Collins
internet-linked
dictionary of

Anagrams

Collins

HarperCollins Publishers
Westerhill Road
Bishopbriggs
Glasgow
G64 2QT

First Edition 2005

© HarperCollins Publishers 2005

UK Edition ISBN 0-00-719467-6

Collins® is a registered trademark of
HarperCollins Publishers Limited

www.collins.co.uk

A catalogue record for this book is
available from the British Library.

Prepared in conjunction with,
and typeset by
Market House Books Ltd,
Aylesbury, England

Printed in Great Britain by Clays Ltd, St Ives plc

Acknowledgements

We would like to thank those authors and
publishers who kindly gave permission for
copyright material to be used in the Collins Word
Web. We would also like to thank Times
Newspapers Ltd for providing valuable data.

EDITORIAL STAFF

EDITORS
Justin Crozier
Cormac McKeown

FOR THE PUBLISHERS
Morven Dooner
Elaine Higgleton
Lorna Knight

Collins internet-linked
dictionary of anagrams

William Collins' dream of knowledge for all began with the publication of his first book in 1819. A self-educated mill worker, he not only enriched millions of lives, but also founded a flourishing publishing house. Today, staying true to this spirit, Collins books are packed with inspiration, innovation, and practical expertise. They place you at the centre of a world of possibility and give you exactly what you need to explore it.

Language is the key to this exploration, and at the heart of Collins Dictionaries is language as it is really used. New words, phrases, and meanings spring up every day, and all of them are captured and analysed by the Collins Word Web. Constantly updated, and with over 2.5 billion entries, this living language resource is unique to our dictionaries.

Words are tools for life. And a Collins Dictionary makes them work for you.

Collins. Do more

CONTENTS

vi
Foreword

vii
Using the internet safely

viii
Tips for safe use of the internet and
chatrooms

1–872
Collins internet-linked dictionary of
Anagrams

1–32
Supplement: Word Play

Whether you're stuck for words on Scrabble, crosswords or, indeed, any word game, Collins *internet-linked Dictionary of Anagrams* is your ideal reference. Packed with words and phrases, and based on Collins' extensive word games list, this book comprises over 100,000 anagrams.

The letter sets in the book are split into sections according to length, from 4-letter words to 15-letter words, and then according to alphabetical order of their component letters (eg all sets containing A come before those with B, but no A). All conceivable anagram solutions for the letter sets are listed next to the letter sets.

In addition to all this, Collins *internet-linked dictionary of Anagrams* contains a useful supplement with handy tips on internet crossword-solving resources, an introduction to solving cryptic crosswords, how to create anagrams and other –grams, and helpful words for word games.

This section offers advice chiefly to parents concerned with the online safety of their children. Hints and tips for safe surfing are provided as is a list of websites dealing with this subject in more detail.

The internet contains an inconceivably large amount of information, much of it free, on a vast range of topics. It does not belong to and is not controlled by any single organization, government, or nation. Although the absence of centralized control is occasionally lamented as anarchic, the lack of a top-down structure provides many benefits.

The internet offers the chance for anyone with a computer and a modem to communicate with and learn from any person, group, or organization similarly equipped. Libraries, museums, art galleries, governments, universities, research institutes, and many other bodies provide open access to their data and links to the online resources of other organizations.

This availability of information and the unparalleled potential for communication and the spread of ideas provides internet users with incalculable benefits, but there are downsides. As the internet is unregulated and decentralized there is no quality-control mechanism; the only barrier preventing someone from setting up a website is technical ability. There is much of little merit on the internet.

More worrying is the potential for criminal misuse. The internet's accessibility and inclusiveness is exploited by those who wish to disseminate hate or obscenity or to take advantage of the vulnerable or gullible. As 70 per cent of UK households with school-age children are online it is important that parents and carers are aware of the potential dangers as well as the benefits.

> Find out as much as possible about the internet, chatrooms, instant messaging, and email. A number of websites dealing with the concerns of parents are listed at the bottom of this section.
> Make internet surfing a family event as often as possible.
> Limit the amount of time your children spend online. Encourage them to maintain their other interests and hobbies.
> Keep the computer in a family room so that you can check how long your children have been using the internet.
> Make sure your child doesn't give out personal details, phone numbers, addresses, or any other information that could be used to identify him or her, such as information about your family or the school he or she goes to.
> Make sure that any chatroom used by your child is monitored to prevent publication of offensive material or personal contact details.
> Online contacts should not be taken at face value. They may not be what they seem.
> Warn children never to arrange to meet someone only ever previously met on the internet without first telling you. Accompany your child to any meetings and make sure they are held in a public place.
> Children should not accept files from people they don't know and trust offline, since the files could contain viruses or self-extracting software which could reveal personal information to the sender.
> Video-conferencing and webcams allow the transmission of voice and live images. Children should be discouraged from using this technology unsupervised and with people they don't know and trust offline.
> Warn your children never to respond directly to anything they find disturbing. Encourage them to log off and report what they found to an adult.
> Consider using internet filtering software and child-friendly search engines. Use your browser's controls, as some offer varying degrees of security for each family member.
> Investigate your internet service provider's (ISP) child-protection services. Do they filter out spam (unwanted email), for instance?
> Investigate internet safety in greater detail at the following websites:

> www.chatdanger.com
> http://safety.ngfl.gov.uk
> www.childnet-int.org/links/index.html
> www.internetcrimeforum.org.uk/chatwise_streetwise.html
> www.nspcc.org.uk/html/home/needadvice/
> helpyourchildsurfinsafety.htm

Four Letters

AABB	abba	**AAGY**	Gaya	**AAMN**	Anam	**ABBO**	boab		beta
	baba	**AAGZ**	Gaza		mana	**ABBR**	barb	**ABEU**	Aube
AABC	abac	**AAHH**	haha	**AAMR**	Aram	**ABBU**	babu		beau
AABH	Ahab	**AAHK**	haka		maar	**ABBY**	baby	**ABEY**	abye
AABI	Abia	**AAHM**	amah		mara	**ABCH**	bach	**ABEZ**	Baez
AABL	alba		Hama		Rama	**ABCK**	back		Beza
	baal	**AAHN**	Naha	**AAMS**	maas	**ABCN**	banc	**ABFL**	flab
	Bala	**AAHR**	haar	**AAMY**	maya	**ABCR**	carb	**ABFR**	barf
AABS	abas	**AAHY**	ayah	**AAMZ**	Zama		crab	**ABGH**	bagh
	baas	**AAIL**	Alai	**AANN**	anna	**ABCS**	cabs	**ABGL**	blag
	Saba	**AAIM**	Maia		naan		scab	**ABGN**	bang
AACM	cama	**AAIP**	Apia		nana	**ABCU**	Cuba	**ABGO**	Gabo
AACN	Cana	**AAIR**	aria	**AANO**	anoa	**ABDE**	abed	**ABGR**	brag
AACP	capa		raia	**AANR**	Aran		bade		garb
	paca	**AAIS**	Asia		Nara		bead		grab
AACS	caas	**AAJP**	jaap	**AANS**	anas	**ABDI**	Bida	**ABGS**	bags
AACV	cava	**AAJR**	ajar		San'a	**ABDL**	bald		gabs
AACW	waac		raja	**AANT**	anta	**ABDN**	band	**ABGY**	gaby
AADD	dada	**AAJV**	java		tana	**ABDO**	doab	**ABHI**	Bhai
AADM	Adam	**AAJX**	Ajax	**AANZ**	azan	**ABDR**	bard	**ABHL**	blah
AADN	Dana	**AAJY**	Jaya	**AAPP**	papa		brad	**ABHS**	bash
	nada	**AAKK**	kaka	**AAPR**	arpa		drab	**ABHT**	baht
AADR	Adar	**AAKL**	kaal		para	**ABDS**	dabs		bath
	Arad	**AAKM**	kama		Pará	**ABDU**	baud	**ABHU**	habu
AADT	data	**AAKN**	kana	**AAPT**	tapa		daub	**ABIK**	Biak
AAEG	Gaea	**AAKR**	arak	**AAPU**	paua	**ABDW**	bawd	**ABIL**	Albi
AAEL	alae		kara	**AAQU**	aqua	**ABEK**	bake		bail
AAER	area	**AAKT**	kata	**AARS**	Aras		beak		Bali
AAFH	haaf		taka		Saar	**ABEL**	Abel	**ABIM**	bima
AAFJ	jafa	**AAKV**	kava	**AART**	rata		able		iamb
AAFL	alfa	**AAKW**	kawa		Tara		bael	**ABIN**	bani
AAFR	afar		waka	**AARU**	aura		bale	**ABIR**	abri
AAFS	faas	**AALM**	lama	**AARV**	vara		Bâle		Bari
AAGG	gaga		mala	**AASV**	Sava		blae		rabi
AAGH	agha	**AALN**	anal		vasa		Elba		riba
AAGI	Gaia	**AALP**	alap	**AATU**	atua		Labe	**ABIS**	bias
AAGJ	jaga		paal	**AATW**	tawa	**ABEM**	beam	**ABIT**	bait
AAGL	alga	**AALR**	alar	**AATX**	taxa		bema	**ABJM**	jamb
	gala		Lara	**AAWW**	wawa	**ABEN**	bane	**ABJO**	Joab
AAGM	agma	**AALS**	alas	**AAWY**	away		bean	**ABJS**	jabs
	gama	**AALT**	taal	**ABBE**	abbe	**ABER**	bare	**ABJU**	juba
AAGN	naga		tala		abbé		bear	**ABKL**	balk
AAGR	agar	**AALV**	Alva		Abbe		brae	**ABKN**	bank
	Agra		lava		babe	**ABES**	base	**ABKO**	boak
	raga		Vaal	**ABBI**	Abib	**ABET**	abet	**ABKR**	bark
AAGS	agas	**AALW**	Waal		Babi		bate		brak
	saga	**AAMM**	mama	**ABBL**	blab		beat		krab

ABKS bask	ecad	**ACIM** mica	octa	mead
kabs	**ACDH** chad	**ACIN** cain	taco	**ADEN** Aden
ABKU Baku	**ACDI** acid	**ACIO** ciao	**ACOX** coax	dean
ABLL ball	cadi	**ACIP** pica	coxa	**ADEO** odea
ABLM balm	**ACDK** dack	**ACIS** Acis	**ACPP** Capp	**ADEP** aped
lamb	**ACDL** clad	asci	**ACPR** carp	**ADER** dare
ABLO bola	**ACDO** coda	Sica	crap	dear
ABLS albs	**ACDR** card	**ACJK** jack	**ACPS** caps	read
labs	drac	**ACKL** calk	**ACPT** pact	**ADES** daes
slab	**ACDS** cads	lack	**ACPY** pacy	sade
ABLT blat	scad	**ACKM** mack	**ACRR** carr	**ADET** date
ABLW bawl	**ACEF** cafe	**ACKP** pack	**ACRS** arcs	**ADEU** Aude
ABLY ably	face	**ACKR** cark	cars	**ADEV** deva
ABMO ambo	**ACEG** cage	rack	scar	Veda
boma	**ACEH** Aceh	**ACKS** cask	**ACRT** cart	**ADEW** awed
Moab	ache	sack	**ACRW** craw	wade
ABMR barm	each	**ACKT** tack	**ACRY** Cary	**ADEX** axed
ABMU Baum	**ACEK** cake	**ACKW** wack	cray	**ADEZ** adze
ABNO bona	**ACEL** alec	**ACKY** caky	racy	daze
Oban	Cela	yack	**ACRZ** czar	**ADFF** daff
ABNR barn	lace	**ACLL** call	**ACSS** sacs	**ADFO** fado
bran	**ACEM** acme	**ACLM** calm	**ACST** acts	**ADFR** fard
ABNS bans	came	clam	cast	**ADFS** fads
nabs	mace	**ACLN** clan	cats	**ADFT** daft
ABNT bant	**ACEN** acne	**ACLO** alco	scat	**ADGL** glad
ABNU buna	ance	coal	**ACSV** vacs	**ADGM** AMDG
ABOR baro	Caen	cola	**ACSW** caws	**ADGN** dang
boar	cane	**ACLP** clap	**ACSY** cays	Gand
bora	**ACEP** cape	**ACLR** carl	**ACTT** tact	**ADGO** dago
ABOS abos	pace	**ACLS** lacs	**ACVY** cavy	goad
boas	**ACER** acer	**ACLT** clat	**ACWY** YWCA	**ADGR** darg
obas	acre	talc	**ADDD** Dadd	drag
soba	care	**ACLU** caul	**ADDE** dead	Gard
ABOT boat	race	**ACLW** claw	Edda	grad
ABOZ Boaz	**ACES** aces	**ACLX** calx	**ADDO** dado	**ADGS** dags
ABPS baps	case	**ACLY** acyl	**ADDS** adds	gads
ABRS bars	**ACET** tace	clay	dads	**ADGU** gaud
bras	**ACEV** cave	lacy	**ADDU** daud	**ADHJ** hadj
ABRT Bart	**ACEW** Wace	**ACMN** Manc	duad	**ADHK** dhak
brat	**ACFF** caff	**ACMO** camo	**ADDY** addy	**ADHL** dahl
ABRU bura	**ACFL** calf	coma	dyad	dhal
ABRW braw	**ACFT** fact	**ACMP** camp	**ADEF** deaf	**ADHN** hand
warb	**ACGL** clag	**ACMR** cram	fade	**ADHO** Doha
ABRY bray	**ACGN** cang	marc	**ADEG** aged	**ADHR** hard
ABSS bass	**ACGR** crag	**ACMS** cams	egad	**ADHS** dahs
ABST bast	**ACGS** cags	macs	gaed	dash
bats	scag	scam	**ADEH** hade	shad
stab	**ACGY** cagy	**ACMY** cyma	haed	**ADHU** haud
tabs	**ACHI** chai	YMCA	head	**ADIK** kadi
ABSW swab	**ACHK** hack	**ACNR** cran	**ADEI** Adie	**ADIL** dali
ABSY abys	**ACHM** cham	narc	aide	dial
bays	mach	**ACNS** cans	idea	laid
ABTT batt	**ACHP** chap	scan	**ADEJ** jade	**ADIM** amid
ABTU abut	**ACHR** arch	**ACNT** cant	**ADEK** Deak	maid
tabu	char	**ACNY** cyan	**ADEL** dale	**ADIP** paid
tuba	**ACHS** Asch	**ACOP** capo	deal	**ADIQ** qadi
ACCE ceca	cash	**ACOR** Caro	lade	**ADIR** arid
ACCO coca	**ACHT** chat	Roca	lead	raid
ACCS SACC	**ACHW** chaw	**ACOS** ocas	Leda	**ADIS** aids
ACDE aced	**ACHY** achy	soca	**ADEM** dame	dais
cade	**ACIL** Cali	**ACOT** Cato	Edam	Dias
dace	laic	coat	made	sadi

	said			**AEHL**	hale		olea		pean
ADIT	adit	**ADRW**	draw		heal	**AELP**	leap	**AENR**	Arne
	dita		ward		Leah		pale		earn
ADIV	avid	**ADRY**	dray	**AEHM**	ahem		peal		near
	diva		yard		haem		plea		rean
ADIW	wadi	**ADST**	tads		hame	**AELR**	earl	**AENS**	sane
ADIZ	Diaz	**ADSU**	Saud		Mahé		lear		sena
ADKN	dank	**ADSW**	daws	**AEHP**	epha		rale	**AENT**	ante
ADKR	dark		wads		heap		real		Aten
ADKS	daks	**ADSY**	days	**AEHR**	hare	**AELS**	ales		etna
ADKU	duka		yads		hear		lase		neat
ADKW	dawk	**ADUV**	Vaud		Hera		leas	**AENV**	nave
ADLN	land	**ADVY**	davy		rhea		sale		Neva
ADLO	load	**ADWY**	wady	**AEHS**	Ashe		Salé		vane
ADLR	lard	**ADYZ**	Yazd		haes		seal		vena
ADLS	dals	**AEEG**	agee		shea	**AELT**	Elat	**AENW**	anew
	lads	**AEEJ**	ajee	**AEHT**	haet		late		wane
ADLU	auld	**AEEK**	akee		hate		leat		wean
	dual	**AEEL**	alee		heat		tael	**AENY**	yean
	laud		Elea	**AEHV**	have		tale	**AENZ**	naze
	Lüda	**AEES**	ease	**AEHW**	whae		teal	**AEOR**	aero
	udal	**AEFK**	fake	**AEHY**	yeah		tela	**AEOT**	toea
ADLY	lady	**AEFL**	feal	**AEHZ**	haze	**AELU**	Laue	**AEOZ**	zoea
ADMN	damn		flea	**AEIL**	Elia	**AELV**	avel	**AEPR**	pare
ADMP	damp		leaf		ilea		lave		Paré
ADMR	dram	**AEFM**	fame	**AEIM**	amie		leva		pear
ADMS	dams	**AEFN**	fane	**AEIN**	eina		vale		Pera
	mads	**AEFR**	fare	**AEIR**	Aire		veal		rape
ADMU	duma		fear	**AEJK**	jake		vela		reap
	maud		frae	**AEJL**	Jael	**AELW**	wale	**AEPS**	apes
ADMW	dwam	**AEFS**	safe	**AEJN**	Jaén		weal		apse
ADNO	dona	**AEFT**	fate		jane	**AELX**	axel		pase
ADNR	darn		feat		jean		axle		peas
	nard		feta		Jena	**AELY**	yale		spae
	rand	**AEFV**	fave	**AEJP**	jape	**AELZ**	laze	**AEPT**	pate
ADNS	dans	**AEFZ**	faze	**AEKL**	kale		zeal		peat
	nads	**AEGG**	gage		lake	**AEMN**	amen		tape
	sand	**AEGL**	gale		leak		mane	**AEPV**	pave
ADNU	Duna	**AEGM**	game	**AEKM**	kame		mean	**AEPX**	apex
ADNW	dawn		mage		make		name	**AEPZ**	Páez
	wand		mega	**AEKN**	Kean	**AEMR**	mare	**AERR**	rare
ADOP	dopa	**AEGN**	agen	**AEKP**	peak		ream		rear
ADOR	Odra		gane	**AEKR**	rake	**AEMS**	mesa	**AERS**	ares
	road		gean	**AEKS**	keas		same		arse
ADOS	sado	**AEGP**	gape		sake		seam		ears
	soda		page	**AEKT**	take	**AEMT**	mate		eras
ADOT	dato		peag		teak		meat		rase
	doat	**AEGR**	areg	**AEKW**	wake		meta		sear
	toad		gear		weak		tame		sera
ADOW	woad		Gera		weka		team	**AERT**	rate
ADPR	drap		rage	**AELL**	leal		Tema		tare
	pard	**AEGS**	ages	**AELM**	Elam	**AEMW**	wame		tear
ADPS	daps		gaes		lame	**AEMX**	exam	**AERU**	Auer
	pads		sage		male	**AEMY**	Aymé		urea
ADQU	quad	**AEGT**	gate		Malé		Eyam	**AERV**	aver
ADRS	Ards	**AEGU**	ague		meal	**AEMZ**	maze		rave
	rads	**AEGV**	gave		mela	**AENN**	Anne	**AERW**	ware
	sard		vega	**AELN**	elan		nane		wear
ADRT	dart	**AEGW**	wage		lane	**AENO**	aeon	**AERY**	aery
	drat	**AEGY**	Gaye		lean	**AENP**	nape		Ayer
	trad	**AEGZ**	gaze		Lena		neap		eyra
ADRU	daur	**AEHK**	hake	**AELO**	aloe		pane		yare

3

	year	**AFLP**	flap		taig	**AGRT**	grat		YMHA
AERZ	Ezra	**AFLR**	farl	**AGIV**	vagi	**AGRU**	gaur	**AHNO**	noah
	raze	**AFLS**	alfs	**AGIY**	yagi		guar	**AHNS**	Nash
AESS	seas	**AFLT**	flat	**AGIZ**	Gîza		ruga		shan
AEST	east	**AFLW**	flaw	**AGJS**	jags		Urga	**AHNT**	tanh
	eats	**AFLX**	flax	**AGKN**	knag	**AGRV**	grav		than
	etas	**AFLY**	flay	**AGKS**	skag	**AGRY**	Gary	**AHNW**	hwan
	sate	**AFMO**	foam	**AGKU**	kagu		gray	**AHOP**	opah
	seat	**AFMR**	farm	**AGKW**	gawk	**AGRZ**	Graz	**AHOR**	hoar
	seta	**AFNS**	fans	**AGLL**	gall	**AGSS**	sags		hora
	taes	**AFNU**	faun	**AGLM**	glam	**AGST**	gats	**AHOT**	oath
	teas	**AFNW**	fawn	**AGLN**	lang		stag	**AHOU**	Oahu
AESU	Esau	**AFOR**	afro	**AGLO**	gaol		tags	**AHOW**	whoa
AESV	aves		faro		goal	**AGSV**	vags	**AHOX**	hoax
	save		fora	**AGLS**	gals	**AGSW**	swag	**AHOY**	ahoy
	vase	**AFOS**	oafs		lags		wags		hoya
AESW	awes		sofa		slag	**AGSY**	gays	**AHPR**	harp
	waes	**AFOY**	ofay	**AGLT**	Galt	**AGUY**	yuga	**AHPS**	haps
AESX	axes		Yafo	**AGLU**	aglu	**AHHN**	Hahn		hasp
	Saxe	**AFPR**	frap		Gaul	**AHHS**	hash		pash
AESY	ayes	**AFRS**	fras	**AGMO**	ogam		shah	**AHPT**	path
	easy	**AFRT**	fart	**AGMP**	gamp	**AHHT**	hath		phat
	eyas		frat	**AGMR**	gram	**AHIJ**	haji		Ptah
AETT	tate		raft		marg	**AHIK**	haik	**AHPU**	hapu
	teat	**AFRU**	faur	**AGMS**	gams	**AHIL**	hail		puha
AETW	twae		frau		mags		hila	**AHPW**	whap
	weta		Urfa	**AGMU**	Guam	**AHIR**	hair	**AHRS**	rash
AETY	yate	**AFRY**	fray	**AGMY**	gamy	**AHIU**	huia	**AHRT**	hart
AETZ	zeta	**AFRZ**	zarf	**AGNO**	agon	**AHIY**	hiya		rath
AEUV	uvea	**AFST**	fast	**AGNP**	pang	**AHJJ**	hajj		tahr
AEVW	wave		fats	**AGNR**	gnar	**AHKL**	lakh		thar
AFFF	faff		saft		gran	**AHKN**	ankh	**AHRZ**	Harz
AFFG	gaff	**AFSX**	Sfax		rang		hank	**AHSS**	sash
AFFN	naff	**AFSY**	fays	**AGNS**	gans		Kahn	**AHST**	hast
AFFO	Offa	**AFTT**	Taft		nags		khan		hats
AFFR	raff	**AFTU**	faut		sang	**AHKO**	koha		shat
AFFW	waff		tufa		snag	**AHKP**	kaph	**AHSW**	haws
AFGL	flag	**AFTW**	waft	**AGNT**	gnat	**AHKR**	hark		shaw
AFGN	fang	**AGGI**	giga		tang	**AHKS**	hask		shwa
AFGR	frag	**AGGJ**	jagg	**AGNU**	gaun	**AHKT**	khat		wash
	Graf	**AGGN**	gang		guan	**AHKW**	hawk	**AHSY**	ashy
AFGS	fags	**AGGO**	agog	**AGNV**	vang	**AHLL**	hall		hays
AFHL	half	**AGGR**	ragg	**AGNW**	gnaw	**AHLM**	halm		shay
AFHS	fash	**AGGS**	gags	**AGNY**	Nagy	**AHLO**	halo	**AHTT**	that
AFHT	haft	**AGHI**	Haig		yang	**AHLR**	harl	**AHTU**	Utah
AFHU	hauf	**AGHN**	hang	**AGOR**	Argo	**AHLS**	Hals	**AHTW**	thaw
AFIK	kaif	**AGHS**	gash	**AGOS**	goas		lahs		what
AFIL	fail		hags		sago		lash	**AHWY**	YWHA
	fila		shag	**AGOT**	goat	**AHLT**	halt	**AHYZ**	hazy
AFIN	fain	**AGHT**	gath		Göta		lath	**AIIL**	ilia
	naif		ghat		toga	**AHLU**	haul		Ilía
AFIP	Piaf	**AGIL**	gila	**AGOY**	Goya		hula	**AIIS**	Iaşi
AFIR	fair		glia		yoga	**AHLY**	hyla	**AIIX**	ixia
AFIS	Safi	**AGIM**	magi	**AGPS**	gaps	**AHMM**	Hamm	**AIJL**	jail
AFIT	fiat	**AGIN**	agin		gasp	**AHMO**	homa	**AIJN**	Jain
AFIW	waif		Agni		spag	**AHMR**	harm	**AIKK**	kaik
AFKL	flak		gain	**AGPU**	gaup	**AHMS**	hams		kaki
AFLL	fall	**AGIO**	agio	**AGPW**	gawp		mash	**AIKL**	ilka
AFLM	flam	**AGIR**	gari	**AGPY**	gapy		sham		kail
AFLN	flan		ragi	**AGQU**	quag	**AHMT**	math		kali
AFLO	foal		Riga	**AGRS**	gars	**AHMW**	wham		laik
	loaf	**AGIT**	gait		rags	**AHMY**	Mahy	**AIKM**	kami

	maik		pina	**AJPU**	jaup	**AKSW**	skaw		sals
AIKN	akin	**AINR**	Iran		puja	**AKSY**	yaks	**ALST**	alts
	ikan		rain	**AJRS**	jars	**AKTY**	kyat		last
	kain		rani	**AJRU**	jura	**AKTZ**	Katz		lats
	kina	**AINS**	ains	**AJSW**	jaws	**AKUW**	wauk		salt
AIKP	pika		anis	**AJSY**	jays	**ALLM**	mall		slat
AIKR	raki		isna	**AJXY**	jaxy	**ALLO**	Lalo	**ALSU**	saul
AIKS	saki		sain	**AJZZ**	jazz		olla	**ALSV**	lavs
	sika		Sian	**AKLN**	lank	**ALLP**	pall	**ALSW**	awls
AIKT	ikat	**AINT**	anti	**AKLO**	alko	**ALLT**	tall		laws
	tika		tain		kola	**ALLW**	wall		slaw
AIKU	kuia	**AINV**	vain	**AKLR**	lark	**ALLY**	ally	**ALSY**	lays
AIKV	kiva		vina	**AKLS**	Salk	**ALMM**	malm		slay
AILM	lima	**AINW**	wain	**AKLT**	talk	**ALMO**	loam		Syal
	mail	**AINX**	Xi'an	**AKLU**	kula		mola	**ALTU**	Lü-ta
	mali	**AINY**	ayin	**AKLW**	walk	**ALMP**	lamp		Tula
AILN	anil	**AINZ**	nazi	**AKLY**	alky		palm	**ALUU**	luau
	lain	**AIOT**	iota		laky	**ALMR**	marl	**ALUW**	waul
	nail		Oita	**AKMO**	amok	**ALMS**	alms	**ALUY**	Yalu
AILO	Liao	**AIOW**	Iowa		mako		lams	**ALWW**	wawl
AILP	lipa	**AIPP**	pipa	**AKMR**	mark		slam	**ALWY**	yawl
	pail	**AIPR**	pair	**AKMS**	maks	**ALMT**	malt	**ALYZ**	lazy
AILR	aril	**AIPS**	Apis		mask	**ALMU**	alum	**AMMO**	ammo
	lair		Pisa	**AKNO**	Kano		luma	**AMMS**	mams
	lari	**AIPT**	pita		kaon		maul	**AMNN**	Mann
	liar	**AIQR**	Iraq		koan	**ALMY**	amyl	**AMNO**	Amon
	lira	**AIRS**	airs	**AKNP**	knap	**ALNO**	loan		moan
	rail		Asir	**AKNR**	knar	**ALNP**	plan		mona
	rial		Isar		nark	**ALNR**	larn		noma
AILS	ails		rais		rank	**ALNU**	luna		Oman
	sail		rias	**AKNS**	sank		ulan	**AMNS**	mans
	sial		sair	**AKNT**	kant		ulna	**AMNU**	Amün
AILT	alit		sari		tank	**ALNW**	lawn		maun
	Atli	**AIRT**	airt	**AKNU**	kuna	**ALOP**	opal	**AMNX**	Manx
	lati		arti	**AKNW**	wank		Pola	**AMNY**	many
	tail	**AIRV**	vair	**AKNY**	yank	**ALOR**	oral		myna
	tali	**AIRY**	airy	**AKOR**	kora	**ALOS**	also	**AMOR**	mora
AILV	vail		Iyar		okra		Laos		Omar
	vial	**AISS**	sais	**AKOS**	koas		sola		roam
AILW	wail		Saïs		oaks	**ALOT**	alto		roma
	wali	**AIST**	aits		okas		lota	**AMOS**	Amos
AILX	axil		Asti		soak		tola		moas
AILZ	zila		Sita	**AKOT**	Kota	**ALOV**	oval		soma
AIMM	imam		tais		okta	**ALOW**	alow	**AMOT**	atom
	maim		Tisa	**AKOY**	kayo		awol		moat
AIMN	amin	**AISV**	Siva		oaky	**ALOZ**	Özal	**AMOU**	ouma
	main		visa		okay		Zola	**AMOX**	moxa
	mani	**AISX**	axis	**AKPR**	park	**ALPP**	palp	**AMOY**	Amoy
	mina	**AITT**	Tati	**AKRS**	arks	**ALPS**	alps		mayo
AIMO	moai	**AITV**	vita		Rask		laps		moya
AIMR	amir	**AITW**	wait		sark		pals	**AMPR**	pram
	rami	**AITX**	taxi	**AKRT**	kart		slap		ramp
AIMS	aims	**AIVV**	viva	**AKRU**	Kura	**ALPT**	plat	**AMPS**	amps
	amis	**AJKS**	jaks	**AKRW**	wark	**ALPU**	paul		maps
	Siam	**AJLR**	jarl	**AKRY**	yark		pula		samp
	sima	**AJMS**	jams	**AKSS**	asks	**ALPW**	pawl		spam
AIMU	Maui	**AJNO**	Joan	**AKST**	kats	**ALPY**	paly	**AMPT**	tamp
AIMX	maxi	**AJOT**	jato		skat		play	**AMPU**	puma
AINO	Iona		jota		task	**ALRU**	Ural	**AMPV**	vamp
	naoi		Tajo	**AKSU**	auks	**ALRY**	aryl	**AMRS**	arms
AINP	nipa	**AJPR**	jarp		skua		lyra		mars
	pain	**AJPS**	japs	**AKSV**	kvas	**ALSS**	lass		rams

AMRT mart, tram

AMRU Amur, arum, Umar

AMRW warm

AMRX Marx

AMRY army, mary

AMSS mass, sams

AMST mast, mats, tams

AMSW maws, swam

AMSX Xmas

AMSY mays, yams

AMTT matt

AMTY maty

AMUX Axum

AMUZ Mazu

AMYZ mazy

ANNO anon, nona

ANNS nans

ANOR Arno, Oran, roan

ANOS naos

ANOT Aton, nota

ANOV Avon, nova

ANOX axon

ANOZ Zoan

ANPS naps, pans, snap, span

ANPT pant

ANPU puna

ANPW pawn

ANRT rant, tarn

ANRW warn

ANRY nary, yarn

ANSS sans

ANST ants, nats, tans

ANSU anus

ANSV vans

ANSW awns, sawn, swan, wans

ANSY nays, Nysa

ANTU aunt, tuan, tuna

ANTW want

ANUU unau

ANUY yuan, Yüan

ANVY navy

ANWY wany, yawn

ANYZ zany

AOPR proa

AOPS soap

AOPT atop

AOPU oupa

AORR orra, roar

AORS oars, osar, Rosa, soar, sora

AORT rato, rota, taro

AORV arvo

AOSS ossa

AOST oast, oats, stoa, tosa

AOSY soya

AOTU auto

AOVW avow

AOVZ Azov

APPS paps

APPU pupa

APRR parr

APRS raps, rasp, spar

APRT part, prat, rapt, tarp, trap

APRU prau

APRW warp, wrap

APRY pray

APSS asps

APST past, pats, spat, taps

APSU upas

APSV pavs

APSW paws, swap, wasp

APSY pays, pyas, spay, yaps

APSZ zaps

APTU patu, tapu, upta

APTY pyat

APUY yaup

APWY yawp

AQUY quay

ARSS ASSR

ARST arts, rats, star, tars, tsar

ARSU Asur, sura, ursa

ARSV vars

ARSW wars

ARSY rays

ARTT tart

ARTW wart

ARTY arty, tray

ARTZ tzar

ARUW waur

ARVY vary

ARWY awry, wary

ARZZ razz

ASSS sass

ASSU Susa

ASSV savs

ASSW saws

ASSY says

ASTT stat, tats

ASTU saut, taus

ASTV tavs, vast, vats

ASTW swat, taws, twas, wast, wats

ASTY stay, tays

ASUV Suva

ASVV vavs

ASWW waws

ASWY sway, ways, yaws

ATTU Attu, taut

ATTW twat, watt

ATUV vatu

AVWY wavy

AWXY waxy

BBBI bibb

BBCO cobb

BBDI DBib

BBEL bleb

BBES ebbs

BBEW Webb

BBIJ jibb

BBIS bibs

BBLO blob

BBLU blub, bulb

BBMO bomb

BBOO boob

BBOS bobs

BBOU bubo

BBSU bubs

BBUU bubu

BCEH Cheb

BCEI bice

BCEK beck

BCEU Cebu, cube

BCHO Cóbh

BCHU chub

BCIR crib

BCKO bock

BCKU buck

BCLO bloc

BCLU club

BCMO comb

BCOS cobs

BCRU curb

BCSU cubs

BDEE bede, debe

BDEI bide

BDEL bled

BDEN bend

BDEO bode

BDER bred

BDES beds, debs

BDET debt

BDEY byde

BDIN bind

BDIR bird

BDIS bids, dibs

BDLO bold

BDMU dumb

BDNO bond

BDNU bund

BDOO doob

BDOR dorb

BDOS bods, dobs

BDOY body, Boyd, doby

BDRU drub

BDRY Byrd

BDSU buds, dubs

BEEF beef

BEEH hebe

BEEL Elbe

BEEN been

BEEP beep

BEER beer, bree

BEES bees

BEET beet

BEGI gibe

BEGR berg

BEGS begs

BEGY gybe

BEHN Behn

BEHR herb

BEHT beth

BEIJ jibe

BEIK bike, kibe

BEIL Biel, bile

BEIN beni, bine

BEIR bier, brei, brie

BEIS bise

BEIT bite

BEIV vibe

BEIX ibex

BEJU jube

BEKO boke, Kobe

BEKR berk, kerb

BEKY byke

BELL bell

BELO bole, lobe, Loeb

BELP pleb

BELR Brel

BELS bels

BELT belt, blet

BELU blue

BELW blew

BEMO mobe

BEMR berm

BENN Benn

BENO bone, Bône, ebon, Nebo

BENR Bern, bren

Code	Words
BENS	bens, nebs
BENT	bent
BENZ	Benz
BEOO	oboe
BEOR	bore, Ebro, robe
BEOS	Bose
BEOT	boet
BEOY	obey, yebo
BEPU	pube
BERR	brer
BERS	rebs, Serb
BERU	rube
BERV	verb
BERW	brew
BERY	brey, byre
BEST	best, bets
BESW	webs
BESY	beys, byes
BETU	bute, tube
BETY	byte
BEUZ	zebu
BEVY	bevy
BFFI	biff
BFFO	boff
BFFU	buff
BFIR	frib
BFIS	fibs
BFMU	bumf
BFOR	forb
BFOS	fobs
BFOY	boyf
BGIL	glib
BGIN	bing
BGIO	Gobi
BGIR	brig
BGIS	bigs, gibs
BGLO	blog, glob
BGNO	bong
BGNU	bung
BGNY	Byng
BGOO	gobo
BGOR	Borg, brog
BGOS	bogs, gobs
BGOY	bogy, goby
BGRU	burg, grub
BGSU	bugs
BHIS	bish
BHLU	buhl
BHMO	Böhm
BHOO	boho, hobo
BHOR	Bohr
BHOS	bosh, hobs
BHOT	both
BHRU	buhr
BHSU	bush, hubs
BIIS	ibis
BIJS	jibs
BIKL	bilk
BIKO	Biko
BIKR	birk, brik
BIKS	bisk
BILL	bill
BILM	limb
BILN	blin
BILO	boil
BILP	blip
BILR	birl
BIMR	brim
BINS	bins, nibs, snib
BINT	bint
BINY	inby
BIOR	brio
BIOS	bios, obis
BIOT	obit
BIOZ	Zibo
BIRR	birr
BIRS	bris, ribs
BIRT	brit
BISS	sibs
BIST	bist, bits
BITT	bitt
BJOS	jobs
BKLO	Blok
BKLU	bulk
BKNO	bonk, knob
BKNU	bunk
BKOO	book, kobs
BKOS	bosk, kobs
BKOY	kybo
BKRU	burk
BKSU	busk
BLLO	boll, Böll
BLLU	bull
BLMU	Blum
BLOO	bolo, bool, lobo, obol
BLOS	lobs, slob
BLOT	blot, bolt
BLOW	blow, bowl
BLRU	blur, burl
BLSU	slub
BMNU	numb
BMOO	boom
BMOR	borm
BMOT	tomb
BMOU	Bomu, umbo
BMOW	womb
BMOY	moby
BMPU	bump
BMSU	bums
BNNO	Bonn
BNOO	boon
BNOR	born, Brno
BNOS	nobs, snob
BNOY	bony
BNRU	burn
BNSU	buns, nubs, snub
BNTU	bunt
BOOR	boor
BOOS	boos
BOOT	boot
BOOY	boyo
BOOZ	bozo
BOPS	bops
BORS	bors, bros, orbs, robs, sorb
BORT	bort
BORW	brow
BORZ	Broz
BOSS	boss, sobs
BOST	bots, stob
BOSW	bows, swob
BOSY	boys, sybo, yobs
BOTT	bott
BOTU	bout
BOTY	toby
BOUY	buoy
BOXY	boxy
BPRU	burp
BPSU	pubs
BRRU	burr
BRSU	burs, rubs
BRTU	brut
BRUY	bury, ruby
BSSU	buss, subs
BSTU	bust, buts, stub, tubs
BSUY	busy, buys
BTTU	butt
BUZZ	buzz
CCHI	chic
CCKO	cock
CCOO	coco
CCOR	croc
CDEE	cede
CDEI	cedi, cide, dice, iced
CDEK	deck
CDEO	code, coed
CDER	cred
CDEU	cued, duce
CDHI	chid, dich
CDIK	dick
CDIO	odic
CDIS	disc
CDKO	dock
CDKU	duck
CDLO	clod, cold
CDOO	doco
CDOR	cord, docs
CDOS	cods, docs
CDOU	douc
CDOY	Cody
CDRU	crud, curd
CDSU	scud
CDTU	duct
CEER	cere, cree
CEET	cete
CEFH	chef
CEFK	feck
CEFL	clef
CEFO	C of E
CEGL	cleg
CEHK	heck
CEHL	lech
CEHO	echo, oche
CEHP	pech
CEHR	cher
CEHS	sech
CEHT	echt, etch, tech
CEHW	chew
CEHZ	chez
CEIL	ceil, Içel, lice
CEIM	mice
CEIN	cine, nice
CEIP	epic, pice
CEIR	cire, eric, rice
CEIS	ices, sice
CEIT	cite
CEIV	vice
CEKK	keck
CEKM	meck
CEKN	neck
CEKO	coke
CEKP	peck
CEKR	reck
CEKY	Eyck
CELL	cell
CELM	clem
CELO	cole
CELS	cels
CELT	celt
CELU	clue, luce
CELW	clew
CEMO	come
CEMY	cyme
CENO	Coen, cone, once
CENT	cent
CEOP	cope
CEOR	cero, core
CEOT	cote
CEOU	Coué
CEOV	cove
CEPS	ceps, pecs, Pécs, spec
CEPU	puce
CERS	recs
CERT	cert
CERU	cure, curé, ecru
CERW	crew

CESS cess	**CIKL** lick	**CLOW** cowl	died	**DEHR** herd
secs	**CIKM** mick	**CLOY** cloy	**DDEO** eddo	**DEHS** edhs
CEST sect	**CIKN** nick	coly	**DDER** redd	shed
tecs	**CIKP** pick	**CLRU** curl	**DDEU** dude	**DEHU** hued
CESU cues	**CIKR** rick	**CLTU** cult	**DDEY** dyed	**DEHY** Hyde
ecus	**CIKS** sick	**CLUY** Lucy	eddy	**DEIJ** jedi
CESY syce	**CIKT** tick	**CMOO** Como	**DDIK** Kidd	**DEIK** dike
CETU cute	**CIKW** wick	coom	**DDIO** dido	**DEIL** deil
CETY cyte	**CIKY** icky	**CMOP** comp	**DDOO** dodo	deli
CEXY Ceyx	**CILL** cill	**CMOR** corm	**DDOS** odds	idle
CFFO coff	**CILO** Clio	**CMOS** coms	**DDOT** Todd	lied
CFFU cuff	coil	**CMSU** scum	**DDRU** rudd	**DEIM** dime
CFHO Foch	loci	**CMSW** cwms	sudd	idem
CFIO C of I	**CILP** clip	**CNNO** conn	**DDSU** duds	**DEIN** deni
coif	**CIMR** crim	**CNOO** coon	**DEEF** feed	dine
fico	**CINO** coin	**CNOR** corn	**DEEG** edge	Enid
foci	coni	**CNOS** cons	geed	nide
CFIS fisc	icon	**CNOU** unco	**DEEH** heed	**DEIP** pied
CFIU fuci	**CINU** unci	**CNOY** cony	**DEEK** deek	**DEIR** dire
CFKU fuck	**CINZ** zinc	**CNSY** sync	deke	Reid
CFLO floc	**CIOR** coir	**CNTU** Cnut	eked	ride
CFOR corf	Cori	cunt	**DEEL** dele	**DEIS** dies
CFOS C of S	**CIOT** coit	**COOP** coop	**DEEM** deem	ides
CFOT coft	otic	poco	deme	side
CGHO chog	**CIOV** Vico	**COOS** coos	meed	**DEIT** diet
CGHU chug	**CIOZ** zoic	**COOT** coot	**DEEN** dene	edit
CGIS cigs	**CIPS** pics	**COPR** crop	Eden	tide
CGKU guck	spic	**COPS** cops	need	tied
CGLO clog	**CIRU** uric	scop	**DEEP** deep	**DEIV** Devi
CGOR crog	**CISS** sics	**COPT** Copt	peed	dive
CGOS cogs	**CIST** cist	**COPU** coup	**DEER** deer	vide
CHIK hick	tics	**COPW** cowp	de re	vied
CHIL lich	**CITY** city	**COPY** copy	dere	**DEIW** wide
CHIM mich	**CJKO** jock	**CORS** orcs	dree	**DEJN** Nejd
CHIN chin	**CJLU** Cluj	rocs	rede	**DEJU** Jude
inch	**CKLO** lock	**CORT** torc	reed	**DEKO** doek
CHIP chip	**CKLU** luck	**CORW** crow	**DEES** dees	**DEKS** desk
CHIR rich	**CKMO** mock	**COSS** coss	seed	keds
CHIT chit	**CKMU** muck	**COST** cost	**DEET** teed	**DEKU** duke
itch	**CKNO** conk	cots	**DEEW** weed	**DEKY** dyke
CHIV chiv	nock	scot	**DEEY** eyed	**DELL** dell
CHKO hock	**CKOO** cook	**COSW** cows	**DEFI** deif	**DELM** meld
Koch	**CKOP** pock	scow	**DEFL** fled	**DELN** lend
CHKU huck	**CKOR** cork	**COSY** cosy	**DEFN** fend	**DELO** delo
CHLO loch	rock	**COYZ** cozy	**DEFO** feod	dole
CHLY lych	**CKOS** sock	**CPSU** cups	**DEFS** feds	lode
CHMU chum	**CKOW** cowk	cusp	**DEFT** deft	**DELP** pled
much	**CKPS** SPCK	scup	**DEFU** feud	**DELS** sled
CHNO chon	**CKPU** puck	**CPUY** Cuyp	**DEFY** defy	**DELU** duel
CHOO coho	**CKRU** ruck	**CRSU** crus	**DEGI** Gide	**DELV** veld
CHOP chop	**CKSU** cusk	curs	gied	**DELW** lewd
CHOS cosh	suck	scur	**DEGL** geld	weld
CHOT coth	**CKTU** tuck	**CRSY** scry	gled	**DELY** yeld
Toc H	**CKUY** yuck	**CRTU** curt	**DEGO** doge	**DEMN** mend
CHOU chou	**CLLU** cull	**CRUX** crux	**DEGR** dreg	**DEMO** demo
ouch	**CLMU** culm	**CSSU** cuss	**DEGS** degs	dome
CHOW chow	**CLOO** cool	**CSTU** cuts	**DEGY** edgy	Edom
CHRU Chur	loco	scut	**DEHI** heid	mode
CHSU cush	**CLOS** cols	**CSTY** cyst	hide	**DEMR** derm
such	**CLOT** clot	**DDDO** Dodd	hied	**DEMY** demy
CHWY wych	colt	**DDEE** deed	**DEHL** held	**DENO** done
CIKK kick		**DDEI** deid	**DEHO** hoed	node

DENP pend	**DFLO** fold	idyl	**DMOS** doms	spud
DENR nerd	**DFNO** fond	**DIMN** mind	mods	**DPUU** pudu
rend	**DFNU** fund	**DIMS** dims	**DMOU** doum	**DRSU** surd
DENS dens	**DFOO** food	mids	**DMPU** dump	urds
ends	**DFOR** ford	**DINO** Indo-	**DMRU** drum	**DRSY** drys
send	**DFRY** fyrd	nodi	**DMSU** muds	**DRTU** turd
sned	**DFUU** Du Fu	Odin	**DNOO** doon	**DSSU** suds
DENT dent	**DFUY** Dufy	**DINR** Drin	Ondo	**DSTU** dust
tend	**DGIL** gild	rind	**DNOP** pond	stud
DENU dune	**DGIN** ding	**DINS** dins	**DNOR** Nord	**DTUY** duty
nude	**DGIR** gird	sind	**DNOS** dons	**DUUW** wudu
DENV vend	grid	**DINT** dint	nods	**EEEP** epee
DENW wend	**DGIS** digs	**DINU** Idun	**DNOU** doun	**EEFJ** jefe
DENY deny	**DGIU** guid	**DINW** wind	udon	**EEFK** keef
dyne	**DGLO** gold	**DIOR** Dior	undo	**EEFL** feel
DENZ Zend	**DGNO** dong	**DIOT** doit	**DNOW** down	flee
DEOP dope	**DGNU** dung	**DIOV** Ovid	**DNOY** yond	**EEFM** feme
oped	**DGOO** good	void	**DNRU** durn	**EEFR** fere
DEOR dero	**DGOS** dogs	**DIPR** drip	nurd	free
doer	gods	**DIPS** dips	**DNSU** duns	reef
dore	**DGOY** dogy	**DIQU** quid	**DNSY** synd	**EEFS** fees
Doré	**DGRU** drug	**DIRS** rids	**DNTU** dunt	**EEFT** feet
Oder	**DGSU** dugs	**DIRT** dirt	**DNWY** wynd	fete
redo	**DHII** Idhi	**DISS** diss	**DOOP** pood	**EEGH** ghee
rode	**DHIN** hind	**DIST** dits	**DOOR** door	**EEGK** geek
DEOS does	**DHIS** dish	**DISV** divs	odor	**EEGL** glee
dose	**DHLO** hold	vids	rood	**EEGN** gene
odes	**DHOO** hood	**DISY** yids	**DOOS** doos	**EEGO** ogee
DEOT dote	**DHOS** dohs	**DITY** tidy	**DOOW** wood	**EEGR** eger
toed	dosh	**DITZ** ditz	**DOPR** dorp	gree
DEOV dove	hods	**DIUW** Wu Di	drop	**EEGS** gees
DEOW owed	shod	**DJLO** Jodl	prod	**EEHL** heel
DEOZ doze	**DHOT** doth	**DJOO** dojo	**DOPS** dops	hele
DEPS sped	**DHOU** Oudh	Jodo	pods	**EEHM** heme
DEPU dupe	**DHOW** dhow	**DJOU** judo	**DOPU** doup	**EEHR** here
DERS reds	**DHOY** yodh	**DJUY** judy	**DOPY** dopy	Rhee
DERU rude	**DHRU** Hurd	**DKNU** dunk	**DOQU** quod	**EEHT** thee
rued	**DHTU** thud	**DKOO** dook	**DORS** dors	**EEHW** whee
urde	**DIIL** Dili	**DKOR** dork	rods	**EEIR** Eire
DERV derv	**DIIM** midi	**DKOU** douk	**DORT** dort	Erie
Revd	**DIIN** nidi	**DKSU** dusk	trod	**EEJP** jeep
DERW drew	**DIIR** irid	**DKUU** kudu	**DORU** dour	**EEJR** jeer
DERY drey	**DIIV** divi	**DLLO** doll	duro	**EEJT** jete
dyer	**DIKN** dink	**DLLU** dull	**DORW** word	**EEKK** keek
DEST teds	kind	**DLMO** mold	**DORY** dory	**EEKL** keel
DESU deus	**DIKR** dirk	**DLNU** Lund	**DOSS** doss	Klee
dues	**DIKS** disk	**DLOP** plod	sods	leek
Duse	kids	**DLOR** lord	**DOST** dost	**EEKM** meek
sued	skid	**DLOS** dols	dots	**EEKN** keen
used	**DILL** dill	sold	tods	knee
DESW dews	**DILM** mild	**DLOT** dolt	**DOSU** duos	**EEKP** keep
weds	**DILN** lind	told	ouds	peek
DESY deys	**DILO** diol	**DLOU** loud	udos	peke
dyes	idol	ludo	**DOSW** dows	**EEKR** reek
DESZ zeds	lido	**DLOW** wold	**DOSY** doys	**EEKS** ekes
DETU duet	Lodi	**DLOY** odyl	yods	seek
DEWY dewy	olid	**DLOZ** Łódź	**DOSZ** dzos	**EEKW** week
DEYZ Yezd	**DILS** lids	**DLSU** luds	**DOTY** tody	**EELN** Néel
DFFO doff	sild	**DLUY** duly	**DOXY** doxy	**EELP** peel
DFFU duff	slid	**DMOO** doom	**DOYZ** dozy	pele
DFIN find	**DILW** wild	mood	**DPSU** dups	Pelé
DFIS fids	**DILY** idly	**DMOR** dorm	puds	**EELR** leer

Code	Word
	reel
EELS	eels
	else
	lees
	seel
EELT	leet
	tele
EELU	Uele
EELW	weel
EELY	eely
EEMM	meme
EEMN	neem
EEMR	mere
EEMS	seem
	seme
EEMT	meet
	mete
	teem
EEMZ	meze
	mzee
EENN	nene
EENP	neep
	peen
	pene
EENR	erne
	reen
EENS	seen
EENT	teen
EENV	even
	neve
EENW	ween
EEPP	peep
EEPR	peer
	pere
EEPS	pees
	seep
EEPV	veep
EEPW	weep
EERS	seer
	sere
EERT	Erté
	rete
	tree
EERU	Eure
EERV	erev
	ever
	veer
EERW	ewer
	weer
	were
EERY	eyre
EESS	esse
	sees
EEST	Este
	tees
EESV	eves
EESW	ewes
	wees
EESX	exes
EESY	eyes
EESZ	zees
EETW	twee
EFFI	fief
	fife
EFFJ	jeff
EFFS	effs
EFFT	teff
EFGN	Genf
EFHT	heft
EFIK	kief
EFIL	file
	lief
	life
EFIN	fine
	nife
EFIR	fier
	fire
	rife
EFIS	seif
EFIV	five
EFIW	wife
EFKR	kerf
EFKY	fyke
EFLL	fell
EFLO	floe
EFLP	pelf
EFLS	self
	left
EFLT	felt
EFLU	flue
	fuel
EFLW	flew
EFLX	flex
EFLY	fley
EFMU	fume
EFNR	fern
EFNS	fens
EFOR	fore
	froe
	orfe
EFOS	foes
EFOX	Foxe
EFRS	refs
	serf
EFRT	fret
	reft
	tref
EFRU	Urfé
EFRY	Frey
EFSS	fess
EFST	efts
	fest
EFSU	feus
	fuse
EFTW	weft
EFUZ	fuze
EGGS	eggs
EGGY	yegg
EGHU	huge
EGIL	glei
EGIN	gien
	Inge
EGIS	egis
	gies
EGIT	gite
EGIV	give
EGKN	Genk
EGKS	kegs
	skeg
EGLN	glen
EGLO	loge
	ogle
EGLS	gels
	legs
EGLT	gelt
EGLU	glue
	luge
EGLY	gley
EGMR	germ
EGMS	gems
EGMU	geum
EGNO	gone
EGNS	engs
	gens
EGNT	gent
EGNU	genu
EGOR	ergo
	goer
	gore
	ogre
	rego
	Roeg
EGOS	egos
	geos
	goes
EGOV	vego
EGPS	pegs
EGPU	Pegu
EGRS	ergs
	Gers
EGRU	grue
	urge
EGRW	grew
EGRX	grex
EGRY	grey
	gyre
EGST	gest
	gets
	tegs
EGTZ	Getz
EGVY	gyve
EHHT	heth
EHIK	hike
EHIR	heir
	hire
EHIS	hies
EHIV	hive
EHJU	jehu
EHKO	hoke
EHKS	kesh
EHKU	kueh
EHLL	hell
EHLM	helm
EHLO	hole
EHLP	help
EHLR	herl
	lehr
EHMO	home
EHMP	hemp
EHMR	herm
EHMS	hems
	mesh
	Shem
EHMT	meth
	them
EHMU	Hume
EHNO	hone
EHNR	hern
EHNS	hens
	nesh
EHNT	hent
	then
EHNW	hewn
	when
EHOP	hope
EHOR	hero
	hoer
EHOS	hoes
	hose
	shoe
EHOT	theo-
EHOV	hove
EHOW	howe
EHPT	hept
EHPW	phew
EHPY	hype
EHRS	hers
	resh
EHSS	Hess
	sesh
	shes
EHST	eths
	hest
	hets
	Seth
EHSU	hues
EHSW	hews
	shew
EHSY	heys
EHTT	teth
EHTW	thew
	whet
EHTY	they
EHWW	whew
EHWY	whey
EIIV	Veii
EIJV	jive
EIKK	kike
EIKL	Kiel
	like
EIKM	mike
EIKN	kine
	Nike
EIKP	kepi
	pike
EIKR	kier
EIKS	Eisk
	seik
	sike
EIKT	kite
	tike
EIKV	Kiev
EIKY	yike
EILM	lime
	mile
EILN	lien
	line
	Nile
EILO	Leo I
EILP	pile
	plie
EILR	lire
	riel
	rile
EILS	Elis
	isle
	leis
	lies
EILT	lite
	tile
EILU	lieu
EILV	evil
	Levi
	live
	veil
	vile
	vlei
EILW	weil
	wile
EILX	ilex
	Leix
EIMM	mime
EIMN	Emin
	mien
	mine
EIMR	emir
	Meir
	mire
	rime
EIMS	mise
	semi
EIMT	emit
	item
	mite
	time
EINN	nine
EINO	onie
EINP	pine
EINR	Erin
	Neri
	rein
	Reni
EINS	sine
EINT	tine
EINU	Niue
EINV	nevi
	vein
	vine
EINW	Wien

	wine	**EKLW**	kewl		leno		neum	**ENRT**	rent
EINZ	zein	**EKLY**	kyle		León	**EMOP**	mope		tern
	zine		yelk		lone		poem	**ENRU**	rune
EIOS	Oise	**EKMO**	moke		noel		pome	**ENRW**	wren
EIPP	pipe	**EKMP**	kemp	**ELNS**	lens	**EMOR**	moer	**ENSS**	ness
EIPR	peri	**EKNO**	keno	**ELNT**	lent		more	**ENST**	nest
	pier	**EKNR**	kern	**ELNU**	lune		omer		nets
	ripe		renk	**ELOO**	oleo		Rome		sent
EIPS	pies	**EKNS**	kens	**ELOP**	lope	**EMOS**	some		sten
	pise		neks		pole	**EMOT**	mote		tens
EIPW	wipe		sken	**ELOR**	lore		tome	**ENSW**	news
EIPZ	pize	**EKNT**	kent		Orel	**EMOU**	moue		sewn
EIRS	Eris	**EKNU**	neuk		orle	**EMOV**	move		wens
	reis		nuke		role	**EMOW**	meow	**ENSY**	nyes
	rise	**EKNW**	knew	**ELOS**	lose	**EMPR**	perm		snye
	sire	**EKOP**	poke		oles	**EMPT**	empt		syne
EIRT	Réti	**EKOR**	kero		sloe		temp		yens
	rite	**EKOS**	Keos		sole	**EMRT**	term	**ENTT**	nett
	tier		okes	**ELOT**	Leto	**EMRU**	mure		tent
	tire		soke		tole	**EMSS**	mess	**ENTU**	tune
EIRV	rive	**EKOT**	keto	**ELOV**	levo	**EMST**	stem	**ENTV**	vent
	vier		toke		love	**EMSU**	emus	**ENTW**	newt
EIRW	weir	**EKOW**	woke		ovel		meus		went
	wire	**EKOY**	yoke		vole		muse	**ENTX**	next
EISS	sies	**EKPR**	perk	**ELOW**	lowe	**EMSW**	mews	**ENTY**	tyne
EIST	site	**EKPS**	keps		Löwe		smew	**ENVY**	envy
	ties		skep	**ELOX**	Leo X	**EMTU**	mute	**EOOS**	oose
EISV	Ives		spek	**ELPT**	lept	**EMTZ**	Metz	**EOOZ**	ooze
	vies	**EKPT**	kept		pelt	**EMZZ**	mezz	**EOPP**	pepo
	vise	**EKPU**	puke	**ELPU**	plue	**ENNO**	neon		poep
EISW	wise	**EKPY**	kype		pule		none		pope
EISZ	size	**EKRR**	Kerr	**ELPW**	plew	**ENNP**	Penn	**EOPR**	pore
EITU	etui	**EKRS**	erks	**ELPY**	yelp	**ENOP**	nope		repo
EITW	wite	**EKRT**	trek	**ELRU**	lure		open		rope
EITX	exit	**EKRU**	Kure		rule		peon	**EOPS**	epos
EITY	yeti	**EKST**	sekt	**ELRY**	lyre		pone		opes
	yite		sket		rely	**ENOR**	Nero		peso
EIVV	vive	**EKSW**	skew		Ryle		oner		pose
EIVW	view	**EKSY**	esky	**ELSS**	less		Orne	**EOPT**	poet
	wive		keys		sels		Reno		tope
EJKO	joke		Skye	**ELST**	lest		rone	**EOPX**	expo
EJKR	jerk	**EKTY**	kyte		lets	**ENOS**	Enos	**EORS**	eros
EJLL	jell		tyke	**ELSU**	lues		eons		ores
EJLO	Joel	**ELLS**	ells		slue		noes		roes
EJOS	joes		sell	**ELSW**	slew		nose		rose
EJOT	Tejo	**ELLT**	tell		Wels		ones		sore
EJOV	Jove	**ELLU**	Elul	**ELSY**	lyes		sone	**EORT**	rote
EJOY	joey	**ELLW**	well		lyse	**ENOT**	Eton		tore
EJSS	jess	**ELLY**	Lely	**ELTU**	lute		note	**EORU**	euro
EJST	jest		Lyle	**ELTW**	welt		Teno		roue
	jets		yell	**ELTY**	lyte		tone	**EORV**	over
EJSU	Jesu	**ELMO**	lome	**ELUX**	luxe	**ENOV**	oven		rove
EJSW	jews		Lomé	**ELUY**	yule	**ENOW**	enow	**EORW**	ower
EJTU	jute		mole	**ELVY**	levy		Owen		owre
EKKS	keks	**ELMR**	merl	**ELWY**	Weyl	**ENOX**	exon		Rowe
EKLM	Melk	**ELMS**	elms	**EMMO**	memo		Nexø		wero
EKLO	koel	**ELMT**	melt	**EMMS**	mems		oxen		wore
EKLP	kelp	**ELMU**	mule	**EMNO**	meno	**ENOZ**	zone	**EORY**	oyer
EKLS	elks	**ELMW**	mewl		nome	**ENPS**	pens		yore
	leks	**ELMY**	lyme		omen	**ENPT**	pent	**EORZ**	zero
EKLT	kelt		ylem	**EMNT**	ment	**ENPU**	Pune	**EOST**	toes
EKLU	luke	**ELNO**	enol	**EMNU**	menu	**ENRS**	erns	**EOSU**	Ouse

EOSV	voes	ESST	sets	FILM	film	FOXY	foxy	GINT	ting
EOSW	owes	ESSU	sues		flim	FRSU	furs	GINW	wing
	woes		uses	FILO	filo		surf	GINZ	zing
EOSY	oyes	ESSW	sews		foil	FRTU	turf	GIOR	giro
EOTT	tote	ESTT	sett	FILP	flip	FRUY	fury	GIOS	gios
EOTV	veto		stet	FILS	fils	FSSU	fuss	GIOV	Vigo
	vote		test	FILT	flit	FSUU	Sufu	GIOY	yogi
EOTY	eyot	ESTU	suet		lift	FTTU	tuft	GIOZ	Zog I
	toey		utes	FIMR	firm	FTUU	Tu Fu	GIPR	grip
EOVW	wove	ESTV	vest	FINN	Finn	FUZZ	fuzz		prig
EOWY	yowe		vets	FINO	fino	GGHO	Gogh	GIPS	gips
EOYZ	oyez	ESTW	stew		foin		hogg		pigs
EPPR	prep		west		info	GGIN	ging	GIRR	girr
	repp		wets	FINR	firn	GGIR	grig	GIRS	gris
EPPS	peps	ESTX	sext	FINS	fins	GGIS	gigs		rigs
EPRS	reps	ESTY	stye	FIPS	spif	GGLU	glug	GIRT	girt
EPRT	pert	ESTZ	zest	FIRS	firs	GGNO	gong		grit
EPRU	Peru	ESUZ	Suez		rifs		nogg		trig
	pure		Zeus	FIRT	frit	GGOO	gogo	GIRY	gyri
EPRV	perv	ESWY	yews		rift		goog	GIST	gist
EPRY	prey	ETTX	text	FIST	fist	GGOR	grog		gits
	pyre	ETTY	yett		fits	GGUV	vugg		tigs
EPST	pest	FFGU	guff		sift	GHHI	high	GISW	swig
	pets	FFHU	huff	FISU	Sufi	GHIN	nigh		wigs
	sept	FFII	fifi	FIZZ	fizz	GHIS	Gish	GITW	twig
	step	FFIJ	jiff	FKLO	folk		sigh	GJNO	jong
EPSU	spue	FFIM	miff	FKNU	funk	GHIW	whig	GJNU	Jung
EPSW	pews	FFIN	niff	FKOR	fork	GHNO	hong	GJOS	jogs
	spew	FFIR	riff	FKOU	Kofu	GHNU	hung	GJSU	jugs
EPSY	espy	FFIT	tiff	FLLU	full	GHOS	gosh	GKNO	gonk
	pyes	FFIY	iffy	FLOO	fool		hogs	GKNU	gunk
	Spey	FFIZ	ziff	FLOP	flop	GHOU	Hugo		Küng
EPTW	wept	FFLU	luff	FLOR	rolf	GHOY	yogh	GKOO	gook
EPTY	pyet	FFMU	muff	FLOT	loft	GHSU	gush	GKOW	gowk
	type	FFOR	Orff	FLOU	foul		hugs	GLLU	gull
ERRS	errs	FFOT	toff	FLOW	flow	GHTU	thug	GLMO	glom
ERRU	ruer	FFPU	puff		fowl	GHUV	vugh	GLMU	glum
ERSS	sers	FFRU	ruff		wolf	GIIR	Rigi	GLNO	long
ERST	erst	FFTU	tuff	FLRU	furl	GIJS	jigs	GLNU	lung
	rest	FGIR	frig	FLUX	flux	GIKN	gink	GLOO	logo
	rets	FGIS	figs	FMOO	mofo		king	GLOS	Glos
ERSU	Reus	FGIT	gift	FMOR	form	GIKO	Kogi		logs
	rues	FGIU	Gifu		from	GILL	gill		slog
	ruse	FGLO	flog	FMUY	fumy	GILM	glim	GLOU	Lugo
	suer		golf	FNOT	font	GILN	ling	GLOW	glow
	sure	FGLU	gulf	FNSU	funs	GILR	girl		gowl
	user	FGNU	fung	FOOP	poof	GILS	ligs	GLOY	logy
ERSV	revs	FGOO	goof	FOOR	roof	GILT	gilt	GLPU	gulp
	vers	FGOR	frog	FOOT	foot	GILU	iglu		plug
ERSY	ryes	FGOS	fogs	FOOW	woof	GIMN	ming	GLSU	lugs
	Yser	FGOY	fogy	FOOY	oofy	GIMP	gimp		slug
ERTT	tret	FGSU	fugs		yoof	GIMR	grim	GLTU	glut
ERTU	true	FHIS	fish	FOPR	prof	GIMS	migs	GLUY	ugly
ERTV	Tver	FHNO	fohn	FOPS	fops	GINO	ingo	GMNO	mong
	vert	FHOO	hoof	FOPU	pouf	GINP	ping	GMNU	mung
ERTW	wert	FHOW	howf	FORT	fort	GINR	girn	GMOR	gorm
ERTY	trey	FIIJ	Fiji	FORU	four		grin	GMOS	mogs
	tyre	FIIN	Ifni	FORW	frow		ring		smog
ERTZ	Retz	FIJU	fuji	FOSS	foss	GINS	gins	GMSU	gums
ERUV	eruv	FIKN	fink	FOST	soft		sign		mugs
ERUY	Urey	FILL	fill	FOTT	toft		sing		smug
ERVY	very			FOTU	tofu		snig	GMSY	gyms

GNNO nong
GNNU Gunn
GNOO goon
GNOP pong
GNOS gons
nogs
snog
song
GNOT tong
GNOU Ogun
GNOW gnow
gown
GNPU pung
GNRU gurn
rung
GNSU gnus
guns
snug
sung
GNTU tung
GNWY Gwyn
GNYY gyny
GOOP goop
pogo
GOOS goos
GOOT Togo
GOPR prog
GOPY pogy
GORS Gros
GORT grot
trog
GORW grow
GORY gory
Györ
gyro
orgy
GORZ Görz
GOSS goss
GOST togs
GOSW wogs
GOSY goys
GOTU gout
GOUZ Zoug
GPSU pugs
spug
GPSY gyps
GRSU rugs
GRTU trug
GRUU guru
GSTU gust
guts
tugs
GSUV guvs
vugs
GSUY guys
HHJV JHVH
HHSU hush
HHUU huhu
HHVY YHVH
HIIM mihi
HIKS kish
Sikh

HIKT kith
HILL hill
HILO Holi
HILT hilt
lith
HIMS Hims
shim
HIMW whim
HINS hins
nish
shin
sinh
HINT hint
thin
HINW whin
HIOO Ohio
HIOP Ipoh
HIOR hori
HIOT thio
HIPS hips
phis
pish
ship
HIPT pith
HIPW whip
HIPZ phiz
HIRW whir
HISS hiss
HIST hist
hits
shit
sith
this
HISV shiv
HISW wish
HITW whit
with
HIWZ whiz
HJNO john
HJOS josh
HKLO kohl
HKLU hulk
HKNO honk
HKNU hunk
HKOO hook
HKOP koph
HKOW howk
HKSU husk
Kush
HLLU hull
HLMO holm
HLOP holp
HLOS hols
HLOT holt
loth
HLOW howl
HLOY holy
HLRU hurl
HLSU lush
shul
HLWY hwyl
HMNY hymn

HMOO homo
HMOR Röhm
HMOS Homs
mhos
mosh
ohms
shmo
HMOT moth
HMOW whom
HMOY homy
HMPU hump
HMSU hums
mush
HMTY myth
HNOO hoon
HNOP phon
HNOR horn
HNOS nosh
HNOT thon
HNSU huns
shun
Thun
HOOP hoop
pooh
HOOS shoo
soho
HOOT hoot
HOPQ qoph
HOPS hops
posh
shop
HOPT phot
HOPW whop
HOPY hypo
HORS rhos
HORT Roth
Thor
thro
HORU hour
HOSS sohs
HOST host
hots
shot
tosh
HOSW hows
show
HOSY hoys
HOSZ zhos
HOTU thou
HPSU push
HPSY hyps
HPTU phut
HPUW whup
HRRU Ruhr
HRSU rhus
rush
HRSY Rhys
HRTU hurt
ruth
thru
HSSU huss

HSTU huts
shut
thus
tush
HSWY whys
HUUW Wuhu
IIKT tiki
IIKW kiwi
IILP pili
IIMN mini
IIMP impi
IIMR miri
IINP I-pin
IINR INRI
IINS nisi
IINT inti
IIPP pipi
IIPT tipi
IIRS iris
IISS Isis
IISW iwis
IITT titi
IIXZ Zi Xi
IJKN jink
IJLL jill
IJLT jilt
IJMS jism
IJNN jinn
IJNO join
IJNR Rijn
IJNX jinx
IJZZ jizz
IKKN kink
IKKR kirk
IKLL kill
IKLM milk
IKLN kiln
link
IKLO kilo
Loki
IKLS ilks
silk
IKLT kilt
IKLU Luik
IKMN mink
IKMO moki
IKMR mirk
IKMS skim
IKNO ikon
kino
oink
IKNP pink
IKNR rink
IKNS inks
kins
sink
skin
IKNT knit
IKNW wink
IKNY inky
IKOR Okri
IKOS oiks

IKPP kipp
IKPS kips
skip
spik
IKRS irks
kris
risk
IKRU kuri
IKSS kiss
skis
IKST kist
kits
skit
IKUV Kivu
ILLM mill
ILLO lilo
ILLP pill
ILLR rill
ILLS ills
sill
ILLT lilt
till
ILLW will
ILLY lily
ILMN limn
ILMO limo
milo
moil
ILMP limp
ILMS mils
slim
ILMT milt
ILMY limy
ILNN linn
ILNO lino
lion
loin
noil
ILNT lint
ILNY inly
liny
ILNZ Linz
ILOO olio
ILOP Li Po
ILOR roil
ILOS oils
silo
soil
soli
ILOT loti
toil
ILOV viol
ILOY oily
ILPS lips
lisp
slip
ILPU puli
ILST list
lits
silt
slit
ILTT tilt

ILTU	litu		tins		Witt	KOPY	poky	LORT	rotl
ILTW	wilt	INSU	unis	ITUW	Wu Ti	KORS	Orsk	LORU	lour
ILVV	Lviv	INSW	wins	ITZZ	tizz	KORU	koru	LORY	lory
ILVY	Livy	INTT	tint	IUWX	Wuxi	KORW	work		Orly
ILWY	wily	INTU	unit	IZZZ	zizz	KORY	york	LOSS	loss
IMMO	momi	INTW	twin	JJUU	juju	KOSU	souk		sols
IMNO	mino	INTY	tiny	JKNU	junk	KOSW	woks	LOST	lost
	Miño	INVY	viny	JKOO	jook	KOUZ	zouk		lots
IMNT	mint	INWY	winy	JKOU	jouk	KRSU	rusk		slot
IMNX	minx	IOPR	Pori	JKOY	joky	KRTU	turk	LOSU	lous
IMOO	mooi	IOPS	pois	JLOO	Jolo	KRUU	kuru		soul
IMOR	Miró	IOPT	topi	JLOS	jols	KSTU	tusk	LOSW	lows
IMOS	miso	IORS	sori	JLOT	jolt	KSUY	kyus		owls
IMOT	omit	IORT	riot	JLOW	jowl	KTUU	kutu		slow
IMOZ	Mo-Zi		roti	JMOO	mojo	LLLO	loll	LOSY	loys
IMPP	pimp		tiro	JMPU	jump	LLLU	lull	LOTU	lout
IMPR	prim		tori	JNOU	Juno	LLMO	moll		tolu
IMPS	imps		trio	JOOT	Tojo	LLMU	mull		Toul
	simp	IOSS	Ossi	JOSS	joss	LLNU	null	LOTV	volt
IMPW	wimp	IOTT	Tito	JOST	jots	LLOP	poll	LOUU	Oulu
IMQU	quim	IOVV	vivo	JOSY	joys	LLOR	roll	LOVV	Lvov
IMRS	rims	IPPS	pips	JRUY	jury	LLOT	toll	LOWW	Lwów
	smir	IPPY	pipy	JSTU	just	LLPU	pull	LOWY	yowl
IMRT	trim	IPQU	quip		juts	LLTU	Tull	LPPU	pulp
IMRU	muir	IPRS	rips	KKOO	kook	LLUU	lulu	LPRU	purl
	rimu	IPRT	trip	KLNO	Köln	LLYY	Lyly	LPSU	plus
IMRV	mirv	IPRU	puir	KLNU	lunk	LMOO	loom		puls
IMRY	miry		puri	KLOO	kolo	LMOS	olms	LRSU	slur
	rimy	IPSS	piss		look	LMOT	molt	LRUY	ruly
	Ymir		psis	KLOP	polk	LMOU	Lomu	LSTU	lust
IMSS	isms		sips	KLOS	skol	LMOY	moly		slut
	miss	IPST	pits	KLOV	volk	LMPU	lump	LSUU	sulu
IMST	mist		spit	KLOY	yolk		plum	LTUZ	lutz
	smit		tips	KLRU	lurk	LMSU	lums	LUUZ	zulu
	stim	IPSV	spiv	KLSU	sulk		slum	MMMU	mumm
IMSW	swim	IPSW	wisp	KMNO	monk	LNNY	Lynn	MMOS	moms
IMTT	mitt	IPSY	yips	KMOO	moko	LNOO	loon	MMPU	mump
IMTU	muti	IPSZ	zips		mook	LNOR	lorn	MMSU	mums
INNS	inns	IPTT	Pitt	KMOS	Omsk	LNOY	Lyon	MNOO	mono
INOP	pion	IPTY	pity	KMRU	murk	LNRU	nurl		moon
INOR	iron	IPUY	Pu-yi	KMRY	Krym	LNUY	luny	MNOR	morn
	noir	IPXY	pixy	KMSU	musk	LNXY	lynx		norm
	nori	IQTU	quit	KNOO	nook	LOOP	loop	MNOS	mons
INOS	ions	IQUZ	quiz	KNOP	knop		polo	MNOU	muon
	Sion	IRRY	yirr	KNOR	nork		pool	MNOW	mown
INOT	into	IRSS	sirs	KNOT	knot	LOOS	loos	MNOY	mony
INOV	vino	IRST	stir		tonk		Oslo	MNTU	munt
INOW	wino	IRTW	writ	KNOW	know		solo	MOOR	moor
INOY	yoni	IRTZ	ritz		wonk		sool		Moro
INOZ	Zion	IRWY	wiry	KNOX	Knox	LOOT	loot		room
INPR	pirn	ISST	sits	KNPU	punk		tool	MOOS	moos
INPS	nips	ISTT	tits	KNRU	knur	LOOW	wool	MOOT	moot
	pins	ISTU	suit	KNSU	sunk	LOPP	plop	MOOZ	zoom
	snip		tuis	KNTU	knut	LOPS	lops	MOPP	pomp
	spin	ISTW	wist	KNUU	Nuuk		slop	MOPR	prom
INPT	pint		wits	KOOP	pook	LOPT	plot		romp
INPY	piny	ISTZ	sitz	KOOR	rook	LOPU	loup	MOPS	mops
INQU	quin		zits	KOOS	sook	LOPW	lowp		poms
INRU	ruin	ISWY	ywis	KOOT	koto		plow	MOPY	mopy
INSS	sins	ISWZ	swiz		took	LOPY	ploy		yomp
INST	nits	ISYZ	sizy	KOPR	pork		poly	MORS	mors
	snit	ITTW	twit	KOPS	kops			MORT	mort

MORW worm	**NOOX** Oxon	**NTXY** Xnty	**OPSY** posy		swot
MOSS moss	**NOOZ** zoon	**OOPP** poop	**OPTT** pott		tows
MOST most	**NOPR** porn	**OOPR** poor	**OPTU** pout		twos
mots	**NOPS** pons	**OOPS** oops	**OPTY** pyot	**OSTY** toys
toms	**NOPT** pont	**OOPT** topo	typo	**OSUX** Oxus
MOSU muso	**NOPU** upon	**OORS** roos	**OPXY** poxy	**OSUY** yous
sumo	**NOPY** pony	**OORT** Oort	**ORRT** rort	**OSVW** vows
MOSW mows	**NORS** sorn	root	torr	**OSWW** wows
MOSY somy	**NORT** torn	roto	**ORSS** Ross	**OTTU** tout
MOTU motu	tron		**ORST** orts	**OTWY** towy
MOUV ovum	**NORW** worn	**OOST** soot	rots	**PPSU** pups
MOXY myxo	**NORZ** Zorn	Soto	sort	**PRRU** purr
MOZZ mozz	**NOSS** sons	**OOSW** woos	tors	**PRSU** spur
MPPU pump	**NOST** snot	**OOSY** oosy	**ORSU** ours	**PRSY** spry
MPRU rump	tons	**OOSZ** zoos	sour	**PRTU** Prut
MPSU sump	**NOSU** nous	**OOTT** otto	**ORSW** rows	**PSST** psst
MPTU tump	onus	toot	**ORSY** rosy	**PSSU** puss
MPUY umpy	Osun	**OOTZ** zoot	Syro-	sups
MRSU smur	**NOSW** owns	**OOUZ** ouzo	**ORTT** tort	**PSTU** puts
MSSU muss	snow	**OOYZ** oozy	trot	tups
sums	sown	**OPPR** prop	**ORTU** rout	**PTTU** putt
MSTU must	wons	**OPPS** pops	tour	**PTUZ** putz
muts	**NOSY** nosy	**OPRS** pros	**ORTW** trow	**QSSU** suqs
smut	**NOTU** toun	**OPRT** port	wort	**RRTY** Tyrr
stum	unto	**OPRU** pour	**ORTY** ryot	**RRUU** ruru
tums	**NOTW** nowt	roup	tory	**RSSU** USSR
MSUW swum	town	**OPRW** prow	troy	**RSTT** Trst
MSUY Sumy	wont	**OPRY** pyro	tyro	**RSTU** rust
MTTU mutt	**NOTY** tony	ropy	**ORUV** vrou	ruts
MUZZ muzz	**NOXY** onyx	yorp	**ORUX** roux	**RSUU** urus
NNNU Nunn	**NPSU** puns		**ORUY** your	**RTUY** yurt
NNOO Nono	spun	**OPSS** poss	**ORXY** oryx	**SSSU** suss
noon	**NPTU** punt	sops	**OSSS** soss	**SSUU** susu
NNOR Norn	**NPUY** puny	**OPST** opts	**OSST** sots	**SSUW** wuss
NNOU noun	**NRSU** runs	post	toss	**STTU** tuts
NNSU nuns	urns	pots	**OSSU** sous	**STXY** Styx
sunn	**NRTU** runt	spot	**OSSW** sows	xyst
NOOP poon	turn	stop	**OSTT** stot	**TTUU** tutu
NOOS soon	**NSSU** suns	tops	tots	
NOOT onto	**NSTU** nuts	**OPSU** opus	**OSTU** oust	
oont	stun	soup	outs	
toon	tuns	**OPSW** pows	**OSTW** stow	
		swop		
		wops		

Five Letters

AAABC	abaca	AABJR	Rajab		kacha	AADIN	Aidan	AAEHK	hakea
	Caaba	AABJU	Abuja	AACHP	pacha		Diana	AAEKL	akela
AAABK	Kaaba	AABKN	banak	AACIR	acari		naiad	AAEKP	apeak
AAABQ	Aqaba		Banka		Arica	AADIS	Saadi	AAEKW	awake
AAADN	Adana	AABKR	Akbar		Caria		Saida	AAELP	palea
AAAGM	agama		bakra	AACIS	Isaac	AADIW	Wadai	AAELR	areal
AAAGN	Agaña		Barak	AACJL	Cajal	AADJJ	Djaja	AAELT	alate
AAAIS	A'asia	AABLN	Alban	AACKL	alack	AADJW	Wajda	AAEMR	maare
AAAMP	Amapá		banal	AACKY	yacka	AADKK	Akkad		marae
AAANS	asana		Laban	AACLL	calla	AADKR	Dakar	AAEMZ	amaze
AAANT	anata		nabla	AACLN	canal		Kádár	AAENP	apnea
AAANZ	Azaña	AABLR	labra		Lacan	AADLN	Aldan		paean
AAARU	Aarau	AABLS	balas	AACLS	scala	AADLS	salad	AAENR	anear
AAASV	Vaasa		balsa	AACLT	Talca	AADLT	datal		arena
AAATT	taata		basal	AACMN	caman	AADLU	Lauda	AAENT	Aetna
AABBR	Babar	AABLT	tabla	AACMO	Macao	AADLW	dwaal		antae
AABBS	abbas	AABMM	mamba	AACMS	camas	AADMM	madam	AAEOZ	zoaea
	babas	AABMP	abamp	AACMU	Macáu	AADMN	adman	AAEQU	aquae
AABBY	yabba	AABMS	samba	AACMW	macaw		daman	AAERS	areas
AABCK	aback	AABNT	Banat	AACNN	canna	AADMO	Damão	AAERU	aurae
AABCL	cabal	AABNW	bwana	AACNT	tacan	AADMR	damar	AAERW	aware
AABCR	barca		nawab	AACNV	Cavan		drama	AAFFJ	Jaffa
AABCS	abacs	AABRR	barra	AACPR	Capra	AADMS	Adams	AAFHI	Haifa
AABCU	Bacău	AABRS	Basra	AACPS	pacas	AADNP	panda	AAFHS	haafs
AABDE	baaed		sabra		scapa	AADNR	Nadar	AAFIL	Faial
	Baeda	AABRT	rabat	AACPU	Capua	AADNV	vanda	AAFIM	mafia
AABDN	banda	AABRU	Aruba	AACRS	sacra		V and A	AAFIT	tafia
AABEK	Bekaa	AABRY	Araby	AACRT	carat	AADNY	dayan	AAFJN	Najaf
AABEM	abeam	AABRZ	bazar	AACSW	waacs	AADOV	Davao	AAFJS	jafas
	ameba	AACCD	Accad	AACUV	vacua	AADOW	Adowa	AAFKK	Kafka
AABES	abase	AACCE	caeca	AADDH	dadah	AADPR	Arpád	AAFKN	nakfa
AABET	abate	AACCO	cacao	AADDX	addax	AADPT	adapt	AAFLL	Falla
AABFT	abaft	AACCR	Accra	AADEF	faaed	AADPU	Padua	AAFLS	alfas
AABGL	Galba	AACCU	Cauca	AADEG	adage	AADRR	radar	AAFLT	fatal
AABGM	gamba	AACCY	yacca	AADEH	ahead	AADRV	Drava	AAFLY	Fayal
AABGR	Braga	AACDE	caaed	AADEN	Danaë	AADRW	award	AAFNU	fauna
	Gabar	AACDH	dacha	AADFR	daraf	AADSS	Assad	AAFRS	Safar
AABHI	Baha'í	AACDI	Dacia		farad	AADST	Sadat	AAFTW	fatwa
	Bahia	AACDU	cauda	AADGG	dagga	AADTW	Waadt	AAGGR	ragga
AABHM	hamba	AACEI	aecia	AADGN	Dagan	AADTY	adyta	AAGGW	wagga
AABHS	abash	AACEN	Canea	AADGR	garda	AADUW	Aduwa	AAGHL	galah
	Sabah	AACEP	apace	AADHK	Dhaka	AAEFN	faena	AAGHN	Ghana
	Shaba	AACER	areca	AADHL	hadal	AAEGL	algae	AAGHR	Hagar
AABIL	labia		Ceará	AADHN	adhan		galea	AAGHS	aghas
AABIR	braai	AACFI	facia		Dahna	AAEGP	agape	AAGHT	Gatha
	Rabia	AACGN	Gäncä	AADHW	dawah	AAEGT	agate	AAGIN	again
AABJN	bajan	AACHK	Chaka	AADIM	Amida	AAEGV	agave	AAGIS	saiga

ABB | 5 letter words

Code	Words
AAGIT	taiga
AAGJN	ganja
AAGJS	jagas
AAGKN	kanga
AAGLL	algal
AAGLN	lagan
AAGLO	Laoag
AAGLR	argal
AAGLS	galas
AAGLV	vagal
AAGLY	gayal
AAGMM	gamma, magma
AAGMN	manga
AAGMR	Agram, grama
AAGMS	agmas
AAGHT	tagma
AAGNP	pagan, panga
AAGNS	nagas, Sagan
AAGNT	tanga
AAGOR	agora
AAGPR	apgar
AAGRS	ragas
AAGSS	sagas
AAGUV	guava
AAHHS	hahas
AAHHT	hatha
AAHIN	Hania
AAHIS	Aisha
AAHJR	rajah
AAHKM	Khama
AAHKS	hakas, kasha, Shaka
AAHLL	Allah, halal
AAHLM	halma, hamal
AAHLN	nahal
AAHLO	aloha
AAHLP	alpha
AAHLR	lahar
AAHLS	Lhasa
AAHLT	latah
AAHLV	halva
AAHMO	Omaha
AAHMR	haram
AAHMS	amahs
AAHMZ	hamza
AAHNN	Hanna
AAHNS	hansa
AAHNU	Hanau
AAHNZ	hazan
AAHOR	aroha
AAHPR	Praha
AAHPS	pasha
AAHRR	Harar
AAHRS	haars, Sarah
AAHRT	arhat, ratha
AAHRV	Varah
AAHRY	rayah
AAHSW	awash
AAHSY	ayahs
AAHWZ	Ahwaz
AAIIL	aalii
AAIKK	kaiak
AAIKS	Kasai, sakai
AAIKT	akita, kiaat
AAIKU	Kauai
AAILM	lamia
AAILN	lanai, liana
AAILR	laari
AAILS	alias
AAILV	avail, Ávila
AAILX	axial
AAIMN	amain, amnia, anima, mania
AAIMR	maria
AAIMT	Amati, matai
AAIMZ	zamia
AAINP	apian
AAINR	Arian, naira
AAINS	Asian
AAINV	avian
AAIPR	Praia
AAIPS	paisa
AAIPV	Pavia
AAIRS	arias, raias
AAIRT	aarti, atria, raita, tiara
AAIRV	varia
AAIRZ	Zaria
AAISS	assai
AAIST	satai
AAISV	Saiva
AAITW	await, tawai
AAJKS	Askja
AAJLP	jalap
AAJNP	japan
AAJNV	Javan
AAJNW	jawan
AAJPS	jaaps
AAJRS	rajas
AAKKS	kakas
AAKKY	kayak, yakka
AAKLO	koala
AAKLP	kalpa
AAKLR	kraal
AAKLS	laksa
AAKLT	Kalat
AAKMR	karma, makar, marka
AAKNN	Nanak
AAKNR	Karan
AAKNT	tanka
AAKNZ	Kazan
AAKOS	Asoka, Osaka
AAKOT	Takao
AAKPP	kappa
AAKPR	parka
AAKPS	Spaak
AAKRS	araks, karas, Sarka
AAKRT	karat, Katar
AAKRW	Kwara
AAKSS	Kassa
AAKST	katas, takas
AAKSV	kavas
AAKSW	wakas
AAKTZ	zakat
AALLM	llama
AALLO	Alloa
AALLU	alula
AALLV	Laval, Valla
AALLW	walla
AALLY	allay
AALMM	malam
AALMO	alamo
AALMP	Palma
AALMR	alarm, malar, Mälar
AALMS	lamas, malas
AALMT	Malta
AALMU	ulama
AALMW	malwa
AALNN	annal
AALNS	nasal
AALNT	natal
AALNV	naval
AALNY	nyala
AALOT	Aalto
AALPP	appal, papal
AALPS	paals, plaas, salpa
AALPT	Plata
AALPU	Palau
AALPY	playa
AALPZ	La Paz, plaza
AALQT	talaq
AALRT	altar, artal, ratal
AALRU	aural
AALRV	larva
AALRY	alary
AALRZ	lazar
AALSS	Lassa, salsa
AALST	Aalst, atlas, Salta, talas
AALTY	Yalta
AALWY	alway
AAMMM	mamma
AAMMN	amman
AAMMS	mamas
AAMNN	Annam, manna
AAMNS	Masan
AAMNT	atman, manat, manta
AAMNX	axman
AAMNY	mayan
AAMOR	aroma
AAMOS	omasa, Samoa
AAMPR	Parma
AAMPT	Tampa
AAMRS	maars, maras, Maraş, Samar
AAMRT	Marat
AAMSS	amass, assam, massa
AAMSY	mayas
AAMTU	amaut
AAMTZ	matza
AANNN	Annan, nanna
AANNS	annas, naans, nanas
AANNW	wanna
AANNY	Yanan
AANOR	Aaron
AANOS	anoas
AANOX	xoana
AANPP	nappa
AANPR	prana
AANPT	Patna
AANPV	pavan
AANPY	Panay
AANRR	Arran
AANRS	saran
AANRT	antra, ratan
AANRV	Narva, navar, varna
AANRY	Arany
AANST	Santa, Satan, tanas, Tsana
AANSU	sauna
AANSW	Aswan
AANSY	Nyasa
AANSZ	azans
AANTT	Tanta
AANTV	avant
AAORT	aorta
AAOST	Aosta
AAPPS	papas
AAPPU	Papua
AAPPW	papaw
AAPPZ	Zappa
AAPRR	parra
AAPRS	paras
AAPRT	apart
AAPST	pasta, tapas
AAPSU	pauas
AAPSY	Pasay
AAPTW	watap
AAQRT	Qatar
AAQRZ	Zarqa
AAQSU	aquas
AARRS	arras
AARRU	Arrau, aurar
AARRY	array
AARST	rasta, ratas
AARSU	auras
AARSV	varas
AARTT	attar, tatar
AARTW	Warta
AARTY	tayra
AARTZ	Taraz, Tzara
AASSY	assay
AASTV	avast
AASTW	tawas
AASTY	satay
AASWW	wawas
AASWY	aways
AATXY	ataxy
AATZZ	tazza
ABBCO	cabob
ABBCY	cabby
ABBDE	abbed
ABBEK	kebab
ABBEL	babel
ABBER	Baber
ABBES	abbes, babes

ABB | 5 letter words

Code	Word	Code	Word	Code	Word	Code	Word	Code	Word
ABBEY	abbey		blade	ABEHJ	hejab		barer	ABHRS	brash
ABBGY	gabby	ABDEN	Baden	ABEHL	belah		barre	ABHRT	Barth
ABBIM	bambi		Benda	ABEHN	Behan		Berar	ABHST	bahts
ABBIR	rabbi	ABDEO	abode	ABEHO	bohea	ABERS	bares		baths
ABBKO	kabob		adobe		obeah		baser	ABHSU	habus
ABBLO	Balbo	ABDER	ardeb	ABEHR	Brahe		bears		subah
ABBLS	blabs		Bader		rehab		braes		subha
ABBLU	babul		barde	ABEHS	saheb		saber	ABIIL	alibi
	bubal		bared		Sheba		sabre		Libia
ABBNO	nabob		beard	ABEHT	bathe	ABERU	Auber	ABIIM	iambi
ABBOS	boabs		bread	ABEIR	Beira	ABERV	brave	ABIIT	tibia
ABBOT	abbot		Breda		Beria	ABERY	barye	ABIIZ	Ibiza
ABBRS	barbs		debar	ABEIS	Basie		yerba	ABIJM	Jambi
ABBRU	Babur	ABDES	based	ABEIZ	baize	ABERZ	braze	ABIKL	kibla
ABBRY	barby		beads	ABEJM	jambe		zebra	ABIKR	Kabir
ABBSU	babus	ABDET	bated	ABEJR	Jerba	ABESS	bases	ABIKT	batik
ABBTY	tabby	ABDEU	daube	ABEKL	Blake	ABEST	abets	ABILN	binal
ABBYY	yabby	ABDEY	bayed		bleak		baste		blain
ABCCY	baccy		beady	ABEKR	baker		bates	ABILQ	Iqbal
ABCEH	beach	ABDHN	bandh		brake		beast		qibla
ABCEI	ceiba	ABDIL	Blida		break		beats	ABILR	Arbil
ABCEK	Baeck	ABDIR	Baird	ABEKS	bakes		betas		Blair
ABCEL	cable		braid		beaks		tabes		brail
ABCER	Barce		rabid	ABEKY	beaky	ABESU	abuse		libra
	brace	ABDIU	Dubai	ABELL	label		beaus	ABILS	bails
	caber	ABDLN	bland	ABELM	amble	ABESY	abyes		basil
ABCHI	Chiba	ABDLO	dobla		blame		bayes	ABILT	balti
ABCHR	brach	ABDLY	badly		Melba	ABETT	betta	ABILU	Libau
ABCHT	batch		baldy	ABELR	abler	ABETU	beaut	ABILY	Libya
ABCIN	cabin	ABDNR	brand		baler		tubae	ABIMR	mbira
ABCIO	cobia	ABDNS	bands		belar	ABETY	beaty	ABIMS	bimas
ABCIR	baric	ABDNU	Dubna		blare	ABEUX	beaux		iambs
	rabic	ABDNY	bandy		blear	ABFFN	Banff		simba
ABCIS	basic		Danby	ABELS	baels	ABFRU	fubar	ABIMT	ambit
ABCJO	Jacob	ABDOR	bardo		bales	ABFRY	Fabry	ABINQ	niqab
ABCKL	black		board		Basel	ABGGR	Bragg	ABINR	bairn
ABCKR	brack		broad		Basle	ABGGY	baggy		brain
ABCKS	backs		dobra		blaes	ABGHN	bhang		Brian
ABCLN	Blanc		dorba		blase	ABGHS	baghs		Rabin
ABCMS	Cambs	ABDOS	doabs		sable	ABGIR	Bragi	ABINS	basin
ABCNO	bacon	ABDRS	bards	ABELT	bleat	ABGLS	blags		nabis
	banco		brads		table	ABGNO	bogan		sabin
ABCNU	Cuban		drabs		Taleb		Gabon	ABINU	nubia
ABCOR	Broca	ABDRY	Darby	ABELU	Belau	ABGNS	bangs	ABIOT	biota
	carbo	ABDSU	bauds	ABELY	bayle	ABGOR	Gabor	ABIQS	Qabis
	carob		daubs		belay		garbo	ABIRR	briar
	cobra	ABDSW	bawds	ABELZ	blaze	ABGRS	brags	ABIRS	abris
ABCOT	Cabot	ABDUY	dauby	ABEMP	Pemba		garbs		rabis
ABCOV	vocab	ABDWY	bawdy	ABEMR	amber		grabs	ABISS	basis
ABCRS	crabs	ABEEL	abele		bream				bassi
ABCRT	bract		albee	ABEMS	beams			ABIST	baits
ABCRY	carby		Beale	ABEMY	beamy				basti
ABCSS	scabs	ABEFL	fable		embay	ABHIJ	bhaji	ABJLU	Jubal
ABCSU	scuba	ABEFR	Fabre		maybe		hijab	ABJMO	jambo
ABDDY	baddy	ABEGI	bagie	ABENO	beano	ABHIM	bimah	ABJMS	jambs
ABDEG	badge	ABEGL	bagel	ABENS	Asben	ABHIO	Bohai	ABJNO	banjo
	begad		belga		banes	ABHIR	Bihar	ABJOT	jabot
	debag		gable		beans	ABHIS	sahib	ABJSU	jubas
ABDEI	abide	ABEGN	began	ABENV	Bevan	ABHIT	habit	ABKLN	blank
ABDEK	baked	ABEGR	barge	ABENY	beany	ABHKL	Balkh	ABKLS	balks
ABDEL	abled	ABEGS	Gabès	ABEOV	above	ABHLS	blahs	ABKLU	baulk
	baled	ABEGT	begat	ABERR	Arber	ABHMO	abohm		Kabul
						ABHOR	abhor		
						ABHOS	basho		
						ABHOT	Botha		

Code	Word
ABKLY	balky
ABKNS	banks
ABKNU	Kuban
ABKOR	borak
ABKOS	boaks
ABKRS	barks
ABKRU	burka
ABKSS	basks
ABKST	Bakst
ABLLS	balls
ABLLU	bulla
ABLLY	bally
ABLMS	balms
	lambs
ABLMU	album
ABLMY	balmy
ABLNU	balun
ABLOR	labor
	lobar
ABLOS	bolas
ABLOT	bloat
ABLOY	boyla
ABLRT	blart
ABLRU	lubra
ABLRW	brawl
ABLSS	slabs
ABLST	blast
	blats
ABLSW	bawls
ABLTU	tubal
ABLWY	bylaw
ABMMO	mambo
ABMOS	ambos
	bomas
	sambo
ABMOT	Tambo
ABMOZ	Zomba
ABMRS	barms
ABMRU	Burma
	rumba
	umbra
ABMRY	ambry
	barmy
ABMSU	Sumba
ABMSY	abysm
ABMTU	Batum
ABMUY	mauby
ABNNS	banns
ABNNU	unban
ABNOR	baron
ABNOT	baton
ABNRS	barns
ABNRT	brant
ABNRU	Braun
	buran
	unbar
	urban
ABNRW	brawn
ABNTU	bantu
	tabun
ABNUY	bunya
ABOOT	taboo
ABOOZ	bazoo
ABORR	arbor
	barro
ABORS	boars
	boras
	Borås
ABORT	abort
	boart
	tabor
ABORV	bravo
ABORX	borax
ABORY	boyar
ABOSS	basso
ABOST	boast
	boats
	sabot
ABOSV	Basov
ABOTU	about
ABOUY	bayou
ABPST	Pabst
ABQRU	burqa
ABQSU	squab
ABRRU	Burra
ABRRY	barry
ABRSS	brass
ABRST	brats
	trabs
ABRSU	Arbus
	Brusa
	buras
	bursa
	Busra
ABRSW	warbs
ABRSY	brays
ABRWY	warby
ABRXY	braxy
ABSST	stabs
ABSSW	swabs
ABSSY	abyss
ABSTT	batts
ABSTU	abuts
	tabus
	tubas
ABTTY	batty
	Byatt
ABUZZ	abuzz
ABWYY	byway
ACCDY	cycad
ACCEH	cache
ACCEL	cecal
ACCEM	mecca
ACCHO	chaco
	coach
ACCHT	catch
ACCIR	circa
	craic
ACCIT	cacti
ACCIW	wicca
ACCKL	clack
ACCKR	crack
ACCKY	cacky
ACCLU	Lucca
ACCMO	occam
ACCNZ	CCANZ
ACCOO	cocoa
ACCOS	cocas
	Sacco
ACCUY	yucca
ACDDY	caddy
ACDEF	decaf
	faced
ACDEG	cadge
	caged
ACDEH	ached
ACDEK	caked
ACDEL	clade
	decal
	laced
ACDEM	maced
ACDEN	caned
	dance
ACDEP	paced
ACDER	acred
	arced
	cadre
	cared
	cedar
	raced
ACDES	cades
	cased
	daces
	ecads
ACDET	acted
	cadet
ACDEV	caved
ACDEW	cawed
ACDEY	decay
ACDHO	chado
ACDHR	chard
ACDHT	Tchad
ACDHY	daych
ACDIN	canid
	nicad
ACDIR	acrid
	caird
	cardi
	daric
	Dirac
ACDIS	acids
	asdic
	cadis
ACDIT	dicta
ACDIY	acidy
ACDIZ	Cádiz
ACDKR	drack
ACDKS	dacks
ACDLS	clads
	scald
ACDLU	cauld
	ducal
ACDNY	candy
ACDOR	draco
ACDOS	codas
ACDOT	octad
ACDRS	cards
ACDRY	cardy
	darcy
ACDSS	scads
ACDSU	scaud
ACDTU	ducat
ACEEK	ackee
ACEEP	peace
ACEES	cease
ACEFH	chafe
ACEFL	fecal
ACEFR	facer
	farce
ACEFS	cafes
	faces
ACEFT	facet
ACEGL	glace
ACEGN	Gance
ACEGR	grace
ACEGS	cages
ACEGY	cagey
ACEHK	cheka
ACEHL	chela
	leach
ACEHN	hance
ACEHP	chape
	cheap
	peach
ACEHR	reach
ACEHS	aches
	chase
ACEHT	cheat
	tache
	teach
	theca
ACEIL	Alice
	ileac
ACEIM	amice
ACEIN	Caine
ACEIR	ceria
	erica
ACEIS	saice
ACEIV	cavie
ACEKL	aleck
ACEKP	Čapek
ACEKR	acker
	crake
	creak
ACEKS	cakes
ACEKW	wacke
ACEKY	cakey
ACELL	cella
	macle
ACELM	camel
ACELN	Celan
	clean
	lance
ACELP	Calpe
	place
ACELR	carle
	Clare
	clear
	lacer
ACELS	alecs
	claes
	laces
	scale
ACELT	cleat
	eclat
ACELV	calve
	cavel
	clave
ACEMO	cameo
	comae
ACEMR	Carme
	Ceram
	cream
	macer
	Merca
ACEMS	acmes
	cames
	maces
ACEMY	cymae
ACENO	canoe
	ocean
ACENP	pecan
ACENR	caner
	Carné
	crane
	nacre
	rance
ACENS	canes
	scena
ACENT	enact
ACEOR	ocrea
ACEOX	coxae
ACEPR	caper
	crape
	pacer
	recap
ACEPS	capes
	paces
	scape
	space
ACEPT	Capet
	epact
ACEPY	pacey
ACERR	carer
	racer
ACERS	acers
	acres
	cares
	carse
	races
	scare
	serac
ACERT	caret
	carte
	cater
	crate
	react
	recta
	trace
ACERV	carve

caver
crave
varec
ACERW Carew
ACERY Carey
ACERZ craze
ACESS cases
ACEST caste
cates
taces
ACESU cause
sauce
ACESV caves
ACESY Cayes
ACETT tacet
ACETU acute
Ceuta
ACETX exact
ACFFH chaff
ACFFS caffs
ACFHU chufa
ACFIL calif
ACFIR farci
ACFKL flack
ACFLO focal
ACFNR franc
ACFNY fancy
ACFRS scarf
ACFRT craft
ACFRU furca
ACFRY farcy
ACFST facts
ACGHN chang
ACGIM gamic
magic
ACGIN acing
ACGIR cigar
craig
ACGLN clang
ACGLS clags
ACGNO conga
ACGNS cangs
ACGOR cargo
ACGOU guaco
ACGRS crags
scrag
ACGSS scags
ACHHT hatch
ACHIK haick
ACHIL Haliç
ACHIM Micah
ACHIN chain
Chian
china
ACHIR chair
Chari
ACHIT aitch
Chita
ACHKL chalk
ACHKS hacks
shack
ACHKW chawk

whack
ACHLO loach
ACHLR larch
ACHLS clash
ACHLT latch
ACHLU luach
ACHMO choma
macho
mocha
ACHMP champ
ACHMR charm
march
ACHMS chams
chasm
ACHMT match
ACHNO nacho
ACHNR ranch
ACHNT chant
natch
nucha
ACHOP poach
ACHOR orach
roach
ACHOS chaos
ACHOT Catho
tacho
ACHOV havoc
ACHPR parch
ACHPS chaps
Pasch
ACHPT patch
ACHRR charr
ACHRS chars
crash
ACHRT chart
ACHRY chary
ACHSS Sachs
ACHST chats
ACHSU sauch
ACHSW chaws
schwa
ACHTW watch
ACHTY yacht
ACHUV vauch
ACIIL cilia
iliac
ACIIN acini
ACILL lilac
ACILM claim
malic
ACILN linac
ACILP plica
ACILR Clair
ACILS laics
salic
ACILT ictal
tical
ACILU aulic
ACILV cavil
ACILX calix
ACILY Lycia

ACIMN manic
ACIMR micra
ACIMS micas
ACINN Cinna
ACINO Ciano
ACINP panic
ACINR cairn
ACINT actin
antic
ACINV vinca
ACIOR Cairo
coria
ACIOT coati
ACIOZ azoic
ACIPR Capri
carpi
ACIPS aspic
Pašić
picas
spica
ACIPZ capiz
ACIRT artic
ACIRU auric
curia
ACIRV vicar
ACIRX Craxi
ACISU Caius
ACITT attic
tacit
ACITU Utica
ACITV vatic
ACJKS jacks
ACJKY jacky
ACJNU cajun
ACKKN knack
ACKLN clank
ACKLO cloak
ACKLR Clark
ACKLS calks
lacks
slack
ACKLU caulk
ACKMS macks
smack
ACKMU amuck
ACKNR crank
ACKNS snack
ACKOR croak
ACKOW wacko
ACKPS packs
ACKPU pucka
ACKQU quack
ACKRS carks
racks
ACKRT track
ACKRW wrack
ACKSS casks
sacks
ACKST stack
tacks
ACKSW wacks
ACKSY yacks

ACKTY tacky
ACKWY wacky
ACLLO local
ACLLS calls
scall
ACLMO cloam
comal
ACLMP clamp
ACLMS calms
clams
ACLNS clans
Lancs
ACLNU Lucan
ACLOP copal
ACLOR carol
claro
coral
Lorca
ACLOS alcos
coals
colas
ACLOT octal
ACLOV vocal
ACLOW cowal
ACLOX coxal
ACLOY coaly
ACLOZ colza
ACLPS claps
clasp
scalp
ACLPU culpa
ACLRS carls
ACLRW crawl
ACLRY clary
ACLSS class
ACLST talcs
ACLSU cauls
Lucas
ACLSW claws
ACLSY clays
scaly
ACLXY calyx
ACMMO comma
ACMNO macon
Mâcon
Nam Co
ACMOP campo
ACMOR carom
macro
Maroc
ACMOS comas
ACMPR cramp
ACMPS camps
scamp
ACMPY campy
ACMRS crams
marcs
scram
ACMRY cymar
ACMSS scams
ACMSU camus
musca

sumac
ACMSY cymas
ACNNO ancon
canon
ACNNY canny
nancy
ACNOP capon
Copán
ACNOR acorn
narco
racon
ACNOS canso
ACNOT acton
canto
cotan
ACNOY cyano
ACNPU pucan
uncap
ACNRS crans
narcs
scran
ACNRY carny
ACNSS scans
ACNST canst
cants
scant
ACNTY canty
ACOPR copra
ACOPS capos
scopa
ACOPT capot
ACORS oscar
ACORT actor
Croat
ACORY oracy
ACOST ascot
coast
coats
costa
octas
tacos
ACOTT cotta
ACPPU cuppa
ACPRS carps
craps
scarp
scrap
ACPRY crapy
ACPST pacts
ACPSU scaup
ACPTU caput
ACRRS carrs
ACRRU crura
ACRRY carry
ACRSS crass
scars
ACRST carts
scart
ACRSU scaur
ACRSW craws
scraw
ACRSY crays

Code	Word
	scary
ACRSZ	czars
ACRTT	tract
ACRTY	Tracy
ACRYZ	crazy
ACSST	casts
	scats
ACSSU	ascus
ACSTU	scuta
ACSUY	saucy
ACTTY	catty
ADDDE	added
ADDDY	daddy
ADDEF	faded
ADDEH	haded
ADDEI	aided
ADDEJ	jaded
	Jedda
ADDEL	addle
	daled
	dedal
	laded
ADDER	adder
	dared
	dread
	readd
ADDET	dated
ADDEW	waded
ADDEZ	dazed
ADDFY	faddy
ADDGI	gadid
ADDIJ	Jidda
ADDIV	David
ADDLY	Lydda
ADDNY	dandy
ADDOS	dados
	saddo
ADDPY	paddy
ADDRY	dryad
ADDSU	dauds
	duads
ADDSY	dyads
ADDWY	waddy
ADEEM	edema
	Meade
	Medea
ADEEN	Deane
ADEER	eared
	Reade
ADEES	aedes
	eased
ADEEV	deave
	evade
ADEFG	fadge
ADEFK	faked
ADEFM	famed
ADEFR	fader
	fared
ADEFS	fades
ADEFT	fated
ADEFX	faxed
ADEFY	fayed
ADEFZ	fazed
ADEGG	gaged
ADEGI	Adige
ADEGL	glade
ADEGM	gamed
ADEGP	gaped
	paged
ADEGR	Edgar
	grade
	radge
	raged
ADEGS	degas
ADEGT	gated
ADEGW	waged
ADEGZ	gazed
ADEHJ	jehad
ADEHK	Kedah
	kheda
ADEHL	haled
ADEHN	Haden
ADEHR	hared
	heard
ADEHS	hades
	heads
	sadhe
	shade
ADEHT	death
	hated
ADEHW	hawed
ADEHX	hexad
ADEHY	hayed
	heady
ADEHZ	hazed
ADEIL	ailed
	ideal
ADEIM	aimed
	amide
	media
ADEIR	aider
	aired
	irade
	redia
ADEIS	aides
	aside
	Desai
	ideas
ADEIU	adieu
ADEIZ	azide
ADEJP	japed
ADEJS	jades
ADEJU	Judea
ADEJW	jawed
ADEKN	knead
	naked
ADEKR	drake
	Radek
	raked
ADEKS	asked
ADELL	ladle
ADELM	lamed
	medal
ADELN	Dalén
	eland
	laden
ADELP	paled
	pedal
	plead
ADELR	Adler
	alder
	lader
ADELS	dales
	deals
	lades
	lased
	leads
ADELT	dealt
	delta
	lated
ADELV	laved
ADELW	dwale
	waled
	weald
ADELY	delay
	leady
ADELZ	lazed
ADEMN	admen
	amend
	deman
	maned
	Medan
	menad
	named
ADEMR	armed
	derma
	dream
ADEMS	dames
	meads
ADEMT	mated
	tamed
ADEMZ	mazed
ADENO	anode
ADENP	paned
	Penda
ADENR	André
	Arden
	denar
	Nader
	redan
ADENS	Andes
	deans
	sedan
	Sedna
	Snead
ADENT	anted
	Dante
ADENU	Auden
ADENV	daven
	vaned
	Venda
ADENW	awned
	dewan
	waned
ADEOR	adore
	oared
	oread
ADEPR	drape
	padre
	pared
	raped
ADEPS	spade
	spaed
ADEPT	adept
	taped
ADEPV	paved
ADEPW	pawed
ADEPY	payed
ADERR	darer
	drear
ADERS	arsed
	dares
	dears
	rased
	reads
ADERT	rated
	tared
	trade
	tread
ADERV	drave
	raved
ADERW	dewar
	wader
	wared
ADERX	raxed
ADERY	deary
	rayed
	ready
ADERZ	razed
ADESS	sades
ADEST	dates
	sated
	stead
	tsade
ADESV	devas
	saved
ADESW	Dawes
	sawed
	wades
ADESZ	adzes
	dazes
ADETW	tawed
ADETX	taxed
ADEVW	waved
ADEWX	waxed
ADEWY	yawed
ADFFR	draff
ADFFS	daffs
ADFFY	daffy
ADFIU	Fuad I
ADFLO	Faldo
ADFNO	fonda
ADFOS	fados
ADFRT	draft
ADFRU	fraud
ADFRW	dwarf
ADGGY	daggy
ADGIL	algid
ADGIU	Gaudí
ADGLN	gland
ADGLS	glads
ADGMO	dogma
ADGNO	Dagon
	donga
	gonad
ADGNR	grand
ADGNW	dwang
ADGNY	gandy
ADGOS	dagos
	goads
ADGOU	Gouda
ADGRS	dargs
	drags
	grads
ADGRU	Durga
	guard
ADGSU	gauds
ADGUY	gaudy
ADHIJ	hadji
	jihad
ADHIK	khadi
ADHIL	halid
ADHIM	Mahdi
ADHIN	Dinah
ADHIO	Idaho
ADHIP	aphid
ADHIS	dashi
ADHJU	Judah
ADHKS	dhaks
ADHLS	dhals
ADHNO	donah
ADHNS	hands
ADHNU	hudna
ADHNY	handy
	Haydn
ADHOR	hoard
ADHRS	hards
	shard
ADHRY	hardy
	hydra
ADHSS	shads
ADHST	hadst
ADHSU	hauds
	sadhu
ADHSY	shady
ADIIL	iliad
ADIIN	Aidin
	India
ADIIO	oidia
ADIIR	radii
ADIKS	kadis
ADIKU	aduki
ADILN	nidal
ADILP	plaid
ADILR	drail
	laird
	liard
ADILS	dials
ADILT	Dalit
	tidal

ADILU dulia
ADILV valid
      Vidal
ADILY daily
      Lydia
ADIMN admin
      mandi
ADIMO amido
ADIMS maids
      Midas
ADIMT admit
ADIMX admix
ADINN Dinan
      dinna
ADINO danio
ADINR dinar
      drain
      Indra
      nadir
ADINV divan
      Dvina
      viand
ADINW diwan
ADINY Aydin
ADIOP podia
ADIOR aroid
      Dario
      radio
ADIOS adios
ADIOU audio
      Douai
      Ouida
ADIOV avoid
ADIOZ diazo
ADIPR rapid
ADIPS sapid
ADIPV pavid
      vapid
ADIQS qadis
ADIRS raids
      Sidra
ADIRT triad
ADIRX radix
ADIRY dairy
      diary
ADIRZ izard
ADISS saids
ADIST adits
      ditas
      staid
ADISU Saudi
ADISV Davis
      divas
ADISY daisy
      sayid
ADITU audit
ADITV davit
ADJNU Dunaj
ADJOU Oujda
ADJSU judas
ADKKU dukka
ADKLS skald

ADKLY alkyd
ADKNR drank
ADKNY kandy
ADKOR Korda
ADKOV vodka
ADKRS darks
ADKRY darky
ADKSU dukas
ADKSW dawks
ADLLO aldol
      allod
ADLLU Udall
ADLLY dally
ADLMO dolma
      modal
ADLMY madly
ADLNO Ndola
      nodal
      Öland
ADLNS lands
ADLNY Dylan
ADLOS loads
ADLOT dotal
ADLOU aloud
      doula
ADLOW waldo
      woald
ADLRS lards
ADLRU dural
ADLRW drawl
ADLRY lardy
      Rydal
ADLSU duals
      lauds
ADLSY sadly
ADLTU adult
ADLUY yauld
ADMNO monad
      nomad
ADMNS damns
ADMNU maund
ADMOR Radom
ADMOU douma
ADMPS damps
ADMRS drams
ADMRU mudra
ADMRY mardy
ADMSU adsum
      dumas
      mauds
ADMSW dwams
ADMTU datum
ADMUW dwaum
ADNNO donna
ADNNY danny
ADNOO doona
ADNOR adorn
      Donar
      radon
ADNOS donas
ADNOU Donau
ADNPY pandy

      Pydna
ADNRS darns
      nards
      rands
ADNRU Durán
ADNRW drawn
ADNRY randy
ADNSS sands
ADNST stand
ADNSU Sudan
ADNSW dawns
      wands
ADNSY sandy
ADNTU daunt
ADOPR Prado
ADOPT adopt
ADORR ardor
ADORS dorsa
      roads
      sarod
ADORT troad
ADORU doura
ADOSS sodas
ADOST datos
      doats
      toads
ADOSV Davos
ADOTY toady
      today
ADPRS draps
      pards
ADPRU purda
ADPSU Padus
ADQSU quads
      squad
ADRRU durra
ADRST darts
      strad
ADRSU daurs
      duras
      Sudra
ADRSW draws
      sward
      wards
ADRSY drays
      yards
ADRTY tardy
ADSTU adust
ADUVZ Vaduz
AEEFZ feaze
AEEGL aglee
      eagle
AEEGP peage
AEEGR agree
      eager
      eagre
AEEHV heave
      hevea
AEEIL Eleia
AEEIR aerie
AEEKN akene
AEEKP Peake

AEEKR rakee
AEEKS akees
AEELN anele
AEELS easel
      lease
AEELT elate
      telae
AEELV leave
AEEMN enema
      Nemea
AEEMR ameer
      ramee
AEENR arene
      ranee
AEENT eaten
      enate
AEENV venae
AEEOZ zoeae
AEEPR perea
AEEPS pease
AEEPY payee
AEERR raree
AEERS easer
      erase
      saree
AEERT arete
      eater
AEERV reave
AEERZ razee
AEESS eases
AEEST setae
      tease
AEESV eaves
AEETX exeat
AEEVW weave
AEFFG gaffe
AEFGN ganef
AEFHS sheaf
AEFIR afire
      feria
AEFKL flake
AEFKN kenaf
AEFKR faker
      freak
AEFKS fakes
AEFLL fella
AEFLM flame
      fleam
AEFLR farle
      feral
      flare
AEFLS false
      fleas
      leafs
AEFLT fetal
AEFLY leafy
AEFMR frame
AEFMS fames
AEFNR frena
AEFNS fanes
AEFOR afore
AEFOV fovea

AEFPR frape
AEFRR farer
AEFRS fares
      fears
      safer
AEFRT after
AEFRU Fauré
AEFRW wafer
AEFRY faery
      fayre
      Freya
AEFSS safes
AEFST fates
      feast
      feats
AEFSX faxes
AEFSZ fazes
AEFUV fauve
AEGGR agger
      eggar
      gager
AEGGS gages
AEGGU gauge
AEGHM Egham
AEGHN Hagen
      Neagh
AEGHP phage
AEGHR gerah
AEGHU Hague
AEGIL agile
AEGIM image
AEGIR Aegir
AEGIS aegis
AEGJR jager
AEGLL Galle
      legal
AEGLM gleam
AEGLN angel
      angle
      Galen
      glean
      Lange
AEGLP plage
AEGLR Alger
      Elgar
      glare
      lager
      large
      regal
AEGLS gales
AEGLT aglet
AEGLV gavel
      Gävle
AEGLY agley
AEGLZ glaze
AEGMM gemma
AEGMN mange
AEGMO omega
AEGMR gamer
      marge
AEGMS games

mages	Lehár	**AEHSV** haves	**AEIRT** irate	**AEKRW** waker
AEGMY gamey	**AEHLS** hales	shave	retia	wreak
AEGNO agone	heals	**AEHSW** hawse	terai	**AEKSS** sakes
genoa	leash	**AEHSY** Hayes	**AEIRU** aurei	**AEKST** Keats
Onega	selah	**AEHSZ** hazes	**AEIRZ** zaire	skate
AEGNR anger	shale	**AEHTT** theta	Zaïre	stake
range	**AEHLT** lathe	**AEHTW** wheat	**AEIST** Saite	steak
AEGNS Agnes	**AEHLV** halve	**AEHVV** heavy	Satie	takes
geans	Havel	**AEIJK** Ikeja	**AEITV** vitae	**AEKSU** ukase
AEGNT agent	**AEHLW** whale	**AEIJX** jaxie	**AEITW** waite	**AEKSW** askew
Tange	wheal	**AEIKL** alike	**AEIVW** waive	wakes
AEGNU genua	**AEHLY** Haley	alkie	**AEJKS** jakes	wekas
AEGNV ganev	Healy	**AEIKN** Aiken	**AEJLV** javel	Wesak
vegan	**AEHLZ** hazel	**AEILL** ileal	**AEJMR** Ajmer	**AEKSY** Askey
AEGNW Agnew	**AEHMR** harem	**AEILM** email	**AEJMS** james	**AEKTW** tweak
AEGNY gynae	herma	**AEILN** alien	**AEJNS** janes	**AELLM** Malle
AEGPR gaper	**AEHMS** hames	aline	jeans	**AELLN** Allen
grape	shame	Laine	**AEJNT** Janet	**AELLP** lapel
pager	Shema	liane	**AEJPR** japer	Pella
AEGPS gapes	**AEHMT** meath	**AEILP** pilea	**AEJPS** japes	**AELLS** Ellás
pages	Mehta	**AEILR** ariel	jaspe	Sella
AEGRS gears	**AEHNN** Henan	**AEILS** aisle	**AEJST** tajes	**AELLU** Luleå
rages	henna	Elias	**AEKKM** Mekka	**AELLY** alley
sarge	**AEHNR** Ahern	**AEILT** Eilat	**AEKLN** ankle	**AELMM** lemma
AEGRT grate	**AEHNS** ashen	telia	**AEKLR** laker	**AELMN** leman
great	hanse	**AEILV** alive	**AEKLS** kales	Léman
targe	Nashe	**AEILX** axile	lakes	**AELMP** ample
terga	**AEHNT** neath	**AEIMN** amine	leaks	maple
AEGRU argue	thane	anime	slake	Palme
auger	**AEHNV** haven	Maine	**AEKLW** kwela	**AELMR** lamer
rugae	**AEHNY** hyena	minae	**AEKLY** leaky	realm
AEGRV grave	**AEHOR** Horae	**AEIMR** Marie	**AEKMN** Ekman	**AELMS** lames
AEGRW wager	**AEHOS** Hosea	ramie	**AEKMR** kerma	males
AEGRY gayer	**AEHOT** Tahoe	**AEIMS** amies	maker	meals
AEGRZ gazer	**AEHOV** hovea	Seami	**AEKMS** kames	melas
graze	**AEHPR** raphe	**AEIMZ** maize	makes	Salem
AEGSS gases	**AEHPS** ephas	Zeami	**AEKMT** Kamet	**AELMT** metal
sages	heaps	**AEINN** inane	**AEKNO** oaken	**AELMU** ulema
AEGST gates	phase	**AEINP** Paine	**AEKNP** pekan	**AELMY** mealy
stage	shape	**AEINS** Aisne	**AEKNR** naker	**AELNO** alone
AEGSU usage	**AEHRS** Asher	anise	**AEKNS** skean	anole
AEGSW swage	hares	isnae	snake	**AELNP** Nepal
wages	hears	Siena	sneak	panel
AEGSZ gazes	rheas	**AEINT** entia	**AEKNT** taken	penal
AEGTT Atget	share	Taine	**AEKNV** knave	plane
AEGTU Taegu	shear	tenia	**AEKNW** waken	plena
AEGUV vague	**AEHRT** earth	tinea	**AEKNY** Kenya	**AELNR** Larne
AEGUZ gauze	Harte	**AEINV** naevi	**AEKOR** Korea	learn
AEHHP ephah	heart	naive	**AEKOW** awoke	neral
AEHHT heath	Herat	**AEINX** xenia	**AEKPR** Perak	renal
AEHJZ Hejaz	rathe	**AEINZ** azine	**AEKPS** peaks	**AELNS** lanes
AEHKL Hekla	Thera	**AEIPS** paise	spake	leans
AEHKS hakes	**AEHRV** haver	sepia	speak	**AELNT** leant
Hašek	Havre	**AEIPT** pieta	**AEKPY** peaky	**AELNU** ulnae
shake	**AEHRW** whare	pietà	**AEKQU** quake	**AELNV** navel
AEHKW Hawke	**AEHRZ** hazer	**AEIPV** Piave	**AEKRR** raker	venal
AEHKY Hayek	**AEHSS** ashes	**AEIRS** aesir	**AEKRS** asker	**AELNY** Lenya
AEHLL Halle	sheas	Aries	eskar	**AELOS** aloes
Hallé	**AEHST** ashet	arise	rakes	**AELOV** laevo
AEHLM hemal	haste	raise	saker	**AELOZ** azole
AEHLP aleph	hates	serai	**AEKRT** taker	**AELPP** appel
AEHLR haler	heats		**AEKRU** Akure	apple

23

pepla	selva	**AEMST** mates	**AENSV** avens	pases
AELPR lepra	slave	meats	Evans	passe
paler	vales	satem	naves	spaes
pearl	valse	steam	Sevan	**AEPST** paste
AELPS lapse	**AELSW** Lawes	tames	vanes	pates
leaps	swale	teams	**AENSW** sewan	peats
pales	wales	**AEMSU** amuse	wanes	septa
peals	weals	**AEMSW** wames	weans	spate
pleas	**AELSX** axels	**AEMSX** exams	**AENSY** yeans	tapes
salep	axles	**AEMSY** samey	**AENSZ** senza	**AEPSU** pause
sepal	**AELSY** lyase	seamy	**AENTX** Texan	**AEPSV** paves
AELPT leapt	**AELSZ** lazes	**AEMSZ** mazes	**AENTZ** zante	**AEPSX** paxes
lepta	**AELTT** latte	smaze	**AENVW** navew	**AEPTU** taupe
petal	**AELTV** valet	**AEMTT** matte	**AENWX** waxen	**AEPTX** expat
plate	**AELTX** exalt	**AEMTY** etyma	**AENWY** waney	**AEPTY** peaty
pleat	latex	matey	Wayne	**AEPVY** peavy
tepal	**AELUV** uveal	meaty	**AENZZ** zazen	**AEQRU** quare
AELPY Paley	value	**AEMUV** mauve	**AEOPR** opera	**AERRR** rarer
AELQU equal	**AELVV** valve	**AEMYZ** mazey	**AEOPS** Aesop	**AERRS** raser
quale	**AELWY** Waley	**AENNP** panne	**AEOPT** potae	rears
AELRS arles	**AELZZ** lezza	penna	**AEORS** arose	Sarre
earls	**AEMMN** Menam	**AENNR** Renan	orate	serra
lares	**AEMMT** Mamet	**AENNS** senna	**AEORT** Erato	**AERRT** terra
laser	**AEMMY** mamey	**AENNT** anent	**AEORV** Évora	**AERRV** raver
rales	**AEMNN** Namen	**AENNX** annex	**AEOSS** oases	verra
reals	Neman	**AENNY** Yenan	**AEOST** Oates	**AERRY** yarer
AELRT alert	**AEMNR** Marne	**AENOP** paeon	stoae	**AERRZ** razer
alter	ramen	**AENOS** aeons	toeas	**AERSS** arses
artel	reman	Saône	**AEOSV** soave	rases
later	**AEMNS** amens	Soane	**AEOSZ** zoeas	rasse
ratel	manes	**AENOT** Aneto	**AEOTV** ovate	saser
taler	manse	atone	**AEOTZ** azote	sears
AELRU ureal	means	oaten	**AEPPR** paper	**AERST** aster
AELRV laver	mensa	**AENOV** novae	rappe	rates
ravel	names	**AENOX** axone	**AEPPU** pupae	reast
Reval	**AEMNT** ament	**AENPP** nappe	**AEPRR** parer	resat
velar	manet	Papen	**AEPRS** asper	stare
AELRW waler	meant	**AENPS** aspen	pares	tares
AELRX relax	**AEMNV** maven	napes	parse	tears
AELRY early	**AEMNX** axmen	neaps	pears	**AERSV** avers
layer	**AEMNY** meany	panes	prase	raves
leary	yamen	peans	presa	saver
relay	**AEMOR** morae	**AENPT** paten	rapes	**AERSW** sawer
AELSS lases	Morea	**AENPZ** Penza	reaps	swear
sales	**AEMOV** voema	**AENQU** quean	spare	wares
seals	**AEMOW** Maewo	**AENRR** reran	spear	wears
AELST least	**AEMRR** rearm	**AENRS** earns	**AEPRT** apter	**AERSX** raxes
leats	**AEMRS** mares	nares	pater	**AERSY** arsey
salet	maser	nears	peart	eyras
setal	reams	reans	Petra	sayer
slate	Seram	saner	prate	years
Staël	smear	snare	taper	**AERSZ** razes
stale	**AEMRT** armet	**AENRT** antre	**AEPRU** Apure	**AERTT** tater
steal	mater	**AENRV** Nerva	pareu	tetra
stela	tamer	raven	**AEPRV** parev	treat
taels	**AEMRW** Mewar	**AENRW** Warne	parve	**AERTU** urate
tales	**AEMRY** Mayer	**AENRY** yearn	paver	**AERTV** avert
teals	**AEMRZ** mazer	**AENSS** Assen	**AEPRY** apery	trave
tesla	**AEMSS** mases	sensa	payer	**AERTW** Ewart
AELSV avels	masse	**AENST** antes	Peary	tawer
laves	mesas	nates	repay	water
salve	seams	stane	**AEPSS** apses	**AERTX** extra

taxer	**AFGRT** graft	**AFLTY** fatly	Omagh	**AGKOP** gopak
AERTY teary	**AFHIR** Farhi	**AFLUW** awful	**AGHNO** hogan	**AGKSU** kagus
AERUZ azure	**AFHIT** faith	**AFLWY** flawy	**AGHNS** gnash	**AGKSW** gawks
AERVV varve	**AFHIZ** hafiz	**AFLXY** flaxy	hangs	**AGKWY** gawky
AERVW waver	**AFHLS** flash	**AFMOR** foram	sangh	**AGLLS** galls
AERWX waxer	**AFHRW** wharf	**AFMOS** foams	Shang	**AGLMU** mulga
AERWY weary	**AFHST** hafts	**AFMOY** foamy		**AGLNO** along
AESSS asses	shaft	**AFMRS** farms	**AGHNW** whang	logan
AESST asset	**AFHSU** haufs	**AFMSU** Musaf	**AGHOT** Gotha	**AGLNR** gnarl
sates	**AFIKL** kalif	**AFMUY** Fayum	**AGHPR** graph	**AGLNS** glans
seats	**AFIKR** fakir	**AFNNO** fanon	**AGHRT** garth	slang
tasse	kafir	**AFNNY** fanny	**AGHSS** shags	**AGLOO** agloo
AESSV saves	**AFILL** flail	**AFNRS** snarf	**AGHST** ghats	**AGLOP** galop
vases	**AFILN** final	**AFNRU** furan	**AGHSU** saugh	**AGLOR** algor
AESSX saxes	**AFILO** folia	**AFNRY** Frayn	ghaut	argol
AESSY essay	Olaf I	**AFNSU** fauns	**AGHUW** waugh	goral
AESSZ assez	**AFILP** pilaf		**AGIIT** atigi	largo
AESTT state	**AFILR** filar	**AFNSW** fawns	**AGIIV** vigia	**AGLOS** gaols
taste	flair	**AFOOT** afoot	**AGIKN** kiang	goals
teats	frail	**AFORS** afros	**AGILL** glial	Lagos
testa	Lifar	sofar	**AGILN** algin	**AGLOT** gloat
AESTU saute	**AFILS** fails	**AFORV** favor	align	**AGLOV** galvo
AESTV stave	**AFINR** infra	**AFORY** foray	Laing	Volga
vesta	**AFINS** fains	**AFORZ** forza	ligan	**AGLOW** aglow
AESTW sweat	naifs	**AFOSS** fossa	linga	**AGLRU** glaur
tawse	**AFINT** faint	sofas	**AGILO** logia	gular
twaes	**AFIOS** Sofia	**AFOST** fatso	**AGILR** argil	**AGLRY** glary
waste	**AFIQR** faqir	softa	glair	gyral
wetas	**AFIRR** friar	**AFOSY** ofays	grail	**AGLSS** glass
AESTX taxes	**AFIRS** fairs	**AFPRS** fraps	**AGILS** glias	slags
texas	**AFIRT** afrit	**AFRSS** frass	sigla	**AGLSU** aglus
AESTY yates	iftar	frats	**AGILU** ugali	**AGLTU** gault
yeast	**AFIRY** fairy	rafts	**AGILW** wilga	**AGLYZ** glazy
Yeats	**AFIST** fiats	**AFRSU** fraus	**AGILY** gaily	**AGMMU** gumma
AESTZ zetas	**AFISW** waifs	**AFRSW** swarf	**AGIMN** gamin	**AGMMY** gammy
AESUV suave	**AFKLN** flank	**AFRSY** frays	**AGIMO** amigo	**AGMNO** among
uveas	**AFKLS** flaks	**AFRSZ** zarfs	imago	mango
AESVW waves	flask	**AFSST** fasts	**AGIMS** agism	ngoma
AESWX waxes	**AFKLY** flaky	**AFSTU** Faust	sigma	**AGMNU** munga
AESXZ zaxes	**AFKNR** frank	fauts	**AGINO** gonia	**AGMNY** mangy
AETTV Evatt	**AFKOT** kofta		ngaio	**AGMOT** magot
AEVWY wavey	**AFKRT** kraft	**AFSTW** wafts	**AGINP** aping	**AGMPS** gamps
AFFFS faffs	**AFLLS** falls	**AFSUV** favus	**AGINR** grain	**AGMRS** grams
AFFGS gaffs	**AFLMS** flams	**AFTTY** fatty	**AGINS** gains	**AGMSU** magus
AFFIX affix	**AFLMY** flamy	**AGGGO** gogga	Siang	**AGMTU** gamut
AFFLO offal	**AFLNS** flans	**AGGIN** aging	**AGINT** giant	**AGNNO** Agnon
AFFLU luffa	**AFLNU** Falun	**AGGIW** wigga	ngati	gonna
AFFNY nyaff	**AFLOO** aloof	**AGGJS** jaggs	tangi	**AGNNW** gnawn
AFFQU quaff	loofa	**AGGJY** jaggy	**AGINW** awing	**AGNOP** ponga
AFFST staff	**AFLOR** flora	**AGGLU** gulag	wigan	**AGNOR** argon
AFFSW waffs	**AFLOS** foals	**AGGMO** Magog	**AGINX** axing	groan
AFFTY taffy	loafs	**AGGMU** mugga	Xiang	nagor
AFGHU faugh	**AFLOT** aloft	**AGGNS** gangs	**AGIOS** agios	orang
AFGLO oflag	float	**AGGOR** aggro	Goiás	organ
AFGLS flags	**AFLOU** afoul	Gogra	**AGIRT** tragi	**AGNOT** tango
AFGLU fugal	**AFLOV** Olaf V	**AGGRS** raggs	**AGIRV** virga	tonga
AFGNO fango	**AFLPS** flaps	**AGGRY** raggy	**AGIST** agist	**AGNOU** guano
ganof	**AFLRS** farls	**AGHHU** haugh	gaits	**AGNOW** gowan
AFGNS fangs	**AFLST** flats	**AGHIN** hangi	taigs	wagon
AFGOR Fargo	**AFLSW** flaws	**AGHIZ** ghazi	**AGISU** Gaius	wonga
AFGOT fagot	**AFLSY** flays	**AGHLU** laugh	**AGJLU** jugal	**AGNOV** agony
AFGRS frags	**AFLTU** fault	**AGHMO** ogham	**AGKNS** knags	**AGNPR** prang

Code	Word		Code	Word		Code	Word		Code	Word		Code	Word
AGNPS	pangs		AHHIS	Shiah		AHKRS	harks		AHOOY	yahoo		AIINS	Sinai
	spang		AHHNS	Shahn			shark		AHOPS	opahs		AIIPU	Piauí
AGNPU	Pan Gu		AHHOS	hohas		AHKSS	hasks		AHORS	Horsa		AIIQR	Iraqi
	punga		AHHOX	Hoxha		AHKST	khats		AHORT	Horta		AIISX	ixias
AGNRS	gnars		AHHPY	hypha		AHKSW	hawks			torah		AIIVZ	Iviza
	grans		AHHRS	harsh		AHKSY	shaky		AHORY	hoary		AIJJN	Jinja
AGNRT	grant		AHHSS	shahs		AHLLO	hallo		AHORZ	Zohar		AIJKN	kanji
AGNRW	wrang		AHIIS	shiai			holla		AHOST	Athos		AIJKT	Kitaj
AGNRY	angry		AHIIT	Haiti		AHLLS	halls			hoast		AIJLS	jails
	rangy		AHIJJ	hajji			shall			hosta		AIJNN	Jinan
AGNSS	sangs		AHIJS	hajis		AHLMS	halms			oaths			ninja
	snags		AHIJZ	Hijaz		AHLMU	haulm			shoat		AIJOR	rioja
AGNST	angst		AHIKK	khaki		AHLNO	halon		AHOSY	hoyas		AIJOU	ouija
	gnats		AHIKM	hakim			lohan		AHOTZ	azoth		AIKKM	kamik
	stang		AHIKS	haiks		AHLNU	uhlan		AHPPY	happy		AIKKS	kaiks
	tangs			Kashi		AHLOR	horal		AHPRS	harps			kakis
AGNSU	Angus		AHIKU	haiku		AHLOS	halos			sharp		AIKKT	tikka
	Gansu		AHIKV	Khiva			shoal		AHPRT	Tharp		AIKLS	kails
	guans		AHIKZ	khazi		AHLOT	loath		AHPRY	harpy			laiks
	sugan		AHILL	Hilla			lotah		AHPSS	hasps			Laski
AGNSV	vangs		AHILP	phial		AHLPS	plash		AHPST	paths		AIKLT	tilak
AGNSW	gnaws		AHILR	hilar		AHLPT	Plath			staph		AIKMO	maiko
AGNTU	gaunt		AHILS	hails		AHLPY	haply		AHPSU	hapus		AIKMS	maiks
AGNTW	twang		AHILT	Lahti			phyla			puhas		AIKMU	umiak
AGNTY	tangy			lathi		AHLRS	harls		AHPSW	pshaw		AIKNS	kinas
AGOOT	Otago			thali		AHLSS	slash			whaps			Nasik
AGORS	Argos		AHIMR	Hiram		AHLST	halts		AHPUW	whaup		AIKNT	takin
AGORT	argot			ihram			laths		AHQSU	quash		AIKNU	nikau
	groat		AHIMS	Amish			shalt		AHRRY	harry		AIKOP	okapi
AGOSS	sagos		AHINO	Hanoi		AHLSU	hauls		AHRST	harts		AIKPP	kippa
AGOST	goats		AHINS	Hsian		AHLSW	shawl			Rasht		AIKPS	pikas
	togas			nashi			Walsh			raths		AIKPU	pikau
AGOSY	yogas		AHINU	Anhui		AHLSY	hylas			tahrs		AIKRR	karri
AGOTT	gotta		AHIOP	Pohai			shaly			thars		AIKRT	krait
AGOTV	gavot		AHIPS	aphis		AHLTY	lathy			trash		AIKRU	kauri
AGOYZ	gyoza			apish		AHMMU	Ummah		AHRSU	Århus		AIKSS	sakis
AGPPY	gappy			spahi		AHMMY	hammy			Ashur			sikas
AGPRS	grasp		AHIRS	hairs		AHMNU	human			shura		AIKST	Sakti
	sprag			Shari			Nahum			surah			sitka
AGPRY	grapy		AHIRT	airth		AHMNY	mynah		AHRSY	syrah		AIKSV	kivas
AGPSS	gasps		AHIRU	rahui		AHMOS	Shamo		AHRTW	wrath		AIKSZ	Ziska
	spags			Uriah		AHMPS	pashm		AHRTY	rhyta		AILLV	villa
AGPSU	gaups		AHIRY	hairy		AHMRS	harms		AHRUW	whaur		AILLZ	zilla
AGPSW	gawps		AHIST	saith			marsh		AHRXY	hyrax		AILMN	Milan
AGQSU	quags			Thaïs		AHMSS	shams		AHSST	stash		AILMS	Islam
AGRSS	grass		AHISU	huias			smash		AHSSU	Susah			mails
AGRSU	argus		AHISV	shiva		AHMST	maths			Ushas			salmi
	gaurs		AHITW	Tihwa		AHMSW	shawm		AHSSW	shaws			Simla
	sugar		AHJNO	Jonah			whams			shwas		AILMU	miaul
AGRSV	gravs		AHJTU	thuja		AHMSY	mashy			swash		AILMY	My Lai
AGRSY	grays		AHKLS	lakhs		AHNNO	honan		AHSSY	shays		AILNO	aloin
AGRUU	augur		AHKMO	Mokha		AHNNU	Hunan		AHSTW	swath		AILNP	plain
AGRVY	gravy		AHKNS	ankhs		AHNOS	noahs			thaws		AILNS	anils
AGSST	stags			hanks		AHNOT	Hotan		AHSTY	hasty			nails
AGSSU	gauss			khans		AHNPT	Panth		AHSWY	washy			slain
AGSSW	swags			shank		AHNSS	shans		AHTUY	thuya			snail
AGSSY	gassy		AHKNT	thank		AHNST	Hants		AIIKR	ariki		AILNT	Latin
AGSTU	Tagus		AHKNY	hanky			snath		AIILM	milia		AILNV	anvil
AGSTY	stagy		AHKOO	hooka		AHNTT	Thant		AIILO	aioli			nival
AGSUV	vagus		AHKOS	kohas		AHNTU	haunt		AIILT	litai		AILNW	lawin
AGTTU	gutta			shako		AHNUW	Wuhan		AIIMM	Miami		AILNY	inlay
AGUYZ	gauzy		AHKPS	kaphs		AHOOW	wahoo		AIINO	Ionia		AILOP	pilao

Code	Word	Code	Word	Code	Word
AILOS	Laois	AIMNV	mavin		Sivan
AILOT	Italo-	AIMNY	Minya		vinas
AILOV	viola	AIMNZ	Mainz	AINSW	swain
AILOZ	Lao Zi		nizam		wains
	Lazio	AIMOR	moira	AINSY	ayins
AILPP	palpi	AIMOU	miaou	AINSZ	nazis
	pipal	AIMOW	miaow	AINTT	taint
AILPS	lapis	AIMOX	axiom		titan
	pails	AIMPR	Priam	AINTU	Uniat
AILPT	plait		prima	AINTW	twain
AILPU	Pauli	AIMRR	marri		witan
	Paul I	AIMRS	amirs	AINUX	auxin
	pilau		simar	AINYZ	zayin
AILPW	pilaw	AIMRT	amrit	AIOPT	patio
AILQU	quail		Tarim	AIORT	ratio
AILRS	arils	AIMRU	mauri	AIORX	orixa
	lairs		Urmia	AIOSS	oasis
	laris	AIMRY	Mary I	AIOST	iotas
	liars	AIMRZ	mirza		ostia
	liras	AIMSS	amiss	AIPPP	pappi
	rails	AIMST	maist	AIPPS	pipas
	rials		tamis	AIPRS	pairs
AILRT	trail	AIMSV	mavis		paris
	trial	AIMSW	swami		Sapir
AILRU	Luria	AIMSX	maxis		Sarpi
AILRV	rival	AIMSY	Mysia	AIPRT	atrip
	viral	AIMTY	amity		tapir
AILRY	lairy	AINNO	anion	AIPRU	Piura
	riyal	AINNP	pinna	AIPSS	apsis
AILRZ	Rizal	AINNS	Nisan	AIPST	tapis
AILSS	lassi	AINOP	piano	AIPSV	Pasvi
	sails	AINOR	noria	AIPTT	Patti
	sisal	AINOW	Iowan		pitta
AILST	litas	AINOX	axion	AIPZZ	pizza
	tails	AINOZ	Anzio	AIQRU	quair
AILSU	Aulis	AINPS	nipas	AIQSU	quasi
	Laius		pains	AIQUY	Yaqui
AILSV	silva		spain	AIRRS	arris
	vails	AINPT	inapt	AIRRW	wirra
	vials		paint	AIRSS	arsis
AILSW	wails		patin		saris
	Wisła		pinta	AIRST	airts
AILSX	axils	AINRS	naris		astir
AILSY	Islay		rains		sitar
AILSZ	zilas		ranis		stair
AILTT	atilt		sarin		stria
AILTV	vital	AINRT	intra		tarsi
AILTY	Italy		riant	AIRSU	Arius
	laity		Tiran	AIRSV	vairs
AIMMS	imams		train	AIRSY	Syria
	maims	AINRV	invar	AIRSZ	sizar
AIMMU	imaum		ravin	AIRTT	trait
AIMMX	maxim		Vanir	AIRVX	varix
AIMNN	Minna	AINRY	rainy	AISSV	Sivas
AIMNO	amino	AINSS	sains		visas
	Naomi		sasin	AISTT	Attis
	Omani	AINST	antis	AISTV	vista
AIMNR	Arnim		saint	AISTW	waist
	Marin		satin		waits
AIMNS	mains		stain	AISTX	taxis
	minas		Tanis	AISTZ	Tisza
AIMNT	matin	AINSV	savin	AISVV	vivas

Code	Word	Code	Word
AITTV	vitta	AKMSS	masks
AITWZ	Waitz	AKMSU	Aksum
AITZZ	izzat	AKNOR	Akron
	Ta'izz		Koran
AJKNR	Kranj		krona
AJKOR	rojak	AKNOS	kaons
AJLOP	jalop		koans
AJLOU	joual	AKNOT	tonka
AJLRS	jarls	AKNOV	Konya
AJLRU	jural	AKNPR	prank
AJMMU	Jammu	AKNPS	knaps
AJMMY	jammy		spank
AJMNU	Jumna	AKNPU	punka
AJMOR	major	AKNRS	knars
AJMRU	jumar		krans
AJNNY	janny		narks
AJNOS	Jason		ranks
AJNOU	Anjou	AKNRY	narky
AJNSU	Janus	AKNST	stank
AJNTU	jaunt		tanks
	junta	AKNSU	ankus
AJOPP	Joppa		Kansu
AJOST	jatos	AKNSW	swank
	jotas		wanks
AJPRS	jarps	AKNSY	snaky
AJPSU	jaups		yanks
	pujas	AKNUZ	kanzu
AJRRY	Jarry	AKNWY	wanky
AJRTU	jurat	AKOOR	karoo
AJRUU	Juruá	AKOOZ	kazoo
AJSSY	Jassy	AKOPP	koppa
AJYZZ	jazzy	AKOPY	yapok
AKKLU	kulak	AKORS	koras
AKKNS	skank		okras
AKKOP	kapok	AKORT	korat
AKKOW	wokka	AKOSS	soaks
AKKPU	pukka	AKOST	oktas
AKLLY	alkyl	AKOSY	kayos
AKLNP	plank		okays
AKLNU	kulan	AKOTY	tokay
AKLNY	lanky	AKPRS	parks
AKLOP	polka		spark
AKLOS	alkos	AKPRY	parky
	kolas	AKPTU	kaput
	skoal	AKPWY	pawky
AKLRS	larks	AKQRU	quark
AKLRT	Trakl	AKQUY	quaky
AKLRY	larky	AKRSS	sarks
AKLSS	Śląsk	AKRST	karst
AKLST	stalk		karts
	talks		stark
AKLSU	kulas	AKRSW	warks
AKLSW	lawks	AKRSY	sarky
	walks	AKRTU	kraut
AKLTU	taluk		kurta
AKLTY	talky	AKSST	tasks
AKLUW	waulk	AKSSU	skuas
AKMNY	manky	AKSSV	kvass
AKMOR	korma	AKSTY	kyats
AKMOS	makos	AKSUW	wauks
AKMOU	oakum	ALLLY	allyl
AKMRS	marks	ALLMO	molal

ALLMS malls
small
ALLMU mulla
ALLMY myall
ALLNO llano
ALLOS ollas
salol
ALLOT allot
atoll
ALLOW allow
ALLOY alloy
loyal
ALLPS palls
spall
ALLPY pally
ALLRY rally
ALLST stall
ALLSU Sulla
ALLSW walls
ALLSY sally
ALLTY tally
ALLWY wally
ALLXY laxly
ALMMO Malmö
ALMNO monal
ALMNY manly
ALMOR molar
moral
ALMOS loams
molas
ALMOT matlo
ALMOX Lomax
ALMOY loamy
ALMPS lamps
palms
plasm
psalm
ALMPY amply
palmy
ALMQU qualm
ALMRS marls
ALMRU larum
mural
ALMRY marly
ALMSS slams
ALMST malts
smalt
ALMSU alums
mauls
ALMTY malty
ALMUX Uxmal
ALNNO Nolan
ALNNU annul
ALNOP nopal
ALNOR Arlon
loran
ALNOS loans
salon
sloan
solan
ALNOT notal
talon

tolan
tonal
ALNOW lowan
ALNOZ zonal
ALNPS plans
ALNPT plant
ALNRS larns
snarl
ALNRU lunar
ulnar
ALNST slant
ALNSU Lanús
ulans
ulnas
ALNSW lawns
yulan
ALNWY Alwyn
lawny
wanly
ALNXY xylan
ALOPR parol
polar
ALOPS opals
Palos
salop
ALOPT Plato
ploat
ALORS orals
solar
ALORT tolar
ALORV valor
volar
ALORY royal
ALOSS lasso
ALOST Alost
altos
lotas
salto
Talos
tolas
ALOSV ovals
salvo
ALOTT total
ALOTV lovat
volta
ALOVV volva
ALPPS palps
ALPPU pupal
ALPPY apply
ALPSS slaps
ALPST plast
plats
splat
ALPSU pulas
ALPSW pawls
ALPSY palsy
plays
splay
ALPTU tulpa
ALPTY aptly
platy

typal
ALPUY layup
ALRRU rural
ALRST slart
ALRSU sural
ALRSY lyras
ALRTU ultra
ALRTW trawl
ALRWY rawly
ALSST lasts
salts
slats
ALSSY lyssa
slays
ALSTU talus
Tulsa
usual
ALSTY salty
slaty
ALSUU luaus
usual
ALSUW wauls
ALSVY sylva
ALSWW wawls
ALSWY yawls
ALTTY lytta
ALTUV vault
ALTWZ waltz
ALUUV uvula
ALUVV vulva
AMMMO momma
AMMMY mammy
AMMNO ammon
AMMOY myoma
AMMRS smarm
AMMRY rammy
AMMSU summa
AMMSY sammy
AMMTY tammy
AMNNU unman
AMNNY Nyman
AMNOR manor
norma
roman
AMNOS mason
moans
monas
nomas
soman
AMNOT toman
AMNOW woman
AMNOY anomy
Mayon
AMNOZ Monza
AMNRU Namur
unarm
AMNSU manus
AMNSY mynas
AMOQR qorma
AMORR armor
Morar
AMORS Maros
moras

roams
AMORU amour
AMORY mayor
moray
AMOSS Samos
somas
AMOST atoms
moats
stoma
AMOSU oumas
AMOTU Omuta
AMOTW amowt
AMOTY atomy
motza
AMOTZ matzo
AMPRS prams
ramps
AMPRT tramp
AMPSS spams
spasm
AMPST stamp
tamps
AMPSU pumas
AMPSV vamps
AMPSW swamp
AMPYY yampy
AMRRU murra
AMRRY marry
AMRST marts
smart
trams
AMRSU musar
ramus
Sarum
AMRSW swarm
warms
AMRTU Murat
AMRTY tryma
AMRUU aurum
AMRUY Maury
AMSST masts
AMSSY massy
AMSTT matts
AMSTU Matsu
AMSTY mayst
AMTTU Tatum
ANNNY nanny
ANNOY annoy
ANNSU sunna
ANOOP Poona
ANOPR apron
ANOPT panto
Paton
ANOPW powan
ANOPY yapon
ANORS arson
roans
sonar
ANORT rotan
trona
ANORW rowan
ANORY rayon

ANOST Aston
ANOSV novas
ANOSX axons
Naxos
Saxon
ANOTT tanto
ANOTU tauon
ANOTW Wotan
ANOTX taxon
ANOTY atony
ayont
ANOUY noyau
ANOWY noway
ANPPY nappy
ANPRW prawn
ANPRY pyran
ANPSS snaps
spans
ANPST pants
ANPSU punas
Pusan
ANPSW pawns
spawn
ANPSY pansy
ANPTU unapt
ANQRU Qur'an
ANQTU quant
ANRST rants
tarns
trans
ANRSW warns
ANRSY yarns
ANRUU Nauru
ANRUY unary
ANSST Stans
ANSSW swans
ANSTU aunts
staun
tuans
tunas
ANSTW wants
ANSTY antsy
nasty
tansy
ANSUU unaus
ANSUY unsay
ANSWY yawns
ANTTU taunt
ANTTY natty
ANTUV vaunt
ANTUY aunty
ANTWY tawny
ANVVY navvy
AOORZ razoo
AOPRS aspro
Páros
proas
sapor
AOPRT aport
porta
Prato

AOPRV	vapor	**APSST**	pasts	**BBBOY**	bobby	**BCENO**	bonce		biled
AOPSS	psoas		spats	**BBCEU**	cubeb	**BCEOY**	Boyce	**BDEIM**	bedim
	soaps	**APSSW**	swaps	**BBCOS**	cobbs	**BCERU**	Bruce		imbed
AOPST	Pasto		wasps	**BBCUY**	cubby		cuber	**BDEIP**	biped
AOPSU	oupas	**APSSY**	Passy	**BBDEE**	ebbed	**BCESU**	cubes	**BDEIR**	breid
AOPSY	soapy		spays	**BBDOU**	dubbo	**BCHIM**	chimb		bride
AOPTU	Taupo	**APSTU**	patus	**BBDOY**	dobby	**BCHIR**	birch		rebid
AOPTY	atopy		sputa	**BBEEL**	Bebel	**BCHIT**	bitch	**BDEIS**	bides
AOPTZ	topaz		stupa	**BBEER**	rebbe	**BCHLO**	Bloch	**BDEIT**	bidet
AOQTU	quota	**APSTY**	pasty	**BBEIL**	bible	**BCHNU**	bunch		debit
AORRS	roars		patsy	**BBEIR**	bribe	**BCHOR**	broch	**BDEKO**	boked
AORRV	Varro		pyats	**BBELS**	blebs	**BCHOS**	Bosch	**BDEKY**	byked
AORRW	arrow	**APSUY**	yaups	**BBEMO**	Bembo	**BCHOT**	botch	**BDELN**	blend
AORRZ	razor	**APSWY**	waspy		bombe	**BCHRU**	Bruch	**BDELU**	blued
AORSS	saros		yawps	**BBEOP**	bebop	**BCHSU**	chubs	**BDEMO**	demob
	soars	**APTTY**	patty	**BBERU**	Buber	**BCHTU**	butch	**BDENO**	boned
	soras	**APZZZ**	pzazz	**BBEWY**	webby	**BCHUU**	buchu	**BDENS**	bends
AORST	Astor	**AQRTU**	quart	**BBGIO**	gobbi	**BCIKR**	brick	**BDENY**	bendy
	roast	**AQSSU**	quass	**BBGIS**	Gibbs	**BCILM**	climb	**BDEOO**	booed
	rotas	**AQSTU**	squat	**BBGOY**	gobby	**BCIOR**	boric	**BDEOR**	bored
	Sarto	**AQSUW**	squaw	**BBHOS**	Hobbs	**BCIPU**	pubic		orbed
	taros	**AQSUY**	quays	**BBHOY**	hobby	**BCIRS**	cribs		robed
	Troas	**ARRST**	starr	**BBHUY**	hubby	**BCITU**	cubit	**BDEOS**	bodes
AORSV	savor	**ARRSU**	surra	**BBIJS**	jibbs	**BCKLO**	block	**BDEOW**	bowed
AORTT	ottar	**ARRTY**	tarry	**BBILO**	bilbo	**BCKOR**	brock	**BDEOX**	boxed
	tarot	**ARSST**	stars	**BBILY**	bilby	**BCKOS**	bocks	**BDERY**	derby
	troat		trass		Libby	**BCKOU**	bucko	**BDEST**	debts
AORVY	ovary		tsars	**BBIMO**	bimbo	**BCKSU**	bucks	**BDESU**	bused
AOSST	oasts	**ARSSU**	Assur	**BBLOO**	bobol	**BCLMO**	clomb		debus
	stoas		suras	**BBLOS**	blobs	**BCLOS**	blocs	**BDESY**	bydes
	Tasso	**ARSTT**	start	**BBLOY**	lobby	**BCLSU**	clubs	**BDETU**	debut
	tosas		tarts	**BBLRU**	blurb	**BCMOO**	combo		tubed
AOSSU	Sousa	**ARSTU**	surat	**BBLSU**	blubs		coomb	**BDFII**	bifid
AOSTT	stoat		sutra		bulbs	**BCMOS**	combs	**BDHIO**	dhobi
	toast	**ARSTW**	straw	**BBMOS**	bombs	**BCMRU**	crumb	**BDHNU**	bundh
AOSTU	autos		swart	**BBNOY**	nobby	**BCNOU**	bunco	**BDIIN**	bindi
AOSVW	avows		warts	**BBNUY**	nubby	**BCORY**	corby	**BDIIR**	Irbid
AOSVY	savoy	**ARSTY**	satyr	**BBOOS**	boobs	**BCRSU**	curbs	**BDILN**	blind
AOTWY	Otway		stray	**BBOOY**	booby		scrub	**BDILU**	build
APPPY	pappy		trays		yobbo	**BDDEI**	bided	**BDINO**	Bondi
APPSU	pupas	**ARSTZ**	tzars	**BBRSU**	burbs	**BDDEO**	boded	**BDINS**	binds
APPSY	sappy	**ARSUV**	varus	**BBRUY**	rubby	**BDDEU**	debud	**BDIOP**	bipod
APPVY	yappy	**ARSUY**	saury	**BBSUU**	bubus	**BDDEY**	byded	**BDIOV**	bovid
APPYZ	zappy	**ARTTU**	Tartu	**BBSUY**	busby	**BDDIY**	biddy	**BDIRS**	birds
APRRS	parrs		tuart	**BBTUY**	tubby	**BDDUY**	buddy		dribs
APRRY	parry	**ARTTY**	ratty	**BCCEO**	bocce	**BDEEL**	bedel	**BDLNO**	blond
APRSS	rasps		tarty	**BCCIO**	bocci		bleed	**BDLOO**	blood
	spars	**ARTWY**	warty	**BCCIU**	cubic	**BDEEM**	embed	**BDMOU**	dumbo
APRST	parts	**ASSSY**	sassy	**BCDEU**	cubed	**BDEER**	brede	**BDNOS**	bonds
	prats	**ASSTU**	sauts	**BCEEH**	beech		breed	**BDNOU**	bound
	sprat	**ASSTW**	swats	**BCEEL**	celeb	**BDEES**	debes	**BDNSU**	bunds
	strap	**ASSTY**	stays	**BCEER**	rebec	**BDEEW**	bedew	**BDNUU**	bundu
	tarps	**ASSWY**	sways	**BCEEX**	xebec		dweeb	**BDNUY**	bundy
	traps	**ASTTW**	twats	**BCEEZ**	zebec	**BDEEY**	debye	**BDOOR**	brood
APRSU	praus		watts	**BCEHL**	belch	**BDEGI**	gibed		droob
	supra	**ASTTY**	tasty	**BCEHN**	bench	**BDEGO**	bodge	**BDORS**	dorbs
APRSW	warps	**ASTUY**	Asyut	**BCEHO**	boche	**BDEGU**	budge	**BDOSU**	Doubs
	wraps	**ASTVY**	vasty	**BCEIR**	Brice		debug	**BDOTU**	doubt
APRSY	prays	**ASVVY**	savvy	**BCEIS**	bices	**BDEGY**	gybed	**BDRSU**	drubs
	raspy	**ATTTY**	tatty	**BCEKS**	becks	**BDEIJ**	jibed	**BDRSY**	Byrds
	spray	**ATTWY**	Wyatt	**BCELO**	coble	**BDEIK**	biked	**BEEFS**	beefs
APRTY	party	**BBBIS**	bibbs	**BCEMO**	combe	**BDEIL**	bield	**BEEFY**	beefy

BEEGI	beige
BEEGL	glebe
BEEGR	Geber
	grebe
BEEGT	beget
BEEHI	Hebei
BEEHP	Phebe
BEEHT	Bethe
	thebe
BEEIL	belie
BEEJL	jebel
BEEJM	jembe
BEEKL	Keble
BEELL	belle
BEELM	Belém
BEELN	leben
BEELP	bleep
	plebe
BEELR	rebel
BEELT	betel
BEELV	bevel
BEELZ	bezel
BEEMR	berme
	ember
BEENN	benne
BEENS	Beneš
BEENT	benet
	Benét
BEENU	Benue
BEEOR	boree
BEEOS	obese
BEEPS	beeps
BEERS	beers
	brees
BEERT	beret
	Ebert
BEERV	breve
BEERW	weber
BEERY	beery
BEEST	beets
	beset
BEETT	Tebet
BEFGO	befog
BEFIR	brief
	fiber
	fibre
BEFIT	befit
BEFOU	boeuf
BEGIL	bilge
BEGIN	begin
	being
	binge
BEGIO	bogie
BEGIR	giber
BEGIS	gibes
BEGLO	bogle
	globe
BEGLU	bugle
	bulge
BEGMU	begum
BEGNU	begun
BEGOT	begot

BEGOY	bogey
BEGRS	bergs
BEGSY	gybes
BEHIU	Hubei
BEHMO	Böhme
BEHOR	Horeb
BEHOT	Bothe
BEHRS	herbs
BEHRT	berth
BEHRY	herby
BEHST	beths
BEIIK	bikie
BEIJR	jiber
BEIJS	jibes
BEIKM	Mbeki
BEIKR	biker
BEIKS	bikes
	kibes
BEILL	libel
BEILO	obeli
BEILR	Erbil
	liber
BEILS	biles
	Eblis
BEILY	Belyi
BEIMO	biome
	mobie
BEIMT	Témbi
BEIMU	imbue
BEINN	Benin
BEINO	Niobe
BEINR	brine
BEINS	benis
	bines
	Ibsen
BEINV	Bevin
BEINX	Benxi
BEIOR	Berio
	Ibero-
BEIOS	Boise
BEIOW	bowie
BEIRR	brier
BEIRS	biers
	breis
	bries
BEIRT	biter
	Ibert
	Tiber
	tribe
BEISS	bises
BEIST	bites
BEISV	vibes
BEITT	Betti
	Tibet
BEITZ	Bizet
	zibet
BEIVV	vibey
BEJSU	jubes
BEKLO	bloke
BEKOR	berko
	broke
BEKOS	bokes

BEKRS	berks
	kerbs
	Krebs
BEKRU	burke
BEKSY	bykes
BELLS	bells
BELLY	belly
BELMU	umbel
	umble
BELNO	Nobel
	noble
BELNT	blent
BELOO	Boole
BELOR	roble
BELOS	boles
	lobes
BELOT	botel
BELOU	boule
BELOW	below
	bowel
	elbow
BELOY	Boyle
BELPS	plebs
BELRT	blert
BELRU	bluer
	brule
	ruble
BELRY	beryl
BELSS	bless
BELST	belts
	blest
	blets
BELSU	blues
BELSY	Selby
BELTU	bluet
BELUY	bluey
BEMOP	pombe
BEMOR	brome
	omber
	ombre
BEMOS	besom
	mobes
BEMOW	embow
BEMRS	berms
BEMRU	brume
	umber
BEMSU	embus
	sebum
BENNO	bonne
BENNY	benny
BENOO	Boone
BENOR	boner
	borne
BENOS	bones
BENOT	bento
BENOW	Bowen
BENOY	Boyne
	ebony
BENOZ	bonze
	Bozen
BENRT	brent
BENST	bents

BEOOS	oboes
BEOOT	Obote
BEOOZ	booze
BEOPR	probe
BEORR	borer
BEORS	bores
	brose
	robes
	sober
BEORW	bower
BEORX	boxer
BEORY	Boyer
	Robey
BEOST	boets
BEOSU	bouse
BEOSW	bowse
BEOSX	boxes
BEOSY	obeys
	syboe
BEOTT	botte
BEOTV	Bovet
BEOTY	Tobey
BEPSU	pubes
BERRS	brers
BERRY	berry
BERST	Brest
BERSU	burse
	rebus
	rubes
BERSV	verbs
BERSW	brews
BERSY	breys
	byres
BERTU	brute
	buret
	rebut
	tuber
BERUY	buyer
BESST	bests
BESSU	buses
BESTU	tubes
BESTY	bytes
BESUV	Beuys
BESUZ	zebus
BETTU	butte
BEVVY	bevvy
BFFIO	biffo
BFFIS	biffs
BFFIU	buffi
BFFLU	bluff
BFFOO	boffo
BFFOU	buffo
BFFSU	buffs
BFIOR	fibro
BFIRS	fribs
BFLYY	flyby
BFOOY	boofy
BFORS	forbs
BFORY	forby
BFOSY	boyfs
BFSUY	fubsy
BGGOY	boggy

BGGUY	buggy
BGHIL	Bligh
BGHIT	bight
BGHOU	bough
BGHRU	burgh
BGIIL	gibli
BGILN	bling
BGILY	bilgy
BGINO	bingo
BGINR	bring
BGINS	bings
BGINY	bingy
BGIOT	bigot
BGIRS	brigs
BGISU	gibus
BGLOS	blogs
	globs
BGLUY	bulgy
BGMOO	gombo
BGMOU	gumbo
BGNOO	bongo
	boong
BGNOS	bongs
BGNSU	bungs
BGNUY	bungy
BGOOR	Bogor
BGOOS	gobos
BGOOY	gooby
BGORS	brogs
BGORU	bourg
BGOSU	bogus
BGRSU	burgs
BGRUY	rugby
BHILU	Hubli
BHIMO	himbo
BHIOS	Bisho
BHIRT	birth
	brith
BHLOO	Bohol
BHLSU	blush
	buhls
BHLTY	Blyth
BHMOR	rhomb
BHMPU	bumph
BHMRU	rhumb
BHMTU	thumb
BHOOS	bohos
	hobos
BHOOT	booth
BHORT	broth
	throb
BHOTY	bothy
BHRSU	brush
	buhrs
	shrub
BHSUY	bushy
BIIKS	Biisk
BIILM	limbi
BIILN	blini
BIILR	Irbil
BIIMN	nimbi

Code	Word
BIINY	Yibin
BIIOR	oribi
BIISU	Sibiu
BIJOU	bijou
BIKLN	blink
BIKLS	bilks
BIKNR	brink
BIKOO	Bioko
BIKRS	birks
	briks
	brisk
BIKSS	bisks
BIKSY	Biysk
BILLR	brill
BILLS	bills
BILLY	billy
BILMO	limbo
BILMP	blimp
BILMS	limbs
BILNY	bliny
BILOO	oboli
BILOR	broil
BILOS	Blois
	boils
BILPS	blips
BILRS	birls
BILSS	bliss
BILST	stilb
BILSY	sibyl
BILTU	built
BILTZ	blitz
BIMOZ	zombi
BIMRS	brims
BINNU	Bunin
BINOR	robin
BINOS	bison
BINRU	bruin
	burin
	rubin
BINRY	briny
BINSS	snibs
BINST	bints
BIOOT	Boito
BIORT	orbit
BIOST	obits
BIOTT	Tobit
BIOZZ	bizzo
BIPSU	pubis
BIQSU	squib
BIRRS	birrs
BIRST	brits
BIRTU	bruit
	Tibur
BISSY	byssi
BISTT	bitts
BISTU	busti
BISVY	Visby
BITTY	bitty
BIVVY	bivvy
BIYZZ	bizzy
BJMOU	jumbo
BKLSU	bulks

Code	Word
BKLUY	bulky
BKMOU	kombu
BKNOS	bonks
	knobs
BKNOU	bunko
	konbu
BKNSU	bunks
BKOOR	brook
BKOOS	books
BKOSS	bosks
BKOSY	bosky
BKRSU	burks
BKSSU	busks
BKSUU	Üsküb
BLLOS	bolls
BLLSU	bulls
BLLUY	bully
BLMOO	bloom
BLMPU	plumb
BLNOW	blown
BLNOY	nobly
BLNTU	blunt
BLOOS	bolos
	bools
	obols
BLOOT	Tobol
BLOOY	looby
BLOSS	slobs
BLOST	blots
	bolts
BLOSU	bolus
BLOSW	blows
	bowls
BLOTU	boult
BLOUW	Bülow
BLOWY	blowy
BLRSU	blurs
	burls
BLRTU	blurt
BLRUY	burly
BLSSU	slubs
BLTUY	butyl
BMMOU	mumbo
BMNSU	numbs
BMOOR	bromo
	broom
BMOOS	booms
	bosom
BMORS	borms
BMOST	tombs
BMOSU	umbos
BMOSW	wombs
BMOTY	Bytom
BMOUX	buxom
BMPSU	bumps
BMPUY	bumpy
BNNOY	bonny
BNNRU	Brünn
BNNUY	bunny
BNOOR	Borno
	boron

Code	Word
BNOOS	boons
	boson
BNORU	bourn
	Bruno
BNORW	brown
BNORX	Bronx
BNORY	Byron
BNOSS	snobs
BNOSU	bonus
	bosun
BNRSU	burns
BNRTU	brunt
	burnt
BNSSU	snubs
BNSTU	bunts
BOORS	boors
	sorbo
BOORT	robot
BOORU	buroo
BOOST	boost
	boots
BOOSY	boyos
BOOSZ	bozos
BOOTY	booty
BOOWX	oxbow
BOOYZ	boozy
BOPUW	upbow
BORRU	burro
BORSS	sorbs
BORSW	brows
BORTU	turbo
BORTY	borty
BORTZ	bortz
BOSST	stobs
BOSSW	swobs
BOSSY	bossy
BOSTT	botts
BOSTU	bouts
BOSUY	buoys
BOSWY	sybow
BOSYY	boysy
BPRSU	burps
BRRSU	burrs
BRRUY	burry
BRSTU	burst
BSSTU	busts
	stubs
BSTTU	butts
BSTUY	busty
BTTUU	butut
BTTUY	butty
CCCIO	cocci
CCDEO	codec
CCEEL	Lecce
CCEER	recce
CCEHK	check
CCEHY	Čechy
CCEHZ	Czech
CCEIL	Cecil
CCEIR	cerci
	ceric
	Circe

Code	Word
CCEKL	cleck
CCELY	cycle
	leccy
CCEMU	cecum
CCEOR	Croce
CCEOS	cosec
	secco
CCERY	Crécy
CCESU	cusec
CCHIK	chick
CCHIN	cinch
CCHIO	chico
CCHKO	chock
CCHKU	chuck
CCHLU	culch
CCHNO	conch
CCHOO	choco
CCHOU	couch
CCHRU	curch
CCHTU	cutch
CCHTW	cwtch
CCIIR	Ricci
CCIIV	civic
CCIKL	click
CCIKR	crick
CCILO	colic
CCIMO	comic
CCIMU	mucic
CCINO	conic
CCINY	cynic
CCIOS	cisco
CCIRS	circs
CCKLO	clock
CCKLU	cluck
CCKOR	crock
CCKOS	cocks
CCKOY	cocky
CCKRU	cruck
CCLOY	cyclo
CCMOY	McCoy
CCOOS	cocos
CCORS	crocs
CCORU	occur
CCOSU	Cusco
CCOUZ	Cuzco
CDDEE	ceded
CDDEI	diced
CDDEO	coded
CDDUY	cuddy
CDEEI	deice
CDEER	ceder
	cered
	creed
CDEES	cedes
CDEEU	deuce
	educe
CDEHI	chide
CDEHN	Dench
CDEIM	medic
CDEIR	cider
	cried
	dicer

Code	Word
	riced
CDEIS	dices
CDEIT	cited
	edict
CDEIV	Vedic
	viced
CDEIY	dicey
CDEKO	coked
CDEKR	dreck
CDEKS	decks
CDELO	dolce
CDELU	clued
CDELY	Clyde
CDEMO	Médoc
CDENO	Condé
	coned
CDENS	scend
CDENU	dunce
CDEOO	cooed
CDEOP	coped
CDEOR	coder
	cored
	credo
	decor
CDEOS	codes
	coeds
CDEOT	coted
CDEOU	coude
	douce
CDEOV	coved
CDEOW	cowed
CDEOX	codex
	coxed
CDERU	crude
	cured
CDERY	cyder
	decry
CDESU	duces
CDETU	educt
CDHIL	child
CDHIT	ditch
CDHOR	chord
CDHTU	dutch
CDHUY	duchy
CDIIO	iodic
CDIIS	disci
CDIKS	dicks
CDIKY	dicky
CDILU	lucid
	ludic
CDIMU	mucid
CDIOS	disco
CDIOT	dicot
CDIPU	cupid
	pudic
CDISS	discs
CDISU	scudi
CDKOS	docks
CDKSU	ducks
CDKUY	ducky
CDLOS	clods

Code	Word	Code	Word	Code	Word	Code	Word	Code	Word
	scold	**CEFIT**	fecit	**CEIKL**	cleik	**CEKRS**	recks	**CEOPU**	coupe
CDLOU	cloud	**CEFKL**	fleck		ickle	**CEKRW**	wreck	**CEORR**	crore
	could	**CEFLS**	clefs	**CEIKT**	Tieck	**CELLO**	cello	**CEORS**	ceros
CDLWY	Clwyd	**CEFLT**	cleft	**CEILM**	clime	**CELLS**	cells		cores
CDNOO	codon	**CEFOR**	force		melic	**CELMO**	celom		corse
	condo	**CEGIN**	genic	**CEILN**	cline	**CELMS**	clems		score
CDOOS	docos	**CEGIR**	grice	**CEILO**	oleic	**CELNO**	Cleon	**CEORT**	recto
CDORS	cords	**CEGKN**	Genck	**CEILR**	relic		clone	**CEORU**	Coeur
	scrod	**CEGKO**	gecko	**CEILS**	ceils	**CELNU**	uncle	**CEORV**	cover
CDORU	duroc	**CEGLS**	clegs		Leics	**CELOR**	ceorl	**CEORW**	cower
CDORW	crowd	**CEGNO**	conge		slice	**CELOS**	close		Crowe
CDOSU	doucs	**CEGOR**	Greco	**CEILT**	telic		coles	**CEORY**	Royce
	scudo	**CEHHT**	cheth	**CEILV**	Clive		socle	**CEORZ**	croze
CDOSY	scody	**CEHIL**	chiel	**CEIMN**	mince	**CELOT**	Colet	**CEOST**	coset
CDRSU	cruds		chile	**CEIMR**	crime		telco		cotes
	curds	**CEHIM**	chime		Meriç	**CELOU**	leuco	**CEOSV**	coves
CDRUY	curdy		hemic	**CEIMS**	mesic	**CELOV**	clove		voces
CDSSU	scuds	**CEHIN**	chine	**CEIMT**	metic	**CELOY**	coley	**CEOSW**	Cowes
CDSTU	ducts		niche	**CEIMX**	cimex	**CELOZ**	cloze	**CEOSX**	coxes
CEEEM	emcee	**CEHIR**	Reich	**CEINR**	nicer	**CELPT**	clept	**CEOTT**	octet
CEEFN	fence	**CEHIT**	ethic	**CEINS**	Cenis	**CELPU**	cupel	**CEOTV**	covet
CEEFS	feces	**CEHIV**	chive		since	**CELPY**	clype	**CEOVY**	covey
CEEHK	cheek	**CEHJU**	Cheju	**CEINW**	wince	**CELRU**	cruel	**CEPRT**	crept
CEEHL	Elche	**CEHKO**	choke	**CEIOR**	Coire		lucre	**CEPRY**	crepy
	leech	**CEHKR**	Kerch	**CEIOV**	voice		ulcer		Percy
CEEHN	hence	**CEHKS**	hecks	**CEIPR**	price	**CELST**	celts	**CEPSS**	specs
CEEHP	cheep	**CEHKT**	ketch	**CEIPS**	epics	**CELSU**	clues	**CEQRS**	Sercq
CEEHR	cheer	**CEHLO**	Chloe		spice		luces	**CERRU**	curer
CEEIN	niece	**CEHLP**	chelp	**CEIPT**	Tepic	**CELSW**	clews		recur
CEEIP	piece	**CEHLT**	letch	**CEIRR**	crier	**CELTU**	culet	**CERSS**	cress
CEEJT	eject	**CEHLW**	welch		ricer	**CELUX**	culex	**CERST**	certs
CEEKL	cleek	**CEHLY**	chyle	**CEIRS**	cires	**CEMOR**	comer		crest
CEEKN	Encke	**CEHMO**	chemo		cries		crome	**CERSU**	cruse
CEEKR	creek	**CEHMY**	chyme		erics	**CEMOS**	comes		cures
CEELL	Celle	**CEHNO**	Cohen		rices	**CEMOT**	comet		curse
CEELP	clepe		Enoch	**CEIRT**	citer		comte		sucre
CEELR	creel	**CEHNT**	tench		recti	**CEMRY**	mercy	**CERSW**	crews
CEELT	elect	**CEHNW**	wench		trice	**CEMSY**	cymes		screw
CEELX	excel	**CEHOP**	epoch	**CEIRU**	curie	**CENNO**	nonce	**CERTU**	cruet
CEELY	lycee	**CEHOR**	chore		ureic	**CENOP**	ponce		curet
CEEMR	creme		ocher	**CEIRX**	xeric	**CENOR**	Creon		cuter
CEENP	pence		ochre	**CEISS**	sices		crone		eruct
CEENS	cense	**CEHOS**	chose	**CEIST**	cites		oncer		truce
	scene		oches	**CEISV**	vices	**CENOS**	cones	**CERUV**	curve
CEEOO	cooee		Soche	**CEITU**	cutie		scone	**CESST**	sects
CEEPR	creep	**CEHPR**	perch	**CEITV**	civet	**CENOT**	cento	**CESSY**	syces
	crepe	**CEHPS**	pechs		evict		conte	**CESTU**	cutes
CEERS	ceres	**CEHRT**	chert	**CEITW**	twice	**CENOU**	Cuneo		scute
	crees		retch	**CEJOY**	Joyce		ounce	**CETUY**	cutey
	scree	**CEHRU**	ruche	**CEKKS**	kecks	**CENOV**	coven	**CFFHU**	chuff
CEERT	Crete	**CEHSS**	chess	**CEKLO**	Locke	**CENOY**	coney	**CFFIL**	cliff
	erect	**CEHST**	chest	**CEKLR**	clerk	**CENOZ**	cozen	**CFFOS**	coffs
	terce		techs	**CEKLY**	Lecky	**CENPU**	punce		scoff
CEERW	crewe	**CEHSW**	chews	**CEKMS**	mecks	**CENST**	cents	**CFFSU**	cuffs
CEEST	cetes	**CEHTU**	chute	**CEKNS**	necks		scent		scuff
CEESY	sycee	**CEHTV**	vetch		sneck	**CEOOR**	cooer	**CFHIL**	filch
CEEUV	cuvee	**CEHTY**	techy	**CEKOO**	Cooke	**CEOOY**	cooey	**CFHIN**	finch
CEFHI	chief		Tyche	**CEKOR**	Korçë	**CEOPR**	coper	**CFHIT**	fitch
	fiche	**CEHVY**	chevy		ocker	**CEOPS**	copes	**CFHIU**	fichu
CEFHS	chefs	**CEHWY**	chewy	**CEKOS**	cokes		copse	**CFHOO**	choof
CEFHT	fecht	**CEIIR**	icier	**CEKPS**	pecks		Pecos	**CFHSU**	Fuchs
	fetch	**CEIJU**	juice		speck		scope	**CFIKL**	flick

CFILO folic	**CHINP** pinch	**CHORT** torch	**CILTY** lytic	**CKMSU** mucks
CFIOS coifs	**CHINS** chins	**CHORY** ochry	**CILXY** cylix	**CKMUY** mucky
CFISS fiscs	**CHINT** nicht	**CHOST** coths	**CIMNO** Cimon	**CKNOR** cronk
CFISU ficus	**CHINW** winch	**CHOSU** hocus	nomic	**CKNOS** conks
CFKLO flock	**CHIOR** chiro	**CHOSW** chows	**CIMNU** cumin	nocks
CFKOR frock	choir	**CHOTT** chott	mucin	**CKNSU** snuck
CFKSU fucks	ichor	**CHOTU** couth	**CIMOR** micro	**CKOOR** crook
CFLOS flocs	**CHIOS** Chios	touch	**CIMOS** osmic	**CKOOS** cooks
CFMOY comfy	Sochi	**CHOUV** vouch	**CIMPR** crimp	**CKOOY** cooky
CFORT croft	**CHIPR** chirp	**CHOUX** choux	**CIMRS** crims	**CKOPS** pocks
CFORU Corfu	**CHIPS** chips	**CHPSY** psych	scrim	Spock
CFOSU focus	**CHIPT** pitch	**CHRRU** churr	**CIMSU** music	**CKOPY** pocky
CFRSU scurf	**CHIRR** chirr	**CHRSU** crush	**CINNO** conin	**CKORS** corks
CFRTU Cruft	**CHIRT** richt	**CHRTW** crwth	**CINOR** orcin	rocks
CFSUU fucus	**CHIRU** chiru	**CHSUY** cushy	**CINOS** coins	**CKORY** corky
CGGIY ciggy	**CHIST** chits	**CIILT** licit	icons	rocky
CGHLU gulch	sicht	**CIILV** civil	scion	**CKOSS** socks
CGHOO Gooch	stich	**CIILY** icily	sonic	**CKOST** stock
CGHOU cough	**CHISU** cuish	**CIIMM** mimic	**CINOT** tonic	**CKOSW** cowks
CGHSU chugs	**CHISV** chivs	**CIINO** ionic	**CINOV** covin	**CKOTY** tocky
CGIIN icing	**CHITW** witch	**CIINR** ricin	**CINOZ** zinco	**CKOUY** yucko
CGILN cling	**CHITY** itchy	**CIINV** Vinci	**CINRU** incur	**CKPSU** pucks
CGILO logic	tichy	vinic	runic	**CKRSU** rucks
CGINO coign	**CHIUX** Chu Xi	**CIIRR** cirri	**CINSU** incus	**CKRTU** truck
CGIOR corgi	**CHIVY** chivy	**CIJUY** juicy	**CINTT** tinct	**CKSSU** cusks
CGIOY yogic	vichy	**CIKKS** kicks	**CINTU** cutin	sucks
CGKLU Gluck	**CHKNU** chunk	**CIKLN** clink	tunic	**CKSTU** stuck
CGLNU clung	**CHKOO** choko	**CIKLS** licks	**CINYZ** zincy	tucks
CGLOO colog	chook	slick	**CIOPT** optic	**CKUYY** yucky
CGLOS clogs	**CHKOS** hocks	**CIKMS** micks	picot	**CLLOY** colly
CGNOO cogon	shock	**CIKMY** micky	topic	**CLLSU** culls
congo	**CHKOW** chowk	**CIKNS** nicks	**CIORS** crios	scull
CGOOR Coorg	**CHKOY** choky	snick	**CIORT** toric	**CLLUY** cully
CGORS crogs	**CHKSU** shuck	**CIKOS** sicko	**CIORU** curio	**CLMOP** clomp
CHHIT hitch	**CHKTU** kutch	**CIKPR** prick	**CIOST** coits	**CLMOU** Colum
CHHIW which	**CHLMU** mulch	**CIKPS** picks	stoic	locum
CHHNU hunch	**CHLNU** lunch	spick	**CIOTX** toxic	**CLMPU** clump
CHHOO hooch	**CHLNY** lynch	**CIKPY** picky	**CIPRS** crisp	**CLMSU** culms
CHHTU hutch	**CHLOS** lochs	**CIKQU** quick	scrip	**CLMTU** mulct
CHIIL chili	**CHLOT** cloth	**CIKRS** ricks	**CIPRY** pricy	**CLNOO** colon
lichi	**CHLRU** churl	**CIKRT** trick	**CIPSS** spics	Colón
CHIKN chink	lurch	**CIKRW** wrick	**CIPSY** spicy	**CLNOW** clown
CHIKO hoick	**CHLSU** schul	**CIKSS** sicks	**CIPTY** typic	**CLNUY** Cluny
Kochi	**CHMNU** munch	**CIKST** stick	**CISST** cists	**CLOOR** color
CHIKS hicks	**CHMOO** choom	ticks	**CISSY** cissy	crool
CHIKT thick	mooch	**CIKSW** wicks	**CISTU** cutis	**CLOOS** cools
CHILL chill	**CHMOP** chomp	**CIKVY** Vicky	ictus	locos
CHILM milch	**CHMOS** schmo	**CILLS** cills	**CIVVY** civvy	**CLOOY** cooly
CHILO choli	**CHMPU** chump	**CILNO** nicol	**CJKOO** jocko	**CLOPS** clops
CHILP pilch	**CHMSU** chums	**CILNS** Lincs	**CJKOS** jocks	**CLOST** clots
CHILT licht	**CHMTU** mutch	**CILNT** clint	**CJNOU** junco	colts
CHILZ zilch	**CHNOT** notch	**CILOS** coils	**CKKNO** knock	**CLOSU** locus
CHIMN Minch	**CHNPU** punch	**CILOT** lotic	**CKLNO** clonk	**CLOSW** cowls
CHIMO ohmic	**CHNRU** churn	**CILOW** wilco	**CKLNU** clunk	scowl
CHIMP chimp	runch	**CILPS** clips	**CKLOP** Płock	**CLOSY** cloys
CHIMR chirm	**CHNSY** synch	**CILPU** picul	**CKLOS** locks	**CLOTU** clout
CHIMS misch	**CHOOP** pooch	Pulci	**CKLPU** pluck	**CLOYY** coyly
CHIMT micht	**CHOOS** cohos	**CILRU** curli	**CKLSU** lucks	**CLPSU** sculp
mitch	**CHOPR** porch	**CILRY** Cyril	**CKLUY** lucky	**CLRSU** curls
CHIMU humic	**CHOPS** chops	lyric	**CKMNO** Monck	**CLRUY** curly
CHINO chino	**CHOPT** potch	**CILSU** sulci	**CKMOS** mocks	**CLSTU** cults
Chino-	**CHOPU** pouch	**CILTU** culti	smock	**CLTUY** culty

33

Code	Word		Code	Word		Code	Word		Code	Word		Code	Word
CMMOO	commo		COSSW	scows		DDIRU	druid			needs		DEFOS	feods
CMMOS	comms		COSTT	Scott		DDIST	didst		DEENU	endue		DEFOX	foxed
CMMOY	commy		COSTU	scout		DDLOY	oddly		DEENY	needy		DEFRU	Freud
CMOOP	compo		CPRTY	crypt		DDMUY	muddy		DEENZ	Enzed		DEFSU	feuds
CMOPS	comps		CPSSU	cusps		DDNOY	noddy		DEEOP	epode			fused
CMORS	corms			scups		DDNUY	nuddy		DEEOR	erode		DEFUZ	fuzed
CMORU	mucor		CPTUU	cutup		DDOOS	dodos		DEEPS	deeps		DEGHY	hedgy
	mucro		CRRUY	curry		DDOPY	poddy			pedes		DEGIL	gelid
CMOSU	comus		CRSTU	crust		DDOSY	soddy			speed			glide
CMPRU	crump			curst		DDOTY	toddy		DEERR	erred		DEGIM	midge
CMRSU	scrum		CRSUY	Cyrus		DDOWY	dowdy		DEERS	deers		DEGIN	deign
CMRUY	Cymru		CRUVY	curvy		DDRSU	rudds			drees			dinge
CMSSU	scums		CSSTU	scuts		DDRUY	ruddy			redes		DEGIO	dogie
CMSUU	mucus		CSSTY	cysts		DEEFF	effed			reeds			geoid
CNNOS	conns		CTTUY	cutty		DEEFO	Defoe			seder		DEGIR	dirge
CNOOR	corno		DDDIY	diddy		DEEFR	defer			sered			gride
	croon		DDEEG	edged			freed		DEERT	deter			ridge
CNOOS	coons		DDEEL	deled		DEEFS	feeds			treed		DEGIU	guide
CNOOT	conto		DDEEN	ended		DEEFT	feted		DEERU	urdee		DEGJU	judge
CNOPY	poncy		DDEER	dreed		DEEGG	egged		DEERV	Verde		DEGLO	Gödel
CNORS	corns			reded		DEEGH	hedge		DEERY	redye			lodge
	scorn		DDEES	deeds		DEEGK	kedge			reedy			ogled
CNORT	tronc		DDEEW	dewed		DEEGL	glede		DEESS	seeds		DEGLS	gelds
CNORU	cornu		DDEFY	Dyfed			gleed		DEEST	steed			gleds
CNORW	crown		DDEGO	dodge			ledge		DEESU	suede		DEGLU	glued
CNORY	corny		DDEHI	hided		DEEGO	geode			swede			luged
	crony		DDEIK	diked		DEEGR	edger		DEESW	sewed		DEGLY	ledgy
CNOSU	conus		DDEIL	idled			greed			swede		DEGMO	modge
	uncos		DDEIN	dined		DEEGS	edges			weeds		DEGNO	Ogden
CNOTU	count		DDEIO	diode			sedge		DEESX	desex		DEGNU	nudge
CNOWY	Conwy		DDEIR	dried		DEEGW	wedge			sexed		DEGOP	podge
CNSSY	syncs			redid		DEEHL	heled		DEESY	seedy		DEGOR	gored
CNSTU	cunts		DDEIS	sided		DEEHR	heder		DEETU	etude		DEGOS	doges
CNSUU	uncus		DDEIT	tided		DEEHS	heeds		DEETW	de Wet		DEGOT	godet
CNTUU	uncut		DDEIV	dived		DEEHW	hewed			tweed		DEGOW	wodge
COOPS	coops		DDEKY	dyked		DEEHX	hexed		DEETY	Teyde		DEGOY	dogey
	scoop		DDELO	doled		DEEIL	edile		DEEUX	exude		DEGPU	pudge
COOPT	coopt		DDEMO	domed			elide		DEEVX	vexed		DEGRS	dregs
COORS	corso		DDENY	neddy		DEEIN	diene		DEEWY	Dewey		DEGRU	grued
COORT	Corot		DDEOP	doped		DEEIR	eider			weedy			urged
COORV	Corvo		DDEOR	odder		DEEIT	Teide		DEFFI	fifed		DEGRY	gyred
COOST	coots			roded		DEEJW	jewed		DEFFO	deffo		DEGSY	sedgy
	scoot		DDEOS	dosed		DEEKN	kneed		DEFGI	fidge		DEGUY	guyed
COPRS	corps		DDEOT	doted		DEEKR	Derek		DEFGU	fudge		DEGVY	gyved
	crops		DDEOW	dowed		DEEKY	keyed		DEFIL	felid		DEGWY	wedgy
COPRU	croup		DDEOZ	dozed		DEELR	elder			field		DEHIK	hiked
COPSS	scops		DDEPU	duped		DEELS	deles			filed		DEHIL	Delhi
COPSU	coups		DDERS	redds			Leeds		DEFIN	fiend		DEHIR	hider
COPSW	cowps		DDERU	udder		DEELU	elude			fined			hired
COPUY	coypu		DDESU	dudes		DEELV	delve		DEFIR	fired		DEHIS	heids
CORRU	cruor		DDETY	teddy			Velde			fried			hides
CORSS	cross		DDGIY	giddy		DEEMN	Emden		DEFIT	fetid			shied
CORST	torcs		DDGOY	dodgy			emend		DEFIX	fixed			sidhe
CORSU	Orcus		DDHUU	hudud		DEEMS	deems		DEFIY	deify		DEHIV	hived
	scour		DDIKY	kiddy			demes			edify		DEHKO	hoked
CORSW	crows		DDILO	dildo			meeds		DEFJL	fjeld		DEHLO	dhole
	Worcs		DDIMX	Middx		DEEMT	meted		DEFLT	delft			holed
CORTU	court		DDIMY	middy		DEEMW	mewed		DEFLU	flued		DEHMO	homed
CORWY	cowry		DDINU	undid		DEENO	donee		DEFLY	Fylde		DEHNO	honed
CORYZ	Orczy		DDINY	d'Indy		DEENR	ender		DEFMR	fremd		DEHNS	shend
COSST	costs			Indy, d'		DEENS	denes		DEFMU	fumed		DEHOP	ephod
	scots		DDIOS	didos			dense		DEFNS	fends			hoped
									DEFNU	unfed			

DEHOR Herod / horde
DEHOS hosed
DEHPT depth
DEHPY hyped
DEHRS herds / sherd / shred
DEHSS sheds
DEHUZ Zhu De
DEIIM imide
DEIIN indie
DEIIV ivied
DEIIX dixie
DEIJR jerid
DEIJV jived
DEIKL liked
DEIKM miked
DEIKN inked
DEIKP piked
DEIKR irked
DEIKS dikes / skied
DEIKT kited
DEIKY yiked
DEILM limed
DEILN lined
DEILO oiled / oldie
DEILP lepid / piled / plied
DEILR idler / riled
DEILS deils / delis / idles / sidle / siled / slide
DEILT tilde / tiled
DEILV devil / lived
DEILW wield / Wilde / wiled
DEILY yield
DEIMM mimed
DEIMN denim / mined
DEIMP imped
DEIMR dimer / mired / rimed
DEIMS deism / dimes
DEIMT demit / timed
DEIMX mixed
DEINO Dione
DEINP pined

DEINR diner / Indre
DEINS Denis / dines / nides / snide
DEINT ident / teind / tined
DEINU indue / Udine
DEINV vined
DEINW Edwin / wined
DEINX index / nixed
DEINZ dizen
DEIOV video
DEIOW dowie
DEIOX doxie / oxide
DEIPP piped
DEIPR pride / pried
DEIPS spied
DEIPT tepid
DEIPW wiped
DEIPZ pized
DEIRR drier / rider
DEIRS dries / rides / sider / sired
DEIRT tired / tried
DEIRV diver / drive / rived / Verdi
DEIRW weird / wider / wired / wried
DEISS sides
DEIST deist / diets / edits / sited / stied / tides
DEISV dives / vised
DEISW wides / wised
DEISZ sized
DEITY deity
DEIVW wived
DEJKO joked
DEJOY joyed
DEKKO dekko

DEKNO kendo
DEKNU nuked
DEKOP poked
DEKOS doeks
DEKOT toked
DEKOY yoked
DEKPU puked
DEKSS desks
DEKSU dukes
DEKSY dykes
DELLN Lendl
DELLS dells
DELLW dwell
DELMO model
DELMS melds
DELNO Eldon / loden / Nolde / olden
DELNS lends
DELOO looed
DELOP loped / poled
DELOR older
DELOS delos / doles / lodes
DELOU loued
DELOV loved
DELOW dowel / lowed
DELOY Doyle / odyle / yodel / yodle
DELPU duple / puled
DELRU lured / ruled
DELRY redly
DELSS sleds
DELSU duels / dulse / slued
DELSV velds
DELSW welds
DELSY lysed
DELTU luted
DELTV veldt
DELTW dwelt
DEMMO modem
DEMNO demon
DEMNS mends
DEMOO mooed
DEMOP moped
DEMOR drome / Drôme
DEMOS demos / domes / modes
DEMOU odeum
DEMOV moved

DEMOW mowed
DEMRS derms
DEMRU demur / mured
DEMSU mused / sedum
DEMTU muted
DENNO donne
DENOO odeon
DENOR drone / redon
DENOS nodes / nosed / sonde
DENOT noted / toned
DENOV devon
DENOW endow / owned / Woden
DENOY doyen
DENOZ dozen / zoned
DENPS pends / spend
DENPU upend
DENRS nerds / rends
DENRT trend
DENRU Düren / under
DENRY nerdy
DENSS sends / sneds
DENST dents / tends
DENSU dunes / nudes
DENSV vends
DENSW wends
DENSY Denys / dynes / syned
DENTU tuned
DENUU undue
DENUW unwed
DEOOR rodeo
DEOOW wooed
DEOOZ oozed
DEOPR pedro / pored / roped
DEOPS dopes / posed / spode
DEOPT depot / opted / toped
DEOPY dopey
DEORR derro / order
DEORS deros / doers / doser / rodes / rosed

DEORT doter / trode
DEORU Duero / uredo
DEORV dover / drove / roved
DEORW dower / rowed
DEORX redox
DEORZ dozer
DEOSS doses
DEOST dotes / Odets
DEOSU douse
DEOSV doves
DEOSW dowse / sowed
DEOSZ dozes
DEOTT toted
DEOTU outed
DEOTV voted
DEOTW towed
DEOTX detox
DEOTY toyed
DEOVW vowed
DEOWW wowed
DEOXY deoxy
DEPPU upped
DEPRU drupe / duper / du Pré / Dupré / perdu / prude
DEPSU dupes / pseud / spued
DEPTY typed
DERRU Dürer / ruder
DERRY derry / dryer / redry / Ryder
DERSS dress
DERSU druse
DERSY dreys / dyers
DERTU trued
DERTY tyred
DESTU duets
DESUX duxes
DETUV duvet
DFFOS doffs
DFFSU duffs
DFFUY Duffy
DFILU fluid

Code	Word	Code	Word	Code	Word	Code	Word	Code	Word
DFINS	finds	DHOOS	hoods	DINSW	winds	DLORY	lordy	DOPRU	proud
DFINU	fundi	DHORY	hydro	DINWY	windy	DLOST	dolts	DOQSU	quods
DFIOR	fiord	DHOSW	dhows	DIOOT	ootid	DLOSW	wolds	DORSS	dross
DFIRT	drift		showd	DIOOV	ovoid	DLOUW	would	DORSU	duros
DFJOR	fjord	DHOSY	yodhs	DIOOZ	zooid	DLOWY	dowly		sudor
DFLOO	flood	DHOWY	howdy	DIOPR	Prodi	DLOYY	doyly	DORSW	sword
DFLOS	folds	DHRSU	hurds	DIOPS	dipso	DLRYY	dryly		words
DFNOR	frond	DHSTU	thuds	DIOPY	pyoid	DMMUY	dummy	DORTU	Tudor
DFNOS	fonds	DIILL	dilli	DIORS	doris	DMNOU	mound	DORTY	dorty
DFNOU	found	DIILP	lipid	DIORT	droit	DMOOS	dooms	DORUY	Oudry
DFNSU	funds	DIILV	livid	DIOST	doits		moods	DORWY	dowry
DFNUY	fundy	DIIMO	idiom	DIOSV	voids		sodom		rowdy
DFOOR	fordo	DIIMS	midis	DIOSY	Doisy	DMOOV	doomy		wordy
DFOOS	foods	DIIMT	timid	DIOTT	ditto		moody	DOTTY	dotty
DFOOY	foody	DIINR	indri	DIOTV	divot	DMORS	dorms	DPPUY	duppy
DFORS	fords	DIINT	nitid	DIOWW	widow	DMORY	dormy	DPSSU	spuds
DFRSY	fyrds	DIIOT	idiot	DIPPY	dippy	DMPSU	dumps	DPSUU	pudus
DGGOO	doggo	DIIVV	vivid	DIPRS	drips	DMPUY	dumpy	DRRUY	durry
DGGOY	daggy	DIJNN	djinn	DIQSU	quids	DMRSU	drums	DRSSU	surds
DGHIT	dight	DIJNO	Dijon		squid	DMRUU	durum	DRSTU	durst
DGHOU	dough	DIKNR	drink	DIRTY	dirty	DNNOU	dunno		turds
DGIIR	rigid	DIKNS	dinks	DIRUZ	durzi	DNNOY	donny	DSSTU	dusts
DGIIT	digit		kinds	DISTY	ditsy	DNNUY	dunny		studs
DGILS	gilds	DIKNY	dinky	DITTY	ditty	DNOOR	donor	DSSUY	sudsy
DGILU	guild		kindy	DITYZ	ditzy		doorn	DSTUY	dusty
DGIMY	midgy	DIKOS	Disko	DIVVY	divvy		rondo		study
DGINO	dingo	DIKRS	dirks	DIYZZ	dizzy	DNOOS	snood	EEEFZ	feeze
	doing	DIKSS	disks	DJNOR	Njord	DNOOT	tondo	EEEGL	gelee
DGINR	grind		skids	DJOOS	dojos	DNOPS	ponds		Gelée
DGINS	dings	DILLR	drill	DKKOO	Kodok	DNOPU	pound	EEEGS	geese
DGINY	dingy	DILLS	dills	DKNOO	donko	DNORU	N'Dour	EEEIR	eerie
	dying	DILLY	dilly		kondo		round	EEELM	melee
DGIRS	girds		idyll	DKNRU	drunk	DNORW	drown	EEELP	Peele
	grids	DILMS	milds	DKNSU	dunks	DNOSU	nodus		Pelée
DGIRY	ridgy	DILMY	dimly	DKOOR	drook		sound	EEELV	levee
DGLOS	golds	DILNO	Dolin	DKOOS	dooks	DNOSW	downs	EEEMS	semee
DGLOU	Gould		indol	DKORS	dorks	DNOSY	Dyson	EEEPS	epees
DGLOY	godly	DILOS	diols	DKORU	drouk		synod	EEEPT	tepee
DGNOO	Ogdon		idols	DKORY	dorky	DNOTU	donut	EEEPV	peeve
DGNOS	dongs		lidos	DKOSU	douks	DNOUW	wound	EEEPW	pewee
DGNSU	dungs		soldi		kudos	DNOWY	downy	EEERV	reeve
DGNUY	dungy		solid	DKSSU	dusks	DNRSU	nurds	EEFGR	Frege
DGOOS	goods	DILOY	doily	DKSUU	kudus	DNRUY	nurdy	EEFHI	Hefei
DGOOY	Godoy	DILRU	lurid	DKSUY	dusky	DNSSY	synds	EEFIL	Eifel
	goody	DILRY	drily	DKUUZ	kudzu	DNSTU	dunts	EEFIR	fiere
DGOPY	podgy	DILSS	silds	DLLOR	droll	DNSWY	wynds	EEFJS	jefes
DGORU	gourd	DILSW	wilds	DLLOS	dolls	DNTUW	Wundt	EEFLR	fleer
DGPUY	pudgy	DILSY	idyls	DLLOY	dolly	DOOPR	droop	EEFLS	feels
DGRSU	drugs	DIMNS	minds		Lloyd	DOOPS	poods		flees
DHIMU	humid	DIMOU	odium	DLLSU	dulls	DOORS	doors	EEFLT	fleet
DHINS	hinds	DIMRU	mudir	DLLUY	dully		odors	EEFMM	femme
DHINU	Hindu	DIMST	midst	DLMOS	molds		roods	EEFMS	femes
DHIOT	dhoti	DIMTU	tumid	DLMOU	mould	DOORU	Douro	EEFRR	freer
DHIOY	hyoid	DINOP	poind	DLMOY	moldy		odour		refer
DHIRT	third	DINOR	Rodin	DLNUY	Lundy	DOOST	stood	EEFRS	feres
DHISY	dishy	DINOS	Sidon	DLOOR	dolor	DOOSW	woods		frees
DHITU	dhuti	DINOT	tondi		drool	DOOTU	outdo		reefs
DHITW	width	DINOX	Dixon	DLOOS	dolos	DOOWY	woody		sefer
DHLLO	dholl	DINRS	rinds		soldo	DOOVZ	doozy	EEFRV	fever
DHLOS	holds	DINST	dints	DLOPS	plods	DOPRS	dorps	EEFRW	fewer
DHNOO	Hondo	DINSU	Indus	DLORS	lords		drops	EEFSS	fesse
DHNOU	hound		nidus	DLORW	world		prods	EEFST	fetes

Code	Word
EEFSU	fusee
EEFUZ	fuzee
EEGGR	egger
EEGHL	Hegel
EEGHN	henge
EEGIL	liege
	Liège
EEGIN	Eigen
	genie
EEGIR	Eiger
EEGIS	siege
EEGIV	vegie
EEGKR	greek
EEGKS	geeks
EEGKY	geeky
EEGLR	leger
	Léger
EEGLS	glees
	leges
EEGLT	gleet
EEGLY	elegy
EEGMR	merge
EEGNR	genre
	green
EEGNS	genes
EEGNT	genet
	tenge
EEGNV	Negev
	venge
EEGNW	ngwee
EEGOS	ogees
EEGRR	Greer
	Reger
EEGRS	grees
	Segrè
	serge
EEGRT	egret
	greet
EEGRV	verge
EEGST	egest
	geest
	geste
EEGSU	segue
EEHIN	Heine
	Henie
EEHLL	Helle
EEHLN	Helen
EEHLS	heels
	heles
EEHLT	lethe
EEHLV	helve
EEHLW	wheel
EEHMR	rehem
	rheme
EEHMT	theme
EEHNR	Herne
EEHNS	sheen
EEHNW	wheen
EEHNZ	Henze
EEHPS	sheep
EEHRS	Esher
	heres
	sheer
EEHRT	ether
	there
	three
EEHRW	hewer
	where
EEHRX	hexer
EEHRY	Heyer
EEHSS	Hesse
EEHST	sheet
	these
EEHSX	hexes
EEHTT	teeth
EEIJT	eejit
EEIJW	jewie
EEILM	elemi
EEILT	elite
EEILX	exile
EEINR	Irene
EEINS	seine
EEINV	nieve
EEINX	exine
EEIPR	Ieper
EEIRS	Isère
EEIRT	retie
	Tiree
EEIRV	reive
EEIRY	eyrie
EEISS	seise
EEISV	sieve
EEISZ	seize
EEITV	evite
EEJLW	jewel
EEJLY	jeely
EEJPS	jeeps
EEJRS	jeers
EEJRZ	Jerez
EEJSS	jesse
EEJST	jetes
EEKKS	keeks
EEKLN	kneel
EEKLR	kerel
EEKLS	keels
	leeks
	sleek
EEKLV	kevel
EEKMP	Kempe
EEKNR	kerne
EEKNS	keens
	knees
EEKNT	kente
EEKOP	pekoe
EEKOV	evoke
EEKPS	keeps
	peeks
	pekes
EEKRS	esker
	reeks
EEKRY	reeky
	rekey
EEKSS	seeks
EEKST	skeet
EEKSW	weeks
EEKSX	kexes
EEKSY	Kesey
EELLV	level
EELMM	Memel
EELMR	merle
EELNO	leone
EELNP	Le Pen
EELNS	lenes
EELNV	Leven
EELNW	newel
EELOP	elope
EELOW	Loewe
EELPR	leper
	repel
EELPS	peels
	sleep
	speel
EELPX	expel
EELRS	leers
	reels
EELRT	relet
EELRU	Euler
EELRV	elver
	lever
	revel
EELRY	leery
EELSS	seels
	seles
EELST	leets
	sleet
	steel
	stele
EELSV	elves
EELSW	Lewes
EELTU	elute
EELTX	telex
EELTY	Leyte
EELTZ	Etzel
	Tezel
EEMMN	Emmen
EEMMR	emmer
EEMMT	emmet
EEMNS	menes
	mesne
	neems
	semen
EEMNU	neume
EEMNY	enemy
	Yemen
EEMOR	Meroë
EEMOT	emote
EEMPT	Tempe
EEMRS	meres
	merse
EEMRT	meter
	metre
EEMRX	remex
EEMRY	emery
EEMSS	seems
EEMST	meets
	metes
	teems
EEMSU	meuse
EEMSZ	mezes
	mzees
EENNP	penne
EENNS	nenes
EENPR	neper
	preen
EENPS	neeps
	peens
	penes
EENQU	queen
EENRS	ernes
	reens
	sneer
EENRT	enter
	rente
	terne
	treen
EENRU	enure
EENRV	erven
	nerve
	never
	Verne
EENRW	newer
	renew
EENSS	Essen
	sense
EENST	steen
	teens
	tense
EENSU	ensue
EENSV	evens
	neves
	seven
EENSW	sewen
	weens
EENSY	Syene
EENTT	tenet
EENTV	event
EENTW	tween
EENTY	teeny
EENUV	venue
EENWY	weeny
EEOPT	topee
EEORS	erose
EEOXY	oxeye
EEPPS	peeps
EEPRS	peers
	peres
	perse
	prese
	speer
	spree
EEPRT	peter
EEPRU	puree
	rupee
EEPRV	perve
EEPSS	seeps
EEPST	steep
EEPSW	sweep
	weeps
EEPWY	weepy
EEQRU	queer
EEQUU	queue
EERSS	seers
	seres
EERST	ester
	reest
	reset
	steer
	stere
	terse
	trees
EERSU	reuse
EERSV	erevs
	serve
	sever
	veers
	verse
EERSW	ewers
	sewer
	sweer
	Weser
EERSX	Xeres
EERSY	eyres
EERTV	evert
	revet
EERTX	exert
EERUV	revue
EERVV	verve
EERVX	vexer
EERVY	every
	veery
EESSX	Essex
	sexes
EESSY	yeses
EESTW	sweet
	weest
EESVX	vexes
EETTU	tutee
EETTV	Tevet
EETTW	tweet
EFFFO	feoff
EFFIR	fifer
EFFIS	fiefs
	fifes
EFFOR	offer
	reffo
EFFRU	ruffe
EFGIN	feign
EFGIR	grief
EFGOR	forge
	gofer
EFGOY	fogey
EFGUU	fugue
EFHIO	Hofei
EFHIT	thief
EFHLS	flesh
	shelf
EFHNO	foehn
EFHPY	Phyfe
EFHRS	fresh
EFHST	hefts

EFHTT	theft	EFMMY	femmy	EGILN	Elgin
EFHTY	hefty	EFMOR	forme		ingle
EFIKN	knife		Frome	EGILO	Egoli
EFILN	elfin	EFMOS	fomes	EGILR	liger
EFILR	filer	EFMRU	femur	EGILS	Giles
	flier		fumer		gleis
	lifer	EFMSU	fumes	EGILT	gilet
	rifle	EFMTU	fumet		legit
EFILS	files	EFNNU	Funen	EGILU	guile
	flies	EFNNY	fenny	EGIMM	gimme
EFILT	filet	EFNOR	freon	EGIMN	minge
	flite	EFNOT	often	EGIMR	grime
EFIMR	fermi	EFNRS	ferns	EGINP	genip
EFIMU	Fiume	EFNRY	ferny	EGINR	niger
EFINR	finer	EFORR	frore		Regin
	infer	EFORS	froes		reign
EFINS	fines		orfes	EGINS	segni
EFINT	feint	EFORT	fetor		singe
EFIOX	foxie		forte	EGINT	tinge
EFIRR	Er Rif	EFORX	forex	EGINV	given
	firer	EFORY	foyer	EGINY	eying
	frier	EFORZ	froze	EGIOV	ogive
EFIRS	fiers	EFOSS	fosse	EGIPR	gripe
	fires	EFOSX	foxes	EGIRT	tiger
	fries	EFOWY	Fowey		Tigré
	frise	EFRRY	ferry	EGIRV	giver
	serif		fryer	EGIST	gites
EFIRT	refit		refry	EGISU	guise
	treif	EFRSS	serfs	EGISV	gives
EFIRV	fiver	EFRST	frets	EGIWZ	Zweig
EFIRX	fixer	EFRUZ	furze	EGKRY	gryke
EFIRY	fiery	EFSST	fests	EGKSS	skegs
	reify	EFSSU	fuses	EGLLY	gelly
EFISV	fives	EFSTU	fetus	EGLMO	golem
EFISX	fixes	EFSTW	wefts		Gomel
EFKLS	skelf	EFSTY	festy	EGLMU	glume
EFKLU	fluke	EFSUZ	fuzes	EGLNN	Glenn
EFKRS	kerfs	EGGIN	ginge	EGLNO	Elgon
EFKSY	fykes	EGGIR	Grieg		longe
EFLLS	fells	EGGIU	gigue	EGLNS	glens
EFLLY	felly	EGGLY	leggy	EGLNU	lunge
EFLMU	flume	EGGNU	gunge	EGLOO	Goole
EFLNO	felon	EGGOP	pogge	EGLOR	ogler
EFLOR	Rolfe	EGGOR	gorge	EGLOS	loges
EFLOS	floes	EGGOU	gouge		ogles
EFLOT	flote	EGGSY	yeggs	EGLOV	glove
EFLOW	Wolfe	EGHIL	Leigh		Vogel
EFLOX	flexo	EGHIN	hinge	EGLOZ	gloze
EFLOY	foley		neigh	EGLRU	gluer
EFLRY	ferly	EGHIT	eight		gruel
	flyer	EGHIW	weigh		luger
EFLST	felts	EGHNT	Ghent	EGLSU	glues
	lefts		thegn		gules
EFLSU	flues	EGHOU	Hogue		luges
	fuels	EGHRU	huger	EGLSY	gleys
	fusel	EGHRY	Gehry	EGLUY	gluey
EFLSW	flews	EGIIN	genii	EGMMY	gemmy
EFLSY	fleys	EGIJR	rejig	EGMNO	genom
EFLTU	flute	EGIKL	klieg		gnome
EFLTY	flyte	EGIKN	eking	EGMNU	Meung
	lefty	EGIKR	grike	EGMOT	gemot
EFLUY	fluey	EGILM	gimel	EGMRS	germs

EGMSU	geums	EHHST	heths
EGNNO	ennog	EHIKR	hiker
EGNOP	pengo	EHIKS	hikes
EGNOR	genro		sheik
	goner	EHILO	helio
	negro	EHILS	shiel
	Norge	EHILT	Leith
EGNOS	segno		lithe
EGNOY	Goyen	EHILW	while
	Yonge	EHILX	helix
EGNPU	unpeg	EHIMN	hemin
EGNRZ	grenz	EHIMO	homie
EGNST	gents	EHINR	Rhein
EGNSU	genus		rhine
	negus	EHINS	Hines
EGNSY	Synge		shine
EGNTW	Gwent	EHINT	thine
EGNUU	Enugu	EHINW	whine
EGOOS	goose	EHIRR	hirer
EGOOY	gooey	EHIRS	heirs
EGOPR	grope		hires
EGOPY	pogey		shier
EGORR	roger		shire
EGORS	goers	EHIRT	ither
	gores		Reith
	gorse		their
	ogres	EHISS	shies
	regos	EHIST	heist
EGORT	ergot		shite
	Grote	EHISV	hives
	Roget		shive
EGORU	rogue	EHITT	tithe
	rouge	EHITW	white
EGORV	grove		withe
EGORW	Gower	EHJLO	Jehol
EGORY	Corey	EHKLW	whelk
EGOSS	gesso	EHKNO	Kohen
	gosse	EHKOO	Hooke
EGOSV	vegos	EHKOS	hokes
EGOUV	vogue	EHKOY	hokey
	vouge	EHLLO	hello
EGPRU	purge	EHLLS	hells
EGPSU	speug		shell
EGPTU	getup	EHLMO	mohel
	Puget	EHLMS	helms
EGPTY	Egypt	EHLMU	Hulme
EGPUY	Péguy	EHLMW	whelm
EGRRU	urger	EHLOS	holes
EGRSU	grues		sheol
	Suger	EHLOT	helot
	surge		hotel
	urges		thole
EGRSY	greys	EHLOV	hovel
	gyres	EHLOW	whole
EGRUW	Gweru	EHLOY	holey
EGSST	gests		hoyle
EGSSU	guess	EHLPS	helps
EGSTU	guest	EHLPW	whelp
EGSVY	gyves	EHLPY	phyle
EGTTY	Getty	EHLRS	herls
EHHOP	Hopeh		lehrs
EHHPU	Hupeh	EHLRZ	Herzl

EHLSW	welsh	EHRSU	usher	EIILL	Lille	EILSS	isles		renin
EHLTU	Thule	EHRSW	shrew	EILLN	Neill		siles	EINNS	Ennis
EHLTY	ethyl		wersh	EILLO	ollie	EILST	islet		nines
EHLXY	hexyl	EHRSY	shyer	EILLR	rille		istle	EINNU	ennui
EHMNY	hymen	EHRTU	Uther	EILLS	Ellis		lites	EINNV	Niven
EHMOR	homer	EHRTW	threw		lisle		stile		venin
	horme	EHRTZ	hertz	EILLW	Weill		tiles	EINNW	Ne Win
EHMOS	homes	EHSST	hests	EILMN	Ilmen	EILSU	ileus	EINOP	opine
EHMOT	metho	EHSSW	shews		limen	EILSV	elvis	EINOS	eosin
EHMOY	homey	EHSTT	teths		Milne		evils		noise
EHMPS	hemps	EHSTU	shute	EILMP	impel		lives	EINOV	envoi
EHMQS	Qeshm	EHSTW	thews	EILMR	miler		veils		ovine
EHMRS	herms		whets	EILMS	limes		vleis	EINPR	repin
EHMRT	therm	EHTWY	thewy		miles	EILSW	lewis		ripen
EHMRU	rheum	EIIJM	Meiji		slime		wiles	EINPS	penis
EHMRY	rhyme	EIIKR	reiki		smile	EILSX	lexis		pines
EHMST	meths	EIILP	pilei	EILMU	ileum		silex		snipe
EHMSY	meshy	EIIMN	imine	EILMY	limey	EILTT	title		spine
EHMTY	thyme	EIINS	nisei	EILNN	Lenin	EILTU	utile	EINPT	inept
EHNOP	phone	EIINX	nixie		linen	EILTX	ixtle		nepit
EHNOR	heron	EIIPX	pixie	EILNO	eloin	EIMMR	mimer	EINQU	quine
	rhone	EIISV	ivies		olein	EIMMS	mimes	EINRS	reins
	Rhône	EIITY	yitie	EILNR	liner	EIMNR	miner		resin
EHNOS	hones	EIJKO	Keijo	EILNS	lenis	EIMNS	miens		rinse
	hosen	EIJRV	jiver		lines		mines		risen
	shone	EIJSV	jives	EILNT	inlet		Nîmes		serin
EHNOY	honey	EIKKS	kikes	EILNV	levin	EIMNV	vimen		siren
EHNRS	herns	EIKLN	inkle		liven	EIMNY	meiny	EINRT	inert
EHNRU	Nehru		Klein	EILNY	liney	EIMNZ	mizen		inter
EHNRY	henry		Kline	EILOR	Loire	EIMOR	moire		niter
EHNST	hents		liken		oiler	EIMOV	movie		nitre
	shent	EIKLR	Rilke		oriel	EIMOX	moxie		Terni
EHNSW	shewn	EIKLS	likes		reoil		oxime		trine
	whens	EIKLY	kiley	EILOT	Eliot	EIMPR	prime	EINRU	inure
EHNTT	tenth		kylie		toile	EIMPT	tempi		urine
EHOOY	hooey	EIKMN	minke	EILOV	olive	EIMPU	umpie	EINRV	Nervi
EHOPR	ephor	EIKMS	mikes		voile	EIMRR	rimer		riven
	hoper	EIKNO	eikon	EILOW	Loewi	EIMRS	emirs		Viren
EHOPS	hopes		koine	EILOX	Leo IX		mires	EINRX	nixer
EHORS	hoers	EIKNP	pekin	EILPP	Lippe		miser	EINSS	sines
	horse		Penki	EILPR	peril		Reims	EINST	inset
	hoser	EIKNR	inker		plier		rimes		stein
	shoer	EIKNS	skein	EILPS	piles	EIMRT	merit		Stine
	shore		Skien		plies		miter		tines
EHORT	other	EIKOP	pokie		Siple		mitre	EINSV	Nevis
	throe	EIKPR	piker		slipe		remit		veins
EHORV	hover	EIKPS	kepis		spiel		timer		vines
EHORW	whore		pikes		spile	EIMRX	mixer	EINSW	sewin
EHOSS	hoses		spike	EILPX	pixel		remix		sinew
	shoes	EIKRS	kiers	EILRS	riels	EIMSS	mises		swine
EHOST	ethos		skier		riles		seism		wines
	shote	EIKRT	kiter		slier		semis	EINSX	nixes
	those		trike	EILRT	liter	EIMST	emits	EINSZ	zeins
EHOSU	house	EIKSS	sikes		litre		items		zines
EHOSV	shove		skies		relit		metis	EINTU	unite
EHOSW	howes	EIKST	kites		tiler		mites		untie
	whose		skite	EILRU	Lurie		smite	EINTW	twine
EHPRT	Perth		tikes		Uriel		times	EINVX	vixen
EHPRY	hyper	EIKSV	skive	EILRV	liver	EIMSX	mixes	EINVY	veiny
EHPSY	hypes	EIKSY	Yeisk		livre	EIMTX	mixte	EINWY	winey
EHRST	Herts		yikes		viler	EINNP	penni	EINWZ	winze
	Resht	EIKTW	Kitwe	EILRY	riley	EINNR	inner		wizen

Code	Word
EIOPS	poise
EIOPZ	piezo
EIORS	osier
EIORV	vireo
EIOSS	Ossie
EIOTW	towie
EIOWY	yowie
EIOZZ	ozzie
EIPPR	piper
EIPPS	pipes
EIPQU	equip
	pique
EIPRR	prier
	riper
EIPRS	peris
	piers
	pries
	prise
	speir
	spier
	spire
EIPRT	piert
	tripe
EIPRV	viper
EIPRW	wiper
EIPRZ	prize
EIPSS	spies
EIPST	piste
	spite
	stipe
EIPSW	swipe
	wipes
EIPSY	yipes
EIPSZ	pizes
EIPTT	petit
EIPTW	pewit
EIPTY	piety
EIPXY	pyxie
EIQRU	quire
EIQTU	quiet
	quite
EIRRS	riser
EIRRT	trier
EIRRV	river
EIRRW	wirer
	wrier
EIRRY	eyrir
EIRSS	rises
	sires
EIRST	resit
	rites
	Siret
	tiers
	tires
	tries
EIRSV	rives
	siver
	viers
	vires
	Vries
EIRSW	sweir
	weirs
	wires
	wiser
	wries
EIRSX	sixer
EIRSZ	sizer
EIRTT	titer
	titre
	trite
EIRTU	uteri
EIRTV	rivet
EIRTW	write
EISSS	sises
EISST	sites
	sties
EISSU	issue
EISSV	vises
EISSW	wises
EISSX	sixes
EISSZ	sizes
EISTU	etuis
EISTX	exist
	exits
	sixte
EISTY	yetis
	yites
EISTZ	Zeist
EISUV	Viseu
EISVW	swive
	views
	wives
EITTW	twite
	Witte
EIVWY	viewy
EJKOP	kopje
EJKOR	joker
EJKOS	jokes
EJKOY	jokey
EJKRS	jerks
EJKRY	jerky
EJLLO	jello
EJLLS	jells
EJLLY	jelly
EJLOP	polje
EJLOU	joule
EJLPU	julep
EJLRU	jurel
EJMMY	jemmy
EJNNY	jenny
EJNOS	jones
EJNOY	enjoy
EJOSY	joeys
EJRRY	jerry
EJRWY	Jewry
EJSST	jests
EJSSU	jesus
EJSTU	jutes
EJTTY	jetty
EKKOP	kopek
EKKRY	kerky
EKLLN	knell
EKLLS	kells
EKLLY	kelly
EKLMS	skelm
EKLNO	Knole
EKLNT	knelt
EKLOS	koels
EKLOY	kyloe
	yokel
EKLPS	skelp
	spelk
EKLPY	kelpy
EKLST	kelts
EKLSY	kyles
	yelks
EKMOS	mokes
	smoke
EKMPS	kemps
EKMPT	kempt
EKMPY	kempy
EKMRS	Krems
EKNNY	Kenny
EKNOR	krone
EKNOS	snoek
EKNOT	token
EKNOW	woken
EKNRS	kerns
EKNSS	skens
EKNSU	neuks
	nukes
EKOOT	Tooke
EKOPR	poker
EKOPS	pokes
	spoke
EKOPY	pokey
EKORT	toker
EKORY	yoker
EKOSS	sokes
EKOST	stoke
	tokes
EKOSY	yokes
EKPRS	perks
EKPRY	perky
EKPSS	skeps
EKPSU	pukes
EKPSY	kypes
	pesky
EKPTU	tupek
EKRRY	kerry
EKRST	treks
EKSST	skets
EKSSW	skews
EKSTY	kytes
	tykes
EKSYY	Yeysk
ELLLY	Lyell
ELLMS	smell
ELLNS	snell
ELLNY	nelly
ELLOR	oller
ELLOS	losel
ELLPS	spell
ELLQU	quell
ELLSS	sells
ELLST	stell
	tells
ELLSW	swell
	wells
ELLSY	yells
ELLSZ	Szell
ELLTU	tulle
ELLTY	telly
ELLWY	welly
ELMMU	lumme
ELMNO	lemon
	melon
ELMNU	lumen
ELMOR	morel
ELMOS	Melos
	moles
ELMOT	metol
	motel
ELMOU	oleum
ELMOY	moyle
ELMPU	plume
ELMRS	merls
ELMRU	lemur
ELMST	melts
	smelt
ELMSU	mules
ELMSW	mewls
ELMUV	velum
ELMUY	muley
ELMXY	xylem
ELNOR	enrol
	loner
	Loren
ELNOS	enols
	lenos
	noels
	Olsen
ELNOT	Elton
	lento
ELNOV	novel
	Venlo
ELNPZ	Plzeň
ELNSU	lunes
ELNWY	newly
ELOOP	Poole
ELOOS	loose
ELOPR	loper
	poler
	prole
ELOPS	lopes
	poles
	slope
ELOPU	loupe
ELOPY	poley
ELOPZ	Lopez
ELORS	lores
	loser
	orles
	roles
	sorel
ELORV	lover
	Vlorë
ELORW	lower
	rowel
ELOSS	loess
	loses
	sloes
	soles
ELOST	stole
ELOSU	louse
	ousel
	Seoul
ELOSV	loves
	ovels
	solve
	voles
ELOSW	lowse
ELOSY	Losey
ELOTV	volte
ELOTW	owlet
	towel
ELOTX	extol
ELOTY	Elyot
ELOUV	ovule
ELOUZ	ouzel
ELOVW	vowel
ELOVY	lovey
ELPRU	puler
ELPRY	reply
ELPST	pelts
	slept
	spelt
ELPSU	plues
	pules
	pulse
ELPSW	plews
ELPSY	slype
	yelps
ELPTU	letup
ELRRU	lurer
	ruler
ELRSU	lures
	luser
	rules
ELRSY	lyres
	slyer
ELRTY	tyler
ELSSU	slues
ELSSW	slews
ELSSY	lyses
	Yssel
ELSTU	lutes
ELSTW	welts
ELSTY	style
ELSUY	yules
ELTUX	exult
ELTWY	Welty
	wetly
EMMOS	memos
	Somme
EMNNO	Menon
	nomen
EMNNU	numen
EMNOS	meson

nomes	EMRUW Mweru	runes	EOPXY epoxy	EPRST prest
omens	EMRUX murex	ENRSW wrens	EOQRU roque	strep
EMNOT Monet	EMSST stems	ENRTT Trent	EOQTU quote	EPRSU purse
monte	EMSSU muses	ENRTU tuner	toque	sprue
EMNOV venom	EMSSW smews	ENRTY entry	EORRR error	spuer
EMNOW women	EMSSY messy	ENRVY nervy	EORRT retro	super
EMNOY money	EMSTU mutes	Verny	EORRV rover	EPRSV pervs
EMNRU rumen	ENNOS nones	ENRWY Newry	EORRW rower	EPRSY preys
EMNSU menus	ENNOT nonet	ENSST nests	EORSS roses	Ypres
neums	tenno	ENSSU Neuss	sores	EPRTU erupt
EMOOR Moore	tenon	ENSSY snyes	EORST resto	upter
romeo	tonne	synes	rotes	EPRTW twerp
EMOOS moose	ENNOX xenon	ENSTT stent	store	EPSST pests
EMOPR moper	ENNOY Yonne	tents	tores	septs
proem	ENNPY penny	ENSTU suent	EORSU euros	steps
EMOPS Epsom	ENOOR roneo	tunes	roues	EPSSU spues
mopes	ENOOS noose	unset	rouse	EPSSW spews
poems	ENOOZ ozone	ENSTV vents	EORSV Évros	EPSTU setup
pomes	ENOPR Perón	ENSTW newts	overs	stupe
EMOPT tempo	ENOPS Nepos	ENSUV nevus	roves	upset
EMOPY myope	opens	venus	servo	EPSTW swept
EMORR ormer	peons	ENSUX nexus	verso	EPSTY pyets
EMORS Moers	pones	unsex	EORSW serow	types
mores	Posen	ENSWY newsy	sower	EPSUY Pusey
morse	snoep	Sweyn	swore	EPSXY pyxes
omers	ENOPY peony	ENTTY netty	worse	EPTTY petty
EMORT metro	ENORS Ensor	EOOPS Espoo	EORSZ zeros	EQRUY query
EMORV mover	Norse	EOOPV poove	EORTT otter	EQSTU quest
vomer	oners	EOORS roose	torte	EQTUU tuque
EMORW mower	rones	EOORW wooer	toter	ERRSU ruers
EMOSS moses	senor	EOOSZ oozes	EORTU outer	surer
EMOST moste	snore	EOPPS pepos	outre	ERRTU truer
motes	ENORT tenor	poeps	route	ERRTY retry
smote	toner	popes	Touré	terry
tomes	ENORU rouen	EOPRR repro	EORTV overt	ERRWY wryer
EMOSU moues	ENORW owner	EOPRS pores	trove	ERSST rests
mouse	rowen	poser	voter	tress
EMOSV moves	ENOSS noses	prose	EORTW tower	ERSSU ruses
EMOSW meows	sones	ropes	wrote	suers
EMOSY mosey	ENOST notes	Soper	EORTX oxter	users
EMOSZ mozes	onset	spore	EORTY toyer	ERSTT trets
EMOTT motet	seton	EOPRT repot	EORVW vower	ERSTU trues
motte	steno	toper	EORXX xerox	ERSTV verst
totem	stone	trope	EOSSU souse	verts
EMOZZ mezzo	tones	EOPRV prove	EOSTT totes	ERSTW strew
EMPRS perms	ENOSV ovens	EOPRW power	EOSTV stove	trews
sperm	ENOSW Owens	EOPRY ropey	votes	wrest
EMPST empts	ENOSX exons	EOPSS pesos	EOSTW Stowe	ERSTY Steyr
temps	ENOSY nosey	poses	EOSTX sexto	treys
EMPSU spume	ENOSZ zones	posse	EOSTY eyots	tyres
EMPTT tempt	ENOVW woven	speos	EOSUY youse	ERSUU Eurus
EMPTY empty	ENOVY envoy	EOPST estop	EOSVV Svevo	ERSUV eruvs
EMRRU murre	ENPRU prune	pesto	EOSWY yowes	ERSVY syver
EMRRY merry	ENPST spent	poets	EOTTV Ovett	ERTTU utter
EMRST terms	ENQRU quern	stoep	EPPPY peppy	ERTUV vertu
EMRSU mures	ENRRU rerun	stope	EPPRS preps	ERTWY twyer
Mureş	ENRST Ernst	topes	EPPRU upper	ERUVY Yurev
muser	rents	EOPSX expos	EPPSY Pepys	ESSTT setts
Remus	stern	poxes	EPRRU purer	stets
serum	terns	EOPSY poesy	EPRRY perry	tests
Sumer	ENRSU nurse	posey	pryer	ESSTV vests
EMRSY Myers		sepoy	EPRSS press	ESSTW stews

ESSTY styes	**FGORS** frogs	**FIRZZ** frizz	**FORTY** forty	**GHLPY** glyph
ESSTZ zests	**FHILT** filth	**FISST** fists	**FOSST** softs	**GHNOS** hongs
ESTTX texts	**FHIRT** firth	sifts	**FOSTT** tofts	**GHNOT** thong
ESTTY testy	frith	**FISTW** swift	**FOSTY** softy	**GHORU** rough
yetts	**FHIST** shift	**FIYZZ** fizzy	**FRRSS** RSFSR	**GHOST** ghost
ESTUY suety	**FHISY** fishy	**FKLNU** flunk	**FRRUY** furry	**GHOSU** sough
ESTYZ zesty	**FHKUU** Khufu	**FKLOO** kloof	**FRSSU** surfs	**GHOSY** yoghs
FFFLU fluff	**FHLSU** flush	**FKLOS** folks	**FRSTU** turfs	**GHOTU** ought
FFGIR griff	**FHOOS** hoofs	**FKLOY** folky	**FRSUY** surfy	tough
FFGRU gruff	**FHOOT** Hooft	**FKLUY** fluky	**FRTUY** turfy	**GHRSU** shrug
FFHIT fifth	**FHORT** forth	**FKNSU** funks	**FRUYZ** furzy	**GHSTU** thugs
froth	**FKNUY** funky	**FSSUY** fussy	**GHSUV** vughs
FFHIW whiff	**FHORW** Whorf	**FKORS** forks	**FSTTU** tufts	**GHSUY** gushy
FFHOU Hofuf	**FHOSW** howfs	**FLLOY** folly	**FSTUY** fusty	**GHUVY** vughy
FFHOW howff	**FHRTU** furth	**FLLSU** fulls	**FTTUY** tufty	**GIILS** sigil
FFHSU huffs	Fürth	**FLLUY** fully	**FUVZZ** fuzzy	**GIILV** vigil
FFHUU Hufuf	**FHSUU** Shufu	**FLNNY** Flynn	**GGGLO** glogg	**GIINP** piing
FFHUY huffy	**FIILO** Ofili	**FLNOW** flown	**GGHOS** hoggs	**GIJNO** Gijón
FFIJS jiffs	**FIINS** finis	**FLOOR** floor	**GGHUY** huggy	jingo
FFIJY jiffy	**FIINX** infix	**FLOOS** fools	**GGIIL** Gigli	**GIKNS** ginks
FFIKS skiff	**FIINZ** Finzi	**FLOOW** Woolf	**GGIJY** jiggy	kings
FFIMS miffs	**FIKLU** kulfi	**FLOPS** flops	**GGILO** Golgi	**GIKOR** Gorki
FFIMY miffy	**FIKNR** Frink	**FLORU** flour	**GGINO** going	**GILLR** grill
FFINS niffs	**FIKNS** finks	fluor	**GGINS** gings	**GILLS** gills
sniff	**FIKRS** frisk	**FLORY** flory	**GGIOT** gigot	**GILLY** gilly
FFINY niffy	**FILLR** frill	**FLOSS** floss	**GGIPY** piggy	**GILMS** glims
FFIQU quiff	**FILLS** fills	**FLOST** lofts	**GGIRS** grigs	**GILNO** lingo
FFIRS riffs	**FILLY** filly	**FLOSU** fouls	**GGLOO** Gogol	login
FFIST stiff	**FILMS** films	**FLOSW** flows	**GGLSU** glugs	**GILNS** lings
tiffs	**FILMU** filum	fowls	**GGMOY** moggy	sling
FFISZ ziffs	**FILMY** filmy	wolfs	**GGMUY** muggy	**GILNT** glint
FFITY fifty	**FILNT** flint	**FLOTU** flout	**GGNOS** gongs	**GILNU** lungi
FFLSU luffs	**FILOO** folio	**FLOTY** lofty	noggs	**GILNY** lingy
sluff	**FILOR** Forlì	**FLRSU** furls	**GGNUY** gungy	lying
FFMSU muffs	**FILOS** filos	**FLTUY** fluty	**GGOOS** googs	**GILOO** igloo
FFNSU snuff	foils	**FMMOR** Fromm	**GGOSY** soggy	**GILOS** Sligo
FFOST toffs	**FILPS** flips	**FMOOS** mofos	**GGPUY** puggy	**GILRS** girls
FFOTY toffy	**FILRT** flirt	**FMORS** forms	**GGSUV** vuggs	**GILRY** girly
FFPSU puffs	**FILST** flits	**FMORU** forum	**GGUVY** vuggy	**GILST** gilts
FFPUY puffy	lifts	**FMORY** FYROM	**GHHIS** highs	**GILSU** iglus
FFRSU ruffs	**FILSU** fusil	**FMPRU** frump	**GHHIT** hight	**GILTU** guilt
FFSTU stuff	**FILTY** fitly	**FNNUY** funny	thigh	**GILTZ** glitz
FGGIR Frigg	**FIMOS** Foism	**FNORS** frons	**GHHOO** Hoogh	**GIMMR** Grimm
FGGOY foggy	**FIMOT** motif	**FNORT** front	**GHHOU** hough	**GIMNY** mingy
FGGUY fuggy	**FIMRS** firms	**FNORW** frown	**GHILT** light	**GIMOS** gismo
FGHIT fight	**FIMTU** mufti	**FNOST** fonts	**GHIMT** might	**GIMOY** goyim
FGILN fling	**FINNY** finny	**FNOTU** fount	**GHINO** hongi	**GIMOZ** gizmo
FGINO gonif	**FINOS** finos	futon	**GHINS** Singh	**GIMPS** gimps
FGINU fungi	foins	**FOOPR** proof	**GHINT** night	**GIMPY** gimpy
FGIOU fugio	**FINRS** firns	**FOOPS** poofs	thing	pigmy
FGIRS frigs	**FINTU** unfit	spoof	**GHINY** hying	**GIMRY** grimy
FGIST gifts	**FINTY** nifty	**FOOPY** poofy	**GHIRT** girth	**GINOP** gipon
FGLNO flong	**FINUX** unfix	**FOORS** roofs	grith	oping
FGLNU flung	**FINUY** unify	**FOOST** foots	right	pingo
FGLOS flogs	**FIOST** foist	**FOOSW** woofs	**GHISS** sighs	**GINOR** giron
golfs	**FIPSS** spifs	**FOOTY** footy	**GHIST** sight	groin
FGLSU gulfs	**FIRRY** firry	**FOPRS** profs	**GHISW** whigs	**GINOT** ingot
FGLUY gulfy	**FIRST** first	**FOPSU** poufs	**GHITT** tight	tigon
FGNOO gonof	frits	**FORRU** furor	**GHITW** wight	toing
FGOOR forgo	rifts	**FORST** forts	**GHLLY** ghyll	**GINOW** owing
FGOOS goofs	**FIRTT** fritt	frost	**GHLOU** ghoul	**GINOY** yogin
FGOOY goofy	**FIRTU** fruit	**FORSU** fours	lough	**GINPS** pings

GINPU	Pugin	GLORW	growl		gyros	HINOT	Othin	HLOSS	slosh
GINRS	girns	GLORY	glory	GORSZ	grosz	HINPU	unhip	HLOST	Holst
	grins	GLOSS	gloss	GORTU	grout	HINSS	shins		holts
	rings		slogs		trugo	HINST	hints		sloth
GINRU	ruing	GLOSW	glows	GOSTU	gouts		thins	HLOSW	howls
	unrig	GLPSU	gulps		gusto	HINSY	shiny	HLOTU	Louth
GINRW	wring		plugs	GOSTV	Vogts	HINWV	whiny	HLOTY	hotly
GINSS	signs	GLPUY	gulpy	GOSTY	stogy	HIOOT	Otho I	HLPSU	plush
	sings	GLRUY	lurgy	GOTUY	gouty	HIOPP	hippo	HLPSY	sylph
	snigs	GLSSU	slugs		guyot	HIOPR	Ophir	HLRSU	hurls
GINST	sting	GLSTU	gluts	GPPUY	guppy	HIOPT	tophi	HLSSU	slush
	tings	GMMUY	gummy	GPSSU	spugs	HIORS	horis	HLSYY	shyly
GINSU	suing	GMNOO	mongo	GPSYY	gypsy	HIORU	houri	HMNOT	month
	using	GMNOS	mongs	GRSTU	trugs	HIOST	hoist	HMNPY	nymph
GINSW	swing	GMNOU	mungo	GRSUU	gurus	HIPPY	hippy	HMNSY	hymns
	wings	GMOOR	groom	GRSUY	gyrus	HIPSS	ships	HMOOP	oomph
GINSZ	zings	GMOSS	smogs	GSSTU	gusts	HIPST	piths	HMOOS	homos
GINTY	tying	GMPRU	grump	GSTUY	gusty	HIPSW	whips	HMOPR	morph
GINUX	Xingú	GMPYY	pygmy		gutsy	HIPTY	pithy	HMORU	humor
GINVY	Vigny	GNNOS	nongs	GTTUY	gutty	HIRRS	shirr		mohur
	vying	GNNUY	gunny	HHISS	shish	HIRRW	whirr	HMOST	moths
GINYZ	zingy	GNOOP	pongo	HHISW	whish	HIRST	Hirst	HMOTU	mouth
GIOPP	gippo	GNOOS	goons	HHMPU	humph		shirt	HMOTY	mothy
GIOPR	pirog		Soong	HHOTT	Thoth	HIRSU	shiur		mytho-
GIORR	rigor	GNOOZ	gonzo	HHSSU	shush	HIRSW	whirs	HMPSU	humps
GIORS	giros	GNOPR	prong	HHSUU	huhus	HISST	shits		sumph
GIORT	griot	GNOPS	pongs	HIIKO	hikoi	HISSU	sushi	HMPTU	thump
GIORV	vigor	GNOPY	pongy	HIILN	nihil	HISSV	shivs	HMPUW	whump
	Virgo	GNORW	grown	HIIRS	Irish	HISSW	swish	HMPUY	humpy
GIOSY	yogis		wrong	HIJNO	John I	HISTW	whist	HMRRY	myrrh
GIPPY	gippy	GNORY	gyron	HIJOS	shoji		wisht	HMRTU	thrum
GIPRS	grips	GNOSS	snogs	HIKLW	whilk	HISTX	sixth	HMSTU	musth
	prigs		songs	HIKNS	knish	HITWY	whity	HMSTY	myths
	sprig	GNOST	tongs	HIKNT	think		withy		Smyth
GIPSY	gipsy	GNOSW	gnows	HIKOS	Khíos	HIWZZ	whizz	HMSUU	humus
GIRRS	girrs		gowns	HIKRS	shirk	HJNOS	johns	HMSUY	mushy
GIRST	girts	GNOUY	young	HIKSW	whisk	HKKOU	hokku	HMTYY	thymy
	grist	GNPSU	pungs	HILLS	hills	HKLSU	hulks	HNOOP	phono
	grits	GNRSU	gurns		shill	HKLUY	hulky	HNOOR	honor
	trigs		rungs	HILLT	thill	HKMOU	hokum	HNOOS	hoons
GISST	gists	GNRTU	grunt	HILLY	hilly	HKNOS	honks		shoon
GISSW	swigs	GNRUW	wrung	HILMU	hilum	HKNOY	honky	HNOOW	nohow
GISTW	twigs	GNSSU	snugs	HILOT	litho	HKNSU	hunks	HNOPS	phons
GJMUU	jugum	GNSTU	stung		thiol	HKNTU	thunk	HNOPY	phony
GJOSU	jougs	GNSUW	swung	HILRT	thirl	HKOOS	hooks	HNORS	horns
GKLNO	klong	GOOPS	goops	HILRW	whirl		shook		shorn
GKOOS	gooks		pogos	HILST	hilts	HKOOY	hooky	HNORT	north
GKORY	Gorky	GOOPY	goopy		liths	HKOPS	kophs		thorn
GKOSW	gowks	GOORS	sorgo	HILSU	hilus	HKOSW	howks	HNORU	Huron
GLLOY	golly	GOORY	goory	HILSY	shily	HKSSU	husks	HNORY	horny
GLLSU	gulls	GOOSY	goosy	HILTT	tilth	HKSUY	husky	HNOSU	Oshun
GLLUY	gully	GOOTU	outgo	HIMNO	Minho	HLLOO	hollo	HNOSW	shown
GLMOO	gloom	GOPPY	gyppo	HIMQS	Qishm	HLLOU	hullo	HNOSY	hyson
GLMOU	mogul	GOPRS	progs	HIMRT	mirth	HLLOY	holly	HNSSU	shuns
GLNOO	logon		sprog	HIMSS	shims	HLLSU	hulls	HNSTU	hunts
GLNOS	longs	GOPRU	group	HIMST	smith	HLMOS	holms		shunt
GLNOU	gluon	GOPRY	porgy	HIMSW	whims	HLMPY	lymph	HOOPS	hoops
GLNSU	lungs	GORSS	gross	HIMTY	thymi	HLNOO	holon		poohs
	slung	GORST	grots	HINNO	Nihon	HLNSU	shuln		posho
GLOOS	logos		trogs	HINNT	ninth	HLOOS	shool	HOOPT	photo
GLOOY	gooly	GORSW	grows	HINNY	hinny	HLOPX	phlox	HOOPW	whoop
	ology	GORSY	gorsy	HINOR	rhino	HLORW	whorl		

HOORT	ortho	**IILLV**	villi	**IKMOS**	mokis	**ILMNS**	limns	**ILSSY**	lysis
HOOSS	shoos	**IILMT**	limit	**IKMPS**	skimp	**ILMNU**	linum	**ILSTT**	stilt
HOOST	hoots	**IILMU**	ilium	**IKMRS**	smirk	**ILMOO**	mooli		tilts
	shoot	**IILNN**	linin	**IKMRY**	mirky	**ILMOS**	limos	**ILSTW**	wilts
	sooth	**IILNO**	Ilion	**IKMSS**	skims		milos	**ILSTY**	silty
HOOSW	whoso	**IILPP**	Lippi	**IKNOP**	pinko		Mílos		styli
	woosh	**IILPS**	pilis	**IKNOS**	ikons		moils	**ILSTZ**	Liszt
HOOTT	tooth	**IIMMN**	minim		nkosi	**ILMPS**	limps	**ILSUU**	Iulus
HOPQS	qophs	**IIMMR**	Mimir	**IKNPR**	prink	**ILMPY**	imply	**IMMOS**	Moism
HOPRT	thorp	**IIMMX**	immix	**IKNPS**	pinks	**ILMSS**	slims	**IMMSY**	mimsy
HOPSS	shops	**IIMNS**	minis		Pinsk	**ILMST**	milts	**IMNOR**	minor
HOPST	phots	**IIMPR**	primi	**IKNPY**	pinky	**ILMSU**	Musil	**IMNOS**	minos
HOPSW	whops	**IIMPS**	impis	**IKNRS**	rinks		simul		Simon
HOPSY	hypos	**IIMRZ**	Izmir	**IKNSS**	sinks	**ILMSY**	slimy	**IMNOU**	onium
	sophy	**IIMST**	Misti		skins	**ILNNS**	linns	**IMNPS**	nimps
HOQTU	quoth		mitis	**IKNST**	knits	**ILNOS**	linos	**IMNRU**	Nurmi
HORST	horst	**IIMTZ**	Izmit		skint		lions	**IMNST**	mints
	short	**IINNO**	inion		stink		loins	**IMNSU**	minus
HORSU	Horus	**IINOX**	Ixion	**IKNSW**	swink	**ILNOW**	Wilno	**IMNTY**	minty
	hours	**IINST**	intis		winks	**ILNPU**	lupin	**IMOPR**	primo
HORSY	horsy	**IIORT**	torii	**IKNTW**	twink	**ILNPY**	Pliny	**IMOPU**	opium
HORTT	troth	**IIPPS**	pipis	**IKNYZ**	zinky	**ILNSY**	lysin	**IMORT**	Timor
HORTU	routh	**IIPPT**	pipit	**IKOOR**	iroko	**ILNTU**	unlit	**IMORZ**	Imroz
HORTW	rowth	**IIPST**	tipis		koori		until	**IMOST**	moist
	throw	**IISTT**	titis	**IKOOT**	Kioto	**ILNTY**	linty		omits
	whort	**IISTV**	visit	**IKORV**	Kirov	**ILNVY**	vinyl	**IMOSU**	Suomi
	worth	**IJKMU**	mujik	**IKPSS**	skips	**ILOOP**	polio	**IMOSX**	sixmo
	wroth	**IJKNS**	jinks		spiks	**ILOOS**	olios	**IMOTV**	vomit
HOSST	hosts	**IJLLS**	jills	**IKPSY**	spiky	**ILOOV**	ovoli	**IMPPR**	primp
	shots	**IJLST**	jilts	**IKPTU**	tupik	**ILOPS**	Pílos	**IMPPS**	pimps
HOSSW	shows	**IJMMY**	jimmy	**IKQRU**	quirk		polis	**IMPRS**	prims
HOSTT	shott	**IJNOS**	joins	**IKRRS**	skirr		spoil		prism
HOSTU	shout	**IJNOT**	joint	**IKRRU**	Rurik	**ILOPT**	pilot	**IMPRU**	purim
	south	**IJOST**	joist	**IKRSS**	risks	**ILOPU**	poilu	**IMPSS**	simps
	thous	**IKKNO**	Nikko	**IKRST**	skirt	**ILOPX**	oxlip	**IMPST**	timps
HOSUY	shoyu	**IKKNS**	kinks		stirk	**ILORS**	loris	**IMPSW**	wimps
HOSWY	showy		skink	**IKRSU**	kuris		roils	**IMPUX**	mixup
HOTTY	hotty	**IKKNY**	kinky	**IKRSY**	risky	**ILORT**	Tirol	**IMPWY**	wimpy
HOTUY	youth	**IKKOS**	kiosk	**IKSST**	kists		triol	**IMQSU**	quims
HOUUW	Wu Hou	**IKKRS**	kirks		skits	**ILORY**	roily	**IMRRS**	smirr
HPSTU	phuts	**IKKRU**	kukri	**IKSSY**	kissy	**ILORZ**	zoril	**IMRRU**	murri
HPSUW	whups	**IKLLR**	krill	**IKTTY**	kitty	**ILOSS**	silos	**IMRSS**	smirs
HPSUY	pushy	**IKLLS**	kills	**ILLMS**	mills		soils	**IMRST**	trims
HRRUY	hurry		skill	**ILLOS**	lilos	**ILOST**	Solti	**IMRSU**	muirs
HRSTU	hurst	**IKLMO**	milko	**ILLPR**	prill		toils		rimus
	hurts	**IKLMS**	milks	**ILLPS**	pills	**ILOSU**	louis	**IMRSV**	mirvs
HRSUY	rushy	**IKLMT**	Klimt		spill	**ILOSV**	viols	**IMRTU**	murti
HRTTU	truth	**IKLMY**	milky	**ILLPU**	pulli	**ILPPU**	pupil		Timur
HRUUU	uhuru	**IKLNP**	plink	**ILLQU**	quill	**ILPPY**	lippy	**IMSST**	mists
HSSTU	shuts	**IKLNS**	kilns	**ILLRS**	rills	**ILPSS**	lisps		stims
HSSUY	hussy		links	**ILLRT**	trill		slips	**IMSSW**	swims
IIJJU	Ujiji		slink	**ILLSS**	sills	**ILPST**	spilt	**IMSSY**	missy
IIJLN	Jilin	**IKLNT**	Klint	**ILLST**	lilts		split	**IMSTT**	mitts
IIJNN	jinni	**IKLNV**	kylin		still	**ILPSU**	pilus	**IMSTY**	misty
IIKKO	kikoi	**IKLOS**	kilos		tills		pulis	**INNNO**	ninon
IIKLM	kilim	**IKLRS**	skirl	**ILLSW**	swill	**ILPTU**	tulip	**INNNY**	ninny
IIKNN	kinin	**IKLSS**	silks		wills	**ILQTU**	quilt	**INNOO**	onion
IIKNR	Kirin	**IKLST**	kilts	**ILLSY**	silly	**ILRSW**	swirl	**INNOR**	ronin
IIKNZ	Iznik	**IKLSY**	silky		slily	**ILRTW**	twirl	**INNOT**	niton
IIKRT	Kríti	**IKLXY**	kylix	**ILLTW**	twill	**ILSST**	lists	**INNOU**	Inönü
IIKST	tikis	**IKMNS**	minks	**ILLTY**	tilly		silts		union
IIKSW	kiwis		Minsk	**ILLWY**	willy		slits	**INNOX**	Nixon

Code	Word		Code	Word		Code	Word		Code	Word		Code	Word
INNPU	unpin		IOPST	posit		ITYZZ	tizzy		KNOST	knots		LLRTU	trull
INNPY	pinny			topis		JJSUU	jujus			stonk		LLSTU	stull
INNQU	Quinn		IOPSU	pious		JKNSU	junks			tonks		LLSUU	lulus
INNRU	inurn		IOPTV	pivot		JKNUY	junky		KNOSW	knows		LLSUY	sully
INNSU	Ninus		IOQTU	Quito		JKOOS	jooks			wonks		LLSYY	slyly
	Sunni			quoit		JKOSU	jouks		KNOSY	yonks		LLTUY	Tully
INNTY	tinny		IORRS	orris		JLLOY	jolly		KNOTU	knout		LLXYY	xylyl
INOOR	Orion		IORST	riots		JLOST	jolts		KNOUY	Yukon		LMMUY	lummy
INOPP	ippon			tiros		JLOSW	jowls		KNOWY	wonky		LMOOS	looms
INOPR	orpin			torsi		JLOTY	jolty		KNPSU	punks		LMOOT	molto
	prion			trios		JMOOS	mojos			spunk		LMORS	slorm
	Ripon		IORSV	visor		JMORU	jorum		KNRRU	knurr		LMOST	molts
INOPS	opsin		IORVY	ivory		JMPSU	jumps		KNRSU	knurs			smolt
	pions		IORVZ	vizor		JMPUY	jumpy		KNRTU	trunk		LMOSU	Mosul
INOPT	pinto		IPPYZ	zippy		JNOPU	jupon		KNSSU	sunks			solum
	piton		IPQSU	quips		JNOTU	jotun		KNSTU	stunk		LMOTU	moult
	point		IPQUU	quipu			junto		KNSUU	Nukus		LMPPU	plump
INOQU	quoin		IPRST	spirt		JORRU	juror		KOOPS	spook		LMPSU	lumps
INORS	irons			sprit		JOSTU	joust		KOORS	rooks			plums
	ornis			strip		KKLSU	skulk		KOORY	rooky			slump
	rosin			trips		KKNSU	skunk		KOOSS	sooks		LMPUY	lumpy
INORT	intro		IPRSU	sirup		KKOOS	kooks		KOOST	kotos			plumy
	Niort		IPRSY	spiry		KKOOY	kooky			stook		LMRUY	rumly
	nitro		IPRTW	twirp		KKRSU	Kursk		KOOTY	Kyoto		LMSSU	slums
INORY	irony		IPRVY	privy		KKUYY	yukky			Tokyo		LNNOY	nylon
INOSV	vinos		IPSST	spits		KLLNO	knoll		KOPRY	porky		LNOOS	loons
INOSW	winos		IPSSV	Ipsus		KLLSU	skull		KOPSV	Pskov			solon
INOSY	noisy		IPSSV	spivs		KLNOP	plonk		KORST	stork		LNOOV	loony
INOTX	toxin		IPSSW	wisps		KLNPU	plunk			torsk		LNOPY	pylon
INOXX	Xixón		IPSTU	situp		KLNRU	knurl		KORSW	works		LNOSY	Lyons
INPPU	pinup		IPSTY	tipsy		KLNSU	slunk		KORSY	yorks		LNOTU	Luton
INPPY	nippy		IPSTZ	spitz		KLNUU	Kulun		KOSSU	souks		LNOUZ	Luzon
INPRS	pirns		IPSUV	Pius V		KLOOP	plook		KPPRU	Krupp		LNRSU	nurls
INPRT	print		IPSUX	Pius X		KLOOS	kolos		KRSSU	rusks		LOOOV	ovolo
INPRU	purin		IPSWY	wispy			looks		KRSTU	turks		LOOPR	orlop
	unrip		IPSXY	pyxis			skool		KRSUU	kurus		LOOPS	loops
INPSS	snips		IPTTU	putti		KLOPU	plouk		KRTUU	Turku			polos
	spins		IQRTU	quirt		KLOSY	yolks		KSSTU	tusks			pools
INPST	pints		IQSTU	quist		KLOVY	yolky		KSTUU	kutus			sloop
INPSY	spiny			quits		KLRSU	lurks		KTTUU	tuktu			spool
INPTU	input			squit		KLSSU	sulks		LLLOS	lolls		LOOPY	loopy
	Putin		IQSUZ	squiz		KLSUY	sulky		LLLOY	lolly		LOORV	Orlov
INPUZ	unzip		IRRSY	yirrs		KLTUZ	klutz		LLLSU	lulls		LOORY	Oryol
INQSU	quins		IRSST	stirs		KMNOO	Nkomo		LLLUY	Lully		LOOSS	solos
INQTU	quint		IRSTW	wrist		KMNOS	monks		LLMOS	molls			sools
INRSU	ruins			writs		KMOOP	Mokpo		LLMOY	molly		LOOST	loots
INRTU	Turin		IRSUV	virus		KMOOS	mokos		LLMSU	mulls			lotos
INSST	snits		IRTUV	virtu			smoko		LLOOP	L'pool			sloot
INSSU	nisus		IRTYZ	ritzy		KMOST	Tomsk		LLOOR	Rollo			stool
	sinus		ISSSU	Issus		KMOSY	smoky		LLOPS	polls			tools
INSTT	stint		ISSSW	swiss		KMRUY	murky		LLOPY	polly		LOOSV	Vólos
	tints		ISSSY	sissy		KMSSU	musks		LLOQU	quoll		LOOSW	wools
INSTU	suint		ISSTU	situs		KMSUY	musky		LLORS	rolls		LOOTT	lotto
	Tunis			suits		KNNOW	known		LLORT	troll		LOOWY	wooly
	units		ISTTU	Titus		KNOOR	kroon		LLOST	tolls		LOPPS	plops
INSTW	twins		ISTTW	twist		KNOOS	nooks		LLOSY	lysol		LOPPY	loppy
INTTY	nitty			twits			snook		LLOTY	tolly			polyp
INTUV	unity		ISTXY	sixty		KNOOV	Kovno			tolyl		LOPRW	prowl
INUXZ	Xun Zi		ISWZZ	swizz		KNOOY	nooky		LLOWY	lowly		LOPSS	slops
IOOPT	topoi		ITTTU	tutti		KNOPS	knops			wolly		LOPST	plots
IOOTT	Otto I		ITTWX	twixt		KNORS	norks		LLOXY	xylol		LOPSU	loups
IOPRR	prior		ITTWY	witty		KNORT	tronk		LLPSU	pulls		LOPSW	lowps

Key	Word
	plows
LOPSY	ploys
	polys
	Pylos
LOPTU	Pluto
	poult
LOPUU	Upolu
LORRY	lorry
LORST	rotls
LORSU	lours
LORTY	Tylor
	Tyrol
LORUX	Luxor
LORWY	lowry
LOSST	slots
LOSSU	solus
	souls
LOSSW	slows
LOSSY	lossy
LOSTU	lotus
	louts
	Soult
LOSTV	volts
LOSTY	stylo
LOSUY	lousy
LOSWY	yowls
LOTYZ	zloty
LPPSU	pulps
LPPUY	pulpy
LPRSU	purls
	slurp
LPSUU	lupus
LRSSU	slurs
LRSUY	surly
LRTUY	truly
LRUUU	Uluru
LRWYY	wryly
LSSTU	lusts
	sluts
LSTUY	lusty
LSUUZ	zulus
LUVVY	luvvy
MMMUY	mummy
MMOPY	pommy
MMOSU	momus
MMOTY	tommy
MMOUY	yummo
MMPSU	mumps
MMRUY	rummy
MMSUY	mumsy
MMTUY	tummy
MMUYY	yummy
MNOOR	moron
MNOOS	monos
	moons
MNOOY	moony
MNORS	morns
	norms
MNORU	mourn
	Munro
MNORY	Myron
MNOSU	muons
MNOTT	Nottm
MNOTU	mount
	notum
MNSTU	munts
MOOPR	promo
MOORR	morro
MOORS	moors
	rooms
MOORT	motor
MOORV	vroom
MOORY	moory
	roomy
MOOSS	mosso
MOOST	moots
MOOSZ	zooms
MOOTT	motto
MOPPS	pomps
MOPRS	proms
	romps
MOPRT	tromp
MOPST	stomp
MOPSY	yomps
MORRU	rumor
MORST	morts
	storm
MORSW	worms
MORTU	tumor
MORUZ	Ormuz
MORWY	wormy
MOSSU	musos
MOSSY	mossy
MOSTU	motus
	smout
MOSTW	smowt
MOSUY	mousy
MOTTY	motty
MOTUZ	Mo-tzu
MPPSU	pumps
MPRSU	rumps
MPSSU	sumps
MPSTU	stump
	tumps
MPSUY	spumy
MRSSU	smurs
MRSTU	strum
MSSTU	musts
	smuts
	stums
MSSUY	mussy
MSTTU	mutts
MSTUV	musty
MSTYY	stymy
MUYZZ	muzzy
NNNUY	nunny
NNOOS	noons
NNOOY	Noyon
NNOSU	nouns
NNOSY	sonny
NNRUY	runny
NNSUY	sunny
NNTUY	tunny
NOOPR	porno
NOOPS	poons
	snoop
	spoon
NOORT	Orton
	roton
NOOST	oonts
	snoot
	toons
NOOSW	swoon
NOOSZ	zoons
NOPST	ponts
NOPTU	puton
NORSS	sorns
NORST	snort
	trons
NORSW	sworn
NORTU	Toruń
NOSST	snots
NOSSW	snows
NOSSY	sonsy
NOSTT	Notts
NOSTU	Notus
	nutso
	snout
	tonus
	touns
NOSTW	nowts
	towns
	wonts
NOSTY	stony
	Tyson
NOSWY	snowy
NOTUZ	Utzon
NOTWY	nowty
	towny
NPRSU	spurn
NPSTU	punts
NPSUU	sunup
NPTUY	punty
NRSTU	runts
	turns
NRTUY	runty
NSSTU	stuns
NSTTU	stunt
NTTUY	nutty
OOOPP	Poopó
OOPPS	poops
OOPPV	Popov
OOPRS	sopor
	spoor
OOPRT	poort
	Porto
	troop
OOPST	stoop
	topos
OOPSW	swoop
OOPTT	potto
OORRT	rotor
OORRU	Oruro
OORST	roost
	roots
	stoor
	torso
OORTU	outro
OORTY	rooty
OOSST	soots
OOSTT	toots
OOSTY	sooty
OOWYZ	woozy
OPPPY	poppy
OPPRS	props
OPPSY	popsy
	soppy
OPRST	ports
	prost
	sport
	strop
OPRSU	pours
	roups
OPRSW	prows
OPRSY	prosy
OPRTU	Prout
OPRUY	roupy
OPRXY	proxy
OPSST	posts
	spots
	stops
OPSSU	soups
OPSSW	swops
OPSSY	sysop
OPSTU	pouts
	spout
	stoup
OPSTW	stowp
OPSTY	pyots
	typos
OPSUY	soupy
OPSWY	Powys
OPTTU	putto
OPTTY	potty
OPTUY	pouty
OPTUZ	Tzu-po
OPYZZ	pozzy
ORRST	rorts
ORRSY	sorry
ORRTU	Truro
ORRTY	rorty
ORRWY	worry
ORSST	sorts
ORSSU	sorus
	sours
ORSTT	torts
	trots
ORSTU	roust
	routs
	stour
	torus
	tours
ORSTW	strow
	trows
	worst
	worts
ORSTY	ryots
	story
	stroy
	tyros
ORSUV	vrous
ORSUY	yours
ORTTU	trout
	tutor
OSSST	stoss
OSSTT	stots
OSSTU	ousts
OSSTW	stows
	swots
OSTTU	stout
	touts
OSUYZ	soyuz
OTTTY	totty
PPPUY	puppy
PPUYY	yuppy
PRRSU	purrs
PRSSU	spurs
PRSTU	spurt
	turps
PRSUU	Purús
	usurp
PRSUY	pursy
	syrup
PSSUY	pussy
PSTTU	putts
PTTUY	putty
RRSUU	rurus
RSSTU	rusts
	truss
RSTTU	strut
	sturt
RSTTY	tryst
RSTUW	wurst
RSTUY	rusty
	yurts
RSUUY	usury
RTTUY	rutty
SSSUU	susus
SSTXY	xysts
SSUWY	wussy
STTUU	tutus
TTTUY	tutty
TTUVY	vutty

Six Letters

<table>
<tr><td>AAABBN</td><td>Banaba</td><td>AAAGIL</td><td>Aglaia</td><td>AAAPPY</td><td>papaya</td><td>AABDRY</td><td>bayard</td></tr>
<tr><td>AAABCL</td><td>cabala</td><td>AAAGLM</td><td>Málaga</td><td>AAAPTZ</td><td>zapata</td><td>AABDSS</td><td>badass</td></tr>
<tr><td>AAABCN</td><td>cabana</td><td>AAAGLN</td><td>Alagna</td><td>AAARRT</td><td>Ararat</td><td>AABEEM</td><td>amebae</td></tr>
<tr><td>AAABCS</td><td>abacas</td><td>AAAGLT</td><td>Galata</td><td>AAARTV</td><td>avatar</td><td>AABEGM</td><td>ambage</td></tr>
<tr><td></td><td>casaba</td><td>AAAGMS</td><td>agamas</td><td>AAARTW</td><td>Tarawa</td><td>AABEGS</td><td>seabag</td></tr>
<tr><td>AAABDN</td><td>Abadan</td><td>AAAGNN</td><td>nagana</td><td>AAASTT</td><td>taatas</td><td>AABEKM</td><td>Makeba</td></tr>
<tr><td>AAABHN</td><td>Habana</td><td>AAAGNR</td><td>Angara</td><td>AAATWY</td><td>Yawata</td><td>AABELM</td><td>mabela</td></tr>
<tr><td>AAABIR</td><td>Arabia</td><td>AAAGRU</td><td>Aargau</td><td>AABBBO</td><td>baobab</td><td>AABELR</td><td>arable</td></tr>
<tr><td>AAABKK</td><td>kabaka</td><td>AAAHIK</td><td>Akhaïa</td><td>AABBCO</td><td>babaco</td><td></td><td>Arbela</td></tr>
<tr><td>AAABKL</td><td>kabala</td><td>AAAHIT</td><td>taiaha</td><td>AABBCY</td><td>abbacy</td><td>AABELT</td><td>ablate</td></tr>
<tr><td>AAABKN</td><td>Abakan</td><td>AAAHKR</td><td>akhara</td><td>AABBDO</td><td>Abbado</td><td>AABELZ</td><td>ablaze</td></tr>
<tr><td>AAABLM</td><td>Ambala</td><td>AAAHMR</td><td>Amhara</td><td>AABBIS</td><td>Abbas I</td><td>AABEMO</td><td>amoeba</td></tr>
<tr><td></td><td>Balaam</td><td>AAAHNV</td><td>Havana</td><td>AABBLL</td><td>lablab</td><td>AABEMS</td><td>amebas</td></tr>
<tr><td>AAABLR</td><td>labara</td><td></td><td>vahana</td><td>AABBLO</td><td>balboa</td><td>AABERU</td><td>bauera</td></tr>
<tr><td>AAABLT</td><td>albata</td><td>AAAHRS</td><td>Sahara</td><td>AABBST</td><td>sabbat</td><td>AABERZ</td><td>zareba</td></tr>
<tr><td></td><td>balata</td><td>AAAHTY</td><td>Yahata</td><td>AABCEO</td><td>cobaea</td><td>AABESS</td><td>abases</td></tr>
<tr><td>AAABNN</td><td>Annaba</td><td>AAAILL</td><td>alalia</td><td>AABCHM</td><td>ambach</td><td>AABEST</td><td>abates</td></tr>
<tr><td></td><td>banana</td><td>AAAILN</td><td>Alania</td><td>AABCHS</td><td>casbah</td><td>AABETU</td><td>bateau</td></tr>
<tr><td>AAABNS</td><td>anabas</td><td>AAAILR</td><td>aralia</td><td>AABCIM</td><td>cambia</td><td>AABFIR</td><td>Biafra</td></tr>
<tr><td>AAABNT</td><td>Bataan</td><td>AAAINZ</td><td>Azania</td><td>AABCIR</td><td>arabic</td><td>AABGGR</td><td>ragbag</td></tr>
<tr><td>AAABRT</td><td>Atbara</td><td>AAAITX</td><td>ataxia</td><td>AABCIU</td><td>Cuiabá</td><td>AABGGS</td><td>gasbag</td></tr>
<tr><td></td><td>braata</td><td>AAAJLP</td><td>Jalapa</td><td>AABCLR</td><td>Cabral</td><td>AABGIM</td><td>gambia</td></tr>
<tr><td>AAABRZ</td><td>baraza</td><td>AAAJMP</td><td>pajama</td><td>AABCLS</td><td>cabals</td><td>AABGIN</td><td>baaing</td></tr>
<tr><td></td><td>bazaar</td><td>AAAJMU</td><td>ujamaa</td><td>AABCLU</td><td>bacula</td><td>AABGKN</td><td>Bangka</td></tr>
<tr><td>AAABTT</td><td>batata</td><td>AAAJRW</td><td>Jawara</td><td>AABCLZ</td><td>Balzac</td><td>AABGMN</td><td>bagman</td></tr>
<tr><td>AAACCI</td><td>acacia</td><td>AAAKKN</td><td>kanaka</td><td>AABCMN</td><td>cabman</td><td>AABGMR</td><td>Bagram</td></tr>
<tr><td>AAACDG</td><td>cadaga</td><td>AAAKLM</td><td>kamala</td><td>AABCMT</td><td>tambac</td><td>AABGMS</td><td>gambas</td></tr>
<tr><td>AAACDI</td><td>Acadia</td><td>AAAKLS</td><td>alaska</td><td>AABCMY</td><td>Cambay</td><td>AABGRT</td><td>ratbag</td></tr>
<tr><td>AAACDN</td><td>canada</td><td>AAAKNR</td><td>Ankara</td><td>AABCRS</td><td>scarab</td><td>AABHJN</td><td>bhajan</td></tr>
<tr><td>AAACEH</td><td>Achaea</td><td></td><td>Kanara</td><td>AABCSU</td><td>abacus</td><td>AABHKS</td><td>kasbah</td></tr>
<tr><td>AAACJN</td><td>jacana</td><td>AAAKRT</td><td>Rakata</td><td>AABCUY</td><td>Cuyabá</td><td></td><td>sabkha</td></tr>
<tr><td>AAACLP</td><td>alpaca</td><td>AAALMS</td><td>masala</td><td>AABDDG</td><td>Bagdad</td><td>AABHLR</td><td>bharal</td></tr>
<tr><td>AAACMP</td><td>Macapá</td><td></td><td>salaam</td><td>AABDER</td><td>abrade</td><td>AABHMR</td><td>brahma</td></tr>
<tr><td>AAACMR</td><td>maraca</td><td>AAALMY</td><td>Malaya</td><td>AABDES</td><td>abased</td><td>AABHMS</td><td>shamba</td></tr>
<tr><td>AAACNN</td><td>Canaan</td><td>AAALQS</td><td>al-Aqsa</td><td>AABDET</td><td>abated</td><td>AABHNS</td><td>Bashan</td></tr>
<tr><td>AAACNR</td><td>arcana</td><td>AAAMMN</td><td>Manama</td><td>AABDEU</td><td>aubade</td><td></td><td>Shaban</td></tr>
<tr><td></td><td>Canara</td><td>AAAMNN</td><td>manana</td><td>AABDGO</td><td>dagoba</td><td>AABHNV</td><td>bhavan</td></tr>
<tr><td>AAACOX</td><td>Oaxaca</td><td>AAAMNP</td><td>panama</td><td>AABDIN</td><td>Ibadan</td><td>AABHNW</td><td>bhawan</td></tr>
<tr><td>AAADGL</td><td>Ala Dağ</td><td>AAAMNT</td><td>ataman</td><td></td><td>indaba</td><td>AABHRT</td><td>Bharat</td></tr>
<tr><td>AAADGM</td><td>Da Gama</td><td>AAAMRS</td><td>Asmara</td><td>AABDIS</td><td>Abdias</td><td>AABHSW</td><td>bashaw</td></tr>
<tr><td>AAADLM</td><td>Almada</td><td></td><td>samara</td><td>AABDLL</td><td>ballad</td><td></td><td>Wabash</td></tr>
<tr><td>AAADMR</td><td>armada</td><td>AAANNS</td><td>ananas</td><td>AABDLM</td><td>lambda</td><td>AABIKL</td><td>Baikal</td></tr>
<tr><td>AAADMS</td><td>Masada</td><td>AAANNT</td><td>Tanana</td><td>AABDMN</td><td>badman</td><td></td><td>Kabila</td></tr>
<tr><td>AAADNN</td><td>Ananda</td><td>AAANPR</td><td>Paraná</td><td>AABDOR</td><td>aboard</td><td>AABIKR</td><td>Kariba</td></tr>
<tr><td>AAADNP</td><td>panada</td><td>AAANRT</td><td>Ratana</td><td></td><td>abroad</td><td>AABILL</td><td>labial</td></tr>
<tr><td>AAAELZ</td><td>azalea</td><td>AAANSS</td><td>asanas</td><td></td><td>Baroda</td><td>AABILR</td><td>Brăila</td></tr>
<tr><td>AAAFRT</td><td>Arafat</td><td>AAANST</td><td>Astana</td><td>AABDRT</td><td>tabard</td><td>AABILU</td><td>abulia</td></tr>
</table>

AABILV Libava	**AACCIN** anicca	**AACGLY** galyac	**AACLOX** coaxal
AABIMR ambari	**AACCLO** cloaca	**AACHIN** Chania	**AACLPR** carpal
Bairam	**AACCLP** calpac	**AACHIT** Ithaca	**AACLPS** pascal
marabi	**AACCLR** calcar	**AACHKR** chakra	**AACLPU** paucal
AABIMZ Zambia	**AACCMO** macaco	charka	**AACLRS** lascar
AABINN banian	**AACCNN** cancan	**AACHKW** kwacha	rascal
AABINT Aintab	**AACCNR** Carnac	**AACHLS** calash	sacral
AABINZ banzai	**AACCOS** cacaos	**AACHMN** machan	scalar
AABIRS arabis	**AACDDU** caudad	**AACHMS** Ascham	**AACLSS** Casals
braais	**AACDEF** facade	Schama	**AACLSU** casual
AABIRT Tabari	**AACDEI** acedia	**AACHNO** Chaoan	causal
AABIST abatis	**AACDEL** alcade	**AACHNR** anarch	**AACLTU** actual
Bastia	**AACDER** arcade	**AACHNS** ashcan	**AACMNR** carman
AABISW Swabia	**AACDFR** cafard	**AACHNT** acanth	**AACMNS** camans
wasabi	**AACDGI** cadagi	Tanach	**AACMNU** Cumaná
AABJNS bajans	**AACDHS** dachas	**AACHNZ** chazan	**AACMNY** cayman
AABJOR Baroja	**AACDHT** datcha	**AACHPS** pachas	**AACMOT** Tacoma
AABKLN Balkan	**AACDHU** Dachau	**AACHRS** charas	**AACMRT** tarmac
AABKLR Barkla	**AACDIN** Candia	**AACHRT** Cathar	**AACMSS** camass
AABKMO Bamako	**AACDIR** acarid	**AACHTT** attach	**AACMSW** macaws
AABKNN kanban	**AACDLU** caudal	**AACHTY** Cathay	**AACNNO** Ancona
AABKNR barkan	**AACDMP** madcap	**AACIIR** Icaria	**AACNNS** cannas
AABKNS banaks	**AACDNR** canard	**AACIJM** jicama	**AACNOV** Canova
AABKRS bakras	cardan	**AACILL** laical	**AACNPR** Carnap
AABLMO Malabo	**AACDOP** da capo	**AACILM** calami	**AACNPT** catnap
AABLMS balsam	**AACEFI** faciae	camail	**AACNRT** arctan
AABLNS nablas	**AACEFL** faecal	**AACILP** apical	**AACNRY** canary
AABLNU Labuan	**AACEFR** carafe	**AACILR** Alaric	**AACNST** sancta
AABLNY Albany	**AACEHP** apache	racial	tacans
AABLOR aboral	**AACEHT** chaeta	**AACILS** Calais	**AACNSV** canvas
AABLOV lavabo	**AACEIN** Nicaea	**AACIMN** caiman	**AACNTT** actant
AABLRU Rabaul	**AACEJR** jacare	maniac	**AACNTV** vacant
AABLSS balsas	**AACELN** anlace	**AACINR** arnica	**AACNUX** Cunaxa
AABLST basalt	**AACELP** palace	carina	**AACPPY** papacy
tablas	**AACELS** Alsace	crania	**AACPRS** Caspar
AABLTU ablaut	**AACELT** acetal	**AACIPS** capias	**AACRST** carats
AABMMS mambas	**AACELY** Celaya	**AACIPT** capita	**AACRSU** acarus
AABMNR barman	**AACEMO** caeoma	**AACIRV** caviar	**AACRTV** cravat
AABMNT bantam	**AACEMR** camera	**AACISS** cassia	**AADDEL** daedal
batman	**AACENN** cannae	**AACITT** Attica	**AADDIL** alidad
AABMRS sambar	**AACENP** canape	**AACITV** atavic	**AADDLN** adland
AABMRY ambary	**AACENR** arcane	**AACITX** ataxic	**AADDMS** Addams
AABMSS sambas	**AACENT** catena	**AACJKL** jackal	**AADDOU** aoudad
AABNNY banyan	**AACEPR** Parcae	**AACJOU** acajou	**AADEFR** afeard
AABNRY Bárány	**AACERS** arecas	**AACKMY** Mackay	**AADEGJ** jagaed
AABNSW nawabs	caesar	**AACKRR** arrack	**AADEGL** gelada
AABNUV Vauban	**AACETV** caveat	**AACKSY** yackas	**AADEGM** damage
AABNYY bayyan	vacate	**AACKTT** attack	**AADEGN** agenda
AABORR arroba	**AACFIL** facial	**AACLLN** callan	**AADEGS** adages
AABORT abator	**AACFIR** Africa	**AACLLO** Callao	**AADEIT** ideata
rabato	**AACFIS** fascia	**AACLLS** callas	**AADEJU** Judaea
AABOSU oubaas	**AACFLU** facula	**AACLLU** calalu	**AADEKW** awaked
AABRRS Barras	faucal	**AACLMN** Alcman	**AADELS** salade
AABRSS sabras	**AACFNT** caftan	**AACLMT** lactam	**AADEMM** madame
AABRSZ bazars	**AACFRS** fracas	**AACLMU** macula	**AADEMN** anadem
AABRTY baryta	**AACFRX** carfax	**AACLNO** canola	maenad
AABTTW abwatt	**AACFVY** Cavafy	**AACLNR** carnal	**AADEMZ** amazed
AACCDI cicada	**AACGGM** cagmag	**AACLNS** canals	**AADENN** Andean
AACCEL caecal	**AACGIM** agamic	**AACLNT** Cantal	**AADENT** adnate
AACCHM chacma	**AACGIN** caaing	**AACLNU** canula	**AADENV** Nevada
AACCIL alcaic	**AACGIR** agaric	lacuna	**AADENX** adnexa
cicala	**AACGIU** guaiac	**AACLOT** catalo	**AADEOR** Oradea

AADEPR	parade	**AADMMR**	dammar	**AAEGLV**	lavage	**AAEMNP** apeman
AADERV	Veadar	**AADMMS**	madams	**AAEGLZ**	Alagez	**AAEMNR** Amen-Ra
AADEWW	wawaed	**AADMNO**	Manado	**AAEGMN**	manage	**AAEMNS** seaman
AADFIR	afraid	**AADMNS**	damans	**AAEGMR**	Gemara	**AAEMNX** axeman
AADFMU	madafu	**AADMOU**	amadou		megara	**AAEMRS** maraes
AADFRS	darafs	**AADMOV**	Adamov	**AAEGNR**	Reagan	**AAEMRU** Rameau
	farads	**AADMRS**	dramas	**AAEGNT**	agnate	**AAEMSZ** amazes
AADGHR	dargah		madras	**AAEGOR**	agorae	**AAENNZ** zenana
AADGIM	agamid	**AADMRU**	Madura	**AAEGPV**	pavage	**AAENOP** apnoea
AADGIO	adagio		maraud	**AAEGRV**	ravage	**AAENPS** España
AADGIR	Agadir	**AADMRZ**	mazard	**AAEGST**	agates		paeans
	gardai	**AADMSS**	admass	**AAEGSV**	agaves	**AAENPV** pavane
AADGLO	Ladoga	**AADMYY**	mayday		savage	**AAENRS** arenas
AADGNN	Da Nang	**AADNNR**	randan	**AAEGTU**	gateau	**AAENST** ansate
AADGNP	padang	**AADNPS**	pandas	**AAEHKP**	pakeha	**AAENSU** nausea
AADGNR	argand	**AADNRU**	Arnaud	**AAEHKS**	hakeas	**AAENSW** seawan
AADGNU	Uganda	**AADNRW**	Rwanda	**AAEHKT**	takahe	**AAEORT** aortae
AADGOP	pagoda	**AADNRY**	Anadyr	**AAEHLM**	haemal	**AAEOSZ** zoaeas
AADGRS	Asgard	**AADNSU**	Danaüs	**AAEHLT**	althea	**AAEPPR** appear
AADGRY	gaydar	**AADNSV**	vandas	**AAEHMT**	athame	**AAEPTT** tapeta
AADHIL	dahlia	**AADNSY**	dayans		hamate	**AAERRT** errata
AADHIM	Amidah	**AADOPS**	posada	**AAEHNT**	Athena	**AAERSX** Araxes
AADHKN	khanda	**AADOPV**	Padova	**AAEHNY**	hyaena	**AAERWX** earwax
AADHMM	dhamma	**AADOSW**	Sadowa	**AAEHPR**	raphae	**AAESTV** Avesta
AADHMR	dharma	**AADPRS**	Prasad	**AAEHRR**	Harare		savate
AADHNR	dharna	**AADPST**	adapts	**AAEHSY**	Ayesha	**AAESWY** seaway
AADHRZ	hazard	**AADPSW**	padsaw	**AAEILM**	amelia	**AAFFIM** maffia
AADILN	Dalian	**AADPYY**	payday		lamiae	**AAFFIR** affair
AADILO	alodia	**AADRRS**	radars	**AAEILR**	aerial		raffia
AADILR	radial		sardar		realia	**AAFFIT** taffia
AADILS	dalasi	**AADRRV**	Vardar	**AAEILX**	alexia	**AAFFJN** Jaffna
AADIMN	maidan	**AADRSW**	awards	**AAEIMN**	anemia	**AAFFRY** affray
AADIMT	Matadi	**AADRTU**	Artaud	**AAEINT**	taenia	**AAFFST** Staffa
AADINO	Adonai		datura	**AAEITV**	aviate	**AAFGHN** afghan
AADINR	Adrian	**AADRTY**	datary	**AAEKLN**	alkane	**AAFGIN** faaing
	radian	**AAEEGL**	galeae	**AAEKLR**	Kerala	**AAFHTW** fatwah
AADINS	naiads	**AAEEGN**	Aegean	**AAEKLS**	akelas	**AAFIKS** sifaka
AADIST	stadia	**AAEEGR**	Graeae	**AAEKNN**	ananke	**AAFILM** Amalfi
AADJLN	jandal	**AAEEGT**	eatage	**AAEKNW**	awaken	**AAFIMT** Fatima
AADJMU	Jumada	**AAEELP**	paleae	**AAEKRT**	karate		Fátima
AADKMS	damask	**AAEENS**	Aeneas	**AAEKSW**	awakes	**AAFINN** Fianna
AADKNU	Kaduna	**AAEEOZ**	zoaeae	**AAELLP**	paella	**AAFINR** farina
	Kaunda	**AAEEPR**	peraea	**AAELLU**	alulae	**AAFINX** Fa Xian
AADKOT	Dakota	**AAEERT**	aerate	**AAELMN**	Alemán	**AAFIRS** safari
AADKPU	padauk	**AAEFGR**	agrafe	**AAELMT**	malate	**AAFIST** fatsia
AADLLS	Dallas	**AAEFLM**	aflame		tamale	**AAFKNS** nafkas
AADLMW	wadmal	**AAEFLV**	favela	**AAELNN**	anneal	**AAFKNT** kaftan
AADLMY	malady	**AAEFNR**	fraena	**AAELNT**	lanate	**AAFLLL** fallal
AADLNO	anodal	**AAEFNS**	faenas	**AAELOR**	areola	**AAFLNU** faunal
	Loanda	**AAEFNU**	faunae	**AAELPP**	appeal	**AAFLOT** afloat
AADLNR	Darlan	**AAEFNZ**	Faenza	**AAELPR**	earlap	**AAFNSU** faunas
AADLNS	sandal	**AAEGGR**	garage	**AAELPS**	salpae	**AAFSTW** fatwas
AADLNU	landau	**AAEGGV**	gavage	**AAELPT**	palate	**AAGGHI** Haggai
	Luanda	**AAEGIN**	Aegina	**AAELPY**	Lepaya	**AAGGLO** galago
AADLNV	vandal	**AAEGIR**	Graiae	**AAELRT**	relata	**AAGGQU** quagga
AADLOP	apodal	**AAEGKR**	Kagera		Valera	**AAGGRS** saggar
AADLOS	Salado	**AAEGLM**	agleam	**AAELRV**	larvae	**AAGGRT** ragtag
AADLOU	Douala	**AAEGLN**	anlage		Valera	**AAGGSW** waggas
AADLRU	radula		galena	**AAELRZ**	Azrael	**AAGHKN** kangha
AADLRY	Layard		lagena	**AAELSW**	Wałęsa		khanga
AADLSS	salads	**AAEGLR**	alegar	**AAELTV**	valeta	**AAGHLS** galahs
AADMMN	madman		laager	**AAELZZ**	Azazel	**AAGHMR** Armagh
				AAEMMM	mammae		

49

	graham
AAGHNP	Pahang
AAGHNR	hangar
AAGHNS	Sangha
AAGHST	aghast
AAGIJW	Jigawa
AAGIKN	kainga
AAGILL	Gallia
AAGILN	agnail
	Anglia
AAGILP	Paglia
	palagi
AAGILR	argali
	garial
AAGILT	Galaţi
AAGILV	gavial
AAGIMN	magian
AAGINN	angina
	inanga
AAGINR	nagari
AAGINU	Guiana
	iguana
AAGINV	vagina
AAGIOS	asiago
AAGIRW	waragi
AAGISS	Agassi
AAGJRU	jaguar
AAGKLN	Kalgan
AAGKLU	Kaluga
AAGKLY	galyak
AAGKNS	kangas
AAGLLN	lalang
AAGLLP	plagal
AAGLMN	Malang
AAGLNO	analog
	angola
AAGLNR	langar
	raglan
AAGLNT	galant
AAGLRS	argals
AAGLRT	tragal
AAGLST	stalag
AAGLSY	gayals
AAGLWY	Galway
AAGLXY	galaxy
AAGMMS	gammas
	magmas
AAGMMT	gammat
AAGMNR	ragman
AAGMNS	gasman
AAGMOT	Gotama
AAGMRW	Wagram
AAGMRY	magyar
	margay
AAGNNO	goanna
	Nagano
AAGNNY	Anyang
AAGNOR	angora
	Aragon
	organa
AAGNOT	taonga
AAGNOY	Nagoya

AAGNPR	parang
AAGNPS	pagans
	pangas
AAGNRS	sangar
AAGNRT	Granta
AAGNRY	angary
AAGNST	satang
	tangas
AAGNTU	taguan
AAGNUV	Ungava
AAGNUY	Guyana
AAGORS	agoras
AAGPPR	grappa
AAGPRS	Gaspar
AAGRRY	garrya
AAGRSU	Ragusa
AAGRSV	Vargas
AAGRUV	avruga
AAGRVY	vagary
AAGSUV	guavas
AAHHJJ	hajjah
AAHHLL	hallah
AAHHLV	halvah
AAHHMZ	hamzah
AAHHNN	Hannah
AAHHPT	aphtha
AAHHWW	Haw-Haw
AAHIIS	Isaiah
AAHIIW	Hawaii
AAHIKN	Khaniá
AAHIKP	pakahi
AAHILT	hiatal
	Thalia
AAHILY	aliyah
AAHIMS	ahimsa
AAHINN	Hainan
	Nanhai
AAHINT	tahina
AAHIOT	taihoa
AAHIPR	pariah
	raphia
AAHIRR	harira
AAHIRS	sharia
AAHITW	tawhai
AAHJKT	jhatka
AAHJRR	jarrah
AAHJRS	rajahs
AAHKKM	Makkah
AAHKKT	kathak
AAHKLS	Khalsa
AAHKLY	khayal
AAHKMO	Oakham
AAHKPS	pashka
AAHKPU	hapuka
AAHKST	Shakta
AAHLLL	hallal
AAHLLO	halloa
AAHLLS	halals
AAHLLW	wallah
AAHLMM	hammal
AAHLMS	hamals
AAHLMT	maltha

AAHLMU	hamaul
AAHLNS	nahals
AAHLNT	Anhalt
AAHLPS	alphas
AAHLRS	ashlar
	lahars
AAHLRT	hartal
AAHLSV	halvas
AAHMMM	hammam
AAHMNS	shaman
AAHMPY	mayhap
AAHMRS	ashram
	harams
AAHMRT	Martha
AAHMST	asthma
AAHMTZ	matzah
AAHNNS	Anshan
AAHNNT	Nathan
AAHNSS	hansas
AAHNSZ	hazans
AAHNTU	Utahan
AAHNTV	Havant
AAHNUW	whanau
AAHNZZ	hazzan
AAHOSW	Oshawa
AAHPPR	paraph
AAHPRS	Parsha
	Saphar
AAHPSS	pashas
AAHPTY	apathy
AAHRSS	harass
AAHRST	arhats
	rathas
AAHRSU	Aarhus
	Ashura
AAHRSY	rayahs
AAHSSY	sashay
AAIIKR	Ikaría
AAIILS	aaliis
AAIILT	Italia
AAIINY	Aíyina
AAIISV	Savaii
AAIJNN	Janina
AAIJNP	Panaji
AAIJRV	Javari
AAIKKS	kaiaks
AAIKLL	alkali
AAIKLM	kalmia
AAIKLN	kalian
AAIKMT	Katmai
AAIKNO	aikona
AAIKRS	askari
AAIKRT	Katari
AAIKRZ	Karzai
AAIKSS	sakais
AAIKST	akitas
	kiaats
AAILLP	pallia
AAILLX	axilla
AAILMN	animal
	lamina
	manila

AAILMP	impala
AAILMS	lamias
	salami
AAILMW	Malawi
AAILNR	narial
AAILNS	lanais
	lianas
	nasial
	salina
AAILNT	antlia
	Latina
AAILNY	inyala
AAILPU	Apulia
AAILQU	Aquila
	qualia
AAILRS	laaris
	Larisa
AAILRT	atrial
	lariat
	latria
AAILSS	assail
AAILSV	avails
	saliva
	salvia
	Valais
AAILTT	Attila
AAILTV	Latvia
AAIMMS	miasma
AAIMMX	maxima
AAIMNR	airman
	Armani
	Marian
	marina
AAIMNS	manias
	Manisa
	Samian
AAIMNY	Yamani
AAIMRR	marari
AAIMRT	amrita
	tamari
AAIMRV	Ma'ariv
AAIMST	matais
AAIMSZ	zamias
AAIMTT	tatami
AAINNT	Tainan
AAINNY	Yanina
AAINOX	anoxia
AAINPP	papain
AAINPR	parian
	pirana
AAINPS	Saipan
AAINPT	patina
	pinata
	taipan
AAINRS	nairas
	Sarnia
AAINRT	antiar
	Tirana
AAINRU	anuria
	urania
AAINST	istana
AAINTT	attain

ABB | 6 letter words

AAINTW	Taiwan	**AAKNSU**	Kaunas	**AALORT**	aortal	**AANORV**	Novara
AAINTY	Yantai	**AAKNWZ**	kwanza	**AALOVW**	avowal	**AANOST**	sonata
AAIOPR	aporia	**AAKOPR**	pakora	**AALPPS**	appals	**AANOSV**	Savona
AAIOTU	Aouita	**AAKPPS**	kappas	**AALPPU**	papula	**AANOTT**	anatto
AAIPRY	apiary	**AAKPRS**	parkas	**AALPRR**	parral	**AANPPS**	nappas
AAIPZZ	piazza	**AAKRST**	karats	**AALPRY**	parlay	**AANPPU**	Papuan
AAIQRT	Qatari	**AAKSST**	Saktas	**AALPSS**	salpas	**AANPRT**	partan
AAIRST	arista	**AAKTVV**	Vyatka	**AALPSU**	pausal		tarpan
	tarsia	**AAKUWY**	Yukawa		Upsala		trapan
	tiaras	**AAKUYZ**	yakuza	**AALPSY**	playas	**AANPRU**	purana
AAIRSV	Vasari	**AALLLN**	lallan	**AALPSZ**	plazas	**AANPSV**	pavans
AAIRUW	wairua	**AALLMM**	mallam	**AALRST**	altars	**AANQTU**	quanta
AAIRVY	aviary	**AALLMS**	llamas		astral	**AANRRT**	arrant
	Yavarí	**AALLNY**	anally		ratals	**AANRRY**	yarran
AAIRWY	airway	**AALLPP**	appall		tarsal	**AANRSS**	sarans
AAIRZZ	razzia		palpal	**AALRSY**	salary	**AANRST**	ratans
AAISSS	assais	**AALLRU**	alular	**AALRSZ**	lazars	**AANRSV**	varnas
AAISST	satais	**AALLRV**	larval	**AALSSS**	salsas	**AANRTT**	rattan
AAISTW	awaits	**AALLSW**	wallas	**AALSSV**	vassal		tantra
	tawais	**AALLSY**	allays	**AALSWY**	always		tartan
AAISVY	Vaisya	**AALMMM**	mammal	**AALTUV**	valuta	**AANRTZ**	tarzan
AAITUY	yautia	**AALMMS**	Lammas	**AALTVV**	Vltava	**AANRUV**	Varuna
AAJKNS	sanjak		malams	**AALWYY**	waylay	**AANRYZ**	Ryazan
AAJLMR	Al Marj	**AALMNP**	napalm	**AAMMMS**	mammas	**AANSSU**	Assuan
AAJLNO	janola	**AALMNT**	Altman	**AAMMRR**	marram		Nassau
AAJLPS	jalaps	**AALMNU**	alumna	**AAMMRT**	tammar		saunas
AAJMNP	jampan		manual	**AAMMUZ**	mazuma	**AANSTV**	savant
AAJMNR	Jarman	**AALMNW**	lawman	**AAMNNR**	Mannar	**AANSTZ**	stanza
AAJMOR	Marajó	**AALMNY**	layman	**AAMNOS**	Manáos	**AANTUV**	avaunt
AAJMPY	pyjama	**AALMOQ**	Aqmola		Samoan	**AANWYY**	anyway
AAJNPR	prajna	**AALMOR**	amoral	**AAMNOZ**	amazon	**AAOPST**	sapota
AAJNPS	japans	**AALMOT**	amatol	**AAMNPS**	sampan	**AAORRU**	aurora
AAJNRT	Trajan	**AALMPR**	palmar	**AAMNPX**	Paxman	**AAORST**	aortas
AAJNRU	Arjuna	**AALMPS**	lampas	**AAMNRT**	mantra		Sorata
AAJNSW	jawans		Palmas	**AAMNST**	mantas	**AAORTT**	totara
AAJPRU	Japurá		plasma		Tasman	**AAOTTV**	ottava
AAJRSW	swaraj	**AALMRS**	alarms	**AAMNSU**	Manaus	**AAOTTW**	Ottawa
AAKKLP	kalpak		malars	**AAMNTU**	mantua	**AAPPSW**	papaws
AAKKMR	markka	**AALMRU**	alarum	**AAMNTX**	taxman	**AAPPWW**	pawpaw
AAKKNR	Karnak	**AALMTY**	Almaty	**AAMOPR**	paramo	**AAPRRS**	parras
AAKKOP	kakapo		amytal	**AAMORS**	aromas	**AAPRST**	Patras
AAKKRU	Krakau	**AALNNS**	annals		Masora		satrap
AAKKSY	kayaks	**AALNNU**	annual	**AAMORV**	Morava		Sparta
AAKLMO	Akmola	**AALNOS**	Solana	**AAMORZ**	Zamora	**AAPRUY**	Yapurá
AAKLMR	Kalmar	**AALNOT**	atonal	**AAMOSS**	samosa	**AAPSST**	pastas
AAKLMU	Makalu		Latona	**AAMOST**	somata	**AAPSTW**	wataps
AAKLOS	koalas	**AALNOV**	Avalon	**AAMOTY**	Toyama	**AAPWXX**	paxwax
AAKLRS	kraals		Avlona	**AAMPPS**	pampas	**AAPZZZ**	pazazz
AAKLSS	laksas		Valona	**AAMQST**	Masqat	**AAQQWW**	Qwaqwa
AAKLSU	Lusaka	**AALNOX**	axonal	**AAMQSU**	squama	**AAQRSU**	quasar
AAKLTU	taluka	**AALNOZ**	azonal	**AAMRSU**	asarum	**AARRSY**	arrays
AAKMNU	manuka	**AALNPR**	planar	**AAMRSW**	aswarm	**AARRTT**	tartar
AAKMRS	makars	**AALNPT**	platan	**AAMRSY**	Ramsay	**AARSST**	sastra
	markas	**AALNRT**	antral	**AAMRTU**	trauma	**AARSTT**	strata
AAKMRU	kumara		tarnal	**AAMSSS**	assams		tatars
AAKMTU	makuta	**AALNRU**	ranula	**AAMSTU**	amauts	**AARSTY**	astray
AAKNNS	Kansan	**AALNRW**	narwal	**AAMSTZ**	matzas		tayras
AAKNOR	anorak	**AALNRX**	larnax	**AAMTTU**	Umtata	**AARSWW**	warsaw
AAKNRT	kantar	**AALNSS**	nasals	**AANNNS**	nannas	**AARTTY**	Tatary
AAKNSS	Kansas	**AALNST**	aslant	**AANNRU**	anuran	**AASSSY**	assays
AAKNST	askant	**AALNSY**	nyalas	**AANNTT**	natant	**AASTZZ**	tazzas
	tankas	**AALOPY**	payola	**AANNYZ**	nyanza	**ABBBEL**	babble

ABB | 6 letter words

ABBCEI cabbie	**ABBRRU** Rubbra	**ABCLOT** cobalt	**ABDEKS** basked
ABBCER Crabbe	**ABBRSU** busbar	**ABCMOP** mobcap	**ABDELL** balled
ABBCIR bicarb	**ABCCIO** boccia	**ABCMOR** crambo	**ABDELM** ambled
ABBCOS cabobs	**ABCCLU** buccal	**ABCMOT** combat	bedlam
ABBCOT bobcat	**ABCDEH** bached	tombac	beldam
ABBCRY crabby	**ABCDEK** backed	**ABCMRS** scramb	blamed
ABBCSY scabby	**ABCDEL** cabled	**ABCNOR** carbon	lambed
ABBDDE dabbed	**ABCDER** braced	corban	**ABDELO** albedo
ABBDEG gabbed	**ABCDIR** bardic	**ABCNOS** bacons	doable
ABBDEI babied	**ABCDTU** abduct	**ABCORS** brasco	**ABDELR** balder
ABBDEJ jabbed	**ABCEEH** Achebe	carobs	blared
ABBDEL dabble	**ABCEEM** became	cobras	**ABDELS** blades
ABBDEN nabbed	**ABCEGO** bocage	**ABCORX** boxcar	**ABDELT** tabled
ABBDER barbed	**ABCEGU** cubage	**ABCORY** carboy	**ABDELW** bawled
dabber	**ABCEHL** bleach	**ABCOSV** vocabs	**ABDELY** dyable
ABBDET tabbed	**ABCEHN** Chenab	**ABCRST** bracts	**ABDELZ** blazed
ABBDEU bedaub	**ABCEHR** Béchar	**ABDDEE** beaded	**ABDEMN** badmen
ABBEEW bawbee	breach	**ABDDEI** abided	**ABDENN** banned
ABBEFU Babeuf	**ABCEHS** baches	baddie	**ABDENP** bedpan
ABBEGL gabble	**ABCEHU** Hecuba	**ABDDEL** bladed	**ABDENU** Danube
ABBEGR gabber	**ABCEIK** backie	**ABDDEN** banded	**ABDEOS** abodes
ABBEIR barbie	**ABCEIM** amebic	**ABDDER** badder	adobes
ABBEIS babies	**ABCEIS** ceibas	barded	**ABDEOT** boated
ABBEIY yabbie	**ABCEJT** abject	**ABDDEU** daubed	**ABDERR** barred
ABBEJR jabber	**ABCEKR** backer	**ABDDEY** daybed	**ABDERS** ardebs
ABBEKS kebabs	**ABCELS** cables	**ABDDHU** buddha	bardes
ABBELR barbel	**ABCELT** cablet	**ABDEEH** behead	beards
rabble	**ABCEMN** cabmen	**ABDEEK** beaked	breads
ABBELS babels	**ABCEMR** camber	debeak	debars
ABBELU bauble	**ABCEMW** webcam	**ABDEEL** beadle	sabred
ABBELW wabble	**ABCENO** beacon	**ABDEEM** beamed	serdab
ABBERR barber	**ABCENU** cubane	**ABDEEN** beaned	**ABDERU** dauber
ABBERT barbet	**ABCERR** bracer	**ABDEER** beared	**ABDERV** adverb
rabbet	**ABCERS** braces	**ABDEES** debase	braved
ABBERY yabber	cabers	**ABDEET** debate	**ABDERY** brayed
ABBESS abbess	**ABCFIR** fabric	**ABDEFL** fabled	**ABDERZ** brazed
ABBESY abbeys	**ABCFNO** confab	**ABDEGG** bagged	**ABDEST** basted
ABBFLY flabby	**ABCHIU** Bauchi	**ABDEGL** gabled	**ABDESU** abused
ABBGMU bumbag	**ABCHLN** blanch	**ABDEGN** banged	daubes
ABBGOR gabbro	**ABCHMO** Cobham	**ABDEGO** bodega	**ABDETT** batted
ABBGRY grabby	**ABCHNR** branch	**ABDEGR** badger	**ABDETU** tabued
ABBHJU jubbah	**ABCHNU** Buchan	barged	**ABDFOR** forbad
ABBHSY shabby	**ABCHOR** broach	garbed	**ABDHNS** bandhs
ABBIJL jilbab	**ABCHPR** Archbp	**ABDEGS** badges	**ABDHOY** hobday
ABBILO Bilbao	**ABCHPU** hubcap	debags	**ABDIJM** Djambi
ABBIMS Babism	**ABCHRU** Baruch	**ABDEHL** blahed	**ABDILR** bridal
bambis	**ABCIIM** iambic	**ABDEHS** bashed	labrid
ABBIOR Robbia	**ABCIJO** Jacobi	**ABDEHT** bathed	ribald
ABBIRS rabbis	**ABCILT** Baltic	**ABDEIL** bailed	**ABDINR** Briand
ABBIRT rabbit	**ABCILU** abulic	**ABDEIR** abider	riband
ABBITW wabbit	**ABCINS** cabins	bardie	**ABDINT** bandit
ABBKOS kabobs	**ABCIOS** cobias	**ABDEIS** abides	**ABDIRR** briard
ABBLRU bulbar	**ABCISS** basics	biased	**ABDIRS** braids
ABBLSU babuls	**ABCISU** Baucis	**ABDEIT** baited	disbar
bubals	**ABCISY** Biscay	**ABDEIZ** baized	**ABDLLY** baldly
ABBLWY wabbly	**ABCKLS** blacks	**ABDEJR** Djerba	**ABDLNO** Boland
ABBMOO bamboo	**ABCKPU** backup	**ABDEKL** balked	**ABDLOS** doblas
ABBMOY Bombay	**ABCKRS** bracks	**ABDEKN** banked	**ABDLRY** drably
ABBNOO baboon	**ABCKRU** buckra	**ABDEKO** boaked	**ABDNOR** Brando
ABBNOS nabobs	**ABCLMY** cymbal	**ABDEKR** barked	roband
ABBORS absorb	**ABCLNO** Balcon	braked	**ABDNOU** abound
ABBOST abbots	blanco	debark	**ABDNRS** brands

ABDNRT	Brandt	**ABEGLU**	beluga	**ABEJMS**	jambes	**ABELSU**	suable
ABDNRU	Dunbar		blague	**ABEJOR**	jerboa		usable
	Durban	**ABEGMN**	bagmen	**ABEJRT**	Béjart	**ABELSY**	basely
ABDNRY	brandy	**ABEGMR**	bregma	**ABEJRU**	abjure		belays
ABDORS	adsorb	**ABEGMU**	Mugabe	**ABEKKZ**	Kazbek	**ABELSZ**	blazes
	boards	**ABEGNR**	banger	**ABEKLM**	kembla	**ABELTT**	battle
	broads		graben	**ABEKLR**	balker		tablet
	dobras	**ABEGOR**	borage	**ABEKLY**	Blakey	**ABELTY**	Batley
	dorbas	**ABEGOZ**	gazebo	**ABEKMN**	embank	**ABELWY**	byelaw
ABDORT	Bardot	**ABEGRS**	barges	**ABEKMR**	embark	**ABEMNO**	bemoan
ABDORY	byroad	**ABEGRZ**	Zagreb	**ABEKNR**	banker	**ABEMNR**	barmen
ABDOSY	Abydos	**ABEGTU**	baguet	**ABEKNT**	banket	**ABEMNT**	batmen
ABDOYY	dayboy	**ABEHIL**	habile	**ABEKOT**	Aktobe	**ABEMOS**	Soemba
ABDRRU	durbar	**ABEHLR**	herbal	**ABEKOU**	Bouaké	**ABEMRS**	ambers
ABDRSU	absurd	**ABEHLS**	belahs	**ABEKRR**	barker		breams
ABDRWY	bawdry	**ABEHLU**	Beulah	**ABEKRS**	bakers		Sambre
ABEEGL	beagle	**ABEHNT**	Theban		brakes	**ABEMRU**	umbrae
ABEEGR	barege	**ABEHOS**	obeahs		breaks	**ABEMSU**	Mabuse
	bargee	**ABEHRS**	basher	**ABEKRY**	bakery	**ABEMSY**	embays
ABEEHV	behave		rehabs	**ABEKST**	basket		maybes
ABEEIL	bailee	**ABEHRT**	bather	**ABELLS**	labels	**ABENNR**	banner
ABEEIN	beanie		bertha	**ABELLT**	ballet	**ABENOR**	borane
ABEEKR	beaker		breath	**ABELLU**	bullae	**ABENOS**	beanos
ABEEKT	betake	**ABEHSS**	bashes	**ABELLY**	Bellay	**ABENOT**	Beaton
ABEELN	baleen		sahebs	**ABELMM**	embalm		onbeat
	enable	**ABEHST**	bathes	**ABELMR**	ambler	**ABENRR**	barren
ABEELS	abeles		Shebat		Balmer	**ABENRS**	Barnes
ABEEMN	bemean	**ABEIIL**	bailie		marble	**ABENRT**	banter
	bename	**ABEIIR**	Iberia		ramble		barnet
ABEEMR	beamer	**ABEIIT**	tibiae	**ABELMS**	ambles	**ABENRU**	urbane
ABEENT	beaten	**ABEIKK**	bakkie		blames	**ABENRY**	barney
ABEENU	Beaune	**ABEILL**	alible	**ABELMW**	wamble		Bayern
ABEEOR	aerobe		Belial	**ABELNR**	branle		nearby
ABEEOU	Euboea		labile	**ABELNU**	nebula	**ABENRZ**	brazen
ABEERR	bearer		liable		unable	**ABENST**	absent
ABEERT	beater	**ABEILM**	lambie	**ABELNY**	bylane		Besant
	berate	**ABEILR**	bailer	**ABELOR**	boreal	**ABENSY**	Naseby
	rebate		librae	**ABELOT**	boatel	**ABENTT**	batten
ABEERV	beaver	**ABEILS**	abseil		lobate	**ABENTU**	butane
ABEERW	beware		isabel		oblate	**ABENTZ**	bezant
ABEERY	Baeyer	**ABEILT**	albeit	**ABELOW**	Lebowa	**ABEORS**	Boreas
ABEFFL	baffle		albite	**ABELPU**	Puebla	**ABEORT**	boater
ABEFHL	behalf	**ABEILV**	viable	**ABELRR**	barrel		borate
ABEFLL	befall	**ABEILW**	bewail	**ABELRS**	Albers		rebato
ABEFLM	flambe	**ABEILY**	bailey		balers	**ABEORZ**	bezoar
ABEFLR	fabler	**ABEIMN**	Namibe		belars	**ABEOSS**	Sasebo
ABEFLS	fables	**ABEINR**	Braine		blares	**ABEPTU**	upbeat
ABEFMR	ferbam	**ABEINS**	sabine		blears	**ABEQRU**	barque
ABEFPR	prefab	**ABEINT**	binate	**ABELRT**	albert		Braque
ABEGGR	beggar	**ABEINZ**	Azbine		labret	**ABEQSU**	basque
ABEGIS	bagies		Ibáñez	**ABELRV**	verbal	**ABERRS**	barres
	gabies	**ABEIOT**	boatie	**ABELRW**	bawler		Barrès
ABEGIU	Ibagué	**ABEIRR**	barrie		warble	**ABERRT**	barret
ABEGLL	Elbląg		Ribera	**ABELRY**	barely		barter
ABEGLM	gamble	**ABEIRS**	braise		barley	**ABERRV**	braver
ABEGLN	bangle		rabies		bleary	**ABERRW**	brawer
	Bengal		Serbia	**ABELRZ**	blazer	**ABERRY**	brayer
ABEGLR	garble	**ABEIRT**	barite	**ABELSS**	sables	**ABERRZ**	brazer
ABEGLS	bagels		terbia	**ABELST**	ablest	**ABERSS**	sabers
	belgas	**ABEISS**	biases		bleats		sabres
	gables	**ABEISZ**	baizes		stable	**ABERST**	barest
ABEGLT	gablet	**ABEJMR**	jamber		tables		breast

	Tarbes	**ABGMNO**	bogman		Albion	**ABLMOO**	abloom
ABERSU	abuser	**ABGNOO**	boonga		Alboin	**ABLMOP**	aplomb
	bursae		gaboon	**ABILNS**	blains		Pombal
	busera	**ABGNOR**	Bangor	**ABILNY**	Libyan	**ABLMOR**	bromal
ABERSV	braves		barong	**ABILOR**	bailor	**ABLMRU**	brumal
ABERSY	baryes		brogan	**ABILRS**	brails		labrum
	yerbas	**ABGNOS**	bogans		brasil		lumbar
ABERSZ	brazes	**ABGOOT**	Bogotá	**ABILRT**	tribal		umbral
	zebras		Tobago	**ABILRU**	burial	**ABLMRY**	marbly
ABERTT	batter	**ABGORS**	garbos	**ABILRZ**	brazil	**ABLMSU**	albums
ABERTX	baxter	**ABGORT**	bogart	**ABILSS**	basils	**ABLMTY**	tymbal
ABERTY	betray	**ABGRSU**	Burgas	**ABILST**	baltis	**ABLMWY**	wambly
ABERUU	bureau	**ABHIIR**	Bihari	**ABILSY**	Baylis	**ABLNOZ**	blazon
ABERUY	Aubrey	**ABHIJS**	bhajis	**ABIMMU**	Mumbai	**ABLNSU**	baluns
ABERWY	bewray	**ABHIKL**	kiblah	**ABIMNN**	binman		Nablus
ABERZZ	Zabrze	**ABHIKT**	bhakti	**ABIMPT**	bitmap	**ABLNTU**	buntal
ABESSS	basses	**ABHIMR**	mihrab	**ABIMRS**	mbiras	**ABLOOR**	robalo
ABESST	basest	**ABHIMS**	bimahs	**ABIMRU**	barium	**ABLORS**	labors
	basset	**ABHINR**	Harbin		Umbria	**ABLORU**	labour
	bastes	**ABHINS**	banish	**ABIMSS**	simbas	**ABLOST**	bloats
	beasts	**ABHIOO**	boohai	**ABIMST**	ambits		oblast
ABESSU	abuses	**ABHIOP**	phobia	**ABIMSU**	iambus	**ABLOSY**	boylas
ABESTT	bettas	**ABHISS**	sahibs	**ABINNU**	Nubian	**ABLOTT**	talbot
ABESTU	beauts	**ABHIST**	habits	**ABINOS**	basion	**ABLOTV**	abvolt
ABETTU	battue	**ABHLOP**	Bhopal		bonsai	**ABLPRU**	burlap
	tubate	**ABHMNO**	bonham		Bosnia	**ABLPYY**	byplay
ABETTY	Beatty	**ABHMOS**	abohms	**ABINOT**	obtain	**ABLRST**	blarts
ABETUY	beauty	**ABHMOT**	Botham	**ABINRS**	bairns	**ABLRSU**	bursal
ABEUXY	Bayeux	**ABHMOU**	Huambo		brains		lubras
ABEZZZ	bezazz	**ABHMRS**	Brahms	**ABINRY**	binary	**ABLRSW**	brawls
ABFGLU	bagful	**ABHMRU**	rhumba		brainy	**ABLRTU**	brutal
ABFILU	fibula	**ABHMSU**	ambush	**ABINSS**	basins	**ABLRWY**	brawly
ABFISY	basify	**ABHNOT**	Naboth		sabins	**ABLSST**	blasts
ABFLRY	barfly	**ABHNRU**	Hurban	**ABINSU**	Anubis	**ABLSTY**	stably
ABFOOR	foobar	**ABHNTU**	Bhutan	**ABIORR**	barrio	**ABLSUY**	usably
ABGGIW	bagwig	**ABHORR**	harbor	**ABIORS**	isobar	**ABLSWY**	bylaws
ABGHTU	hagbut	**ABHORS**	abhors	**ABIOST**	biotas	**ABMMOO**	Moomba
ABGIKN	baking	**ABHORT**	Hobart	**ABIRRS**	briars	**ABMMOS**	mambos
ABGIKT	kitbag	**ABHOST**	bathos	**ABIRRY**	briary	**ABMNOW**	bowman
ABGILM	gimbal	**ABHOTX**	hatbox	**ABIRSU**	airbus	**ABMNRU**	Barnum
ABGILN	baling	**ABHOXY**	haybox	**ABIRTZ**	Tabriz	**ABMNSU**	busman
ABGIMR	gambir	**ABHPTY**	bypath	**ABISST**	bastis	**ABMNTU**	numbat
ABGIMT	gambit	**ABHRSY**	brashy	**ABISSU**	Bissau		Tubman
ABGIMY	bigamy	**ABHSSU**	subahs	**ABJJOO**	jojoba	**ABMOSS**	sambos
ABGINO	bagnio	**ABIIKL**	Bialik	**ABJLMU**	jumbal	**ABMOTV**	Tambov
	gabion		Bikila	**ABJLNU**	Banjul	**ABMOTW**	wombat
	Gobian	**ABIILS**	alibis	**ABJNOS**	banjos	**ABMRSU**	sambur
ABGINR	baring		Basil I	**ABJNPU**	Punjab		umbras
	Gibran	**ABIILT**	tibial	**ABJOST**	jabots	**ABMRUY**	aumbry
ABGINS	basing	**ABIINN**	bainin	**ABKLNS**	blanks	**ABMSSY**	abysms
ABGINT	bating	**ABIIST**	tibias	**ABKLSU**	baulks	**ABNNUY**	Bunyan
ABGINU	Bangui	**ABIJRS**	Srbija	**ABKLSY**	skylab	**ABNORS**	barons
ABGINY	abying	**ABIJRU**	jabiru	**ABKLUY**	baulky	**ABNORT**	barton
	baying	**ABIKKU**	kabuki	**ABKNRS**	branks	**ABNORY**	barony
ABGIOR	Borgia	**ABIKLS**	Balkis	**ABKORS**	boraks		baryon
ABGIOS	biogas	**ABIKMO**	akimbo	**ABKORT**	Bartók	**ABNOST**	batons
ABGIOU	baguio	**ABIKRS**	Biskra	**ABKRSU**	burkas	**ABNOTY**	botany
ABGKOO	bogoak	**ABIKTT**	battik	**ABKUUV**	Bukavu	**ABNRST**	brants
ABGLLO	global	**ABILLO**	Baliol	**ABLLOO**	lobola	**ABNRSU**	burans
ABGLMO	gambol	**ABILMT**	timbal	**ABLLOT**	ballot		unbars
ABGLOR	Ålborg	**ABILMU**	labium	**ABLLPU**	ballup	**ABNRTU**	turban
	brolga	**ABILNO**	albino	**ABLLSY**	ballsy	**ABNRTY**	Bryant

ABNRUU	auburn	**ACCENU**	Cuenca	**ACDEFH**	chafed	**ACDEPP**	capped
ABNRUY	anbury	**ACCEPT**	accept	**ACDEFR**	farced	**ACDEPR**	carped
ABNRWY	brawny	**ACCERS**	scarce	**ACDEGR**	cadger		craped
ABNSTU	bantus	**ACCERU**	accrue		graced		redcap
ABNSUY	bunyas	**ACCESS**	access	**ACDEGS**	cadges	**ACDEPS**	scaped
ABNTYZ	byzant	**ACCESU**	accuse	**ACDEGT**	gedact		spaced
ABOOST	taboos	**ACCGNO**	cognac	**ACDEHK**	hacked	**ACDERR**	carder
ABOOSZ	bazoos	**ACCHIK**	chiack	**ACDEHR**	arched	**ACDERS**	cadres
ABOOTU	Baotou	**ACCHIR**	Chirac		echard		cedars
ABORRS	arbors	**ACCHKY**	chyack	**ACDEHS**	chased		sacred
	Barros	**ACCHNO**	concha	**ACDEHT**	detach		scared
ABORRU	arbour	**ACCHNY**	chancy	**ACDEHW**	chawed	**ACDERT**	carted
ABORRW	barrow	**ACCHOU**	cachou	**ACDEIN**	decani		crated
ABORSS	Brassó	**ACCHRT**	cratch	**ACDEIR**	cardie		redact
ABORST	aborts	**ACCHSU**	succah	**ACDEIS**	de Sica		traced
	Strabo	**ACCHTY**	catchy	**ACDEIV**	advice	**ACDERV**	carved
	tabors	**ACCHUY**	Cauchy	**ACDEJK**	jacked		craved
ABORSV	Braşov	**ACCIIN**	acinic	**ACDEKL**	calked	**ACDERZ**	crazed
	bravos	**ACCILO**	calico		lacked	**ACDEST**	cadets
ABORSY	boyars	**ACCILT**	lactic	**ACDEKP**	packed	**ACDESU**	caused
ABORTU	rubato	**ACCINO**	cocain	**ACDEKR**	arcked		sauced
	tabour	**ACCINT**	cantic		carked	**ACDESY**	decays
ABORTW	towbar	**ACCINY**	cyanic		racked	**ACDETT**	catted
ABORTY	tarboy	**ACCIOT**	ocicat	**ACDEKS**	sacked	**ACDEUX**	caudex
	Torbay	**ACCIPR**	capric	**ACDEKT**	tacked	**ACDHIR**	chadri
ABOSSS	bassos	**ACCIRR**	ricrac	**ACDEKY**	yacked		diarch
ABOSST	boasts	**ACCIRS**	siccar	**ACDELL**	called	**ACDHMR**	drachm
	sabots	**ACCIRT**	arctic	**ACDELM**	calmed	**ACDHOR**	chador
ABOSUY	bayous	**ACCITT**	tactic	**ACDELN**	candle	**ACDHRS**	chards
ABOSWW	bowsaw	**ACCKLO**	Alcock		lanced	**ACDIIM**	amidic
ABPRTU	abrupt	**ACCKLS**	clacks	**ACDELO**	coaled	**ACDIIP**	adipic
ABPSSY	bypass	**ACCKRS**	cracks	**ACDELP**	placed	**ACDIJU**	Judaic
ABPSTY	bypast	**ACCKSU**	Cusack	**ACDELR**	Calder	**ACDILM**	Mladic
ABQSSU	squabs	**ACCLNY**	Clancy		cradle	**ACDILP**	placid
ABRRSU	bursar	**ACCLOU**	coucal		credal	**ACDILS**	discal
ABRSSU	bursas	**ACCNNU**	Cancún	**ACDELS**	clades	**ACDILY**	acidly
ABRSSY	brassy	**ACCORS**	arccos		decals	**ACDINO**	anodic
ABSUWY	subway		corsac		scaled	**ACDINR**	Andrić
ABSWYY	byways	**ACCORW**	Cracow	**ACDELT**	talced		Cardin
ACCCIL	calcic	**ACCOST**	accost	**ACDELU**	caudle		rancid
ACCCLO	coccal	**ACCRUY**	curacy		Claude	**ACDINY**	cyanid
ACCDEE	accede	**ACCSTU**	cactus	**ACDELV**	calved	**ACDIOT**	dacoit
ACCDEH	cached	**ACCSUU**	caucus	**ACDELW**	clawed	**ACDIOZ**	zodiac
ACCDEN	Deccan	**ACCSUY**	yuccas	**ACDELY**	clayed	**ACDIPR**	Picard
ACCDII	acidic	**ACCTUU**	Cúcuta	**ACDEMN**	Camden	**ACDIPS**	capsid
ACCDOR	accord	**ACDDEE**	decade	**ACDEMP**	camped	**ACDIRS**	cairds
ACCDSY	cycads	**ACDDEG**	cadged		decamp		darics
ACCEHN	chance	**ACDDEI**	caddie	**ACDENN**	canned	**ACDIST**	dicast
ACCEHS	caches	**ACDDEN**	danced	**ACDENO**	acnode	**ACDLNU**	unclad
ACCEHT	cachet	**ACDDER**	carded		canoed	**ACDLSS**	scalds
ACCEIL	celiac	**ACDDEU**	adduce		deacon	**ACDLTY**	dactyl
	cicale	**ACDDII**	diacid	**ACDENR**	craned	**ACDMSU**	Cadmus
ACCEIP	icecap	**ACDDIN**	candid		dancer	**ACDMTU**	mudcat
	ipecac	**ACDDIS**	caddis		nacred	**ACDNNU**	Duncan
ACCEIT	acetic	**ACDDIT**	addict	**ACDENS**	ascend	**ACDNOR**	candor
ACCEKL	cackle	**ACDDIY**	dyadic		dances		Conrad
ACCELN	cancel	**ACDDTU**	adduct	**ACDENT**	cadent	**ACDNRY**	Drancy
ACCELR	cercal	**ACDEEF**	deface		canted	**ACDORR**	Rocard
ACCELS	calces	**ACDEEN**	decane		decant	**ACDORS**	Dorcas
ACCEMU	caecum	**ACDEEP**	peaced	**ACDENY**	dancey		dracos
ACCENR	cancer	**ACDEER**	decare	**ACDEOT**	coated	**ACDORW**	coward
ACCENT	accent	**ACDEES**	ceased	**ACDEOX**	coaxed	**ACDORY**	Corday

ACDOST	octads	**ACEFTU**	faucet		Thrace		Neckar
ACDPRU	Duparc	**ACEGHN**	change	**ACEHRW**	chawer	**ACEKPR**	packer
ACDRSU	Cardus	**ACEGHR**	charge	**ACEHRX**	exarch		repack
ACDSSU	scauds	**ACEGHU**	gauche	**ACEHSS**	chases	**ACEKPT**	packet
ACDSTU	ducats	**ACEGIL**	Gaelic		chasse	**ACEKRR**	racker
ACEEFF	efface	**ACEGIR**	cagier	**ACEHST**	chaste	**ACEKRS**	crakes
ACEEFN	enface	**ACEGLN**	glance		cheats		creaks
ACEEFR	reface	**ACEGLS**	glaces		sachet		sacker
ACEEFS	faeces	**ACEGLU**	Glauce		scathe		screak
ACEEGN	encage	**ACEGLY**	legacy		taches	**ACEKRT**	racket
ACEEHL	chelae	**ACEGNU**	cangue	**ACEHSU**	Huesca		tacker
ACEEHN	achene	**ACEGNY**	agency	**ACEHSW**	cashew	**ACEKRW**	wacker
ACEEHT	Hecate		Cagney	**ACEILM**	maleic	**ACEKRY**	creaky
	thecae	**ACEGOS**	socage		malice		yacker
ACEEIP	apiece	**ACEGOW**	cowage	**ACEILN**	inlace	**ACEKST**	casket
ACEEJT	ejecta	**ACEGRS**	graces	**ACEILP**	plaice	**ACEKSW**	wackes
ACEEKS	ackees	**ACEHHS**	Shache		plicae	**ACEKTT**	tacket
ACEELL	cellae	**ACEHHT**	chetah	**ACEILR**	eclair	**ACEKTY**	tackey
ACEELN	enlace	**ACEHIK**	hackie		lacier	**ACELLO**	locale
ACEELR	alerce	**ACEHIM**	haemic	**ACEIMN**	anemic	**ACELLR**	caller
	cereal	**ACEHIP**	phaeic		cinema		cellar
ACEELV	cleave	**ACEHIR**	achier		iceman		recall
ACEEMN	menace		cahier	**ACEIMO**	Maceió	**ACELLV**	Cavell
ACEEMR	amerce		eriach	**ACEIMR**	Crimea	**ACELMR**	calmer
	careme	**ACEHIS**	chaise		Mercia		Carmel
	Carême	**ACEHKL**	hackle	**ACEIMS**	amices		marcel
	raceme	**ACEHKR**	hacker		camise	**ACELMS**	camels
ACEEMZ	eczema	**ACEHLM**	Machel	**ACEIMU**	aecium		mascle
ACEENR	careen	**ACEHLN**	Chanel	**ACEINN**	canine		mescal
ACEENS	Cesena	**ACEHLP**	chapel		neanic	**ACELMT**	camlet
	encase		pleach	**ACEINR**	carnie	**ACELMU**	almuce
	seance	**ACEHLR**	Rachel		Racine		macule
	seneca	**ACEHLS**	chelas	**ACEINS**	casein	**ACELMZ**	mezcal
ACEENT	cetane		laches		incase	**ACELNN**	cannel
	tenace	**ACEHLT**	chalet	**ACEINT**	centai	**ACELNR**	lancer
ACEEOR	ocreae		thecal		enatic	**ACELNS**	cleans
ACEEOT	coatee	**ACEHLV**	cheval	**ACEINX**	axenic		lances
ACEEPS	escape	**ACEHMN**	manche	**ACEIPR**	pacier		Senlac
	peaces	**ACEHMR**	macher	**ACEIPS**	apices	**ACELNT**	cantle
ACEERR	career		Marche		spicae		cental
ACEERS	crease	**ACEHMS**	sachem	**ACEIQU**	caique		lancet
ACEERT	cerate		schema	**ACEIRR**	racier	**ACELNU**	cuneal
	create	**ACEHNS**	encash	**ACEIRS**	caries		launce
	ecarte		hances	**ACEIRU**	curiae		unlace
ACEESS	ceases	**ACEHNU**	nuchae	**ACEISS**	saices	**ACELOR**	coaler
ACEFFT	affect	**ACEHOP**	cheapo	**ACEISV**	cavies		oracle
ACEFHR	chafer	**ACEHOR**	chorea		vesica	**ACELOS**	solace
ACEFHS	chafes		Horace	**ACEITT**	cattie	**ACELOT**	Alecto
ACEFIL	facile		ochrea	**ACEITV**	active		locate
ACEFIN	fiance		orache		Cavite	**ACELOV**	alcove
ACEFIR	fiacre	**ACEHPR**	eparch	**ACEIVV**	vivace		coeval
ACEFIS	facies		preach	**ACEJKT**	jacket	**ACELPR**	carpel
ACEFLU	fecula	**ACEHPS**	chapes	**ACEJLO**	cajole		parcel
ACEFNR	France		Pesach	**ACEKLM**	mackle		placer
ACEFRS	facers	**ACEHPT**	hepcat	**ACEKLR**	calker	**ACELPS**	places
	farces	**ACEHPY**	peachy		Clarke	**ACELPT**	caplet
	Scarfe	**ACEHRR**	archer		lacker		placet
ACEFRU	furcae	**ACEHRS**	arches	**ACEKLS**	alecks	**ACELPU**	culpae
ACEFSS	fasces		chaser	**ACEKLT**	tackle	**ACELQU**	calque
ACEFST	facets		eschar	**ACEKLY**	lackey		claque
ACEFSU	fauces		search	**ACEKMN**	McKean	**ACELRR**	carrel
ACEFSY	casefy	**ACEHRT**	Cather	**ACEKNR**	canker	**ACELRS**	carles

	clears		recant		crases	**ACGHOU**	gaucho
	lacers		trance		scares	**ACGHRU**	curagh
	scaler	**ACENRV**	carven		seracs	**ACGHTU**	caught
	sclera		cavern	**ACERST**	carets	**ACGIKN**	caking
ACELRT	cartel		craven		caster	**ACGILL**	gallic
	claret	**ACENRY**	carney		caters	**ACGILN**	lacing
	rectal	**ACENST**	ascent		crates	**ACGILR**	garlic
ACELRV	carvel		centas		reacts	**ACGILS**	glacis
	claver		enacts		recast	**ACGILY**	cagily
ACELRW	clawer		secant		traces	**ACGIMN**	macing
ACELSS	Cassel		stance	**ACERSU**	causer	**ACGIMS**	magics
	scales	**ACENSU**	usance		cesura	**ACGINN**	caning
ACELST	castle	**ACENTU**	Canute		saucer	**ACGINO**	agonic
	cleats	**ACEOPS**	scopae	**ACERSV**	carves	**ACGINP**	pacing
ACELSU	caules	**ACEOPT**	capote		cavers	**ACGINR**	arcing
	clause		toecap		craves		caring
	Leucas	**ACEOPW**	cowpea	**ACERSY**	carsey		racing
ACELSV	calves	**ACEORR**	correa		creasy	**ACGINS**	casing
	cavels	**ACEORS**	Açôres	**ACERSZ**	crazes		Signac
	claves		coarse	**ACERTU**	curate	**ACGINT**	acting
ACELSX	calxes		rosace	**ACESST**	castes	**ACGINV**	caving
ACELTT	cattle	**ACEORW**	crowea	**ACESSU**	causes	**ACGINW**	cawing
ACELTY	acetyl	**ACEORX**	coaxer		sauces	**ACGIOR**	Gorica
ACELWY	Cawley	**ACEOST**	coates	**ACESTT**	stacte	**ACGIRS**	cigars
ACELYY	Cayley		costae		tacets		craigs
	clayey	**ACEOSW**	ECOWAS	**ACESTU**	acutes	**ACGIRT**	tragic
ACEMNP	encamp	**ACEOSX**	coaxes		cuesta	**ACGIUU**	Iguaçú
ACEMNR	carmen	**ACEOSY**	O'Casey		Escaut	**ACGLNS**	clangs
ACEMNU	acumen	**ACEOTV**	avocet	**ACESTX**	exacts	**ACGLNU**	glucan
ACEMNW	McEwan		octave	**ACESUY**	causey	**ACGNOR**	garcon
ACEMOP	pomace	**ACEPPR**	capper		cayuse	**ACGNOS**	congas
ACEMOS	cameos	**ACEPRR**	carper	**ACFFHS**	chaffs		gascon
ACEMOT	comate	**ACEPRS**	capers	**ACFFHY**	chaffy	**ACGNOU**	cougan
ACEMPR	camper		crapes	**ACFFLS**	sclaff	**ACGORS**	cargos
ACEMRS	creams		escarp	**ACFGIN**	facing	**ACGORU**	cougar
	macers		pacers	**ACFHLN**	flanch	**ACGOSU**	guacos
	scream		parsec	**ACFHRT**	fratch	**ACGOWY**	cogway
ACEMRT	mercat		recaps	**ACFHSU**	chufas	**ACGRSS**	scrags
ACEMRY	creamy		scrape	**ACFILS**	califs	**ACGTTU**	catgut
ACEMSU	muscae		spacer		fiscal	**ACHHNU**	haunch
ACEMTU	acetum	**ACEPRT**	carpet	**ACFIOS**	fiasco	**ACHHTT**	thatch
ACEMUX	exacum	**ACEPRU**	apercu	**ACFIPY**	pacify	**ACHIIS**	ischia
ACENNO	ancone	**ACEPSS**	scapes	**ACFISS**	fascis	**ACHIJK**	hijack
ACENNR	canner		spaces	**ACFKLS**	flacks	**ACHIKO**	kochia
ACENNS	Cannes	**ACEPST**	aspect	**ACFKNR**	Franck	**ACHIKS**	haicks
ACENNU	nuance		epacts	**ACFLNO**	falcon	**ACHIKW**	Hawick
ACENNY	Annecy	**ACEPSY**	spacey		flacon	**ACHILM**	l'chaim
ACENOP	Capone	**ACEPTU**	teacup	**ACFLNU**	canful	**ACHILO**	lochia
ACENOR	cornea	**ACEQSU**	casque	**ACFLRU**	fulcra	**ACHILP**	caliph
ACENOS	canoes		sacque		furcal	**ACHILR**	archil
	oceans	**ACERRS**	carers	**ACFNOR**	franco		chiral
ACENOT	octane		racers	**ACFNRS**	francs	**ACHILT**	chital
ACENPR	prance		scarer	**ACFORT**	factor	**ACHIMN**	Mincha
ACENPS	pecans	**ACERRT**	carter	**ACFRSS**	scarfs	**ACHIMR**	chimar
ACENRS	caners		crater	**ACFRST**	crafts	**ACHIMS**	chiasm
	casern		tracer	**ACFRTY**	crafty	**ACHINN**	Chinan
	cranes	**ACERRU**	curare	**ACGGIN**	caging	**ACHINR**	inarch
ACENRT	canter	**ACERRV**	carver	**ACGGIO**	agogic		Ranchi
	carnet		craver	**ACGGLY**	claggy	**ACHINS**	chains
	centra	**ACERRY**	Carrey	**ACGGRY**	craggy		chinas
	Cretan	**ACERSS**	caress	**ACGHIN**	aching	**ACHINT**	canthi
	nectar		carses		Ichang	**ACHIPS**	phasic

ACHIPT	haptic	**ACHTTY**	chatty	**ACIMTU**	Actium	**ACKNRY**	cranky
	pathic	**ACIILS**	sialic	**ACINNT**	tannic	**ACKNSS**	snacks
	phatic		silica	**ACINNY**	cyanin	**ACKNTU**	untack
ACHIQU	quaich	**ACIILT**	italic	**ACINOP**	Pacino	**ACKORS**	croaks
ACHIRS	chairs	**ACIINN**	niacin	**ACINOS**	casino	**ACKORY**	croaky
	rachis	**ACIINS**	Nicias	**ACINOT**	action	**ACKOSW**	wackos
ACHKKU	chukka	**ACIIRT**	iatric		atonic	**ACKQSU**	quacks
ACHKLS	chalks	**ACIIST**	Saitic		cation	**ACKRST**	tracks
ACHKLY	chalky	**ACIKLN**	calkin	**ACINOX**	anoxic	**ACKRSW**	wracks
ACHKMO	Ockham	**ACIKMR**	karmic	**ACINPS**	panics	**ACKSST**	stacks
ACHKOS	shacko	**ACIKNT**	catkin	**ACINPT**	catnip	**ACLLMY**	calmly
ACHKOW	whacko	**ACIKPX**	pickax	**ACINRS**	arcsin	**ACLLNO**	clonal
ACHKRU	chukar	**ACILLN**	clinal		cairns	**ACLLOO**	alcool
ACHKSS	shacks	**ACILLP**	plical	**ACINRT**	Cintra	**ACLLOP**	callop
ACHKSW	chawks	**ACILLS**	lilacs	**ACINRU**	uranic	**ACLLOR**	collar
	whacks		scilla	**ACINST**	antics	**ACLLOS**	Laclos
ACHKTW	thwack	**ACILLY**	lacily		nastic		locals
ACHKWY	whacky	**ACILMO**	Colima	**ACINSU**	acinus	**ACLLOW**	callow
ACHLLO	cholla	**ACILMS**	claims	**ACINSV**	vincas	**ACLLSS**	scalls
ACHLMU	Culham	**ACILMX**	climax	**ACINTT**	intact	**ACLLSU**	callus
ACHLNO	lochan	**ACILNO**	alnico	**ACINTU**	tunica	**ACLLSY**	scally
ACHLNU	launch		oilcan	**ACINUV**	vicuna		Scylla
	nuchal	**ACILNP**	caplin	**ACIOPT**	atopic	**ACLMMY**	clammy
ACHLOR	choral	**ACILNR**	carlin		copita	**ACLMOP**	copalm
ACHLRY	archly	**ACILNS**	linacs	**ACIORS**	scoria	**ACLMOR**	clamor
ACHLTU	Clutha	**ACILNT**	tincal	**ACIORT**	aortic		Colmar
ACHMMY	chammy	**ACILNU**	Alcuin	**ACIOST**	coatis	**ACLMPS**	clamps
ACHMOR	chroma		Lucian		scotia	**ACLMTU**	talcum
	morcha		Lucina	**ACIOSV**	ovisac	**ACLNOT**	coltan
ACHMOS	machos		uncial	**ACIOTZ**	azotic	**ACLNOX**	claxon
ACHMPS	champs	**ACILNV**	Calvin	**ACIPRS**	capris	**ACLNOY**	Lycaon
ACHMRS	charms	**ACILNY**	Lycian	**ACIPRY**	piracy	**ACLNUV**	vulcan
ACHMSS	chasms	**ACILOR**	caroli	**ACIPSS**	aspics	**ACLNUY**	lunacy
ACHMST	smatch		lorica		spicas	**ACLOPU**	copula
ACHMSU	sumach	**ACILOS**	social	**ACIPTT**	tipcat		cupola
ACHNOR	anchor	**ACILOT**	coital	**ACIQTU**	acquit	**ACLORR**	corral
	archon	**ACILOX**	oxalic	**ACIRRU**	curari	**ACLORS**	Carlos
	Charon	**ACILRT**	citral	**ACIRSS**	crasis		carols
	rancho		rictal		crissa		claros
ACHNOS	nachos	**ACILRU**	curial	**ACIRST**	artics		corals
ACHNOT	Can Tho		lauric		crista	**ACLORT**	crotal
ACHNPU	paunch		uracil		racist	**ACLORU**	ocular
ACHNRU	raunch	**ACILRY**	racily	**ACIRSU**	Icarus	**ACLORW**	Carlow
ACHNST	chants	**ACILST**	ticals	**ACIRSV**	vicars	**ACLORY**	calory
	snatch	**ACILSU**	caulis	**ACIRTU**	uratic	**ACLOST**	costal
	stanch	**ACILSV**	cavils	**ACISSS**	cassis	**ACLOSU**	oscula
ACHNSU	Usnach	**ACIMNO**	anomic	**ACISTT**	attics	**ACLOSV**	vocals
ACHNTU	chaunt		camion		static	**ACLOSW**	cowals
	nautch		manioc	**ACITUY**	acuity	**ACLOTT**	Alcott
ACHNTY	chanty	**ACIMNP**	Campin	**ACITVY**	cavity	**ACLOTU**	Toluca
ACHOPR	carhop	**ACIMNS**	manics	**ACJKSY**	jacksy	**ACLPSS**	clasps
ACHOSV	havocs	**ACIMNT**	mantic	**ACKKNS**	knacks		scalps
ACHOUV	avouch	**ACIMOO**	oomiac	**ACKLNP**	Planck	**ACLPUU**	cupula
ACHPTY	patchy	**ACIMOS**	mosaic	**ACKLNS**	clanks	**ACLRRU**	crural
ACHRRS	charrs	**ACIMOT**	atomic	**ACKLOS**	cloaks	**ACLRST**	clarts
ACHRST	charts	**ACIMPS**	scampi	**ACKLSS**	slacks	**ACLRSW**	crawls
	starch	**ACIMPT**	impact	**ACKLSU**	caulks		scrawl
ACHSSU	sauchs	**ACIMRS**	racism		Lukács	**ACLRTU**	curtal
ACHSSW	schwas	**ACIMRT**	matric	**ACKMSS**	smacks	**ACLRTY**	clarty
ACHSTU	cushat	**ACIMRU**	Murcia	**ACKNOR**	Cranko	**ACLRWY**	crawly
ACHSTW	swatch	**ACIMRY**	myrica	**ACKNPU**	unpack	**ACLSSY**	classy
ACHSTY	yachts	**ACIMST**	mastic	**ACKNRS**	cranks	**ACMMOS**	commas

ACMNOO Monaco	**ACORRT** carrot	laddie	**ADDGOR** Godard
ACMNOR macron	trocar	**ADDEIM** diadem	**ADDGRU** du Gard
ACMNOS mascon	**ACORSS** across	mediad	**ADDHOO** doodah
socman	oscars	**ADDEIR** raided	**ADDHOS** Ashdod
ACMNOT Cotman	**ACORST** actors	**ADDEIS** addies	**ADDHSU** saddhu
ACMNOW cowman	castor	**ADDEKR** darked	**ADDIIV** David I
ACMOPS campos	Castro	**ADDELL** ladled	**ADDIMR** Madrid
ACMORS caroms	costar	**ADDELN** dandle	**ADDIMS** misadd
macros	scrota	landed	**ADDIMY** midday
Marcos	**ACORSU** Caruso	**ADDELO** loaded	**ADDLNO** Donald
ACMOST mascot	**ACORTT** cottar	**ADDELP** paddle	**ADDLWY** waddly
scamto	**ACORTU** turaco	**ADDELR** ladder	**ADDMOO** Dodoma
ACMOSU mucosa	**ACORTV** cavort	larded	**ADDNOO** Dodona
ACMPRS cramps	**ACORUV** Cavour	raddle	**ADDOOR** dorado
ACMPSS scamps	**ACORYZ** coryza	**ADDELS** addles	**ADDORS** dorsad
ACMPSU campus	**ACOSST** ascots	daleds	**ADDORT** dotard
ACMRSS scrams	coasts	saddle	**ADDRSY** dryads
ACMRSU sacrum	**ACOSTT** cottas	**ADDELU** lauded	**ADDSWY** swaddy
ACMRSY cymars	**ACOSZZ** scozza	**ADDELW** dawdle	**ADEEFL** leafed
ACMSSU sumacs	**ACOTTU** outact	waddle	**ADEEFM** defame
ACMSTU muscat	**ACPPSU** cuppas	**ADDELY** deadly	**ADEEFN** deafen
ACMUUV vacuum	**ACPRSS** scarps	**ADDEMM** dammed	**ADEEFR** deafer
ACNNNO cannon	scraps	**ADDEMN** damned	feared
ACNNOS canons	**ACPRSU** carpus	demand	**ADEEFT** defeat
ACNNOT cannot	**ACPRSW** scrawp	madden	**ADEEFZ** feazed
canton	**ACPSSU** scaups	**ADDEMP** damped	**ADEEGG** degage
ACNNOY canyon	**ACPSTU** catsup	**ADDEMR** madder	**ADEEGR** agreed
ACNNRY cranny	upcast	**ADDENR** dander	dragee
ACNOOR corona	**ACRRTU** cratur	darned	geared
racoon	**ACRSST** scarts	**ADDENS** dedans	**ADEEHL** Hadlee
ACNOPS capons	**ACRSSU** scaurs	sadden	healed
ACNOPY canopy	**ACRSSW** scraws	sanded	**ADEEHP** heaped
ACNORR carron	**ACRSTT** tracts	**ADDENU** undead	**ADEEHR** adhere
rancor	**ACSTTY** scatty	**ADDENW** dawned	header
ACNORS acorns	**ADDDEG** gadded	**ADDEOR** adored	hedera
Carson	**ADDDEL** addled	deodar	**ADEEHT** heated
racons	**ADDDEM** madded	**ADDEOS** dadoes	**ADEEHV** heaved
ACNORT cantor	**ADDDEN** addend	**ADDEOT** doated	**ADEEIL** aedile
Carnot	**ADDDEO** dadoed	**ADDEOW** woaded	Eliade
carton	**ADDDEP** padded	**ADDEPP** dapped	**ADEEIM** mediae
contra	**ADDDEW** wadded	**ADDEPR** draped	**ADEEIR** dearie
craton	**ADDDOO** doodad	**ADDEPS** spaded	rediae
ACNORU cornua	**ADDEEH** headed	**ADDERR** radder	**ADEEIS** easied
ACNORY crayon	**ADDEEL** leaded	**ADDERS** adders	**ADEEIT** ideate
ACNOSS Casson	**ADDEEN** deaden	dreads	**ADEEJY** deejay
ACNOST actons	**ADDEER** Eadred	readds	**ADEEKL** leaked
cantos	**ADDEEV** deaved	sadder	**ADEEKP** peaked
octans	evaded	**ADDERT** darted	**ADEELN** aneled
ACNOTT octant	**ADDEFF** daffed	traded	leaden
ACNOTU toucan	**ADDEFG** fadged	**ADDERU** daured	leaned
ACNOTX Caxton	**ADDEFN** Fadden	**ADDERW** Edward	**ADEELP** leaped
ACNPSU pucans	**ADDEGG** dagged	wadder	pealed
uncaps	**ADDEGO** goaded	warded	**ADEELR** dealer
ACNSST scants	**ADDEGR** gadder	**ADDERY** yarded	leader
ACNSTU cantus	graded	**ADDETU** Daudet	**ADEELS** leased
ACNSTY scanty	**ADDEHI** haddie	**ADDGIN** adding	sealed
ACOOTV octavo	**ADDEHK** keddah	**ADDGIO** gadoid	**ADEELT** delate
ACOPRS copras	**ADDEHN** handed	**ADDGIP** giddap	elated
ACOPRT captor	**ADDEHS** dashed	**ADDGIS** gadids	**ADEELV** leaved
ACOPSS scopas	shaded	**ADDGIY** gidday	**ADEEMN** amende
ACOPST capots	**ADDEHU** hauded	**ADDGHO** goddam	demean
ACOPTW cowpat	**ADDEIL** dialed	**ADDGOO** ogdoad	**ADEEMO** oedema

ADEEMR reamed	**ADEFNW** fawned	**ADEGPW** gawped	red hat
remade	**ADEFOR** fedora	**ADEGRR** garred	thread
ADEEMS seamed	**ADEFRS** faders	Gérard	**ADEHRY** hydrae
ADEEMT teamed	**ADEFRT** dafter	grader	**ADEHSS** dashes
ADEENN ennead	farted	regard	sadhes
ADEENR earned	rafted	**ADEGRS** grades	sashed
endear	**ADEFRY** defray	**ADEGRT** grated	shades
neared	frayed	**ADEGRU** argued	**ADEHST** deaths
ADEENT anteed	**ADEFST** fasted	**ADEGRV** graved	hasted
ADEENW weaned	**ADEFTT** fatted	**ADEGRY** grayed	**ADEHSV** shaved
ADEENY yeaned	**ADEFTU** fauted	**ADEGRZ** grazed	**ADEHSW** hawsed
ADEEPR reaped	**ADEFTW** wafted	**ADEGSS** gassed	shawed
ADEEPS pesade	**ADEGGG** gagged	**ADEGST** staged	washed
ADEEPT pedate	**ADEGGI** gadgie	**ADEGSW** swaged	**ADEHSX** hexads
ADEERR dearer	**ADEGGJ** jagged	**ADEHHK** khedah	**ADEHSY** Hyades
reader	**ADEGGL** lagged	**ADEHHS** hashed	**ADEHTT** hatted
reared	**ADEGGM** magged	**ADEHIL** hailed	**ADEHTW** thawed
reread	**ADEGGN** ganged	halide	**ADEHYY** heyday
ADEERS erased	nagged	**ADEHIR** haired	**ADEIJL** jailed
Red Sea	**ADEGGR** dagger	Hardie	**ADEIKL** laiked
reseda	ragged	**ADEHJS** hadjes	**ADEIKN** Deakin
seared	**ADEGGS** sagged	jehads	**ADEIKR** darkie
ADEERT derate	**ADEGGT** gadget	**ADEHJZ** Hedjaz	**ADEILL** allied
ADEERV evader	tagged	**ADEHKN** hanked	Lleida
reaved	**ADEGGU** gauged	**ADEHKR** harked	**ADEILM** mailed
ADEERW drawee	**ADEGGV** vagged	**ADEHKS** khedas	medial
ADEERX exedra	**ADEGGW** wagged	**ADEHKW** hawked	**ADEILN** Aldine
ADEERZ razeed	**ADEGHN** hanged	**ADEHLM** lamedh	alined
ADEESS Edessa	**ADEGHS** gashed	**ADEHLN** Handel	Daniel
ADEEST seated	**ADEGIL** Gilead	handle	Delian
sedate	**ADEGIM** imaged	**ADEHLO** haloed	denial
teased	**ADEGIN** daeing	**ADEHLR** harled	nailed
ADEESV deaves	gained	herald	**ADEILO** eidola
evades	**ADEGIT** gaited	**ADEHLS** lashed	**ADEILP** aliped
ADEESX axseed	**ADEGIW** Eadwig	**ADEHLT** daleth	elapid
ADEEVW weaved	**ADEGKN** Kang-de	halted	pleiad
ADEFFF faffed	**ADEGKW** gawked	lathed	**ADEILR** derail
ADEFFG gaffed	**ADEGLL** galled	**ADEHLU** hauled	laired
ADEFFW waffed	**ADEGLN** angled	**ADEHLV** halved	Lérida
ADEFGG fagged	dangle	**ADEHLW** whaled	railed
ADEFGN fanged	**ADEGLO** gaoled	**ADEHMM** hammed	redial
ADEFGS fadges	**ADEGLR** glared	**ADEHMR** harmed	relaid
ADEFHS fashed	**ADEGLS** glades	**ADEHMS** mashed	**ADEILS** aisled
ADEFHT hafted	**ADEGLZ** glazed	shamed	deasil
ADEFIL afield	**ADEGMM** gammed	**ADEHNP** daphne	ideals
failed	**ADEGNN** ganned	**ADEHNR** harden	ladies
ADEFIR faired	**ADEGNO** Ogaden	**ADEHNU** hauden	sailed
ADEFKL flaked	**ADEGNR** danger	**ADEHOX** hoaxed	**ADEILT** detail
ADEFLM flamed	gander	**ADEHPP** happed	dilate
ADEFLO foaled	garden	**ADEHPR** harped	tailed
loafed	ranged	**ADEHPS** hasped	**ADEILU** audile
ADEFLR fardel	**ADEGNU** augend	pashed	**ADEILV** vailed
flared	**ADEGNW** gnawed	phased	**ADEILW** wailed
ADEFLU feudal	**ADEGOR** dogear	shaped	**ADEIMM** maimed
ADEFLW flawed	**ADEGOS** dagoes	**ADEHPT** heptad	**ADEIMN** Damien
ADEFLY deafly	dosage	**ADEHRR** Erhard	maiden
flayed	seadog	harder	median
ADEFMO foamed	**ADEGOT** dotage	**ADEHRS** dasher	medina
ADEFMR farmed	togaed	Ershad	**ADEIMR** admire
framed	**ADEGPP** gapped	shared	Mérida
ADEFMT mafted	**ADEGPS** gasped	**ADEHRT** dearth	**ADEIMS** amides
ADEFNN fanned	**ADEGPU** gauped	hatred	mesiad

ADEINO	Oneida	**ADEKNT**	tanked	**ADELRR**	larder	**ADENNP**	panned
ADEINP	pained	**ADEKNW**	wanked	**ADELRS**	alders	**ADENNT**	tanned
ADEINR	Dairen	**ADEKNY**	yanked		laders	**ADENNU**	duenna
	Darien	**ADEKOS**	soaked	**ADELRU**	aulder	**ADENNW**	wanned
	Derain	**ADEKOY**	kayoed		Éluard	**ADENOS**	anodes
	rained		okayed		lauder	**ADENOT**	atoned
	read in	**ADEKPR**	parked	**ADELRY**	dearly		donate
ADEINS	sained	**ADEKPY**	keypad	**ADELST**	deltas	**ADENOY**	noyade
	Sendai	**ADEKQU**	quaked		desalt	**ADENPP**	append
ADEINT	detain	**ADEKRR**	darker		lasted		napped
ADEINV	invade	**ADEKRS**	drakes		salted	**ADENPR**	pander
ADEINZ	Zidane	**ADEKRY**	darkey		slated		repand
ADEIOR	roadie	**ADEKST**	skated		staled	**ADENPT**	panted
ADEIOT	iodate		staked	**ADELSV**	salved		pedant
ADEIPR	diaper		tasked		slaved		pentad
	paired	**ADEKUW**	wauked	**ADELSW**	wealds	**ADENPW**	pawned
	repaid	**ADELLP**	palled	**ADELSY**	delays	**ADENPX**	expand
ADEIRR	raider	**ADELLR**	ladler	**ADELUV**	valued	**ADENRR**	darner
ADEIRS	aiders	**ADELLS**	dalles	**ADELUW**	wauled		errand
	irades		ladles	**ADELWW**	wawled	**ADENRS**	denars
	raised	**ADELLU**	allude	**ADELWY**	yawled		redans
ADEIRT	tirade		aludel	**ADELZZ**	dazzle		sander
ADEIRU	uredia	**ADELLW**	walled	**ADEMMN**	madmen		snared
ADEIRV	varied	**ADELMM**	lammed	**ADEMMR**	dammer	**ADENRT**	ardent
ADEISS	asides	**ADELMO**	loamed		rammed		Arendt
	daises	**ADELMP**	palmed	**ADEMMS**	sammed		ranted
	dassie	**ADELMR**	Del Mar	**ADEMNN**	manned	**ADENRU**	Neruda
ADEISU	adieus		dermal	**ADEMNO**	daemon		unread
ADEISV	advise		marled		Menado	**ADENRW**	Andrew
	davies		medlar		moaned		wander
	visaed	**ADELMS**	damsel		modena		warden
ADEISW	wadies		lameds	**ADEMNP**	dampen		warned
ADEISZ	azides		medals	**ADEMNR**	randem	**ADENRY**	denary
ADEITV	dative	**ADELMT**	malted		remand		yarned
ADEITW	waited	**ADELMU**	dumela	**ADEMNS**	amends	**ADENRZ**	zander
ADEITX	taxied		mauled		demans	**ADENSS**	sedans
ADEIUX	adieux	**ADELNO**	loaned		desman	**ADENSU**	sundae
ADEIVV	vivaed	**ADELNP**	planed		menads	**ADENSV**	davens
ADEIVW	waived	**ADELNR**	darnel	**ADEMNT**	tandem	**ADENSW**	dewans
ADEJMM	jammed		lander	**ADEMNU**	unmade	**ADENTT**	attend
ADEJOU	Judaeo-		larned	**ADEMOP**	pomade	**ADENTV**	advent
ADEJPR	jarped	**ADELNS**	elands	**ADEMOR**	radome	**ADENTW**	wanted
ADEJPU	jauped		landes		roamed	**ADENUY**	Yaunde
ADEJRR	jarred		sendal	**ADEMOT**	moated	**ADENWY**	dawney
ADEJRU	adjure	**ADELNT**	dental	**ADEMOW**	meadow		yawned
ADEJZZ	jazzed	**ADELNU**	unlade	**ADEMPP**	mapped	**ADEOPS**	soaped
ADEKKY	yakked		unlead	**ADEMPR**	damper	**ADEORR**	adorer
ADEKLN	Kendal	**ADELOP**	pedalo		ramped		roared
ADEKLR	darkle	**ADELOR**	Laredo	**ADEMPT**	tamped	**ADEORS**	adores
	larked		loader	**ADEMPV**	vamped		oreads
ADEKLS	slaked		ordeal	**ADEMRR**	marred		soared
ADEKLT	talked		reload	**ADEMRS**	dermas	**ADEORT**	doater
ADEKLW	walked	**ADELOS**	aldose		dreams		orated
ADEKMR	marked	**ADELPP**	dapple	**ADEMRT**	dreamt	**ADEORW**	redowa
ADEKMS	masked		lapped	**ADEMRW**	warmed	**ADEOSS**	Odessa
ADEKNR	danker	**ADELPR**	pedlar	**ADEMRY**	dreamy	**ADEOSV**	vadose
	darken	**ADELPS**	lapsed	**ADEMSS**	massed	**ADEOVW**	avowed
	narked		pedals	**ADEMST**	masted	**ADEPPR**	dapper
	ranked		pleads	**ADEMSU**	amused		rapped
ADEKNS	kneads	**ADELPT**	plated		medusa	**ADEPPS**	sapped
	sandek	**ADELPW**	dewlap	**ADEMTT**	matted	**ADEPPT**	tapped
	Sendak	**ADELPY**	played	**ADEMWY**	Medway	**ADEPPY**	yapped

ADEPPZ	zapped	ADETTT	tatted	ADGRTU	Utgard	ADIJNO	adjoin
ADEPRR	draper	ADETTV	vatted	ADHHIT	hadith	ADIKKO	Kodiak
ADEPRS	drapes	ADFFOR	afford	ADHHIW	whidah	ADIKKS	Skikda
	padres	ADFFRS	draffs	ADHHKU	duhkha	ADIKMN	Kidman
	parsed	ADFFRY	draffy	ADHHOU	houdah	ADIKMO	mikado
	rasped	ADFGIN	fading	ADHHOW	howdah	ADIKNO	daikon
	spader	ADFGLY	gadfly	ADHHWY	whydah	ADIKNP	kidnap
	spared	ADFGRU	Fugard	ADHIIJ	jihadi	ADIKSU	adsuki
	spread	ADFHSU	shaduf	ADHIJS	hadjis	ADIKTT	diktat
ADEPRT	depart	ADFILY	ladify		jadish	ADIKUZ	adzuki
	parted	ADFIRT	adrift		jihads	ADILLP	pallid
	petard	ADFLTY	daftly	ADHIKU	haiduk	ADILMO	amidol
	prated	ADFLYY	dayfly	ADHILO	haloid	ADILMS	dismal
ADEPRW	warped		ladyfy	ADHILS	halids	ADILMY	milady
ADEPRY	prayed	ADFNOT	fantod	ADHIMR	dirham	ADILNN	inland
ADEPSS	passed	ADFRRU	Darfur	ADHINS	danish	ADILNO	dolina
	spades	ADFRST	drafts		sandhi		ladino
ADEPST	adepts	ADFRSU	frauds	ADHIOO	hoodia	ADILNR	aldrin
	pasted	ADFRSW	dwarfs	ADHIOR	hairdo	ADILNS	island
ADEPSU	paused	ADFRTY	drafty	ADHIPS	aphids	ADILNT	tindal
ADEPSY	spayed	ADGGRY	draggy	ADHIRS	radish	ADILNU	unlaid
ADEPTT	patted	ADGHIN	Gandhi		Rashid	ADILNV	Lydian
ADEPTU	update		hading	ADHIRY	hydria	ADILPS	plaids
ADEPUY	yauped	ADGHRU	durgah		Riyadh	ADILRS	drails
ADEPWY	yawped	ADGIIN	aiding	ADHISS	Hassid		lairds
ADERRS	darers	ADGIJN	jading	ADHKKU	dukkah		liards
ADERRT	darter	ADGIJO	adjigo		dukkha	ADILRY	aridly
	retard	ADGILN	lading	ADHLMO	Oldham	ADILRZ	lizard
	tarred		ligand	ADHLNU	Uhland	ADILSS	Aldiss
	trader	ADGILO	algoid	ADHLRY	hardly	ADILST	distal
ADERRW	drawer		dialog	ADHMNO	hodman	ADILVY	avidly
	redraw	ADGIMY	digamy	ADHMNU	numdah	ADIMMT	dammit
	reward	ADGINO	ganoid	ADHMRU	Durham	ADIMNO	daimon
	warder	ADGINR	daring	ADHNNU	unhand		domain
	warred		gradin	ADHNOO	Doohan	ADIMNR	mandir
ADERRY	dreary	ADGINT	dating	ADHNOR	hadron	ADIMNS	admins
ADERSS	Esdras	ADGINW	wading	ADHNOS	donahs		mandis
ADERST	stared	ADGINY	Gdynia	ADHNOU	houdan	ADIMNT	mantid
	trades	ADGINZ	Danzig	ADHNOY	Haydon	ADIMOT	diatom
	treads		dazing	ADHNRU	dhurna	ADIMOY	daimyo
ADERSW	sawder	ADGIOV	Godiva	ADHNSY	shandy	ADIMRS	disarm
	Seward	ADGIRU	Giraud	ADHORS	hoards	ADIMRU	radium
	waders		Guardi	ADHORU	dourah	ADIMRY	myriad
ADERTT	ratted	ADGIRV	gravid	ADHORW	Howard	ADIMSS	sadism
	tetrad	ADGKMO	Domagk	ADHOSW	shadow	ADIMST	admits
ADERTV	advert	ADGKNS	Gdańsk	ADHPRU	purdah		amidst
ADERTW	warted	ADGLLY	gladly	ADHRSS	shards	ADIMSY	dismay
ADERZZ	razzed	ADGLNS	glands	ADHRSY	hydras	ADIMWY	midway
ADESSS	sassed	ADGLOP	lapdog	ADHSSU	sadhus	ADINNP	pindan
ADESST	steads	ADGMNO	dogman	ADIIKO	aikido	ADINNT	Dinant
	tsades		God man	ADIILM	miladi	ADINNU	induna
ADESSU	Dessau	ADGMOS	dogmas	ADIILN	inlaid	ADINOR	inroad
ADESTT	stated	ADGNNO	Andong	ADIILW	Diwali		ordain
	tasted	ADGNOP	dognap	ADIIMN	Midian	ADINOS	adonis
ADESTU	sauted	ADGNOR	dragon	ADIIMO	daimio		danios
ADESTV	staved		Gondar	ADIIMR	midair	ADINOX	dioxan
ADESTW	tawsed	ADGNOS	dongas	ADIINN	Indian	ADINPR	Pindar
	wadset		gonads	ADIINV	avidin	ADINPT	pandit
	wasted	ADGNRS	grands	ADIINZ	diazin	ADINPU	unpaid
ADESTY	stayed	ADGNSW	dwangs	ADIIPR	diapir	ADINQR	qindar
	steady	ADGRSU	gradus	ADIJLS	Djilas	ADINRS	dinars
ADESWY	swayed		guards	ADIJMS	masjid		drains

	nadirs		Roland	**ADOPST**	adopts	**AEEGSU**	Aegeus
ADINRU	durian	**ADLNOS**	soldan	**ADORRU**	ardour	**AEEGSW**	sewage
ADINRW	Darwin	**ADLNOT**	dalton	**ADORSS**	sarods	**AEEHHW**	heehaw
	inward	**ADLNOU**	unload	**ADORSU**	Sardou	**AEEHKM**	hakeem
ADINSU	unsaid	**ADLNPU**	upland	**ADORTW**	toward	**AEEHKT**	Hekate
ADINSV	divans	**ADLNRU**	lurdan	**ADPRSU**	purdas	**AEEHLN**	Helena
	viands	**ADLNSU**	Lasdun	**ADPRUW**	upward	**AEEHLR**	healer
ADINSW	diwans	**ADLOPU**	upload	**ADQSSU**	squads	**AEEHLW**	awheel
ADINTY	dainty	**ADLORS**	dorsal	**ADRSST**	strads	**AEEHLX**	exhale
ADIORS	radios	**ADLOSS**	dossal	**ADRSSW**	swards	**AEEHLY**	Healey
ADIORT	adroit	**ADLOSU**	doulas	**ADRTWY**	tawdry	**AEEHMR**	hareem
	Doráti	**ADLOSW**	Oswald	**AEEEHL**	healee		hermae
ADIOSV	avoids		waldos	**AEEEST**	Aeëtes	**AEEHMU**	heaume
ADIOSZ	diazos	**ADLRSW**	drawls	**AEEFIR**	faerie	**AEEHNP**	peahen
ADIPRS	rapids	**ADLRWY**	drawly		feriae	**AEEHNT**	ethane
	sparid	**ADLSTU**	adults	**AEEFKR**	fakeer	**AEEHNV**	heaven
ADIPSX	spadix	**ADMNOR**	random	**AEEFLM**	female	**AEEHNX**	hexane
ADIRRS	sirdar	**ADMNOS**	damson	**AEEFOV**	foveae	**AEEHNY**	Heaney
ADIRSS	Sardis		monads	**AEEFRR**	fearer	**AEEHPR**	heaper
ADIRST	triads		nomads	**AEEFRT**	afreet	**AEEHPS**	spahee
ADIRSU	radius	**ADMNOY**	dynamo		feater	**AEEHRR**	hearer
ADIRSZ	izards	**ADMNSU**	maunds	**AEEFSZ**	feazes		rehear
ADIRTZ	Tizard	**ADMNUY**	maundy	**AEEGGN**	engage	**AEEHRS**	haeres
ADIRVZ	vizard	**ADMORR**	ramrod	**AEEGGR**	raggee		hearse
ADIRWZ	wizard	**ADMORT**	Tadmor		reggae	**AEEHRT**	aether
ADIRZZ	izzard	**ADMORU**	maduro	**AEEGHZ**	geezah		heater
ADISST	sadist	**ADMORZ**	Ormazd	**AEEGIR**	Ariège		hereat
ADISSY	sayids	**ADMOSU**	doumas	**AEEGJR**	jaeger		reheat
ADISTU	audits	**ADMRSU**	mudras	**AEEGKN**	Keegan	**AEEHRV**	heaver
ADISTV	davits	**ADMSUW**	dwaums	**AEEGLL**	allege	**AEEHSV**	heaves
ADISYY	sayyid	**ADMTUY**	adytum	**AEEGLP**	pelage		heveas
ADJKOU	judoka		Dumyat	**AEEGLR**	galere		sheave
ADJNOR	jordan	**ADNNOS**	donnas		regale	**AEEILM**	mealie
ADJSTU	adjust	**ADNNOT**	danton	**AEEGLS**	eagles	**AEEIMN**	meanie
ADKKNO	Kokand	**ADNNOU**	adnoun		Le Sage	**AEEINT**	teniae
ADKLNY	dankly	**ADNNTU**	Dunant	**AEEGLT**	eaglet	**AEEIRR**	aerier
ADKLOY	Kodály	**ADNOOR**	Adorno		legate	**AEEIRS**	aeries
ADKLRY	darkly		nardoo		telega		easier
ADKLSS	skalds	**ADNOOS**	doonas	**AEEGLU**	league	**AEEISS**	easies
ADKMRU	Marduk	**ADNOOW**	wandoo	**AEEGMM**	gemmae	**AEEKLN**	alkene
ADKNRU	Durkan	**ADNOPR**	pardon	**AEEGMN**	manege	**AEEKLR**	leaker
ADKOPS	padkos	**ADNOPT**	dopant		menage	**AEEKLY**	Leakey
ADKOPU	padouk	**ADNORS**	adorns	**AEEGMR**	meager	**AEEKMR**	remake
ADKORV	Dvořák		Andros		meagre	**AEEKMZ**	kameez
ADKOSV	vodkas		nadors	**AEEGMT**	gamete	**AEEKNS**	akenes
ADLLOR	dollar	**ADNORU**	around		metage	**AEEKNW**	weaken
ADLLOS	aldols		Nordau	**AEEGNN**	ennage	**AEEKRT**	retake
	allods	**ADNORV**	Vardon	**AEEGNR**	enrage	**AEEKRU**	eureka
ADLLUY	dually	**ADNORW**	onward		genera	**AEEKRW**	rewake
ADLMNO	almond	**ADNOSU**	soudan	**AEEGNS**	senega		weaker
	dolman	**ADNOSW**	Dawson	**AEEGNT**	negate	**AEELLL**	allele
	Maldon	**ADNOTY**	Dayton	**AEEGNV**	avenge	**AEELLM**	mallee
	old man	**ADNRST**	strand		geneva	**AEELLR**	lealer
ADLMOS	dolmas	**ADNRTU**	tundra	**AEEGNW**	New Age	**AEELLS**	sallee
ADLMOU	Moldau	**ADNRUW**	undraw	**AEEGOP**	apogee	**AEELMN**	enamel
ADLMPY	damply	**ADNSST**	stands	**AEEGOT**	goatee	**AEELMP**	empale
ADLMTU	talmud	**ADNSTU**	daunts	**AEEGRS**	agrees	**AEELNR**	leaner
ADLNOO	doolan	**ADNSTY**	dynast		eagers	**AEELNS**	aneles
ADLNOP	Poland	**ADNSUY**	Sunday		eagres	**AEELNT**	lateen
ADLNOR	Arnold	**ADOOTW**	Atwood		grease	**AEELNV**	leaven
	Landor	**ADOPRT**	Dorpat	**AEEGRV**	greave	**AEELOR**	areole
	lardon	**ADOPRY**	parody	**AEEGST**	egesta	**AEELOT**	oleate

AEELPR leaper / repeal
AEELPS asleep / elapse / please / sapele
AEELRS leaser / reales / resale / reseal / sealer / Searle
AEELRT elater / relate / Tralee
AEELRV leaver / reveal / vealer
AEELSS easels / leases
AEELST elates / stelae / teasel
AEELSV leaves / sleave
AEELSW weasel
AEELSZ sleaze
AEELTT Attlee
AEELTU eluate
AEELTV velate / veleta
AEELTZ teazel / teazle
AEELWY leeway
AEEMMM mammee
AEEMNN Nemean
AEEMNP apemen
AEEMNR meaner / rename
AEEMNS enemas / mensae / seamen
AEEMNX axemen / examen
AEEMPR ampere / Ampère
AEEMRR reamer
AEEMRS ameers / seamer
AEEMSS sesame
AEEMTX taxeme
AEENNP pennae
AEENNT neaten
AEENNX annexe
AEENPR paneer
AEENPT nepeta
AEENPU eupnea
AEENPW pawnee
AEENRR earner / nearer
AEENRS arenes / ranees

AEENRT entera / neater / rateen
AEENRV Erevan
AEENRW weaner
AEENST enates / Santee / sateen / senate
AEENSU unease
AEENSW Swanee
AEENTW atween
AEENUV avenue
AEEPPR rappee
AEEPRR reaper
AEEPRS Parsee / Pearse / serape
AEEPRT repeat
AEEPRV pareve / repave
AEEPST peseta
AEEPSV Pavese
AEEPSW pesewa
AEEPSX apexes
AEEPSY payees
AEEPTT pattee
AEEPVY peavey
AEEQRU quaere
AEEQTU equate
AEERRR rearer
AEERRS eraser / serrae
AEERRT tearer
AEERRW wearer
AEERSS easers / erases / sarees
AEERST aretes / easter / eaters / reseat / seater / teaser / Teresa
AEERSU reseau / urease
AEERSV averse / reaves / Varese / Varèse
AEERSZ razees
AEERTY eatery
AEERVW weaver
AEESST teases
AEESSW seesaw
AEESSY eyases
AEESTT estate / testae
AEESTX exeats
AEESVW weaves
AEEWXY waxeye

AEFFGR gaffer
AEFFGS gaffes
AEFFIN affine
AEFFIP piaffe
AEFFLR raffle
AEFFLW waffle
AEFFLY yaffle
AEFFNR naffer
AEFFRZ zaffer / zaffre
AEFGLN flange
AEFGNS ganefs
AEFGOR forage
AEFHKR Khafre
AEFHLL fellah
AEFHRS afresh
AEFHRT father / hafter
AEFHSS fashes
AEFIJO feijoa
AEFILL faille
AEFILN finale
AEFILR ferial
AEFILS Feisal
AEFILT fetial
AEFIMN famine
AEFINN fainne / Fenian
AEFINR infare
AEFIRR fairer
AEFIRS ferias / fraise
AEFIRT treifa
AEFIRY aerify
AEFIST fastie / fiesta
AEFITX fixate
AEFJNT fanjet
AEFKLN fankle
AEFKLR flaker
AEFKLS flakes
AEFKLY flakey
AEFKNS kenafs
AEFKRS fakers / freaks
AEFKRY fakery / freaky
AEFKSW Fawkes
AEFLLN fallen
AEFLLR faller
AEFLLS fellas
AEFLMN flamen
AEFLMR flamer
AEFLMS flames / fleams
AEFLNU Le Fanu
AEFLNV Alfvén
AEFLNX flaxen
AEFLOR florae / loafer
AEFLOT foetal
AEFLOV foveal

AEFLRS falser / farles / flares
AEFLRT falter
AEFLRU earful / ferula
AEFLRY flayer
AEFLST festal
AEFLSY safely
AEFLTY fealty / featly
AEFMNO foeman
AEFMOR femora
AEFMRR farmer / framer
AEFMRS frames
AEFMRT Fermat
AEFNNR fanner
AEFNRW fawner
AEFNST fasten
AEFNSU unsafe
AEFNTT fatten
AEFNZZ Fezzan
AEFORS Faroes
AEFOSS fossae
AEFOSV favose
AEFPPR frappe
AEFRRR Ferrar
AEFRRS farers / Fraser
AEFRRT frater / rafter
AEFRRU faurer
AEFRRY rarefy
AEFRRZ Frazer
AEFRST afters / faster / safter / strafe
AEFRSU feuars
AEFRSW wafers
AEFRTT fatter
AEFRTW wafter
AEFRWY wafery
AEFSST feasts / safest
AEFSTY safety
AEFSUV fauves
AEGGGL gaggle
AEGGGR gagger
AEGGHL haggle
AEGGIM maggie
AEGGIN ageing
AEGGJR jagger
AEGGLR gargle / raggle
AEGGLW waggle
AEGGNR ganger / grange / nagger
AEGGNS Ganges
AEGGNU gangue

AEGGRS	aggers	**AEGIST**	ageist	**AEGMNS**	gasmen	**AEGRRY**	grayer
	eggars	**AEGISV**	visage	**AEGMNT**	magnet	**AEGRRZ**	grazer
	gagers	**AEGITU**	augite	**AEGMNY**	mangey	**AEGRSS**	gasser
	sagger	**AEGITY**	gaiety	**AEGMOS**	omegas	**AEGRST**	grates
AEGGRT	garget	**AEGJLN**	jangle	**AEGMPS**	sepmag		greats
AEGGRU	gauger	**AEGJRS**	jagers	**AEGMRS**	marges		stager
AEGGSU	gauges	**AEGJTU**	jugate	**AEGMRU**	mauger		targes
AEGGWW	gewgaw	**AEGKNS**	Skagen		maugre	**AEGRSU**	argues
AEGHIN	haeing	**AEGKST**	gasket		murage		augers
AEGHIR	hegira	**AEGLLN**	Angell	**AEGMRW**	mawger		sauger
AEGHIS	geisha	**AEGLLU**	Gaulle	**AEGMSS**	megass	**AEGRSV**	graves
AEGHIW	aweigh		ullage	**AEGMST**	gamest	**AEGRSW**	swager
AEGHIY	Hygeia	**AEGLLY**	galley	**AEGMUY**	maguey		wagers
AEGHMO	homage	**AEGLMN**	legman	**AEGMUZ**	zeugma	**AEGRSY**	greasy
	ohmage		mangel	**AEGNNO**	nonage	**AEGRSZ**	gazers
AEGHNR	hanger		mangle	**AEGNNP**	penang		grazes
	rehang	**AEGLMS**	gleams	**AEGNNT**	gannet	**AEGRTT**	target
AEGHNS	Ganesh	**AEGLMV**	maglev	**AEGNOR**	Gerona	**AEGRTU**	rugate
AEGHNW	Hwange	**AEGLMY**	gamely		onager	**AEGRTY**	gyrate
AEGHOR	gherao		gleamy		orange	**AEGRUV**	vaguer
AEGHPS	phages	**AEGLNR**	Algren	**AEGNOS**	agones	**AEGRVY**	garvey
AEGHRS	gerahs		angler		genoas	**AEGSSS**	gasses
AEGHRT	gather		erlang	**AEGNOV**	Genova	**AEGSST**	stages
AEGHSS	gashes		langer	**AEGNRR**	garner	**AEGSSU**	usages
AEGILM	milage		largen		ranger	**AEGSSW**	swages
AEGILN	genial		regnal	**AEGNRS**	angers	**AEGSTY**	gayest
	linage	**AEGLNS**	angels		ranges		stagey
AEGILO	goalie		angles		sanger	**AEGSUZ**	gauzes
AEGILP	paigle		gleans		serang	**AEGTTU**	guttae
AEGILS	ligase	**AEGLNT**	tangle	**AEGNRT**	argent	**AEGTYY**	gayety
	silage	**AEGLNU**	lagune		garnet	**AEHHJV**	Jahveh
AEGILT	aiglet		langue	**AEGNRV**	graven	**AEHHLT**	health
	ligate	**AEGLNW**	wangle	**AEGNRW**	gnawer	**AEHHMS**	HaShem
AEGILV	glaive	**AEGLOR**	galore		Wagner	**AEHHPS**	ephahs
AEGILZ	El Gîza		gaoler	**AEGNRY**	anergy	**AEHHPY**	hyphae
AEGIMN	enigma	**AEGLOT**	legato	**AEGNST**	agents	**AEHHRS**	rehash
	gamine	**AEGLOV**	lovage		vegans	**AEHHRT**	hearth
AEGIMP	magpie	**AEGLPS**	plages	**AEGNSV**	ganevs	**AEHHSS**	hashes
AEGIMR	gamier	**AEGLPU**	plague	**AEGNSY**	gansey	**AEHHST**	heaths
	maigre	**AEGLRR**	larger	**AEGOPT**	potage		sheath
	mirage	**AEGLRS**	glares	**AEGORT**	orgeat	**AEHHTY**	heathy
AEGIMS	ageism		Glaser		Ortega	**AEHHWY**	Yahweh
	images		lagers		Tagore	**AEHIIW**	Weihai
AEGINR	earing		regals		toerag	**AEHIJL**	Elijah
	gainer	**AEGLRT**	tergal	**AEGORU**	aerugo	**AEHIJR**	hejira
	reagin	**AEGLRV**	gravel	**AEGOTU**	outage	**AEHIKN**	hankie
	regain	**AEGLRY**	argyle	**AEGOTW**	towage	**AEHILM**	hiemal
	regina	**AEGLRZ**	glazer	**AEGOVY**	voyage		lehaim
AEGINS	Agnesi	**AEGLST**	aglets	**AEGPRS**	gapers	**AEHILN**	inhale
	easing	**AEGLSV**	gavels		gasper	**AEHILP**	Philae
AEGINT	eating	**AEGLSY**	sagely		grapes	**AEHILR**	hailer
	tagine	**AEGLSZ**	glazes		pagers	**AEHILS**	Elisha
AEGINU	guinea	**AEGLTU**	Tugela		sparge		Ilesha
AEGIPP	pipage	**AEGLTW**	talweg	**AEGPRT**	parget		sheila
AEGIPT	Piaget	**AEGMMR**	gammer	**AEGPRU**	Prague	**AEHILT**	halite
AEGIRT	aigret		gramme	**AEGPRW**	gawper	**AEHILW**	awhile
	gaiter	**AEGMMS**	smegma	**AEGPRY**	grapey	**AEHIMM**	maihem
	triage	**AEGMNO**	gamone	**AEGRRT**	garret	**AEHIMN**	haemin
AEGIRV	Argive	**AEGMNR**	engram		garter	**AEHIMR**	hermai
	rivage		german		grater	**AEHIMS**	mashie
AEGIRW	earwig		manger	**AEGRRU**	arguer	**AEHINR**	hernia
AEGIRZ	Gezira		ragmen	**AEGRRV**	graver	**AEHINW**	wahine

AEHIRS	ashier	**AEHMNR**	Arnhem
	sheria		Mähren
AEHIRZ	hazier	**AEHMNT**	anthem
AEHIST	Hestia		hetman
	saithe	**AEHMNU**	humane
AEHJJS	hajjes	**AEHMNW**	Newham
AEHKLT	Khelat	**AEHMPR**	hamper
AEHKMS	samekh	**AEHMRR**	harmer
AEHKNR	hanker	**AEHMRS**	harems
	harken		masher
AEHKNS	shaken	**AEHMSS**	mashes
AEHKRS	kasher		shames
	shaker	**AEHMST**	Thames
AEHKRW	hawker	**AEHMUW**	mahewu
AEHKSS	shakes	**AEHMMY**	Mayhew
AEHKSY	ashkey	**AEHNNS**	hennas
AEHKWY	hawkey	**AEHNPP**	happen
AEHLLL	hallel	**AEHNPT**	hapten
AEHLLR	Haller	**AEHNRT**	anther
AEHLLS	Hellas		Tehran
AEHLLT	lethal		thenar
AEHLLY	Halley	**AEHNSS**	hanses
AEHLMN	Hameln	**AEHNST**	Athens
AEHLMP	pelham		hasten
AEHLMR	Harlem		snathe
	Mahler		thanes
AEHLMT	hamlet	**AEHNSV**	havens
AEHLNS	hansel		shaven
AEHLOR	Lahore	**AEHNSW**	whenas
AEHLOS	haloes	**AEHNSY**	hyenas
AEHLOT	loathe		Seyhan
AEHLPS	alephs	**AEHNTT**	Thanet
AEHLPY	phylae	**AEHNUW**	whenua
AEHLRS	ashler	**AEHORS**	ashore
	halers		hoarse
	lasher	**AEHORX**	hoaxer
AEHLRT	halter	**AEHOSV**	hoveas
	lather	**AEHOSX**	hoaxes
	thaler	**AEHPRR**	harper
	Thrale	**AEHPRS**	phrase
AEHLRU	haleru		seraph
	hauler		shaper
AEHLRW	whaler		sherpa
AEHLRY	Harley	**AEHPRT**	tephra
AEHLSS	hassle		teraph
	lashes		threap
	shales	**AEHPSS**	pashes
AEHLST	haslet		phases
	lathes		shapes
	shelta	**AEHPST**	spathe
	Thales	**AEHRRR**	Harrer
AEHLSV	halves	**AEHRRS**	rasher
AEHLSW	whales		sharer
	wheals	**AEHRRT**	rather
AEHLSY	Ashley	**AEHRSS**	rashes
AEHLSZ	hazels		shares
AEHLTW	wealth		shears
AEHLTY	hyetal	**AEHRST**	earths
AEHLUV	Huelva		Hearst
AEHLVY	Halévy		hearts
AEHMMR	hammer		Sarthe
AEHMMY	mayhem	**AEHRSV**	havers

	shaver	**AEILMP**	impale
AEHRSW	hawser	**AEILMR**	mailer
	rewash		remail
	washer	**AEILMS**	emails
	whares		mesial
AEHRSZ	hazers		samiel
AEHRTT	hatter	**AEILNO**	eolian
	threat	**AEILNP**	alpine
AEHRTV	thrave		Nepali
AEHRTW	thawer		pineal
	wreath	**AEILNR**	aliner
AEHRTY	earthy		larine
	hearty		linear
AEHRVW	wharve		nailer
AEHRVY	Harvey	**AEILNS**	aliens
AEHSSS	sashes		alines
AEHSST	ashets		lianes
	hastes		saline
AEHSSV	shaves	**AEILNT**	entail
AEHSSW	hawses		tineal
	washes	**AEILNV**	alevin
AEHSTT	thetas		alvine
AEHSTV	Shevat		valine
AEHSTW	swathe		veinal
	wheats		venial
AEIILR	Leiria	**AEILNX**	alexin
AEIILS	liaise		xenial
AEIIPR	Pieria	**AEILOS**	Aeolis
AEIIPT	Taipei	**AEILPS**	espial
AEIIRR	airier		laipse
AEIJKR	Rijeka		lipase
AEIJLR	jailer		Pelias
AEIJMS	James I		pileas
AEIJNR	injera	**AEILPT**	aplite
AEIJNT	Netaji		Pilate
	tajine	**AEILQU**	equali
AEIJRV	jarvie	**AEILRR**	railer
AEIJSX	jaxies	**AEILRS**	ariels
AEIKLR	lakier		Israel
AEIKLS	alkies		sailer
	alsike		serail
AEIKLT	talkie		serial
AEIKNS	Eakins	**AEILRT**	retail
	kinase		retial
AEIKNT	Aitken	**AEILRW**	wailer
	intake	**AEILRZ**	lazier
	kentia	**AEILSS**	aisles
AEIKNW	Wankie		lassie
AEIKNZ	kaizen	**AEILST**	saltie
AEIKOR	oakier	**AEILSV**	Leavis
AEIKOS	oakies		silvae
AEIKPR	parkie		valise
AEIKRS	kaiser	**AEILSY**	easily
AEIKRV	Kaveri	**AEILUV**	eluvia
AEILLM	mallei	**AEIMMM**	mammie
AEILLN	lienal	**AEIMMN**	ammine
	lineal	**AEIMMR**	maimer
AEILLR	Allier	**AEIMNO**	anomie
AEILLS	allies	**AEIMNP**	pieman
AEILLT	taille	**AEIMNR**	airmen
	telial		marine
AEILMN	menial		Namier

	remain
AEIMNS	Amiens
	amines
	animes
AEIMNT	etamin
	inmate
AEIMNX	Xiamen
AEIMNY	Niamey
AEIMPY	pyemia
AEIMRS	armies
	maries
	sarmie
AEIMRT	imaret
	matier
AEIMRU	uremia
AEIMRW	Weimar
AEIMRY	rimaye
AEIMRZ	mazier
AEIMST	maties
	samite
AEIMXX	maxixe
AEINNO	eonian
AEINNP	pennia
	pinnae
AEINNR	narine
AEINNS	inanes
	insane
	sienna
AEINNT	innate
	tannie
AEINNU	Niuean
AEINNV	Vienna
AEINOS	Naoise
AEINPR	Napier
	rapine
AEINPT	patine
	Pétain
	pineta
AEINRS	arisen
	arsine
	sarnie
AEINRT	ratine
	retain
	retina
AEINRV	Erivan
	ravine
	vainer
AEINRZ	zanier
AEINSS	sanies
	sasine
AEINST	tisane
AEINSV	naives
	navies
	savine
AEINSZ	azines
	zanies
AEINTU	auntie
AEINTV	native
AEINTY	Yentai
AEIOPR	Peoria
AEIOPS	soapie
AEIOPT	opiate

AEIOPZ	epizoa
AEIORS	ariose
AEIORV	Aveiro
AEIOSV	Savoie
AEIOVV	Évvoia
AEIPPT	Petipa
AEIPRR	pairer
	rapier
	repair
AEIPRS	aspire
	paries
	Persia
	praise
	spirea
AEIPRT	pirate
AEIPSS	sepias
AEIPST	petsai
	pietas
AEIPSV	pavise
AEIRRS	arsier
	raiser
	sairer
	sierra
AEIRRT	artier
AEIRRV	arrive
	Rivera
AEIRRW	warier
AEIRSS	arises
	raises
	serais
	Sisera
AEIRST	satire
	striae
	terais
AEIRSV	Servia
	varies
AEIRTT	attire
	ratite
AEIRTW	waiter
AEIRVW	waiver
	wavier
AEIRVX	Xavier
AEIRWX	waxier
AEISST	siesta
	tassie
AEISSU	Aussie
AEISSX	axises
AEISSZ	assize
AEISTX	taxies
AEISTY	aseity
AEISUY	Ieyasu
AEISVW	waives
AEITTT	tattie
AEITTV	vittae
AEJMMR	jammer
AEJMRT	ramjet
AEJMST	jetsam
AEJMSV	James V
AEJNNS	Jansen
AEJNOT	Taejon
AEJNST	sejant
AEJNUU	Juneau

AEJPRS	japers
	jasper
AEJPRY	japery
AEJRSU	Jaurès
AEJRUZ	Juárez
AEJRVY	jarvey
AEJRZZ	jazzer
AEJSZZ	jazzes
AEKKNR	kraken
AEKKRY	yakker
AEKLNR	lanker
	rankle
AEKLNS	ankles
AEKLNT	anklet
AEKLNW	knawel
AEKLNY	alkyne
AEKLOY	Oakley
AEKLPS	splake
AEKLRR	larker
AEKLRS	lakers
	Lasker
	slaker
AEKLRT	talker
AEKLRW	walker
AEKLSS	Kassel
	slakes
AEKLST	lasket
AEKLSU	Leukas
AEKLSV	Levkás
AEKLTU	auklet
AEKLWY	weakly
AEKMNR	Kerman
AEKMNU	unmake
AEKMOT	matoke
AEKMPU	makeup
AEKMRR	marker
	remark
AEKMRS	kermas
	makers
	masker
AEKMRT	market
AEKMRU	kumera
AEKNNY	Kenyan
AEKNOR	Korean
AEKNOT	Keaton
AEKNOW	awoken
AEKNPS	pekans
AEKNRR	ranker
AEKNRS	nakers
AEKNRT	tanker
AEKNRW	Newark
	wanker
AEKNSS	skeans
	snakes
	sneaks
AEKNSV	knaves
AEKNSW	wakens
AEKNSY	Sankey
	sneaky
AEKOPT	Topeka
AEKORS	arkose
	soaker

AEKOSY	kayoes
AEKPRR	parker
AEKPRS	Parkes
AEKPSS	speaks
AEKPTU	takeup
	uptake
AEKQRU	quaker
AEKQSU	quakes
	squeak
AEKRRS	rakers
AEKRSS	askers
	eskars
	sakers
AEKRST	skater
	strake
	streak
	takers
	tasker
AEKRSW	wakers
	wreaks
AEKSST	skates
	stakes
	steaks
AEKSSU	ukases
AEKSTW	tweaks
AEKTWY	tweaky
AEKWYY	keyway
AELLLY	leally
AELLMO	Almelo
AELLMT	mallet
AELLMU	Lemalu
AELLMY	lamely
AELLNY	leanly
AELLPS	lapels
AELLPT	pallet
AELLPY	palely
AELLRT	taller
AELLRU	allure
	laurel
AELLRW	waller
AELLRY	really
AELLST	sallet
AELLSY	alleys
AELLTT	tallet
AELLTU	luteal
AELLTW	wallet
AELLTY	lately
	lealty
AELLVW	Wavell
AELLVY	valley
AELMMR	rammel
	rammle
AELMMS	lemmas
AELMNO	melano
AELMNS	Anselm
	lemans
	Le Mans
	mensal
AELMNT	lament
	mantel
	mantle
	mental

Key	Word
AELMNW	lawmen
AELMNY	laymen
	Manley
	meanly
	namely
AELMOR	morale
AELMOS	Salome
AELMPR	lamper
	palmer
AELMPS	maples
	sample
AELMPU	ampule
AELMRS	realms
AELMRT	armlet
	martel
AELMRU	mauler
AELMRV	marvel
AELMRY	Marley
AELMST	lamest
	metals
AELMSU	Samuel
	ulemas
AELMSY	measly
AELMTU	amulet
	muleta
AELMTY	tamely
AELNNR	lanner
AELNOR	loaner
	reloan
AELNOS	anoles
	lanose
AELNOT	etalon
	tolane
AELNPR	planer
	replan
AELNPS	Naples
	panels
	planes
AELNPT	planet
	platen
AELNPU	Plauen
AELNRS	learns
	nerals
AELNRT	antler
	learnt
	rental
AELNRU	Lauren
	neural
	unreal
AELNRV	nerval
	verlan
	vernal
AELNRY	larney
	nearly
AELNSU	unseal
AELNSV	navels
	Valens
AELNSY	sanely
AELNTT	latent
	latten
	talent
AELNTU	eluant

Key	Word
	lunate
AELNTV	levant
AELNTY	neatly
AELOPP	Aleppo
AELOPR	parole
AELOPS	aslope
	El Paso
AELOPT	pelota
AELOPX	poleax
AELORS	solera
AELOST	osteal
AELOSU	Aeolus
AELOSV	loaves
AELOSZ	azoles
AELOTZ	zealot
AELOVV	volvae
AELPPR	lapper
	rappel
AELPPS	appels
	apples
AELPPT	applet
	lappet
AELPPU	papule
AELPPY	appley
AELPQU	plaque
AELPRR	parrel
AELPRS	lapser
	pearls
AELPRT	palter
	plater
AELPRU	pleura
AELPRY	parley
	pearly
	player
	replay
AELPSS	lapses
	passel
	sepals
AELPST	palest
	pastel
	petals
	plates
	pleats
	septal
	staple
	tepals
AELPTT	Platte
AELQSU	equals
	squeal
AELQUY	Quayle
AELQUZ	quezal
AELRRT	retral
AELRRY	rarely
AELRSS	lasers
AELRST	alerts
	alters
	artels
	estral
	laster
	ratels
	salter
	slater

Key	Word
	staler
	stelar
	talers
AELRSU	saurel
AELRSV	lavers
	ravels
	salver
	serval
	slaver
AELRSW	walers
	warsle
AELRSY	layers
	relays
	slayer
AELRTT	latter
	rattle
AELRTV	travel
	varlet
AELRTW	Walter
AELRTY	elytra
	lyrate
	raylet
	realty
AELRUV	valuer
AELRVY	Valéry
AELRWY	lawyer
	Warley
AELRYY	yarely
	yearly
AELRZZ	razzle
AELSSS	Elsass
	lasses
AELSST	salets
	slates
	stales
	steals
	tassel
	teslas
AELSSV	salves
	selvas
	slaves
	valses
AELSSW	awless
	swales
AELSTT	latest
	lattes
AELSTU	salute
AELSTV	valets
	vestal
AELSTX	exalts
AELSTY	slatey
AELSUV	values
AELSUX	sexual
AELSVV	valves
AELSVY	slavey
	sylvae
AELSYZ	sleazy
AELTTT	tattle
AELTTW	wattle
AELTTY	lyttae
AELTUX	luxate
AELUUV	uvulae

Key	Word
AELUVV	vulvae
AEMMMT	mammet
AEMMNR	merman
AEMMOR	Mamoré
AEMMRR	rammer
AEMMRY	yammer
AEMMRZ	mamzer
AEMMST	stemma
AEMMSU	summae
AEMMSY	mameys
AEMMTU	maumet
AEMNNP	penman
AEMNNR	manner
AEMNNW	Newman
AEMNNY	Nyeman
AEMNOP	mopane
AEMNOR	enamor
	Merano
	moaner
AEMNOT	omenta
AEMNOU	Nouméa
AEMNOY	yeoman
AEMNPU	pneuma
AEMNQU	manque
AEMNRS	Mearns
	remans
AEMNRT	marten
AEMNRU	manure
AEMNSS	manses
AEMNST	aments
	mantes
	stamen
AEMNSU	unseam
AEMNSV	mavens
AEMNSY	yamens
AEMNTX	taxmen
AEMORR	remora
	roamer
AEMORS	ramose
AEMORT	omerta
AEMORU	Moreau
AEMORW	womera
AEMORX	xeroma
AEMPPR	mapper
	pamper
	preamp
AEMPRR	prearm
AEMPRT	tamper
AEMPRV	revamp
	vamper
AEMQRU	marque
AEMQSU	masque
AEMRRR	marrer
AEMRRS	rearms
AEMRRU	armure
AEMRRW	rewarm
	warmer
AEMRSS	masers
	Ramses
	smears
AEMRST	armets
	master

maters
stream
tamers
AEMRSU Maseru
AEMRSY Ramsey
smeary
AEMRSZ mazers
AEMRTT matter
AEMRTU mature
Mutare
AEMSSS masses
AEMSST steams
AEMSSU amuses
assume
AEMSSY Massey
AEMSSZ smazes
AEMSTT mattes
tamest
AEMSTU meatus
AEMSTY mayest
steamy
AEMSUV mauves
AEMSYZ zymase
AEMTTU mutate
AENNNS Nansen
AENNOV novena
AENNOY anyone
AENNRS Sarnen
Sennar
AENNRT tanner
AENNRV Vänern
AENNRW wanner
AENNSS sennas
AENNST Nantes
AENNTT tenant
AENOPS paeons
AENOPW weapon
AENOPY paeony
AENORS reason
senora
AENORT atoner
ornate
AENORV Averno
Verona
AENOSS season
AENOST atones
AENOSX axones
AENOTT notate
AENOTZ zonate
AENPPR napper
parpen
AENPPS nappes
AENPRT arpent
entrap
parent
trepan
AENPRW enwrap
AENPRY napery
AENPRZ panzer
AENPSS aspens
AENPST patens
AENPTT patent
patten
AENPTU peanut
AENQSU queans
AENRRS snarer
AENRRT errant
ranter
AENRRW warner
warren
AENRSS Nasser
sarsen
snares
AENRST antres
astern
Santer
sterna
AENRSV Anvers
ravens
AENRSW answer
AENRSY senary
yearns
AENRTT natter
AENRTU nature
AENRTV tavern
Traven
AENRTW wanter
AENRWY yawner
AENSST assent
sanest
stanes
AENSSU anuses
AENSTU Austen
unseat
AENSTX sextan
AENSUV naevus
AENSUY uneasy
AENSVW navews
AENSWY sawney
AENTTU attune
tauten
Tetuán
AENTTX extant
AENTTY tetany
AENTWY tawney
AEOPPS appose
AEOPQU opaque
AEOPRS operas
Pesaro
AEOPRT Pareto
protea
AEOPRU Europa
AEOPSS Pessoa
AEOPST potaes
AEOPTT teapot
AEOPTY teapoy
AEORRR roarer
AEORRS soarer
AEORSS serosa
soares
AEORST orates
AEORSU arouse
Roseau
AEORSZ Azores
AEORTT rotate
AEORVW avower
AEORZZ Arezzo
AEOSTZ azotes
AEOTTU outate
outeat
AEOUVZ zouave
AEPPRR rapper
AEPPRS papers
sapper
AEPPRT tapper
AEPPRU pauper
AEPPRY papery
prepay
yapper
AEPPTT tappet
AEPPTU pupate
AEPRRS parers
parser
rasper
sparer
AEPRRT prater
AEPRRU parure
uprear
AEPRRW prewar
rewrap
warper
AEPRRY prayer
AEPRSS aspers
parses
repass
spares
sparse
spears
AEPRST paters
prates
repast
tapers
trapes
AEPRSU pareus
pauser
AEPRSV pavers
AEPRSX praxes
AEPRSY payers
repays
AEPRTT patter
AEPRTU uprate
AEPRUY yauper
AEPRWY yawper
AEPSSS passes
AEPSST pastes
spates
stapes
AEPSSU pauses
upases
AEPSTT aptest
AEPSTX expats
AEPSUX auspex
AEQRRU quarer
AEQRSU square
AEQRTU quarte
quatre
AEQRUV quaver
AEQSUY queasy
AEQTTU Quetta
AERRSS rasers
AERRST arrest
rarest
raster
Sartre
starer
AERRSV ravers
AERRSZ razers
AERRTT ratter
AERRTY artery
AERSSS rasses
sasers
AERSST assert
asters
reasts
stares
AERSSU assure
AERSSV savers
AERSSW sawers
swears
wrasse
AERSSY sayers
AERSTT stater
taster
taters
tetras
treats
AERSTU Atreus
Seurat
urates
AERSTV averts
starve
traves
vaster
AERSTW tawers
waster
waters
AERSTX extras
taxers
AERSTY estray
stayer
yarest
AERSTZ ersatz
AERSUU aureus
uraeus
AERSUV suaver
AERSUZ azures
Suárez
AERSVV varves
AERSVW wavers
AERSVY Savery
AERSWX waxers
AERSWY sawyer
swayer
AERSZZ razzes
AERTTT tatter
AERTTY treaty
yatter
AERTUU auteur

AERTWY	watery	AFGRST	grafts	AFKLSS	flasks	AGGIZZ	zigzag
AERTYZ	azerty	AFGRUY	argufy	AFKNRS	franks	AGGLNY	gangly
AESSSS	assess	AFHIIR	hairif	AFKOST	koftas	AGGLSY	slaggy
	sasses	AFHIKL	khalif	AFLLOR	floral	AGGLWY	waggly
AESSST	assets	AFHIKR	kharif	AFLLOW	fallow	AGGMOT	maggot
	tasses	AFHIMS	famish	AFLLPU	lapful	AGGMRU	muggar
AESSSY	essays	AFHIOS	oafish	AFLLTY	flatly	AGGNOW	waggon
AESSTT	states	AFHIRS	sharif	AFLLUW	lawful	AGGNRU	nuggar
	tasset	AFHIST	faiths	AFLMNU	manful	AGGNSY	snaggy
	tastes	AFHLMU	fulham	AFLMNY	flyman	AGGQUY	quaggy
AESSTU	sautes	AFHLOO	loofah	AFLMOR	formal	AGHHSU	haughs
AESSTV	staves	AFHLSY	flashy	AFLMOU	Malouf	AGHILN	haling
	vestas	AFHMOT	fathom	AFLMRU	armful	AGHILT	alight
AESSTW	sweats	AFHNOS	Foshan		fulmar	AGHINR	haring
	tawses	AFHORS	shofar	AFLMYY	mayfly	AGHINS	hangis
	wastes	AFHRSW	wharfs	AFLNOT	fontal		Hsiang
AESSTY	yeasts	AFHSST	shafts	AFLNPU	panful	AGHINT	hating
AESTTT	attest	AFIIJN	Fijian	AFLNTU	flaunt	AGHINV	having
AESTTU	astute	AFIILL	filial	AFLOOS	loofas	AGHINW	hawing
	statue	AFIILN	finial	AFLORS	floras	AGHINY	haying
AESTWY	sweaty	AFIILO	Olaf II	AFLORV	flavor	AGHINZ	hazing
AESTYY	yeasty	AFIIMN	infima	AFLOST	floats	AGHIPS	Pisgah
AESVWY	waveys	AFIJNU	Fujian	AFLOTY	floaty	AGHIQU	quaigh
AFFGUW	guffaw	AFIKLS	kalifs	AFLRTU	artful	AGHIRR	gharri
AFFHIO	Offiah	AFIKRS	fakirs	AFLSTU	faults	AGHIRS	garish
AFFIKR	kaffir		kafirs		flatus	AGHIRT	aright
AFFILP	pilaff	AFIKRU	Faruk I	AFLSWY	sawfly	AGHISU	aguish
AFFIMR	affirm	AFILLS	flails	AFLTUY	faulty	AGHISZ	ghazis
AFFINR	Fafnir	AFILMU	famuli	AFLWYY	flyway	AGHKNU	Hanguk
AFFIRT	tariff	AFILMY	family	AFMNOR	Forman	AGHLNY	Lynagh
AFFLOY	layoff	AFILNS	finals	AFMNOT	fantom	AGHLSU	laughs
	Offaly	AFILNU	infula	AFMOOS	samfoo	AGHNNU	hungan
AFFLSU	luffas	AFILNV	flavin	AFMORT	format	AGHNOS	hogans
AFFLUX	afflux	AFILNY	Finlay	AFMOSU	famous		Shango
AFFLWY	waffly		naifly	AFNNOS	fanons	AGHNPU	hangup
AFFNSY	nyaffs	AFILOR	foliar	AFNPRY	frypan	AGHNRT	thrang
AFFOPY	payoff	AFILRS	flairs	AFNRSS	snarfs	AGHNSW	whangs
AFFORR	Forfar		frails	AFNSUU	Faunus	AGHNTU	naught
AFFQSU	quaffs	AFILRY	fairly	AFORRW	farrow	AGHNUY	gunyah
AFFSST	staffs	AFILRZ	frazil	AFORRY	orfray	AGHOQU	quahog
AFGGIO	Foggia	AFILSY	salify	AFORSV	favors	AGHPRS	graphs
AFGGLY	flaggy	AFIMNR	firman	AFORSY	forays	AGHRRY	gharry
AFGGOT	faggot	AFIMNY	infamy	AFORSZ	Sforza	AGHRST	garths
AFGIJM	figjam	AFIMRT	maftir	AFORUV	favour	AGHSSU	saughs
AFGIKN	faking	AFIMRY	ramify	AFOSSS	fossas	AGHSTU	aughts
AFGIMN	faming	AFIMSS	massif	AFOSST	fatsos		ghauts
AFGINO	Fangio	AFIMUY	Faiyûm		softas	AGHTTU	taught
AFGINR	faring	AFIMUZ	umfazi	AFRSTU	frusta	AGIIJN	gaijin
AFGINT	fating	AFINNN	finnan	AGGGIN	gaging	AGIIKL	Kigali
AFGINX	faxing	AFINNO	fanion	AGGGOS	goggas	AGIILN	ailing
AFGINY	faying	AFINNT	infant	AGGHIS	haggis		Iligan
AFGINZ	fazing	AFINRU	unfair	AGGHSY	shaggy		nilgai
AFGISY	gasify	AFINST	faints	AGGIIL	gilgai	AGIIMN	aiming
AFGLNO	flagon	AFINSU	fusain	AGGILO	loggia	AGIINR	airing
AFGLNU	fungal	AFINYZ	nazify	AGGIMN	gaming	AGIIST	atigis
AFGLOS	oflags	AFIQRS	faqirs	AGGINP	gaping	AGIISV	vigias
AFGLRU	frugal	AFIRRS	friars		paging	AGIIUX	Xia Gui
AFGMNU	Fa Ngum	AFIRRY	friary	AGGINR	raging	AGIJNP	japing
AFGNOS	ganofs	AFIRST	afrits	AGGINT	gating	AGIJNW	jawing
AFGORT	forgat	AFIRTY	ratify	AGGINW	waging	AGIJSW	jigsaw
AFGOST	fagots	AFJLRU	jarful	AGGINZ	gazing	AGIKLN	Glinka
AFGOTU	fugato	AFKLNS	flanks	AGGIWW	wigwag	AGIKMN	making

AGIKNN	Anking	AGINPT	taping	AGLNOY	Loyang		wagons
AGIKNR	raking	AGINPV	paving	AGLNRS	gnarls	AGNOTU	nougat
AGIKNS	asking	AGINPW	pawing	AGLNRU	langur	AGNOWY	gowany
	gaskin	AGINPY	paying	AGLNRY	gnarly	AGNPRS	prangs
	kiangs	AGINRR	raring	AGLNSS	slangs		sprang
	Sikang	AGINRS	arsing	AGLNSY	slangy	AGNPRU	Nagpur
AGIKNT	taking		grains	AGLNTY	tangly	AGNPSU	pungas
AGIKNW	waking		rasing	AGLNUU	ungual	AGNRST	grants
AGILLU	ligula	AGINRT	gratin		ungula	AGNRSW	wrangs
AGILMN	laming		rating	AGLOOS	agloos	AGNRTY	gantry
	lingam		taring	AGLOOT	galoot	AGNSST	stangs
	malign	AGINRV	raving	AGLOPS	galops	AGNSSU	sugans
AGILMO	glioma	AGINRW	waring	AGLORS	argols	AGNSTW	twangs
AGILMP	magilp	AGINRX	raxing		gorals	AGNSTY	angsty
AGILMY	gamily	AGINRY	grainy		Goslar	AGNTUY	Tanguy
AGILNP	paling		raying		largos	AGNTWY	twangy
AGILNS	algins	AGINRZ	razing	AGLOSS	glossa	AGOORT	agorot
	aligns	AGINSS	assign	AGLOST	gloats	AGORST	argots
	lasing	AGINST	gainst	AGLOSV	galvos		groats
	lingas		giants	AGLOWY	logway	AGORSY	argosy
	signal		sating	AGLPUY	plaguy	AGORTU	ragout
AGILNU	lingua		tangis	AGLRSU	Glarus	AGOSTU	outgas
AGILNV	laving	AGINSV	saving	AGLRUV	vulgar	AGOSTV	gavots
AGILNW	lawing	AGINSW	sawing	AGLRUY	glaury	AGOSYZ	gyozas
	waling	AGINSY	saying	AGLRYY	grayly	AGOTTU	tautog
AGILNY	gainly	AGINTW	tawing	AGLSSY	glassy	AGPRSS	grasps
	laying	AGINTX	taxing	AGLSUV	valgus		sprags
AGILNZ	lazing	AGINVW	waving	AGMMNO	gammon	AGRSSU	sugars
AGILOR	gloria	AGINWX	waxing	AGMMNU	magnum	AGRSSY	grassy
AGILOS	oilgas	AGINWY	yawing	AGMMSU	gummas	AGRSTU	tragus
AGILOT	galiot	AGIORU	giaour	AGMNNU	gunman	AGRSUU	augurs
AGILOV	ogival	AGIORV	virago	AGMNOR	morgan	AGRSUY	sugary
AGILPU	Puglia	AGIOTU	agouti	AGMNOS	mangos	AGRUUY	augury
AGILRS	glairs	AGIRST	gratis		ngomas	AGSTUU	august
AGILRY	glairy	AGIRSV	virgas	AGMNOX	magnox	AHHIJR	hijrah
AGILSS	siglas	AGIRTU	guitar	AGMNSU	magnus	AHHISV	shivah
AGILSW	wilgas	AGISST	agists		mungas	AHHKOO	hookah
AGIMNN	naming	AGJLMO	logjam	AGMNUY	maungy	AHHLPY	hyphal
AGIMNR	arming	AGJLSU	jugals	AGMOOY	oogamy	AHHOOR	hoorah
	margin	AGJNOR	jargon	AGMORS	orgasm	AHHORT	Hathor
AGIMNS	gamins	AGKLNO	kalong	AGMORV	vagrom	AHHORW	Howrah
AGIMNT	mating	AGKLOT	kgotla	AGMOST	magots	AHHPPU	huppah
	taming	AGKLOU	kagoul	AGMOYZ	zygoma	AHHRRU	hurrah
AGIMNY	maying	AGKNOR	Angkor	AGMPUZ	gazump	AHHRST	thrash
AGIMNZ	mazing	AGKNRU	kurgan	AGMRTU	Targum	AHHUZZ	huzzah
AGIMOS	amigos	AGKOPS	gopaks	AGMSTU	gamuts	AHIILT	lithia
AGIMSS	sigmas	AGLLNO	gallon	AGNNOY	Yangon	AHIINT	tahini
AGIMST	stigma	AGLLOP	gallop	AGNNRU	Gunnar	AHIISS	shiais
AGIMWW	wigwam	AGLLPU	Gallup	AGNNRY	granny	AHIITT	Tahiti
AGINNP	paning	AGLLSU	gallus	AGNNTU	Antung	AHIJJS	hajjis
AGINNQ	Anqing	AGLMMO	Glomma	AGNOPS	pongas	AHIJNN	Jinnah
AGINNT	anting	AGLMOR	glamor	AGNOQU	quango	AHIJNS	Jhansi
AGINNW	awning	AGLMSU	mulgas	AGNORR	garron	AHIJOS	Josiah
	waning	AGLNNO	longan	AGNORS	groans	AHIKKS	khakis
AGINOR	Girona	AGLNNU	lungan		nagors	AHIKMO	Kohima
	oaring	AGLNOO	lagoon		orangs	AHIKMS	hakims
	onagri	AGLNOP	Pagnol		organs	AHIKMV	mikvah
	origan	AGLNOS	logans		sarong	AHIKOW	kowhai
AGINOS	ngaios		slogan	AGNOST	sontag	AHIKRS	rakish
	Saigon	AGLNOT	Galton		tangos		shikar
AGINPR	paring	AGLNOU	lanugo		tongas	AHIKSS	shiksa
	raping		Lugano	AGNOSW	gowans	AHIKST	Shakti

AHIKSZ	khazis	AHKKSU	sukkah	AHMOSV	moshav	AHSSTW	swaths
AHILLP	phalli	AHKLNU	Khulna	AHMOTU	mahout	AHSTUY	thuyas
AHILLT	thalli	AHKMOS	moksha	AHMOTZ	matzoh	AIIJSV	Sivaji
AHILLZ	zillah	AHKMOW	mohawk	AHMOWY	haymow	AIIKLS	Likasi
AHILMP	Imphal	AHKNOT	Khotan	AHMPSU	mashup	AIILMN	limina
AHILMU	hamuli	AHKNOW	Hankow	AHMRSY	marshy	AIILRY	airily
AHILNR	rhinal	AHKNPU	punkah	AHMRTW	warmth	AIIMMN	minima
AHILNU	inhaul	AHKNRS	shrank	AHMSSU	samshu	AIIMMR	Miriam
AHILNY	hyalin	AHKNSS	shanks		shamus	AIIMNS	simian
	linhay	AHKNST	thanks	AHMSSW	shawms	AIIMNT	intima
AHILOS	Lashio	AHKOOS	hookas	AHNNSY	shanny	AIIMNV	vimina
AHILPS	palish	AHKOSS	shakos	AHNOPR	orphan	AIIMOR	moirai
	phials	AHKPUU	hapuku	AHNOPY	aphony	AIIMPR	impair
AHILPT	Lapith	AHKRSS	sharks	AHNORS	sharon	AIIMRY	Mary II
AHILPZ	Zilpah	AHKRTU	khurta		shoran	AIIMST	samiti
AHILST	lathis	AHLLMO	mollah	AHNOST	Ashton	AIINNN	Ninian
	latish	AHLLMU	mullah	AHNOWY	anyhow	AIINNO	Ionian
	tahsil	AHLLNU	nullah	AHNRTW	thrawn	AIINNZ	zinnia
AHILSV	lavish	AHLLOO	halloo	AHNRVY	hryvna	AIINRS	raisin
AHILTW	withal		holloa	AHNSST	snaths	AIINRZ	Rinzai
AHILYZ	hazily	AHLLOS	hallos	AHNSTU	haunts	AIINST	isatin
AHIMNO	Namhoi		hollas		sunhat	AIINSX	sixain
AHIMNS	Mishna	AHLLOT	hallot		Ushant	AIINTT	titian
AHIMOR	mohair	AHLLOW	hallow	AHNSTY	shanty	AIINVV	Ivan IV
AHIMPS	mishap	AHLLRT	thrall	AHNTTU	U Thant		Vivian
AHIMRS	ihrams	AHLLUX	hallux	AHOORS	shoora	AIIORS	ariosi
	marish	AHLMNY	Hamlyn	AHOORY	hooray	AIIPTW	wapiti
	Shamir		hymnal	AHOOSW	wahoos	AIIRST	Istria
AHINPT	hatpin	AHLMOO	moolah	AHOOSY	yahoos	AIIRTV	trivia
AHINRS	Shinar	AHLMOS	shalom	AHOPPS	Paphos	AIISSS	Assisi
AHINRU	unhair	AHLMSU	haulms		Sappho	AIITUW	tauiwi
AHINSS	nashis	AHLNOS	halons	AHOPRS	pharos	AIJJNU	Ujjain
	Shansi		lohans		phasor	AIJKNS	kanjis
AHINSU	Husain	AHLNOT	Halton	AHOPST	pathos	AIJLMS	majlis
AHINSV	vanish	AHLNSU	uhlans		potash	AIJLNU	Julian
AHINSW	washin		unlash	AHOQTU	quotha	AIJLOR	jailor
AHINSX	Shanxi	AHLOOP	hoopla	AHORRW	harrow	AIJLOV	jovial
AHIOPS	Sophia	AHLORT	harlot	AHORRY	horary	AIJMNP	Panjim
AHIORS	orisha	AHLORW	Harlow	AHORTT	throat	AIJMOR	romaji
AHIORT	thoria		Warhol	AHORTU	author	AIJNNS	ninjas
AHIOST	Taisho	AHLOSS	shoals	AHORTX	thorax	AIJNOV	Jovian
AHIPRS	parish	AHLOST	lotahs	AHOSST	hoasts	AIJPRU	Jaipur
	raphis	AHLOSY	shoaly		hostas	AIKLMN	malkin
AHIPRU	rupiah	AHLPSS	splash		shoats	AIKLNO	kaolin
AHIPSS	spahis	AHLPSU	sulpha		Thásos	AIKLNR	Larkin
AHIPTY	Pythia	AHLPSY	plashy	AHOTWZ	howzat	AIKLST	tilaks
AHIRRS	arrish	AHLRSY	rashly	AHPRRY	Pyrrha	AIKLSU	saluki
	Harris	AHLSSW	shawls	AHPRSS	sharps	AIKLSZ	Kalisz
	sirrah	AHLTUZ	halutz	AHPSUW	washup	AIKLTU	likuta
AHIRRW	wirrah	AHMMSY	shammy		whaups	AIKMNS	kamsin
AHIRST	airths	AHMMWY	whammy	AHQSSU	squash	AIKMNW	mawkin
	Ishtar	AHMNNU	numnah	AHRRTU	Arthur	AIKMOO	oomiak
AHIRSV	ravish	AHMNOS	hansom	AHRRUY	hurray	AIKMOP	Maikop
AHIRSW	rawish	AHMNPY	nympha	AHRSSU	Asshur	AIKMOT	Komati
	wairsh	AHMNSU	Hamsun		hussar	AIKMSU	Kumasi
AHIRSZ	Shiraz		humans	AHRSTT	strath		umiaks
AHIRTW	wraith	AHMNSY	mynahs	AHRSTW	swarth	AIKNNN	nankin
AHISSW	siwash	AHMNTU	Uthman		wraths	AIKNNP	napkin
AHISTU	hiatus	AHMOOP	oompah	AHRSTY	trashy	AIKNPR	kirpan
AHISTV	Vashti	AHMORY	moryah	AHRTTW	thwart		parkin
AHJOSU	Joshua	AHMORZ	mahzor	AHRTWY	wrathy	AIKNRT	kirtan
AHJSTU	thujas	AHMOST	Thomas	AHSSTU	tussah	AIKNRU	Kiruna

AIKNRV	Narvik	**AILNRT**	ratlin	**AIMNST**	mantis	**AINQTU**	quaint
AIKNST	Atkins		trinal		matins		quinta
	Kistna	**AILNRU**	urinal	**AIMNSU**	animus	**AINRST**	instar
	takins	**AILNSS**	snails	**AIMNSV**	mavins		Sintra
AIKNSU	nikaus	**AILNST**	instal	**AIMNSY**	Mysian		strain
	Suakin		Stalin	**AIMNSZ**	nizams		trains
AIKOPS	okapis	**AILNSU**	insula	**AIMNTT**	mattin	**AINRSV**	ravins
AIKOPT	katipo	**AILNSV**	anvils		titman	**AINRSY**	Syrian
AIKORT	troika		silvan	**AIMNTU**	manitu	**AINRTU**	nutria
AIKOTW	kwaito	**AILNSY**	inlays	**AIMNUZ**	mizuna	**AINSSS**	sasins
AIKPPS	kippas	**AILNTY**	litany	**AIMOPT**	optima	**AINSST**	saints
AIKPSU	pikaus	**AILNVY**	vainly	**AIMOPY**	myopia		satins
AIKRRS	karris	**AILNYZ**	zanily	**AIMOST**	Taoism		stains
AIKRST	kraits	**AILOPS**	pilaos	**AIMOSU**	miaous	**AINSSW**	swains
AIKRSU	kauris	**AILORS**	sailor	**AIMOSV**	Asimov	**AINSTT**	statin
AIKSST	sitkas	**AILORT**	rialto	**AIMOSW**	miaows		taints
AIKTUW	Kuwait		tailor	**AIMOSX**	axioms		tanist
AILLMU	allium	**AILORU**	Auriol	**AIMPRS**	Pamirs		titans
AILLMY	Millay	**AILOSS**	assoil	**AIMPRT**	armpit	**AINSTU**	Austin
AILLPR	pillar	**AILOSV**	Valois		impart	**AINSTW**	witans
AILLST	tallis		violas	**AIMPSS**	passim	**AINSTY**	sanity
AILLSV	villas	**AILOSX**	oxalis	**AIMQSU**	maquis		satiny
AILLSW	Wallis	**AILOTX**	oxtail	**AIMRRS**	marris	**AINSYZ**	zayins
AILLSZ	zillas	**AILPPS**	pipals	**AIMRSS**	simars	**AINTVY**	vanity
AILLTT	tallit	**AILPRS**	spiral	**AIMRST**	amrits	**AIOORS**	arioso
AILLUZ	lazuli	**AILPST**	pastil		Marist	**AIOPRV**	pavior
AILLYZ	lazily		plaits	**AIMRSU**	Marius	**AIOPST**	patios
AILMNO	Molina		spital		mauris		patois
	oilman	**AILPUV**	Paul VI	**AIMRSW**	Wismar	**AIOPTU**	utopia
AILMNR	marlin	**AILQSU**	quails	**AIMRSZ**	mirzas	**AIORSS**	Orissa
AILMNU	alumni	**AILRRW**	Wirral	**AIMRTU**	atrium	**AIORST**	aorist
	lumina	**AILRST**	trails		Timaru		aristo
AILMNY	mainly		trials	**AIMRTX**	matrix		Artois
AILMOP	lipoma	**AILRSV**	rivals	**AIMSSW**	swamis		ratios
AILMOS	Siloam	**AILRSY**	riyals	**AIMSTU**	autism		satori
	Somali	**AILRTU**	ritual	**AINNNT**	tannin	**AIORSV**	savior
AILMOT	maloti	**AILRWY**	warily	**AINNOS**	anions	**AIORSX**	orixas
	Tolima	**AILSSS**	sisals		nasion	**AIORTV**	viator
AILMPR	primal	**AILSSV**	silvas	**AINNOT**	anoint	**AIOSYZ**	zoysia
AILMRT	mitral	**AILSSY**	Lysias		nation	**AIPPRR**	riprap
	ramtil	**AILSTU**	situla	**AINNPS**	inspan	**AIPPRY**	papyri
AILMSS	missal	**AILSTV**	vitals		pinnas	**AIPPST**	papist
	salmis	**AILSUV**	visual	**AINNST**	Tsinan	**AIPRST**	rapist
AILMST	mistal	**AILSVZ**	vizsla	**AINOPR**	porina		tapirs
	smalti	**AILTXY**	laxity	**AINOPS**	pianos	**AIPRSV**	parvis
AILMSU	miauls	**AILVWY**	wavily		Pisano	**AIPRSW**	ripsaw
AILMSX	smilax	**AILWXY**	waxily	**AINOQU**	Aquino	**AIPRSX**	praxis
AILMSY	mislay	**AIMMOS**	mimosa	**AINORS**	norias	**AIPRTY**	parity
AILMTU	Latium	**AIMMSU**	imaums	**AINORT**	aroint	**AIPRUY**	pyuria
	ultima	**AIMMSX**	maxims		ration	**AIPSST**	pastis
	Umtali	**AIMNNO**	amnion	**AINORZ**	Azorín	**AIPSTW**	pitsaw
AILMYZ	mazily		nomina	**AINOSS**	Ossian		sawpit
AILNNU	annuli	**AIMNNU**	numina	**AINOSX**	axions	**AIPSZZ**	pizzas
AILNOP	Napoli	**AIMNNY**	minyan	**AINPRS**	sprain	**AIPZZZ**	pizazz
AILNOS	alison	**AIMNOP**	mopani	**AINPRW**	inwrap	**AIQRSU**	quairs
AILNOT	latino	**AIMNOS**	Osman I	**AINPST**	paints	**AIRRTY**	rarity
	talion	**AIMNOT**	manito		patins	**AIRSST**	sistra
AILNPS	plains	**AIMNPT**	pitman		ptisan		sitars
	spinal	**AIMNPY**	paynim	**AINPSV**	spavin		stairs
AILNPT	plaint	**AIMNRT**	Antrim	**AINPTU**	tipuna	**AIRSSU**	russia
	pliant		martin	**AINPTY**	painty	**AIRSSZ**	sizars
AILNPU	Ulpian	**AIMNRU**	rumina	**AINQRT**	qintar	**AIRSTT**	artist

	strait	**AKNPRU**	Kanpur	**ALMMUY**	amylum	**ALORSY**	royals
	strati	**AKNPSS**	spanks	**ALMNOR**	Molnár	**ALORTU**	Latour
	traits	**AKNPSU**	punkas		normal		La Tour
AIRSTU	aurist	**AKNRRY**	knarry	**ALMNOS**	monals	**ALORTY**	Taylor
AIRSTY	Styria	**AKNRSY**	snarky		salmon	**ALORUV**	louvar
AIRTTT	attrit	**AKNRUU**	Nakuru	**ALMNOU**	monaul		ovular
AIRTTY	yttria	**AKNSST**	stanks	**ALMNTU**	Multan		valour
AISSST	assist	**AKNSSW**	swanks	**ALMORS**	molars	**ALOSSS**	lassos
	stasis	**AKNSUZ**	kanzus		morals	**ALOSSV**	salvos
AISSTU	Assiut	**AKNSWY**	swanky	**ALMORT**	mortal	**ALOSTT**	totals
AISSTV	vistas	**AKOORR**	karroo	**ALMORU**	morula	**ALOSVV**	volvas
AISSTW	waists	**AKOORS**	karoos	**ALMORY**	Malory	**ALOTUW**	outlaw
AJKNSY	jansky	**AKOOSZ**	kazoos	**ALMOST**	almost	**ALOTUY**	layout
AJKORS	rojaks	**AKOPPS**	koppas		matlos		outlay
AJKORT	Rajkot	**AKOPRV**	Karpov		smalto	**ALPPSU**	palpus
AJLOPS	jalops	**AKOPSY**	yapoks	**ALMOTW**	matlow	**ALPRRU**	larrup
AJLOPY	jalopy	**AKORSS**	kaross	**ALMPSS**	plasms	**ALPRSU**	pulsar
AJMORS	majors	**AKORSU**	kouras		psalms	**ALPRSW**	sprawl
AJMRSU	jumars	**AKOSTY**	tokays	**ALMQSU**	qualms	**ALPRTY**	paltry
AJNSTU	jaunts	**AKOTWY**	towkay	**ALMRSU**	larums		partly
	juntas	**AKPRSS**	sparks		murals		raptly
AJNTUY	jaunty	**AKPRSY**	sparky	**ALMRWY**	warmly	**ALPSST**	splats
AJORRW	Jarrow	**AKPSSU**	Puskas	**ALMSUY**	asylum	**ALPSSU**	lapsus
AJPRTU	Rajput	**AKQRSU**	quarks	**ALMTUU**	mutual	**ALPSSY**	splays
AJRSTU	jurats	**AKQSUW**	squawk		umlaut	**ALPSTY**	platys
AKKKOO	kokako	**AKRSTU**	krauts	**ALNNOU**	nounal	**ALRSST**	slarts
AKKLSU	kulaks		kurtas	**ALNNSU**	annuls	**ALRSTU**	lustra
AKKNSS	skanks			**ALNOOS**	saloon		ultras
AKKNSY	skanky	**ALLMOS**	slalom	**ALNOOZ**	zoonal	**ALRSTW**	trawls
AKKOOP	pakoko	**ALLMOW**	mallow	**ALNOPS**	nopals	**ALRSTY**	stylar
AKKOQU	quokka	**ALLMSS**	smalls	**ALNORS**	lorans	**ALRSUU**	Ursula
AKKORU	Kokura	**ALLMSU**	mullas	**ALNOSS**	salons	**ALRSUW**	walrus
AKKORW	Kraków	**ALLMSY**	myalls		solans	**ALRTTY**	rattly
AKLLNY	lankly	**ALLMUV**	vallum	**ALNOST**	talons		tartly
AKLLSY	alkyls	**ALLNOP**	pollan	**ALNOSW**	Lawson	**ALRUUV**	uvular
AKLMOR	Kolmar	**ALLNOS**	llanos		lowans	**ALRUVV**	vulvar
AKLMOY	Kolyma	**ALLNUU**	lunula	**ALNOTV**	volant	**ALSSSU**	lassus
AKLMUU	Maluku	**ALLOOP**	apollo	**ALNOTW**	Walton	**ALSSTU**	saltus
AKLNOX	klaxon		palolo	**ALNPST**	plants		tussal
AKLNPS	planks	**ALLOOY**	Loyola	**ALNRSS**	snarls	**ALSSUU**	usuals
AKLNRY	rankly	**ALLOPR**	pallor	**ALNRSY**	snarly	**ALSSVY**	sylvas
AKLNSU	kulans	**ALLOPW**	wallop	**ALNRUY**	uranyl	**ALSTTY**	lyttas
AKLOPS	polkas	**ALLORY**	orally	**ALNRXY**	larynx	**ALSTUV**	vaults
	Polska	**ALLOSS**	salols	**ALNSST**	slants	**ALSTVY**	vastly
AKLOSV	Slovak	**ALLOST**	allots	**ALNSTU**	sultan	**ALSUUV**	uvulas
AKLOVY	Kvaløy		atolls	**ALNSUY**	unlays	**ALSUVV**	vulvas
AKLPTU	uptalk	**ALLOSW**	allows		yulans	**ALTTUY**	tautly
AKLPUW	walkup		sallow	**ALNSVY**	sylvan	**ALTUUV**	Tuvalu
AKLRVY	valkyr	**ALLOSY**	alloys	**ALNTUW**	walnut	**AMMMNO**	mammon
AKLSST	stalks	**ALLOTW**	tallow	**ALOOPS**	saloop	**AMMMOS**	mommas
AKLSTU	taluks	**ALLOUU**	allyou	**ALOPPR**	poplar	**AMMORT**	marmot
AKLSTY	stalky	**ALLOVV**	ovally	**ALOPPT**	laptop	**AMMOSU**	omasum
AKLSUW	waulks	**ALLOWW**	wallow	**ALOPRR**	parlor	**AMMOSY**	myomas
AKMNSU	unmask	**ALLPRU**	plural	**ALOPRS**	parols	**AMMOXY**	myxoma
AKMORS	kormas	**ALLPSS**	spalls	**ALOPRT**	patrol	**AMMPUW**	wampum
AKMOSV	Moskva	**ALLPSY**	psylla		portal	**AMMRSS**	smarms
AKMPRU	markup	**ALLQSU**	squall	**ALOPST**	ploats	**AMMRSY**	smarmy
AKNNNO	Kannon	**ALLRUY**	lauryl		postal	**AMMSTU**	summat
AKNNOO	nanook	**ALLSST**	stalls	**ALOPVV**	Pavlov	**AMMTUZ**	Tammuz
AKNORU	koruna	**ALLSTY**	lastly	**ALOQTU**	loquat	**AMNNOR**	norman
AKNORY	ryokan	**ALLUVV**	vulval	**ALORST**	sortal	**AMNNOS**	Manson
AKNPRS	pranks	**ALMMOW**	Mowlam	**ALORSV**	salvor	**AMNNOY**	anonym
		ALMMUW	wammul				

AMNNSU unmans
AMNOOP Pomona
AMNOOR maroon
    romano
AMNOPT potman
    tampon
AMNORR marron
AMNORS manors
    ransom
    romans
AMNORT matron
AMNORY mornay
AMNOSS masons
    Samson
AMNOST Nam Tso
    tomans
AMNOSW Mawson
    womans
AMNOTU amount
    outman
AMNPTU Putnam
AMNPTY tympan
AMNQRU Qumran
AMNRSU Mansur
    unarms
AMNRSY Smyrna
AMNRTU antrum
    Truman
AMNSSU Samsun
AMNTTU mutant
AMNTUU autumn
AMOOTT tomato
AMOPST Patmos
AMOPTU Maputo
AMOQRS qormas
AMORRS armors
AMORRT mortar
AMORRU armour
AMORRW marrow
AMORRY armory
AMORSS morass
AMORST stroma
AMORSU amours
    ramous
AMORSY mayors
    morays
AMORTU Outram
AMORTZ Mozart
AMOSTW amowts
AMOSTZ matzos
    motzas
AMPRRU Rampur
AMPRST tramps
AMPRUW warmup
AMPSSS spasms
AMPSST stamps
AMPSSW swamps
AMPSWY swampy
AMRRTY martyr
AMRRUY murray
AMRSST smarts
AMRSSU musars

AMRSSW swarms
AMRSTU struma
AMRSTY smarty
AMRTTU Muttra
AMSSSY Massys
AMSSTY Matsys
ANNNUY Yünnan
ANNOOX xoanon
ANNOPZ Poznań
ANNORT natron
ANNOST sonant
ANNOSW Wönsan
ANNOSY annoys
ANNOTW wanton
ANNOTY Antony
    tannoy
ANNPSU pannus
    unsnap
ANNRTY tranny
ANNSTU suntan
ANNTTU nutant
ANOORS Sonora
ANOORT ratoon
ANOPRS aprons
    parson
    sanpro
ANOPRT parton
    patron
    tarpon
ANOPST pantos
ANOPSW powans
ANOPSY yapons
ANOPTT Patton
ANOPTX Paxton
ANOPTY Payton
ANOPUV yaupon
ANORRW narrow
ANORSS sonars
ANORST rotans
ANORSV sovran
ANORSW rowans
ANORSY rayons
ANORTT attorn
ANORTU outran
ANORTW Tarnów
    Warton
ANORTY notary
ANORWY Norway
ANORYZ zonary
ANOSST santos
ANOSTU tauons
ANOSTW Watson
ANOSUY noyaus
ANOSWY noways
ANOSXY saxony
ANPPSY snappy
ANPRSW prawns
ANPRTY pantry
    trypan
ANPRUW unwrap
ANPSSW spawns
ANPTUU tupuna

ANQSTU quants
ANRSTU Saturn
ANRSUU Uranus
ANRSUY sunray
ANRSYZ Syzran
ANRTTU truant
ANRTTY tyrant
ANRUWY runway
    unwary
ANSSTU stauns
ANSSUY unsays
ANSTTU taunts
    tutsan
ANSTUV vaunts
ANSTXY syntax
ANSYZZ snazzy
AOOPTT potato
AOOPTW Paotow
AOORRT orator
AOORRY arroyo
AOORSZ razoos
AOOTTT tattoo
AOPPRT apport
AOPRRT parrot
    raptor
AOPRRU uproar
AOPRRW prowar
AOPRSS aspros
    sapors
AOPRST pastor
    portas
AOPRSU parous
AOPRSV vapors
AOPRUV vapour
AOPRVY vapory
AOPTUY payout
AOQRTU quarto
AOQSTU quotas
AORRST rostra
    sartor
AORRSW arrows
AORRSY rosary
AORRSZ razors
AORRTY rotary
AORRWY yarrow
AORSST assort
    roasts
AORSSV savors
AORSTT stator
    tarots
    troats
AORSTU soutar
AORSTX storax
AORSUU aurous
AORSUV savour
AORSVY savory
AORTVY votary
AOSSTT stoats
    toasts
AOSSVY savoys
AOSTTU outsat
AOSTTY toasty

AOSTWW Swatow
APPPSU pappus
APRRSY sparry
APRSST sprats
    straps
APRSSY sprays
APRSTY pastry
APSSSU passus
APSSTU stupas
APSSUW wassup
AQRRUY quarry
AQRSTU quarts
AQRTUZ quartz
AQSSTU squats
AQSSUW squaws
AQUYZZ quazzy
ARRSTY starry
ARSSST strass
ARSSTT starts
ARSSTU Straus
    sutras
    tarsus
ARSSTW straws
ARSSTY satyrs
    strays
ARSTTU Stuart
    tuarts
ARSTUU Taurus
ARSTUX surtax
ARSTWY strawy
ARSTXY styrax
ASSTTU status
BBBDEI bibbed
BBBDEO bobbed
BBBEIL bibble
BBBEIR bibber
BBBELO bobble
BBBELU bubble
BBBELY blebby
BBBHUU hubbub
BBBINO bobbin
BBBLOY blobby
BBBLUY bubbly
BBCDEO cobbed
BBCDEU cubbed
BBCEIR Cibber
BBCELO cobble
BBCEOR cobber
BBCEOW cobweb
BBCESU cubebs
BBCHUY chubby
BBCLUY clubby
BBDDEI dibbed
BBDDEO dobbed
BBDDEU dubbed
BBDEEW webbed
BBDEFI fibbed
BBDEFO fobbed
BBDEGI gibbed
BBDEGO gobbed
BBDEGU bedbug
BBDEHO hobbed

BBDEIJ jibbed	**BBEMOS** bombes	**BCEELY** Cybele	**BCHSUU** buchus
BBDEIL dibble	**BBENOW** Benbow	**BCEEMO** become	**BCIILM** limbic
BBDEIN nibbed	**BBEORR** robber	**BCEEQU** Quebec	**BCIINO** bionic
BBDEIR bribed	**BBEORS** sobber	**BCEERS** rebecs	niobic
dibber	**BBEOSU** buboes	**BCEESX** xebecs	**BCIINU** incubi
ribbed	**BBERRU** rubber	**BCEESZ** zebecs	**BCIIOP** biopic
BBDEJO jobbed	**BBERTU** tubber	**BCEHLN** blench	**BCIIOT** biotic
BBDELO lobbed	**BBGINO** gibbon	**BCEHNU** Bunche	**BCIKNO** kincob
BBDEMO bombed	**BBGRUY** grubby	**BCEHNY** benchy	**BCIKRS** bricks
mobbed	**BBHIOT** hobbit	**BCEHOR** broche	**BCIKRY** bricky
BBDEOO boobed	**BBHNOO** hobnob	**BCEHOS** boches	**BCILMO** Imbolc
BBDEOR dobber	**BBIIOO** Bío-Bío	**BCEHRT** Brecht	**BCILMS** climbs
robbed	**BBIIUU** buibui	**BCEHRU** cherub	**BCILPU** public
BBDEOS sobbed	**BBIKOS** skibob	**BCEIIK** bickie	**BCIMOR** bromic
BBDEPU pubbed	**BBILLU** bulbil	**BCEIIS** ibices	**BCIMSU** cubism
BBDERU rubbed	**BBILOS** bilbos	**BCEIKR** bicker	**BCINOR** bicorn
BBDESU subbed	**BBIMOS** bimbos	**BCEIKU** buckie	**BCIORS** borsic
BBDETU tubbed	**BBINNU** nubbin	**BCEIKW** Bewick	sorbic
BBDIKU dibbuk	**BBINOR** ribbon	**BCEIOR** corbie	**BCIRRU** rubric
BBDINO dobbin	robbin	**BCEIOX** icebox	**BCISTU** cubist
BBDINU dubbin	**BBKNOY** knobby	**BCEIPS** biceps	cubits
BBDKUY dybbuk	**BBLLUU** bulbul	**BCEIRS** scribe	**BCKLOS** blocks
BBDOSU dubbos	**BBLNUY** nubbly	**BCEIRT** terbic	**BCKLOY** blocky
BBEEHL Hebbel	**BBLOOS** bobols	**BCEIST** bisect	**BCKORS** brocks
BBEEIW webbie	**BBLOWY** blowby	**BCEJOT** object	**BCMOOS** combos
BBEELP pebble	wobbly	**BCEKLU** buckle	coombs
BBEERS rebbes	**BBLRSU** blurbs	Lübeck	**BCMORY** corymb
BBEFIR fibber	**BBLRUY** rubbly	**BCEKNO** beckon	**BCMRSU** crumbs
BBEGIN Big Ben	**BBMRUY** brumby	**BCEKRU** bucker	**BCMRUY** crumby
ebbing	Bumbry	**BCEKTU** bucket	**BCNOOR** bronco
BBEGIR gibber	**BBNNOO** bonbon	**BCELLO** Belloc	**BCNOSU** buncos
BBEGIT gibbet	**BBNOOO** bonobo	**BCELOR** corbel	**BCNOTU** cobnut
BBEGLO gobble	**BBNOSY** snobby	**BCELOS** cobles	**BCNOUY** bouncy
BBEGNU Bengbu	**BBNOTU** nobbut	**BCELOU** boucle	**BCOOSY** scooby
BBEGOT gobbet	**BBNSUY** snubby	**BCEMOO** coombe	**BCOOWY** cowboy
BBEHLO hobble	**BBOOOO** booboo	**BCEMOR** comber	**BCORSY** Crosby
BBEHLU Hubble	**BBOOSY** yobbos	**BCEMOS** combes	**BCRSSU** scrubs
BBEHOS Hobbes	**BBOOUU** boubou	**BCEMRU** cumber	**BDDDEE** bedded
BBEIIM imbibe	**BBORTU** burbot	**BCENOR** Brecon	**BDDDEU** budded
BBEIJR jibber	**BBOSUY** busboy	**BCENOS** bonces	**BDDEER** bedder
BBEIKL kibble	**BBRSUU** suburb	**BCENOU** bounce	breded
BBEILN nibble	**BBSSTU** Stubbs	**BCEOTT** obtect	**BDDEGO** bodged
BBEILR Ribble	**BBSTUY** stubby	**BCERSU** cubers	**BDDEGU** budged
BBEILS bibles	**BCCEIO** boccie	**BCGINU** cubing	**BDDEIL** Biddle
BBEILW wibble	**BCDEEK** bedeck	**BCGORU** coburg	**BDDEIN** bidden
BBEIRR briber	**BCDEIO** bodice	**BCGORY** cyborg	**BDDEIO** bodied
BBEIRS bribes	**BCDEKO** bocked	**BCHILO** chibol	**BDDEIR** bidder
BBEJOR jobber	**BCDEKU** bucked	**BCHIMS** chimbs	**BDDELU** buddle
BBELLU bulbel	Dubček	**BCHINY** Binchy	**BDDENO** bonded
BBELMU bumble	**BCDEMO** combed	**BCHIOP** phobic	**BDDERU** redbud
BBELNO nobble	**BCDENO** Cobden	**BCHIRT** bricht	**BDDESU** debuds
BBELNU nubble	**BCDERU** curbed	**BCHITY** bitchy	**BDDISU** disbud
BBELOT boblet	**BCDIOU** cuboid	**BCHLOT** blotch	**BDEEEF** beefed
BBELOW wobble	**BCEEHR** breech	**BCHLSU** schlub	**BDEEEN** bendee
BBELPY pebbly	**BCEEHT** Bechet	**BCHMOU** Bochum	**BDEEEP** beeped
plebby	**BCEEHY** beechy	**BCHNRU** brunch	**BDEEGG** begged
BBELRU burble	**BCEEIR** Bierce	**BCHNUY** bunchy	**BDEEGR** Edberg
lubber	**BCEEKR** Becker	**BCHOOR** brocho	**BDEEHL** beheld
rubble	rebeck	brooch	**BDEEIL** belied
BBEMNU benumb	**BCEEKT** becket	**BCHORS** borsch	edible
BBEMOR bomber	**BCEEKZ** zebeck	brochs	**BDEEIR** bredie
mobber	**BCEELS** celebs	**BCHOTY** botchy	**BDEEIS** beside

BDEEIT betide
BDEEJL djebel
BDEEJM djembe
BDEEKR kerbed
BDEELL bedell
    belled
BDEELN blende
BDEELS bedels
    bleeds
BDEELT belted
BDEEMS embeds
BDEENR bender
BDEEOY obeyed
BDEERS bredes
    breeds
BDEERW brewed
BDEERY breyed
BDEEST bested
BDEESW bedews
    dweebs
BDEETT betted
BDEEWY dweeby
BDEFFI biffed
BDEFFU buffed
BDEFIR fibred
BDEGGI bigged
BDEGGO bogged
BDEGGU bugged
BDEGIL bilged
BDEGIN binged
BDEGIO bodgie
    bogied
BDEGIR begird
    bridge
BDEGIU budgie
BDEGLO globed
BDEGLU bludge
    bugled
    bulged
BDEGNO bonged
BDEGNU bunged
BDEGOR bodger
BDEGOS bodges
BDEGRU redbug
BDEGSU budges
    debugs
BDEGTU budget
BDEHIN behind
BDEHLO behold
BDEHOT hotbed
BDEHSU bushed
BDEIIR birdie
    bridie
BDEIKL bilked
BDEILL billed
BDEILM limbed
BDEILO boiled
    bolide
BDEILR birled
    bridle
BDEILS bields
BDEIMS bedims

    imbeds
BDEIMU imbued
BDEINN binned
BDEINR binder
    brined
    inbred
    rebind
BDEINU beduin
BDEIOR boride
BDEIOS bodies
BDEIPS bipeds
BDEIRR birder
    birred
BDEIRS breids
    brides
    debris
    rebids
BDEIRU buried
BDEIRV verbid
BDEIST bedsit
    bidets
    debits
BDEISU busied
BDEITT bitted
BDEKLU bulked
BDEKNO bonked
BDEKNU bunked
    debunk
BDEKOO booked
BDEKRU burked
BDEKSU busked
BDELLO Dobell
BDELLU bulled
BDELNO blonde
    bolden
BDELNS blends
BDELNU bundle
BDELOO boodle
    booled
BDELOR bolder
    bordel
BDELOT bolted
BDELOU double
BDELOW blowed
    bowled
BDELRU burled
BDEMMU bummed
BDEMNU numbed
BDEMOO boomed
BDEMOR bormed
BDEMOS demobs
BDEMOT tombed
BDEMOW wombed
BDEMOY embody
BDEMPU bumped
BDEMRU dumber
BDENNU unbend
BDENOR bonder
BDENOY beyond
BDENRU burden
    burned
    unbred

BDENTU bunted
BDEOOT booted
BDEOOZ boozed
BDEOPP bopped
BDEOPR probed
BDEORR border
BDEORS desorb
BDEORT Bordet
    debtor
BDEORW browed
BDEOSS bossed
BDEOSU boused
BDEOSW bowsed
BDEOTT botted
BDEOUY buoyed
BDEPRU burped
BDERRU burred
    deburr
BDESSU bussed
BDESTU busted
    debuts
BDESUU subdue
BDETTU butted
BDEUZZ buzzed
BDFIOR forbid
BDGIIN biding
BDGIIR Brigid
BDGINO boding
BDGINY byding
BDHIIN bhindi
    bindhi
BDHIOS dhobis
BDHIRY hybrid
BDHNSU bundhs
BDIILO libido
BDIIMR midrib
BDIITT tidbit
BDIKNO bodkin
BDILNS blinds
BDILNU Dublin
BDILOY bodily
BDILSU builds
BDIMNO Bodmin
BDIMOR morbid
BDINNU unbind
BDINOU boudin
BDIOOT biodot
BDIOPS bipods
BDIOSU Dubois
BDIOSV bovids
BDIOTU outbid
BDIRTU turbid
BDKLOO kobold
BDLLOY boldly
BDLMUY dumbly
BDLNOO doblon
BDLNOS blonds
BDLOOS bloods
BDLOOY bloody
BDLOUY doubly
BDNOOY nobody
BDNORY Drobny

BDNOSU bounds
BDNOTU obtund
BDOORS broods
    droobs
BDOORY broody
BDORWY byword
BDOSTU doubts
BEEEFL feeble
BEEEHP ephebe
BEEELT beetle
BEEEMS beseem
BEEEPR beeper
BEEERZ beezer
    breeze
BEEESV beeves
BEEFIL belief
BEEFLL befell
BEEFLY feebly
BEEFOR before
BEEFRT bereft
BEEGHR Gheber
BEEGIL beigel
BEEGIS beiges
BEEGIY bigeye
BEEGLS glebes
BEEGNO begone
BEEGNR bergen
BEEGOR greebo
BEEGRS grebes
BEEGRT Egbert
BEEGRU burgee
BEEGST begets
BEEHLT bethel
BEEHMS Shembe
BEEHOP phoebe
BEEHOV behove
BEEHRT Hébert
BEEHRY hereby
BEEHST behest
    Thebes
BEEIKL belike
BEEILR belier
BEEILS belies
BEEILZ Belize
BEEIMR bemire
    bireme
BEEINN Bienne
BEEINW newbie
BEEIST betise
BEEISV bevies
BEEISX ibexes
BEEJLS jebels
BEEJMS jembes
BEEKLM Kemble
BEEKLR Kléber
BEEKOR reebok
BEEKRS breeks
BEEKRU rebuke
BEEKSY Békésy
BEELLS belles
BEELMM emblem
BEELNO Leoben

BEELNS	Belsen	**BEFLRY**	belfry	**BEHMRU**	Humber	**BEIOST**	sobeit
BEELNV	Veblen	**BEFORS**	Forbes	**BEHNOR**	Hebron		tobies
BEELPS	bleeps	**BEFORY**	forbye	**BEHOOS**	hoboes	**BEIOSW**	bowies
	plebes	**BEFRUY**	rubefy	**BEHORT**	bother		bowsie
BEELRS	rebels	**BEGGIR**	bigger	**BEHOSS**	boshes	**BEIPPU**	buppie
BEELRT	belter	**BEGGLO**	boggle	**BEHRST**	berths	**BEIQSU**	bisque
	Elbert	**BEGGOR**	bogger	**BEHSSU**	bushes	**BEIRRS**	briers
	treble	**BEGGRU**	bugger	**BEIIKR**	birkie	**BEIRRU**	burier
BEELRY	berley	**BEGIIL**	Liebig	**BEIIKS**	bikies	**BEIRRV**	briery
BEELSS	Bessel	**BEGILN**	bingle	**BEIIRS**	iberis	**BEIRSS**	brises
BEELSV	bevels	**BEGILO**	oblige	**BEIIRV**	vibier	**BEIRST**	bestir
BEELSZ	bezels	**BEGILR**	gerbil	**BEIISS**	ibises		bister
BEELXY	Bexley	**BEGILS**	bilges	**BEIJLR**	jerbil		bistre
BEEMMR	member	**BEGINN**	benign	**BEIJRS**	jibers		biters
BEEMNR	Bremen		Bingen	**BEIKLR**	bilker		bitser
BEEMRS	bermes	**BEGINO**	biogen	**BEIKOO**	bookie		breist
	embers		Gibeon	**BEIKRS**	bikers		tribes
BEEMRU	embrue	**BEGINR**	Bering	**BEILLR**	biller	**BEIRSU**	bruise
BEEMSU	bemuse	**BEGINS**	begins	**BEILLS**	libels		buries
BEENNT	bennet		beings	**BEILLT**	billet		busier
BEENOR	boreen		binges	**BEILMN**	nimble		rubies
	enrobe	**BEGINU**	beguin	**BEILMO**	emboli	**BEIRSV**	brevis
BEENOT	beento	**BEGIOO**	boogie		mobile	**BEIRSW**	brewis
	Beeton	**BEGIOS**	bogies	**BEILMR**	limber	**BEIRTT**	bitter
BEENRU	Reuben		gobies	**BEILMW**	wimble	**BEIRTU**	Beirut
BEENRW	Webern	**BEGIOU**	bougie	**BEILMY**	blimey	**BEISSU**	busies
BEENTU	butene	**BEGIRS**	gibers	**BEILNO**	boline	**BEISTZ**	zibets
BEEOOT	bootee	**BEGIRT**	begirt		Nobile	**BEITUY**	ubiety
BEEOPP	bopeep	**BEGLNO**	belong	**BEILNR**	berlin	**BEJJUU**	jujube
BEEORR	rebore	**BEGLNU**	blunge	**BEILNU**	nubile	**BEJLMU**	jumble
BEEORS	borees		bungle	**BEILNX**	Blixen	**BEJORU**	objure
BEEORY	obeyer	**BEGLOR**	Bolger	**BEILNY**	byline	**BEKKRY**	brekky
BEERRU	Breuer	**BEGLOS**	bogles	**BEILOR**	boiler	**BEKLOS**	blokes
BEERRV	reverb		globes		libero	**BEKLOY**	blokey
BEERRW	brewer	**BEGLOT**	goblet		reboil	**BEKLRU**	bulker
BEERST	berets	**BEGLOW**	weblog	**BEILOT**	boleti	**BEKNOR**	broken
	breest	**BEGLRU**	bugler	**BEILOW**	blowie	**BEKNRU**	bunker
BEERSU	Erebus		burgle	**BEILSY**	Bisley	**BEKOOR**	booker
BEERSV	breves	**BEGLSU**	bugles	**BEIMNN**	binmen		Brooke
BEERSW	webers		bulges	**BEIMOS**	biomes	**BEKOOT**	betook
BEERTT	better	**BEGMNO**	bogmen		mobies	**BEKORR**	broker
BEERTV	brevet	**BEGMSU**	begums	**BEIMOZ**	zombie	**BEKOST**	bosket
BEERYZ	breezy	**BEGNOY**	bygone	**BEIMRT**	timber	**BEKRSU**	burkes
BEESST	besets	**BEGNRU**	bunger		timbre		busker
BEESTU	bustee	**BEGOOR**	goober	**BEIMRU**	erbium	**BELLOU**	boulle
BEFFIR	biffer	**BEGOOS**	goboes		imbrue		lobule
BEFFOU	bouffe	**BEGORS**	Borges	**BEIMSU**	imbues	**BELLOW**	bellow
BEFFRU	buffer	**BEGORU**	brogue	**BEINNO**	Benoni	**BELLTU**	bullet
	rebuff	**BEGOSY**	bogeys	**BEINNZ**	benzin	**BELLUY**	bluely
BEFFTU	buffet	**BEGRRU**	burger	**BEINOR**	bonier	**BELMMU**	mumble
BEFGOS	befogs		Bürger		O'Brien	**BELMOY**	emboly
BEFHOO	behoof	**BEGRSU**	Bruges	**BEINOV**	bovine	**BELMRU**	lumber
BEFILM	fimble	**BEHILT**	blithe	**BEINOX**	bonxie		rumble
BEFILO	foible	**BEHINT**	henbit	**BEINRS**	brines	**BELMSU**	umbels
BEFIRS	briefs	**BEHISS**	bishes	**BEINRU**	Brunei		umbles
	fibers	**BEHIST**	Thisbe	**BEINRY**	byrnie	**BELMTU**	tumble
	fibres	**BEHISU**	bushie	**BEINST**	Nesbit	**BELNNY**	blenny
BEFIRT	bifter	**BEHKOR**	rhebok	**BEINTT**	bitten	**BELNOR**	nobler
BEFIST	befits	**BEHLMU**	humble	**BEINVZ**	Ben-Zvi	**BELNOS**	nobles
BEFLMU	fumble	**BEHLRU**	burhel	**BEIOOT**	bootie	**BELNOY**	Boleyn
BEFLOO	befool	**BEHLSU**	bushel	**BEIORS**	ribose	**BELNOZ**	benzol
BEFLOU	befoul	**BEHMOR**	hombre	**BEIORX**	boxier	**BELNRU**	Brunel

	Lebrun	**BENNTU**	bunnet		tubers		gibson
BELNTU	unbelt		unbent	**BERSUX**	exurbs	**BGINOW**	bowing
BELNUU	Buñuel	**BENOOR**	Borneo	**BERSUY**	buyers	**BGINOX**	boxing
BELNYZ	benzyl		Oberon	**BERTTU**	butter	**BGINRS**	brings
BELOOR	bolero	**BENORR**	reborn	**BERUZZ**	buzzer	**BGINSU**	busing
BELOOS	sobole	**BENORS**	boners	**BESSSU**	busses	**BGINTU**	tubing
BELOOT	Bootle	**BENORT**	breton	**BESSTU**	subset	**BGINUY**	buying
BELOOV	Belovo		Brontë	**BESTTU**	buttes	**BGIORV**	Viborg
BELOPU	pueblo	**BENORU**	bourne	**BESUZZ**	buzzes	**BGIOST**	bigots
BELORS	robles	**BENORW**	Browne	**BFFIIN**	biffin	**BGLMOO**	moblog
BELORT	bolter	**BENORZ**	bonzer	**BFFINO**	boffin	**BGLNOO**	oblong
BELORU	rouble		bronze	**BFFLSU**	bluffs	**BGLOSU**	globus
BELORW	blower	**BENOST**	bentos	**BFFNOU**	Buffon	**BGLRUU**	bulgur
	bowler	**BENOSZ**	bonzes	**BFFORU**	ruboff	**BGMOOS**	gombos
BELOSS	lesbos	**BENOTY**	betony	**BFFOSU**	buffos	**BGMOSU**	gumbos
BELOST	botels	**BENRRU**	burner	**BFGOOW**	fogbow	**BGNOOS**	bongos
BELOSU	blouse		Burren	**BFIILR**	fibril		boongs
	boules	**BENRST**	brents	**BFIINR**	fibrin	**BGNTUU**	Butung
	obelus	**BENRSU**	Rubens	**BFIMOR**	biform	**BGOORU**	burgoo
BELOSW	bowels	**BENRTU**	brunet	**BFINOW**	bowfin	**BGORSU**	bourgs
	Bowles		burnet	**BFIORS**	rosbif		Burgos
	elbows	**BENRUY**	Burney	**BFLOTY**	botfly	**BGORVY**	Vyborg
BELOTT	bottle	**BEOORR**	Örebro	**BFLOUX**	boxful	**BHHIKU**	bhikhu
BELOUZ	Boulez	**BEOORT**	reboot	**BFLSYY**	flybys	**BHIKOS**	kibosh
BELRRU	burler	**BEOORZ**	boozer	**BFLTUU**	tubful	**BHILPY**	Philby
BELRST	blerts		rebozo	**BFMORY**	Formby	**BHILSU**	bluish
BELRSU	Elbrus	**BEOOSZ**	boozes	**BGGIIN**	biggin	**BHIMOR**	rhombi
	rubles	**BEOPPR**	bopper		gibing	**BHIMTU**	Thimbu
BELRSY	beryls	**BEOPRR**	prober	**BGGIIW**	bigwig	**BHIOPS**	bishop
BELRTU	butler	**BEOPRS**	probes	**BGGINO**	biggon	**BHIOSY**	boyish
BELRTY	trebly	**BEORRS**	borers	**BGGINY**	gybing	**BHIRST**	births
BELRUY	burley		resorb	**BGGIRS**	Briggs		briths
BELSTU	bluest	**BEORSS**	sobers	**BGGNOO**	bogong	**BHIRSU**	hubris
	bluets	**BEORST**	sorbet	**BGGNOU**	bugong	**BHIRSY**	hybris
	bustle		strobe	**BGHIIL**	ghibli	**BHITWY**	Whitby
	sublet	**BEORSU**	bourse	**BGHIIN**	binghi	**BHKNOU**	bohunk
	subtle	**BEORSW**	bowers	**BGHILT**	blight	**BHKOSY**	kybosh
BELSUY	bluesy		bowser	**BGHIRT**	bright	**BHLMUY**	humbly
	blueys		browse	**BGHIST**	bights	**BHLOSY**	bolshy
BELTUU	tubule	**BEORSX**	boxers	**BGHMUU**	humbug	**BHMORS**	rhombs
BEMMRU	bummer	**BEORTT**	bettor	**BGHOSU**	boughs	**BHMRSU**	rhumbs
BEMNOT	entomb	**BEORTV**	obvert	**BGHOTU**	bought	**BHMSTU**	thumbs
BEMNOW	bowmen	**BEORVV**	bovver	**BGHRSU**	burghs	**BHNORY**	Hornby
	enwomb	**BEORWY**	bowery	**BGIIJN**	jibing	**BHOOOO**	boohoo
BEMNRU	number		bowyer	**BGIIKN**	biking	**BHOOST**	booths
BEMOOR	boomer	**BEOSSS**	bosses	**BGIILN**	biling	**BHORST**	broths
BEMOPS	pombes		obsess	**BGIILS**	giblis		throbs
BEMORS	bromes	**BEOSST**	bosset	**BGIINN**	Binnig	**BHOTTU**	Bhutto
	somber	**BEOSSU**	bouses	**BGIINT**	biting	**BHRSSU**	shrubs
	sombre	**BEOSSW**	bowses	**BGIKNO**	boking	**BHRSUY**	brushy
BEMORY	embryo	**BEOSSY**	syboes	**BGIKNY**	byking	**BIIIKN**	bikini
BEMOSS	besoms	**BEOSTT**	bottes	**BGILLY**	glibly	**BIIKTZ**	kibitz
	emboss		obtest	**BGILNO**	globin	**BIILNS**	blinis
BEMOSW	embows	**BEOSTU**	obtuse		goblin	**BIILTW**	twibil
BEMPRU	bumper	**BEOSTW**	bestow	**BGILNU**	bluing	**BIIMOS**	obiism
BEMRSU	brumes	**BEPRSU**	superb	**BGINNO**	boning	**BIIMOZ**	imbizo
	umbers	**BERRUY**	rebury		Ningbo	**BIINOT**	biotin
BENNOS	Benson	**BERSSU**	burses	**BGINOO**	booing	**BIINOU**	biniou
	bonnes	**BERSTU**	brutes	**BGINOR**	boring	**BIIORS**	Boris I
BENNOT	Benton		burets		orbing		oribis
	bonnet		buster		robing	**BIIORV**	vibrio
BENNSU	bunsen		rebuts	**BGINOS**	bingos	**BIISTV**	vibist

BIITTT	titbit	BKOOSY	booksy
BIJLOT	Bitolj	BKORTU	Korbut
BIJOUX	bijoux		Tobruk
BIKKRY	Kirkby	BKOSXY	skybox
BIKLNS	blinks	BLLOOO	lobolo
BIKMNU	bumkin	BLLORY	brolly
BIKNRS	brinks	BLMNUY	numbly
BIKNSU	buskin	BLMOOS	blooms
BIKRSS	brisks	BLMOOY	bloomy
BILLNO	billon	BLMOSY	symbol
BILLNU	Lublin	BLMPSU	plumbs
BILLOW	billow	BLNOOS	bolson
BILLOX	bollix	BLNOOT	Bolton
BILLOY	billyo	BLNOTU	unbolt
BILLRS	brills	BLNOTY	Blyton
BILMNY	nimbly	BLNSTU	blunts
BILMOS	limbos	BLOOSU	obolus
BILMPS	blimps	BLOOTT	blotto
BILMSU	limbus	BLOOWY	lowboy
BILNOS	Lisbon	BLOPUW	blowup
BILNTZ	blintz	BLOSTU	boults
BILOOT	Lobito	BLOSWY	blowsy
BILORS	broils	BLOWYZ	blowzy
BILRTY	trilby	BLRRUY	blurry
BILSST	stilbs	BLRSTU	blurts
BILSSY	sibyls	BLSTUY	subtly
BILSUY	busily	BMOORS	brooms
BIMMOO	miombo	BMOOSS	bosoms
BIMNOS	bonism	BMOOSY	bosomy
BIMNSU	nimbus	BMOOTT	bottom
BIMORS	Imbros	BMOOTY	tomboy
BIMOSZ	zombis	BMOTUU	Mobutu
BIMSTU	submit	BNNORU	unborn
BINNOR	inborn	BNOORS	Robson
BINNOU	bunion	BNOOSS	bosons
BINNOY	Binyon	BNOOST	boston
BINNRY	brinny	BNORSU	bourns
BINOOT	bonito		suborn
BINORS	robins	BNORSW	browns
BINORY	briony	BNORTU	Bruton
BINOST	bonist		burton
BINPUY	bunyip	BNORWY	browny
BINRSU	bruins	BNORYY	bryony
	burins	BNORYZ	bronzy
BIOORZ	borzoi	BNOSSU	bosuns
BIOOST	oboist	BNOSUW	sunbow
BIOPSY	biopsy	BNOTTU	button
BIORST	bistro	BNOTUX	Buxton
	orbits	BNOTUY	bounty
BIOSTU	subito	BNRSTU	brunts
BIOSZZ	bizzos	BNRTUY	Tyburn
BIQSSU	squibs	BOOPTY	potboy
BIRSTU	bruits	BOORRW	borrow
BIRTTU	turbit	BOORRY	Rob Roy
BISSTU	bustis	BOORST	robots
BJLMUY	jumbly	BOORSU	buroos
BJMOSU	jumbos	BOOSST	boosts
BKLMOO	Lombok	BOOSWX	oxbows
BKMNUU	bunkum	BOOTUX	outbox
BKNOSU	bunkos	BOOWWW	bowwow
	konbus	BORRSU	burros
BKOORS	brooks	BORRUW	burrow

BORSTU	robust	CCHHRU	church
BORTTU	turbot	CCHIKS	chicks
BORTUU	rubout	CCHILN	clinch
BOSSWY	sybows	CCHILO	cholic
BOTUUY	buyout	CCHILY	chicly
BRSSTU	bursts		Clichy
BRSTUU	Brutus	CCHINO	cochin
BSSSUY	byssus	CCHIOR	choric
BSTTUU	bututs	CCHIOS	chicos
CCCCIO	coccic	CCHIPU	hiccup
CCCDIO	coccid	CCHKOO	chocko
CCCHOY	choccy	CCHKOS	chocks
CCCILY	cyclic	CCHKSU	chucks
CCCOSU	coccus	CCHLTU	clutch
CCCOXY	coccyx		cultch
CCDEER	recced	CCHNOS	conchs
CCDEKO	cocked	CCHNOY	conchy
CCDELY	cycled	CCHNRU	crunch
CCDEOS	codecs	CCHOOS	chocos
CCDEOT	decoct	CCHOOT	cootch
CCEEHR	creche	CCHORS	scorch
	crèche	CCHORT	crotch
CCEELS	Eccles	CCHORU	crouch
CCEEOR	coerce	CCHOST	scotch
CCEERS	recces	CCHRTU	crutch
CCEHIL	chicle	CCHSTU	scutch
	cliche	CCIILN	clinic
CCEHIO	choice	CCIILT	clitic
	echoic	CCIINO	iconic
CCEHIT	hectic	CCIINP	picnic
CCEHKS	checks	CCIINZ	zincic
CCEHKY	checky	CCIIOR	Riccio
CCEHLN	clench	CCIIPR	picric
CCEHLO	cloche	CCIIRT	citric
CCEHOS	cosech		critic
CCEIIL	cilice	CCIISV	civics
	icicle	CCIKLS	clicks
CCEILR	circle	CCIKRS	cricks
	cleric	CCILNO	clonic
CCEILY	cicely	CCILTU	cultic
CCEINS	scenic	CCIMOS	comics
CCEIOR	cicero		cosmic
CCEIPT	pectic	CCIMRY	Cymric
CCEIRS	cercis	CCINOS	conics
CCEIRT	cretic	CCINSY	cynics
CCEITY	cecity	CCIOPT	Coptic
CCEKLO	cockle	CCIOSS	ciscos
CCEKLS	clecks	CCIPRU	cupric
CCEKLY	clecky	CCIRSU	circus
CCEKOP	copeck	CCISTY	cystic
CCEKOR	cocker	CCKLOS	clocks
CCELRY	cycler	CCKLSU	clucks
CCELSY	cycles	CCKLUY	clucky
CCENOS	sconce	CCKOOU	cuckoo
CCEORS	soccer	CCKOPU	cockup
CCEOSS	seccos	CCKORS	crocks
CCERSU	cercus	CCKRSU	crucks
	cruces	CCLOTU	occult
CCESSU	cusecs	CCNOOO	cocoon
CCFILO	flocci	CCNORU	concur
CCHHII	chichi	CCOOOR	rococo
CCHHIN	chinch	CCOPUY	occupy

CCORSU	crocus	**CDEENR**	decern	**CDEILS**	sliced	**CDEMOY**	comedy
	occurs	**CDEENS**	censed	**CDEILT**	delict	**CDENNO**	conned
	succor	**CDEENT**	decent		deltic	**CDENOP**	ponced
CCOSTU	stucco	**CDEEOO**	cooeed	**CDEILU**	Euclid	**CDENOR**	corned
CCSSUU	cuscus	**CDEEPR**	creped	**CDEIMN**	minced	**CDENOS**	second
CDDDEO	codded	**CDEERS**	ceders	**CDEIMO**	medico	**CDENOT**	docent
CDDEEI	decide		creeds	**CDEIMR**	dermic	**CDENPU**	punced
	deiced		screed	**CDEIMS**	medics	**CDENRU**	Cruden
CDDEEK	decked	**CDEERU**	reduce	**CDEINO**	coined	**CDENSS**	scends
CDDEEO	decode	**CDEERW**	crewed	**CDEINR**	cinder	**CDENSU**	dunces
CDDEEU	deduce	**CDEESS**	cessed	**CDEINU**	induce		secund
	deuced	**CDEESU**	deuces	**CDEINW**	winced	**CDENSY**	synced
	educed		educes	**CDEIOP**	copied	**CDEOOP**	cooped
CDDEHI	chided		seduce	**CDEIOT**	coedit	**CDEOPP**	copped
CDDEIS	disced	**CDEETT**	detect	**CDEIOV**	voiced	**CDEOPU**	couped
CDDEIU	cuddie	**CDEFFO**	coffed	**CDEIPR**	priced	**CDEOPW**	cowped
CDDEKO	docked	**CDEFFU**	cuffed	**CDEIPS**	spiced	**CDEORR**	corder
CDDEKU	ducked	**CDEFII**	deific	**CDEIPT**	depict		record
CDDELO	coddle	**CDEFKU**	fucked	**CDEIRS**	ciders	**CDEORS**	coders
CDDELU	cuddle	**CDEFNU**	fecund		dicers		credos
CDDEOR	codder	**CDEFOR**	forced		scried		decors
	corded	**CDEGGO**	cogged	**CDEIRT**	credit		scored
CDDERU	curded	**CDEGIN**	ceding		direct	**CDEORW**	crowed
CDDETU	deduct	**CDEGIO**	geodic		triced	**CDEOST**	costed
CDDHUY	chuddy	**CDEGLU**	cudgel	**CDEIRV**	cervid	**CDEOSU**	escudo
CDDLOY	cloddy	**CDEGOR**	codger	**CDEIST**	edicts	**CDEOSY**	decoys
CDDLUY	cuddly	**CDEHIL**	childe	**CDEKLO**	locked	**CDEOTT**	cotted
CDDRUY	cruddy	**CDEHIM**	chimed	**CDEKLU**	lucked	**CDEOYZ**	zydeco
CDEEEM	emceed		miched	**CDEKMO**	mocked	**CDEPPU**	cupped
CDEEER	decree	**CDEHIN**	chined	**CDEKMU**	mucked	**CDEPSU**	cusped
	recede		inched	**CDEKNO**	conked	**CDERRU**	cruder
CDEEES	secede		niched		docken	**CDERSU**	cursed
CDEEEX	exceed	**CDEHIR**	chider		nocked	**CDERSY**	cyders
CDEEFN	fenced		dreich	**CDEKOO**	cooked		descry
CDEEFT	defect		herdic	**CDEKOR**	corked	**CDERUV**	curved
CDEEHL	leched	**CDEHIS**	chides		docker	**CDERUY**	decury
CDEEHO	echoed	**CDEHIT**	itched		redock	**CDESSU**	cussed
CDEEHP	peched	**CDEHKO**	choked		rocked	**CDESTU**	educts
CDEEHR	cheder		hocked	**CDEKOS**	socked	**CDFINU**	fundic
CDEEHT	etched	**CDEHNR**	drench	**CDEKOT**	docket	**CDFIOU**	fucoid
CDEEHW	chewed	**CDEHOR**	ochred	**CDEKOW**	cowked	**CDFIOY**	codify
CDEEIL	ceiled	**CDEHOS**	coshed	**CDEKPU**	pucked	**CDGIIN**	dicing
	decile	**CDEHOU**	douche	**CDEKRS**	drecks	**CDGINO**	coding
CDEEIN	edenic	**CDEIIL**	Lidice	**CDEKRU**	ducker	**CDHIOR**	orchid
CDEEIP	pieced	**CDEIIM**	Medici		rucked		rhodic
CDEEIR	deicer	**CDEIIR**	dicier	**CDEKRY**	drecky	**CDHIRY**	hydric
CDEEIS	deices	**CDEIJU**	juiced	**CDEKSU**	sucked	**CDHORS**	chords
CDEEIT	deceit	**CDEIKK**	kicked	**CDEKTU**	tucked	**CDIIIM**	imidic
CDEEIV	device	**CDEIKL**	licked	**CDELLU**	culled	**CDIIIR**	iridic
CDEEIX	excide	**CDEIKM**	medick	**CDELNO**	cloned	**CDIINT**	indict
CDEEJT	deject	**CDEIKN**	nicked	**CDELOO**	cooled	**CDIIOY**	idiocy
CDEEKK	kecked	**CDEIKP**	picked		locoed	**CDIISV**	viscid
CDEEKL	deckel	**CDEIKR**	dicker	**CDELOR**	colder	**CDILNO**	codlin
	deckle		ricked	**CDELOS**	closed	**CDIMOU**	mucoid
CDEEKN	necked	**CDEIKS**	sicked	**CDELOW**	cowled	**CDIMOY**	cymoid
CDEEKO	decoke	**CDEIKT**	ticked	**CDELOY**	cloyed	**CDIMSU**	muscid
CDEEKP	pecked	**CDEIKU**	duckie	**CDELPY**	clyped	**CDIMTU**	dictum
CDEEKR	decker	**CDEIKW**	wicked	**CDELRU**	curdle	**CDINOO**	conoid
	recked	**CDEIKY**	dickey		curled	**CDINOR**	nordic
CDEELP	cleped	**CDEILO**	coiled	**CDELTU**	dulcet	**CDINSU**	Cnidus
CDEELW	clewed		coldie	**CDEMOO**	comedo	**CDINSY**	syndic
CDEENO	encode		docile	**CDEMOP**	comped	**CDINTU**	induct

CDIOSS discos	**CEEHRU** euchre	**CEENOR** encore	**CEFIRR** ferric
CDIOTT cottid	**CEEHRV** chevre	**CEENOS** Enesco	**CEFKLS** flecks
CDIPSU cuspid	**CEEHRW** chewer	**CEENOT** cenote	**CEFKRU** fucker
CDISSU discus	**CEEHRY** cheery	**CEENPS** spence	**CEFLST** clefts
CDJNOU jocund	**CEEHST** etches	**CEENPT** pecten	**CEFNOR** confer
CDLLOY coldly	**CEEHSW** eschew	**CEENRS** censer	**CEFORR** forcer
CDLOSS scolds	**CEEHSY** cheesy	screen	**CEFORS** forces
CDLOSU clouds	**CEEHTV** chevet	secern	fresco
CDLOUY cloudy	**CEEIKL** Kielce	**CEENRT** center	**CEFRUW** curfew
CDMNOO condom	**CEEILN** Céline	centre	**CEGGLO** coggle
CDMOOO comodo	**CEEILS** siecle	recent	**CEGGPU** eggcup
CDMOOT dotcom	**CEEIMT** emetic	tenrec	**CEGHIO** chigoe
CDNOOR condor	**CEEINN** Nicene	**CEENRY** Cyrene	**CEGINO** coigne
cordon	**CEEINP** Niepce	**CEENSS** censes	**CEGINR** cering
CDNOOS codons	**CEEINS** nieces	scenes	cringe
condos	**CEEINT** entice	**CEEOOS** cooees	**CEGINU** cueing
CDNSUY Cydnus	**CEEINV** evince	**CEEORV** corvee	**CEGIRR** gricer
CDOORT doctor	Venice	**CEEPRS** creeps	**CEGIRS** grices
CDOORY corody	**CEEIPR** Peirce	crepes	**CEGKOS** geckos
CDORSS scrods	piecer	**CEEPRT** recept	**CEGLRY** clergy
CDORSU durocs	pierce	**CEEPRY** creepy	**CEGNOR** conger
CDORSW crowds	recipe	crepey	**CEGNOS** conges
CEEEFL fleece	**CEEIPS** pieces	**CEEPTX** except	**CEGNOT** cogent
CEEEGR greece	specie	expect	**CEGNSU** scunge
CEEEHS cheese	**CEEIRS** cerise	**CEEPTY** ectype	**CEGNTY** cygnet
CEEELS Cleese	**CEEIRT** recite	**CEEPUY** eyecup	**CEGORR** grocer
CEEEMS emcees	tierce	**CEERSS** cesser	**CEHHSU** sheuch
CEEERS creese	**CEEIRU** ecurie	recess	**CEHHTU** Chu Teh
CEEFFO coffee	**CEEISS** ecesis	screes	**CEHIIN** echini
CEEFFT effect	**CEEISX** excise	**CEERST** certes	**CEHIKY** hickey
CEEFHL fleche	**CEEITV** Ecevit	erects	**CEHILN** lichen
CEEFIR fierce	**CEEITX** excite	resect	**CEHILS** chiels
Recife	**CEEJRT** reject	screet	chiles
CEEFLY fleecy	**CEEJST** ejects	secret	chisel
CEEFNN fennec	**CEEKLS** cleeks	**CEERSU** cereus	**CEHIMR** chimer
CEEFNR fencer	**CEEKNR** necker	ceruse	**CEHIMS** chimes
CEEFNS fences	**CEEKNU** Eucken	Creuse	miches
CEEFSU fescue	**CEEKPR** pecker	rescue	**CEHIMU** echium
CEEHIL eliche	**CEEKRS** creeks	secure	**CEHINP** Penchi
lichee	**CEEKRT** Eckert	**CEERTT** tercet	**CEHINR** enrich
CEEHIS seiche	**CEELMO** cleome	**CEERTU** Teucer	**CEHINS** chines
CEEHIT techie	**CEELNP** pencel	**CEESSS** cesses	inches
CEEHIW chewie	**CEELNR** crenel	**CEESSX** excess	niches
CEEHKL heckle	**CEELOR** creole	**CEESSY** cyeses	**CEHINT** ethnic
CEEHKS cheeks	**CEELOU** coulee	**CEESTX** exsect	**CEHINY** hyenic
CEEHKY cheeky	**CEELOV** veloce	**CEESUV** cuvees	**CEHIOR** coheir
CEEHLR lecher	**CEELPS** clepes	**CEESUX** excuse	heroic
CEEHLS leches	**CEELRS** creels	**CEFFIO** office	**CEHIPR** cipher
CEEHLY lychee	sclere	**CEFFLO** coffle	**CEHIQU** quiche
CEEHMS scheme	**CEELRT** tercel	**CEFFOR** coffer	**CEHIRR** chirre
smeech	**CEELRV** clever	**CEFHIS** chiefs	richer
CEEHNT thence	**CEELRW** crewel	fiches	**CEHIRS** riches
CEEHNW whence	**CEELRY** celery	**CEFHIT** fetich	**CEHIRT** cither
CEEHNY Cheney	**CEELST** elects	Fichte	thrice
CEEHOR cohere	select	**CEFHLN** flench	**CEHIST** ethics
reecho	**CEELSX** excels	**CEFHLT** fletch	itches
CEEHOS echoes	**CEELSY** lycees	**CEFHNR** french	**CEHISU** cushie
CEEHPS cheeps	**CEEMNT** cement	**CEFHOO** Chefoo	**CEHISV** chives
speech	**CEEMNY** cymene	**CEFHST** fechts	**CEHITT** thetic
CEEHQU cheque	**CEEMRR** mercer	**CEFIKL** fickle	**CEHKLO** hockle
CEEHRS cheers	**CEEMRS** cremes	**CEFINT** infect	**CEHKLU** huckle
CEEHRT etcher	**CEEMRT** cermet	**CEFIOS** ficoes	**CEHKNU** kuchen

CEHKOR choker	**CEIINS** incise	**CEILRT** relict	**CEIOSS** cosies
hocker	**CEIINT** incite	**CEILSS** slices	cossie
CEHKOS chokes	**CEIIST** cities	**CEILSU** sluice	**CEIOSV** voices
CEHKOY chokey	iciest	**CEILSV** clevis	**CEIOSZ** cozies
hockey	**CEIISV** civies	**CEILTU** luetic	**CEIOTX** exotic
CEHKST sketch	**CEIJMO** Méjico	**CEIMMO** commie	**CEIPPT** peptic
CEHKTV kvetch	**CEIJNT** inject	**CEIMNO** income	**CEIPRR** pricer
CEHLMO Molech	**CEIJRU** juicer	**CEIMNR** mincer	**CEIPRS** cripes
CEHLOR choler	**CEIJSU** juices	**CEIMNS** cnemis	precis
CEHLOT clothe	**CEIKKR** kicker	minces	prices
CEHLOU louche	**CEIKLM** melick	**CEIMNU** neumic	spicer
CEHLPS chelps	mickle	**CEIMOX** Mexico	**CEIPRY** pricey
schlep	**CEIKLN** nickel	**CEIMPU** pumice	**CEIPSS** Pisces
CEHLPU pleuch	**CEIKLP** pickle	**CEIMPY** pyemic	spices
CEHLSY lyches	**CEIKLR** licker	**CEIMRS** crimes	**CEIPST** septic
CEHMMY chemmy	rickle	**CEIMRT** metric	**CEIQRU** cirque
CEHMOR chrome	**CEIKLS** cleiks	**CEIMRU** cerium	**CEIRRS** criers
CEHNOO ochone	sickle	uremic	ricers
CEHNOS chosen	**CEIKLT** tickle	**CEIMST** metics	**CEIRSS** crises
CEHNOT techno	**CEIKMY** mickey	**CEIMSU** cesium	scries
CEHNOU cohune	**CEIKNR** nicker	miscue	**CEIRST** citers
CEHNQU quench	**CEIKNS** sicken	**CEINNO** conine	steric
CEHNRT trench	**CEIKOO** cookie	**CEINOR** coiner	trices
CEHNRW wrench	**CEIKOS** Košice	orcein	**CEIRSU** cruise
CEHNST stench	**CEIKPR** picker	recoin	crusie
CEHNUU eunuch	**CEIKPT** picket	**CEINOS** conies	curies
CEHOOS choose	**CEIKRR** ricker	cosine	**CEIRTU** uretic
CEHOPS Cheops	**CEIKRS** sicker	oscine	**CEIRUV** Cuvier
epochs	**CEIKRT** ticker	**CEINOT** noetic	**CEIRUZ** cruzie
CEHORS chores	**CEIKRW** wicker	notice	**CEIRVX** cervix
cosher	**CEIKRY** crikey	**CEINOV** novice	**CEISSU** cuisse
ochers	rickey	**CEINOX** exonic	**CEISSY** cyesis
ochres	**CEIKTT** ticket	**CEINPR** pincer	**CEISTU** cuties
CEHORT hector	**CEIKTW** wicket	prince	**CEISTV** civets
rochet	**CEIKTY** tickey	**CEINPT** incept	evicts
tocher	**CEILLM** micell	pectin	**CEJKOY** jockey
troche	**CEILLO** collie	**CEINQU** cinque	**CEJNOU** jounce
CEHORU rouche	ocelli	quince	**CEJOOS** jocose
CEHORY ochery	**CEILLR** Çiller	**CEINRT** cretin	**CEKKOP** kopeck
CEHOSS choses	**CEILMS** climes	**CEINRU** Runcie	**CEKLMU** muckle
coshes	**CEILNO** cineol	**CEINRV** Cervin	**CEKLOR** locker
CEHOSU ouches	enolic	**CEINRW** wincer	**CEKLOT** locket
CEHOTU touche	**CEILNP** pencil	**CEINST** incest	**CEKLRS** clerks
CEHPRY chypre	**CEILNS** clines	insect	**CEKLRU** ruckle
cypher	**CEILNT** client	nicest	**CEKLSU** suckle
CEHPSY psyche	lectin	**CEINSU** incuse	**CEKMOR** mocker
CEHRRY cherry	lentic	**CEINSW** winces	**CEKMRU** mucker
CEHRSU ruches	**CEILNU** leucin	**CEINTY** nicety	**CEKMRX** Merckx
CEHRTW wretch	nuclei	**CEINWY** wincey	**CEKNOR** conker
CEHRTY cherty	**CEILNY** nicely	**CEIOOR** coorie	reckon
CEHSST chests	**CEILOO** coolie	**CEIOOT** cootie	**CEKNSS** snecks
CEHSTU chutes	**CEILOP** police	**CEIOPR** copier	**CEKOOR** cooker
tusche	**CEILOR** coiler	**CEIOPS** copies	**CEKOPT** pocket
CEHSTY chesty	recoil	**CEIOPT** poetic	**CEKORR** corker
scythe	**CEILOS** colies	**CEIORR** corrie	rocker
CEHTTY tetchy	**CEILOT** citole	orrice	**CEKORS** ockers
CEIIKR ickier	**CEILPS** splice	**CEIORS** cosier	**CEKORT** rocket
CEIIKS Ciskei	**CEILPV** pelvic	**CEIORT** erotic	**CEKOST** socket
sickie	**CEILPY** clypei	**CEIORU** courie	**CEKPRU** pucker
CEIILT elicit	**CEILQU** clique	**CEIORV** voicer	**CEKPSS** specks
CEIILX exilic	**CEILRS** relics	**CEIORW** cowrie	**CEKRSU** sucker
CEIINR irenic	slicer	**CEIORZ** cozier	**CEKRSW** wrecks

CEKRTU	tucker	**CEMNOS**	socmen	**CEORRW**	crower		cuteys
CEKTTU	tucket	**CEMNOW**	cowmen	**CEORSS**	corses	**CFFHIS**	Schiff
CELLNU	Cullen	**CEMNTU**	centum		crosse	**CFFHSU**	chuffs
CELLOS	cellos	**CEMOOS**	comose		scores	**CFFHUY**	chuffy
CELLOT	collet	**CEMOPR**	comper	**CEORST**	corset	**CFFILS**	cliffs
CELLOU	locule	**CEMORR**	Cromer		Cortés	**CFFILY**	cliffy
CELLOW	Cowell	**CEMORS**	comers		coster	**CFFINO**	coffin
CELLRU	culler		scrome		escort	**CFFOSS**	scoffs
CELLTU	cullet	**CEMOST**	comets		rectos	**CFFOTU**	cutoff
CELMOO	coelom	**CEMOSU**	mucose		scoter		offcut
CELMOP	compel	**CEMOSY**	cymose	**CEORSU**	cerous	**CFFRSU**	scruff
CELMOR	cormel	**CEMOTU**	Temuco		course	**CFFRUY**	Cruyff
CELMOS	celoms	**CEMRTU**	rectum		crouse	**CFFSSU**	scuffs
CELMOY	comely	**CENNOS**	nonces		source	**CFGINU**	fungic
CELMSU	muscle	**CENOOP**	poonce	**CEORSV**	corves	**CFHILN**	flinch
CELMUY	lyceum	**CENOPR**	Procne		covers	**CFHILT**	flitch
CELNNU	nuncle	**CENOPS**	ponces	**CEORSW**	cowers	**CFHIRS**	Frisch
CELNOR	cornel	**CENOPU**	pounce		escrow	**CFHISU**	fichus
CELNOS	clones	**CENOPY**	poncey	**CEORSY**	corsey	**CFHLSY**	flysch
CELNOV	cloven	**CENORR**	corner	**CEORSZ**	crozes	**CFHOOS**	choofs
CELNOY	Ceylon	**CENORS**	censor	**CEORTT**	cotter	**CFHOUU**	Fu-chou
CELNSU	uncles		crones	**CEORTU**	croute	**CFIILM**	filmic
CELNTU	lucent		oncers	**CEORTV**	covert	**CFIINO**	Ficino
CELOOR	cooler	**CENORT**	cornet		vector	**CFIINU**	unific
CELOOT	ocelot	**CENORU**	conure	**CEORTX**	cortex	**CFIIST**	fistic
CELOPU	couple		uncoer	**CEOSSS**	cosses	**CFIITY**	citify
CELOPY	Copley	**CENOSS**	scones	**CEOSST**	cestos	**CFIKLS**	flicks
	Coypel	**CENOST**	centos		cosets	**CFILOR**	frolic
CELOQU	cloque		contes		cosset	**CFIMOR**	formic
CELORS	ceorls	**CENOSU**	ounces	**CEOSSU**	scouse	**CFIMOT**	comfit
	closer	**CENOSV**	covens	**CEOSTT**	octets	**CFINOT**	confit
	cresol	**CENOSY**	coneys	**CEOSTV**	covets	**CFISTU**	fustic
CELORT	colter	**CENOSZ**	cozens	**CEOSVY**	coveys	**CFITYY**	cityfy
	lector	**CENOVX**	convex	**CEPPRU**	cupper	**CFKLOS**	flocks
CELORU	colure	**CENOVY**	convey	**CEPRSU**	spruce	**CFKLOY**	flocky
CELORV	clover	**CENPSU**	punces	**CEPRSY**	cypres	**CFKORS**	frocks
CELOSS	closes	**CENRYZ**	Czerny	**CERRSU**	curers	**CFKPUU**	fuckup
	socles	**CENSST**	scents		curser	**CFLPUU**	cupful
CELOST	closet	**CENSSU**	census		recurs	**CFORST**	crofts
	telcos	**CENSTY**	encyst	**CERSST**	crests	**CFOSUU**	fucous
CELOSU	coleus	**CENSUU**	cuneus	**CERSSU**	cruses	**CFRSUY**	scurfy
CELOSV	cloves	**CEOOPR**	cooper		curses	**CGGLOY**	cloggy
CELOSX	scolex	**CEOORS**	cooers		sucres		coggly
CELOSY	coleys	**CEOOSY**	cooeys	**CERSSW**	screws	**CGGORY**	croggy
CELOTU	Clouet	**CEOOTY**	coyote	**CERSSY**	Cressy	**CGHHOU**	chough
CELOWY	Cowley		oocyte	**CERSTU**	cruets	**CGHIIN**	I Ching
CELPSU	cupels	**CEOPPR**	copper		curets	**CGHILT**	glitch
CELPSY	clypes	**CEOPRS**	copers		Custer	**CGHINR**	grinch
CELPTY	yclept		corpse		eructs	**CGHIOT**	gothic
CELPUU	cupule	**CEOPRT**	copter		rectus	**CGHLOU**	clough
CELRRU	curler	**CEOPRU**	croupe		truces	**CGHORU**	grouch
CELRSU	cruels		recoup	**CERSUV**	curves	**CGHOSU**	coughs
	ulcers	**CEOPRW**	Cowper	**CERSUX**	cruxes	**CGIILT**	tiglic
CELRTU	cutler	**CEOPRY**	recopy	**CERSWY**	screwy	**CGIINO**	congii
	reluct	**CEOPSS**	copses	**CERTTU**	cutter	**CGIINR**	ricing
CELRUU	curule		scopes	**CERTUV**	curvet	**CGIINS**	icings
CELRUV	culver	**CEOPSU**	coupes	**CESSSU**	cusses	**CGIINT**	citing
CELRUW	curlew	**CEOPTY**	cotype	**CESSTU**	cestus	**CGIINV**	vicing
CELSTU	culets	**CEOQTU**	coquet		scutes	**CGIKNO**	coking
CELTTU	cutlet	**CEORRS**	crores	**CESTTU**	cutest	**CGILNS**	clings
	cuttle		scorer	**CESTUY**	cutesy	**CGILNU**	cluing
CELTUY	cutely	**CEORRT**	rector			**CGILNY**	clingy

CGIMNO	coming		thymic	**CHLSSU**	schuls	**CIKNPU**	unpick
	gnomic	**CHINNO**	Inchon	**CHLSTU**	slutch	**CIKNPY**	pyknic
CGINNO	coning	**CHINOP**	chopin	**CHMMUY**	chummy	**CIKNSS**	snicks
CGINOO	cooing		phonic	**CHMOOR**	chromo	**CIKNYZ**	zincky
CGINOP	coping	**CHINOR**	Chiron	**CHMOOS**	chooms	**CIKOSS**	sickos
	picong	**CHINOS**	chinos		smooch	**CIKOSY**	yoicks
CGINOR	coring	**CHINOT**	chiton	**CHMOPS**	chomps	**CIKPPU**	pickup
CGINOS	coigns	**CHINRU**	urchin	**CHMPSU**	chumps	**CIKPRS**	pricks
CGINOT	coting	**CHINST**	nichts	**CHMSTU**	smutch	**CIKPSS**	spicks
CGINOV	coving		snitch	**CHNOOP**	poncho	**CIKPTU**	uptick
CGINOW	cowing	**CHINTZ**	chintz	**CHNOOS**	Chosŏn	**CIKQSU**	quicks
CGINOX	coxing	**CHIOPR**	orphic	**CHNOTY**	notchy	**CIKRST**	strick
CGINRU	curing	**CHIOPS**	Phocis	**CHNPUY**	punchy		tricks
CGINRY	crying	**CHIOPT**	photic	**CHNRSU**	churns	**CIKRSW**	wricks
CGIOOT	cogito	**CHIORS**	chiros	**CHNSSY**	synchs	**CIKRTY**	tricky
CGIORS	corgis		choirs	**CHNTUU**	tuchun	**CIKSST**	sticks
CGLLOY	glycol		ichors	**CHOORT**	cohort	**CIKSTY**	sticky
CGLNOU	unclog		orchis	**CHOOSS**	scoosh	**CIKWYZ**	Zwicky
CGLOOU	colugo	**CHIORT**	rhotic	**CHOOSY**	choosy	**CILLOU**	loculi
CGNOOS	cogons		thoric	**CHOPPY**	choppy	**CILLSU**	cullis
	congos	**CHIOSY**	coyish	**CHOPSY**	psycho	**CILMUU**	cumuli
CGNOOU	congou	**CHIOSZ**	schizo	**CHOPUY**	pouchy	**CILNOU**	uncoil
CGNSUY	scungy	**CHIPPY**	chippy	**CHORSU**	chorus	**CILNST**	clints
CHHIIL	Chihli	**CHIPRS**	chirps	**CHORTU**	trouch	**CILNTU**	incult
CHHNOO	honcho	**CHIPRY**	chirpy	**CHOSTT**	chotts	**CILOPU**	oilcup
CHHOOS	cohosh	**CHIPSY**	physic	**CHOSUU**	Su-chou	**CILOPY**	policy
CHHOOT	hootch		scyphi	**CHOSUW**	Süchow	**CILORS**	Locris
CHIILL	chilli	**CHIPTY**	pitchy	**CHOTUY**	couthy	**CILORT**	lictor
	Illich	**CHIQTU**	quitch		touchy	**CILOSU**	coulis
CHIILS	lichis	**CHIRRS**	chirrs	**CHPSSY**	psychs	**CILOSV**	clovis
CHIILT	litchi	**CHIRST**	Christ	**CHPSTU**	putsch	**CILOSY**	cosily
	lithic		richts	**CHRRSU**	churrs	**CILOTU**	toluic
CHIINS	nicish	**CHIRSU**	chirus	**CHRSTW**	crwths	**CILOYZ**	cozily
CHIINT	chitin	**CHIRUZ**	Zürich	**CHSSSU**	schuss	**CILPSU**	piculs
CHIKKO	Hickok	**CHISST**	schist	**CHSTUY**	cushty	**CILQUY**	cliquy
CHIKNS	chinks		sichts	**CHSTUZ**	Schütz	**CILRSY**	lyrics
CHIKNY	chinky		stichs	**CHSWYZ**	Schwyz	**CIMMNU**	cummin
CHIKOS	hoicks	**CHISTT**	stitch	**CIIIRT**	iritic	**CIMMOS**	commis
CHIKOT	thicko	**CHISTW**	switch	**CIIKNP**	pickin	**CIMMOT**	commit
CHIKOX	Hickox	**CHITTW**	twitch	**CIILMU**	cilium	**CIMMOX**	commix
CHIKRS	kirsch	**CHITTY**	chitty	**CIILOP**	lipoic	**CIMNOR**	micron
CHIKST	kitsch		titchy	**CIILSY**	Sicily	**CIMNOS**	cosmin
	shtick	**CHIVVY**	chivvy	**CIIMMS**	mimics	**CIMNOU**	conium
	skitch	**CHJMOU**	Jochum	**CIIMOT**	miotic		muonic
CHIKTY	thicky	**CHJNOU**	Chŏnju	**CIIMSV**	civism	**CIMNRU**	crinum
CHILLS	chills	**CHKLOO**	klooch	**CIIMTV**	victim	**CIMNSU**	mucins
CHILLY	chilly	**CHKNSU**	chunks	**CIINNU**	uncini	**CIMOPY**	myopic
CHILMO	holmic	**CHKNUY**	chunky	**CIINOR**	ironic	**CIMORS**	micros
CHILOR	orchil	**CHKOOS**	chokos	**CIINOS**	ionics	**CIMORU**	corium
CHILOS	cholis		chooks	**CIINOT**	Ticino	**CIMOST**	sitcom
CHILPY	phylic	**CHKOSS**	shocks	**CIINQU**	quinic	**CIMOTY**	comity
CHILRY	richly	**CHKOSW**	chowks	**CIINRT**	citrin		myotic
CHILST	lichts	**CHKSSU**	shucks		nitric	**CIMPRS**	crimps
CHIMNU	Munich	**CHLMOO**	moloch	**CIIOPS**	Scipio		scrimp
CHIMNY	hymnic	**CHLNOO**	Cholon	**CIIPRS**	Crispi	**CIMPRY**	crimpy
CHIMOR	hormic	**CHLOOS**	school	**CIIRSS**	crisis	**CIMRSS**	scrims
CHIMPS	chimps	**CHLOOT**	Clotho	**CIIRTV**	vitric	**CIMRUU**	curium
CHIMRS	chirms		coolth	**CIKKPU**	kickup	**CIMSTY**	mystic
	chrism	**CHLORS**	schorl	**CIKLNS**	clinks	**CINNOR**	Cronin
	smirch	**CHLOST**	cloths	**CIKLSS**	slicks	**CINNOU**	nuncio
CHIMSS	schism	**CHLOSU**	slouch	**CIKLSY**	sickly	**CINOOZ**	ozonic
CHIMTY	mythic	**CHLRSU**	churls	**CIKLTY**	tickly	**CINOPT**	pontic

CINORT	citron	CLLOOP	collop	CNORSW	crowns	DDEEEN	needed
CINORZ	zircon	CLLOOY	coolly	CNORSY	synroc	DDEEER	reeded
CINOSS	scions	CLLORS	scroll	CNORUW	Curnow	DDEEES	seeded
	sonics	CLLSSU	sculls	CNORUZ	Curzon	DDEEEW	weeded
CINOST	tocsin	CLMNOU	column	CNOSTU	counts	DDEEFI	de fide
	tonics	CLMOPS	clomps		Tucson		defied
CINOSU	cousin	CLMOPY	comply	CNOTUY	county	DDEEFN	defend
CINOSV	covins	CLMOSU	locums	COOORZ	corozo		fended
CINOSY	Sicyon	CLMPSU	clumps		Orozco	DDEEFU	feuded
CINOSZ	zincos	CLMPUY	clumpy	COOPRS	scroop	DDEEGG	degged
CINPSU	Pincus	CLMSTU	mulcts	COOPSS	scoops	DDEEGH	hedged
CINRSU	incurs	CLMSUY	clumsy	COOPST	coopts	DDEEGK	kedged
CINRTU	Curtin		muscly	COOPWX	cowpox	DDEEGL	gelded
CINSTT	tincts	CLNOOS	colons	COORTT	Cortot		ledged
CINSTU	cutins	CLNOOU	uncool	COORUU	roucou	DDEEGR	dredge
	tunics	CLNOOY	colony	COOSST	scoots	DDEEGW	wedged
CIOORT	octroi	CLNOSU	clonus	COOSTY	oocyst	DDEEHL	heddle
CIOPRT	tropic		consul	COPRRS	scrorp	DDEEHR	herded
CIOPST	optics	CLNOSW	clowns	COPRSU	corpus	DDEEIL	elided
	picots	CLNRUU	uncurl		croups	DDEEIN	denied
	topics	CLOORS	colors	COPRTY	crypto		indeed
CIOPTT	ptotic		crools	COPRUY	croupy	DDEEIR	deride
CIOPWY	wicopy	CLOORU	colour	COPSSU	Scopus		diedre
CIORSU	curios	CLOORY	colory	COPSUY	coypus	DDEEIS	eddies
CIORTT	tricot	CLOSSW	scowls	CORRSU	cursor	DDEEIT	dieted
CIORTV	victor	CLOSTU	clouts	CORSSU	scours		edited
CIOSST	stoics		locust	CORSSY	Scyros	DDEELM	meddle
CIOSTU	coitus	CLOSTY	costly	CORSTU	courts		melded
CIPPRS	Cripps	CLPSSU	sculps	CORSUV	corvus	DDEELP	peddle
CIPRSS	crisps	CLPSTU	sculpt	CORTUY	outcry	DDEELR	reddle
	scrips	CLRTUY	curtly	COSSTU	custos	DDEELS	sledded
CIPRST	script	CLSSUU	sulcus		Scotus	DDEELU	delude
CIPRSY	crispy	CLSTUU	cultus		scouts		dueled
CIRRSU	cirrus	CMMNOO	common	COSTTU	cottus		eluded
CIRSTT	strict	CMMOOR	romcom	COTTUU	cutout	DDEELV	delved
CIRSTU	citrus	CMMOOS	commos	CPRSTY	crypts	DDEELW	welded
	rictus	CMMRUY	crummy	CPRSUY	cyprus	DDEEMN	mended
	rustic	CMMSUY	scummy	CPSTUU	cutups	DDEEMO	demode
CIRTTY	yttric	CMNNOO	noncom	CRRSUY	scurry	DDEENN	denned
CISSSU	cissus	CMNOSY	syncom	CRSSTU	crusts	DDEENP	depend
CISSTU	cistus	CMOOPS	compos	CRSTUY	crusty		pended
CISSUV	viscus	CMOOSS	cosmos		curtsy	DDEENR	redden
CJKOOS	jockos	CMOOSW	Moscow	CRSUVY	scurvy	DDEENT	dented
CJNOSU	juncos	CMOSTU	custom	CSUYZZ	scuzzy		tended
CKKNOS	knocks	CMOSUU	mucous	DDDEEE	deeded	DDEENU	denude
CKLNOS	clonks	CMPRSU	crumps	DDDEEI	eddied		dudeen
CKLNOU	unlock		scrump	DDDEER	redded		Dundee
CKLNSU	clunks	CMPRUU	cuprum	DDDEET	tedded		endued
CKLNUY	clunky	CMRSSU	scrums	DDDEEW	wedded	DDEENV	vended
CKLOPU	lockup	CMSTUU	scutum	DDDEIK	kidded	DDEENW	wended
CKLPSU	plucks	CNOOPU	coupon	DDDEIL	diddle	DDEEOR	eroded
CKLPUY	plucky	CNOORS	croons		lidded	DDEEOS	eddoes
CKMOPU	mockup	CNOORT	croton	DDDEIR	ridded	DDEERR	redder
CKMOSS	smocks	CNOOST	contos	DDDELO	doddle	DDEERT	tedder
CKNORU	uncork		nostoc	DDDEMU	mudded	DDEERY	Eddery
CKNTUU	untuck		oncost	DDDENO	nodded		redyed
CKOORS	crooks	CNOOTT	cotton	DDDEOP	podded	DDEEUV	de Duve
CKOSST	stocks	CNOOTY	tycoon	DDDEOR	dodder	DDEEUX	exuded
CKOSTY	stocky	CNOOVY	convoy	DDDEOS	sodded	DDEFFO	doffed
CKRSTU	struck	CNORSS	scorns	DDEEEH	heeded	DDEFFU	duffed
	trucks	CNORST	troncs	DDEEEM	deemed	DDEFGI	fidged
CKRSUU	ruckus	CNORSU	Cronus			DDEFGU	fudged

DDEFIL	fiddle	DDEIPP	dipped
DDEFLO	folded	DDEIPR	prided
DDEFLU	fuddle	DDEIRR	ridder
DDEFNU	funded	DDEISS	dissed
DDEFOR	fodder	DDEJRU	judder
	forded	DDEKNU	dunked
DDEGGI	digged	DDEKOO	dooked
DDEGGO	dogged	DDEKOU	douked
DDEGIL	gilded	DDEKSU	dusked
	glided	DDELLO	dolled
DDEGIN	dinged	DDELLU	dulled
DDEGIR	girded	DDELMO	molded
	grided	DDELMU	muddle
	ridged	DDELNO	noddle
DDEGIT	geddit	DDELOO	doodle
DDEGIU	guided	DDELOP	poddle
DDEGJU	judged	DDELOT	toddle
DDEGLO	lodged	DDELPU	puddle
DDEGLU	guddle	DDELRU	ruddle
DDEGMO	dodgem	DDELUY	Dudley
	modged	DDEMNU	Edmund
DDEGNO	donged	DDEMOO	doomed
DDEGNU	dinged	DDEMOR	Modred
	nudged	DDEMPU	dumped
DDEGOR	dodger	DDENNO	donned
DDEGOS	dodges	DDENNU	dunned
DDEGRU	drudge	DDENOR	donder
DDEHIN	hidden		droned
DDEHIS	dished	DDENOS	Seddon
DDEHLU	huddle		sodden
DDEHNO	hodden	DDENOW	downed
DDEHOO	hooded	DDENOY	dynode
DDEHOR	horded	DDENRY	Dryden
DDEIIK	kiddie	DDENSU	sudden
DDEIIO	iodide	DDENSY	synded
DDEIIT	tidied	DDENTU	dunted
DDEIIV	divide	DDENUY	undyed
DDEIKL	kiddle	DDEOOS	dodoes
DDEIKN	dinked	DDEOOW	wooded
DDEIKR	dirked	DDEORV	droved
	kidder	DDEORW	worded
DDEIKS	disked	DDEOSS	dossed
DDEILM	middle	DDEOST	oddest
DDEILO	dildoe	DDEOSU	doused
DDEILP	piddle	DDEOSW	dowsed
DDEILR	riddle	DDEOTT	dotted
DDEILS	sidled	DDEPPU	dupped
DDEILW	widdle	DDERRU	rudder
DDEIMM	dimmed	DDERSU	udders
DDEIMN	midden	DDESTU	dusted
	minded	DDFILY	fiddly
DDEIMS	desmid	DDFIOR	fordid
DDEINN	dinned	DDHINO	hoddin
DDEINR	ridden	DDHISU	dudish
DDEINT	dinted	DDHOSY	shoddy
DDEINU	indued	DDIIKK	dikdik
DDEINW	winded	DDIKSY	skiddy
DDEIOS	didoes	DDILNR	dirndl
	diodes	DDILOS	dildos
DDEIOT	doited	DDILTY	tiddly
DDEIOV	devoid	DDIOPY	dipody
	voided	DDIORS	sordid

DDIOTU	outdid	DEEFUZ	defuze
DDIOTY	oddity	DEEFZZ	fezzed
DDIRSU	druids	DEEGGI	gidgee
	siddur	DEEGGL	legged
DDLMUY	muddly	DEEGGP	pegged
DDLPUY	puddly	DEEGGV	vegged
DDMMUU	dumdum	DEEGHR	hedger
DEEEFR	feeder	DEEGHS	hedges
	reefed	DEEGIJ	gidjee
DEEEFZ	feezed	DEEGIN	deeing
DEEEGR	degree	DEEGIR	edgier
DEEEHL	heeled	DEEGIS	sieged
DEEEHR	heeder	DEEGKS	kedges
DEEEJR	jeered	DEEGLL	gelled
	jereed	DEEGLN	legend
DEEEKK	keeked	DEEGLP	pledge
DEEEKL	keeled	DEEGLR	gelder
DEEEKN	keened		ledger
DEEEKP	peeked		redleg
DEEEKR	reeked	DEEGLS	gledes
DEEELN	needle		ledges
DEEELP	peeled		sledge
DEEELR	leered	DEEGLU	deluge
	reeled	DEEGMM	gemmed
DEEELS	seeled	DEEGMR	merged
DEEELT	delete	DEEGNR	gender
DEEEMR	redeem	DEEGNU	dengue
DEEEMS	seemed	DEEGNV	venged
DEEEMT	teemed	DEEGOS	geodes
DEEENP	deepen	DEEGRS	edgers
	peened		greeds
DEEENV	evened	DEEGRV	verged
	vendee	DEEGRY	greedy
	Vendée		greyed
DEEENW	weened	DEEGSS	sedges
DEEEPP	peeped	DEEGSU	segued
DEEEPR	deeper	DEEGSW	wedges
	peered	DEEGSZ	Szeged
DEEEPS	seeped	DEEHLM	helmed
DEEEPV	peeved	DEEHLP	helped
DEEERS	seeder	DEEHLV	helved
DEEERV	reeved	DEEHMM	hemmed
	veered	DEEHMS	meshed
DEEERW	weeder	DEEHMT	themed
DEEERY	redeye	DEEHNT	hented
DEEFGL	fledge	DEEHRR	herder
DEEFHT	hefted	DEEHSW	shewed
DEEFIL	defile	DEEILN	Leiden
DEEFIN	define	DEEILR	lieder
DEEFIR	defier		relied
	deifer	DEEILS	diesel
DEEFIS	defies		ediles
DEEFLL	felled		elides
DEEFLT	felted	DEEILV	levied
DEEFLU	fueled		veiled
DEEFLX	flexed	DEEILX	exiled
DEEFLY	fleyed	DEEILY	eyelid
DEEFNR	fender	DEEIMP	impede
DEEFRS	defers	DEEIMS	demies
DEEFRT	defter		demise
DEEFRY	redefy	DEEIMT	itemed
DEEFSU	defuse	DEEINN	indene

DEEINR	denier	**DEELRW**	lewder	**DEENTV**	vented	**DEFFNO**	offend
	Edirne		reweld	**DEENTX**	dentex	**DEFFOR**	doffer
	nereid		welder		extend	**DEFFPU**	puffed
	reined	**DEELST**	eldest	**DEENUV**	vendue	**DEFFRU**	duffer
DEEINS	denies	**DEELSU**	eludes	**DEEOPS**	depose		ruffed
	dienes	**DEELSV**	delves		epodes	**DEFGGI**	figged
	seined	**DEELSW**	slewed		speedo	**DEFGGO**	fogged
DEEINV	Devine	**DEELTT**	letted	**DEEORS**	erodes	**DEFGIR**	fridge
	endive	**DEELTU**	eluted		redoes	**DEFGIS**	fidges
	envied		teledu	**DEEORT**	teredo	**DEFGIT**	fidget
	veined	**DEELTW**	welted	**DEEORV**	devore		gifted
DEEIPP	Dieppe	**DEELUX**	deluxe	**DEEORZ**	zeroed	**DEFGLO**	Geldof
DEEIPS	espied	**DEEMNO**	omened	**DEEOTV**	devote		golfed
DEEIRS	desire	**DEEMNR**	mender		vetoed	**DEFGLU**	gulfed
	eiders		remend	**DEEPPP**	pepped	**DEFGLY**	fledgy
	reside	**DEEMNS**	emends	**DEEPPR**	repped	**DEFGOO**	goofed
DEEIRT	dieter		Mendes	**DEEPRU**	perdue	**DEFGOR**	forged
	reedit	**DEEMNT**	dement		pureed	**DEFGSU**	fudges
	retied	**DEEMOT**	demote	**DEEPRV**	perved	**DEFHIS**	fished
	tiered		emoted	**DEEPRY**	preyed	**DEFHOO**	hoofed
DEEIRU	ureide	**DEEMOW**	meowed	**DEEPSS**	speeds	**DEFIKN**	finked
DEEIRV	derive	**DEEMPR**	permed	**DEEPSW**	spewed		knifed
	reived		premed	**DEEPSY**	speedy	**DEFILL**	filled
DEEIRW	dewier	**DEEMPT**	empted	**DEEPTT**	petted	**DEFILM**	filmed
DEEISS	dieses		temped	**DEEPTU**	depute	**DEFILO**	foiled
	seised	**DEEMRT**	termed	**DEEQUU**	queued	**DEFILR**	rifled
DEEISV	devise	**DEEMRU**	demure	**DEERRW**	redrew	**DEFILS**	fields
	sieved	**DEEMRY**	remedy	**DEERSS**	seders	**DEFILT**	flited
DEEISZ	seized	**DEEMSS**	messed	**DEERST**	desert		lifted
DEEITV	evited	**DEEMTU**	Te Deum		deters	**DEFIMR**	firmed
DEEITX	exited	**DEENNO**	donnee		rested	**DEFINN**	finned
DEEIVW	viewed	**DEENNP**	penned	**DEERSU**	reused	**DEFINO**	foined
DEEJKR	jerked	**DEENNY**	yenned	**DEERSV**	served	**DEFINR**	finder
DEEJLL	jelled	**DEENOP**	depone		versed		friend
DEEJSS	jessed		opened	**DEERSY**	redyes		redfin
DEEJST	jested	**DEENOR**	redone	**DEERTT**	retted	**DEFINS**	fiends
DEEJTT	jetted	**DEENOS**	donees	**DEERTX**	dexter	**DEFINU**	fundie
DEEKKR	Dekker		Odense	**DEERVV**	revved	**DEFIOO**	foodie
DEEKNN	kenned	**DEENOT**	denote	**DEESST**	steeds	**DEFIOT**	foetid
DEEKNR	kerned	**DEENOV**	ovened	**DEESSW**	swedes	**DEFIRT**	rifted
DEEKOV	evoked	**DEENPX**	expend	**DEESTT**	detest	**DEFIRV**	fervid
DEEKPR	perked	**DEENRR**	render		tested	**DEFIST**	fisted
DEEKSW	skewed	**DEENRS**	denser	**DEESTU**	etudes		sifted
DEELLR	Deller		enders	**DEESTV**	devest	**DEFITT**	fitted
DEELLW	welled		sender		vested	**DEFIZZ**	fizzed
DEELLY	yelled	**DEENRT**	rented	**DEESTW**	stewed	**DEFJLS**	fjelds
DEELMN	Mendel		tender		tweeds	**DEFKLU**	fluked
DEELMT	melted	**DEENRU**	Deurne	**DEESTZ**	zested	**DEFKNU**	funked
DEELMW	mewled		endure	**DEESUX**	exudes	**DEFKOR**	forked
DEELMY	medley		enured	**DEETTV**	vetted	**DEFLLU**	fulled
DEELNR	lender	**DEENRV**	Denver	**DEETTW**	wetted	**DEFLMU**	flumed
DEELNS	Selden		nerved	**DEETWY**	tweedy	**DEFLMY**	medfly
DEELNW	wedeln		vender	**DEFFHU**	huffed	**DEFLNO**	enfold
DEELNY	Leyden	**DEENSS**	sensed	**DEFFIM**	miffed		fondle
DEELOP	eloped	**DEENST**	nested	**DEFFIN**	niffed	**DEFLOO**	fooled
DEELPR	pedler		tensed	**DEFFIR**	differ	**DEFLOR**	folder
DEELPT	pelted	**DEENSU**	endues		riffed		refold
DEELPY	deeply		ensued	**DEFFIT**	tiffed	**DEFLOT**	lofted
	yelped	**DEENSW**	Sweden	**DEFFLU**	duffel	**DEFLOU**	fouled
DEELRS	elders	**DEENTT**	detent		duffle	**DEFLOW**	flowed
DEELRU	eluder		netted		luffed		fowled
DEELRV	delver		tented	**DEFFMU**	muffed		wolfed

DEFLRU	furled		glider		monged	DEHITW	whited
DEFLTU	fluted		regild	DEGMOS	modges		withed
DEFLTY	deftly		ridgel	DEGMSU	smudge	DEHJOS	joshed
	flyted	DEGILS	glides	DEGNNU	gunned	DEHKLU	hulked
DEFLUX	fluxed	DEGILY	edgily	DEGNOP	ponged	DEHKNO	honked
DEFMOR	deform	DEGIMR	grimed	DEGNOT	tonged	DEHKOO	hooked
	formed	DEGIMS	midges	DEGNOW	gowned	DEHKOW	howked
DEFNNU	funned		smidge	DEGNRU	dunger	DEHKSU	husked
DEFNOR	fonder	DEGIMT	midget		gerund	DEHLLU	hulled
DEFNOU	fondue	DEGINN	ending		gurned	DEHLNO	holden
DEFNRU	funder		ginned		nudger	DEHLOR	holder
	refund	DEGINO	Gideon	DEGNSU	nudges	DEHLOS	dholes
DEFOOR	foredo	DEGINP	pinged	DEGOOP	pogoed	DEHLOT	tholed
	roofed	DEGINR	dinger	DEGOOS	goosed	DEHLOW	howled
DEFOOT	footed		girned	DEGOPR	groped	DEHLPU	upheld
DEFOOW	woofed		reding	DEGOPS	podges	DEHLRU	hurdle
DEFORU	Froude		ringed	DEGORS	sodger		hurled
DEFRRU	furred	DEGINS	deigns	DEGORU	drogue	DEHLSU	lushed
DEFRSU	surfed		design		gourde	DEHMMU	hummed
DEFRTU	turfed		dinges		rogued	DEHMNO	hodmen
DEFSSU	fussed		signed		rouged	DEHMNY	hymned
DEFTTU	tufted		singed	DEGOSS	gossed	DEHMOS	moshed
DEFUZZ	fuzzed	DEGINT	tinged	DEGOST	godets	DEHMOT	method
DEGGGI	gigged	DEGINW	dewing		stodge	DEHMPU	humped
DEGGHO	hogged		winged	DEGOSW	wodges	DEHMRY	rhymed
DEGGHU	hugged	DEGINY	dingey	DEGOSY	dogeys	DEHMSU	mushed
DEGGIJ	jigged		dyeing	DEGPPY	gypped	DEHNOP	phoned
DEGGIL	ligged	DEGINZ	zinged	DEGPRU	purged	DEHNOR	dehorn
DEGGIN	edging	DEGIOS	dogies	DEGPSU	pudges		horned
DEGGIO	doggie		geoids	DEGRSU	surged	DEHNOS	noshed
DEGGIP	pigged	DEGIPP	gipped	DEGRTU	trudge	DEHNOY	hoyden
DEGGIR	digger	DEGIPR	griped	DEGSTU	degust	DEHNRY	Hendry
	rigged	DEGIRR	girder		gusted	DEHNSS	shends
DEGGIT	tigged	DEGIRS	dirges	DEGTTU	gutted	DEHNSU	unshed
DEGGIW	wigged		grides	DEHHSU	hushed	DEHNTU	hunted
DEGGJO	jogged		ridges	DEHILL	hilled	DEHOOP	hooped
DEGGJU	jugged	DEGIRT	girted	DEHILP	Delphi	DEHOOS	shooed
DEGGLO	dogleg	DEGIRU	guider	DEHILS	shield	DEHOOT	hooted
	logged	DEGIST	digest	DEHILT	hilted	DEHOPP	hopped
DEGGLU	lugged	DEGISU	guides	DEHILW	whiled	DEHOPS	ephods
DEGGMU	mugged		guised	DEHIMN	mehndi	DEHORS	hordes
DEGGNO	gonged	DEGITU	dugite	DEHIMO	hemoid		horsed
DEGGNU	gunged	DEGITW	widget	DEHINO	hoiden		reshod
DEGGOR	dogger	DEGJRU	judger		honied		Rhodes
	gorged	DEGJSU	judges	DEHINR	hinder		shored
DEGGOT	togged	DEGLLU	gulled	DEHINS	shined	DEHORW	whored
DEGGOU	gouged	DEGLNO	dongle	DEHINT	hinted	DEHOST	hosted
DEGGPU	pugged		golden	DEHINW	whined	DEHOSU	housed
DEGGRU	grudge		longed	DEHIOO	hoodie	DEHOSV	shoved
	rugged	DEGLNU	gulden	DEHIOS	Hesiod	DEHOSW	showed
DEGGRY	dreggy		lunged	DEHIOX	oxhide	DEHOTT	hotted
DEGGTU	tugged	DEGLOP	plodge	DEHIPP	hipped	DEHPST	depths
DEGHIN	hinged	DEGLOR	dogrel	DEHIPS	pished	DEHPSU	pushed
DEGHIR	dreigh		lodger	DEHIPT	pithed	DEHRSS	sherds
DEGHIS	sighed	DEGLOS	lodges	DEHIRS	hiders		shreds
DEGHSU	gushed	DEGLOV	gloved		shired	DEHRSU	rushed
DEGIIW	widgie	DEGLOW	glowed	DEHIRT	dither	DEHRSW	shrewd
DEGIKN	kinged	DEGLOZ	glozed	DEHISS	dishes	DEHTTU	hutted
DEGILL	gilled	DEGLPU	gulped		hissed	DEIIKN	dinkie
DEGILN	dingle	DEGLSU	sludge	DEHIST	shited		kindie
DEGILR	gilder	DEGMMU	gummed	DEHISW	wished	DEIIKR	Kediri
	girdle	DEGMNO	dogmen	DEHITT	tithed	DEIILP	lipide

DEIIMS	imides	**DEILNO**	doline		demits	triode
DEIINO	iodine		indole		misted	**DEIORV** voider
DEIINS	indies	**DEILNT**	dentil	**DEIMTU**	tedium	**DEIORW** dowier
	inside		Tilden	**DEINNP**	pinned	weirdo
DEIINT	indite	**DEILOP**	diploe	**DEINNR**	dinner	**DEIORZ** dozier
	tineid		dipole	**DEINNS**	Dennis	**DEIOST** todies
DEIINV	divine	**DEILOR**	roiled		sinned	**DEIOSV** videos
DEIIOS	iodise	**DEILOS**	Isolde	**DEINNT**	dentin	**DEIOSX** doxies
DEIIOZ	iodize		oldies		indent	oxides
DEIIPT	pitied		soiled		intend	**DEIPPP** pipped
DEIIRS	irides	**DEILOT**	toiled		tinned	**DEIPPR** dipper
DEIIRT	tidier	**DEILOV**	livedo	**DEINNU**	undine	ripped
DEIISS	diesis	**DEILPP**	lipped	**DEINNW**	enwind	**DEIPPS** sipped
DEIIST	tidies	**DEILPS**	dispel	**DEINOP**	opined	**DEIPPT** tipped
DEIISX	deixis		lisped	**DEINOR**	De Niro	**DEIPPZ** zipped
	dixies		spiled		Indore	**DEIPQU** piqued
DEIJKN	jinked	**DEILPX**	diplex		ironed	**DEIPRS** prides
DEIJLT	jilted	**DEILRS**	idlers	**DEINOS**	Edison	prised
DEIJNO	joined		sidler		noised	spider
DEIJNX	jinxed		slider		onside	spired
DEIJRS	jerids	**DEILRV**	drivel	**DEINOV**	nevoid	**DEIPRZ** prized
DEIJSU	judies	**DEILRW**	wilder	**DEINOZ**	D'Inzeo	**DEIPSS** pissed
DEIKLL	killed	**DEILRY**	direly	**DEINPP**	nipped	**DEIPST** spited
DEIKLM	milked		ridley	**DEINPS**	sniped	**DEIPSU** upside
DEIKLN	kilned	**DEILSS**	sidles		spined	**DEIPSV** vespid
	kindle		slides	**DEINRS**	diners	**DEIPSW** swiped
	linked	**DEILST**	delist		rinsed	wisped
DEIKLO	keloid		idlest		snider	**DEIPTT** pitted
DEIKLS	silked		listed	**DEINRT**	rident	**DEIRRS** derris
DEIKLT	kilted		silted		tinder	driers
DEIKNP	pinked		tildes	**DEINRU**	inured	riders
DEIKNR	kinder	**DEILSU**	Delius		ruined	**DEIRRU** durrie
DEIKNW	winked	**DEILSV**	devils	**DEINRV**	driven	**DEIRRV** driver
DEIKNY	kidney	**DEILSW**	wields		verdin	**DEIRRY** yirred
DEIKPP	kipped	**DEILSY**	yields	**DEINRW**	rewind	**DEIRST** driest
DEIKPS	spiked	**DEILTT**	tilted		winder	stride
DEIKPU	Updike		titled	**DEINST**	teinds	**DEIRSU** diseur
DEIKRS	risked	**DEILTU**	dilute	**DEINSU**	indues	**DEIRSV** divers
DEIKRU	duiker	**DEILTW**	wilted		undies	drives
DEIKSS	kissed	**DEILWY**	dewily	**DEINSW**	widens	**DEIRSW** weirds
DEIKST	skited		widely		Widnes	**DEIRTV** divert
DEIKSV	skived		wieldy		Wisden	**DEISSS** disses
DEIKTT	kitted	**DEIMMR**	dimmer	**DEINSY**	Disney	**DEISST** deists
DEILLM	milled		rimmed		Sidney	desist
DEILLP	pilled	**DEIMMU**	medium		snidey	**DEISSU** disuse
DEILLT	lilted	**DEIMNO**	monied	**DEINSZ**	dizens	issued
	tilled	**DEIMNP**	impend	**DEINTT**	tinted	**DEISTU** duties
DEILLU	illude	**DEIMNR**	minder	**DEINTU**	dunite	suited
DEILLW	willed		remind		united	**DEISTV** divest
DEILMN	limned	**DEIMNS**	denims		untied	**DEISTW** widest
	milden	**DEIMNT**	minted	**DEINTW**	de Wint	**DEISVW** swived
DEILMO	meloid	**DEIMOR**	dormie		twined	**DEITTW** de Witt
	moiled		moider	**DEIOOR**	oroide	witted
DEILMP	dimple	**DEIMOW**	mowdie	**DEIOOV**	Oviedo	**DEIZZZ** zizzed
	limped	**DEIMPP**	pimped	**DEIOPR**	dopier	**DEJKNU** junked
DEILMR	milder	**DEIMPR**	primed		Pedro I	**DEJKOO** jooked
DEILMS	misled	**DEIMPW**	wimped		period	**DEJKOU** jouked
	slimed	**DEIMRS**	dermis	**DEIOPS**	poised	**DEJLLO** jolled
	smiled		dimers	**DEIORS**	dories	**DEJLOT** jolted
DEILMT	milted	**DEIMRT**	mitred	**DEIORT**	editor	**DEJLOW** jowled
DEILMW	mildew	**DEIMSS**	missed		rioted	**DEJMPU** jumped
DEILNN	linden	**DEIMST**	demist		tierod	**DEJOTT** jotted

DEJTTU jutted
DEKKOS dekkos
DEKLOO looked
DEKLRU lurked
DEKLSU sulked
DEKMNU Mukden
DEKMOS smoked
DEKNOR Kedron
DEKNOY donkey
DEKNOZ zonked
DEKNRU dunker
DEKOOR rooked
DEKOOS sooked
DEKOOT dooket
DEKOPS spoked
DEKORW worked
DEKORY yorked
DEKOST stoked
DEKOSU souked
DEKRUY duyker
DEKSTU tusked
DELLLO lolled
DELLLU lulled
DELLMU mulled
DELLOP polled
DELLOR rolled
DELLOT tolled
DELLOU duello
DELLOW Dowell
DELLPU pulled
DELLRU duller
DELLSU Dulles
DELLSW dwells
DELLWY lewdly
DELMNO dolmen
DELMOO loomed
DELMOR molder
DELMOS models / seldom
DELMOT molted
DELMOU module
DELMOY melody
DELMPU lumped / plumed
DELNOO noodle
DELNOR rondel
DELNOU louden / nodule
DELNOV Vondel
DELNOW Weldon
DELNRU nurled / rundle
DELNUY nudely
DELOOP looped / poodle / pooled
DELOOS loosed / oodles / soloed / sooled
DELOOT looted / toledo / tooled

DELOPP lopped
DELOPR polder
DELOPS sloped
DELOPU louped
DELOPW lowped / plowed
DELOPY deploy
DELORS Delors / resold / solder
DELORT retold
DELORU louder / loured
DELORW weldor
DELORY yodler
DELOSS dossel
DELOST oldest
DELOSU loused
DELOSV solved
DELOSW dowels / lowsed / slowed
DELOSY yodels / yodles
DELOTT dottel / dottle / lotted
DELOTU louted
DELOWY yowled
DELOYY doyley
DELPPU pulped
DELPRU drupel / purled
DELPSU pulsed
DELPTU duplet
DELPUX duplex
DELRUY rudely
DELSSU dulses
DELSTU lusted
DELSTV veldts
DELSTY styled
DEMMMU mummed
DEMMOS modems
DEMMPU mumped
DEMMSU summed
DEMNOO mooned
DEMNOR modern
DEMNOS demons
DEMOOR moored / roomed
DEMOOT mooted
DEMOOZ zoomed
DEMOPP mopped
DEMOPR romped
DEMOPS mopeds
DEMOPY yomped
DEMORR dormer
DEMORW wormed
DEMOST modest
DEMOTT domett
DEMPPU pumped

DEMPRU dumper
DEMPSU spumed
DEMRRU murder
DEMRSU demurs
DEMSSU mussed / sedums
DEMUZZ muzzed
DENNOS donnes
DENNOT Denton / tendon
DENNOU undone
DENNOW wonned
DENNPU punned
DENNRU dunner
DENNSU sunned
DENNTU tunned
DENOOS nodose / noosed / odeons
DENOOW wooden
DENOPR ponder
DENOPT Top End
DENORS drones / snored / sorned
DENORT rodent
DENORU undoer
DENORV vendor
DENORW downer / wonder
DENORY Rodney / yonder
DENOSS sondes
DENOST Donets / Ostend / stoned
DENOSU undoes
DENOSV devons
DENOSW endows / snowed
DENOSY doyens
DENOSZ dozens
DENOTW wonted
DENPRU pruned
DENPSS spends
DENPSU sendup / upends
DENPTU punted
DENRST trends
DENRSU nursed / sunder
DENRTU turned
DENRTY trendy
DENRUV Verdun
DENRUW undrew
DENSTU Undset
DENSUU unused
DENSUW sundew
DENSYY Sydney
DENTTU nutted
DEOOPP pooped
DEOORS rodeos / roosed

DEOORT rooted
DEOORV overdo
DEOOST De Soto / sooted
DEOOTT tooted
DEOPPP popped
DEOPPR dopper
DEOPPS sopped
DEOPPT topped
DEOPPW wopped
DEOPRS prosed / spored
DEOPRT deport / ported / redtop
DEOPRU poured / rouped
DEOPRV proved
DEOPRW powder
DEOPSS possed
DEOPST depots / despot / posted / stoped
DEOPSU pseudo
DEOPTT potted
DEOPTU pouted
DEOQTU quoted
DEORRS derros / orders
DEORRT retrod
DEORRU ordure
DEORRV drover
DEORRW reword
DEORSS dosers / dosser / sordes
DEORST Dorset / doters / sorted / stored / strode
DEORSU douser / roused / soured
DEORSV droves
DEORSW dowers / dowser / drowse
DEORSZ dozers
DEORTT dotter / rotted
DEORTU detour / routed / toured
DEORTW trowed
DEORTX dextro
DEORUV devour
DEOSSS dosses
DEOSST tossed
DEOSSU douses

	soused	**DFOOSU**	doofus	**DGORSU**	gourds	**DIKKOP**	dikkop
DEOSSW	dowses	**DGGNOU**	dugong	**DGOSTY**	stodgy	**DIKLNY**	kindly
DEOSTU	ousted		gundog	**DGOTUU**	dugout	**DIKLTU**	kidult
DEOSTV	stoved	**DGGRUY**	druggy	**DHIIPS**	hispid	**DIKMNU**	dinkum
DEOSTW	stowed	**DGHIIN**	hiding	**DHIISW**	widish	**DIKNNU**	unkind
DEOSUX	exodus	**DGHINY**	dinghy	**DHIJTU**	Judith	**DIKNOR**	Kidron
DEOSXY	desoxy	**DGHIST**	dights	**DHILOS**	Dhilos	**DIKNRS**	drinks
DEOTTT	totted	**DGHOOT**	hotdog		oldish	**DIKNSV**	Dvinsk
DEOTTU	touted	**DGHOSU**	doughs	**DHIMOS**	modish	**DIKOOS**	skidoo
DEOTUV	devout	**DGHOTU**	dought	**DHINOO**	Hindoo	**DILLMY**	mildly
DEOTUX	tuxedo	**DGHOUY**	doughy	**DHINSY**	shindy	**DILLRS**	drills
DEPPPU	pupped	**DGIIKN**	diking	**DHIOOT**	dhooti	**DILLSY**	idylls
DEPPSU	supped	**DGIILN**	idling	**DHIOPY**	hypoid	**DILLWY**	wildly
DEPPTU	tupped	**DGIINN**	dining	**DHIORR**	horrid	**DILMOR**	milord
DEPRRU	purred		indign	**DHIOST**	dhotis	**DILMOU**	idolum
DEPRSU	drupes	**DGIINO**	indigo	**DHIOSV**	dovish		moduli
	dupers	**DGIINP**	pidgin	**DHIOSY**	hyoids	**DILMPY**	dimply
	perdus	**DGIINR**	riding	**DHIRST**	thirds	**DILNNU**	dunlin
	prudes	**DGIINS**	siding	**DHIRSU**	rudish	**DILNTU**	indult
	pursed	**DGIINT**	tiding	**DHISTU**	dhutis	**DILNUU**	Ulundi
DEPRUY	dupery	**DGIINV**	diving	**DHISTW**	widths	**DILOPY**	dopily
DEPSSU	pseuds	**DGIIST**	digits	**DHLLOS**	dholls		ploidy
DEPSUY	pudsey	**DGIJOU**	judogi	**DHLOPU**	holdup	**DILOSS**	solids
DEPTTU	putted	**DGIKNY**	dyking		uphold	**DILOST**	stolid
DEPTUY	deputy	**DGILNO**	doling	**DHLOSU**	should	**DILOXY**	xyloid
DERRSU	Durrës	**DGILOT**	diglot	**DHLTUU**	Duluth	**DILOYZ**	dozily
DERRSY	dryers	**DGILSU**	guilds	**DHNOOU**	Houdon	**DIMNOO**	domino
DERRTV	Rt Revd	**DGIMNO**	doming	**DHNORT**	Northd	**DIMNOR**	nimrod
DERRUY	rudery	**DGIMOO**	omigod	**DHNOSU**	hounds	**DIMNRU**	Nimrud
DERSSU	druses	**DGIMTU**	midgut		Hudson	**DIMNSU**	nudism
	duress	**DGINOP**	doping		unshod	**DIMOPU**	podium
DERSSY	dressy		pongid	**DHOOOO**	hoodoo	**DIMOSU**	sodium
DERSTU	duster	**DGINOR**	roding	**DHOORS**	Rhodos	**DIMOSW**	wisdom
	rudest	**DGINOS**	doings		Ródhos	**DIMOSY**	disomy
	rusted		dosing	**DHOORT**	hotrod	**DIMPSY**	dimpsy
DERSTY	dryest	**DGINOT**	doting	**DHORSU**	shroud	**DIMRSU**	mudirs
DERTTU	rutted	**DGINOU**	guidon	**DHORSY**	hydros	**DINNUW**	unwind
DESSSU	sussed	**DGINOW**	dowing	**DHORTU**	drouth	**DINOOR**	indoor
DESTUV	duvets		Godwin	**DHOSSW**	showds	**DINOPS**	poinds
DETTTU	tutted	**DGINOZ**	dozing	**DIIJNN**	djinni	**DINOPU**	dupion
DFGGOO	fogdog	**DGINPU**	duping	**DIILMP**	limpid		unipod
DFGIIR	frigid	**DGINRS**	grinds	**DIILOP**	lipoid	**DINORU**	durion
DFGILU	fulgid	**DGINRU**	during	**DIILOS**	solidi	**DINOSU**	Dunois
DFIINY	nidify	**DGINRY**	drying	**DIILPS**	lipids	**DINOSW**	disown
DFIIRT	trifid	**DGIOTW**	godwit	**DIILQU**	liquid	**DINOTZ**	Dönitz
DFILNO	infold	**DGIRSU**	Sigurd	**DIILST**	distil	**DINOWW**	window
DFILOR	florid	**DGIRTU**	turgid	**DIILTY**	tidily	**DINPSU**	Pindus
DFILSU	fluids	**DGLOOU**	duolog	**DIIMNU**	indium	**DINPTU**	pundit
DFIMOY	modify	**DGLOOY**	goodly	**DIIMOS**	idioms	**DINPUW**	upwind
DFINSU	fundis	**DGLSUY**	sludgy		iodism		windup
DFIORS	fiords	**DGMSUY**	smudgy	**DIIMOU**	oidium	**DINRUU**	Urundi
DFIRST	drifts	**DGNOOR**	Dorgon	**DIIMTW**	dimwit	**DINSTU**	nudist
DFIRTY	drifty		drongo	**DIIMTY**	dimity	**DINTUV**	nudity
DFJORS	fjords		Gordon	**DIINOX**	dioxin		untidy
DFLNOU	unfold		Grodno	**DIINRS**	indris	**DIOOPP**	doppio
DFLNOY	fondly	**DGNOOS**	godson	**DIIOOP**	opioid	**DIOOPS**	isopod
DFLOOS	floods	**DGNOOU**	Gounod	**DIIORV**	viroid	**DIOORT**	toroid
DFLORU	Rudolf	**DGNOOW**	godown	**DIIOST**	idiots	**DIOOST**	ootids
DFNORS	fronds	**DGNORU**	ground	**DIIOTT**	doitit	**DIOOSU**	iodous
DFNOSU	founds	**DGNOSU**	sundog	**DIJMSU**	musjid		odious
DFNSUU	fundus		sun-god	**DIJNNY**	djinny	**DIOOSV**	ovoids
DFOORX	oxford	**DGNRUU**	Gudrun	**DIKKLU**	kudlik	**DIOOSZ**	zooids

DIOOTX	toxoid		untrod	EEELNV	eleven	EEFLLR	feller
DIOPRT	torpid	DNOSSU	sounds	EEELPR	peeler	EEFLNN	fennel
	tripod	DNOSSY	synods	EEELRR	reeler	EEFLNS	flense
DIORRT	torrid	DNOSTU	donuts	EEELSS	lessee	EEFLRS	fleers
DIORST	droits		stound	EEELST	Steele	EEFLRT	reflet
DIOSTT	dittos	DNOSUW	swound	EEELSV	levees		telfer
DIOSTU	studio		wounds		sleeve		Terfel
DIOSTV	divots	DNOSUZ	zounds	EEELSY	Elysée	EEFLRU	ferule
DIOSWW	widows	DNOTTU	Dutton	EEELTV	eyelet		fueler
DIPPRY	drippy	DNRSUY	sundry	EEEMMS	sememe		refuel
DIPRTU	putrid	DOOOOV	voodoo	EEEMNR	meneer	EEFLRW	Werfel
DIPSTU	stupid	DOOPRS	droops	EEEMRS	seemer	EEFLRX	reflex
DIQSSU	squids	DOOPRU	uropod	EEEMRT	meeter	EEFLRY	freely
DIRSUZ	durzis	DOOPRY	droopy		teemer	EEFLST	fleets
DJNNOO	donjon	DOORSU	odours	EEEMST	esteem	EEFLSX	flexes
DKNOOP	pondok	DOOSWY	woodsy		mestee	EEFLTT	fettle
DKNOOS	donkos	DOPRSY	dropsy	EEENRS	serene	EEFLUY	eyeful
	kondos	DORSSW	swords	EEENRT	entree	EEFMMS	femmes
DKNRSU	drunks	DORSSY	drossy		eterne	EEFMNO	foemen
DKOOOO	koodoo	DORSTU	stroud		retene	EEFPRR	prefer
DKOORS	drooks	DORSWY	drowsy	EEENRV	evener	EEFPTY	tepefy
DKORSU	drouks	DPSTUU	dustup		veneer	EEFRRS	refers
DKORSY	drosky	DRSTUY	sturdy	EEENSS	Essene	EEFRRT	ferret
DLLOOP	dollop	EEEEPT	teepee	EEENSZ	sneeze	EEFRST	fester
DLLORY	drolly	EEEEPW	peewee	EEEOPP	epopee		freest
	lordly	EEEEWW	weewee	EEEPPR	peeper	EEFRSU	refuse
DLLOUW	Ludlow	EEEFFT	effete	EEEPRV	peever	EEFRSV	fevers
DLLOUY	loudly	EEEFLR	feeler	EEEPRW	weeper	EEFRTT	fetter
DLMNOO	Lomond	EEEFRR	reefer	EEEPST	tepees	EEFRTU	refute
DLMOSU	moulds	EEEFRZ	freeze	EEEPSV	peeves	EEFSSS	fesses
DLMOUY	mouldy	EEEFSZ	feezes	EEEPSW	pewees	EEFSSU	fusees
DLNNOO	London	EEEGMR	emerge	EEERRV	revere	EEFSTW	fewest
DLNOPU	Dunlop	EEEGNR	Greene	EEERSV	reeves	EEFSUZ	fuzees
DLNOSU	unsold		renege		severe	EEFSZZ	fezzes
DLNOTU	untold	EEEGNU	Eugène	EEERTT	teeter	EEGGGI	geggie
DLNOUV	Völund	EEEGNV	Genève		terete	EEGGIN	geeing
DLNUUY	unduly	EEEGRS	Seeger	EEERTV	Tevere	EEGGIR	Geiger
DLOOPS	podsol	EEEGRZ	geezer	EEERTX	Exeter		greige
DLOOPZ	podzol	EEEHLR	heeler	EEERVW	weever	EEGGIV	veggie
DLOORS	drools		reheel	EEESTT	settee	EEGGLR	eggler
DLOORU	dolour	EEEHNS	Sheene	EEESTV	steeve	EEGGOR	George
DLORSW	worlds	EEEHNT	ethene	EEETWZ	tweeze	EEGGRS	eggers
DLORUY	dourly	EEEHST	seethe	EEFFIL	Eiffel	EEGGSV	vegges
DMMRUY	drummy	EEEHTT	teethe	EEFFOT	toffee	EEGHNS	henges
DMNOOR	dromon	EEEHWZ	wheeze	EEFFSU	effuse	EEGHOT	Goethe
DMNOOY	monody	EEEIJL	jeelie	EEFGIN	feeing	EEGIIK	Geikie
DMNOSU	mounds	EEEIKL	keelie	EEFGRU	refuge	EEGILS	lieges
	osmund	EEEILS	seelie	EEFHIR	heifer	EEGIMR	emigre
DMNOTU	Du Mont	EEEINW	weenie	EEFHOR	hereof		regime
DMOOSS	sodoms	EEEIPR	peerie	EEFHRT	hefter	EEGINN	engine
DMOOSY	sodomy	EEEIRR	eerier	EEFILN	feline	EEGINP	peeing
DMORSU	dorsum	EEEJRR	jeerer		fleein	EEGINS	genies
DNNOOU	Dunoon	EEEKLU	ekuele	EEFILR	ferlie		seeing
DNOORS	donors	EEEKMR	meeker		refile		Siegen
	rondos	EEEKNR	keener		relief	EEGINT	teeing
DNOOSS	snoods	EEEKNT	ketene	EEFINR	ferine	EEGINW	weeing
DNOOSU	nodous	EEEKPR	keeper		refine	EEGINY	eyeing
DNOOSW	Dowson	EEEKRS	seeker	EEFINW	Newfie	EEGIRV	grieve
DNOPSU	pounds	EEELMS	melees	EEFIRR	refire	EEGISS	sieges
DNORSU	rounds		Semele	EEFIRS	fieres	EEGKLR	kegler
DNORSW	drowns	EEELMX	lexeme	EEFIRZ	frieze	EEGLMN	legmen
DNORTU	rotund	EEELNS	Selene	EEFLLO	felloe	EEGLMU	legume

EEGLNS	Engels	**EEHLWY**	wheely	**EEIKSS**	eskies	**EEINSV**	envies
EEGLNT	gentle	**EEHMMR**	hemmer	**EEILLL**	Lillee		nieves
EEGLNU	lungee	**EEHMNP**	hempen	**EEILMS**	elemis	**EEINSX**	exines
EEGLRT	reglet	**EEHMNS**	enmesh		Méliès	**EEINTT**	nettie
EEGLRU	reglue	**EEHMPT**	tempeh	**EEILNP**	penile	**EEINTV**	venite
EEGLST	gleets	**EEHMRS**	Hermes	**EEILNR**	lierne	**EEINTX**	extine
EEGLTY	gleety		rehems		reline	**EEINTZ**	Iténez
EEGMNO	genome	**EEHMSS**	meshes	**EEILNS**	enisle	**EEIORS**	soiree
EEGMNR	germen	**EEHMST**	themes		ensile	**EEIPPT**	tippee
EEGMNT	tegmen	**EEHMUX**	exhume		senile	**EEIPPY**	yippee
EEGMOT	gemote	**EEHNOR**	hereon		silene	**EEIPQU**	equipe
EEGMRR	merger	**EEHNOX**	hexone	**EEILOR**	loerie	**EEIPRR**	Pierre
EEGMRS	merges	**EEHNPS**	sphene	**EEILPT**	pelite	**EEIPRS**	espier
EEGNNT	gennet	**EEHNPW**	nephew	**EEILRS**	relies	**EEIPRT**	Peter I
EEGNOP	pongee	**EEHNRT**	nether		resile		Petrie
EEGNRS	genres	**EEHNRZ**	Herzen	**EEILRV**	levier	**EEIPRX**	expire
	greens	**EEHNSS**	sheens		relive	**EEIPSS**	espies
EEGNRT	gerent	**EEHNSY**	sheeny		revile	**EEIPTT**	petite
	regent	**EEHNTV**	ethyne		veiler	**EEIPTW**	peewit
EEGNRY	energy	**EEHNWW**	whenwe	**EEILRY**	eerily	**EEIRRS**	sirree
	greeny	**EEHOPS**	sheepo	**EEILST**	elites	**EEIRRT**	etrier
	Ygerne	**EEHORS**	heroes	**EEILSV**	levies		retire
EEGNST	genets		reshoe	**EEILSW**	Wiesel	**EEIRRV**	reiver
	gentes	**EEHORT**	hereto	**EEILSX**	exiles	**EEIRRW**	rewire
EEGNSV	venges		hetero		ilexes	**EEIRSS**	seiser
EEGPRU	pugree		Hotere	**EEILTV**	levite		series
EEGRRT	regret	**EEHOSX**	hexose	**EEILVW**	weevil	**EEIRST**	resite
EEGRRV	verger	**EEHOTW**	towhee	**EEILZZ**	lezzie		reties
EEGRRW	regrew	**EEHPPR**	hepper	**EEIMMN**	Eminem		Steier
EEGRRY	greyer	**EEHPRS**	herpes	**EEIMNN**	Niemen	**EEIRSV**	reives
EEGRSS	egress		sphere	**EEIMNP**	piemen		revise
EEGRST	egrets	**EEHPRT**	threep	**EEIMNR**	ermine	**EEIRSX**	sexier
	greets	**EEHRSS**	reshes	**EEIMNT**	emetin	**EEIRSY**	eyries
EEGRSV	verges		sheers	**EEIMNY**	Yemeni	**EEIRTV**	verite
EEGRSX	grexes	**EEHRST**	Esther	**EEIMPR**	empire	**EEIRVV**	revive
EEGRSY	geyser		threes		epimer	**EEIRVW**	review
EEGRTT	getter	**EEHRSW**	hewers		permie		viewer
EEGRUZ	Greuze		shewer		premie	**EEISSS**	seises
EEGSST	egests		wheres	**EEIMRS**	Mieres	**EEISSV**	sieves
	geests	**EEHRSX**	hexers		misere	**EEISSY**	Sieyès
	gestes	**EEHRSY**	heresy		remise	**EEISSZ**	seizes
EEGSSU	segues	**EEHRTT**	tether	**EEIMRT**	metier	**EEISTV**	evites
EEHHSS	sheesh	**EEHRTW**	wether		tremie	**EEITTW**	wettie
EEHHSW	wheesh	**EEHSST**	sheets	**EEIMSS**	emesis	**EEITTY**	yettie
EEHINR	herein		theses	**EEINNP**	pinene	**EEJJNU**	jejune
	inhere	**EEHSVY**	Hevesy	**EEINNR**	nerine	**EEJKRR**	jerker
EEHINT	theine	**EEHWYY**	wheyey		Rennie	**EEJLSW**	jewels
EEHIRR	rehire	**EEHWYZ**	wheezy	**EEINNS**	Esenin	**EEJMOR**	Jerome
EEHIRT	either	**EEIIKK**	kiekie	**EEINNV**	Vienne	**EEJNNR**	Jenner
EEHIST	sithee	**EEIILM**	mielie	**EEINOS**	eosine	**EEJNNS**	Jensen
EEHITV	thieve	**EEIIMN**	meinie	**EEINPR**	repine	**EEJNNT**	jennet
EEHKLS	shekel	**EEIINW**	wienie	**EEINQU**	equine	**EEJRST**	jester
EEHLLN	Hellen	**EEIJNN**	jinnee	**EEINRS**	nereis	**EEJRSY**	jersey
EEHLLR	heller	**EEIJSS**	jessie		serein	**EEJSSS**	jesses
EEHLLS	Helles	**EEIJST**	eejits		serine	**EEJSSW**	Jewess
EEHLMR	helmer	**EEIJSW**	jewies	**EEINRT**	entire	**EEKKLR**	lekker
EEHLMT	helmet	**EEIKLP**	kelpie		triene	**EEKKNO**	koneke
EEHLPR	helper	**EEIKLS**	selkie	**EEINRV**	envier	**EEKLLR**	Keller
EEHLQS	sheqel	**EEIKLT**	Keitel		Nièvre	**EEKLMY**	meekly
EEHLSV	helves	**EEIKPW**	kewpie	**EEINRW**	wiener	**EEKLNN**	kennel
	shelve	**EEIKRS**	seiker	**EEINSS**	Neisse	**EEKLNR**	kernel
EEHLSW	wheels				seines	**EEKLNS**	kneels

EEKLNY	keenly	EELNRU	unreel	EEMNNP	penmen		nester
EEKLPR	Kepler	EELNSS	lenses	EEMNOR	moreen		resent
EEKLRS	kerels		lessen	EEMNOT	toneme		Sterne
EEKLRT	kelter	EELNST	nestle	EEMNOY	yeomen		tenser
EEKLRW	kewler	EELNSV	Velsen	EEMNSS	menses	EENRSU	ensure
EEKLSS	sleeks	EELNSW	newels	EEMNSU	neumes		enures
EEKLSV	kevels	EELNTT	nettle	EEMNTU	unmeet		Nereus
EEKLSY	sleeky	EELNTU	eluent	EEMNYZ	enzyme	EENRSV	nerves
EEKLTT	kettle	EELNUV	Leuven	EEMOPT	metope		Nevers
EEKLWY	weekly		venule	EEMORS	Oresme		Severn
EEKMNS	Meknès	EELNVY	Evelyn	EEMORT	emoter	EENRSW	renews
EEKMRR	Kremer		evenly		meteor	EENRSY	sneery
EEKMRS	kermes	EELNXY	xylene		remote	EENRTT	tenter
EEKNOT	ketone	EELOPP	people	EEMORV	remove	EENRTU	neuter
EEKNRR	renker	EELOPR	eloper	EEMOST	emotes		retune
EEKNRS	kernes	EELOPS	elopes	EEMPRS	sempre		tenure
EEKNST	kentes	EELORS	resole	EEMPRT	temper		tureen
EEKNSY	Keynes	EELORZ	Lozère	EEMPRY	empery	EENRTV	venter
EEKORV	evoker	EELOVV	evolve	EEMPTX	exempt	EENRTX	extern
	revoke	EELPPU	peepul	EEMRRT	termer	EENRVY	venery
EEKORW	rewoke	EELPRS	lepers	EEMRRU	murree	EENSSS	nesses
EEKOST	ketose		repels	EEMRSS	merses		senses
EEKOSV	evokes	EELPRT	pelter	EEMRST	merest	EENSST	tenses
EEKPPU	upkeep		petrel		mester	EENSSU	ensues
EEKPRU	peruke	EELPRY	yelper		meters	EENSSV	sevens
EEKRSS	eskers	EELPSS	sleeps		metres	EENSSW	sewens
EEKRSW	skewer		speels	EEMRSU	resume	EENSTT	tenets
	Wesker	EELPST	pestle		Semeru	EENSTU	tenues
EEKRSY	kersey	EELPSU	Peleus	EEMRSV	vermes	EENSTV	events
	rekeys	EELPSV	pelves	EEMRSY	Mersey	EENSTW	newest
EELLPS	Pelles	EELPSX	expels	EEMRTU	Meerut	EENSUV	venues
EELLPT	pellet	EELPSY	sleepy	EEMSSS	messes	EENSVW	sweven
EELLRS	resell	EELQSU	sequel	EEMSTU	mustee	EENSWY	sweeny
	seller	EELRSS	lesser	EENNOO	Oenone		weensy
EELLRT	retell	EELRST	relets	EENNPY	Penney	EENSYZ	sneezy
	teller		streel	EENNRS	rennes	EENTTX	extent
EELLRY	yeller	EELRSV	elvers	EENNRT	rennet	EENTUX	exeunt
EELLSV	levels		levers		tenner	EENTWY	tweeny
EELLSW	Sewell		revels	EENNST	sennet	EEOOTT	toetoe
	Welles	EELRTT	letter	EENNSU	unseen	EEOPRS	repose
EELMOT	omelet	EELRTU	Teruel	EENNUV	uneven	EEOPRU	Europe
EELMPR	Lemper	EELRTW	welter	EENNUY	ennuye	EEOPST	topees
EELMPT	pelmet	EELRUV	velure	EENOPR	opener	EEOPSX	expose
	temple	EELSST	sleets		reopen	EEOPTU	toupee
EELMRS	merles		steels		repone	EEOPTY	peyote
EELMRT	melter		steles	EENOPT	poteen	EEORST	stereo
	remelt	EELSSV	selves	EENORS	Orense	EEORSV	soever
EELMRU	relume		vessel	EENORZ	rezone	EEORSZ	zeroes
EELMRW	mewler	EELSTT	settle	EENOSV	venose	EEORTV	vetoer
EELMRY	merely	EELSTU	elutes	EENOTV	Veneto	EEORUV	oeuvre
EELMSY	seemly	EELSTV	svelte	EENOTW	townee	EEOSST	setose
EELMTT	mettle	EELSTY	sleety	EENOVZ	evzone	EEOSSV	Seveso
EELMTY	meetly		steely	EENPRS	nepers	EEOSTV	vetoes
EELNNT	lenten	EELSWY	Wesley		preens	EEOSXY	oxeyes
EELNNV	vennel	EELTTZ	Tetzel	EENPRT	repent	EEPPPR	pepper
EELNOS	leones	EELTVV	velvet	EENPRY	pyrene	EEPPST	steppe
EELNOV	elevon	EELTVW	twelve	EENPSU	Peneus	EEPPRY	preyer
EELNPS	pensel	EELTWY	tweely	EENQSU	queens	EEPRSS	speers
	spleen	EEMMNO	moneme	EENRRT	renter		sprees
EELNPV	Pleven	EEMMNR	mermen	EENRRW	Werner	EEPRST	pester
EELNRR	Lerner	EEMMRY	yemmer	EENRSS	sneers		peters
EELNRT	relent	EEMMST	emmets	EENRST	enters		preset

	Streep	**EERTUY**	tuyere	**EFHLSS**	shelfs	**EFIRST**	refits
EEPRSU	peruse	**EERTVV**	vervet	**EFHLSY**	fleshy		sifter
	purees	**EERTVX**	vertex	**EFHOOR**	hoofer		strife
	rupees	**EERUVX**	Évreux	**EFHRRU**	fuhrer	**EFIRSU**	furies
EEPRSV	perves	**EESSTT**	sestet	**EFHSTT**	thefts		surfie
	vesper		testes	**EFIINT**	finite	**EFIRSV**	fivers
EEPRSW	spewer	**EESSTW**	sweets	**EFIKLO**	folkie	**EFIRSX**	fixers
EEPRSY	Speyer	**EESSWX**	Wessex	**EFIKNO**	Fokine	**EFIRTT**	fitter
EEPRTT	petter	**EESTTU**	suttee	**EFIKNR**	knifer		titfer
EEPRTU	repute		tutees	**EFIKNS**	knifes	**EFIRTY**	ferity
EEPRTW	pewter	**EESTTW**	tweets	**EFIKSV**	five Ks	**EFIRVY**	verify
EEPRTX	expert	**EESTTX**	sextet	**EFILLR**	filler	**EFIRZZ**	fizzer
EEPRTY	retype	**EFFFOS**	feoffs		refill	**EFISTY**	feisty
EEPRUV	prevue	**EFFGIN**	effing	**EFILLT**	fillet	**EFISZZ**	fizzes
EEPSST	steeps	**EFFGIR**	griffe	**EFILMR**	refilm	**EFKKOR**	Fokker
EEPSSW	sweeps	**EFFGIY**	effigy	**EFILNO**	olefin	**EFKLSS**	skelfs
EEPSTT	septet	**EFFGOR**	goffer	**EFILNY**	finely	**EFKLSU**	flukes
EEPSWY	sweepy	**EFFIIR**	iffier	**EFILOS**	filose	**EFKLUY**	flukey
EEPTTU	puttee	**EFFILP**	piffle	**EFILOU**	foulie	**EFKNRU**	funker
EEQRSU	queers	**EFFILR**	riffle	**EFILPP**	fipple	**EFLLOT**	flotel
EEQSUU	queues	**EFFILY**	Liffey	**EFILPR**	pilfer	**EFLLOW**	fellow
EERRST	rester	**EFFIMO**	moffie	**EFILRR**	rifler	**EFLLRU**	fuller
	terser	**EFFIRS**	fifers	**EFILRS**	filers	**EFLMNY**	flymen
EERRSV	revers	**EFFJOR**	Joffre		fliers	**EFLMSU**	flumes
	server	**EFFKOY**	offkey		lifers	**EFLMSY**	myself
EERRTT	terret	**EFFLMU**	muffle		rifles	**EFLNNU**	funnel
EERRTU	Reuter	**EFFLRU**	ruffle	**EFILRT**	filter	**EFLNOS**	felons
	ureter	**EFFLUX**	efflux		lifter	**EFLNOY**	felony
EERRTV	revert	**EFFOPU**	pouffe		trifle	**EFLNTU**	fluent
EERRVY	revery	**EFFORS**	offers	**EFILRU**	ireful		unfelt
EERSST	esters		reffos	**EFILRY**	rifely	**EFLOOT**	footle
	reests	**EFFORT**	effort	**EFILST**	filets	**EFLOOZ**	foozle
	resets	**EFFORX**	forfex		flites	**EFLORR**	Ferrol
	steers	**EFFOST**	offset		itself	**EFLORS**	Flores
	steres		setoff		stifle	**EFLORT**	floret
EERSSU	reuses	**EFFPRU**	puffer	**EFILSU**	Fuseli		lofter
EERSSV	serves	**EFFRSU**	ruffes		fusile	**EFLORU**	fouler
	severs		suffer	**EFILTU**	futile	**EFLORW**	flower
	verses	**EFFTTU**	tuffet	**EFILWY**	wifely		fowler
EERSSW	sewers	**EFGGRU**	Fugger	**EFILZZ**	fizzle		wolfer
	sweers	**EFGINR**	finger	**EFIMRR**	firmer	**EFLORX**	flexor
EERSTT	retest		fringe	**EFIMRS**	fermis	**EFLORY**	Florey
	setter	**EFGINS**	feigns	**EFINNR**	finner	**EFLOSW**	Fowles
	street	**EFGINT**	feting	**EFINNS**	Finsen	**EFLOSY**	foleys
	tester	**EFGIOS**	fogies	**EFINNY**	Finney	**EFLOUW**	woeful
EERSTU	retuse	**EFGIRS**	griefs	**EFINPR**	perfin	**EFLPRU**	purfle
	Tereus	**EFGIRU**	figure	**EFINRR**	Fenrir	**EFLRRU**	furler
EERSTV	everts	**EFGLNU**	engulf	**EFINRS**	infers	**EFLRSY**	flyers
	revest	**EFGLOR**	golfer	**EFINRY**	finery	**EFLRTU**	fluter
	revets	**EFGOOR**	forego	**EFINST**	feints	**EFLRUU**	rueful
	Trèves	**EFGORR**	forger		finest	**EFLRUX**	reflux
EERSTW	wester	**EFGORS**	forges		infest	**EFLRUY**	fleury
EERSTX	exerts		gofers	**EFINSU**	infuse	**EFLSTU**	flutes
	exsert	**EFGORT**	forget	**EFIOOT**	footie	**EFLSTY**	flyest
EERSTY	yester	**EFGOSY**	fogeys	**EFIOPT**	Petöfi		flytes
EERSTZ	zester	**EFGRSU**	Fergus	**EFIORX**	foxier	**EFLSUU**	useful
EERSUV	revues	**EFGSUU**	fugues	**EFIOST**	softie	**EFLSUX**	fluxes
EERSVU	swerve	**EFHILS**	elfish	**EFIOSX**	foxies	**EFMNOT**	foment
EERSVX	vexers	**EFHIRS**	fisher	**EFIPRX**	prefix	**EFMNRU**	frenum
EERTTT	tetter		sherif	**EFIRRS**	firers	**EFMORR**	Fermor
EERTTW	wetter	**EFHISS**	fishes		friers		former
EERTTX	texter	**EFHIST**	fetish	**EFIRSS**	serifs		reform

EFMORS	formes	EGGLOR	logger	EGIILT	Ligeti	EGINPP	Epping
EFMRSU	femurs	EGGLOT	goglet	EGIIMN	gemini		pigpen
	fumers		toggle	EGIINP	pieing	EGINPR	pinger
EFMSTU	fumets	EGGLOW	woggle	EGIINT	ignite	EGINPS	genips
EFMTUY	tumefy	EGGLRU	gurgle	EGIJLN	jingle	EGINRR	erring
EFNNOT	Fenton		lugger	EGIJNW	jewing		ringer
EFNORS	Fresno	EGGLTU	guglet	EGIJRS	rejigs	EGINRS	Ingres
EFNORZ	frozen	EGGMRU	mugger	EGIKLS	kliegs		reigns
EFNOST	Sefton	EGGNRU	grunge	EGIKNP	Peking		resign
	soften	EGGNSU	gunges	EGIKNY	keying		sering
EFNRUZ	Frunze	EGGNTU	nugget	EGIKRS	grikes		signer
EFNRYZ	frenzy	EGGOPS	pogges	EGIKRS	grikes		singer
EFOORR	reroof	EGGORR	gorger	EGILLR	grille	EGINRW	Wigner
	roofer	EGGORS	gorges	EGILLU	ligule		winger
EFOORT	foetor	EGGORT	gorget	EGILMN	mingle	EGINSS	gneiss
	footer		togger	EGILMP	megilp		singes
EFOORW	woofer	EGGORU	gouger	EGILMS	gimels	EGINST	ingest
EFOQUU	Fouqué	EGGOSU	gouges	EGILMT	gimlet		signet
EFORRU	furore	EGGPRY	preggy	EGILNN	ginnel		tinges
EFORRV	fervor	EGGRRU	rugger	EGILNO	eloign	EGINSU	genius
EFORST	fetors	EGGRTU	tugger		legion	EGINSV	givens
	forest	EGHHIR	higher	EGILNP	Li Peng	EGINSW	sewing
	fortes	EGHHIT	eighth	EGILNR	linger		swinge
	foster		height	EGILNS	ingles	EGINSX	sexing
	softer	EGHHSU	Hughes		single	EGINTU	gunite
EFORSY	foyers		sheugh	EGILNT	tingle	EGINTW	twinge
EFORTU	fouter	EGHIIN	hieing	EGILOO	goolie	EGINVX	vexing
EFOSSS	fosses	EGHILN	heling	EGILOR	logier	EGIOOR	gooier
EFOSTU	foetus	EGHILS	sleigh	EGILPT	piglet		goorie
EFRRSU	surfer	EGHINO	hoeing	EGILRS	grilse	EGIOPS	pogies
EFRRSY	fryers	EGHINR	Hering		ligers	EGIORR	gorier
EFRRTU	Erfurt	EGHINS	hinges	EGILRU	gluier	EGIORS	orgies
	returf		neighs		ligure	EGIORT	goiter
EFRSSU	fusser	EGHINW	hewing		reguli		goitre
EFRTTU	tufter		whinge		uglier	EGIOST	egoist
EFRTUU	future	EGHINX	hexing	EGILRV	Vergil	EGIOSV	ogives
EFSSSU	fusses	EGHIOT	hogtie	EGILST	gilets	EGIPPR	grippe
EFSUZZ	fuzzes	EGHIRS	sigher		legist	EGIPRR	griper
EGGGIL	giggle	EGHIST	eights	EGILSU	guiles	EGIPRS	gripes
EGGGIN	egging	EGHISW	weighs		uglies	EGIRST	tigers
EGGGLO	goggle	EGHITW	weight	EGILTU	glutei	EGIRSU	guiser
EGGGNO	eggnog	EGHITY	eighty	EGIMMR	megrim		regius
EGGHIL	higgle	EGHLMP	phlegm	EGIMNR	mering	EGIRSV	givers
EGGHOR	hogger	EGHLNT	length		minger	EGIRTV	grivet
EGGHOT	hogget	EGHLPU	Guelph	EGIMNS	minges	EGISSU	guises
EGGHRU	hugger		pleugh	EGIMNT	meting	EGJLNU	jungle
EGGIIN	gieing	EGHLUV	hugely	EGIMNW	mewing	EGKMNO	Mekong
EGGIJL	jiggle	EGHMMO	megohm	EGIMNZ	Mengzi	EGKMSU	muskeg
EGGIJR	jigger	EGHNOS	Goshen	EGIMOS	egoism	EGKRRU	Kruger
EGGILN	niggle	EGHNOU	enough	EGIMPU	guimpe	EGKRSY	grykes
EGGILO	loggie	EGHNPU	Penghu	EGIMPY	gympie	EGLLTU	gullet
EGGILR	ligger	EGHNRU	hunger	EGIMRS	grimes	EGLLUY	gulley
EGGILW	wiggle		rehung	EGINNR	ginner	EGLMOS	golems
EGGINR	ginger	EGHNST	thegns	EGINNS	ensign	EGLMSU	glumes
	nigger	EGHOPR	gopher	EGINOP	epigon	EGLNNU	gunnel
EGGIRR	rigger	EGHORZ	Herzog		pigeon	EGLNOR	longer
EGGIRW	wigger	EGHOTT	ghetto	EGINOR	eringo	EGLNOS	longes
EGGISU	gigues	EGHRSU	gusher		ignore	EGLNOU	lounge
EGGJLO	joggle	EGHSSU	gushes		Origen	EGLNPU	plunge
EGGJLU	juggle	EGHSTU	hugest		region	EGLNRU	lunger
EGGJOR	jogger	EGIILL	gillie	EGINOS	soigne	EGLNSU	gunsel
EGGLOO	google	EGIILR	girlie	EGINOT	toeing		lunges
				EGINOW	wigeon		

EGLNTU	englut	**EGOOOU**	Ogooué		holies	**EHIRTW**	whiter
	gluten	**EGOOPR**	pogoer		isohel		wither
EGLNTY	gently	**EGOORV**	groove	**EHILOT**	eolith		writhe
EGLOPR	proleg	**EGOOSS**	gooses	**EHILPR**	hirple	**EHIRTZ**	zither
EGLOPS	gospel	**EGOOST**	stooge	**EHILRS**	hirsel	**EHISSS**	hisses
EGLORS	oglers	**EGOOSY**	goosey		relish	**EHISST**	heists
EGLORU	regulo	**EGOPRR**	groper	**EHILRT**	Hitler		shiest
EGLORV	glover	**EGOPRS**	gropes	**EHILSS**	shiels		shites
	grovel	**EGOPSY**	pogeys	**EHILSV**	elvish		thesis
EGLORW	glower	**EGORRS**	rogers	**EHILSW**	whiles	**EHISSV**	shives
EGLOSV	gloves	**EGORRW**	grower	**EHIMMS**	immesh	**EHISSW**	wishes
EGLOSZ	glozes		regrow	**EHIMNR**	menhir	**EHISTT**	theist
EGLOUY	eulogy	**EGORSS**	gorses	**EHIMNS**	inmesh		Thetis
EGLPRU	gulper		ogress	**EHIMNU**	inhume		tithes
EGLRSU	gluers	**EGORST**	goster	**EHIMOR**	homier	**EHISTW**	whites
	gruels	**EGORSU**	grouse	**EHIMOS**	homies		withes
	lugers		rogues	**EHIMRS**	Rheims	**EHITTW**	Hewitt
EGLRYV	greyly		rouges	**EHIMRT**	hermit	**EHITWY**	whitey
EGLUZZ	guzzle		rugose		mither	**EHJLMU**	Jhelum
EGMNNU	gunmen	**EGORSV**	groves	**EHIMRU**	humeri	**EHJOOR**	Johore
EGMNOO	mongoe	**EGORSY**	gyrose	**EHIMST**	theism	**EHJOPS**	joseph
EGMNOR	monger	**EGORTV**	grovet		Themis	**EHJORS**	josher
	morgen	**EGOSSV**	Vosges	**EHINOR**	heroin	**EHJORT**	Jethro
EGMNOS	genoms	**EGOSTY**	stogey	**EHINOT**	Hotien	**EHJOSS**	joshes
	gnomes	**EGOSUV**	vouges	**EHINPX**	phenix	**EHKLOR**	Köhler
EGMNOT	Egmont	**EGOSYZ**	zygose	**EHINRS**	shiner	**EHKLPT**	klepht
EGMNOU	eumong	**EGOTYZ**	zygote		shrine	**EHKLSW**	whelks
EGMNTU	nutmeg	**EGPRRU**	purger	**EHINRT**	hinter	**EHKLWY**	whelky
EGMNUU	eumung	**EGPRSU**	purges		nither	**EHKNOR**	honker
EGMOOS	smooge		spurge	**EHINRW**	whiner	**EHKNRU**	hunker
EGMORU	morgue	**EGPSSU**	speugs	**EHINRY**	Henry I	**EHKOOR**	hooker
EGMOST	gemots	**EGPSTU**	getups	**EHINSS**	Shensi	**EHKOOY**	hookey
EGMRTU	tergum	**EGRRSU**	surger		shines	**EHKORS**	kosher
EGNNOO	nonego		urgers	**EHINSW**	newish	**EHKORY**	horkey
EGNNOS	ennogs	**EGRSSU**	surges		whines	**EHKPTU**	Phuket
EGNNOU	guenon	**EGRSTU**	gutser	**EHINTW**	whiten	**EHKRSU**	husker
EGNNRU	gunner	**EGRTTU**	gutter	**EHINTZ**	zenith	**EHLLOR**	holler
EGNOOR	Oregon	**EGSSTU**	guests	**EHIOPR**	ephori	**EHLLOS**	hellos
	orgone		gusset	**EHIOPT**	ophite	**EHLLRU**	huller
EGNOOT	gentoo	**EHHIKS**	sheikh	**EHIORS**	hosier	**EHLLSS**	shells
EGNOOY	gooney	**EHHIRT**	hither	**EHIORT**	heriot	**EHLLSY**	shelly
EGNOPS	pengos	**EHHISW**	Hewish	**EHIOST**	hostie	**EHLMMU**	hummel
	sponge	**EHHNPY**	hyphen	**EHIOTT**	hottie	**EHLMNU**	unhelm
EGNORS	goners	**EHHRST**	thresh	**EHIPPR**	hipper	**EHLMOP**	phloem
	Negros	**EHHSSU**	hushes	**EHIPRS**	perish	**EHLMOS**	Holmes
EGNORV	govern	**EHIIJM**	Himeji		reship		mohels
EGNORY	eryngo	**EHIIPP**	hippie		seriph	**EHLMOY**	homely
	Geryon	**EHIIST**	Shiite	**EHIPSS**	pishes	**EHLMSW**	whelms
	groyne	**EHIKKS**	kishke	**EHIPSZ**	phizes	**EHLMTY**	methyl
EGNOSS	gnoses	**EHIKMV**	mikveh	**EHIRRS**	hirers	**EHLNOP**	holpen
EGNOTT	gotten	**EHIKRS**	hikers	**EHIRSS**	hisser		phenol
EGNOTU	tongue		shriek		shiers	**EHLNPY**	phenyl
EGNOXY	oxygen		shrike		shires	**EHLOOY**	hooley
EGNPPU	Pengpu	**EHIKSS**	sheiks	**EHIRST**	theirs	**EHLOPP**	hopple
EGNPRU	repugn	**EHILLL**	Hillel		Thiers	**EHLORW**	howler
EGNPSU	unpegs	**EHILLR**	hiller	**EHIRSV**	shiver		Wöhler
EGNRTU	gunter	**EHILMO**	Elohim		shrive	**EHLOSS**	Sholes
	gurnet	**EHILMU**	helium	**EHIRSW**	wisher	**EHLOST**	helots
	urgent	**EHILNN**	Linnhe	**EHIRSX**	rhexis		hostel
EGNRTY	gentry	**EHILOO**	hoolie	**EHIRTT**	hitter		hotels
EGNRUY	gurney	**EHILOR**	holier		tither		tholes
EGNSUU	ungues	**EHILOS**	helios	**EHIRTV**	thrive	**EHLOSU**	housel

EHLOSV	hovels	**EHOPRU**	uphroe	**EIILOT**	iolite	**EIKLNU**	unlike
	shovel	**EHOPTT**	Tophet	**EIILPP**	lippie	**EIKLNV**	kelvin
EHLOSW	wholes	**EHOPUV**	uphove	**EIILRV**	virile	**EIKLNW**	welkin
EHLOTW	howlet	**EHORRT**	rhetor	**EIILRW**	wilier		winkle
EHLPSW	whelps	**EHORSS**	horses	**EIILRX**	elixir	**EIKLRT**	kilter
EHLRRU	hurler		hosers	**EIIMNS**	imines		kirtle
EHLRTU	hurtle		shoers	**EIIMPS**	impies	**EIKLSS**	kissel
	Luther		shores	**EIIMRR**	rimier	**EIKLST**	Kleist
EHLRUY	hurley	**EHORST**	others	**EIINNT**	intine	**EIKLSV**	Kislev
EHLSSU	lushes		throes		tinnie	**EIKLSW**	Wilkes
EHLSTT	shtetl	**EHORSV**	hovers	**EIINOS**	ionise	**EIKLSY**	kileys
EHLSTU	hustle		shover	**EIINOZ**	ionize		kylies
	sleuth		shrove	**EIINPR**	pinier	**EIKLTT**	kittel
EHLSTY	shelty	**EHORSW**	shower	**EIINPT**	pinite		kittle
EHLUXY	Huxley		whores		tiepin	**EIKMNR**	merkin
EHMMRU	hummer	**EHORSY**	horsey	**EIINRT**	tinier	**EIKMOR**	Mörike
EHMNOP	phenom	**EHORTT**	hotter	**EIINRV**	Irvine	**EIKMPS**	Kempis
EHMNOR	Hermon		tother	**EIINRW**	winier	**EIKMRS**	kermis
EHMNSY	hymens	**EHORTV**	throve	**EIINRZ**	Rienzi	**EIKMST**	kismet
EHMORS	homers	**EHORTX**	exhort	**EIINSS**	niseis	**EIKMSU**	muskie
EHMORT	mother	**EHORTY**	theory		seisin	**EIKMTU**	kumite
EHMOSS	moshes	**EHORTZ**	zeroth	**EIINSX**	nixies	**EIKNOO**	nookie
	shmoes	**EHOSST**	shotes	**EIINSZ**	seizin	**EIKNOS**	eikons
EHMOST	methos	**EHOSSU**	houses	**EIINTV**	invite	**EIKNOV**	invoke
EHMRRY	rhymer		shouse	**EIIPRS**	pieris	**EIKNPR**	perkin
EHMRST	therms	**EHOSSV**	shoves	**EIIPRU**	euripi		Pernik
EHMRSU	musher	**EHPRSU**	pusher	**EIIPST**	pities	**EIKNRS**	inkers
	rheums	**EHPRSY**	hypers	**EIIPSX**	pixies		sinker
EHMRSY	rhymes		sphery	**EIIRRW**	wirier	**EIKNRT**	tinker
EHMRUY	rheumy		sypher	**EIIRSS**	irises	**EIKNRW**	winker
EHMSSU	mushes	**EHPRYZ**	zephyr	**EIIRVZ**	vizier		Wrekin
EHNNUW	unhewn	**EHPSSU**	pushes	**EIISTY**	yities	**EIKNSS**	skeins
EHNOPR	phoner	**EHRRSU**	rusher	**EIJKNR**	jerkin	**EIKNSV**	knives
EHNOPS	phones	**EHRRSY**	sherry		jinker		Nevski
EHNOPY	phoney	**EHRRTU**	hurter	**EIJKNT**	inkjet	**EIKNSY**	Kinsey
EHNORS	herons	**EHRRWY**	wherry	**EIJKNU**	junkie	**EIKNTT**	kitten
	nosher	**EHRSSU**	rhesus	**EIJKOR**	jokier	**EIKOOR**	rookie
EHNORT	hornet		rushes	**EIJKOS**	Osijek	**EIKOPP**	koppie
	Theron		ushers	**EIJLRT**	jilter	**EIKOPR**	pokier
	throne		Ussher	**EIJLSS**	IJssel	**EIKOPS**	pokies
EHNOSS	noshes	**EHRSSW**	shrews	**EIJNNO**	enjoin	**EIKORY**	yorkie
EHNOST	honest	**EHRSSY**	shyers	**EIJNOR**	joiner	**EIKOTW**	Koweit
	Stheno	**EHRSTY**	thyrse		rejoin	**EIKPPR**	kipper
EHNOSY	honeys	**EHSSSU**	Sesshu	**EIJNRU**	injure	**EIKPPT**	keppit
EHNPRY	Phryne	**EHSSTU**	tushes	**EIJNSX**	jinxes	**EIKPRS**	pikers
EHNRSY	henrys	**EHSSTY**	shyest	**EIJNTY**	jitney	**EIKPSS**	spikes
EHNRTU	hunter	**EHSTTY**	Tethys	**EIJRSU**	juries	**EIKRRS**	risker
EHNRVY	Henry V	**EIIILO**	Leo III	**EIJRSV**	jivers	**EIKRSS**	kisser
EHNSTT	tenths	**EIIKLS**	silkie	**EIJRTT**	jitter		krises
EHOOOP	hoopoe	**EIIKNP**	pinkie	**EIJSTU**	jesuit		skiers
EHOOPR	hooper	**EIIKNR**	inkier	**EIJSZZ**	jizzes	**EIKRST**	kiters
EHOOPY	phooey	**EIILLN**	nielli	**EIKKOO**	kookie		strike
EHOORT	hooter	**EIILLP**	pillie	**EIKKRS**	skrike		trikes
EHOORV	hoover	**EIILLS**	lilies	**EIKLLR**	killer	**EIKRSV**	skiver
EHOOST	soothe	**EIILLT**	illite	**EIKLLY**	Ilkley	**EIKSSS**	kisses
EHOOSV	hooves	**EIILLW**	willie		likely	**EIKSST**	skites
EHOPPR	hopper	**EIILMR**	limier	**EIKLMR**	milker	**EIKSSV**	skives
EHOPRS	ephors	**EIILMS**	simile	**EIKLNO**	Elikón	**EIKSTW**	weskit
	hopers	**EIILMU**	milieu	**EIKLNR**	linker	**EILLMR**	miller
	posher	**EIILNR**	inlier	**EIKLNS**	likens	**EILLMT**	millet
EHOPRT	pother	**EIILNT**	lintie		silken	**EILLMU**	illume
	thorpe	**EIILOR**	oilier	**EIKLNT**	tinkle	**EILLNO**	niello

	O'Neill
EILLNP	penill
EILLNT	lentil
	lintel
	tellin
EILLOT	tollie
EILLPU	pilule
EILLRS	rilles
	siller
EILLRT	rillet
	tiller
EILLRW	willer
EILLST	listel
EILLTT	little
EILLTW	willet
EILLTY	Tilley
EILLVY	evilly
	lively
	vilely
EILMNO	moline
	oilmen
EILMNR	limner
	merlin
EILMNS	limens
	simnel
EILMNY	myelin
EILMOR	moiler
EILMOS	molies
	Molise
EILMOT	motile
EILMPP	pimple
EILMPR	limper
EILMPS	impels
	simple
EILMPT	limpet
EILMPU	pileum
EILMPW	wimple
EILMRS	milers
	smiler
EILMRT	milter
EILMSS	missel
	slimes
	smiles
EILMST	mistle
EILMSU	muesli
EILMSY	limeys
	smiley
EILMTU	telium
EILMTY	timely
EILMZZ	mizzle
EILNNO	online
EILNNS	linens
EILNNT	linnet
EILNNY	linney
EILNOO	loonie
EILNOP	Pelion
	pinole
EILNOR	neroli
EILNOS	eloins
	insole
	lesion
	Silone

EILNOT	entoil
EILNPP	nipple
EILNPS	pensil
	Pilsen
	spinel
	spline
EILNPT	leptin
	pintle
EILNPU	lineup
	lupine
EILNRS	liners
EILNRT	linter
EILNRU	lunier
EILNST	enlist
	inlets
	listen
	silent
	tinsel
EILNSU	lunies
EILNSV	livens
	snivel
EILNSY	lysine
EILNTU	lutein
EILNTY	lenity
EILNUV	unlive
	unveil
EILOOR	oriole
EILOOT	oolite
EILOPS	pilose
	poleis
EILOPT	piolet
	polite
EILORS	lories
	oilers
	oriels
	reoils
	Serlio
EILORT	Loiret
	loiter
	toiler
EILORU	lourie
EILORV	oliver
EILORW	lowrie
EILOST	toiles
EILOSV	lovies
	olives
	voiles
EILOSX	isolex
EILOTT	toilet
EILOTV	violet
EILPPR	ripple
EILPPT	tipple
EILPPU	pileup
EILPRS	lisper
	perils
	Perlis
	pliers
EILPRT	triple
EILPRY	ripely
	Ripley
EILPSS	plisse
	slipes

	spiels
	spiles
EILPST	stipel
EILPSU	epulis
	pileus
EILPSV	pelvis
EILPSW	swiple
EILPSX	pixels
EILPZZ	pizzle
EILRST	lister
	liters
	litres
	relist
	tilers
EILRSV	livers
	livres
	silver
	sliver
EILRSW	swiler
EILRTT	litter
	tilter
EILRTU	rutile
EILRUW	wurlie
EILRVY	livery
	verily
EILSST	islets
	sliest
	stiles
EILSSY	Sisley
EILSTT	titles
EILSTU	Iseult
EILSTV	vilest
EILSTX	ixtles
EILSTY	Elytis
	stylie
EILSVW	swivel
EILSWY	wisely
EILSXY	sexily
EILSZZ	sizzle
EILTTT	tittle
EILTTU	lutite
EILTTV	vittle
EILTVY	levity
EILUVV	luvvie
EIMMNU	immune
EIMMOR	memoir
EIMMRS	mimers
	simmer
EIMMRU	immure
EIMMRZ	zimmer
EIMMST	semmit
EIMNNX	meninx
EIMNOO	Moonie
EIMNOR	merino
EIMNOS	eonism
	Miseno
	monies
	Simeon
EIMNPT	pitmen
EIMNRS	Mersin
	miners
EIMNRT	minter

	remint
EIMNRU	murine
EIMNRV	vermin
EIMNSX	minxes
EIMNSZ	mizens
EIMNTT	mitten
	titmen
EIMNTU	minuet
	minute
EIMNTY	enmity
EIMNZZ	mizzen
EIMOPS	impose
EIMORS	isomer
	moires
	rimose
EIMOSS	mioses
	mossie
EIMOST	somite
EIMOSV	movies
EIMOSX	oximes
EIMOTV	motive
EIMOTY	moiety
EIMOZZ	mozzie
EIMPRR	primer
EIMPRS	primes
	simper
EIMPRT	permit
EIMPRU	impure
	umpire
EIMPRX	premix
EIMPSU	umpies
EIMPTU	impute
	uptime
EIMRRS	rimers
EIMRRT	retrim
	trimer
EIMRSS	misers
	remiss
EIMRST	merits
	mister
	miters
	mitres
	remits
	smiter
	timers
EIMRSV	verism
	vermis
EIMRSX	mixers
EIMRSY	misery
EIMSSS	misses
	seisms
EIMSST	smites
	tmesis
EIMSSU	misuse
EIMSSX	sexism
EIMSTY	stymie
EINNNR	rennin
EINNOO	ionone
EINNOT	intone
EINNOY	yonnie
EINNPR	pinner
EINNPS	pennis

EINNPT tenpin	**EINQUU** unique	**EIORSS** osiers	wirers
EINNRS inners	**EINQUZ** quinze	**EIORST** sortie	**EIRRTT** triter
sinner	**EINRRS** rinser	tories	**EIRRTW** writer
EINNRT intern	**EINRRU** ruiner	triose	**EIRSST** resist
tinner	**EINRSS** resins	**EIORSV** vireos	resits
EINNRW winner	rinses	**EIORTU** tourie	sister
EINNST sennit	serins	**EIOSTV** soviet	**EIRSSU** issuer
tennis	sirens	**EIOTTT** tottie	**EIRSSW** sweirs
EINNSU Ennius	**EINRST** estrin	**EIOTVV** votive	**EIRSSX** sixers
EINNSV venins	insert	**EIPPRR** ripper	**EIRSSZ** sizers
EINNTT intent	inters	**EIPPRS** pipers	**EIRSTT** sitter
EINNTV invent	sinter	sipper	titers
EINNTY ninety	trines	**EIPPRT** Pripet	titres
EINOOT toonie	**EINRSU** erinus	tipper	triste
EINOPR orpine	insure	**EIPPRZ** zipper	**EIRSTU** suiter
Pinero	inures	**EIPPST** sippet	**EIRSTV** rivets
EINOPS opines	ursine	**EIPPSU** Peipus	stiver
ponies	**EINRSX** nixers	**EIPPTT** tippet	strive
EINOPT pointe	**EINRTT** tinter	**EIPPUY** yuppie	verist
EINORR ironer	Trient	**EIPQSU** equips	**EIRSTW** wriest
Renoir	**EINRTU** triune	piques	writes
EINORS nosier	uniter	**EIPQTU** piquet	**EIRTTT** titter
senior	**EINRTV** invert	**EIPRRS** priers	**EIRTTV** trivet
EINORT Ireton	**EINRTW** twiner	sprier	**EIRTTW** witter
norite	winter	**EIPRRU** puirer	**EIRTUV** virtue
orient	**EINRVW** wivern	**EIPRSS** pisser	**EIRTVY** verity
tonier	**EINRVY** vinery	prises	**EISSSU** issues
EINORV enviro	**EINRWY** winery	speirs	Suisse
renvoi	**EINSST** insets	spiers	**EISSSW** wisses
EINOSS enosis	steins	spires	**EISSTT** testis
noesis	Tessin	**EIPRST** esprit	**EISSTU** suites
noises	**EINSSW** sewins	priest	tissue
ossein	sinews	ripest	**EISSTW** wisest
sonsie	swines	sprite	**EISSTX** exists
EINOST tonies	**EINSTU** tenuis	stripe	sexist
EINOSV envois	unites	**EIPRSU** Epirus	**EISSVW** swives
EINOSW nowise	unties	uprise	**EISTTW** twites
EINOTW townie	**EINSTV** invest	**EIPRSV** vipers	**EISTZZ** tizzes
twonie	**EINSTW** twines	**EIPRSW** wipers	**EISUXZ** Zeuxis
EINOVW inwove	wisent	**EIPRSZ** prizes	**EISWZZ** wizzes
EINPPR nipper	**EINSUW** unwise	**EIPRTV** privet	**EISZZZ** zizzes
EINPPS pepsin	**EINSUX** unisex	**EIPRTY** pyrite	**EJKLLY** Jekyll
EINPRR Perrin	**EINSVX** vixens	**EIPRXY** expiry	**EJKNRU** junker
EINPRS repins	**EINSWY** sinewy	**EIPSSS** pisses	**EJKNTU** junket
ripens	**EINSWZ** winzes	sepsis	**EJKOPS** kopjes
sniper	wizens	speiss	Skopje
EINPRT Pinter	**EINTTY** entity	**EIPSST** pistes	**EJKORS** jokers
EINPRU punier	yitten	spites	**EJLLOS** jellos
purine	**EIOORT** toorie	stipes	**EJLOPS** poljes
unripe	**EIOORZ** oozier	**EIPSSW** swipes	**EJLORT** jolter
EINPRV Previn	**EIOOST** otiose	**EIPSTW** pewits	**EJLOST** jostle
EINPRY pinery	**EIOPPT** potpie	**EIPSXY** pyxies	**EJLOSU** joules
EINPSS snipes	**EIOPRR** ropier	**EIQRSU** quires	**EJLPSU** juleps
spines	**EIOPRX** poxier	risque	**EJLRSU** jurels
EINPST instep	**EIOPSS** poises	squire	**EJLSTU** justle
nepits	posies	**EIQRUV** quiver	Sutlej
spinet	possie	**EIQSTU** quiets	**EJMOOS** mojoes
EINPSU puisne	**EIOPST** postie	**EIQTUY** equity	**EJMOST** jetsom
supine	**EIOPTT** tiptoe	**EIRRSS** risers	**EJMPRU** jumper
EINQSU quines	**EIORRS** rosier	**EIRRST** triers	**EJNOSV** Jevons
sequin	**EIORRT** rioter	**EIRRSV** rivers	**EJNOSY** enjoys
EINQTU quinte	**EIORRW** Owerri	**EIRRSW** werris	**EJNOTT** jetton

EJOPRT	projet		Müller	**ELMPPU**	peplum	**ELOPPP**	popple
EJORSS	josser	**ELLMSS**	smells	**ELMPRU**	lumper	**ELOPPR**	lopper
EJORTT	jotter	**ELLMSY**	smelly		rumple		propel
EJOSSS	josses	**ELLMTU**	mullet	**ELMPSU**	plumes	**ELOPPS**	Pelops
EJOTTW	Jowett	**ELLMUV**	vellum	**ELMRSU**	lemurs		peplos
EKKOPS	kopeks	**ELLMUY**	mulley	**ELMRTY**	myrtle	**ELOPPT**	topple
EKKOPU	pukeko	**ELLNOP**	pollen		termly	**ELOPRS**	lopers
EKLLNS	knells	**ELLNOR**	enroll	**ELMSST**	smelts		polers
EKLLSY	skelly	**ELLNOV**	lonely	**ELMSSU**	mussel		proles
EKLMMU	kummel	**ELLNSU**	sullen	**ELMSUY**	muleys		sloper
EKLMOT	Moltke	**ELLNUU**	lunule	**ELMTUU**	mutuel		splore
EKLMOW	Welkom	**ELLNUW**	unwell		mutule	**ELOPRT**	petrol
EKLMSS	skelms	**ELLOPW**	Powell	**ELMTUW**	umwelt	**ELOPRV**	plover
EKLNOS	kelson	**ELLOPX**	pollex	**ELMTUY**	mutely	**ELOPRW**	plower
EKLOOR	looker	**ELLORR**	roller	**ELMUZZ**	muzzle	**ELOPRX**	plexor
EKLOSY	kyloes	**ELLORT**	toller	**ELNNOR**	Lennon	**ELOPSS**	slopes
	yokels	**ELLORW**	Orwell	**ELNNOS**	nelson	**ELOPSU**	loupes
EKLPSS	skelps	**ELLOSS**	losels	**ELNNRU**	runnel	**ELOPTT**	pottle
	spelks	**ELLOSY**	solely	**ELNNTU**	tunnel	**ELOPTU**	tupelo
EKLRRU	lurker	**ELLOTX**	extoll	**ELNOOS**	loosen	**ELORRS**	sorrel
EKLRSU	sulker	**ELLOVY**	lovely	**ELNOOV**	Leonov	**ELORSS**	lessor
EKMNOY	monkey		volley	**ELNOOW**	woolen		losers
EKMOOP	mopoke	**ELLOWY**	yellow	**ELNOOY**	looney	**ELORST**	Ortles
EKMORS	smoker	**ELLPRU**	puller	**ELNOPT**	lepton		ostler
EKMOSS	smokes	**ELLPSS**	spells	**ELNOPY**	openly		sterol
EKMSTU	musket	**ELLPTU**	pullet		poleyn	**ELORSU**	louser
EKNNOR	kronen	**ELLPUY**	pulley	**ELNORS**	enrols	**ELORSV**	lovers
EKNNOT	nekton	**ELLQSU**	quells		loners		solver
EKNNSU	sunken	**ELLSSW**	swells	**ELNORZ**	Lorenz	**ELORSW**	lowers
EKNNTU	unkent	**ELLSTU**	tellus	**ELNOSS**	lesson		lowser
EKNOPS	spoken	**ELMMOP**	pommel	**ELNOST**	lentos		rowels
EKNORR	kroner	**ELMMOR**	Rommel		Solent		slower
EKNORW	knower	**ELMMOS**	Moslem		stolen	**ELORSY**	sorely
EKNORY	Orkney	**ELMMPU**	pummel		telson	**ELORTV**	revolt
EKNOSS	snoeks	**ELMNOR**	merlon	**ELNOSU**	ensoul	**ELORTW**	trowel
EKNOST	tokens	**ELMNOS**	Lemnos	**ELNOSV**	novels	**ELORUV**	louver
EKNOUY	unyoke		lemons		sloven		louvre
EKNPTU	unkept		melons	**ELNOUZ**	zonule		velour
EKOORR	korero		solemn	**ELNOZZ**	nozzle	**ELORVW**	wolver
EKOORT	retook	**ELMNOT**	loment	**ELNPTU**	n-tuple	**ELORVY**	overly
EKOPRR	porker		melton		penult	**ELORWY**	Rowley
EKOPRS	pokers		molten	**ELNPTY**	pentyl		yowler
EKOPSS	spokes	**ELMNOY**	lemony		plenty	**ELOSSS**	losses
EKOPSY	pokeys	**ELMNPU**	lumpen	**ELNRTU**	runlet	**ELOSST**	stoles
EKORRW	rework		plenum	**ELNRUZ**	luzern	**ELOSSU**	louses
	worker	**ELMNSU**	lumens	**ELNSSU**	unless		ousels
EKORRY	yorker	**ELMOOP**	pomelo	**ELNSSY**	selsyn	**ELOSSV**	solves
EKORST	stoker	**ELMOPR**	Plomer	**ELNSXY**	lynxes	**ELOSSW**	lowses
	stroke	**ELMOPY**	employ	**ELNTTU**	nutlet	**ELOSTU**	solute
EKORSY	yokers	**ELMORS**	morels	**ELNTTY**	nettly		tousle
EKOSST	stokes		morsel	**ELNTUZ**	Lützen	**ELOSTV**	voltes
EKPSTU	tupeks	**ELMORT**	merlot	**ELNUZZ**	nuzzle	**ELOSTW**	lowest
EKRRSY	skerry		molter	**ELOOOT**	O'Toole		towels
EKRSTU	tusker	**ELMORY**	Morley	**ELOOPR**	looper	**ELOSTX**	extols
EKRTUY	turkey	**ELMOST**	molest	**ELOOPT**	pootle	**ELOSUV**	ovules
ELLLOR	loller		motels	**ELOORS**	looser	**ELOSUZ**	ouzels
ELLLOV	Lovell	**ELMOSU**	oleums	**ELOORT**	looter	**ELOSVW**	vowels
ELLLOW	Lowell	**ELMOSY**	Mosley		retool		wolves
ELLMNU	mullen	**ELMOTT**	mottle		rootle	**ELOSWY**	Wolsey
ELLMOW	mellow	**ELMOTY**	motley		tooler	**ELOSXY**	xylose
ELLMPU	pellum	**ELMOUV**	volume	**ELOOSS**	looses		
ELLMRU	muller	**ELMOZZ**	mozzle	**ELOOTT**	tootle		

Code	Word
ELOTTU	outlet
ELOTUV	volute
ELOTUZ	touzle
ELOTWY	owelty
ELPPRU	pulper
	purple
ELPPSU	peplus
	supple
ELPQUU	pulque
ELPRRU	purler
ELPRSU	pulers
ELPRTY	peltry
	pertly
ELPRUY	purely
ELPSSU	pluses
	pulses
ELPSSY	slypes
ELPSTU	letups
ELPSUX	plexus
	suplex
ELPUZZ	puzzle
ELRRSU	lurers
	rulers
ELRSSU	lusers
ELRSTU	luster
	lustre
	result
	rustle
	Sluter
	sutler
	ulster
ELRSTY	styler
ELRSUY	surely
ELRTTU	turtle
ELRTTY	tetryl
ELRUWY	wurley
ELSSTU	tussle
ELSSTY	slyest
	styles
ELSTTY	stylet
ELSTUX	exults
ELSTUY	Yseult
EMMMRU	mummer
EMMNNO	Memnon
EMMNOT	moment
EMMORY	memory
EMMOST	mestom
EMMRRU	rummer
EMMRSU	summer
EMMSUU	museum
EMNNOT	Menton
	Monnet
EMNOOR	Monroe
EMNOPS	Empson
EMNOPT	potmen
EMNOPY	eponym
EMNORS	sermon
EMNORT	mentor
	Merton
EMNORY	Romney
EMNOSS	mesons
EMNOST	montes
EMNOSV	venoms
EMNOSY	moneys
EMNOTY	etymon
EMNOTZ	Montez
EMNOXY	exonym
EMNRSU	rumens
EMNRTU	munter
EMNSSU	sensum
EMNTUY	Tyumen
EMOORR	roomer
EMOORS	morose
	romeos
EMOORT	mooter
EMOORX	Exmoor
EMOOSS	osmose
EMOPPT	moppet
EMOPPY	pompey
EMOPRR	romper
EMOPRS	mopers
	proems
EMOPRT	trompe
EMOPST	tempos
EMOPSY	myopes
EMOQSU	mosque
EMOQUY	Quemoy
EMORRS	ormers
EMORRT	termor
	tremor
EMORRW	wormer
EMORSS	morses
EMORST	metros
	motser
EMORSU	mouser
EMORSV	movers
	vomers
EMORSW	mowers
EMORSY	Mysore
EMORUV	mevrou
EMOSSS	mosses
EMOSSU	mousse
EMOSSY	moseys
	myoses
EMOSTT	motets
	mottes
	totems
EMOSUY	mousey
EMOSZZ	mezzos
	mozzes
EMPPTU	muppet
EMPRSS	sperms
EMPRSU	spumes
EMPSTT	tempts
EMPSTU	septum
EMRRSU	murres
EMRRUY	murrey
EMRSSU	musers
	serums
EMRSTU	estrum
	muster
	stumer
	Sumter
EMRTTU	mutter
EMSSSU	musses
EMSSTU	Musset
EMSSTY	Metsys
	system
EMSUZZ	muzzes
ENNNOP	pennon
ENNOPU	unopen
ENNORU	neuron
ENNORW	renown
ENNOST	nonets
	sonnet
	tennos
	tenons
	tonnes
ENNOSU	nonuse
ENNOTW	newton
ENNPRU	punner
ENNPRY	Prynne
ENNPTU	punnet
ENNRRU	runner
ENNRST	Nernst
ENNTUY	Tunney
ENOOPR	operon
ENOORS	roneos
	sooner
ENOORT	enroot
ENOORY	Rooney
ENOOSS	nooses
ENOOSZ	snooze
ENOPRR	perron
ENOPRS	person
ENOPRT	Repton
ENOPRV	proven
ENOPRY	pyrone
ENOPST	pontes
ENOPTT	potent
ENORRS	snorer
ENORRY	ornery
ENORSS	senors
	sensor
	snores
ENORST	nestor
	stoner
	tenors
	tensor
	toners
ENORSW	owners
	rowens
	worsen
ENORTT	rotten
	Trento
ENORTY	Tyrone
ENORUV	unrove
ENOSST	onsets
	stenos
	stones
ENOSSU	onuses
ENOSSW	sowens
ENOSTT	teston
ENOSTW	Townes
ENOSTX	sexton
ENOSTY	stoney
ENOSUV	venous
ENOSVY	envoys
ENOTTU	tenuto
ENPPRU	prenup
ENPRRU	pruner
ENPRSU	prunes
ENPRTU	punter
ENPRUY	penury
ENPSTU	unstep
ENPTUU	tuneup
ENPTUW	unwept
ENQRSU	querns
ENRRSU	reruns
ENRRTU	return
	turner
ENRSST	sterns
ENRSSU	nurses
ENRSTU	tuners
	unrest
ENRSTW	strewn
ENRSTY	sentry
ENRSUU	unsure
ENRTTU	nutter
ENRTUU	untrue
ENRVWY	wyvern
ENSSSU	Nessus
ENSSTU	sunset
ENTTWY	twenty
EOOPPS	oppose
EOOPRR	poorer
EOOPSV	pooves
EOORRS	rooser
EOORRT	rooter
	torero
EOORSS	rooses
EOORST	torose
EOORSW	wooers
EOORTT	tooter
EOOSTV	Eötvös
EOOSTW	Soweto
EOPPPR	popper
EOPPPT	poppet
EOPPRR	proper
EOPPRT	topper
EOPPRY	popery
	pyrope
	yopper
EOPRRS	repros
EOPRRT	porter
	pretor
	report
EOPRRU	pourer
EOPRSS	posers
	posser
	proses
	spores
EOPRST	poster
	presto
	repots
	topers
	tropes
EOPRSU	poseur

	uprose		strove	**ERSSTU**	estrus	**FFOPTU**	putoff
EOPRSV	proves		troves		russet	**FFRRUU**	furfur
EOPRSW	powers		voters		surest	**FFSSTU**	stuffs
EOPRSY	osprey	**EORSTW**	towers		tusser	**FFSTUY**	stuffy
EOPRTT	potter	**EORSTX**	oxters	**ERSSTV**	versts	**FGGIIZ**	fizgig
EOPRTU	pouter	**EORSTY**	oyster	**ERSSTW**	strews	**FGGORY**	froggy
	troupe		storey		wrests	**FGHILT**	flight
EOPRTX	export		toyers	**ERSSTY**	tressy	**FGHIRT**	fright
EOPRTY	poetry		Troyes	**ERSSUU**	uruses	**FGHIST**	fights
EOPRXY	peroxy	**EORSTZ**	zoster	**ERSSUV**	versus	**FGHOTU**	fought
EOPSSS	posses	**EORSVW**	vowers	**ERSSVY**	syvers	**FGIILN**	filing
EOPSST	estops	**EORSWW**	wowser	**ERSTTU**	truest	**FGIINN**	fining
	posset	**EORSXY**	oryxes		utters	**FGIINR**	firing
	ptoses	**EORTTT**	totter	**ERSTUU**	suture	**FGIINX**	fixing
	stoeps	**EORTTU**	touter		uterus	**FGILNS**	flings
	stopes	**EORTTX**	extort	**ERSTUV**	Struve	**FGILNU**	ingulf
EOPSSU	opuses	**EORTVX**	vortex		turves	**FGILNY**	flying
	spouse	**EORUVY**	voyeur		vertus	**FGILUY**	uglify
EOPSSY	sepoys	**EOSSST**	Sestos	**ERSTUY**	surety	**FGIMNU**	fuming
EOPSTX	sexpot		tosses	**ERSTVY**	vestry	**FGINOS**	gonifs
EOQRTU	roquet	**EOSSSU**	souses	**ERSTWY**	twyers	**FGINOX**	foxing
	torque		Sousse		wryest	**FGINRY**	fringy
EOQSTU	quotes	**EOSSTV**	stoves	**ERSTXY**	xyster		frying
	toques	**EOSSTX**	sextos	**ERSUVY**	survey	**FGINSU**	fusing
EORRRS	errors	**EOSTTU**	outset	**ERTTUX**	urtext	**FGINUZ**	fuzing
EORRRT	rorter		setout	**ESSSSU**	susses	**FGIOSU**	fugios
	terror	**EOSUUV**	uveous	**ESSSUW**	wusses	**FGJLUU**	jugful
EORRRY	orrery	**EOSVYY**	Voysey	**ESSSUX**	Sussex	**FGLMUU**	mugful
EORRST	resort	**EPPPRY**	preppy	**FFFLSU**	fluffs	**FGLNOS**	flongs
	retros	**EPPPTU**	puppet	**FFFLUY**	fluffy	**FGNOOS**	gonofs
	roster	**EPPRSU**	supper	**FFGIIN**	fifing	**FGNSUU**	fungus
	sorter		uppers	**FFGINO**	offing	**FGOORT**	forgot
EORRSU	rouser	**EPRRSU**	purser	**FFGLOO**	logoff	**FHHISU**	Fushih
EORRSV	rovers	**EPRRSY**	pryers	**FFHIOS**	offish	**FHIINS**	finish
EORRSW	rowers		spryer	**FFHIST**	fifths	**FHILTY**	filthy
	worser	**EPRRTU**	Rupert	**FFHISW**	whiffs	**FHIMUY**	humify
EORRSY	rosery	**EPRSST**	prests	**FFHIWY**	whiffy	**FHIRST**	firths
EORRTT	retort		streps	**FFHORS**	shroff		friths
	rotter	**EPRSSU**	purses	**FFHOSW**	howffs		shrift
EORRTU	router		sprues	**FFIINT**	tiffin	**FHIRTT**	thrift
	tourer		spuers	**FFIIUZ**	Uffizi	**FHISST**	shifts
EORRTV	Trevor		supers	**FFIKSS**	skiffs	**FHISTU**	shufti
	trover	**EPRSTU**	erupts	**FFILLU**	fulfil	**FHISTY**	shifty
EORRZZ	rozzer		purest	**FFILPS**	spliff	**FHNSUU**	Fushun
EORSST	restos	**EPRSTW**	twerps	**FFILTU**	fitful	**FHORST**	froths
	stores	**EPRSUU**	pursue	**FFIMNU**	muffin	**FHORTU**	fourth
	tosser	**EPRTTU**	putter	**FFINPU**	puffin	**FHORTY**	frothy
EORSSU	rouses	**EPRTTY**	pretty	**FFINSS**	sniffs	**FHORWY**	forwhy
	serous	**EPRTUZ**	Perutz	**FFINSY**	sniffy	**FHOUUZ**	Fuzhou
EORSSV	servos	**EPRUVY**	purvey	**FFIOPR**	ripoff	**FHPRUY**	furphy
	versos	**EPSSSU**	pusses	**FFIOPT**	tipoff	**FHSTUY**	shufty
EORSSW	serows	**EPSSTU**	setups	**FFIOST**	soffit	**FIIKNR**	firkin
	sowers		stupes	**FFIPSY**	spiffy	**FIILLN**	infill
EORSTT	otters		upsets	**FFIQSU**	quiffs	**FIILLP**	fillip
	tortes	**EQRTWY**	qwerty	**FFISST**	stiffs	**FIILRU**	Friuli
	toters	**EQSSTU**	quests	**FFISTY**	stiffy	**FIILST**	Tiflis
EORSTU	ouster	**EQSTUU**	tuques	**FFISUX**	suffix	**FIILVY**	vilify
	outers	**ERRSSU**	usurer	**FFLOTY**	fylfot	**FIIMNR**	infirm
	routes	**ERRSUY**	surrey	**FFLSSU**	sluffs	**FIIMNY**	minify
	souter	**ERRTTU**	turret	**FFNORU**	runoff	**FIIMST**	misfit
	trouse	**ERRTUY**	Ruyter	**FFNSSU**	snuffs	**FIINOR**	fiorin
EORSTV	stover	**ERSSST**	stress	**FFNSUY**	snuffy	**FIITXY**	fixity

FIIVVY vivify	**FLNOTU** Fulton	**GGINUY** guying	**GHOORS** sorgho
FIJLOR frijol	**FLNRUU** unfurl	**GGINVY** gyving	**GHORSU** roughs
FIKLSU kulfis	**FLOORS** floors	**GGIOOR** gorgio	**GHORTU** trough
FIKRSS frisks	**FLOOTW** Flotow	**GGIOST** gigots	**GHORTW** growth
FIKRSY frisky	**FLOOYZ** floozy	**GGITWY** twiggy	**GHOSST** ghosts
FILLRS frills	**FLOPPY** floppy	**GGLLOO** loglog	**GHOSSU** soughs
FILLRY frilly	**FLOPTU** potful	**GGLOOO** googol	**GHOSTU** oughts
FILLUW wilful	**FLORSU** flours	**GGLOOY** googly	sought
FILMOU folium	**FLORUY** floury	**GGMOSY** smoggy	toughs
FILMRY firmly	**FLOSSY** flossy	**GGMRUU** muggur	**GHRSSU** shrugs
FILMSY flimsy	**FLOSTU** flouts	**GGNOOR** gorgon	**GIIJNV** jiving
FILNOR florin	**FLOSTY** softly	**GGNOOY** gongyo	**GIIKLN** liking
FILNOW inflow	**FLOTUY** outfly	**GGNRUY** grungy	**GIIKMN** miking
FILNST flints	**FLRRUY** flurry	**GGPSUY** spuggy	**GIIKNN** inking
FILNSU sinful	**FLRSUU** sulfur	**GGRRUU** grugru	**GIIKNP** piking
FILNTU tinful	**FMORSU** forums	**GHHILY** highly	**GIIKNR** irking
FILNTY flinty	**FMPRSU** frumps	**GHHIST** thighs	**GIIKNS** Siking
FILNUX influx	**FMPRUY** frumpy	**GHHOSU** houghs	skiing
FILOOR Florio	**FNORST** fronts	**GHHOTU** though	**GIIKNT** kiting
FILOOS folios	**FNORSW** frowns	**GHIIKN** hiking	**GIIKNV** viking
FILORV frivol	**FNOSTU** founts	**GHIINR** hiring	**GIIKNY** yiking
FILOSS fossil	futons	**GHIINV** hiving	**GIILMN** liming
FILOTW Wolfit	**FOOPRS** proofs	**GHIKNO** hoking	**GIILNN** lignin
FILOXY foxily	**FOOPSS** spoofs	**GHIKNT** knight	lining
FILPPY flippy	**FOOTUX** outfox	**GHILNO** holing	**GIILNO** oiling
FILPTU uplift	**FORRSU** furors	**GHILPT** plight	**GIILNP** piling
FILRST flirts	**FORRUW** furrow	**GHILST** lights	**GIILNR** riling
FILRTY flirty	**FORSST** frosts	slight	**GIILNS** siling
FILSSU fusils	**FORSTW** frowst	**GHIMNO** homing	**GIILNT** tiling
FIMNOR inform	**FORSTY** frosty	**GHIMTY** mighty	**GIILNU** Guilin
FIMOST motifs	**FORSUU** rufous	**GHINNO** honing	**GIILNV** living
FIMSSU Sufism	**FORSWY** frowsy	**GHINOP** hoping	**GIILNW** wiling
FIMSTU muftis	**FORUYZ** frouzy	**GHINOS** hosing	**GIILOS** sigloi
FINOOS foison	**FORWYZ** frowzy	**GHINPY** hyping	**GIILRV** Virgil
FINORT forint		**GHINST** nights	**GIILSS** sigils
FINORX fornix	**GGGILY** giggly	things	**GIILSV** vigils
FINOSU fusion	**GGGLOS** gloggs	**GHINSY** shying	**GIIMMN** miming
FINOTY notify	**GGGLOY** goggly	**GHINTY** nighty	**GIIMNN** mining
FINSTU unfits	**GGGORY** groggy	**GHIOPZ** phizog	**GIIMNP** imping
FIOPRT profit	**GGHINO** hoggin	**GHIORT** righto	**GIIMNR** miring
FIORST fortis	**GGHORU** grough	**GHIOSY** goyish	riming
FIOSST foists	**GGHSUY** shuggy	**GHIRST** girths	**GIIMNT** timing
FIOSSY ossify	**GGIINP** piggin	griths	**GIIMNX** mixing
FIOTTU outfit	**GGIINV** giving	rights	**GIINNN** inning
FIPRUY purify	**GGIIRR** grigri	**GHIRTW** wright	**GIINNP** pining
FIPTYY typify	**GGIJLY** jiggly	**GHISST** sights	**GIINNS** sining
FIRSST firsts	**GGIKNO** gingko	**GHISTT** tights	**GIINNW** wining
FIRSTT fritts	gingko	**GHISTW** wights	**GIINNX** nixing
FIRSTU fruits	**GGILNO** ogling	**GHLLSY** ghylls	Xining
FIRTUY fruity	**GGILNU** gluing	**GHLOPU** plough	**GIINOR** origin
FIRYZZ frizzy	luging	**GHLOSU** ghouls	**GIINOY** yogini
FISSTW swifts	**GGILNY** niggly	loughs	**GIINPP** piping
FISTWY swifty	**GGILOO** gigolo	slough	**GIINPW** wiping
FJLOUY joyful	**GGILWY** wiggly	**GHLPSY** glyphs	**GIINPZ** pizing
FKLNSU flunks	**GGINNO** noggin	**GHNORT** throng	**GIINRS** rising
FKLNUY flunky	**GGINOQ** qigong	**GHNOST** thongs	siring
FKLOOS kloofs	**GGINOR** goring	**GHNOSU** shogun	**GIINRT** tiring
FKLOSY folksy	Göring	**GHNOTU** hognut	**GIINRV** Irving
FLLOOW follow	gringo	nought	riving
FLLOUY foully	**GGINOS** goings	**GHNOUW** Hong-wu	virgin
FLMOOR formol	**GGINOZ** Zigong	**GHNRUY** hungry	**GIINRW** wiring
FLMORY formyl	**GGINRU** urging	**GHNUUW** Hung-wu	**GIINST** siting
	GGINRY gyring		

GIINSV	vising	**GIMNOW**	mowing	**GINRTY**	trying	**GMPSUY**	gypsum
GIINSW	wising	**GIMNPU**	impugn		tyring	**GNNOOR**	rognon
GIINSZ	sizing	**GIMNRU**	muring	**GINRWY**	wrying	**GNNSUU**	unsung
GIINVW	wiving	**GIMNSU**	Mingus	**GINSST**	stings	**GNOOPS**	pongos
GIIOPR	pirogi		musing	**GINSSW**	swings	**GNOORT**	Gorton
GIIRST	Tigris	**GIMNTU**	muting	**GINSTY**	stingy		trogon
GIJKNO	joking	**GIMOSS**	gismos		stying	**GNOPPU**	oppugn
GIJLNO	Jilong	**GIMOSZ**	gizmos	**GINSUU**	unguis		popgun
GIJLNY	jingly	**GIMOTU**	gomuti	**GINSWY**	swingy	**GNOPRS**	prongs
GIJNOY	joying	**GINNOO**	gonion	**GIOORV**	vigoro	**GNOPSY**	spongy
GIKLNU	Kilung	**GINNOS**	nosing	**GIOOTT**	Giotto	**GNORST**	strong
	Lungki	**GINNOT**	noting	**GIOPSS**	gossip	**GNORSW**	wrongs
GIKLNY	kingly		toning	**GIOPST**	spigot	**GNORSY**	gyrons
GIKNNU	nuking	**GINNOW**	owning	**GIOPTU**	pigout	**GNORYZ**	Grozny
GIKNOP	poking	**GINNOZ**	zoning	**GIORRS**	rigors	**GNOTUU**	outgun
GIKNOT	toking	**GINNRU**	urning	**GIORRU**	rigour	**GNPRSU**	sprung
GIKNOW	Woking	**GINNSY**	syning	**GIORST**	griots	**GNQRUU**	Qungur
GIKNOY	yoking	**GINNTU**	tuning	**GIORTU**	rigout	**GNRSTU**	grunts
GIKNOZ	Kong Zi	**GINOOS**	isogon	**GIORUV**	vigour		strung
GIKNPU	puking	**GINOOW**	wooing	**GIOSTT**	Tostig	**GNRTUU**	Guntur
GIKNSY	skying	**GINOOZ**	oozing	**GIOSTU**	giusto	**GOORSS**	sorgos
GIKRTU	tugrik	**GINOPR**	poring	**GIOTUZ**	Guizot	**GOORTT**	grotto
GILLOO	Gilolo		roping	**GIPRSS**	sprigs	**GOORVY**	groovy
GILLRS	grills	**GINOPS**	gipons	**GIPSTY**	pigsty	**GOPRSS**	sprogs
GILLUY	uglily		pingos	**GIRTTY**	gritty	**GOPRSU**	groups
GILMNU	lignum		posing	**GIRTUY**	Guitry	**GORRTU**	turgor
GILMRY	grimly	**GINOPT**	opting	**GJLNUY**	jungly	**GORSTU**	grouts
GILNOO	logion		toping	**GJMSUU**	jugums	**GORSUU**	rugous
	looing	**GINORS**	girons	**GJNOOU**	goujon	**GORSYZ**	groszy
GILNOP	loping		grison	**GJNRUU**	gurjun	**GORTTU**	rotgut
	poling		groins	**GKLNOS**	klongs		Turgot
GILNOS	losing		rosing	**GKNRUU**	Kungur	**GORTTY**	grotty
GILNOT	tiglon		signor	**GLLMUY**	glumly	**GORTUY**	grouty
GILNOU	louing	**GINORT**	trigon	**GLLOOP**	gollop		yogurt
GILNOV	loving	**GINORV**	roving	**GLMNOO**	mongol	**GOSTUY**	guyots
GILNOW	lowing	**GINORW**	rowing	**GLMOOS**	glooms	**GSYVYZ**	syzygy
GILNPU	puling	**GINOSS**	gnosis	**GLMOOY**	gloomy	**HHHOOT**	Hohhot
GILNPY	plying	**GINOST**	ingots	**GLMOSU**	moguls	**HHILOS**	Shiloh
GILNRU	luring		stingo	**GLMSUY**	smugly	**HHISTW**	whisht
	ruling		tigons	**GLNOOO**	oolong	**HHMRTY**	rhythm
GILNSS	slings		toings	**GLNOOY**	Yong Lo	**HHNOSU**	Honshu
GILNST	glints	**GINOSW**	sowing	**GLNOSU**	gluons	**HHOOSW**	whoosh
GILNSU	lungis	**GINOTT**	toting		Longus	**HHORTY**	Horthy
	nisgul	**GINOTU**	outing	**GLNOUY**	Yung-lo	**HHRSTU**	thrush
GILNSY	lysing	**GINOTV**	voting	**GLNPUU**	unplug	**HIIJNO**	John II
	singly	**GINOTW**	towing	**GLNSUY**	snugly	**HIILLT**	Lilith
GILNTU	luting	**GINOTY**	toying	**GLOOOY**	oology	**HIILPP**	Philip
GILNTY	tingly	**GINOVW**	vowing	**GLOOPR**	prolog	**HIIMMS**	mishmi
GILOOS	igloos	**GINOWW**	wowing	**GLOOTU**	logout	**HIIMPS**	impish
GILOOY	gooily	**GINPPU**	upping	**GLOPTU**	putlog	**HIIMSS**	Shiism
GILORY	gorily	**GINPRS**	spring	**GLORSW**	growls	**HIIMST**	isthmi
GILOSS	siglos	**GINPRY**	prying	**GLOSSY**	glossy		mishit
GILRSY	grisly	**GINPSU**	spuing	**GMNNOO**	gnomon	**HIINTW**	within
GILRTY	trigly	**GINPSY**	spying	**GMNOOS**	mongos	**HIIOPT**	pithoi
GILSTU	guilts	**GINPTU**	pignut	**GMNOST**	mongst	**HIIRST**	Tishri
GILTUY	guilty	**GINPTY**	typing	**GMNOSU**	mungos	**HIITZZ**	zizith
GILTYZ	glitzy	**GINRRU**	runrig	**GMNTUU**	gumnut	**HIJNOV**	John IV
GIMNNO	mignon	**GINRST**	string	**GMNUUZ**	mzungu		John VI
GIMNOO	mooing	**GINRSU**	unrigs	**GMOOPR**	pogrom	**HIJNSU**	shinju
GIMNOP	moping	**GINRSW**	wrings	**GMOORS**	grooms	**HIJOSS**	shojis
GIMNOU	gonium	**GINRTU**	truing	**GMPRSU**	grumps	**HIKMUZ**	muzhik
GIMNOV	moving		Turing	**GMPRUY**	grumpy	**HIKNRS**	shrink

Code	Word	Code	Word	Code	Word	Code	Word
HIKNST	thinks	HIRRSW	whirrs	HMPRUY	murphy	HPPSUU	pushup
HIKRSS	shirks	HIRSST	shirts	HMPSSU	sumphs	HPRSUU	uprush
HIKSSW	whisks	HIRSTT	thirst	HMPSTU	thumps	HPSTUY	typhus
HIKSUU	Kiushu	HIRSTY	Irtysh	HMPTUY	humpty	HRSSTU	hursts
HIKSWY	whisky		shirty	HMRSTU	thrums	HRSTTU	thrust
HILLOY	holily		thyrsi	HMSTUY	thymus		truths
HILLPU	uphill	HIRTTY	thirty	HNNOOP	phonon	HSTUUX	Xuthus
HILLRS	shrill	HISSTW	whists	HNOOPT	photon	IIIMNR	Rimini
HILLRT	thrill	HISSTX	sixths	HNOORS	honors	IIIPSU	Pius II
HILLSS	shills	HISSWY	swishy	HNOORT	thoron	IIIRST	iritis
HILLST	thills	HISTTY	shitty	HNOORU	honour	IIKKMS	Sikkim
HILMOS	holism		stithy	HNOPSY	Hypnos	IIKKOS	kikois
HILMOW	whilom	HIWYZZ	whizzy		syphon	IIKLMS	kilims
HILMOY	homily	HJNNOY	johnny	HNOPTY	phyton	IIKNNS	kinins
HILMSU	mulish	HKNOOU	unhook		python	IIKNPP	pipkin
HILNOT	Hilton	HKNOSY	shonky		typhon	IIKNSS	siskin
HILNPT	plinth	HKNRSU	shrunk	HNORST	norths	IIKPUW	wikiup
HILNTY	thinly	HKOOPU	hookup		thorns	IIKRTT	Tikrit
HILOOT	oolith	HKOORT	Rothko	HNORSU	onrush	IILLMU	limuli
	tholoi	HKOOSS	shooks	HNORTW	thrown	IILLOO	Iloilo
HILOPS	polish	HKOUVZ	Zhukov	HNORTY	rhyton	IILLOY	oilily
HILOST	lithos	HKSUUY	Kyushu		thorny	IILLSW	Willis
	thiols	HLLOOS	hollos	HNOSTU	Huston	IILMMU	milium
HILOSW	owlish	HLLOOW	hollow	HNOTTU	Hutton	IILMST	limits
HILRST	thirls	HLLOPY	phyllo	HNRTUU	unhurt	IILNNS	linins
HILRSW	whirls	HLLOSU	hullos	HNSSTU	shunts	IILNNU	inulin
HILSTW	whilst	HLLOWY	wholly	HNSSTY	synths	IILNOP	Pílion
HIMMSY	shimmy	HLLSUY	lushly	HOOOOR	hooroo	IILNOR	Ilorin
HIMNOY	hominy	HLMOTY	thymol	HOOPSS	poshos	IILNOV	violin
HIMORS	morish	HLMPUY	phylum	HOOPST	photos	IILNST	instil
	Romish	HLNOOS	holons	HOOPSW	whoops	IILNTY	tinily
HIMOTY	mythoi	HLNOUY	unholy	HOOPSY	shypoo	IILOSU	Louis I
HIMPRS	shrimp	HLNSUU	Lüshun	HOOPTT	hotpot	IILOTV	Tivoli
HIMSST	smiths	HLOOSS	shools	HOORRR	horror	IILPST	pistil
HIMSTY	smithy	HLOOST	tholos	HOOSST	shoots	IILRWY	wirily
HIMSWY	whimsy	HLOPSS	splosh		sooths	IILSTT	Tilsit
HINNST	ninths	HLOPSU	Ophüls	HOOSSW	swoosh	IILTTW	twilit
HINNSY	shinny	HLORSW	whorls	HOOSTT	tooths	IIMMNS	minims
HINNTU	Ithunn	HLORUY	hourly	HOOTTY	toothy	IIMMNU	minium
HINNWY	whinny	HLOSST	sloths	HOPRRY	Pyrrho	IIMNNO	minion
HINOPS	siphon	HLOSSY	sloshy	HOPRST	thorps	IIMNOU	ionium
HINORS	rhinos	HLPSSY	sylphs	HOPRTY	trophy	IIMNTZ	Nimitz
HINOST	Shinto	HLPSUY	plushy	HOPSSY	hyssop	IIMOSS	miosis
HINPSU	punish	HLPSYY	sylphy		phossy	IIMRST	smriti
	unship	HLSSUY	slushy	HOPSTU	tophus	IIMRSU	surimi
HINPSX	sphinx	HMMSUU	hummus		upshot	IIMSSS	missis
HINRSU	inrush	HMNOPY	nympho	HORSST	horsts	IINNOP	pinion
HINSTY	shinty	HMNOST	months		shorts	IINNOS	inions
HINSUV	Vishnu	HMNPSY	nymphs	HORSTT	troths	IINNPY	pinyin
HINSUW	unwish	HMOOPR	morpho	HORSTU	rouths	IINOPS	Piniós
HIOPPS	hippos	HMOOST	shtoom	HORSTW	rowths	IINOPT	poitin
	popish		smooth		throws	IINORS	Orsini
HIOPST	pithos	HMOPRS	morphs		worths	IINORV	virino
HIOPSY	physio	HMOPRY	Morphy	HORSTY	shorty		virion
HIORSU	houris	HMORSU	humors	HORTWY	worthy	IINOSV	vision
HIOSST	hoists		mohurs	HOSSTT	shotts	IINPPP	pippin
HIOTTU	outhit	HMORUU	humour	HOSSTU	shouts	IINPTX	pinxit
HIOTWZ	howzit	HMORUZ	Hormuz		stoush	IINSST	insist
HIPPSU	uppish	HMOSTU	mouths	HOSTUY	shouty	IINTTU	intuit
HIPRST	thrips	HMOSTY	mythos		youths	IINTTW	nitwit
HIQSSU	squish	HMOSUU	houmus	HOSUUZ	Suzhou	IIOOTT	toitoi
HIRRSS	shirrs	HMOTUY	mouthy	HOUUXZ	Xuzhou	IIOPZZ	Piozzi

IIORSS	Osiris	IKNSTW	twinks	ILNPST	splint
IIORZZ	Rizzio	IKNSTY	stinky	ILNPSU	lupins
IIOSTT	otitis	IKOOPU	Kuopio	ILNPUY	punily
IIPPST	pipits	IKOORS	irokos	ILNSSY	lysins
IIPPUU	piupiu	IKORSS	Skíros	ILNSTU	insult
IIPRRU	puriri	IKORYZ	Yizkor		sunlit
IIPRST	spirit	IKPRSU	prusik	ILNSVY	vinyls
IIPRTU	pituri		spruik	ILOOYZ	oozily
IIPSUV	Pius IV	IKPSTU	tupiks	ILOPPY	polypi
	Pius VI	IKQRSU	quirks	ILOPRX	prolix
IIPSUX	Pius IX	IKQRUY	quirky	ILOPRY	pylori
	Pius XI	IKRRSS	skirrs		ropily
IISSTV	visits	IKRRUY	Ryurik	ILOPSS	spoils
IJKMOU	moujik	IKRSST	skirts	ILOPST	pilots
IJKMSU	mujiks		stirks		pistol
IJLLOO	Jilolo	IKSUUV	Suu Kyi		postil
IJLNOP	Joplin	IKSVVY	skivvy		spoilt
IJMNOS	jimson	ILLMPY	limply	ILOPSU	pilous
IJMOSS	jissom	ILLMSY	slimly		poilus
IJNOPS	Jospin	ILLNOV	Villon	ILOPSX	oxlips
IJNORU	junior	ILLOPW	pillow	ILOPTY	polity
IJNOST	joints	ILLOWW	willow	ILOQRU	liquor
IJNRUY	injury	ILLPRS	prills	ILORRS	Lorris
IJNSUU	Junius	ILLPSS	spills	ILORST	triols
IJOSST	joists	ILLQSU	quills	ILORSY	rosily
IJRSTU	jurist		squill	ILORSZ	zorils
IKKKRU	Kirkuk	ILLRST	trills	ILOSUV	Louis V
IKKNSS	skinks	ILLSST	stills	ILOTTW	wittol
IKKOSS	kiosks	ILLSSW	swills	ILPPRY	ripply
IKKRSU	kukris	ILLSTW	twills	ILPPSU	pupils
IKKUUY	kikuyu	ILLSTY	stilly		slipup
IKLLSS	skills	ILLSUV	villus	ILPPSY	slippy
IKLLSY	skilly	ILMMSU	Muslim	ILPPTU	pulpit
IKLMOS	milkos	ILMNOS	Límnos	ILPRTY	triply
IKLNNU	unlink	ILMNOT	Milton	ILPSST	splits
IKLNPS	plinks	ILMNOU	moulin	ILPSTU	tulips
IKLNPU	linkup	ILMNSU	muslin	ILPTTU	uptilt
	uplink	ILMOOS	moolis	ILQSTU	quilts
IKLNSS	slinks	ILMOOV	moolvi	ILRSSW	swirls
IKLNSY	kylins	ILMOSS	lissom	ILRSTW	twirls
	slinky	ILMOSZ	Miłosz	ILRSTY	lyrist
IKLNTY	tinkly	ILMOTU	ultimo	ILRSWY	swirly
IKLOPY	pokily	ILMPPY	pimply	ILSSTT	stilts
IKLRSS	skirls	ILMPRY	primly	ILSTTU	lutist
IKLSSU	suslik	ILMPSY	simply	IMMMOS	momism
IKMNOO	kimono	ILMRSY	lyrism	IMMNOS	monism
IKMOSU	koumis	ILMRTY	trimly		nomism
IKMPSS	skimps	ILMSSU	simuls	IMMOOS	simoom
IKMPSY	skimpy	ILMSSY	slimsy	IMMOSU	osmium
IKMRSS	smirks	ILMSTU	litmus	IMMOTW	wommit
IKMSSU	kumiss	ILMTUU	tumuli	IMMSTU	mutism
IKMSUU	Kisumu	ILMYZZ	mizzly		summit
IKNNOT	Tonkin	ILNOOT	lotion	IMNNOW	minnow
IKNNSY	skinny	ILNOPP	poplin	IMNNTU	muntin
IKNNTU	unknit	ILNOPT	pontil	IMNOOR	morion
IKNOOR	krooni	ILNOQU	quinol		Moroni
IKNOPS	pinkos	ILNOST	Liston	IMNOOS	simoon
IKNOST	stinko		tonsil	IMNOOT	motion
IKNPRS	prinks	ILNOSU	insoul	IMNORS	minors
IKNRSU	Ruskin	ILNOSW	Wilson	IMNOST	inmost
IKNSST	stinks	ILNOSY	nosily		monist
IKNSSW	swinks	ILNPRU	purlin	IMNOSY	myosin
	simony				
IMNTUY	mutiny				
IMOPRS	porism				
	primos				
IMOPRT	import				
IMOPRV	improv				
IMOPST	impost				
IMORRR	mirror				
IMORRS	morris				
IMOSSX	sixmos				
IMOSSY	myosis				
IMOSTU	ostium				
IMOSTV	vomits				
IMOTTT	tomtit				
IMPPRS	primps				
IMPRSS	prisms				
IMPRSU	primus				
	purims				
	purism				
IMPSUX	mixups				
IMQRSU	squirm				
IMRRSS	smirrs				
IMRRSU	murris				
IMRSTU	murtis				
	truism				
IMSSSU	missus				
INNNOS	ninons				
INNOOS	onions				
INNOOT	notion				
INNOOY	oniony				
INNOPP	Nippon				
INNOPZ	Pinzón				
INNORS	ronins				
INNORT	intron				
INNOSU	unions				
	unison				
INNOWW	winnow				
INNPSU	unpins				
INNRSU	inurns				
INOOPS	poison				
INOOPT	option				
	potion				
INOORS	orison				
INOORT	Torino				
INOPPS	ippons				
INOPRS	orpins				
	prions				
	prison				
INOPST	pintos				
	piston				
	pitons				
	points				
INOPTT	tinpot				
INOPTY	pointy				
INOQSU	quoins				
INORSS	rosins				
INORST	intros				
INORSY	rosiny				
INORTT	triton				
INORTU	turion				
INOSTT	stotin				
INOSTX	toxins				

INOSUV	vinous	**IQSSTU**	quists	**KNPSUY**	spunky	stools
INPPRU	Nippur		squits	**KNRRSU**	knurrs	**LOOSTV** volost
INPPSU	pinups	**IRSSTW**	wrists	**KNRSTU**	trunks	**LOOVVX** volvox
INPPSY	snippy	**IRSSTY**	syrtis	**KOOOST**	Sokoto	**LOPPRY** propyl
INPRST	prints	**IRSSUU**	Ussuri	**KOOOSV**	Kosovo	**LOPPSY** polyps
	sprint	**IRSTWY**	wristy	**KOOPSS**	spooks	sloppy
INPRSU	unrips	**ISSSTU**	tussis	**KOOPSY**	spooky	**LOPRSW** prowls
INPRTU	turnip	**ISSTTW**	twists	**KOORUU**	Kourou	**LOPRTY** portly
	Turpin	**ISTTWY**	twisty	**KOORVV**	Kovrov	protyl
INPSTU	inputs	**JLLOOP**	jollop	**KOOSST**	stooks	**LOPSTU** poults
INPSUZ	unzips	**JLNOOS**	Jolson	**KOOTTU**	tuktoo	**LORSUY** sourly
INQSTU	quints	**JLSTUY**	justly	**KOOTWW**	kowtow	**LORTTY** trotyl
	squint	**JMORSU**	jorums	**KOPRUW**	workup	**LOSTYZ** zlotys
INQSUY	quinsy	**JNNOOS**	Jonson	**KORSST**	storks	**LPPRUY** purply
INRSXY	syrinx	**JNNOTU**	jotunn		torsks	**LPPSUY** supply
INRTWY	wintry	**JNOORU**	journo	**KORSSY**	Skyros	**LPRRUY** plurry
INSSTT	stints	**JNOPSU**	jupons	**KSTTUU**	tuktus	**LPRSSU** slurps
INSTUW	Wutsin	**JNOSTU**	jotuns	**LLLOOP**	lollop	**LPRSYY** spryly
IOOPST	Potosí		juntos	**LLNORU**	unroll	**LPSTUU** Plutus
IOOPTU	Poitou	**JNSTUU**	unjust	**LLOOTU**	toluol	**LRRSUY** slurry
IOOTTV	Otto IV	**JOOPPY**	joypop	**LLOOWY**	woolly	**LRSTUY** sultry
IOPPTT	tiptop	**JOOSUY**	joyous	**LLOPUX**	Pollux	**LRUUXY** luxury
IOPRRS	priors	**JORRSU**	jurors	**LLORST**	stroll	**LSSTUY** stylus
IOPRRY	priory	**JOSSTU**	jousts		trolls	**MMNOOR** Mormon
IOPRST	prosit	**KKLMUU**	mukluk	**LLOSWY**	slowly	**MMNOSU** summon
	ripost	**KKLOOZ**	kolkoz	**LLOSXY**	xylols	**MMOOPP** pompom
	tripos	**KKLSSU**	skulks	**LLOTUY**	toluyl	**MMOOTT** motmot
IOPSST	posits	**KKMTUU**	muktuk	**LLPPUU**	pullup	**MMRRUU** murmur
	ptosis	**KKNSSU**	skunks	**LLPSUU**	pullus	**MMUUUU** muumuu
IOPSSY	pyosis	**KKOTUU**	kotuku	**LLRSTU**	trulls	**MNNOUW** unmown
IOPSTV	pivots	**KKLLNOS** knolls		**LLSSTU**	stulls	**MNOOPP** pompon
IOQSTU	quoits	**KLLNOY**	knolly	**LLSXYY**	xylyls	**MNOORS** morons
IORRTW	worrit	**KLLOSY**	skolly	**LMMOUX**	lummox	**MNOORT** Morton
IORSSV	visors	**KLLSSU**	skulls	**LMMPUY**	plummy	**MNOORU** unmoor
IORSTU	suitor	**KLNNUU**	Kunlun	**LMMSUY**	slummy	**MNOOTU** mouton
IORSVZ	vizors	**KLNOOP**	plonko	**LMOOOO**	mooloo	**MNORSU** mourns
IOSSTT	Tissot	**KLNOPS**	plonks	**LMOOOP**	Molopo	**MNOSSU** Somnus
	tsotsi	**KLNPSU**	plunks	**LMOORU**	ormolu	**MNOSSY** Symons
IOSTTU	outsit	**KLNRSU**	knurls	**LMORSS**	slorms	**MNOSTU** mounts
IOTTUW	outwit	**KLNRUY**	knurly	**LMOSST**	smolts	**MNOTTU** mutton
IPPQUU	quippu	**KLOOPS**	plooks	**LMOSSU**	solums	**MNPTUY** numpty
IPPRTY	trippy	**KLOOPU**	lookup	**LMOSTU**	moults	**MOOPRS** promos
IPPTUY	uppity	**KLOOPY**	plooky	**LMOSTY**	mostly	**MOORRS** morros
IPQSUU	quipus	**KLOOSS**	skools	**LMOTUZ**	Olmütz	**MOORRW** morrow
IPRRTU	irrupt	**KLOPSU**	plouks	**LMPPSU**	plumps	**MOORST** motors
IPRSST	spirts	**KLOPUY**	plouky	**LMPRUY**	rumply	Tromsø
	sprits	**KLRTUU**	kultur	**LMPSSU**	slumps	**MOOSSU** osmous
	stirps	**KLTUYZ**	klutzy	**LMTTUU**	tumult	**MOOSTT** mottos
	strips	**KMOOOR**	mokoro	**LNNOSY**	nylons	**MOOTVY** yom tov
IPRSSU	sirups	**KMOOSS**	smokos	**LNOOPY**	polony	**MOPPRT** prompt
IPRSSY	prissy	**KNNOTU**	unknot	**LNOOST**	stolon	**MOPSST** stomps
IPRSTU	purist	**KNOORR**	kronor	**LNOOTU**	Toulon	**MOPSSU** possum
	spruit	**KNOORS**	Kronos	**LNOPSY**	pylons	**MOPSTU** upmost
IPRSTW	twirps		kroons	**LNOPTU**	pluton	**MOQRUU** quorum
IPRSTY	stripy	**KNOOSS**	snooks	**LNOTTY**	Lytton	**MORRSU** rumors
IPRTUY	purity	**KNORRU**	kronur	**LNRUUY**	unruly	**MORRUU** rumour
IPSSTU	situps	**KNORST**	tronks	**LOOPPT**	Pol Pot	**MORSST** storms
IPSTTY	typist	**KNORUY**	koruny	**LOOPRS**	orlops	**MORSTU** tumors
IPSVVY	spivvy	**KNOSST**	stonks	**LOOPRY**	poorly	**MORSTY** stormy
IPTTTU	tittup	**KNOSTU**	knouts	**LOOPSS**	sloops	**MORTUU** tumour
IQRSTU	quirts	**KNOTTY**	knotty		spools	**MOSSTU** smouts
	squirt	**KNPSSU**	spunks	**LOOSST**	sloots	**MOSSTW** smowts

MOSTTU	utmost	**NOOSTY**	snooty	**OOPRSU**	porous	**OPSSTW**	stowps
MPRSTU	trumps	**NOOSYZ**	snoozy	**OOPRTU**	uproot	**OPSTTY**	spotty
MPRSUU	rumpus	**NOOTTW**	Wotton	**OOPSST**	stoops	**OPTTUU**	output
MPSSTU	stumps	**NOPSTU**	Pontus	**OOPSSW**	swoops		putout
MPSTUU	sputum		putons	**OOPSTT**	pottos	**ORSSTU**	rousts
MPSTUY	stumpy		unstop	**OOPWWW**	powwow		stours
MRSSTU	strums	**NOPTUW**	uptown	**OORRST**	rotors	**ORSSTW**	strows
MSTTUY	smutty	**NORSST**	snorts	**OORRSW**	sorrow		worsts
NNOORT	Norton	**NORSTW**	strown	**OORSST**	roosts	**ORSSTY**	stroys
NNOOTW	wonton	**NORTUU**	outrun		stoors	**ORSTTU**	trouts
NNORUW	unworn		runout		torsos		tutors
NNORUY	Runyon	**NOSSTU**	snouts	**OORSTU**	outros	**ORTTUY**	tryout
NNOSUW	unsown	**NOSTTU**	Sutton		torous	**OSSTTU**	stouts
NOOPRS	Porson	**NOSTTY**	snotty	**OORSTV**	Rostov	**OSSTXY**	xystos
NOOPRT	pronto	**NPRSSU**	spurns	**OORSTY**	rootsy	**OSTTWY**	swotty
	proton	**NPRTUU**	turnup	**OOSTTY**	tootsy	**PRRSUY**	spurry
NOOPSS	snoops		upturn	**OPPSSY**	psyops	**PRSSTU**	spurts
	spoons	**NPSSUU**	sunups	**OPRSST**	sports	**PRSSUU**	usurps
NOOPSY	snoopy	**NSSTTU**	stunts		strops	**PRSSUY**	syrups
	spoony	**OOOPRT**	Oporto	**OPRSTU**	Proust	**PRSUYY**	syrupy
NOORST	nostro	**OOPPRT**	troppo		sprout	**RSSTTU**	struts
	rotons	**OOPRRT**	torpor		stupor		trusts
NOORTU	notour	**OOPRSS**	sopors	**OPRSTY**	sporty	**RSSTTY**	trysts
	unroot		spoors	**OPSSTU**	spouts	**RSSTUW**	wursts
NOOSST	snoots	**OOPRST**	poorts		stoups	**RSTTUY**	trusty
NOOSSW	swoons		troops		tossup	**SSTUXY**	xystus

Seven Letters

AAAABLM Alabama
AAAALMT Alma-Ata
AAABBCL cabbala
AAABBKL kabbala
AAABBLS babalas
AAABBNN Banaban
AAABCIR arabica
AAABCLR Calabar
AAABCLS cabalas
AAABCLV baclava
AAABCNS cabanas
AAABCOR carabao
AAABCSS casabas
        cassaba
AAABCTW catawba
AAABDFR abfarad
AAABDLM lambada
AAABDLR Aldabra
AAABDNN bandana
AAABDNR Narbada
AAABENS Sabaean
AAABFLL falbala
AAABHJL Halabja
AAABHLQ qabalah
AAABHMR Abraham
AAABHMS Bahamas
AAABILN Albania
AAABILX abaxial
AAABINR Arabian
AAABIPR Paraíba
AAABIRV Bavaria
AAABITV batavia
AAABKKS kabakas
AAABKLR Karbala
AAABKLS kabalas
AAABKLV baklava
AAABKPS baaskap
AAABLLU Lualaba
AAABLST balatas
AAABMNR Anambra
AAABMOS abomasa
AAABMST mastaba
AAABNNS bananas
AAABNRS Banaras
AAABORR araroba
AAABRST braatas
AAABRSX abrasax

        abraxas
AAABRSZ barazas
        bazaars
AAABSTT batatas
AAACCIS acacias
AAACCLM malacca
AAACCLP alpacca
AAACCLR caracal
AAACCRS Caracas
        cascara
AAACDGS cadagas
AAACDIN Acadian
AAACDIR arcadia
AAACDLU acaudal
AAACDMM macadam
AAACENP panacea
AAACHHL halacha
AAACHLZ chalaza
AAACHRY acharya
AAACIJM Jamaica
AAACILM malacia
AAACINT Catania
AAACJMR jacamar
AAACJNS jacanas
AAACJRU Aracajú
AAACLLS La Scala
AAACLLV cavalla
AAACLMN almanac
AAACLNT Alacant
        cantala
        Catalan
AAACLPS alpacas
AAACLPT catalpa
AAACLRZ alcazar
AAACMRS maracas
        marasca
        mascara
AAACMRY Maracay
AAACNPU Capuana
AAACNRS arcanas
AAACNRV caravan
AAACNST canasta
AAACNTT cantata
AAACRRR Carrara
AAACRWY caraway
AAACSST cassata
AAACSSV cassava

AAADDMO amadoda
AAADELM alameda
AAADFRY faraday
AAADGGH Aggadah
AAADGHL Galahad
AAADGNR Granada
AAADGUV Daugava
AAADHHS shahada
AAADHMN Hamadān
AAADHNS sadhana
AAADHWY hadaway
AAADILX adaxial
AAADIRT radiata
AAADLLN Laaland
AAADLMN amandla
        mandala
AAADMNR Narmada
        Ramadan
AAADMNT adamant
AAADMNZ Zaandam
AAADMRS armadas
        madrasa
AAADWYY awayday
AAAEGLT galatea
AAAEGNP apanage
AAAEHLT althaea
AAAEIMN anaemia
AAAEKRS Kara Sea
AAAELPT Plataea
AAAELRS Aral Sea
AAAELSZ azaleas
AAAENST anatase
AAAERWY areaway
AAAFFLL alfalfa
AAAFHLS Falasha
AAAFIRT ratafia
AAAFRWY faraway
AAAGHIP aphagia
AAAGHKN Aga Khan
AAAGHNT ataghan
AAAGHPR agrapha
AAAGILN analgia
AAAGILT Galatia
AAAGINR Niagara
AAAGINZ gazania
AAAGIPT patagia
AAAGISS assagai

AAAGKNN Kananga
AAAGKNR karanga
AAAGKNT Katanga
AAAGLMM amalgam
AAAGLNS lasagna
AAAGLOS Alagoas
AAAGMMT magmata
AAAGMNR anagram
AAAGMNU Managua
AAAGMTT tagmata
AAAGMTU Gautama
AAAGNRR ngarara
AAAGNRT tanagra
AAAGRST Aragats
AAAHHKL halakha
AAAHHLV halavah
AAAHIKP aphakia
AAAHIKW kahawai
AAAHIPS aphasia
AAAHIST taiahas
AAAHKRS akharas
AAAHLNN alannah
AAAHMMT mahatma
AAAHMST Athamas
        tamasha
AAAHNRS Saharan
AAAHNRY Haryana
AAAHNSV vahanas
AAAHPPR Harappa
AAAHPRT paratha
AAAHRTW waratah
AAAIKKR karakia
AAAIKLT latakia
AAAIKRS akrasia
AAAILMR malaria
AAAILNX anaxial
AAAILPS aplasia
AAAILPT Patiala
AAAILRT talaria
AAAILST Alsatia
AAAIMNT amanita
AAAIMRS Samaria
AAAINNS Ananias
AAAINNZ Azanian
AAAIPRX apraxia
AAAIPSS Aspasia
AAAIQRU aquaria

111

AAAJKNR	Karajan	AABBDRU	Barbuda
AAAJKRT	Jakarta	AABBEGN	beanbag
AAAJMPS	pajamas	AABBEKL	Baalbek
AAAKKMR	markkaa	AABBEMN	Mbabane
AAAKKNS	kanakas	AABBERR	Barbera
AAAKLLV	Kaválla	AABBERT	barbate
AAAKLMP	Kampala	AABBHMR	Brabham
AAAKLMR	Alkmaar	AABBHST	sabbath
AAAKLMS	kamalas		Shabbat
AAAKLNS	Alaskan	AABBLLS	lablabs
AAAKLSS	Kassala	AABBLOS	balboas
AAAKMOY	Okayama	AABBNRT	Brabant
AAAKMPR	Karmapa	AABBRRY	Barbary
AAAKMRS	Makasar	AABBSST	sabbats
AAAKNRS	Sankara	AABBSSU	babassu
AAAKNTY	Antakya	AABCCEH	Bacchae
AAAKPPU	kaupapa	AABCCET	baccate
AAAKRSW	Sarawak	AABCDIN	Cabinda
AAALLMP	La Palma	AABCDIR	carabid
AAALLPT	La Plata	AABCEFR	facebar
	palatal	AABCELL	Caballé
AAALMNY	Malayan	AABCELN	balance
AAALMRS	marsala	AABCELP	capable
AAALMSS	salaams	AABCELT	actable
AAALMTY	Malatya	AABCEMR	macabre
AAALNNT	lantana	AABCEMS	ambsace
AAALNPW	Palawan	AABCEOS	cobaeas
AAALNTT	Atlanta	AABCERT	abreact
AAALNTY	Antalya		bearcat
AAALRRY	arrayal		cabaret
AAALRSZ	Salazar	AABCFKT	fatback
AAALWYY	layaway	AABCHHR	brachah
AAAMMPR	mampara	AABCHIL	Laibach
AAAMMRR	Marmara	AABCHIR	brachia
AAAMNNT	anatman	AABCHMT	ambatch
AAAMNPS	panamas	AABCHNR	barchan
AAAMNPT	Matapan	AABCHOR	abroach
AAAMNRT	maranta	AABCHSS	casbahs
AAAMNST	atamans	AABCIIP	Picabia
AAAMORT	tamarao	AABCILM	cambial
AAAMRSS	samaras	AABCIMR	Cambrai
	samsara		Cambria
AAAMRTU	tamarau	AABCIMS	Cabimas
AAAMSSW	Massawa	AABCINR	carabin
AAANNRY	Narayan	AABCIOP	copaiba
AAANNSV	savanna	AABCIRT	Bactria
AAANPPY	papayan	AABCITX	taxicab
AAANRTT	tantara	AABCKLY	layback
AAAOPRZ	parazoa	AABCKPY	backpay
AAAPPRT	apparat		payback
AAAPPSY	papayas	AABCKRR	barrack
AAAPSST	passata	AABCKSW	backsaw
AAARRST	Tarrasa	AABCLPY	capably
AAARSTV	avatars	AABCLRY	Barclay
AAARTTT	ratatat	AABCMMU	macumba
AAARTTU	tuatara	AABCORT	acrobat
AAARTXY	ataraxy	AABCOST	Tabasco
AABBBEG	Babbage	AABCOTT	catboat
AABBBOS	baobabs	AABCRSS	scarabs
AABBCEG	cabbage	AABDDER	abraded
AABBCOS	babacos	AABDDGH	Baghdad
AABBDIS	Abbasid	AABDDIK	kabaddi

AABDDNO	Abaddon	AABEGGG	baggage
AABDDNS	sanddab	AABEGGR	garbage
AABDEFL	fadable	AABEGLR	algebra
AABDEGM	gambade	AABEGMS	ambages
AABDEGN	bandage	AABEGRR	barrage
AABDEHS	abashed	AABEGSS	bagasse
AABDEIR	braaied	AABEHLT	hatable
AABDEIS	diabase	AABEHRS	earbash
AABDEKW	dawbake	AABEHSS	abashes
AABDELL	ballade	AABEIKN	ikebana
AABDELR	Abelard	AABEILM	amiable
AABDELT	ablated	AABEILN	abelian
	datable	AABEILT	labiate
AABDELW	wadable	AABEIOR	aerobia
AABDEMS	sambaed	AABEIRS	airbase
AABDENU	bandeau	AABEJLL	jellaba
AABDERR	abrader	AABEJMU	jambeau
AABDERS	abrades	AABEKLM	makable
AABDESU	aubades	AABEKLT	takable
AABDEWZ	Bezwada	AABEKRY	kerbaya
AABDGHN	handbag	AABELLL	labella
AABDGMO	gambado	AABELLN	balneal
AABDGNS	sandbag	AABELLR	earball
AABDGNU	Buganda	AABELLS	salable
AABDGOS	dagobas	AABELMN	namable
AABDHIO	Obadiah	AABELMT	tamable
AABDHNT	hatband	AABELNO	abalone
AABDHRU	bahadur	AABELNS	bansela
AABDIIS	basidia	AABELPR	parable
AABDIJN	Abidjan	AABELPY	payable
AABDIKR	bidarka	AABELRS	arables
AABDIMR	barmaid	AABELRT	Alberta
AABDINS	indabas		ratable
AABDINT	tabanid	AABELSS	balases
AABDIOT	biodata	AABELST	ablates
AABDJOZ	Badajoz		astable
AABDLLR	Ballard	AABELTT	abettal
AABDLLS	ballads	AABELTU	tableau
AABDLMS	lambdas	AABELTX	taxable
AABDLRW	bradawl	AABEMNS	baseman
AABDLRY	Arblay, d'	AABEMOS	amoebas
	d'Arblay	AABEMRR	Braemar
AABDLSU	Salduba	AABEMST	Masbate
AABDMNR	armband	AABENNW	wannabe
	Bradman	AABENRT	antbear
AABDNNO	abandon	AABENRV	Barnave
AABDNRR	Barnard	AABENTY	abeyant
AABDNRS	sandbar	AABERST	abreast
AABDORV	bravado	AABERSU	subarea
AABDRRW	drawbar	AABERSZ	zarebas
AABDRST	bastard	AABERTT	tabaret
	tabards	AABETUX	bateaux
AABDRSU	subadar	AABFFLY	affably
AABDRSY	bayards	AABFILU	fabliau
AABEELT	eatable	AABFINR	Biafran
AABEEMO	amoebae	AABGGRS	ragbags
AABEERZ	zareeba	AABGGSS	gasbags
AABEFFL	affable	AABGHNR	bhangra
AABEFGL	fleabag		Branagh
AABEFNR	Aberfan	AABGHSW	bagwash
AABEFNS	fanbase	AABGIIL	abigail

AABGILM	mailbag	AABLLSY	basally
AABGIMN	Gambian		salably
AABGINR	bargain	AABLLWY	wallaby
AABGINS	abasing	AABLMOS	Absalom
AABGINT	abating	AABLMRU	labarum
AABGLOR	Aalborg	AABLMSS	balsams
AABGRST	ratbags	AABLMST	lambast
AABHHIW	Wahhabi	AABLMSY	abysmal
AABHIMS	Baha'ísm		balsamy
AABHINR	Bahrain	AABLNOT	Balaton
AABHITT	habitat	AABLNRU	Barnaul
AABHKNR	barkhan	AABLNSS	San Blas
AABHKOR	Bokhara	AABLNTT	blatant
AABHKRS	Bhaskar	AABLORT	ablator
AABHKRU	Bukhara	AABLOSV	lavabos
AABHKSS	kasbahs	AABLRTU	tabular
	sabkhas	AABLRTY	ratably
AABHLRS	bharals	AABLSST	basalts
AABHLTY	bathyal	AABLSSY	abyssal
AABHMNR	Brahman	AABLTTU	abuttal
AABHMRS	brahmas	AABLTXY	taxably
AABHMSS	shambas	AABMMOS	Mombasa
AABHNSV	bhavans	AABMNOT	boatman
AABHNSW	bhawans	AABMNOY	amboyna
AABHOST	Sabaoth		Bayamón
AABHSSW	bashaws	AABMNST	bantams
AABIILX	biaxial		batsman
AABIIMN	Namibia	AABMORT	Tambora
AABIKNS	banksia	AABMORU	marabou
AABILLR	barilla	AABMRSS	sambars
AABILLS	labials	AABMSUW	Sumbawa
AABILMN	Balmain	AABNNOZ	bonanza
AABILMY	amiably	AABNNSY	banyans
AABILNS	Basilan	AABNOSY	sabayon
AABILNT	Taliban	AABORRS	arrobas
AABILOU	aboulia		rasbora
AABILRS	basilar	AABORST	abators
AABIMMR	marimba		rabatos
AABIMNO	amboina	AABOTTY	attaboy
AABIMNZ	Zambian	AABQSUU	subaqua
AABIMRS	ambaris	AABRRUV	bravura
AABIMST	basmati	AABSSSY	sassaby
AABINNS	banians	AABSTTW	abwatts
AABINOU	ouabain	AACCDEI	cicadae
AABINST	abstain	AACCDES	cascade
AABINSW	Swabian		saccade
AABIORT	airboat	AACCDIR	cardiac
AABIORZ	Orizaba	AACCDIS	cicadas
AABIRSS	Brassaï	AACCDOR	Accardo
AABIRST	barista	AACCELO	cloacae
	bartsia	AACCERS	carcase
AABISSY	Bisayas	AACCEST	saccate
AABISTT	abattis	AACCHIR	archaic
	Batista	AACCHLN	clachan
AABJMRT	jambart	AACCHLS	Calchas
AABKMRU	Mubarak	AACCHMP	champac
AABKNPR	Brakpan	AACCHMS	chacmas
AABKNRS	barkans	AACCHNR	Cranach
AABKNRT	tanbark	AACCHPU	Pachuca
AABKOOZ	bazooka	AACCIJO	Ajaccio
AABLLNY	banally	AACCILM	acclaim
AABLLST	ballast	AACCILS	alcaics

	cicalas		calando
AACCILU	acicula	AACDLNS	scandal
AACCIOR	carioca	AACDLOS	scalado
AACCITT	atactic	AACDLPR	placard
AACCJKR	carjack	AACDMPS	madcaps
AACCKLP	calpack	AACDNRS	canards
AACCKRR	carrack		cardans
AACCLLO	cloacal	AACDOOV	avocado
AACCLLT	catcall	AACDPRU	crapaud
AACCLOP	polacca	AACDRSZ	czardas
AACCLOR	caracol	AACEEGR	acreage
AACCLPS	calpacs	AACEEHR	earache
AACCLRU	accrual	AACEEHT	chaetae
	caracul	AACEEKT	teacake
AACCLSU	accusal	AACEELN	anelace
AACCMOS	macacos	AACEEMN	Camenae
AACCNNS	cancans	AACEEMR	camerae
AACCNVY	vacancy	AACEEMS	amesace
AACCORU	curacao	AACEENT	catenae
	Curaçao	AACEERT	acerate
AACCOTT	toccata	AACEESS	casease
AACCRSS	carcass	AACEEST	caseate
AACDDEL	decadal	AACEETT	acetate
AACDDIN	candida	AACEFIS	fasciae
AACDEEM	academe	AACEFLT	falcate
AACDEFS	facades	AACEFLU	faculae
AACDEHL	Chaldea	AACEFRR	carfare
AACDEHM	chamade	AACEFRS	carafes
AACDEHR	charade	AACEGKP	package
AACDEHT	cathead	AACEGLS	scalage
AACDEII	aecidia	AACEGNR	caganer
AACDEIL	alcaide		carnage
AACDELL	alcalde		cranage
AACDELN	canaled	AACEGRT	cartage
	candela	AACEHLP	acaleph
	decanal	AACEHLR	alchera
AACDELR	caldera	AACEHNP	panache
AACDELS	alcades	AACEHNR	Arachne
	scalade	AACEHOP	Phocaea
AACDEMY	academy	AACEHPS	apaches
AACDENV	advance	AACEHPU	chapeau
AACDENZ	cadenza	AACEHRT	trachea
AACDERS	arcades	AACEHST	achates
AACDERV	cadaver	AACEHTT	attache
AACDERY	daycare	AACEHTU	chateau
AACDETU	caudate	AACEILN	Caelian
AACDETV	vacated	AACEIMN	anaemic
AACDFIR	faradic	AACEIMR	America
AACDGIS	cadagis	AACEINN	Nicaean
AACDHMO	Machado	AACEINO	Oceania
AACDHMR	drachma	AACEINR	carinae
AACDHST	datchas	AACEIRV	avarice
AACDIIS	ascidia		caviare
AACDIJU	Judaica	AACEIST	ectasia
AACDILR	radical	AACEJKN	Janáček
AACDINT	antacid	AACEJRS	jacares
AACDINV	vanadic	AACEKNP	pancake
AACDIOR	acaroid	AACEKNS	askance
AACDIRS	acarids	AACEKOT	oatcake
	ascarid	AACELLN	canella
AACDJKW	jackdaw	AACELLP	Laplace
AACDLNO	acnodal	AACELLT	lacteal

113

AACELLW	Wallace	AACGHNN	Changan	AACIIST	Asiatic	AACLLNU	lacunal
AACELMN	Maclean	AACGIIL	Galicia	AACIITV	viatica	AACLLOO	calaloo
	manacle	AACGILL	glacial	AACIJLP	jalapic	AACLLSU	clausal
AACELMR	cameral	AACGILM	magical	AACIKLL	alkalic	AACLLVY	cavally
	caramel	AACGINT	agnatic	AACIKLR	clarkia	AACLMNT	clamant
	ceramal	AACGIRS	agarics	AACIKNN	canakin	AACLMRU	macular
	maceral	AACGLOT	catalog	AACIKPR	Rapacki	AACLMST	lactams
AACELMU	maculae	AACGLOU	coagula	AACIKRT	akratic	AACLMSU	calamus
AACELNS	anlaces	AACGLRV	Calgary	AACILLS	callais	AACLNNO	anconal
AACELNU	canulae	AACGLSY	galyacs	AACILMR	mailcar	AACLNNU	cannula
	lacunae	AACGNOR	Orcagna	AACILMS	camails	AACLNOR	Alarcón
AACELNV	valance	AACGNOU	guanaco	AACILNO	Laconia		Alcoran
AACELPR	carpale	AACHHKR	charkha	AACILNR	cranial	AACLNPY	claypan
AACELPS	palaces	AACHHLL	challah	AACILNT	actinal	AACLNRU	canular
AACELPT	placate	AACHHMT	Chatham		antical		lacunar
AACELRS	scalare	AACHIKN	kachina	AACILNU	Lucania	AACLNSU	canulas
AACELRV	caravel	AACHIKR	Karachi	AACILOS	asocial		lacunas
AACELST	acetals	AACHILM	Malachi	AACILOX	coaxial	AACLOPR	caporal
	lactase	AACHILR	rachial	AACILPS	spacial		crapola
AACELSU	Alcaeus	AACHILT	calathi	AACILPT	capital	AACLORT	Carlota
AACELTT	lactate	AACHIMR	machair	AACILRR	railcar		coaltar
AACELTV	clavate	AACHIMS	chiasma	AACILUY	Ucayali	AACLOST	catalos
AACEMMR	macrame	AACHINT	acanthi	AACIMNO	manioca		coastal
AACEMNV	caveman		Ithacan	AACIMNS	caimans	AACLOTT	cattalo
AACEMQU	macaque		tachina		maniacs	AACLPRS	carpals
AACEMRS	cameras	AACHIPR	charpai	AACIMOR	acromia	AACLPRT	caltrap
AACEMRU	Marceau	AACHIPS	aphasic	AACIMRU	Mauriac	AACLPSS	pascals
AACENOT	Actaeon		Chiapas	AACIMTY	cymatia	AACLPSU	paucals
	Caetano	AACHIPT	chapati	AACINNT	cantina		scapula
AACENPS	canapes	AACHIRT	cithara	AACINOR	Aaronic	AACLPTY	playact
AACENRT	cateran	AACHKMN	Hackman		ocarina	AACLRSS	lascars
AACENTY	cyanate	AACHKMP	champak	AACINPT	captain		rascals
AACEOPT	peacoat	AACHKMR	Rackham	AACINRS	arnicas		scalars
AACEORS	rosacea	AACHKNR	Harnack		carinas	AACLRTY	lactary
AACEPRS	Pescara	AACHKRS	chakras	AACINRZ	czarina	AACLRVY	calvary
AACEPWY	paceway		charkas	AACINST	satanic		cavalry
AACEQTU	Caquetá	AACHKRY	hayrack	AACINTV	Vatican	AACLSSU	casuals
AACERSS	caesars	AACHKSW	hacksaw	AACIOPT	tapioca	AACLSTU	actuals
AACERST	Caserta		kwachas	AACIOPV	copaiva	AACLSUV	vascula
AACERSU	caesura	AACHLLN	Lachlan	AACIORT	Croatia	AACLSUX	Lascaux
AACERSZ	sazerac	AACHLMS	chasmal	AACIORV	Craiova	AACLTTU	tactual
AACERTT	teacart	AACHLMY	Malachy	AACIOTV	Octavia	AACMNNO	Monacan
AACERTU	arcuate	AACHLNT	canthal	AACIPRX	apraxic	AACMNRU	arcanum
AACERWY	raceway	AACHLPP	chappal	AACIQTU	aquatic	AACMNSY	caymans
AACESTV	caveats	AACHLPS	paschal	AACIRSV	caviars	AACMORR	camorra
	vacates	AACHMNP	chapman	AACISSS	cassias	AACMORS	sarcoma
AACETTU	actuate	AACHMNR	Cam Ranh	AACISTT	astatic	AACMORT	marcato
AACFILS	facials	AACHMNS	machans	AACJKLS	jackals	AACMRRT	tramcar
	fascial	AACHMSY	yashmac	AACJKMN	manjack	AACMRSS	sarcasm
AACFILU	faucial	AACHMTU	Machaut	AACJKSS	jackass	AACMRST	tarmacs
AACFINR	African	AACHNOP	panocha	AACJMOR	Majorca	AACNNOZ	canzona
AACFINT	fanatic	AACHNPX	panchax	AACJOST	Jocasta	AACNORU	A Coruña
AACFLLT	catfall	AACHNRS	anarchs	AACJOSU	acajous	AACNOSS	Canossa
AACFLLU	falcula	AACHNRY	anarchy	AACKKLO	Kaolack	AACNOST	sacaton
AACFLLY	fallacy	AACHNSU	anchusa	AACKLMR	Lamarck		Toscana
AACFLPT	flatcap	AACHNSZ	chazans	AACKLTW	catwalk	AACNPST	capstan
AACFLRT	fractal	AACHRRT	catarrh	AACKNRS	ransack		catnaps
AACFLRU	facular	AACHRSU	Huáscar	AACKPRR	carpark	AACNRTU	curtana
AACFLTU	factual	AACHRSW	Crashaw	AACKPRT	ratpack	AACNSSV	canvass
AACFNST	caftans	AACHRWY	archway	AACKSTT	attacks	AACNSTT	actants
AACGGMS	cagmags	AACIINR	Icarian	AACLLNS	callans	AACNTUY	Yucatán
AACGHLL	Chagall	AACIINT	actinia	AACLLNT	callant	AACOPPR	apocarp

AACPSTW catspaw	vedalia	AADGLLW gadwall	AADJLNS jandals
AACRSTV cravats	AADEIMR madeira	AADGLNO gonadal	AADKLNO Oakland
AACRTTT attract	AADEINR araneid	AADGLNR garland	AADKMNR Danmark
AACRTUY actuary	Ariadne	AADGLRU gradual	AADKMSS damasks
AACSSTT Cassatt	AADEINS naiades	AADGMNR grandam	AADKNOT Dakotan
AACTUWY cutaway	AADEIRT radiate	grandma	AADKNRT tankard
AADDDEN addenda	tiaraed	AADGMOT dogmata	AADKNRY Yarkand
AADDEES Dead Sea	AADEITV aviated	AADGMRS smaragd	AADKPSU padauks
AADDEGM damaged	AADEITW awaited	AADGNNU Ugandan	AADKRWW awkward
AADDEHH hadedah	AADEJMR jemadar	AADGNPR grandpa	AADLLMR mallard
AADDEIL alidade	AADEJNU Judaean	AADGNPS Dapsang	AADLLNP Lapland
AADDEMN deadman	AADEKLR kraaled	padangs	AADLLPU paludal
AADDENP deadpan	AADEKMR kamerad	AADGNRT gardant	AADLMMU Malamud
AADDEPR paraded	AADEKPR parkade	AADGOPR podagra	AADLMNO mandola
AADDEPT adapted	AADELLY allayed	AADGOPS pagodas	AADLMNU ladanum
AADDERW awarded	AADELMN Almadén	AADGRSY gaydars	AADLNRY lanyard
AADDESX addaxes	Mandela	AADHHMS Mashhad	AADLNSS sandals
AADDFGI Gaddafi	AADELMO alamode	AADHHNR Dhahran	AADLNSU landaus
AADDFIQ Qaddafi	AADELMR alarmed	AADHHRT hardhat	AADLNSV vandals
AADDGNR grandad	AADELNR adrenal	AADHILR Harald I	AADLNWY Wayland
AADDHKR khaddar	AADELNW danelaw	AADHILS dahlias	AADLOPY payload
AADDIIK didakai	AADELNX adnexal	AADHIMR hadarim	AADLPPU applaud
AADDILS alidads	AADELNZ Zealand	AADHIMS samadhi	AADLRRU radular
AADDIMN Miandad	AADELRU radulae	AADHINO Idahoan	AADLRWY Aylward
AADDIMS dadaism	AADELRY already	AADHINP daphnia	AADMNNO madonna
AADDIST dadaist	AADELSS salades	AADHINR Hadrian	AADMNNS sandman
AADDLYY Lady Day	AADELTU adulate	AADHKNS dhansak	AADMNOR madrona
AADDMOR Damodar	AADEMMN manmade	khandas	monarda
AADDNVV dvandva	AADEMNO adenoma	AADHLRV halyard	AADMNRS mansard
AADDOSU aoudads	AADEMNS anadems	AADHMNR hardman	AADMNTU tamandu
AADDRST dastard	maenads	AADHNPR hardpan	AADMORT matador
AADEEFR afeared	AADEMNT mandate	AADHNSW handsaw	AADMOYY Omayyad
AADEELT dealate	AADEMNY name day	AADHOYY Ayodhya	AADMRRY yardarm
AADEEMT edemata	AADEMRW Medawar	AADHRSZ hazards	AADMRSU marauds
AADEERT aerated	AADEMSS amassed	AADHRWY hayward	AADMRSZ mazards
AADEERW awardee	AADENNP Pandean	AADHSWY washday	AADMRZZ mazzard
AADEFHT fathead	AADENNT andante	AADIINN Indiana	AADMUYY Umayyad
AADEFLY al Fayed	AADENRU Dunărea	AADIINO dianoia	AADNNRS randans
AADEGGR aggrade	AADENRV veranda	AADIIPS adipsia	AADNNRW Rwandan
garaged	AADENSW weasand	AADILLO alodial	AADNOPR pandora
AADEGHN Den Haag	AADENTV Vedanta	AADILMR admiral	AADNORR Andorra
AADEGLS geladas	AADEPRR parader	AADILMT matilda	AADNORY anyroad
AADEGMN managed	AADEPRS parades	AADILNP paladin	AADNRVW vanward
AADEGMR damager	AADEPRT adapter	AADILNR laniard	AADOPRR parador
AADEGMS damages	readapt	AADILNS Saladin	AADOPRS parados
AADEGNR Grenada	AADEPSS passade	AADILNU Laudian	AADOPRT adaptor
AADEGNS agendas	AADERRW awarder	AADILPS apsidal	AADOPRX paradox
Sandage	AADERRY arrayed	AADILRS radials	AADOPSS posadas
AADEGRT gradate	AADERSW seaward	AADILSS dalasis	AADORWY roadway
AADEGRV ravaged	AADESSY assayed	AADILTV datival	AADOSTT tostada
AADEGRY drayage	AADFHOS Fashoda	AADILWY waylaid	AADPSSW padsaws
yardage	AADGGHR haggard	AADIMNR Miranda	AADPSYY paydays
AADEGSV savaged	AADGGLR laggard	AADIMNS maidans	AADPTTU dupatta
AADEHIR airhead	AADGHNZ Gandzha	AADIMOR diorama	AADQRTU quadrat
AADEHLN Haldane	AADGHOR darogha	AADIMOT domatia	AADRRSS sardars
AADEHMN headman	AADGHRS dargahs	AADIMRU Madurai	AADRSTU daturas
AADEHMS ashamed	AADGIKZ Kaz Daği	AADINRS radians	AADRSTY daystar
AADEHPR Phaedra	AADGIMM digamma	AADINRT radiant	AADRWWY wayward
AADEHPS saphead	AADGIMR diagram	AADINRV Andvari	AAEEFGL leafage
AADEHRW warhead	AADGIMS agamids	AADINRW wardian	AAEEFRT ratafee
AADEHWY headway	AADGINN Dingaan	AADIRSU sudaria	AAEEGKL leakage
AADEILV availed	AADGIOS adagios	AADISST stadias	AAEEGLT galeate

AAEEGMR	Megaera	AAEGLRV	Algarve	AAEIKLN	akenial	AAELMNU	alumnae
AAEEGMT	agamete	AAEGLSV	lavages	AAEIKLR	Karelia	AAELMOT	oatmeal
AAEEGNO	Neogaea		salvage	AAEIKLU	Kilauea	AAELMPT	palmate
AAEEGRV	average	AAEGMNR	manager	AAEIKRT	Karaite	AAELMST	malates
AAEEHRT	hetaera	AAEGMNS	manages	AAEILLN	La Línea		maltase
AAEEINT	taeniae	AAEGMNT	magenta	AAEILLX	axillae		tamales
AAEEKLS	seakale		magnate	AAEILMN	Alamein	AAELMSY	amylase
AAEELMT	maleate	AAEGMPR	rampage		laminae	AAELNNS	anneals
AAEELOR	areolae	AAEGMRT	Margate	AAEILMR	Almería	AAELNRS	arsenal
AAEEMNT	emanate	AAEGMSS	massage	AAEILMS	malaise	AAELNRT	Lateran
	enemata	AAEGNNP	pannage	AAEILNN	alanine	AAELNST	sealant
	manatee	AAEGNNT	tannage	AAEILNO	aeolian	AAELNSY	analyse
AAEEMRT	amreeta	AAEGNOP	apogean	AAEILNT	antliae	AAELNTT	tetanal
AAEEMTX	meataxe	AAEGNPT	pageant	AAEILNU	El Aaiún	AAELNYZ	analyze
AAEEPPS	appease	AAEGNPW	pawnage	AAEILOR	olearia	AAELORR	areolar
AAEERST	aerates	AAEGNRR	arrange	AAEILOT	Aetolia	AAELORS	areolas
AAEERSW	seaware	AAEGNRT	tanager	AAEILRS	aerials	AAELORU	aureola
AAEERTU	aureate	AAEGNST	agnates	AAEILRV	velaria	AAELOTX	oxalate
AAEERTX	exarate	AAEGNSU	guanase	AAEILSS	aliases	AAELPPR	apparel
AAEFFGR	agraffe	AAEGNTV	vantage	AAEIMMT	imamate	AAELPPS	appeals
AAEFFIR	affaire	AAEGPRR	parerga	AAEIMNR	Armenia	AAELPPT	palpate
AAEFFLL	falafel	AAEGPRW	warpage	AAEIMNS	amnesia	AAELPPU	papulae
AAEFFNR	fanfare	AAEGPSS	passage	AAEIMNT	amentia	AAELPRS	earlaps
AAEFFTT	taffeta	AAEGQUY	quayage		animate	AAELPRT	apteral
AAEFGNR	Fergana	AAEGRRV	ravager	AAEIMPY	pyaemia	AAELPRV	palaver
AAEFGRS	agrafes	AAEGRST	teargas	AAEIMRR	armeria	AAELPSS	plaases
AAEFGTW	waftage	AAEGRSV	ravages	AAEIMRT	amirate	AAELPST	palates
AAEFHMR	Fareham	AAEGRTT	regatta	AAEIMRU	uraemia	AAELPTT	tapetal
AAEFHNS	Eşfahān	AAEGRUV	Guevara	AAEIMTV	amative	AAELPTU	plateau
AAEFKLO	oakleaf	AAEGSSU	assuage	AAEINNO	aeonian	AAELPTY	apetaly
AAEFLPR	earflap		sausage	AAEINPR	Pienaar	AAELRST	tarseal
AAEFLSV	favelas	AAEGSSV	savages	AAEINPT	patinae	AAELRTZ	lazaret
AAEFMRT	fermata	AAEGSTW	wastage	AAEINST	entasia	AAELRVZ	Alvarez
AAEFNST	Santa Fe	AAEGTTW	wattage	AAEIPRR	pareira	AAELSST	atlases
AAEFRRR	Ferrara	AAEGTUX	gateaux	AAEIPRS	spiraea	AAELSTV	valetas
AAEFRRW	warfare	AAEGTWY	gateway	AAEIPRT	Tarpeia	AAELSUX	asexual
AAEFRST	Far East		getaway	AAEIPTT	apatite	AAELTTV	Valetta
AAEGGNO	anagoge	AAEHHIL	Hialeah	AAEIRST	aristae	AAELTUV	valuate
AAEGGRS	garages	AAEHHPT	aphthae		Astaire	AAELTVV	valvate
AAEGHLU	haulage	AAEHILP	aphelia		atresia	AAEMMMR	maremma
AAEGHMR	Grahame	AAEHIMN	Anaheim	AAEIRSU	Eurasia	AAEMNPP	pampean
AAEGHNT	thanage	AAEHIRT	hetaira	AAEIRTT	arietta	AAEMNRS	Manresa
AAEGILR	Algeria		Rhaetia	AAEIRTV	variate	AAEMNRT	ramenta
	lairage	AAEHKNT	khanate	AAEISTT	satiate	AAEMNSS	Masséna
	regalia	AAEHKPS	pakehas	AAEISTV	aviates	AAEMNST	Eastman
AAEGILS	algesia	AAEHKST	takahes	AAEITUX	eutaxia		Smetana
AAEGINV	vaginae	AAEHLLL	allheal	AAEJOPR	aparejo	AAEMNTU	manteau
AAEGISS	assegai	AAEHLMR	Haarlem	AAEKKOR	karaoke	AAEMQSU	squamae
AAEGISU	ageusia	AAEHLNT	ethanal	AAEKLNS	alkanes	AAEMRSS	amasser
AAEGITT	agitate	AAEHLPR	Raphael	AAEKLNT	alkanet	AAEMRTU	amateur
AAEGKNT	tankage	AAEHLPS	phaseal	AAEKMRR	earmark	AAEMSSS	amasses
AAEGKOS	soakage	AAEHLPX	hexapla	AAEKMRS	seamark	AAENNNT	antenna
AAEGLLT	tallage	AAEHLRT	trehala	AAEKNSW	awakens	AAENNRV	Ravenna
AAEGLMN	gamelan	AAEHLST	altheas	AAEKPRT	partake	AAENNST	annates
AAEGLMT	gametal	AAEHMST	athames	AAELLLM	lamella	AAENNSZ	zenanas
AAEGLNN	anlagen	AAEHNPR	hanaper	AAELLLS	La Salle	AAENNTT	tannate
AAEGLNS	anlages	AAEHNPS	saphena	AAELLPS	paellas	AAENPST	anapest
	lagenas	AAEHNSY	hyaenas	AAELLPT	patella		peasant
	lasagne	AAEHRRT	Earhart	AAELLRT	lateral	AAENPSV	pavanes
AAEGLNU	leguaan	AAEHRSY	hearsay	AAELLSW	seawall	AAENPTT	epatant
AAEGLRR	realgar	AAEHSTT	hastate	AAELMMR	almemar	AAENRRT	narrate
AAEGLRS	laagers	AAEIJLP	Liepāja	AAELMMT	lemmata	AAENRRV	Navarre

AAENRSZ	Sarazen	AAGGILN	ganglia	AAGINSY	gainsay	AAHHNPT	naphtha
AAENRTU	taurean	AAGGINR	Gagarin	AAGINTU	Antigua	AAHHOPR	pharaoh
AAENRTV	taverna	AAGGIZZ	Zagazig	AAGINWW	wawaing	AAHIIKW	Hawaiki
AAENRUW	unaware	AAGGJRY	jaggary	AAGIOTT	agitato	AAHIIMT	himatia
AAENSST	Nastase	AAGGLMO	magalog	AAGIPPR	Agrippa	AAHIINT	Haitian
AAENSSW	Swansea	AAGGLOS	galagos	AAGIPRU	piragua	AAHIJNR	harijan
AAENSTU	Antaeus	AAGGLRY	graylag	AAGIRST	Artigas	AAHIKMT	Khatami
AAENSTV	Avestan	AAGGNOY	anagogy		Stagira	AAHIKPS	pakahis
	savante	AAGGNST	gangsta	AAGISSZ	Agassiz	AAHIKRT	kithara
AAEORRT	aerator	AAGGNWY	gangway	AAGISTT	sagitta	AAHILMT	thalami
AAEORRU	aurorae	AAGGQSU	quaggas	AAGJMNU	Majunga	AAHILPV	pahlavi
AAEPPRS	appears	AAGGRSS	saggars	AAGJRSU	jaguars	AAHIMNO	mahonia
AAEPPRT	parapet	AAGHHZZ	Ghazzah	AAGJRTU	Gujarat	AAHIMNR	Ahriman
AAERRRS	arrears	AAGHILR	Aligarh	AAGKLSY	galyaks	AAHIMNS	Samhain
AAERRSS	arrases		gharial	AAGKNRS	Angarsk		shamina
AAERRTT	tartare	AAGHILZ	Ghazali	AAGLLNT	gallant	AAHIMNZ	hazanim
AAERSSY	assayer	AAGHINN	anhinga	AAGLNNO	Angolan	AAHIMRT	Marathi
AAERSTT	Astarte	AAGHITU	Gauhati	AAGLNOS	analogs	AAHINNU	Huainan
AAESSTV	savates	AAGHKNS	kanghas	AAGLNOY	analogy	AAHINOP	aphonia
AAESSWY	seaways		khangas	AAGLNPS	lapsang	AAHINOR	Honiara
AAETTUW	Watteau	AAGHKNT	thangka	AAGLNRS	langars	AAHINPP	paphian
AAFFINS	saffian	AAGHLNT	gnathal		raglans	AAHINPR	piranha
AAFFINT	affiant	AAGHLSU	Agulhas	AAGLNRU	angular	AAHINST	Ashanti
AAFFIRS	affairs	AAGHMMU	Maugham	AAGLNTY	galanty		shaitan
	raffias	AAGHMNN	hangman	AAGLRUU	arugula	AAHINSX	Shaanxi
AAFFIRX	Fairfax	AAGHMRS	grahams		augural	AAHINTU	Hainaut
AAFFRSY	affrays	AAGHNNY	Hanyang	AAGLRVX	gravlax	AAHINTW	taniwha
AAFGHIN	afghani	AAGHNRS	hangars	AAGLSST	stalags	AAHIPRS	pariahs
AAFGHNS	afghans	AAGHNST	sanghat	AAGMMNS	magsman		raphias
AAFGLMN	flagman	AAGHNUV	Vaughan	AAGMMRR	grammar	AAHIPRT	Parthia
AAFGORR	farrago	AAGHRSW	washrag	AAGMMST	gammats	AAHIPTY	Hypatia
AAFHILX	Halifax	AAGIINO	Goiânia	AAGMMTU	gummata	AAHIRRS	hariras
AAFHINS	Isfahan	AAGIINT	Niigata	AAGMMUY	mamaguy	AAHISTW	tawhais
AAFHLWY	halfway	AAGIKNS	kaingas	AAGMNOR	Romagna	AAHJRRS	jarrahs
AAFHMNR	Farnham	AAGIKNT	tikanga	AAGMNOS	sangoma	AAHKLRS	lashkar
AAFHNST	Fatshan	AAGIKNW	awaking	AAGMNOT	agamont	AAHKMMR	Markham
AAFHSTW	fatwahs	AAGILMY	myalgia	AAGMNPR	pangram	AAHKMSY	yashmak
AAFIILR	filaria	AAGILNN	anginal	AAGMNRT	tangram	AAHKMYY	Khayyám
AAFIILS	Faisal I	AAGILNP	paginal	AAGMNSW	swagman	AAHKNPU	Punakha
AAFIJST	fajitas	AAGILNS	agnails	AAGMOPY	apogamy	AAHKNRS	Shankar
AAFIKSS	sifakas	AAGILNV	Galvani	AAGMRRY	gramary	AAHKNSY	Sankhya
AAFILNT	fantail		vaginal	AAGMRSY	margays	AAHKPSS	pashkas
	tailfan	AAGILOT	otalgia	AAGNNOS	goannas	AAHKPSU	hapukas
AAFIMRY	Mayfair	AAGILPS	palagis	AAGNOPR	paragon	AAHLLLS	hallals
AAFINNT	infanta	AAGILRS	argalis	AAGNORS	angoras	AAHLLOS	halloas
AAFIPRT	parfait		garials	AAGNORZ	organza	AAHLLSW	wallahs
AAFIRSS	safaris	AAGILSV	gavials	AAGNOST	taongas	AAHLLWY	hallway
AAFIRUY	rufiyaa	AAGILTW	wagtail	AAGNPRS	parangs		Whyalla
AAFIRWY	fairway	AAGIMNO	angioma	AAGNRRY	granary	AAHLMMS	hammals
AAFISST	fatsias	AAGIMNS	siamang	AAGNRSS	sangars	AAHLMPR	Ramphal
AAFJLOR	alforja	AAGIMNZ	amazing	AAGNRTT	Grattan	AAHLMRS	marshal
AAFKMNU	Kaufman	AAGINNS	inangas	AAGNRTV	vagrant	AAHLMRU	hamular
AAFKNST	kaftans	AAGINOS	agnosia	AAGNSTU	taguans	AAHLMST	malthas
AAFLLLS	fallals	AAGINRR	arraign	AAGOPSS	sapsago	AAHLMSU	hamauls
AAFLLTY	fatally	AAGINRS	sangria	AAGORSU	saguaro	AAHLNPX	phalanx
AAFLMNX	Flaxman		sarangi	AAGPPRS	grappas	AAHLNRW	narwhal
AAFLNUU	faunula	AAGINRT	Gratian	AAGRRSY	garryas	AAHLPRS	phrasal
AAFLWYY	flyaway	AAGINRU	guarani	AAGSTUU	Augusta	AAHLPST	asphalt
AAFMNST	fantasm	AAGINRZ	zingara	AAHHJJS	hajjahs	AAHLRSS	ashlars
AAFNSTT	fantast	AAGINST	against	AAHHLLS	hallahs	AAHLRSW	shalwar
AAFNSTY	fantasy	AAGINSU	iguanas	AAHHLSV	halvahs	AAHLSWW	Shawwal
AAGGIJN	jagaing	AAGINSV	vaginas	AAHHMSS	Shamash	AAHMNNU	hanuman

117

AAHMNSS	shamans	**AAILMOS**	Somalia	**AAINPRS**	parians	**AAKLWWY**	walkway
AAHMOPR	amphora	**AAILMPR**	Palmira		piranas	**AAKMNSU**	manukas
AAHMQSU	quamash	**AAILMPS**	impalas	**AAINPRT**	Trapani	**AAKMNSW**	Waksman
AAHMRSS	ashrams	**AAILMRR**	Ar Rimal	**AAINPRU**	Rapa Nui	**AAKMNUU**	Manukau
AAHMRTU	Mathura	**AAILMRT**	marital	**AAINPST**	patinas	**AAKMORV**	Markova
AAHMSTZ	matzahs		martial		taipans	**AAKMOSU**	mousaka
AAHNNNS	Nan Shan	**AAILMSS**	salamis	**AAINQRW**	Qairwan	**AAKMRSU**	kumaras
AAHNNOS	hosanna	**AAILNOS**	Sinaloa	**AAINQSU**	Aquinas	**AAKMRSY**	Masaryk
AAHNRTX	anthrax	**AAILNOT**	Laotian	**AAINRST**	antiars	**AAKMRUZ**	mazurka
AAHNRTY	rhatany	**AAILNOV**	valonia		artisan	**AAKMRWY**	waymark
AAHNSUW	whanaus	**AAILNPT**	platina		Sinatra	**AAKNNTU**	nunatak
AAHNSZZ	hazzans	**AAILNPU**	Naipaul		tsarina	**AAKNORS**	anoraks
AAHORSU	sahuaro	**AAILNRV**	laniary	**AAINRSU**	saurian	**AAKNRSS**	Saransk
AAHPPRS	paraphs	**AAILNSS**	salinas	**AAINRTV**	variant	**AAKNRST**	kantars
AAHPRTW	warpath	**AAILNSY**	inyalas	**AAINRTW**	antiwar	**AAKNRTU**	Turkana
AAHPTWY	pathway	**AAILNTV**	Latvian	**AAINRTY**	Nayarit	**AAKNSWZ**	kwanzas
AAHRSST	shastra		valiant	**AAINSST**	istanas	**AAKOOPP**	pakapoo
AAHRSTY	ashtray	**AAILORS**	solaria	**AAINSSY**	sanyasi	**AAKOPRS**	pakoras
AAHRTTW	athwart	**AAILORV**	variola	**AAINSTT**	attains	**AAKPRWY**	parkway
AAHSSSY	sashays	**AAILOST**	solatia	**AAINTTT**	attaint	**AAKRTTU**	Atatürk
AAIIKNR	Nikaria	**AAILPRT**	partial	**AAINTUY**	Taiyuan	**AAKRTUY**	autarky
AAIILMN	Iliamna		patrial	**AAIOPRS**	aporias	**AALLLNS**	lallans
AAIILMR	airmail	**AAILPRY**	airplay	**AAIORRS**	rosaria	**AALLLSW**	Walsall
AAIILNT	Italian	**AAILPST**	spatial	**AAIORST**	Astoria	**AALLMMS**	mallams
AAIILPT	tilapia	**AAILQWW**	qawwali	**AAIORTV**	aviator	**AALLMPU**	ampulla
AAIINNR	Iranian	**AAILRRV**	arrival	**AAIPPRU**	puparia	**AALLNPU**	planula
AAIINRZ	Zaïrian	**AAILRST**	Al Sirat	**AAIPPTT**	pitapat	**AALLNSY**	nasally
AAIINTT	titania		lariats	**AAIPRTT**	partita	**AALLOPR**	Rapallo
AAIIRSU	Isauria	**AAILRTT**	rattail	**AAIPRTV**	Parvati	**AALLORW**	Oral Law
AAIIRVV	vivaria	**AAILRTV**	travail	**AAIPSZZ**	piazzas	**AALLOTV**	lavolta
AAIJLNU	Juliana	**AAILRWY**	railway	**AAIQQZZ**	Zaqaziq	**AALLOWY**	Alloway
AAIJNTU	Tijuana	**AAILSSS**	assails	**AAIQSSU**	quassia	**AALLPPS**	appalls
AAIKLLS	alkalis	**AAILSSV**	salvias	**AAIQTUV**	aquavit	**AALLPPY**	papally
AAIKLMS	kalmias	**AAILSSW**	wassail	**AAIRSSS**	Sassari	**AALLRUY**	aurally
AAIKLNP	palinka	**AAILSTU**	Lusatia	**AAIRSST**	tarsias	**AALMMMS**	mammals
AAIKLNS	kalians	**AAIMMNO**	ammonia	**AAIRSSY**	Assyria	**AALMMNO**	ammonal
AAIKLPR	palikar	**AAIMMSS**	miasmas	**AAIRSTU**	Austria	**AALMMNS**	almsman
AAIKMNN	manakin	**AAIMNOR**	Romania	**AAIRSWY**	airways	**AALMNOY**	anomaly
AAIKNNT	Kantian	**AAIMNOS**	anosmia	**AAIRSZZ**	razzias		Layamon
AAIKNOW	Okinawa	**AAIMNOT**	animato	**AAISTTV**	atavist	**AALMNPS**	napalms
AAIKNST	Katsina	**AAIMNRS**	marinas	**AAISTUY**	yautias	**AALMNSU**	manuals
AAIKOTW	Waikato	**AAIMNRT**	martian	**AAITWXY**	taxiway	**AALMOPR**	Palomar
AAIKPPR	paprika		tamarin	**AAJKLWY**	jaywalk	**AALMORY**	mayoral
AAIKPTZ	Kapitza	**AAIMNRU**	Rumania	**AAJKNSS**	sanjaks	**AALMPRY**	palmary
AAIKRSS	askaris	**AAIMNRZ**	Mazarin	**AAJMNPS**	jampans		palmyra
AAIKTVV	akvavit	**AAIMNST**	stamina	**AAJMPSY**	pyjamas	**AALMRSU**	alarums
AAILLMM	mamilla	**AAIMORR**	Roraima	**AAJNNSU**	San Juan	**AALMRTU**	Umar Tal
AAILLMN	manilla	**AAIMORV**	Moravia	**AAJOPST**	Tapajós	**AALMRUX**	Malraux
AAILLMX	maxilla	**AAIMRRS**	mararis	**AAJOPSU**	sapajou	**AALNNRU**	annular
AAILLNV	vanilla	**AAIMRST**	amritas	**AAKKLOT**	Kolkata	**AALNNSU**	annuals
AAILLPP	papilla		Maritsa	**AAKKLPS**	kalpaks	**AALNOUV**	Ulanova
AAILLRX	axillar	**AAIMRSU**	Masuria	**AAKKLRU**	karakul	**AALNPRT**	plantar
AAILLXY	axially		samurai	**AAKKMOT**	tokamak	**AALNPST**	platans
AAILMMN	mailman	**AAIMSTT**	tatamis	**AAKKMRU**	Kara Kum		saltpan
AAILMMS	Lamaism	**AAIMSTV**	atavism	**AAKKOPS**	kakapos	**AALNQTU**	quantal
	miasmal	**AAINNRU**	uranian	**AAKKSUZ**	zakuska	**AALNRSW**	narwals
AAILMMX	maximal	**AAINNRV**	navarin	**AAKLMRY**	malarky	**AALNRTU**	natural
AAILMNR	laminar		nirvana	**AAKLNOR**	Alkoran	**AALNSTT**	saltant
AAILMNS	animals	**AAINNWX**	Wanxian	**AAKLOOP**	palooka	**AALNSTU**	sultana
	laminas	**AAINOPS**	paisano	**AAKLOOT**	talooka	**AALNSTY**	analyst
AAILMNT	matinal	**AAINORV**	ovarian	**AAKLRSU**	kursaal	**AALOPRS**	parasol
AAILMNU	alumina	**AAINORZ**	Arizona	**AAKLSTU**	talukas	**AALOPST**	Spalato

AALOPSY	payolas	AANNOTT	annatto
AALOPTV	Poltava	AANNRSU	anurans
AALOPVV	pavlova	AANNRUU	Nauruan
AALORRU	auroral	AANNSSU	Susanna
AALORSU	arousal	AANNSYZ	nyanzas
AALOSTT	Astolat	AANNTUY	Yuan Tan
AALOSVW	avowals	AANORTT	Taranto
AALPPRU	papular	AANOSST	sonatas
AALPPSU	Uppsala	AANOSTT	anattos
AALPRRS	parrals	AANPRST	partans
AALPRSY	parlays		spartan
AALPRTY	laptray		tarpans
AALPSTU	spatula		trapans
AALRSST	tarsals	AANPRUU	Uruapan
AALRSTT	stratal	AANPSST	passant
AALRSTU	austral	AANQRTU	quartan
AALRSTY	astylar	AANRRSY	yarrans
AALRSUZ	Lazarus	AANRRTW	warrant
AALSSSV	vassals	AANRSTT	rattans
AALSSTU	assault		tartans
AALSTUV	valutas	AANRSTZ	tarzans
AALSWYY	waylays	AANRUWY	runaway
AAMMMRY	mammary	AANSSTT	tsantsa
AAMMNNX	Manxman	AANSSTV	savants
AAMMNRY	Myanmar	AANSSTZ	stanzas
AAMMOTY	myomata	AANSTTT	statant
AAMMRST	ramstam	AANSWYY	anyways
	tammars	AANTUUV	Vanuatu
AAMNNOR	Marañón	AAOPSST	sapotas
AAMNNOT	Montana	AAORRSU	auroras
AAMNORR	marrano	AAORSTT	totaras
	orraman	AAORSTV	Ostrava
AAMNORS	oarsman		Saratov
AAMNORZ	romanza	AAORSVV	vavasor
AAMNOSZ	amazons	AAOSTTV	ottavas
AAMNOTV	Mantova	AAOTTUY	tatouay
AAMNOTY	anatomy	AAPPSWW	pawpaws
AAMNPRT	mantrap	AAPRRTT	rattrap
	rampant	AAPRSST	satraps
AAMNPSS	sampans	AAPRSTY	satrapy
AAMNPTY	tympana	AAPRTUU	raupatu
AAMNRST	Mansart	AAPRTWY	partway
	mantras	AAPZZZZ	pazzazz
AAMNRSU	Mansûra	AAQRSSU	quasars
AAMNSTU	mantuas	AARRSTT	tartars
AAMOPRS	paramos	AARRTTY	Tartary
AAMORSV	samovar	AARSSST	sastras
AAMORTU	Utamaro	ABBBDEL	babbled
AAMORTY	amatory		blabbed
AAMOSSS	samosas	ABBBELR	babbler
AAMOSTT	stomata		blabber
AAMOTTU	automat		brabble
AAMPRRT	rampart	ABBBELS	babbles
AAMPRSS	Sampras	ABBBITT	babbitt
AAMRRSU	Maurras	ABBCDER	crabbed
AAMRRTY	Marryat	ABBCDES	scabbed
AAMRSST	matrass	ABBCEHI	babiche
AAMRSTU	sumatra	ABBCEIS	cabbies
	traumas	ABBCELS	scabble
AAMRTTY	trymata	ABBCERR	crabber
AAMRTWY	tramway	ABBCIKT	backbit
AAMSSTU	satsuma	ABBCKUY	buyback

ABBCOST	bobcats	ABBERSY	yabbers
ABBCOTY	abbotcy	ABBESSU	subbase
ABBCRYY	crybaby	ABBGGIN	gabbing
ABBDDEL	dabbled	ABBGIJN	jabbing
ABBDDER	drabbed	ABBGINN	nabbing
ABBDEGL	gabbled	ABBGINR	barbing
ABBDEGR	grabbed	ABBGINT	tabbing
ABBDEIY	yabbied	ABBGINY	babying
ABBDELR	dabbler	ABBGOOU	bugaboo
	drabble	ABBGORS	gabbros
	rabbled	ABBHISY	babyish
ABBDELS	dabbles	ABBHJSU	jubbahs
	slabbed	ABBHRRU	rhubarb
ABBDELW	wabbled	ABBHTTU	bathtub
ABBDERR	drabber	ABBIIMN	bambini
ABBDERS	dabbers	ABBIJLS	jilbabs
ABBDERT	drabbet	ABBILOT	bobtail
ABBDEST	stabbed	ABBILSU	bubalis
ABBDESU	bedaubs	ABBIMNO	bambino
ABBDESW	swabbed	ABBIORT	rabbito
ABBDGIN	dabbing	ABBIRST	rabbits
ABBDILO	Boabdil	ABBKLOU	blaubok
ABBDINR	ribband	ABBLLTU	bullbat
ABBDMOR	bombard	ABBLMRY	brambly
ABBDNOX	bandbox	ABBLNOY	Babylon
ABBEERR	Berbera	ABBMOOR	bombora
ABBEESW	bawbees	ABBMOOS	bamboos
ABBEGIR	gabbier	ABBMOST	bombast
ABBEGLR	gabbler	ABBMOTU	bumboat
	grabble	ABBNOOS	baboons
ABBEGLS	gabbles	ABBNRUY	Banbury
ABBEGMR	Bamberg	ABBOORU	rubaboo
ABBEGNO	bogbean	ABBORRU	Barbour
ABBEGNU	bugbane	ABBORSS	absorbs
ABBEGPR	grabber	ABBOSTY	bobstay
ABBEGRS	gabbers	ABBQSUY	squabby
ABBEGRU	bugbear	ABBRSSU	busbars
	Burbage	ABBSSSU	subbass
ABBEHMO	Hobbema	ABCCCHI	bacchic
ABBEINT	Babinet	ABCCEER	Rebecca
ABBEIRS	barbies	ABCCEIR	acerbic
ABBEIST	tabbies		breccia
ABBEISY	yabbies	ABCCEIS	baccies
ABBEJRS	jabbers		sebacic
ABBEKRU	Abu-Bekr	ABCCHII	bacchii
ABBELLR	barbell	ABCCHSU	Bacchus
ABBELMR	bramble	ABCCHTY	bycatch
ABBELOR	belabor	ABCCILU	cubical
ABBELRR	rabbler	ABCCIMR	cambric
ABBELRS	barbels	ABCCIOR	boracic
	rabbles	ABCCKOW	bawcock
	slabber	ABCCKTU	cutback
ABBELRU	barbule	ABCCOOT	tobacco
ABBELRW	wabbler	ABCCSUU	succuba
ABBELSU	baubles	ABCDEEH	beached
ABBELSW	wabbles	ABCDEEL	debacle
ABBEOTX	beatbox	ABCDEHT	batched
ABBERRS	barbers	ABCDEHU	debauch
ABBERST	barbets	ABCDEIK	dieback
	rabbets	ABCDEIN	cabined
	stabber	ABCDEIP	pedicab
ABBERSW	swabber	ABCDEIR	carbide

ABCDEKL	blacked	ABCEKRW	Warbeck	ABCIKLT	backlit	ABDDINS	disband
ABCDEKR	redback	ABCEKST	setback	ABCIKSY	sickbay	ABDDLLO	oddball
ABCDEOR	brocade	ABCEKTW	wetback	ABCILRS	scribal	ABDEEFG	feedbag
ABCDERU	cudbear	ABCELLN	Leblanc	ABCILST	Baltics	ABDEEGL	beagled
ABCDIIS	dibasic	ABCELLU	bullace	ABCILTU	cubital	ABDEEGR	rebadge
ABCDILR	baldric	ABCELMO	cembalo	ABCIMMU	cambium	ABDEEHS	beheads
ABCDIRS	scabrid	ABCELMR	cambrel	ABCIMOR	Coimbra	ABDEEHV	behaved
ABCDIRT	catbird		clamber	ABCIMRU	Cumbria	ABDEEIR	beadier
ABCDISU	subacid	ABCELOP	placebo	ABCIMST	cambist	ABDEELL	labeled
ABCDLOO	Bacolod	ABCELOV	vocable	ABCINOT	botanic	ABDEELM	beldame
ABCDNOS	abscond	ABCELPU	bluecap	ABCIOOR	Cariboo	ABDEELN	enabled
ABCDOOR	cordoba	ABCELRU	curable	ABCIORU	caribou	ABDEELR	bleared
	Córdoba	ABCELST	cablets	ABCIOUV	bivouac	ABDEELS	beadles
ABCDRUY	Cadbury	ABCELSU	bascule	ABCIRTY	barytic	ABDEELT	belated
ABCDSTU	abducts	ABCEMRS	cambers	ABCJOSU	jacobus		bleated
ABCEEHM	Beecham	ABCEMSW	webcams	ABCKLLY	blackly	ABDEELY	belayed
ABCEEHS	beaches	ABCENOR	baconer	ABCKLOT	backlot		dyeable
ABCEEMR	embrace	ABCENOS	beacons	ABCKMRU	buckram	ABDEEMN	benamed
ABCEENR	carbeen	ABCENOW	cowbane	ABCKMUZ	zambuck	ABDEEMR	breamed
	carbene	ABCENOZ	cabezon	ABCKNNO	bannock	ABDEEMY	embayed
ABCEENS	absence	ABCENRU	unbrace	ABCKNOT	Bantock	ABDEENR	Bardeen
ABCEERR	cerebra	ABCEOOS	caboose	ABCKOSW	sowback	ABDEERR	barreed
ABCEESU	because	ABCEORS	boraces	ABCKOTU	backout	ABDEERS	debaser
ABCEGIR	ribcage	ABCEORV	cabover		outback		sabered
ABCEGOS	boscage	ABCERRS	bracers	ABCKSTU	sackbut	ABDEERT	berated
ABCEHIL	Labiche	ABCERSU	subrace	ABCKSUW	bucksaw		debater
ABCEHIT	Thebaic	ABCESSS	abscess		sawbuck		rebated
ABCEHKM	Beckham	ABCESTW	webcast	ABCLLOY	callboy	ABDEERW	bewared
ABCEHLO	chaebol	ABCESTY	Catesby	ABCLMNU	clubman	ABDEESS	debases
ABCEHLU	bauchle	ABCFIKN	finback	ABCLMOU	Columba	ABDEEST	bestead
ABCEHMR	chamber	ABCFILO	bifocal	ABCLMOY	cymbalo		debates
	chambre	ABCFIOT	biofact	ABCLMSY	cymbals	ABDEETT	abetted
ABCEHMT	Macbeth	ABCFIRS	fabrics	ABCLMUU	baculum	ABDEFFL	baffled
ABCEHRS	braches	ABCFKLY	flyback	ABCLNOY	balcony	ABDEFLT	flatbed
ABCEHRT	brachet	ABCFLOO	cobloaf	ABCLNSU	subclan	ABDEFOR	forbade
ABCEHST	batches	ABCFNOS	confabs	ABCLOVY	vocably	ABDEFST	bedfast
ABCEIIT	abietic	ABCGHIN	baching	ABCLRUY	curably	ABDEGGL	blagged
ABCEIKS	backies	ABCGHKO	hogback	ABCMNRW	Cwmbran	ABDEGGR	bragged
ABCEIKT	tieback	ABCGIKN	backing	ABCMOPS	mobcaps	ABDEGHI	bighead
ABCEILM	alembic	ABCGILN	cabling	ABCMOST	combats	ABDEGHR	beghard
	cembali	ABCGINR	bracing	ABCMRSS	scrambs	ABDEGIN	beading
ABCEILR	caliber	ABCGKLO	backlog	ABCNORS	carbons	ABDEGIR	abridge
	calibre	ABCGMSU	scumbag		corbans		brigade
ABCEILT	citable	ABCHHII	hibachi	ABCORRW	crowbar	ABDEGLM	gambled
ABCEIMO	amoebic	ABCHILS	chablis	ABCORSS	brascos	ABDEGLR	garbled
ABCEIMU	Cimabue	ABCHILU	Baluchi	ABCORSX	boxcars	ABDEGNO	bondage
ABCEINR	carbine	ABCHIOT	cohabit	ABCORSY	carboys		dogbane
ABCEINT	cabinet	ABCHKTU	hackbut	ABDDEER	bearded	ABDEGOR	Beograd
ABCEIOR	aerobic	ABCHLOR	Chabrol		breaded		Bogarde
ABCEIOT	iceboat	ABCHNRU	Churban	ABDDEES	debased	ABDEGOS	bodegas
ABCEIRS	ascribe	ABCHNRY	branchy	ABDDEET	debated	ABDEGRS	badgers
	Brescia	ABCHOTT	chatbot	ABDDEIN	bandied	ABDEHIL	hidable
	carbies	ABCHPSU	hubcaps	ABDDEIR	braided	ABDEHIT	habited
ABCEIRZ	zebraic	ABCIILL	bacilli	ABDDEIS	baddies		Thebaid
ABCEISS	abscise	ABCIILN	albinic	ABDDELR	bladder	ABDEHLR	halberd
	scabies	ABCIILS	basilic	ABDDENR	branded	ABDEHOR	Deborah
ABCEITT	tabetic	ABCIILT	albitic	ABDDEOR	boarded	ABDEHOW	bowhead
ABCEKLN	blacken	ABCIIMN	minicab		roadbed	ABDEHRT	breadth
ABCEKLR	blacker	ABCIIMS	iambics	ABDDEOY	deadboy	ABDEHSU	subhead
ABCEKNR	bracken	ABCIIOR	ciboria	ABDDEST	baddest	ABDEIIL	alibied
ABCEKRS	backers	ABCIIOT	abiotic	ABDDHIS	baddish	ABDEILP	bipedal
ABCEKRT	bracket	ABCIJNO	jacobin	ABDDHSU	buddhas		piebald

ABDEILR	bedrail		broader	**ABDLNOY**	Blaydon
	brailed	**ABDEORT**	aborted	**ABDLORY**	broadly
	ridable		borated	**ABDLOYY**	ladyboy
ABDEILS	baldies	**ABDEOST**	boasted	**ABDLRUY**	durably
	disable	**ABDEOTU**	boutade	**ABDLSUU**	subdual
ABDEILU	audible	**ABDERSS**	serdabs	**ABDNNOR**	Bonnard
ABDEILY	beadily	**ABDERST**	dabster	**ABDNOPR**	proband
ABDEIMO	ameboid	**ABDERSU**	daubers	**ABDNORS**	robands
ABDEINR	bandier	**ABDERSV**	adverbs	**ABDNOSS**	Donbass
	brained	**ABDERUY**	daubery	**ABDNOSU**	abounds
ABDEINS	bandies	**ABDETTU**	abutted	**ABDNOSX**	sandbox
ABDEIRR	braider	**ABDGIIN**	abiding	**ABDNOSY**	sandboy
ABDEIRS	abiders	**ABDGILN**	balding	**ABDNOUU**	Audubon
	bardies		blading	**ABDNOYY**	anybody
	braised	**ABDGINN**	banding	**ABDNSTY**	standby
	darbies	**ABDGINO**	Baoding	**ABDOOWY**	baywood
	seabird	**ABDGINR**	barding	**ABDORSS**	adsorbs
ABDEIRT	tribade		brigand	**ABDORSY**	byroads
ABDEIRW	bawdier	**ABDGINT**	dingbat	**ABDOSYY**	dayboys
ABDEIRX	axebird	**ABDGINU**	daubing	**ABDRRSU**	durbars
ABDEISS	biassed	**ABDGINW**	windbag	**ABDRRUY**	du Barry
ABDEJRU	abjured	**ABDGLNO**	Bagnold	**ABDRSTU**	bustard
ABDEKLN	blanked	**ABDGLUY**	ladybug	**ABDRUZZ**	buzzard
ABDEKLU	baulked	**ABDGNNU**	Bandung	**ABEEELS**	seeable
ABDEKRS	debarks	**ABDHIIT**	adhibit	**ABEEERV**	bereave
ABDELMR	marbled	**ABDHILS**	baldish	**ABEEFFL**	effable
	rambled	**ABDHMTU**	mudbath	**ABEEFGR**	Fabergé
ABDELMS	bedlams	**ABDHNOR**	bodhran	**ABEEFLM**	flambee
	beldams	**ABDHNSU**	husband	**ABEEGHR**	herbage
ABDELMW	wambled	**ABDHOSY**	hobdays	**ABEEGLL**	gabelle
ABDELNR	blander	**ABDIINO**	anobiid	**ABEEGLS**	beagles
ABDELOR	labored	**ABDIKOR**	Kobarid	**ABEEGLT**	getable
ABDELOS	albedos	**ABDILMO**	bimodal	**ABEEGRR**	gerbera
ABDELOT	bloated	**ABDILNW**	Baldwin	**ABEEGRS**	bargees
	lobated	**ABDILOO**	diabolo	**ABEEGRU**	auberge
ABDELOW	dowable	**ABDILOR**	labroid	**ABEEGRW**	brewage
ABDELPU	dupable	**ABDILOT**	tabloid	**ABEEHNN**	henbane
ABDELRT	blarted	**ABDILRS**	bridals	**ABEEHNS**	banshee
ABDELRU	durable		labrids		shebean
ABDELRW	brawled		ribalds	**ABEEHNT**	beneath
	warbled	**ABDILRV**	rabidly	**ABEEHRT**	breathe
ABDELRY	Bradley	**ABDILTU**	Bidault	**ABEEHSV**	behaves
	dryable	**ABDILUY**	audibly	**ABEEHTY**	eyebath
ABDELST	baldest	**ABDILWY**	bawdily	**ABEEILN**	Abilene
	blasted	**ABDIMNR**	birdman	**ABEEILS**	bailees
	stabled	**ABDIMOR**	ambroid	**ABEEINS**	beanies
ABDELTT	battled	**ABDIMRU**	Rimbaud	**ABEEINT**	betaine
	blatted	**ABDINOR**	inboard	**ABEEIRT**	beatier
ABDEMMO	mamboed	**ABDINRS**	ribands	**ABEEIST**	beastie
ABDEMNO	abdomen	**ABDINRT**	antbird	**ABEEKLR**	bleaker
ABDEMRU	Bermuda	**ABDINST**	bandits		Kerbela
ABDENOR	bandore	**ABDINSU**	ibn-Saud	**ABEEKNT**	betaken
	broaden	**ABDIOOR**	Boiardo	**ABEEKNV**	eyebank
ABDENPS	bedpans	**ABDIPRU**	upbraid	**ABEEKPS**	bespeak
ABDENRR	Bernard	**ABDIRRS**	briards	**ABEEKRR**	breaker
	brander	**ABDIRSS**	disbars	**ABEEKRS**	beakers
	rebrand	**ABDIRSU**	subarid	**ABEEKST**	betakes
ABDENSS	badness	**ABDJORU**	Dobruja	**ABEELLR**	relabel
ABDENTU	unbated	**ABDKOOY**	daybook	**ABEELLY**	eyeball
ABDEOOT	tabooed	**ABDLLNY**	blandly	**ABEELMZ**	emblaze
ABDEOPY	Peabody	**ABDLLOR**	bollard	**ABEELNR**	enabler
ABDEORR	boarder	**ABDLMOR**	Lombard	**ABEELNS**	enables

ABEELNT	Beltane
	tenable
ABEELNU	nebulae
ABEELOR	earlobe
ABEELQU	equable
ABEELRR	blearer
ABEELRT	bleater
	retable
ABEELSU	useable
ABEEMNS	basemen
	bemeans
	benames
ABEEMRS	beamers
	besmear
ABEENNW	bawneen
ABEENOU	Euboean
ABEENRS	Benares
ABEENRV	verbena
ABEENRY	beanery
ABEEORS	aerobes
ABEERRS	bearers
ABEERRT	rebater
ABEERST	beaters
	berates
	rebates
ABEERSV	beavers
ABEERSW	bewares
ABEERTT	abetter
ABEESWX	beeswax
ABEFFIS	baffies
ABEFFLR	baffler
ABEFFLS	baffles
ABEFFOT	offbeat
ABEFGST	gabfest
ABEFILN	finable
ABEFILR	friable
ABEFILU	fibulae
ABEFILX	fixable
ABEFITY	beatify
ABEFLLS	befalls
ABEFLLU	baleful
ABEFLLY	flyable
ABEFLMS	flambes
ABEFLNU	baneful
ABEFLRS	fablers
ABEFLST	Belfast
ABEFORR	forbear
ABEFPRS	prefabs
ABEGGIR	baggier
ABEGGIS	baggies
ABEGGLR	blagger
ABEGGMO	gamboge
ABEGGRR	bragger
ABEGGRS	beggars
ABEGGRU	burgage
ABEGGRY	beggary
ABEGHMR	Maghreb
ABEGHNS	shebang
ABEGHOT	Bagehot
ABEGHRU	bearhug
ABEGILN	Belgian
	Bengali

ABEGILR Gabriel	**ABEIILL** baillie	**ABEIOOT** Boeotia	**ABELMRR** marbler
ABEGILV givable	**ABEIILR** Liberia	**ABEIOST** boaties	rambler
ABEGIMN beaming	**ABEIILS** bailies	**ABEIOTV** obviate	**ABELMRS** amblers
ABEGIMR gambier	**ABEIINR** Iberian	**ABEIPST** baptise	marbles
ABEGIMT megabit	**ABEIINT** bainite	**ABEIPTZ** baptize	rambles
ABEGINN beaning	**ABEIIRS** Siberia	**ABEIRRR** barrier	**ABELMRT** lambert
ABEGINO begonia	**ABEIJNS** basenji	**ABEIRRS** barries	**ABELMSW** wambles
ABEGINR bearing	**ABEIKKS** bakkies	brasier	**ABELMTU** mutable
ABEGINT beating	**ABEIKLL** likable	**ABEIRRT** arbiter	**ABELNNO** Lebanon
ABEGIPP bagpipe	**ABEIKLR** balkier	rarebit	**ABELNOS** Abelson
ABEGKOS boskage	**ABEIKLS** skiable	**ABEIRRW** warbier	bonsela
ABEGLMR gambler	**ABEIKLT** batlike	**ABEIRRZ** bizarre	**ABELNOT** notable
gambrel	**ABEIKNR** Bikaner	brazier	**ABELNOY** baloney
ABEGLMS gambles	**ABEIKNT** beatnik	**ABEIRSS** braises	**ABELNRS** branles
ABEGLMU Belgaum	**ABEILLN** linable	brassie	**ABELNRU** nebular
ABEGLNS bangles	**ABEILLO** lobelia	**ABEIRST** terbias	**ABELNRY** blarney
ABEGLOT globate	**ABEILLP** pliable	**ABEIRTT** battier	**ABELNSU** nebulas
ABEGLRR Arlberg	**ABEILLR** braille	biretta	**ABELNSY** bylanes
garbler	liberal	ratbite	**ABELNTU** tunable
ABEGLRS garbles	**ABEILLV** livable	**ABEIRTV** vibrate	**ABELNTY** tenably
ABEGLRU blaguer	**ABEILMN** minable	**ABEIRTX** Beatrix	**ABELOPR** ropable
ABEGLSS bagless	**ABEILMR** balmier	**ABEIRUX** exurbia	**ABELOPT** potable
ABEGLST gablets	remblai	**ABEISSS** biasses	**ABELORR** laborer
ABEGLSU belugas	**ABEILMS** ableism	**ABEISTT** batiste	**ABELORT** bloater
ABEGMNR Bergman	lambies	**ABEISUV** abusive	**ABELORU** rubeola
ABEGMOR Bergamo	**ABEILMT** limbate	**ABEITUX** bauxite	**ABELOSS** bolases
embargo	timbale	**ABEJLUY** bluejay	**ABELOST** boatels
ABEGMRU umbrage	**ABEILMX** mixable	**ABEJMRS** jambers	oblates
ABEGNOS nosebag	**ABEILNP** biplane	**ABEJNOS** banjoes	**ABELOSV** absolve
ABEGNRS bangers	**ABEILNS** lesbian	**ABEJNOW** jawbone	**ABELOSW** sowable
grabens	**ABEILNZ** Albéniz	**ABEJORS** jerboas	**ABELOTV** votable
ABEGOPY pageboy	**ABEILOU** Boileau	**ABEJRRU** abjurer	**ABELOTW** towable
ABEGORR begorra	**ABEILRS** bailers	**ABEJRSU** abjures	**ABELPPY** Appleby
ABEGORS borages	**ABEILRT** Alberti	**ABEKLLY** bleakly	**ABELQUY** equably
Seaborg	Albert I	**ABEKLNR** blanker	**ABELRRS** barrels
ABEGORX gearbox	librate	**ABEKLNT** blanket	**ABELRRW** brawler
ABEGOSZ gazebos	triable	**ABEKLRS** balkers	warbler
ABEGOUY buoyage	**ABEILSS** abseils	**ABEKLRU** baulker	**ABELRST** alberts
ABEGSTU baguets	**ABEILST** astilbe	**ABEKMNS** embanks	blaster
ABEHILR hirable	bestial	**ABEKMRS** embarks	labrets
ABEHIMO bohemia	stabile	**ABEKNRS** bankers	**ABELRSU** Belarus
ABEHINO Bien Hoa	**ABEILSW** bewails	**ABEKNSU** sunbake	Breslau
ABEHIRS bearish	**ABEILSY** baileys	**ABEKPRU** breakup	**ABELRSV** verbals
ABEHITU habitue	**ABEILSZ** sizable	**ABEKRRS** barkers	**ABELRSW** bawlers
ABEHKRU hauberk	**ABEILVV** bivalve	**ABEKRST** Stębark	warbles
ABEHKTU ketubah	**ABEIMNT** ambient	**ABEKSST** baskets	**ABELRSY** barleys
ABEHLMS shamble	**ABEIMOS** Amboise	**ABELLMN** bellman	**ABELRSZ** blazers
ABEHLMT Lambeth	**ABEIMOT** Moabite	**ABELLMY** Bellamy	**ABELRTT** battler
ABEHLNT benthal	**ABEIMRR** barmier	**ABELLNO** Bellona	**ABELRVY** bravely
ABEHLRS herbals	**ABEIMRS** ambries	**ABELLNT** netball	**ABELSST** stables
ABEHLRT blather	**ABEIMSU** maubies	**ABELLNY** Allenby	**ABELSSU** subsale
halbert	**ABEIMZZ** Zambezi	**ABELLOS** losable	**ABELSTT** battels
ABEHMNT Bentham	**ABEINNR** Bernina	**ABELLOV** lovable	battles
ABEHNRY abhenry	**ABEINOR** Bonaire	**ABELLRU** rubella	tablets
ABEHNTY Bethany	**ABEINOZ** Zenobia	rulable	**ABELSTU** Setúbal
ABEHRRS brasher	**ABEINRS** Serbian	**ABELLST** ballets	**ABELSTY** beastly
ABEHRSS bashers	**ABEINRT** atebrin	**ABELLTU** bullate	**ABELSUY** useably
ABEHRST Barthes	**ABEINRZ** ibn-Ezra	**ABELMMS** embalms	**ABELSWY** byelaws
bathers	**ABEINSS** Bassein	**ABELMNT** beltman	**ABELTWY** beltway
berthas	sabines	lambent	**ABEMNOS** ambones
breaths	**ABEINST** Antibes	**ABELMNU** albumen	bemoans
ABEHRTY breathy	basinet	**ABELMOV** movable	**ABEMNOT** boatmen

ABEMNST	batsmen	**ABERSUU**	bureaus	**ABGIMST**	gambits	**ABHLSTU**	Balthus
ABEMNSU	sunbeam	**ABERSWY**	bewrays	**ABGINNN**	banning	**ABHMNOS**	bonhams
ABEMORS	Ambrose	**ABERTTU**	abutter	**ABGINNT**	banting	**ABHMNSU**	bushman
ABEMORT	bromate	**ABERTTY**	battery	**ABGINOS**	bagnios	**ABHMRSU**	rhumbas
ABEMRRT	Rambert	**ABERUUX**	bureaux		gabions	**ABHNSTU**	sunbath
ABEMSSY	embassy	**ABERUVY**	Avebury	**ABGINOT**	boating	**ABHORRS**	harbors
ABENNNR	Brennan	**ABESSST**	bassets	**ABGINRR**	barring	**ABHORRU**	harbour
ABENNOR	Bornean	**ABESSSY**	abysses	**ABGINRS**	sabring	**ABHOTUY**	hautboy
ABENNOY	Bayonne	**ABESTTU**	battues	**ABGINRV**	braving	**ABHPSTY**	bypaths
ABENNRS	banners	**ABFFIIL**	bailiff	**ABGINRY**	braying	**ABHRSTU**	tarbush
ABENORS	boranes	**ABFFINO**	banoffi	**ABGINRZ**	brazing	**ABHSTUW**	washtub
ABENORT	baronet	**ABFFLOU**	buffalo	**ABGINST**	basting	**ABIIINR**	biriani
ABENOST	onbeats	**ABFGILN**	fabling	**ABGINSU**	abusing	**ABIIKKT**	kibitka
ABENOSY	soybean	**ABFGLSU**	bagfuls	**ABGINTT**	batting	**ABIILMU**	bulimia
ABENOTY	bayonet	**ABFHIST**	batfish	**ABGINTU**	tabuing	**ABIILNO**	Lin Biao
ABENQTU	banquet	**ABFHLSU**	bashful	**ABGINTW**	batwing	**ABIILNQ**	inqilab
ABENRRS	barrens	**ABFIILR**	bifilar	**ABGITTU**	Bugatti	**ABIILOV**	bolivia
ABENRRU	Raeburn	**ABFIIMR**	fimbria	**ABGKKNO**	bangkok	**ABIILRV**	biliary
ABENRST	banters	**ABFIKNR**	Firbank	**ABGKORW**	workbag	**ABIILST**	stibial
	barnets	**ABFILRU**	fibular	**ABGLMNU**	Balmung	**ABIILTY**	ability
ABENRSY	barneys	**ABFILSU**	fibulas	**ABGLMOS**	gambols	**ABIIMNR**	minibar
ABENRSZ	brazens	**ABFIMOR**	fibroma	**ABGLMOU**	lumbago	**ABIINNS**	bainins
ABENRUX	exurban	**ABFLORU**	Balfour	**ABGLNOO**	bologna		ibn-Sina
ABENSST	absents	**ABFLOTW**	batfowl	**ABGLORS**	brolgas	**ABIINOR**	Nairobi
ABENSTT	battens	**ABFLOTY**	flyboat		Gorbals		robinia
ABENSTZ	bezants	**ABFOOTY**	foyboat	**ABGLORT**	ragbolt	**ABIINRT**	Britain
ABENTUZ	Bautzen	**ABGGGIN**	bagging	**ABGLORU**	Borlaug	**ABIINRU**	Urban II
ABENTZZ	bezzant	**ABGGILY**	baggily	**ABGLRRU**	burglar	**ABIINRY**	biryani
ABEOOTV	obovate	**ABGGINN**	banging	**ABGMORW**	bagworm	**ABIIOSS**	abiosis
ABEOPRS	saprobe	**ABGGINR**	barging	**ABGMRRU**	Marburg	**ABIJLNR**	brinjal
ABEOPRT	probate		garbing	**ABGNOOS**	boongas	**ABIJNPU**	Punjabi
ABEOQRU	baroque	**ABGGISW**	bagwigs		gaboons	**ABIJPRU**	Bijapur
ABEORRT	taborer	**ABGGORT**	boggart	**ABGNOPR**	probang	**ABIJRSU**	jabirus
ABEORST	boaster	**ABGHILN**	blahing	**ABGNORS**	barongs	**ABIKLLY**	balkily
	boaters	**ABGHINS**	bashing		brogans	**ABIKLMN**	lambkin
	borates	**ABGHINT**	bathing	**ABGNOTU**	gunboat	**ABIKNNU**	Bakunin
	rebatos	**ABGHLRU**	burghal	**ABGOORT**	botargo	**ABIKRST**	britska
ABEORSV	bravoes	**ABGHMRU**	hamburg	**ABGOPST**	postbag	**ABIKRTZ**	britzka
ABEORSX	boraxes	**ABGHOTU**	abought	**ABGORST**	bogarts	**ABILLLO**	Balliol
ABEORSY	rosebay	**ABGHSTU**	hagbuts	**ABGOTTU**	tugboat	**ABILLMY**	balmily
ABEORSZ	bezoars	**ABGIILN**	bailing	**ABGRRUW**	Warburg	**ABILLNP**	pinball
ABEORTT	abettor	**ABGIINS**	biasing	**ABHHKTU**	khutbah	**ABILLPY**	pliably
	taboret	**ABGIINT**	baiting	**ABHHSUY**	hushaby	**ABILLSW**	sawbill
ABEPRTY	typebar	**ABGIINZ**	baizing	**ABHIINT**	inhabit	**ABILLSY**	syllabi
ABEPSTU	upbeats	**ABGIKLN**	balking	**ABHIKTW**	hawkbit	**ABILLWX**	waxbill
ABEQRSU	barques	**ABGIKNN**	banking	**ABHILNO**	hobnail	**ABILLWY**	waybill
ABEQSSU	basques	**ABGIKNO**	boaking	**ABHILOS**	abolish	**ABILMNU**	albumin
ABERRST	barrets	**ABGIKNR**	barking	**ABHILTU**	halibut	**ABILMOX**	mailbox
	barters		braking	**ABHIMNR**	Brahmin	**ABILMST**	timbals
ABERRSY	brayers	**ABGIKNS**	bakings	**ABHIMRS**	mihrabs	**ABILNOS**	albinos
ABERRSZ	brazers		basking	**ABHINOT**	Bothnia	**ABILNQU**	Blanqui
ABERRVY	bravery	**ABGIKST**	kitbags	**ABHINRS**	Bas-Rhin	**ABILNSU**	Albinus
ABERSSS	brasses	**ABGILLN**	balling	**ABHINST**	absinth	**ABILOPR**	bipolar
ABERSST	breasts	**ABGILMN**	ambling	**ABHIOOS**	boohais		parboil
ABERSSU	abusers		blaming	**ABHIOPS**	phobias	**ABILORS**	bailors
	buseras		lambing	**ABHIORS**	boarish	**ABILORT**	Bartoli
	surbase	**ABGILMS**	gimbals	**ABHIOST**	isobath		orbital
ABERSTT	batters	**ABGILNR**	blaring	**ABHIOSU**	haubois	**ABILORV**	bolivar
ABERSTV	bravest	**ABGILNT**	tabling	**ABHIRTY**	Yathrib	**ABILOTU**	bailout
ABERSTW	brawest	**ABGILNW**	bawling	**ABHISTU**	habitus	**ABILRRY**	library
ABERSTY	barytes	**ABGILNZ**	blazing	**ABHLOUX**	boxhaul	**ABILRSS**	brasils
	betrays	**ABGILOR**	garboil	**ABHLRSY**	brashly	**ABILRSU**	burials

ABILRSZ	brazils	ABLORSU	labours	ACCDFIL	flaccid	ACCEKPU	cupcake
ABILSYZ	sizably		suboral	ACCDHIL	chalcid	ACCEKRR	cracker
ABIMNRU	Umbrian	ABLORTT	Rotblat	ACCDILS	scaldic	ACCEKRT	cracket
ABIMORR	Maribor	ABLOSST	oblasts	ACCDINS	scandic	ACCELLY	calycle
ABIMOSS	biomass	ABLOSTT	talbots	ACCDIOT	octadic	ACCELNO	conceal
ABIMPST	baptism	ABLOSTV	abvolts	ACCDIPR	Piccard	ACCELNS	cancels
	bitmaps	ABLOSTX	saltbox	ACCDLOY	cacodyl	ACCELOR	coracle
ABIMRTT	trimtab	ABLPRSU	burlaps	ACCDORS	accords	ACCELSU	saccule
ABINNOS	Bosnian	ABLPSYY	byplays	ACCEEHL	caleche	ACCELSY	calyces
ABINOOR	boronia	ABLRTUU	tubular	ACCEEHO	coachee	ACCENOR	conacre
ABINORT	taborin	ABMNNOR	Bormann	ACCEELN	cenacle	ACCENOV	concave
ABINORW	rainbow	ABMNSTU	numbats	ACCEERS	Cáceres	ACCENPT	peccant
ABINOSS	basions	ABMOORR	barroom	ACCEERT	accrete	ACCENRS	cancers
ABINOST	bastion	ABMORTU	tambour	ACCEFIT	factice	ACCENST	accents
	obtains	ABMOSTW	wombats	ACCEFLU	felucca	ACCEOPY	cacoepy
ABINRST	brisant	ABMRSSU	samburs	ACCEHIL	caliche	ACCEOTU	Cocteau
ABINRTV	vibrant	ABNNORS	Branson		chalice	ACCEPRY	peccary
ABINRUV	Urban VI	ABNOORZ	borazon	ACCEHIN	chicane	ACCEPST	accepts
ABIORRS	barrios	ABNOOSS	bassoon	ACCEHLN	chancel	ACCERRS	scarcer
ABIORSS	isobars	ABNORST	bartons	ACCEHLO	cochlea	ACCERSU	accrues
ABIORTV	vibrato	ABNORSY	baryons	ACCEHNO	conchae		accuser
ABIORUX	Roubaix	ABNORTY	baryton	ACCEHNR	chancer	ACCESSU	accuses
ABIORZZ	Barozzi	ABNORTZ	Trabzon		chancre	ACCFIIP	pacific
ABIPSTT	baptist	ABNOTUY	buoyant	ACCEHNS	chances	ACCFILY	calcify
ABIRSSY	Sybaris	ABNRSTU	turbans	ACCEHNY	chancey	ACCGHIN	caching
ABIRUZZ	Abruzzi	ABNSTYZ	byzants	ACCEHOR	caroche	ACCGHIO	Chicago
ABISSST	bassist	ABOOPSS	soapbox		coacher	ACCGNOS	cognacs
ABJJOOS	jojobas	ABOORRT	Borotra	ACCEHOS	coaches	ACCHIKS	chiacks
ABJKMOS	sjambok	ABOORTW	rowboat	ACCEHPU	capuche	ACCHILS	Chalcis
ABJLMSU	jumbals	ABOOTTW	towboat	ACCEHRT	catcher	ACCHIMS	chasmic
ABKLLNY	blankly	ABORRSU	arbours	ACCEHRU	Chaucer	ACCHINO	chicano
ABKLOTX	talkbox	ABORRSW	barrows	ACCEHST	cachets	ACCHIOT	chaotic
ABKLRUW	bulwark	ABORSTU	robusta		catches	ACCHIOU	acouchi
ABKNOOV	Nabokov		rubatos	ACCEHTU	catechu	ACCHKNO	Hancock
ABKNRSY	Bryansk		tabours	ACCEHXY	cachexy	ACCHKOY	haycock
ABKNRUU	bunraku	ABORSTW	towbars	ACCEIIL	Cecilia	ACCHKSY	chyacks
ABLLLOW	lowball	ABOSSWW	bowsaws	ACCEIKP	icepack	ACCHLNO	conchal
ABLLLUY	lullaby	ABPRSTU	subpart	ACCEIKR	cackier	ACCHNRU	craunch
ABLLNOO	balloon	ABRRSSU	bursars	ACCEILL	calicle	ACCHOPU	capouch
ABLLOOS	lobolas	ABRRSUY	bursary	ACCEILN	calcine		pachuco
ABLLORR	rollbar	ABRRTUY	turbary	ACCEILO	coeliac	ACCHORT	Charcot
ABLLORU	lobular	ABRSTUU	arbutus	ACCEILS	calices	ACCHOSU	cachous
ABLLOST	ballots	ABRSTUY	Astbury	ACCEILT	calcite	ACCHOTW	choctaw
ABLLOTY	tallboy	ABSSUWY	subways	ACCEIMR	ceramic	ACCHOUY	acouchy
ABLLOVY	lovably	ACCCILY	acyclic		racemic	ACCHPTU	catchup
ABLLPSU	ballups	ACCDDEE	acceded	ACCEINO	cocaine	ACCHRRU	currach
ABLMMOU	bummalo	ACCDDEI	caddice		oceanic	ACCHRST	scratch
ABLMMUU	Lumumba	ACCDEEN	cadence	ACCEINV	vaccine	ACCHSSU	succahs
ABLMNOU	umbonal	ACCDEER	acceder	ACCEIPR	caprice	ACCIIIL	Cilicia
ABLMOOT	tombola	ACCDEES	accedes	ACCEIPS	icecaps	ACCIILN	aclinic
ABLMOVY	movably	ACCDEHN	chanced		ipecacs	ACCIINT	actinic
ABLMPUU	pabulum	ACCDEHO	coached	ACCEIPV	peccavi	ACCIIST	ascitic
ABLMSTU	Stambul	ACCDEII	accidie	ACCEIQU	cacique		sciatic
ABLMSTY	tymbals	ACCDEIU	caducei	ACCEIST	ascetic	ACCIKRR	carrick
ABLMTUY	mutably	ACCDEKL	cackled	ACCEITT	ectatic	ACCIKRS	carsick
ABLNOOZ	Bolzano		clacked	ACCEKLO	Leacock	ACCILLU	calculi
ABLNOSZ	blazons	ACCDEKO	cockade	ACCEKLR	cackler	ACCILMO	comical
ABLNOTU	butanol	ACCDEKR	cracked		clacker	ACCILMU	calcium
ABLNOTY	notably	ACCDENY	cadency		crackle	ACCILNO	conical
ABLOORS	robalos	ACCDEOP	Cape Cod	ACCEKLS	cackles		laconic
ABLOPYY	playboy	ACCDERU	accrued	ACCEKOP	peacock	ACCILNU	Cluniac
ABLORST	borstal	ACCDESU	accused	ACCEKOS	seacock	ACCILNY	cynical

ACCILOR	caloric	ACDDHRU	chuddar	ACDEGKO	dockage		dancier
ACCILOS	calicos	ACDDIIS	diacids	ACDEGLN	clanged	ACDEINS	candies
ACCILOV	vocalic	ACDDIRS	discard		glanced		incased
ACCILRU	crucial	ACDDIRY	dryadic	ACDEGNO	congaed	ACDEINY	cyanide
ACCILRY	acrylic	ACDDIST	addicts		decagon	ACDEIPR	peracid
ACCILSS	classic	ACDDISY	dyadics	ACDEGNU	uncaged	ACDEIRR	carried
ACCILST	clastic	ACDDKOP	paddock	ACDEGOR	cordage	ACDEIRS	cardies
ACCILSU	sacculi	ACDDSTU	adducts	ACDEGRS	cadgers		darcies
ACCILTU	Calicut	ACDEEES	decease	ACDEGST	gedacts		radices
ACCINNO	canonic	ACDEEFF	effaced	ACDEHHT	hatched		sidecar
ACCINRU	crucian	ACDEEFN	enfaced	ACDEHIN	chained	ACDEISV	advices
ACCIOPR	caproic	ACDEEFR	defacer		echidna	ACDEITT	dictate
ACCIORS	Corsica		refaced	ACDEHIP	edaphic	ACDEITY	edacity
ACCIOST	ocicats	ACDEEFS	defaces	ACDEHIR	chaired	ACDEJLO	cajoled
ACCIRRS	ricracs	ACDEEFT	faceted	ACDEHIX	hexadic	ACDEKKN	knacked
ACCIRST	arctics	ACDEEGL	glaceed	ACDEHKL	hackled	ACDEKLM	mackled
ACCISTT	tactics	ACDEEGN	encaged	ACDEHKS	shacked	ACDEKLN	clanked
ACCISTU	caustic	ACDEEHL	leached	ACDEHKW	whacked	ACDEKLO	cloaked
ACCKNNO	Cannock	ACDEEHP	peached	ACDEHLS	clashed	ACDEKLS	slacked
ACCKOPR	caprock	ACDEEHR	Ardèche	ACDEHMP	champed	ACDEKLT	tackled
ACCKOSS	cassock		reached	ACDEHMR	charmed		talcked
	cossack	ACDEEHT	cheated		marched	ACDEKLU	caulked
ACCKPRU	crackup	ACDEEIR	deciare	ACDEHMT	matched	ACDEKMS	smacked
ACCKTTU	Cuttack	ACDEEJT	dejecta	ACDEHNR	endarch	ACDEKNR	cranked
ACCLNOT	Clacton	ACDEEKR	creaked		ranched	ACDEKNS	snacked
ACCLOSU	coucals	ACDEELL	cadelle	ACDEHNT	chanted	ACDEKOR	croaked
ACCMOOY	cocoyam	ACDEELN	cleaned	ACDEHOP	poached	ACDEKQU	quacked
ACCMOPT	compact		enlaced	ACDEHOR	roached	ACDEKRT	tracked
ACCMRUU	curcuma	ACDEELR	cleared	ACDEHOT	cathode	ACDEKRW	wracked
ACCNNOO	cooncan		creedal	ACDEHPP	chapped	ACDEKST	stacked
ACCNOOP	cocopan		declare	ACDEHPR	parched	ACDEKSW	swacked
ACCNOOR	raccoon	ACDEELS	descale	ACDEHPT	patched	ACDELLN	Cleland
ACCNOTT	contact	ACDEELT	cleated	ACDEHRR	charred	ACDELLS	scalled
ACCNOTU	account	ACDEELV	cleaved	ACDEHRS	crashed	ACDELLU	Claudel
ACCOPTY	copycat	ACDEEMN	menaced	ACDEHRT	charted	ACDELMM	clammed
ACCOQSU	squacco	ACDEEMR	amerced	ACDEHSS	chassed	ACDELMO	Macleod
ACCORRY	Corcyra		creamed	ACDEHST	scathed	ACDELMP	clamped
ACCORSS	corsacs	ACDEEMV	medevac	ACDEHSY	dayches	ACDELNO	celadon
ACCOSST	accosts	ACDEENS	encased	ACDEHTT	chatted	ACDELNR	candler
ACCRSTU	accurst	ACDEENT	enacted	ACDEHTW	watched	ACDELNS	calends
ACDDDEI	caddied	ACDEENV	vendace	ACDEHTY	yachted		candles
ACDDDEU	adduced	ACDEEPR	capered	ACDEILL	cedilla	ACDELNU	unlaced
ACDDEEF	defaced	ACDEEPS	escaped	ACDEILM	camelid	ACDELOP	pedocal
ACDDEEL	decaled	ACDEERS	creased		claimed	ACDELOR	caroled
ACDDEES	decades		decares		decimal	ACDELOS	solaced
ACDDEEY	decayed	ACDEERT	catered		declaim	ACDELOT	located
ACDDEHI	Didache		cerated		medical	ACDELPP	clapped
ACDDEHR	cheddar		created	ACDEILN	Iceland	ACDELPS	clasped
ACDDEHY	dayched		reacted		inlaced		scalped
ACDDEIN	candied	ACDEETT	taceted	ACDEILR	decrial	ACDELQU	calqued
ACDDEIS	caddies	ACDEETU	educate		radicel	ACDELRR	cradler
ACDDEIU	decidua	ACDEETX	exacted		radicle	ACDELRS	cradles
ACDDELN	candled	ACDEFFH	chaffed	ACDEILS	Alcides		scalder
ACDDELO	cladode	ACDEFIN	fancied	ACDEILT	citadel	ACDELRU	caulder
ACDDELR	cradled	ACDEFRS	scarfed		deltaic	ACDELRW	crawled
ACDDELS	scalded	ACDEFRT	crafted		dialect	ACDELSS	classed
ACDDEOP	decapod	ACDEGGL	clagged		edictal		declass
ACDDESU	adduces	ACDEGGR	cragged	ACDEILV	caviled	ACDELST	castled
	scauded	ACDEGGS	scagged	ACDEIMV	medivac	ACDELWW	dewclaw
ACDDHHU	chuddah	ACDEGHN	Changde	ACDEIMY	mediacy	ACDEMMR	crammed
ACDDHIS	caddish		changed	ACDEINO	oceanid	ACDEMMS	scammed
ACDDHKO	haddock	ACDEGHR	charged	ACDEINR	carnied	ACDEMNO	Cædmon

125

	Macedon	**ACDHLOR**	chordal	**ACDLNOR**	caldron	**ACEELMN**	Alcmene
ACDEMOR	comrade	**ACDHMPU**	Duchamp	**ACDLSTY**	dactyls	**ACEELMP**	emplace
ACDEMPR	cramped	**ACDHMRS**	drachms	**ACDMMNO**	command	**ACEELMR**	reclame
ACDEMPS	decamps	**ACDHNOW**	cowhand	**ACDMOOW**	camwood	**ACEELNN**	Laënnec
	scamped	**ACDHOPR**	pochard	**ACDMORZ**	czardom	**ACEELNO**	Celaeno
ACDENNS	scanned	**ACDHORR**	orchard	**ACDMSTU**	mudcats	**ACEELNR**	cleaner
ACDENNT	candent	**ACDHORS**	chadors	**ACDNOOR**	cardoon	**ACEELNS**	cleanse
ACDENOR	dracone	**ACDHRYY**	dyarchy	**ACDNORU**	candour		enlaces
ACDENOS	acnodes	**ACDIIIN**	indicia	**ACDOORS**	Cardoso		scalene
	deacons	**ACDIINN**	indican	**ACDOORV**	Cordova	**ACEELNV**	enclave
ACDENOT	tacnode	**ACDIINO**	conidia	**ACDORST**	costard		valence
ACDENPR	pranced	**ACDIINV**	da Vinci	**ACDORSU**	crusado	**ACEELPR**	percale
ACDENPT	pandect	**ACDIIRT**	arctiid	**ACDORSW**	cowards		replace
ACDENRS	dancers		triacid	**ACDORUZ**	cruzado	**ACEELRR**	clearer
ACDENRT	Tancred		triadic	**ACDRSTU**	custard		Le Carré
	tranced	**ACDIITY**	acidity	**ACEEEPS**	escapee	**ACEELRS**	alerces
ACDENRU	Cernuda	**ACDIKLS**	skaldic	**ACEEEUV**	evacuee		cereals
	durance	**ACDILMO**	domical	**ACEEFFR**	effacer	**ACEELRT**	Electra
ACDENRY	ardency	**ACDILMS**	cladism	**ACEEFFS**	effaces		treacle
ACDENSS	ascends	**ACDILNO**	nodical	**ACEEFIN**	faience	**ACEELRV**	cleaver
ACDENST	decants	**ACDILNU**	incudal		fiancee	**ACEELST**	celesta
	descant	**ACDILOP**	placoid	**ACEEFLU**	feculae		selecta
	scanted	**ACDILOR**	cordial	**ACEEFNS**	enfaces	**ACEELSV**	cleaves
ACDENTU	unacted	**ACDILOT**	cotidal	**ACEEFPR**	preface	**ACEELVX**	exclave
ACDEOOR	Odoacer	**ACDILRY**	acridly	**ACEEFRS**	refaces	**ACEEMNR**	menacer
ACDEOPS	peascod	**ACDILST**	cladist	**ACEEGIL**	elegiac	**ACEEMNS**	menaces
ACDEORR	corrade	**ACDILTW**	wildcat	**ACEEGNS**	encages	**ACEEMNV**	cavemen
ACDEORT	cordate	**ACDIMMU**	cadmium	**ACEEGSU**	escuage	**ACEEMNY**	Mayence
	redcoat	**ACDIMNO**	monacid	**ACEEHHT**	cheetah		Mycenae
ACDEORU	Ecuador		monadic	**ACEEHIV**	achieve	**ACEEMPS**	Campese
ACDEOST	coasted		nomadic	**ACEEHKL**	Haeckel	**ACEEMRR**	amercer
ACDEOUV	couvade	**ACDIMNY**	dynamic	**ACEEHLR**	leacher		creamer
ACDEPPR	crapped	**ACDIMOO**	camoodi	**ACEEHLS**	Chelsea	**ACEEMRS**	amerces
ACDEPRS	redcaps	**ACDINNU**	Duncan I		leaches		racemes
	scarped	**ACDINOT**	Candiot	**ACEEHLT**	chelate	**ACEEMRT**	cremate
	scraped	**ACDINRU**	iracund	**ACEEHMR**	machree	**ACEENNP**	penance
ACDEQSU	casqued	**ACDINST**	discant	**ACEEHMT**	machete	**ACEENNR**	narceen
ACDERRS	carders	**ACDINSU**	Sudanic	**ACEEHNN**	enhance	**ACEENNT**	canteen
	scarred	**ACDINSY**	cyanids	**ACEEHNP**	cheapen	**ACEENNY**	cayenne
ACDERST	redacts	**ACDIOPR**	parodic	**ACEEHNS**	achenes	**ACEENNZ**	Cézanne
	scarted		picador		enchase	**ACEENOR**	corneae
ACDERSU	crusade	**ACDIORR**	corrida	**ACEEHOR**	ochreae	**ACEENOT**	acetone
ACDERTT	detract		Ricardo	**ACEEHPR**	cheaper	**ACEENRS**	careens
ACDERTU	Decatur	**ACDIORS**	sarcoid		peacher		caserne
	traduce	**ACDIORT**	carotid	**ACEEHPS**	peaches	**ACEENRT**	centare
ACDERWY	Cawdrey	**ACDIOST**	dacoits	**ACEEHRR**	reacher		crenate
ACDESTT	scatted	**ACDIOSZ**	zodiacs	**ACEEHRS**	reaches		reenact
ACDFFIR	Cardiff	**ACDIOTY**	dacoity	**ACEEHRT**	cheater	**ACEENRV**	cervena
ACDFIIT	fatidic	**ACDIOXY**	oxyacid		hectare	**ACEENSS**	encases
ACDFIIY	acidify	**ACDIPRY**	Picardy		reteach		seances
ACDFIOT	factoid	**ACDIPSS**	capsids		teacher		senecas
ACDGGIN	cadging	**ACDIQRU**	quadric	**ACEEHST**	escheat	**ACEENST**	tenaces
ACDGINN	dancing	**ACDIRST**	drastic		teaches	**ACEENTU**	cuneate
ACDGINO	gonadic	**ACDISST**	dicasts	**ACEEHTT**	thecate	**ACEEORS**	acerose
ACDGINR	carding	**ACDITUV**	viaduct	**ACEEILP**	calipee	**ACEEORT**	ocreate
ACDGKLO	daglock	**ACDJNTU**	adjunct	**ACEEILT**	Eleatic	**ACEEOSS**	caseose
ACDGORT	dogcart	**ACDKLOP**	padlock	**ACEEINR**	Cairene	**ACEEOST**	acetose
ACDHIIL	chiliad	**ACDKMPU**	mudpack	**ACEEINU**	eucaine		coatees
ACDHINR	Chardin	**ACDKNVY**	Van Dyck	**ACEEISV**	vesicae	**ACEEPRR**	caperer
ACDHIRR	Richard	**ACDLLOR**	collard	**ACEEJKN**	jackeen	**ACEEPRS**	escaper
ACDHIRY	diarchy	**ACDLLUY**	ducally	**ACEEKNP**	kneecap	**ACEEPSS**	escapes
ACDHISS	Chassid	**ACDLNOP**	Copland	**ACEELLN**	nacelle	**ACEEPST**	pectase

ACEEPTT	pectate	**ACEGIMR**	grimace	**ACEHISS**	chaises	**ACEHNST**	chasten
ACEERRS	careers	**ACEGIMT**	gametic	**ACEHIST**	achiest	**ACEHNSU**	nauches
	creaser	**ACEGINO**	coinage		aitches	**ACEHNTT**	etchant
ACEERRT	caterer	**ACEGINP**	peacing	**ACEHITY**	yachtie	**ACEHNTU**	unteach
	retrace	**ACEGINR**	anergic	**ACEHKLR**	hackler	**ACEHNTY**	chantey
	terrace		grecian	**ACEHKLS**	hackles	**ACEHOOT**	ootheca
ACEERSS	creases	**ACEGINS**	ceasing		shackle	**ACEHOPR**	Pechora
ACEERST	creates	**ACEGINY**	gynecia	**ACEHKNY**	hackney		poacher
ACEERSU	cesurae	**ACEGIRT**	cigaret	**ACEHKRS**	hackers	**ACEHOPS**	cheapos
ACEERSV	Versace	**ACEGIST**	cagiest	**ACEHKRT**	Eckhart		poaches
ACEERTX	exacter	**ACEGKLO**	lockage	**ACEHKRW**	whacker	**ACEHORS**	choreas
	excreta	**ACEGKLR**	grackle	**ACEHKRY**	hackery		oraches
ACEESSS	asceses	**ACEGKOR**	corkage	**ACEHLLS**	shellac		roaches
ACEFFHI	affiche	**ACEGLLO**	collage	**ACEHLLT**	hellcat	**ACEHOTY**	chayote
ACEFFHR	chaffer	**ACEGLNO**	congeal	**ACEHLMY**	alchemy	**ACEHPPS**	schappe
ACEFFIN	caffein	**ACEGLNR**	clanger	**ACEHLNN**	channel	**ACEHPRS**	eparchs
ACEFFST	affects	**ACEGLNS**	glances	**ACEHLNO**	chalone		parches
ACEFGIP	pigface	**ACEGLOU**	cagoule	**ACEHLNR**	charnel	**ACEHPRT**	chapter
ACEFHMR	chamfer	**ACEGNOR**	acrogen	**ACEHLOP**	epochal		patcher
ACEFHRS	chafers	**ACEGNOT**	cognate	**ACEHLOR**	cholera	**ACEHPRY**	eparchy
ACEFHRU	chaufer	**ACEGNSU**	cangues		chorale		preachy
ACEFILL	icefall	**ACEGORS**	cargoes		choreal	**ACEHPSS**	chapess
ACEFILM	malefic		corsage	**ACEHLOS**	loaches	**ACEHPST**	hepcats
ACEFINN	finance		socager	**ACEHLOT**	cathole		patches
ACEFINR	fancier	**ACEGORU**	courage	**ACEHLPS**	chapels	**ACEHRRS**	archers
ACEFINS	fancies	**ACEGOTT**	cottage	**ACEHLPT**	chaplet		crasher
	fascine	**ACEGSTU**	scutage	**ACEHLPY**	cheaply	**ACEHRRT**	charter
	fiances	**ACEHHLR**	Harlech	**ACEHLRS**	Charles		rechart
ACEFIRS	farcies	**ACEHHLT**	hatchel		clasher	**ACEHRRV**	charver
	fiacres	**ACEHHMS**	Meshach		larches	**ACEHRRX**	xerarch
ACEFITV	factive	**ACEHHRT**	hatcher	**ACEHLRY**	charley	**ACEHRRY**	archery
ACEFITY	acetify	**ACEHHRU**	hachure	**ACEHLSS**	clashes	**ACEHRSS**	chasers
ACEFLRU	careful	**ACEHHST**	chetahs	**ACEHLST**	chalets		crashes
ACEFNNO	faconne		hatches		latches		eschars
ACEFNOS	Fonseca	**ACEHHTT**	hatchet		satchel	**ACEHRSW**	chawers
ACEFNRU	furnace	**ACEHIKS**	hackies	**ACEHLSV**	chevals	**ACEHRSX**	exarchs
ACEFOTU	outface	**ACEHILL**	challie	**ACEHLTT**	chattel	**ACEHRSY**	hyraces
ACEFRRT	refract		helical		latchet	**ACEHRTT**	chatter
ACEFRRU	farceur	**ACEHILM**	lechaim	**ACEHMNP**	chapmen		ratchet
ACEFRSU	surface		Meilhac	**ACEHMPR**	champer	**ACEHRTW**	watcher
ACEFRTU	facture		Michael	**ACEHMPS**	Sempach	**ACEHRTY**	Cythera
	furcate	**ACEHILN**	Chilean	**ACEHMRR**	charmer	**ACEHRXY**	exarchy
ACEFSTU	faucets	**ACEHILR**	charlie		marcher	**ACEHSSS**	chasses
ACEFTTW	Fawcett	**ACEHILT**	alethic	**ACEHMRS**	machers	**ACEHSST**	sachets
ACEGHNR	changer		ethical		marches		scathes
ACEGHNS	changes	**ACEHIMN**	machine		mesarch	**ACEHSSW**	cashews
ACEGHOU	gouache	**ACEHIMP**	impeach		schmear	**ACEHSTW**	watches
ACEGHOW	cowhage	**ACEHIMR**	chimera	**ACEHMRT**	matcher	**ACEIILS**	laicise
ACEGHRR	charger	**ACEHIMT**	hematic		rematch	**ACEIILT**	ciliate
ACEGHRS	Chagres	**ACEHINN**	Chennai	**ACEHMSS**	sachems	**ACEIILZ**	laicize
	charges		enchain	**ACEHMST**	matches	**ACEIJKS**	jackies
ACEGIIR	Craigie	**ACEHINR**	archine	**ACEHMTT**	matchet		jacksie
ACEGILN	angelic	**ACEHINY**	hyaenic	**ACEHMTY**	ecthyma	**ACEIKLS**	saclike
	anglice	**ACEHIPP**	chappie	**ACEHMTZ**	chametz	**ACEIKLT**	catlike
	galenic	**ACEHIPT**	aphetic	**ACEHNNT**	enchant	**ACEIKMR**	keramic
	Legnica		hepatic	**ACEHNOR**	Acheron	**ACEIKPX**	pickaxe
ACEGILP	pelagic	**ACEHIRR**	charier	**ACEHNOS**	Acheson	**ACEIKRT**	tackier
ACEGILR	glacier	**ACEHIRS**	cahiers	**ACEHNRR**	rancher	**ACEIKRW**	wackier
	gracile		cashier	**ACEHNRS**	ranches	**ACEIKSS**	seasick
ACEGILS	algesic		eriachs	**ACEHNRT**	chanter	**ACEIKST**	tackies
ACEGILT	algetic	**ACEHIRT**	theriac		tranche	**ACEILLL**	allelic
ACEGIMO	camogie	**ACEHIRV**	archive	**ACEHNSS**	Sachsen	**ACEILLM**	micella

ACEILLX	lexical		nancies	**ACEISST**	ascites		recalls
ACEILMN	cnemial	**ACEINNT**	ancient		ectasis	**ACELLRY**	Carlyle
	melanic	**ACEINNY**	cyanine	**ACEISTT**	catties		clearly
ACEILMR	claimer	**ACEINOP**	paeonic		statice	**ACELMNO**	Coleman
	miracle	**ACEINOS**	acinose	**ACEISTV**	actives	**ACELMOT**	camelot
	reclaim	**ACEINOT**	aconite	**ACEITTV**	cavetti	**ACELMOU**	leucoma
ACEILMT	climate	**ACEINPR**	caprine	**ACEJKST**	jackets	**ACELMPR**	clamper
ACEILMX	exclaim	**ACEINPS**	inscape	**ACEJLOR**	cajoler	**ACELMRS**	marcels
ACEILMY	mycelia	**ACEINRS**	arsenic	**ACEJLOS**	cajoles	**ACELMSS**	mascles
ACEILNP	capelin		carnies	**ACEJNOT**	jaconet		mescals
	panicle	**ACEINRT**	cantier	**ACEJNOY**	joyance	**ACELMST**	calmest
	pelican		ceratin	**ACEJPTU**	cajeput		camlets
ACEILNR	carline		certain	**ACEJRTT**	traject	**ACELMSU**	almuces
	Linacre		creatin	**ACEKKNR**	knacker		macules
ACEILNS	inlaces	**ACEINSS**	incases	**ACEKLMS**	mackles	**ACELMSZ**	mezcals
	sanicle	**ACEINTT**	Canetti	**ACEKLNS**	slacken	**ACELMTU**	calumet
	scaleni		nictate	**ACEKLPT**	placket	**ACELNNO**	alencon
ACEILNU	cauline		tetanic	**ACEKLRS**	calkers		Alençon
ACEILOR	calorie	**ACEINTV**	venatic		lackers	**ACELNNU**	unclean
	cariole	**ACEINTX**	inexact		slacker	**ACELNNY**	lyncean
	loricae	**ACEINTY**	cyanite	**ACEKLRT**	tackler	**ACELNOR**	corneal
ACEILOS	celosia	**ACEINTZ**	zincate	**ACEKLRU**	caulker	**ACELNOT**	lactone
ACEILOT	aloetic	**ACEINVZ**	Vicenza	**ACEKLST**	tackles	**ACELNOY**	Alcyone
ACEILPR	caliper	**ACEIOPT**	ectopia	**ACEKLSY**	lackeys	**ACELNOZ**	calzone
	replica	**ACEIORS**	cariose	**ACEKMNN**	McKenna	**ACELNPS**	enclasp
ACEILPS	plaices		scoriae	**ACEKMRS**	smacker		spancel
	special	**ACEIORT**	erotica	**ACEKNRR**	cranker	**ACELNPT**	clapnet
ACEILPT	plicate	**ACEIOTX**	exotica	**ACEKNRS**	cankers	**ACELNPU**	cleanup
ACEILRS	claries	**ACEIPPR**	crappie	**ACEKNVY**	van Eyck	**ACELNRS**	lancers
	eclairs		epicarp	**ACEKORR**	croaker	**ACELNRT**	central
	scalier	**ACEIPRS**	scrapie	**ACEKORU**	Kerouac	**ACELNRU**	lucarne
ACEILRT	article		spacier	**ACEKPPR**	prepack		nuclear
	recital	**ACEIPRT**	paretic	**ACEKPRS**	packers		unclear
ACEILRU	auricle		picrate		repacks	**ACELNRY**	larceny
ACEILRV	clavier	**ACEIPST**	aseptic	**ACEKPST**	packets	**ACELNST**	cantles
	valeric		paciest	**ACEKRRS**	rackers		centals
ACEILST	Castile		spicate	**ACEKRRT**	tracker		lancets
	elastic	**ACEIPSU**	auspice	**ACEKRSS**	sackers	**ACELNSU**	censual
	laciest	**ACEIPSZ**	capizes		screaks		launces
	latices		capsize	**ACEKRST**	rackets		unlaces
	salicet	**ACEIPTV**	captive		restack	**ACELNTY**	latency
ACEILSV	vesical	**ACEIQRU**	acquire		stacker	**ACELNVY**	valency
ACEILTT	lattice		Quercia		tackers	**ACELOPR**	polacre
	tactile	**ACEIQSU**	caiques	**ACEKRSW**	wackers	**ACELOPT**	polecat
ACEIMNO	encomia	**ACEIQUZ**	cazique	**ACEKRSY**	screaky	**ACELOPU**	copulae
ACEIMNP	pemican	**ACEIRRR**	carrier	**ACEKRTY**	rackety	**ACELOQU**	coequal
ACEIMNR	carmine	**ACEIRRS**	carries	**ACEKSST**	caskets	**ACELORR**	caroler
	Crimean		scarier	**ACEKSTT**	tackets	**ACELORS**	claroes
ACEIMNS	amnesic	**ACEIRRT**	Cartier	**ACEKTTY**	tackety		coalers
	cinemas		cirrate	**ACELLMO**	calomel		escolar
ACEIMNT	nematic		erratic	**ACELLMY**	mycella		oracles
ACEIMNX	Mexican	**ACEIRRW**	aircrew	**ACELLNY**	cleanly		solacer
ACEIMPR	campier	**ACEIRRZ**	crazier	**ACELLOR**	corella	**ACELORT**	locater
ACEIMPY	pyaemic	**ACEIRST**	cristae		ocellar	**ACELORY**	caloyer
ACEIMRU	Maurice		raciest	**ACELLOS**	callose	**ACELOSS**	solaces
	uraemic		stearic		locales	**ACELOST**	alecost
ACEIMST	sematic	**ACEIRSU**	saucier	**ACELLOT**	collate		lactose
ACEIMSU	caesium	**ACEIRSV**	varices	**ACELLPS**	scalpel		locates
ACEIMTX	taxemic		viscera	**ACELLPY**	clypeal		talcose
ACEINNP	pinnace	**ACEIRTT**	cattier	**ACELLRR**	carrell	**ACELOSV**	alcoves
ACEINNR	cannier		citrate	**ACELLRS**	callers		coevals
ACEINNS	canines	**ACEISSS**	ascesis		cellars	**ACELOTT**	calotte

ACELOTU oculate	**ACEMRST** mercats	**ACEOSTU** acetous	**ACFFIKM** maffick
ACELOTY acolyte	**ACEMRSU** Marcuse	**ACEOSTV** avocets	**ACFFILT** afflict
ACELOUV vacuole	**ACEMSUX** exacums	octaves	**ACFFIRT** traffic
ACELPPR clapper	**ACENNOS** ancones	**ACEOTTV** cavetto	**ACFFLSS** sclaffs
ACELPRS carpels	sonance	**ACEOTUU** autocue	**ACFFLTU** factful
clasper	**ACENNOT** connate	couteau	**ACFFOST** castoff
parcels	**ACENNOZ** canzone	**ACEPPRS** cappers	**ACFGHIN** chafing
scalper	**ACENNRS** canners	**ACEPRRS** carpers	**ACFGINR** farcing
ACELPRT plectra	scanner	scarper	**ACFGINS** facings
ACELPRY prelacy	**ACENNRY** cannery	scraper	**ACFHIST** catfish
ACELPST placets	**ACENNST** nascent	**ACEPRSS** escarps	**ACFHISU** fuchsia
ACELPSU capsule	**ACENNSU** nuances	parsecs	**ACFHLNU** flaunch
specula	**ACENNTY** tenancy	scrapes	Funchal
upscale	**ACENOOR** coronae	spacers	**ACFHRTU** futharc
ACELPSY cypsela	**ACENORS** coarsen	**ACEPRST** carpets	**ACFHRTY** fratchy
ACELPTY ectypal	corneas	precast	**ACFIILN** finical
ACELQRU lacquer	**ACENORT** enactor	spectra	**ACFILNO** folacin
ACELQSU calques	**ACENOSU** Oceanus	**ACEPRSU** apercus	**ACFILNY** fancily
claques	**ACENOSZ** Cosenza	scauper	**ACFILRY** clarify
ACELQUY lacquey	**ACENOTV** centavo	**ACEPRTU** capture	**ACFILSS** fiscals
ACELRRS carrels	**ACENPRR** prancer	**ACEPSST** aspects	**ACFIMRU** fumaric
ACELRRW crawler	**ACENPRS** prances	**ACEPSTU** cuspate	**ACFIMSS** fascism
ACELRSS classer	**ACENPTY** patency	teacups	**ACFINNY** infancy
scalers	**ACENRRY** errancy	**ACEQRTU** racquet	**ACFINOT** faction
ACELRST cartels	**ACENRSS** caserns	**ACEQSSU** casques	**ACFINRS** Francis
clarets	**ACENRST** canters	sacques	**ACFINRT** frantic
scarlet	carnets	**ACERRSS** scarers	infarct
ACELRSU cesural	Castner	**ACERRST** carters	infract
secular	nectars	craters	**ACFINRY** carnify
ACELRSV carvels	recants	tracers	**ACFIOSS** fiascos
clavers	trances	**ACERRSU** curares	**ACFIRSY** scarify
ACELRSW clawers	**ACENRSV** caverns	**ACERRSV** carvers	**ACFISST** fascist
ACELRTT clatter	cravens	cravers	**ACFKLSU** sackful
ACELRTU Lautrec	**ACENRSY** carneys	**ACERRTT** retract	**ACFLLOY** focally
Leuctra	**ACENRTU** centaur	**ACERRTY** tracery	**ACFLNOS** falcons
ACELRTV Calvert	**ACENRTY** nectary	**ACERRUV** verruca	flacons
ACELRTY treacly	**ACENSST** ascents	**ACERRVY** carvery	**ACFLNSU** canfuls
ACELRWY Crawley	stances	**ACERSST** actress	**ACFLRTU** cartful
ACELSSS classes	**ACENSSU** usances	casters	**ACFLRUU** furcula
ACELSST castles	**ACENSTU** nutcase	recasts	**ACFLTTU** tactful
ACELSSU clauses	**ACEOOPP** apocope	**ACERSSU** causers	**ACFLTUY** faculty
ACELSTU sulcate	**ACEOPRX** exocarp	cesuras	**ACFNRTU** fructan
ACELSUU aculeus	**ACEOPSS** scapose	saucers	**ACFORST** factors
ACELSXY calyxes	**ACEOPST** capotes	sucrase	**ACFORTY** factory
ACELTUY acutely	toecaps	**ACERSSV** scarves	**ACGGINR** gracing
ACELTXY exactly	**ACEOPSW** cowpeas	**ACERSSY** carseys	**ACGGRSY** scraggy
ACEMMRR crammer	**ACEOPTU** outpace	**ACERSTT** scatter	**ACGHIKN** hacking
ACEMMRS scammer	**ACEORRS** coarser	**ACERSTU** curates	**ACGHINR** arching
ACEMNOR Cameron	correas	**ACERSTY** sectary	chagrin
cremona	**ACEORRT** acroter	**ACERTTU** curtate	charing
Menorca	creator	**ACERTTX** extract	**ACGHINS** chasing
romance	reactor	**ACERTTY** cattery	**ACGHINT** gnathic
ACEMNOS Camoëns	**ACEORSS** rosaces	**ACERTUY** cautery	**ACGHINW** chawing
ACEMNPS encamps	**ACEORST** coaster	**ACERUVY** Cauvery	chinwag
ACEMNRR Cranmer	**ACEORSU** acerous	**ACESSTU** caestus	**ACGHINY** Yichang
ACEMOPR compare	carouse	cuestas	**ACGHIOR** choragi
ACEMORU morceau	**ACEORSX** coaxers	**ACESSTY** ecstasy	**ACGHIPR** graphic
ACEMOSU mucosae	**ACEORTU** outrace	**ACESSUY** causeys	**ACGHLOY** Chogyal
ACEMPRR cramper	**ACEORTV** overact	cayuses	**ACGHMRT** McGrath
ACEMPRS campers	**ACEORTX** exactor	**ACESTTU** scutate	**ACGHNRU** graunch
scamper	**ACEOSSU** caseous	**ACESTTY** testacy	**ACGHNUW** Wuchang
ACEMRSS screams	**ACEOSTT** costate	**ACFFIIT** caitiff	**ACGHOSU** gauchos

ACGHRRU	curragh	**ACGIORT**	argotic		haricot	**ACHNSTY**	snatchy
ACGHRSU	curaghs	**ACGIRST**	gastric	**ACHIOST**	isotach	**ACHOOST**	cahoots
ACGIILN	alginic	**ACGKLLO**	gallock	**ACHIPPS**	sapphic	**ACHOPRS**	carhops
ACGIITU	augitic	**ACGLNOR**	clangor	**ACHIPST**	pathics	**ACHOPRT**	toparch
ACGIJKN	jacking	**ACGLNSU**	glucans		spathic	**ACHOPRY**	charpoy
ACGIKLN	calking	**ACGNOOT**	octagon	**ACHIQRU**	charqui	**ACHORSU**	aurochs
	lacking	**ACGNNOR**	crannog	**ACHIQSU**	quaichs	**ACHRSTY**	starchy
ACGIKNP	packing	**ACGNORS**	garcons	**ACHIRTU**	haircut	**ACHSSTU**	cushats
ACGIKNR	arcking	**ACGNOSS**	gascons	**ACHIRTY**	charity	**ACHSSTY**	stachys
	carking	**ACGNOSU**	cougans	**ACHISSS**	chassis	**ACIIILS**	Sicilia
	racking	**ACGNOSY**	Gascony	**ACHISTT**	cattish	**ACIIKNN**	canikin
ACGIKNS	sacking	**ACGORSU**	cougars	**ACHISTY**	Scythia	**ACIIKRS**	airsick
ACGIKNT	tacking	**ACGOSWY**	cogways	**ACHKKSU**	chukkas	**ACIILMS**	laicism
ACGIKNY	yacking	**ACHHIIT**	Hitachi	**ACHKLOV**	Chkalov	**ACIILNO**	Nicolai
ACGIKRR	Garrick	**ACHHIRS**	rhachis	**ACHKMMO**	hammock	**ACIILNR**	clarini
ACGILLN	calling	**ACHHIRW**	Harwich	**ACHKOPS**	hopsack	**ACIILNS**	salicin
ACGILLO	logical	**ACHHMSU**	chumash	**ACHKOSS**	hassock	**ACIILNV**	vicinal
ACGILMN	calming	**ACHHPPU**	chuppah		shackos	**ACIILOR**	Carol II
ACGILMY	myalgic	**ACHHTTY**	thatchy	**ACHKRSU**	chukars	**ACIILPT**	aplitic
ACGILNN	lancing	**ACHIILS**	ischial	**ACHKSTW**	thwacks	**ACIILRY**	ciliary
ACGILNO	coaling	**ACHIIMS**	chiasmi	**ACHLLOO**	alcohol	**ACIILST**	italics
ACGILNP	placing	**ACHIINT**	chianti	**ACHLLOR**	chloral	**ACIIMMS**	miasmic
ACGILNR	carling	**ACHIIPS**	pachisi	**ACHLLOS**	chollas	**ACIIMOT**	comitia
ACGILNS	lacings	**ACHIITW**	Wichita	**ACHLLOU**	Cholula	**ACIIMST**	simatic
	scaling	**ACHIJKS**	hijacks	**ACHLMNU**	McLuhan	**ACIINNO**	anionic
ACGILNT	catling	**ACHIJMO**	Joachim	**ACHLMSZ**	schmalz	**ACIINOS**	Nicosia
	talcing	**ACHIJNT**	jacinth	**ACHLNOS**	lochans	**ACIINOV**	avionic
ACGILNU	cingula	**ACHIKLN**	Nalchik	**ACHLNOW**	Lanchow	**ACIINPS**	piscina
ACGILNV	calving	**ACHIKOS**	kochias	**ACHLNOY**	halcyon	**ACIINSS**	Cassini
ACGILNW	clawing	**ACHIKRS**	ricksha	**ACHLNTU**	unlatch	**ACIINTT**	titanic
ACGILNY	claying	**ACHIKRY**	hayrick	**ACHLORS**	chorals	**ACIIORS**	Oscar II
ACGIMNO	coaming	**ACHILLN**	Chillán		scholar	**ACIIPPR**	priapic
ACGIMNP	camping	**ACHILLO**	lochial	**ACHLORT**	trochal	**ACIIPRT**	piratic
ACGIMRS	Gramsci	**ACHILLP**	phallic	**ACHLOSW**	salchow	**ACIIRST**	satiric
ACGINNN	canning	**ACHILLS**	challis	**ACHLTUZ**	chalutz	**ACIJKLN**	Jacklin
ACGINNR	craning	**ACHILLT**	thallic	**ACHMMNO**	McMahon	**ACIJLOS**	Jalisco
ACGINNS	canings	**ACHILLV**	Villach	**ACHMNOR**	monarch	**ACIJUZZ**	jacuzzi
ACGINNT	canting	**ACHILNP**	Chaplin		nomarch	**ACIKLNS**	calkins
ACGINOP	Cipango	**ACHILOR**	chorial	**ACHMNSU**	Schuman	**ACIKLOR**	airlock
ACGINOR	organic	**ACHILOS**	scholia	**ACHMOPR**	camphor	**ACIKLTY**	tackily
ACGINOS	agnosic	**ACHILOV**	Covilhã	**ACHMORS**	chromas	**ACIKLWY**	wackily
ACGINOT	coating	**ACHILPS**	caliphs		morchas	**ACIKNPY**	panicky
	cotinga	**ACHILRS**	archils	**ACHMORZ**	machzor	**ACIKNST**	catkins
ACGINOX	coaxing	**ACHILRY**	charily	**ACHMOST**	stomach	**ACIKPRT**	patrick
ACGINPP	capping	**ACHILST**	chitals	**ACHMPTU**	matchup	**ACIKRST**	karstic
ACGINPR	carping	**ACHILSY**	clayish	**ACHMSSU**	sumachs	**ACIKRWW**	Warwick
	craping	**ACHIMNO**	mohican	**ACHMSUW**	cumshaw	**ACIKUWZ**	Zwickau
ACGINPS	scaping	**ACHIMOS**	chamois	**ACHNNSW**	Schwann	**ACILLMS**	miscall
	spacing	**ACHIMRS**	charism	**ACHNOOY**	chanoyo	**ACILLRY**	lyrical
ACGINRS	sacring		chimars	**ACHNORS**	anchors	**ACILLSS**	scillas
	scaring	**ACHIMSS**	chiasms		archons	**ACILMNO**	limacon
ACGINRT	carting	**ACHINNU**	unchain		ranchos		malonic
	crating	**ACHINOP**	aphonic	**ACHNOTY**	tachyon	**ACILMPS**	plasmic
	tracing	**ACHINOT**	Antioch	**ACHNOUY**	chanoyu		psalmic
ACGINRV	carving	**ACHINOY**	onychia	**ACHNOVY**	anchovy	**ACILMSU**	musical
	craving	**ACHINPS**	spinach	**ACHNPSS**	schnaps	**ACILNNY**	cannily
ACGINRZ	crazing	**ACHINSU**	Sichuan	**ACHNPUY**	paunchy	**ACILNOR**	clarino
ACGINSS	casings	**ACHINTX**	xanthic	**ACHNRTY**	chantry		clarion
ACGINST	casting	**ACHINTY**	Cynthia	**ACHNRUY**	raunchy		Locrian
ACGINSU	causing	**ACHIOPS**	isopach	**ACHNSTU**	canthus	**ACILNOS**	oilcans
	saucing	**ACHIOPT**	aphotic		chaunts	**ACILNOU**	inocula
ACGINTT	catting	**ACHIORT**	chariot		staunch	**ACILNOV**	Calvino

ACILNPS	caplins	**ACINORS**	saronic	**ACKLLOP**	pollack	**ACLPRUU**	cupular
ACILNPY	pliancy	**ACINORT**	carotin	**ACKLLOR**	Rockall	**ACLRSSW**	scrawls
ACILNRS	carlins	**ACINOSS**	caisson	**ACKLLSY**	slackly	**ACLRSSY**	crassly
ACILNST	tincals		casinos	**ACKLMOT**	Matlock	**ACLRSTU**	crustal
ACILNSU	uncials		cassino	**ACKLOOR**	oarlock		curtals
ACILNTU	lunatic	**ACINOST**	actions	**ACKLORW**	warlock	**ACLRSTY**	crystal
ACILNTY	cantily		atonics	**ACKMMMO**	mammock	**ACLRSWY**	scrawly
ACILNUV	vincula		cations	**ACKMNRU**	ruckman	**ACLSSTU**	cutlass
ACILOPT	capitol	**ACINOSU**	acinous	**ACKMOST**	stomack	**ACMNOPR**	crampon
	optical	**ACINOSY**	syconia	**ACKMOTT**	mattock	**ACMNOPY**	company
	topical	**ACINOTT**	taction	**ACKNORY**	Conakry	**ACMNORS**	macrons
ACILOSS	socials	**ACINOTU**	auction	**ACKNPSU**	unpacks	**ACMNORY**	acronym
ACILOST	stoical		caution	**ACKNSTU**	untacks	**ACMNOSS**	mascons
ACILOTV	voltaic	**ACINPRT**	cantrip	**ACKOWZZ**	wazzock	**ACMNSTU**	sanctum
ACILPRT	clipart	**ACINPRU**	puranic	**ACLLLOY**	locally	**ACMNTUU**	Tucumán
ACILPST	plastic	**ACINPRY**	cyprian	**ACLLMMO**	Malcolm	**ACMOOPT**	Potomac
ACILPSU	spicula	**ACINQTU**	quantic	**ACLLOOR**	corolla	**ACMOOST**	scotoma
ACILPTY	typical	**ACINRTT**	tantric	**ACLLOOS**	alcools	**ACMOPSS**	compass
ACILRSS	crissal	**ACINRTU**	curtain	**ACLLOPS**	callops	**ACMORTW**	catworm
ACILRTU	curtail	**ACINSUV**	vicunas		scallop	**ACMOSST**	mascots
	trucial	**ACIOPRS**	prosaic	**ACLLORR**	Carroll	**ACMQTUU**	cumquat
ACILRTY	clarity	**ACIOPRT**	apricot	**ACLLORS**	collars	**ACMSSTU**	muscats
ACILRVY	vicarly		aprotic	**ACLLORU**	locular	**ACMSUUV**	vacuums
ACILRYZ	crazily		parotic	**ACLLOSU**	callous	**ACNNNOS**	cannons
ACILSSS	classis	**ACIOPSS**	Picasso	**ACLLOVY**	vocally	**ACNNNUY**	uncanny
ACILSUY	saucily	**ACIOPST**	copitas	**ACLLRYY**	acrylyl	**ACNNORU**	Corunna
ACILTTY	cattily	**ACIOPTY**	opacity	**ACLMNOO**	locoman	**ACNNORY**	canonry
	tacitly	**ACIORRS**	corsair	**ACLMNUY**	calumny	**ACNNOST**	cantons
ACILTUV	victual	**ACIORSU**	carious	**ACLMOPS**	copalms	**ACNNOSY**	canyons
ACIMMNO	ammonic		curiosa	**ACLMORS**	clamors	**ACNOORS**	coronas
ACIMNOP	campion	**ACIORTT**	ricotta	**ACLMORU**	clamour		racoons
ACIMNOR	marconi	**ACIOSST**	scotias	**ACLMOSU**	mucosal	**ACNOORT**	cartoon
	minorca	**ACIOSSV**	ovisacs	**ACLNOOO**	Laocoon		coranto
ACIMNOS	anosmic	**ACIPRSS**	casspir	**ACLNOOR**	coronal		Cortona
	camions	**ACIPRSY**	piscary		Locarno	**ACNOPSU**	Canopus
	masonic	**ACIPRVY**	privacy	**ACLNOOT**	coolant	**ACNOPSW**	snowcap
ACIMNRS	narcism	**ACIPSST**	spastic	**ACLNOOV**	volcano	**ACNORRS**	Scarron
ACIMNRU	cranium	**ACIPTUY**	paucity	**ACLNOPT**	Clapton	**ACNORRU**	rancour
	cumarin	**ACIQRTU**	quartic	**ACLNORT**	Carlton	**ACNORRY**	carryon
ACIMNTT	catmint	**ACIQSTU**	acquits	**ACLNORU**	cornual	**ACNORST**	cantors
ACIMOOS	oomiacs	**ACIRRSU**	curaris		courlan		cartons
ACIMOPT	apomict	**ACIRSST**	racists	**ACLNOSX**	claxons		cratons
	potamic		sacrist	**ACLNPSU**	unclasp	**ACNORSY**	crayons
	Tampico	**ACIRSSU**	cuirass	**ACLNSTY**	scantly	**ACNOSTT**	octants
ACIMOSS	mosaics	**ACIRSTT**	astrict	**ACLOOPP**	alcopop	**ACNOSTU**	conatus
ACIMOST	somatic	**ACIRSTU**	Scutari		Coppola		toucans
ACIMPRY	primacy	**ACIRSTY**	satyric	**ACLOPRT**	caltrop	**ACNPRSY**	syncarp
ACIMPST	impacts	**ACIRSTZ**	czarist	**ACLOPRU**	copular	**ACNRRTU**	currant
ACIMRSS	racisms	**ACIRTUY**	raucity	**ACLOPSU**	copulas	**ACNRSWY**	scrawny
ACIMRST	matrics	**ACISSTT**	statics		cupolas	**ACNRTUY**	truancy
ACIMRSZ	czarism	**ACISSTU**	casuist		scopula	**ACNSSTU**	Sanctus
ACIMSST	mastics	**ACISTTU**	catsuit	**ACLOPSY**	calypso	**ACNSSUU**	Cusanus
	miscast		Tacitus	**ACLORRS**	corrals	**ACNSTUY**	Tuscany
ACINNOT	actinon	**ACITUVY**	vacuity	**ACLORST**	crotals	**ACOOPRR**	corpora
	contain	**ACJKKSY**	skyjack		scrotal	**ACOOPTT**	topcoat
ACINNOZ	canzoni	**ACJKLOW**	lockjaw	**ACLORSU**	carolus	**ACOORST**	Socotra
ACINNST	stannic	**ACJKNNO**	jannock		oculars	**ACOORTU**	touraco
ACINNSY	cyanins	**ACJKNOS**	Jackson		oscular	**ACOOSTV**	octavos
ACINOPT	caption	**ACJKOPT**	jackpot	**ACLORWW**	Wrocław	**ACOPPRR**	procarp
	Pontiac	**ACJLORU**	jocular	**ACLOSTU**	talcous	**ACOPRRT**	carport
ACINOQU	coquina	**ACJMNTU**	muntjac	**ACLOTTW**	Walcott	**ACOPRST**	captors
ACINORR	carrion	**ACJPTUU**	cajuput	**ACLPRTY**	cryptal	**ACOPSTW**	cowpats

ACORRST	carrots	**ADDEGHO**	godhead		waddles	**ADDILNY**	dandily
	trocars	**ADDEGIL**	gladdie	**ADDELTW**	twaddle	**ADDIMNO**	diamond
ACORRTT	tractor	**ADDEGJU**	adjudge	**ADDELYZ**	dazedly	**ADDIMSS**	misadds
ACORRTU	curator	**ADDEGLN**	dangled	**ADDELZZ**	dazzled	**ADDINOR**	android
ACORRTY	carroty		gladden	**ADDEMMW**	dwammed	**ADDINOS**	Addison
ACORSST	castors	**ADDEGLO**	Delgado	**ADDEMNS**	demands	**ADDKLNU**	Dundalk
	costars	**ADDEGLR**	gladder		maddens	**ADDLLRU**	dullard
ACORSSU	sarcous	**ADDEGRS**	gadders	**ADDEMOP**	pomaded	**ADDLNOO**	Dandolo
ACORSTT	cottars	**ADDEGRU**	guarded	**ADDEMRY**	dramedy	**ADDLNOW**	Dowland
ACORSTU	surcoat	**ADDEHIO**	Hodeida	**ADDEMST**	maddest	**ADDNNOR**	donnard
	turacos	**ADDEHIR**	diehard	**ADDEMUW**	dwaumed	**ADDOORS**	dorados
ACORSTV	cavorts	**ADDEHKS**	keddahs	**ADDENOR**	adorned	**ADDORST**	dotards
ACORSUU	raucous	**ADDEHLN**	handled	**ADDENOT**	donated	**ADDQSUY**	squaddy
ACOSSZZ	scozzas	**ADDEHOR**	hoarded	**ADDENOU**	duodena	**ADEEEFY**	fedayee
ACOSTTU	outacts	**ADDEIIS**	daisied	**ADDENPU**	pudenda	**ADEEESW**	seaweed
	outcast	**ADDEILL**	dallied	**ADDENRS**	danders	**ADEEFKR**	freaked
ACOSUUV	vacuous		dialled	**ADDENSS**	saddens	**ADEEFLR**	federal
ACPPRSY	scrappy	**ADDEILR**	drailed	**ADDENTU**	daunted	**ADEEFLT**	deflate
ACPSSTU	catsups	**ADDEILS**	laddies		undated	**ADEEFMR**	defamer
	upcasts	**ADDEILT**	dilated	**ADDEOPT**	adopted	**ADEEFMS**	defames
ACRRSTU	craturs	**ADDEIMR**	admired	**ADDEORS**	deodars	**ADEEFNS**	deafens
ACRSSSU	Crassus	**ADDEIMS**	diadems	**ADDEPTU**	updated	**ADEEFRT**	draftee
ADDDEEL	Deledda	**ADDEIMX**	admixed	**ADDERSS**	address	**ADEEFRW**	wafered
ADDDEER	dreaded	**ADDEINO**	adenoid	**ADDERST**	addrest	**ADEEFST**	deafest
	readded	**ADDEINP**	pandied		raddest		defeats
ADDDEGL	gladded	**ADDEINR**	dandier	**ADDERSW**	Edwards		feasted
ADDDEIS	daddies		drained		swarded	**ADEEFUY**	Feydeau
ADDDEIW	waddied	**ADDEINS**	dandies		wadders	**ADEEGGH**	egghead
ADDDELN	dandled	**ADDEINU**	unaided	**ADDERSY**	dryades	**ADEEGGN**	engaged
ADDDELP	paddled	**ADDEINV**	invaded	**ADDERTT**	dratted	**ADEEGLL**	alleged
ADDDELR	raddled	**ADDEIOR**	radioed	**ADDERVW**	Edward V	**ADEEGLM**	gleamed
ADDDELS	saddled	**ADDEIOT**	iodated	**ADDESST**	saddest	**ADEEGLN**	gleaned
ADDDELW	dawdled		toadied	**ADDFHIS**	faddish	**ADEEGLR**	lagered
	waddled	**ADDEIOV**	avoided	**ADDFIMS**	faddism		regaled
ADDDENO	deodand	**ADDEIPS**	paddies	**ADDFINY**	dandify	**ADEEGLU**	leagued
ADDDENS	addends	**ADDEIRR**	Derrida	**ADDFIST**	faddist	**ADEEGLZ**	deglaze
ADDDGOR	Goddard	**ADDEIRW**	Edward I	**ADDGGIN**	gadding	**ADEEGMN**	endgame
ADDDOOS	doodads	**ADDEISV**	advised	**ADDGILN**	addling	**ADEEGNR**	angered
ADDEEEY	deadeye	**ADDEISW**	swaddie	**ADDGIMN**	madding		derange
ADDEEFM	defamed		waddies	**ADDGIMR**	Midgard		enraged
ADDEEGR	degrade	**ADDEITU**	audited	**ADDGINO**	dadoing		grandee
ADDEEHR	adhered	**ADDEJLY**	jadedly	**ADDGINP**	padding		grenade
	redhead	**ADDEJRU**	adjured	**ADDGINW**	wadding	**ADEEGNT**	negated
ADDEEKN	kneaded	**ADDEKLR**	darkled	**ADDGIOS**	gadoids	**ADEEGNV**	avenged
ADDEELM	medaled	**ADDELLU**	alluded	**ADDGLNO**	gladdon	**ADEEGOT**	goateed
ADDEELP	pedaled		dualled	**ADDGMNO**	goddamn	**ADEEGRR**	regrade
	pleaded	**ADDELNR**	dandler	**ADDGNNO**	Dandong	**ADEEGRS**	dragees
ADDEELT	delated	**ADDELNS**	dandles	**ADDGOOS**	ogdoads		greased
ADDEELY	delayed	**ADDELNU**	unladed	**ADDGOSY**	dogdays	**ADEEGRU**	guardee
ADDEEMN	amended	**ADDELPP**	dappled	**ADDHIKS**	kaddish	**ADEEGRV**	greaved
	deadmen	**ADDELPR**	paddler	**ADDHILS**	laddish	**ADEEGRW**	ragweed
ADDEEMR	dreamed	**ADDELPS**	paddles	**ADDHIMS**	maddish		wagered
ADDEENS	deadens	**ADDELRS**	ladders	**ADDHIQS**	Qaddish	**ADEEGSS**	degases
ADDEERT	derated		raddles	**ADDHITY**	hydatid	**ADEEHIR**	headier
ADDEEST	sedated		saddler	**ADDHNOR**	Rhondda	**ADEEHLS**	leashed
	steaded	**ADDELRW**	dawdler	**ADDHOOS**	doodahs	**ADEEHLX**	exhaled
ADDEFHN	handfed		drawled	**ADDHOTY**	athodyd	**ADEEHMN**	headmen
ADDEFIR	faddier		waddler	**ADDHSSU**	saddhus	**ADEEHNN**	hennaed
ADDEFRT	drafted	**ADDELSS**	saddles	**ADDIIIV**	David II	**ADEEHNS**	dasheen
ADDEFRU	defraud	**ADDELST**	staddle	**ADDIINS**	disdain	**ADEEHNT**	nethead
ADDEFRW	dwarfed	**ADDELSW**	dawdles	**ADDIKTY**	katydid	**ADEEHNV**	havened
ADDEGGR	dragged		swaddle	**ADDILMN**	midland	**ADEEHPR**	ephedra

ADEEHRR reheard
ADEEHRS adheres
        headers
        sheared
ADEEHRT earthed
        hearted
ADEEHRV havered
ADEEHSS Édhessa
ADEEHST headset
ADEEHSV sheaved
ADEEHSY hayseed
ADEEIJT jadeite
ADEEILM emailed
        limeade
ADEEILN aliened
        delaine
ADEEILS aediles
ADEEIMT mediate
ADEEINN adenine
ADEEINS aniseed
ADEEIRR readier
ADEEIRS dearies
        readies
ADEEIRW wearied
ADEEISS disease
        seaside
ADEEITV deviate
ADEEJSY deejays
ADEEKNP kneepad
ADEEKNR kneader
ADEEKNS sneaked
ADEEKNW wakened
ADEEKRW rewaked
        wreaked
ADEEKTW tweaked
ADEEKWY weekday
ADEELLN Allende
ADEELLS allseed
ADEELMN Edelman
ADEELMP empaled
ADEELMR emerald
ADEELMS measled
ADEELMT metaled
ADEELNP deplane
        paneled
ADEELNR Leander
        learned
ADEELNS Seeland
ADEELNZ Zeeland
ADEELPR pearled
        pleader
ADEELPS elapsed
        pleased
ADEELPT pleated
ADEELQU equaled
ADEELRS dealers
        leaders
ADEELRT alerted
        altered
        related
        treadle
ADEELRV raveled

ADEELRW leeward
ADEELRX relaxed
ADEELRY delayer
        layered
        relayed
ADEELST delates
ADEELSV sleaved
ADEELTT ladette
ADEELTV valeted
ADEELTX exalted
ADEELTZ teazled
ADEELUV devalue
        Uvedale
ADEELYZ laydeez
ADEEMNR amender
        meander
        reedman
        renamed
ADEEMNS demeans
ADEEMRR dreamer
        rearmed
ADEEMRS smeared
ADEEMST steamed
ADEEMSU medusae
ADEEMWY mayweed
ADEENNS enneads
ADEENNX annexed
ADEENRS endears
ADEENRV ravened
ADEENRY deanery
        yearned
ADEENST East End
        standee
ADEENTT dentate
ADEEOPT adoptee
ADEEORW oarweed
ADEEPPR papered
ADEEPRS speared
ADEEPRT predate
        tapered
ADEEPRV deprave
        pervade
        repaved
ADEEPSS pesades
ADEEQTU equated
ADEERRS readers
        rereads
ADEERRT retread
        treader
ADEERRV averred
ADEERRW redware
ADEERSS resedas
ADEERST dearest
        derates
        estrade
        reasted
ADEERSV adverse
        evaders
ADEERSW drawees
ADEERTT treated
ADEERTV averted
ADEERTW watered

ADEERVW wavered
ADEESST sedates
ADEESSY essayed
ADEESTU sauteed
ADEESTW sweated
ADEESTY yeasted
ADEETUX exudate
ADEFFIN affined
ADEFFIR daffier
ADEFFIX affixed
ADEFFLO leadoff
ADEFFLR raffled
ADEFFLW waffled
ADEFFQU quaffed
ADEFFST staffed
ADEFGGL flagged
ADEFGGR fragged
ADEFGLN flanged
ADEFGOR foraged
ADEFGOT fagoted
ADEFGRT grafted
ADEFHLS flashed
ADEFHRW wharfed
ADEFHST shafted
ADEFILL flailed
ADEFINR Friedan
ADEFINT defiant
        fainted
ADEFITX fixated
ADEFKLN fankled
        flanked
ADEFKNR franked
ADEFLLN elfland
ADEFLMM flammed
ADEFLOT floated
ADEFLPP flapped
ADEFLRS fardels
ADEFLTT flatted
ADEFLTU default
        faulted
ADEFNRS snarfed
ADEFNSU snafued
ADEFNUZ unfazed
ADEFOOS seafood
ADEFORS fedoras
ADEFORV favored
ADEFORY forayed
ADEFPPR frapped
ADEFRRT drafter
        redraft
ADEFRST strafed
ADEFRSY defrays
ADEFSTT daftest
ADEGGGL gaggled
ADEGGHL haggled
ADEGGHS shagged
ADEGGIR daggier
ADEGGLR draggle
        gargled
ADEGGLS slagged
ADEGGLW waggled
ADEGGMO demagog

ADEGGNS snagged
ADEGGOP pedagog
ADEGGPS spagged
ADEGGRS daggers
ADEGGRV raggedy
ADEGGST gadgets
        stagged
ADEGGSW swagged
ADEGGTY gadgety
ADEGHIN heading
ADEGHLU laughed
ADEGHMO homaged
ADEGHNS gnashed
ADEGHNW whanged
ADEGHPR graphed
ADEGILN aligned
        dealing
        leading
ADEGILR glaired
ADEGILT ligated
ADEGILV glaived
ADEGINR deraign
        gradine
        grained
        reading
ADEGINV deaving
        evading
ADEGINW windage
ADEGIOT godetia
ADEGIRU gaudier
ADEGIRV Rig-Veda
ADEGIST agisted
ADEGISU gaudies
ADEGISV visaged
ADEGJLN jangled
ADEGLLU ullaged
ADEGLMN mangled
ADEGLNN England
ADEGLNO Donegal
ADEGLNR dangler
        gnarled
ADEGLNS dangles
        glandes
        slanged
ADEGLNT tangled
ADEGLNW wangled
ADEGLOT gloated
ADEGLPU plagued
ADEGLRY gradely
ADEGLSS glassed
ADEGLTY dalgyte
        Lydgate
ADEGMNU agendum
ADEGNNU dunnage
ADEGNOR groaned
ADEGNOS sondage
ADEGNOT tangoed
ADEGNOV dogvane
ADEGNOW gowaned
ADEGNPR pranged
ADEGNPU unpaged
ADEGNRR Gardner

	gnarred	**ADEHLMN**	Helmand	**ADEIJUZ**	Judaize	**ADEIMOW**	miaowed
	grander	**ADEHLMS**	lamedhs	**ADEIKLR**	Kildare	**ADEIMPR**	dampier
ADEGNRS	dangers	**ADEHLMU**	Duhamel	**ADEIKRS**	darkies	**ADEIMRR**	admirer
	ganders	**ADEHLNR**	handler	**ADEILLR**	dallier		married
	gardens	**ADEHLNS**	handles		dialler	**ADEIMRS**	admires
ADEGNRT	dragnet		handsel		rallied		misread
	granted	**ADEHLOS**	shoaled	**ADEILLS**	dallies	**ADEIMRT**	readmit
ADEGNRW	wranged	**ADEHLOT**	loathed		sallied	**ADEIMRU**	Daumier
ADEGNST	stanged	**ADEHLPS**	plashed	**ADEILLT**	tallied	**ADEIMRY**	midyear
ADEGNSU	augends	**ADEHLRS**	heralds	**ADEILLY**	ideally	**ADEIMST**	Mideast
ADEGNTW	twanged	**ADEHLSS**	hassled	**ADEILMM**	dilemma		misdate
ADEGNUW	unwaged		slashed	**ADEILMP**	impaled	**ADEIMSX**	admixes
ADEGNWY	Weygand	**ADEHLST**	daleths		implead	**ADEIMTU**	ideatum
ADEGORS	dogears	**ADEHLTY**	deathly	**ADEILMR**	Daimler	**ADEIMTY**	daytime
ADEGORW	dowager	**ADEHMMS**	shammed	**ADEILMS**	medials	**ADEINNN**	nannied
	wordage	**ADEHMMW**	whammed		misdeal	**ADEINNS**	dannies
ADEGOSS	dosages	**ADEHMNP**	Hampden		mislead	**ADEINOR**	aneroid
	seadogs	**ADEHMOY**	Dahomey	**ADEILMU**	miauled	**ADEINOS**	anodise
ADEGOST	dotages	**ADEHMSS**	smashed	**ADEILNN**	annelid	**ADEINOV**	naevoid
ADEGOVY	voyaged	**ADEHNPS**	daphnes		lindane	**ADEINOX**	dioxane
ADEGPRS	grasped	**ADEHNRS**	hardens	**ADEILNP**	plained	**ADEINOZ**	anodize
	spadger	**ADEHNRU**	unheard	**ADEILNR**	Ireland	**ADEINPS**	pandies
	sparged	**ADEHNST**	handset	**ADEILNS**	denials	**ADEINPT**	painted
ADEGPRU	upgrade	**ADEHNTU**	haunted	**ADEILNU**	aliunde	**ADEINRR**	drainer
ADEGRRS	graders	**ADEHNUY**	Da Yunhe		unideal		randier
	regards	**ADEHOPT**	pothead	**ADEILNW**	Wieland	**ADEINRS**	randies
ADEGRRU	guarder	**ADEHOPX**	hexapod	**ADEILOP**	oedipal		sandier
ADEGRSS	grassed	**ADEHORR**	hoarder	**ADEILOR**	dariole		sardine
ADEGRSU	sugared	**ADEHOST**	hoasted	**ADEILOZ**	diazole	**ADEINRT**	detrain
ADEGRTY	gyrated	**ADEHOTW**	towhead	**ADEILPP**	applied		trained
	tragedy	**ADEHPPW**	whapped	**ADEILPR**	predial	**ADEINRU**	unaired
ADEGRUU	augured	**ADEHPRS**	phrased	**ADEILPS**	alipeds		uranide
ADEGRUY	gaudery		sharped		elapids	**ADEINRV**	invader
ADEGSSU	degauss		Shepard		laipsed		ravined
ADEHHKS	khedahs	**ADEHPST**	heptads	**ADEILPT**	plaited	**ADEINST**	detains
ADEHHOP	hophead		spathed		taliped		instead
ADEHHOT	hothead	**ADEHQSU**	quashed	**ADEILQU**	quailed		sainted
ADEHILL	Delilah	**ADEHRSS**	dashers	**ADEILRS**	derails		stained
ADEHILN	hieland	**ADEHRST**	dearths		redials	**ADEINSV**	invades
	inhaled		hardest	**ADEILRT**	dilater	**ADEINTT**	tainted
ADEHILP	helipad		hatreds		trailed	**ADEINTV**	deviant
ADEHILS	halides		threads	**ADEILRU**	uredial	**ADEIOPS**	adipose
ADEHILY	headily		trashed	**ADEILRV**	rivaled	**ADEIOPT**	opiated
ADEHIMO	haemoid	**ADEHRTY**	hydrate	**ADEILRY**	readily	**ADEIORS**	roadies
ADEHINP	headpin		thready	**ADEILSS**	deasils		soredia
	pinhead	**ADEHSST**	stashed	**ADEILSU**	audiles	**ADEIORV**	avoider
ADEHINR	handier	**ADEHSSW**	swashed	**ADEILSV**	devisal	**ADEIORX**	exordia
ADEHIPR	raphide	**ADEHSTW**	swathed	**ADEILSY**	dialyse	**ADEIOST**	iodates
ADEHIPS	aphides	**ADEHSYY**	heydays	**ADEILYZ**	dialyze		toadies
	diphase	**ADEIILR**	deliria	**ADEIMMR**	mermaid	**ADEIOSX**	oxidase
ADEHIPT	pithead	**ADEIILS**	dailies	**ADEIMMT**	tammied	**ADEIOSZ**	diazoes
ADEHIRR	hardier		liaised	**ADEIMNS**	maidens	**ADEIOTX**	oxidate
	harried		sedilia		medians	**ADEIPPR**	drappie
ADEHIRS	hardies	**ADEIIMN**	diamine		medinas		prepaid
	shadier	**ADEIINR**	denarii		sideman	**ADEIPRR**	parried
ADEHIRW	rawhide	**ADEIINZ**	diazine	**ADEIMNT**	mediant	**ADEIPRS**	aspired
ADEHKNS	shanked	**ADEIIPR**	peridia	**ADEIMNU**	unaimed		despair
ADEHKNT	thanked	**ADEIIRR**	Airdrie	**ADEIMOU**	miaoued		diapers
ADEHKRS	sharked	**ADEIIRS**	airside				praised
ADEHLLO	halloed		dairies			**ADEIPRT**	partied
	hollaed		diaries				pirated
ADEHLLP	lapheld	**ADEIISS**	daisies			**ADEIPSS**	apsides

ADEIRRS raiders	**ADELLRU** allured	**ADELPST** stapled	**ADEMRRU** eardrum
ADEIRRT tardier	**ADELLST** stalled	**ADELPSW** dewlaps	**ADEMRST** smarted
tarried	**ADELLSU** alludes	**ADELPSY** splayed	**ADEMRSW** swarmed
ADEIRRV arrived	aludels	**ADELPTT** platted	**ADEMRTU** matured
ADEIRST astride	**ADELMMS** slammed	**ADELPTY** adeptly	**ADEMSSU** assumed
diaster	**ADELMMY** Malmédy	**ADELRRS** larders	medusas
disrate	**ADELMNO** Mondale	**ADELRRU** ruderal	**ADEMSTU** Admetus
tirades	**ADELMNR** mandrel	**ADELRRW** drawler	**ADEMTTU** mutated
ADEIRSU residua	**ADELMNT** mantled	**ADELRST** slarted	**ADENNOY** annoyed
ADEIRSV adviser	**ADELMOR** earldom	**ADELRSU** lauders	anodyne
ADEIRSX radixes	**ADELMOS** damosel	**ADELRSW** warsled	**ADENNPS** spanned
ADEIRTT attired	**ADELMOZ** damozel	**ADELRTT** rattled	**ADENNPT** pendant
ADEIRTY dietary	**ADELMPS** sampled	**ADELRTW** trawled	**ADENNSU** duennas
ADEISSS dassies	**ADELMRS** medlars	**ADELRTX** dextral	**ADENNSW** swanned
ADEISSV advises	**ADELMSS** damsels	**ADELRTY** lyrated	**ADENOPR** aproned
ADEISTV datives	**ADELNNP** planned	**ADELSST** desalts	operand
vistaed	**ADELNNU** unladen	**ADELSTT** slatted	padrone
ADEISTW waisted	**ADELNOR** ladrone	**ADELSTU** auldest	pandore
ADEISVV savvied	Leonard	saluted	**ADENOPS** dapsone
ADEISWY wayside	**ADELNOT** taloned	**ADELSZZ** dazzles	**ADENOPT** Da Ponte
ADEITUZ deutzia	**ADELNPT** planted	**ADELTTT** tattled	notepad
ADEITWY tideway	**ADELNPY** endplay	**ADELTTW** wattled	**ADENORR** Reardon
ADEJMOR majored	**ADELNRR** Lardner	**ADELTUV** vaulted	**ADENORU** rondeau
ADEJMRU jumared	**ADELNRS** darnels	**ADELTUX** luxated	**ADENOST** donates
mudejar	slander	**ADELTWZ** waltzed	**ADENOSY** noyades
ADEJNTU jaunted	snarled	**ADELUVX** Delvaux	**ADENOTT** notated
ADEJRRU adjurer	**ADELNRU** Arundel	**ADEMMNR** Drammen	**ADENOTZ** zonated
ADEJRSU adjures	launder	**ADEMMPS** spammed	**ADENOUY** Yaoundé
ADEJSSU judases	rundale	**ADEMMRS** smarmed	**ADENPPR** parpend
ADEKKNS skanked	**ADELNRY** Darnley	**ADEMMRT** trammed	**ADENPPS** appends
ADEKLLN Kendall	**ADELNSS** sendals	**ADEMNNS** sandmen	snapped
ADEKLNP planked	**ADELNST** dentals	**ADEMNNU** mundane	**ADENPRR** pardner
ADEKLNR rankled	slanted	unnamed	**ADENPRS** panders
ADEKLNS kalends	**ADELNSU** Ålesund	**ADEMNOR** madrone	**ADENPST** pedants
ADEKLNY nakedly	unlades	**ADEMNOS** daemons	pentads
ADEKLOP polkaed	unleads	masoned	**ADENPSW** spawned
ADEKLRS darkles	**ADELNTU** lunated	monades	**ADENPSX** expands
ADEKLST stalked	**ADELNTW** wetland	**ADEMNOW** womaned	spandex
ADEKLUW waulked	**ADELNTY** Tyndale	**ADEMNOZ** Mendoza	**ADENPSY** dyspnea
ADEKMNR Denmark	**ADELNTZ** Zetland	**ADEMNPS** dampens	**ADENPUV** unpaved
ADEKNPP knapped	**ADELNUU** Ulan-Ude	**ADEMNRS** randems	**ADENQTU** quanted
ADEKNPR pranked	**ADELOPR** leopard	remands	**ADENRRS** darners
ADEKNPS spanked	paroled	**ADEMNRU** duramen	errands
ADEKNRR knarred	**ADELOPS** deposal	manured	Randers
ADEKNRS darkens	pedalos	maunder	**ADENRRW** redrawn
ADEKNRU Kundera	**ADELOPT** ploated	unarmed	**ADENRRY** reynard
ADEKNSS sandeks	tadpole	**ADEMNSS** desmans	**ADENRSS** sanders
ADEKNST dankest	**ADELORS** loaders	madness	**ADENRST** stander
stanked	ordeals	**ADEMNST** tandems	**ADENRSU** asunder
ADEKNSU unasked	reloads	**ADEMNSU** medusan	danseur
ADEKNSW swanked	**ADELORT** delator	**ADEMNTU** untamed	**ADENRSW** Andrews
ADEKNVY vandyke	leotard	**ADEMOPS** pomades	wanders
ADEKPRS sparked	**ADELORU** roulade	**ADEMORR** armored	wardens
ADEKPSY keypads	**ADELORX** Axelrod	**ADEMORS** radomes	**ADENRSZ** zanders
ADEKRST darkest	**ADELOSS** aldoses	**ADEMOSW** meadows	**ADENRTU** daunter
ADEKRSY darkeys	lassoed	**ADEMOSY** someday	Durante
ADELLMU medulla	**ADELOSW** waldoes	**ADEMOWY** meadowy	untread
ADELLNR landler	**ADELOTT** totaled	**ADEMPRS** dampers	**ADENRTV** verdant
ADELLOW allowed	**ADELPPR** Leppard	**ADEMPRT** tramped	**ADENRTX** dextran
ADELLOY alloyed	**ADELPPS** dapples	**ADEMPST** dampest	**ADENRUY** Reynaud
ADELLPS spalled	slapped	stamped	unready
ADELLRS ladlers	**ADELPRS** pedlars	**ADEMPSW** swamped	**ADENSSS** sadness

ADENSSU	sundaes
ADENSTT	attends
ADENSTU	stauned
	unsated
ADENSTV	advents
ADENSUV	unsaved
ADENSWY	endways
ADENTTU	attuned
	taunted
ADENTUV	vaunted
ADENTUX	untaxed
ADENUWX	unwaxed
ADEOPPS	apposed
ADEOPQU	opaqued
ADEOPRR	eardrop
ADEOPRT	readopt
ADEOPRV	vapored
ADEOPST	podesta
ADEORRS	adorers
ADEORST	doaters
	roasted
	torsade
ADEORSU	aroused
ADEORSV	savored
ADEORTT	rotated
	troated
ADEORTU	outdare
	readout
ADEORYZ	zedoary
ADEOSTT	toasted
ADEOTTU	outdate
ADEPPRT	trapped
ADEPPRW	wrapped
ADEPPSW	swapped
ADEPPTU	pupated
ADEPRRS	drapers
	sparred
ADEPRRY	drapery
ADEPRSS	spaders
	spreads
ADEPRST	departs
	petards
ADEPRSY	sprayed
ADEPRTU	updater
	uprated
ADEPSTT	spatted
ADEPSTU	updates
ADEQRSU	squared
ADERRST	darters
	retards
	starred
	traders
ADERRSW	drawers
	redraws
	rewards
	warders
ADERSSU	assured
ADERSSW	sawders
ADERSTT	started
	tetrads
ADERSTV	adverts
	starved
ADERSTW	steward
	strawed
ADERSTY	strayed
ADERSUY	dasyure
ADERSVW	dwarves
ADERTUU	Trudeau
ADESSTW	wadsets
ADESTTU	statued
ADESTTW	swatted
ADFFGIN	daffing
ADFFHNO	handoff
	offhand
ADFFIST	distaff
ADFFLOO	offload
ADFFORS	affords
ADFGGIN	fadging
ADFGINS	fadings
ADFHLNU	handful
ADFHLNY	flyhand
ADFHOOS	shadoof
ADFHORS	Ashford
ADFHSSU	shadufs
ADFILLU	fluidal
ADFILNN	Finland
ADFILOR	Florida
ADFIMNY	damnify
ADFINRT	indraft
ADFLMTU	mudflat
ADFLNOP	plafond
ADFLNSY	sandfly
ADFLORS	Salford
ADFLORT	Altdorf
ADFLORU	foulard
ADFNNOT	fondant
ADFNOST	fantods
ADFOOPT	footpad
ADFORRW	forward
	froward
ADFORTW	Watford
ADGGGIN	dagging
ADGGHNO	hangdog
ADGGINO	goading
ADGGINR	grading
	niggard
ADGHILO	hidalgo
ADGHINN	handing
ADGHINR	Harding
ADGHINS	dashing
	shading
ADGHINU	hauding
ADGHIPR	digraph
ADGHNNU	handgun
ADGHNOS	sandhog
ADGHRSU	durgahs
ADGHRTU	draught
ADGIILN	dialing
	gliadin
ADGIILT	digital
ADGIINO	gonidia
ADGIINR	raiding
ADGIINU	iguanid
ADGIIPY	pygidia
ADGIJOS	adjigos
ADGIKNR	darking
ADGILLN	ladling
ADGILNN	landing
ADGILNO	digonal
	loading
ADGILNR	darling
	larding
ADGILNS	ligands
ADGILNU	languid
	lauding
ADGILOR	goliard
ADGILOS	dialogs
ADGILUY	gaudily
ADGIMMN	damming
ADGIMNN	damning
ADGIMNP	damping
ADGIMNR	mridang
ADGINNR	darning
ADGINNS	sanding
ADGINNW	dawning
ADGINOQ	Qingdao
ADGINOR	adoring
ADGINOS	ganoids
	Sogdian
ADGINOT	doating
ADGINPP	dapping
ADGINPR	draping
ADGINPS	spading
ADGINRS	gradins
ADGINRT	darting
	trading
ADGINRU	dauring
ADGINRW	drawing
	warding
ADGINRY	yarding
ADGINST	datings
ADGINWY	gwyniad
ADGIPRU	pagurid
ADGIRZZ	gizzard
ADGLMNO	mangold
ADGLNOO	dongola
	gondola
ADGLNOR	goldarn
ADGLNOT	Gotland
ADGLNOY	daylong
ADGLNRY	grandly
ADGLOOV	Vologda
ADGLOPS	lapdogs
ADGLOSU	Douglas
ADGMNOO	goodman
ADGMNOR	gormand
ADGMOOR	Mogador
ADGNOOR	dragoon
	gadroon
ADGNORS	dragons
ADGNORU	aground
	Durango
ADGNORY	organdy
ADGNRRU	gurnard
ADGOOPS	gospoda
ADHHISW	whidahs
ADHHMOS	shahdom
ADHHOSU	houdahs
ADHHOSW	howdahs
ADHHSWY	whydahs
ADHIIKS	dashiki
ADHIIMS	maidish
ADHIIPS	Phidias
ADHIJMS	Jamshid
ADHIKRS	darkish
ADHIKSU	haiduks
ADHILMO	halidom
ADHILMU	Milhaud
ADHILNY	handily
ADHILOP	haploid
ADHILOR	Harold I
ADHILOS	haloids
ADHILOY	holiday
	hyaloid
	hyoidal
ADHILRY	hardily
ADHILSY	shadily
ADHIMPS	dampish
	phasmid
ADHIMQS	Dimashq
ADHIMRS	dirhams
	midrash
ADHINOR	Rhodian
ADHINPS	Daphnis
	dishpan
ADHINPU	dauphin
ADHINSS	sandhis
ADHINUY	Hunyadi
ADHIOOS	hoodias
ADHIORS	hairdos
ADHIOST	toadish
ADHJKNU	Khujand
ADHLLLO	holdall
ADHLLNO	holland
ADHLOYY	holy day
	holyday
ADHMMNO	Hammond
ADHMNOO	manhood
ADHMNOU	Mahound
ADHMNSU	numdahs
ADHMNWY	Wyndham
ADHMORY	hydroma
ADHNNSU	unhands
ADHNNUY	unhandy
ADHNORS	hadrons
ADHNOSU	houdans
ADHNOSW	Ashdown
ADHNOTU	handout
ADHNOVZ	Zhdanov
ADHNRTY	hydrant
ADHOPRT	hardtop
ADHOPST	dashpot
ADHOSSW	shadows
ADHOSWY	shadowy
ADHPRSU	purdahs
ADIIJNU	Jundiaí
ADIILMS	mislaid
ADIILNO	lianoid

ADIILNV	invalid		Szilard	ADIRSWZ	wizards	ADMNOQU	quondam

ADIILNV invalid
ADIILOS sialoid
ADIILRW wirilda
ADIILUV diluvia
ADIILVV Vivaldi
ADIIMNU Numidia
ADIIMOS daimios
ADIINSU indusia
ADIINSZ diazins
ADIIPRS diapirs
ADIIPXY pyxidia
ADIIRST diarist
ADIIRSU Darius I
ADIIRTY aridity
ADIITVY avidity
ADIJMSS masjids
ADIJMSU Judaism
ADIJNOS adjoins
ADIJNOT adjoint
ADIKLOS odalisk
ADIKMNN mankind
ADIKMOS mikados
ADIKMOU daimoku
ADIKMRU Makurdi
ADIKNPS kidnaps
        skidpan
ADIKNSW Dawkins
ADIKSTT diktats
ADIKSWY skidway
ADILLMM milldam
ADILLTY tidally
ADILLVY validly
ADILLYY daylily
ADILMNO mondial
ADILMNR mandril
ADILMNU maudlin
ADILMOP diploma
ADILMOU alodium
ADILMOY amyloid
ADILMPS plasmid
ADILMSU dualism
ADILNNV Vinland
ADILNOR ordinal
ADILNOS dolinas
        ladinos
ADILNRU diurnal
ADILNRY randily
ADILNSS islands
ADILNSU sundial
ADILNSY Lindsay
ADILOOZ zooidal
ADILOPR dipolar
ADILORT dilator
ADILOTU outlaid
ADILPRY pyralid
        rapidly
ADILPST plastid
ADILPSY display
ADILPTU plaudit
ADILPVY vapidly
ADILQSU squalid
ADILRSZ lizards

        Szilard
ADILRTY tardily
ADILSTU dualist
ADILSTY staidly
ADILTUV duality
ADIMNNO mondain
ADIMNOS daimons
        domains
        madison
ADIMNRS mandirs
ADIMORR mirador
ADIMOST diatoms
        mastoid
ADIMOSY daimyos
ADIMOTT mattoid
ADIMPRY pyramid
ADIMRSS disarms
ADIMRSY myriads
ADIMSST dismast
ADIMSSY dismays
ADIMSTU stadium
ADIMSWY midways
ADINNOP dipnoan
ADINNOR andiron
ADINNPS pindans
ADINNRS innards
ADINNRW indrawn
        winnard
ADINNSU indunas
ADINOPP oppidan
ADINOPR padroni
        poniard
ADINOPT pintado
ADINORS inroads
        Nidaros
        ordains
        sadiron
ADINOSV Novi Sad
ADINOTX oxidant
ADINPST pandits
        sandpit
ADINQRS qindars
ADINRSU durians
ADINRSW inwards
ADINSTT distant
ADINTTY dittany
ADIOOSW woodsia
ADIOPRR airdrop
ADIOPRS sparoid
ADIOPRT parotid
ADIORST astroid
ADIORSV advisor
ADIORTU auditor
ADIOSUV Vaudois
ADIOSVW disavow
ADIPRSS sparids
ADIPRUU Udaipur
ADIRRSS sirdars
ADIRSSU sardius
ADIRSTY satyrid
ADIRSUY dysuria
ADIRSVZ vizards

ADIRSWZ wizards
ADIRSZZ izzards
ADISSST sadists
ADISSYY sayyids
ADJKOSU judokas
ADJLLNY Jylland
ADJLMOR jarldom
ADJLNTU Jutland
ADJNNOU Don Juan
ADJNORU adjourn
ADJORRU adjuror
ADJSSTU adjusts
ADKLMRU mudlark
ADKLNRU Kurland
ADKOPSU padouks
ADKORWY workday
ADKORYY Aykroyd
ADKRSUU Üsküdar
ADKRSWY skyward
ADLLLNO Lolland
ADLLMOY modally
ADLLNOR Rolland
ADLLNOW lowland
ADLLNOY nodally
ADLLNTY Tyndall
ADLLOPR pollard
ADLLORS dollars
ADLMNOS almonds
        dolmans
ADLMOOV Moldova
ADLMORU modular
ADLMNOR norland
ADLNOOR lardoon
        Orlando
ADLNOOS doolans
ADLNOPU poundal
ADLNORS lardons
ADLNORU nodular
ADLNOSS soldans
ADLNOST daltons
        sandlot
ADLNOSU unloads
ADLNOSY synodal
ADLNOTU outland
ADLNPRT Prandtl
ADLNPSU uplands
ADLNRSU lurdans
ADLNRTU Rutland
ADLNRUY laundry
ADLNSYY Lyndsay
ADLOORW Larwood
ADLOPRU poulard
ADLORRW warlord
ADLORSU sudoral
ADLORUY Our Lady
ADLOSSS dossals
ADLOSTW Ostwald
ADMMNSU summand
ADMNOOR doorman
        madrono
ADMNOOW woodman
ADMNOOZ madzoon

ADMNOQU quondam
ADMNORT dormant
        mordant
ADMNORY Ormandy
ADMNOSS damsons
ADMNOSU osmunda
ADMNOSY dynamos
ADMNSTU dustman
ADMOORT doormat
ADMOORY dayroom
ADMOPST Potsdam
ADMORRS ramrods
ADMORST stardom
        tsardom
ADMORSU maduros
ADMORTW madwort
ADMRSTU durmast
        mustard
ADNNOOY noonday
ADNNOSU adnouns
ADNNRTU dunnart
ADNNRUW undrawn
ADNNSTU Dunstan
ADNNSUY Dunsany
ADNOORS nardoos
ADNOORT donator
        tandoor
        tornado
ADNOOSW wandoos
ADNOPRS pardons
ADNOPRU pandour
ADNOPST dopants
ADNORRS Ronsard
ADNORST Rostand
ADNORSW onwards
ADNORTU rotunda
ADNORTY Drayton
ADNOSTU astound
        Donatus
ADNPSTU dustpan
        standup
ADNRSST strands
ADNRSUW sunward
        undraws
ADNSSTY dynasts
ADNSTYY dynasty
ADOOPSU apodous
ADOOPSW sapwood
ADOORWY doorway
ADOOSTT tostado
ADORSTW towards
ADORSUU arduous
ADORTUW outward
ADORUZZ Durazzo
ADPRSUW upwards
ADSSTUU Tussaud
ADSSTUW sawdust
AEEEGGN engagee
AEEEGKL keelage
AEEEGLT legatee
AEEEGNT teenage
AEEEGPR peerage

AEEEGPS	seepage	**AEEGLNS**	Senegal	**AEEHHST**	sheathe	**AEEILRR**	earlier
AEEEGRT	etagere	**AEEGLNT**	elegant	**AEEHHINR**	herniae		learier
AEEEHLS	healees	**AEEGLNU**	euglena	**AEEHIRV**	heavier	**AEEILRS**	realise
AEEEILN	alienee	**AEEGLNV**	evangel	**AEEHISV**	heavies	**AEEILRT**	atelier
AEEEIRT	eaterie	**AEEGLOR**	aerogel	**AEEHKMS**	hakeems	**AEEILRZ**	realize
AEEEELRS	release	**AEEGLPS**	pelages	**AEEHKNR**	hearken	**AEEILTV**	elative
AEEELTV	elevate	**AEEGLRS**	galeres	**AEEHLNT**	lethean	**AEEIMNS**	meanies
AEEEPPT	Papeete		regales	**AEEHLPT**	heeltap		nemesia
AEEFFLL	felafel	**AEEGLRU**	leaguer	**AEEHLRS**	healers	**AEEIMNT**	etamine
AEEFHRT	feather	**AEEGLRY**	eagerly	**AEEHLRT**	haltere		matinee
AEEFILR	leafier	**AEEGLRZ**	reglaze		leather	**AEEIMNX**	examine
AEEFILW	alewife	**AEEGLSS**	ageless	**AEEHLRV**	Le Havre	**AEEIMRS**	seamier
AEEFIRS	faeries	**AEEGLST**	eaglets	**AEEHLSS**	leashes		seriema
	freesia		legates	**AEEHLSX**	exhales	**AEEIMRT**	emirate
AEEFKRS	fakeers		telegas	**AEEHLSY**	eyelash		meatier
AEEFLLT	fellate	**AEEGLSU**	leagues	**AEEHLTT**	athlete	**AEEIMSS**	siamese
	leaflet	**AEEGLSV**	selvage	**AEEHMNT**	methane	**AEEIMST**	steamie
AEEFLMS	females	**AEEGLTV**	vegetal	**AEEHMRS**	hareems	**AEEINPR**	perinea
AEEFLRT	reflate	**AEEGMMT**	gemmate		mahseer	**AEEINRT**	Aintree
AEEFLRU	ferulae		tagmeme	**AEEHMRT**	thermae		arenite
AEEFLRW	welfare	**AEEGMNR**	germane	**AEEHMSU**	heaumes		retinae
AEEFLSU	easeful	**AEEGMNS**	maneges	**AEEHMSV**	Evesham		trainee
AEEFMNR	freeman		menages	**AEEHNPS**	peahens	**AEEINST**	etesian
AEEFMRR	reframe	**AEEGMSS**	megasse	**AEEHNPT**	haptene	**AEEINTV**	naivete
AEEFMRT	fermate		message		heptane		Venetia
AEEFNRS	Farnese	**AEEGMST**	gametes	**AEEHNRT**	earthen	**AEEINVW**	inweave
AEEFNRU	Freneau		metages		hearten	**AEEINVZ**	Venezia
AEEFORS	Faeroes	**AEEGNNS**	ennages	**AEEHNSV**	heavens	**AEEIORT**	etaerio
	Faroese	**AEEGNNV**	Genevan	**AEEHNTW**	wheaten	**AEEIPRR**	pereira
AEEFOTV	foveate	**AEEGNOP**	peonage	**AEEHPRS**	heapers	**AEEIPRS**	aperies
AEEFRRS	fearers	**AEEGNPP**	genappe		reshape	**AEEIPSV**	peavies
AEEFRRT	ferrate	**AEEGNRS**	enrages	**AEEHPRT**	preheat	**AEEIPTX**	expiate
AEEFRST	afreets	**AEEGNRT**	grantee	**AEEHPSS**	spahees	**AEEIRRT**	Eretria
	feaster		greaten	**AEEHPUV**	upheave		Eritrea
AEEFRTU	feature		negater	**AEEHRRS**	hearers		tearier
AEEFRWY	freeway		reagent		rehears	**AEEIRRW**	wearier
AEEFSTT	featest	**AEEGNRV**	avenger		shearer	**AEEIRST**	aeriest
AEEGGLT	gateleg		engrave	**AEEHRSS**	hearses		seriate
AEEGGNR	engager	**AEEGNST**	negates	**AEEHRST**	aethers	**AEEIRSW**	wearies
AEEGGNS	engages	**AEEGNSV**	avenges		heaters	**AEEIRTT**	ariette
AEEGGRU	regauge	**AEEGNTT**	tentage		reheats		iterate
AEEGHNN	Gehenna	**AEEGNTV**	ventage		Theresa	**AEEISST**	easiest
AEEGHNW	whangee	**AEEGNTW**	Newgate	**AEEHRSV**	heavers	**AEEISVV**	evasive
AEEGHSZ	geezahs	**AEEGOPS**	apogees	**AEEHRSW**	whereas	**AEEIUVX**	exuviae
AEEGILL	galilee	**AEEGORV**	overage	**AEEHRTT**	theater	**AEEJKSS**	jakeses
AEEGILM	mileage	**AEEGOST**	goatees		theatre	**AEEJNST**	sejeant
AEEGILN	lineage	**AEEGPRS**	presage		thereat	**AEEKKNO**	kokanee
AEEGILP	epigeal	**AEEGPRU**	pugaree	**AEEHRTW**	weather	**AEEKLNS**	alkenes
AEEGILW	weigela	**AEEGRRS**	greaser		whereat	**AEEKLRS**	leakers
AEEGINP	epigean	**AEEGRRT**	greater		wreathe	**AEEKMNS**	kamseen
AEEGINR	Erigena		regrate	**AEEHSSV**	sheaves	**AEEKMRS**	remakes
AEEGIRT	Reigate	**AEEGRRU**	reargue	**AEEHSWY**	eyewash	**AEEKMRT**	meerkat
AEEGIRU	eugarie	**AEEGRRW**	wagerer	**AEEIKLP**	apelike	**AEEKNNN**	nankeen
AEEGJRS	jaegers	**AEEGRSS**	greases		pealike	**AEEKNNP**	kneepan
AEEGLLS	alleges	**AEEGRST**	restage	**AEEIKLR**	earlike	**AEEKNRT**	retaken
AEEGLLZ	gazelle	**AEEGRSV**	greaves		leakier	**AEEKNRW**	rewaken
AEEGLMN	gleeman	**AEEGRUZ**	guereza	**AEEILMR**	Lamerie		wakener
	melange	**AEEGSTT**	gestate		mealier	**AEEKNSW**	weakens
AEEGLMT	meltage		tagetes	**AEEILMS**	mealies	**AEEKPRS**	speaker
AEEGLNR	enlarge	**AEEGTTZ**	gazette	**AEEILNT**	lineate	**AEEKRRT**	retaker
	general	**AEEHHNT**	heathen	**AEEILPT**	epilate	**AEEKRRW**	wreaker
	gleaner	**AEEHHRT**	heather		pileate	**AEEKRST**	retakes

AEEKRSW rewakes
AEEKRTW tweaker
AEEKSTW weakest
AEELLLS alleles
AEELLMS mallees
AEELLPS Apelles
AEELLSS sallees
AEELLST lealest
AEELLWY walleye
AEELMNP empanel
        emplane
AEELMNR reelman
AEELMNS enamels
AEELMNV velamen
AEELMNY amylene
AEELMPR empaler
AEELMPS empales
AEELMPX example
        exempla
AEELMSS measles
AEELMST Maltese
AEELMTU emulate
AEELNNP enplane
AEELNPS spelean
AEELNRR learner
        relearn
AEELNRT enteral
        eternal
        teleran
AEELNRW renewal
AEELNST leanest
AEELNSV enslave
        leavens
AEELNSW Salween
AEELOPR parolee
AEELOPX poleaxe
AEELORS areoles
AEELORU aureole
AEELOST oleates
AEELPRR pearler
AEELPRS leapers
        pleaser
        presale
        relapse
        repeals
AEELPRT pleater
        prelate
AEELPRU pleurae
AEELPSS elapses
        pleases
AEELPTT palette
        peltate
AEELPTU epaulet
AEELQRU lequear
AEELQSU sequela
AEELRRT realter
        relater
AEELRRX relaxer
AEELRSS earless
        leasers
        resales
        reseals

        sealers
AEELRST elaters
        Laertes
        relates
        stealer
AEELRSV leavers
        reveals
        several
        vealers
AEELRSX relaxes
AEELRSY sealery
AEELRTX exalter
AEELRUV revalue
AEELRUY Euryale
AEELSST teasels
AEELSSV sleaves
AEELSSW aweless
        weasels
AEELSTT Seattle
AEELSTU eluates
AEELSTV veletas
AEELSTX latexes
AEELSTZ teazels
        teazles
AEELTTY layette
AEELTVW wavelet
AEEMMMR maremme
AEEMMMS mammees
AEEMMPY empyema
AEEMMRT ammeter
        metamer
AEEMNNO anemone
AEEMNNP penname
AEEMNNY Mayenne
AEEMNRS renames
AEEMNST meanest
AEEMNSX examens
AEEMORT erotema
AEEMOSW awesome
AEEMPRS amperes
AEEMPRT Tampere
        tempera
AEEMPTU amputee
AEEMQRU marquee
AEEMRRS reamers
        smearer
AEEMRSS Rameses
        seamers
AEEMRST steamer
AEEMRSU measure
AEEMSTX taxemes
AEENNOT neonate
AEENNOV novenae
AEENNPT pennate
        pentane
AEENNRS ensnare
AEENNST neatens
AEENNSX annexes
AEENNTU uneaten
AEENOPU eupnoea
AEENOSU aeneous
AEENPST nepetas

        penates
AEENPSW pawnees
AEENPSX expanse
AEENQUU Queneau
AEENRRS earners
AEENRRT terrane
AEENRRV ravener
AEENRRY yearner
AEENRST earnest
        eastern
AEENRSW weaners
AEENRTT entreat
        ratteen
        ternate
AEENRTV nervate
        Tavener
        veteran
AEENRVY Yerevan
AEENSST entases
        sateens
        senates
        sensate
AEENSTT neatest
AEENSUV avenues
AEEOPRT operate
AEEORST roseate
AEEORSV oversea
AEEORTV overate
        overeat
AEEORVW overawe
AEEPPRR paperer
        prepare
        repaper
AEEPRRS reapers
        spearer
AEEPRRT taperer
AEEPRSS asperse
        pareses
        serapes
AEEPRST repeats
AEEPRSV repaves
AEEPRTZ trapeze
AEEPSST pesetas
AEEPSSW pesewas
AEEPSTT septate
AEEPSVY peaveys
AEEQRSU quaeres
AEEQSTU equates
AEERRRS rearers
AEERRSS erasers
AEERRST serrate
        tearers
AEERRSU erasure
AEERRSW swearer
        wearers
AEERRTT retreat
        treater
AEERRTW waterer
AEERRUX Auxerre
AEERRVW waverer
AEERSST easters

        reseats
        teasers
        tessera
AEERSSU reseaus
AEERSTT estreat
        restate
AEERSTU austere
AEERSTW sweater
AEERSUX reseaux
AEERSVW weavers
AEESSSW seesaws
AEESSTT estates
AEESTTT testate
AEESWXY waxeyes
AEFFGIL fig leaf
AEFFGIR giraffe
AEFFGRS gaffers
AEFFGRU gauffer
AEFFHRS Shaffer
AEFFIPS piaffes
AEFFIST taffies
AEFFISX affixes
AEFFKOP offpeak
AEFFKOR rakeoff
AEFFKOT takeoff
AEFFLLY flyleaf
AEFFLNS snaffle
AEFFLRR raffler
AEFFLRS raffles
AEFFLRU fearful
AEFFLRW waffler
AEFFLSW waffles
AEFFLSY yaffles
AEFFLTU fateful
AEFFMRU earmuff
AEFFNST naffest
AEFFOVW waveoff
AEFFQRU quaffer
AEFFRST restaff
        staffer
AEFGGGO foggage
AEFGGLR flagger
AEFGIKN Kaifeng
AEFGILN finagle
        leafing
AEFGILO foliage
AEFGILR fragile
AEFGINR fearing
AEFGINU Fuegian
AEFGINZ feazing
AEFGIRT frigate
AEFGIRU refugia
AEFGITU fatigue
AEFGLMN flagmen
AEFGLNR flanger
AEFGLNS flanges
AEFGLOT flotage
AEFGLOW flowage
AEFGNRR franger
AEFGNRT engraft
AEFGOOT footage
AEFGORR forager

AEFGORS	forages	**AEFKLNS**	fankles	**AEFOPRW**	forepaw	**AEGHILR** Raleigh
AEFGORV	forgave	**AEFKLOS**	Lefkoşa	**AEFORRV**	favorer	**AEGHINP** heaping
AEFGRRT	grafter	**AEFKLRS**	flakers		overfar	**AEGHINR** hearing
AEFGRTY	Freytag	**AEFKLRT**	fartlek	**AEFORRY**	forayer	**AEGHINT** gahnite
AEFHINS	Fa-hsien	**AEFKLST**	flasket	**AEFORSW**	foresaw	heating
AEFHIRT	faither	**AEFKLUW**	wakeful	**AEFOSST**	fatsoes	**AEGHINV** heaving
AEFHIRW	wharfie	**AEFKNRR**	franker	**AEFPPRS**	frappes	**AEGHINZ** genizah
AEFHLLS	fellahs	**AEFKORS**	forsake	**AEFRRST**	fraters	**AEGHIRS** hegiras
AEFHLRS	flasher	**AEFLLNN**	flannel		rafters	**AEGHISS** geishas
AEFHLSS	flashes	**AEFLLOT**	floatel		strafer	**AEGHLNO** halogen
AEFHLTU	hateful	**AEFLLRR**	Farrell	**AEFRSST**	fasters	**AEGHLOU** La Hogue
AEFHRRT	farther	**AEFLLRS**	fallers		strafes	**AEGHLRU** laugher
AEFHRST	fathers	**AEFLLSY**	falsely	**AEFRSTU**	faurest	**AEGHLTW** thalweg
	hafters	**AEFLLTT**	flatlet	**AEFRSTW**	fretsaw	**AEGHMNN** hangmen
AEFIILR	Alfieri	**AEFLMNS**	flamens		wafters	**AEGHMOS** homages
	Falerii	**AEFLMOR**	femoral	**AEFRTTU**	tartufe	ohmages
AEFIILT	filiate	**AEFLMRS**	flamers	**AEFRTUW**	wafture	**AEGHMRS** Gresham
AEFIIRS	fairies	**AEFLNOV**	flavone	**AEFRWYZ**	frawzey	**AEGHMSU** meshuga
AEFIJOS	feijoas	**AEFLNRU**	flaneur	**AEFSSTT**	fastest	**AEGHNOX** hexagon
AEFIKLN	fanlike		frenula		saftest	**AEGHNRS** hangers
AEFIKLR	flakier		funeral	**AEFSTTT**	fattest	rehangs
AEFIKLT	fatlike	**AEFLNTT**	flatten	**AEGGGLS**	gaggles	sherang
AEFILLM	famille	**AEFLNUU**	faunule	**AEGGGLU**	luggage	**AEGHNSS** gnashes
AEFILMN	inflame	**AEFLOOV**	foveola	**AEGGGRS**	gaggers	**AEGHNST** stengah
AEFILNS	finales	**AEFLOPW**	peafowl	**AEGGGRY**	gaggery	**AEGHOPY** hypogea
AEFILNT	inflate	**AEFLORS**	loafers	**AEGGHLR**	haggler	**AEGHORS** gheraos
AEFILNU	infulae		safrole	**AEGGHLS**	haggles	**AEGHOST** hostage
AEFILNV	flavine	**AEFLORT**	floater	**AEGGHMO**	hemagog	**AEGHRST** gathers
AEFILOT	foliate		floreat	**AEGGIJR**	jaggier	**AEGIIMN** imagine
AEFILPT	fleapit		refloat	**AEGGIMS**	maggies	**AEGIINR** Igraine
AEFILRR	frailer	**AEFLPPR**	flapper	**AEGGINR**	gearing	Nigeria
AEFILRU	failure	**AEFLPRS**	felspar	**AEGGINS**	signage	**AEGIKLN** leaking
AEFILRV	favrile	**AEFLPRY**	palfrey	**AEGGIOR**	Georgia	linkage
AEFILSS	falsies	**AEFLRST**	Falster	**AEGGIOS**	isagoge	**AEGIKLT** glaiket
AEFILTT	flattie		falters	**AEGGIRU**	garigue	**AEGIKNP** peaking
AEFIMNR	fireman	**AEFLRSU**	ferulas	**AEGGISW**	swaggie	**AEGIKNS** sinkage
AEFIMNS	famines		refusal	**AEGGJRY**	jaggery	**AEGIKNT** Keating
AEFIMOR	foamier	**AEFLRSY**	flayers	**AEGGLNO**	agelong	**AEGIKPR** garpike
AEFIMRR	firearm	**AEFLRTT**	flatter	**AEGGLNR**	gangrel	**AEGIKRW** gawkier
AEFINNS	fainnes	**AEFLRTU**	tearful	**AEGGLRR**	gargler	**AEGILLL** illegal
	fannies	**AEFLRZZ**	frazzle	**AEGGLRS**	gargles	**AEGILLN** nigella
AEFINNT	infante	**AEFLSST**	falsest		raggles	**AEGILLO** Galileo
AEFINNZ	fanzine		fatless	**AEGGLRW**	waggler	**AEGILLP** pillage
AEFINPR	firepan	**AEFMNNY**	Feynman	**AEGGLRY**	greylag	**AEGILLR** Allegri
AEFINRR	refrain	**AEFMNOR**	foramen	**AEGGLSW**	waggles	**AEGILLT** tillage
AEFINRS	infares		foreman	**AEGGNRS**	gangers	**AEGILLU** ligulae
AEFINRT	fainter	**AEFMNRU**	fraenum		granges	**AEGILLV** village
AEFINTX	antefix	**AEFMORR**	forearm		naggers	**AEGILLY** agilely
AEFIQRU	aquifer	**AEFMORT**	formate	**AEGGNTU**	Gauteng	**AEGILMR** gremial
AEFIRRR	farrier	**AEFMRRS**	farmers	**AEGGRSS**	aggress	**AEGILMS** milages
	Ferrari		framers		saggers	**AEGILNN** aneling
AEFIRRZ	Frazier	**AEFNNOT**	Fontane	**AEGGRST**	stagger	leaning
AEFIRSS	fraises	**AEFNNRS**	fanners		taggers	**AEGILNP** leaping
AEFIRST	fairest	**AEFNOPR**	profane	**AEGGRSU**	gaugers	pealing
AEFIRTT	fattier	**AEFNORR**	foreran	**AEGGRSW**	swagger	**AEGILNR** engrail
AEFISST	fasties	**AEFNORT**	Torfaen	**AEGGRTY**	gargety	nargile
	fiestas	**AEFNRSS**	farness	**AEGGRWY**	waggery	realign
AEFISTT	fatties	**AEFNRSW**	fawners	**AEGGSWW**	gewgaws	**AEGILNS** leasing
AEFISTX	fixates	**AEFNSST**	fastens	**AEGHHNU**	Huang He	sealing
AEFJNST	fanjets		fatness	**AEGHHUY**	Haughey	**AEGILNT** elating
AEFKLNR	Falkner	**AEFNSSU**	snafues	**AEGHIKL**	haglike	gelatin
	flanker	**AEFNSTT**	fattens	**AEGHILN**	healing	genital

AEGILNU	linguae
AEGILNV	leaving
AEGILOS	goalies
	soilage
AEGILOU	eulogia
AEGILPS	Legaspi
	paigles
AEGILRR	glarier
AEGILRS	Algiers
AEGILRZ	glazier
AEGILSS	ligases
AEGILST	aiglets
	ligates
AEGILSV	glaives
AEGILTU	glutaei
AEGIMMR	gammier
AEGIMNN	meaning
	Meninga
AEGIMNR	germina
	mangier
	reaming
AEGIMNS	enigmas
	gamines
	seaming
AEGIMNT	mintage
	teaming
	tegmina
AEGIMOS	imagoes
AEGIMPR	epigram
	primage
AEGIMPS	magpies
AEGIMPT	pigmeat
AEGIMRR	armiger
AEGIMRS	gisarme
	mirages
AEGIMRT	migrate
	ragtime
AEGIMRY	imagery
AEGIMST	gamiest
	sigmate
AEGIMSV	misgave
AEGINNR	earning
	engrain
	grannie
	nearing
AEGINNT	anteing
	antigen
	gentian
AEGINNU	anguine
	guanine
AEGINNV	Angevin
AEGINNW	weaning
AEGINNY	yeaning
AEGINOR	iron age
AEGINOS	agonies
	agonise
AEGINOZ	agonize
AEGINPP	genipap
AEGINPR	reaping
AEGINPS	spaeing
AEGINRR	angrier
	earring

	grainer
	rangier
	rearing
AEGINRS	earings
	erasing
	gainers
	regains
	searing
	seringa
AEGINRT	granite
	ingrate
	tangier
	tearing
AEGINRV	reaving
	vinegar
AEGINRW	wearing
AEGINRZ	zingare
AEGINST	easting
	ingesta
	seating
	teasing
AEGINSU	guineas
AEGINSY	easying
AEGINTV	vintage
AEGINTW	Wingate
AEGINTZ	tzigane
AEGINVW	weaving
AEGIORV	Argovie
AEGIOSV	Segovia
AEGIPPR	gappier
AEGIPRR	grapier
AEGIPRS	prisage
AEGIPRU	Perugia
AEGIRRZ	grazier
AEGIRSS	gassier
AEGIRST	aigrets
	gaiters
	seagirt
	stagier
AEGIRSV	Gervais
	gravies
	rivages
AEGIRSW	earwigs
AEGIRTU	Gautier
AEGIRTV	virgate
AEGIRUY	yugarie
AEGIRUZ	gauzier
AEGISST	ageists
AEGISSV	visages
AEGJLNR	jangler
AEGJLNS	jangles
AEGKLLS	Gaskell
AEGKLOU	kagoule
AEGKMRY	kerygma
AEGKNOS	Kaesŏng
AEGKSST	gaskets
AEGLLLY	legally
AEGLLNO	galleon
AEGLLNR	langrel
AEGLLNY	langley
AEGLLOR	allegro
AEGLLOT	tollage

AEGLLRY	allergy
	gallery
	largely
	regally
AEGLLSU	seagull
	sullage
	ullages
AEGLLSY	galleys
AEGLLTU	gluteal
AEGLMNR	mangler
AEGLMNS	mangels
	mangles
AEGLMPU	plumage
AEGLMSV	maglevs
AEGLNOT	tangelo
AEGLNOU	Angelou
AEGLNPR	grapnel
AEGLNPS	spangle
AEGLNRS	anglers
	erlangs
	largens
AEGLNRT	tangler
AEGLNRU	granule
AEGLNRW	wangler
	wrangle
AEGLNST	langest
	tangles
AEGLNSU	angelus
	lagunes
AEGLNSW	wangles
AEGLNTT	gantlet
AEGLNTU	languet
AEGLNUU	ungulae
AEGLNUW	gunwale
AEGLOPR	pergola
AEGLORS	gaolers
AEGLORT	gloater
	legator
	Ortegal
AEGLORV	vorlage
AEGLOSS	glossae
AEGLOST	legatos
AEGLOTV	voltage
AEGLPPR	grapple
AEGLPRU	earplug
	graupel
	plaguer
AEGLPSS	gapless
AEGLPSU	plagues
AEGLPUY	plaguey
AEGLRRU	regular
AEGLRSS	largess
AEGLRST	largest
AEGLRSV	gravels
	verglas
AEGLRSY	argyles
AEGLRSZ	glazers
AEGLRTU	tegular
AEGLRTY	greatly
AEGLRVY	gravely
AEGLSSS	gasless
	glasses

AEGLSTT	gestalt
AEGLSTW	talwegs
AEGLTUV	vulgate
AEGLUUY	guayule
AEGLUVY	vaguely
AEGMMRS	gammers
	grammes
AEGMMRU	rummage
AEGMNNO	agnomen
AEGMNOR	marengo
	megaron
AEGMNOS	gamones
	mangoes
AEGMNOT	magneto
	megaton
	montage
AEGMNPY	pygmean
AEGMNRS	engrams
	germans
	mangers
AEGMNRT	garment
	margent
AEGMNRY	Germany
AEGMNST	magnets
AEGMNSW	swagmen
AEGMNTU	augment
	mutagen
AEGMOOR	moorage
AEGMOXY	exogamy
AEGMRSU	murages
AEGMSUY	magueys
AEGMSUZ	zeugmas
AEGNNOR	Argonne
	Garonne
AEGNNOT	tonnage
AEGNNRT	regnant
AEGNNRU	gunnera
AEGNNST	gannets
AEGNNTT	tangent
AEGNNTU	tunnage
AEGNOOR	oregano
AEGNORR	groaner
AEGNORS	onagers
	oranges
AEGNORT	negator
AEGNORW	wagoner
AEGNOST	tangoes
AEGNOSY	nosegay
AEGNPRT	trepang
AEGNRRS	garners
	rangers
AEGNRRT	granter
AEGNRST	garnets
	Sargent
	strange
AEGNRSW	gnawers
AEGNRTT	Garnett
AEGNSSY	ganseys
	gayness
AEGNTYZ	Yangtze
AEGOPRT	portage
	potager

AEGOPRU	Guaporé	AEHILMO	hemiola
AEGOPST	gestapo	AEHILMS	Ishmael
	postage	AEHILNR	hernial
AEGOPTT	pottage		inhaler
AEGORRT	garrote	AEHILNS	inhales
AEGORST	storage	AEHILNT	Antheil
	toerags	AEHILNY	hyaline
AEGORTT	garotte	AEHILOR	airhole
AEGORTU	outrage	AEHILPR	harelip
AEGORVV	voyager	AEHILPT	haplite
AEGOSSU	gaseous	AEHILRS	hailers
AEGOSTU	outages	AEHILRT	lathier
AEGOSTW	stowage	AEHILRU	haulier
	towages	AEHILSS	sheilas
AEGOSVY	voyages	AEHILSW	shawlie
AEGOTTV	gavotte	AEHILTY	hyalite
AEGPRRS	grasper	AEHILUV	vihuela
	sparger	AEHILVY	heavily
AEGPRSS	gaspers	AEHIMMR	hammier
	sparges	AEHIMNR	Manhire
AEGPRST	pargets	AEHIMNS	Hsia-men
AEGPRSW	gawpers	AEHIMNT	hematin
AEGPSSU	pegasus	AEHIMNY	hymenia
AEGPSTU	upstage	AEHIMPR	Ephraim
AEGRRST	garrets	AEHIMPS	phaeism
	garters	AEHIMRS	mishear
	graters	AEHIMSS	mashies
AEGRRSU	arguers		messiah
AEGRRSV	gravers	AEHIMST	atheism
AEGRRSZ	grazers	AEHINPR	heparin
AEGRRTT	Garrett	AEHINPS	Pahsien
AEGRRUV	gravure	AEHINRS	hernias
AEGRSSS	gassers	AEHINRT	hairnet
	grasses		inearth
AEGRSST	stagers	AEHINSS	hessian
AEGRSSU	arguses	AEHINSV	evanish
	saugers	AEHINSW	wahines
AEGRSSW	swagers	AEHIORR	hoarier
AEGRSTT	targets	AEHIPPR	happier
AEGRSTV	gravest	AEHIPPT	epitaph
AEGRSTY	grayest	AEHIPRS	harpies
	gyrates		sharpie
AEGRSUZ	Zagreus	AEHIPSS	aphesis
AEGSTUU	auguste	AEHIQSU	quashie
AEGSTUV	vaguest	AEHIRRR	harrier
AEGTTTU	guttate	AEHIRRS	harries
AEHHJOV	Jehovah	AEHIRST	hastier
AEHHJPT	Japheth	AEHIRSU	Herisau
AEHHLTY	healthy	AEHIRSW	washier
AEHHMSY	Heysham	AEHIRWY	haywire
AEHHNSV	Heshvan	AEHISST	ashiest
AEHHRRS	harsher		saithes
AEHHRST	hearths		stashie
AEHHSST	sheaths	AEHISTT	atheist
AEHIIRR	hairier	AEHISTZ	haziest
AEHIJRS	hejiras	AEHISVY	yeshiva
AEHIKLT	hatlike	AEHITTW	thwaite
AEHIKNS	hankies	AEHKLOY	Hoylake
AEHIKPS	peakish	AEHKMSS	samekhs
AEHIKRS	shakier	AEHKMWY	Wykeham
AEHIKST	shitake	AEHKNRS	hankers
AEHIKSW	weakish		harkens

AEHKOSS	shakoes	AEHMNPY	nymphae
AEHKPSU	shakeup	AEHMNRS	Sherman
AEHKRSS	kashers	AEHMNST	anthems
	shakers		hetmans
AEHKRSW	hawkers	AEHMOPT	apothem
AEHKRTY	Kythera	AEHMPRS	hampers
AEHKSSY	ashkeys	AEHMPTY	empathy
AEHLLMN	Hellman	AEHMRRS	harmers
AEHLLRW	Harwell	AEHMRSS	marshes
AEHLLUV	helluva		mashers
AEHLMNN	Lehmann		smasher
AEHLMNO	manhole	AEHMRST	Amherst
AEHLMNY	hymenal		hamster
AEHLMOP	Omphale	AEHMRWX	Wrexham
AEHLMOR	armhole	AEHMSSS	smashes
AEHLMPS	pelhams	AEHMSTT	shmatte
AEHLMRT	thermal	AEHMTTW	Matthew
AEHLMRU	humeral	AEHMUZZ	mezuzah
AEHLMST	hamlets	AEHNOPT	phaeton
AEHLNOT	ethanol		phonate
AEHLNRT	enthral	AEHNORS	hoarsen
AEHLNSS	hansels	AEHNORT	another
AEHLNSU	unleash	AEHNORV	Hanover
AEHLOPR	ephoral	AEHNOSX	hexosan
AEHLOPT	taphole	AEHNPPS	happens
AEHLORT	loather	AEHNPRS	sharpen
AEHLOSS	asshole	AEHNPRT	panther
AEHLOST	loathes	AEHNRSS	harness
AEHLPRS	spheral	AEHNRST	anthers
AEHLPSS	hapless		thenars
	plashes	AEHNRTU	haunter
AEHLPSU	Alpheus		unearth
AEHLPSY	shapely		urethan
	Shapley	AEHNRTX	narthex
AEHLRSS	ashlers	AEHNSST	hastens
	lashers		snathes
	slasher	AEHNSTW	Tshwane
AEHLRST	halters	AEHNSTY	astheny
	harslet		shantey
	lathers	AEHOORT	toheroa
	slather	AEHOPST	teashop
	thalers	AEHORRS	hoarser
AEHLRSU	haulers	AEHORST	earshot
AEHLRSW	whalers	AEHORSX	hoaxers
AEHLRTU	Hérault	AEHORTU	Thoreau
AEHLRTY	earthly	AEHPPRS	perhaps
	Hartley	AEHPPSU	shapeup
	lathery	AEHPRRS	harpers
AEHLSSS	hassles		sharper
	slashes	AEHPRSS	phrases
AEHLSST	haslets		seraphs
	Hasselt		shapers
	hatless		sherpas
AEHLSTT	stealth	AEHPRST	threaps
AEHLTWY	wealthy	AEHPRSW	prewash
AEHMMOT	Mahomet	AEHPRTY	therapy
AEHMMRS	hammers	AEHPSST	spathes
	shammer	AEHPSTY	Pytheas
AEHMMSS	shammes	AEHQSSU	quashes
AEHMMTT	Hammett	AEHRRSS	rashers
AEHMNNR	Hermann		sharers
AEHMNOR	menorah	AEHRRTU	urethra

AEHRSST	shaster	AEIKLMR	armlike	AEILMMS	melisma	AEILNSV	alevins
	trashes	AEIKLNO	kaoline	AEILMNN	Lemnian		valines
AEHRSSV	shavers	AEIKLNR	lankier		lineman	AEILNSY	elysian
AEHRSSW	hawsers	AEIKLNT	antlike		melanin	AEILNTU	alunite
	washers	AEIKLNU	unalike	AEILMNP	impanel	AEILNTV	ventail
AEHRSTT	hatters	AEIKLOR	oarlike		maniple	AEILNVY	naively
	shatter	AEIKLOT	keitloa	AEILMNR	manlier	AEILOPR	peloria
	threats	AEIKLRR	larkier		marline	AEILORV	variole
AEHRSTV	harvest	AEIKLRT	ratlike		mineral	AEILOST	isolate
	thraves		talkier	AEILMNS	malines	AEILOTV	violate
AEHRSTW	thawers	AEIKLRW	warlike		menials	AEILPPR	applier
	wreaths	AEIKLST	lakiest		seminal	AEILPPS	applies
AEHRSVW	wharves		talkies	AEILMNT	ailment	AEILPRT	platier
AEHRSWY	washery	AEIKLSW	sawlike		aliment	AEILPRV	prevail
AEHRSXY	hyraxes	AEIKLWX	waxlike	AEILMNU	Manuel I	AEILPSS	espials
AEHRTUU	hauteur	AEIKMNP	pikeman	AEILMNY	El Minya		lipases
AEHSSST	stashes	AEIKMNR	mankier	AEILMOR	Morelia		palsies
AEHSSSW	swashes		ramekin	AEILMPR	impaler	AEILPST	platies
AEHSSTW	swathes	AEIKMST	mistake		impearl		talipes
AEHSTUX	exhaust	AEIKNRR	narkier		lempira	AEILPSY	paisley
AEIIJMS	James II	AEIKNRS	snakier		palmier	AEILQTU	liquate
AEIIKNT	kainite	AEIKNRT	Katrine	AEILMPS	impales		tequila
AEIIKWZ	Azikiwe		Kénitra	AEILMRS	mailers	AEILRRS	railers
AEIILMP	lipemia		keratin		realism	AEILRRT	retiral
AEIILNN	aniline	AEIKNRU	Ukraine		remails		retrial
AEIILNR	airline	AEIKNSS	kinases	AEILMRT	Latimer		trailer
AEIILNX	exilian	AEIKNST	intakes		maltier	AEILRRU	Laurier
AEIILRR	lairier		kentias		marlite	AEILRSS	airless
AEIILRS	Israeli	AEIKNSX	Xenakis	AEILMSS	aimless		sailers
	Salieri	AEIKNSY	kyanise		samiels		serails
AEIILSS	liaises	AEIKNTY	kyanite	AEILMTY	meatily		serials
	silesia	AEIKNYZ	kyanize	AEILNNY	inanely	AEILRST	realist
AEIIMNT	intimae	AEIKOST	oakiest	AEILNOP	opaline		retails
AEIIMPR	imperia	AEIKPRR	parkier	AEILNOR	aileron		saltier
AEIIMRT	airtime	AEIKPRW	pawkier		alienor		saltire
AEIIMRV	viremia	AEIKQRU	quakier	AEILNOS	anisole		slatier
AEIIMST	amities	AEIKRRS	sarkier	AEILNOT	elation	AEILRSV	revisal
AEIIMTT	imitate	AEIKRSS	kaisers		toenail	AEILRSW	wailers
AEIINNR	Aneirin	AEIKRSY	Kayseri	AEILNPR	plainer	AEILRTT	tertial
AEIINNS	asinine	AEILLLM	Melilla		praline	AEILRTU	uralite
AEIINPR	Pierian	AEILLMN	manille	AEILNPS	alpines	AEILRTY	irately
AEIINRR	rainier	AEILLNR	ralline		spaniel		reality
AEIINRT	inertia	AEILLNU	uillean	AEILNPT	pantile		tearily
AEIINST	isatine	AEILLOV	alveoli	AEILNPU	Pauline	AEILRVV	revival
AEIINTX	axinite	AEILLPR	pallier	AEILNPX	explain	AEILRVY	virelay
AEIIPRR	prairie	AEILLPY	epyllia	AEILNRS	aliners	AEILRWY	wearily
AEIIRRV	riviera	AEILLQU	Lalique		Linares	AEILSSS	lassies
AEIIRST	airiest	AEILLRR	rallier		nailers	AEILSSV	valises
AEIISSV	Eivissa	AEILLRS	rallies	AEILNRT	latrine	AEILSTU	situlae
AEIITTV	vitiate		sallier		ratline	AEILSTV	estival
AEIJKLW	jawlike	AEILLRT	literal		reliant	AEILSTZ	laziest
AEIJKMN	Eijkman		tallier		retinal	AEILTTU	Lutetia
AEIJLNV	javelin		triella		trenail	AEILTUV	Lietuva
AEIJLRS	jailers	AEILLSS	sallies	AEILNRV	ravelin	AEILTVV	Tel Aviv
AEIJMMR	jammier	AEILLST	Liestal	AEILNRX	relaxin	AEILTVY	vilayet
AEIJMNS	jasmine		sitella	AEILNRY	inlayer	AEILUVX	exuvial
AEIJMSV	James IV		tailles	AEILNST	elastin	AEIMMNS	mammies
	James VI		tallies		entails	AEIMMNS	misname
AEIJRSV	jarvies	AEILLSW	wallies		nailset	AEIMMPS	spammie
AEIJRZZ	jazzier	AEILLUV	eluvial		salient	AEIMMRS	maimers
AEIKKST	takkies	AEILLVX	vexilla		slainte		rammies
AEIKLMN	manlike	AEILMMN	mailmen	AEILNSU	insulae	AEIMMRT	marmite

	trammie
AEIMMSS	sammies
AEIMMST	tammies
AEIMNNR	Riemann
AEIMNNT	mannite
AEIMNOR	moraine
	romaine
AEIMNOT	amniote
AEIMNRR	mariner
AEIMNRS	marines
	remains
	seminar
AEIMNRT	meranti
	minaret
	raiment
AEIMNRV	Minerva
AEIMNRW	wireman
AEIMNSS	Massine
	Messina
	samisen
AEIMNST	inmates
AEIMNSW	Wiseman
AEIMNTV	Vietnam
AEIMNTY	amenity
AEIMOOP	ipomoea
AEIMOPR	emporia
AEIMORR	armoire
AEIMOST	atomies
	atomise
AEIMOTX	toxemia
AEIMOTZ	atomize
AEIMPRS	impresa
AEIMPRT	primate
AEIMPRV	vampire
AEIMPSS	impasse
AEIMPST	impaste
	pastime
AEIMRRR	marrier
AEIMRRS	marries
AEIMRSS	massier
	sarmies
AEIMRST	Artemis
	imarets
	maestri
	Maistre
	smartie
AEIMRSY	rimayes
AEIMRTU	muriate
AEIMRTW	wartime
AEIMSST	Matisse
	tamises
AEIMSSV	massive
	mavises
AEIMSSW	swamies
AEIMSSY	myiases
AEIMSTT	matiest
AEIMSTZ	maziest
	mestiza
AEIMSXX	maxixes
AEINNNS	nannies
AEINNPR	pannier
AEINNPT	pinnate

AEINNRS	insnare
AEINNRT	entrain
	trannie
AEINNRU	aneurin
AEINNSW	swannie
AEINOPZ	epizoan
AEINORS	erasion
AEINORT	Aretino
AEINOST	Estonia
AEINOSV	evasion
AEINOXZ	oxazine
AEINPPR	nappier
AEINPPS	nappies
AEINPRT	painter
	pertain
	repaint
AEINPSS	pansies
AEINPST	panties
	patines
	sapient
AEINPSZ	Penzias
AEINPTT	patient
AEINPTU	petunia
AEINQTU	antique
	quinate
AEINRRS	sierran
AEINRRT	retrain
	terrain
	trainer
AEINRSS	Resnais
	sarnies
AEINRST	antsier
	nastier
	retains
	retinas
	retsina
	stainer
	stearin
AEINRSV	ravines
	Servian
AEINRTT	intreat
	iterant
	nattier
	nitrate
	tertian
AEINRTU	taurine
	uranite
	urinate
AEINRTW	tinware
AEINRVV	vervain
AEINSST	entasis
	nasties
	sestina
	Staines
	tansies
	tisanes
AEINSSV	vinasse
AEINSTT	instate
	satinet
AEINSTU	aunties
	sinuate
AEINSTV	natives

	vainest
AEINSTX	sextain
AEINSTZ	zaniest
AEINSVV	navvies
AEINSWY	anywise
AEINTVY	naivety
AEINTXY	anxiety
AEIOPRS	soapier
AEIOPST	opiates
AEIOQSU	sequoia
AEIORSV	ovaries
AEIOSST	Ossetia
	sosatie
AEIOSTT	toastie
AEIOSTZ	azotise
AEIOTZZ	azotize
AEIPPPR	pappier
AEIPPPS	pappies
AEIPPRS	apprise
	sappier
AEIPPRT	periapt
AEIPPRZ	apprize
	zappier
AEIPRRS	aspirer
	parries
	praiser
	rapiers
	repairs
AEIPRSS	aspires
	paresis
	praises
	Serapis
AEIPRST	pairest
	parties
	pastier
	piaster
	piastre
	pirates
	traipse
AEIPRSU	Piraeus
	upraise
AEIPRSV	parvise
AEIPRTT	partite
AEIPRTV	private
AEIPRTW	wiretap
AEIPRXY	pyrexia
AEIPSSS	asepsis
AEIPSST	pasties
	patsies
AEIPSSV	passive
	pavises
AEIPSTT	patties
AEIPTXY	epitaxy
AEIRRRT	tarrier
AEIRRRV	arriver
AEIRRSS	arrises
	raisers
	sierras
AEIRRST	tarries
	tarsier
AEIRRSV	arrives
AEIRRTT	rattier

	tartier
AEIRRTU	Etruria
AEIRRTY	retiary
AEIRSSS	sassier
AEIRSST	arsiest
	sairest
	satires
AEIRSSU	sauries
AEIRSTT	artiest
	artiste
	attires
	ratites
	striate
	tastier
AEIRSTV	vastier
AEIRSTW	waiters
	wariest
AEIRSVV	savvier
AEIRSVW	waivers
AEIRTTT	tattier
	titrate
AEIRTUZ	azurite
AEIRTVY	variety
AEISSST	siestas
	tassies
AEISSSW	wiseass
AEISSSZ	assizes
AEISSUV	suasive
AEISSUX	auxesis
AEISSVV	savvies
AEISTTT	tatties
AEISTTU	situate
AEISTTV	stative
AEISTTY	satiety
AEISTVW	waviest
AEISTWX	waxiest
AEISUYY	Iyeyasu
AEITTTV	vittate
AEJJLNU	jejunal
AEJLLOV	Vallejo
AEJLNUV	juvenal
AEJLOSU	jalouse
	jealous
AEJMMRS	jammers
AEJMNOS	Jameson
AEJMRST	ramjets
AEJMSTY	majesty
AEJNNOS	joannes
AEJNORT	Tanjore
AEJNOSS	San Jose
	San José
AEJPRSS	jaspers
AEJRRTT	Jarrett
AEJRSVY	jarveys
AEJRSZZ	jazzers
AEKKNRS	krakens
AEKKRRY	Kérkyra
AEKLNRS	rankles
AEKLNST	anklets
	lankest
AEKLNSY	alkynes
AEKLOST	skatole

AEKLOTU	Tokelau	**AELLNVY**	venally	**AELMPSS**	mapless	**AELNSTV**	levants
AEKLPRS	sparkle	**AELLOPW**	Walpole		samples	**AELNSTY**	Stanley
AEKLPSS	splakes	**AELLORS**	rosella	**AELMPSU**	ampules	**AELOORS**	aerosol
AEKLRRS	larkers	**AELLORT**	reallot	**AELMPTU**	plumate		roseola
AEKLRSS	slakers	**AELLORV**	allover	**AELMRSS**	armless	**AELOPRS**	paroles
AEKLRST	stalker		overall	**AELMRST**	armlets		reposal
	talkers	**AELLOSS**	loessal	**AELMRSU**	maulers	**AELOPRT**	prolate
AEKLRSW	walkers	**AELLPRU**	pleural		serumal	**AELOPRV**	overlap
AEKLSST	laskets	**AELLPST**	pallets	**AELMRSV**	marvels	**AELOPST**	apostle
AEKLSTU	auklets	**AELLPTY**	playlet	**AELMRTT**	martlet		pelotas
AEKMNOS	sokeman	**AELLQUV**	equally	**AELMRTU**	relatum	**AELOPSX**	exposal
AEKMNRU	Kamerun	**AELLRRU**	allurer	**AELMSST**	matless	**AELOPTT**	paletot
	unmaker	**AELLRST**	stellar	**AELMSTU**	amulets	**AELOPTU**	outleap
AEKMNSU	unmakes	**AELLRSU**	allures		muletas	**AELORRT**	realtor
AEKMPSU	makeups		laurels	**AELNNPR**	planner		relator
AEKMRRS	markers			**AELNNRS**	lanners	**AELORSS**	lassoer
	remarks	**AELLRTY**	alertly	**AELNNRT**	lantern		oarless
AEKMRSS	maskers	**AELLRVY**	ravelly	**AELNNRU**	unlearn	**AELORST**	Oastler
AEKMRST	markets	**AELLSST**	sallets	**AELNNTU**	annulet		oestral
AEKMRSU	kumeras	**AELLSSW**	lawless	**AELNOPT**	Lepanto	**AELORTV**	levator
AEKNNRT	Kärnten	**AELLSTT**	tallest		polenta	**AELORUU**	rouleau
AEKNOPS	Spokane	**AELLSTW**	wallets	**AELNOPU**	apolune	**AELORVY**	layover
AEKNPPR	knapper	**AELLSTY**	stalely	**AELNORS**	loaners		overlay
AEKNPRS	spanker	**AELLSVY**	valleys		orleans	**AELOSSS**	lassoes
AEKNPSU	unspeak	**AELLTUU**	ululate		Orléans	**AELOSSV**	salvoes
AEKNRRS	rankers	**AELLUVV**	valvule		reloans	**AELOSTV**	solvate
AEKNRSS	kranses				Salerno	**AELOSTZ**	zealots
AEKNRST	rankest	**AELMMNO**	mamelon	**AELNORU**	aleuron	**AELOSUZ**	zealous
	tankers	**AELMMNS**	almsmen	**AELNORV**	veronal	**AELOSVY**	saveloy
AEKNRSW	wankers	**AELMMOY**	myeloma	**AELNOST**	etalons	**AELOTTU**	toluate
AEKNRVY	knavery	**AELMMRS**	slammer	**AELNOUV**	von Laue	**AELOTUV**	ovulate
AEKNSSU	ankuses	**AELMMRT**	trammel	**AELNPPR**	preplan	**AELOTVV**	volvate
AEKOPRS	presoak	**AELMMST**	stammel	**AELNPPY**	playpen	**AELOTVY**	ovately
AEKOPTZ	Zátopek	**AELMMSY**	malmsey	**AELNPRS**	planers	**AELPPRS**	lappers
AEKORSS	soakers	**AELMNOR**	almoner		replans		rappels
AEKOSTV	voetsak	**AELMNOT**	lomenta	**AELNPRT**	planter		slapper
AEKOTTU	outtake		Montale		replant	**AELPPRY**	reapply
	takeout		telamon	**AELNPRY**	plenary	**AELPPST**	lappets
AEKPSSY	passkey	**AELMNPR**	lampern	**AELNPST**	planets	**AELPPSU**	appulse
AEKPSTU	uptakes		Perlman		platens		papules
AEKQRSU	quakers	**AELMNRU**	numeral	**AELNPTX**	explant	**AELPQSU**	plaques
AEKQSSU	squeaks	**AELMNRV**	Malvern	**AELNPTY**	aplenty	**AELPRRS**	parrels
AEKQSUY	squeaky	**AELMNSS**	manless		penalty	**AELPRSS**	lapsers
AEKRRST	starker	**AELMNST**	laments	**AELNQUU**	unequal	**AELPRST**	palters
AEKRSST	skaters		mantels	**AELNRRS**	snarler		persalt
	strakes		mantles	**AELNRST**	antlers		plaster
	streaks	**AELMNTT**	mantlet		rentals		platers
	taskers	**AELMOPR**	Palermo		saltern		psalter
AEKRSTY	Starkey	**AELMOPU**	ampoule		slanter		stapler
	streaky	**AELMOPY**	maypole		sternal	**AELPRSU**	perusal
AEKSWYY	keyways	**AELMORT**	molerat	**AELNRSY**	larneys	**AELPRSY**	parleys
AELLMNS	Mansell	**AELMORU**	morulae	**AELNRTU**	neutral		parsley
AELLMNU	lumenal	**AELMORV**	removal	**AELNRTV**	ventral		players
AELLMRS	smaller	**AELMORW**	Marlowe	**AELNRUV**	unravel		replays
AELLMRV	Marvell	**AELMOSS**	molasse		venular		sparely
AELLMST	mallets	**AELMOST**	maltose	**AELNSSU**	sensual	**AELPRTT**	partlet
AELLMSU	malleus	**AELMOSY**	amylose		unseals		platter
AELLMWX	maxwell	**AELMOTT**	matelot	**AELNSSW**	awnless		prattle
AELLNOV	novella	**AELMPRS**	lampers	**AELNSSX**	laxness	**AELPRTY**	peartly
AELLNPR	Parnell		palmers	**AELNSTT**	talents		pteryla
AELLNPY	penally		sampler	**AELNSTU**	eluants	**AELPSSS**	passels
AELLNUU	lunulae	**AELMPRT**	templar		lunates		sapless
			trample				
		AELMPRY	lamprey				

AELPSST	pastels	**AEMMMST**	mammets	**AEMORSW**	womeras	**AENOPRT**	operant
	staples	**AEMMNOT**	momenta	**AEMOSWY**	someway		pronate
AELPSSY	Plassey	**AEMMNTU**	amentum	**AEMOTTY**	Mayotte		protean
AELPSTT	peltast	**AEMMOPR**	mampoer	**AEMOTTZ**	mozetta	**AENOPSW**	weapons
AELPSTU	pulsate	**AEMMPRS**	spammer	**AEMPPRS**	mappers	**AENORRV**	overran
AELQRRU	quarrel	**AEMMRRS**	rammers		pampers	**AENORSS**	reasons
AELQRSU	Quarles	**AEMMRST**	stammer	**AEMPRRS**	prearms		senoras
AELQSSU	squeals	**AEMMRSY**	yammers	**AEMPRRT**	tramper	**AENORST**	atoners
AELQSSU	squeals	**AEMMRSZ**	mamzers	**AEMPRRW**	prewarm		senator
AELQSUZ	quezals	**AEMMSST**	stemmas	**AEMPRST**	stamper		treason
AELQTUZ	quetzal	**AEMMSTU**	maumets		tampers	**AENORSY**	Reynosa
AELRRSU	surreal	**AEMNNNU**	Neumann	**AEMPRSV**	revamps	**AENORTU**	Tourane
AELRRSW	warsler	**AEMNNOS**	mannose		vampers	**AENORVY**	Aveyron
AELRRTT	rattler	**AEMNNOT**	montane	**AEMPRSW**	swamper	**AENORWZ**	warzone
AELRRTW	trawler	**AEMNNOU**	noumena	**AEMPRTU**	tempura	**AENOSSS**	seasons
AELRSST	artless	**AEMNNOY**	many-one	**AEMPSTU**	Paestum	**AENOSTT**	notates
	lasters		one-many	**AEMPTTT**	attempt	**AENOSTU**	soutane
	salters			**AEMPTTU**	tapetum	**AENOUUV**	nouveau
	slaters	**AEMNNRS**	manners	**AEMQRSU**	marques	**AENPPRS**	nappers
AELRSSU	saurels	**AEMNNRT**	remnant		masquer		parpens
AELRSSV	salvers	**AEMNNSW**	newsman	**AEMQRUZ**	Márquez		snapper
	servals	**AEMNNTU**	unmeant	**AEMQSSU**	masques	**AENPRRT**	partner
	slavers	**AEMNOPP**	pampoen	**AEMRRRS**	marrers	**AENPRRW**	prawner
AELRSSW	warsles	**AEMNOPR**	manrope	**AEMRRRY**	remarry	**AENPRST**	arpents
AELRSSY	rayless	**AEMNOPS**	mopanes	**AEMRRST**	armrest		entraps
	slayers	**AEMNORR**	orramen		smarter		parents
AELRSTT	rattles	**AEMNORS**	enamors	**AEMRRSW**	rewarms		pastern
	starlet		moaners		warmers		trepans
	startle		oarsmen	**AEMRRTU**	erratum	**AENPRSW**	enwraps
AELRSTU	saluter		Ransome	**AEMRSST**	masters		spawner
AELRSTV	travels		San Remo		streams	**AENPRSZ**	panzers
	varlets	**AEMNORT**	tonearm	**AEMRSSU**	assumer	**AENPRTT**	pattern
	vestral	**AEMNORU**	enamour		Erasmus		reptant
AELRSTW	warstle		neuroma		masseur	**AENPRTW**	Antwerp
	wastrel	**AEMNORV**	overman	**AEMRSTT**	matters	**AENPRUV**	parvenu
AELRSTY	raylets	**AEMNORY**	anymore		smatter	**AENPSST**	aptness
AELRSUV	valuers	**AEMNOTT**	tomenta	**AEMRSTU**	matures	**AENPSSY**	synapse
AELRSVY	slavery	**AEMNPSU**	pneumas		strumae	**AENPSTT**	patents
AELRSWY	lawyers	**AEMNPTU**	putamen	**AEMRSTW**	warmest		pattens
AELRTTT	tartlet	**AEMNPTY**	payment	**AEMRSTY**	mastery	**AENPSTU**	peanuts
	tattler	**AEMNRRU**	manurer		streamy	**AENQSUY**	Quesnay
AELRTTU	tutelar	**AEMNRST**	martens	**AEMRTTY**	mattery	**AENRRSS**	snarers
AELRTUV	vaulter		smarten	**AEMRTTZ**	Zermatt	**AENRRST**	ranters
AELRTWZ	waltzer	**AEMNRSU**	manures	**AEMRTUU**	trumeau	**AENRRSW**	warners
AELSSST	tassels		surname	**AEMSSSU**	assumes		warrens
AELSSTT	stalest	**AEMNRTU**	trueman	**AEMSTTU**	mutates	**AENRRTY**	ternary
AELSSTU	salutes	**AEMNSST**	stamens	**AENNNPT**	pennant	**AENRSSS**	sarsens
	taluses	**AEMNSSU**	unseams	**AENNORY**	annoyer	**AENRSSW**	answers
AELSSTV	vestals	**AEMNSTY**	amnesty	**AENNOTU**	tonneau		rawness
AELSSTX	taxless	**AEMOORT**	tearoom	**AENNPRS**	spanner	**AENRSTT**	natters
AELSSUU	Sulu Sea	**AEMOORW**	woomera	**AENNRST**	tanners	**AENRSTU**	natures
AELSSVY	slaveys	**AEMOOST**	osteoma	**AENNRTT**	entrant		saunter
AELSTTT	tattles	**AEMOOSV**	vamoose	**AENNRTY**	tannery	**AENRSTV**	servant
AELSTTW	wattles	**AEMOPPR**	pampero	**AENNSSW**	wanness		taverns
AELSTTY	stately	**AEMOPRS**	Pasmore	**AENNSTT**	tannest		versant
AELSTUX	luxates	**AEMOPRT**	Patmore		tenants	**AENRSTW**	wanters
AELSTWZ	waltzes	**AEMOPST**	Petsamo			**AENRSUW**	unswear
AELSUVY	suavely	**AEMORRR**	armorer	**AENNSTW**	wannest	**AENRSWY**	yawners
AELSWZZ	swazzle	**AEMORRS**	remoras	**AENOOTZ**	entozoa	**AENRTTU**	taunter
AELTTTW	twattle		roamers	**AENOPPR**	propane	**AENRTTV**	Vättern
AELTTUX	textual	**AEMORRV**	overarm	**AENOPRS**	Pearson	**AENRTUV**	vaunter
AELTUVV	vulvate	**AEMORRW**	earworm		persona	**AENRUWY**	unweary
AELTUYY	Lyautey	**AEMORST**	maestro		Porsena		

Code	Word
AENSSST	assents
AENSSTU	unseats
AENSSTX	sextans
AENSSWY	sawneys
AENSTTU	attunes
	tautens
	tetanus
AENSTTX	sextant
AENSTUZ	Neusatz
AEOOPPS	papoose
AEOPPPS	pappose
AEOPPRV	approve
AEOPPSS	apposes
AEOPQSU	opaques
AEOPRRT	praetor
	prorate
AEOPRRV	vaporer
AEOPRST	esparto
	proteas
	seaport
AEOPRVY	overpay
AEOPSST	petasos
AEOPSTT	teapots
AEOPSTY	teapoys
AEOPSTZ	topazes
AEOQRTU	equator
	quorate
AEOQSUU	aqueous
AEORRRS	roarers
AEORRSS	soarers
AEORRST	roaster
AEORRSU	arouser
AEORSSS	Ross Sea
	saroses
	serosas
AEORSSU	arouses
AEORSTT	Rosetta
	rotates
	toaster
AEORSVW	avowers
	oversaw
AEORTUW	outwear
AEORTVX	overtax
AEOSTTU	outeats
AEOSUVZ	zouaves
AEPPRRS	rappers
AEPPRRT	trapper
AEPPRRW	wrapper
AEPPRSS	sappers
AEPPRST	tappers
AEPPRSU	paupers
AEPPRSW	swapper
AEPPRSY	prepays
	yappers
AEPPSTT	tappets
AEPPSTU	pasteup
	pupates
AEPQRTU	parquet
AEPRRSS	parsers
	raspers
	sparers
	sparser
AEPRRST	praters
AEPRRSU	parures
	uprears
AEPRRSW	rewraps
	warpers
AEPRRSY	prayers
	respray
	sprayer
AEPRRTU	rapture
AEPRSST	repasts
AEPRSSU	pausers
AEPRSSY	pessary
AEPRSTT	patters
	spatter
	tapster
AEPRSTU	Pasteur
	pasture
	uprates
AEPRSUX	aruspex
AEPRSUY	yaupers
AEPRSWY	yawpers
AEPRTXY	apteryx
AEPSSTU	petasus
AEPSTTU	upstate
AEQRRSU	squarer
AEQRRTU	quarter
AEQRSSU	squares
AEQRSTU	quarest
	quatres
AEQRSUV	quavers
AEQRTTU	quartet
AEQRUVY	quavery
AERRSST	arrests
	rasters
	starers
AERRSSU	assurer
AERRSTT	ratters
	restart
	starter
AERRSTV	starver
	Travers
AERRSTY	strayer
AERSSST	asserts
AERSSSU	assures
AERSSSW	wrasses
AERSSTT	staters
	tasters
AERSSTV	starves
AERSSTW	wasters
AERSSTY	estrays
	stayers
AERSSWY	sawyers
	swayers
AERSTTT	stretta
	tatters
AERSTTU	stature
AERSTTW	Stewart
	swatter
AERSTTY	yatters
AERSTUU	auteurs
AERSTUY	estuary
AERSTVY	strayve
AESSSTT	tassets
AESSTTT	attests
AESSTTU	statues
AESSTTV	vastest
AESSTUV	suavest
AESSTUY	eustasy
AESTTTU	statute
AFFFGIN	faffing
AFFFLLO	falloff
AFFGGIN	gaffing
AFFGINW	waffing
AFFGSUW	guffaws
AFFHIRS	raffish
AFFHLUU	Al Hufuf
AFFHMNO	Hoffman
AFFIKRS	kaffirs
AFFILOR	riffola
AFFILSY	falsify
AFFIMRS	affirms
AFFIMST	mastiff
AFFINRU	funfair
	ruffian
AFFINTY	tiffany
AFFIRST	tariffs
AFFKLOR	Karloff
AFFLOPY	playoff
AFFLOSY	layoffs
AFFNORS	saffron
AFFNORT	affront
AFFNOYZ	Zoffany
AFFOPSY	payoffs
AFGGGIN	fagging
AFGGOST	faggots
AFGGOTY	faggoty
AFGHFIS	hagfish
AFGHINS	fashing
AFGHINT	hafting
AFGHIRS	garfish
AFGHRTU	fraught
AFGIILN	failing
AFGIINR	fairing
AFGIJMS	figjams
AFGIKLN	flaking
AFGILLN	falling
AFGILMN	flaming
AFGILNO	foaling
	loafing
AFGILNR	flaring
AFGILNT	fatling
AFGILNU	gainful
AFGILNW	flawing
AFGILNY	anglify
	flaying
AFGILRU	figural
AFGIMNO	foaming
AFGIMNR	farming
	framing
AFGIMNY	magnify
AFGINNN	fanning
AFGINNW	fawning
AFGINRT	farting
	ingraft
	rafting
AFGINRY	fraying
AFGINST	fasting
AFGINTT	fatting
AFGINTU	fauting
AFGINTW	wafting
AFGIRTY	gratify
AFGKORT	koftgar
AFGLLLY	gallfly
AFGLLUY	fugally
AFGLNOS	flagons
AFGMNOR	frogman
AFGNOPU	Pang-fou
AFGORTY	Fogarty
AFGOSTU	fugatos
AFHIIRS	fairish
AFHIKLS	khalifs
AFHIKRS	kharifs
AFHIKUY	kufiyah
AFHILTW	halfwit
AFHIMNU	hafnium
AFHINOS	fashion
AFHIORS	oarfish
AFHIRST	ratfish
AFHISSW	sawfish
AFHISTT	fattish
AFHISWY	fishway
AFHKORY	hayfork
AFHKRTU	futhark
AFHLMRU	harmful
AFHLOOS	loofahs
AFHMNNO	Hofmann
AFHMOST	fathoms
AFHMOUZ	Mahfouz
AFHORSS	shofars
AFIILNS	finials
AFIILOR	airfoil
AFIILRS	Israfil
AFIILRT	airlift
AFIIMOS	mafiosi
AFIINRS	Frisian
AFIKKLR	Falkirk
AFIKLLY	flakily
AFIKLOT	flokati
AFIKNRT	ratfink
AFIKORU	Farouk I
AFILLNP	pinfall
AFILLNY	finally
AFILLPT	pitfall
AFILLPU	pailful
AFILLRY	frailly
AFILLSU	Ulfilas
AFILLUV	fluvial
AFILLUW	wailful
	Wulfila
AFILMNT	liftman
AFILMOR	aliform
AFILMOY	foamily
AFILMPY	amplify
AFILNPU	painful
AFILNTY	faintly
AFILORW	airflow

AFILOTX	foxtail	AFMORST	formats	AGGISZZ	zigzags	AGHIPRY	Phrygia
AFILQUY	qualify	AFMORTU	foumart	AGGKNOT	Gangtok	AGHIQSU	quaighs
AFILRRY	friarly	AFMOSTU	sfumato	AGGLOSW	Glasgow	AGHIRSY	grayish
AFILRTY	frailty	AFNORTU	Fortuna	AGGMORR	grogram	AGHJMNO	mahjong
AFILSSY	salsify	AFNPRSY	frypans	AGGMOST	maggots	AGHKOSW	goshawk
AFILSTU	fistula	AFNSSTU	sunfast	AGGMOTY	maggoty	AGHLLUZ	Zaghlul
AFILSTY	falsity	AFOOTWY	footway	AGGMRSU	muggars	AGHLMPU	galumph
AFILTTY	fattily	AFORRSW	farrows	AGGNOSU	Angus Og	AGHLNUY	nylghau
AFIMNRS	firmans	AFORRSY	orfrays	AGGNOSW	waggons	AGHLOOS	gasohol
AFIMOOS	mafioso	AFORSUV	favours	AGGNRSU	nuggars	AGHLOSU	goulash
AFIMRST	maftirs	AFOSTUU	fatuous	AGHHINS	hashing	AGHLSTY	ghastly
AFIMSSS	massifs	AGGGGIN	gagging	AGHHIWY	highway	AGHMNNU	Hungnam
AFIMSTT	fattism	AGGGIJN	jagging	AGHHMNU	Hamhung	AGHMORY	hygroma
AFIMSUV	fauvism	AGGGILN	lagging	AGHHNOW	Hwang Ho	AGHMRRU	murragh
AFIMSUZ	umfazis	AGGGIMN	magging	AGHHORT	Hogarth	AGHNNOU	houngan
AFIMTTY	mattify	AGGGINN	ganging	AGHHOSW	hogwash	AGHNNSU	hungans
AFINNOS	fanions		nagging	AGHHTUY	haughty	AGHNOSU	Songhua
AFINNOT	fontina	AGGGINR	ragging	AGHIILN	hailing	AGHNOTU	hangout
AFINNST	infants	AGGGINS	sagging	AGHIINQ	Qinghai		tohunga
AFINSSU	fusains	AGGGINT	tagging	AGHIKNN	hanking	AGHNPSU	hangups
AFINSTU	fustian	AGGGINU	gauging	AGHIKNR	harking	AGHNRST	thrangs
AFIORTU	faitour	AGGGINV	vagging	AGHIKNS	shaking	AGHNRUY	Hungary
AFISSTT	sitfast	AGGGINW	wagging	AGHIKNW	hawking	AGHNSTU	naughts
AFISSTY	satisfy	AGGHHIS	haggish	AGHIKSW	gawkish	AGHNSUY	gunyahs
AFISTTT	fattist	AGGHIMN	gingham	AGHILNO	haloing	AGHNTUY	naughty
AFISTUV	fauvist	AGGHINN	hanging	AGHILNR	harling	AGHOQSU	quahogs
AFITTUV	fatuity	AGGHINS	gashing	AGHILNS	lashing	AGHORTW	warthog
AFKKOUU	Fukuoka	AGGHISW	waggish	AGHILNT	halting	AGHRTUU	Thurgau
AFKLNRY	frankly	AGGHNOV	Van Gogh		lathing	AGIIJLN	jailing
AFKLNTU	tankful	AGGIILS	gilgais	AGHILNU	hauling	AGIIJNX	Jiangxi
AFKRRTU	fraktur	AGGIIMN	imaging		nilghau	AGIIKLN	laiking
AFLLOOY	aloofly	AGGIINN	gaining	AGHILNV	halving	AGIIKLT	glaikit
AFLLORU	florula	AGGIINT	gaiting	AGHILNW	whaling	AGIIKNS	Kiangsi
AFLLOSW	fallows	AGGIINV	gingiva	AGHILOT	Goliath		Si Kiang
AFLLOTU	fallout	AGGIKNW	gawking	AGHILRS	largish	AGIILMN	mailing
	outfall	AGGILLN	galling	AGHILRT	alright	AGIILNN	alining
AFLLPSU	lapfuls	AGGILNN	angling	AGHILST	alights		nailing
AFLLPUY	playful	AGGILNO	gaoling	AGHIMMN	hamming	AGIILNR	lairing
AFLLUWY	awfully	AGGILNR	glaring	AGHIMNR	harming		railing
AFLMNOU	moanful	AGGILNZ	glazing	AGHIMNS	mashing	AGIILNS	nilgais
AFLMORU	formula	AGGILOS	loggias		shaming		sailing
AFLMORW	wolfram	AGGIMMN	gamming	AGHIMRS	Grisham	AGIILNT	intagli
AFLMOST	flotsam	AGGINNN	ganning	AGHINOX	hoaxing		tailing
AFLMRSU	armfuls	AGGINNR	ranging	AGHINPP	happing	AGIILNV	vailing
	fulmars	AGGINNW	gnawing	AGHINPR	harping	AGIILNW	wailing
AFLMSUU	famulus	AGGINPP	gapping	AGHINPS	hasping	AGIILPT	pigtail
AFLNORT	frontal	AGGINPS	gasping		pashing	AGIILRU	Liguria
AFLNPSU	panfuls	AGGINPU	gauping		phasing	AGIILTY	agility
AFLNSTU	flaunts	AGGINPW	gawping		shaping	AGIIMMN	maiming
AFLNTUY	flaunty	AGGINRR	garring	AGHINRS	garnish	AGIIMMS	imagism
AFLOOTW	woolfat	AGGINRT	grating		sharing	AGIIMOR	origami
AFLOPTT	flattop	AGGINRU	arguing	AGHINRT	Granthi	AGIIMST	imagist
AFLORSV	flavors	AGGINRV	graving	AGHINSS	sashing	AGIINNP	paining
AFLORUV	flavour	AGGINRY	graying	AGHINST	hasting	AGIINNR	ingrain
AFLPRTY	flytrap	AGGINRZ	grazing	AGHINSU	anguish		raining
AFLPSTY	flypast	AGGINSS	gassing	AGHINSV	shaving	AGIINNS	Ningsia
AFLSUWY	swayful	AGGINST	staging	AGHINSW	hawsing		saining
AFMNOOT	footman	AGGINSW	swaging		shawing	AGIINPR	pairing
AFMNORT	formant	AGGINUU	Gauguin		washing	AGIINRS	airings
AFMNOST	fantoms	AGGINUY	Guiyang	AGHINTT	hatting		arising
AFMNRTU	turfman	AGGIORS	gorgias	AGHINTW	thawing		raising
AFMOORS	Formosa	AGGISWW	wigwags	AGHIOST	goatish	AGIINRZ	zingari

AGIINSV	visaing	AGILMNY	mangily
AGIINTW	waiting	AGILMOS	gliomas
AGIINTX	taxiing	AGILNNO	loaning
AGIINVV	vivaing	AGILNNP	planing
AGIINVW	waiving	AGILNNR	larning
AGIIORZ	Gorizia	AGILNNS	Lansing
AGIJMMN	jamming		linsang
AGIJNNN	Nanjing	AGILNOT	antilog
AGIJNNU	Nu Jiang	AGILNOV	Vignola
AGIJNPR	jarping	AGILNPP	lapping
AGIJNPU	jauping	AGILNPS	lapsing
AGIJNRR	jarring		palings
AGIJNSU	Jiangsu		sapling
AGIJNZZ	jazzing	AGILNPT	plating
AGIJSSW	jigsaws	AGILNPU	Pauling
AGIKKNY	yakking	AGILNPW	lapwing
AGIKLNR	larking	AGILNPY	playing
AGIKLNS	slaking	AGILNRY	angrily
AGIKLNT	talking		rangily
AGIKLNW	walking	AGILNSS	signals
AGIKLWY	gawkily	AGILNST	anglist
AGIKMNR	marking		lasting
AGIKMNS	makings		salting
	masking		slating
AGIKNNR	narking		staling
	ranking	AGILNSV	salving
AGIKNNT	tanking		slaving
AGIKNNW	wanking	AGILNSY	slaying
AGIKNNY	yanking	AGILNUV	valuing
AGIKNOS	soaking	AGILNUW	wauling
AGIKNOY	kayoing	AGILNWW	wawling
	okaying	AGILNWY	yawling
AGIKNPR	parking	AGILOPT	galipot
AGIKNQU	quaking	AGILORS	Argolis
AGIKNRS	sarking		girasol
AGIKNRT	karting		glorias
AGIKNSS	gaskins	AGILORW	airglow
AGIKNST	skating		Gwalior
	staking	AGILOST	galiots
	takings	AGILSTY	stagily
	tasking	AGILUYZ	gauzily
AGIKNSU	Kiangsu	AGIMMNR	ramming
AGIKNUW	wauking	AGIMMNS	samming
AGILLMU	gallium	AGIMNNN	manning
AGILLNP	palling	AGIMNNO	moaning
AGILLNU	lingual	AGIMNNW	wingman
AGILLNW	walling	AGIMNOR	roaming
AGILLNY	allying	AGIMNOT	moating
AGILLOR	gorilla	AGIMNPP	mapping
AGILLOT	galliot	AGIMNPR	ramping
AGILLRU	ligular	AGIMNPT	tamping
AGILLRY	Gillray	AGIMNPV	vamping
AGILLSU	ligulas	AGIMNRR	marring
	lugsail	AGIMNRS	armings
AGILMMN	lamming		margins
AGILMNO	loaming	AGIMNRT	migrant
AGILMNP	palming	AGIMNRW	warming
AGILMNR	marling	AGIMNSS	massing
AGILMNS	lingams	AGIMNST	masting
	maligns	AGIMNSU	amusing
AGILMNT	malting	AGIMNTT	matting
AGILMNU	mauling	AGIMORS	isogram

AGIMORU	gourami	AGINRTW	ringtaw
AGIMOSY	isogamy	AGINRVY	varying
AGIMSST	stigmas	AGINRZZ	razzing
AGIMSWW	wigwams	AGINSSS	assigns
AGINNNN	Nanning		sassing
AGINNNP	panning	AGINSST	Sitsang
AGINNNT	tanning	AGINSSV	savings
AGINNNW	wanning	AGINSSY	sayings
AGINNOT	atoning	AGINSTT	stating
AGINNOV	Avignon		tasting
AGINNPP	napping	AGINSTU	sauting
AGINNPT	panting	AGINSTV	staving
AGINNPW	pawning	AGINSTW	tawsing
AGINNRS	snaring		wasting
AGINNRT	ranting	AGINSTY	staying
AGINNRW	warning		stygian
AGINNRY	yarning	AGINSVY	Savigny
AGINNSW	awnings	AGINSWY	swaying
AGINNTW	wanting	AGINTTT	tatting
AGINNWY	yawning	AGINTTV	vatting
AGINOOO	oogonia	AGINTXY	taxying
AGINOOP	pogonia	AGINWWX	waxwing
AGINOPR	porangi	AGIOPPT	agitpop
AGINOPS	soaping	AGIORSU	giaours
AGINOPT	Paoting	AGIORSV	viragos
AGINORR	roaring	AGIOSTU	agoutis
AGINORS	signora	AGIOUUY	ouguiya
	soaring	AGIRSTU	guitars
AGINORT	orating	AGIRTVV	gravity
AGINORZ	zingaro	AGJKNUW	Kwangju
AGINOST	agonist	AGJLRUU	jugular
AGINOVW	avowing	AGJNOOR	jargoon
AGINPPR	rapping	AGJNORS	jargons
AGINPPS	sapping	AGKLMOU	Gomulka
AGINPPT	tapping	AGKLNOS	kalongs
AGINPPY	yapping	AGKLNSU	Lugansk
AGINPPZ	zapping	AGKLOSU	kagouls
AGINPRS	parings	AGKMNOP	kampong
	parsing	AGLLNOO	galloon
	rasping	AGLLNOS	gallons
	sparing	AGLLNTU	gallnut
AGINPRT	parting		nutgall
	prating	AGLLOOR	rogallo
AGINPRW	warping	AGLLOOT	galloot
AGINPRY	praying	AGLLOPS	gallops
AGINPSS	passing	AGLLOSS	glossal
AGINPST	pasting	AGLLOSU	gallous
AGINPSU	pausing	AGLLOSW	gallows
AGINPSY	spaying	AGLLOTT	glottal
AGINPTT	patting	AGLLPTY	glyptal
AGINPUY	yauping	AGLLRYY	gyrally
AGINPUZ	Zipangu	AGLMORU	glamour
AGINPWY	yawping	AGLNNOS	longans
AGINRRT	tarring	AGLNNOT	Langton
AGINRRW	warring	AGLNNSU	lungans
AGINRST	gastrin	AGLNOOO	ologoan
	ratings	AGLNOOS	lagoons
	staring	AGLNORU	languor
AGINRSU	Sungari	AGLNOSS	slogans
AGINRSV	ravings	AGLNOSU	lanugos
AGINRSY	syringa	AGLNOUV	Luoyang
AGINRTT	ratting	AGLNPSY	spangly

AGLNPUY	gunplay	AHHORTW	Haworth	AHIMNPS	shipman	AHLLOPS	shallop
AGLNRSU	langurs	AHHPPSU	huppahs	AHIMNTW	Whitman	AHLLOST	shallot
AGLNRTY	Langtry	AHHPTUZ	hutzpah	AHIMOPR	morphia	AHLLOSW	hallows
AGLNRUU	ungular	AHHRRSU	hurrahs	AHIMPSS	mishaps		shallow
AGLNTUY	gauntly	AHHSUZZ	huzzahs	AHIMPSV	vampish	AHLLOTY	loathly
AGLOOPY	apology	AHIIKNT	Haitink	AHIMRST	Mithras		tallyho
AGLOOST	galoots	AHIIKOT	Akihito	AHIMRSW	warmish	AHLLPSU	phallus
AGLOSSS	glossas	AHIIKRS	shikari	AHIMSSU	hassium	AHLLPYY	aphylly
AGLOSWY	logways	AHIIKRT	Kíthira	AHIMSWY	Yahwism	AHLLRST	thralls
AGLSYYZ	syzygal	AHIIMMS	Mishima	AHIMTUZ	azimuth	AHLLSTU	thallus
AGMMNOS	gammons	AHIIMNT	thiamin	AHIMTVZ	mitzvah	AHLMNPY	nymphal
AGMMNSU	magnums	AHIIMSS	sashimi	AHINNST	tannish	AHLMNSY	hymnals
AGMMORY	myogram	AHIIMST	samithi	AHINNTX	xanthin	AHLMNUY	humanly
AGMNNOR	grannom	AHIINPR	hairpin	AHINOST	Onitsha	AHLMORU	humoral
AGMNORS	morgans	AHIIPRS	airship	AHINOTZ	hoatzin	AHLMSTU	Malthus
AGMNORU	organum	AHIIQQR	Qiqihar	AHINPRS	harpins	AHLMSUU	hamulus
AGMNOST	amongst	AHIJMSW	Jahwism	AHINPSS	Spanish	AHLNOPR	alphorn
AGMNOTU	Montagu	AHIJOUZ	Jiazhou	AHINPST	hatpins	AHLNOPT	haplont
AGMNSTU	mustang	AHIJSTV	Jahvist	AHINPTY	Pythian	AHLNORT	althorn
AGMNSTY	gymnast	AHIKKLS	Khalkís	AHINRST	tarnish	AHLNOUZ	Lanzhou
	syntagm	AHIKLMS	Lakshmi	AHINRSU	unhairs	AHLOOPS	hooplas
AGMNSYY	syngamy	AHIKLRS	larkish	AHINRSV	varnish	AHLORST	harlots
AGMOPRR	program	AHIKLSY	shakily	AHINSSU	Hussain	AHLOTUU	outhaul
AGMORRW	ragworm	AHIKMNS	khamsin	AHINSSW	washins	AHLPRSY	sharply
AGMORSS	orgasms	AHIKMRS	kashmir	AHIOOST	atishoo	AHLPSSY	splashy
AGMORSV	vagroms	AHIKMSV	mikvahs	AHIOPXY	hypoxia	AHMMMOT	mammoth
AGMPRSU	grampus	AHIKMSW	mawkish	AHIORSS	orishas	AHMMTUZ	Thammuz
AGMPSUZ	gazumps	AHIKNRS	Krishna	AHIORSW	airshow	AHMNNSU	numnahs
AGNNNOO	nonagon	AHIKNSV	knavish	AHIPRSS	raspish	AHMNNTU	manhunt
AGNNNOT	Nantong	AHIKNSW	Hawkins	AHIPRST	harpist	AHMNNUU	unhuman
AGNNOOR	argonon	AHIKORS	karoshi	AHIPRSU	rupiahs	AHMNOPT	Hampton
	organon	AHIKOSU	Hokusai	AHIPRSW	warship		phantom
	Rangoon	AHIKOSW	kowhais	AHIPSSW	waspish	AHMNORY	harmony
AGNNTTU	Tan-tung	AHIKRSS	shikars	AHIPSTY	Pythias	AHMNOSS	hansoms
AGNOQSU	quangos	AHIKSSS	shiksas	AHIPSWW	whipsaw	AHMNOSU	Housman
AGNORRS	garrons	AHILLNT	anthill	AHIPSWY	shipway	AHMNOSW	showman
AGNORRT	grantor	AHILLRY	Hillary	AHIQSTU	Asquith	AHMNSTY	Nasmyth
AGNORSS	sarongs	AHILLSZ	zillahs	AHIRRSW	wirrahs	AHMOOPS	shampoo
AGNOSTU	nougats	AHILLTT	tallith	AHIRSTT	athirst	AHMOSTU	mahouts
	outsang	AHILMOP	omphali		rattish	AHMOSTZ	matzohs
	Sagunto	AHILMOU	haloumi		tartish	AHMOSWY	haymows
AGNRTUY	gauntry	AHILMTW	Whitlam	AHIRSTW	trishaw	AHMOTTZ	matzoth
AGOPPST	stopgap	AHILNOU	Anouilh		wraiths	AHMPSSU	smashup
AGORRTW	ragwort	AHILNPS	planish	AHISSTU	shiatsu	AHNNNOS	Shannon
AGORRTY	gyrator	AHILNSU	inhauls	AHISTTW	whatsit	AHNNOTY	Anthony
AGORSTU	ragouts	AHILNSY	linhays	AHISTWY	Yahwist	AHNOOPR	harpoon
AGORTTU	Tortuga	AHILORY	hoarily	AHKKORV	Kharkov	AHNOPRS	orphans
AGOSTTU	tautogs	AHILOTY	aliyoth	AHKKSSU	sukkahs	AHNORSS	shorans
AGOSUYZ	azygous	AHILOTZ	thiazol	AHKLNSY	Shankly	AHNORSX	saxhorn
AGRUUUY	Uruguay	AHILPPY	happily	AHKLTUY	Hakluyt	AHNORTW	Wharton
AGSSTUU	augusts	AHILPRT	philtra	AHKMNRU	Nkrumah	AHNOSTU	Shantou
AHHHISS	hashish	AHILPSY	apishly	AHKMORR	markhor	AHNOTTW	whatnot
AHHIKSW	hawkish	AHILSST	saltish	AHKMOSW	mohawks	AHNPPUY	unhappy
AHHIMNU	hahnium		tahsils	AHKNPSU	punkahs	AHNPRXY	pharynx
AHHISSV	shivahs	AHILSSV	slavish	AHKPSUU	hapukus	AHNRSVY	hryvnas
AHHISTT	shittah	AHILSTY	hastily	AHKRSTU	kashrut	AHNRVYY	hryvnya
AHHKOOS	hookahs	AHILSWY	washily		khurtas	AHNSSTU	sunhats
AHHKSTY	Shakhty	AHILTTZ	Hazlitt	AHLLMOS	mollahs	AHNSTUX	Xanthus
AHHLRSY	harshly	AHIMMRS	rammish	AHLLMSU	mullahs	AHOORSY	hoorays
AHHNSSU	Shushan	AHIMNNS	mannish	AHLLNSU	nullahs	AHOPRSS	phasors
AHHOORS	hoorahs	AHIMNNU	inhuman	AHLLOOS	halloos	AHOPRTY	atrophy
AHHOPRS	shophar	AHIMNOT	Othman I		holloas	AHOPTTW	towpath

AHORRSW	harrows	**AIILRST**	liatris	**AIKLSSU**	salukis	**AILMSSS**	missals
AHORSTT	throats	**AIILRTV**	trivial	**AIKLSSY**	skysail	**AILMSST**	mistals
AHORSTU	authors	**AIIMMNS**	animism	**AIKMNNS**	kinsman	**AILMSSY**	mislays
	Suharto	**AIIMMNX**	maximin	**AIKMNSS**	kamsins	**AILMSTU**	ultimas
AHORTTY	throaty		minimax	**AIKMNSW**	mawkins	**AILMSTY**	myalist
AHOSTUV	Shavuot	**AIIMNNV**	minivan	**AIKMOOS**	oomiaks	**AILNNOT**	antlion
AHOSTUW	outwash	**AIIMNOR**	amorini	**AIKMRUY**	Kumayri	**AILNNPU**	pinnula
	washout	**AIIMNPS**	pianism	**AIKMSUY**	Kismayu	**AILNORR**	Lorrain
AHPRRTY	phratry	**AIIMNPT**	timpani	**AIKNNNS**	nankins	**AILNOSS**	alisons
AHPSSTU	Thapsus	**AIIMNRT**	martini	**AIKNNPS**	napkins	**AILNOST**	latinos
AHQSSUY	squashy	**AIIMNSS**	simians	**AIKNNUY**	Kuan Yin		Saint-Lô
AHRRSUY	hurrays	**AIIMNST**	animist	**AIKNOSY**	Soyinka	**AILNOSV**	Novalis
AHRSSSU	hussars	**AIIMNTU**	minutia	**AIKNPRS**	kirpans	**AILNOUV**	Louvain
AHRSSTT	straths	**AIIMNTV**	vitamin		parkins	**AILNPST**	plaints
AHRSTTW	thwarts	**AIIMNZZ**	Mazzini	**AIKOORT**	rooikat	**AILNPSX**	salpinx
AHRSTWY	swarthy	**AIIMPRS**	impairs	**AIKOPST**	katipos	**AILNPTU**	nuptial
AHSSSTU	tussahs	**AIIMRST**	simitar	**AIKORST**	troikas	**AILNPTY**	inaptly
AIIIINV	Ivan III	**AIIMRUW**	Aruwimi	**AIKRTUZ**	zikurat		ptyalin
AIIIKKW	Waikiki	**AIIMSST**	samitis	**AILLLMO**	Maillol	**AILNQTU**	quintal
AIIILMS	Ismaili	**AIIMSSV**	Sivaism	**AILLLNO**	linalol	**AILNRST**	ratlins
AIIILMT	militia	**AIIMSSY**	myiasis	**AILLMNU**	luminal	**AILNRSU**	insular
AIIILNT	initial	**AIINNSZ**	zinnias	**AILLMOT**	maillot		urinals
AIIILPU	Paul III	**AIINNTY**	inanity	**AILLMPU**	Illampu	**AILNRTY**	riantly
AIIILVX	lixivia	**AIINORV**	Ivorian		pallium	**AILNSST**	instals
AIIJMNS	Jainism	**AIINOTT**	notitia	**AILLMSU**	alliums	**AILNSSV**	silvans
AIIJMOW	Iwo Jima	**AIINPRS**	aspirin	**AILLMSW**	sawmill	**AILNSTY**	nastily
AIIJNNT	Tianjin	**AIINPRT**	Patinir	**AILLNNO**	lanolin		saintly
AIIKLNN	Kalinin	**AIINPST**	pianist	**AILLNNT**	Tallinn	**AILNTTY**	nattily
AIIKMMS	skimmia	**AIINRSS**	raisins	**AILLNPY**	plainly	**AILOORW**	woorali
AIIKMNN	manikin	**AIINRST**	Istrian	**AILLNST**	install	**AILOPST**	apostil
AIIKNNT	tankini	**AIINRSY**	raisiny	**AILLORZ**	zorilla		topsail
AIIKOTW	Kowaiti	**AIINRTV**	vitrain	**AILLPRS**	pillars	**AILOPSY**	soapily
AIIKRRU	rauriki	**AIINRTZ**	triazin	**AILLPRU**	pilular	**AILOPTT**	talipot
AIIKSTU	Kutaisi	**AIINSST**	isatins	**AILLPUV**	pluvial	**AILOPTV**	pivotal
AIIKTUW	Kuwaiti	**AIINSSX**	sixains	**AILLQSU**	squilla	**AILOQTU**	aliquot
AIILLLP	lapilli	**AIINSTU**	Tunisia	**AILLRSV**	Villars	**AILORSS**	sailors
AIILLMN	liminal	**AIIOOTV**	Voiotia	**AILLSTY**	saltily	**AILORST**	rialtos
AIILLMS	Millais	**AIIOPRR**	a priori	**AILLTVY**	vitally		sliotar
AIILLMW	William	**AIIOPST**	Pistoia	**AILMMOR**	immoral		tailors
AIILLNV	villain	**AIIORTV**	Vitoria	**AILMMSY**	myalism	**AILORUX**	uxorial
AIILLQU	quillai		Vitória	**AILMMUW**	mwalimu	**AILORVY**	olivary
AIILLRY	Illyria	**AIIPSTW**	wapitis	**AILMNNO**	nominal	**AILOSSS**	assoils
AIILMMN	minimal	**AIJJMMS**	jimjams	**AILMNOP**	lampion	**AILOSSU**	São Luís
AIILMNT	intimal	**AIJLORS**	jailors	**AILMNOS**	malison	**AILOSTT**	altoist
AIILMNV	viminal	**AIJLORT**	tolarji		Soliman	**AILOTVY**	ovality
AIILMRS	similar	**AIJLYZZ**	jazzily	**AILMNOY**	alimony	**AILOVVV**	Vavilov
AIILMRY	miliary	**AIJNORT**	janitor	**AILMNPS**	plasmin	**AILPPSY**	sappily
AIILNOP	Lin Piao	**AIKKMNR**	kirkman	**AILMNPT**	implant	**AILPQSU**	pasquil
AIILNOS	liaison	**AIKKMOT**	komatik	**AILMNRS**	marlins	**AILPRSS**	spirals
AIILNOV	Livonia	**AIKKOPV**	kopiyka	**AILMOOV**	moviola	**AILPRSU**	parulis
AIILNPT	pintail	**AIKKSUZ**	zakuski	**AILMOPS**	lipomas		spirula
	Platini	**AIKLLNY**	lankily	**AILMOPT**	optimal	**AILPSST**	pastils
AIILNPU	nauplii	**AIKLMMN**	milkman	**AILMOPY**	Olympia		spitals
AIILNRY	rainily	**AIKLMNN**	linkman	**AILMOST**	somital	**AILPSSY**	Palissy
AIILNTU	nautili	**AIKLMNS**	malkins	**AILMOSY**	isoamyl	**AILPSTU**	Pilatus
AIILNTY	anility	**AIKLMOO**	Molokai	**AILMOZZ**	Milazzo	**AILPSTY**	pastily
AIILOPT	Li T'ai-	**AIKLNST**	Slatkin	**AILMPRU**	primula	**AILPSWY**	slipway
po		**AIKLNSY**	snakily	**AILMPST**	palmist		waspily
AIILORV	ravioli	**AIKLOST**	Sialkot	**AILMPSY**	misplay	**AILQTUY**	quality
AIILPRU	lipuria	**AIKLPWY**	pawkily	**AILMRST**	mistral	**AILRRVY**	rivalry
AIILQSU	siliqua	**AIKLQUY**	quakily		ramtils	**AILRSTT**	starlit
AIILQTU	Iqaluit	**AIKLRTT**	titlark	**AILMRSU**	simular	**AILRSTU**	rituals

151

AILRSTY	trysail	**AINNNST**	tannins
AILRTTU	titular	**AINNOOX**	Oxonian
AILRTTY	rattily	**AINNOPS**	saponin
AILRTUV	virtual	**AINNOSS**	nasions
AILSSSY	sassily	**AINNOST**	anoints
AILSSUV	visuals		nations
AILSSVZ	vizslas		onanist
AILSTTY	tastily	**AINNPSS**	inspans
AILSTUV	Vistula	**AINNPST**	snaptin
AILSTUW	lawsuit	**AINNQTU**	quinnat
AILTTTY	tattily		quintan
AILTTUU	Tutuila	**AINNRTU**	urinant
AIMMMUX	maximum	**AINNSTT**	instant
AIMMNSU	Samnium	**AINNTUY**	annuity
AIMMNTU	manumit	**AINOORT**	Ontario
AIMMORZ	Mizoram		oration
AIMMOSS	mimosas	**AINOOTV**	ovation
AIMMOST	atomism	**AINOOVV**	Ivanovo
AIMMSUX	maximus	**AINOPPT**	appoint
AIMNNOS	amnions	**AINOPRS**	parison
	mansion		porinas
	onanism		soprani
AIMNNOZ	Manzoni	**AINOPRT**	atropin
AIMNNSY	minyans	**AINOPSS**	passion
AIMNOOR	amorino	**AINOPSZ**	Spinoza
AIMNOPR	rampion	**AINOPTU**	opuntia
AIMNOPS	mopanis		utopian
AIMNOPT	maintop	**AINORST**	rations
	ptomain	**AINORSW**	warison
	tampion	**AINORTU**	rainout
AIMNORS	Romains		Tournai
AIMNOST	manitos	**AINOSSS**	Onassis
AIMNOTU	manitou	**AINOSSU**	suasion
	tinamou	**AINOSTT**	station
AIMNPRU	Manipur	**AINOSUX**	anxious
AIMNPSY	paynims	**AINOSVY**	synovia
AIMNPTY	tympani	**AINPPRS**	parsnip
AIMNRRU	murrain	**AINPQTU**	piquant
AIMNRST	martins	**AINPRSS**	sprains
AIMNRSU	Surinam	**AINPRST**	spirant
	uranism		spraint
AIMNRTU	Martinů	**AINPRSW**	inwraps
	natrium	**AINPRTU**	puritan
AIMNRTV	Martin V	**AINQRST**	qintars
	varmint	**AINQRTU**	Tarquin
AIMNRUU	uranium	**AINQRUY**	quinary
AIMNSTT	mattins	**AINQSTU**	asquint
AIMNSTU	manitus	**AINRRTY**	trinary
	tsunami	**AINRRUY**	urinary
AIMNSYZ	zanyism	**AINRSST**	instars
AIMOPST	impasto		strains
AIMORST	amorist	**AINRSSU**	Russian
AIMORSU	Maurois	**AINRSTT**	transit
AIMOSTT	atomist		Tristan
AIMPRRY	primary	**AINRSTU**	nutrias
AIMPRST	armpits	**AINRTTT**	titrant
	imparts	**AINRTUY**	unitary
AIMQRSU	marquis	**AINSSTT**	tanists
AIMRSST	tsarism	**AINSSTU**	issuant
AIMRSTU	Maurist		sustain
AIMRSTZ	tzarism	**AINSUUV**	Suiyüan
AIMSSTT	statism	**AINTTVY**	tantivy

AIOORRS	Rosario	**AKLRSVY**	valkyrs
AIOORSS	ariosos	**AKLUUWZ**	KwaZulu
AIOORST	Ariosto	**AKMNORW**	workman
AIOPRRT	airport	**AKMNSSU**	unmasks
AIOPRRU	Porirua	**AKMORST**	ostmark
AIOPRRZ	Pizarro	**AKMPRSU**	markups
AIOPRSV	paviors	**AKMQTUU**	kumquat
AIOPRTT	patriot	**AKMRSTU**	muskrat
AIOPRTY	topiary	**AKNNOOS**	nanooks
AIOPRUV	paviour	**AKNORSU**	korunas
AIOPSTU	utopias		Sukarno
AIORRRW	warrior	**AKNORSY**	ryokans
AIORRTT	traitor	**AKNORTU**	outrank
AIORSSV	saviors	**AKOOPRT**	partook
AIORSSY	Rossiya	**AKOORRS**	karroos
AIORSTV	travois	**AKOORST**	Sokotra
AIORSTY	ostiary	**AKORRTW**	artwork
AIORSUV	saviour	**AKORWWX**	waxwork
	various	**AKOSTWY**	towkays
AIPPRSU	priapus	**AKOUVYZ**	Yuzovka
AIPPSST	papists	**AKPSSSY**	Spassky
AIPRRTU	Tripura	**AKQSSUW**	squawks
AIPRSST	rapists	**ALLLOYY**	loyally
AIPRSSU	Prussia	**ALLMNOY**	allonym
AIPRSSW	ripsaws	**ALLMNPU**	pullman
AIPSSTW	pitsaws	**ALLMORY**	morally
	sawpits	**ALLMOSS**	slaloms
AIPZZZZ	pizzazz	**ALLMOSW**	mallows
AIRSSTT	artists	**ALLNOPS**	pollans
	straits	**ALLNOST**	Allston
	tsarist	**ALLNOTY**	tonally
AIRSSTU	aurists	**ALLNOYZ**	zonally
AIRSTTT	attrits	**ALLNRUU**	lunular
AIRSTVY	varsity	**ALLNSTY**	slantly
AISSSST	assists	**ALLNTUU**	ululant
AISSTTT	statist	**ALLOOPS**	apollos
AISSTTU	Statius	**ALLOOTX**	axolotl
AISTTVY	vastity	**ALLOPRS**	pallors
AISTUVY	suavity	**ALLOPRY**	payroll
AJKMNNU	junkman	**ALLOPSW**	wallops
AJKMNTU	muntjak	**ALLORWY**	rollway
AJKNSSY	janskys	**ALLORYY**	royally
AJLLRUY	jurally	**ALLOSSW**	sallows
AJLMORY	majorly	**ALLOSTW**	tallows
AJLNORU	journal	**ALLOSWW**	swallow
AJLOPPY	jaloppy		wallows
AJMNRUY	juryman	**ALLOSWY**	sallowy
AKKKOOS	kokakos	**ALLOTTY**	totally
AKKLRSY	skylark	**ALLOTWY**	tallowy
AKKNORY	Konakry	**ALLOTYY**	loyalty
AKKOOPS	pakokos	**ALLPRSU**	plurals
AKKOQSU	quokkas	**ALLPSSY**	psyllas
AKKSTUY	Yakutsk	**ALLQSSU**	squalls
AKLMNOO	Kolomna	**ALLQSUY**	squally
AKLNOSX	klaxons	**ALLRRUY**	rurally
AKLOSVV	Slavkov	**ALLRSTU**	lustral
AKLOTTU	outtalk	**ALLSSTU**	Sallust
AKLOTUW	outwalk	**ALLSUUY**	usually
	walkout	**ALMNNUY**	unmanly
AKLPSTU	uptalks	**ALMNOOP**	lampoon
AKLPSUW	walkups	**ALMNOPS**	plasmon
AKLRSTY	starkly	**ALMNOPW**	plowman

ALMNORU	unmoral		outlays
ALMNORY	almonry	ALOSTXY	oxysalt
ALMNOSS	salmons	ALOTTUU	Tutuola
ALMNOSU	monauls	ALPRRSU	larrups
	solanum	ALPRSSU	pulsars
ALMNOSY	Solyman	ALPRSSW	sprawls
ALMNOWY	womanly	ALPRSWY	sprawly
ALMNPSU	sunlamp	ALPSTUU	Plautus
ALMNSUU	alumnus	ALQSTUY	squatly
ALMOPPT	palmtop	ALRSSUU	russula
ALMORRU	morular	ALRSTUU	sutural
ALMORST	mortals	ALRSUUV	uvulars
ALMORSU	morulas	AMMNRUY	nummary
ALMORTU	tumoral	AMMOPTU	pomatum
ALMOSST	smaltos	AMMORST	marmots
ALMOSSW	Low Mass	AMMOSXY	myxomas
ALMOSTW	matlows	AMMRSUY	summary
ALMOTTU	mulatto	AMNNORS	normans
ALMRSTY	smartly	AMNNOSW	snowman
ALMRTUU	tumular	AMNNOSY	anonyms
ALMSSUY	alyssum	AMNNOTY	antonym
	asylums	AMNNOUU	Unamuno
ALMSTUU	umlauts	AMNNSTU	stannum
ALNNRSU	unsnarl	AMNOOPP	pompano
ALNNSUU	annulus	AMNOORS	maroons
ALNOOPT	platoon	AMNOORV	Romanov
ALNOORT	ortolan	AMNOOTT	ottoman
ALNOOSS	saloons	AMNOOTZ	matzoon
ALNOPPY	panoply	AMNOPPR	propman
ALNOPYY	polynya	AMNOPRY	paronym
ALNORUZ	zonular	AMNOPST	postman
ALNPTUY	unaptly		tampons
ALNSSTU	sultans	AMNOPTU	pantoum
ALNSSVY	sylvans	AMNORRS	marrons
ALNSTUW	walnuts	AMNORSS	ramsons
ALNSUUU	unusual		ransoms
ALOOPSS	saloops	AMNORST	Marston
ALOORTT	Tortola		matrons
ALOPPRS	poplars		transom
ALOPPRU	popular	AMNORSY	masonry
ALOPPRY	propyla	AMNORTU	romaunt
ALOPRRS	parlors	AMNOSTU	amounts
ALOPRRU	parlour		outmans
ALOPRST	patrols	AMNPSTY	tympans
	portals	AMNPTTU	Puttnam
ALOPRSU	parlous	AMNPTYY	tympany
ALOPRTW	Paltrow	AMNQTUU	quantum
ALOPSSU	spousal	AMNRTTU	tantrum
ALOPTUY	outplay	AMNSTTU	mutants
ALOQRRU	rorqual	AMNSTUU	autumns
ALOQRSU	squalor	AMOOORS	amoroso
ALOQSTU	loquats	AMOOPRS	prosoma
ALORRST	rostral	AMOOPRT	taproom
ALORSST	sortals	AMOORSU	amorous
ALORSSV	salvors	AMOORXY	oxymora
ALORSUV	louvars	AMOPSTT	topmast
ALORTUU	Rouault	AMORRST	mortars
ALORTWW	awlwort	AMORRSU	armours
ALORTYY	royalty	AMORRSW	marrows
ALOSTTU	outlast	AMORRUY	armoury
ALOSTUW	outlaws	AMORRWY	marrowy
ALOSTUY	layouts	AMPRSUW	warmups

AMRRSTY	martyrs		payouts
AMRRTYY	martyry	AOPTTUU	autoput
AMRSTTU	stratum	AOQRSTU	quartos
ANNOSST	sonants	AOQRTUY	Torquay
ANNOSTW	wantons	AORRSST	sartors
ANNOSTY	tannoys	AORRSWY	yarrows
ANNOTTU	Taunton	AORSSST	assorts
ANNPSSU	unsnaps	AORSSTT	stators
ANNRTYY	tyranny	AORSSTU	soutars
ANNSSTU	suntans	AORSSUV	savours
ANNTUUV	Nunavut	AORSSUY	ossuary
ANOOPRS	soprano	AORSUVY	savoury
ANOOPRT	patroon	AORUVVY	vouvray
ANOORST	ratoons	AOSTTUY	outstay
ANOORTT	Otranto	APPRRUU	purpura
	rattoon	APPRSUY	papyrus
ANOOSSS	Sassoon	APRSSSU	surpass
ANOPRRS	sporran	APRSTTU	startup
ANOPRSS	parsons		upstart
ANOPRST	partons	AQRSTUU	Suqutra
	patrons	AQSTTUY	squatty
	tarpons	ARSSSTU	Strauss
ANOPSTU	outspan	ARSSTTU	stratus
ANOPSUY	yaupons	BBBDELO	blobbed
ANORRSW	narrows		bobbled
ANORSSV	sovrans	BBBDELU	blubbed
ANORSTT	attorns		bubbled
ANORSUU	anurous	BBBEILS	bibbles
	uranous	BBBEIOS	bobbies
ANORWWY	wayworn	BBBEIRS	bibbers
ANPRSTU	suntrap	BBBELOS	bobbles
	unstrap	BBBELRU	blubber
ANPRSUW	unwraps		bubbler
ANRSSTU	sunstar	BBBELSU	bubbles
ANRSSUY	sunrays	BBBEORY	bobbery
ANRSTTU	truants	BBBGIIN	bibbing
ANRSTTY	tyrants	BBBGINO	bobbing
ANRSUWY	runways	BBBHSUU	hubbubs
AOOPPRS	apropos	BBBINOS	bobbins
	Sapporo	BBCCIKO	bibcock
AOOPRST	Atropos	BBCDEIR	cribbed
AOOPRTT	taproot	BBCDELO	cobbled
AOORRST	orators	BBCDELU	clubbed
AOORRSY	arroyos	BBCEEIR	berbice
AOORRTT	rotator	BBCEIRR	cribber
AOORRTU	Rotorua	BBCEKRU	Brubeck
AOORRTY	oratory	BBCELOR	clobber
AOOSTTT	tattoos		cobbler
AOPPPSU	pappous	BBCELOS	cobbles
AOPPRRT	rapport	BBCELRU	clubber
AOPPRST	apports	BBCEORS	cobbers
AOPRRST	parrots	BBCEOSW	cobwebs
	raptors	BBCEOTT	Cobbett
AOPRRSU	uproars	BBCGINO	cobbing
AOPRRSW	sparrow	BBCGINU	cubbing
AOPRRTY	portray	BBCHISU	cubbish
AOPRSST	pastors	BBCINOU	bubonic
AOPRSTW	postwar	BBCKLOU	Lubbock
AOPRSUV	vapours	BBCRSUY	scrubby
AOPRUVY	vapoury	BBDDEIL	dibbled
AOPSSTU	passout	BBDDERU	drubbed
AOPSTUY	autopsy	BBDEELP	pebbled

BBDEGIR Gibberd	**BBEIJRS** jibbers	mobbing	**BCDEHOT** botched
BBDEGLO gobbled	**BBEIKLS** kibbles	**BBGINOO** boobing	**BCDEHOU** debouch
BBDEGRU grubbed	**BBEILNR** nibbler	**BBGINOR** robbing	**BCDEIIO** biocide
BBDEGSU bedbugs	**BBEILNS** nibbles	**BBGINOS** gibbons	**BCDEIKR** bricked
BBDEHLO hobbled	**BBEILOS** bilboes	sobbing	**BCDEILM** climbed
BBDEIIM imbibed	lobbies	**BBGINPU** pubbing	**BCDEIMR** McBride
BBDEIKL kibbled	**BBEILOT** bibelot	**BBGINRU** rubbing	**BCDEIOS** bodices
BBDEILN nibbled	**BBEILQU** quibble	**BBGINSU** gubbins	**BCDEIRS** scribed
BBDEILO bilobed	**BBEILSW** wibbles	subbing	**BCDEKLO** blocked
lobbied	**BBEIMOS** bimboes	**BBGINTU** tubbing	**BCDEKLU** buckled
BBDEILR dibbler	**BBEIOOS** boobies	**BBGIOSU** gibbous	**BCDEKOR** bedrock
dribble	**BBEIOOT** bobotie	**BBHIMOS** Hobbism	**BCDEKOY** bockedy
BBDEILS dibbles	**BBEIRRS** bribers	mobbish	**BCDELOU** becloud
BBDEILW wibbled	**BBEIRRY** bribery	**BBHIOST** hobbits	**BCDEMRU** crumbed
BBDEINS snibbed	**BBEIRSU** rubbies	**BBHIOSY** yobbish	**BCDENOU** bounced
BBDEIOS dobbies	**BBEIRTU** tubbier	**BBHIRSU** rubbish	buncoed
BBDEIRS dibbers	**BBEISSU** busbies	**BBHNOOS** hobnobs	**BCDIIRU** rubidic
BBDEKNO knobbed	**BBEISTU** stubbie	**BBHRSUY** shrubby	**BCDINOW** cowbind
BBDELMU bumbled	**BBEJORS** jobbers	**BBIILST** biblist	**BCDIORW** cowbird
BBDELNO nobbled	**BBEJORY** jobbery	**BBIISUU** buibuis	**BCDIOSU** cuboids
BBDELOS bobsled	**BBEKLOS** blesbok	**BBIJMOO** jibboom	**BCDKORU** burdock
BBDELOW wobbled	**BBELLOY** bellboy	**BBIJNOS** jibbons	**BCDSTUU** subduct
BBDELRU burbled	**BBELLSU** bulbels	**BBIKOSS** skibobs	**BCEEEHN** beechen
BBDELSU slubbed	**BBELMRU** bumbler	**BBIKTUZ** kibbutz	**BCEEEHR** Beecher
BBDENSU snubbed	**BBELMSU** bumbles	**BBILLSU** bulbils	**BCEEEHS** beeches
BBDEORS dobbers	**BBELNOR** nobbler	**BBILNOY** nobbily	beseech
BBDEOSW swobbed	**BBELNOS** nobbles	**BBINNSU** nubbins	**BCEEELS** Celebes
BBDERRU drubber	**BBELNSU** nubbles	**BBINORS** ribbons	**BCEEFIN** benefic
BBDESTU stubbed	**BBELORS** slobber	robbins	**BCEEGIR** iceberg
BBDGIIN dibbing	**BBELORU** boerbul	**BBINORY** ribbony	**BCEEHIP** ephebic
BBDGINO dobbing	**BBELORW** wobbler	**BBIRTUY** rubbity	**BCEEHIT** hebetic
BBDGINU dubbing	**BBELORY** lobbyer	**BBJLOOW** blowjob	**BCEEHLS** belches
BBDIKSU dibbuks	**BBELOST** boblets	**BBKLNOY** knobbly	**BCEEHNR** bencher
BBDILRY dribbly	**BBELOSW** wobbles	**BBKOOOO** boobook	**BCEEHNS** benches
BBDINOS dobbins	**BBELRRU** burbler	**BBLLSUU** bulbuls	**BCEEHOU** bouchee
BBDIRUY rubbidy	**BBELRSU** burbles	**BBLOSUU** bulbous	**BCEEILR** Liberec
BBDKSUY dybbuks	lubbers	**BBLSTUY** stubbly	**BCEEIRS** escribe
BBEEENT Entebbe	**BBELSTU** stubble	**BBNNOOS** bonbons	**BCEEIRT** terebic
BBEEERR berbere	**BBEMNSU** benumbs	**BBNOOOS** bonobos	**BCEEKNU** buckeen
BBEEERU bebeeru	**BBEMORS** bombers	**BBNOORU** bourbon	**BCEEKRS** rebecks
BBEEIRW webbier	mobbers	**BBOOOOS** booboos	**BCEEKST** beckets
BBEELPS pebbles	**BBENRSU** snubber	**BBOOSSY** bossboy	**BCEEKSZ** zebecks
BBEFILR fribble	**BBEORRS** robbers	**BBOOSUU** boubous	**BCEEKTT** Beckett
BBEFIRS fibbers	**BBEORRY** robbery	**BBORSTU** burbots	**BCEEKUY** buckeye
BBEGILR glibber	**BBEORSS** sobbers	**BBRSSUU** suburbs	**BCEELOU** bouclee
gribble	**BBEORYY** yobbery	**BCCEILO** ecbolic	**BCEEMOS** becomes
BBEGINW webbing	**BBEPRUW** brewpub	**BCCEILU** cubicle	**BCEENOS** obscene
BBEGIOS gibbose	**BBERRSU** rubbers	**BCCEILY** bicycle	**BCEHINR** birchen
BBEGIRS gibbers	**BBERRUY** rubbery	**BCCEMOR** crombec	**BCEHINT** benthic
BBEGIST gibbets	**BBERSTU** tubbers	**BCCILOU** bucolic	**BCEHIOR** brioche
BBEGLOR gobbler	**BBFGIIN** fibbing	**BCCINOO** obconic	**BCEHIOT** biotech
BBEGLOS gobbles	**BBFGINO** fobbing	**BCCISUU** succubi	**BCEHIRS** birches
BBEGMOR Bomberg	**BBGGIIN** gibbing	**BCCMOOX** coxcomb	**BCEHIST** bitches
BBEGOST gobbets	**BBGGINO** gobbing	**BCCMSUU** succumb	**BCEHISW** Wisbech
BBEGRRU grubber	**BBGHINO** hobbing	**BCCNOOR** corncob	**BCEHITW** bewitch
BBEHIOS hobbies	**BBGIIJN** jibbing	**BCDEEHL** belched	**BCEHLRU** blucher
BBEHISU hubbies	**BBGIINN** nibbing	**BCDEEHN** benched	Blücher
BBEHLOR hobbler	**BBGIINR** bribing	**BCDEEIL** decibel	**BCEHNRU** Buchner
BBEHLOS hobbles	ribbing	**BCDEEKS** bedecks	Büchner
BBEIILS bilbies	**BBGIJNO** jobbing	**BCDEHIR** birched	**BCEHNSU** bunches
BBEIIMR imbiber	**BBGILNO** lobbing	**BCDEHIT** bitched	**BCEHORT** botcher
BBEIIMS imbibes	**BBGIMNO** bombing	**BCDEHNU** bunched	**BCEHORU** Boucher

BCEHORW	cowherb	BCGIMNO	combing	BDDEFOR	Bedford	BDEELOW	elbowed
BCEHOST	botches	BCGINRU	curbing	BDDEGIN	bedding	BDEELRT	trebled
BCEHOSU	subecho	BCGORSU	coburgs	BDDEGIR	bridged	BDEELSS	blessed
BCEHRSU	cherubs	BCGORSY	cyborgs	BDDEGLU	bludged	BDEEMOS	besomed
BCEHRTU	butcher	BCHHORS	borshch	BDDEIIR	birdied	BDEEMOW	embowed
BCEHSTU	butches	BCHIIOP	biochip	BDDEIIS	biddies	BDEEMRU	embrued
BCEIIKR	brickie	BCHIKOU	chibouk	BDDEILN	blinded	BDEEMSU	bemused
BCEIIKS	bickies	BCHIKSU	buckish	BDDEILR	bridled		embused
BCEIKLO	blockie	BCHIMOR	rhombic	BDDEIRR	redbird	BDEENOR	enrobed
BCEIKLR	brickle	BCHINOR	bronchi	BDDEIRS	bidders	BDEENPR	prebend
BCEIKRS	bickers	BCHIOPR	pibroch	BDDEISU	buddies	BDEENRS	benders
BCEIKRW	Berwick	BCHIOPS	phobics	BDDELNU	bundled	BDEENRT	Derbent
BCEIKSU	buckies	BCHLOTY	blotchy	BDDELOO	bloodled	BDEEORR	rebored
BCEILMO	embolic	BCHNOOR	broncho		boodled	BDEEORS	bedsore
BCEILMR	climber	BCHORST	borscht	BDDELOR	broddle		sobered
BCEILOR	bricole	BCIIKLN	niblick	BDDELOU	doubled	BDEERUW	burweed
	corbeil	BCIILMU	bulimic	BDDELSU	buddles	BDEESSU	debuses
BCEIMNO	combine	BCIILSY	sibylic	BDDENOU	bounded	BDEFFLU	bluffed
BCEIMOR	microbe	BCIINOS	bionics	BDDEOOR	brooded	BDEFLMU	fumbled
BCEINOZ	benzoic	BCIIOPS	biopics	BDDEOTU	doubted	BDEGGLO	boggled
BCEINRU	brucine	BCIIOPT	bioptic	BDDERSU	redbuds	BDEGHIT	bedight
BCEIORS	corbies	BCIISTU	biscuit	BDDESUU	subdued		bighted
BCEIRRS	scriber	BCIKKRU	Kubrick	BDDGIIN	bidding	BDEGILO	obliged
BCEIRSS	scribes	BCIKNOS	kincobs	BDDGINU	budding	BDEGINN	bending
BCEIRSU	suberic	BCILMPU	plumbic	BDDISSU	disbuds	BDEGINO	Bendigo
BCEISST	bisects	BCILOOR	bicolor	BDEEEEZ	Zebedee	BDEGINR	breding
BCEJOST	objects	BCIMNOU	umbonic	BDEEELP	bleeped	BDEGIOO	boogied
BCEJSTU	subject	BCINORU	rubicon	BDEEELR	bleeder	BDEGIOS	bodgies
BCEKLLO	bellock	BCINSUU	incubus	BDEEELT	beetled	BDEGIOT	bigoted
BCEKLOR	blocker	BCIOORT	robotic	BDEEELV	beveled	BDEGIRS	begirds
BCEKLRU	buckler	BCIORST	strobic	BDEEERR	breeder		bridges
BCEKLSU	buckles	BCIRRSU	rubrics	BDEEERZ	breezed	BDEGIRT	Bridget
BCEKNOR	Brocken	BCIRTUV	butyric	BDEEFIR	briefed	BDEGISU	budgies
BCEKNOS	beckons	BCISSTU	cubists		debrief	BDEGLNU	blunged
BCEKORT	brocket	BCJKMUU	jumbuck		fibered		bungled
BCEKORU	roebuck	BCKLLOU	bullock	BDEEGOY	bogeyed	BDEGLRU	bludger
BCEKOSU	buckoes	BCKLNOU	unblock	BDEEHOV	behoved		burgled
BCEKRSU	buckers	BCKOTTU	buttock	BDEEHRT	berthed	BDEGLSU	bludges
BCEKSTU	buckets	BCLMOOO	Colombo	BDEEILL	bellied	BDEGOOY	goodbye
BCELLOW	cowbell	BCLMOOU	coulomb		libeled	BDEGRSU	redbugs
BCELLSU	subcell	BCLMRUY	crumbly	BDEEILO	El Obeid	BDEGSTU	budgets
BCELMNU	clubmen	BCLOOSU	colobus	BDEEILS	Delibes	BDEHINS	behinds
BCELMRU	clumber	BCMORSY	corymbs		edibles	BDEHINT	Beth Din
	crumble	BCMOSTU	combust	BDEEILV	bedevil	BDEHIRT	birthed
BCELMSU	scumble	BCNOORS	broncos	BDEEIMR	bemired	BDEHLMU	humbled
BCELNOZ	Coblenz	BCNOSTU	cobnuts	BDEEIMT	bedtime	BDEHLOS	beholds
BCELORS	corbels	BCOOSWY	cowboys	BDEEINR	bendier	BDEHLSU	blushed
BCELORT	Colbert	BCOOTTY	boycott		inbreed	BDEHMTU	thumbed
BCELOSU	boucles	BCOSTTU	Cottbus	BDEEINZ	bedizen	BDEHOST	hotbeds
BCEMNOW	Newcomb	BDDDEIU	buddied	BDEEIRR	berried	BDEHRSU	brushed
BCEMOOS	coombes	BDDDELU	buddled	BDEEIRS	bredies	BDEIIRS	birdies
BCEMORS	combers	BDDEEES	seedbed		derbies		bridies
BCEMRRU	crumber	BDDEEEW	bedewed	BDEEISS	besides	BDEIKLN	blinked
BCEMRSU	cumbers	BDDEEIL	bielded	BDEEIST	betides	BDEIKRS	brisked
BCENORU	bouncer	BDDEEIS	bedside	BDEEIVV	bevvied	BDEILLU	bullied
BCENOSU	bounces	BDDEEIT	betided	BDEEJLS	djebels	BDEILMW	wimbled
BCEORSU	obscure		debited	BDEEKRU	rebuked	BDEILNR	blinder
BCEORTU	Courbet	BDDEELN	blended	BDEELLS	bedells		brindle
BCESSTU	subsect	BDDEEOS	Beddoes	BDEELNR	blender	BDEILOR	broiled
BCFSSUU	subfusc	BDDEERS	bedders		Brendel	BDEILOS	bolides
BCGIKNO	bocking	BDDEESU	debused	BDEELNS	blendes	BDEILPP	blipped
BCGIKNU	bucking	BDDEETU	debuted	BDEELOV	beloved	BDEILRR	bridler

155

BDEILRS	bridles
BDEILRT	driblet
BDEILRU	builder
	rebuild
BDEILTZ	blitzed
BDEIMMR	brimmed
BDEIMNR	birdmen
BDEIMOR	bromide
BDEIMRU	imbrued
BDEINOU	bedouin
BDEINRS	binders
	rebinds
BDEINRY	bindery
BDEINSU	beduins
	bundies
BDEIORR	broider
BDEIORS	borides
	disrobe
BDEIORT	orbited
BDEIORV	overbid
BDEIORZ	zebroid
BDEIOSY	disobey
BDEIRRS	birders
BDEIRST	bestrid
BDEIRSU	bruised
BDEIRSV	verbids
BDEIRTU	bruited
BDEISST	bedsits
BDEISSU	subside
BDEISTU	subedit
BDEISUW	Budweis
BDEITUY	dubiety
BDEJLMU	jumbled
BDEJORU	objured
BDEKNOO	bookend
BDEKNOU	bunkoed
BDEKNSU	debunks
BDEKOOR	brooked
BDELLOR	bedroll
BDELMMU	mumbled
BDELMOO	bloomed
BDELMPU	plumbed
BDELMRU	rumbled
BDELMTU	tumbled
BDELNNU	Blunden
BDELNOR	blonder
BDELNOS	blondes
BDELNRU	blunder
	bundler
BDELNSU	bundles
BDELNTU	blunted
BDELOOS	boodles
BDELORS	bordels
BDELORU	boulder
	doubler
BDELORW	lowbred
BDELOST	boldest
BDELOSU	bloused
	doubles
BDELOTT	blotted
	bottled
BDELOTU	boulted
	doublet
BDELRRU	blurred
BDELRTU	blurted
BDELSTU	bustled
BDEMOOR	bedroom
	boredom
	broomed
BDEMOOS	bosomed
BDEMSTU	dumbest
BDENNOU	bounden
	unboned
BDENNSU	unbends
BDENORU	bounder
	rebound
BDENORW	browned
BDENORZ	bronzed
BDENOUW	unbowed
BDENRSU	burdens
BDENSTU	subtend
BDEOORR	brooder
BDEOOST	boosted
BDEOPST	bedpost
BDEORRS	borders
BDEORRU	bordure
BDEORSS	desorbs
BDEORST	debtors
	strobed
BDEORSU	rosebud
BDEORSW	browsed
BDEORTU	doubter
	obtrude
	outbred
	redoubt
BDEORUV	overdub
BDERRSU	deburrs
BDESSUU	subdues
BDESSUY	Debussy
BDFIILY	bifidly
BDFIIOR	fibroid
BDFIORS	forbids
BDGGINO	bodging
BDGGINU	budging
BDGGLOU	goldbug
BDGIINN	binding
BDGIINR	birding
BDGIIOO	gobioid
BDGILOO	globoid
BDGINNO	bonding
BDGINOS	bodings
BDGINOY	bodying
BDGLLOU	bulldog
BDGOOOW	bogwood
BDHIINS	bhindis
	bindhis
BDHIOSU	bushido
BDHIRSY	hybrids
BDHOOOY	boyhood
BDIILOR	oilbird
BDIILOS	libidos
BDIIMRS	midribs
BDIISTT	tidbits
BDIKNOS	bodkins
BDILLNY	blindly
BDILNNO	Blondin
BDILPUU	buildup
	upbuild
BDIMNPU	dumpbin
BDIMNUU	dubnium
BDINNOU	inbound
BDINNSU	unbinds
BDINOOR	Borodin
	bridoon
BDINOSU	boudins
BDINRSU	sunbird
BDINRUU	Burundi
BDINSTU	dustbin
BDIOOOV	obovoid
BDIOORU	boudoir
BDIOOST	biodots
BDIOSTU	outbids
BDIOSUU	dubious
BDIRSTU	disturb
BDISSUY	subsidy
BDKLOOS	kobolds
BDKORSY	Brodsky
BDLNOOS	doblons
BDLOOOX	oxblood
BDNNOUU	unbound
BDNOORU	bourdon
BDNOOWW	downbow
BDNORUW	rubdown
BDNOSTU	obtunds
BDOOOWX	boxwood
BDOORRY	Boyd Orr
BDORSWY	bywords
BDRSUUY	Sudbury
BEEEFIR	beefier
	freebie
BEEEFLR	feebler
BEEEFTW	webfeet
BEEEGIS	besiege
BEEEGKL	geelbek
BEEEGNR	breenge
BEEEGRR	bergere
BEEEHIV	beehive
BEEEHNS	shebeen
BEEEHPS	ephebes
BEEEILL	libelee
BEEEILN	beeline
BEEEILV	believe
BEEEIRR	beerier
BEEEJLW	bejewel
BEEEJLZ	jezebel
BEEEKLL	belleek
BEEELPR	bleeper
BEEELPS	Peebles
BEEELRV	beveler
BEEELST	beetles
BEEEMRS	berseem
BEEEMSS	beseems
BEEENNZ	benzene
BEEENTW	between
BEEEPRS	beepers
BEEERSZ	beezers
	breezes
BEEFGIN	beefing
BEEFILR	febrile
BEEFILS	beliefs
BEEFILY	beefily
BEEFINT	benefit
BEEFIRR	briefer
BEEFLOR	Froebel
BEEFLTY	beetfly
BEEGGNU	geebung
BEEGILL	legible
BEEGILO	obligee
BEEGILS	beigels
BEEGILU	beguile
BEEGIMR	begrime
BEEGINP	beeping
BEEGINR	bigener
	breinge
BEEGINT	beignet
BEEGINU	beguine
BEEGISY	bigeyes
BEEGJRS	Esbjerg
BEEGLMR	Lemberg
BEEGNRS	bergens
BEEGNRZ	Bregenz
BEEGRSU	burgees
BEEHIRR	herbier
BEEHLRT	blether
BEEHNRS	Behrens
BEEHNTU	Beuthen
BEEHOOV	behoove
BEEHOPS	phoebes
BEEHOSV	behoves
BEEHRRT	Herbert
BEEHRST	sherbet
BEEHRSW	beshrew
	Hebrews
BEEHRTY	thereby
BEEHRWY	whereby
BEEHSST	behests
BEEHSTY	bheesty
BEEIJLU	jubilee
BEEIKLW	weblike
BEEILLS	bellies
BEEILMP	epiblem
BEEILNR	berline
BEEILOS	obelise
BEEILOZ	obelize
BEEILRS	beliers
BEEILRY	beerily
BEEIMRS	bemires
	biremes
BEEIMST	betimes
BEEINNS	bennies
BEEINNZ	benzine
BEEINOS	ebonies
	ebonise
BEEINOT	ebonite
BEEINOZ	ebonize
BEEINRZ	zebrine
BEEIOSU	Eusebio
BEEIQUZ	bezique

BEEIRRS	berries		subsere	BEGILNT	belting	BEHILRT	Hilbert
BEEIRRV	brevier	BEERSTT	betters	BEGILNU	blueing	BEHILSU	blueish
BEEIRSZ	Béziers	BEERSTV	brevets	BEGILNY	belying	BEHILSW	weblish
BEEIRTZ	Bizerte	BEERSTW	bestrew	BEGILOR	Broglie	BEHIMOR	bioherm
BEEISTW	website		webster		obliger	BEHINOP	hipbone
BEEISVV	bevvies	BEERTTU	burette	BEGILOS	obliges	BEHINOR	Hiberno-
BEEJMOR	Bermejo	BEESSTU	bustees	BEGILRS	gerbils	BEHINRU	Niebuhr
BEEJSSU	bejesus	BEFFIRS	biffers	BEGILRT	gilbert	BEHINST	henbits
BEEKNOT	betoken	BEFFLRU	bluffer	BEGILST	giblets	BEHIOST	bothies
BEEKOPS	bespoke	BEFFRSU	buffers	BEGINOS	biogens	BEHIOTW	howbeit
BEEKORS	reeboks		rebuffs	BEGINOY	obeying	BEHIRRT	rebirth
BEEKRRS	berserk	BEFFSTU	buffets	BEGINNR	bringer	BEHIRSU	bushier
BEEKRRU	rebuker	BEFGIIL	filibeg	BEGINRW	brewing		Bushire
BEEKRSU	rebukes	BEFGIIR	Fibiger	BEGINRY	breying	BEHISSU	bushies
BEELLMN	bellmen	BEFGIRU	firebug	BEGINSS	bigness	BEHKKOO	kokobeh
BEELMMS	emblems	BEFILMS	fimbles	BEGINST	besting	BEHKNOO	Hoboken
BEELMOW	embowel	BEFILNU	bluefin	BEGINSU	beguins	BEHKORS	rheboks
BEELMRT	tremble	BEFILOS	foibles	BEGINTT	betting	BEHLLOP	bellhop
BEELMWY	Wembley	BEFILOU	biofuel	BEGIOOS	boogies	BEHLLOX	hellbox
BEELNNO	ennoble	BEFILRT	filbert		goobies	BEHLMRU	humbler
BEELNOZ	benzole	BEFILRY	briefly	BEGIOSU	bougies	BEHLMSU	humbles
BEELNTY	Bentley	BEFILSU	fusible	BEGIRSU	Bergius	BEHLORT	brothel
BEELNUX	Benelux		subfile	BEGISSU	gibuses	BEHLRSU	blusher
BEELOTY	eyebolt	BEFINOR	bonfire	BEGKMOS	gemsbok		burhels
BEELRST	belters	BEFIOOR	boofier	BEGLLOU	globule	BEHLSSU	blushes
	trebles	BEFIORX	firebox	BEGLMRU	grumble		bushels
BEELRSY	berleys	BEFIRST	bifters	BEGLMUU	bluegum	BEHMNSU	bushmen
BEELSSS	blesses	BEFIRSU	fubsier	BEGLNOS	belongs	BEHMOOY	homeboy
BEELSSW	webless	BEFIRVY	verbify	BEGLNRU	blunger	BEHMORS	hombres
BEEMMRS	members	BEFITUX	tubifex		bungler	BEHMOST	Tshombe
BEEMNPT	benempt	BEFLLWY	flyblew	BEGLNSU	blunges	BEHMNOT	benthon
BEEMORW	embower	BEFLMRU	fumbler		bungles	BEHNORU	Bonheur
BEEMRSU	Burmese	BEFLMSU	fumbles	BEGLOOS	globose	BEHNOST	benthos
	embrues	BEFLOOS	befools	BEGLOOT	bootleg	BEHNPRU	Hepburn
BEEMSSU	bemuses	BEFLORT	Belfort	BEGLOST	goblets	BEHNRTU	burthen
	embuses	BEFLOSU	befouls	BEGLOSW	bowlegs	BEHOORT	theorbo
BEENNST	bennets	BEFOORR	forbore		weblogs	BEHOPRT	potherb
BEENNTT	Bennett	BEFOOTW	webfoot	BEGLOUY	Beyoğlu	BEHOPSU	phoebus
BEENORR	enrober	BEGGGIN	begging	BEGLRSU	buglers	BEHORRT	brother
BEENORS	boreens	BEGGIOR	boggier		burgles	BEHORST	bothers
	enrobes	BEGGIRU	buggier	BEGMORR	Romberg	BEHORTT	betroth
BEENOST	beentos	BEGGIST	biggest	BEGNNOY	Bonynge	BEHRRSU	brusher
	boneset	BEGGISU	buggies	BEGNOOS	bongoes	BEHRRTU	Thurber
BEENOTY	Toynbee	BEGGLOS	boggles	BEGNORS	Bergson	BEHRSSU	brushes
BEENSTU	subteen	BEGGMOR	Gomberg	BEGNORU	burgeon	BEIIKLN	niblike
BEENSUV	subvene	BEGGORS	boggers	BEGNOSY	bygones	BEIIKLR	riblike
BEEOOST	bootees	BEGGRSU	buggers	BEGNOTT	bettong	BEIIKRS	birkies
BEEOPPS	bopeeps	BEGGRUY	buggery	BEGNRSU	bungers	BEIILLN	Bellini
BEEORRS	rebores	BEGHINR	Behring	BEGNRSU	bungers	BEIILLS	billies
	soberer	BEGHLOR	Holberg	BEGOORS	goobers	BEIILRS	risible
BEEORRU	bourree	BEGHRRU	burgher	BEGORSU	Bourges	BEIILSV	visible
BEEORSV	observe	BEGIIJN	Beijing		brogues	BEIINNR	Bernini
	obverse	BEGIILR	bilgier	BEGRRSU	burgers	BEIINOT	niobite
	verbose	BEGIINN	inbeing	BEGRSSU	burgess	BEIINRR	brinier
BEEORSY	obeyers	BEGIINR	breiing	BEHIITX	exhibit	BEIINST	stibine
BEEORWY	eyebrow	BEGIINS	bingies	BEHIKKS	Bishkek	BEIIOTT	biotite
BEEQSTU	bequest	BEGIKNR	kerbing	BEHIKLO	hoblike	BEIIRTT	bittier
BEERRSV	reverbs	BEGILLN	belling	BEHIKNT	bethink	BEIISTT	Tibesti
BEERRSW	brewers	BEGILLY	legibly	BEHILLX	Bexhill	BEIISTV	vibiest
BEERRWY	brewery	BEGILMU	Belgium	BEHILMS	blemish	BEIISVV	bivvies
BEERSST	breests	BEGILNO	ignoble	BEHILMT	thimble	BEIISZZ	bizzies
BEERSSU	rebuses	BEGILNS	bingles	BEHILNO	Holbein	BEIJLRS	jerbils
				BEHILOS	bolshie		

BEIKKLU	Kubelik	**BEINNOR**	bonnier	**BEKORRS**	brokers	**BELOSTU**	boletus
BEIKLNR	blinker	**BEINNOS**	benison	**BEKOSST**	boskets	**BELRRSU**	burlers
BEIKLOS	obelisk	**BEINNOZ**	benzoin	**BEKRSSU**	buskers	**BELRSTU**	bluster
BEIKLOX	boxlike	**BEINNSU**	bunnies	**BELLNPU**	bullpen		bustler
BEIKLRS	bilkers	**BEINOOT**	eobiont	**BELLOSU**	boulles		butlers
BEIKLRU	bulkier	**BEINORT**	bornite		lobules		subtler
BEIKNRS	brisken	**BEINORW**	brownie		soluble	**BELRSUU**	subrule
BEIKOOS	bookies	**BEINOST**	boniest	**BELLOSW**	bellows	**BELRSUY**	burleys
BEIKORS	boskier	**BEINOSV**	bovines		Boswell	**BELRTUY**	butlery
BEIKRRS	brisker	**BEINOSX**	bonxies	**BELLOUV**	voluble	**BELSSTU**	bustles
BEIKRST	brisket	**BEINOTT**	bottine	**BELLRRU**	burrell		sublets
BEIKSTV	Vitebsk	**BEINRSU**	suberin	**BELLSSU**	Bussell	**BELSTUU**	tubules
BEILLST	billets	**BEINRSY**	byrnies	**BELLSTU**	bullets	**BEMMOOS**	embosom
BEILLSU	bullies	**BEINRTT**	bittern	**BELMMRU**	mumbler	**BEMMRSU**	bummers
BEILMNR	nimbler		Britten	**BELMMSU**	mumbles	**BEMNOST**	entombs
BEILMOR	embroil	**BEINRTU**	tribune	**BELMNOS**	nombles	**BEMNOSU**	umbones
BEILMOS	mobiles		turbine	**BELMNOU**	nelumbo	**BEMNOSW**	enwombs
BEILMRS	limbers	**BEIOOPT**	biotope	**BELMNOY**	benomyl	**BEMNRSU**	numbers
BEILMRT	timbrel	**BEIOORZ**	boozier	**BELMNSU**	numbles	**BEMOORS**	boomers
	Trimble	**BEIOOST**	booties	**BELMOOR**	bloomer	**BEMORST**	mobster
BEILMSU	sublime	**BEIOPTY**	biotype	**BELMOPR**	problem	**BEMORSY**	embryos
BEILMSW	wimbles	**BEIORRT**	bortier	**BELMORT**	temblor	**BEMPRSU**	bumpers
BEILNOS	bolines		orbiter	**BELMORY**	Bromley	**BEMSSUU**	subsume
BEILNOW	bowline		Robert I	**BELMOSU**	embolus	**BENNORT**	Brenton
BEILNRS	berlins	**BEIORSS**	bossier	**BELMPRU**	plumber	**BENNORW**	newborn
BEILNSY	bylines	**BEIORSY**	boysier	**BELMRRU**	rumbler	**BENNOST**	bonnets
BEILNTZ	blintze	**BEIORUV**	bouvier	**BELMRSU**	lumbers	**BENNSTU**	bunnets
BEILOOS	loobies	**BEIOSSU**	soubise		rumbles	**BENOORS**	Osborne
BEILOPR	preboil	**BEIOSSW**	bowsies		slumber		Robeson
BEILOPY	epiboly	**BEIOSTX**	boxiest	**BELMRTU**	tumbler	**BENORRW**	browner
BEILOQU	oblique	**BEIOSTY**	obesity		tumbrel	**BENORRZ**	bronzer
BEILORR	broiler	**BEIQRTU**	briquet	**BELMRTY**	trembly	**BENORSS**	Bresson
BEILORS	boilers	**BEIQSSU**	bisques	**BELMSTU**	stumble	**BENORST**	bretons
	liberos	**BEIRRRU**	burrier		tumbles	**BENORSU**	bournes
	reboils	**BEIRRSU**	bruiser	**BELNOOR**	borneol	**BENORSZ**	bronzes
BEILORT	Blériot		buriers	**BELNOOY**	boloney	**BENOSSU**	bonuses
BEILORW	blowier	**BEIRSST**	bestirs	**BELNOST**	noblest	**BENOSWY**	newsboy
BEILORZ	Berlioz		bisters	**BELNOYZ**	benzoyl	**BENRRSU**	burners
BEILOSW	blowies		bistres	**BELNRTU**	blunter	**BENRSSU**	brussen
BEILRRU	burlier	**BEIRSSU**	bruises	**BELNRUY**	Burnley	**BENRSTU**	burnets
BEILRSS	ribless		bitsers	**BELNSTU**	sunbelt	**BENRTTU**	Burnett
BEILRST	blister		breists		unbelts	**BENRUWY**	Newbury
	bristle	**BEIRSSU**	bruises	**BELNUUZ**	Zebulun	**BEOORSS**	sorbose
BEILRTT	brittle	**BEIRSTT**	bitters	**BELOOPR**	blooper	**BEOORST**	booster
	triblet	**BEIRSTU**	bustier	**BELOORS**	boleros		reboots
BEILRTU	rebuilt	**BEIRTTU**	tribute	**BELOOSS**	soboles	**BEOORSZ**	boozers
BEILRTY	liberty	**BEIRTVY**	brevity	**BELOOVY**	Byelovo		rebozos
BEILSSS	blisses	**BEISSTU**	busiest	**BELOPSU**	pueblos	**BEOPPRS**	boppers
BEILSTU	subtile	**BEISTTU**	butties	**BELORST**	bolster	**BEOPRRS**	probers
BEILSTW	blewits	**BEITTWX**	betwixt		bolters	**BEOPRRV**	proverb
BEILSTZ	blitzes	**BEJJSUU**	jujubes		lobster	**BEOQSTU**	bosquet
BEILTTU	bluetit	**BEJKOUX**	jukebox	**BELORSU**	roubles	**BEOQSUY**	obsequy
BEIMMRR	brimmer	**BEJLMRU**	jumbler	**BELORSW**	blowers	**BEOQTUU**	bouquet
BEIMNOR	bromine	**BEJLMSU**	jumbles		bowlers	**BEORRSS**	resorbs
BEIMNTU	bitumen	**BEJLOSS**	jobless	**BELORSY**	soberly	**BEORRST**	Roberts
BEIMOSZ	zombies	**BEJORSU**	objures	**BELORTT**	blotter	**BEORRSW**	browser
BEIMPRU	bumpier	**BEKLNOZ**	Koblenz		bottler	**BEORSST**	sorbets
BEIMRST	timbers	**BEKLOOT**	booklet	**BELORTU**	boulter		strobes
	timbres	**BEKLRSU**	bulkers		trouble	**BEORSSU**	bourses
BEIMRSU	imbrues		burlesk	**BELOSSU**	blouses	**BEORSSW**	bowsers
BEIMRTU	terbium	**BEKNORS**	bonkers		boluses		browses
BEIMSTU	subitem	**BEKNRSU**	bunkers	**BELOSTT**	bottles	**BEORSTT**	bettors

BEORSTV	obverts	BGGINOS	biggons	BGINOPP	bopping	BIIIKNS	bikinis
BEORSUZ	subzero	BGGNOOS	bogongs	BGINOPR	probing	BIIILST	Tbilisi
BEORSWY	bowyers	BGGNOSU	bugongs	BGINORS	borings	BIIJOTU	Jibouti
BEORUVY	overbuy	BGHHIOY	highboy	BGINORZ	zorbing	BIILLNO	billion
BEOSSST	bossets	BGHIILS	ghiblis	BGINOSS	bossing	BIILLTW	twibill
BEOSSTT	obtests	BGHIINS	binghis		gibsons	BIILNTU	inbuilt
BEOSSTU	Bossuet	BGHILST	blights	BGINOSU	bousing	BIILOSU	bilious
BEOSSTW	bestows	BGHILTY	blighty	BGINOSW	bowsing	BIILRSY	risibly
BEPRRTU	perturb	BGHINOR	bighorn	BGINOTT	botting	BIILSTW	twibils
BEPRTUY	puberty	BGHINSU	bushing	BGINOUY	buoying	BIILSVY	visibly
BEQRSUU	brusque	BGHIPSU	bushpig	BGINOWW	wingbow	BIIMNOU	niobium
BERRSTU	burster	BGHIRST	brights	BGINPRU	burping	BIIMNSU	minibus
BERSSTU	busters	BGHLRUU	burghul	BGINRRU	burring	BIIMPRS	biprism
BERSTTU	butters	BGHMORU	homburg	BGINRUY	burying	BIIMSTU	stibium
BERSTUV	subvert	BGHMSUU	humbugs	BGINSSU	bussing	BIINOSU	binious
BERSUZZ	buzzers	BGHOOOS	Oshogbo	BGINSTU	busting	BIINSTU	Bisitun
BERTTUY	buttery	BGHOORU	borough	BGINSUY	busying	BIIORSV	vibrios
BESSSTU	subsets	BGHORTU	brought	BGINTTU	butting	BIISSTV	vibists
BESTTUX	subtext	BGIIKLN	bilking	BGINUZZ	buzzing	BIISTTT	titbits
BFFGIIN	biffing	BGIILLN	billing	BGIORTY	bigotry	BIJNOSU	subjoin
BFFGINU	buffing	BGIILNO	boiling	BGKLOOO	logbook	BIKLLUY	bulkily
BFFIINS	biffins	BGIILNR	birling	BGKORSY	grysbok	BIKLNOT	inkblot
BFFILOO	boiloff	BGIILNS	sibling	BGLMORU	Borglum	BIKLNOY	linkboy
BFFINOS	boffins	BGIIMNU	imbuing	BGLMRUY	grumbly	BIKLRSY	briskly
BFFLLUY	bluffly	BGIINNN	binning	BGLNOOS	oblongs	BIKMNOO	boomkin
BFFLOOW	blowoff	BGIINNR	brining	BGLNOOW	longbow	BIKMNPU	bumpkin
BFFNOOU	buffoon	BGIINRR	birring	BGLNOUW	blowgun	BIKMNSU	bumkins
BFGIORT	frogbit	BGIINTT	bitting	BGLOOSU	globous	BIKNRSY	Rybinsk
BFHIOSX	boxfish	BGIKLNU	bulking	BGLOSSU	bugloss	BIKNSSU	buskins
BFHIRSU	furbish	BGIKNNO	bonking	BGLOSUY	bogusly	BILLNOS	billons
BFHLSUY	bushfly	BGIKNNU	bunking	BGNOSSU	subsong	BILLNOU	bullion
BFIILRS	fibrils	BGIKNOO	booking	BGOORSU	burgoos	BILLNUY	Lyublin
BFIINOR	fibroin	BGIKNOR	broking	BHHIIST	bhishti	BILLOPX	pillbox
BFILMRU	brimful	BGIKNRU	burking	BHHIKSU	bhikhus	BILLOSW	billows
BFILOTY	liftboy	BGIKNSU	busking	BHIIINT	inhibit	BILLOWY	billowy
BFILSUY	fusibly	BGILLNU	bulling	BHIINRS	brinish	BILLRWY	wrybill
BFINOSW	bowfins	BGILMOU	gumboil	BHIIPSS	sibship	BILMNOR	nombril
BFIORSS	rosbifs	BGILMRU	Limburg	BHIKLOS	blokish	BILMOOS	Ólimbos
BFIORST	Bifrost	BGILNOO	booling	BHIKOOS	bookish	BILMPUY	bumpily
BFIORSU	fibrous	BGILNOS	goblins	BHILLOY	billyoh	BILMRTU	tumbril
BFIRTUY	brutify	BGILNOT	biltong	BHILLSU	bullish	BILNNOY	bonnily
BFKLOOY	flybook		bolting	BHILOTU	holibut	BILNOTU	botulin
BFLLOUW	bowlful	BGILNOW	blowing	BHILPSU	publish	BILNRSU	Lisburn
BFLLOWY	blowfly		bowling	BHILSUY	bushily	BILNTUU	unbuilt
	flyblow	BGILNOY	ignobly	BHIMOOS	hoboism	BILORST	bristol
BFLOSUX	boxfuls	BGILNRU	burling	BHIMOPR	bimorph	BILOSSU	subsoil
BFLSTUU	tubfuls	BGILNSU	bluings	BHIMORT	thrombi	BILOSSY	bossily
BFOOOTY	footboy	BGILOOR	obligor	BHIMORU	bohrium	BILPTUU	upbuilt
BGGGIIN	bigging	BGILOOY	biology	BHIMSTU	bismuth	BILRSTY	bristly
BGGGINO	bogging	BGILRTU	Tilburg	BHINRSU	burnish	BILRTTY	brittly
BGGGINU	bugging	BGIMMNU	bumming	BHIOORS	boorish	BILRTUY	tilbury
BGGHIIS	biggish	BGIMNNU	numbing	BHIOOST	booshit	BIMMOOS	miombos
BGGIILN	bilging	BGIMNOO	booming	BHIOPSS	bishops	BIMMORS	bromism
BGGIINN	binging	BGIMNOR	borming	BHIOSWZ	showbiz	BIMNOSU	omnibus
BGGIINS	biggins	BGIMNOT	tombing	BHIRSTU	brutish	BIMOSSS	bossism
BGGIISW	bigwigs	BGIMNPU	bumping	BHISTTU	bushtit	BIMRSUX	bruxism
BGGILNO	globing	BGIMRSY	Grimsby	BHKNOSU	bohunks	BIMSSSU	submiss
BGGILNU	bugling	BGINNRU	Brüning	BHLNOSU	bulrush	BIMSSTU	submits
	bulging		burning	BHMORSU	rhombus	BINNOSU	bunions
BGGINNO	bonging	BGINNTU	bunting	BHOOOOS	boohoos	BINOORS	Orbison
BGGINNU	bunging	BGINOOT	booting	BHOOSTW	bowshot	BINOOST	bonitos
		BGINOOZ	boozing	BHPRSUU	brushup	BINOOSU	niobous

BINOSST	bonists	BOOPRTT	Bottrop	CCEEKOV	cockeye		orectic
BINPSUY	bunyips	BOOPSTX	postbox	CCEELRY	recycle	CCEIOSS	ciscoes
BINRTUY	butyrin	BOOPSTY	postboy	CCEENRY	recency	CCEIPST	sceptic
BINSTUU	Bisutun		potboys	CCEEORR	coercer	CCEIRST	cretics
	subunit	BOORRSW	borrows	CCEEORS	coerces	CCEISSU	succise
BIOOORS	rooibos	BOORRTY	robotry	CCEERSY	secrecy	CCEKLOR	clocker
BIOORSZ	borzois	BOOSWWW	bowwows	CCEFHRU	curchef	CCEKLOS	cockles
BIOOSST	oboists	BOPSSTU	postbus	CCEFNOT	confect	CCEKNOV	cockney
BIOOSUV	obvious	BORRSUW	burrows	CCEGNOY	cogency	CCEKOPS	copecks
BIOPRTY	probity	BORSTTU	turbots	CCEHIKN	chicken	CCEKOPT	petcock
BIORRTU	burrito	BOSTUUY	buyouts	CCEHIKU	chuckie	CCEKORS	cockers
BIORRTW	ribwort	CCCDIOO	coccoid	CCEHILS	cliches	CCEKORT	crocket
BIORSST	bistros	CCCDIOS	coccids	CCEHILU	culchie	CCELLOT	collect
	Brissot	CCCNOOT	concoct	CCEHINO	conchie	CCELLOU	Uccello
BIORSTT	bistort	CCCOOSU	coccous	CCEHINS	cinches	CCELNOY	cyclone
BIORSTW	Bristow	CCDEEER	recceed	CCEHINT	technic	CCELRSY	cyclers
BIORSUU	rubious	CCDEEHK	checked	CCEHIOR	choicer	CCENNOR	concern
BIRSTTU	turbits	CCDEEIM	ecdemic		choreic	CCENNOT	concent
BISSSTU	subsist	CCDEEIO	ecocide	CCEHIOS	choices		connect
BISTUUU	busuuti	CCDEEKL	clecked		Cochise	CCENOPT	concept
BKLOOST	Tobolsk	CCDEENO	concede	CCEHIRS	screich	CCENORT	concert
BKNOOTW	bowknot	CCDEENY	decency	CCEHIST	hectics	CCENOSS	sconces
BKOORWX	workbox	CCDEEOR	coerced	CCEHKLU	chuckle	CCEOOTT	cocotte
BLLNTUY	bluntly	CCDEESU	succeed	CCEHKOR	chocker	CCEOPRS	Cecrops
BLLOOOS	lobolos	CCDEHIL	cliched	CCEHKPU	checkup	CCEORRT	correct
BLLOSUY	solubly	CCDEHIN	cinched	CCEHKRU	chucker	CCEORRU	reoccur
BLLOUVY	volubly	CCDEHKO	chocked	CCEHLOS	cloches	CCEORTW	twoccer
BLMMPUU	plumbum	CCDEHKU	chucked	CCEHLRU	cleruch	CCESSSU	success
BLMOOOT	tombolo	CCDEHOU	couched	CCEHNOS	conches	CCFIRUY	crucify
BLMOORW	lobworm	CCDEHTW	cwtched	CCEHORT	crochet	CCFLOSU	floccus
BLMOOSS	blossom	CCDEIIL	icicled	CCEHORU	coucher	CCGHINO	gnocchi
BLMOSSY	symbols	CCDEIIT	deictic	CCEHOSU	couches	CCGIKNO	cocking
BLMOUXY	buxomly	CCDEIKL	clicked	CCEHRSU	curches	CCGIKNU	cucking
BLNNOUW	unblown	CCDEILR	circled	CCEHSTW	cwtches	CCGILNY	cycling
BLNOORW	lowborn	CCDEIMO	comedic	CCEIILS	cilices	CCGKOOR	gorcock
BLNOOSS	bolsons	CCDEIOS	codices		icicles	CCHHIIS	chichis
BLNOOSU	blouson	CCDEKLO	clocked	CCEIIMS	cimices	CCHHRUY	churchy
BLNOOTU	Boulton		cockled	CCEIIRT	icteric	CCHIIOR	Chirico
BLNOSTU	unbolts	CCDEKLU	clucked	CCEIKLR	clicker	CCHIIST	stichic
BLOOPWY	plowboy	CCDEKOR	crocked	CCEIKOR	cockier	CCHIKLS	Schlick
BLOOQUY	obloquy	CCDELOU	occlude	CCEIKOS	cockies	CCHIKST	schtick
BLOORWW	lowbrow	CCDENOS	sconced	CCEIKRT	cricket	CCHILOR	chloric
BLOOSWY	lowboys	CCDENOU	conduce	CCEILMO	celomic	CCHILOS	Colchis
BLOOTUW	blowout	CCDEOST	decocts	CCEILNU	nucleic	CCHIMOR	chromic
BLOPSTU	subplot	CCDHIIL	cichlid	CCEILRR	circler	CCHINOR	chronic
BLOPSUW	blowups	CCDIILO	codicil	CCEILRS	circles	CCHIORY	chicory
BLORUVY	Rublyov	CCDIILU	culicid		clerics	CCHIOTW	cowitch
BMNOOSU	unbosom	CCDIIOR	cricoid	CCEILRT	circlet	CCHIPSU	hiccups
BMOOORX	boxroom	CCDILOY	cycloid	CCEILSU	culices	CCHIPSY	psychic
BMOOSTT	bottoms	CCDKLOU	cuckold	CCEILSY	cylices	CCHKLOS	schlock
BMOOSTY	tomboys	CCDNOOR	concord	CCEILTU	cuticle	CCHKMSU	schmuck
BMORSUU	brumous	CCDNOTU	conduct	CCEIMOT	cometic	CCHKOOS	chockos
BNNRSUU	sunburn	CCEEHKR	checker	CCEIMST	smectic	CCHKOSY	cockshy
BNOORYZ	Broonzy		recheck	CCEINOR	cornice	CCHNRSU	scrunch
BNOOSST	bostons	CCEEHOR	ecorche		crocein	CCHNRUY	crunchy
BNORSSU	suborns	CCEEHRS	creches	CCEINOS	concise	CCHOORS	scrooch
BNORSTU	burtons		screech	CCEINOT	conceit	CCHOSTU	succoth
BNORSUU	burnous	CCEEILN	licence	CCEINRT	centric	CCIIILS	silicic
BNORTUU	burnout	CCEEINR	eccrine	CCEIOPP	coppice	CCIILNS	clinics
BNOSSUW	sunbows	CCEEINS	science	CCEIOPT	ectopic	CCIILOT	colitic
BNOSTTU	buttons	CCEEIRV	crevice	CCEIORS	ciceros	CCIILPR	circlip
BNOTTUY	buttony			CCEIORT	cerotic	CCIILST	clitics

CCIINPS	picnics	CDDEHRU	chudder	CDEEHPR	perched	CDEERSU	reduces
CCIINPU	Puccini	CDDEINU	induced	CDEEHRS	cheders		rescued
CCIIRST	critics	CDDEIOT	de dicto	CDEEHRT	retched		secured
CCIIRTU	circuit	CDDEISU	cuddies	CDEEHRU	euchred		seducer
CCIKLOW	cowlick	CDDELOR	coddler	CDEEHST	chested	CDEERSW	screwed
CCIKLOY	cockily	CDDELOS	coddles	CDEEIIT	eidetic	CDEERTU	eructed
	colicky		scolded	CDEEILN	decline	CDEESSU	seduces
CCIKOPT	cockpit	CDDELOU	clouded	CDEEILP	pedicel	CDEESSY	ecdyses
CCILNOO	colonic	CDDELRU	curdled		pedicle	CDEESTT	detects
CCILNOU	council	CDDELSU	cuddles	CDEEILS	deciles	CDEESUX	excused
CCILOOP	piccolo	CDDEORS	codders	CDEEIMN	endemic	CDEFFHU	chuffed
CCILSTY	cyclist	CDDEORW	crowded	CDEEINO	codeine	CDEFFIO	coiffed
CCIMOTY	mycotic	CDDESTU	deducts	CDEEINT	enticed	CDEFFOS	scoffed
CCINOTV	convict	CDDGINO	codding	CDEEINV	evinced	CDEFFSU	scuffed
CCIOORS	sirocco	CDDIIKN	niddick	CDEEIOS	diocese	CDEFHIL	filched
CCIOPTU	occiput	CDDIIOS	discoid	CDEEIOV	devoice	CDEFHOO	choofed
CCIPRTY	cryptic	CDDIIOY	didicoy	CDEEIPR	pierced	CDEFIIT	deficit
CCISUYZ	Cyzicus	CDDIIRU	druidic	CDEEIRR	decrier	CDEFIKL	flicked
CCKOOSU	cuckoos	CDDIKOP	piddock	CDEEIRS	decries	CDEFINO	confide
CCKOPSU	cockups	CDDIKOR	Roddick		deicers	CDEFKLO	flocked
CCLOPSY	cyclops	CDDIORS	discord	CDEEIRT	recited	CDEFKOR	defrock
CCLOSTU	occults	CDDKOPU	puddock	CDEEIST	deceits		frocked
CCMOOOR	morocco	CDDKORU	ruddock	CDEEISV	devices	CDEFNTU	defunct
CCNOOOS	cocoons	CDEEEFL	fleeced	CDEEISX	excides	CDEFOSU	focused
CCNOOPU	puccoon	CDEEEFN	defence		excised	CDEGGHU	chugged
CCNOOTU	coconut	CDEEEHK	cheeked	CDEEITV	evicted	CDEGGLO	clogged
CCNORSU	concurs	CDEEEHL	leeched	CDEEITX	excited		coggled
CCNORSU	concurs	CDEEEHP	cheeped	CDEEJST	dejects	CDEGGOR	crogged
CCNOSSU	concuss	CDEEEHR	cheered	CDEEKLS	deckels	CDEGHNU	Chengdu
CCORSSU	succors	CDEEEHS	cheesed		deckles	CDEGHOU	coughed
CCORSUU	succour	CDEEEIV	deceive	CDEEKNR	redneck	CDEGIIN	deicing
CCORSUY	succory	CDEEEJT	ejected	CDEEKNS	snecked	CDEGIKN	decking
CCOSSTU	stuccos	CDEEELT	elected	CDEEKOS	decokes	CDEGINR	cringed
CCSSSUU	succuss	CDEEEPR	precede	CDEEKPS	specked	CDEGINU	educing
CDDDEEI	decided	CDEEERR	decreer	CDEEKRS	deckers	CDEGLSU	cudgels
CDDDEEO	decoded	CDEEERS	decrees	CDEEKRW	wrecked	CDEGNSU	scunged
CDDDEEU	deduced		recedes	CDEELMM	clemmed	CDEGORS	codgers
CDDDELO	coddled		seceder	CDEELPU	cupeled	CDEHHIT	hitched
CDDDELU	cuddled	CDEEERT	decreet		decuple	CDEHHNU	hunched
CDDDESU	scudded		erected	CDEELPY	ycleped	CDEHHTU	hutched
CDDEEER	decreed	CDEEESS	secedes	CDEELSU	seclude	CDEHIIL	ceilidh
	receded	CDEEESX	exceeds	CDEELUX	exclude	CDEHIIV	chivied
CDDEEES	seceded	CDEEFHT	fetched	CDEENOR	encoder	CDEHIKN	chinked
CDDEEII	deicide	CDEEFII	edifice		encored	CDEHIKO	hoicked
CDDEEIR	decider	CDEEFKL	flecked	CDEENOS	encodes	CDEHILL	chilled
	decried	CDEEFLT	clefted		seconde	CDEHILO	cheloid
CDDEEIS	decides		deflect	CDEENOZ	cozened	CDEHILP	delphic
CDDEEIX	excided	CDEEFOR	deforce	CDEENRS	decerns	CDEHILR	eldrich
CDDEEKO	decoked	CDEEFST	defects	CDEENRT	centred	CDEHIMR	chirmed
CDDEENO	encoded	CDEEGHN	Chengde		credent	CDEHIMT	mitched
CDDEENS	descend	CDEEGKT	gedeckt	CDEENST	descent	CDEHINN	chinned
	scended	CDEEHIP	cepheid		scented	CDEHINO	hedonic
CDDEEOR	decoder	CDEEHIS	dehisce	CDEEOOY	cooeyed	CDEHINP	pinched
CDDEEOS	decodes	CDEEHIV	chevied	CDEEOPR	proceed	CDEHINW	winched
CDDEEOY	decoyed	CDEEHKL	heckled	CDEEORV	covered	CDEHIOW	cowhide
CDDEERU	reduced	CDEEHLP	chelped	CDEEORW	cowered	CDEHIPP	chipped
CDDEESU	deduces	CDEEHLT	letched	CDEEORY	decoyer	CDEHIPR	chirped
	seduced	CDEEHLW	welched	CDEEOST	cestode	CDEHIPT	pitched
CDDEEUW	cudweed	CDEEHMS	schemed	CDEEOTV	coveted	CDEHIRR	chirred
CDDEHIN	chidden	CDEEHNW	wenched	CDEERRU	reducer	CDEHIRS	chiders
CDDEHIT	ditched	CDEEHOR	cohered	CDEERSS	screeds		Driesch
CDDEHOR	chorded		ochered	CDEERST	crested		herdics
CDDEHOU	douched						

CDEHIRT	ditcher		snicked	CDEIRTV	verdict	CDENOSS	seconds
CDEHIST	ditches	CDEIKPR	pricked	CDEISST	dissect	CDENOST	docents
	sichted	CDEIKRR	derrick	CDEISSY	ecdysis	CDENOTU	counted
CDEHISU	duchies	CDEIKRS	dickers	CDEJNOU	jounced	CDENPUY	pudency
CDEHITW	witched	CDEIKRT	tricked	CDEKKNO	knocked	CDENRUU	uncured
CDEHIVV	chivved	CDEIKRU	duckier	CDEKLNO	clonked	CDEOOPP	copepod
CDEHKLO	hockled	CDEIKRW	wricked	CDEKLNU	clunked	CDEOOPS	scooped
CDEHKOO	chooked	CDEIKST	sticked	CDEKLOW	wedlock	CDEOOPT	coopted
CDEHKOS	shocked	CDEIKSU	duckies	CDEKLPU	plucked	CDEOORR	corrode
CDEHKSU	shucked	CDEIKSY	dickeys	CDEKLRU	ruckled	CDEOORT	Côte-d'Or
CDEHKUY	heyduck	CDEILLO	collide	CDEKLSU	suckled	CDEOORV	vocoder
CDEHLMU	mulched		collied	CDEKMOS	smocked	CDEOOST	scooted
CDEHLNU	lunched	CDEILMO	melodic	CDEKNOR	dorneck	CDEOOTV	dovecot
CDEHLNY	lynched	CDEILNU	include	CDEKNOS	dockens	CDEOPPR	cropped
CDEHLOT	clothed		nuclide	CDEKNSU	sundeck	CDEOPRS	corpsed
CDEHLRU	lurched	CDEILOP	policed	CDEKOOR	crooked	CDEOPRU	crouped
CDEHLST	Scheldt	CDEILOS	coldies	CDEKORS	dockers		produce
CDEHMMU	chummed	CDEILPP	clipped		redocks	CDEORRS	corders
CDEHMNU	munched	CDEILPS	spliced	CDEKOST	destock		records
CDEHMOO	mooched	CDEILPU	clupeid		dockets	CDEORRW	crowder
CDEHMOP	chomped	CDEILSU	sluiced		stocked	CDEORSS	crossed
CDEHMOR	chromed	CDEILTU	ductile	CDEKRSU	duckers	CDEORSU	coursed
CDEHMPU	chumped	CDEIMNO	demonic	CDEKRTU	trucked		scoured
CDEHMTU	mutched		McIndoe	CDELLOU	collude		sourced
CDEHNOT	notched	CDEIMOR	dormice	CDELLSU	sculled	CDEORTU	courted
CDEHNPU	punched	CDEIMOS	medicos	CDELMPU	clumped	CDEORUU	douceur
CDEHNRU	chunder	CDEIMOT	demotic	CDELMSU	muscled	CDEORWY	Cowdrey
	churned	CDEIMPR	crimped	CDELMTU	mulcted	CDEOSSU	escudos
CDEHNSY	synched	CDEIMPU	pumiced	CDELNOO	condole	CDEOSTU	scouted
CDEHOPP	chopped	CDEIMSU	miscued	CDELNOW	clowned	CDEPRTY	decrypt
CDEHOPU	pouched	CDEINOS	secondi	CDELNOY	condyle	CDERSTU	crudest
CDEHORW	chowder	CDEINOT	ctenoid	CDELOOR	colored		crusted
	cowherd		deontic		crooled	CDFHIOS	codfish
CDEHOSU	douches		noticed	CDELOPP	clopped	CDFIILU	fluidic
	hocused	CDEINRS	cinders	CDELOPU	coupled	CDFILUY	dulcify
CDEHOTU	touched		discern	CDELORS	scolder	CDFIOSU	fucoids
CDEHOUV	vouched		rescind	CDELOST	coldest	CDGHIIN	chiding
CDEHPSY	psyched	CDEINRU	inducer	CDELOSW	scowled	CDGIINO	gonidic
CDEHRRU	churred	CDEINRY	cindery	CDELOTT	clotted	CDGIINS	discing
CDEHRSU	crushed	CDEINSU	incudes	CDELOUY	doucely	CDGIKNO	docking
CDEHSSU	duchess		incused	CDELPSU	sculped	CDGIKNU	ducking
CDEHSTU	Deutsch		induces	CDELRRU	curdler	CDGILNO	codling
	dutches	CDEINSX	exscind	CDELRSU	curdles		lingcod
CDEHSTY	scythed	CDEINTT	tincted	CDELRUY	crudely	CDGINNO	condign
CDEIIKR	dickier	CDEIOOR	cooried	CDELTUU	ductule	CDGINOR	cording
CDEIIKS	dickies	CDEIOPR	percoid	CDEMMNO	commend	CDGINRU	curding
CDEIINR	dineric	CDEIORR	Roderic	CDEMMOO	commode	CDHIINT	chindit
CDEIINS	incised	CDEIORS	scodier	CDEMMSU	scummed	CDHIIST	distich
	indices	CDEIORT	cordite	CDEMNNO	condemn	CDHILLY	childly
CDEIINT	identic	CDEIORU	couried	CDEMOOS	comedos	CDHILOS	coldish
	incited	CDEIORV	divorce	CDEMORS	scromed	CDHILUW	Dulwich
CDEIIOR	ericoid	CDEIORW	crowdie	CDEMORU	decorum	CDHIMST	Schmidt
CDEIIST	deistic	CDEIOST	cestoid	CDEMPRU	crumped	CDHINOR	chondri
	diciest		coedits	CDENNOO	condone	CDHIOOR	choroid
CDEIISU	suicide	CDEIPRS	crisped	CDENNOT	contend		ochroid
CDEIJST	disject	CDEIPRT	predict	CDENOOP	poonced	CDHIORS	orchids
CDEIKLN	clinked	CDEIPST	depicts	CDENOOR	crooned	CDHIPTY	diptych
CDEIKLP	pickled	CDEIRRU	curried	CDENOOS	secondo	CDHMORU	Murdoch
CDEIKLS	slicked	CDEIRST	credits	CDENOPU	pounced	CDIIIOT	idiotic
CDEIKLT	tickled		directs	CDENORS	scorned	CDIIJRU	juridic
CDEIKMS	medicks	CDEIRSU	cruised	CDENORU	crunode	CDIILLY	idyllic
CDEIKNS	dickens	CDEIRSV	cervids	CDENORW	crowned	CDIILMO	domicil

CDIILNY	dicliny	CEEEHSS	cheeses
CDIIMNO	Dominic	CEEEINP	epicene
CDIIMOS	disomic	CEEEIPR	creepie
CDIINOR	crinoid	CEEEIRV	receive
CDIINOT	diction	CEEEITV	evictee
CDIINOV	vidicon	CEEELRT	reelect
CDIINOZ	zincoid	CEEELST	celeste
CDIINST	indicts	CEEENRT	Terence
CDIIORS	cirsoid	CEEENSS	essence
CDIIORX	corixid	CEEEOTZ	Coetzee
CDIIOSS	cissoid	CEEEPRR	creeper
CDIIOSV	viscoid	CEEERRT	erecter
CDIKLNO	Old Nick		reerect
CDIKNOR	dornick	CEEERSS	creeses
CDILLOO	colloid	CEEERST	secrete
CDILLUV	lucidly	CEEERTX	excrete
CDILNOS	codlins	CEEETUX	execute
CDILOTU	dulotic	CEEFFNO	offence
CDILOTZ	Colditz	CEEFFOS	coffees
CDILPPU	Cudlipp	CEEFFST	effects
CDIMMOU	modicum	CEEFHLS	fleches
CDIMNOO	monodic	CEEFHNR	Fechner
CDIMOOS	cosmoid	CEEFHRT	fechter
CDIMSSU	muscids		fetcher
CDIMSTU	dictums	CEEFHST	fetches
CDINOOS	conoids	CEEFIRR	fiercer
CDINOSY	synodic	CEEFKLR	flecker
CDINOTU	conduit		freckle
	noctuid	CEEFLRT	reflect
CDINSSY	syndics	CEEFNNS	fennecs
CDINSTU	inducts	CEEFNOR	enforce
CDIOPRR	ripcord	CEEFNRS	fencers
CDIOSTT	cottids	CEEFPRT	perfect
CDIOSTY	cystoid		prefect
CDIOTUV	oviduct	CEEFSSU	fescues
CDIPSSU	cuspids	CEEGINR	generic
CDIRSUY	dysuric	CEEGINT	genetic
CDIRTUY	crudity	CEEGINU	eugenic
CDISSSU	discuss	CEEGIRZ	grecize
CDKNNOU	dunnock	CEEGKOS	geckoes
CDLOOPY	lycopod	CEEGLLO	college
CDLOSTU	couldst	CEEGLNO	Glencoe
CDMMOOO	commodo	CEEGLNT	neglect
CDMNOOS	condoms	CEEGLOR	El Greco
CDMOOST	dotcoms	CEEGLOU	eclogue
CDNOORS	condors	CEEGNRY	regency
	cordons	CEEGORT	cortege
CDNOORY	Croydon	CEEHHMS	Shechem
CDNOTUW	cutdown	CEEHILN	elenchi
CDOOOPT	octopod	CEEHILR	Eichler
CDOORRY	corrody	CEEHILS	helices
CDOORST	doctors		lichees
CDOOTUW	woodcut		Schiele
CDOPRTU	product	CEEHILV	vehicle
CDOSTUY	custody	CEEHIMR	chimere
CEEEFIL	fleecie	CEEHIMS	chemise
CEEEFLS	fleeces	CEEHINR	Chénier
CEEEHLS	leeches	CEEHINS	chinese
	Scheele	CEEHIOR	cheerio
CEEEHPR	cheeper	CEEHIRT	etheric
CEEEHRR	cheerer		heretic
CEEEHRV	Cheever		techier

CEEHIRW	chewier	CEEILSS	iceless
CEEHISS	seiches		siecles
CEEHIST	techies	CEEILST	sectile
CEEHISV	chevies	CEEILSV	vesicle
CEEHKLR	heckler	CEEILTU	leucite
CEEHKLS	heckles	CEEIMNT	centime
CEEHKNP	henpeck	CEEIMRS	mercies
CEEHKST	ketches	CEEIMRX	excimer
CEEHLNO	chelone	CEEIMST	emetics
	echelon	CEEINNS	incense
CEEHLRS	lechers	CEEINOS	senecio
CEEHLRW	welcher	CEEINPU	eupneic
CEEHLRY	cheerly	CEEINRS	ceresin
	lechery		sincere
CEEHLSS	chessel	CEEINRT	enteric
CEEHLST	letches		enticer
CEEHLSW	welches	CEEINRV	cervine
CEEHLSY	lychees	CEEINST	entices
CEEHMRS	schemer	CEEINSV	evinces
	schmeer	CEEINTV	Vicente
CEEHMRT	merchet	CEEIOPT	picotee
CEEHMSS	schemes	CEEIORT	coterie
CEEHNPU	penuche	CEEIORV	revoice
CEEHNRW	wencher	CEEIPRR	piercer
CEEHNST	tenches		reprice
CEEHNSW	wenches	CEEIPRS	piecers
CEEHORR	coherer		pierces
CEEHORS	coheres		precise
CEEHORT	trochee		recipes
CEEHPRR	percher	CEEIPRT	receipt
CEEHPRS	perches	CEEIPRU	epicure
CEEHPSU	Cepheus	CEEIPSS	species
CEEHQRU	chequer	CEEIPST	pectise
CEEHQSU	cheques	CEEIPTZ	pectize
CEEHRST	Chester	CEEIRRT	reciter
	etchers	CEEIRST	recites
	retches	CEEIRSU	ecuries
CEEHRSU	euchres	CEEIRSV	service
CEEHRSV	chevres	CEEIRTX	exciter
CEEHRSW	chewers	CEEISSX	excises
CEEHSSS	chesses	CEEISTX	excites
CEEHSSW	eschews	CEEITTZ	zetetic
CEEHSTV	chevets	CEEJORT	ejector
	vetches	CEEJRST	rejects
CEEIIKL	icelike	CEEKLNT	necklet
CEEIINR	eirenic	CEEKLPS	speckle
CEEIINW	icewine	CEEKMNN	Mencken
CEEIIPR	epeiric	CEEKNRS	neckers
CEEIJNT	Cetinje	CEEKNSY	Eysenck
CEEIJOR	rejoice	CEEKOSY	sockeye
CEEIKNT	necktie	CEEKPRS	peckers
CEEILLM	micelle	CEEKRRW	wrecker
CEEILNO	cineole	CEELLLU	cellule
CEEILNR	recline	CEELLNO	colleen
CEEILNS	license	CEELLOS	cellose
	selenic	CEELMNS	Clemens
	silence	CEELMNT	clement
CEEILNT	centile		Tlemcen
CEEILNU	leucine	CEELMOS	cleomes
CEEILPS	eclipse	CEELMOT	telecom
CEEILRT	reticle	CEELMOW	welcome
	tiercel	CEELNOS	enclose

CEELNPS	pencels	**CEEPPRT**	percept		rectify	**CEGIRRS**	gricers
CEELNRS	crenels		precept	**CEFISSU**	ficuses	**CEGKLOR**	grockle
CEELNRT	lectern	**CEEPPRU**	prepuce	**CEFKLLO**	elflock	**CEGLNOO**	cologne
CEELNRU	lucerne	**CEEPRSS**	precess	**CEFKLOT**	fetlock	**CEGLOOY**	ecology
CEELORS	creoles	**CEEPRST**	recepts	**CEFKLRY**	freckly	**CEGLOSU**	glucose
CEELORT	elector		respect	**CEFKRSU**	fuckers	**CEGLOSY**	glycose
	electro		scepter	**CEFLNOU**	flounce	**CEGNORS**	congers
CEELOSU	coulees		sceptre	**CEFLNUY**	fluency	**CEGNORY**	cryogen
CEELOTT	Colette		specter	**CEFMORY**	comfrey	**CEGNOST**	congest
CEELOTU	elocute		spectre	**CEFNORS**	confers	**CEGNRUY**	urgency
CEELPRT	prelect	**CEEPRTX**	excerpt	**CEFNOSS**	confess	**CEGNSSU**	scunges
CEELRRU	crueler	**CEEPSTX**	expects	**CEFNOSU**	confuse	**CEGNSTY**	cygnets
CEELRSS	scleres	**CEEPSTY**	ectypes	**CEFNOTU**	confute	**CEGOORS**	scrooge
CEELRST	tercels	**CEEPSUY**	eyecups	**CEFOPRS**	forceps	**CEGORRS**	grocers
CEELRSU	recluse	**CEERRSU**	rescuer	**CEFORRS**	forcers	**CEGORRY**	grocery
CEELRTU	lecture		securer	**CEFORRT**	crofter	**CEGORSU**	scourge
CEELRTY	erectly	**CEERRSW**	screwer	**CEFORSS**	frescos		scrouge
CEELSST	selects	**CEERRUV**	recurve	**CEFORSU**	focuser	**CEHHILR**	Ehrlich
CEELTTU	lettuce	**CEERSSS**	cessers		refocus	**CEHHIRS**	cherish
CEEMMOR	commere		cresses	**CEFOSSU**	focuses	**CEHHIRT**	hitcher
CEEMNOR	McEnroe	**CEERSST**	cresset	**CEFRSUW**	curfews	**CEHHIST**	hitches
CEEMNQU	McQueen		resects	**CEFSSUU**	fucuses	**CEHHITU**	hutchie
CEEMNRU	cerumen		screets	**CEGGHIR**	chigger	**CEHHKOV**	Chekhov
CEEMNST	cements		secrets	**CEGGIIS**	ciggies	**CEHHNSU**	hunches
CEEMOPR	compeer	**CEERSSU**	rescues	**CEGGIOR**	georgic	**CEHHOST**	shochet
	compere		secures	**CEGGLOS**	coggles	**CEHHSSU**	sheuchs
CEEMOPT	compete	**CEERSTT**	tercets	**CEGHILN**	leching	**CEHHSTU**	hutches
CEEMRRS	mercers	**CEERTTU**	curette	**CEGHINO**	echoing	**CEHIIKT**	thickie
CEEMRRY	mercery	**CEESSTX**	exsects	**CEGHINP**	peching	**CEHIILS**	chilies
CEEMRST	cermets	**CEESSUX**	excuses	**CEGHINT**	etching	**CEHIINR**	hircine
CEEMSTY	mycetes	**CEETTUV**	cuvette	**CEGHINW**	chewing	**CEHIINT**	ichnite
CEENNOU	enounce	**CEFFIOR**	officer	**CEGHIOS**	chigoes	**CEHIIPP**	chippie
CEENNOV	convene	**CEFFIOS**	offices	**CEGHIRS**	screigh	**CEHIIRT**	itchier
CEENNRT	centner	**CEFFISU**	suffice	**CEGHITU**	guichet		tichier
CEENOOT	ecotone	**CEFFLOS**	coffles	**CEGHLSU**	gulches	**CEHIISV**	chivies
CEENOPT	potence	**CEFFLSU**	scuffle	**CEGHORU**	cougher	**CEHIJOR**	Jericho
CEENORS	encores	**CEFFORS**	coffers	**CEGIILN**	ceiling	**CEHIKNT**	chetnik
	necrose		scoffer	**CEGIILW**	Gliwice		kitchen
CEENORZ	cozener	**CEFGINN**	fencing	**CEGIINP**	piecing		thicken
CEENOST	cenotes	**CEFHILR**	filcher	**CEGIKKN**	kecking	**CEHIKOO**	chookie
CEENPRS	spencer	**CEFHILS**	filches	**CEGIKNN**	necking	**CEHIKOR**	chokier
CEENPRT	percent	**CEFHILY**	chiefly	**CEGIKNP**	pecking	**CEHIKOS**	chokies
CEENPSS	spences		Chifley	**CEGIKNR**	recking	**CEHIKPS**	peckish
CEENPST	pectens	**CEFHINS**	finches	**CEGIKOR**	Górecki	**CEHIKRR**	Herrick
CEENRSS	censers	**CEFHIRS**	Fischer	**CEGILMP**	gemclip	**CEHIKRS**	shicker
	screens	**CEFHIST**	fitches	**CEGILNP**	cleping	**CEHIKRT**	thicker
	secerns	**CEFHITT**	fitchet	**CEGILNR**	clinger	**CEHIKRW**	whicker
CEENRST	centers	**CEFHITW**	fitchew		cringle	**CEHIKSY**	hickeys
	centres	**CEFIILT**	fictile	**CEGILNW**	clewing	**CEHIKTT**	thicket
	tenrecs	**CEFIIOR**	orifice	**CEGILNY**	glycine	**CEHILLR**	chiller
CEENRSU	censure	**CEFIITV**	fictive	**CEGIMNO**	genomic	**CEHILMN**	Mechlin
CEENRSY	scenery	**CEFIKLR**	flicker	**CEGIMNU**	mucigen	**CEHILNO**	choline
CEEOPST	pectose	**CEFILNT**	inflect	**CEGIMRW**	McGwire		helicon
CEEOPTY	ecotype	**CEFILNU**	funicle	**CEGINNS**	censing	**CEHILNS**	lichens
CEEORRT	erector	**CEFILRU**	lucifer	**CEGINOS**	cognise	**CEHILPS**	pilches
CEEORRV	coverer	**CEFIMOR**	comfier		coignes	**CEHILRR**	Richler
	recover	**CEFINNO**	confine	**CEGINOZ**	cognize	**CEHILRV**	chervil
CEEORRZ	Corrèze	**CEFINOR**	conifer	**CEGINPR**	creping	**CEHILSS**	chisels
CEEORSV	corvees	**CEFINST**	infects	**CEGINRR**	cringer	**CEHILTY**	ethylic
CEEORTV	coveter	**CEFIPSY**	specify	**CEGINRS**	cringes		lecythi
CEEORTW	cowtree	**CEFIRSS**	sferics	**CEGINRW**	crewing		techily
CEEOTTT	octette	**CEFIRTY**	certify	**CEGINSS**	cessing	**CEHIMMS**	chemism

CEHIMNY	chimney	CEHLNNU	chunnel
CEHIMOS	echoism	CEHLNOT	cholent
CEHIMRS	chimers	CEHLNRU	luncher
CEHIMRT	thermic	CEHLNRY	lyncher
CEHIMST	chemist	CEHLNSU	lunches
	mitches	CEHLNSY	lynches
CEHIMSU	echiums	CEHLNTY	lynchet
CEHINOP	chopine	CEHLORT	chortle
	phocine	CEHLORY	Chorley
CEHINOR	Cheiron	CEHLOST	clothes
CEHINPR	phrenic	CEHLPSS	schleps
CEHINPS	pinches	CEHLPSU	pleuchs
	sphenic	CEHLQSU	squelch
CEHINRT	cithern	CEHLRRU	lurcher
CEHINRW	wincher	CEHLRSU	lurches
CEHINST	ethnics	CEHMNNU	München
	sthenic	CEHMNRU	muncher
CEHINSU	echinus	CEHMNSU	munches
CEHINSW	winches	CEHMOOR	moocher
CEHIOPS	hospice	CEHMOOS	mooches
CEHIOPT	potiche	CEHMORS	chromes
CEHIORR	chorrie	CEHMOSS	schmoes
CEHIORS	coheirs	CEHMOTZ	chometz
	heroics	CEHMSTU	mutches
CEHIOTU	couthie	CEHNOOP	hencoop
CEHIOTV	cheviot	CEHNORV	chevron
CEHIPPR	chipper	CEHNOST	notches
CEHIPRR	chirper	CEHNOSU	cohunes
CEHIPRS	ciphers	CEHNPRU	puncher
	spheric	CEHNPSU	punches
CEHIPRT	pitcher	CEHNRRU	churner
CEHIPST	pitches	CEHNRTU	chunter
CEHIQSU	quiches	CEHNSUU	eunuchs
CEHIRRS	chirres	CEHNTUY	chutney
CEHIRRT	richter	CEHOOPS	pooches
CEHIRST	cithers	CEHOORS	chooser
	richest	CEHOORT	cheroot
CEHIRSU	cushier	CEHOOSS	chooses
CEHIRSZ	scherzi	CEHOPPR	chopper
CEHIRTT	chitter	CEHOPRS	porches
CEHISSU	cuishes	CEHOPST	potches
	cushies	CEHOPSU	pouches
CEHISTW	witches	CEHORSS	coshers
CEHISWZ	Schweiz	CEHORST	hectors
CEHKKRU	chukker		rochets
CEHKLMO	hemlock		tochers
CEHKLOS	hockles		torches
CEHKLSU	huckles		troches
CEHKNOY	Hockney	CEHORSU	rouches
CEHKORS	chokers	CEHORSZ	scherzo
	hockers	CEHORTU	retouch
	shocker		toucher
CEHKOSY	chokeys	CEHORTW	wotcher
	hockeys	CEHORUV	voucher
CEHKPTU	ketchup	CEHOSSU	hocuses
CEHKRSU	shucker	CEHOSTU	touches
CEHKRUY	huckery	CEHOSUV	vouches
CEHKSTY	sketchy	CEHPRSY	cyphers
CEHKTVY	kvetchy	CEHPSSY	psyches
CEHLLPU	chellup	CEHRRSU	crusher
CEHLMOR	chromel	CEHRSSU	crushes
CEHLMSU	mulches	CEHRSTT	stretch

CEHRTTU	Utrecht	CEIKLPU	cuplike
CEHSSTY	scythes	CEIKLRS	lickers
CEIIJRU	juicier		rickles
CEIIKNT	kinetic		slicker
CEIIKPR	pickier	CEIKLRT	tickler
CEIIKQU	quickie		trickle
CEIIKSS	sickies	CEIKLRU	luckier
CEIIKST	ekistic	CEIKLRW	Lerwick
	ickiest	CEIKLSS	sickles
CEIILLN	Cellini	CEIKLST	stickle
CEIILLS	silicle		tickles
CEIILNN	incline	CEIKMRU	muckier
CEIILPP	clippie	CEIKMSY	mickeys
CEIILPT	pelitic	CEIKNOT	kenotic
CEIILST	elicits		ketonic
CEIILTV	levitic	CEIKNQU	quicken
CEIIMMT	mimetic	CEIKNRS	nickers
CEIIMNS	menisci		snicker
CEIIMOT	meiotic	CEIKNSS	sickens
CEIIMPR	empiric	CEIKNST	snicket
CEIIMSS	seismic	CEIKOOS	cookies
CEIIMTT	titmice	CEIKOPS	pockies
CEIINNO	coniine	CEIKORR	rockier
CEIINNR	cinerin	CEIKORS	Rockies
CEIINOR	oneiric	CEIKORT	tockier
CEIINOS	eosinic	CEIKPRR	pricker
CEIINOV	invoice	CEIKPRS	pickers
CEIINPS	piscine	CEIKPRT	pricket
CEIINRS	irenics	CEIKPST	pickets
	sericin		skeptic
CEIINRT	citrine	CEIKQRU	quicker
	crinite	CEIKRRS	rickers
	inciter	CEIKRRT	tricker
	neritic	CEIKRST	rickets
CEIINSS	iciness		Sickert
	incises		sticker
CEIINST	incites		tickers
CEIINSU	cuisine	CEIKRSW	wickers
CEIINTZ	citizen	CEIKRSY	rickeys
	zincite	CEIKRTU	truckie
CEIIOPZ	epizoic	CEIKRTY	rickety
CEIIPRR	pricier	CEIKRUY	yuckier
CEIIPRS	spicier	CEIKSST	sickest
CEIIPRT	picrite	CEIKSTT	tickets
CEIIRST	eristic	CEIKSTW	wickets
CEIIRUZ	cruizie	CEIKSTY	tickeys
CEIIRVX	Eric XIV	CEILLMS	micells
CEIISSS	cissies	CEILLNU	nucelli
CEIISVV	civvies	CEILLOR	collier
CEIITUV	uveitic		Corelli
CEIJNST	injects	CEILLOS	collies
CEIJRSU	juicers	CEILLST	cellist
CEIJSTU	justice	CEILLSU	cullies
CEIKKRS	kickers	CEILMOP	compile
CEIKKSW	Keswick		polemic
CEIKLMS	melicks	CEILMPR	crimple
CEIKLNR	clinker	CEILNNU	nuclein
	crinkle	CEILNOP	pinocle
CEIKLNS	nickels	CEILNOS	inclose
CEIKLPR	pickler	CEILNOT	lection
	prickle	CEILNOX	lexicon
CEIKLPS	pickles	CEILNPS	pencils

	splenic		Ericson	**CEIOSTZ**	coziest	**CEKOORS**	cookers
CEILNST	clients		recoins	**CEIPQTU**	picquet		Crookes
	lectins	**CEINORU**	coenuri	**CEIPRRS**	crisper	**CEKOORY**	cookery
	stencil	**CEINORV**	corvine		pricers	**CEKOPST**	pockets
CEILNTU	tunicle	**CEINOSS**	cession	**CEIPRSS**	spicers	**CEKORRS**	corkers
CEILOOS	coolies		cosines	**CEIPRST**	triceps		rockers
CEILOPR	peloric	**CEINOST**	notices	**CEIPRSY**	spicery	**CEKORRY**	rockery
CEILOPS	polices		section	**CEIPRTU**	cuprite	**CEKORST**	restock
CEILORS	coilers	**CEINOSV**	novices		picture		rockets
	recoils	**CEINOTT**	tonetic	**CEIPRTY**	pyretic		stocker
CEILOSS	ossicle	**CEINOTX**	exciton	**CEIPRXY**	pyrexic	**CEKORTW**	twocker
CEILOST	citoles	**CEINOUV**	unvoice	**CEIPSST**	cesspit	**CEKOSST**	sockets
CEILOTT	coletit	**CEINPPR**	Crippen		septics	**CEKPRSU**	puckers
CEILPPR	clipper	**CEINPRS**	pincers	**CEIQRSU**	cirques	**CEKRRTU**	trucker
	cripple		princes	**CEIRRRU**	currier	**CEKRSSU**	suckers
CEILPRS	splicer	**CEINPST**	incepts	**CEIRRSU**	cruiser	**CEKRSTU**	tuckers
CEILPSS	splices		inspect		curries	**CEKSTTU**	tuckets
CEILPSU	spicule		pectins	**CEIRRTT**	critter	**CELLMNO**	Clonmel
CEILQSU	cliques	**CEINQSU**	cinques	**CEIRRTU**	recruit	**CELLNNO**	Connell
CEILQUY	cliquey		quinces	**CEIRRTX**	rectrix	**CELLNOO**	colonel
CEILRRU	curlier	**CEINRRU**	reincur	**CEIRRUV**	curvier	**CELLOST**	collets
CEILRSS	slicers	**CEINRST**	cistern	**CEIRSSU**	cruises	**CELLOSU**	locules
CEILRST	relicts		cretins		crusies		ocellus
CEILRTU	cultier	**CEINRSW**	wincers	**CEIRSTT**	trisect	**CELLOSY**	closely
	utricle	**CEINRTT**	cittern	**CEIRSTU**	icterus	**CELLPRU**	Purcell
CEILSSS	scissel	**CEINRUV**	incurve	**CEIRSUV**	cursive	**CELLRRU**	cruller
CEILSSU	sluices	**CEINSST**	incests	**CEIRSUZ**	cruzies	**CELLRSU**	cullers
CEIMMOS	commies		insects	**CEIRTTX**	tectrix		sculler
CEIMMRR	crimmer	**CEINSSU**	incuses	**CEISSSU**	cuisses	**CELLRUY**	cruelly
CEIMNOR	incomer	**CEINSTY**	cystine	**CEISSTU**	cutises	**CELMNOO**	locomen
CEIMNOS	Comines	**CEINSWY**	winceys		ictuses		monocle
	cosmine	**CEINTTX**	extinct	**CEISTTU**	cutties	**CELMOOS**	coeloms
	incomes	**CEIOORS**	coories	**CEJKOSY**	jockeys	**CELMOPS**	compels
	mesonic	**CEIOOST**	cooties	**CEJNOOS**	cojones	**CELMOPX**	complex
CEIMNOT	centimo	**CEIOPRS**	copiers	**CEJNORU**	conjure	**CELMORS**	cormels
	entomic	**CEIOPST**	poetics	**CEJNOSU**	jounces	**CELMPRU**	crumple
	tonemic	**CEIOPSU**	piceous		juncoes	**CELMSSU**	muscles
CEIMNRS	mincers	**CEIORRS**	cirrose	**CEJOPRT**	project	**CELMSUY**	lyceums
CEIMNRU	numeric		corries	**CEKKLNU**	knuckle	**CELMTUU**	cumulet
CEIMNSU	Mencius		crosier	**CEKKNOR**	knocker	**CELNNOU**	nucleon
CEIMNYZ	enzymic	**CEIORRU**	courier	**CEKKOPS**	kopecks	**CELNNSU**	nuncles
CEIMOPT	metopic		Ricoeur	**CEKLLRY**	clerkly	**CELNOOS**	Colenso
CEIMORT	mortice	**CEIORRZ**	crozier	**CEKLNRU**	clunker		colones
CEIMOSX	exosmic	**CEIORST**	erotics	**CEKLORS**	lockers		console
CEIMOTT	totemic	**CEIORSU**	couries	**CEKLORY**	Lockyer	**CELNOOY**	Clooney
CEIMOTV	vicomte	**CEIORSV**	voicers	**CEKLOST**	lockets	**CELNOPU**	Poulenc
CEIMOTX	toxemic	**CEIORSW**	cowries	**CEKLOTY**	tockley	**CELNORS**	cornels
CEIMPRR	crimper	**CEIORTT**	cottier	**CEKLPRU**	plucker	**CELNOSU**	counsel
CEIMPRS	spermic	**CEIORTV**	evictor	**CEKLRSU**	ruckles		unclose
CEIMPSU	pumices	**CEIORTX**	excitor		suckler	**CELNOTU**	noctule
CEIMRST	metrics		xerotic	**CEKLRTU**	truckle	**CELNSUU**	nucleus
CEIMRSU	murices	**CEIORVY**	viceroy	**CEKLSSU**	suckles	**CELOORR**	colorer
CEIMSSU	miscues	**CEIOSSS**	cossies	**CEKMNOY**	mockney	**CELOORS**	coolers
CEINNOV	connive	**CEIOSST**	cosiest	**CEKMORS**	mockers		creosol
CEINOOS	Ionesco		Ossetic	**CEKMORY**	mockery	**CELOOST**	coolest
CEINOOT	coontie	**CEIOSSU**	cesious	**CEKMRSU**	muckers		ocelots
CEINOPR	porcine	**CEIOSSV**	viscose	**CEKNOOV**	convoke	**CELOPRU**	coupler
CEINOPT	entopic	**CEIOSTT**	scottie	**CEKNORS**	conkers	**CELOPSU**	couples
	nepotic	**CEIOSTV**	costive		reckons	**CELOPTU**	couplet
CEINORR	cornier	**CEIOSTX**	coexist	**CEKNRWY**	wryneck		octuple
CEINORS	coiners		exotics	**CEKOOPR**	precook	**CELORSS**	closers
	cronies	**CEIOSTY**	society	**CEKOOPW**	cowpoke	**CELORST**	colters

	corslet		Crotone	**CEORRSU** courser	**CFIKNNO** finnock
	costrel	**CENOPRU** pouncer	cruores	**CFIKOSS** fossick
	lectors	**CENOPSU** pounces	scourer	**CFIKTUW** fuckwit
CELORSU closure	**CENOPSY** syncope	**CEORRSW** crowers	**CFILORS** frolics
colures	**CENOPTU** pouncet	**CEORRSY** sorcery	**CFILORU** fluoric
CELORSV clovers	**CENOPTY** potency	**CEORRTY** rectory	**CFIMNOR** confirm
CELORSW scowler	**CENOQRU** conquer	**CEORSSS** crosses	**CFIMOST** comfits
CELORTT crottle	**CENORRS** corners	**CEORSST** corsets	**CFIORSY** scorify
CELORTU cloture	scorner	costers	**CFISSTU** fustics
clouter	**CENORRW** crowner	escorts	**CFKNORU** unfrock
coulter	recrown	scoters	**CFKOTTU** futtock
CELOSST closest	**CENORSS** censors	sectors	**CFLMRUU** fulcrum
closets	**CENORST** cornets	**CEORSSU** courses	**CFLNOUX** conflux
CELOSSX coxless	Costner	Croesus	**CFLOOOS** Foscolo
CELPRSU scruple	**CENORSU** conures	scouser	**CFLOOPW** cowflop
CELPSUU cupules	**CENORTT** cornett	sources	**CFMNOOR** conform
CELPSUY clypeus	**CENORTU** cornute	sucrose	**CFMOORT** comfort
CELRRSU curlers	counter	**CEORSSW** escrows	**CFOSSUU** fuscous
CELRSTU cluster	recount	**CEORSSY** corseys	**CGGGINO** cogging
cutlers	trounce	**CEORSTT** cotters	**CGGIINR** gricing
relucts	**CENORTV** convert	**CEORSTU** croutes	**CGHHOSU** choughs
CELRSTY clyster	**CENORUV** uncover	scouter	**CGHIILM** milchig
CELRSUV culvers	**CENOSSY** coyness	**CEORSTV** coverts	**CGHIIMN** chiming
CELRSUW curlews	**CENOSTT** Consett	vectors	miching
CELRTTU clutter	contest	**CEORTUU** couture	**CGHIINN** chining
CELRTUU culture	**CENOSTU** contuse	**CEORTUV** couvert	inching
CELRTUV culvert	uncoest	**CEOSSST** cossets	niching
CELRTUY cruelty	**CENOSVY** conveys	**CEOSSSU** scouses	**CGHIINT** itching
cutlery	**CENOTTX** context	**CEPPRRU** crupper	**CGHIKNO** choking
CELSTTU cutlets	**CENPRTY** encrypt	**CEPPRSU** cuppers	hocking
cuttles	**CENRRTU** current	scupper	**CGHIKNU** chi kung
scuttle	**CENRSTU** encrust	**CEPRRSU** sprucer	Kuching
CEMMNOT comment	**CENRSUW** unscrew	**CEPRSSU** percuss	**CGHILNU** Chilung
CEMMNOU commune	**CENRTUY** century	spruces	**CGHILPY** glyphic
CEMMOOV commove	**CENSSTY** encysts	**CEPRSSY** cypress	**CGHINNO** chignon
CEMMOTU commute	**CEOOPRS** coopers	**CEPRSUW** screwup	**CGHINOR** ochring
CEMMRSU scummer	scooper	**CEPSSTU** suspect	**CGHINOS** coshing
CEMNNOT contemn	**CEOOPRY** coopery	**CERRSSU** cursers	**CGHINOU** Noguchi
CEMNOOP compone	**CEOORST** scooter	**CERSTTU** cutters	**CGHINRU** ruching
CEMNOOY economy	**CEOOSTY** coyotes	scutter	**CGHINSU** Cushing
CEMNOSU consume	oocytes	**CERSTUV** curvets	**CGHIOST** gothics
CEMNRTU centrum	**CEOPPRR** cropper	**CERSTUY** curtsey	**CGHLNOS** schlong
CEMOOPS compose	**CEOPPRS** coppers	**CFFGINO** coffing	**CGHLOSU** cloughs
CEMOOPT compote	**CEOPPRY** coppery	**CFFGINU** cuffing	**CGHORUY** grouchy
CEMOOTU outcome	**CEOPRRS** scorper	**CFFHINO** chiffon	**CGIIJNU** juicing
CEMOPRS compers	**CEOPRRT** porrect	**CFFIKKO** kickoff	**CGIIKKN** kicking
CEMOPTU compute	**CEOPRRU** procure	**CFFIKOP** pickoff	**CGIIKLN** licking
CEMORSS scromes	**CEOPRSS** corpses	**CFFINOS** coffins	**CGIIKMM** gimmick
CEMOSTU costume	process	**CFFOSTU** cutoffs	**CGIIKNN** nicking
CEMPRTU crumpet	**CEOPRST** copters	offcuts	**CGIIKNP** picking
CEMRRUY mercury	Spector	**CFFRSSU** scruffs	**CGIIKNR** ricking
CEMRSTU rectums	**CEOPRSU** croupes	**CFFRSUY** scruffy	**CGIIKNS** sicking
CENNOOT connote	recoups	**CFGIKNU** fucking	**CGIIKNT** ticking
CENNORY Connery	**CEOPRTT** protect	**CFGINOR** forcing	**CGIIKNW** wicking
CENNOST consent	**CEOPRUV** coverup	**CFHINSU** fuchsin	**CGIILLO** illogic
CENNOTT content	**CEOPSTY** cotypes	**CFHIOSW** cowfish	**CGIILNO** coiling
CENNOTV convent	**CEOQRTU** croquet	**CFHOOOW** Foochow	**CGIILNS** slicing
CENNRSU scunner	**CEOQSTU** coquets	**CFHORTU** futhorc	**CGIIMMN** mincing
CENOOPS poonces	**CEORRSS** crosser	**CFIIKNY** finicky	**CGIINNO** coining
CENOORR coroner	recross	**CFIILNT** inflict	**CGIINNW** wincing
crooner	scorers	**CFIIMNO** omnific	**CGIINOV** voicing
CENOORT coronet	**CEORRST** rectors	**CFIINOT** fiction	**CGIINPR** pricing

CGIINPS	spicing	**CGLNOSU**	unclogs	**CHIPRRU**	chirrup	**CIIMNNO**	nimonic
CGIINRT	tricing	**CGLOOSU**	colugos	**CHIPRRY**	pyrrhic	**CIIMNOU**	Iconium
CGIINSS	cissing	**CHHINOR**	rhonchi	**CHIPSSY**	physics	**CIIMOOS**	Cosimo I
CGIKLNO	locking	**CHHINTU**	unhitch	**CHIRRSU**	currish	**CIIMOST**	somitic
CGIKLNU	lucking	**CHHNOOS**	honchos	**CHIRSTY**	christy	**CIIMOTT**	mitotic
CGIKMNO	mocking	**CHHOSUU**	Hsü-chou	**CHISSST**	schists	**CIIMRST**	trismic
CGIKMNU	mucking	**CHHRTTU**	thrutch	**CHISTTU**	chutist	**CIIMSTV**	victims
CGIKNNO	conking	**CHIIKLM**	milchik	**CHITTWY**	twitchy	**CIINOOT**	coition
	nocking	**CHIIKSS**	sickish	**CHKLOOT**	klootch	**CIINOPR**	porcini
CGIKNOO	cooking	**CHIILLT**	Tillich	**CHKLOSY**	shylock	**CIINORS**	incisor
CGIKNOR	corking	**CHIILST**	litchis	**CHKMMOU**	hummock	**CIINPRS**	crispin
	rocking	**CHIIMSU**	ischium	**CHKMOSY**	Chomsky	**CIINQTU**	quintic
CGIKNOS	socking	**CHIINOT**	thionic	**CHKNOOS**	schnook	**CIINSTU**	Ictinus
CGIKNOW	cowking	**CHIIOPT**	ophitic	**CHLMOOS**	molochs	**CIIORST**	soritic
CGIKNPU	kingcup	**CHIIPSW**	Ipswich	**CHLMORY**	chromyl	**CIIOSUV**	vicious
	pucking	**CHIIRRS**	scirrhi	**CHLOOSS**	schools	**CIIPRTY**	pyritic
CGIKNRU	rucking	**CHIKLLO**	hillock	**CHLOPST**	splotch	**CIJNNOO**	conjoin
CGIKNSU	sucking	**CHIKLTY**	thickly	**CHLOSUY**	chylous	**CIJNNTU**	injunct
CGIKNTU	tucking	**CHIKNOO**	chinook		slouchy	**CIKKLLO**	killock
CGILLNU	culling	**CHIKORY**	hickory	**CHLSTUY**	slutchy	**CIKKNNO**	Kinnock
CGILNNO	cloning	**CHIKOST**	thickos	**CHMOORS**	chromos	**CIKLLOP**	pillock
CGILNOO	cooling	**CHIKPSU**	puckish	**CHMOSUY**	chymous	**CIKLLOR**	rollick
	locoing	**CHIKSST**	shticks	**CHMSTUY**	smutchy	**CIKLLSY**	slickly
CGILNOS	closing	**CHIKSTY**	kitschy	**CHNNOOR**	chronon	**CIKLLUY**	luckily
CGILNOW	cowling	**CHILLMU**	chillum	**CHNNOPY**	Pynchon	**CIKLMOS**	Miskolc
CGILNOY	cloying	**CHILLNO**	Chillon	**CHNNOSU**	nonsuch	**CIKLMUY**	muckily
	Coligny	**CHILNOO**	holonic	**CHNOOPS**	ponchos	**CIKLNRY**	crinkly
CGILNPY	clyping	**CHILNOR**	chlorin	**CHNOORT**	torchon	**CIKLORY**	rockily
CGILNRU	curling	**CHILNOS**	Nichols	**CHNORSY**	synchro	**CIKLOWW**	Wicklow
CGILORW	cowgirl	**CHILNSY**	lychnis	**CHNORTU**	cothurn	**CIKLPRY**	prickly
CGILOTT	glottic	**CHILOOS**	coolish	**CHNOTUU**	uncouth	**CIKLQUY**	quickly
CGILPTY	glyptic	**CHILORS**	orchils	**CHNSTUU**	tuchuns	**CIKLRTY**	trickly
CGIMNOP	comping	**CHILOST**	coltish	**CHOOOSW**	Soochow	**CIKMORR**	rimrock
CGIMNOS	comings	**CHILPSY**	sylphic	**CHOOPPS**	copshop	**CIKNOSW**	cowskin
CGINNNO	conning	**CHILSTU**	cultish	**CHOOPST**	post hoc	**CIKNPSU**	unpicks
CGINNNU	cunning	**CHIMMTU**	Mitchum	**CHOORST**	cohorts	**CIKNSTU**	unstick
CGINNOP	poncing	**CHIMOPR**	morphic	**CHOORSU**	ochrous	**CIKOSTU**	sickout
CGINNOR	corning	**CHIMORS**	chrisom	**CHOORWZ**	Chorzów	**CIKPPSU**	pickups
CGINNOS	consign	**CHIMRUU**	Urumchi	**CHOPSSY**	psychos	**CIKPSTU**	stickup
CGINNPU	puncing	**CHIMSSS**	schisms	**CHOPTUU**	touchup	**CIKPUWY**	wickyup
CGINNSY	syncing	**CHIMSTY**	tychism	**CHPSSUY**	scyphus	**CIKRSTY**	tricksy
CGINOOP	cooping	**CHINOOR**	chorion	**CIIILLT**	illicit	**CIKRSWY**	Ryswick
CGINOPP	copping	**CHINOPS**	chopins	**CIIINPT**	incipit	**CILLNNO**	Lincoln
CGINOPS	picongs		phonics	**CIIJLUY**	juicily	**CILLNOS**	collins
CGINOPU	couping	**CHINORS**	Cornish	**CIIKKLL**	killick	**CILLNSU**	Scullin
CGINOPW	cowping	**CHINORT**	Corinth	**CIIKLPY**	pickily	**CILLOOR**	criollo
CGINOPY	copying	**CHINORW**	Norwich	**CIIKNPS**	pickins	**CILMNOP**	complin
CGINORS	scoring	**CHINOST**	chitons	**CIIKPUW**	wickiup	**CILMOOS**	locoism
CGINORW	crowing	**CHINOSU**	cushion	**CIILLTY**	licitly	**CILMSTU**	cultism
CGINOST	costing	**CHINQSU**	squinch	**CIILLVY**	civilly	**CILNNOT**	Clinton
	gnostic	**CHINRSU**	urchins	**CIILNOP**	cipolin	**CILNOOR**	orcinol
CGINOSU	congius	**CHINSTY**	snitchy	**CIILNOS**	silicon	**CILNOSU**	uncoils
CGINOTT	cotting	**CHINTYZ**	chintzy	**CIILNOT**	Nilotic	**CILNOTU**	linocut
CGINPPU	cupping	**CHIOORS**	isochor	**CIILNUV**	uncivil	**CILNPSU**	sculpin
CGINRSU	cursing	**CHIOORZ**	chorizo	**CIILOOT**	oolitic	**CILNSTU**	linctus
CGINRSY	scrying	**CHIOPRT**	trophic	**CIILOPT**	politic	**CILOOPT**	copilot
CGINRUV	curving	**CHIOPXY**	hypoxic	**CIILOST**	colitis	**CILOORU**	couloir
CGINSSU	cussing	**CHIORST**	Christo		solicit	**CILOOSS**	colossi
CGINTTU	cutting		Christo-	**CIILOSV**	Clovis I	**CILOPRY**	pyloric
CGIOTYZ	zygotic		ostrich	**CIILPSY**	spicily	**CILOPSU**	oilcups
CGKLNOU	gunlock	**CHIORVW**	Virchow	**CIIMMNO**	minicom	**CILOPSW**	cowslip
CGLLOSY	glycols	**CHIOSSZ**	schizos	**CIIMMRY**	mimicry	**CILORST**	lictors

CILOSTU	oculist	CIORSUU	curious	CMNNOOT	Moncton	DDDEFLU	fuddled
CILPRSY	crisply	CIORTVY	victory	CMNOOOT	monocot	DDDEGII	giddied
CILPRTU	culprit	CIOSSSY	sycosis	CMNOOPT	Compton	DDDEGIR	gridded
CILSTTU	cultist	CIOSSUV	viscous	CMNOOPY	compony	DDDEGLU	guddled
CIMMOST	commits	CIPRSST	scripts	CMOOORS	Comoros	DDDEGRU	drudged
CIMNOOR	Comorin	CIPRSSU	prussic	CMOOPRT	comport	DDDEHLU	huddled
	moronic	CIPRTTY	tryptic	CMOOPST	compost	DDDEHTU	thudded
	omicron	CIPRUVY	pyruvic	CMOORSU	cormous	DDDEIIS	diddies
CIMNORS	crimson	CIPSTTY	styptic	CMORSTU	scrotum	DDDEIIV	divided
	microns	CIRSSTU	rustics	CMORTUW	cutworm	DDDEIKS	skidded
CIMNORU	Noricum	CJKNNOO	jonnock	CMOSSTU	customs	DDDEILM	middled
CIMNOSU	coniums	CKKLNUY	knuckly	CMOSUVY	Muscovy	DDDEILP	piddled
CIMNRSU	crinums	CKLLMOU	mullock	CMPRSSU	scrumps	DDDEILR	diddler
CIMOORS	morisco	CKLLOOP	pollock	CMPRSUY	scrumpy		riddled
CIMOOST	osmotic	CKLNOSU	unlocks	CNNOOOR	O'Connor	DDDEILS	diddles
CIMOPSY	miscopy	CKLNOTU	locknut	CNNOORS	Connors	DDDEIMU	muddied
CIMOSST	Scotism	CKLNOUW	Lucknow	CNNORRU	Runcorn	DDDELMU	muddled
	sitcoms	CKLNUUY	unlucky	CNNORTU	nocturn	DDDELNO	noddled
CIMOSSY	mycosis	CKLOORW	rowlock	CNNORUW	uncrown	DDDELOO	doodled
CIMOTYZ	zymotic	CKLOOTU	lockout	CNOOOTU	Cotonou	DDDELOP	plodded
CIMPRSS	scrimps	CKLOPSU	lockups	CNOOPPR	popcorn		poddled
CIMPRSY	scrimpy	CKLOPTU	potluck	CNOOPSU	coupons	DDDELOS	doddles
CIMRSSU	crissum		putlock		soupcon	DDDELOT	toddled
CIMSSTY	mystics	CKMOPSU	mockups	CNOORRW	cornrow	DDDELPU	puddled
CINNNOU	inconnu	CKNOOOR	rockoon	CNOORST	consort	DDDELRU	ruddled
CINNORU	unicorn	CKNOOOS	Cookson		crotons	DDDEOPR	prodded
CINNOSU	nuncios	CKNORSU	uncorks	CNOORTT	contort	DDDEORS	dodders
CINNOTU	unction	CKNSTUU	unstuck	CNOORTU	contour	DDDEORY	doddery
CINNSUU	uncinus		untucks		crouton	DDDEPSU	spudded
CINOOOR	Orinoco	CKOOOPT	cooktop	CNOOSST	oncosts	DDDESTU	studded
CINOOPR	porcino	CKOOOTU	cookout	CNOOSTT	cottons	DDEEELN	needled
CINOOPS	opsonic	CKOORST	Rostock	CNOOSTY	tycoons	DDEEELT	deleted
CINORRT	tricorn	CKORTUW	cutwork	CNOOSUU	nocuous	DDEEEMN	emended
CINORSS	incross	CKOSSTU	tussock	CNOOSVY	convoys	DDEEEPS	speeded
CINORST	cistron	CLLMOSU	mollusc	CNOOTTY	cottony	DDEEERR	Red Deer
	citrons	CLLOOPS	collops	CNORSSU	uncross	DDEEESX	desexed
CINORSZ	zircons		scollop	CNORTUY	country	DDEEFGL	fledged
CINORTU	ruction	CLLORSS	scrolls	CNOSSSU	Cnossus	DDEEFII	deified
CINORTY	tyronic	CLLOSUU	loculus	COOORSZ	corozos		edified
CINOSST	consist	CLMNOSU	columns	COOPRRT	proctor	DDEEFIL	defiled
	tocsins	CLMOOOU	Olomouc	COOPRSS	scroops		fielded
CINOSSU	cousins	CLMOOPT	complot	COOPRTU	outcrop	DDEEFIN	defined
	Socinus	CLMOSUU	osculum	COOPSTU	octopus	DDEEFNS	defends
CINOSTU	suction	CLMPRUY	crumply	COORSUU	roucous	DDEEFSU	defused
CINOSUZ	zincous	CLMSUUU	cumulus	COOSTTY	otocyst	DDEEFUZ	defuzed
CINOTXY	oxyntic	CLNOORT	control	COPRRSS	scrorps	DDEEGIN	deeding
CINRSTU	incrust	CLNOOSS	consols	COPRRTU	corrupt		deigned
CIOOPRS	Scorpio	CLNOSSU	consuls	COPRSSU	cuprous	DDEEGLP	pledged
CIOOPRT	portico	CLNOSTU	consult	CORRSSU	cursors	DDEEGLS	sledged
CIOOPSU	copious	CLNRSUU	uncurls	CORRSSU	cursory	DDEEGLU	deluged
CIOOQTU	coquito	CLOORSU	colours	COSTTUU	cutouts	DDEEGRR	dredger
CIOORST	octrois	CLOORUY	coloury	DDDDEIL	diddled	DDEEGRS	dredges
CIOORSU	corious	CLOOSTY	cytosol	DDDEEGR	dredged	DDEEHLS	heddles
CIOPRST	tropics	CLOPRSU	Proclus	DDDEEHS	shedded	DDEEHRS	shedder
CIOPRTY	Cypriot	CLORSSY	crossly	DDDEEIR	derided	DDEEILV	deviled
CIOPSTY	copyist	CLORTUY	courtly	DDDEELM	meddled	DDEEILW	wielded
CIORRSU	cirrous	CLOSSTU	locusts	DDDEELP	peddled	DDEEILY	yielded
CIORSSS	scissor	CLPSSTU	sculpts	DDDEELR	reddled	DDEEIMP	impeded
CIORSSU	Roscius	CMMNOOS	commons	DDDEELU	deluded	DDEEIMS	demised
CIORSTT	tricots	CMMOORS	romcoms	DDDEENS	snedded		misdeed
CIORSTU	citrous	CMMRSUY	scrummy	DDDEENU	denuded	DDEEINS	neddies
CIORSTV	victors	CMNNOOS	noncoms	DDDEFIL	fiddled	DDEEINT	teinded

Code	Word
DDEEINW	widened
DDEEINX	deindex
	indexed
DDEEINZ	dizened
DDEEIOV	videoed
DDEEIPS	depside
DDEEIRR	Deirdre
	derider
	redried
DDEEIRS	derides
	desired
	diedres
	resided
DDEEIRV	derived
DDEEIRW	weirded
DDEEIST	teddies
DDEEISV	devised
DDEELLU	duelled
DDEELLW	dwelled
DDEELMO	modeled
DDEELMR	meddler
DDEELMS	meddles
DDEELOY	yodeled
DDEELPR	peddler
DDEELPS	peddles
DDEELRS	reddles
DDEELRU	deluder
DDEELSU	deludes
DDEEMOT	demoted
DDEENOP	deponed
DDEENOT	denoted
DDEENOW	endowed
DDEENPS	depends
DDEENPU	upended
DDEENRS	Dresden
	reddens
DDEENRT	trended
DDEENRU	denuder
	endured
DDEENSU	denudes
	dudeens
DDEEOPS	deposed
	seedpod
DDEEORR	ordered
DDEEORW	dowered
DDEEOTV	devoted
DDEEOTX	detoxed
DDEEPTU	deputed
DDEERRS	redders
DDEERSS	dressed
DDEERST	reddest
	tedders
DDEERTU	detrude
DDEETTU	duetted
DDEFILR	fiddler
DDEFILS	fiddles
DDEFIOR	foredid
DDEFIRT	drifted
DDEFLNO	Flodden
	fondled
DDEFLOO	flooded
DDEFLSU	fuddles
DDEFNOR	fronded
DDEFNOU	founded
DDEFORR	Redford
DDEFORS	fodders
DDEGGRU	drugged
	grudged
DDEGHIT	dighted
DDEGIIR	giddier
DDEGIIS	giddies
DDEGILR	girdled
	griddle
DDEGIMO	demigod
	Megiddo
DDEGINO	dingoed
DDEGINR	redding
DDEGINT	tedding
DDEGINW	wedding
DDEGINY	eddying
DDEGIOR	dodgier
DDEGLOP	plodged
DDEGLOS	dogsled
DDEGLSU	guddles
DDEGMOS	dodgems
DDEGMSU	smudged
DDEGNOS	godsend
DDEGNOU	dudgeon
DDEGNWY	Gwynedd
DDEGORS	dodgers
	gorsedd
DDEGOSS	goddess
DDEGOST	stodged
DDEGRRU	drudger
DDEGRSU	drudges
DDEGRTU	trudged
DDEHIRS	reddish
DDEHIRY	hydride
DDEHLRU	huddler
	hurdled
DDEHLSU	huddles
DDEHNOU	hounded
DDEHNRU	hundred
DDEHOSW	showded
DDEHRSU	shudder
DDEIIKS	kiddies
DDEIIMS	middies
DDEIINT	indited
DDEIINV	divined
DDEIIOS	iodides
	iodised
DDEIIOX	dioxide
DDEIIOZ	iodized
DDEIIRT	dirtied
DDEIIRV	divider
DDEIISV	divides
DDEIIZZ	dizzied
DDEIKLN	kindled
DDEIKLS	kiddles
DDEIKNR	kindred
DDEIKRS	kidders
DDEILLO	dollied
DDEILLR	drilled
DDEILLU	illuded
DDEILMP	dimpled
DDEILMS	middles
DDEILNS	slidden
DDEILNW	dwindle
DDEILOS	dildoes
DDEILOT	deltoid
DDEILPR	piddler
DDEILPS	piddles
DDEILRR	riddler
DDEILRS	riddles
DDEILRT	tiddler
DDEILTU	diluted
DDEILTW	twiddle
DDEILTY	lyddite
DDEIMMU	dummied
DDEIMNS	middens
DDEIMNU	Edmund I
DDEIMOR	dermoid
DDEIMOS	desmoid
DDEIMRU	muddier
DDEIMSS	desmids
DDEIMSU	muddies
DDEINNU	Dunedin
DDEINOP	poinded
DDEINOS	noddies
DDEINOT	dentoid
DDEINPS	dispend
DDEINST	distend
DDEINSW	swidden
DDEIOPR	Perdido
DDEIOPS	poddies
DDEIORT	Diderot
DDEIORV	overdid
DDEIORW	dowdier
DDEIOST	toddies
DDEIOSW	dowdies
DDEIOTT	dittoed
DDEIOWW	widowed
DDEIPPR	dripped
DDEIRRS	ridders
DDEIRRU	ruddier
DDEISSU	disused
DDEISTU	studied
DDEJRSU	judders
DDEKMOU	dukedom
DDEKOOR	drooked
DDEKORU	drouked
DDELMOT	Detmold
DDELMOU	moulded
DDELMRU	muddler
DDELMSU	muddles
DDELNOO	noodled
DDELNOS	noddles
DDELOOR	doodler
	drooled
DDELOOS	doodles
DDELOPR	plodder
DDELOPS	poddles
DDELORT	toddler
DDELOST	toddles
DDELPRU	puddler
DDELPSU	puddles
	spuddle
DDELRSU	ruddles
DDEMMRU	drummed
DDEMMSU	smeddum
DDEMNOR	Redmond
DDEMNOS	Desmond
DDEMNOT	oddment
DDEMNOU	mounded
DDEMORR	Mordred
DDENNOR	dendron
DDENOOS	desnood
	snooded
DDENOPS	despond
DDENOPU	pounded
DDENORS	donders
DDENORT	trodden
DDENORU	redound
	rounded
	underdo
DDENORW	drowned
DDENOSS	oddness
	soddens
DDENOSU	sounded
DDENOSY	dynodes
DDENOUW	wounded
DDENSSU	suddens
DDEOOPR	drooped
DDEOORW	redwood
DDEOOWY	dyewood
DDEOPPR	dropped
DDEOPRR	prodder
DDEOPRW	dewdrop
DDEORSW	drowsed
DDEPRSU	spudder
DDERRSU	rudders
DDGGINO	dodging
DDGHOOO	godhood
DDGIIKN	kidding
DDGIILY	giddily
DDGIINR	ridding
DDGIMNU	mudding
DDGINNO	nodding
DDGINOP	podding
DDGINOS	sodding
DDGINOW	Dowding
DDGINPU	pudding
DDGIPUY	giddyup
DDGNOOS	Dodgson
DDGOOOW	dogwood
DDHIKSU	kiddush
DDHIORY	hydroid
DDIIKKS	dikdiks
DDIIKLS	skidlid
DDIILOP	diploid
DDILMUY	muddily
DDILNRS	dirndls
DDILOWY	dowdily
DDILRUY	ruddily
DDIMOOS	dodoism
DDINOSS	Siddons
DDIRSSU	siddurs

DDMMSUU	dumdums	DEEENSV	vendees	DEEFLLU	fuelled	DEEHIRR	rehired
DDMNOOR	dromond	DEEENSZ	sneezed	DEEFLNS	flensed	DEEHIST	heisted
DEEEEWW	weeweed	DEEENTT	detente	DEEFLNU	needful	DEEHITV	thieved
DEEEFLR	fleered	DEEENTV	evented	DEEFLOT	feedlot	DEEHLLS	shelled
DEEEFLT	fleeted	DEEENUV	Deneuve	DEEFLRU	feruled	DEEHLMW	whelmed
DEEEFNS	defense	DEEEOTV	devotee	DEEFLTT	fettled	DEEHLOV	hoveled
DEEEFRS	feeders	DEEEPRS	speeder	DEEFMOR	freedom	DEEHLPW	whelped
DEEEFRV	fevered		speered	DEEFNRS	fenders	DEEHLSV	shelved
DEEEGLP	pledgee	DEEEPRT	petered	DEEFORV	overfed	DEEHLSW	welshed
DEEEGMR	demerge	DEEEPST	deepest	DEEFRSU	refused	DEEHMUX	exhumed
	emerged		steeped	DEEFRTT	fretted	DEEHNOY	honeyed
DEEEGNR	greened	DEEEQRU	queered	DEEFRTU	refuted	DEEHNRT	Drenthe
	reneged	DEEERRV	revered	DEEFSSU	defuses	DEEHNVZ	Dezhnev
DEEEGRS	degrees	DEEERSS	seeders	DEEFSTT	deftest	DEEHORV	hovered
DEEEGRT	deterge	DEEERST	reested	DEEFSUZ	defuzes	DEEHPRS	sphered
	greeted		steered	DEEGGIS	gidgees	DEEHRRS	herders
DEEEGST	egested	DEEERSV	deserve	DEEGHIN	heeding	DEEHRSU	ushered
DEEEHLW	wheedle		severed		neighed	DEEHTTW	whetted
	wheeled	DEEERSW	sewered	DEEGHIW	weighed	DEEIIRW	weirdie
DEEEHNS	sheened		sweered	DEEGHOW	hogweed	DEEIIST	deities
DEEEHRS	heeders		weeders	DEEGHRS	hedgers	DEEIJLL	jellied
	heredes	DEEERSY	redeyes	DEEGIJS	gidjees	DEEIJMM	jemmied
	sheered	DEEERTV	everted	DEEGILN	deleing	DEEIKLN	kneidel
DEEEHST	seethed	DEEERTX	exerted	DEEGIMN	deeming		likened
	sheeted	DEEESSX	desexes	DEEGIMV	demiveg	DEEIKMW	midweek
DEEEHTT	teethed	DEEESTV	steeved	DEEGINN	needing	DEEIKOV	dovekie
DEEEHWZ	wheezed	DEEETTV	vedette	DEEGINR	dreeing	DEEILLM	De Mille
DEEEINR	needier	DEEETTW	tweeted		energid	DEEILMR	Demirel
DEEEIRR	reedier	DEEETWZ	tweezed		reeding	DEEILNO	eloined
DEEEIRS	seedier	DEEFFFO	feoffed		reigned	DEEILNR	redline
DEEEIRW	weedier	DEEFFIN	effendi	DEEGINS	seeding		relined
DEEEISV	devisee	DEEFFOR	offered	DEEGINW	weeding	DEEILNS	enisled
DEEEJLW	jeweled	DEEFFSU	effused	DEEGIPW	pigweed		ensiled
DEEEJRR	jerreed	DEEFGIN	feeding	DEEGIRV	diverge		linseed
DEEEJRS	jereeds		feigned		grieved	DEEILNV	livened
DEEEKLN	kneeled	DEEFGLS	fledges	DEEGIRW	wedgier	DEEILNY	dyeline
DEEEKLS	sleeked	DEEFGRU	refuged	DEEGIST	edgiest	DEEILOR	reoiled
DEEEKNW	weekend	DEEFHLS	fleshed	DEEGJRU	rejudge	DEEILPR	replied
DEEEKRY	rekeyed		shelfed	DEEGLNR	Grendel	DEEILPS	spieled
DEEELLV	leveled	DEEFHLU	heedful	DEEGLNS	legends	DEEILRS	resiled
DEEELNS	needles	DEEFHRS	freshed	DEEGLNT	gentled	DEEILRV	deliver
DEEELPT	deplete	DEEFIIR	deifier	DEEGLOY	goldeye		relived
DEEELRV	levered		edifier	DEEGLPR	pledger		reviled
	reveled		reified	DEEGLPS	pledges	DEEILRW	wielder
DEEELST	deletes	DEEFIIS	deifies	DEEGLPT	pledget	DEEILRY	reedily
	sleeted		edifies	DEEGLRS	gelders		yielder
	steeled	DEEFILN	Enfield		ledgers	DEEILSS	diesels
DEEELSV	sleeved	DEEFILR	defiler		redlegs	DEEILSY	eyelids
DEEELTX	telexed		ferlied		sledger		seedily
DEEEMNR	reedmen		fielder	DEEGLRU	reglued	DEEILTU	dilutee
DEEEMNS	demesne		refiled	DEEGLRW	wergeld	DEEILWY	weedily
DEEEMRS	emersed	DEEFILS	defiles	DEEGLSS	sledges	DEEIMNO	dominee
	medrese	DEEFINR	definer	DEEGLSU	deluges	DEEIMNS	sidemen
	redeems		refined	DEEGMUW	gumweed	DEEIMOT	Edomite
DEEEMRT	Demeter	DEEFINS	defines	DEEGNNO	endogen	DEEIMPR	demirep
	metered	DEEFINT	feinted	DEEGNRS	genders		impeder
DEEENPR	preened	DEEFIRR	ferried	DEEGORR	rogered	DEEIMPS	impedes
DEEENPS	deepens		refired	DEEGOSY	geodesy	DEEIMPT	emptied
DEEENQU	queened		refried	DEEGSSU	guessed	DEEIMRS	remised
DEEENRS	sneered	DEEFIRS	defiers	DEEGSTU	guested	DEEIMRT	demerit
DEEENRT	entered	DEEFIST	deifest	DEEHIKV	khedive		dimeter
DEEENRW	renewed	DEEFKLR	Krefeld	DEEHINR	inhered		merited

	mitered	DEEIRVV	revived	DEELRSV	delvers	DEEOPPY	popeyed
DEEIMRX	remixed	DEEISSU	diseuse	DEELRSW	rewelds	DEEOPRS	deposer
DEEIMSS	demises	DEEISSV	devises		welders		reposed
DEEIMTT	emitted	DEEISTW	dewiest	DEELSTT	settled	DEEOPRW	powered
DEEINNS	Dinesen	DEEISTX	existed	DEELSTU	teledus	DEEOPSS	deposes
DEEINNT	dentine	DEEISVZ	Devizes	DEELSTW	lewdest		speedos
DEEINNU	ennuied	DEEITTV	vidette	DEELTUX	exulted	DEEOPSX	exposed
DEEINNZ	denizen	DEEJNOY	enjoyed	DEELVXY	vexedly	DEEORRR	orderer
DEEINPR	Dnieper	DEEKKLR	de Klerk	DEEMMST	stemmed		reorder
	repined	DEEKKRT	trekked	DEEMNOR	moderne	DEEORRS	reredos
	ripened	DEEKLLN	knelled	DEEMNOU	eudemon	DEEORST	oersted
DEEINRS	deniers	DEEKLPS	skelped	DEEMNOV	Vendôme		teredos
	resined	DEEKNNS	skenned	DEEMNOY	moneyed	DEEORSV	devores
DEEINRW	rewiden	DEEKNNY	Kennedy	DEEMNRS	menders	DEEORTT	ottered
	widener	DEEKNOT	tokened		remends		tetrode
DEEINRX	indexer	DEEKNRW	Kendrew	DEEMNST	dements	DEEORTW	towered
DEEINST	destine	DEEKORV	revoked	DEEMORV	removed	DEEORUV	overdue
DEEINSV	endives	DEEKOVY	dovekey	DEEMORX	exoderm	DEEORVY	overdye
DEEINSW	endwise	DEEKSTT	sketted	DEEMOSS	demoses	DEEORXX	xeroxed
DEEINSX	indexes	DEELLMS	smelled	DEEMOST	demotes	DEEOSTV	devotes
DEEINTT	dinette	DEELLNR	Rendell	DEEMOSY	moseyed	DEEOSTX	detoxes
DEEINTU	detinue	DEELLPS	spelled	DEEMPRS	premeds	DEEPPPR	prepped
DEEINTV	evident	DEELLQU	quelled	DEEMPSY	Dempsey	DEEPPST	stepped
DEEINWZ	wizened	DEELLRU	dueller	DEEMPTT	tempted	DEEPPSU	speedup
DEEIOPS	episode	DEELLRW	dweller	DEEMRSU	resumed	DEEPRSS	depress
DEEIOPT	epidote	DEELLRY	elderly	DEENNOS	donnees		des Prés
DEEIOPX	epoxide	DEELLSW	swelled	DEENNOT	tenoned		pressed
DEEIPPT	peptide	DEELMOR	Delorme	DEENNOY	doyenne	DEEPRSU	perdues
DEEIPRS	preside		modeler	DEENNPT	pendent		perused
	speired		remodel	DEENNUY	ennuyed	DEEPRTU	erupted
DEEIPRV	deprive	DEELMPT	templed	DEENOOR	roneoed		reputed
DEEIPRX	expired	DEELMPU	deplume	DEENOPR	reponed	DEEPRTY	retyped
DEEIPSS	despise	DEELMRU	relumed	DEENOPS	depones	DEEPRUV	prevued
DEEIPST	despite	DEELMST	smelted		spondee	DEEPSTU	deputes
DEEIQRU	queried	DEELMSU	mulesed	DEENOPT	pentode	DEEQSTU	quested
DEEIQTU	quieted	DEELMSY	medleys	DEENORS	endorse	DEERRSS	dresser
DEEIRRS	derries	DEELMTT	mettled	DEENORT	erodent		redress
	desirer	DEELNOT	dolente	DEENORW	endower	DEERRUV	verdure
	Dreiser	DEELNPU	pendule		reendow	DEERSSS	dresses
	redries	DEELNRS	lenders	DEENORZ	rezoned	DEERSST	deserts
	resider		slender	DEENOST	denotes		dessert
	serried	DEELNSS	endless		Tenedos		tressed
DEEIRRT	retired	DEELNST	nestled	DEENPPR	perpend	DEERSTW	strewed
	retried	DEELNSW	wedelns	DEENPRS	spender		wrested
DEEIRRV	deriver	DEELNSY	densely	DEENPRT	pretend	DEERSTX	dexters
DEEIRRW	rewired	DEELNTT	nettled	DEENPSX	expends	DEERSVW	swerved
	weirder	DEELOPP	peopled	DEENRRS	renders	DEERTTU	uttered
DEEIRSS	desires	DEELOPR	deplore	DEENRSS	redness	DEERTUX	extrude
	resides	DEELOPV	develop		senders	DEESSTT	detests
DEEIRST	dieters	DEELOPX	explode	DEENRST	tenders	DEESSTU	Sudetes
	reedits	DEELORS	resoled	DEENRSU	endures	DEESSTV	devests
	resited	DEELORU	urodele		ensured	DEESTTT	stetted
DEEIRSU	residue	DEELORW	lowered	DEENRSV	venders	DEFFFLU	fluffed
	ureides		roweled	DEENRTU	denture	DEFFHIW	whiffed
DEEIRSV	derives	DEELOSU	delouse		tenured	DEFFILP	piffled
	deviser	DEELOTW	toweled	DEENRTW	Derwent	DEFFILR	riffled
	De Vries	DEELOVV	devolve	DEENSST	densest	DEFFIMO	fiefdom
	diverse		evolved	DEENSTT	detents	DEFFINS	sniffed
	revised	DEELPRS	pedlers	DEENSTW	West End	DEFFIOS	offside
DEEIRSW	sweired	DEELPRU	prelude	DEENSTX	extends	DEFFIRS	differs
DEEIRTU	erudite	DEELPST	pestled	DEENSUV	vendues	DEFFIST	stiffed
DEEIRTV	riveted	DEELRSU	eluders	DEENSUX	unsexed	DEFFISU	diffuse

DEFFLMU	muffled	**DEFIRZZ**	frizzed		slogged		regilds
DEFFLRU	ruffled	**DEFISTU**	feudist	**DEGGLOT**	toggled		ridgels
DEFFLSU	sluffed	**DEFKLNU**	flunked	**DEGGLPU**	plugged	**DEGILRU**	guilder
DEFFNOR	forfend	**DEFLLOU**	doleful	**DEGGLRU**	gurgled	**DEGILRW**	wergild
DEFFNOS	offends	**DEFLNOR**	fondler	**DEGGLSU**	slugged	**DEGILUV**	divulge
	sendoff	**DEFLNOS**	enfolds	**DEGGNOO**	doggone	**DEGIMNN**	mending
DEFFNSU	snuffed		fondles	**DEGGNOS**	snogged	**DEGIMNS**	smidgen
DEFFORS	doffers	**DEFLNOT**	tenfold	**DEGGNOU**	gudgeon	**DEGIMST**	midgets
DEFFRSU	duffers	**DEFLOOR**	flooder	**DEGGNSU**	snugged	**DEGINNN**	denning
DEFFSTU	duffest		floored	**DEGGOPR**	progged	**DEGINNP**	pending
	stuffed		reflood	**DEGGORS**	doggers	**DEGINNR**	grinned
DEFGGIR	frigged	**DEFLOOT**	footled	**DEGGORT**	trogged		rending
DEFGGLO	flogged	**DEFLOOZ**	foozled	**DEGGORY**	doggery	**DEGINNS**	endings
DEFGGOR	frogged	**DEFLOPP**	flopped	**DEGGRRU**	grudger		sending
DEFGINN	fending	**DEFLORS**	folders	**DEGGRSU**	grudges	**DEGINNT**	denting
DEFGINR	fringed		refolds	**DEGGRTU**	drugget		tending
DEFGINU	feuding	**DEFLORT**	telford	**DEGHHOU**	houghed	**DEGINNU**	enduing
DEFGINY	defying	**DEFLORU**	floured	**DEGHILT**	delight	**DEGINNV**	vending
DEFGIOR	firedog	**DEFLOTU**	flouted		lighted	**DEGINNW**	wending
DEFGIRS	fridges	**DEFLPRU**	purfled	**DEGHINR**	herding	**DEGINNY**	denying
DEFGIRU	figured	**DEFLRUU**	Duruflé	**DEGHINW**	whinged	**DEGINOR**	eroding
DEFGIST	fidgets	**DEFMORS**	deforms	**DEGHIOT**	hogtied		Gironde
DEFGITY	fidgety		serfdom	**DEGHIRT**	girthed		groined
DEFHIRS	redfish	**DEFNOOR**	fordone		righted		ignored
DEFHIST	shifted	**DEFNORT**	fronted	**DEGHIST**	sighted		negroid
DEFHLSU	flushed	**DEFNORU**	founder	**DEGHORU**	roughed		redoing
DEFHORT	frothed	**DEFNORW**	frowned	**DEGHOST**	ghosted	**DEGINOS**	dingoes
DEFIILM	midlife	**DEFNOST**	fondest	**DEGHOSU**	soughed	**DEGINOT**	ingoted
DEFIILN	infidel	**DEFNOSU**	fondues	**DEGHOTU**	toughed	**DEGINOW**	wendigo
	infield	**DEFNRSU**	refunds	**DEGIILN**	eliding		widgeon
DEFIIMS	fideism	**DEFOOPR**	proofed	**DEGIINN**	indigen	**DEGINRR**	grinder
DEFIIMW	midwife	**DEFOOPS**	spoofed	**DEGIINR**	dingier	**DEGINRW**	redwing
DEFIINU	unified	**DEFOORS**	fordoes	**DEGIINT**	dieting	**DEGINSS**	designs
DEFIINX	infixed	**DEFOORT**	redfoot		editing	**DEGINSW**	swinged
DEFIIST	fideist	**DEFORST**	defrost		ignited	**DEGINSY**	dingeys
DEFIKRS	frisked		frosted	**DEGIISW**	widgies	**DEGINTW**	twinged
DEFILLR	frilled	**DEFORWX**	Wexford	**DEGIJLN**	jingled	**DEGINUX**	exuding
DEFILNT	flinted	**DEFRSUY**	Dreyfus	**DEGIKLO**	doglike	**DEGIOOS**	goodies
DEFILOO	folioed	**DEGGGIL**	giggled		godlike	**DEGIOPR**	podgier
DEFILOW	oldwife	**DEGGGIN**	degging	**DEGILLO**	gollied	**DEGIORT**	goitred
DEFILPP	flipped	**DEGGGLO**	goggled	**DEGILLR**	grilled	**DEGIPPR**	gripped
DEFILRT	flirted	**DEGGHIL**	higgled	**DEGILLU**	gullied	**DEGIPRU**	pudgier
	trifled	**DEGGHIN**	hedging	**DEGILLY**	gelidly	**DEGIRRS**	girders
DEFILRU	direful	**DEGGIJL**	jiggled	**DEGILMN**	melding	**DEGIRSS**	digress
DEFILST	stifled	**DEGGIKN**	kedging		mingled	**DEGIRSU**	guiders
DEFILTT	flitted	**DEGGILN**	gelding	**DEGILNN**	lending	**DEGIRTT**	gritted
DEFILTY	fetidly		niggled	**DEGILNO**	glenoid	**DEGISST**	digests
DEFILXY	fixedly	**DEGGILU**	Gielgud	**DEGILNS**	dingles	**DEGISTU**	dugites
DEFILZZ	fizzled	**DEGGILW**	wiggled		singled	**DEGISTW**	widgets
DEFIMOR	deiform	**DEGGINS**	edgings	**DEGILNT**	glinted	**DEGJRSU**	judgers
DEFINRS	finders		snigged		tingled	**DEGLMOO**	gloomed
	friends	**DEGGINW**	wedging	**DEGILNU**	dueling	**DEGLNNO**	endlong
	redfins	**DEGGIOS**	doggies		eluding	**DEGLNOS**	dongles
DEFINRU	unfired	**DEGGIPR**	prigged		indulge	**DEGLNOU**	lounged
DEFINSU	infused	**DEGGIRS**	diggers	**DEGILNV**	delving	**DEGLNPU**	plunged
DEFINUX	unfixed	**DEGGIRT**	trigged	**DEGILNW**	welding	**DEGLNSU**	guldens
DEFIOOS	foodies	**DEGGIRU**	druggie	**DEGILOR**	gloried	**DEGLOPR**	pledgor
DEFIOST	foisted	**DEGGISW**	swigged		godlier	**DEGLOPS**	plodges
DEFIPRY	perfidy	**DEGGITW**	twigged	**DEGILRR**	girdler		splodge
DEFIRRT	drifter	**DEGGJLO**	joggled	**DEGILRS**	gilders	**DEGLORS**	lodgers
DEFIRTT	fritted	**DEGGJLU**	juggled		girdles	**DEGLORW**	growled
DEFIRTU	fruited	**DEGGLOS**	doglegs		gliders	**DEGLOSS**	glossed

	godless	**DEHIORT** theroid	**DEHOSTT** shotted
DEGLSSU	sludges	**DEHIOST** hoisted	**DEHOSTU** shouted
DEGLTTU	glutted	**DEHIOSU** hideous	**DEHPPUW** whupped
DEGLUZZ	guzzled	**DEHIOSX** oxhides	**DEIIJMM** jimmied
DEGMNOO	goodmen	**DEHIOTU** hideout	**DEIIKKL** kidlike
DEGMOOR	groomed	**DEHIPPS** shipped	**DEIIKLS** dislike
DEGMOOS	smoodge	**DEHIPPW** whipped	**DEIIKNR** dinkier
	smooged	**DEHIRRS** shirred	**DEIIKNS** dinkies
DEGMPRU	grumped	**DEHIRRU** hurried		kindies
DEGMSSU	smudges	**DEHIRRW** whirred	**DEIILLS** dillies
DEGNNOU	dungeon	**DEHIRST** dithers	**DEIILMP** implied
DEGNOPR	pronged	**DEHIRSU** hurdies	**DEIILMT** delimit
DEGNOPS	sponged		Rushdie		limited
DEGNORU	guerdon	**DEHIRSV** dervish	**DEIILOS** doilies
	undergo		shrived		idolise
DEGNORW	wronged	**DEHIRTV** thrived	**DEIILOZ** idolize
DEGNOTU	tongued	**DEHIRTW** writhed	**DEIILPS** lipides
DEGNRSU	dungers	**DEHIRTY** dithery	**DEIIMMX** immixed
	gerunds	**DEHISSW** Swedish	**DEIIMNO** dominie
	nudgers		swished	**DEIINOS** ionised
DEGNRTU	grunted	**DEHISTT** shitted	**DEIINOT** edition
	trudgen	**DEHISTW** whisted	**DEIINOZ** ionized
DEGOORV	grooved	**DEHISVV** shivved	**DEIINRS** insider
DEGOOST	stooged	**DEHIWZZ** whizzed	**DEIINRT** inditer
DEGOPRU	grouped	**DEHKORS** Shkodër		nitride
DEGORRS	Rodgers	**DEHLLOO** holloed	**DEIINRU** uridine
DEGORSS	grossed	**DEHLLOU** hulloed	**DEIINRV** diviner
	sodgers	**DEHLOOT** toehold	**DEIINRW** windier
DEGORSU	drogues	**DEHLOPP** hoppled	**DEIINSS** insides
	gourdes	**DEHLORS** holders	**DEIINST** indites
	groused	**DEHLORW** whorled		tineids
DEGORTU	grouted	**DEHLOSS** sloshed	**DEIINSV** divines
DEGOSST	stodges	**DEHLRRU** hurdler	**DEIINTV** invited
DEGRRTU	trudger	**DEHLRSU** hurdles	**DEIIOPR** Pedro II
DEGRSTU	trudges	**DEHLRTU** hurtled	**DEIIORS** iodiser
DEGSSTU	degusts	**DEHLSSU** slushed	**DEIIORT** diorite
DEHHSSU	shushed	**DEHLSTU** hustled	**DEIIORZ** iodizer
DEHIINN	hinnied	**DEHMORU** humored	**DEIIOSS** iodises
DEHIIRS	dishier	**DEHMOST** methods	**DEIIOSX** oxidise
DEHIKRS	shirked	**DEHMOTU** mouthed	**DEIIOSZ** iodizes
DEHIKSW	whisked	**DEHMPTU** thumped	**DEIIOXZ** oxidize
DEHILPR	hirpled	**DEHNNSU** shunned	**DEIIPPR** dippier
DEHILRT	thirled	**DEHNOOR** honored	**DEIIPRT** riptide
DEHILRW	whirled	**DEHNOOW** hoedown		tiderip
DEHILSS	shields		woodhen	**DEIIRRT** dirtier
DEHILTY	diethyl	**DEHNORR** Hordern	**DEIIRST** dirties
DEHIMMS	shimmed	**DEHNORS** dehorns		ditsier
DEHIMNU	inhumed	**DEHNORT** thonder	**DEIIRTZ** ditzier
DEHIMOP	hemipod		throned	**DEIIRZZ** dizzier
DEHIMOR	heirdom	**DEHNORU** hounder	**DEIISTT** ditties
DEHIMOT	ethmoid	**DEHNOSY** hoydens		tidiest
DEHIMUX	humidex	**DEHNOTZ** dozenth	**DEIISTV** visited
DEHINNS	shinned	**DEHNRTU** thunder	**DEIISVV** divvies
DEHINNT	thinned	**DEHNSTU** shunted	**DEIISYZ** Yezidis
DEHINOR	hordein	**DEHOOPW** whooped	**DEIISZZ** dizzies
DEHINOS	hoidens	**DEHOOST** soothed	**DEIJLLO** jollied
DEHINRS	hinders	**DEHOOSW** wooshed	**DEIJNOR** joinder
	nerdish	**DEHOOTT** toothed	**DEIJNOT** jointed
	shrined	**DEHOOWY** Heywood	**DEIJNRU** injured
DEHINRX	Hendrix	**DEHOPPS** shopped	**DEIJORY** joyride
DEHIOOS	hoodies	**DEHOPPW** whopped	**DEIJOST** joisted
DEHIOOT	dhootie	**DEHORTW** worthed	**DEIKLLS** deskill

	skilled
DEIKLNP	plinked
DEIKLNR	kindler
DEIKLNS	kindles
DEIKLNT	tinkled
DEIKLNW	winkled
DEIKLOR	rodlike
DEIKLOS	keloids
DEIKLRS	skirled
DEIKLTT	kittled
DEIKMMS	skimmed
DEIKMPS	skimped
DEIKMRS	smirked
DEIKNNS	skinned
DEIKNOS	doeskin
	Sekondi
DEIKNOV	invoked
DEIKNPR	prinked
DEIKNRR	drinker
DEIKNRS	redskin
DEIKNST	kindest
DEIKNSW	swinked
DEIKNSY	kidneys
DEIKNTT	knitted
DEIKPPS	skipped
DEIKRRS	skirred
DEIKRST	skirted
DEIKRSU	duikers
	duskier
DEIKSVY	skydive
DEILLMU	illumed
DEILLNW	indwell
DEILLOS	dollies
DEILLPR	prilled
DEILLPS	spilled
DEILLQU	quilled
DEILLRR	driller
	redrill
DEILLRT	trilled
DEILLSS	lidless
DEILLST	stilled
DEILLSU	illudes
	sullied
DEILLSW	swilled
DEILLTW	twilled
DEILMMS	slimmed
DEILMNS	mildens
DEILMOP	implode
DEILMOR	moldier
DEILMOS	meloids
	midsole
DEILMOY	myeloid
DEILMPP	pimpled
DEILMPS	dimples
	mispled
DEILMPW	wimpled
DEILMST	mildest
DEILMSW	mildews
DEILMWY	mildewy
DEILMXY	mixedly
DEILMZZ	mizzled
DEILNNS	lindens

DEILNNU	unlined		reminds	**DEINSTT**	dentist	**DEIPTTU**	puttied
DEILNOO	eidolon	**DEIMNSS**	dimness		stinted	**DEIQRSU**	squired
DEILNOS	dolines	**DEIMNST**	mindset	**DEINSTY**	density	**DEIQRTU**	quirted
DEILNOT	lentoid	**DEIMNTU**	minuted		destiny	**DEIQTTU**	quitted
DEILNPS	spindle	**DEIMNUX**	unmixed	**DEINSUZ**	unsized	**DEIRRST**	stirred
	splined	**DEIMOOR**	moidore	**DEIOORW**	woodier		strider
DEILNRT	tendril		moodier	**DEIOOSS**	isodose	**DEIRRSU**	durries
DEILNST	dentils	**DEIMOPR**	impedor	**DEIOOST**	osteoid	**DEIRRSV**	drivers
DEILNSW	swindle	**DEIMOPS**	imposed	**DEIOPPP**	poppied	**DEIRRST**	strides
DEILNSY	Lindsey	**DEIMORS**	moiders	**DEIOPRS**	periods	**DEIRRSU**	diseurs
	snidely	**DEIMOST**	modiste	**DEIOPRT**	diopter	**DEIRSTU**	dustier
DEILNTU	diluent	**DEIMOSW**	mowdies		dioptre	**DEIRSTV**	diverts
DEILNTW	indwelt	**DEIMOTT**	omitted		peridot	**DEISSST**	desists
DEILNUV	unlived	**DEIMOTV**	motived	**DEIOPRV**	provide	**DEISSSU**	disuses
DEILOPR	leporid		vomited	**DEIOPSS**	dispose	**DEISSTU**	studies
DEILOPS	despoil	**DEIMPPR**	primped	**DEIOPST**	deposit		tissued
	diploes	**DEIMPRU**	dumpier		dopiest	**DEISSTV**	divests
	dipoles		umpired		posited	**DEISTTW**	twisted
	spoiled	**DEIMPTU**	imputed		topside	**DEITTTW**	twitted
DEILOPT	piloted	**DEIMRRS**	smirred	**DEIOPSU**	Oedipus	**DEJLOST**	jostled
DEILOPU	euploid	**DEIMRSY**	semidry		Opus Dei	**DEJLSTU**	justled
DEILORS	soldier	**DEIMRUU**	uredium	**DEIOPTT**	tiptoed	**DEJMOUZ**	Judezmo
DEILORW	dowlier	**DEIMSST**	demists	**DEIOPTV**	pivoted	**DEJOORV**	joyrode
DEILOSV	livedos	**DEIMSSU**	misused	**DEIORRT**	dortier	**DEJOSTU**	jousted
DEILOSY	doylies	**DEIMSTW**	Midwest	**DEIORRW**	rowdier	**DEKKLSU**	skulked
DEILPPR	rippled	**DEIMSTY**	stymied		wordier	**DEKLLNO**	knolled
DEILPPS	slipped	**DEINNOS**	donnies		worried	**DEKLNOP**	plonked
DEILPPT	tippled	**DEINNOT**	intoned	**DEIORSS**	dossier	**DEKLNPU**	plunked
DEILPRT	tripled	**DEINNRS**	dinners	**DEIORST**	editors	**DEKLNRU**	knurled
DEILPSS	dispels	**DEINNRU**	inurned		sortied	**DEKNNRU**	drunken
DEILPSU	Lepidus	**DEINNST**	indents		steroid	**DEKNOST**	Donetsk
DEILPTY	tepidly		intends		storied		stonked
DEILPUX	Dupleix	**DEINNSU**	dunnies		triodes	**DEKNOSY**	donkeys
DEILQTU	quilted		undines	**DEIORSV**	devisor	**DEKNOTT**	knotted
DEILRSS	sidlers	**DEINNSW**	enwinds		devoirs	**DEKNOUY**	unyoked
	sliders	**DEINNTU**	dunnite		visored	**DEKNRRU**	drunker
DEILRSV	drivels	**DEINNTW**	twinned		voiders	**DEKNRSU**	dunkers
DEILRSW	swirled	**DEINOOZ**	ozonide	**DEIORSW**	dowries	**DEKOOPS**	spooked
	wilders	**DEINOPS**	spinode		rowdies	**DEKOOST**	dookets
DEILRTU	diluter	**DEINOPT**	pointed		weirdos		stooked
DEILRTW	twirled	**DEINORS**	indorse	**DEIORTT**	Detroit	**DEKOPST**	desktop
DEILRTY	tiredly		rosined		dottier	**DEKORST**	stroked
DEILRVY	devilry	**DEINORU**	dourine	**DEIORTU**	outride	**DEKORWY**	keyword
DEILRWY	weirdly	**DEINORW**	downier	**DEIORVZ**	vizored	**DEKOSVY**	skydove
DEILRZZ	drizzle	**DEINOTZ**	Doenitz	**DEIORWW**	widower	**DEKRSUY**	duykers
DEILSTT	stilted	**DEINPPS**	snipped	**DEIOSTU**	outside	**DELLOOW**	woolled
DEILSTU	dilutes	**DEINPRT**	printed		tedious	**DELLOPR**	redpoll
DEILSTW	wildest	**DEINRRU**	nurdier	**DEIOSTW**	dowiest	**DELLORT**	trolled
DEILSZZ	sizzled	**DEINRSU**	insured	**DEIOSTZ**	doziest	**DELLOSU**	duellos
DEIMMPR	primmed	**DEINRSV**	verdins	**DEIOSUV**	devious	**DELLOVW**	lowveld
DEIMMRS	dimmers	**DEINRSW**	rewinds	**DEIPPQU**	quipped	**DELLRRU**	Durrell
DEIMMRT	midterm		winders	**DEIPPRS**	dippers	**DELLSTU**	dullest
	trimmed	**DEINRTT**	trident	**DEIPPRT**	tripped	**DELMMSU**	slummed
DEIMMRU	immured	**DEINRTU**	intrude	**DEIPPSU**	duppies	**DELMNOS**	dolmens
DEIMMST	dimmest		turdine	**DEIPRSS**	spiders	**DELMORS**	molders
DEIMMSU	dummies		untried	**DEIPRST**	striped		slormed
	mediums	**DEINRTX**	dextrin	**DEIPRSY**	spidery		smolder
DEIMNNU	minuend	**DEINRTY**	tindery	**DEIPSSU**	upsides	**DELMORU**	moulder
DEIMNOR	minored	**DEINSST**	dissent	**DEIPSSV**	vespids		remould
DEIMNPS	impends		snidest	**DEIPSTT**	spitted	**DELMOSU**	modules
	Mendips	**DEINSSY**	endysis	**DEIPSTU**	dispute	**DELMOTT**	mottled
DEIMNRS	minders			**DEIPSXY**	pyxides		

175

DELMOTU	moulted
DELMOUV	volumed
DELMPPU	plumped
DELMPRU	rumpled
DELMPSU	slumped
DELMUZZ	muzzled
DELNOOS	noodles
DELNORS	rondels
DELNORU	roundel
DELNOSS	oldness
DELNOSU	loudens
	nodules
DELNOTW	letdown
DELNOTY	notedly
DELNOUV	unloved
DELNPRU	plunder
DELNRSU	rundles
DELNRTU	rundlet
	trundle
DELNRUU	unruled
DELNSSU	dulness
DELNUZZ	nuzzled
DELOOPP	pleopod
DELOOPS	poodles
	spooled
DELOOPT	pootled
DELOORT	rootled
DELOOSS	dolosse
DELOOST	stooled
DELOOTT	tootled
DELOPPP	plopped
	poppled
DELOPPS	slopped
DELOPPT	toppled
DELOPRS	polders
	presold
DELOPRT	droplet
DELOPRW	prowled
DELOPSY	deploys
DELOPTT	plotted
DELORRY	orderly
DELORSS	solders
DELORST	oldster
DELORSU	Lourdes
DELORSW	weldors
DELORSY	yodlers
DELORTT	dottrel
DELORUV	louvred
DELOSSS	dossels
DELOSTT	dottels
	dottles
	slotted
DELOSTU	loudest
	tousled
DELOSYY	doyleys
DELOSZZ	sozzled
DELOTUV	voluted
DELOTUZ	touzled
DELPPSU	suppled
DELPRSU	drupels
	slurped
DELPSTU	duplets
DELPUZZ	puzzled
DELRRSU	slurred
DELRSTU	lustred
	rustled
	strudel
DELRTTU	turtled
DELSSTU	tussled
DEMMRRU	drummer
DEMMSTU	stummed
DEMNOOR	doormen
	Ormonde
DEMNOOW	woodmen
DEMNORS	moderns
DEMNORT	mordent
DEMNORU	mourned
DEMNOST	endmost
DEMNOTU	demount
	mounted
DEMNOUV	unmoved
DEMNSTU	dustmen
DEMOOPP	popedom
DEMOOPR	predoom
DEMOORT	motored
DEMOOSS	osmosed
DEMOPST	stomped
DEMORRS	dormers
DEMORRU	rumored
DEMORST	stormed
DEMOSTY	modesty
DEMPRSU	dumpers
DEMPRTU	trumped
DEMPSTU	stumped
DEMRRSU	murders
	smurred
DEMSTTU	smutted
DENNORT	donnert
DENNOST	tendons
DENNOUW	enwound
	unowned
DENNSTU	dunnest
	stunned
DENOOPS	snooped
	spooned
DENOOSW	swooned
	woodens
DENOOSZ	snoozed
DENOOTU	duotone
	outdone
DENOPPR	propend
DENOPRS	ponders
	respond
DENOPRT	portend
DENOPRU	pounder
DENOPSU	unposed
DENOPUX	expound
DENORRU	rondure
	rounder
DENORRW	drowner
DENORST	rodents
	snorted
DENORSU	Øresund
	resound
	sounder
	undoers
DENORSV	vendors
DENORSW	downers
	wonders
DENORUW	rewound
	wounder
DENOSTU	snouted
DENPRSU	spurned
DENPRTU	prudent
DENPSSU	sendups
	suspend
DENRSSU	sunders
	undress
DENRSSY	dryness
DENSSUW	sundews
DENSTTU	student
	stunted
DENTUVY	duvetyn
DEOOPPS	opposed
DEOOPRS	spoored
DEOOPRT	torpedo
	trooped
DEOOPST	stooped
DEOOPSW	swooped
DEOORRT	redroot
DEOORST	roosted
DEOORTU	outrode
DEOOSTU	outdoes
DEOPPPR	propped
DEOPPRR	dropper
DEOPPRS	doppers
DEOPPST	stopped
DEOPPSW	swopped
DEOPRRU	prouder
DEOPRST	deports
	sported
DEOPRSW	powders
DEOPRTU	trouped
DEOPRWY	powdery
DEOPSST	despots
DEOPSSU	spoused
DEOPSTT	spotted
DEOPSTU	spouted
DEORRSV	drovers
DEORRSW	rewords
DEORSSS	dossers
DEORSSU	dousers
DEORSSW	dowsers
	drowses
DEORSTT	dotters
DEORSTU	detours
	rousted
DEORSTW	strowed
	worsted
DEORSTY	destroy
	stroyed
DEORSUV	devours
DEORTTT	trotted
DEORTTU	tutored
DEOSSYY	odyssey
DEOSTTT	stotted
DEOSTTU	testudo
DEOSTTW	swotted
DEOSTUU	duteous
DEOSTUX	tuxedos
DEPRRSU	spurred
DEPRRUY	prudery
DEPRSTU	spurted
DEPRSUU	pursued
	usurped
DEPRSUY	syruped
DERSSTU	dusters
	trussed
DERSTTU	trusted
DERSTTY	trysted
DERSTUU	sutured
DFFGINO	doffing
DFFGINU	duffing
DFFIIMR	midriff
DFFIIRT	triffid
DFFILOR	Lifford
DFGGIIN	fidging
DFGGINU	fudging
DFGHIOS	dogfish
DFGIINN	finding
DFGIINY	dignify
DFGILNO	folding
DFGINNU	funding
DFGINOR	fording
	Fröding
DFGINOU	fungoid
DFHILSU	dishful
DFHIMSU	mudfish
DFIILRW	Wilfrid
DFILLUY	fluidly
DFILMNU	mindful
DFILNOP	pinfold
DFILNOS	infolds
DFILORT	trifold
DFILORU	Rudolf I
DFILOSX	sixfold
DFILTUU	dutiful
DFLMOUW	mudflow
DFLNOSU	unfolds
DFLOOTU	foldout
DFLOOTW	twofold
DFMMORU	Mumford
DFMORRU	Rumford
DFNNOUU	unfound
DFNORUY	foundry
DGGGIIN	digging
DGGGINO	dogging
DGGHIOS	doggish
DGGIILN	gilding
	gliding
DGGIINN	dinging
DGGIINR	girding
	griding
	ridging
DGGIINU	guiding
DGGIJNU	judging
DGGILNO	Golding
	lodging

DGGIMNO	modging
DGGINNO	donging
DGGINNU	dunging
	nudging
DGGNOSU	dugongs
DGHIINS	dishing
	hidings
	shindig
DGHIKNO	Hodgkin
DGHILNO	holding
DGHINOO	hooding
DGHINOR	hording
DGHINTU	hindgut
DGHIOOS	goodish
DGHOOOW	Hogwood
DGHOOST	hotdogs
DGHORTU	drought
DGHOTUY	doughty
DGIIKNN	dinking
DGIIKNR	dirking
DGIIKNS	disking
DGIILNS	sidling
	sliding
DGIILNW	wilding
DGIILNY	dingily
DGIILRY	rigidly
DGIIMMN	dimming
DGIIMNN	minding
DGIIMNS	smidgin
DGIIMOS	sigmoid
DGIINNN	dinning
DGIINNT	dinting
DGIINNU	induing
DGIINNW	winding
DGIINOS	indigos
DGIINOV	voiding
DGIINOW	windigo
DGIINOX	digoxin
DGIINPP	dipping
DGIINPR	priding
DGIINPS	pidgins
DGIINPU	pinguid
DGIINRS	ridings
DGIINRV	driving
DGIINSS	dissing
	sidings
DGIINST	tidings
DGIINTY	dignity
	tidying
DGIJOSU	judogis
DGIKLNO	Kolding
DGIKMNO	kingdom
DGIKNNU	dunking
DGIKNOO	dooking
DGIKNOU	douking
DGIKNSU	dusking
DGILLNO	dolling
DGILLNU	dulling
DGILMNO	molding
DGILNOO	Goldoni
DGILNOR	lording
DGILOPY	podgily

DGILOST	diglots
DGILPUY	pudgily
DGIMNOO	Domingo
	dooming
DGIMNPU	dumping
DGIMNSU	Sigmund
DGIMSTU	midguts
DGINNNO	donning
DGINNNU	dunning
DGINNOR	droning
DGINNOU	undoing
DGINNOW	downing
DGINNSY	synding
DGINNTU	dunting
DGINNUY	undying
DGINOOW	wooding
DGINOPS	pongids
DGINORS	rodings
DGINORV	droving
DGINORW	wording
DGINOSS	dossing
DGINOSU	dousing
	guidons
DGINOSW	dowsing
DGINOTT	dotting
DGINPPU	dupping
DGINSTU	dusting
DGIOORR	Rodrigo
DGIOPRY	prodigy
DGIOSTW	godwits
DGIQSUY	squidgy
DGISSTU	disgust
DGLNOUY	ungodly
DGLOOOW	logwood
DGLOOST	godslot
DGLOOSU	duologs
DGLOPSY	splodgy
DGMOOUW	gumwood
DGMOPRU	gumdrop
DGNOOOP	gonopod
DGNOOOR	godroon
DGNOORS	drongos
DGNOOSS	godsons
DGNOOSW	godowns
DGNOOUV	Godunov
DGNORSU	grounds
DGNOSSU	sundogs
DGOORTT	dogtrot
DGOPRRU	prodrug
DGOSTUU	dugouts
DHIILOT	lithoid
DHIILSW	wildish
DHIIMNO	hominid
DHIIMPS	midship
DHIINOU	Houdini
DHIINRU	hirudin
DHIIOPX	xiphoid
DHIIORZ	rhizoid
DHIIOST	histoid
DHILLOS	dollish
DHILLPY	phyllid
DHILLSU	dullish

DHILMUY	humidly
DHILNOP	dolphin
DHILOST	doltish
DHILOSU	loudish
DHILRTY	thirdly
DHIMOPR	dimorph
DHIMORU	humidor
	rhodium
DHIMPSU	dumpish
DHINNOS	donnish
DHINOPY	hypnoid
DHINORS	dronish
DHINRSU	nurdish
DHIOOST	dhootis
DHIOPTY	typhoid
DHIORTY	thyroid
DHIPRSU	prudish
DHIPRSY	syrphid
DHJOPRU	jodhpur
DHKORSY	droshky
DHLMOOU	hoodlum
DHLOOTU	holdout
DHLOPSU	holdups
	upholds
DHMMRUU	humdrum
DHMNOYY	hymnody
DHNNOOU	nunhood
DHNOPRU	Prud'hon
DHOOOOS	hoodoos
DHOPRSU	pushrod
DHORSSU	shrouds
DHORSTU	drouths
DHORSUY	hydrous
DHORTUY	drouthy
DHORXYY	hydroxy
DIIIMRU	iridium
DIIINPS	insipid
DIIJNOS	disjoin
DIIKKNS	kidskin
DIILLST	distill
DIILLVY	lividly
DIILMNS	dislimn
DIILMOO	modioli
DIILMOS	idolism
DIILMTY	timidly
DIILNNU	indulin
DIILNWY	windily
DIILOPS	lipoids
DIILOST	idolist
DIILQSU	liquids
DIILRSU	silurid
DIILRTY	dirtily
DIILSST	distils
DIILSTY	idylist
DIILVVY	vividly
DIILYZZ	dizzily
DIIMNOR	midiron
DIIMSSS	dismiss
DIIMSTW	dimwits
DIINOQU	quinoid
DIINORS	sordini
DIINOSX	dioxins

DIIOOPS	opioids
DIIOPRS	spiroid
DIIORSV	divisor
	viroids
DIIRSTX	distrix
DIJMSSU	musjids
DIJOSTU	judoist
DIKKLSU	kudliks
DIKKOPS	dikkops
DIKLSUY	duskily
DIKNOOR	Doornik
DIKOORT	drookit
DIKORTU	droukit
DILLOSY	solidly
DILLPSY	psyllid
DILLRUY	luridly
DILMNRU	drumlin
DILMOOY	doomily
	moodily
DILMORS	milords
DILMPUY	dumpily
DILMTUY	tumidly
DILNNSU	dunlins
DILNOPT	diplont
DILNOXY	indoxyl
DILNPSY	spindly
DILNSTU	indults
DILOPVV	Plovdiv
DILORWY	rowdily
	wordily
DILOSSU	dulosis
	solidus
DILOSTY	styloid
DILOTTY	dottily
DILRYZZ	drizzly
DILSTUY	dustily
DIMMOST	midmost
DIMNOOR	Mindoro
DIMNOOS	dominos
DIMNOPU	impound
DIMNOSU	Dominus
DIMNOTW	midtown
DIMNOWX	mixdown
DIMOPSU	podiums
DIMOSSW	wisdoms
DIMRTUU	triduum
DIMRUUV	duumvir
DINNOPR	nondrip
DINNOPW	pindown
DINNOSW	Swindon
DINNSUW	unwinds
DINOORS	indoors
	sordino
DINOPSU	unipods
DINORSU	durions
DINORSW	Windsor
DINORWW	windrow
DINOSSW	disowns
DINOSWW	windows
DINPSTU	pundits
DINPSUW	windups
DINSSTU	nudists

DIOOPPS	doppios	**EEEFLRS**	feelers	**EEEINRS**	eserine	**EEENPRR**	preener
DIOOPSS	isopods	**EEEFLRT**	fleeter	**EEEINRT**	teenier	**EEENPRT**	preteen
DIOORST	toroids	**EEEFLSS**	feeless	**EEEINRW**	weenier		terpene
DIOORTT	ridotto	**EEEFMNR**	freemen	**EEEINSW**	weenies	**EEENPST**	steepen
DIOOSTX	toxoids	**EEEFORS**	foresee	**EEEINTW**	tweenie	**EEENPSX**	expense
DIOPRST	disport	**EEEFRRS**	reefers	**EEEIPRS**	peeries	**EEENRRS**	sneerer
	tripods	**EEEFRRZ**	freezer	**EEEIPRW**	weepier	**EEENRRT**	enterer
DIOPRTY	tripody	**EEEFRSZ**	freezes	**EEEIPST**	epeeist		reenter
DIORRST	stridor	**EEEGIKR**	geekier	**EEEIPSW**	weepies	**EEENRRW**	renewer
DIORSTT	distort	**EEEGILN**	gleenie	**EEEIRRT**	retiree	**EEENRRY**	Nyerere
DIOSSTU	studios	**EEEGILS**	elegies	**EEEIRRV**	reverie	**EEENRST**	entrees
DIPRSTU	disrupt		elegise	**EEEIRST**	eeriest	**EEENRSV**	eveners
DIPSSTU	stupids	**EEEGILZ**	elegize	**EEEIRSV**	veeries		veneers
DJNNOOS	donjons	**EEEGINP**	epigene	**EEEISTW**	sweetie	**EEENRSZ**	sneezer
DKLOOPS	Podolsk	**EEEGINR**	greenie	**EEEJLRW**	jeweler	**EEENRTV**	eventer
DKNOOPS	pondoks	**EEEGINU**	Eugénie	**EEEJLRZ**	Jezreel		evernet
DKOOOOS	koodoos	**EEEGIPR**	perigee	**EEEJPRS**	jeepers	**EEENRTX**	externe
DLLOOPS	dollops	**EEEGKLR**	kegeler	**EEEJRRS**	jeerers	**EEENRUV**	revenue
DLLORWY	worldly	**EEEGLMN**	gleemen	**EEEKLLU**	ukelele		unreeve
DLMNOOU	Muldoon	**EEEGLNT**	genteel	**EEEKLNR**	kneeler		
DLMOSUU	modulus	**EEEGLRY**	Greeley	**EEEKLPW**	ekpwele	**EEENSSZ**	sneezes
DLNOOWW	lowdown	**EEEGMRS**	emerges	**EEEKLRS**	sleeker	**EEENSTW**	sweeten
DLNORUY	roundly	**EEEGNOS**	Genoese	**EEEKLSW**	Weelkes	**EEEOPPS**	epopees
DLNOSUY	soundly	**EEEGNPR**	epergne	**EEEKMST**	meekest	**EEEORSV**	oversee
DLOOOTW	woodlot	**EEEGNRR**	greener	**EEEKNPT**	keepnet	**EEEORSY**	eyesore
DLOOPPY	polypod		reneger	**EEEKNRS**	keeners	**EEEPPRS**	peepers
DLOOPTY	tylopod	**EEEGNRS**	reneges	**EEEKNST**	keenest	**EEEPRSS**	peeress
DLOOPUY	duopoly	**EEEGNRU**	renegue		ketenes	**EEEPRST**	steeper
DLOOPWY	plywood	**EEEGNRV**	revenge	**EEEKPRS**	keepers	**EEEPRSV**	peevers
DLOOSTU	outsold	**EEEGNRW**	Wegener	**EEEKRSS**	seekers	**EEEPRSW**	sweeper
DLOPRUY	proudly	**EEEGNSS**	geneses	**EEEKRST**	keester		weepers
DLOSTUW	wouldst	**EEEGNTT**	genette	**EEELLRV**	leveler	**EEEPRTU**	Euterpe
DMNOORS	dromons	**EEEGRRT**	greeter	**EEELMNT**	element	**EEEQRRU**	queerer
DMNOSSU	osmunds	**EEEGRSZ**	geezers	**EEELMSX**	lexemes	**EEEQSUZ**	squeeze
DMNOSSY	Symonds	**EEEGRUX**	exergue	**EEELNSV**	elevens	**EEERRRV**	reverer
DNNOOSW	Snowdon	**EEEHILW**	wheelie	**EEELPRS**	peelers	**EEERRST**	steerer
DNNORUW	rundown	**EEEHLNR**	Heerlen		sleeper	**EEERRSV**	reserve
DNNOSUU	unsound	**EEEHLOY**	eyehole	**EEELPRT**	replete		reveres
DNNOSUW	sundown	**EEEHLRS**	heelers	**EEELPST**	steeple		reverse
DNNOUUW	unwound		reheels	**EEELRRS**	reelers	**EEERRSW**	sweerer
DNOORTU	orotund	**EEEHLRW**	wheeler	**EEELRTV**	leveret	**EEERSSS**	seeress
DNOOTUW	nutwood	**EEEHRRS**	sheerer	**EEELSSS**	lessees	**EEERSTT**	teeters
DNOPRUU	roundup	**EEEHRWZ**	wheezer	**EEELSSV**	sleeves	**EEERSTV**	Everest
DNOSSTU	stounds	**EEEHSST**	seethes	**EEELSSY**	eyeless	**EEERSTW**	sweeter
DNOSSUW	swounds	**EEEHSTT**	esthete	**EEELSTX**	telexes	**EEERSVW**	weevers
DOOOOSV	voodoos		teethes	**EEELSTY**	eyelets	**EEERTTW**	tweeter
DOOORSU	odorous	**EEEHSWZ**	wheezes	**EEELTTX**	teletex	**EEERTWZ**	tweezer
DOOORTU	outdoor	**EEEIJLS**	jeelies	**EEEMMSS**	meseems	**EEESSTT**	settees
DOOPRSU	uropods	**EEEIKLL**	eellike		sememes	**EEESSTV**	steeves
DOOPRSY	prosody	**EEEIKLS**	keelies	**EEEMNRS**	meneers	**EEESTWZ**	tweezes
DOOPRTU	dropout	**EEEIKLV**	eyelike	**EEEMNSS**	Messene	**EEFFFNO**	enfeoff
DPSSTUU	dustups	**EEEIKLZ**	Ezekiel		nemeses	**EEFFFOR**	feoffer
EEEEFRR	referee	**EEEILRR**	leerier	**EEEMORT**	eroteme	**EEFFINT**	fifteen
EEEEFRW	Wee Free	**EEEILRV**	relieve	**EEEMRRV**	Vermeer	**EEFFJRY**	Jeffrey
EEEEGTX	exegete	**EEEILVV**	evil eye	**EEEMRSS**	seemers	**EEFFNOS**	offense
EEEEPST	teepees	**EEEIMMR**	Mérimée	**EEEMRST**	meeters	**EEFFORR**	offerer
EEEEPSW	peewees	**EEEIMNS**	enemies		teemers	**EEFFOST**	toffees
EEEESHW	weewees	**EEEIMNT**	emetine	**EEEMRTX**	extreme	**EEFFSSU**	effuses
EEEFFFO	feoffee	**EEEIMPR**	epimere	**EEEMSST**	esteems	**EEFGILN**	feeling
EEEFFKO	O'Keeffe		preemie		mestees		fleeing
EEEFGRU	refugee	**EEEIMRT**	eremite	**EEENNPT**	pentene	**EEFGILT**	gefilte
EEEFHRS	shereef	**EEEINNT**	Étienne	**EEENNTT**	entente	**EEFGINR**	feigner

	freeing		fresnel	**EEGIKLL**	leglike	**EEGLNOR** erelong
	reefing	**EEFLNSS**	flenses	**EEGIKLM**	gemlike	**EEGLNOU** eugenol
EEFGINZ	feezing	**EEFLRRU**	ferrule	**EEGIKLN**	keeling	**EEGLNOZ** lozenge
EEFGLLU	gleeful	**EEFLRST**	reflets	**EEGIKNN**	keening	**EEGLNRT** gentler
EEFGLOR	foreleg		telfers		kneeing	**EEGLNRY** greenly
EEFGLOS	solfege	**EEFLRSU**	ferules	**EEGIKNP**	keeping	**EEGLNST** gentles
EEFGORR	reforge		fuelers		peeking	**EEGLNSU** lungees
EEFGRSU	refuges		refuels	**EEGIKNR**	reeking	**EEGLRST** reglets
EEFHIRS	heifers			**EEGIKNS**	seeking	**EEGLRSU** reglues
EEFHIRT	heftier	**EEFLRTT**	fettler	**EEGIKNT**	kitenge	**EEGMNOS** genomes
EEFHISY	fisheye	**EEFLRTU**	fleuret	**EEGILNN**	Glennie	**EEGMNRS** germens
EEFHITZ	Heifetz	**EEFLRUX**	flexure	**EEGILNP**	peeling	**EEGMNST** segment
EEFHLRS	flesher	**EEFLSTT**	fettles	**EEGILNR**	leering	**EEGMOST** gemotes
	herself	**EEFLSUY**	eyefuls		reeling	**EEGMRRS** mergers
EEFHLSS	fleshes	**EEFMNOR**	foremen	**EEGILNS**	seeling	**EEGMRTU** gumtree
EEFHNRS	freshen	**EEFMNRT**	ferment	**EEGILNT**	gentile	**EEGNNST** gennets
EEFHORT	thereof	**EEFMOTT**	mofette	**EEGILRV**	veliger	**EEGNNUY** Guyenne
EEFHORW	whereof	**EEFMPRU**	perfume	**EEGILST**	elegist	**EEGNORS** negroes
EEFHRRS	fresher	**EEFNRRW**	Renfrew	**EEGIMMR**	immerge	**EEGNPUX** expunge
	refresh	**EEFNRRY**	fernery	**EEGIMNR**	regimen	**EEGNRSS** negress
EEFHRRU	fuehrer	**EEFNRTV**	fervent	**EEGIMNS**	seeming	**EEGNRST** gerents
EEFHRSS	freshes	**EEFNSSW**	fewness	**EEGIMNT**	meeting		regents
EEFHRST	freshet	**EEFNSSY**	feyness		teeming	**EEGNRSZ** grenzes
	hefters	**EEFNSTU**	Fuentes	**EEGIMRS**	emigres	**EEGNSSU** genuses
EEFIIRR	fierier	**EEFORRV**	forever		regimes		neguses
	reifier	**EEFORRZ**	refroze		remiges	**EEGOPRT** protege
EEFIIRS	reifies	**EEFOTTU**	fouette	**EEGINNP**	peening	**EEGPRSU** pugrees
EEFIKLL	elflike	**EEFPRRS**	prefers	**EEGINNS**	engines	**EEGRRSS** regress
EEFILLS	fellies	**EEFPRSU**	perfuse	**EEGINNU**	genuine	**EEGRRST** regrets
EEFILLX	flexile	**EEFRRST**	ferrets		Guienne	**EEGRRSU** resurge
EEFILNO	olefine	**EEFRRSU**	refuser		ingenue	**EEGRRSV** vergers
EEFILOS	Fiesole	**EEFRRTU**	refuter	**EEGINNV**	evening	**EEGRRUY** gruyere
EEFILRS	ferlies	**EEFRRTY**	ferrety	**EEGINNW**	weening	**EEGRSSU** guesser
	refiles	**EEFRSST**	festers	**EEGINOP**	epigone	**EEGRSSY** geysers
	reliefs	**EEFRSSU**	refuses	**EEGINOS**	soignee	**EEGRSTT** getters
EEFILRT	fertile	**EEFRSTT**	fetters	**EEGINPP**	peeping	**EEGRSTU** gesture
EEFILST	felsite	**EEFRSTU**	refutes	**EEGINPR**	peering	**EEGRSTY** greyest
	lefties	**EEFSSTU**	fetuses	**EEGINPS**	seeping	**EEGSSSU** guesses
EEFIMMR	femmier	**EEGGGIS**	geggies	**EEGINPV**	peeving	**EEHHRTW** whether
EEFIMNR	firemen	**EEGGHTU**	thuggee	**EEGINPW**	weeping	**EEHHSTW** wheesht
EEFINNS	Fiennes	**EEGGILN**	neglige	**EEGINRS**	greisen	**EEHIKLN** Heinkel
EEFINRR	refiner	**EEGGILR**	leggier	**EEGINRT**	integer	**EEHIKLO** hoelike
EEFINRS	refines	**EEGGINR**	greeing			treeing	**EEHILMN** hemline
EEFINRZ	Firenze	**EEGGIOR**	George I	**EEGINRV**	reeving	**EEHILOS** Héloïse
EEFINSS	finesse	**EEGGIRV**	Gergiev		veering	**EEHILRT** Heitler
EEFIRRR	Ferrier	**EEGGISV**	veggies	**EEGINSS**	genesis		Theiler
EEFIRRS	ferries	**EEGGLNO**	Geelong		Giessen	**EEHILST** sheltie
	refires	**EEGGLRS**	egglers	**EEGINSV**	Sévigné	**EEHILSX** helixes
	refries	**EEGGNOR**	engorge	**EEGINTX**	exigent	**EEHINNV** Nineveh
EEFIRRT	ferrite	**EEGGORR**	regorge	**EEGIPRS**	Sergipe	**EEHINOR** heroine
EEFIRSS	Seferis	**EEGGORV**	George V	**EEGIRRV**	griever	**EEHINOS** Hesione
EEFIRST	festier	**EEGGPRU**	puggree	**EEGIRSV**	grieves	**EEHINRR** errhine
	Seifert	**EEGHILN**	heeling		Sverige	**EEHINRS** henries
EEFIRSZ	friezes	**EEGHINR**	rehinge	**EEGISTV**	vestige		inheres
EEFISTV	festive	**EEGHINY**	hygiene	**EEGKLNU**	Keelung	**EEHINRT** neither
EEFLLOS	felloes	**EEGHIRW**	reweigh	**EEGKLRS**	keglers		therein
EEFLLRS	fellers		weigher	**EEGKNOR**	kerogen	**EEHINRW** wherein
EEFLLRU	fueller	**EEGHKMO**	Okeghem	**EEGKNRU**	gerenuk	**EEHIPRT** prithee
EEFLLTY	fleetly	**EEGHLNO**	Hengelo	**EEGLLNN**	Lenglen	**EEHIPSV** peevish
EEFLNNO	Fénelon	**EEGHMNU**	hegumen	**EEGLLSS**	legless	**EEHIPTT** epithet
EEFLNOS	oneself	**EEGHNRY**	greyhen	**EEGLMMU**	gemmule	**EEHIRRS** rehires
EEFLNRS	flenser	**EEGIJNR**	jeering	**EEGLMSU**	legumes	**EEHIRSS** heiress
		EEGIKKN	keeking			

179

Key	Word
EEHIRST	heister
EEHIRSV	shrieve
EEHISST	hessite
EEHISTV	thieves
EEHKLOY	keyhole
EEHKLSS	shekels
EEHKOOY	eyehook
EEHKORT	Roethke
EEHLLMP	phellem
EEHLLRS	hellers
EEHLLRY	hellery
EEHLLSY	Shelley
EEHLMRS	helmers
EEHLMST	helmets
EEHLORY	holeyer
EEHLOSY	Holy See
EEHLPRS	helpers
EEHLPRT	telpher
EEHLRST	shelter
EEHLRSV	shelver
EEHLRSW	welsher
EEHLRSY	sheerly
EEHLSSV	shelves
EEHLSSW	welshes
EEHMMRS	hemmers
EEHMNOP	phoneme
EEHMNRY	mynheer
EEHMORT	theorem
EEHMRUX	exhumer
EEHMSUX	exhumes
EEHNNOS	shoneen
EEHNNRY	hennery
EEHNOPT	potheen
EEHNORT	thereon
EEHNORW	nowhere
	whereon
EEHNPST	Stephen
EEHNPSW	nephews
EEHNSTU	enthuse
EEHNSTV	seventh
EEHOOPW	whoopee
EEHOPRU	euphroe
EEHOPSS	sheepos
EEHOPST	heptose
EEHORRV	hoverer
EEHORSS	reshoes
EEHORST	heteros
EEHORSU	rehouse
EEHORTT	thereto
EEHORTW	whereto
EEHORVW	however
	whoever
EEHOSTW	towhees
EEHOSTY	eyeshot
EEHPPST	heppest
EEHPPSY	Sheppey
EEHPRSS	spheres
EEHPRST	threeps
EEHPSSU	Ephesus
EEHRRSW	wersher
EEHRRTW	wherret
EEHRSSW	shewers
EEHRSTT	tethers
EEHRSTW	wethers
EEHRTTW	whetter
EEHSSTU	Theseus
EEHSTUY	shuteye
EEIIKKS	kiekies
EEIILMS	mielies
EEIIMNS	meinies
EEIIMPR	riempie
EEIIMST	itemise
EEIIMTZ	itemize
EEIINNS	neineis
EEIINRT	niterie
EEIINSW	wienies
EEIINSY	Yenisei
EEIIPST	pieties
EEIIRRV	riviere
EEIIRVW	viewier
EEIJKRR	jerkier
EEIJLLS	jellies
EEIJMMS	jemmies
EEIJMNZ	Jiménez
EEIJNNS	jennies
EEIJRRS	jerries
EEIJSSS	jessies
EEIJSTT	jetties
EEIKKRR	kerkier
EEIKLNR	Lineker
EEIKLOT	toelike
EEIKLPS	kelpies
EEIKLPT	pikelet
EEIKLSS	selkies
EEIKLST	sleekit
EEIKMNP	pikemen
EEIKMPR	kempier
EEIKNPY	pinkeye
EEIKNRS	Erskine
EEIKNRT	kernite
EEIKPPR	perkier
EEIKPRS	peskier
EEIKPSW	kewpies
EEIKRRS	kerries
EEIKRST	keister
EEIKSST	seikest
EEIKTTT	tektite
EEILLNS	nellies
EEILLOR	Lorelei
EEILLPS	ellipse
EEILLRS	rellies
EEILLST	tellies
EEILLSV	Seville
EEILLSW	wellies
EEILMMT	meltemi
EEILMNN	linemen
EEILMNY	myeline
EEILMOR	Molière
EEILMRU	Lumière
EEILMRV	vermeil
EEILNNO	leonine
EEILNNS	Nielsen
EEILNNT	lenient
	Tenniel
EEILNNV	enliven
EEILNOR	eloiner
EEILNOV	Evil One
EEILNPS	pensile
EEILNRS	liernes
	relines
EEILNRV	livener
EEILNSS	enisles
	ensiles
	silenes
EEILNST	setline
	tensile
EEILNTT	entitle
EEILNTV	veinlet
EEILNUV	veinule
EEILOPT	petiole
EEILORS	loeries
EEILORV	overlie
	relievo
EEILOTZ	zeolite
EEILPRR	replier
EEILPRS	replies
	spieler
EEILPRT	perlite
	reptile
EEILPRU	puerile
EEILPSS	pelisse
EEILPST	epistle
	pelites
EEILPWY	weepily
EEILQRU	relique
EEILRRV	reviler
EEILRSS	ireless
	resiles
EEILRST	leister
	sterile
EEILRSU	leisure
EEILRSV	leviers
	relives
	reviles
	servile
	veilers
EEILRTT	retitle
EEILRVY	liveyer
EEILSSS	sessile
EEILSST	telesis
EEILSSU	Eleusis
EEILSSV	Elevsís
EEILSSW	lewises
EEILSTV	levites
	velites
EEILSTX	sextile
EEILSUV	elusive
EEILSVW	weevils
EEILTTX	textile
EEILVWY	weevily
EEIMMNS	immense
EEIMMRS	immerse
EEIMNNO	nominee
EEIMNNT	eminent
EEIMNOT	onetime
EEIMNRS	ermines
EEIMNRT	Meitner
EEIMNRW	wiremen
EEIMNSS	Meissen
	nemesis
	siemens
EEIMNSX	Ximenes
EEIMNSZ	Menzies
EEIMOPS	episome
EEIMOPT	epitome
EEIMOSS	meioses
EEIMOTV	emotive
EEIMPRR	premier
EEIMPRS	empires
	emprise
	epimers
	imprese
	premies
	premise
	spireme
EEIMPRT	emptier
EEIMPST	empties
	septime
EEIMQRU	requiem
EEIMRRR	merrier
EEIMRRT	trireme
EEIMRSS	messier
	miseres
	remises
EEIMRST	meister
	metiers
	tremies
EEIMRSX	remixes
EEIMRTT	emitter
	termite
EEIMSST	metisse
EEINNNP	pennine
EEINNPS	pennies
	pinenes
EEINNRS	nerines
EEINNRT	interne
EEINNRV	innerve
	nervine
EEINNST	intense
EEINNSY	Yesenin
EEINNTW	entwine
EEINNTZ	netizen
EEINOPR	pioneer
EEINOPS	peonies
EEINPPS	pepsine
EEINPRR	ripener
EEINPRS	erepsin
	repines
EEINPRT	Petrine
EEINPSS	penises
EEINPST	Epstein
EEINPSV	pensive
	vespine
EEINQRU	enquire
EEINQTU	quieten
EEINRRT	reinter
	rentier
	terrine

EEINRRV	nervier		reversi	**EELLMRS**	smeller	**EELORSY**	erosely
	vernier		reviser	**EELLNOV**	novelle	**EELORVV**	evolver
EEINRST	entries	**EEIRRSW**	rewires	**EELLNUV**	unlevel		revolve
	Steiner		sweirer	**EELLORV**	Vellore	**EELOSTT**	teleost
	Teniers	**EEIRRTV**	riveter	**EELLPRS**	presell	**EELOSVV**	evolves
	trienes	**EEIRRTW**	rewrite		speller	**EELOTUV**	evolute
EEINRSV	enviers	**EEIRRVV**	reviver	**EELLPST**	pellets		veloute
	inverse	**EEIRSSS**	seisers	**EELLQRU**	queller	**EELPPRX**	perplex
EEINRSW	newsier	**EEIRSST**	resites	**EELLRSS**	resells	**EELPPSU**	peepuls
	wieners	**EEIRSSU**	reissue		sellers	**EELPQRU**	prequel
EEINRSY	Erinyes	**EEIRSSV**	revises	**EELLRST**	retells	**EELPRST**	pelters
EEINRTU	retinue	**EEIRSTT**	testier		tellers		petrels
	reunite		Trieste	**EELLRSY**	yellers		spelter
	uterine	**EEIRSTV**	restive	**EELLSWZ**	Wellesz	**EELPRSU**	repulse
EEINSTT	netties		sievert	**EELMNOO**	oenomel	**EELPRSY**	Presley
EEINSTV	tensive		veriest	**EELMOPY**	employe		yelpers
EEINSTX	extines	**EEIRSUZ**	seizure	**EELMORW**	eelworm	**EELPRTZ**	pretzel
	sixteen	**EEIRSVV**	revives	**EELMOST**	omelets	**EELPRVY**	replevy
EEINSTY	syenite	**EEIRSVW**	reviews	**EELMOSY**	Moseley	**EELPSSS**	Lesseps
EEIOPPT	epitope		viewers	**EELMPST**	pelmets	**EELPSST**	pestles
EEIOPSS	poesies	**EEIRSXX**	Xerxes I		temples	**EELPSTY**	steeply
EEIOPST	poetise	**EEIRTVV**	vetiver	**EELMPTT**	templet	**EELQRUY**	queerly
EEIOPSX	epoxies	**EEISSTX**	sexiest	**EELMRST**	melters	**EELQSSU**	sequels
EEIOPTZ	poetize	**EEISTTW**	wetties		remelts	**EELRRVY**	revelry
EEIORSS	soirees	**EEISTTY**	yetties		smelter	**EELRSST**	streels
EEIORSV	erosive	**EEJKRRS**	jerkers	**EELMRSU**	lemures	**EELRSTT**	letters
EEIPPPR	peppier	**EEJLRWY**	jewelry		relumes		settler
EEIPPST	peptise	**EEJNNST**	jennets	**EELMRSW**	mewlers		sterlet
EEIPPTT	pipette	**EEJNORY**	enjoyer	**EELMSSU**	muleses		trestle
EEIPPTZ	peptize	**EEJPRRU**	perjure	**EELNNSV**	vennels	**EELRSTW**	swelter
EEIPQRU	perique	**EEJRSST**	jesters	**EELNOPV**	envelop		welters
	reequip	**EEJRSSY**	jerseys	**EELNOPY**	polyene		wrestle
	repique	**EEKKNOS**	konekes	**EELNORT**	Le Nôtre	**EELRSTY**	restyle
EEIPQSU	equipes	**EEKKRRT**	trekker	**EELNOSV**	elevons		tersely
EEIPRRR	perrier	**EEKLLNR**	Kneller		Slovene	**EELRSTZ**	seltzer
EEIPRRS	perries	**EEKLLSY**	sleekly	**EELNOTT**	notelet	**EELRSUV**	velures
	prisere	**EEKLLUU**	ukulele	**EELNOTU**	toluene	**EELSSSU**	useless
	reprise	**EEKLMRZ**	klezmer	**EELNPSS**	pensels	**EELSSSV**	vessels
	respire	**EEKLNNS**	kennels		spleens	**EELSSSX**	sexless
EEIPRRX	expirer	**EEKLNOS**	keelson	**EELNPSY**	spleeny	**EELSSTT**	settles
EEIPRSS	espiers	**EEKLNRS**	kernels	**EELNQUY**	queenly	**EELSTVV**	velvets
	pressie	**EEKLRST**	kestrel	**EELNRST**	nestler	**EELSTVW**	twelves
EEIPRST	respite	**EEKLSSY**	keyless		relents	**EELSTWY**	sweetly
EEIPRSV	previse	**EEKLSTT**	kettles		slenter	**EELTVVY**	velvety
EEIPRSX	expires	**EEKLSTW**	kewlest	**EELNRSU**	unreels	**EEMMNOS**	monemes
EEIPRTT	pettier	**EEKMNOS**	sokemen	**EELNSSS**	lessens	**EEMMNOT**	memento
EEIPRVW	preview	**EEKMRUZ**	Kurzeme	**EELNSST**	nestles	**EEMMOST**	mestome
EEIPRZZ	prezzie	**EEKNNTT**	kennett	**EELNSTT**	nettles	**EEMMRST**	stemmer
EEIPSTW	peewits	**EEKNOST**	ketones	**EELNSTU**	eluents	**EEMNNOV**	envenom
EEIQRRU	require	**EEKNOTY**	keynote		unsteel	**EEMNOOS**	someone
EEIQRSU	esquire	**EEKNRST**	renkest	**EELNSTY**	tensely	**EEMNOOY**	mooneye
	queries	**EEKNSST**	knesset	**EELNSUV**	venules	**EEMNORS**	Emerson
EEIQRTU	quieter	**EEKNSTU**	netsuke	**EELNSXY**	xylenes	**EEMNORV**	overmen
	requite	**EEKORRV**	revoker	**EELNTTU**	lunette	**EEMNORY**	moneyer
EEIQSTU	equites	**EEKORSV**	evokers	**EELOPPS**	peoples	**EEMNOST**	tonemes
EEIRRRT	retirer		revokes	**EELOPRS**	elopers	**EEMNPTU**	umpteen
	terrier	**EEKOSTV**	voetsek		leprose	**EEMNSYZ**	enzymes
EEIRRST	etriers	**EEKPRSU**	perukes	**EELOPRX**	explore	**EEMOPRR**	emperor
	retires	**EEKRRUZ**	kreuzer	**EELOPTU**	eelpout	**EEMOPRW**	empower
	retries	**EEKRSSW**	skewers	**EELORSS**	resoles	**EEMOPST**	metopes
	terries	**EELLLVY**	levelly	**EELORSU**	Soleure	**EEMORRS**	remorse
EEIRRSV	reivers	**EELLMOS**	Moselle	**EELORSV**	resolve	**EEMORRT**	remoter

Code	Word
EEMORRV	remover
EEMORST	emoters
	meteors
EEMORSV	removes
EEMPPRT	preempt
EEMPRRT	preterm
EEMPRSS	empress
EEMPRST	tempers
EEMPRSU	presume
	supreme
EEMPRTT	tempter
EEMPRTU	permute
EEMPSTT	tempest
EEMPSTX	exempts
EEMRRST	termers
EEMRRSU	murrees
	resumer
EEMRSST	mesters
EEMRSSU	resumes
EEMSSTU	mustees
EEMSTTU	musette
EENNORT	enteron
	tenoner
EENNORU	neurone
EENNOSS	Essonne
	oneness
EENNOTY	neoteny
EENNPTU	Neptune
EENNRST	tenners
EENNRTU	Turenne
EENNRUV	unnerve
EENNSST	sennets
EENNSSU	unseens
EENNSSW	newness
EENNSTT	Sennett
EENOPPR	prepone
	propene
EENOPPT	peptone
EENOPRS	openers
	Penrose
	reopens
	repones
EENOPST	open set
	pentose
EENOPTY	neotype
EENORSS	senores
EENORST	estrone
EENORSZ	rezones
EENOSTV	ventose
EENOSTW	townees
EENOSVZ	evzones
EENPPRT	perpent
EENPRSS	Spenser
EENPRST	present
	repents
	serpent
EENPRSV	Pevsner
EENPRSY	pyrenes
EENPRTV	prevent
EENPRTY	perenty
EENQSTU	sequent
EENRRST	renters
	sterner
EENRRSU	ensurer
EENRRTY	reentry
EENRRUV	nervure
EENRSST	nesters
	resents
EENRSSU	ensures
EENRSTT	tenters
EENRSTU	neuters
	tenures
	tureens
EENRSTV	venters
EENRSTW	western
EENRSTX	externs
EENRSTY	styrene
	yestern
EENRTUV	venture
EENRUVY	Nureyev
EENSSTT	tensest
EENSSTV	stevens
EENSSTW	wetness
EENSSUX	unsexes
EENSSVW	swevens
EENSTTX	extents
EENSTVY	seventy
EENTTWY	Wynette
EEOOPRS	operose
EEOOSTT	toetoes
EEOPPTT	popette
EEOPRRS	reposer
EEOPRRV	reprove
EEOPRSS	reposes
EEOPSSS	speoses
EEOPSST	poetess
EEOPSSU	espouse
EEOPSSX	exposes
EEOPSTU	toupees
EEOPSTY	eyespot
EEORRST	restore
EEORRSV	reverso
EEORRTU	reroute
EEORRTV	evertor
EEORRTW	rewrote
EEORSST	Orestes
	stereos
EEORSTT	rosette
EEORSTV	overset
	vetoers
EEORSUV	oeuvres
	overuse
EEORSVW	oversew
EEORSXX	xeroxes
EEPPPRS	peppers
EEPPPRY	peppery
EEPPRST	stepper
EEPPSST	steppes
EEPPSUW	upsweep
EEPPSUY	eupepsy
EEPRRSS	repress
EEPRRSU	peruser
EEPRRSV	preyers
EEPRRTV	pervert
	Prévert
EEPRSSS	presses
EEPRSST	pesters
	presets
EEPRSSU	Perseus
	peruses
EEPRSSV	vespers
EEPRSSW	spewers
EEPRSSX	express
EEPRSTT	petters
	pretest
EEPRSTU	reputes
EEPRSTX	experts
	sexpert
EEPRSTY	retypes
EEPRSUV	prevues
EEPRTTX	pretext
EEPSSTT	septets
EEPSTTU	puttees
EEPSTTY	typeset
EEQRRUY	equerry
EEQRSTU	quester
	request
EERRSST	resters
EERRSSV	servers
EERRSTT	terrets
EERRSTU	ureters
EERRSTV	reverts
EERRSTW	strewer
	wrester
EERRSVW	swerver
EERRTTU	utterer
EERSSST	tresses
EERSSTT	retests
	setters
	streets
	tersest
	testers
EERSSTU	Surtees
EERSSTV	revests
EERSSTW	westers
EERSSTX	exserts
EERSSUV	Severus
EERSSVW	swerves
EERSTTT	tetters
EERSTTU	trustee
EERSTTW	wetters
EERSTTX	texters
EERSTUV	vesture
EERSTUY	tuyeres
EERSTVV	vervets
EERTTUX	texture
EESSSTT	sestets
EESSTTU	suttees
EESSTTX	sextets
EESTTTW	wettest
EFFFLRU	fluffer
EFFFOOR	feoffor
EFFGINS	effings
EFFGIRS	griffes
EFFGORS	goffers
EFFGRRU	gruffer
EFFHILW	whiffle
EFFHIRS	sheriff
EFFHIRU	huffier
EFFHIRW	whiffer
EFFHLSU	shuffle
EFFIIJS	jiffies
EFFIIMR	miffier
EFFIINR	niffier
EFFIIST	fifties
	iffiest
EFFIKLS	skiffle
EFFILNO	offline
EFFILNS	sniffle
EFFILPS	piffles
EFFILRR	riffler
EFFILRS	riffles
EFFILRY	firefly
EFFIMOS	moffies
EFFINRS	sniffer
EFFINST	stiffen
EFFIORT	forfeit
EFFIORX	foxfire
EFFIOST	toffies
EFFIPRU	puffier
EFFIRST	stiffer
EFFLMRU	muffler
EFFLMSU	muffles
EFFLNSU	snuffle
EFFLOSU	souffle
EFFLRRU	ruffler
EFFLRSU	ruffles
EFFLRTU	fretful
	truffle
EFFNRSU	snuffer
EFFOORR	offeror
EFFOPRR	proffer
EFFOPSU	pouffes
EFFORST	efforts
EFFOSST	offsets
	setoffs
EFFPRSU	puffers
EFFPRUY	puffery
EFFRSSU	suffers
EFFRSTU	stuffer
EFFSSUU	suffuse
EFFSTTU	tuffets
EFGGIOR	foggier
EFGGIRU	fuggier
EFGGLOR	flogger
EFGHIMS	gemfish
EFGHINT	hefting
EFGHIRT	fighter
	freight
EFGILLN	felling
EFGILMN	fleming
EFGILNR	flinger
EFGILNT	felting
EFGILNU	fueling
EFGILNX	flexing
EFGILNY	fleying
EFGIMNT	figment

EFGINNP	pfennig	**EFIKLRU**	flukier	**EFIOOST**	footsie	**EFLORTU**	flouter
EFGINOR	foreign	**EFIKNRS**	knifers	**EFIORRT**	rotifer	**EFLORTW**	felwort
EFGINPR	perfing	**EFIKNRU**	funkier	**EFIORRU**	Fourier	**EFLORVY**	flyover
EFGINRS	fingers	**EFIKRRS**	frisker	**EFIORST**	forties		overfly
	fringes	**EFIKRST**	frisket	**EFIOSST**	softies	**EFLORWY**	flowery
EFGINRU	gunfire	**EFILLOS**	follies	**EFIOSTX**	foxiest	**EFLOSTU**	foulest
EFGIOOR	goofier	**EFILLOW**	lowlife	**EFIPPRT**	frippet	**EFLOTUW**	outflew
EFGIORV	forgive	**EFILLRS**	fillers	**EFIPRST**	presift	**EFLPRSU**	purfles
EFGIRRU	figurer		refills	**EFIPRTY**	petrify	**EFLRRSU**	furlers
EFGIRSU	figures	**EFILLST**	fillets	**EFIRRRU**	furrier	**EFLRSSU**	furless
EFGLNSU	engulfs	**EFILMNT**	liftmen	**EFIRRSU**	friseur	**EFLRSTU**	fluster
EFGLNTU	fulgent	**EFILMRS**	refilms	**EFIRRTT**	fritter		fluters
EFGLORS	golfers	**EFILMST**	filmset	**EFIRRTU**	fruiter		restful
EFGMNOR	frogmen		leftism		turfier	**EFLRTTU**	flutter
EFGNOOR	forgone	**EFILNOS**	olefins	**EFIRRTY**	terrify	**EFLSSUU**	usefuls
EFGOORR	forgoer	**EFILNOX**	flexion	**EFIRRZZ**	frizzer	**EFLSTUZ**	zestful
EFGOORS	forgoes	**EFILNSS**	finless	**EFIRSST**	sifters	**EFMNOOT**	footmen
EFGORRS	forgers	**EFILOOS**	floosie	**EFIRSSU**	fissure	**EFMNOST**	foments
EFGORRY	forgery		foliose		fussier	**EFMNRTU**	turfmen
EFGORST	forgets	**EFILOOZ**	floozie		surfies	**EFMOPRR**	perform
EFGORTU	foregut	**EFILOPR**	profile	**EFIRSTT**	fitters		preform
EFHIIRS	fishier	**EFILORT**	loftier		titfers	**EFMOPRT**	pomfret
EFHIJSW	jewfish		trefoil	**EFIRSTU**	fustier	**EFMORRS**	formers
EFHILMS	flemish	**EFILOSU**	foulies		surfeit		reforms
	himself	**EFILPPR**	flipper	**EFIRSTW**	swifter	**EFMRTUY**	furmety
EFHILSS	selfish	**EFILPPS**	fipples	**EFIRSVY**	versify	**EFNNOTY**	Fonteyn
EFHILTY	heftily	**EFILPPU**	pipeful	**EFIRSZZ**	fizzers	**EFNOOST**	festoon
EFHINST	fishnet	**EFILPRS**	pilfers		frizzes	**EFNORRU**	forerun
EFHIRSS	fishers	**EFILQUY**	liquefy	**EFIRTTU**	turfite	**EFNORRW**	frowner
EFHIRST	shifter	**EFILRRS**	riflers	**EFIRTUV**	furtive	**EFNORST**	frontes
EFHIRSY	fishery	**EFILRRT**	flirter	**EFIRTUX**	fixture	**EFNORTU**	fortune
EFHISUW	huswife		trifler	**EFIRUZZ**	fuzzier	**EFNORTW**	forwent
EFHLLPU	helpful	**EFILRRY**	riflery	**EFISTTT**	fittest	**EFNORUZ**	unfroze
EFHLLSY	fleshly	**EFILRST**	filters	**EFISTTY**	testify	**EFNOSST**	softens
EFHLOOX	foxhole		lifters	**EFJLSTU**	jestful	**EFNRSSU**	Furness
EFHLOPU	hopeful		stifler	**EFKLMNO**	menfolk	**EFOOPRR**	reproof
EFHLRSU	flusher		trifles	**EFKLNUY**	flunkey	**EFOOPRS**	spoofer
EFHLRSY	freshly	**EFILRTT**	flitter	**EFKNRSU**	funkers	**EFOOPRT**	foretop
EFHLSSU	flushes	**EFILRVV**	flivver	**EFLLORU**	florule		poofter
EFHLSTY	thyself	**EFILRZZ**	frizzle	**EFLLOST**	flotels	**EFOORRS**	reroofs
EFHLTTW	twelfth	**EFILSST**	stifles	**EFLLOSW**	fellows		roofers
EFHRRSU	fuhrers	**EFILSTT**	leftist	**EFLLRSU**	fullers	**EFOORST**	foetors
EFHRRTU	further	**EFILSZZ**	fizzles	**EFLLSSY**	flyless		footers
EFIILLN	Fellini	**EFIMMRU**	fermium	**EFLLSTU**	fullest	**EFOORSW**	woofers
EFIILLS	fillies	**EFIMNOR**	fermion	**EFLMOSU**	fulsome	**EFOORTW**	woofter
EFIILMR	filmier	**EFIMNTT**	fitment	**EFLMSUU**	museful	**EFOPPRY**	foppery
EFIILMS	misfile	**EFIMOST**	fomites	**EFLNNSU**	funnels	**EFOPRSS**	profess
EFIILRY	fierily	**EFIMRST**	firmest	**EFLNORU**	fleuron	**EFOPRSU**	profuse
EFIILSS	fissile	**EFIMRTY**	metrify	**EFLNORY**	felonry	**EFOQTUU**	Fouquet
EFIIMRR	rimfire	**EFINNOR**	inferno	**EFLNSSU**	fulness	**EFORRST**	Forrest
EFIIMRS	misfire	**EFINNRS**	finners	**EFLNTUU**	tuneful		Forster
EFIINNR	finnier	**EFINNRU**	funnier	**EFLOORY**	foolery	**EFORRSU**	ferrous
EFIINPV	fivepin	**EFINNSU**	funnies	**EFLOORZ**	foozler		furores
EFIINRT	niftier	**EFINPRS**	perfins	**EFLOOST**	footles	**EFORRSV**	fervors
EFIINRU	unifier	**EFINRST**	snifter	**EFLOOSZ**	foozles	**EFORRTY**	torrefy
EFIINSU	unifies	**EFINRSU**	infuser	**EFLORST**	florets	**EFORRUV**	fervour
EFIINSX	infixes	**EFINRUY**	reunify		lofters	**EFORSST**	forests
EFIISTW	swiftie	**EFINSST**	fitness	**EFLORSU**	ourself		fosters
EFIJLLY	jellify		infests	**EFLORSW**	flowers	**EFORSTU**	fouters
EFIJLOT	jetfoil	**EFINSSU**	infuses		fowlers	**EFOSSTT**	softest
EFIKLOS	folkies	**EFINSUX**	unfixes		wolfers	**EFPRTUY**	putrefy
EFIKLOX	foxlike	**EFIOOPR**	poofier	**EFLORSX**	flexors	**EFPSTUY**	stupefy

EFRRSSU	surfers	EGGLOOY	geology	EGHIOST	hogties	EGIINSV	sieving
EFRRSTU	returfs	EGGLORS	loggers	EGHIOTT	gothite	EGIINSZ	seizing
EFRSSSU	fussers		slogger	EGHIOTV	eightvo	EGIINTV	eviting
EFRSTTU	tufters	EGGLORT	toggler	EGHIRRT	righter	EGIINTX	exiting
EFRSTUU	futures	EGGLOST	goglets	EGHIRSS	sighers	EGIINVW	viewing
EGGGILN	legging		toggles	EGHIRST	sighter	EGIIORR	Roger II
EGGGILR	giggler	EGGLOSW	woggles	EGHIRSU	gushier	EGIIPPS	gippies
EGGGILS	giggles	EGGLPRU	plugger	EGHIRSY	greyish	EGIIPRW	periwig
EGGGINP	pegging	EGGLRSU	gurgles	EGHIRTT	tighter	EGIIPSS	gipsies
EGGGINV	vegging		luggers	EGHIRTU	Guthrie	EGIJKNR	jerking
EGGGLOS	goggles		slugger	EGHISTW	weights	EGIJLLN	jelling
EGGGNOS	eggnogs	EGGLRTU	gurglet	EGHISTY	hygeist	EGIJLNR	jingler
EGGHILR	higgler	EGGLSTU	guglets	EGHITWY	weighty	EGIJLNS	jingles
EGGHILS	higgles	EGGMRSU	muggers	EGHLLOU	lughole	EGIJNOS	jingoes
EGGHIRU	huggier		smugger	EGHLMPY	phlegmy	EGIJNSS	jessing
EGGHORS	hoggers	EGGNRSU	snugger	EGHLNOR	leghorn	EGIJNST	jesting
EGGHOST	hoggets	EGGNSTU	nuggets	EGHLNST	lengths	EGIJNTT	jetting
EGGHRSU	huggers	EGGNTUY	nuggety	EGHLNTY	lengthy	EGIKLMU	gumlike
EGGIIJR	jiggier	EGGORRS	gorgers	EGHLOOS	shoogle	EGIKLNR	erlking
EGGIINS	sieging	EGGORRY	Gregory	EGHLPSU	pleughs	EGIKLNT	kinglet
EGGIIPR	piggier	EGGORST	gorgets	EGHMMOS	megohms	EGIKLRU	ruglike
EGGIIPS	piggies		toggers	EGHMOSU	gumshoe	EGIKLTU	gutlike
EGGIJLS	jiggles	EGGORSU	gougers	EGHNOOS	hognose	EGIKNNN	kenning
EGGIJRS	jiggers	EGGORTY	toggery	EGHNORS	Senghor	EGIKNNR	kerning
EGGILLN	gelling	EGGRSTU	tuggers	EGHNORU	roughen	EGIKNOV	evoking
EGGILNR	niggler	EGGSSTU	suggest	EGHNOTU	toughen	EGIKNPP	kepping
EGGILNS	niggles	EGHHIRS	highers	EGHNRSU	hungers	EGIKNPR	perking
	sniggle	EGHHIST	eighths	EGHNRTU	Gunther	EGIKNSW	skewing
EGGILNU	glueing		heights	EGHNSUY	Huygens	EGILLMU	Guillem
EGGILRS	liggers		highest	EGHOPRS	gophers	EGILLNS	selling
EGGILRW	wiggler	EGHHSSU	sheughs	EGHORRU	rougher	EGILLNT	gillnet
	wriggle	EGHIILL	ghillie	EGHORTU	tougher		telling
EGGILSW	wiggles	EGHIINT	nightie	EGHORTZ	Hertzog	EGILLNW	welling
EGGIMMN	gemming	EGHIINV	inveigh	EGHOSTT	ghettos	EGILLNY	yelling
EGGIMNR	merging	EGHIKLO	hoglike	EGHOSUU	hugeous	EGILLOR	girolle
EGGIMOS	moggies	EGHIKNR	gherkin	EGHRSSU	gushers	EGILLOS	gollies
EGGIMRU	muggier	EGHILMN	helming	EGHRTUY	theurgy	EGILLRR	griller
EGGINNS	ginseng	EGHILNP	helping	EGIIKLW	wiglike	EGILLRS	grilles
EGGINNV	venging	EGHILNS	english	EGIILLS	gillies	EGILLSU	gullies
EGGINOR	Goering		shingle	EGIILNT	lignite		ligules
EGGINRS	gingers	EGHILNT	lighten	EGIILNV	veiling	EGILMMN	lemming
	niggers	EGHILNV	helving	EGIILNX	exiling		Memling
	snigger	EGHILRT	lighter	EGIILPZ	Leipzig	EGILMMR	glimmer
EGGINRU	grueing		relight	EGIILRS	girlies	EGILMNR	gremlin
	gungier	EGHILSS	sleighs	EGIIMNP	impinge		mingler
EGGINRV	verging	EGHILST	sleight	EGIIMNR	mingier	EGILMNS	mingles
EGGINRY	gingery	EGHIMMN	hemming	EGIIMNT	iteming	EGILMNT	melting
	greying	EGHIMNS	meshing	EGIIMPR	gimpier	EGILMNU	legumin
EGGINTT	getting	EGHIMNT	theming	EGIIMPS	pigmies	EGILMNW	mewling
EGGIORS	soggier	EGHINNT	henting	EGIIMRR	grimier	EGILMOR	gomeril
EGGIPRU	puggier	EGHINNU	unhinge	EGIIMSV	misgive	EGILMOS	Limoges
EGGIPRY	piggery	EGHINOS	shoeing	EGIINNR	reining	EGILMOV	Mogilev
EGGIRRS	riggers	EGHINRR	herring	EGIINNS	insigne	EGILMPS	glimpse
EGGIRRT	trigger	EGHINRT	Enright		seining	EGILMST	gimlets
EGGIRSW	swigger		righten	EGIINNV	veining	EGILNNS	ginnels
EGGJLOR	joggler	EGHINRW	whinger	EGIINOP	epigoni	EGILNOP	eloping
EGGJLOS	joggles	EGHINST	Hengist	EGIINRT	igniter	EGILNOS	eloigns
EGGJLRU	juggler	EGHINSW	shewing		tiering		legions
EGGJLSU	juggles		whinges	EGIINRV	reiving		lingoes
EGGJORS	joggers	EGHINTT	tighten	EGIINRZ	zingier	EGILNOT	lentigo
EGGLMSU	smuggle	EGHIORS	ogreish	EGIINSS	seising	EGILNPS	spignel
EGGLNSU	snuggle	EGHIORU	roughie	EGIINST	ignites	EGILNPT	pelting

EGILNPY	yelping	EGINNOP	opening	EGINRTY	retying	EGLNOST	longest
EGILNRS	lingers	EGINNOV	ovening	EGINRVV	revving	EGLNOSU	lounges
	slinger	EGINNPU	penguin	EGINSST	ingests	EGLNOYZ	lozengy
EGILNRT	ringlet	EGINNRR	grinner		signets	EGLNPRU	plunger
	tingler	EGINNRS	ginners	EGINSSW	swinges	EGLNPSU	plunges
EGILNRY	relying	EGINNRT	renting	EGINSTT	setting	EGLNRSU	lungers
EGILNSS	Lessing		ringent		testing	EGLNSSU	gunsels
	singles	EGINNRU	enuring	EGINSTV	vesting	EGLNSTU	engluts
EGILNST	glisten	EGINNRV	nerving	EGINSTW	stewing	EGLOORS	regosol
	singlet	EGINNSS	ensigns		twinges	EGLOPRS	prolegs
	tingles		sensing		westing	EGLOPSS	gospels
EGILNSU	slueing	EGINNST	nesting	EGINSTZ	zesting	EGLORRW	growler
EGILNSW	slewing		tensing	EGINTTV	vetting	EGLORSS	glosser
	swingle	EGINNSU	ensuing	EGINTTW	wetting	EGLORSV	glovers
EGILNTT	letting		gunnies	EGIOOPR	goopier		grovels
EGILNTU	eluting	EGINNTT	netting	EGIOORS	goories	EGLORSW	glowers
EGILNTW	welting		tenting		goosier	EGLOSSS	glosses
	winglet	EGINNTV	venting	EGIOOST	gooiest	EGLPRSU	gulpers
EGILNVY	levying	EGINNVY	envying	EGIOPPS	gippoes		splurge
EGILOOS	goolies	EGINOOS	isogone	EGIOPRS	porgies	EGLRSUU	regulus
	ologies	EGINOPR	perigon		serpigo	EGLRUZZ	guzzler
EGILORS	glories		pongier	EGIOPRU	groupie	EGLSSTU	gutless
EGILOST	logiest	EGINOPS	epigons		pirogue	EGLSTUU	gluteus
EGILPST	piglets		pigeons	EGIORST	goiters	EGLSUZZ	guzzles
EGILRSS	grilses	EGINORR	ignorer		goitres	EGMMORT	grommet
EGILRST	glister	EGINORS	eringos		goriest	EGMMOSU	gummose
	gristle		ignores	EGIORTU	goutier	EGMMRTU	grummet
EGILRSU	ligures		regions	EGIORTV	vertigo	EGMNOOS	mongoes
	lurgies		signore	EGIOSST	egoists	EGMNORS	mongers
EGILRTT	glitter	EGINORT	genitor		stogies		morgens
EGILRUV	virgule	EGINORZ	zeroing	EGIOSTT	egotist	EGMNOSU	eumongs
EGILRZZ	grizzle	EGINOSU	igneous	EGIPPRR	gripper	EGMNOYZ	zymogen
EGILSST	legists	EGINOSW	wigeons	EGIPPSU	guppies	EGMNSTU	nutmegs
EGILSSV	Slesvig	EGINOSY	isogeny	EGIPRRS	gripers	EGMNSUU	eumungs
EGILSSW	wigless	EGINOTV	vetoing	EGIPRUU	guipure	EGMOORR	groomer
EGILSTU	gluiest	EGINPPP	pepping	EGIPSSY	gypsies	EGMOOSS	smooges
	ugliest	EGINPPS	pigpens	EGIRRRU	gurrier	EGMOPRS	Gompers
EGIMMRR	grimmer	EGINPRS	pingers	EGIRRTT	gritter	EGMORSU	grumose
EGIMMRS	megrims		springe	EGIRSST	tigress		morgues
EGIMMRU	gummier	EGINPRV	perving	EGIRSSU	guisers	EGMORTU	gourmet
EGIMMSU	gummies	EGINPRY	preying	EGIRSTU	gustier	EGNNORT	rontgen
EGIMMTU	gummite	EGINPSW	spewing		gutsier		Röntgen
EGIMNNO	omening	EGINPSY	espying	EGIRSTV	grivets	EGNNOSU	guenons
EGIMNNW	wingmen	EGINPTT	petting	EGIRTTU	turgite	EGNNPTU	pungent
EGIMNOT	emoting	EGINPYY	epigyny	EGISTTU	gutties	EGNNRSU	gunners
	mitogen	EGINQUU	queuing	EGJLNSU	jungles	EGNNRUY	gunnery
EGIMNOU	Minogue	EGINRRS	ringers	EGKLORW	legwork	EGNNTUU	unguent
EGIMNOW	meowing	EGINRRW	wringer	EGKMSSU	muskegs	EGNOORY	orogeny
EGIMNPR	perming	EGINRSS	ingress	EGKNTUZ	Tzekung	EGNOOST	gentoos
EGIMNPT	empting		resigns	EGKRTYZ	Gretzky	EGNOOTU	outgone
	pigment		signers	EGLLNNU	Gunnell	EGNOPRS	sponger
	temping		singers	EGLLOUY	yule log	EGNOPRY	progeny
EGIMNRS	merings	EGINRST	resting	EGLLSTU	gullets		pyrogen
	mingers		stinger	EGLLSUY	gulleys	EGNOPSS	sponges
EGIMNRT	terming	EGINRSU	reusing	EGLMMRU	glummer	EGNORRW	regrown
EGIMNSS	messing	EGINRSV	serving	EGLMNOR	mongrel		wronger
EGIMOST	egotism		versing	EGLMOOR	legroom	EGNORSS	engross
EGIMPSU	guimpes	EGINRSW	swinger	EGLMSSU	gumless	EGNORSU	surgeon
EGIMPSY	gympies		wingers	EGLNNSU	gunnels	EGNORSV	governs
	pygmies	EGINRSY	syringe	EGLNOOY	enology	EGNORSY	eryngos
EGINNNP	penning	EGINRTT	gittern		neology		groynes
EGINNNY	yenning		retting	EGLNORU	lounger	EGNORUY	younger

EGNOSTU	tongues	**EHIKKSS**	kishkes	**EHIMPRW**	whimper		writher
EGNPRSU	repugns	**EHIKLTU**	hutlike	**EHIMPSU**	humpies	**EHIRSSS**	hissers
EGNRRTU	grunter	**EHIKMSV**	mikvehs	**EHIMRST**	hermits	**EHIRSSV**	shivers
EGNRSTU	gurnets	**EHIKNOS**	honkies		mithers		shrives
EGNRSUY	gurneys	**EHIKNRT**	rethink	**EHIMRSU**	mushier	**EHIRSSW**	swisher
EGNRSYY	synergy		thinker	**EHIMSWY**	whimsey		wishers
EGNRTTU	grutten	**EHIKNSS**	knishes	**EHINNRT**	thinner	**EHIRSTT**	hitters
	turgent	**EHIKPPS**	Pishpek	**EHINOPR**	phonier		tithers
EGOOPRS	pogoers	**EHIKRRS**	shirker	**EHINOPS**	phonies	**EHIRSTU**	hirsute
EGOORSV	grooves	**EHIKRSS**	shrieks	**EHINOPX**	phoenix	**EHIRSTV**	thrives
EGOOSST	stooges		shrikes	**EHINORR**	hornier	**EHIRSTW**	swither
EGOOSTU	outgoes	**EHIKRSU**	huskier	**EHINORS**	inshore		withers
EGOPRRS	gropers	**EHIKRSW**	whisker	**EHINOST**	histone		writhes
EGOPRRU	grouper	**EHIKSSU**	huskies	**EHINOSU**	heinous	**EHIRSTZ**	zithers
	regroup	**EHIKSVZ**	Izhevsk	**EHINPRT**	Penrith	**EHIRSVY**	shivery
EGORRSS	grosser	**EHIKSWY**	whiskey	**EHINRSS**	shiners	**EHIRTTW**	whitter
EGORRSU	grouser	**EHILLNO**	hellion		shrines	**EHISSSU**	hussies
EGORRSW	growers	**EHILLOS**	hollies	**EHINRST**	hinters	**EHISSSW**	swishes
	regrows	**EHILLRS**	hillers	**EHINRSV**	shriven	**EHISSTT**	theists
EGORRTU	grouter	**EHILLTY**	lithely	**EHINRSW**	whiners	**EHISSTU**	Hussite
EGORRUY	roguery	**EHILMMR**	Himmler	**EHINRTV**	thriven		stushie
EGORSSS	grosses	**EHILNOP**	pinhole	**EHINRTW**	writhen	**EHISTTW**	wettish
EGORSST	gosters	**EHILNOT**	hotline	**EHINRVY**	Henry IV		whitest
EGORSSU	grouses		neolith		Henry VI	**EHISTWY**	whiteys
EGORSTV	grovets	**EHILNPS**	plenish	**EHINSSU**	Hussein	**EHISWZZ**	whizzes
EGORTUW	outgrew	**EHILOOS**	hoolies	**EHINSTW**	whitens	**EHJKNOT**	Khojent
EGOSTYZ	zygotes	**EHILOPT**	hoplite	**EHINSTZ**	zeniths	**EHJLOOV**	Holy Joe
EGPRRSU	purgers	**EHILOSS**	isohels	**EHINSUW**	Wuhsien	**EHJOPSS**	josephs
EGPRSSU	spurges	**EHILOST**	Elohist	**EHINTWY**	Whitney	**EHJORSS**	joshers
EGPRSUU	upsurge		eoliths	**EHIOOST**	tooshie	**EHKLPST**	klephts
EGRRSSU	surgers		holiest	**EHIOPRS**	rosehip	**EHKMOOS**	smokeho
EGRRSUY	surgery		hostile	**EHIOPSS**	sophies	**EHKNORS**	honkers
EGRSSTU	gutsers		Sithole	**EHIOPST**	ophites		Kherson
EGRSTTU	gutters	**EHILOUZ**	Leizhou	**EHIORRS**	horsier	**EHKNRSU**	hunkers
EGSSSTU	gussets	**EHILPRS**	hirples	**EHIORRT**	heritor	**EHKOORS**	hookers
EHHHOTU	Huhehot	**EHILPRT**	philter		Herriot	**EHKRSSU**	huskers
EHHIKSS	sheikhs		philtre	**EHIORSS**	hosiers	**EHLLORS**	hollers
EHHILLS	hellish	**EHILPSS**	hipless	**EHIORST**	heriots	**EHLLRSU**	hullers
EHHIMRS	Rhemish	**EHILRRW**	whirler		hoister	**EHLMNOT**	Helmont
EHHINRS	Rhenish	**EHILRST**	slither		shortie		menthol
EHHIRTT	thither	**EHILRSV**	shrivel	**EHIORSW**	showier	**EHLMNSU**	unhelms
EHHIRTW	whither	**EHILSTT**	thistle	**EHIORSY**	hosiery	**EHLMSTY**	methyls
EHHISSW	whishes	**EHILSTW**	whistle	**EHIORTT**	thorite	**EHLNOPS**	phenols
EHHISWY	wheyish	**EHILTTW**	whittle	**EHIOSST**	hosties	**EHLNRTU**	luthern
EHHMOSS	Moshesh	**EHILTWY**	whitely	**EHIOSTT**	hotties	**EHLNTTY**	tenthly
EHHNPSY	hyphens	**EHIMMPS**	Memphis	**EHIOSTY**	isohyet	**EHLOOPT**	pothole
EHHSSSU	shushes	**EHIMMRS**	shimmer	**EHIPPRS**	shipper	**EHLOOST**	Lesotho
EHIIIKT	heitiki	**EHIMNNU**	Menuhin	**EHIPPRW**	whipper	**EHLOOSY**	hooleys
EHIIKLP	hiplike	**EHIMNPS**	shipmen	**EHIPPST**	hippest	**EHLOPPR**	hoppler
EHIILLR	hillier	**EHIMNRS**	menhirs	**EHIPPTW**	whippet	**EHLOPPS**	hopples
EHIINNS	hinnies	**EHIMNRU**	inhumer	**EHIPRSS**	reships	**EHLOPSX**	phloxes
EHIINRS	shinier		rhenium		seriphs	**EHLOPSY**	spyhole
EHIINRT	inherit	**EHIMNSU**	inhumes	**EHIPRST**	hipster	**EHLORST**	holster
EHIINRW	whinier	**EHIMNTY**	thymine	**EHIPRSU**	pushier		hostler
EHIINRY	Henry II	**EHIMOPT**	Imhotep	**EHIPRSW**	whisper	**EHLORSW**	howlers
EHIIPPR	hippier	**EHIMORS**	heroism	**EHIPSST**	Thespis	**EHLORTY**	helotry
EHIIPPS	hippies		moreish	**EHIPSTT**	pettish	**EHLOSSS**	sloshes
	shippie	**EHIMORT**	moither	**EHIRRSU**	hurries	**EHLOSST**	hostels
EHIIPRT	pithier		mothier		rushier	**EHLOSSU**	housels
EHIISST	stishie	**EHIMORZ**	rhizome	**EHIRRSV**	shriver	**EHLOSSV**	shovels
EHIISTW	whities	**EHIMOST**	homiest	**EHIRRTV**	thriver	**EHLOSTW**	howlets
	withies	**EHIMPRU**	humpier	**EHIRRTW**	wherrit	**EHLRRSU**	hurlers

Code	Word
EHLRSSU	Husserl
EHLRSTU	hurtles
	hustler
EHLRSUY	hurleys
EHLSSSU	slushes
EHLSSTU	hustles
	sleuths
EHLSTTU	shuttle
EHMMRSU	hummers
EHMNOOR	hormone
	moorhen
EHMNOSW	showmen
EHMNPTY	nymphet
EHMNTTU	hutment
EHMOOSW	somehow
EHMOPRT	Morpeth
EHMORST	mothers
	smother
	thermos
EHMORTU	mouther
EHMORTY	mothery
EHMOTUX	Exmouth
EHMPRTU	thumper
EHMRRSY	rhymers
EHMRRTU	murther
EHMRSSU	mushers
EHMRSUU	humerus
EHNNOPR	nephron
EHNNRSU	shunner
EHNOORR	honorer
EHNOORS	onshore
EHNOPRS	phoners
EHNOPRY	hyperon
EHNOPSY	phoneys
EHNOPUY	euphony
EHNOPXY	phenoxy
EHNORRT	norther
EHNORRY	heronry
EHNORSS	Horsens
	noshers
EHNORST	hornets
	shorten
	thrones
EHNORSU	unhorse
EHNORSY	noshery
EHNOSST	hotness
EHNOSTT	shotten
EHNOSTY	honesty
EHNOUWZ	Wenzhou
EHNPRSY	phrensy
EHNRSTU	hunters
	shunter
EHNSSSY	shyness
EHOOOPS	hoopoes
EHOOPRS	hoopers
EHOOPRW	whooper
EHOOPTY	oophyte
EHOORST	hooters
	shooter
	soother
EHOORSV	hoovers
EHOOSST	soothes
EHOOSSW	wooshes
EHOPPRS	hoppers
	shopper
EHOPPRT	prophet
EHOPPRW	whopper
EHOPRRY	orphrey
EHOPRST	pothers
	strophe
	thorpes
EHOPRSU	Orpheus
	uphroes
EHOPRSY	phoresy
EHOPSST	poshest
EHORRST	rhetors
	shorter
EHORRTW	thrower
EHORSSV	shovers
EHORSSW	showers
EHORSTU	shouter
	souther
EHORSTX	exhorts
EHORSWY	showery
EHORTUX	Theroux
EHOSSST	hostess
EHOSSSU	shouses
EHOSTTT	hottest
EHOSTUY	Southey
EHPRSSU	pushers
EHPRSSY	syphers
EHPRSYZ	zephyrs
EHPRTTU	turpeth
EHRRSSU	rushers
EHRRSTU	hurters
EHRSSTY	shyster
	thyrses
EHRSTTU	shutter
EHRSTTW	strewth
EIIILOX	Leo XIII
EIIILRV	rilievi
EIIILST	ileitis
EIIINPR	ripieni
EIIJMMS	jimmies
EIIKKNR	kinkier
EIIKLLP	liplike
EIIKLMR	milkier
EIIKLMS	mislike
EIIKLNT	tinlike
EIIKLNW	Kweilin
EIIKLRS	silkier
EIIKLSS	silkies
EIIKLVY	ivylike
EIIKNPS	pinkies
EIIKNSS	kinesis
EIIKNST	inkiest
EIIKPRS	spikier
EIIKRRS	riskier
EIIKSTT	kitties
EIIKSUW	Kweisui
EIILLMM	millime
EIILLMN	milline
EIILLNV	villein
EIILLPS	pillies
EIILLRS	sillier
EIILLSS	sillies
EIILLSW	willies
EIILLTT	littlie
EIILLTV	vitelli
EIILMPR	imperil
EIILMPS	implies
EIILMPT	limepit
EIILMRS	milreis
	slimier
EIILMRT	Leitrim
	limiter
EIILMSS	missile
	similes
EIILMST	elitism
	El Misti
	limiest
	limites
EIILMSU	milieus
EIILMUX	milieux
EIILNOS	elision
	isoline
	lionise
EIILNOV	olivine
EIILNOZ	lionize
EIILNPS	splenii
EIILNRS	inliers
EIILNRT	nitrile
EIILNST	linties
EIILNTU	inutile
EIILORR	roilier
EIILORV	Olivier
	rilievo
EIILOST	oiliest
EIILPPR	lippier
EIILPPS	lippies
EIILQSU	silique
EIILRSX	elixirs
EIILSTT	elitist
EIILSTU	utilise
EIILSTW	wiliest
EIILSUX	Lisieux
EIILTUZ	utilize
EIIMMSS	mimesis
EIIMMST	mistime
EIIMMSX	immixes
EIIMNPR	primine
EIIMNRT	interim
	mintier
	termini
EIIMNRV	miniver
EIIMNTV	minivet
EIIMNTY	nimiety
EIIMOPP	Pompeii
EIIMOSS	meiosis
EIIMPRS	pismire
EIIMPRW	wimpier
EIIMPST	pietism
EIIMPTY	impiety
EIIMRST	mistier
	rimiest
EIIMSSS	missies
EIIMSSV	missive
EIIMSSZ	sizeism
EIINNNP	ninepin
EIINNNS	ninnies
EIINNPS	pinnies
EIINNQU	quinine
EIINNRT	tinnier
EIINNST	intines
	tinnies
EIINNTW	intwine
EIINOPR	ripieno
EIINORS	ioniser
	ironies
	ironise
	noisier
EIINORT	Niterói
EIINORZ	ionizer
	ironize
EIINOSS	ionises
EIINOSZ	ionizes
EIINPPR	nippier
EIINPRS	inspire
	spinier
EIINPST	piniest
	tiepins
EIINPTT	pentiti
EIINQRU	inquire
EIINQTU	inquiet
EIINRTT	nitrite
	nittier
EIINRTV	inviter
	vitrine
EIINSSS	seisins
EIINSSZ	seizins
EIINSTT	tiniest
EIINSTU	unities
	unitise
EIINSTV	invites
EIINSTW	winiest
EIINTUV	unitive
EIINTUZ	unitize
EIIOPTT	petitio
EIIORSV	ivories
EIIOSTZ	zoisite
EIIPPRZ	zippier
EIIPPRV	privier
EIIPRST	tipsier
EIIPRSV	privies
EIIPRSW	wispier
EIIPSTT	pietist
EIIQQUU	Iquique
EIIRRTZ	ritzier
EIIRSTV	revisit
EIIRSTW	wiriest
EIIRSVZ	viziers
EIIRTTW	wittier
EIISSSS	sissies
EIISSTX	sixties
EIISTUV	uveitis
EIISTZZ	tizzies
EIJKKSU	jukskei
EIJKLRY	jerkily

EIJKNNS Jenkins	**EIKLRTV** Kilvert	**EILLMNU** mullein	**EILMSSU** mueslis
EIJKNPR perjink	**EIKLSSU** sulkies	**EILLMOS** mollies	**EILMSSY** messily
EIJKNRS jerkins	**EIKLSTT** kittels	**EILLMOT** melilot	**EILMSTT** smittle
jinkers	kittles	**EILLMOU** mouille	**EILMSTU** Miletus
EIJKNSU junkies	skittle	**EILLMRS** millers	**EILMSUY** Elysium
EIJKOST jokiest		**EILLMST** millets	**EILMSZZ** mizzles
EIJLLOR jollier	**EIKMMRR** krimmer	**EILLMSU** illumes	**EILMUUV** eluvium
EIJLLOS jollies	**EIKMMRS** skimmer	**EILLMTT** Millett	**EILNNOR** onliner
EIJLLOT Jolliet	**EIKMMNS** kinsmen	**EILLMTU** mullite	**EILNNPU** pinnule
EIJLORT joltier	**EIKMNOR** moniker	**EILLNOS** niellos	**EILNNRY** innerly
EIJLRST jilters	**EIKMNRS** merkins	**EILLNSS** illness	**EILNNST** linnets
EIJMPRU jumpier	**EIKMORS** irksome	**EILLNST** lentils	**EILNOOR** loonier
EIJNNOS enjoins	smokier	lintels	**EILNOOS** loonies
EIJNORS joiners	**EIKMOSS** smokies	tellins	**EILNOOV** violone
rejoins	**EIKMRRS** smirker	**EILLORW** lowlier	**EILNOPR** plerion
EIJNORT jointer	**EIKMRRU** murkier	**EILLORZ** zorille	proline
EIJNORY joinery	**EIKMRSS** kirmess	**EILLOST** tollies	**EILNOPS** epsilon
EIJNPRU juniper	**EIKMRSU** muskier	**EILLOSW** wollies	**EILNORR** loriner
EIJNRRU injurer	**EIKMSSU** muskies	**EILLPRS** spiller	**EILNORT** Lorient
EIJNRSU injures	**EIKNNOR** einkorn	**EILLPSS** lipless	retinol
EIJNSTY jitneys	**EIKNNRS** skinner	**EILLPSU** pilules	**EILNOSS** insoles
EIJPRTU Jupiter	**EIKNOOR** rooinek	**EILLQTU** quillet	lesions
EIJRSTT jitters	**EIKNOOS** nookies	**EILLRST** rillets	lioness
EIJRTTY jittery	**EIKNOPS** pinkoes	stiller	**EILNOST** entoils
EIJSSTU jesuits	**EIKNORV** invoker	tillers	**EILNOSU** elusion
EIJSSUV jussive	**EIKNORW** wonkier	trellis	**EILNOTU** elution
EIKKLRS Selkirk	**EIKNOSS** kenosis	**EILLRSW** swiller	outline
EIKKLSY kylikes	**EIKNOSV** invokes	willers	**EILNOTV** violent
skylike	**EIKNPRR** prinker	**EILLRTT** littler	**EILNOTW** towline
EIKKMNR kirkmen	**EIKNPRS** perkins	**EILLSST** listels	**EILNOVV** involve
EIKKOOR kookier	**EIKNRSS** sinkers	**EILLSSU** sullies	**EILNPPS** nipples
EIKKOPS Kopeisk	**EIKNRST** stinker	**EILLSTW** Sitwell	**EILNPRS** pilsner
EIKKRUY yukkier	tinkers	willets	**EILNPRU** purline
EIKLLNW inkwell	**EIKNRSW** swinker	**EILMMRS** slimmer	**EILNPSS** pensils
EIKLLOS skollie	winkers	**EILMNRS** limners	splines
EIKLLOW owllike	**EIKNRTT** knitter	merlins	**EILNPST** leptins
EIKLLRS killers	trinket	**EILMOOV** moolvie	pintles
reskill	**EIKNSTT** kittens	**EILMOPR** implore	**EILNPSU** lineups
EIKLLST skillet	**EIKNTUZ** kunzite	**EILMORR** lorimer	lupines
EIKLMMN milkmen	**EIKOORR** rookier	**EILMORS** moilers	spinule
EIKLMNN linkmen	**EIKOORS** koories	**EILMOSS** lissome	**EILNPTY** ineptly
EIKLMNR kremlin	rookies	**EILMOST** motiles	**EILNPUV** vulpine
EIKLMRS milkers	**EIKOOST** stookie	**EILMPPS** pimples	**EILNRST** linters
EIKLNNU nunlike	**EIKOPPR** porkpie	**EILMPRS** limpers	slinter
EIKLNOS sonlike	**EIKOPPS** koppies	prelims	**EILNRSV** silvern
EIKLNOT Tolkien	**EIKOPRR** porkier	simpler	**EILNRTY** inertly
EIKLNRS linkers	**EIKOPRS** porkies	**EILMPRU** lumpier	**EILNRVY** nervily
EIKLNRU urnlike	**EIKOPST** pokiest	plumier	**EILNSSS** sinless
EIKLNRW wrinkle	**EIKORSY** yorkies	**EILMPRY** primely	**EILNSST** enlists
EIKLNST tinkles	**EIKOSST** ketosis	**EILMPSS** simples	listens
EIKLNSU sunlike	**EIKPPRS** kippers	**EILMPST** limpest	silents
EIKLNSV kelvins	skipper	limpets	tinsels
EIKLNSW winkles	**EIKPPST** skippet	**EILMPSU** impulse	**EILNSSU** silenus
EIKLNSY skyline	**EIKRRSS** riskers	**EILMPSW** wimples	**EILNSSV** snivels
EIKLNTU nutlike	**EIKRRST** skirret	**EILMPSX** simplex	**EILNSTU** luniest
EIKLNTW twinkle	skirter	**EILMPTY** emptily	utensil
EIKLOTY toylike	striker	**EILMQSU** Quilmes	**EILNSTW** Winslet
EIKLPRY perkily	**EIKRSSS** kissers	**EILMRRY** merrily	**EILNSTY** Yeltsin
EIKLPST Lipetsk	**EIKRSST** strikes	**EILMRSS** smilers	**EILNSUV** unlives
EIKLPSY peskily	**EIKRSSV** skivers	**EILMRST** milters	unveils
EIKLRST kirtles	**EIKRSTT** skitter	**EILMRSU** misrule	**EILNSVY** sylvine
EIKLRSU sulkier	**EIKSSTW** weskits	**EILMRSY** miserly	**EILNVXY** vixenly
	EILLLOS lollies		

EILOOPR loopier	**EILRSSV** silvers	**EIMNRSU** murines	**EIMSSSU** misuses
EILOOPT Tiepolo	slivers	**EIMNSSU** minuses	**EIMSSTY** stymies
EILOORS orioles	**EILRSSW** swilers	**EIMNSTT** mittens	**EINNOOS** ionones
EILOORW woolier	**EILRSTT** litters	smitten	**EINNOPS** pension
EILOOSS loosies	slitter	**EIMNSTU** minuets	**EINNOPT** pontine
EILOOST oolites	tilters	minutes	**EINNOQU** quinone
ostiole	**EILRSTU** lustier	**EIMNSZZ** mizzens	**EINNORT** intoner
EILOOSW woolies	**EILRSUW** wurlies	**EIMNUZZ** muezzin	nointer
EILOPRS spoiler	**EILRSVY** silvery	**EIMOORR** roomier	ternion
EILOPST piolets	**EILRSZZ** sizzler	**EIMOPRR** primero	**EINNORU** reunion
pistole	**EILRTTY** tritely	**EIMOPRS** imposer	Réunion
Ploeşti	**EILRTUV** rivulet	promise	**EINNORV** environ
EILOPSU pileous	**EILSSTW** witless	semipro	**EINNOSS** sonnies
EILOPSV plosive	**EILSSTY** stylise	**EIMOPRV** improve	**EINNOST** intones
EILOPTX exploit	**EILSSVW** swivels	**EIMOPRW** impower	tension
EILORRS lorries	**EILSSZZ** sizzles	**EIMOPSS** imposes	**EINNOSV** venison
EILORSS rissole	**EILSTTT** tittles	**EIMOPST** stompie	**EINNOSY** yonnies
EILORST Estoril	**EILSTTU** lutites	**EIMORRW** wormier	**EINNOTT** tontine
estriol	**EILSTTV** vittles	**EIMORSS** isomers	**EINNOVW** inwoven
loiters	**EILSTTY** stylite	mossier	**EINNPRS** pinners
toilers	testily	**EIMORST** erotism	spinner
EILORSU louries	**EILSTVY** sylvite	mortise	**EINNPRT** enprint
lousier	**EILSTYZ** stylize	**EIMORSU** mousier	**EINNPST** Pinsent
soilure	**EILSUVV** luvvies	**EIMORSV** verismo	tenpins
EILORSW lowries	**EILSWZZ** swizzle	**EIMORTT** omitter	**EINNPSY** spinney
EILORTT tortile	**EIMMMSU** mummies	**EIMORTV** vomiter	**EINNRRU** runnier
triolet	**EIMMNSU** immunes	**EIMOSSS** mossies	**EINNRSS** sinners
EILORTU outlier	**EIMMOPS** pommies	**EIMOSST** somites	**EINNRST** interns
EILOSTT litotes	**EIMMORS** memoirs	**EIMOSTT** motties	tinners
toilets	**EIMMOST** tommies	**EIMOSTU** timeous	**EINNRSU** sunnier
EILOSTV violets	**EIMMPRR** primmer	**EIMOSTV** motives	**EINNRSW** winners
EILOTUV outlive	**EIMMPRU** premium	**EIMOSTZ** mestizo	**EINNRTV** vintner
EILPPPY peppily	**EIMMRRT** trimmer	**EIMOSYZ** isozyme	**EINNSST** sennits
EILPPRR rippler	**EIMMRRU** rummier	**EIMOSZZ** mozzies	**EINNSSU** sunnies
EILPPRS ripples	**EIMMRSS** simmers	**EIMOTTU** timeout	**EINNSTT** intents
slipper	**EIMMRST** misterm	**EIMPQRU** Quimper	**EINNSTU** Sunnite
EILPPRT ripplet	**EIMMRSU** immures	**EIMPRRS** primers	tunnies
tippler	mumsier	**EIMPRRU** impurer	**EINNSTV** invents
EILPPRU pulpier	rummies	**EIMPRSS** impress	**EINNSWY** Swinney
EILPPST stipple	**EIMMRSW** swimmer	premiss	**EINNTUW** untwine
tipples	**EIMMRSZ** zimmers	simpers	**EINOOPZ** epizoon
EILPPSU pileups	**EIMMRUY** yummier	**EIMPRST** imprest	**EINOORS** erosion
EILPPSW swipple	**EIMMSST** semmits	permits	**EINOOST** isotone
EILPRSS lispers	**EIMMSTU** tummies	**EIMPRSU** umpires	toonies
EILPRST triples	**EIMNNOS** Simenon	**EIMPRTU** imputer	**EINOOSZ** ozonise
EILPRTT triplet	**EIMNNOT** mention	**EIMPSST** misstep	**EINOOZZ** ozonize
EILPRTX triplex	**EIMNOOR** moonier	**EIMPSTU** impetus	**EINOPRS** orpines
EILPRUU purlieu	**EIMNOOS** isonome	imputes	**EINOPRT** pointer
EILPSST stipels	moonies	**EIMPSTY** mistype	protein
tipless	noisome	**EIMQSTU** mesquit	repoint
EILPSSW swiples	**EIMNOOT** emotion	**EIMRRST** retrims	tropine
EILPSTT spittle	**EIMNOPS** peonism	trimers	**EINOPSS** spinose
EILPSTU stipule	**EIMNOPT** pimento	**EIMRSST** misters	**EINOPST** pointes
EILPSZZ pizzles	**EIMNORS** merinos	smiters	**EINOPTT** in petto
EILPTTY pettily	**EIMNOST** moisten	**EIMRSSU** misuser	pentito
EILQRTU quilter	**EIMNOSW** winsome	mussier	**EINOPTU** poutine
EILQRUU liqueur	**EIMNOTT** Menotti	surmise	**EINOQUX** equinox
EILQTUY quietly	**EIMNPTU** pinetum	**EIMRSTT** metrist	**EINORRS** ironers
EILRRSU surlier	**EIMNRRU** murrine	**EIMRSTU** mustier	rosiner
EILRRTW twirler	**EIMNRST** minster	**EIMRTTU** tertium	**EINORSS** seniors
EILRSST listers	minters	**EIMRTUX** mixture	sonsier
relists	remints	**EIMRUZZ** muzzier	**EINORST** norites

	oestrin		witness	**EIPPSTT**	tippets	**EISSSTX**	sexists
	orients	**EINSSUW**	sunwise	**EIPPSUY**	yuppies	**EISSSUW**	wussies
	stonier	**EINSTTT**	Stettin	**EIPPTTT**	Tippett	**EISSTUV**	tussive
EINORSU	urinose	**EINSTTW**	twinset	**EIPRRST**	striper	**EISSWZZ**	swizzes
EINORSV	enviros	**EINSTTY**	tensity	**EIPRRUV**	upriver	**EJJMNUU**	jejunum
	version	**EINTTTW**	twitten	**EIPRSSS**	pissers	**EJKMNNU**	junkmen
EINORSW	snowier	**EINTTUY**	tenuity	**EIPRSST**	persist	**EJKNRSU**	junkers
EINORTT	tritone	**EIOOPST**	isotope		priests	**EJKNSTU**	junkets
EINORTU	routine	**EIOORST**	sootier		spriest	**EJLORST**	jolters
EINORTV	Trevino		toories		sprites		jostler
EINORTW	nowtier	**EIOORTV**	Orvieto		stirpes	**EJLOSST**	jostles
EINOSSS	session	**EIOORWZ**	woozier		stripes	**EJLOSSY**	joyless
EINOSST	nosiest	**EIOOSTT**	tootsie	**EIPRSSU**	pussier	**EJLSSTU**	justles
EINOSTT	toniest	**EIOOSTZ**	ooziest		suspire	**EJMNRUY**	jurymen
EINOSTU	Soutine	**EIOPPPS**	poppies		uprises	**EJMPRSU**	jumpers
EINOSTW	townies	**EIOPPRS**	soppier	**EIPRSTT**	spitter	**EJNORUY**	journey
	twonies	**EIOPPSS**	popsies		tipster	**EJNOSTT**	jettons
EINOSUV	envious	**EIOPPST**	potpies	**EIPRSTU**	puirest	**EJOORVY**	overjoy
	niveous	**EIOPRRS**	prosier	**EIPRSTV**	privets	**EJOPPRT**	propjet
EINPPRS	nippers	**EIOPRRT**	pierrot	**EIPRSTY**	pyrites	**EJOPRST**	projets
EINPPST	snippet	**EIOPRST**	reposit		stripey	**EJOPRTT**	jetport
EINPRRT	printer		riposte	**EIPRSUU**	euripus	**EJORSSS**	jossers
	reprint		ropiest	**EIPRUVW**	purview	**EJORSTT**	jotters
EINPRSS	snipers	**EIOPRSU**	soupier	**EIPRUZZ**	Peruzzi	**EJORSTU**	jouster
EINPRSU	uprisen	**EIOPRSX**	proxies	**EIPSSSU**	pussies	**EJPRRUY**	perjury
EINPSST	insteps	**EIOPRTT**	pottier	**EIPSSTZ**	spitzes	**EKKLRSU**	skulker
	spinets	**EIOPSSS**	possies	**EIPSTTU**	putties	**EKKOPSU**	pukekos
EINPSSU	supines	**EIOPSST**	posties	**EIQRSSU**	squires	**EKLLMSU**	skellum
EINPSTU	puniest	**EIOPSTT**	potties	**EIQRSTU**	querist	**EKLLNOR**	knoller
	punties		spottie	**EIQRSUV**	quivers	**EKLLRRU**	kruller
EINPTTY	tintype		tiptoes	**EIQRTTU**	quitter	**EKLNNUU**	Kuenlun
EINQRUY	enquiry	**EIOPSTU**	piteous	**EIQRUVY**	quivery	**EKLNOPR**	plonker
EINQSSU	sequins	**EIOPSTX**	poxiest	**EIQRUZZ**	quizzer	**EKLNORS**	snorkel
EINQSTU	inquest	**EIOPSZZ**	pozzies	**EIQSTUU**	quietus	**EKLNOSS**	kelsons
EINQTTU	quintet	**EIOPTUW**	wipeout	**EIQSUZZ**	quizzes	**EKLNOST**	Skelton
EINQTUU	unquiet	**EIOQTUX**	quixote	**EIRRRST**	stirrer	**EKLNOSW**	Knowles
EINRRSS	rinsers	**EIORRRS**	sorrier	**EIRRSTU**	rustier	**EKLNOSY**	Lysenko
EINRRSU	insurer	**EIORRRT**	terroir	**EIRRSTV**	striver	**EKLNPTU**	Plunket
	ruiners	**EIORRST**	rioters	**EIRRSTW**	writers	**EKLOORS**	lookers
EINRSST	inserts		roister	**EIRRTTU**	ruttier	**EKLOSSZ**	Slezsko
	sinters	**EIORRSW**	worries	**EIRSSST**	resists	**EKLOSTV**	stokvel
EINRSSU	insures	**EIORSST**	rosiest		sisters	**EKLRRSU**	lurkers
	sunrise		siroset	**EIRSSSU**	issuers	**EKLRSSU**	sulkers
EINRSTT	stinter		sorites	**EIRSSTT**	sitters	**EKLSTUZ**	klutzes
	tinters		sorties	**EIRSSTV**	stivers	**EKMNORW**	workmen
EINRSTU	triunes		stories		strives	**EKMNORY**	monkery
	uniters	**EIORSSU**	serious		verists	**EKMNOSY**	monkeys
EINRSTV	inverts	**EIORSSX**	xerosis	**EIRSSUU**	usuries	**EKMNPTU**	unkempt
	striven	**EIORSTU**	touries	**EIRSSUV**	viruses	**EKMOOPS**	mopokes
	Ventris	**EIORSTV**	Treviso	**EIRSTTT**	stretti	**EKMORSS**	smokers
EINRSTW	twiners	**EIOSSTV**	soviets		titters	**EKMSSTU**	muskets
	winters		stovies		tritest	**EKNNSSU**	Knussen
EINRSVW	wiverns	**EIOSTTT**	stottie	**EIRSTTV**	trivets	**EKNOORS**	snooker
EINRTTU	nuttier	**EIOSTUZ**	outsize	**EIRSTTW**	retwist	**EKNOPSU**	unspoke
EINRTTW	written	**EIPPPSU**	puppies		twister	**EKNORSW**	knowers
EINRTUV	venturi	**EIPPRRS**	rippers		witters	**EKNORSY**	yonkers
EINRTWY	wintery	**EIPPRRT**	tripper	**EIRSTUV**	virtues	**EKNORTT**	knotter
EINSSSU	Senussi	**EIPPRST**	tippers	**EIRSUVV**	survive	**EKNORTW**	network
	sinuses	**EIPPRSZ**	zippers	**EIRTTTW**	twitter	**EKNORUY**	younker
EINSSSY	synesis	**EIPPRTT**	trippet	**EIRTTUV**	vuttier		Yukoner
EINSSTV	invests	**EIPPSST**	sippets	**EISSSTU**	tissues	**EKNORWY**	New York
EINSSTW	wisents					**EKNOSUY**	unyokes

EKNRTUY	turnkey	ELMOORT	tremolo	ELOORST	looters	ELOSSVW	vowless
EKNSTUZ	Kuznets	ELMOPRY	polymer		retools	ELOSTTU	outlets
EKOOPRV	provoke	ELMOPSU	plumose		rootles	ELOSTUU	luteous
EKOORRS	koreros	ELMOPSY	employs		toolers	ELOSTUV	volutes
EKOORRY	rookery	ELMOPTY	Ptolemy	ELOORTT	rootlet	ELOSTUZ	touzles
EKOORST	stooker	ELMORSS	morsels		tootler	ELOSWZZ	swozzle
EKOPRRS	porkers	ELMORTU	moulter	ELOOSST	loosest	ELPPRSU	pulpers
EKOPRUY	kouprey	ELMOSST	molests		lotoses		purples
EKORRSW	reworks	ELMOSTT	mottles	ELOOSTT	tootles	ELPPSSU	supples
	workers	ELMOSTY	motleys	ELOOSTU	outsole	ELPQSUU	pulques
EKORRSY	yorkers	ELMOSUU	emulous	ELOPPPS	popples	ELPRRSU	purlers
EKORSST	stokers	ELMOSUV	volumes	ELOPPRS	loppers	ELPRUZZ	puzzler
	strokes	ELMPPRU	plumper		propels	ELPSTUU	pustule
EKOSSTV	Sovetsk	ELMPPSU	peplums	ELOPPST	stopple	ELPSUZZ	puzzles
EKPPSUU	seppuku	ELMPRSU	lumpers		topples	ELRRSTU	rustler
EKRSSTU	tuskers		rumples	ELOPRRW	prowler	ELRRTTU	turtler
EKRSTUY	turkeys	ELMRSTY	myrtles	ELOPRRY	pyrrole	ELRSSTU	lusters
ELLLORS	lollers	ELMRTUU	multure	ELOPRSS	plessor		lustres
ELLMNSU	mullens	ELMRTUY	elytrum		slopers		results
ELLMOOR	morello	ELMRUZZ	muzzler		splores		rustles
ELLMORR	morrell	ELMSSSU	mussels	ELOPRSU	leprous		sutlers
ELLMOSW	mellows	ELMSTUU	mutuels		pelorus		ulsters
ELLMPUU	plumule		mutules		sporule	ELRSSTY	stylers
ELLMRSU	mullers	ELMSTUW	umwelts	ELOPRSV	plovers	ELRSTTU	turtles
ELLMSTU	mullets	ELMSUZZ	muzzles	ELOPRSW	plowers	ELRSUWY	wurleys
ELLMSUY	mulleys	ELNNOSS	nelsons	ELOPRSX	plexors	ELRTTUY	utterly
ELLNOOV	Novello	ELNNRSU	runnels	ELOPRSY	leprosy	ELRTUUV	vulture
ELLNOOW	woollen	ELNNRTU	trunnel	ELOPRTT	plotter	ELSSSTU	tussles
ELLNORS	enrolls	ELNNSTU	tunnels	ELOPRTU	plouter	ELSSSUY	Ulysses
ELLNOST	stollen	ELNOOPT	peloton	ELOPRTW	plowter	ELSSTTY	stylets
ELLNOSW	swollen	ELNOOSS	loosens	ELOPRTY	protyle	EMMMNOS	Mommsen
ELLNSSU	sullens	ELNOOSU	unloose	ELOPSST	topless	EMMMRSU	mummers
ELLNSUU	lunules	ELNOOSW	woolens	ELOPSTT	pottles	EMMMRUY	mummery
ELLOOSY	loosely	ELNOOSY	looneys	ELOPSTU	tupelos	EMMNOOR	monomer
ELLOOWY	Woolley	ELNOPRU	pleuron	ELOPTUV	Tupolev	EMMNOPR	Pommern
ELLOPTU	pollute	ELNOPRY	pronely	ELORRSS	sorrels	EMMNORY	meronym
ELLORRS	rollers	ELNOPST	leptons	ELORRSU	Roulers	EMMNOST	moments
ELLORRT	troller	ELNOPSY	poleyns	ELORSSS	lessors	EMMNOTU	omentum
ELLORTY	trolley	ELNOPTU	opulent	ELORSST	ostlers	EMMNOTY	metonym
ELLOSTU	outsell	ELNORTY	elytron		sterols	EMMOOTY	myotome
	sellout	ELNORTZ	Lorentz	ELORSSU	lousers	EMMOSST	mestoms
ELLOSTX	extolls	ELNOSSS	lessons	ELORSSV	solvers	EMMOSSU	momuses
ELLOSVY	volleys		sonless	ELORSTT	settlor	EMMRRSU	rummers
ELLOSWY	yellows	ELNOSST	telsons		slotter	EMMRSSU	summers
ELLOWYY	yellowy	ELNOSSU	ensouls	ELORSTV	revolts	EMMRSTU	rummest
ELLPRSU	pullers	ELNOSSV	slovens	ELORSTW	trowels	EMMRSUY	summery
ELLPSTU	pullets	ELNOSSW	lowness	ELORSUV	louvers	EMMSSUU	museums
ELLPSUW	upswell	ELNOSTV	solvent		louvres	EMMNOSW	snowmen
ELLPSUY	pulleys	ELNOSUZ	zonules		velours	EMNOORT	montero
ELLRSSU	Russell	ELNOSZZ	nozzles	ELORSUY	elusory	EMNOOST	moonset
ELMMOPS	pommels	ELNOTVY	novelty	ELORSVW	wolvers	EMNOPPR	propmen
ELMMORT	trommel	ELNPSTU	penults	ELORSWY	yowlers	EMNOPST	postmen
ELMMPSU	pummels	ELNRSTU	runlets	ELORTTY	lottery	EMNOPSU	spumone
ELMMPTU	plummet	ELNRSTY	sternly	ELORTVY	overtly	EMNOPSY	eponyms
ELMMRSU	slummer	ELNSSSU	sunless	ELOSSTU	lotuses	EMNOPYY	eponymy
ELMMRTU	tummler	ELNSSSY	selsyns		solutes	EMNORRU	mourner
ELMNOPW	plowmen		slyness		tousles	EMNORSS	sermons
ELMNORS	merlons	ELNSTTU	nutlets	ELOSSTW	lowsest	EMNORST	mentors
ELMNOST	loments	ELNSTUY	Lutyens		slowest		monster
ELMNPSU	plenums	ELNSUZZ	nuzzles	ELOSSTY	systole	EMNORTT	torment
ELMOOPS	pomelos	ELOOPRS	loopers		toyless	EMNORTU	mounter
ELMOORS	Morelos	ELOOPST	pootles		tyloses		remount

EMNORTV	Vermont	**ENNRSTU**	stunner		nutters	**EOPSSSU**	spouses
EMNOSST	stemson	**ENOOPPR**	propone	**ENRSVWY**	wyverns	**EOPSSTX**	sexpots
EMNOSTY	etymons	**ENOOPRS**	operons	**ENSSSTU**	sunsets	**EOPSTTU**	outstep
EMNOSXY	exonyms		snooper	**EOOOPRS**	oospore	**EOQRSTU**	questor
EMNOTUX	Monteux	**ENOOPSY**	spooney	**EOOOPRS**	opposer		roquets
EMNRSSU	rumness	**ENOORRT**	Torreón		propose		torques
EMNRSTU	munster	**ENOORST**	enroots	**EOOPPRV**	popover	**EORRRST**	terrors
	Münster		Orontes	**EOOPPSS**	opposes	**EORRSST**	resorts
	munters	**ENOORSU**	onerous	**EOOPRRS**	spoorer		rosters
	sternum	**ENOORSZ**	snoozer	**EOOPRRT**	trooper		sorters
EMNRTUZ	Müntzer	**ENOOSST**	soonest	**EOOPRST**	poorest	**EORRSSU**	rousers
EMOOPRS	oosperm	**ENOOSSZ**	snoozes		stooper	**EORRSTT**	retorts
EMOOPRT	promote	**ENOOSTT**	testoon	**EOOPRTV**	overtop		rotters
EMOOPRZ	Pomorze	**ENOOTXY**	oxytone	**EOOPRTW**	towrope		stertor
EMOORRS	roomers	**ENOPRRS**	perrons	**EOORRSS**	roosers	**EORRSTU**	routers
EMOORST	mooters	**ENOPRSS**	persons	**EOORRST**	rooster		tourers
EMOOSSS	osmoses	**ENOPRST**	postern		rooters		trouser
EMOOSTT	mottoes		Preston		toreros	**EORRSTV**	Vorster
EMOOSTW	twosome	**ENOPRSY**	pyrones	**EOORRVW**	rowover	**EORRSTY**	stroyer
EMOOSTY	myosote	**ENOPRTT**	portent	**EOORSSS**	soroses	**EORRSZZ**	rozzers
EMOPPST	moppets	**ENOPRTW**	Newport	**EOORSTT**	tooters	**EORRTTT**	trotter
EMOPRRS	rompers	**ENOPRTY**	entropy	**EOORTUW**	outwore	**EORRTTU**	torture
EMOPRST	stomper	**ENOPSST**	stepson	**EOOSSSU**	osseous	**EORSSST**	tossers
	trompes	**ENOQTUU**	unquote	**EOOSSTT**	tootses	**EORSSTU**	estrous
EMOPRSU	supremo	**ENORRSS**	snorers	**EOOTTUV**	outvote		oestrus
EMOQSSU	mosques	**ENORRST**	snorter	**EOPPPRS**	poppers		ousters
EMORRST	stormer		Torrens	**EOPPPST**	poppets		souters
	termors	**ENORRTT**	torrent	**EOPPRRS**	prosper		tussore
	tremors	**ENORRUV**	overrun	**EOPPRSS**	oppress	**EORSSTV**	votress
EMORRSW	wormers		runover	**EOPPRST**	popster	**EORSSTY**	oysters
EMORRWY	wormery	**ENORSSS**	sensors		stopper		storeys
EMORSST	motsers	**ENORSST**	stoners		toppers	**EORSSWW**	wowsers
EMORSSU	mousers		tensors	**EOPPRSU**	purpose	**EORSTTT**	stotter
EMORSUV	mevrous	**ENORSSW**	worsens	**EOPPRSW**	swopper		stretto
EMORSUY	Seymour	**ENORSSY**	sensory	**EOPPRSY**	yoppers		totters
EMOSSSU	mousses	**ENORSTT**	snotter	**EOPPSSU**	suppose	**EORSTTU**	outsert
EMOSSYZ	zymoses		stentor	**EOPRRSS**	pressor		stouter
EMOSTVZ	zemstvo	**ENORSTU**	tonsure	**EOPRRST**	porters		touters
EMPPSTU	muppets	**ENORSUV**	nervous		pretors	**EORSTTW**	swotter
EMPRSTU	stumper	**ENORSUW**	unswore		reports	**EORSTTX**	extorts
	sumpter	**ENORTUY**	tourney		sporter	**EORSUVY**	voyeurs
EMPRTTU	trumpet	**ENOSSSU**	Souness	**EOPRRSU**	pourers	**EORTTTY**	tottery
EMRRSTU	sturmer	**ENOSSTT**	stetson	**EOPRRTU**	trouper	**EOSSTTU**	outsets
EMRRUUZ	Erzurum		testons	**EOPRSST**	posters	**EPPPSTU**	puppets
EMRSSTU	musters	**ENOSSTU**	outness		prestos	**EPPRRUU**	purpure
	stumers	**ENOSSTX**	sextons	**EOPRSSU**	poseurs	**EPPRSSU**	suppers
EMRSTTU	mutters	**ENOSTUU**	tenuous	**EOPRSSW**	prowess	**EPPSTUW**	upswept
EMRSTYY	mystery	**ENOTTUW**	outwent	**EOPRSSY**	ospreys	**EPRRSSU**	pursers
EMSSSTY	systems	**ENPPRSU**	prenups	**EOPRSTT**	potters	**EPRRSUU**	pursuer
ENNNOPS	pennons	**ENPRRSU**	pruners		protest		usurper
ENNNRUY	nunnery		spurner		spotter	**EPRRSUY**	spurrey
ENNORSU	neurons	**ENPRSTU**	punster	**EOPRSTU**	petrous	**EPRRTUU**	rupture
	nonuser		punters		posture	**EPRSSTY**	spryest
ENNORTT	Trenton	**ENPSSTU**	unsteps		pouters	**EPRSSUU**	pursues
ENNORTU	neutron	**ENPSTUU**	tuneups		proteus	**EPRSTTU**	putters
ENNOSST	sonnets	**ENRRSTU**	returns		spouter		sputter
ENNOSTU	neuston		turners		troupes	**EPRSUVY**	purveys
ENNOSTW	newtons	**ENRRSUY**	nursery	**EOPRSTX**	exports	**ERRSSTU**	trusser
ENNOTWW	Newtown	**ENRRTUU**	nurture	**EOPRSUU**	uprouse	**ERRSSUU**	usurers
ENNPRSU	punners	**ENRRTUY**	turnery	**EOPRTTY**	pottery	**ERRSSUY**	surreys
ENNPSTU	punnets	**ENRSSWY**	wryness	**EOPRTVY**	poverty	**ERRSTTU**	truster
ENNRRSU	runners	**ENRSTTU**	entrust	**EOPSSSS**	possess		turrets

ERRSTTY	tryster	**FGGHIIS**	fishgig	**FGINOSX**	foxings	**FILNNUY**	funnily
ERSSSTU	russets	**FGGIINT**	gifting	**FGINRRU**	furring	**FILNORS**	florins
	trusses	**FGGIISZ**	fizgigs	**FGINRSU**	surfing	**FILNORU**	fluorin
	tussers	**FGGILNO**	golfing	**FGINRTU**	turfing	**FILNOSW**	inflows
ERSSTUU	sutures	**FGGILNU**	gulfing	**FGINSSU**	fussing	**FILNOUX**	fluxion
ERSSTUY	russety	**FGGILOY**	foggily	**FGINTTU**	tufting	**FILNSTU**	tinfuls
ERSSTXY	xysters	**FGGINOO**	goofing	**FGINUZZ**	fuzzing	**FILNTUY**	unfitly
ERSSUVY	surveys	**FGGINOR**	forging	**FGIORTW**	figwort	**FILORST**	florist
ERSTTTU	stutter	**FGHHIOS**	hogfish	**FGISTUU**	fuguist	**FILORSV**	frivols
ERSTTUX	urtexts	**FGHIINS**	fishing	**FGJLSUU**	jugfuls	**FILORTU**	floruit
FFFILOT	liftoff	**FGHIIPS**	pigfish	**FGLMSUU**	mugfuls	**FILOSSS**	fossils
FFGHINU	huffing	**FGHILST**	flights	**FGLNORU**	furlong	**FILPSTU**	uplifts
FFGIIMN	miffing	**FGHILTY**	flighty	**FGLNOSU**	songful	**FILRRUY**	furrily
FFGIINN	niffing	**FGHINOO**	hoofing	**FGLOOUY**	ufology	**FILRSTY**	firstly
FFGIINR	griffin	**FGHIOSY**	fogyish	**FGNOORU**	fourgon	**FILRYZZ**	frizzly
	riffing	**FGHIRST**	frights	**FGNOSUU**	fungous	**FILSSUY**	fussily
FFGIINT	tiffing	**FGHNOOR**	foghorn	**FHIILSY**	fishily	**FILSTTU**	flutist
FFGILNU	luffing	**FGIIKNN**	finking	**FHIINNS**	Finnish	**FILSTUW**	wistful
FFGIMNU	muffing		knifing	**FHIINPS**	pinfish	**FILSTUY**	fustily
FFGINOR	griffon	**FGIILLN**	filling	**FHIKLOS**	folkish	**FILSTWY**	swiftly
FFGINOS	offings	**FGIILMN**	filming	**FHILOOS**	foolish	**FILUYZZ**	fuzzily
FFGINPU	puffing	**FGIILNO**	foiling	**FHILOSW**	wolfish	**FIMMMUY**	mummify
FFGLRUY	gruffly	**FGIILNR**	rifling	**FHILSUW**	wishful	**FIMNORS**	informs
FFHHISU	huffish	**FGIILNS**	filings	**FHINRSU**	furnish	**FIMNORU**	uniform
FFHILTY	fifthly	**FGIILNT**	fliting	**FHINSSU**	sunfish	**FIMOORV**	oviform
FFHILUY	huffily		lifting	**FHIOPPS**	foppish	**FIMORTY**	mortify
FFHIOST	toffish	**FGIILNY**	lignify	**FHIORRY**	horrify	**FIMRTUY**	furmity
FFHOOSW	showoff	**FGIIMNR**	firming	**FHIRSTT**	thrifts	**FIMSTYY**	mystify
FFHORSS	shroffs	**FGIINNN**	finning	**FHIRTTY**	thrifty	**FINOOSS**	foisons
FFHOSTU	shutoff	**FGIINNO**	foining	**FHKORTU**	futhork	**FINOPSU**	soupfin
FFIILMY	miffily	**FGIINRS**	firings	**FHLOOSY**	shoofly	**FINOPTY**	pontify
FFIINST	tiffins	**FGIINRT**	rifting	**FHLRTUU**	hurtful	**FINORSS**	frisson
FFILLLU	fulfill	**FGIINST**	fisting		ruthful	**FINORST**	forints
FFILLSU	fulfils		sifting	**FHNOTUX**	foxhunt	**FINOSSU**	fusions
FFILNSY	sniffly	**FGIINSX**	fixings	**FHOOOTT**	hotfoot	**FIOORSU**	furioso
FFILPSS	spliffs	**FGIINSY**	signify	**FHORSTU**	fourths	**FINORSU**	furious
FFILPUY	puffily	**FGIINTT**	fitting	**FHORSTY**	Forsyth	**FIOPRST**	profits
FFILRTY	fritfly	**FGIINZZ**	fizzing	**FIIKNRS**	firkins	**FIOPSTX**	postfix
FFILSTU	fistful	**FGIKLNU**	fluking	**FIILLMO**	milfoil	**FIORSUU**	furious
FFILSTY	stiffly	**FGIKLNU**	funking	**FIILLMY**	filmily	**FIOSTTU**	outfits
FFIMNSU	muffins	**FGIKNOR**	forking	**FIILLNS**	infills	**FIPPUYY**	yuppify
FFINOOT	finfoot	**FGILLNU**	fulling	**FIILLPS**	fillips	**FIRSSUY**	russify
FFINOPS	spinoff	**FGILMNU**	fluming	**FIILNOT**	tinfoil	**FKLMOOT**	folkmot
FFINOPT	pontiff	**FGILNOO**	fooling	**FIILNTY**	niftily	**FKLNOOR**	Norfolk
FFINPSU	puffins	**FGILNOT**	lofting	**FIILPTU**	pitiful	**FKOOORS**	forsook
FFIOPRS	ripoffs	**FGILNOU**	fouling	**FIIMMNU**	infimum	**FLLOOSW**	follows
FFIOPST	tipoffs	**FGILNOW**	flowing	**FIIMSST**	misfits	**FLLOPTU**	topfull
FFIORTY	fortify		fowling	**FIINOSS**	fission	**FLLOSUU**	soulful
FFIOSST	soffits		wolfing	**FIINRTY**	nitrify	**FLLSTUU**	lustful
FFIQSUY	squiffy	**FGILNRU**	furling	**FIIOPST**	positif	**FLMMOUX**	flummox
FFJMOPU	jumpoff	**FGILNSU**	ingulfs	**FIIRTVY**	vitrify	**FLMNOOU**	mouflon
FFKLORU	forkful	**FGILNTU**	fluting	**FIJLLOY**	jollify	**FLMOOOT**	tomfool
FFKLOSU	Suffolk	**FGILNTY**	flyting	**FIJSTUY**	justify	**FLMOORU**	roomful
FFKOOSS	Kossoff	**FGILNUX**	fluxing	**FIKKLNO**	kinfolk	**FLMORWY**	wormfly
FFLNSUY	snuffly	**FGILOOY**	goofily	**FIKLLSU**	skilful	**FLNOORR**	forlorn
FFLOSTY	fylfots	**FGILORY**	glorify	**FIKLNSU**	skinful	**FLNRSUU**	unfurls
FFNORSU	runoffs	**FGIMNOR**	forming	**FILLLUW**	willful	**FLOOTUW**	outflow
FFNORTU	turnoff	**FGIMOSY**	fogyism	**FILLMOY**	mollify	**FLOPSTU**	potfuls
FFOOPST	stopoff	**FGINNNU**	funning	**FILLNUY**	nullify	**FLOSUUV**	fulvous
FFOPSTU	putoffs	**FGINOOR**	roofing	**FILLOTU**	toilful	**FMOOPRU**	Profumo
FGGGIIN	figging	**FGINOOT**	footing	**FILLOTY**	loftily	**FMRSTUU**	frustum
FGGGINO	fogging	**FGINOOW**	woofing	**FILMNOO**	monofil	**FNNNUUY**	unfunny
						FNNOORT	fronton

193

FNOORRW	forworn	**GGIINPS**	piggins	**GHIINNW**	whining	**GHINOTU**	houting
FNOORSU	sunroof	**GGIINRT**	girting	**GHIINPS**	pishing	**GHINPSU**	pushing
FNOPRTU	upfront		ringgit	**GHIINPT**	pithing	**GHINRSU**	Grishun
FNSSUUY	unfussy	**GGIINSS**	Gissing	**GHIINRS**	shiring		rushing
FOOOPRT	rooftop	**GGIINSU**	guising	**GHIINSS**	hissing	**GHINRTU**	hurting
FOOORTT	footrot	**GGIIRRS**	grigris	**GHIINST**	insight	**GHINTTU**	hutting
FOOOTTU	outfoot	**GGIJNSU**	juggins		shiting	**GHIOPSZ**	phizogs
FOORTTX	foxtrot	**GGILLNU**	gulling	**GHIINSW**	wishing	**GHIORSU**	roguish
FOPSSTU	fusspot	**GGILMUY**	muggily	**GHIINTT**	hitting	**GHIOSUV**	voguish
FORRSUW	furrows	**GGILNNO**	longing		tithing	**GHIOUUZ**	Guizhou
FORRUWY	furrowy	**GGILNNU**	lunging	**GHIINTW**	whiting	**GHIPRTU**	upright
FORSSTW	frowsts	**GGILNOS**	gosling		withing	**GHIPTTU**	uptight
FORSTWY	frowsty	**GGILNOV**	gloving	**GHIIRST**	tigrish	**GHIRSTW**	wrights
GGGGIIN	gigging	**GGILNOW**	glowing	**GHIJNOS**	joshing	**GHLMOOO**	homolog
GGGHINO	hogging	**GGILNOZ**	glozing	**GHIKLNU**	hulking	**GHLOOSY**	shoogly
GGGHINU	hugging	**GGILNPU**	gulping	**GHIKNNO**	honking	**GHLOPSU**	ploughs
GGGIIJN	jigging	**GGILOOS**	gigolos	**GHIKNOO**	hooking	**GHLORUY**	roughly
GGGIILN	ligging	**GGILOSY**	soggily	**GHIKNOW**	howking	**GHLOSSU**	sloughs
GGGIINP	pigging	**GGILRWY**	wriggly	**GHIKNST**	knights	**GHLOSTY**	ghostly
GGGIINR	rigging	**GGIMMNU**	gumming	**GHIKNSU**	husking	**GHLOSUY**	sloughy
GGGIINT	tigging	**GGIMNSU**	muggins	**GHIKRTU**	tughrik	**GHLOTUY**	toughly
GGGIINW	wigging	**GGINNNU**	gunning	**GHILLNU**	hulling	**GHMORSU**	sorghum
GGGIJNO	jogging	**GGINNOO**	ongoing	**GHILLTY**	lightly	**GHNOOTW**	Hogtown
GGGIJNU	jugging	**GGINNOP**	ponging	**GHILNOS**	longish	**GHNOPRY**	gryphon
GGGILNO	logging	**GGINNOS**	noggins	**GHILNOT**	tholing	**GHNORST**	throngs
GGGILNU	lugging	**GGINNOT**	tonging	**GHILNOU**	Holguín	**GHNOSSU**	shoguns
GGGIMNU	mugging	**GGINNOW**	gowning	**GHILNOW**	howling	**GHNOSTU**	gunshot
GGGINNO	gonging	**GGINNRU**	gurning	**GHILNRU**	hurling		hognuts
	nogging	**GGINOOP**	pogoing	**GHILNSU**	lushing		noughts
GGGINNU	gunging	**GGINOOS**	goosing	**GHILNSY**	shingly		shotgun
GGGINOR	gorging	**GGINOPR**	groping	**GHILNTY**	nightly	**GHNRTUU**	Guthrun
GGGINOT	togging	**GGINORS**	gringos	**GHILPST**	plights	**GHOOOSW**	hoosgow
GGGINOU	gouging	**GGINORU**	roguing	**GHILRTY**	rightly	**GHOORSS**	sorghos
GGGINPU	pugging		roguing	**GHILSST**	slights	**GHORSTU**	troughs
GGGINSU	sugging	**GGINORW**	growing	**GHILSTY**	sightly	**GHORSTW**	growths
GGGINTU	tugging	**GGINORZ**	grozing	**GHILSUY**	gushily	**GHORTUW**	wrought
GGHHIOS	hoggish	**GGINOSS**	gossing	**GHILTTY**	tightly	**GHORTUY**	yoghurt
GGHIINN	hinging	**GGINPPY**	gypping	**GHIMMNU**	humming	**GIIILNU**	Giulini
GGHIINS	Higgins	**GGINPRU**	purging	**GHIMNNY**	hymning	**GIIJKNN**	jinking
	sighing	**GGINRSU**	surging	**GHIMNOS**	gnomish	**GIIJLNT**	jilting
GGHIIPS	piggish	**GGINSTU**	gusting		moshing	**GIIJNNO**	joining
GGHINSU	gushing	**GGINTTU**	gutting	**GHIMNPU**	humping	**GIIJNNX**	jinxing
	Huggins	**GGIOORS**	gorgios	**GHIMNRY**	rhyming	**GIIKLLN**	killing
GGHIPSU	puggish	**GGIOPTT**	Piggott	**GHIMNSU**	mushing	**GIIKLMN**	milking
GGHORSU	groughs	**GGIPRSY**	spriggy	**GHINNOP**	phoning	**GIIKLNN**	inkling
GGIIILN	gingili	**GGLLOOS**	loglogs	**GHINNOR**	horning		kilning
GGIIKNN	kinging	**GGLOOOS**	googols	**GHINNOS**	noshing		linking
GGIILLN	gilling	**GGMRSUU**	muggurs	**GHINNOT**	nothing	**GIIKLNP**	Kipling
GGIIHMN	minging	**GGNOORS**	gorgons	**GHINNTU**	hunting	**GIIKLNS**	silking
GGIIMNR	griming	**GGNOOSY**	gongyos	**GHINOOP**	hooping	**GIIKLNT**	kilting
GGIINNN	ginning	**GGRRSUU**	grugrus	**GHINOOS**	shooing	**GIIKNNP**	kingpin
GGIINNO	ingoing	**GHHINSU**	hushing	**GHINOOT**	hooting		pinking
GGIINNP	pinging	**GHHLOOY**	Hooghly	**GHINOPP**	hopping	**GIIKNNS**	sinking
GGIINNR	girning	**GHHORTU**	through	**GHINORS**	horsing	**GIIKNNW**	winking
	ringing	**GHHOTTU**	thought		shoring	**GIIKNPP**	kipping
GGIINNS	signing	**GHIILLN**	hilling	**GHINORW**	whoring	**GIIKNPS**	pigskin
	singing	**GHIILNT**	hilting	**GHINOST**	hosting		spiking
GGIINNT	tinging	**GHIILNW**	whiling	**GHINOSU**	housing	**GIIKNRS**	griskin
GGIINNW	winging	**GHIILRS**	girlish	**GHINOSV**	shoving		risking
GGIINNZ	zinging	**GHIINNS**	Hsining	**GHINOSW**	showing	**GIIKNSS**	kissing
GGIINPP	gipping		shining	**GHINOTT**	hotting	**GIIKNST**	kitings
GGIINPR	griping	**GHIINNT**	hinting		tonight		skiting

GIIKNSV	skiving	**GIINOPS**	poising	**GILLLNO**	lolling		rooming
	vikings	**GIINORS**	origins	**GILLLNU**	lulling	**GIMNOOT**	mooting
GIIKNTT	kitting		signior	**GILLMNU**	mulling	**GIMNOOZ**	zooming
GIILLMN	milling		signori	**GILLNOP**	polling	**GIMNOPP**	mopping
GIILLNO	gillion	**GIINORT**	rioting	**GILLNOR**	rolling	**GIMNOPR**	romping
GIILLNP	pilling	**GIINOSY**	yoginis	**GILLNOT**	tolling	**GIMNOPY**	yomping
GIILLNT	lilting	**GIINPPP**	pipping	**GILLNPU**	pulling	**GIMNORW**	worming
	tilting	**GIINPPR**	ripping	**GILMMUY**	gummily	**GIMNOSU**	mousing
GIILLNW	willing	**GIINPPS**	sipping	**GILMNOO**	looming	**GIMNOWY**	Wyoming
GIILMNN	limning	**GIINPPT**	tipping	**GILMNOT**	molting	**GIMNPPU**	pumping
GIILMNO	moiling	**GIINPPZ**	zipping	**GILMNPU**	lumping	**GIMNPSU**	impugns
GIILMNP	limping	**GIINPQU**	piquing		pluming		spuming
GIILMNS	sliming	**GIINPRS**	prising	**GILMNSU**	lignums	**GIMNSSU**	mussing
	smiling		spiring	**GILMPSY**	gymslip	**GIMNUZZ**	muzzing
GIILMNT	milting	**GIINPRZ**	prizing	**GILNNRU**	nurling	**GIMOSTU**	gomutis
GIILMPR	pilgrim	**GIINPSS**	pissing	**GILNNSU**	unsling	**GINNNOO**	nooning
GIILNNS	linings	**GIINPST**	spiting	**GILNOOP**	looping	**GINNNOW**	wonning
GIILNNY	inlying	**GIINPSW**	swiping		pooling	**GINNNPU**	punning
GIILNOR	ligroin		wisping	**GILNOOS**	loosing	**GINNNRU**	running
	roiling	**GIINPTT**	pitting		soloing	**GINNNSU**	sunning
GIILNOS	soiling	**GIINPTW**	wingtip		sooling	**GINNNTU**	tunning
GIILNOT	toiling	**GIINPTY**	pitying	**GILNOOT**	looting	**GINNOOS**	noosing
GIILNPP	lipping	**GIINRRY**	yirring		tooling	**GINNOPS**	spongin
GIILNPS	lisping	**GIINRSS**	risings	**GILNOPP**	lopping	**GINNORS**	snoring
	spiling	**GIINRSV**	virgins	**GILNOPS**	sloping		sorning
GIILNST	listing	**GIINRTW**	writing	**GILNOPU**	louping	**GINNORU**	grunion
	silting	**GIINSSU**	issuing	**GILNOPW**	lowping	**GINNORW**	ingrown
GIILNSV	livings	**GIINSSW**	wissing		plowing	**GINNORY**	gironny
GIILNTT	tilting	**GIINSTT**	sitting	**GILNORU**	louring	**GINNOSS**	nosings
	titling	**GIINSTU**	suiting	**GILNORW**	Rowling	**GINNOST**	stoning
GIILNTW	wilting	**GIINSVW**	swiving	**GILNOSS**	losings	**GINNOSW**	snowing
	witling	**GIINTTW**	witting	**GILNOST**	tiglons	**GINNOSZ**	zonings
GIILNWZ	Zwingli	**GIINZZZ**	zizzing	**GILNOSU**	lousing	**GINNOTW**	wonting
GIILRST	strigil	**GIJKNNU**	junking	**GILNOSV**	solving	**GINNPPU**	pruning
GIIMMNR	rimming	**GIJKNOO**	jooking	**GILNOSW**	lowsing	**GINNPTU**	punting
GIIMNNT	minting	**GIJKNOU**	jouking		slowing	**GINNRSU**	nursing
GIIMNPP	pimping	**GIJLLNO**	jolling	**GILNOTT**	lotting		urnings
GIIMNPR	priming	**GIJLNOT**	jolting	**GILNOTU**	louting	**GINNRTU**	turning
GIIMNPW	wimping	**GIJMNPU**	jumping	**GILNOWY**	yowling	**GINNTTU**	nutting
GIIMNRT	mitring	**GIJNOTT**	jotting	**GILNPPU**	pulping	**GINNTUY**	untying
GIIMNSS	missing	**GIJNTTU**	jutting	**GILNPRU**	purling	**GINOOPP**	pooping
GIIMNST	misting	**GIKLNOO**	looking	**GILNPSU**	pulsing	**GINOORS**	roosing
	smiting	**GIKLNRU**	lurking	**GILNRSU**	rulings	**GINOORT**	rooting
	timings	**GIKLNSU**	sulking	**GILNSSU**	nisguls	**GINOOSS**	isogons
GIINNNP	pinning	**GIKMNNU**	Kunming	**GILNSTU**	lusting	**GINOOST**	sooting
GIINNNS	innings	**GIKMNOS**	smoking	**GILNSTY**	styling	**GINOOSW**	wooings
	sinning	**GIKNNOO**	kongoni	**GILNVVY**	vyingly	**GINOOTT**	tooting
GIINNNT	tinning		Kooning	**GILOORS**	girosol	**GINOPPP**	popping
GIINNNW	winning	**GIKNNOW**	knowing	**GILORTY**	trilogy	**GINOPPS**	sopping
GIINNOP	Nipigon	**GIKNNSU**	Sun King	**GILORTZ**	Görlitz	**GINOPPT**	topping
	opining	**GIKNOOR**	rooking	**GILOSTT**	glottis	**GINOPPW**	wopping
GIINNOR	ironing	**GIKNOOS**	Song Koi	**GILOTUY**	goutily	**GINOPRS**	prosing
GIINNOS	noising		sooking	**GILRSTY**	gristly		sporing
GIINNPP	nipping	**GIKNOPS**	spoking	**GILRTUY**	liturgy	**GINOPRT**	porting
GIINNPS	sniping	**GIKNORW**	working	**GILRYZZ**	grizzly	**GINOPRU**	ingroup
GIINNRS	rinsing	**GIKNORY**	yorking	**GILSTUY**	gustily		pouring
GIINNRU	inuring	**GIKNOST**	stoking	**GIMMMNU**	mumming		rouping
	ruining	**GIKNOSU**	souking	**GIMMNPU**	mumping	**GINOPRV**	proving
GIINNSW	inswing	**GIKNOSY**	Kosygin	**GIMMNSU**	summing	**GINOPSS**	possing
GIINNTT	tinting	**GIKNOUY**	Yingkou	**GIMNNOO**	mooning	**GINOPST**	posting
GIINNTU	uniting	**GIKNSTU**	tusking	**GIMNNOR**	morning		stoping
GIINNTW	twining	**GIKRSTU**	tugriks	**GIMNOOR**	mooring	**GINOPTT**	potting

195

GINOPTU	pouting	**GLNNSUU**	unslung	**HIIMNSX**	minxish	**HINNORT**	tinhorn
GINOQTU	quoting	**GLNOOOR**	Logroño	**HIIMPSW**	wimpish	**HINOORZ**	horizon
GINORSS	grisons	**GLNOOPR**	prolong	**HIIMRSU**	shiurim	**HINOPSS**	siphons
	signors	**GLNOOPY**	polygon	**HIIMSST**	mishits	**HINORSU**	nourish
GINORST	sorting	**GLNORWY**	wrongly	**HIIMSTT**	shittim	**HINOSTW**	townish
	storing	**GLNOSUV**	Volsung	**HIINNOT**	thionin	**HINPPSU**	pushpin
	trigons	**GLNOSUW**	sunglow	**HIINSSW**	swinish	**HINPSSU**	unships
GINORSU	rousing	**GLNOTTU**	glutton	**HIINSTW**	Swithin	**HINRSTU**	runtish
	souring	**GLNPSUU**	unplugs	**HIIOPRW**	powhiri	**HINSTUW**	Whitsun
GINORSY	signory	**GLOOORY**	orology	**HIJNOUZ**	Jinzhou	**HIOPRSW**	worship
GINORTT	rotting	**GLOOOTY**	otology	**HIKKOSU**	Shikoku	**HIOPSST**	sophist
GINORTU	routing	**GLOOOYZ**	zoology	**HIKLSUY**	huskily	**HIOPSSY**	physios
	touring	**GLOOPRS**	prologs	**HIKMNOS**	monkish	**HIOPSTW**	Sopwith
GINORTW	trowing	**GLOORUY**	urology	**HIKMSUU**	Sukhumi	**HIORSSU**	sourish
GINOSST	stingos	**GLOPSTU**	putlogs	**HIKMSUZ**	muzhiks	**HIORSTY**	history
	tossing	**GLORSSY**	grossly	**HIKNNOR**	inkhorn	**HIOSSTT**	sottish
GINOSSU	sousing	**GMMOSUU**	gummous	**HIKNNTU**	unthink	**HIOSTTU**	outhits
GINOSTU	ousting	**GMMPUUW**	mugwump	**HIKNOOU**	hokonui	**HIOTTUW**	outwith
	outings	**GMNNOOS**	gnomons	**HIKNOPS**	Hopkins		without
	outsing	**GMNOORU**	gunroom	**HIKNPSU**	punkish		
GINOSTV	stoving	**GMNOORW**	morwong		Pushkin	**HIPRSUX**	Phrixus
GINOSTW	stowing	**GMNSUUZ**	mzungus	**HIKNRSS**	shrinks	**HIQSSUY**	squishy
GINOTTT	totting	**GMOOPRS**	pogroms	**HIKOVVZ**	Zhivkov	**HIRSSTT**	thirsts
GINOTTU	touting	**GMORSUU**	grumous	**HILLPSU**	uphills	**HIRSTTU**	ruttish
GINPPPU	pupping	**GMORTUW**	mugwort	**HILLRSS**	shrills	**HIRSTTY**	thirsty
GINPPSU	supping	**GMRUYYZ**	zymurgy	**HILLRST**	thrills	**HJNNOOS**	Johnson
GINPPTU	tupping	**GNNOORS**	rognons	**HILLRSY**	shrilly	**HKKLOOS**	kolkhos
GINPRRU	purring	**GNNORYY**	gyronny	**HILLTUU**	Luthuli	**HKKLOOZ**	kolkhoz
GINPRSS	springs	**GNOOOSS**	gossoon	**HILMMOU**	holmium	**HKKOOST**	Okhotsk
GINPRSU	pursing	**GNOORST**	trogons	**HILMPSU**	lumpish	**HKKOSTU**	sukkoth
GINPRSY	springy	**GNOPPSU**	oppugns	**HILMSUY**	mushily	**HKNOOSU**	unhooks
GINPSTU	pignuts		popguns	**HILMTUU**	thulium	**HKNOOWW**	knowhow
GINPSUW	upswing	**GNOPRUW**	grownup	**HILNNTY**	ninthly	**HKOOOPT**	pothook
GINPTTU	putting	**GNOSTUU**	outguns	**HILNORY**	hornily	**HKOOPSU**	hookups
GINRSST	strings		outsung	**HILNOTY**	thionyl	**HKOOSVZ**	sovkhoz
GINRSTU	rusting	**GNPSUUW**	upswung	**HILNPST**	plinths	**HKORSWY**	workshy
GINRSTY	stringy	**GOOPRST**	gosport	**HILOOST**	ooliths	**HKOSSTU**	Kossuth
GINRTTU	rutting	**GOORSTT**	grottos	**HILOOTT**	otolith	**HLLOOSW**	hollows
GINSSSU	sussing	**GOORTUW**	outgrow	**HILORSY**	horsily	**HLLPSUY**	plushly
GINTTTU	tutting	**GORSTTU**	rotguts	**HILORTU**	urolith	**HLMNOTY**	monthly
GIOPRRU	prurigo	**GORSTUY**	yogurts	**HILOSTU**	loutish	**HLOOPSS**	sploosh
GIOPRSU	Gropius	**HHIISTW**	whitish	**HILOSWY**	showily	**HLOOSTY**	soothly
GIOPSSS	gossips	**HHINNSU**	hunnish	**HILOTWW**	whitlow	**HLORSTY**	shortly
GIOPSST	spigots	**HHIORSW**	whorish	**HILPSUY**	pushily	**HLPRSUU**	sulphur
GIOPSSY	gossipy	**HHIOSTT**	hottish	**HILSSTY**	stylish	**HMMNOOY**	homonym
GIORRSU	rigours	**HHISSTW**	whishts	**HILSTTY**	thistly	**HMMOOSU**	hoummos
GIORSTU	Grotius	**HHMRSTY**	rhythms	**HILSTXY**	sixthly	**HMNOOST**	Thomson
	rigouts	**HHOOSTT**	hotshot	**HIMMMTU**	Thummim	**HMNOPSY**	nymphos
GIOSSYZ	zygosis	**HIIIJNO**	John III	**HIMMOST**	Thomism	**HMNOPYY**	hyponym
GISWWYY	wysiwyg	**HIIIKRS**	rikishi	**HIMMPSU**	mumpish	**HMOOSST**	smooths
GJNOOSU	goujons	**HIIILPP**	Philip I	**HIMNSTY**	hymnist	**HMOOSTY**	smoothy
GJNRSUU	gurjuns	**HIIJKNS**	hijinks	**HIMOORS**	moorish	**HMOOSUU**	houmous
GJOORTT	jogtrot	**HIIKNNS**	shinkin	**HIMOPRS**	Orphism	**HMORSUU**	humours
GKKNOOS	songkok	**HIIKNNS**	kinship		rompish	**HNNOOPS**	phonons
GKMOORY	Gromyko		pinkish	**HIMOPSS**	sophism	**HNOOPST**	photons
GLLLOOR	logroll	**HIILLPP**	Phillip	**HIMOPST**	moshpit	**HNOOPTY**	typhoon
GLLOOPS	gollops	**HIILMTU**	lithium	**HIMORSW**	wormish	**HNOORSU**	honours
GLMNOOS	mongols	**HIILPPV**	Philip V	**HIMORTU**	thorium	**HNOOSTU**	Houston
GLMNUUU	umlungu	**HIILPST**	shilpit	**HIMOTTY**	timothy	**HNOPSSY**	syphons
GLMOOVY	myology	**HIILPTY**	pithily	**HIMPRSS**	shrimps	**HNOPSTY**	phytons
GLMORUW	lugworm	**HIILRTT**	trilith	**HIMPRTU**	triumph		pythons
GLNNOOR	lorgnon	**HIIMMSS**	mishmis	**HIMSSTU**	isthmus	**HNRTTUU**	untruth
						HNSTUUZ	Hsün-tzu

HOOPSSY	shypoos
HOOPSTT	hotpots
	potshot
HOORRRS	horrors
HOOSTTU	outshot
HOPRSTU	hotspur
HOPRTUW	upthrow
HOPSSSY	hyssops
HOPSSTU	upshots
HOPSTTU	shotput
HOPSTUY	typhous
HORSTUU	outrush
HOSTTUU	shutout
HPPSSUU	pushups
HPRRSUY	Pyrrhus
HRSSTTU	thrusts
HRSSTUY	thyrsus
IIIKMNN	minikin
IIILOSU	Louis II
IIIPRUV	Viipuri
IIIPSUV	Pius VII
IIIPSUX	Pius XII
IIJLLNO	jillion
IIJNSUU	Sinŭiju
IIKKLNY	kinkily
IIKKNPS	kipskin
IIKLLMY	milkily
IIKLLSY	silkily
IIKLMNP	limpkin
IIKLMRY	mirkily
IIKLNOS	oilskin
IIKLNSW	Wilkins
IIKLPSY	spikily
IIKLRSY	riskily
IIKMOUZ	Koizumi
IIKNPPS	pipkins
IIKNSSS	siskins
IIKPSUW	wikiups
IILLMNO	million
IILLMSY	slimily
IILLNOP	pillion
IILLNOZ	zillion
IILLNST	instill
IILMSTU	stimuli
IILMSTY	mistily
IILNNSU	insulin
IILNNTY	tinnily
IILNORS	sirloin
IILNOSV	violins
IILNOSY	noisily
IILNPPY	nippily
IILNPUV	pulvini
IILNSST	instils
IILNSUV	Vilnius
IILOPRT	tripoli
IILORTV	vitriol
IILOSTV	violist
IILOSUV	Louis IV
IILOSUX	Louis IX
	Louis XI
IILPRVY	privily
IILPSST	pistils
IILPSTY	tipsily
IILPSWY	wispily
IILRTYZ	ritzily
IILTTUY	utility
IILTTWY	wittily
IIMMMNU	minimum
IIMMNSU	minimus
IIMNNOS	minions
IIMNOSS	mission
IIMNOSZ	Zionism
IIMNPRT	imprint
IIMOPSU	impious
IIMOSST	mitosis
IIMOSSU	simious
IIMOSTT	Imittós
IIMRSST	smritis
IIMRTTU	tritium
IIMRTUV	trivium
IINNOOP	opinion
IINNOPS	pinions
IINOPSS	isospin
IINORSS	Rossini
IINORST	ironist
IINORSV	virinos
	virions
IINORTT	introit
IINOSSV	visions
IINOTTU	tuition
IINPPPS	pippins
IINQRUY	inquiry
IINRTTY	trinity
IINSSST	insists
IINSTTU	intuits
IINSTTW	nitwits
IIOOSTT	toitois
IIOPRSS	pissoir
IIOQSTU	Iquitos
IIORSTV	visitor
IIPPSUU	piupius
IIPRRSU	puriris
IIPRSST	spirits
IIPRSTU	pituris
IIPRTTZ	Tirpitz
IIPRTVY	privity
IITTTZZ	tzitzit
IJJMSUU	jujuism
IJJSTUU	jujitsu
	jujuist
IJKLLOY	killjoy
IJKMOSU	moujiks
IJLLOTY	jollity
IJLMPUY	jumpily
IJLNOQU	jonquil
IJLNOTY	jointly
IJNORSU	juniors
IJRSSTU	jurists
IKKMNOU	kikumon
IKKRSTU	Irkutsk
IKKSUUY	kikuyus
IKLLPSU	upskill
IKLLSUY	sulkily
IKLMOOS	lookism
IKLMOPS	milksop
IKLMOSY	smokily
IKLMRUY	murkily
IKLNNSU	unlinks
IKLNOOT	kiloton
IKLNPSU	linkups
	uplinks
IKLNRWY	wrinkly
IKLOOTT	toolkit
IKLOSSU	souslik
IKLSSSU	susliks
IKMNOOS	kimonos
	Míkonos
	monoski
IKMNPPU	pumpkin
IKMOOST	mistook
IKMOSSU	koumiss
IKNNSTU	unknits
IKNOPRW	pinwork
IKNOPST	Skipton
IKNORTW	tinwork
IKNPSTU	sputnik
IKPRSSU	prusiks
	spruiks
ILLMNOU	mullion
ILLMNRU	millrun
ILLMORU	Murillo
ILLMPUY	lumpily
ILLMSUU	limulus
ILLNOQU	quillon
ILLNORS	Rollins
ILLNPUU	lupulin
ILLNTUY	nullity
ILLOPRY	pillory
ILLOPSW	pillows
ILLORTU	Utrillo
ILLOSUV	villous
ILLOSUY	lousily
ILLOSWW	willows
ILLOWWY	willowy
ILLPPUY	pulpily
ILLQSSU	squills
ILLRSUY	surlily
ILLSTUY	lustily
ILMMSUU	mimulus
ILMNOOT	moonlit
ILMNOOY	moonily
ILMNOSU	moulins
ILMNSSU	muslins
ILMOOPP	Limpopo
ILMOORY	roomily
ILMOOSV	moolvis
ILMORTU	turmoil
ILMOSTY	moistly
ILMOSUY	mousily
ILMRSSY	lyrisms
ILMSSUY	mussily
ILMSTUY	mustily
ILMUYZZ	muzzily
ILNNOPS	nonslip
ILNNOSS	Nilsson
ILNNSUY	sunnily
ILNOOPS	plosion
ILNOORS	rosinol
ILNOORV	Livorno
ILNOOST	lotions
	soliton
ILNOPRU	purloin
ILNOPST	pontils
ILNOPSU	upsilon
ILNORST	nostril
ILNOSST	tonsils
ILNOSSU	insouls
ILNOSTY	stonily
ILNOSWY	snowily
ILNPRSU	purlins
ILNPSST	splints
ILNSSTU	insults
ILNTTUY	nuttily
ILOOPST	topsoil
ILOOSST	soloist
ILOOSTY	sootily
ILOOWYZ	woozily
ILOPPSY	soppily
ILOPRSY	prosily
ILOPSST	pistols
	postils
ILOPSTT	spotlit
ILOPSUY	piously
ILOQRSU	liquors
ILORRSY	sorrily
ILORSTU	troilus
ILOSSTY	tylosis
ILOSTTW	wittols
ILOSUVX	Louis XV
ILPPSSU	slipups
ILPPSTU	pulpits
ILPSTTU	uptilts
ILRSSTY	lyrists
ILRSTUY	rustily
ILRTTUY	ruttily
ILSSTTU	lutists
ILSSTTY	stylist
ILSTTUU	titulus
IMMOOSS	simooms
IMMOPTU	optimum
IMMOSTU	stomium
IMMSSTU	summits
IMNNNOU	munnion
IMNNOSW	minnows
IMNNSTU	muntins
IMNOOPT	tompion
IMNOORS	morions
IMNOORT	monitor
IMNOOSS	simoons
IMNOOST	motions
IMNOOSU	ominous
IMNOOSY	isonomy
IMNOOUX	oxonium
IMNOPRW	pinworm
IMNOPSS	Simpson
IMNOPSU	spumoni
IMNORST	Strimon
IMNOSST	monists

Code	Word
IMOOPRX	proximo
IMOORST	Morisot
IMOOSSS	osmosis
IMOOSSU	osmious
IMOPRST	imports
	tropism
IMOPRTU	protium
IMOPSST	imposts
IMORRRS	mirrors
IMORSTU	tourism
IMORSTY	trisomy
IMOSSTU	missout
IMOSSYZ	zymosis
IMOSTTT	tomtits
IMOSTUV	vomitus
IMQRSSU	squirms
IMQRSUY	squirmy
IMRSSTU	sistrum
	trismus
	truisms
IMRTTUY	yttrium
INNNOOR	noniron
INNOOPS	opsonin
INNOOST	notions
INNORST	introns
INNOSTU	nonsuit
INNOSTW	Winston
INNOSWW	winnows
INOOPRT	portion
INOOPSS	poisons
	poisson
INOOPST	options
	potions
INOORSS	orisons
INOORST	isotron
	nitroso
	torsion
INOORTT	tortoni
INOOSUX	noxious
INOPPST	topspin
INOPRSS	prisons
INOPSST	pistons
INOPSSU	poussin
	spinous
INOPSTU	spinout
INORSTT	tritons
INORSTU	nitrous
	turions
INORSUU	ruinous
	urinous
INOSSUU	sinuous
INOSTUV	Ustinov
INPRSST	sprints
INPRSTU	turnips
INPRSTY	trypsin
INQSSTU	squints
INQSTUY	squinty
INRSTTU	intrust
INSSTUU	sunsuit
INSTTUW	untwist
IOOPRSV	proviso
IOOPSTY	isotopy
IOORSSS	sorosis
IOORSTT	risotto
IOORSTU	riotous
IOOSSST	ostosis
IOPRSST	riposts
IOPRSSY	pyrosis
IOPRSTT	protist
IOQRTTU	quittor
IORRSTW	worrits
IORSSTU	suitors
IORSTTU	tourist
IOSSSTT	tsotsis
IOSSTTU	outsits
IOSTTUW	outwits
IPPQSUU	quippus
IPRRSTU	irrupts
	stirrup
IPRSSTU	purists
	spruits
IPRSTUU	pursuit
IPSSSTY	stypsis
IPSSTTY	typists
IPSTTTU	tittups
IQRSTTU	squirts
ISSTUVX	Sixtus V
JJSTUUU	jujutsu
JLLOOPS	jollops
JMOPTUU	outjump
JNNORUY	nonjury
JNNOSTU	jotunns
JNOORSU	journos
	sojourn
JOOPPSY	joypops
KKLMSUU	mukluks
KKMOOSU	skookum
KKNOOOR	Koko Nor
KKNORUU	Kuku Nor
KLLMOSU	mollusk
KLNOOOW	Kowloon
KLNOOPS	plonkos
KLOOOTU	lookout
	outlook
KMNOOSY	Mykonos
KMOOORS	mokoros
KMOSSUY	koumyss
KNNNOUW	unknown
KNNOSTU	unknots
KNOOPTT	topknot
KNOOSSS	Knossos
KNOPRTY	krypton
KNORRTY	krytron
KOOPRSW	Worksop
KOOPRTW	worktop
KOORTUW	outwork
	workout
KOOSSUU	soukous
KOOSTTU	tuktoos
KOOSTWW	kowtows
KORSTTY	Trotsky
KOTUUVZ	Kutuzov
LLLOOPS	lollops
LLMOOPR	rollmop
LLMPPUY	plumply
LLNORSU	unrolls
LLOOPRT	rolltop
	trollop
LLOORTU	rollout
LLOPTUU	pullout
LLORSST	strolls
LLPPSUU	pullups
LMNOOOS	Solomon
LMOOOOS	mooloos
LMOOOTV	Molotov
LMOPSUY	Olympus
LMORSUU	Romulus
LMRSTUU	lustrum
LMSTTUU	tumults
LMSTUUU	tumulus
LNNOPSU	nonplus
LNOOSST	stolons
LNOPSTU	plutons
LNOSTYZ	Olsztyn
LNRTUUY	untruly
LOOOORS	oloroso
LOOSSTV	volosts
LOOSTTY	Tolstoy
LOPPSUY	polypus
LOPRSUY	pylorus
LOPRTUY	poultry
LOPSSTY	stylops
LOSTTUY	stoutly
LPRSSUU	surplus
MMNNOOY	mononym
MMNOSSU	summons
MMOOPPS	pompoms
MMOOSTT	motmots
MMOPSTY	symptom
MMRRSUU	murmurs
MMSUUUU	muumuus
MNNOOOS	monsoon
MNNOSYY	synonym
MNOOPPS	pompons
MNOOPTY	toponym
MNOORSU	sunroom
	unmoors
MNOOSUY	onymous
MNORSTU	nostrum
	Urmston
MNORSTY	Strymon
MNOTTUY	muttony
MOOOTYZ	zootomy
MOOPPSU	pompous
MOOPSSU	opossum
MOOPSTT	topmost
MOORRSW	morrows
MOOSTTU	outmost
MOPPRST	prompts
MOPSSSU	possums
MOPSSUU	spumous
MOQRSUU	quorums
MORRSTU	rostrum
MORRSUU	rumours
MORSTUU	tumours
NNOOOPT	pontoon
NNOOPRS	nonpros
NNOOPRU	pronoun
NNOOPSS	sponson
NNOOPST	nonstop
NNOOSTW	wontons
NNORSUW	unsworn
NOOORTT	Toronto
NOOOSUZ	ozonous
NOOOTTW	Wootton
NOOPRSS	sponsor
NOOPRST	protons
NOOPSYZ	Pozsony
NOORSTU	unroots
NOORTUW	outworn
NOOTTWY	toytown
NOPSSTU	sunspot
	unstops
NORSTUU	outruns
	runouts
NORTTUU	outturn
	turnout
NPRSTUU	turnups
	upturns
NRSSTUU	untruss
OOOOPRT	potoroo
OOORTTU	outroot
OOPRSSU	soursop
OOPRSTU	uproots
OOPRSTV	provost
OOPRTTU	outport
OOPRTUU	outpour
OOPSSTT	tosspot
OOPSTTU	outpost
OOPSWWW	powwows
OORRSSW	sorrows
OORSUVV	Suvorov
OPPRRTU	purport
OPPRSTU	support
OPPRSTY	stroppy
OPRSSTU	sprouts
	stupors
OPSSSTU	tossups
OPSTTUU	outputs
	putouts
ORSTTUU	surtout
ORSTTUY	tryouts
RSTTUUY	Ustyurt

Eight Letters

AAAAABENN	anabaena	AAABDENS	Banda Sea	AAACCISU	Caucasia
AAAAABKTW	Kawabata	AAABDEST	database	AAACCLMS	malaccas
AAAAACCRR	caracara	AAABDFRS	abfarads	AAACCLPS	alpaccas
AAAAACNRS	anasarca	AAABDHHI	dahabiah	AAACCLRS	caracals
AAAADMTV	amadavat	AAABDHLL	Abd Allah	AAACCRSS	cascaras
AAAADTVV	avadavat	AAABDKNT	databank	AAACCRTT	cataract
AAAAEMNR	Aramaean	AAABDKSZ	Szabadka	AAACDEIM	academia
AAAAGIRU	Araguaia	AAABDLMS	lambadas	AAACDELM	aceldama
AAAAGLRT	Agartala	AAABDLNO	Badalona	AAACDENR	dracaena
AAAAGMTY	Yamagata	AAABDNNN	bandanna	AAACDEQU	aquacade
AAAAHJMR	maharaja	AAABDNNS	bandanas	AAACDETU	acaudate
AAAAHMNY	Mahayana	AAABDNRS	saraband	AAACDFIR	faradaic
AAAAIMPR	arapaima	AAABDNRT	abradant	AAACDILR	caldaria
AAAAINPY	Ayia Napa	AAABEHNR	habanera	AAACDINN	Canadian
AAAAIRTX	ataraxia	AAABEHRT	barathea	AAACDINR	acaridan
AAAAKKNT	katakana	AAABENSS	anabases		arcadian
AAAAKKWW	kawakawa	AAABFILR	al-Farabi	AAACDKLY	lackaday
AAAAKMWY	Wakayama	AAABFLLS	falbalas	AAACDNNO	anaconda
AAAAKNWZ	Kanazawa	AAABGLNY	bangalay	AAACDNRS	sandarac
AAAALLVV	lavalava	AAABGLOR	algaroba	AAACDOTV	advocaat
AAAALNTT	Atalanta	AAABGMNQ	mbaqanga	AAACEERS	Caesarea
AAAAMMTT	matamata	AAABGNST	Batangas	AAACEHLT	calathea
AAAAMNRY	Ramayana	AAABGRTU	rutabaga	AAACEHLZ	chalazae
AAAANNST	Santa Ana	AAABHIKZ	Abkhazia	AAACELNT	analecta
AAABBBRS	Barabbas	AAABHIMN	Bahamian	AAACELST	catalase
AAABBCLS	cabbalas	AAABHIMT	Amitabha	AAACENNP	panacean
AAABBHKL	kabbalah	AAABHJLV	Jhabvala	AAACENPS	panaceas
AAABBILT	abbatial	AAABHLMR	Alhambra	AAACGHNR	charanga
AAABBKLS	kabbalas	AAABHMNR	Brahmana	AAACGLSW	scalawag
AAABBNRS	Barnabas	AAABHMST	mastabah	AAACGMNP	campagna
AAABCCMW	maccabaw	AAABHPRT	Bhatpara	AAACGMNR	armagnac
AAABCCRT	baccarat	AAABINPR	Parnaíba	AAACGNRU	Rancagua
AAABCDOZ	Bozcaada	AAABINRV	Bavarian	AAACHILW	Walachia
AAABCENT	Ecbatana	AAABINSS	anabasis	AAACHIPS	aphasiac
AAABCHLS	calabash	AAABINTV	Batavian		Caiaphas
AAABCILP	abapical	AAABIPSS	piassaba	AAACHLLZ	chalazal
AAABCILR	Calabria	AAABISTV	batavias	AAACHLMN	La Mancha
AAABCINT	anabatic	AAABKLSV	baklavas	AAACHLSZ	chalazas
AAABCITT	ciabatta	AAABKPSS	baasskap	AAACHRSY	acharyas
AAABCLSV	baclavas	AAABLLRT	Ballarat	AAACIJMN	Jamaican
AAABCNRR	barranca	AAABLOPR	parabola	AAACILMN	maniacal
AAABCNRU	carnauba	AAABMNRT	Martaban	AAACILMR	calamari
AAABCORS	carabaos	AAABMSST	mastabas	AAACILRV	calvaria
AAABCPRY	capybara	AAABORRS	ararobas	AAACILST	Castalia
AAABCSSS	cassabas	AAABRSUY	Surabaya	AAACILSY	calisaya
AAABCSTW	catawbas	AAACCEPR	carapace	AAACIMNP	Campania
AAABDEHH	dahabeah	AAACCILR	calcaria	AAACINSU	Nausicaä

AAACINTV	cavatina	**AAAEHLST**	althaeas	**AAAHHPRS**	parashah
AAACIRRS	sacraria	**AAAEHMNT**	anathema	**AAAHHSTT**	tatahash
AAACIRTX	ataraxic	**AAAEHNPS**	anaphase	**AAAHHTWY**	Hathaway
AAACJMRS	jacamars	**AAAEIMRV**	Ave Maria	**AAAHIINW**	Hawaiian
AAACKLMN	almanack	**AAAEKKRT**	karateka	**AAAHIKLR**	Kalahari
AAACKMRT	tamarack	**AAAEKLLV**	Kalevala	**AAAHIKSW**	kahawais
AAACLLSV	cavallas	**AAAEKMNU**	Mauna Kea	**AAAHILPS**	Ali Pasha
AAACLLTX	Tlaxcala	**AAAEKNTW**	Te Kanawa	**AAAHIMNR**	maharani
AAACLMNS	almanacs	**AAAEKTWY**	takeaway	**AAAHIMRT**	hamartia
AAACLMUY	Macaulay	**AAAELMMN**	analemma		Mata Hari
AAACLNST	cantalas	**AAAELRTV**	lavatera	**AAAHIMRV**	Mahavira
AAACLPST	catalpas	**AAAEMTTV**	Tamatave	**AAAHINNY**	Hinayana
AAACLRSZ	alcazars	**AAAENNSS**	ananases	**AAAHJLMT**	Taj Mahal
AAACLRTZ	Alcatraz	**AAAENPRV**	paravane	**AAAHLLLV**	Valhalla
AAACMRSS	macassar	**AAAENPST**	anapaest	**AAAHLLLW**	Walhalla
	marascas	**AAAEOORT**	Aotearoa	**AAAHLLMR**	Ramallah
AAACNOSV	Casanova	**AAAERSWY**	areaways	**AAAHMMST**	mahatmas
AAACNRSV	caravans	**AAAERTWY**	tearaway	**AAAHMNOR**	Maranhão
AAACNSTT	cantatas	**AAAFFLLS**	alfalfas	**AAAHMNRT**	amaranth
AAACRSWY	caraways	**AAAFHHRT**	haftarah	**AAAHMSST**	tamashas
AAACSSSV	cassavas	**AAAFINST**	fantasia	**AAAHNNSV**	savannah
AAACSTWY	castaway	**AAAFINUV**	avifauna	**AAAHNOPR**	anaphora
AAADDORV	Vadodara	**AAAFIRST**	ratafias	**AAAHNPPR**	Harappan
AAADELMS	alamedas	**AAAFLLWY**	fallaway	**AAAHRSTW**	waratahs
	salaamed	**AAAGGJLN**	Ganga jal	**AAAHSWWY**	washaway
AAADEMNN	Mandaean	**AAAGGLLN**	galangal	**AAAIINPR**	apiarian
AAADEMSV	Sama-Veda	**AAAGHINN**	Ghanaian	**AAAIJNTU**	Tia Juana
AAADENPS	Pasadena	**AAAGHINR**	hiragana	**AAAIKKSW**	Kawasaki
AAADENTV	vanadate	**AAAGHIPR**	agraphia	**AAAIKMSY**	Yamasaki
AAADEPRT	tapadera	**AAAGHNNT**	agnathan	**AAAIKNTY**	Antakiya
AAADFRSY	faradays	**AAAGHNST**	ataghans	**AAAILLMR**	malarial
AAADGGHH	haggadah	**AAAGHNTY**	yataghan	**AAAILLPT**	palatial
AAADGGHS	haggadas	**AAAGIKNS**	Nagasaki	**AAAILMNR**	malarian
AAADGIMM	gammadia	**AAAGILNT**	Galatian	**AAAILMNW**	Malawian
AAADGINU	Guadiana	**AAAGILRU**	La Guaira	**AAAILMRT**	Altamira
AAADGLMY	amygdala	**AAAGINRR**	agrarian	**AAAILMSV**	malvasia
AAADGLNN	Nagaland	**AAAGINSZ**	gazanias	**AAAILMSY**	Malaysia
AAADHHLV	havdalah	**AAAGISSS**	assagais	**AAAILNOT**	Anatolia
AAADHIMN	Mahanadi	**AAAGJLNR**	La Granja	**AAAILNST**	Alsatian
AAADHKNR	Kandahar	**AAAGJMNR**	Jamnagar	**AAAILPRX**	paraxial
AAADHMRS	madrasah	**AAAGJORY**	raja yoga	**AAAILRSU**	Laurasia
AAADIKLS	Kalidasa	**AAAGKNNO**	Okanagan	**AAAIMMST**	miasmata
AAADILMT	Dalmatia	**AAAGKRSV**	Gavaskar	**AAAIMNOR**	Marianao
AAADILRU	adularia	**AAAGLMMS**	amalgams	**AAAIMNOZ**	Amazonia
AAADIMNY	adynamia	**AAAGLMSY**	Malagasy	**AAAIMNST**	amanitas
AAADIRST	radiatas	**AAAGLNRW**	Warangal		Tasmania
AAADJKRT	Djakarta	**AAAGLNSS**	lasagnas	**AAAIMRST**	Sarmatia
AAADKNNS	Sandakan	**AAAGLNTV**	galavant	**AAAIMRTV**	Amravati
AAADKRRV	aardvark	**AAAGLRST**	astragal	**AAAINNST**	Antisana
AAADLLLN	La-La land	**AAAGMNNN**	Namangan	**AAAINNTZ**	Tanzania
AAADLMNS	mandalas	**AAAGMNRS**	anagrams	**AAAINOPR**	paranoia
AAADLMNY	Mandalay		Samarang	**AAAINQRU**	aquarian
AAADLNRS	Saarland	**AAAGMNRT**	Ramat Gan	**AAAINRSV**	Varanasi
AAADMNOR	Maradona	**AAAGMORS**	Saramago	**AAAIPSSV**	piassava
AAADMNST	adamants	**AAAGNPRS**	parasang	**AAAJMNRU**	Ramanuja
AAADMNTU	tamandua	**AAAGNRRS**	ngararas	**AAAJPRUY**	Jayapura
AAADMRUY	Amu Darya	**AAAGNRTU**	Tauranga	**AAAKKMRU**	Kamakura
AAADNSTZ	Zaanstad	**AAAGORZZ**	Zaragoza	**AAAKKORT**	Krakatoa
AAADSWYY	awaydays	**AAAGPRUY**	Paraguay	**AAAKLWWY**	walkaway
AAAEGNPP	appanage	**AAAHHITW**	Hiawatha	**AAAKMNRS**	namaskar
AAAEGNPS	apanages	**AAAHHKLS**	halakhas	**AAAKMTUU**	kaumatua
AAAEHLMT	Amalthea	**AAAHHLSV**	halavahs	**AAAKNNRS**	Arkansan

AAAKNRSS	Arkansas	AABBOORR	Bora Bora	AABCELST	castable
AAAKOSWY	soakaway	AABBSSSU	babassus	AABCELSU	causable
AAALLPRX	parallax	AABCCEHK	backache	AABCELWY	cableway
AAALLPST	palatals	AABCCEIR	Beccaria	AABCEMRV	vambrace
AAALMNOU	Mauna Loa	AABCCELS	cascabel	AABCEMSS	ambsaces
AAALMNTZ	Mazatlán	AABCCERT	braccate	AABCENRR	Canberra
AAALNNST	lantanas	AABCCHKS	cashback	AABCERST	abreacts
AAALNPRT	rataplan	AABCCHKT	backchat		bearcats
AAALNRTT	tarlatan	AABCCHNT	bacchant		cabarets
AAALRRSY	arrayals	AABCCIMR	carbamic	AABCERTT	cabretta
AAAMMPRS	mamparas	AABCCINN	cannabic	AABCESSU	abacuses
AAAMNOPR	panorama	AABCCKKP	backpack	AABCFHKL	halfback
AAAMNOSZ	Amazonas	AABCCKLP	blackcap	AABCFIIL	bifacial
AAAMNRRY	yarraman	AABCCKLW	clawback	AABCFKLL	fallback
AAAMNRST	marantas	AABCCMOT	catacomb	AABCFKST	fastback
AAAMNSSS	Manassas	AABCCMOY	maccaboy		fatbacks
AAAMNSTZ	Matanzas	AABCDEIN	abidance	AABCGIMO	cambogia
AAAMORST	tamaraos	AABCDEIO	Boadicea	AABCGKRY	grayback
AAAMOTTU	automata	AABCDEIT	abdicate	AABCHILR	brachial
AAAMRSTU	tamaraus	AABCDEKT	backdate	AABCHINR	branchia
AAAMRTTU	traumata	AABCDELL	caballed	AABCHKLS	backlash
AAANNPRU	Anapurna	AABCDELN	balanced	AABCHKSW	backwash
AAANNSSV	savannas	AABCDHKN	backhand	AABCHLOO	coolabah
AAANOPRZ	parazoan	AABCDHKR	hardback	AABCHMRY	chambray
AAANQTUU	aquanaut	AABCDIIS	diabasic	AABCHNNU	Buchanan
AAANRSTT	tantaras	AABCDIMO	Cambodia	AABCHNRS	barchans
AAANSTXY	Astyanax	AABCDIRS	carabids	AABCIILR	biracial
AAAORSWY	soaraway	AABCDKRW	backward	AABCIILS	basilica
AAAPPRST	apparats		drawback	AABCIINR	brainiac
AAAPQRTU	paraquat	AABCDKRY	backyard	AABCIKLT	tailback
AAAPSTTU	taupatas	AABCDLRS	Carlsbad	AABCILLR	bacillar
AAARSTTT	ratatats	AABCEEFL	faceable		cabrilla
AAARSTTU	tuataras	AABCEELT	Albacete	AABCILMS	balsamic
AABBCDEG	cabbaged	AABCEENY	abeyance		cabalism
AABBCDRS	scabbard	AABCEERT	acerbate	AABCILMY	amicably
AABBCEGS	cabbages	AABCEFRS	facebars	AABCILNN	cannibal
AABBCEIS	abbacies	AABCEGOT	cabotage	AABCILNO	anabolic
AABBCEKR	bareback	AABCEHLS	cashable	AABCILST	basaltic
AABBCEKT	backbeat	AABCEHMS	ambaches		cabalist
AABBCINR	barbican	AABCEHNR	barchane	AABCINNN	cannabin
AABBCIRR	barbaric	AABCEHRU	Auerbach	AABCINNO	Baconian
AABBCIST	sabbatic	AABCEILM	amicable	AABCINNR	cinnabar
AABBDENS	baseband	AABCEIMN	ambiance	AABCINNS	cannabis
AABBDHIU	Abu Dhabi	AABCEINR	carabine	AABCINRS	carabins
AABBDORS	Barbados	AABCEIRT	bacteria	AABCINRT	Bactrian
AABBEELR	bearable	AABCEKLM	clambake	AABCINSU	banausic
AABBEELT	beatable	AABCEKLP	packable	AABCIRSS	brassica
AABBEGNS	beanbags	AABCEKLR	lacebark	AABCISSS	abscissa
AABBEILL	bailable	AABCEKLS	Black Sea	AABCISTX	taxicabs
AABBEKLN	bankable		sackable	AABCKKLT	talkback
AABBELLM	blamable	AABCEKST	backseat	AABCKLNO	loanback
AABBELLS	baseball	AABCELLL	callable	AABCKLNY	claybank
AABBELOS	baalebos	AABCELLN	Ballance	AABCKLPY	playback
AABBELRY	bearably	AABCELLP	placable	AABCKLRT	black art
AABBELTY	Table Bay	AABCELLS	scalable	AABCKNPS	snapback
AABBHKSU	babushka	AABCELNR	balancer	AABCKPRT	bratpack
AABBHSST	sabbaths		barnacle	AABCKPSY	paybacks
AABBIILL	bilabial	AABCELNS	balances	AABCKRRS	barracks
AABBILRT	barbital	AABCELOR	albacore	AABCKSTY	backstay
AABBIRSU	babirusa	AABCELPS	spacelab	AABCKSWY	swayback
AABBIRSY	Baybars I	AABCELRT	bracteal	AABCLLPY	placably
AABBLLMY	blamably		cartable	AABCLLSY	scalably

AABCLNTY blatancy	**AABDGNOV** vagabond	**AABEELRS** erasable
AABCLRRY carbaryl	**AABDGNSS** sandbags	**AABEELRT** rateable
AABCNORR barranco	**AABDGORR** garboard	tearable
AABCNOSU Casaubon	**AABDGOTU** gadabout	**AABEELRW** wearable
AABCOORS Sorocaba	**AABDHLLN** handball	**AABEELST** eatables
AABCORST acrobats	**AABDHLLR** hardball	**AABEELSV** saveable
AABCOSTT catboats	**AABDHLLU** Abdullah	**AABEEMNO** amoebean
AABCRSTT abstract	**AABDHNST** hatbands	**AABEEMNT** entameba
AABDDEET deadbeat	**AABDHRSU** bahadurs	**AABEEMPR** abampere
AABDDEGN bandaged	subahdar	**AABEENNW** wannabee
AABDDEHL baldhead	**AABDHRUY** Buraydah	**AABEENOR** anaerobe
AABDDEHN headband	**AABDIILR** biradial	**AABEERSZ** zareebas
AABDDINZ zindabad	**AABDIILS** basidial	**AABEERTT** trabeate
AABDDLNS badlands	**AABDIKRS** bidarkas	**AABEFGLS** fleabags
Bad Lands	**AABDIMRS** barmaids	**AABEFHKL** halfbeak
AABDDMRU murdabad	**AABDINNR** rainband	**AABEFLLL** flabella
AABDEELR readable	**AABDINNU** Danubian	**AABEFLMR** farmable
AABDEELT dateable	**AABDINST** tabanids	framable
AABDEELV evadable	**AABDINVY** Dvina Bay	**AABEFLMU** flambeau
AABDEELW wadeable	**AABDKNNS** sandbank	**AABEFLSY** False Bay
AABDEEMN endameba	**AABDLLRY** balladry	**AABEFNSS** fanbases
AABDEERR Aberdare	**AABDLLUY** laudably	**AABEGGGS** baggages
AABDEERT teabread	**AABDLMNU** labdanum	**AABEGGLY** gageably
AABDEERY bayadere	**AABDLMNY** damnably	**AABEGILN** gainable
AABDEGHN headbang	**AABDLMRU** adumbral	**AABEGLLL** glabella
AABDEGIN badinage	**AABDLOOT** boatload	**AABEGLLM** ballgame
AABDEGLR gradable	**AABDLOPR** lapboard	**AABEGLNW** gnawable
AABDEGMS gambades	**AABDLORR** labrador	**AABEGLRS** algebras
AABDEGNS bandages	larboard	**AABEGLRT** glabrate
AABDEGRR barraged	**AABDLORY** adorably	**AABEGLRU** arguable
AABDEHKN Bankhead	**AABDLRSV** Svalbard	Balaguer
AABDEHKR hardbake	**AABDLRSW** bradawls	**AABEGMNR** bargeman
AABDEIOU aboideau	**AABDMNNS** bandsman	**AABEGMNY** mangabey
AABDEISS diabases	**AABDMNRS** armbands	**AABEGMRT** bregmata
AABDEJLL djellaba	**AABDNNOS** abandons	**AABEGMTT** gambetta
AABDEKRY daybreak	**AABDNNTU** abundant	**AABEGNOR** baronage
AABDEKSW dawbakes	**AABDNORR** Barnardo	**AABEGORT** abrogate
AABDELLS ballades	**AABDNPSS** passband	**AABEGOST** sabotage
Sabadell	**AABDNRRY** barnyard	**AABEGRRS** barrages
AABDELLU laudable	**AABDORSV** bravados	**AABEHIMS** Maebashi
AABDELMN damnable	**AABDORWY** broadway	**AABEHIRR** herbaria
AABDELOR adorable	**AABDRRSS** brassard	**AABEHJLL** jellabah
AABDELPR drapable	**AABDRRSW** drawbars	**AABEHKLS** shakable
AABDELPT baldpate	**AABDRSST** bastards	**AABEHLMS** shamable
AABDELRT tradable	**AABDRSSU** subadars	**AABEHLPS** shapable
AABDELRW drawable	**AABDRSTY** bastardy	**AABEHLPT** alphabet
AABDELRY readably	**AABEEFLN** fleabane	**AABEHLRS** sharable
AABDEMNS beadsman	**AABEEGGL** gageable	**AABEHLSV** shavable
AABDENST Banstead	**AABEEGKR** breakage	**AABEHLSW** washable
AABDENTU unabated	**AABEEGNT** abnegate	**AABEHMRS** Habermas
AABDENUX bandeaux	**AABEEHLL** healable	**AABEILLM** mailable
AABDENVW waveband	**AABEEHLR** hearable	**AABEILLS** isabella
AABDEORS seaboard	**AABEEHLT** hateable	sailable
AABDERRS abraders	**AABEEHMR** harambee	**AABEILRS** Rabelais
AABDFHIT bad faith	**AABEEKLT** takeable	raisable
AABDFHLN fahlband	**AABEELLS** leasable	**AABEILRV** variable
AABDGHNS handbags	saleable	**AABEILST** labiates
AABDGHOT Godthaab	sealable	satiable
AABDGHOV Bodh Gaya	**AABEELMN** amenable	**AABEILTV** ablative
AABDGINR abrading	nameable	**AABEIMRS** ambaries
AABDGLNR landgrab	**AABEELMT** tameable	**AABEIMRU** Mirabeau
AABDGMOS gambados	**AABEELPR** reapable	**AABEINST** basanite

AABEIOTU	aboiteau	**AABEMNRT**	Bramante	**AABILLRS**	barillas
AABEIRST	Sabatier	**AABEMOSW**	Soembawa	**AABILLST**	ballista
AABEIRSV	abrasive	**AABENNSW**	wannabes	**AABILMNS**	bailsman
AABEIRTU	aubretia	**AABENRRT**	aberrant	**AABILMNU**	bimanual
	aubrieta	**AABENRST**	ratsbane	**AABILNNU**	biannual
AABEISST	abatises		Strabane	**AABILNOR**	baronial
AABEISUV	Beauvais	**AABEORRT**	arboreta	**AABILNOT**	ablation
AABEJLLS	jellabas	**AABEOSSU**	oubaases	**AABILNRU**	binaural
AABEJMSY	James Bay	**AABERSSU**	subareas	**AABILNTY**	banality
AABEJMUX	jambeaux	**AABFILUX**	fabliaux	**AABILOST**	sailboat
AABEKLLS	slakable	**AABFLLST**	fastball	**AABILRRT**	arbitral
AABEKLLT	talkable	**AABFLOTT**	faltboat	**AABILRST**	arbalist
AABEKLLW	walkable		flatboat	**AABILRSY**	basilary
AABEKMNR	brakeman	**AABGGGNN**	gangbang	**AABILRVY**	variably
AABEKNRS	Nebraska	**AABGGRRT**	braggart	**AABILSTY**	satiably
AABEKOTU	Abeokuta	**AABGHINS**	abashing	**AABIMMRS**	marimbas
AABEKRRS	baresark	**AABGHKRS**	shagbark	**AABIMNOT**	Manitoba
AABEKRSY	kerbayas	**AABGIILS**	abigails	**AABIMNRU**	manubria
AABELLMR	Marbella	**AABGIINR**	braaiing	**AABIMORS**	ambrosia
AABELLMT	meatball	**AABGILMS**	mailbags	**AABIMRSU**	simaruba
AABELLNO	loanable	**AABGILNT**	ablating	**AABINNPR**	brainpan
AABELLPP	palpable		bangtail	**AABINORS**	abrasion
AABELLPS	lapsable	**AABGILRU**	Bulgaria	**AABINRTT**	Brattain
AABELLPY	playable	**AABGIMNS**	sambaing	**AABINRTZ**	bartizan
AABELLRS	earballs	**AABGINRS**	bargains	**AABINRZZ**	Zanzibar
AABELLSV	salvable	**AABGLLLO**	goalball	**AABINSST**	abstains
AABELLSY	saleably	**AABGLLRY**	ballyrag	**AABIORST**	airboats
AABELLUV	valuable	**AABGLMNU**	galbanum	**AABIORSV**	bavarois
AABELMNY	amenably	**AABGLNOW**	bangalow	**AABIORTT**	abattoir
AABELMPP	mappable	**AABGLRUY**	arguably	**AABIOSSY**	bioassay
AABELMST	blastema	**AABGMORR**	barogram	**AABIOSTV**	Boa Vista
	lambaste	**AABGNNOU**	Nobunaga	**AABIRSST**	baristas
AABELMSU	amusable	**AABGNORZ**	garbanzo		bartsias
AABELMTU	ambulate	**AABHHKLS**	Balkhash	**AABIRTUY**	rubaiyat
AABELNNT	tannable	**AABHHORU**	brouhaha	**AABISTUZ**	zaibatsu
AABELNOS	abalones	**AABHIIKS**	Baisakhi	**AABJLPRU**	Jabalpur
AABELNOT	atonable	**AABHIINR**	Bahraini	**AABJMRST**	jambarts
AABELNPS	anableps	**AABHIINU**	bauhinia	**AABJNOOS**	Obasanjo
AABELNRT	Albertan	**AABHILLR**	hairball	**AABKLLPR**	ballpark
AABELNRY	balneary	**AABHILNN**	Hannibal	**AABKMNNS**	banksman
AABELNSS	banselas	**AABHILTU**	habitual	**AABKOOSZ**	bazookas
AABELORR	arboreal	**AABHILTY**	Bat Hayil	**AABKOPRS**	soapbark
AABELOSV	lavaboes	**AABHIMNR**	Brahmani	**AABKORTU**	Kotabaru
AABELOVW	avowable	**AABHINTT**	habitant	**AABLLMOR**	balmoral
AABELPPT	tappable	**AABHISTT**	habitats	**AABLLPPY**	palpably
AABELPRS	parables	**AABHKKKU**	Habakkuk	**AABLLSST**	ballasts
	parsable	**AABHKNRS**	barkhans	**AABLLSTU**	blastula
	sparable	**AABHKNUY**	Ayub Khan	**AABLLSVY**	salvably
AABELPSS	passable	**AABHMMOT**	Mmabatho	**AABLLUVY**	valuably
AABELRST	arbalest	**AABHMSWY**	Byam Shaw	**AABLMNOR**	abnormal
AABELRTT	Barletta	**AABHNOTU**	autobahn	**AABLMNTU**	ambulant
AABELRTY	betrayal	**AABHORRT**	Arbroath	**AABLMOST**	blastoma
	rateably	**AABIIJLT**	jailbait	**AABLMSST**	lambasts
AABELSTT	abettals	**AABIILNS**	Basilian	**AABLNORW**	Bonar Law
	statable	**AABIILRS**	Brasília	**AABLORST**	ablators
	tastable	**AABIIMNN**	Namibian	**AABLORTY**	altar boy
AABELSTU	tableaus	**AABIKLMS**	kabalism	**AABLOTUY**	layabout
AABELSTW	wastable	**AABIKLNU**	Kinabalu	**AABLOUWY**	Bulawayo
AABELSTX	taxables	**AABIKLST**	kabalist	**AABLPSSY**	passably
AABELSWY	swayable	**AABIKNSS**	banksias	**AABLRRTU**	Barrault
AABELTTU	tabulate	**AABIKOSS**	Bokassa I	**AABLSTTU**	abuttals
AABELTUX	tableaux	**AABILLLY**	labially	**AABMMOSU**	abomasum

AABMNOTW	batwoman	**AACCILMS**	acclaims	**AACDEKNP**	pancaked
AABMNRTU	rambutan	**AACCILNU**	Culiacán	**AACDEKTT**	attacked
AABMORSU	marabous	**AACCILNV**	vaccinal	**AACDELLN**	canalled
AABMORTU	marabout	**AACCILRU**	acicular	**AACDELLS**	alcaldes
	tamboura	**AACCILTT**	tactical	**AACDELMN**	manacled
AABNNORR	Ann Arbor	**AACCIMOS**	Masaccio	**AACDELNR**	calendar
AABNNOST	absonant	**AACCINRT**	Carnatic		Cardenal
AABNNOSZ	bonanzas	**AACCIORS**	cariocas		landrace
AABNOSSY	sabayons	**AACCIPRT**	apractic	**AACDELNS**	candelas
AABNOSTW	Botswana	**AACCIPTY**	capacity	**AACDELNV**	valanced
AABNRRUZ	Zurbarán	**AACCIRTY**	caryatic	**AACDELOS**	caseload
AABORRRT	barrator	**AACCJKRS**	carjacks	**AACDELPT**	placated
AABORRSS	rasboras	**AACCJKRW**	crackjaw	**AACDELRS**	calderas
AABORSTT	barostat	**AACCJORU**	carcajou	**AACDELSS**	scalades
AABRRRTY	barratry	**AACCKKPS**	packsack	**AACDELTT**	lactated
AABRRSST	brassart	**AACCKLPS**	calpacks	**AACDEMRY**	Macready
AACCCFIO	focaccia	**AACCKRRS**	carracks	**AACDENRS**	Cárdenas
AACCCHHU	cachucha	**AACCLLST**	catcalls	**AACDENRV**	advancer
AACCCIRR	Carracci	**AACCLOPS**	polaccas	**AACDENSV**	advances
AACCCRUY	accuracy	**AACCLOPU**	Acapulco	**AACDENSZ**	cadenzas
AACCDDES	cascaded	**AACCLORS**	caracols	**AACDEOTU**	autocade
AACCDEIM	academic	**AACCLPRS**	calcspar	**AACDEOTV**	advocate
AACCDELO	accolade	**AACCLRSU**	caraculs	**AACDEQUY**	adequacy
AACCDERR	racecard		saccular	**AACDERST**	cadaster
AACCDESS	cascades	**AACCLSSU**	accusals		cadastre
	saccades	**AACCLTTU**	Calcutta	**AACDERSV**	cadavers
AACCDHIR	characid	**AACCOPRS**	ascocarp	**AACDERTU**	arcuated
AACCDIRS	cardiacs	**AACCOSTT**	staccato	**AACDETTU**	actuated
AACCDOVY	advocacy		toccatas	**AACDGGHI**	haggadic
AACCEENT	cetacean	**AACCSSUU**	Caucasus	**AACDGINR**	carangid
AACCEFLO	coalface	**AACDDEHI**	acidhead		cardigan
AACCEHIX	cachexia	**AACDDEIL**	daedalic	**AACDHHKR**	hardhack
AACCEILN	calcanei	**AACDDENV**	advanced	**AACDHHNS**	shadchan
AACCEILU	aciculae	**AACDDETU**	caudated	**AACDHHRS**	shadrach
AACCEIRR	cercaria	**AACDDINR**	radicand	**AACDHIIS**	dichasia
AACCELOR	caracole	**AACDDINS**	candidas	**AACDHILR**	diarchal
AACCELTY	calycate	**AACDEEHH**	headache	**AACDHIMR**	chadarim
AACCEMNU	cumacean	**AACDEEHR**	headrace	**AACDHINP**	handicap
AACCENRT	carcanet	**AACDEEHS**	headcase	**AACDHINR**	arachnid
AACCENTU	acutance	**AACDEELS**	escalade	**AACDHKRT**	hardtack
AACCERSS	carcases	**AACDEEMS**	academes	**AACDHLOT**	cathodal
AACCERTU	accurate	**AACDEEPS**	escapade	**AACDHLRY**	charlady
AACCFILR	farcical	**AACDEEST**	caseated		dyarchal
AACCFLTU	calctufa	**AACDEETT**	acetated	**AACDHMRS**	drachmas
AACCGILT	galactic	**AACDEGKP**	packaged	**AACDHNRT**	handcart
AACCHILP	pachalic	**AACDEHHY**	headachy	**AACDHPRS**	crashpad
AACCHINR	anarchic	**AACDEHIN**	hacienda	**AACDIINS**	ascidian
	characin	**AACDEHLP**	cephalad	**AACDIIRT**	Adriatic
AACCHISV	viscacha	**AACDEHMR**	drachmae	**AACDIKRZ**	Karadžić
AACCHIVZ	vizcacha	**AACDEHMS**	chamades	**AACDILLP**	palladic
AACCHLLT	catchall	**AACDEHRS**	charades	**AACDILMT**	dalmatic
AACCHLNS	clachans	**AACDEHRT**	cathedra	**AACDILMU**	caladium
AACCHLOR	charcoal	**AACDEHST**	catheads	**AACDILNO**	diaconal
AACCHLOT	cachalot	**AACDEHTT**	attached	**AACDILNR**	cardinal
AACCHLRS	clarsach	**AACDEILO**	Laodicea	**AACDILNU**	dulciana
AACCHMNO	coachman	**AACDEILS**	alcaides	**AACDILNV**	vandalic
AACCHMPS	champacs		sidalcea	**AACDILOZ**	zodiacal
AACCHOUY	Ayacucho	**AACDEIMN**	maenadic	**AACDILRR**	railcard
AACCIINV	vaccinia	**AACDEIMS**	camisade	**AACDILRS**	radicals
AACCIIST	sciatica	**AACDEIMT**	acetamid	**AACDIMNY**	adynamic
AACCIITT	Titicaca	**AACDEINR**	radiance		cyanamid
AACCIKMN	Mackinac	**AACDEJNT**	adjacent	**AACDIMOS**	camisado

AACDIMRT	dramatic	**AACEFIST**	fasciate	**AACEILOP**	alopecia
AACDINRY	radiancy	**AACEFLLU**	falculae	**AACEILRT**	tailrace
AACDINST	antacids	**AACEFRRS**	carfares	**AACEILRV**	cavalier
AACDIOTU	autacoid	**AACEFRSX**	carfaxes	**AACEIMNR**	American
AACDIRSS	ascarids	**AACEFRTT**	artefact	**AACEIMNS**	amnesiac
AACDIRTY	caryatid	**AACEGHRT**	Carthage	**AACEIMTT**	catamite
AACDITUY	audacity	**AACEGILN**	angelica	**AACEINNO**	Oceanian
AACDJKSW	jackdaws	**AACEGILT**	glaciate	**AACEINNV**	Avicenna
AACDJQRU	jacquard	**AACEGINR**	canaigre	**AACEINPZ**	Piacenza
AACDKLNU	Auckland	**AACEGINY**	gynaecia	**AACEINRS**	canaries
AACDLLUY	caudally	**AACEGIRR**	carriage		cesarian
AACDLNRT	Cartland	**AACEGIRV**	vicarage	**AACEINRT**	carinate
AACDLNSS	scandals	**AACEGKPR**	packager		craniate
AACDLORT	cartload	**AACEGKPS**	packages	**AACEINRV**	variance
AACDLOSS	scalados	**AACEGLSS**	scalages	**AACEINST**	estancia
AACDLOSV	calvados	**AACEGMRU**	Camargue	**AACEINTV**	cavatine
AACDLPRS	placards	**AACEGMUY**	Camagüey	**AACEIOPR**	capoeira
AACDMMOR	cardamom	**AACEGNRS**	caganers	**AACEIPPS**	papacies
AACDMMRU	cardamum	**AACEGTTT**	Cattegat	**AACEIPRS**	airspace
AACDMNOR	cardamon	**AACEHILL**	achillea	**AACEIPSS**	capiases
AACDMSSU	Damascus		heliacal	**AACEIPTT**	apatetic
AACDOORV	Odovacar	**AACEHILN**	achenial		capitate
AACDOOSV	avocados	**AACEHILP**	phacelia	**AACEIRSV**	caviares
AACDORRT	cartroad	**AACEHIMR**	chimaera	**AACEITTV**	activate
AACDPRSU	crapauds	**AACEHIMT**	haematic	**AACEKKLW**	cakewalk
AACEEFIT	facetiae	**AACEHINS**	China Sea	**AACEKNPS**	pancakes
AACEEFLP	paleface	**AACEHIPT**	hepatica	**AACEKOST**	oatcakes
AACEEGLV	cleavage	**AACEHIRS**	archaise	**AACEKRTT**	attacker
AACEEGNR	carageen	**AACEHIRZ**	archaize	**AACELLOT**	allocate
AACEEGNY	gynaecea	**AACEHLMN**	La Manche	**AACELLST**	lacteals
AACEEGRS	acreages	**AACEHLNU**	eulachan	**AACELLTY**	alleycat
AACEEHLR	Heraclea	**AACEHLPS**	acalephs	**AACELMNP**	placeman
AACEEHLT	leachate	**AACEHLRT**	tracheal	**AACELMNS**	manacles
AACEEHRS	earaches	**AACEHLRX**	exarchal	**AACELMRS**	caramels
AACEEHRT	tracheae	**AACEHLSS**	calashes		ceramals
AACEEIMT	emaciate	**AACEHLST**	alcahest		macerals
AACEEINN	encaenia	**AACEHMRS**	marchesa	**AACELMTU**	maculate
AACEEIRT	acierate	**AACEHMST**	schemata	**AACELNNO**	anconeal
AACEEKST	teacakes	**AACEHNPS**	panaches	**AACELNNU**	cannulae
AACEELNS	anelaces	**AACEHPSU**	chapeaus	**AACELNPR**	parlance
AACEELRT	lacerate	**AACEHPUX**	chapeaux	**AACELNPT**	placenta
AACEELST	escalate	**AACEHRTT**	attacher	**AACELNPY**	anyplace
AACEELTU	aculeate		reattach	**AACELNRT**	lacerant
	Le Cateau	**AACEHSTT**	attaches	**AACELNRV**	arcanely
AACEEMNS	Maecenas	**AACEHSTU**	chateaus	**AACELNST**	analects
AACEEMRT	macerate	**AACEHTUX**	chateaux	**AACELNSV**	valances
AACEEMSS	amesaces	**AACEIINT**	actiniae	**AACELNTU**	canulate
AACEEMST	casemate	**AACEIKMT**	kamacite		tenacula
AACEENNT	catenane	**AACEILLM**	camellia	**AACELORS**	Coral Sea
AACEENRS	cesarean	**AACEILLN**	alliance	**AACELOST**	cataloes
AACEENTT	catenate		canaille	**AACELOSU**	acaulose
AACEEPSS	seascape	**AACEILMN**	analcime	**AACELPRS**	carpales
AACEEPST	East Cape		calamine	**AACELPST**	placates
AACEERSU	caesurae	**AACEILMT**	calamite	**AACELPSU**	scapulae
AACEERTV	acervate	**AACEILNP**	Palencia	**AACELRSS**	scalares
AACEESST	caseates	**AACEILNS**	canalise	**AACELRSU**	caesural
AACEESTT	acetates	**AACEILNT**	Alicante	**AACELRSV**	caravels
AACEETUV	evacuate		analcite	**AACELRWY**	clearway
AACEETVX	excavate	**AACEILNU**	acauline	**AACELSST**	lactases
AACEFFIN	affiance	**AACEILNV**	valencia	**AACELSTT**	lactates
AACEFILM	facemail		valiance	**AACELSTY**	catalyse
AACEFILT	califate	**AACEILNZ**	canalize	**AACELTTY**	cattleya

AACELTYZ	catalyze	**AACGILRT**	tragical	**AACHMMNO**	Macmahon
AACEMNPS	spaceman	**AACGIMMT**	magmatic	**AACHMNOU**	Ancohuma
AACEMQSU	macaques	**AACGIMNN**	manganic	**AACHMNTW**	watchman
AACEMRSS	massacre	**AACGIMNP**	campaign	**AACHMNUY**	naumachy
AACENNOR	Anacreon	**AACGIMNS**	Mascagni	**AACHMORT**	achromat
AACENPRS	pancreas	**AACGIMOP**	apogamic		trachoma
AACENPSU	saucepan	**AACGIMRR**	margaric	**AACHMPRY**	pharmacy
AACENPTT	pancetta	**AACGIMUU**	guaiacum	**AACHMSSY**	yashmacs
AACENRST	canaster	**AACGINOT**	contagia	**AACHNNUW**	Wanchüan
	caterans	**AACGINTV**	vacating	**AACHNPRS**	sarpanch
AACENRTT	reactant	**AACGISTY**	sagacity	**AACHNRST**	trashcan
AACENRTY	catenary	**AACGLMOU**	glaucoma	**AACHNSSU**	anchusas
AACENRVZ	czarevna	**AACGLOST**	catalogs	**AACHNSTU**	acanthus
AACENSSV	canvases	**AACGMNRS**	cragsman	**AACHOPPR**	approach
AACENSTY	cyanates	**AACGNOSU**	guanacos	**AACHRSWY**	archways
AACENTUV	evacuant	**AACGNRVY**	vagrancy	**AACHRTUY**	autarchy
AACEOPST	peacoats	**AACHHILR**	rhachial	**AACIILMO**	maiolica
AACEORSU	araceous	**AACHHIMS**	mashiach	**AACIILRT**	iatrical
AACEORTV	caveator	**AACHHKNU**	Chanukah	**AACIILRV**	vicarial
AACEOSST	seacoast	**AACHHKRS**	charkhas	**AACIILTV**	viatical
AACEPSWY	paceways	**AACHHLLS**	challahs	**AACIINST**	actinias
AACERRRS	Carreras	**AACHHTWY**	hatchway	**AACIIRSV**	viscaria
AACERRTU	arcature	**AACHIIMR**	mariachi	**AACIJLMO**	majolica
AACERSSU	caesuras	**AACHIKNS**	kachinas	**AACIJNOP**	japonica
AACERSSZ	sazeracs	**AACHILLR**	rachilla	**AACIKLMS**	mailsack
AACERSTT	castrate	**AACHILMS**	chiasmal	**AACIKLRS**	clarkias
	teacarts	**AACHILMT**	thalamic	**AACIKMNW**	mackinaw
AACERSWY	raceways	**AACHILNP**	chaplain	**AACIKNNS**	canakins
AACERTTT	tractate	**AACHILOU**	Coahuila	**AACIKRTU**	autarkic
AACESTTU	actuates	**AACHILPS**	calipash	**AACILLLY**	laically
AACESUWY	causeway		pashalic	**AACILLMR**	lacrimal
AACESUXY	Aux Cayes	**AACHILRV**	archival	**AACILLMT**	climatal
AACFFGHR	Chargaff	**AACHIMNN**	chainman	**AACILLPY**	apically
AACFHMST	camshaft	**AACHIMNR**	chairman	**AACILLRY**	racially
AACFILLY	facially	**AACHIMNS**	shamanic	**AACILMNT**	calamint
AACFINST	fanatics	**AACHIMNZ**	chazanim		claimant
AACFIRRT	aircraft	**AACHIMRR**	armchair	**AACILMRS**	mailcars
AACFIRST	frascati	**AACHIMRS**	archaism	**AACILMTY**	calamity
AACFIRTT	artifact		charisma	**AACILNNO**	Laconian
AACFJKLP	flapjack		machairs	**AACILNOR**	Carniola
AACFKLPT	flatpack	**AACHIMSS**	chiasmas		Carolina
AACFLLST	catfalls	**AACHINNO**	Noachian	**AACILNOY**	Lycaonia
AACFLNNR	Lanfranc	**AACHINRY**	Hyrcania	**AACILNRV**	carnival
AACFLRST	fractals	**AACHINSW**	chainsaw	**AACILNTT**	Atlantic
AACGGINO	anagogic	**AACHIOTU**	Ouachita		tantalic
AACGHHNS	Changsha	**AACHIPRS**	charpais	**AACILNTU**	nautical
AACGHLLO	agalloch	**AACHIPSS**	aphasics	**AACILNTY**	analytic
AACGHNNN	Nanchang	**AACHIPST**	chapatis	**AACILNVY**	valiancy
AACGHOPZ	gazpacho	**AACHIPTT**	chapatti	**AACILOTT**	coattail
AACGHORU	guacharo	**AACHIRSS**	Issachar		tailcoat
AACGIILN	Galician	**AACHIRST**	archaist	**AACILPRU**	piacular
AACGIILR	Cagliari		citharas	**AACILPST**	aplastic
AACGIIMN	magician	**AACHKKOZ**	kazachok		capitals
AACGILLN	gallican	**AACHKMPS**	champaks	**AACILPSZ**	capsizal
AACGILLU	Caligula	**AACHKNSW**	hacksawn	**AACILPTU**	capitula
AACGILNN	Anglican	**AACHKRSY**	hayracks	**AACILPTY**	atypical
	canaling	**AACHKSSW**	hacksaws	**AACILRRS**	railcars
AACGILNO	analogic	**AACHKSTY**	haystack	**AACILRTY**	alacrity
AACGILNV	galvanic	**AACHLMNO**	monachal	**AACILRUU**	auricula
AACGILOR	Agricola	**AACHLMOS**	chloasma	**AACILSTT**	statical
AACGILOU	guaiacol	**AACHLPPS**	chappals	**AACILSTY**	salacity
AACGILOX	coxalgia	**AACHLSTU**	calathus	**AACIMMNO**	ammoniac

AACIMMRS	marasmic	**AACLORSU**	carousal	**AADDNRST**	standard
AACIMNOR	macaroni	**AACLORUV**	vacuolar	**AADDNRSU**	Dardanus
	Marciano	**AACLPPRT**	claptrap	**AADDNSVV**	dvandvas
	marocain	**AACLPRST**	caltraps	**AADDRSST**	dastards
AACIMNPS	Campinas	**AACLPRSU**	scapular	**AADEEGHR**	headgear
AACIMORR	Armorica	**AACLPRSU**	scapular	**AADEEGHT**	headgate
AACIMORS	Cimarosa	**AACLPRTY**	calyptra	**AADEEGLR**	laagered
AACIMORT	aromatic	**AACLPSSU**	scapulas	**AADEEGLT**	galeated
AACIMPRU	Apurimac	**AACLPSTY**	playacts	**AADEEGMN**	endamage
AACIMRST	Sarmatic	**AACLPTTU**	catapult	**AADEEGNR**	gadarene
AACINNST	cantinas	**AACLRSUV**	vascular	**AADEEGRV**	averaged
AACINOPR	paranoic	**AACLSTTY**	catalyst	**AADEEIRT**	eradiate
AACINORS	ocarinas	**AACLSTUY**	casualty	**AADEEKNW**	awakened
AACINORT	Croatian	**AACMNOOR**	macaroon	**AADEELMR**	de la Mare
	raincoat	**AACMNPRY**	rampancy	**AADEELNN**	annealed
AACINOTV	Octavian	**AACMNRRU**	macruran	**AADEELPP**	appealed
	vacation	**AACMORRS**	camorras	**AADEELRV**	de Valera
AACINPST	captains	**AACMORSS**	sarcomas	**AADEELRW**	Delaware
AACINQTU	acquaint	**AACMRRST**	tramcars	**AADEEMNR**	Maeander
AACINRSZ	czarinas	**AACNNOSZ**	canzonas	**AADEEMNT**	emanated
AACINSSU	Ascanius	**AACNPSST**	capstans	**AADEEMOT**	oedemata
AACINSTZ	stanzaic	**AACNRSTT**	transact	**AADEEMRR**	demerara
AACIPRST	aspartic	**AACNRSTU**	curtanas	**AADEENPT**	tapenade
AACIPRTY	rapacity	**AACOPPRS**	apocarps	**AADEENRU**	Adenauer
AACIQSTU	aquatics	**AACOPRSU**	acarpous	**AADEENTT**	antedate
AACIRRTT	tartaric	**AACOPSTV**	postcava	**AADEEPPR**	appeared
AACIRSSU	Siracusa	**AACORRTV**	varactor	**AADEEPPS**	appeased
AACIRSTT	castrati	**AACORSTT**	castrato	**AADEEQTU**	adequate
AACIRTZZ	czaritza	**AACORTTU**	actuator	**AADEERSW**	awardees
AACJKLPS	slapjack		autocrat	**AADEFFRY**	affrayed
AACJKOOR	jackaroo	**AACPSSTW**	catspaws	**AADEFHLT**	flathead
AACJKSTY	jackstay	**AACRSTTT**	attracts	**AADEFHST**	fatheads
AACKKNPS	knapsack	**AACSTUWY**	cutaways		headfast
AACKLOWY	lockaway	**AADDDEEH**	deadhead		
AACKLSTW	catwalks	**AADDDGNR**	granddad	**AADEFILR**	fairlead
AACKMNRT	trackman	**AADDEEIL**	Adelaide	**AADEFIRS**	faradise
AACKMNST	tacksman	**AADDEELT**	dealated	**AADEFIRZ**	faradize
AACKNRSS	ransacks	**AADDEFLL**	deadfall	**AADEFLLR**	falderal
AACKORWY	rockaway	**AADDEGGR**	aggraded	**AADEFLRY**	defrayal
AACKPRST	ratpacks	**AADDEGRT**	gradated	**AADEGGRS**	aggrades
AACLLMOR	Mallorca	**AADDEHHS**	hadedahs	**AADEGHLN**	danelagh
AACLLMRY	lacrymal	**AADDEHLN**	headland	**AADEGHMN**	Dagenham
AACLLNRY	carnally	**AADDEHMN**	handmade	**AADEGILL**	diallage
AACLLNST	callants	**AADDEHRW**	headward	**AADEGILT**	gladiate
AACLLRRY	carryall	**AADDEHRZ**	hazarded	**AADEGINR**	drainage
AACLLRSY	rascally	**AADDEILR**	Daladier		gardenia
AACLLSUY	casually	**AADDEILS**	alidades	**AADEGITT**	agitated
	causally	**AADDEINS**	Danaides	**AADEGITV**	divagate
AACLLTUY	actually	**AADDEIRT**	radiated	**AADEGLLT**	tallaged
AACLMNNS	clansman	**AADDEKMS**	damasked	**AADEGLMN**	magdalen
AACLMOTU	comatula	**AADDELSU**	Daedalus	**AADEGLMY**	amygdale
AACLMRRU	macrural	**AADDELTU**	adulated	**AADEGLOP**	galopade
AACLNNOT	cantonal	**AADDEMNT**	mandated	**AADEGLSV**	salvaged
AACLNNOW	canon law	**AADDEMRU**	marauded	**AADEGMNR**	grandame
AACLNNRU	cannular	**AADDEMRY**	daydream	**AADEGMPR**	rampaged
AACLNNSU	cannulas	**AADDGNRS**	grandads	**AADEGMRS**	damagers
AACLNOPR	coplanar	**AADDGNRU**	graduand	**AADEGMSS**	massaged
AACLNRUÑ	La Coruña	**AADDHILU**	Id-ul-Adha	**AADEGNRR**	arranged
AACLNRSU	lacunars	**AADDHIMN**	handmaid	**AADEGNRS**	Sardegna
AACLNRUY	lacunary	**AADDIIKS**	didakais	**AADEGPSS**	passaged
AACLNTVY	vacantly	**AADDISST**	dadaists	**AADEGRST**	gradates
AACLORRU	oracular	**AADDLLNY**	landlady	**AADEGRTU**	graduate
		AADDLNRW	landward	**AADEGSSU**	assuaged

AADEHILN	nailhead
AADEHILR	headrail
	railhead
AADEHILS	headsail
AADEHIRR	diarrhea
AADEHIRS	airheads
AADEHIWY	hideaway
AADEHKOT	Hakodate
AADEHLLL	halalled
AADEHLLO	halloaed
AADEHLMO	Almohade
AADEHLMP	headlamp
AADEHLNR	anhedral
AADEHLPS	slaphead
AADEHMNS	headsman
AADEHMST	masthead
AADEHNRV	verandah
AADEHPSS	sapheads
AADEHRRW	hardware
AADEHRSS	Dassehra
	harassed
AADEHRSW	warheads
AADEHSSY	sashayed
AADEIINR	Deianira
AADEIKLP	Klaipeda
AADEILMR	Armidale
AADEILMS	maladies
AADEILNT	dentalia
AADEILPR	praedial
AADEILPS	palisade
AADEILPT	lapidate
AADEILRS	salaried
AADEILSS	assailed
AADEILSV	vedalias
AADEILTV	validate
AADEIMNR	marinade
AADEIMNT	animated
	diamante
AADEIMPZ	diazepam
AADEIMRV	maravedi
AADEIMST	adamsite
	diastema
AADEIMTT	Damietta
AADEINRS	araneids
AADEINTT	attained
AADEIPRS	paradise
AADEIPSU	diapause
AADEIPTV	adaptive
AADEIRST	dataries
	radiates
AADEISST	diastase
AADEISTT	astatide
	satiated
AADEITVW	viewdata
AADEJMNN	Ndjamena
AADEJMRS	jemadars
AADEJNNP	japanned
AADEJNOT	Ondaatje
AADEKLLN	lakeland
AADEKLRV	kaleyard
AADEKMNR	mandrake
AADEKMRS	kamerads

AADEKPRS	parkades
AADELLPP	appalled
AADELMNP	napalmed
AADELMNR	alderman
AADELMNS	dalesman
	leadsman
AADELMOS	alamodes
AADELMPT	palmated
AADELNPT	peatland
AADELNRS	adrenals
AADELNSU	Aalesund
AADELNSY	analysed
AADELNUY	Delaunay
AADELNYZ	analyzed
AADELPPT	palpated
AADELPRY	parlayed
AADELRRW	De La Warr
AADELRSY	saleyard
AADELSTU	adulates
AADELTUV	valuated
AADEMNOS	adenomas
AADEMNST	mandates
AADEMRRU	marauder
AADEMRRS	madrases
AADEMWZZ	zamzawed
AADENNST	andantes
AADENNTV	Davenant
AADENRRT	narrated
AADENRSV	verandas
AADENRTT	tartaned
AADENSSW	weasands
AADENSTY	asyndeta
AADENSTZ	stanzaed
AADEPPRT	preadapt
AADEPRRS	paraders
AADEPRST	adapters
	readapts
AADEQRTU	quadrate
AADERRRW	rearward
AADERRSW	awarders
AADERSSW	seawards
AADERSTW	eastward
AADERUVY	ayurveda
AADFFLLN	Llandaff
AADFGLST	Flagstad
AADFGNOO	fandango
AADFHMNR	farmhand
AADFHNST	handfast
AADFIINT	intifada
AADFIMRS	faradism
AADFINRU	unafraid
AADFLLLN	landfall
AADFLMNR	farmland
AADFLORW	aardwolf
AADFLOTW	dataflow
AADFLOTX	toadflax
AADFLOWY	foldaway
AADFMRYY	farmyard
AADGGHRS	haggards
AADGGIMN	damaging
AADGGLNN	gangland
AADGGLRS	laggards

AADGGRST	staggard
AADGHIPR	diagraph
AADGHJNU	Junagadh
AADGHORS	daroghas
	Sargodha
AADGIINS	gainsaid
AADGILLO	gladiola
AADGILLR	gaillard
	galliard
AADGILMR	madrigal
AADGILNO	diagonal
	gonadial
AADGIMMS	digammas
AADGIMPR	paradigm
AADGIMRS	diagrams
AADGINOS	Sogdiana
AADGINPR	parading
AADGINPT	adapting
AADGINRR	darraign
AADGINRU	guardian
AADGINRW	awarding
AADGIORV	Godavari
AADGIQRU	quadriga
AADGLLNN	Langland
AADGLLSW	gadwalls
AADGLNRS	garlands
AADGLOPR	podagral
AADGLRSU	graduals
AADGMNOP	pagandom
AADGMNOR	dragoman
AADGMNRS	grandams
	grandmas
AADGMRSS	smaragds
AADGNNOO	Onondaga
AADGNNQU	quandang
AADGNORS	Granados
AADGNPRS	grandpas
AADGNRTU	guardant
AADGNRUV	vanguard
AADGNRWY	drangway
AADGOORV	Avogadro
AADGRRUW	gurdwara
AADHHIJK	Khadijah
AADHHIPS	padishah
AADHIINP	aphidian
AADHILLR	halliard
AADHILNR	handrail
AADHILNT	Thailand
AADHILNU	Ludhiana
AADHILRV	havildar
AADHINNZ	Andizhan
AADHINOT	anthodia
AADHINPS	daphnias
AADHINRR	harridan
AADHKNSS	dhansaks
AADHLMST	Halmstad
AADHLPSS	slapdash
AADHLRSY	halyards
AADHMMMU	Muhammad
AADHMNNY	handyman
AADHMNOU	omadhaun
AADHMNRU	Damanhûr

AADHNSSW	handsaws	**AADLMNUU**	laudanum	**AAEEJNPS**	Japanese
AADHNSTT	hatstand	**AADLNOPR**	parlando	**AAEEJNSV**	Javanese
AADHRSWY	haywards	**AADLNRSY**	lanyards	**AAEEJPVY**	Vajpayee
AADHSSWY	washdays	**AADLOPRV**	Pavlodar	**AAEEKMNS**	namesake
AADIILVV	Valdivia	**AADLOPSY**	payloads	**AAEEKMRT**	teamaker
AADIINRS	Sardinia	**AADLORST**	loadstar	**AAEEKNRW**	reawaken
AADIINRV	Adrian IV	**AADLORSV**	Salvador	**AAEEKPRT**	parakeet
AADIKLLO	alkaloid	**AADLORTU**	adulator	**AAEEKQSU**	seaquake
AADIKLRY	kailyard	**AADLPPSU**	applauds	**AAEELLLM**	lamellae
AADIKNQR	qindarka	**AADMMNOW**	madwoman	**AAEELLMR**	amarelle
AADIKORT	Takoradi	**AADMMNSU**	mandamus	**AAEELLPT**	patellae
AADILLLO	allodial	**AADMNORS**	madronas	**AAEELMMT**	metamale
AADILLNR	landrail		monardas	**AAEELMST**	maleates
AADILLOP	Palladio	**AADMNORT**	mandator	**AAEELNNR**	annealer
AADILLRY	radially	**AADMNQRU**	Marquand	**AAEELNPS**	seaplane
AADILLSY	dyslalia	**AADMNRSS**	mansards		spelaean
AADILMNN	mainland	**AADMNSTU**	tamandus	**AAEELNST**	elastane
AADILMNT	Maitland	**AADMORRT**	tramroad	**AAEELORT**	areolate
AADILMOV	Moldavia	**AADMORST**	matadors	**AAEELPPR**	appealer
AADILMRS	admirals	**AADMRRSY**	yardarms	**AAEELRTU**	laureate
AADILMVY	Limavady	**AADMRSZZ**	mazzards	**AAEELSST**	elastase
AADILNPR	prandial	**AADNNORR**	Andorran	**AAEELTUV**	evaluate
AADILNPS	paladins	**AADNNORS**	Sarandon	**AAEELVWY**	wayleave
AADILNRS	laniards	**AADNNPSU**	pandanus	**AAEEMMTT**	teammate
AADILNTT	dilatant	**AADNOPRS**	pandoras	**AAEEMNNS**	Annamese
AADILORR	railroad	**AADNOPSS**	sandsoap	**AAEEMNPT**	nametape
AADILPRY	lapidary	**AADNOSUV**	vanadous	**AAEEMNST**	emanates
AADILRST	diastral	**AADNOSWY**	nowadays		manatees
AADIMMSZ	Mazdaism	**AADNPRSU**	Pandarus	**AAEEMRST**	amreetas
AADIMNNO	Mindanao	**AADNPSTT**	standpat	**AAEEMSSS**	Assamese
AADIMNNR	mandarin	**AADNPSUY**	Paysandú	**AAEEMSTX**	meataxes
AADIMNOT	manatoid	**AADNQRTU**	quadrant	**AAEENNNT**	antennae
AADIMNRT	tamarind	**AADNQRUY**	quandary	**AAEENNRZ**	Nazarene
AADIMNRY	dairyman	**AADNRSSY**	Andrássy	**AAEENRST**	arsenate
	mainyard	**AADOPPRR**	paradrop		Near East
AADIMNRZ	zamindar	**AADOPRRS**	paradors		serenata
AADIMNUV	vanadium	**AADOPRST**	adaptors	**AAEENRTT**	anteater
AADIMORS	dioramas	**AADOPSUY**	paduasoy	**AAEENSTU**	nauseate
AADIMPST	misadapt	**AADORSVY**	savoyard	**AAEEPPRR**	rapparee
AADIMSTZ	samizdat	**AADORSWY**	roadways		reappear
AADINOPR	paranoid	**AADPSTTU**	dupattas	**AAEEPPRS**	appeaser
AADINOPS	diapason	**AADQRSTU**	quadrats	**AAEEPPSS**	appeases
AADINOPT	adaption	**AADRRSSY**	Syr Darya	**AAEEPRST**	asperate
AADINOTV	avoidant	**AADRSSTU**	Adrastus		separate
AADINRST	radiants	**AAEEEHRT**	hetaerae	**AAEEPSTT**	aseptate
AADIOPRS	diaspora	**AAEEFRRS**	seafarer	**AAEERSTT**	stearate
AADIORRT	radiator	**AAEEFRST**	ratafees	**AAEFFGRS**	agraffes
AADIRRSY	disarray	**AAEEGILN**	alienage	**AAEFFIRS**	affaires
AADISTXY	dystaxia	**AAEEGKLS**	leakages	**AAEFFLLS**	falafels
AADJNTTU	adjutant	**AAEEGMPR**	amperage	**AAEFFNRS**	fanfares
AADJNTUV	adjuvant	**AAEEGMST**	agametes	**AAEFFSTT**	taffetas
AADKLMNR	landmark	**AAEEGNNO**	Neogaean	**AAEFGHRW**	wharfage
AADKLNPR	parkland	**AAEEGNRS**	sangaree	**AAEFGLLL**	flagella
AADKMNTU	Katmandu	**AAEEGNRT**	tagareen	**AAEFGLOT**	floatage
AADKNRST	tankards	**AAEEGRSV**	averages	**AAEFIILR**	filariae
AADKORWY	workaday	**AAEEGRTW**	waterage	**AAEFIKLT**	kalifate
AADLLMRS	mallards	**AAEEHIMR**	haeremai	**AAEFILTY**	fayalite
AADLMNNS	landsman	**AAEEHLMR**	ahemeral	**AAEFIMRR**	airframe
AADLMNOR	mandorla	**AAEEHNPS**	saphenae	**AAEFINNT**	faineant
AADLMNOS	mandolas	**AAEEHRTW**	aweather	**AAEFINTX**	antefixa
AADLMNRY	Maryland		wheatear	**AAEFKMST**	makefast
AADLMNSS	landmass	**AAEEILNT**	alienate	**AAEFLMTT**	flatmate

AAEFLNUU	faunulae	**AAEGLPRV**	Palgrave	**AAEHINST**	asthenia
AAEFLPRS	earflaps	**AAEGLRST**	agrestal	**AAEHIPPS**	Pasiphaë
AAEFLRTW	flatware	**AAEGLRSV**	salvager	**AAEHKLST**	alkahest
AAEFMRST	fermatas	**AAEGLSSV**	Las Vegas	**AAEHKMRV**	haymaker
AAEFRRWY	wayfarer		salvages	**AAEHKNST**	khanates
AAEGGIOT	agiotage	**AAEGLSVY**	savagely	**AAEHLLLS**	allheals
AAEGGLNR	Lagrange	**AAEGMMNS**	gamesman	**AAEHLMNT**	methanal
	langrage	**AAEGMNNT**	Mantegna	**AAEHLMNW**	whaleman
AAEGGLNU	language	**AAEGMNPY**	pygmaean	**AAEHLMSY**	sealyham
AAEGGMMR	grammage	**AAEGMNRS**	managers	**AAEHLMTU**	hamulate
AAEGGNOS	anagoges		Semarang	**AAEHLNRT**	antheral
AAEGGNRY	garganey	**AAEGMNRT**	magnetar	**AAEHLNRW**	narwhale
AAEGGOPR	paragoge	**AAEGMNRV**	gravamen	**AAEHLNTX**	exhalant
AAEGHIRS	Hargeisa	**AAEGMNST**	magnates	**AAEHLPRS**	pearlash
AAEGHLNP	phalange	**AAEGMORR**	aerogram	**AAEHLPRX**	hexaplar
AAEGHLSU	haulages	**AAEGMORS**	sagamore	**AAEHLPUV**	upheaval
AAEGHMRX	hexagram	**AAEGMPRR**	rampager	**AAEHMMOT**	hematoma
AAEGHNRU	harangue	**AAEGMPRS**	rampages	**AAEHMNRT**	earthman
AAEGILLN	Galilean	**AAEGMRRT**	Margaret	**AAEHMNSS**	Manasseh
AAEGILLR	galleria	**AAEGMRRV**	margrave	**AAEHMOPR**	amphorae
AAEGILNP	pelagian	**AAEGMRRY**	gramarye	**AAEHMORT**	atheroma
AAEGILNR	Algerian	**AAEGMRSS**	massager	**AAEHNPRS**	hanapers
	geranial	**AAEGMRST**	megastar	**AAEHNPST**	pheasant
AAEGILNT	agential		Ramsgate	**AAEHNRTU**	Rathenau
	alginate	**AAEGMRTU**	ageratum	**AAEHNRTZ**	Nazareth
AAEGILRS	lairages	**AAEGMSSS**	massages	**AAEHNTTX**	xanthate
AAEGILSX	galaxies	**AAEGMTTW**	megawatt	**AAEHPRSW**	Peshawar
AAEGILTT	tailgate	**AAEGMUYZ**	Mayagüez	**AAEHRSSS**	harasses
AAEGIMNO	egomania	**AAEGNNST**	tannages	**AAEHRSTT**	Hatteras
AAEGIMNS	magnesia	**AAEGNOOT**	Notogaea	**AAEHRSTU**	arethusa
AAEGIMNT	agminate	**AAEGNPST**	pageants	**AAEHRTWX**	earthwax
AAEGIMNZ	magazine	**AAEGNRPR**	arranger	**AAEIILMP**	lipaemia
AAEGIMRR	marriage	**AAEGNRRS**	arranges	**AAEIILMP**	lipaemia
AAEGIMRT	Armitage	**AAEGNRST**	tanagers	**AAEIILQU**	Aquileia
	maritage	**AAEGNRTU**	runagate	**AAEIIMRV**	viraemia
AAEGINPS	paganise	**AAEGNSTT**	stagnate	**AAEIIPRS**	apiaries
AAEGINPT	paginate	**AAEGNSTV**	vantages	**AAEIIRSV**	aviaries
AAEGINPZ	paganize	**AAEGNSUY**	Saguenay	**AAEIJNRT**	naartjie
AAEGINRT	aerating	**AAEGORRT**	arrogate	**AAEIKKMZ**	kamikaze
AAEGINTV	navigate	**AAEGORTT**	aegrotat	**AAEIKLLN**	alkaline
	vaginate	**AAEGPSSS**	passages	**AAEIKLLS**	alkalies
AAEGIRSV	vagaries	**AAEGQSUV**	quayages		alkalise
AAEGISSS	assegais	**AAEGRRSV**	ravagers	**AAEIKLLZ**	alkalize
AAEGISTT	agitates	**AAEGRSSU**	assuager	**AAEIKLNR**	Karelian
AAEGIVWY	giveaway	**AAEGRSTT**	regattas	**AAEIKMRR**	krameria
AAEGKNNW	KaNgwane	**AAEGRSTZ**	stargaze	**AAEILLLU**	alleluia
AAEGKOSS	soakages	**AAEGRSVY**	savagery	**AAEILLMM**	mamillae
AAEGKTTT	Kattegat	**AAEGSSSU**	assuages	**AAEILLMX**	maxillae
AAEGLLMN	Magellan		sausages	**AAEILLNT**	allanite
AAEGLLMS	smallage	**AAEGSTTW**	wattages	**AAEILLPP**	papillae
AAEGLLPR	pellagra	**AAEGSTWY**	gateways	**AAEILLPT**	palliate
AAEGLLSS	galleass		getaways	**AAEILLRT**	arillate
AAEGLLST	tallages	**AAEHIIMR**	Ihimaera	**AAEILMMX**	axilemma
AAEGLLTU	glutaeal	**AAEHIIRT**	hetairai	**AAEILMNT**	laminate
AAEGLMNS	gamelans	**AAEHILNP**	aphelian	**AAEILMNV**	velamina
AAEGLMPY	gameplay	**AAEHILNT**	anthelia	**AAEILMRT**	material
AAEGLMST	almagest	**AAEHILPR**	parhelia	**AAEILNPR**	airplane
AAEGLNOU	analogue	**AAEHIMNT**	anthemia	**AAEILNPT**	palatine
AAEGLNPP	lagnappe		haematin	**AAEILNRU**	aurelian
AAEGLNSS	lasagnes	**AAEHINNT**	Athenian	**AAEILNRV**	valerian
AAEGLNSU	leguaans	**AAEHINPT**	aphanite	**AAEILNSS**	nasalise
AAEGLNTU	angulate	**AAEHINRT**	Rhaetian		Salesian
				AAEILNSZ	nasalize

AAEILNTU	Aleutian	**AAEJMNRV**	maryjane	**AAELNSSY**	analyses
AAEILOTU	Alaouite	**AAEJOPRS**	aparejos	**AAELNSTT**	atlantes
AAEILPRT	parietal	**AAEJORSV**	Sarajevo	**AAELNSYZ**	analyzes
AAEILPRX	preaxial	**AAEJRSTX**	Jaxartes	**AAELOPRS**	psoralea
AAEILPST	stapelia	**AAEKKMNR**	Akkerman	**AAELORSU**	aureolas
AAEILPSZ	La Spezia	**AAEKLMRW**	lawmaker	**AAELORTY**	aleatory
AAEILRRT	arterial	**AAEKLMRY**	malarkey	**AAELOSTX**	oxalates
AAEILRSS	assailer	**AAEKLNNT**	Kelantan	**AAELPPRS**	apparels
	salaries	**AAEKLNRS**	larnakes	**AAELPPRT**	La Trappe
AAEILRTV	varietal	**AAEKLNST**	alkanets	**AAELPPST**	palpates
AAEILSTV	aestival	**AAEKMRRS**	earmarks	**AAELPPSU**	applause
	salivate	**AAEKMRSS**	seamarks	**AAELPRST**	palestra
AAEILSTX	saxatile	**AAEKNPRT**	partaken	**AAELPRSV**	palavers
AAEILTVX	laxative	**AAEKNTTY**	Kenyatta	**AAELPRSY**	paralyse
AAEIMMST	imamates	**AAEKORTY**	akaryote	**AAELPRYZ**	paralyze
AAEIMNNR	Armenian	**AAEKPRRT**	partaker	**AAELPSTU**	plateaus
AAEIMNNT	Mantinea	**AAEKPRST**	partakes	**AAELPSTV**	palstave
AAEIMNOX	anoxemia	**AAELLLMR**	lamellar	**AAELPTUX**	plateaux
AAEIMNPR	pearmain	**AAELLLMS**	lamellas	**AAELRSST**	tarseals
AAEIMNRT	animater	**AAELLLPR**	parallel	**AAELRSTZ**	lazarets
	marinate	**AAELLLSS**	Lassalle	**AAELRSVY**	Vasarely
AAEIMNST	animates	**AAELLMMR**	Mallarmé	**AAELRUZZ**	zarzuela
AAEIMNTT	Antietam	**AAELLMPU**	ampullae	**AAELRWYY**	waylayer
AAEIMOTX	toxaemia	**AAELLNNV**	Van Allen	**AAELSTUV**	valuates
AAEIMOTZ	azotemia	**AAELLNPU**	planulae	**AAEMMNOT**	ammonate
AAEIMPRS	aspermia	**AAELLORV**	alveolar	**AAEMMNRT**	armament
AAEIMRST	amirates	**AAELLPRT**	patellar	**AAEMMOST**	metasoma
AAEIMRTY	Maitreya	**AAELLRST**	laterals	**AAEMNORT**	emanator
AAEINNRS	Saarinen	**AAELLSWY**	Wallasey	**AAEMNOTZ**	metazoan
AAEINORT	aeration	**AAELLTTV**	Valletta	**AAEMNPRS**	Parmesan
AAEINORX	anorexia	**AAELLWWY**	wellaway		spearman
AAEINPPR	priapean	**AAELLWVY**	alleyway	**AAEMNPRT**	parament
AAEINRRW	rainwear	**AAELMMNO**	melanoma	**AAEMNRRY**	yarramen
AAEINRST	antisera	**AAELMMOX**	axolemma	**AAEMNRST**	Santarém
	artesian	**AAELMMRS**	almemars	**AAEMNRTW**	waterman
	Santeria	**AAELMMTU**	malamute	**AAEMNSTU**	manteaus
AAEINRTT	reattain	**AAELMNRT**	maternal	**AAEMNTUX**	manteaux
AAEINRTZ	atrazine	**AAELMNSS**	salesman	**AAEMORTT**	amaretto
	Nazarite	**AAELMNST**	talesman		teratoma
AAEINSST	entasias	**AAELMNSY**	seamanly	**AAEMOTTU**	automate
AAEINSTT	astatine	**AAELMOSU**	mausolea	**AAEMPTTU**	amputate
AAEINSTV	sanative	**AAELMPRT**	malapert	**AAEMQSTU**	squamate
AAEINTTT	titanate	**AAELMPTY**	playmate	**AAEMRRTU**	armature
AAEIPPRS	appraise	**AAELMRSY**	lamasery	**AAEMRSSS**	amassers
AAEIPQRU	Arequipa	**AAELMRTT**	maltreat	**AAEMRSTU**	amateurs
AAEIPRST	aspirate	**AAELMSSY**	amylases	**AAEMRTTU**	maturate
	parasite	**AAELNNNT**	antennal	**AAENNNST**	antennas
	septaria	**AAELNNOT**	neonatal	**AAENNOTT**	annotate
AAEIPRTT	patriate	**AAELNNSU**	Lausanne	**AAENNSTT**	tannates
AAEIPRTZ	trapezia	**AAELNNTU**	annulate	**AAENORTU**	aeronaut
AAEIPRXY	apyrexia	**AAELNOSS**	seasonal	**AAENPPRT**	apparent
AAEIRRRT	terraria	**AAELNPRT**	parental		trappean
AAEIRRST	taraires		paternal	**AAENPRTY**	prytanea
AAEIRSTT	ariettas		prenatal	**AAENPSST**	anapests
	aristate	**AAELNPRW**	warplane		peasants
AAEIRSTV	variates	**AAELNPST**	pleasant	**AAENPSTY**	peasanty
AAEIRSVW	airwaves	**AAELNRSS**	arsenals	**AAENRRST**	narrates
AAEIRTTZ	zaratite	**AAELNRST**	asternal	**AAENRSTV**	tavernas
AAEISSTT	satiates	**AAELNRSY**	analyser		tsarevna
AAEJLNOP	jalapeno	**AAELNRTX**	relaxant	**AAENRSUW**	unawares
AAEJLNPU	Jean Paul	**AAELNRYZ**	analyzer	**AAENSSTV**	savantes
AAEJMNNY	Jan Mayen	**AAELNSST**	sealants	**AAEOPSTT**	apostate

AAEORRST	aerators	**AAFMOPRR**	paraform	**AAGILNTV**	galivant
AAEORSTT	aerostat	**AAFMORST**	Amfortas	**AAGILOOP**	apologia
AAEORTTV	rotavate	**AAFNSSTT**	fantasts	**AAGILOPT**	topalgia
AAEPPRST	parapets	**AAGGGHNS**	gangshag	**AAGILOSS**	aglossia
AAEPPSTT	appestat	**AAGGGINR**	garaging	**AAGILPRY**	plagiary
AAEPRTXY	taxpayer	**AAGGILLN**	ganglial	**AAGILRRW**	warrigal
AAEPSWXX	paxwaxes	**AAGGILNR**	gangliar	**AAGILSTT**	sagittal
AAERRSTU	Sarraute	**AAGGIMNN**	managing	**AAGILSTW**	wagtails
AAERRTTT	tartrate	**AAGGIMNR**	maraging	**AAGIMMRR**	marigram
AAERSSSY	assayers	**AAGGINRV**	ravaging	**AAGIMNNO**	agnomina
AAERSSTV	Västerås	**AAGGINSV**	savaging	**AAGIMNOS**	angiomas
AAERSTTU	saturate	**AAGGLLLY**	lallygag	**AAGIMNPS**	paganism
AAERTWWY	waterway	**AAGGLRSY**	graylags	**AAGIMNSS**	amassing
AAFFGILS	gaffsail	**AAGGNORT**	Taganrog		siamangs
AAFFILRT	taffrail	**AAGGNSST**	gangstas	**AAGIMNSY**	gymnasia
AAFFINPR	paraffin	**AAGGNSWY**	gangways	**AAGIMPTU**	patagium
AAFFINST	affiants	**AAGGOOPP**	Pago Pago	**AAGIMSTT**	stigmata
AAFFLSTU	afflatus	**AAGHHINS**	shanghai	**AAGINNNY**	nannygai
AAFFMNST	staffman	**AAGHHINU**	Huang Hai	**AAGINNOT**	agnation
AAFGHINS	afghanis	**AAGHHINW**	Hwang Hai	**AAGINNST**	Siangtan
AAFGHNRU	fraughan	**AAGHHNOS**	oanshagh	**AAGINNTU**	Antiguan
AAFGLLNU	langlauf	**AAGHHNUU**	Huang Hua	**AAGINNTX**	Xiangtan
AAFGLNRT	flagrant	**AAGHILNN**	hangnail	**AAGINNUW**	Wanganui
AAFGNRRT	fragrant	**AAGHILRS**	gharials	**AAGINORR**	rangiora
AAFGORRS	farragos	**AAGHINNS**	anhingas	**AAGINOST**	Santiago
AAFHIRST	airshaft	**AAGHINPS**	paganish	**AAGINPRU**	pagurian
AAFHJLLU	Fallujah	**AAGHKMNY**	gymkhana	**AAGINPST**	paganist
AAFHLSTY	layshaft	**AAGHKNST**	thangkas	**AAGINRRS**	arraigns
AAFHQRRU	Farquhar	**AAGHLNPY**	anaglyph		Srinagar
AAFHRSUU	hausfrau	**AAGHMNNO**	Monaghan	**AAGINRRY**	arraying
AAFIIILS	Faisal II	**AAGHMNOY**	hogmanay	**AAGINRSS**	sangrias
AAFIIKLR	Faliraki		mahogany		sarangis
AAFIILLM	familial	**AAGHMNRT**	Grantham	**AAGINRSU**	guaranis
AAFIILLR	filarial	**AAGHNNRT**	Nha Trang	**AAGINRTT**	Rattigan
AAFIILMR	familiar	**AAGHNNST**	Tangshan	**AAGINRUZ**	Zungaria
AAFIILNR	filarian	**AAGHNPRY**	phrygana	**AAGINSST**	assignat
AAFIKLLY	alkalify	**AAGHNSST**	sanghats	**AAGINSSU**	gaussian
AAFILLNR	rainfall	**AAGHRSSW**	washrags	**AAGINSSY**	assaying
AAFILMST	fatalism	**AAGIILMN**	imaginal		gainsays
AAFILNST	fantails	**AAGIILNS**	aliasing	**AAGIORTT**	agitator
AAFILPRS	Parsifal	**AAGIILNV**	availing	**AAGIPRSU**	piraguas
AAFILSTT	fatalist	**AAGIIMNN**	magainin	**AAGIRSTV**	gravitas
AAFILTTY	fatality	**AAGIIMST**	astigmia		stravaig
AAFIMNOR	foramina	**AAGIINNP**	Paganini	**AAGKNOOR**	kangaroo
AAFINNOV	favonian	**AAGIINNU**	iguanian	**AAGKNOOV**	Okavango
AAFINNRS	safranin	**AAGIINTV**	aviating	**AAGKNORR**	Ragnarök
AAFINNST	infantas	**AAGIINTW**	awaiting	**AAGLLMOY**	allogamy
AAFINRRW	warfarin	**AAGIJRTU**	Gujarati	**AAGLLNRY**	laryngal
AAFINSTU	faustian	**AAGIKLNO**	kaoliang	**AAGLLNST**	gallants
AAFIPRST	parfaits	**AAGIKLNR**	kraaling	**AAGLLOPY**	polygala
AAFIRSUY	rufiyaas	**AAGIKLUV**	Kaliyuga	**AAGLLOSS**	aglossal
AAFIRSWY	fairways	**AAGILLNU**	Anguilla	**AAGLLOWY**	Galloway
AAFIRTTT	frittata	**AAGILLNY**	allaying	**AAGLMNSS**	glassman
AAFJLORS	alforjas	**AAGILLSS**	galliass	**AAGLNQUU**	aqualung
AAFKMUUY	Fukuyama	**AAGILMNO**	magnolia	**AAGLNRRU**	granular
AAFKORTU	Karafuto	**AAGILMNR**	alarming	**AAGLRSTU**	gastrula
AAFLLNUY	faunally		marginal	**AAGMMRRS**	grammars
AAFLLPRT	pratfall	**AAGILMOT**	gliomata	**AAGMMSUY**	mamaguys
AAFLNNOT	nonfatal	**AAGILNOT**	galtonia	**AAGMNORT**	martagon
AAFLSTWY	flatways	**AAGILNOV**	Liaoyang	**AAGMNOSS**	sangomas
AAFLSWYY	flyaways	**AAGILNRR**	larrigan	**AAGMNOST**	agamonts
AAFMNSST	fantasms	**AAGILNRS**	Sangrail	**AAGMNRST**	tangrams

AAGMNSTY	syntagma	**AAHKMSSY**	yashmaks	**AAIKLNOS**	Salonika
AAGMORTY	Gayomart	**AAHKORSV**	Sakharov	**AAIKLNRS**	Sri Lanka
AAGMOTUY	autogamy	**AAHKRSTV**	Hrvatska	**AAIKLORU**	Liákoura
AAGMOTYZ	zygomata	**AAHLLMRS**	marshall	**AAIKLOSV**	Slovakia
AAGMRSST	matgrass	**AAHLLOPT**	allopath	**AAIKLPRS**	palikars
AAGNNSTT	stagnant	**AAHLLSWY**	hallways	**AAIKMNNS**	manakins
AAGNNUXZ	Xuan Zang	**AAHLLUVX**	Vauxhall	**AAIKMRST**	tamarisk
AAGNOPRS	paragons	**AAHLMRSS**	marshals	**AAIKNNTT**	antitank
AAGNOPRT	tragopan	**AAHLMSTU**	thalamus	**AAIKNORU**	Kairouan
AAGNORRT	arrogant	**AAHLNNSU**	An Lu Shan	**AAIKNPST**	Pakistan
	tarragon	**AAHLNPST**	ashplant	**AAIKSSTW**	swastika
AAGNORSZ	organzas	**AAHLNRSW**	narwhals	**AAIKSTVV**	akvavits
AAGNORTU	argonaut	**AAHLPSST**	asphalts	**AAILLLUV**	alluvial
AAGNRSTV	vagrants	**AAHMMORR**	Moharram	**AAILLMMM**	mammilla
AAGNRTUY	guaranty	**AAHMMRRU**	Muharram	**AAILLMNS**	manillas
AAGORSSS	sargasso	**AAHMNNSU**	hanumans	**AAILLMNT**	mantilla
AAGORSSU	saguaros	**AAHMNORT**	marathon	**AAILLMOR**	Amarillo
AAGRSSTU	sastruga	**AAHMNOTX**	xanthoma	**AAILLMPT**	taillamp
AAGRSTUZ	zastruga	**AAHMNPST**	phantasm	**AAILLMRX**	maxillar
AAHHIJLR	Al Hijrah	**AAHMOPRS**	amphoras	**AAILLNSV**	vanillas
AAHHIKNU	hanukiah	**AAHMRSST**	stramash	**AAILLRXY**	axillary
AAHHKKNU	Hanukkah	**AAHNNOSS**	hosannas	**AAILMMNU**	Maulmain
AAHHKMRS	hashmark	**AAHNNSTY**	Tyan-Shan	**AAILMMRS**	alarmism
AAHHMMSS	shammash	**AAHNOPTW**	Powhatan	**AAILMNOR**	manorial
AAHHNPST	naphthas	**AAHNOSTT**	thanatos		morainal
AAHHOPRS	pharaohs	**AAHNPSTY**	phantasy	**AAILMNOS**	Somalian
AAHIIKRR	hari-kari	**AAHNRTTY**	Hanratty	**AAILMNOX**	monaxial
AAHIIKRT	tarakihi	**AAHNTUWY**	huntaway	**AAILMNST**	staminal
AAHIILRT	hairtail	**AAHOPRTU**	autoharp		talisman
AAHIINPS	Hispania	**AAHOQSUW**	aquashow	**AAILMNSV**	Malvinas
AAHIINSS	Hassan II	**AAHORSSU**	sahuaros	**AAILMOPT**	lipomata
AAHIINTT	Tahitian	**AAHPRSTW**	warpaths	**AAILMORR**	armorial
AAHIJNRS	harijans	**AAHPSTWY**	pathways	**AAILMRSS**	Marsalis
AAHIKLNS	Sakhalin	**AAHRSSTY**	ashtrays	**AAILMRST**	alarmist
AAHIKLPS	pashalik	**AAIIILMR**	miliaria	**AAILMTTU**	ultimata
AAHIKNOV	Haakon IV	**AAIIILMS**	Ismailia	**AAILNNOT**	national
AAHIKNSS	Kinshasa	**AAIIJJPP**	jipijapa	**AAILNNPT**	plantain
AAHIKRST	kitharas	**AAIILMNS**	mainsail	**AAILNNRU**	lunarian
AAHILLLS	shillala	**AAIILMRS**	airmails	**AAILNNST**	annalist
AAHILMRY	Hail Mary	**AAIILNRZ**	alizarin	**AAILNOPS**	salopian
AAHILNNT	inhalant	**AAIILNUX**	uniaxial	**AAILNOPT**	talapoin
AAHILNOT	halation	**AAIILPST**	tilapias	**AAILNORS**	orinasal
AAHILNPT	Naphtali	**AAIILRTX**	triaxial	**AAILNORT**	notarial
AAHILQUZ	Zia ul Haq	**AAIILTXY**	axiality		rational
AAHIMNOS	mahonias	**AAIIMNNR**	Arminian	**AAILNOSV**	Slavonia
AAHIMNPS	pashmina	**AAIIMNNT**	maintain	**AAILNOTV**	lavation
AAHIMNRR	Harriman	**AAIIMNPX**	panmixia	**AAILNOTX**	laxation
AAHIMNZZ	hazzanim	**AAIIMNQS**	Si-ma Qian	**AAILNQTU**	aliquant
AAHIMSTT	Matthias	**AAIIMNRS**	Arianism	**AAILNSSY**	analysis
AAHINNST	Tian Shan	**AAIIMNRT**	Maritain	**AAILNSTT**	Atlantis
AAHINNTX	Xanthian	**AAIINNNO**	Ioánnina	**AAILNSTU**	Lusatian
AAHINPRS	piranhas	**AAIINOTV**	aviation	**AAILNSTY**	nasality
AAHINPRT	Parthian	**AAIINPRR**	riparian	**AAILNTTY**	natality
AAHINSST	shaitans	**AAIINPRS**	Parisian	**AAILORRS**	rasorial
AAHIPPRS	Sapphira	**AAIINRST**	intarsia	**AAILORRV**	variolar
AAHIPSXY	asphyxia	**AAIINRSU**	Isaurian	**AAILPPRU**	puparial
AAHJNNOT	Jonathan	**AAIIPRST**	apiarist	**AAILPRST**	partials
AAHKLLMR	hallmark	**AAIIRSTV**	aviarist		patrials
AAHKLMOO	Oklahoma	**AAIIRTVX**	aviatrix	**AAILPRSY**	airplays
AAHKLOOS	Koolhaas	**AAIJNRYZ**	janizary	**AAILPRVZ**	Parzival
AAHKMOOY	Yokohama	**AAIKKNOS**	skokiaan	**AAILQRSU**	squarial
AAHKMOTW	tomahawk	**AAIKLNNN**	alkannin	**AAILQSWW**	qawwalis

AAILRRSV	arrivals	**AAINSTTT**	attaints	**AALNOORS**	oronasal
AAILRSTT	rattails	**AAINSTTV**	avantist	**AALNOPRT**	patronal
AAILRSTV	travails	**AAIOPRSU**	parousia	**AALNOPST**	postanal
AAILRSVY	salivary	**AAIORSTV**	aviators	**AALNPSST**	saltpans
AAILRSWY	railways	**AAIPPSTT**	pitapats	**AALNPTWX**	waxplant
AAILSSSW	wassails	**AAIPRSSX**	sparaxis	**AALNRRTY**	arrantly
AAILSSTY	staysail	**AAIPRSTT**	partitas	**AALNRSTU**	naturals
AAIMMNOS	ammonias	**AAIQRSTU**	aquarist	**AALNSSTU**	sultanas
AAIMMNST	mainmast	**AAIQRSUU**	Aquarius	**AALNSSTY**	analysts
AAIMMRSU	samarium	**AAIQSSSU**	quassias	**AALNSTTU**	tantalus
AAIMNNOR	Romanian	**AAIRSSTT**	tsaritsa	**AALNTUUV**	Tuvaluan
AAIMNNRU	Rumanian	**AAIRSSTU**	Asturias	**AALOOPSU**	São Paulo
AAIMNNTU	Numantia	**AAIRSTWY**	stairway	**AALOPPRV**	approval
AAIMNORT	animator	**AAISSTTV**	atavists	**AALOPPST**	apoplast
AAIMNORU	Roumania	**AAISTWXY**	taxiways	**AALOPRSS**	parasols
AAIMNORV	Moravian	**AAJKLSWY**	jaywalks	**AALOPRST**	pastoral
AAIMNORW	airwoman	**AAJMMORR**	marjoram	**AALOPSVV**	pavlovas
AAIMNOTT	antiatom	**AAKKLRSU**	karakuls	**AALORSSU**	arousals
AAIMNPRZ	marzipan	**AAKKMOST**	tokamaks	**AALORTUV**	valuator
AAIMNPTU	putamina	**AAKKOSUZ**	zakouska	**AALORTVY**	lavatory
AAIMNRRT	trimaran	**AAKLOOPS**	palookas	**AALPRSTU**	spatular
AAIMNRST	martians	**AAKLOOST**	talookas	**AALPRSTY**	laptrays
	tamarins	**AAKLRSSU**	kursaals	**AALPSSTU**	spatulas
AAIMNRSU	Masurian	**AAKLSWWY**	walkways	**AALRSTTW**	stalwart
AAIMNSST	mantissa	**AAKMMNRS**	marksman	**AALRSTUY**	salutary
	satanism	**AAKMORUZ**	mazourka	**AALSSSTU**	assaults
AAIMNSTY	mainstay	**AAKMOSSU**	mousakas	**AAMMOTXY**	myxomata
AAIMNTYZ	Zamyatin		moussaka	**AAMMRSSU**	marasmus
AAIMOPRS	mariposa	**AAKMRSUZ**	mazurkas	**AAMNNNOT**	Montanan
	parosmia	**AAKMRSWY**	waymarks	**AAMNORRS**	marranos
AAIMPRST	pastrami	**AAKNNSTU**	nunataks	**AAMNORSZ**	romanzas
AAIMPRSU	marsupia	**AAKOOPPS**	pakapoos	**AAMNPRST**	mantraps
AAIMQRUU	aquarium	**AAKOPRSV**	Kasparov	**AAMNQSUW**	squawman
AAIMRRST	Amritsar	**AAKORSUW**	Kurosawa	**AAMNRSTU**	Sumatran
AAIMRUVX	Marivaux	**AAKPRSWY**	parkways	**AAMOPRRU**	paramour
AAIMSSTV	atavisms	**AALLLLMP**	Pall Mall	**AAMORSSU**	mosasaur
AAINNNOP	Pannonia	**AALLMNTY**	tallyman	**AAMORSSV**	samovars
AAINNORT	Ontarian	**AALLMNUY**	manually	**AAMORSTT**	stromata
	Taínaron	**AALLMORY**	amorally	**AAMOSTTU**	automats
AAINNORV	Navarino	**AALLMPRU**	ampullar	**AAMPRRST**	ramparts
AAINNOST	sonatina	**AALLNNUY**	annually	**AAMRSSTT**	mattrass
AAINNOTT	natation	**AALLNOTY**	atonally	**AAMRSTWY**	tramways
AAINNRSV	navarins	**AALLNPRU**	planular	**AAMSSSTU**	satsumas
AAINNSST	naissant	**AALLNRTY**	tarnally	**AANNOSST**	assonant
AAINNSSY	sannyasi	**AALLOOPT**	Palo Alto	**AANNOSTT**	annattos
AAINOPSS	paisanos	**AALLOORW**	wallaroo	**AANNRSTY**	stannary
AAINORRS	rosarian	**AALLORSU**	allosaur	**AANORRRT**	narrator
AAINOTTX	taxation	**AALLORWY**	rollaway	**AANORTTY**	natatory
AAINPRST	aspirant	**AALLPRST**	plastral	**AANPPTTY**	pattypan
	partisan	**AALLRSTY**	astrally	**AANPRSST**	spartans
AAINPRTZ	partizan	**AALLRUVV**	valvular	**AANRRSTW**	warrants
AAINQRRU	quarrian	**AALMNOPP**	Pamplona	**AANRRTTY**	tartanry
AAINQRTU	quatrain	**AALMNORT**	matronal	**AANRRTWY**	warranty
AAINQTTU	aquatint	**AALMNORU**	monaural	**AANRSTTU**	saturant
AAINRSST	artisans	**AALMNOWY**	laywoman	**AANRSUWY**	runaways
	tsarinas	**AALMNTTU**	tantalum	**AAOPSSTY**	apostasy
AAINRSSU	saurians	**AALMNTUU**	autumnal	**AAORSSVV**	vavasors
AAINRSTU	Austrian	**AALMOPPR**	malaprop		vavassor
AAINRSTV	variants	**AALMOSTT**	stomatal	**AAORSUVV**	vavasour
AAINRSTY	sanitary	**AALMPPSU**	paspalum	**AAOSTTUY**	tatouays
AAINSSSS	assassin	**AALMPRSY**	palmyras	**AAOSTWWY**	stowaway
AAINSSTT	satanist	**AALNNOST**	sonantal	**AAPRRSTT**	rattraps

AARRSTTU	Tartarus	**ABBDGINR**	drabbing	**ABBGGINR**	grabbing
AARSTTUY	statuary	**ABBDHIRT**	birdbath	**ABBGHRSU**	Habsburg
ABBBDELR	brabbled	**ABBDHOOY**	babyhood	**ABBGILNR**	rabbling
ABBBEILR	bribable	**ABBDILNO**	bailbond	**ABBGILNS**	slabbing
ABBBELRR	brabbler	**ABBDINRS**	ribbands	**ABBGILNW**	wabbling
ABBBELRS	babblers	**ABBDMORS**	bombards	**ABBGINST**	stabbing
	blabbers	**ABBDNORW**	browband	**ABBGINSW**	swabbing
	brabbles	**ABBDOORX**	boxboard	**ABBGINYY**	yabbying
ABBBELTU	tubbable	**ABBDRRUY**	Bradbury	**ABBGOOSU**	bugaboos
ABBBGILN	babbling	**ABBEEJRR**	jabberer	**ABBHILSY**	shabbily
	blabbing	**ABBEEJRS**	bejabers	**ABBHINOS**	nabobish
ABBBHSUY	bushbaby	**ABBEELLN**	Ben Bella	**ABBHIORT**	rabbitoh
ABBBISTT	babbitts	**ABBEELTU**	bluebeat	**ABBHRRSU**	rhubarbs
ABBBOSTU	subabbot	**ABBEELVW**	Ebbw Vale	**ABBHSTTU**	bathtubs
ABBCCKMO	backcomb	**ABBEERTT**	barbette	**ABBILLOT**	boatbill
ABBCDEKN	backbend	**ABBEESSS**	abbesses	**ABBILLSU**	sillabub
ABBCDELS	scabbled	**ABBEFILR**	flabbier	**ABBILOST**	bobtails
ABBCEERU	barbecue	**ABBEGIST**	gabbiest	**ABBILOTU**	tabbouli
ABBCEGIR	cribbage	**ABBEGLRR**	grabbler	**ABBIMNOS**	bambinos
ABBCEHIS	babiches	**ABBEGLRS**	gabblers		nabobism
ABBCEHTU	bathcube		grabbles	**ABBINORX**	brainbox
ABBCEIKT	backbite	**ABBEGNOS**	bogbeans	**ABBIORST**	rabbitos
ABBCEILR	barbicel	**ABBEGNSU**	bugbanes	**ABBIRRTY**	rabbitry
ABBCEIRR	crabbier	**ABBEGRRS**	grabbers	**ABBIRSUU**	suburbia
ABBCEIRS	scabbier	**ABBEGRSU**	bugbears	**ABBKKNOO**	bankbook
ABBCEKNO	backbone	**ABBEHIRS**	shabbier	**ABBKLOSU**	blauboks
ABBCEKNU	buckbean	**ABBEHORT**	bathrobe	**ABBLLRSU**	bullbars
ABBCELLU	clubable	**ABBEILLO**	boilable	**ABBLLSTU**	bullbats
ABBCELRS	scrabble	**ABBEILNU**	bubaline	**ABBLLSUY**	syllabub
ABBCELSS	scabbles	**ABBEILOT**	bilobate	**ABBLOPRY**	probably
ABBCERRS	crabbers	**ABBEILRW**	wabblier	**ABBMOORS**	bomboras
ABBCGINR	crabbing	**ABBEILST**	bistable	**ABBMOSST**	bombasts
ABBCGINS	scabbing	**ABBEIMRU**	berimbau	**ABBMOSTU**	bumboats
ABBCGIOR	gabbroic	**ABBEIMWZ**	Zimbabwe	**ABBNRSUU**	suburban
ABBCIILL	biblical	**ABBEINRS**	Brisbane	**ABBOSSTY**	bobstays
ABBCIINR	rabbinic	**ABBEIRRT**	rabbiter	**ABCCDHIK**	dabchick
ABBCIKRT	brickbat	**ABBEIRRW**	barbwire	**ABCCDIOU**	Boudicca
ABBCILSY	scabbily	**ABBELLRS**	barbells	**ABCCEEHN**	bechance
ABBCKLOW	blowback	**ABBELMRS**	brambles	**ABCCEELP**	peccable
ABBCKLOY	blackboy	**ABBELOPR**	probable	**ABCCEILY**	celibacy
ABBCKNRU	backburn	**ABBELORS**	belabors	**ABCCEIRS**	breccias
ABBCKSUY	buybacks	**ABBELORU**	belabour	**ABCCEKMO**	comeback
ABBDDEEL	beddable	**ABBELQSU**	squabble	**ABCCESUU**	succubae
ABBDDEEU	bedaubed	**ABBELRRS**	rabblers	**ABCCHISU**	bacchius
ABBDDEIL	biddable	**ABBELRSS**	slabbers	**ABCCHNOO**	cabochon
ABBDDELR	drabbled	**ABBELRSU**	barbules	**ABCCIKKK**	kickback
ABBDDILY	biddably	**ABBELRSW**	wabblers	**ABCCILOR**	carbolic
ABBDEEER	beebread	**ABBELRSY**	slabbery	**ABCCILOT**	cobaltic
ABBDEEJR	jabbered	**ABBENORS**	baseborn	**ABCCILUU**	cubicula
ABBDEERR	barbered	**ABBENORY**	nabobery	**ABCCINOR**	carbonic
ABBDEERT	rabbeted	**ABBEORRS**	absorber	**ABCCIORS**	ascorbic
ABBDEGLR	grabbled		reabsorb	**ABCCKLLO**	ballcock
ABBDEHOO	boobhead	**ABBEORTW**	browbeat	**ABCCKOOT**	cockboat
ABBDEIRT	rabbited	**ABBERRRY**	barberry	**ABCCKOSW**	bawcocks
ABBDELMR	brambled	**ABBERRYY**	bayberry	**ABCCKSTU**	cutbacks
ABBDELRS	dabblers	**ABBERSST**	stabbers	**ABCCMOOY**	maccoboy
	drabbles	**ABBERSSU**	Barbusse	**ABCCOOST**	tobaccos
ABBDEMOR	bombarde	**ABBERSSW**	swabbers	**ABCDDEOR**	brocaded
ABBDEORS	absorbed	**ABBESSSU**	subbases	**ABCDDETU**	abducted
ABBDERST	drabbest	**ABBFILLY**	flabbily	**ABCDEEFK**	feedback
	drabbets	**ABBFLOOT**	bobfloat	**ABCDEEHL**	bleached
ABBDGILN	dabbling	**ABBGGILN**	gabbling	**ABCDEEHR**	breached

ABCDEELM	becalmed	
ABCDEELS	debacles	
ABCDEELU	educable	
ABCDEEMR	cambered	
	embraced	
ABCDEENO	beaconed	
ABCDEFLO	boldface	
ABCDEGIR	birdcage	
ABCDEGKL	Gladbeck	
ABCDEHLN	blanched	
ABCDEHNR	branched	
ABCDEHOR	broached	
ABCDEIIT	diabetic	
ABCDEIKS	backside	
ABCDEILR	calibred	
ABCDEIMR	MacBride	
ABCDEIPS	pedicabs	
ABCDEIRS	ascribed	
ABCDEISS	abscised	
ABCDEKLO	blockade	
ABCDEKLV	backveld	
ABCDEKNN	neckband	
ABCDEKNU	unbacked	
ABCDEKRS	redbacks	
ABCDELOO	caboodle	
ABCDEMNU	dumbcane	
ABCDEMOT	combated	
ABCDEMRS	scrambed	
ABCDENRU	unbraced	
ABCDENSU	abducens	
ABCDENTU	abducent	
ABCDEORS	brocades	
ABCDFKLO	foldback	
ABCDHKLO	holdback	
ABCDHLNU	clubhand	
ABCDHMOR	Chambord	
ABCDIILO	biocidal	
	diabolic	
ABCDIIRT	tribadic	
ABCDIKLS	backslid	
ABCDILLR	birdcall	
ABCDILOU	cuboidal	
ABCDILRS	baldrics	
ABCDIRST	catbirds	
ABCDKLNU	Buckland	
ABCDKNOW	backdown	
ABCDKOOR	backdoor	
ABCDKOPR	backdrop	
ABCDKORW	backword	
ABCDLLNU	clubland	
ABCDNOSS	absconds	
ABCDOORS	cordobas	
ABCDOORW	crabwood	
ABCDOPRU	cupboard	
ABCDORTU	abductor	
ABCDORUY	obduracy	
ABCEEEFK	beefcake	
ABCEEGRR	Bergerac	
ABCEEHLM	bechamel	
ABCEEHLR	bleacher	
ABCEEHLS	bleaches	
ABCEEHLW	chewable	
ABCEEHRS	breaches	
ABCEEILT	celibate	
	citeable	
ABCEEIMN	ambience	
ABCEEKLY	eyeblack	
ABCEELOV	evocable	
ABCEELRR	cerebral	
ABCEELRT	bracelet	
ABCEEMRR	embracer	
ABCEEMRS	embraces	
ABCEENOZ	cabezone	
ABCEENRS	carbeens	
	carbenes	
ABCEENSS	absences	
ABCEFIIT	beatific	
ABCEFIKL	backfile	
ABCEFIKR	backfire	
	fireback	
ABCEFINO	boniface	
ABCEGHIN	beaching	
ABCEGIRS	ribcages	
ABCEGKLL	blackleg	
ABCEGKLO	blockage	
ABCEGKMU	megabuck	
ABCEGKRY	greyback	
ABCEHILR	Alberich	
ABCEHIRR	Chabrier	
ABCEHITT	bathetic	
ABCEHLNS	blanches	
	Schnabel	
ABCEHLOR	bachelor	
ABCEHLOS	chaebols	
ABCEHLSU	bauchles	
	chasuble	
ABCEHMOT	hecatomb	
ABCEHMRS	chambers	
ABCEHMRY	Chambéry	
ABCEHNRS	branches	
ABCEHNSW	Schwaben	
ABCEHOOT	cohobate	
ABCEHORR	broacher	
ABCEHORS	broaches	
ABCEHORU	barouche	
ABCEHRST	brachets	
ABCEIIRT	rabietic	
ABCEIJOT	Jacobite	
ABCEIKKL	kickable	
ABCEIKLP	pickable	
ABCEIKLS	scablike	
ABCEIKST	tiebacks	
ABCEIKWZ	zwieback	
ABCEILLR	cribella	
ABCEILLT	balletic	
ABCEILMS	alembics	
ABCEILNN	binnacle	
ABCEILNO	coinable	
ABCEILOR	cabriole	
ABCEILOS	sociable	
ABCEILRS	calibers	
	calibres	
ABCEIMRW	micawber	
ABCEINRS	brisance	
	carbines	
ABCEINRT	bacterin	
ABCEINST	bascinet	
	cabinets	
ABCEINTU	incubate	
ABCEIORS	aerobics	
ABCEIORT	boracite	
ABCEIOST	iceboats	
ABCEIRRT	catbrier	
ABCEIRSS	ascribes	
ABCEIRSW	crabwise	
ABCEIRTT	brattice	
ABCEIRTY	acerbity	
ABCEISSS	abscises	
ABCEJLTY	abjectly	
ABCEJNOS	Jacobsen	
ABCEKKSW	skewback	
ABCEKLLO	lockable	
ABCEKLMO	mockable	
ABCEKLNS	blackens	
ABCEKLOO	cookable	
ABCEKLSS	backless	
ABCEKLST	blackest	
ABCEKLTT	Blackett	
ABCEKMNN	Beckmann	
ABCEKNRS	brackens	
ABCEKOOS	bookcase	
	casebook	
ABCEKRST	backrest	
	brackets	
ABCEKSST	setbacks	
ABCEKSTW	wetbacks	
ABCELLMP	Campbell	
ABCELLPU	culpable	
ABCELLSU	bullaces	
ABCELMNY	lambency	
ABCELMOS	cembalos	
ABCELMRS	cambrels	
	clambers	
	scramble	
ABCELMRU	La Cumbre	
ABCELMRY	cymbaler	
ABCELNUU	nubecula	
ABCELOOT	bootlace	
ABCELOPS	placebos	
ABCELORT	brocatel	
ABCELOST	obstacle	
ABCELOSV	vocables	
ABCELPSU	bluecaps	
ABCELRTT	bractlet	
ABCELSSU	bascules	
ABCEMOOS	camboose	
ABCEMORT	combater	
ABCEMORU	Eboracum	
ABCEMSSY	Cambyses	
ABCENNOS	Besançon	
ABCENORS	baconers	
ABCENOSW	cowbanes	
ABCENOSZ	cabezons	
ABCENRSU	unbraces	
ABCEOOSS	cabooses	
ABCEOSUX	saucebox	

ABCERRTU	carburet	ABCIMMSU	cambiums	ABDDEHMO	hebdomad
ABCERRWY	cyberwar	ABCIMNRU	Cumbrian	ABDDEHOY	hobdayed
ABCERSSU	subraces	ABCIMSST	cambists	ABDDEILS	disabled
ABCERTUU	cubature	ABCINNOS	nonbasic	ABDDEILU	buddleia
ABCESSTW	webcasts	ABCINORY	baryonic	ABDDEINS	sideband
ABCESTUU	subacute	ABCINOST	botanics	ABDDELRS	bladders
ABCFIKLL	backfill	ABCINOUV	Bucovina	ABDDELRY	bladdery
ABCFIKNS	finbacks	ABCINRSU	Brancusi	ABDDENOU	abounded
ABCFILOS	bifocals	ABCINRVY	vibrancy	ABDDEORS	adsorbed
ABCFIOST	biofacts	ABCIOPRS	saprobic		roadbeds
ABCFKLLU	fullback	ABCIORSU	caribous	ABDDEOSY	deadboys
ABCFKLLY	blackfly	ABCIOSSU	scabious	ABDDFORR	Bradford
ABCFKLSY	flybacks	ABCIOSTU	Subotica	ABDDILMO	lambdoid
ABCGHINT	batching	ABCIOSUV	bivouacs	ABDDILRY	ladybird
ABCGHKOS	hogbacks	ABCJKOOT	bootjack	ABDDIMNO	bondmaid
ABCGHNPU	punchbag		jackboot	ABDDINSS	disbands
ABCGIINN	cabining			ABDDIRRY	yardbird
ABCGIKLN	blacking	ABCKLLOS	ballocks	ABDDLLOS	oddballs
ABCGIKNS	backings	ABCKLLPU	pullback	ABDDLNRY	Byrd Land
ABCGINRS	bracings	ABCKLOPT	blacktop	ABDDLUWY	bulwaddy
ABCGKLMU	blackgum	ABCKLOST	backlots	ABDEEEFL	feedable
ABCGKLOS	backlogs	ABCKLOTU	blackout	ABDEEEMN	bemeaned
ABCGMSSU	scumbags	ABCKMOOR	backroom	ABDEEENR	Aberdeen
ABCHHIIS	hibachis	ABCKMOSS	mossback	ABDEEERV	beavered
ABCHIIPS	biphasic	ABCKMOST	backmost		bereaved
ABCHIKLS	blackish	ABCKMRSU	buckrams	ABDEEFGS	feedbags
ABCHIKRS	brackish	ABCKMSUZ	zambucks	ABDEEFLM	flambeed
ABCHILOO	coolibah	ABCKNNOS	bannocks	ABDEEGGR	beggared
ABCHIMOR	choriamb	ABCKOORR	roorback	ABDEEGLL	gabelled
ABCHIMRU	brachium	ABCKOORU	buckaroo	ABDEEGLR	Belgrade
ABCHINOR	bronchia	ABCKOPST	backstop	ABDEEGNO	Abednego
ABCHIOST	cohabits	ABCKOSSW	sowbacks	ABDEEHIR	braeheid
ABCHIRRT	tribrach	ABCKSSTU	sackbuts	ABDEEHLS	shedable
ABCHKLOW	howlback	ABCKSSUW	bucksaws	ABDEEHNO	bonehead
ABCHKMPU	humpback		sawbucks	ABDEEHRR	Eberhard
ABCHKOOP	chapbook	ABCLLNOR	cornball	ABDEEHRT	breathed
ABCHKOOS	cashbook	ABCLLOSY	callboys	ABDEEHST	bethesda
ABCHKSTU	hackbuts	ABCLLPUY	culpably	ABDEEIKR	bidarkee
ABCHLLUU	clubhaul	ABCLMMOV	cymbalom	ABDEEILN	deniable
ABCHMOTX	matchbox	ABCLMOOO	coloboma	ABDEEILR	rideable
ABCHOSTT	chatbots	ABCLMOSY	cymbalos	ABDEEILS	abseiled
ABCIIKRR	airbrick	ABCLMSUU	baculums	ABDEEILW	bewailed
ABCIIMNS	minicabs	ABCLNORY	carbonyl	ABDEEIST	beadiest
ABCIINRS	Scriabin	ABCLNSSU	subclans		diabetes
ABCIIORS	isobaric	ABCLORXY	carboxyl	ABDEEJMN	enjambed
ABCIIRST	tribasic	ABCLSSSU	subclass	ABDEEKMN	embanked
ABCIIRTU	Curitiba	ABCMOORT	mobocrat	ABDEEKMR	embarked
ABCIISTY	basicity	ABCNORTY	corybant	ABDEELLL	labelled
ABCIJNOS	jacobins	ABCNOUVY	buoyancy	ABDEELLW	weldable
ABCIKLST	backlist	ABCORRSS	crossbar	ABDEELMM	embalmed
ABCIKMRS	Bismarck	ABCORRSW	crowbars	ABDEELMN	mendable
ABCIKNPS	backspin	ABCORRTU	turbocar	ABDEELMS	beldames
ABCIKSSY	sickbays	ABCORSSU	scabrous	ABDEELMZ	emblazed
ABCILLNY	billycan	ABCRSTTU	subtract	ABDEELNS	sendable
ABCILLSU	bacillus	ABDDEEEH	beheaded	ABDEELOR	leeboard
ABCILLSY	syllabic	ABDDEEGG	debagged	ABDEELPT	bedplate
ABCILMMO	cimbalom	ABDDEEGR	badgered	ABDEELRR	barreled
ABCILMOO	Colombia	ABDDEEHT	deathbed	ABDEELZZ	bedazzle
ABCILMOU	Columbia	ABDDEEKR	debarked	ABDEEMNO	bemoaned
ABCILNPU	publican	ABDDEERR	debarred	ABDEEMNS	beadsmen
ABCILOSY	sociably	ABDDEEST	bedstead		bedesman
ABCILRRU	rubrical	ABDDEGIR	abridged	ABDEENNR	bannered
			brigaded		

ABDEENRT	bantered	**ABDEILMN**	mandible	**ABDENRRS**	branders
ABDEENRY	barneyed	**ABDEILNN**	bin Laden	**ABDENRRU**	unbarred
ABDEENRZ	brazened	**ABDEILNR**	bilander	**ABDENRSS**	drabness
ABDEENST	absented	**ABDEILNW**	windable	**ABDENRTU**	breadnut
ABDEENTT	battened	**ABDEILNY**	deniably		turbaned
ABDEEPRS	bespread	**ABDEILOV**	voidable	**ABDENTTU**	debutant
ABDEERRT	bartered	**ABDEILPS**	piebalds	**ABDEOORW**	bearwood
ABDEERRY	ryebread	**ABDEILRS**	bedrails	**ABDEOPRT**	probated
ABDEERSS	debasers	**ABDEILRT**	librated	**ABDEORRS**	boarders
ABDEERST	breasted	**ABDEILRV**	drivable	**ABDEORRW**	wardrobe
	debaters	**ABDEILSS**	disables	**ABDEORST**	broadest
ABDEERTT	battered	**ABDEILSU**	audibles	**ABDEORSW**	sowbread
ABDEERTW	waterbed	**ABDEILTU**	dutiable	**ABDEORTU**	obdurate
ABDEERTY	betrayed	**ABDEIMOO**	amoeboid	**ABDEORUX**	bordeaux
ABDEERWY	bewrayed	**ABDEIMOR**	amberoid	**ABDEOSTU**	boutades
ABDEERWY	bewrayed	**ABDEINNR**	endbrain	**ABDEPSSY**	bypassed
ABDEESST	basseted	**ABDEINOR**	debonair	**ABDEPSTU**	Budapest
	besteads	**ABDEINOT**	obtained	**ABDERSST**	dabsters
ABDEFHOO	boofhead	**ABDEINRS**	brandies	**ABDERSSU**	surbased
ABDEFIIS	basified	**ABDEINST**	bandiest	**ABDERSTW**	bedstraw
ABDEFILN	findable	**ABDEINSU**	unbiased	**ABDERTUW**	drawtube
ABDEFLLO	foldable	**ABDEIOST**	beastoid	**ABDFLOOT**	foldboat
ABDEFLOR	fordable	**ABDEIOTV**	obviated	**ABDGHINR**	hangbird
ABDEGHIS	bigheads	**ABDEIPST**	baptised	**ABDGIINR**	braiding
ABDEGHRS	beghards	**ABDEIPTZ**	baptized	**ABDGILOO**	Badoglio
ABDEGILN	blindage	**ABDEIRRS**	braiders	**ABDGILOR**	gaolbird
ABDEGILU	guidable	**ABDEIRST**	braidest	**ABDGIMNR**	Bridgman
ABDEGINR	bearding		tribades	**ABDGINNO**	Abingdon
	breading	**ABDEIRSX**	axebirds	**ABDGINNR**	branding
ABDEGINS	beadings	**ABDEIRTV**	vibrated	**ABDGINNY**	bandying
	debasing	**ABDEISSU**	disabuse	**ABDGINOR**	boarding
ABDEGINT	debating	**ABDEISTW**	bawdiest	**ABDGINRS**	brigands
ABDEGIRR	abridger	**ABDEJNOW**	jawboned	**ABDGINST**	dingbats
ABDEGIRS	abridges	**ABDEKLSW**	skewbald	**ABDGINSW**	windbags
	brigades	**ABDEKNSU**	sunbaked	**ABDGINUY**	Daubigny
ABDEGLMO	gamboled	**ABDEKORW**	beadwork	**ABDGLSUY**	ladybugs
ABDEGLOT	globated	**ABDEKORY**	keyboard	**ABDGNRSU**	Sandburg
ABDEGLSU	slugabed	**ABDELLMO**	moldable	**ABDGNRUU**	Dünaburg
ABDEGNOS	bondages	**ABDELLOR**	beadroll	**ABDHHSSU**	shadbush
	dogbanes	**ABDELLOT**	balloted	**ABDHIIST**	adhibits
ABDEGOPR	pegboard	**ABDELLUY**	du Bellay	**ABDHILLN**	handbill
ABDEGORT	bogarted	**ABDELNOR**	banderol	**ABDHILNS**	blandish
ABDEGRSU	subgrade		Oberland	**ABDHINRS**	brandish
ABDEHINS	banished	**ABDELNOZ**	blazoned	**ABDHIRTY**	birthday
ABDEHITU	habitude	**ABDELNSS**	baldness	**ABDHKNOO**	handbook
ABDEHKLU	bulkhead	**ABDELNST**	blandest	**ABDHLMUZ**	Dzhambul
ABDEHKNO	knobhead	**ABDELORU**	laboured	**ABDHLORW**	blowhard
ABDEHLLN	handbell	**ABDELOSV**	absolved	**ABDHLOST**	Shadbolt
ABDEHLLO	holdable	**ABDELOSW**	dowsabel	**ABDHMOTU**	badmouth
ABDEHLLU	bullhead	**ABDELRSU**	durables	**ABDHNORS**	bodhrans
ABDEHLMS	shambled	**ABDEMNNS**	bandsmen	**ABDHNSSU**	husbands
ABDEHLRS	halberds	**ABDEMNOS**	abdomens	**ABDIIJLR**	jailbird
ABDEHMSU	ambushed	**ABDEMORT**	bromated	**ABDIILLR**	billiard
ABDEHNSU	Dushanbe	**ABDEMRSU**	bermudas	**ABDIILNW**	Baldwin I
ABDEHORR	abhorred	**ABDEMRTU**	drumbeat	**ABDIIMNR**	midbrain
	harbored	**ABDENNOS**	noseband	**ABDIIMSU**	basidium
ABDEHOSW	bowheads	**ABDENORR**	Dearborn	**ABDIINOS**	anobiids
ABDEHRST	breadths	**ABDENORS**	bandores		obsidian
ABDEHSSU	subheads		broadens	**ABDIINNR**	rainbird
ABDEIIRT	diatribe	**ABDENORW**	rawboned	**ABDIINTT**	banditti
ABDEIKNU	baudekin	**ABDENORY**	boneyard	**ABDIIRTY**	rabidity
ABDEILLR	brailled	**ABDENOTW**	downbeat	**ABDILLRY**	ribaldly
ABDEILLS	slidable				

ABDILMOR	Lombardi	ABEEGRSU	auberges	ABEELLLS	sellable
ABDILNOS	Basildon	ABEEGRSW	brewages	ABEELLLT	tellable
ABDILOOS	diabolos	ABEEGTTU	baguette	ABEELLMT	meltable
ABDILORS	labroids	ABEEHILR	hireable	ABEELLOV	loveable
ABDILOST	tabloids	ABEEHINT	thebaine	ABEELLRS	relabels
ABDILRRY	ribaldry	ABEEHIRZ	hebraize	ABEELLSY	eyeballs
ABDILRZZ	blizzard	ABEEHLLL	heelball	ABEELMMR	embalmer
ABDINOTY	antibody	ABEEHLLP	helpable	ABEELMNO	bonemeal
ABDINRTY	banditry	ABEEHLLR	harebell	ABEELMOV	moveable
ABDIPRSU	upbraids	ABEEHLMR	Malherbe	ABEELMPR	preamble
ABDJMOOR	doorjamb	ABEEHLPT	aleph-bet	ABEELMSS	assemble
ABDKOOSY	daybooks	ABEEHNSS	banshees		beamless
ABDLLNUW	bundwall		shebeans	ABEELMSZ	emblazes
ABDLLORS	bollards	ABEEHORS	rheobase	ABEELMTT	embattle
ABDLMORY	Lombardy	ABEEHQTU	bequeath	ABEELNOP	beanpole
ABDLOSYY	ladyboys	ABEEHRRT	breather		openable
ABDLRSUU	subdural	ABEEHRST	breathes	ABEELNOV	ovenable
ABDLRSUY	absurdly	ABEEHSTY	eyebaths	ABEELNRS	enablers
ABDMNNOS	bondsman	ABEEIKKL	beaklike	ABEELNRT	rentable
ABDMOOPR	mopboard	ABEEIKLL	likeable	ABEELNTU	tuneable
ABDNOPRS	probands	ABEEIKLM	beamlike	ABEELOPR	operable
ABDNORUY	boundary	ABEEIKRS	bakeries		ropeable
ABDNOSSY	sandboys	ABEEILLN	lineable	ABEELORX	exorable
ABDNSSTY	standbys	ABEEILLR	reliable	ABEELOTV	voteable
ABDNSTUU	butsudan	ABEEILLV	leviable	ABEELRST	blearest
ABDOORTU	outboard		liveable		bleaters
ABDOOSSW	basswood	ABEEILMN	mineable		retables
ABDRSSTU	bustards	ABEEILNP	plebeian	ABEELRSU	reusable
ABDRSUZZ	buzzards	ABEEILNS	Balinese	ABEELRSV	servable
ABEEEFRS	freebase		baseline	ABEELRTU	bateleur
ABEEEGRV	beverage	ABEEILNU	banlieue	ABEELSSS	baseless
ABEEEHTT	hebetate	ABEEILNV	enviable	ABEELSSU	sublease
ABEEELLR	reelable	ABEEILNZ	Belizean	ABEELSTT	testable
ABEEELNS	Lebanese	ABEEILPX	expiable	ABEELTTW	wettable
ABEEENRT	tenebrae	ABEEILRR	blearier	ABEEMMNR	membrane
ABEEENST	absentee	ABEEILRT	liberate	ABEEMMRU	bummaree
ABEEERSV	bereaves	ABEEILRW	bewailer	ABEEMNQU	Queen Mab
ABEEFFNO	banoffee	ABEEILSS	seisable	ABEEMNRS	Seremban
ABEEFILN	fineable	ABEEILST	seablite	ABEEMNST	basement
ABEEFILR	afebrile	ABEEILSZ	seizable	ABEEMNTT	abetment
	balefire		sizeable	ABEEMRSS	besmears
	fireable	ABEEILTV	evitable	ABEENNRT	banneret
ABEEFILS	feasible	ABEEILUU	Beaulieu	ABEENNSW	bawneens
ABEEFILT	fleabite	ABEEILVW	viewable	ABEENNTU	unbeaten
ABEEFLLL	fellable	ABEEINRZ	Berezina	ABEENORS	seaborne
ABEEFLLN	befallen	ABEEINST	betaines	ABEENOTZ	benzoate
ABEEFLMS	flambees	ABEEISST	beasties	ABEENRRT	banterer
ABEEFORR	forebear	ABEEISTT	beatiest	ABEENRSS	bareness
ABEEGILV	giveable	ABEEISTU	beauties	ABEENRST	absenter
ABEEGIRV	verbiage	ABEEJMNT	Betjeman	ABEENSV	verbenas
ABEEGLLS	gabelles	ABEEJMOR	jamboree	ABEENSSS	baseness
ABEEGLNU	Benguela	ABEEKLLW	Bakewell	ABEEORRV	overbear
ABEEGLTT	gettable	ABEEKLOT	keelboat	ABEERRRT	barterer
ABEEGMNR	bargemen	ABEEKLSS	beakless	ABEERRST	rebaters
ABEEGMTY	megabyte	ABEEKLST	bleakest	ABEERRTT	barrette
ABEEGMUU	Maubeuge	ABEEKMNR	brakemen		batterer
ABEEGNOS	Gabonese	ABEEKMRR	reembark		berretta
ABEEGNNR	Béranger	ABEEKNSY	eyebanks	ABEERRTV	vertebra
ABEEGNRT	Bretagne	ABEEKOOP	peekaboo	ABEERRTY	betrayer
ABEEGNTT	bagnette	ABEEKPSS	bespeaks		teaberry
ABEEGOSZ	gazeboes	ABEEKRRS	breakers	ABEERRWY	bewrayer
ABEEGRRS	gerberas	ABEELLLR	labeller	ABEERSTT	abetters

ABEFFKOR	breakoff	**ABEGINOS**	begonias	**ABEIILMT**	imitable
ABEFFLRS	bafflers	**ABEGINRR**	barreing	**ABEIILNN**	biennial
ABEFFOST	offbeats		berrigan	**ABEIILNR**	bilinear
ABEFGSST	gabfests	**ABEGINRS**	bearings		Liberian
ABEFHILS	fishable		sabering	**ABEIILNV**	inviable
ABEFIIMR	fimbriae	**ABEGINRT**	berating	**ABEIILPT**	pitiable
ABEFIISS	basifies		rebating	**ABEIILRT**	Albert II
ABEFILLL	fallible	**ABEGINRU**	Rugbeian	**ABEIILST**	sibilate
ABEFILLO	foilable	**ABEGINRW**	bewaring	**ABEIILTV**	vitiable
ABEFILLR	fireball	**ABEGINST**	beatings	**ABEIINRR**	brainier
ABEFILLT	liftable	**ABEGINTT**	abetting	**ABEIINRS**	binaries
ABEFILOT	lifeboat	**ABEGINTW**	wingbeat		Siberian
ABEFILRS	barflies	**ABEGIOSS**	biogases	**ABEIIRST**	Tiberias
ABEFILSY	feasibly	**ABEGIPPS**	bagpipes	**ABEIJLNO**	joinable
ABEFILTT	fittable	**ABEGKORS**	grosbeak	**ABEIJLTU**	jubilate
ABEFIORT	biforate	**ABEGLMOR**	Lag b'Omer	**ABEIJMNN**	benjamin
	fireboat	**ABEGLMRS**	gamblers	**ABEIJNSS**	basenjis
ABEFIRRT	firebrat		gambrels	**ABEIKLLM**	balmlike
ABEFITUY	beautify	**ABEGLMUY**	mealybug		lamblike
ABEFKLNT	Left Bank	**ABEGLORU**	Uleåborg	**ABEIKLLN**	balkline
ABEFLLMU	blameful	**ABEGLORW**	growable		linkable
ABEFLLRU	furlable	**ABEGLRRS**	garblers	**ABEIKLNS**	sinkable
ABEFLLTU	tableful	**ABEGLRSS**	garbless	**ABEIKLRU**	baulkier
ABEFLMOR	formable	**ABEGLRSU**	blaguers	**ABEIKLSS**	kissable
ABEFLRSU	surfable	**ABEGMNOS**	gambeson	**ABEIKLST**	balkiest
ABEFLRTU	Flaubert	**ABEGMNOY**	bogeyman	**ABEIKNRS**	bearskin
ABEFOORT	barefoot	**ABEGMORT**	bergamot	**ABEIKNST**	beatniks
ABEFORRS	forbears	**ABEGMRSU**	umbrages	**ABEILLLM**	millable
ABEFORTU	Beaufort	**ABEGNOOR**	Gaborone	**ABEILLLT**	tillable
ABEGGHLU	huggable	**ABEGNOSS**	nosebags	**ABEILLLW**	willable
ABEGGILN	beagling	**ABEGNOST**	Bastogne	**ABEILLMS**	mislabel
ABEGGIST	baggiest	**ABEGNSTU**	subagent	**ABEILLNT**	libelant
ABEGGITY	gigabyte	**ABEGOPSY**	pageboys	**ABEILLNV**	Banville
ABEGGLRS	blaggers	**ABEGOSUY**	buoyages	**ABEILLOS**	isolable
ABEGGLRY	beggarly	**ABEGRRUV**	burgrave		lobelias
ABEGGMOS	gamboges	**ABEGSSTU**	substage	**ABEILLOV**	violable
ABEGGRRS	braggers	**ABEHIINR**	Hibernia	**ABEILLPS**	lapsible
ABEGHIMR	Maghrebi	**ABEHILNR**	hibernal	**ABEILLRS**	brailles
ABEGHINS	Siegbahn	**ABEHILTT**	tithable		liberals
ABEGHINV	behaving	**ABEHIMMS**	memsahib	**ABEILLRY**	Bareilly
ABEGHINZ	Benghazi	**ABEHIMNO**	bohemian		blearily
ABEGHNSS	shebangs	**ABEHINSS**	banishes		reliably
ABEGIILR	Gabrieli	**ABEHINST**	absinthe	**ABEILLST**	bastille
ABEGIIMS	bigamies	**ABEHIORV**	behavior		listable
ABEGIJTU	bijugate	**ABEHIRRS**	brashier	**ABEILMNS**	bailsmen
ABEGIKNR	breaking	**ABEHISTU**	habitues	**ABEILMNT**	bailment
ABEGIKNT	betaking	**ABEHKRSU**	hauberks	**ABEILMRW**	wamblier
ABEGILLN	labeling	**ABEHKSTU**	ketubahs	**ABEILMSS**	missable
ABEGILNN	enabling	**ABEHLMNS**	shambles	**ABEILMST**	balmiest
ABEGILNR	blearing	**ABEHLRST**	blathers		timbales
ABEGILNS	signable		halberts	**ABEILNNW**	winnable
	singable	**ABEHMNOR**	hornbeam	**ABEILNPS**	biplanes
ABEGILNT	bleating	**ABEHMOOR**	rehoboam	**ABEILNRS**	rinsable
	tangible	**ABEHMSSU**	ambushes	**ABEILNRU**	ruinable
ABEGILNY	belaying	**ABEHMSTU**	bushmeat	**ABEILNSS**	lesbians
ABEGILOT	obligate	**ABEHNSTU**	sunbathe	**ABEILNST**	instable
ABEGILPP	Big Apple	**ABEHORRR**	abhorrer	**ABEILNSU**	sabuline
ABEGIMNN	benaming		harborer	**ABEILNTV**	bivalent
ABEGIMNR	breaming	**ABEHOSTX**	hatboxes	**ABEILNTY**	binately
ABEGIMNS	beamings	**ABEHOSXY**	hayboxes	**ABEILNUV**	unviable
ABEGIMNY	embaying	**ABEHRSST**	brashest	**ABEILNVY**	enviably
ABEGIMST	megabits	**ABEHRTUY**	Bayreuth	**ABEILPPR**	rippable

ABEILPPT	tippable	**ABEIRSTW**	warbiest	**ABELNRUY**	urbanely
ABEILPRT	partible	**ABEIRSTY**	bestiary	**ABELNRYZ**	brazenly
ABEILPSS	passible		sybarite	**ABELNSTU**	unstable
ABEILPST	epiblast	**ABEIRTTY**	ytterbia	**ABELNSTY**	absently
ABEILRRU	reburial	**ABEISTTT**	battiest	**ABELNSUU**	unusable
ABEILRST	librates	**ABEJKLOU**	kabeljou	**ABELOPRT**	portable
ABEILRTW	writable	**ABEJLMPU**	jumpable	**ABELOPRV**	provable
ABEILRVY	biyearly	**ABEJMOOR**	jeroboam	**ABELOPRY**	operably
ABEILSST	astilbes	**ABEJNOSW**	jawbones	**ABELOPST**	potables
	stabiles	**ABEJRRSU**	abjurers	**ABELOQTU**	quotable
ABEILSSU	issuable	**ABEKLMOS**	abelmosk	**ABELORRS**	laborers
ABEILSTU	suitable		smokable	**ABELORRU**	labourer
ABEILSUX	bisexual	**ABEKLNOW**	knowable		rubeolar
ABEILSVV	bivalves	**ABEKLNST**	blankest	**ABELORST**	bloaters
ABEILSYZ	sizeably		blankets		sortable
ABEIMORU	aerobium	**ABEKLNTY**	blankety		storable
ABEIMRST	barmiest	**ABEKLORW**	workable	**ABELORSV**	absolver
ABEIMRSU	aumbries	**ABEKLRSU**	baulkers	**ABELOSSU**	sabulose
ABEIMRTV	ambivert	**ABEKMNNS**	banksmen	**ABELOSSV**	absolves
	verbatim	**ABEKNNOT**	banknote	**ABELOSTU**	absolute
ABEIMSSU	iambuses	**ABEKNSSU**	sunbakes	**ABELOSTW**	bestowal
ABEINNOZ	bezonian	**ABEKNSTW**	West Bank	**ABELPRTU**	pubertal
ABEINNRU	inurbane	**ABEKOORY**	yearbook	**ABELRRSW**	brawlers
ABEINOOT	Boeotian	**ABEKORST**	Stabroek		warblers
ABEINORR	airborne	**ABEKORTU**	breakout	**ABELRSST**	blasters
ABEINORS	baronies		outbreak	**ABELRSTT**	battlers
	searobin	**ABEKPRSU**	breakups	**ABELRSTU**	baluster
ABEINORT	baritone	**ABEKRSTY**	basketry	**ABELRTTU**	rebuttal
	obtainer	**ABELLLMU**	labellum	**ABELSSSU**	subsales
ABEINOST	botanies	**ABELLLSY**	syllable	**ABELSTUU**	subulate
	botanise	**ABELLMRU**	umbellar	**ABELSTWY**	beltways
	obeisant		umbrella	**ABELTTUU**	tubulate
ABEINOTZ	botanize	**ABELLNOT**	ballonet	**ABEMMNOO**	moonbeam
ABEINRRW	brawnier	**ABELLNST**	netballs	**ABEMNOTU**	Beaumont
ABEINRSU	anburies	**ABELLOSV**	solvable		umbonate
	urbanise	**ABELLOTU**	lobulate	**ABEMNOTW**	batwomen
ABEINRTU	braunite	**ABELLOTY**	lobately	**ABEMNPRU**	penumbra
	urbanite		oblately	**ABEMNRRY**	Berryman
ABEINRUZ	urbanize	**ABELLOVY**	loveably	**ABEMNSSU**	sunbeams
ABEINSST	basinets	**ABELLRVY**	verbally	**ABEMNSUY**	sunbeamy
	bassinet	**ABELMNNO**	nobleman	**ABEMNTTU**	abutment
ABEINTTU	intubate	**ABELMNOP**	Belmopan	**ABEMORST**	bromates
ABEIORTV	abortive	**ABELMNOZ**	emblazon	**ABENNNOR**	Narbonne
ABEIORUV	Beauvoir	**ABELMNSU**	albumens	**ABENNORS**	Bernanos
ABEIOSTV	obviates	**ABELMOSU**	albumose	**ABENNORT**	Brentano
ABEIPRRS	sparerib	**ABELMOSV**	movables	**ABENNOTU**	butanone
ABEIPSST	baptises	**ABELMOTY**	metaboly	**ABENNRUV**	Van Buren
ABEIPSTZ	baptizes	**ABELMRRS**	marblers	**ABENOPSU**	subpoena
ABEIRRRS	barriers		ramblers	**ABENORSS**	baroness
ABEIRRSS	brasiers	**ABELMRST**	lamberts	**ABENORST**	baronets
	brassier	**ABELMSSY**	assembly	**ABENORTT**	betatron
ABEIRRST	arbiters	**ABELNNOR**	bannerol	**ABENORTV**	bevatron
	rarebits	**ABELNORZ**	blazoner	**ABENORTY**	barytone
ABEIRRSU	Briareus	**ABELNOSS**	bonselas	**ABENOSSW**	sawbones
ABEIRRSZ	braziers	**ABELNOST**	notables	**ABENOSSY**	soybeans
ABEIRRVY	breviary		stonable	**ABENOSTY**	bayonets
ABEIRRYZ	braziery	**ABELNOSY**	baloneys	**ABENQSTU**	banquets
ABEIRSSS	brassies	**ABELNPRU**	prunable	**ABENSTZZ**	bezzants
ABEIRSSU	airbuses	**ABELNRRY**	barrenly	**ABEOPPRY**	paperboy
ABEIRSTT	birettas	**ABELNRSY**	Barnsley	**ABEOPRSS**	saprobes
	ratbites		blarneys	**ABEOPRST**	probates
ABEIRSTV	vibrates	**ABELNRTU**	turnable	**ABEOQRSU**	baroques

ABEORRST	taborers	**ABGHMRSU**	hamburgs	**ABGLORSU**	glabrous
ABEORRTU	tabourer	**ABGHNRUV**	Vanbrugh	**ABGLRRSU**	burglars
ABEORSST	boasters	**ABGHORTU**	broughta	**ABGLRRUY**	burglary
ABEORSSY	rosebays	**ABGHPRSU**	Hapsburg	**ABGLRSUZ**	Salzburg
ABEORSTT	abettors	**ABGIIILN**	alibiing	**ABGMORSW**	bagworms
	taborets	**ABGIILNR**	brailing	**ABGNOORV**	boongary
ABEORSTU	saboteur	**ABGIILOT**	obligati	**ABGNOPRS**	probangs
ABEORTTU	obturate	**ABGIIMST**	bigamist	**ABGNORSU**	osnaburg
	tabouret	**ABGIINNO**	bignonia	**ABGNOSTU**	gunboats
ABEORTUV	outbrave	**ABGIINNR**	braining	**ABGNOSWY**	bowyangs
ABEOSSST	asbestos	**ABGIINRS**	braising	**ABGOORST**	botargos
ABEOSTWX	sweatbox	**ABGIINSS**	biassing	**ABGOPSST**	postbags
ABEPRSSY	passerby	**ABGIIRTT**	Birgitta	**ABGOSTTU**	tugboats
ABEPRSTY	typebars	**ABGIJNRU**	abjuring	**ABGRRTUW**	Wartburg
ABEPSSSY	bypasses	**ABGIKLNN**	blanking	**ABHHOSTU**	Shabuoth
ABEQRSUU	arquebus	**ABGIKLNU**	baulking	**ABHIINST**	inhabits
ABERRRTY	barretry	**ABGIKNNS**	bankings	**ABHIINTY**	Bithynia
ABERRTYY	tayberry	**ABGIKNRR**	ringbark	**ABHIIORZ**	rhizobia
ABERRWXY	waxberry	**ABGILMNR**	marbling	**ABHIKLLW**	hawkbill
ABERSSSU	surbases		rambling	**ABHIKLOR**	kohlrabi
ABERSSTU	abstruse	**ABGILMNS**	lambings	**ABHIKNRU**	Bukharin
ABERSTTU	abutters	**ABGILMNW**	wambling	**ABHIKSTW**	hawkbits
ABERTTUY	butyrate	**ABGILMNT**	bantling	**ABHIKSUZ**	buzkashi
ABFFGILN	baffling	**ABGILNNU**	Bulganin	**ABHILNOS**	hobnails
ABFFIILS	bailiffs	**ABGILNOR**	laboring	**ABHILNOT**	biathlon
ABFFINOS	banoffis	**ABGILNOT**	bloating	**ABHILOPS**	basophil
ABFFLLPU	puffball	**ABGILNRT**	blarting	**ABHILSST**	stablish
ABFFLOST	blastoff	**ABGILNRW**	brawling	**ABHILSTU**	halibuts
ABFFLOSU	buffalos		warbling	**ABHIMNOR**	Morbihan
ABFFNOTU	bouffant	**ABGILNST**	blasting	**ABHIOSST**	isobaths
ABFGLLOO	goofball		stabling	**ABHIOSTU**	hautbois
ABFGORUU	faubourg	**ABGILNSW**	bawlings	**ABHIRRSU**	airbrush
ABFHIORS	boarfish	**ABGILNTT**	battling	**ABHKOOOT**	boathook
ABFIILLR	fibrilla		blatting	**ABHLLMOT**	mothball
ABFIILMR	fimbrial	**ABGILNTY**	tangibly	**ABHLLOOY**	ballyhoo
ABFIILRR	fibrilar	**ABGILOOT**	obligato	**ABHLLPSU**	pushball
ABFILLLY	fallibly	**ABGILORS**	garboils	**ABHLOSUX**	boxhauls
ABFILNSU	basinful	**ABGILORW**	brigalow	**ABHLOSWW**	washbowl
ABFILSTU	fabulist	**ABGIMMNO**	mamboing	**ABHLPSUY**	subphyla
ABFIMORS	fibromas	**ABGIMOSU**	bigamous	**ABHLSSTU**	saltbush
ABFKLLOR	korfball		subimago	**ABHMNSUU**	subhuman
ABFLLOOT	football	**ABGINNOR**	aborning	**ABHMOORT**	bathroom
ABFLLOST	softball	**ABGINNRT**	Branting	**ABHOORST**	tarboosh
ABFLOSTU	boastful	**ABGINNST**	bantings	**ABHOOSTW**	showboat
ABFLOSTW	batfowls	**ABGINOOT**	tabooing	**ABHORRSU**	harbours
ABFLOSTY	flyboats	**ABGINORT**	aborting	**ABHOSTUY**	hautboys
ABFLOSUU	fabulous		borating	**ABHRSTTU**	Bathurst
ABFNORTU	turbofan	**ABGINOST**	boasting	**ABHSSTUW**	washtubs
ABFOOSTY	foyboats	**ABGINOUU**	Oubangui	**ABIIIKRT**	Kiribati
ABFORSTU	surfboat	**ABGINNTTU**	abutting	**ABIIINRS**	birianis
ABGGGILN	blagging	**ABGIRRSS**	ribgrass	**ABIIKKST**	kibitkas
ABGGGINR	bragging	**ABGKLOUV**	Bulgakov	**ABIIKLSS**	basilisk
ABGGILMN	gambling	**ABGKOOYZ**	Boğazköy	**ABIILLMR**	millibar
ABGGILNR	garbling	**ABGKORSW**	workbags	**ABIILLTY**	lability
ABGGNOOT	toboggan	**ABGLLLOY**	globally	**ABIILMNO**	binomial
ABGGORST	boggarts	**ABGLLNUW**	bungwall	**ABIILMNS**	albinism
ABGGRSUU	Augsburg	**ABGLLORU**	globular	**ABIILNNO**	Albinoni
ABGHHILL	highball	**ABGLLRUY**	bullyrag	**ABIILNOT**	libation
ABGHIINT	habiting	**ABGLMOPU**	plumbago	**ABIILNOV**	Bolivian
ABGHINWZ	whizbang	**ABGLNOOT**	longboat	**ABIILNRS**	brasilin
ABGHMORU	brougham	**ABGLNOUW**	bungalow	**ABIILNRY**	brainily
ABGHMOTU	Tombaugh	**ABGLORST**	ragbolts	**ABIILNRZ**	brazilin

ABIILNST	sibilant
ABIILNVY	inviably
ABIILPTY	pitiably
ABIIMNOT	ambition
ABIIMNRS	minibars
ABIINORS	robinias
ABIINRSY	biryanis
ABIIQQUU	Qu Qiu Bai
ABIIRRRU	Ibarruri
ABIIRRTZ	Biarritz
ABIIRSSV	vibrissa
ABIJLNRS	brinjals
ABIJLNTU	jubilant
ABIJNOST	banjoist
ABIKLLUY	baulkily
ABIKLMNS	lambkins
	lambskin
ABIKLMOU	kumbaloi
ABIKNORR	ironbark
ABIKNORU	Baikonur
ABIKNOUV	Bukovina
ABIKNRSY	Skryabin
ABIKRSST	britskas
ABIKRSTZ	britzkas
ABILLLPY	playbill
ABILLOVY	violably
ABILLRTY	tribally
ABILLSSW	sawbills
ABILLSWX	waxbills
ABILLSWY	waybills
ABILMNOU	olibanum
ABILMNSU	albumins
ABILMORS	laborism
ABILMPSU	Ipsambul
ABILNOOT	boltonia
	oblation
ABILNOTU	ablution
	abutilon
ABILNRTU	tribunal
	turbinal
ABILNRWY	brawnily
ABILNSTU	Istanbul
ABILOPRS	parboils
ABILORST	laborist
	orbitals
	strobila
ABILORSV	bolivars
ABILRSSY	brassily
ABILRSTU	subviral
ABILSSUY	issuably
ABILSTUY	suitably
ABIMNOSU	bimanous
ABIMNRSU	urbanism
ABIMORSU	biramous
ABIMPSST	baptisms
ABINOORS	boronias
ABINOORT	abortion
ABINOPTX	paintbox
ABINORST	Ratisbon
	taborins
ABINORSW	rainbows

ABINORTU	tabourin
ABINOSST	bastions
ABINOSTT	botanist
ABINRSTV	vibrants
ABINRTTY	Brittany
ABINRTUY	urbanity
ABIOORRV	Río Bravo
ABIOPRSU	biparous
ABIOPSTU	subtopia
ABIORRST	arborist
ABIORRTV	vibrator
ABIORSTV	vibratos
ABIORTUY	obituary
ABIPSSTT	baptists
ABIRRSTU	airburst
ABISSSST	bassists
ABJKMOSS	sjamboks
ABJKNOOS	Jakobson
ABKKMOOR	bookmark
ABKLLNOR	bankroll
ABKLOOPY	playbook
ABKLRSUW	bulwarks
ABKNOPST	stopbank
ABKNPRTU	bankrupt
ABKOOPSS	passbook
ABLLMOOR	ballroom
ABLLMOPW	blowlamp
ABLLMOSY	smallboy
ABLLNOOS	balloons
ABLLNOSW	snowball
ABLLORRS	rollbars
ABLLOSTY	tallboys
ABLLRTUY	brutally
ABLLSSUY	syllabus
ABLMNNTU	Bultmann
ABLMNRUU	alburnum
	laburnum
ABLNORYZ	blazonry
ABLNRSUY	Lansbury
ABLNSTUY	unstably
ABLOORTY	oblatory
ABLOPRSU	subpolar
ABLOPRTY	portably
ABLOPRVY	provably
ABLOPSYY	playboys
ABLORSST	borstals
ABLORSSU	subsolar
ABLORSTY	sortably
ABLOSSUU	sabulous
ABLOSTTU	subtotal
ABLPRTUY	abruptly
ABMOORRS	barrooms
ABMORSTU	tambours
ABMRRSUY	burramys
ABMRSUUU	Usumbura
ABNNORUV	von Braun
ABNOORRT	roborant
ABNOORYZ	bryozoan
ABNOOSSS	bassoons
ABNORSTY	barytons
ABNORTUU	runabout
ABNOSSUU	Aubusson

ABOORSTW	rowboats
ABOOSTTU	outboast
ABOOSTTW	towboats
ABPRSSTU	subparts
ACCCDILY	Cycladic
ACCCDIRU	Carducci
ACCCENPY	peccancy
ACCCFIIL	calcific
ACCCIILT	calcitic
ACCCIIPR	capricci
ACCCILLY	cyclical
ACCDDEKO	cockaded
ACCDDEOR	accorded
ACCDDIII	diacidic
ACCDDIIT	didactic
ACCDEEER	reaccede
ACCDEELN	canceled
ACCDEENS	cadences
ACCDEENT	accented
ACCDEEPT	accepted
ACCDEERS	acceders
ACCDEERT	accreted
ACCDEESS	accessed
ACCDEGIN	acceding
ACCDEHIK	chiacked
ACCDEHIL	chaliced
ACCDEHIN	chicaned
ACCDEHKY	chyacked
ACCDEILN	calcined
ACCDEILY	delicacy
ACCDEINO	decanoic
ACCDEINT	accident
ACCDEIRT	accredit
ACCDEISU	caudices
ACCDEKLR	crackled
ACCDEKOS	cockades
ACCDELSY	Cyclades
ACCDENOV	concaved
ACCDEORR	accorder
ACCDEOST	accosted
ACCDERSU	accursed
ACCDESUU	caduceus
	caucused
ACCDGHOO	coachdog
ACCDHIIR	diarchic
ACCDHIKW	Chadwick
ACCDHILS	chalcids
ACCDHIOT	cathodic
ACCDHIRY	dyarchic
ACCDIIOT	acidotic
ACCDIIST	dicastic
ACCDILTY	dactylic
ACCDINOR	cancroid
	draconic
ACCDIOOR	coracoid
ACCDITUY	caducity
ACCDOSUU	caducous
ACCEEHLO	cochleae
ACCEEHLS	caleches
ACCEEHMP	Campeche
ACCEEILR	celeriac
ACCEEILS	ecclesia

ACCEEIMN	MacNeice	**ACCEINRT**	acentric	**ACCHHOOW**	Chaochow
ACCEEKLN	necklace	**ACCEINRY**	Cyrenaic	**ACCHIIMS**	chiasmic
ACCEELNO	coenacle	**ACCEINSV**	vaccines	**ACCHIIRT**	rachitic
ACCEELNR	canceler	**ACCEIOPR**	cecropia	**ACCHIIST**	chiastic
	clarence	**ACCEIOTV**	coactive	**ACCHILNY**	chancily
ACCEELNS	cenacles	**ACCEIPRS**	caprices	**ACCHILOT**	catholic
ACCEELOS	coalesce	**ACCEIPRT**	practice	**ACCHILOY**	Chiclayo
ACCEELRT	calcrete	**ACCEIPSV**	peccavis	**ACCHIMOR**	achromic
ACCEENNS	nascence	**ACCEIQSU**	caciques	**ACCHINNO**	cinchona
ACCEENRT	reaccent	**ACCEIRRR**	ricercar	**ACCHINOS**	chicanos
ACCEENST	acescent	**ACCEIRSU**	curacies	**ACCHINPU**	capuchin
ACCEEPRT	accepter	**ACCEIRTU**	cruciate	**ACCHIORT**	thoracic
	reaccept	**ACCEISST**	ascetics		trochaic
ACCEERST	accretes	**ACCEISTT**	ecstatic	**ACCHIOSU**	acouchis
ACCEESSS	accesses	**ACCEKLNR**	cracknel	**ACCHKLOR**	charlock
ACCEFFIY	efficacy	**ACCEKLRS**	cacklers	**ACCHKOSY**	haycocks
ACCEFILS	fascicle		clackers	**ACCHMNOY**	Maconchy
ACCEFLSU	feluccas		crackles	**ACCHMRTY**	McCarthy
ACCEGKMO	gamecock	**ACCEKNOY**	Cockayne	**ACCHNNOT**	Connacht
ACCEHIKP	chickpea	**ACCEKOPS**	peacocks	**ACCHNNUY**	unchancy
ACCEHILM	alchemic	**ACCEKOSS**	seacocks	**ACCHNOOR**	coronach
	chemical	**ACCEKPSU**	cupcakes	**ACCHNOTU**	couchant
ACCEHILP	cephalic	**ACCEKRRS**	crackers	**ACCHNRUY**	craunchy
ACCEHILS	caliches	**ACCEKRST**	crackets	**ACCHOPSU**	pachucos
	chalices	**ACCELMNY**	cyclamen	**ACCHORTU**	cartouch
ACCEHIMN	mechanic	**ACCELNOS**	conceals	**ACCHORTY**	octarchy
ACCEHIMS	sachemic	**ACCELNOV**	conclave	**ACCHOSTW**	choctaws
ACCEHINO	anechoic	**ACCELNRU**	caruncle	**ACCHPSTU**	catchups
ACCEHINR	chancier	**ACCELORS**	coracles	**ACCHRRSU**	currachs
	chicaner	**ACCELRSY**	scarcely	**ACCHRSTY**	scratchy
ACCEHINS	chicanes	**ACCELSSU**	saccules	**ACCIIILN**	Cilician
ACCEHINT	catechin	**ACCENNSY**	nascency	**ACCIILLN**	clinical
ACCEHIRT	catchier	**ACCENORS**	conacres	**ACCIILMT**	climatic
ACCEHLNS	chancels	**ACCENORT**	accentor	**ACCIILNO**	iconical
ACCEHLOR	cochlear	**ACCENOST**	cosecant	**ACCIILRT**	critical
ACCEHLOT	catechol	**ACCENOSV**	concaves	**ACCIIMNN**	cinnamic
ACCEHMNO	coachmen	**ACCEOPRT**	acceptor	**ACCIINNO**	aniconic
ACCEHNNO	chaconne	**ACCEORST**	ectosarc	**ACCIINNP**	piccanin
ACCEHNOR	encroach	**ACCEORTU**	accouter	**ACCIINOT**	aconitic
ACCEHNRS	chancers		accoutre		cationic
	chancres	**ACCERSST**	scarcest		itaconic
ACCEHNRY	chancery	**ACCERSSU**	accusers	**ACCIINTY**	cyanitic
ACCEHOPT	cachepot	**ACCESSTU**	cactuses	**ACCIIOPT**	occipita
ACCEHORS	caroches	**ACCESSUU**	caucuses	**ACCIIRTX**	cicatrix
	coachers	**ACCFFLTU**	calctuff	**ACCIKKNN**	nicknack
ACCEHPSU	capuches	**ACCFHLTY**	catchfly	**ACCIKKRR**	rickrack
ACCEHRST	catchers	**ACCFLNOO**	confocal	**ACCIKKTT**	ticktack
	cratches	**ACCFOORT**	cofactor	**ACCIKLOT**	cocktail
ACCEIKLT	ticklace	**ACCGHINN**	chancing	**ACCIKRRS**	carricks
ACCEIKST	cackiest	**ACCGHINO**	coaching	**ACCILMUU**	aciculum
ACCEILLR	clerical	**ACCGHINT**	catching	**ACCILNOT**	lactonic
ACCEILLU	caulicle	**ACCGHIOR**	choragic	**ACCILNOV**	volcanic
ACCEILLV	clavicle	**ACCGHRSU**	Gracchus	**ACCILORT**	cortical
ACCEILNS	calcines	**ACCGIKLN**	cackling	**ACCILRRU**	circular
ACCEILNT	canticle		clacking	**ACCILSSS**	classics
ACCEILNY	calycine	**ACCGIKMR**	gimcrack	**ACCILTUU**	cuticula
ACCEILOS	calicoes	**ACCGIKNR**	cracking	**ACCIMNOS**	moccasin
ACCEILRV	cervical	**ACCGILOX**	coxalgic	**ACCIMORU**	coumaric
ACCEILTY	acetylic	**ACCGINRU**	accruing	**ACCIMPSU**	capsicum
ACCEIMNO	Comaneci	**ACCGINSU**	accusing	**ACCINOOS**	occasion
ACCEIMRS	ceramics	**ACCGLOOY**	cacology	**ACCINOOT**	coaction
ACCEINOT	acetonic	**ACCHHITT**	chitchat	**ACCINORS**	Corsican

ACCINORT	cratonic	**ACDDEILU**	decidual	**ACDEEIMR**	ceramide
	narcotic	**ACDDEINR**	riddance		medicare
ACCINORV	cavicorn	**ACDDEISU**	deciduas	**ACDEEIMT**	decimate
ACCINOTY	cyanotic	**ACDDEITT**	dictated		medicate
ACCINRSU	crucians	**ACDDEKLO**	deadlock	**ACDEEINN**	decennia
ACCIOPST	spiccato	**ACDDELOS**	cladodes		enneadic
ACCIORST	acrostic	**ACDDENTU**	adducent	**ACDEEINU**	audience
	Socratic	**ACDDEOPS**	decapods	**ACDEEINV**	deviance
ACCIORSY	isocracy	**ACDDEORR**	corraded	**ACDEEIRS**	deciares
ACCIOSTU	acoustic	**ACDDERSU**	crusaded	**ACDEEJKT**	jacketed
ACCIRRTT	trictrac	**ACDDERTU**	traduced	**ACDEEKLR**	lackered
ACCIRSTY	scarcity	**ACDDGILN**	cladding	**ACDEEKLY**	lackeyed
ACCISSTU	caustics	**ACDDGINU**	adducing	**ACDEEKNR**	cankered
ACCKKRSU	rucksack	**ACDDGINY**	caddying	**ACDEEKPR**	repacked
ACCKOOOT	cockatoo	**ACDDHHSU**	chuddahs	**ACDEEKRS**	screaked
ACCKOPRT	crackpot	**ACDDHIIO**	diadochi	**ACDEEKRT**	racketed
ACCKORST	stockcar	**ACDDHIOY**	diadochy	**ACDEELLR**	cellared
ACCKOSSS	cassocks	**ACDDHIRY**	hydracid		recalled
	cossacks	**ACDDHKOS**	haddocks	**ACDEELLS**	cadelles
ACCKPRSU	crackups		shaddock	**ACDEELMP**	emplaced
ACCLLNOY	cyclonal	**ACDDHRSU**	chuddars	**ACDEELNR**	calender
ACCLLOSU	occlusal	**ACDDIIOR**	cardioid	**ACDEELNS**	cleansed
ACCLLSUU	calculus	**ACDDILNY**	candidly	**ACDEELNT**	lanceted
ACCLMOSU	Moluccas	**ACDDILTY**	didactyl	**ACDEELPR**	parceled
ACCLSSUU	sacculus	**ACDDIRSS**	discards		replaced
ACCMNOOR	Moroccan	**ACDDKLNO**	dockland	**ACDEELRR**	declarer
ACCMOOSY	cocoyams	**ACDDKOPS**	paddocks	**ACDEELRS**	declares
ACCMOPST	compacts	**ACDDKORY**	dockyard	**ACDEELRT**	decretal
ACCMOSTU	accustom	**ACDDLMNO**	McDonald	**ACDEELRV**	clavered
ACCMRSUU	curcumas	**ACDDORTU**	adductor	**ACDEELSS**	declasse
ACCNOOPS	cocopans	**ACDEEEFT**	defecate		descales
ACCNOORS	raccoons	**ACDEEEKS**	seedcake	**ACDEEMNO**	codename
ACCNOOTU	cocoanut	**ACDEEEMR**	reedmace	**ACDEEMNP**	encamped
ACCNOPTU	occupant	**ACDEEENR**	careened	**ACDEEMRS**	screamed
ACCNORTT	contract	**ACDEEENT**	antecede	**ACDEEMRT**	cremated
ACCNOSTT	contacts	**ACDEEERR**	careered	**ACDEENNP**	penanced
ACCNOSTU	accounts	**ACDEEERS**	decrease	**ACDEENNT**	tendance
ACCOPSTY	copycats	**ACDEEESS**	deceases	**ACDEENOT**	anecdote
ACCOQSSU	squaccos		seedcase	**ACDEENRS**	ascender
ACCORRTY	carrycot	**ACDEEFFT**	affected		reascend
ACDDDEIT	addicted	**ACDEEFIN**	defiance	**ACDEENRT**	cantered
ACDDDETU	adducted	**ACDEEFIS**	casefied		crenated
ACDDEEES	deceased	**ACDEEFPR**	prefaced		decanter
ACDDEEHT	detached	**ACDEEFRS**	defacers		recanted
ACDDEEIT	dedicate	**ACDEEFTT**	facetted	**ACDEENRV**	caverned
ACDDEEIU	deciduae	**ACDEEGLY**	delegacy	**ACDEENRY**	carneyed
ACDDEELL	decalled	**ACDEEHIN**	echidnae		decenary
ACDDEELR	declared	**ACDEEHIR**	charidee	**ACDEENRZ**	credenza
ACDDEELS	descaled	**ACDEEHIV**	achieved	**ACDEENSV**	vendaces
ACDDEEMP	decamped	**ACDEEHLP**	pleached	**ACDEENTT**	dancette
ACDDEENR	credenda	**ACDEEHLT**	chelated	**ACDEEOPS**	peasecod
ACDDEENS	ascended	**ACDEEHMR**	demarche	**ACDEEORT**	decorate
ACDDEENT	decadent	**ACDEEHNN**	enhanced	**ACDEEPPR**	recapped
	decanted	**ACDEEHNS**	encashed	**ACDEEPRS**	escarped
ACDDEERT	redacted		enchased	**ACDEEPRT**	carpeted
ACDDEESU	Sadducee	**ACDEEHPR**	preached	**ACDEERRT**	cratered
ACDDEETU	educated	**ACDEEHRS**	searched		retraced
ACDDEHIK	dickhead	**ACDEEHRT**	detacher		terraced
ACDDEHKN	deckhand	**ACDEEHST**	detaches	**ACDEERSS**	caressed
ACDDEHRS	cheddars	**ACDEEIIP**	epicedia	**ACDEESTU**	educates
ACDDEIIL	deicidal	**ACDEEILT**	delicate	**ACDEESUX**	caudexes
ACDDEIIM	medicaid	**ACDEEILU**	aedicule	**ACDEFFLS**	sclaffed

ACDEFGIN	defacing	**ACDEIINR**	acridine	**ACDEIPSZ**	capsized
ACDEFHKU	headfuck	**ACDEIINS**	sciaenid	**ACDEIQRU**	acquired
ACDEFIIP	pacified	**ACDEIINT**	actinide	**ACDEIRSS**	Cressida
ACDEFILN	canfield		ctenidia		sidecars
ACDEFILR	filecard		indicate	**ACDEIRTT**	tetracid
ACDEFINN	financed	**ACDEIITV**	vaticide	**ACDEISTT**	dictates
ACDEFNOW	facedown	**ACDEIJNU**	jaundice	**ACDEKNPU**	unpacked
ACDEFORT	factored	**ACDEIKNP**	panicked	**ACDEKNTU**	untacked
ACDEFOTU	outfaced	**ACDEIKPX**	pickaxed	**ACDEKOST**	stockade
ACDEFRSU	surfaced	**ACDEILLM**	medallic	**ACDELLLW**	Caldwell
ACDEFRTU	furcated	**ACDEILLS**	cedillas	**ACDELLNO**	Candolle
ACDEGGRS	scragged	**ACDEILLV**	cavilled	**ACDELLOR**	carolled
ACDEGIIL	algicide	**ACDEILMS**	decimals		collared
ACDEGIKM	magicked		declaims	**ACDELLOT**	collated
ACDEGILN	decaling		medicals	**ACDELLSU**	callused
ACDEGIMR	grimaced	**ACDEILMT**	maledict	**ACDELMOR**	clamored
ACDEGINU	guidance	**ACDEILMX**	climaxed	**ACDELMOS**	Damocles
ACDEGINY	decaying	**ACDEILNP**	panicled	**ACDELMSU**	muscadel
ACDEGIRS	disgrace	**ACDEILNU**	dulcinea	**ACDELNOO**	canoodle
ACDEGKOS	dockages	**ACDEILNY**	adenylic	**ACDELNOR**	colander
ACDEGNOS	decagons	**ACDEILPS**	displace	**ACDELNPU**	unplaced
ACDEGORS	God's acre	**ACDEILPT**	plicated	**ACDELNRS**	candlers
ACDEHHNU	haunched	**ACDEILRS**	decrials	**ACDELOPT**	clodpate
ACDEHHRU	hachured		radicels	**ACDELRRS**	cradlers
ACDEHHTT	thatched		radicles	**ACDELRSS**	scalders
ACDEHIJK	hijacked	**ACDEILRT**	articled	**ACDELRSW**	scrawled
ACDEHILR	Heraclid	**ACDEILRU**	auricled	**ACDELRSY**	sacredly
	heraldic	**ACDEILST**	citadels	**ACDELSTU**	cauldest
ACDEHIMM	chammied		dialects	**ACDELSWW**	dewclaws
ACDEHIMN	machined	**ACDEILSY**	ecdysial	**ACDEMMRS**	scrammed
ACDEHIMS	schiedam	**ACDEILTT**	latticed	**ACDEMNOR**	romanced
ACDEHINR	inarched	**ACDEIMNO**	comedian	**ACDEMOPR**	compadre
	Red China		daemonic		compared
ACDEHINS	echidnas		demoniac	**ACDEMORS**	comrades
ACDEHIRS	rachides	**ACDEIMNP**	pandemic	**ACDEMORT**	democrat
ACDEHIRT	tracheid	**ACDEIMOR**	Mordecai	**ACDEMSTU**	muscadet
ACDEHIRV	archived	**ACDEIMPT**	impacted	**ACDEMUUV**	vacuumed
ACDEHKLO	headlock	**ACDEIMRT**	timecard	**ACDENNNO**	cannoned
ACDEHKLS	shackled	**ACDEIMSV**	medivacs	**ACDENNOR**	ordnance
ACDEHKOV	havocked	**ACDEINNR**	crannied	**ACDENNOT**	cantoned
ACDEHKRU	archduke	**ACDEINOP**	canopied	**ACDENNST**	scandent
ACDEHKTW	thwacked	**ACDEINOS**	diocesan	**ACDENOPR**	endocarp
ACDEHLNR	chandler		oceanids	**ACDENORS**	dracones
ACDEHLNU	launched	**ACDEINOT**	actioned	**ACDENORT**	cartoned
ACDEHLOR	Rochdale		catenoid	**ACDENORY**	crayoned
ACDEHNOR	anchored	**ACDEINOV**	voidance		deaconry
ACDEHNPU	paunched	**ACDEINPT**	pedantic	**ACDENOST**	endocast
ACDEHNST	snatched	**ACDEINRT**	dicentra		tacnodes
	stanched	**ACDEINSS**	acidness	**ACDENOTU**	outdance
ACDEHNSU	uncashed	**ACDEINST**	danciest	**ACDENPPU**	uncapped
ACDEHORR	hardcore		distance	**ACDENPST**	pandects
ACDEHORT	chordate	**ACDEINSY**	cyanides	**ACDENRSU**	durances
ACDEHOST	cathodes	**ACDEINTT**	nictated	**ACDENRTU**	underact
ACDEHOUV	avouched	**ACDEINTU**	incudate		untraced
ACDEHPST	despatch	**ACDEINVY**	deviancy	**ACDENRVY**	verdancy
ACDEHRRS	chresard	**ACDEIOPS**	diascope	**ACDENSST**	descants
ACDEHRST	starched	**ACDEIORS**	idocrase	**ACDENSUU**	uncaused
ACDEIILN	alcidine	**ACDEIORT**	ceratoid	**ACDEOORS**	doorcase
ACDEIILS	laicised	**ACDEIOSS**	acidoses	**ACDEOPRY**	copyread
ACDEIILT	ciliated	**ACDEIOSU**	edacious	**ACDEOPSS**	peascods
ACDEIILZ	laicized	**ACDEIPRS**	peracids	**ACDEOPTU**	outpaced
ACDEIIMU	aecidium	**ACDEIPSS**	spadices	**ACDEORRS**	corrades

ACDEORRT	redactor	**ACDIIILN**	indicial	**ACDIRSTT**	distract
ACDEORST	redcoats	**ACDIIJLU**	judicial	**ACDISTUV**	viaducts
ACDEORSU	caroused	**ACDIILMS**	disclaim	**ACDJNSTU**	adjuncts
ACDEORTU	educator	**ACDIILNO**	conidial	**ACDKLOPS**	padlocks
	outraced	**ACDIILSU**	suicidal	**ACDKMPSU**	mudpacks
ACDEORTV	cavorted	**ACDIILTY**	dialytic	**ACDLLORS**	collards
ACDEOTTU	outacted	**ACDIIMNO**	daimonic	**ACDLNOPU**	Coupland
ACDEPPRS	scrapped		Dominica	**ACDLNORS**	caldrons
ACDEPRSW	scrawped	**ACDIIMOR**	dioramic		Crosland
ACDEPRTU	captured	**ACDIIMOT**	diatomic	**ACDLNORU**	cauldron
ACDEPSTU	cuspated	**ACDIIMSU**	ascidium		Courland
ACDEQTUU	aqueduct	**ACDIINNO**	conidian	**ACDLNORY**	condylar
ACDERRSU	crusader	**ACDIINNT**	indicant	**ACDLNOST**	Scotland
ACDERRTU	traducer	**ACDIINOT**	actinoid	**ACDLOOOR**	colorado
ACDERSSU	crusades		diatonic	**ACDLOORT**	doctoral
ACDERSTT	detracts	**ACDIINPY**	pycnidia	**ACDLORWY**	cowardly
ACDERSTU	traduces	**ACDIIOPR**	DiCaprio	**ACDMMNOO**	commando
ACDFFHNU	handcuff	**ACDIIOSS**	acidosis	**ACDMMNOS**	commands
ACDFFIRT	diffract	**ACDIIRST**	arctiids	**ACDMNORY**	dormancy
ACDFFLOS	scaffold		carditis		mordancy
ACDFIILU	fiducial	**ACDIIRTY**	acridity	**ACDMOOSW**	camwoods
ACDFILOU	fucoidal	**ACDIISST**	sadistic	**ACDMORSZ**	czardoms
ACDFINOR	fricando	**ACDILLOT**	Clotilda	**ACDNNORU**	Cournand
ACDFIOST	factoids	**ACDILLOU**	caudillo	**ACDNOORS**	cardoons
ACDFORRW	Crawford	**ACDILLPY**	placidly	**ACDNOORT**	acrodont
ACDGHINY	dayching	**ACDILMOU**	mucoidal	**ACDNOORV**	cordovan
ACDGHOTW	dogwatch	**ACDILMSS**	cladisms	**ACDNOSTW**	downcast
	watchdog	**ACDILMTU**	talmudic	**ACDOORST**	ostracod
ACDGIILO	dialogic	**ACDILNOO**	conoidal	**ACDOPRST**	postcard
ACDGILNN	candling	**ACDILNOR**	ironclad	**ACDORSST**	costards
ACDGILNR	cradling	**ACDILNOT**	daltonic	**ACDORSSU**	crusados
ACDGILNS	scalding	**ACDILNSY**	syndical	**ACDORSUZ**	cruzados
ACDGIMOT	dogmatic	**ACDILNUU**	nudicaul	**ACDRSSTU**	custards
ACDGINNY	candying	**ACDILOPY**	polyadic	**ACDRSTTU**	dustcart
ACDGINRS	cardings	**ACDILORS**	cordials	**ACEEEFRR**	carefree
ACDGINSU	scauding	**ACDILORT**	dicrotal	**ACEEEGLN**	elegance
ACDGIOPR	podagric	**ACDILOUV**	oviducal	**ACEEEIPR**	earpiece
ACDGIRSU	Guiscard	**ACDILPSU**	cuspidal	**ACEEELMR**	cameleer
ACDGKLOS	daglocks	**ACDILSST**	cladists	**ACEEENRR**	careener
ACDGLNOO	golconda	**ACDILSTW**	wildcats	**ACEEENSV**	evanesce
ACDGORST	dogcarts	**ACDILSUU**	Claudius	**ACEEEPSS**	escapees
ACDHIILS	chiliads	**ACDIMNOO**	codomain	**ACEEERRT**	recreate
ACDHIIPS	diphasic		monoacid	**ACEEERTT**	etcetera
ACDHIIRR	Richard I	**ACDIMNSU**	scandium	**ACEEERTX**	execrate
ACDHIKNP	handpick	**ACDIMNSY**	dynamics	**ACEEESUV**	evacuees
ACDHILPR	pilchard	**ACDIMOOS**	camoodis	**ACEEFFIN**	caffeine
ACDHINOR	hadronic	**ACDINOPS**	spondaic	**ACEEFFRS**	effacers
ACDHINSW	sandwich	**ACDINORS**	sardonic	**ACEEFHWY**	wheyface
ACDHIOPS	scaphoid	**ACDINORT**	tornadic	**ACEEFINS**	fiancees
ACDHIORY	hyracoid	**ACDINORW**	cordwain	**ACEEFISS**	casefies
ACDHIPST	dispatch	**ACDINSST**	discants	**ACEEFLPU**	peaceful
ACDHIQRU	charquid	**ACDINSTY**	dynastic	**ACEEFLSS**	faceless
ACDHIRRS	Richards	**ACDIOPRS**	picadors	**ACEEFPRR**	prefacer
ACDHKORR	hardrock		sporadic	**ACEEFPRS**	prefaces
ACDHLNOR	chaldron	**ACDIORRS**	corridas	**ACEEFPRT**	praefect
	chlordan	**ACDIORSS**	sarcoids	**ACEEFPTY**	typeface
	chondral	**ACDIORST**	carotids	**ACEEFRSU**	farceuse
ACDHMNTU	dutchman	**ACDIORTT**	dictator	**ACEEGHNP**	Pechenga
ACDHNOSW	cowhands	**ACDIOSTX**	doxastic	**ACEEGHNX**	exchange
ACDHOOTW	woodchat	**ACDIOSTY**	dystocia	**ACEEGHRR**	recharge
ACDHOPRS	pochards	**ACDIOSXY**	oxyacids	**ACEEGILS**	elegiacs
ACDHORRS	orchards	**ACDIQRSU**	quadrics		legacies

227

ACEEGINR	Carnegie		reliance	**ACEELPTU**	peculate
ACEEGINS	agencies	**ACEEILNS**	salience	**ACEELPTY**	clypeate
ACEEGINT	agenetic	**ACEEILPS**	especial	**ACEELRRS**	clearers
ACEEGIRZ	graecize	**ACEEILSU**	Seleucia	**ACEELRSS**	careless
ACEEGKRW	wreckage	**ACEEIMRR**	creamier	**ACEELRST**	clearest
ACEEGLNY	elegancy		rearmice		treacles
ACEEGNOZ	cozenage	**ACEEIMRS**	casimere	**ACEELRSV**	cleavers
ACEEGNSV	scavenge		racemise	**ACEELRTU**	ulcerate
ACEEGORR	racegoer	**ACEEIMRZ**	racemize	**ACEELRTV**	cervelat
ACEEGORV	coverage	**ACEEINNR**	narceine	**ACEELRTX**	excretal
ACEEGSSU	escuages	**ACEEINPS**	sapience	**ACEELSST**	celestas
ACEEHHRU	heuchera	**ACEEINPT**	patience		selectas
ACEEHHST	cheetahs	**ACEEINRS**	increase	**ACEELSSY**	Les Cayes
ACEEHILM	Aleichem	**ACEEINRT**	centiare	**ACEELSTT**	telecast
ACEEHINS	Eisenach		creatine	**ACEELSVX**	exclaves
ACEEHINT	echinate		increate	**ACEEMNPS**	spacemen
ACEEHIPR	peachier		iterance	**ACEEMNRS**	menacers
ACEEHIPT	epitheca	**ACEEINST**	cineaste	**ACEEMNST**	casement
	petechia	**ACEEINTV**	enactive	**ACEEMOPR**	camporee
ACEEHIRT	hetaeric	**ACEEINTX**	exitance	**ACEEMORS**	racemose
ACEEHIRV	achiever	**ACEEIPST**	speciate	**ACEEMORV**	overcame
	chivaree	**ACEEIRRT**	Terceira	**ACEEMRRS**	amercers
ACEEHISV	achieves	**ACEEIRSU**	causerie		creamers
ACEEHKTT	hackette	**ACEEIRSW**	wiseacre		screamer
ACEEHLOS	shoelace	**ACEEIRTV**	creative	**ACEEMRRY**	creamery
ACEEHLPS	pleaches		reactive	**ACEEMRST**	cremates
ACEEHLRS	Heracles	**ACEEISTV**	vesicate	**ACEEMRTW**	crewmate
	leachers	**ACEEJKNS**	jackeens	**ACEENNPS**	penances
ACEEHLST	chelates	**ACEEKLMR**	mackerel	**ACEENNPZ**	Penzance
ACEEHLSW	eschewal	**ACEEKNPS**	kneecaps	**ACEENNRT**	entrance
ACEEHMNP	camphene	**ACEEKNRW**	neckwear	**ACEENNST**	canteens
ACEEHMNR	menarche	**ACEELLNS**	nacelles	**ACEENORT**	carotene
ACEEHMRS	cashmere	**ACEELLNT**	lancelet	**ACEENOST**	notecase
	marchese	**ACEELLOT**	ocellate	**ACEENPRR**	parcener
ACEEHMST	machetes	**ACEELLOV**	Lovelace	**ACEENRRT**	recanter
ACEEHNNR	enhancer	**ACEELLRR**	cellarer		recreant
ACEEHNNS	enhances	**ACEELLRT**	cellaret	**ACEENRSS**	casernes
ACEEHNPS	cheapens	**ACEELMNP**	placemen	**ACEENRST**	centares
ACEEHNRS	enchaser	**ACEELMPS**	emplaces		encastre
ACEEHNRT	Charente	**ACEELNOR**	Caerleon		reascent
ACEEHNSS	encashes	**ACEELNPR**	preclean		reenacts
	enchases	**ACEELNPT**	pentacle		sarcenet
ACEEHOOT	oothecae	**ACEELNRR**	larcener	**ACEENRSV**	cervenas
ACEEHPRR	preacher	**ACEELNRS**	cleaners	**ACEEPRRS**	caperers
ACEEHPRS	peachers		cleanser	**ACEEPRSS**	escapers
	preaches	**ACEELNRU**	cerulean	**ACEEPSTT**	spectate
ACEEHPST	cheapest	**ACEELNRW**	Lawrence	**ACEEPSTY**	typecase
ACEEHRRS	reachers	**ACEELNSS**	cleanses	**ACEERRSS**	caresser
	research	**ACEELNST**	cleanest		creasers
	searcher	**ACEELNSU**	nuclease	**ACEERRST**	caterers
ACEEHRSS	searches	**ACEELNSV**	enclaves		retraces
ACEEHRST	cheaters		valences		terraces
	hectares	**ACEELNTT**	tentacle	**ACEERRSU**	ecraseur
	teachers	**ACEELNTU**	nucleate	**ACEERRTT**	Carteret
ACEEHRTT	catheter	**ACEELOPS**	escalope	**ACEERRTU**	creature
ACEEHRTY	Cytherea		opalesce	**ACEERRUV**	verrucae
ACEEHSST	escheats	**ACEELORS**	escarole	**ACEERSSS**	caresses
ACEEHSTX	cathexes	**ACEELORT**	relocate	**ACEERSSS**	cerastes
ACEEIKLL	lacelike	**ACEELPRR**	replacer	**ACEERSSU**	surcease
ACEEIKRR	creakier	**ACEELPRS**	replaces	**ACEERSSV**	crevasse
ACEEILMR	Calimere	**ACEELPRV**	Perceval	**ACEERSTX**	exacters
ACEEILNR	careline	**ACEELPSY**	cypselae	**ACEERTTU**	eructate

ACEESSTT	cassette	**ACEGHIIT**	chigetai	**ACEGKLOS**	lockages
ACEFFGIN	effacing	**ACEGHIKN**	Chekiang	**ACEGKLRS**	grackles
ACEFFHIS	affiches	**ACEGHILN**	leaching	**ACEGKRTU**	truckage
ACEFFHRS	chaffers	**ACEGHILT**	lichgate	**ACEGLLNO**	collagen
ACEFFHRU	chauffer	**ACEGHINP**	peaching	**ACEGLLOS**	collages
ACEFFILY	Aycliffe	**ACEGHINR**	reaching	**ACEGLNOS**	congeals
ACEFFLLU	fullface	**ACEGHINT**	cheating		longcase
ACEFFLRS	sclaffer		teaching	**ACEGLNOT**	octangle
ACEFGINN	enfacing	**ACEGHIRR**	Argerich	**ACEGLNRS**	clangers
ACEFGINR	refacing	**ACEGHLTY**	lychgate	**ACEGLOSU**	cagoules
ACEFGINT	faceting	**ACEGHLUY**	gauchely	**ACEGMNOY**	geomancy
ACEFGIPS	pigfaces	**ACEGHNRS**	changers	**ACEGMNRS**	cragsmen
ACEFGLRU	graceful	**ACEGHOSU**	gouaches	**ACEGMOPS**	compages
ACEFHISV	cavefish	**ACEGHRRS**	chargers	**ACEGMRRY**	gramercy
ACEFHLNS	flanches	**ACEGIIMP**	epigamic	**ACEGNNOR**	crannoge
ACEFHMRS	chamfers	**ACEGIINV**	vicinage	**ACEGNNOY**	cyanogen
ACEFHORU	farouche	**ACEGIIRS**	Gaiseric	**ACEGNNRY**	regnancy
ACEFHRSU	chaufers	**ACEGIKNR**	creaking	**ACEGNNTY**	tangency
ACEFIIPR	pacifier	**ACEGILLO**	collegia	**ACEGNORS**	acrogens
ACEFIIPS	pacifies	**ACEGILLR**	allergic	**ACEGNOST**	cognates
ACEFIIRT	artifice	**ACEGILMU**	mucilage	**ACEGOPRY**	geocarpy
ACEFILLS	icefalls	**ACEGILNN**	cleaning	**ACEGORSS**	corsages
ACEFILLY	facilely		enlacing		socagers
ACEFILOP	epifocal	**ACEGILNO**	Angelico	**ACEGORST**	escargot
ACEFILOS	focalise	**ACEGILNR**	clearing	**ACEGORSV**	Cosgrave
ACEFILOZ	focalize	**ACEGILNT**	cleating	**ACEGORTT**	cottager
ACEFILRY	fireclay	**ACEGILNV**	cleaving	**ACEGORTY**	category
ACEFIMPR	campfire	**ACEGILNW**	lacewing	**ACEGOSTT**	cottages
ACEFINNS	finances	**ACEGILRS**	glaciers	**ACEGSSTU**	scutages
ACEFINRS	fanciers		Scaliger	**ACEHHINS**	Shechina
ACEFINSS	fascines	**ACEGILSS**	glacises	**ACEHHIPS**	cheapish
ACEFINST	fanciest	**ACEGIMMT**	tagmemic	**ACEHHIRR**	hierarch
ACEFIOSS	fiascoes	**ACEGIMNN**	menacing	**ACEHHIST**	shechita
ACEFIRRT	craftier	**ACEGIMNR**	amercing	**ACEHHLST**	hatchels
ACEFIRTT	trifecta		creaming	**ACEHHMNN**	henchman
ACEFLMNO	flamenco		germanic	**ACEHHNRT**	ethnarch
ACEFLNOR	falconer	**ACEGIMNS**	magnesic	**ACEHHNSU**	haunches
ACEFLNOT	conflate	**ACEGIMNT**	magnetic	**ACEHHNSV**	Cheshvan
	falconet	**ACEGIMOX**	exogamic	**ACEHHPRT**	heptarch
ACEFLNRY	cranefly	**ACEGIMRR**	grimacer	**ACEHHRST**	hatchers
ACEFLORS	alfresco	**ACEGIMRS**	grimaces	**ACEHHRSU**	hachures
ACEFLRTU	crateful	**ACEGIMTY**	megacity	**ACEHHRTT**	thatcher
ACEFLRUU	furculae	**ACEGINNO**	canoeing	**ACEHHRTY**	hatchery
ACEFNNOS	faconnes	**ACEGINNS**	encasing		thearchy
ACEFNORV	conferva	**ACEGINNT**	enacting	**ACEHHSTT**	hatchets
ACEFNRSU	furnaces	**ACEGINOS**	coinages		thatches
ACEFOOPT	footpace	**ACEGINOV**	gynoecia	**ACEHIIMS**	ischemia
ACEFORST	forecast	**ACEGINPR**	capering	**ACEHIIRT**	hetairic
ACEFOSTU	outfaces	**ACEGINPS**	escaping		hieratic
ACEFRRST	refracts	**ACEGINRS**	creasing	**ACEHIJKR**	hijacker
ACEFRRSU	farceurs		grecians	**ACEHIKLR**	chalkier
	surfacer	**ACEGINRT**	argentic	**ACEHIKRW**	whackier
ACEFRRTU	fracture		catering	**ACEHILLS**	Achilles
ACEFRSSU	surfaces		creating	**ACEHILMN**	inchmeal
ACEFRSTU	furcates		reacting	**ACEHILMS**	Macleish
ACEGGILN	cageling	**ACEGINRU**	Guernica	**ACEHILMV**	Malevich
	glaceing	**ACEGINSS**	caginess	**ACEHILNP**	cephalin
ACEGGILR	claggier	**ACEGINTT**	taceting	**ACEHILNT**	chatline
ACEGGINN	encaging	**ACEGINTX**	exacting		ethnical
ACEGGINT	Gangetic	**ACEGIOTT**	cogitate	**ACEHILOR**	heroical
ACEGGIRR	craggier	**ACEGIRST**	agrestic	**ACEHILPR**	parhelic
ACEGHHNT	Changteh		cigarets	**ACEHILPY**	peachily

ACEHILRS	Charles I	**ACEHLLST**	hellcats	**ACEHNSUZ**	Szechuan
	charlies	**ACEHLMNU**	Mulhacén	**ACEHNUVX**	Cuxhaven
ACEHILSS	Lachesis	**ACEHLNNS**	channels	**ACEHOPRR**	reproach
ACEHILTT	athletic	**ACEHLNOS**	chalones	**ACEHOPRS**	poachers
ACEHIMMS	chammies	**ACEHLNOU**	eulachon	**ACEHORRV**	overarch
ACEHIMNN	chainmen	**ACEHLNOY**	Halcyone	**ACEHORST**	thoraces
	Eichmann	**ACEHLNPT**	planchet	**ACEHORTT**	theocrat
ACEHIMNR	chairmen	**ACEHLNRS**	charnels	**ACEHORTU**	outreach
ACEHIMNS	machines	**ACEHLNRU**	launcher	**ACEHOSSW**	showcase
ACEHIMNT	anthemic		relaunch	**ACEHOSTU**	cathouse
ACEHIMPR	camphire	**ACEHLNRY**	Charnley		soutache
ACEHIMPT	empathic	**ACEHLNSU**	launches	**ACEHOSTY**	chayotes
	emphatic	**ACEHLOOT**	oothecal	**ACEHOSUV**	avouches
ACEHIMRS	chimeras	**ACEHLORS**	chorales	**ACEHPRRT**	Petrarch
	marchesi	**ACEHLORT**	chlorate	**ACEHPRST**	chapters
ACEHIMST	hematics		trochlea		patchers
	misteach	**ACEHLOST**	eschalot	**ACEHPRSU**	purchase
	tachisme	**ACEHLOSU**	Achelous	**ACEHRRSS**	crashers
ACEHIMTT	thematic	**ACEHLPRV**	chapelry	**ACEHRRST**	charters
ACEHINNS	enchains	**ACEHLPST**	chaplets		Chartres
ACEHINOT	ethanoic	**ACEHLRSS**	clashers		recharts
	inchoate	**ACEHLRSV**	Charles V		starcher
ACEHINOX	hexanoic	**ACEHLRSX**	Charles X	**ACEHRRSV**	charvers
ACEHINRS	archines	**ACEHLRSY**	charleys	**ACEHRRTT**	tetrarch
	inarches	**ACEHLRTU**	trauchle	**ACEHRSST**	starches
ACEHINRV	vacherin	**ACEHLSSS**	cashless	**ACEHRSSU**	chasseur
ACEHINSS	Anchises	**ACEHLSST**	satchels	**ACEHRSTT**	chatters
ACEHINST	asthenic	**ACEHLSTT**	chattels		ratchets
	chanties		latchets	**ACEHRSTW**	watchers
ACEHIPPS	chappies	**ACEHLSTY**	chastely	**ACEHRSTY**	Strachey
ACEHIPRS	seraphic	**ACEHMNRT**	merchant	**ACEHRTTY**	chattery
ACEHIPRT	chapiter	**ACEHMNSS**	chessman		trachyte
	patchier	**ACEHMNTW**	watchmen	**ACEHSSSU**	chausses
	phreatic	**ACEHMORT**	chromate	**ACEHSSTW**	swatches
ACEHIPST	hepatics	**ACEHMPRS**	champers	**ACEIILMN**	limacine
	pastiche	**ACEHMRRS**	charmers	**ACEIILMX**	Mexicali
ACEHIPTT	pathetic		marchers	**ACEIILNR**	irenical
ACEHIPTW	whitecap	**ACEHMRST**	matchers	**ACEIILNS**	salicine
ACEHIRSS	cashiers	**ACEHMSST**	smatches	**ACEIILNT**	Catiline
	rachises	**ACEHMSTT**	matchets	**ACEIILNX**	alexinic
ACEHIRST	chariest	**ACEHMSTU**	mustache	**ACEIILSS**	laicises
ACEHIRSU	eucharis	**ACEHNNPT**	penchant	**ACEIILST**	ciliates
ACEHIRSV	archives	**ACEHNNST**	enchants		silicate
ACEHIRTT	chattier	**ACEHNOPR**	Cape Horn	**ACEIILSZ**	laicizes
ACEHISST	chastise		chaperon	**ACEIIMSS**	aseismic
ACEHISTX	cathexis	**ACEHNOPT**	cenotaph	**ACEIIMTU**	maieutic
ACEHISTY	yachties	**ACEHNORR**	ranchero	**ACEIINPS**	piscinae
ACEHKLOV	havelock	**ACEHNPSU**	paunches	**ACEIINRT**	arenitic
ACEHKLPR	kreplach	**ACEHNRRS**	ranchers	**ACEIINTV**	inactive
ACEHKLRS	hacklers	**ACEHNRSS**	archness	**ACEIIPRS**	piracies
	shackler	**ACEHNRST**	chanters	**ACEIIRRT**	criteria
ACEHKLSS	shackles		snatcher	**ACEIISTV**	cavities
ACEHKLSV	Alchevsk		stancher	**ACEIJKSS**	jacksies
ACEHKLTY	latchkey		tranches	**ACEIJMST**	majestic
ACEHKNSY	hackneys	**ACEHNRTU**	chaunter	**ACEIKKLS**	sacklike
ACEHKORV	havocker	**ACEHNSST**	chastens	**ACEIKLLY**	claylike
ACEHKOSS	shackoes		snatches	**ACEIKLRY**	creakily
ACEHKRSW	whackers		stanches	**ACEIKMNN**	nickname
ACEHKRTW	thwacker	**ACEHNSTT**	etchants	**ACEIKMRS**	keramics
ACEHLLOO	coalhole	**ACEHNSTU**	nautches	**ACEIKMRV**	maverick
ACEHLLPP	Chappell		unchaste	**ACEIKNPS**	capeskin
ACEHLLSS	shellacs	**ACEHNSTY**	chanteys	**ACEIKNRR**	crankier

ACEIKOTW	Katowice	**ACEILOTV**	locative	**ACEINNST**	ancients
ACEIKPSX	pickaxes	**ACEILOVZ**	vocalize		canniest
ACEIKSTT	tackiest	**ACEILPPY**	pipeclay		insectan
ACEIKSTW	wackiest	**ACEILPRS**	calipers		instance
ACEILLLT	clitella		replicas	**ACEINNSU**	nuisance
ACEILLMR	micellar		spiracle	**ACEINNSY**	cyanines
	millrace	**ACEILPRT**	particle	**ACEINNTU**	uncinate
ACEILLMS	micellas		prelatic	**ACEINOPR**	apocrine
ACEILLMT	metallic	**ACEILPRU**	peculiar		Poincaré
ACEILLMY	mycelial	**ACEILPRV**	Percival		procaine
ACEILLNT	cliental	**ACEILPSS**	slipcase	**ACEINOPS**	canopies
ACEILLOP	calliope		specials		caponise
ACEILLOR	rocaille	**ACEILPST**	tieclasp	**ACEINOPZ**	caponize
ACEILLOS	localise	**ACEILPXY**	epicalyx	**ACEINORS**	scenario
ACEILLOT	teocalli	**ACEILRRT**	clartier	**ACEINORT**	actioner
ACEILLOZ	localize	**ACEILRRW**	crawlier		creation
ACEILLPR	calliper	**ACEILRSS**	classier		reaction
ACEILLPS	allspice	**ACEILRST**	altrices	**ACEINORV**	veronica
ACEILLRS	Carlisle		articles	**ACEINORX**	anorexic
ACEILLRV	caviller		recitals	**ACEINOST**	aconites
ACEILLSS	scallies		sterical		canoeist
ACEILMMO	camomile	**ACEILRSU**	auricles	**ACEINOTT**	taconite
ACEILMMR	clammier		Escurial	**ACEINOTV**	conative
ACEILMNP	manciple	**ACEILRSV**	claviers		invocate
ACEILMNS	mescalin		visceral	**ACEINOTX**	exaction
ACEILMOS	camisole	**ACEILRTT**	tractile	**ACEINPSS**	inscapes
ACEILMPS	misplace	**ACEILRTU**	Lucretia	**ACEINPTT**	pittance
ACEILMRS	claimers		reticula	**ACEINPUY**	picayune
	miracles	**ACEILRTV**	vertical	**ACEINRRU**	curarine
	reclaims	**ACEILRTY**	literacy	**ACEINRRY**	cinerary
ACEILMRT	metrical	**ACEILSST**	Alcestis	**ACEINRSS**	raciness
ACEILMRY	creamily		elastics	**ACEINRST**	canister
ACEILMST	clematis		salicets		cisterna
	climates		scaliest		scantier
ACEILMSU	musicale	**ACEILSTT**	lattices	**ACEINRTT**	interact
ACEILMSX	climaxes	**ACEILTVY**	actively	**ACEINRTU**	Cernăuţi
	exclaims	**ACEIMMNP**	pemmican	**ACEINRTV**	navicert
ACEILNNP	pinnacle	**ACEIMMOS**	semicoma	**ACEINRVY**	vicenary
ACEILNOR	acrolein	**ACEIMMRS**	racemism	**ACEINSSU**	issuance
	lonicera	**ACEIMMTT**	metamict	**ACEINSTT**	cantiest
ACEILNPS	capelins	**ACEIMNOX**	anoxemic		nictates
	panicles	**ACEIMNPS**	pemicans		tetanics
	pelicans	**ACEIMNRU**	manicure	**ACEINSTV**	vesicant
ACEILNRS	carlines	**ACEIMNSS**	amnesics	**ACEINSTZ**	zincates
ACEILNRT	clarinet	**ACEIMNST**	semantic	**ACEINTTU**	tunicate
ACEILNSS	laciness	**ACEIMNSY**	sycamine	**ACEINTTX**	excitant
	sanicles	**ACEIMOTX**	toxaemic	**ACEINTTY**	tenacity
ACEILNSU	lunacies	**ACEIMOTZ**	azotemic	**ACEIOPRT**	aporetic
ACEILNSY	saliency		metazoic		operatic
ACEILOPR	capriole	**ACEIMPSS**	escapism	**ACEIORSS**	scariose
ACEILOPT	poetical	**ACEIMPST**	campiest	**ACEIORSV**	varicose
ACEILORR	carriole		campsite	**ACEIOSSU**	caesious
ACEILORS	calories	**ACEIMRST**	ceramist	**ACEIOTVV**	vocative
	carioles		matrices	**ACEIPPRR**	pericarp
	Escorial	**ACEIMRTU**	muricate	**ACEIPPRS**	crappies
ACEILORT	erotical	**ACEIMSTU**	autecism		epicarps
	loricate	**ACEIMTTU**	muticate	**ACEIPRRS**	perisarc
ACEILORZ	calorize	**ACEINNOS**	canonise	**ACEIPRST**	crispate
ACEILOSS	celosias	**ACEINNOT**	enaction		picrates
ACEILOST	societal	**ACEINNOZ**	canonize		practise
ACEILOSV	vocalise	**ACEINNPS**	pinnaces	**ACEIPRTY**	apyretic
ACEILOSX	saxicole	**ACEINNRS**	crannies	**ACEIPSST**	escapist

	spaciest		stackers		lacrosse
ACEIPSSU	auspices	**ACELLLRU**	cellular		solacers
ACEIPSSZ	capsizes	**ACELLNOT**	Lancelot	**ACELORST**	locaters
ACEIPSTV	captives	**ACELLNRU**	nucellar		sectoral
ACEIQRRU	acquirer	**ACELLNRW**	Cranwell	**ACELORSU**	carousel
ACEIQRSU	acquires	**ACELLOPS**	collapse	**ACELORSY**	caloyers
ACEIQSUZ	caziques		escallop		coarsely
ACEIRRRS	carriers	**ACELLORR**	caroller	**ACELOSST**	alecosts
ACEIRRSS	Cassirer	**ACELLORS**	corellas	**ACELOSTT**	calottes
ACEIRRST	erratics	**ACELLORV**	coverall	**ACELOSTU**	osculate
ACEIRRSU	curarise		overcall	**ACELOSTY**	acolytes
ACEIRRSW	aircrews	**ACELLOST**	collates	**ACELOSUV**	vacuoles
	airscrew	**ACELLOSW**	coleslaw	**ACELOTTY**	catolyte
ACEIRRTX	creatrix	**ACELLOTU**	loculate	**ACELPPRS**	clappers
ACEIRRUZ	curarize	**ACELLOVY**	coevally		scrapple
ACEIRSST	Castries	**ACELLPSS**	scalpels	**ACELPRSS**	claspers
	scariest	**ACELLRRS**	carrells		scalpers
ACEIRSTT	citrates	**ACELLRTY**	rectally	**ACELPRST**	spectral
	cristate	**ACELLSSU**	calluses	**ACELPRSU**	specular
	scattier	**ACELLSSW**	clawless	**ACELPSSU**	capsules
ACEIRSTU	suricate	**ACELLSTU**	scutella	**ACELPTUU**	cupulate
ACEIRSTZ	craziest	**ACELMNNS**	clansmen	**ACELPTUY**	eucalypt
ACEIRTTU	urticate	**ACELMNOR**	cornmeal	**ACELQRSU**	lacquers
ACEIRTTV	tractive	**ACELMNSS**	calmness	**ACELQSUY**	lacqueys
ACEIRTUV	curative	**ACELMOPT**	compleat	**ACELRRSW**	crawlers
ACEIRTVY	veracity	**ACELMORR**	clamorer		scrawler
ACEISSTU	sauciest	**ACELMORS**	scleroma	**ACELRSSS**	classers
	suitcase	**ACELMORY**	claymore	**ACELRSSU**	seculars
ACEISTTT	cattiest	**ACELMOSU**	leucomas	**ACELRSTT**	clatters
ACEISTTU	eustatic	**ACELMPRS**	clampers	**ACELRTTU**	cultrate
ACEJKOOR	jackeroo	**ACELMSTU**	calumets	**ACELRTTY**	clattery
ACEJLORS	cajolers		muscatel	**ACELSSTT**	tactless
ACEJLORY	cajolery	**ACELMTUU**	cumulate	**ACELSUUV**	Vaucluse
ACEJNOST	jaconets	**ACELNNRS**	scrannel	**ACEMMOTY**	mycetoma
ACEJNOSY	joyances	**ACELNOOT**	ecotonal	**ACEMMRRS**	crammers
ACEJNRRY	jerrycan	**ACELNORT**	Coltrane	**ACEMMRSS**	scammers
ACEJPSTU	cajeputs	**ACELNORV**	novercal	**ACEMNOOR**	Cameroon
ACEJRSTT	trajects	**ACELNOST**	lactones	**ACEMNORR**	romancer
ACEKKMRU	muckrake	**ACELNOSU**	lacunose	**ACEMNORS**	romances
ACEKKNRS	knackers	**ACELNOSZ**	calzones	**ACEMNORU**	Cameroun
ACEKKNRY	knackery	**ACELNOTV**	covalent	**ACEMNRUY**	numeracy
ACEKLNSS	slackens	**ACELNPSS**	enclasps	**ACEMOOST**	comatose
ACEKLORV	laverock		spancels	**ACEMOPRR**	comparer
ACEKLPST	plackets	**ACELNPST**	clapnets	**ACEMOPRS**	compares
ACEKLRSS	slackers	**ACELNPSU**	cleanups		mesocarp
ACEKLRST	tacklers	**ACELNRSU**	lucarnes	**ACEMOPRT**	mercapto
ACEKLRSU	caulkers	**ACELNRVY**	cravenly	**ACEMORRT**	cremator
ACEKLSST	slackest	**ACELNSSU**	scalenus		Mercator
	tackless	**ACELNSTY**	secantly	**ACEMORSU**	racemous
ACEKMNRT	trackmen	**ACELOOSS**	Colossae	**ACEMORSW**	caseworm
ACEKMNST	tacksmen	**ACELOPPU**	populace	**ACEMORSY**	sycamore
ACEKMRSS	smackers	**ACELOPRS**	parclose	**ACEMORTY**	cometary
ACEKNPRU	unpacker		polacres	**ACEMORUX**	morceaux
ACEKNRST	crankest	**ACELOPRT**	pectoral	**ACEMPRRS**	crampers
ACEKOPRY	Cape York	**ACELOPRU**	opercula	**ACEMPRSS**	scampers
ACEKORRS	croakers	**ACELOPST**	polecats	**ACEMPSSU**	campuses
ACEKORSW	casework	**ACELOPSU**	scopulae	**ACEMRSST**	scamster
ACEKPPRS	prepacks	**ACELOPTU**	calotype	**ACENNNOU**	announce
ACEKPSSY	skyscape	**ACELOPTY**	calotype	**ACENNOSS**	canoness
ACEKQRUY	quackery	**ACELOQSU**	coequals	**ACENNOTT**	cotenant
ACEKRRST	trackers	**ACELORRS**	carolers	**ACENNOTV**	covenant
ACEKRSST	restacks	**ACELORSS**	escolars	**ACENNOTZ**	canzonet

ACENNRSS	scanners	ACERRSTT	retracts	ACFLORSU	scrofula
ACENOPRW	Cawnpore	ACERRSUV	verrucas	ACFLOTTU	floatcut
ACENOPST	capstone	ACERRUVZ	Veracruz	ACFLOTUU	Foucault
	opencast	ACERSSTT	scatters	ACFLRSTU	cartfuls
ACENOPTW	Cape Town	ACERSSTY	actressy	ACFMOTTU	factotum
ACENOQTU	cotquean	ACERSSUY	Syracuse	ACGGGILN	clagging
ACENORRT	Torrance	ACERSTTX	extracts	ACGGGINS	scagging
ACENORRW	careworn	ACERSTTY	cytaster	ACGGHINN	changing
ACENORSS	coarsens	ACERTTUW	cutwater	ACGGHINR	charging
ACENORST	ancestor	ACFFGHIN	chaffing	ACGGIINT	gigantic
	enactors	ACFFIILO	official	ACGGIIOS	isagogic
ACENORSU	nacreous	ACFFIIST	caitiffs	ACGGILNN	clanging
ACENORTU	courante	ACFFIKMS	mafficks		glancing
ACENORTY	enactory	ACFFILNU	fanciful	ACGGILRY	craggily
ACENOSSV	cavesson	ACFFILST	afflicts	ACGGINNO	congaing
ACENOSTV	centavos	ACFFIRST	traffics	ACGGLNOU	glucagon
ACENPRRS	prancers	ACFFLOSW	scofflaw	ACGGLRSY	scraggly
ACENPTTU	punctate	ACFFOSST	castoffs	ACGHHIIN	Chinghai
ACENRSTT	transect	ACFGHITT	catfight	ACGHHIJK	highjack
ACENRSTU	centaurs	ACFGIIMN	magnific	ACGHHINT	hatching
	recusant	ACFGIIPR	caprifig	ACGHHNOW	Hangchow
ACENRSTY	ancestry	ACFGINNY	fancying	ACGHIIMN	michigan
ACENRTTU	truncate	ACFGINRS	scarfing	ACGHIINN	chaining
ACENRTUY	centaury	ACFGINRT	crafting	ACGHIINR	chairing
ACENSSTU	nutcases	ACFGITUY	fugacity	ACGHIKLN	hackling
ACENSSTW	newscast	ACFHHINW	hawfinch	ACGHIKNS	shacking
ACEOOPSU	poaceous	ACFHIJKS	jackfish	ACGHIKNU	Chu Kiang
ACEOORTV	evocator	ACFHILNO	falchion	ACGHIKNW	whacking
	overcoat	ACFHILOS	coalfish	ACGHILNS	clashing
ACEOPPRS	copperas	ACFHIRSW	crawfish	ACGHILNY	achingly
ACEOPRSX	exocarps	ACFHIRSY	crayfish	ACGHILOR	oligarch
ACEOPRTT	attercop	ACFHISSU	fuchsias	ACGHIMNP	champing
ACEOPSTU	outpaces	ACFHLTUW	watchful	ACGHIMNR	charming
ACEORRST	acroters	ACFHMNOR	chamfron		marching
	creators	ACFHNNOR	chanfron	ACGHIMNT	matching
	reactors	ACFHORST	Ashcroft	ACGHINNN	Nan-ching
ACEORRSU	carouser	ACFHRSTU	futharcs	ACGHINNR	ranching
ACEORRTT	retroact	ACFIILTY	facility	ACGHINNT	chanting
ACEORRTU	eurocrat	ACFIIMPS	pacifism	ACGHINOP	poaching
ACEORRTV	cavorter	ACFIINRS	Francis I	ACGHINOT	Chingtao
ACEORSST	coarsest	ACFIIPST	pacifist	ACGHINPP	chapping
	coasters	ACFIKLNS	calfskin	ACGHINPR	parching
	Socrates	ACFILLSY	fiscally	ACGHINPT	nightcap
ACEORSSU	carouses	ACFILNOR	fornical		patching
ACEORSTU	outraces	ACFILNOT	califont	ACGHINRR	charring
ACEORSTV	overacts	ACFILORT	trifocal	ACGHINRS	chagrins
	overcast	ACFILRTY	craftily		crashing
ACEORSTX	exactors	ACFILSSY	classify	ACGHINRT	charting
ACEOSTTU	outcaste	ACFIMNRU	francium	ACGHINRU	churinga
ACEOSTUU	autocues	ACFINORT	fraction	ACGHINST	scathing
	Cousteau	ACFINOST	factions	ACGHINSW	chinwags
ACEOTUUX	couteaux	ACFINRST	infarcts	ACGHINTT	chatting
ACEOTUXY	auxocyte		infracts	ACGHINTU	Taichung
ACEPRRSS	scarpers	ACFINSTY	sanctify	ACGHINTW	watching
	scrapers	ACFIOSTU	factious	ACGHINTY	yachting
ACEPRRSU	supercar	ACFISSST	fascists	ACGHIPRS	graphics
ACEPRRTU	capturer	ACFKLOST	lockfast	ACGHLLOR	gralloch
ACEPRSST	precasts	ACFKLSSU	sackfuls	ACGHLOOY	chaology
ACEPRSSU	scaupers	ACFKOSTT	fatstock	ACGHNRVY	gynarchy
ACEPRSTU	captures	ACFLMNOO	mooncalf	ACGHNTUU	uncaught
ACEPSTTY	typecast	ACFLNORY	falconry	ACGHOPUV	Pugachov
ACEQRSTU	racquets	ACFLOOPS	foolscap	ACGHORSU	choragus

ACGHRRSU	curraghs	**ACGINORS**	organics	**ACHIKRSS**	rickshas
ACGIILMN	claiming	**ACGINOST**	agnostic	**ACHIKRSW**	rickshaw
ACGIILNN	inlacing		coasting	**ACHIKRSY**	hayricks
ACGIILNO	logician		coatings	**ACHILMRS**	chrismal
ACGIILNV	caviling		cotingas	**ACHILMTY**	mythical
ACGIINNS	incasing	**ACGINPPR**	crapping	**ACHILNNS**	clannish
ACGIINRT	granitic	**ACGINPRS**	scarping	**ACHILNOS**	Nicholas
ACGIJLNO	cajoling		scraping	**ACHILOPU**	pachouli
ACGIKLMN	mackling	**ACGINPSS**	spacings	**ACHILORT**	acrolith
ACGIKLNN	clanking	**ACGINRRS**	scarring	**ACHILPSY**	physical
ACGIKLNO	cloaking	**ACGINRRY**	carrying	**ACHILPTY**	patchily
ACGIKLNS	slacking	**ACGINRST**	scarting	**ACHILRVY**	chivalry
ACGIKLNT	tackling		tracings	**ACHILTTY**	chattily
	talcking	**ACGINRSU**	Granicus	**ACHIMMOS**	machismo
ACGIKLNU	caulking	**ACGINRSV**	carvings	**ACHIMMST**	mismatch
ACGIKLRY	garlicky		cravings	**ACHIMNOP**	champion
ACGIKMNS	smacking	**ACGINSST**	castings	**ACHIMNOR**	harmonic
ACGIKNNR	cranking	**ACGINSTT**	scatting	**ACHIMNOS**	mohicans
ACGIKNNS	snacking	**ACGIOORS**	gracioso	**ACHIMNOX**	Chamonix
ACGIKNOR	croaking	**ACGIORST**	orgastic	**ACHIMNPT**	pitchman
ACGIKNPS	packings	**ACGIORSU**	gracious	**ACHIMNSU**	inasmuch
ACGIKNQU	quacking	**ACGIPRSY**	spagyric	**ACHIMOPR**	amphoric
ACGIKNRT	tracking	**ACGJLNOU**	conjugal	**ACHIMPSS**	scampish
ACGIKNRW	wracking	**ACGLMOUU**	coagulum	**ACHIMRSS**	charisms
ACGIKNST	stacking	**ACGLNORS**	clangors	**ACHIMRST**	chartism
ACGILLNS	callings	**ACGLNORU**	clangour	**ACHIMSSU**	chiasmus
ACGILLRS	Scargill	**ACGLOOPS**	Glooscap	**ACHINNSU**	anchusin
ACGILMMN	clamming	**ACGLOSUU**	glaucous		unchains
ACGILMNO	gnomical	**ACGLSSTU**	cutglass	**ACHINNUY**	Yinchuan
ACGILMNP	clamping	**ACGNNOOT**	contango	**ACHINORS**	Niarchos
ACGILMTU	glutamic	**ACGNNORS**	crannogs	**ACHINORT**	anorthic
ACGILNNU	unlacing	**ACGNOOST**	octagons	**ACHINOTZ**	hoactzin
ACGILNOP	Polignac	**ACGNORST**	congrats	**ACHINSTY**	Scythian
ACGILNOR	caroling	**ACHHIIMS**	Chishima	**ACHIOPRT**	atrophic
ACGILNOS	solacing	**ACHHILMS**	Hamlisch	**ACHIOPSS**	isopachs
ACGILNOT	locating	**ACHHILPT**	phthalic	**ACHIORST**	chariots
ACGILNPP	clapping	**ACHHINRU**	Nurhachi		haricots
ACGILNPS	clasping	**ACHHINTW**	whinchat	**ACHIORTV**	tovarich
	scalping	**ACHHINTY**	hyacinth	**ACHIOSST**	isotachs
ACGILNQU	calquing	**ACHHIPPR**	hipparch	**ACHIPPSS**	sapphics
ACGILNRS	carlings	**ACHHLLOT**	challoth	**ACHIPRRT**	parritch
ACGILNRW	crawling	**ACHHLNOR**	rhonchal		phratric
ACGILNSS	classing	**ACHHLORY**	holarchy	**ACHIPTTU**	chupatti
ACGILNST	castling	**ACHHNTTU**	nuthatch	**ACHIRRTY**	triarchy
	catlings	**ACHHOOUZ**	Chaozhou	**ACHIRSTT**	chartist
ACGILNUY	guanylic	**ACHHPPSU**	chuppahs	**ACHIRSTU**	haircuts
ACGILRSU	surgical	**ACHHPTUZ**	chutzpah	**ACHISTTY**	chastity
ACGIMMNR	cramming	**ACHIILMS**	chiliasm	**ACHKKORW**	hackwork
ACGIMMNS	scamming	**ACHIILPT**	haplitic	**ACHKMMOS**	hammocks
ACGIMNOS	coamings	**ACHIILST**	chiliast	**ACHKMORS**	shamrock
ACGIMNPR	cramping	**ACHIINPS**	Hispanic	**ACHKNOOT**	canthook
ACGIMNPS	campings	**ACHIINRT**	trichina	**ACHKOSSS**	hassocks
	scamping	**ACHIINST**	chiantis	**ACHLLOOS**	alcohols
ACGIMNSY	syngamic	**ACHIINSU**	Chișinău	**ACHLLORY**	chorally
ACGIMORS	orgasmic	**ACHIIRST**	rachitis	**ACHLMSTZ**	schmaltz
ACGIMOUU	guaiocum	**ACHIJNST**	jacinths	**ACHLNORT**	Charlton
ACGINNNS	cannings	**ACHIKKSW**	kickshaw	**ACHLNOSY**	halcyons
	scanning	**ACHIKLMV**	hickymal	**ACHLOPRT**	calthrop
ACGINNPR	prancing	**ACHIKLPT**	chalkpit	**ACHLOPTT**	potlatch
ACGINNRT	trancing	**ACHIKNOP**	pachinko	**ACHLORSS**	scholars
ACGINNRY	carnying	**ACHIKOOW**	Kiaochow	**ACHLOSSW**	salchows
ACGINNST	scanting	**ACHIKQSU**	quackish	**ACHLOTWX**	waxcloth

ACHLPRTU	Plutarch	ACIIMTUV	viaticum	ACILNORS	clarinos
ACHMNNSU	Schumann	ACIINNOS	Socinian		clarions
ACHMNORS	monarchs	ACIINNOT	inaction	ACILNORT	cilantro
	nomarchs	ACIINNQU	cinquain		contrail
ACHMNORY	monarchy	ACIINNRV	nirvanic	ACILNOSU	unsocial
	nomarchy	ACIINOPT	optician	ACILNOUV	univocal
ACHMOORT	chatroom	ACIINORZ	zirconia	ACILNRSU	cislunar
ACHMOSST	stomachs	ACIINOSV	avionics	ACILNRUY	culinary
ACHMOSTY	stomachy	ACIINOTT	citation		uranylic
ACHMOTTU	outmatch	ACIINPRS	Priscian	ACILNSTU	lunatics
ACHMSSUW	cumshaws	ACIINPSS	piscinas		sultanic
ACHNORXY	chronaxy	ACIINRSS	narcissi	ACILNSTY	scantily
ACHNOSTY	tachyons	ACIINRTU	uranitic	ACILOPRT	tropical
ACHNPPSS	schnapps	ACIIORST	aoristic	ACILOPST	postical
ACHNRSYY	synarchy		Iscariot	ACILORRV	corrival
ACHOORTU	coauthor	ACIIORTV	victoria	ACILORTV	vortical
ACHOPRST	toparchs	ACIIPPST	papistic	ACILOSTV	vocalist
ACHOPRSY	charpoys	ACIIRSTT	artistic	ACILOTVY	vocality
ACHOPRTY	toparchy	ACIISTTT	atticist	ACILPSST	plastics
ACHOTTUW	watchout	ACIISTTU	autistic	ACILRSTU	curtails
ACHPRSTU	pushcart	ACIISTTV	activist	ACILRTUV	cultivar
ACHPTTUY	chupatty	ACIITTVY	activity	ACILSSST	classist
ACHRRTUY	craythur	ACIITVVY	vivacity	ACILSSUU	Clausius
ACIIILMN	inimical	ACIJKKPS	skipjack	ACILSTTY	scattily
ACIIILNS	Sicilian	ACIJSUZZ	jacuzzis	ACILSTUV	victuals
ACIIILNV	civilian	ACIKLMNV	Vlaminck	ACILSTVY	sylvatic
ACIIINST	isatinic	ACIKLNOT	antilock	ACIMMTUY	cymatium
	Sinaitic	ACIKLNRY	crankily	ACIMNNNO	cinnamon
ACIIKLNO	kaolinic	ACIKLNSU	Nicklaus	ACIMNNOR	Minorcan
ACIIKNNN	cannikin	ACIKLORS	airlocks	ACIMNOOR	acromion
ACIIKNNS	canikins	ACIKLORY	croakily	ACIMNOPS	campions
ACIIKNTY	kyanitic	ACIKNNPR	crankpin	ACIMNORT	romantic
ACIIKPRT	paitrick	ACILLLNY	clinally	ACIMNORU	coumarin
ACIILLNV	vanillic	ACILLLOP	pollical	ACIMNORY	acrimony
ACIILLSU	silicula	ACILLMMN	McMillan	ACIMNOST	monastic
ACIILLTV	villatic	ACILLMMY	clammily	ACIMNOTU	aconitum
ACIILMNR	criminal	ACILLMOS	localism	ACIMNPTY	tympanic
ACIILMOT	comitial	ACILLMSS	miscalls	ACIMNRSU	craniums
ACIILMPT	palmitic	ACILLNOO	colonial	ACIMOPST	apomicts
ACIILMSS	laicisms	ACILLNOR	carillon	ACIMORSY	cramoisy
ACIILNOR	ironical	ACILLNOS	scallion	ACIMOSST	massicot
ACIILNPS	piscinal	ACILLNUY	uncially	ACIMOSTT	stomatic
ACIILNPT	platinic	ACILLOQU	coquilla	ACIMRRSY	miscarry
ACIILNRS	Sinclair	ACILLORT	clitoral	ACIMSSST	miscasts
ACIILRTU	uralitic	ACILLORY	collyria	ACINNNOO	nonanoic
ACIILSST	silastic	ACILLOST	Callisto	ACINNOOT	conation
ACIIMNNT	mannitic		localist	ACINNOQU	conquian
ACIIMNOR	morainic	ACILLOSY	socially	ACINNOSS	scansion
ACIIMNOS	simoniac	ACILLOTY	locality	ACINNOST	actinons
ACIIMNOT	amniotic	ACILLOUV	colluvia		canonist
ACIIMNST	actinism	ACILLSSY	classily		contains
ACIIMNSU	musician	ACILMNOP	complain		sanction
ACIIMNTU	actinium	ACILMNOS	laconism		sonantic
ACIIMNTY	intimacy		limacons	ACINNOSU	Asunción
	minacity	ACILMOPR	proclaim	ACINNOTU	continua
ACIIMOST	iotacism	ACILMOSV	vocalism	ACINNRTY	tyrannic
ACIIMOTT	amitotic	ACILMSSS	classism	ACINNSTY	instancy
ACIIMPRV	vampiric	ACILMSSU	musicals	ACINOOPR	picaroon
ACIIMRST	scimitar	ACILMSTY	mystical	ACINOOTV	vocation
ACIIMRTU	muriatic	ACILNOOT	location	ACINOPPT	panoptic
ACIIMSTT	atticism	ACILNOPS	salpicon	ACINOPRS	parsonic
ACIIMSTV	activism	ACILNOPT	platonic	ACINOPST	captions

ACINOPTU	acupoint	**ACKMOSTT**	mattocks	**ACNNORST**	Scranton
ACINORSS	narcosis	**ACKOPRRT**	traprock	**ACNNOSTT**	constant
ACINORST	cantoris	**ACLLLNOY**	clonally	**ACNOOORT**	octaroon
	carotins	**ACLLMMOX**	Malcolm X	**ACNOORRY**	coronary
ACINORTT	traction	**ACLLNNOO**	nonlocal	**ACNOORST**	cartoons
ACINOSSS	caissons	**ACLLNORW**	Cornwall		corantos
ACINOSSY	cyanosis	**ACLLOORT**	collator		ostracon
ACINOSTT	oscitant	**ACLLOOSS**	colossal	**ACNOORSU**	canorous
	tactions	**ACLLOPSS**	scallops	**ACNOORTY**	octonary
ACINOSTU	auctions	**ACLLORUY**	ocularly	**ACNOPSSW**	snowcaps
	cautions	**ACLLRTUU**	cultural	**ACNORRSY**	carryons
ACINOSTW	wainscot	**ACLLSTUU**	Catullus	**ACNORRTY**	contrary
ACINOSWX	coxswain	**ACLMMNOT**	Montcalm	**ACNORSTT**	contrast
ACINOTTX	toxicant	**ACLMMNOU**	communal	**ACNORTTU**	turncoat
ACINPQUY	piquancy	**ACLMMORW**	clamworm	**ACNPRSSY**	syncarps
ACINPRST	cantrips	**ACLMNOOO**	coolamon	**ACNPRSYY**	syncarpy
ACINPRSY	cyprians	**ACLMNORU**	columnar	**ACNRRSTU**	currants
ACINPSTY	synaptic	**ACLMNORY**	normalcy	**ACOOPSTT**	topcoats
ACINQSTU	quantics	**ACLMORSU**	clamours	**ACOORSTU**	touracos
ACINRSTU	curtains	**ACLMRSUU**	muscular	**ACOPPRRS**	procarps
ACINRTTU	taciturn	**ACLMSTUU**	custumal	**ACOPRRST**	carports
	urticant	**ACLMSUUV**	vasculum	**ACOPRRTT**	protract
ACINSTTY	sanctity	**ACLNNOOV**	nonvocal	**ACORRSTT**	tractors
ACINSTYY	syncytia	**ACLNOORS**	coronals	**ACORRSTU**	curators
ACIOOPST	scotopia	**ACLNOORT**	colorant	**ACORRTUY**	carryout
ACIOOPTX	Cotopaxi	**ACLNOOST**	coolants	**ACORSSTU**	surcoats
ACIOPRST	apricots	**ACLNOOSV**	volcanos	**ACORSSUW**	curassow
ACIOPRTT	protatic	**ACLNOOSY**	Colonsay	**ACORSSWY**	crossway
ACIOPSST	potassic	**ACLNOPSY**	syncopal	**ACORSTTY**	cryostat
ACIOPSSU	spacious	**ACLNORSU**	consular	**ACOSSTTU**	outcasts
ACIOPSTU	captious		courlans	**ACPSSTUY**	pussycat
ACIORSSS	corsairs	**ACLNORTU**	calutron	**ADDDEEEN**	deadened
ACIORRTU	Courtrai	**ACLNOSTU**	osculant	**ADDDEEGR**	degraded
ACIORSSU	scarious	**ACLNPSSU**	unclasps	**ADDDEEIM**	diademed
ACIORTTY	atrocity	**ACLNPTUU**	punctual	**ADDDEELR**	laddered
	citatory	**ACLNSTUU**	Tuscular	**ADDDEEMN**	demanded
ACIORTVY	voracity	**ACLOOPPS**	alcopops		maddened
ACIOSTUU	cautious	**ACLOOPRR**	corporal	**ADDDEENR**	dandered
ACIPRSSS	casspirs	**ACLOPPRY**	Polycarp	**ADDDEENS**	saddened
ACIPSSST	spastics	**ACLOPRRU**	procural	**ADDDEGJU**	adjudged
ACIQRSTU	quartics	**ACLOPRST**	caltrops	**ADDDEIMS**	misadded
ACIRSSST	sacrists	**ACLOPRXY**	xylocarp	**ADDDELSW**	swaddled
ACIRSSTT	astricts	**ACLOPSSU**	scopulas	**ADDDELTW**	twaddled
ACIRSSTY	sacristy	**ACLOPSSY**	calypsos	**ADDDEMNU**	addendum
ACIRSSTZ	czarists	**ACLOSSTU**	outclass	**ADDDENOS**	deodands
ACISSSTU	casuists	**ACLRSSTY**	crystals	**ADDDEOOW**	deadwood
ACISSTTU	catsuits	**ACMMNOSY**	scammony	**ADDEEEFN**	deafened
ACJKKSSY	skyjacks	**ACMNOOPR**	monocarp	**ADDEEEFT**	defeated
ACJKOPST	jackpots	**ACMNOORT**	monocrat	**ADDEEEMN**	demeaned
ACJMNSTU	muntjacs	**ACMNOPRS**	corpsman	**ADDEEENR**	deadener
ACJPSTUU	cajuputs		crampons		endeared
ACKKMOPR	pockmark	**ACMNORSS**	Crossman	**ADDEEESY**	deadeyes
ACKLLOPS	pollacks	**ACMNORSY**	acronyms	**ADDEEFHN**	handfeed
ACKLLPSU	skullcap	**ACMNSSTU**	sanctums	**ADDEEFIL**	defilade
ACKLNORS	Clarkson	**ACMOOPRS**	coprosma	**ADDEEFLT**	deflated
ACKLOOPW	woolpack	**ACMOORRT**	motorcar	**ADDEEFRY**	defrayed
ACKLOORS	oarlocks	**ACMOOSST**	scotomas	**ADDEEGGR**	daggered
ACKLOOSW	woolsack	**ACMORSTW**	catworms	**ADDEEGHR**	hardedge
ACKLORSW	warlocks		wormcast	**ADDEEGLN**	danegeld
ACKMMOSS	mammocks	**ACMORSTY**	costmary	**ADDEEGNR**	deranged
ACKMNOST	stockman	**ACMQSTUU**	cumquats		gardened
ACKMOSST	stomacks	**ACNNNORY**	cannonry	**ADDEEGOR**	dogeared

ADDEEEGRR	degrader	**ADDEGJSU**	adjudges	**ADDELPRS**	paddlers
	regarded	**ADDEGLNS**	gladdens	**ADDELRSS**	saddlers
	regraded	**ADDEGLST**	gladdest	**ADDELRST**	straddle
ADDEEGRS	degrades	**ADDEGNRU**	ungraded	**ADDELRSW**	dawdlers
ADDEEGSS	degassed	**ADDEGPRU**	upgraded		waddlers
ADDEEHLR	heralded	**ADDEHHLN**	handheld	**ADDELRSY**	Drysdale
ADDEEHLV	aldehyde	**ADDEHILR**	dihedral		saddlery
ADDEEHNR	hardened	**ADDEHINW**	headwind	**ADDELRTW**	twaddler
ADDEEHRS	redheads	**ADDEHIRS**	diehards	**ADDELSST**	staddles
ADDEEHRT	threaded	**ADDEHLOS**	shedload	**ADDELSSW**	swaddles
ADDEEILN	deadline	**ADDEHLOW**	Howel Dda	**ADDELSTW**	twaddles
ADDEEILR	deadlier	**ADDEHLWY**	Hywel Dda	**ADDEMNPU**	undamped
	derailed	**ADDEHMRU**	drumhead	**ADDEMOSY**	domesday
ADDEEILT	detailed	**ADDEHNNU**	unhanded	**ADDENOPR**	pardoned
ADDEEIMT	mediated	**ADDEHNRU**	Dehra Dun	**ADDENPRU**	undraped
ADDEEINT	detained	**ADDEHNSU**	unshaded	**ADDENRST**	stranded
ADDEEIPR	diapered	**ADDEHOPR**	drophead	**ADDEORTU**	outdared
ADDEEISS	diseased	**ADDEHORW**	headword	**ADDEOTTU**	outdated
ADDEEIST	steadied	**ADDEHOSW**	shadowed	**ADDEPRSU**	superadd
ADDEEITV	deviated	**ADDEHRTY**	hydrated	**ADDFFILO**	daffodil
ADDEEKNR	darkened	**ADDEHSTU**	Thaddeus	**ADDFFINR**	dandriff
ADDEELLM	medalled	**ADDEIIRW**	Edward II	**ADDFFNRU**	dandruff
ADDEELLP	pedalled	**ADDEIITV**	additive	**ADDFIRSU**	Safid Rud
ADDEELNP	deplaned	**ADDEIJNO**	adjoined	**ADDFISST**	faddists
ADDEELNU	unleaded	**ADDEIKNP**	kidnaped	**ADDFORRT**	Dartford
ADDEELOR	reloaded	**ADDEILNS**	islanded	**ADDGGILN**	gladding
ADDEELRT	treadled		landside	**ADDGILNN**	dandling
ADDEELST	desalted	**ADDEILNT**	tideland	**ADDGILNP**	paddling
ADDEELUV	devalued	**ADDEILSY**	dialysed	**ADDGILNR**	raddling
ADDEEMNN	demanned	**ADDEILYZ**	dialyzed	**ADDGILNS**	saddling
ADDEEMNP	dampened	**ADDEIMOS**	sodamide	**ADDGILNW**	dawdling
ADDEEMNR	demander	**ADDEIMRS**	disarmed		waddling
	redemand	**ADDEIMST**	misdated	**ADDGINSW**	waddings
	remanded	**ADDEIMSY**	dismayed	**ADDGINWY**	waddying
ADDEEMNV	Demavend	**ADDEIMTT**	admitted	**ADDGLNOS**	gladdons
ADDEENPP	appended	**ADDEINOR**	ordained	**ADDGMRUU**	mudguard
ADDEENPR	pandered	**ADDEINOS**	adenoids	**ADDGOQSU**	godsquad
ADDEENPX	expanded		anodised	**ADDHHLNO**	handhold
ADDEENRW	wandered	**ADDEINOZ**	anodized	**ADDHINSY**	dandyish
ADDEENSS	deadness	**ADDEINPR**	drepanid	**ADDHISTY**	hydatids
ADDEENTT	attended	**ADDEINST**	dandiest	**ADDHOORW**	hardwood
ADDEENTU	denudate	**ADDEIOPR**	parodied	**ADDHOSTY**	athodyds
ADDEENUV	unevaded	**ADDEIORS**	sideroad	**ADDIINOT**	addition
ADDEEPRT	departed	**ADDEIOTX**	oxidated	**ADDIINRT**	Trinidad
	predated	**ADDEIQSU**	squaddie	**ADDIINSS**	disdains
ADDEEPRV	depraved	**ADDEIRST**	disrated	**ADDIKSTY**	katydids
	pervaded	**ADDEIRSW**	sideward	**ADDILMNS**	midlands
ADDEERRT	retarded	**ADDEIRVW**	Edward IV	**ADDIMNOS**	diamonds
ADDEERRW	rewarded		Edward VI	**ADDIMNSY**	dandyism
ADDEERSW	sawdered	**ADDEIRVZ**	vizarded	**ADDINNOR**	ordinand
ADDEERTV	adverted	**ADDEISSU**	dissuade	**ADDINORS**	androids
ADDEFFOR	afforded	**ADDEISSW**	swaddies	**ADDINRWW**	windward
ADDEFIIL	ladified	**ADDEJSTU**	adjusted	**ADDKLNOR**	Dorkland
ADDEFILY	ladyfied	**ADDELMOS**	dolmades	**ADDKNRRU**	drunkard
ADDEFIST	faddiest	**ADDELNNS**	Land's End	**ADDLLNOR**	landlord
ADDEFLRU	dreadful	**ADDELNOU**	duodenal	**ADDLLRSU**	dullards
ADDEFRSU	defrauds		unloaded	**ADDLNNOW**	downland
ADDEGGLR	draggled	**ADDELNPU**	pudendal	**ADDLNOOW**	download
ADDEGHOR	Drogheda	**ADDELNRS**	dandlers		woodland
ADDEGILS	gladdies	**ADDELNSU**	unsaddle	**ADDLNORR**	randlord
ADDEGINR	dreading	**ADDELOOR**	eldorado	**ADDLORSY**	Lord's Day
	readding		El Dorado	**ADDLORTY**	dotardly

ADDMOOSY	doomsday	**ADEEFRTU**	featured	**ADEEHLNR**	rehandle
ADDNOPWY	pandowdy	**ADEEGGHS**	eggheads	**ADEEHLNS**	hanseled
ADDNORWW	downward	**ADEEGGRU**	regauged	**ADEEHLNU**	unhealed
ADDOORRY	dooryard	**ADEEGHRT**	gathered	**ADEEHLRT**	haltered
ADDOORWW	woodward	**ADEEGINN**	Engadine		lathered
ADDOORWY	woodyard	**ADEEGINR**	regained	**ADEEHLSS**	headless
ADEEEFNY	fedayeen	**ADEEGIRS**	disagree	**ADEEHLTY**	heatedly
ADEEEFRT	defeater	**ADEEGLLU**	de Gaulle	**ADEEHMMO**	homemade
	federate	**ADEEGLNR**	enlarged	**ADEEHMMR**	hammered
ADEEEGLT	delegate		largened	**ADEEHMNN**	menhaden
ADEEEGNR	renegade	**ADEEGLNT**	danegelt	**ADEEHMNS**	headsmen
ADEEEGNT	teenaged	**ADEEGLRV**	graveled	**ADEEHMPR**	hampered
ADEEEGRS	degrease	**ADEEGLRZ**	reglazed	**ADEEHMST**	stemhead
ADEEEGUW	agueweed	**ADEEGLSV**	selvaged	**ADEEHNPP**	happened
ADEEEHRS	haeredes	**ADEEGMMT**	gemmated	**ADEEHNRR**	hardener
ADEEEHRT	reheated	**ADEEGMNR**	gendarme		reharden
ADEEEHSY	eyeshade	**ADEEGMNS**	endgames	**ADEEHNRT**	adherent
ADEEEINT	detainee	**ADEEGMNY**	ganymede	**ADEEHNSS**	dasheens
ADEEEKNW	weakened	**ADEEGMOP**	megapode	**ADEEHNST**	hastened
ADEEELMN	enameled	**ADEEGMOS**	megadose		netheads
ADEEELNV	leavened	**ADEEGMSS**	messaged	**ADEEHNTU**	unheated
ADEEELPR	repealed	**ADEEGNNR**	endanger	**ADEEHORS**	sorehead
ADEEELRS	released	**ADEEGNOR**	renegado	**ADEEHORV**	overhead
	resealed	**ADEEGNRR**	gardener	**ADEEHPRS**	reshaped
ADEEELRV	revealed		garnered	**ADEEHPRT**	threaped
ADEEELST	teaseled	**ADEEGNRS**	deranges	**ADEEHPUV**	upheaved
ADEEELSW	weaseled		grandees	**ADEEHRRT**	rethread
ADEEELTV	elevated		grenades		threader
ADEEELTZ	teazeled	**ADEEGNRU**	dungaree	**ADEEHRRW**	Hereward
ADEEENNT	neatened		underage	**ADEEHRST**	headrest
ADEEENRS	serenade	**ADEEGNRV**	engraved	**ADEEHRSW**	rewashed
ADEEENTT	attendee	**ADEEGORT**	derogate	**ADEEHRTT**	threated
	edentate	**ADEEGPRS**	presaged	**ADEEHRTW**	wreathed
ADEEEPRS	rapeseed	**ADEEGPRT**	pargeted	**ADEEHSST**	headsets
ADEEEPRT	repeated	**ADEEGRRS**	regrades	**ADEEHSSY**	hayseeds
ADEEERST	reseated	**ADEEGRRT**	gartered	**ADEEIILS**	idealise
ADEEESSW	seesawed		regrated	**ADEEIILZ**	idealize
ADEEFHNR	freehand	**ADEEGRRU**	Daguerre	**ADEEIIRS**	Dies Irae
ADEEFHOR	forehead		reargued	**ADEEIJKL**	jadelike
ADEEFHRT	fathered	**ADEEGRRV**	Redgrave	**ADEEIJMR**	jeremiad
ADEEFIIR	aerified	**ADEEGRSS**	degasser	**ADEEIJST**	jadeites
ADEEFILN	enfilade		dressage	**ADEEILLO**	oeillade
ADEEFIMS	semideaf	**ADEEGRST**	restaged	**ADEEILMN**	endemial
ADEEFIRR	rarefied	**ADEEGRSU**	guardees	**ADEEILMR**	remailed
ADEEFLLT	fellated	**ADEEGRSW**	ragweeds		remedial
ADEEFLOR	freeload	**ADEEGRTT**	targeted	**ADEEILMS**	limeades
ADEEFLPR	pedalfer	**ADEEGSSS**	degasses	**ADEEILMV**	medieval
ADEEFLRR	deferral	**ADEEGSTT**	gestated	**ADEEILNS**	delaines
ADEEFLRT	faltered	**ADEEGSWY**	edgeways	**ADEEILNT**	dateline
	reflated	**ADEEGTTZ**	gazetted		entailed
ADEEFLSS	fadeless	**ADEEHHRS**	rehashed		lineated
ADEEFLST	deflates	**ADEEHHST**	sheathed	**ADEEILPS**	pleiades
ADEEFLSX	flaxseed	**ADEEHIKL**	headlike	**ADEEILPT**	depilate
ADEEFMNR	freedman	**ADEEHIKZ**	Zedekiah		epilated
ADEEFMRR	reframed	**ADEEHILN**	headline		pileated
ADEEFMRS	defamers	**ADEEHIST**	headiest	**ADEEILRR**	derailer
ADEEFNSS	deafness	**ADEEHISV**	adhesive	**ADEEILRS**	realised
ADEEFNST	fastened	**ADEEHKNR**	hankered		sidereal
ADEEFNTT	fattened		harkened	**ADEEILRT**	elaterid
ADEEFOTV	foveated	**ADEEHKWW**	hawkweed		retailed
ADEEFRRY	defrayer	**ADEEHKWY**	hawkeyed	**ADEEILRZ**	realized
ADEEFRST	draftees	**ADEEHLLW**	wellhead	**ADEEILSS**	idealess

ADEEIMNR	remained	**ADEELMPX**	exampled	**ADEEMPST**	stampede
ADEEIMNT	dementia	**ADEELMRS**	demersal		stepdame
ADEEIMNX	examined		emeralds	**ADEEMRRS**	dreamers
ADEEIMRR	dreamier	**ADEELMRV**	marveled	**ADEEMRRW**	rewarmed
ADEEIMRT	diameter	**ADEELMTU**	emulated	**ADEEMRST**	mastered
ADEEIMST	mediates	**ADEELNNP**	enplaned		streamed
	Tameside	**ADEELNNU**	unaneled	**ADEEMRSU**	Madurese
ADEEIMTT	meditate	**ADEELNOR**	oleander		measured
ADEEINNS	adenines		reloaned	**ADEEMRTT**	mattered
	andesine	**ADEELNPS**	deplanes	**ADEEMSWY**	mayweeds
ADEEINOP	oedipean	**ADEELNPT**	endplate	**ADEENNPT**	pennated
ADEEINPT	diapente	**ADEELNRS**	Landseer	**ADEENNRS**	Andersen
ADEEINRS	arsenide	**ADEELNRV**	lavender		Ardennes
	nearside	**ADEELNRY**	Alderney		ensnared
ADEEINRT	detainer	**ADEELNSU**	unleased	**ADEENNRU**	unearned
	retained		unsealed	**ADEENNTT**	tenanted
ADEEINRV	reinvade	**ADEELNSV**	enslaved	**ADEENNUW**	unweaned
ADEEINST	andesite	**ADEELNTT**	talented	**ADEENOPW**	weaponed
ADEEINVW	inweaved	**ADEELNTV**	levantine	**ADEENORS**	reasoned
ADEEIPRR	repaired	**ADEELOPS**	pedaloes	**ADEENORV**	endeavor
ADEEIPRS	airspeed	**ADEELOPX**	poleaxed	**ADEENORY**	aerodyne
ADEEIPTX	expiated	**ADEELOST**	desolate	**ADEENOSS**	seasoned
ADEEIRRR	drearier	**ADEELPPT**	lappeted	**ADEENOST**	endostea
ADEEIRST	readiest	**ADEELPRS**	pleaders	**ADEENOTT**	detonate
	steadier		relapsed	**ADEENPPR**	endpaper
ADEEIRTT	iterated	**ADEELPRT**	paltered	**ADEENPRR**	panderer
ADEEISSS	diseases	**ADEELPRY**	parleyed	**ADEENPRX**	expander
ADEEISST	steadies		replayed	**ADEENPTT**	patented
ADEEISTV	deviates	**ADEELPST**	pedestal	**ADEENRRW**	wanderer
	sedative	**ADEELPTY**	pedately	**ADEENRSS**	dearness
ADEEKKRR	Kerkrade	**ADEELQSU**	squealed	**ADEENRSU**	undersea
ADEEKMRR	remarked	**ADEELRRT**	treadler	**ADEENRSW**	Andrewes
ADEEKMRT	demarket	**ADEELRST**	treadles		answered
	marketed	**ADEELRSV**	slavered	**ADEENRTT**	attender
ADEEKNPS	kneepads	**ADEELRSY**	delayers		nattered
ADEEKNPW	knapweed	**ADEELRTV**	traveled	**ADEENRTU**	denature
ADEEKNRR	darkener	**ADEELRUV**	revalued		underate
ADEEKNRS	kneaders	**ADEELSST**	dateless		undereat
ADEEKQSU	squeaked		tasseled	**ADEENSST**	assented
ADEEKRST	streaked	**ADEELSTU**	adultese		standees
ADEEKSWY	weekdays	**ADEELSTY**	sedately	**ADEENSSU**	danseuse
ADEELLLP	lapelled	**ADEELSUV**	devalues		Sudanese
ADEELLMT	metalled	**ADEEMMRY**	yammered	**ADEENSTU**	unseated
ADEELLMU	medullae	**ADEEMMSS**	mesdames	**ADEENTTU**	tautened
ADEELLNP	panelled	**ADEEMMXY**	myxedema	**ADEENTTV**	vendetta
ADEELLNY	leadenly	**ADEEMNNR**	mannered	**ADEEOPRT**	operated
ADEELLPR	predella		Menander	**ADEEOPST**	adoptees
ADEELLPS	sepalled		remanned	**ADEEORSW**	oarweeds
ADEELLPT	petalled	**ADEEMNOR**	demeanor	**ADEEORVW**	overawed
ADEELLQU	equalled		enamored	**ADEEPPRR**	prepared
ADEELLRU	laureled	**ADEEMNOT**	nematode	**ADEEPRRS**	spreader
ADEELLRV	ravelled	**ADEEMNOU**	eudaemon	**ADEEPRRU**	upreared
ADEELLSS	allseeds	**ADEEMNPR**	dampener	**ADEEPRRV**	depraver
	leadless	**ADEEMNPY**	ependyma		pervader
ADEELLTY	elatedly	**ADEEMNRS**	amenders	**ADEEPRSS**	aspersed
ADEELLWY	walleyed		meanders		repassed
ADEELMNSU	lemonade	**ADEEMNSU**	unseamed	**ADEEPRST**	pederast
ADEELMNP	emplaned	**ADEEMORT**	moderate		predates
ADEELMNR	aldermen	**ADEEMPPR**	pampered		repasted
ADEELMNS	dalesmen	**ADEEMPRR**	prearmed		trapesed
	leadsmen	**ADEEMPRT**	tampered	**ADEEPRSU**	persuade
ADEELMNT	lamented	**ADEEMPRV**	revamped	**ADEEPRSV**	depraves

	pervades	**ADEFIRRT**	draftier		signaled
ADEEPRTT	pattered	**ADEFKSST**	deskfast	**ADEGILNT**	delating
ADEEPRTU	depurate	**ADEFLLLU**	ladleful	**ADEGILNY**	delaying
ADEEPSST	stapedes	**ADEFLLOR**	falderol	**ADEGILOU**	dialogue
ADEEPSWY	speedway	**ADEFLLOW**	fallowed	**ADEGILSS**	glissade
ADEEQRUV	quavered	**ADEFLLRY**	alderfly	**ADEGIMNN**	amending
ADEERRRT	retarder	**ADEFLMRU**	dreamful	**ADEGIMNR**	dreaming
ADEERRRW	rewarder	**ADEFLNOR**	foreland		margined
ADEERRST	arrested	**ADEFLNRS**	Flanders	**ADEGIMNT**	Mitnaged
	retreads	**ADEFLNTU**	flaunted	**ADEGIMOR**	ideogram
	serrated	**ADEFLORT**	deflator	**ADEGIMRT**	migrated
	treaders	**ADEFLORV**	flavored	**ADEGINOR**	organdie
ADEERRTW	redwater	**ADEFLPRS**	feldspar	**ADEGINOS**	agonised
ADEERSST	asserted	**ADEFLRTW**	leftward		diagnose
	estrades	**ADEFLRZZ**	frazzled		San Diego
ADEERSTT	restated	**ADEFLSTU**	defaults	**ADEGINOZ**	agonized
ADEERTTT	tattered	**ADEFMNRU**	unframed	**ADEGINRR**	Gardiner
ADEERTTY	yattered	**ADEFNOPR**	profaned	**ADEGINRS**	deraigns
ADEERVYY	everyday	**ADEFNSST**	daftness		gradines
ADEESSSS	assessed	**ADEFORRW**	farrowed		readings
ADEESTTT	attested	**ADEFORRY**	foreyard	**ADEGINRT**	derating
ADEFFGUW	guffawed	**ADEFORUV**	favoured		gradient
ADEFFIMR	affirmed	**ADEFRRST**	drafters		treading
ADEFFIRT	tariffed		redrafts	**ADEGINSS**	assigned
ADEFFIST	daffiest	**ADEFSSTT**	stedfast		Gassendi
ADEFFLNS	snaffled	**ADEGGIRR**	draggier	**ADEGINST**	sedating
ADEFFLOS	leadoffs	**ADEGGIST**	daggiest		steading
ADEFFORT	tradeoff	**ADEGGJLY**	jaggedly	**ADEGINSU**	Agnus Dei
ADEFGGOT	faggoted	**ADEGGLNU**	angledug	**ADEGINSW**	windages
ADEFGIIS	gasified	**ADEGGLRS**	draggles	**ADEGINTV**	vintaged
ADEFGILN	finagled	**ADEGGLRY**	raggedly	**ADEGIOST**	godetias
ADEFGILO	foliaged	**ADEGGMOS**	demagogs	**ADEGIRTU**	Radiguet
ADEFGILR	Garfield	**ADEGGMOY**	demagogy	**ADEGIRWY**	ridgeway
ADEFGILS	gadflies	**ADEGGOPS**	pedagogs	**ADEGISTU**	gaudiest
ADEFGIMN	defaming	**ADEGGOPY**	pedagogy	**ADEGJNOR**	jargoned
ADEFGIRT	driftage	**ADEGGRTY**	gadgetry	**ADEGLLNU**	glandule
ADEFGIRU	argufied	**ADEGHHOS**	hogshead	**ADEGLLOP**	galloped
ADEFGITU	fatigued	**ADEGHILT**	alighted	**ADEGLMOS**	gladsome
ADEFGLOT	gatefold		gilthead	**ADEGLMUY**	amygdule
ADEFHILS	dealfish	**ADEGHINR**	adhering	**ADEGLNPS**	spangled
ADEFHILT	Hatfield		Hardinge	**ADEGLNRS**	danglers
ADEFHIMS	famished	**ADEGHINS**	headings		glanders
ADEFHMOT	fathomed		sheading	**ADEGLNRW**	wrangled
ADEFHNOR	forehand	**ADEGHLNO**	headlong	**ADEGLNSS**	gladness
ADEFIILN	finialed	**ADEGHNRT**	thranged	**ADEGLNUZ**	unglazed
ADEFIILR	airfield	**ADEGHORT**	goatherd	**ADEGLOSU**	Gesualdo
ADEFIILS	ladifies	**ADEGHRTU**	daughter	**ADEGLPPR**	grappled
	salified	**ADEGIILN**	gliadine	**ADEGLSTY**	dalgytes
ADEFIILT	filiated	**ADEGIILP**	diplegia	**ADEGMMNO**	gammoned
ADEFIIMR	ramified	**ADEGIIMN**	imagined	**ADEGMMRU**	rummaged
ADEFIINZ	nazified	**ADEGIIMS**	digamies	**ADEGMNOR**	dragomen
ADEFIIRT	ratified	**ADEGIIRT**	digerati	**ADEGMNOY**	endogamy
ADEFILMN	inflamed	**ADEGIITT**	digitate	**ADEGMNSU**	agendums
ADEFILNT	inflated	**ADEGIKLO**	goadlike	**ADEGMORW**	wordgame
ADEFILOT	foliated	**ADEGIKNN**	kneading	**ADEGMPUZ**	gazumped
ADEFILSY	dayflies	**ADEGILLP**	pillaged	**ADEGNNOR**	androgen
	ladyfies	**ADEGILMN**	maligned	**ADEGNOPU**	poundage
ADEFIMNR	Friedman		medaling	**ADEGNORT**	dragonet
ADEFIMPR	firedamp	**ADEGILNP**	pedaling	**ADEGNOSS**	sondages
ADEFINRR	infrared		pleading	**ADEGNOSV**	dogvanes
ADEFINYZ	denazify	**ADEGILNR**	dragline	**ADEGNPRR**	Grand Pré
ADEFIORS	foresaid	**ADEGILNS**	dealings	**ADEGNRRU**	grandeur

ADEGNRST	dragnets	**ADEHIRRT**	trihedra	**ADEHPRSU**	Phaedrus
	grandest	**ADEHIRSS**	radishes	**ADEHQSSU**	squashed
ADEGNRUZ	gazunder	**ADEHIRST**	hardiest	**ADEHRRUY**	hurrayed
ADEGOORY	goodyear	**ADEHIRSV**	ravished	**ADEHRSTY**	hydrates
ADEGOPRR	dragrope	**ADEHIRSW**	rawhides	**ADEHRTTW**	thwarted
ADEGOPRT	portaged	**ADEHISST**	shadiest	**ADEIILMS**	idealism
ADEGORRT	garroted	**ADEHISSW**	siwashed		miladies
ADEGORSW	dowagers	**ADEHKNRS**	redshank	**ADEIILRS**	Disraeli
ADEGORTT	garotted	**ADEHKORW**	headwork	**ADEIILST**	idealist
ADEGORTU	outraged	**ADEHKPRY**	Hyde Park	**ADEIILTV**	dilative
	ragouted	**ADEHLLOO**	hallooed	**ADEIILTY**	ideality
ADEGORTW	waterdog		holloaed	**ADEIIMNN**	indamine
ADEGPRRU	upgrader	**ADEHLLOW**	hallowed	**ADEIIMNR**	meridian
ADEGPRSU	upgrades	**ADEHLLRT**	thralled	**ADEIIMNS**	diamines
ADEGPSTU	upstaged	**ADEHLLSW**	Shadwell	**ADEIIMPR**	impaired
ADEGRRST	dragster	**ADEHLLSY**	dayshell	**ADEIIMRS**	semiarid
ADEGRRSU	guarders	**ADEHLMNO**	homeland	**ADEIIMTT**	imitated
ADEGRSSU	graduses	**ADEHLNRS**	handlers	**ADEIINNS**	sanidine
ADEGTTTU	guttated	**ADEHLNSS**	handless	**ADEIINRT**	daintier
ADEHHIPS	headship		handsels	**ADEIINRU**	uredinia
ADEHHIST	shithead	**ADEHLNST**	shetland	**ADEIINST**	adenitis
ADEHHLOY	Holyhead		Stendhal		dainties
ADEHHOOR	hoorahed	**ADEHLNSU**	unlashed	**ADEIINSZ**	diazines
ADEHHOPS	hopheads	**ADEHLOPS**	asphodel	**ADEIIPRS**	presidia
ADEHHOST	hotheads	**ADEHLPSS**	splashed	**ADEIIRSS**	airsides
ADEHHRRU	hurrahed	**ADEHLRRY**	heraldry	**ADEIITTV**	vitiated
ADEHHRST	thrashed	**ADEHMMMO**	Mohammed	**ADEIITUV**	auditive
ADEHHUZZ	huzzahed	**ADEHMNNY**	handymen	**ADEIKLLO**	keloidal
ADEHIKLN	handlike	**ADEHMNOS**	handsome	**ADEIKLLR**	lardlike
ADEHIKLV	khedival	**ADEHMNOT**	methadon	**ADEIKLLY**	ladylike
ADEHIKNS	skinhead	**ADEHMNRS**	herdsman	**ADEIKLNS**	sandlike
ADEHILLM	Heimdall	**ADEHMNRU**	unharmed	**ADEIKLNW**	dawnlike
ADEHILMW	Waldheim	**ADEHMOOR**	headroom		wandlike
ADEHILNR	hardline	**ADEHMORW**	homeward	**ADEIKLOT**	toadlike
ADEHILNU	unhailed	**ADEHMOST**	headmost	**ADEIKLPV**	Kapil Dev
ADEHILPS	helipads	**ADEHMOSU**	madhouse	**ADEIKLSW**	sidewalk
ADEHILRY	Hyder Ali	**ADEHNOPR**	orphaned	**ADEIKMRT**	tidemark
ADEHILSV	lavished	**ADEHNOPT**	phonated	**ADEIKNPR**	kidnaper
ADEHIMOT	hematoid	**ADEHNORV**	handover	**ADEIKNSY**	kyanised
ADEHIMRS	misheard		overhand	**ADEIKNYZ**	kyanized
	semihard	**ADEHNOSS**	sandshoe	**ADEIKORT**	keratoid
ADEHINOP	diaphone	**ADEHNRSS**	hardness	**ADEILLMY**	medially
ADEHINOS	adhesion	**ADEHNRSU**	unshared	**ADEILLNN**	landline
ADEHINOY	hyoidean	**ADEHNRSW**	swanherd	**ADEILLNU**	unallied
ADEHINPS	deanship	**ADEHNRTU**	unthread	**ADEILLNY**	leylandi
	headpins	**ADEHNSST**	handsets	**ADEILLOR**	arillode
	pinheads	**ADEHNSSU**	sunshade	**ADEILLPR**	pillared
ADEHINPU	dauphine	**ADEHNSUV**	unshaved	**ADEILLPS**	spadille
	Dauphiné	**ADEHNSUW**	unwashed	**ADEILLRS**	dalliers
ADEHINRS	Sheridan	**ADEHOORT**	Theodora		diallers
ADEHINRU	unhaired	**ADEHOORW**	harewood	**ADEILLRT**	trialled
ADEHINSS	shandies	**ADEHOORY**	hoorayed	**ADEILLRV**	rivalled
ADEHINST	handiest	**ADEHOPRS**	rhapsode	**ADEILLSW**	sidewall
ADEHINSV	vanished	**ADEHOPST**	potheads	**ADEILMMS**	dilemmas
ADEHIORS	Herodias	**ADEHOPSX**	hexapods	**ADEILMNO**	de Molina
	Rhodesia	**ADEHOPXY**	hexapody		melanoid
ADEHIOTT	athetoid	**ADEHORRS**	hoarders	**ADEILMNY**	maidenly
ADEHIPRS	raphides	**ADEHORRW**	harrowed		medianly
	Sephardi	**ADEHORSW**	shadower	**ADEILMOX**	aldoxime
ADEHIPSS	pisshead	**ADEHORTU**	authored	**ADEILMPS**	impleads
ADEHIPST	pitheads	**ADEHOSTW**	towheads		misplead
	Spithead	**ADEHPPRS**	Sheppard	**ADEILMRY**	dreamily

241

ADEILMSS	misdeals	**ADEIMNOT**	dominate	**ADEINRTU**	indurate
	misleads	**ADEIMNOZ**	nomadize		urinated
ADEILMST	medalist	**ADEIMNRV**	dairymen	**ADEINRUV**	unvaried
	misdealt	**ADEIMNRZ**	zemindar	**ADEINRVV**	vineyard
ADEILMSV	Maldives	**ADEIMNSS**	sidesman	**ADEINSST**	sandiest
ADEILNNR	inlander	**ADEIMNST**	mediants	**ADEINSSV**	vanessid
ADEILNNS	annelids	**ADEIMNSU**	maundies	**ADEINSTT**	instated
ADEILNNT	dentinal	**ADEIMNTY**	dynamite	**ADEINSTU**	sinuated
ADEILNNV	Vineland	**ADEIMORR**	airdrome	**ADEINSTV**	deviants
ADEILNOP	palinode	**ADEIMORT**	mediator	**ADEIOPRS**	diaspore
ADEILNOS	Leonidas	**ADEIMOSS**	sesamoid		parodies
ADEILNOT	delation	**ADEIMOST**	atomised	**ADEIOPRV**	overpaid
ADEILNRS	islander	**ADEIMOTZ**	atomized	**ADEIOPST**	dioptase
ADEILNTV	divalent	**ADEIMPRT**	imparted	**ADEIOPTV**	adoptive
ADEILOPR	Leopardi	**ADEIMPST**	impasted	**ADEIORST**	asteroid
ADEILOPS	sepaloid	**ADEIMRRS**	admirers	**ADEIORSV**	avoiders
ADEILOPT	petaloid		disarmer	**ADEIORTT**	teratoid
ADEILORT	idolater		marrieds	**ADEIORTV**	deviator
	tailored	**ADEIMRSS**	misreads	**ADEIOSTX**	oxidates
ADEILORV	overlaid		sidearms	**ADEIOSTZ**	azotised
ADEILORX	exordial	**ADEIMRST**	readmits	**ADEIOTZZ**	azotized
ADEILOSS	assoiled	**ADEIMSST**	misdates	**ADEIPPRS**	apprised
ADEILOST	diastole	**ADEIMSTY**	daytimes		drappies
	isolated	**ADEINNOT**	anointed	**ADEIPPRZ**	apprized
	sodalite		antinode	**ADEIPRSS**	despairs
ADEILOSV	de Valois	**ADEINNOV**	Devonian	**ADEIPRST**	traipsed
	Val-d'Oise	**ADEINNPT**	pinnated	**ADEIPRSU**	upraised
ADEILOSZ	diazoles	**ADEINNRS**	insnared	**ADEIPRTU**	eupatrid
ADEILOTT	datolite	**ADEINNRZ**	rendzina	**ADEIPTTU**	aptitude
ADEILOTV	dovetail	**ADEINNTU**	antidune	**ADEIQORU**	quarried
	violated		inundate	**ADEIQSUY**	quayside
ADEILPPP	pedipalp	**ADEINOPT**	antipode	**ADEIRRTW**	tawdrier
ADEILPRS	spiraled	**ADEINORR**	ordainer	**ADEIRRWW**	wiredraw
ADEILPRT	dipteral	**ADEINORT**	deration	**ADEIRSST**	disaster
ADEILPRU	epidural		ordinate		disrates
ADEILPRV	deprival		rationed	**ADEIRSSU**	radiuses
ADEILPST	talipeds	**ADEINOSS**	anodises	**ADEIRSSV**	advisers
ADEILQTU	liquated	**ADEINOST**	astonied	**ADEIRSTT**	striated
ADEILRRY	drearily		sedation		tardiest
ADEILRST	dilaters	**ADEINOSZ**	anodizes	**ADEIRTTT**	titrated
ADEILRSU	residual	**ADEINOTT**	antidote	**ADEIRTUV**	durative
	Ruisdael		tetanoid	**ADEIRVWY**	driveway
ADEILRSY	dialyser	**ADEINOTV**	donative	**ADEISSST**	assisted
ADEILRTT	detrital	**ADEINPPX**	appendix	**ADEISSTT**	distaste
ADEILRUV	Duvalier	**ADEINPRS**	sprained	**ADEISSWY**	sideways
ADEILRVY	variedly	**ADEINPRT**	dipteran		waysides
ADEILRYZ	dialyzer	**ADEINPRU**	unpaired	**ADEISTTU**	situated
ADEILSSV	devisals	**ADEINPSV**	spavined	**ADEISTUZ**	deutzias
ADEILSSY	dialyses	**ADEINQTU**	antiqued	**ADEISTWY**	tideways
ADEILSTY	diastyle	**ADEINRRS**	drainers	**ADEITTTU**	attitude
	steadily		serranid	**ADEJLOSU**	jaloused
ADEILSWY	Day-Lewis	**ADEINRSS**	aridness	**ADEJNORS**	Jordaens
ADEILSXY	dyslexia		sardines	**ADEJOPRY**	jeopardy
ADEILSYZ	dialyzes	**ADEINRST**	detrains	**ADEJRRSU**	adjurers
ADEILTTU	altitude		randiest	**ADEJRSTU**	adjuster
	latitude		strained		readjust
ADEILTVY	datively	**ADEINRSU**	denarius	**ADEKLMRY**	markedly
ADEIMMNS	misnamed		unraised	**ADEKLNSU**	unslaked
ADEIMMRS	mermaids		uranides	**ADEKLPRS**	sparkled
ADEIMNNO	mondaine	**ADEINRSV**	invaders	**ADEKMNRU**	unmarked
ADEIMNOP	dopamine	**ADEINRTT**	Andretti	**ADEKMNSU**	unmasked
ADEIMNOS	nomadise		nitrated	**ADEKMORS**	darksome

ADEKNNSS	dankness	
ADEKNOTW	takedown	
ADEKNRSS	darkness	
ADEKQSUW	squawked	
ADEKRTYZ	Radetzky	
ADELLMOS	slalomed	
ADELLMRU	medullar	
ADELLMSU	medullas	
ADELLNNU	annulled	
ADELLNRS	landlers	
ADELLNSS	landless	
ADELLNSW	Sandwell	
	wallsend	
ADELLOPW	walloped	
ADELLOSU	sallowed	
ADELLOTT	allotted	
	totalled	
ADELLOTW	tallowed	
ADELLOVY	ladylove	
ADELLOWW	wallowed	
ADELLQSU	squalled	
ADELLTUU	ululated	
ADELMNNS	landsmen	
ADELMNOO	Laomedon	
ADELMNRS	mandrels	
ADELMOPS	malposed	
ADELMORS	earldoms	
ADELMOSS	damosels	
ADELMOSZ	damozels	
ADELMOTU	modulate	
ADELMPRT	trampled	
ADELMRRU	demurral	
ADELMSSY	massedly	
ADELNNSW	Newlands	
ADELNORS	solander	
ADELNORU	unloader	
ADELNORV	overland	
	rondavel	
ADELNOVY	Donleavy	
ADELNPRS	spandrel	
ADELNPRY	repandly	
ADELNPSY	dyspneal	
	endplays	
ADELNPUY	unplayed	
ADELNRSS	slanders	
ADELNRSU	launders	
ADELNRSY	Lysander	
ADELNRTY	ardently	
ADELNRUY	underlay	
ADELNSTU	unsalted	
ADELNSTW	wetlands	
ADELNTUU	undulate	
ADELNUUV	unvalued	
ADELOOPV	levodopa	
ADELOORV	overload	
ADELOPRS	leopards	
ADELOPRU	poularde	
ADELOPSS	deposals	
ADELOPST	tadpoles	
ADELOPTY	petalody	
ADELORSS	roadless	
ADELORST	delators	
	del Sarto	
	leotards	
	lodestar	
ADELORSU	roulades	
ADELORTW	leadwort	
ADELOSTV	solvated	
ADELOTUV	ovulated	
ADELOTUW	outlawed	
ADELOVWY	avowedly	
ADELPPRY	dapperly	
ADELPRSW	sprawled	
ADELPRTT	prattled	
ADELPRTU	preadult	
ADELPSTU	pulsated	
ADELRRSU	ruderals	
ADELRRSW	drawlers	
ADELRRTU	ultrared	
ADELRSSW	wardless	
ADELRSTT	startled	
ADELRSTW	warstled	
ADELRSUY	Ruysdael	
ADELRTUY	adultery	
ADEMMNOW	madwomen	
ADEMNNNU	unmanned	
ADEMNNSU	Amundsen	
ADEMNOOR	marooned	
ADEMNOPR	pomander	
ADEMNOPT	tamponed	
ADEMNORS	madrones	
	ransomed	
ADEMNOTU	amounted	
ADEMNPSS	dampness	
ADEMNRRU	underarm	
	unmarred	
ADEMNRSU	maunders	
	surnamed	
ADEMNRTU	undreamt	
ADEMNRUW	unwarmed	
ADEMNSSU	medusans	
ADEMNSUU	unamused	
ADEMOORT	moderato	
ADEMOOST	stomodea	
ADEMOOSV	vamoosed	
ADEMOPRY	pyoderma	
ADEMORRT	mortared	
ADEMORRU	armoured	
ADEMORTW	damewort	
	wardmote	
ADEMOSSU	Asmodeus	
ADEMRRSU	eardrums	
ADEMRRTY	martyred	
ADENNORS	Anderson	
ADENNOSY	anodynes	
ADENNOTU	unatoned	
ADENNOTW	wantoned	
ADENNPST	pendants	
ADENNRUW	unwarned	
ADENNTUW	unwanted	
ADENOORT	ratooned	
ADENOORW	wanderoo	
ADENOPRR	pardoner	
ADENOPRS	operands	
	padrones	
	pandores	
	Sarpedon	
ADENOPRT	pronated	
ADENOPST	notepads	
ADENOPSY	dyspnoea	
ADENORRW	narrowed	
ADENORTT	attorned	
ADENORTW	danewort	
	teardown	
ADENORUX	rondeaux	
ADENORUY	Dounreay	
ADENOTUY	autodyne	
ADENPPRS	parpends	
ADENPPTU	untapped	
ADENPRRS	pardners	
ADENPRTY	pedantry	
ADENPRUY	underpay	
ADENQRSU	squander	
ADENRRWY	wardenry	
ADENRSST	standers	
ADENRSSU	danseurs	
	Saunders	
ADENRSTU	daunters	
	transude	
	untreads	
ADENRSTX	dextrans	
ADENRTTU	truanted	
ADENRTVY	Daventry	
ADENRUWY	underway	
ADENSTTU	unstated	
	untasted	
ADENSTUY	unsteady	
ADENSUWY	unswayed	
ADEOOPSS	apodoses	
ADEOORRT	toreador	
ADEOOSTW	Eastwood	
ADEOOTTT	tattooed	
ADEOPPRV	approved	
ADEOPRRS	eardrops	
ADEOPRRT	parroted	
	predator	
	prorated	
	teardrop	
ADEOPRSS	Sporades	
ADEOPRST	readopts	
ADEOPRTT	tetrapod	
ADEOPRUV	vapoured	
ADEOPSST	podestas	
ADEOPSTT	postdate	
ADEORRST	roadster	
ADEORRVW	overdraw	
ADEORSST	assorted	
	torsades	
ADEORSTU	outdares	
	readouts	
ADEORSTX	extrados	
ADEORSUV	savoured	
ADEOSTTU	outdates	
ADEPPRST	strapped	
ADEPRRTU	raptured	
ADEPRSTU	pastured	

	updaters
ADEQSTTU	squatted
ADERRSSW	wardress
ADERRSTT	redstart
ADERSSTW	stewards
ADERSSUY	dasyures
ADERSTUX	surtaxed
ADERSTVY	strayved
ADERSTWW	westward
ADFFHNOS	handoffs
ADFFISST	distaffs
ADFFLOOS	offloads
ADFFNOST	standoff
ADFFORRT	Trafford
ADFFORST	Stafford
ADFGINNU	unfading
ADFGINRT	drafting
ADFGINRW	dwarfing
ADFGMNOO	man of God
ADFHIOST	toadfish
ADFHIRSW	dwarfish
ADFHLNSU	handfuls
ADFHLNSY	flyhands
ADFHLOST	holdfast
ADFHOOSS	shadoofs
ADFHORRT	Hartford
ADFIILPY	lapidify
ADFIIRSU	Firdausi
ADFILLLN	landfill
ADFILLNW	windfall
ADFILMNO	manifold
ADFILRTY	draftily
ADFIMRSW	dwarfism
ADFINRST	indrafts
ADFIORSV	disfavor
ADFKNOOR	Kordofan
ADFLLNOW	downfall
ADFLMNOR	landform
ADFLNOPS	plafonds
ADFLORSU	foulards
ADFMORST	Stamford
ADFNNOST	fondants
ADFNOORZ	forzando
ADFNORST	Stanford
ADFOOPST	footpads
ADFORRSW	forwards
ADGGGINR	dragging
ADGGHNOS	hangdogs
ADGGIIMO	DiMaggio
ADGGILNN	dangling
ADGGINRS	niggards
ADGGINRU	guarding
ADGGLRSU	sluggard
ADGHHILN	highland
ADGHHIOR	highroad
ADGHILLL	gildhall
ADGHILLS	Dalglish
ADGHILNN	handling
ADGHILOS	hidalgos
ADGHILTY	daylight
ADGHINOR	hoarding
ADGHINPR	handgrip

ADGHINSS	shadings
ADGHIPRS	digraphs
ADGHITTW	tightwad
ADGHLNNO	longhand
ADGHNNOS	Shandong
ADGHNNSU	handguns
ADGHNOSS	sandhogs
ADGHRSTU	draughts
ADGHRTUY	draughty
ADGIIIRT	tigridia
ADGIILLN	dialling
ADGIILLO	gladioli
ADGIILMR	Grimaldi
ADGIILNO	gonidial
ADGIILNR	drailing
ADGIILNS	gliadins
ADGIILNT	dilating
ADGIILPY	pygidial
ADGIILRS	Igdrasil
ADGIILST	digitals
ADGIILTY	algidity
ADGIIMNR	admiring
ADGIIMNX	admixing
ADGIIMOR	idiogram
ADGIIMST	digamist
ADGIINNR	draining
ADGIINNU	guanidin
ADGIINNV	invading
ADGIINOR	radioing
ADGIINOT	iodating
ADGIINOV	avoiding
ADGIINRY	dairying
ADGIINSU	iguanids
ADGIINSV	advising
ADGIINTU	auditing
ADGIJNRU	adjuring
ADGIKLNR	darkling
ADGILLNU	alluding
	dualling
ADGILLNW	windgall
ADGILLNY	dallying
ADGILLOT	goldtail
ADGILMNS	gildsman
ADGILMOR	marigold
ADGILNNS	landings
ADGILNNU	unlading
ADGILNOS	loadings
ADGILNPP	dappling
ADGILNPS	Spalding
ADGILNRS	darlings
ADGILNRW	drawling
ADGILNRY	daringly
ADGILNZZ	dazzling
ADGILOOS	solidago
ADGILOPR	prodigal
ADGILORS	goliards
ADGILRVY	gravidly
ADGIMMNW	dwamming
ADGIMNOP	pomading
ADGIMNRS	mridangs
ADGIMNUW	dwauming
ADGIMOSU	digamous

ADGINNOR	adorning
ADGINNOT	donating
ADGINNPY	pandying
ADGINNST	standing
ADGINNTU	daunting
ADGINOOR	rigadoon
ADGINOPT	adopting
ADGINORU	rigaudon
ADGINOTY	toadying
ADGINPTU	updating
ADGINRSW	drawings
	swarding
ADGINRSY	yardings
ADGINSWY	gwyniads
ADGIORTT	Titograd
ADGIPRSU	pagurids
ADGIRSZZ	gizzards
ADGKOOSZ	gadzooks
ADGLMNOS	mangolds
ADGLMNSU	gumlands
ADGLNNOR	Grønland
ADGLNOOS	gondolas
ADGLNOOT	Togoland
ADGMNORS	gormands
ADGMNORU	gourmand
ADGNNOQU	quandong
ADGNNORS	grandson
ADGNNRVY	gynandry
ADGNOORS	dragoons
	gadroons
ADGNRRSU	gurnards
ADGPRRUU	Durgapur
ADHHIPRS	hardship
ADHHLOOV	havdoloh
ADHHMOSS	shahdoms
ADHHNRTY	hydranth
ADHIIJMS	jihadism
ADHIIKSS	dashikis
ADHIILLR	Hilliard
ADHIILOR	Harold II
ADHIINOP	ophidian
ADHIJLSY	jadishly
ADHIKKOO	Hokkaido
ADHILLOT	thalloid
ADHILLRY	hydrilla
ADHILMOS	halidoms
ADHILNOR	rhodinal
ADHILOOW	Hailwood
ADHILOPS	haploids
	shipload
ADHILOPY	haploidy
ADHILOSY	holidays
ADHILPSY	ladyship
ADHIMNOS	admonish
ADHIMNOU	humanoid
ADHIMOPP	amphipod
ADHIMPSS	phasmids
ADHINNOV	Dohnányi
ADHINOPY	diaphony
ADHINPSS	dishpans
ADHINPSU	dauphins
ADHINSST	standish

ADHINSTU	dianthus	**ADIIRSTT**	distrait	**ADILSSTU**	dualists
ADHINTUV	Hindutva	**ADIJLLOO**	Djailolo	**ADIMMNOS**	monadism
ADHIOSTY	toadyish	**ADIJNOST**	adjoints		nomadism
ADHIPRSW	wardship	**ADIKLLOR**	roadkill	**ADIMMNSY**	dynamism
ADHIPRSY	shipyard	**ADIKLOSS**	odalisks	**ADIMMOTU**	domatium
ADHIRTWW	withdraw	**ADIKMOSU**	daimokus	**ADIMNNOR**	Mondrian
ADHKNORW	handwork	**ADIKNNNU**	dunnakin	**ADIMNNOS**	mondains
ADHLLLOS	holdalls	**ADIKNNST**	inkstand	**ADIMNNOT**	dominant
ADHLLNOS	hollands	**ADIKNOPY**	pyinkado	**ADIMNOSS**	madisons
ADHLLNOY	Holy Land	**ADIKNPSS**	skidpans	**ADIMNOST**	donatism
ADHLMORT	thraldom	**ADIKSSWY**	skidways		saintdom
ADHLNOPR	Randolph	**ADILLLNW**	Lindwall	**ADIMNRSY**	misandry
ADHLNOTU	duathlon	**ADILLLPY**	pallidly	**ADIMNSTY**	dynamist
ADHLNOUW	downhaul	**ADILLMMS**	milldams	**ADIMOPRY**	myriapod
ADHLNSTU	Landshut	**ADILLMNR**	mandrill	**ADIMOPSY**	sympodia
ADHLORRY	Old Harry	**ADILLMOU**	allodium	**ADIMORRS**	miradors
ADHMORSY	hydromas	**ADILLMSY**	dismally	**ADIMOSST**	mastoids
ADHNNORU	Honduran	**ADILLNPS**	landslip	**ADIMOSTT**	mattoids
ADHNNORSU	Honduras	**ADILLOSW**	disallow	**ADIMOSTY**	toadyism
ADHNOSTU	handouts	**ADILLOSY**	disloyal	**ADIMPRSY**	pyramids
	thousand	**ADILLRUV**	Vuillard	**ADIMRSUU**	sudarium
ADHNOSWW	downwash	**ADILLSTY**	distally	**ADIMSSST**	dismasts
ADHNRSTY	hydrants	**ADILMNNO**	mandolin	**ADIMSSTU**	stadiums
ADHOOPRS	hospodar	**ADILMNOS**	salmonid	**ADINNNTU**	inundant
ADHOORSW	roadshow	**ADILMNRS**	mandrils	**ADINNOOR**	Rondônia
ADHOPRST	hardtops	**ADILMOPS**	diplomas	**ADINNOOT**	donation
	potshard		plasmoid	**ADINNOPS**	dipnoans
ADHOPRSY	rhapsody	**ADILMOPT**	diplomat	**ADINNORS**	andirons
ADHOPSST	dashpots	**ADILMOPY**	olympiad	**ADINNRSW**	winnards
ADHORRTY	hydrator	**ADILMOSY**	amyloids	**ADINOOPS**	isopodan
ADIIINRV	viridian	**ADILMOTY**	modality	**ADINOOPT**	adoption
ADIIIQRU	daiquiri	**ADILMPSS**	plasmids	**ADINOORT**	tandoori
ADIIKLMM	milkmaid	**ADILMPSU**	paludism	**ADINOOTT**	dotation
ADIIKLST	tailskid	**ADILNNOR**	Londrina	**ADINOPPS**	oppidans
ADIIKNST	antiskid	**ADILNNSU**	disannul	**ADINOPRS**	poniards
ADIILLMR	milliard	**ADILNOOR**	doornail	**ADINOPST**	satinpod
ADIILLOP	lipoidal	**ADILNOOV**	vindaloo	**ADINORRY**	ordinary
ADIILLUV	diluvial	**ADILNORS**	ordinals	**ADINORSS**	sadirons
ADIILMRV	Vladimir	**ADILNOTY**	nodality	**ADINORST**	intrados
ADIILNOT	dilation	**ADILNPRS**	spandril	**ADINORSU**	dinosaur
ADIILNSU	indusial	**ADILNPST**	displant	**ADINORTU**	duration
ADIILNSV	invalids	**ADILNRSU**	diurnals	**ADINOSSV**	Davisson
ADIILNSW	windsail	**ADILNRWY**	inwardly	**ADINOSTT**	Donatist
ADIILNTW	tailwind	**ADILNSSU**	sundials	**ADINOSTX**	oxidants
ADIILNTY	daintily	**ADILNSSW**	windlass	**ADINOSTY**	dystonia
ADIILNUV	diluvian	**ADILOORT**	toroidal	**ADINPSST**	sandpits
ADIILOPP	diplopia	**ADILOPRT**	dioptral	**ADIOOPRT**	parotoid
ADIILSSY	dialysis		tripodal	**ADIOOPSS**	apodosis
ADIILTVY	validity	**ADILOPSS**	disposal	**ADIOOSSW**	woodsias
ADIIMNNU	Numidian	**ADILORST**	dilators	**ADIOPPST**	postpaid
ADIIMNOT	Domitian	**ADILORSY**	solidary	**ADIOPRRS**	airdrops
ADIIMRST	triadism	**ADILORTY**	adroitly	**ADIOPRSS**	sparoids
ADIINNOS	Sidonian		dilatory	**ADIOPRST**	parodist
ADIINNOT	nidation		idolatry		parotids
ADIINOOT	iodation	**ADILOSTY**	sodality		Port Said
ADIINOSY	Dionysia	**ADILPRSY**	pyralids	**ADIOPRTY**	podiatry
ADIINOTU	audition	**ADILPSST**	plastids	**ADIOPSTY**	dystopia
ADIINRST	distrain	**ADILPSSY**	displays	**ADIORRTT**	traditor
ADIIPRTY	rapidity	**ADILPSTU**	plaudits	**ADIORSST**	astroids
ADIIPSTY	sapidity	**ADILRTTY**	tiltyard	**ADIORSSV**	advisors
ADIIPTVY	vapidity	**ADILRTWY**	tawdrily	**ADIORSTU**	auditors
ADIIRSST	diarists	**ADILRWYZ**	wizardly	**ADIORSVY**	advisory

245

ADIORTUY	auditory	**ADNNOOSY**	noondays	**AEEELNPS**	Nepalese
ADIOSSVW	disavows	**ADNNORTY**	dynatron	**AEEEELNRV**	venereal
ADIRRWYZ	wizardry	**ADNOOPRV**	Andropov	**AEEEELNST**	selenate
ADIRSSTY	satyrids	**ADNOOQRU**	quadroon	**AEEELPRR**	repealer
ADJKNRUY	junkyard	**ADNOORST**	donators	**AEEEELQSU**	sequelae
ADJLMORS	jarldoms		tandoors	**AEEELRRS**	releaser
ADJNORSU	adjourns		tornados	**AEEEELRRV**	revealer
ADJORRSU	adjurors	**ADNOOSVW**	advowson	**AEEELRSS**	releases
ADKLMRSU	mudlarks	**ADNOPRSU**	pandours	**AEEEELRTX**	axletree
ADKLOORW	woodlark	**ADNOQRSU**	squadron	**AEEEELSTV**	elevates
	workload	**ADNORSTU**	rotundas	**AEEEMMRT**	metamere
ADKMNORW	markdown	**ADNORSTW**	sandwort	**AEEEMNST**	easement
ADKMOORR	darkroom	**ADNORSXY**	sardonyx	**AEEEMPRT**	permeate
ADKNORTU	outdrank	**ADNORTUW**	untoward	**AEEEENPTT**	patentee
ADKOORRW	roadwork	**ADNOSSTU**	astounds	**AEEEENRTV**	enervate
ADKORSWY	workdays	**ADNOSTTU**	outstand		venerate
ADKRSSWY	skywards		standout	**AEEEPRRT**	repartee
ADLLLOOY	doolally	**ADNPSSTU**	dustpans		repeater
ADLLNOSW	lowlands	**ADNRSSUW**	sunwards	**AEEEPSTW**	sweetpea
ADLLNUUZ	Zululand	**ADOOPPRU**	pauropod	**AEEEERRTW**	treeware
ADLLOPRS	pollards	**ADOOPRRT**	trapdoor	**AEEERSST**	esterase
ADLLORSY	dorsally	**ADOOPRSU**	sauropod		tesserae
ADLMNOOR	moorland	**ADOORSWY**	doorways	**AEEFFLLS**	felafels
ADLMNOOV	Moldovan	**ADOOSSSW**	sasswood	**AEEFFLTT**	flatfeet
ADLMNORY	randomly	**ADOPPRST**	Stoppard	**AEEFFNRT**	afferent
ADLMOPSY	psalmody	**ADOPRSSW**	password	**AEEFGILR**	filagree
ADLNNORS	norlands	**ADOPSSSU**	soapsuds	**AEEFGIRR**	ferriage
ADLNNOTW	townland	**ADORSTUW**	outwards	**AEEFGLSU**	fuselage
ADLNNTUU	undulant	**ADORSTUY**	sudatory	**AEEFHLLS**	selfheal
ADLNOORS	lardoons	**ADRSSTTU**	stardust	**AEEFHRST**	feathers
ADLNOORW	loanword	**AEEEFORS**	Faeroese	**AEEFHRTY**	feathery
ADLNOPRT	portland	**AEEEFRRW**	freeware	**AEEFIIRS**	aerifies
ADLNOPRU	pauldron	**AEEEGGNR**	reengage	**AEEFIKLL**	leaflike
ADLNOPSU	poundals	**AEEEGHNS**	Seahenge	**AEEFIKRR**	freakier
ADLNOPWY	downplay	**AEEEGLLS**	legalese	**AEEFIKRW**	wakerife
	playdown	**AEEEGLMR**	Meleager	**AEEFILMN**	filename
ADLNOSTU	outlands	**AEEEGLRT**	regelate	**AEEFILNR**	flanerie
ADLOOPRU	uropodal		relegate	**AEEFILST**	fealties
ADLOPRSU	poulards	**AEEEGLRV**	leverage		fetiales
ADLOPRWY	wordplay	**AEEEGLST**	legatees		leafiest
ADLOQSUW	oldsquaw	**AEEEGNRT**	generate	**AEEFIPSW**	spaewife
ADLORRSW	warlords		teenager	**AEEFIRRR**	rarefier
ADLORTWY	towardly	**AEEEGNSS**	ageneses	**AEEFIRRS**	rarefies
ADLPRUWY	upwardly	**AEEEGPRS**	peerages	**AEEFIRSS**	freesias
ADMMNORU	Omdurman	**AEEEGPSS**	seepages	**AEEFISST**	safeties
ADMMNSSU	summands	**AEEEGRST**	etageres	**AEEFKOPR**	forepeak
ADMNNORY	monandry		steerage	**AEEFLLLM**	Flémalle
	Normandy	**AEEEGRSW**	sewerage	**AEEFLLMT**	flamelet
ADMNOORS	madronos	**AEEEGTTV**	vegetate	**AEEFLLNV**	evenfall
ADMNOOST	mastodon	**AEEEHLRT**	ethereal	**AEEFLLRW**	farewell
ADMNOOSW	woodsman	**AEEEHMPR**	ephemera	**AEEFLLSS**	leafless
ADMNORST	mordants	**AEEEHRRS**	rehearse	**AEEFLLST**	fellates
ADMNORSW	sandworm	**AEEEHRRT**	reheater		leaflets
ADMNOSSU	osmundas	**AEEEHSTT**	aesthete	**AEEFLMSS**	fameless
ADMOOPPP	poppadom	**AEEEILNS**	alienees		selfsame
ADMOORRT	Dartmoor	**AEEEIMNX**	examinee	**AEEFLNRU**	funereal
ADMOORRW	wardroom	**AEEEIRST**	eateries	**AEEFLOOV**	foveolae
ADMOORST	doormats	**AEEEKKPS**	keepsake	**AEEFLORV**	overleaf
ADMOPPPU	poppadum	**AEEEKNRW**	weakener	**AEEFLRRR**	referral
ADMORSST	tsardoms	**AEEEKNTW**	Enewetak	**AEEFLRRT**	falterer
ADMRSSTU	durmasts	**AEEELLPP**	appellee	**AEEFLRSS**	fearless
	mustards	**AEEELMNR**	enameler	**AEEFLRST**	reflates

AEEFLTTT	flatette	AEEGIRSU	eugaries	AEEGNSTV	ventages
AEEFMNOR	forename	AEEGIRTT	aigrette	AEEGNSUY	Guyanese
AEEFMORS	fearsome	AEEGIRTV	ergative	AEEGOPRV	overpage
AEEFMRRS	reframes	AEEGISTY	gayeties	AEEGORRV	overgear
AEEFNRST	fastener	AEEGKMRR	regmaker	AEEGPRRS	presager
	fenestra	AEEGLLNR	allergen	AEEGPRSS	asperges
	refasten	AEEGLLSZ	gazelles		presages
AEEFNRTT	fattener	AEEGLMNS	melanges	AEEGPRSU	pugarees
AEEFNSSS	safeness	AEEGLMOS	mesoglea	AEEGRRRT	regrater
AEEFRRST	ferrates	AEEGLMPX	megaplex	AEEGRRSS	greasers
AEEFRSTU	feasters	AEEGLMRT	telegram	AEEGRRST	regrates
AEEFRSTU	features	AEEGLMRY	meagerly	AEEGRRSU	reargues
AEEFRSWY	freeways		meagrely	AEEGRRSW	wagerers
AEEGGINR	agreeing	AEEGLNNO	Angeleno	AEEGRSST	restages
AEEGGIRV	aggrieve	AEEGLNNR	Erlangen	AEEGRSTT	greatest
AEEGGNNR	gangrene	AEEGLNNT	entangle	AEEGRSUZ	guerezas
AEEGGNRS	engagers	AEEGLNOS	gasolene	AEEGSSTT	gestates
AEEGGPRU	puggaree	AEEGLNOT	elongate	AEEGSTTZ	gazettes
AEEGGRSU	regauges	AEEGLNRR	enlarger	AEEHHHSS	hasheesh
AEEGHILN	Hegelian		Erlanger	AEEHHIKZ	Hezekiah
AEEGHIRT	heritage	AEEGLNRS	enlarges	AEEHHIMN	Nehemiah
AEEGHLOT	helotage		generals	AEEHHLNZ	hazelhen
AEEGHMPR	grapheme		gleaners	AEEHHNST	heathens
AEEGHNRS	shagreen	AEEGLNRT	regental	AEEHHRST	heathers
AEEGHNSW	whangees	AEEGLNSV	evangels	AEEHHRTY	heathery
AEEGHRRT	gatherer	AEEGLNSY	Anglesey	AEEHHSST	sheaths
	regather	AEEGLRSS	eelgrass	AEEHIJMR	Jeremiah
AEEGIIST	gaieties		gearless	AEEHIKLN	Alekhine
AEEGIKLM	gamelike		largesse	AEEHIKLR	harelike
AEEGIKLT	gatelike	AEEGLRSU	leaguers	AEEHIKMN	Khamenei
AEEGILLS	galilees	AEEGLRSZ	reglazes	AEEHIKRS	shikaree
	legalise	AEEGLRTU	regulate	AEEHILRS	shiralee
AEEGILLZ	legalize	AEEGLRUX	exergual	AEEHILTV	Helvetia
AEEGILMN	liegeman	AEEGLSST	gateless	AEEHIMNT	hematein
AEEGILMR	gleamier	AEEGLSSV	selvages	AEEHIMNX	hexamine
AEEGILMS	gelsemia	AEEGLSSW	wageless	AEEHIMTT	hematite
	mileages	AEEGLSSY	eyeglass	AEEHIPRS	Hesperia
AEEGILNR	algerine	AEEGLTTU	tutelage		pharisee
AEEGILNS	ensilage	AEEGMMNS	gamesmen		sphairee
	lineages	AEEGMMOS	gamesome	AEEHIRRT	earthier
AEEGILNT	galenite	AEEGMMST	gemmates		heartier
	gelatine		tagmemes	AEEHIRST	hearties
	legatine	AEEGMNSS	gameness	AEEHIRSV	shivaree
AEEGILPR	perigeal	AEEGMRRS	Grasmere	AEEHISST	esthesia
AEEGILRS	gaselier	AEEGMRSS	Messager	AEEHISTT	hesitate
AEEGILSW	weigelas	AEEGMRST	gamester	AEEHISTV	heaviest
AEEGILTV	levigate	AEEGMSSS	messages	AEEHISTW	White Sea
AEEGIMNT	geminate	AEEGMSSU	messuage	AEEHKLLR	rakehell
AEEGIMRT	emigrate	AEEGNNNO	enneagon	AEEHKLLU	keelhaul
AEEGINPR	perigean	AEEGNPPS	genappes	AEEHKNRR	harkener
AEEGINRR	regainer	AEEGNRRV	engraver	AEEHKNRS	hearkens
AEEGINRS	gesneria	AEEGNRST	estrange	AEEHLLSS	seashell
AEEGINRZ	razeeing		grantees	AEEHLMNW	whalemen
AEEGINSS	agenesis		greatens		wheelman
	assignee		negaters	AEEHLMNY	hymeneal
AEEGINSU	Guianese		reagents	AEEHLMPT	helpmate
AEEGINSV	envisage		sergeant	AEEHLNOT	anethole
AEEGINTV	agentive	AEEGNRSV	avengers	AEEHLNPT	elephant
	negative		engraves	AEEHLNRT	leathern
AEEGIPQU	equipage	AEEGNRUV	Auvergne	AEEHLNSS	haleness
AEEGIRRS	greasier	AEEGNSSS	sageness	AEEHLNVY	heavenly
AEEGIRSS	greasies	AEEGNSTT	tentages		

AEEHLORS	arsehole	**AEEIKNRS**	sneakier	**AEEIMORV**	Aviemore
	halosere	**AEEIKNRT**	ankerite	**AEEIMRSS**	seriemas
AEEHLOSU	alehouse	**AEEIKNTW**	Keewatin	**AEEIMRST**	emirates
AEEHLPST	heeltaps	**AEEILLNT**	tenaille		steamier
AEEHLPTT	telepath	**AEEILLRT**	laetrile	**AEEIMSST**	seamiest
AEEHLRST	halteres	**AEEILMMN**	melamine		steamies
	leathers	**AEEILMNT**	melanite	**AEEIMSTT**	estimate
AEEHLRTY	leathery	**AEEILMRS**	measlier		meatiest
AEEHLSST	heatless	**AEEILMRT**	Lemaître	**AEEINNRS**	anserine
AEEHLSTT	athletes		materiel	**AEEINNTV**	Aventine
AEEHLTTY	ethylate		realtime		venetian
AEEHMMRR	hammerer	**AEEILMST**	mealiest	**AEEINOPS**	paeonies
AEEHMNRT	earthmen	**AEEILMTZ**	metalize	**AEEINPRS**	naperies
AEEHMNTU	atheneum	**AEEILNPR**	perineal	**AEEINPRT**	aperient
AEEHMNTX	exanthem	**AEEILNPS**	penalise		Patenier
AEEHMORW	homeware		sepaline	**AEEINRRT**	Arretine
AEEHMPRR	hamperer	**AEEILNPT**	petaline		Eritrean
AEEHMPSS	emphases		tapeline		retainer
AEEHMRSS	mahseers	**AEEILNPZ**	penalize	**AEEINRSS**	Asnières
AEEHMRTY	erythema	**AEEILNRT**	elaterin	**AEEINRST**	arenites
AEEHNNTX	xanthene		entailer		arsenite
AEEHNNVW	Newhaven		treenail		resinate
	New Haven	**AEEILNRV**	Verlaine		stearine
AEEHNOPR	earphone	**AEEILORT**	aerolite		Teresina
AEEHNRRT	Traherne	**AEEILOTT**	etiolate		trainees
AEEHNRST	hastener	**AEEILPRR**	pearlier	**AEEINRSU**	uneasier
	heartens	**AEEILPRS**	espalier	**AEEINSSS**	easiness
AEEHNRTT	threaten		pearlies	**AEEINSTT**	anisette
AEEHNRTU	urethane	**AEEILPRT**	pearlite		tetanise
AEEHNRTW	enwreath	**AEEILPST**	epilates	**AEEINSTV**	naivetes
	waterhen	**AEEILQSU**	equalise	**AEEINSVW**	inweaves
AEEHNRWY	anywhere	**AEEILQUZ**	equalize	**AEEINTTZ**	tetanize
AEEHNSTW	enswathe	**AEEILRRS**	realiser	**AEEIOOPP**	epopoeia
AEEHOPRT	ephorate	**AEEILRRT**	retailer	**AEEIORST**	etaerios
AEEHORRV	overhear	**AEEILRRZ**	realizer	**AEEIPPSU**	eupepsia
AEEHORSS	sea horse	**AEEILRSS**	realises	**AEEIPPTT**	appetite
	seahorse	**AEEILRST**	ateliers	**AEEIPRRR**	rareripe
	seashore		earliest		repairer
AEEHORTV	overheat		leariest	**AEEIPRST**	parietes
AEEHOSTU	teahouse	**AEEILRSV**	velarise	**AEEIPRSU**	Peiraeus
AEEHPPRS	preshape	**AEEILRSY**	yearlies	**AEEIPSST**	epitases
AEEHPRRS	rephrase	**AEEILRSZ**	realizes	**AEEIPSTX**	expiates
AEEHPRRT	threaper		sleazier	**AEEIQRSU**	queasier
AEEHPRSS	reshapes	**AEEILRTT**	laterite	**AEEIQSTU**	equiseta
AEEHPRST	preheats		literate	**AEEIRRST**	arteries
AEEHPSUV	upheaves	**AEEILRTV**	levirate	**AEEIRSTT**	ariettes
AEEHRRSS	shearers		relative		iterates
AEEHRRTU	urethrae	**AEEILRVW**	liveware		teariest
AEEHRSSW	rewashes		reviewal		treaties
AEEHRSTT	theaters	**AEEILRVZ**	velarize		treatise
	theatres	**AEEILSTV**	elatives	**AEEIRSTW**	sweatier
AEEHRSTW	weathers	**AEEILSVW**	alewives		weariest
	wreathes	**AEEILTTV**	levitate	**AEEIRSTY**	yeastier
AEEHRTVW	whatever	**AEEIMMNT**	meantime	**AEEIRSVV**	aversive
AEEIKLLS	seallike	**AEEIMNRT**	antimere	**AEEISTTT**	steatite
AEEIKLMU	leukemia	**AEEIMNRX**	examiner	**AEEISTTV**	estivate
AEEIKLMZ	mazelike	**AEEIMNSS**	Messenia	**AEEITUVX**	exuviate
AEEIKLPT	tapelike		Messiaen	**AEEJLNPT**	jetplane
AEEIKLRW	weaklier		nemesias	**AEEJMPPS**	Jemappes
AEEIKLST	leakiest	**AEEIMNST**	matinees	**AEEJNRST**	serjeant
AEEIKLVW	wavelike	**AEEIMNSX**	examines	**AEEJORSV**	Serajevo
AEEIKMNT	ketamine	**AEEIMNUV**	mauveine	**AEEKKLWY**	lykewake

AEEKKNOS	kokanees	**AEELMPSX**	examples	**AEELRRSX**	relaxers
AEEKLLNY	Keneally	**AEELMPTT**	palmette	**AEELRRTU**	ureteral
AEEKLLST	skeletal		template	**AEELRRTV**	traveler
AEEKLMMU	mameluke	**AEELMRTX**	extremal	**AEELRSST**	stealers
AEEKLMRT	telemark	**AEELMSSS**	seamless		tearless
AEEKLMSS	makeless	**AEELMSST**	mateless		tesseral
AEEKLSSW	wakeless		meatless	**AEELRSTX**	exalters
AEEKLSTY	eyestalk		tameless	**AEELRSTY**	easterly
AEEKMMRR	Kammerer	**AEELMSTU**	emulates	**AEELRSUV**	revalues
AEEKMNSS	kamseens	**AEELNNPS**	enplanes	**AEELRSVY**	aversely
AEEKMORV	makeover	**AEELNNRT**	lanneret	**AEELSSST**	seatless
AEEKMRRR	remarker	**AEELNNSS**	leanness	**AEELSSWV**	waveless
AEEKMRRT	marketer	**AEELNOPR**	peroneal	**AEELSTTT**	statelet
AEEKMRST	meerkats	**AEELNOPT**	antelope	**AEELSTTY**	layettes
AEEKNNNS	nankeens	**AEELNORU**	aleurone	**AEELSTVW**	wavelets
AEEKNNPS	kneepans	**AEELNPPS**	spalpeen	**AEEMMNTZ**	mazement
AEEKNPSW	newspeak	**AEELNPQU**	Palenque	**AEEMMPSY**	empyemas
AEEKNRSS	sneakers	**AEELNPSS**	paleness	**AEEMMRRY**	yammerer
AEEKNRSW	rewakens	**AEELNQSU**	squalene	**AEEMMRST**	ammeters
	wakeners	**AEELNRRS**	learners		metamers
AEEKNSSW	weakness		relearns	**AEEMMSST**	messmate
AEEKORST	keratose	**AEELNRSS**	realness	**AEEMNNOS**	anemones
AEEKORTV	overtake	**AEELNRST**	telerans	**AEEMNNRT**	remanent
	takeover	**AEELNRSV**	enslaver	**AEEMNNST**	meanness
AEEKPRSS	speakers	**AEELNRSW**	renewals	**AEEMNPRS**	spearmen
AEEKPRTT	parkette	**AEELNRTV**	levanter	**AEEMNPRT**	permeant
AEEKQRSU	squeaker		relevant		peterman
AEEKRRST	retakers	**AEELNRTX**	external	**AEEMNPRY**	empyrean
	streaker	**AEELNSST**	lateness	**AEEMNPTV**	pavement
AEEKRRSW	wreakers	**AEELNSSV**	enslaves	**AEEMNRST**	Ansermet
AEEKRSTW	tweakers		vaneless	**AEEMNRSW**	menswear
AEELLLTT	telltale	**AEELNSWY**	Wesleyan	**AEEMNRTU**	numerate
AEELLMSS	mealless	**AEELNTUV**	eventual	**AEEMNRTV**	averment
AEELLOTT	allottee	**AEELOPRS**	parolees	**AEEMNRTW**	watermen
AEELLPPY	Alleppey	**AEELOPRV**	overleap	**AEEMNRUV**	maneuver
AEELLPTT	platelet	**AEELOPSX**	poleaxes	**AEEMNRVY**	everyman
AEELLRRV	raveller	**AEELORST**	oleaster	**AEEMNSSS**	sameness
AEELLSTT	stellate	**AEELORSU**	aureoles	**AEEMNSST**	Massenet
AEELLSWY	walleyes	**AEELORTT**	tolerate		tameness
	weaselly	**AEELORTV**	elevator	**AEEMNSTW**	sweetman
AEELLTVV	valvelet	**AEELOTTT**	teetotal	**AEEMORST**	Masorete
AEELMMNU	Emmanuel	**AEELPRRS**	pearlers	**AEEMPPPR**	pamperer
AEELMMTU	malemute		relapser	**AEEMPRRT**	tamperer
AEELMNNT	Telemann	**AEELPRRT**	palterer	**AEEMPRRV**	revamper
AEELMNOT	Manolete	**AEELPRRY**	parleyer	**AEEMPRST**	temperas
AEELMNPR	Perelman	**AEELPRSS**	pleasers	**AEEMPRTT**	attemper
AEELMNPS	empanels		relapses	**AEEMPSTU**	amputees
	emplanes	**AEELPRST**	pleaters	**AEEMQRRU**	remarque
	ensample		prelates	**AEEMQRSU**	marquees
AEELMNRT	lamenter	**AEELPRSU**	pleasure	**AEEMQTTU**	maquette
AEELMNSS	lameness	**AEELPRSV**	vesperal	**AEEMRRSS**	smearers
	maleness	**AEELPRTY**	pterylae	**AEEMRRST**	remaster
	maneless	**AEELPSST**	spatlese		streamer
	nameless	**AEELPSTT**	palettes	**AEEMRRSU**	measurer
	salesmen	**AEELPSTU**	epaulets	**AEEMRSST**	masseter
AEELMNST	talesmen	**AEELQRSU**	lequears		steamers
AEELMNSU	Menelaus		squealer	**AEEMRSSU**	measures
AEELMNTT	mantelet	**AEELQSUZ**	quezales		reassume
AEELMOTT	matelote	**AEELRRST**	realters	**AEEMRSTT**	teamster
AEELMPRS	empalers		relaters	**AEEMRSTV**	Temesvár
AEELMPRX	exemplar	**AEELRRSV**	reversal	**AEEMRSTW**	stemware
AEELMPRY	empyreal		slaverer	**AEEMSSSU**	masseuse

AEEMSSTU	meatuses	**AEERRRST**	arrester	**AEFGIRST**	frigates
AEENNOST	neonates		rearrest	**AEFGIRSU**	argufies
AEENNPRY	Pyrenean	**AEERRSST**	asserter	**AEFGIRTU**	figurate
AEENNRRS	ensnarer		reassert		fruitage
AEENNRRT	Nanterre		serrates	**AEFGISTU**	fatigues
AEENNRSS	ensnares	**AEERRSSU**	erasures	**AEFGLLNO**	longleaf
	nearness		reassure	**AEFGLLOP**	flagpole
AEENNRTV	revenant	**AEERRSSW**	swearers	**AEFGLLOR**	Lagerlöf
AEENNSSS	saneness	**AEERRSTT**	retreats	**AEFGLLSS**	flagless
AEENNSST	neatness		treaters	**AEFGLMNU**	fugleman
AEENNSTT	setenant	**AEERRSTU**	treasure	**AEFGLMOP**	megaflop
AEENNSUW	Suwannee	**AEERRSTV**	traverse	**AEFGLNRS**	flangers
AEENOPRS	personae	**AEERRSTW**	waterers	**AEFGLNSS**	fangless
AEENORRS	reasoner	**AEERRSVW**	waverers	**AEFGLOOR**	floorage
AEENORSS	seasoner	**AEERSSSS**	reassess	**AEFGLOPR**	leapfrog
AEENORST	resonate	**AEERSSTT**	estreats	**AEFGLORU**	Laforgue
AEENORTV	renovate		restates	**AEFGLRTU**	grateful
AEENORVW	ovenware	**AEERSSTW**	sweaters	**AEFGMNRT**	fragment
AEENOTTU	outeaten	**AEERSSUU**	uraeuses	**AEFGNORT**	frontage
AEENPQTU	petanque	**AEERSTTT**	attester	**AEFGNRRS**	frangers
AEENPRUV	parvenue	**AEESSSSS**	assesses	**AEFGNRST**	engrafts
AEENPSSX	expanses	**AEESSTTT**	testates	**AEFGOORT**	footgear
AEENPTTY	antetype	**AEFFGIIL**	effigial	**AEFGOOST**	footages
AEENRRRW	warrener	**AEFFGIRS**	giraffes	**AEFGORRS**	foragers
AEENRRSS	rareness	**AEFFGOST**	offstage	**AEFGORTT**	frottage
AEENRRST	terranes	**AEFFGRSU**	gauffers	**AEFGRRST**	grafters
AEENRRSV	raveners		suffrage	**AEFHIKRS**	freakish
AEENRRSY	yearners	**AEFFHIKY**	kaffiyeh	**AEFHIKSW**	weakfish
AEENRRTT	natterer	**AEFFHILL**	halflife	**AEFHILLN**	fellahin
AEENRRTV	taverner	**AEFFIIPT**	Ipatieff	**AEFHILLR**	firehall
AEENRSST	earnests	**AEFFILUV**	effluvia	**AEFHILLT**	tefillah
	sarsenet	**AEFFIMRR**	affirmer	**AEFHILMS**	fishmeal
AEENRSTT	entreats		reaffirm	**AEFHILMT**	halftime
AEENRSTV	veterans	**AEFFKORS**	rakeoffs	**AEFHILNS**	shinleaf
AEENRSTW	Westenra	**AEFFKOST**	takeoffs	**AEFHILRS**	flashier
AEENRTTV	antevert	**AEFFLNSS**	snaffles	**AEFHIMSS**	famishes
AEENRTTX	extranet	**AEFFLNTU**	affluent	**AEFHINUZ**	Han Fei Zu
AEENRTTY	entreaty	**AEFFLRRS**	rafflers	**AEFHIRST**	faithers
AEEOPRRT	perorate	**AEFFLRSW**	wafflers	**AEFHIRSW**	wharfies
AEEOPRST	operates	**AEFFLSTU**	sufflate	**AEFHLMSU**	shameful
	protease	**AEFFLSUX**	affluxes	**AEFHLNOT**	halftone
AEEOPRTT	operetta	**AEFFMNST**	staffmen	**AEFHLRRU**	Harfleur
AEEORRSU	rearouse	**AEFFMRSU**	earmuffs	**AEFHLRSS**	flashers
AEEORRSV	Averroës	**AEFFNNSS**	naffness	**AEFHLRTY**	fatherly
AEEORRTV	overrate	**AEFFORST**	afforest		Flaherty
AEEORSSV	overseas	**AEFFOSVW**	waveoffs	**AEFHLSTU**	hasteful
AEEORSTV	overeats	**AEFFQRSU**	quaffers	**AEFHMNOZ**	Zamenhof
AEEORSVW	overawes	**AEFFRSST**	restaffs	**AEFHMNRS**	freshman
AEEPPRRR	preparer		staffers	**AEFHMORT**	fathomer
AEEPPRRS	paperers	**AEFFRTTU**	tartuffe	**AEFHRSTT**	farthest
	prepares	**AEFGGLRS**	flaggers	**AEFIIKLW**	waiflike
	repapers	**AEFGIIRS**	gasifier	**AEFIILLN**	nailfile
AEEPRRRT	parterre	**AEFGIISS**	gasifies	**AEFIILMS**	families
AEEPRRSS	asperser	**AEFGIKLN**	fanglike	**AEFIILNS**	finalise
	spearers	**AEFGIKMN**	Mafeking	**AEFIILNZ**	finalize
AEEPRRST	taperers		Mafikeng	**AEFIILSS**	salifies
AEEPRRTU	aperture	**AEFGIKNR**	freaking	**AEFIILST**	filiates
AEEPRSSS	asperses	**AEFGILNR**	finagler	**AEFIIMNS**	infamies
	repasses	**AEFGILNS**	finagles		infamise
AEEPRSST	trapeses	**AEFGIMTU**	fumigate	**AEFIIMNZ**	infamize
AEEPRSTZ	trapezes	**AEFGINRW**	wafering	**AEFIIMRS**	ramifies
AEEQRRUV	quaverer	**AEFGINST**	feasting	**AEFIINST**	fainites

AEFIINSZ	nazifies	**AEFINRSS**	fairness	**AEFLPRSY**	palfreys
AEFIIPRT	aperitif		sanserif	**AEFLRSSU**	refusals
AEFIIRRS	friaries	**AEFINRST**	fainters	**AEFLRSTT**	flatters
AEFIIRRT	ratifier	**AEFINSTT**	faintest	**AEFLRSZZ**	frazzles
AEFIIRST	ratifies	**AEFIORTV**	favorite	**AEFLRTTU**	aflutter
AEFIITVX	fixative	**AEFIPRRT**	firetrap	**AEFLRTTY**	flattery
AEFIKKLV	Keflavík	**AEFIQRSU**	aquifers	**AEFLSSTU**	flatuses
AEFIKLMO	foamlike	**AEFIRRRS**	farriers	**AEFLSTTT**	flattest
AEFIKLNU	faunlike	**AEFIRRRY**	farriery	**AEFLSTTU**	tasteful
AEFIKLNW	fawnlike	**AEFISTTT**	fattiest	**AEFLSTUW**	wasteful
AEFIKLRY	freakily	**AEFKLLOT**	folktale	**AEFMNORS**	foramens
AEFIKLST	flakiest	**AEFKLLST**	self-talk	**AEFMORRS**	forearms
AEFIKRUW	waukrife	**AEFKLNRS**	flankers	**AEFMORST**	foremast
AEFILLLN	Fall Line	**AEFKLNRU**	Faulkner		formates
AEFILLNT	flatline	**AEFKLSST**	flaskets		mortsafe
AEFILLOT	fellatio	**AEFKNORS**	forsaken	**AEFMORVW**	waveform
AEFILLRW	firewall	**AEFKNRST**	frankest	**AEFNNSTU**	unfasten
AEFILLTT	Tafilelt	**AEFKOPRS**	forspeak	**AEFNOPRR**	profaner
AEFILMNR	inflamer	**AEFKORRS**	forsaker	**AEFNOPRS**	profanes
	rifleman	**AEFKORRW**	workfare	**AEFNORRW**	forewarn
AEFILMNS	flamines	**AEFKORSS**	forsakes	**AEFNORST**	seafront
	inflames	**AEFKORTU**	freakout	**AEFNRRST**	transfer
AEFILMNT	filament	**AEFLLNNS**	flannels	**AEFNRRUY**	funerary
AEFILMSY	mayflies	**AEFLLORT**	fellator	**AEFNRSTU**	aftersun
AEFILMUY	El Faiyûm	**AEFLLORU**	florulae	**AEFNSSST**	fastness
AEFILNNR	infernal	**AEFLLORV**	overfall		saftness
AEFILNPS	lifespan	**AEFLLOST**	floatels	**AEFOORTW**	footwear
AEFILNRT	inflater	**AEFLLPTU**	plateful	**AEFOPRRT**	forepart
AEFILNRU	fraulein	**AEFLLRUX**	flexural	**AEFOPRSW**	forepaws
AEFILNST	inflates	**AEFLLSSW**	flawless	**AEFORRSV**	favorers
AEFILOOR	aerofoil	**AEFLLSTT**	flatlets	**AEFORRSW**	forswear
AEFILORS	foresail	**AEFLLSTY**	festally	**AEFORRSY**	forayers
AEFILORT	floatier	**AEFLMORU**	formulae	**AEFORRUV**	favourer
AEFILOST	foliates		fumarole	**AEFORSTW**	software
AEFILPRX	prefixal	**AEFLMOSS**	foamless	**AEFORSTY**	forestay
AEFILPST	fleapits	**AEFLMOSY**	flaysome	**AEFOSSWY**	Fosse Way
AEFILRST	frailest	**AEFLMOTU**	flameout	**AEFRRSST**	strafers
AEFILRSU	failures	**AEFLNNOT**	fontanel	**AEFRSTTU**	tartufes
AEFILRTT	filtrate	**AEFLNNTY**	fentanyl	**AEFRSTUW**	waftures
AEFILRTU	faultier	**AEFLNOPT**	pantofle	**AEFRSWYZ**	frawzeys
	filature	**AEFLNORS**	farnesol	**AEGGGINN**	engaging
AEFILRUW	weariful	**AEFLNORT**	floreant	**AEGGHIRS**	shaggier
AEFILSSW	sawflies	**AEFLNRSU**	flaneurs	**AEGGHISS**	haggises
AEFILSTT	flatties		funerals	**AEGGHJRY**	jagghery
AEFILSTU	fistulae	**AEFLNRTU**	flaunter	**AEGGHLRS**	hagglers
AEFILSTV	festival	**AEFLNSST**	flatness	**AEGGHMOS**	hemagogs
AEFILSTW	flatwise	**AEFLNSTT**	flattens	**AEGGHNNY**	Hengyang
AEFILTUU	fauteuil	**AEFLNSUU**	faunules	**AEGGHOPY**	geophagy
AEFIMNST	manifest	**AEFLOORS**	seafloor	**AEGGHORU**	roughage
AEFIMORR	aeriform	**AEFLOORV**	foveolar	**AEGGIINV**	gingivae
AEFIMOST	foamiest	**AEFLOPRT**	teraflop	**AEGGIJST**	jaggiest
AEFIMRRS	firearms	**AEFLOPRY**	foreplay	**AEGGILLN**	alleging
AEFIMRRW	firmware	**AEFLOPSW**	peafowls	**AEGGILLR**	grillage
AEFINNNS	Anfinsen	**AEFLORRV**	flavorer	**AEGGILMN**	gleaming
AEFINNSS	naifness	**AEFLORST**	floaters	**AEGGILNN**	gleaning
AEFINNST	infantes		forestal	**AEGGILNR**	lagering
AEFINNSZ	fanzines		refloats		regaling
AEFINOPR	pinafore	**AEFLORTW**	fleawort	**AEGGILNU**	leaguing
AEFINORS	farinose	**AEFLOSTT**	falsetto	**AEGGIMOR**	Maggiore
AEFINOTT	fetation	**AEFLPPRS**	flappers	**AEGGIMSU**	misgauge
AEFINPRS	firepans	**AEFLPPRY**	flypaper	**AEGGINNR**	angering
AEFINRRS	refrains	**AEFLPRSS**	felspars		enraging

AEGGINNT	negating	**AEGHMOPT**	apothegm	**AEGILMNP**	empaling
AEGGINNV	avenging	**AEGHNNSY**	Shenyang	**AEGILMNR**	germinal
AEGGINOR	Georgian	**AEGHNOPT**	heptagon		maligner
AEGGINOS	seagoing		pathogen		malinger
AEGGINRR	Grainger	**AEGHNORV**	hangover	**AEGILMNT**	ligament
AEGGINRS	gearings		overhang		metaling
	greasing	**AEGHNOSX**	hexagons		tegminal
AEGGINRW	wagering	**AEGHNRSS**	gnashers	**AEGILMRS**	gremials
AEGGIOPR	arpeggio		sherangs	**AEGILMRX**	lexigram
AEGGIOSS	isagoges	**AEGHNSST**	stengahs	**AEGILNNP**	paneling
AEGGIQRU	quaggier	**AEGHOPPR**	prophage	**AEGILNNR**	learning
AEGGIRRU	garrigue	**AEGHOPPY**	apophyge	**AEGILNNS**	leanings
AEGGISSW	swaggies	**AEGHORST**	shortage	**AEGILNNT**	gantline
AEGGLNPT	eggplant	**AEGHOSST**	hostages	**AEGILNNW**	weanling
AEGGLNRS	gangrels	**AEGHRTTU**	retaught	**AEGILNNY**	yeanling
AEGGLORY	gargoyle	**AEGIILLU**	aiguille	**AEGILNOR**	geraniol
AEGGLOWY	wayleggo	**AEGIILMN**	emailing		regional
AEGGLRRS	garglers	**AEGIILMO**	oligemia	**AEGILNOS**	gasoline
AEGGLRST	straggle	**AEGIILMR**	remigial	**AEGILNOT**	gelation
AEGGLRSW	wagglers	**AEGIILNN**	aliening		legation
AEGGLRSY	greylags	**AEGIILNR**	gainlier	**AEGILNPR**	pearling
AEGGMORT	mortgage	**AEGIILTT**	litigate	**AEGILNPS**	elapsing
AEGGNORW	waggoner	**AEGIILTV**	ligative		pleasing
AEGGNRST	gangster	**AEGIIMNR**	imaginer	**AEGILNPT**	pleating
AEGGRSST	staggers		migraine	**AEGILNQU**	equaling
AEGGRSSW	swaggers	**AEGIIMNS**	imagines	**AEGILNRS**	engrails
AEGHIJNZ	Zhejiang	**AEGIIMTT**	mitigate		nargiles
AEGHILLM	megillah	**AEGIINNR**	arginine		realigns
AEGHILLS	shigella		Nigerian		Salinger
AEGHILMT	megalith	**AEGIINRR**	grainier		signaler
AEGHILNR	narghile	**AEGIINTV**	Ignatiev	**AEGILNRT**	alerting
	nargileh	**AEGIIRRT**	irrigate		altering
AEGHILNS	healings	**AEGIKLNS**	linkages		integral
	leashing		snaglike		relating
AEGHILNT	atheling	**AEGIKLNT**	gnatlike		teraglin
AEGHILNX	exhaling	**AEGIKLNW**	weakling		triangle
AEGHILRT	litharge	**AEGIKLOT**	goatlike	**AEGILNRV**	raveling
	thirlage	**AEGIKMNR**	remaking	**AEGILNRX**	relaxing
AEGHILRY	Rayleigh	**AEGIKNNS**	sneaking	**AEGILNRY**	layering
AEGHINNN	hennaing	**AEGIKNNW**	wakening		relaying
AEGHINNV	havening	**AEGIKNPS**	speaking		yearling
AEGHINRS	hearings	**AEGIKNRT**	retaking	**AEGILNSS**	glassine
	shearing	**AEGIKNRW**	rewaking	**AEGILNST**	gelatins
AEGHINRT	earthing		wreaking		genitals
	hearting	**AEGIKNTW**	tweaking		stealing
	ingather	**AEGIKNNWY**	Kweiyang	**AEGILNSV**	leavings
AEGHINRV	havering	**AEGIKPRS**	garpikes		sleaving
AEGHINRY	Haringey	**AEGIKSTW**	gawkiest	**AEGILNTV**	valeting
AEGHINSV	sheaving	**AEGILLLS**	illegals	**AEGILNTX**	exalting
AEGHINSZ	genizahs	**AEGILLMS**	legalism	**AEGILNTZ**	teazling
AEGHINTT	gnathite	**AEGILLNY**	genially	**AEGILOPS**	spoilage
AEGHIOPS	esophagi	**AEGILLPR**	pillager	**AEGILOPT**	pilotage
AEGHIPPR	epigraph	**AEGILLPS**	pillages	**AEGILORS**	gasolier
AEGHIPRT	graphite		spillage		girasole
AEGHIRRS	gharries	**AEGILLRU**	guerilla		seraglio
AEGHLNOS	halogens	**AEGILLRV**	villager	**AEGILOSS**	oilgases
AEGHLOPY	hypogeal	**AEGILLST**	legalist	**AEGILPPS**	slippage
AEGHLOSS	galoshes		stillage	**AEGILPPU**	pupilage
AEGHLRSU	laughers	**AEGILLSV**	villages	**AEGILPSU**	Pelagius
AEGHLRTU	laughter	**AEGILLTU**	ligulate	**AEGILRRU**	glaurier
AEGHLRTY	lethargy	**AEGILLTY**	legality	**AEGILRSS**	glassier
AEGHLSTW	thalwegs	**AEGILMMR**	aglimmer	**AEGILRST**	glariest

AEGILRSU	Galerius		reassign	AEGLMNSS	glassmen
AEGILRSY	greasily		seringas	AEGLMNTU	gunmetal
AEGILRSZ	glaziers	AEGINRST	angriest	AEGLMOTV	megavolt
AEGILRTT	aglitter		angstier	AEGLMSSU	gaumless
AEGILRTU	Gaultier		ganister	AEGLNNPT	plangent
	ligature		gantries	AEGLNNSY	langsyne
AEGILRTY	regality		granites	AEGLNNTU	untangle
AEGILRVW	lawgiver		ingrates	AEGLNORS	Selangor
AEGILRYZ	glaziery		rangiest	AEGLNORY	yearlong
AEGIMMST	gammiest		reasting	AEGLNOST	tangelos
AEGIMNNR	renaming	AEGINRSV	vinegars	AEGLNOZZ	González
AEGIMNNS	meanings	AEGINRSW	swearing	AEGLNPRS	grapnels
AEGIMNRR	rearming	AEGINRTT	treating	AEGLNPSS	spangles
AEGIMNRS	smearing	AEGINRTV	averting	AEGLNRRW	wrangler
AEGIMNRT	emigrant		vintager	AEGLNRST	strangle
AEGIMNRU	geranium	AEGINRTW	watering		tanglers
	maungier	AEGINRVW	wavering	AEGLNRSU	granules
AEGIMNSS	gaminess	AEGINRVY	vinegary	AEGLNRSW	wanglers
AEGIMNST	mangiest	AEGINRWY	wearying		wrangles
	mintages	AEGINSST	eastings	AEGLNRSY	larynges
	steaming		giantess	AEGLNSTT	gantlets
AEGIMPRS	epigrams	AEGINSSY	essaying	AEGLNSTU	languets
AEGIMPRU	umpirage	AEGINSTT	tangiest	AEGLNSUW	gunwales
AEGIMQRU	quagmire	AEGINSTU	sauteing	AEGLNTTU	gauntlet
AEGIMRRS	armigers	AEGINSTV	vintages	AEGLNTUU	ungulate
AEGIMRSS	gisarmes	AEGINSTW	sweating	AEGLOOOZ	zoogloea
AEGIMRST	migrates	AEGINSTY	yeasting	AEGLOOPU	apologue
	sterigma	AEGINSTZ	tziganes	AEGLOORY	aerology
AEGIMRTT	Magritte	AEGIOPRR	progeria	AEGLOPRS	pergolas
AEGIMSSU	misusage	AEGIORSS	argosies	AEGLOPRY	playgoer
AEGINNNX	annexing	AEGIORSV	viragoes	AEGLORST	gloaters
AEGINNOS	anginose	AEGIOSTU	agouties		legators
AEGINNOT	Antigone	AEGIOSTX	geotaxis	AEGLORTV	travelog
	negation	AEGIPPRT	griptape	AEGLOSTV	voltages
AEGINNRS	earnings	AEGIPPST	gappiest	AEGLPPRR	grappler
	engrains	AEGIPRST	grapiest	AEGLPPRS	grapples
	grannies	AEGIRRSS	grassier	AEGLPRSU	earplugs
AEGINNRV	ravening	AEGIRRSZ	graziers		plaguers
AEGINNRY	yearning	AEGIRSTV	virgates	AEGLRRSS	regulars
AEGINNST	antigens	AEGIRSUU	auguries	AEGLRSTU	gestural
	gentians	AEGIRSUY	yugaries	AEGLSSTT	gestalts
AEGINNSU	sanguine	AEGISSST	gassiest	AEGLSTUU	glutaeus
AEGINOPT	pinotage	AEGISSTT	stagiest	AEGLSTUV	vulgates
AEGINORS	organise	AEGISTUZ	gauziest	AEGLSUUV	guayules
AEGINORT	Iron Gate	AEGJLNRS	janglers	AEGMMNOR	gammoner
AEGINORZ	organize	AEGJLTUU	jugulate	AEGMMPRU	Pergamum
AEGINOSS	agonises	AEGKLLOT	lekgotla	AEGMMRRU	rummager
AEGINOSV	Gonaïves	AEGKLOSU	kagoules	AEGMMRSU	rummages
AEGINOSZ	agonizes	AEGLLMNN	Gell-Mann	AEGMNNOT	magneton
AEGINPRS	papering	AEGLLNOS	galleons	AEGMNORV	mangrove
AEGINPPS	genipaps	AEGLLNRW	Wrangell	AEGMNOST	magnetos
AEGINPRS	spearing	AEGLLOPR	galloper		megatons
AEGINPRT	tapering	AEGLLORS	allegros		montages
AEGINPRV	repaving	AEGLLORY	allegory	AEGMNOXY	xenogamy
AEGINPRY	repaying	AEGLLOSS	gaolless	AEGMNRST	garments
AEGINPTY	egyptian		goalless		margents
AEGINQTU	equating	AEGLLOTT	tollgate	AEGMNRTU	argentum
AEGINRRS	earrings	AEGLLRVY	gravelly		argument
	grainers	AEGLLSSU	galluses	AEGMNSTU	augments
AEGINRRU	Guarneri		seagulls		mutagens
AEGINRRV	averring	AEGLMNNO	mangonel	AEGMOORS	moorages
AEGINRSS	assigner	AEGLMNRS	manglers	AEGMOPRW	gapeworm

AEGMORSS	gossamer	**AEHIIKRT**	terakihi	xanthine
AEGMPRUZ	gazumper	**AEHIIKST**	shiitake	**AEHINORT** antihero
AEGMPSTU	stumpage	**AEHIIKSU**	Hsia Kuei	**AEHINOST** Esthonia
AEGMRSUV	Musgrave	**AEHIILMO**	hemiolia	**AEHINOTT** thionate
AEGNNOPT	pentagon	**AEHIILNR**	hairline	**AEHINPPY** epiphany
AEGNNORT	negatron	**AEHIIMNT**	thiamine	**AEHINPRT** perianth
AEGNNOST	tonnages	**AEHIINTZ**	thiazine	**AEHINPST** thespian
AEGNNPRT	pregnant	**AEHIIOPT**	Ethiopia	**AEHINRST** hairnets
AEGNNRSU	gunneras	**AEHIIRSS**	Irish Sea	inearths
AEGNNSTT	tangents	**AEHIIRST**	hairiest	**AEHINRSV** vanisher
AEGNNSTU	tunnages	**AEHIKKLW**	hawklike	**AEHINRSW** sherwani
AEGNOPRR	parergon	**AEHIKLLL**	El Khalil	**AEHINRTU** Ruthenia
AEGNORRS	groaners	**AEHIKLLO**	halolike	**AEHINRTW** tarwhine
AEGNORRY	orangery	**AEHIKLLT**	lathlike	**AEHINSSS** hessians
AEGNORSS	Sargeson	**AEHIKLNP**	kephalin	**AEHINSST** anthesis
AEGNORST	estragon	**AEHIKLRS**	rashlike	shanties
	negators	**AEHIKRTW**	Whitaker	**AEHINSSV** vanishes
	ragstone	**AEHIKSST**	shakiest	**AEHINSSZ** haziness
AEGNORSW	wagoners	**AEHILMSW**	Lewisham	**AEHINSTT** hesitant
AEGNORTT	tetragon		limewash	**AEHIOPRS** aphorise
AEGNORTU	outrange	**AEHILNOP**	aphelion	**AEHIOPRU** euphoria
AEGNOSSY	nosegays	**AEHILNRS**	inhalers	**AEHIOPRZ** aphorize
AEGNOTUY	autogeny	**AEHILNRU**	inhauler	**AEHIORST** hoariest
AEGNPPRU	gunpaper	**AEHILNSY**	hyalines	**AEHIORTU** thiourea
AEGNPRST	trepangs	**AEHILNTX**	anthelix	**AEHIPPRS** sapphire
AEGNPRSU	speargun	**AEHILNTZ**	zenithal	**AEHIPPST** epitaphs
AEGNRRST	granters	**AEHILOTZ**	thiazole	happiest
	stranger	**AEHILPRS**	harelips	**AEHIPRSS** parishes
AEGNRSSY	grayness		plashier	sharpies
AEGNRSYY	asynergy	**AEHILRSS**	hairless	**AEHIPSTT** Peshitta
AEGOPPST	stoppage	**AEHILRSU**	hauliers	**AEHIQSSU** quashies
AEGOPRST	portages	**AEHILRSV**	lavisher	**AEHIRRRS** harriers
	potagers		shrieval	**AEHIRRST** trashier
AEGOPSTT	gatepost	**AEHILRTY**	earthily	**AEHIRRSV** ravisher
AEGORRRT	garroter		heartily	**AEHIRRSW** wairsher
AEGORRST	garrotes	**AEHILSSV**	lavishes	**AEHIRSRY** Ayrshire
AEGORRTT	garotter	**AEHILSSW**	shawlies	**AEHIRSSV** ravishes
	garrotte	**AEHILSTT**	lathiest	**AEHIRSTU** thesauri
AEGORSTT	garottes	**AEHILSUV**	vihuelas	**AEHIRSTW** waterish
AEGORSTU	outrages	**AEHILTWW**	Whitelaw	**AEHIRSTY** hysteria
AEGORSVY	voyagers	**AEHIMMNN**	Mannheim	**AEHIRTYZ** yahrzeit
AEGORTTU	tutorage	**AEHIMMSS**	shammies	**AEHISSST** stashies
AEGORUVY	voyageur	**AEHIMMST**	hammiest	**AEHISSSW** siwashes
AEGOSSTU	outgases	**AEHIMMSW**	whammies	**AEHISSTT** atheists
AEGOSSTW	stowages	**AEHIMNNU**	inhumane	hastiest
AEGOSTTV	gavottes	**AEHIMNSU**	humanise	**AEHISSTU** hiatuses
AEGPRRSS	graspers	**AEHIMNUZ**	humanize	**AEHISSTW** washiest
	spargers	**AEHIMPRS**	samphire	**AEHISTTW** thwaites
AEGPSSTU	upstages		seraphim	**AEHJNNOS** johannes
AEGPSTUY	Aegyptus	**AEHIMPRT**	teraphim	**AEHKLOOY** Holyoake
AEGRRSSY	ryegrass	**AEHIMPSS**	emphasis	**AEHKNNSU** unshaken
AEGRRSUV	gravures		misshape	**AEHKNSTT** Tashkent
AEGRSTTY	strategy	**AEHIMPST**	mateship	**AEHKNSWW** newshawk
AEGSSTUU	augustes		shipmate	**AEHKOSTU** shakeout
AEHHHJPT	Jephthah	**AEHIMRRS**	marshier	**AEHKPSSU** shakeups
AEHHIKNS	Shekinah	**AEHIMRSS**	mishears	**AEHLLLTY** lethally
AEHHINPR	Ha-erh-pin	**AEHIMSSS**	messiahs	**AEHLLMTY** methylal
AEHHNOPT	Phaëthon	**AEHIMTUY**	euthymia	**AEHLLNRT** enthrall
AEHHRRST	thrasher	**AEHINNSS**	shannies	Hartnell
AEHHRSST	harshest	**AEHINNST**	Tien Shan	**AEHLLORW** hallower
	thrashes	**AEHINNSW**	Wanhsien	**AEHLMMNS** helmsman
AEHIIKLR	hairlike	**AEHINNTX**	xanthein	**AEHLMNNP** Helpmann

AEHLMNOS	manholes	AEHNOPPY	hypopnea	AEIILNRT	inertial
AEHLMNOT	methanol		payphone	AEIILNSS	Silesian
AEHLMNSW	Welshman	AEHNOPRT	hapteron	AEIILNST	alienist
AEHLMNUV	humanely	AEHNOPST	phaetons		litanies
AEHLMORS	armholes		phonates		Taliesin
AEHLMOSU	hamulose		stanhope	AEIILNTZ	latinize
AEHLMPPT	pamphlet	AEHNORSS	hoarsens	AEIILPPT	tailpipe
AEHLMRSS	harmless	AEHNORST	North Sea	AEIILQSU	siliquae
AEHLMRST	thermals		Sheraton	AEIILRST	lairiest
AEHLMSUW	Hume's law	AEHNORTT	Atherton		listeria
AEHLNOTY	ethanoyl	AEHNOSSX	hexosans	AEIILRTT	literati
AEHLNPRS	shrapnel	AEHNPRSS	sharpens	AEIILSTV	vitalise
AEHLNPTY	enthalpy	AEHNPRST	panthers	AEIILTVZ	vitalize
AEHLNRST	enthrals	AEHNRSSS	rashness	AEIIMMRT	maritime
AEHLNRTU	Lutheran	AEHNRSTU	haunters	AEIIMMSX	maximise
AEHLNSST	nathless		unearths	AEIIMMXZ	maximize
AEHLNSSU	unlashes	AEHNRTTU	earthnut	AEIIMNTT	intimate
AEHLNTUZ	hazelnut	AEHNSSTY	shanteys	AEIIMNTU	minutiae
AEHLOPRT	plethora	AEHNSTUW	unswathe	AEIIMOSS	ameiosis
AEHLOPST	tapholes	AEHOORST	toheroas	AEIIMPRR	impairer
AEHLOPTT	hotplate	AEHOPPRS	prophase	AEIIMPSY	epimysia
AEHLORST	loathers	AEHOPRRY	pyorrhea	AEIIMRSS	Ramses II
AEHLORSY	hoarsely	AEHOPSST	spathose	AEIIMRST	seriatim
AEHLORUV	overhaul		teashops	AEIIMSTT	imitates
AEHLORYY	Holy Year	AEHOPSTU	phaseout	AEIINNRS	sirenian
AEHLOSSS	assholes		taphouse	AEIINNRT	triennia
AEHLPPRT	thrapple	AEHORRRW	harrower	AEIINPRS	Piranesi
AEHLPRSS	splasher	AEHORRSW	warhorse	AEIINRSS	airiness
AEHLPSSS	splashes	AEHORSST	hoarsest	AEIINRST	rainiest
AEHLPSST	pathless	AEHORSSW	sawhorse	AEIINRTZ	triazine
AEHLPSTU	sulphate	AEHORSTT	rheostat	AEIINSST	isatines
AEHLRRTU	urethral	AEHORSTU	rathouse		sanitise
AEHLRSSS	slashers	AEHORSTX	thoraxes		teniasis
AEHLRSST	harslets	AEHORSTY	Rothesay	AEIINSTV	vanities
	slathers	AEHPPSSU	shapeups	AEIINSTZ	sanitize
AEHLSSTW	thawless	AEHPRRSS	sharpers	AEIINSVV	invasive
AEHLSSTY	Thessaly	AEHPRSST	sharpest	AEIINTTT	titanite
AEHLSTTY	stealthy	AEHPRSUX	haruspex	AEIIPPRS	prairies
AEHMMRSS	shammers	AEHPRSUY	euphrasy	AEIIPRST	parities
AEHMNNPY	nymphean	AEHQRSSU	squasher	AEIIPRZZ	pizzeria
AEHMNOPR	morphean	AEHQSSSU	squashes	AEIIPSST	epitasis
AEHMNORS	horseman	AEHRRSTU	urethras	AEIIPSTX	epitaxis
	menorahs	AEHRRSTY	trashery	AEIIRRST	rarities
AEHMNOSU	houseman	AEHRRTTW	thwarter	AEIIRRTT	irritate
AEHMNPRU	prehuman	AEHRSSTT	shatters	AEIIRSST	satirise
AEHMOPRT	metaphor	AEHRSSTV	harvests		Tiresias
AEHMOPST	apothems	AEHSSTUX	exhausts	AEIIRSTW	wisteria
AEHMOSTT	hemostat	AEIIIJMS	James III	AEIIRSTZ	satirize
AEHMOSTW	somewhat	AEIIINTT	initiate	AEIIRTTT	tritiate
AEHMPPRY	pamphrey	AEIIIPRT	retiarii	AEIISTTV	vitiates
AEHMRSSS	smashers	AEIIJMSV	James VII	AEIITTTV	titivate
AEHMRSST	hamsters	AEIIKLLT	taillike	AEIJLLSS	jailless
AEHMSSSU	shamuses	AEIIKRTY	teriyaki	AEIJLNSV	javelins
AEHMSSTT	shmattes	AEIILLTV	illative	AEIJLOPS	jalopies
AEHMSTTW	Matthews	AEIILMNN	mainline	AEIJLOSU	jalousie
AEHMSTTY	amethyst	AEIILMNS	alienism	AEIJMMST	jammiest
AEHMSUZZ	mezuzahs	AEIILMPR	imperial	AEIJMNSS	jasmines
AEHNNOPT	pantheon	AEIILMSZ	Islamize	AEIJNRTU	jauntier
AEHNNORV	Hannover	AEIILMTT	militate	AEIJORST	jarosite
AEHNNPSU	unshapen	AEIILNQU	aquiline	AEIJSTZZ	jazziest
AEHNNSUV	unshaven	AEIILNRR	airliner	AEIKKLMS	masklike
AEHNOOPT	hanepoot	AEIILNRS	airlines	AEIKKLNT	tanklike

AEIKKKLPR	parklike	AEILLPST	palliest	AEILNNPU	pinnulae
AEIKLLOV	Oakville		pastille	AEILNNRT	internal
AEIKLLST	saltlike	AEILLQSU	squillae	AEILNNSU	Linnaeus
AEIKLMST	mastlike	AEILLRRS	ralliers	AEILNNSY	insanely
AEIKLNPS	skiplane	AEILLRRY	raillery	AEILNNTY	innately
AEIKLNSS	sealskin	AEILLRSS	railless	AEILNOPS	opalines
AEIKLNST	lankiest		salliers	AEILNORR	Lorraine
AEIKLNSW	swanlike	AEILLRST	literals	AEILNORS	ailerons
AEIKLNSY	sneakily		talliers		alienors
AEIKLOPS	soaplike		triellas	AEILNORT	oriental
AEIKLOST	keitloas	AEILLRSY	serially		relation
AEIKLOSV	Levkosia	AEILLRVX	vexillar		Tirolean
AEIKLPRT	traplike	AEILLSSS	sailless	AEILNORV	overlain
AEIKLPSW	wasplike	AEILLSST	sitellas	AEILNOST	insolate
AEIKLRST	larkiest		tailless		toenails
	stalkier	AEILLSTT	sittella	AEILNOSV	Slovenia
	starlike		tallites	AEILNOSX	siloxane
AEIKLRTW	wartlike	AEILLSUV	allusive	AEILNPRS	pralines
AEIKLRVY	valkyrie	AEILLSYZ	sleazily	AEILNPRT	interlap
AEIKLRWY	walkyrie	AEILLTUZ	lazulite		triplane
AEIKLSTT	talkiest	AEILMMNS	melanism	AEILNPSS	painless
AEIKMNNR	Inkerman	AEILMMNU	Immanuel		spaniels
AEIKMNRS	ramekins	AEILMMOR	memorial	AEILNPST	panelist
AEIKMNST	mankiest	AEILMMOT	immolate		pantiles
	mistaken	AEILMMRT	trilemma		plainest
AEIKMRST	mistaker	AEILMMSS	melismas	AEILNPSX	explains
	sitkamer	AEILMNNO	minneola	AEILNPTT	tinplate
AEIKMSST	mistakes	AEILMNNS	linesman	AEILNRSS	rainless
AEIKNRST	narkiest	AEILMNOS	laminose	AEILNRST	entrails
	Transkei		semolina		latrines
AEIKNRSW	swankier	AEILMNPS	impanels		ratlines
AEIKNRTW	knitwear		maniples		reinstal
AEIKNSST	snakiest	AEILMNRS	marlines		trenails
AEIKNSSY	kyanises		minerals	AEILNRSV	ravelins
AEIKNSYZ	kyanizes	AEILMNRT	terminal	AEILNRSX	relaxins
AEIKPRRS	sparkier		tramline	AEILNRSY	inlayers
AEIKPRST	parkiest	AEILMNST	ailments	AEILNRTU	tenurial
AEIKPSTW	pawkiest		aliments	AEILNRTV	interval
AEIKQSTU	quakiest		manliest	AEILNRTY	interlay
AEIKRSST	asterisk	AEILMOPR	proemial	AEILNSST	salients
	sarkiest	AEILMORS	moralise	AEILNSSZ	laziness
AEIKRSTV	Kristeva	AEILMORZ	moralize	AEILNSTU	insulate
AEILLLLN	Llanelli	AEILMPRS	impalers	AEILNSTV	ventails
AEILLLMO	malleoli		impearls	AEILNSUY	uneasily
AEILLLMS	allelism		lempiras	AEILNTVY	natively
AEILLLNY	lineally	AEILMPRV	primeval		venality
AEILLMNS	manilles	AEILMPST	palmiest	AEILNUVV	univalve
AEILLMNY	menially	AEILMPTY	playtime	AEILOPPT	oppilate
AEILLMSS	mailless	AEILMRSS	realisms	AEILOPRS	polarise
AEILLMSY	mesially	AEILMRSY	mislayer	AEILOPRT	epilator
AEILLNNO	lanoline		smearily	AEILOPRZ	polarize
AEILLNPS	Spillane	AEILMRTT	remittal	AEILOPST	spoliate
	splenial	AEILMRUV	velarium	AEILORSS	solarise
AEILLNQU	quinella	AEILMSTT	maltiest	AEILORSV	Olivares
AEILLNRY	linearly		metalist		valorise
AEILLNSS	nailless		smaltite		varioles
	sensilla	AEILMSTU	simulate	AEILORSZ	solarize
AEILLNST	Antilles	AEILMSTY	steamily	AEILORTV	violater
AEILLNUV	laevulin	AEILMSUV	misvalue		Voltaire
AEILLNVY	venially	AEILMTTU	mutilate	AEILORTZ	triazole
AEILLOSS	loessial		ultimate	AEILORVZ	valorize
AEILLOTV	volatile	AEILNNOS	solanine	AEILOSST	isolates

AEILOSTT	totalise		romanise	**AEINNOST**	Estonian
AEILOSTV	violates	**AEIMNORT**	Maronite	**AEINNOTT**	intonate
AEILOTTZ	totalize	**AEIMNORW**	airwomen	**AEINNOTV**	innovate
AEILPPQU	applique	**AEIMNORZ**	Marenzio		venation
AEILPPRS	appliers		romanize	**AEINNPRS**	panniers
AEILPRRS	reprisal	**AEIMNOST**	amniotes	**AEINNRRS**	insnarer
AEILPRRT	paltrier	**AEIMNOSW**	womanise	**AEINNRRT**	inerrant
AEILPRST	pilaster	**AEIMNOTZ**	monazite	**AEINNRSS**	insnares
	plaister	**AEIMNOWZ**	womanize	**AEINNRST**	entrains
AEILPRSV	prevails	**AEIMNQRU**	ramequin		trannies
AEILPRSW	slipware	**AEIMNRRR**	Marriner	**AEINNRTT**	intranet
AEILPRTV	livetrap	**AEIMNRRS**	mariners	**AEINNSSV**	vainness
AEILPRXY	pyrexial	**AEIMNRSS**	seminars	**AEINNSSZ**	zaniness
AEILPSSY	paisleys	**AEIMNRST**	minarets	**AEINNSTT**	stannite
AEILPSTT	platiest	**AEIMNRSU**	aneurism	**AEINOPPT**	antipope
AEILPSUU	Apuleius		Sumerian	**AEINOPRT**	atropine
AEILPSUV	plausive	**AEIMNRSY**	seminary	**AEINOPST**	saponite
AEILQRTU	quartile	**AEIMNRTT**	martinet	**AEINOQTU**	equation
	requital	**AEIMNRTU**	ruminate	**AEINORRT**	anterior
AEILQSTU	liquates	**AEIMNRTY**	tyramine	**AEINORRW**	ironware
	tequilas	**AEIMNSSS**	samisens	**AEINORSS**	erasions
AEILQSUY	queasily	**AEIMNSST**	mantises		sensoria
AEILQTUV	equality		matiness	**AEINORST**	notaries
AEILRRST	retirals	**AEIMNSSZ**	maziness		notarise
	retrials	**AEIMOOPS**	ipomoeas		senorita
	trailers	**AEIMOPSX**	apomixes	**AEINORSV**	aversion
AEILRRSU	ruralise	**AEIMORRS**	armoires	**AEINORTU**	Touraine
AEILRRTT	rattlier		armories	**AEINORTZ**	notarize
AEILRRTY	literary	**AEIMORST**	amortise	**AEINOSSV**	evasions
AEILRRUZ	ruralize		atomiser	**AEINOSXZ**	oxazines
AEILRSST	realists		Timor Sea	**AEINOTVX**	vexation
	saltiers	**AEIMORTT**	amoretti	**AEINPPPS**	panpipes
	saltires	**AEIMORTZ**	amortize	**AEINPPRS**	snappier
	slaister		atomizer	**AEINPPST**	nappiest
AEILRSSV	revisals	**AEIMOSST**	atomises	**AEINPRRT**	terrapin
AEILRSTU	uralites	**AEIMOSTZ**	atomizes	**AEINPRRU**	unrepair
AEILRSUU	Aurelius	**AEIMOTTV**	motivate	**AEINPRST**	painters
AEILRSVV	revivals	**AEIMPRRT**	imparter		pantries
AEILRSVY	virelays	**AEIMPRSS**	impresas		pertains
AEILRTUZ	lazurite	**AEIMPRST**	apterism		pinaster
AEILSSTT	saltiest		primates		repaints
	slatiest	**AEIMPRSV**	vampires	**AEINPRTT**	triptane
AEILSSUV	Vesalius	**AEIMPRSW**	swampier	**AEINPRUV**	Peruvian
AEILSSUW	Sulawesi	**AEIMPSSS**	impasses	**AEINPSST**	steapsin
AEILSTVY	vilayets	**AEIMPSST**	impastes	**AEINPSSU**	apneusis
AEILSTWY	sweatily		pastimes	**AEINPSTT**	patients
AEILSTYY	yeastily	**AEIMQRSU**	marquise	**AEINPSTU**	petunias
AEIMMNNT	immanent	**AEIMRRRS**	marriers		supinate
AEIMMNOS	seminoma	**AEIMRRTU**	Arretium	**AEINPSTY**	epinasty
AEIMMNOT	ammonite	**AEIMRSST**	asterism	**AEINPTTY**	antitype
AEIMMNSS	misnames		smarties	**AEINQRTU**	quainter
AEIMMPST	psammite	**AEIMRSSY**	emissary	**AEINQSTU**	antiques
AEIMMRRS	smarmier	**AEIMRSTT**	mistreat		quantise
AEIMMRST	marmites		teratism	**AEINQTTU**	equitant
	trammies	**AEIMRSTU**	muriates	**AEINQTUY**	antiquey
AEIMMRTU	immature	**AEIMRSTX**	matrixes	**AEINQTUZ**	quantize
AEIMNNOT	nominate	**AEIMSSST**	massiest	**AEINRRST**	restrain
AEIMNNRS	reinsman	**AEIMSSTT**	misstate		retrains
AEIMNNNWZ	Weizmann	**AEIMSSTZ**	mestizas		strainer
AEIMNOPT	ptomaine	**AEIMTTUV**	mutative		terrains
AEIMNORS	moraines	**AEINNOPV**	pavonine		trainers
	romaines	**AEINNORT**	anointer	**AEINRRTV**	veratrin

AEINRRTW	interwar			**AEKNNRSS**	rankness
AEINRSST	artiness		traipses	**AEKNOORS**	Soekarno
	stainers	**AEIPRSSU**	upraises	**AEKNOOTY**	Kootenay
AEINRSSU	anuresis	**AEIPRSSV**	parvises	**AEKNORSV**	Nekrasov
AEINRSSW	wariness	**AEIPRSSX**	praxises	**AEKNPPRS**	knappers
AEINRSTT	intreats	**AEIPRSTV**	privates	**AEKNPPSS**	spanspek
	nitrates	**AEIPRSTW**	wiretaps	**AEKNPRSS**	spankers
	straiten	**AEIPRSTY**	asperity	**AEKNPSSU**	unspeaks
	tertians	**AEIPRSVY**	vespiary	**AEKOPRSS**	presoaks
AEINRSTU	Neustria	**AEIPRTVY**	varitype	**AEKOPSTU**	outspeak
	uranites	**AEIPSSSV**	passives		speakout
	urinates	**AEIPSSTT**	pastiest	**AEKORRWW**	workwear
AEINRSUZ	suzerain	**AEIPTTUV**	putative	**AEKORSSS**	karosses
AEINRSVV	vervains	**AEIQRRRU**	quarrier	**AEKORSTV**	overtask
AEINRSZZ	snazzier	**AEIQRRSU**	quarries	**AEKOSTTU**	outtakes
AEINSSST	sestinas	**AEIQRUZZ**	quazzier		stakeout
AEINSSSV	vinasses	**AEIRRRST**	starrier		takeouts
AEINSSTT	antsiest		tarriers	**AEKPSSSY**	passkeys
	instates	**AEIRRRSV**	arrivers	**AEKQRSUW**	squawker
	nastiest	**AEIRRSST**	tarsiers	**AEKRRSST**	starkers
	titaness	**AEIRRSTW**	strawier	**AEKRSSTT**	starkest
AEINSSTX	sextains	**AEIRRTTY**	tertiary	**AELLMNOO**	allomone
AEINSSVW	waviness	**AEIRSSST**	assister	**AELLMNTY**	mentally
AEINSSWX	waxiness	**AEIRSSTT**	artistes		tallymen
AEINSTTT	nattiest		striates	**AELLMORT**	martello
AEINSTWY	Steinway	**AEIRSSTW**	waitress	**AELLMOTY**	tomalley
AEINSUVV	vesuvian	**AEIRSTTT**	rattiest	**AELLMOYZ**	allozyme
AEINTTUU	autunite		tartiest	**AELLMSST**	smallest
AEINTTVZ	Vanzetti		titrates	**AELLMSWX**	maxwells
AEIOPPST	apposite		tristate	**AELLNOSV**	novellas
AEIOPRRT	Pretoria	**AEIRSTVY**	vestiary	**AELLNPRU**	prunella
	priorate	**AEIRSVZZ**	Svizzera	**AELLNRUY**	neurally
AEIOPRRW	airpower	**AEISSSST**	sassiest		unreally
AEIOPRSV	vaporise	**AEISSSTY**	essayist	**AELLNRVY**	vernally
AEIOPRTX	expiator	**AEISSTTT**	tastiest	**AELLNSST**	tallness
AEIOPRVZ	vaporize	**AEISSTTU**	situates	**AELLNTTY**	latently
AEIOPSST	soapiest	**AEISSTTV**	statives	**AELLNTUU**	lunulate
AEIOPTTV	optative		vastiest	**AELLOPRT**	preallot
AEIOQSSU	sequoias	**AEISSTVY**	savviest	**AELLOPRW**	walloper
AEIORRSS	rosaries	**AEISTTTT**	tattiest	**AELLOPTY**	allotype
AEIORRST	rotaries	**AEJLOSSU**	jalouses	**AELLORSS**	rosellas
AEIORSSV	savories	**AEJLOSUY**	jealousy	**AELLORST**	reallots
AEIORSTV	viatores	**AEJMOOSW**	Moose Jaw		rostella
	votaries	**AEKKMNOO**	kakemono	**AELLORSV**	overalls
AEIORTTV	rotative	**AEKLMNOV**	Malenkov	**AELLORSW**	Rosewall
AEIOSSST	sosaties	**AEKLMRUW**	lukewarm	**AELLORWW**	wallower
AEIOSSTT	toasties	**AEKLMRUY**	yarmulke	**AELLOSUV**	alveolus
AEIOSSTZ	azotises	**AEKLNNSS**	lankness	**AELLPSTY**	playlets
AEIOSTZZ	azotizes	**AEKLNOSY**	ankylose	**AELLQRSU**	squaller
AEIPPPST	pappiest	**AEKLNSST**	tankless	**AELLRRSU**	allurers
AEIPPRSS	apprises	**AEKLOPRW**	ropewalk	**AELLRRTY**	retrally
AEIPPRST	periapts	**AEKLORVW**	walkover	**AELLRTTY**	latterly
AEIPPRSZ	apprizes	**AEKLPRRS**	sparkler	**AELLRTVY**	trevally
AEIPPSST	sappiest	**AEKLPRSS**	sparkles	**AELLRTYY**	lyrately
AEIPPSTZ	zappiest	**AEKLRSST**	stalkers	**AELLSSST**	saltless
AEIPQRTU	pratique	**AEKLSSST**	taskless	**AELLSSTY**	tasselly
AEIPRRSS	aspirers	**AEKMMNRS**	marksmen	**AELLSTUU**	ululates
	praisers	**AEKMNRSU**	unmakers	**AELLSUVV**	valvules
AEIPRRSU	upraiser		unmasker	**AELLSUXY**	sexually
AEIPRSST	pastries	**AEKMNRUZ**	Zukerman	**AELMMNOS**	mamelons
	piasters	**AEKMORTW**	teamwork	**AELMMORW**	mealworm
	piastres		workmate		
		AEKMPRTU	upmarket		

AELMMOSY	myelomas	AELNPPSY	playpens	AELOSTUV	ovulates
AELMMRSS	slammers	AELNPRST	planters	AELOSTUY	autolyse
AELMMRST	trammels		replants	AELOTUUV	outvalue
AELMNNOT	nonmetal	AELNPRSU	purslane	AELOTUYZ	autolyze
AELMNNOU	noumenal		supernal	AELPPRSS	slappers
AELMNNRY	mannerly	AELNPSSS	snapless	AELPPSSU	appulses
AELMNOPS	neoplasm	AELNPSSU	spansule	AELPQRTU	Quelpart
	pleonasm	AELNPSTX	explants	AELPRRRU	larruper
AELMNORS	almoners	AELNPTTU	petulant	AELPRRSW	sprawler
AELMNORT	Montreal	AELNPTTY	patently	AELPRRTT	prattler
AELMNOST	telamons	AELNRRSS	snarlers	AELPRRTU	Perrault
AELMNOSU	melanous	AELNRRTY	errantly	AELPRSST	persalts
AELMNOWY	laywomen	AELNRSST	salterns		plasters
AELMNOYY	yeomanly		slanters		psalters
AELMNPRS	lamperns	AELNRSTT	slattern		staplers
AELMNRSU	mensural	AELNRSTU	neutrals	AELPRSSU	perusals
	numerals	AELNRSUV	unravels	AELPRSSY	parsleys
AELMNSTT	mantlets	AELNRSXY	larynxes		sparsely
AELMNSTY	mesnalty	AELNRTTW	trawlnet	AELPRSTT	partlets
AELMOORS	saleroom	AELNSSST	saltness		platters
AELMOPRR	premolar	AELNTTUX	exultant		prattles
AELMOPRT	temporal	AELOORRS	roseolar		splatter
AELMOPSU	ampoules	AELOORSS	aerosols	AELPRSTY	plastery
AELMOPSX	exoplasm		roseolas		psaltery
AELMOPSY	maypoles	AELOORTW	waterloo	AELPSSTT	peltasts
AELMOPTT	palmetto	AELOORTZ	zoolater	AELPSSTU	pulsates
AELMORSU	ramulose	AELOPPRS	prolapse	AELQRRSU	quarrels
AELMORSV	removals		sapropel	AELQRSUV	servqual
AELMORSY	ramosely	AELOPPTU	populate	AELQRSUY	squarely
AELMORTU	emulator	AELOPPXY	apoplexy	AELQSTUZ	quetzals
AELMOSSS	molasses	AELOPQUY	opaquely	AELRRSSW	warslers
AELMOSTT	matelots	AELOPRRV	reproval	AELRRSTT	rattlers
AELMPRRT	trampler	AELOPRSS	reposals		startler
AELMPRSS	samplers	AELOPRST	petrosal	AELRRSTW	trawlers
AELMPRST	templars		polestar		warstler
	tramples	AELOPRSV	overlaps	AELRRTVY	varletry
AELMPRSY	lampreys	AELOPRVY	overplay	AELRSSST	starless
AELMRSST	tramless	AELOPRYZ	pyrazole	AELRSSTT	starlets
AELMRSTT	maltster	AELOPSSS	soapless		startles
	martlets	AELOPSST	apostles	AELRSSTU	saluters
AELMRSTY	masterly	AELOPSSU	espousal	AELRSSTW	warstles
AELMRTUY	maturely		sepalous		wastrels
AELMSSST	mastless	AELOPSSX	exposals	AELRSSUU	russulae
AELNNOOP	napoleon	AELOPSTT	paletots	AELRSSUW	walruses
AELNNOOX	naloxone	AELOPSTU	outleaps	AELRSTTT	tartlets
AELNNOQU	nonequal		petalous		tattlers
AELNNORU	neuronal	AELOPTTU	outleapt	AELRSTTU	lustrate
AELNNOSU	annulose	AELORRST	realtors		tutelars
AELNNPRS	planners		relators	AELRSTUV	vaulters
AELNNRST	lanterns	AELORSSS	lassoers		vestural
AELNNRSU	unlearns	AELORSSU	Larousse	AELRSTWZ	waltzers
AELNNRTU	unlearnt	AELORSTV	levators	AELRTTUX	textural
AELNNSTU	annulets	AELORSUU	rouleaus	AELRTTUY	tutelary
AELNOPPT	Appleton	AELORSVY	layovers	AELSSSTU	saltuses
AELNOPRS	personal		overlays	AELSTTUY	astutely
AELNOPST	Tonle Sap	AELORTYZ	zealotry	AEMMNRTU	ramentum
AELNOPSU	apolunes	AELORUUX	rouleaux	AEMMOORT	roommate
AELNOPXY	Polyxena	AELOSSTV	solvates	AEMMORST	marmoset
AELNORTT	tolerant	AELOSSTY	asystole	AEMMRSST	stammers
AELNORTY	ornately	AELOSSVY	saveloys	AEMMRTUY	maumetry
AELNOSSV	ovalness	AELOSTTU	toluates	AEMNNORT	ornament
AELNPPRS	preplans	AELOSTTW	wastelot	AEMNNRST	remnants

AEMNOORT	anteroom		smartest	**AENSSTTU**	tautness
AEMNOORY	aeronomy		smatters	**AENSSTTX**	sextants
AEMNOPPS	pampoens	**AEMRSSUU**	Sarum use	**AENSSTXY**	syntaxes
AEMNOPRS	manropes	**AEMRTUUX**	trumeaux	**AEOOPPPS**	pappoose
AEMNOPRW	manpower	**AENNNOTU**	Nuneaton	**AEOOPPSS**	papooses
AEMNORRS	ransomer	**AENNNPST**	pennants	**AEOOPRRT**	operator
AEMNORST	monstera	**AENNOOTZ**	entozoan	**AEOOPSTT**	potatoes
AEMNORSU	enamours	**AENNOPRT**	patronne	**AEOORRST**	sororate
	neuromas	**AENNOPST**	pentosan	**AEOORTTT**	tattooer
AEMNORSV	overmans	**AENNORST**	resonant	**AEOORTTV**	rotovate
AEMNORTY	monetary	**AENNORSU**	unreason	**AEOPPRSV**	approves
AEMNORVY	overmany	**AENNORSY**	annoyers	**AEOPRRST**	praetors
AEMNORYY	yeomanry	**AENNORTW**	wantoner		prorates
AEMNOSTU	seamount	**AENNOSTU**	tonneaus	**AEOPRRSV**	vaporers
AEMNPRSS	pressman	**AENNOSTV**	Evanston	**AEOPRRUV**	vapourer
AEMNPRSU	superman	**AENNOTUX**	tonneaux	**AEOPRRVW**	wrapover
AEMNPSTY	payments	**AENNPRSS**	spanners	**AEOPRSST**	espartos
AEMNRRSU	manurers	**AENNRSTT**	entrants		protases
	surnamer	**AENNRSWY**	swannery		seaports
AEMNRRUY	numerary	**AENNRTTY**	tenantry	**AEOPRSSU**	asperous
AEMNRSST	smartens	**AENOOPST**	teaspoon	**AEOPRSSV**	overpass
AEMNRSSU	surnames	**AENOPRSS**	responsa		passover
AEMNRSSW	warmness	**AENOPRST**	operants	**AEOPRSTT**	prostate
AEMNRSTU	menstrua		Paterson	**AEOPRSTU**	apterous
AEMNRSUY	aneurysm		pronates	**AEOPRSTV**	overpast
AEMNRTTU	Tarentum	**AENOPRTT**	patentor	**AEOPRSVY**	overpays
AEMOORST	tearooms	**AENOPRWY**	weaponry	**AEOPTTUY**	autotype
AEMOORSW	woomeras	**AENORRRW**	narrower	**AEOQRSTU**	equators
AEMOORTT	amoretto	**AENORRST**	antrorse		quaestor
AEMOOSST	maestoso	**AENORSST**	assentor	**AEOQRTTU**	torquate
	osteomas		senators	**AEORRSST**	assertor
AEMOOSSV	vamooses		treasons		assorter
AEMOOSTT	tomatoes	**AENORSSU**	anserous		roasters
AEMOOSTU	autosome		arsenous	**AEORRSSU**	arousers
AEMOPPRS	pamperos	**AENORSUV**	ravenous	**AEORRSTT**	rostrate
AEMOPRTW	tapeworm	**AENORSWZ**	warzones	**AEORRTZZ**	terrazzo
AEMOQSSU	squamose	**AENORTTY**	attorney	**AEORSSSS**	assessor
AEMORRRS	armorers	**AENOSSTU**	Ouessant	**AEORSSTT**	toasters
AEMORRRU	armourer		soutanes	**AEORSSTV**	votaress
AEMORRST	rearmost	**AENOSSUU**	nauseous	**AEORSSUU**	rousseau
AEMORRSY	rosemary	**AENOUUVX**	nouveaux	**AEORSTTT**	attestor
AEMORSSS	morasses	**AENPPRSS**	snappers		testator
AEMORSST	maestros	**AENPRRST**	partners	**AEORSTTU**	outstare
AEMORSSY	mayoress	**AENPRRSW**	prawners	**AEORSTUW**	outwears
AEMORTTU	tautomer	**AENPRSST**	pasterns	**AEORSTVY**	overstay
AEMORUWZ	Muzorewa	**AENPRSSW**	spawners	**AEPPRRST**	strapper
AEMOSTTZ	mozettas	**AENPRSTT**	patterns		trappers
AEMOTTZZ	mozzetta		transept	**AEPPRRSW**	wrappers
AEMPRRST	trampers	**AENPRSUV**	parvenus	**AEPPRSSW**	swappers
AEMPRRSW	prewarms	**AENPSSSY**	synapses	**AEPPSSTU**	pasteups
AEMPRRSY	spermary	**AENQRRTU**	quartern	**AEPQRSTU**	parquets
AEMPRSST	stampers	**AENRRRTY**	errantry	**AEPRRSSY**	resprays
AEMPRSSW	swampers	**AENRSSTT**	tartness		sprayers
AEMPRSTU	upstream	**AENRSSTU**	anestrus	**AEPRRSTU**	raptures
AEMPRSUX	supermax		saunters	**AEPRSSST**	sparsest
AEMPSTTT	attempts	**AENRSSTV**	servants		trespass
AEMQRSSU	marquess		versants	**AEPRSTTT**	spatters
	masquers	**AENRSSUW**	unswears		tapsters
AEMRRSST	armrests	**AENRSTTU**	taunters	**AEPRSSTU**	pastures
AEMRSSSU	assumers	**AENRSTUV**	vaunters	**AEPRSTTU**	upstater
	masseurs	**AENRSTWY**	sternway	**AEPRSTTY**	tapestry
AEMRSSTT	mattress	**AENSSSTV**	vastness	**AEPRSTUX**	supertax

AEPSSSSU	passuses	**AFGHINRT**	farthing	**AFIILLLY**	filially
AEPSSTTU	upstates	**AFGHINRW**	wharfing	**AFIILMMS**	familism
AEQRRSSU	squarers	**AFGHINST**	shafting	**AFIILMNS**	finalism
AEQRRSTU	quarters	**AFGHIOST**	goatfish	**AFIILMST**	Familist
AEQRSTTU	quartets	**AFGHLNSU**	flashgun	**AFIILNRU**	Friulian
	squatter	**AFGIILLN**	flailing		unifilar
AEQRSTUZ	quartzes	**AFGIILNS**	failings	**AFIILNST**	finalist
AERRSSSU	assurers	**AFGIINNT**	fainting	**AFIILNTY**	finality
AERRSSTT	restarts	**AFGIINRS**	fairings	**AFIILORS**	airfoils
	starters	**AFGIINTX**	fixating	**AFIILRST**	airlifts
AERRSSTV	starvers	**AFGIKLNN**	fankling	**AFIIMNPR**	rifampin
AERRSSTY	strayers		flanking	**AFIINNOS**	sainfoin
AERRSTUY	treasury	**AFGIKNNR**	franking		sinfonia
AERSSSST	strasses	**AFGIKORT**	koftgari	**AFIINOTX**	fixation
AERSSSUU	Saussure	**AFGILLNT**	flatling	**AFIIORRT**	triforia
AERSSTTT	strettas	**AFGILMMN**	flamming	**AFIJKRTU**	jakfruit
AERSSTTU	statures	**AFGILMNO**	flamingo	**AFIKLNNR**	franklin
AERSSTTW	swatters	**AFGILNOT**	floating	**AFIKLOST**	flokatis
AERSSTUX	surtaxes	**AFGILNOW**	Fowliang	**AFIKMNNR**	finnmark
AERSSTVY	strayves	**AFGILNPP**	flapping	**AFIKNNPU**	Panufnik
AERSTTVY	travesty	**AFGILNST**	fatlings	**AFIKNRST**	ratfinks
AERTTUXY	textuary	**AFGILNTT**	flatting	**AFILLLOT**	flotilla
AESSSTTU	statuses	**AFGILNTU**	faulting	**AFILLNPS**	pinfalls
AESSTTTU	statutes	**AFGIMNRS**	framings	**AFILLPST**	pitfalls
AFFFFIRR	riffraff	**AFGIMNTU**	fumigant	**AFILLPSU**	pailfuls
AFFGHIRT	affright	**AFGIMORS**	gasiform	**AFILLTUY**	faultily
AFFGIINX	affixing	**AFGINNRS**	snarfing	**AFILMNOR**	formalin
AFFGIIRT	graffiti	**AFGINNSU**	snafuing		informal
AFFGILNR	raffling	**AFGINORV**	favoring	**AFILMNOS**	foilsman
AFFGILNW	waffling	**AFGINORY**	foraying	**AFILMRUU**	Mufulira
AFFGINQU	quaffing	**AFGINPPR**	frapping	**AFILNORT**	flatiron
AFFGINST	staffing	**AFGINRST**	ingrafts		inflator
AFFGIORT	graffito		strafing	**AFILNPPT**	flippant
AFFHILLS	fallfish	**AFGINRTU**	figurant	**AFILNRUY**	unfairly
AFFHILST	flatfish	**AFGIPRTW**	giftwrap	**AFILORSW**	airflows
AFFHILTU	faithful	**AFGJNRUU**	Jungfrau	**AFILOSTX**	foxtails
AFFHNOTV	van't Hoff	**AFGKORST**	koftgars	**AFILRSTU**	fistular
AFFIINTY	affinity	**AFGLLRUY**	frugally	**AFILSSTU**	fistulas
AFFILLMM	flimflam	**AFGLLSSU**	glassful	**AFILSTTU**	flautist
AFFILSUX	suffixal	**AFGLNNOO**	gonfalon	**AFIMMNOY**	ammonify
AFFIMSST	mastiffs	**AFGNNNOO**	gonfanon	**AFIMMORR**	ramiform
AFFINOSU	affusion	**AFHIILSS**	sailfish	**AFIMNOPR**	napiform
AFFINRSU	funfairs	**AFHIILST**	fishtail	**AFIMNOSU**	infamous
	ruffians	**AFHIINST**	faintish	**AFIMOOSS**	mafiosos
AFFIPSTT	tipstaff	**AFHIKSUY**	kufiyahs	**AFIMORRU**	auriform
AFFLLOOT	footfall	**AFHILLSY**	flashily	**AFIMORRV**	variform
AFFLOOTT	flatfoot	**AFHILOSY**	oafishly	**AFINNOTU**	fountain
AFFLOPSY	playoffs	**AFHILSST**	saltfish	**AFINNRTY**	infantry
AFFLRUUU	furfural	**AFHILSTT**	flattish	**AFINOPSY**	saponify
AFFNORST	affronts	**AFHILSTW**	halfwits	**AFINQTUY**	quantify
AFFNRUUU	furfuran	**AFHINOSS**	fashions	**AFINRSTX**	transfix
AFFRTTUU	Truffaut	**AFHINOSY**	fashiony	**AFIORSTU**	faitours
AFGGGILN	flagging	**AFHIRSST**	starfish	**AFIRSTTY**	stratify
AFGGGINR	fragging	**AFHISSWY**	fishways	**AFISSSTT**	sitfasts
AFGGILNN	flanging	**AFHKLNTU**	thankful	**AFISSTUV**	fauvists
AFGGILOP	gigaflop	**AFHKORSY**	hayforks	**AFKLNOTU**	outflank
AFGGINOR	foraging	**AFHKRSTU**	futharks	**AFKLNSTU**	tankfuls
AFGGINOT	fagoting	**AFHLMOTU**	Falmouth	**AFKLOSWY**	folkways
AFGGINRT	grafting	**AFHLRTUW**	wrathful	**AFKMOORT**	footmark
AFGHILNS	flashing	**AFHNOOST**	fantoosh	**AFLLLORY**	florally
AFGHILNT	fanlight	**AFHNORRT**	Far North	**AFLLLUWY**	lawfully
AFGHILPS	flagship	**AFHOOPTT**	footpath	**AFLLMNUY**	manfully

AFLLMORY	formally	
AFLLNOOV	flavonol	
AFLLNOSW	snowfall	
AFLLNUUW	unlawful	
AFLLOOTW	footwall	
AFLLOSTU	outfalls	
AFLLRTUY	artfully	
AFLMNOPR	planform	
AFLMNOST	loftsman	
AFLMOPRT	platform	
AFLMORSU	formulas	
AFLMORTW	flatworm	
AFLMORTY	Fort Lamy	
AFLMOSUY	famously	
AFLNORST	frontals	
AFLOPSTT	flattops	
AFLORSUV	flavours	
AFLPRSTY	flytraps	
AFLPSSTY	flypasts	
AFMNNOOS	Son of Man	
AFMNNORT	frontman	
AFMNORST	formants	
AFMOOPRR	proforma	
AFMORSTU	foumarts	
AFMORTUY	fumatory	
AFMOSSTU	sfumatos	
AFNNOTTY	nonfatty	
AFOORSTZ	sforzato	
AFOOSTWY	footways	
AGGGGILN	gaggling	
AGGGHILN	haggling	
AGGGHINS	shagging	
AGGGILNN	gangling	
AGGGILNR	gargling	
AGGGILNS	slagging	
AGGGILNW	waggling	
AGGGINNS	snagging	
AGGGINPS	spagging	
AGGGINST	stagging	
AGGGINSW	swagging	
AGGHILNU	laughing	
AGGHILST	gaslight	
AGGHILSY	shaggily	
AGGHIMNO	homaging	
AGGHINNS	gnashing	
	hangings	
AGGHINNW	whanging	
AGGHINPR	graphing	
AGGHISTT	gastight	
AGGHJMNO	mahjongg	
AGGHLOOT	golgotha	
AGGIILNN	aligning	
AGGIILNR	glairing	
AGGIILNT	ligating	
AGGIILNV	gingival	
AGGIINNR	graining	
AGGIINNS	gainings	
AGGIINST	agisting	
AGGIJLNN	jangling	
AGGILLNU	ullaging	
AGGILMNN	mangling	
AGGILMNO	gloaming	

AGGILNNO	ganglion	
AGGILNNR	gnarling	
AGGILNNS	slanging	
AGGILNNT	tangling	
AGGILNNW	wangling	
AGGILNOT	gloating	
AGGILNPU	plaguing	
AGGILNPY	gapingly	
AGGILNRY	grayling	
AGGILNSS	glassing	
AGGINNOR	groaning	
AGGINNOT	tangoing	
AGGINNPR	pranging	
AGGINNRR	gnarring	
AGGINNRT	granting	
AGGINNRW	wranging	
AGGINNST	stanging	
AGGINNSW	gnawings	
AGGINNTW	twanging	
AGGINOOX	Gaoxiong	
AGGINOVY	voyaging	
AGGINPRS	grasping	
	sparging	
AGGINRSS	grassing	
AGGINRST	gratings	
AGGINRSU	sugaring	
AGGINRSZ	grazings	
AGGINRTY	gyrating	
AGGINRUU	auguring	
AGGINSSS	gassings	
AGGINSST	stagings	
AGGIRTUZ	ziggurat	
AGGLLLOV	lollygag	
AGGLLOOY	algology	
AGGLMOOR	logogram	
AGGLOORY	agrology	
AGGLRSTY	straggly	
AGGMORRS	grograms	
AGGNUWZZ	zugzwang	
AGHHIILT	hightail	
AGHHIMSS	High Mass	
AGHHINOP	Haiphong	
AGHHISWY	highways	
AGHHLOTU	although	
AGHHNOUZ	Hangzhou	
AGHIILMP	Malpighi	
AGHIILNN	inhaling	
AGHIILOS	Laoighis	
AGHIINST	Tsinghai	
AGHIIPRR	hairgrip	
AGHIIRTT	airtight	
AGHIJNRT	nightjar	
AGHIJNUZ	Zhu Jiang	
AGHIKNNS	shanking	
AGHIKNNT	thanking	
AGHIKNRS	sharking	
AGHILLNO	halloing	
	hollaing	
AGHILMTY	almighty	
AGHILNOO	hooligan	
AGHILNOS	shoaling	
AGHILNOT	loathing	

AGHILNPS	plashing	
AGHILNRS	harlings	
	ringhals	
AGHILNSS	hassling	
	lashings	
	slashing	
AGHILNSU	languish	
	nilghaus	
AGHILRSY	garishly	
AGHIMMNS	shamming	
AGHIMMNW	whamming	
AGHIMNPR	pharming	
AGHIMNRS	Ram Singh	
AGHIMNSS	smashing	
AGHINNOT	gnathion	
AGHINNTU	haunting	
AGHINNTY	anything	
AGHINOST	hoasting	
AGHINPPW	whapping	
AGHINPRS	harpings	
	phrasing	
	sharping	
AGHINPSS	phasings	
AGHINQSU	quashing	
AGHINRRY	harrying	
AGHINRST	trashing	
AGHINSST	hastings	
	stashing	
AGHINSSV	shavings	
AGHINSSW	swashing	
	washings	
AGHINSTW	swathing	
AGHINUZZ	Zhuangzi	
AGHIPRRT	trigraph	
AGHIRSTT	straight	
AGHISSTT	tightass	
AGHISSTW	sightsaw	
AGHJRTUU	Jugurtha	
AGHKNOPT	pakthong	
AGHKOSSW	goshawks	
AGHLMOOR	hologram	
AGHLMPSU	galumphs	
AGHLNOSU	shogunal	
AGHLNOTU	Laughton	
AGHLNSUY	nylghaus	
AGHLOOSS	gasohols	
AGHLOTUU	outlaugh	
AGHMMOOY	homogamy	
AGHMNPSU	sphagnum	
AGHMOOPY	omophagy	
AGHMOORR	Gomorrah	
AGHMOPRY	myograph	
AGHMORSY	hygromas	
AGHMRRSU	murraghs	
AGHNNOSU	houngans	
AGHNNSTU	shantung	
AGHNOORS	shagroon	
AGHNORST	staghorn	
AGHNOSTU	hangouts	
	tohungas	
AGHNTTUU	untaught	
AGHORSTW	warthogs	

AGIIIKMR	kirigami	AGIKLNNR	rankling	AGILNOST	antilogs
AGIIILNS	liaising	AGIKLNOP	polkaing	AGILNOTT	totaling
AGIIINNS	insignia	AGIKLNST	stalking	AGILNOTY	antilogy
AGIIINRV	Virginia	AGIKLNTY	takingly	AGILNPPS	slapping
AGIIJJNN	Jinjiang	AGIKLNUW	waulking	AGILNPPY	applying
AGIILLMN	Milligan	AGIKMNNU	unmaking	AGILNPRS	sparling
AGIILMNP	impaling	AGIKMNRS	markings	AGILNPSS	saplings
AGIILMNS	misalign	AGIKMNPP	knapping	AGILNPST	platings
AGIILMNU	miauling	AGIKNNPR	pranking		stapling
AGIILNNO	Liaoning	AGIKNNPS	spanking	AGILNPSW	lapwings
AGIILNNP	plaining	AGIKNNRS	rankings	AGILNPSY	palsying
AGIILNNU	inguinal	AGIKNNST	stanking		splaying
AGIILNNY	inlaying	AGIKNNSW	swanking	AGILNPTT	platting
AGIILNOR	original	AGIKNOSS	soakings	AGILNRST	slarting
AGIILNOT	intaglio	AGIKNOST	goatskin		starling
	ligation	AGIKNPRS	sparking	AGILNRSU	singular
	taglioni	AGIKNRSS	sarkings	AGILNRSW	warsling
AGIILNOX	gloxinia	AGILLMNU	mulligan	AGILNRTT	rattling
AGIILNPS	laipsing	AGILLMNY	malignly	AGILNRTW	trawling
AGIILNPT	plaiting	AGILLNOW	allowing	AGILNRVY	ravingly
AGIILNQU	quailing	AGILLNOY	alloying	AGILNSST	anglists
AGIILNRS	railings	AGILLNPS	spalling		lastings
AGIILNRT	ringtail	AGILLNRU	alluring		saltings
	trailing	AGILLNRY	rallying		slatings
AGIILNRU	Ligurian	AGILLNST	stalling	AGILNSTT	slatting
AGIILNRV	rivaling	AGILLNSU	linguals	AGILNSTU	saluting
	virginal	AGILLNSY	sallying	AGILNSVY	savingly
AGIILNSS	sailings		signally	AGILNTTT	tattling
AGIILNST	tailings		slangily	AGILNTTW	wattling
AGIILNTT	litigant	AGILLNTY	tallying	AGILNTUV	vaulting
AGIILNTV	vigilant	AGILLOPT	gallipot	AGILNTUX	luxating
AGIILORU	oliguria	AGILLORS	gorillas	AGILNTWZ	waltzing
AGIILPST	pigtails	AGILLOST	galliots	AGILNTXY	taxingly
AGIIMNOU	miaouing	AGILLPUY	plaguily	AGILOORS	gloriosa
AGIIMNOW	miaowing	AGILLSSU	lugsails	AGILOOXY	axiology
AGIIMNST	giantism	AGILLSSY	glassily	AGILOPST	galipots
AGIIMSST	imagists	AGILMMNS	slamming	AGILORSS	girasols
AGIINNNO	Annigoni	AGILMNNT	mantling	AGILSYYZ	syzygial
AGIINNPT	painting	AGILMNOO	Mongolia	AGIMMNPS	spamming
AGIINNRS	ingrains	AGILMNPS	sampling	AGIMMNRS	smarming
AGIINNRT	training	AGILMNRS	marlings	AGIMMNRT	tramming
AGIINNRV	ravining	AGILMNRU	Langmuir	AGIMMNTY	tammying
AGIINNST	sainting	AGILMNST	maltings	AGIMMOSY	misogamy
	staining	AGILMOPR	lipogram	AGIMNNOS	masoning
AGIINNTT	tainting	AGILMORS	algorism	AGIMNNOW	womaning
AGIINOPT	opiating		Margolis	AGIMNNRU	manuring
AGIINORS	Sargon II	AGILNNNP	planning		unarming
AGIINORT	rigatoni	AGILNNOP	pangolin	AGIMNORR	armoring
AGIINOST	Agostini	AGILNNOQ	Qian Long		roarming
AGIINPRS	aspiring	AGILNNOS	loanings	AGIMNORS	organism
	praising	AGILNNPT	planting	AGIMNORU	origanum
AGIINPRT	pirating	AGILNNRS	snarling	AGIMNORY	agrimony
AGIINRRV	arriving	AGILNNSS	linsangs	AGIMNPPS	mappings
AGIINRTT	attiring	AGILNNST	slanting	AGIMNPRT	tramping
AGIINSTU	Ignatius	AGILNNUY	ungainly	AGIMNPST	stamping
AGIJLNPY	japingly		unlaying	AGIMNPSW	swamping
AGIJMNOR	majoring	AGILNOOO	oogonial	AGIMNRRY	marrying
AGIJMNRU	jumaring	AGILNOOS	isogonal	AGIMNRST	migrants
AGIJNNTU	jaunting	AGILNOPR	paroling		smarting
AGIKKNNS	skanking	AGILNOPT	ploating	AGIMNRSW	swarming
AGIKLMOR	kilogram	AGILNORT	trigonal	AGIMNRTU	maturing
AGIKLNNP	planking	AGILNOSS	lassoing	AGIMNSSU	assuming

263

AGIMNSTT	mattings	AGINRRST	starring	AGMOOTVY	vagotomy
AGIMNTTU	mutating	AGINRRTY	tarrying	AGMOPRRS	programs
AGIMORRT	migrator	AGINRSST	gastrins	AGMORRSW	ragworms
AGIMORSS	isograms	AGINRSSU	assuring	AGNNNOOS	nonagons
AGIMORSU	gouramis	AGINRSSY	syringas	AGNNOORS	argonons
AGINNNNY	nannying	AGINRSTT	starting		organons
AGINNNOY	annoying	AGINRSTV	starving	AGNNOQTU	quantong
AGINNNPS	spanning	AGINRSTW	strawing	AGNNOSSW	swan song
AGINNNSW	swanning	AGINRSTY	stingray	AGNNOTUX	Xuan-tong
AGINNOPR	aproning		straying	AGNNOUXZ	Xuan Zong
AGINNOPT	Paignton	AGINRTVY	gyniatry	AGNORRST	grantors
	poignant	AGINSTTT	tattings	AGNORTUY	nugatory
AGINNORT	ignorant	AGINSTTW	swatting	AGNPPRSU	upsprang
AGINNOSU	anginous	AGINSVVY	savvying	AGOORRTY	rogatory
AGINNOTT	notating	AGINSWWX	waxwings	AGOORTUY	autogyro
AGINNPPS	snapping	AGIOORTU	autogiro	AGOPPSST	stopgaps
AGINNPSW	spawning	AGIOPPRT	agitprop	AGORRSTW	ragworts
	wingspan	AGIRSSTU	sastrugi	AGORRSTY	gyrators
AGINNQTU	quanting	AGIRTTUY	gratuity	AGORRTYY	gyratory
AGINNRST	rantings	AGJLOSUV	Jugoslav	AGORSTTY	gyrostat
AGINNRSW	warnings	AGJLRSUU	jugulars	AGSSTUUU	Augustus
AGINNSTU	stauning	AGJNOORS	jargoons	AHHIKLSS	shashlik
AGINNSUY	unsaying	AGKLOORV	Gorlovka	AHHILPSW	whiplash
AGINNTTU	attuning	AGKMNOPS	kampongs	AHHIMMSS	mishmash
	taunting	AGKNOOOV	Okovango	AHHINRTU	Haut-Rhin
AGINNTUV	vaunting	AGKNSTUU	Tunguska	AHHIPRSS	sharpish
AGINOOPS	pogonias	AGKORSSW	gasworks	AHHIRSST	Tarshish
AGINOORT	rogation	AGLLMOPW	glowlamp	AHHISSTT	shittahs
AGINOPPS	apposing	AGLLNOOS	galloons	AHHKMOTW	hawkmoth
AGINOPQU	opaquing	AGLLNSTU	gallnuts	AHHKRSTU	kashruth
AGINOPRV	vaporing		nutgalls	AHHLNOPT	naphthol
AGINORRS	garrison	AGLLOORS	rogallos	AHHLNPTY	naphthyl
AGINORSS	assignor	AGLLOOST	galloots	AHHMPRRU	harrumph
	signoras	AGLLPSTY	glyptals	AHHNORTW	hawthorn
AGINORST	organist	AGLLRUVY	vulgarly	AHHOPRSS	shophars
	roasting	AGLMOPYY	polygamy	AHHOPSTU	aphthous
AGINORSU	arousing	AGLNOOOS	ologoans	AHIIILMN	malihini
AGINORSV	savoring	AGLNOSST	glasnost	AHIIKMRS	Kashmiri
AGINORTT	rotating	AGLNOSWY	longways	AHIIKRSS	shikaris
	troating	AGLNOUVZ	Glazunov	AHIILORT	Lothair I
AGINORTV	graviton	AGLNSSSU	sunglass	AHIILRTY	hilarity
AGINORTY	gyration	AGLOOPST	goalpost	AHIIMNOT	himation
AGINOSST	agonists	AGLOPRTU	Portugal	AHIIMNRU	manuhiri
AGINOSTT	tangoist	AGLORSSY	glossary	AHIIMNST	isthmian
	toasting	AGLOSUVY	Yugoslav	AHIIMOPX	amphioxi
	Tsingtao	AGLPSSSY	spyglass	AHIIMSST	samithis
AGINPPRS	rappings	AGLRTTUU	guttural	AHIINPRS	hairpins
AGINPPRT	trapping	AGLSTUUY	augustly	AHIINSSW	swainish
AGINPPRW	wrapping	AGMMNOOR	monogram	AHIIOPST	hospitia
AGINPPSW	swapping		nomogram	AHIIPRSS	airships
AGINPPTU	pupating	AGMMNOOY	monogamy	AHIIRSTW	tawhiris
AGINPRRS	sparring	AGMMORSY	myograms	AHIKLNRS	rinkhals
AGINPRRY	parrying	AGMMNORS	grannoms	AHIKLRSY	rakishly
AGINPRSS	raspings	AGMNOORS	sonogram	AHIKMNSS	khamsins
AGINPRST	partings	AGMNOORY	agronomy	AHIKNNOT	Ikhnaton
AGINPRSY	spraying	AGMNORST	angstrom	AHIKNOSU	Sihanouk
AGINPRTU	uprating		Ångström	AHIKNPRS	prankish
AGINPRTY	partying	AGMNORSU	organums	AHIKORSS	karoshis
AGINPSSS	passings	AGMNSSTU	mustangs	AHIKORST	Oistrakh
AGINPSST	pastings	AGMNSSTY	gymnasts	AHIKOSUZ	Shizuoka
AGINPSTT	spatting		syntagms	AHIKPRSS	sparkish
AGINQRSU	squaring	AGMOOOSU	oogamous	AHILLMOU	halloumi

AHILLMPS	phallism
AHILLMSS	smallish
AHILLMTU	thallium
AHILLPST	phallist
AHILLSVY	lavishly
AHILMNOT	Hamilton
AHILMOST	mailshot
AHILMOSU	haloumis
AHILMQSU	qualmish
AHILMTUZ	halutzim
AHILNOPS	siphonal
AHILNOPT	oliphant
AHILNORT	horntail
AHILNOST	Lothians
AHILOORT	lotario
AHILOPSS	alphosis
	haplosis
AHILOPST	hospital
AHILPSSY	physalis
AHILRSTY	trashily
AHIMMNSU	humanism
AHIMMORZ	mahzorim
AHIMMOSV	moshavim
AHIMNOSW	womanish
AHIMNSTU	humanist
AHIMNSTX	xanthism
AHIMNTUY	humanity
AHIMOOSY	yahooism
AHIMOPRS	aphorism
AHIMOPST	opsimath
AHIMORRW	hairworm
AHIMPPSS	sapphism
AHIMPRST	trampish
AHIMPSSW	swampish
AHIMRSST	smartish
AHIMSSTU	Tsushima
AHIMSTUZ	azimuths
AHIMSTVZ	mitzvahs
AHINNOPT	antiphon
AHINNSTX	xanthins
AHINORRS	Harrison
AHINOSST	astonish
AHINOSTZ	hoatzins
AHINPPSS	snappish
AHINPRST	tranship
AHINPRSU	Nishapur
AHINPSWW	whipsawn
AHINQSUV	vanquish
AHINSTUU	tauhinus
AHIOOPST	photopia
AHIOPPRT	Potiphar
AHIOPRST	aphorist
AHIOPRSV	vaporish
AHIORSSW	airshows
AHIORSTV	tovarish
AHIPRSST	harpists
AHIPRSSW	warships
AHIPSSWW	whipsaws
AHIPSSWY	shipways
AHIQRSSU	squarish
AHIRSSTW	trishaws
AHISSTTW	whatsits

AHKLOPRU	Kolhapur
AHKLOPST	shoptalk
AHKMOORR	markhoor
AHKMORRS	markhors
AHKMORTU	Khartoum
AHKNOTUY	thankyou
AHLLNOOS	shalloon
AHLLNOTW	townhall
AHLLNOUW	unhallow
AHLLOPSS	shallops
AHLLOSST	shallots
AHLLOSSW	shallows
AHLLOSTU	thallous
AHLLOSTY	tallyhos
AHLMMOPY	lymphoma
AHLMNNRU	Luhrmann
AHLMNOOR	hormonal
AHLMNOST	Mansholt
AHLMOOPS	omphalos
AHLMOPTY	polymath
AHLMOSUU	hamulous
AHLNNORT	lanthorn
AHLNOPRS	alphorns
AHLNOPST	haplonts
AHLNORST	althorns
AHLOPRSU	Sholapur
AHLOPSST	slapshot
AHLORRTY	harlotry
AHLOSTUU	outhauls
AHMMMOST	mammoths
AHMNNNOU	nonhuman
AHMNNSTU	huntsman
	manhunts
AHMNOPST	phantoms
AHMNORRS	ramshorn
AHMNSSUY	Huysmans
AHMOOPPT	photomap
AHMOOPSS	shampoos
AHMOORSW	washroom
AHMOPTYY	myopathy
AHMORTTW	tamworth
AHMORTUY	Yarmouth
AHMPSSSU	smashups
AHMPSTYY	sympathy
AHMQSSUU	musquash
AHNOOPRS	harpoons
AHNOORRY	honorary
AHNOPPSW	pawnshop
AHNOPPSY	pansophy
AHNOPSST	snapshot
AHNORSSX	saxhorns
AHNORSTV	Tórshavn
AHNOSTTW	whatnots
AHNOSTUX	xanthous
AHNRSVYY	hryvnyas
AHOOSSTY	soothsay
AHOOSTTW	sawtooth
AHOPSTTW	towpaths
AHOPSTUW	southpaw
AHORTTUW	watthour
AHOSSTUW	washouts
AHQRRTUU	Urquhart

AIIILLMN	Illimani
AIIILLMW	William I
AIIILLVX	lixivial
AIIILMST	militias
AIIILNST	initials
AIIILRVZ	vizirial
AIIKKSUY	sukiyaki
AIIKLLMN	Millikan
AIIKLNOR	Iráklion
AIIKLNRR	larrikin
AIIKMMSS	skimmias
AIIKMNNN	mannikin
AIIKMNNS	manikins
AIIKNNNP	pannikin
AIIKNNST	tankinis
AIIKORTY	yakitori
AIIKRRSU	raurikis
AIIKTTZZ	tzatziki
AIILLLUV	illuvial
AIILLMNO	monilial
AIILLMRY	milliary
AIILLMSW	Williams
AIILLNNV	vanillin
AIILLNOP	pollinia
AIILLNOT	illation
AIILLNPT	antipill
AIILLNRY	Illyrian
AIILLNSV	villains
AIILLNVY	villainy
AIILLPRS	sliprail
	spirilla
AIILLQSU	quillais
AIILLWWW	williwaw
AIILMNPS	alpinism
AIILMNPT	palmitin
AIILMNTT	militant
AIILMRST	mistrial
AIILMRTY	limitary
	military
AIILMSST	Islamist
AIILMSTV	vitalism
AIILNNOV	Livonian
AIILNOPS	Pasolini
AIILNOPT	Politian
AIILNOPV	pavilion
AIILNOSS	liaisons
AIILNOSV	visional
AIILNPST	alpinist
	pintails
	tailspin
AIILNQRU	Quirinal
AIILNSTY	salinity
AIILNTTY	latinity
AIILORTT	Littoria
AIILQSSU	siliquas
AIILRSTT	trialist
AIILSTTV	vitalist
AIILTTVY	vitality
AIIMMNNY	minyanim
AIIMMNRU	Ariminum
AIIMNNOS	insomnia
AIIMNPSS	sinapism

AIIMNPSX	panmixis	AIKLSSSY	skysails	AILMNRUY	luminary
AIIMNRST	martinis	AIKMRSTZ	sitzmark	AILMNSTU	simulant
AIIMNRSU	Arminius	AIKNNOOS	nainsook	AILMOOSV	moviolas
AIIMNSST	animists	AIKNNOST	Atkinson	AILMOPRU	Mariupol
AIIMNSTT	titanism	AIKNNSSW	swanskin	AILMOPRX	proximal
AIIMNSTV	nativism	AIKNORTY	karyotin	AILMORSS	solarism
	vitamins	AIKNOSTT	stotinka	AILMORST	moralist
AIIMNTTU	titanium	AIKOORST	rooikats	AILMORSU	solarium
AIIMOPSX	apomixis	AIKPTTUU	patutuki	AILMORSY	royalism
AIIMORTT	imitator	AIKRSTUZ	zikurats	AILMORTY	molarity
AIIMOSST	amitosis	AILLLNOO	linalool		morality
AIIMPPRS	priapism	AILLLOST	Saltillo	AILMOSTU	solatium
AIIMPRTY	imparity	AILLLPSU	lapillus	AILMOSTV	voltaism
AIIMRSST	simitars	AILLMOSS	Limassol	AILMPPSY	misapply
AIIMRSTU	tiramisu	AILLMOST	maillots	AILMPRSU	primulas
AIIMRUVV	vivarium	AILLMOSY	loyalism	AILMPSST	palmists
AIIMSSTT	mastitis	AILLMOTY	molality		psalmist
AIINNOSV	invasion	AILLMPSU	palliums	AILMPSSY	misplays
AIINNOTV	nivation	AILLMSSW	sawmills	AILMPSTY	ptyalism
AIINNQTU	quintain	AILLMUUV	alluvium	AILMRRSU	ruralism
AIINNSTU	Tunisian	AILLNOPP	papillon	AILMRSSU	simulars
AIINNSTV	Vinnitsa	AILLNORT	antiroll	AILMRSTU	altruism
AIINNSTY	insanity	AILLNOST	stallion		muralist
AIINORTT	antiriot	AILLNOSU	allusion		ultraism
	tritonia	AILLNOUV	alluvion	AILMSSTY	myalists
AIINOSTT	notitias	AILLNPSY	spinally	AILNNOOT	notional
AIINPRSS	aspirins	AILLNPTY	pliantly	AILNNOST	antlions
AIINPRST	Priština	AILLNSST	installs	AILNNOSU	unisonal
AIINPSST	pianists	AILLNSUV	Sullivan	AILNNOSY	Lyonnais
AIINRRTT	irritant	AILLORSY	sailorly	AILNNOTU	lunation
AIINRSTV	vitrains	AILLORSZ	zorillas	AILNNPRU	pinnular
AIINSTTV	nativist	AILLORTT	littoral	AILNNSTU	insulant
	visitant		tortilla	AILNOOPT	optional
AIINTTVY	nativity	AILLOSTY	loyalist	AILNOOST	solation
AIIORRST	sartorii	AILLOTTT	tallitot	AILNOPRU	unipolar
AIIORSTT	aortitis	AILLPRSY	spirally	AILNOPTY	ponytail
AIIORSTV	ovaritis	AILLPRTY	paltrily	AILNOSTY	lanosity
AIIORTTV	vitiator	AILLPSSY	playlist	AILNOSUV	avulsion
AIIPRRST	airstrip	AILLPSUV	pluvials	AILNOSVY	synovial
AIIPRVVY	vivipary	AILLPSWY	spillway	AILNOTTV	volitant
AIIRSSTT	satirist	AILLQSSU	squillas	AILNOTTY	tonality
	sitarist	AILLRTUY	ritually	AILNOTUX	luxation
AIJKKNOU	kinkajou	AILLSUVY	visually	AILNPPSY	snappily
AIJLLOOR	jillaroo	AILMMNOO	monomial	AILNPSTU	nuptials
AIJLLOVY	jovially	AILMMNUU	aluminum	AILNPSUU	nauplius
AIJLNTUY	jauntily	AILMMORS	moralism		Paulinus
AIJMORTY	majority	AILMMORT	immortal	AILNQRTU	tranquil
AIJNOPPY	popinjay	AILMMRSY	smarmily	AILNQSTU	quintals
AIJNORST	janitors	AILMMSTU	summital	AILNQTUY	quaintly
AIKKLLRW	Kirkwall	AILMMSUW	mwalimus	AILNRSSU	insulars
AIKKMOST	komatiks	AILMNNOS	nominals	AILNRTTU	rutilant
AIKKOOSW	kokowais	AILMNNOT	mannitol	AILNRUWY	unwarily
AIKKOPSY	kopiykas	AILMNNPP	Lippmann	AILNSSTU	stunsail
AIKKOSUZ	zakouski	AILMNOOP	palomino	AILNSSUV	Silvanus
AIKKRTUZ	zikkurat	AILMNOOR	monorail	AILNSTTU	lutanist
AIKLLSTY	stalkily	AILMNOOT	motional	AILNSTUU	nautilus
AIKLNNPS	snaplink	AILMNOPS	lampions	AILNSYZZ	snazzily
AIKLNOPS	Polanski	AILMNOPY	Olympian	AILOOPZZ	Paolozzi
AIKLNSST	Stalinsk		palimony	AILOORST	isolator
AIKLNSWY	swankily	AILMNOSS	malisons		ostiolar
AIKLOTTW	kilowatt	AILMNPST	implants	AILOORTV	violator
AIKLRSTT	titlarks	AILMNPTU	platinum	AILOPRTU	troupial

AILOPRTY	polarity	**AIMNRSTU**	naturism	**AIOPRRSS**	Pissarro
AILOPRUY	polyuria	**AIMNRSTV**	varmints	**AIOPRRST**	airports
AILOPSST	apostils	**AIMNSSTU**	tsunamis	**AIOPRRTT**	portrait
	topsails	**AIMNSTUU**	Manutius	**AIOPRSST**	prosaist
AILOQSTU	aliquots	**AIMOPRSS**	prosaism		protasis
AILORSST	sliotars	**AIMOPSSY**	symposia	**AIOPRSTT**	patriots
	solarist	**AIMORRST**	armorist	**AIOPRSUV**	paviours
AILORSTY	royalist	**AIMORRSU**	rosarium	**AIORRRSW**	warriors
	solitary	**AIMORRUV**	variorum	**AIORRSTT**	traitors
AILORSVY	savorily	**AIMORSST**	amorists	**AIORRSTV**	varistor
AILORTTU	tutorial	**AIMORSTY**	ramosity	**AIORSSUV**	saviours
AILORTUV	outrival	**AIMOSSTT**	atomists	**AIORSTTV**	votarist
AILOSSTT	altoists	**AIMPPRUU**	puparium	**AIOSSSTY**	isostasy
AILOSSUY	Aloysius	**AIMRTTUY**	maturity	**AIPPRSTT**	Trappist
AILOTTTY	totality	**AINNNOST**	santonin	**AIPPRSTY**	papistry
AILPPRUY	pupilary	**AINNOOTT**	notation	**AIPRSSTU**	upstairs
AILPQSSU	pasquils	**AINNOOTV**	novation	**AIPRSSTY**	sparsity
AILPRSSU	spirulas	**AINNOOTZ**	zonation	**AIRRSTTY**	artistry
AILPRSTU	stipular	**AINNOPSS**	saponins	**AIRSSSTT**	tsarists
AILPSSWY	slipways	**AINNOSST**	onanists	**AISSSTTT**	statists
AILPSTUY	playsuit	**AINNOSTU**	Antonius	**AJKMNSTU**	muntjaks
AILRRSTU	ruralist	**AINNOTTU**	nutation	**AJLNORSU**	journals
AILRRSTY	starrily	**AINNPSST**	snaptins	**AJORRTUY**	juratory
AILRRTUY	rurality	**AINNRSTU**	Nuristan	**AKKLRSSY**	skylarks
AILRSSTY	trysails	**AINNSSTT**	instants	**AKKOOSUY**	Yokosuka
AILRSTTU	altruist	**AINNSTTY**	nystatin	**AKKORSTW**	taskwork
	titulars	**AINOOPTT**	potation	**AKLNNOPT**	plankton
	ultraist	**AINOORST**	orations	**AKLOSTTU**	outtalks
AILRSTTY	straitly	**AINOORTT**	rotation	**AKLOSTUW**	outwalks
AILRSUVV	survival	**AINOOSTT**	ostinato		walkouts
AILRTTUY	titulary	**AINOOSTV**	ovations	**AKLPRRSU**	larkspur
AILSSTUW	lawsuits	**AINOPPST**	appoints	**AKMMNOOR**	monomark
AIMMMNOU	ammonium	**AINOPPTU**	pupation	**AKMMNRSU**	Murmansk
AIMMMSUX	maximums	**AINOPRSS**	parisons	**AKMMOOTU**	Kumamoto
AIMMNORS	Romanism	**AINOPSSS**	passions	**AKMNOOPU**	mokopuna
AIMMNORT	mortmain	**AINOPSTU**	opuntias	**AKMOORST**	Kostroma
AIMMNSTU	manumits		utopians	**AKMOPRST**	postmark
AIMMOSST	atomisms	**AINOPSTW**	swaption	**AKMORSST**	ostmarks
AIMMRSUU	masurium	**AINOQRRU**	quarrion	**AKMQSTUU**	kumquats
AIMNNOPT	pointman	**AINORSST**	arsonist	**AKMRSSTU**	muskrats
AIMNNOSS	mansions	**AINORSSW**	warisons	**AKNNOSTZ**	Konstanz
AIMNNOTU	antimuon	**AINORSTT**	strontia	**AKNOOUYZ**	yokozuna
	mountain	**AINOSSTT**	stations	**AKNOPSTW**	swankpot
AIMNNOTY	antimony	**AINOSSUU**	Ausonius	**AKNORSTU**	outranks
	antinomy	**AINOSTTU**	titanous	**AKOPRRTW**	partwork
AIMNNRTU	ruminant	**AINPPRSS**	parsnips	**AKORSWWX**	waxworks
AIMNOORV	Monrovia	**AINPRSST**	spirants	**ALLLOSWY**	sallowly
AIMNOOTY	myotonia		spraints	**ALLLPRUY**	Lyallpur
AIMNOPRS	rampions	**AINPRSSU**	Prussian		plurally
AIMNOPST	maintops	**AINPRSTU**	puritans	**ALLMNORY**	normally
	ptomains		Rasputin	**ALLMNOSY**	allonyms
	tampions	**AINPSSSY**	synapsis	**ALLMNPSU**	pullmans
AIMNOQRU	maroquin	**AINPSSTU**	puissant	**ALLMOPSX**	smallpox
AIMNORST	Romanist	**AINPSTTU**	pantsuit	**ALLMORTY**	mortally
AIMNORTU	Minotaur	**AINQTTUY**	quantity	**ALLMOUWY**	mulloway
AIMNORTY	minatory	**AINRSSTT**	transits	**ALLMTUUY**	mutually
AIMNOSTU	manitous	**AINRSTTT**	titrants	**ALLNNOUY**	nounally
	Mount Isa	**AINRSTTU**	antirust	**ALLNOOPS**	planosol
	tinamous		naturist	**ALLNOOPY**	Apollyon
AIMNOTTU	mutation	**AINRSTTY**	tanistry	**ALLOOSTX**	axolotls
AIMNRSTT	Tantrism	**AINSSSTU**	sustains	**ALLOPRSY**	payrolls
	transmit	**AIOOORRT**	oratorio	**ALLOPSTY**	postally

ALLORSST	allsorts	AMNOOPPS	pompanos	APRSSTTU	upstarts
ALLORSWY	rollways	AMNOOSTT	ottomans	BBBCEOWY	cobwebby
ALLOSSWW	swallows	AMNOOTUY	autonomy	BBBEILOR	blobbier
ALLRUUVY	uvularly	AMNOOTXY	taxonomy	BBBEILRU	bubblier
ALMMNRUU	nummular	AMNOPRSY	paronyms	BBBEINOT	bobbinet
ALMNNOOR	nonmoral	AMNOPSTU	pantoums	BBBELRSU	blubbers
ALMNOOPS	lampoons	AMNORSST	transoms		bubblers
ALMNOPSS	plasmons	AMNORSTU	romaunts	BBBELRUY	blubbery
ALMNORTY	matronly	AMNOTTUY	tautonym	BBBGILNO	blobbing
ALMNOSSU	solanums	AMNRSTTU	tantrums		bobbling
ALMOOPRY	playroom	AMOOPRSS	prosomas	BBBGILNU	blubbing
ALMOORTU	alumroot	AMOOPRST	taprooms		bubbling
ALMOPPST	lamppost	AMOORRTY	moratory	BBCCIKOS	bibcocks
	palmtops	AMOORTWY	motorway	BBCDERSU	scrubbed
ALMORSUU	ramulous	AMOOTTUY	autotomy	BBCDIMOY	bombycid
ALMORSUY	ramously	AMOPRSXY	paroxysm	BBCEEIRS	berbices
ALMOSTTU	mulattos	AMOPSSTT	topmasts	BBCEHIRU	chubbier
ALMPSSTY	symplast	AMOPTUUY	Putumayo	BBCEIKKR	Birkbeck
ALMSSSUU	alyssums	AMOQSSUU	squamous	BBCEILRS	scribble
ALNNORRU	nonrural	AMORRTUY	mortuary	BBCEILRU	clubbier
ALNNOTWY	wantonly	AMORSTTU	outsmart	BBCEIRRS	cribbers
ALNNRSSU	unsnarls	AMRSSTTU	stratums	BBCEKLSU	blesbuck
ALNOOPRT	Tarnopol	ANNOORST	sonorant	BBCEKLUU	bluebuck
ALNOOPST	platoons	ANNOPRTY	nonparty	BBCELORS	clobbers
ALNOOPYZ	polyzoan	ANNOSSTU	stannous		cobblers
ALNOORST	ortolans	ANNPRSUY	spunyarn	BBCELRSU	clubbers
ALNOPRST	plastron	ANOOPRRT	pronator	BBCEMNOU	buncombe
ALNOPRTY	patronly	ANOOPRSS	sopranos	BBCERRSU	scrubber
ALNOPSYY	polynyas	ANOOPRST	patroons	BBCGIINR	cribbing
ALNORRWY	narrowly	ANOORSTT	rattoons	BBCGILNO	cobbling
ALNORSVY	sovranly	ANOPRRSS	sporrans	BBCGILNU	clubbing
ALNPPSTU	supplant	ANOPRTTU	trapunto	BBCHKOOS	boschbok
ALNSSUVY	Sylvanus	ANOPSSTU	outspans	BBCHKSUU	bushbuck
ALOOPPRS	proposal	ANORSSTW	Strawson	BBCILLUY	clubbily
ALOOPRST	postoral	ANORSTVY	sovranty	BBCILRSY	scribbly
ALOORSUV	valorous	ANORSUVY	unsavory	BBDDEEIR	dibbered
ALOORTYZ	zoolatry	ANPRSSTU	suntraps	BBDDEEMO	demobbed
ALOPPRSU	populars		unstraps	BBDDEILR	dribbled
ALOPPRYY	polypary	ANPRSTUU	pursuant	BBDEEGIR	gibbered
ALOPRRSU	parlours	ANRRSTUY	unstarry	BBDEEGIT	gibbeted
ALOPRSTU	postural	ANRSSSTU	sunstars	BBDEEMNU	benumbed
	pulsator	AOOOPRTZ	protozoa	BBDEERSU	subbreed
ALOPSSSU	spousals	AOOPPRSY	apospory	BBDEFILR	fribbled
ALOPSTUU	patulous	AOOPRSSU	saporous	BBDEHORT	throbbed
ALOPSTUY	outplays	AOOPRSTT	taproots	BBDEILLR	bellbird
ALOQRRSU	rorquals	AOOPRSTW	soapwort	BBDEILMY	Dimbleby
ALORSTTW	saltwort	AOOPRSUV	vaporous	BBDEILQU	quibbled
ALORSTWW	awlworts	AOOPRTTY	potatory	BBDEILRR	dribbler
ALORTUWY	outlawry	AOORRSTT	rotators	BBDEILRS	dribblers
ALOSSTTU	outlasts	AOORRTTY	rotatory		dribbles
ALOSSTXY	oxysalts	AOORSSUV	savorous	BBDEILRT	dribblet
ALOSTTUZ	Zlatoust	AOPPRRST	rapports	BBDEILRU	bluebird
ALPPSTUY	platypus	AOPPRSST	passport	BBDEIMOV	divebomb
ALPRSTUU	pustular	AOPRRRTY	parrotry	BBDEINOR	ribboned
ALRSSSUU	russulas	AOPRRSSW	sparrows	BBDEIQSU	squibbed
AMMNOORT	motorman	AOPRRSTY	portrays	BBDELLMU	dumbbell
AMMNPTUY	tympanum	AOPRSTTY	pyrostat	BBDELLOO	bobolled
AMMOPSTU	pomatums	AOPSTTUU	autoputs	BBDELOSS	bobsleds
AMMORRWY	armyworm	AOPTTUYY	autotypy	BBDELSTU	stubbled
AMNNOSTW	townsman	AORRSTTW	starwort	BBDERRSU	drubbers
AMNNOSTY	antonyms	AORSUVVY	vouvrays	BBDERSUU	suburbed
AMNNSTTU	stuntman	AOSSTTUY	outstays	BBDGIILN	dibbling

BBDGINRU	drubbing	**BBEORRXY**	boxberry	**BCCILOOR**	broccoli
BBDOSUYY	busybody	**BBGGILNO**	gobbling	**BCCILOSU**	bucolics
BBEEERSU	bebeerus	**BBGGINRU**	grubbing	**BCCINORR**	corncrib
BBEEGLOS	Goebbels	**BBGHILNO**	hobbling	**BCCIRTUU**	cucurbit
BBEEHMOR	Beerbohm	**BBGIIIMN**	imbibing	**BCCMOOSX**	coxcombs
BBEEIIRR	beriberi	**BBGIIKLN**	kibbling	**BCCMSSUU**	succumbs
BBEEILPR	plebbier	**BBGIILNN**	nibbling	**BCCNOORS**	corncobs
BBEEIRRS	berberis	**BBGIILNW**	wibbling	**BCCSSUUU**	succubus
BBEEISTW	webbiest	**BBGIINNS**	snibbing	**BCDEEEK**	bedecked
BBEELLLU	bluebell	**BBGIINRS**	ribbings	**BCDDEHIL**	childbed
BBEEOPPR	bebopper	**BBGIKNNO**	knobbing	**BCDEEEHR**	breeched
BBEFILRR	fribbler	**BBGILMNU**	bumbling	**BCDEEENR**	Debrecen
BBEFILRS	fribbles	**BBGILNNO**	nobbling	**BCDEEHLN**	blenched
BBEFILRT	flibbert	**BBGILNOW**	wobbling	**BCDEEHOU**	debouche
BBEFIMOR	firebomb	**BBGILNOY**	lobbying	**BCDEEIKR**	bickered
BBEGIIST	gibbsite	**BBGILNRU**	burbling	**BCDEEILR**	credible
BBEGILNP	pebbling	**BBGILNSU**	slubbing	**BCDEEILS**	decibels
BBEGILRS	gribbles	**BBGILRUY**	grubbily	**BCDEEILU**	educible
BBEGILST	glibbest	**BBGINNSU**	snubbing	**BCDEEINT**	benedict
BBEGINSW	webbings	**BBGINOSW**	swobbing	**BCDEEIRS**	describe
BBEGIRRU	grubbier	**BBGINRSU**	rubbings		escribed
BBEGLMRU	Blumberg	**BBGINSTU**	stubbing	**BCDEEIST**	bisected
BBEGLORS	gobblers	**BBHILOSS**	slobbish	**BCDEEJOT**	objected
BBEGMORR	Bromberg	**BBHINOSS**	snobbish	**BCDEEKNO**	beckoned
BBEGRRSU	grubbers	**BBHIORTY**	hobbitry	**BCDEEKRU**	reedbuck
BBEHIOTW	bobwhite	**BBHIOSTY**	hobbyist	**BCDEEKTU**	bucketed
BBEHLORS	hobblers	**BBHIRSUY**	rubbishy	**BCDEELOR**	corbeled
BBEHLSUU	bluebush	**BBHRSSUU**	subshrub	**BCDEEMRU**	cumbered
BBEIIMRS	imbibers	**BBIILSST**	biblists	**BCDEEOTT**	obtected
BBEIKNOR	knobbier	**BBIKLNOO**	bobolink	**BCDEFKOR**	Beckford
BBEILLLU	bluebill	**BBIKORSU**	Bobruisk	**BCDEHLOT**	blotched
BBEILNRS	nibblers	**BBILMOSY**	lobbyism	**BCDEHNOS**	Den Bosch
BBEILORW	wobblier	**BBILOSTY**	lobbyist	**BCDEIIOS**	biocides
BBEILOST	bibelots	**BBILOSUU**	bibulous	**BCDEIIRR**	ricebird
BBEILOSW	wobblies	**BBILSTUY**	stubbily	**BCDEIKRR**	redbrick
BBEILQRU	quibbler	**BBIMNOSS**	snobbism	**BCDEILRY**	credibly
BBEILQSU	quibbles	**BBKOOOOS**	boobooks	**BCDEIMNO**	combined
BBEILRRY	bilberry	**BBLLNNUU**	bulnbuln	**BCDEINOU**	icebound
BBEIMOST	bombsite	**BBLLOUYY**	bullyboy	**BCDEKLRU**	Delbrück
BBEIMRSU	brumbies	**BBNOORSU**	bourbons	**BCDEKORS**	bedrocks
BBEIOOST	boboties	**BBNORSTU**	stubborn	**BCDELMRU**	crumbled
BBEIRSTU	stubbier	**BBOOSSSY**	bossboys	**BCDELMSU**	scumbled
	subtribe	**BCCCIILY**	bicyclic	**BCDELOSU**	beclouds
BBEISSTU	stubbies	**BCCDEILY**	bicycled	**BCDEMNOU**	uncombed
BBEISTTU	tubbiest	**BCCDELOU**	Dulbecco	**BCDEMORY**	corymbed
BBEKLOOU	bluebook	**BCCEEIRR**	cerebric	**BCDENRUU**	uncurbed
BBEKLOSS	blesboks	**BCCEHIRU**	cherubic	**BCDEORSU**	obscured
BBEKNOOT	bontebok	**BCCEIIIS**	cicisbei	**BCDIIMOR**	bromidic
BBELLOSY	bellboys	**BCCEIILO**	libeccio	**BCDIIPSU**	bicuspid
BBELLRUY	lubberly	**BCCEIIOS**	cicisbeo	**BCDIKLLU**	duckbill
BBELMRSU	bumblers	**BCCEILOS**	ecbolics	**BCDILMOY**	molybdic
BBELNORS	nobblers	**BCCEILOY**	biocycle	**BCDILORU**	colubrid
BBELOORW	bobowler	**BCCEILRU**	crucible	**BCDINOSW**	cowbinds
BBELORSS	slobbers	**BCCEILRY**	bicycler	**BCDINRUU**	rubicund
BBELORSU	boerbuls	**BCCEILSU**	cubicles	**BCDIORSW**	cowbirds
BBELORSW	wobblers	**BCCEILSY**	bicycles	**BCDKORSU**	burdocks
BBELORSY	lobbyers	**BCCEMORS**	crombecs	**BCDSSTUU**	subducts
	slobbery	**BCCEMRUU**	cucumber	**BCEEEFIN**	benefice
BBELOTUW	blowtube	**BCCIIMOR**	microbic	**BCEEEHRS**	breeches
BBELRRSU	burblers	**BCCIINOO**	Boccioni	**BCEEERSU**	berceuse
BBENORSY	snobbery	**BCCIISTU**	cubistic	**BCEEFILN**	fencible
BBENRSSU	snubbers	**BCCILMOU**	columbic	**BCEEGIRS**	icebergs

BCEEHINR	benchier	**BCEIILOP**	epibolic	**BCGINRSU**	curbings
BCEEHKSU	buckshee	**BCEIINRS**	inscribe	**BCHIILTY**	bitchily
BCEEHLNS	blenches	**BCEIKLOO**	booklice	**BCHIISSU**	hibiscus
BCEEHNRS	benchers	**BCEIKNNT**	Bentinck	**BCHIKLOS**	blockish
BCEEHNTU	beechnut	**BCEILMRS**	climbers	**BCHIKOSU**	chibouks
BCEEHOSU	bouchees	**BCEILMRU**	Mulciber	**BCHILOTY**	botchily
BCEEIILM	imbecile	**BCEILNRU**	runcible	**BCHILRTU**	Ulbricht
BCEEIKRR	bickerer	**BCEILORS**	bricoles	**BCHILSTU**	Lubitsch
BCEEILNR	bernicle		corbeils	**BCHIOORY**	choirboy
BCEEINOT	cenobite	**BCEILPRU**	republic	**BCHIOPRS**	pibrochs
BCEEIOSX	iceboxes	**BCEIMNOR**	combiner	**BCHKNORU**	buckhorn
BCEEIRSS	escribes	**BCEIMNOS**	combines	**BCHKOSTU**	buckshot
BCEEKNOR	beckoner	**BCEIMNRU**	incumber	**BCHLNOUX**	lunchbox
BCEEKNSU	buckeens	**BCEIMORS**	microbes	**BCHNOORS**	bronchos
BCEEKSUY	buckeyes	**BCEIMRRU**	crumbier	**BCHNORSU**	bronchus
BCEELOOR	borecole	**BCEINORU**	bouncier	**BCIIILMU**	umbilici
BCEELOSU	bouclees	**BCEINOVX**	biconvex	**BCIIIOTT**	biotitic
BCEELRTU	tubercle	**BCEIOOPS**	bioscope	**BCIIKLNS**	niblicks
BCEEMNOW	Newcombe	**BCEIOOSS**	scoobies	**BCIILLSY**	sibyllic
BCEEMNRU	encumber	**BCEIORRS**	cribrose	**BCIILMSU**	bulimics
BCEEMRRU	cerebrum	**BCEIORST**	bisector	**BCIILOTY**	biolytic
	cumberer	**BCEIRSSS**	scribers	**BCIIMNOO**	bionomic
BCEEPRTY	cyberpet	**BCEJSSTU**	subjects	**BCIIMORU**	ciborium
BCEERRSU	Cerberus	**BCEKLLOS**	bellocks	**BCIINORV**	vibronic
BCEERSXY	cybersex	**BCEKLORS**	blockers	**BCIIOPTY**	biotypic
BCEERTVY	brevetcy	**BCEKLRSU**	bucklers	**BCIISSTU**	biscuits
BCEFFIIR	febrific		subclerk	**BCIKKNSU**	buckskin
BCEFHISU	subchief	**BCEKNRRU**	Bruckner	**BCIKLOOT**	bootlick
BCEFILOR	forcible	**BCEKORST**	brockets	**BCIKORRW**	cribwork
BCEGHILN	belching	**BCEKORSU**	roebucks	**BCIKOSTT**	bitstock
BCEGHINN	benching	**BCELLOSW**	cowbells	**BCILLPUY**	publicly
BCEGIINO	biogenic	**BCELLSSU**	subcells	**BCILMOSY**	symbolic
BCEGIMNO	becoming	**BCELMOOS**	Colombes	**BCILNOUY**	bouncily
BCEGKMSU	gemsbuck	**BCELMRSU**	crumbles	**BCILOORU**	bicolour
BCEHIIRT	bitchier	**BCELMSSU**	scumbles	**BCINORSU**	bursicon
BCEHIMOT	Chimbote	**BCEMRRSU**	crumbers	**BCINOSSU**	subsonic
BCEHIMRS	besmirch	**BCENORSU**	bouncers	**BCINOSTU**	subtonic
BCEHIMRU	cherubim	**BCEORRSU**	obscurer	**BCINOSUU**	incubous
BCEHINOR	Cheribon	**BCEORRWY**	cowberry	**BCIOOPSY**	bioscopy
BCEHINRU	bunchier	**BCEORSSU**	obscures	**BCIOORST**	robotics
BCEHIORS	brioches	**BCESSSTU**	subsects	**BCIOPSTU**	subtopic
BCEHIORT	botchier	**BCFIIMOR**	morbific	**BCIORRSU**	cribrous
BCEHIRRT	brichter	**BCFIIORT**	fibrotic	**BCJKMSUU**	jumbucks
BCEHIRST	britches	**BCFILORY**	forcibly	**BCKKOOOO**	cookbook
BCEHLOST	blotches	**BCFIMORU**	cubiform	**BCKLLOOS**	bollocks
BCEEHLRSU	bluchers	**BCFLOOTU**	clubfoot	**BCKLLOSU**	bullocks
BCEHNRSU	brunches	**BCGHIINR**	birching	**BCKLLOUY**	bullocky
BCEHOORS	brooches	**BCGHIINT**	bitching	**BCKLNOSU**	sunblock
BCEHOPSU	subepoch	**BCGHINNU**	bunching		unblocks
BCEHORRT	Ter Borch	**BCGHINOT**	botching	**BCKOOOPY**	copybook
BCEHORRU	brochure	**BCGIIKNR**	bricking	**BCKOSTTU**	buttocks
BCEHORST	botchers	**BCGIILMN**	climbing	**BCLMOOSU**	coulombs
BCEHRSTU	butchers	**BCGIILOO**	biologic	**BCLMOSUU**	Columbus
	Schubert	**BCGIINRS**	scribing	**BCLOORTU**	clubroot
BCEHRTTU	Cuthbert	**BCGIKLNO**	blocking	**BCMORSUU**	cumbrous
BCEHRTUY	butchery	**BCGIKLNU**	buckling	**BCMOSSTU**	combusts
BCEHSTTU	butchest	**BCGIMNOS**	combings	**BCOOORTW**	crowboot
BCEIIKLN	iceblink	**BCGIMNRU**	crumbing	**BCOORSSW**	crossbow
BCEIIKRR	brickier	**BCGIMNUU**	cumbungi	**BCOOSTTY**	boycotts
BCEIIKRS	brickies	**BCGINNOU**	bouncing	**BCORSTTU**	obstruct
BCEIILMS	miscible		buncoing	**BDDDDEEU**	debudded
BCEIILNV	vincible			**BDDDEEEM**	embedded

BDDDEEIM	imbedded	**BDEEFITT**	befitted	**BDEELRUY**	burleyed
BDDDELOR	broddled	**BDEEFLOO**	befooled	**BDEELSST**	debtless
BDDEEESS	seedbeds	**BDEEFLOU**	befouled	**BDEEMNOT**	bodement
BDDEEFLU	befuddle	**BDEEFOOR**	forebode		entombed
BDDEEGGU	debugged	**BDEEFOOW**	beefwood	**BDEEMNOW**	enwombed
BDDEEGIR	begirded	**BDEEGGRU**	begrudge	**BDEEMNRU**	numbered
BDDEEGTU	budgeted		buggered	**BDEEMOSS**	embossed
BDDEEIMM	bedimmed	**BDEEGILN**	bleeding	**BDEEMPRU**	bumpered
BDDEEIMO	embodied	**BDEEGILU**	beguiled	**BDEEMSSU**	embussed
BDDEEINT	indebted	**BDEEGIMR**	begrimed	**BDEENPRS**	prebends
BDDEEINW	bindweed	**BDEEGINR**	breeding	**BDEENSUV**	subvened
BDDEEIRR	reedbird		breinged	**BDEEOORT**	rebooted
BDDEEIRS	birdseed	**BDEEGINW**	bedewing	**BDEEOORR**	borderer
BDDEEISS	bedsides	**BDEEGLNO**	belonged	**BDEEORRS**	resorbed
BDDEEKNU	debunked	**BDEEHIRS**	Hebrides	**BDEEORSS**	bedsores
BDDEENRU	burdened	**BDEEHLNO**	beholden	**BDEEORST**	bestrode
BDDEEORR	bordered	**BDEEHLOR**	beholder	**BDEEORSV**	observed
BDDEEORS	desorbed	**BDEEHLSU**	busheled	**BDEEORTU**	outbreed
BDDEERRU	deburred	**BDEEHMOR**	homebred	**BDEEORTV**	obverted
BDDEESSU	debussed	**BDEEHOOV**	behooved	**BDEEOSSS**	obsessed
BDDEGINR	Bridgend	**BDEEHORT**	bothered	**BDEEOSTT**	besotted
BDDEGINS	beddings	**BDEEIILL**	elidible		obtested
BDDEILNR	brindled	**BDEEIILN**	inedible	**BDEEOSTW**	bestowed
BDDEILOO	bloodied	**BDEEIKRS**	kerbside	**BDEEPRRU**	purebred
BDDEINNU	unbidden	**BDEEILLL**	libelled	**BDEERRWY**	dewberry
BDDEINRU	underbid	**BDEEILLT**	billeted	**BDEERSUW**	burweeds
BDDEIORS	disrobed	**BDEEILMR**	limbered	**BDEERTTU**	buttered
BDDEIOWY	widebody	**BDEEILNR**	rendible		rebutted
BDDEISSU	subsided	**BDEEILNU**	unedible	**BDEESSSU**	debusses
BDDELOOR	bloodred	**BDEEILNV**	vendible	**BDEFFTUU**	Dubuffet
BDDELORS	broddles	**BDEEILOR**	erodible	**BDEFIIRR**	firebird
BDDENOTU	obtunded		reboiled	**BDEFIMOR**	biformed
BDDEORTU	obtruded	**BDEEILOS**	obelised	**BDEFINRR**	fernbird
BDDGILNU	buddling	**BDEEILOZ**	obelized	**BDEGHILT**	blighted
BDDGINUY	buddying	**BDEEILRW**	bewilder	**BDEGHIST**	bedights
BDDGOOSY	dogsbody	**BDEEILSV**	bedevils	**BDEGIILN**	bielding
BDDHIIRY	dihybrid	**BDEEIMOS**	embodies	**BDEGIINT**	betiding
BDDHIMSU	Buddhism	**BDEEIMRT**	timbered		debiting
BDEEEEMS	beseemed	**BDEEIMST**	bedtimes	**BDEGILNN**	blending
BDEEEGIS	besieged	**BDEEINOS**	ebonised	**BDEGINSU**	debusing
BDEEEGNR	breenged	**BDEEINOT**	obedient	**BDEGINTU**	debuting
BDEEEHTU	hebetude	**BDEEINOZ**	ebonized	**BDEGIRUX**	Uxbridge
BDEEEILV	believed	**BDEEINRS**	inbreeds	**BDEGLMRU**	grumbled
BDEEEIRV	Bedivere	**BDEEINST**	bendiest	**BDEGLNOU**	bludgeon
BDEEEIRW	dweebier	**BDEEINSZ**	bedizens	**BDEGLRSU**	bludgers
BDEEELLR	rebelled	**BDEEIRRU**	reburied	**BDEGOOSY**	goodbyes
BDEEELLV	bevelled	**BDEEIRST**	bestride	**BDEGORRY**	dogberry
BDEEELRS	bleeders	**BDEEIRSY**	birdseye	**BDEHIKOS**	kiboshed
BDEEELRY	berleyed	**BDEEIRTT**	bittered	**BDEHLSUV**	bushveld
BDEEELUW	blueweed	**BDEEKNRU**	bunkered	**BDEHMOOY**	homebody
BDEEEMNS	bedesmen		debunker	**BDEHOOOO**	boohooed
BDEEENOS	Bodensee	**BDEEKORR**	brokered	**BDEHORTW**	Bedworth
BDEEERRS	breeders	**BDEELLOW**	bellowed	**BDEIIKLR**	birdlike
BDEEERTT	bettered	**BDEELMNO**	embolden	**BDEIIKTZ**	kibitzed
BDEEERTV	breveted	**BDEELMOR**	rebeldom	**BDEIILMR**	birdlime
BDEEFFRU	buffered	**BDEELMRT**	trembled	**BDEIILTY**	debility
	rebuffed	**BDEELMRU**	lumbered	**BDEIIRTU**	Itúrbide
BDEEFFTU	buffeted	**BDEELNNO**	ennobled	**BDEILLMU**	bdellium
BDEEFGGO	befogged	**BDEELNRS**	blenders	**BDEILLOW**	billowed
BDEEFINR	befriend	**BDEELNTU**	unbelted	**BDEILLOX**	bollixed
BDEEFIRS	debriefs	**BDEELORU**	redouble	**BDEILMOS**	semibold
BDEEFIRU	rubefied	**BDEELOSV**	beloveds	**BDEILMSU**	sublimed

BDEILNOY bodyline	**BDEMOOSY** somebody	**BDGKOOOO** Good Book
BDEILNRS blinders	**BDEMOOTT** bottomed	**BDGLLOSU** bulldogs
brindles	**BDEMSSUU** subsumed	**BDGNRUUY** burgundy
BDEILNRU Dubliner	**BDENNOTU** dubonnet	**BDGOOOSW** bogwoods
unbridle	**BDENNRUU** unburden	**BDHIIPRW** whipbird
BDEILNRY Brindley	**BDENOORU** eurobond	**BDHILNRU** Brunhild
BDEILNST blindest	**BDENOOTW** bentwood	**BDHILNRY** Brynhild
BDEILOOR bloodier	**BDENORSU** bounders	**BDHIMOOR** rhomboid
BDEILOOS bloodies		rebounds	**BDHINRSU** ibn-Rushd
BDEILOQU obliqued		suborned	**BDHIORST** birdshot
BDEILORV lovebird	**BDENOTTU** buttoned	**BDHKOORU** Dukhobor
BDEILOSS bodiless	**BDENRUUY** underbuy	**BDHLMOTU** Humboldt
BDEILRRS bridlers	**BDENSSTU** subtends	**BDHOOOSY** boyhoods
BDEILRRY lyrebird	**BDEOORRS** brooders	**BDIIINRS** brindisi
BDEILRST bristled	**BDEOORRW** borrowed	**BDIIIORV** vibrioid
driblets	**BDEOOTUX** outboxed	**BDIIJOTU** Djibouti
BDEILRSU builders	**BDEOOWWW** bowwowed	**BDIILLNW** windbill
rebuilds	**BDEOPSST** bedposts	**BDIILORS** oilbirds
BDEIMNOR Benidorm	**BDEOPSTU** subdepot	**BDIIMRUU** rubidium
BDEIMNSU nimbused	**BDEORRSU** bordures	**BDILLOOV** bloodily
BDEIMNUU unimbued	suborder	**BDILMORY** morbidly
BDEIMORS bromides	**BDEORRTU** obtruder	**BDILNNSU** sunblind
BDEIMORY embryoid	**BDEORRUW** burrowed	**BDILNPRU** purblind
BDEINOOS nobodies	**BDEORSSU** rosebuds	**BDILPSUU** buildups
BDEINOOW woodbine	**BDEORSTU** doubters	upbuilds
BDEINORV ovenbird	obtrudes	**BDILRTUY** turbidly
BDEINOSU bedouins	redoubts	**BDIMNORU** moribund
BDEINRUU unburied	**BDEORSUV** overdubs	**BDIMOSTU** misdoubt
BDEINSUX subindex	**BDERSUWY** Dewsbury	**BDINNORR** Dornbirn
BDEIOORR broodier	**BDFFIPRU** puffbird	**BDINNRUW** windburn
BDEIORRS broiders	**BDFGNOOU** fogbound	**BDINOOOR** Borodino
disrober	**BDFIIITY** bifidity	**BDINOORS** bridoons
BDEIORSS disrobes	**BDFIIORS** fibroids	**BDINORSW** snowbird
BDEIORSV overbids	**BDFILLLO** billfold	**BDINRSSU** sunbirds
BDEIOSSY disobeys	**BDFILNOO** bloodfin	**BDINSSTU** dustbins
BDEIOSUX suboxide	**BDFIRRSU** surfbird	**BDIOORSU** boudoirs
BDEIRSSU disburse	**BDFLOTUU** doubtful	**BDIORUZZ** burdizzo
subsider	**BDFORSUY** bodysurf	**BDIOSTUY** bodysuit
BDEISSSU subsides	**BDGGIINR** bridging	**BDIRSSTU** disturbs
BDEISSTU subedits	**BDGGILNU** bludging	**BDKOOORW** wordbook
BDELLOOR bordello	**BDGGLOSU** goldbugs	**BDKOORWY** bodywork
BDELLORS bedrolls	**BDGHOOUY** doughboy	**BDKOOSTU** studbook
BDELLOUZ bulldoze	**BDGIIKNR** kingbird	**BDLLSTUU** bulldust
BDELMNOO Belmondo	**BDGIILNN** blinding	**BDLNOOOU** doubloon
BDELMOSY symboled	**BDGIILNR** bridling	**BDLNOOWW** blowdown
BDELMSTU stumbled	**BDGIILNU** building	**BDLOSTUW** Dust Bowl
BDELNNUU unbundle	**BDGIINNS** bindings	**BDNNOOTU** bunodont
BDELNOSS boldness	**BDGIIOOS** gobioids	**BDNOORSU** bourdons
BDELNOST blondest	**BDGILNNO** blonding	**BDNOOSUX** soundbox
BDELNOTU unbolted	**BDGILNNU** bundling	**BDNOOSWW** downbows
BDELNRSU blunders	**BDGILNOO** blooding	**BDNOOTUU** outbound
bundlers	boodling	**BDNORSUW** rubdowns
BDELOORV overbold	**BDGILNOU** doubling	**BDOOOSWX** boxwoods
BDELORSU boulders	**BDGILOOS** globoids	**BDORUWZZ** buzzword
doublers	**BDGINNOS** bondings	**BEEEEFLN** enfeeble
BDELORTU troubled	**BDGINNOU** bounding	**BEEEENRT** terebene
BDELORUU doublure	**BDGINOOR** brooding	**BEEEFIRS** freebies
BDELORUY bouldery	**BDGINORS** birdsong	**BEEEFIST** beefiest
BDELOSTU doublets	songbird	**BEEEFLNT** Benfleet
BDEMNNOS bondsmen	**BDGINOTU** doubting	**BEEEFLST** feeblest
BDEMNSSU dumbness	**BDGINSUU** subduing	**BEEEGIRS** besieger
BDEMOORS bedrooms	**BDGIRSUU** Duisburg	**BEEEGISS** besieges

BEEEGKLS	geelbeks	**BEEGLNOR**	Grenoble	**BEEIRRSU**	reburies
BEEEGNRS	breenges	**BEEGMNOY**	bogeymen	**BEEIRRSV**	breviers
BEEEGORS	greeboes	**BEEGMRSU**	submerge	**BEEIRRTT**	bitterer
BEEEGRRS	bergeres	**BEEGNOTT**	begotten	**BEEIRSSU**	suberise
BEEEGRTT	begetter	**BEEGNRRU**	Erenburg	**BEEIRSSV**	brevises
BEEEHISV	beehives		Runeberg	**BEEIRSUZ**	suberize
BEEEHLWW	webwheel	**BEEGNRSU**	sungrebe	**BEEISSTW**	websites
BEEEHNOY	honeybee	**BEEHHMOT**	behemoth	**BEEISSUU**	Eusebius
BEEEHNSS	shebeens	**BEEHIKLR**	herblike	**BEEKMOPR**	pembroke
BEEEILLL	libellee	**BEEHILMN**	Blenheim	**BEEKNOPS**	bespoken
BEEEILLS	libelees	**BEEHIMOT**	boehmite	**BEEKNOST**	betokens
BEEEILLT	billetee	**BEEHIRST**	herbiest		steenbok
BEEEILNS	beelines	**BEEHLLNT**	hellbent	**BEEKRRSS**	berserks
BEEEILRV	believer	**BEEHLOOR**	borehole	**BEEKRRSU**	rebukers
BEEEILSV	believes	**BEEHLRST**	blethers	**BEELLORW**	bellower
BEEEINNS	Beninese	**BEEHLRSU**	busheler		rebellow
BEEEIRRZ	breezier	**BEEHNOOP**	neophobe	**BEELMNNO**	noblemen
BEEEIRST	beeriest	**BEEHNRRT**	brethren	**BEELMOSW**	embowels
BEEEJLSW	bejewels	**BEEHNRVZ**	Brezhnev	**BEELMRRT**	trembler
BEEEJLSZ	jezebels	**BEEHOOSV**	behooves	**BEELMRRU**	lumberer
BEEEKLRY	Berkeley	**BEEHRSST**	sherbets	**BEELMRST**	trembles
BEEELLRV	beveller	**BEEHRSSW**	beshrews	**BEELNNOR**	ennobler
BEEELMNS	ensemble	**BEEIILNZ**	zibeline	**BEELNNOS**	ennobles
BEEELMRS	resemble	**BEEIIRSS**	iberises	**BEELNOSS**	boneless
BEEELMZZ	embezzle	**BEEIJLSU**	jubilees		nobless
BEEELPRS	bleepers	**BEEIKKRS**	brekkies	**BEELNOSU**	bluenose
BEEELRSV	bevelers	**BEEIKLTU**	tubelike	**BEELNSSU**	blueness
BEEELRVY	Beverley	**BEEIKLWY**	biweekly	**BEELNTTU**	betelnut
BEEEMMRR	remember	**BEEIKORS**	broekies	**BEELNTUY**	butylene
BEEERSTT	besetter	**BEEILLLR**	libeller	**BEELOOST**	obsolete
BEEFFRTU	buffeter	**BEEILLNO**	lobeline	**BEELORVW**	overblew
BEEFILLT	lifebelt	**BEEILLRT**	billeter	**BEELOSTY**	eyebolts
BEEFILLX	flexible	**BEEILLTT**	belittle	**BEELRSSV**	verbless
BEEFILNU	unbelief	**BEEILLTU**	tullibee	**BEELRTUU**	trueblue
BEEFILRS	belfries	**BEEILMOS**	embolies	**BEELSSTU**	tubeless
BEEFINST	benefits		embolise	**BEEMNRRU**	renumber
BEEFIRST	briefest	**BEEILMOZ**	embolize	**BEEMOPRT**	obtemper
BEEFIRSU	rubefies	**BEEILMPR**	periblem	**BEEMORSS**	embosser
BEEFLORU	befouler	**BEEILMPS**	epiblems	**BEEMORSW**	embowers
BEEFNORR	freeborn	**BEEILNNS**	blennies	**BEEMOSSS**	embosses
BEEFOORT	freeboot	**BEEILNRR**	Berliner	**BEEMQSUU**	embusque
BEEGGNSU	geebungs	**BEEILNRS**	berlines	**BEEMRSSU**	submerse
BEEGHLRU	Breughel	**BEEILNRY**	beryline	**BEEMSSSU**	embusses
	Brueghel	**BEEILNSS**	sensible	**BEENNORS**	Berenson
BEEGHORS	Borghese	**BEEILNST**	stilbene	**BEENOPTY**	teenybop
BEEGIILL	eligible		tensible	**BEENORRS**	enrobers
BEEGIILX	exigible	**BEEILNSU**	nebulise	**BEENORTV**	verboten
BEEGILLR	gerbille	**BEEILNUZ**	nebulize	**BEENOSST**	bonesets
BEEGILNP	bleeping	**BEEILOSS**	obelises	**BEENPRST**	besprent
BEEGILNT	beetling	**BEEILOSZ**	obelizes	**BEENRSTW**	bestrewn
BEEGILNV	beveling	**BEEILOTV**	lovebite	**BEENRTTU**	brunette
BEEGILOS	obligees	**BEEILRRT**	terrible	**BEENSSTU**	subteens
BEEGILRU	beguiler	**BEEILRSU**	bluesier	**BEENSSUV**	subvenes
BEEGILSU	beguiles	**BEEILRYZ**	breezily	**BEEOORRV**	overbore
BEEGIMRS	begrimes	**BEEIMRTT**	embitter	**BEEOORTT**	beetroot
BEEGINNR	beginner	**BEEINNSV**	Ben Nevis	**BEEORRSU**	bourrees
BEEGINRS	bigeners	**BEEINOSS**	ebonises	**BEEORRSV**	observer
	breinges	**BEEINOST**	betonies	**BEEORRSY**	Rosebery
BEEGINRW	Weinberg	**BEEINOSZ**	ebonizes	**BEEORSST**	soberest
BEEGINRZ	breezing	**BEEIORTV**	overbite	**BEEORSSU**	suberose
BEEGINSU	beguines	**BEEIQSUZ**	beziques	**BEEORSSV**	observes
BEEGINSW	beeswing				obverses

BEEORSTU	tuberose	**BEGIILLN**	libeling	**BEHILMRW**	whimbrel
BEEORSTW	bestower	**BEGIILLY**	eligibly	**BEHILMST**	thimbles
BEEORSWY	eyebrows	**BEGIILST**	bilgiest	**BEHILNPY**	biphenyl
BEEOSSSS	obsesses	**BEGIIMNR**	bemiring	**BEHILORR**	horrible
BEEQSSTU	bequests	**BEGIKNRS**	kerbings	**BEHILORS**	bolshier
BEERRSTW	brewster	**BEGIKNRU**	rebuking	**BEHILOSS**	bolshies
BEERRTTU	rebutter	**BEGILLLU**	bluegill	**BEHILRTU**	thurible
BEERSSSU	subseres		gullible	**BEHIMNOO**	bonhomie
BEERSSTW	bestrews	**BEGILLNY**	bellying	**BEHIMORS**	bioherms
	websters	**BEGILLOU**	Gelibolu	**BEHINNOS**	shinbone
BEERSSUV	subserve	**BEGILNNU**	Nibelung	**BEHINOPS**	hipbones
BEERSTTU	burettes	**BEGILNNY**	benignly	**BEHINOSW**	wishbone
BEERSTTY	bystreet	**BEGILNOW**	elbowing	**BEHINSTU**	Behistun
BEFFLRSU	bluffers	**BEGILNRT**	trebling	**BEHIOSTU**	Boethius
BEFFLSTU	bluffest	**BEGILNSS**	blessing	**BEHIRRST**	rebirths
BEFGIILL	fillibeg		glibness	**BEHIRRSU**	brushier
BEFGIILS	filibegs	**BEGILNST**	beltings	**BEHISSTU**	bushiest
BEFGIINR	briefing	**BEGILNSU**	blueings	**BEHLLOOT**	bolthole
BEFGILNU	fungible	**BEGILNTU**	Belitung	**BEHLLOOW**	blowhole
BEFGIRRU	Freiburg	**BEGILORS**	obligers	**BEHLLOPS**	bellhops
BEFGIRSU	firebugs	**BEGILRST**	gilberts	**BEHLLOTW**	Bothwell
BEFHILSU	bluefish	**BEGIMNOS**	besoming	**BEHLLPSU**	bellpush
BEFHINOS	bonefish	**BEGIMNOW**	embowing	**BEHLMRSU**	humblers
BEFHIRSU	bushfire	**BEGIMNRU**	embruing	**BEHLMSTU**	humblest
BEFILLXY	flexibly	**BEGIMNSU**	bemusing	**BEHLORST**	brothels
BEFILMOR	forelimb		embusing	**BEHLRSSU**	blushers
BEFILOST	botflies	**BEGIMOST**	misbegot	**BEHMOOSY**	homeboys
BEFILOSU	biofuels	**BEGINNNO**	nonbeing	**BEHNNOUY**	honeybun
BEFILOUV	lifebuoy	**BEGINNOR**	enrobing	**BEHNRSTU**	burthens
BEFILRST	filberts		ringbone	**BEHOORST**	theorbos
BEFILSSU	subfiles	**BEGINNTU**	Tübingen	**BEHOORSX**	horsebox
BEFINORS	bonfires	**BEGINORR**	reboring	**BEHOOSUY**	houseboy
BEFIOOST	boofiest	**BEGINORS**	Gisborne	**BEHOPRST**	potherbs
BEFISSTU	fubsiest		sobering	**BEHORRST**	brothers
BEFLLLUY	bellyful	**BEGINRRS**	bringers	**BEHORSTT**	betroths
BEFLMRSU	fumblers	**BEGINRRY**	berrying	**BEHORTUY**	Beyrouth
BEFLORUW	furbelow	**BEGINRSW**	brewings	**BEHRRSSU**	brushers
BEFNOORR	forborne	**BEGINRVY**	bevvying	**BEIIKRTZ**	kibitzer
BEGGIINN	bingeing	**BEGKMOSS**	gemsboks	**BEIIKSTZ**	kibitzes
BEGGIINO	bogieing	**BEGLLOSU**	globules	**BEIILLST**	libelist
BEGGINOY	bogeying	**BEGLMRRU**	grumbler	**BEIILMMO**	immobile
BEGGINRS	Ginsberg	**BEGLMRSU**	grumbles	**BEIILMOS**	mobilise
BEGGIOST	boggiest	**BEGLNOOU**	Boulogne	**BEIILMOZ**	mobilize
BEGGISTU	buggiest	**BEGLNRSU**	blungers	**BEIILNRS**	rinsible
BEGGOOOS	goosegob		bunglers	**BEIILNTZ**	Leibnitz
BEGGOORT	Göteborg	**BEGLNRUU**	Lüneburg	**BEIILRST**	trilbies
BEGHIILP	philibeg	**BEGLOOST**	bootlegs	**BEIILRTT**	libretti
BEGHIIRT	Ghiberti	**BEGNNRRU**	Nürnberg	**BEIILSSU**	Sibelius
BEGHILRT	blighter	**BEGNOORU**	bourgeon	**BEIILSSV**	visibles
BEGHILRU	Burleigh	**BEGNORRU**	Orenburg	**BEIILSTT**	stilbite
BEGHINOR	neighbor	**BEGNORSU**	burgeons	**BEIIMNNR**	renminbi
BEGHINOV	behoving	**BEGNORTU**	burgonet	**BEIINNRS**	brinnies
BEGHINRT	berthing	**BEGNORUY**	Burgoyne	**BEIINORS**	brionies
	brighten	**BEGNOSTT**	bettongs	**BEIINOST**	niobites
BEGHIOST	gobshite	**BEGNSSUU**	subgenus	**BEIINRST**	briniest
BEGHIRRT	brighter	**BEGPRSUU**	superbug	**BEIINSTT**	stibnite
BEGHLNOU	bunghole	**BEHIISTX**	exhibits	**BEIIOPSS**	biopsies
BEGHLRUY	Burghley	**BEHIKLOS**	blokeish	**BEIIORRT**	Robert II
BEGHNOTU	boughten	**BEHIKNST**	bethinks	**BEIIOSTT**	biotites
BEGHOSTU	besought	**BEHIKOSS**	kiboshes	**BEIIRSTU**	Tiberius
BEGHOSUU	bughouse	**BEHILLOS**	shoebill	**BEIISSTU**	subitise
BEGHRRSU	burghers	**BEHILLTY**	blithely	**BEIISTTT**	bittiest

BEIISTUZ	subitize	**BEILRSTU**	burliest	**BELLLLPU**	bellpull
BEIJMOSU	jumboise		subtiler	**BELLMMRU**	Brummell
BEIJMOUZ	jumboize	**BEILRSTY**	blistery	**BELLNORW**	wellborn
BEIJNORT	Tjirebon	**BEILRTTY**	bitterly	**BELLNOSU**	bullnose
BEIKKLNO	knoblike	**BEILSTTU**	bluetits	**BELLNPSU**	bullpens
BEIKLMOT	tomblike		subtitle	**BELLOOSU**	lobulose
BEIKLMOW	womblike	**BEIMMRRS**	brimmers	**BELLOPTY**	potbelly
BEIKLNRS	blinkers	**BEIMNSSU**	nimbuses	**BELLORTW**	bellwort
BEIKLOSS	obelisks	**BEIMNSTU**	bitumens	**BELMMRSU**	mumblers
BEIKLOTY	kilobyte	**BEIMOORS**	ribosome	**BELMNOSU**	nelumbos
BEIKLRUY	rubylike	**BEIMORTU**	Umberto I	**BELMOORS**	bloomers
BEIKLSTU	bulkiest	**BEIMORTY**	biometry	**BELMOORY**	bloomery
BEIKNOST	steinbok	**BEIMORYZ**	ribozyme	**BELMOPRS**	problems
BEIKNRRY	inkberry	**BEIMPSTU**	bumpiest	**BELMORST**	temblors
BEIKNRSS	briskens	**BEIMRSTU**	resubmit	**BELMORSY**	somberly
BEIKOORT	brookite	**BEIMSSTU**	subitems		sombrely
BEIKOSST	boskiest	**BEINNOSS**	benisons	**BELMPRSU**	plumbers
BEIKRSST	briskest		boniness	**BELMPRUY**	plumbery
	briskets	**BEINNOST**	bonniest	**BELMRRSU**	rumblers
BEILLMRY	limberly	**BEINNOSZ**	benzoins	**BELMRRUY**	mulberry
BEILLMSS	limbless	**BEINOOST**	eobionts	**BELMRSSU**	slumbers
BEILLNRU	Lilburne	**BEINOQRU**	Quiberon	**BELMRSTU**	stumbler
BEILLNTU	bulletin	**BEINORSW**	brownies		tumblers
BEILLORS	brollies	**BEINORSY**	bryonies		tumbrels
BEILLOSU	libelous	**BEINORTZ**	bronzite	**BELMSSTU**	stumbles
BEILLOSX	bollixes	**BEINOSTT**	bottines	**BELNOOSY**	boloneys
BEILMMOS	embolism	**BEINOSTU**	bounties	**BELNOSUU**	nebulous
BEILMNOR	bromelin	**BEINRSTT**	bitterns	**BELNSTTU**	bluntest
BEILMNOU	nobelium	**BEINRSTU**	tribunes	**BELNSTUU**	unsubtle
BEILMNRU	unlimber		turbines	**BELOOOSX**	loosebox
BEILMNST	nimblest	**BEINSSSU**	business	**BELOOPRS**	bloopers
BEILMOOR	bloomier	**BEIOOPST**	biotopes	**BELOOPRT**	boltrope
BEILMORS	embroils	**BEIOORST**	robotise	**BELOORVW**	overblow
BEILMRSS	brimless	**BEIOORTZ**	robotize	**BELOOSST**	bootless
BEILMRST	timbrels	**BEIOOSTZ**	booziest	**BELOOTUV**	obvolute
BEILMSSU	sublimes	**BEIOPSTY**	biotypes	**BELORRTU**	troubler
BEILNNTU	buntline	**BEIOQTUU**	boutique	**BELORSST**	bolsters
BEILNOPS	bonspiel	**BEIORRST**	orbiters		lobsters
BEILNOSW	bowlines	**BEIORSTT**	bortiest	**BELORSTT**	blotters
BEILNOVY	bovinely	**BEIORSTY**	sobriety		bottlers
BEILNSSY	sensibly	**BEIORSUV**	bouviers	**BELORSTU**	boulters
BEILNSTY	tensibly	**BEIOSSST**	bossiest		troubles
BEILNSTZ	blintzes	**BEIOSSTY**	boysiest	**BELOSTUY**	obtusely
BEILOORV	boilover	**BEIQRSTU**	briquets	**BELPRSUY**	superbly
BEILOPPW	blowpipe	**BEIRRSSU**	bruisers	**BELRSSSU**	Brussels
BEILOPRS	preboils	**BEIRRSTU**	burriest	**BELRSSTU**	blusters
BEILOPSS	possible	**BEIRSSTU**	bustiers		bustlers
BEILOQSU	obliques	**BEIRSTTU**	tributes	**BELRSSUU**	subrules
BEILORRS	broilers	**BEISSTTU**	bustiest	**BELRSTUY**	blustery
BEILORST	strobile	**BEJLMRSU**	jumblers	**BELSSTTU**	subtlest
BEILORSW	blowsier	**BEJORTTU**	turbojet	**BELSTTUY**	subtlety
BEILORTT	libretto	**BEKLNORY**	brokenly	**BEMMOOSS**	embosoms
BEILORWZ	blowzier	**BEKLNTTU**	Blunkett	**BEMNNSSU**	numbness
BEILOSTW	blowiest	**BEKLOORT**	brooklet	**BEMNOORT**	trombone
BEILPRTV	blipvert	**BEKLOOST**	Belostok	**BEMOORRS**	sombrero
BEILRRRU	blurrier		booklets	**BEMORSST**	mobsters
BEILRRTT	brittler	**BEKLRSSU**	burlesks	**BEMRSSTU**	bumsters
BEILRRTY	terribly	**BEKNNORU**	unbroken	**BEMSSSUU**	subsumes
BEILRSST	blisters	**BEKNOOOT**	notebook	**BENNNOTU**	unbonnet
	bristles	**BEKNOORR**	Brookner	**BENNOORS**	Sorbonne
BEILRSTT	brittles	**BEKOOORV**	overbook	**BENNOPYY**	pennyboy
	triblets	**BEKOOTTX**	textbook	**BENOORSU**	burnoose

BENORRSU	suborner	
BENORRTU	trueborn	
BENORSTU	burstone	
	rubstone	
BENORSTW	brownest	
BENORSUU	burnouse	
BENORTTU	buttoner	
	rebutton	
BENOSSWY	newsboys	
BENRSTUY	subentry	
BENSSSUY	busyness	
BEOOORTV	overboot	
BEOORRRW	borrower	
BEOORSST	boosters	
BEOORSTY	botryose	
BEOOSTUX	outboxes	
BEOPRRSV	proverbs	
BEOQSSTU	bosquets	
BEOQSTUU	bouquets	
BEORRRUW	burrower	
BEORRSSW	browsers	
BEORSTUU	tuberous	
BEORSUVY	overbusy	
	overbuys	
BEPRRSTU	perturbs	
BEPSSTUY	subtypes	
BERRSSTU	bursters	
BERSSTTU	buttress	
BERSSTUV	subverts	
BESSSSUY	byssuses	
BFFFLMUU	bumfluff	
BFFGILNU	bluffing	
BFFHORSU	brushoff	
BFFLOOSW	blowoffs	
BFFLOTUU	outbluff	
BFFNOOSU	buffoons	
BFFNOSUX	snuffbox	
BFGHINTU	bunfight	
BFGILMNU	fumbling	
BFGIORRU	Fribourg	
BFGIORST	frogbits	
BFGLLORU	bullfrog	
BFHIILLS	billfish	
BFHILOST	fishbolt	
BFHILOSW	blowfish	
	fishbowl	
BFHIMNSU	numbfish	
BFHLLSUU	blushful	
BFIIORSS	fibrosis	
BFILLMRU	brimfull	
BFILLSSU	blissful	
BFILOSTY	liftboys	
BFIMORTU	tubiform	
BFKLOOSY	flybooks	
BFLLNOWY	flyblown	
BFLLOSUW	bowlfuls	
BFLLOSWY	flyblows	
BFLOORSU	subfloor	
BFOOOSTY	footboys	
BGGGILNO	boggling	
BGGHIINT	bighting	
BGGIILNO	obliging	

BGGIILNY	gibingly	
BGGIINNR	bringing	
BGGILNNU	blunging	
	bungling	
BGGILNRU	burgling	
BGGINRUZ	Ginzburg	
BGHHINOR	highborn	
BGHHIORW	highbrow	
BGHHIOSY	highboys	
BGHIINRT	birthing	
BGHILMNU	humbling	
BGHILNSU	blushing	
BGHILRTY	brightly	
BGHIMNTU	thumbing	
BGHIMOTU	bigmouth	
BGHINORS	bighorns	
BGHINORT	Brighton	
BGHINRSU	brushing	
BGHIPSSU	bushpigs	
BGHMORSU	homburgs	
BGHOORSU	boroughs	
BGIIJLNY	jibingly	
BGIIKLNN	blinking	
BGIIKNRS	brisking	
BGIILLNS	billings	
BGIILMNW	wimbling	
BGIILNOR	broiling	
BGIILNOS	boilings	
BGIILNPP	blipping	
BGIILNRS	brisling	
BGIILNSS	siblings	
BGIILNTY	bitingly	
BGIILNTZ	blitzing	
BGIIMMNR	brimming	
BGIIMNRU	imbruing	
BGIINORT	orbiting	
BGIINRSU	bruising	
BGIINRTU	bruiting	
BGIJLMNU	jumbling	
BGIJNORU	objuring	
BGIJOSUU	bijugous	
BGIKLNOT	kingbolt	
BGIKNNOS	bonkings	
BGIKNNOU	bunkoing	
BGIKNNOY	Nykøbing	
BGIKNOOR	brooking	
BGIKNOOS	bookings	
BGIKNSTU	stinkbug	
BGILLLUY	gullibly	
BGILLNOU	globulin	
BGILLNRU	bullring	
BGILLNUY	bullying	
BGILMMNU	mumbling	
BGILMNOO	blooming	
BGILMNPU	plumbing	
BGILMNRU	rumbling	
BGILMNTU	tumbling	
BGILMORU	Limbourg	
BGILMOSU	gumboils	
BGILMOTU	gumbotil	
BGILNNTU	blunting	
BGILNORT	ringbolt	

BGILNORY	boringly	
BGILNOSU	blousing	
BGILNOTT	blotting	
	bottling	
BGILNOTU	boulting	
BGILNRRU	blurring	
BGILNRTU	blurting	
BGILNSTU	bustling	
BGILOORS	obligors	
BGIMNOOR	brooming	
BGIMNOOS	bosoming	
BGIMNORW	ringwomb	
BGINNORW	browning	
BGINNORZ	bronzing	
BGINNRSU	burnings	
BGINOOST	boosting	
BGINORST	strobing	
BGINORSW	browsing	
BGINRSTU	bursting	
BGINSUZZ	buzzings	
BGKLOOOS	logbooks	
BGKORSSY	grysboks	
BGLNOOSW	longbows	
BGLNOSUW	blowguns	
BGLOORYY	bryology	
BGMNOOOR	gombroon	
BGMOOSTU	gumboots	
BGOPRSUU	subgroup	
BGRRUUWZ	Würzburg	
BHIIINST	inhibits	
BHIIOPRT	prohibit	
BHIIPSSS	sibships	
BHIKLLOO	billhook	
BHILLNOR	hornbill	
BHILLPUW	bullwhip	
BHILLSTU	bullshit	
BHILORRY	horribly	
BHILOSTU	holibuts	
BHILOSYY	boyishly	
BHIMNORT	thrombin	
BHIMOPRS	bimorphs	
BHINORSW	brownish	
BHINORTU	Thonburi	
BHIOOPRT	biotroph	
BHISSTTU	bushtits	
BHKMNOOY	hymn book	
		hymnbook
BHKNOOOR	hornbook	
BHLLNORU	bullhorn	
BHLMNOOR	Bornholm	
BHLOOOTT	tolbooth	
BHMMOTTU	Tom Thumb	
BHMNTTUU	thumbnut	
BHMORSTU	thrombus	
BHNOOOST	bosthoon	
BHNOORTX	boxthorn	
BHOOSSTW	bowshots	
BHPRSSUU	brushups	
BIIKMRSS	Simbirsk	
BIILLMOR	morbilli	
BIILLNOS	billions	
BIILLNOT	Billiton	

BIILLSTW	twibills	BLLMOORW	bollworm	CCDEHKLU	chuckled
BIILMOTY	mobility	BLMOOORS	Lombroso	CCDEHLTU	clutched
BIILNOOV	oblivion	BLMOOOST	tombolos		declutch
BIILNORU	urobilin	BLMOOOTY	lobotomy	CCDEHNRU	crunched
BIILNOTY	nobility	BLMOORSW	lobworms	CCDEHOOT	cootched
BIILNTUY	nubility	BLMOOSSS	blossoms	CCDEHORS	scorched
BIILORST	strobili	BLMOOSSY	blossomy	CCDEHORT	crotched
BIILOSSY	biolysis	BLMOPSUU	plumbous	CCDEHORU	crouched
BIILSTTW	witblits	BLNOOSSU	blousons	CCDEHOST	scotched
BIIMMNSY	nimbyism	BLOOPSWY	plowboys	CCDEHRTU	crutched
BIIMMOSZ	zombiism	BLOORSWW	lowbrows	CCDEHSTU	scutched
BIIMNOSU	niobiums	BLOOSSTY	slyboots	CCDEIILO	cleidoic
BIIMPRSS	biprisms	BLOOSTUW	blowouts	CCDEIINO	coincide
BIIMSSTU	stibiums	BLOPSSTU	subplots	CCDEINOR	corniced
BIIQTUUY	ubiquity	BLORSTUY	robustly	CCDEINOT	occident
BIIRSSTU	bursitis	BLOSTUUU	tubulous	CCDEIOPP	coppiced
BIJNOSSU	subjoins	BMNOOORW	monobrow	CCDEIOPU	occupied
BIKLNOST	inkblots	BMNOOOTW	boomtown	CCDEKOOU	cuckooed
BIKLNOSY	linkboys	BMNOORRU	moorburn	CCDELNOU	conclude
BIKMNOOS	boomkins	BMNOOSSU	unbosoms	CCDELOSU	occludes
BIKMNPSU	bumpkins	BMNORTUW	mowburnt	CCDELOTU	occulted
BIKMTTUU	Timbuktu	BMOOORSX	boxrooms	CCDENOOO	cocooned
BIKOOUUZ	bouzouki	BMOORSSU	sombrous	CCDENORU	conducer
BILLNOOU	bouillon	BMOORSTU	motorbus	CCDENOSU	conduces
BILLOSWY	blowsily	BMOORTTY	bottomry	CCDEORRU	occurred
BILLOWYZ	blowzily	BNNORTUW	nutbrown	CCDEORSU	succored
BILLRSWY	wrybills	BNNOTTUU	unbutton	CCDEOSTU	stuccoed
BILLSTUU	Tibullus	BNNRSTUU	sunburnt	CCDHIILO	cichloid
BILMMPSU	plumbism	BNOOOSUY	sonobuoy	CCDHIILS	cichlids
BILMNORS	nombrils	BNOORTUW	brownout	CCDHIIOR	dichroic
BILMOSTU	botulism	BNORSTUU	burnouts	CCDHIIOT	dichotic
BILMRSTU	tumbrils	BNRSSTUU	sunburst	CCDHINOO	conchoid
BILNOSTU	botulins	BOOPRSSU	Bosporus	CCDIILOS	codicils
BILOORST	sorbitol	BOOPSSTY	postboys	CCDIILSU	culicids
BILOORTT	borlotti	BORSTTUU	outburst	CCDIINOS	scincoid
BILOPSSY	possibly	CCCDIILY	dicyclic	CCDIIORS	cricoids
BILOPSUY	Polybius	CCCEEILT	eclectic	CCDIIORT	dicrotic
BILORSST	bristols	CCCEGOSY	coccyges	CCDILOSY	cycloids
BILOSSSU	subsoils	CCCEILNY	encyclic	CCDKLOSU	cuckolds
BILSTTUY	subtilty	CCCHIORY	chiccory	CCDKOOOW	woodcock
BIMNOSTY	symbiont	CCCIINSU	succinic	CCDNOORS	concords
BIMNRRUU	muirburn	CCCILNOY	cyclonic	CCDNOSTU	conducts
BIMNRUUV	viburnum	CCCINSTU	succinct	CCEEGINR	recceing
BIMOORST	robotism	CCCKOORW	cockcrow	CCEEHKNS	schnecke
BINNOORS	Robinson	CCCNOOST	concocts	CCEEHKPR	precheck
BINNOORZ	Bronzino	CCDDEENO	conceded	CCEEHKRS	checkers
BINOOPRT	Bonporti	CCDDEEOT	decocted		rechecks
BINORSTW	Brownist	CCDDELOU	occluded	CCEEHLNS	clenches
BINSSTUU	subunits	CCDDENOU	conduced	CCEEHMOO	Ecce Homo
BIOPRSTW	bowsprit	CCDEEENR	credence	CCEEHORS	ecorches
BIORRSTU	burritos	CCDEEHLN	clenched	CCEEHRSY	screechy
BIORSSTT	bistorts	CCDEEIOP	codpiece	CCEEIILS	cicelies
BIORSTTY	botrytis	CCDEEIOS	ecocides	CCEEIKLR	cleckier
BIORSTUY	bistoury	CCDEEKOR	cockered	CCEEILNR	encircle
BISSSSTU	subsists	CCDEEKOY	cockeyed	CCEEILNS	licences
BISSTUUU	busuutis	CCDEELRY	recycled	CCEEILNT	elenctic
BJNNOORS	Bjørnson	CCDEENOR	conceder	CCEEILPY	epicycle
BKKOOORW	workbook	CCDEENOS	concedes	CCEEILRT	electric
BKLNOORY	Brooklyn	CCDEESSU	succeeds	CCEEIMNU	ecumenic
BKMOOORW	bookworm	CCDEHHRU	churched	CCEEINOR	cicerone
BKNOOSTW	bowknots	CCDEHILN	clinched	CCEEINOV	conceive
BLLLLOOY	loblolly	CCDEHIPU	hiccuped	CCEEINSS	sciences

CCEEIORV	coercive	**CCEHORST**	crochets	**CCEKORSU**	cocksure
CCEEIRSS	cercises		crotches	**CCEKORTT**	Crockett
CCEEIRSV	cervices	**CCEHORSU**	couchers	**CCELLOST**	collects
	crevices		crouches	**CCELMOPT**	complect
CCEEITTU	eutectic	**CCEHORTT**	crotchet	**CCELNOSY**	cyclones
CCEEKLOR	cockerel	**CCEHOSST**	scotches	**CCELOPSY**	cyclopes
CCEEKNRW	crewneck	**CCEHRSTU**	crutches	**CCELOSSY**	cycloses
CCEEKOSY	cockeyes		scutcher	**CCENNORS**	concerns
CCEELMNY	clemency	**CCEHSSTU**	scutches	**CCENNOST**	concents
CCEELOSS	scoleces	**CCEIIKLN**	nickelic		connects
CCEELRSY	recycles	**CCEIILNT**	enclitic	**CCENOORT**	concerto
CCEEMMNO	commence	**CCEIILOR**	licorice	**CCENOPST**	concepts
CCEEMMOR	commerce	**CCEIILPT**	ecliptic	**CCENORST**	concerts
CCEENNOS	ensconce	**CCEIILST**	scilicet	**CCENORTY**	cornetcy
CCEENORT	concrete	**CCEIILTU**	leucitic	**CCENRRUY**	currency
CCEENRST	crescent	**CCEIINNO**	conicine	**CCEOOSTT**	cocottes
CCEEORRS	coercers	**CCEIINOR**	ciceroni	**CCEOPRUY**	reoccupy
CCEFFHKO	checkoff	**CCEIINTU**	cicutine	**CCEORRST**	corrects
CCEFHRSU	curchefs	**CCEIKLRS**	clickers	**CCEORRSU**	reoccurs
CCEFIIPS	specific	**CCEIKOST**	cockiest		succorer
CCEFIRRU	crucifer	**CCEIKRST**	crickets	**CCEORSSU**	crocuses
CCEFLLOU	floccule	**CCEILMOO**	coelomic	**CCEORSTU**	stuccoer
CCEFLOOS	floccose	**CCEILMOP**	complice	**CCEOSSTU**	stuccoes
CCEFNOST	confects	**CCEILNUY**	unicycle	**CCESSSUU**	cuscuses
CCEGHIKN	checking	**CCEILOSS**	scolices	**CCFIIRUX**	crucifix
CCEGIKLN	clecking	**CCEILRRS**	circlers	**CCFIKNOY**	cocknify
CCEGILRY	glyceric	**CCEILRRU**	curricle	**CCFILLOU**	flocculi
CCEGINNO	congenic	**CCEILRST**	circlets	**CCFILNOT**	conflict
CCEGINOR	coercing	**CCEILRSY**	cresylic	**CCFKLOOT**	cockloft
CCEHHINS	chinches	**CCEILRTY**	tricycle	**CCGHHIOU**	hiccough
CCEHHRSU	churches	**CCEILRUU**	curlicue	**CCGHIINN**	cinching
CCEHIIMR	chimeric	**CCEILSTU**	cuticles	**CCGHIKNO**	chocking
CCEHIIMS	ischemic	**CCEIMNNO**	economic	**CCGHIKNU**	chucking
CCEHIINZ	zecchini	**CCEIMOST**	cosmetic	**CCGHINOU**	couching
CCEHIKNS	chickens	**CCEIMRRU**	mercuric	**CCGHINTW**	cwtching
CCEHIKSU	chuckies	**CCEIMRUV**	cervicum	**CCGIIKLN**	clicking
CCEHILNR	clincher	**CCEINNOV**	convince	**CCGIIKNR**	cricking
CCEHILNS	clinches	**CCEINOOR**	coercion	**CCGIILNR**	circling
CCEHILOR	choleric	**CCEINORS**	cornices	**CCGIKLNO**	clocking
CCEHILOY	choicely		croceins		cockling
CCEHILSU	culchies	**CCEINORT**	concerti	**CCGIKLNU**	clucking
CCEHINOR	corniche		necrotic	**CCGIKNOR**	crocking
	enchoric	**CCEINOST**	conceits	**CCGILLOY**	glycolic
CCEHINOS	conchies	**CCEINOTT**	tectonic	**CCGILOSU**	glucosic
CCEHINOZ	zecchino	**CCEINPRT**	precinct	**CCGINNOS**	sconcing
CCEHINRU	crunchie	**CCEINRTU**	cincture	**CCGINOTW**	twoccing
CCEHINST	technics	**CCEINSZZ**	Szczecin	**CCGKOORS**	gorcocks
CCEHIORT	ricochet	**CCEIOORT**	crocoite	**CCHHIITY**	ichthyic
CCEHIOST	choicest	**CCEIOPPS**	coppices	**CCHHINOT**	chthonic
CCEHKLRU	chuckler	**CCEIOPRU**	occupier	**CCHHINOU**	Chin-Chou
CCEHKLSU	chuckles	**CCEIOPSU**	occupies	**CCHHLRUY**	churchly
CCEHKORW	checkrow	**CCEIOPTY**	ecotypic	**CCHHNRUU**	unchurch
CCEHKOTU	checkout	**CCEIORST**	cortices	**CCHHOOWW**	chowchow
CCEHKPSU	checkups	**CCEIPSST**	sceptics	**CCHIINUZ**	zucchini
CCEHLMOR	cromlech	**CCEIPSUV**	Vespucci	**CCHIIORT**	orchitic
CCEHLRSU	cleruchs	**CCEIRRSU**	circuses	**CCHINORT**	Crichton
CCEHLRUY	cleruchy	**CCEKLORS**	clockers	**CCHIPSSY**	psychics
CCEHLSTU	clutches	**CCEKNOSY**	cockneys	**CCHKMSSU**	schmucks
CCEHNRSU	crunches	**CCEKOPST**	petcocks	**CCHKOOST**	cockshot
CCEHOOST	cootches	**CCEKORRY**	crockery	**CCIILPRS**	circlips
CCEHORRS	scorcher	**CCEKORST**	crockets	**CCIIMNSY**	cynicism
CCEHORSS	scorches			**CCIINORZ**	zirconic

CCIIRSTU	circuits
CCIIRTUY	circuity
CCIKKLOP	picklock
CCIKKOTT	ticktock
CCIKLOSW	cowlicks
CCIKOPST	cockpits
CCILNOOS	colonics
CCILNOSU	councils
CCILOOPS	piccolos
CCILORUU	curculio
CCILOSSY	cyclosis
CCILSSTY	cyclists
CCINOORT	crotonic
CCINOPSY	syncopic
CCINORSY	cryonics
CCINOSTV	convicts
CCIOOPST	scotopic
CCIOORSS	siroccos
CCIOOTXY	oxytocic
CCIOPSTU	occiputs
CCJNNOTU	conjunct
CCKMMORU	crummock
CCKMOOOR	moorcock
CCKNORTU	turncock
CCKOOPST	stopcock
CCKOPRSU	cockspur
CCLLOTUY	occultly
CCNOOPSU	puccoons
CCNOOSTU	coconuts
CCOOSSUU	couscous
CCOOTTUU	tucotuco
CCORSSTU	crosscut
CCORSSUU	succours
CCTTUUUU	tucutucu
CDDDEETU	deducted
CDDDIIOY	diddicoy
CDDEEEEX	exceeded
CDDEEEFT	defected
CDDEEEIV	deceived
CDDEEEJT	dejected
CDDEEENR	decerned
CDDEEENT	decedent
CDDEEEPR	preceded
CDDEEETT	detected
CDDEEFOR	deforced
CDDEEGLU	cudgeled
CDDEEHIS	dehisced
CDDEEHIT	cheddite
CDDEEHNR	drenched
CDDEEIIS	deicides
CDDEEIKR	dickered
CDDEEILN	declined
CDDEEINR	cindered
CDDEEIOT	coedited
CDDEEIOV	devoiced
CDDEEIPT	depicted
CDDEEIRS	deciders
	descried
CDDEEIRT	credited
	directed
CDDEEKNU	undecked
CDDEEKOR	redocked

CDDEEKOT	docketed
CDDEEKUW	duckweed
CDDEELPU	decupled
CDDEELSU	secluded
CDDEELUX	excluded
CDDEELUY	deucedly
CDDEENOS	seconded
CDDEENSS	descends
CDDEEORR	recorded
CDDEEORS	decoders
CDDEERUV	decurved
CDDEESUW	cudweeds
CDDEFIIO	codified
CDDEFINO	confided
CDDEGIIN	deciding
CDDEGINO	decoding
CDDEGINU	deducing
CDDEHIRT	Redditch
CDDEHISU	chuddies
CDDEHRSU	chudders
CDDEIINT	indicted
CDDEILLO	collided
CDDEILNU	included
CDDEILOR	cloddier
CDDEINTU	inducted
CDDEIORV	divorced
CDDEIRRU	cruddier
CDDELLOU	colluded
CDDELNOO	condoled
CDDELORS	coddlers
CDDENNOO	condoned
CDDENOOR	cordoned
CDDEOORR	corroded
CDDEOORT	doctored
CDDEOORW	codeword
CDDEOPRU	produced
CDDGHILO	godchild
CDDGILNO	coddling
CDDGILNU	cuddling
CDDGINSU	scudding
CDDHHISU	shidduch
CDDHIIRY	dihydric
CDDHILOS	cloddish
CDDIIKNS	niddicks
CDDIIOSS	discoids
CDDIIOSY	didicoys
CDDIISTY	dytiscid
CDDIKOPS	piddocks
CDDIORSS	discords
CDDKOPSU	puddocks
CDDKORSU	ruddocks
CDDOOORW	cordwood
CDEEEERX	exceeder
CDEEEFFT	effected
CDEEEFNS	defences
CDEEEHNS	Enschede
CDEEEHOR	reechoed
CDEEEHSW	eschewed
CDEEEINV	evidence
CDEEEIRV	deceiver
	received
CDEEEISV	deceives

CDEEEJRT	rejected
CDEEELLX	excelled
CDEEELST	deselect
	selected
CDEEEMNT	cemented
CDEEENOS	secondee
CDEEENRS	screened
	secerned
CDEEENRT	centered
CDEEEPRS	precedes
CDEEEPTX	expected
CDEEERRS	decreers
CDEEERSS	recessed
	seceders
CDEEERST	decreets
	resected
	screeted
	secreted
CDEEERTT	detecter
CDEEERTX	excreted
CDEEESTX	exsected
CDEEETUX	executed
CDEEFHLN	flenched
CDEEFHLT	fletched
CDEEFIIL	icefield
CDEEFIIS	edifices
CDEEFIIT	feticide
CDEEFINT	infected
CDEEFKLR	freckled
CDEEFKOR	foredeck
CDEEFLST	deflects
CDEEFNOR	enforced
CDEEFORS	deforces
CDEEFORT	defector
CDEEGIIR	regicide
CDEEGINO	genocide
CDEEGINR	receding
CDEEGINS	seceding
CDEEGIOS	geodesic
CDEEGIOT	geodetic
CDEEGIRU	cudgerie
CDEEGIRZ	grecized
CDEEGKST	gedeckts
CDEEHIKL	helideck
CDEEHILN	lichened
CDEEHILS	chiseled
CDEEHINR	enriched
CDEEHIPR	ciphered
	decipher
CDEEHISS	dehisces
CDEEHKST	sketched
CDEEHLPU	pleuched
CDEEHLSU	schedule
CDEEHNQU	quenched
CDEEHNRR	drencher
CDEEHNRS	drenches
CDEEHNRT	trenched
CDEEHNRW	wrenched
CDEEHORS	coshered
CDEEHORT	hectored
	tochered
CDEEHPRY	cyphered

279

CDEEHRTW	wretched	CDEEIRUY	Eurydice		escorted
CDEEIILT	elicited	CDEEITUV	eductive	CDEEORSV	coversed
CDEEIIMN	medicine	CDEEJKOY	jockeyed	CDEEORSW	escrowed
CDEEIIMP	epidemic	CDEEKLPS	speckled	CDEEORSY	decoyers
CDEEIINT	indictee	CDEEKNOR	reckoned	CDEEORTT	cottered
CDEEIIRT	dieretic	CDEEKNRS	rednecks		detector
CDEEIISV	decisive	CDEEKOPT	pocketed	CDEEORTV	vectored
CDEEIITT	dietetic	CDEEKORT	rocketed	CDEEOSST	cestodes
CDEEIJNT	injected	CDEEKORW	rockweed		cosseted
CDEEIJOR	rejoiced	CDEEKOST	socketed	CDEEPRST	sceptred
CDEEIKLN	nickeled	CDEEKPRU	puckered	CDEERRRU	recurred
CDEEIKNR	nickered	CDEEKRSU	suckered	CDEERRSU	reducers
CDEEIKNS	sickened	CDEEKRTU	tuckered	CDEERRUV	recurved
CDEEIKPT	picketed	CDEELLOT	colleted	CDEERSSU	seducers
CDEEIKRW	wickeder	CDEELLPU	cupelled	CDEERTTU	curetted
CDEEIKTT	ticketed	CDEELMOW	welcomed	CDEERTUV	curveted
CDEEILNP	penciled	CDEELNOS	enclosed	CDEFFISU	sufficed
CDEEILNR	decliner	CDEELNPU	peduncle	CDEFFLSU	scuffled
	reclined	CDEELNTY	decently	CDEFHILN	flinched
CDEEILNS	declines	CDEELOOW	locoweed	CDEFHILT	flitched
	licensed	CDEELOPU	decouple	CDEFIIIL	filicide
	silenced	CDEELOST	closeted	CDEFIIIT	citified
CDEEILNT	denticle	CDEELOTU	elocuted	CDEFIIOR	codifier
CDEEILNV	Cliveden	CDEELPRU	preclude	CDEFIIOS	codifies
CDEEILOR	recoiled	CDEELPSU	decuples	CDEFIIST	deficits
CDEEILPS	eclipsed	CDEELRTU	lectured	CDEFIITY	cityfied
	pedicels		relucted	CDEFILOS	Scofield
	pedicles	CDEELRUX	excluder	CDEFINNO	confined
CDEEILRT	derelict	CDEELSSU	secludes	CDEFINNU	infecund
CDEEILSU	Seleucid	CDEELSUX	excludes	CDEFINOR	confider
CDEEIMNR	endermic	CDEEMNPR	compered	CDEFINOS	confides
CDEEIMOR	mediocre	CDEEMOPT	competed	CDEFIORY	recodify
CDEEIMOS	comedies	CDEEMORT	ectoderm	CDEFKORS	defrocks
CDEEIMPR	premedic	CDEEMRTU	Decretum	CDEFLNOU	flounced
CDEEIMRV	decemvir	CDEENNOS	condense	CDEFLORY	forcedly
CDEEINNS	incensed	CDEENNOU	denounce	CDEFNORU	unforced
CDEEINNT	indecent		enounced	CDEFNOSU	confused
CDEEINOR	recoined	CDEENNOV	convened	CDEFNOTU	confuted
CDEEINPT	incepted	CDEENNPY	pendency	CDEFOSSU	focussed
CDEEINRU	reinduce	CDEENNTY	tendency	CDEGHIOR	Goderich
CDEEINTU	inductee	CDEENORR	cornered	CDEGHORU	grouched
CDEEIOPR	recopied	CDEENORS	censored	CDEGIILP	diplegic
CDEEIORV	divorcee		encoders	CDEGIINX	exciding
	revoiced		necrosed	CDEGIKNO	decoking
CDEEIOSS	dioceses		seconder	CDEGIKSW	Sedgwick
CDEEIOSV	devoices	CDEENOSY	ecdysone	CDEGILOO	Coolidge
CDEEIPRR	repriced	CDEENOTX	coextend	CDEGINNO	encoding
CDEEIPRS	precised	CDEENOVX	convexed	CDEGINNS	scending
CDEEIPRT	decrepit	CDEENOVY	conveyed	CDEGINOS	cognised
	depicter	CDEENPRU	prudence	CDEGINOY	decoying
CDEEIPRU	pedicure	CDEENRSU	censured		gynecoid
CDEEIPST	pectised	CDEENRUV	verecund	CDEGINOZ	cognized
CDEEIPTZ	pectized	CDEENSST	descents	CDEGINRU	reducing
CDEEIRRS	decriers	CDEENSTY	encysted	CDEGINRY	decrying
	descrier	CDEEOOPR	coopered	CDEGINSU	seducing
CDEEIRRT	redirect	CDEEOOTV	dovecote	CDEGINSY	dysgenic
CDEEIRSS	descries	CDEEOPPR	coppered	CDEGORSU	scourged
CDEEIRST	discreet	CDEEOPRS	proceeds		scrouged
	discrete	CDEEOPRU	recouped	CDEHHNOO	honchoed
CDEEIRSU	decuries	CDEEORRR	recorder	CDEHIILO	helicoid
CDEEIRSV	serviced		rerecord	CDEHIILS	ceilidhs
CDEEIRSY	Criseyde	CDEEORST	corseted	CDEHIIMO	homicide

CDEHIINO	echinoid	CDEIIOSU	diecious	CDEINRUV	incurved
CDEHIIRT	Dietrich	CDEIIPRR	cirriped	CDEINSSX	exscinds
CDEHIIVV	chivvied	CDEIIRTU	diuretic	CDEINSTY	syndetic
CDEHIKRW	herdwick	CDEIISSU	suicides	CDEIOORS	corodies
CDEHIKST	skitched	CDEIJSST	disjects	CDEIOORT	coeditor
CDEHILNR	children	CDEIKLNR	crinkled	CDEIOPRS	percoids
CDEHILOR	chloride	CDEIKLOR	cordlike	CDEIOPRT	depictor
CDEHILOS	cheloids	CDEIKLPR	prickled	CDEIOPST	despotic
CDEHILRS	Childers	CDEIKLRT	trickled	CDEIOPTY	copyedit
CDEHILRT	eldritch	CDEIKLRU	luderick	CDEIORRT	creditor
CDEHIMOT	methodic	CDEIKLST	stickled		director
CDEHIMRS	smirched	CDEIKLWY	wickedly	CDEIORRV	codriver
CDEHINOS	hedonics	CDEIKNPU	unpicked		divorcer
CDEHINST	snitched	CDEIKOST	diestock	CDEIORST	cordites
CDEHIOSW	cowhides	CDEIKRRS	derricks	CDEIORSV	discover
CDEHIOTY	theodicy	CDEIKRSTU	duckiest		divorces
CDEHIRST	ditchers	CDEILLOR	collider	CDEIORTU	outcried
CDEHISTT	stitched	CDEILLOS	collides	CDEIOSST	scodiest
CDEHISTW	switched	CDEILLOU	lodicule	CDEIPRST	predicts
CDEHITTW	twitched	CDEILLOY	docilely		scripted
CDEHKLSU	shelduck	CDEILLPU	pellucid	CDEIPRTU	pictured
CDEHKSUY	heyducks	CDEILMOP	compiled	CDEIRRSU	scurried
CDEHLOOS	deschool		complied	CDEIRSTU	crudites
	schooled	CDEILMOY	myceloid		curtsied
CDEHLORT	chortled	CDEILMPR	crimpled	CDEIRSTV	verdicts
CDEHLOSU	slouched	CDEILMRU	dulcimer	CDEISSST	dissects
CDEHMNTU	dutchmen	CDEILNOS	inclosed	CDEISSSU	discuses
CDEHMOOS	smooched	CDEILNOU	uncoiled	CDEJNORU	conjured
CDEHMSTU	smutched	CDEILNRV	cylinder	CDEKKLNU	knuckled
CDEHNOOP	chenopod	CDEILNSU	includes	CDEKLMOR	clerkdom
CDEHNRSU	chunders		nuclides	CDEKLNOU	unlocked
CDEHOOSS	scooshed	CDEILOOW	woodlice	CDEKLRTU	truckled
CDEHORRS	Schröder	CDEILOPU	clupeoid	CDEKNOOU	uncooked
CDEHORSU	chorused	CDEILORS	scleroid	CDEKNOOV	convoked
CDEHORSW	chowders	CDEILORU	cloudier	CDEKNORU	uncorked
	cowherds	CDEILOSS	disclose	CDEKNTUU	untucked
CDEHOSSU	hocussed	CDEILPPR	crippled	CDEKOPSY	copydesk
CDEHSSSU	schussed	CDEILPSU	clupeids	CDEKOSST	destocks
CDEIIILS	silicide	CDEILRTY	directly	CDELLNOU	Culloden
CDEIIIMT	miticide	CDEILSXY	dyslexic	CDELLOOP	clodpole
CDEIIIOS	idiocies	CDEIMMOT	decommit	CDELLORS	scrolled
CDEIIKKS	sidekick	CDEIMMOX	commixed	CDELLORU	colluder
CDEIIKMM	mimicked	CDEIMORT	morticed	CDELLOSU	colludes
CDEIIKST	dickiest	CDEIMOST	Docetism	CDELLOTU	cloudlet
	stickied		domestic	CDELLTUY	dulcetly
CDEIILMM	dilemmic	CDEIMPRS	scrimped	CDELMNOO	monocled
CDEIILMO	domicile	CDEINNOU	uncoined	CDELMNOU	columned
CDEIILNN	inclined	CDEINNOV	connived	CDELMPRU	crumpled
CDEIILNO	indocile	CDEINOOZ	endozoic	CDELNOOR	condoler
CDEIILOT	idiolect	CDEINORS	consider	CDELNOOS	condoles
CDEIILPS	disciple	CDEINORT	centroid		consoled
CDEIILRU	ridicule		doctrine	CDELNOSS	coldness
CDEIIMRT	dimetric	CDEINORU	decurion	CDELNOSU	unclosed
CDEIINNT	incident	CDEINOTU	eduction	CDELNOSY	condyles
CDEIINOS	decision	CDEINOUV	unvoiced		secondly
CDEIINOV	invoiced	CDEINPRS	prescind	CDELNRUU	uncurled
CDEIINRT	indicter	CDEINPRU	unpriced	CDELNSUY	secundly
	indirect	CDEINPSY	dyspneic	CDELOORU	coloured
CDEIINTY	cytidine	CDEINRRU	incurred		decolour
CDEIIOPR	periodic	CDEINRSS	discerns	CDELOPTU	octupled
CDEIIOPS	episodic		rescinds	CDELORSS	cordless
CDEIIOPT	epidotic	CDEINRSU	inducers		scolders

CDELORSU	closured	**CDGHIINT**	ditching	**CDIKKOPR**	dropkick
CDELORTU	clotured	**CDGHILOW**	Chlodwig	**CDIKNORS**	dornicks
CDELORZZ	crozzled	**CDGHINOR**	chording	**CDIKNOSW**	windsock
CDELPRSU	scrupled	**CDGHINOU**	douching	**CDILLOOS**	colloids
CDELPSTU	sculpted	**CDGIINNU**	inducing	**CDILLOUY**	cloudily
CDELRRSU	curdlers	**CDGIKLNU**	duckling	**CDILOOPS**	podsolic
CDELRSUY	cursedly	**CDGIKLOR**	gridlock	**CDILOOPZ**	podzolic
CDELRTUU	cultured	**CDGILNOS**	codlings	**CDILOORS**	discolor
CDELRUVY	curvedly		lingcods	**CDILOORT**	lordotic
CDELSSTU	ductless		scolding	**CDILOOTY**	cotyloid
CDELSSUY	cussedly	**CDGILNOU**	clouding	**CDIMMOSU**	modicums
CDELSTTU	scuttled	**CDGILNRU**	curdling	**CDIMOORT**	microdot
CDELSTUU	ductules	**CDGINORW**	crowding	**CDINNQUU**	quidnunc
CDEMMNOS	commends	**CDGLOOOY**	codology	**CDINORTU**	inductor
CDEMMNOU	communed	**CDGNOOTU**	gonoduct	**CDINOSTU**	conduits
CDEMMOOS	commodes	**CDHHIILS**	childish		discount
CDEMMOOV	commoved	**CDHIINNW**	Chindwin		noctuids
CDEMMOTU	commuted	**CDHIINST**	chindits	**CDIOOPRS**	prosodic
CDEMMRSU	scrummed	**CDHIIOOR**	chorioid	**CDIOORRR**	corridor
CDEMNNOS	condemns	**CDHIIORT**	hidrotic	**CDIOPRRS**	ripcords
CDEMNOOW	comedown		trichoid	**CDIOPRSU**	cuspidor
	downcome	**CDHIIOSZ**	schizoid	**CDIOSSTY**	cystoids
CDEMNOSU	consumed	**CDHIISST**	distichs	**CDIOSTUV**	oviducts
CDEMNOTU	document	**CDHILOOP**	chilopod	**CDJLNOUY**	jocundly
CDEMOOPS	composed	**CDHIMNOR**	Richmond	**CDKLOOOS**	ockodols
CDEMOPTU	computed	**CDHINNOR**	chondrin	**CDKNNOSU**	dunnocks
CDEMOSTU	costumed	**CDHIOORS**	choroids	**CDKOOORW**	corkwood
CDEMPRSU	scrumped	**CDHIOORT**	trochoid	**CDLLLOOP**	clodpoll
CDENNOOR	condoner	**CDHIOPRW**	whipcord	**CDLOOPSY**	lycopods
CDENNOOS	condones	**CDHIPSTY**	diptychs	**CDMMOOSU**	Commodus
CDENNOOT	connoted	**CDHLOOPY**	copyhold	**CDMNOOPU**	compound
CDENNOST	contends	**CDHOOOPW**	woodchop	**CDMNORUU**	corundum
CDENOORT	creodont	**CDHOORRU**	urochord	**CDNNOOOT**	conodont
CDENOOVY	convoyed	**CDHORTUW**	Cudworth	**CDNNOOTY**	cynodont
CDENORSU	crunodes	**CDIIIMNS**	minidisc	**CDOOOPST**	octopods
CDENORTU	cornuted	**CDIIIMNU**	indicium	**CDOORRUY**	corduroy
	trounced	**CDIIIORT**	dioritic	**CDOOSTUW**	woodcuts
CDENOSTU	contused	**CDIIKPST**	dipstick	**CDOPRSTU**	products
CDENRTUU	undercut	**CDIILMOS**	domicils	**CEEEEIPY**	eyepiece
CDEOOPPS	copepods	**CDIILOPP**	diplopic	**CEEEELST**	selectee
CDEOOPRS	scrooped	**CDIILOTY**	docility	**CEEEFFRT**	effecter
CDEOOPST	postcode	**CDIILRUY**	uridylic	**CEEEFILR**	fleecier
CDEOORRR	corroder	**CDIILSVY**	viscidly	**CEEEFILS**	fleecies
CDEOORRS	corrodes	**CDIILTUY**	lucidity	**CEEEFNOR**	conferee
CDEOORSU	decorous	**CDIIMNOU**	conidium	**CEEEGIMN**	emceeing
CDEOORSV	vocoders	**CDIIMTUY**	mucidity	**CEEEGINX**	exigence
CDEOOSTV	dovecots	**CDIINORS**	crinoids	**CEEEGITX**	exegetic
CDEOPRRU	procured	**CDIINORT**	indictor	**CEEEGMNR**	mergence
	producer	**CDIINOST**	dictions	**CEEEGNRV**	vergence
CDEOPRSU	produces	**CDIINOSV**	vidicons	**CEEEHIKR**	cheekier
CDEORRSW	crowders	**CDIINPRY**	cyprinid	**CEEEHIRR**	cheerier
CDEORSUU	douceurs	**CDIINSTT**	distinct	**CEEEHIRS**	cheesier
CDEOSSTU	custodes	**CDIIOOSU**	dioicous	**CEEEHLMN**	Mechelen
CDEPRSTY	decrypts	**CDIIOPRT**	dioptric	**CEEEHNNY**	Cheyenne
CDERSTTU	destruct	**CDIIORSU**	Dioscuri	**CEEEHORS**	reechoes
CDFIILSU	fluidics		sciuroid	**CEEEHPRS**	cheepers
CDFIKMNU	mindfuck	**CDIIORSX**	corixids	**CEEEHPSS**	speeches
CDFIKOPR	Pickford	**CDIIOSSS**	cissoids	**CEEEHRRS**	cheerers
CDFIKORS	disfrock	**CDIIPTUY**	cupidity	**CEEEHRSW**	eschewer
CDFKOORR	Rockford	**CDIIRSTT**	district	**CEEEIJTV**	ejective
CDFKOOTU	duckfoot	**CDIJNSTU**	disjunct	**CEEEILNN**	lenience
CDFNNOOU	confound	**CDIKKNOW**	kickdown	**CEEEILNS**	licensee

CEEEILNT	telecine	CEEFINRT	frenetic		Michelet
CEEEILRT	erectile		infecter	CEEHILRW	clerihew
CEEEILTV	cleveite		reinfect	CEEHILRY	cheerily
	elective	CEEFIRST	fiercest	CEEHILSV	vehicles
CEEEIMNN	eminence	CEEFKLRS	freckles	CEEHILSW	Weichsel
CEEEIMRR	reremice	CEEFKLSS	feckless	CEEHILTV	Helvetic
CEEEINNT	enceinte	CEEFLNOR	florence	CEEHIMRS	chimeres
CEEEINPS	epicenes	CEEFLNTU	feculent	CEEHIMRT	hermetic
CEEEIPRR	creepier	CEEFLRST	reflects	CEEHIMSS	chemises
	creperie	CEEFNORR	confrere	CEEHINPR	encipher
CEEEIPRS	creepies		enforcer	CEEHINPT	phenetic
CEEEIPRV	perceive	CEEFNORS	enforces	CEEHINRR	enricher
CEEEIRRV	receiver	CEEFNRVY	fervency	CEEHINRS	enriches
CEEEIRSV	receives	CEEFOPRR	perforce	CEEHINRT	Chrétien
CEEEIRSX	exercise	CEEFOPRT	perfecto	CEEHINTT	enthetic
CEEEJRRT	rejecter	CEEFORSS	frescoes	CEEHIORS	cheerios
CEEELLNR	crenelle	CEEFORTW	crowfeet	CEEHIOSV	cohesive
CEEELOST	Eteocles	CEEFPRST	perfects	CEEHIPRT	herpetic
CEEELPRT	preelect		prefects	CEEHIRRS	cherries
CEEELRRV	cleverer	CEEGHIKN	cheeking	CEEHIRST	chestier
CEEELRST	reelects	CEEGHILN	leeching		heretics
	reselect	CEEGHINP	cheeping	CEEHIRTT	tetchier
CEEELRTT	electret	CEEGHINR	cheering	CEEHISTT	esthetic
CEEELSST	celestes	CEEGHINS	cheesing		techiest
CEEEMNRT	cementer	CEEGHKMO	Ockeghem	CEEHISTW	chewiest
	cerement	CEEGHLLS	Schlegel	CEEHKLRS	hecklers
CEEEMORT	ectomere	CEEGHLOW	cogwheel	CEEHKNOR	Honecker
CEEEMRTY	cemetery	CEEGIJNT	ejecting	CEEHKNPS	henpecks
CEEENNST	sentence	CEEGIKRU	Guericke	CEEHKRST	sketcher
CEEENNSV	Cévennes	CEEGILNT	electing	CEEHKSST	sketches
CEEENPRS	presence	CEEGILOT	eclogite	CEEHLLRW	Cherwell
CEEENPRT	pretence	CEEGILRS	clergies	CEEHLMOO	hemocoel
CEEENQSU	sequence	CEEGINOO	cooeeing	CEEHLNOS	chelones
CEEENRRS	screener	CEEGINOR	erogenic		echelons
CEEENRRT	reentres	CEEGINPR	creeping	CEEHLNPU	penuchle
CEEENSSS	essences	CEEGINRS	Genseric	CEEHLNSU	elenchus
CEEEPRRS	creepers	CEEGINRT	erecting	CEEHLORT	reclothe
CEEERRST	erecters	CEEGINST	genetics	CEEHLOSS	echoless
	reerects	CEEGINSU	eugenics	CEEHLRSU	hercules
CEEERRTX	excreter	CEEGINXY	exigency	CEEHLRSW	welchers
CEEERSSS	recesses	CEEGIORX	exoergic	CEEHLSSS	chessels
CEEERSST	secretes	CEEGIRSZ	grecizes	CEEHMNSS	chessmen
	sesterce	CEEGKNOR	Greenock	CEEHMOTY	hemocyte
CEEERSSU	cereuses	CEEGLLOS	colleges	CEEHMRSS	schemers
CEEERSTX	excretes	CEEGLNST	neglects	CEEHMRST	merchets
CEEERTUX	executer	CEEGLOSU	eclogues	CEEHMSTU	Tecumseh
CEEESSSX	excesses	CEEGMNOY	cymogene	CEEHNNOW	nowhence
CEEESTUX	executes	CEEGNNOO	oncogene	CEEHNNRT	entrench
CEEFFNOS	offences	CEEGNNOR	congener	CEEHNORT	coherent
CEEFFORT	effector	CEEGNORV	Congreve	CEEHNQRU	quencher
CEEFGILN	fleecing		converge	CEEHNQSU	quenches
CEEFHIKR	kerchief	CEEGORST	corteges	CEEHNRRT	retrench
CEEFHIST	fetiches	CEEHHIRS	Cheshire		trencher
CEEFHLNR	flencher	CEEHHLRS	Herschel	CEEHNRST	trenches
CEEFHLNS	flenches	CEEHHMNN	henchmen	CEEHNRSW	wenchers
CEEFHLRT	fletcher	CEEHHNPR	Chephren		wrenches
CEEFHLRU	cheerful	CEEHIIST	ethicise	CEEHNSST	stenches
CEEFHLST	fletches	CEEHIITZ	ethicize	CEEHOPRY	coryphee
CEEFHRST	fechters	CEEHIKLY	cheekily	CEEHOPTT	pochette
	fetchers	CEEHILLN	chenille	CEEHORRS	coherers
CEEFILLY	fleecily		Hellenic	CEEHORRT	torchere
CEEFILRT	telferic	CEEHILMT	Melchite		
CEEFILRY	fiercely				

CEEHORST	trochees	**CEEIMNST**	centimes	**CEEKLLMN**	McKellen
CEEHPRRS	perchers		tenesmic	**CEEKLNPU**	penuckle
CEEHPRRY	perchery	**CEEIMORT**	meteoric	**CEEKLNST**	necklets
CEEHQRSU	chequers	**CEEIMOTY**	meiocyte	**CEEKLPSS**	speckles
CEEHRSTW	wretches	**CEEIMRSX**	excimers	**CEEKLRSS**	clerkess
CEEHRSTY	Chertsey	**CEEIMSTT**	smectite		reckless
CEEHRTTU	teuchter	**CEEINNOP**	pinecone	**CEEKNORR**	reckoner
CEEIIKLV	vicelike	**CEEINNOT**	neotenic	**CEEKNORV**	Cerenkov
CEEIIMPR	epimeric	**CEEINNSS**	incenses	**CEEKOPRX**	oxpecker
CEEIIMRT	eremitic		niceness	**CEEKORRT**	corktree
CEEIINST	niceties	**CEEINNST**	nescient	**CEEKOSSY**	sockeyes
CEEIINSW	icewines	**CEEINOPU**	eupnoeic	**CEEKRRSW**	wreckers
CEEIINVV	evincive	**CEEINORT**	erection	**CEELLLSU**	cellules
CEEIJLLO	Jellicoe		neoteric	**CEELLMOU**	molecule
CEEIJNOT	ejection	**CEEINORV**	overnice	**CEELLNOS**	colleens
CEEIJORR	rejoicer	**CEEINORX**	exocrine	**CEELLNOU**	nucleole
CEEIJORS	rejoices	**CEEINOSS**	senecios	**CEELLPRU**	cupeller
CEEIJRUV	verjuice	**CEEINOST**	seicento	**CEELLRRU**	crueller
CEEIKLNN	neckline	**CEEINOTV**	evection	**CEELLRVY**	cleverly
CEEIKLPR	pickerel	**CEEINPRT**	prentice	**CEELLSSU**	clueless
CEEIKNRS	sickener		terpenic	**CEELLSTY**	selectly
CEEIKNST	neckties	**CEEINPST**	pectines	**CEELMNTV**	Clement V
CEEIKPRT	picketer	**CEEINPSX**	sixpence	**CEELMOPT**	complete
CEEILLLP	pellicle	**CEEINQRU**	quercine	**CEELMORW**	welcomer
CEEILLMS	micelles	**CEEINRST**	enticers	**CEELMOST**	telecoms
CEEILLNT	lenticel		scienter	**CEELMOSW**	welcomes
	lenticle		secretin	**CEELMRTU**	electrum
CEEILLRV	Vercelli	**CEEINRSU**	insecure	**CEELNOPU**	opulence
CEEILMNT	Clement I		sinecure	**CEELNORS**	encloser
CEEILMOR	comelier	**CEEINRTT**	reticent	**CEELNORT**	electron
CEEILMPS	semplice	**CEEINRTU**	enuretic	**CEELNOSS**	encloses
CEEILNNY	leniency	**CEEINSTY**	cysteine	**CEELNPTU**	centuple
CEEILNOT	election	**CEEIOPPR**	pericope	**CEELNRST**	lecterns
CEEILNOV	violence	**CEEIOPPS**	episcope	**CEELNRTU**	relucent
CEEILNPR	penciler	**CEEIOPRS**	recopies	**CEELNRTY**	recently
CEEILNRR	recliner	**CEEIOPST**	picotees	**CEELNSTU**	esculent
CEEILNRS	licenser	**CEEIORST**	coteries	**CEELORSS**	coreless
	reclines		esoteric	**CEELORST**	corselet
	silencer	**CEEIORSV**	revoices		electors
CEEILNSS	licenses	**CEEIORSX**	exorcise		electros
	silences	**CEEIORTT**	erotetic		selector
CEEILNST	centiles	**CEEIORTX**	exoteric	**CEELORTV**	coverlet
CEEILORR	recoiler	**CEEIORXZ**	exorcize	**CEELOSSU**	coleuses
CEEILPRS	eclipser	**CEEIPPTU**	eupeptic	**CEELOSTU**	elocutes
	Pericles	**CEEIPRRS**	piercers	**CEELPPRU**	Culpeper
CEEILPRY	creepily		reprices	**CEELPRST**	prelects
CEEILPSS	eclipses	**CEEIPRSS**	precises	**CEELRRTU**	lecturer
CEEILQSU	liquesce	**CEEIPRST**	receipts	**CEELRSSU**	cureless
CEEILRST	reticles	**CEEIPRSU**	epicures		recluses
	sclerite	**CEEIPSST**	pectises	**CEELRSTU**	cruelest
	tiercels	**CEEIPSTZ**	pectizes		lectures
CEEILRSV	versicle	**CEEIRRST**	reciters	**CEELRSTY**	secretly
CEEILRTU	reticule	**CEEIRRSW**	screwier	**CEELRSUY**	securely
CEEILRTY	celerity	**CEEIRRTU**	ureteric	**CEELSTTU**	lettuces
CEEILSSV	clevises	**CEEIRSSV**	services	**CEEMMNTU**	cementum
	vesicles	**CEEIRSTU**	cerusite	**CEEMMORS**	commeres
	viceless		cutesier	**CEEMNNOW**	Newcomen
CEEILSTT	testicle	**CEEIRSTV**	vertices	**CEEMNORW**	newcomer
CEEIMMPY	empyemic	**CEEIRSTX**	exciters	**CEEMNORY**	ceremony
CEEIMMRS	mesmeric	**CEEIRSVX**	cervixes	**CEEMNOYZ**	coenzyme
CEEIMNNY	eminency	**CEEJORRT**	rejector	**CEEMOORV**	comeover
CEEIMNPS	specimen	**CEEJORST**	ejectors		overcome

CEEMOOTY	oomycete	CEERSTTU	curettes
CEEMOPRS	compeers	CEESSSTU	cestuses
	comperes	CEESTTUV	cuvettes
CEEMOPST	competes	CEFFHIRU	chuffier
CEEENORT	cretonne	CEFFILWY	Wycliffe
CEENNORU	renounce	CEFFIORS	officers
CEENNORV	convener	CEFFIORU	coiffeur
CEENNOSU	enounces		coiffure
CEENNOSV	convenes	CEFFIRSU	sufficer
CEENNRST	centners	CEFFISSU	suffices
CEENOOST	ecotones	CEFFLORU	forceful
CEENOPRV	Provence	CEFFLSSU	scuffles
CEENOPST	potences	CEFFORSS	scoffers
CEENOPTW	twopence	CEFGHINT	fechting
CEENORSS	necroses		fetching
CEENORSV	conserve	CEFGIKLN	flecking
	converse	CEFGILNT	clefting
CEENORSZ	cozeners	CEFHIIMS	mischief
CEENORTT	trecento	CEFHILNR	flincher
CEENORVY	conveyer	CEFHILNS	flinches
	reconvey	CEFHILNY	Finchley
CEENOSVX	convexes	CEFHILRS	filchers
CEENPPTU	tuppence	CEFHILST	flitches
CEENPRSS	spencers	CEFHINSU	fuchsine
CEENRRSU	censurer	CEFHISTT	fitchets
CEENRSST	Cressent	CEFHISTW	fitchews
CEENRSSU	censures	CEFHKOOR	forehock
CEENSSSU	censuses	CEFHLSTU	chestful
CEENSSTU	cuteness	CEFIIIST	citifies
CEEOORST	creosote	CEFIILLM	mellific
CEEOPRRT	receptor	CEFIILNO	olefinic
CEEOPRTY	cerotype	CEFIILST	felsitic
CEEOPSTY	ecotypes	CEFIILTY	felicity
CEEOQTTU	coquette	CEFIIORS	orifices
CEEORRRS	sorcerer	CEFIIRRT	terrific
CEEORRST	erectors	CEFIISTY	cityfies
	secretor	CEFIKLOR	firelock
CEEORRSU	recourse	CEFIKLRS	flickers
	resource	CEFIKLRY	flickery
CEEORRSV	coverers	CEFILLLO	follicle
	recovers	CEFILMRU	merciful
CEEORRVY	recovery	CEFILNOT	flection
CEEORSSS	Scorsese	CEFILNST	inflects
CEEORSTV	coveters	CEFILNSU	funicles
CEEORTTV	corvette	CEFILOUV	voiceful
CEEORTUX	executor	CEFILRSU	lucifers
CEEOSTTT	octettes	CEFIMOST	comfiest
CEEPPRST	percepts	CEFINNOR	confiner
	precepts	CEFINNOS	confines
CEEPPRSU	prepuces	CEFINORS	conifers
CEEPRSST	respects		forensic
	scepters		fornices
	sceptres	CEFINORT	infector
	specters	CEFINOTT	confetti
	spectres	CEFIOPRS	forcipes
CEEPRSTX	excerpts	CEFIORTY	ferocity
CEERRSSU	rescuers	CEFKLLOS	elflocks
	securers	CEFKLOOR	forelock
CEERRSSW	screwers	CEFKLOST	fetlocks
CEERRSUV	recurves	CEFKLPSY	flyspeck
CEERSSST	cressets	CEFKLRUW	wreckful
CEERSSTW	setscrew	CEFLNOSU	flounces

CEFLNRUU	furuncle
CEFLNUWY	Cynewulf
CEFMORSY	comfreys
CEFNORTU	confuter
CEFNOSSU	confuses
CEFNOSTU	confutes
CEFOQTUU	Foucquet
CEFORRST	crofters
CEFORSSU	focusers
CEFORSTU	fructose
CEGGHIRS	chiggers
CEGGILOO	geologic
CEGGIORS	croggies
	georgics
CEGGLNOY	glycogen
CEGGMORR	McGregor
CEGHIINY	hygienic
CEGHIKLN	heckling
CEGHILLW	Chigwell
CEGHILNP	chelping
CEGHILNT	letching
CEGHILNW	welching
CEGHILST	glitches
CEGHIMNS	scheming
CEGHINNW	wenching
CEGHINOR	cohering
	ochering
CEGHINPR	perching
CEGHINRT	retching
CEGHINRU	euchring
CEGHINST	etchings
CEGHINVY	chevying
CEGHIRSS	screighs
CEGHIRTU	theurgic
CEGHISTU	guichets
CEGHMRUY	chemurgy
CEGHNORS	groschen
CEGHORSU	coughers
	grouches
CEGIILMO	oligemic
CEGIILNS	ceilings
CEGIINNT	enticing
CEGIINNV	evincing
CEGIINOS	isogenic
CEGIINPR	piercing
CEGIINRT	reciting
CEGIINSS	gneissic
CEGIINSX	excising
CEGIINTV	evicting
CEGIINTX	exciting
CEGIIOST	egoistic
CEGIKNNS	snecking
CEGIKNPS	specking
CEGIKNRW	wrecking
CEGILMMN	clemming
CEGILMPS	gemclips
CEGILNPU	cupeling
CEGILNRS	clingers
	cringles
CEGILNRY	glycerin
CEGILNSU	Guesclin
CEGILNTU	cultigen

CEGILRSY	lysergic
CEGIMNOS	genomics
CEGIMNOY	myogenic
CEGIMNUY	gynecium
CEGINNOR	encoring
CEGINNOZ	cozening
CEGINNRT	centring
CEGINNST	scenting
CEGINNSY	ensigncy
CEGINOOP	geoponic
CEGINOOR	orogenic
CEGINOOV	cooeying
CEGINOPY	pyogenic
CEGINORT	gerontic
CEGINORV	covering
CEGINORW	cowering
CEGINOSS	cognises
CEGINOSZ	cognizes
CEGINOTV	coveting
CEGINOXY	oxygenic
CEGINRRS	cringers
CEGINRST	cresting
CEGINRSU	rescuing
	scungier
	securing
CEGINRSW	screwing
CEGINRSY	synergic
CEGINRTU	eructing
CEGINSUX	excusing
CEGKLORS	grockles
CEGLLOOU	collogue
CEGLLORY	glycerol
CEGLLRYY	glyceryl
CEGLNOOS	colognes
CEGLNOTY	cogently
CEGLOOOY	oecology
CEGLOOTY	cetology
CEGLOSSY	glycoses
CEGMNNOO	cognomen
CEGNNPUY	pungency
CEGNOOTY	gonocyte
CEGNORSS	congress
CEGNORSU	scrounge
CEGNOSST	congests
CEGNOTYY	cytogeny
CEGOORSS	scrooges
CEGORRSU	scourger
CEGORSSU	scourges
	scrouges
CEHHIRST	hitchers
CEHHISTU	hutchies
CEHHNSTU	Cheshunt
CEHHOOSS	cohoshes
CEHHOPTY	hypothec
CEHHOSST	shochets
CEHIIKNS	chinkies
CEHIIKST	thickies
CEHIILLR	chillier
CEHIILLS	chillies
CEHIILMN	Michelin
CEHIILMO	hemiolic
CEHIILNN	lichenin

CEHIILNT	lecithin
CEHIILOT	eolithic
CEHIILTY	helicity
CEHIIMOS	isocheim
	isochime
CEHIIMPT	mephitic
CEHIIMRT	hermitic
CEHIINNR	Nichiren
CEHIINST	ichnites
CEHIIPPR	chippier
CEHIIPPS	chippies
CEHIIPRR	chirpier
CEHIIPRT	pitchier
CEHIIRST	christie
CEHIIRTT	titchier
	trichite
CEHIISTT	chitties
	ethicist
	itchiest
	theistic
	tichiest
CEHIISVV	chivvies
CEHIKLNY	Hinckley
CEHIKLPT	klephtic
CEHIKLRS	clerkish
CEHIKLSU	suchlike
CEHIKMNT	Chimkent
CEHIKMOS	homesick
CEHIKNRR	Kirchner
CEHIKNRU	chunkier
CEHIKNST	chetniks
	kitchens
	thickens
CEHIKOOS	chookies
CEHIKOST	chokiest
	thickoes
CEHIKOWW	Kweichow
CEHIKRSW	whickers
CEHIKSST	skitches
CEHIKSTT	thickest
	thickets
	thickset
CEHILLMT	Mitchell
CEHILLPR	prechill
CEHILLRS	chillers
	schiller
CEHILMOR	Melchior
CEHILMOU	humicole
CEHILMTY	methylic
CEHILNOP	phenolic
	pinochle
CEHILNOR	chlorine
CEHILNOS	helicons
CEHILNRU	Reuchlin
CEHILNSS	chinless
CEHILOOS	schoolie
CEHILORS	ceorlish
CEHILORT	chlorite
	clothier
CEHILOSU	Choiseul
CEHILPTY	phyletic
CEHILRSV	chervils

CEHILTTY	tetchily
CEHIMMRU	chummier
CEHIMMSS	chemisms
CEHIMNOP	phonemic
CEHIMNPT	pitchmen
CEHIMNSU	munchies
CEHIMNSY	chimneys
CEHIMNTZ	Chemnitz
CEHIMORT	chromite
	trichome
CEHIMRRS	smircher
CEHIMRSS	smirches
CEHIMSST	chemists
CEHINNRT	intrench
CEHINOOS	cohesion
CEHINOPS	chopines
CEHINOPT	phonetic
	Pinochet
CEHINOPU	euphonic
CEHINORU	unheroic
CEHINOSY	hyoscine
CEHINPRU	punchier
CEHINRSS	richness
CEHINRST	christen
	citherns
	snitcher
CEHINRSW	Schwerin
	winchers
CEHINRTU	ruthenic
CEHINSST	snitches
CEHIOORS	choosier
	isochore
CEHIOPPR	choppier
CEHIOPRU	euphoric
CEHIOPSS	hospices
CEHIOPST	postiche
	potiches
CEHIOPTU	euphotic
CEHIORRS	chorries
CEHIORRT	rhetoric
	torchier
CEHIORRV	overrich
CEHIORSS	orchises
CEHIORTU	touchier
CEHIOSTV	cheviots
CEHIPPRS	chippers
CEHIPRRS	chirpers
CEHIPRSS	spherics
CEHIPRST	pitchers
CEHIRSTT	chitters
	stitcher
CEHIRSTW	switcher
CEHIRSTY	hysteric
CEHIRTTW	twitcher
CEHIRTWY	witchery
CEHISSTT	stitches
CEHISSTU	cushiest
CEHISSTW	switches
CEHISTTW	twitches
CEHKKRSU	chukkers
CEHKLMOS	hemlocks
CEHKLOOS	klooches

CEHKLOSY	Shockley	**CEIIKLMR**	limerick	**CEIINSTZ**	citizens
CEHKNPUY	keypunch	**CEIIKLRS**	sicklier		zincites
CEHKORSS	shockers	**CEIIKMMR**	mimicker	**CEIINTUZ**	cutinize
CEHKPSTU	ketchups	**CEIIKNSS**	ickiness	**CEIIOPRT**	periotic
CEHKRSSU	shuckers		kinesics	**CEIIOPSW**	wicopies
CEHKRSTU	huckster	**CEIIKNST**	kinetics	**CEIIOSTT**	osteitic
CEHLLORS	chollers	**CEIIKPST**	pickiest	**CEIIPRRS**	crispier
CEHLLPSU	chellups	**CEIIKQSU**	quickies	**CEIIPRST**	priciest
CEHLMOPU	Chemulpo	**CEIIKRRT**	trickier	**CEIIPSST**	spiciest
CEHLNNOU	luncheon	**CEIIKRST**	stickier	**CEIIQRTU**	critique
CEHLNOST	cholents	**CEIIKSST**	ekistics	**CEIIRSST**	eristics
CEHLNOTU	unclothe		stickies	**CEIIRSTV**	veristic
CEHLNRSU	lunchers	**CEIILLNO**	linoleic	**CEIIRSUZ**	cruizies
CEHLNRSY	lynchers	**CEIILLPT**	elliptic	**CEIISTVV**	vivisect
CEHLNSTY	lynchets	**CEIILLSS**	silicles	**CEIJNORT**	injector
CEHLORRT	chortler	**CEIILLSU**	silicule	**CEIJNOUV**	cunjevoi
CEHLORST	chortles	**CEIILMNS**	lemnisci	**CEIJSSTU**	justices
CEHLORSU	sloucher	**CEIILMNT**	limnetic	**CEIKKLOR**	corklike
CEHLOSSU	slouches	**CEIILMNY**	myelinic	**CEIKKNRS**	knickers
CEHLQSUY	squelchy	**CEIILNNR**	incliner	**CEIKKRRS**	skerrick
CEHLRRSU	lurchers	**CEIILNNS**	inclines	**CEIKLMNY**	McKinley
CEHLSTUY	lecythus	**CEIILNOP**	picoline	**CEIKLMSU**	scumlike
CEHMNRSU	munchers	**CEIILNOS**	isocline	**CEIKLNRS**	clinkers
CEHMNSSU	muchness		silicone		crinkles
CEHMOORS	moochers	**CEIILOPS**	policies	**CEIKLNRU**	clunkier
CEHMOOSS	smooches	**CEIILORT**	elicitor	**CEIKLNSZ**	Selznick
CEHMOOSZ	schmooze	**CEIILOTZ**	zeolitic	**CEIKLOSV**	lovesick
CEHMORUV	overmuch	**CEIILPPS**	clippies	**CEIKLPRS**	picklers
CEHMSSTU	smutches	**CEIILPRT**	perlitic		prickles
CEHNNOPU	puncheon	**CEIILPSS**	eclipsis	**CEIKLPRU**	pluckier
CEHNNOSU	nonesuch	**CEIILPTX**	explicit	**CEIKLRSS**	slickers
	unchosen	**CEIILPTY**	pyelitic	**CEIKLRST**	stickler
CEHNOOPS	hencoops	**CEIILRTV**	verticil		strickle
CEHNOORS	schooner	**CEIILSSS**	scissile		ticklers
CEHNORSV	chevrons	**CEIIMOPT**	epitomic		trickles
CEHNPRSU	punchers	**CEIIMORS**	isomeric	**CEIKLSST**	slickest
CEHNRRSU	churners	**CEIIMOST**	comities		stickles
CEHNRSTU	chunters		semiotic	**CEIKLSTU**	luckiest
CEHNSTTU	chestnut	**CEIIMOSW**	Oświęcim	**CEIKMNOR**	monicker
CEHNSTUY	chutneys	**CEIIMPRS**	empirics	**CEIKMSTU**	muckiest
CEHOOORZ	zoochore	**CEIIMRRT**	trimeric	**CEIKNNOT**	nektonic
CEHOORSS	choosers	**CEIIMRST**	meristic	**CEIKNNPY**	Pinckney
CEHOORST	cheroots	**CEIIMRTT**	termitic	**CEIKNOTY**	cytokine
CEHOORSU	ocherous	**CEIINNOP**	nepionic	**CEIKNQSU**	quickens
	ochreous	**CEIINNOR**	irenicon	**CEIKNRSS**	snickers
CEHOOSSS	scooshes	**CEIINNOT**	nicotine	**CEIKNRST**	stricken
CEHOPPRS	choppers	**CEIINNRS**	cinerins	**CEIKNSSS**	sickness
CEHOPPRY	prophecy	**CEIINORS**	recision	**CEIKNSST**	snickets
CEHOPSTW	Chepstow		soricine	**CEIKORST**	rockiest
CEHORSSU	choruses	**CEIINOSV**	invoices		stockier
CEHORSSZ	scherzos	**CEIINOSX**	excision	**CEIKOSTT**	tockiest
CEHORSTU	touchers	**CEIINOTV**	eviction	**CEIKPRRS**	prickers
CEHORSUV	vouchers	**CEIINPPR**	principe	**CEIKPRST**	prickets
CEHPSSTU	putsches		Príncipe	**CEIKPSST**	skeptics
CEHRRSSU	crushers	**CEIINRST**	citrines	**CEIKQSTU**	quickest
CEHRSTTY	stretchy		crinites		quickset
CEHSSSSU	schusses		inciters	**CEIKRRST**	trickers
CEIIILSV	civilise	**CEIINRSU**	incisure	**CEIKRRTY**	trickery
CEIIILVZ	civilize		sciurine	**CEIKRSST**	stickers
CEIIINSV	incisive	**CEIINRTU**	neuritic	**CEIKRSTU**	truckies
CEIIJSTU	jesuitic	**CEIINSTU**	cutinise	**CEIKSTUY**	yuckiest
	juiciest	**CEIINSTY**	syenitic	**CEILLNOU**	nucleoli

CEILLOPS	pollices	CEIMMNOS	Commines	CEINRRSU	reincurs
CEILLOQU	coquille	CEIMMNOU	encomium	CEINRSST	cisterns
CEILLORS	colliers		meconium	CEINRSTT	centrist
CEILLORY	colliery	CEIMMORT	recommit		citterns
CEILLRTU	telluric	CEIMMOSX	commixes	CEINRSUV	incurves
CEILLSST	cellists	CEIMMRRU	crummier	CEINRTTU	intercut
CEILLSSU	cullises	CEIMMRSU	crummies		tincture
CEILMMUY	mycelium	CEIMNNOY	neomycin	CEIOOTXX	exotoxic
CEILMNOP	compline	CEIMNOOT	emoticon	CEIOPRRU	croupier
CEILMOPR	compiler	CEIMNOPT	pentomic	CEIOPRSU	precious
	complier	CEIMNOPY	eponymic	CEIOPSSU	specious
CEILMOPS	compiles	CEIMNORS	incomers	CEIORRSS	crosiers
	complies		sermonic	CEIORRSU	couriers
	polemics	CEIMNORT	intercom	CEIORRSZ	croziers
CEILMOSS	solecism	CEIMNOST	centimos	CEIORRTU	courtier
CEILMOSU	coliseum	CEIMNOSU	Comenius	CEIORRUZ	cruzeiro
CEILMPRS	crimples	CEIMNRST	centrism	CEIORSTT	cottiers
CEILMPUU	peculium	CEIMNSSU	meniscus	CEIORSTU	citreous
CEILMRSU	clumsier	CEIMOPRS	comprise		outcries
CEILMTUU	lutecium	CEIMORRU	Mercouri	CEIORSTV	evictors
CEILNNSU	nucleins	CEIMORST	mortices		vortices
CEILNNSY	syncline	CEIMORSX	exorcism	CEIORSTX	excitors
CEILNOOS	colonies	CEIMOSTV	vicomtes		exorcist
	colonise	CEIMPRRS	crimpers	CEIORSVY	viceroys
	eclosion	CEIMRRTU	turmeric	CEIORTTU	toreutic
CEILNOOZ	colonize	CEIMSSTY	systemic	CEIOSSTT	scotties
CEILNOPR	replicon	CEINNNOT	innocent	CEIOSSTX	coexists
CEILNOPT	leptonic	CEINNNRU	neuronic	CEIPQSTU	picquets
CEILNORS	incloser	CEINNORV	conniver	CEIPRRSS	crispers
	licensor	CEINNOSV	connives	CEIPRRST	rescript
CEILNOSS	incloses	CEINNOTU	continue		scripter
CEILNOST	lections	CEINOOPR	pecorino	CEIPRSST	crispest
	telsonic	CEINOOST	coonties	CEIPRSTU	crepitus
CEILNOSX	lexicons	CEINOOTZ	entozoic		pictures
CEILNPRY	princely		enzootic		piecrust
CEILNRUV	culverin	CEINOPPT	peptonic	CEIPRSUU	Epicurus
CEILNSST	stencils	CEINOPRS	conspire	CEIPSSST	cesspits
CEILNSTU	tunicles	CEINOPRT	inceptor	CEIRRRSU	curriers
CEILOORZ	colorize		pretonic	CEIRRRUY	curriery
CEILOPRT	petrolic	CEINOPRU	Couperin	CEIRRSSU	cruisers
CEILOPTU	poultice	CEINOPRV	province		scurries
CEILOPTY	epicotyl	CEINOPTT	entoptic	CEIRRSTT	critters
CEILORST	cloister	CEINOPTU	unpoetic		restrict
	costlier	CEINORRT	tricorne		stricter
CEILORTY	cryolite	CEINORSS	necrosis	CEIRRSTU	crustier
CEILOSSS	ossicles	CEINORST	corniest		recruits
CEILOSST	solecist	CEINORSU	coinsure	CEIRRSUV	scurvier
	solstice	CEINORTT	contrite	CEIRSSSU	scissure
CEILOSSU	coulisse	CEINORTU	neurotic	CEIRSSTT	trisects
CEILOSSV	clovises	CEINORTV	contrive	CEIRSSTU	citruses
CEILOSTT	coletits	CEINOSSS	cessions		crusties
CEILOTVY	velocity		cosiness		curtsies
CEILPPRR	crippler	CEINOSST	sections		rictuses
CEILPPRS	clippers	CEINOSSZ	coziness	CEIRSSUV	cursives
	cripples	CEINOSTT	stenotic	CEIRSTUV	curviest
CEILPRSS	splicers	CEINOSTU	counties	CEIRSTUY	security
CEILPRSU	surplice	CEINOSTX	excitons	CEIRSUZZ	scuzzier
CEILPSSU	spicules	CEINOSTY	cytosine	CEISSSSU	cissuses
CEILRSTU	curliest	CEINOSUV	unvoices	CEISSSTU	cistuses
	utricles	CEINPRSS	princess	CEJLOOSY	jocosely
CEILSTTU	cultiest	CEINPRST	spectrin	CEJNORRU	conjurer
CEIMMNNO	mnemonic	CEINPSST	inspects	CEJNORSU	conjures

CEJNRTUU	juncture	
CEJOPRST	projects	
CEKKLNSU	knuckles	
CEKKNORS	knockers	
CEKKNTUY	Kentucky	
CEKLLNOR	rollneck	
CEKLLOOV	lovelock	
CEKLLORW	Rockwell	
CEKLLSSU	luckless	
CEKLOPST	lockstep	
CEKLPRSU	pluckers	
CEKLRRTU	truckler	
CEKLRSSU	sucklers	
CEKLRSTU	truckles	
CEKLSSSU	suckless	
CEKMNOST	stockmen	
CEKMNOSY	mockneys	
CEKNOORV	convoker	
CEKNOOSV	convokes	
CEKNOPST	penstock	
CEKNRSWY	wrynecks	
CEKOOORV	overcook	
CEKOOPRS	precooks	
CEKOOPSW	cowpokes	
CEKOORRS	rockrose	
CEKOORRW	coworker	
CEKOPRST	sprocket	
CEKORRTY	rocketry	
CEKORSST	restocks	
	stockers	
CEKORSTW	twockers	
CEKRRSTU	truckers	
CEKRSSUU	ruckuses	
CELLLOVY	Clovelly	
CELLMORW	Cromwell	
CELLNNOO	O'Connell	
CELLNOOS	colonels	
CELLNORW	Cornwell	
CELLNSUU	nucellus	
CELLNTUU	luculent	
CELLNTUY	lucently	
CELLOOST	Costello	
CELLRRSU	crullers	
CELLRSSU	scullers	
CELLRSUY	scullery	
CELMNOOS	monocles	
CELMOSYY	cymosely	
CELMPRSU	crumples	
	scrumple	
CELMPRTU	plectrum	
CELMPSUU	speculum	
CELMSTUU	cumulets	
CELNNOSU	nucleons	
CELNOORS	consoler	
CELNOOSS	consoles	
	coolness	
CELNOOVV	convolve	
CELNOPRT	plectron	
CELNOPUU	uncouple	
CELNOPUY	opulency	
CELNORWY	clownery	
CELNOSSU	clonuses	

	counsels	
	uncloses	
CELNOSTU	noctules	
CELNOSUV	convulse	
CELNOSVY	solvency	
CELNOVXY	convexly	
CELOOORV	overcool	
CELOOPSS	cesspool	
CELOORRS	colorers	
CELOORTW	colewort	
CELOOSTU	closeout	
CELOPRSU	couplers	
CELOPSTU	couplets	
	octuples	
CELOPSUU	opuscule	
CELORSST	corslets	
	costrels	
	crosslet	
CELORSSU	closures	
	sclerous	
CELORSSW	scowlers	
CELORSTT	crottles	
CELORSTU	clotures	
	clouters	
	coulters	
CELORSUU	ulcerous	
CELORTVY	covertly	
CELOSSST	costless	
CELOSTTU	culottes	
CELPRSSU	scruples	
CELPRSUY	sprucely	
CELRSSTU	clusters	
CELRSSTY	clysters	
CELRSTTU	clutters	
CELRSTUU	cultures	
CELRSTUV	culverts	
CELRSTUY	clustery	
CELSSTTU	scuttles	
CELSSTUU	cultuses	
CEMMNOOR	commoner	
CEMMNOOS	consomme	
CEMMNOST	comments	
CEMMNOSU	communes	
CEMMOOSV	commoves	
CEMMORTU	commuter	
CEMMOSTU	commutes	
CEMMRSSU	scummers	
CEMNNOST	contemns	
CEMNOOTY	monocyte	
CEMNOPRS	corpsmen	
CEMNOPTT	contempt	
CEMNORSU	consumer	
	mucrones	
CEMNOSSU	consumes	
CEMNRSTU	centrums	
CEMOOPRS	composer	
CEMOOPSS	composes	
CEMOOPST	compotes	
CEMOORSY	sycomore	
CEMOOSSS	cosmoses	
CEMOOSTU	outcomes	
CEMOPRSS	compress	

CEMOPRTU	computer	
CEMOPSTU	computes	
CEMORSTU	costumer	
	customer	
CEMOSSTU	costumes	
CEMPRSTU	crumpets	
	spectrum	
CENNOOPR	cornpone	
CENNOORV	convenor	
CENNOOST	connotes	
CENNORTU	nocturne	
CENNOSST	consents	
CENNOSTT	contents	
CENNOSTV	convents	
CENNRSSU	scunners	
CENOORRS	coroners	
	crooners	
CENOORST	coronets	
CENOORSU	corneous	
CENOORVY	conveyor	
CENOPRSU	pouncers	
CENOPRSY	necropsy	
CENOPSSY	syncopes	
CENOQRSU	conquers	
CENOQSTU	conquest	
CENORRSS	scorners	
CENORRSW	crowners	
	recrowns	
CENORSTT	cornetts	
CENORSTU	construe	
	counters	
	recounts	
	trounces	
CENORSTV	converts	
CENORSUU	cernuous	
	coenurus	
CENORSUV	uncovers	
CENORSUY	cynosure	
CENORTVY	Coventry	
CENOSSTT	contests	
CENOSSTU	contuses	
	countess	
CENOSTTX	contexts	
CENPRSTY	encrypts	
CENPRTUU	puncture	
CENRRSTU	currents	
CENRSSTU	curtness	
	encrusts	
CENRSSUW	unscrews	
CEOOOPST	otoscope	
CEOOPRRV	overcrop	
CEOOPRSS	scoopers	
CEOORSST	scooters	
CEOOSTUV	covetous	
CEOPPRRS	croppers	
CEOPPRST	prospect	
CEOPRRRU	procurer	
CEOPRRSS	scorpers	
CEOPRRSU	procures	
CEOPRSTT	Prescott	
	protects	
CEOPRSTW	crowstep	

	screwtop
CEOPRSUU	cupreous
CEOPRSUV	coverups
CEOQRSTU	croquets
CEOQRTUY	coquetry
CEORRSSS	crossers
CEORRSSU	coursers
	scourers
CEORRSTY	corsetry
CEORSSSU	scousers
CEORSSTU	crustose
	scouters
CEORSTUV	couverts
CEORSTUY	courtesy
CEOSSTTU	cottuses
CEPPRRSU	cruppers
CEPPRSSU	scuppers
CEPPRTUU	uppercut
CEPRSSTU	sprucest
CEPRSTUU	cutpurse
CEPSSSTU	suspects
CERSSTTU	scutters
CERSSTUY	curtseys
CERSSUUX	excursus
CFFGHINU	chuffing
CFFGIINO	coiffing
CFFGINOS	scoffing
CFFGINSU	scuffing
CFFHINOY	chiffony
CFFIKKOS	kickoffs
CFFIRTUY	fructify
CFFKKNOO	knockoff
CFGHIILN	filching
CFGHINOO	choofing
CFGIIKLN	flicking
CFGIIKNR	fricking
CFGIKLNO	flocking
CFGIKNOR	frocking
CFGINORT	crofting
CFGINOSU	focusing
CFHIINOO	finochio
CFHIIORR	horrific
CFHIKORS	rockfish
CFHIKSSU	suckfish
CFHORSTU	futhorcs
CFIIILSY	silicify
CFIILMNU	fulminic
CFIILNST	inflicts
CFIILNUU	funiculi
CFIILOPR	prolific
CFIIMNOS	somnific
CFIINORT	friction
CFIINOST	fictions
CFIKLORY	frolicky
CFIKLSTU	stickful
CFIKNNOS	finnocks
CFIKOSSS	fossicks
CFIKSTUW	fuckwits
CFILMOOR	coliform
CFILRSUU	sulfuric
CFIMNORS	confirms
CFIMNORU	unciform

CFINNOTU	function
CFKNORSU	unfrocks
CFKOSTTU	futtocks
CFLLOORU	colorful
CFLMRSUU	fulcrums
CFLMRUUU	furculum
CFLNORSU	scornful
CFLOOPSU	scoopful
CFMNOORS	conforms
CFMOORST	comforts
CFNNOORT	confront
CFOOORTW	crowfoot
CFRSTUUU	usufruct
CGGGHINU	chugging
CGGGILNO	clogging
	coggling
CGGGINOR	crogging
CGGHINOU	coughing
CGGIILNN	clinging
CGGIINNR	cringing
CGGINNSU	scunging
CGGINORS	scroggin
CGHHIINT	hitching
CGHHINNU	hunching
CGHHINTU	hutching
CGHIIKNN	chinking
CGHIIKNO	hoicking
CGHIILLN	chilling
CGHIIMNR	chirming
CGHIIMNT	mitching
CGHIINNN	chinning
CGHIINNP	pinching
CGHIINNW	winching
CGHIINPP	chipping
CGHIINPR	chirping
CGHIINPT	pitching
CGHIINRR	chirring
CGHIINST	sichting
CGHIINTW	witching
CGHIINVV	chivving
CGHIINVY	chivying
CGHIJNNO	Chŏngjin
CGHIJNNU	Chungjin
CGHIKLNO	hockling
CGHIKNNU	chunking
CGHIKNOO	chooking
CGHIKNOS	shocking
CGHIKNSU	shucking
CGHILMNU	mulching
CGHILNNU	lunching
CGHILNNY	lynching
CGHILNOT	clothing
CGHILNRU	lurching
CGHIMMNU	chumming
CGHIMNNU	munching
CGHIMNOO	mooching
CGHIMNOP	chomping
CGHIMNOR	chroming
CGHIMNPU	chumping
CGHIMNTU	mutching
CGHIMPSY	sphygmic
CGHINNOS	chignons

CGHINNOT	notching
CGHINNPU	punching
CGHINNRU	churning
CGHINNSY	synching
CGHINOOS	choosing
CGHINOPP	chopping
CGHINOPU	pouching
CGHINOSU	hocusing
CGHINOTU	touching
CGHINOUV	vouching
CGHINPSY	psyching
CGHINRRU	churring
CGHINRSU	crushing
	ruchings
CGHINSTY	scything
CGHLNOSS	schlongs
CGHNOOSU	souchong
CGIIILNT	lignitic
CGIIINNS	incising
CGIIINNT	inciting
CGIIKLNN	clinking
CGIIKLNP	pickling
CGIIKLNS	lickings
	slicking
CGIIKLNT	tickling
CGIIKMMS	gimmicks
CGIIKMMY	gimmicky
CGIIKNNS	snicking
CGIIKNPR	pricking
CGIIKNPS	pickings
CGIIKNRT	tricking
CGIIKNRW	wricking
CGIIKNST	sticking
CGIIKNSW	wickings
CGIIKPST	pigstick
CGIILMOS	logicism
CGIILNOP	policing
CGIILNPP	clipping
CGIILNPS	splicing
CGIILNSU	sluicing
CGIILOST	logistic
CGIILRTU	liturgic
CGIIMNNO	incoming
CGIIMNPR	crimping
CGIIMNPU	pumicing
CGIIMNSU	miscuing
CGIINNOT	noticing
CGIINNSU	incusing
CGIINNTT	tincting
CGIINOOS	isogonic
CGIINPRS	crisping
CGIINRSU	cruising
CGIJNNOU	jouncing
CGIKKNNO	knocking
CGIKLNNO	clonking
CGIKLNNU	clunking
CGIKLNOR	rockling
CGIKLNPU	plucking
CGIKLNRU	ruckling
CGIKLNSU	suckling
CGIKMNOS	smocking
CGIKNOOR	crooking

CGIKNORW	corkwing	**CGLOOOTY**	tocology	**CHINOPTY**	hypnotic
CGIKNOST	stocking	**CGLOOTYY**	cytology		pythonic
CGIKNOTW	twocking	**CGLRSUUY**	Lycurgus		typhonic
CGIKNPSU	kingcups	**CGNOORTU**	Goncourt	**CHINORTU**	cothurni
CGIKNRTU	trucking	**CHHHHOTU**	Hochhuth	**CHINOSSU**	cushions
CGIKPSTU	pigstuck	**CHHIIKST**	thickish	**CHINOSTZ**	schizont
CGILLNOY	collying	**CHHIIPST**	phthisic	**CHINOSUY**	cushiony
CGILLNSU	sculling	**CHHILRSU**	churlish	**CHIOOPPT**	photopic
CGILMNPU	clumping	**CHHIMRTY**	rhythmic	**CHIOOPTY**	oophytic
CGILMNSU	muscling	**CHHNORSU**	rhonchus	**CHIOORSS**	isochors
CGILMNTU	mulcting	**CHHOOPTT**	hotchpot	**CHIOORSU**	ichorous
CGILMNUU	cingulum	**CHIIINRT**	rhinitic	**CHIOORSZ**	chorizos
	glucinum	**CHIIKLST**	ticklish	**CHIOPRST**	strophic
CGILMOOY	myologic	**CHIILNNP**	linchpin	**CHIOSSTT**	Scottish
CGILNNOW	clowning	**CHIILNST**	chitlins	**CHIPRRSU**	chirrups
CGILNOOR	coloring	**CHIILOPT**	hoplitic	**CHIPRRSY**	pyrrhics
	crooling	**CHIILORT**	trochili	**CHIPRRUY**	chirrupy
CGILNOOY	cooingly	**CHIILOST**	holistic	**CHIPRTTY**	triptych
CGILNOPP	clopping		Stilicho	**CHIRRSSU**	scirrhus
CGILNOPU	coupling	**CHIILPRY**	chirpily	**CHISSTTU**	chutists
CGILNOSW	cowlings	**CHIILPTZ**	Lipchitz	**CHKLOSSY**	shylocks
	scowling	**CHIILQSU**	cliquish	**CHKMMOSU**	hummocks
CGILNOTT	clotting	**CHINOPS**	siphonic	**CHKMMOUY**	hummocky
CGILNPSU	sculping	**CHIINORT**	ornithic	**CHKNOOSS**	schnooks
CGILOORU	urologic	**CHIIORST**	historic	**CHKNORSU**	cornhusk
CGILORSW	cowgirls		orchitis	**CHKOOOPS**	cookshop
CGILPSTY	glyptics	**CHIIPPRU**	hippuric	**CHKOPSTU**	tuckshop
CGIMMNSU	Cummings	**CHIIRSTT**	tristich	**CHKORRTU**	Thurrock
	scumming	**CHIKLLOS**	hillocks	**CHLNOOOP**	colophon
CGIMNNOO	gnomonic	**CHIKLLOY**	hillocky	**CHLOORSU**	chlorous
	oncoming	**CHIKLNUY**	chunkily	**CHLOPSTY**	splotchy
CGIMNOPU	upcoming	**CHIKLORS**	horlicks	**CHMNORRU**	crumhorn
CGIMNORS	scroming	**CHIKMNNU**	munchkin	**CHMOORSU**	chromous
CGIMNPRU	crumping	**CHIKMNPU**	chipmunk	**CHNNOORS**	chronons
CGIMRRUY	micrurgy	**CHIKMNTU**	mutchkin	**CHNOOPTT**	topnotch
CGINNOOP	pooncing	**CHIKNOOR**	Korchnoi	**CHNORSSY**	synchros
CGINNOOR	crooning	**CHIKNOOS**	chinooks	**CHNORSTU**	cothurns
CGINNOPU	pouncing	**CHIKOPTY**	kyphotic	**CHOPSTUU**	touchups
CGINNORS	scorning	**CHIKOSST**	stockish	**CHORSTTU**	shortcut
CGINNORW	crowning	**CHIKPSYY**	physicky	**CIIILMPT**	implicit
CGINNOSS	consigns	**CHILLMSU**	chillums	**CIIILMSU**	silicium
CGINNOTU	counting	**CHILLOOT**	oilcloth	**CIIILTVY**	civility
CGINOOPS	scooping	**CHILMMUY**	chummily	**CIIINNOS**	incision
CGINOOPT	coopting	**CHILMOSU**	scholium	**CIIINTVY**	vicinity
CGINOOST	scooting	**CHILMPSU**	clumpish	**CIIJRSTU**	juristic
CGINOPPR	cropping	**CHILNNPY**	lynchpin	**CIIKKLLS**	killicks
CGINOPRS	corpsing	**CHILNOSW**	clownish	**CIIKLPST**	lipstick
CGINOPRU	crouping	**CHILNPUY**	punchily	**CIIKLRTY**	trickily
CGINORSS	crossing	**CHILOOOZ**	holozoic	**CIIKLSTY**	stickily
CGINORSU	coursing	**CHILOOYZ**	hylozoic	**CIIKNPPR**	pinprick
	scouring	**CHILOPPY**	choppily	**CIIKNPST**	stickpin
	sourcing	**CHILOSTT**	clottish	**CIIKPSUW**	wickiups
CGINORTU	courting	**CHILOTUY**	touchily	**CIILLMTU**	tillicum
CGINOSTU	scouting	**CHILOTYY**	Holy City	**CIILLNOP**	pollinic
CGINRRUY	currying	**CHIMMORU**	chromium	**CIILLSUU**	Lucilius
CGINRSTU	crusting	**CHIMNORW**	inchworm	**CIILMOPY**	impolicy
CGINSTTU	cuttings	**CHIMNOSU**	insomuch	**CIILMOSS**	sciolism
	tungstic	**CHIMNOSY**	chymosin	**CIILMRSY**	lyricism
CGKLNOSU	gunlocks	**CHIMORSS**	chrisoms	**CIILOOPT**	politico
CGKNOSTU	gunstock	**CHINOORS**	chorions	**CIILOPST**	colpitis
CGLMOOVY	mycology		isochron		politics
CGLNOOOY	oncology	**CHINOORT**	orthicon	**CIILORST**	clitoris

CIILOSST	sciolist	**CILMPSUU**	spiculum	**CIORSSSS**	scissors
	solicits	**CILNNOOS**	Nicolson	**CIPPRRUU**	purpuric
CIILPRSY	crispily	**CILNOORU**	unicolor	**CIPSSTTY**	styptics
CIILRSTY	lyricist	**CILNOOST**	colonist	**CIRSSTUY**	citrussy
CIILRTUU	utriculi	**CILNOOTU**	locution	**CJNOORRU**	conjuror
CIILSTTY	stylitic	**CILNOPTU**	plutonic	**CKKNOOTU**	knockout
CIIMMNOS	minicoms	**CILNOSTU**	linocuts	**CKLLMOSU**	mullocks
CIIMNOOS	isonomic	**CILNOSUY**	cousinly	**CKLLMOUY**	mullocky
CIIMNOST	monistic	**CILNPSSU**	sculpins	**CKLLOOPS**	pollocks
	nomistic	**CILOOPST**	copilots	**CKLMMOOS**	slommock
CIIMORST	trisomic	**CILOOPYZ**	polyzoic	**CKLNOSTU**	locknuts
CIIMOSST	stoicism	**CILOORRT**	tricolor	**CKLOORSW**	rowlocks
CIIMOSVZ	isozymic	**CILOORST**	colorist	**CKLOOSTU**	lockouts
CIIMRTTU	triticum		cortisol	**CKLOPSTU**	putlocks
CIINNSTT	instinct	**CILOORSU**	couloirs	**CKMMORUW**	muckworm
CIINOOST	isotonic	**CILOPRRY**	pyrrolic	**CKNOOORS**	rockoons
CIINORSS	incisors	**CILOPRUY**	polyuric	**CKNOOSTT**	Stockton
CIINORST	crostini	**CILOPSSW**	cowslips	**CKOOOSTU**	cookouts
CIINOSSS	scission	**CILOSSTU**	oculists	**CKOOPSTT**	stockpot
CIINOSTT	stiction	**CILOSSTY**	systolic	**CKOSSSTU**	tussocks
CIINOSTV	Visconti	**CILOSSUU**	luscious	**CKOSSTUY**	tussocky
CIINOTTY	tonicity	**CILPRSTU**	culprits	**CLLLSUUU**	Lucullus
CIINPSTU	sinciput	**CILPSSTU**	sculpsit	**CLLMOSSU**	molluscs
CIIOOPST	isotopic	**CILRSTTY**	strictly	**CLLNNOOY**	Connolly
CIIOQTUX	quixotic	**CILRSTUY**	crustily	**CLLOOPSS**	scollops
CIIOTTXY	toxicity	**CILRSUVY**	scurvily	**CLLOOQUY**	colloquy
CIIPRRTU	pruritic	**CILSSTTU**	cultists	**CLMMNOOY**	commonly
CIIPRSTU	puristic	**CIMNOORS**	omicrons	**CLMOOOTY**	colotomy
CIIRSTTU	truistic	**CIMNOOTY**	myotonic	**CLMOOPST**	complots
CIISSTTY	cystitis	**CIMNORSS**	crimsons	**CLMOSUUU**	cumulous
CIJKOSTY	joystick	**CIMNORSY**	cronyism	**CLMSTUUU**	Tusculum
CIJNNOOS	conjoins	**CIMNOSTU**	miscount	**CLNOORST**	controls
CIJNNOOT	conjoint	**CIMNOSUU**	mucinous	**CLNOSSTU**	consults
CIJNNOTU	junction	**CIMNOSUY**	syconium	**CLOOOPRT**	protocol
CIJOOSTY	jocosity	**CIMOOOTZ**	zootomic	**CLOOSSSU**	colossus
CIKKLLOS	killocks	**CIMOORSS**	moriscos	**CLOPRSTU**	sculptor
CIKLLOPS	pillocks	**CIMOSTUU**	muticous	**CMMNNOOU**	uncommon
CIKLLORS	rollicks	**CIMOSTUY**	mucosity	**CMNOOOCS**	monocots
CIKLLPUY	pluckily	**CINNOOTU**	continuo	**CMNOOPRT**	Crompton
CIKLNOST	linstock	**CINNOOTX**	nontoxic	**CMOOPRST**	comports
CIKLOPSU	liposuck	**CINNORSU**	unicorns	**CMOOPSST**	composts
CIKLOSTY	stockily	**CINNOSTU**	unctions	**CMORSSTU**	scrotums
CIKMNNNO	McKinnon	**CINNOSTY**	syntonic	**CMORSTUW**	cutworms
CIKMOORS	sickroom	**CINNQUUX**	quincunx	**CNNORSTU**	nocturns
CIKNNOOS	coonskin	**CINOOOPT**	cooption	**CNNORSUW**	uncrowns
CIKNNOST	nonstick	**CINOOPRS**	scorpion	**CNOOOORT**	octoroon
CIKNOSSW	cowskins	**CINOOPRT**	protonic	**CNOOPSSU**	soupcons
CIKNSSTU	unsticks	**CINOOTXY**	oxytocin	**CNOORRTY**	cryotron
CIKOSSTT	stockist	**CINOPSTY**	synoptic	**CNOORSST**	consorts
CIKOSSTU	sickouts	**CINORRST**	tricorns	**CNOORSTT**	contorts
CIKOSTTU	stickout	**CINORSST**	cistrons	**CNOORSTU**	contours
CIKPSSTU	stickups	**CINORSTU**	ructions		croutons
CIKPSUWY	wickyups	**CINOSSST**	consists	**CNOSTUUU**	unctuous
CILLMSUY	clumsily	**CINOSTUV**	viscount	**COOPRRST**	proctors
CILLNOOT	cotillon	**CINRSSTU**	incrusts	**COOPRSTU**	outcrops
CILLNOSU	scullion	**CINRSTTU**	instruct	**COOPRSUU**	croupous
CILLOOOT	ocotillo	**CINRSTUY**	scrutiny	**COOPRSUY**	uroscopy
CILLOORS	criollos	**CIOOOPRS**	oosporic	**COORSSTU**	outcross
CILMNOPU	pulmonic	**CIOOOTXZ**	zootoxic	**COOSSTTY**	otocysts
CILMNOUU	inoculum	**CIOOPRST**	porticos	**COPRRSTU**	corrupts
CILMNUUV	vinculum	**CIOOQSTU**	coquitos	**DDDDEEOR**	doddered
CILMOPSY	olympics	**CIOPSSTY**	copyists	**DDDEEEFN**	defended

DDDEEEENP	depended	**DDEEGIST**	digested	**DDEENNOR**	donnered
DDDEEEENR	reddened	**DDEEGJRU**	rejudged	**DDEENNTU**	untended
DDDEEFOR	foddered	**DDEEGOPS**	godspeed	**DDEENOOW**	woodened
DDDEEHRS	shredded	**DDEEGORS**	sodgered	**DDEENOPR**	pondered
DDDEEIKN	Dedekind	**DDEEGRRS**	dredgers	**DDEENOPW**	pondweed
DDDEEJRU	juddered	**DDEEGSTU**	degusted	**DDEENORS**	endorsed
DDDEENOR	dondered	**DDEEHILS**	shielded	**DDEENORW**	wondered
DDDEENOS	soddened	**DDEEHINR**	hindered	**DDEENRSU**	denuders
DDDEENUW	unwedded	**DDEEHIRT**	dithered		sundered
DDDEEORR	dodderer	**DDEEHNOR**	dehorned	**DDEEOPRT**	deported
DDDEERTU	detruded	**DDEEHRRS**	shredder	**DDEEOPRW**	powdered
DDDEGILR	griddled	**DDEEHRSS**	shedders	**DDEEORRW**	reworded
DDDEIINV	dividend	**DDEEIINT**	inedited	**DDEEORTU**	detoured
DDDEILNW	dwindled	**DDEEIIRV**	redivide	**DDEEORUV**	devoured
DDDEILRS	diddlers	**DDEEIKNW**	Wedekind	**DDEEORVY**	overdyed
DDDEILTW	twiddled	**DDEEILLV**	devilled	**DDEERRUV**	verdured
DDDEINOR	dendroid	**DDEEILMN**	mildened	**DDEERSTU**	detrudes
DDDEINRU	underdid	**DDEEILMW**	mildewed	**DDEERTUX**	extruded
DDDEIQSU	squidded	**DDEEILNR**	redlined	**DDEFFISU**	diffused
DDDGIILN	diddling	**DDEEILRV**	driveled	**DDEFIIIN**	nidified
DDDEEEEMR	redeemed	**DDEEILRW**	wildered	**DDEFIILM**	midfield
DDEEEENP	deepened	**DDEEIMNP**	impended	**DDEFIILR**	fiddlier
DDEEEFIR	redefied	**DDEEIMNR**	reminded	**DDEFIIMO**	modified
DDEEEFLX	deflexed	**DDEEIMOR**	moidered	**DDEFILLO**	Oldfield
DDEEEFNR	defender	**DDEEIMOS**	Diomedes	**DDEFILNO**	infolded
	fendered	**DDEEIMSS**	misdeeds	**DDEFILRS**	fiddlers
DDEEEFRR	deferred	**DDEEIMST**	demisted	**DDEFLNOU**	unfolded
DDEEEGLR	ledgered	**DDEEIMTT**	demitted	**DDEFNNUU**	unfunded
DDEEEGMR	demerged	**DDEEINNT**	indented	**DDEFOPRT**	Deptford
DDEEEGRT	deterged		intended	**DDEGGINR**	dredging
DDEEEHLW	wheedled	**DDEEINNU**	undenied	**DDEGGLOY**	doggedly
DDEEEHNU	unheeded	**DDEEINRT**	dendrite	**DDEGGNOO**	doggoned
DDEEEIMR	remedied	**DDEEINST**	destined	**DDEGHINS**	shedding
DDEEEIRT	reedited	**DDEEINTU**	unedited	**DDEGIINR**	deriding
DDEEELPT	depleted	**DDEEIPRS**	presided	**DDEGIIST**	giddiest
DDEEELRW	rewelded	**DDEEIPRV**	deprived	**DDEGILMN**	meddling
DDEEEMNR	remended	**DDEEIPSS**	depsides	**DDEGILNP**	peddling
DDEEEMNT	demented		despised	**DDEGILNR**	reddling
DDEEENNU	unneeded	**DDEEIPST**	despited	**DDEGILNU**	deluding
DDEEENPX	expended	**DDEEIRRS**	deriders		indulged
DDEEENRR	rendered	**DDEEIRTV**	diverted	**DDEGILOS**	dislodge
DDEEENRT	tendered	**DDEEISST**	desisted	**DDEGILRS**	griddles
DDEEENSU	unseeded	**DDEEISTV**	divested	**DDEGILUV**	divulged
DDEEENTX	extended	**DDEELLMO**	modelled	**DDEGIMOS**	demigods
DDEEENUW	unweeded	**DDEELLOY**	yodelled	**DDEGINNS**	snedding
DDEEERRT	deterred	**DDEELMOR**	moldered	**DDEGINNU**	denuding
DDEEERST	deserted	**DDEELMPU**	deplumed	**DDEGINSW**	weddings
DDEEERSV	deserved	**DDEELMRS**	meddlers	**DDEGINUU**	unguided
DDEEESTT	detested	**DDEELNOU**	loudened	**DDEGIOST**	dodgiest
DDEEESTV	devested	**DDEELOPR**	deplored	**DDEGLOPS**	splodged
DDEEFFIR	differed	**DDEELOPX**	exploded	**DDEGLOSS**	dogsleds
DDEEFFNO	offended	**DDEELOPY**	deployed	**DDEGMOOS**	smoodged
DDEEFGIT	fidgeted	**DDEELORS**	soldered	**DDEGNOOR**	Dordogne
DDEEFINR	friended	**DDEELOSU**	deloused	**DDEGNORU**	grounded
DDEEFLNO	enfolded	**DDEELOVV**	devolved		underdog
DDEEFLOR	refolded	**DDEELPRS**	peddlers	**DDEGNOSS**	godsends
DDEEFMOR	deformed	**DDEELPRU**	preluded	**DDEGNOSU**	dudgeons
DDEEFNRU	refunded	**DDEELRSU**	deluders	**DDEGOOTU**	outdodge
	underfed	**DDEEMNNU**	unmended	**DDEGOOWW**	Wedgwood
DDEEGILR	regilded	**DDEEMNOR**	endoderm	**DDEGORSS**	gorsedds
DDEEGINS	designed	**DDEEMRRU**	demurred	**DDEGRRSU**	drudgers
DDEEGIRV	diverged		murdered	**DDEGRRUY**	drudgery

DDEHILLO	Old Delhi	DDEIORRS	disorder	DDGLORRU	druglord
DDEHILNY	hiddenly	DDEIOSTW	dowdiest	DDGOOOOW	Goodwood
DDEHINOR	dihedron	DDEIPSTU	disputed	DDHILOSY	shoddily
DDEHIORS	shoddier	DDEIRSSU	druidess	DDHILSUY	dudishly
DDEHIOSS	shoddies	DDEIRSTU	ruddiest	DDHIORSY	hydroids
DDEHIRSY	hydrides		sturdied	DDHIOSWY	dowdyish
DDEHLRSU	huddlers	DDEKMOSU	dukedoms	DDIIIIVV	dividivi
DDEHNRSU	hundreds	DDELLOOP	dolloped	DDIIKLSS	skidlids
DDEHO000	hoodooed	DDELMRSU	muddlers	DDIILOPS	diploids
DDEHOOSW	woodshed	DDELNOSY	soddenly	DDIILOPY	diploidy
DDEHORSU	shrouded	DDELNRTU	trundled	DDIIMMUY	didymium
DDEHRSSU	shudders	DDELNSUY	suddenly	DDIIMRSU	druidism
DDEHRSUY	shuddery	DDELOORS	doodlers		siddurim
DDEIIKLS	disliked	DDELOPRS	plodders	DDIINOPU	dupondii
DDEIILNR	dieldrin	DDELORST	toddlers	DDIIQTUY	quiddity
DDEIILOS	idolised	DDELPRSU	puddlers	DDILOOPP	diplopod
DDEIILOZ	idolized	DDELPSSU	spuddles	DDILOOWW	wildwood
DDEIILRT	tiddlier	DDEMNOST	oddments	DDILORSY	sordidly
DDEIIMNU	Edmund II	DDEMNOUU	duodenum	DDIMOSUY	didymous
DDEIINTU	untidied	DDEMNPUU	pudendum	DDINNOWW	downwind
DDEIIOPS	diopside	DDEMOOTU	outmoded	DDINOOOT	odontoid
	dipodies	DDENNORS	dendrons	DDINOOWW	woodwind
DDEIIOST	oddities	DDENOOSS	desnoods	DDLMORSU	doldrums
DDEIIOSX	dioxides	DDENOOUW	unwooded	DDMNOORS	dromonds
	oxidised	DDENOPSS	desponds	DDMNORTU	Dortmund
DDEIIOXZ	oxidized	DDENORSU	redounds	DDNOORTW	downtrod
DDEIIRSV	dividers	DDENOSUW	swounded	DEEEEFRR	refereed
DDEIIRUV	reduviid	DDEOOOOV	voodooed	DEEEEGKR	kedgeree
DDEIKSVY	skydived	DDEOORSW	redwoods	DEEEEHLR	reheeled
DDEILMOP	imploded	DDEOOSWY	dyewoods	DEEEEMMS	meseemed
DDEILNPS	spindled	DDEOPRRS	prodders	DEEEEMRR	redeemer
	splendid	DDEOPRSW	dewdrops	DEEEEMST	esteemed
DDEILNRU	unriddle	DDEPRSSU	spudders	DEEEENPR	deepener
DDEILNSW	dwindles	DDFGIILN	fiddling	DEEEENRV	veneered
	swindled	DDFGILNU	fuddling	DEEEERTT	teetered
DDEILOPS	displode	DDFMNOUU	dumfound	DEEEFHST	sheetfed
	lopsided	DDGGIINY	giddying	DEEEFINR	redefine
DDEILOST	deltoids	DDGGILNU	guddling	DEEEFIPT	tepefied
DDEILPRS	piddlers	DDGGINNO	dingdong	DEEEFIRS	redefies
DDEILRRS	riddlers	DDGGINRU	drudging	DEEEFIRW	fireweed
DDEILRST	tiddlers	DDGHILNU	huddling	DEEEFKST	keftedes
DDEILRTW	twiddler	DDGHINTU	thudding	DEEEFLRU	refueled
DDEILRZZ	drizzled	DDGIIINO	indigoid	DEEEFLRX	reflexed
DDEILSTW	twiddles	DDGIIINV	dividing	DEEEFMNR	freedmen
DDEIMMNU	undimmed	DDGIIKNS	skidding	DEEEFNRT	deferent
DDEIMORS	dermoids	DDGIILMN	middling	DEEEFNSS	defenses
DDEIMOSS	desmoids	DDGIILNP	piddling	DEEEFORV	overfeed
DDEIMOSU	medusoid	DDGIILNR	riddling	DEEEFRRR	deferrer
DDEIMSTU	muddiest	DDGILMNU	muddling		referred
DDEINNRU	unridden	DDGILNNO	noddling	DEEEFRRT	ferreted
DDEINORS	indorsed	DDGILNOO	doodling	DEEEFRST	festered
DDEINOSW	disendow	DDGILNOP	plodding	DEEEFRTT	fettered
	disowned		poddling	DEEEGILS	elegised
	downside	DDGILNOT	toddling	DEEEGILZ	elegized
DDEINOWW	windowed	DDGILNPU	puddling	DEEEGIPR	pedigree
DDEINPSS	dispends	DDGILNRU	ruddling	DEEEGIRR	greedier
DDEINRST	stridden	DDGIMNUY	muddying	DEEEGISW	edgewise
DDEINRTU	intruded	DDGINOPR	prodding	DEEEGLNR	Legendre
DDEINSST	distends	DDGINPSU	puddings	DEEEGLPS	pledgees
DDEIOPRS	dropsied		spudding	DEEEGLSS	edgeless
DDEIOPRV	provided	DDGINPUY	puddingy	DEEEGLSV	selvedge
DDEIOPSS	disposed	DDGINSTU	studding	DEEEGMRR	demerger

DEEEEGMRS	demerges	**DEEEMPTX**	exempted
DEEEGNNR	engender	**DEEEMRSS**	medreses
DEEEGNRU	renegued	**DEEEMRST**	deemster
DEEEGNRV	revenged	**DEEENOPR**	reopened
DEEEGRSS	egressed	**DEEENORS**	endorsee
DEEEGRST	deterges	**DEEENPRT**	repented
DEEEGRTT	gettered		repetend
DEEEHHSW	wheeshed	**DEEENPRX**	expender
DEEEHLMT	helmeted	**DEEENPSS**	deepness
DEEEHLRW	wheedler	**DEEENPSX**	expensed
DEEEHLSS	heedless	**DEEENRRR**	renderer
DEEEHLSW	wheedles	**DEEENRRT**	tenderer
DEEEHMMR	rehemmed	**DEEENRRV**	reverend
DEEEHMNS	enmeshed	**DEEENRST**	resented
DEEEHPRT	threeped	**DEEENRTT**	tentered
DEEEHRTT	tethered	**DEEENRTU**	neutered
DEEEIKLS	seedlike	**DEEENRTV**	Deventer
DEEEIKLW	weedlike	**DEEENRTX**	extender
DEEEILRV	relieved	**DEEENRUV**	revenued
DEEEIMRS	remedies		unreeved
DEEEINRR	reindeer	**DEEENSTT**	detentes
DEEEINRS	nereides	**DEEENSTX**	dentexes
DEEEINST	neediest	**DEEEOPRT**	deportee
DEEEINTV	eventide	**DEEEOSTV**	devotees
DEEEIPRS	speedier	**DEEEPPPR**	peppered
DEEEIPTX	expedite	**DEEEPRSS**	speeders
DEEEIRRR	derriere	**DEEEPRST**	pestered
DEEEIRSS	diereses	**DEEEQSUZ**	squeezed
DEEEIRST	reediest	**DEEERRRV**	verderer
DEEEIRTW	tweedier	**DEEERRST**	deserter
DEEEIRVW	reviewed	**DEEERRSV**	deserver
DEEEISST	seediest		reserved
	Teesside		reversed
DEEEISSV	devisees	**DEEERRTV**	reverted
DEEEISTW	weediest	**DEEERSSV**	deserves
DEEEJLLW	jewelled	**DEEERSTT**	detester
DEEEJRRS	jerreeds		retested
DEEEKLNN	kenneled		streeted
DEEEKLNR	kerneled	**DEEERSTV**	revested
DEEEKNSW	weekends	**DEEERSTW**	westered
DEEEKOPW	pokeweed	**DEEERSTX**	exserted
DEEEKRSW	skewered	**DEEERTTV**	revetted
DEEELLLV	levelled	**DEEERUVX**	Devereux
DEEELLPR	predelle	**DEEESTTV**	vedettes
	repelled	**DEEFFGOR**	goffered
DEEELLPT	pelleted	**DEEFFINS**	effendis
DEEELLPX	expelled	**DEEFFNOR**	forefend
DEEELLRV	revelled		offender
DEEELMRT	remelted	**DEEFFRSU**	suffered
DEEELNRT	relented	**DEEFGILR**	fledgier
DEEELNRU	unreeled	**DEEFGILZ**	Ziegfeld
DEEELNSS	lessened	**DEEFGINR**	fingered
	needless	**DEEFGLNU**	engulfed
DEEELPST	depletes	**DEEFGLOO**	feelgood
	steepled	**DEEFGLUW**	gulfweed
DEEELRTT	lettered	**DEEFGORR**	reforged
DEEELRTW	weltered	**DEEFHLOR**	freehold
DEEELSSS	seedless	**DEEFHLRS**	feldsher
DEEELSSW	weedless	**DEEFHORR**	Hereford
DEEEMNRS	Menderes	**DEEFIINT**	definite
DEEEMNSS	demesnes	**DEEFIIRS**	deifiers
DEEEMPRT	tempered		edifiers

	fireside
DEEFIIRV	verified
DEEFILLR	refilled
DEEFILLT	filleted
DEEFILMR	refilmed
DEEFILMS	medflies
DEEFILNX	inflexed
DEEFILPR	pilfered
DEEFILRS	defilers
	fielders
DEEFILRT	filtered
DEEFIMTU	tumefied
DEEFINRR	inferred
DEEFINRS	definers
DEEFINRZ	frenzied
DEEFINSS	finessed
DEEFINST	infested
DEEFIORS	foreside
DEEFIPRX	prefixed
DEEFIRTT	refitted
DEEFLLOW	fellowed
DEEFLLRU	fullered
DEEFLNNU	funneled
DEEFLNOR	enfolder
DEEFLORW	deflower
	flowered
DEEFLOST	feedlots
DEEFLRRU	ferruled
DEEFLRUX	refluxed
DEEFMNOT	fomented
DEEFMORR	deformer
	reformed
DEEFMORS	freedoms
DEEFMPRU	perfumed
DEEFNOOR	foredone
DEEFNOST	softened
DEEFNRRU	refunder
DEEFNSST	deftness
DEEFOORR	reroofed
DEEFOORS	foredoes
DEEFOORT	footered
DEEFOORW	woodfree
DEEFORST	deforest
	De Forest
	forested
	fostered
DEEFORTU	foutered
DEEFPRSU	perfused
DEEFRRTU	returfed
DEEGGHHO	hedgehog
DEEGGIJR	jiggered
	rejigged
DEEGGINR	gingered
DEEGGIRR	dreggier
DEEGGLOR	doggerel
DEEGGNOR	engorged
DEEGGNPU	unpegged
DEEGGORR	regorged
DEEGGORT	gorgeted
DEEGHHOP	hedgehop
DEEGHILL	Edgehill
DEEGHILS	sleighed

DEEGHINR rehinged	**DEEGRRSU** resurged	**DEEIIPRU** priedieu
DEEGHITW weighted	**DEEGRSTU** gestured	**DEEIIRSS** dieresis
DEEGHLPU pleughed	**DEEGRTTU** guttered	**DEEIIRST** siderite
DEEGHNRU hungered	**DEEGSSTU** gusseted	**DEEIIRSV** derisive
DEEGHOPS sheepdog	**DEEHHNPY** hyphened	**DEEIIRSW** weirdies
DEEGHORW hedgerow	**DEEHHPRS** shepherd	**DEEIISSS** disseise
DEEGHOSW hogweeds	**DEEHHRST** threshed	**DEEIISSZ** disseize
DEEGHOTT dogteeth	**DEEHIKLS** shedlike	**DEEIJNNO** enjoined
DEEGIINN indigene	**DEEHIKRS** shrieked	**DEEIJNOR** rejoined
DEEGILMT gimleted	**DEEHILNW** New Delhi	**DEEIJRTT** jittered
DEEGILNN needling	**DEEHILRS** relished	**DEEIKLLR** killdeer
DEEGILNO eloigned		shielder	**DEEIKLLS** skellied
DEEGILNR lingered	**DEEHILSS** hideless	**DEEIKLMO** domelike
	reedling	**DEEHILSV** dishevel	**DEEIKLMW** milkweed
DEEGILNS seedling	**DEEHIMMS** immeshed	**DEEIKLNN** enkindle
DEEGILNT deleting	**DEEHIMNS** inmeshed	**DEEIKLNR** rekindle
DEEGILRW weregild	**DEEHIMOP** hemipode	**DEEIKLOV** dovelike
DEEGILRY greedily	**DEEHIMRT** Meredith	**DEEIKLSW** silkweed
DEEGIMMR immerged	**DEEHINPR** ephedrin	**DEEIKNRS** deerskin
DEEGIMNN emending	**DEEHINRR** hinderer	**DEEIKNRT** tinkered
DEEGIMRU demiurge	**DEEHINRS** drisheen	**DEEIKOSV** dovekies
DEEGINOS Diogenes	**DEEHINTW** whitened	**DEEIKPPR** kippered
DEEGINPS speeding	**DEEHIOTX** ethoxide	**DEEIKSTT** diskette
DEEGINRR deringer	**DEEHIPRS** perished	**DEEILLMN** Medellín
DEEGINRS designer	**DEEHIRRT** ditherer	**DEEILLMP** impelled
	energids	**DEEHIRSV** shivered		milleped
	redesign	**DEEHIRSW** shrewdie	**DEEILLNO** nielloed
	reedings	**DEEHIRTW** withered	**DEEILLRT** tillered
	resigned	**DEEHIRTY** heredity	**DEEILLVY** veiledly
DEEGINSS edginess	**DEEHKNOS** keeshond	**DEEILMNU** demilune
DEEGINST ingested	**DEEHKNRU** hunkered	**DEEILMOS** melodies
	signeted	**DEEHLLOR** hollered		melodise
DEEGINSX desexing	**DEEHLLOV** hovelled	**DEEILMOZ** melodize
DEEGIORT goitered	**DEEHLMNU** unhelmed	**DEEILNOT** deletion
DEEGIPSW pigweeds	**DEEHLNPU** unhelped		entoiled
DEEGIRST digester	**DEEHLOSU** houseled	**DEEILNRS** redlines
	redigest	**DEEHLOSV** shoveled	**DEEILNRU** underlie
DEEGIRSV diverges	**DEEHLSTU** sleuthed	**DEEILNSS** idleness
DEEGISTW wedgiest	**DEEHMNRS** herdsmen	**DEEILNST** enlisted
DEEGJPRU prejudge	**DEEHMORT** mothered		listened
DEEGJRSU rejudges	**DEEHNORR** dehorner		tinseled
DEEGLLUY gulleyed	**DEEHNORT** dethrone	**DEEILNSV** sniveled
DEEGLNOZ lozenged		threnode	**DEEILNTT** entitled
DEEGLNRY legendry	**DEEHNOWY** honeydew	**DEEILNUV** unveiled
DEEGLOPR pledgeor	**DEEHNSTU** enthused	**DEEILOPT** lepidote
DEEGLORV groveled	**DEEHOOVR** hoovered	**DEEILORT** dolerite
DEEGLORW glowered	**DEEHOPRT** pothered		loitered
DEEGLOSY goldeyes	**DEEHORSU** rehoused	**DEEILORV** evildoer
DEEGLPRS pledgers	**DEEHORSW** showered	**DEEILPRX** diplexer
DEEGLPST pledgets	**DEEHORTX** exhorted	**DEEILPSY** speedily
DEEGLRSS sledgers	**DEEHPRSY** syphered	**DEEILRST** relisted
DEEGLRSU Guelders	**DEEHRRSW** shrewder	**DEEILRSU** leisured
DEEGLRSW wergelds	**DEEIIKLT** tidelike	**DEEILRSV** delivers
DEEGMSUW gumweeds	**DEEIILNS** sideline		silvered
DEEGNNOS endogens	**DEEIILRV** liveried		slivered
DEEGNNOY endogeny	**DEEIILRW** wieldier	**DEEILRSW** wielders
DEEGNOPU geepound	**DEEIIMRS** dimerise	**DEEILRSY** yielders
DEEGNORV governed	**DEEIIMRZ** dimerize	**DEEILRTT** littered
DEEGNPRU repugned	**DEEIIMST** itemised		retitled
DEEGNPUX expunged	**DEEIIMTZ** itemized	**DEEILRVY** delivery
DEEGORST gostered	**DEEIINOZ** deionize	**DEEILSST** tideless
DEEGOTUW goutweed	**DEEIIPRS** Pierides	**DEEILSTU** dilutees

DEEILSUV	delusive		wideness	DEEISSSU	diseuses
DEEILSVW	swiveled	DEEINSTT	dinettes	DEEISTTV	videttes
DEEIMMNS	endemism	DEEINSTU	detinues	DEEJKNTU	junketed
DEEIMMOS	semidome	DEEINSTV	invested	DEEJPRRU	perjured
DEEIMMRS	immersed	DEEINSTY	Tyneside	DEEKKOOY	okeydoke
	simmered	DEEINTUV	duvetine	DEEKMNOY	monkeyed
DEEIMNOR	domineer	DEEIOPRX	peroxide	DEEKNNNU	unkenned
DEEIMNOS	demonise	DEEIOPSS	episodes	DEEKNOTW	knotweed
	dominees	DEEIOPST	poetised	DEEKNOTY	keynoted
DEEIMNOZ	demonize	DEEIOPSX	epoxides	DEEKORRW	reworked
DEEIMNPT	pediment	DEEIOPTZ	poetized	DEEKOSVY	dovekeys
DEEIMNRR	reminder	DEEIORRV	override	DEELLMOR	modeller
DEEIMNRT	reminted	DEEIORSV	overside	DEELLMOW	mellowed
DEEIMNSS	sidesmen	DEEIOTVX	videotex	DEELLMRU	mullered
DEEIMNST	sediment	DEEIPPQU	equipped	DEELLNOR	enrolled
DEEIMNSU	seminude	DEEIPPRZ	zippered	DEELLORW	rowelled
DEEIMPRR	periderm	DEEIPPST	peptides	DEELLORY	yodeller
DEEIMPRS	demireps		peptised	DEELLOTW	towelled
	impeders	DEEIPPTT	pipetted	DEELLOTX	extolled
	premised	DEEIPPTZ	peptized	DEELLOVY	volleyed
	simpered	DEEIPQRU	repiqued	DEELLOWY	yellowed
DEEIMPRX	premixed	DEEIPRRS	presider	DEELLRSU	duellers
DEEIMRST	demerits		reprised	DEELLRSW	dwellers
	demister		respired	DEELLSSW	weldless
	dimeters	DEEIPRRV	depriver	DEELMMOP	pommeled
	mistered	DEEIPRSS	despiser	DEELMMPU	pummeled
DEEIMRTT	remitted		disperse	DEELMNOO	melodeon
DEEINNPR	repinned		presides	DEELMNTU	unmelted
DEEINNRT	indenter	DEEIPRST	Depretis	DEELMOOS	dolesome
	intender		priested	DEELMOPR	empolder
	interned		respited	DEELMOPY	employed
DEEINNRV	innerved	DEEIPRSV	deprives	DEELMORS	modelers
DEEINNST	desinent		prevised		remodels
DEEINNSZ	denizens	DEEIPRTT	prettied	DEELMOST	molested
DEEINNTV	invented	DEEIPSSS	despises	DEELMPSU	deplumes
DEEINNTW	entwined	DEEIPSST	despites	DEELMRUY	demurely
DEEINORS	indorsee		sidestep	DEELNNTU	tunneled
DEEINORT	oriented	DEEIPSTU	deputies	DEELNOOS	loosened
DEEINOSV	nosedive		deputise	DEELNORT	redolent
DEEINPSS	dispense	DEEIPTUZ	deputize		rondelet
DEEINQRU	enquired	DEEIQRRU	required	DEELNOSS	lessoned
DEEINQSU	sequined	DEEIQRSU	esquired	DEELNOSU	ensouled
DEEINRRT	interred	DEEIQRTU	requited	DEELNPSU	pendules
	trendier	DEEIQRUV	quivered	DEELNRTU	underlet
DEEINRRW	rewinder	DEEIQTUU	quietude	DEELNRTY	tenderly
DEEINRSS	direness	DEEIRRRV	Red River	DEELNSSW	lewdness
DEEINRST	Dniester	DEEIRRSS	derrises	DEELNWWY	newlywed
	inserted		desirers	DEELOORT	retooled
	resident		dressier	DEELOPRR	deplorer
	sintered		residers	DEELOPRS	deplores
	trendies	DEEIRRST	destrier	DEELOPRV	preloved
DEEINRSU	uredines	DEEIRRSV	derivers	DEELOPRX	exploder
DEEINRSW	rewidens	DEEIRRTV	diverter		explored
	wideners	DEEIRRWW	wiredrew	DEELOPRY	redeploy
DEEINRSX	indexers	DEEIRSST	resisted	DEELOPSV	develops
DEEINRTU	retinued	DEEIRSSU	residues	DEELOPSX	explodes
	reunited	DEEIRSSV	devisers	DEELORRS	solderer
DEEINRTV	inverted		disserve	DEELORSU	urodeles
DEEINRTW	wintered		dissever	DEELORSV	resolved
DEEINRTX	dextrine	DEEIRSTW	weirdest	DEELORTT	dotterel
DEEINSST	destines	DEEIRTTT	tittered	DEELORTV	revolted
DEEINSSW	dewiness	DEEIRTTW	wittered	DEELORTW	troweled

DEELORUV	louvered	
DEELORVV	revolved	
DEELOSSU	delouses	
DEELOSVV	devolves	
DEELPRRU	preluder	
DEELPRSU	preludes	
	repulsed	
DEELPRTU	drupelet	
DEELPSUX	duplexes	
DEELRSTU	lustered	
	resulted	
DEELRSTW	wrestled	
DEELRSTY	restyled	
DEEMMORS	mesoderm	
DEEMMRSU	summered	
DEEMNOOS	moonseed	
DEEMNOQU	queendom	
DEEMNORT	entoderm	
DEEMOORT	odometer	
DEEMORRT	tremored	
DEEMORSW	wormseed	
DEEMORSX	exoderms	
DEEMORTU	udometer	
DEEMPRST	dempster	
DEEMPRSU	presumed	
DEEMPRTU	permuted	
DEEMRRRU	demurrer	
	murderer	
DEEMRSTU	mustered	
DEEMRTTU	muttered	
DEENNOPT	deponent	
DEENNOPU	unopened	
DEENNORW	renowned	
DEENNOST	sonneted	
DEENNOSY	doyennes	
DEENNPST	pendents	
DEENNRTU	unrented	
DEENNRUV	unnerved	
DEENNSSU	nudeness	
DEENOORT	enrooted	
DEENOORV	overdone	
DEENOOST	Oostende	
DEENOPSS	spondees	
DEENOPST	pentodes	
DEENORRS	endorser	
DEENORRW	wonderer	
DEENORSS	endorses	
DEENORST	erodents	
DEENORSW	endowers	
	reendows	
	worsened	
DEENORTU	deuteron	
DEENPPRS	perpends	
DEENPRSS	spenders	
DEENPRST	pretends	
DEENRRSU	sunderer	
DEENRRTU	returned	
DEENRSSU	rudeness	
DEENRSTU	dentures	
	sederunt	
	underset	
	unrested	

DEENRSUV	unserved	
	unversed	
DEENRTUV	ventured	
DEENSTTU	untested	
DEENTUVY	duvetyne	
DEEOORRV	overrode	
DEEOORSV	overdoes	
	overdose	
DEEOPPST	estopped	
DEEOPRRT	portered	
	reported	
DEEOPRRV	reproved	
DEEOPRRW	powderer	
DEEOPRSS	deposers	
DEEOPRST	dopester	
	reedstop	
DEEOPRTT	pottered	
	repotted	
DEEOPRTX	exported	
DEEOPSSU	espoused	
DEEOQRTU	roqueted	
DEEORRRS	orderers	
	reorders	
DEEORRST	resorted	
	restored	
	rostered	
DEEORRTT	retorted	
DEEORRTU	rerouted	
DEEORRUV	devourer	
DEEORRVW	overdrew	
	Verwoerd	
DEEORSST	oersteds	
DEEORSTT	tetrodes	
DEEORSTX	dextrose	
DEEORSTY	oystered	
	storeyed	
DEEORSUV	overused	
DEEORSVY	overdyes	
DEEORTTT	tottered	
DEEORTTX	extorted	
DEEOSSUX	exoduses	
DEEPPRSU	suppered	
DEEPPSSU	speedups	
DEEPRTTU	puttered	
DEEPRUVY	purveyed	
DEERRSSS	dressers	
DEERRSUV	verdures	
DEERRTTU	turreted	
DEERSSST	desserts	
	stressed	
DEERSTUV	vestured	
DEERSTUX	extrudes	
DEERSUVY	surveyed	
DEERTTUX	textured	
DEFFHILW	whiffled	
DEFFHLSU	shuffled	
DEFFHORS	shroffed	
DEFFILNS	sniffled	
DEFFILNU	Nuffield	
DEFFILOV	fivefold	
DEFFIMOS	fiefdoms	
DEFFIORS	offsider	

DEFFIOSS	offsides	
DEFFIQSU	squiffed	
DEFFIRSU	diffuser	
DEFFISSU	diffuses	
DEFFISUX	suffixed	
DEFFLNSU	snuffled	
DEFFNORS	forfends	
DEFFNOSS	sendoffs	
DEFFSSUU	suffused	
DEFFSTUY	dyestuff	
DEFGGILN	fledging	
DEFGHILT	flighted	
DEFGHIRT	frighted	
DEFGIILN	defiling	
	fielding	
DEFGIILU	uglified	
DEFGIINN	defining	
DEFGIINY	deifying	
	edifying	
DEFGIIST	digestif	
DEFGILNU	ingulfed	
DEFGILRU	dirgeful	
DEFGILTY	giftedly	
DEFGINSU	defusing	
DEFGINUZ	defuzing	
DEFGIOOW	goodwife	
DEFGIORS	firedogs	
DEFGJORU	forjudge	
DEFHIIMU	humified	
DEFHIINS	fiendish	
	finished	
DEFHIOOW	wifehood	
DEFHIRST	redshift	
DEFHLOOS	selfhood	
DEFHOORS	serfhood	
DEFHORRT	Hertford	
DEFIIILV	vilified	
DEFIIIMN	minified	
DEFIIINS	nidifies	
DEFIIIVV	vivified	
DEFIILLO	oilfield	
DEFIILLP	filliped	
DEFIILLW	wildlife	
DEFIILMS	misfiled	
DEFIILNS	infidels	
	infields	
DEFIILOR	oilfired	
DEFIILRW	wildfire	
DEFIILSU	fluidise	
DEFIILTY	fidelity	
DEFIILUZ	fluidize	
DEFIIMOR	modifier	
DEFIIMOS	modifies	
DEFIIMRS	misfired	
DEFIINOT	notified	
DEFIINTY	identify	
DEFIIOSS	ossified	
DEFIIOTV	videofit	
DEFIIPRU	purified	
DEFIIPSS	fissiped	
DEFIIPTY	typified	
DEFIISST	fideists	

DEFILLNU	unfilled	DEGGILNS	geldings	DEGIINST	dingiest
DEFILNNO	ninefold		sledging	DEGIINSV	devising
DEFILNOR	infolder		sniggled	DEGIISSU	disguise
DEFILNRS	flinders	DEGGILNU	deluging	DEGIJMSU	misjudge
DEFILNRU	unrifled	DEGGILRW	wriggled	DEGIKLOV	kidglove
	urnfield	DEGGINRU	unrigged	DEGILLNU	duelling
DEFILNRY	friendly	DEGGIORS	disgorge	DEGILLNW	dwelling
DEFILOPR	profiled	DEGGIPRS	sprigged	DEGILMNO	modeling
DEFILORU	fluoride	DEGGIRSU	druggies	DEGILMNS	gildsmen
DEFILORV	frivoled	DEGGLMSU	smuggled	DEGILMPS	glimpsed
DEFILOTU	outfield	DEGGLNSU	snuggled	DEGILNOS	sidelong
DEFILOTY	foetidly	DEGGLRUY	ruggedly	DEGILNOW	doweling
DEFILPRU	prideful	DEGGNOSU	gudgeons	DEGILNOY	yodeling
DEFILPTU	uplifted	DEGGRRSU	grudgers	DEGILNRU	indulger
DEFILRRU	flurried	DEGHHILV	highveld	DEGILNSU	indulges
DEFILRVY	fervidly	DEGHIINS	dinghies	DEGILNSW	swingled
DEFILRZZ	frizzled	DEGHIKNT	knighted	DEGILOOR	goodlier
DEFIMNOR	informed	DEGHILNS	shingled	DEGILOOY	ideology
DEFIMOPR	pediform	DEGHILPT	plighted	DEGILOST	godliest
DEFIMORY	remodify	DEGHILST	delights	DEGILRRS	girdlers
DEFIMRRU	drumfire		slighted	DEGILRSU	guilders
DEFIMRSU	Dumfries	DEGHINNS	shending	DEGILRSW	wergilds
DEFINORW	forewind	DEGHINNU	unhinged	DEGILRUV	divulger
DEFINRTY	trendify	DEGHINOT	Deighton	DEGILRZZ	grizzled
DEFINTTU	unfitted	DEGHIOPS	dogeship	DEGILSUV	divulges
DEFIOPRT	profited	DEGHIORU	doughier	DEGIMNNS	mendings
DEFIOTXY	detoxify	DEGHLOOS	shoogled	DEGIMNOT	demoting
DEFIRRST	drifters	DEGHLOPU	ploughed	DEGIMNPU	impugned
DEFIRSSU	fissured	DEGHLORY	hydrogel	DEGIMNSS	smidgens
DEFISSTU	feudists	DEGHLOSU	sloughed	DEGIMOOT	goodtime
DEFKLORY	forkedly	DEGHMOSU	gumshoed	DEGIMORR	Gordimer
DEFLLOOR	folderol	DEGHNOOS	hognosed	DEGINNNU	unending
DEFLLOOW	followed	DEGHNORT	thronged	DEGINNOP	deponing
DEFLMRSU	Rumsfeld	DEGHNORY	hydrogen	DEGINNOT	denoting
DEFLNORS	fondlers	DEGHOOOP	Good Hope	DEGINNOW	endowing
DEFLNORU	flounder	DEGHOOSU	doghouse	DEGINNPS	spending
	unfolder	DEGIIIST	digitise	DEGINNPU	upending
DEFLNRUU	unfurled	DEGIIITZ	digitize	DEGINNRT	trending
DEFLOORS	flooders	DEGIILNT	diligent	DEGINNRU	enduring
	refloods	DEGIILNV	deviling	DEGINNSU	unsigned
DEFLOORT	foretold	DEGIILNW	wielding	DEGINNTU	untinged
DEFLOORV	overfold	DEGIILNY	yielding	DEGINOPS	deposing
DEFLOOSS	foodless	DEGIILTU	digitule	DEGINORR	ordering
DEFMNORU	unformed	DEGIILTY	gelidity	DEGINORS	negroids
DEFMOOOR	foredoom	DEGIIMNP	impeding	DEGINORV	ringdove
DEFNNOSS	fondness		impinged	DEGINORW	dowering
DEFNNOUW	newfound	DEGIIMNS	demising	DEGINOSW	widgeons
DEFNOOPS	spoonfed	DEGIIMSU	misguide	DEGINOTV	devoting
DEFNOORS	frondose	DEGIINNR	nidering	DEGINOTX	detoxing
DEFNOORV	overfond	DEGIINNS	indigens	DEGINPRS	springed
DEFNORRU	frondeur	DEGIINNT	indigent	DEGINPTU	deputing
DEFNORSU	founders		teinding	DEGINRRS	grinders
DEFNORTU	fortuned	DEGIINNW	widening	DEGINRRY	grindery
DEFNRRUU	underfur	DEGIINNX	indexing		redrying
DEFOORRW	foreword	DEGIINNZ	dizening	DEGINRSS	dressing
DEFOOTUX	outfoxed	DEGIINOS	indigoes	DEGINRST	stringed
DEFORRUW	furrowed	DEGIINOV	videoing	DEGINRSU	grundies
DEFORSST	defrosts	DEGIINRS	desiring	DEGINRSW	redwings
DEGGHINS	hedgings		residing	DEGINRSY	syringed
DEGGHRSU	shrugged		ringside	DEGINTTU	duetting
DEGGIINN	deigning	DEGIINRV	deriving	DEGIOPRR	porridge
DEGGILNP	pledging	DEGIINRW	weirding	DEGIOPSS	gossiped

DEGIOPST	podgiest
DEGIORST	stodgier
DEGIPSTU	pudgiest
DEGJMNTU	judgment
DEGLLNOY	goldenly
DEGLLOOP	golloped
DEGLMNOT	lodgment
DEGLNRTU	gruntled
DEGLOOPR	prologed
DEGLOOPY	pedology
DEGLOOUU	duologue
DEGLOPRS	pledgors
DEGLOPSS	splodges
DEGLPRSU	splurged
DEGMOOSS	smoodges
DEGNNOSU	dungeons
DEGNOOSS	goodness
DEGNOOST	stegodon
DEGNOPPU	oppugned
DEGNORSU	guerdons
DEGNORYY	gyrodyne
DEGPRSUU	upsurged
DEGRRSTU	trudgers
DEHHILTW	withheld
DEHHISTW	whishted
DEHHOOSW	whooshed
DEHIIKLS	dishlike
DEHIILSV	devilish
DEHIIMMS	shimmied
DEHIIMST	ditheism
DEHIINNS	shinnied
DEHIINNW	whinnied
DEHIINSS	shindies
DEHIINST	shintied
DEHIISST	dishiest
DEHIISTT	ditheist
	stithied
DEHIJMNO	demijohn
DEHIKLOO	hoodlike
DEHIKMOS	sheikdom
DEHIKMRU	Durkheim
DEHIKNOW	Windhoek
DEHILLRS	shrilled
DEHILLRT	thrilled
DEHILMOS	demolish
DEHILNOV	honiedly
DEHILNPY	diphenyl
DEHILOOR	heliodor
DEHILOPS	polished
DEHILOTY	holytide
DEHILPSU	sulphide
DEHILSTW	whistled
DEHILTTW	whittled
DEHIMNOS	hedonism
	Sondheim
DEHIMOPS	hemipods
DEHIMOST	ethmoids
DEHIMPRS	shrimped
DEHINOPS	siphoned
	sphenoid
DEHINOST	hedonist
DEHINPSU	punished

DEHINSUW	unwished
DEHIOOST	dhooties
DEHIOPRS	spheroid
DEHIOSSW	sideshow
DEHIOSTU	hideouts
DEHIQSSU	squished
DEHIRSTT	thirsted
DEHIRTWW	withdrew
DEHKLNOU	elkhound
DEHKNOOU	unhooked
DEHLLOOW	hollowed
DEHLLOPY	phyllode
DEHLMORY	hydromel
DEHLNOOW	downhole
DEHLNTUY	huntedly
DEHLOORV	holdover
DEHLOOSS	hoodless
DEHLOOST	toeholds
	toolshed
DEHLOOSW	woolshed
DEHLOPRU	upholder
DEHLOPSS	sploshed
DEHLORSU	shoulder
DEHLRRSU	hurdlers
DEHLRSWY	shrewdly
DEHLSTTU	shuttled
DEHMMRTU	thrummed
DEHMNRUY	unrhymed
DEHMOORW	whoredom
DEHMOOST	smoothed
DEHMOPRY	hypoderm
DEHMORUU	humoured
DEHNOORU	honoured
DEHNOOSW	hoedowns
	woodhens
DEHNOPSY	syphoned
DEHNORSU	enshroud
	hounders
	unhorsed
DEHNORTY	threnody
DEHNOSSW	snowshed
DEHNOSUU	unhoused
DEHNRSTU	thunders
DEHNRTUY	thundery
DEHOOPRT	theropod
DEHOORSW	Sherwood
DEHOOSSW	swooshed
DEHOPRST	potsherd
DEHOSSTU	stoushed
DEIIIMST	dimities
DEIIINSV	divinise
DEIIINVZ	divinize
DEIIISVV	divisive
DEIIKLMS	misliked
DEIIKLNR	kindlier
DEIIKLSS	dislikes
DEIIKNST	dinkiest
DEIIKSVV	skivvied
DEIILMRU	delirium
DEIILMST	delimits
DEIILNNU	induline
DEIILNOS	lionised

DEIILNOT	tolidine
DEIILNOZ	lionized
DEIILNPV	vilipend
DEIILNVY	divinely
DEIILNXY	xylidine
DEIILORS	idoliser
DEIILORZ	idolizer
DEIILOSS	idolises
DEIILOSZ	idolizes
DEIILPSS	sideslip
DEIILSTU	utilised
DEIILTUZ	utilized
DEIIMMRS	dimerism
DEIIMMST	mistimed
DEIIMNOS	dominies
DEIIMNRT	diriment
DEIIMNTU	mutinied
DEIIMOSS	disomies
DEIIMPRU	peridium
DEIIMSVW	midwives
DEIINNOP	pinioned
DEIINNPP	pinniped
DEIINNTW	intwined
DEIINORS	derision
	ironised
	ironside
	resinoid
DEIINORZ	ironized
DEIINOST	editions
	sedition
DEIINOSV	visioned
DEIINPPW	windpipe
DEIINPRS	inspired
DEIINPRT	intrepid
DEIINPRY	pyridine
DEIINPTU	unpitied
DEIINQRU	inquired
DEIINRSS	insiders
DEIINRST	disinter
	inditers
	nitrides
DEIINRSV	diviners
DEIINRTU	untidier
DEIINSST	insisted
	tidiness
DEIINSTU	disunite
	nudities
	unitised
	untidies
DEIINSTW	windiest
DEIINTTU	intuited
DEIINTTY	identity
DEIINTUZ	unitized
DEIIOPRS	presidio
DEIIORSS	iodisers
DEIIORST	diorites
DEIIORSX	oxidiser
DEIIORSZ	iodizers
DEIIORTX	trioxide
DEIIORXZ	oxidizer
DEIIOSSX	oxidises
DEIIOSXZ	oxidizes

DEIIPPRR	drippier	
DEIIPPST	dippiest	
DEIIPRST	riptides	
	spirited	
	tiderips	
DEIIPRSZ	disprize	
DEIIPTTY	tepidity	
DEIIQSTU	disquiet	
DEIIRSSU	diuresis	
DEIIRSTT	dirtiest	
DEIISSTT	ditsiest	
DEIISTTZ	ditziest	
DEIISTZZ	dizziest	
DEIJNNOU	unjoined	
DEIJNORS	joinders	
DEIJORRY	joyrider	
DEIJORSY	joyrides	
DEIKKLNO	klondike	
DEIKLLOR	lordlike	
DEIKLLSS	deskills	
DEIKLNNU	unlinked	
DEIKLNOR	Kol Nidre	
DEIKLNRS	kindlers	
DEIKLNRW	wrinkled	
DEIKLNSS	kindless	
DEIKLNTW	twinkled	
DEIKLORS	Roskilde	
DEIKMNOO	kimonoed	
DEIKNNRU	unkinder	
DEIKNNSS	kindness	
DEIKNORU	Iron Duke	
DEIKNOSS	doeskins	
DEIKNRRS	drinkers	
DEIKNRSS	redskins	
DEIKNSSU	unkissed	
DEIKORSS	droskies	
DEIKPRSU	prusiked	
	spruiked	
DEIKRSVY	skydiver	
DEIKSSTU	duskiest	
DEIKSSVY	skydives	
DEILLNSW	indwells	
DEILLNTU	untilled	
DEILLNUW	unwilled	
DEILLOOP	Leopold I	
DEILLOPW	pillowed	
DEILLORR	lordlier	
DEILLRRS	drillers	
	redrills	
DEILLSTU	duellist	
DEILMNOO	melodion	
DEILMNSS	mildness	
	mindless	
DEILMOOT	dolomite	
DEILMOPR	implored	
	impolder	
DEILMOPS	implodes	
DEILMORU	lemuroid	
	mouldier	
DEILMOST	melodist	
	moldiest	
DEILMOSU	emulsoid	

DEILMOTV	demivolt	
DEILMPTU	multiped	
DEILMRSU	misruled	
DEILNNOT	indolent	
DEILNOOS	eidolons	
	solenoid	
DEILNOSU	delusion	
	insouled	
	unsoiled	
DEILNOTU	outlined	
DEILNOVV	involved	
DEILNPSS	spindles	
DEILNPST	splinted	
DEILNRST	tendrils	
DEILNRSW	swindler	
DEILNRTY	trendily	
DEILNSST	dintless	
DEILNSSW	swindles	
	wildness	
	windless	
DEILNSTU	diluents	
	insulted	
	unlisted	
DEILNTTU	untitled	
DEILNTUY	unitedly	
DEILNUWY	unwieldy	
DEILOOPW	woodpile	
DEILOPRS	leporids	
DEILOPSS	despoils	
DEILOPST	pistoled	
	postiled	
DEILOPSU	euploids	
DEILOPUY	euploidy	
DEILOQRU	liquored	
DEILORSS	soldiers	
DEILORSY	soldiery	
DEILORTY	elytroid	
DEILOSSV	dissolve	
DEILOSTU	solitude	
DEILOSTW	dowliest	
DEILOSVW	oldwives	
DEILOTUV	outlived	
DEILPPST	stippled	
DEILPPSU	supplied	
DEILPRSU	serpulid	
DEILPTTU	uptilted	
DEILRSSY	dressily	
DEILRSTU	diluters	
DEILRSZZ	drizzles	
DEILRTUZ	Lüderitz	
DEILRTVY	deviltry	
DEILSSTY	stylised	
DEILSTUY	sedulity	
DEILSTYZ	stylized	
DEILSWZZ	swizzled	
DEIMMNOS	demonism	
DEIMMOST	immodest	
DEIMMRST	midterms	
DEIMMRSU	drummies	
DEIMNNOY	Endymion	
DEIMNNSU	minuends	
DEIMNOOS	dominoes	

		monodies
DEIMNOOT	demotion	
	motioned	
DEIMNOOX	monoxide	
DEIMNOPT	piedmont	
DEIMNOST	demonist	
DEIMNOTW	downtime	
DEIMNPSS	misspend	
DEIMNPTU	impudent	
DEIMNRTU	rudiment	
DEIMNSST	mindsets	
DEIMOORS	moidores	
DEIMOOSS	sodomise	
DEIMOOST	moodiest	
	sodomite	
DEIMOOSZ	sodomize	
DEIMOPRS	impedors	
	promised	
DEIMOPRT	imported	
DEIMOPRV	improved	
DEIMOPST	imposted	
DEIMORRR	mirrored	
DEIMORST	mortised	
DEIMORSU	dimerous	
	soredium	
DEIMORUX	exordium	
DEIMOSST	modistes	
DEIMOSTT	demotist	
DEIMPSTU	dumpiest	
DEIMPSTY	mistyped	
DEIMQRSU	squirmed	
DEIMRSSU	surmised	
DEIMRSUU	residuum	
DEINNNOU	innuendo	
DEINNNPU	unpinned	
DEINNOOT	noontide	
DEINNOPT	endpoint	
DEINNORT	indentor	
DEINNORU	unironed	
DEINNOWW	winnowed	
DEINNPRU	underpin	
DEINNRUW	unwinder	
DEINNTUW	untwined	
DEINOOPS	poisoned	
	Poseidon	
DEINOOPT	optioned	
DEINOOSZ	ozonides	
	ozonised	
DEINOOTV	devotion	
DEINOOZZ	ozonized	
DEINOPPW	downpipe	
DEINOPRT	dipteron	
DEINOPRY	pyrenoid	
DEINOPSS	dopiness	
	spinodes	
DEINOPSU	unpoised	
DEINOPTW	dewpoint	
DEINORRS	indorser	
DEINORSS	indorses	
DEINORSU	sourdine	
DEINORSW	disowner	
	windrose	

DEINORVW overwind	**DEIRRSTU** sturdier	**DELOTUVY** devoutly
DEINOSSV voidness	**DEIRSSST** distress	**DELRSSTU** strudels
DEINOSSZ doziness	**DEIRSSTU** diestrus	**DELSSSTU** dustless
DEINOSTW downiest	**DEIRSTTU** detritus	**DEMMNOOO** monomode
DEINOSWZ downsize	**DEIRSUVV** survived	**DEMMNOSU** summoned
DEINPPRU unripped	**DEISSTTU** dustiest	**DEMMRRSU** drummers
DEINPPUZ unzipped	**DEISTTTU** duettist	**DEMMRRUU** murmured
DEINPRST sprinted	**DEKNORUW** unworked	**DEMMRSTU** strummed
DEINPSST stipends	**DEKNRSTU** drunkest	**DEMMNOOT** Edmonton
DEINQSTU squinted	**DEKOOPRV** provoked	**DEMNOOOP** monopode
DEINRRTU intruder	**DEKOOTWW** kowtowed	**DEMNOORU** unmoored
DEINRRSU sundries	**DEKOPSST** desktops	**DEMNOOSW** woodsmen
DEINRSTT strident	**DEKORSWY** keywords	**DEMNORST** mordents
tridents	**DELLLOOP** lolloped	**DEMNORSY** syndrome
DEINRSTU intrudes	**DELLNNOY** Donnelly	**DEMNOSTU** demounts
nurdiest	**DELLNOPU** unpolled	mudstone
DEINRSTX dextrins	**DELLNORU** unrolled	**DEMOOPPS** popedoms
DEINSSST dissents	**DELLNSSU** dullness	**DEMOOPRR** prodrome
DEINSSSY syndesis	**DELLOORS** Sordello	**DEMOOPRS** predooms
DEINSSTT dentists	**DELLOPRS** redpolls	**DEMOOPRT** promoted
DEINSTUU unsuited	**DELLOPTU** polluted	**DEMOORST** doomster
DEIOOORR Río de Oro	**DELLORRY** drollery	**DEMOORSU** dormouse
DEIOORSW woodsier	**DELLORSS** lordless	**DEMOORTY** odometry
DEIOOSSS isodoses	**DELLORST** strolled	**DEMOPPRT** prompted
DEIOOSTW woodiest	**DELLOSTY** oldstyle	**DEMORRUU** rumoured
DEIOPRRV provider	**DELMNORY** modernly	**DENNOSTY** syndeton
DEIOPRSS disposer	**DELMNOTW** meltdown	**DENNOTUW** unwonted
DEIOPRST diopters	**DELMNPUU** pendulum	**DENNRTUU** unturned
dioptres	**DELMORSS** smolders	**DENOOOTW** woodnote
riposted	**DELMORSU** moulders	**DENOOPPR** proponed
DEIOPRSV disprove	remoulds	**DENOORRS** endorsor
provides	smoulder	**DENOORTU** unrooted
DEIOPSSS disposes	**DELMOSTY** modestly	**DENOORTX** nextdoor
DEIOPSST deposits	**DELNNOOR** Londoner	**DENOOSTU** duotones
topsides	**DELNOOSU** nodulose	**DENOPPRS** propends
DEIORRSW drowsier	unloosed	**DENOPRSS** responds
DEIORRSY derisory	**DELNOOWY** woodenly	**DENOPRST** portends
DEIORRTU outrider	**DELNOPRS** splendor	**DENOPRSU** pounders
DEIORRTW worrited	**DELNORSU** roundels	**DENOPRUV** unproved
DEIORSSS dossiers	**DELNORSY** Reynolds	**DENOPSUX** expounds
DEIORSST steroids	**DELNORTU** roundlet	**DENOQTUU** unquoted
DEIORSSU desirous	**DELNORWW** New World	**DENORRSU** rondures
DEIORSSV devisors	**DELNOSSU** loudness	rounders
DEIORSTT dortiest	**DELNOSTW** letdowns	**DENORRSW** drowners
DEIORSTU outrides	**DELNOSUV** unsolved	**DENORSSU** dourness
outsider	**DELNPRSU** plunders	resounds
DEIORSTW rowdiest	**DELNRRTU** trundler	sounders
wordiest	**DELNRSTU** rundlets	**DENORSTU** roundest
DEIORSWW widowers	trundles	tonsured
DEIORTTX tetroxid	**DELOOPPS** pleopods	unsorted
DEIOSSTU outsides	**DELOORRV** overlord	**DENORSTY** drystone
DEIOSTTT dottiest	**DELOORSS** odorless	**DENORSUW** wounders
DEIOSTUZ outsized	**DELOORSV** oversold	**DENORTUW** undertow
DEIPPRST stripped	**DELOOSSW** woodless	**DENOSSTU** soundest
DEIPRRTU irrupted	**DELOPPST** stoppled	**DENPRTUU** upturned
DEIPRSSU suspired	**DELOPRST** droplets	**DENPSSSU** suspends
DEIPRSTU disputer	**DELOPSTU** postlude	**DENRRTUU** nurtured
stupider	**DELORSST** oldsters	**DENRSSSU** sundress
DEIPSSTU disputes	**DELORSSW** wordless	**DENSSTTU** students
DEIPTTTU tittuped	**DELORSTT** dottrels	**DENSTTUY** studenty
DEIQRSTU squirted	**DELORSUY** delusory	**DEOOORSW** rosewood
DEIRRSST striders	**DELOSSUU** sedulous	**DEOOPPRS** proposed

DEOOPPRT	pteropod	DFIOOPRS	disproof	DGIINORT	digitron
DEOOPRST	doorstep	DFLLOSSU	Dollfuss	DGIINOSX	digoxins
DEOOPRTU	uprooted	DFLMOSUW	mudflows	DGIINOTT	dittoing
DEOOPWWW	powwowed	DFLOOSTU	foldouts	DGIINOWW	widowing
DEOORRST	redroots	DFNOOPRU	profound	DGIINPPR	dripping
DEOORRSW	sorrowed	DFNOORSU	frondous	DGIINRST	striding
DEOORRVW	overword	DFOOOSTW	softwood	DGIINRTY	dirtying
DEOOSTWW	Westwood	DGGGIINS	diggings	DGIINVVY	divvying
DEOOTTUV	outvoted	DGGGINRU	drugging	DGIINYZZ	dizzying
DEOPPRRS	droppers		grudging	DGIJKNNO	Jongkind
DEOPPRST	stropped	DGGHIINT	dighting	DGIKLOOY	kidology
DEOPPRSU	purposed	DGGIILNR	girdling	DGIKMNOS	kingdoms
DEOPPSSU	supposed		ridgling	DGIKNOOR	drooking
DEOPRRTU	protrude	DGGIINNO	dingoing	DGIKNOOW	kingwood
DEOPRSTU	postured	DGGIINNR	grinding	DGIKNORU	drouking
	proudest	DGGIINNW	wingding	DGILLNOR	lordling
	sprouted	DGGIINSU	guidings	DGILLNOY	dollying
DEOPRSUU	uproused	DGGILNOP	plodding	DGILLOOW	goodwill
DEORRTTU	tortured	DGGILNOS	lodgings	DGILMNOS	moldings
DEORSSTW	worsteds	DGGIMNSU	smudging	DGILMNOU	moulding
DEORSSTY	destroys	DGGINNOT	Dongting	DGILMNPU	dumpling
DEORSTUX	dextrous	DGGINOST	stodging	DGILMSUY	smudgily
DEOSSSSU	Odysseus	DGGINRTU	trudging	DGILNNOO	noodling
DEOSSSYY	odysseys	DGGIRSTU	druggist	DGILNOOR	drooling
DEPPSSYY	dyspepsy	DGHIIMNT	midnight	DGILNORS	lordings
DEPRRTUU	ruptured	DGHIINSS	shindigs	DGILOSTY	stodgily
DERSTTTU	strutted	DGHIKNOO	kinghood	DGILRTUY	turgidly
DFFIIMRS	midriffs	DGHILLNU	dunghill	DGIMMNRU	drumming
DFFIIRST	triffids	DGHILNOS	holdings	DGIMMNUY	dummying
DFFIORSU	diffusor	DGHILNRU	hurdling	DGIMNNOU	mounding
DFFLOORU	fourfold	DGHILOOR	girlhood	DGIMNNOU	mounding
DFFOORUW	woodruff	DGHINNOU	hounding	DGINNOOS	snooding
DFGGHIOT	dogfight	DGHINOSW	showding	DGINNOPU	pounding
DFGHILOS	goldfish	DGHINSTU	hindguts	DGINNORU	rounding
DFGIIIRY	rigidify	DGHNOTUU	doughnut	DGINNORW	drowning
DFGIILRY	frigidly	DGHOOOTT	dogtooth	DGINNOSU	sounding
DFGIINNS	findings	DGHORRUY	roughdry		undoings
DFGIINRT	drifting	DGHORSTU	droughts	DGINNOUW	wounding
DFGILNNO	fondling	DGHORTUY	droughty	DGINOOPR	drooping
DFGILNOO	flooding	DGIIINNT	inditing	DGINOOPS	gospodin
DFGINNOU	founding	DGIIINNV	divining	DGINOOTU	outdoing
DFGINOOR	fordoing	DGIIINOS	iodising	DGINOPPR	dropping
DFGLNOOR	Longford	DGIIINOZ	iodizing	DGINORSW	drowsing
DFGNOOOS	son of God	DGIIIRTY	rigidity		wordings
DFHIIMUY	humidify	DGIIKLNN	kindling	DGINSSTU	dustings
DFHILSSU	dishfuls	DGIIKNNR	drinking	DGINSTUY	studying
DFHIMRSU	drumfish	DGIILLNR	drilling	DGISSSTU	disgusts
DFHLOOOT	foothold	DGIILLNU	illuding	DGLOOOSW	logwoods
DFHNOOUX	foxhound	DGIILLNW	wildling	DGLOOOXY	doxology
DFIILMTU	multifid	DGIILLOU	liguloid	DGLOOSST	godslots
DFIILOSY	solidify	DGIILMNP	dimpling	DGMOPRSU	gumdrops
DFIILRTU	Id-ul-Fitr	DGIILNNP	pindling	DGMOPSYY	gypsydom
DFIILTUY	fluidity	DGIILNSW	wildings	DGNOOOPS	gonopods
DFIINPRT	driftpin	DGIILNTU	diluting	DGNOOORS	godroons
DFIKNOOS	skinfood	DGIIMNOU	gonidium	DGNOOORV	Novgorod
DFILLOOT	floodlit	DGIIMNSS	smidgins	DHHILOTW	withhold
DFILLORY	floridly	DGIIMOSS	sigmoids	DHIIIMNS	diminish
DFILLOWW	wildfowl	DGIIMPUY	pygidium		minidish
DFILNNOU	nonfluid	DGIINNOP	poinding	DHIIMNOO	hominoid
DFILNOPS	pinfolds	DGIINNOR	nonrigid	DHIIMNOS	hominids
DFIMOOOR	iodoform	DGIINNSW	windings	DHIIMNSU	Hinduism
DFINRSUW	windsurf	DGIINORR	gridiron	DHIIMOST	isthmoid
				DHIIMPSS	midships

DHIIMTUY humidity	**DIILLSTY** idyllist	**DINOORRS** indorsor
DHIIOPSX xiphoids	**DIILMNSS** dislimns	**DINOOSTY** nodosity
DHIIORSS hidrosis	**DIILMOPP** pompilid	**DINOPRTY** drypoint
DHIIORSZ rhizoids	**DIILMUUV** diluvium	**DINORSWW** windrows
DHIJOPRU Jodhpuri	**DIILNNSU** indulins	**DINOSSUY** Dionysus
DHIKNOOW hoodwink	**DIILNOTU** dilution	**DINPRTUY** punditry
DHIKORSY hydroski	**DIILNTUY** untidily	**DINRSTUY** industry
DHILLNOW downhill	**DIILOPRT** triploid	**DIOORSTT** ridottos
DHILLOPY phylloid	**DIILOPSS** diplosis	**DIOPRSST** disports
DHILLPSY phyllids	**DIILORTU** utilidor	**DIORRSST** stridors
DHILMOPY lymphoid	**DIILOSST** idolists	**DIORSSTT** distorts
DHILMOSY modishly	**DIILOSTY** solidity	**DIOSSTUU** studious
DHILNOPS dolphins	**DIILRSSU** silurids	**DIPRSSTU** disrupts
DHILOPRS lordship	**DIILSSTY** idylists	**DIRSSTTU** distrust
DHILOPSS slipshod	**DIIMMNOU** dominium	**DKLNOOOW** lookdown
DHILORRY horridly	**DIIMMNOO** dominion	**DKMNOOOR** komondor
DHIMNOST hindmost	**DIIMNOPT** midpoint	**DKNORTUU** outdrunk
DHIMOPRS dimorphs	**DIIMNORS** midirons	**DKOOORWW** woodwork
DHIMORSU humidors	**DIIMNOSS** Sismondi	**DKORSTUW** studwork
DHIMOSTU Sidmouth	**DIIMNSUU** indusium	**DLLMORSU** slumlord
DHINOORS dishonor	**DIIMOPRS** prismoid	**DLNOOSUU** nodulous
DHINORSU roundish	**DIIMPUXY** pyxidium	**DLNOOSWW** lowdowns
DHINOTUW whodunit	**DIIMRUUV** duumviri	slowdown
DHINTUWY whydunit	**DIIMTTUY** tumidity	**DLNORTUY** rotundly
DHIOOPRZ rhizopod	**DIINNOSU** disunion	**DLOOOORS** doloroso
DHIORSTY thyroids	**DIINOOPS** iodopsin	**DLOOORSU** dolorous
thyrsoid	**DIINOSSU** sinusoid	**DLOOOSTW** woodlots
DHIPRSSY syrphids	**DIINSTUY** disunity	**DLOOPPSY** polypods
DHJOPRSU jodhpurs	**DIIORSST** sistroid	**DLOOPPUW** pulpwood
DHKMNOOO monkhood	**DIIORSSV** divisors	**DLOOPPYY** polypody
DHLMOOSU hoodlums	**DIJOSSTU** judoists	**DLOOPSTY** tylopods
DHLOOORY holy rood	**DIKLNNUY** unkindly	**DMNNOOOT** monodont
DHLOORSY hydrosol	**DIKNOPUV** Pudovkin	**DMOOORWW** woodworm
DHLOOSTU holdouts	**DIKNORTU** outdrink	wormwood
DHLORXYV hydroxyl	**DILLMNOP** millpond	**DMPPPUUY** mudpuppy
DHLOSSTU shouldst	**DILLOORS** doorsill	**DNNOORTU** Duntroon
DHMMRSUU humdrums	**DILLOSTY** stolidly	**DNNOOTWW** downtown
DHMNOOOT homodont	**DILLPSSY** psyllids	**DNNORSUW** rundowns
DHNNOOSU nunhoods	**DILMNOSW** slimdown	**DNNORTUW** downturn
DHNOOPRU Proudhon	**DILMNRSU** drumlins	turndown
DHNOOSWW showdown	**DILMOOSU** modiolus	**DNNOSSUW** sundowns
DHNOSTUW shutdown	**DILNOPST** diplonts	**DNOOPPRU** propound
DHOOORTX orthodox	**DILOOPPY** polypoid	**DNOOPRSW** snowdrop
DHOOPRST dropshot	**DILOOPRY** droopily	**DNOOPRSW** downpour
DHOORSUW woodrush	**DILOORSS** lordosis	**DNOORSUW** wondrous
DHOPRSSU pushrods	**DILOOSUY** odiously	**DNOOSTUW** nutwoods
DIIILLQU illiquid	**DILOPRTY** torpidly	**DNOPRSUU** roundups
DIIILTVY lividity	**DILORRTY** torridly	**DNORRSUU** surround
DIIIMOST idiotism	**DILORSWY** drowsily	**DOOOPRST** doorpost
DIIIMTTY timidity	**DILPRTUY** putridly	doorstop
DIIINOSV division	**DILPSTUY** stupidly	**DOOORSTU** outdoors
DIIINTVY divinity	**DILRSTUY** sturdily	**DOOORSUW** sourwood
DIIIPRST dispirit	**DIMMNORY** myrmidon	**DOOOSTTU** outstood
DIIIRTVY viridity	**DIMNOOST** monodist	**DOOPRRTW** dropwort
DIIJNOSS disjoins	**DIMNOPSU** impounds	**DOOPRSTU** dropouts
DIIJNOST disjoint	**DIMNOSTU** dismount	**EEEEFRRS** referees
DIIKKNSS kidskins	**DIMNOSWX** mixdowns	**EEEEFRRZ** refreeze
DIILLMNR millrind	**DIMOOPPU** Pompidou	**EEEEGGRR** greegree
DIILLMNW windmill	**DIMORSWY** rowdyism	**EEEEGHRT** Etherege
DIILLMPY limpidly	**DIMRSTUU** triduums	**EEEEGMRR** reemerge
DIILLQUY liquidly	**DIMRSUUV** duumvirs	**EEEEGQSU** squeegee
DIILLSST distills	**DINOOORW** ironwood	**EEEEGSSX** exegeses

EEEEGSTX	exegetes	EEEEGRSUX	exergues	EEEINRSW	weensier
EEEEHTTY	eyeteeth	EEEHHSSW	wheeshes	EEEINRTZ	eternize
EEEELLPX	expellee	EEEHILRW	erewhile	EEEINSTT	teeniest
EEEELLVY	eyelevel	EEEHILSW	wheelies	EEEINSTV	ventise
EEEELNSV	sleeveen	EEEHINSS	sheenies	EEEINSTW	tweenies
EEEELPRT	Peterlee	EEEHIRSS	heresies		weeniest
EEEENRRV	veneerer	EEEHIRST	etherise	EEEINTUX	euxenite
EEEEPTTW	peetweet	EEEHIRTZ	etherize	EEEINTVZ	eventize
EEEFFFOS	feoffees	EEEHIRWZ	wheezier	EEEIPRRV	reprieve
EEEFFLTY	effetely	EEEHKLNO	kneehole	EEEIPSST	epeeists
EEEFFNRT	efferent	EEEHLLSS	heelless	EEEIPSTW	weepiest
EEEFFORT	forefeet	EEEHLMPT	helpmeet	EEEIQSUX	exequies
EEEFFRVW	feverfew	EEEHLNTV	eleventh	EEEIRRST	retirees
EEEFGRSU	refugees	EEEHLNTY	ethylene	EEEIRRSV	reveries
EEEFINRT	Tenerife	EEEHLOPP	peephole	EEEIRRTV	retrieve
EEEFIPST	tepefies	EEEHLOSY	eyeholes	EEEIRRVW	reviewer
EEEFLRSX	reflexes	EEEHLRSW	wheelers	EEEIRTVX	exertive
EEEFLSST	feetless	EEEHMNSS	enmeshes	EEEISSTW	sweeties
EEEFNORS	foreseen	EEEHMNTV	vehement	EEEJKKNR	kneejerk
EEEFNRRT	referent	EEEHNNPT	nepenthe	EEEJLLRW	jeweller
EEEFNRSS	freeness	EEEHNNQU	henequen	EEEJLRSW	jewelers
EEEFNRUZ	unfreeze	EEEHNPRS	ensphere	EEEKLLSS	keelless
EEEFORRS	foreseer	EEEHNRVW	whenever	EEEKLLSU	ukeleles
EEEFORSS	foresees	EEEHORST	shoetree	EEEKLNRS	kneelers
EEEFRRRR	referrer	EEEHPRRT	threeper	EEEKLSST	sleekest
EEEFRRRT	ferreter	EEEHRRVW	wherever	EEEKMNSS	meekness
EEEFRRSZ	freezers	EEEHRSST	sheerest	EEEKNNSS	keenness
EEEFRRTT	fetterer	EEEHRSWZ	wheezers	EEEKNORS	kerosene
EEEGGILN	negligee	EEEHSSTT	esthetes	EEEKNPST	keepnets
EEEGHINT	eighteen	EEEIKLRT	treelike	EEEKNSTV	Kesteven
EEEGIKST	geekiest	EEEIKLSW	weeklies	EEEKRSST	keesters
EEEGILMN	liegemen	EEEILLRV	reveille	EEELLLRV	leveller
EEEGILNS	gleenies	EEEILMRS	seemlier	EEELLLSW	sewellel
EEEGILRT	gleetier	EEEILNPR	pelerine	EEELLNOU	enrollee
EEEGILSS	elegises	EEEILNRY	eyeliner	EEELLNQU	quenelle
EEEGILSZ	elegizes	EEEILNST	selenite	EEELLPRR	repeller
EEEGINNR	engineer	EEEILNSU	unseelie	EEELLPRX	expeller
EEEGINRS	energies	EEEILPRS	sleepier	EEELLRRV	reveller
	energise	EEEILRRV	reliever	EEELLRSV	levelers
	greenies	EEEILRST	leeriest	EEELMNST	elements
EEEGINRZ	energize	EEEILRSV	relieves	EEELMOPY	employee
EEEGIPRS	perigees	EEEILRVY	liveyere	EEELMOTT	omelette
EEEGIRTY	tigereye	EEEILSTV	televise	EEELMRTU	muleteer
EEEGISSX	exegesis	EEEIMNRU	meuniere	EEELNOPP	Penelope
EEEGISTV	egestive	EEEIMNRY	Niemeyer	EEELNOPV	envelope
EEEGKLRS	kegelers	EEEIMPRR	premiere	EEELNOSV	novelese
EEEGLNRT	greenlet	EEEIMPRS	emperies	EEELNRSW	newsreel
EEEGMNRT	emergent		epimeres	EEELNRSY	serenely
EEEGMNRU	merengue		preemies	EEELOPPR	repeople
EEEGMORT	geometer	EEEIMRRS	miserere	EEELPRSS	peerless
EEEGNPRS	epergnes	EEEIMRST	eremites		sleepers
EEEGNRRS	renegers	EEEIMRSZ	Mézières	EEELPSST	steeples
EEEGNRRU	reneguer	EEEIMRTT	remittee	EEELRRTT	letterer
EEEGNRRV	revenger	EEEINNNT	nineteen	EEELRSST	treeless
EEEGNRRY	greenery	EEEINNRT	internee	EEELRSTT	resettle
EEEGNRST	greenest		retinene	EEELRSTV	leverets
EEEGNRSU	renegues	EEEINNST	Estienne	EEELRSVY	severely
EEEGNRSV	revenges	EEEINNSV	Viennese	EEELTTTX	teletext
EEEGNSTT	genettes	EEEINPRT	perentie	EEEMMRUZ	mezereum
EEEGOPRT	protegee	EEEINRRS	sneerier	EEEMNNTT	tenement
EEEGRRST	greeters	EEEINRSS	eeriness	EEEMNORZ	mezereon
EEEGRSSS	egresses	EEEINRST	eternise	EEEMNPRT	petermen

EEEMNSTW	sweetmen	**EEERSTTW**	tweeters	**EEFIIMNZ**	feminize
EEEMORRV	evermore	**EEERSTVX**	vertexes	**EEFIINRS**	fineries
EEEMORST	stereome	**EEERSTWZ**	tweezers	**EEFIIRRS**	reifiers
EEEMPRRT	temperer	**EEESSTTW**	sweetest	**EEFIIRRV**	verifier
EEEMRSST	semester	**EEESTTTX**	sextette	**EEFIIRST**	feistier
EEEMRSTX	extremes	**EEFFFNOS**	enfeoffs		ferities
EEENNOPR	neoprene	**EEFFFORS**	feoffers		fieriest
EEENNOSV	venenose	**EEFFGIIS**	effigies	**EEFIIRSV**	verifies
EEENNSSV	evenness	**EEFFHIKY**	keffiyeh	**EEFIKLMU**	fumelike
EEENNSTT	ententes	**EEFFINST**	fifteens	**EEFIKLNR**	fernlike
EEENORSV	overseen	**EEFFISUV**	effusive	**EEFIKLRS**	serflike
	Veronese	**EEFFJRSY**	Jeffreys	**EEFIKNNP**	penknife
EEENORVY	everyone	**EEFFLNTU**	effluent	**EEFILLNY**	felinely
EEENPPRS	prepense	**EEFFMORR**	freeform	**EEFILLRW**	free will
EEENPRRS	preeners	**EEFFNOSS**	offenses		freewill
EEENPRRT	repenter	**EEFFORRS**	offerers	**EEFILLSS**	lifeless
EEENPRST	pretense	**EEFFORSX**	forfexes	**EEFILMNR**	riflemen
	terpenes	**EEFFRRSU**	sufferer	**EEFILMST**	fistmele
EEENPRSY	Pyrenees	**EEFGIILR**	filigree	**EEFILMTX**	flextime
EEENPSST	steepens	**EEFGILNR**	fleering	**EEFILNOS**	felonies
EEENPSSX	expenses	**EEFGILNS**	feelings		olefines
EEENRSS	sneerers	**EEFGILNT**	fleeting	**EEFILPRR**	pilferer
EEENRRST	enterers	**EEFGINNP**	pfennige	**EEFILRRT**	refilter
	reenters	**EEFGINNR**	fingerer	**EEFILRSS**	fireless
	terrenes	**EEFGINRS**	feigners	**EEFILRSU**	fusileer
EEENRRSW	renewers	**EEFGINRV**	fevering	**EEFILSST**	felsites
EEENRRTU	returnee	**EEFGINRZ**	freezing	**EEFILSSW**	wifeless
EEENRRTV	reverent	**EEFGLLNR**	Grenfell	**EEFIMMST**	femmiest
EEENRRUV	revenuer	**EEFGLLTU**	gefullte	**EEFIMORT**	foretime
EEENRSSZ	sneezers	**EEFGLMNU**	fuglemen	**EEFIMSTU**	tumefies
EEENRSTV	eventers	**EEFGLNRY**	greenfly	**EEFINNSS**	fineness
EEENRSTX	externes	**EEFGLNUV**	vengeful	**EEFINRRR**	inferrer
EEENRSTY	yestreen	**EEFGLORS**	forelegs	**EEFINRRS**	refiners
EEENRSUV	revenues	**EEFGLOSS**	solfeges	**EEFINRRY**	refinery
	unreeves	**EEFGNOOR**	foregone	**EEFINRSS**	rifeness
EEENSSTW	sweetens	**EEFGOORR**	foregoer	**EEFINRST**	infester
	tweeness	**EEFGOORS**	foregoes	**EEFINRSU**	reinfuse
EEEOPPSY	popeseye	**EEFGORRS**	reforges	**EEFINRSZ**	frenzies
EEEORRSV	overseer	**EEFHILLR**	hellfire	**EEFINSSS**	finesses
EEEORRSX	xerosere	**EEFHILRS**	fleshier	**EEFIPRSX**	prefixes
EEEORSSV	oversees	**EEFHIRSV**	feverish	**EEFIRRST**	ferrites
EEEORSSY	eyesores	**EEFHIRTY**	etherify	**EEFIRRSU**	surefire
EEEPRRST	pesterer	**EEFHISST**	fetishes	**EEFIRRVY**	reverify
EEEPRRSV	perverse	**EEFHISTT**	heftiest	**EEFIRSTT**	frisette
	preserve	**EEFHLLWY**	flywheel	**EEFIRSTY**	esterify
EEEPRRTW	pewterer	**EEFHLMST**	themself	**EEFIRTTZ**	frizette
EEEPRSST	steepers	**EEFHLRSS**	fleshers	**EEFISSTT**	festiest
EEEPRSSW	sweepers	**EEFHMNRS**	freshmen	**EEFKNORW**	foreknew
EEEPSSTT	steepest	**EEFHMORY**	Meyerhof	**EEFLLLNU**	fluellen
EEEPSTTT	septette	**EEFHNRSS**	freshens	**EEFLLNSS**	fellness
EEEQRSTU	queerest	**EEFHORRT**	therefor	**EEFLLORR**	El Ferrol
EEEQRSUZ	squeezer	**EEFHRRSS**	freshers	**EEFLLORT**	foretell
EEEQSSUZ	squeezes	**EEFHRRSU**	fuehrers	**EEFLLRSU**	fuellers
EEERRRSV	reserver	**EEFHRSST**	freshest	**EEFLLSSS**	selfless
	reverers		freshets	**EEFLMSSU**	fumeless
	reverser	**EEFIIKLL**	lifelike	**EEFLNORU**	fluorene
EEERRRTV	reverter	**EEFIIKLW**	wifelike	**EEFLNOST**	felstone
EEERRSST	steerers	**EEFIILLN**	lifeline	**EEFLNRSS**	flensers
EEERRSSV	reserves	**EEFIILMT**	lifetime		fresnels
	reverses	**EEFIIMNN**	feminine	**EEFLNRSU**	sneerful
EEERRSTT	resetter	**EEFIIMNS**	feminise	**EEFLNRTU**	refluent
EEERSSTW	sweerest			**EEFLNTUV**	eventful

EEFLORRW	flowerer	EEGHIIST	eighties		eulogise
	reflower	EEGHIKLY	Keighley	EEGILOUZ	eulogize
EEFLORTV	leftover	EEGHILNW	wheeling	EEGILQSU	squilgee
EEFLORTW	floweret	EEGHILRS	sleigher	EEGILRSV	veligers
EEFLORVW	overflew	EEGHINNS	sheening	EEGILRSV	verligte
EEFLORWW	werewolf	EEGHINRS	greenish	EEGILRTV	elegists
EEFLOSUX	flexuose		rehinges	EEGILSST	immerges
EEFLRRSU	ferrules		sheering	EEGIMMRS	meninges
EEFLRSST	fretless	EEGHINST	seething	EEGIMNNS	Nimwegen
EEFLRSTT	fettlers		sheeting	EEGIMNNW	regimens
EEFLRSTU	fleurets	EEGHINTT	teething	EEGIMNRS	metering
EEFLRSUX	flexures	EEGHINWZ	wheezing	EEGIMNRT	regiment
	refluxes	EEGHIOTT	goethite		meringue
EEFLSSSU	fuseless	EEGHIRST	Thesiger	EEGIMNRU	meetings
EEFMNORT	fomenter	EEGHIRSW	reweighs	EEGIMNST	preening
EEFMNRST	ferments		weighers	EEGINNPR	queening
EEFMORRR	reformer	EEGHIRTW	weighter	EEGINNQU	sneering
EEFMOSTT	mofettes	EEGHISST	sightsee	EEGINNRS	entering
EEFMPRRU	perfumer	EEGHISTY	eyesight	EEGINNRT	renewing
EEFMPRSU	perfumes	EEGHLNNT	lengthen	EEGINNRW	enginery
EEFNORRZ	refrozen	EEGHMNOY	hegemony	EEGINNRY	ingenues
EEFNORST	softener	EEGHMNSU	hegumens	EEGINNSU	unseeing
EEFNORTU	fourteen	EEGHMORT	geotherm		evenings
EEFNORTW	forewent	EEGHNOPS	phosgene	EEGINNSV	sneezing
	Freetown	EEGHNOPY	hypogene	EEGINNSZ	eventing
EEFNQRTU	frequent	EEGHNRSY	greyhens	EEGINNTV	epigones
EEFNRTTU	unfetter	EEGHNSTU	hugeness	EEGINOPS	erigeron
EEFOORRT	rooftree	EEGHOPTY	geophyte	EEGINORR	eringoes
EEFOPRRZ	prefroze	EEGHORTT	together	EEGINORS	egestion
EEFORRST	forester	EEGHOSTT	ghettoes	EEGINOST	speering
	fosterer	EEGIILNR	lingerie	EEGINPRS	petering
	reforest	EEGIILNV	inveigle	EEGINPRT	pureeing
EEFORRSU	ferreous	EEGIINNR	Nigerien	EEGINPRU	steeping
EEFORRTY	feretory	EEGIINNT	reignite	EEGINPST	sweeping
EEFORSUV	feverous	EEGIINTV	genitive	EEGINPSW	queering
EEFOSSTT	fossette	EEGIJLNW	jeweling	EEGINQRU	queueing
EEFOSSTU	foetuses	EEGIJMNN	Nijmegen	EEGINQUU	resigner
EEFOSTTU	fouettes	EEGIJNRS	jeerings	EEGINRRS	revering
EEFPRSSU	perfuses	EEGIJOPR	jerepigo	EEGINRRV	gentries
EEFRRSSU	refusers	EEGIKLLN	glenlike	EEGINRST	integers
EEFRRSTU	refuters	EEGIKLLU	gluelike		reesting
EEGGHLLS	eggshell	EEGIKLNN	kneeling		steering
EEGGHNOR	Honegger	EEGIKLNS	sleeking	EEGINRSU	seigneur
EEGGHSTU	thuggees	EEGIKNRY	rekeying	EEGINRSV	severing
EEGGIIOR	George II	EEGIKNST	kitenges	EEGINRSW	sewering
EEGGIJRR	rejigger	EEGILLNV	leveling		sweering
EEGGILNS	negliges	EEGILLRV	Greville	EEGINRTV	everting
EEGGILST	leggiest	EEGILNOR	eloigner	EEGINRTX	exerting
EEGGIMNR	emerging	EEGILNPS	peelings	EEGINSSU	geniuses
EEGGINNR	greening		sleeping	EEGINSTU	eugenist
	reneging	EEGILNRR	lingerer	EEGINSTV	steeving
EEGGINRT	greeting	EEGILNRS	leerings	EEGINSTW	sweeting
EEGGINST	egesting	EEGILNRU	reguline	EEGINTTW	tweeting
EEGGINSU	segueing	EEGILNRV	levering	EEGINTWZ	tweezing
EEGGIORV	George IV		reveling	EEGIOPSU	epigeous
	George VI	EEGILNST	gentiles	EEGIPRST	prestige
EEGGLOOR	geologer		sleeting	EEGIRRST	register
EEGGNORS	engorges		steeling	EEGIRRSV	grievers
EEGGORRS	regorges	EEGILNSV	sleeving	EEGIRSTT	grisette
EEGGPRRS	preggers	EEGILNTX	telexing	EEGISSTV	vestiges
EEGGPRSU	puggrees	EEGILOPU	epilogue	EEGKNORS	kerogens
EEGHHINT	heighten	EEGILOSU	eulogies		

EEGKNRSU	gerenuks		relishes	EEHLSSTW	thewless
EEGLMMSU	gemmules	EEHILSST	shelties	EEHMMOPR	morpheme
EEGLMNOR	Glen More	EEHILSUV	Hevelius	EEHMMORT	ohmmeter
EEGLMOSS	glosseme	EEHILTWY	Whiteley	EEHMNOPS	phonemes
EEGLNOPY	polygene	EEHILWYZ	wheezily	EEHMNORS	horsemen
EEGLNOSZ	lozenges	EEHIMMSS	immeshes	EEHMNOSU	housemen
EEGLNOTY	telegony	EEHIMNRT	theremin	EEHMNRSY	mynheers
EEGLNPRS	Spengler	EEHIMNSS	inmeshes	EEHMORST	theorems
EEGLNSTT	gentlest	EEHIMRRU	rheumier	EEHMORVW	whomever
EEGLOOST	Togolese	EEHIMRST	erethism	EEHMRSUX	exhumers
EEGMNOST	gemstone	EEHIMRTT	thermite	EEHNNOOT	ethonone
EEGMNSST	segments	EEHINNQU	henequin	EEHNNORT	enthrone
EEGMNTTU	tegument		heniquen	EEHNNOSS	shoneens
EEGMORSU	gruesome	EEHINNRS	enshrine	EEHNOPRU	hereupon
EEGMORSW	grewsome	EEHINNRT	inherent	EEHNOPTY	neophyte
EEGMORTY	geometry	EEHINORS	heroines	EEHNORST	Hortense
EEGMRSTU	gumtrees		nosherie	EEHNORTU	hereunto
EEGNNORT	roentgen	EEHINORT	hereinto	EEHNPRSU	unsphere
EEGNNOSV	evensong	EEHINPRS	insphere	EEHNPSTU	Pentheus
EEGNOPTY	genotype	EEHINPRT	nephrite	EEHNSSTU	enthuses
EEGNORST	estrogen		trephine	EEHNSSTV	sevenths
EEGNORSU	generous	EEHINPSX	phenixes	EEHOOPRS	oosphere
EEGNORSY	eryngoes	EEHINRRS	errhines	EEHOOPSW	whoopees
EEGNOTYZ	zygotene	EEHINRTT	thirteen	EEHOORSV	overshoe
EEGNPRUX	expunger	EEHINRTW	whitener	EEHOOTTY	eyetooth
EEGNPSUX	expunges	EEHIORST	isothere	EEHOPPSW	peepshow
EEGNRSSY	greyness		theories	EEHOPRSU	euphroes
EEGNRSUY	guernsey		theorise	EEHORRSV	hoverers
EEGNRTUV	Turgenev	EEHIORTZ	theorize	EEHORRTX	exhorter
EEGOPRST	proteges	EEHIPPST	psephite	EEHORSSU	rehouses
EEGOPRSU	superego	EEHIPPTY	epiphyte	EEHPRSTU	superhet
EEGORRRU	Guerrero	EEHIPRSS	perishes	EEHPRSTY	hypester
EEGORRVW	overgrew	EEHIPRTT	tephrite	EEHRRSTW	wherrets
EEGORSSS	ogresses	EEHIPSTT	epithets	EEHRSSTW	wershest
EEGRRSSU	resurges	EEHIQRSU	queerish	EEHRSTTW	whetters
EEGRRSTU	gesturer	EEHIRRSS	sherries	EEHSSTTY	Thyestes
EEGRRSUY	gruyeres	EEHIRRSV	shiverer	EEIIIPRT	Peter III
EEGRSSSU	guessers	EEHIRRSW	wherries	EEIIKLLN	linelike
EEGRSSTU	gestures	EEHIRRTW	witherer	EEIIKLLR	likelier
EEHHIPSS	sheepish	EEHIRSST	heisters	EEIIKLLV	veillike
EEHHIRTW	herewith	EEHIRSSV	shrieves	EEIIKLNV	veinlike
EEHHKLOT	Koheleth	EEHIRTVY	thievery		vinelike
EEHHLLLO	hellhole	EEHISSTW	sweetish	EEIIKLRW	wirelike
EEHHNOSU	henhouse	EEHKLOSY	keyholes	EEIIKLSV	viselike
EEHHRRST	thresher	EEHKLOWY	Holy Week	EEIIKLSW	likewise
EEHHRSST	threshes	EEHKOOSY	eyehooks	EEIILLMM	millieme
EEHHSSTW	wheeshts	EEHLLMSS	helmless	EEIILLOP	eolipile
EEHIIKLV	hivelike	EEHLLPSS	helpless	EEIILLRV	livelier
EEHIKLMO	homelike	EEHLMMNS	helmsmen	EEIILMNT	ilmenite
EEHIKLMP	hemplike	EEHLMOSS	homeless		melinite
EEHIKLWY	wheylike	EEHLNOSW	Henslowe		menilite
EEHIKNNT	Kenneth I	EEHLNOTT	telethon		timeline
EEHIKRRS	shrieker	EEHLOPSS	hopeless	EEIILMRT	timelier
EEHILLMS	shlemiel	EEHLOPST	heelpost	EEIILNPP	pipeline
EEHILLNP	helpline	EEHLORST	hosteler	EEIILNST	lenities
EEHILMNS	hemlines	EEHLORSV	shoveler	EEIILNTV	lenitive
EEHILMNU	helenium	EEHLOSTY	holeyest	EEIILRSV	liveries
EEHILMOR	homelier	EEHLPRST	telphers	EEIILSTV	levities
EEHILNPW	pinwheel	EEHLPRSU	spherule	EEIILSTW	lewisite
EEHILORT	hotelier	EEHLRSST	shelters	EEIIMMTT	mimetite
EEHILPRT	herptile	EEHLRSSV	shelvers	EEIIMNST	enmities
EEHILRSS	heirless	EEHLRSSW	welshers	EEIIMOST	moieties

EEIIMPRS	riempies	EEILLLMV	Melville	EEILPPSS	pipeless
EEIIMRSS	miseries	EEILLMPR	impeller	EEILPPSY	epilepsy
EEIIMRTZ	itemizer	EEILLMRS	smellier	EEILPRRS	repliers
EEIIMSST	itemises	EEILLMSS	smellies	EEILPRSS	spielers
EEIIMSSV	emissive	EEILLNOR	lonelier	EEILPRST	epistler
EEIIMSTZ	itemizes	EEILLNSY	senilely		peltries
EEIINNST	einstein	EEILLORV	lovelier		reptiles
	nineties	EEILLOSV	lovelies		spirelet
EEIINNTV	Ninevite	EEILLPSS	ellipses	EEILPSSS	pelisses
EEIINPPR	piperine	EEILLPSY	sleepily	EEILPSST	epistles
EEIINPRS	pineries	EEILLSSV	veilless	EEILPSSV	pelvises
EEIINPRV	viperine	EEILLTVY	velleity	EEILPSTY	epistyle
EEIINRRV	riverine	EEILMNNO	limonene	EEILQRSU	reliques
EEIINRST	niteries	EEILMNNS	linesmen	EEILRRSV	revilers
EEIINRSV	vineries	EEILMNRU	lemurine		silverer
EEIINRSW	wineries		relumine	EEILRSST	leisters
EEIINRTT	retinite	EEILMNSU	selenium		tireless
EEIINRTV	reinvite	EEILMNTY	Mytilene	EEILRSSW	wireless
EEIINSSV	inessive	EEILMRSS	rimeless	EEILRSTT	retitles
EEIINSTT	entities	EEILMSST	timeless	EEILRSVY	liveyers
EEIIOPTZ	epizoite	EEILMSUV	emulsive	EEILSSTX	sextiles
EEIIPRSX	expiries	EEILNNST	sentinel	EEILSSVW	viewless
EEIIQSTU	equities	EEILNNSV	enlivens	EEILSTTX	textiles
EEIIRRSV	rivieres	EEILNOPR	leporine	EEIMMORS	memories
EEIIRSTV	verities	EEILNORS	eloiners		memorise
EEIISTVW	viewiest		Elsinore	EEIMMORZ	memorize
EEIJKRST	jerkiest	EEILNOSV	novelise	EEIMMOST	sometime
EEIJLNNU	julienne	EEILNOVZ	novelize	EEIMMRRS	immerser
EEIJLNRT	jetliner	EEILNPPZ	zeppelin	EEIMMRSS	immerses
EEIJLNUV	juvenile	EEILNPRS	pilsener	EEIMMRST	meristem
EEIJNNOR	enjoiner	EEILNPRU	perilune	EEIMNNOS	nominees
EEIKKLRS	Kirklees	EEILNPRV	replevin	EEIMNNRS	reinsmen
EEIKKNRS	Kerenski	EEILNPST	plenties	EEIMNOPT	Piemonte
EEIKKRST	kerkiest	EEILNQUY	equinely	EEIMNORS	emersion
EEIKLLSS	skellies	EEILNRST	enlister	EEIMNORV	vomerine
EEIKLMST	stemlike		Leinster	EEIMNOST	monetise
EEIKLNOS	noselike		listener		semitone
EEIKLNOV	ovenlike	EEILNRSV	liveners	EEIMNOTZ	monetize
EEIKLNSS	likeness	EEILNRTY	entirely		zonetime
EEIKLNST	nestlike		lientery	EEIMNPRS	spermine
EEIKLNTT	tentlike	EEILNSST	setlines	EEIMNPRU	perineum
EEIKLORS	roselike	EEILNSSV	evilness	EEIMNRTU	mutineer
EEIKLORT	lorikeet		veinless	EEIMNRTV	virement
EEIKLPST	pikelets		vileness	EEIMNSUV	Museveni
	spikelet		vineless	EEIMOPRS	promisee
	steplike	EEILNSSW	wineless		reimpose
EEIKLRRS	Kreisler	EEILNSTT	entitles	EEIMOPSS	episomes
EEIKLRST	triskele	EEILNSTV	veinlets	EEIMOPST	epitomes
EEIKLSTV	vestlike	EEILNSUV	veinules	EEIMORST	tiresome
EEIKMOTX	ketoxime	EEILNSVY	Yvelines	EEIMORTV	overtime
EEIKMPST	kempiest	EEILOPST	petioles	EEIMOSSW	somewise
EEIKNORS	kerosine	EEILORRT	loiterer	EEIMPRRS	premiers
EEIKNORV	reinvoke	EEILORST	Tirolese		simperer
EEIKNOTW	Eniwetok	EEILORSV	overlies	EEIMPRSS	emprises
EEIKNPSY	pinkeyes		relievos		impreses
EEIKNRRT	tinkerer	EEILORVV	overlive		premises
EEIKOQUV	equivoke	EEILOSSX	isolexes		spiremes
EEIKPRST	perkiest	EEILOSTW	owelties	EEIMPRST	emptiers
EEIKPSST	peskiest	EEILOSTZ	zeolites	EEIMPRSX	premixes
EEIKRRSS	skerries	EEILOSVW	vowelise	EEIMPSTT	emptiest
EEIKRSST	keisters	EEILOTTT	toilette	EEIMQRSU	requiems
EEIKSTTT	tektites	EEILOVWZ	vowelize	EEIMQSTU	mesquite

EEIMRRST	merriest	**EEINRSTX**	intersex	**EEIRRSST**	resister
	rimester	**EEINRSTY**	serenity	**EEIRRSSV**	revisers
	triremes	**EEINRSUV**	universe	**EEIRRSTV**	riveters
EEIMRRTT	remitter	**EEINRTTY**	entirety	**EEIRRSTW**	rewrites
	trimeter		eternity	**EEIRRSVV**	revivers
EEIMRSTT	emitters	**EEINSSSW**	wiseness	**EEIRRTTT**	titterer
	termites	**EEINSSSX**	sexiness	**EEIRSSSU**	reissues
EEIMRSTU	emeritus	**EEINSSTW**	newsiest	**EEIRSSTU**	sureties
EEIMRTTY	temerity	**EEINSSTX**	sixteens	**EEIRSSTV**	sieverts
EEIMSSST	messiest	**EEINSTTW**	twenties		vestries
	metisses	**EEINSTTX**	existent	**EEIRSSTW**	sweirest
EEINNNPS	pennines	**EEIOPRRT**	portiere	**EEIRSSUZ**	seizures
EEINNPTT	penitent	**EEIOPRRV**	overripe	**EEIRSTVV**	vetivers
EEINNRST	intenser	**EEIOPSST**	poetises	**EEIRSTVY**	severity
	internes	**EEIOPSTZ**	poetizes	**EEIRTTTZ**	terzetti
EEINNRSV	innerves	**EEIORRRS**	orreries	**EEISSTTT**	testiest
	nervines	**EEIORRSS**	roseries	**EEJJLNUY**	jejunely
EEINNRTT	renitent	**EEIORRTV**	overtire	**EEJKNRTU**	junketer
EEINNRTV	reinvent	**EEIORRTX**	exterior	**EEJLPSTU**	pulsejet
EEINNSTT	sentient	**EEIORSST**	erotesis	**EEJNORSY**	enjoyers
EEINNSTW	entwines	**EEIORSVW**	overwise	**EEJPRRRU**	perjurer
EEINOPPR	ronepipe	**EEIORSVZ**	oversize	**EEJPRRSU**	perjures
EEINOPRS	isoprene	**EEIORVVW**	overview	**EEKKKNNO**	Kekkonen
	pioneers	**EEIORVWW**	wirewove	**EEKKORWW**	workweek
EEINORRT	reorient	**EEIPPPRS**	preppies	**EEKKRRST**	trekkers
EEINORST	serotine	**EEIPPPST**	peppiest	**EEKLLNNY**	Kennelly
EEINORSV	eversion	**EEIPPQRU**	equipper	**EEKLLSUU**	ukuleles
EEINORTT	tenorite	**EEIPPRRS**	perspire	**EEKLNNNU**	unkennel
EEINORTX	exertion	**EEIPPRST**	peptiser	**EEKLNOSS**	keelsons
EEINOSST	essonite	**EEIPPRTY**	peripety	**EEKLNOST**	skeleton
EEINOSTT	noisette	**EEIPPRTZ**	peptizer	**EEKLORST**	Koestler
	teosinte	**EEIPPSST**	peptises	**EEKLOSSY**	yokeless
EEINPRRS	ripeners	**EEIPPSTT**	pipettes	**EEKLRSST**	kestrels
EEINPRSS	ripeness	**EEIPPSTZ**	peptizes	**EEKMOORV**	Kemerovo
EEINPRSU	resupine	**EEIPQRSU**	reequips	**EEKNNSTT**	kennetts
EEINPRTX	inexpert		repiques	**EEKNOSTY**	keynotes
EEINQRRU	enquirer	**EEIPRRRS**	perriers		keystone
EEINQRSU	enquires	**EEIPRRSS**	priseres	**EEKNSSSW**	skewness
	squireen		reprises	**EEKNSSTU**	netsukes
EEINQSTU	quietens		respires	**EEKORRSV**	revokers
EEINRRST	inserter	**EEIPRRSX**	expirers	**EEKRRSUZ**	kreuzers
	reinsert	**EEIPRRTT**	preterit	**EEKRRTUZ**	kreutzer
	reinters		prettier	**EELLLLMP**	pellmell
	rentiers	**EEIPRSSS**	pressies	**EELLMORW**	mellower
	terrines	**EEIPRSST**	respites	**EELLMRSS**	smellers
EEINRRSU	reinsure	**EEIPRSSV**	previses	**EELLNORR**	enroller
EEINRRSV	verniers	**EEIPRSTT**	pretties	**EELLNPRU**	prunelle
EEINRRTU	reuniter	**EEIPRSTX**	preexist	**EELLNSSW**	wellness
EEINRRTV	inverter	**EEIPRSVW**	previews	**EELLNSTU**	entellus
EEINRRTW	winterer	**EEIPRSZZ**	prezzies	**EELLORST**	solleret
EEINRRTX	interrex	**EEIPRTUV**	eruptive	**EELLORSV**	oversell
EEINRSST	sentries	**EEIPSSTW**	stepwise	**EELLORTX**	extoller
EEINRSSU	enuresis	**EEIPSTTT**	pettiest	**EELLORVY**	volleyer
EEINRSSV	inverses	**EEIQRRRU**	requirer	**EELLORWY**	yellower
EEINRSTT	insetter	**EEIQRRSU**	requires	**EELLOSSS**	soleless
	interest	**EEIQRRTU**	requiter	**EELLOSSV**	loveless
EEINRSTU	esurient	**EEIQRRUV**	quiverer	**EELLOSWY**	Wolseley
	retinues	**EEIQRSSU**	esquires	**EELLPRSS**	presells
	reunites	**EEIQRSTU**	requites		spellers
EEINRSTV	nerviest	**EEIQSTTU**	quietest	**EELLQRSU**	quellers
	reinvest	**EEIRRRST**	retirers	**EELMMPUX**	exemplum
	sirvente		terriers	**EELMNOOS**	lonesome

	oenomels	**EELOSSTT**	teleosts	**EEMPRSTT**	tempters
EELMNSUY	unseemly	**EELOSSTV**	vetoless	**EEMPRSTU**	permutes
EELMNTUY	unmeetly		voteless	**EEMPSSTT**	tempests
EELMOPRY	employer	**EELOSTUV**	evolutes	**EEMRRSSU**	resumers
	reemploy		veloutes	**EEMRRTTU**	mutterer
EELMOPSY	employes	**EELPPSSU**	pepluses	**EEMSSTTU**	musettes
EELMORST	molester	**EELPPSTU**	septuple	**EENNNOSS**	nonsense
EELMORSW	eelworms	**EELPQRSU**	prequels	**EENNNOTV**	nonevent
EELMORTY	remotely	**EELPRRSU**	repulser	**EENNNPTY**	tenpenny
EELMOTVW	twelvemo	**EELPRSSU**	repulses	**EENNOORT**	rotenone
EELMPSTT	templets	**EELPRSTZ**	pretzels	**EENNOPSS**	openness
EELMRRTU	murrelet	**EELPRTXY**	expertly	**EENNOPTX**	exponent
EELMRSST	smelters	**EELPSSUX**	plexuses	**EENNORST**	tenoners
	termless		suplexes	**EENNORSU**	neurones
EELMRSTY	smeltery	**EELPSTUX**	sextuple	**EENNRSUV**	unnerves
EELNNOSS	loneness	**EELRRSTW**	wrestler	**EENOORST**	oestrone
EELNNRTU	tunneler	**EELRSSST**	restless	**EENOORTU**	euronote
EELNNUVY	unevenly	**EELRSSTT**	settlers	**EENOORTV**	overtone
EELNOORS	loosener		sterlets	**EENOPPST**	peptones
EELNOPPU	unpeople		trestles	**EENOPRSS**	response
EELNOPRT	petronel	**EELRSSTU**	streusel	**EENOPRST**	Peterson
EELNOPSV	envelops	**EELRSSTW**	swelters	**EENOPRTT**	entrepot
EELNOPSY	polyenes		wrestles	**EENOPRXY**	pyroxene
EELNOPTY	polytene	**EELRSSTY**	restyles	**EENOPSST**	pentoses
EELNOQTU	eloquent	**EELRSTWY**	westerly	**EENOPSTY**	neotypes
EELNORST	entresol	**EELSSSTV**	vestless	**EENORSSS**	soreness
EELNORUV	von Euler	**EELSSSTZ**	zestless	**EENORSSU**	neuroses
EELNOSSS	noseless	**EELSSTTX**	textless	**EENORSTX**	extensor
	soleness	**EEMMNORT**	Mentmore	**EENORSVW**	oversewn
EELNOSST	noteless	**EEMMNOST**	mementos	**EENOSSST**	stenoses
	toneless	**EEMMNOTV**	movement	**EENOSTUV**	ventouse
EELNOSSU	selenous	**EEMMNRRY**	merrymen	**EENPPRST**	perpents
EELNOSTT	notelets	**EEMMOSST**	mestomes	**EENPRSST**	pertness
EELNRSST	nestlers	**EEMMRSST**	stemmers		presents
	slenters	**EEMMNOPR**	prenomen		serpents
EELNSSSW	newsless	**EEMNNOSV**	envenoms	**EENPRSSU**	Preussen
EELNSSTT	tentless	**EEMNOOSY**	mooneyes		pureness
	unsteels	**EEMNORSY**	moneyers	**EENPRSTV**	prevents
EELNSSTV	ventless	**EEMNORTY**	Monterey	**EENPSSSU**	suspense
EELNSTTU	lunettes	**EEMNPRSS**	pressmen	**EENPSTTU**	petuntse
	unsettle	**EEMNPRSU**	supermen	**EENPTTUZ**	petuntze
EELOPPSS	peploses	**EEMNPRTU**	erumpent	**EENQSSTU**	sequents
EELOPPST	estoppel	**EEMNRSTU**	muenster	**EENRRRTU**	returner
EELOPRRX	explorer	**EEMNSSTU**	muteness	**EENRRSSU**	ensurers
EELOPRSX	explores		tenesmus	**EENRRSUV**	nervures
EELOPRTT	teleport	**EEMNSTTV**	vestment	**EENRRTUV**	venturer
EELOPSTU	eelpouts	**EEMOOPRT**	proteome	**EENRSSSU**	sureness
	sleepout	**EEMOORRT**	orometer	**EENRSSTT**	sternest
EELORRSV	resolver	**EEMOORRV**	moreover	**EENRSSTU**	trueness
EELORRTV	revolter	**EEMOORTT**	roomette	**EENRSSTW**	westerns
EELORRTW	troweler	**EEMOPRRS**	emperors	**EENRSTUV**	ventures
EELORRUV	overrule		premorse	**EEOOPRST**	proteose
EELORRVV	revolver	**EEMOPRSW**	empowers	**EEOOPRSX**	exospore
EELORSSV	resolves	**EEMOQRSU**	moresque	**EEOOPRTZ**	zoetrope
EELORSTU	resolute	**EEMOQTTU**	moquette	**EEOPPSTT**	popettes
EELORSTY	Tyrolese	**EEMORRSV**	removers	**EEOPRRRT**	reporter
EELORSVV	evolvers	**EEMORSST**	somerset	**EEOPRRRV**	reprover
	revolves	**EEMORSTT**	remotest	**EEOPRRSS**	reposers
EELORTTU	roulette	**EEMOTTTU**	teetotum	**EEOPRRSV**	reproves
EELORTUV	revolute	**EEMPPRST**	preempts	**EEOPRRTT**	potterer
	truelove	**EEMPRRSU**	presumer	**EEOPRRTX**	exporter
		EEMPRSSU	presumes		reexport

EEOPRSSS	espresso	EFFHIILS	filefish	EFGIILRU	uglifier
EEOPRSSU	espouser	EFFHIIRW	whiffier	EFGIILSU	uglifies
	repousse	EFFHIISW	fishwife	EFGIINNR	infringe
EEOPRSSX	exposers	EFFHIITT	fiftieth		refining
	expresso	EFFHILRW	whiffler	EFGIINNT	feinting
EEOPRSTV	overstep	EFFHILSW	whiffles	EFGIINRR	refiring
EEOPRSTY	serotype	EFFHIRRS	Sherriff	EFGIINRU	figurine
EEOPRSUX	exposure	EFFHIRSS	sheriffs	EFGIINRY	reifying
EEOPSSSU	espouses	EFFHIRSW	whiffers	EFGIITUV	fugitive
EEOPSSTW	sweetsop	EFFHISTU	huffiest	EFGIKLLU	gulflike
EEOPSSTY	eyespots	EFFHLRSU	shuffler	EFGILLNO	lifelong
EEORRRST	resorter	EFFHLSSU	shuffles	EFGILLNU	fuelling
	restorer	EFFHOORS	offshore	EFGILLUU	guileful
	retrorse	EFFIIMST	miffiest	EFGILNNS	flensing
EEORRRTT	retorter	EFFIINRS	sniffier	EFGILNOR	florigen
EEORRSST	restores	EFFIINST	niffiest	EFGILNRS	flingers
EEORRSSV	reversos	EFFIIPRS	spiffier	EFGILNRU	feruling
EEORRSTU	reroutes	EFFIKLRU	rufflike	EFGILNRY	ferlying
EEORRSTV	evertors	EFFILNRS	sniffler	EFGILNTT	fettling
EEORRSTX	extrorse	EFFILNSS	sniffles	EFGILNTW	leftwing
EEORRTTT	totterer	EFFILRRS	rifflers	EFGILPRU	fireplug
EEORRTTX	extorter	EFFINOSU	effusion	EFGILSST	giftless
EEORRTUV	overture	EFFINRSS	sniffers	EFGIMNST	figments
	trouvere	EFFINRSU	snuffier	EFGIMOSY	fogeyism
EEORSSTT	rosettes	EFFINSST	stiffens	EFGIMRUU	refugium
EEORSSTV	estovers	EFFIORST	forfeits	EFGINNPS	pfennigs
	oversets	EFFIPSTU	puffiest	EFGINORV	forgiven
EEORSSUV	overuses	EFFIRSTU	stuffier	EFGINORW	forewing
EEORSSVW	oversews	EFFISSTT	stiffest	EFGINRRY	ferrying
EEORSTVX	vortexes	EFFISSUX	suffixes		refrying
EEORTTTZ	terzetto	EFFLMNUU	unmuffle	EFGINRSU	refusing
EEPPRSST	steppers	EFFLMRSU	mufflers	EFGINRTT	fretting
EEPPSSUW	upsweeps	EFFLNRSU	snuffler	EFGINRTU	refuting
EEPRRSSU	perusers	EFFLNSSU	snuffles	EFGIOOST	goofiest
	pressure	EFFLOSSU	souffles	EFGIOPTT	pettifog
EEPRRSTV	perverts	EFFLRRSU	rufflers	EFGIORRV	forgiver
EEPRRTTU	putterer	EFFLRSTU	truffles	EFGIORSV	forgives
EEPRSSTT	pretests	EFFNRSSU	snuffers	EFGIRRSU	figurers
EEPRSSUX	supersex	EFFOOORT	forefoot	EFGLOOVX	foxglove
EEPRSTTU	upsetter	EFFOORRS	offerors	EFGNORSU	Ferguson
EEPRSTTX	pretexts	EFFOPRRS	proffers	EFGNSSUU	funguses
EEPSSTTY	typesets	EFFRRSUU	furfures	EFGOORRS	forgoers
EEQRSSTU	questers	EFFRSSTU	stuffers	EFGORSTU	foreguts
	requests	EFFSSSUU	suffuses	EFHIIKLS	fishlike
EERRSSTU	tressure	EFGGIINN	feigning		fleishik
EERRSSTW	strewers	EFGGILOS	solfeggi	EFHIILMN	Niflheim
	wresters	EFGGINRU	refuging	EFHIILRT	filthier
EERRSSVW	swervers	EFGGIOST	foggiest	EFHIILST	tilefish
EERRSTTU	utterers	EFGGISTU	fuggiest	EFHIIMSU	humifies
EERRSUVY	resurvey	EFGGLORS	floggers	EFHIINRS	finisher
EERSSSST	stresses	EFGHHIIL	highlife		refinish
EERSSTTU	trustees	EFGHIILS	fleishig	EFHIINSS	finishes
EERSSTUV	Servetus	EFGHILNS	fleshing	EFHIIPPS	pipefish
	vestures		shelfing	EFHIIPRS	fireship
EERSTTUX	textures	EFGHINRS	freshing	EFHIIRST	shiftier
EFFFGINO	feoffing	EFGHINRT	frighten	EFHIISST	fishiest
EFFFILRU	fluffier	EFGHINSU	feng shui	EFHIKLOO	hooflike
EFFFLRSU	fluffers	EFGHIOSY	fogeyish	EFHILLSY	elfishly
EFFFOORS	feoffors	EFGHIRST	fighters	EFHILTWY	whitefly
EFFGINOR	offering		freights	EFHINSST	fishnets
EFFGINSU	effusing	EFGIILNR	refiling	EFHIORRT	frothier
EFFGRSTU	gruffest	EFGIILNU	figuline	EFHIORSS	rosefish

EFHIORSV	overfish	EFIKLLOW	wolflike	EFIMOSST	semisoft
EFHIORTT	fortieth	EFIKLMOR	foremilk	EFIMOSTT	ofttimes
EFHIPRSU	furphies	EFIKLNSU	flunkies	EFIMRSTU	fremitus
EFHIRRTU	thurifer	EFIKLOOR	rooflike	EFINNORS	infernos
EFHIRSST	shifters	EFIKLORS	folksier	EFINNPSU	finespun
EFHISSTU	shufties	EFIKLRSU	surflike	EFINNSTU	funniest
EFHKLNOU	funkhole	EFIKLSTU	flukiest	EFINOPTX	pontifex
EFHLNORS	hornfels	EFIKNORS	foreskin	EFINORRT	frontier
EFHLOOSS	hoofless	EFIKNRSU	refusnik	EFINORRU	Fournier
EFHLOOSX	foxholes	EFIKNSTU	funkiest	EFINORTY	renotify
EFHLOPSU	hopefuls	EFIKORRW	firework	EFINOSSX	foxiness
EFHLORSY	horsefly	EFIKRRSS	friskers	EFINRSST	snifters
EFHLOSUU	houseful	EFIKRSST	friskets	EFINRSSU	infusers
EFHLOSUY	housefly	EFILLLNU	fluellin	EFIOOPST	poofiest
EFHLRSSU	flushers	EFILLMOR	Fillmore	EFIOPRRT	portfire
EFHLSTTW	twelfths	EFILLORV	overfill		profiter
EFHOORSW	foreshow	EFILLOSW	lowlifes	EFIORRST	frostier
EFHRRSTU	furthers	EFILLRUY	irefully		rotifers
EFHRSTTU	furthest	EFILLSTY	stellify	EFIORRSW	frowsier
EFIIILRV	vilifier	EFILLTUY	futilely	EFIORRTT	retrofit
EFIIILSV	vilifies	EFILMNOS	foilsmen	EFIORRUZ	frouzier
EFIIIMNS	minifies	EFILMSST	filmsets	EFIORRWZ	frowzier
EFIIINNT	infinite	EFILMSUY	emulsify	EFIPPRRY	frippery
EFIIIRVV	vivifier	EFILNNTU	influent	EFIPPRST	frippets
EFIIISTX	fixities	EFILNORU	fluorine	EFIPPRUY	repurify
EFIIISVV	vivifies	EFILNSUX	influxes	EFIPRSST	presifts
EFIIKRRS	friskier	EFILOOSS	floosies	EFIPRSUX	superfix
EFIILLNT	tefillin	EFILOOSZ	floozies	EFIPRTTY	prettify
EFIILMRS	flimsier	EFILOPPR	floppier	EFIRRRSU	furriers
EFIILMST	filmiest	EFILOPPS	floppies	EFIRRRUY	furriery
EFIILNRT	flintier	EFILOPRR	profiler	EFIRRSSU	friseurs
EFIILNTY	felinity	EFILOPRS	profiles	EFIRRSTT	fritters
	finitely	EFILORRV	frivoler	EFIRRSTU	fruiters
EFIILRST	filister	EFILORSS	flossier		furriest
EFIILRSU	fusilier	EFILORST	trefoils	EFIRRSZZ	frizzers
EFIIMMNS	feminism	EFILORTU	fluorite	EFIRSSSU	fissures
EFIIMNST	feminist	EFILOSTT	loftiest	EFIRSSTU	surfeits
EFIIMRSS	misfires	EFILOSTU	outflies	EFIRSSTW	swifters
EFIINNOS	sinfonie	EFILPPRS	flippers	EFIRSTTU	turfiest
EFIINNST	finniest	EFILPPSU	pipefuls		turfites
EFIINORR	inferior	EFILPRTU	uplifter	EFIRSTUX	fixtures
EFIINORT	notifier	EFILPSTU	spiteful	EFISSSTU	fussiest
EFIINOST	notifies	EFILRRST	flirters	EFISSTTU	fustiest
EFIINPSV	fivepins		triflers	EFISSTTW	swiftest
EFIINPSX	spinifex	EFILRRSU	flurries	EFISTUZZ	fuzziest
EFIINRRT	ferritin	EFILRRVY	Fly River	EFKLLOOR	folklore
EFIINRSU	unifiers	EFILRRZZ	frizzler	EFKLMNOS	menfolks
EFIINSTT	niftiest	EFILRSST	stiflers	EFKLMOOT	folkmote
EFIINSUV	infusive	EFILRSTT	flitters	EFKLNSUY	flunkeys
EFIIORSS	ossifier	EFILRSUV	flivvers	EFKLNUWY	Kynewulf
EFIIOSSS	ossifies	EFILRSZZ	frizzles	EFKNOORW	foreknow
EFIIPRRU	purifier	EFILSSTT	leftists	EFKNRSTU	funkster
EFIIPRST	spitfire	EFILSTTW	swiftlet	EFKOOPRS	forspoke
EFIIPRSU	purifies	EFIMNORR	informer	EFKORRTW	fretwork
EFIIPRTY	typifier		reinform	EFLLLOOW	woolfell
EFIIPSTY	typifies		reniform	EFLLNSSU	fullness
EFIIRRTU	fruitier	EFIMNORS	ensiform	EFLLNTUY	fluently
EFIIRRZZ	frizzier		fermions	EFLLOORW	follower
EFIIRVVY	revivify	EFIMNRSS	firmness	EFLLORSU	florules
EFIISSTW	swifties	EFIMNSTT	fitments	EFLLORUV	overfull
EFIJLORS	frijoles	EFIMORRT	retiform	EFLLOUWY	woefully
		EFIMORST	setiform	EFLLRUUY	ruefully

EFLLSUUY usefully	**EGGGILRS** gigglers	**EGGLMOOY** gemology
EFLMMRUY flummery	**EGGGIORR** groggier	**EGGLMRSU** smuggler
EFLMNOST loftsmen	**EGGGNNOR** ronggeng	**EGGLMSSU** smuggles
EFLMNRUU frenulum	**EGGGOOOS** goosegog	**EGGLNSSU** snuggles
EFLMORRY formerly	**EGGHHIINN** neighing	**EGGLORSS** sloggers
EFLMORSS formless	**EGGHIINW** weighing	**EGGLORST** togglers
EFLNORSU fleurons	**EGGHIKSW** eggwhisk	**EGGLPRSU** pluggers
EFLNORTT frontlet	**EGGHILRS** higglers	**EGGLRSSU** sluggers
EFLNORYZ frozenly	**EGGHIORU** Gheorgiu	**EGGLRSTU** gurglets
EFLNOSSU foulness	**EGGHISSU** shuggies	struggle
EFLNOSTY stonefly	**EGGHISTU** huggiest	**EGGMRSUY** smuggery
EFLOORSS roofless	**EGGHRTUY** thuggery	**EGGMSSTU** smuggest
EFLOORSZ foozlers	**EGGIIJLR** jigglier	**EGGNOOSY** geognosy
EFLOORTU footrule	**EGGIIJST** jiggiest	**EGGNRSUY** snuggery
EFLOORVW overflow	**EGGIILLN** gingelli	**EGGNSSTU** snuggest
EFLOOSST footless	**EGGIILNR** nigglier	**EGGOORSU** gorgeous
EFLOPRUW powerful	**EGGIILRW** wigglier	**EGGSSSTU** suggests
EFLORSTU flouters	**EGGIINNR** reigning	**EGHHILTY** eighthly
EFLORSUY yourself	**EGGIINNS** singeing	**EGHHINSS** highness
EFLORSVY flyovers	**EGGIINNT** tingeing	**EGHHORUW** roughhew
EFLOSUUX flexuous	**EGGIINRT** Girgenti	**EGHIILLS** ghillies
EFLRSSTU flusters	**EGGIINRV** grieving	**EGHIILNR** hireling
EFLRSTTU flutters	**EGGIIPST** piggiest	**EGHIILNS** shieling
EFLRSTUU frustule	**EGGIIRTW** twiggier	**EGHIIMRT** mightier
EFLRTTUY fluttery	**EGGIKLNO** gonglike	**EGHIINNR** inhering
EFMNORTY fromenty	**EGGIKNOS** gingkoes	**EGHIINRR** rehiring
EFMNRTUY frumenty	ginkgoes	**EGHIINST** heisting
furmenty	**EGGILLNY** gingelly	nighties
EFMOORST foremost	**EGGILNNT** gentling	**EGHIINSV** inveighs
EFMOORSU foursome	**EGGILNRS** nigglers	**EGHIINTV** thieving
EFMOPRRS performs	sniggler	**EGHIIPRS** Respighi
preforms	**EGGILNRU** grueling	**EGHIIRST** tigerish
EFMOPRST pomfrets	regluing	**EGHIISTY** hygieist
EFNNOOOR forenoon	**EGGILNRY** gingerly	**EGHIKNRS** gherkins
EFNNORST fornenst	**EGGILNSS** sniggles	**EGHILLNS** shelling
EFNNORUZ unfrozen	**EGGILOOS** googlies	**EGHILLOR** Holliger
EFNOOOTT footnote	**EGGILQSU** squiggle	**EGHILMNW** whelming
EFNOORRW foreworn	**EGGILRRW** wriggler	**EGHILMOR** homegirl
EFNOOSST eftsoons	**EGGILRSW** wigglers	**EGHILNOT** Leighton
festoons	wriggles	**EGHILNOV** hoveling
EFNOPRST forspent	**EGGIMSTU** muggiest	**EGHILNPS** helpings
EFNORRSU foreruns	**EGGINNOR** Groening	**EGHILNPW** whelping
EFNORRSW frowners	**EGGINNSS** ginsengs	**EGHILNRS** shingler
EFNORSTU fortunes	**EGGINORR** gorgerin	**EGHILNSS** shingles
EFNOSSST softness	rogering	**EGHILNST** lightens
EFOOOPRT footrope	**EGGINOUV** vogueing	**EGHILNSV** shelving
EFOOORST footsore	**EGGINRRU** grungier	**EGHILNSW** welshing
EFOOPRRS reproofs	**EGGINRSS** sniggers	**EGHILNUW** gluhwein
EFOOPRSS spoofers	**EGGINSSU** guessing	**EGHILORT** regolith
EFOOPRST foretops	**EGGINSTU** guesting	**EGHILPRT** plighter
poofters	gungiest	**EGHILRST** lighters
EFOOPSTT footstep	**EGGIORRY** Gregory I	relights
EFOORRSW forswore	**EGGIOSST** soggiest	slighter
EFOORSTT footrest	**EGGIPRRS** sprigger	**EGHILSTT** lightest
EFOORSTW woofters	**EGGIPRRY** priggery	**EGHIMNUX** exhuming
EFOOSTUX outfoxes	**EGGIPSSU** spuggies	**EGHINNOY** honeying
EFORRRUW furrower	**EGGIPSTU** puggiest	**EGHINNST** sennight
EFORRSST fortress	**EGGIRRST** triggers	**EGHINNSU** unhinges
EFORRSTY forestry	**EGGIRSSW** swiggers	**EGHINORV** hovering
EFORRSUV fervours	**EGGJLORS** jogglers	**EGHINOST** histogen
EGGGIILR gigglier	**EGGJLRSU** jugglers	**EGHINPRS** Pershing
EGGGILNS leggings	**EGGJLRUY** jugglery	sphering

EGHINPSS	sphinges	EGIILRRS	grislier	EGIKLNST	kinglets
EGHINRRS	herrings	EGIILRSS	grislies	EGIKLNSY	Kingsley
EGHINRRU	hungrier	EGIILRTU	guiltier	EGIKNNNS	kennings
EGHINRST	rightens	EGIILRTZ	glitzier		skenning
EGHINRSU	ushering	EGIILTWZ	Gleiwitz	EGIKNNOT	tokening
EGHINRSW	Gershwin	EGIIMNPR	impinger	EGIKNORV	revoking
	whingers	EGIIMNPS	impinges	EGIKNSTT	sketting
EGHINSTT	tightens	EGIIMNRS	remising	EGILLMNS	smelling
EGHINTTW	whetting	EGIIMNRT	meriting	EGILLNOV	livelong
EGHIOPSU	pishogue		mitering	EGILLNOW	Lilongwe
EGHIORSU	roughies	EGIIMNRX	remixing	EGILLNPS	spelling
EGHIOSTV	eightvos	EGIIMNST	mingiest	EGILLNQU	quelling
EGHIOTUW	outweigh	EGIIMNSV	misgiven	EGILLNSW	swelling
EGHIRRST	righters	EGIIMNTT	emitting	EGILLNTU	glutelin
EGHIRSST	sighters	EGIIMOPT	impetigo	EGILLOOR	gloriole
EGHISSTU	gushiest	EGIIMORR	grimoire	EGILLORS	girolles
EGHISSTY	hygeists	EGIIMPST	gimpiest	EGILLRRS	grillers
EGHISTTT	tightest	EGIIMRST	grimiest	EGILMMNS	lemmings
EGHLLOPU	plughole	EGIIMSSV	misgives	EGILMMRS	glimmers
EGHLLOSU	lugholes	EGIINNPR	repining	EGILMNOT	longtime
EGHLNORS	leghorns		ripening	EGILMNRS	gremlins
EGHLOOOR	horologe	EGIINNPW	Winnipeg		minglers
EGHLOORY	rheology	EGIINNRS	resining	EGILMNRU	reluming
EGHLOOSS	goloshes	EGIINNSV	veinings	EGILMNST	smelting
	shoogles	EGIINNWZ	wizening	EGILMNSU	mulesing
EGHLOOTY	ethology	EGIINOPR	peignoir	EGILMOOR	gloomier
	theology	EGIINORS	seignior		oligomer
EGHLOPRU	plougher	EGIINPRS	speiring	EGILMORS	gomerils
EGHMNOOY	homogeny	EGIINPRX	expiring	EGILMOUU	eulogium
EGHMOPUY	hypogeum	EGIINQTU	quieting	EGILMPRS	glimpser
EGHMOSSU	gumshoes	EGIINRRT	retiring	EGILMPSS	glimpses
EGHNOOTY	theogony	EGIINRRW	rewiring	EGILNNOS	Solingen
EGHNORSU	roughens	EGIINRST	igniters	EGILNNST	nestling
EGHNORUV	overhung		resiting	EGILNNTT	nettling
EGHNOSTU	toughens		stingier	EGILNOPP	peopling
EGHNOTUU	Huguenot	EGIINRSV	revising	EGILNORS	resoling
EGHNRSTT	strength	EGIINRSW	sweiring	EGILNORW	lowering
EGHOOOSW	hoosegow		swingier		roweling
EGHORRTW	regrowth	EGIINRTU	intrigue	EGILNOSS	loginess
EGHORSTU	roughest	EGIINRTV	riveting	EGILNOSU	ligneous
EGHOSTTU	toughest	EGIINRVV	reviving	EGILNOSW	longwise
EGIIJLNR	jinglier	EGIINSST	stingies	EGILNOTW	toweling
EGIIKKLN	kinglike	EGIINSSZ	seizings	EGILNOVV	evolving
EGIIKLNN	likening	EGIINSTX	existing	EGILNPRY	replying
EGIIKLNR	kinglier	EGIINSTZ	zingiest	EGILNPSS	spignels
EGIIKLNW	winglike	EGIINSVW	viewings	EGILNPST	pestling
EGIIKLTW	twiglike	EGIIPRSW	periwigs	EGILNRSS	slingers
EGIILMMN	immingle	EGIIPSST	pigsties	EGILNRST	ringlets
EGIILNNO	eloining	EGIIRRTT	grittier		sterling
EGIILNNR	relining	EGIIRRTTU	te igitur		tinglers
EGIILNNS	enisling	EGIITUXY	exiguity	EGILNRSW	newsgirl
	ensiling	EGIJKNRS	jerkings	EGILNSST	glistens
EGIILNNU	linguine	EGIJLLNY	jellying		singlets
EGIILNNV	livening	EGIJLNRS	jinglers	EGILNSSU	ugliness
EGIILNOR	religion	EGIJLNRU	junglier	EGILNSSW	swingles
	reoiling	EGIJMMNY	jemmying		wingless
EGIILNPS	spieling	EGIJNNOY	enjoying	EGILNSTT	settling
EGIILNRS	resiling	EGIKKNRT	trekking	EGILNSTW	winglets
	riesling	EGIKLLNN	knelling	EGILNTUX	exulting
EGIILNRV	reliving	EGIKLNOS	songlike	EGILNVXY	vexingly
	reviling	EGIKLNPS	skelping	EGILOOSU	isologue
EGIILNTZ	Liegnitz	EGIKLNSS	kingless	EGILOOTY	etiology

EGILORSS	glossier	**EGINORXX**	xeroxing	**EGLMNSSU**	glumness
EGILOSSS	glossies	**EGINPPPR**	prepping	**EGLMOPRU**	promulge
EGILOSTU	eulogist	**EGINPPST**	stepping	**EGLMORSS**	gormless
EGILRRZZ	grizzler	**EGINPPRS**	springer	**EGLNNOOR**	longeron
EGILRSST	glisters	**EGINPRSS**	pressing	**EGLNOOOY**	oenology
	gristles		springes	**EGLNOOPR**	prolonge
	gritless	**EGINPRSU**	perusing	**EGLNOOPY**	penology
EGILRSTT	glitters	**EGINPRTU**	erupting	**EGLNOORV**	overlong
EGILRSTY	greylist		reputing	**EGLNORSU**	loungers
EGILRSUV	virgules	**EGINPRTY**	retyping	**EGLNORUU**	longueur
EGILRSZZ	grizzles	**EGINPRUV**	prevuing	**EGLNOSYY**	lysogeny
EGILRTTY	glittery	**EGINPRVY**	perigyny	**EGLNPRSU**	plungers
EGIMMNST	stemming	**EGINQRUY**	querying	**EGLNRSSU**	rungless
EGIMMRST	grimmest	**EGINQSTU**	questing	**EGLNRTUY**	urgently
EGIMMSTU	gummiest	**EGINRRST**	restring	**EGLOOPRU**	prologue
EGIMNNNO	mignonne		ringster	**EGLOOPTY**	logotype
EGIMNOOR	Geronimo		stringer	**EGLOORSY**	serology
EGIMNORS	negroism	**EGINRRSW**	wringers	**EGLOOSXY**	sexology
EGIMNORV	removing	**EGINRRTY**	retrying	**EGLORRSW**	growlers
EGIMNOST	mitogens	**EGINRSST**	stingers	**EGLORSSS**	glossers
EGIMNOSY	moseying		tressing	**EGLORSUY**	rugosely
EGIMNPRU	impugner		trigness	**EGLPRSSU**	splurges
EGIMNPST	pigments	**EGINRSSV**	servings	**EGLRSUZZ**	guzzlers
EGIMNPTT	tempting	**EGINRSSW**	swingers	**EGMMORST**	grommets
EGIMNPTY	emptying	**EGINRSSY**	syringes	**EGMMRSTU**	grummets
EGIMNRSS	grimness	**EGINRSTT**	gitterns	**EGMNNOOY**	monogeny
EGIMNRSU	resuming	**EGINRSTW**	strewing	**EGMNOOOS**	gonosome
EGIMNRUY	eryngium		wresting		mongoose
EGIMORST	ergotism	**EGINRSVW**	swerving	**EGMNOSYZ**	zymogens
EGIMPRRU	grumpier	**EGINRTTU**	uttering	**EGMNSSSU**	smugness
EGINNNOT	tenoning	**EGINSSTT**	settings	**EGMOORRS**	groomers
EGINNOOR	roneoing	**EGINSSTW**	westings	**EGNNOOTY**	ontogeny
EGINNOPR	reponing	**EGINSTTT**	stetting	**EGNNORST**	rontgens
EGINNOPS	openings	**EGIOOPST**	goopiest	**EGNNOTTU**	ungotten
EGINNORT	nitrogen	**EGIOORRV**	groovier	**EGNNOTUV**	Vonnegut
EGINNORV	vigneron	**EGIOOSST**	goosiest	**EGNNSSSU**	snugness
EGINNORZ	rezoning	**EGIOPRSS**	gossiper	**EGNNSTTU**	tungsten
EGINNPSU	penguins	**EGIOPRSU**	groupies	**EGNNSTUU**	unguents
EGINNRRS	grinners		pirogues	**EGNOOOPR**	gonopore
EGINNRRU	unerring	**EGIORRTT**	grottier	**EGNOORRV**	governor
EGINNRSU	ensuring	**EGIORRTU**	groutier	**EGNOOSSS**	Goossens
EGINNRSV	nervings	**EGIORSST**	strigose	**EGNOOTUX**	oxtongue
EGINNSSU	Guinness	**EGIORSSU**	griseous	**EGNOPPRU**	oppugner
EGINNSUX	unsexing	**EGIORSUV**	grievous	**EGNOPRSS**	spongers
EGINOORR	Río Negro	**EGIOSSTT**	egotists	**EGNOPRSY**	pyrogens
EGINOOSS	isogones	**EGIOSTTU**	goutiest	**EGNORRST**	stronger
EGINOPRS	perigons	**EGIOSUUX**	exiguous	**EGNORRSW**	wrongers
	reposing	**EGIPPRRS**	grippers	**EGNORSST**	songster
	spongier	**EGIPRSUU**	guipures	**EGNORSSU**	surgeons
EGINOPRU	Perugino	**EGIRRRSU**	gurriers	**EGNORSTU**	sturgeon
EGINOPRW	powering	**EGIRRSTT**	gritters	**EGNOSTUY**	youngest
EGINOPST	pongiest	**EGIRRSTY**	registry	**EGNRRSTU**	grunters
EGINOPSX	exposing	**EGISSTTU**	gustiest		restrung
EGINORRS	Grierson		gutsiest	**EGNRSTUU**	Ten Gurus
	ignorers	**EGISSYYZ**	syzygies	**EGOOPRRU**	prorogue
EGINORSS	goriness	**EGJLNORU**	jongleur	**EGOORRVW**	overgrow
EGINORST	genitors	**EGJLNOTU**	jelutong	**EGOORSTT**	grottoes
	Signoret	**EGLLMORW**	gromwell	**EGOPRRSS**	progress
EGINORTT	ottering	**EGLLOOPR**	golloper	**EGOPRRSU**	groupers
EGINORTU	routeing	**EGLMMSTU**	glummest		regroups
EGINORTW	towering	**EGLMNOOY**	menology	**EGOPSSUY**	gypseous
EGINORVW	wingover	**EGLMNORS**	mongrels	**EGORRSSU**	grousers

EGORRSTU	grouters	EHIKLMNY	hymnlike	EHIMMNUY	hymenium
EGORSSST	grossest	EHIKLMPU	humplike	EHIMMRSS	shimmers
EGOSSTUU	outguess	EHIKLNOR	hornlike	EHIMMRSY	shimmery
EGPRSSUU	upsurges	EHIKLNOS	sinkhole	EHIMNOPR	morphine
EHHIIPRS	heirship	EHIKLOOP	hooplike	EHIMNORT	thermion
EHHIISTV	thievish	EHIKLOSY	yokelish	EHIMNOSS	hominess
EHHILMNT	helminth	EHIKLRSU	rushlike	EHIMNOTT	monteith
EHHINOPT	thiophen	EHIKMNST	methinks	EHIMNPST	shipment
EHHIORTT	hitherto	EHIKNORS	shonkier	EHIMNRRU	murrhine
EHHIRSSW	shrewish	EHIKNRRS	shrinker	EHIMNRSU	inhumers
EHHLOOST	shothole	EHIKNRST	rethinks	EHIMOOST	smoothie
EHHMPRUY	Humphrey		thinkers	EHIMORST	isotherm
EHHNOORS	shoehorn	EHIKRRSS	shirkers		moithers
EHHOOSSW	whooshes	EHIKRSSW	whiskers		Stroheim
EHHOOSTU	hothouse	EHIKRSWY	whiskery	EHIMORSZ	rhizomes
EHHOPRTW	Hepworth	EHIKSSTU	huskiest	EHIMORTU	mouthier
EHHRSSTU	thrushes	EHIKSSWY	whiskeys	EHIMOSTT	mothiest
EHIIIKST	heitikis	EHILLLMO	molehill	EHIMPRRS	shrimper
EHIIINRY	Henry III	EHILLMOP	philomel	EHIMPRSU	murphies
EHIIJOPS	Joseph II	EHILLNOS	hellions	EHIMPRSW	whimpers
EHIIKLNS	Helsinki	EHILLPTY	phyllite	EHIMPSTU	humpiest
EHIIKLPW	whiplike	EHILLRRS	shriller		humpties
EHIIKMNO	Khomeini	EHILLRRT	thriller	EHIMPSUU	euphuism
EHIIKNSV	Kishinev	EHILLSVY	elvishly	EHIMRSTY	smithery
EHIIKSSW	whiskies	EHILMNOP	Philemon	EHIMSSTU	mushiest
EHIILLMW	Wilhelm I	EHILMNOS	lemonish	EHIMSSWY	whimseys
EHIILLST	hilliest	EHILMOOR	heirloom	EHINNRST	thinners
EHIILMOS	homilies	EHILMOST	helotism	EHINNSST	thinness
EHIILRSV	liverish	EHILMPSY	symphile	EHINNSSU	sunshine
EHIIMMSS	shimmies	EHILNOPS	pinholes	EHINNSTT	thinnest
EHIIMPST	mephitis	EHILNOPT	tholepin	EHINOOPS	isophone
EHIIMRSW	whimsier	EHILNORU	unholier	EHINOPPR	hornpipe
EHIIMSST	smithies	EHILNOSS	holiness	EHINOPRY	Hyperion
EHIIMSSW	whimsies	EHILNOST	holstein	EHINOPST	phoniest
EHIINNOS	inhesion		hotlines	EHINORRT	thornier
EHIINNOT	thionine		neoliths	EHINORST	horniest
EHIINNRS	inshrine	EHILNOTX	xenolith	EHINOSST	histones
EHIINNSS	shinnies	EHILNSWY	newishly	EHINOSTU	outshine
EHIINNSW	whinnies	EHILOOPZ	zoophile	EHINPPRU	unhipper
EHIINRST	inherits	EHILOPRS	polisher	EHINPRSU	punisher
EHIINRVY	Henry VII		repolish	EHINPSSU	punishes
EHIINSST	shiniest	EHILOPRT	heliport	EHINPSSX	sphinxes
	shinties	EHILOPSS	polishes	EHINRSSU	inrushes
EHIINSTW	whiniest	EHILOPST	hoplites	EHINSSUW	unwishes
EHIINSVX	vixenish		isopleth	EHIOOPST	isophote
EHIIPPSS	shippies	EHILORTY	rhyolite	EHIOORTT	toothier
EHIIPPST	hippiest	EHILOSST	hostiles	EHIOOSST	stooshie
EHIIPRSV	viperish	EHILPRST	philters	EHIOPPSU	eohippus
EHIIPSTT	pithiest		philtres	EHIOPRSS	poserish
EHIIRRST	shirtier	EHILPSTU	sulphite		rosehips
EHIIRRTX	heritrix	EHILRRSW	whirlers	EHIOPRST	trophies
EHIIRSTT	shittier	EHILRSST	slithers	EHIORRST	heritors
	thirties	EHILRSSU	slushier	EHIORRTW	worthier
EHIIRTTW	Whittier	EHILRSSV	shrivels	EHIORSST	hoisters
EHIIRWZZ	whizzier	EHILRSTW	whistler		horsiest
EHIISSST	stishies	EHILRSTY	slithery		shorties
EHIISSTT	stithies	EHILRTTW	whittler	EHIORSTT	theorist
EHIISTTX	sixtieth	EHILSSSU	slushies	EHIORSTU	shoutier
EHIJNNOS	johnnies	EHILSSSW	wishless	EHIORSTW	worthies
EHIJOSTV	Jehovist	EHILSSTT	thistles	EHIORTWZ	howitzer
EHIKKLOO	hooklike	EHILSSTW	whistles	EHIOSSTU	housesit
EHIKKLSU	husklike	EHILSTTW	whittles		stoushie

EHIOSSTW	showiest	**EHMNOORS**	hormones	**EHOPPRST**	prophets
EHIOSSTY	isohyets		moorhens	**EHOPPRSW**	whoppers
EHIOTTUW	whiteout	**EHMNOOST**	smoothen	**EHOPPRSY**	prophesy
EHIPPRSS	shippers	**EHMNOOTY**	theonomy	**EHOPRRSY**	orphreys
EHIPPRSW	whippers	**EHMNOPSU**	homespun	**EHOPRSST**	hotpress
EHIPPSTW	whippets	**EHMNPRVY**	hypernym		strophes
EHIPQSUY	physique	**EHMNPSTY**	nymphets	**EHOPRSUV**	pushover
EHIPRSST	hipsters	**EHMNSTTU**	hutments	**EHOPRTUY**	eutrophy
EHIPRSSW	whispers	**EHMOORST**	smoother	**EHOPSTUY**	Typhoeus
EHIPRSTW	whipster	**EHMOPRSU**	Morpheus	**EHORRSTW**	throwers
EHIPSSTU	pushiest	**EHMORRSU**	Rushmore	**EHORRSTY**	herstory
EHIPSTUU	euphuist	**EHMORSST**	smothers	**EHORSSTT**	shortest
EHIQSSSU	squishes	**EHMORSTU**	mouthers	**EHORSSTU**	shouters
EHIRRSSV	shrivers	**EHMORSTY**	smothery		southers
EHIRRSTT	thirster	**EHMORTUV**	vermouth	**EHOSSSTU**	stoushes
EHIRRSTV	thrivers	**EHMOTUWY**	Weymouth	**EHPRSSUU**	uprushes
EHIRRSTW	wherrits	**EHMOTUZZ**	mezuzoth	**EHPRSTTU**	turpeths
	writhers	**EHMPRSTU**	thumpers	**EHPRSUYZ**	Zephyrus
EHIRSSSW	swishers	**EHMRRSTU**	murthers	**EHRRSTTU**	thruster
EHIRSSTU	rushiest	**EHMRTUYY**	eurythmy	**EHRSSSTY**	shysters
EHIRSSTW	swithers	**EHMSSTUY**	thymuses	**EHRSSTTU**	shutters
EHIRSTTW	whitters	**EHMSTTUY**	Hymettus	**EHRSSTUY**	tusherys
EHIRTTTW	whittret	**EHNNOOPX**	Xenophon	**EHRSTTTU**	truth set
EHISSSTU	stushies	**EHNNOPRS**	nephrons	**EIIILPPR**	liripipe
EHISSUVW	huswives	**EHNNORRT**	northern	**EIIIMMNS**	minimise
EHJOPSSU	Josephus		thronner	**EIIIMMNZ**	minimize
EHKLNOOT	knothole	**EHNNORSY**	Henryson	**EIIJNRSU**	injuries
EHKLOOSS	hookless	**EHNNORTU**	unthrone	**EIIKKLLS**	silklike
EHKMOORW	homework	**EHNNRSSU**	shunners	**EIIKKLLT**	kiltlike
EHKMOOSS	smokehos	**EHNOOPTY**	honeypot	**EIIKKLNS**	skinlike
EHKNNRSU	shrunken	**EHNOORRS**	honorers	**EIIKKNST**	kinkiest
EHKNOOOS	hooknose	**EHNOORRU**	honourer	**EIIKLLLY**	lilylike
EHLLMOPY	phyllome	**EHNOORSW**	whoreson	**EIIKLLMN**	limekiln
EHLLNSTU	nutshell	**EHNOORTW**	honewort	**EIIKLLSS**	skillies
EHLLOOOP	loophole	**EHNOORVZ**	Voronezh	**EIIKLMRS**	misliker
EHLMOORW	wormhole	**EHNOOSSW**	snowshoe	**EIIKLMSS**	mislikes
EHLMORTY	motherly	**EHNOOSTU**	outshone	**EIIKLMST**	milkiest
EHLMOSUU	Mulhouse	**EHNOPRSY**	hyperons	**EIIKLNOR**	ironlike
EHLNOPSU	sulphone	**EHNOPSSY**	hypnoses	**EIIKLNRS**	slinkier
EHLNORSS	hornless	**EHNORRST**	northers	**EIIKLPSW**	wisplike
EHLNOSST	lothness	**EHNORSST**	shortens	**EIIKLSST**	silkiest
EHLNOSTY	honestly	**EHNORSSU**	onrushes	**EIIKLSTU**	suitlike
EHLNRSTU	lutherns		unhorses	**EIIKMPRS**	skimpier
EHLNSSSU	lushness	**EHNORSTU**	southern	**EIIKMRST**	mirkiest
EHLOOPRT	porthole	**EHNOSTUU**	nuthouse	**EIIKNNOS**	noisenik
	potholer	**EHNOSTUW**	New South	**EIIKNNRS**	skinnier
EHLOOPST	potholes	**EHNRSSTU**	huntress	**EIIKNNSS**	inkiness
EHLOOPTY	holotype		shunters	**EIIKNNSW**	wineskin
EHLOPPRS	hopplers	**EHOOPRRT**	horopter	**EIIKPSST**	spikiest
EHLOPSSS	sploshes	**EHOOPRSW**	whoopers	**EIIKQRRU**	quirkier
EHLOPSSY	spyholes	**EHOOPRTY**	orthoepy	**EIIKRSST**	riskiest
EHLORSST	holsters	**EHOOPSTT**	photoset	**EIIKSSVV**	skivvies
	hostlers	**EHOOPSTU**	housetop	**EIILLLVY**	livelily
EHLORSTT	throstle		pothouse	**EIILLMNN**	Minnelli
EHLORSTY	hostelry	**EHOOPSTY**	oophytes	**EIILLMNR**	milliner
EHLORTTT	throttle	**EHOOPTYZ**	zoophyte	**EIILLMNS**	millines
EHLRSSTU	hustlers	**EHOORSST**	shooters		slimline
	ruthless		soothers	**EIILLMNU**	illumine
EHLSSTTU	shuttles	**EHOORSTV**	overshot	**EIILLNST**	niellist
EHMMRRTU	thrummer	**EHOOSSSW**	swooshes	**EIILLNSV**	villeins
EHMNNOPP	Pnom Penh	**EHOOSTUU**	outhouse	**EIILLNTV**	vitellin
EHMNNSTU	huntsmen	**EHOPPRSS**	shoppers	**EIILLOST**	Sillitoe

EIILLPSS	ellipsis	**EIIMNRTT**	intermit	**EIINSSTU**	unitises
EIILLRSV	Villiers	**EIIMNRTX**	intermix	**EIINSTTT**	nittiest
EIILLSST	silliest	**EIIMNSTT**	mintiest	**EIINSTTZ**	Steinitz
EIILLSTT	littlies	**EIIMNSTU**	mutinies	**EIINSTUZ**	unitizes
EIILLSUV	illusive	**EIIMNSTV**	minivets	**EIIOPRRS**	priories
EIILMMOT	immotile	**EIIMOPRX**	mirepoix	**EIIOPRST**	Poitiers
EIILMNNT	liniment	**EIIMOPST**	optimise	**EIIOPSTV**	positive
EIILMNOT	limonite	**EIIMOPSZ**	epizoism	**EIIOSSTT**	osteitis
EIILMNSS	liminess	**EIIMOPTZ**	optimize	**EIIOSSTZ**	zoisites
EIILMNST	Milstein	**EIIMOSSV**	omissive	**EIIPPSTZ**	zippiest
EIILMOPT	impolite	**EIIMOSUX**	eximious	**EIIPPRSS**	prissier
EIILMPRS	imperils	**EIIMOTVV**	vomitive	**EIIPRRST**	stripier
EIILMRSS	slimsier	**EIIMPRSS**	misprise	**EIIPRRTW**	tripwire
EIILMRST	limiters		pismires	**EIIPRSTV**	priviest
EIILMSSS	missiles	**EIIMPRSZ**	misprize	**EIIPSSTT**	pietists
EIILMSST	slimiest	**EIIMPSTW**	wimpiest		stipites
EIILMSTT	mistitle	**EIIMQSTU**	quietism		tipsiest
EIILMSTY	myelitis	**EIIMRSTT**	metritis	**EIIPSSTW**	wispiest
EIILNORS	lioniser	**EIIMSSSV**	missives	**EIIQSTTU**	quietist
EIILNORT	triolein	**EIIMSSTT**	mistiest	**EIIRRSTW**	wristier
EIILNORZ	lionizer		semitist	**EIIRSSTV**	revisits
EIILNOSS	elisions	**EIINNNPS**	ninepins	**EIIRSTTZ**	ritziest
	isolines	**EIINNOSU**	unionise	**EIISTTTW**	wittiest
	lionises	**EIINNOSV**	envision	**EIJJNTUY**	jejunity
	oiliness	**EIINNOUZ**	unionize	**EIJKORRS**	skijorer
EIILNOSV	olivines	**EIINNSST**	tininess	**EIJLLOST**	jolliest
EIILNOSZ	lionizes	**EIINNSTT**	Tientsin	**EIJLOSTT**	joltiest
EIILNQTU	quintile		tinniest	**EIJMPSTU**	jumpiest
EIILNRST	nitriles	**EIINNSTW**	intwines	**EIJNORST**	jointers
EIILNSSW	wiliness	**EIINOPRS**	ripienos	**EIJNORTU**	jointure
EIILNSTY	senility	**EIINOPRT**	pointier	**EIJNOSTT**	jettison
EIILNTTU	intitule		poitrine	**EIJNPRSU**	junipers
EIILNTUV	vituline	**EIINOPTT**	petition	**EIJNRRSU**	injurers
EIILOPST	pisolite	**EIINORRT**	interior	**EIJRSTUY**	jesuitry
	polities	**EIINORSS**	ionisers	**EIKKLNNY**	Kilkenny
EIILORST	roiliest		ironises	**EIKKLNOT**	knotlike
EIILOTVV	volitive		sironise	**EIKKLSTU**	tusklike
EIILPPRS	slippier	**EIINORSV**	revision	**EIKKOOST**	kookiest
EIILPPST	lippiest	**EIINORSZ**	ionizers	**EIKKSTUY**	yukkiest
EIILPSST	pitiless		ironizes	**EIKLLMNU**	Mulliken
EIILPSTY	pyelitis		sironize	**EIKLLMPU**	plumlike
EIILQSSU	siliques	**EIINOSST**	noisiest	**EIKLLNSW**	inkwells
EIILRSSS	Isserlis	**EIINOVVZ**	Zinoviev	**EIKLLNUY**	unlikely
EIILRSTU	utiliser	**EIINPPRS**	snippier	**EIKLLNXY**	lynxlike
EIILRTUZ	utilizer	**EIINPPST**	nippiest	**EIKLLOOW**	woollike
EIILSSTT	elitists	**EIINPRRS**	inspirer	**EIKLLORV**	overkill
EIILSSTU	utilises	**EIINPRSS**	inspires	**EIKLLOSS**	skollies
EIILSTUZ	utilizes	**EIINPRST**	pristine	**EIKLLOSU**	soullike
EIILTUVV	Viti Levu	**EIINPSST**	spiniest	**EIKLLRSS**	reskills
EIIMMNNO	menomini	**EIINPSTZ**	pintsize	**EIKLLSSS**	skilless
EIIMMNNT	imminent	**EIINPTUV**	punitive	**EIKLLSST**	skillets
EIIMMNSU	immunise	**EIINQRRU**	inquirer	**EIKLMNOS**	moleskin
EIIMMNUZ	immunize	**EIINQRSU**	inquires	**EIKLMNRS**	kremlins
EIIMMPRU	imperium	**EIINQTUY**	inequity	**EIKLMORW**	wormlike
EIIMMSST	mistimes	**EIINRRTW**	wintrier	**EIKLMOSS**	mosslike
EIIMNOPT	pimiento	**EIINRSST**	insister	**EIKLNOST**	Ilkeston
EIIMNORT	Minorite		sinister	**EIKLNOSW**	snowlike
EIIMNOSS	emission	**EIINRSSW**	wiriness	**EIKLNPRS**	sprinkle
EIIMNPRS	primines	**EIINRSTT**	nitrites	**EIKLNRRU**	knurlier
EIIMNRSS	miriness	**EIINRSTU**	neuritis	**EIKLNRSW**	wrinkles
EIIMNRST	interims	**EIINRSTV**	inviters	**EIKLNRTW**	twinkler
	minister		vitrines	**EIKLNSSS**	skinless

EIKLNSTW	twinkles	**EILLPRSS**	spillers	**EILNOSTV**	novelist
EIKLOORT	rootlike	**EILLPSSS**	slipless	**EILNOSTW**	towlines
EIKLOSYY	Yeşilköy	**EILLQSTU**	quillets	**EILNOSUV**	evulsion
EIKLRTUZ	klutzier	**EILLRRSW**	swillers	**EILNOSVV**	involves
EIKLSSTT	skittles	**EILLSSST**	listless	**EILNOTUV**	involute
EIKLSSTU	sulkiest	**EILLSSTT**	stillest	**EILNPRST**	splinter
EIKMMRSS	skimmers	**EILLSTTT**	littlest	**EILNPRSU**	purlines
EIKMNOPT	Potemkin	**EILLSTUV**	vitellus	**EILNPSSU**	spinules
EIKMNORS	monikers	**EILMMNOU**	Moulmein		splenius
EIKMNOST	tokenism	**EILMMPRU**	plummier	**EILNPSUY**	supinely
EIKMORTW	timework	**EILMMRRS**	slimmers	**EILNQUUY**	uniquely
EIKMOSST	smokiest	**EILMMSST**	slimmest	**EILNRRUU**	unrulier
EIKMRRSS	smirkers	**EILMNOQU**	Miquelon	**EILNRSST**	slinters
EIKMRSTU	murkiest	**EILMNOSU**	emulsion	**EILNRSTU**	insulter
EIKMSSTU	muskiest	**EILMNOTY**	mylonite	**EILNRSUU**	Ursuline
EIKNNPSS	pinkness	**EILMNPSS**	limpness	**EILNRTUV**	virulent
EIKNNRSS	skinners	**EILMNPTU**	tumpline	**EILNRTWY**	winterly
EIKNOORS	rooineks	**EILMNRST**	minstrel	**EILNSSTU**	utensils
EIKNOPSS	pokiness	**EILMNSSS**	slimness	**EILNSTTU**	lutenist
EIKNORSS	Eriksson	**EILMNTUY**	minutely	**EILNSUWY**	unwisely
EIKNORSV	invokers		untimely	**EILOOPST**	loopiest
EIKNORTT	knottier	**EILMOOPS**	liposome	**EILOORST**	oestriol
EIKNOSTW	wonkiest	**EILMOOSS**	Solimões	**EILOOSST**	ostioles
EIKNPRRS	prinkers	**EILMOOST**	toilsome	**EILOOSTW**	wooliest
EIKNPRSU	spunkier	**EILMOOSV**	moolvies	**EILOPPRS**	sloppier
EIKNPRTU	turnpike	**EILMOPRR**	implorer	**EILOPRRT**	portlier
EIKNRRST	stinkers	**EILMOPRS**	implores	**EILOPRSS**	spoilers
EIKNRSSW	swinkers	**EILMOPST**	milepost	**EILOPRSU**	perilous
EIKNRSTT	knitters		polemist	**EILOPRSV**	slipover
	trinkets	**EILMOPTY**	Ptolemy I	**EILOPRTW**	pilewort
EIKNSSTT	skintest	**EILMORRS**	lorimers	**EILOPSST**	pistoles
EIKOOPRS	spookier	**EILMORSY**	rimosely	**EILOPSSV**	plosives
EIKOORST	rookiest	**EILMPRUY**	impurely	**EILOPSTX**	exploits
EIKOOSST	stookies	**EILMPSST**	misspelt	**EILOPSUV**	pluviose
EIKOPRST	porkiest		simplest	**EILORRTU**	ulterior
EIKORRWW	wirework	**EILMPSSU**	impulses	**EILORSSS**	rissoles
EIKPPRSS	skippers	**EILMPSTU**	lumpiest	**EILORSSU**	soilures
EIKPPSST	skippets		plumiest	**EILORSTT**	triolets
EIKPRRSU	spruiker	**EILMRSSU**	misrules	**EILORSTU**	outliers
EIKRRSST	skirrets	**EILMRSSY**	remissly	**EILORTTY**	toiletry
	skirters	**EILMTTUU**	lutetium	**EILOSSTU**	lousiest
	strikers	**EILMTTUY**	multeity	**EILOSTTT**	stiletto
EIKRSSTT	skitters	**EILNNORS**	onliners	**EILOSTUV**	outlives
EILLLSTW	Stilwell	**EILNNOST**	insolent	**EILOTVVY**	votively
EILLMNOU	linoleum	**EILNNOSW**	snowline	**EILPPRRS**	ripplers
EILLMNSU	mulleins	**EILNNPSU**	pinnules	**EILPPRSS**	slippers
EILLMOPS	plimsole	**EILNNSSU**	luniness	**EILPPRST**	ripplets
EILLMOST	melilots	**EILNNTTY**	intently		stippler
EILLMPSS	misspell	**EILNOOPS**	polonies		tipplers
EILLMPTU	multiple	**EILNOOST**	looniest	**EILPPRSU**	supplier
EILLMUVX	vexillum		oilstone	**EILPPRSY**	slippery
EILLNOPY	epyllion	**EILNOOSV**	violones	**EILPPSST**	stipples
EILLNOTU	luteolin	**EILNOPRS**	plerions	**EILPPSSU**	supplies
EILLNPSW	pinswell	**EILNOPRU**	neuropil	**EILPPSSW**	swipples
EILLNSTY	silently	**EILNOPSS**	epsilons	**EILPPSTU**	pulpiest
	tinselly	**EILNORRS**	loriners	**EILPRSTT**	splitter
EILLNSVY	snivelly	**EILNORSS**	ironless		triplets
EILLOORW	woollier	**EILNORTT**	trotline	**EILPRSTY**	priestly
EILLOOSW	woollies	**EILNORVV**	involver	**EILPRSUU**	purlieus
EILLOPTY	politely	**EILNOSSU**	elusions	**EILPRSUY**	pleurisy
EILLORSZ	zorilles	**EILNOSSW**	lewisson	**EILPRTTY**	prettily
EILLOSTW	lowliest	**EILNOSTU**	outlines	**EILPRTUZ**	Pulitzer

EILPSSTU	stipules	EIMOORST	motorise	EINNORWW	winnower
EILQRRSU	squirrel		roomiest	EINNOSSS	nosiness
EILQRSTU	quilters	EIMOORTZ	motorize	EINNOSST	tensions
EILQRSUU	liqueurs	EIMOPPRR	improper	EINNOSTT	tinstone
EILRRSSU	slurries	EIMOPRRS	primrose		tontines
EILRRSTU	sultrier		promiser	EINNPRSS	spinners
EILRRSTW	twirlers	EIMOPRRT	importer	EINNPRST	enprints
EILRRTWY	writerly		reimport	EINNPSSU	puniness
EILRSSTT	slitters	EIMOPRRV	improver	EINNPSSY	spinneys
EILRSSTU	surliest	EIMOPRSS	imposers	EINNPSXY	sixpenny
EILRSSTV	listserv		promises	EINNRRSTU	runniest
EILRSSTY	sisterly		semipros	EINNRSTV	vintners
	styliser	EIMOPRST	imposter	EINNRTTU	nutrient
EILRSSZZ	sizzlers	EIMOPRSV	improves	EINNSSTU	sunniest
EILRSTTW	wristlet	EIMOPRSW	impowers	EINNSTUW	untwines
EILRSTUV	rivulets	EIMOPRUU	europium	EINOOPRS	poisoner
EILRSTYZ	stylizer	EIMOPSST	stompies		spoonier
EILRSUUX	luxuries	EIMOQSTU	misquote	EINOOPSS	opsonise
EILSSSTY	stylises	EIMORRST	mortiser		spoonies
EILSSTTU	lustiest		stormier	EINOOPSZ	opsonize
EILSSTTY	stylites	EIMORRTT	remittor	EINOORSS	erosions
EILSSTYZ	stylizes	EIMORRWW	wireworm	EINOORST	snootier
EILSSWZZ	swizzles	EIMORSST	mortises	EINOORSZ	ozoniser
EIMMNNTU	muniment	EIMORSTT	omitters	EINOORZZ	ozonizer
EIMMNORS	misnomer	EIMORSTU	moisture	EINOOSST	isotones
EIMMOPRU	emporium	EIMORSTV	vomiters	EINOOSSZ	ooziness
EIMMORRT	Mortimer	EIMORSTW	wormiest		ozonises
EIMMOSTT	totemism	EIMORSTY	isometry	EINOOSZZ	ozonizes
EIMMPRST	primmest	EIMOSSST	mossiest	EINOOTXX	exotoxin
EIMMPRSU	premiums	EIMOSSTU	mousiest	EINOPRRS	prisoner
EIMMRRST	trimmers	EIMOSSTZ	mestizos	EINOPRRS	ropiness
EIMMRSST	misterms	EIMOSSYZ	isozymes	EINOPRST	pointers
EIMMRSSW	swimmers	EIMOSTTT	totemist		proteins
EIMMRSTT	trimmest	EIMOSTTU	timeouts		repoints
EIMMRSTU	rummiest		titmouse	EINOPRSU	pruinose
EIMMSSTU	mumsiest	EIMPRSST	imprests	EINOPRTU	eruption
EIMMSTUY	yummiest	EIMPRSSU	primuses	EINOPSTT	nepotist
EIMNNOOT	noontime	EIMPRSTU	impurest	EINOPSTU	poutines
EIMNNOPT	imponent		stumpier	EINOPSWX	swinepox
EIMNNOST	mentions	EIMPSSST	missteps	EINOQSTU	question
EIMNNOTT	ointment	EIMPSSTY	mistypes	EINOQTTU	quotient
EIMNOOPS	empoison	EIMPSSUY	Puseyism	EINORRSS	rosiners
EIMNOORS	moonrise	EIMQRRSU	squirmer	EINORRST	introrse
EIMNOORV	omnivore	EIMQSSTU	mesquits	EINORRTV	invertor
EIMNOOSS	isonomes	EIMQSTUY	mystique	EINORSSS	rosiness
EIMNOOST	emotions	EIMRRSSU	surmiser	EINORSST	oestrins
	mooniest	EIMRRSTU	mistress	EINORSSU	neurosis
EIMNOPRT	orpiment	EIMRSSSU	misusers		resinous
EIMNOPST	nepotism		surmises	EINORSSV	versions
	pimentos	EIMRSSTT	metrists	EINORSTT	snottier
EIMNOPTT	impotent	EIMRSTTU	smuttier		tritones
EIMNORSU	monsieur	EIMRSTUX	mixtures	EINORSTU	routines
EIMNORTW	timeworn	EIMSSSTU	mussiest	EINORSTV	investor
EIMNORTY	enormity	EIMSSTTU	mustiest	EINORSTY	tyrosine
EIMNOSST	moistens	EIMSTUZZ	muzziest	EINORSUV	souvenir
EIMNPRSS	primness	EINNOPSS	pensions	EINORTTU	ritenuto
EIMNPSST	misspent	EINNORST	intoners	EINOSSSS	sessions
EIMNRSST	minsters		ternions	EINOSSST	sonsiest
	trimness	EINNORSU	reunions		stenosis
EIMNRSTU	terminus	EINNORSV	environs	EINOSSTT	snotties
EIMNRSTY	entryism	EINNORTU	neutrino		stoniest
EIMNSUZZ	muezzins	EINNORTV	inventor	EINOSSTW	snowiest

EINOSTTW	nowtiest	**EIPPRSTT**	trippets	**EKNNOPSU**	unspoken
EINOSTVY	venosity	**EIPQRSTU**	quipster	**EKNOOPRW**	openwork
EINPPSST	snippets	**EIPRRRSU**	spurrier	**EKNOORSS**	snookers
EINPPSTY	snippety	**EIPRRSST**	stripers	**EKNORSTT**	knotters
EINPRRST	printers	**EIPRRRSU**	spurries	**EKNORSTW**	networks
	reprints		surprise	**EKNORSUY**	younkers
	sprinter		uprisers	**EKNRSTUY**	turnkeys
EINPRRTU	prurient	**EIPRRSTZ**	spritzer	**EKOOOPRT**	pokeroot
EINPRRTY	printery	**EIPRSSST**	persists	**EKOOORTV**	overtook
EINPRSST	spinster	**EIPRSSSU**	suspires	**EKOOPRSV**	provokes
EINPSTTY	tintypes	**EIPRSSTT**	spitters	**EKOOPSTU**	outspoke
EINQRSTU	squinter		tipsters	**EKOORRVW**	overwork
EINQRTTU	quitrent	**EIPRSUVW**	purviews	**EKOORSST**	stookers
EINQSSTU	inquests	**EIPSSSTU**	pussiest	**EKOORTWW**	kowtower
EINQSTTU	quintets	**EIQRRSTU**	squirter	**EKOPRSTU**	upstroke
EINRRSSU	insurers	**EIQRSSTU**	querists	**EKOPRSTV**	Petrovsk
EINRSSSU	sunrises	**EIQRSTTU**	quitters	**EKOPRSUY**	koupreys
EINRSSTT	stinters	**EIQRSUZZ**	quizzers	**ELLLMOWY**	mellowly
EINRSSXY	syrinxes	**EIQSSUZZ**	squizzes	**ELLLNSUY**	sullenly
EINRSTTY	entryist	**EIRRRSST**	stirrers	**ELLLOWYY**	yellowly
EINSSTTW	twinsets	**EIRRSSTV**	strivers	**ELLMNOSY**	solemnly
EINSTTTU	nuttiest	**EIRRSTTU**	trustier	**ELLMOORS**	morellos
EIOOPPRS	porpoise	**EIRSSTTU**	rustiest	**ELLMORRS**	morrells
EIOOPPST	opposite		trusties	**ELLMOSTT**	Smollett
EIOOPSST	isotopes	**EIRSSTTW**	retwists	**ELLMPSUU**	plumules
EIOORSTT	tortoise		twisters	**ELLNOORV**	lovelorn
EIOOSSTT	sootiest	**EIRSSUVV**	survives	**ELLNOOSW**	woollens
	tootsies	**EIRSTTTU**	ruttiest	**ELLNOPRU**	prunello
EIOOSTWZ	wooziest	**EIRSTTTW**	twitters	**ELLNOSST**	stollens
EIOPPRTW	pipewort	**EIRTTTWY**	twittery	**ELLNOSVY**	slovenly
EIOPPSST	soppiest	**EISSSSTU**	tussises	**ELLNOUVY**	unlovely
EIOPRRSS	prioress	**EISSUUVV**	Vesuvius	**ELLOOPRT**	Trollope
EIOPRRST	pierrots	**EISTTTUV**	vuttiest	**ELLOORRV**	rollover
	sportier	**EJLOPSTU**	pulsojet	**ELLOOSST**	toolless
EIOPRRSU	superior	**EJLORSST**	jostlers	**ELLOPRST**	pollster
EIOPRSST	prosiest	**EJNNOSWY**	Wyn Jones	**ELLOPRTU**	polluter
	reposits	**EJNORSUY**	journeys	**ELLOPRUV**	pullover
	ripostes	**EJNSSSTU**	justness	**ELLOPSTU**	pollutes
	triposes	**EJOORSVY**	overjoys	**ELLORRST**	stroller
EIOPRSTT	spottier	**EJOPPRST**	propjets		trollers
EIOPRSTV	sportive	**EJOPRSTT**	jetports	**ELLORSTY**	trolleys
EIOPRSUV	pervious	**EJORSSTU**	jousters	**ELLOSSSU**	soulless
	previous	**EKKLOOSZ**	kolkozes	**ELLOSSTU**	outsells
	viperous	**EKKLRSSU**	skulkers	**ELLPPSUY**	supplely
EIOPSSTT	spotties	**EKKMORSY**	kromesky	**ELLPSSUW**	upswells
EIOPSSTU	soupiest	**EKLLMSSU**	skellums	**ELMMNOTU**	lomentum
EIOPSTTT	pottiest	**EKLLNORS**	knollers	**ELMMNOTY**	momently
EIOPSTUW	wipeouts	**EKLLOSSY**	yolkless	**ELMMORST**	trommels
EIORRRST	terroirs	**EKLLRRSU**	krullers	**ELMMOSUX**	lummoxes
EIORRSST	resistor	**EKLMNOSS**	Smolensk	**ELMMPSTU**	plummets
	roisters	**EKLNOOOR**	onlooker	**ELMMRSSU**	slummers
	sorriest	**EKLNOPRS**	plonkers	**ELMMRSUY**	summerly
EIORRSTV	servitor	**EKLNORSS**	snorkels	**ELMNOOOP**	monopole
EIORRSVY	revisory	**EKLNOSST**	knotless	**ELMNOOSS**	moonless
EIORRSTT	Rossetti	**EKLNOSWY**	Knowsley	**ELMNORUY**	Mulroney
EIORRSTY	serosity	**EKLOOORV**	lookover	**ELMNUUZZ**	unmuzzle
EIORSTTW	swottier		overlook	**ELMOOPSY**	polysome
EIORSTUV	vitreous	**EKLOOPSW**	slowpoke	**ELMOORST**	tremolos
EIOSSTTT	stotties	**EKLORSSW**	workless	**ELMOORSY**	morosely
EIOSSTUZ	outsizes	**EKLOSSTV**	stokvels	**ELMOOSSY**	lysosome
EIPPRRST	stripper	**EKMOOPRR**	morepork	**ELMOPRSY**	polymers
	trippers	**EKMRSTUY**	musketry	**ELMOPSYY**	polysemy

ELMORSTU	moulters	EMMMNOTU	momentum	ENNOORTV	nonvoter
ELMOSTUU	tumulose	EMMNNOTU	monument	ENNOPRSU	unperson
ELMOSYYZ	lysozyme	EMMNOOOS	monosome	ENNOPRUV	unproven
ELMPPRSU	plumpers	EMMNOORS	monomers	ENNOPTWY	twopenny
ELMPPSTU	plumpest	EMMNOORT	motormen	ENNORSST	sternson
ELMPRSSU	rumpless	EMMNOOSY	monosemy	ENNORSSU	nonusers
ELMPRSVYZ	Przemyśl	EMMNORSU	resummon	ENNORSSW	wornness
ELMRSTUU	multures	EMMNOSTY	metonyms	ENNORSTU	neutrons
ELMRSUZZ	muzzlers	EMMNOTTU	tomentum	ENNOSSTU	sunstone
ELNNOOSU	unloosen	EMMNOTYY	metonymy	ENNPPTUY	tuppenny
ELNNORSS	lornness	EMMOOSTY	myotomes	ENNRSSTU	stunners
ELNNOSSU	nounless	EMMRRRUU	murmurer	ENOOOSSZ	zoonoses
ELNNRSTU	trunnels	EMMRRSTU	strummer	ENOOPPRS	propones
ELNOOPRT	Ternopol	EMMRSTYY	symmetry	ENOOPPST	postpone
ELNOOPST	pelotons	EMMNNOOU	noumenon	ENOOPRSS	poorness
ELNOOSST	solonets	EMMNOOOT	monotone		snoopers
ELNOOSSU	unlooses	EMMNOSTW	townsmen	ENOOPSTT	potstone
ELNOOSTZ	solonetz	EMMNSTTU	stuntmen	ENOORRST	Sorrento
ELNOPRVY	provenly	EMNOOPTY	monotype	ENOORSSZ	snoozers
ELNOPSTU	pleuston	EMNOORST	mesotron	ENOOSSTT	testoons
ELNOPTTY	potently		monteros	ENOPRSST	posterns
ELNORSTU	turnsole		Montrose	ENOPRSTT	portents
ELNORTTY	rottenly	EMNOORSU	enormous	ENOPRTUW	uptowner
ELNOSSSW	slowness	EMNOORSW	newsroom	ENOPSSST	stepsons
	snowless	EMNOOSUV	venomous	ENOPSSSY	synopses
ELNOSSTV	solvents	EMNOOTTY	tenotomy	ENOQSTUU	unquotes
ELNOSSTW	townless	EMNORRSU	mourners	ENORRSST	snorters
ELNOSUVY	venously	EMNORSST	monsters	ENORRSTT	torrents
ELNPRTUU	purulent	EMNORSTT	torments	ENORRSUV	overruns
ELOOPRSU	superloo	EMNORSTU	mounters	ENORRTUU	Tourneur
ELOORSST	rootless		remounts	ENORRTUV	overturn
ELOORSTT	rootlets	EMNORSUU	numerous		turnover
	tootlers	EMNORTUX	Montreux	ENORSSSU	sourness
ELOOSSTU	outsoles	EMNOSSST	stemsons	ENORSSTT	snotters
ELOOSTUU	Toulouse	EMNOSUUY	euonymus		stentors
ELOPPRRY	properly	EMNOSUVY	evonymus	ENORSSTU	tonsures
ELOPPSST	stopples	EMNRSSTU	sternums	ENORSTUY	tourneys
ELOPRRSW	prowlers	EMOOPRRT	promoter	ENOSSSTT	stetsons
ELOPRSSS	plessors	EMOOPRSS	oosperms	ENOSSSUU	sensuous
ELOPRSSU	sporules	EMOOPRST	promotes	ENPRRSSU	spurners
ELOPRSTT	plotters	EMOOPRSZ	zoosperm	ENPRSSSY	spryness
ELOPRSTU	plouters	EMOORRST	restroom	ENPRSSTU	punsters
ELOPRSTW	plowters	EMOORTYZ	zoometry	ENRRRTUU	nurturer
ELOPRSTY	prostyle	EMOOSSTW	twosomes	ENRRSTUU	nurtures
ELOPRSUV	overplus	EMOOSSTY	myosotes	ENRRSTTU	entrusts
ELOPRSVY	pyrolyse	EMOPPRRT	prompter	EOOOPRSS	oospores
ELOPRYYZ	pyrolyze	EMOPRSST	stompers	EOOOPRSZ	zoospore
ELOPSSST	spotless	EMOPRSSU	spermous	EOOORRST	roseroot
ELOPSSTY	stylopes		supremos	EOOPPRRS	proposer
ELORSSTT	settlors	EMORRSST	stormers	EOOPPRSS	opposers
	slotters	EMORSSTU	strumose		proposes
ELORSTUY	elytrous	EMOSSTVZ	zemstvos	EOOPPRSV	popovers
	urostyle	EMPRRTUY	trumpery	EOOPPTTY	topotype
ELPPRSUY	resupply	EMPRSSTU	stumpers	EOOPRRSS	spoorers
ELPRSTTU	splutter		sumpters	EOOPRRST	troopers
ELPRSUZZ	puzzlers	EMPRSSUU	rumpuses	EOOPRRTU	uprooter
ELPSSTUU	pustules	EMPRSTTU	strumpet	EOOPRSST	stoopers
ELRRSSTU	rustlers		trumpets	EOOPRSTV	overtops
ELRRSTTU	turtlers	EMRRSSTU	sturmers		stopover
ELRSSSTU	rustless	ENNNOSTY	Tennyson	EOOPRSTW	towropes
ELRSTUUV	vultures	ENNOOOTZ	entozoon	EOOPSTTV	stovetop
ELSSSTUY	styluses	ENNOOPPT	opponent	EOORRRSW	sorrower

323

EOORRSST	roosters	FFGILNRU	ruffling	FGIILNRS	riflings
EOORRSVW	rowovers	FFGILNSU	sluffing	FGIILNRT	flirting
EOORSSTU	oestrous	FFGINNSU	snuffing		trifling
EOOSTTUV	outvotes	FFGINORS	griffons	FGIILNST	stifling
EOPPRRSS	prospers	FFGINOSW	swoffing	FGIILNTT	flitting
EOPPRRTY	property	FFGINSTU	stuffing	FGIILNZZ	fizzling
EOPPRSST	popsters	FFHIISST	stiffish	FGIINNSU	infusing
	stoppers	FFHILOSW	wolffish	FGIINNUX	unfixing
EOPPRSSU	purposes	FFHILOSY	offishly	FGIINNUV	unifying
	supposer	FFHOOOST	offshoot	FGIINOST	foisting
EOPPSSSU	supposes	FFHOOSSW	showoffs	FGIINRTT	fritting
EOPRRSST	portress	FFHOSSTU	shutoffs	FGIINRTU	fruiting
	sporters	FFIILMOR	filiform	FGIINRZZ	frizzing
EOPRRSTU	posturer	FFIILNSY	sniffily	FGIINSST	siftings
	troupers	FFIILPSY	spiffily	FGIINSTT	fittings
EOPRRUVY	purveyor	FFIKLORT	forklift	FGIKLNNU	flunking
EOPRSSTT	protests	FFILLLSU	fulfills	FGILMNUY	fumingly
	spotters	FFILLTUY	fitfully	FGILNOOR	flooring
EOPRSSTU	postures	FFILRTUU	fruitful	FGILNOOT	footling
	spouters	FFILSSTU	fistfuls	FGILNOOZ	foozling
EOPRSSUU	uprouses	FFILSTUY	stuffily	FGILNOPP	flopping
EOPSSTTU	outsteps	FFIMORSU	fusiform	FGILNORU	flouring
EOQRSSTU	questors	FFINOOST	finfoots	FGILNOTU	flouting
EORRRTTU	torturer	FFINOPRT	offprint	FGILNPRU	purfling
EORRSSST	stressor	FFINOPSS	spinoffs	FGILNSTU	flutings
EORRSSTU	trousers	FFINOPST	pontiffs	FGINNORT	fronting
EORRSSTY	stroyers	FFJMOPSU	jumpoffs	FGINNORW	frowning
EORRSTTT	trotters	FFKLORSU	forkfuls	FGINOOPR	proofing
EORRSTTU	tortures	FFLMNOOU	moufflon	FGINOOPS	spoofing
EORRSUVY	surveyor	FFNORSTU	turnoffs	FGINOOST	footings
EORRTUUV	trouveur	FFOOPSST	stopoffs	FGINORST	frosting
EORSSSTU	tussores	FFOORRUU	froufrou	FGINRRSU	furrings
EORSSTTT	stotters	FGGGIINR	frigging	FGIORSTW	figworts
	strettos	FGGGILNO	flogging	FGISSTUU	fuguists
EORSSTTU	outserts	FGGGINOR	frogging	FGLLMOOU	gloomful
EORSSTTW	swotters	FGGHIINT	fighting	FGLNORSU	furlongs
EOSSTTTU	stoutest	FGGHIISS	fishgigs	FGLNORUW	wrongful
EPPPRTUY	puppetry	FGGHINTU	gunfight	FGLOOOST	footslog
EPPRSSSU	suppress	FGGIILNN	flinging	FGNOORSU	fourgons
EPRRSSUU	pursuers	FGGIINNR	fringing	FHHIKOOS	fishhook
	usurpers	FGGIINRU	figuring		fish-hook
EPRRSTUU	ruptures	FGGINOOR	forgoing	FHHOORST	shofroth
EPRSSTTU	sputters	FGGINORS	forgings	FHIIKLMS	milkfish
ERRSSSTU	trussers	FGHIIKNS	kingfish	FHIIKNSS	fishskin
ERRSSTTU	trusters	FGHIILNT	inflight	FHIILLTY	filthily
ERRSSTTY	trysters	FGHIINST	shifting	FHIILNOS	lionfish
ERRSTTTU	strutter	FGHIITTW	Whitgift	FHIILSTY	shiftily
ERSSTTTU	stutters	FGHILNSU	flushing	FHIKMNOS	monkfish
FFFGILNU	fluffing		lungfish	FHILLOOT	foothill
FFFILLUY	fluffily	FGHILRTU	rightful	FHILLORT	hillfort
FFFILOST	liftoffs	FGHINORT	frothing	FHILMPSU	lumpfish
FFGHIINW	whiffing	FGHIOTTU	outfight	FHILMRTU	mirthful
FFGHIIRT	Griffith	FGHLORUU	furlough	FHILORSU	flourish
FFGHIORS	frogfish	FGHNOORS	foghorns	FHILORTY	frothily
FFGHIRSU	gruffish	FGHNOTUU	unfought	FHIMNOOS	moonfish
FFGIILNP	piffling	FGIIINNX	infixing	FHIMPRSU	frumpish
FFGIILNR	riffling	FGIIKNRS	frisking	FHIOOPTT	photofit
FFGIINNS	sniffing	FGIILLNR	frilling	FHKORSTU	futhorks
FFGIINPS	spiffing	FGIILLNS	fillings	FHLLOSTU	slothful
FFGIINRS	griffins	FGIILNNT	flinting	FHLMORUU	humorful
FFGIINST	stiffing	FGIILNOO	folioing	FHLMOTUU	mouthful
FFGILMNU	muffling	FGIILNPP	flipping		

FHLORTUY	fourthly	FLMOORSU	roomfuls	GGIILLNR	grilling
FHLOTUUY	youthful	FLNOOPSU	spoonful	GGIILMNN	mingling
FHLRTTUU	truthful	FLNOOTUW	outflown	GGIILMNY	ginglymi
FHOOORST	forsooth	FLOOPTTY	toplofty	GGIILNNS	singling
FHOOOSTT	hotfoots	FLOOSTUW	outflows		slinging
FIIILNOP	Filipino	FLOPRSTU	sportful	GGIILNNT	glinting
FIIIMNST	finitism	FLRSTTUU	trustful		tingling
FIIINNOX	infixion	FMNOORTT	Montfort	GGIIMPRS	priggism
FIIINNTY	infinity	FMRSSTUU	frustums	GGIINNNR	grinning
FIIKLRSY	friskily	FNNOORST	frontons	GGIINNOR	groining
FIILLMOS	milfoils	FNOOORTW	footworn		ignoring
FIILLMSY	flimsily	FNOORRSW	forsworn	GGIINNOS	ingoings
FIILLNTY	flintily	FNOORSSU	sunroofs	GGIINNOT	ingoting
FIILMNRY	infirmly	FOOOPRST	rooftops	GGIINNRW	wringing
FIILMOPR	piliform	FOOOSTTU	outfoots	GGIINNSS	Sing Sing
FIILMPSY	simplify	FOORSTTX	foxtrots	GGIINNST	stinging
FIILRTUY	fruitily	FOPSSSTU	fusspots	GGIINNSW	swinging
FIILRYZZ	frizzily	GGGGIILN	giggling	GGIINNTW	twinging
FIILTTUY	futility	GGGGILNO	goggling	GGIINPPR	gripping
FIIMOPRS	pisiform	GGHIIILN	higgling	GGIINRST	ringgits
FIINNOSU	infusion	GGGIIJLN	jiggling	GGIINRTT	gritting
FIINORTU	fruition	GGIILLNN	niggling	GGIIRRSS	grisgris
FIINOSSS	fissions	GGIILLNW	wiggling		gris-gris
FIIOPSST	positifs	GGGIINNS	snigging	GGILLNOY	gollying
FIKKLNOS	kinsfolk	GGGIINPR	prigging	GGILLNUY	gullying
FIKLLLSU	skillful	GGGIINRS	riggings	GGILLOOW	golliwog
FIKLNSSU	skinfuls	GGGIINRT	trigging	GGILMNOO	glooming
FILLLUWY	wilfully	GGGIINSW	swigging	GGILNNOS	longings
FILLNSUY	sinfully		wiggings	GGILNNOU	lounging
FILLOPPY	floppily	GGGIINTW	twigging	GGILNNPU	plunging
FILMNOOS	monofils	GGGIJLNO	joggling	GGILNORW	growling
FILMPRUY	frumpily	GGGIJLNU	juggling	GGILNORY	glorying
FILNOSUX	fluxions	GGGILNOS	slogging	GGILNOSS	glossing
FILORSST	florists	GGGILNOT	toggling		goslings
FILORSTY	frostily	GGGILNPU	plugging	GGILNTTU	glutting
FILORUYZ	frouzily	GGGILNRU	gurgling	GGILNUZZ	guzzling
FILRSTTU	tristful	GGGILNSU	slugging	GGILQSUY	squiggly
FILSSTTU	flutists	GGGILORY	groggily	GGIMNOOR	grooming
FILSTTUY	stultify	GGGINNOS	noggings	GGIMNOOS	smooging
FIMNORSU	uniforms		snogging	GGIMNPRU	grumping
FIMOPRRY	pyriform	GGGINNSU	snugging	GGINNNSU	gunnings
FIMORTUY	fumitory	GGGINOPR	progging	GGINNOOS	ongoings
FIMRSTUU	futurism	GGGINORT	trogging	GGINNOPR	pronging
FINOOPSY	opsonify	GGHHINOU	houghing	GGINNOPS	sponging
FINOPSSU	soupfins	GGHHISTU	thuggish	GGINNORW	wronging
FINORSSS	frissons	GGHIILNT	lighting	GGINNOSS	singsong
FIOORSSU	furiosos	GGHIINOS	O'Higgins	GGINNOTU	tonguing
FIORTTUY	fortuity	GGHIINRT	girthing	GGINNRTU	grunting
FIRSTTUU	futurist		righting	GGINNRTU	Tungting
FIRTTUUY	futurity	GGHIINST	sighting	GGINOORV	grooving
FJLLOUYY	joyfully	GGHIIPRS	priggish	GGINOOST	stooging
FKKLOORW	workfolk	GGHILSSU	sluggish	GGINOOTU	outgoing
FKLMOOOT	folkmoot	GGHINORU	roughing	GGINOPRU	grouping
FKLMOOST	folkmots	GGHINOST	ghosting	GGINORSS	grossing
FKLNRTUU	trunkful	GGHINOSU	soughing	GGINORSU	grousing
FKMOORRW	formwork	GGHINOTU	toughing	GGINORTU	grouting
FKNOORTX	Fort Knox	GGHINOTY	hogtying	GGLLPUUY	pluggugly
FKOOORTW	footwork	GGHKNNOO	Hong Kong	GHHIILST	lightish
FLMNOOSU	mouflons	GGHOOPRS	grogshop	GHHIIRST	rightish
FLMNORUU	mournful	GGIIINNT	igniting	GHHILOSU	ghoulish
FLMOOORW	moorfowl	GGIIINOR	Grigioni	GHHINSSU	shushing
FLMOOOST	tomfools	GGIIJLNN	jingling	GHHIOPST	highspot

GHHIORSU roughish	**GHIMNORU** humoring	**GIIINNOZ** ionizing
GHHIOSTU toughish	**GHIMNOTU** mouthing	**GIIINNTV** inviting
GHHOORTU thorough	**GHIMNPTU** thumping	**GIIINORS** signiori
GHHOSTTU thoughts	**GHIMNSTU** gunsmith	**GIIINSTV** visiting
GHIIJNOS jingoish	**GHIMPRSU** grumpish	**GIIJMMNY** jimmying
GHIIKNNS Hsinking	**GHINNNSU** shunning	**GIIJMNOS** jingoism
GHIIKNNT thinking	**GHINNOOR** honoring	**GIIJNNOT** jointing
GHIIKNPS kingship	**GHINNOQU** Qui Nhong	**GIIJNNRU** injuring
GHIIKNRS shirking	**GHINNORT** northing	**GIIJNOST** jingoist
GHIIKNSW whisking	throning	joisting
GHIILLNS shilling	**GHINNOST** nothings	**GIIKKLNP** kingklip
GHIILMTY mightily	**GHINNSTU** shunting	**GIIKLLNS** killings
GHIILNPR hirpling	**GHINOOPW** whooping	skilling
GHIILNRT thirling	**GHINOOST** shooting	**GIIKLNNP** plinking
GHIILNRW whirling	soothing	**GIIKLNNS** inklings
GHIILTTW twilight	**GHINOOSW** wooshing	slinking
GHIIMMNS shimming	**GHINOOTT** toothing	**GIIKLNNT** tinkling
GHIIMNNU inhuming	**GHINOPPS** hoppings	**GIIKLNNW** winkling
GHIIMRST rightism	shopping	**GIIKLNRS** skirling
GHIINNNS shinning	**GHINOPPW** whopping	**GIIKLNTT** kittling
GHIINNNT thinning	**GHINORTW** ingrowth	**GIIKMMNS** skimming
GHIINNNY hinnying	throwing	**GIIKMNPS** skimping
GHIINNRS shrining	worthing	**GIIKMNRS** smirking
GHIINNST hintings	**GHINOSSU** housings	**GIIKNNNS** skinning
GHIINOST hoisting	**GHINOSSW** showings	**GIIKNNOV** invoking
GHIINPPS shipping	**GHINOSTT** shotting	**GIIKNNPR** prinking
GHIINPPW whipping	**GHINOSTU** houtings	**GIIKNNPS** kingpins
GHIINRRS shirring	shouting	**GIIKNNST** stinking
GHIINRRW whirring	southing	**GIIKNNSW** swinking
GHIINRST shirting	**GHINOSUY** youngish	**GIIKNNTT** knitting
GHIINRSV shriving	**GHINPPUW** whupping	**GIIKNPPS** skipping
GHIINRTV thriving	**GHINRRUY** hurrying	**GIIKNPSS** pigskins
GHIINRTW writhing	**GHINSSTU** hustings	**GIIKNRRS** skirring
GHIINSST insights	**GHINSTTU** shutting	**GIIKNRSS** griskins
GHIINSSW swishing	**GHIORTTU** outright	**GIIKNRST** skirting
GHIINSTT shitting	**GHIPRSTU** uprights	striking
tithings	**GHIPRSUU** guruship	**GIILLMNS** millings
GHIINSTW whisting	**GHIPSSYY** gypsyish	**GIILLMNU** illuming
whitings	**GHLMOOOS** homologs	**GIILLNOR** grillion
GHIINSVV shivving	**GHLMOOOY** homology	**GIILLNOS** gillions
GHIINWZZ whizzing	**GHLNNOOR** longhorn	**GIILLNPR** prilling
GHIIORSU Ishiguro	**GHLNOORU** hourlong	**GIILLNPS** spilling
GHIIRSTT rightist	**GHLOOORY** horology	**GIILLNQU** quilling
GHIKLNTY knightly	**GHLORTUU** turlough	**GIILLNRT** trilling
GHIKLSTY skylight	**GHMNOOOY** homogony	**GIILLNST** stilling
GHIKRSTU tughriks	**GHMORSSU** sorghums	**GIILLNSW** swilling
GHILLNOO holloing	**GHNNOOOZ** gohonzon	**GIILLNTW** twilling
GHILLNOS Shillong	**GHNOPRSY** gryphons	**GIILLPSW** pigswill
GHILLNOU hulloing	**GHNOPYYY** hypogyny	**GIILLTUY** guiltily
GHILLOTW lowlight	**GHNOSSTU** gunshots	**GIILMMNS** slimming
GHILLSTY slightly	shotguns	**GIILMNPW** wimpling
GHILNOPP hoppling	**GHNOSTUU** unsought	**GIILMNPY** implying
GHILNOPS longship	**GHOOOSSW** hoosgows	**GIILMNZZ** mizzling
GHILNOSS sloshing	**GHOORTUY** yoghourt	**GIILMPRS** pilgrims
GHILNRTU hurtling	**GHOPRTUW** upgrowth	**GIILMPSU** pugilism
GHILNRUY hungrily	**GHORSTUY** yoghurts	**GIILNNPS** splining
GHILNSSU slushing	**GIIILMNT** limiting	**GIILNNUV** unliving
GHILNSTU hustling	**GIIILNNU** linguini	**GIILNOPS** spoiling
sunlight	**GIIILOTV** vitiligo	**GIILNOPT** piloting
GHILORSW showgirl	**GIIIMMNX** immixing	**GIILNPPR** rippling
GHILPRTY triglyph	**GIIINNOS** ionising	**GIILNPPS** slipping
GHIMNNOPR morphing	**GIIINNOT** ignition	**GIILNPPT** tippling

GIILNPRT	tripling	GIINQRTU	quirting	GILNOOSS	loosings
GIILNPSS	lispings	GIINQTTU	quitting	GILNOOST	stooling
GIILNQSU	quisling	GIINQUZZ	quizzing	GILNOOSY	sinology
GIILNQTU	quilting	GIINRRST	stirring	GILNOOTT	tootling
GIILNRST	Stirling	GIINRSTV	striving	GILNOPPP	plopping
GIILNRSW	swirling	GIINRSTW	writings		poppling
GIILNRTW	twirling	GIINSSTT	sittings	GILNOPPS	slopping
GIILNSST	listings	GIINSSTU	tissuing	GILNOPPT	toppling
GIILNSTT	slitting	GIINSTTW	twisting	GILNOPRW	prowling
	stilting	GIINTTTW	twitting	GILNOPSY	spongily
GIILNSTU	linguist	GIIORRST	rigorist	GILNOPTT	plotting
GIILNSTW	witlings	GIIPRSTZ	spritzig	GILNOSTT	slotting
GIILNSTY	stingily	GIJKLNOV	jokingly	GILNOSTU	tousling
GIILNSZZ	sizzling	GIJLLNOV	jollying	GILNOTUY	outlying
GIILPSTU	pugilist	GIJLNOST	jostling	GILNOTUZ	touzling
GIILRSST	strigils	GIJLNSTU	justling	GILNPPSU	suppling
GIILRTTY	grittily	GIJNOSTT	jottings	GILNPRSU	slurping
GIIMMNPR	primming	GIJNOSTU	jousting	GILNPUZZ	puzzling
GIIMMNRT	trimming	GIKKLNSU	skulking	GILNRRSU	slurring
GIIMMNRU	immuring	GIKLLNNO	knolling	GILNRSTU	lustring
GIIMMNSW	swimming	GIKLNNOP	plonking		rustling
GIIMMNNOR	minoring	GIKLNNPU	plunking	GILNRTTU	turtling
GIIMNNOY	ignominy	GIKLNNRU	knurling	GILNRTYY	tryingly
GIIMNNTU	minuting	GIKLNNUY	unkingly	GILNSSTU	tussling
GIIMNOPS	imposing	GIKNNOST	Kingston	GILOOOST	oologist
GIIMNOTT	omitting		stonking	GILOORSS	girosols
GIIMNOTV	motiving	GIKNNOTT	knotting	GILOORSU	glorious
	vomiting	GIKNNOUY	unyoking	GILOORVY	virology
GIIMNPPR	primping	GIKNNRTU	trunking	GILOOSSS	isogloss
GIIMNPRS	primings	GIKNOOPS	spooking	GILOOSTY	sitology
GIIMNPRU	umpiring	GIKNOOST	stooking	GILOSSST	glossist
GIIMNPTU	imputing	GIKNOPST	kingpost	GILOSTUY	gulosity
GIIMNRRS	smirring	GIKNORST	stroking	GIMMNSTU	stumming
GIIMNSSU	misusing	GIKNORSW	workings	GIMMOSSU	gummosis
GIIMORRS	rigorism	GILLMOOY	gloomily	GIMNNNSU	Munnings
GIINNNOT	intoning	GILLNORS	rollings	GIMNNORS	mornings
GIINNNPS	spinning	GILLNORT	trolling	GIMNNORU	mourning
GIINNNRU	inurning	GILLNOVY	lovingly	GIMNNOTU	mounting
GIINNNSW	winnings	GILLNSUY	sullying	GIMNNOUV	unmoving
GIINNNTW	twinning	GILLOOPW	polliwog	GIMNOOOU	oogonium
GIINNOPT	pointing	GILLOSSY	glossily	GIMNOORS	moorings
GIINNORS	ironings	GILMMNSU	slumming	GIMNOORT	motoring
	nigrosin	GILMMTUY	multigym	GIMNOOSS	osmosing
	rosining	GILMNORS	slorming	GIMNOPST	stomping
GIINNORT	ignitron	GILMNOTT	mottling	GIMNOPTU	gumption
GIINNPPS	snipping	GILMNOTU	moulting	GIMNORRU	rumoring
GIINNPRT	printing	GILMNOVY	movingly	GIMNORRW	ringworm
GIINNRSU	insuring	GILMNPPU	plumping	GIMNORST	storming
GIINNRTU	untiring	GILMNPRU	rumpling	GIMNOSSU	mousings
GIINNSTT	stinting	GILMNPSU	slumping	GIMNOSYY	misogyny
GIINOPST	positing	GILMNUZZ	muzzling	GIMNPRTU	trumping
GIINOPTV	pivoting	GILMOOSY	misology	GIMNPSTU	stumping
GIINORSS	signiors	GILMPRUY	grumpily	GIMNRRSU	smurring
GIINORSV	visoring	GILMPSSY	gymslips	GIMNSTTU	smutting
GIINORVZ	vizoring	GILNNOSU	Longinus	GIMNSTYY	stymying
GIINPPQU	quipping	GILNNOUV	unloving	GINNNOOS	noonings
GIINPPRT	tripping	GILNNRSU	nursling	GINNNSTU	stunning
GIINPRST	striping	GILNNSSU	unslings	GINNOOPS	snooping
GIINPRSU	uprising	GILNNUZZ	nuzzling		spooning
GIINPSTT	spitting	GILNOOPS	spooling	GINNOOSW	swooning
GIINPTTU	tituping	GILNOOPT	pootling	GINNOOSZ	snoozing
GIINQRSU	squiring	GILNOORT	rootling	GINNOPTU	gunpoint

GINNOPTY	poynting	GLMNORUW	lungworm	HIILMPSY	impishly
GINNORST	snorting	GLMNRTUU	ngultrum	HIILMTUY	humility
GINNORSU	grunions	GLMNSUUU	umlungus	HIILNSUY	Ilyushin
GINNPRSU	spurning	GLMOOOPY	pomology	HIILPSSY	syphilis
GINNRSTU	turnings	GLMOORWW	glowworm	HIILRSTT	triliths
	unstring	GLMOOVYZ	zymology	HIILRSTY	shirtily
GINNSTTU	nuttings	GLMORSUW	lugworms	HIILSTTY	shittily
	stunting	GLNNOORS	lorgnons	HIIMNSTT	tinsmith
GINOOPPS	opposing	GLNOOOSY	nosology	HIIMOPSS	phimosis
GINOOPRS	spooring	GLNOOOTY	ontology	HIIMORTZ	Zhitomir
GINOOPRT	trooping	GLNOOPRS	prolongs	HIINNNSY	ninnyish
GINOOPST	stooping	GLNOOPSY	polygons	HIIPRTTU	puirtith
GINOOPSW	swooping	GLNOPRSU	longspur	HIISSTTT	tsitsith
GINOORST	roosting	GLNOPVYY	polygyny	HIKKNSUU	inukshuk
GINOPPPR	propping	GLNORSTY	strongly	HIKNNORS	inkhorns
GINOPPST	stopping		strongyl	HIKNNSTU	unthinks
	toppings	GLNORTUW	lungwort	HIKNOOSU	hokonuis
GINOPPSW	swopping	GLNOSSUW	sunglows	HIKNOTTU	outthink
GINOPRST	sporting	GLNOSTTU	gluttons	HIKOOPRZ	pirozhok
GINOPRSU	ingroups	GLNOTTUY	gluttony	HIKOOPSS	spookish
GINOPRTU	trouping	GLOOOPSY	posology	HIKOORSU	Kuroshio
GINOPSST	postings	GLOOOPTY	topology	HIKOPSSY	kyphosis
	signpost	GLOOPSSY	gossypol	HILLLOSU	Solihull
GINOPSSU	spousing	GLOOPTYY	logotypy	HILLMSUY	mulishly
GINOPSTT	spotting		typology	HILLOOPT	lopolith
GINOPSTU	spouting	GLOORSUU	orgulous	HILLOOST	lithosol
GINORRWY	worrying	GMMPSUUW	mugwumps	HILLOSWY	owlishly
GINORSTU	rousting	GMNNOOYY	monogyny	HILMNOOT	monolith
GINORSTW	strowing	GMNOORSW	morwongs	HILMOPYY	myophily
	worsting	GMNOORTU	Gourmont	HILMPRTU	philtrum
GINORSTY	storying	GMORSTUW	mugworts	HILNORTY	thornily
	stroying	GNNRSTUU	unstrung	HILOOSTT	otoliths
GINORTTT	trotting	GNOOOSSS	gossoons	HILOOTTY	toothily
GINORTTU	tutoring	GNOORTUW	outgrown	HILOPPSY	popishly
GINOSSTU	outsings	GNOPRSUW	grownups	HILORSTU	uroliths
GINOSTTT	stotting	GNPPRSUU	upsprung	HILORSUU	urushiol
GINOSTTW	swotting	GOOPRTUU	outgroup	HILORTWY	Holy Writ
GINOSTUW	outswing	GOORSTUW	outgrows		worthily
GINPPRSU	upspring	HHIIOORT	Hirohito	HILOSTWW	whitlows
GINPRRSU	spurring	HHIIPSST	phthisis	HILPPRSU	purplish
GINPRSTU	spurting	HHILMOSS	shloshim	HILPPSUY	uppishly
GINPRSUU	pursuing	HHILPSSY	sylphish	HILSSTTU	sluttish
	usurping	HHKKSSUU	khuskhus	HIMMOPRU	phormium
GINPRSUY	syruping	HHLOORUY	Holy Hour	HIMNOSST	Smithson
GINPSSUW	upswings	HHOOPPRS	phosphor	HIMNSSTY	hymnists
GINPTTUY	puttying	HHOOSSTT	hotshots	HIMOOPRS	isomorph
GINRSSTU	trussing	HIIIILPP	Philip II	HIMOPRRT	trimorph
GINRSTTU	trusting	HIIILMNS	nihilism	HIMOPRSW	shipworm
GINRSTTY	trysting	HIIILNST	nihilist	HIMOPRWW	whipworm
GINRSTUU	suturing	HIIILNTY	nihility	HIMOPSSS	sophisms
GIOORRSU	rigorous	HIIILPPP	Philippi	HIMOPSST	moshpits
GIOORSTU	goitrous	HIIILPPV	Philip IV	HIMORSTU	humorist
GIOORSUV	vigorous		Philip VI	HIMOTTVZ	mitzvoth
GIORSTUY	rugosity	HIIINRST	rhinitis	HIMPRSTU	triumphs
GJOORSTT	jogtrots	HIIJNOXX	John XXII	HINNORST	tinhorns
GKKNOOSS	songkoks	HIIKMRSS	skirmish	HINNSSUY	sunshiny
GKLOOOTY	tokology	HIIKNNSS	shinkins	HINOORSZ	horizons
GLLLOORS	logrolls	HIIKOPRS	piroshki	HINOPRTW	Winthrop
GLLOOPTY	polyglot	HIIKOPRZ	pirozhki	HINOPSSY	hypnosis
GLLOOPWY	pollywog	HIIKSSTT	skittish	HINOPSTW	township
GLMNOOOY	monology	HIILLPPS	Phillips	HINORTXY	thyroxin
	nomology	HIILMOST	homilist	HINOSTTU	Tithonus

HINPPSSU	pushpins	IIJJJSTUU	jiujitsu	IIMOPSTT	optimist
HIOOPRTT	poortith	IIJKNNSY	Nijinsky	IIMORSSU	Missouri
HIOORSST	orthosis	IIJLLNOS	jillions	IIMORSTY	rimosity
HIOORTWZ	Horowitz	IIKKNPSS	kipskins	IIMOTTVY	motivity
HIOPRSSW	worships	IIKKORSS	Sikorski	IIMPRTUY	impurity
HIOPRSUZ	rhizopus	IIKLLNOS	skillion	IIMRRTTU	Trimurti
HIOPSSST	sophists	IIKLLNSY	slinkily	IIMRRTUV	triumvir
HIOSSTTU	stoutish	IIKLMNPS	limpkins	IIMSSTUW	swimsuit
HIPPPSUY	puppyish	IIKLMPSY	skimpily	IINNOOPS	opinions
HIPSSSUY	Sisyphus	IIKLNOSS	oilskins	IINNOPPT	pinpoint
HKMOOORW	hookworm	IIKLQRUY	quirkily	IINNOSTU	unionist
HKOOOPST	pothooks	IIKNOSTT	stotinki	IINNPSST	tinsnips
HKOOPRSW	workshop	IILLLPUV	pulvilli	IINNSTTU	tinnitus
HKOOSVVZ	sovkhozy	IILLMNOS	millions	IINOOPST	position
HLLLOOWY	hollowly	IILLMRTU	trillium	IINOPSSS	isospins
HLLMNOOU	monohull	IILLMUUV	illuvium	IINORSST	ironists
HLLNOOUU	Honolulu	IILLNOPS	pillions	IINORSTT	introits
HLMOOSTY	smoothly	IILLNORT	trillion	IINOSTVY	vinosity
HLMOPTUY	Plymouth	IILLNOSU	illusion	IINQRSUU	Quirinus
HLNOOOTU	Luton Hoo	IILLNOSZ	zillions	IINRTTUY	triunity
HLNOOSUW	Hounslow	IILLNSST	instills	IIOOPSTV	oviposit
HLNOSTUY	Olynthus	IILMMNOS	Molinism	IIOORRRR	riroriro
HMMNOOSY	homonyms	IILMMPSS	simplism	IIOOSTTY	otiosity
HMMNOOTU	Monmouth	IILMNORT	mirliton	IIOPRRTY	priority
HMMNOOYY	homonymy	IILMNOSU	Limousin	IIOPRSSS	pissoirs
HMMOORSU	mushroom	IILMORST	troilism	IIORSSTV	visitors
HMNOOOST	moonshot	IILMOTTY	motility	IIORSTUV	virtuosi
HMNOOPST	Thompson	IILMRSSY	missilry	IISSTUVX	Sixtus IV
HMNOPSYY	hyponyms	IILNOOST	inositol	IJJMSSUU	jujuisms
	symphony	IILNOOTV	volition	IJJSSTUU	jujuists
HMNOPYYY	hyponymy	IILNORSS	sirloins	IJJSTUUU	jiujutsu
HMOOORSW	showroom	IILNPPSY	snippily	IJKKORRT	Kortrijk
HMOORSUU	humorous	IILNRTWY	wintrily	IJKLLOSY	killjoys
HNOOPRSW	shopworn	IILOOPPR	liripoop	IJLLORTU	Trujillo
HNOOPSTY	typhoons	IILOPRST	tripolis	IJLNOQSU	jonquils
HNOORRTW	hornwort	IILOPSTY	pilosity	IJMPSTUU	jumpsuit
HNOORSTU	southron	IILORSTT	troilist	IKKLNORW	linkwork
HNORTUWY	unworthy	IILORSTV	vitriols	IKKLNOSY	kolinsky
HNRSTTUU	untruths	IILOSSTV	violists	IKKLSSUY	Issyk-Kul
HOOOSTTU	outshoot	IILOSUVX	Louis XIV	IKKMNOSU	kikumons
	shootout		Louis XVI	IKKORSSY	sikorsky
HOPPRRYY	porphyry	IILPRSSY	prissily	IKLLMORW	millwork
HOPRSSTU	hotspurs	IILSTUUV	uvulitis	IKLLOOTV	kilovolt
HOPRSTUW	upthrows	IILSTUVV	vulvitis	IKLLOTWZ	Kollwitz
HOSSTTUU	shutouts	IIMMMNSU	minimums	IKLLPSSU	upskills
HPRSTTUU	upthrust	IIMMNTUY	immunity	IKLMOPSS	milksops
IIIILMNT	Mitilíni	IIMMOPST	optimism	IKLMORSW	silkworm
IIIJLSUU	Julius II	IIMMOPSU	opiumism	IKLMORTW	milkwort
IIIKLNPS	spilikin	IIMMSTTU	mittimus	IKLNOOST	kilotons
IIIKMNNS	minikins	IIMNNOOT	monition	IKLNOPST	slipknot
IIILLMNP	minipill	IIMNNOSU	unionism	IKLNOTTY	knottily
IIILLMNU	illinium	IIMNNOTU	munition	IKLNPSUY	spunkily
IIILLNOS	Illinois	IIMNOOSS	omission	IKLOOPST	Topolski
IIILMRSV	virilism	IIMNOPRS	imprison	IKLOOPSY	spookily
IIILMUVX	lixivium	IIMNORTT	intromit	IKLOSSSU	sousliks
IIILOSUV	Louis VII	IIMNORTY	minority	IKMNOOSS	monoskis
IIILOSUX	Louis XII	IIMNOSSS	missions	IKMNPPSU	pumpkins
IIILRTVY	virility	IIMNOSST	simonist	IKNOOPRT	pinkroot
IIIMMPRS	imprimis	IIMNPRST	imprints	IKNOORRW	ironwork
IIINPRST	inspirit		misprint	IKNOPSTT	stinkpot
IIINQTUY	iniquity	IIMNPTUY	impunity	IKNORSTW	tinworks
IIJJKRSW	Rijswijk	IIMNRSTY	ministry	IKNORWYZ	Zworykin

IKORSSTU	kurtosis	IMNOPRSW	pinworms	IPRSSTUU	pursuits
ILLLMOPS	plimsoll	IMNOSTUU	mutinous	JLNSTUUY	unjustly
ILLLOOPP	lollipop	IMOOPRRS	promisor	JLOOSUYY	joyously
ILLLOOWY	woollily	IMOOPRST	impostor	JMOPSTUU	outjumps
ILLMNOSU	mullions	IMOOQSTU	mosquito	JNNOORRU	nonjuror
ILLMNRSU	millruns	IMOORSTT	motorist	JNOORSSU	sojourns
ILLMOSSY	lissomly	IMOORSTU	timorous	KKLMUVYZ	Kyzyl Kum
ILLMPSUY	psyllium	IMOORTVY	vomitory	KKNOORTW	knotwork
ILLMPTUY	multiply	IMOOSSTY	myosotis	KLLMNSUU	numskull
ILLNOQSU	quillons	IMOOSTUV	vomitous	KLLMOSSU	mollusks
ILLOPPSS	slipslop	IMOPPRRU	proprium	KLNORSTY	klystron
ILLOPPSY	sloppily	IMRSSTTU	mistrust	KLOOOSTU	lookouts
ILLOPRTW	pillwort	INNNNOOU	nonunion		outlooks
ILLOPRXY	prolixly	INNNORTU	trunnion	KLOOPRSW	slopwork
ILLORSTU	trollius	INNOOPRU	prounion	KMOOORRW	workroom
ILLORSUV	illusory	INNOOPSS	sponsion	KNNNOSUW	unknowns
ILLOSSVY	lyolysis	INNOORST	notornis	KNOOPSTT	topknots
ILLRSTUY	sultrily	INNOSSTU	nonsuits	KNOORTWY	Yorktown
ILMNOOPU	polonium	INOOOSSZ	zoonosis	KOOORSTV	voorskot
ILMNOSUU	luminous	INOOOTXZ	zootoxin	KOOPRSTW	worktops
ILMOPPSU	populism	INOOPRST	portions	KOORSTUW	outworks
ILMORSTU	turmoils		positron		workouts
ILMORSTY	stormily		sorption	LLMOOPRS	rollmops
ILMPPTUU	pulpitum	INOOPSTT	spittoon	LLMOPRUU	pullorum
ILMSSTUU	stimulus	INOOPTTU	outpoint	LLOOPRST	trollops
ILMSTTUY	smuttily	INOORSST	isotrons	LLOOPRTY	trollopy
ILNOOPSS	plosions	INOORSTY	sonority	LLOORSTU	rollouts
ILNOOSTU	solution	INOOSSSS	Soissons	LLOPSTUU	pullouts
ILNOOSTY	snootily	INOPRTTU	printout	LLOSUUVV	volvulus
ILNOOTUV	volution	INOPRTUY	punitory	LMNOOOPY	monopoly
ILNOPRSU	purloins	INOPSSSU	poussins	LMOOOOPR	poolroom
ILNOPSSU	upsilons	INOPSSSY	synopsis	LMOOOORT	toolroom
ILNOPSTU	Plotinus	INOPSSTU	spinouts	LMOOPRTU	pulmotor
	unspoilt	INPPRRUU	purpurin	LMOORSWW	slowworm
ILNOPSTY	Stolypin	INPRRSTU	surprint	LMOOTXYY	xylotomy
ILNORSST	nostrils	INPRSTTU	turnspit	LMOPPRTY	promptly
ILNORSTY	nitrosyl	INRSSTTU	intrusts	LMOSTUUU	tumulous
ILNOSTTY	snottily	INSSSTUU	sunsuits	LMRSSTUU	lustrums
ILNPSUUV	pulvinus	INSSTTUW	untwists	LNOOOPRT	poltroon
ILOOPPRS	propolis	IOOPRSSV	provisos	LNOOPPRY	propylon
ILOOPSST	topsoils	IOOPRSTY	isotropy	LNOORTUV	Volturno
ILOOPUZZ	Pozzuoli		porosity	LOOOORSS	olorosos
ILOOSSST	soloists	IOORRSTY	sorority	LOOPPSUU	populous
ILOPPSTU	populist	IOORSSTT	risottos	LOOPPSUY	polypous
ILOPRSTY	sportily	IOORSSUV	voussoir	LOOPRSUY	porously
ILOPSTTY	spottily	IOORSTTU	tortious	LORSSTUU	lustrous
ILOPSUUV	pluvious	IOORSTTY	torosity	MMNNOOSY	mononyms
ILOQRTUU	loquitur	IOORSTUV	virtuoso	MMOORTTY	tommyrot
ILPPSSUY	Lysippus	IOORSUUX	uxorious	MMOPSSTY	symptoms
ILRSTTUY	trustily	IOOSSTTU	stotious	MNNOOOSS	monsoons
ILSSSTTY	stylists	IOPRRSUV	provirus	MNNOOOTY	monotony
IMMNOORS	moronism	IOPRSSTT	protists	MNNOSSYY	synonyms
IMMOPSTU	optimums	IOPRSSUU	spurious	MNNOSYYY	synonymy
IMMRSTUY	summitry	IOPRSTTU	outstrip	MNOOOPRT	Pontormo
IMNNNOSU	munnions	IOPRSTUY	pyritous	MNOOORTW	moonwort
IMNNOOTT	monotint	IORRSUVV	survivor	MNOOORXY	oxymoron
IMNNOSUU	numinous	IORSSTTU	tourists	MNOOPRTU	pronotum
IMNOOPST	tompions	IORSSUUU	usurious	MNOOPSTY	toponyms
IMNOORRS	Morrison	IORSTTUY	touristy	MNOOPTYY	toponymy
IMNOORST	monitors	IORSTUUV	virtuous	MNOORSTT	Stormont
IMNOORTY	monitory	IPRRSSTU	stirrups	MNORSSTU	nostrums
	moronity	IPRRSTUU	pruritus	MNORSTUU	surmount

MOOORRTW	moorwort	**NOOORSSU**	sonorous	**OOPRSTUU**	outpours
	tomorrow	**NOOPRSSS**	sponsors	**OOPSSSTT**	tosspots
MOOPSSSU	opossums	**NOPSSSTU**	sunspots	**OOPSSTTU**	outposts
MOORSTUU	tumorous	**NORSTTUU**	outturns	**OORSTTUU**	tortuous
MORRSSTU	rostrums		turnouts	**OPPRRSTU**	purports
MORSSTUU	strumous	**OOOOPRST**	potoroos	**OPPRSSTU**	supports
NNOOOPST	pontoons	**OOORSTTU**	outroots	**OPRSSSUU**	sourpuss
	spontoon	**OOPRSSSU**	soursops	**ORSSTTUU**	surtouts
NNOOPRSU	pronouns	**OOPRSSTV**	provosts	**RRSSSUUU**	susurrus
NNOOPSSS	sponsons	**OOPRSTTU**	outports		

Nine Letters

AAAABCLLV	balaclava	**AAAAMPRTT**	paramatta	**AAABEILLV**	available
AAAABCLMN	balmacaan	**AAAANNSTY**	Santayana	**AAABEINOR**	anaerobia
AAAABDHLL	Allahabad	**AAABBDINR**	Barbadian	**AAABEJORS**	Soerabaja
AAAABDJLL	Jalalabad	**AAABBINRR**	barbarian	**AAABEKPRR**	parabrake
AAAABENNS	anabaenas	**AAABCCEMN**	Maccabean	**AAABEKRRS**	Skara Brae
AAAABGNRU	Guanabara	**AAABCCHHR**	bacharach	**AAABEKRHY**	breakaway
AAAABHKST	Athabaska	**AAABCCHLN**	bacchanal	**AAABEKSST**	katabases
AAAABIKLL	balalaika	**AAABCCHNR**	charabanc	**AAABELLPT**	palatable
AAAABILMN	Alabamian	**AAABCCITT**	catabatic	**AAABELRST**	alabaster
AAAABJLMY	jambalaya	**AAABCDEHN**	Banda Aceh	**AAABELSSY**	assayable
AAAABKLLV	Balaklava	**AAABCDIIT**	adiabatic	**AAABEPRSS**	parabases
AAAACCHMT	tacamahac	**AAABCDRRU**	barracuda	**AAABERSST**	braatases
AAAACCLLR	Caracalla	**AAABCEIRS**	scarabaei	**AAABGHNRV**	Bhavnagar
AAAACCRRS	caracaras	**AAABCELTU**	acetabula	**AAABGLLNO**	Alba Longa
AAAACDIMM	macadamia	**AAABCELTV**	vacatable	**AAABGLNSY**	bangalays
AAAACDJNR	jacaranda	**AAABCEMRT**	carbamate	**AAABGLORR**	algarroba
AAAACDKLY	alackaday	**AAABCESST**	catabases	**AAABGLORS**	algarobas
AAAACDMNR	Maracanda	**AAABCHNNR**	anabranch	**AAABGMNOZ**	Zamboanga
AAAACGILT	agalactia	**AAABCIKTT**	katabatic	**AAABGRSTU**	rutabagas
AAAACHILS	achalasia	**AAABCILNR**	Calabrian	**AAABHHLLU**	Baha'ullah
AAAACHKKL	chakalaka	**AAABCILNT**	abactinal	**AAABHINNS**	Nana Sahib
AAAACHSUY	ayahuasca	**AAABCIMOR**	Maracaibo	**AAABHKNRT**	Bakhtaran
AAAACINRU	Araucania	**AAABCISST**	catabasis	**AAABHLRTZ**	balthazar
AAAACIRRU	araucaria	**AAABCISTT**	ciabattas	**AAABHMSST**	mastabahs
AAAACLMNS	Salamanca	**AAABCLMOR**	carambola	**AAABIKSST**	katabasis
AAAACLNRT	Alcántara	**AAABCLMRU**	ambulacra	**AAABILLVY**	availably
AAAACMNRT	catamaran	**AAABCNNRS**	barrancas	**AAABILMNY**	Manila Bay
AAAADGIMR	Madariaga	**AAABCNRSU**	carnaubas	**AAABILMRS**	Salambria
AAAADGKNR	Karaganda	**AAABCPRSY**	capybaras	**AAABIPRSS**	parabasis
AAAADILLM	Dalai Lama	**AAABDDEHM**	Ahmedabad	**AAABIPSSS**	piassabas
AAAADMSTV	amadavats	**AAABDDFIR**	Faridabad	**AAABJKLNU**	Banja Luka
AAAADSTVV	avadavats	**AAABDDMOR**	Moradabad	**AAABLLPTY**	palatably
AAAAEHKLL	Haleakala	**AAABDEHHS**	dahabeahs	**AAABLOPRS**	parabolas
AAAAGHJMN	Mahajanga	**AAABDELPT**	adaptable	**AAABLPRST**	parablast
AAAAGIKMS	Amagasaki	**AAABDELRW**	awardable	**AAABMNRTU**	marabunta
AAAAHHJMR	maharajah	**AAABDENRS**	sarabande	**AAACCDEIM**	Accademia
AAAAHJMRS	maharajas	**AAABDESST**	databases	**AAACCDELV**	cavalcade
AAAAHKPPW	whakapapa	**AAABDHHIS**	dahabiahs	**AAACCELLN**	calcaneal
AAAAHLPTU	Atahualpa	**AAABDHHKS**	Ashkhabad	**AAACCELNN**	calcanean
AAAAILLPR	paralalia	**AAABDILLS**	sabadilla	**AAACCESTZ**	Zacatecas
AAAAILNPS	anaplasia	**AAABDILMS**	Islamabad	**AAACCGNOU**	Aconcagua
AAAAIMPRS	arapaimas	**AAABDINNT**	anabantid	**AAACCHKMT**	tacmahack
AAAAINSST	Anastasia	**AAABDNNNS**	bandannas	**AAACCILLU**	acalculia
AAAAJNRVY	Vajrayana	**AAABDNRSS**	sarabands	**AAACCINSU**	Caucasian
AAAAKKNRT	Karnataka	**AAABDNRST**	abradants	**AAACCIRTT**	ataractic
AAAAKKSWW	kawakawas	**AAABEEMNO**	amoebaean	**AAACCLMNO**	calamanco
AAAALLSVV	lavalavas	**AAABEHNRS**	habaneras	**AAACCRSTT**	cataracts

AAAACCRSTU	Caratacus	**AAACIRSTX**	ataraxics	**AAAEGLLPR**	paralegal
AAACDEHRZ	azedarach	**AAACKLMNS**	almanacks	**AAAEGLMNU**	malaguena
AAACDEQSU	aquacades	**AAACKMRST**	tamaracks	**AAAEGLMTU**	Guatemala
AAACDHIKT	kadaitcha	**AAACLMNPU**	campanula	**AAAEGLSSV**	vassalage
AAACDHNRS	sandarach	**AAACLMPST**	cataplasm	**AAAEGMNNT**	manganate
AAACDILNR	calandria	**AAACLRSUV**	avascular	**AAAEGNPPS**	appanages
AAACDINRS	acaridans	**AAACMORST**	sarcomata	**AAAEHHLMR**	Halmahera
	arcadians	**AAACMRTUX**	taraxacum	**AAAEHIKKT**	kahikatea
AAACDLRST	cadastral	**AAACNORTZ**	Catanzaro	**AAAEHIMRT**	Arimathea
AAACDNNOS	anacondas	**AAACSSTWY**	castaways	**AAAEHLNNT**	Nathanael
AAACDNRSS	Cassandra	**AAADDEILN**	daedalian	**AAAEHMMOT**	haematoma
	sandaracs	**AAADDHHMRY**	hamadryad	**AAAEHMNST**	anathemas
AAACDOSTV	advocaats	**AAADEFIST**	asafetida	**AAAEHNPSS**	anaphases
AAACEENRS	caesarean	**AAADEGLMN**	Magdalena	**AAAEIKLPR**	parakelia
AAACEGNRT	Cartagena	**AAADEGLMY**	amygdalae	**AAAEILPRX**	paralexia
AAACEGORT	Arctogaea	**AAADEGNTV**	advantage	**AAAEILTUV**	Auliye-Ata
AAACEHINP	Phaeacian	**AAADEHRTV**	Theravada	**AAAEIMNOX**	anoxaemia
AAACEHLNV	avalanche	**AAADELMMR**	marmalade	**AAAEIMOTZ**	azotaemia
AAACEHLST	calatheas	**AAADELNRX**	Alexandra	**AAAEIMPRS**	sapraemia
AAACEIMNT	catamenia	**AAADEMNOT**	adenomata	**AAAEKKRST**	karatekas
AAACEIMPR	paramecia	**AAADENSTV**	vanadates	**AAAEKSTWY**	takeaways
AAACEINNT	Canaanite	**AAADEOPTZ**	zapateado	**AAAELLNPT**	panatella
AAACEINOR	oceanaria	**AAADEPRST**	tapaderas	**AAAELMMNS**	analemmas
AAACEINRS	caesarian	**AAADFHILW**	Wadi Halfa	**AAAELMSTT**	Malatesta
AAACELNRV	Canaveral	**AAADGGHHS**	haggadahs	**AAAELNNTT**	antenatal
AAACEMMNR	cameraman	**AAADGILRU**	La Guardia		Atlantean
AAACFILNT	fanatical	**AAADGLMNR**	Grand Lama	**AAAELNPQU**	aquaplane
AAACGHLLN	Callaghan	**AAADGLRVX**	gravadlax	**AAAELNTTT**	tantalate
AAACGHMTT	Chattagam	**AAADGMMNR**	grandmama	**AAAELPRST**	palaestra
AAACGILSU	causalgia	**AAADGNPPR**	grandpapa	**AAAELRSTV**	lavateras
AAACGINRV	Nicaragua	**AAADGNRVY**	Nagyvárad	**AAAEMNPRT**	paramenta
AAACGLLSW	scallawag	**AAADHHMNR**	Rhamadhan	**AAAEMNSST**	Tasman Sea
AAACGLSSW	scalawags	**AAADHHPRZ**	haphazard	**AAAEMPRST**	aspartame
AAACGMNPS	campagnas	**AAADHIILR**	Haidar Ali	**AAAENPRSV**	paravanes
AAACHIKKN	Aniakchak	**AAADHILMN**	Al Madinah	**AAAENPSST**	anapaests
AAACHILLW	Wallachia	**AAADHJLNR**	Jalandhar	**AAAENRRTT**	Tartarean
AAACHILNW	Walachian	**AAADHMRSS**	madrasahs	**AAAERSTWY**	tearaways
AAACHIMNU	naumachia	**AAADHMRSY**	hamadryas	**AAAFFIKRR**	Kaffraria
AAACHIMST	chiasmata	**AAADILLNP**	Palladian	**AAAFGLRRT**	Trafalgar
AAACHIPSS	aphasiacs	**AAADILMNT**	dalmatian	**AAAFGMSTU**	Famagusta
AAACHIRSZ	Zacharias	**AAADILNSU**	Andalusia	**AAAFHHRST**	haftarahs
AAACHKKMT	Kamchatka	**AAADILPRS**	paradisal	**AAAFIILLR**	alfilaria
AAACHKPRR	pracharak	**AAADILRSU**	adularias	**AAAFILNUV**	avifaunal
AAACHLNRT	charlatan	**AAADIOPPR**	parapodia	**AAAFINSST**	fantasias
AAACHLPRR	chaparral	**AAADJJPRU**	Djajapura	**AAAFIRRST**	Ras Tafari
AAACHLRRT	catarrhal	**AAADKMNRS**	Samarkand	**AAAFLMNST**	fantasmal
AAACHNPTY	panchayat	**AAADKRRSV**	aardvarks	**AAAFLORST**	solfatara
AAACHNRSU	Huascarán	**AAADLMMOR**	Marmolada	**AAAFRSSSS**	sassafras
AAACHOPRT	cataphora	**AAADLMNTY**	adamantly	**AAAGGLLNS**	galangals
AAACIIRSS	acariasis	**AAADLNNSY**	analysand	**AAAGGLOPS**	galapagos
AAACILLMR	camarilla		Nyasaland	**AAAGHHOTY**	hatha yoga
AAACILLNN	anaclinal	**AAADMNRTY**	mandatary	**AAAGHIKNV**	Aga Khan IV
AAACILNOT	Catalonia	**AAADMNSTU**	tamanduas	**AAAGHJNNT**	Jagannath
AAACILNPT	aplanatic	**AAAEEEGNS**	Aegean Sea	**AAAGHNNST**	agnathans
AAACILNRU	lacunaria	**AAAEEGRRR**	arrearage	**AAAGHNSTY**	yataghans
AAACILNST	satanical	**AAAEEGRTW**	agateware	**AAAGHPPRR**	paragraph
AAACILRSV	calvarias	**AAAEEHMNR**	maharanee	**AAAGILMNS**	salaaming
AAACILRTU	actuarial	**AAAEFGMNU**	megafauna	**AAAGILNST**	Galatians
AAACINOPR	paranoiac	**AAAEFNNST**	Santa Fean	**AAAGILRST**	astragali
AAACINOTT	catatonia	**AAAEGGRTV**	aggravate	**AAAGIMNNU**	Guamanian
AAACINPRT	pancratia	**AAAEGHLMY**	Meghalaya	**AAAGIMNOT**	angiomata
AAACINRSU	casuarina	**AAAEGILNS**	analgesia	**AAAGIMNRV**	gravamina

AAAGIMRRT	margarita		saponaria	**AABBEIILT**	bilabiate
AAAGINOPT	Patagonia	**AAAÏNORST**	sanatoria	**AABBEINRT**	rabbinate
AAAGINRRS	agrarians	**AAAINORTT**	natatoria	**AABBEIRRS**	barbarise
AAAGINRRT	rangatira	**AAAINPPWY**	Appian Way	**AABBEIRRZ**	barbarize
AAAGJNNRU	Nagarjuna	**AAAINPSSU**	Pausanias	**AABBELLMY**	blameably
AAAGLNSTV	galavants	**AAAINPSTV**	vanaspati	**AABBELLSS**	baseballs
AAAGLRSST	astragals	**AAAINQRSU**	aquarians	**AABBELLTU**	tabulable
AAAGNORRT	Tarragona	**AAAINRRTV**	Navaratri	**AABBFFINY**	Baffin Bay
AAAGNPRSS	parasangs	**AAAIPPRZZ**	paparazzi	**AABBHILTY**	habitably
AAAGORSSS	Saragossa	**AAAIPRSTX**	parataxis	**AABBHKSSU**	babushkas
AAAGPRSSU	asparagus	**AAAIPSSVV**	piassavas	**AABBIILLS**	bilabials
AAAHHHJNS	Shah Jahan	**AAAIRSSTU**	Austrasia	**AABBIKLMS**	kabbalism
AAAHHHPRT	Haphtarah	**AAAIRSSTV**	Sarasvati	**AABBIKLST**	kabbalist
AAAHIKKLT	kathakali	**AAAJNPRTU**	Rajputana	**AABBIKRUY**	Abukir Bay
AAAHIKRTW	Kathiawar	**AAAJPRTUY**	Putrajaya	**AABBILLOO**	boobialla
AAAHILMNV	Himalayan	**AAAKKMORR**	Karakoram	**AABBILNOY**	Babylonia
AAAHILMST	Tashi Lama	**AAAKLMOOZ**	Kalamazoo	**AABBIMRRS**	barbarism
AAAHILMSY	Himalayas	**AAAKMSTTU**	Takamatsu	**AABBINTTU**	ibn-Batuta
AAAHIMNRS	maharanis	**AAAKOSSWY**	soakaways	**AABBIRRTY**	barbarity
AAAHIMNRU	marihuana	**AAAKRRSTU**	Surakarta	**AABBIRSSU**	babirusas
AAAHIMRST	hamartias	**AAALLLPTY**	palatally	**AABBNOTVY**	Botany Bay
AAAHIMSTY	Yamashita	**AAALLMPSS**	Las Palmas	**AABBORRSU**	barbarous
AAAHINRRT	anarthria	**AAALMNRSY**	salaryman	**AABCCEEMS**	Maccabees
AAAHINSVV	Vaishnava	**AAALNPSTY**	anaplasty	**AABCCEFKL**	blackface
AAAHJNRST	Rajasthan	**AAALNRSTV**	Transvaal	**AABCCEHKS**	backaches
AAAHKMOTV	Akhmatova	**AAALNRTTU**	tarantula	**AABCCEHLT**	catchable
AAAHKNRST	astrakhan	**AAAMMSTUY**	Matsuyama	**AABCCEHNT**	bacchante
AAAHLLOTY	ayatollah	**AAAMNOPRS**	panoramas	**AABCCEKPS**	backspace
AAAHMMSTU	Hamamatsu	**AAAMNRRSY**	yarramans	**AABCCELSS**	cascabels
AAAHMNNTT	manhattan	**AAANNPRRU**	Annapurna	**AABCCHHKT**	hatchback
AAAHMNRST	amaranths	**AAANQSTUU**	aquanauts	**AABCCHKKU**	huckaback
AAAHMNRTT	harmattan	**AAANRSSTT**	tarantass	**AABCCHKSS**	cashbacks
AAAHNNSSV	savannahs	**AAAOPPRZZ**	paparazzo	**AABCCHNST**	bacchants
AAAHNOPRS	anaphoras	**AAAPPRSTU**	apparatus	**AABCCIKKP**	pickaback
AAAHSSWWY	washaways	**AABBBEJNO**	bobbejaan	**AABCCILOT**	catabolic
AAAHTTUVY	Ayutthaya	**AABBCCIRR**	bricabrac	**AABCCIORT**	acrobatic
AAAIIJNRY	Irian Jaya	**AABBCDEIL**	abdicable	**AABCCJKKL**	blackjack
AAAIILLLP	palilalia	**AABBCDKOR**	backboard	**AABCCKKPS**	backpacks
AAAIILMNR	laminaria	**AABBCDRSS**	scabbards	**AABCCKKRT**	backtrack
AAAIINRST	sanitaria	**AABBCEINR**	Caribbean	**AABCCKLPS**	blackcaps
AAAIJMNRU	marijuana	**AABBCEKST**	backbeats	**AABCCKLSW**	clawbacks
AAAIKLLNT	antalkali	**AABBCGGIN**	cabbaging	**AABCCKRRY**	carryback
AAAILLNPS	Sillanpää	**AABBCHKOR**	Bar Kochba	**AABCCMOST**	catacombs
AAAILLRRW	Illawarra	**AABBCILMS**	cabbalism	**AABCDDEFL**	baldfaced
AAAILMMMN	mammalian	**AABBCILST**	cabbalist	**AABCDDEIT**	abdicated
AAAILMNSV	malvasian	**AABBCINRS**	barbicans	**AABCDDEKT**	backdated
AAAILMNSY	Malaysian	**AABBCKLLL**	blackball	**AABCDDORR**	cardboard
AAAILMORT	amatorial	**AABBCKMRR**	barmbrack	**AABCDEEFR**	barefaced
AAAILNNOT	Anatolian	**AABBCKNRR**	barnbrack	**AABCDEEHH**	beachhead
AAAILNNPR	planarian	**AABBDDNOR**	broadband	**AABCDEELN**	danceable
AAAILNRST	artisanal	**AABBDEELT**	debatable	**AABCDEELY**	decayable
AAAILNSST	assailant	**AABBDELOR**	boardable	**AABCDEERT**	abreacted
AAAILPPRS	appraisal	**AABBDELST**	beadblast		acerbated
AAAILRSTU	Australia	**AABBDENSS**	basebands	**AABCDEHKL**	blackhead
AAAIMNNOZ	amazonian	**AABBDEORS**	baseboard	**AABCDEIMR**	carbamide
AAAIMNNST	Tasmanian		bosberaad	**AABCDEIRR**	barricade
AAAIMNORT	inamorata	**AABBEEKLR**	breakable	**AABCDEIST**	abdicates
AAAIMNOST	Toamasina	**AABBEEKRT**	breakbeat	**AABCDEKLL**	blacklead
AAAIMNRST	samaritan	**AABBEELLM**	blameable	**AABCDEKLP**	backpedal
	Sarmatian	**AABBEELRT**	rebatable	**AABCDEKRR**	barracked
AAAINNNTZ	Tanzanian	**AABBEHHST**	Bathsheba	**AABCDEKST**	backdates
AAAINOPRS	paranoias	**AABBEHILT**	habitable	**AABCDELNR**	barnacled

AABCDEMRV	vambraced	**AABCEILMR**	bicameral	**AABCIILSS**	basilicas
AABCDEMSU	ambuscade	**AABCEILNP**	incapable	**AABCIINOT**	anabiotic
AABCDENNO	abondance	**AABCEILNT**	cantabile	**AABCIINRS**	brainiacs
AABCDENNU	abundance	**AABCEILRT**	bacterial	**AABCIKLLM**	blackmail
AABCDENOR	carbonade		calibrate	**AABCIKLLT**	blacktail
AABCDENPS	spaceband	**AABCEILST**	Baltic Sea	**AABCIKLOT**	katabolic
AABCDHILN	baldachin	**AABCEIMNR**	mainbrace	**AABCIKLST**	tailbacks
AABCDHKNS	backhands	**AABCEINOR**	anaerobic	**AABCIKRST**	backstair
AABCDHKRS	hardbacks	**AABCEINRR**	carabiner	**AABCILLRS**	cabrillas
AABCDHNTW	watchband	**AABCEINRS**	carabines	**AABCILLRY**	bacillary
AABCDIMNO	Cambodian	**AABCEIORT**	aerobatic	**AABCILLSY**	asyllabic
AABCDIORS	scaraboid	**AABCEISSS**	abscissae		basically
AABCDIORT	abdicator	**AABCEJKMR**	amberjack	**AABCILNNS**	cannibals
AABCDKLMP	blackdamp	**AABCEKLMS**	clambakes	**AABCILNOT**	botanical
AABCDKRSW	backwards	**AABCEKLRS**	lacebarks	**AABCILNPY**	incapably
	drawbacks	**AABCEKLRT**	trackable	**AABCILNTU**	Tubal-cain
AABCDLNSS	scablands	**AABCEKLST**	stackable	**AABCILOPR**	parabolic
AABCDLOPR	clapboard	**AABCEKPPR**	paperback	**AABCILOST**	bicoastal
AABCDNOOR	carbonado	**AABCEKRRR**	barracker	**AABCILRUV**	vibracula
AABCDORST	broadcast	**AABCEKRTW**	backwater	**AABCILSST**	cabalists
AABCEEELP	peaceable	**AABCEKSST**	backseats	**AABCINNOR**	carbanion
AABCEEHLR	reachable	**AABCELLOR**	caballero	**AABCINNRS**	cinnabars
AABCEEHLS	chaseable	**AABCELLOT**	locatable	**AABCIRSSS**	brassicas
AABCEEHLT	cheatable	**AABCELLSS**	classable	**AABCISSSS**	abscissas
	teachable	**AABCELMNU**	ambulance	**AABCKLLMP**	lampblack
AABCEEKLS	leaseback	**AABCELMRY**	macabrely	**AABCKLLRT**	trackball
AABCEEKNR	canebrake	**AABCELNNS**	scannable	**AABCKLMSS**	black mass
AABCEELLN	cleanable	**AABCELNNU**	unbalance	**AABCKLNOS**	loanbacks
AABCEELLR	clearable	**AABCELNOR**	Barcelona	**AABCKLPSY**	playbacks
	lacerable	**AABCELNRS**	balancers	**AABCKNPSS**	snapbacks
AABCEELLV	cleavable		barnacles	**AABCKORRZ**	razorback
AABCEELNT	enactable	**AABCELOOS**	calaboose	**AABCKPRST**	bratpacks
AABCEELPS	escapable	**AABCELORR**	barcarole	**AABCKSSTY**	backstays
AABCEELPY	peaceably	**AABCELORS**	albacores	**AABCLRTTY**	tractably
AABCEELRS	calabrese	**AABCELORZ**	carbazole	**AABCMNOTT**	combatant
AABCEELRT	creatable	**AABCELPRS**	scrapable	**AABCNOORR**	barracoon
	traceable	**AABCELPSS**	spacelabs	**AABCNORRS**	barrancos
AABCEELTX	exactable	**AABCELRST**	Castlebar	**AABCRSSTT**	abstracts
AABCEENRR	aberrance	**AABCELRTT**	tractable	**AABDDEEST**	deadbeats
AABCEERST	acerbates	**AABCELRTU**	trabecula	**AABDDEGLS**	saddlebag
AABCEERTT	bracteate	**AABCELRTY**	traceably	**AABDDEHLS**	baldheads
AABCEFIRT	fabricate	**AABCELSWY**	cableways	**AABDDEHNS**	headbands
AABCEFOSU	fabaceous	**AABCEMRSV**	vambraces	**AABDDEHOR**	headboard
AABCEGILR	algebraic	**AABCENORT**	carbonate	**AABDDEHRY**	Hyderabad
AABCEGKLM	blackgame	**AABCENRRY**	aberrancy	**AABDDEINR**	braindead
AABCEGKST	backstage	**AABCEOSTU**	sauceboat	**AABDDENNO**	abandoned
AABCEGLMR	cablegram	**AABCFHKLS**	flashback	**AABDDGHUY**	Buddh Gaya
AABCEGPRT	carpetbag		halfbacks	**AABDDHORR**	hardboard
AABCEHHLT	hatchable	**AABCFINRT**	fabricant	**AABDDHORS**	dashboard
AABCEHINR	branchiae	**AABCFKSST**	fastbacks	**AABDDNNST**	bandstand
AABCEHIRT	brachiate	**AABCGILLN**	caballing	**AABDDORRT**	dartboard
AABCEHITZ	chabazite	**AABCGILNN**	balancing	**AABDEEEMN**	endamebae
AABCEHKLW	whaleback	**AABCGKRSY**	graybacks	**AABDEEGNT**	abnegated
AABCEHLMP	Palm Beach	**AABCGLOSU**	calabogus	**AABDEEHRS**	earbashed
AABCEHLMT	matchable	**AABCGRRSS**	crabgrass	**AABDEELLP**	pleadable
AABCEHLPT	patchable	**AABCHIKRY**	hairyback	**AABDEELLR**	balladeer
AABCEHLRT	chartable	**AABCHILNR**	branchial	**AABDEELLS**	Bleasdale
AABCEHLTW	watchable	**AABCHILTY**	Bat Chayil	**AABDEELMN**	amendable
AABCEHMST	ambatches	**AABCHIORS**	barachois	**AABDEELPR**	drapeable
AABCEHNRS	barchanes	**AABCHKLSS**	backslash	**AABDEELRT**	tradeable
AABCEILLM	claimable	**AABCHLOOS**	coolabahs	**AABDEEMNO**	endamoeba
AABCEILMN	imbalance	**AABCIILNS**	basilican	**AABDEEMNS**	endamebas

AABDEENNO	abandonee	**AABDIJNOR**	jaborandi		relatable
AABDEERST	teabreads	**AABDIKORV**	Kirovabad	**AABEELLRX**	relaxable
AABDEERSY	bayaderes	**AABDILMNO**	abdominal	**AABEELMNR**	Lambaréné
AABDEERTT	trabeated	**AABDILMRY**	admirably	**AABEELMSU**	amuseable
AABDEFLOR	broadleaf	**AABDILNQU**	baldaquin	**AABEELNNX**	annexable
AABDEFLRT	flatbread	**AABDILORS**	sailboard	**AABEELNOT**	atoneable
AABDEGGGS	gasbagged	**AABDILORT**	broadtail	**AABEELNTU**	uneatable
AABDEGHNS	headbangs		tailboard	**AABEELORT**	elaborate
AABDEGINO	gabionade	**AABDILOVY**	avoidably	**AABEELPRR**	reparable
AABDEGINR	bargained	**AABDILSSU**	disabusal	**AABEELPRS**	separable
	gabardine	**AABDILSVY**	advisably	**AABEELPRY**	repayable
AABDEGLRS	gradables	**AABDINNRT**	trainband	**AABEELQTU**	equatable
AABDEGLRU	guardable	**AABDINOST**	bastinado	**AABEELRSW**	wearables
AABDEGMOS	gambadoes	**AABDINSTW**	waistband	**AABEELRTT**	treatable
AABDEGORT	abrogated	**AABDKLORW**	boardwalk	**AABEELRTV**	avertable
AABDEGOST	sabotaged	**AABDKNNSS**	sandbanks	**AABEELRTW**	tableware
AABDEGRRY	graybeard	**AABDLLORW**	wallboard	**AABEELSTT**	stateable
AABDEHIST	Bethsaida	**AABDLNSST**	sandblast	**AABEEMNOT**	entamoeba
AABDEHJLL	djellabah	**AABDLOOST**	boatloads	**AABEEMNST**	abasement
AABDEHKNR	handbrake	**AABDLOOSW**	balsawood		entamebas
AABDEHLNR	handlebar	**AABDLOPRS**	lapboards	**AABEEMNTT**	abatement
AABDEHLSY	abashedly	**AABDLORRS**	labradors	**AABEEMPRS**	abamperes
AABDEHNSU	unabashed	**AABDLRSTY**	bastardly	**AABEENNSW**	wannabees
AABDEILLT	dilatable	**AABDNRRSY**	barnyards	**AABEENORS**	anaerobes
AABDEILMR	admirable	**AABDORRST**	starboard	**AABEEQRSU**	arabesque
AABDEILNN	Leninabad	**AABDRRSSS**	brassards	**AABEERSTT**	Battersea
AABDEILNR	drainable	**AABDRRSTY**	bastardry	**AABEFFLQU**	quaffable
AABDEILNV	invadable	**AABEEEGLR**	agreeable	**AABEFGILT**	fatigable
AABDEILOV	avoidable	**AABEEEMNT**	entamebae	**AABEFHKLS**	halfbeaks
AABDEILRV	adverbial	**AABEEFLMR**	frameable	**AABEFIMRS**	frambesia
AABDEILSV	advisable	**AABEEFLNS**	fleabanes	**AABEFKLNR**	frankable
AABDEIMNR	Marienbad	**AABEEFNST**	beanfeast	**AABEFKRST**	breakfast
AABDEINST	abstained	**AABEEGGLU**	gaugeable	**AABEFLLMM**	flammable
AABDEIOSU	aboideaus	**AABEEGILM**	imageable	**AABEFLLOT**	floatable
AABDEIOUX	aboideaux	**AABEEGKRS**	breakages	**AABEFLMSU**	flambeaus
AABDELLNT	tableland	**AABEEGLLL**	glabellae	**AABEFLMUX**	flambeaux
AABDELLST	ballasted	**AABEEGLLN**	gleanable	**AABEFLORV**	favorable
AABDELMST	lambasted	**AABEEGLLT**	bagatelle	**AABEGGHLS**	shaggable
AABDELMTU	ambulated	**AABEEGLRY**	agreeably	**AABEGGLUY**	gaugeably
AABDELORT	dolabrate	**AABEEGLTT**	getatable	**AABEGHLLU**	laughable
AABDELPST	baldpates	**AABEEGNST**	abnegates	**AABEGHORR**	harborage
AABDELTTU	tabulated	**AABEEHKLS**	shakeable	**AABEGHSSW**	bagwashes
AABDELTWY	twayblade	**AABEEHLLX**	exhalable	**AABEGILNV**	navigable
AABDEMORT	dreamboat	**AABEEHLMS**	shameable	**AABEGILRV**	Belgravia
AABDEMRTU	adumbrate	**AABEEHLPS**	shapeable	**AABEGINRR**	bargainer
AABDENSTW	sweatband	**AABEEHLRS**	shareable	**AABEGIRRT**	arbitrage
AABDENSVW	wavebands	**AABEEHLSV**	shaveable	**AABEGIRRU**	bigarreau
AABDEORSS	seaboards	**AABEEHMRS**	harambees	**AABEGKLOR**	gaolbreak
AABDEORST	adsorbate	**AABEEHRRS**	earbasher	**AABEGLLLR**	glabellar
AABDEORSV	bravadoes	**AABEEHRSS**	earbashes	**AABEGLMNP**	Palembang
AABDGGINN	bandaging	**AABEEHRTT**	heartbeat	**AABEGLNOR**	Bangalore
AABDGHLRU	Bradlaugh	**AABEEILLN**	alienable	**AABEGLNRT**	grantable
AABDGIILR	garibaldi	**AABEEILRS**	raiseable	**AABEGLPRS**	graspable
AABDGNNOW	bandwagon	**AABEEINRS**	bearnaise	**AABEGMNSY**	mangabeys
AABDGNOSV	vagabonds	**AABEEKLLS**	slakeable	**AABEGNORS**	baronages
AABDGORRS	garboards	**AABEEKLPP**	bakeapple	**AABEGNORT**	abnegator
AABDGOSTU	gadabouts	**AABEEKLPS**	speakable	**AABEGNRUZ**	Aurangzeb
AABDHIORZ	biohazard	**AABEELLLM**	malleable	**AABEGORST**	abrogates
AABDHLLNS	handballs	**AABEELLNR**	learnable	**AABEGOSST**	sabotages
AABDHLRSU	Hasdrubal	**AABEELLPS**	pleasable	**AABEHILRR**	herbarial
AABDHORSW	washboard	**AABEELLRS**	resalable	**AABEHIMNN**	Inhambane
AABDHRSSU	subahdars	**AABEELLRT**	alterable	**AABEHINNS**	Beni Hasan

AABEHITTU	habituate	**AABELMNNU**	unnamable	**AABHIMMRU**	Hammurabi
AABEHJLLS	jellabahs	**AABELMNST**	stableman	**AABHINRSW**	brainwash
AABEHLMSS	smashable	**AABELMNTU**	untamable	**AABHINSSW**	washbasin
AABEHLOTW	whaleboat	**AABELMSST**	blastemas	**AABHINSTT**	habitants
AABEHLPST	alphabets		lambastes	**AABHIPRRV**	vibraharp
AABEHLSTW	swathable	**AABELMSSU**	assumable	**AABHKORTU**	Kota Bharu
AABEHMNST	abashment	**AABELMSTU**	ambulates	**AABHNOSTU**	autobahns
AABEIILLS	Isabella I	**AABELNPPS**	snappable	**AABIILLMS**	labialism
	labialise	**AABELNSUY**	unsayable	**AABIILLTY**	labiality
AABEIILLZ	labialize	**AABELOPPS**	apposable	**AABIILNRR**	librarian
AABEIIRTU	aubrietia	**AABELOPRV**	vaporable	**AABIILNRZ**	Brazilian
AABEIIRTV	bivariate	**AABELORST**	astrolabe	**AABIILNST**	balanitis
AABEIJKLR	jailbreak	**AABELORTT**	rotatable	**AABIINNRT**	Britannia
AABEIKLNS	balkanise	**AABELPRRY**	reparably	**AABIINOSS**	anabiosis
AABEIKLNZ	balkanize	**AABELPRSS**	sparables	**AABIINRZZ**	Zanzibari
AABEIKLRV	Balakirev	**AABELPRSY**	separably	**AABIINSSY**	Abyssinia
AABEIKNRR	karabiner	**AABELRSST**	arbalests	**AABIKLSST**	kabalists
AABEILLMN	laminable	**AABELRSSU**	assurable	**AABILLNPT**	paintball
AABEILLNR	ballerina	**AABELRSTU**	saturable	**AABILLORS**	isallobar
AABEILLRT	bilateral	**AABELRSTY**	betrayals	**AABILMNOS**	anabolism
AABEILLST	ballistae	**AABELRTTU**	tablature	**AABILMNRU**	manubrial
AABEILLSW	wallabies	**AABELSTTU**	tabulates	**AABILMOPR**	ambipolar
AABEILMNR	lamebrain	**AABEMOSTT**	steamboat	**AABILMOPY**	amblyopia
AABEILMNU	unamiable	**AABEMRRSS**	embarrass	**AABILMORS**	ambrosial
AABEILNOT	anabolite	**AABENOPRT**	Bonaparte	**AABILMPST**	baptismal
AABEILNRT	trainable	**AABEOPPRT**	approbate	**AABILNOST**	ablations
AABEILNST	stainable	**AABFGILSU**	basifugal	**AABILNOTT**	battalion
AABEILPST	basipetal	**AABFIKNRS**	Fairbanks	**AABILOSST**	sailboats
AABEILRSV	variables	**AABFIMORT**	fibromata	**AABILRRSU**	bursarial
AABEILSTV	ablatives	**AABFLORVY**	favorably	**AABILRSST**	arbalists
AABEILTVV	bivalvate	**AABFLOSTT**	faltboats	**AABILSVWY**	Walvis Bay
AABEIMNOT	abominate		flatboats	**AABIMNNOT**	Manitoban
AABEIMNZZ	Zambezian	**AABGGGNNS**	gangbangs	**AABIMNORS**	ambrosian
AABEIMRSU	Beaumaris	**AABGGIMNO**	gambogian	**AABIMORSS**	ambrosias
AABEINORS	arabinose	**AABGGINRR**	barraging	**AABIMORSU**	simarouba
AABEINOSS	anabioses	**AABGGRRST**	braggarts	**AABINNPRS**	brainpans
AABEINRST	abstainer	**AABGHILRT**	Galbraith	**AABINORSS**	abrasions
AABEINRVW	brainwave	**AABGHKRSS**	shagbarks	**AABINOSTW**	boatswain
AABEINSST	Sebastian	**AABGHLLUV**	laughably	**AABINRSTZ**	bartizans
AABEIOSTU	aboiteaus	**AABGHLPRU**	Bhagalpur	**AABIORSTT**	abattoirs
AABEIOTUX	aboiteaux	**AABGHNOUY**	Hu Yaobang	**AABIOSSSY**	bioassays
AABEIRPRT	arbitrate	**AABGHOPRR**	barograph	**AABIRRRTY**	arbitrary
AABEIRSSV	abrasives	**AABGILNRU**	Bulgarian	**AABJJLLNU**	Ljubljana
AABEIRSTU	aubretias	**AABGILNST**	bangtails	**AABKLLPRS**	ballparks
	aubrietas	**AABGILNVY**	navigably	**AABKLOTUW**	walkabout
AABEISSSS	sassabies	**AABGILRRT**	Gibraltar	**AABKLSTVY**	Blavatsky
AABEISSTT	abattises	**AABGIMOSU**	ambagious	**AABKOPRSS**	soapbarks
AABEKLNST	beanstalk	**AABGINNOR**	born-again	**AABLLLOWY**	allowably
AABEKMNRS	brakesman	**AABGLLLOS**	goalballs	**AABLLMORS**	balmorals
AABEKNNRS	Nebraskan	**AABGLLRSY**	ballyrags	**AABLLMSYY**	abysmally
AABEKPPRR	paperbark	**AABGLNOSW**	bangalows	**AABLLNTTY**	blatantly
AABELLLMY	malleably	**AABGMORRS**	barograms	**AABLLRSTU**	blastular
AABELLLOW	allowable	**AABGNORSZ**	garbanzos	**AABLLRSYY**	syllabary
AABELLMNY	Ballymena	**AABGNRRUW**	burrawang	**AABLLRTUY**	tabularly
AABELLMST	meatballs	**AABGOORRT**	abrogator	**AABLLSSTU**	blastulas
AABELLNPT	plantable	**AABHHIKSU**	hibakusha	**AABLMNORY**	myrobalan
AABELLNSU	unsalable	**AABHHISTV**	Tishah b'Av	**AABLMOSST**	blastomas
AABELLOPR	parolable	**AABHHORSU**	brouhahas	**AABLNOPSS**	Bolan Pass
AABELLPPR	palpebral	**AABHIILRZ**	bilharzia	**AABLNORTU**	Ulan Bator
AABELLRTY	alterably	**AABHIIMNP**	amphibian	**AABLORSST**	albatross
AABELLSTU	blastulae	**AABHIINSU**	bauhinias	**AABLORTTU**	tabulator
AABELLSUV	valuables	**AABHILLRS**	hairballs	**AABLOSTUY**	layabouts

AABLRSSTU	subastral	**AACCELNSU**	calcaneus	**AACCLNORY**	acronycal
AABMNNOTU	Montauban	**AACCELNTU**	accentual	**AACCMNOPY**	accompany
AABMNRSTU	rambutans	**AACCELORS**	caracoles	**AACCOPRRS**	sarcocarp
AABMORSTU	marabouts	**AACCELSTU**	sacculate	**AACCOPRSS**	ascocarps
	tambouras	**AACCEMNSU**	cumaceans	**AACCORTUY**	autocracy
AABORRRST	barrators	**AACCENPTT**	acceptant	**AACDDEEGH**	Dedéagach
AABORSSTT	barostats	**AACCENRST**	carcanets	**AACDDEELS**	escaladed
AABRRSSST	brassarts	**AACCEORTT**	coarctate	**AACDDEHIS**	acidheads
AABRSSTTU	substrata	**AACCERSSS**	carcasses	**AACDDEINT**	candidate
AACCCFIOS	focaccias	**AACCERSSY**	accessary	**AACDDELNS**	scandaled
AACCCHHSU	cachuchas	**AACCGHNOR**	Gran Chaco	**AACDDELOP**	decapodal
AACCCHIRS	saccharic	**AACCHILMO**	mailcoach	**AACDDELPR**	placarded
AACCCIOPR	carpaccio	**AACCHILPS**	pachalics	**AACDDENOP**	decapodan
AACCDDINY	candidacy	**AACCHIMNO**	Michoacán	**AACDDEOTV**	advocated
AACCDEHKR	crackhead	**AACCHIMOT**	macchiato	**AACDDIIST**	dadaistic
AACCDEIIR	acaricide	**AACCHIMSY**	sciamachy	**AACDDIMPV**	Camp David
AACCDEILM	acclaimed	**AACCHINRS**	characins	**AACDDINRS**	radicands
AACCDEIMS	academics		saccharin	**AACDDKPWY**	paddywack
AACCDEIRV	cadaveric	**AACCHIPRR**	archicarp	**AACDDLMNO**	Macdonald
AACCDEJNY	adjacency	**AACCHIRTT**	cathartic		MacDonald
AACCDELLT	catcalled	**AACCHIRTU**	autarchic	**AACDDMORU**	docudrama
AACCDELOR	caracoled	**AACCHISSV**	viscachas	**AACDEEEFT**	defaecate
AACCDELOS	accolades	**AACCHISVZ**	vizcachas	**AACDEEFLT**	defalcate
AACCDERRS	racecards	**AACCHLLST**	catchalls	**AACDEEHHR**	headreach
AACCDGINS	cascading	**AACCHLORS**	charcoals	**AACDEEHHS**	headaches
AACCDHIRS	characids	**AACCHLOST**	cachalots	**AACDEEHHY**	headachey
AACCDHLRU	archducal	**AACCHLRSS**	clarsachs	**AACDEEHRS**	headraces
AACCDHORY	adhocracy	**AACCHNNWY**	wanchancy	**AACDEEHSS**	headcases
AACCDIINR	circadian	**AACCIILNT**	anaclitic	**AACDEEIMS**	academies
AACCDNORT	accordant	**AACCIILNV**	vaccinial	**AACDEEIMT**	acetamide
AACCEEHIN	echinacea	**AACCIINPS**	capsaicin		emaciated
AACCEEIRR	cercariae	**AACCIINTT**	tactician	**AACDEEIRT**	acierated
AACCEELNR	clearance	**AACCIIRSS**	Circassia		eradicate
AACCEENRT	reactance	**AACCILLNO**	laconical	**AACDEELRS**	escalader
AACCEENST	cetaceans	**AACCILLNY**	calycinal	**AACDEELRT**	lacerated
AACCEFHKL	chalkface	**AACCILLRU**	calicular	**AACDEELSS**	escalades
AACCEFLOS	coalfaces	**AACCILLSS**	classical	**AACDEELST**	escalated
AACCEFNRS	Francesca	**AACCILMNU**	cacuminal	**AACDEELTU**	aculeated
AACCEHILL	cailleach	**AACCILNNO**	canonical	**AACDEEMNS**	damascene
AACCEHJKP	cheapjack	**AACCILNOR**	acronical	**AACDEEMRT**	demarcate
AACCEHRRT	character	**AACCILNRU**	canicular		macerated
AACCEHSTW	watchcase	**AACCILPRT**	practical	**AACDEEMST**	casemated
AACCEIILN	caecilian	**AACCILSTU**	caustical	**AACDEENTT**	catenated
AACCEIINR	Cirenaica	**AACCILTTY**	catalytic	**AACDEEPSS**	escapades
AACCEILMR	acclaimer	**AACCIMNOR**	carcinoma	**AACDEETUV**	evacuated
AACCEILMT	acclimate		macaronic	**AACDEETUX**	excaudate
AACCEILNT	analectic		maccaroni	**AACDEETVX**	excavated
AACCEILRR	cercarial	**AACCINOTT**	catatonic	**AACDEFFIN**	affianced
AACCEILST	ascetical	**AACCINPRT**	pancratic	**AACDEFFIR**	fairfaced
AACCEILTU	aciculate	**AACCINPTY**	captaincy	**AACDEFHRS**	headscarf
AACCEINRR	cercarian	**AACCINRTT**	antarctic	**AACDEFIST**	fasciated
AACCEINRY	Cyrenaica	**AACCIOPRT**	capacitor	**AACDEGGGM**	cagmagged
AACCEINSV	vacancies	**AACCIOPSU**	capacious	**AACDEGILT**	glaciated
AACCEINTV	vaccinate	**AACCIORST**	Costa Rica	**AACDEGLNO**	decagonal
AACCEJKLN	lancejack	**AACCIRSST**	sarcastic	**AACDEGLOT**	cataloged
AACCEJKRR	carjacker	**AACCJKRSW**	crackjaws	**AACDEGNOS**	gasconade
AACCEKNRS	crankcase	**AACCJORSU**	carcajous	**AACDEHILN**	enchilada
AACCEKRRT	racetrack	**AACCKKPSS**	packsacks	**AACDEHINS**	haciendas
AACCELLRT	catcaller	**AACCKMNRS**	cracksman	**AACDEHIRS**	archaised
AACCELLTU	calculate	**AACCLLRUY**	calycular	**AACDEHIRZ**	archaized
AACCELMNU	calcaneum	**AACCLMORY**	cyclorama	**AACDEHKMS**	smackhead
AACCELMTY	cyclamate	**AACCLMSTY**	cataclysm	**AACDEHKSW**	hacksawed

AACDEHLLN	dancehall		cadastres	**AACDMMRSU**	cardamums
AACDEHLRT	cathedral	**AACDERSTT**	castrated	**AACDMNORS**	cardamons
	clarthead	**AACDERTTT**	attracted	**AACDMOSUV**	muscavado
AACDEHORT	octahedra	**AACDFHNRT**	handcraft	**AACEEEGNR**	careenage
AACDEHRST	cathedras	**AACDFIILT**	fatidical	**AACEEFINN**	faineance
AACDEIIPR	epicardia	**AACDFIOPR**	picofarad	**AACEEFIRT**	cafeteria
AACDEILLN	dalliance	**AACDGINNV**	advancing	**AACEEFLPS**	palefaces
AACDEILLT	dialectal	**AACDGINOR**	carangoid	**AACEEFLPT**	faceplate
AACDEILMR	creamlaid	**AACDGINRS**	carangids	**AACEEFMRT**	farcemeat
AACDEILNO	Caledonia		cardigans	**AACEEFRRT**	aftercare
	laodicean	**AACDGLMOR**	cladogram	**AACEEGKPR**	repackage
AACDEILNS	canalised	**AACDHHKRS**	hardhacks	**AACEEGLLR**	cellarage
AACDEILNZ	canalized	**AACDHHNSS**	shadchans	**AACEEGLSV**	cleavages
AACDEILPS	asclepiad	**AACDHIILL**	chiliadal	**AACEEGNRR**	carrageen
AACDEILSS	sidalceas	**AACDHIILR**	rachidial	**AACEEHHRT**	heartache
AACDEILTU	acidulate	**AACDHIILS**	dichasial	**AACEEHLNP**	encephala
AACDEIMMS	academism	**AACDHILMY**	chlamydia	**AACEEHLPS**	acalephes
AACDEIMNO	Macedonia	**AACDHINOR**	arachnoid	**AACEEHNOR**	Chaeronea
AACDEIMNY	cyanamide	**AACDHINOT**	acanthoid	**AACEEHPRT**	eparchate
AACDEIMPR	paramedic	**AACDHINPS**	handicaps	**AACEEHRTT**	tracheate
	preadamic	**AACDHINRS**	arachnids	**AACEEHRTX**	exarchate
AACDEIMSS	camisades	**AACDHINRT**	cantharid	**AACEEILNR**	Erie Canal
AACDEIMST	steadicam	**AACDHKRST**	hardtacks	**AACEEIMST**	emaciates
AACDEINOR	androecia	**AACDHLMNR**	marchland	**AACEEINRT**	ecarinate
AACDEINOT	diaconate	**AACDHLNPS**	handclasp	**AACEEIRST**	acierates
AACDEINOV	avoidance	**AACDHLNPU**	launchpad	**AACEEJLTU**	ejaculate
AACDEINPS	cispadane	**AACDHLNRS**	crashland	**AACEEKMPR**	pacemaker
AACDEINPT	captained	**AACDHNRST**	handcarts	**AACEEKRRT**	caretaker
AACDEINRS	radiances	**AACDHPRRS**	cardsharp	**AACEELLMU**	melaleuca
AACDEINRT	carinated	**AACDIIIMR**	miracidia	**AACEELNPS**	pleasance
AACDEITTV	activated	**AACDIINNR**	cnidarian	**AACEELNPT**	placentae
AACDEJNST	adjacents	**AACDIINSS**	ascidians	**AACEELNST**	elastance
AACDEKMRT	tarmacked	**AACDIISST**	diastasic	**AACEELPRT**	paraclete
AACDEKNRS	ransacked	**AACDIISTT**	diastatic	**AACEELRST**	lacerates
AACDELLNU	calendula	**AACDILLRY**	radically	**AACEELRTT**	altercate
AACDELLNY	decanally	**AACDILMNO**	monadical	**AACEELSST**	escalates
AACDELLOT	allocated	**AACDILMNY**	dynamical	**AACEELTTY**	acetylate
AACDELMNS	Candlemas	**AACDILMRU**	caldarium	**AACEEMMNR**	cameramen
AACDELMTU	maculated	**AACDILMST**	dalmatics	**AACEEMPST**	meatspace
AACDELNOT	anecdotal	**AACDILMSU**	caladiums	**AACEEMRRT**	macerater
AACDELNPS	landscape	**AACDILNRS**	cardinals	**AACEEMRRW**	creamware
AACDELNRS	calendars	**AACDILNSU**	dulcianas	**AACEEMRST**	macerates
AACDELNRT	declarant	**AACDILNTY**	dilatancy	**AACEEMSST**	casemates
AACDELNTU	canulated	**AACDILOPR**	parodical	**AACEENNST**	catenanes
AACDELOPS	loadspace	**AACDILORT**	carotidal	**AACEENRTU**	centaurea
AACDELOSS	caseloads	**AACDILOTU**	autocidal	**AACEENSTT**	catenates
AACDELPTY	playacted	**AACDILRRS**	railcards	**AACEEOPRS**	aerospace
AACDELSTY	catalysed	**AACDIMORY**	myocardia	**AACEEPRSS**	cassareep
AACDELTYZ	catalyzed	**AACDIMOSS**	camisados	**AACEEPSSS**	seascapes
AACDEMNRS	Scamander	**AACDIMRST**	dramatics	**AACEESTUV**	evacuates
AACDEMNTU	manducate	**AACDINNOR**	draconian	**AACEESTVX**	excavates
AACDEMRSS	massacred	**AACDINOTU**	caudation	**AACEFFINS**	affiances
AACDENNNO	cannonade	**AACDINRTU**	traducian	**AACEFFIRT**	affricate
AACDENNST	ascendant	**AACDIOSTU**	autacoids	**AACEFGLNR**	flagrance
AACDENORR	carronade	**AACDIOSUU**	audacious	**AACEFGNRR**	fragrance
AACDENOTU	coadunate	**AACDIQRTU**	quadratic	**AACEFGORT**	factorage
AACDENPPT	catnapped	**AACDIRSSY**	dyscrasia	**AACEFGOSU**	fagaceous
AACDENRSV	advancers	**AACDIRSTY**	caryatids	**AACEFILLS**	fallacies
AACDENSSV	canvassed	**AACDJNTUY**	adjutancy	**AACEFILST**	califates
AACDEOSTU	autocades	**AACDJQRSU**	jacquards	**AACEFINNY**	faineancy
AACDEOSTV	advocates	**AACDLORST**	cartloads	**AACEFINST**	fascinate
AACDERSST	cadasters	**AACDMMORS**	cardamoms	**AACEFKMPR**	packframe

AACEFLLTU	falculate	**AACEHKLNO**	kalanchoe	**AACEIMNSS**	amnesiacs
AACEFLPST	Cape Flats	**AACEHKMOR**	hackamore	**AACEIMNTU**	acuminate
AACEFRSTT	artefacts	**AACEHKMPU**	Kampuchea	**AACEIMOTZ**	azotaemic
AACEGHHMU	gamahuche	**AACEHKMRR**	Marrakech	**AACEIMPRS**	sapraemic
AACEGHIMR	archimage	**AACEHKRSV**	haversack	**AACEIMPRT**	metacarpi
AACEGHLNR	archangel	**AACEHKRTY**	Thackeray	**AACEIMQRU**	Macquarie
AACEGHLTT	Gaeltacht	**AACEHLNSU**	eulachans	**AACEIMRST**	marcasite
AACEGHMNP	champagne	**AACEHLRTT**	clathrate	**AACEIMSTT**	catamites
AACEGHMRU	gamaruche	**AACEHMNPR**	marchpane		masticate
AACEGHNOR	anchorage	**AACEHNNSV**	Chavannes	**AACEINNRT**	incarnate
AACEGHRST	gatecrash	**AACEHNOTV**	anchoveta	**AACEINOST**	caseation
AACEGILLN	angelical	**AACEHNPSX**	panchaxes	**AACEINPST**	anapestic
	englacial	**AACEHNPTY**	tachypnea	**AACEINRRT**	tarriance
	galenical	**AACEHNRST**	anthraces	**AACEINRST**	ascertain
AACEGILNS	analgesic	**AACEHPPRS**	scrapheap		Cartesian
	angelicas	**AACEHPRTU**	parachute		sectarian
AACEGILRS	Algeciras	**AACEHRSST**	catharses	**AACEINRSV**	variances
AACEGILRT	cartilage	**AACEHRSTT**	attachers	**AACEINSST**	estancias
AACEGILST	glaciates	**AACEIILNT**	laciniate	**AACEIOSST**	associate
AACEGIMNO	egomaniac	**AACEIILRS**	racialise	**AACEIPRSS**	airspaces
AACEGINST	caseating	**AACEIILRZ**	racialize	**AACEIPSTU**	auspicate
AACEGIRRS	carriages	**AACEIINRR**	cineraria	**AACEIPTTV**	captivate
AACEGIRSV	vicarages	**AACEIIRTV**	vicariate	**AACEIRSST**	staircase
AACEGISTT	castigate	**AACEIKNTW**	antwackie	**AACEIRSTU**	actuaries
AACEGKPRS	packagers	**AACEILLMS**	camellias	**AACEISTTV**	activates
AACEGKRWY	graywacke	**AACEILLNS**	alliances	**AACEISTUV**	causative
AACEGLMOU	guacamole	**AACEILLPT**	capitella	**AACEJKLPP**	applejack
AACEGLOST	galactose	**AACEILLRV**	varicella	**AACEJKSSS**	jackasses
AACEGLOSU	coagulase	**AACEILLSV**	cavallies	**AACEKKLSW**	cakewalks
AACEGLOTU	catalogue	**AACEILLTV**	vacillate	**AACEKLLMR**	Mackellar
	coagulate	**AACEILMNP**	campanile	**AACEKLPSW**	spacewalk
AACEGNNST	stagnance	**AACEILMPS**	eclampsia	**AACEKMRRS**	Mackerras
AACEGNORR	arrogance	**AACEILMST**	calamites	**AACEKNRRS**	ransacker
AACEGNRSU	sugarcane	**AACEILMTV**	calmative	**AACEKRSTT**	attackers
AACEGOPST	scapegoat	**AACEILNNR**	carnelian	**AACELLLRU**	acellular
AACEGORTT	greatcoat	**AACEILNNT**	cantilena	**AACELLLTY**	lacteally
AACEHHIRZ	Zechariah		lancinate	**AACELLLUV**	vallecula
AACEHIIMS	ischaemia	**AACEILNPP**	appliance	**AACELLNOR**	olecranal
AACEHILLO	echolalia	**AACEILNPT**	analeptic	**AACELLNOW**	allowance
AACEHILLS	achilleas		aplanetic	**AACELLNPT**	placental
AACEHILLT	alecithal		El Capitan	**AACELLNST**	castellan
AACEHILMT	malachite	**AACEILNRS**	arsenical	**AACELLOST**	allocates
AACEHILNS	selachian	**AACEILNRT**	lacertian	**AACELLTVY**	clavately
AACEHILNT	chatelain		nectarial	**AACELMNTT**	cattleman
AACEHILPR	eparchial	**AACEILNSS**	canalises	**AACELMOTU**	comatulae
AACEHILPS	phacelias	**AACEILNSZ**	canalizes	**AACELMSST**	classmate
AACEHILPT	caliphate	**AACEILNTV**	venatical	**AACELMSTU**	maculates
AACEHIMNT	machinate	**AACEILORT**	aleatoric	**AACELNNOZ**	Canal Zone
AACEHIMRS	chimaeras	**AACEILPRX**	paralexic	**AACELNNTU**	cannulate
AACEHIMST	haematics	**AACEILPSS**	asclepias	**AACELNOTT**	Canaletto
AACEHIMTT	athematic	**AACEILPTU**	apiculate	**AACELNPRS**	parlances
AACEHINNT	acanthine	**AACEILPTV**	placative	**AACELNPST**	placentas
AACEHINRW	chinaware	**AACEILRST**	tailraces	**AACELNRST**	ancestral
AACEHIOPT	apothecia	**AACEILRSV**	calvaries		Lancaster
AACEHIOST	taoiseach		cavaliers	**AACELNSTU**	canulates
AACEHIPST	chapaties		cavalries	**AACELNSUZ**	Suez Canal
	hepaticas	**AACEILRUU**	auriculae	**AACELOPRT**	acropetal
AACEHIPTT	apathetic	**AACEILSTU**	actualise		cleopatra
AACEHIRRS	archaiser	**AACEILTTU**	actualite	**AACELORST**	escalator
AACEHIRRZ	archaizer	**AACEILTUZ**	actualize	**AACELOSTT**	cattaloes
AACEHIRSS	archaises	**AACEIMNOX**	anoxaemic	**AACELOTUV**	autoclave
AACEHIRSZ	archaizes	**AACEIMNRR**	Ermanaric		vacuolate

AACELPPRT applecart	**AACFJNOOR** Joan of Arc	**AACHILPST** asphaltic
AACELPSTU aspectual	**AACFLLTUY** factually	**AACHILSST** thalassic
capsulate	**AACFLOPSW** Scapa Flow	**AACHIMNOR** harmonica
AACELPSTY catalepsy	**AACFLRRTU** fractural	**AACHIMNRR** Charminar
AACELPTXY cataplexy	**AACFMNRST** craftsman	**AACHIMNRS** anarchism
AACELRRTU creatural	**AACGGIKNP** packaging	**AACHIMNRU** Manchuria
AACELRSTY catalyser	**AACGGIOPR** paragogic	**AACHIMRRS** armchairs
AACELRSWY clearways	**AACGHHIRY** hagiarchy	**AACHIMRRT** matriarch
AACELRTUW caterwaul	**AACGHILPR** graphical	**AACHIMRSS** archaisms
AACELRTUX curtalaxe	**AACGHIMNP** champaign	charismas
AACELRTUV arcuately	**AACGHINTT** attaching	**AACHIMSTT** asthmatic
AACELRTYZ catalyzer	**AACGHLLOS** agallochs	**AACHINNRY** Hyrcanian
AACELSSTY catalyses	**AACGHMORT** tachogram	**AACHINOPR** anaphoric
AACELSTTY cattleyas	**AACGHOPRR** arcograph	pharaonic
AACELSTYZ catalyzes	**AACGHOPSZ** gazpachos	**AACHINRST** anarchist
AACEMNNOR Connemara	**AACGHORSU** guacharos	cantharis
AACEMNPRT mercaptan	**AACGIIMNS** magicians	**AACHIPRRT** patriarch
AACEMNPRU Capernaum	**AACGIKNNP** pancaking	**AACHIPSTT** chapattis
AACEMNRST sacrament	**AACGIKNTT** attacking	**AACHIRSST** archaists
AACEMORRT macerator	**AACGILLLY** glacially	catharsis
AACEMRRSS massacrer	**AACGILLMY** magically	**AACHKMMRT** matchmark
AACEMRSSS massacres	**AACGILLNN** canalling	**AACHKSSTY** haystacks
AACENNNOY annoyance	**AACGILLOS** scagliola	**AACHLLMRY** lachrymal
AACENNOSS assonance	**AACGILMNN** manacling	**AACHLLPTY** cataphyll
AACENPRRY parcenary	**AACGILMOR** macroglia	**AACHLMNOR** monarchal
AACENPSSU saucepans	**AACGILNPT** placating	**AACHLMRSY** marshalcy
AACENPSTT pancettas	**AACGILNTT** lactating	**AACHMNNOR** anchorman
AACENRSSU anacruses	**AACGIMNPS** campaigns	**AACHMNORW** charwoman
assurance	**AACGIMOTU** autogamic	**AACHMNSTY** yachtsman
AACENRSSV canvasser	**AACGIMPRT** pragmatic	**AACHMORST** achromats
AACENRSTT reactants	**AACGIMSUU** guaiacums	**AACHMRRTU** Macarthur
AACENRSVZ czarevnas	**AACGINOOS** ascogonia	MacArthur
AACENRTTU cauterant	**AACGINORV** Craigavon	**AACHNNOTY** anthocyan
AACENSSSV canvasses	**AACGINTTU** actuating	**AACHNOSTU** acanthous
AACENSSTT castanets	**AACGIOSSU** sagacious	**AACHNOTTY** chatoyant
AACENSTUV evacuants	**AACGLLSWY** scallywag	**AACHOPPRY** apocrypha
AACEOOPPT apocopate	**AACGLNOOT** octagonal	**AACHQSSTU** sasquatch
AACEORSTV caveators	**AACGLNOTU** coagulant	**AACIILLNV** Cavallini
AACEORTUV excavator	**AACGLOORY** acarology	**AACIILLRT** altricial
AACEORTVX excavator	**AACGLSSUY** Gay-Lussac	**AACIILMRS** racialism
AACEOSSST seacoasts	**AACGMORRT** cartogram	**AACIILMST** lamaistic
AACEOSTUX taxaceous	**AACGNNSTY** stagnancy	**AACIILNPT** ancipital
AACERRSTU arcatures	**AACGORSTU** sugarcoat	**AACIILNSS** anaclisis
AACERRTTT attracter	**AACHHHIUU** chihuahua	**AACIILNST** Castilian
AACERSSTT castrates	**AACHHIKNU** chanukiah	**AACIILNTV** vaticinal
AACERSSTT tractates	**AACHHILLR** rhachilla	**AACIILPRT** piratical
AACESSUWY causeways	**AACHHIRSS** Shacharis	**AACIILRST** racialist
AACFGLNRY flagrancy	**AACHHSTWY** hatchways	satirical
AACFGNRRY fragrancy	**AACHIILNP** Chaliapin	**AACIIMMST** miasmatic
AACFHIMNR chamfrain	**AACHIILPT** aliphatic	**AACIIMOTX** axiomatic
AACFHJKST jackshaft	**AACHIIMRS** mariachis	**AACIINNOP** poinciana
AACFHMSST camshafts	**AACHIINRT** Carinthia	**AACIINNOT** nicotiana
AACFIILNN financial	**AACHIIPRS** pharisaic	**AACIINPRT** patrician
AACFIILRT trifacial	**AACHIIRRV** charivari	**AACIINRRT** Trinacria
AACFILNOT factional	**AACHIKMSY** skiamachy	**AACIINRTV** vicariant
AACFILORT factorial	**AACHILLPS** callipash	**AACIIPRST** parasitic
AACFILORV varifocal	**AACHILMNP** Champlain	**AACIIRRTU** urticaria
AACFIMNST fantasmic	**AACHILNOZ** chalazion	**AACIIRSSV** viscarias
AACFINNOR Franconia	**AACHILNPS** chaplains	**AACIISTTV** atavistic
AACFINSTT fantastic	**AACHILOPR** parochial	**AACIJNOPS** japonicas
AACFIRSTT artifacts	**AACHILOPT** chipolata	**AACIJNOTT** jactation
AACFJKLPS flapjacks	**AACHILPSS** pashalics	**AACIKLMSS** mailsacks

AACIKMNNY	kanamycin	**AACINNOST**	santonica	**AADDDEEHS**	deadheads
AACIKMNSW	mackinaws	**AACINOOTV**	avocation	**AADDDGNRS**	granddads
AACIKORTY	akaryotic	**AACINOPRS**	caparison	**AADDDGNRY**	grandaddy
AACILLMMN	Macmillan		paranoics	**AADDEEFHT**	fatheaded
	MacMillan	**AACINOPRT**	paratonic	**AADDEEGMN**	endamaged
AACILLNOT	allantoic	**AACINORST**	raincoats	**AADDEEHPS**	sapheaded
AACILLNRY	ancillary	**AACINORTU**	arcuation	**AADDEEHRT**	Dead Heart
	cranially	**AACINOSST**	cassation	**AADDEEIRT**	eradiated
AACILLNTU	lunatical	**AACINOSTU**	causation	**AADDEEMRY**	readymade
AACILLNTV	vacillant	**AACINOSTV**	vacations	**AADDEENRV**	verandaed
AACILLNTY	actinally	**AACINOTTU**	actuation	**AADDEENTT**	antedated
AACILLPRY	capillary	**AACINQSTU**	acquaints	**AADDEEPRT**	readapted
AACILLPTY	capitally	**AACINRSST**	sacristan	**AADDEFIRS**	faradised
AACILMMNO	ammonical	**AACINRSSU**	anacrusis	**AADDEFIRZ**	faradized
AACILMNST	calamints	**AACINRSTU**	Naucratis	**AADDEFLLS**	deadfalls
	claimants		rusticana	**AADDEGIMR**	diagramed
AACILMOSW	Mosaic law	**AACIOPRSU**	rapacious	**AADDEGITV**	divagated
AACILMPST	plasmatic	**AACIORTTV**	activator	**AADDEGLNR**	garlanded
AACILMRSU	simulacra	**AACIOSTTW**	waistcoat	**AADDEGMNU**	undamaged
AACILNNOR	nonracial	**AACIRSTZZ**	czaritzas	**AADDEGRTU**	graduated
AACILNNUV	vulcanian	**AACJKLPSS**	slapjacks	**AADDEHHRS**	hardheads
AACILNOPT	placation	**AACJKOORS**	jackaroos	**AADDEHILU**	Eid-ul-Adha
AACILNORR	carnaroli	**AACJKSSTY**	jackstays	**AADDEHLNS**	headlands
AACILNORT	cantorial	**AACKKNPSS**	knapsacks	**AADDEHNST**	headstand
AACILNOTT	lactation	**AACKORSWY**	rockaways	**AADDEHRSW**	headwards
AACILNOTY	acylation	**AACLLOPRS**	collapsar	**AADDEILNO**	adenoidal
	claytonia	**AACLLOSTY**	coastally	**AADDEILPS**	palisaded
AACILNPPT	applicant	**AACLLRRSY**	carryalls	**AADDEILPT**	lapidated
AACILNRST	carnalist	**AACLLRSTU**	claustral	**AADDEILTV**	validated
AACILNRSV	carnivals	**AACLLTTUY**	tactually	**AADDEIMNR**	marinaded
AACILNRTY	carnality	**AACLNNOSU**	noncausal	**AADDEIMNW**	Wad Medani
AACILNRUV	navicular	**AACLNOOSS**	Soo Canals	**AADDEINNV**	Nanda Devi
AACILNSTU	actual sin	**AACLNOPTU**	cantaloup	**AADDEINRT**	andradite
AACILORTU	auctorial	**AACLNRUUV**	avuncular	**AADDELLNS**	sandalled
AACILOSSU	salacious	**AACLOPRTU**	portulaca	**AADDELMNR**	dreamland
AACILOSTT	coattails	**AACLOPRTY**	placatory	**AADDELPPU**	applauded
AACILPRTU	capitular	**AACLOPSTV**	postcaval	**AADDELRST**	astraddle
AACILPRTY	paralytic	**AACLORSSU**	carousals	**AADDEMNNT**	demandant
AACILPSSZ	capsizals	**AACLPRSSU**	scapulars	**AADDEMNOR**	andromeda
AACILQTTU	acquittal	**AACLPRSTY**	calyptras	**AADDEMRSY**	daydreams
AACILRRTU	articular	**AACLPRSUY**	scapulary	**AADDEMRVY**	daydreamy
AACILRRUU	auricular	**AACLPSTTU**	catapults	**AADDENPTU**	unadapted
AACILRSTT	Scarlatti	**AACLRRTUY**	cartulary	**AADDEORST**	roadstead
AACILRSTY	rascality	**AACLSSTTY**	catalysts	**AADDEQRTU**	quadrated
	satyrical	**AACMNOORS**	macaroons	**AADDGNRSU**	graduands
AACILRSUU	auriculas	**AACMNOTTU**	catamount	**AADDHIMNS**	handmaids
AACILSSTY	catalysis	**AACMNRRSU**	macrurans	**AADDHNNST**	handstand
AACILSTUY	causality	**AACMOOSTT**	scotomata	**AADDIIMRV**	dairymaid
AACILTTUY	actuality	**AACNNORRV**	Carnarvon	**AADDINPRT**	dandiprat
AACIMNNNU	Mancunian	**AACNNOSTT**	Constanţa	**AADDIRRWY**	Irrawaddy
AACIMNOPR	panoramic	**AACNRSSTT**	transacts	**AADDLNRSW**	landwards
AACIMNORR	Armorican	**AACNRSTUY**	sanctuary	**AADDLRSTY**	dastardly
AACIMNORS	macaronis	**AACNRSTUZ**	Santa Cruz	**AADDMRSTT**	Darmstadt
	marocains	**AACOOPSTT**	capotasto	**AADDNRSST**	standards
AACIMNOST	anosmatic	**AACORRSTT**	castrator	**AADEEGHMT**	megadeath
AACIMOPRS	macropsia	**AACORRSTV**	varactors	**AADEEGHNP**	phagedena
AACIMORST	aromatics	**AACORRTTT**	attractor	**AADEEGHST**	Gateshead
AACIMORTU	amaurotic	**AACORSSTT**	castratos	**AADEEGLMN**	magdalene
AACIMOTTU	automatic	**AACORSSWY**	cassowary	**AADEEGMNS**	endamages
AACIMRRSU	sacrarium	**AACORSTTU**	actuators	**AADEEGNOR**	orangeade
AACIMRTTU	traumatic		autocrats	**AADEEGNPP**	appendage
AACINNORT	carnation	**AACPRSSTU**	Spartacus	**AADEEHHRX**	hexahedra

AADEEHKNS	snakehead	**AADEGINTV**	navigated	**AADEILMRT**	diametral
AADEEHPRS	spearhead	**AADEGIPRS**	disparage	**AADEILMRV**	Valdemar I
AADEEIKWW	wideawake	**AADEGIQRU**	quadrigae	**AADEILMRW**	Waldemar I
AADEEILMV	mediaeval	**AADEGISTV**	divagates	**AADEILNNN**	annelidan
AADEEILNT	alienated	**AADEGLLNT**	gallanted	**AADEILNNR**	adrenalin
AADEEIMNT	deaminate	**AADEGLLOP**	gallopade	**AADEILNNS**	Inland Sea
AADEEIRST	eradiates	**AADEGLMNS**	magdalens	**AADEILNOT**	dealation
AADEEKMRR	earmarked	**AADEGLMSY**	amygdales	**AADEILNSS**	nasalised
AADEEKMRY	makeready	**AADEGLNNR**	rangeland	**AADEILNSV**	vandalise
AADEELLMN	allemande	**AADEGLNRV**	landgrave	**AADEILNSZ**	nasalized
AADEELNPS	esplanade	**AADEGLNTU**	angulated	**AADEILNVZ**	vandalize
AADEELNRX	alexander	**AADEGLOPS**	galopades	**AADEILPSS**	palisades
AADEELPPR	appareled	**AADEGLRVW**	waldgrave	**AADEILPST**	lapidates
AADEELPRV	palavered	**AADEGMMUY**	mamaguyed		stapedial
AADEELRRY	lay reader	**AADEGMNRS**	grandames	**AADEILRTV**	travailed
AADEELTUV	devaluate	**AADEGMOSV**	savagedom	**AADEILSSW**	wassailed
	evaluated	**AADEGNOPR**	paragoned	**AADEILSTV**	salivated
AADEEMNRT	tradename	**AADEGNRRT**	regardant		validates
AADEEMRRS	demeraras	**AADEGNSTT**	stagnated	**AADEILTUV**	laudative
AADEEMRSU	admeasure	**AADEGORRT**	arrogated	**AADEIMMNS**	maenadism
AADEENSTT	antedates	**AADEGRRRU**	rearguard	**AADEIMNRS**	marinades
AADEENSTU	nauseated	**AADEGRRVY**	graveyard	**AADEIMNRT**	marinated
AADEEORTT	toadeater	**AADEGRSTU**	graduates	**AADEIMRST**	dramatise
AADEEPRST	paederast	**AADEGRSTZ**	stargazed	**AADEIMRSV**	maravedis
	separated	**AADEHHKNS**	handshake	**AADEIMRTZ**	dramatize
AADEERRTT	retardate	**AADEHILNS**	nailheads	**AADEIMSST**	adamsites
AADEESTTV	devastate	**AADEHILRR**	diarrheal	**AADEINPRT**	pintadera
AADEFGLNN	fandangle	**AADEHILRS**	headrails	**AADEINRST**	steradian
AADEFGRSU	safeguard		railheads	**AADEINRTT**	attainder
AADEFHLST	flatheads	**AADEHILSS**	headsails	**AADEINTTT**	attainted
AADEFHSST	headfasts	**AADEHIMOT**	haematoid	**AADEIPPRS**	appraised
AADEFILNT	fantailed	**AADEHIORR**	diarrhoea		disappear
AADEFILRS	fairleads	**AADEHIPRT**	apartheid	**AADEIPRSS**	paradises
AADEFINST	fantasied	**AADEHIRST**	stairhead	**AADEIPRST**	aspirated
AADEFIORS	aforesaid	**AADEHISWY**	hideaways		disparate
AADEFIRRS	faradiser	**AADEHLLLL**	hallalled	**AADEIPSSU**	diapauses
AADEFIRRZ	faradizer	**AADEHLLST**	headstall	**AADEISSST**	diastases
AADEFIRSS	faradises	**AADEHLMNN**	manhandle	**AADEJKLWY**	jaywalked
AADEFIRSZ	faradizes	**AADEHLMPS**	headlamps	**AADEJLLNS**	Sjælland
AADEFLLRS	falderals	**AADEHLMRS**	marshaled	**AADEJRUVY**	Yajur-Veda
AADEFLNOR	farandole	**AADEHLMSY**	ashamedly	**AADEKLRSY**	kaleyards
AADEFLRSY	defrayals	**AADEHLNNP**	panhandle	**AADEKMNRS**	mandrakes
AADEFMPRT	afterdamp	**AADEHLNRT**	heartland	**AADEKMRRT**	trademark
AADEFMRST	farmstead	**AADEHLPSS**	slapheads	**AADEKMRWY**	waymarked
AADEFOSWY	Days of Awe	**AADEHLPST**	asphalted	**AADELLNOT**	lanolated
AADEFRRTW	afterward	**AADEHMNSU**	unashamed	**AADELLNTU**	landaulet
AADEFSSTT	steadfast	**AADEHMPST**	Hampstead	**AADELLNUY**	unallayed
AADEGHNRU	harangued	**AADEHMSST**	mastheads	**AADELLQRU**	quadrella
AADEGHNRY	hydrangea	**AADEHNRSV**	verandahs	**AADELLSSY**	saleslady
AADEGHNST	stagehand	**AADEHORRW**	arrowhead	**AADELMMOR**	melodrama
AADEGIIRT	Dei gratia	**AADEHPRTT**	deathtrap	**AADELMNOR**	ealdorman
AADEGILRT	taligrade	**AADEHRRTW**	earthward	**AADELMNRS**	malanders
AADEGILTT	tailgated	**AADEHRSVW**	drawshave	**AADELMPSU**	Lampedusa
AADEGIMNT	diamagnet	**AADEIILMR**	airmailed	**AADELNNTU**	annulated
AADEGINNR	Grenadian	**AADEIIPRS**	praesidia	**AADELNPST**	peatlands
AADEGINPS	paganised	**AADEIIRRT**	irradiate	**AADELNRRU**	rural dean
AADEGINPT	paginated	**AADEIIRTV**	radiative	**AADELNSTW**	wasteland
AADEGINPZ	paganized	**AADEIKLLS**	alkalised	**AADELOPRT**	pardalote
AADEGINRR	arraigned	**AADEIKLLZ**	alkalized	**AADELPPRU**	applauder
AADEGINRS	drainages	**AADEILLPT**	palliated	**AADELPRSY**	paralysed
	gardenias	**AADEILMNN**	almandine	**AADELPRTW**	drawplate
AADEGINRT	tragedian	**AADEILMNT**	laminated	**AADELPRYZ**	paralyzed

AADELRSSY saleyards	**AADGILNOS** diagonals	**AADIKLRSY** kailyards
AADELSSTU assaulted	**AADGILNTU** adulating	**AADILLMOR** armadillo
AADEMMNNOR memoranda	**AADGILORT** gladiator	**AADILLMPU** palladium
AADEMMRST Amsterdam	**AADGILRRU** guardrail	**AADILLOPS** sapodilla
AADEMNPRS ampersand	**AADGIMMNO** gammadion	**AADILMNNO** adnominal
AADEMNRST tradesman	**AADGIMNNT** mandating	**AADILMNOR** Māoriland
AADEMOOST stomodaea	**AADGIMNRU** marauding	**AADILMNOV** Moldavian
AADEMOTTU automated	**AADGIMORR** radiogram	**AADILMNSV** vandalism
AADEMPRRT ramparted	**AADGIMORU** audiogram	**AADILMNTU** Tamil Nadu
AADEMPTTU amputated	**AADGIMPRS** paradigms	**AADILMOPS** plasmodia
AADEMRRSU marauders	**AADGINORT** gradation	**AADILMORT** maladroit
AADEMRTTU maturated	**AADGINRRS** darraigns	**AADILMPRY** pyramidal
AADENNOTT annotated	**AADGINRSU** guardians	**AADILMRTY** admiralty
AADENNPPT appendant	**AADGINRUZ** Dzungaria	**AADILNNOT** antinodal
AADENNPRT trapanned	**AADGIQRSU** quadrigas	**AADILNOPT** antipodal
AADENNRST Santander	**AADGJPRUU** Durga Puja	**AADILNOTT** antidotal
AADENNTTT attendant	**AADGLLNRU** glandular	**AADILNOTU** adulation
AADENOWWX woadwaxen	**AADGLLRUY** gradually	laudation
AADENPPRS sandpaper	**AADGLNOOW** wagonload	
AADENPRTU pandurate	**AADGLNRSS** grassland	**AADILNRTY** radiantly
AADENRRTT retardant	**AADGLNSSS** sandglass	**AADILNSTT** dilatants
AADENRRTW warranted	**AADGMNORS** dragomans	**AADILNSWZ** Swaziland
AADEOPRRS paradores	**AADGMNRSU** guardsman	**AADILORRS** railroads
AADEOPRSS paradoses	**AADGMRRTU** dramaturg	**AADILORTT** dilatator
AADEOPRSX paradoxes	**AADGNNQSU** quandangs	**AADILOSVW** disavowal
AADEORTTV rotavated	**AADGNNRTU** grandaunt	**AADILPSSY** dysplasia
AADEPPRST preadapts	**AADGNRSUV** vanguards	**AADIMNNOT** damnation
AADEQRSTU quadrates	**AADGNRSWY** drangways	**AADIMNNRS** mandarins
AADERRRSW rearwards	**AADGORRTU** graduator	**AADIMNRST** tamarinds
AADERRSVY adversary	**AADGRRSUW** gurdwaras	**AADIMNRSZ** zamindars
AADERRTTT tartrated	**AADHHJKNR** Jharkhand	**AADIMNUVZ** avizandum
AADERSSTW eastwards	**AADHIIILR** Harald III	**AADIMPSST** misadapts
AADERSTTU saturated	**AADHIINPS** aphidians	**AADIMRSTT** dramatist
AADFFIITV affidavit	**AADHILLNO** Hollandia	**AADINNNOT** andantino
AADFGIRUU Guardafui	**AADHILLRS** halliards	**AADINNOOT** anodontia
AADFGNNOS fandangos	**AADHILNRS** handrails	**AADINOORT** adoration
AADFGNORR Fragonard	**AADHILNSV** vandalish	**AADINOPRS** paranoids
AADFHNSST handfasts	**AADHILRST** tahsildar	**AADINOPSS** diapasons
AADFILNRY fairyland	**AADHILRSV** havildars	**AADINOPST** adaptions
AADFLLLNS landfalls	**AADHINNOT** danthonia	**AADINSSTY** saint's day
AADFLOSTW dataflows	**AADHINPSU** Upanishad	**AADIORRST** radiators
AADFMNRST draftsman	**AADHINRRS** harridans	**AADIORRTY** radiatory
AADFMRRSY farmyards	**AADHIORRT** arthrodia	**AADIORSTU** sudatoria
AADGGGINR aggrading	**AADHIPSSY** dysphasia	**AADIPRSXY** dyspraxia
AADGGHHOT haggadoth	**AADHKLNRS** landshark	**AADIPSSUY** upsadaisy
AADGGHIST haggadist	**AADHLLNST** hallstand	**AADIRRSSY** disarrays
AADGGHLRY haggardly	**AADHLMNRS** marshland	**AADJNSTTU** adjutants
AADGGINRT gradating	**AADHMNOSU** omadhauns	**AADJNSTUV** adjuvants
AADGGLLRY laggardly	**AADHNSSTW** washstand	**AADKLMNRS** landmarks
AADGGRSST staggards	**AADHORRSU** hadrosaur	**AADKLNOSW** Landowska
AADGHIMPR diaphragm	**AADHORSUZ** hazardous	**AADKLNPRS** parklands
AADGHINRT Adi Granth	**AADIIINNN** Indianian	**AADKLORSV** volksraad
AADGHINRZ hazarding	**AADIILMNV** Maldivian	**AADKLRWWY** awkwardly
AADGHIPRS diagraphs	**AADIIMMOT** ommatidia	**AADKNORRS** Krasnodar
AADGHIPSY dysphagia	**AADIIMNRZ** zamindari	**AADLLOPSU** palladous
AADGIINRT radiating	**AADIINORT** radiation	**AADLMNORS** mandorlas
AADGIKMNS damasking	**AADIINRRT** irradiant	**AADLMNPSW** swampland
AADGILLOS gladiolas	**AADIIORTU** auditoria	**AADLMOORV** Almodóvar
AADGILLRS galliards	**AADIIQRUV** quadrivia	**AADLORSST** loadstars
AADGILMNY amygdalin	**AADIISSST** diastasis	**AADLORSTU** adulators
AADGILMRS madrigals	**AADIJNNOR** Jordanian	**AADLORTUY** adulatory
AADGILNOR girandola	**AADIKLLOS** alkaloids	laudatory

AADLRWWYY	waywardly	AAEEKMNSS	namesakes	AAEFFINRT	raffinate
AADMMNOOR	monodrama	AAEEKMRST	teamakers	AAEFFLNUZ	affluenza
AADMNORST	mandators	AAEEKNPTW	wapentake	AAEFGHMNR	Fermanagh
AADMNORTY	damnatory	AAEEKNRSW	reawakens	AAEFGHRWS	wharfages
	mandatory	AAEEKPRRT	parrakeet	AAEFGINRS	seafaring
AADMORRST	tramroads	AAEEKPRST	parakeets	AAEFGIRSX	saxifrage
AADNNORSU	anandrous	AAEEKPSSY	speakeasy	AAEFGLLLR	flagellar
AADNOOPSW	sapanwood	AAEEKQSSU	seaquakes	AAEFGORRS	farragoes
AADNOORRS	Aaron's rod	AAEELLLMT	lamellate	AAEFHLRST	flatshare
AADNQRSTU	quadrants	AAEELLMRS	amarelles	AAEFHMRTT	aftermath
AADOPPRRS	paradrops	AAEELLOTV	alveolate	AAEFIILLR	alfileria
AADOPPRST	strappado	AAEELLPPT	appellate	AAEFIKLST	kalifates
AADOPSSUY	paduasoys	AAEELLPTT	patellate	AAEFILNTX	antefixal
AADORSSVY	savoyards	AAEELLQRU	aquarelle	AAEFILRTY	fairytale
AAEEEHLRT	aethereal	AAEELMMRT	metameral	AAEFIMMNR	mainframe
AAEEFHRTT	afterheat	AAEELMMST	metamales	AAEFIMNOU	meiofauna
AAEEFKPRT	afterpeak	AAEELMNPT	nameplate	AAEFIMRRS	airframes
AAEEFLOTV	faveolate	AAEELMNRT	Tamerlane	AAEFINNRS	safranine
AAEEFLTTY	Lafayette	AAEELMSST	matelasse	AAEFINNST	faineants
AAEEFRRSS	seafarers	AAEELMSTT	stalemate	AAEFINSST	fantasies
AAEEGGGRT	aggregate	AAEELNNRS	annealers		fantasise
AAEEGINTV	evaginate	AAEELNOPR	aeroplane	AAEFINSTZ	fantasize
AAEEGIRTV	variegate	AAEELNPSS	seaplanes	AAEFINTTU	infatuate
AAEEGLRVY	averagely	AAEELNRTT	alternate	AAEFKLLST	leafstalk
AAEEGMNNS	manganese	AAEELNSST	elastanes	AAEFKLNRR	farnarkel
AAEEGMPRS	amperages	AAEELPPRS	appealers	AAEFKMSST	makefasts
AAEEGNORS	Aragonese	AAEELPRST	palestrae	AAEFLLLRY	fallalery
AAEEGNPRT	parentage	AAEELPSTV	Laptev Sea	AAEFLLRTW	waterfall
AAEEGNRRR	rearrange	AAEELRSTU	laureates	AAEFLMSTT	flatmates
AAEEGNRSS	sangarees	AAEELRTTZ	lazarette	AAEFLNRRT	fraternal
AAEEGNRST	tagareens	AAEELRTUV	revaluate	AAEFLORTZ	Fortaleza
AAEEGNRTU	guarantee	AAEELRTUY	aureately	AAEFMNSTY	safetyman
AAEEGNRHW	Greenaway	AAEELSTUV	evaluates	AAEFRRSWY	wayfarers
AAEEGPRSU	gaspereau	AAEELSVWY	wayleaves	AAEGGHIOP	geophagia
AAEEHIMNT	haematein	AAEEMMNTZ	amazement	AAEGGILLN	galingale
AAEEHIMTT	haematite	AAEEMMPTY	empyemata	AAEGGILNR	laagering
AAEEHISST	aesthesia	AAEEMMPTZ	temazepam	AAEGGILNW	Galwegian
AAEEHKNNT	Akhenaten	AAEEMMNST	teammates	AAEGGINOS	anagogies
AAEEHLMRX	hexameral	AAEEMMNNS	anamneses	AAEGGINRV	averaging
AAEEHLMTW	wheatmeal	AAEEMNPST	nametapes	AAEGGLLNO	gallonage
AAEEHLRRS	rehearsal	AAEEMPRRT	parameter	AAEGGLMOU	magalogue
AAEEHMNTU	athenaeum	AAEENPPRT	parapente	AAEGGLNSU	languages
AAEEHMNTX	exanthema	AAEENRRTW	warrantee	AAEGGMMRS	grammages
AAEEHMPST	metaphase	AAEENRSST	arsenates	AAEGGNRSY	garganeys
AAEEHRRSW	shareware		serenatas	AAEGGOPRS	paragoges
AAEEHRSTW	wheatears	AAEENRSSW	awareness	AAEGGOPRU	paragogue
AAEEIKLMT	Amalekite	AAEENRSTT	anteaters	AAEGHIILM	hemialgia
AAEEIKLMU	leukaemia	AAEENSSTU	nauseates	AAEGHILNS	Saghalien
AAEEILLMN	El Alamein	AAEENTTTU	attenuate	AAEGHINRW	Whangarei
AAEEILLTV	alleviate	AAEEOPRSU	aeropause	AAEGHLLPY	hypallage
AAEEILMNS	Melanesia	AAEEOPRTV	evaporate	AAEGHLNOX	hexagonal
AAEEILNST	alienates	AAEEPPRRS	rapparees	AAEGHLNPR	phalanger
AAEEILRTT	aliterate		reappears	AAEGHLNPS	phalanges
	retaliate	AAEEPPRSS	appeasers	AAEGHMRSX	hexagrams
AAEEIMNRT	reanimate	AAEEPRRTY	ratepayer	AAEGHNOPR	orphanage
AAEEIMNTV	emanative	AAEEPRSST	separates	AAEGHNORS	angashore
AAEEIMNTX	exanimate	AAEERRSWW	rewarewas	AAEGHNRRU	haranguer
AAEEINSTW	Taiwanese	AAEERSSTT	stearates	AAEGHNRSU	harangues
AAEEIPTTX	expatiate	AAEESTTVV	Tsvetaeva	AAEGHOPRY	aerophagy
AAEEISTTV	aestivate	AAEFFIILT	affiliate	AAEGHORRT	Harrogate
AAEEKKMVY	Makeyevka	AAEFFILRS	rafflesia	AAEGIILMO	oligaemia
AAEEKLNNP	palankeen	AAEFFINPR	paraffine	AAEGIILNT	genitalia

AAEGIILQU	aquilegia	**AAEGLOSST**	aglossate	**AAEHMMNOT**	Mahometan
AAEGIKNNW	awakening	**AAEGLPRSV**	palsgrave	**AAEHMMOST**	hematomas
AAEGILLRS	gallerias	**AAEGLRSSV**	salvagers	**AAEHMNRSW**	washerman
AAEGILLRV	Gällivare	**AAEGLRSSW**	glassware	**AAEHMOOTZ**	hematozoa
AAEGILMNS	magnesial	**AAEGLRSTU**	gastrulae	**AAEHMORST**	atheromas
AAEGILMRT	metralgia	**AAEGLRTTU**	gratulate	**AAEHMOSTT**	haemostat
AAEGILNNN	annealing	**AAEGMMNNO**	Agamemnon	**AAEHMQSSU**	quamashes
AAEGILNNT	galantine	**AAEGMNOPT**	tamponage	**AAEHMRSTU**	shamateur
AAEGILNOS	analogies	**AAEGMNORT**	matronage	**AAEHNNTUY**	Netanyahu
	analogise	**AAEGMNPRT**	pentagram	**AAEHNPSST**	pheasants
AAEGILNOZ	analogize	**AAEGMNRST**	magnetars	**AAEHNSSTT**	Shan State
AAEGILNPP	appealing	**AAEGMNRTT**	termagant	**AAEHNSTTX**	xanthates
	lagniappe	**AAEGMORRS**	aerograms	**AAEHRRSTT**	earthstar
AAEGILNPS	pelagians	**AAEGMORSS**	sagamores	**AAEHRSSTU**	arethusas
AAEGILNRU	neuralgia	**AAEGMPRRS**	rampagers	**AAEHRSSUU**	Ahasuerus
AAEGILNST	agentials	**AAEGMRRSV**	margraves	**AAEIILMNR**	animalier
	alginates	**AAEGMRRTT**	tetragram	**AAEIILMNS**	animalise
AAEGILNSV	galvanise	**AAEGMRSSS**	massagers	**AAEIILMNZ**	animalize
AAEGILNVZ	galvanize	**AAEGMRSST**	megastars	**AAEIILMRT**	latimeria
AAEGILRTT	tailgater	**AAEGMRSTT**	stratagem	**AAEIILNNT**	antialien
AAEGILSTT	tailgates	**AAEGMRSTU**	ageratums	**AAEIILNRS**	laniaries
AAEGIMMNS	mismanage	**AAEGMSTTW**	megawatts	**AAEIILPTX**	epitaxial
AAEGIMNNS	magnesian	**AAEGNNOOT**	Notogaean	**AAEIILRST**	aerialist
AAEGIMNNT	emanating	**AAEGNOPRS**	parsonage	**AAEIILRSV**	Rea Silvia
	manganite	**AAEGNOPRT**	patronage	**AAEIIMNNT**	inanimate
AAEGIMNRR	margarine	**AAEGNPRTY**	pageantry	**AAEIIMRST**	artemisia
AAEGIMNRT	marginate	**AAEGNRRRS**	arrangers	**AAEIINNOS**	Ionian Sea
AAEGIMNSZ	magazines	**AAEGNRSTU**	runagates	**AAEIINQTU**	Aquitaine
AAEGIMRRS	marriages	**AAEGNRSTV**	Stavanger	**AAEIINSST**	taeniasis
AAEGIMRRT	margarite	**AAEGNSSTT**	stagnates	**AAEIINSTT**	insatiate
AAEGIMRST	maritages	**AAEGOPPRT**	propagate	**AAEIJKLNW**	Kwajalein
AAEGINNRT	Argentina	**AAEGOPRSU**	Areopagus	**AAEIJNRST**	naartjies
AAEGINORT	aragonite	**AAEGORRST**	arrogates	**AAEIKKMSZ**	kamikazes
AAEGINPPR	appearing	**AAEGORSTT**	aegrotats	**AAEIKLLSS**	alkalises
AAEGINPPS	appeasing	**AAEGPRSTU**	pasturage	**AAEIKLLSZ**	alkalizes
AAEGINPRS	paganiser	**AAEGRRSTZ**	stargazer	**AAEIKLNNN**	Leninakan
AAEGINPRZ	paganizer	**AAEGRSSSU**	assuagers	**AAEIKLTTV**	talkative
AAEGINPSS	paganises	**AAEGRSSTZ**	stargazes	**AAEIKMNRR**	rainmaker
AAEGINPST	paginates	**AAEHHINPZ**	Zephaniah	**AAEIKMRRS**	kramerias
AAEGINPSZ	paganizes	**AAEHHLNOT**	halothane	**AAEIKRSTU**	autarkies
AAEGINPTZ	Gaziantep	**AAEHHLPTT**	phthalate	**AAEILLLSU**	alleluias
AAEGINRRR	arraigner	**AAEHHMMNNN**	Hahnemann	**AAEILLMMM**	mammillae
AAEGINRRS	granaries	**AAEHILMMS**	hamamelis	**AAEILLMMT**	mamillate
AAEGINRSY	asynergia	**AAEHILNTV**	leviathan	**AAEILLMNT**	alimental
	gainsayer	**AAEHILRST**	harestail	**AAEILLNPR**	enalapril
AAEGINSTV	navigates	**AAEHIMMNR**	Mariehamn	**AAEILLNPS**	sailplane
AAEGIRTTV	gravitate	**AAEHIMNOT**	theomania	**AAEILLNPT**	tailplane
AAEGISTTT	sagittate	**AAEHIMRTU**	hematuria	**AAEILLNTV**	élan vital
AAEGISVWY	giveaways	**AAEHINPST**	aphanites	**AAEILLPPT**	papillate
AAEGKKRRS	Skagerrak	**AAEHINRST**	rhatanies	**AAEILLPSS**	paillasse
AAEGKLNTU	Gatún Lake	**AAEHKMRSY**	haymakers		palliasse
AAEGLLMPS	plasmagel	**AAEHKNSYZ**	Ashkenazy	**AAEILLPST**	palliates
AAEGLLNRY	laryngeal	**AAEHLLNOP**	allophane	**AAEILMMRS**	marmalise
AAEGLMNOR	Mangalore	**AAEHLLSTU**	haustella	**AAEILMMRZ**	marmalize
AAEGLMNTU	mangulate	**AAEHLMRRS**	marshaler	**AAEILMMST**	melismata
AAEGLMPSY	gameplays	**AAEHLNPSX**	phalanxes	**AAEILMMSX**	axilemmas
AAEGLMSST	almagests	**AAEHLNPSY**	synalepha	**AAEILMNOS**	anomalies
AAEGLMTTU	glutamate	**AAEHLNRSW**	narwhales	**AAEILMNRT**	Lamartine
AAEGLNOSU	analogues	**AAEHLNSTT**	Athelstan	**AAEILMNSS**	Messalina
AAEGLNPPS	lagnappes	**AAEHLNSTX**	exhalants	**AAEILMNST**	laminates
AAEGLNRTU	granulate	**AAEHLOPPR**	phalarope	**AAEILMNSZ**	Manizales
AAEGLNSTU	angulates	**AAEHLPSUV**	upheavals	**AAEILMNTU**	aluminate

AAEILMPRV	primaeval
	verapamil
AAEILMPTT	palmitate
AAEILMRST	materials
AAEILMRTU	tularemia
AAEILMTVY	amatively
AAEILNNSU	annualise
AAEILNNUZ	annualize
AAEILNORS	Orléanais
AAEILNORT	alienator
	rationale
AAEILNPRS	airplanes
AAEILNPRT	perinatal
AAEILNPST	palatines
AAEILNPTX	taxiplane
AAEILNRSV	valerians
AAEILNSSS	nasalises
AAEILNSSZ	nasalizes
AAEILNSTT	tantalise
AAEILNTTT	tantalite
AAEILNTTZ	tantalize
AAEILORTV	variolate
AAEILPPTT	palpitate
AAEILPRST	parietals
	psalteria
AAEILPRTZ	trapezial
AAEILPSST	stapelias
AAEILRSSS	assailers
AAEILRSSW	wassailer
AAEILRSTU	estuarial
AAEILRSTV	varietals
AAEILSSSV	vassalise
AAEILSSTV	salivates
AAEILSSVZ	vassalize
AAEILSTUVX	laxatives
AAEIMMNOT	ammoniate
AAEIMNNOT	anamniote
	emanation
AAEIMNNSS	amnesiass
AAEIMNOPR	Pomerania
AAEIMNOST	anatomies
	anatomise
AAEIMNOTZ	amazonite
	anatomize
AAEIMNPRR	repairman
AAEIMNPRS	pearmains
AAEIMNRST	animaters
	marinates
AAEIMNRTU	Martineau
AAEIMNSTT	staminate
AAEIMOPRT	ametropia
AAEIMORST	aromatise
AAEIMORTZ	aromatize
AAEIMPRST	spermatia
AAEIMRRST	airstream
AAEIMRSTT	metatarsi
AAEINPPRT	appertain
AAEINPRST	septarian
AAEINPRTT	Antipater
AAEINPSSV	Vespasian
AAEINQTTU	antiquate
AAEINRRTV	narrative

AAEINRRTW	rainwater
AAEINRRVY	Inveraray
AAEINRSTT	reattains
AAEINSTTT	titanates
AAEIORSSU	Essaouira
AAEIPPRRS	appraiser
AAEIPPRSS	appraises
AAEIPRSST	aspirates
	parasites
	satrapies
AAEIPSSTV	passivate
AAEIRRSTT	tartarise
AAEIRRTTZ	tartarize
AAEIRSSTU	Aristaeus
AAEIRSSTV	aviatress
AAEIRSTTZ	zaratites
AAEISSSUV	assuasive
AAEJKLRWY	jaywalker
AAEJLNOPS	jalapenos
AAEKLMPRT	platemark
AAEKLMPRY	playmaker
AAEKLMRSW	lawmakers
AAEKLPRST	lapstrake
	lapstreak
AAEKMRRTW	watermark
AAEKNPRST	Pasternak
AAEKORSTY	akaryotes
AAEKPRRST	partakers
AAELLLMOR	malleolar
AAELLLPRS	parallels
AAELLLRTY	laterally
AAELLNPPT	appellant
AAELLORSV	alveolars
AAELLPPRW	wallpaper
AAELLSSUX	asexually
AAELLSWYY	alleyways
AAELMMNOS	melanomas
AAELMMORR	marmoreal
AAELMMOSX	axolemmas
AAELMMOTY	myelomata
AAELMMPST	metaplasm
AAELMMSTU	malamutes
AAELMNOSU	mausolean
AAELMNPPU	Pampeluna
AAELMNRSU	El Mansûra
AAELMNRSY	salarymen
AAELMPRST	malaperts
AAELMPSTY	playmates
AAELMRSTT	maltreats
AAELNNRTT	alternant
AAELNOPRT	rotaplane
AAELNORTZ	Lanzarote
AAELNPRST	prenatals
AAELNPRSW	warplanes
AAELNPRTY	planetary
AAELNPSTT	pantalets
AAELNRSSY	analysers
AAELNRSTT	translate
AAELNRSTX	relaxants
AAELNRSYZ	analyzers
AAELNRUWY	unawarely
AAELNSTTU	sultanate

AAELNUUVV	Vanua Levu
AAELOOPRT	tropaeola
AAELOPPRY	propylaea
AAELOPRSS	psoraleas
AAELOPRST	pastorale
AAELOPSSU	asepalous
AAELOPSTU	apetalous
AAELORRSU	rearousal
AAELORSTT	attolaser
AAELORTTZ	lazaretto
AAELORTUV	evaluator
AAELPRRSY	paralyser
AAELPRRYZ	paralyzer
AAELPRSST	palestras
AAELPRSSY	paralyses
AAELPRSYZ	paralyzes
AAELPSSTV	palstaves
AAELPSTTU	spatulate
AAELRRSTV	traversal
AAELRSSTU	assaulter
	australes
	saleratus
AAELRSTTW	saltwater
AAELRSUZZ	zarzuelas
AAELRSWYY	waylayers
AAELSSTWY	leastways
AAEMMNORR	marmorean
AAEMMNOST	ammonates
AAEMMNRST	armaments
AAEMMORTT	mattamore
AAEMMOSST	metasomas
AAEMNORST	emanators
AAEMNORTU	neuromata
AAEMNORTY	emanatory
AAEMNOSTZ	metazoans
AAEMNPRST	paraments
AAEMNPRTT	apartment
AAEMNQRSU	Marquesan
AAEMNSSTT	statesman
AAEMOOSTT	osteomata
AAEMORSSU	amauroses
AAEMORSTT	amarettos
	teratomas
AAEMOSTTU	automates
AAEMPRSTY	paymaster
AAEMPSTTU	amputates
AAEMRRSST	smartarse
AAEMRRSTU	armatures
AAEMRSSST	matrasses
AAEMRSTTU	maturates
AAENNNRTY	antennary
AAENNOSTT	annotates
AAENNPRRT	trapanner
AAENNTTTU	attenuant
AAENORRVZ	Verrazano
AAENORSTU	aeronauts
AAENPRSTY	peasantry
AAENPSTXY	anaptyxes
AAENRRRST	Stranraer
AAENRRRTW	warranter
AAENRSSTV	tsarevnas
AAENSTTTT	attestant

347

AAEOPRRST	separator
AAEOPRSTT	pastorate
AAEOPSSTT	apostates
AAEORSSTT	aerostats
AAEORSTTV	rotavates
AAEPPSSTT	appestats
AAEPRSTXY	taxpayers
AAERRSTTT	tartrates
AAERRSTTU	saturater
AAERSSTTU	saturates
AAERSTTWW	Wast Water
AAERSTWWY	waterways
AAFFFGLST	flagstaff
AAFFGILSS	gaffsails
AAFFGINRY	affraying
AAFFGNRSU	suffragan
AAFFILRST	taffrails
AAFFIMNRT	affirmant
AAFFINPRS	paraffins
AAFFKMNNU	Kauffmann
AAFGHNRSU	fraughans
AAFGILNRS	franglais
AAFGILNST	falangist
AAFGINRWY	wayfaring
AAFGLLORT	allograft
AAFGLORSU	sugarloaf
AAFGORTTU	autograft
AAFHHORTT	haftaroth
AAFHLSSTY	layshafts
AAFHMRRSU	Musharraf
AAFHRSSUU	hausfraus
AAFILLNRS	rainfalls
AAFILMNOR	foraminal
AAFILNOTX	aflatoxin
AAFILORUW	rauwolfia
AAFILSSTT	fatalists
AAFIMORTU	fumatoria
AAFINNRSS	safranins
AAFINSSTT	fantasist
AAFKLNOUU	Nuku'alofa
AAFLLPRST	pratfalls
AAFMORRTW	marrowfat
AAGGGHNSS	gangshags
AAGGGINRS	garagings
AAGGIINTT	agitating
AAGGILLNT	tallaging
AAGGILNSV	salvaging
AAGGIMNOR	angiogram
AAGGIMNPR	rampaging
AAGGIMNSS	massaging
AAGGINNRR	arranging
AAGGINPSS	passaging
AAGGINSSU	assuaging
AAGGKLNNP	gangplank
AAGGLLLSY	lallygags
AAGGLMNOR	Glamorgan
AAGGLNOSY	synagogal
AAGGMNOOY	agamogony
AAGHHILRT	high altar
AAGHHINSS	shanghais
AAGHHIRTT	High Tatra
AAGHHNOSS	oanshaghs

AAGHIKMNY	haymaking
AAGHIKMOS	Kagoshima
AAGHILLLN	halalling
AAGHILLMN	Allingham
AAGHILLNO	halloaing
AAGHILNNS	hangnails
AAGHILNRS	ashlaring
AAGHILPSU	ispaghula
AAGHIMOOP	omophagia
AAGHIMPRR	marigraph
AAGHINNRU	Hungarian
AAGHINNSW	Wang An Shi
AAGHINRSS	harassing
AAGHINSSY	sashaying
AAGHKMNSY	gymkhanas
AAGHLLOPR	allograph
AAGHLNPRY	pharyngal
AAGHLNPSY	anaglyphs
AAGHLNPYY	anaglyphy
AAGHMNOSY	hogmanays
AAGHNOOPR	angophora
AAGHNOSTU	agnathous
AAGHOPRTU	autograph
AAGIIKNNS	Kisangani
AAGIIKNRY	Kirinyaga
AAGIILNSS	assailing
AAGIIMNNS	magainins
AAGIIMNNT	animating
AAGIIMNRY	imaginary
AAGIINNSU	iguanians
AAGIINNTT	attaining
AAGIINOTT	agitation
AAGIINPPR	Agrippina
AAGIINRTT	antitragi
AAGIINSTT	satiating
AAGIJNNNP	japanning
AAGIKLNOS	kaoliangs
AAGIKMRSS	kissagram
AAGIKNPRT	partaking
AAGILLNPP	appalling
AAGILLNST	Saint Gall
AAGILLNTV	gallivant
AAGILLORT	alligator
AAGILLPSW	galliwasp
AAGILMNNO	agnominal
AAGILMNNP	napalming
AAGILMNNS	signalman
AAGILMNNT	malignant
AAGILMNOS	magnolias
AAGILMNRS	marginals
AAGILMNSV	galvanism
AAGILMNYZ	amazingly
AAGILMRST	magistral
AAGILNNSY	analysing
AAGILNNYZ	analyzing
AAGILNOST	analogist
	galtonias
	nostalgia
AAGILNPPT	palpating
AAGILNPRY	parlaying
AAGILNRRS	larrigans
AAGILNRSY	salarying

AAGILNRUU	inaugural
AAGILNRUV	vulgarian
AAGILNSTV	galivants
AAGILNTUV	valuating
AAGILNWYY	waylaying
AAGILOOPS	apologias
AAGILQUUY	Guayaquil
AAGILRRSW	warrigals
AAGIMMMST	magmatism
AAGIMMRRS	marigrams
AAGIMNOSY	anisogamy
AAGIMNPRT	ptarmigan
AAGIMORTU	matagouri
AAGIMSSST	massagist
AAGINNNSY	nannygais
AAGINNRRT	narrating
AAGINOOTV	vagotonia
AAGINOPRS	sporangia
AAGINORRS	rangioras
AAGINORTV	navigator
AAGINPRSU	pagurians
AAGINPSST	paganists
AAGINPTXY	taxpaying
AAGINSTTU	sitatunga
AAGIORSTT	agitators
AAGIORSUV	vagarious
AAGIPRSTZ	Gaza Strip
AAGIRSSTV	stravaigs
AAGKLNUUZ	Gazankulu
AAGKMORRY	karyogram
AAGKMORVY	karyogamy
AAGKNNRUU	Guru Nanak
AAGKNOORS	kangaroos
AAGLLLNTY	gallantly
AAGLLNNTU	ungallant
AAGLLNRTY	gallantry
AAGLLNRUY	angularly
AAGLLOPSY	polygalas
AAGLMMMOY	mammalogy
AAGLMNORU	granuloma
AAGLNNNOO	nonagonal
AAGLNOOSU	analogous
AAGLNQSUU	aqualungs
AAGLNRTTU	gratulant
AAGLNRTVY	vagrantly
AAGLRRSTU	gastrular
AAGLRSSTU	gastrulas
AAGMMMMOR	mammogram
AAGMNNOSU	manganous
AAGMNNORST	martagons
AAGMOOPSU	apogamous
AAGMRSSSU	sargassum
AAGNNORTU	orangutan
AAGNOORRT	Rarotonga
AAGNOPRST	tragopans
AAGNORRTU	guarantor
AAGNORSTU	angostura
	argonauts
AAGNRUUUV	Uruguayan
AAGOORRRT	arrogator
AAGORSSSS	sargassos
AAHHIIMRS	maharishi

AAHHIKNSU	hanukiahs
AAHHILLNS	inshallah
AAHHIMPPT	amphipath
AAHHINPTY	hypanthia
AAHHOPRST	parashoth
AAHIIKNOV	Haakon VII
AAHIIKRST	tarakihis
AAHIILNTU	Lithuania
AAHIILRST	hairtails
AAHIIMUWY	Mu'awiyah I
AAHIINRSY	Nasiriyah
AAHIKLPSS	pashaliks
AAHIKMNNR	Imran Khan
AAHIKRSTY	Kshatriya
AAHILLLSS	shillalas
AAHILMNOT	malathion
AAHILMPPY	Pamphylia
AAHILMTUZ	azimuthal
AAHILNNST	inhalants
AAHILNORT	inhalator
AAHILNSTU	ailanthus
AAHILORTU	authorial
AAHILPSXY	asphyxial
AAHIMMNSS	shamanism
AAHIMNOPY	hypomania
AAHIMNSST	shamanist
AAHIMNSTU	amianthus
AAHINOORR	honoraria
AAHINOPRT	parathion
AAHINPTTY	antipathy
AAHINRRTU	Arthurian
AAHIOPPSS	apophasis
AAHIORSTU	haustoria
AAHIPRRSY	hairspray
AAHJNRTUV	Thanjavur
AAHKLLMRS	hallmarks
AAHKLMNOO	Oklahoman
AAHKMOSTW	tomahawks
AAHLLMOSW	Hallowmas
AAHLLOPST	allopaths
AAHLLOPTY	allopathy
AAHLLPRSY	phrasally
AAHLMNNTU	lanthanum
AAHLNNNOT	lanthanon
AAHLNPSST	ashplants
AAHLPPPSY	slaphappy
AAHLPRSSU	Pharsalus
AAHMNNPTU	Hauptmann
AAHMNNSSU	Haussmann
AAHMNORST	marathons
AAHMNOSWW	washwoman
AAHMNPPRY	paranymph
AAHMNPSST	phantasms
AAHMOPPRR	paramorph
AAHNNOOTZ	anthozoan
AAHNNOSTU	ananthous
AAHNOTTXY	anthotaxy
AAHNSTUWY	huntaways
AAHOPRSTU	autoharps
AAHOQSSUW	aquashows
AAHORTHWY	throwaway
AAIIILMRT	militaria
AAIIJJPPS	jipijapas
AAIIKNNRU	Ukrainian
AAIIKNPST	Pakistani
AAIIKPRTT	tripitaka
AAIILLMST	tallaisim
AAIILMMNS	animalism
AAIILMNNR	laminarin
AAIILMNOS	islomania
AAIILMNSS	mainsails
AAIILMNST	animalist
AAIILMNTY	animality
AAIILMPRT	impartial
	primatial
AAIILNOPP	palinopia
AAIILNOSU	Louisiana
AAIILNRTV	antiviral
AAIILNSTU	Lusitania
AAIILRUXY	auxiliary
AAIIMMNST	animatism
AAIIMNNOT	animation
AAIIMNNST	maintains
AAIIMNORS	Asia Minor
AAIIMNRTU	Mauritian
AAIIMNSSS	Masinissa
AAIIMORST	Timișoara
AAIIMPPRR	primipara
AAIINNRTU	unitarian
AAIINNRTV	invariant
AAIINOPRT	topiarian
AAIINORTV	variation
AAIINOSTT	satiation
AAIINPRRS	riparians
AAIINRRTU	Ruritania
AAIINRSST	intarsias
AAIIPRSST	apiarists
AAIIRSSTV	aviarists
AAIJMRSSW	swarajism
AAIJNRSSY	janissary
AAIJRSSTW	swarajist
AAIKKNOSS	skokiaans
AAIKLLOSS	alkalosis
AAIKLNNNS	alkannins
AAIKLNNRS	Sri Lankan
AAIKLNOSV	Slovakian
AAIKLOSUV	souvlakia
AAIKMNSUY	Sakyamuni
AAIKMRSST	tamarisks
AAIKNNOPT	pontianak
AAIKNOTTU	taikonaut
AAIKNQRTU	antiquark
AAIKRSTTU	autarkist
AAIKSSSTW	swastikas
AAILLLNOT	lallation
AAILLLSUV	alluvials
AAILLMMRV	mamillary
AAILLMMXY	maximally
AAILLMNST	mantillas
AAILLMOPP	papilloma
AAILLMORT	tamarillo
AAILLMPST	taillamps
AAILLMRRY	armillary
AAILLMRSY	amaryllis
AAILLMRTY	maritally
	martially
AAILLMRXY	maxillary
AAILLNOPT	altiplano
AAILLNOST	allantois
AAILLNOTV	vallation
AAILLNPRU	nullipara
AAILLNPSW	Aspinwall
AAILLNTVY	valiantly
AAILLOPRT	palliator
AAILLPPRY	papillary
AAILLPRTY	partially
AAILLPSTY	spatially
AAILMNNPS	plainsman
AAILMNOPT	palmation
AAILMNORT	laminator
AAILMNOST	atonalism
AAILMNPRU	manipular
AAILMNSST	talismans
AAILMNTTU	matutinal
AAILMORRS	armorials
AAILMORSU	malarious
AAILMORTY	amorality
AAILMPRSU	marsupial
AAILMPRTU	multipara
AAILMRSST	alarmists
AAILNNOPS	Annapolis
AAILNNOPT	planation
AAILNNOST	nationals
	santolina
AAILNNOSV	Slavonian
AAILNNPQU	palanquin
AAILNNPRU	uniplanar
AAILNNPST	plantains
AAILNNRSU	lunarians
AAILNNSST	annalists
AAILNOOTV	ovational
AAILNOPPT	palpation
AAILNOPSS	passional
AAILNOPST	talapoins
AAILNOPUW	paulownia
AAILNORSS	orinasals
AAILNORST	rationals
AAILNOSTT	saltation
AAILNOSTV	lavations
	salvation
AAILNOTTY	atonality
AAILNOTUV	valuation
AAILNPPTT	palpitant
AAILNPRTU	tarpaulin
AAILNPRTY	planarity
AAILNPSTU	Saint Paul
AAILNSSTW	Stanisław
AAILOPPRY	polyparia
AAILOPRRT	raptorial
AAILOPSTX	postaxial
AAILORRST	sartorial
AAILPRSSY	paralysis
AAILQRSSU	squarials
AAILSSSTY	staysails
AAIMMNNOO	monomania
AAIMMNRST	Martinmas

AAIMMNNSST	mainmasts	**AAKNOOSST**	saskatoon	**ABBBDEELR**	blabbered
AAIMMRSSU	samariums	**AAKNOPSTV**	Návpaktos	**ABBBDEITT**	babbitted
AAIMNNNTU	Numantian	**AALLMOOSS**	Los Alamos	**ABBBEEILR**	bribeable
AAIMNNORS	San Marino	**AALLMOPSS**	plasmasol	**ABBBELRRS**	brabblers
AAIMNNORU	Roumanian	**AALLMPRUY**	ampullary	**ABBBGILNR**	brabbling
AAIMNNRST	San Martín	**AALLMRSYY**	Sally Army	**ABBBGILNS**	babblings
AAIMNOORT	inamorato	**AALLNNOPY**	pollyanna		blabbings
AAIMNOOTY	amyotonia	**AALLNNRUY**	annularly	**ABBBOSSTU**	subabbots
AAIMNOPRY	pyromania	**AALLNRTUY**	naturally	**ABBCCKKLO**	backblock
AAIMNORST	animators	**AALLOORSW**	wallaroos	**ABBCCKKLU**	blackbuck
AAIMNOSTT	anatomist	**AALLORRUY**	aurorally	**ABBCCKMOS**	backcombs
AAIMNPRSU	marsupian	**AALLORSAU**	allosaurs	**ABBCDEERU**	barbecued
AAIMNNRRST	trimarans	**AALLORSVY**	Yaroslavl	**ABBCDEFNO**	confabbed
AAIMNRSTT	tarantism	**AALMMNOSW**	almswoman	**ABBCDEKNS**	backbends
AAIMNSSST	mantissas	**AALMNNPST**	plantsman	**ABBCDELRS**	scrabbled
AAIMNSSTY	mainstays	**AALMNOOSU**	anomalous	**ABBCDELRY**	crabbedly
AAIMOORRT	moratoria	**AALMNOPRT**	patrolman	**ABBCDIKLR**	blackbird
AAIMOPRSS	mariposas	**AALMNPRTY**	rampantly	**ABBCDKLOY**	blackbody
	parosmias	**AALMOOSTU**	autosomal	**ABBCDKORU**	buckboard
AAIMORSSU	amaurosis	**AALMOQSSU**	squamosal	**ABBCEEIRS**	Caribbees
	mosasauri	**AALMORTYY**	mayoralty	**ABBCEERSU**	barbecues
AAIMOSSST	Massasoit	**AALMPPSSU**	paspalums	**ABBCEIKRT**	backbiter
AAIMQRSUU	aquariums	**AALNNOOPT**	pantaloon	**ABBCEIKST**	backbites
AAINNNSSY	sannyasin	**AALNNRTUU**	unnatural	**ABBCEILLM**	climbable
AAINNNTTU	annuitant	**AALNOOPZZ**	pozzolana	**ABBCEILRS**	barbicels
AAINNORRT	narration	**AALNOPSST**	postnasal	**ABBCEIOST**	abbotcies
AAINNORTT	Tarantino	**AALNOPSTT**	postnatal	**ABBCEIRST**	crabbiest
	tarnation	**AALNOPUZZ**	puzzolana	**ABBCEIRSY**	crybabies
AAINNOSST	sonatinas	**AALNOSTTU**	tantalous	**ABBCEISST**	scabbiest
AAINNOSTT	natations	**AALNPSTWX**	waxplants	**ABBCEKLLT**	black belt
AAINNRSTU	Saturnian	**AALNSSTWY**	slantways	**ABBCEKLNO**	boneblack
AAINNSSSY	sannyasis	**AALOPPRSV**	approvals	**ABBCEKNOS**	backbones
AAINOORRT	oratorian	**AALOPPSST**	apoplasts	**ABBCEKNSU**	buckbeans
AAINOPQRU	aquaporin	**AALOPRRTY**	portrayal	**ABBCELRRS**	scrabbler
AAINOPRST	antipasto	**AALOPRSST**	pastorals	**ABBCELRSS**	scrabbles
AAINORRSS	rosarians	**AALOPSSVY**	Savoy Alps	**ABBCGILNS**	scabbling
AAINOSTTX	taxations	**AALORSTTY**	saltatory	**ABBCHNRSU**	subbranch
AAINPRSST	aspirants	**AALORSTUV**	valuators	**ABBCIINRS**	rabbinics
	partisans	**AALRSSTTW**	stalwarts	**ABBCIMOST**	bombastic
AAINPRSTZ	partizans	**AAMMOORST**	Matamoros	**ABBCKLLUY**	buckyball
AAINPSSSY	asynapsis	**AAMNOOTTU**	automaton	**ABBCKLNRU**	Blackburn
AAINPSTXY	anaptyxis	**AAMNOPRTU**	paramount	**ABBCKLOOT**	bootblack
AAINQRRSU	quarrians	**AAMNQRRUY**	quarryman	**ABBCKLOSW**	blowbacks
AAINQRSTU	quatrains	**AAMOOPRST**	prosomata	**ABBCKLOSY**	blackboys
AAINQRTUY	antiquary	**AAMOPRRSU**	paramours	**ABBCKLTTU**	blackbutt
AAINQSTTU	aquatints	**AAMOPRTTU**	amputator	**ABBCKNRSU**	backburns
AAINSSSSS	assassins	**AAMORSSSU**	mosasaurs	**ABBCLMOOU**	abcoulomb
AAINSSSTT	assistant	**AANNOORTT**	annotator	**ABBDDEMOR**	bombarded
	satanists	**AANNOSSST**	assonants	**ABBDDOORY**	bodyboard
AAINSSTTV	avantists	**AANORRRST**	narrators	**ABBDEELOR**	belabored
AAIOPPRRT	apparitor	**AANORRRTW**	warrantor	**ABBDEELRS**	slabbered
AAIOPRRST	aspirator	**AANORSTTU**	astronaut	**ABBDEELRU**	bluebeard
AAIOPRTTV	Pavarotti	**AANPRSSSU**	Parnassus	**ABBDEGINR**	Banbridge
AAIOPSTTU	autopista	**AANRSSTTU**	saturants	**ABBDEGINU**	bedaubing
AAIORRTTT	trattoria	**AAOORRTTV**	rotavator	**ABBDEGNRU**	Bundaberg
AAIQRSSTU	aquarists	**AAOPRRSTY**	raspatory	**ABBDEHOOS**	boobheads
AAIRSSSTT	tsaritsas	**AAORRSTTU**	saturator	**ABBDEHRRU**	rhubarbed
AAIRSSTWY	stairways		tartarous	**ABBDEILLU**	buildable
AAJNORRTW	Trojan War	**AAORSSSSV**	vavassors	**ABBDEILOT**	bobtailed
AAKKMORRU	Karakorum	**AAORSSUUV**	vavasours	**ABBDEILTU**	dubitable
AAKMORSUZ	mazourkas	**AAOSSTWWY**	stowaways	**ABBDELLNY**	bellyband
AAKMOSSSU	moussakas	**ABBBCELLU**	clubbable	**ABBDELOTU**	doubtable

ABBDELQSU	squabbled
ABBDELSUU	subduable
ABBDEMORS	bombardes
ABBDENOSX	bandboxes
ABBDGILNR	drabbling
ABBDHIRST	birdbaths
ABBDHLOOT	bloodbath
ABBDILLOR	billboard
	broadbill
ABBDILTUY	dubitably
ABBDIMORR	broadbrim
ABBDLOTUY	doubtably
ABBDLSUUY	subduably
ABBDMNOOR	bombardon
ABBDNORSW	browbands
ABBDNOSTU	bandobust
ABBEEEHRS	Beersheba
ABBEEILLV	Abbeville
ABBEEJRRS	jabberers
ABBEEKLRU	rebukable
ABBEEKNOR	breakbone
ABBEELLMS	semblable
ABBEELOPR	probeable
ABBEELRRS	slabberer
ABBEELRRY	blaeberry
ABBEENRRY	baneberry
ABBEEOSTX	beatboxes
ABBEERRRY	bearberry
ABBEERSTT	barbettes
ABBEFILST	flabbiest
ABBEGIJNR	jabbering
ABBEGILLO	obligable
ABBEGINRR	barbering
ABBEGINRT	rabbeting
ABBEGLRRS	grabblers
ABBEHINOS	Hobbesian
ABBEHISST	shabbiest
ABBEHLOTU	tabbouleh
ABBEHORST	bathrobes
ABBEIKNRU	Burkinabé
ABBEILMOT	bombilate
ABBEILMRR	bramblier
ABBEILMSU	Abu Simbel
ABBEILSST	bistables
ABBEILSSU	bubalises
ABBEILSTW	wabbliest
ABBEIMNOR	Barenboim
ABBEIMNOS	bombasine
ABBEIMNOT	bombinate
ABBEIMNOZ	bombazine
ABBEIMRSU	berimbaus
ABBEINORT	barbitone
ABBEIRRST	rabbiters
ABBEKLOOR	brookable
ABBELLMPU	plumbable
ABBELLMSY	semblably
ABBELMOOZ	bamboozle
ABBELOPRS	probables
ABBELORSU	belabours
ABBELOSTY	stableboy
ABBELQRSU	squabbler
ABBELQSSU	squabbles

ABBELSTTU	battlebus
ABBENORST	absorbent
ABBEORRSS	absorbers
	reabsorbs
ABBEORSTW	browbeats
ABBERSUUU	subbureau
ABBESSSSU	subbasses
ABBFHLLSU	flashbulb
ABBFLOOST	bobfloats
ABBGGILNR	grabbling
ABBGIILOT	obbligati
ABBGIINRT	rabbiting
ABBGIJLNY	jabbingly
ABBGILLNO	billabong
ABBGILMNR	brambling
ABBGILOOT	obbligato
ABBGINNOT	Babington
ABBGINORS	absorbing
ABBGIORUU	Bourguiba
ABBHIINRT	B'nai B'rith
ABBHIOPST	abbotship
ABBHIORST	rabbitohs
ABBIIMNRS	rabbinism
ABBIINRST	rabbinist
ABBILLOST	boatbills
ABBILLSSU	sillabubs
ABBINNORU	Brian Boru
ABBJMRUUU	Bujumbura
ABBKKNOOS	bankbooks
ABBLLSSUY	syllabubs
ABBNNRSSU	suburbans
ABCCCCIOO	Boccaccio
ABCCCEFIO	beccafico
ABCCCKKLO	blackcock
ABCCDEEHN	bechanced
ABCCDHIKS	dabchicks
ABCCEEFRY	cybercafe
ABCCEEHKL	checkable
ABCCEEHNS	bechances
ABCCEENRU	buccaneer
ABCCEIIST	scabietic
ABCCEIKLL	clickable
ABCCEINOV	biconcave
ABCCEKMOS	comebacks
ABCCELNRU	carbuncle
ABCCELORY	cryocable
ABCCEMNRU	cumbrance
ABCCEMNTU	accumbent
ABCCEOOST	tobaccoes
ABCCFIINO	Fibonacci
ABCCFIMOR	bacciform
ABCCHHKNU	hunchback
ABCCHIOOR	Barocchio
ABCCHKLOT	backcloth
ABCCHKOTU	touchback
ABCCHNOOR	Conchobar
ABCCHNOOS	cabochons
ABCCIKKKS	kickbacks
ABCCIKRST	crabstick
ABCCILLOU	bucolical
ABCCILLUY	cubically
ABCCILNOO	obconical

ABCCILORU	corbicula
ABCCIRSTU	subarctic
ABCCKKOOR	crookback
ABCCKNOTU	countback
ABCCKOOST	cockboats
ABCCKORSS	backcross
ABCCKORTU	backcourt
ABCCMOORY	mobocracy
ABCDDEEHU	debauched
ABCDDEEIL	decidable
ABCDDEILU	adducible
ABCDDEKLO	blockaded
ABCDDENOS	absconded
ABCDDKORU	duckboard
ABCDEEEHL	de la Beche
ABCDEEEHU	debauchee
ABCDEEHMR	chambered
ABCDEEHRU	debaucher
ABCDEEHSU	debauches
ABCDEEILM	medicable
ABCDEEILR	calibered
ABCDEEKLN	blackened
ABCDEEKRT	bracketed
ABCDEELMR	clambered
ABCDEESSS	abscessed
ABCDEFIKL	backfield
ABCDEFIKR	backfired
ABCDEGIKR	ridgeback
ABCDEGIMR	Cambridge
ABCDEGIRS	birdcages
ABCDEHIOT	cohabited
ABCDEHKLO	blockhead
ABCDEHOOT	cohobated
ABCDEIIST	diabetics
ABCDEIJLU	judicable
ABCDEIKLS	backslide
ABCDEIKRU	rudbeckia
ABCDEIKSS	backsides
ABCDEILMY	medicably
ABCDEILNO	balconied
ABCDEILTU	decubital
ABCDEINTU	incubated
ABCDEIORT	bacteroid
ABCDEIPRU	Pardubice
ABCDEIRTT	bratticed
ABCDEKLNY	Clydebank
ABCDEKLOR	blockader
ABCDEKLOS	blockades
ABCDEKMRU	buckramed
ABCDEKNNS	neckbands
ABCDELLOS	scoldable
ABCDELMNO	Candomblé
ABCDELMRS	scrambled
ABCDEMNSU	dumbcanes
ABCDENORR	cornbread
ABCDENORS	absconder
ABCDENOSU	casebound
	subdeacon
ABCDEOORT	obcordate
ABCDGINOR	brocading
ABCDGINTU	abducting
ABCDHINRS	disbranch

ABCDHIOPR	chipboard
ABCDHIRSY	Charybdis
ABCDHKLOS	holdbacks
ABCDIKRRY	brickyard
ABCDILOPR	clipboard
ABCDILSUY	subacidly
ABCDINOOT	bandicoot
ABCDINOTU	abduction
ABCDIOOSU	bodacious
ABCDKLOOR	roadblock
ABCDKLOOW	blackwood
ABCDKNOSW	backdowns
ABCDKOORR	corkboard
ABCDKOOSW	backwoods
ABCDKOPRS	backdrops
ABCDKORSW	backsword
	backwords
ABCDLNRSU	scrubland
ABCDOORSW	crabwoods
ABCDOPRSU	cupboards
ABCDORSTU	abductors
ABCEEEELLR	cerebella
ABCEEEELLT	electable
ABCEEEELRT	celebrate
	erectable
ABCEEEELRX	execrable
ABCEEENNR	cerberean
ABCEEEERRT	cerebrate
ABCEEFHRU	Feuerbach
ABCEEFIRS	briefcase
ABCEEFLOR	forceable
ABCEEGKNR	greenback
ABCEEHIOT	cohabitee
ABCEEHIRT	Rechabite
ABCEEHKLO	chokeable
ABCEEHLLP	Pachelbel
ABCEEHLLY	bellyache
ABCEEHLRS	bleachers
ABCEEILLS	sliceable
ABCEEILNV	bivalence
ABCEEILRT	recitable
ABCEEILST	celibates
ABCEEILSX	excisable
ABCEEILTX	excitable
ABCEEIMMS	misbecame
ABCEEINOS	obeisance
ABCEEINNR	carbineer
ABCEEKKNR	breakneck
ABCEEKPSW	sweepback
ABCEELMNS	semblance
ABCEELMRR	clamberer
ABCEELMRY	cymbaleer
ABCEELNRT	celebrant
ABCEELNST	albescent
ABCEELNUU	nubeculae
ABCEELOPS	placeboes
ABCEELORT	bracteole
ABCEELORV	coverable
	revocable
ABCEELOTV	covetable
ABCEELRRS	cerebrals
ABCEELRST	bracelets

ABCEELRSU	rescuable
	securable
ABCEELRXY	execrably
ABCEELSUX	excusable
ABCEEMMOR	Morecambe
ABCEEMORR	embraceor
ABCEEMORT	embrocate
ABCEEMOTY	amebocyte
ABCEEMRRS	embracers
ABCEEMRRY	embracery
ABCEENORY	Conybeare
ABCEENOSZ	cabezones
ABCEENRTY	cybernate
ABCEENSTT	tabescent
ABCEEORST	obsecrate
ABCEEOSSU	sebaceous
ABCEEPRRU	cupbearer
ABCEESSSS	abscesses
ABCEFFHNO	Offenbach
ABCEFHLSU	flashcube
ABCEFIKLS	backfiles
ABCEFIKRS	backfires
	firebacks
ABCEFIRTU	bifurcate
ABCEFLOSU	focusable
ABCEFOSTU	obfuscate
ABCEGHINN	bleaching
ABCEGHINR	breaching
ABCEGHLNO	Long Beach
ABCEGILOR	bricolage
ABCEGILOT	cogitable
ABCEGIMNR	cambering
	embracing
ABCEGINNO	beaconing
ABCEGKLLS	blacklegs
ABCEGKLOS	blockages
ABCEGKMSU	megabucks
ABCEGKRSY	greybacks
ABCEGKRTU	tuckerbag
ABCEHILTY	chalybite
ABCEHINOT	aitchbone
ABCEHIORT	cohabiter
ABCEHKLLS	shellback
ABCEHKLOS	shockable
	shoeblack
ABCEHKMNR	benchmark
ABCEHKORS	horseback
ABCEHKRRY	hackberry
ABCEHKTUW	buckwheat
ABCEHLNTT	Blanchett
ABCEHLORS	bachelors
ABCEHLOTU	touchable
ABCEHLRSU	crushable
ABCEHLSSU	chasubles
ABCEHMOST	hecatombs
ABCEHOOST	cohobates
ABCEHOQRU	quebracho
ABCEHORRS	broachers
ABCEHORSU	barouches
ABCEHORTU	tarbouche
ABCEHRSTU	Bucharest
ABCEIILNS	sibilance

ABCEIILRS	irascible
ABCEIIMRT	imbricate
ABCEIJLNU	jubilance
ABCEIJNOT	abjection
ABCEIKLLS	Black Isle
ABCEIKRRV	Back River
ABCEIKSWZ	zwiebacks
ABCEILLOS	obeliscal
ABCEILLPP	clippable
ABCEILMOT	metabolic
ABCEILMST	blastemic
	cembalist
ABCEILNNS	binnacles
ABCEILNOS	balconies
ABCEILNOT	cobaltine
ABCEILNOV	invocable
ABCEILNRU	binuclear
	incurable
ABCEILNVY	bivalency
ABCEILORS	cabrioles
	carbolise
ABCEILORT	cabriolet
ABCEILORZ	carbolize
ABCEILOTT	cobaltite
ABCEILRTU	lubricate
ABCEILRUX	Excalibur
ABCEILSTU	bisulcate
ABCEILTXY	excitably
ABCEIMOTV	combative
ABCEIMRSW	micawbers
ABCEIMRTU	bacterium
ABCEINORS	carbonise
ABCEINORT	bicornate
ABCEINORZ	carbonize
ABCEINRRS	brisances
ABCEINRST	bacterins
ABCEINSST	bascinets
ABCEINSTU	incubates
ABCEIOPTT	betatopic
ABCEIPRRSU	carburise
ABCEIRRTU	rubricate
ABCEIRRUZ	carburize
ABCEIRSTT	brattices
ABCEJNSTU	subjacent
ABCEJOSSU	jacobuses
ABCEKKSSW	skewbacks
ABCEKLLNR	Bracknell
ABCEKLMOR	Blackmore
ABCEKLNSS	blackness
ABCEKLPRU	parbuckle
ABCEKOOSS	bookcases
	casebooks
ABCEKPSTW	backswept
	sweptback
ABCEKRTUW	waterbuck
ABCELLOOR	colorable
ABCELLRSU	subcellar
ABCELLRSW	screwball
ABCELLRUV	curveball
ABCELMOOR	rocambole
ABCELMRRS	scrambler
ABCELMRSS	scrambles

ABCELMRSY	cymbalers	**ABCHKOOPS**	chapbooks	**ABCKOOPRS**	scrapbook
ABCELNOST	constable	**ABCHKOOSS**	cashbooks	**ABCKOORRS**	roorbacks
ABCELNOTU	countable	**ABCHKORSV**	boschvark	**ABCKOORSU**	buckaroos
ABCELOOST	bootlaces	**ABCHKORTW**	throwback	**ABCKOPSST**	backstops
ABCELORVY	revocably	**ABCHLLNPU**	punchball	**ABCLLNORS**	cornballs
ABCELOSST	obstacles	**ABCHLLSUU**	clubhauls	**ABCLMMOSY**	cymbaloms
ABCELOSTT	ectoblast	**ABCHLRWYZ**	Wałbrzych	**ABCLMNNOT**	Mont Blanc
ABCELRSST	bractless	**ABCIIIKLW**	bailiwick	**ABCLMNOUW**	clubwoman
ABCELRSTT	bractlets	**ABCIIILPT**	bicipital	**ABCLMOOOS**	colobomas
ABCELRSTU	scrutable	**ABCIIKNRS**	brainsick	**ABCLNORSY**	carbonyls
ABCELRTUU	lucubrate	**ABCIIKRRS**	airbricks	**ABCLNOWYY**	Colwyn Bay
ABCELSSUU	subclause	**ABCIILLMU**	umbilical	**ABCLOOSTU**	cobaltous
ABCELSUXY	excusably	**ABCIILLST**	ballistic	**ABCMOORST**	mobocrats
ABCEMOOSS	cambooses	**ABCIILMOR**	microbial	**ABCMOSSUU**	submucosa
ABCEMORSS	crossbeam	**ABCIILNOT**	albinotic	**ABCNOORSU**	carbonous
ABCEMORST	combaters	**ABCIILNSY**	sibilancy	**ABCNORSTU**	obscurant
ABCEMRSUV	verbascum	**ABCIILORU**	Roubiliac	**ABCNORSTY**	corybants
ABCENORTY	baronetcy	**ABCIILRSY**	irascibly	**ABCORRSSS**	crossbars
ABCENRRRY	cranberry	**ABCIIMNOR**	microbian	**ABCORRSTU**	turbocars
ABCENRTUU	bucentaur	**ABCIINRRU**	rubrician	**ABCRSSTTU**	subtracts
ABCENSSTU	substance	**ABCIIOPRY**	biopiracy	**ABDDDEELR**	bladdered
ABCEOOPRS	baroscope	**ABCIIOSTT**	biostatic	**ABDDDEINS**	disbanded
ABCEOPRRY	reprobacy	**ABCIIRSTY**	sybaritic	**ABDDEEEST**	besteaded
ABCERRSTU	carburets	**ABCIJLNUY**	jubilancy	**ABDDEEGHI**	bigheaded
ABCERRSWY	cyberwars	**ABCIKLLST**	blacklist	**ABDDEEGHL**	sheddable
ABCFGHIKT	fightback	**ABCILLMRU**	lumbrical	**ABDDEEHST**	deathbeds
ABCFHIKLS	blackfish	**ABCILLNSY**	billycans	**ABDDEELLU**	deludable
ABCFHRSTU	bushcraft	**ABCILLORU**	bilocular	**ABDDEELMO**	beadledom
ABCFIKLLS	backfills	**ABCILLSSY**	syllabics	**ABDDEELUW**	bulwaddee
ABCFKLLSU	fullbacks	**ABCILMMOS**	cimbaloms	**ABDDEELZZ**	bedazzled
ABCGGIKPY	piggyback	**ABCILMNOO**	Colombian	**ABDDEENOR**	broadened
ABCGHIKLT	backlight	**ABCILMNOU**	Columbian	**ABDDEENRR**	rebranded
ABCGHIKST	backsight	**ABCILMOPY**	amblyopic	**ABDDEEPRS**	bedspread
ABCGHILNN	blanching	**ABCILMSTY**	cymbalist	**ABDDEESST**	bedsteads
ABCGHINNR	branching	**ABCILMSUX**	subclimax	**ABDDEFILN**	deafblind
ABCGHINOR	broaching	**ABCILNNOU**	connubial	**ABDDEGLLO**	dodgeball
ABCGHNPSU	punchbags	**ABCILNORU**	binocular	**ABDDEHIIT**	adhibited
ABCGHOORV	Gorbachov	**ABCILNPSU**	publicans	**ABDDEHMOS**	hebdomads
ABCGIINRS	ascribing	**ABCILNRTU**	lubricant	**ABDDEHNSU**	husbanded
ABCGIINSS	abscising	**ABCILNRUY**	incurably	**ABDDEIILV**	dividable
ABCGIKLNS	blackings	**ABCILOPSY**	polybasic	**ABDDEILSU**	buddleias
	slingback	**ABCILORRU**	courbaril	**ABDDEINSS**	sidebands
ABCGILNRY	bracingly		orbicular	**ABDDEIORS**	broadside
ABCGIMNOT	combating	**ABCILOSSU**	subsocial		sideboard
ABCGIMNRS	scrambing	**ABCIMNOOS**	monobasic	**ABDDEIPRU**	upbraided
ABCGINNRU	unbracing	**ABCIMNORU**	carbonium	**ABDDEIRRS**	disbarred
ABCHHIKRU	Kuch Bihar	**ABCIMOSTU**	subatomic	**ABDDEISSU**	disabused
ABCHHKSUW	bushwhack	**ABCIMRSTY**	cambistry	**ABDDELOSW**	saddlebow
ABCHIILLN	chilblain	**ABCINOORR**	Rio Branco	**ABDDGORUY**	bodyguard
ABCHIIMOR	choriambi	**ABCINORTU**	incubator	**ABDDHINTW**	bandwidth
ABCHIIOST	isobathic	**ABCINOSTY**	obstinacy	**ABDDHNORU**	hardbound
ABCHIIRSU	Suribachi	**ABCJKOOST**	bootjacks	**ABDDILRSY**	ladybirds
ABCHILMOS	shambolic		jackboots	**ABDDIMNOS**	bondmaids
ABCHILNOR	bronchial	**ABCKKLMNO**	Black Monk	**ABDDIRRSY**	yardbirds
ABCHILOOS	coolibahs	**ABCKLLLOP**	blackpoll	**ABDDLLUWY**	bullwaddy
ABCHIMORS	choriambs	**ABCKLLOOP**	Blackpool	**ABDDLMOOR**	moldboard
ABCHIRRST	tribrachs	**ABCKLLPSU**	pullbacks	**ABDEEEFLR**	deferable
ABCHKLOSW	howlbacks	**ABCKLOPST**	blacktops	**ABDEEEFRS**	freebased
ABCHKMPSU	humpbacks	**ABCKLOSTU**	blackouts	**ABDEEEGLL**	delegable
ABCHKMRSU	marshbuck	**ABCKMOSSS**	mossbacks	**ABDEEEHTT**	hebetated
ABCHKMTTU	thumbtack	**ABCKNORSU**	Osnabrück	**ABDEEELLR**	relabeled
ABCHKNORT	thornback	**ABCKNORUY**	Ayckbourn	**ABDEEELMN**	emendable

ABDEEEELRV	bleareyed	**ABDEELPST**	bedplates	**ABDEIILNU**	inaudible
ABDEEEMRS	besmeared	**ABDEELRSS**	beardless	**ABDEIILNV**	divinable
ABDEEESWX	beeswaxed	**ABDEELRSY**	Beardsley	**ABDEIILOS**	diabolise
ABDEEFHIR	Faidherbe	**ABDEELSSU**	subleased	**ABDEIILOZ**	diabolize
ABDEEFIIT	beatified	**ABDEELSZZ**	bedazzles	**ABDEIILST**	sibilated
ABDEEFILN	definable	**ABDEEMNRT**	debarment	**ABDEIIRST**	diatribes
ABDEEFORR	freeboard	**ABDEEMNSU**	sunbeamed	**ABDEIJLTU**	jubilated
ABDEEGGLR	bedraggle	**ABDEEMRRW**	bedwarmer	**ABDEIKLMR**	Abd-el-Krim
ABDEEGHIN	beheading	**ABDEEMRSY**	Ember days	**ABDEIKLNR**	drinkable
ABDEEGINR	gaberdine	**ABDEENOTY**	bayoneted	**ABDEIKMRS**	disembark
ABDEEGJLU	judgeable	**ABDEENQTU**	banqueted	**ABDEIKNRS**	snakebird
ABDEEGLLO	lodgeable	**ABDEENRRT**	bartender	**ABDEIKNRW**	windbreak
ABDEEGLLP	pledgable	**ABDEENTTU**	debutante	**ABDEIKNSU**	baudekins
ABDEEGMOR	embargoed	**ABDEEOPST**	speedboat	**ABDEILLLO**	labelloid
ABDEEGORR	garderobe	**ABDEEORRU**	bordereau	**ABDEILLLR**	drillable
ABDEEGRRV	greybeard	**ABDEEPRSS**	bespreads	**ABDEILLLU**	lullabied
ABDEEHINR	Hebridean	**ABDEERRST**	redbreast	**ABDEILMNS**	mandibles
ABDEEHIRS	braeheids	**ABDEERVVY**	Berdyayev	**ABDEILMOR**	bromeliad
ABDEEHIRZ	hebraized	**ABDEFFLOU**	buffaloed	**ABDEILNNO**	bandoline
ABDEEHLRT	blathered	**ABDEFHOOS**	boofheads	**ABDEILNOR**	bandolier
ABDEEHNOS	boneheads	**ABDEFIISX**	basifixed	**ABDEILNRS**	bilanders
ABDEEHRSW	shewbread	**ABDEFILNY**	definably	**ABDEILOPR**	parboiled
ABDEEHSST	bethesdas	**ABDEFINRR**	firebrand	**ABDEILRSY**	desirably
ABDEEIILR	diablerie	**ABDEFLLOO**	floodable	**ABDEIMNRU**	Bermudian
ABDEEIINR	badinerie	**ABDEFLOTW**	batfowled	**ABDEINNRS**	endbrains
ABDEEIKRS	bidarkees	**ABDEFORRT**	fretboard	**ABDEINOST**	botanised
ABDEEILLW	wieldable	**ABDEFORTY**	afterbody	**ABDEINOSY**	anybodies
ABDEEILLY	yieldable	**ABDEGGGIN**	debagging	**ABDEINOTZ**	botanized
ABDEEILMS	Ambleside	**ABDEGGINR**	badgering	**ABDEINRSS**	rabidness
	demisable	**ABDEGGMOR**	beggardom	**ABDEINRSU**	urbanised
ABDEEILMT	bedlamite	**ABDEGGMRU**	Magdeburg	**ABDEINRUZ**	urbanized
ABDEEILNR	breadline	**ABDEGHLRU**	Aldeburgh	**ABDEINSSU**	unbiassed
ABDEEILNS	disenable	**ABDEGIINU**	biguanide	**ABDEINSSW**	bawdiness
ABDEEILRS	desirable	**ABDEGIIRR**	brigadier	**ABDEINTTU**	intubated
ABDEEILRT	liberated	**ABDEGIKNR**	debarking	**ABDEIOSST**	beastoids
ABDEEILRV	derivable	**ABDEGILOT**	obligated	**ABDEIPRRU**	upbraider
	driveable	**ABDEGINRR**	debarring	**ABDEIRRTW**	waterbird
ABDEEILSV	devisable	**ABDEGIRRS**	abridgers	**ABDEISSSU**	disabuses
ABDEEINSS	beadiness	**ABDEGLLMO**	gambolled	**ABDEKLRUW**	bulwarked
ABDEEINSW	Wiesbaden	**ABDEGLSSU**	slugabeds	**ABDEKLSSW**	skewbalds
ABDEEINTT	bidentate	**ABDEGOPRS**	pegboards	**ABDEKNORW**	breakdown
ABDEEINTU	butadiene	**ABDEGRSSU**	subgrades	**ABDEKORRW**	wordbreak
ABDEEIRSU	dauberies	**ABDEGRTUY**	budgetary	**ABDEKORSY**	keyboards
ABDEEITTU	beatitude	**ABDEHIINT**	inhabited	**ABDELLLSY**	syllabled
ABDEELLLY	Leadbelly	**ABDEHILNO**	hobnailed	**ABDELLMOU**	mouldable
ABDEELLPS	speedball	**ABDEHILOS**	abolished	**ABDELLNOO**	ballooned
ABDEELLRR	barrelled	**ABDEHIRTW**	Whitbread	**ABDELLORS**	beadrolls
ABDEELLRV	verballed	**ABDEHISTU**	habitudes	**ABDELLORY**	laboredly
ABDEELLTY	belatedly	**ABDEHKLSU**	bulkheads	**ABDELLOTU**	lobulated
ABDEELMRT	Alembert, d'	**ABDEHKNOS**	knobheads	**ABDELMNOY**	baldmoney
	d'Alembert	**ABDEHLLNS**	handbells	**ABDELMOTY**	molybdate
ABDEELMSS	assembled	**ABDEHLLSU**	bullheads	**ABDELNNSS**	blandness
ABDEELMTT	embattled	**ABDEHLOOT**	bloodheat	**ABDELNORS**	banderols
ABDEELNOR	banderole	**ABDEHLOTW**	deathblow	**ABDELNOST**	endoblast
	bandoleer	**ABDEHLOUX**	boxhauled	**ABDELNOSU**	soundable
ABDEELNOT	denotable	**ABDEHNRRT**	Bernhardt	**ABDELNOUW**	woundable
ABDEELNPR	prebendal	**ABDEHNRSU**	husbander	**ABDELNRUY**	endurably
ABDEELNPS	spendable	**ABDEHNSTU**	sunbathed	**ABDELNSTU**	Dunstable
ABDEELNRU	endurable	**ABDEHORRU**	harboured	**ABDELORUV**	boulevard
ABDEELNRY	blarneyed	**ABDEHORSW**	showbread	**ABDELOSSW**	dowsabels
ABDEELOPS	deposable	**ABDEHRRSY**	shadberry	**ABDELTTUU**	tubulated
ABDEELORS	leeboards	**ABDEIIIYZ**	Bayezid II	**ABDEMNRRT**	Rembrandt

ABDEMORTU	tamboured
ABDEMRSTU	drumbeats
ABDENNNOO	bandoneon
ABDENNOSS	nosebands
ABDENNTTU	Butenandt
ABDENOPRR	Paderborn
ABDENORSS	broadness
ABDENORST	adsorbent
ABDENORSY	boneyards
ABDENOSSX	sandboxes
ABDENOSTU	eastbound
ABDENOSTW	downbeats
ABDENRSTU	breadnuts
ABDENRSTY	bystander
ABDEOORRT	breadroot
ABDEOORRV	overboard
ABDEOORSW	bearwoods
ABDEOORWZ	zebrawood
ABDEORRSW	wardrobes
ABDEORTTU	obturated
ABDEORTUV	outbraved
ABDERSSTW	bedstraws
ABDERSTUW	drawtubes
ABDFGLMOO	Lamb of God
ABDFIIRRR	friarbird
ABDFLOOST	foldboats
ABDFNORRT	Brantford
ABDFOOORT	footboard
ABDFORRSU	surfboard
ABDGGIINR	abridging
	brigading
ABDGHINOV	hobdaying
ABDGHINRS	hangbirds
ABDGIILNS	disabling
ABDGIILNY	abidingly
ABDGIINRS	braidings
ABDGILNNR	brandling
ABDGILORS	gaolbirds
ABDGINNOU	abounding
ABDGINORS	adsorbing
	boardings
	signboard
ABDGINRRY	brigandry
ABDGLOPRU	plugboard
ABDHIINNR	hindbrain
ABDHILLNS	handbills
ABDHILORT	Bartholdi
ABDHIMORY	hybridoma
ABDHIMRTY	dithyramb
ABDHIOPRS	shipboard
ABDHIRSTY	birthdays
ABDHKNOOS	handbooks
ABDHLORSW	blowhards
ABDHMOSTU	badmouths
ABDHNOSUY	Hudson Bay
ABDHNRSUY	husbandry
ABDHOOSWX	shadowbox
ABDIIILLN	libidinal
ABDIIJLRS	jailbirds
ABDIILLRS	billiards
ABDIILMOS	diabolism
ABDIILNUY	inaudibly

ABDIILOST	diabolist
	idioblast
ABDIIMNRS	midbrains
ABDIIMPRV	bipyramid
ABDIIMRST	tribadism
ABDIINOUU	Baudouin I
ABDIINRRS	rainbirds
ABDIKMORS	skimboard
ABDILLMOR	millboard
ABDILRSZZ	blizzards
ABDIMNNOT	badminton
ABDINNOSU	Nabonidus
ABDINNRUU	Burundian
ABDINORUY	duobinary
ABDINRSTW	wristband
ABDIOORRW	briarwood
ABDIRSTUY	absurdity
ABDJMOORS	doorjambs
ABDLLNSUW	bundwalls
ABDLMOOOR	broadloom
ABDLORSSU	subdorsal
ABDMMNOSU	ombudsman
ABDMNORTU	Dumbarton
ABDMOOORR	boardroom
	Broadmoor
ABDNOORSW	snowboard
ABDNSSTUU	butsudans
ABDOORSTU	outboards
ABDOOSSSW	basswoods
ABEEEEFRT	beefeater
ABEEEFKST	beefsteak
ABEEEFLRR	referable
ABEEEFLRZ	freezable
ABEEEFRSS	freebases
ABEEEGGRT	eggbeater
ABEEEGLNR	generable
ABEEEGLRU	beleaguer
ABEEEGLTV	vegetable
ABEEEGRSV	beverages
ABEEEHLSW	wheelbase
ABEEEHSTT	hebetates
ABEEEINRS	beaneries
ABEEEKNRV	breakeven
ABEEEKPRR	barkeeper
ABEEELMPR	permeable
ABEEELNRT	enterable
ABEEELNRV	venerable
ABEEELNRW	renewable
ABEEELRRV	reverable
ABEEELRST	steerable
ABEEELRSV	serveable
	severable
ABEEENSST	absentees
ABEEERRTT	terebrate
ABEEERRTV	vertebrae
ABEEERTUX	exuberate
ABEEERWYZ	breezeway
ABEEESSWX	beeswaxes
ABEEFFILN	ineffable
ABEEFFNOS	banoffees
ABEEFGLOR	forgeable
ABEEFIIST	beatifies

ABEEFIKRR	firebreak
ABEEFILNR	inferable
	refinable
ABEEFILRS	balefires
ABEEFILST	fleabites
ABEEFLRSU	refusable
ABEEFLRTU	refutable
ABEEFORRR	forbearer
ABEEFORRS	forebears
ABEEGGLOR	gorgeable
ABEEGHILW	weighable
ABEEGHNOR	habergeon
ABEEGHRTU	hagbuteer
ABEEGILNN	bengaline
ABEEGIMNN	bemeaning
ABEEGINRS	Bering Sea
ABEEGINRU	aubergine
ABEEGINRV	beavering
	bereaving
ABEEGKORR	brokerage
ABEEGLLRU	regulable
ABEEGLMNR	embrangle
ABEEGLNPR	pregnable
ABEEGLNPS	bespangle
ABEEGLOPR	bargepole
	porbeagle
ABEEGLRTT	Great Belt
ABEEGLSSU	guessable
ABEEGMNRW	wambenger
ABEEGMORS	embargoes
ABEEGMSTY	megabytes
ABEEGNORS	Boanerges
	Gaberones
ABEEGNORZ	bronze age
ABEEGNRSU	subgenera
ABEEGNSTT	bagnettes
ABEEGORSX	gearboxes
ABEEGSTTU	baguettes
ABEEHHKSS	baksheesh
ABEEHILRT	heritable
ABEEHILST	Elisabeth
ABEEHILTZ	Elizabeth
ABEEHIMSV	misbehave
ABEEHIMTW	whitebeam
ABEEHINRS	abhenries
ABEEHINRT	hibernate
	inbreathe
ABEEHIRRT	breathier
ABEEHIRSZ	hebraizes
ABEEHKOSU	bakehouse
ABEEHLLRS	harebells
ABEEHLMPS	blaspheme
ABEEHLNOW	whalebone
ABEEHNORS	horsebean
ABEEHNRTY	abernethy
ABEEHNSTU	Bhutanese
ABEEHORRS	seborrhea
ABEEHORSS	rheobases
ABEEHORTU	hereabout
ABEEHQSTU	bequeaths
ABEEHRRST	breathers
ABEEHRSTT	hartbeest

ABEEIINRT	inebriate
ABEEIIRST	biseriate
ABEEIKNST	snakebite
ABEEILLMR	mirabelle
ABEEILLRV	relivable
ABEEILMPT	emptiable
ABEEILMRS	miserable
ABEEILMST	estimable
ABEEILMTT	timetable
ABEEILNPS	plebeians
ABEEILNQU	inequable
ABEEILNRR	inerrable
ABEEILNSS	baselines
ABEEILNSU	banlieues
ABEEILQTU	equitable
ABEEILRRW	rewirable
ABEEILRST	beastlier
	bleariest
	liberates
ABEEILRSV	revisable
	verbalise
ABEEILRSW	bewailers
ABEEILRTT	albertite
ABEEILRTV	avertible
	veritable
ABEEILRVV	revivable
ABEEILRVZ	verbalize
ABEEIMSSS	embassies
ABEEINSST	asbestine
ABEEIPRST	rebaptise
ABEEIPRTZ	rebaptize
ABEEIRRSS	brasserie
	brassiere
ABEEIRRST	biserrate
ABEEIRSTT	batteries
ABEEJLLNY	jellybean
ABEEJLMSU	Jebel Musa
ABEEJLNOY	enjoyable
ABEEJMORS	jamborees
ABEEKLMOS	smokeable
ABEEKLNNO	anklebone
ABEEKLNSS	bleakness
ABEEKLORV	revokable
ABEEKLOST	keelboats
ABEEKLRSS	brakeless
ABEEKMNRS	brakesmen
ABEEKMRRS	reembarks
ABEELLLPS	spellable
ABEELLLRS	labellers
ABEELLMSS	blameless
ABEELLMTU	umbellate
ABEELLNRT	netballer
ABEELLORT	tolerable
ABEELLORW	lowerable
ABEELLOVV	evolvable
ABEELLSST	tableless
ABEELMMOR	memorable
ABEELMMRS	embalmers
ABEELMNRU	numerable
ABEELMNST	stablemen
ABEELMORV	removable
ABEELMOSV	moveables

ABEELMPRS	preambles
ABEELMPRY	permeably
ABEELMPTT	temptable
ABEELMRSS	assembler
ABEELMRSU	resumable
ABEELMSSS	assembles
ABEELMSTT	embattles
ABEELNNTU	untenable
ABEELNOPS	beanpoles
ABEELNOST	stoneable
ABEELNRVY	venerably
ABEELOPSX	exposable
ABEELPRRV	preverbal
ABEELPRSU	superable
ABEELPRTU	reputable
ABEELRRTV	vertebral
ABEELRRUY	La Bruyère
ABEELRSVW	swervable
ABEELRTTU	utterable
ABEELSSSU	subleases
ABEEMMNRS	membranes
ABEEMMNTY	embayment
ABEEMMRSU	bummarees
ABEEMNPRU	penumbrae
ABEEMNSST	basements
ABEEMNSTT	abetments
ABEEMNTTT	battement
ABEEMORRT	barometer
ABEEMRRSU	embrasure
ABEEMRSTW	webmaster
ABEENNRST	bannerets
ABEENOSTZ	benzoates
ABEENQRTU	banqueter
ABEENQTTU	banquette
ABEENRRST	banterers
ABEENRRSY	naseberry
ABEENRSST	absenters
	steenbras
ABEENRSSV	braveness
ABEENRTUX	exuberant
ABEEOPRRT	perborate
	reprobate
ABEEORRSV	overbears
ABEEOSTUU	beauteous
ABEEPRSTT	bespatter
ABEERRRST	barterers
ABEERRSTT	barrettes
	batterers
	berrettas
ABEERRSTV	vertebras
ABEERRSTY	betrayers
ABEERRSWY	bewrayers
ABEERSTTY	Bay Street
ABEFFILNY	ineffably
ABEFFKORS	breakoffs
ABEFFLOSU	buffaloes
ABEFGILLN	befalling
ABEFGILNR	frangible
ABEFHISST	batfishes
ABEFIILLR	fibrillae
ABEFIILNU	unifiable
ABEFIILOT	bifoliate

ABEFIIMRT	fimbriate
ABEFILLRS	fireballs
ABEFILLRT	filtrable
ABEFILNRU	funebrial
ABEFILNRY	inferably
ABEFILOST	lifeboats
ABEFILTUU	beautiful
ABEFIMORS	framboise
ABEFINORR	forebrain
ABEFINOSX	Foxe Basin
ABEFIORST	fireboats
ABEFIOSTY	biosafety
ABEFIRRST	firebrats
ABEFKLSTU	basketful
ABEFLLLMU	flabellum
ABEFLLLUY	balefully
ABEFLLNUY	banefully
ABEFLLRRU	barrelful
ABEFLLSTU	tablefuls
ABEFLNOSW	wolfsbane
ABEFLORTW	batfowler
ABEFLRTUY	refutably
ABEFORRTY	ferryboat
ABEFRTTTU	butterfat
ABEGGGINR	beggaring
ABEGGGLLU	gluggable
ABEGGINSS	bagginess
ABEGGISTY	gigabytes
ABEGGNOPS	spongebag
ABEGHILRT	rightable
ABEGHILST	sightable
ABEGHINRR	harbinger
ABEGHINRT	breathing
ABEGHMRRU	hamburger
ABEGHRSSU	sagebrush
ABEGHRTTU	hagbutter
ABEGIILLT	litigable
ABEGIILMT	mitigable
ABEGIILNS	abseiling
ABEGIILNT	ignitable
ABEGIILNW	bewailing
ABEGIILRR	irrigable
ABEGIINOR	aborigine
ABEGIKMNN	embanking
ABEGIKMNR	embarking
ABEGILLLN	labelling
ABEGILLOS	globalise
ABEGILLOZ	globalize
ABEGILMMN	embalming
ABEGILMNZ	emblazing
ABEGILNOR	ignorable
ABEGILNRR	barreling
ABEGILNST	bleatings
	tangibles
ABEGILOST	obligates
ABEGIMNNO	bemoaning
ABEGIMRRS	ambergris
ABEGINNNT	benignant
ABEGINNOW	Winnebago
ABEGINNRT	bantering
ABEGINNRY	barneying
ABEGINNRZ	brazening

ABEGINNST	absenting	
ABEGINNTT	battening	
ABEGINRRS	berrigans	
ABEGINRRT	bartering	
ABEGINRST	breasting	
ABEGINRTT	battering	
ABEGINRTY	betraying	
ABEGINRUY	guberniya	
ABEGINRWY	bewraying	
ABEGINSST	basseting	
	beastings	
ABEGINSTW	swingbeat	
ABEGJORTU	objurgate	
ABEGJSTUU	subjugate	
ABEGKORSS	grosbeaks	
ABEGKRSTU	grubstake	
ABEGLLNNY	Glen Albyn	
ABEGLLNOU	Lobengula	
ABEGLNORU	Boulanger	
ABEGLNUUW	Bangweulu	
ABEGLRSSU	bluegrass	
ABEGMMMRU	brummagem	
ABEGMNOOR	boomerang	
ABEGMNOSS	gambesons	
ABEGMNOSY	moneybags	
ABEGMORST	bergamots	
ABEGNSSTU	subagents	
ABEGOORST	botargoes	
ABEGORSTU	subrogate	
ABEGRRSUV	burgraves	
ABEGSSSTU	substages	
ABEHHISSU	hushabies	
ABEHHLLOZ	Hezbollah	
ABEHHOSTU	bathhouse	
ABEHIINNR	Hibernian	
ABEHIITTW	whitebait	
ABEHIKLNT	thinkable	
ABEHILMOP	amphibole	
ABEHILOPR	barophile	
ABEHILOPS	basophile	
ABEHILORS	abolisher	
ABEHILOSS	abolishes	
ABEHILOTT	batholite	
ABEHILPPS	shippable	
ABEHILRST	herbalist	
ABEHILRSY	bearishly	
ABEHILRTY	breathily	
	heritably	
ABEHILSST	establish	
ABEHIMMSS	memsahibs	
ABEHIMNOS	bohemians	
ABEHIMRRU	herbarium	
ABEHINOOP	neophobia	
ABEHIOPRU	euphorbia	
ABEHIORSV	behaviors	
ABEHIORUV	behaviour	
ABEHIRRTT	birthrate	
ABEHIRSST	brashiest	
ABEHKLLRS	shellbark	
ABEHKLMMU	Kumbh Mela	
ABEHKNNOV	København	
ABEHLLNWY	Newby Hall	

ABEHLMNSU	bushelman	
ABEHLMPSY	blasphemy	
ABEHLNNSU	shunnable	
ABEHLNOOR	honorable	
ABEHLOPRY	hyperbola	
ABEHLORTT	betrothal	
ABEHMNORS	hornbeams	
ABEHMOORS	rehoboams	
ABEHNORRT	abhorrent	
	earthborn	
ABEHNRRTU	heartburn	
ABEHNRSSS	brashness	
ABEHNRSTU	sunbather	
ABEHNSSTU	sunbathes	
ABEHOOSTU	boathouse	
	houseboat	
ABEHORRRS	abhorrers	
	harborers	
ABEHORRRU	harbourer	
ABEHQRSUU	harquebus	
ABEHRSSTU	tarbushes	
ABEIIILST	abilities	
ABEIILLLR	illiberal	
ABEIILLMT	limitable	
ABEIILNNS	biennials	
ABEIILNOS	ionisable	
ABEIILNOZ	ionizable	
ABEIILNRS	brasilein	
ABEIILNRT	nailbiter	
ABEIILNRZ	brazilein	
ABEIILRRS	libraries	
ABEIILRRT	irritable	
ABEIILRTV	vibratile	
ABEIILSST	sibilates	
	stabilise	
ABEIILSTV	visitable	
ABEIILSTZ	stabilize	
ABEIIMMNO	meibomian	
ABEIINNPT	bipinnate	
ABEIINNRT	inebriant	
ABEIINRST	brainiest	
ABEIIPRTT	bipartite	
ABEIIRSSV	vibrissae	
ABEIIRTVV	vibrative	
ABEIJLNRU	injurable	
ABEIJLSTU	jubilates	
ABEIJMNNS	benjamins	
ABEIJRSVY	Jervis Bay	
ABEIKLLNU	unlikable	
ABEIKLNRT	Treblinka	
ABEIKLNSS	balkiness	
ABEIKLNTT	knittable	
ABEIKLSTU	baulkiest	
ABEIKMORR	biomarker	
ABEIKNNRT	interbank	
ABEIKNRSS	bearskins	
ABEILLLMS	slimeball	
ABEILLLNT	libellant	
ABEILLLRY	liberally	
ABEILLLST	labellist	
ABEILLLSU	lullabies	
	sulliable	

ABEILLMSS	mislabels	
ABEILLNST	libelants	
ABEILLNUV	unlivable	
ABEILLPSU	plausible	
ABEILLSTY	bestially	
ABEILMMOV	immovable	
ABEILMMSW	swimmable	
ABEILMMTU	immutable	
ABEILMNSS	balminess	
ABEILMNST	bailments	
ABEILMOPS	imposable	
ABEILMORT	Baltimore	
ABEILMOSX	mailboxes	
ABEILMPTU	imputable	
ABEILMRSV	verbalism	
ABEILMRSY	miserably	
ABEILMSTU	sublimate	
ABEILMSTW	wambliest	
ABEILMSTY	estimably	
ABEILNPRT	printable	
ABEILNPSU	subalpine	
ABEILNRRY	inerrably	
ABEILNRSS	brainless	
ABEILNRSU	insurable	
ABEILNSTV	bivalents	
ABEILOQSU	obsequial	
ABEILORRT	liberator	
ABEILORST	strobilae	
ABEILORSV	bolivares	
ABEILORTT	trilobate	
ABEILPSST	epiblasts	
ABEILQTUY	equitably	
ABEILRRST	stirrable	
ABEILRRSU	reburials	
ABEILRRYZ	bizarrely	
ABEILRSTU	brutalise	
ABEILRSTV	verbalist	
ABEILRTUZ	brutalize	
ABEILRTVY	veritably	
ABEILRVVY	revivably	
ABEILSSUX	bisexuals	
ABEILSTTW	twistable	
ABEILSUVY	abusively	
ABEIMMNRT	timberman	
ABEIMNORT	brominate	
ABEIMNRST	brainstem	
	tribesman	
ABEIMNRSU	submarine	
ABEIMOSSS	biomasses	
ABEIMPRST	rebaptism	
ABEIMRSTV	ambiverts	
ABEINNOST	sanbenito	
ABEINNOSZ	bezonians	
ABEINNRST	bannister	
ABEINNSTT	abstinent	
ABEINNTYZ	byzantine	
ABEINOOPW	bioweapon	
ABEINORST	baritones	
	obtainers	
ABEINOSST	botanises	
ABEINOSTT	obstinate	
ABEINOSTZ	botanizes	

357

ABEINPRST	breastpin	**ABELOPSTT**	spottable	**ABFILNSSU**	basinfuls
ABEINRSST	banisters	**ABELORRSU**	labourers	**ABFILSSTU**	fabulists
ABEINRSSU	urbanises	**ABELORSSV**	absolvers	**ABFLLOOST**	footballs
ABEINRSTU	urbanites	**ABELORTTX**	rattlebox	**ABFLLOSST**	softballs
ABEINRSTW	brawniest	**ABELOSSTU**	absolutes	**ABFLOOTTX**	Fox Talbot
ABEINRSUZ	urbanizes	**ABELOSSTX**	saltboxes	**ABFLORRUW**	barrowful
ABEINRTTU	tribunate	**ABELOSTTY**	stylobate	**ABFNORSTU**	turbofans
	turbinate	**ABELPRSUY**	superably	**ABFORSSTU**	surfboats
ABEINSSST	bassinets	**ABELPRTTU**	prebuttal	**ABGGGINRS**	braggings
ABEINSTTU	intubates	**ABELPRTUY**	reputably	**ABGGILMNO**	gamboling
ABEIOORSV	Beriosova	**ABELRSSTU**	balusters	**ABGGINORT**	bogarting
ABEIOPRTV	probative	**ABELRSTTU**	rebuttals	**ABGGLOORY**	garbology
ABEIPRRSS	spareribs		trustable	**ABGGNOOST**	toboggans
ABEIRRRST	barrister	**ABELRSUYY**	Aylesbury	**ABGHHILLS**	highballs
ABEIRRSST	arbitress	**ABELSTTUU**	tubulates	**ABGHIINNS**	banishing
ABEIRRSSU	bursaries	**ABELSTUUX**	subluxate	**ABGHILMNS**	shambling
ABEIRRSTU	turbaries	**ABEMMNOOS**	moonbeams	**ABGHILRTY**	rightably
ABEIRSSST	brassiest	**ABEMNPRSU**	penumbras	**ABGHIMNSU**	ambushing
ABEIRSSTY	sybarites	**ABEMNSTTU**	abutments	**ABGHINORR**	abhorring
ABEIRTTTU	attribute	**ABEMOOPRR**	broomrape		harboring
ABEJLNOVY	enjoyably	**ABEMOPRTY**	ambrotype	**ABGHINSWZ**	whizbangs
ABEJMOORS	jeroboams	**ABEMORRRY**	Barrymore	**ABGHINWZZ**	whizzbang
ABEKKMOOR	bookmaker	**ABEMORRTU**	arboretum	**ABGHIOPRY**	biography
ABEKLMOSS	abelmosks	**ABEMORRTY**	barometry	**ABGHMORSU**	broughams
ABEKLNNSS	blankness	**ABENNORTW**	warbonnet	**ABGHORSTU**	broughtas
ABEKLOOPT	bookplate	**ABENNSTTU**	subtenant	**ABGIILLNR**	brailling
ABEKLORTW	worktable	**ABENOOSTT**	stoneboat	**ABGIILLNU**	bilingual
ABEKLORVY	revokably	**ABENOPRRS**	barperson	**ABGIILNRT**	librating
ABEKLOSTX	talkboxes	**ABENOPSSU**	subpoenas	**ABGIIMSST**	bigamists
ABEKNNOST	banknotes	**ABENORSTT**	betatrons	**ABGIIMTUY**	ambiguity
ABEKOORSY	yearbooks	**ABENORSTV**	bevatrons	**ABGIINNOS**	bignonias
ABEKORSTU	breakouts		observant	**ABGIINNOT**	obtaining
	outbreaks	**ABENORSTY**	barytones	**ABGIINOTV**	obviating
ABELLLSSY	syllables	**ABEOOPRTW**	powerboat	**ABGIINPST**	baptising
ABELLMNTY	lambently	**ABEOOPSSX**	soapboxes	**ABGIINPTZ**	baptizing
ABELLMRSU	umbrellas	**ABEOORRSU**	arboreous	**ABGIINRTV**	vibrating
ABELLNOST	ballonets	**ABEOPPRSY**	paperboys	**ABGIJNNOW**	jawboning
ABELLNOUV	unlovable	**ABEOPRRSY**	soapberry	**ABGIKNNSU**	sunbaking
ABELLORTY	tolerably	**ABEORRSTU**	tabourers	**ABGIKNRRS**	ringbarks
ABELMMORY	memorably	**ABEORSSTU**	saboteurs	**ABGILLNOT**	balloting
ABELMNORY	embryonal	**ABEORSSTU**	obturates	**ABGILMNRS**	ramblings
ABELMNOSZ	emblazons		tabourets	**ABGILNNOZ**	blazoning
ABELMNOTU	mountable	**ABEORSTUV**	outbraves	**ABGILNNST**	bantlings
ABELMNOUV	unmovable	**ABEPRRRSY**	raspberry	**ABGILNORU**	labouring
ABELMNPRU	penumbral	**ABEPRSSSY**	passersby	**ABGILNOSV**	absolving
ABELMNRUY	numerably	**ABERSSTTU**	substrate	**ABGILNRSW**	brawlings
ABELMNSTU	submental	**ABERSSTUU**	arbutuses	**ABGILNSST**	stablings
ABELMOORT	motorable	**ABERSTTUY**	butyrates	**ABGILOORT**	obligator
ABELMORVY	removably	**ABFFLLPSU**	puffballs	**ABGILOOST**	obligatos
ABELMOSST	mesoblast	**ABFFLOSST**	blastoffs	**ABGILORSW**	brigalows
ABELMOSSU	albumoses	**ABFFNOSTU**	bouffants	**ABGIMNORT**	bromating
ABELNNORS	bannerols	**ABFGIINSY**	basifying	**ABGIMNRSU**	Gambrinus
ABELNNORV	nonverbal	**ABFGIOPSY**	Bay of Pigs	**ABGIMOSUU**	ambiguous
ABELNNTUY	untenably	**ABFGLLOOS**	goofballs	**ABGINNRRU**	unbarring
ABELNORSZ	blazoners	**ABFGORSUU**	faubourgs	**ABGINOPRT**	probating
ABELNOSTT	entoblast	**ABFHLLSUY**	bashfully	**ABGINOSST**	boastings
ABELNOSYZ	lazybones	**ABFIILLRR**	fibrillar	**ABGINOSTW**	swingboat
ABELNRSTU	subaltern	**ABFIILLRY**	bifilarly	**ABGINPSSY**	bypassing
ABELNRTTU	turntable	**ABFIIORSU**	bifarious	**ABGLLNSUW**	bungwalls
ABELOOPPS	opposable	**ABFILLSYY**	syllabify	**ABGLLRSUY**	bullyrags
ABELOPPST	stoppable	**ABFILMSUY**	subfamily	**ABGLMNOOS**	boomslang
ABELOPRST	portables	**ABFILNOTU**	bufotalin	**ABGLMOPSU**	plumbagos

ABGLNOOST	longboats	ABIINOOTV	obviation	ABKNOPSST	stopbanks
ABGLNOSUW	bungalows	ABIINORTV	vibration	ABKNPRSTU	bankrupts
ABHHIIRUV	bahuvrihi	ABIJNOSST	banjoists	ABKOOPSSS	passbooks
ABHHILLOZ	Hizbollah	ABIKLMNSS	lambskins	ABLLLOOST	stoolball
ABHHILOTT	batholith	ABIKLOSTY	Białystok	ABLLMOORS	ballrooms
ABHHIRRSU	hairbrush	ABIKNORRS	ironbarks	ABLLMOPSW	blowlamps
ABHIIILOP	biophilia	ABILLLPSY	playbills	ABLLMOSSY	smallboys
ABHIILLMS	bismillah	ABILLMSSY	syllabism	ABLLNOSSW	snowballs
ABHIILMRT	brit milah	ABILLNOPT	ballpoint	ABLLRTUUY	tubularly
ABHIIPSTU	Tipu Sahib	ABILLORRZ	razorbill	ABLMNNOTZ	Boltzmann
ABHIKLLSW	hawkbills	ABILLORTY	orbitally	ABLMNORSU	subnormal
	hawksbill	ABILLPSUY	plausibly	ABLMNRSUU	laburnums
ABHIKMRRT	birthmark	ABILMMOVY	immovably	ABLNRSUUY	sublunary
ABHILMNTU	thumbnail	ABILMMTUV	immutably	ABLOOPPSY	opposably
ABHILMOPY	amphiboly	ABILMOORS	ribosomal	ABLOOPRST	blastopor
ABHILMSTU	bismuthal	ABILMORSU	labourism	ABLORTTUU	tubulator
ABHILNOOT	halobiont	ABILMORXY	xylorimba	ABLOSSTTU	subtotals
ABHILNOST	biathlons	ABILMPTUY	imputably	ABMNORRST	barnstorm
ABHILNRSU	nailbrush	ABILMRSTU	brutalism	ABMOOOOTW	Toowoomba
ABHILNRTY	labyrinth	ABILMSTTU	submittal	ABMOORRTT	motorboat
ABHILOPSS	basophils	ABILNOOST	boltonias	ABNOORRST	roborants
ABHILORSY	boarishly		oblations	ABNOORSYZ	bryozoans
ABHIOOOPZ	zoophobia	ABILNORUV	binovular	ABNOORTUZ	zorbonaut
ABHKMRRSU	brushmark	ABILNOSTU	ablutions	ABNORSTUU	runabouts
ABHKOOOST	boathooks		abutilons	ABNORTTUU	turnabout
ABHLLMOST	mothballs	ABILNRSTU	tribunals	ABOOPRRTY	probatory
ABHLLOOSY	ballyhoos		turbinals	ABOOPRSST	bootstrap
ABHLNOORY	honorably	ABILNRTVY	vibrantly	ABOORRTTU	obturator
ABHLOPSTY	hypoblast	ABILOORSU	laborious	ABOOSSTTU	outboasts
ABHLOSSWW	washbowls	ABILOPRRT	Port Blair	ABRRSSTTU	starburst
ABHLPRSUY	subphylar	ABILORRTY	libratory	ABRRSTTUW	bratwurst
ABHMOORST	bathrooms	ABILORSST	laborists	ACCCCEHIT	cachectic
ABHNORTTU	Arbuthnot	ABILORSTU	labourist	ACCCDEEEN	accedence
ABHOOSSTW	showboats	ABILRSSUY	Salisbury	ACCCDEEIN	accidence
ABIIILLTY	liability	ABILRSTTU	brutalist	ACCCDILOY	cacodylic
ABIIILNTY	inability	ABILRSTUY	salubrity	ACCCEEENS	acescence
ABIIILTVY	viability	ABILRTTUY	brutality	ACCCEENSY	acescency
ABIIINRUV	Urban VIII	ABIMMNRUU	manubrium	ACCCEGINO	cacogenic
ABIIJMMUY	Mbujimayi	ABIMNORTU	tambourin	ACCCEGLOY	coccygeal
ABIIKLSSS	basilisks	ABIMNTUYZ	Byzantium	ACCCEHIOT	cacoethic
ABIILLMRS	millibars	ABINOOPRT	probation	ACCCEHITT	cathectic
ABIILLNOT	ballotini	ABINOOPST	spoonbait	ACCCEILLO	calcicole
ABIILLNRT	brilliant	ABINOORST	abortions	ACCCEIOPT	copacetic
ABIILMNNO	binominal	ABINOPRTU	abruption	ACCCHKOOR	cockroach
ABIILMNOS	binomials	ABINOPSTU	subtopian	ACCCIILLY	alicyclic
ABIILMNSS	albinisms	ABINORSTU	tabourins	ACCCIILMT	climactic
ABIILMRST	tribalism	ABINOSSTT	botanists	ACCCIIOPR	capriccio
ABIILNOOT	abolition	ABINRRTUY	tribunary	ACCCKMMOR	McCormack
ABIILNOOV	boliviano	ABINRSSUY	Sainsbury	ACCCNOPUY	occupancy
ABIILNORT	libration	ABIOORNRT	briarroot	ACCDDEEEN	decadence
ABIILNORY	nobiliary	ABIORRSST	arborists	ACCDDEEER	reacceded
ABIILNOST	libations	ABIORRSTV	vibrators	ACCDDEENY	decadency
ABIILNSST	sibilants	ABIORRSUV	arbovirus	ACCDDEILS	discalced
ABIILRRTY	irritably	ABIORRTVY	vibratory	ACCDDIIST	didactics
ABIILRSSV	vibrissal	ABIORSTTU	stirabout	ACCDDIORS	disaccord
ABIILRSTT	tribalist	ABIPRSTTY	baptistry	ACCDEEERS	reaccedes
ABIILSTTY	stability	ABIRRSSTU	airbursts	ACCDEEHIK	chickadee
ABIILSTUY	suability	ABIRRTTUY	tributary	ACCDEEINS	cadencies
	usability	ABJLLOOTY	jollyboat	ACCDEEIST	desiccate
ABIIMNOST	ambitions	ABKKMOORS	bookmarks	ACCDEEKOP	peacocked
ABIIMORSS	isobarism	ABKLLNORS	bankrolls	ACCDEELLN	cancelled
ABIIMOSTU	ambitious	ABKLLOOST	bookstall	ACCDEELNO	concealed

ACCDEELOS	coalesced
ACCDEFIIL	calcified
ACCDEFILS	fascicled
ACCDEFILY	decalcify
ACCDEHIKR	deckchair
ACCDEHILR	childcare
ACCDEHNRU	craunched
ACCDEHRST	scratched
ACCDEIILN	Icelandic
ACCDEIILT	dialectic
ACCDEILNR	calendric
ACCDEINOT	anecdotic
ACCDEINST	accidents
	desiccant
ACCDEIORW	cowardice
ACCDEIPRT	practiced
ACCDEIRST	accredits
ACCDEKOSS	cassocked
ACCDEMNOO	cacodemon
ACCDEMOPT	compacted
ACCDEMORR	camcorder
ACCDEMORY	democracy
ACCDENOTT	contacted
ACCDENOTU	accounted
ACCDEORRS	accorders
	scorecard
ACCDEORTU	accoutred
ACCDFILLY	flaccidly
ACCDGINOR	according
ACCDHHRUY	archduchy
ACCDHIIIL	chiliadic
ACCDHIIOR	radicchio
ACCDHINOR	chancroid
ACCDHNPRU	cardpunch
ACCDHOOOW	coachwood
ACCDHOORT	octachord
ACCDHORTW	catchword
ACCDIIINT	diactinic
ACCDIIIRT	diacritic
ACCDIIMNO	monacidic
ACCDIIOPT	apodictic
ACCDILLNO	Condillac
ACCDILLOY	cycloidal
ACCDILSTY	dactylics
ACCDINOOR	accordion
ACCDINORS	cancroids
ACCDIOORS	coracoids
ACCDKNORW	crackdown
ACCDNOORT	concordat
ACCDOOORV	Corcovado
ACCEEEILS	ecclesiae
ACCEEELRS	recalesce
ACCEEENRR	recreance
ACCEEGLMV	megacycle
ACCEEHIKR	chickaree
ACCEEHILR	chelicera
ACCEEHIST	catechise
ACCEEHITY	haecceity
ACCEEHITZ	catechize
ACCEEHKMN	namecheck
ACCEEHKMT	checkmate
ACCEEHLOT	cochleate

ACCEEHNPR	perchance
ACCEEHOST	cacoethes
ACCEEHPST	speech act
ACCEEILST	Celtic Sea
ACCEEIPRS	peccaries
ACCEEIQSU	acquiesce
ACCEEIRRR	ricercare
ACCEEIRTV	accretive
ACCEEISTX	exsiccate
ACCEEKLNS	necklaces
ACCEEKLOT	cockateel
ACCEELLNR	canceller
ACCEELLOR	clearcole
ACCEELNOR	concealer
ACCEELNOS	coenacles
ACCEELNOV	covalence
ACCEELNPR	precancel
ACCEELNRS	cancelers
	clarences
ACCEELOSS	coalesces
ACCEELPST	spectacle
ACCEENNSS	nascences
ACCEENNST	canescent
ACCEENRRY	recreancy
ACCEENRST	reaccents
ACCEENRSU	recusance
ACCEEOPSU	cepaceous
ACCEEORSU	ceraceous
ACCEEOSTU	cetaceous
ACCEEPRST	accepters
	reaccepts
ACCEESSUU	Ceauşescu
ACCEFGILU	calcifuge
ACCEFHLNU	chanceful
ACCEFHLOT	facecloth
ACCEFIILS	calcifies
ACCEFIIRS	sacrifice
ACCEFILSS	fascicles
ACCEFILSU	fascicule
ACCEGHLNO	chalcogen
ACCEGIKNO	Cockaigne
ACCEGILNN	canceling
ACCEGINNT	accenting
ACCEGINOR	acrogenic
ACCEGINPT	accepting
ACCEGINRT	accreting
ACCEGINSS	accessing
ACCEGIORT	categoric
ACCEGIOTT	geotactic
ACCEGKMOS	gamecocks
ACCEHHIRT	thearchic
ACCEHHKOT	heathcock
ACCEHIIMS	ischaemic
ACCEHIKLR	checkrail
ACCEHIKNR	raincheck
ACCEHIKPS	chickpeas
ACCEHILLO	echolalic
ACCEHILMS	chemicals
ACCEHILNO	coachline
	cochineal
ACCEHILNT	technical
ACCEHILOT	chicalote

ACCEHIMNS	mechanics
	mischance
ACCEHIMST	catechism
	schematic
ACCEHINRS	chicaners
ACCEHINRY	chicanery
ACCEHINST	catechins
	chanciest
ACCEHIOSU	acouchies
ACCEHIRST	scratchie
ACCEHIRTT	architect
ACCEHISTT	catchiest
	catechist
ACCEHLNOR	chloracne
ACCEHLOOT	chocolate
ACCEHLOPT	catchpole
ACCEHMMNU	mumchance
ACCEHMNTT	catchment
ACCEHNNOS	chaconnes
ACCEHNRSU	craunches
ACCEHOPST	cachepots
ACCEHOPSU	capouches
ACCEHORTU	cartouche
ACCEHORTY	theocracy
ACCEHRRST	scratcher
ACCEHRSST	scratches
ACCEIILMN	calcimine
ACCEIIMNT	cinematic
ACCEIINOS	cocainise
ACCEIINOZ	cocainize
ACCEIINRT	circinate
ACCEIIPRT	accipiter
ACCEIIRRR	ricercari
ACCEIIRST	cicatrise
ACCEIIRTZ	cicatrize
ACCEIISTV	siccative
ACCEIKKLP	placekick
ACCEIKLOT	cockatiel
ACCEIKLST	ticklaces
ACCEIKRSW	wisecrack
ACCEIKRTT	Catterick
ACCEILLOT	laccolite
ACCEILLRS	clericals
ACCEILLSU	caulicles
ACCEILLSV	clavicles
ACCEILMOX	cacomixle
ACCEILMPT	eclamptic
ACCEILNRT	centrical
ACCEILNST	canticles
ACCEILNTU	inculcate
ACCEILOPR	precocial
ACCEILPST	sceptical
ACCEILRTU	circulate
ACCEILTUU	cuticulae
ACCEIMNPT	impeccant
ACCEIMOSU	micaceous
ACCEINORT	accretion
	anorectic
ACCEINOSS	accession
ACCEINOST	oscitance
ACCEINSTU	encaustic
	succinate

ACCEIOPST	copasetic	**ACCHILLOT**	laccolith	**ACCILRRUU**	curricula
ACCEIORTT	corticate	**ACCHILNOY**	halcyonic	**ACCILRTUU**	cuticular
ACCEIPRST	practices	**ACCHILNUU**	Cuchulain	**ACCIMNORY**	acronymic
ACCEIPSTY	cityscape	**ACCHILOST**	catholics	**ACCIMNOSS**	moccasins
ACCEIRRRS	ricercars	**ACCHILPSY**	psychical	**ACCIMNOSY**	sciomancy
ACCEISSTT	ecstatics	**ACCHIMNOR**	monarchic	**ACCIMOORS**	crocosmia
ACCEJKRSW	jackscrew	**ACCHIMOPR**	camphoric	**ACCIMORTY**	timocracy
ACCEKLNRS	cracknels	**ACCHIMORT**	chromatic	**ACCIMPSSU**	capsicums
ACCEKMNRS	cracksmen	**ACCHIMOST**	stomachic	**ACCINOOSS**	occasions
ACCEKNORR	corncrake	**ACCHIMOSY**	sciomachy	**ACCINOOST**	coactions
ACCELLOOT	collocate	**ACCHINNOS**	cinchonas	**ACCINOPRR**	Capricorn
ACCELLTUU	cucullate	**ACCHINPSU**	capuchins	**ACCINORST**	narcotics
ACCELMNSY	cyclamens	**ACCHIORST**	trochaics	**ACCINOSTY**	oscitancy
ACCELNOPY	cyclopean	**ACCHIRTTY**	trachytic	**ACCINOTVY**	concavity
ACCELNOSV	conclaves	**ACCHKLMOT**	matchlock	**ACCINSTTY**	syntactic
ACCELNOVY	concavely	**ACCHKLORS**	charlocks	**ACCIOPRTT**	catoptric
	covalency	**ACCHKLOST**	sackcloth	**ACCIORSST**	acrostics
ACCELNPTY	peccantly	**ACCHKLSTU**	saltchuck	**ACCIOSSTU**	acoustics
ACCELNRSU	caruncles	**ACCHKOORW**	coachwork	**ACCJKORSS**	crossjack
ACCELOTUY	autocycle	**ACCHLLOPT**	catchpoll	**ACCKKMMUU**	muckamuck
ACCEMNRTY	McCartney	**ACCHLOORT**	colcothar	**ACCKKRSSU**	rucksacks
ACCEMOPRT	compacter		ochlocrat	**ACCKOOOST**	cockatoos
ACCEMORTY	macrocyte	**ACCHLOOSW**	slowcoach	**ACCKOPRST**	crackpots
ACCEMPRSU	creamcups	**ACCHLOOTY**	chocolaty	**ACCLLOSUU**	calculous
ACCENNOST	Constance	**ACCHNOOPY**	cacophony	**ACCLLSUUY**	calyculus
ACCENNOTY	cotenancy	**ACCHNOORS**	coronachs	**ACCLMOPTY**	compactly
ACCENOORS	coenosarc	**ACCHNORSU**	chancrous	**ACCLNNNOO**	colcannon
ACCENOPRY	coparceny	**ACCHOSSTU**	succotash	**ACCLRSSUU**	succursal
ACCENORST	accentors	**ACCIIILNN**	clinician	**ACCMMOORS**	macrocosm
ACCENORSU	cancerous	**ACCIILLSY**	salicylic	**ACCMNOORY**	monocracy
ACCENOSST	cosecants	**ACCIILLVY**	civically		nomocracy
ACCENRSUY	recusancy	**ACCIILNOR**	conciliar	**ACCMNOTUY**	contumacy
ACCEOPRST	acceptors	**ACCIILOPT**	occipital	**ACCMORSTY**	macrocyst
ACCEORRSW	scarecrow	**ACCIILOST**	cloacitis	**ACCMOSSTU**	accustoms
ACCEORSSY	accessory	**ACCIILRTU**	circuital	**ACCNNOSTY**	constancy
ACCEORSTU	accouters	**ACCIILTVY**	acclivity	**ACCNOORTT**	contactor
	accoutres	**ACCIIMNOS**	cocainism	**ACCNOOSTU**	cocoanuts
	coruscate	**ACCIIMNPT**	panmictic	**ACCNOPSTU**	occupants
ACCFFHHIN	chaffinch	**ACCIIMOPT**	apomictic	**ACCNORSTT**	contracts
ACCFIILOR	calorific	**ACCIIMQSU**	caciquism	**ACCNORTTU**	cunctator
ACCFIILSU	fasciculi	**ACCIINNPS**	piccanins	**ACCOPRRUY**	procuracy
ACCFIISST	fascistic	**ACCIINOSY**	isocyanic	**ACCOPRSTY**	cystocarp
ACCFINNOU	Confucian	**ACCIINRTY**	intricacy	**ACCORRSTY**	carrycots
ACCFOORST	cofactors	**ACCIIOPST**	pasticcio	**ACDDDEEIT**	dedicated
ACCGHHINU	Chu Chiang	**ACCIIORST**	isocratic	**ACDDDEIRS**	discarded
ACCGHHNNU	Changchun	**ACCIIOSTT**	isotactic	**ACDDDEKOP**	paddocked
ACCGHHNOW	Changchow	**ACCIISSTU**	casuistic	**ACDDEEEFT**	defecated
ACCGHIIKN	chiacking	**ACCIKKNNS**	nicknacks	**ACDDEEEIT**	dedicatee
ACCGHIINN	chicaning	**ACCIKKRRS**	rickracks	**ACDDEEENT**	anteceded
ACCGHIKNY	chyacking	**ACCIKKSTT**	ticktacks	**ACDDEEERS**	decreased
ACCGIILNN	calcining	**ACCIKLOST**	cocktails	**ACDDEEILM**	declaimed
ACCGIKLNR	crackling	**ACCIKNOSW**	cockswain	**ACDDEEIMT**	decimated
ACCGIKMRS	gimcracks	**ACCILLMOY**	comically		medicated
ACCGINNOV	concaving	**ACCILLNOY**	conically	**ACDDEEIST**	dedicates
ACCGINOST	accosting	**ACCILLNVY**	cynically	**ACDDEEITU**	deciduate
ACCGINSUU	caucusing	**ACCILLRUY**	crucially	**ACDDEELSS**	declassed
ACCHHISTT	chitchats	**ACCILMSUU**	aciculums	**ACDDEELWW**	dewclawed
ACCHHMNRU	churchman	**ACCILNORV**	clavicorn	**ACDDEENST**	decadents
ACCHIILRV	chivalric	**ACCILNOTU**	noctiluca	**ACDDEEORT**	decorated
ACCHIINNP	chincapin	**ACCILOSUV**	acclivous	**ACDDEERTT**	detracted
ACCHIKPST	chapstick	**ACCILPRTY**	cryptical	**ACDDEFIII**	acidified
ACCHILLOO	alcoholic	**ACCILRRSU**	circulars	**ACDDEGIRS**	disgraced

ACDDEGNOO dodecagon	**ACDEEGHNX** exchanged	**ACDEEITUV** educative
ACDDEHIKS dickheads	**ACDEEGHRR** recharged	**ACDEEJRTT** trajected
ACDDEHILY aldehydic	**ACDEEGINS** deceasing	**ACDEEKKNR** knackered
ACDDEIINT indicated	**ACDEEGIRZ** graecized	**ACDEEKLNS** slackened
ACDDEIITV addictive	**ACDEEGLNO** congealed	**ACDEEKPPR** prepacked
ACDDEIIJNU jaundiced	**ACDEEGLOU** decalogue	**ACDEEKRST** restacked
ACDDEILPS displaced	**ACDEEGNSV** scavenged	**ACDEELLMR** marcelled
ACDDEINST discanted	**ACDEEGOPU** decoupage	**ACDEELLNV** Cleveland
distanced	**ACDEEHHLT** hatcheled	**ACDEELLOT** decollate
ACDDEIORT dedicator	**ACDEEHIMP** impeached	ocellated
ACDDEIRRS discarder	**ACDEEHINN** enchained	**ACDEELLPR** parcelled
ACDDEKLOP padlocked	**ACDEEHINT** echinated	**ACDEELNNU** uncleaned
ACDDEKLOS deadlocks	**ACDEEHIRS** cashiered	**ACDEELNPS** enclasped
ACDDEKOST deadstock	charidees	spanceled
stockaded	**ACDEEHIRT** tracheide	**ACDEELNRS** calenders
ACDDELNOO canoodled	**ACDEEHKNY** hackneyed	**ACDEELNSU** Enceladus
ACDDELNRU underclad	**ACDEEHLLN** chandelle	**ACDEELNTT** tentacled
ACDDEMMNO commanded	**ACDEEHLNN** channeled	**ACDEELNTU** nucleated
ACDDENOTU outdanced	**ACDEEHLOR** Delaroche	**ACDEELOPS** opalesced
ACDDGIINT addicting	**ACDEEHLPT** chapleted	**ACDEELORT** relocated
ACDDGINTU adducting	**ACDEEHMRS** demarches	**ACDEELORV** Coverdale
ACDDHHNSU dachshund	**ACDEEHMRT** rematched	**ACDEELPTU** peculated
ACDDHIRSY hydracids	**ACDEEHNNT** enchanted	**ACDEELQRU** lacquered
ACDDHKOSS shaddocks	**ACDEEHNST** chastened	**ACDEELRRS** declarers
ACDDIILOS discoidal	**ACDEEHRRT** chartered	**ACDEELRST** decretals
ACDDIILRU druidical	recharted	**ACDEELRSW** leadscrew
ACDDIINOT addiction	**ACDEEHRST** detachers	**ACDEELRTT** clattered
ACDDIIORS cardioids	**ACDEEHRTT** chattered	**ACDEELRTU** ulcerated
ACDDINOTU adduction	**ACDEEIINT** teniacide	**ACDEELSSS** declasses
ACDDKLNOS docklands	**ACDEEIIRT** diaeretic	**ACDEELSTY** decastyle
ACDDKORSY dockyards	**ACDEEIJTV** adjective	**ACDEEMNOS** codenames
ACDDLLNOU cloudland	**ACDEEILMN** endemical	**ACDEEMPRS** scampered
ACDDORSTU adductors	**ACDEEILMR** declaimer	**ACDEENNRT** entranced
ACDEEEFST defecates	reclaimed	**ACDEENNRU** endurance
ACDEEEHIP headpiece	**ACDEEILMX** exclaimed	**ACDEENNRY** decennary
ACDEEEHNP cheapened	**ACDEEILNN** celandine	**ACDEENNST** ascendent
ACDEEEHNR adherence	decennial	**ACDEENORS** coarsened
ACDEEEHST escheated	**ACDEEILNT** declinate	**ACDEENOSS** deaconess
ACDEEEKSS seedcakes	**ACDEEILNU** euclidean	**ACDEENOST** anecdotes
ACDEEELSS declassee	**ACDEEILPR** calipered	**ACDEENRSS** ascenders
ACDEEEMRT decameter	**ACDEEILRT** decaliter	reascends
decametre	decalitre	**ACDEENRST** decanters
ACDEEENRT reenacted	**ACDEEILST** delicates	descanter
ACDEEENST antecedes	**ACDEEILSU** aedicules	**ACDEENRSU** ascendeur
ACDEEENSV evanesced	**ACDEEILTU** elucidate	**ACDEENRSZ** credenzas
ACDEEEPRT deprecate	**ACDEEILTY** acetylide	**ACDEENRTY** daycentre
ACDEEEPRV Cape Verde	**ACDEEIMNO** macedoine	**ACDEENSTT** dancettes
ACDEEERRT recreated	**ACDEEIMNP** impedance	**ACDEEOPSS** peasecods
ACDEEERSS decreases	**ACDEEIMRS** ceramides	**ACDEEORST** decorates
ACDEEERST desecrate	racemised	**ACDEEORTV** overacted
ACDEEERTU reeducate	**ACDEEIMRZ** racemized	**ACDEEPRRS** scarpered
ACDEEERTX execrated	**ACDEEIMST** decimates	**ACDEEPSTT** spectated
ACDEEESSS seedcases	medicates	**ACDEEQRTU** racqueted
ACDEEFFHR chaffered	**ACDEEINOS** oceanides	**ACDEERRTT** retracted
ACDEEFHMR chamfered	**ACDEEINRS** increased	**ACDEERSST** Descartes
ACDEEFHWY wheyfaced	**ACDEEINSU** audiences	**ACDEERSSU** surceased
ACDEEFIIT acetified	**ACDEEINSV** deviances	**ACDEERSSV** crevassed
ACDEEFINS defiances	**ACDEEIOPR** adipocere	**ACDEERSTT** scattered
ACDEEFKRT afterdeck	**ACDEEIPRT** predicate	**ACDEERSTU** reductase
ACDEEFNTU fecundate	**ACDEEIPST** speciated	**ACDEERTTU** eructated
ACDEEFORT defecator	**ACDEEIRRT** traceried	**ACDEERTTX** extracted
ACDEEFRRT refracted	**ACDEEISTV** vesicated	**ACDEESSTU** decussate

ACDEFFIKM	mafficked	**ACDEHILLO**	cheloidal	**ACDEIIOPR**	aperiodic
ACDEFFILR	Radcliffe	**ACDEHINNR**	hindrance	**ACDEIIOST**	dacoities
ACDEFFILT	afflicted	**ACDEHINNU**	unchained	**ACDEIIPRR**	parricide
ACDEFFIST	disaffect	**ACDEHINOT**	inchoated	**ACDEIIPRT**	patricide
ACDEFFMOR	cofferdam	**ACDEHINSV**	cavendish		pediatric
ACDEFHINR	archfiend	**ACDEHIOPX**	hexapodic	**ACDEIISTV**	vaticides
ACDEFHLRS	feldschar	**ACDEHIPRY**	hyperacid	**ACDEIJNSU**	jaundices
ACDEFIIIL	edificial	**ACDEHIPST**	cadetship	**ACDEIKLNN**	calkinned
ACDEFIIIR	acidifier	**ACDEHIRST**	tracheids	**ACDEIKMNN**	nicknamed
ACDEFIIIS	acidifies	**ACDEHIRSY**	dyarchies	**ACDEIKMNR**	Mackinder
ACDEFIILR	clarified	**ACDEHISST**	chastised	**ACDEIKRST**	sidetrack
ACDEFIILT	feticidal	**ACDEHKLOS**	headlocks	**ACDEILLMS**	miscalled
ACDEFIINR	carnified	**ACDEHKMOP**	chokedamp	**ACDEILLMY**	decimally
ACDEFIIRS	scarified	**ACDEHKMPU**	chempaduk		medically
ACDEFILLO	coalfield	**ACDEHKOST**	headstock	**ACDEILLOS**	localised
ACDEFILLU	Caulfield	**ACDEHKRSU**	archdukes	**ACDEILLOZ**	localized
ACDEFILOS	focalised	**ACDEHLNOR**	chlordane	**ACDEILLTY**	edictally
ACDEFILOZ	focalized	**ACDEHLNOT**	decathlon	**ACDEILMNU**	unclaimed
ACDEFILRS	filecards	**ACDEHLNRS**	chandlers	**ACDEILMPS**	misplaced
ACDEFILRU	cauldrife	**ACDEHLNRY**	chandlery	**ACDEILMST**	maledicts
ACDEFINRT	infarcted	**ACDEHLNTU**	unlatched	**ACDEILNNP**	candlepin
	infracted	**ACDEHLRSU**	schedular		pinnacled
ACDEFLNOT	conflated	**ACDEHLRTU**	trauchled	**ACDEILNOR**	clarioned
ACDEFMNOO	moonfaced	**ACDEHMNNU**	unmatched	**ACDEILNOU**	Deucalion
ACDEFRRTU	fractured	**ACDEHMOST**	stomached	**ACDEILNSU**	dulcineas
ACDEGGIMO	demagogic	**ACDEHMPRY**	pachyderm	**ACDEILNSW**	Windscale
ACDEGGIOP	pedagogic	**ACDEHMPSS**	Deschamps	**ACDEILNTU**	acidulent
ACDEGGIRT	catrigged	**ACDEHMSTU**	mustached	**ACDEILNVY**	divalency
ACDEGHINR	chagrined	**ACDEHNOPR**	cardphone	**ACDEILOPR**	caprioled
ACDEGHINT	detaching		phonecard	**ACDEILOPT**	petalodic
ACDEGHIRS	discharge	**ACDEHNRRT**	trenchard	**ACDEILORT**	loricated
ACDEGHNNU	unchanged	**ACDEHNRTU**	uncharted	**ACDEILORX**	Delacroix
ACDEGHNRU	graunched	**ACDEHNSTU**	staunched	**ACDEILORZ**	calorized
	uncharged		unscathed	**ACDEILOST**	dislocate
ACDEGIILR	regicidal	**ACDEHNTUW**	unwatched	**ACDEILOSV**	vocalised
ACDEGIILS	algicides	**ACDEHOOPT**	chaetopod	**ACDEILOVZ**	vocalized
ACDEGILLN	decalling	**ACDEHORRV**	hardcover	**ACDEILPRS**	displacer
ACDEGILNO	genocidal	**ACDEHORSS**	crosshead	**ACDEILPRU**	pedicular
ACDEGILNR	declaring	**ACDEHORST**	chordates	**ACDEILPSS**	displaces
ACDEGILNS	descaling	**ACDEHOSSW**	showcased	**ACDEILPTU**	duplicate
ACDEGILOO	logaoedic	**ACDEHPRSU**	purchased	**ACDEILRSS**	laserdisc
ACDEGIMNO	endogamic	**ACDEHRRSS**	chresards	**ACDEILRTU**	curtailed
ACDEGIMNP	decamping	**ACDEIIINT**	dietician	**ACDEILTUV**	victualed
ACDEGINNS	ascending	**ACDEIIIST**	acidities	**ACDEIMNNO**	dominance
ACDEGINNT	decanting	**ACDEIILMN**	adminicle	**ACDEIMNNT**	mendicant
ACDEGINOY	gynaecoid		medicinal	**ACDEIMNOP**	companied
ACDEGINRT	redacting	**ACDEIILNO**	lidocaine		compendia
ACDEGINTU	educating	**ACDEIILNT**	identical	**ACDEIMNOS**	comedians
ACDEGIOTT	cogitated	**ACDEIILNU**	euclidian		demoniacs
ACDEGIRRS	disgracer	**ACDEIILNX**	indexical	**ACDEIMNPS**	pandemics
ACDEGIRRT	cartridge	**ACDEIILRV**	larvicide	**ACDEIMNRU**	manicured
ACDEGIRSS	disgraces		veridical	**ACDEIMNSU**	muscadine
ACDEGLNOR	clangored	**ACDEIILST**	deistical	**ACDEIMNTY**	mendacity
ACDEGLMOU	Languedoc	**ACDEIIMMY**	immediacy	**ACDEIMORT**	decimator
ACDEGNNOU	undecagon	**ACDEIIMRT**	diametric	**ACDEIMRST**	timecards
ACDEHHIKT	thickhead		matricide	**ACDEIMRTU**	muricated
ACDEHHIRS	rhachides	**ACDEIINOS**	sciaenoid	**ACDEINNOR**	ordinance
ACDEHHNTU	unhatched	**ACDEIINOT**	dianoetic	**ACDEINNOS**	canonised
ACDEHHORX	hexachord	**ACDEIINSS**	sciaenids	**ACDEINNOT**	contained
ACDEHIIRR	diarrheic	**ACDEIINST**	actinides	**ACDEINNOZ**	canonized
ACDEHIIRS	diarchies		indicates	**ACDEINNST**	instanced
ACDEHIITT	diathetic	**ACDEIINTV**	vindicate	**ACDEINOPS**	caponised

ACDEINOPT	captioned	ACDELNOTU	unlocated	ACDFOORTW	woodcraft
ACDEINOPZ	caponized	ACDELNPSU	unclasped	ACDGHIILO	glochidia
ACDEINORR	coriander	ACDELNRUY	underclay	ACDGHIIPR	digraphic
ACDEINORS	dinoceras	ACDELOPST	clodpates	ACDGHIMOY	dichogamy
ACDEINORT	redaction	ACDELOPTU	copulated	ACDGHIPSY	dysphagic
ACDEINOSS	diocesans		cupolated	ACDGHOSTW	watchdogs
ACDEINOST	catenoids	ACDELORTY	cordately	ACDGIILNO	gadolinic
ACDEINOSV	voidances	ACDELOSTU	osculated	ACDGIILOR	goliardic
ACDEINOTU	auctioned	ACDELPRSY	clepsydra	ACDGIINNY	cyaniding
	cautioned	ACDELRTTU	cultrated	ACDGIINTT	dictating
	education	ACDEMMMNO	commendam	ACDGIIRST	digastric
ACDEINOTV	advection	ACDEMMNOR	commander	ACDGILNRS	cradlings
	invocated	ACDEMNOPR	compander	ACDGIMOST	dogmatics
ACDEINPRT	predicant		cramponed	ACDGINORR	corrading
ACDEINRSS	acridness	ACDEMOORR	acrodrome	ACDGINRSU	crusading
ACDEINRST	discanter	ACDEMOORT	motorcade	ACDGINRTU	traducing
ACDEINRTU	curtained	ACDEMOPRS	compadres	ACDGIOOPR	Podgorica
ACDEINSST	distances	ACDEMOPSS	compassed	ACDGLOOST	Gold Coast
ACDEINSSY	anecdysis	ACDEMORST	democrats	ACDGORRSS	cordgrass
ACDEINSTY	asyndetic	ACDENNNOU	announced	ACDHIIIRR	Richard II
	syndicate	ACDENNNSU	unscanned	ACDHIILMO	homicidal
ACDEINTTU	tunicated	ACDENNRST	transcend	ACDHIILOP	acidophil
ACDEIOPSS	diascopes	ACDENOOOW	canoewood		haploidic
ACDEIOPTY	adipocyte	ACDENOOTT	cottonade	ACDHIILST	distichal
ACDEIPRST	crispated	ACDENOPRS	endocarps	ACDHIIMRS	midrashic
	practised	ACDENORST	Doncaster	ACDHIIMSU	dichasium
ACDEIPRTY	predacity	ACDENORSY	secondary	ACDHIINNO	Indochina
ACDEIPSTU	cuspidate	ACDENORTU	undercoat	ACDHIINOP	diaphonic
ACDEIQTTU	acquitted	ACDENOSST	endocasts	ACDHIKNPS	handpicks
ACDEIRRSU	curarised	ACDENOSTU	outdances	ACDHILPRS	pilchards
ACDEIRRUZ	curarized	ACDENPTTU	punctated	ACDHILRSY	chrysalid
ACDEIRSSU	cuirassed	ACDENRRSU	unscarred	ACDHILRUY	hydraulic
ACDEIRSTT	astricted	ACDENRRTU	undercart	ACDHIMORT	chromatid
	cristated	ACDENRSTU	underacts	ACDHIOPRS	rhapsodic
ACDEIRSTY	dicastery	ACDENRTTU	truncated	ACDHIORSY	hyracoids
ACDEIRTTU	urticated	ACDEOORRT	decorator	ACDHIORYZ	hydrazoic
ACDEIRUVY	ayurvedic	ACDEOORSS	doorcases	ACDHIPSSY	dysphasic
ACDEISSTY	ecdysiast	ACDEOORTT	doctorate	ACDHIRRSU	churidars
ACDEJKKSY	skyjacked	ACDEOPRSY	copyreads	ACDHKORRS	hardrocks
ACDEKKMRU	muckraked	ACDEORRST	costarred	ACDHLNORS	chaldrons
ACDEKMMMO	mammocked		redactors	ACDHMNOOR	chondroma
ACDEKNRTU	untracked	ACDEORRTT	detractor	ACDHMOOTW	doomwatch
ACDEKOSST	stockades	ACDEORSST	coatdress		matchwood
ACDELLOPS	collapsed	ACDEORSSU	crusadoes	ACDHOOPPS	scaphopod
	scalloped	ACDEORSTU	ceratodus	ACDHOOSTW	woodchats
ACDELLORR	corralled		educators	ACDHORTTW	watchword
ACDELLOST	Oldcastle	ACDEORSUU	rudaceous	ACDIIILMT	miticidal
ACDELLOSU	calloused	ACDEORSUZ	cruzadoes	ACDIIIMOT	idiomatic
ACDELMOPR	placoderm	ACDEORTUY	educatory	ACDIIJLRU	juridical
ACDELMORU	clamoured	ACDEORTUZ	Côte d'Azur	ACDIIJRUY	judiciary
ACDELMORY	comradely	ACDEOSTTU	outcasted	ACDIILMNO	dominical
ACDELMSSU	muscadels	ACDEQSTUU	aqueducts	ACDIILMSS	disclaims
ACDELMTUU	cumulated	ACDERRSSU	crusaders	ACDIILMSX	disclimax
ACDELNNOO	colonnade	ACDERRSTU	traducers	ACDIILNOR	crinoidal
ACDELNNOR	clarendon	ACDFFHNSU	handcuffs	ACDIILOSS	dissocial
ACDELNNTU	candlenut	ACDFFIRST	diffracts	ACDIILOST	diastolic
ACDELNNUU	undulance	ACDFFLOSS	scaffolds	ACDIILOSV	viscoidal
ACDELNOOR	canoodler	ACDFHILSS	scaldfish	ACDIILPTY	placidity
ACDELNOOS	canoodles	ACDFIIILL	filicidal	ACDIILSTU	dualistic
ACDELNOOW	lancewood	ACDFIIRUY	fiduciary	ACDIIMNNO	Dominican
ACDELNORS	Androcles	ACDFINNOT	confidant	ACDIIMPRY	pyramidic
	colanders	ACDFNTTUY	candytuft	ACDIIMRTY	mydriatic

ACDIINNST	indicants	ACDORRTUY	courtyard	ACEEGHNSX	exchanges
ACDIINORS	radionics	ACDRSSTTU	dustcarts	ACEEGHRRS	recharges
ACDIINORT	indicator	ACEEEFIRT	cafetiere	ACEEGILNR	generical
ACDIINOSY	Dionysiac	ACEEEFLNR	freelance	ACEEGILNT	clientage
ACDIINOTT	dictation	ACEEEGHPR	repechage		genetical
ACDIINRTY	rancidity	ACEEEGLNS	elegances	ACEEGILRS	sacrilege
ACDIIOPRT	diatropic	ACEEEGNNV	vengeance	ACEEGILRV	viceregal
	podiatric	ACEEEHIPT	epithecae		viceregal
ACDIIRTTX	dictatrix		petechiae	ACEEGIMNT	metagenic
ACDIJORTU	judicator	ACEEEHIRV	echeveria	ACEEGINNR	careening
ACDIKKLRY	Kirkcaldy	ACEEEHNPR	cheapener	ACEEGINRR	careering
ACDIKKNST	kickstand	ACEEEHRST	reteaches	ACEEGINRV	grievance
ACDIKNQSU	quicksand	ACEEEILMP	piecemeal	ACEEGIRRV	caregiver
ACDIKRSTY	yardstick	ACEEEIMPT	peacetime	ACEEGIRSZ	graecizes
ACDILLLOO	colloidal	ACEEEIPRS	earpieces	ACEEGIRTT	cigarette
ACDILLOOR	coralloid	ACEEEKNQU	queencake	ACEEGKRSW	wreckages
ACDILLORY	cordially	ACEEEKRRT	racketeer	ACEEGKRWY	greywacke
ACDILLOSU	caudillos	ACEEELMRS	cameleers	ACEEGLLOU	colleague
ACDILMNOO	monodical	ACEEELNPS	Pleasence	ACEEGLNOR	congealer
ACDILMOPS	psalmodic	ACEEELNRT	crenelate	ACEEGLNRT	rectangle
ACDILMOPY	diplomacy	ACEEELNRV	relevance	ACEEGLRSS	graceless
ACDILMOTU	comatulid	ACEEELNTU	enucleate	ACEEGMNOR	geomancer
ACDILNOOR	coordinal	ACEEELNTY	acetylene	ACEEGMNUY	gynaeceum
ACDILNORS	ironclads	ACEEELSSS	ceaseless	ACEEGNORU	encourage
ACDILNORT	doctrinal	ACEEEMNNR	remanence	ACEEGNRSV	scavenger
ACDILNOSY	synodical	ACEEEMNPR	permeance	ACEEGNRSY	sergeancy
ACDILOORT	doctorial	ACEEENPPT	appetence	ACEEGNSSV	scavenges
ACDILOPRS	dropsical	ACEEENPRS	esperance	ACEEGOOPR	cooperage
ACDILORSY	corydalis	ACEEENRRS	careeners	ACEEGORRS	racegoers
ACDILOSTU	custodial	ACEEENRSV	severance	ACEEGRTTU	curettage
ACDILOSTY	dystocial	ACEEENSSV	evanesces	ACEEHHRSU	heucheras
ACDILOSUU	acidulous	ACEEERRST	recreates	ACEEHHTUX	Hexateuch
ACDILOTUV	oviductal	ACEEERSTT	etceteras	ACEEHIIPR	hairpiece
ACDILRTTY	tridactyl	ACEEERSTX	execrates	ACEEHILMS	alchemies
ACDIMNOOS	codomains	ACEEFFHRR	chafferer		alchemise
ACDIMNOOS	codomains	ACEEFFHRU	rechauffe	ACEEHILMZ	alchemize
ACDIMOPSS	spasmodic	ACEEFFITV	affective	ACEEHILPT	petechial
ACDIMORRU	macruroid	ACEEFFLNU	affluence	ACEEHILRT	heretical
ACDIMORTY	mordacity	ACEEFFLTU	effectual	ACEEHILRV	chevalier
ACDINOOPT	actinopod	ACEEFHLNP	halfpence	ACEEHIMNS	achimenes
ACDINOSTU	custodian	ACEEFHLPR	parfleche		mechanise
ACDIORSTT	dictators	ACEEFHMRR	chamferer	ACEEHIMNZ	mechanize
ACDIRSSTT	distracts	ACEEFHORR	forereach	ACEEHIMPR	impeacher
ACDJLNTUY	adjunctly	ACEEFHSTT	factsheet	ACEEHIMPS	impeaches
ACDJOORTU	coadjutor	ACEEFHSWY	wheyfaces	ACEEHINNV	enhancive
ACDKLORTU	truckload	ACEEFIITR	acetifier	ACEEHINPT	phenacite
ACDKMNNOO	monadnock	ACEEFIIST	acetifies	ACEEHINRR	rancherie
ACDKORSTY	stockyard	ACEEFILPR	fireplace	ACEEHINRT	Catherine
ACDLMNOOY	condyloma	ACEEFINRT	interface	ACEEHINSS	Aeschines
ACDLMNOPW	clampdown	ACEEFIRSS	fricassee	ACEEHINST	hesitance
ACDLNNORW	crownland	ACEEFMORT	forcemeat	ACEEHIPRR	preachier
ACDLNORSU	cauldrons	ACEEFNNRW	New France	ACEEHIPRS	eparchies
ACDLNSTYY	syndactyl	ACEEFNORV	confervae		parcheesi
ACDMMNOOS	commandos	ACEEFPRRS	prefacers	ACEEHIPRT	apheretic
ACDMMNORU	communard	ACEEFPRST	praefects	ACEEHIPST	peachiest
ACDMOOPRR	comprador	ACEEFPSTY	typefaces	ACEEHIRSV	achievers
ACDMOOSUV	muscovado	ACEEFRRSU	resurface		chivarees
ACDNOORRT	corrodant	ACEEFRSSU	farceuses	ACEEHIRSX	exarchies
ACDNOORSV	cordovans	ACEEGHIOR	heroic age	ACEEHISTT	aesthetic
ACDNOSSTW	downcasts	ACEEGHIRU	gaucherie	ACEEHLMNO	chameleon
ACDOORRSS	crossroad	ACEEGHLLN	challenge	ACEEHLMOO	haemocoel
ACDOORSST	ostracods	ACEEGHNRX	exchanger	ACEEHLMPV	champleve
ACDOPRSST	postcards				

ACEEHLNRU	herculean	ACEEILNSV	valencies	ACEELLNST	lancelets
ACEEHLNRW	Walcheren	ACEEILPRS	periclase	ACEELLORT	electoral
ACEEHLNSS	seneschal		prelacies	ACEELLPSS	placeless
ACEEHLNST	Cleanthes	ACEEILPRT	replicate	ACEELLRRS	cellarers
ACEEHLNTU	Neuchâtel	ACEEILPTX	explicate	ACEELLRST	cellarets
ACEEHLORT	trochleae	ACEEILRST	cartelise	ACEELMNPT	placement
ACEEHLOSS	shoelaces	ACEEILRTZ	cartelize	ACEELMNST	selectman
ACEEHLPSS	chapeless	ACEEIMMNN	immanence	ACEELMNTT	cattlemen
ACEEHLRTW	cartwheel	ACEEIMMNT	mincemeat	ACEELMOPS	someplace
ACEEHMMRT	machmeter	ACEEIMMRT	metameric	ACEELMORT	latecomer
ACEEHMNRY	archenemy	ACEEIMNPR	mepacrine	ACEELNNRU	cannelure
ACEEHMOTY	haemocyte	ACEEIMNSX	exciseman	ACEELNNSS	cleanness
ACEEHMRST	rematches	ACEEIMPRT	imprecate	ACEELNORT	coeternal
ACEEHMRSU	charmeuse	ACEEIMRRS	careerism		tolerance
ACEEHNNRS	enhancers	ACEEIMRSS	cassimere	ACEELNPRS	precleans
ACEEHNNRT	enchanter		racemises	ACEELNPST	pentacles
ACEEHNOPR	chaperone	ACEEIMRST	creamiest	ACEELNPTU	petulance
ACEEHNPSS	cheapness		miscreate	ACEELNRRS	larceners
ACEEHNPTY	pachytene	ACEEIMRSZ	racemizes	ACEELNRSS	cleansers
ACEEHNRSS	enchasers	ACEEIMRTT	metricate		clearness
ACEEHNRST	chastener	ACEEIMRVW	crimewave	ACEELNRTU	calenture
ACEEHNRTT	entrechat	ACEEINNRS	canneries		crenulate
ACEEHNSTU	chanteuse	ACEEINNRT	nectarine	ACEELNRTY	crenately
	unteaches	ACEEINNST	insectean	ACEELNRVY	relevancy
ACEEHORRS	racehorse		tenancies	ACEELNRVV	insectean
ACEEHORRV	overreach	ACEEINNTU	enunciate	ACEELNSSU	nucleases
ACEEHOSTU	theaceous	ACEEINPRU	epicurean	ACEELNSTT	tentacles
ACEEHPRRS	preachers	ACEEINPTT	pectinate	ACEELNSTU	nucleates
ACEEHPRTY	archetype	ACEEINRRS	errancies	ACEELNSTW	Newcastle
ACEEHPSSS	chapesses		increaser	ACEELNTUX	exultance
ACEEHRRRT	charterer	ACEEINRSS	increases	ACEELNTUV	cuneately
	recharter	ACEEINRST	centiares	ACEELOOSU	oleaceous
ACEEHRRSS	searchers		cisternae	ACEELOPRT	percolate
ACEEHRRTT	chatterer		iterances	ACEELOPSS	escalopes
ACEEHRRTY	treachery		nectaries		opalesces
ACEEHRSTT	catheters	ACEEINSST	cineastes	ACEELORRT	correlate
ACEEIILNR	eirenical	ACEEIORTX	excoriate	ACEELORSS	casserole
ACEEIILPT	tailpiece	ACEEIOSSS	ecossaise	ACEELORST	relocates
ACEEIJQRU	jacquerie	ACEEIOTVV	evocative	ACEELORSW	lowercase
ACEEIKLLS	scalelike	ACEEIPRTT	crepitate	ACEELORTT	lectorate
ACEEIKLMR	creamlike	ACEEIPRTV	precative	ACEELORTU	urceolate
ACEEIKMNZ	Mackenzie	ACEEIPSST	speciates	ACEELPRRS	replacers
ACEEIKRST	creakiest	ACEEIQRRU	reacquire	ACEELPSSS	spaceless
ACEEILLMS	limescale	ACEEIRRST	careerist	ACEELPSTU	peculates
ACEEILLNR	cleanlier		traceries		speculate
ACEEILLST	celestial	ACEEIRRSV	carveries	ACEELPTUX	exculpate
ACEEILLTV	vellicate	ACEEIRSST	sectaries	ACEELQRRU	lacquerer
ACEEILMNS	mescaline	ACEEIRSSU	causeries	ACEELRRTT	clatterer
ACEEILMNZ	mezcaline	ACEEIRSSW	wiseacres	ACEELRSST	traceless
ACEEILMRR	reclaimer	ACEEIRSTT	catteries	ACEELRSTU	ulcerates
ACEEILMRT	carmelite	ACEEIRSTU	cauteries	ACEELRSTV	cervelats
ACEEILMRX	exclaimer		cauterise	ACEELRTUY	electuary
ACEEILMST	timescale	ACEEIRSTV	creatives	ACEELSSSU	causeless
ACEEILMTT	telematic	ACEEIRTTX	extricate		sauceless
ACEEILNTTX	telematic	ACEEIRTUZ	cauterize	ACEELSSTT	telecasts
ACEEILNOR	Coleraine	ACEEISSST	ecstasies	ACEEMMOOT	ammocoete
ACEEILNPR	percaline	ACEEISSTT	testacies	ACEEMMORR	macromere
ACEEILNRS	carelines	ACEEISSTV	vesicates	ACEEMNNTT	enactment
	larcenies	ACEEKLMRS	mackerels	ACEEMNRRY	mercenary
	reliances	ACEEKNSTT	snackette	ACEEMNSST	casements
ACEEILNRT	interlace	ACEELLLSU	cellulase	ACEEMOPRS	camporees
	reclinate	ACEELLMRR	marceller		capsomere
ACEEILNST	latencies			ACEEMORRS	sarcomere

ACEEMORTT	octameter	**ACEFFIORT**	forficate	**ACEFMNRST**	craftsmen
ACEEMORVW	creamwove	**ACEFFLRSS**	sclaffers	**ACEFNNORT**	Frontenac
ACEEMPRRS	scamperer	**ACEFFOSTU**	suffocate	**ACEFNORSV**	confervas
ACEEMRRSS	screamers	**ACEFGHILT**	lightface	**ACEFNRSTT**	transfect
ACEEMRRTU	mercurate	**ACEFGHLNU**	changeful	**ACEFOOPRS**	roofscape
ACEEMRSTY	mercy seat	**ACEFGINPR**	prefacing	**ACEFOOPST**	footpaces
ACEENNNOR	cannoneer	**ACEFGINSY**	casefying	**ACEFORRRT**	refractor
ACEENNORS	resonance	**ACEFGINTT**	facetting	**ACEFORRRU**	carrefour
ACEENNOST	Cantonese	**ACEFGLNOR**	gerfalcon	**ACEFORSST**	forecasts
ACEENNRST	entrances	**ACEFHIINT**	chieftain	**ACEFOSTUU**	tufaceous
	renascent	**ACEFHIKLT**	thickleaf	**ACEFRRSSU**	surfacers
ACEENNRTY	centenary	**ACEFHINRS**	franchise	**ACEFRRSTU**	fractures
ACEENORST	carotenes	**ACEFHIPRY**	preachify	**ACEGGILNS**	cagelings
ACEENOSST	notecases	**ACEFHIRRT**	fratchier	**ACEGGILST**	claggiest
ACEENPPTY	appetency	**ACEFHISST**	catfishes	**ACEGGINOS**	Gascoigne
ACEENPRRS	parceners	**ACEFHLNSU**	flaunches	**ACEGGIRRS**	scraggier
ACEENPRRT	carpenter	**ACEFHOSUV**	vouchsafe	**ACEGGIRST**	craggiest
ACEENPTTX	expectant	**ACEFIILMS**	facsimile	**ACEGGMORR**	MacGregor
ACEENRRST	recanters	**ACEFIILRR**	clarifier	**ACEGHHILP**	high place
	recreants	**ACEFIILRS**	clarifies	**ACEGHHPTU**	Hugh Capet
ACEENRRTU	crenature	**ACEFIILRT**	laticifer	**ACEGHIIMN**	Chiengmai
ACEENRSST	reascents	**ACEFIINNR**	financier	**ACEGHIINV**	achieving
ACEENRSSY	necessary	**ACEFIINNS**	infancies	**ACEGHIIST**	chigetais
ACEENRSTV	Cervantes	**ACEFIINRS**	carnifies	**ACEGHILNP**	pleaching
ACEENRTTU	utterance	**ACEFIIPRS**	pacifiers	**ACEGHILNT**	chelating
ACEENSSTU	acuteness	**ACEFIIRRS**	scarifier	**ACEGHILRT**	lethargic
ACEENSSTX	exactness	**ACEFIIRRT**	artificer	**ACEGHINNN**	enhancing
ACEENTTUX	executant	**ACEFIIRSS**	scarifies	**ACEGHINNS**	encashing
ACEEOOPRT	cooperate	**ACEFIIRST**	artifices		enchasing
ACEEOPRRT	procreate	**ACEFIIRTV**	fricative	**ACEGHINPR**	preaching
ACEEORRRT	recreator	**ACEFIISST**	satisfice	**ACEGHINRS**	searching
ACEEORRTT	rectorate	**ACEFIITTV**	factitive	**ACEGHINSS**	chasseing
ACEEORRTV	overreact	**ACEFIJKKN**	jackknife	**ACEGHINST**	teachings
ACEEORTUV	eucaryote	**ACEFIKRTU**	fruitcake	**ACEGHIRST**	Reichstag
ACEEOSSTU	setaceous	**ACEFILNNO**	falconine	**ACEGHMNOS**	cheongsam
ACEEPPRSU	uppercase	**ACEFILORT**	fortalice	**ACEGHMORT**	hectogram
ACEEPRRTU	recapture	**ACEFILOSS**	focalises	**ACEGHNRSU**	graunches
ACEEPSSTT	spectates	**ACEFILOSZ**	focalizes	**ACEGHOPRY**	creophagy
ACEEPSSTY	typecases	**ACEFILSTU**	faculties	**ACEGHOPTY**	phagocyte
ACEERRSSS	caressers	**ACEFIMORT**	formicate	**ACEGHRRSU**	surcharge
ACEERRSST	creatress	**ACEFIMPRS**	campfires	**ACEGIILLS**	gallicise
ACEERRSSU	ecraseurs	**ACEFINNSS**	fanciness	**ACEGIILLZ**	gallicize
ACEERRSTT	scatterer	**ACEFINORT**	fornicate	**ACEGIILMO**	oligaemic
	streetcar	**ACEFINPRT**	faceprint	**ACEGIILNS**	anglicise
ACEERRSTU	creatures	**ACEFINSTU**	infuscate	**ACEGIILNT**	genitalic
ACEERRSTY	secretary	**ACEFINTTV**	ventifact	**ACEGIILNV**	vigilance
ACEERRTUV	recurvate	**ACEFIORST**	factories	**ACEGIILNZ**	anglicize
ACEERSSST	actresses		factorise	**ACEGIIMNT**	enigmatic
ACEERSSSU	surceases	**ACEFIORTZ**	factorize	**ACEGIINNT**	antigenic
ACEERSSSV	crevasses	**ACEFIOSTU**	facetious	**ACEGIINSV**	vicinages
ACEERSSTU	secateurs	**ACEFIRSTT**	craftiest	**ACEGIIRRT**	geriatric
ACEERSTTU	eructates	**ACEFLLRUY**	carefully	**ACEGIJKNT**	jacketing
ACEERTUXY	executary	**ACEFLMNOS**	flamencos	**ACEGIKLNR**	lackering
ACEESSSTT	cassettes	**ACEFLNORR**	conferral	**ACEGIKLNY**	lackeying
ACEESSSTU	caestuses	**ACEFLNORS**	falconers	**ACEGIKNNR**	cankering
ACEFFFLRU	carfuffle	**ACEFLNORV**	conferval	**ACEGIKNPR**	repacking
ACEFFGINT	affecting	**ACEFLNOST**	conflates	**ACEGIKNRS**	screaking
ACEFFHRSU	chauffers		falconets	**ACEGIKNRT**	racketing
ACEFFHRUU	chauffeur	**ACEFLPTUU**	teacupful	**ACEGIKPRR**	ragpicker
ACEFFIIOT	officiate	**ACEFLRSTU**	cratefuls	**ACEGILLLO**	collegial
ACEFFIKMR	mafficker	**ACEFLRSUU**	saucerful	**ACEGILLNO**	collegian
ACEFFINOT	affection	**ACEFLTTUU**	fluctuate	**ACEGILLNR**	cellaring

	recalling	**ACEGLNOTY**	cognately	Charles VI
ACEGILLOR	allegoric	**ACEGMMNOO**	commonage	**ACEHILRSX** Charles IX
ACEGILLOT	colligate	**ACEGMMRSU**	scrummage	Charles XI
ACEGILMNP	emplacing	**ACEGNNORS**	crannoges	**ACEHILRUV** vehicular
ACEGILMSU	mucilages	**ACEGNNOTT**	cotangent	**ACEHILSTT** athletics
ACEGILNNO	congenial	**ACEGNNPRY**	pregnancy	**ACEHILTTY** tachylite
ACEGILNNS	cleansing	**ACEGORRTU**	corrugate	**ACEHIMMNS** mechanism
ACEGILNPR	parceling	**ACEGORSST**	escargots	**ACEHIMNOT** methanoic
	replacing	**ACEGORSTT**	cottagers	**ACEHIMNRV** machinery
ACEGILNRS	clearings	**ACEHHHIST**	shechitah	**ACEHIMNST** mechanist
ACEGILNRU	genicular	**ACEHHILPS**	chelaship	**ACEHIMPST** emphatics
	neuralgic	**ACEHHIRRS**	hierarchs	**ACEHIMRTU** hematuric
ACEGILNRV	clavering	**ACEHHIRRY**	hierarchy	rheumatic
ACEGILNRW	clearwing	**ACEHHIRSS**	rhachises	**ACEHIMSTT** thematics
ACEGILNSW	lacewings	**ACEHHISTX**	hexastich	**ACEHINORT** anchorite
ACEGILNTU	cingulate	**ACEHHLLST**	shtetlach	antechoir
ACEGILOOR	aerologic	**ACEHHMNTT**	hatchment	**ACEHINORX** chronaxie
ACEGILRTU	curtilage	**ACEHHMOTY**	theomachy	**ACEHINOST** inchoates
	Géricault	**ACEHHNRST**	ethnarchs	**ACEHINOSV** anchovies
	graticule	**ACEHHNRTY**	ethnarchy	**ACEHINPST** cathepsin
ACEGIMMNR	engrammic	**ACEHHOOTT**	toothache	**ACEHINRRU** hurricane
ACEGIMMRS	scrimmage	**ACEHHOPTY**	hypotheca	raunchier
ACEGIMMST	tagmemics	**ACEHHPRST**	heptarchs	**ACEHINRSS** chariness
ACEGIMNNP	encamping	**ACEHHPRTY**	heptarchy	**ACEHINRST** chantries
ACEGIMNOT	geomantic	**ACEHHRSTT**	thatchers	snatchier
	megatonic	**ACEHHSSTY**	Hesychast	**ACEHINRSV** vacherins
ACEGIMNRS	screaming	**ACEHIILRS**	Charles II	**ACEHINSST** asthenics
ACEGIMNRT	centigram	**ACEHIIMNT**	hematinic	Caithness
	cremating	**ACEHIIMSS**	ischemias	**ACEHINSTY** hesitancy
ACEGIMNST	magnetics	**ACEHIIMTT**	hematitic	**ACEHINTTU** authentic
ACEGIMNTU	mutagenic	**ACEHIINOP**	Phoenicia	**ACEHIOPRY** coryphaei
ACEGIMNUY	gynaecium	**ACEHIINPP**	epiphanic	**ACEHIPPSS** spaceship
ACEGIMRRS	grimacers	**ACEHIINPT**	epicanthi	**ACEHIPRST** chapiters
ACEGIMTUZ	zeugmatic	**ACEHIINRT**	trichinae	**ACEHIPRUY** eucryphia
ACEGINNPR	penancing	**ACEHIINST**	Han Cities	**ACEHIPSST** pastiches
ACEGINNOP	poignance	**ACEHIIPPT**	epitaphic	**ACEHIPSTT** patchiest
ACEGINNOR	ignorance	**ACEHIIRST**	charities	**ACEHIPSTW** whitecaps
ACEGINNRT	cantering	**ACEHIISTT**	atheistic	**ACEHIRRRT** trierarch
	recanting	**ACEHIJKRS**	hijackers	**ACEHIRRST** Charteris
ACEGINNRV	caverning	**ACEHIKKLL**	chalklike	starchier
ACEGINNRY	carneying	**ACEHIKLPT**	Pitch Lake	**ACEHIRSST** chastiser
ACEGINNSU	unceasing	**ACEHIKLST**	chalkiest	**ACEHIRSTT** theatrics
ACEGINOTU	autogenic	**ACEHIKNPP**	Peckinpah	**ACEHIRSTU** Eucharist
ACEGINPPR	recapping	**ACEHIKORT**	artichoke	**ACEHISSST** chastises
ACEGINPRS	escarping	**ACEHIKRST**	heartsick	**ACEHISTTT** chattiest
ACEGINPRT	carpeting	**ACEHIKSTW**	whackiest	**ACEHKLOSV** havelocks
ACEGINPRY	panegyric	**ACEHILLLY**	helically	**ACEHKLRSS** shacklers
ACEGINRRT	cratering	**ACEHILLTY**	ethically	**ACEHKLSTY** latchkeys
	retracing	**ACEHILMMO**	chamomile	**ACEHKMORY** chromakey
	terracing	**ACEHILMST**	alchemist	**ACEHKOPRS** packhorse
ACEGINRSS	caressing	**ACEHILNNO**	chelonian	**ACEHKORST** shortcake
ACEGINRST	caterings	**ACEHILNOR**	enchorial	**ACEHKORSV** havockers
	recasting	**ACEHILNOT**	chelation	**ACEHKRSTW** thwackers
ACEGIOPRR	paregoric	**ACEHILNOU**	Chou En-lai	**ACEHLLLMS** clamshell
ACEGIOSTT	cogitates	**ACEHILNST**	chatlines	**ACEHLLLOR** chlorella
	geostatic	**ACEHILNTU**	unethical	**ACEHLLOPY** epochally
ACEGIRSTT	strategic	**ACEHILNTY**	thylacine	holy place
ACEGJNOTU	conjugate	**ACEHILORR**	Charleroi	**ACEHLLRTW** Chartwell
ACEGKRSTU	truckages	**ACEHILPRS**	clipshear	**ACEHLMOPR** polemarch
ACEGLMNRY	clergyman		spherical	**ACEHLMOST** moschatel
ACEGLNNPY	plangency	**ACEHILRSU**	Heraclius	**ACEHLMSST** matchless
ACEGLNOST	octangles	**ACEHILRSV**	Charles IV	**ACEHLNOSU** eulachons

ACEHLNOSY	anchylose		soutaches	**ACEIKNPSS**	capeskins
ACEHLNPST	planchets	**ACEHOSTWY**	Cetshwayo	**ACEIKNRST**	crankiest
ACEHLNPTY	phlyctena	**ACEHPRRSU**	purchaser	**ACEIKNSST**	tackiness
ACEHLNRSU	launchers	**ACEHPRSSU**	purchases	**ACEIKNSSW**	wackiness
ACEHLNSTU	unlatches	**ACEHPRTTT**	Pratchett	**ACEIKOPSS**	skiascope
ACEHLOPSU	cephalous	**ACEHRRSST**	starchers	**ACEIKPRRT**	peritrack
ACEHLOPSW	showplace	**ACEHRRSTT**	tetrarchs	**ACEILLLNY**	cleanlily
ACEHLORRT	trochlear	**ACEHRRTTY**	tetrarchy	**ACEILLLXY**	lexically
ACEHLORST	chlorates	**ACEHRSSSU**	chasseurs	**ACEILLMOP**	polemical
ACEHLORSU	housecarl	**ACEIIILST**	italicise	**ACEILLMOR**	allomeric
ACEHLORTT	charlotte	**ACEIIILTZ**	italicize	**ACEILLMOT**	collimate
ACEHLOSST	eschalots	**ACEIIKLST**	ekistical	**ACEILLMRS**	millraces
ACEHLOTTY	catholyte	**ACEIIKMNT**	kinematic		miscaller
ACEHLRSST	chartless	**ACEIIILLOT**	ciliolate	**ACEILLMSY**	mesically
ACEHLSSUV	Aeschylus	**ACEIILLTV**	levitical	**ACEILLNOR**	collinear
ACEHLTTYY	tachylyte	**ACEIILMPR**	empirical		coralline
ACEHMNNOR	anchormen	**ACEIILMPT**	implicate	**ACEILLNPS**	spellican
ACEHMNOPY	cymophane	**ACEIILMSS**	seismical	**ACEILLOPS**	calliopes
ACEHMNORT	metarchon	**ACEIILNNT**	anticline	**ACEILLORS**	localiser
ACEHMNORW	charwomen	**ACEIILNNV**	vicennial	**ACEILLORT**	corallite
ACEHMNOTY	theomancy	**ACEIILNPS**	cisalpine	**ACEILLORZ**	localizer
ACEHMNPRT	parchment	**ACEIILNST**	inelastic	**ACEILLOSS**	localises
ACEHMNRST	merchants		sciential	**ACEILLOST**	oscillate
ACEHMNSTY	yachtsmen	**ACEIILORT**	aerolitic		teocallis
ACEHMNTTU	humectant	**ACEIILOSS**	socialise	**ACEILLOSZ**	localizes
ACEHMORST	chromates	**ACEIILOST**	socialite	**ACEILLOTV**	collative
	stomacher	**ACEIILOSZ**	socialize	**ACEILLPRS**	callipers
ACEHMORTV	overmatch	**ACEIILPRT**	pearlitic	**ACEILLPSS**	allspices
ACEHMOSTT	chemostat	**ACEIILRST**	eristical	**ACEILLPSY**	specially
ACEHMOSTU	moustache		realistic	**ACEILLPTY**	plicately
ACEHMPRTY	champerty	**ACEIILRTT**	lateritic	**ACEILLRSV**	cavillers
ACEHMSSTU	mustaches		triticale	**ACEILLRXY**	xerically
ACEHNNPST	penchants	**ACEIILRTV**	leviratic	**ACEILMMOS**	camomiles
ACEHNNRTT	trenchant	**ACEIILSST**	silicates	**ACEILMMST**	clammiest
ACEHNOPRS	chaperons	**ACEIILSTV**	calvities	**ACEILMNNU**	luminance
ACEHNOPRT	North Cape	**ACEIIMMNR**	Cimmerian	**ACEILMNOP**	policeman
ACEHNOPST	cenotaphs	**ACEIIMMRU**	americium	**ACEILMNOT**	melanotic
ACEHNORRS	rancheros	**ACEIIMNRT**	antimeric	**ACEILMNPS**	manciples
ACEHNORSS	anchoress		criminate	**ACEILMNRU**	numerical
ACEHNOSTT	stonechat	**ACEIIMNSS**	messianic	**ACEILMNSU**	calumnies
ACEHNOSTU	ceanothus	**ACEIIMORS**	cramoisie		masculine
ACEHNPPRS	schnapper	**ACEIIMPRS**	primacies	**ACEILMNTU**	culminate
ACEHNPRTY	pentarchy	**ACEIIMPTV**	impactive	**ACEILMOSS**	camisoles
ACEHNRSST	snatchers	**ACEIIMRST**	armistice		coseismal
	stanchers	**ACEIINOTV**	noviciate	**ACEILMOSV**	semivocal
ACEHNRSTU	chaunters	**ACEIINPRS**	precisian	**ACEILMPSS**	misplaces
	stauncher	**ACEIINPST**	epinastic	**ACEILMRRU**	mercurial
ACEHNRSUZ	schnauzer	**ACEIINRTT**	intricate	**ACEILMRTU**	tularemic
ACEHNSSTU	staunches	**ACEIINRTY**	itineracy	**ACEILMSSU**	musicales
ACEHOOSTU	housecoat	**ACEIINTTT**	nictitate	**ACEILNNNO**	canneloni
ACEHOPPRR	hoppercar	**ACEIIOPST**	opacities	**ACEILNNOR**	cornelian
ACEHOPRRS	sharecrop	**ACEIIPRSS**	piscaries	**ACEILNNOT**	octennial
ACEHOPRTY	pothecary	**ACEIIPSTT**	epistatic	**ACEILNNPS**	pinnacles
ACEHOPSST	chassepot	**ACEIIRSTV**	variscite	**ACEILNNTY**	anciently
ACEHORRST	carthorse	**ACEIISTTT**	steatitic	**ACEILNOPR**	porcelain
	orchestra	**ACEIISTUV**	vacuities	**ACEILNORS**	censorial
ACEHORSTT	theocrats	**ACEIJKNPS**	jacksnipe	**ACEILNORT**	clarionet
ACEHORSTY	theocrasy	**ACEIKLLSV**	Sackville	**ACEILNOST**	coastline
ACEHORTTU	rotachute	**ACEIKLNNS**	cleanskin		sectional
ACEHORTVW	overwatch	**ACEIKLPST**	skeptical	**ACEILNOSV**	volcanise
ACEHOSSSW	showcases	**ACEIKMNNS**	nicknames	**ACEILNOTU**	inoculate
ACEHOSSTU	cathouses	**ACEIKMRSV**	mavericks	**ACEILNOVZ**	volcanize

ACEILNPTU	inculpate	**ACEIMNRST**	miscreant	**ACEINQTTU**	quittance
ACEILNRST	cisternal	**ACEIMNRSU**	manicures	**ACEINRRSW**	scrawnier
	clarinets		muscarine	**ACEINRSST**	canisters
	larcenist	**ACEIMNSST**	semantics		scenarist
ACEILNRTU	centurial	**ACEIMNSSY**	sycamines	**ACEINRSSZ**	craziness
ACEILNRTY	certainly	**ACEIMNTYZ**	enzymatic	**ACEINRSTT**	interacts
ACEILNSSS	scaliness	**ACEIMORST**	Masoretic	**ACEINRSTU**	truancies
ACEILNSUV	vulcanise	**ACEIMORVW**	microwave	**ACEINRSTV**	navicerts
ACEILNTUV	vulcanite	**ACEIMOSTU**	autoecism	**ACEINRSTY**	insectary
ACEILNTXY	inexactly	**ACEIMPRST**	spermatic	**ACEINRTTY**	certainty
ACEILNUVZ	vulcanize	**ACEIMRSST**	ceramists	**ACEINRTUV**	incurvate
ACEILOPPS	episcopal	**ACEIMRTTU**	micturate	**ACEINSSSU**	issuances
ACEILOPRS	caprioles	**ACEINNNRU**	uncannier		sauciness
ACEILOPRS	caprioles	**ACEINNNSS**	canniness	**ACEINSSTT**	cattiness
ACEILOPST	scapolite	**ACEINNOOV**	novocaine		scantiest
ACEILOQUV	equivocal	**ACEINNOPT**	pentanoic		tacitness
ACEILORRS	carrioles	**ACEINNORS**	canonries	**ACEINSSTV**	vesicants
ACEILORRT	rectorial	**ACEINNORT**	container	**ACEINSTTU**	tunicates
ACEILORST	sclerotia		crenation	**ACEINSTTX**	excitants
	sectorial	**ACEINNOSS**	ascension	**ACEINSTTY**	intestacy
ACEILORSV	vocaliser		canonises	**ACEIOPRRS**	acrospire
ACEILORSZ	calorizes	**ACEINNOST**	enactions	**ACEIOPRSU**	auriscope
ACEILORTT	tectorial	**ACEINNOSZ**	canonizes	**ACEIOPRTV**	proactive
ACEILORTV	vectorial	**ACEINNRRY**	inerrancy	**ACEIOPSTV**	vitascope
ACEILORVZ	vocalizer	**ACEINNRSU**	insurance	**ACEIOPTTT**	petticoat
ACEILOSSV	vocalises	**ACEINNRTU**	runcinate	**ACEIORRSV**	corrasive
ACEILOSVZ	vocalizes		uncertain	**ACEIORSST**	Isocrates
ACEILOTVY	coevality	**ACEINNSST**	cantiness		ostracise
ACEILPPPR	paperclip		incessant	**ACEIORSTZ**	ostracize
ACEILPPSY	pipeclays		instances	**ACEIORSUV**	veracious
ACEILPRSS	spiracles	**ACEINNSSU**	nuisances	**ACEIOSTUU**	autecious
ACEILPRST	particles	**ACEINOOST**	isooctane	**ACEIOSTUV**	vitaceous
ACEILPRSU	peculiars	**ACEINOOTV**	evocation	**ACEIOSTVV**	vocatives
ACEILPRTU	plicature	**ACEINOPRS**	proscenia	**ACEIOTTUU**	autocutie
ACEILPSSS	slipcases	**ACEINOPRT**	recaption	**ACEIPPRRS**	pericarps
ACEILPSSU	Asclepius	**ACEINOPSS**	caponises		scrappier
	capsulise	**ACEINOPSU**	pinaceous	**ACEIPRRSS**	perisarcs
ACEILPSTU	euplastic	**ACEINOPSZ**	caponizes	**ACEIPRSST**	practises
	spiculate	**ACEINORRT**	cinerator	**ACEIPRSSU**	aruspices
ACEILPSTY	specialty	**ACEINORRV**	carnivore	**ACEIPSSST**	escapists
ACEILPSUZ	capsulize	**ACEINORSS**	scenarios	**ACEIPSSTU**	spacesuit
ACEILPTUY	eucalypti	**ACEINORST**	actioners	**ACEIQRRSU**	acquirers
ACEILRRTU	curtailer		creations	**ACEIQRRSU**	acquirers
	reticular		narcotise	**ACEIQRTTU**	acquitter
ACEILRSTT	clartiest		reactions	**ACEIQSTUY**	sequacity
ACEILRSTU	sterculia	**ACEINORSV**	veronicas	**ACEIRRSSU**	curarises
ACEILRSTV	verticals	**ACEINORSX**	anorexics	**ACEIRRSSW**	airscrews
ACEILRSTW	crawliest	**ACEINORTT**	carnotite	**ACEIRRSUZ**	curarizes
ACEILRSUV	vesicular	**ACEINORTU**	cautioner	**ACEIRSSSU**	cuirasses
ACEILRTUV	lucrative	**ACEINORTZ**	narcotize	**ACEIRSSTU**	suricates
	revictual	**ACEINOSST**	canoeists	**ACEIRSTTU**	rusticate
ACEILSSST	classiest		cessation		urticates
ACEILSUWY	sluiceway	**ACEINOSTU**	tenacious	**ACEIRSTUV**	curatives
ACEILTTUV	cultivate	**ACEINOSTV**	invocates	**ACEIRSUWY**	cruiseway
ACEIMMNNY	immanency	**ACEINOSTX**	exactions	**ACEISSSTU**	suitcases
ACEIMMNPS	pemmicans	**ACEINOSUV**	vinaceous	**ACEISSTTT**	scattiest
ACEIMMOSS	semicomas	**ACEINPRTT**	crepitant	**ACEJKKMOS**	smokejack
ACEIMNOPS	companies	**ACEINPRUY**	pecuniary	**ACEJKKRSY**	skyjacker
ACEIMNORT	cremation	**ACEINPSSU**	puissance	**ACEJKLMST**	jacksmelt
	manticore	**ACEINPSTT**	pittances	**ACEJKNOST**	jackstone
ACEIMNOST	encomiast	**ACEINPSTU**	apneustic	**ACEJKOORS**	jackeroos
ACEIMNPTU	pneumatic	**ACEINPSUY**	picayunes	**ACEJLMSUU**	majuscule
				ACEKKMRRU	muckraker

ACEKKMRSU	muckrakes		corporeal	**ACENOSSSV**	cavessons
ACEKLLMMU	mallemuck	**ACELOOSTT**	coelostat	**ACENOSSTT**	stonecast
ACEKLNSSS	slackness	**ACELOPRRU**	opercular	**ACENOSTUU**	cutaneous
ACEKLOPRW	workplace	**ACELOPRSS**	parcloses	**ACENPRRTY**	carpentry
ACEKLORSV	laverocks	**ACELOPRST**	pectorals	**ACENPRSUU**	pursuance
ACEKLRSST	trackless	**ACELOPRTU**	peculator	**ACENPTTUU**	punctuate
ACEKMNRUZ	Zuckerman	**ACELOPSTU**	copulates	**ACENRSSSS**	crassness
ACEKMSTUW	mucksweat		scopulate	**ACENRSSTT**	transects
ACEKNNTTU	Nantucket	**ACELOPSTY**	calotypes	**ACENRSSTU**	recusants
ACEKNORSU	cankerous	**ACELORRSU**	carrousel	**ACENRSSTZ**	Carstensz
ACEKNPRSU	unpackers	**ACELORSSU**	caroluses	**ACENRSTTU**	truncates
ACEKOPRRT	retropack		carousels	**ACENSSSTW**	newscasts
ACEKOPRTY	copytaker	**ACELOSSTU**	cassoulet	**ACEOORPRT**	corporate
ACEKORRSY	Ayers Rock		osculates	**ACEOOPRSS**	ascospore
ACEKPRSSU	sapsucker	**ACELOSTTY**	catolytes	**ACEOOPRTT**	Caporetto
ACEKPSSSY	skyscapes	**ACELPPRRU**	curlpaper	**ACEOORSSU**	rosaceous
ACEKRSTUW	awestruck	**ACELPSTUY**	eucalypts	**ACEOORSTV**	evocators
ACELLLMOU	columella	**ACELRRSSW**	scrawlers		overcoats
ACELLMORU	molecular	**ACELSSSTU**	cutlasses	**ACEOPPRST**	spaceport
ACELLMRSU	Marcellus	**ACEMMOSTY**	mycetomas	**ACEOPRRTY**	precatory
ACELLNNUY	uncleanly	**ACEMMOTTU**	commutate	**ACEOPRSSY**	caryopses
ACELLNORU	nucleolar	**ACEMNOOPS**	moonscape	**ACEOPRSTT**	spectator
ACELLNOSS	localness	**ACEMNOORU**	coumarone	**ACEORRRTT**	retractor
ACELLNRTY	centrally	**ACEMNOPSS**	encompass	**ACEORRRVY**	carryover
ACELLNRUY	unclearly	**ACEMNORRS**	romancers	**ACEORRSSU**	carousers
ACELLOPRS	scalloper	**ACEMNORTU**	mucronate	**ACEORRSTT**	retroacts
ACELLOPSS	collapses	**ACEMOOPSU**	pomaceous	**ACEORRSTU**	craterous
	escallops	**ACEMOORSU**	moraceous		eurocrats
ACELLOQUY	coequally	**ACEMOPRRS**	comparers	**ACEORRSTV**	cavorters
ACELLORRS	carollers	**ACEMOPRSS**	mesocarps	**ACEORRTTX**	extractor
ACELLORSS	sclerosal	**ACEMOPSSS**	compasses	**ACEORSSTV**	overcasts
ACELLORSV	coveralls	**ACEMORRST**	cremators	**ACEORSTTY**	astrocyte
	overcalls	**ACEMORRTY**	crematory	**ACEORSTUU**	rutaceous
ACELLOSSU	callouses	**ACEMORSSW**	caseworms	**ACEOSSTTU**	outcastes
ACELLRSTU	scutellar	**ACEMORSSY**	sycamores	**ACEOSTUXY**	auxocytes
ACELLRSUY	secularly	**ACEMOSSUU**	musaceous	**ACEPRRSTU**	capturers
ACELLSSSS	classless	**ACEMOSTVY**	vasectomy	**ACEPSSTTY**	typecasts
ACELMMNOS	commensal	**ACEMPRSUY**	supremacy	**ACERRTUUV**	curvature
ACELMMNSU	muscleman	**ACEMRSSST**	scamsters	**ACERSSTTY**	cytasters
ACELMNTUU	tenaculum	**ACENNNORU**	announcer	**ACERSTTUW**	cutwaters
ACELMOPST	ectoplasm	**ACENNNOSU**	announces	**ACFFGILNS**	sclaffing
ACELMORRS	clamorers	**ACENNOSTT**	cotenants	**ACFFIILNO**	officinal
ACELMORRU	clamourer	**ACENNOSTU**	Antonescu	**ACFFIILOS**	officials
ACELMORSS	scleromas	**ACENNOSTV**	covenants	**ACFFIINOT**	officiant
ACELMORSY	claymores	**ACENNOSTZ**	canzonets	**ACFFIIORY**	officiary
ACELMOSUU	ulmaceous	**ACENNSSST**	scantness	**ACFFIKRTY**	trafficky
ACELMSSTU	muscatels	**ACENOPRRT**	copartner	**ACFFILMOR**	falciform
ACELMSTUU	cumulates		procreant	**ACFFLOSSW**	scofflaws
ACELNNOOR	olecranon	**ACENOPSST**	capstones	**ACFGHMORR**	frogmarch
ACELNNOTY	connately	**ACENOPSTW**	townscape	**ACFGIIMNO**	magnifico
ACELNOOSV	volcanoes	**ACENOPSTY**	syncopate	**ACFGIINNN**	financing
ACELNOPRV	Provençal	**ACENOPTYY**	cyanotype	**ACFGIINPY**	pacifying
ACELNORSU	larcenous	**ACENOQSTU**	cotqueans	**ACFGIIPRS**	caprifigs
ACELNORTU	nucleator	**ACENORRTU**	raconteur	**ACFGIKNRT**	kingcraft
	recountal	**ACENORRUY**	Yourcenar	**ACFGINORT**	factoring
ACELNOSTU	consulate	**ACENORSST**	ancestors	**ACFGINOTU**	outfacing
ACELNOSTY	claystone	**ACENORSTU**	courantes	**ACFGINRSU**	surfacing
ACELNPRTU	crapulent		courtesan	**ACFGINRTU**	furcating
ACELNPTUY	petulancy		nectarous	**ACFGIOSUU**	fugacious
ACELNRTTU	reluctant	**ACENORSUV**	cavernous	**ACFGLNORY**	gyrfalcon
ACELNTUXY	exultancy	**ACENORTUZ**	courtezan	**ACFHIILRT**	chairlift
ACELOOPRR	corporale	**ACENORUVV**	Vancouver	**ACFHILNOS**	falchions

ACFHKORST	rockshaft	**ACGHIJKLT**	jacklight	**ACGILLNOR**	carolling
ACFHLORTW	flowchart	**ACGHIKLNS**	shackling		collaring
ACFHMNORS	chamfrons	**ACGHIKNOV**	havocking	**ACGILLNOT**	collating
ACFHMORSU	forasmuch	**ACGHIKNTW**	thwacking	**ACGILLNSU**	callusing
ACFHNNORS	chanfrons	**ACGHILNNU**	launching	**ACGILLOOO**	oological
ACFIIINRS	Francis II	**ACGHILORS**	oligarchs	**ACGILLOST**	collagist
ACFIIISST	fasciitis	**ACGHILORY**	oligarchy	**ACGILMNOR**	clamoring
ACFIILLNV	finically	**ACGHILPRY**	graphicly	**ACGILNNST**	scantling
ACFIILNOT	fictional	**ACGHIMMNY**	chammying	**ACGILNNTY**	cantingly
ACFIIMNOR	aciniform	**ACGHIMOOP**	omophagic	**ACGILNORS**	carolings
ACFIIOPRS	saporific	**ACGHINNOR**	anchoring	**ACGILNOST**	gnostical
ACFIIOPRV	vaporific	**ACGHINNOT**	gnathonic		nostalgic
ACFIIPSST	pacifists	**ACGHINNPU**	paunching	**ACGILNOXY**	coaxingly
ACFIJKRTU	jackfruit	**ACGHINNST**	snatching	**ACGILNPRY**	carpingly
ACFIKLNSS	calfskins		stanching	**ACGILNRSW**	scrawling
ACFIKNRSS	scarfskin	**ACGHINNUY**	Ch'ing-yüan	**ACGIMMNRS**	scramming
ACFIKRRTU	Friar Tuck	**ACGHINOUV**	avouching	**ACGIMNNOO**	cognomina
ACFILMORU	formulaic	**ACGHINPST**	nightcaps	**ACGIMNNOR**	romancing
	fumarolic	**ACGHINRST**	starching	**ACGIMNOOR**	agronomic
ACFILMORV	claviform	**ACGHINRSU**	churingas	**ACGIMNOPR**	comparing
ACFILNNOR	francolin	**ACGHKNOWW**	Kwangchow	**ACGIMNORR**	cairngorm
ACFILNOOT	olfaction	**ACGHLLORS**	grallochs	**ACGIMNOTU**	contagium
ACFILNOST	califonts	**ACGHLMOOY**	logomachy	**ACGIMNSTY**	gymnastic
ACFILNPPY	flippancy	**ACGHMOPRY**	cymograph		syntagmic
ACFILNRTY	franticly	**ACGHNNOTU**	Connaught	**ACGIMNUUV**	vacuuming
ACFILNRUU	funicular	**ACGHNOORV**	Goncharov	**ACGIMOPRT**	pictogram
ACFILORST	trifocals	**ACGHNTUUZ**	Chuang-tzu	**ACGIMOSUU**	guaiocums
ACFIMORRY	formicary	**ACGHOPPRY**	copygraph	**ACGIMOTYZ**	zygomatic
ACFINORRT	infractor	**ACGHORSTU**	roughcast	**ACGINNNNO**	cannoning
ACFINORST	fractions	**ACGIIILNS**	laicising	**ACGINNNOT**	cantoning
ACFINORTU	furcation	**ACGIIILNZ**	laicizing	**ACGINNOOT**	cognation
ACFIORSTU	fractious	**ACGIIIMST**	imagistic		contagion
ACFJKORST	Jack Frost	**ACGIIKNNP**	panicking	**ACGINNOPY**	canopying
ACFKNORWY	fancywork	**ACGIIKNPX**	pickaxing		poignancy
ACFLLTTUY	tactfully	**ACGIILLLO**	illogical	**ACGINNORT**	cartoning
ACFLMNOOR	conformal	**ACGIILLMS**	gallicism	**ACGINNORV**	crayoning
ACFLNTTUU	fluctuant	**ACGIILLNV**	cavilling	**ACGINNOST**	cognisant
	untactful	**ACGIILLOR**	cigarillo	**ACGINNOTZ**	cognizant
ACFLOOPSS	foolscaps	**ACGIILLPR**	pilgarlic	**ACGINNPPU**	uncapping
ACFLOORTY	olfactory	**ACGIILMNS**	anglicism	**ACGINOPTU**	outpacing
ACFMOSTTU	factotums	**ACGIILMNX**	climaxing	**ACGINORSU**	carousing
ACFOOSTUU	autofocus	**ACGIILMOR**	microglia	**ACGINORTU**	outracing
ACGGGINRS	scragging	**ACGIILNOS**	gasolinic	**ACGINORTV**	cavorting
ACGGIIKMN	magicking		logicians	**ACGINOSST**	agnostics
ACGGIIMNR	grimacing	**ACGIILNRT**	articling	**ACGINOTTU**	outacting
ACGGIIOSS	isagogics	**ACGIILNST**	anglicist	**ACGINPPRS**	scrapping
ACGGILRSY	scraggily	**ACGIILNTT**	latticing	**ACGINPRSS**	scrapings
ACGGINOTT	cottaging	**ACGIILRTY**	gracility	**ACGINPRSW**	scrawping
ACGHHHIIR	highchair	**ACGIIMNPT**	impacting	**ACGINPRTU**	capturing
ACGHHIJKS	highjacks	**ACGIIMSTT**	stigmatic	**ACGINPSTU**	upcasting
ACGHHILNT	hatchling	**ACGIINNOR**	inorganic	**ACGINPTUY**	pugnacity
ACGHHINOT	hoatching	**ACGIINNOT**	actioning	**ACGIOORSS**	graciosos
ACGHHINRU	hachuring		incognita	**ACGIOORTT**	cogitator
ACGHHINST	hatchings	**ACGIINNTT**	nictating	**ACGJNNOTU**	conjugant
ACGHHINTT	thatching	**ACGIINOST**	agonistic	**ACGJNORRU**	currajong
ACGHIIJKN	hijacking	**ACGIINPSZ**	capsizing	**ACGKNNSUY**	gunnysack
ACGHIIKNN	Chinkiang	**ACGIINQRU**	acquiring	**ACGLNORSU**	clangours
ACGHIIMNN	machining	**ACGIIORST**	orgiastic	**ACGLOOPRY**	carpology
ACGHIIMNS	michigans	**ACGIIRSTT**	gastritic	**ACGLOOSTY**	scatology
ACGHIINNR	inarching	**ACGIKNNPU**	unpacking	**ACGMOPRTY**	cryptogam
ACGHIINRV	archiving	**ACGIKNNTU**	untacking	**ACGNNOOST**	contangos
ACGHIIPRT	graphitic	**ACGILLLOY**	logically	**ACGNORRUW**	currawong

ACGORRSUY surrogacy	monachist	**ACIIKNNNS** cannikins
ACHHIKLSS shashlick	**ACHIMNSTW** switchman	**ACIIKPRST** paitricks
ACHHILNOR rhonchial	**ACHIMOOTX** homotaxic	**ACIILLNOS** collinsia
ACHHILORT haircloth	**ACHIMOPSU** Pachomius	isoclinal
ACHHINNOT chthonian	**ACHIMORST** rhotacism	**ACIILLNST** scintilla
ACHHINOST chainshot	**ACHIMORYZ** mycorhiza	**ACIILLOPT** political
ACHHINSTW whinchats	**ACHIMOSST** masochist	**ACIILLSSU** siliculas
ACHHINSTY hyacinths	**ACHIMOSTU** mustachio	**ACIILMNPU** municipal
ACHHIPPRS hipparchs	**ACHIMRSST** Christmas	**ACIILMNRS** criminals
ACHHIPRSU pushchair	**ACHIMRSSW** scrimshaw	**ACIILMNSV** Calvinism
ACHHLOSTW washcloth	**ACHINNOST** stanchion	**ACIILMNTY** militancy
ACHIIIMOS Chisimaio	**ACHINNOTW** Chinatown	**ACIILMOSS** socialism
ACHIIKNNP chinkapin	**ACHINNSSU** anchusins	**ACIILMOSU** malicious
ACHIILMOS isochimal	**ACHINOPPS** pansophic	**ACIILMQTU** quitclaim
ACHIILMSW whimsical	**ACHINOPRT** anthropic	**ACIILNNOT** clintonia
ACHIILNOS Nicholas I	**ACHINOPST** cashpoint	**ACIILNOOT** coalition
ACHIILRTY chirality	**ACHINOSTZ** hoactzins	**ACIILNOPT** plication
ACHIILSST chiliasts	**ACHIOOPST** sociopath	**ACIILNOVV** convivial
ACHIIMNST machinist	**ACHIOPPRS** hippocras	**ACIILNOVY** inviolacy
ACHIINPSY physician	**ACHIORSTT** rhotacist	**ACIILNPPR** principal
ACHIINRST Christian	**ACHIORSTV** tovarisch	**ACIILNPST** cisplatin
Christina	**ACHIPRSUY** haruspicy	**ACIILNRSU** incisural
ACHIIOPST pistachio	**ACHIPSTTU** chupattis	**ACIILOPRT** pictorial
ACHIIORST ahistoric	**ACHIRSSTT** chartists	**ACIILORST** soritical
ACHIIPRSV vicarship	**ACHISTUWZ** Auschwitz	**ACIILORTZ** triazolic
ACHIIRRTT arthritic	**ACHKKKOOS** Kokoschka	**ACIILOSST** socialist
ACHIIRSTV archivist	**ACHKLNOOS** solonchak	**ACIILOSTY** sociality
ACHIISTWY Yahwistic	**ACHKMNOUU** Manchukuo	**ACIILQUZZ** quizzical
ACHIKKSSW kickshaws	**ACHKMORSS** shamrocks	**ACIILTTTY** tactility
ACHIKLMST mahlstick	**ACHKMORTU** touchmark	**ACIIMMNOT** ammonitic
ACHIKLMSY hickymals	**ACHKNORRW** hornwrack	**ACIIMMPST** psammitic
ACHIKLPST chalkpits	**ACHKOPRTW** patchwork	**ACIIMNNOS** insomniac
ACHIKNOST antishock	**ACHLLORSY** scholarly	**ACIIMNNOT** antimonic
ACHIKRSSW rickshaws	**ACHLMNOOS** schoolman	antinomic
ACHILLNTY Chantilly	**ACHLMSTYZ** schmaltzy	**ACIIMNOPT** impaction
ACHILLOST sailcloth	**ACHLNSTUY** staunchly	**ACIIMNORT** mortician
ACHILMOPU mailpouch	**ACHLOOSTU** holocaust	**ACIIMNOSS** simoniacs
ACHILMPTY lymphatic	**ACHLOPRST** calthrops	**ACIIMNOSU** minacious
ACHILMTUZ chalutzim	**ACHLOPRYY** polyarchy	**ACIIMNOTT** manicotti
ACHILNOPT haplontic	**ACHLOPTUY** patchouly	**ACIIMNSSU** musicians
ACHILNORT antichlor	**ACHMOORST** chatrooms	**ACIIMOPRS** micropsia
ACHILNOSV Nicholas V	**ACHMOORSU** achromous	**ACIIMOPST** simpatico
ACHILNRUY raunchily	**ACHNOPSTY** sycophant	**ACIIMORTT** triatomic
ACHILNSTU clianthus	**ACHNSTUYZ** Zacynthus	**ACIIMOSST** mosaicist
ACHILNSTY snatchily	**ACHOORSTU** coauthors	**ACIIMOSTT** atomistic
ACHILOPSU pachoulis	**ACHOPSTTW** stopwatch	**ACIIMOTTY** atomicity
ACHILOPTU patchouli	**ACHOPSTUY** hypocaust	**ACIIMPRST** prismatic
ACHILORST acroliths	**ACHORSSST** Trossachs	**ACIIMRSST** scimitars
ACHILORTV archivolt	**ACHORTTTU** cutthroat	**ACIIMSSTT** atticisms
ACHILOSST scholiast	**ACHPRSSTU** pushcarts	**ACIIMSTUV** viaticums
ACHILPSSY physicals	**ACHRRSTUY** craythurs	**ACIINNOST** onanistic
ACHILRSSY chrysalis	**ACIIILNOS** siciliano	Toscanini
ACHILRSTY starchily	**ACIIILNOT** ciliation	**ACIINNOTT** nictation
ACHILSTTY cattishly	**ACIIILNRT** triclinia	**ACIINNOTU** incaution
ACHIMMNOS monachism	**ACIIILNSV** civilians	**ACIINNQSU** cinquains
ACHIMMORZ machzorim	**ACIIIMNST** animistic	**ACIINOPST** opticians
ACHIMMOSS masochism	**ACIIIMNTV** vitaminic	**ACIINORTV** Victorian
ACHIMNOPS champions	**ACIIIMRSV** Casimir IV	**ACIINOSTT** Anticosti
ACHIMNOPY hypomanic	**ACIIINPPR** principia	citations
ACHIMNORS harmonics	**ACIIINPST** pianistic	**ACIINOTTX** antitoxic
ACHIMNORT chromatin	sincipita	**ACIINOTTY** atonicity
ACHIMNOST macintosh	**ACIIJRSTU** justiciar	**ACIINPRTU** Paricutín

	puritanic	**ACILMNSUU**	unmusical	**ACIMORSTT**	stromatic
ACIINPTTY	antitypic	**ACILMNSUV**	vulcanism	**ACIMPRSTY**	sympatric
ACIINRRTY	irritancy	**ACILMOOPY**	Pilcomayo	**ACIMRSTTU**	strumatic
ACIIOPRST	psoriatic	**ACILMOPRS**	comprisal	**ACINNORST**	constrain
ACIIOPRTT	parotitic		proclaims		transonic
	patriotic	**ACILMOSSV**	vocalisms	**ACINNOSSS**	scansions
ACIIOPTZZ	pizzicato	**ACILMPTUU**	capitulum	**ACINNOSST**	canonists
ACIIORSSV	varicosis	**ACILMSSTU**	masculist		sanctions
ACIIORSTV	victorias		simulcast	**ACINNOSTT**	Tocantins
ACIIORSTY	cariosity	**ACILNNNUY**	uncannily	**ACINOOPPR**	propanoic
ACIIORSUV	vicarious	**ACILNNOOS**	nonsocial	**ACINOOPRS**	picaroons
ACIIOSSTT	isostatic	**ACILNNOTU**	continual	**ACINOOPRT**	proaction
ACIIOSUVV	vivacious		inoculant	**ACINOOPTZ**	panzootic
ACIIPRSTT	patristic	**ACILNNQTU**	clinquant	**ACINOORRS**	corrasion
ACIIPTTVY	captivity	**ACILNNRUU**	ranunculi	**ACINOORST**	consortia
ACIISSTTT	atticists	**ACILNOOSS**	Colossian	**ACINOORTV**	invocator
	statistic	**ACILNOOST**	locations	**ACINOOSST**	iconostas
ACIISSTTU	autistics	**ACILNOPRT**	prolactin	**ACINOOSTV**	vocations
ACIISSTTV	activists	**ACILNOPSS**	salpicons	**ACINOOTUX**	auxotonic
ACIJKKPSS	skipjacks	**ACILNOPSY**	isopycnal	**ACINOPSTU**	acupoints
ACIJLMNUU	Janiculum	**ACILNORST**	contrails	**ACINORSST**	croissant
ACIJNNORT	Corantijn	**ACILNORTT**	contralti	**ACINORSTY**	crayonist
ACIKKNNOT	antiknock	**ACILNOSTT**	clinostat	**ACINOSSTW**	wainscots
ACIKLMPTU	multipack	**ACILNOSTU**	suctional	**ACINOSSWX**	coxswains
ACIKLMSTU	maulstick		sulcation	**ACINOSTTU**	scutation
ACIKLNOTY	ankylotic	**ACILNOSUV**	univocals	**ACINOSTTX**	toxicants
ACIKLOSTT	tailstock	**ACILNPTUY**	untypical	**ACINRSSSU**	narcissus
ACIKLPSST	slapstick	**ACILNRSTU**	lincrusta	**ACIOOPRSU**	paroicous
ACIKLPSTY	plasticky	**ACILNRSWY**	scrawnily	**ACIOOPRSZ**	saprozoic
ACIKNNPRS	crankpins	**ACILNSTYY**	syncytial	**ACIOORSTU**	atrocious
ACIKNOOPR	pickaroon	**ACILOOPRS**	acropolis	**ACIOORSUV**	voracious
ACIKNOSTU	Kostunica	**ACILOOPST**	apostolic	**ACIOOSTUU**	autoicous
ACIKOPSSY	skiascopy	**ACILOPPRT**	captopril	**ACIOOTTUX**	autotoxic
ACIKRSTTU	tracksuit	**ACILOQTUY**	loquacity	**ACIOPRSSY**	caryopsis
ACILLLOUV	colluvial	**ACILORRSU**	cursorial	**ACIOPRSTT**	prostatic
ACILLLRVY	lyrically	**ACILORRSV**	corrivals	**ACIOPRSTY**	piscatory
ACILLMOSS	localisms	**ACILORRSU**	ossicular	**ACIOPTTUY**	autotypic
ACILLMSUY	musically	**ACILORSTU**	ocularist	**ACIOSTTXY**	cytotaxis
ACILLNNSY	synclinal		suctorial	**ACIRSSTUY**	casuistry
ACILLNOOS	colonials	**ACILOSSTV**	vocalists	**ACJKOPRST**	jockstrap
ACILLNOOT	collation	**ACILOSSTY**	asystolic	**ACJLLORUY**	jocularly
ACILLNORS	carillons	**ACILOTTUY**	autolytic	**ACKKMOPRS**	pockmarks
ACILLNOSS	scallions	**ACILPPRSY**	scrappily	**ACKLLPSSU**	skullcaps
ACILLNOTY	tonically	**ACILRRTUU**	utricular	**ACKLMOOOR**	cloakroom
ACILLOOQU	colloquia	**ACILRSTUV**	cultivars	**ACKLNORST**	cornstalk
ACILLOPTY	optically	**ACILSSTTY**	systaltic	**ACKLOOPSW**	woolpacks
	topically	**ACIMMNOOT**	monatomic	**ACKLOOSSW**	woolsacks
ACILLORST	cloistral	**ACIMMORSS**	commissar	**ACKLORSST**	crosstalk
ACILLORYZ	zircalloy	**ACIMNNNOS**	cinnamons	**ACKLORSSW**	crosswalk
ACILLOSST	localists	**ACIMNNOOP**	companion	**ACLLLOSUY**	callously
ACILLOSTY	callosity	**ACIMNOOST**	onomastic	**ACLLMNOSU**	molluscan
	stoically	**ACIMNOOTU**	autonomic	**ACLLOORRY**	corollary
ACILLOTXY	toxically	**ACIMNOOTX**	taxonomic	**ACLLOORST**	collators
ACILLPTYY	typically	**ACIMNOPRY**	paronymic		colostral
ACILMMOTT	committal	**ACIMNORST**	narcotism	**ACLMMORSW**	clamworms
ACILMNNTU	culminant		romantics	**ACLMNOOOS**	coolamons
ACILMNOPS	complains	**ACIMNOSST**	monastics	**ACLMNOORU**	colourman
ACILMNOPT	complaint	**ACIMNOSTU**	aconitums		monocular
	compliant	**ACIMNOSUU**	acuminous	**ACLMOOOPR**	Marco Polo
ACILMNOSS	laconisms	**ACIMOOTTU**	autotomic	**ACLMOORSS**	classroom
ACILMNOSV	volcanism	**ACIMOPSSY**	symposiac	**ACLMOORSU**	clamorous
ACILMNPRT	McPartlin	**ACIMORSST**	ostracism	**ACLMOPSTY**	cytoplasm

ACLMSSUUV	vasculums
ACLNNORTU	nocturnal
ACLNOORST	colorants
ACLNOORTT	contralto
ACLNORSTU	calutrons
ACLNORSUY	cynosural
ACLOOOORRT	coralroot
ACLOOPRRS	corporals
ACLOORUWY	colourway
ACLOPPRVY	polycarpy
ACLOPRRSU	procurals
ACLOPRSTU	Patroclus
ACLOPRSUU	crapulous
	opuscular
ACLOPRSXY	xylocarps
ACLOPRTTU	plutocrat
ACLORSUUY	raucously
ACLOSTUUY	Autolycus
ACLOSUUVY	vacuously
ACMNOOPRS	monocarps
ACMNOOPSY	manoscopy
ACMNOORRT	cormorant
ACMNOORST	monocrats
ACMNOOSTU	cosmonaut
ACMNOPRVY	pyromancy
ACMNORSTU	sanctorum
ACMOOPRSS	coprosmas
ACMOORRST	motorcars
ACMOORSTU	macrotous
ACMORRSUU	macrurous
ACMORSSTW	wormcasts
ACMORSTUV	customary
ACNNNOOST	consonant
ACNNOSSTT	constants
ACNOOOORST	octaroons
ACNOOPRST	corposant
ACNOORRSU	rancorous
ACNOORSST	ostracons
ACNORSSTT	contrasts
ACNORSTTU	turncoats
ACNORSTTY	contrasty
ACOOPPRRS	sporocarp
ACOORSSTU	autocross
ACOPRRSTT	protracts
ACORRSTTU	scrutator
ACORRSTUY	carryouts
ACORSSSUW	curassows
ACORSSSWY	crossways
ACORSSTTY	cryostats
ACOSSTTTY	statocyst
ACPSSSTUY	pussycats
ADDDEEEHR	redheaded
ADDDEEFIL	defiladed
ADDDEEFRU	defrauded
ADDDEEGLN	gladdened
ADDDEEHNR	redhanded
ADDDEEKLS	skedaddle
ADDDEENTU	denudated
ADDDEERSS	addressed
ADDDEFIIN	dandified
ADDDEGMNO	goddamned
ADDDEIINS	disdained

ADDDEIMNO	diamonded
ADDDEISSU	dissuaded
ADDDELNSU	unsaddled
ADDDELRST	straddled
ADDEEEFRT	federated
ADDEEEGLT	delegated
ADDEEEGRS	degreased
ADDEEELTW	Tweeddale
ADDEEEMNR	meandered
ADDEEENRS	deadeners
	serenaded
ADDEEENWZ	Waddenzee
ADDEEEPRT	depredate
ADDEEERRT	retreaded
ADDEEERSS	addressee
ADDEEFHNS	handfeeds
ADDEEFILN	enfiladed
ADDEEFILS	defilades
ADDEEFLTU	defaulted
ADDEEFNNT	defendant
ADDEEFNSS	fadedness
ADDEEFRRT	redrafted
ADDEEFRRU	defrauder
ADDEEGHIP	pigheaded
ADDEEGINN	deadening
ADDEEGINR	deraigned
ADDEEGIRS	disagreed
ADDEEGLNR	gladdener
	glandered
ADDEEGORT	derogated
ADDEEGRRS	degraders
ADDEEGSSU	degaussed
ADDEEHHOT	hotheaded
ADDEEHINP	pinheaded
ADDEEHLNR	rehandled
ADDEEHLNS	handseled
ADDEEHLSY	aldehydes
ADDEEHOTW	towheaded
ADDEEHRSS	headdress
ADDEEHRTY	dehydrate
ADDEEIILS	idealised
ADDEEIILZ	idealized
ADDEEIILLR	redialled
ADDEEILMP	impleaded
ADDEEILNS	deadlines
ADDEEILPT	depilated
ADDEEILRV	daredevil
ADDEEILST	deadliest
ADDEEIMTT	meditated
ADDEEINRT	detrained
ADDEEINRV	reinvaded
ADDEEIPRR	draperied
ADDEEIPRS	despaired
ADDEEIPRU	Depardieu
ADDEEJNSS	jadedness
ADDEELNNR	Nederland
ADDEELNPY	endplayed
ADDEELNRS	slandered
ADDEELNRU	laundered
ADDEELOST	desolated
ADDEELPPW	dewlapped
ADDEEMNRS	demanders

	redemands
ADDEEMNRU	maundered
	undreamed
ADDEEMNST	damnedest
ADDEEMORT	moderated
ADDEEMPST	stampeded
ADDEENNPT	dependant
ADDEENOTT	detonated
ADDEENRST	darnedest
ADDEENRTU	denatured
ADDEENSTU	denudates
ADDEEOPRS	desperado
ADDEEOPRT	readopted
ADDEEPRSU	persuaded
ADDEEPRTU	depurated
ADDEERRSS	addresser
	readdress
ADDEERSSS	addresses
ADDEERSTW	stewarded
ADDEESTTW	wadsetted
ADDEFFHNO	offhanded
ADDEFFLOO	offloaded
ADDEFIINN	damnified
ADDEFIINS	dandifies
ADDEFIIPT	pedatifid
ADDEFINNR	Ferdinand
ADDEFORRW	forwarded
ADDEGGINR	degrading
ADDEGHILT	deadlight
ADDEGHINR	hagridden
ADDEGIIMN	diademing
ADDEGIITT	digitated
ADDEGILNR	laddering
ADDEGILOU	dialogued
ADDEGILSS	glissaded
ADDEGIMNN	demanding
	maddening
ADDEGINNR	dandering
ADDEGINNS	saddening
ADDEGINOS	diagnosed
ADDEGIRRS	disregard
ADDEGLRUY	guardedly
ADDEGNOOR	dragooned
	gadrooned
ADDEGNORW	downgrade
ADDEGNRRU	undergrad
ADDEGNRUU	unguarded
ADDEHHOTY	hydathode
ADDEHILOY	holidayed
ADDEHILRS	dihedrals
ADDEHINRY	anhydride
ADDEHINSW	headwinds
ADDEHINSY	hendiadys
ADDEHIRRW	hardwired
ADDEHIRYZ	hydrazide
ADDEHLOSS	shedloads
ADDEHMRSU	drumheads
ADDEHNNRU	underhand
ADDEHNORS	hardnosed
ADDEHORSW	headwords
ADDEIIIMT	dimidiate
ADDEIIIRW	Edward III

ADDEIILNV	invalided	**ADDFIIQRU**	quadrifid	**ADEEEINRS**	deaneries
ADDEIILNX	Dixieland	**ADDFLNNOO**	land of Nod	**ADEEEINST**	detainees
ADDEIIMNS	desmidian	**ADDGGIJNU**	adjudging	**ADEEEIRSS**	diaereses
ADDEIIRVW	Edward VII	**ADDGHNORU**	draghound	**ADEEEKNRW**	rewakened
ADDEIISTV	additives	**ADDGIIMNS**	misadding	**ADEEEKNSW**	snakeweed
ADDEIKNPP	kidnapped	**ADDGILMNY**	maddingly	**ADEEELLMN**	enamelled
ADDEILLNS	landslide	**ADDGILNSW**	swaddling	**ADEEELLST**	teaselled
ADDEILMMN	middleman	**ADDGILNTW**	twaddling	**ADEEELLSW**	weaselled
ADDEILMNR	Midlander	**ADDGINNOT**	Addington	**ADEEELLTZ**	teazelled
ADDEILNNO	dandelion	**ADDGMRSUU**	mudguards	**ADEEELMNP**	empaneled
ADDEILNRU	underlaid	**ADDGOQSSU**	godsquads	**ADEEELNRR**	relearned
ADDEILNST	tidelands	**ADDHHIOOR**	hardihood	**ADEEELNRZ**	Zeelander
ADDEILPSY	displayed	**ADDHHLNOS**	handholds	**ADEEELRRT**	realtered
ADDEILSVY	advisedly	**ADDHIIKMS**	kaddishim	**ADEEEMNRR**	meanderer
ADDEIMNOS	nomadised	**ADDHLOOTU**	adulthood	**ADEEEMOST**	edematose
ADDEIMNOT	demantoid	**ADDHNNORU**	roundhand	**ADEEEMPRT**	permeated
	dominated	**ADDHOORSW**	hardwoods	**ADEEEMRSV**	Mesa Verde
ADDEIMNOZ	nomadized	**ADDIINOST**	additions	**ADEEENRRS**	serenader
ADDEIMNTY	dynamited	**ADDINNNOU**	Dundonian	**ADEEENRSS**	serenades
ADDEIMORT	dermatoid	**ADDINNORS**	ordinands	**ADEEENRST**	East Ender
ADDEIMPRY	pyramided	**ADDINORSU**	diandrous	**ADEEENRTT**	entreated
ADDEIMSST	dismasted	**ADDKNRRSU**	drunkards	**ADEEENRTV**	denervate
ADDEINNRU	undrained	**ADDLLNNOU**	Llandudno		enervated
ADDEINNTU	inundated	**ADDLLNORS**	landlords		venerated
ADDEINOPR	poniarded	**ADDLNNOOP**	Pondoland	**ADEEENSTT**	edentates
ADDEINPRS	drepanids	**ADDLNOOSW**	downloads	**ADEEEPPRR**	repapered
ADDEINPRU	underpaid		woodlands	**ADEEEPRSS**	rapeseeds
ADDEINRTT	dittander	**ADDLNORRS**	randlords	**ADEEEPRST**	desperate
ADDEINRTU	indurated	**ADDLNORST**	landdrost	**ADEEERRTT**	retreated
ADDEINSUV	unadvised	**ADDNORSWW**	downwards	**ADEEERSTT**	estreated
ADDEIORSS	sideroads	**ADDOORRSY**	dooryards	**ADEEERTTU**	deuterate
ADDEIOSVW	disavowed	**ADDOORSWY**	woodyards	**ADEEERTWW**	waterweed
ADDEIQSSU	squaddies	**ADEEEFHRT**	feathered	**ADEEFFGRU**	gauffered
ADDEIRSSU	dissuader	**ADEEEFLLT**	leafleted	**ADEEFFILR**	fieldfare
ADDEIRSSW	sidewards	**ADEEEFNRR**	referenda	**ADEEFFRST**	restaffed
ADDEISSSU	dissuades	**ADEEEFRST**	defeaters	**ADEEFGILR**	filagreed
ADDEISSTT	distasted		federates	**ADEEFGINN**	deafening
ADDEJNORU	adjourned	**ADEEEFRTW**	feedwater	**ADEEFGINT**	defeating
ADDEKNRSU	underdaks	**ADEEEGGNR**	reengaged	**ADEEFGLLR**	Lagerfeld
ADDELLOPR	pollarded	**ADEEEGGRT**	gadgeteer	**ADEEFGNRT**	engrafted
ADDELMOTU	modulated	**ADEEEGHNR**	greenhead	**ADEEFHORS**	foreheads
ADDELNSSU	unsaddles	**ADEEEGLRT**	regelated	**ADEEFIKLW**	Wakefield
ADDELNTUU	undulated		relegated	**ADEEFIKRR**	firedrake
ADDELRRST	straddler	**ADEEEGLRV**	leveraged	**ADEEFILMS**	Masefield
ADDELRSST	straddles	**ADEEEGLST**	delegates	**ADEEFILNS**	enfilades
ADDELRSTW	twaddlers	**ADEEEGNRS**	renegades	**ADEEFILOT**	defoliate
ADDEMNORT	mordanted	**ADEEEGNRT**	generated	**ADEEFILSU**	feudalise
ADDEMORRY	dromedary		greatened	**ADEEFILUZ**	feudalize
ADDENNORU	unadorned	**ADEEEGRSS**	degreases	**ADEEFIMST**	defeatism
ADDENNRTU	redundant	**ADEEEGSUW**	agueweeds	**ADEEFINRR**	refrained
ADDENNTUU	undaunted	**ADEEEGTTV**	vegetated	**ADEEFISTT**	defeatist
ADDENOORT	deodorant	**ADEEEHHRT**	heathered	**ADEEFLLNN**	flanneled
ADDENOPTU	unadopted	**ADEEEHKNR**	hearkened	**ADEEFLLRY**	federally
ADDENORUY	duodenary	**ADEEEHLRT**	leathered	**ADEEFLMST**	Flamsteed
ADDENOSTU	astounded	**ADEEEHLST**	steelhead	**ADEEFLNNR**	Fernandel
ADDENRSTU	transuded	**ADEEEHNRT**	heartened	**ADEEFLNRU**	underleaf
ADDEOPSTT	postdated	**ADEEEHPRT**	preheated	**ADEEFLNTT**	flattened
ADDEORRSS	addressor	**ADEEEHRRS**	rehearsed	**ADEEFLORS**	freeloads
ADDEPQRUU	quadruped	**ADEEEHRTW**	weathered	**ADEEFLORT**	floreated
ADDEPRSSU	superadds	**ADEEEHSSY**	eyeshades		refloated
ADDFFILOS	daffodils	**ADEEEILMN**	madeleine	**ADEEFLRRS**	deferrals
ADDFFNRUY	dandruffy	**ADEEEILNT**	delineate	**ADEEFLRTT**	flattered

ADEEFLRTU	defaulter	ADEEGMOSS	megadoses	ADEEHRRST	rethreads
ADEEFLRTW	delftware	ADEEGMRRU	demurrage		threaders
ADEEFLSSX	flaxseeds	ADEEGNNRS	endangers	ADEEHRSST	headrests
ADEEFMNOR	forenamed		greensand	ADEEHRSTT	shattered
ADEEFMORR	forearmed	ADEEGNNUV	unavenged	ADEEHRSTV	harvested
ADEEFMORT	fadometer	ADEEGNORS	renegados	ADEEHRSTW	watershed
ADEEFRRSY	defrayers	ADEEGNRRS	gardeners	ADEEHSTUX	exhausted
ADEEGGINR	degearing	ADEEGNRST	estranged	ADEEIILRS	idealiser
ADEEGGINS	disengage	ADEEGNRSU	dungarees	ADEEIILRZ	idealizer
ADEEGGIRV	aggrieved	ADEEGNRSV	Gravesend	ADEEIILSS	idealises
ADEEGGIRW	earwigged	ADEEGORST	derogates	ADEEIILSZ	idealizes
ADEEGGLNO	golden age	ADEEGRRSS	deergrass	ADEEIIMMT	immediate
ADEEGGLNY	engagedly	ADEEGRSSS	degassers	ADEEIIMNS	deaminise
ADEEGGMOU	demagogue	ADEEGSSSU	degausses	ADEEIIMNZ	deaminize
ADEEGGNNR	gangrened	ADEEGSTTU	degustate	ADEEIIMST	mediatise
ADEEGGNNU	unengaged	ADEEHHITW	whitehead	ADEEIIMTV	mediative
ADEEGGOPU	pedagogue	ADEEHHLRY	Heyerdahl	ADEEIIMTZ	mediatize
ADEEGGRSS	aggressed	ADEEHIISV	Heaviside	ADEEIIRSS	diaeresis
ADEEGGRST	staggered	ADEEHIKTV	khedivate	ADEEIIRST	dietaries
ADEEGGRSW	swaggered	ADEEHILNR	headliner	ADEEIJMRS	jeremiads
ADEEGIILT	Gileadite	ADEEHILNS	headlines	ADEEIKLMR	dreamlike
ADEEGIKLL	gladelike	ADEEHIMNV	Midheaven	ADEEILLOS	oeillades
ADEEGILLR	galleried	ADEEHINRT	herniated	ADEEILLUV	Deauville
ADEEGILLS	legalised		inearthed	ADEEILMNP	impaneled
ADEEGILLZ	legalized	ADEEHINSS	headiness	ADEEILMNR	madrilene
ADEEGILNR	engrailed	ADEEHINSV	evanished	ADEEILMNT	alimented
	realigned	ADEEHIRRT	threadier	ADEEILMPR	epidermal
ADEEGILRR	gradelier	ADEEHISST	diatheses		impearled
ADEEGILTV	levigated	ADEEHISSV	adhesives		impleader
ADEEGIMNN	demeaning	ADEEHISTT	hesitated	ADEEILMRS	misdealer
ADEEGIMNT	geminated	ADEEHKLRS	sheldrake		misleader
ADEEGIMRT	emigrated	ADEEHKSWW	hawkweeds	ADEEILMTY	mediately
ADEEGINNR	endearing	ADEEHLLNS	hanselled	ADEEILMTZ	metalized
	engrained	ADEEHLLOS	leasehold	ADEEILNOT	toenailed
	grenadine	ADEEHLLSW	wellheads	ADEEILNPS	penalised
ADEEGINRR	grenadier	ADEEHLNRS	rehandles	ADEEILNPX	explained
	rereading	ADEEHLNSU	unleashed	ADEEILNPZ	penalized
ADEEGINRT	denigrate	ADEEHLRST	slathered	ADEEILNSS	idealness
ADEEGINST	designate	ADEEHLSSS	shadeless	ADEEILNST	datelines
ADEEGINSV	envisaged	ADEEHLSST	deathless	ADEEILOTT	etiolated
ADEEGINTV	negatived	ADEEHLTTY	ethylated	ADEEILPPR	reapplied
ADEEGIPRS	De Gasperi	ADEEHMNOT	methadone	ADEEILPRS	pearlised
ADEEGIRSS	disagrees	ADEEHMOST	homestead	ADEEILPRV	prevailed
ADEEGIRST	tragedies	ADEEHMSST	stemheads	ADEEILPRZ	pearlized
ADEEGIRSU	gauderies	ADEEHNORS	hoarsened	ADEEILPSS	displease
ADEEGIUVW	waveguide	ADEEHNOST	headstone	ADEEILPST	depilates
ADEEGLLLY	allegedly	ADEEHNPPR	apprehend	ADEEILQSU	equalised
ADEEGLLRV	gravelled	ADEEHNPRS	sharpened	ADEEILQUZ	equalized
ADEEGLNNR	Greenland	ADEEHNRRS	hardeners	ADEEILRRS	derailers
ADEEGLNNT	entangled		rehardens	ADEEILRST	elaterids
ADEEGLNOT	elongated	ADEEHNRSS	harnessed	ADEEILRSV	velarised
ADEEGLNRW	Wergeland	ADEEHNRST	adherents	ADEEILRVZ	velarized
ADEEGLNRY	enragedly	ADEEHNRTU	unearthed	ADEEILTTV	levitated
	legendary	ADEEHNSTW	enswathed	ADEEIMMNS	misdemean
ADEEGLOOW	eaglewood	ADEEHORRV	overheard	ADEEIMMRT	dreamtime
ADEEGLRTU	regulated	ADEEHORSS	soreheads	ADEEIMNNO	menadione
ADEEGMNRR	germander	ADEEHORSV	overheads	ADEEIMNOU	eudemonia
ADEEGMNRS	gendarmes	ADEEHOSWY	eyeshadow	ADEEIMNRR	remainder
ADEEGMNRT	garmented	ADEEHPPRS	preshaped	ADEEIMNRT	minareted
	margented	ADEEHPRRS	rephrased	ADEEIMNST	amnestied
ADEEGMNTU	augmented	ADEEHPRST	spreathed	ADEEIMRRR	remarried
ADEEGMOPS	megapodes	ADEEHPRSW	prewashed	ADEEIMRST	diameters

377

	dreamiest	**ADEELMNPY**	ependymal		stepdames
ADEEIMSST	demitasse	**ADEELMORU**	remoulade	**ADEEMPSTU**	despumate
ADEEIMSTT	estimated	**ADEELMRSS**	dreamless	**ADEEMPTTT**	attempted
	meditates	**ADEELNNPR**	replanned	**ADEEMRSSU**	reassumed
ADEEINNOS	adenosine	**ADEELNNRU**	unlearned	**ADEEMRSTT**	smattered
ADEEINNRT	entrained	**ADEELNORS**	Esdraelon	**ADEENNORR**	nonreader
ADEEINPRT	pertained		oleanders	**ADEENNPRT**	trepanned
	repainted	**ADEELNORV**	overladen	**ADEENNPRU**	depanneur
ADEEINRRT	retrained	**ADEELNOST**	endosteal	**ADEENNRSS**	Anderssen
ADEEINRSS	nearsides	**ADEELNPRT**	replanted	**ADEENORST**	resonated
	readiness	**ADEELNPST**	endplates	**ADEENORSV**	endeavors
ADEEINRST	detainers	**ADEELNPTX**	explanted	**ADEENORSY**	aerodynes
	resinated	**ADEELNQUU**	unequaled	**ADEENORTV**	renovated
ADEEINRSV	reinvades	**ADEELNRRS**	slanderer	**ADEENORUV**	endeavour
ADEEINRTT	denitrate	**ADEELNRRU**	launderer	**ADEENOSTT**	detonates
	intreated	**ADEELNRSU**	underseal	**ADEENPPRS**	endpapers
ADEEINRUW	unwearied	**ADEELNRTU**	unaltered	**ADEENPPRT**	entrapped
ADEEINSTT	tetanised		unrelated	**ADEENPPRW**	enwrapped
ADEEINTTZ	tetanized	**ADEELNRUV**	unraveled	**ADEENPRRS**	panderers
ADEEINTVV	adventive	**ADEELNSSW**	Waldenses	**ADEENPRRT**	partnered
ADEEIOPRT	periodate	**ADEELNTTY**	dentately	**ADEENPRSX**	expanders
ADEEIOPTV	videotape	**ADEELOPTU**	outleaped	**ADEENPRTT**	patterned
ADEEIORSZ	zedoaries	**ADEELORST**	desolater	**ADEENPSST**	adeptness
ADEEIPPSS	passepied	**ADEELORTT**	tolerated	**ADEENRRSW**	wanderers
ADEEIPPST	peptidase	**ADEELOSST**	desolates	**ADEENRRSW**	wanderers
ADEEIPRRS	draperies	**ADEELPRST**	plastered	**ADEENRRTU**	underrate
ADEEIPRSS	airspeeds	**ADEELPRSU**	pleasured	**ADEENRRUW**	underwear
ADEEIPRTU	repudiate	**ADEELPSST**	pedestals	**ADEENRSSU**	underseas
ADEEIRRST	dreariest	**ADEELQRRU**	quarreled	**ADEENRSTT**	attenders
ADEEIRSST	steadiers	**ADEELRRST**	treadlers	**ADEENRSTU**	denatures
ADEEIRSTV	advertise	**ADEELRRTU**	adulterer		sauntered
ADEEIRSTW	waterside	**ADEELRSST**	tradeless		undereats
ADEEIRTTW	tidewater	**ADEELRSTY**	steelyard	**ADEENRSTY**	sedentary
ADEEIRTTX	extradite	**ADEELRSVY**	adversely	**ADEENRTTU**	untreated
ADEEIRTVZ	advertize	**ADEEMMNNT**	amendment	**ADEENRTTV**	advertent
ADEEISSTT	stateside	**ADEEMMORT**	dermatome	**ADEENRTUV**	adventure
	steadiest	**ADEEMMOXY**	myxoedema	**ADEENSSSU**	danseuses
ADEEISSTV	sedatives	**ADEEMMRST**	stammered	**ADEENSTTV**	vendettas
ADEEISTTV	estivated	**ADEEMNOPR**	promenade	**ADEEOPRRT**	perorated
ADEEITUVX	exudative	**ADEEMNORS**	demeanors	**ADEEOPRSV**	eavesdrop
	exuviated	**ADEEMNORT**	emendator	**ADEEOORSU**	rearoused
ADEEJMRSU	mudejares		Notre Dame	**ADEEORRTV**	overrated
ADEEKMRST	demarkets	**ADEEMNORU**	demeanour		overtrade
ADEEKNNSS	nakedness		enamoured	**ADEEORTVX**	overtaxed
ADEEKNPSW	knapweeds	**ADEEMNOST**	nematodes	**ADEEPPRRW**	rewrapped
ADEEKNRRS	darkeners	**ADEEMNPRS**	dampeners	**ADEEPPRSS**	appressed
ADEEKNRTU	undertake	**ADEEMNPSY**	ependymas	**ADEEPQRTU**	parqueted
ADEEKOPRS	presoaked	**ADEEMNRRU**	maunderer	**ADEEPRRSS**	spreaders
ADEELLLRU	laurelled	**ADEEMNRST**	smartened	**ADEEPRRSU**	persuader
ADEELLMRV	marvelled		tradesmen	**ADEEPRRSV**	depravers
ADEELLNRY	learnedly	**ADEEMNRTU**	numerated		pervaders
ADEELLPPR	rappelled	**ADEEMNRTY**	dynameter	**ADEEPRRSY**	resprayed
ADEELLPSY	pleasedly	**ADEEMNSSS**	madnesses	**ADEEPRRTU**	departure
ADEELLRTV	travelled	**ADEEMOORR**	aerodrome	**ADEEPRSST**	pederasts
ADEELLRXY	relaxedly	**ADEEMOPRR**	madrepore	**ADEEPRSSU**	persuades
ADEELLSST	tasselled	**ADEEMORRX**	xeroderma	**ADEEPRSTT**	spattered
ADEELLSTT	stellated	**ADEEMORST**	moderates	**ADEEPRSTU**	depasture
ADEELLTXY	exaltedly	**ADEEMORTT**	trematode		depurates
ADEELMMRT	trammeled	**ADEEMOSTU**	edematous	**ADEEPRSTY**	pederasty
ADEELMNOP	pademelon	**ADEEMPRRW**	prewarmed	**ADEEPSSUX**	pseudaxes
ADEELMNOR	ealdormen	**ADEEMPRST**	stampeder	**ADEEPSSWY**	speedways
ADEELMNOS	lemonades	**ADEEMPSST**	stampedes	**ADEEQRRTU**	quartered
				ADEERRRST	retarders

ADEERRRSW	rewarders	ADEFLLLSU	ladlefuls		grindelia
ADEERRSSU	reassured	ADEFLLMSY	damselfly	ADEGIILNS	gliadines
ADEERRSTT	restarted	ADEFLLNOV	Flevoland	ADEGIILNT	detailing
ADEERRSTU	treasured	ADEFLLORS	falderols	ADEGIILOS	dialogise
ADEERRSTV	traversed	ADEFLMMOR	malformed	ADEGIILOZ	dialogize
ADEERSTYY	yesterday	ADEFLNORS	forelands	ADEGIILPT	pigtailed
ADEFFIILS	falsified	ADEFLORRT	Altdorfer	ADEGIILTT	litigated
ADEFFLSTU	sufflated	ADEFLORST	deflators	ADEGIIMNT	mediating
ADEFFNORT	affronted	ADEFLORUV	flavoured	ADEGIIMTT	mitigated
ADEFFORST	tradeoffs	ADEFLORWY	dayflower	ADEGIINNR	ingrained
ADEFGGOPW	powfagged	ADEFLPRSS	feldspars	ADEGIINNT	detaining
ADEFGHORT	godfather	ADEFLRSTW	leftwards	ADEGIINNU	guanidine
ADEFGIILN	anglified	ADEFMNNTU	fundament	ADEGIINPR	diapering
ADEFGIIMN	magnified	ADEFMNRST	draftsmen	ADEGIINTV	deviating
ADEFGIIRT	gratified	ADEFMOORR	doorframe	ADEGIIRRT	irrigated
ADEFGILNT	deflating	ADEFMORTT	formatted	ADEGIKLLN	glandlike
ADEFGILRU	lifeguard	ADEFNORUV	unfavored	ADEGIKLNV	gavelkind
ADEFGIMTU	fumigated	ADEFOOPRR	proofread	ADEGIKLRU	guardlike
ADEFGINRT	ingrafted	ADEFORRRW	forwarder	ADEGIKNNR	darkening
ADEFGINRY	defraying	ADEFORRSY	foreyards	ADEGILLMN	medalling
ADEFGIRRU	fireguard	ADEFORRTV	overdraft	ADEGILLNP	pedalling
ADEFGLOOT	floodgate	ADEFORRTW	afterword	ADEGILLNS	signalled
ADEFGLOST	gatefolds		Waterford	ADEGILLNY	leadingly
ADEFGLRRU	regardful	ADEFORTUY	feudatory	ADEGILNNP	deplaning
ADEFHINOS	fashioned	ADEFRRSTU	fraudster	ADEGILNNR	Ingerland
ADEFHINRT	threadfin	ADEGGGINR	daggering		Leningrad
ADEFHIPSS	spadefish	ADEGGGIWW	wigwagged	ADEGILNNU	unaligned
ADEFHIRST	headfirst	ADEGGGIZZ	zigzagged		unleading
ADEFHLOOS	falsehood	ADEGGIITZ	dziggetai	ADEGILNOR	girandole
ADEFHNORS	forehands	ADEGGILNR	langridge		reloading
ADEFIILMP	amplified	ADEGGIMSU	misgauged	ADEGILNOS	alongside
ADEFIILNS	finalised	ADEGGINNR	deranging	ADEGILNPS	pleadings
ADEFIILNZ	finalized		gardening	ADEGILNRS	draglines
ADEFIILQU	qualified	ADEGGINOR	dogearing	ADEGILNRT	treadling
ADEFIILRS	airfields	ADEGGINRR	regarding		triangled
ADEFIILRT	airlifted		regrading	ADEGILNRU	gerundial
ADEFIIMNS	damnifies	ADEGGINSS	degassing	ADEGILNST	desalting
	infamised	ADEGGIRST	draggiest	ADEGILNUV	devaluing
ADEFIIMNZ	infamized	ADEGGLNSU	angledugs	ADEGILNVY	evadingly
ADEFIIMTT	mattified	ADEGGLORY	gargoyled	ADEGILORU	dialoguer
ADEFIISST	satisfied	ADEGGLRST	straggled	ADEGILOSU	dialogues
ADEFIKNRW	drawknife	ADEGGMORT	mortgaged	ADEGILRRS	rigsdaler
ADEFILLNT	flatlined	ADEGGNORU	groundage	ADEGILRSS	glissader
ADEFILLSU	fusillade	ADEGHHILT	headlight	ADEGILRTU	ligatured
ADEFILMNS	fieldsman	ADEGHHOSS	hogsheads	ADEGILSSS	glissades
	Mansfield	ADEGHIILV	Diaghilev	ADEGILTUV	divulgate
ADEFILMSU	feudalism	ADEGHILNR	heralding	ADEGIMNNN	demanning
ADEFILNNZ	zinfandel	ADEGHILST	giltheads	ADEGIMNNP	dampening
ADEFILNOT	deflation	ADEGHINNR	hardening	ADEGIMNNR	remanding
	defoliant	ADEGHINRS	garnished	ADEGIMNTU	magnitude
ADEFILNRS	Friesland	ADEGHINRT	threading	ADEGIMORS	ideograms
ADEFILNSS	sandflies	ADEGHINSS	sheadings	ADEGIMOST	dogmatise
ADEFILNTY	defiantly	ADEGHINSU	anguished	ADEGIMOTZ	dogmatize
ADEFILORT	floriated	ADEGHIOPR	ideograph	ADEGINNPP	appending
ADEFILRTT	filtrated	ADEGHLLNO	Helgoland	ADEGINNPR	pandering
ADEFILSTU	feudalist	ADEGHLMPU	galumphed	ADEGINNPX	expanding
ADEFILTUY	feudality	ADEGHLORS	gasholder	ADEGINNRT	integrand
ADEFINOST	Di Stéfano	ADEGHNOUZ	gazehound	ADEGINNRW	wandering
ADEFINRSU	fundraise	ADEGHORST	goatherds	ADEGINNTT	attending
ADEFIRSTT	draftiest	ADEGHRRTU	draughter	ADEGINORR	Rio Grande
ADEFKNNRU	unfranked	ADEGHRSTU	daughters	ADEGINORS	grandiose
ADEFKSSST	deskfasts	ADEGIILNR	derailing		organdies

379

	organised
ADEGINORZ	organized
ADEGINOSS	diagnoses
ADEGINPRS	spreading
ADEGINPRT	departing
	predating
ADEGINPRV	depraving
	pervading
ADEGINRRS	grandsire
ADEGINRRT	retarding
ADEGINRRW	redrawing
	rewarding
ADEGINRST	gradients
ADEGINRSW	sawdering
ADEGINRTV	adverting
ADEGINSST	steadings
ADEGINSSU	gaudiness
ADEGINSTT	digestant
ADEGINSTY	steadying
ADEGIPRRT	partridge
ADEGIRSWY	ridgeways
ADEGIRTTU	gratitude
ADEGJLTUU	jugulated
ADEGLLLOU	Dolgellau
ADEGLLNOO	gallooned
ADEGLLNSU	glandules
ADEGLNNTU	untangled
ADEGLNOOO	ologoaned
ADEGLNOST	gladstone
ADEGLNRST	strangled
ADEGLNRUW	Grünewald
ADEGLOOPY	paedology
ADEGLRSSU	guardless
ADEGMNRSU	guardsmen
ADEGMOPRR	deprogram
ADEGNNOPR	pendragon
ADEGNNORS	androgens
ADEGNNORW	downrange
ADEGNNORY	androgyne
ADEGNNRSS	grandness
ADEGNOORS	goosander
ADEGNOPPR	dognapper
ADEGNOPRT	godparent
ADEGNORSS	dragoness
ADEGNORST	dragonets
ADEGNORSU	dangerous
ADEGNORTU	outranged
ADEGNOSTW	downstage
ADEGNRRSU	grandeurs
ADEGNRSUZ	gazunders
ADEGOPRRS	dragropes
ADEGOPRRT	Petrograd
ADEGORRTT	garrotted
ADEGOSSTU	outgassed
ADEGPRRSU	upgraders
ADEGRRSST	dragsters
ADEHHISST	shitheads
ADEHHLLRS	hardshell
ADEHIIKLV	khedivial
ADEHIILNP	delphinia
ADEHIIMNS	maidenish
ADEHIINPR	nephridia

ADEHIIRRR	hairdrier
ADEHIISST	diathesis
ADEHIKKLS	Kikládhes
ADEHIKNPS	handspike
ADEHIKNSS	skinheads
ADEHIKNSW	windshake
ADEHIKRRS	shikarred
ADEHILMNS	mishandle
ADEHILMOT	ethmoidal
ADEHILNNR	Rheinland
	Rhineland
ADEHILNPR	philander
ADEHILNPS	planished
ADEHILNRR	hardliner
ADEHILOSU	Dalhousie
ADEHILRRT	trihedral
ADEHILRST	heraldist
ADEHIMNOR	rhodamine
ADEHIMNRS	mindshare
ADEHIMNSU	humanised
ADEHIMNUZ	humanized
ADEHIMOSU	housemaid
ADEHIMPSS	misshaped
ADEHIMPTW	whitedamp
ADEHIMRTY	diathermy
ADEHINNRS	Sanhedrin
ADEHINNSS	handiness
ADEHINOPS	diaphones
ADEHINOPU	audiphone
ADEHINORS	Rhodesian
ADEHINOSS	adhesions
ADEHINPRT	printhead
ADEHINPSS	deanships
ADEHINPSU	dauphines
ADEHINRRT	Reinhardt
ADEHINRSS	hardiness
ADEHINRST	tarnished
ADEHINRSV	varnished
ADEHINRTY	anhydrite
ADEHINRYZ	hydrazine
ADEHINSSS	shadiness
ADEHIOPRS	aphorised
ADEHIOPRT	Aphrodite
	atrophied
ADEHIOPRZ	aphorized
ADEHIPRST	therapsid
ADEHIPSSS	pissheads
ADEHIPSSY	diaphyses
ADEHIPSWW	whipsawed
ADEHIRRRY	hairdryer
ADEHIRSTW	dishwater
ADEHKNNTU	unthanked
ADEHKNOSW	shakedown
ADEHKNRSS	redshanks
ADEHLLOSW	shallowed
ADEHLLOTY	tallyhoed
ADEHLLSSY	dayshells
ADEHLMNOS	homelands
ADEHLOPRY	polyhedra
ADEHLOPSS	asphodels
ADEHLORST	Aldershot
ADEHLORSY	hydrolase

ADEHLPPRT	thrappled
ADEHLPSTU	sulphated
ADEHMNORS	handsomer
ADEHMOOPS	shampooed
ADEHMOORV	Hoover Dam
ADEHMORSW	homewards
ADEHMOSSU	madhouses
ADEHNOOPR	harpooned
ADEHNOORS	overhands
	overhands
ADEHNORVY	hydrovane
ADEHNOSSS	sandshoes
ADEHNRSSW	swanherds
ADEHNRSTU	unthreads
ADEHNSSSU	sunshades
ADEHNSTUW	unswathed
ADEHOORSU	roadhouse
ADEHOORTW	heartwood
ADEHOOSTT	statehood
ADEHOPPPY	poppyhead
ADEHOPRSS	rhapsodes
ADEHORRSW	shoreward
ADEHORRSY	drayhorse
ADEHORSSW	shadowers
ADEHORSTU	Stourhead
ADEIIILNT	initialed
ADEIIINTT	dietitian
	initiated
ADEIIILNY	leylandii
ADEIIILMNN	mainlined
ADEIIILMOZ	imidazole
ADEIIILMST	Miltiades
ADEIIILMTT	militated
ADEIIILNRT	deliriant
	interlaid
ADEIIILNST	disentail
ADEIIILNTZ	latinized
ADEIIILORT	editorial
ADEIIILORV	D'Oliviera
ADEIIILPTX	pixilated
ADEIIILQTU	liquidate
ADEIIILSST	idealists
ADEIIILSTU	dualities
ADEIIILSTV	vitalised
ADEIIILTVZ	vitalized
ADEIIIMMSX	maximised
ADEIIIMMXZ	maximized
ADEIIIMNNS	indamines
ADEIIIMNOT	mediation
ADEIIIMNRS	meridians
ADEIIIMNRZ	zemindari
ADEIIIMNTT	intimated
ADEIIIMOTT	diatomite
ADEIIIMSSV	admissive
ADEIIINNOS	Indonesia
ADEIIINOTV	deviation
ADEIIINPPR	drainpipe
ADEIIINSST	sanitised
ADEIIINSTT	daintiest
	dittanies
ADEIIINSTZ	sanitized
ADEIIIOSTZ	diazotise

ADEIIOTVX	oxidative	
ADEIIOTZZ	diazotize	
ADEIIPRRS	disrepair	
ADEIIPRSS	dispraise	
ADEIIPSST	dissipate	
ADEIIRRTT	irritated	
ADEIIRSST	Aristides	
	satirised	
ADEIIRSTZ	satirized	
ADEIIRTTT	tritiated	
ADEIITTTV	titivated	
ADEIKKSST	kidstakes	
ADEIKLRSS	laserdisk	
ADEIKLSSW	sidewalks	
ADEIKMORS	kaiserdom	
ADEIKMRST	tidemarks	
ADEIKNPPR	kidnapper	
ADEIKNPRS	spikenard	
ADEIKNPRT	predikant	
ADEILLMNO	medallion	
ADEILLMOT	metalloid	
ADEILLMRT	treadmill	
ADEILLMST	medallist	
ADEILLNOU	andouille	
ADEILLNST	installed	
ADEILLORS	arillodes	
ADEILLPRS	spiralled	
ADEILLPRU	preludial	
ADEILLPSS	spadilles	
ADEILLQRU	quadrille	
ADEILLSSW	sidewalls	
ADEILMMOT	immolated	
ADEILMNNN	Lindemann	
ADEILMNNO	mandoline	
ADEILMNOP	diplonema	
ADEILMNPT	implanted	
ADEILMNST	dismantle	
ADEILMNTU	dentalium	
ADEILMOPT	diplomate	
ADEILMOPY	polyamide	
ADEILMORS	moralised	
ADEILMORZ	moralized	
ADEILMOSX	aldoximes	
ADEILMOTV	moldavite	
ADEILMPSS	mispleads	
ADEILMPSY	misplayed	
ADEILMPTU	amplitude	
ADEILMSST	medalists	
ADEILMSTU	simulated	
ADEILMSUV	misvalued	
ADEILMTTU	mutilated	
ADEILNNRS	inlanders	
ADEILNNRU	underlain	
ADEILNOPP	panoplied	
ADEILNOPS	palinodes	
ADEILNOPT	planetoid	
ADEILNOPU	aneuploid	
ADEILNOST	delations	
	insolated	
ADEILNPPU	unapplied	
ADEILNPTT	tinplated	
ADEILNRRT	interlard	

ADEILNRSS	islanders	
ADEILNRSU	laundries	
ADEILNRTT	tridental	
ADEILNRTU	uitlander	
ADEILNRUV	unrivaled	
ADEILNRUY	unreadily	
ADEILNSSV	validness	
ADEILNSTU	insulated	
ADEILNSTW	Waldstein	
ADEILOPPT	oppilated	
ADEILOPRS	polarised	
ADEILOPRT	depilator	
ADEILOPRZ	polarized	
ADEILOPST	spoliated	
ADEILOQSU	odalisque	
ADEILORSS	solarised	
ADEILORST	estradiol	
	idolaters	
	steroidal	
ADEILORSV	valorised	
ADEILORSZ	solarized	
ADEILORVZ	valorized	
ADEILOSTT	datolites	
	totalised	
ADEILOSTV	dovetails	
ADEILOTTZ	totalized	
ADEILPPPS	pedipalps	
ADEILPPQU	appliqued	
ADEILPRSS	dispersal	
ADEILPRSU	epidurals	
	parulides	
ADEILPRSV	deprivals	
ADEILPRSY	displayer	
ADEILPTTU	platitude	
ADEILRRSU	ruralised	
ADEILRRUZ	ruralized	
ADEILRSSU	residuals	
ADEILRSSY	dialysers	
ADEILRSYZ	dialyzers	
ADEILRTTU	rutilated	
ADEILSSTU	lassitude	
ADEILSSTY	diastyles	
ADEILSTTU	altitudes	
	latitudes	
ADEIMMRST	midstream	
ADEIMNNOS	mondaines	
ADEIMNNOT	nominated	
ADEIMNNTU	indumenta	
ADEIMNOPT	ademption	
ADEIMNORS	randomise	
	romanised	
ADEIMNORZ	randomize	
	romanized	
ADEIMNOSS	nomadises	
ADEIMNOST	dominates	
	Maidstone	
	staminode	
ADEIMNOSW	womanised	
ADEIMNOSZ	nomadizes	
ADEIMNOWZ	womanized	
ADEIMNPRR	reprimand	
ADEIMNPRS	spiderman	

ADEIMNRRU	unmarried	
ADEIMNRSU	nursemaid	
ADEIMNRSZ	zemindars	
ADEIMNRTU	ruminated	
ADEIMNRTY	dynamiter	
ADEIMNSTY	dynamites	
ADEIMORRS	airdromes	
ADEIMORST	amortised	
	mediators	
ADEIMORTT	meditator	
ADEIMORTY	mediatory	
ADEIMORTZ	amortized	
ADEIMOTTV	motivated	
ADEIMPRST	spermatid	
ADEIMRRSS	disarmers	
ADEIMRRUU	Du Maurier	
ADEIMRTUX	admixture	
ADEIMRTXY	taxidermy	
ADEIMSSTT	misstated	
ADEINNNPS	inspanned	
ADEINNNSU	Dunsinane	
ADEINNNTT	intendant	
ADEINNOST	antinodes	
ADEINNOTT	dentation	
	intonated	
ADEINNOTV	innovated	
ADEINNRSS	randiness	
ADEINNRTU	untrained	
ADEINNSSS	sandiness	
ADEINNSTU	antidunes	
	inundates	
	unstained	
ADEINNTTU	untainted	
ADEINOOTX	exodontia	
ADEINOPPT	appointed	
ADEINOPRR	preordain	
ADEINOPRT	predation	
ADEINOPST	antipodes	
ADEINORRS	ordainers	
	serranoid	
ADEINORST	derations	
	notarised	
	ordinates	
ADEINORTY	arytenoid	
ADEINORTZ	notarized	
ADEINOSST	sedations	
ADEINOSTT	antidotes	
	stationed	
ADEINOSTV	donatives	
ADEINOTUX	exudation	
ADEINPPRS	sandpiper	
ADEINPPRW	inwrapped	
ADEINPPST	standpipe	
ADEINPRSS	rapidness	
ADEINPRST	dipterans	
ADEINPSSS	sapidness	
ADEINPSSV	vapidness	
ADEINPSTU	supinated	
ADEINQSTU	quantised	
ADEINQTUZ	quantized	
ADEINRRSS	serranids	
ADEINRRWW	wiredrawn	

ADEINRSST	Streisand	**ADELMNOOP**	lampooned	**ADENNOSTY**	asyndeton
	tardiness	**ADELMNOPS**	endoplasm	**ADENNPPSU**	unsnapped
ADEINRSTT	transited	**ADELMOOST**	stomodeal	**ADENNSSTW**	newsstand
ADEINRSTU	indurates	**ADELMOSTU**	modulates	**ADENOORST**	tornadoes
ADEINRSVY	vineyards	**ADELMRRSU**	demurrals	**ADENOORSW**	wanderoos
ADEINSSST	staidness	**ADELNNNPU**	unplanned	**ADENOORTT**	detonator
ADEINSSSV	vanessids	**ADELNNORW**	landowner		rattooned
ADEINSSTU	sustained	**ADELNNOSW**	Lansdowne	**ADENOOSTT**	toadstone
ADEINSSTY	dynasties	**ADELNNPTU**	unplanted	**ADENOOWWX**	woodwaxen
ADEINSTTV	Adventist	**ADELNNRSU**	unsnarled	**ADENOPRRS**	pardoners
ADEIOPRSV	vaporised	**ADELNOOPR**	Apeldoorn	**ADENOPRTV**	davenport
ADEIOPRTZ	trapezoid	**ADELNOOST**	loadstone	**ADENORRVW**	overdrawn
ADEIOPRVZ	vaporized	**ADELNOPSY**	dyspnoeal	**ADENORSTV**	standover
ADEIOPSST	dioptases	**ADELNORSS**	solanders	**ADENOSTTW**	downstate
ADEIORSST	asteroids	**ADELNORSU**	unloaders	**ADENOTTWY**	wyandotte
ADEIORSTT	storiated	**ADELNORSV**	overlands	**ADENPPRUW**	unwrapped
ADEIORSTV	deviators		rondavels	**ADENPRRTU**	underpart
ADEIORSVW	disavower	**ADELNORTU**	outlander	**ADENPRSSU**	underpass
ADEIORTVY	deviatory	**ADELNORUY**	roundelay	**ADENPRSUY**	underpays
ADEIPPSSY	dyspepsia	**ADELNPRSS**	spandrels	**ADENQRSSU**	squanders
ADEIPRSTU	eupatrids	**ADELNPRUY**	underplay	**ADENRRSTW**	sternward
ADEIPRSUU	Epidaurus	**ADELNRRUY**	Drury Lane	**ADENRSSTU**	transudes
ADEIPRTVY	depravity	**ADELNRSSU**	laundress	**ADENRSTUY**	Tyndareus
	varityped	**ADELNRSUY**	underlays	**ADEOOPRTT**	taprooted
ADEIPSSUX	pseudaxis	**ADELNRTVY**	verdantly	**ADEOORRST**	toreadors
ADEIPSTTU	aptitudes	**ADELNSSTU**	dauntless	**ADEOORTTV**	rotovated
ADEIQSSUY	quaysides	**ADELNSTUU**	undulates	**ADEOPRRST**	predators
ADEIRRSUY	residuary	**ADELOORST**	desolator		teardrops
ADEIRRSWW	wiredraws	**ADELOORSV**	overloads	**ADEOPRRTU**	depurator
ADEIRSSST	disasters	**ADELOPPRS**	prolapsed	**ADEOPRRTY**	portrayed
ADEIRSSSU	sardiuses	**ADELOPPTU**	populated		predatory
ADEIRSTTW	tawdriest	**ADELOPRSU**	poulardes	**ADEOPRSTT**	tetrapods
ADEIRSTUV	duratives		superload	**ADEOPRSTU**	outspread
ADEIRSTUY	adversity	**ADELOPTUY**	outplayed	**ADEOPRTTY**	tetrapody
ADEIRSVWY	driveways	**ADELORSST**	lodestars	**ADEOPSSTT**	postdates
ADEIRTTTT	attritted	**ADELORSTW**	leadworts	**ADEORRSST**	roadsters
ADEISSSTT	distastes	**ADELOSTTU**	outlasted	**ADEORRSVW**	overdraws
ADEISTTTU	attitudes	**ADELOSTUY**	autolysed	**ADEORRSWW**	swearword
ADEISTTUV	vastitude	**ADELOTUUV**	outvalued	**ADEORSTTU**	outstared
ADEJLNRTU	Jutlander	**ADELOTUYZ**	autolyzed	**ADEOSTTUY**	outstayed
ADEJRSSTU	adjusters	**ADELPPRRU**	larrupped	**ADEPRSSSU**	surpassed
	readjusts	**ADELPQRUU**	quadruple	**ADEPRSTTU**	upstarted
ADEKKLRSY	skylarked	**ADELRRSTY**	drysalter	**ADERRSSTT**	redstarts
ADEKLNOSY	ankylosed	**ADELRSSUY**	assuredly	**ADERSSTWW**	westwards
ADEKLNRTU	Tendulkar	**ADELRSTTU**	lustrated	**ADFFGINOR**	affording
ADEKLOTTU	outtalked	**ADEMMORST**	masterdom	**ADFFIIMRS**	disaffirm
ADEKLOTUW	outwalked	**ADEMMNORT**	adornment	**ADFFNOSST**	standoffs
ADEKNORRV	overdrank	**ADEMMNOTU**	outmanned	**ADFFORRST**	Strafford
ADEKNORTU	outranked	**ADEMNOPRS**	pomanders	**ADFGHIRSU**	Fishguard
ADEKOPRSW	spadework	**ADEMNORST**	transomed	**ADFGIILNY**	ladifying
ADELLLOWY	allowedly	**ADEMNORSU**	meandrous	**ADFGILNVY**	ladyfying
ADELLMRUY	medullary	**ADEMNPSTU**	unstamped	**ADFGINORS**	sangfroid
ADELLNOOT	Donatello	**ADEMNRTUU**	unmatured	**ADFGLNORY**	dragonfly
ADELLNOPR	landloper	**ADEMNSSUU**	unassumed	**ADFHINRST**	firsthand
ADELLNORW	lowlander	**ADEMOORRT**	moderator	**ADFHLOORY**	foolhardy
ADELLNOUY	unalloyed	**ADEMOORST**	astrodome	**ADFHLOSST**	holdfasts
ADELLNTUU	lunulated	**ADEMOPRSY**	pyodermas	**ADFIILNOR**	Floridian
ADELLOPRT	patrolled	**ADEMORRTT**	Rotterdam	**ADFILLLUY**	fluidally
ADELLOSVY	ladyloves	**ADEMORSTW**	wardmotes	**ADFILLNSW**	windfalls
ADELLOSWW	swallowed	**ADENNNSTU**	suntanned	**ADFILMNOS**	manifolds
ADELLRTXY	dextrally	**ADENNORSS**	Sanderson	**ADFILNOOV**	flavonoid
ADELMNNUY	mundanely	**ADENNOSST**	sandstone	**ADFIORSSV**	disfavors

ADFIORSUV	disfavour	**ADGIINNOZ**	anodizing	**ADHILMNPY**	nymphalid
ADFLLNOSW	downfalls	**ADGIINORT**	granitoid	**ADHILMSTY**	Ladysmith
ADFLLOOST	faldstool	**ADGIINOSS**	diagnosis	**ADHILNOPY**	hypnoidal
ADFLMNORS	landforms	**ADGIINOTX**	oxidating	**ADHILOPSS**	shiploads
ADFLORRWY	forwardly	**ADGIINRST**	disrating	**ADHILOPTY**	typhoidal
	frowardly	**ADGIINRTY**	dignitary	**ADHILPSSY**	ladyships
ADFNOORSZ	forzandos	**ADGIIRTVY**	gravidity	**ADHILSTTU**	Dasht-i-Lut
	sforzando	**ADGIJNSTU**	adjusting	**ADHIMNOSU**	humanoids
ADFNORRTW	frontward	**ADGILLNSW**	windgalls	**ADHIMNOTU**	anthodium
ADGGGILNR	draggling	**ADGILLNUV**	languidly	**ADHIMOPPS**	amphipods
ADGGGNNOU	Guangdong	**ADGILLOST**	goldtails	**ADHIMSTYY**	dysthymia
ADGGILNRY	niggardly	**ADGILLOSU**	gladiolus	**ADHINNNOTY**	hydantoin
ADGGILRSY	Yggdrasil	**ADGILMNSU**	guildsman	**ADHINNSTU**	Hindustan
ADGGINNOP	dognaping	**ADGILMORS**	marigolds	**ADHINOOST**	sainthood
ADGGINPRU	upgrading	**ADGILNNOT**	Aldington	**ADHINOPSY**	dysphonia
ADGGLOORV	Volgograd	**ADGILNNOU**	unloading	**ADHINORTY**	hydration
ADGGLRSSU	sluggards	**ADGILNORY**	adoringly	**ADHINRTWW**	withdrawn
ADGHHILNS	highlands	**ADGILNOSS**	glissando	**ADHINSTTW**	withstand
ADGHHIORS	highroads	**ADGILNPPS**	Gippsland	**ADHIOOSST**	soothsaid
ADGHHOOPR	hodograph	**ADGILNRTY**	dartingly	**ADHIOPRSY**	dysphoria
ADGHILLLS	gildhalls	**ADGILOORY**	radiology	**ADHIPRSSW**	wardships
ADGHILLLU	guildhall	**ADGILOOSS**	solidagos	**ADHIPRSSY**	shipyards
ADGHILNNS	handlings	**ADGILOOUV**	audiology	**ADHIRRSSTY**	hydrastis
ADGHILNSY	dashingly	**ADGILOPRS**	prodigals	**ADHIRSTWW**	withdraws
ADGHILSTY	daylights	**ADGIMMOST**	dogmatism	**ADHISTWWY**	widthways
ADGHIMOSU	Mogadishu	**ADGIMOSTT**	dogmatist	**ADHKNORTW**	Dankworth
ADGHINNNU	unhanding	**ADGINNOOU**	iguanodon	**ADHLLMORT**	thralldom
ADGHINORS	dragonish	**ADGINNOPR**	pardoning	**ADHLNNORT**	northland
	hoardings	**ADGINNNRST**	stranding	**ADHLNOSTU**	duathlons
ADGHINOSW	shadowing	**ADGINNRUW**	undrawing	**ADHLNOSUW**	downhauls
ADGHINPRS	handgrips	**ADGINNSST**	standings	**ADHMNOOOW**	womanhood
ADGHINRTU	indraught	**ADGINOORS**	grandioso	**ADHMOORSY**	hydrosoma
ADGHINRTY	hydrating	**ADGINOPRY**	parodying	**ADHMORTTU**	Dartmouth
ADGHIRRTW	rightward	**ADGINORTU**	outdaring	**ADHNOORYZ**	hydrozoan
ADGHISTTW	tightwads	**ADGINOTTU**	outdating	**ADHNORRTW**	northward
ADGHNOOPR	ondograph	**ADGINPRSY**	dayspring	**ADHNORSUY**	anhydrous
ADGHNOSTU	staghound	**ADGIORUUX**	Giraudoux	**ADHNORTUY**	hydronaut
ADGHPRTUU	updraught	**ADGLNOORY**	andrology	**ADHNOSSTU**	thousands
ADGIIILNT	digitalin	**ADGMNORSU**	gourmands	**ADHNRSSTU**	Sandhurst
ADGIIILST	digitalis	**ADGMOORRU**	guardroom	**ADHOOPRRT**	arthropod
ADGIIJNNO	adjoining	**ADGNNNNOU**	Dungannon	**ADHOOPRSS**	hospodars
ADGIIKNNP	kidnaping	**ADGNNOQSU**	quandongs	**ADHOOPRST**	potshards
ADGIILLTY	digitally	**ADGNNORSS**	grandsons	**ADHORRSTY**	hydrators
ADGIILMOS	dialogism	**ADGNNORYY**	androgyny	**ADHORSTTY**	hydrostat
	sigmoidal	**ADGOOPRST**	gastropod	**ADHORSTUW**	southward
ADGIILNNS	islanding	**ADGOOPRSU**	podagrous	**ADIIIIRSU**	Darius III
ADGIILNPS	Pig Island	**ADHHIPRSS**	hardships	**ADIIINOSZ**	isoniazid
ADGIILNSS	glissandi	**ADHHNOORU**	hoarhound	**ADIIINRSV**	viridians
ADGIILNSY	dialysing	**ADHHNORST**	shorthand	**ADIIIQRSU**	daiquiris
ADGIILNYZ	dialyzing	**ADHHNRSTY**	hydranths	**ADIIKLMMS**	milkmaids
ADGIILOSS	diglossia	**ADHHOPRTY**	hydropath	**ADIIKLNNU**	kundalini
ADGIILOST	dialogist	**ADHIILLOT**	lithoidal	**ADIIKLSST**	tailskids
ADGIIMNRS	disarming	**ADHIILORZ**	rhizoidal	**ADIILLMRS**	milliards
ADGIIMNST	misdating	**ADHIIMMRS**	midrashim	**ADIILLNTU**	lunitidal
ADGIIMNSY	dismaying	**ADHIIMPSS**	amidships	**ADIILLNVY**	invalidly
ADGIIMNTT	admitting	**ADHIINOPS**	ophidians	**ADIILLPTY**	pallidity
ADGIIMORS	idiograms	**ADHIIOPSU**	aphidious	**ADIILMOPS**	idioplasm
ADGIIMRUU	Maiduguri	**ADHIIOPTY**	idiopathy	**ADIILMSSS**	dismissal
ADGIIMSST	digamists	**ADHIIPSSY**	diaphysis	**ADIILNOPT**	platinoid
ADGIINNNT	indignant	**ADHIKMNNU**	humankind	**ADIILNOST**	dilations
ADGIINNOR	ordaining	**ADHIKNORW**	handiwork	**ADIILNOTU**	nautiloid
ADGIINNOS	anodising	**ADHILLRSY**	hydrillas	**ADIILNSSW**	windsails

ADIILNSTW	tailwinds	ADIMNSSTY	dynamists	ADNOPRRTY	protandry
ADIILOORV	varioloid	ADIMOOQSU	Quasimodo	ADNOPRRUW	wrapround
ADIIMNOSS	admission	ADIMOPRSY	myriapods	ADNOPRSTU	Port Sudan
ADIIMNOUZ	diazonium	ADINNNOUZ	D'Annunzio	ADNOQRSSU	squadrons
ADIIMOPRR	primordia	ADINNNOOST	donations	ADNORSSTW	sandworts
ADIIMRSSY	mydriasis	ADINNOOSW	Snowdonia	ADNOSSTTU	outstands
ADIINNOST	nidations	ADINNORTU	inundator		standouts
ADIINNOSY	Dionysian	ADINNOSST	dissonant	ADOOOORRWW	arrowwood
ADIINOOST	iodations	ADINOOPST	adoptions	ADOOPPRSU	pauropods
ADIINOOTX	oxidation	ADINOOSTW	satinwood	ADOOPRRST	trapdoors
ADIINOQTU	quotidian	ADINOPSY	dystopian	ADOOPRSSU	sauropods
ADIINORSS	anidrosis	ADINORSSU	dinosaurs	ADOOPSSSS	Dos Passos
ADIINORTT	tradition	ADINORSTU	durations	ADOPRSSSW	passwords
ADIINOSTU	auditions	ADINPSTTU	disputant	ADOPSSSUY	soapsudsy
ADIINRSST	distrains	ADIOOPRST	parotoids	AEEEEHMPR	ephemerae
ADIINRSTT	distraint	ADIOPRSST	parodists	AEEEEFGLRT	telferage
ADIINRSTU	saturniid	ADIORRSTT	traditors	AEEEEFHLLN	fellaheen
ADIIPRSTY	disparity	ADIOSSSUU	assiduous	AEEEEFHRRT	hereafter
ADIISSTUY	assiduity	ADJKNRSUY	junkyards	AEEEEFLLRT	leafleter
ADIJNOOVV	Vojvodina	ADJMMOOOR	majordomo	AEEEEFNRST	fenestrae
ADIKKNNSY	Kandinsky	ADKLOORSW	woodlarks	AEEEEFRRSW	freewares
ADIKLLORS	roadkills		workloads	AEEEEFRSTT	Free State
ADIKMNNOW	womankind	ADKMNORSW	markdowns	AEEEGGGNR	greengage
ADIKNNNSU	dunnakins	ADKMOORRS	darkrooms	AEEEEGGNRS	reengages
ADIKNNSST	inkstands	ADKNORRWW	drawnwork	AEEEGGRST	segregate
ADIKNOPSY	pyinkados	ADKNORSTT	Kronstadt	AEEEGHLRW	gearwheel
ADIKNRSTU	Kurdistan	ADKOORRSW	roadworks	AEEEGHMRT	megathere
ADILLMNRS	mandrills	ADLLNSSUV	Sundsvall	AEEEGIMNR	menagerie
ADILLMNUY	maudlinly	ADLMNOORS	moorlands	AEEEGKRTW	Great Week
ADILLNPSS	landslips	ADLMNORTY	mordantly	AEEEGLRST	regelates
ADILLNRUY	diurnally	ADLMOOPRR	prodromal		relegates
ADILLOSSW	disallows	ADLMOORTU	modulator	AEEEGMNNP	empennage
ADILLQSUY	squalidly	ADLMOPRUW	mouldwarp	AEEEGMNRT	agreement
ADILMMSTU	talmudism	ADLNNOORW	nanoworld	AEEEGNRSS	eagerness
ADILMNNOS	mandolins	ADLNNOSTW	townlands	AEEEGNRST	generates
ADILMNOOS	salmonoid	ADLNOPRSU	pauldrons		teenagers
ADILMNOSS	salmonids	ADLNOPRVY	polyandry	AEEEGNRTW	tweenager
ADILMNOST	daltonism	ADLNOPSWY	downplays	AEEEGNSTV	Stevenage
ADILMNRUU	duralumin	ADLNORTUU	undulator	AEEEGORRV	overeager
ADILMOPSS	plasmoids	ADLNOSUWY	Low Sunday	AEEEGRTTZ	gazetteer
ADILMOPST	diplomats	ADLNRSSTU	Stralsund	AEEEGSTTV	vegetates
ADILMOPSY	olympiads	ADLOOOSTT	toadstool	AEEEHKNRR	hearkener
	sympodial	ADLOPRSWY	swordplay	AEEEHLMPR	ephemeral
ADILMSTTU	Talmudist	ADLORSUUY	arduously	AEEEHLSSY	eyelashes
ADILNNSSU	disannuls	ADLORTUWY	outwardly	AEEEHMPRS	ephemeras
ADILNOORS	doornails	ADLPQRUUV	quadruply	AEEEHMRTX	hexameter
ADILNOOSV	vindaloos	ADMMORRTY	martyrdom	AEEEHNRRV	Verhaeren
ADILNORTW	antiworld	ADMNNORSU	roundsman	AEEEHRRRS	rehearser
ADILNPRSS	spandrils	ADMNOORTY	dynamotor	AEEEHRRSS	rehearses
ADILNPSST	displants	ADMNOOSST	mastodons	AEEEHRRST	reheaters
ADILNSTTY	distantly	ADMNORSST	sandstorm	AEEEHRRTW	weatherer
ADILOPRSV	disproval	ADMNORSSW	sandworms	AEEEHRSTT	tearsheet
ADILOPRXY	pyridoxal		swordsman	AEEEHSSTT	aesthetes
ADILOPSSS	disposals	ADMOOPPPS	poppadoms	AEEEILRSS	sealeries
ADILORSTW	swordtail	ADMOOPPRU	pompadour	AEEEILRTT	elaterite
ADILRSTTY	tiltyards	ADMOORRSW	wardrooms	AEEEIMNRX	reexamine
ADIMMNOST	dominants	ADMOPPPSU	poppadums	AEEEIMNSX	examinees
ADIMNNTUY	mundanity	ADNNORRUU	runaround	AEEEINSUX	Euxine Sea
ADIMNOOOP	monopodia	ADNNOSSWW	swansdown	AEEEIPPRT	papeterie
ADIMNOORT	admonitor	ADNOOPRTW	Portadown	AEEEIRRTT	reiterate
	dominator	ADNOOQRSU	quadroons	AEEEKKPSS	keepsakes
ADIMNOSTY	staminody	ADNOOSSVW	advowsons	AEEEKLTTT	teakettle

AEEEKMRRT	marketeer	AEEFILOTX	exfoliate	AEEGHOSTU	gatehouse
AEEEKNRSW	weakeners	AEEFILRSV	lifesaver	AEEGHRRST	gatherers
AEEELLMNR	enameller	AEEFIMORT	aforetime		regathers
AEEELLMNT	elemental	AEEFINRRR	refrainer	AEEGIIMRS	imageries
AEEELLPPS	appellees	AEEFINSTX	antefixes	AEEGIKLPR	grapelike
AEEELLRST	teaseller	AEEFIRRRS	rarefiers	AEEGIKNNW	weakening
AEEELLSST	telesales	AEEFIRRTW	firewater	AEEGILLRS	allergies
AEEELMNRS	enamelers	AEEFKOPRS	forepeaks		galleries
AEEELMSTW	sweetmeal		forespeak	AEEGILLRT	treillage
AEEELNNPP	peneplane	AEEFLLMSS	flameless	AEEGILLRV	grevillea
AEEELNSST	selenates	AEEFLLMST	flamelets	AEEGILLSS	legalises
AEEELNUVZ	Venezuela	AEEFLLRSW	farewells	AEEGILLST	legislate
AEEELORRS	Roeselare	AEEFLLSUY	easefully	AEEGILLSZ	legalizes
AEEELPRRS	repealers	AEEFLLSVY	flyleaves	AEEGILMNN	enameling
AEEELPTTU	epaulette	AEEFLMNRT	Fremantle		meningeal
AEEELRRSS	releasers	AEEFLMRSS	frameless	AEEGILMNR	greenmail
AEEELRRSV	revealers	AEEFLNRST	fenestral	AEEGILMSS	imageless
AEEELRSTX	axletrees	AEEFLNRTT	flattener	AEEGILMST	gleamiest
AEEEMMNST	semanteme	AEEFLNSSS	falseness	AEEGILNNT	eglantine
AEEEMMRST	metameres	AEEFLNSTW	Westfalen		inelegant
AEEEMNNRT	nemertean	AEEFLOOTV	foveolate	AEEGILNNV	leavening
AEEEMNRST	mesentera	AEEFLORSS	Flores Sea	AEEGILNPR	repealing
AEEEMNRTU	enumerate	AEEFLORST	foresteal	AEEGILNRS	algerines
AEEEMNSST	easements	AEEFLOSTV	love feast		releasing
AEEEMORRT	aerometer	AEEFLPSTY	splayfeet		resealing
AEEEMPRST	permeates	AEEFLRRRS	referrals	AEEGILNRV	revealing
AEEEMPRTT	temperate	AEEFLRRST	falterers	AEEGILNST	anglesite
AEEEMRRSU	remeasure	AEEFLRRTT	flatterer		gelatines
AEEEMRTVW	wavemeter	AEEFLSTTT	flatettes		teaseling
AEEEMSTTW	sweetmeat	AEEFMNORS	forenames	AEEGILNSW	weaseling
AEEENNPRT	perennate		freemason	AEEGILNTV	elevating
AEEENOPRW	weaponeer	AEEFMNSTY	safetymen	AEEGILNTZ	teazeling
AEEENORTV	overeaten	AEEFNRSST	fasteners	AEEGILRSS	gaseliers
AEEENORTX	exonerate		refastens	AEEGILRSV	silver age
AEEENPRRT	penetrate	AEEFNRSTT	fatteners	AEEGILRTU	gauleiter
AEEENPRTT	penetrate	AEEFOPRRT	perforate	AEEGILSTV	levigates
AEEENPSTT	patentees	AEEFORSTT	foretaste	AEEGIMNRT	germanite
AEEENRRST	easterner	AEEGGHMOU	hemagogue		germinate
AEEENRRTW	treenware	AEEGGILLR	Gelligaer	AEEGIMNRZ	germanize
AEEENRSTV	enervates	AEEGGINRR	gregarine	AEEGIMNST	geminates
	venerates	AEEGGIRSV	aggrieves		magnesite
AEEENTTUV	eventuate	AEEGGLNOY	genealogy		magnetise
AEEENTTUX	extenuate	AEEGGLNRT	Great Glen	AEEGIMNTT	magnetite
AEEEPRRST	repartees	AEEGGMORT	mortgagee	AEEGIMNTZ	magnetize
	repeaters	AEEGGNNRS	gangrenes	AEEGIMOST	isogamete
AEEERSSST	esterases	AEEGGPRSU	puggarees	AEEGIMPTT	pegmatite
AEEFFILRT	afterlife	AEEGGRRST	staggerer	AEEGIMRRT	remigrate
AEEFGILLR	fillagree	AEEGGRRSW	swaggerer	AEEGIMRST	emigrates
AEEFGILPR	pilferage	AEEGGRSSS	aggresses	AEEGINNNT	neatening
AEEFGILRS	filagrees	AEEGHILST	Eastleigh	AEEGINNRT	argentine
AEEFGINRS	farseeing	AEEGHIMRT	hermitage		tangerine
AEEFGINTU	teniafuge	AEEGHINRR	rehearing	AEEGINNUW	New Guinea
AEEFGLLOT	flageolet	AEEGHINRS	garnishee	AEEGINOPS	espionage
AEEFGLORW	flowerage	AEEGHINRT	reheating	AEEGINOTT	negotiate
AEEFGLSSU	fuselages	AEEGHIRST	heritages	AEEGINPRT	interpage
AEEFGORST	fosterage	AEEGHLPRT	telegraph		repeating
AEEFHLLSS	selfheals	AEEGHLRSS	shearlegs	AEEGINPRV	grapevine
AEEFHLRTT	heartfelt	AEEGHMNOP	megaphone	AEEGINRRS	regainers
AEEFIKLLM	flamelike	AEEGHMPRS	graphemes	AEEGINRSS	gesnerias
AEEFIKRST	freakiest	AEEGHMRTZ	megahertz	AEEGINRST	reseating
AEEFILMNS	filenames	AEEGHNOPT	pathogene		stingaree
AEEFILNRT	interleaf	AEEGHNRSW	greenwash	AEEGINRTT	argentite
AEEFILNSS	leafiness				

	integrate	**AEEGNRSSV**	graveness	**AEEHKMMOR**	homemaker
AEEGINSSS	assignees	**AEEGNSSUV**	vagueness	**AEEHKMORS**	shoemaker
AEEGINSSV	envisages	**AEEGOPPST**	estoppage	**AEEHKNRRS**	harkeners
AEEGINSSW	seesawing	**AEEGOPRRT**	porterage	**AEEHLLMOW**	wholemeal
AEEGINSTU	sauteeing		reportage	**AEEHLLNOW**	Halloween
AEEGINSTV	agentives	**AEEGORRSV**	overgears	**AEEHLLOSW**	wholesale
	negatives	**AEEGORRVZ**	overgraze	**AEEHLLSSS**	seashells
AEEGIPQSU	equipages	**AEEGORSTU**	Great Ouse	**AEEHLMNSW**	wheelsman
AEEGIRSST	greasiest	**AEEGPRRSS**	presagers	**AEEHLMNSY**	hymeneals
AEEGIRSTT	aigrettes	**AEEGPRTUX**	expurgate	**AEEHLMPRY**	melaphyre
AEEGIRSTV	ergatives	**AEEGRRRST**	regraters	**AEEHLMPST**	helpmates
AEEGISTTV	gestative	**AEEGRSSTT**	greatests	**AEEHLMRTY**	erythemal
AEEGKMRRS	regmakers	**AEEHHIKLT**	heathlike		hemelytra
AEEGLLNOR	organelle	**AEEHHILRT**	healthier	**AEEHLMSSS**	shameless
AEEGLLNRS	allergens	**AEEHHLNSZ**	hazelhens	**AEEHLMTTY**	methylate
AEEGLLNRY	generally	**AEEHHLOSW**	hawsehole	**AEEHLNOPS**	anopheles
AEEGLLNTY	elegantly	**AEEHHNNPT**	naphthene	**AEEHLNOPT**	phenolate
AEEGLLRSS	glareless	**AEEHHNPTY**	hyphenate	**AEEHLNOSW**	Halesowen
AEEGLMNNT	gentleman	**AEEHHNRTY**	heathenry	**AEEHLNPST**	elephants
AEEGLMNRY	germanely	**AEEHHNSTU**	unsheathe	**AEEHLNSST**	natheless
AEEGLMNST	segmental	**AEEHIILPR**	perihelia	**AEEHLNSSU**	unleashes
AEEGLMOOS	mesogloea	**AEEHIILPT**	epithelia	**AEEHLNSSV**	havenless
AEEGLMORT	algometer	**AEEHIKNPT**	phenakite	**AEEHLOPST**	telophase
	glomerate	**AEEHIKRSS**	shikarees	**AEEHLORSS**	arseholes
AEEGLMRRW	legwarmer	**AEEHILLTW**	tailwheel		haloseres
AEEGLMRST	telegrams	**AEEHILMNW**	meanwhile	**AEEHLORST**	trehalose
AEEGLNNPT	pentangle	**AEEHILNTV**	Helvetian	**AEEHLOSSU**	alehouses
AEEGLNNRT	entangler	**AEEHILPRS**	shapelier	**AEEHLPRRV**	hyperreal
AEEGLNNST	entangles	**AEEHILRRT**	earthlier	**AEEHLPSSS**	phaseless
AEEGLNORS	sloganeer	**AEEHILRSS**	shiralees		shapeless
AEEGLNOST	elongates	**AEEHILRTW**	wealthier	**AEEHLPSTT**	telepaths
AEEGLNRRS	enlargers	**AEEHIMNST**	mainsheet	**AEEHLPTTY**	telepathy
AEEGLNRSS	largeness	**AEEHIMPRY**	hyperemia	**AEEHLRSST**	heartless
AEEGLNSSU	angeluses	**AEEHIMPSS**	emphasise	**AEEHLRTWY**	weatherly
AEEGLNSTT	gestalten	**AEEHIMPST**	empathise	**AEEHLSTTY**	ethylates
AEEGLORRV	overlarge	**AEEHIMPSZ**	emphasize	**AEEHLSTXY**	hexastyle
AEEGLORVZ	overglaze	**AEEHIMPTZ**	empathize	**AEEHMMORT**	hammertoe
AEEGLPRSS	grapeless	**AEEHIMRST**	hetaerism	**AEEHMMPSY**	emphysema
AEEGLRSSS	largesses	**AEEHINNPZ**	phenazine	**AEEHMMRRS**	hammerers
AEEGLRSSV	verglases	**AEEHINPRS**	Hesperian	**AEEHMNNOP**	phenomena
AEEGLRSTU	regulates	**AEEHINPSS**	Ephesians	**AEEHMNRSW**	washermen
AEEGMNRRS	merganser	**AEEHINRSV**	haversine	**AEEHMNSTU**	atheneums
AEEGMNRTU	augmenter	**AEEHINRTU**	eutherian	**AEEHMNSTX**	exanthems
AEEGMOPRS	megaspore	**AEEHINRTZ**	Therezina	**AEEHMOPRS**	semaphore
AEEGMORST	gasometer	**AEEHINSSV**	evanishes	**AEEHMORST**	heartsome
AEEGMRSST	gamesters		heaviness	**AEEHMORSW**	homewares
AEEGMSSSU	messuages	**AEEHIPPSW**	hawsepipe	**AEEHMOSST**	hematoses
AEEGNNNOS	enneagons	**AEEHIPRSS**	apheresis	**AEEHMOSTU**	housemate
AEEGNNRST	transgene		pharisees	**AEEHMPPRS**	hamperers
AEEGNNSTW	newsagent	**AEEHIPRST**	therapies	**AEEHMPRRS**	petersham
AEEGNOPRS	personage	**AEEHIRRST**	earthrise	**AEEHMSTTW**	Westmeath
AEEGNORRT	generator	**AEEHIRSSV**	shivarees	**AEEHNOORT**	oenothera
AEEGNORTT	teratogen	**AEEHIRSSW**	washeries	**AEEHNOPRS**	earphones
AEEGNORTU	entourage	**AEEHIRSTT**	earthiest	**AEEHNOPTX**	toxaphene
AEEGNOTTW	wagonette		heartiest	**AEEHNPPRY**	hyperpnea
AEEGNOTXY	oxygenate		hesitater	**AEEHNPRRS**	sharpener
AEEGNPRSS	passenger		hetaerist	**AEEHNRRSS**	harnesser
AEEGNRRST	estranger	**AEEHISSTT**	hesitates	**AEEHNRSSS**	harnesses
AEEGNRRSV	engravers	**AEEHKLLRS**	rakehells	**AEEHNRSST**	hasteners
AEEGNRSST	estranges	**AEEHKLLRY**	rakehelly	**AEEHNRSTT**	threatens
	greatness	**AEEHKLLSU**	keelhauls	**AEEHNRSTW**	enwreaths
	sergeants	**AEEHKLPSW**	sheepwalk	**AEEHNRSTX**	narthexes

AEEHNRSWY	anywheres	
AEEHNSSTW	enswathes	
AEEHOPRST	ephorates	
AEEHOPRTY	aerophyte	
AEEHORRSV	overhears	
AEEHORSSS	seashores	
AEEHORSTV	overheats	
AEEHORSUW	warehouse	
AEEHOSSTU	teahouses	
AEEHPPRSS	preshapes	
AEEHPRRSS	rephrases	
AEEHPRRST	threapers	
AEEHPRSSW	prewashes	
AEEHPRSTU	Euphrates	
	superheat	
AEEHRRSTT	shatterer	
AEEHRRSTV	harvester	
AEEHRSTUX	exhauster	
AEEHRSTYZ	Esterházy	
AEEIILLOP	aeolipile	
AEEIILMNT	eliminate	
AEEIILQRU	reliquiae	
AEEIILRSS	serialise	
AEEIILRST	Israelite	
	realities	
AEEIILRSZ	serialize	
AEEIIMNST	amenities	
AEEIINNTV	Vientiane	
AEEIINRTT	itinerate	
AEEIINSTV	naiveties	
AEEIINSTX	anxieties	
AEEIIPPRT	peripetia	
AEEIIRSTV	varieties	
AEEIIRTTV	iterative	
AEEIIRTVZ	vizierate	
AEEIJMNSS	jessamine	
AEEIJMSST	majesties	
AEEIKKLNS	snakelike	
AEEIKKPPS	Pikes Peak	
AEEIKLLNS	silkalene	
AEEIKLLPT	petallike	
AEEIKLLVV	valvelike	
AEEIKLMUW	Milwaukee	
AEEIKLNNP	Lenin Peak	
AEEIKLNSS	leakiness	
AEEIKLPRS	sprekelia	
AEEIKLSTW	weakliest	
AEEIKLSTY	yeastlike	
AEEIKMNOT	ketonemia	
AEEIKNRSV	knaveries	
AEEIKNSST	sneakiest	
AEEIKQRSU	squeakier	
AEEIKRRST	streakier	
AEEILLMNT	metalline	
AEEILLMRS	marseille	
AEEILLMST	metallise	
AEEILLMTZ	metallize	
AEEILLNOT	lineolate	
	linoleate	
AEEILLNST	tenailles	
AEEILLPPS	Apple Isle	
AEEILLPST	palletise	

AEEILLPTT	paillette	
AEEILLPTZ	palletize	
AEEILLRST	laetriles	
AEEILLSSS	aisleless	
AEEILLSTT	satellite	
AEEILLTVW	wavellite	
AEEILLTVX	vexillate	
AEEILMMST	lemmatise	
AEEILMMTZ	lemmatize	
AEEILMNNT	alinement	
	lineament	
AEEILMNRY	minelayer	
AEEILMNSS	mealiness	
	messaline	
AEEILMNST	enamelist	
AEEILMOOS	elaiosome	
AEEILMORT	meliorate	
AEEILMRST	misrelate	
	salimeter	
AEEILMRTT	altimeter	
AEEILMRTU	elaterium	
AEEILMRTW	limewater	
AEEILMSST	measliest	
AEEILMSTZ	metalizes	
AEEILMTUV	emulative	
AEEILNNPP	peneplain	
AEEILNNPR	perennial	
AEEILNNSX	sexennial	
AEEILNNTV	levantine	
	valentine	
AEEILNOTV	elevation	
AEEILNPPP	pineapple	
AEEILNPRS	plenaries	
AEEILNPRX	explainer	
AEEILNPSS	penalises	
AEEILNPST	Palestine	
	penalties	
	tapelines	
AEEILNPSX	expansile	
AEEILNPSZ	penalizes	
AEEILNRSS	earliness	
	leariness	
AEEILNRST	entailers	
	treenails	
AEEILNRSV	vernalise	
AEEILNRTW	waterline	
AEEILNRVZ	vernalize	
AEEILNSST	essential	
AEEILNSSV	aliveness	
AEEILNTTV	ventilate	
AEEILOPTT	petiolate	
AEEILORRT	arteriole	
AEEILORST	aerolites	
AEEILOSTT	etiolates	
AEEILPPRS	reapplies	
AEEILPRRV	prevailer	
AEEILPRSS	espaliers	
AEEILPRST	pearliest	
AEEILQRSU	equaliser	
AEEILQRUZ	equalizer	
AEEILQSSU	equalises	
AEEILQSUZ	equalizes	

AEEILRRSS	realisers	
AEEILRRST	retailers	
AEEILRRSZ	realizers	
AEEILRRTV	retrieval	
AEEILRSSV	velarises	
AEEILRSSW	weariless	
AEEILRSTT	laterites	
	literates	
	statelier	
AEEILRSTV	levirates	
	relatives	
	versatile	
AEEILRSTY	seriately	
AEEILRSVW	reviewals	
AEEILRSVZ	velarizes	
AEEILRTTU	elutriate	
AEEILSSTW	leastwise	
AEEILSSTZ	sleaziest	
AEEILSSUX	sexualise	
AEEILSTTV	levitates	
AEEILSUXZ	sexualize	
AEEILSVVY	evasively	
AEEIMNNPT	impennate	
AEEIMNNRV	venireman	
AEEIMNNZZ	mezzanine	
AEEIMNPRR	repairmen	
AEEIMNRST	antimeres	
	Trasimene	
AEEIMNRSX	examiners	
AEEIMNRTT	terminate	
AEEIMNSSS	seaminess	
AEEIMNSST	amnesties	
	meatiness	
AEEIMNSTT	estaminet	
AEEIMOPPR	peperomia	
AEEIMORSS	isomerase	
AEEIMORSW	wearisome	
AEEIMPRTT	impetrate	
AEEIMRRRS	remarries	
AEEIMRRST	streamier	
AEEIMRSST	masteries	
AEEIMRSTT	tasimeter	
AEEIMRTTX	taximeter	
AEEIMSSTT	estimates	
	steamiest	
AEEINNNPS	Apennines	
AEEINNPST	septennia	
AEEINNRST	tanneries	
AEEINNRTT	entertain	
AEEINNRTV	innervate	
AEEINNSST	insensate	
AEEINNSSV	naiveness	
AEEINNSTV	venetians	
AEEINOPPT	appointee	
AEEINOPRT	peritonea	
AEEINOPSW	weaponise	
AEEINOPWZ	weaponize	
AEEINORTT	orientate	
AEEINPRTT	pepsinate	
AEEINPRSS	passerine	
AEEINPRST	aperients	
	episterna	

	pistareen	**AEEKLNRST**	Lankester	**AEELNOPTX**	exoplanet
	sparteine	**AEEKLSSTY**	eyestalks	**AEELNPPSS**	spalpeens
AEEINPSVX	expansive	**AEEKMNRTW**	newmarket	**AEELNPRTV**	prevalent
AEEINRRST	retainers	**AEEKMORSV**	makeovers	**AEELNRSSS**	snareless
	ternaries	**AEEKMRRRS**	remarkers	**AEELNRSST**	alertness
AEEINRRTT	reiterant	**AEEKMRRST**	marketers	**AEELNRSSV**	enslavers
AEEINRRTV	veratrine	**AEEKNORTV**	overtaken	**AEELNRSTV**	levanters
AEEINRSST	arsenites	**AEEKORSTV**	overtakes	**AEELNRSTX**	externals
	resinates		takeovers	**AEELNRSTY**	earnestly
AEEINRSSW	weariness	**AEEKORTUY**	eukaryote	**AEELNRTTV**	tervalent
AEEINRSTT	reinstate	**AEEKPRSTT**	parkettes	**AEELNRTTY**	ternately
AEEINRSTU	estuarine	**AEEKQRSSU**	squeakers	**AEELNRTVY**	Trevelyan
AEEINRSTV	invertase	**AEEKRRSST**	streakers	**AEELNSSST**	staleness
AEEINRSTY	eyestrain	**AEELLLMOS**	lamellose	**AEELNSSTY**	sensately
AEEINSSTT	tetanises	**AEELLLSTT**	telltales	**AEELOPPSV**	overleaps
AEEINSSTU	uneasiest	**AEELLNPPZ**	Appenzell	**AEELOPRTV**	overleapt
AEEINSTTT	enstatite	**AEELLNPRT**	repellant	**AEELORSST**	oleasters
	intestate	**AEELLNPTX**	expellant	**AEELORSTT**	tolerates
	satinette	**AEELLNRTY**	enterally	**AEELORSTV**	elevators
AEEINSTTU	austenite		eternally	**AEELORSTY**	roseately
AEEINSTTZ	tetanizes	**AEELLOPST**	sellotape	**AEELORTVY**	elevatory
AEEINTTTV	attentive		soleplate	**AEELORUVV**	overvalue
	tentative	**AEELLOSTT**	allottees	**AEELPPRRU**	puerperal
AEEIOOPPS	epopoeias	**AEELLOSUV**	laevulose	**AEELPPRSS**	paperless
AEEIOPRST	operatise	**AEELLOSWY**	Yellow Sea	**AEELPPRTU**	perpetual
	periostea	**AEELLPSTT**	platelets	**AEELPPRSS**	relapsers
AEEIOPRTV	evaporite	**AEELLPTTY**	peltately	**AEELPPRST**	palterers
	operative	**AEELLRRSV**	ravellers		plasterer
AEEIOPRTZ	operatize	**AEELLRRTV**	traveller	**AEELPRRSY**	parleyers
AEEIPPRST	appetiser	**AEELLRSVY**	severally	**AEELPRRTU**	prelature
AEEIPPRSU	pauperise	**AEELLRTTU**	tellurate	**AEELPRSSU**	pleasures
AEEIPPRTZ	appetizer	**AEELLSSUV**	valueless	**AEELPRSSV**	vesperals
AEEIPPRUZ	pauperize	**AEELLSSVV**	valveless	**AEELPRSTT**	saltpeter
AEEIPPSTT	appetites	**AEELLSTVV**	saltpetre		saltpetre
AEEIPRRRS	rareripes	**AEELMMNRT**	entrammel	**AEELQRRRU**	quarreler
	repairers	**AEELMMRRT**	trammeler	**AEELQRSSU**	squealers
AEEIPRRTV	privateer	**AEELMMSTU**	malemutes	**AEELQSTUZ**	quetzales
AEEIPRSSS	pessaries	**AEELMMTXY**	metaxylem	**AEELQUVZZ**	Velázquez
AEEIPRSSV	aspersive	**AEELMNOST**	telamones	**AEELRRSSV**	reversals
AEEIPRSVV	pervasive	**AEELMNPRT**	parlement		slaverers
AEEIPRTTX	extirpate	**AEELMNPSS**	ampleness	**AEELRRSTU**	serrulate
AEEIPSSVW	spaewives		ensamples	**AEELRRSTV**	travelers
AEEIQSSTU	queasiest	**AEELMNRST**	lamenters	**AEELRSSTW**	waterless
AEEIRSSTT	sestertia	**AEELMNRTV**	ravelment	**AEELRSTUY**	austerely
	treatises	**AEELMNSTT**	mantelets	**AEELRSTVY**	severalty
AEEIRSSTU	estuaries	**AEELMORST**	elastomer	**AEELSSSTT**	stateless
AEEIRSSTV	assertive	**AEELMOSTT**	matelotes		tasteless
AEEIRSTWW	wasteweir	**AEELMOSWY**	awesomely	**AEELSSSTW**	sweatless
AEEISSTTV	estivates	**AEELMOTTT**	matelotte	**AEELSSSTY**	yeastless
AEEISSTTW	sweatiest	**AEELMPRSU**	supermale	**AEELSSTTT**	statelets
AEEISSTTY	yeastiest	**AEELMPRSX**	exemplars	**AEEMMNORT**	manometer
AEEISTUVX	exuviates	**AEELMPRXY**	exemplary	**AEEMMNSTU**	amusement
AEEJKRRTW	jerkwater	**AEELMPSTT**	palmettes	**AEEMMORTT**	atmometer
AEEJLMRSU	Jerusalem		templates	**AEEMMPRUV**	empyreuma
AEEJMORTT	majorette	**AEELMRSST**	semestral	**AEEMMRRST**	stammerer
AEEJMRSTT	jetstream	**AEELMRSTT**	streamlet	**AEEMMRRSY**	yammerers
AEEJNOSTZ	Zeta-Jones	**AEELMRSTX**	extremals	**AEEMMSSST**	messmates
AEEJNRSST	serjeants	**AEELMRTTW**	meltwater	**AEEMNNOPR**	praenomen
AEEKKLSWY	lykewakes	**AEELNNNTU**	antennule	**AEEMNNORT**	nanometre
AEEKLLPSW	sleepwalk	**AEELNNPSS**	planeness	**AEEMNNOTT**	atonement
AEEKLMMSU	mamelukes	**AEELNNRST**	lannerets	**AEEMNNPRT**	permanent
AEEKLMRST	telemarks	**AEELNOPST**	antelopes	**AEEMNOPRT**	treponema

AEEMNOPSU menopause	**AEENPRSTY** septenary	**AEFFLNOPT** pantoffle
AEEMNOPYZ apoenzyme	**AEENPRSUV** parvenues	**AEFFLNSTU** affluents
AEEMNORUV manoeuvre	**AEENPSTTY** antetypes	**AEFFLORSW** safflower
AEEMNPRTY repayment	**AEENNRRSW** warreners	**AEFFLSSTU** sufflates
AEEMNPSTV pavements	**AEENRRSTT** natterers	**AEFFNOOSS** offseason
AEEMNRSST steersman	**AEENRRSTU** saunterer	**AEFFORSST** afforests
AEEMNRSTU numerates	**AEENRRSTV** taverners	**AEFFORSTV** overstaff
AEEMNRSTV averments	**AEENRRTUV** nervature	**AEFFRSTTU** tartuffes
AEEMNRSUV maneuvers	**AEENRSSTU** sauternes	**AEFGHHISS** hagfishes
AEEMNRTTT treatment	**AEENRSTTV** anteverts	**AEFGHILNS** angelfish
AEEMNSSTT statesmen	**AEENSSSUV** suaveness	**AEFGHILST** safelight
AEEMNSSTY mateyness	**AEEOOPRTZ** azeotrope	**AEFGHINRT** fathering
AEEMNSTTT statement	**AEEOPPRSU** peasouper	**AEFGHIRSS** garfishes
testament	**AEEOPRRST** perorates	**AEFGHIRST** gearshift
AEEMOPSSU mesopause	**AEEOPRSST** proteases	**AEFGHORRT** forgather
AEEMORRSU rearmouse	**AEEOPRSTT** operettas	**AEFGIILNS** anglifies
AEEMORRTT rotameter	poetaster	**AEFGIIMNR** magnifier
AEEMORRTY aerometry	**AEEOPSSST** petasoses	**AEFGIIMNS** magnifies
AEEMORSST Massorete	**AEEOQRRTU** Querétaro	**AEFGIINRY** aerifying
AEEMORTTU autometer	**AEEOORSSU** rearouses	**AEFGIIRRT** gratifier
AEEMPPRRS pamperers	**AEEOORSTV** overrates	**AEFGIIRSS** gasifiers
AEEMPRRST tamperers	**AEEOORSTW** rosewater	**AEFGIIRST** gratifies
AEEMPRRSV revampers	**AEEOORRTVW** overwater	**AEFGILLLN** flagellin
AEEMPRRTU premature	**AEEOORSTTV** overstate	**AEFGILLLS** gallflies
AEEMPRSTT attempers	**AEEOORSTTW** twoseater	**AEFGILLNT** fellating
AEEMPRTTT attempter	**AEEOORSTVX** overtaxes	**AEFGILLRY** fragilely
reattempt	**AEEPPRRRS** preparers	**AEFGILMOR** galeiform
AEEMPRTTU permutate	**AEEPRRRST** parterres	**AEFGILNRS** finaglers
AEEMQRRSU remarques	**AEEPRRSSS** aspersers	**AEFGILNRT** faltering
AEEMQRTTU Marquette	**AEEPRRSTU** apertures	reflating
AEEMQSTXY maquettes	**AEEPRSTXY** apteryxes	**AEFGIMNRR** reframing
AEEMRRSST remasters	**AEEPSSSTU** petasuses	**AEFGIMSTU** fumigates
streamers	**AEEQRRSUV** quaverers	**AEFGINNST** fastening
AEEMRRSSU measurers	**AEEQRSSTU** sequestra	**AEFGINNTT** fattening
AEEMRRSTT smatterer	**AEEQRTTTU** quartette	**AEFGINRRY** rarefying
AEEMRSSST masseters	**AEEQRTUUX** exequatur	**AEFGINRTU** featuring
AEEMRSSSU reassumes	**AEERRRSST** arresters	figurante
AEEMRSSTT teamsters	rearrests	**AEFGIORSS** ossifrage
AEEMRTTTW wattmeter	**AEERRRSSU** reassurer	**AEFGIRRRY** Grey Friar
AEEMSSSSU masseuses	**AEERRRSTU** serrature	**AEFGISTTU** fustigate
AEENNOPTT panettone	treasurer	**AEFGLLLMU** flagellum
AEENNPRRT trepanner	**AEERRRSTV** traverser	**AEFGLLOPS** flagpoles
AEENNPRTT penetrant	**AEERRSSST** asserters	**AEFGLMOPS** megaflops
repentant	reasserts	**AEFGLNOST** flagstone
AEENNRRSS ensnarers	**AEERRSSSU** reassures	**AEFGLOPRS** leapfrogs
AEENNRRTT reentrant	**AEERRSSTU** treasures	**AEFGLORTW** afterglow
AEENNRSTV revenants	**AEERRSSTV** traverses	**AEFGLRTUU** fulgurate
AEENOPPRT notepaper	**AEERRTTVX** extravert	**AEFGMNRST** fragments
AEENOPRST personate	**AEERSSTTT** attesters	**AEFGNORST** frontages
AEENOPTTT potentate	**AEESTTTTU** statuette	**AEFGNORTX** xenograft
AEENORRSS reasoners	**AEFFGRSSU** suffrages	**AEFHHISST** sheatfish
AEENORRTV enervator	**AEFFHIKSY** kaffiyehs	**AEFHHLLTU** healthful
venerator	**AEFFIILRS** falsifier	**AEFHHLOTW** heathfowl
AEENORSSS seasoners	**AEFFIILSS** falsifies	**AEFHIKMST** makeshift
AEENORSST resonates	**AEFFIKPST** pikestaff	**AEFHILMSS** fishmeals
AEENORSTV renovates	**AEFFILLUV** effluvial	**AEFHILMST** halftimes
AEENORSTW stoneware	**AEFFIMRRS** affirmers	**AEFHILPST** fishplate
AEENPPRRT entrapper	reaffirms	**AEFHILSST** faithless
AEENPPRSW newspaper	**AEFFINORS** raffinose	flashiest
AEENPRRTU enrapture	**AEFFIRTUX** affixture	**AEFHIMNRS** fisherman
AEENPRSSS spareness	**AEFFLLRUY** fearfully	**AEFHINORS** fashioner
AEENPRSST peartness	**AEFFLLTUY** fatefully	refashion

AEFHINTTT	antitheft	**AEFILORSS**	foresails	**AEFLOSSTT**	falsettos
AEFHIORSS	oarfishes	**AEFILOSTT**	floatiest	**AEFLPPRSY**	flypapers
AEFHIPRSS	spearfish	**AEFILRSTT**	filtrates	**AEFLPRRUY**	prayerful
AEFHIRSST	ratfishes	**AEFILRSTU**	filatures	**AEFMNOORW**	forewoman
AEFHISSSW	sawfishes	**AEFILRSTW**	welfarist	**AEFMORSST**	foremasts
AEFHKNORS	foreshank	**AEFILSSTV**	festivals		mortsafes
AEFHLLTUY	hatefully	**AEFILSTTU**	faultiest	**AEFMORSTT**	aftermost
AEFHLNNPY	halfpenny		fistulate	**AEFMORSVW**	waveforms
AEFHLNOST	halftones	**AEFILSTUU**	fauteuils	**AEFNNOORT**	afternoon
AEFHLNSSW	newsflash	**AEFIMMNRT**	firmament	**AEFNNSSTU**	unfastens
AEFHLORSV	flashover	**AEFIMNOSS**	foaminess	**AEFNOPRRS**	profaners
AEFHLORTY	O'Flaherty	**AEFIMNOST**	manifesto	**AEFNORRSW**	forewarns
AEFHMORST	fathomers	**AEFIMNOTX**	tamoxifen	**AEFNORSST**	seafronts
AEFHMORSU	farmhouse	**AEFIMNSST**	manifests	**AEFNORTTU**	fortunate
AEFHORRTU	Our Father	**AEFIMORSS**	misfeasor	**AEFNORTVW**	wavefront
AEFHORSTW	aftershow	**AEFIMORTV**	formative	**AEFNORTWY**	Fort Wayne
AEFIIKLRY	fairylike	**AEFINNSST**	faintness	**AEFNRRSST**	transfers
AEFIILLNS	nailfiles	**AEFINOOTT**	foetation	**AEFNRSSTU**	aftersuns
AEFIILMNS	semifinal	**AEFINOPRR**	poriferan		transfuse
AEFIILMPR	amplifier	**AEFINOPRS**	pinafores	**AEFOOPRRW**	wearproof
AEFIILMPS	amplifies	**AEFINORSU**	nefarious	**AEFOPRRST**	foreparts
AEFIILNNT	infantile	**AEFINOSTY**	Sainte Foy	**AEFOPRRTY**	prefatory
AEFIILNSS	finalises	**AEFINRTZZ**	frizzante	**AEFOPSSTT**	softpaste
AEFIILNSZ	finalizes	**AEFINSSTT**	fattiness	**AEFORRSSW**	forswears
AEFIILQRU	qualifier	**AEFIORSTV**	favorites	**AEFORRSUV**	favourers
AEFIILQSU	qualifies	**AEFIORTUV**	favourite	**AEFORSSTY**	forestays
AEFIILRST	frailties	**AEFIPRRST**	firetraps	**AEFRRSTTU**	frustrate
AEFIILSSS	salsifies	**AEFIPRSUW**	superwaif	**AEGGGINRU**	regauging
AEFIILSST	falsities	**AEFKLLUWY**	wakefully	**AEGGGIRWW**	wigwagger
AEFIIMNSS	infamises	**AEFKLNOSW**	snowflake	**AEGGHILMS**	Gilgamesh
AEFIIMNSZ	infamizes	**AEFKLORSW**	falsework	**AEGGHINNR**	rehanging
AEFIIMSTT	mattifies	**AEFKMORRW**	framework	**AEGGHINRT**	gathering
AEFIINRTU	infuriate	**AEFKNNRSS**	frankness	**AEGGHIRTZ**	gigahertz
AEFIIPRST	aperitifs	**AEFKOPRSS**	forspeaks	**AEGGHISST**	shaggiest
AEFIIRRST	ratifiers	**AEFKORRSS**	forsakers	**AEGGHOPRR**	ergograph
AEFIIRSST	satisfier	**AEFLLLNNY**	flannelly	**AEGGHOPRY**	geography
AEFIISSST	satisfies	**AEFLLNTTU**	flatulent	**AEGGIINNR**	regaining
AEFIISTTU	fatuities	**AEFLLORST**	fellators	**AEGGIIORV**	Viareggio
AEFIISTVX	fixatives		forestall	**AEGGILLRS**	grillages
AEFIKLNSS	flakiness	**AEFLLORSV**	overfalls	**AEGGILNNR**	enlarging
AEFILLNOT	fellation	**AEFLLPSTU**	platefuls		largening
AEFILLNOX	flexional	**AEFLLRTUY**	tearfully	**AEGGILNNS**	gleanings
AEFILLNST	flatlines	**AEFLLSSTU**	faultless	**AEGGILNRV**	graveling
AEFILLOOT	foliolate	**AEFLMORSU**	fumaroles	**AEGGILNRZ**	reglazing
AEFILLRSW	firewalls	**AEFLMORTU**	formulate	**AEGGIMMNT**	gemmating
AEFILLRTX	fellatrix	**AEFLMORWY**	mayflower	**AEGGIMNSS**	messaging
AEFILMMOR	oriflamme	**AEFLMOSTU**	flameouts	**AEGGIMSSU**	misgauges
AEFILMNOS	Isle of Man	**AEFLMRSTU**	masterful	**AEGGINNRR**	garnering
AEFILMNRS	inflamers	**AEFLNNOST**	fontanels	**AEGGINNRV**	engraving
AEFILMNST	filaments	**AEFLNNSTY**	fentanyls	**AEGGINOOR**	gorgoneia
AEFILMNTU	fulminate	**AEFLNOOSS**	aloofness	**AEGGINORR**	Gregorian
AEFILMORS	formalise	**AEFLNOPRY**	profanely	**AEGGINORT**	Agrigento
AEFILMORZ	formalize	**AEFLNOPST**	pantofles	**AEGGINOSY**	easygoing
AEFILMRSW	welfarism	**AEFLNOPTU**	pantoufle	**AEGGINPRS**	presaging
AEFILNNUZ	influenza	**AEFLNRSTU**	flaunters	**AEGGINPRT**	pargeting
AEFILNORT	reflation	**AEFLNSSUW**	awfulness	**AEGGINRRT**	gartering
AEFILNRSS	frailness	**AEFLOOPTT**	footplate		regrating
AEFILNRST	inflaters	**AEFLOORSS**	seafloors	**AEGGINRRU**	rearguing
AEFILNRSU	frauleins	**AEFLORRSV**	flavorers	**AEGGINRST**	restaging
AEFILNRTU	flauntier	**AEFLORRUV**	flavourer	**AEGGINRTT**	targeting
AEFILOORS	aerofoils	**AEFLORSTW**	fleaworts	**AEGGINSTT**	gestating
AEFILORRT	rotiferal	**AEFLORTWW**	waterfowl	**AEGGINTTZ**	gazetting

AEGGIOPRS	arpeggios	
AEGGIQSTU	quaggiest	
AEGGLNPST	eggplants	
AEGGLNRRY	glengarry	
AEGGLORSY	gargoyles	
AEGGLRRST	straggler	
AEGGLRSST	straggles	
AEGGMORRT	mortgager	
AEGGMORST	mortgages	
AEGGNNRTU	Trengganu	
AEGGNORSW	waggoners	
AEGGNOSUY	synagogue	
AEGGNRSST	gangsters	
AEGGORRSS	aggressor	
AEGHHINRS	rehashing	
AEGHHINST	sheathing	
AEGHHIRTU	haughtier	
AEGHHOPTY	theophagy	
AEGHIIINP	Iphigenia	
AEGHIKNNR	hankering	
	harkening	
AEGHIKNPR	phreaking	
AEGHIKNRS	shrinkage	
AEGHILLMS	megillahs	
AEGHILLSS	shigellas	
AEGHILMST	megaliths	
AEGHILNNS	hanseling	
AEGHILNRS	narghiles	
	nargilehs	
	shearling	
AEGHILNRT	earthling	
	haltering	
	lathering	
AEGHILNST	athelings	
AEGHILNSV	shaveling	
AEGHILRST	ghastlier	
	thirlages	
AEGHILRSV	gravelish	
AEGHIMMNR	hammering	
AEGHIMNPR	hampering	
AEGHIMNRT	nightmare	
AEGHIMNWY	Hemingway	
AEGHIMORR	hierogram	
AEGHIMPPR	epiphragm	
AEGHINNPP	happening	
AEGHINNST	hastening	
AEGHINOPS	siphonage	
AEGHINPRS	reshaping	
AEGHINPRT	threaping	
AEGHINPUV	upheaving	
AEGHINRRS	garnisher	
AEGHINRSS	garnishes	
AEGHINRST	ingathers	
AEGHINRSW	rewashing	
AEGHINRTT	threating	
AEGHINRTU	naughtier	
AEGHINRTW	nightwear	
	wreathing	
AEGHINSSU	anguishes	
AEGHINSTT	gnathites	
AEGHINSTU	naughties	
AEGHIOOPS	oesophagi	
AEGHIPPRS	epigraphs	
AEGHIPPRY	epigraphy	
AEGHIPRRS	serigraph	
AEGHIPSTT	spaghetti	
AEGHISSTU	Aegisthus	
AEGHLLMPY	megaphyll	
AEGHLMNNT	lengthman	
AEGHLOOPR	oleograph	
AEGHLOORR	logorrhea	
AEGHLORTT	larghetto	
AEGHLOSSU	goulashes	
AEGHLRSTU	slaughter	
AEGHMNOPR	nephogram	
AEGHMOPST	apothegms	
AEGHMPRVY	hypergamy	
AEGHNNOOR	gonorrhea	
AEGHNOPST	heptagons	
	pathogens	
AEGHNOPTY	pathogeny	
AEGHNORSV	hangovers	
	overhangs	
AEGHNOSTU	shogunate	
AEGHNPRSY	pharynges	
AEGHOPPRS	prophages	
AEGHOPPSY	apophyges	
AEGHOPRST	grapeshot	
AEGHOPSSU	esophagus	
AEGHORSST	shortages	
AEGIIKLNT	giantlike	
AEGIILLNN	lilangeni	
AEGIILLRS	grisaille	
AEGIILLRT	argillite	
AEGIILLSU	aiguilles	
AEGIILMNR	remailing	
AEGIILMSV	vigesimal	
AEGIILNNT	entailing	
AEGIILNPT	epilating	
AEGIILNRR	rerailing	
AEGIILNRS	realising	
AEGIILNRT	retailing	
AEGIILNRZ	realizing	
AEGIILNSS	signalise	
AEGIILNST	gainliest	
AEGIILNSZ	signalize	
AEGIILNTV	genitival	
	vigilante	
AEGIILNTY	geniality	
AEGIILSTT	litigates	
AEGIILSTV	vestigial	
AEGIIMMRT	immigrate	
AEGIIMMTT	migmatite	
AEGIIMMNR	remaining	
AEGIIMNNX	examining	
AEGIIMNRS	imaginers	
	migraines	
AEGIIMOSS	isogamies	
AEGIIMSTT	mitigates	
AEGIINNRT	retaining	
AEGIINNVW	inweaving	
AEGIINORT	originate	
AEGIINOTT	goniatite	
AEGIINPRR	repairing	
AEGIINPTX	expiating	
AEGIINRST	grainiest	
AEGIINRTT	granitite	
	iterating	
AEGIINSTT	instigate	
AEGIIRRST	irrigates	
AEGIIRSTT	Stagirite	
AEGIIRSTV	gravities	
AEGIISSTV	visagiste	
AEGIJNORS	jargonise	
AEGIJNORZ	jargonize	
AEGIJNTUU	unijugate	
AEGIKKMNR	kingmaker	
AEGIKLLSS	glasslike	
AEGIKLLST	Gaitskell	
AEGIKLNSW	weaklings	
AEGIKLRSS	grasslike	
AEGIKMNRR	remarking	
AEGIKMNRT	marketing	
AEGIKNQSU	squeaking	
AEGIKNRST	streaking	
AEGIKNSSW	gawkiness	
AEGILLLLY	illegally	
AEGILLLNU	gallinule	
AEGILLMNT	metalling	
AEGILLNNP	panelling	
AEGILLNOS	lignaloes	
AEGILLNQU	equalling	
AEGILLNRS	signaller	
AEGILLNRU	laureling	
AEGILLNRV	Granville	
	ravelling	
AEGILLNTU	lingulate	
AEGILLPPR	Grappelli	
AEGILLPPU	pupillage	
AEGILLPRS	aspergill	
	pillagers	
AEGILLPSS	spillages	
AEGILLRRU	guerrilla	
AEGILLRSS	salesgirl	
AEGILLRST	allergist	
	gallerist	
AEGILLRSU	guerillas	
AEGILLRSV	villagers	
AEGILLSST	legalists	
	stillages	
AEGILMNNP	emplaning	
AEGILMNNS	signalmen	
AEGILMNNT	alignment	
	lamenting	
AEGILMNPX	exampling	
AEGILMNRS	maligners	
	malingers	
AEGILMNRV	marveling	
AEGILMNST	ligaments	
AEGILMNTU	emulating	
	glutamine	
AEGILMORR	rigmarole	
AEGILMORS	glamorise	
AEGILMORZ	glamorize	
AEGILMOSU	São Miguel	
AEGILMRSX	lexigrams	

AEGILNNNP	enplaning	**AEGIMMNSU**	magnesium	**AEGINOSTT**	gestation
AEGILNNOR	reloaning	**AEGIMMNNR**	remanning	**AEGINOTTU**	outeating
AEGILNNRS	learnings	**AEGIMMNNU**	unmeaning	**AEGINPPRR**	preparing
AEGILNNST	gantlines	**AEGIMMNNO**	enamoring	**AEGINPPRY**	prepaying
AEGILNNSU	unsealing		omnirange	**AEGINPRRU**	uprearing
AEGILNNSV	enslaving	**AEGIMMNNOT**	Montaigne	**AEGINPRSS**	aspersing
AEGILNNSW	weanlings	**AEGIMMNNRT**	germinant		preassign
AEGILNNSY	yeanlings	**AEGIMMNNSS**	manginess		repassing
AEGILNNTV	levanting	**AEGIMMNNSU**	unseaming	**AEGINPRST**	repasting
AEGILNOPX	poleaxing	**AEGIMMNORT**	morganite		trapesing
AEGILNORU	neuroglia	**AEGIMMNOSZ**	Egas Moniz	**AEGINPRTT**	pattering
AEGILNORY	legionary	**AEGIMMNPPR**	pampering	**AEGINPSTY**	egyptians
AEGILNOST	gelations	**AEGIMMNPRR**	prearming	**AEGINQRUV**	quavering
	legations	**AEGIMMNPRT**	tampering	**AEGINRRST**	arresting
AEGILNPRS	relapsing	**AEGIMMNPRV**	revamping		serrating
AEGILNPRT	paltering	**AEGIMMNRRW**	rewarming	**AEGINRRTU**	garniture
AEGILNPRY	parleying	**AEGIMMNRSS**	Massinger	**AEGINRSSS**	assigners
	replaying	**AEGIMMNRST**	emigrants		reassigns
AEGILNPSS	salpinges		mastering	**AEGINRSST**	asserting
AEGILNQSU	squealing		streaming	**AEGINRSTT**	restating
AEGILNRSS	grainless	**AEGIMMNRSU**	geraniums	**AEGINRSTU**	gauntries
	signalers		measuring		signature
AEGILNRST	integrals	**AEGIMMNRTT**	mattering	**AEGINRSTV**	vintagers
	teraglins	**AEGIMMNSTT**	magnetist	**AEGINRTTT**	tattering
	triangles	**AEGIMMNSTU**	maungiest	**AEGINRTTU**	Ungaretti
AEGILNRSV	slavering	**AEGIMMOSTY**	stegomyia	**AEGINRTTY**	yattering
AEGILNRSY	layerings	**AEGIMMQRSU**	quagmires	**AEGINSSSS**	assessing
	syringeal	**AEGIMMRSST**	sterigmas		gassiness
	yearlings	**AEGIMMRSTY**	magistery	**AEGINSSST**	staginess
AEGILNRTU	granulite	**AEGIMMSSSU**	misusages	**AEGINSSTT**	angstiest
AEGILNRTV	traveling	**AEGINNNRS**	ensnaring	**AEGINSSUZ**	gauziness
AEGILNRTY	ingrately	**AEGINNNTT**	tenanting	**AEGINSTTT**	attesting
AEGILNRUV	revaluing	**AEGINNORS**	reasoning	**AEGINSTUU**	Augustine
AEGILNRWY	wearingly	**AEGINNORW**	Norwegian	**AEGIPRTUV**	purgative
AEGILNSST	tasseling	**AEGINNORZ**	organzine	**AEGIRRRST**	registrar
AEGILNSSW	wineglass	**AEGINNOSS**	seasoning	**AEGIRSSST**	grassiest
AEGILNSTY	teasingly	**AEGINNOST**	negations	**AEGISTTUV**	gustative
AEGILOOPS	apologies	**AEGINNOSU**	guanosine	**AEGJLSTUU**	jugulates
	apologise	**AEGINNOTT**	negotiant	**AEGKLNOOP**	pokelogan
AEGILOOPZ	apologize	**AEGINNPPR**	Perpignan	**AEGKLNOPS**	Longs Peak
AEGILOOTY	aetiology	**AEGINNPRT**	parenting	**AEGKORSTT**	agterskot
AEGILOPSS	spoilages	**AEGINNPTT**	patenting	**AEGLLNOPW**	alpenglow
AEGILORSS	gasoliers	**AEGINNRSS**	ranginess	**AEGLLNOST**	gallstone
	girasoles	**AEGINNRST**	gannister	**AEGLLOOOZ**	zoogloeal
	seraglios	**AEGINNRSW**	answering	**AEGLLOPRS**	gallopers
AEGILORSU	glaireous	**AEGINNRSY**	yearnings	**AEGLLOSSW**	gallowses
AEGILORTV	levigator	**AEGINNRTT**	integrant	**AEGLLOSTT**	tollgates
AEGILPPRR	papergirl		nattering	**AEGLLRRUY**	regularly
AEGILPPSS	slippages	**AEGINNSST**	assenting	**AEGLLRTUY**	tegularly
AEGILPRTY	pterygial	**AEGINNSSU**	sanguines	**AEGLLSSSS**	glassless
AEGILRRRU	irregular	**AEGINNSTU**	unseating	**AEGLMMORY**	myelogram
AEGILRSTU	glauriest	**AEGINNTTU**	tautening	**AEGLMNNOS**	mangonels
	ligatures	**AEGINOPRS**	Singapore	**AEGLMNOOY**	anemology
AEGILRSUV	vulgarise	**AEGINOPRT**	operating	**AEGLMNORW**	angleworm
AEGILRSVW	lawgivers	**AEGINOPST**	pinotages	**AEGLMORTY**	algometry
AEGILRTUV	virgulate	**AEGINORRS**	organiser	**AEGLMOSTV**	megavolts
AEGILRUVZ	vulgarize	**AEGINORRV**	granivore	**AEGLNNOOT**	Long Eaton
AEGILSSST	glassiest	**AEGINORRZ**	organizer	**AEGLNNSTU**	untangles
AEGIMMNOT	gemmation	**AEGINORSS**	organises	**AEGLNOPRY**	gyroplane
AEGIMMNRU	germanium	**AEGINORSZ**	organizes	**AEGLNORSU**	granulose
AEGIMMNRY	yammering	**AEGINORTT**	gittarone	**AEGLNOSSW**	wagonless
AEGIMMNST	magnetism	**AEGINORVW**	overawing	**AEGLNOSTU**	langouste

AEGLNRRST	strangler	AEGPRRRUY	prayer rug	AEHILORST	horsetail
AEGLNRRSW	wranglers	AEHHHILLOP	halophile		isotheral
AEGLNRSST	strangles	AEHHHILLPT	tephillah	AEHILOSTT	heliostat
AEGLNRSTY	strangely	AEHHHILLTW	Whitehall	AEHILPPTY	epiphytal
AEGLNSTTU	gauntlets	AEHHHILLTY	healthily	AEHILPRSS	splashier
AEGLNSTUU	ungulates	AEHHHILMST	healthism	AEHILPSST	plashiest
AEGLOOOSZ	zoogloeas	AEHHHILNPT	phthalein	AEHILRSSV	lavishers
AEGLOOPSU	apologues	AEHHHIMPRS	Hampshire	AEHILRSTY	hairstyle
AEGLOPPRU	propagule	AEHHHIORRS	horsehair	AEHIMNNOT	anthemion
AEGLOPRSY	playgoers	AEHHHIPPSS	shipshape	AEHIMNORS	harmonies
AEGLORRTU	regulator	AEHHHISSVY	yeshivahs		harmonise
AEGLORSTV	travelogs	AEHHHISTWW	whitewash	AEHIMNORZ	harmonize
AEGLORTTY	tetralogy	AEHHHLNTUY	unhealthy	AEHIMNPSS	misshapen
AEGLPPRRS	grapplers	AEHHHLOPTY	halophyte	AEHIMNPST	pantheism
AEGLRSSSS	grassless	AEHHHLPRTY	hypethral	AEHIMNRSU	humaniser
AEGLRSSSU	sugarless	AEHHHMOOPT	homeopath	AEHIMNRUZ	humanizer
AEGMMNNORS	gammoners	AEHHHMORRT	Rotherham	AEHIMNSSU	humanises
AEGMMOPRR	programme	AEHHHNOPTY	theophany	AEHIMNSUZ	humanizes
AEGMMRRSU	rummagers	AEHHHNORTW	Hawthorne	AEHIMNTTY	Hymettian
AEGMNNORT	magnetron	AEHHHNRSSS	harshness	AEHIMOSST	hematosis
AEGMNNOST	magnetons	AEHHHOPPST	phosphate	AEHIMPSSS	misshapes
AEGMNORRW	warmonger	AEHHHOPTTY	theopathy	AEHIMPSST	shipmates
AEGMNORSU	germanous	AEHHHORSTT	Ashtoreth		steamship
AEGMNORSV	mangroves	AEHHHOSSUW	washhouse	AEHIMPSTT	empathist
AEGMNORTU	augmentor	AEHHHRRSST	thrashers	AEHIMQSSU	squeamish
AEGMNOTTU	mangetout	AEHIIKRST	terakihis	AEHIMRSST	marshiest
AEGMNRSTU	arguments	AEHIILMTU	humiliate	AEHINNRTU	Ruthenian
AEGMOOSUX	exogamous	AEHIILNOP	neophilia	AEHINNSTX	xanthines
AEGMOPRSW	gapeworms	AEHIILNRS	hairlines	AEHINOPST	pantihose
AEGMORSSS	gossamers	AEHIILNTX	antihelix	AEHINORSS	hoariness
AEGMORSSY	gossamery	AEHIIMNST	histamine	AEHINORTT	anorthite
AEGMORSTY	gasometry	AEHIIMRST	hetairism	AEHINOSTT	thionates
AEGMPRSSU	grampuses	AEHIIMRTY	Himyarite	AEHINPPRU	unhappier
AEGMPRSUZ	gazumpers	AEHIINOPT	Ethiopian	AEHINPPSS	happiness
AEGMPSSTU	stumpages	AEHIINRSS	hairiness	AEHINPPTX	Xanthippe
AEGNNOPST	pentagons	AEHIIPSTT	hepatitis	AEHINPRST	perianths
AEGNNORST	negatrons	AEHIIRSTT	hetairist	AEHINPRUW	wharepuni
AEGNNORSY	nongreasy	AEHIJLOSU	jailhouse	AEHINPSSS	apishness
AEGNNPRTU	repugnant	AEHIKKLRS	sharklike	AEHINPSST	thespians
AEGNNSSTU	gauntness	AEHIKLMNU	humanlike	AEHINPSSY	Sisyphean
AEGNORRWY	garryowen	AEHIKLMRS	marshlike	AEHINPSTT	pantheist
AEGNORSST	ragstones	AEHIKLSWY	weakishly	AEHINRRST	tarnisher
AEGNORSTT	tetragons	AEHIKNSSS	shakiness	AEHINRRSU	Arrhenius
AEGNORSTU	argentous	AEHILLMOP	philomela	AEHINRRSV	varnisher
	outranges	AEHILLNRT	allethrin	AEHINRRST	tarnishes
AEGNRRSST	strangers	AEHILLNSV	Nashville	AEHINRSSV	vanishers
AEGNRSSTT	strangest	AEHILLPTY	philately		varnishes
AEGNRSSTU	assurgent	AEHILLSTT	tallithes	AEHINRSSW	sherwanis
AEGNSTTTU	tungstate	AEHILLTTY	lethality	AEHINRSTW	tarwhines
AEGOOSWYZ	wayzgoose	AEHILLTWW	whitewall	AEHINSSST	hastiness
AEGOPPSST	stoppages	AEHILLTWY	wealthily	AEHINSSSW	washiness
AEGOPRRUW	groupware	AEHILMNOP	nemophila	AEHIOPPRY	hyperopia
AEGOPSSTT	gateposts	AEHILMSTU	Shulamite	AEHIOPRSS	aphorises
AEGORRNST	garroters	AEHILNNOT	anthelion	AEHIOPRST	atrophies
AEGORRRTT	garrotter	AEHILNOOZ	heliozoan	AEHIOPRSZ	aphorizes
AEGORRSTT	garotters	AEHILNOPR	parhelion	AEHIORRTT	throatier
	garrottes	AEHILNOST	hailstone	AEHIORSTT	hesitator
AEGORRSTU	surrogate	AEHILNOUZ	Zhou En Lai	AEHIORSTU	authorise
AEGORSSTU	stegosaur	AEHILNPRS	planisher	AEHIORSTX	rheotaxis
AEGORSTTY	gestatory	AEHILNPSS	planishes	AEHIORTTV	hortative
AEGORSUVY	voyageurs	AEHILNQRU	harlequin	AEHIORTUZ	authorize
AEGOSSSTU	outgasses	AEHILNRSU	inhaulers	AEHIOSSTT	athetosis

AEHIPPRSS	sapphires	AEHNNOPRT	Parthenon	AEIIILLRST	listerial
AEHIPRRST	phratries	AEHNNOPST	pantheons	AEIIILLSTV	illatives
AEHIPRSTT	therapist	AEHNNRSSU	unharness	AEIIILLTTT	titillate
AEHIQRSSU	squashier	AEHNOOPPV	hypopnoea	AEIIILMNNR	mainliner
AEHIRRSSV	ravishers	AEHNOOPPR	harpooner	AEIIILMNNS	mainlines
AEHIRRSTW	swarthier	AEHNOOPSX	saxophone	AEIIILMNNT	eliminant
AEHIRSSTT	trashiest	AEHNOPPSY	payphones	AEIIILMNOS	alimonies
AEHIRSSTW	wairshest	AEHNOPRST	hapterons	AEIIILMNOZ	iminazole
AEHIRSSTY	hysterias		Parthenos	AEIIILMNSU	aluminise
AEHJLLNOS	Hall-Jones	AEHNOPRTU	neuropath		Suleiman I
AEHKLNOPV	Plekhanov	AEHNOPRTY	honeytrap	AEIIILMNUZ	aluminize
AEHKLNSST	thankless	AEHNOPSST	stanhopes	AEIIILMOSV	malvoisie
AEHKLRRSU	Karlsruhe	AEHNOPSSU	saphenous	AEIIILMPRS	imperials
AEHKNSSWW	newshawks	AEHNOPSTY	pantyhose	AEIIILMRSS	serialism
AEHKORRTW	earthwork	AEHNORSTT	northeast	AEIIILMRTT	literatim
AEHKOSSTU	shakeouts	AEHNPRSSS	sharpness	AEIIILMSTT	militates
AEHLLLMPS	lampshell	AEHNPRSXY	pharynxes	AEIIILNNOT	lineation
AEHLLMRTY	thermally	AEHNRSTTU	earthnuts	AEIIILNNRT	triennial
AEHLLNNOT	nonlethal	AEHNSSTUW	unswathes	AEIIILNNSV	venial sin
AEHLLNOOP	allophone	AEHOOOORRT	otorrhoea	AEIIILNNSY	asininely
AEHLLNRST	enthralls	AEHOOPRRY	pyorrhoea	AEIIILNOPT	epilation
AEHLLORSW	hallowers	AEHOOPSTT	osteopath	AEIIILNOTV	inviolate
	shallower	AEHOOSSTU	oasthouse	AEIIILNPRT	reptilian
AEHLLPSSU	phalluses	AEHOPPSSY	apophyses	AEIIILNPST	platinise
AEHLLPSSY	haplessly	AEHOPSSTT	posthaste	AEIIILNPTV	plaintive
AEHLLSSTU	thalluses	AEHOPSSTU	phaseouts	AEIIILNPTZ	platinize
AEHLMOOST	loathsome		taphouses	AEIIILNRRS	airliners
AEHLMOSSU	almshouse	AEHOPSSTW	sweatshop	AEIIILNRRT	trilinear
AEHLMPPST	pamphlets	AEHOPTTUY	autophyte	AEIIILNRST	saintlier
AEHLNNOPR	alpenhorn	AEHORRRSW	harrowers	AEIIILNRSU	uniserial
AEHLNNOSST	loathness	AEHORRSSW	warhorses	AEIIILNRTY	linearity
AEHLNPSUY	unshapely	AEHORSSSW	sawhorses	AEIIILNSST	alienists
AEHLNRTUY	unearthly	AEHORSSTT	rheostats	AEIIILNSTW	waistline
AEHLNSTUZ	hazelnuts	AEHORSSTU	authoress	AEIIILNSTZ	latinizes
AEHLOPPSY	polyphase		rathouses	AEIIILNTVY	veniality
AEHLOPRRY	pyorrheal	AEHORSTVW	shortwave	AEIIILORST	solitaire
AEHLOPRSW	plowshare	AEHORSTVY	overhasty	AEIIILORSV	Lavoisier
AEHLOPRSY	horseplay	AEHORSTWY	seaworthy	AEIIILORTV	variolite
AEHLOPSTT	hotplates	AEHOSSSTU	South Seas	AEIIILOSTV	isolative
AEHLOPSUY	playhouse	AEHOSSTTU	southeast	AEIIILOTVV	violative
AEHLORSUV	overhauls	AEHQRSSSU	squashers	AEIIILPPST	tailpipes
AEHLORTUU	outhauler	AEHRRSTTW	thwarters	AEIIILQSTU	qualities
AEHLORTWY	holy water	AEHRSSTUU	thesaurus	AEIIILRRST	triserial
AEHLPPRST	thrapples	AEIIILNRT	initialer	AEIIILRRSV	rivalries
AEHLPRRSU	spherular	AEIIILRVZ	vizierial	AEIIILRSTU	ritualise
AEHLPRSSS	splashers	AEIIILTVX	lixiviate	AEIIILRSTV	vitaliser
AEHLPSSTU	sulphates	AEIIIMRSS	Ramses III	AEIIILRTUZ	ritualize
AEHLRSSTU	Althusser	AEIIIMTTV	imitative	AEIIILRTVZ	vitalizer
AEHLRSSTW	wrathless	AEIIINNST	inanities	AEIIILSSTV	vitalises
AEHMMOORT	harmotome	AEIIINSTT	initiates	AEIIILSSUV	visualise
AEHMNNRTU	manhunter	AEIIJLNUV	juvenilia	AEIIILSTVZ	vitalizes
AEHMNNSSU	humanness	AEIIKKTTW	kittiwake	AEIIILSUVZ	visualize
AEHMNOSWW	washwomen	AEIIKLLNS	silkaline	AEIIMMNSX	minimaxes
AEHMNRRWY	wherryman		snaillike	AEIIMMRSS	Semiramis
AEHMOOPRS	shampooer	AEIIKLNOT	kaolinite	AEIIMMRSX	maximiser
AEHMOPRST	metaphors	AEIIKLNOZ	kaolinize	AEIIMMRXZ	maximizer
AEHMORRTW	earthworm	AEIIKLNST	saintlike	AEIIMMSSX	maximises
	heartworm	AEIIKLRST	triskelia	AEIIMMSXZ	maximizes
AEHMORTWW	wheatworm	AEIIKMRSS	kaiserism	AEIIMNNRT	nitramine
AEHMOSSTT	hemostats	AEIIKRSTT	keratitis	AEIIMNOPP	Pompeiian
AEHMPPRSY	pamphreys	AEIILLMNN	millennia	AEIIMNORU	iminourea
AEHMSSTTY	amethysts	AEIILLMRS	ramillies	AEIIMNPST	impatiens

AEIIMNPTT	impatient	**AEIIJNSSZZ**	jazziness	**AEIILLRSTW**	stairwell
AEIIMNRTT	intimater	**AEIIJNSTTU**	jauntiest	**AEIILLRTWY**	waterlily
	Marinetti	**AEIIJORSST**	jarosites	**AEIILLRVXY**	vexillary
AEIIMNRTU	miniature	**AEIKKLLOO**	lookalike	**AEIILLSSTT**	sittellas
AEIIMNSTT	intimates	**AEIKKLLST**	stalklike	**AEIILMMNPS**	pelmanism
AEIIMPRRS	impairers	**AEIKKNNSS**	snakeskin	**AEIILMMNST**	mentalism
	primaries	**AEIKLLNPT**	plantlike	**AEIILMMORS**	memorials
AEIIMPRSY	perimysia	**AEIKLLNRY**	Killarney	**AEIILMMOST**	immolates
AEIIMPSSV	impassive	**AEIKLLTUV**	vaultlike	**AEIILMMRST**	trilemmas
AEIIMRRSV	arrivisme	**AEIKLLTWZ**	waltzlike	**AEIILMNNOS**	minneolas
AEIINNNTV	antivenin	**AEIKLMNOS**	kalsomine	**AEIILMNNOT**	melatonin
AEIINNOST	antinoise	**AEIKLMNOW**	womanlike	**AEIILMNNPS**	plainsmen
AEIINNPTT	inpatient	**AEIKLNNSS**	lankiness	**AEIILMNNSS**	manliness
AEIINNRSS	raininess	**AEIKLNOVY**	Nikolayev	**AEIILMNOOT**	emotional
	sirenians	**AEIKLNPSS**	skiplanes	**AEIILMNOPR**	prolamine
AEIINNRSV	Nivernais	**AEIKLNSSS**	sealskins	**AEIILMNORS**	almonries
AEIINNRTT	itinerant	**AEIKLQSUY**	squeakily		normalise
AEIINNRTU	uraninite	**AEIKLRSTW**	strawlike	**AEIILMNORT**	mentorial
AEIINNSTU	annuities	**AEIKLRSTY**	streakily	**AEIILMNORZ**	normalize
	insinuate	**AEIKLRSVY**	valkyries	**AEIILMNOSS**	loaminess
AEIINOPTX	expiation	**AEIKLRSWY**	walkyries		melanosis
AEIINORTT	iteration	**AEIKLSSTT**	stalkiest	**AEIILMNOTU**	emulation
AEIINOTTV	novitiate	**AEIKMRSST**	mistakers	**AEIILMNPRT**	implanter
AEIINQRSU	quinaries		sitkamers	**AEIILMNPSU**	asplenium
AEIINNRRSU	urinaries	**AEIKNNPRS**	spinnaker	**AEIILMNPSY**	manyplies
AEIINRRTY	itinerary	**AEIKNNSSS**	snakiness	**AEIILMNPTU**	penultima
AEIINRSTW	West Irian	**AEIKNORTU**	ketonuria	**AEIILMNRST**	terminals
AEIINRTUV	urinative	**AEIKNPRSS**	Speranski		tramlines
AEIINSSST	sanitises	**AEIKNPSSW**	pawkiness	**AEIILMNRSU**	semilunar
AEIINSSTZ	sanitizes	**AEIKNQSSU**	quakiness	**AEIILMNRVY**	liveryman
AEIINSTTT	titanites	**AEIKNSSTW**	swankiest	**AEIILMNSST**	maltiness
AEIINSTTV	tantivies	**AEIKORSST**	keratosis	**AEIILMNSTT**	mentalist
AEIIOPRST	topiaries	**AEIKPPQSU**	pipsqueak	**AEIILMNTTY**	mentality
AEIIORSST	ostiaries	**AEIKPRSST**	sparkiest	**AEIILMOPRS**	semipolar
AEIIPRPSTV	privatise	**AEIKRSSST**	asterisks	**AEIILMORRS**	moraliser
AEIIPRSZZ	pizzerias	**AEIILLLMSS**	allelisms	**AEIILMORRZ**	moralizer
AEIIPRTTV	partitive	**AEIILLLRTY**	literally	**AEIILMORSS**	moralises
AEIIPRTVV	privative	**AEIILLMNRY**	millenary	**AEIILMORSZ**	moralizes
AEIIPRTVZ	privatize	**AEIILLMNSY**	seminally	**AEIILMOSTU**	mousetail
AEIIPSSST	epistasis	**AEIILLMSSY**	aimlessly	**AEIILMPRST**	prelatism
AEIIPSSTX	epistaxis	**AEIILLMSTT**	metallist	**AEIILMPSTY**	playtimes
AEIIPSTTT	stipitate	**AEIILLNOPS**	Pisanello	**AEIILMRRSU**	semirural
AEIIRRSST	satiriser	**AEIILLNOPT**	pollinate	**AEIILMRSSY**	mislayers
AEIIRRSTT	arteritis	**AEIILLNPRY**	plenarily	**AEIILMRSTT**	remittals
	irritates	**AEIILLNPST**	panellist	**AEIILMRSTY**	salimetry
AEIIRRSTU	retiarius	**AEIILLNPTT**	petillant	**AEIILMRTTY**	altimetry
AEIIRRSTV	arriviste	**AEIILLNRST**	installer	**AEIILMSSTT**	metalists
AEIIRRSTZ	satirizer		reinstall	**AEIILMSSTU**	simulates
AEIIRSSST	satirises	**AEIILLNRTU**	tellurian	**AEIILMSSUV**	misvalues
AEIIRSSTV	varsities	**AEIILLNRTY**	reliantly	**AEIILMSSVY**	massively
AEIIRSSTW	wisterias	**AEIILLNSTY**	saliently	**AEIILMSTTU**	mutilates
AEIIRSSTZ	satirizes	**AEIILLOPPS**	papillose		stimulate
AEIIRSTTT	tritiates	**AEIILLOPPT**	papillote		ultimates
AEIIRTTTV	attritive		popliteal	**AEIILMSTUU**	mutualise
AEIISSSTV	assistive	**AEIILLOSTV**	volatiles	**AEIILMTUUZ**	mutualize
AEIISTTTV	titivates	**AEIILLOSTY**	loyalties	**AEIILNNNOR**	nonlinear
AEIITTTTV	tittivate	**AEIILLPRSU**	pluralise	**AEIILNNOOP**	Napoleon I
AEIJKKRVY	Reykjavik	**AEIILLPRUZ**	pluralize	**AEIILNNOPR**	nonpareil
AEIJLOPPS	jaloppies	**AEIILLPSST**	pastilles	**AEIILNNOST**	tensional
AEIJLOSSU	jalousies	**AEIILLPSTU**	pulsatile	**AEIILNNOSY**	lyonnaise
AEIJMNNSS	Jansenism	**AEIILLRRTY**	artillery	**AEIILNNOTV**	antinovel
AEIJNRSST	janitress	**AEIILLRSST**	trailless		Valentino

AEILNNPSS	plainness	**AEILOPSST**	spoliates	**AEIMNNOTT**	mentation
AEILNNPSU	peninsula	**AEILORRTT**	literator	**AEIMNNOYZ**	anonymize
AEILNNPTY	pinnately	**AEILORSSS**	solarises	**AEIMNNRST**	mannerist
AEILNNRST	internals	**AEILORSSV**	valorises	**AEIMNOPRT**	protamine
AEILNNTUV	univalent	**AEILORSSZ**	solarizes	**AEIMNOPST**	ptomaines
AEILNOOPS	polonaise	**AEILORSTT**	aristotle	**AEIMNORSS**	masonries
AEILNOORS	erosional		totaliser		romanises
AEILNOPPR	piperonal	**AEILORSTV**	violaters	**AEIMNORSU**	uniramose
AEILNOPPS	panoplies	**AEILORSTY**	royalties	**AEIMNORSW**	womaniser
AEILNOPST	sealpoint	**AEILORSVZ**	valorizes	**AEIMNORSZ**	romanizes
AEILNOPSY	Polynesia	**AEILORTTV**	levitator	**AEIMNORTV**	normative
AEILNOPTT	peltation	**AEILORTTZ**	totalizer	**AEIMNORTW**	tirewoman
	potential	**AEILOSSTT**	totalises	**AEIMNORWZ**	womanizer
AEILNORSS	sensorial	**AEILOSTTZ**	totalizes	**AEIMNOSSW**	womanises
AEILNORST	orientals	**AEILPPQSU**	appliques	**AEIMNOSWZ**	womanizes
	relations	**AEILPPRTU**	preputial	**AEIMNPRST**	spearmint
	serotinal	**AEILPPSUV**	appulsive	**AEIMNPSTY**	tympanies
	tensorial	**AEILPRRSS**	reprisals	**AEIMNQRSU**	ramequins
AEILNORSV	versional	**AEILPRSST**	pilasters	**AEIMNRSSU**	aneurisms
AEILNORTT	natrolite	**AEILPRSTT**	paltriest	**AEIMNRSTT**	martinets
AEILNOSSS	sessional		prelatist	**AEIMNRSTU**	antiserum
AEILNOSST	insolates	**AEILPRSTV**	livetraps		ruminates
AEILNOSSX	siloxanes	**AEILPRTVY**	privately	**AEIMNRTTY**	maternity
AEILNPRST	interlaps	**AEILPSSTT**	pastelist	**AEIMNSSSS**	massiness
	strapline	**AEILPSSVY**	passively	**AEIMOOPPT**	pampootie
	triplanes	**AEILPSTTU**	stipulate	**AEIMOPRRT**	imperator
AEILNPRTY	interplay	**AEILPSTUV**	pulsative	**AEIMOPRTX**	proximate
	painterly	**AEILQRRUV**	reliquary	**AEIMORRSU**	armouries
AEILNPSST	panelists	**AEILQRSTU**	quartiles	**AEIMORRSV**	Averroism
AEILNPSTT	tinplates		requitals	**AEIMORSST**	amortises
AEILNPSTV	sapiently	**AEILRRSSU**	ruralises		atomisers
AEILNPTTX	plaintext	**AEILRRSUZ**	ruralizes	**AEIMORSTT**	East Timor
AEILNPTTY	patiently	**AEILRSSST**	slaisters		estimator
AEILNPTUV	pulvinate	**AEILRSSTT**	last rites	**AEIMORSTZ**	amortizes
AEILNRSST	reinstals	**AEILRSSTY**	lay sister		atomizers
	trainless	**AEILRSTTT**	rattliest	**AEIMORTTU**	autotimer
AEILNRSTT	sterilant	**AEILRTUUX**	luxuriate	**AEIMOSTTV**	motivates
AEILNRSTV	intervals	**AEILSSSTV**	vistaless	**AEIMPPRSU**	pauperism
AEILNRSTY	interlays	**AEILSSSTW**	waistless	**AEIMPRRST**	imparters
AEILNRSUV	universal	**AEILSTUXY**	sexuality	**AEIMPRSTU**	septarium
AEILNRTTV	trivalent	**AEIMMMNOT**	mammonite	**AEIMPRTUZ**	trapezium
AEILNRTUV	avirulent	**AEIMMNNOO**	monoamine	**AEIMPSSTW**	swampiest
AEILNRTUY	unreality	**AEIMMNNRS**	mannerism	**AEIMQRSSU**	marquises
AEILNSSST	saintless	**AEIMMNNTU**	minuteman	**AEIMRRRTU**	terrarium
	saltiness	**AEIMMNOPT**	pantomime	**AEIMRRSTY**	martyries
	slatiness	**AEIMMNOSS**	seminomas		martyrise
	stainless	**AEIMMNOST**	ammonites	**AEIMRRTYZ**	martyrize
AEILNSSTT	taintless	**AEIMMNSTZ**	mizenmast	**AEIMRSSST**	asterisms
AEILNSSTU	insulates	**AEIMMPSST**	psammites	**AEIMRSSTT**	mistreats
AEILNSSTW	slantwise	**AEIMMRSST**	smarmiest		teratisms
AEILNSTUY	sinuately	**AEIMMRSSU**	summaries	**AEIMRSTTY**	tasimetry
AEILNSTVY	sylvanite		summarise	**AEIMSSSTT**	misstates
AEILNSUUX	unisexual	**AEIMMRSTX**	mixmaster	**AEINNNOTV**	nonnative
AEILNSUVV	univalves	**AEIMMRSUZ**	summarize	**AEINNNPTU**	Neptunian
AEILOOSTT	ostiolate	**AEIMMSTUV**	summative	**AEINNOPSX**	expansion
AEILOPPST	oppilates	**AEIMNNNOT**	Maintenon	**AEINNOPTT**	panettoni
AEILOPRRS	polariser	**AEIMNNNQU**	mannequin	**AEINNORST**	anointers
AEILOPRRZ	polarizer	**AEIMNNOPR**	prenomina	**AEINNORTV**	nervation
AEILOPRSS	polarises	**AEIMNNOPU**	pneumonia		vernation
AEILOPRST	epilators	**AEIMNNOST**	Minnesota	**AEINNOSST**	sensation
	saprolite		nominates	**AEINNOSTT**	intonates
AEILOPRSZ	polarizes	**AEIMNNOSY**	anonymise	**AEINNOSTU**	Saint-Ouen

AEINNOSTV	innovates	**AEINRRSTT**	restraint	**AEKLNOOPW**	Polokwane
	venations	**AEINRRTTV**	travertin	**AEKLNOSSY**	ankyloses
AEINNOTTT	attention	**AEINRSSTT**	rattiness	**AEKLOPRSW**	ropewalks
	tentation		resistant	**AEKLORSVW**	walkovers
AEINNPPSS	nappiness		straitens	**AEKLPRRSS**	sparklers
AEINNPSST	inaptness	**AEINRSSTU**	sustainer	**AEKMNNORY**	Orkneyman
AEINNRRSS	insnarers	**AEINRSSUZ**	suzerains	**AEKMNOOQU**	moonquake
AEINNRSTT	instanter	**AEINSSSSS**	sassiness	**AEKMNOORR**	moonraker
	intranets	**AEINSSSTT**	tastiness	**AEKMNOPSS**	spokesman
	transient	**AEINSSTTT**	tattiness	**AEKMNRSSU**	unmaskers
AEINNRSTU	Neustrian	**AEINSSTZZ**	snazziest	**AEKMOORRV**	voorkamer
	saturnine	**AEINSSUVV**	vesuvians	**AEKMOORSY**	karyosome
AEINNRSTY	tyrannies	**AEIOORRST**	oratories	**AEKMORSTW**	workmates
	tyrannise	**AEIOPRRST**	priorates	**AEKMPRRSS**	pressmark
AEINNRTUV	aventurin	**AEIOPRRSV**	vaporiser	**AEKNOORST**	snakeroot
AEINNRTVZ	tyrannize	**AEIOPRRVZ**	vaporizer	**AEKNPPSSS**	spanspeks
AEINNSSST	nastiness	**AEIOPRSSV**	vaporises	**AEKNPRRST**	prankster
AEINNSSTT	nattiness	**AEIOPRSTX**	expiators	**AEKNRSSST**	starkness
AEINNSSTW	tawniness	**AEIOPRSVZ**	vaporizes	**AEKNRSTTU**	Turkestan
AEINOOPRT	operation	**AEIOPRTTV**	portative	**AEKOPPRRW**	paperwork
AEINOOPSU	ionopause		vaporetti	**AEKOPRTYY**	karyotype
AEINOPPPR	Popperian	**AEIOPRTXY**	expiatory	**AEKOPSSTU**	outspeaks
AEINOPPRT	appointer	**AEIOPSSTU**	autopsies	**AEKORRWWX**	waxworker
	reappoint	**AEIOPSTTV**	optatives	**AEKORSSTV**	overtasks
AEINOPPST	antipopes	**AEIORSSSU**	ossuaries	**AEKOSSTTU**	stakeouts
AEINOPRSS	aspersion	**AEIORSSTV**	assortive	**AEKQRSSUW**	squawkers
AEINOPRST	patronise	**AEIORSSUV**	savouries	**AELLLMOSU**	malleolus
	Petrosian	**AEIORSTTV**	estivator	**AELLLPTUU**	pullulate
AEINOPRSV	pervasion	**AEIORTUVV**	uvarovite	**AELLLRSTU**	stellular
AEINOPRSY	aepyornis	**AEIOSTUVX**	vexatious	**AELLLSSWY**	lawlessly
AEINOPRTZ	patronize	**AEIPPRRTY**	Tipperary	**AELLMMRUX**	Max Müller
AEINOPSSS	soapiness	**AEIPPRSTU**	peripatus	**AELLMNOOS**	allomones
AEINOQRTU	inquorate	**AEIPRRSSU**	upraisers	**AELLMNOTT**	allotment
	ortanique	**AEIPRSSTU**	prussiate	**AELLMNSSS**	smallness
AEINOQSTU	equations	**AEIPRSTTU**	petaurist	**AELLMOPRY**	permalloy
AEINOQTTU	totaquine	**AEIPRSTUZ**	trapezius	**AELLMORST**	martellos
AEINORRST	serration	**AEIPRSTVY**	varitypes	**AELLMORTU**	Tullamore
AEINORRTV	overtrain	**AEIQRRRSU**	quarriers	**AELLMORTY**	allometry
AEINORSST	assertion	**AEIQRTTUZ**	quartzite	**AELLMOSYZ**	allozymes
	notarises	**AEIQSTUZZ**	quazziest	**AELLNNOTW**	Allentown
	senoritas	**AEIRRSSTT**	starriest	**AELLNOSSY**	loyalness
AEINORSSU	arsenious		traitress	**AELLNOSTW**	stonewall
AEINORSSV	aversions	**AEIRRTTTU**	triturate	**AELLNQUUY**	unequally
AEINORSTT	stationer	**AEIRSSSST**	assisters	**AELLNRTUY**	neutrally
AEINORSTZ	notarizes	**AEIRSSTTU**	tessitura	**AELLNRTVY**	ventrally
AEINOSTVX	vexations	**AEIRSSTTW**	strawiest	**AELLNSSUY**	sensually
AEINPPSSS	sappiness	**AEIRSTTTX**	testatrix	**AELLOOPRT**	allotrope
AEINPPSST	snappiest	**AEIRSTTUU**	auteurist	**AELLOPRRT**	patroller
AEINPRRST	terrapins	**AEIRSTTUY**	austerity	**AELLOPRST**	preallots
	transpire	**AEISSSSTY**	essayists	**AELLOPRSW**	wallopers
AEINPRSST	pinasters	**AEISSTTUW**	sweatsuit	**AELLOPRTW**	potwaller
AEINPRTTY	paternity	**AEJLLOSUY**	jealously	**AELLOPRTY**	prolately
AEINPSSST	pastiness	**AEJMMORRT**	major term	**AELLOPSTY**	allotypes
AEINPSSSW	waspiness	**AEJMNOSTW**	Jamestown	**AELLORRST**	rostellar
AEINPSSTU	supinates	**AEJOPSTUX**	juxtapose	**AELLORSWW**	swallower
AEINPSTTY	antitypes	**AEKKLRRSY**	skylarker		wallowers
AEINQSSTU	quantises	**AEKKMNOOS**	kakemonos	**AELLOSSTW**	sallowest
AEINQSTTU	quaintest	**AEKLLSSST**	stalkless	**AELLOSUYZ**	zealously
AEINQSTUZ	quantizes	**AEKLMOORT**	toolmaker	**AELLQRSSU**	squallers
AEINRRSST	restrains	**AEKLMORSS**	lossmaker	**AELLRSSTY**	artlessly
	strainers	**AEKLMORTW**	metalwork	**AELLRSSYY**	raylessly
	tarriness	**AEKLMRSUY**	yarmulkes	**AELLRSTUW**	Ullswater

AELLTTUXY	textually	**AELORSSSV**	savorless	**AENNOSTTW**	wantonest
AELMMNOSW	almswomen	**AELOSSTTW**	wastelots	**AENNPSSTU**	unaptness
AELMMORST	maelstrom	**AELOSSTUY**	autolyses	**AENNRSTTU**	transeunt
AELMMORSW	mealworms	**AELOSTUUV**	outvalues	**AENNSSTUY**	Sun Yat-sen
AELMMOSUU	mausoleum	**AELOSTUYZ**	autolyzes	**AENOOPSST**	soapstone
AELMNNNTU	annulment	**AELPPRTUW**	Wuppertal		teaspoons
AELMNNOOP	monoplane	**AELPRRRSU**	larrupers	**AENOORRST**	resonator
AELMNNOST	nonmetals	**AELPRRSSW**	sprawlers	**AENOORRTV**	renovator
AELMNNPST	plantsmen	**AELPRRSTT**	prattlers	**AENOPRRST**	prosterna
AELMNOOPR	lampooner	**AELPRSSST**	strapless	**AENOPRSST**	patroness
AELMNOORT	monolater	**AELPRSSTT**	splatters		transpose
AELMNOORY	monolayer	**AELPRSSTU**	pertussal	**AENOPRSTT**	patentors
AELMNOPRT	patrolmen	**AELPSTTUU**	pustulate	**AENOPRSUV**	supernova
AELMNOPSS	neoplasms	**AELQRRTUY**	quarterly	**AENORRSTW**	narrowest
	pleonasms	**AELQRSSUV**	servquals	**AENORRTWW**	waterworn
AELMNOPTU	pulmonate	**AELRRSSTT**	startlers	**AENORSSST**	assentors
AELMNORST	marlstone	**AELRRSSTW**	warstlers	**AENORSSTU**	anestrous
	mestranol	**AELRSSTTU**	lustrates		anoestrus
AELMNORWW	lawnmower	**AEMMNORTY**	manometry	**AENORSTTY**	attorneys
AELMNOSSW	womanless		momentary	**AENPRSSTT**	transepts
AELMNRSTU	menstrual	**AEMMOORST**	roommates	**AENQRRSTU**	quarterns
AELMNRTTU	tremulant	**AEMMORSST**	marmosets	**AENQSSSTU**	squatness
AELMOORSS	salerooms	**AEMMORTTY**	atmometry	**AENRSSSTW**	swartness
	salesroom	**AEMMRSTYY**	asymmetry	**AEOOPPPSS**	pappooses
AELMOPRRS	premolars	**AEMMNNOPST**	Montespan	**AEOOPRRST**	operators
AELMOPSTT	palmettos	**AEMMNNORST**	ornaments	**AEOOPRSTU**	autospore
AELMORSTU	emulators	**AEMMNNORTT**	remontant	**AEOOPRSUX**	auxospore
AELMORSUV	marvelous	**AEMMNNOSWW**	newswoman	**AEOOPRTTV**	vaporetto
AELMOSSTY	atmolyses	**AEMMNOOPRT**	monoptera	**AEOORRSTV**	overroast
AELMOSTTU	mulattoes		protonema	**AEOORRSTZ**	Zoroaster
AELMPPRRST	tramplers	**AEMMNOORST**	anterooms	**AEOORSTTT**	tattooers
AELMPSSSW	swampless	**AEMMNOORTX**	taxonomer	**AEOORSTTV**	rotovates
AELMRSSTT	maltsters	**AEMMNORRSS**	ransomers	**AEOORTTUU**	autoroute
AELNNOOPS	napoleons	**AEMMNORRTU**	numerator	**AEOPRRRTY**	portrayer
AELNNOOSX	naloxones	**AEMMNORSST**	monsteras	**AEOPRRSTT**	prostrate
AELNNOSUX	nonsexual		Sorenstam	**AEOPRRSTU**	pterosaur
AELNNSSUU	annuluses	**AEMMNORSTY**	monastery	**AEOPRRSTW**	spearwort
AELNOPRSS	personals		oysterman	**AEOPRRSUV**	vapourers
AELNOPRSY	layperson	**AEMMNOSSTU**	seamounts	**AEOPRRSVW**	wrapovers
AELNOPSTY	neoplasty	**AEMMNPRTUY**	prytaneum	**AEOPRSSSV**	passovers
AELNORTVW	navelwort	**AEMMNQRRUY**	quarrymen	**AEOPRSSTT**	prostates
AELNPRSSU	purslanes	**AEMMNRSSU**	surnamers	**AEOPSTTUY**	autotypes
AELNPSSSU	spansules	**AEMMNRSSST**	smartness	**AEOQRRSSU**	squarrose
AELNRRUVY	vulnerary	**AEMMNRSSSU**	Rasmussen	**AEOQRSSTU**	quaestors
AELNRSSTT	slatterns	**AEMMNRSSUY**	aneurysms	**AEORRSSST**	assertors
AELNRSTTU	resultant	**AEMMNRSTTU**	transmute		assorters
AELNSSSTU	sultaness	**AEMMNRSTVY**	vestryman	**AEORRSTZZ**	terrazzos
AELNSSSUU	usualness	**AEMOORSTT**	stateroom	**AEORSSSSS**	assessors
AELOOPRVY	parleyvoo	**AEMOOSSST**	maestosos	**AEORSSTTT**	attestors
AELOORRTT	tolerator	**AEMOOSSTU**	autosomes		testators
AELOORSTZ	zoolaters	**AEMOPRRTY**	temporary	**AEORSSTTU**	outstares
AELOPPRSS	prolapses	**AEMOPRSTU**	mousetrap	**AEORSSTUU**	trousseau
AELOPPSTU	populates	**AEMOPRSTW**	tapeworms	**AEORSSTVY**	overstays
AELOPRRSV	reprovals	**AEMOPSTTY**	asymptote	**AEPPRRSST**	strappers
AELOPRRTW	pearlwort	**AEMORRRSU**	armourers	**AEPPRSSUY**	papyruses
AELOPRRTY	proletary	**AEMORSTTU**	tautomers	**AEPPRSTUU**	suppurate
AELOPRSSV	vaporless	**AEMOSTTZZ**	mozzettas	**AEPQRRTUY**	parquetry
AELOPRSTU	sporulate	**AEMQRRTUY**	marquetry	**AEPRRSSTU**	superstar
AELOPRSVY	overplays	**AENNOPRST**	patronnes	**AEPRSSSSU**	surpasses
AELOPSSSU	espousals	**AENNOPSST**	pentosans	**AEPRSSSTT**	tapstress
AELOPSTTU	postulate	**AENNORRST**	resnatron	**AEPRSSTTU**	upstaters
AELORRSTX	extrorsal	**AENNORSSU**	unreasons	**AEQRSSTTU**	squatters

AERRSSTUU	susurrate	
AFFGGINUW	guffawing	
AFFGHIRST	affrights	
AFFGIIMNR	affirming	
AFFGIINRT	tariffing	
AFFGIIRST	sgraffiti	
AFFGILNNS	snaffling	
AFFGILNSW	wafflings	
AFFGIORST	sgraffito	
AFFHILRSY	raffishly	
AFFIILNPT	plaintiff	
AFFIKLOOP	Poliakoff	
AFFILLMMS	flimflams	
AFFILNRUY	ruffianly	
AFFINOSSU	affusions	
AFFIPSSTT	tipstaffs	
AFFKNORRT	Frankfort	
AFFKNRRTU	frankfurt	
AFFLLOOST	footfalls	
AFFLLORUV	flavorful	
AFFLOOSTT	flatfoots	
AFFLOOTTU	footfault	
AFFLOPSTW	plowstaff	
AFGGGINOT	faggoting	
AFGGGINRS	fraggings	
AFGGIILNN	finagling	
AFGGIINSY	gasifying	
AFGGIINTU	fatiguing	
AFGGILOPS	gigaflops	
AFGGINRST	graftings	
AFGGINRUY	argufying	
AFGGLNNOU	Falun Gong	
AFGHIILNZ	Fang Lizhi	
AFGHIIMNS	famishing	
AFGHILLNT	nightfall	
AFGHILNST	fanlights	
AFGHILPSS	flagships	
AFGHILSTT	lightfast	
AFGHIMNOT	fathoming	
AFGHINRST	farthings	
AFGHINSST	shaftings	
AFGHMOORT	homograft	
AFGIIILNT	filiating	
AFGIILLNY	failingly	
AFGIILMNN	inflaming	
AFGIILNNT	inflating	
AFGIILNNU	unfailing	
AFGIILNOT	foliating	
AFGIILNSY	salifying	
AFGIILRTY	fragility	
AFGIIMNRY	ramifying	
AFGIINNYZ	nazifying	
AFGIINRTY	ratifying	
AFGIKNORS	forsaking	
AFGILLMNY	flamingly	
AFGILLNOW	fallowing	
AFGILLNST	flatlings	
AFGILLNUY	gainfully	
AFGILMNOS	flamingos	
AFGILNNTU	flaunting	
AFGILNNWY	fawningly	
AFGILNORV	flavoring	

AFGILNRZZ	frazzling	
AFGILRTUY	frugality	
AFGIMNSTU	fumigants	
AFGIMORTU	fumigator	
AFGINNOPR	profaning	
AFGINORRW	farrowing	
AFGINORUV	favouring	
AFGINRSTU	figurants	
AFGINSTTU	fungistat	
AFGIPRSTW	giftwraps	
AFGLLSSSU	glassfuls	
AFGLNNOOS	gonfalons	
AFGLNRTUU	fulgurant	
AFGNNNOOS	gonfanons	
AFGNOPRSW	frogspawn	
AFHIIKNOP	kniphofia	
AFHIILNSS	snailfish	
AFHIILNTU	hifalutin	
AFHIILSST	fishtails	
AFHIKMSUU	Fukushima	
AFHIKNRST	rankshift	
AFHINORTU	thiofuran	
AFHIORSTY	forsythia	
AFHLLMRUY	harmfully	
AFHLLORST	shortfall	
AFHLMNRUU	unharmful	
AFHOOPSTT	footpaths	
AFHOORRST	hoarfrost	
AFHOOSSTT	soothfast	
AFIIILNOT	filiation	
AFIILMNSU	Flaminius	
AFIILNNOT	inflation	
AFIILNOOT	foliation	
AFIILNSST	finalists	
AFIILORRT	triforial	
AFIIMNRRY	infirmary	
AFIINOSTX	fixations	
AFIIORRTU	fioritura	
AFIIORTVZ	Fitzrovia	
AFIJKRSTU	jakfruits	
AFIKLNNRS	franklins	
AFILLLOST	flotillas	
AFILLLUWY	wailfully	
AFILLNOUX	fluxional	
AFILLNPUY	painfully	
AFILLNRUV	Furnivall	
AFILLNTUY	flauntily	
AFILMMORS	formalism	
AFILMNNTU	fulminant	
AFILMOPRS	salpiform	
AFILMORST	formalist	
AFILMORTY	formality	
AFILNOOSV	Alfonso VI	
AFILNOOTT	flotation	
AFILNORST	flatirons	
	inflators	
AFILOORSS	fossorial	
AFILSSTTU	flautists	
AFIMNNORT	informant	
AFIMNOORT	formation	
AFINNOSTU	fountains	
AFINOOPRR	rainproof	

AFINOPRTY	profanity	
AFINRSTTX	transfixt	
AFIORRSST	Froissart	
AFIOSTTUU	fatuitous	
AFIRRSTTU	starfruit	
AFKLNOSTU	outflanks	
AFKLOOSTT	footstalk	
AFKMOORST	footmarks	
AFLLLPUVY	playfully	
AFLLNORTY	frontally	
AFLLNOSSW	snowfalls	
AFLLOOSTT	footstall	
AFLLOOSTW	footwalls	
AFLMNOPRS	planforms	
AFLMOPRST	platforms	
AFLMORRUY	formulary	
AFLMORSTW	flatworms	
AFLOOPSTY	splayfoot	
AFLOORSUV	flavorous	
AFLOPRRSU	fluorspar	
AFLOSTUUY	fatuously	
AFMNORRST	transform	
AFMOORSTY	styrofoam	
AFOORSSTZ	sforzatos	
AGGGILNNY	naggingly	
AGGGILNSS	slaggings	
AGGGLNOOU	Goolagong	
AGGHHILSY	haggishly	
AGGHIILNT	alighting	
AGGHILOOY	hagiology	
AGGHILSST	gaslights	
AGGHILSWY	waggishly	
AGGHINNRT	thranging	
AGGHLOOPR	logograph	
AGGHNOUUZ	Guangzhou	
AGGIIIMNN	imagining	
AGGIIJNNQ	Jiang Qing	
AGGIILLNP	pillaging	
AGGIILMNN	maligning	
AGGIILNNS	signaling	
AGGIILNVW	lawgiving	
AGGIIMNNR	margining	
AGGIIMNRT	migrating	
AGGIIMNST	gigantism	
AGGIINNOS	agonising	
AGGIINNOZ	agonizing	
AGGIINNSS	assigning	
AGGIINNTV	vintaging	
AGGIJNNOR	jargoning	
AGGIKNNSU	Sungkiang	
AGGILLLNY	gallingly	
AGGILLNOP	galloping	
AGGILLNRY	glaringly	
AGGILNNOS	ganglions	
	singalong	
AGGILNNPS	spangling	
AGGILNNRW	wrangling	
AGGILNNWY	gnawingly	
AGGILNOOY	angiology	
AGGILNPPR	grappling	
AGGILNPSY	gaspingly	
AGGILNRSY	graylings	

AGGILNRTY	gratingly	**AGHILNORT**	granolith	**AGIIINSTV**	vaginitis
AGGILNRYZ	grazingly	**AGHILNOST**	loathings	**AGIIINTTV**	vitiating
AGGIMMNNO	gammoning	**AGHILNPSS**	splashing	**AGIIKLMNR**	grimalkin
AGGIMMNRU	rummaging	**AGHILNPTY**	plaything	**AGIIKMNST**	mistaking
AGGIMNPUZ	gazumping	**AGHILNTUV**	naughtily	**AGIIKNNSY**	kyanising
AGGINNOOR	gorgonian	**AGHILOOOR**	horologia	**AGIIKNNYZ**	kyanizing
AGGINNORS	groanings	**AGHILOSTY**	goatishly	**AGIILLLOP**	Gallipoli
AGGINOPRT	portaging	**AGHILRSTT**	starlight	**AGIILLMMR**	milligram
AGGINORRS	grosgrain	**AGHIMNRST**	hamstring	**AGIILLNOR**	gorillian
AGGINORRT	garroting	**AGHIMOPRY**	amphigory	**AGIILLNPR**	pillaring
AGGINORTT	garotting	**AGHIMORST**	histogram	**AGIILLNRT**	trialling
AGGINORTU	outraging	**AGHIMSTTU**	mistaught	**AGIILLNRV**	rivalling
	ragouting	**AGHINNOPR**	orphaning	**AGIILLRSY**	sigillary
AGGINPSTU	upstaging	**AGHINNOPT**	phonating	**AGIILMNSS**	misaligns
AGGIRSTUZ	ziggurats	**AGHINNOST**	gnathions	**AGIILMNSY**	mislaying
AGGKNNTUW	Kwangtung	**AGHINNRSY**	grannyish	**AGIILMNTY**	malignity
AGGLLLOSY	lollygags	**AGHINOORY**	hooraying	**AGIILMSSV**	Vigil Mass
AGGLMOORS	logograms	**AGHINORRW**	harrowing	**AGIILNNSU**	anilingus
AGGMOORRT	mortgagor	**AGHINORTU**	authoring	**AGIILNNWZ**	Zwinglian
AGGMOSTYY	mystagogy	**AGHINQSSU**	squashing	**AGIILNORS**	originals
AGGNNOPYY	Pyongyang	**AGHINRRUY**	hurraying	**AGIILNORT**	tailoring
AGGNSUWZZ	zugzwangs	**AGHINRTTW**	thwarting	**AGIILNOSS**	assoiling
AGHHIILST	hightails	**AGHIOSTTU**	outasight	**AGIILNOST**	intaglios
AGHHIKNTW	nighthawk	**AGHIPRRST**	trigraphs		isolating
AGHHILRTU	ultrahigh	**AGHIPRSUU**	augurship		ligations
AGHHILTUV	haughtily	**AGHIRSSTT**	straights	**AGIILNOSX**	gloxinias
AGHHINOOR	hoorahing	**AGHKMOPRY**	kymograph	**AGIILNOTV**	violating
AGHHINRRU	hurrahing	**AGHKNOPST**	pakthongs	**AGIILNPRS**	spiraling
AGHHINRST	thrashing	**AGHKOORSS**	grasshook	**AGIILNQTU**	liquating
AGHHINUZZ	huzzahing	**AGHKOPRRU**	Gorakhpur	**AGIILNRST**	ringtails
AGHHLOOPR	holograph	**AGHLLOOPY**	haplology	**AGIILNRSV**	virginals
AGHHMOOPR	homograph	**AGHLMNOPU**	ploughman	**AGIILNSSS**	isinglass
AGHHNOUZZ	Zhangzhou	**AGHLMOOPR**	lagomorph	**AGIILNSTT**	litigants
AGHIIIKRZ	Kirghizia	**AGHLMOORS**	holograms	**AGIILORTT**	litigator
AGHIIILLTT	taillight	**AGHLMOOTU**	goalmouth	**AGIILOTTT**	Togliatti
AGHIILNSV	lavishing	**AGHLNOOTY**	anthology	**AGIIMMNNS**	misnaming
AGHIIMMMN	Immingham	**AGHLNOSTU**	onslaught	**AGIIMMNRT**	immigrant
AGHIINNRU	unhairing	**AGHLOOPTY**	pathology	**AGIIMMNRT**	immigrant
AGHIINNSV	vanishing	**AGHLOPPRY**	polygraph	**AGIIMNORT**	migration
AGHIINPRT	thraiping	**AGHLOPRXY**	xylograph	**AGIIMNOST**	atomising
AGHIINRSV	ravishing	**AGHLORSSU**	hourglass		sigmation
AGHIINRTT	raintight	**AGHLOSTUU**	outlaughs	**AGIIMNOTZ**	atomizing
AGHIINRTU	Thuringia	**AGHMNOOPR**	monograph	**AGIIMNPRT**	imparting
AGHIINSSW	siwashing		nomograph	**AGIIMNPST**	impasting
AGHIIPRRS	hairgrips		phonogram	**AGIIMORTT**	mitigator
AGHIJNRST	nightjars	**AGHMNOOPY**	monophagy	**AGIINNNOT**	anointing
AGHIKLSWY	gawkishly	**AGHMNRSTU**	hamstrung	**AGIINNNRS**	insnaring
AGHIKMNOW	Wokingham	**AGHMOOPRT**	photogram	**AGIINNORS**	signorina
AGHIKNOSU	Kaohsiung	**AGHMOPRSY**	myographs	**AGIINNORT**	rationing
AGHIKRRTW	Arkwright	**AGHMOPRYY**	myography	**AGIINNPRS**	spraining
AGHILLNOO	hallooing	**AGHNNSTUU**	Hsüan T'ung	**AGIINNPST**	paintings
	holloaing	**AGHNOORSS**	shagroons	**AGIINNQTU**	antiquing
AGHILLNOP	anglophil	**AGHNOPSSU**	sphagnous	**AGIINNRST**	straining
AGHILLNOW	hallowing	**AGHNORSST**	staghorns	**AGIINNRRT**	intrigant
AGHILLNRT	thralling	**AGHOOPRRY**	orography		nitrating
AGHILLNSY	lashingly	**AGHOOPRVZ**	zoography	**AGIINNRTU**	urinating
AGHILLNTY	haltingly	**AGHOPRRUY**	urography	**AGIINNSTT**	instating
AGHILLORY	Holy Grail	**AGHORSTTY**	hygrostat	**AGIINORTV**	grivation
AGHILMORT	algorithm	**AGIIIMNPR**	impairing	**AGIINOSTZ**	azotising
	logarithm	**AGIIIMNTT**	imitating	**AGIINOTZZ**	azotizing
AGHILNNSU	unlashing	**AGIIINNRV**	Virginian	**AGIINPPRS**	apprising
AGHILNOOS	hooligans	**AGIIINNSS**	insignias	**AGIINPPRZ**	apprizing

AGIINPRST	traipsing	
AGIINPRSU	upraising	
AGIINRSTT	striating	
AGIINRTTT	titrating	
AGIINSSST	assisting	
AGIINSTTU	situating	
AGIIORRRT	irrigator	
AGIIRSSTT	gastritis	
AGIIRSTTU	guitarist	
AGIJLNOSU	jalousing	
AGIJLNRRY	jarringly	
AGIKLMORS	kilograms	
AGIKLNPRS	sparkling	
AGIKMNNSU	unmasking	
AGIKNNPSS	spankings	
AGIKNOSST	goatskins	
AGIKNQSUW	squawking	
AGILLLNUY	lingually	
AGILLMNOS	slaloming	
AGILLMNRU	Mullingar	
AGILLMNSU	mulligans	
AGILLNNNU	annulling	
AGILLNOPW	walloping	
AGILLNOSW	sallowing	
AGILLNOTT	allotting	
	totalling	
AGILLNOTW	tallowing	
AGILLNOWW	wallowing	
AGILLNQSU	squalling	
AGILLNSTY	lastingly	
AGILLNTUU	ululating	
AGILLOPST	gallipots	
AGILMNNOO	mongolian	
AGILMNNOT	lamington	
AGILMNNOY	moaningly	
AGILMNNST	mantlings	
AGILMNOPY	Pygmalion	
AGILMNPRT	trampling	
AGILMNPSS	samplings	
AGILMNSUY	amusingly	
AGILMOORY	Mariology	
AGILMOPRS	lipograms	
AGILMORSS	algorisms	
AGILMRSUV	vulgarism	
AGILNNOPS	pangolins	
	plainsong	
AGILNNORT	Arlington	
AGILNNRTY	rantingly	
AGILNNRWY	warningly	
AGILNNWYY	yawningly	
AGILNOOSS	isogonals	
AGILNORRY	roaringly	
AGILNORVY	vainglory	
AGILNOSTV	solvating	
AGILNOTUV	ovulating	
AGILNOTUW	outlawing	
AGILNOTUY	outlaying	
AGILNPRSS	sparlings	
AGILNPRSW	sprawling	
AGILNPRSY	sparingly	
AGILNPRTT	prattling	
AGILNPRTY	pratingly	
AGILNPSTU	pulsating	
AGILNRSST	starlings	
AGILNRSSU	singulars	
AGILNRSTT	startling	
AGILNRSTW	warstling	
AGILNRSUY	singulary	
AGILNRVYY	varyingly	
AGILNSTWY	wastingly	
AGILOOPST	apologist	
AGILOORSS	gloriosas	
AGILOPRUY	uropygial	
AGILRRTUY	garrulity	
AGILRTUVY	vulgarity	
AGIMMNSUY	gymnasium	
AGIMNNNNU	unmanning	
AGIMNNOOR	marooning	
AGIMNNOPT	tamponing	
AGIMNNORS	ransoming	
AGIMNNOTU	amounting	
AGIMNNRSU	surnaming	
AGIMNOOSV	vamoosing	
AGIMNORRT	mortaring	
AGIMNORRU	armouring	
AGIMNORSS	organisms	
AGIMNORSU	ignoramus	
AGIMNRRTY	martyring	
AGIMOOSSU	isogamous	
AGIMORRST	migrators	
AGIMORRTY	migratory	
AGINNNOPY	nonpaying	
AGINNNOTW	wantoning	
AGINNOORT	organotin	
	ratooning	
AGINNOPRT	pronating	
AGINNORRW	narrowing	
AGINNORTT	attorning	
AGINNPRSU	unsparing	
AGINNPSSW	wingspans	
AGINNRTTU	truanting	
AGINNRUVY	unvarying	
AGINNSTUY	Tsingyuan	
AGINOORST	rogations	
AGINOOTTT	tattooing	
AGINOPPRV	approving	
AGINOPRRT	parroting	
	prorating	
AGINOPRTU	purgation	
AGINOPRUV	vapouring	
AGINORRSS	garrisons	
AGINORSSS	assignors	
AGINORSST	assorting	
	organists	
	roastings	
AGINORSTV	gravitons	
AGINORSTY	gyrations	
	signatory	
AGINORSUV	savouring	
AGINOSSTT	tangoists	
AGINOSTTU	gustation	
AGINOTTTU	guttation	
AGINPPRST	strapping	
	trappings	
AGINPPRSW	wrappings	
AGINPRRTU	rapturing	
AGINPRSTU	pasturing	
AGINQRRUY	quarrying	
AGINQSTTU	squatting	
AGINRSSTY	stingrays	
AGINRSTUX	surtaxing	
AGINRSTVY	strayving	
AGIOORSTU	autogiros	
AGIOPRRSY	spirogyra	
AGIQRSSTU	grassquit	
AGISSTUUV	Gustavus I	
AGJKNORRU	kurrajong	
AGKLOORYY	karyology	
AGKLORSSW	glasswork	
AGKLPPRSU	sparkplug	
AGKNORSST	knotgrass	
AGLLNOOPY	polygonal	
AGLMOORSU	glamorous	
AGLMOORYY	Maryology	
AGLMPRSUU	sugarplum	
AGLOOPRTY	patrology	
AGLOOPSST	goalposts	
AGLOORSST	glossator	
AGLOORSTY	astrology	
AGLOOTTUY	tautology	
AGLOPPRUY	playgroup	
AGLORRSUU	garrulous	
AGLORSSTW	glasswort	
AGLRSTTUU	gutturals	
AGMMNOORS	groomsman	
	monograms	
	nomograms	
AGMMOSTUU	gummatous	
AGMMNORST	strongman	
AGMNOORSS	sonograms	
AGMNORRST	Armstrong	
	strongarm	
AGMNORSST	angstroms	
AGMNOSSUY	syngamous	
AGMNSSTUY	nystagmus	
AGNNOPPTU	oppugnant	
AGNNOQSTU	quantongs	
AGNOPTTUU	Tupungato	
AGNRRSTUY	strangury	
AGOORSTUY	autogyros	
AGOPRRTUY	purgatory	
AGORSSTTY	gyrostats	
AGORSTTUV	gustatory	
AGRSTTTTU	Stuttgart	
AHHHOOSST	shahtoosh	
AHHIIMORS	Hiroshima	
AHHIKLSSS	shashliks	
AHHMOSTUW	mouthwash	
AHHMPRRSU	harrumphs	
AHHNORRST	hartshorn	
AHHNORSTV	Thorshavn	
AHHNORSTW	hawthorns	
AHIIILMNS	malihinis	
AHIIILORT	Lothair II	
AHIIILPST	philistia	
AHIIILSST	lithiasis	

AHIIJKNRS	jinriksha	**AHIMOPSUX**	amphioxus	**AIIIMNOTT**	imitation
AHIILOOPZ	zoophilia	**AHIMORRSW**	hairworms	**AIIINNNOT**	inanition
AHIILOQSU	Liu Shao Qi	**AHINNOOPT**	phonation	**AIIINNSTY**	asininity
AHIILORSU	hilarious	**AHINNOPST**	antiphons	**AIIINORTT**	initiator
AHIILOSST	halitosis	**AHINNOPTY**	antiphony	**AIIINOTTV**	vitiation
AHIILRSTT	shirttail	**AHINOOPRR**	orpharion	**AIIJLOTVY**	joviality
AHIIMMRST	Mithraism	**AHINOORTT**	hortation	**AIIKLNRRS**	larrikins
AHIIMPRSV	vampirish	**AHINOOSTU**	houstonia	**AIIKMNNNS**	mannikins
AHIINORST	historian	**AHINPRSST**	tranships	**AIIKNNNPS**	pannikins
AHIIPRSSZ	sizarship		transship	**AIILLMMNY**	minimally
AHIIRRSTT	arthritis	**AHIOPPRRY**	porphyria	**AIILLMRSY**	similarly
AHIIRSSTT	Tsitsihar	**AHIOPPSSY**	apophysis	**AIILLNOST**	illations
AHIJLNOPU	John Paul I	**AHIOPRSST**	aphorists	**AIILLNSTY**	saintlily
AHIJMOPRS	majorship	**AHIOPRSUV**	vapourish	**AIILLPRRS**	spirillar
AHIJNNOST	Saint John	**AHIOPSTXY**	hypotaxis	**AIILLRSTT**	triallist
AHIKKKNRSS	sharkskin	**AHIORRTWY**	airworthy	**AIILLRTVY**	trivially
AHIKKTTWY	Kitty Hawk	**AHIORTTUY**	authority	**AIILLSWWW**	williwaws
AHIKLMSWY	mawkishly	**AHKLLMOWY**	mollyhawk	**AIILMMNUU**	aluminium
AHIKLNSVY	knavishly	**AHKMOORRS**	markhoors	**AIILMNORT**	trinomial
AHIKNOSTZ	Zákinthos	**AHKMOORSW**	Hawksmoor	**AIILMNSTT**	militants
AHILLOPRT	prothalli	**AHKNPRSTU**	Pankhurst	**AIILMOSST**	altissimo
AHILLOSSW	sallowish	**AHKORSTUW**	Southwark	**AIILMPRRY**	primarily
AHILLOTTT	tallitoth	**AHLLLOSWY**	shallowly	**AIILMRSST**	mistrials
AHILLPSST	phallists	**AHLLMOOPR**	allomorph	**AIILMRSTU**	ritualism
AHILLPSSY	splashily	**AHLLNOSUW**	unhallows	**AIILNNORS**	rosanilin
AHILLPSTW	whipstall	**AHLLOPSUY**	aphyllous	**AIILNOOST**	isolation
AHILLQSSU	squallish	**AHLMMOSYY**	lymphomas	**AIILNOOTV**	violation
AHILLSSVY	slavishly	**AHLMOOOPR**	homopolar	**AIILNOPSV**	pavilions
AHILMMRSY	rammishly	**AHLMOOPSY**	homoplasy	**AIILNOQTU**	liquation
AHILMNNSY	mannishly	**AHLMOPSTY**	polymaths	**AIILNORSV**	livraison
AHILMNNUY	inhumanly	**AHLMOPTYY**	polymathy	**AIILNORTT**	introital
AHILMOPSY	syphiloma	**AHLMORSTY**	solar myth	**AIILNOSTT**	siltation
AHILMORST	hailstorm	**AHLNNORST**	lanthorns	**AIILNOTTU**	tuitional
AHILMOSST	mailshots	**AHLOPSSST**	slapshots	**AIILNPRSU**	spirulina
AHILMPRTU	triumphal	**AHMNOOPTY**	taphonomy	**AIILNPSST**	alpinists
AHILMPTTU	multipath	**AHMOOPPST**	photomaps		tailspins
AHILMRSTY	lathyrism	**AHMOOPRSU**	amorphous	**AIILNPSTY**	Ypsilanti
AHILNORST	horntails	**AHMOORSSW**	washrooms	**AIILNRSST**	sinistral
AHILNORTT	triathlon	**AHMOPRTTU**	mouthpart	**AIILPRSST**	spritsail
AHILNPPUY	unhappily	**AHMORRSTW**	marshwort	**AIILPRSTU**	spiritual
AHILOORST	lotharios	**AHMORSTTW**	tamworths	**AIILRSSTT**	trialists
AHILOPPTY	Hippolyta	**AHNNNOOTY**	hootnanny	**AIILRSTTU**	ritualist
AHILOPSST	hospitals	**AHNNORSTT**	Northants	**AIILSSTTV**	vitalists
AHILORTTY	throatily	**AHNOOPRTY**	phonatory	**AIIMMPRSV**	vampirism
AHILOSTTT	statolith	**AHNOPPSSW**	pawnshops	**AIIMNNOSS**	insomnias
AHILPSSWY	waspishly	**AHNOPSSST**	snapshots	**AIIMNNTUY**	unanimity
AHILQSSUY	squashily	**AHNOPSTYY**	hyponasty	**AIIMNOPRS**	prosimian
AHILRSTTY	tartishly	**AHNORRSTY**	Strayhorn	**AIIMNOPSS**	impassion
AHILRSTWY	swarthily	**AHNORRTTY**	thyratron	**AIIMNOSTY**	animosity
AHIMMMNOS	mammonish	**AHOOPPRRT**	prothorax	**AIIMNPSTT**	timpanist
AHIMMMOSS	shammosim	**AHOOPRTTU**	autotroph	**AIIMOPRRS**	apriorism
AHIMMNORU	harmonium	**AHOOPRTUX**	auxotroph	**AIIMORSTT**	imitators
AHIMMOPRS	amorphism	**AHOOPSTTT**	photostat	**AIIMPSSSV**	passivism
AHIMNORST	harmonist	**AHOOPTTXY**	phototaxy	**AIIMRSTUU**	Mauritius
AHIMNPSTY	sympathin	**AHOORRTTY**	hortatory	**AIIMRSUVV**	vivariums
AHIMNRTUU	anthurium	**AHOOSSSTY**	soothsays	**AIINNNOOT**	Antonioni
AHIMNSSTU	humanists	**AHOPSSTUW**	southpaws	**AIINNNOPT**	pinnation
AHIMOOSTX	homotaxis	**AHORSTTUW**	watthours	**AIINNORTT**	nitration
AHIMOPRSS	aphorisms	**AIIIILLMW**	William II	**AIINNORTU**	ruination
AHIMOPRSY	mayorship	**AIIILLMW**	William IV		urination
AHIMOPSST	opsimaths	**AIIILLNTY**	initially	**AIINNOSSV**	invasions
AHIMOPSTY	opsimathy	**AIIILMNST**	laminitis	**AIINNOSTU**	sinuation

AIINNOSTV	nivations	**AILLOPPST**	lipoplast	**AILNSSTTU**	lutanists
AIINNOTTX	antitoxin	**AILLOPTVY**	pivotally	**AILOOPTTU**	autopilot
AIINNQSTU	quintains	**AILLORSTT**	littorals	**AILOORSST**	isolators
AIINOPRTT	partition		tortillas	**AILOORSTV**	violators
AIINOPRTV	privation	**AILLORUXY**	uxorially	**AILOORSUV**	variolous
AIINORSTT	striation	**AILLOSSTY**	loyalists	**AILOPRSTU**	troupials
AIINORSVY	visionary	**AILLPPRUY**	pupillary	**AILOPRSTV**	postviral
AIINORTTT	attrition	**AILLPRSTU**	pluralist	**AILORRSUV**	rivalrous
	titration	**AILLPRTUY**	plurality	**AILORSSST**	solarists
AIINOSTTU	situation	**AILLPSSWY**	spillways	**AILORSSTY**	royalists
AIINQTTUY	antiquity	**AILLRTTUY**	titularly	**AILORSTTU**	tutorials
AIINRRSTT	irritants	**AILLRTUVY**	virtually	**AILORSTUV**	outrivals
AIINRSTUV	antivirus	**AILMMNOOS**	monomials	**AILORSUVY**	savourily
AIINSSTTV	nativists	**AILMMOORT**	immolator		variously
	visitants	**AILMMORST**	immortals	**AILOSSTUY**	autolysis
AIIOPRRTY	apriority	**AILMMRSUY**	summarily	**AILPRRSSU**	surprisal
AIIOPRSSS	psoriasis	**AILMMSTUU**	mutualism	**AILPSSTUY**	playsuits
AIIOPRSTT	parotitis	**AILMMTTUU**	ultimatum	**AILRRSSTU**	ruralists
	topiarist	**AILMNNOTY**	antimonyl	**AILRSSTTU**	altruists
AIIOPRTVY	oviparity	**AILMNOOPS**	palominos		ultraists
AIIOPSSTT	pastitsio	**AILMNOORS**	monorails	**AILRSSUVV**	survivals
AIIORRRTT	irritator	**AILMNOPSS**	spoilsman	**AIMMMMNOS**	mammonism
AIIORSTTV	vitiators	**AILMNOPST**	Platonism	**AIMMMNOST**	mammonist
AIIORTTTV	titivator	**AILMNOPSY**	amylopsin	**AIMMNORTY**	matrimony
AIIPRRSST	airstrips	**AILMNORST**	mortal sin	**AIMMNOSTU**	summation
AIIPRTTUY	pituitary	**AILMNORTY**	normality	**AIMMPRSUU**	marsupium
AIIPSSSTV	passivist	**AILMNOSUU**	aluminous	**AIMMRSSTU**	summarist
AIIPSSTVY	passivity	**AILMNSTTU**	stimulant	**AIMNNOORT**	nominator
AIIRSSSTT	satirists	**AILMORSST**	moralists	**AIMNNOPST**	pointsman
	sitarists	**AILMORSSU**	solariums	**AIMNNORUV**	mavournin
AIJKKNOSU	kinkajous	**AILMORSTU**	simulator	**AIMNNOSTU**	antimuons
AIJLLOORS	jillaroos	**AILMORTTU**	mutilator		mountains
AIJNOPPSY	popinjays	**AILMORTTY**	mortality	**AIMNNOSUU**	unanimous
AIJNSSTTU	Saint-Just	**AILMOSSTY**	atmolysis	**AIMNNOTYY**	anonymity
AIKKLMNOS	Akmolinsk	**AILMPRSTY**	palmistry	**AIMNNRSTU**	ruminants
AIKKRSTUZ	zikkurats	**AILMPSSST**	psalmists	**AIMNOPRSY**	parsimony
AIKLMOSTT	milktoast	**AILMRSSTU**	muralists	**AIMNOPRTT**	important
AIKLMSTTU	multitask		ultraisms	**AIMNOPRTY**	patrimony
AIKLNNPSS	snaplinks	**AILMSTTUU**	mutualist	**AIMNORRST**	rainstorm
AIKLNOSSY	ankylosis	**AILMTTUUY**	mutuality	**AIMNORRTU**	ruminator
AIKLOSTTW	kilowatts	**AILNNOPTU**	plutonian	**AIMNORSUU**	uniramous
AIKMNNOSW	kinswoman	**AILNNOSTU**	lunations	**AIMNOSTTU**	mutations
AIKMRSSTZ	sitzmarks	**AILNNSSTU**	insulants	**AIMNPSTTY**	tympanist
AIKNNOOSS	nainsooks	**AILNNSTTY**	instantly	**AIMNRSSTT**	transmits
AIKNNSSSW	swanskins	**AILNNSTUY**	unsaintly	**AIMNRSSTU**	saturnism
AIKNOPRTW	paintwork	**AILNOORST**	tonsorial	**AIMOOPRST**	prostomia
AIKNSSUUY	San Suu Kyi		torsional	**AIMOPRSSS**	prosaisms
AIKPSTTUU	patutukis	**AILNOOSST**	solations	**AIMOPSSTU**	potassium
AILLMMORY	immorally	**AILNOOSTV**	solvation	**AIMORRSST**	armorists
AILLMNNOY	nominally	**AILNOOTUV**	ovulation	**AIMORRSSU**	rosariums
AILLMOPTY	optimally	**AILNOPSTU**	platinous	**AIMORRSUV**	variorums
AILLMPRSU	pluralism		pulsation	**AIMPSSSTU**	assumpsit
AILLMSUUV	alluviums	**AILNOPSTY**	ponytails	**AINNNOSTU**	Antoninus
AILLNOPPS	papillons	**AILNORSTU**	insulator		unisonant
AILLNORST	tonsillar	**AILNOSSUV**	avulsions	**AINNOOPRS**	sopranino
AILLNORSU	lunisolar	**AILNOSTUX**	luxations	**AINNOOPRT**	pronation
AILLNOSST	stallions	**AILNOSTUY**	autolysin	**AINNOORTV**	innovator
AILLNOSSU	allusions	**AILNOSUXY**	anxiously	**AINNOOSTT**	notations
AILLNOSUV	alluvions	**AILNPPSTU**	suppliant	**AINNOOSTV**	novations
AILLNOTUU	ululation	**AILNPQTUY**	piquantly	**AINNOOSTZ**	zonations
AILLNPTUY	nuptially	**AILNRTUUX**	luxuriant	**AINNORSTT**	strontian
AILLNRSUY	insularly	**AILNSSSTU**	stunsails	**AINNOSTTU**	nutations

AINOOPPRT	appointor	
	apportion	
AINOOPRRT	proration	
AINOOPST	potations	
AINOOPSTT	potations	
AINOOQTTU	quotation	
AINOORSTT	rotations	
AINOOSSTT	ostinatos	
AINOOTTUX	autotoxin	
AINOPPSTU	pupations	
AINOPRSTU	supinator	
AINOPRSU	uniparous	
AINOPSSTW	swaptions	
AINOQRRSU	quarrions	
AINORSSST	arsonists	
AINPSSTTU	pantsuits	
AINRSSTTU	naturists	
AINRSSTTY	Tsaritsyn	
AINRSTTTU	antitrust	
AIOOORRST	oratorios	
AIOOOPPRST	proposita	
AIOOPPSST	apoptosis	
AIOOPRSUV	apivorous	
	oviparous	
AIOOSTTTT	tattooist	
AIOPRRSTT	portraits	
AIOPRSSST	prosaists	
AIOPRTTTY	tyropitta	
AIORRSSTU	sartorius	
AIORRSSTV	varistors	
AIORRSTUV	rotavirus	
AIORSSTTV	votarists	
AJMMNNOPU	Panmunjom	
AJMNORUWY	jurywoman	
AKKORSTVV	Tarkovsky	
AKKRSTVVY	Syktyvkar	
AKLLMMOWY	mollymawk	
AKLLMNOSU	molluskan	
AKLMNORWY	workmanly	
AKLNOSUVY	Ulyanovsk	
AKLOORSTT	rootstalk	
AKLOORSVZ	Kolozsvár	
AKLORSSTW	saltworks	
AKLPRRSSU	larkspurs	
AKMMNOORS	monomarks	
AKMNOOPSU	mokopunas	
AKMOPRSST	postmarks	
AKNNORSYY	synkaryon	
AKNOOPRRY	prokaryon	
AKNOPSSTW	swankpots	
ALLMNORUY	unmorally	
ALLMOOSSY	lysosomal	
ALLMOSUWY	mulloways	
ALLNOOPTY	polytonal	
ALLNOPTTU	pollutant	
ALLNSUUUY	unusually	
ALLOOPRTY	allotropy	
ALLOPPRUY	popularly	
ALLOPRSTY	sallyport	
ALLOPRSUY	parlously	
ALLOPSSUY	spousally	
ALLRSTUUY	suturally	
ALMMNSSUU	Mussulman	

ALMNNOOOS	monsoonal	
ALMNOORTY	monolatry	
ALMNOPRUY	pulmonary	
ALMOOPRSY	playrooms	
ALMOORSTU	alumroots	
ALMOORSUY	amorously	
ALMOPPSST	lampposts	
ALMPSSSTY	symplasts	
ALNOOPSTT	tonoplast	
ALNOOPSYZ	polyzoans	
ALNOPPRUU	unpopular	
ALNOPRSST	plastrons	
ALNOPSTTU	postulant	
ALNORTUVY	voluntary	
ALNPPSSTU	supplants	
ALNPSTTUU	pustulant	
ALOOPPRSS	proposals	
ALOOPRRTY	Port Royal	
ALOOPRSTV	Stavropol	
ALOOPSTYZ	zooplasty	
ALOPPRSSU	prolapsus	
ALOPRSSTU	pulsators	
ALOPRSTUY	pulsatory	
ALORSSTTW	saltworts	
AMMNPSTUY	tympanums	
AMMOOSTUY	myomatous	
AMMNNOSUY	anonymous	
AMNOOPSTW	postwoman	
AMNOORSTY	astronomy	
AMNOPRSST	sportsman	
AMNOSTTUY	tautonyms	
AMNOTTUVY	tautonymy	
AMOOORSTV	vasomotor	
AMOORRRWW	arrowworm	
AMOORSTWY	motorways	
AMOOSSTTU	stomatous	
AMOPRSSXY	paroxysms	
AMORRSTWW	strawworm	
AMORSSTTU	outsmarts	
AMPRSTUUY	sumptuary	
ANNOOPRSU	nonparous	
ANNOORSST	sonorants	
ANNORSTUY	tyrannous	
ANOOOPRSZ	sporozoan	
ANOOOPRTZ	protozoan	
ANOOPRRST	pronators	
ANOORSTWY	Stornoway	
ANOPRRSTT	transport	
ANOPRSTTU	trapuntos	
ANORSUUVY	unsavoury	
ANRRSSTUU	susurrant	
AOOOORRTW	arrowroot	
AOOORRTTV	rotovator	
AOOPRRSTT	protostar	
AOOPRSSTW	soapworts	
AOPPRSSST	passports	
AOPRRSTUU	rapturous	
AOPRSSTTY	pyrostats	
AORRRTWWY	worrywart	
AORRSSTTW	starworts	
AORSTTTUY	statutory	
BBBCDEEOW	cobwebbed	

BBBDEELRU	blubbered	
BBBDEHNOO	hobnobbed	
BBBEEELMU	bumblebee	
BBBEEELUZ	Beelzebub	
BBBEEIORS	bobberies	
BBBEELRRU	blubberer	
BBBEGLMUU	bubblegum	
BBBEIKORS	skibobber	
BBBEILOST	blobbiest	
BBBEILSTU	bubbliest	
BBBEINOST	bobbinets	
BBCDEELOR	clobbered	
BBCDEILRS	scribbled	
BBCDIMOSY	bombycids	
BBCEHISTU	chubbiest	
BBCEHLOUY	cubbyhole	
BBCEILRRS	scribbler	
BBCEILRSS	scribbles	
BBCEILSTU	clubbiest	
BBCEIRRSU	scrubbier	
BBCEIRSSU	subscribe	
BBCEKLSSU	blesbucks	
BBCEKTUUY	buckytube	
BBCERRSSU	scrubbers	
BBCGILNSU	clubbings	
BBCGINRSU	scrubbing	
BBCHILSUY	cubbishly	
BBCHKOOSS	boschboks	
BBCHKSSUU	bushbucks	
BBCIIILST	biblicist	
BBDEELORS	slobbered	
BBDEERSSU	subbreeds	
BBDEGIINR	dibbering	
BBDEGIMNO	demobbing	
BBDEHIRSU	rubbished	
BBDEIIRSU	rubbidies	
BBDEILLRS	bellbirds	
BBDEILRRS	dribblers	
BBDEILRST	dribblets	
BBDEILRSU	bluebirds	
BBDEIMOSV	divebombs	
BBDEIORRW	bowerbird	
BBDELLMSU	dumbbells	
BBDELMMOU	bumbledom	
BBDGIILNR	dribbling	
BBDGINRSU	drubbings	
BBDIIKKMU	dibbukkim	
BBDIKKMUY	dybbukkim	
BBDNOSTUU	bundobust	
BBEEEINR	bebeerine	
BBEEEHLMU	humblebee	
BBEEEINRR	berberine	
BBEEIIRRS	briberies	
BBEEILPST	plebbiest	
BBEEINRTZ	rebbetzin	
BBEEIORRS	robberies	
BBEEIORSY	yobberies	
BBEEIRRSU	rubberise	
BBEEIRRUZ	rubberize	
BBEELLLSU	bluebells	
BBEELORRS	slobberer	
BBEELRRUY	blueberry	

BBEEOPPRS	beboppers	**BCCEIINOT**	cenobitic	**BCDIKLLSU**	duckbills
BBEFILRRS	fribblers	**BCCEILOSY**	biocycles	**BCDILORSU**	colubrids
BBEFILRST	flibberts	**BCCEILRSU**	crucibles	**BCDIMOORS**	scombroid
BBEFIMORS	firebombs	**BCCEILRSY**	bicyclers	**BCDKLOOOW**	woodblock
BBEGGIINR	gibbering	**BCCEINNOU**	concubine	**BCDKNOOOS**	boondocks
BBEGGIINT	gibbeting	**BCCEKLORU**	cocklebur	**BCDKNOORU**	rockbound
BBEGGNOOW	wobbegong	**BCCEMRSUU**	cucumbers	**BCEEEEHRS**	beseecher
BBEGHIIRS	gibberish		succumber	**BCEEEEHSS**	beseeches
BBEGHILOS	bobsleigh	**BCCGIILNY**	bicycling	**BCEEEFINS**	benefices
BBEGHIOTW	bobweight	**BCCIILSTY**	bicyclist	**BCEEEHKNO**	cheekbone
BBEGIMNNU	benumbing	**BCCIKLLOY**	billycock	**BCEEELQRU**	becquerel
BBEGINNOT	Bebington	**BCCILMUUU**	cubiculum	**BCEEENQUW**	New Quebec
BBEGINSSU	gubbinses	**BCCINORRS**	corncribs	**BCEEERSSU**	berceuses
BBEGIRSTU	grubbiest	**BCCIORSTU**	scorbutic	**BCEEFILNS**	fencibles
BBEHILLOY	Holy Bible	**BCCIRSTUU**	cucurbits	**BCEEGHINR**	breeching
BBEHIOSTW	bobwhites	**BCCMOORXY**	coxcombry	**BCEEGIINR**	bigeneric
BBEHIRRSU	shrubbier	**BCCMORRUY**	currycomb	**BCEEHINST**	Bechstein
BBEHIRSSU	rubbishes	**BCCOSSUUU**	succubous		benchiest
BBEHLLMOS	bombshell	**BCDDEEHOU**	debouched	**BCEEHISTW**	bewitches
BBEHRRSUY	shrubbery	**BCDDEEILU**	deducible	**BCEEHKLNU**	lebkuchen
BBEIIRSTU	rubbities	**BCDDEEIRS**	described	**BCEEHKOOR**	chokebore
BBEIKLNOR	knobblier	**BCDDEELOU**	beclouded	**BCEEHKTTU**	buckteeth
BBEIKNOST	knobbiest	**BCDDESTUU**	subducted	**BCEEHNNSTU**	beechnuts
BBEILLLSU	bluebills	**BCDDIIKRY**	dickybird	**BCEEHORTT**	brochette
BBEILOSTW	wobbliest	**BCDEEEEHS**	beseeched	**BCEEHOSSU**	subechoes
BBEILQRSU	quibblers	**BCDEEEFIN**	beneficed	**BCEEHPRUY**	hypercube
BBEINSSTU	tubbiness	**BCDEEEINO**	obedience	**BCEEHRTTU**	trebuchet
BBEIRSSTU	subtribes	**BCDEEGIKN**	bedecking	**BCEEIIJTV**	bijective
BBEISSTTU	stubbiest	**BCDEEHIIR**	herbicide	**BCEEIILMS**	imbeciles
BBEKLOOSU	bluebooks	**BCDEEHITW**	bewitched	**BCEEIILNV**	evincible
BBEKNOOST	bonteboks	**BCDEEHOSU**	debouches	**BCEEIJOTV**	objective
BBELOORSW	bobowlers	**BCDEEHRTU**	butchered	**BCEEIKLOR**	Lockerbie
BBERRTTUU	butterbur	**BCDEEILRU**	reducible	**BCEEIKNST**	Steinbeck
BBFGIILNR	fribbling	**BCDEEILSU**	seducible	**BCEEIKRRS**	bickerers
BBGHILLTU	lightbulb	**BCDEEIORR**	cerebroid	**BCEEILLOR**	corbeille
BBGHILNOO	hobgoblin	**BCDEEIRRS**	describer	**BCEEILLOS**	bellicose
BBGHIMOST	bombsight	**BCDEEIRSS**	describes	**BCEEILMNY**	Cymbeline
BBGHINORT	throbbing	**BCDEEJSTU**	subjected	**BCEEILRTY**	celebrity
BBGIILNQU	quibbling	**BCDEEKLLO**	bellocked	**BCEEIMMOS**	misbecome
BBGIINNOR	ribboning	**BCDEEKLRU**	bucklered	**BCEEIMNOR**	recombine
BBGIINQSU	squibbing	**BCDEEKRSU**	reedbucks	**BCEEINOOT**	coenobite
BBGIIOSTY	gibbosity	**BCDEELLOR**	corbelled	**BCEEINOST**	cenobites
BBGILLNOO	bobolling	**BCDEEMNTU**	decumbent	**BCEEIORSX**	boxercise
BBGILMNSU	bumblings	**BCDEHINPT**	pitchbend	**BCEEIPRRS**	prescribe
BBGILOSUY	gibbously	**BCDEIILNU**	inducible	**BCEEJNORT**	jobcentre
BBHIOSSTY	hobbyists	**BCDEIINRS**	inscribed	**BCEEKNORS**	beckoners
BBHRSSSUU	subshrubs	**BCDEIIRRS**	ricebirds	**BCEEKRTTU**	trebucket
BBIIILNRU	bilirubin	**BCDEILOOR**	bicolored	**BCEELNOSY**	obscenely
BBIIKMTUZ	kibbutzim	**BCDEILOSU**	Bois-le-Duc	**BCEELOORS**	borecoles
BBIKLNOOS	bobolinks	**BCDEILRUY**	reducibly	**BCEELOOSS**	obsolesce
BBILOSSTY	lobbyists	**BCDEISTUU**	decubitus	**BCEELRSTU**	tubercles
BBLLNNSUU	bulnbulns	**BCDEKLLOU**	bullocked	**BCEELRUUY**	burleycue
BBLLOSUUY	bulbously	**BCDEKLNOU**	unblocked	**BCEEMNRSU**	encumbers
BBLLOSUYY	bullyboys	**BCDEKLNUU**	unbuckled	**BCEEMNRTU**	recumbent
BCCCKMOOS	cockscomb	**BCDEMOSTU**	combusted	**BCEEMRRSU**	cerebrums
BCCDEHKOY	bodycheck	**BCDEOOTTY**	boycotted		cumberers
BCCDEMSUU	succumbed	**BCDEORRSS**	crossbred	**BCEENPSTU**	pubescent
BCCEEILOR	coercible	**BCDGIKLOR**	goldbrick	**BCEENRSTU**	rubescent
BCCEHIILO	libecchio	**BCDGOSYZZ**	Bydgoszcz	**BCEEPRSTY**	cyberpets
BCCEHIKNP	pinchbeck	**BCDHKNOUU**	buckhound	**BCEFFIOSU**	suboffice
BCCEHKKOO	checkbook	**BCDIILOOS**	discoboli	**BCEFHISSU**	subchiefs
BCCEIIILM	imbecilic	**BCDIIPSSU**	bicuspids	**BCEFHISTT**	bitchfest

BCEFIIKRR	firebrick
BCEFIIRTY	febricity
BCEFIJOTY	objectify
BCEFKLTUU	bucketful
BCEGHILNN	blenching
BCEGHNORS	Schönberg
BCEGHORRU	Cherbourg
BCEGIIKNR	bickering
BCEGIINRS	escribing
BCEGIINST	bisecting
BCEGIJNOT	objecting
BCEGIKNNO	beckoning
BCEGIKNTU	bucketing
BCEGILNOR	corbeling
BCEGIMNOS	becomings
BCEGIMNRU	cumbering
BCEGKMSSU	gemsbucks
BCEGKTTUU	gutbucket
BCEHHORSS	borshches
BCEHIILPT	phlebitic
BCEHIINRU	Cherubini
BCEHIIOST	bioethics
BCEHIISTT	bitchiest
BCEHILORT	blotchier
BCEHIMORS	chemisorb
BCEHINNOT	benthonic
BCEHINOOP	neophobic
BCEHINSTU	bunchiest
BCEHIOQUU	chibouque
BCEHIOSTT	botchiest
BCEHIPSSU	spicebush
BCEHIRSTT	brichtest
BCEHKLMRU	Lehmbruck
BCEHKMRUU	humbucker
BCEHKNORW	workbench
BCEHLNORV	Chernobyl
BCEHLOSUU	clubhouse
BCEHMNOOY	honeycomb
BCEHMOORS	chemosorb
BCEHOPSSU	subepochs
BCEHORRSU	brochures
BCEIIIOPT	epibiotic
BCEIIJNOT	bijection
BCEIIKLNS	iceblinks
BCEIIKRST	brickiest
BCEIILNOT	bilection
BCEIILPSU	publicise
BCEIILPUZ	publicize
BCEIIMORT	biometric
BCEIINNTY	Benin City
BCEIINOST	bisection
BCEIINRRS	inscriber
BCEIINRSS	inscribes
BCEIIRSTX	bisectrix
BCEIJNOOT	objection
BCEIKNOST	steinbock
BCEILLMRU	cribellum
BCEILMNOU	columbine
BCEILMOTU	columbite
BCEILMRRU	crumblier
BCEILNOOT	bolection
BCEILNORU	colubrine

BCEILNRTU	interclub
BCEILPRSU	republics
BCEIMNNTU	incumbent
BCEIMNORS	combiners
BCEIMNORY	embryonic
BCEIMNRSU	incumbers
BCEIMRSTU	crumbiest
BCEINOSTU	bounciest
BCEINOSTY	obscenity
BCEINSSUU	incubuses
BCEIOOPSS	bioscopes
BCEIOPRRS	proscribe
BCEIORRSU	Corbusier
BCEIORSST	bisectors
BCEIORSTT	obstetric
BCEIRSTUU	Bucureşti
BCEKLNSUU	unbuckles
BCEKLRSSU	subclerks
BCEKMRSUU	bumsucker
BCEKNPRUY	cyberpunk
BCEKORTUX	tuckerbox
BCELMNOUW	clubwomen
BCELMOOTY	lobectomy
BCELOOSSU	colobuses
	lobscouse
BCELORSUY	obscurely
BCEMOORSY	corymbose
BCENOORRR	cornborer
BCENORSTU	curbstone
BCEORRRWY	crowberry
BCEORSSTU	obscurest
BCEORSTUX	subcortex
BCEPRTTUU	buttercup
BCFHILLNU	bullfinch
BCGHILNOT	blotching
BCGHILNTU	nightclub
BCGIILOOS	biologics
BCGIIMNNO	combining
BCGIKLNSU	bucklings
BCGIKRSUV	Vicksburg
BCGILMNRU	crumbling
BCGILMNSU	scumbling
BCGINORSU	obscuring
BCHIIMSTU	bismuthic
BCHIIOPRS	bishopric
BCHIIRSTU	hubristic
BCHIIRSTY	hybristic
BCHIKLSUY	buckishly
BCHILLOTY	blotchily
BCHILOOPY	lyophobic
BCHIOORSY	choirboys
BCHKNORSU	buckhorns
BCHKNORTU	buckthorn
BCHKOOTTU	bucktooth
BCHKOSSTU	buckshots
BCHLNOPUW	punchbowl
BCHLOOOSY	schoolboy
BCHLOORTW	blowtorch
BCIILMSUU	umbilicus
BCIILPSTU	publicist
BCIILPTUY	publicity
BCIILRTUY	lubricity

BCIIMNOOS	bionomics
BCIIMOSTY	symbiotic
BCIIOOOTZ	zoobiotic
BCIIOOPRT	probiotic
BCIKKNOST	knobstick
BCIKKNSSU	buckskins
BCIKKORRW	brickwork
BCIKLOOST	bootlicks
BCIKNNRSU	Innsbruck
BCIKNRSUW	Brunswick
BCIKORRSW	cribworks
BCIKORSSW	bitstocks
BCILLORSS	crossbill
BCILMMOUU	columbium
BCILORSUU	lubricous
BCIMNOOTY	mycobiont
BCINOSSTU	subtonics
BCIOOPRSS	proboscis
BCIOPSSTU	subtopics
BCIORSTUY	obscurity
BCIPRSSTU	subscript
BCKKOOOOS	cookbooks
BCKOOOPSY	copybooks
BCLMOOSUU	columbous
BCMNOOORR	broomcorn
BCMOORSTU	combustor
BCMOORSUY	corymbous
BCOOORSTW	crowboots
BCOORSSSW	crossbows
BCORSSTTU	obstructs
BDDDEEISU	disbudded
BDDDEEFLU	befuddled
BDDDEEINR	bedridden
BDDDEGINU	debudding
BDDEEEFIR	debriefed
BDDEEEILV	bedeviled
BDDEEEINZ	bedizened
BDDEEFLSU	befuddles
BDDEEFOOR	foreboded
BDDEEGGRU	begrudged
BDDEEGHIT	bedighted
BDDEEGIMN	embedding
BDDEEGIRR	Redbridge
BDDEEINSW	bindweeds
BDDEEIORR	broidered
BDDEEIOSY	disobeyed
BDDEEIRRS	reedbirds
BDDEEISTU	subedited
BDDEELNRU	blundered
BDDEELORU	redoubled
BDDEENORU	rebounded
BDDEENRRU	underbred
BDDEENSTU	subtended
BDDEFINOR	forbidden
BDDEFIORR	forbidder
BDDEGIIMN	imbedding
BDDEGIINR	rebidding
BDDEGLOOU	doodlebug
BDDEHINOU	hidebound
BDDEHLOOS	bloodshed
BDDEIILMR	birdlimed
BDDEIILNS	blindside

BDDEIIMOR	dibromide
BDDEIISUV	subdivide
BDDEILNRU	unbridled
BDDEIMOSY	disembody
BDDEINOTU	outbidden
BDDEINRSU	disburden
	underbids
BDDEIRSSU	disbursed
BDDEIRSTU	disturbed
BDDEKNOSU	deskbound
BDDELLOUZ	bulldozed
BDDELNNUU	unbundled
BDDELSUUY	subduedly
BDDENNOUU	unbounded
BDDENORUY	underbody
BDDENOTUU	undoubted
BDDENSUUU	unsubdued
BDDFILLNO	blindfold
BDDFMNOUU	dumbfound
BDDGILNOR	broddling
BDDHIIRSY	dihybrids
BDDINNOUW	windbound
BDDLOOOOW	bloodwood
BDEEEEFLN	enfeebled
BDEEEEJLW	bejeweled
BDEEEELRV	belvedere
BDEEEFILL	Bielefeld
BDEEEFINT	benefited
BDEEEGIRV	Beveridge
BDEEEGLRR	Lederberg
BDEEEGLUW	bugleweed
BDEEEHLRT	blethered
BDEEEHRSW	beshrewed
BDEEEISTW	dweebiest
BDEEEKNOT	betokened
BDEEEELMRS	resembled
BDEEELMZZ	embezzled
BDEEEELNOS	nosebleed
BDEEELSUW	blueweeds
BDEEEMMNT	embedment
BDEEEMORW	embowered
BDEEENRTU	debenture
BDEEERSTW	bestrewed
BDEEERTTV	brevetted
BDEEFIILS	disbelief
BDEEFIIRV	verbified
BDEEFINRS	befriends
BDEEFLLOW	bedfellow
BDEEFLORW	flowerbed
BDEEFOORR	foreboder
BDEEFOORS	forebodes
BDEEFOOSW	beefwoods
BDEEFOOTW	webfooted
BDEEGGLOW	bowlegged
BDEEGGORS	Godesberg
BDEEGGRSU	begrudges
BDEEGHINT	benighted
BDEEGILOR	de Broglie
BDEEGMRSU	submerged
BDEEGNORU	burgeoned
BDEEHIITX	exhibited
BDEEHILMS	blemished

BDEEHIORT	Bodhi Tree
BDEEHLLSU	bushelled
BDEEHLORS	beholders
BDEEHORTT	betrothed
BDEEHTUUX	Buxtehude
BDEEIILLN	indelible
BDEEIILOS	biodiesel
BDEEIILRS	derisible
BDEEIINNZ	benzidine
BDEEIINRS	binderies
BDEEIISTU	dubieties
BDEEIKLNR	blinkered
BDEEIKNRS	briskened
BDEEIILLRW	bridewell
BDEEIILLTT	belittled
BDEEILMNO	belemnoid
BDEEILMOR	embroiled
BDEEILMOS	embolised
BDEEILMOZ	embolized
BDEEILMSS	dissemble
BDEEILNNO	nonedible
BDEEILNSU	nebulised
BDEEILNSV	vendibles
BDEEILNUZ	nebulized
BDEEILOPR	preboiled
BDEEILRST	blistered
BDEEILRSW	bewilders
BDEEIMMRS	dismember
BDEEIMORR	embroider
BDEEINRRT	interbred
BDEEIORSY	disobeyer
BDEEIQRTU	briqueted
BDEEIRRST	bestirred
BDEEIRSST	bestrides
BDEEIRSSU	suberised
BDEEIRSTT	bedsitter
BDEEIRSUZ	suberized
BDEEKNRSU	debunkers
BDEEKNRUU	unrebuked
BDEEKOORW	brookweed
BDEELLNRU	Brudenell
BDEELLSSY	blessedly
BDEELMNOS	emboldens
BDEELMRSU	slumbered
BDEELMSUY	bemusedly
BDEELNRRU	blunderer
BDEELNSSU	unblessed
BDEELORST	bolstered
BDEELORSU	redoubles
BDEELRSTU	blustered
BDEEMMOOS	embosomed
BDEEMNOST	bodements
BDEEMRSSU	submersed
BDEEOPRRV	proverbed
BDEEORRRS	borderers
BDEEORSTU	outbreeds
BDEEORVVY	everybody
BDEEPPRSU	purebreds
BDEEPRRTU	perturbed
BDEERSSUV	subserved
BDEERSTUV	subverted
BDEFHIRSU	furbished

BDEFIILRR	riflebird
BDEFIIRRS	firebirds
BDEFIIRTU	brutified
BDEFILLOO	lifeblood
BDEFINORY	boyfriend
BDEFINRRS	fernbirds
BDEGGGINU	debugging
BDEGGHMUU	humbugged
BDEGGIINR	begirding
BDEGGINTU	budgeting
BDEGHILNO	beholding
BDEGHILNR	Lindbergh
BDEGHINRU	Edinburgh
BDEGIIILR	dirigible
BDEGIIINR	birdieing
BDEGIILOS	disoblige
BDEGIIMMN	bedimming
BDEGIINNR	rebinding
BDEGIKNNU	debunking
BDEGIKOOU	guidebook
BDEGIMNOY	embodying
BDEGIMRUY	Muybridge
BDEGINNNU	unbending
BDEGINNRU	burdening
BDEGINORR	bordering
BDEGINORS	desorbing
BDEGINORT	Tonbridge
BDEGINRRU	deburring
BDEGINSSU	debussing
BDEGLNORU	Oldenburg
BDEGLNOSU	bludgeons
BDEHIIINT	inhibited
BDEHIILMN	Blindheim
BDEHIIRSY	hybridise
BDEHIIRYZ	hybridize
BDEHILPSU	published
BDEHIMNOO	Bohemond I
BDEHINRSU	burnished
BDEHIORRS	shorebird
BDEHIORSU	birdhouse
BDEHLLOSY	bodyshell
BDEHNOSTU	South Bend
BDEHNRSUU	unbrushed
	underbush
BDEIIILSV	divisible
BDEIIILTY	edibility
BDEIIKLNS	Libeskind
BDEIILLNY	indelibly
BDEIILMOS	mobilised
BDEIILMOZ	mobilized
BDEIILMRS	birdlimes
BDEIILNNO	blennioid
BDEIIRTTU	turbidite
BDEIISSSU	subsidies
	subsidise
BDEIISSTU	subitised
BDEIISSUZ	subsidize
BDEIISTUZ	subitized
BDEIJMOSU	jumboised
BDEIJMOUZ	jumboized
BDEIJNOSU	subjoined
BDEIKKORU	duikerbok

BDEILLMSU	bdelliums	
BDEILLNOO	bloodline	
BDEILLNPS	spellbind	
BDEILMNOW	Wimbledon	
BDEILMOSS	semibolds	
BDEILNNSS	blindness	
BDEILNRSU	unbridles	
BDEILOOST	bloodiest	
BDEILOQTU	quodlibet	
BDEILORSV	lovebirds	
BDEILORUV	overbuild	
BDEILOSSU	subsoiled	
BDEILPRUU	upbuilder	
BDEILRRSY	lyrebirds	
BDEILSTTU	subtitled	
BDEIMNOST	disentomb	
BDEIMORSU	mousebird	
BDEIMSTTU	submitted	
BDEINNORW	windborne	
BDEINORSV	ovenbirds	
BDEINORTX	tinderbox	
BDEINORTZ	Trebizond	
BDEINOSTU	soundbite	
BDEINRSSU	burnsides	
	sideburns	
BDEINRSUU	unbruised	
BDEIOORRW	brierwood	
BDEIOORST	broodiest	
	robotised	
BDEIOORTZ	robotized	
BDEIORRSS	disrobers	
BDEIORSTU	subeditor	
BDEIOSSUX	suboxides	
BDEIPRSTU	buprestid	
BDEIRRSSU	disburser	
BDEIRRSTU	disturber	
BDEIRSSSU	disburses	
	subsiders	
BDEISSSTU	subsisted	
BDELLMOSY	symbolled	
BDELLOORS	bordellos	
BDELLOOSS	bloodless	
BDELLORUZ	bulldozer	
BDELLOSUZ	bulldozes	
BDELLRRUY	blurredly	
BDELMNNOO	Ben Lomond	
BDELMNPUU	unplumbed	
BDELMOOSS	blossomed	
BDELNNOSS	blondness	
BDELNNSUU	unbundles	
BDELNOOTU	doubleton	
BDELNOSSU	boundless	
BDELOORHW	lowbrowed	
BDELOPRSU	superbold	
BDELORSUU	doublures	
BDELOSSTU	doubtless	
BDEMMNNOU	ombudsmen	
BDEMNOOSU	unbosomed	
BDENNOOST	bondstone	
BDENNOSTU	dubonnets	
BDENNOTTU	obtundent	
BDENNRSUU	sunburned	

	unburdens	
BDENOORSU	burnoosed	
	eurobonds	
BDENOORTW	Brentwood	
BDENORSUU	burnoused	
BDENOSTUW	westbound	
BDENRSUUY	underbuys	
BDEOOORRW	woodborer	
BDEOPSSTU	subdepots	
BDEOORRSU	suborders	
BDEOORRSTU	obtruders	
BDFFIPRSU	puffbirds	
BDFHIILNS	blindfish	
BDFHNOOOU	hoofbound	
BDFILLLOS	billfolds	
BDFILNOOS	bloodfins	
BDFIRRSSU	surfbirds	
BDFLNOOSY	dobsonfly	
BDFORSSUY	bodysurfs	
BDGHOOSUY	doughboys	
BDGIIKNRS	kingbirds	
BDGIILNNS	blindings	
BDGIILNSU	buildings	
BDGIINNNU	unbinding	
BDGIINORS	disrobing	
BDGIINSSU	subsiding	
BDGILNNOS	blondings	
BDGILNOOY	bloodying	
BDGINNORW	bringdown	
BDGINNOTU	obtunding	
BDGINOORS	broodings	
BDGINORSS	birdsongs	
	songbirds	
BDGINORTU	obtruding	
BDHIIMRSY	hybridism	
BDHIIRTYY	hybridity	
BDHIMOORS	rhomboids	
BDHINOOOR	Robin Hood	
BDHKOOORU	Doukhobor	
BDHLOOOST	bloodshot	
BDHOOORTY	Boothroyd	
BDHOORSUW	brushwood	
BDIIILSVY	divisibly	
BDIILLNSW	windbills	
BDIIMORTY	morbidity	
BDIIOSTUY	dubiosity	
BDIIRTTUY	turbidity	
BDIKNORUV	Dubrovnik	
BDILLORSW	swordbill	
BDILMNNOO	moonblind	
BDILMNORW	blindworm	
BDILNNOWW	windblown	
BDILOSUUY	dubiously	
BDIMOSSTU	misdoubts	
BDINNOORU	ironbound	
BDINNRTUW	windburnt	
BDINORSSW	snowbirds	
BDIORRSTU	subtorrid	
BDIORSUZZ	burdizzos	
BDIOSSTUY	bodysuits	
BDKOOORSW	wordbooks	
BDKOOSSTU	studbooks	

BDLMOOORW	bloodworm	
BDLMOOSUY	molybdous	
BDLNOOOSU	doubloons	
BDLNOOSWW	blowdowns	
BDLOOOORT	bloodroot	
BDNNOOSUW	snowbound	
BDNORSTUW	downburst	
BEEEEEKPR	beekeeper	
BEEEEFLNR	enfeebler	
BEEEEFLNS	enfeebles	
BEEEEKMRW	Ember week	
BEEEEMRRY	Meyerbeer	
BEEEFILST	beetflies	
BEEEFINSS	beefiness	
BEEEGGRUZ	Zeebrugge	
BEEEGIMNS	beseeming	
BEEEGIRSS	besiegers	
BEEEGLNRT	greenbelt	
BEEEGNNOR	greenbone	
BEEEGNOOW	woebegone	
BEEEGRSTT	begetters	
BEEEHHLMT	Bethlehem	
BEEEHISST	bheesties	
BEEEHLLOR	hellebore	
BEEEHLRTT	Ethelbert	
BEEEHLSWW	webwheels	
BEEEHNOSY	honeybees	
BEEEHNOTV	Beethoven	
BEEEILLLS	Belle Isle	
	libellees	
BEEEILLST	billetees	
BEEEILMMS	emblemise	
BEEEILMMZ	emblemize	
BEEEILMNT	belemnite	
BEEEILRSV	believers	
	eversible	
BEEEIMRSV	semibreve	
BEEEINRSS	beeriness	
BEEEIRRSW	breweries	
BEEEIRSTZ	breeziest	
BEEEKRRRS	berserker	
BEEELLRSV	bevellers	
BEEELMNSS	ensembles	
BEEELMRRS	resembler	
BEEELMRSS	resembles	
BEEELMRRZ	embezzler	
BEEELMSZZ	embezzles	
BEEELSSSU	sublessee	
BEEEMMRRS	remembers	
BEEENNOTV	Benevento	
BEEENOSSS	obeseness	
BEEERSSTT	besetters	
BEEFFGIRU	febrifuge	
BEEFFRSTU	buffeters	
BEEFIILMS	misbelief	
BEEFIILNR	inferible	
BEEFIIRSV	verbifies	
BEEFILRSS	briefless	
	fiberless	
	fibreless	
BEEFINRSS	briefness	
BEEFIORSX	fireboxes	

BEEFISTUX	tubifexes	**BEEIILRST**	liberties		rebellows
BEEFLORSU	befoulers	**BEEIINRTY**	inebriety	**BEELLRSUX**	Bruxelles
BEEFOORST	freeboots	**BEEIIRSTV**	brevities	**BEELMNORU**	Melbourne
BEEGGIINS	besieging	**BEEIKLMRU**	berkelium	**BEELMOORT**	bolometer
BEEGGINNR	breenging	**BEEIKLMRY**	Kimberley	**BEELMORST**	temblores
BEEGGINTT	begetting	**BEEIKPRSU**	superbike	**BEELMRRST**	tremblers
BEEGGNRTU	Gutenberg	**BEEILLLRS**	libellers	**BEELMRRSU**	lumberers
BEEGHIRTY	eyebright	**BEEILLMSU**	emulsible		slumberer
BEEGHNRRU	Ehrenburg	**BEEILLNOR**	rebellion	**BEELNNORS**	ennoblers
BEEGIIILLL	illegible	**BEEILLNTU**	ebullient	**BEELNNOSS**	nobleness
BEEGIILNV	believing	**BEEILLRST**	billeters	**BEELNOSSU**	bluenoses
BEEGIINOT	Gibeonite	**BEEILLRTT**	belittler	**BEELNOSTU**	bluestone
BEEGIKLLO	globelike	**BEEILLRTU**	rubellite	**BEELORRST**	bolsterer
BEEGILLNR	rebelling	**BEEILLSTT**	belittles	**BEELORSVY**	obversely
BEEGILLNV	bevelling	**BEEILMORR**	embroiler		verbosely
BEEGILLNW	wellbeing	**BEEILMOSS**	embolises	**BEELORTTX**	letterbox
BEEGILLRS	gerbilles	**BEEILMOSZ**	embolizes	**BEELOSSTU**	boletuses
BEEGILNRS	inselberg	**BEEILMPRS**	periblems	**BEELQRSUU**	burlesque
BEEGILNRY	berleying	**BEEILNOST**	bilestone	**BEELRRSTU**	blusterer
BEEGILPRS	Spielberg	**BEEILNRSU**	nebuliser	**BEELRSTUU**	trueblues
BEEGILRSU	beguilers	**BEEILNRUZ**	nebulizer	**BEEMMNNOR**	nonmember
BEEGINNRR	Nirenberg	**BEEILNSSS**	sensibles	**BEEMMNOTW**	embowment
BEEGINNRS	beginners	**BEEILNSSU**	nebulises	**BEEMMNRTU**	Number Ten
BEEGINNRT	Tinbergen	**BEEILNSUZ**	nebulizes	**BEEMNRRSU**	renumbers
BEEGINRTT	bettering	**BEEILORTT**	briolette	**BEEMOPRST**	obtempers
BEEGINRTV	breveting	**BEEILOSTV**	lovebites	**BEEMORSSS**	embossers
BEEGINSST	beestings	**BEEILOTTU**	oubliette	**BEEMQSSUU**	embusques
BEEGINSSW	beeswings	**BEEILPRTU**	eruptible	**BEEMRSSSU**	submerses
BEEGINSTT	besetting	**BEEILRSST**	tribeless	**BEENOORRV**	overborne
BEEGLNOOS	Bolognese	**BEEILRSTU**	butleries	**BEENOQSTU**	obsequent
BEEGMNRRU	Nuremberg	**BEEILRSUZ**	Berzelius	**BEENORRST**	resorbent
BEEGMRRSU	Merseburg	**BEEILSSTU**	bluesiest	**BEENORSST**	soberness
BEEGMRSSU	submerges	**BEEILSTUV**	vestibule	**BEENORSTU**	tenebrous
BEEGNORRS	Rosenberg	**BEEIMMNRT**	timbermen	**BEENRSTTU**	brunettes
BEEGNRRST	Sternberg	**BEEIMMNTU**	imbuement	**BEEOORRSW**	boerewors
BEEGNRSSU	sungrebes	**BEEIMNRST**	tenebrism	**BEEOORSTT**	beetroots
BEEGNRSUV	Venusberg		tribesmen	**BEEORRSSV**	observers
BEEGRSSSU	burgesses	**BEEIMRRSU**	reimburse	**BEEORSSTU**	tuberoses
BEEHHMOST	behemoths	**BEEIMRSTT**	embitters	**BEEORSSTW**	bestowers
BEEHIKRRS	Berkshire	**BEEINNOTT**	bentonite	**BEEORSSUU**	subereous
BEEHILLMS	embellish	**BEEINNRST**	Bernstein	**BEEORSTTU**	soubrette
BEEHILMS	blemishes	**BEEINRRWY**	wineberry	**BEEPRRSTY**	presbyter
BEEHILTUZ	Buthelezi	**BEEINRSTT**	tenebrist	**BEERRSTTU**	rebutters
BEEHINRTT	terebinth	**BEEINRTTU**	butterine	**BEERRSTUV**	subverter
BEEHIOPRS	biosphere	**BEEIOQSSU**	Essequibo	**BEERSSSUV**	subserves
BEEHIORRV	herbivore		obsequies	**BEERSSTTY**	bystreets
BEEHIRSTU	Buteshire	**BEEIORSTV**	overbites	**BEFFGINRU**	buffering
BEEHLLOSX	hellboxes	**BEEIOSSSV**	obsessive		rebuffing
BEEHLLRSU	busheller	**BEEIQRTTU**	briquette	**BEFFGINTU**	buffeting
BEEHLMNSU	bushelmen	**BEEIRSSSU**	suberises	**BEFFIILLR**	fiberfill
BEEHLNRSU	Shelburne		subserises		fibrefill
BEEHLOORS	boreholes	**BEEIRSSUZ**	suberizes	**BEFFLNSSU**	bluffness
BEEHLOPRY	hyperbole	**BEEIRSTTT**	bitterest	**BEFGGGINO**	befogging
BEEHLRSSU	bushelers	**BEEIRSTTU**	butteries	**BEFGHILOS**	globefish
BEEHNOOPS	neophobes	**BEEIRTTTY**	ytterbite	**BEFGIILLS**	fillibegs
BEEHNOOPX	xenophobe	**BEEJKOSUX**	jukeboxes	**BEFGIINRS**	briefings
BEEHNNORS	Sherborne	**BEEKNORST**	kerbstone	**BEFGIINTT**	befitting
BEEIIKNRZ	Berezniki	**BEEKNOSST**	steenboks	**BEFGILNOO**	befooling
BEEIILLRV	Iberville	**BEEKOPRRY**	pokeberry	**BEFGILNOU**	befouling
BEEIILNRT	libertine	**BEELLLMUU**	umbellule	**BEFGILNSU**	fungibles
BEEIILNSZ	zibelines	**BEELLORSU**	resoluble	**BEFGINRUY**	rubefying
BEEIILOPS	epibolies	**BEELLORSW**	bellowers	**BEFGLNRSU**	Flensburg

BEFHILSSU	bushflies	
BEFHILSTU	blueshift	
BEFHIORRS	Frobisher	
BEFHIOSSX	boxfishes	
BEFHIRRSU	brushfire	
	furbisher	
	refurbish	
BEFHIRSSU	bushfires	
	furbishes	
BEFIILNSU	infusible	
BEFIILORT	fibrolite	
BEFIILRTY	febrility	
BEFIIRSTU	brutifies	
BEFILLOSW	blowflies	
BEFILMORS	forelimbs	
BEFINOPRU	ibuprofen	
BEFIORSTT	frostbite	
BEFLLLSUY	bellyfuls	
BEFLLOTTU	bottleful	
BEFLORSUW	furbelows	
BEFLRTTUY	butterfly	
BEGGGINRU	buggering	
BEGGGLOOX	gogglebox	
BEGGHMRUU	humbugger	
BEGGIILNU	beguiling	
BEGGIIMNR	begriming	
BEGGIINNN	beginning	
BEGGIINNR	breinging	
BEGGIINOO	boogieing	
BEGGILNNO	belonging	
BEGGINOSS	bogginess	
BEGGINSSU	bugginess	
BEGGNOORU	Bourgogne	
BEGGOOOSS	goosegobs	
BEGHHINOT	thighbone	
BEGHHOTTU	bethought	
BEGHIILPS	philibegs	
BEGHIILST	blighties	
BEGHILNSU	busheling	
BEGHILRST	blighters	
BEGHINOOV	behooving	
BEGHINORS	neighbors	
BEGHINORT	bothering	
BEGHINORU	neighbour	
BEGHINRST	brightens	
BEGHIORSU	Brighouse	
BEGHIOSST	gobshites	
BEGHIRSTT	brightest	
BEGHLNOSU	bungholes	
BEGHOSSUU	bughouses	
BEGIIILNT	ignitible	
BEGIILLLN	libelling	
BEGIILLLY	illegibly	
BEGIILLNT	billeting	
BEGIILMNR	limbering	
BEGIILNOR	reboiling	
BEGIILNOS	obelising	
BEGIILNOZ	obelizing	
BEGIILOOS	biologies	
BEGIIMNRT	timbering	
BEGIINNOS	ebonising	
BEGIINNOZ	ebonizing	

BEGIINNTY	benignity	
BEGIINRTT	bittering	
BEGIINSST	biestings	
BEGIIORST	bigotries	
BEGIJRTTU	jitterbug	
BEGIKNNRU	bunkering	
BEGIKNORR	brokering	
BEGILLLSU	bluegills	
BEGILLNOW	bellowing	
BEGILMNRT	trembling	
BEGILMNRU	lumbering	
BEGILMORY	gorblimey	
BEGILNNNO	ennobling	
BEGILNNTU	unbelting	
BEGILNRUY	burleying	
BEGILNSSS	blessings	
BEGILNSSU	bulginess	
BEGILRTTU	litterbug	
BEGIMNNOT	entombing	
BEGIMNNOW	enwombing	
BEGIMNNOW	enwombing	
BEGIMNNRU	numbering	
BEGIMNOSS	embossing	
BEGIMNPRU	bumpering	
BEGIMNSSU	embussing	
BEGINNNOS	nonbeings	
BEGINNORS	ringbones	
BEGINNORU	Ben-Gurion	
BEGINNSUV	subvening	
BEGINOORT	rebooting	
BEGINOOSU	biogenous	
BEGINORRS	resorbing	
BEGINORSU	subregion	
BEGINORSV	observing	
BEGINORTV	obverting	
BEGINOSSS	obsessing	
BEGINOSTT	obtesting	
BEGINOSTW	bestowing	
BEGINRRUY	reburying	
BEGINRTTU	buttering	
	rebutting	
BEGIOORSU	bourgeois	
BEGLLOOSY	globosely	
BEGLMRRSU	grumblers	
BEGLMRUUX	Luxemburg	
BEGMORRST	Bergström	
BEGNOORSU	bourgeons	
BEGNORSTU	burgonets	
BEGNOSSSU	bogusness	
BEGPRRSSU	Pressburg	
BEGPRSSUU	superbugs	
BEHHMOOOP	homophobe	
BEHIIINRT	inhibiter	
BEHIILPST	phlebitis	
BEHIIMNOY	yohimbine	
BEHIIORTX	exhibitor	
BEHIKLMTU	thumblike	
BEHIKLOSV	bolshevik	
BEHIKLRSU	brushlike	
	shrublike	
BEHIKLTUZ	Kitzbühel	
BEHIKSUVY	Kuibyshev	
BEHILLOSS	shoebills	

BEHILMRSW	whimbrels	
BEHILNNOR	Heilbronn	
BEHILNPSY	biphenyls	
BEHILOSST	bolshiest	
BEHILPRSU	publisher	
	republish	
BEHILPSSU	publishes	
BEHILRSTU	thuribles	
BEHINNOSS	shinbones	
BEHINOSSW	wishbones	
BEHINRRSU	burnisher	
BEHINRSSU	burnishes	
BEHINSSSU	bushiness	
BEHIORSTT	theorbist	
BEHIRSSTU	brushiest	
BEHKNOSUU	bunkhouse	
BEHLLOOSW	blowholes	
BEHLLRUVY	Lévy-Bruhl	
BEHLMSSTU	thumbless	
BEHLORRTY	brotherly	
BEHLRSSUU	bulrushes	
BEHMOORST	thrombose	
BEHMORSSU	rhombuses	
BEHNNRTUU	unburthen	
BEHNORSTU	buhrstone	
BEHOOPTTU	phototube	
BEHOOSSUY	houseboys	
BEHOPRTYV	bryophyte	
BEIIILNSV	invisible	
BEIIIOPSS	epibiosis	
BEIIIORRT	Robert III	
BEIIKRSTZ	kibitzers	
BEIILLNSY	sibylline	
BEIILLSST	libelists	
BEIILMNTW	nimblewit	
BEIILMOSS	mobilises	
	omissible	
BEIILMOSZ	mobilizes	
BEIILORTT	trilobite	
BEIILOTVZ	Leibovitz	
BEIILRRST	bristlier	
BEIILRSTU	tilburies	
BEIILSSTU	subtilise	
BEIILSTUZ	subtilize	
BEIIMNSSU	minibuses	
BEIIMORTU	Umberto II	
BEIINNRSS	brininess	
BEIINSSTT	bittiness	
BEIISSSTU	subitises	
BEIISSTUZ	subitizes	
BEIJMOSSU	jumboises	
BEIJMOSUZ	jumboizes	
BEIKLMOOR	brooklime	
BEIKLNSSU	bulkiness	
BEIKLOSTY	kilobytes	
BEIKMOORT	motorbike	
BEIKNNOST	steinboks	
BEIKNRSSS	briskness	
BEILLLOSU	libellous	
BEILLMRUY	beryllium	
BEILLMSUY	sublimely	
BEILLNORU	Bernoulli	

BEILLNOSU	insoluble	**BEKLOORST**	brooklets	**BFIILMORR**	libriform
BEILLNSTU	bulletins	**BEKLOOSTY**	Byelostok	**BFIINORSU**	fibrinous
BEILLOPSX	pillboxes		stylebook	**BFILNOTUU**	bountiful
BEILLOQUY	obliquely	**BEKNNNOUW**	unbeknown	**BFILORSUY**	fibrously
BEILLRTTY	brittlely	**BEKNOOOST**	notebooks	**BFIMORRSU**	bursiform
BEILLSSSS	blissless	**BEKOOOORSV**	overbooks	**BFINORRST**	firstborn
BEILLSTUY	subtilely	**BEKOOSTTX**	textbooks	**BFLOORSSU**	subfloors
BEILMMOSS	embolisms	**BELLNOSSU**	bullnoses	**BFMMOOORR**	bromoform
BEILMNRSU	unlimbers	**BELLORSTW**	bellworts	**BGGHIILNT**	blighting
BEILMOOST	bloomiest	**BELMOOORW**	elbowroom	**BGGILLNUY**	bulgingly
BEILMOSSY	symbolise	**BELMOORTY**	bolometry	**BGGILMNRU**	grumbling
BEILMOSYZ	symbolize	**BELMOPSUU**	plumbeous	**BGHHIORSW**	highbrows
BEILNNSTU	buntlines	**BELMRSSTU**	stumblers	**BGHIIKNOS**	kiboshing
BEILNOPSS	bonspiels	**BELNNSSTU**	bluntness	**BGHIKLOOT**	booklight
BEILNPRTU	blueprint	**BELNOORVW**	overblown	**BGHILMNSU**	humblings
BEILNRRSU	burliness	**BELNRTTUU**	turbulent	**BGHIMOSTU**	bigmouths
BEILOOPRT	potboiler	**BELOOPRST**	boltropes	**BGHINOOOO**	boohooing
BEILOOQSU	obloquies	**BELOORSVW**	overblows	**BGHLOOPUY**	ploughboy
BEILOORSV	boilovers	**BELORRSTU**	troublers	**BGHMOOOOS**	Ogbomosho
BEILOPPSW	blowpipes	**BELORSSSU**	sublessor	**BGHORRSUU**	Burroughs
BEILOPSSS	possibles	**BELQRSUUY**	brusquely	**BGIIIKNTZ**	kibitzing
BEILORSST	strobiles	**BEMNOORST**	trombones	**BGIILLNOW**	billowing
BEILORSSU	subsoiler	**BEMNOORSU**	unbosomer	**BGIILLNOX**	bollixing
BEILORSTT	librettos	**BEMNOOSTT**	tombstone	**BGIILMNSU**	subliming
BEILORTUV	overbuilt	**BEMNORTUU**	outnumber	**BGIILMOOR**	imbroglio
BEILOSSTW	blowsiest	**BEMNOSSUX**	buxomness	**BGIILNOQU**	obliquing
BEILOSTWZ	blowziest	**BEMOORRSS**	sombreros	**BGIILNRSS**	brislings
BEILPRSTV	blipverts	**BEMOOSTTT**	bottomset	**BGIILNRST**	bristling
BEILRRSTU	blurriest	**BEMSSSTUY**	subsystem	**BGIILOOST**	biologist
BEILRSTTT	brittlest	**BENNNOSTU**	sunbonnet	**BGIINRSSU**	bruisings
BEILSSTTU	subtilest		unbonnets	**BGIKLNOST**	kingbolts
	subtitles	**BENNOORSW**	brownnose	**BGIKNOPRS**	springbok
BEIMMNNORR	merbromin	**BENNOPSYY**	pennyboys	**BGILLNOSU**	globulins
BEIMNOORS	bromeosin	**BENNORSSW**	brownness	**BGILLNRSU**	bullrings
BEIMNORST	brimstone	**BENOORRST**	Robertson	**BGILMNOOY**	myoglobin
BEIMNOSSU	omnibuses	**BENOORSSU**	burnooses	**BGILMNOSY**	symboling
BEIMNPSSU	bumpiness	**BENOOSTUU**	bounteous	**BGILMNSTU**	stumbling
BEIMOORSS	ribosomes	**BENORRSSU**	suborners	**BGILMOSTU**	gumbotils
BEIMOORST	biostrome	**BENORRSTU**	burrstone	**BGILNNOTU**	unbolting
BEIMRSSTU	resubmits	**BENORRSWY**	snowberry	**BGILNNRUY**	burningly
BEIMRSTTU	submitter	**BENORRTTU**	Otterburn	**BGILNORST**	ringbolts
BEIMRTTUY	ytterbium	**BENORSSTU**	burstones	**BGILNORTU**	troubling
BEINNNRSUW	Swinburne		rubstones	**BGILOORTY**	tribology
BEINOOPRT	obreption	**BENORSSUU**	burnouses	**BGILOOSTY**	globosity
BEINOORSV	obversion	**BENORSTTU**	buttoners	**BGIMNOOTT**	bottoming
BEINOOSSS	obsession		obstruent	**BGIMNSSUU**	subsuming
BEINOOSSZ	booziness		rebuttons	**BGINNNOOT**	Bonington
BEINOSSSS	bossiness	**BENRTTTUU**	butternut	**BGINNORSU**	suborning
BEINRRRTWY	twinberry	**BEOOORSTV**	overboots	**BGINNORSW**	brownings
BEINRTTTU	bitternut	**BEOOPSSTX**	postboxes	**BGINNORTU**	binturong
BEINSSSSUY	businessy	**BEOORRRSW**	borrowers	**BGINNOTTU**	buttoning
BEIOOPRRU	pourboire	**BEOPSSSTU**	postbuses	**BGINOORRW**	borrowing
BEIOORRRT	brierroot	**BEORRRSUW**	burrowers	**BGINOOTUX**	outboxing
BEIOORSST	robotises	**BFFHORSSU**	brushoffs	**BGINOOWWW**	bowwowing
BEIOORSTZ	robotizes	**BFFIIMORR**	fibriform	**BGINORRUW**	burrowing
BEIOQRSTU	sobriquet	**BFFLOSTUU**	outbluffs	**BGINORSTW**	bowstring
BEIOQSTUU	boutiques	**BFGHILLTU**	bullfight	**BGLLOOSUU**	globulous
BEIORSTUV	obtrusive	**BFGHINSTU**	bunfights	**BGLMOOSYY**	symbology
BEIORSTVY	verbosity	**BFGLLORSU**	bullfrogs	**BGNOORSTX**	strongbox
BEIRSSSTU	subsister	**BFGLORSUW**	Wolfsburg	**BGOPRSSUU**	subgroups
BEJORSTTU	turbojets	**BFHILOSST**	fishbolts	**BHHIIKKNU**	bhikkhuni
BEKLOOOSU	booklouse	**BFHILOSSW**	fishbowls	**BHHIMORTY**	biorhythm

BHIIINORT	inhibitor	BKKOOORSW	workbooks	CCDEFIIRU	crucified
BHIILLLLY	hillbilly	BKLLMNSUU	numbskull	CCDEGINNO	conceding
BHIILLNOT	billionth	BKMOOORSW	bookworms	CCDEGINOT	decocting
BHIIMORUZ	rhizobium	BKOOORSTY	storybook	CCDEHIPPU	hiccupped
BHIIOPRST	prohibits	BLLMOORSW	bollworms	CCDEHNRSU	scrunched
BHIKLLOOS	billhooks	BLOORSTUU	troublous	CCDEIIIPT	epidictic
BHIKLOOSY	bookishly	BNNOSTTUU	unbuttons	CCDEIIKNP	picnicked
BHILLNORS	hornbills	BNOOOSSUY	sonobuoys	CCDEIINOS	coincides
BHILLNORT	thornbill	BNOORSTUW	brownouts	CCDEIIRTU	circuited
BHILLPSUW	bullwhips	BNRSSSTUU	sunbursts	CCDEILOOR	crocodile
BHILLSSTU	bullshits	BOOPPRRTU	turboprop	CCDEILRTY	tricycled
BHILMNOTY	bimonthly	BORSSTTUU	outbursts	CCDEILSTY	dyslectic
BHILOORSY	boorishly	CCCDENOOT	concocted	CCDEINNOV	convinced
BHILRSTUY	brutishly	CCCEEINRT	eccentric	CCDEINOOT	decoction
BHIMOOSTY	tomboyish	CCCEIILPY	epicyclic	CCDEINOTV	convicted
BHIOOPRST	biotrophs	CCCENOORT	concocter	CCDEINOUV	conducive
BHIOORRTT	birthroot	CCCFKOORT	Cockcroft	CCDELNORU	concluder
BHIORRTTW	birthwort	CCCGINOOO	gonococci	CCDELNOSU	concludes
BHJOORSTW	jobsworth	CCCHHIKOT	Hitchcock	CCDELNOTU	occludent
BHKNOOORS	hornbooks	CCCHIINNO	cinchonic	CCDENOORT	Condorcet
BHKORRSUW	brushwork	CCCHIKNOP	pinchcock	CCDENORRU	concurred
BHLLNORSU	bullhorns	CCCHILMOU	colchicum	CCDENORSU	conducers
BHLLOOOTT	tollbooth	CCCHILOOT	coccolith	CCDENOSSU	concussed
BHLMPSUUY	subphylum	CCCIILRTY	tricyclic	CCDEORSUU	succoured
BHLOOOSTT	tolbooths	CCCIKMMOR	McCormick	CCDESSSUU	succussed
BHMNOOOSU	bonhomous	CCCKOORSW	cockcrows	CCDFKOORR	Crockford
BHMNSTTUU	thumbnuts	CCCNOOORT	concoctor	CCDGILNOU	occluding
BHNOOOSST	bosthoons	CCDDEEESU	succeeded	CCDGINNOU	conducing
BHNOORSTX	boxthorns	CCDDEIINO	coincided	CCDHIILOR	chloridic
BIIILNSVY	invisibly	CCDDEKLOU	cuckolded	CCDHIIMOR	dichromic
BIIKNNOTV	Botvinnik	CCDDELNOU	concluded	CCDHIIOPT	dichoptic
BIILMSTUY	sublimity	CCDDENOTU	conducted	CCDHINOOS	conchoids
BIILNOOSV	oblivions	CCDEEEHKR	checkered	CCDHKOOUW	woodchuck
BIILOOSUV	oblivious		rechecked	CCDIILNRY	cylindric
BIILOQTUY	obliquity	CCDEEEHRS	screeched	CCDIILTYY	cytidylic
BIILSTTUY	subtility	CCDEEEINS	decencies	CCDIINOSS	scincoids
BIIMMNORS	brominism	CCDEEENRS	credences	CCDIIOORT	corticoid
BIIMMOSSZ	zombiisms	CCDEEERSU	succeeder	CCDKLORUY	cuckoldry
BIIMNOORR	Borromini	CCDEEFNOT	confected	CCDKOOOSW	woodcocks
BIIMNOOST	bionomist	CCDEEHIKW	chickweed	CCDNOORTU	conductor
BIIMOPRTY	improbity	CCDEEHIRS	screiched	CCDOOOSUW	cocuswood
BIIMOSSSY	symbiosis	CCDEEHKNU	unchecked	CCEEEFLNU	feculence
BIKKORSYZ	Korzybski	CCDEEHORT	crocheted	CCEEEHHRR	recherche
BIKLNNOSW	snowblink	CCDEEIINN	incidence	CCEEEHNOR	coherence
BIKOOSUUZ	bouzoukis	CCDEEIKRT	cricketed	CCEEEHRRS	screecher
BILLNOOPS	spoonbill	CCDEEILNR	encircled	CCEEEHRSS	screeches
BILLNOOSU	bouillons	CCDEEILOW	colicweed	CCEEEIKNP	neckpiece
BILLNORST	stillborn	CCDEEINNY	indecency	CCEEEINNS	nescience
BILLNOSUY	insolubly	CCDEEINOT	conceited	CCEEEINRT	reticence
BILMMOSSY	symbolism	CCDEEINOV	conceived	CCEEEIRSS	secrecies
BILMOORST	Stromboli	CCDEEINRS	crescendi	CCEEELORT	rectocele
BILMOSSTY	symbolist	CCDEEIOPS	codpieces	CCEEEMMOR	ecommerce
BILNOSTUU	botulinus	CCDEELLOT	collected	CCEEGINOR	concierge
BILOOPRTU	politburo	CCDEEMMNO	commenced	CCEEGINOT	ectogenic
BILOOSUVY	obviously	CCDEENNOR	concerned	CCEEHIKNR	checkrein
BILORSSTU	strobilus	CCDEENNOS	ensconced	CCEEHILMY	hemicycle
BIMNOSSTY	symbionts	CCDEENNOT	connected	CCEEHIRSS	screiches
BIMNRSUUV	viburnums	CCDEENORS	conceders	CCEEHKNNS	schnecken
BIMOPSTUU	bumptious		crescendo	CCEEHKORV	overcheck
BINOOOSUX	obnoxious	CCDEENORT	concerted	CCEEHKPRS	prechecks
BINOORSTU	obtrusion		concreted	CCEEHLORT	cerecloth
BIOPRSSTW	bowsprits	CCDEEORRT	corrected	CCEEHNORY	coherency

CCEEHORRT	crocheter	**CCEHIKOSS**	cockshies	**CCEINRSTU**	cinctures
CCEEHOTTU	couchette	**CCEHILNOR**	chronicle	**CCEINRSTY**	syncretic
CCEEIIPPR	precipice	**CCEHILNRS**	clinchers	**CCEINSSTY**	synectics
CCEEIKLST	cleckiest	**CCEHINORS**	corniches	**CCEIOORST**	creosotic
CCEEIKRRT	cricketer	**CCEHINRRU**	crunchier	**CCEIOPRSU**	occupiers
CCEEILNOR	reconcile	**CCEHINRSU**	crunchies	**CCEIOPRTY**	precocity
CCEEILNRS	encircles		scrunchie	**CCEIORSSU**	succories
CCEEILOST	scolecite	**CCEEHIORST**	ricochets	**CCEKORRSS**	rockcress
CCEEILPRY	pericycle	**CCEHKLNOT**	neckcloth	**CCEKORRSW**	corkscrew
CCEEILPSY	epicycles	**CCEHKLRSU**	chucklers	**CCELLMNNO**	McConnell
CCEEILRST	electrics	**CCEHKMOOR**	checkroom	**CCELLMRSU**	McCullers
CCEEIMNOU	oecumenic	**CCEHKOORS**	cockhorse	**CCELLNOOY**	colonelcy
CCEEIMORT	ectomeric	**CCEHKORSW**	checkrows	**CCELLOORT**	collector
CCEEINNNO	innocence	**CCEHKOSTU**	checkouts	**CCELMNOOY**	monocycle
CCEEINORS	cicerones	**CCEHLMORS**	cromlechs	**CCELMOOTY**	colectomy
CCEEINORT	ectocrine	**CCEEHLOSTY**	cholecyst	**CCELMOPST**	complects
CCEEINORV	conceiver	**CCEHNNOSU**	scuncheon	**CCELNSTUU**	succulent
CCEEINOSV	conceives	**CCEHNOSTU**	scutcheon	**CCELOPRSU**	corpuscle
CCEEIOPST	copesetic	**CCEHNRSSU**	scrunches	**CCELORRTY**	correctly
CCEEIQRTU	quercetic	**CCEHORRSS**	scorchers	**CCENNNORU**	unconcern
CCEEIRRST	rectrices	**CCEHORSTT**	crotchets	**CCENNOORT**	connector
CCEEIRSTT	tectrices	**CCEHORTTY**	crotchety	**CCENOORST**	concertos
CCEEISTTU	eutectics	**CCEHOTTUZ**	zucchetto	**CCENOORSU**	concourse
CCEEKLLOR	Cockerell	**CCEHRRTUY**	cutcherry	**CCENOORTV**	convector
CCEEKLORS	cockerels	**CCEHRSSTU**	scutchers	**CCENORRTU**	occurrent
CCEEKLORT	cockleert	**CCEIIIPRT**	epicritic	**CCENORSTU**	succentor
CCEELLORT	recollect	**CCEIIIRST**	criticise	**CCENOSSSU**	concusses
CCEELOSTY	cystocele	**CCEIIIRTZ**	criticize	**CCEOOPRSY**	cryoscope
CCEELOTUY	leucocyte	**CCEIIKNPR**	picnicker	**CCEOOPRTT**	ectoproct
CCEEMMNOR	commencer	**CCEIILNOT**	niccolite	**CCEOORRRT**	corrector
CCEEMMNOS	commences	**CCEIILNST**	enclitics	**CCEOPPRUY**	preoccupy
CCEENNORT	concenter	**CCEIILRST**	scleritic	**CCEORRSSU**	succorers
	concentre	**CCEIIMOSS**	coseismic	**CCEORRSUU**	succourer
	connecter	**CCEIINSTY**	cysteinic	**CCEORSSSU**	successor
	reconnect	**CCEIIOPPR**	pericopic	**CCEORSSTU**	stuccoers
CCEENNOSS	ensconces	**CCEIKKLLO**	clocklike	**CCESSSSUU**	succusses
CCEENOOTY	coenocyte	**CCEIKLLOY**	kilocycle	**CCFGHIKOT**	cockfight
CCEENORST	concretes	**CCEIKLOSW**	clockwise	**CCFHIINOO**	finocchio
CCEENRSST	crescents	**CCEIKNOSS**	cockiness	**CCFIILOOR**	colorific
CCEESSSSU	successes	**CCEILMOPS**	complices	**CCFILNOST**	conflicts
CCEFFHKOS	checkoffs	**CCEILNNOU**	nucleonic	**CCFIMORRU**	cruciform
CCEFFIIIL	felicific	**CCEILNOSY**	concisely	**CCFINOSUU**	Confucius
CCEFIIPSS	specifics	**CCEILNOTY**	cyclonite	**CCFKLOOST**	cocklofts
CCEFIIRRU	crucifier	**CCEILNSUY**	unicycles	**CCFKOOOST**	cocksfoot
CCEFIIRSU	crucifies	**CCEILORST**	sclerotic	**CCFLLOSUU**	flocculus
CCEFIRRSU	crucifers	**CCEILOSUV**	occlusive	**CCGHHINOU**	chincough
CCEFKNOYY	cockneyfy	**CCEILRRSU**	curricles	**CCGHHINOU**	churching
CCEFLLOSU	floccules	**CCEILRSTY**	tricycles	**CCGHHIOSU**	hiccoughs
CCEGHHNOW	Chengchow	**CCEILRSUU**	curlicues	**CCGHIILNN**	clinching
CCEGHHNOW	Chengchow	**CCEIMNOOS**	economics	**CCGHIINPU**	hiccuping
CCEGHILNN	clenching	**CCEIMORTY**	microcyte	**CCGHIKLNU**	chuckling
CCEGHIMRU	chemurgic	**CCEIMOSST**	cosmetics	**CCGHILNTU**	clutching
CCEGIKNOR	cockering	**CCEIMRSUV**	cervicums	**CCGHILOOP**	choplogic
CCEGILNRY	recycling	**CCEINNNOY**	innocency	**CCGHINNRU**	crunching
CCEGINNOO	oncogenic	**CCEINNORV**	convincer	**CCGHINOOT**	cootching
CCEGINORY	cryogenic	**CCEINNOSV**	convinces	**CCGHINORS**	scorching
CCEHHIRRU	churchier	**CCEINOORS**	coercions	**CCGHINORU**	crouching
CCEHHMNRU	churchmen	**CCEINOOSS**	consocies	**CCGHINOST**	scotching
CCEHHNRUW	New Church	**CCEINORRT**	incorrect	**CCGHINOSU**	couchings
CCEHIILRS	schlieric	**CCEINORTV**	reconvict	**CCGHINRTU**	crutching
CCEHIIORS	chicories	**CCEINOSTT**	tectonics	**CCGHINSTU**	scutching
CCEHIKLOO	chokecoil	**CCEINPRST**	precincts	**CCGIINNOR**	cornicing
CCEHIKLST	checklist				

413

CCGIINOPP	coppicing
CCGIKNOOU	cuckooing
CCGILLLOY	glycollic
CCGILMOOV	mycologic
CCGILNOTU	occulting
CCGILOORY	cyclogiro
CCGINNOOO	cocooning
CCGINOPUY	occupying
CCGINORRU	occurring
CCGINORSU	succoring
CCGINOSTU	stuccoing
CCHHILLRU	Churchill
CCHHLORUW	Low Church
CCHHOOPST	hopscotch
CCHHOOSWW	chowchows
CCHIIIRTT	trichitic
CCHIILORT	chloritic
CCHIIMOPR	microchip
CCHIIMORT	trichomic
CCHIINOOR	chorionic
CCHIINSUZ	zucchinis
CCHIIOORS	isochoric
CCHIIORRT	cirrhotic
	trichroic
CCHILNRUY	crunchily
CCHILOORT	chlorotic
CCHINNOOR	cornichon
CCHINRSTY	strychnic
CCHIOPSTY	psychotic
CCHKOOSST	cockshots
CCHLNOOTY	colocynth
CCIIILNOP	picolinic
CCIIILNOS	isoclinic
CCIIILNRT	triclinic
CCIIIMRST	criticism
CCIIINNOT	nicotinic
CCIILLLOU	colliculi
CCIILNOTY	clonicity
CCIILOOST	scoliotic
CCIILOPRT	proclitic
CCIIMNSSY	cynicisms
CCIINNOOS	concision
CCIINOPSY	isopycnic
CCIIORRTT	tricrotic
CCIIRRTUY	circuitry
CCIKKLOPS	picklocks
CCIKKOSTT	ticktocks
CCILMOSTU	occultism
CCILNOOPY	polyconic
CCILNOORU	councilor
CCILNOOSU	occlusion
CCILOOORT	colicroot
CCILORSUU	curculios
CCILOSTTU	occultist
CCILOTTYY	cytolytic
CCIMMOORS	microcosm
CCIMNOOTY	monocytic
CCIMOOPRY	microcopy
CCINOOSSU	conscious
CCINOPRST	conscript
CCINORSTT	constrict
CCIOOOPRZ	coprozoic

CCIOOOPST	otoscopic
CCIOOPRSU	uroscopic
CCIOOSTTV	otocystic
CCIOOSTXY	oxytocics
CCIOOTTXY	cytotoxic
CCJNNOSTU	conjuncts
CCKKLOORW	clockwork
CCKKLOOST	stocklock
CCKMOOORS	moorcocks
CCKNORSTU	turncocks
CCKOOPPPY	poppycock
CCKOOPSST	stopcocks
CCKOPRSSU	cockspurs
CCLNOORTY	cyclotron
CCNORSTTU	construct
CCOOPRSYY	cryoscopy
CCOOSTTUU	tucotucos
CCORSSSTU	crosscuts
CCSTTUUUU	tucutucus
CDDDEEENS	descended
CDDDEEILY	decidedly
CDDDEEINU	undecided
CDDDEIORS	discorded
CDDDIIOSY	diddicoys
CDDEEEFLT	deflected
CDDEEEINV	evidenced
CDDEEENRS	descender
	redescend
CDDEEENST	decedents
CDDEEEOPR	proceeded
CDDEEFKOR	defrocked
CDDEEGLLU	cudgelled
CDDEEHLSU	scheduled
CDDEEHNRU	chundered
CDDEEHSSU	duchessed
CDDEEIJST	disjected
CDDEEIKRR	derricked
CDDEEINRS	discerned
	rescinded
CDDEEINRU	reinduced
CDDEEINSX	exscinded
CDDEEIPRT	predicted
CDDEEISST	dissected
CDDEEITUV	deductive
CDDEEKOST	destocked
CDDEELNPU	peduncled
CDDEELOPU	decoupled
CDDEELPRU	precluded
CDDEEMMNO	commended
CDDEEMNNO	condemned
CDDEEMNRU	credendum
CDDEENNOS	condensed
CDDEENNOT	contended
CDDEENNOU	denounced
CDDEENSUU	unseduced
CDDEEPRTY	decrypted
CDDEFIILU	dulcified
CDDEGINTU	deducting
CDDEGIOTY	Dodge City
CDDEHORRT	Dordrecht
CDDEIILMO	domiciled
CDDEIILRU	ridiculed

CDDEIINRT	dendritic
CDDEIIOSV	videodisc
CDDEIIRST	discredit
CDDEILOSS	disclosed
CDDEILOST	cloddiest
CDDEIMOOU	duodecimo
CDDEINOTU	deduction
CDDEIOSUU	deciduous
CDDEIRSTU	cruddiest
CDDEISSSU	discussed
CDDELNOUU	unclouded
CDDELORWY	crowdedly
CDDENORUW	uncrowded
CDDEOORSW	codewords
CDDHHILOO	childhood
CDDHIIORY	hydriodic
CDDHIIQTU	quidditch
CDDIIILOP	diploidic
CDDIISSTY	dytiscids
CDDILNOOY	condyloid
CDEEEEFNR	deference
CDEEEELRT	reelected
CDEEEERRT	reerected
CDEEEERSX	exceeders
CDEEEFITV	defective
CDEEEFLRT	reflected
CDEEEFPRT	perfected
CDEEEGINR	decreeing
CDEEEGINX	exceeding
CDEEEGLNT	neglected
CDEEEHKNP	henpecked
CDEEEHLNO	echeloned
CDEEEHQRU	chequered
CDEEEIMRT	decimeter
	decimetre
CDEEEINNS	desinence
CDEEEINPT	centipede
CDEEEINRS	residence
CDEEEINRT	intercede
CDEEEINSV	evidences
CDEEEINUV	undeceive
CDEEEIPRT	receipted
CDEEEIPRV	perceived
CDEEEIPTV	deceptive
CDEEEIRSV	deceivers
CDEEEIRSX	exercised
CDEEEITTV	detective
CDEEELLOT	decollete
CDEEELNOR	redolence
CDEEELORT	electrode
CDEEELPRT	prelected
CDEEELSST	deselects
CDEEEMNRT	decrement
CDEEENNST	sentenced
CDEEENPRT	precedent
CDEEENQSU	sequenced
CDEEEOPRR	proceeder
CDEEEORRT	retrocede
CDEEEORRV	recovered
CDEEEPRSS	precessed
CDEEEPRST	respected
	sceptered

CDEEEPRTX	excerpted	CDEEHLQSU	squelched	CDEEINRST	stridence
CDEEERSTT	detecters	CDEEHLSSU	schedules	CDEEINRSU	reinduces
CDEEFFIOR	officered	CDEEHNRRS	drenchers	CDEEINRSY	residency
CDEEFGINT	defecting	CDEEHNRTU	chuntered	CDEEINSTU	inductees
CDEEFHLRS	feldscher	CDEEHORTU	retouched	CDEEINTUX	unexcited
CDEEFIILM	fieldmice	CDEEHRSTT	stretched	CDEEIORSV	divorcees
CDEEFIINT	deficient	CDEEHSSSU	duchesses	CDEEIORSX	exorcised
CDEEFIIOT	foeticide	CDEEIILRT	deciliter	CDEEIORXZ	exorcized
CDEEFIIPS	specified		decilitre	CDEEIOSTX	coexisted
CDEEFIIRT	certified	CDEEIILTV	videlicet	CDEEIOTTU	eutectoid
	rectified	CDEEIIMNS	medicines	CDEEIPRST	depicters
CDEEFIIST	feticides	CDEEIIMPR	epidermic	CDEEIPRSU	pedicures
CDEEFIKLR	flickered	CDEEIIMPS	epidemics	CDEEIPRTU	depicture
CDEEFILNT	inflected	CDEEIIMPU	epicedium	CDEEIRRSS	descriers
CDEEFILTU	deceitful	CDEEIIMRT	cetrimide	CDEEIRRST	redirects
CDEEFINOT	defection	CDEEIIMRV	decemviri	CDEEIRRTU	recruited
CDEEFIRTY	decertify		vermicide	CDEEIRSTT	trisected
CDEEFKORS	foredecks	CDEEIINST	indictees	CDEEIRTTU	certitude
CDEEFKOST	feedstock	CDEEIIPRR	cirripede		rectitude
CDEEFLORT	deflector	CDEEIIPST	pesticide	CDEEIRTUV	reductive
CDEEFNORR	conferred	CDEEIIPTV	depictive	CDEEISTUV	seductive
CDEEFNOSS	confessed	CDEEIIRTV	directive	CDEEJOPRT	projected
CDEEFORST	defectors	CDEEIISTT	dietetics	CDEEKOOPR	precooked
CDEEFORSU	refocused	CDEEIJNOT	dejection	CDEEKORST	restocked
CDEEGHIRS	screighed	CDEEIJPRU	prejudice	CDEEKORSW	rockweeds
CDEEGIILN	diligence	CDEEIJRUV	verjuiced	CDEELLMOP	compelled
CDEEGIIMR	germicide	CDEEIKLLN	nickelled	CDEELLNRU	cullender
CDEEGIINN	indigence	CDEEIKLNR	clinkered	CDEELMNTU	demulcent
CDEEGIINT	digenetic	CDEEIKLNU	duncelike	CDEELMOPT	completed
CDEEGIINV	deceiving	CDEEIKLRS	slickered	CDEELNORY	redolency
CDEEGIIRS	regicides	CDEEIKNQU	quickened	CDEELNOSU	counseled
CDEEGIJNT	dejecting	CDEEIKNRS	snickered	CDEELNPSU	peduncles
CDEEGILOR	Coleridge	CDEEIKSST	stickseed	CDEELNPTU	centupled
CDEEGILRY	glyceride	CDEEIKSTW	stickweed	CDEELOPPY	pelecypod
CDEEGINNR	decerning		wickedest	CDEELOPSU	decouples
CDEEGINOR	endoergic	CDEEILLNP	pencilled	CDEELORSS	sclerosed
CDEEGINOS	genocides	CDEEILNNO	indolence	CDEELPRSU	precludes
CDEEGINPR	preceding	CDEEILNRS	decliners	CDEELRSTU	clustered
CDEEGINTT	detecting	CDEEILNST	denticles	CDEELRSUX	excluders
CDEEGIOSS	geodesics		stenciled	CDEELRTTU	cluttered
CDEEGIOST	geodetics	CDEEILORR	Cordelier		declutter
CDEEGIRSU	cudgeries	CDEEILORS	creolised		
CDEEGLLRU	cudgeller	CDEEILORZ	creolized	CDEEMMNOR	recommend
CDEEGNORV	converged	CDEEILQSU	liquesced	CDEEMMNOT	commented
CDEEGNOST	congested	CDEEILRST	derelicts	CDEEMNNOR	condemner
CDEEHHIRS	cherished	CDEEILTXY	excitedly	CDEEMNNOT	contemned
CDEEHIIST	ethicised	CDEEIMMXY	myxedemic	CDEEMNOOS	comedones
CDEEHIITZ	ethicized	CDEEIMNNU	decennium	CDEEMOOPS	decompose
CDEEHIKLS	helidecks	CDEEIMNOU	eudemonic	CDEEMORST	ectoderms
CDEEHIKNT	thickened	CDEEIMNPU	impudence	CDEENNORS	condenser
CDEEHIKRS	shickered	CDEEIMPRS	premedics	CDEENNORT	contender
CDEEHIKRW	whickered	CDEEIMRSV	decemvirs	CDEENNORU	denouncer
CDEEHILLS	chiselled	CDEEINNOR	endocrine		renounced
CDEEHIMRS	Remscheid	CDEEINNSU	secundine	CDEENNOSS	condenses
CDEEHINST	dehiscent	CDEEINOPT	deception	CDEENNOST	consented
CDEEHIPRS	deciphers	CDEEINORT	recondite	CDEENNOSU	denounces
CDEEHIRTT	chittered	CDEEINOST	sectioned	CDEENNOTT	contented
CDEEHITWW	witchweed	CDEEINOTT	detection	CDEENNRSU	scunnered
CDEEHKOSU	deckhouse	CDEEINPST	inspected	CDEENNSTU	unscented
CDEEHLORT	reclothed	CDEEINQUY	De Quincey	CDEENOOPS	endoscope
CDEEHLORY	hydrocele	CDEEINRRS	discerner	CDEENOORT	coroneted
CDEEHLPPS	schlepped		rescinder	CDEENOQRU	conquered
				CDEENORRW	recrowned

CDEENORSS	seconders
CDEENORSV	conserved
	conversed
CDEENORTU	countered
	recounted
CDEENORTV	converted
CDEENORUV	uncovered
CDEENOSTT	contested
CDEENOSTX	coextends
CDEENPRTY	encrypted
CDEENRRTU	decurrent
CDEENRSSU	crudeness
CDEENRSTU	encrusted
CDEENRSUU	unsecured
CDEENRSUW	unscrewed
CDEENSUUX	unexcused
CDEEOORST	creosoted
CDEEOOSTV	dovecotes
CDEEOPRRR	prerecord
CDEEOPRRU	procedure
	reproduce
CDEEOPRSS	processed
CDEEOPRTT	protected
CDEEOQRTU	croqueted
CDEEOQTTU	coquetted
CDEEORRRS	recorders
	rerecords
CDEEORRSS	recrossed
CDEEORSTT	detectors
CDEEPPRSU	scuppered
CDEEPRSSU	percussed
CDEEPSSTU	suspected
CDEERSTTU	scuttered
CDEERSTUY	curtseyed
CDEERTTUV	curvetted
CDEFFIORU	coiffured
CDEFGIINU	fungicide
CDEFGINOR	deforcing
CDEFHIILL	Lichfield
CDEFHIIRR	Friedrich
CDEFHIOSS	codfishes
CDEFIIILS	filicides
CDEFIIISS	cissified
CDEFIIIST	fideistic
CDEFIILNT	inflicted
CDEFIILSU	dulcifies
CDEFIINST	disinfect
CDEFIIORS	codifiers
	scorified
CDEFIKLOR	frolicked
CDEFIKOSS	fossicked
CDEFILNOR	cornfield
CDEFIMNOR	confirmed
CDEFINNOT	confident
CDEFINORS	confiders
CDEFINTUY	fecundity
CDEFKNORU	unfrocked
CDEFMNOOR	conformed
CDEFMOORT	comforted
CDEFNOORW	downforce
CDEGGILNU	cudgeling
CDEGGLNOU	unclogged

CDEGHIINS	dehiscing
CDEGHINNO	chignoned
CDEGHINNR	drenching
CDEGHOSTT	Gottsched
CDEGIIKNR	dickering
CDEGIILNN	declining
CDEGIILOO	ideologic
CDEGIIMRU	demiurgic
CDEGIINNR	cindering
CDEGIINOT	coediting
CDEGIINOV	devoicing
CDEGIINPT	depicting
CDEGIINRT	crediting
	directing
CDEGIKNOR	redocking
CDEGIKNOT	docketing
CDEGILNPU	decupling
CDEGILNSU	secluding
CDEGILNUX	excluding
CDEGILOOP	logopedic
CDEGILOSU	glucoside
CDEGILOSY	glycoside
CDEGINNOS	consigned
	seconding
CDEGINORR	recording
CDEGINRSY	descrying
CDEGINSSY	dysgenics
CDEGLLOOU	collogued
CDEGLORST	goldcrest
CDEGNORSU	scrounged
CDEHHINTU	unhitched
CDEHIIKLL	childlike
CDEHIILNO	lichenoid
CDEHIILOS	helicoids
CDEHIILRT	Dirichlet
CDEHIIMOS	homicides
CDEHIINOS	echinoids
CDEHIIORT	dichroite
CDEHIKLLO	hillocked
CDEHIKOOY	doohickey
CDEHIKPSY	physicked
CDEHIKRSW	herdwicks
CDEHILLSS	childless
CDEHILOOR	choleroid
CDEHILORS	chlorides
CDEHILPST	stepchild
CDEHILSST	ditchless
CDEHINORT	chondrite
	threnodic
CDEHINOSU	cushioned
CDEHIOORT	Theodoric
CDEHIORRS	cirrhosed
CDEHIORSW	chordwise
CDEHIORTW	dowitcher
CDEHKLSSU	shelducks
CDEHKNOOR	Rodchenko
CDEHKOSUV	duckshove
CDEHLMOST	Dolmetsch
CDEHLNORU	chondrule
CDEHLNOTU	unclothed
CDEHLOOSS	deschools
CDEHMOOSZ	schmoozed

CDEHNOOPS	chenopods
CDEHNOOTT	thecodont
CDEHNOTUU	untouched
CDEHOOOPS	hodoscope
CDEIIILSS	silicides
CDEIIILSV	civilised
CDEIIILVZ	civilized
CDEIIIMST	miticides
CDEIIIRST	sideritic
CDEIIKSS	sidekicks
CDEIILLNO	celloidin
	decillion
CDEIILMOS	domiciles
CDEIILMTU	multicide
CDEIILNTU	inductile
CDEIILORT	doleritic
CDEIILOST	idiolects
	solicited
CDEIILOSU	delicious
CDEIILPSS	disciples
CDEIILRRU	ridiculer
CDEIILRSU	ridicules
CDEIILTVY	declivity
CDEIIMNOS	meniscoid
CDEIIMNTU	ctenidium
CDEIIMNTY	mendicity
CDEIIMOPS	miscopied
CDEIIMRST	misdirect
CDEIINNOT	incondite
	nicotined
CDEIINNST	incidents
CDEIINOPT	depiction
CDEIINORT	cretinoid
	direction
CDEIINOSS	decisions
CDEIINRST	indicters
CDEIINRTT	interdict
CDEIINSTU	cutinised
CDEIINTUV	inductive
CDEIINTUZ	cutinized
CDEIIOOSU	dioecious
CDEIIORST	siderotic
CDEIIORTY	iridocyte
CDEIIORUX	uxoricide
CDEIIORVV	divorcive
CDEIIPRRS	cirripeds
CDEIIRRTX	directrix
CDEIIRSTU	diuretics
CDEIJNNOO	conjoined
CDEIKLLOR	rollicked
CDEIKLLOU	cloudlike
CDEIKLLRS	drecksill
CDEIKLRST	strickled
CDEIKLRSU	ludericks
CDEIKOSST	diestocks
CDEILLLOU	celluloid
CDEILLORS	colliders
CDEILLOSU	lodicules
CDEILLTUY	ductilely
CDEILMOPY	polydemic
CDEILMRSU	dulcimers
CDEILNOOS	colonised

CDEILNOOZ	colonized
CDEILNRSY	cylinders
CDEILNSSU	lucidness
CDEILOORZ	colorized
CDEILOPSU	clupeoids
CDEILORSS	discloser
CDEILOSSS	discloses
CDEILOSTU	cloudiest
CDEILPRSU	surpliced
CDEILRTUY	credulity
CDEIMMNOO	incommode
CDEIMMOTT	committed
CDEIMNNOT	condiment
CDEIMNOPR	princedom
CDEIMNORS	crimsoned
CDEIMNORU	indecorum
CDEIMNOSU	Nicodemus
CDEIMNPUY	impudency
CDEIMNSSU	mucidness
CDEIMOPRS	comprised
CDEIMOSST	domestics
CDEINNOTU	continued
	unnoticed
CDEINOOTX	endotoxic
CDEINOPRS	conspired
CDEINOPSY	dyspnoeic
CDEINORSS	considers
	incrossed
CDEINORST	centroids
	doctrines
CDEINORSU	coinsured
	decurions
CDEINORTU	introduce
	reduction
CDEINORTV	contrived
CDEINOSST	consisted
CDEINOSTU	eductions
	seduction
CDEINPRSS	prescinds
CDEINRSSU	curdiness
CDEINRSTU	incrusted
CDEINRSTY	stridency
CDEINRTTU	tinctured
CDEIOORRS	corrodies
CDEIOORST	coeditors
CDEIOPRRT	predictor
CDEIOPRST	depictors
CDEIOPSTY	copyedits
CDEIORRST	creditors
	directors
CDEIORRSV	codrivers
	divorcers
CDEIORRTY	directory
CDEIORSSS	scissored
CDEIORSST	dissector
CDEIORSSU	discourse
CDEIORSSV	discovers
CDEIORSTV	discovert
CDEIORSVY	discovery
CDEIOSSTU	custodies
CDEIPPSTY	dyspeptic
CDEIRSSSU	discusser

CDEISSSSU	discusses
CDEKLMORS	clerkdoms
CDEKLNPUU	unplucked
CDEKLOORY	crookedly
CDEKNOORU	undercook
CDEKOOPRU	puckerood
CDELLOOPS	clodpoles
	scolloped
CDELLORSU	colluders
CDELLOSSU	cloudless
CDELLOSTU	cloudlets
CDELMOOPU	coupledom
CDELMPRSU	scrumpled
CDELNOORS	condolers
CDELNOORT	decontrol
CDELNOORU	undercool
CDELNOOSW	closedown
CDELNOOTY	cotyledon
CDELNOOVV	convolved
CDELNOPUU	uncoupled
CDELNORSU	scoundrel
CDELNOSTU	consulted
CDELNOSUV	convulsed
CDELOORSU	coloureds
	decolours
CDELOORUV	overcloud
CDELORSUU	credulous
CDEMMOOOR	commodore
CDEMMOORT	dotcommer
CDEMNOORW	downcomer
CDEMNOOSW	comedowns
	downcomes
CDEMNOSTU	documents
CDEMOOPRT	comported
CDEMOOPST	composted
CDENNOORS	condoners
CDENNORUW	uncrowned
CDENNOTUU	uncounted
CDENOOPSY	endoscopy
CDENOORRT	corrodent
CDENOORST	consorted
	creodonts
CDENOORTT	contorted
CDENOORTU	contoured
CDENORSSU	uncrossed
CDENORSTU	construed
CDENPRTUU	punctured
CDENRSTUU	undercuts
CDEOOPRRT	proctored
CDEOOPSST	postcodes
CDEOOORRS	corroders
CDEOOORRVW	overcrowd
CDEOORSWW	woodscrew
CDEOPRRSU	producers
CDEOPRRTU	corrupted
CDEORSTTU	destructo
CDEORSTUV	dustcover
CDERSSTTU	destructs
CDFFIILTU	difficult
CDFGHILNO	goldfinch
CDFGIINNO	confiding
CDFGIINOY	codifying

CDFGIOOTY	City of God
CDFHINORY	chondrify
CDFIIMOST	discomfit
CDFIIORSU	sudorific
CDFIKORSS	disfrocks
CDFIMOORR	cordiform
CDFNNOOSU	confounds
CDGHIILNY	chidingly
CDGIIINNT	indicting
CDGIIINOT	indigotic
CDGIILLNO	colliding
CDGIILNNU	including
CDGIILOTT	diglottic
CDGIINNTU	inducting
CDGIINORV	divorcing
CDGIKLNSU	ducklings
CDGIKLORS	gridlocks
CDGILLNOU	colluding
CDGILNNOO	condoling
CDGILNNOY	condignly
CDGILNOSS	scoldings
CDGILOOSY	discology
CDGINNNOO	condoning
CDGINNOOR	cordoning
CDGINOORR	corroding
CDGINOORT	doctoring
CDGINOPRU	producing
CDGNOOSTU	gonoducts
CDHHIIOTY	ichthyoid
CDHHILOST	dishcloth
CDHIIINOT	chitinoid
CDHIILLNW	windchill
CDHIIMOPR	dimorphic
CDHIIMORS	dichroism
CDHIIOORS	chorioids
CDHIIORRS	scirrhoid
CDHIIORSY	isohydric
CDHIIOSSZ	schizoids
CDHIIRRTY	trihydric
CDHILMNOO	Moon Child
CDHILOOPS	chilopods
CDHILOSTU	dishclout
CDHIMNOOR	monorchid
CDHIMOOTY	dichotomy
CDHIMSTYY	dysthymic
CDHINOPSY	dysphonic
CDHIOOPRY	chiropody
CDHIOOPSZ	schizopod
CDHIOORST	trochoids
CDHIOPRSW	whipcords
CDHIOPRSY	dysphoric
CDHLOOPSY	copyholds
CDHMNOOOR	monochord
CDHNNOOOU	coonhound
CDHNOOORT	notochord
CDHNOOTUW	touchdown
CDHOOOPSW	woodchops
CDHOOORTW	torchwood
CDHOOOTUW	touchwood
CDHOORRSU	urochords
CDIIILMNS	diclinism
CDIIIMNSS	minidiscs

417

CDIIINNOT	indiction	CEEEEFNRR	reference	CEEEIMRRS	merceries
CDIIISTVY	viscidity	CEEEEGMNR	emergence		mercerise
CDIIJOSUU	judicious	CEEEEHILP	heelpiece	CEEEIMRRZ	mercerize
CDIIKNNOS	Dickinson	CEEEEHMNV	vehemence	CEEEIMRST	semierect
CDIIKPSST	dipsticks	CEEEEIPSY	eyepieces	CEEEINNPT	penitence
CDIILMOOT	dolomitic	CEEEELSST	selectees	CEEEINNRT	renitence
CDIILNOPT	diplontic	CEEEENRRV	reverence	CEEEINNST	enceintes
CDIILNOSU	diclinous	CEEEFFITV	effective		sentience
CDIILOOPZ	diplozoic	CEEEFFLNU	effluence	CEEEINOPS	nosepiece
CDIILPTUY	duplicity	CEEEFFRST	effecters	CEEEINPRT	epicenter
CDIILTTUY	ductility	CEEEFHLTT	flechette		epicentre
CDIIMNPUY	pycnidium	CEEEFIKLN	fencelike	CEEEINRSS	sceneries
CDIIMORST	dicrotism	CEEEFILST	fleeciest	CEEEINRSU	esurience
CDIINNOOT	condition	CEEEFINNR	inference	CEEEINSTX	existence
CDIINNOTU	induction	CEEEFLNRU	refluence	CEEEIPRRS	creperies
CDIINOPRY	cyprinoid	CEEEFLNSS	fenceless	CEEEIPRRV	perceiver
CDIINORST	indictors	CEEEFNORR	conferree	CEEEIPRST	creepiest
CDIINPRSY	cyprinids		ferrocene	CEEEIPRSV	perceives
CDIINTWYY	Windy City		reenforce	CEEEIPRTV	receptive
CDIIOOPRS	scorpioid	CEEEFNORS	conferees	CEEEIPTVX	exceptive
CDIIOPRST	dioptrics	CEEEFNQRU	frequence	CEEEIRRSV	receivers
CDIIORRTT	tortricid	CEEEFPRRT	perfecter	CEEEIRRSX	exerciser
CDIIPRSTU	tricuspid	CEEEGILNT	telegenic	CEEEIRSSV	recessive
CDIIRSSTT	districts	CEEEGINRS	regencies	CEEEIRSSX	exercises
CDIJNOTUY	jocundity	CEEEGINRT	energetic		sexercise
CDIJNSSTU	disjuncts	CEEEGINSX	exigences	CEEEIRSTV	secretive
CDIKKOPRS	dropkicks	CEEEGISTX	exegetics	CEEEIRTVX	excretive
CDIKMRSTU	drumstick	CEEEGLNRT	neglecter	CEEEISSVX	excessive
CDIKNOSSW	windsocks	CEEEGMNRY	emergency	CEEEITUVX	executive
CDILLMOOU	collodium	CEEEGNRSV	vergences	CEEEJMNTT	ejectment
CDILLNOOO	collodion	CEEEHIKLL	leechlike	CEEEJRRST	rejecters
CDILOORSS	discolors	CEEEHIKST	cheekiest	CEEEKKMST	Kecskemét
CDILOORSU	discolour	CEEEHILRS	lecheries	CEEEKORRT	rocketeer
CDILOOSTY	cotyloids	CEEEHILST	scheelite	CEEELLNRS	crenelles
CDILORSUU	ludicrous	CEEEHINRN	inherence	CEEELLNTX	excellent
CDIMMNOOS	discommon	CEEEHIRST	cheeriest	CEEELMNST	selectmen
CDIMMOOTY	commodity	CEEEHISST	cheesiest	CEEELNOQU	eloquence
CDIMNOORT	microdont	CEEEHKLSS	cheekless	CEEELNOSY	Ceylonese
CDIMNOORU	doronicum	CEEEHLNTY	entelechy	CEEELOPST	telescope
CDIMNORSY	syndromic	CEEEHLRSS	cheerless	CEEELPRST	preelects
CDIMOOPRR	prodromic	CEEEHOPRS	ecosphere		preselect
CDIMOOPST	microdots	CEEEHOPST	sheepcote	CEEELRSST	reselects
CDINNQSUU	quidnuncs	CEEEHQRUX	exchequer	CEEELRSTT	electrets
CDINORSSW	crosswind	CEEEHRSSW	eschewers	CEEELRSTV	cleverest
CDINORSTU	inductors	CEEEHRTTV	chevrette	CEEEMNRRT	recrement
CDINOSSTU	discounts	CEEEIIMPT	timepiece	CEEEMNRST	cementers
CDIOORRRS	corridors	CEEEIINRV	viceriene		cerements
CDIOPRSSU	cuspidors	CEEEIJRTV	rejective	CEEEMNRTX	excrement
CDIRRSTUU	duricrust	CEEEIJSTV	ejectives	CEEEMORST	ectomeres
CDKKNNOOW	knockdown	CEEEILLNT	clientele	CEEENNORV	reconvene
CDKKNOOOR	doorknock	CEEEILNRS	relicense	CEEENNSST	senescent
CDKOOORSW	corkwoods	CEEEILNSS	licensees		sentences
CDKOOOSTW	Stockwood	CEEEILNST	celestine	CEEENORTT	entrecote
	Woodstock		telecines	CEEENOSTY	synoecete
CDLOOSSTW	Cotswolds	CEEEILPSS	epicleses	CEEENPRSS	presences
CDMNNORUU	conundrum	CEEEILRST	Leicester	CEEENPRST	pretences
CDMNOOPSU	compounds	CEEEILSTT	celestite	CEEENQRSU	sequencer
CDNNOOOST	conodonts	CEEEILSTV	electives	CEEENQSSU	sequences
CDNNOOTUW	countdown		selective	CEEENRRSS	screeners
CDOORRSSW	crossword	CEEEIMNNS	eminences	CEEENRSST	erectness
CDOORRSUY	corduroys	CEEEIMNSX	excisemen	CEEEOPRRU	eurocreep
CEEEEFFNR	efference	CEEEIMNTT	cementite	CEEEORRRV	recoverer

CEEEPRRST	respecter	**CEEGILLNX**	excelling	**CEEHILRSW**	clerihews
CEEEPRSSS	precesses	**CEEGILNOT**	telegonic	**CEEHILSTT**	telestich
CEEEPRSTU	persecute	**CEEGILNRY**	glycerine	**CEEHIMORT**	theoremic
CEEERRSTX	excreters	**CEEGILNST**	selecting	**CEEHIMPRV**	hyperemic
CEEERSSST	sesterces	**CEEGIMNNT**	cementing	**CEEHIMRSW**	shrewmice
CEEERSTUX	executers	**CEEGIMNOP**	Compiègne	**CEEHINNRY**	inherency
CEEFFGINT	effecting	**CEEGIMORT**	geometric	**CEEHINPRS**	enciphers
CEEFFIINT	efficient	**CEEGINNOS**	consignee	**CEEHINPRT**	phrenetic
CEEFFIORS	Escoffier	**CEEGINNOX**	xenogenic	**CEEHINPST**	phenetics
CEEFFIOSU	coiffeuse	**CEEGINNRS**	screening	**CEEHINQTU**	technique
CEEFFOOPT	coffeepot		secerning	**CEEHINRRS**	enrichers
CEEFFORST	effectors	**CEEGINNRT**	centering		Schreiner
CEEFGLNTU	genuflect	**CEEGINNST**	ignescent	**CEEHINSST**	techiness
CEEFHIKRS	kerchiefs	**CEEGINOOR**	ecoregion	**CEEHINSTU**	euthenics
CEEFHIPSY	speechify	**CEEGINOOT**	oogenetic	**CEEHINSTZ**	Nietzsche
CEEFHLNRS	flenchers	**CEEGINORS**	congeries	**CEEHIOPSW**	showpiece
CEEFHLRST	fletchers		recognise	**CEEHIORRT**	torchiere
CEEFIINTV	infective	**CEEGINORX**	exergonic	**CEEHIORSS**	coheiress
CEEFIIPRS	specifier	**CEEGINORZ**	recognize	**CEEHIORTT**	theoretic
CEEFIIPSS	specifies	**CEEGINPTX**	excepting	**CEEHIPRST**	herpetics
CEEFIIRRT	certifier		expecting	**CEEHIRRST**	Streicher
	rectifier	**CEEGINRSS**	recessing	**CEEHISSTT**	chestiest
CEEFIIRST	certifies	**CEEGINRST**	resecting		esthetics
	rectifies		screeting	**CEEHISTTT**	tetchiest
CEEFILNNU	influence		secreting	**CEEHKNNOR**	Chernenko
CEEFILRTY	electrify	**CEEGINRSU**	urgencies	**CEEHKNORV**	Cherenkov
CEEFIMPRT	imperfect	**CEEGINRTX**	excreting	**CEEHKRSST**	sketchers
CEEFINORR	reinforce	**CEEGINSTX**	exsecting	**CEEHLLNOP**	cellphone
CEEFINORT	refection	**CEEGINTUX**	executing	**CEEHLMOOS**	hemocoels
CEEFINRST	infecters	**CEEGIORSS**	groceries	**CEEHLORST**	reclothes
	reinfects	**CEEGKNOOS**	gooseneck	**CEEHLORSU**	lecherous
CEEFINTTU	fettucine	**CEEGLMNRY**	clergymen	**CEEHLPRSU**	sepulcher
CEEFIRRST	firecrest	**CEEGLNOOS**	Congolese		sepulchre
CEEFLNRSU	screenful	**CEEGLNORT**	neglector	**CEEHLQRSU**	squelcher
CEEFLNRSY	flyscreen	**CEEGNNOOS**	oncogenes	**CEEHLQSSU**	squelches
CEEFLOORS	foreclose	**CEEGNNORS**	congeners	**CEEHLRWYY**	Wycherley
CEEFLORRT	reflector	**CEEGNORSV**	converges	**CEEHMNORZ**	chernozem
CEEFLORSS	forceless	**CEEGORRSU**	Courrèges	**CEEHMOSTY**	hemocytes
CEEFLORSU	fluoresce	**CEEGORTTU**	courgette	**CEEHNOPRR**	percheron
CEEFLPRTY	perfectly	**CEEHHIRRS**	cherisher	**CEEHNQRSU**	quenchers
CEEFMOORT	focometer	**CEEHHIRSS**	cherishes	**CEEHNRRST**	trenchers
CEEFNOPRU	fourpence	**CEEHHIRVW**	whichever	**CEEHOPRSY**	coryphees
CEEFNORRR	conferrer	**CEEHIILLN**	helicline	**CEEHOPSTT**	pochettes
CEEFNORRS	confreres	**CEEHIILRU**	Richelieu	**CEEHOPTTY**	ectophyte
	enforcers	**CEEHIIPTT**	epithetic	**CEEHORRST**	Rochester
CEEFNOSSS	confesses	**CEEHIIRTT**	erethitic		torcheres
CEEFNQRUY	frequency	**CEEHIISST**	ethicises	**CEEHORRTU**	retoucher
CEEFNRSTU	rufescent	**CEEHIISTZ**	ethicizes	**CEEHORSTU**	retouches
CEEFOOPST	fetoscope	**CEEHIKNRT**	kitchener	**CEEHRRSTT**	stretcher
CEEFOPRRT	perfector		thickener	**CEEHRSSTT**	stretches
CEEFOPRST	perfectos	**CEEHIKNTT**	kitchenet	**CEEHRSTTU**	teuchters
CEEFORRTY	refectory	**CEEHIKPPR**	pikeperch	**CEEIIJNTV**	injective
CEEFORSSU	refocuses	**CEEHIKRST**	sketchier	**CEEIIKLNN**	nickeline
CEEGHIMNO	hegemonic	**CEEHILLMS**	schlemiel	**CEEIILNPR**	pericline
CEEGHINOR	reechoing	**CEEHILLNS**	chenilles	**CEEIILNRT**	lienteric
CEEGHINRW	Greenwich	**CEEHILLRS**	chiseller	**CEEIILNST**	insectile
CEEGHINSW	eschewing	**CEEHILNOS**	lichenose	**CEEIILPPT**	epileptic
CEEGHLOSW	cogwheels	**CEEHILNRS**	schlieren	**CEEIILPRX**	preexilic
CEEGIINRV	receiving	**CEEHILNSS**	Schlesien	**CEEIILPSS**	epiclesis
CEEGIJNRT	rejecting	**CEEHILNTY**	ethylenic	**CEEIIMMNN**	imminence
CEEGIKNOT	ketogenic	**CEEHILPRT**	telpheric	**CEEIIMNPS**	epicenism
CEEGIKNRS	greensick	**CEEHILRSV**	cleverish	**CEEIIMNRS**	reminisce

CEEIIMOST	semeiotic	CEEILNRUV	virulence	CEEINQSTU	quiescent
CEEIIMPRS	imprecise	CEEILORRS	recoilers	CEEINRRSV	scrivener
CEEIIMPST	epistemic	CEEILORSX	excelsior	CEEINRRSU	sinecures
CEEIINNOR	eirenicon	CEEILOSSS	isosceles	CEEINRSTT	intersect
CEEIINNRS	insincere	CEEILOSSV	voiceless	CEEINRSTU	centuries
CEEIINNRT	encrinite	CEEILPRSS	eclipsers	CEEINRSTV	virescent
CEEIINNTV	incentive		priceless	CEEINRSUY	esuriency
CEEIINPRT	recipient	CEEILPRSY	precisely	CEEINSSTY	necessity
CEEIINPTV	inceptive	CEEILQSSU	liquesces	CEEIOOPRS	cooperies
CEEIINPTX	excipient	CEEILRSST	sclerites	CEEIOORTZ	ozocerite
CEEIINTVV	invective	CEEILRSSV	versicles	CEEIOPPRS	pericopes
CEEIIOPST	poeticise	CEEILRSTU	cruelties		periscope
CEEIIOPTZ	poeticize		reticules	CEEIOPPSS	episcopes
CEEIIORST	eroticise	CEEILRSTW	crewelist	CEEIOPRRT	receiptor
CEEIIORTZ	eroticize	CEEILRSUV	reclusive	CEEIOPRRV	overprice
CEEIIOSST	societies	CEEILRSTT	testicles	CEEIOPSST	cespitose
CEEIIPRRS	epicrises	CEEILSSUU	Seleucus I	CEEIORRSS	sorceries
	spiceries	CEEILSSUV	seclusive	CEEIORRST	corsetier
CEEIJLSSU	juiceless	CEEILSUVX	exclusive		rectories
CEEIJNORT	rejection	CEEIMMNSU	ecumenism	CEEIORRSX	exorciser
CEEIJNOST	ejections	CEEIMMORR	micromere	CEEIORRXZ	exorcizer
CEEIJNRTT	interject	CEEIMMOTT	committee	CEEIORSSU	sericeous
CEEIJORRS	rejoicers	CEEIMNNRT	increment	CEEIORSSX	exorcises
CEEIJRSUV	verjuices	CEEIMNOOS	economies	CEEIORSXZ	exorcizes
CEEIKLLRR	clerklier		economise	CEEIPRSST	tricepses
CEEIKLNNS	necklines	CEEIMNOOZ	economize	CEEIPSTTU	Epictetus
CEEIKLNSW	Sweelinck	CEEIMNOPT	impotence	CEEIRRRTU	recruiter
CEEIKLPRS	pickerels	CEEIMNORR	merocrine	CEEIRRSUV	recursive
CEEIKLRSW	screwlike	CEEIMNOST	centesimo	CEEIRSSTU	cerussite
CEEIKMORS	mockeries	CEEIMNOWX	New Mexico	CEEIRSSTW	screwiest
CEEIKNOPS	kinescope	CEEIMNPSS	specimens	CEEIRSUVX	excursive
CEEIKNQRU	requicken	CEEIMNSTU	intumesce	CEEIRTUXX	executrix
CEEIKNRSS	sickeners	CEEIMOSTY	meiocytes	CEEISSTTU	cutesiest
CEEIKOORS	cookeries	CEEIMRRSU	mercuries	CEEJORRST	rejectors
CEEIKOPRW	piecework	CEEIMSSTT	smectites	CEEJORRTT	retroject
	workpiece	CEEINNNSV	Vincennes	CEEKLOTUY	leukocyte
CEEIKORRS	rockeries	CEEINNORS	recension	CEEKNORRS	reckoners
CEEIKPRST	picketers	CEEINNRTY	renitency	CEEKOPRSX	oxpeckers
CEEILLLPS	pellicles	CEEINNSTY	sentiency	CEELLLOSU	cellulose
CEEILLLTU	cellulite	CEEINOPRS	preconise	CEELLMNTY	clemently
CEEILLNOR	Corneille	CEEINOPRT	reception	CEELLMOPR	compeller
CEEILLNPR	penciller	CEEINOPRZ	preconize	CEELLMOSU	molecules
CEEILLNST	lenticels	CEEINOPST	potencies	CEELLMOWY	welcomely
	lenticles	CEEINOPTX	exception	CEELLNOSU	nucleoles
CEEILLNTT	intellect	CEEINORSS	recession	CEELLPRSU	cupellers
CEEILMNNT	inclement	CEEINORST	erections	CEELLRSTU	cruellest
CEEILMNOP	policemen		neoterics	CEELMMNSU	musclemen
CEEILMNSU	luminesce		resection	CEELMNOUW	unwelcome
CEEILMOST	comeliest		secretion	CEELMOPRT	completer
CEEILMRSS	merciless	CEEINORSU	cinereous	CEELMOPST	completes
CEEILNNOS	insolence	CEEINORSX	exocrines	CEELMOPSX	complexes
CEEILNORT	centriole	CEEINORTX	excretion	CEELMORSW	welcomers
CEEILNOST	elections	CEEINOSSS	secession	CEELMOTYY	myelocyte
	selection	CEEINOSTX	exsection	CEELNORSS	enclosers
CEEILNPRS	pencilers	CEEINOTUX	execution	CEELNORST	electrons
CEEILNPRT	princelet	CEEINPRRU	prurience	CEELNORSU	enclosure
CEEILNPST	splenetic	CEEINPRST	prentices	CEELNOSSS	closeness
CEEILNRRS	recliners		prescient	CEELNPRUU	purulence
CEEILNRSS	licensers		reinspect	CEELNPSTU	centuples
	silencers	CEEINPRTT	intercept	CEELNRSSU	cruelness
CEEILNRSY	sincerely	CEEINPSSX	sixpences	CEELNSSST	scentless
CEEILNRTV	ventricle	CEEINQRTU	quercetin	CEELNSSUU	nucleuses

CEELOOPRT	coleopter		sorceress	CEFINORST	infectors
CEELOPRRT	prelector	CEEORRSST	crosstree	CEFINORTU	confiture
CEELOPSTY	telescopy		secretors	CEFIOORSU	ferocious
CEELORSSS	scleroses	CEEORRSSU	recourses	CEFIORRSS	crossfire
CEELORSST	corselets		resources	CEFIORSTU	fruticose
	selectors	CEEORRSTW	worcester	CEFKLOORS	forelocks
CEELORSSV	coverless	CEEORRSTY	secretory	CEFKLOPTU	pocketful
CEELORSTU	Le Creusot	CEEORRSUV	verrucose	CEFKLPSSY	flyspecks
CEELORSTV	coverlets	CEEORRTUV	coverture	CEFKOORRW	workforce
CEELORSUX	exclosure	CEEORRTXY	excretory	CEFLNNOTU	confluent
CEELRRSTU	lecturers	CEEORSTTV	corvettes	CEFLNOSUX	confluxes
CEELRSSST	crestless	CEEORSTUX	executors	CEFLNRSUU	furuncles
CEEMMNORT	commenter	CEEORTUXY	executory	CEFMNOORR	conformer
CEEMNNORT	contemner	CEEPRSSSU	percusses	CEFMOORRT	comforter
CEEMNOPTT	competent	CEEPRSSSY	cypresses	CEFNOORSS	confessor
CEEMNORSW	newcomers	CEEPRSSTU	suspecter	CEFNORSTU	confuters
CEEMNOSYZ	coenzymes	CEERRRSTU	resurrect	CEFOOPSTY	fetoscopy
CEEMNSTTU	tumescent	CEERSSSTW	setscrews	CEFOORRSU	fourscore
CEEMOOPRS	recompose	CEFFHINRY	frenchify	CEFOORRTU	forecourt
CEEMOORSV	comeovers	CEFFHISTU	chuffiest	CEFOORSTV	softcover
	overcomes	CEFFHNOOR	forfochen	CEGGIINRZ	grecizing
CEEMORRTY	cryometer	CEFFIIKLW	Wickliffe	CEGGIOORR	Correggio
CEEMOSSTY	ecosystem	CEFFILSTU	Sutcliffe	CEGGLNOSY	glycogens
CEENNORRT	rencontre	CEFFIORSU	coiffeurs	CEGHIILNS	chiseling
CEENNORRU	renouncer		coiffures	CEGHIINNR	enriching
CEENNORST	consenter	CEFFIRRSU	scruffier	CEGHIINPR	ciphering
CEENNORSU	renounces	CEFFIRSSU	sufficers	CEGHIINSY	hygienics
CEENNORSV	conveners	CEFGHILNN	flenching	CEGHIIOST	gothicise
CEENNORTU	encounter	CEFGHILNT	fletching	CEGHIIOTZ	gothicize
CEENNRSSU	sunscreen	CEFGIINNT	infecting	CEGHIKNST	sketching
CEENOOPST	copestone	CEFGIKLNR	freckling	CEGHILLNS	Schelling
CEENOPRRS	precensor	CEFGINNOR	enforcing	CEGHILLOU	guilloche
CEENOPRRT	precentor	CEFHIIMSS	mischiefs	CEGHILMTU	gemutlich
CEENOPSTT	Pentecost	CEFHIIMST	fetichism	CEGHILNNU	Ch'ien-lung
CEENOPSTW	twopences	CEFHIISTT	fetichist	CEGHILNPU	pleuching
CEENOQRRU	reconquer	CEFHIKRSW	wreckfish	CEGHILNTV	vetchling
CEENORRSV	conserver	CEFHILMOR	cheliform	CEGHILSSW	Schleswig
	converser	CEFHILNRS	flinchers	CEGHIMNSS	schemings
CEENORRTV	converter	CEFHIOSSW	cowfishes	CEGHINNQU	quenching
	reconvert	CEFHKOORS	forehocks	CEGHINNRT	trenching
CEENORSSV	conserves		foreshock	CEGHINNRW	wrenching
	converses	CEFHLSSTU	chestfuls	CEGHINOOT	neogothic
CEENORSTT	contester	CEFHPRRSU	surfperch		theogonic
CEENORSTW	sweetcorn	CEFIILNRT	inflicter	CEGHINOPY	hypogenic
CEENORSVY	conveyers	CEFIILNRU	luciferin	CEGHINORS	coshering
	reconveys	CEFIILTVY	fictively	CEGHINORT	hectoring
CEENPPSTU	tuppences	CEFIINNOT	infection		tochering
CEENRRRTU	recurrent	CEFIINTTU	fettucini	CEGHINORV	Chernigov
CEENRRSSU	censurers	CEFIIORRS	scorifier	CEGHINPRY	cyphering
CEENRRTUX	excurrent	CEFIIORSS	scorifies	CEGHIOPTY	geophytic
CEEOORRSV	overscore	CEFIKLORR	frolicker	CEGHIORRU	grouchier
CEEOORSST	creosotes	CEFIKLORS	firelocks	CEGHKNORU	roughneck
CEEOPPRRT	preceptor	CEFIKORSS	fossicker	CEGHMNOOR	chromogen
CEEOPRRSS	reprocess	CEFILLLOS	follicles	CEGIIILNT	eliciting
CEEOPRRST	receptors	CEFILNORT	inflector	CEGIIJNNT	injecting
CEEOPRRTX	excerptor	CEFILNOST	flections	CEGIIJNOR	rejoicing
CEEOPRSSS	processes	CEFIMNORR	confirmer	CEGIIKLNN	nickeling
CEEOPRSTU	prosecute		reconfirm	CEGIIKNNR	nickering
CEEOQRTTU	croquette	CEFIMNORU	cuneiform	CEGIIKNNS	sickening
CEEOQSTTU	coquettes	CEFINNORS	confiners	CEGIIKNPR	Pickering
CEEORRRSS	sorcerers	CEFINOORT	confiteor	CEGIIKNPT	picketing
CEEORRSSS	recrosses	CEFINORSS	forensics	CEGIIKNTT	ticketing

CEGIILLNO	lignicole	CEGINNNRSU	censuring	CEHIINPRT	nephritic
CEGIILNNP	penciling	CEGINNSTY	encysting		phrenitic
CEGIILNNR	reclining	CEGINOOPR	coopering	CEHIINRST	snitchier
CEGIILNNS	licensing	CEGINOOPS	geoponics	CEHIINRTZ	chintzier
	silencing	CEGINOPPR	coppering	CEHIINSST	itchiness
CEGIILNOR	recoiling	CEGINOPRU	recouping	CEHIINTTY	ethnicity
CEGIILNPS	eclipsing	CEGINOPRY	pyrogenic	CEHIIPPPT	pitchpipe
CEGIIMNOT	mitogenic		recopying	CEHIIPPST	chippiest
CEGIINNNS	incensing	CEGINOPTY	genotypic		psephitic
CEGIINNOR	recoining	CEGINORST	corseting	CEHIIPPTY	epiphytic
CEGIINNPT	incepting		escorting	CEHIIPRRT	peritrich
CEGIINOOR	coorieing	CEGINORSV	coverings	CEHIIPRST	chirpiest
CEGIINORU	courieing	CEGINORSW	escrowing	CEHIIPRTT	tephritic
CEGIINORV	revoicing	CEGINORTT	cottering	CEHIIPSTT	pitchiest
CEGIINOTV	cognitive	CEGINORTV	vectoring	CEHIIRSST	christies
CEGIINPRR	repricing	CEGINOSST	cosseting	CEHIIRSTU	heuristic
CEGIINPRS	precising	CEGINPRST	sceptring	CEHIISSTT	ethicists
CEGIINPST	pectising	CEGINRRRU	recurring	CEHIISTTT	titchiest
CEGIINPTZ	pectizing	CEGINRRUV	recurving	CEHIKLORT	torchlike
CEGIINRSV	servicing	CEGINRSST	crestings	CEHIKLPRS	clerkship
CEGIIOSTT	egotistic	CEGINRTTU	curetting	CEHIKLSTY	sketchily
CEGIJKNOY	jockeying	CEGINRTUV	curveting	CEHIKMRSU	muckerish
CEGIKLNPS	speckling	CEGINSSTU	scungiest	CEHIKNNOT	technikon
CEGIKNNOR	reckoning	CEGIOOPRT	geotropic	CEHIKNSST	thickness
CEGIKNOPT	pocketing	CEGISTYYZ	syzygetic	CEHIKNSTT	Schnittke
CEGIKNORT	rocketing	CEGKMRSUU	gumsucker	CEHIKNSTU	chunkiest
CEGIKNOST	socketing	CEGLLOOSU	colloques	CEHIKORTW	work ethic
CEGIKNPRU	puckering	CEGLNOORY	necrology	CEHIKPRSW	shipwreck
CEGIKNRSU	suckering	CEGMNNOOS	cognomens	CEHIKSSTT	thicksets
CEGIKNRTU	tuckering	CEGNNORTU	congruent	CEHILLNSS	chillness
CEGILLMOU	collegium	CEGNOOSTY	gonocytes	CEHILLPRS	prechills
CEGILLNOT	colleting	CEGNORRSU	scrounger	CEHILMNOS	Michelson
CEGILLNPU	cupelling	CEGNORSSU	scrounges	CEHILMNTU	lunchtime
CEGILMMNO	commingle	CEGNORSUY	surgeoncy	CEHILMOSU	humicoles
CEGILMNOW	welcoming	CEGOOPRSY	gyroscope	CEHILMOTY	hemolytic
CEGILNNOS	enclosing	CEGORRSSU	scourgers	CEHILNOOR	holocrine
CEGILNOPY	polygenic	CEHHHIIKT	hitchhike	CEHILNORU	euchlorin
CEGILNOST	closeting	CEHHIIMST	hemistich	CEHILNOSU	lichenous
CEGILNOSY	lysogenic	CEHHIINNS	Chin-Hsien	CEHILNOTU	touchline
CEGILNOTU	elocuting	CEHHILLMS	schlemihl	CEHILNSTZ	schnitzel
CEGILNRSU	surcingle	CEHHIMOST	shochetim	CEHILOOSS	schoolies
CEGILNRTU	lecturing	CEHHIMSTT	hemstitch	CEHILOPRT	plethoric
	relucting	CEHHINSTU	unhitches	CEHILORST	chlorites
CEGILNSTU	cultigens	CEHHLOOTU	touchhole		clothiers
CEGILOORS	serologic	CEHHNOSTU	Hutcheson	CEHILRSTU	slutchier
CEGILOOST	ecologist	CEHHOOPSU	chophouse	CEHIMMOPR	morphemic
CEGIMNNOO	monogenic	CEHHOPSTY	hypothecs	CEHIMMSTU	chummiest
CEGIMNOOR	ergonomic	CEHIIILPT	epilithic	CEHIMNNOU	ichneumon
CEGIMNOPR	compering	CEHIIKLOR	choirlike	CEHIMNOPS	phonemics
CEGIMNOPT	competing	CEHIIKLRS	lickerish	CEHIMNSTW	switchmen
CEGIMNOUY	gynoecium	CEHIIKLTW	witchlike	CEHIMORST	trichomes
CEGIMNOYZ	zymogenic	CEHIIKORS	hickories	CEHIMPRUY	hypericum
CEGINNNOU	enouncing	CEHIILLST	chilliest	CEHIMRRSS	smirchers
CEGINNNOV	convening	CEHIILMOT	homiletic	CEHIMRSTY	chemistry
CEGINNOOT	ontogenic	CEHIILNOT	ichnolite	CEHIMRTUY	eurythmic
CEGINNORR	cornering		neolithic	CEHINOORS	isochrone
CEGINNORS	censoring	CEHIILNST	lecithins	CEHINOPRT	nephrotic
	consigner	CEHIIMOSS	isocheims	CEHINOPRU	neurochip
	necrosing		isochimes	CEHINOPST	Ctesiphon
CEGINNOVX	convexing	CEHIIMSTY	mythicise		phonetics
CEGINNOVY	conveying	CEHIIMTYZ	mythicize	CEHINOPTY	neophytic
CEGINNRST	centrings	CEHIINPPT	pitchpine	CEHINORTY	Nictheroy

CEHINPRST	sphincter	CEHNNORTU	truncheon	CEIIMORST	eroticism
CEHINPSTU	punchiest	CEHNOOPPY	phenocopy		isometric
CEHINQSSU	squinches	CEHNOORSS	schooners		microsite
CEHINRSST	christens	CEHNOOTTU	touchtone	CEIIMOSST	semiotics
	snitchers	CEHNORRRS	schnorrer	CEIIMOSTX	exoticism
CEHINSTTY	synthetic	CEHNSSTTU	chestnuts	CEIIMPRSU	epicurism
CEHIOOPRT	orthoepic	CEHOOOPRS	horoscope	CEIIMRRTT	trimetric
CEHIOOPRX	exophoric	CEHOOORSZ	zoochores	CEIINNOPT	inception
CEHIOORSS	isochores	CEHOPRTYY	cryophyte	CEIINNORS	irenicons
CEHIOOSST	choosiest	CEHOPSSSY	psychoses	CEIINNORT	incretion
CEHIOPPRT	prophetic	CEIIILRSV	civiliser	CEIINOPRS	precision
CEHIOPPRY	hyperopic	CEIIILRVZ	civilizer	CEIINOPRT	proteinic
CEHIOPPST	choppiest	CEIIILSSV	civilises	CEIINORRT	criterion
CEHIOPRRT	chiropter	CEIIILSVZ	civilizes	CEIINORSS	recisions
CEHIOPRRY	pyorrheic	CEIIIMMRS	mimicries	CEIINORTT	tricotine
CEHIOPRTT	prothetic	CEIIIMSTV	victimise	CEIINOSSX	excisions
CEHIOPRTU	eutrophic	CEIIIMTVZ	victimize	CEIINOSTV	evictions
CEHIOPRTV	overpitch	CEIIINNPT	incipient	CEIINPSSS	spiciness
CEHIOPRTY	hypocrite	CEIIIPRSS	epicrisis	CEIINQRTU	quercitin
CEHIOPSST	postiches	CEIIIPSTT	pietistic	CEIINRSSU	incisures
CEHIOPSTY	sciophyte	CEIIJNNOT	injection		sciurines
CEHIORRST	chorister	CEIIJNSSU	juiciness	CEIINRSTX	extrinsic
	rhetorics	CEIIJNSTU	injustice	CEIINRSTY	sincerity
	torchiers	CEIIKLMPS	mispickel	CEIINRSUV	incursive
CEHIORSST	ostriches	CEIIKLMQU	quicklime	CEIINRTTY	intercity
CEHIORSUV	echovirus	CEIIKLMRS	limericks	CEIINRTYZ	citizenry
CEHIOSSST	schistose	CEIIKLNRS	crinklies	CEIINSSTT	scientist
CEHIOSTTU	touchiest	CEIIKLPRR	pricklier	CEIINSSTU	cutinises
CEHIPRRRU	chirruper	CEIIKLSST	sickliest	CEIINSTUZ	cutinizes
CEHIPRRSU	superrich	CEIIKMMRS	mimickers	CEIIOOPTZ	epizootic
CEHIPRSTW	Prestwich	CEIIKNNPR	princekin	CEIIORSST	isosteric
CEHIPRTTT	Pritchett	CEIIKNPRT	nitpicker	CEIIORSTU	triecious
CEHIRSSTT	stitchers	CEIIKNPSS	pickiness	CEIIORSTV	victories
CEHIRSSTW	switchers	CEIIKRRST	tricksier	CEIIPRSST	crispiest
CEHIRSSTY	hysterics	CEIIKRSTT	trickiest	CEIIPSTTY	septicity
CEHIRSTTW	twitchers	CEIIKSSTT	stickiest	CEIIQRSTU	critiques
CEHIRSTTY	stitchery	CEIILLNNO	linolenic	CEIISSTVV	vivisects
CEHITTTWY	witchetty	CEIILLSSU	silicules	CEIJNNOOR	conjoiner
CEHKLNORS	schnorkel	CEIILMORT	microlite	CEIJNORST	injectors
CEHKLOOST	klootches	CEIILMOSV	Milošević	CEIJNORTT	introject
CEHKOOOSU	cookhouse	CEIILNNOR	crinoline	CEIJNOSUV	cunjevois
CEHKRSSTU	hucksters	CEIILNNRS	incliners	CEIKKLMOS	smocklike
CEHLLOOPT	photocell	CEIILNOSS	isoclines	CEIKKLNRU	knucklier
CEHLMNOOS	schoolmen		silicones	CEIKKRRSS	skerricks
CEHLMNOUU	homuncule	CEIILNPPR	principle	CEIKLLORS	sollicker
CEHLMOOPY	phocomely	CEIILNSST	licitness	CEIKLNOOT	Cook Inlet
CEHLNNOSU	luncheons	CEIILNSSV	civilness	CEIKLNOPV	clovepink
CEHLNOSTU	unclothes	CEIILNSUV	inclusive	CEIKLNORT	interlock
CEHLNOSZZ	schnozzle	CEIILNTYZ	citizenly	CEIKLNOSU	nickelous
CEHLOOPRS	preschool	CEIILOQRU	liquorice	CEIKLNRUU	unluckier
CEHLOOPSS	Sophocles	CEIILORST	elicitors	CEIKLNSSS	slickness
CEHLOPSST	splotches	CEIILOSSU	siliceous	CEIKLNSSU	luckiness
CEHLORRST	chortlers	CEIILPRTU	pleuritic	CEIKLNSTU	clunkiest
CEHLORSSU	slouchers	CEIILRSST	scleritis	CEIKLOPST	stockpile
CEHLOSSTU	touchless	CEIILRSTV	verticils	CEIKLOSTV	livestock
CEHMNOPRS	McPherson	CEIILSTTY	sectility	CEIKLPSTU	pluckiest
CEHMOOPRT	ectomorph	CEIILSTUV	Leviticus	CEIKLRSST	sticklers
CEHMOORRU	urochrome	CEIIMMNNY	imminency		strickles
CEHMOOSSZ	schmoozes	CEIIMNOST	semitonic		trickless
CEHMOTTYY	thymocyte	CEIIMNRST	cretinism	CEIKMNORS	monickers
CEHMRSTTU	schmutter	CEIIMNSST	scientism	CEIKMNSSU	muckiness
CEHNNOPSU	puncheons	CEIIMOPSS	miscopies	CEIKNORSS	rockiness

CEIKNOSTT	stockinet	**CEILORSST**	cloisters	**CEINNRRTU**	incurrent
CEIKNOSTY	cytokines	**CEILOSSST**	solecists	**CEINOORST**	cortisone
CEIKNQSSU	quickness		solstices	**CEINOOSSW**	Sosnowiec
CEIKORRTV	overtrick	**CEILOSSSU**	coulisses	**CEINOPPRU**	porcupine
CEIKOSSTT	stockiest	**CEILOSSTT**	costliest	**CEINOPRRS**	conspirer
CEIKPQSTU	quickstep	**CEILOSTVY**	costively	**CEINOPRRT**	intercrop
CEIKPRSTW	Prestwick	**CEILPPRRS**	cripplers	**CEINOPRSS**	conspires
CEIKQSSTU	quicksets	**CEILPPSUU**	Leucippus	**CEINOPRST**	inceptors
CEIKRRSTT	trickster	**CEILPRSSU**	surplices		inspector
CEILLLMTU	clitellum	**CEILRSTUU**	Lucretius	**CEINOPRSV**	provinces
CEILLNOSS	collinses	**CEILRSUVY**	cursively	**CEINOPRXY**	pyroxenic
CEILLNOUV	involucel	**CEIMMNNOS**	mnemonics	**CEINOPSTU**	pectinous
CEILLOPTU	pollucite	**CEIMMNOOR**	monomeric	**CEINORRST**	tricornes
CEILLOQSU	coquilles	**CEIMMNOOS**	economism	**CEINORRSU**	coinsurer
CEILLOSUV	collusive	**CEIMMNOSU**	communise		recursion
CEILLPSTY	sylleptic		encomiums	**CEINORRTV**	contriver
CEILMNNOO	monocline	**CEIMMNOTU**	comminute	**CEINORRTY**	incretory
CEILMNOOS	semicolon	**CEIMMNOTY**	metonymic	**CEINORSSS**	incrosses
CEILMNOTU	monticule	**CEIMMNOUZ**	communize	**CEINORSSU**	coinsures
CEILMNSSU	lemniscus	**CEIMMOORS**	microsome	**CEINORSTT**	cornetist
CEILMNSUU	minuscule	**CEIMMOORT**	microtome	**CEINORSTU**	countries
CEILMOPRS	compilers	**CEIMMORST**	recommits		cretinous
	compliers	**CEIMMORTT**	committer		neurotics
CEILMOPRY	micropyle	**CEIMMRSTU**	crummiest	**CEINORSTV**	contrives
	polymeric	**CEIMMRSTY**	symmetric	**CEINORSUX**	excursion
CEILMOSSS	solecisms	**CEIMNNOPU**	pneumonic	**CEINOSSUY**	synecious
CEILMOSSU	coliseums	**CEIMNNORT**	nonmetric	**CEINOSTUV**	contusive
CEILMRTUU	reticulum	**CEIMNNOST**	Mont Cenis	**CEINOTVXY**	convexity
CEILMSSTU	clumsiest	**CEIMNOOPT**	coemption	**CEINPRSSS**	crispness
CEILNNOOS	cloisonne	**CEIMNOORT**	microtone	**CEINRSSTT**	centrists
CEILNNSSY	synclines	**CEIMNOOST**	economist	**CEINRSTTU**	intercuts
CEILNOOPS	scopoline	**CEIMNOOSU**	monecious		tinctures
CEILNOORS	coloniser	**CEIMNOPTY**	impotency	**CEIOOPRSS**	coreopsis
CEILNOORZ	colonizer	**CEIMNORST**	intercoms	**CEIOOPRST**	porticoes
CEILNOOSS	colonises	**CEIMNRSST**	centrisms	**CEIOORRSV**	corrosive
CEILNOOSZ	colonizes	**CEIMOOPRR**	poromeric	**CEIOORSTV**	vorticose
CEILNOOTU	elocution	**CEIMOOPST**	composite	**CEIOOSSTX**	toxicoses
CEILNOPRU	pronuclei	**CEIMOORSS**	moriscoes	**CEIOPRRSU**	croupiers
CEILNOPSY	Polynices	**CEIMOORTZ**	zoometric	**CEIOPRTUY**	eurytopic
CEILNORSS	inclosers	**CEIMOOSTX**	exosmotic	**CEIORRSTT**	trisector
	licensors	**CEIMOPRSS**	comprises	**CEIORRSTU**	courtiers
CEILNORST	sclerotin	**CEIMOPRSX**	proxemics	**CEIORRSUZ**	cruzeiros
CEILNORSU	inclosure	**CEIMOPSUU**	pumiceous	**CEIORRTUU**	couturier
	reclusion	**CEIMORSSX**	exorcisms	**CEIORSSSW**	crosswise
CEILNORUV	involucre	**CEIMORSTU**	costumier	**CEIORSSTX**	exorcists
CEILNOSSU	seclusion	**CEIMORSTV**	Meštrović	**CEIORSTTU**	toreutics
CEILNOSUX	exclusion	**CEIMOSSTU**	customise	**CEIPPRRST**	prescript
CEILNRSSU	curliness	**CEIMOSTUV**	muscovite	**CEIPPRSST**	rescripts
CEILNRSUV	culverins	**CEIMOSTUZ**	customize	**CEIPRRSTU**	scripture
CEILNRUVY	virulency	**CEIMSSSTY**	systemics	**CEIRRSSTT**	restricts
CEILNSSTU	linctuses	**CEINNNOOX**	connexion	**CEIRRSTTU**	stricture
CEILOOPRT	coprolite	**CEINNNOST**	innocents	**CEIRSSSSU**	scissures
CEILOORSU	colourise	**CEINNNOTT**	continent	**CEIRSSTTT**	strictest
CEILOORSZ	colorizes	**CEINNNOTV**	connivent	**CEIRSSTTU**	crustiest
CEILOORUZ	colourize	**CEINNOOTV**	connotive	**CEIRSSTUV**	scurviest
CEILOPPRT	proleptic	**CEINNOPRT**	Princeton	**CEISSTUZZ**	scuzziest
CEILOPRSV	coverslip	**CEINNORSV**	connivers	**CEJKOOTUY**	outjockey
	slipcover	**CEINNORSY**	incensory	**CEJNORRSU**	conjurers
CEILOPSTU	poultices	**CEINNORTU**	centurion	**CEJNRSTUU**	junctures
CEILOPSTY	epicotyls		continuer	**CEJOOPRRT**	projector
CEILORRTU	courtlier	**CEINNOSTU**	continues	**CEKKORSTY**	skyrocket
CEILORSSS	sclerosis		neustonic	**CEKLLNORS**	rollnecks

CEKLLOOSV	lovelocks	CEMOPRSTU	computers	CFGIINTYY	cityfying
CEKLNNPUY	luckpenny	CEMORRSUU	mercurous	CFGILNNOU	flouncing
CEKLRRSTU	trucklers	CEMORRSWW	screwworm	CFGILNORY	forcingly
CEKMNORTU	mockernut	CEMORRTYY	cryometry	CFGINNOSU	confusing
CEKNOORSV	convokers	CEMORSSTU	costumers	CFGINNOTU	confuting
CEKNOPSST	penstocks		customers	CFGINOSSU	focussing
CEKOOORSV	overcooks	CENNOOPPY	opponency	CFHIINOOR	honorific
CEKOORRSS	rockroses	CENNOOPRU	pronounce	CFHIKOPRT.	pitchfork
CEKOORRSW	coworkers	CENNOORST	cornstone	CFHIKOSST	stockfish
CEKOORSTV	overstock	CENNOORSV	convenors	CFHLOOOTT	footcloth
CEKOPRSST	sprockets	CENNORSTU	nocturnes	CFHNOORRT	Cornforth
CELLMOPXY	complexly	CENNOSSSU	consensus	CFIIKKLNS	skinflick
CELLMSTUU	scutellum	CENOOPRST	stonecrop	CFIILMMOR	microfilm
CELLNOSUU	nucleolus	CENOOQRRU	conqueror	CFIILNORT	inflictor
CELLOOPTY	collotype	CENOOORRST	consorter	CFIILORST	floristic
CELLOORSS	colorless	CENOORRTV	convertor	CFIINORST	frictions
CELMNOORU	colourmen	CENOORSVY	conveyors	CFIIOOPRS	soporific
CELMNOTUY	contumely	CENOQSSTU	conquests	CFIKLLNOT	flintlock
CELMOOPRY	copolymer	CENORRSTU	construer	CFIKLLOOR	folkloric
CELMOOSSU	colosseum	CENORSSSS	crossness	CFIKLSSTU	stickfuls
CELMOOTUY	leucotomy	CENORSSSU	uncrosses	CFILNSUUU	funiculus
CELMOPRUU	operculum	CENORSSTU	construes	CFIMMOORR	microform
CELMPRSSU	scrumples	CENORSSUY	cynosures	CFIMNORSU	unciforms
CELMPRSTU	plectrums	CENORSTXY	xenocryst	CFIMORSTU	scutiform
CELMPSSUU	speculums	CENPRRTUU	puncturer	CFINNOOSU	confusion
CELNNOTTY	contently	CENPRSTUU	punctures	CFINNOSTU	functions
CELNOORSS	consolers	CEOOOPSST	otoscopes	CFKOOOSST	footstock
CELNOORSU	counselor	CEOOPRRSS	processor	CFLLOORUU	colourful
CELNOOSTU	consolute	CEOOPRRST	prosector	CFLNOORRU	cornflour
CELNOOSVV	convolves	CEOOPRRSV	overcrops	CFLOOOSTT	coltsfoot
CELNOOTUV	convolute	CEOOPRRTT	protector	CFLOOPSSU	scoopfuls
CELNOPRST	plectrons	CEOOPRSTY	sporocyte	CFNNOORST	confronts
CELNOPRTU	corpulent	CEOOPSSTU	octopuses	CFOOORSTW	crowfoots
CELNOPSUU	uncouples	CEOORRSSU	sorcerous	CFORSTUUU	fructuous
CELNORSSW	crownless	CEOORRSSV	crossover	CGGHIKNNU	Chungking
CELNORSTU	consulter	CEOORSTUU	courteous	CGGHINNOQ	Chongqing
CELNOSSTU	countless		outsource	CGGHINORU	grouching
CELNOSSUV	convulses	CEOPPRSST	prospects	CGGIINNOS	cognising
CELNPRUUY	purulency	CEOPRRRSU	precursor	CGGIINNOZ	cognizing
CELNRRTUY	currently		procurers	CGGINORSS	scroggins
CELNRTTUU	truculent	CEOPRRRTU	corrupter	CGGINORSU	scourging
CELOOORSV	overcools	CEOPRRSSU	percussor		scrouging
CELOOPRSU	supercool		procuress	CGHHINNOO	honchoing
CELOOPSSS	cesspools	CEOPRSSTW	screwtops	CGHIIKNST	skitching
CELOORSTW	coleworts	CEORRSUUV	verrucous	CGHIIKNTW	wickthing
CELOPSSUU	opuscules	CEPPRSTUU	uppercuts	CGHIILLNS	schilling
CELORSSST	crosslets	CEPRSSSUU	cupressus	CGHIILNST	chitlings
CELORSSUU	surculose	CEPRSSTUU	cutpurses	CGHIIMNRS	smirching
CELPRSTUU	sculpture	CERRSTTUU	structure	CGHIIMOUZ	Mizoguchi
CEMMNOORS	commoners	CFFGIINSU	sufficing	CGHIINNST	snitching
CEMMNOOST	commonest	CFFGILNSU	scuffling	CGHIINPPS	chippings
CEMMORSTU	commuters	CFFHHIKOR	Kirchhoff	CGHIINSTT	stitching
CEMMNOOPT	component	CFFHIORST	Christoff	CGHIINSTW	switching
CEMNOOOQU	monocoque	CFFIIOOSU	officious		witchings
CEMNOOORS	monoceros	CFFORRSSU	crossruff	CGHIINTTW	twitching
CEMNOORTY	necrotomy	CFGHIILNN	flinching	CGHIINVVY	chivvying
CEMNOOSTY	monocytes	CFGHIILNS	clingfish	CGHIKNNSU	chunkings
CEMNOPSTT	contempts	CFGHIILNT	flitching	CGHILMOOO	homologic
CEMNORSSU	consumers	CFGIIIKNN	finicking	CGHILNNSY	lynchings
CEMNORTUY	emunctory	CFGIIINTY	citifying	CGHILNOOS	schooling
CEMOOPRSS	composers	CFGIILLMN	clingfilm	CGHILNOOY	ichnology
CEMOOPRSU	composure	CFGIINNNO	confining	CGHILNORT	chortling

CGHILNOSU	slouching	
CGHILOOOR	horologic	
CGHILORUY	grouchily	
CGHIMNOOS	smooching	
CGHIMNSTU	smutching	
CGHINNRSU	churnings	
CGHINOOSS	scooshing	
CGHINORSU	chorusing	
CGHINOSSU	hocussing	
CGHINSSSU	schussing	
CGHIOPRTY	copyright	
CGHLLNOOT	longcloth	
CGHLOOORY	chorology	
CGHLOOPYY	phycology	
CGIIIKMMN	mimicking	
CGIIILNNN	inclining	
CGIIINNOV	invoicing	
CGIIKLNNR	crinkling	
CGIIKLNPR	prickling	
CGIIKLNRT	trickling	
CGIIKLNST	stickling	
CGIIKMMRY	gimmickry	
CGIIKNNPU	unpicking	
CGIIKNSTY	stickying	
CGIIKPSST	pigsticks	
CGIILMNNY	mincingly	
CGIILMNOP	compiling	
CGIILMNPR	crimpling	
CGIILMNUU	glucinium	
CGIILNNOS	inclosing	
CGIILNNOU	uncoiling	
CGIILNPPR	crippling	
CGIILNPPS	clippings	
CGIILOSST	glossitic	
	logistics	
CGIILRSTU	liturgics	
CGIIMMNOX	commixing	
CGIIMMNOS	incomings	
CGIIMNORT	morticing	
CGIIMNPRS	scrimping	
CGIIINNNOV	conniving	
CGIINNOOT	cognition	
	incognito	
CGIINNOUV	unvoicing	
CGIINNRRU	incurring	
CGIINNRUV	incurving	
CGIINOOSS	isogonics	
CGIINPRST	scripting	
CGIINPRTU	picturing	
CGIJNNORU	conjuring	
CGIKKLNNU	knuckling	
CGIKLMNOY	mockingly	
CGIKLNNOU	unlocking	
CGIKLNORS	rocklings	
CGIKLNRTU	truckling	
CGIKLNSSU	sucklings	
CGIKLOSTW	glowstick	
CGIKNNOOV	convoking	
CGIKNNORU	uncorking	
CGIKNNTUU	untucking	
CGIKNORSW	corkwings	
CGIKNOSST	stockings	

CGILLNOOY	coolingly	
CGILLNORS	scrolling	
CGILLNOYY	cloyingly	
CGILMNOOO	monologic	
CGILMNOPY	complying	
CGILMNPRU	crumpling	
CGILMOOYZ	zymologic	
CGILNNNUY	cunningly	
CGILNNOOR	longicorn	
CGILNNOOS	consoling	
CGILNNOSU	unclosing	
CGILNNRUU	uncurling	
CGILNOOOY	coniology	
	iconology	
CGILNOORS	colorings	
CGILNOORU	colouring	
CGILNOPSU	couplings	
CGILNOPTU	octupling	
CGILNORSU	closuring	
CGILNORTU	cloturing	
CGILNORWY	crowingly	
CGILNPRSU	scrupling	
CGILNPSTU	sculpting	
CGILNRTUU	culturing	
CGILNSTTU	scuttling	
CGILNTTUY	cuttingly	
CGILOOOPT	topologic	
CGILOOOSY	sociology	
CGILOOPTY	typologic	
CGIMMNNOU	communing	
CGIMMNOOV	commoving	
CGIMMNOTU	commuting	
CGIMMNRSU	scrumming	
CGIMNNOOS	oncomings	
CGIMNNOSU	consuming	
CGIMNOOPS	composing	
CGIMNOPTU	computing	
CGIMNOSTU	costuming	
CGIMNPRSU	scrumping	
CGINNNOOT	connoting	
CGINNOORS	consignor	
CGINNOOVY	convoying	
CGINNORSW	crownings	
CGINNORTU	trouncing	
CGINNOSTU	contusing	
CGINOOPRS	scrooping	
CGINOORTU	Tourcoing	
CGINOPRRU	procuring	
CGINORSSS	crossings	
CGINORSSU	scourings	
CGINORTUY	congruity	
	outcrying	
CGINRRSUY	scurrying	
CGINRSTUY	curtsying	
CGKNOSSTU	gunstocks	
CGLMOOOSY	cosmology	
CGLOOOPRY	coprology	
CGMNOOOSY	cosmogony	
CGNNOOTTU	guncotton	
CGNOORSUU	congruous	
CHHHIIMNO	Ho Chi Minh	
CHHIILLNS	Chin Hills	

CHHIMRSTY	rhythmics	
CHHINORTW	Northwich	
CHHKLLOOY	hollyhock	
CHIIILPPP	philippic	
CHIIILRTT	trilithic	
CHIIIMRRT	Tirich Mir	
CHIILLOPY	lyophilic	
CHIILLPTY	phyllitic	
CHIILMORT	microlith	
CHIILNNPS	linchpins	
CHIILOOPZ	zoophilic	
CHIILOOTT	otolithic	
CHIILORTU	urolithic	
CHIILORTY	rhyolitic	
CHIILPSTU	sulphitic	
CHIILPTTY	typhlitic	
CHIIMSTTY	mythicist	
CHIINOSTU	chitinous	
CHIIOPSST	sophistic	
CHIIORRSS	cirrhosis	
CHIIORSST	trichosis	
CHIIORTTY	rhoticity	
CHIIPSSTY	physicist	
CHIIRSSTT	tristichs	
CHIKLMOST	locksmith	
CHIKMNNSU	munchkins	
CHIKMNPSU	chipmunks	
CHIKMNSTU	mutchkins	
CHIKOOPTT	toothpick	
CHIKOPSTW	whipstock	
CHILLMOPY	phyllomic	
CHILLNOOT	loincloth	
CHILLOOST	oilcloths	
CHILLOSTY	coltishly	
CHILLOSUY	slouchily	
CHILLSTUY	cultishly	
CHILMNOUU	homunculi	
CHILMOOTY	homolytic	
CHILMUUUW	Wu-lu-mu-ch'i	
CHILNNOSU	Nicholson	
CHILNNPSY	lynchpins	
CHILNOPSU	sulphonic	
CHILOOPTY	holotypic	
CHILOORSS	chlorosis	
CHILORSTU	trochilus	
CHILORTUY	ulotrichy	
CHILOSTTY	cystolith	
CHILPRSUU	sulphuric	
CHILRRSUY	currishly	
CHIMMNOOY	homonymic	
CHIMNOOST	monostich	
CHIMNOPSY	symphonic	
CHIMNORSU	Murchison	
CHIMNORSW	inchworms	
CHIMOOPRT	morphotic	
CHIMPSTYY	symphytic	
CHINNOORT	nonrhotic	
CHINOOPST	photonics	
CHINOOPTY	hypotonic	
CHINOORST	orthicons	
CHINOPSTU	countship	
CHINOPSTY	hypnotics	

CHINOSSTZ	schizonts	CIIMOOSST	isosmotic	CIMMMNOSU	communism
CHIOOPRTT	orthoptic	CIIMORSTV	vorticism	CIMMNNOOU	communion
CHIOOPTYZ	zoophytic	CIINNNOTU	inunction	CIMMNOOOS	monosomic
CHIOORSTT	orthotics	CIINNORSU	incursion	CIMMNOOOT	commotion
CHIOPRSTU	courtship	CIINNOSSW	Wisconsin	CIMMNOSTU	communist
CHIOPRSYY	hypocrisy	CIINNOTUY	innocuity	CIMMNOTUY	community
CHIOPSSSY	psychosis	CIINNSSTT	instincts	CIMMOORTY	microtomy
CHIORRSSU	scirrhous	CIINOOPPR	propionic	CIMNNOOOT	monotonic
CHIPRSTTY	triptychs	CIINOOPRT	inotropic	CIMNNOSYY	synonymic
CHKLMOOST	Stockholm	CIINOPSSU	suspicion	CIMNNOTUU	continuum
CHKNORSSU	cornhusks	CIINORSTT	striction	CIMNOOOSU	monoicous
CHLMNOORU	lunchroom	CIINORSUU	incurious	CIMNOOPTY	monotypic
CHLNOOOPS	colophons	CIINOSTVY	synovitic		toponymic
CHLNOOOPY	colophony	CIINPSSTU	sinciputs	CIMNOOTXY	mycotoxin
CHLNOTUUY	uncouthly	CIIOOPRST	isotropic	CIMNOSSTU	miscounts
CHLOOPTYY	hypocotyl	CIIOOSSTX	toxicosis	CIMNSTUYY	syncytium
CHLOPPTYY	polyptych	CIIOPRSTT	tropistic	CINNOOSTU	continuos
CHMNORRSU	crumhorns	CIIORSTTU	touristic		contusion
CHNNORSYY	synchrony	CIIORSTTV	vorticist	CINNOOSUU	innocuous
CHNORSTUU	cothurnus	CIIORSTUV	virtuosic	CINOOOPST	cooptions
CHOOOPPTY	photocopy	CIIORSTUY	curiosity	CINOOORRS	corrosion
CHOOOPRSY	horoscopy	CIIOSSTVY	viscosity	CINOOPRSS	scorpions
CHOOSTTTU	Southcott	CIIRSTTUY	rusticity	CINOOSSUY	synoicous
CHORSSTTU	shortcuts	CIJKOSSTY	joysticks	CINOOTTXY	cytotoxin
CIIILLLTY	illicitly	CIJNNOSTU	junctions	CINOPPRUY	porcupiny
CIIILMNOT	limonitic	CIKKOOSSU	Kosciusko	CINOPRRTU	incorrupt
CIIILMOPT	impolitic	CIKLLNUUY	unluckily	CINOPSSTY	synoptics
CIIILMPTY	implicity	CIKLNOSST	linstocks	CINOSSTUV	viscounts
CIIILOPST	pisolitic	CIKLOORSU	cokuloris	CINOSTUVY	viscounty
CIIILORTV	vitriolic	CIKLOPSSU	liposucks	CINRSSTTU	instructs
CIIILOSSS	silicosis	CIKLORSTW	wristlock	CIOOOPRRT	Porto Rico
CIIILOSSU	silicious	CIKMOORSS	sickrooms	CIOOOPRSZ	zoosporic
CIIIMSTTW	witticism	CIKNNOOSS	coonskins	CIOOOPRTZ	protozoic
CIIINNOSS	incisions	CIKOSSSTT	stockists	CIOOPPRSU	Procopius
CIIINNRST	intrinsic	CILLMORYU	collyrium	CIOOPSSTU	posticous
CIIKLPSST	lipsticks	CILLMOUUV	colluvium	CJNOORRSU	conjurors
CIIKNNOPT	nickpoint	CILLNOOST	cotillons	CKKLOOPST	Klopstock
CIIKNNOTY	cytokinin	CILLNOOSU	collusion	CKKNOOSTU	knockouts
CIIKNPPRS	pinpricks	CILLNOSSU	scullions	CKLMMOOSS	slommocks
CIILLMRUY	Illyricum	CILLOOOST	ocotillos	CKMMORSUW	muckworms
CIILLMSTU	tillicums	CILLOOOTY	coyotillo	CKMOOORST	stockroom
CIILLNOOS	collision	CILMNOPSU	pulmonics	CKNOOOSTW	Cookstown
CIILLNOOT	cotillion	CILMNOSTU	columnist	CKNOORRHW	crownwork
	octillion	CILMOOPSY	polysomic	CKOOORSTT	rootstock
CIILLNUVY	uncivilly	CILMOTYYZ	zymolytic	CKOOPRSTT	Stockport
CIILLOPTY	lipolytic	CILNOORUU	unicolour	CKOOPSSTT	stockpots
	politicly	CILNOOSST	colonists	CLLOOOTTW	Woollcott
CIILMPRSY	scrimpily	CILNOOSTU	locutions	CLMNNOOTU	Montluçon
CIILMRSSY	lyricisms	CILNOSTYY	cytolysin	CLMOOOORT	locomotor
CIILNNOSU	inclusion	CILOOPSUY	copiously	CLMOOOPTY	colpotomy
CIILNOOST	colonitis	CILOORRST	tricolors	CLMOOOSTY	colostomy
CIILNOPTU	punctilio	CILOORRTU	tricolour	CLMOORSTU	colostrum
	unpolitic	CILOORSST	colorists	CLNOOPRSU	proconsul
CIILOOPST	politicos	CILOORSTU	colourist	CLNOORSTU	consultor
CIILOORST	solicitor	CILOPPTYY	polytypic	CLNOOSUUY	nocuously
CIILOOSSS	scoliosis	CILOPRTYY	pyrolytic	CLNORTUUY	uncourtly
CIILOSSST	sciolists	CILORRSUY	cursorily	CLOOOPRST	protocols
CIILOSUVY	viciously	CILORRSUU	curiously	CLOPRRTUY	corruptly
CIILRSSTY	lyricists	CILOSSTYY	cytolysis	CLOPRSSTU	sculptors
CIILSSTTY	stylistic	CILOSSUVY	viscously	CMMNOOORS	Roscommon
CIIMMSSTY	mysticism	CILRSTTUU	culturist	CMNOOORST	cosmotron
CIIMNORUZ	zirconium	CILRSTUUU	utriculus	CMOOORRTU	courtroom

CMOOORSST motocross	**DDEEGJPRU** prejudged	**DDEEMOOPR** predoomed
CMOOOSTTY costotomy	**DDEEGLNPU** unpledged	**DDEEMOPUY** Puy de Dôme
CMOOSTTVY cystotomy	**DDEEGNORU** guerdoned	**DDEENNORU** underdone
CNNNOOTUU count noun	**DDEEGOSSS** goddesses	**DDEENNOUW** unendowed
CNOOOORST octoroons	**DDEEHIINT** hiddenite	**DDEENOPPR** propended
CNOORRSTY cryotrons	**DDEEHNORT** dethroned	**DDEENOPRS** responded
CNOORSSTW crosstown	**DDEEHNORU** deerhound	**DDEENOPRT** portended
CNOPRTUUY upcountry	**DDEEHNRTU** thundered	**DDEENOPUX** expounded
COOPRRRTU corruptor	**DDEEHRRSS** shredders	**DDEENORRT** retrodden
COOPRSSTY sporocyst	**DDEEIILMT** delimited	**DDEENORSU** resounded
COORRSSTW crosswort	**DDEEIILNS** sidelined	underdoes
DDDEEEINX deindexed	**DDEEIIMRS** dimerised	**DDEENOSSS** oddnesses
DDDEEHRSU shuddered	**DDEEIIMRZ** dimerized	**DDEENPSSU** suspended
DDDEEIIRV redivided	**DDEEIINOZ** deionized	**DDEENRSSU** undressed
DDDEEINPS dispended	**DDEEIIOSX** deoxidise	**DDEEOOPRT** torpedoed
DDDEEINST distended	**DDEEIIOXZ** deoxidize	**DDEEOORSV** overdosed
DDDEENOOS desnooded	**DDEEIIPPT** dipeptide	**DDEEORSTY** destroyed
DDDEENORU redounded	**DDEEIIRSV** redivides	**DDEFFIINT** diffident
DDDEEORRS dodderers	**DDEEIISSS** disseised	**DDEFGIIIN** dignified
DDDEGILOS dislodged	**DDEEIISSZ** disseized	**DDEFGINOR** foddering
DDDEGINOR doddering	**DDEEIKLLS** deskilled	**DDEFGJORU** forjudged
DDDEGOOTU outdodged	**DDEEIKLNN** enkindled	**DDEFIILST** fiddliest
DDDEIILVY dividedly	**DDEEIKLNR** rekindled	**DDEFIILSU** fluidised
DDDEIINSV dividends	**DDEEILLPS** dispelled	**DDEFIILUZ** fluidized
DDDEIINUV undivided	**DDEEILLRR** redrilled	**DDEFILNOP** pinfolded
DDDEILNMN unriddled	**DDEEILLRV** drivelled	**DDEFNNOUU** unfounded
DDDEILOPS disploded	**DDEEILMMN** middlemen	**DDEGGHOOT** hotdogged
DDEEEEKNW weekended	**DDEEILMOS** melodised	**DDEGGIORS** disgorged
DDEEEFINR redefined	**DDEEILMOZ** melodized	**DDEGHINRS** shredding
DDEEEFNRS defenders	**DDEEILMSX** Middlesex	**DDEGHINSS** sheddings
DDEEEFNRU underfeed	**DDEEILOPS** despoiled	**DDEGIIIST** digitised
DDEEEGIPR pedigreed	**DDEEILORS** soldiered	**DDEGIIITZ** digitized
DDEEEHLNR Den Helder	**DDEEIMMNO** demimonde	**DDEGIIMSU** misguided
DDEEEILRV delivered	**DDEEIMNOS** demonised	**DDEGIINNR** niddering
DDEEEINRW rewidened	**DDEEIMNOZ** demonized	**DDEGIINSS** giddiness
DDEEEINSX deindexes	**DDEEIMNPU** unimpeded	**DDEGIISSU** disguised
DDEEEIPTX expedited	**DDEEIMRST** dermestid	**DDEGIJMSU** misjudged
DDEEEIRTU deuteride	**DDEEINNST** intendeds	**DDEGIJNRU** juddering
DDEEELOPV developed	**DDEEINORW** eiderdown	**DDEGILOSS** dislodges
DDEEENNPT dependent	**DDEEINOSV** nosedived	**DDEGINNOR** dondering
DDEEENORW reendowed	**DDEEINPSS** dispensed	**DDEGINNOS** soddening
DDEEENPPR perpended	**DDEEINRST** dendrites	**DDEGINNOT** Eddington
DDEEENPRT pretended	distender	**DDEGINRRU** undergird
DDEEEORRR reordered	**DDEEINRSU** underside	**DDEGINRTU** detruding
DDEEEPRSS depressed	undesired	**DDEGISSTU** disgusted
DDEEERRSS redressed	**DDEEINSST** dissented	**DDEGLMSUY** smudgedly
DDEEESTUU desuetude	**DDEEIOORS** deodorise	**DDEGLNOOR** goldenrod
DDEEFFNOR forfended	**DDEEIOORZ** deodorize	**DDEGNOOOR** godrooned
DDEEFGINN defending	**DDEEIOPRX** peroxided	**DDEGNORSU** underdogs
DDEEFGLNU unfledged	**DDEEIOPST** deposited	**DDEGOOSTU** outdodges
DDEEFILNU undefiled	**DDEEIPRSS** dispersed	**DDEHHNRTU** hundredth
DDEEFINNU undefined	**DDEEIPSTU** deputised	**DDEHIIRSY** Yiddisher
DDEEFLOOR reflooded	**DDEEIPTUZ** deputized	**DDEHILRSY** reddishly
DDEEFNORU foundered	**DDEEIRSSS** sidedress	**DDEHINORS** dihedrons
DDEEFORST defrosted	**DDEEIRRSV** disserved	**DDEHIORXY** hydroxide
DDEEGGGLO doglegged	**DDEELMORS** smoldered	**DDEHIOSST** shoddiest
DDEEGGNOU gudgeoned	**DDEELMORU** mouldered	**DDEHOOSSW** woodsheds
DDEEGHILT delighted	remoulded	**DDEIIINSV** divinised
DDEEGINNP depending	**DDEELNPRU** plundered	**DDEIIINVZ** divinized
DDEEGINNR reddening	**DDEELOTVY** devotedly	**DDEIIJNOS** disjoined
DDEEGIRSS digressed	**DDEEMNORS** endoderms	**DDEIIKOSV** videodisk
	DDEEMNOTU demounted	**DDEIILLST** distilled

DDEIILMNS	dislimned		shoreweed
DDEIILSTT	tiddliest	**DDIIIISVV**	dividivis	**DEEEEILLMP**	millepede
DDEIIMSSS	dismissed	**DDILOOPPS**	diplopods	**DEEEEILNNV**	enlivened
DDEIINSST	dissident	**DDILOOSWW**	wildwoods	**DEEEEILPRV**	replevied
DDEIINSTU	disunited	**DDINOPSUU**	dupondius	**DEEEEILPTV**	depletive
DDEIIOPSS	diopsides	**DDNOOORUW**	roundwood	**DEEEEILRRV**	deliverer
DDEIIPRSZ	disprized	**DEEEEGKRS**	kedgerees		redeliver
DDEIIRSUV	reduviids	**DEEEEGMRR**	reemerged	**DEEEEILRST**	leistered
DDEIJNORY	joyridden	**DEEEEGQSU**	squeegeed	**DEEEEILSSW**	edelweiss
DDEIKLNNU	unkindled	**DEEEEKNRW**	weekender	**DEEEEILSTV**	televised
DDEILMNOT	Middleton	**DEEEEMRRS**	redeemers	**DEEEEIMNRT**	determine
DDEILNRRU	unriddler	**DEEEENPRS**	deepeners	**DEEEEIMNSU**	Eumenides
DDEILNRSU	unriddles	**DEEEENPST**	steepened	**DEEEEIMPRR**	premiered
DDEILNTUU	undiluted	**DEEEENRRT**	reentered	**DEEEEIMSST**	disesteem
DDEILOPSS	displodes	**DEEEENSTW**	sweetened	**DEEEEINNSS**	neediness
DDEILORWW	worldwide	**DEEEEFFNO**	enfeoffed	**DEEEEINOPR**	pioneered
DDEILOSSV	dissolved	**DEEEEFHNRS**	freshened	**DEEEEINPTX**	expedient
DDEILRSTW	twiddlers	**DEEEEFHRRS**	refreshed	**DEEEEINQTU**	quietened
DDEILSTUY	studiedly	**DEEEEFINRS**	redefines	**DEEEEINRRS**	reindeers
DDEIMNLPU	impounded	**DEEEEFINSV**	defensive	**DEEEEINRSS**	reediness
DDEIMNSSU	muddiness	**DEEEEFLLNU**	needleful	**DEEEEINRST**	eternised
DDEIMOOSS	sodomised	**DEEEEFLLRU**	refuelled		tenderise
DDEIMOOSZ	sodomized	**DEEEEFMNRT**	deferment		teredines
DDEIMOSSU	medusoids		fermented	**DEEEEINRTZ**	eternized
DDEINORTU	outridden	**DEEEEFNRST**	deferents		tenderize
DDEINORWW	windrowed	**DEEEEFORSV**	overfeeds	**DEEEEINSSS**	seediness
DDEINOSSW	disendows	**DEEEEFPRRR**	preferred	**DEEEEINSSW**	weediness
	dowdiness	**DEEEEFRRRS**	deferrers	**DEEEEIPRRV**	reprieved
	downsides	**DEEEEGGHIR**	Heidegger	**DEEEEIPRTX**	expediter
DDEINOSWZ	downsized	**DEEEEGHIRW**	reweighed	**DEEEEIPRVW**	previewed
DDEINRSSU	ruddiness	**DEEEEGIKLW**	wedgelike	**DEEEEIPSST**	speediest
DDEINSTUU	unstudied	**DEEEEGIMNR**	redeeming	**DEEEEIPSTX**	expedites
DDEIOPRST	disported	**DEEEEGINNP**	deepening	**DEEEEIRRRS**	derrieres
DDEIOPRSV	disproved	**DEEEEGINRS**	energised	**DEEEEIRRTV**	retrieved
DDEIORNSS	disorders	**DEEEEGINRZ**	energized	**DEEEEIRSTV**	detersive
DDEIORSTT	distorted	**DEEEEGINSS**	digeneses	**DEEEEIRUZZ**	Zuider Zee
DDEIPRSTU	disrupted	**DEEEEGIPRS**	pedigrees	**DEEEEISTTW**	tweediest
DDELMNOUU	unmoulded	**DEEEEGIRRT**	ridgetree	**DEEEEKLLNN**	kennelled
DDELNORSU	undersold	**DEEEEGIRST**	greediest	**DEEEEKLLNR**	kernelled
DDELNORUY	roundedly	**DEEEEGKLNT**	kentledge	**DEEEEKNNTT**	kennetted
DDEMNOSUU	duodenums	**DEEEEGLNOY**	goldeneye	**DEEEELLPSW**	speedwell
DDENNORTU	untrodden	**DEEEEGLRSS**	greedless	**DEEEELNOPV**	enveloped
DDENNORUU	unrounded	**DEEEEGLSSV**	selvedges	**DEEEELNSTU**	unsteeled
DDENNORUW	down under	**DEEEEGMNST**	segmented	**DEEEELOPPR**	repeopled
DDENNOUUW	unwounded	**DEEEEGMRRS**	demergers	**DEEEELOPRV**	developer
DDENOOPRS	dropsonde	**DEEEEGNNRS**	engenders		redevelop
DDENOORUW	underwood	**DEEEEGNRTT**	detergent	**DEEEELPPRX**	perplexed
DDENRSTTU	Rundstedt	**DEEEEGRRSS**	regressed	**DEEEELPSSS**	de Lesseps
DDEOPRRTU	protruded	**DEEEEGRRTT**	regretted	**DEEEELRSTT**	resettled
DDFGILORU	Guildford	**DEEEEHHSTW**	wheeshted	**DEEEELRSTW**	sweltered
DDFIOORTW	driftwood	**DEEEEHILRT**	Ethelred I	**DEEEEMNNOV**	envenomed
DDFMNOSUU	dumfounds	**DEEEEHILSW**	sidewheel	**DEEEEMNRTT**	determent
DDGGIILNR	griddling	**DEEEEHIMPR**	ephemerid	**DEEEEMOORT**	oedometer
DDGGINNOS	dingdongs	**DEEEEHINPR**	ephedrine	**DEEEEMOPRT**	pedometer
DDGIIINOS	indigoids	**DEEEEHIRST**	etherised	**DEEEEMOPRW**	empowered
DDGIIKLNY	kiddingly	**DEEEEHIRTZ**	etherized	**DEEEEMORST**	dosemeter
DDGIILMNS	middlings	**DEEEEHLPRT**	telphered	**DEEEEMPPRT**	preempted
DDGIILNNW	dwindling	**DEEEEHLRST**	sheltered	**DEEEEMPSTT**	tempested
DDGIILNTW	twiddling	**DEEEEHLRSW**	wheedlers	**DEEEEMRSST**	deemsters
DDGIINQSU	squidding	**DEEEEHNPRR**	reprehend	**DEEEENNRTU**	unentered
DDGLORRSU	druglords	**DEEEEHNPRS**	ensphered	**DEEEENNRUW**	unrenewed
DDHIOOOWW	widowhood	**DEEEEHNRRU**	hereunder	**DEEEENNSSS**	denseness
		DEEEEHORSW	horseweed		

DEEENORSS	endorsees	**DEEFHRRTU**	furthered	**DEEGGIORS**	doggeries
DEEENPRRT	pretender	**DEEFIIJLL**	jellified	**DEEGGIRRT**	triggered
DEEENPRSS	Despenser	**DEEFIIKLN**	fiendlike	**DEEGGIRST**	dreggiest
DEEENPRST	presented	**DEEFIILMN**	minefield	**DEEGGIRSU**	ruggedise
	repetends	**DEEFIILNR**	infielder	**DEEGGIRUZ**	ruggedize
DEEENPRSX	expenders	**DEEFIILQU**	liquefied	**DEEGGMNTU**	nutmegged
DEEENPRTV	prevented	**DEEFIIMNS**	feminised	**DEEGGNTTU**	nuggetted
DEEENRRRS	renderers		misdefine	**DEEGGSSTU**	suggested
DEEENRRST	tenderers	**DEEFIIMNZ**	feminized	**DEEGHHOPS**	hedgehops
DEEENRRSV	reverends	**DEEFIIMRT**	metrified	**DEEGHIINV**	inveighed
DEEENRRTT	deterrent	**DEEFIINNS**	definiens	**DEEGHILNT**	lightened
DEEENRSTT	tenderest	**DEEFIINRU**	reunified	**DEEGHILNW**	wheedling
DEEENRSTX	extenders	**DEEFIIPRS**	perfidies	**DEEGHILRT**	delighter
DEEENSSVX	vexedness	**DEEFIIPRT**	petrified		relighted
DEEEOPRST	deportees	**DEEFIIRRT**	terrified	**DEEGHINNU**	unheeding
DEEEORRSS	reredoses	**DEEFIIRRS**	firesides	**DEEGHINRT**	rightened
DEEEORSTV	stevedore	**DEEFIIRSV**	versified	**DEEGHINTT**	tightened
DEEEORSVW	oversewed	**DEEFIISTT**	testified	**DEEGHINUW**	unweighed
DEEEORSVX	oversexed	**DEEFILLRU**	fulleride	**DEEGHNORU**	roughened
DEEEPRRSS	repressed	**DEEFILMNS**	fieldsmen	**DEEGHNOTU**	toughened
DEEEPRRSV	preserved	**DEEFILNOX**	deflexion	**DEEGHOPSS**	sheepdogs
DEEEPRRTV	perverted	**DEEFILORT**	trefoiled	**DEEGHORSW**	hedgerows
DEEEPRSSS	depresses	**DEEFILRTT**	flittered	**DEEGHORTW**	Edgeworth
DEEEPRSST	speedster	**DEEFIMRSU**	frusemide	**DEEGIIKLR**	ridgelike
DEEEPRSSU	superseed	**DEEFINNRU**	unrefined	**DEEGIILNU**	guideline
DEEEPRSSX	expressed	**DEEFINRSU**	reinfused	**DEEGIILNV**	inveigled
DEEEPRSTT	pretested	**DEEFINRTW**	winterfed	**DEEGIINNS**	indigenes
DEEEPRSUW	superweed	**DEEFINSST**	fetidness	**DEEGIINRT**	reediting
DEEEQRSTU	requested	**DEEFINSSX**	fixedness		reignited
DEEERRRSS	redresser	**DEEFIORRT**	torrefied	**DEEGIINSS**	digenesis
DEEERRRSV	verderers	**DEEFIORSS**	foresides	**DEEGIISTV**	digestive
DEEERRSSS	redresses	**DEEFIPRRV**	perfervid	**DEEGIJKLU**	judgelike
DEEERRSST	deserters	**DEEFIPRST**	presifted	**DEEGILMMR**	glimmered
DEEERRSSV	deservers	**DEEFIPRTU**	putrefied	**DEEGILNOU**	euglenoid
DEEERSSTT	detesters	**DEEFIPSTU**	stupefied	**DEEGILNPT**	depleting
DEEERUYZZ	Zuyder Zee	**DEEFIRRTT**	frittered	**DEEGILNRS**	reedlings
DEEFFFSTU	feedstuff	**DEEFIRSTU**	surfeited	**DEEGILNRT**	ringleted
DEEFFHILS	Sheffield	**DEEFLLNNU**	funnelled	**DEEGILNRW**	rewelding
DEEFFINRT	different	**DEEFLLNUY**	needfully	**DEEGILNSS**	gelidness
DEEFFINST	stiffened	**DEEFLNNUU**	unneedful		seedlings
DEEFFIORT	forfeited	**DEEFLNORS**	enfolders	**DEEGILNST**	glistened
DEEFFLOSU	souffleed	**DEEFLNOSV**	sevenfold	**DEEGILOOU**	ideologue
DEEFFNORS	forefends	**DEEFLNRTU**	underfelt	**DEEGILOPR**	ridgepole
	offenders	**DEEFLOOTW**	Fleetwood	**DEEGILOSU**	eulogised
DEEFFNORU	unoffered	**DEEFLORSW**	deflowers	**DEEGILOUZ**	eulogized
DEEFFOPRR	proffered	**DEEFLRSTU**	flustered	**DEEGILQSU**	squilgeed
DEEFGHIRT	freighted	**DEEFLRTTU**	fluttered	**DEEGILRST**	glistered
DEEFGIILR	filigreed	**DEEFMOPRR**	performed	**DEEGILRSW**	weregilds
DEEFGIIRS	Siegfried		preformed	**DEEGILRTT**	glittered
DEEFGILST	fledgiest	**DEEFMORRS**	deformers	**DEEGILSSU**	guideless
DEEFGINNU	unfeigned	**DEEFNOOST**	festooned	**DEEGIMNNR**	remending
DEEFGINRR	deferring	**DEEFNRRSU**	refunders	**DEEGIMNNT**	dementing
DEEFGINRY	redefying	**DEEFOOPRR**	reproofed	**DEEGIMNRY**	remedying
DEEFGJORU	forejudge	**DEEFOPRSS**	professed	**DEEGIMORT**	geometrid
DEEFGLSUW	gulfweeds	**DEEFORRST**	defroster	**DEEGIMRSU**	demiurges
DEEFHIRSS	redfishes	**DEEFORSST**	deforests	**DEEGINNPX**	expending
DEEFHLLUY	heedfully	**DEEGGGILN**	legginged	**DEEGINNRR**	rendering
DEEFHLNUU	unheedful	**DEEGGHHOS**	hedgehogs	**DEEGINNRT**	tendering
DEEFHLOPS	sheepfold	**DEEGGILNR**	ledgering	**DEEGINNTX**	extending
DEEFHLORS	freeholds	**DEEGGIMNR**	demerging	**DEEGINORT**	redingote
DEEFHLORT	threefold	**DEEGGINRS**	sniggered	**DEEGINPRS**	predesign
DEEFHLRSS	feldshers	**DEEGGINRT**	deterging	**DEEGINRRR**	derringer

DEEGINRRS	deringers	**DEEHINOPX**	phenoxide	**DEEIIPPPR**	Pied Piper
DEEGINRRT	deterring	**DEEHINORT**	dinothere	**DEEIIPRSU**	Euripides
DEEGINRSS	designers	**DEEHINPRS**	insphered		priedieus
	redesigns		phrensied	**DEEIIPRUX**	priedieux
DEEGINRST	deserting	**DEEHINPRT**	trephined	**DEEIIPSSW**	sideswipe
DEEGINRSV	deserving	**DEEHINRRS**	hinderers	**DEEIIRRSV**	riverside
DEEGINRTU	negritude	**DEEHINRSS**	drisheens	**DEEIIRSTV**	revisited
DEEGINRTV	divergent	**DEEHINRSW**	swineherd	**DEEIIRTVV**	divertive
DEEGINRUV	gerundive	**DEEHIOORT**	Theodore I	**DEEIISSSS**	disseises
DEEGINSTT	detesting	**DEEHIORST**	theorised	**DEEIISSSZ**	disseizes
DEEGINSTV	devesting	**DEEHIORTZ**	theorized	**DEEIJNORR**	rejoinder
DEEGINTTV	vignetted	**DEEHIOSTX**	ethoxides	**DEEIKLLRS**	killdeers
DEEGIOSST	geodesist	**DEEHIPPRS**	reshipped		reskilled
DEEGIPRST	predigest	**DEEHIPRSW**	whispered	**DEEIKLMSW**	milkweeds
DEEGIRRSS	digresser	**DEEHIRRST**	ditherers	**DEEIKLMWY**	midweekly
DEEGIRSSU	digresses	**DEEHIRSSV**	dervishes	**DEEIKLNNR**	enkindler
DEEGIRSST	digesters	**DEEHIRSSW**	shrewdies	**DEEIKLNNS**	enkindles
	redigests	**DEEHIRSTW**	swithered	**DEEIKLNRS**	rekindles
DEEGJLSSU	judgeless	**DEEHIRTTW**	whittered	**DEEIKLNSX**	sexlinked
DEEGJMNTU	judgement	**DEEHKNOSS**	keeshonds	**DEEIKLSSW**	silkweeds
DEEGJPRRU	prejudger	**DEEHLLNSU**	unshelled	**DEEIKNORV**	reinvoked
DEEGJPRSU	prejudges	**DEEHLLOSU**	houselled	**DEEIKNRSS**	deerskins
DEEGKLNOW	knowledge	**DEEHLLOSV**	shovelled	**DEEIKNSTW**	stinkweed
DEEGLLORV	grovelled	**DEEHLMORY**	Meyerhold	**DEEIKPPRS**	skippered
DEEGLMNOT	lodgement	**DEEHLNOYY**	honeyedly	**DEEIKRSTT**	skittered
DEEGLNORW	Glendower	**DEEHLORST**	holstered	**DEEIKSSTT**	diskettes
DEEGLNTTU	englutted	**DEEHMOORT**	hodometer	**DEEILLMPS**	millepeds
DEEGLOPRS	pledgeors	**DEEHMORST**	smothered	**DEEILLNRW**	indweller
DEEGMOORS	Sedgemoor	**DEEHMRRTU**	murthered	**DEEILLNST**	tinselled
DEEGNNORU	undergone	**DEEHNNORS**	Henderson	**DEEILLNSV**	snivelled
DEEGNNSSU	Dungeness	**DEEHNNORT**	enthroned	**DEEILLPRS**	dispeller
DEEGNOORW	greenwood	**DEEHNOPTY**	endophyte	**DEEILLRRV**	driveller
DEEGNOPSU	geepounds	**DEEHNORRS**	dehorners	**DEEILLRST**	trellised
DEEGNORRU	guerdoner	**DEEHNORRT**	dethroner	**DEEILLRTU**	telluride
	undergoer	**DEEHNORST**	dethrones	**DEEILLSVW**	swivelled
DEEGNORSS	engrossed		shortened	**DEEILMNRU**	relumined
DEEGNORSU	undergoes		threnodes	**DEEILMNSU**	demilunes
DEEGOPRRU	regrouped	**DEEHNOSWY**	honeydews	**DEEILMNTV**	devilment
DEEHHIORS	horsehide	**DEEHNPRSU**	unsphered	**DEEILMORS**	melodiser
DEEHHPRSS	shepherds	**DEEHNRRTU**	thunderer	**DEEILMORZ**	melodizer
DEEHIINPT	pethidine	**DEEHOORTX**	heterodox	**DEEILMOSS**	melodises
DEEHIINRT	inherited	**DEEHOOSUW**	Wodehouse	**DEEILMOSZ**	melodizes
DEEHIKRSW	whiskered	**DEEHOPSTU**	Deep South	**DEEILMOTV**	demivolte
DEEHILLRV	helldiver	**DEEHORRSY**	hydrosere	**DEEILMPTU**	multipede
DEEHILNPS	plenished	**DEEHRSSTW**	shrewdest	**DEEILNNRU**	underline
DEEHILOPP	pedophile	**DEEHRSTTU**	shuttered	**DEEILNNSS**	Lindesnes
DEEHILORU	hierodule	**DEEHSSTTU**	dustsheet	**DEEILNOPT**	depletion
DEEHILPRS	eldership	**DEEIIINPR**	pieridine		diplotene
DEEHILRSS	shielders	**DEEIILLMP**	millipede	**DEEILNOST**	deletions
DEEHILRST	slithered	**DEEIILMPR**	imperiled	**DEEILNOSV**	novelised
DEEHILRSV	shriveled	**DEEIILNPP**	pipelined	**DEEILNOVZ**	novelized
DEEHILSSV	dishevels	**DEEIILNSS**	sidelines	**DEEILNPRT**	interpled
DEEHIMMRS	shimmered	**DEEIILRSV**	devilries	**DEEILNPTU**	plenitude
DEEHIMOPS	hemipodes	**DEEIILSTW**	wieldiest	**DEEILNRRU**	underlier
DEEHIMORT	moithered	**DEEIIMNTT**	midinette	**DEEILNRSU**	underlies
DEEHIMOST	methodise	**DEEIIMPRS**	epidermis	**DEEILNRTU**	interlude
DEEHIMOTX	methoxide	**DEEIIMRSS**	dimerises	**DEEILNSSX**	indexless
DEEHIMOTZ	methodize	**DEEIIMRSZ**	dimerizes	**DEEILNTVY**	evidently
DEEHIMPRW	whimpered	**DEEIINOSZ**	deionizes	**DEEILOPRS**	despoiler
DEEHIMSUX	humidexes	**DEEIINRTV**	reinvited	**DEEILOPTX**	exploited
DEEHINNOV	Eindhoven	**DEEIINSST**	densities	**DEEILORRS**	orderlies
DEEHINNRS	enshrined		destinies	**DEEILORST**	dolerites

DEEILORSV	evildoers
DEEILORVV	overlived
DEEILOSVW	vowelised
DEEILOVWZ	vowelized
DEEILPPRS	slippered
DEEILPRSX	diplexers
DEEILRRSS	riderless
DEEILRSVY	diversely
DEEILRTUY	eruditely
DEEIMMORS	memorised
DEEIMMORZ	memorized
DEEIMMOSS	semidomes
DEEIMMRRT	retrimmed
DEEIMMRST	mistermed
DEEIMNNOT	mentioned
DEEIMNNRU	undermine
DEEIMNNTZ	dizenment
DEEIMNORS	domineers
	modernise
DEEIMNORZ	modernize
DEEIMNOSS	demonises
	Des Moines
DEEIMNOST	moistened
	monetised
DEEIMNOSU	Idomeneus
DEEIMNOSZ	demonizes
DEEIMNOTZ	monetized
DEEIMNPRS	spidermen
DEEIMNPST	pediments
DEEIMNPTU	unemptied
DEEIMNRRS	reminders
DEEIMNRTT	detriment
DEEIMNRTU	undertime
	unmerited
DEEIMNSST	sediments
DEEIMNSSX	mixedness
DEEIMOORT	meteoroid
DEEIMOPRS	reimposed
DEEIMOPRW	impowered
DEEIMORST	dosimeter
DEEIMORTV	overtimed
DEEIMOSST	modesties
DEEIMPRRS	periderms
DEEIMPRSS	impressed
DEEIMPRST	distemper
DEEIMPRTT	permitted
DEEIMRSST	demisters
DEEIMRTUU	deuterium
DEEINNOPS	pensioned
DEEINNORT	internode
DEEINNORV	environed
DEEINNOTT	detention
DEEINNPRU	unripened
DEEINNRST	indenters
	intenders
DEEINNRTU	indenture
DEEINNSSS	snideness
DEEINOPRT	repointed
DEEINOPTX	pentoxide
DEEINORSS	indorsees
DEEINORST	desertion
DEEINORSW	rosinweed

DEEINOSSV	nosedives
DEEINPRRT	reprinted
DEEINPRSS	dispenser
DEEINPRST	president
DEEINPRUX	unexpired
DEEINPSSS	dispenses
DEEINPSST	tepidness
DEEINRRSU	reinsured
DEEINRRSW	rewinders
DEEINRSST	dissenter
	residents
	tiredness
DEEINRSSW	weirdness
DEEINRSTT	trendiest
DEEINRSTX	dextrines
DEEINRSUV	unrevised
DEEINSSTW	witnessed
DEEIOPRRT	portiered
DEEIOPRST	redeposit
	reposited
DEEIOPRSX	peroxides
DEEIOPRTX	expeditor
DEEIORRRV	overrider
DEEIORRST	roistered
DEEIORRSV	overrides
DEEIORRTV	overtired
DEEIORRVV	overdrive
DEEIORSVZ	oversized
DEEIORTTX	tetroxide
DEEIOTTVX	videotext
DEEIPPRRS	perspired
DEEIPRRSS	disperser
	presiders
DEEIPRRSV	deprivers
DEEIPRSSS	despisers
	disperses
DEEIPRSST	persisted
DEEIPRSTU	disrepute
DEEIPSSST	sidesteps
DEEIPSSTU	deputises
DEEIPSTUZ	deputizes
DEEIRRSST	destriers
DEEIRRSTV	diverters
DEEIRSSST	dressiest
DEEIRSSSV	disserves
	dissevers
DEEIRSTTW	retwisted
DEEIRSTUV	divesture
	servitude
DEEIRTTTW	twittered
DEEIRTTXY	dexterity
DEEISTTTU	destitute
DEEJKNTTU	junketted
DEEJNORUY	journeyed
DEEJOORVY	overjoyed
DEEKKNSUW	skunkweed
DEEKKOOYY	okeydokey
DEEKLNORS	snorkeled
DEEKLNOSV	veldskoen
DEEKNOORS	snookered
DEEKNORST	stonkered
DEEKNORUV	unrevoked

DEEKNOSTW	knotweeds
DEEKNQRUU	Dunkerque
DEELLMMOP	pommelled
DEELLMMPU	pummelled
DEELLMORS	modellers
DEELLNNTU	tunnelled
DEELLNQUU	unquelled
DEELLNRSU	undersell
DEELLNRSY	slenderly
DEELLNSSY	endlessly
DEELLOPPR	propelled
DEELLORSY	yodellers
DEELLORTW	trowelled
DEELLPSUW	upswelled
DEELMMPTU	plummeted
DEELMNOOS	melodeons
DEELMOORV	velodrome
DEELMOPRS	empolders
DEELNNPST	splendent
DEELNNPTY	pendently
DEELNOOST	lodestone
DEELNOPPU	unpeopled
DEELNORST	rondelets
DEELNPRRU	plunderer
DEELNRSTU	underlets
DEELNSTTU	unsettled
DEELNSWWY	newlyweds
DEELOPRRS	deplorers
DEELOPRSX	exploders
DEELOPRSY	redeploys
DEELOPRTU	ploutered
DEELOPRTW	plowtered
DEELOPRTY	depletory
DEELORRSS	orderless
	solderers
DEELORRUV	overruled
DEELORSSW	dowerless
DEELORSTT	dotterels
DEELORTTU	rouletted
DEELPPSTU	septupled
DEELPRRSU	preluders
DEELPRSTU	drupelets
DEELPRTUY	reputedly
DEEMMOOSS	desmosome
DEEMNNOTW	endowment
DEEMNNRUY	Runnymede
DEEMNOPRS	endosperm
DEEMNOPSU	spodumene
DEEMNORST	entoderms
DEEMNORTT	tormented
DEEMNORTU	remounted
DEEMNOSTU	endosteum
DEEMNPTTU	untempted
DEEMOORST	odometers
DEEMORSSW	wormseeds
DEEMORSTU	udometers
DEEMPRSST	dempsters
DEEMPRTTU	trumpeted
DEEMRRRSU	demurrers
	murderers
DEEMRRSSU	murderess
DEENNOPRS	personned

DEENNOPST	deponents	**DEFFNOPRU**	Pufendorf	**DEFILNRSU**	urnfields
DEENNORTU	undertone	**DEFFSSTUY**	dyestuffs	**DEFILNSSU**	fluidness
DEENNRTUW	underwent	**DEFGGIINT**	fidgeting	**DEFILORSU**	fluorides
DEENOOPRS	endospore	**DEFGGILLN**	fledgling	**DEFILOSTU**	outfields
DEENOPRRS	responder	**DEFGHILOT**	eightfold	**DEFIMNORT**	dentiform
DEENOPRRV	provender	**DEFGHIOSS**	dogfishes	**DEFIMNORU**	uniformed
DEENOPRSV	overspend	**DEFGIIILN**	lignified	**DEFIMORTY**	deformity
DEENOPRUX	expounder	**DEFGIIINS**	dignifies	**DEFIMSTYY**	demystify
DEENOPSUX	unexposed		signified	**DEFINORSU**	foundries
DEENORRSS	endorsers	**DEFGIILOR**	glorified	**DEFINORSW**	forewinds
DEENORRSW	wonderers	**DEFGIINNR**	friending	**DEFIOPSTX**	postfixed
DEENORSTT	snottered		infringed	**DEFIORSST**	disforest
DEENORSTU	deuterons	**DEFGIIRSU**	disfigure	**DEFIORTTU**	fortitude
DEENORTUY	tourneyed	**DEFGIISST**	digestifs	**DEFIOTTTU**	outfitted
DEENPPSTU	unstepped	**DEFGILNNO**	enfolding	**DEFLLLOUY**	dolefully
DEENPRSSU	suspender	**DEFGILNOR**	refolding	**DEFLLOORS**	folderols
	unpressed	**DEFGIMNOR**	deforming	**DEFLLOOSS**	floodless
DEENRRRSU	surrender	**DEFGINNRU**	refunding	**DEFLMMOUX**	flummoxed
DEENRRSSU	sunderers	**DEFGINOOR**	foredoing	**DEFLNORSS**	frondless
DEENRSSSU	undresses	**DEFGJORSU**	forjudges	**DEFLNORSU**	flounders
DEENRSSTU	sederunts	**DEFHIILSV**	devilfish		unfolders
	undersets	**DEFHIIORR**	horrified	**DEFLNORUW**	underflow
DEENRSTTU	entrusted	**DEFHIMSSU**	mudfishes		wonderful
DEENRSTUV	undervest	**DEFHINRSU**	furnished	**DEFLOORSV**	overfolds
DEENRSTYY	dysentery	**DEFHLOOOW**	wholefood	**DEFMOOORS**	foredooms
DEENRTTUU	unuttered	**DEFHOOOTT**	hotfooted	**DEFNOOOTT**	footnoted
DEEOOPRST	torpedoes	**DEFIIINRT**	nitrified	**DEFNOORTU**	underfoot
DEEOORRVV	overdrove	**DEFIIIRTV**	vitrified	**DEFNRRSUU**	underfurs
DEEOORSSV	overdoses	**DEFIIISSS**	sissified	**DEFOOOTTU**	outfooted
DEEOPPRRS	prospered	**DEFIIJLLO**	jollified	**DEFOORRSW**	forewords
DEEOPPRSS	oppressed	**DEFIIJSTU**	justified	**DEFORRSTT**	Stretford
DEEOPPRST	stoppered	**DEFIILLMO**	mollified	**DEGGIILNR**	regilding
DEEOPRRSS	depressor	**DEFIILLNU**	nullified		ridgeling
DEEOPRRSW	powderers	**DEFIILLOS**	oilfields	**DEGGIINNS**	designing
DEEOPRSST	dopesters	**DEFIILMSU**	semifluid	**DEGGIINRV**	diverging
DEEOPRSTT	protested	**DEFIILRSU**	fluidiser	**DEGGIINST**	digesting
DEEOPRSUZ	douzepers	**DEFIILRTU**	Eid-ul-Fitr	**DEGGIJNRU**	rejudging
DEEOPSSSS	possessed	**DEFIILRUZ**	fluidizer	**DEGGILQSU**	squiggled
DEEORRRSS	redressor	**DEFIILSSU**	fluidises	**DEGGINORS**	sodgering
DEEORRSSV	overdress	**DEFIILSUZ**	fluidizes	**DEGGINSTU**	degusting
DEEORRSTU	trousered	**DEFIIMMMU**	mummified	**DEGGIORSS**	disgorger
DEEORRSTX	dextrorse	**DEFIIMNNY**	indemnify	**DEGGIORSS**	disgorges
DEEORRSTY	destroyer	**DEFIIMORS**	modifiers	**DEGGLNPUU**	unplugged
DEEORRSUV	devourers	**DEFIIMORT**	mortified	**DEGGLRSTU**	struggled
DEEORRTUV	overtured	**DEFIIMRWY**	midwifery	**DEGHIILNS**	shielding
DEEORSTTT	stottered	**DEFIIMSTT**	misfitted	**DEGHIILST**	sidelight
DEEORSTUX	dexterous	**DEFIIMSTY**	mystified	**DEGHIINNR**	hindering
DEEPRRSSU	pressured	**DEFIINOPT**	pontified	**DEGHIINRT**	dithering
DEEPRSTTU	sputtered	**DEFIINRTY**	denitrify	**DEGHIJPSU**	judgeship
DEERRSSTU	tressured	**DEFIINSST**	disinfest	**DEGHILMSU**	gumshield
DEERSTTTU	stuttered	**DEFIIPPUY**	yuppified	**DEGHILNTU**	unlighted
DEFFGIINR	differing	**DEFIIPSSS**	fissipeds	**DEGHIMNRU**	humdinger
DEFFGIJRU	Gurdjieff	**DEFIIRSSU**	russified	**DEGHINNOR**	dehorning
DEFFGINNO	offending	**DEFIIRSVY**	diversify	**DEGHINSTU**	unsighted
DEFFIIORT	fortified	**DEFIIRTVY**	devitrify	**DEGHIOPSS**	dogeships
DEFFIISUV	diffusive	**DEFIKLORW**	fieldwork	**DEGHIORTU**	doughtier
DEFFILLLU	fulfilled	**DEFILLORV**	frivolled	**DEGHIOSTU**	doughiest
DEFFILSUY	diffusely	**DEFILMNRU**	remindful	**DEGHIPRTU**	uprighted
DEFFIORSS	offsiders	**DEFILMSUY**	demulsify	**DEGHMOORT**	godmother
DEFFIRSSU	diffusers	**DEFILNORS**	infolders	**DEGHNNRUU**	underhung
DEFFLMNUU	unmuffled	**DEFILNORT**	interfold	**DEGHNOORU**	gorehound
DEFFLNRUU	unruffled	**DEFILNOSW**	snowfield	**DEGHNORUY**	greyhound

DEGHOOSSU	doghouses
DEGIIIMRS	dirigisme
	semirigid
DEGIIINST	dignities
DEGIIIRST	digitiser
	dirigiste
DEGIIIRTZ	digitizer
DEGIIISST	digitises
DEGIIISTZ	digitizes
DEGIILLNV	devilling
DEGIILMMN	immingled
DEGIILMNN	mildening
DEGIILMNW	mildewing
DEGIILNNR	redlining
DEGIILNOV	evildoing
DEGIILNRV	driveling
DEGIILNRW	wildering
DEGIILSTU	digitules
DEGIIMNNP	impending
DEGIIMNNR	reminding
DEGIIMNOR	moidering
DEGIIMNST	demisting
DEGIIMNTT	demitting
DEGIIMRSU	misguider
DEGIIMSSU	misguides
DEGIINNNT	indenting
	intending
DEGIINNNW	enwinding
DEGIINNRS	niderings
DEGIINNRW	rewinding
DEGIINNSS	dinginess
DEGIINNST	destining
	indigents
DEGIINOSS	gneissoid
DEGIINOST	digestion
DEGIINPRS	presiding
DEGIINPRV	depriving
DEGIINPSS	despising
DEGIINPST	despiting
DEGIINRSS	rigidness
	ringsides
DEGIINRTU	intrigued
	nigritude
DEGIINRTV	diverting
DEGIINSST	desisting
DEGIINSTU	distingue
DEGIINSTV	divesting
DEGIIOPRS	prodigies
DEGIIQRSU	squidgier
DEGIIRRSV	verdigris
DEGIIRSSU	disguiser
DEGIISSSU	disguises
DEGIJMRSU	misjudger
DEGIJMSSU	misjudges
DEGIKLORU	gourdlike
DEGIKNNOO	de Kooning
DEGILLMNO	modelling
DEGILLNOW	dowelling
DEGILLNOY	yodelling
DEGILLNSW	dwellings
DEGILMNNU	unmingled
DEGILMNOR	goldminer

	moldering
DEGILMNOS	singledom
DEGILMNPU	depluming
DEGILMNSU	guildsmen
DEGILNNOU	loudening
DEGILNNRU	underling
DEGILNNTU	indulgent
DEGILNOOR	gondolier
DEGILNOPR	deploring
DEGILNOPX	exploding
DEGILNOPY	deploying
DEGILNORS	soldering
DEGILNORU	ungodlier
DEGILNOSS	godliness
DEGILNOSU	delousing
DEGILNOTU	longitude
DEGILNOVV	devolving
DEGILNPRU	preluding
DEGILNRSU	indulgers
DEGILOOST	goodliest
DEGILOSTT	glottides
DEGILRSUV	divulgers
DEGIMNRRU	demurring
	murdering
DEGINNOOW	woodening
DEGINNOPR	pondering
DEGINNORS	endorsing
DEGINNORW	wondering
DEGINNRSU	sundering
DEGINNRUW	underwing
DEGINOORV	overdoing
DEGINOPRT	deporting
DEGINOPRW	powdering
DEGINOPSS	podginess
DEGINORRW	rewording
DEGINORSV	ringdoves
DEGINORTU	detouring
DEGINORUV	devouring
DEGINPSSU	pudginess
DEGINRRTU	undergirt
DEGINRSSS	dressings
DEGINRTUX	extruding
DEGIOOSVW	goodwives
DEGIOPRTY	pterygoid
DEGIOPSTU	guidepost
DEGIOSSTT	stodgiest
DEGJMNSTU	judgments
DEGLLLOOR	logrolled
DEGLLOSSY	godlessly
DEGLMNOST	lodgments
DEGLMOPRU	promulged
DEGLNOOPR	prolonged
DEGLNOOST	goldstone
DEGLNOSU	groundsel
DEGLOOPRU	prologued
DEGLOOSUU	duologues
DEGNNOTUU	outgunned
DEGNOORRW	wrongdoer
DEGNOOSST	stegodons
DEGNOOSTT	stegodont
DEGNOPRUW	gunpowder
DEGNORSVY	gyrodynes

DEGOOPRRU	prorogued
DEGORRSTU	drugstore
DEHHIIMNT	Hindemith
DEHHIINOS	hoidenish
DEHHIKMOS	sheikhdom
DEHHILNOS	Holinshed
DEHHINOSY	hoydenish
DEHHIOPPS	phosphide
DEHHLLNOU	hellhound
DEHHLOOSU	household
DEHHLORST	threshold
DEHHNOORU	horehound
DEHIIINST	histidine
DEHIIKLMR	Kriemhild
DEHIILRSS	disrelish
DEHIIMNTY	thymidine
DEHIINNRS	inshrined
DEHIINNRU	hirundine
DEHIINOOP	idiophone
DEHIIOSTY	hideosity
DEHIISSTT	ditheists
DEHIISTWW	widthwise
DEHIJMNOS	demijohns
DEHIKKOOZ	Kozhikode
DEHIKMOSS	sheikdoms
DEHIKNORT	Thorndike
DEHIKORSS	droshkies
DEHILLNOR	Hölderlin
DEHILOORT	rhodolite
DEHILOSTW	dishtowel
DEHILOSTY	holytides
DEHILOSUY	hideously
DEHILPSSU	sulphides
DEHILRRUY	hurriedly
DEHIMMOST	methodism
DEHIMNORT	Trondheim
DEHIMNSSU	humidness
DEHIMORRT	thermidor
DEHIMOSTT	methodist
DEHIMOSTU	Methodius
DEHIMPRTU	triumphed
DEHINNOPR	endorphin
DEHINOORT	rhodonite
DEHINOPSS	sphenoids
DEHINORRT	trihedron
DEHINORSU	nourished
DEHINORVW	windhover
DEHINOSST	dishonest
	hedonists
DEHINPPSU	unshipped
DEHINRRUU	unhurried
DEHIOORSW	Isherwood
DEHIOOTWW	howtowdie
	whitewood
DEHIOPRSS	spheroids
DEHIOPRSW	worshiped
DEHIORSTY	hysteroid
DEHIOSSSW	sideshows
DEHKLNOSU	elkhounds
DEHKLOOST	stokehold
DEHKNOOOS	hooknosed
DEHKNOOVZ	Dovzhenko

DEHLLOOOP loopholed	**DEIILORSU** delirious	**DEIIORSTX** trioxides
DEHLLOPSY phyllodes	**DEIILORSZ** idolizers	**DEIIORSXZ** oxidizers
DEHLMNOPY endolymph	**DEIILORTV** vitrioled	**DEIIOSSTU** seditious
DEHLMOORU hordeolum	**DEIILPSSS** sideslips	**DEIIPPRST** drippiest
DEHLMOORW wormholed	**DEIILRRZZ** drizzlier	**DEIIPRSSZ** disprizes
DEHLOOPSS splooshed	**DEIILSUVV** divulsive	**DEIIQSSTU** disquiets
DEHLOORSV holdovers	**DEIIMMNSU** immunised	**DEIIRSTVY** diversity
DEHLOOSSW woolsheds	**DEIIMMNUZ** immunized	**DEIIRSUVV** redivivus
DEHLOPRSU upholders	**DEIIMNNOS** dimension	**DEIJLNOTY** jointedly
DEHLORSSU shoulders	**DEIIMNNTY** indemnity	**DEIJNNOTU** unjointed
DEHLORSVY hydrolyse	**DEIIMNOSS** demission	**DEIJNNRUU** uninjured
DEHLORTTT throttled		missioned	**DEIJORRSY** joyriders
DEHLORTVY hydrolyte		Simonides	**DEIKKLNOR** klondiker
DEHLORYYZ hydrolyze	**DEIIMNPRT** imprinted	**DEIKKNOOP** pondokkie
DEHLOSSTU shouldest	**DEIIMNRSS** minidress	**DEIKLLNSU** unskilled
DEHMNOOPR endomorph	**DEIIMNRTW** midwinter	**DEIKLLOSV** volkslied
DEHMOORSY hydrosome	**DEIIMNRUU** uredinium	**DEIKLLPSU** upskilled
DEHMOORTY hodometry	**DEIIMNSST** timidness	**DEIKLNPRS** sprinkled
DEHNNOOPS sphenodon	**DEIIMOPST** optimised	**DEIKLORSW** swordlike
DEHNNORTU unthroned	**DEIIMOPTZ** optimized	**DEIKNNNSTU** unkindest
DEHNNOSTW Townshend	**DEIIMPRSS** misprised	**DEIKNNTTU** unknitted
DEHNNOSUW newshound	**DEIIMPRSU** presidium	**DEIKNORRV** overdrink
DEHNOOSSW snowshoed	**DEIIMPRSZ** misprized	**DEIKNSSSU** duskiness
DEHNORSSU enshrouds	**DEIIMSSSS** dismisses	**DEIKRSSVY** skydivers
DEHNORSTU undershot	**DEIINNNOT** indention	**DEILLMNOU** mullioned
DEHNOSSSW snowsheds	**DEIINNORT** rendition	**DEILLNSUU** unsullied
DEHOOPRST theropods	**DEIINNOSU** unionised	**DEILLNUWY** unwieldly
DEHOORSTU Herodotus	**DEIINNOTT** dentition	**DEILLOOTT** Doolittle
DEHOOSSSU dosshouse	**DEIINNOTV** vendition	**DEILLOOVW** Woodville
DEHOPRSST potsherds	**DEIINNOUZ** unionized	**DEILLOPST** pistolled
DEHORSSTU studhorse	**DEIINNPPS** pinnipeds		postilled
DEIIIKNTT identikit	**DEIINNRTW** interwind	**DEILLORRW** worldlier
DEIIILQSU liquidise	**DEIINNSSW** windiness	**DEILLORST** lordliest
DEIIILQUZ liquidize	**DEIINNTUV** uninvited	**DEILLORSY** soldierly
DEIIIMMNS minimised	**DEIINOPRT** perdition	**DEILLSSTU** duellists
DEIIIMMNZ minimized	**DEIINOPSS** indispose	**DEILLSTTY** stiltedly
DEIIINNQU quinidine	**DEIINORSS** ironsides	**DEILMNOOS** melodions
DEIIINSSS disseisin		resinoids	**DEILMNOSS** moldiness
DEIIINSSV divinises		sironised	**DEILMOOST** dolomites
DEIIINSSZ disseizin	**DEIINORST** disorient	**DEILMOOSU** melodious
DEIIINSVZ divinizes	**DEIINORSV** diversion	**DEILMOPRS** impolders
DEIIKKLNR kilderkin	**DEIINORSZ** sironized	**DEILMORSU** lemuroids
DEIIKLNST kindliest	**DEIINORTT** detrition	**DEILMORTU** turmoiled
DEIIILLMNU illumined	**DEIINORTU** erudition	**DEILMOSST** melodists
DEIIILLMPY impliedly	**DEIINOSST** seditions	**DEILMOSSU** emulsoids
DEIIILLMTY limitedly	**DEIINOTTZ** Donizetti	**DEILMOSTU** mouldiest
DEIIILLNST instilled	**DEIINPPSW** windpipes	**DEILMOSTV** demivolts
DEIIILLOOP Leopold II	**DEIINRSST** dirtiness	**DEILMPSTU** multipeds
DEIIILLOPR pilloried		disinters	**DEILMTTUU** multitude
DEIIILLOPS ellipsoid	**DEIINRSTU** disuniter	**DEILNOOSS** solenoids
DEIIILLRST distiller	**DEIINSSTU** disunites	**DEILNOPRU** purloined
DEIIILMNTU unlimited	**DEIINSSTV** disinvest	**DEILNOPSU** unspoiled
DEIIILMOSS semisolid	**DEIINSSVV** vividness	**DEILNOPTY** pointedly
DEIIILMRSU deliriums	**DEIINSSZZ** dizziness	**DEILNORSU** undersoil
DEIIILMSTT mistitled	**DEIINSTTU** untidiest	**DEILNOSSS** solidness
DEIIILNNSU indulines	**DEIINSTUV** unvisited	**DEILNOSSU** delusions
DEIIILNOTU toluidine	**DEIIOPRSS** presidios	**DEILNOTUV** involuted
DEIIILNPRS spindlier	**DEIIOPRST** tripodies	**DEILNRSSU** luridness
DEIIILNPSV vilipends	**DEIIORSSS** disseisor	**DEILNRSSW** swindlers
DEIIILNSSV lividness		siderosis	**DEILOOPSS** podsolise
DEIIILNTTU intituled	**DEIIORSSX** oxidisers	**DEILOOPST** topsoiled
DEIIILORSS idolisers	**DEIIORSSZ** disseizor	**DEILOOPSU** duopolies

DEILOOPSW	woodpiles	DEINOOPSS	opsonised	DEKOORTUW	outworked
DEILOOPSZ	podsolize	DEINOOPSZ	opsonized	DELLNORSS	drollness
	podzolise	DEINOOSSW	woodiness	DELMNOOOW	lemonwood
DEILOOPZZ	podzolize	DEINOOSTV	devotions	DELMNOSTW	meltdowns
DEILORRWY	worriedly	DEINOPPRR	properdin	DELMNPSUU	pendulums
DEILORSSV	dissolver	DEINOPPSW	downpipes	DELMNUUZZ	unmuzzled
DEILORVWW	worldview	DEINOPRST	dipterons	DELMORSSU	smoulders
	world-view		dripstone	DELNNOOOS	solenodon
DEILOSSSV	dissolves	DEINOPRSY	pyrenoids	DELNNOPSU	nonplused
DEILOSSTU	dissolute	DEINOPRTV	provident	DELNOOOST	dolostone
	solitudes	DEINORRSS	indorsers	DELNOPRSS	splendors
DEILOSTUY	tediously	DEINORRWU	unworried	DELNOPRSU	splendour
DEILOSUVY	deviously	DEINORRWW	windrower	DELNOPRTU	underplot
DEILPRSSU	serpulids	DEINORSST	dortiness	DELNOPSUU	pendulous
DEILPTUXY	duplexity	DEINORSSU	sourdines	DELNORSTU	roundlets
DEIMMMRSU	midsummer	DEINORSSW	disowners	DELNOSSSU	soundless
DEIMMNORS	modernism		rowdiness	DELNOSSUW	woundless
DEIMMNOUY	neodymium		wordiness	DELNPRTUY	prudently
DEIMMOSTY	immodesty	DEINORSTU	detrusion	DELNRRSTU	trundlers
DEIMNOORT	monitored	DEINORSVW	overwinds	DELOOOSUW	woodlouse
DEIMNOOSS	moodiness	DEINOSSTT	dottiness	DELOORRSV	overlords
DEIMNOOST	demotions	DEINOSSWZ	downsizes	DELOORSSU	odourless
DEIMNOOSX	monoxides	DEINPRSTU	unstriped	DELOPRSYY	pyrolysed
DEIMNOPRU	impounder	DEINPSTWW	windswept	DELOPRYYZ	pyrolyzed
DEIMNORST	modernist	DEINRRSTU	intruders	DELOPSSTU	postludes
DEIMNORTY	modernity	DEINRSTTU	intrusted	DELORSSSW	swordless
DEIMNOSST	demonists	DEINRSTTY	dentistry	DELORSTUY	desultory
DEIMNOSTW	downtimes	DEINSSSTU	dustiness	DELOSTUUY	duteously
DEIMNPRTU	imprudent	DEINSTTUW	untwisted	DEMMNOSSU	summonsed
DEIMNPSSS	misspends	DEIOOPRST	depositor	DEMMOOSTU	stomodeum
DEIMNPSSU	dumpiness	DEIOOPRTX	protoxide	DEMNNORSU	roundsmen
DEIMNRSTU	rudiments	DEIOORRSU	uredosori	DEMNNORUU	unmourned
DEIMNRTTU	Tridentum	DEIOOSSTW	woodsiest	DEMNNOTUU	unmounted
DEIMNSSTU	tumidness	DEIOPRRST	postrider	DEMNOOOPS	monopodes
DEIMOOORT	ideomotor	DEIOPRRSV	providers	DEMNOPSUY	pseudonym
DEIMOORST	motorised	DEIOPRSSS	disposers	DEMNORSSW	swordsmen
DEIMOORTY	iodometry	DEIOPRSSU	disposure	DEMNORSSY	syndromes
DEIMOORTZ	motorized	DEIOPRSSV	disproves	DEMNORSTU	undermost
DEIMOOSSS	sodomises	DEIOPRSTU	dipterous	DEMOOPRRS	prodromes
DEIMOOSST	sodomites	DEIORRSTT	distorter	DEMOORSST	doomsters
DEIMOOSSZ	sodomizes	DEIORRSTU	outriders	DEMORRSUU	murderous
DEIMOPPUY	yuppiedom	DEIORSSTU	dioestrus	DENNORSSU	roundness
DEIMOPSST	despotism		outsiders	DENNORSUW	sundowner
DEIMOQSTU	misquoted	DEIORSSTW	drowsiest	DENNOSSSU	soundness
DEIMORSTY	dosimetry	DEIORSTTX	tetroxids	DENNOSSTY	syndetons
DEIMORSUX	exordiums	DEIOTTTUW	outwitted	DENOOOPTW	woodentop
DEIMOSSTT	demotists	DEIPPTTTU	tittupped	DENOOOSTW	woodnotes
DEINNNOSU	innuendos	DEIPRRSSU	surprised	DENOOPPST	postponed
DEINNOOST	noontides	DEIPRRSTU	disrupter	DENOOPPSU	unopposed
DEINNOOTX	endotoxin	DEIPRSSTU	disputers	DENOOPRSS	sponsored
DEINNOPTU	unpointed	DEIPRTTUU	turpitude	DENOOPRSU	ponderous
DEINNORRV	nondriver	DEIPSSTTU	stupidest	DENOORRSS	endorsors
DEINNORST	indentors	DEIRSSTTU	sturdiest	DENOORSTU	tournedos
DEINNOSSW	downiness	DEISSTTTU	duettists	DENOORUVW	overwound
DEINNOSTU	nonsuited	DEJMOPTUU	outjumped	DENOPPRRU	underprop
	tendinous	DEJNOORSU	sojourned	DENOPPSTU	unstopped
DEINNPRSU	underpins	DEJOOPPPY	joypopped	DENOPRSSU	proudness
DEINNRSUU	uninsured	DEKKLNORY	klondyker	DENOPSTTU	unspotted
DEINNRSUW	unwinders	DEKLNNRUY	drunkenly	DENORSTUW	undertows
DEINNRTTU	undertint	DEKNNOTTU	unknotted	DENORTTUU	untutored
DEINNSTTU	unstinted	DEKNOORTU	undertook	DENRSSTUU	untrussed
DEINOOPRT	portioned	DEKNORRUV	overdrunk	DEOOORSSW	rosewoods

DEOOORTTU	outrooted	**DGHILLNSU**	dunghills	**DGINNOSWW**	downswing
DEOOPPRST	pteropods	**DGHILMOST**	goldsmith	**DGINOOOOV**	voodooing
DEOOPRRUV	overproud	**DGHILNOOP**	Godolphin	**DGINOPPRS**	droppings
DEOOPRSST	doorsteps	**DGHILNOPU**	upholding	**DGNNORTUU**	groundnut
DEOOPRTUU	outpoured	**DGHILOPRT**	droplight	**DHHIKNSUU**	Hindu Kush
DEOORRSVW	overwords	**DGHILOTUY**	doughtily	**DHHILOSTW**	withholds
DEOPPRRTU	purported	**DGHIMOPSY**	sphygmoid	**DHHLOORST**	shorthold
DEOPPRSTU	supported	**DGHINOOOO**	hoodooing	**DHIIIPSTY**	hispidity
DEOPRRSTU	protrudes	**DGHINORSU**	shrouding	**DHIILNRWW**	whirlwind
DEOPTTTUU	outputted	**DGHINORTW**	downright	**DHIILOPSY**	syphiloid
DEORRSUUV	verdurous	**DGHLOORYV**	hydrology	**DHIIMNOOS**	hominoids
DFFFOOSTU	foodstuff	**DGHNOSTUU**	doughnuts	**DHIINNNRY**	ninhydrin
DFFGIINSU	diffusing	**DGHOORSUU**	sourdough	**DHIINOPTY**	typhoidin
DFFIINOSU	diffusion	**DGIIIKLNS**	disliking	**DHIKNOOSW**	hoodwinks
DFFIORSSU	diffusors	**DGIIILNOS**	idolising	**DHIKORSSY**	hydroskis
DFFOORSUW	woodruffs	**DGIIILNOZ**	idolizing	**DHILLLOSY**	dollishly
DFGGHIOST	dogfights	**DGIIINNOT**	indigotin	**DHILLNOSW**	downhills
DFGIIINNY	nidifying	**DGIIINNRT**	nitriding	**DHILLOSTY**	doltishly
DFGIIIRTY	frigidity	**DGIIINNTY**	indignity	**DHILNNOSY**	donnishly
DFGIILNNO	infolding	**DGIIINOSX**	oxidising	**DHILOOPPY**	hypoploid
DFGIIMNOY	modifying	**DGIIINOTX**	digitoxin	**DHILOPRSS**	lordships
DFGILNNOU	foundling	**DGIIINOXZ**	oxidizing	**DHILPRSUY**	prudishly
	unfolding	**DGIIJNORY**	joyriding	**DHIMNORUY**	hydronium
DFGILNNOY	goldfinny	**DGIIKNSVY**	skydiving	**DHIMNOSTY**	hymnodist
DFHHINOSU	houndfish	**DGIILLNSW**	wildlings	**DHIMOOOOS**	hoodooism
DFHILOORY	hydrofoil	**DGIILLOOR**	gorilloid	**DHIMORSTW**	wordsmith
DFHIORSSW	swordfish	**DGIILMNOP**	imploding	**DHINNOTUW**	whodunnit
DFHLNOOUW	wolfhound	**DGIILNNPS**	spindling	**DHINNTUWY**	whydunnit
DFHLOOOST	footholds	**DGIILNNSW**	swindling	**DHINOOPRS**	donorship
DFHNOOSUX	foxhounds	**DGIILNNWY**	windingly		rhodopsin
DFIILORTY	floridity	**DGIILNRZZ**	drizzling	**DHINOORSS**	dishonors
DFIINPRST	driftpins	**DGIILOORY**	iridology	**DHINOORSU**	dishonour
	spindrift	**DGIIMNSSU**	Sigismund	**DHINOSTUW**	whodunits
DFIKLNOPY	Pink Floyd	**DGIINNNUW**	unwinding	**DHINSTUWY**	whydunits
DFIKOOPRS	skidproof	**DGIINNORS**	indorsing	**DHIOOPRSZ**	rhizopods
DFILLMNUY	mindfully	**DGIINNOSW**	disowning	**DHIOOSTTW**	withstood
DFILLMOTU	multifold	**DGIINNOWW**	windowing	**DHKMNOOOS**	monkshood
DFILLOSWW	wildfowls	**DGIINNRTU**	intruding	**DHLLOOOWY**	Hollywood
DFILLTUUY	dutifully	**DGIINNTUY**	untidying	**DHLMOOTUU**	loudmouth
DFILMNNUU	unmindful	**DGIINOPRV**	providing	**DHLNOORUW**	howlround
DFILNTUUU	undutiful	**DGIINOPSS**	disposing	**DHLNOOSYY**	holy synod
DFINORSTW	snowdrift	**DGIINORRS**	gridirons	**DHLOORSSY**	hydrosols
DFINRSSUW	windsurfs	**DGIINORST**	digitrons	**DHMNOOPWY**	wood nymph
DFNOOPRSU	profounds	**DGIINORTU**	outriding	**DHNNOORTW**	North Down
DFOOOSSTW	softwoods	**DGIINPPRS**	drippings	**DHNOORTWW**	downthrow
DGGHILOSY	doggishly	**DGIINPSTU**	disputing	**DHNOOSSWW**	showdowns
DGGHINOOT	goodnight	**DGIIRTTUY**	turgidity	**DHNOSSTUW**	shutdowns
DGGHNOORU	groundhog	**DGIKNOOSW**	kingwoods	**DHOOORTXY**	orthodoxy
DGGIILLNY	glidingly	**DGILLNOOP**	dolloping	**DHOOPPPUY**	puppyhood
DGGIILNNU	indulging	**DGILLNORS**	lordlings	**DHOPRSTYY**	dystrophy
DGGIILNRS	ridglings	**DGILLNORW**	worldling	**DIIILMPTY**	limpidity
DGGIILNUV	divulging	**DGILLOOSW**	goodwills	**DIIILNPSY**	insipidly
DGGIINNSW	wingdings	**DGILMNOOO**	mongoloid	**DIIILQTUY**	liquidity
DGGIJLNUY	judgingly	**DGILMNOSU**	mouldings	**DIIIMOSST**	idiotisms
DGGILNOPS	splodging	**DGILMNPSU**	dumplings	**DIIINOSSU**	insidious
DGGIMNOOS	smoodging	**DGILNNORY**	droningly	**DIIINOSSV**	divisions
DGGINNORU	grounding	**DGILNNOSY**	goldsinny	**DIIINOSUV**	invidious
DGGIRSSTU	druggists	**DGILNNRTU**	trundling	**DIIIPRSST**	dispirits
DGHHIINST	hindsight	**DGILNNUYY**	undyingly	**DIIJNOSST**	disjoints
DGHHINOPT	diphthong	**DGIMNOSYZ**	Zsigmondy	**DIIKLPSSU**	Piłsudski
DGHHOORSU	roughshod	**DGINNOSSU**	soundings	**DIILLMNOO**	modillion
DGHIKNOOS	kinghoods	**DGINNOSUW**	swounding	**DIILLMNRS**	millrinds

DIILLMNSW	windmills	DNNORRTUU	turnround	EEEFLRTTU	fleurette
DIILLSSTY	idyllists	DNNORSTUW	downturns	EEEFMNRRT	fermenter
DIILMOPPS	pompilids	DNOOPPRSU	propounds	EEEFNORST	freestone
DIILNOSTU	dilutions	DNOOPRSSW	snowdrops	EEEFNORTT	Nofretete
DIILNOSUV	divulsion	DNOOPRSUW	downpours	EEEFNRRST	referents
DIILOPRST	triploids	DNOOPSSTU	soundpost	EEEFNRSUZ	unfreezes
DIILOSTTY	stolidity	DNOOPSTUW	downspout	EEEFORRSS	foreseers
DIIMMNNOSU	dominiums	DNOORTUWW	woundwort	EEEFPRRRR	preferrer
DIIMMNNOOS	dominions	DNORRSSUU	surrounds	EEEFRRRRS	referrers
DIIMNOPST	midpoints	DOOOPRSST	doorposts	EEEFRRRST	ferreters
DIIMOORTV	Dimitrovo		doorstops	EEEFRRSTT	fetterers
DIIMOORTY	iridotomy	DOOOPRSUU	uropodous	EEEGGILNS	negligees
DIIMOPRSS	prismoids	DOOORSTUY	outdoorsy	EEEGGORTT	georgette
DIIMORSSY	dimissory	DOOPRRSTW	dropworts	EEEGHILNR	reheeling
DIINNOOQU	quinonoid	EEEEELRTY	eyeleteer	EEEGHILNT	gehlenite
DIINNOSSU	disunions	EEEEFGNRS	Genfersee	EEEGHINST	eighteens
DIINOSSSU	sinusoids	EEEEFHLRW	freewheel	EEEGHLRSS	sheerlegs
DIINOSSUY	Dionysius	EEEEFHRST	freesheet	EEEGHOPRS	geosphere
DIIOPRTTY	torpidity	EEEEFPRRZ	prefreeze	EEEGIISSS	eisegesis
DIIORRTTY	torridity	EEEEFRRSZ	refreezes	EEEGILSTT	gleetiest
DIIPRTTUY	putridity	EEEEGGRRS	greegrees	EEEGIMNST	esteeming
DIIPSTTUY	stupidity	EEEEGINVV	Geneviève	EEEGINNOT	eigentone
DIKNOOSTW	stinkwood	EEEEGINHW	weeweeing	EEEGINNRS	engineers
DIKNORSTU	outdrinks	EEEEGISSS	eisegeses	EEEGINNRV	veneering
DILLMNOPS	millponds	EEEEGLNRT	genteeler	EEEGINPRR	peregrine
DILLOOPPY	polyploid	EEEEGMRRS	reemerges	EEEGINRRS	energiser
DILLOORSS	doorsills	EEEEGNRRV	evergreen	EEEGINRRZ	energizer
DILMNOOOP	monoploid	EEEEGQSSU	squeegees	EEEGINRSS	energises
DILMNOSSW	slimdowns	EEEEHLRSW	elsewhere	EEEGINRSZ	energizes
DILMNPUUU	impundulu	EEEEHLRSW	expellees	EEEGINRTT	teetering
DILNOPSUX	spondulix	EEEELMRTT	telemeter	EEEGINRUV	Guinevere
DILOOPTUW	tulipwood	EEEELNOPT	eleoptene	EEEGIRSTY	geyserite
DIMMNORSY	myrmidons	EEEELNSSV	elevenses	EEEGISTTX	exegetist
DIMMOPSUY	sympodium		sleeveens	EEEGKLNRU	Kerguelen
DIMNOOSST	monodists	EEEELNTVV	velveteen	EEEGLLNTY	genteelly
DIMNOPRUU	purdonium	EEEENNSST	Tennessee	EEEGLLRWZ	Zellweger
DIMNORSTW	windstorm	EEEENNSTV	seventeen	EEEGLMNNT	gentlemen
DIMNOSSTU	dismounts	EEEENPRST	presentee	EEEGLNRST	greenlets
DIMOOOOSV	voodooism	EEEENRRSV	veneerers	EEEGMNNRU	energumen
DIMOORRTY	dormitory	EEEENRSTW	sweetener	EEEGMNORS	greensome
DINOOORSU	inodorous	EEEEPRRSV	persevere	EEEGMNRSS	messenger
DINOOORSW	ironwoods	EEEEPRSSS	peeresses	EEEGMNRSU	merengues
DINOOPRTW	woodprint	EEEEPSTTW	peetweets	EEEGMORRT	ergometer
DINOORSS	indorsors	EEEERSSSS	seeresses	EEEGMORST	geometers
DINORTTUY	rotundity	EEEFFIJRS	Jefferies	EEEGNNRSS	greenness
DIOOOOSTV	voodooist	EEEFFRSVW	feverfews	EEEGNOOSS	oogeneses
DIOOOPSSU	isopodous	EEEFGKNRU	fenugreek	EEEGNRRSU	reneguers
DIOOORVWY	ivorywood	EEEFHNOPR	freephone	EEEGNRRSV	revengers
DIOOPRSST	prosodist	EEEFHNRRS	freshener	EEEGNRSSS	negresses
DIOPRRSTU	disruptor	EEEFHORRT	therefore	EEEGOPRST	protegees
DIRSSSTTU	distrusts	EEEFHORRW	wherefore	EEEGRRRTT	regretter
DJLLNRUUU	Jullundur	EEEFHORST	foresheet	EEEGRRSSS	regresses
DKMNOOORS	komondors	EEEFHORTT	foreteeth	EEEHIKLPS	sheeplike
DKORSSTUW	studworks	EEEFHRRRS	refresher	EEEHILLNS	hellenise
DLLMORSSU	slumlords	EEEFHRRSS	refreshes	EEEHILLNZ	hellenize
DLLNORUWY	unworldly	EEEFILRVX	reflexive	EEEHILNNP	nepheline
DLMOOORXY	loxodromy	EEEFINRRS	ferneries	EEEHILNPT	nephelite
DLNNOSUUY	unsoundly	EEEFINRRT	interfere	EEEHILNST	Heseltine
DLNOOSSWW	slowdowns	EEEFLLNRU	fullerene	EEEHILRSW	erewhiles
DLOOORSUY	odorously	EEEFLNSST	fleetness	EEEHIMPRS	ephemeris
DMNOORRUW	roundworm	EEEFLRSSV	feverless	EEEHIMPSU	euphemise
DMOOORSWW	woodworms	EEEFLRSTY	freestyle	EEEHIMPUZ	euphemize

EEEHINNRS	henneries	EEEIMORTT	meteorite	EEELMOSTT	omelettes
EEEHIRRST	etheriser	EEEIMPRRS	premieres	EEELMRSTU	muleteers
EEEHIRRTZ	etherizer	EEEIMPRRT	perimeter	EEELMRTTY	telemetry
EEEHIRSSS	heiresses	EEEIMRRSS	misereres	EEELMRTXY	extremely
EEEHIRSST	etherises	EEEIMRSTT	remittees	EEELNOPSV	envelopes
EEEHIRSTZ	etherizes	EEEIMSSTW	semisweet	EEELNOPTT	leptotene
EEEHISTWZ	wheeziest	EEEINNNST	nineteens	EEELNOSTT	solenette
EEEHKLNOS	kneeholes	EEEINNRST	internees	EEELNOTTV	novelette
EEEHKLOSU	houseleek	EEEINNRTV	intervene	EEELNRRTY	terrenely
EEEHLLSSW	wheelless	EEEINORRT	orienteer	EEELNRSSV	nerveless
EEEHLMNSW	wheelsmen	EEEINPRRS	reserpine	EEELNRSSW	newsreels
EEEHLMNTY	methylene	EEEINPRST	perenties	EEELNSSSS	senseless
EEEHLMPST	helpmeets	EEEINPSSW	weepiness	EEELNSSST	tenseless
EEEHLMSST	themeless	EEEINPSVX	expensive	EEELOPPRS	repeoples
EEEHLNOPT	phenetole	EEEINRRST	reentries	EEELOPRSV	oversleep
	telephone	EEEINRRTW	wernerite		sleepover
EEEHLNOSW	nosewheel	EEEINRSST	eternises	EEELPPRSX	perplexes
EEEHLNSTV	elevenths		sneeriest	EEELRRSTT	letterers
EEEHLOPPS	peepholes	EEEINRSTZ	eternizes	EEELRRSVY	reversely
EEEHLRRST	shelterer	EEEINRTTV	retentive	EEELRSSTT	resettles
EEEHMMNTY	enthymeme	EEEINSSTV	seventies	EEELRSTTT	letterset
EEEHMNOPR	ephemeron	EEEINSSTW	weensiest	EEEMMNOST	mementoes
EEEHMORRT	rheometer	EEEINSTVX	extensive	EEEMMNNRTU	enurement
EEEHMORST	motherese	EEEIPRRRV	repriever	EEEMNNSTT	tenements
	threesome	EEEIPRRSV	reprieves	EEEMNOPRT	treponeme
EEEHMORSW	somewhere	EEEIPRRTT	preterite	EEEMNORRV	nevermore
EEEHMRTTT	thermette	EEEIPRSTX	expertise	EEEMNORSZ	mezereons
EEEHNNPST	nepenthes	EEEIPRTXZ	expertize	EEEMNOXYZ	exoenzyme
EEEHNNQSU	henequens	EEEIQRRSU	equerries	EEEMNRSST	steersmen
EEEHNPRSS	enspheres	EEEIQTTTU	etiquette	EEEMNRSTT	entremets
EEEHNRSSS	sheerness	EEEIRRRTV	retriever	EEEMNRSTY	mesentery
EEEHOPRSX	exosphere	EEEIRRSTV	retrieves	EEEMNRTTV	revetment
EEEHORSST	shoetrees	EEEIRRSVW	reviewers	EEEMOPRTX	extempore
EEEHRSTTU	usherette	EEEIRSTTV	serviette	EEEMORRSU	reremouse
EEEIIKLSV	sievelike	EEEJKNRTU	junketeer	EEEMORSST	stereomes
EEEIIKRST	kieserite	EEEJLLRSW	jewellers	EEEMPRRST	temperers
EEEIJKLLW	jewellike	EEEJLLRWY	jewellery	EEEMPRSSS	empresses
EEEIKNNPR	innkeeper	EEEJNPRSS	Jespersen	EEEMRSSST	semesters
EEEILLPRT	Pelletier	EEEJNRSWY	New Jersey	EEENNOPRS	neoprenes
EEEILLRSV	reveilles	EEEKLMPRR	Klemperer	EEENNORST	sonneteer
EEEILMSST	seemliest	EEEKLNSSS	sleekness	EEENNSSST	tenseness
EEEILNNRV	enlivener	EEEKMORST	smoketree	EEENPRRST	presenter
EEEILNPRS	pelerines	EEEKMRSTU	musketeer		repenters
	presenile	EEEKNOSTY	synoekete		represent
EEEILNQRU	queenlier	EEELLLRSV	levellers	EEENPRRTV	preventer
EEEILNRSS	leeriness	EEELLLSSW	sewellels	EEENPRSST	pretenses
EEEILNRSY	eyeliners	EEELLLSWY	Wellesley	EEENPRSUV	supervene
EEEILNSTX	extensile	EEELLNORS	enrollees	EEENPSSST	steepness
EEEILPRSV	replevies	EEELLNPRT	repellent	EEENQRSSU	queerness
EEEILPSST	sleepiest	EEELLNPTX	expellent	EEENRRSTU	returnees
EEEILPTVX	expletive	EEELLNQSU	quenelles	EEENRRSTW	westerner
EEEILRRRV	Leverrier	EEELLNSSV	levelness	EEENRRSUV	revenuers
EEEILRRSV	relievers	EEELLPRRS	repellers	EEENRSSST	terseness
	revelries	EEELLPRSX	expellers	EEENSSSTW	sweetness
EEEILRSTX	exsertile	EEELLPRTY	repletely	EEEOPSSST	poetesses
EEEILRSVY	liveyeres	EEELLPSSS	sleepless	EEEORRSSV	overseers
EEEILSSTV	televises	EEELLRRSV	revellers	EEEORRSSX	xeroseres
EEEIMMNNO	menominee	EEELMMNOP	Melpomene	EEEORRSTV	oversteer
EEEIMMRSS	mesmerise	EEELMNOPR	perlemoen	EEEORRTVX	overexert
EEEIMMRSZ	mesmerize	EEELMNOPT	elopement	EEEPPPRTU	puppeteer
EEEIMNNRT	nemertine	EEELMNRTV	revelment	EEEPRRRSS	represser
EEEIMNNRV	veniremen	EEELMOPSY	employees	EEEPRRRSV	preserver

EEEPRRRTV	perverter	**EEFHIJSSW**	jewfishes	**EEFILOORS**	fooleries
EEEPRRSSS	represses	**EEFHIKLLS**	shelflike	**EEFILORSV**	overflies
EEEPRRSST	pesterers	**EEFHILLRS**	fleshlier	**EEFILORTU**	outrelief
EEEPRRSSV	preserves		shellfire	**EEFILPRRS**	pilferers
EEEPRRSSX	expresser	**EEFHILSST**	fleshiest	**EEFILRRST**	refilters
EEEPRRSTW	pewterers	**EEFHIMNRS**	fishermen	**EEFILRSSU**	fusileers
EEEPRSSSX	expresses	**EEFHINPRV**	hyperfine	**EEFILSTVY**	festively
EEEPRSTTU	superette	**EEFHINSST**	heftiness	**EEFIMNRTT**	refitment
EEEPSSTTT	septettes	**EEFHIORSU**	firehouse	**EEFIMPRRU**	perfumier
EEEQRRSTU	requester	**EEFHIOSUW**	housewife	**EEFIMRSTU**	furmeties
EEEQRSSTU	sequester	**EEFHLLSWY**	flywheels	**EEFINNPVY**	fivepenny
EEEQRSSUZ	squeezers	**EEFHLLTUW**	Ethelwulf	**EEFINORST**	firestone
EEERRRSSV	reservers	**EEFHLMOTU**	mouthfeel	**EEFINPRSU**	superfine
	reversers	**EEFHLSSTT**	theftless	**EEFINRRRS**	inferrers
EEERRRSTV	reverters	**EEFHMORRT**	therefrom	**EEFINRSST**	infesters
EEERRSSTT	resetters	**EEFHMORRW**	wherefrom	**EEFINRSSU**	reinfuses
EEESSTTTX	sextettes	**EEFHNRSSS**	freshness	**EEFINRSTU**	interfuse
EEFFFKLRU	kerfuffle	**EEFHOORRS**	foreshore	**EEFIOPPRS**	fopperies
EEFFFMNOT	feoffment	**EEFHRRRTU**	furtherer	**EEFIOPRRT**	profiteer
EEFFGLNTU	effulgent	**EEFIIJLLS**	jellifies	**EEFIOPRRW**	firepower
EEFFHIKSY	keffiyehs	**EEFIIKKLN**	knifelike	**EEFIORRRT**	retrofire
EEFFHINTT	fifteenth	**EEFIILLNS**	lifelines	**EEFIORRST**	torrefies
EEFFHLRSU	reshuffle	**EEFIILMST**	lifetimes	**EEFIORRSU**	Soufrière
EEFFIILRS	fireflies	**EEFIILMTX**	flexitime	**EEFIPRRTU**	putrefier
EEFFINOSV	offensive	**EEFIILNRT**	infertile	**EEFIPRSTU**	putrefies
EEFFINRST	stiffener		interfile		stupefier
EEFFIORRT	forfeiter	**EEFIILQRU**	liquefier	**EEFIPRSUV**	perfusive
EEFFIPRSU	pufferies	**EEFIILQSU**	liquefies	**EEFIPSSTU**	stupefies
EEFFJNORS	Jefferson	**EEFIILRST**	fertilise	**EEFIRRRTT**	fritterer
EEFFLNSTU	effluents	**EEFIILRTZ**	fertilize	**EEFIRRRTU**	fruiterer
EEFFOPRRR	profferer	**EEFIIMNSS**	feminises	**EEFIRRSTU**	surfeiter
EEFFRRSSU	sufferers	**EEFIIMNSZ**	feminizes	**EEFIRSSTT**	frisettes
EEFGHIMSS	gemfishes	**EEFIIMNTY**	femineity	**EEFIRSTTZ**	frizettes
EEFGHIRRT	freighter	**EEFIIMRRT**	metrifier	**EEFKNOORT**	foretoken
EEFGIILRS	filigrees	**EEFIIMRST**	metrifies	**EEFKOOPRS**	forespoke
EEFGIINNR	Feininger	**EEFIINRSS**	fieriness	**EEFLLLNSU**	fluellens
EEFGIKLUU	fuguelike	**EEFIINRST**	Finistère	**EEFLLNPSU**	spleenful
EEFGILLNY	feelingly	**EEFIINRSU**	reunifies	**EEFLLORST**	foretells
EEFGILNNU	unfeeling	**EEFIINRTT**	Nefertiti	**EEFLMORTW**	flowmeter
EEFGILNRU	refueling	**EEFIIPRRT**	petrifier	**EEFLMRTUX**	fluxmeter
EEFGILNRX	reflexing	**EEFIIPRST**	petrifies	**EEFLNOSST**	felstones
EEFGILRSS	griefless	**EEFIIRRRT**	terrifier	**EEFLNRSTU**	resentful
EEFGIMRUV	vermifuge	**EEFIIRRST**	terrifies	**EEFLNRTVY**	fervently
EEFGINORR	foreigner	**EEFIIRRSV**	verifiers	**EEFLOPRSU**	reposeful
EEFGINPTY	tepefying		versifier	**EEFLORRSW**	flowerers
EEFGINRRR	referring	**EEFIIRSSV**	versifies		reflowers
EEFGINRRS	fingerers	**EEFIIRSTT**	testifier	**EEFLORRTX**	retroflex
EEFGINRRT	ferreting	**EEFIISSTT**	feistiest	**EEFLORSTV**	leftovers
EEFGINRST	festering		testifies	**EEFLORSTW**	flowerets
EEFGINRTT	fettering	**EEFIKLLTU**	flutelike	**EEFLRRTTU**	flutterer
EEFGIORRS	forgeries	**EEFIKNRST**	kniferest	**EEFMNOORW**	forewomen
EEFGIPRRU	prefigure	**EEFIKNRSU**	refusenik	**EEFMNORST**	fomenters
EEFGLLLUY	gleefully	**EEFILLLOS**	filoselle	**EEFMOPRRR**	performer
EEFGLLTUY	Leyte Gulf	**EEFILLRST**	fillester	**EEFMORRRS**	reformers
EEFGLNRTU	refulgent	**EEFILLRTU**	fullerite	**EEFMPRRSU**	perfumers
EEFGLRRTU	regretful	**EEFILLRTY**	fertilely	**EEFMPRRUY**	perfumery
EEFGOORRS	foregoers	**EEFILLSTY**	lifestyle	**EEFNOPRRZ**	prefrozen
EEFGORRTT	forgetter	**EEFILMPXY**	exemplify	**EEFNOPRST**	forespent
EEFHIIRSS	fisheries	**EEFILMSST**	fistmeles	**EEFNORSST**	softeners
EEFHIISST	fetishise	**EEFILNORS**	felonries	**EEFNORSTU**	fourteens
EEFHIISTZ	fetishize	**EEFILNORX**	reflexion	**EEFNORSTW**	New Forest
EEFHIJLSW	jewelfish	**EEFILNTUW**	wulfenite	**EEFNQRSTU**	frequents

EEFNRSTTU	unfetters	EEGHLMNNT	lengthmen	EEGILOPSU	epilogues
EEFOORRST	rooftrees	EEGHLNNST	lengthens	EEGILORST	sortilege
EEFOPRRTY	ferrotype	EEGHMNOSU	hegumenos	EEGILORSU	eulogiser
EEFOPRSSS	professes	EEGHMORST	geotherms	EEGILORUZ	eulogizer
EEFORRSST	foresters	EEGHNNORR	greenhorn	EEGILOSSU	eulogises
	fosterers	EEGHNNOTY	ethnogeny	EEGILOSUZ	eulogizes
	reforests	EEGHNOOPT	photogene	EEGILQSSU	squilgees
EEFORRTVW	feverwort	EEGHOPSTY	geophytes	EEGILRSTV	verligtes
EEFOSSSTT	fossettes	EEGIIKLRT	tigerlike	EEGIMNPRR	Preminger
EEFPRSSUU	superfuse	EEGIILLPS	Gillespie	EEGIMNPRT	tempering
EEGGHLLSS	eggshells	EEGIILNRV	inveigler	EEGIMNPTX	exempting
EEGGHNORU	Greenough		relieving	EEGIMNRST	regiments
EEGGIIIOR	George III	EEGIILNSV	inveigles	EEGIMNRSU	meringues
EEGGIILNS	elegising	EEGIILORS	religiose	EEGINNOPR	reopening
EEGGIILNT	gelignite	EEGIILPRV	privilege	EEGINNPRT	repenting
EEGGIILNZ	elegizing	EEGIILRUX	religieux	EEGINNPSX	expensing
EEGGIIPRS	piggeries	EEGIINPST	epigenist	EEGINNRST	resenting
EEGGIJRRS	rejiggers	EEGIINRST	reignites	EEGINNRTT	tentering
EEGGILNNR	greenling	EEGIINRVW	reviewing	EEGINNRTU	neutering
EEGGILNNT	negligent	EEGIINSTV	genitives	EEGINNRUV	unreeving
EEGGILNSS	legginess		ingestive	EEGINOOSS	oogenesis
EEGGILOOS	geologies	EEGIISTTZ	zeitgeist	EEGINOPRS	progenies
	geologise	EEGIJLLNW	jewelling	EEGINOPRY	epirogeny
EEGGILOOZ	geologize	EEGIJLNRY	jeeringly	EEGINOPSU	epigenous
EEGGINNRS	greenings	EEGIJOPRS	jerepigos	EEGINORRS	erigerons
EEGGINNRU	reneguing	EEGIKLLMU	glumelike	EEGINORSS	egression
EEGGINNRV	revenging	EEGIKLNNN	kenneling	EEGINORSV	sovereign
EEGGINRSS	egressing	EEGIKLNNR	kerneling	EEGINOSSS	gneissose
EEGGINRST	greetings	EEGIKLNRY	reekingly	EEGINOSST	egestions
EEGGINRTT	gettering	EEGIKNRSW	skewering	EEGINOSXY	oxygenise
EEGGIORSU	egregious	EEGIKNRTT	Kettering	EEGINOXYZ	oxygenize
EEGGLOORS	geologers	EEGILLLNV	levelling	EEGINPPPR	peppering
EEGGRSSTU	suggester	EEGILLMTU	guillemet	EEGINPRST	pestering
EEGHHIITT	eightieth	EEGILLNPR	repelling	EEGINPSSW	sweepings
EEGHHINST	heightens	EEGILLNPT	pelleting	EEGINQSUZ	squeezing
EEGHHINSW	wheeshing	EEGILLNPX	expelling	EEGINRRSS	resigners
EEGHIIKLN	hingelike	EEGILLNRS	reselling	EEGINRRSV	reserving
EEGHIINRV	inveigher	EEGILLNRT	retelling		reversing
EEGHIIRTW	weightier	EEGILLNRV	Grenville	EEGINRRTV	reverting
EEGHIKNTW	weeknight		revelling	EEGINRSSS	ingresses
EEGHILMNT	metheglin	EEGILLNRY	leeringly	EEGINRSSU	seigneurs
EEGHILNNT	enlighten	EEGILLSSU	guileless	EEGINRSSY	synergies
EEGHILNOR	rhigolene	EEGILMMSU	gelsemium	EEGINRSTT	resetting
EEGHILNRT	lengthier	EEGILMNRT	remelting		retesting
EEGHILNSS	hingeless	EEGILMNSY	seemingly		streeting
EEGHILRSS	sleighers	EEGILMRSY	Lyme Regis	EEGINRSTV	revesting
EEGHIMMNR	rehemming	EEGILNNRT	relenting	EEGINRSTW	westering
EEGHIMNNS	enmeshing	EEGILNNRU	unreeling	EEGINRSTX	exserting
EEGHIMOST	eightsome	EEGILNNSS	Esslingen	EEGINRSUY	seigneury
EEGHINORS	reshoeing		lessening	EEGINRTTV	revetting
EEGHINPRT	threeping	EEGILNNUY	genuinely	EEGINSSTU	eugenists
EEGHINRTT	tethering	EEGILNOOS	neologies	EEGINSSTW	sweetings
	tightener		neologise	EEGINSTTV	vignettes
EEGHINSST	sightseen	EEGILNOOZ	neologize	EEGIORRSU	rogueries
EEGHIORVW	overweigh	EEGILNORS	eloigners	EEGIORSTV	vertigoes
EEGHIOSTT	ghettoise	EEGILNPWY	weepingly	EEGIPRUUX	Périgueux
EEGHIOTTZ	ghettoize	EEGILNRRS	lingerers	EEGIRRSST	registers
EEGHIRSST	sightseer	EEGILNRTT	lettering	EEGIRRSSU	regisseur
EEGHIRSTU	theurgies		reletting		surgeries
EEGHIRSTW	weighters	EEGILNRTW	weltering	EEGIRSSST	tigresses
EEGHISSST	sightsees	EEGILNTXY	exigently	EEGIRSSTT	grisettes
EEGHLLNOP	phellogen	EEGILOPRS	Pergolesi	EEGLLMORU	glomerule

EEGLLOOTY	teleology	EEHILNORS	shoreline	EEHIRTTTU	Hutterite
EEGLLOPRS	gospeller	EEHILNOSU	houseline	EEHKLOOST	stokehole
EEGLLORRV	groveller	EEHILNPRS	plenisher	EEHKLORWW	wheelwork
EEGLLOSSV	gloveless		replenish	EEHKORSTW	worksheet
EEGLMNNOU	melungeon	EEHILNPSS	plenishes	EEHLLLNVY	Helvellyn
EEGLMOORY	mereology		spleenish	EEHLLORST	hosteller
EEGLMOSSS	glossemes	EEHILNPSW	pinwheels	EEHLLORSV	shoveller
EEGLNOPSY	polygenes	EEHILNSST	litheness	EEHLMOOSW	wholesome
EEGLNORTT	lorgnette	EEHILOPRX	xerophile	EEHLMORVW	overwhelm
EEGLNOSTU	Telegonus	EEHILOPTY	heliotype	EEHLMOSSY	hemolyses
EEGLPRSUU	superglue	EEHILORST	helotries	EEHLMOSZZ	shemozzle
EEGLRSSSU	surgeless		hoteliers	EEHLMRSSY	rhymeless
EEGLRSSUU	reguluses	EEHILPSST	slipsheet	EEHLNOPTY	polythene
EEGMNOORR	greenroom	EEHILPSVY	peevishly		telephony
EEGMNOSST	gemstones	EEHILRSTW	erstwhile	EEHLNOSSW	wholeness
EEGMNSTTU	teguments	EEHILSTUV	Helvétius	EEHLNOSTT	telethons
EEGNNORST	roentgens	EEHIMMPSU	euphemism	EEHLNSTVY	seventhly
EEGNNOSSV	evensongs	EEHIMNRST	intermesh	EEHLOOPTT	telephoto
EEGNOORST	oestrogen	EEHIMOPRT	hemitrope	EEHLOPSST	heelposts
EEGNOORSU	erogenous	EEHIMPRRW	whimperer	EEHLORSSS	horseless
EEGNOOSUX	exogenous	EEHIMRSTU	rheumiest		shoreless
EEGNOPSTY	genotypes	EEHINNORT	threonine	EEHLORSST	hostelers
EEGNORRSS	engrosser	EEHINNOTV	Einthoven	EEHLORSSV	shovelers
EEGNORSSS	engrosses	EEHINNQSU	henequins	EEHLOSSSU	houseless
EEGNORSSV	governess		heniquens	EEHLPRSSU	spherules
EEGNOSTYZ	zygotenes	EEHINNRSS	enshrines	EEHMMOPRS	morphemes
EEGNPRSUX	expungers	EEHINOPSU	euphonies	EEHMMORST	ohmmeters
EEGNRRSTU	resurgent		euphonise	EEHMNOOPR	pheromone
EEGNRSSUY	guernseys	EEHINOPSX	phoenixes	EEHMNOORW	homeowner
EEGOPRSSU	superegos	EEHINOPUZ	euphonize	EEHMNORTY	heteronym
EEGOQRSTU	grotesque	EEHINORRS	heronries	EEHMNOSSY	homeyness
EEGORRRSS	regressor	EEHINORTT	thereinto	EEHMNPTTU	umpteenth
EEGRRSSTU	gesturers	EEHINORTW	whereinto	EEHMNRRWY	wherrymen
EEHHHLNOO	Hohenlohe	EEHINOSST	hessonite	EEHMOPSTY	mesophyte
EEHHILMOP	hemophile		honesties	EEHMORRTY	rheometry
EEHHINOPT	thiophene	EEHINPRSS	inspheres	EEHMORSST	thermoses
EEHHINOSS	shoeshine		phrensies	EEHMRRRTU	murtherer
EEHHIRTTW	therewith	EEHINPRST	nephrites	EEHMRRSTY	rhymester
EEHHIRTWW	wherewith		trephines	EEHNNOOST	ethonones
EEHHLLLOS	hellholes	EEHINRSTT	thirteens	EEHNNORST	enthrones
EEHHLOPTY	helophyte	EEHINRSTW	whiteners	EEHNOOPRS	noosphere
EEHHNOPPS	phosphene	EEHINSSTW	whiteness	EEHNNOPTY	phenotype
EEHHNOSSU	henhouses	EEHINSTTU	euthenist	EEHNOPRTU	thereupon
EEHHOORSS	horseshoe	EEHINSTTX	sixteenth	EEHNOPRUW	whereupon
EEHHRRSST	threshers	EEHINTTTW	twentieth	EEHNOPSTU	penthouse
EEHIIKRSS	Eskişehir	EEHIORRST	theoriser	EEHNOPSTY	neophytes
EEHIILNTW	White Nile	EEHIORRTZ	theorizer	EEHNOPTTY	entophyte
EEHIINNTT	ninetieth	EEHIORSST	heterosis	EEHNORRST	shortener
EEHIIRTTW	witherite		isotheres	EEHNORSST	otherness
EEHIJNOPS	Josephine		theorises	EEHNORTUW	whereunto
EEHIKLORS	horselike	EEHIORSTW	otherwise	EEHNOSTTW	whetstone
EEHIKNPSS	sheepskin	EEHIORSTZ	theorizes	EEHNPPRSU	penpusher
EEHIKRRSS	shriekers	EEHIPPRRY	periphery	EEHNPRSSU	unspheres
EEHILLLMW	millwheel	EEHIPPSST	psephites	EEHNSSSTY	syntheses
EEHILLNPS	helplines	EEHIPPSSY	epiphyses	EEHOOPRSS	oospheres
EEHILMNSU	heleniums	EEHIPPSTY	epiphytes	EEHOORSSV	overshoes
EEHILMOPS	mesophile	EEHIPRRSW	whisperer	EEHOORSVW	howsoever
EEHILMOST	homeliest	EEHIRRSST	heritress		whosoever
	lithesome	EEHIRRSSV	shiverers	EEHOPPSSW	peepshows
EEHILMRRT	Thirlmere	EEHIRRSTW	witherers	EEHOPRRSU	superhero
EEHILNOOP	oenophile	EEHIRRTTY	erythrite	EEHOPRTXY	xerophyte
EEHILNOPX	xenophile	EEHIRSSTT	Thersites	EEHOPSSTU	pesthouse

EEHOPSSTW	sweetshop	**EEIINSSVW**	viewiness	**EEILLSUVY**	elusively
EEHORRSTX	exhorters	**EEIIOPQSU**	equipoise	**EEILMMNPT**	implement
EEHORRTVW	overthrew	**EEIIOPSTZ**	epizoites	**EEILMMNSY**	immensely
EEHORSTTY	set theory	**EEIIOSSTV**	sovietise	**EEILMMORS**	sommelier
EEHOSSSST	hostesses	**EEIIOSTVZ**	sovietize	**EEILMMORT**	milometer
EEHPRSSTU	superhets	**EEIIQRSTU**	requisite	**EEILMNNOT**	eloinment
EEHPRSSTY	hypesters	**EEIIQSTUX**	exquisite	**EEILMNNTY**	eminently
EEHPRTTXY	hypertext	**EEIIRSSTV**	resistive	**EEILMNOSS**	solemnise
EEIIIKLMN	Menelik II	**EEIJKLLLY**	jellylike	**EEILMNOST**	limestone
EEIIIMNST	nimieties	**EEIJKNRSS**	jerkiness		milestone
EEIIIMPST	impieties	**EEIJLNNSU**	juliennes	**EEILMNOSZ**	solemnize
EEIIKKMSS	Sikkimese	**EEIJLNRST**	jetliners	**EEILMNPPR**	pimpernel
EEIIKLLST	likeliest	**EEIJLNSUV**	juveniles	**EEILMNRSU**	lemurines
EEIIKLNPS	snipelike	**EEIJNNORS**	enjoiners		relumines
EEIIKLNSW	swinelike	**EEIJNSSTT**	jettiness	**EEILMNRVY**	liverymen
EEIIKNNTZ	zinkenite	**EEIJPRRSU**	perjuries	**EEILMNSTU**	musteline
EEIILLMMS	milliemes	**EEIJQRTUY**	jequerity	**EEILMORTT**	tremolite
EEIILLMRT	millerite	**EEIKLLMPU**	plumelike	**EEILMOSTT**	mistletoe
EEIILLMTW	willemite	**EEIKLMORT**	kilometer	**EEILMOSVW**	semivowel
EEIILLNTV	vitelline		kilometre	**EEILMOTVY**	emotively
EEIILLOPS	eolipiles	**EEIKLMOSU**	mouselike	**EEILMPSSX**	simplexes
EEIILLSTV	liveliest	**EEIKLNOST**	stonelike	**EEILMRSST**	meritless
EEIILMRSS	missileer	**EEIKLOPRS**	proselike	**EEILMRSTY**	lysimeter
EEIILMSTT	timeliest	**EEIKLORST**	lorikeets	**EEILNNPSS**	penniless
EEIILNNRT	interline	**EEIKLPSST**	spikelets	**EEILNNSST**	sentinels
EEIILNOTV	olivenite	**EEIKLRSST**	triskeles	**EEILNNSTY**	intensely
EEIILNPPS	pipelines	**EEIKLRTWY**	triweekly	**EEILNOORS**	oleoresin
EEIILNQSU	Esquiline	**EEIKMNORS**	monkeries	**EEILNOPRT**	repletion
EEIILNRST	resilient	**EEIKMNORT**	konimeter		terpineol
EEIILNSTV	lenitives	**EEIKMOSTX**	ketoximes	**EEILNOPTT**	telepoint
EEIILOPST	sepiolite	**EEIKNNPSV**	penknives	**EEILNORVV**	reinvolve
EEIILRSST	sterilise	**EEIKNORSV**	reinvokes	**EEILNORVW**	wolverine
EEIILRSTU	Tuileries	**EEIKNPRSS**	perkiness	**EEILNOSSS**	lionesses
EEIILRSTZ	sterilize	**EEIKNPSSS**	peskiness		noiseless
EEIILRTUZ	reutilize	**EEIKNRRST**	tinkerers	**EEILNOSSU**	selenious
EEIIMMPRS	epimerism	**EEIKOORRS**	rookeries	**EEILNOSSV**	novelises
EEIIMMPRT	primetime	**EEIKOORTZ**	ozokerite	**EEILNOSTV**	novelties
EEIIMMRST	eremitism	**EEIKOQSUV**	equivokes	**EEILNOSVZ**	novelizes
EEIIMMRSV	immersive	**EEILLLNUV**	Lunéville		Venizélos
EEIIMOPST	epitomise	**EEILLLNWV**	Llewelyn I	**EEILNPPSZ**	zeppelins
EEIIMOPTZ	epitomize	**EEILLMNOR**	Niemöller	**EEILNPRSU**	perilunes
EEIIMORSS	isomerise	**EEILLMNOT**	emollient	**EEILNPRSV**	replevins
EEIIMORSZ	isomerize	**EEILLMNPT**	impellent	**EEILNPSSS**	spineless
EEIIMRSSV	remissive	**EEILLMOPR**	millepore	**EEILNPSTT**	pestilent
EEIIMRSTZ	itemizers	**EEILLMPRS**	impellers	**EEILNPSVY**	pensively
EEIINNNPT	penninite	**EEILLMSST**	smelliest	**EEILNRSST**	enlisters
EEIINNSTT	intestine	**EEILLNNTY**	leniently		listeners
EEIINNSTV	intensive	**EEILLNOST**	loneliest	**EEILNRSTU**	unsterile
EEIINNTVV	inventive	**EEILLNRSV**	sniveller	**EEILNRSVY**	inversely
EEIINQRSU	enquiries	**EEILLNSSS**	illnesses	**EEILNSSSW**	sinewless
EEIINRRVV	viverrine	**EEILLNSTY**	tensilely	**EEILOPRST**	epistoler
EEIINRSTT	enteritis	**EEILLOPTU**	petiolule		pistoleer
	retinites	**EEILLOSTV**	loveliest	**EEILOPSST**	politesse
EEIINRSTV	reinvites	**EEILLPRUY**	puerilely	**EEILOPSVX**	explosive
EEIINRSTW	winterise	**EEILLRSST**	trellises	**EEILORRST**	loiterers
EEIINRSVV	inversive	**EEILLRSSV**	liverless	**EEILORRTT**	Tortelier
EEIINRTVW	interview	**EEILLRSTU**	tellurise	**EEILORSTT**	lotteries
EEIINRTWZ	winterize	**EEILLRSTY**	sterilely	**EEILORSVV**	overlives
EEIINSSST	sensitise	**EEILLRSUY**	leisurely	**EEILOSSVW**	vowelises
EEIINSSTT	tensities	**EEILLRSVY**	servilely	**EEILOSTTT**	toilettes
EEIINSSTV	sensitive	**EEILLRTTU**	tellurite	**EEILOSVWZ**	vowelizes
EEIINSSTZ	sensitize	**EEILLRTUZ**	tellurize	**EEILOTUVV**	evolutive

EEILPRSST	epistlers
	spirelets
EEILPRSTY	peristyle
	Priestley
EEILPRSUV	prelusive
	pulverise
	repulsive
EEILPRUVZ	pulverize
EEILPSSTY	epistyles
EEILPSUVX	expulsive
EEILRRSSV	riverless
	silverers
EEILRSTVY	restively
EEILRSUVV	revulsive
EEILSSSSU	issueless
EEIMMMRSS	mesmerism
EEIMMMRSU	mummeries
EEIMMNNTU	minutemen
EEIMMNRRT	merriment
EEIMMORRS	memoriser
EEIMMORRZ	memorizer
EEIMMORSS	memorises
EEIMMORST	meteorism
EEIMMORSZ	memorizes
EEIMMOSST	sometimes
EEIMMRRSS	immersers
EEIMMRSST	meristems
	mesmerist
EEIMMRSTU	summiteer
EEIMMRSTW	swimmeret
EEIMMRSTX	extremism
EEIMNNNOT	Mennonite
EEIMNNORT	mentioner
EEIMNNRTT	interment
EEIMNNRTU	inurement
EEIMNNSTT	sentiment
EEIMNOPTX	exemption
EEIMNORSS	emersions
	sermonise
EEIMNORST	moistener
EEIMNORSZ	sermonize
EEIMNORTW	tirewomen
EEIMNOSST	monetises
	semitones
EEIMNOSTX	sixteenmo
EEIMNOSTZ	monetizes
	zonetimes
EEIMNOSYZ	isoenzyme
EEIMNPQTU	equipment
EEIMNPRSS	primeness
EEIMNPSST	emptiness
EEIMNRRSS	merriness
EEIMNRSTU	mutineers
EEIMNRSTV	virements
EEIMNRTTT	remittent
EEIMNSSSS	messiness
EEIMOOPRS	meiospore
EEIMOORTZ	merozoite
EEIMOPRSS	promisees
	reimposes
EEIMOPRST	peristome
	temporise

EEIMOPRTZ	temporize
EEIMORRSW	wormeries
EEIMORSTV	overtimes
EEIMOSSTZ	mestizoes
EEIMPPRRS	perisperm
EEIMPRRSS	impresser
	simperers
EEIMPRRTT	permitter
	pretermit
EEIMPRRTY	perimetry
EEIMPRSSS	impresses
EEIMPSSTU	impetuses
EEIMQSSTU	mesquites
EEIMQSTUU	equisetum
EEIMRRSST	rimesters
EEIMRRSTT	remitters
	trimester
	trimeters
EEIMRSSSU	messieurs
EEIMRSSTY	mysteries
EEIMRSTTX	extremist
EEIMRTTXY	extremity
EEIMSSSTY	systemise
EEIMSSTTU	sutteeism
EEIMSSTYZ	systemize
EEINNNRSS	innerness
EEINNNRSU	nunneries
EEINNOPPS	Nipponese
EEINNOPRS	pensioner
EEINNORTT	retention
EEINNOSTV	veinstone
EEINNOSTX	extension
EEINNPRST	spinneret
EEINNPRTT	pertinent
EEINNPSST	ineptness
EEINNPSTT	penitents
EEINNRSST	inertness
EEINNRSSV	inverness
	nerviness
EEINNRSTV	reinvents
EEINNSSSW	newsiness
EEINNSSTT	intensest
	sentients
EEINOPPPR	pepperoni
EEINOPPRS	ronepipes
EEINOPPST	peptonise
	pipestone
EEINOPPTZ	peptonize
EEINOPRST	entropies
	interpose
EEINOQSUX	equinoxes
EEINORRST	reorients
EEINORRSV	reversion
EEINORSSV	eversions
EEINORSTX	exertions
	exsertion
EEINORTVW	interwove
EEINOSSTT	noisettes
EEINOSSTV	ostensive
EEINOTTUZ	teutonize
EEINPPPSS	peppiness
EEINPRRRT	reprinter

EEINPRRTT	interpret
EEINPRSSW	winepress
EEINPSSTT	pettiness
EEINQRRSU	enquirers
EEINQRSSU	squireens
EEINQSSTU	quietness
EEINQTTTU	quintette
EEINRRRSU	reinsurer
EEINRRSST	inserters
	reinserts
EEINRRSSU	nurseries
	reinsures
EEINRRSTU	reuniters
	turneries
EEINRRSTV	inverters
EEINRRSTW	winterers
EEINRRTTW	rewritten
EEINRSSSY	syneresis
EEINRSSTT	insetters
	interests
	triteness
EEINRSSTV	sirventes
EEINRSSTW	witnesser
EEINRSSUV	universes
EEINSSSTT	testiness
EEINSSSTW	witnesses
EEINSSTTX	existents
EEINSTTXY	extensity
EEIOPPSTV	stovepipe
EEIOPRRST	portieres
EEIOPRSTT	potteries
EEIOPRTTU	pirouette
EEIOPSTTT	pettitoes
EEIOQQUUV	equivoque
EEIORRRST	roisterer
	terrorise
EEIORRRSV	reservoir
EEIORRRTZ	terrorize
EEIORRSTV	overtires
EEIORRSTX	exteriors
EEIORRTTU	tourtiere
EEIORRTVW	overwrite
EEIORSSUV	overissue
EEIORSSVZ	oversizes
EEIORTTVX	extortive
EEIPPQRSU	equippers
EEIPPRRSS	perspires
EEIPPRSST	peptisers
EEIPPRSTZ	peptizers
EEIPRRSST	persister
EEIPRRSTT	preterits
EEIPRSSST	priestess
EEIPRSSTX	preexists
EEIPRSSUV	supervise
EEIPRSTTT	prettiest
EEIPRTTWY	typewrite
EEIQRRRSU	requirers
EEIQRRSTU	requiters
EEIQRRSUV	quiverers
EEIQSSTUU	quietuses
EEIRRSSST	resisters
EEIRRSSTV	reservist

EEIRRSTTT	titterers	EELNOPPRY	propylene	EEMOOPRST	proteomes
EEIRRTTTW	twitterer	EELNOPPSU	unpeoples	EEMOOPRTT	optometer
EEIRSTUVX	extrusive	EELNOPRST	petronels		potometer
EEJKNRSTU	junketers	EELNOPSTU	plenteous	EEMOORRST	orometers
EEJKNRTTU	junketter	EELNORSST	entresols	EEMOORSTT	roomettes
EEJLNOSST	Jesselton		tenorless	EEMOPPRRT	preemptor
EEJLPSSTU	pulsejets	EELNORSTV	resolvent	EEMOPRRTY	pyrometer
EEJMNNOTY	enjoyment	EELNORTUV	volunteer	EEMOQRSSU	moresques
EEJNOQSUU	Junoesque	EELNOSSST	stoneless	EEMOSTTTU	teetotums
EEJNORRUY	journeyer	EELNPRSTY	presently	EEMPRRSSU	presumers
EEJPRRRSU	perjurers	EELNQSTUY	sequently	EEMPRRTTU	trumpeter
EEKKORSTY	keystroke	EELNSSTTU	unsettles	EEMPRSSTT	temptress
EEKKORSWW	workweeks	EELOOPRSY	operosely	EEMRRSTTU	mutterers
EEKLLNNOS	Nollekens	EELOORSTV	Roosevelt	EEMRSSTTU	metestrus
EEKLMOSSS	smokeless	EELOPPRSS	prolepses	EENNNOSTV	nonevents
EEKLNNNSU	unkennels	EELOPRRSX	explorers	EENNOOSTU	neotenous
EEKLNOSST	skeletons	EELOPRRTU	poulterer	EENNOPRSS	proneness
EEKLNPRSU	spelunker	EELOPRRSU	peloruses	EENNOPSTX	exponents
EEKLORSTW	steelwork	EELOPRSSW	powerless	EENNOSSTV	Stevenson
EEKMNOPSS	spokesmen	EELOPRSTT	teleports	EENNRSSST	sternness
EEKNORRTW	networker	EELOPRSTV	overslept	EENOORRSU	erroneous
EEKNORRWY	New Yorker	EELOPRSTY	polyester	EENOORSTU	euronotes
EEKNOSSTY	keystones		proselyte	EENOORSTV	overtones
EEKRRSTUZ	kreutzers	EELOPRTXY	expletory	EENOPPRTT	prepotent
EELLLLNWY	Llewellyn	EELOPSSTU	sleepouts	EENOPRRSS	responser
EELLMOSTW	mellowest	EELORRSSV	resolvers	EENOPRSSS	responses
EELLMPSSU	plumeless	EELORRSTV	revolters	EENOPRSTT	entrepots
EELLNNRTU	tunneller	EELORRSTW	trowelers	EENOPRSTV	overspent
EELLNORRS	enrollers	EELORRSUV	overrules	EENOPRSXY	pyroxenes
EELLOPPRR	propeller	EELORRSVV	revolvers	EENOPSTTY	stenotype
EELLORRTW	troweller	EELORSSUV	ourselves	EENORRTUY	tourneyer
EELLORSST	sollerets	EELORSTTU	roulettes	EENORSSTV	overtness
EELLORSSV	oversells	EELORSTUV	trueloves	EENORSSTX	extensors
EELLORSTX	extollers	EELPPSSTU	septuples	EENORTTTU	neutretto
EELLORSVY	volleyers	EELPPSTTU	septuplet	EENOSSTUV	ventouses
EELLOSSVW	vowelless	EELPRRSSU	repulsers	EENPRSSSU	suspenser
EELLOSTWY	yellowest	EELPRSSXY	expressly	EENRRRSTU	returners
EELLPSSSU	pulseless	EELPRSTUU	sepulture	EENRRSTUV	venturers
EELLPSSTY	syllepses	EELPSSTUX	sextuples	EEOORPRWV	overpower
EELLSSSUY	uselessly	EELPSTTUX	sextuplet	EEOOPRRSST	proteoses
EELLSSSXY	sexlessly	EELRRSSTW	wrestlers	EEOOPRSSX	exospores
EELMMNOTU	emolument	EELRSSTTU	utterless	EEOOPRSTZ	zoetropes
EELMNNORT	enrolment	EEMMNNOSY	Mnemosyne	EEOORRTWW	overwrote
EELMNOSSS	solemness	EEMMNOORT	metronome	EEOOSSSTX	exostosis
EELMNOSSV	venomless		monometer	EEOOSSTTV	ovotestes
EELMNOTTX	extolment		monotreme	EEOPPRSSS	oppresses
EELMOOPST	leptosome	EEMMNOSTV	movements	EEOPPRSSU	superpose
EELMOPRSY	employers	EEMMOORST	osmometer	EEOPRRRSS	repressor
	reemploys	EEMMORTYZ	zymometer	EEOPRRRST	reporters
EELMOPRTU	petroleum	EEMMNOPRS	prenomens	EEOPRRRSV	reprovers
EELMORSST	molesters	EEMMNOPST	penstemon	EEOPRRRTY	repertory
EELMORTTV	voltmeter	EEMMNORWY	New Romney	EEOPRRSTT	potterers
EELMORTUV	volumeter	EEMNOORTT	tonometer		protester
EELMOSTVW	twelvemos	EEMNOOSTT	tomentose	EEOPRRSTX	exporters
EELMPRSUY	supremely	EEMNOPRYZ	proenzyme		reexports
EELMRRSTU	murrelets	EEMNORRTT	tormenter	EEOPRSSSS	espressos
EELNNOOUV	Nuevo León	EEMNORRTV	Vermonter		repossess
EELNNOPRS	personnel	EEMNORRTY	Monterrey	EEOPRSSSU	espousers
EELNNOSSY	Lyonnesse	EEMNORSTY	oystermen		repousses
EELNNRSTU	tunnelers	EEMNRSTVY	vestrymen	EEOPRSSSX	expressos
EELNOORSS	looseners	EEMNSSTTV	vestments	EEOPRSSTV	oversteps
EELNOOSSS	looseness	EEMOOOSTT	osteotome	EEOPRSSUX	exposures

EEOPRTTWV	typewrote	**EFGGIINNR**	fingering	**EFGINORSW**	forewings
EEOPSSSSS	possesses	**EFGGILNNU**	engulfing	**EFGINORTU**	foutering
EEOPSSSTW	sweetsops	**EFGGILOOS**	solfeggio	**EFGINPRSU**	perfusing
EEOPSSTTU	poussette	**EFGGINOOR**	foregoing	**EFGINRRTU**	returfing
EEOQRSSTU	torqueses	**EFGGINORR**	reforging	**EFGIOPSTT**	pettifogs
EEORRRSST	resorters	**EFGGINOSS**	fogginess	**EFGIORRSV**	forgivers
	restorers	**EFGHHIILR**	highflier	**EFGKNSTUU**	K'ung Fu-tse
EEORRRSTT	retorters	**EFGHHILRY**	highflyer	**EFGLLNTUY**	fulgently
EEORRRSTU	retrousse	**EFGHHIOSS**	hogfishes	**EFGLOOSVX**	foxgloves
EEORRSSTT	totterers	**EFGHIILNT**	nightlife	**EFGNOORTT**	forgotten
EEORRSSTX	extorters	**EFGHIILRT**	flightier	**EFGOOOOST**	goosefoot
EEORRSTUV	overtures	**EFGHIINRT**	infighter	**EFHHIISTW**	whitefish
	trouveres	**EFGHIIPSS**	pigfishes	**EFHHILLSS**	shellfish
EEORRTTVX	extrovert	**EFGHILNSS**	fleshings	**EFHIILSTT**	filthiest
EEORSSSTV	votresses	**EFGHILPRT**	preflight	**EFHIIMSST**	fetishism
EEORSTTTZ	terzettos	**EFGHILTWY**	flyweight	**EFHIINPSS**	pinfishes
EEPRRSSST	prestress	**EFGHINRST**	frightens		snipefish
EEPRRSSSU	pressures	**EFGHIOOSS**	goosefish	**EFHIINRSS**	finishers
EEPRRSTTU	putterers	**EFGHIORST**	foresight	**EFHIINSSS**	fishiness
	sputterer	**EFGIIILNS**	lignifies	**EFHIIORRS**	horrifies
EEPRSSTTU	upsetters	**EFGIIINRS**	signifier	**EFHIIRRTT**	thriftier
EERRSSSTU	tressures	**EFGIIINSS**	signifies	**EFHIISSTT**	fetishist
EERRSSUVY	resurveys	**EFGIILLNR**	refilling		shiftiest
EERRSTTTU	stutterer	**EFGIILLNT**	filleting	**EFHIISSVW**	fishwives
EFFFILSTU	fluffiest	**EFGIILMNR**	refilming	**EFHIJLLSY**	jellyfish
EFFFKLRUU	kurfuffle	**EFGIILNPR**	pilfering	**EFHILLSSW**	swellfish
EFFFLORTU	effortful	**EFGIILNRT**	filtering	**EFHILLSSY**	selfishly
EFFGGINOR	goffering	**EFGIILNSU**	figulines	**EFHILMNOS**	lemonfish
EFFGHIIRT	firefight	**EFGIILORR**	glorifier	**EFHILNSSU**	unselfish
EFFGINORS	offerings	**EFGIILORS**	glorifies	**EFHILSSST**	shiftless
EFFGINRSU	suffering	**EFGIILRSU**	uglifiers	**EFHIMOPRZ**	Pforzheim
EFFGLORTU	forgetful	**EFGIINNRR**	inferring	**EFHINORRT**	firethorn
EFFGNRSSU	gruffness		infringer	**EFHINOSST**	stonefish
EFFHIISTT	fiftieths	**EFGIINNRS**	infringes	**EFHINRRSU**	furnisher
EFFHIISTW	whiffiest	**EFGIINNSS**	finessing		refurnish
EFFHIKSWW	skewwhiff	**EFGIINNST**	infesting	**EFHINRSSU**	furnishes
EFFHILRSW	whifflers	**EFGIINPRT**	fingertip	**EFHINSSSU**	sunfishes
EFFHINSSU	huffiness	**EFGIINPRX**	prefixing	**EFHIORSTT**	fortieths
EFFHLRSSU	shufflers	**EFGIINRSU**	figurines		frothiest
EFFIIMNSS	miffiness	**EFGIINRTT**	refitting	**EFHIORRSTU**	thurifers
EFFIINSST	sniffiest	**EFGIINRVY**	verifying	**EFHLLLPUY**	helpfully
EFFIIORRT	fortifier	**EFGIISTUV**	fugitives	**EFHLLNPUU**	unhelpful
EFFIIORST	fortifies	**EFGILLNOW**	fellowing	**EFHLLOPUY**	hopefully
EFFIIPSST	spiffiest	**EFGILLNRU**	fullering	**EFHLLOSST**	softshell
EFFIIQRSU	squiffier	**EFGILNNNU**	funneling	**EFHLLOSUV**	shovelful
EFFILLLRU	fulfiller	**EFGILNORW**	flowering	**EFHLNSSSU**	flushness
EFFILMUUV	effluvium	**EFGILNORY**	foreignly	**EFHLOOPSU**	flophouse
EFFILNRSS	snifflers	**EFGILNRRU**	ferruling	**EFHLOPSST**	fleshpots
EFFINOSSU	effusions	**EFGILNRUX**	refluxing	**EFHNOORSW**	foreshown
EFFINPRSU	puffiness	**EFGILPRSU**	fireplugs	**EFHNORTUX**	foxhunter
EFFINSSST	stiffness	**EFGILRTUU**	fulgurite	**EFHOOORTT**	foretooth
EFFINSSTU	snuffiest	**EFGIMNNOT**	fomenting	**EFHOORSSW**	foreshows
EFFIOOPRR	fireproof	**EFGIMNORR**	reforming	**EFIIILRSV**	vilifiers
EFFIORRTY	refortify	**EFGIMNPRU**	perfuming	**EFIIINRST**	nitrifies
EFFISSTTU	stuffiest	**EFGIMNTUY**	tumefying	**EFIIIRSTV**	vitrifies
EFFISSUUV	suffusive	**EFGINNOST**	softening	**EFIIIRSVV**	vivifiers
EFFLLRTUY	fretfully	**EFGINNRYZ**	frenzying	**EFIIJLLOS**	jollifies
EFFLMNSUU	unmuffles	**EFGINOORR**	reroofing	**EFIIJRSTU**	justifier
EFFLNRSSU	snufflers	**EFGINOORT**	footering	**EFIIJSSTU**	justifies
EFFNOORRT	forefront	**EFGINOOSS**	goofiness	**EFIIKLRTU**	fruitlike
EFFOORRTY	offertory	**EFGINORST**	foresting	**EFIIKRSST**	friskiest
EFFORSTUV	overstuff		fostering	**EFIILLMOR**	mollifier

EFIILLMOS	mollifies	EFILNOSST	loftiness	EFLNORSTT	frontlets
EFIILLNRU	nullifier	EFILOPPST	floppiest	EFLNORSUW	sunflower
EFIILLNSU	nullifies	EFILOPRRS	profilers	EFLOOOOST	footloose
EFIILLRST	fillister	EFILORRSV	frivolers	EFLOOPRTW	flowerpot
EFIILMNSS	filminess	EFILOSSST	flossiest	EFLOORSVW	overflows
EFIILMOTT	leitmotif	EFILPRSTU	uplifters	EFLOOSTTW	Lowestoft
EFIILMSST	flimsiest	EFILQRUUV	quiverful	EFLOPRSUY	profusely
EFIILNNOX	inflexion	EFILRRSZZ	frizzlers	EFLORRRTU	terrorful
EFIILNSTT	flintiest	EFILRSSTU	fruitless	EFLRSSSTU	stressful
EFIILOPSV	spoilfive	EFILRTUVY	furtively	EFLRSSTUU	frustules
EFIILOSSS	fossilise	EFILSSTTW	swiftlets	EFMOOPRRR	proreform
EFIILOSSZ	fossilize	EFIMMORRS	reformism	EFMOORSSU	foursomes
EFIILRRZZ	frizzlier	EFIMMORRV	vermiform	EFNNOOORS	forenoons
EFIILRSST	filisters	EFIMNORRS	informers	EFNNOPRUY	fourpenny
EFIILRSSU	fusiliers		reinforms	EFNOOOSTT	footnotes
EFIILRTTY	fertility	EFIMORRRS	serriform	EFOOOPRST	footropes
EFIIMMMSU	mummifies	EFIMORRST	firestorm	EFOOPRRSS	professor
EFIIMNSST	feminists		reformist	EFOOPSSTT	footsteps
EFIIMORRT	mortifier		restiform	EFOORSSTT	footrests
EFIIMORST	mortifies	EFINNNSSU	funniness	EFORRRSUW	furrowers
EFIIMRSTU	mortifies	EFINNSSTU	unfitness	EGGGIIJNR	rejigging
EFIIMRSTY	mystifier	EFINOPRSU	perfusion	EGGGIILST	giggliest
EFIIMSSTY	mystifies	EFINOPRSY	personify	EGGGIINNR	gingering
EFIINNNOT	nonfinite	EFINORRST	frontiers	EGGGIINOR	engorging
EFIINNSST	niftiness	EFINOSTVW	Five Towns	EGGGINNPU	unpegging
EFIINNSTY	intensify	EFINRRSSU	furriness	EGGGINORR	regorging
EFIINOPRX	prefixion	EFINRRTUU	furniture	EGGGIORST	groggiest
EFIINOPST	pontifies	EFINRSSTU	turfiness	EGGGOOOSS	goosegogs
EFIINORRS	inferiors	EFINRSSUU	unfussier	EGGHIILNS	sleighing
EFIINORST	notifiers	EFINSSSSU	fussiness	EGGHIINNR	rehinging
EFIINSSZZ	fizziness	EFINSSSTU	fustiness	EGGHIINNW	whingeing
EFIIORRTU	fioriture	EFINSSSTW	swiftness	EGGHIINTW	weighting
EFIIORSSS	ossifiers	EFINSSUZZ	fuzziness	EGGHIKSSW	eggwhisks
EFIIPPSUY	yuppifies	EFIOORSUV	oviferous	EGGHILNPU	pleughing
EFIIPRRSU	purifiers	EFIOPRRST	portfires	EGGHINNRU	hungering
EFIIPRSST	spitfires		profiters	EGGIIJLST	jiggliest
EFIIPRSTY	typifiers	EFIOPSSTX	postfixes	EGGIILMNT	gimleting
EFIIRSSSU	russifies	EFIORRSTT	retrofits	EGGIILNNO	eloigning
EFIIRSTTU	fruitiest	EFIORRSTW	frowstier	EGGIILNNR	lingering
EFIIRSTZZ	frizziest	EFIORSSTT	frostiest	EGGIILNST	niggliest
EFIISTTVY	festivity	EFIORSSTW	frowsiest	EGGIILSTW	wiggliest
EFIKLNSSU	flukiness	EFIORSTUZ	frouziest	EGGIIMMNR	immerging
EFIKLORST	frostlike	EFIORSTWZ	frowziest	EGGIINNRS	resigning
EFIKLOSST	folksiest	EFIORTTTU	outfitter	EGGIINNST	ingesting
EFIKLRSTY	flystrike	EFKLMNOOW	womenfolk		signeting
EFIKNORSS	foreskins	EFKLMOOST	folkmotes	EGGIINNSW	swingeing
EFIKNRSSU	refusniks	EFKNNOORW	foreknown	EGGIINOOR	Giorgione
EFIKOOPRV	Prokofiev	EFKNOOPRS	forspoken	EGGIINOPR	Prigogine
EFIKORRSW	fireworks	EFKNOORSW	foreknows	EGGIINRSV	grievings
EFILLLNSU	fluellins	EFKNRSSTU	funksters	EGGIISTTW	twiggiest
EFILLMOPU	filoplume	EFLLLOOSW	woolfells	EGGIJNSSU	jugginses
EFILLNPTU	plentiful	EFLLMOSUY	fulsomely	EGGILLNRU	gruelling
EFILLORRV	frivoller	EFLLMSUUY	musefully	EGGILLNUY	gulleying
EFILLORSV	overfills	EFLLNTUUY	tunefully	EGGILNORV	groveling
EFILMNORT	lentiform	EFLLOORSW	followers	EGGILNORW	glowering
EFILMNOSY	solemnify	EFLLRSTUY	restfully	EGGILNRSS	snigglers
EFILMOPRX	plexiform	EFLLSTUYZ	zestfully	EGGILNRSU	gruelings
EFILMORSW	wormflies	EFLMMOSUX	flummoxes	EGGILOOST	geologist
EFILNNORT	frontline	EFLNNTUUU	untuneful	EGGILQRSU	squiggler
EFILNNSTU	influents	EFLNOORVW	overflown	EGGILQSSU	squiggles
EFILNOORS	solferino	EFLNOPRTU	profluent	EGGILRRSW	wrigglers
EFILNOOSU	felonious	EFLNORSST	frontless	EGGIMNNOR	mongering
EFILNORTW	interflow				

EGGIMNSSU	mugginess	**EGHILNNOR**	Lohengrin	**EGHNOSSTU**	toughness
EGGINNNOR	Groningen	**EGHILNOPR**	negrophil	**EGHNRSSTT**	strengths
EGGINNORV	governing	**EGHILNORS**	Helsingør	**EGHOOOSSW**	hoosegows
EGGINNOTT	Göttingen	**EGHILNOST**	hosteling	**EGHOOPSUY**	hypogeous
EGGINNPRU	repugning	**EGHILNOSU**	houseling	**EGHOPTYYZ**	zygophyte
EGGINNPUX	expunging	**EGHILNOSV**	shoveling	**EGHORRSTW**	regrowths
EGGINORRS	gorgerins	**EGHILNRSS**	shinglers	**EGIIIMNST**	itemising
EGGINORRW	regrowing	**EGHILNSST**	lightness	**EGIIIMNTZ**	itemizing
EGGINORST	gostering		nightless	**EGIIJLNST**	jingliest
EGGINOSSS	sogginess	**EGHILNSTU**	sleuthing	**EGIIJNNNO**	enjoining
EGGINRRSU	resurging	**EGHILNSUW**	gluhweins	**EGIIJNNOR**	rejoining
EGGINRSTU	gesturing	**EGHILOORS**	shooglier	**EGIIJNRTT**	jittering
	grungiest	**EGHILOORV**	hierology	**EGIIKLNST**	kingliest
EGGINRTTU	guttering	**EGHILORST**	ghostlier	**EGIIKNNRT**	tinkering
EGGINSSTU	gusseting	**EGHILPRST**	plighters	**EGIIKNPPR**	kippering
EGGIORRTU	outrigger	**EGHILPRTU**	uplighter	**EGIIKNRSS**	Kissinger
EGGIORRXY	Gregory IX	**EGHILSSST**	sightless	**EGIIKRSTZ**	sitzkrieg
EGGIPRRSS	spriggers	**EGHILSSTT**	slightest	**EGIILLMNP**	impelling
EGGLMMOOY	gemmology	**EGHIMNORT**	mothering	**EGIILLNNO**	nielloing
EGGLMRSSU	smugglers	**EGHIMNOST**	something	**EGIILLNOR**	gorilline
EGGLRRSTU	struggler	**EGHIMPPSU**	pemphigus	**EGIILLNRT**	tillering
EGGLRSSTU	struggles	**EGHINNSST**	sennights	**EGIILMMNS**	immingles
EGHHIIORS	Hiroshige	**EGHINNSTU**	enthusing	**EGIILNNOT**	entoiling
EGHHINNPY	hyphening	**EGHINOORV**	hoovering	**EGIILNNST**	enlisting
EGHHINRST	threshing	**EGHINOPRT**	pothering		listening
EGHHIPRSU	superhigh	**EGHINORSU**	rehousing		tinseling
EGHHMOTTU	methought	**EGHINORSW**	showering	**EGIILNNSV**	sniveling
EGHHNORUW	roughhewn	**EGHINORTV**	overnight	**EGIILNNTT**	entitling
EGHHNOUZZ	Zhengzhou	**EGHINORTX**	exhorting		inletting
EGHHOPPVY	hypophyge	**EGHINOSST**	histogens	**EGIILNNUV**	unveiling
EGHHORSUW	roughhews	**EGHINOSTU**	noughties	**EGIILNORS**	religions
EGHHORTTU	rethought	**EGHINOSTY**	histogeny	**EGIILNORT**	loitering
EGHIIKLNT	nightlike	**EGHINPRSY**	syphering	**EGIILNOST**	gilsonite
EGHIIKNRS	shrieking	**EGHINRSST**	rightness	**EGIILNPSS**	singspiel
EGHIILLMT	limelight	**EGHINRSTU**	hungriest	**EGIILNRSS**	rieslings
EGHIILNRS	hirelings	**EGHINRTUW**	wuthering	**EGIILNRST**	relisting
	relishing	**EGHINSSSU**	gushiness	**EGIILNRSV**	silvering
EGHIILNSS	shielings	**EGHINSSTT**	tightness		slivering
EGHIILNST	sightline	**EGHIOPRTT**	tightrope	**EGIILNRTT**	littering
EGHIILRST	sightlier	**EGHIORRST**	righteous		retitling
EGHIILTWY	weightily	**EGHIORSTV**	oversight	**EGIILNSVW**	swiveling
EGHIIMMNS	immeshing	**EGHIOSTUW**	outweighs	**EGIILNTTY**	gentility
EGHIIMNNS	inmeshing	**EGHIRSTTU**	theurgist	**EGIILOPST**	epilogist
EGHIIMNTT	nighttime	**EGHLLOPSU**	plugholes	**EGIILORST**	trilogies
EGHIIMSTT	mightiest	**EGHLMNOPU**	ploughmen	**EGIILORSU**	religious
EGHIINNTW	whitening	**EGHLMOOOU**	homologue	**EGIILRRST**	gristlier
EGHIINPRS	perishing	**EGHLNOOPY**	nephology	**EGIILRRZZ**	grizzlier
EGHIINRSV	shivering		phenology	**EGIILRSST**	grisliest
EGHIINRTW	withering	**EGHLNOORS**	longshore	**EGIILRSTU**	liturgies
EGHIINSTY	hygienist	**EGHLNOOSU**	longhouse	**EGIILRSZZ**	grizzlies
EGHIIRSTZ	rightsize	**EGHLNOOTY**	ethnology	**EGIILSTTU**	guiltiest
EGHIISSTY	hygieists	**EGHLNOPYY**	phylogeny	**EGIILSTTZ**	glitziest
EGHIKLOST	ghostlike	**EGHLOOORR**	horologer		Stieglitz
EGHIKNNRU	hunkering	**EGHLOOORS**	horologes	**EGIIMMNRS**	immersing
EGHILLMOT	megilloth	**EGHLOPRSU**	ploughers		simmering
EGHILLNOR	hollering	**EGHLORSTU**	Gütersloh	**EGIIMNNRT**	reminting
EGHILLNOV	hovelling	**EGHMNOORW**	homegrown	**EGIIMNPRS**	impingers
EGHILLNTY	lengthily	**EGHMOOPSS**	gomphoses		premising
EGHILLSST	lightless	**EGHNOOOPR**	gonophore		simpering
EGHILMNNU	unhelming	**EGHNOOPRY**	gynophore	**EGIIMNPRX**	premixing
EGHILMORS	homegirls	**EGHNOPTYY**	phytogeny	**EGIIMNRSS**	griminess
EGHILMOST	lightsome	**EGHNORSSU**	roughness	**EGIIMNRST**	mistering

EGIIMNRTT	remitting	**EGIIJLNSTY**	jestingly	**EGILNRSTU**	lustering
EGIIMNSTY	stymieing	**EGIJNPRRU**	perjuring		resulting
EGIIHOPST	impetigos	**EGIKLLNSY**	skellying	**EGILNRSTW**	wrestling
EGIIMORRS	grimoires	**EGIKLNN00**	inglenook	**EGILNRSTY**	restyling
EGIINNNPR	repinning	**EGIKMNNOV**	monkeying	**EGILNSSTT**	settlings
EGIINNNRT	interning	**EGIKNNOTY**	keynoting	**EGIL000SZ**	zoologies
EGIINNNRV	innerving	**EGIKNORRW**	reworking	**EGIL00SSU**	isologues
EGIINNNTV	inventing	**EGILLLNTY**	tellingly	**EGILOSSST**	glossiest
EGIINNNTW	entwining	**EGILLMNOW**	mellowing	**EGILOSSTT**	glottises
EGIINNORS	nigrosine	**EGILLMNTY**	meltingly	**EGILOSSTU**	eulogists
	signorine	**EGILLMORU**	glomeruli	**EGILRRSZZ**	grizzlers
EGIINNORT	orienting	**EGILLMOTU**	guillemot	**EGILRSSTY**	greylists
EGIINNOST	ingestion	**EGILLNNOR**	enrolling	**EGIMMNNOU**	immunogen
EGIINNOSU	ingenious	**EGILLNNOT**	Ellington	**EGIMMNRSU**	summering
EGIINNQRU	enquiring	**EGILLNORW**	rowelling	**EGIMMNSSU**	gumminess
EGIINNRRT	interring	**EGILLNOTW**	towelling	**EGIMNNORT**	mentoring
EGIINNRST	inserting	**EGILLNOTX**	extolling	**EGIMNORRT**	tremoring
	sintering	**EGILLNOUU**	Longueuil	**EGIMNORST**	Germiston
EGIINNRSW	inswinger	**EGILLNOVY**	volleying	**EGIMNORSV**	misgovern
EGIINNRTU	reuniting	**EGILLNOWY**	yellowing	**EGIMNPRSU**	impugners
EGIINNRTV	inverting	**EGILLNPSS**	spellings		presuming
EGIINNRTW	wintering	**EGILLNSSW**	swellings	**EGIMNPRTU**	permuting
EGIINNSTT	insetting	**EGILLNSTU**	glutelins	**EGIMNRSSY**	synergism
EGIINNSTV	investing	**EGILL00RS**	glorioles	**EGIMNRSTU**	mustering
EGIINNTUY	ingenuity	**EGILLOSSY**	syllogise	**EGIMNRSUY**	eryngiums
EGIINOPRS	peignoirs	**EGILLOSYZ**	syllogize	**EGIMNRTTU**	muttering
EGIINOPST	poetising	**EGILLSSTU**	guiltless	**EGIMPRSTU**	grumpiest
EGIINOPTT	tiptoeing	**EGILMMNOP**	pommeling	**EGINNNOST**	sonneting
EGIINOPTZ	poetizing	**EGILMMNPU**	pummeling	**EGINNNRRU**	rerunning
EGIINORSS	seigniors	**EGILMN00S**	neologism	**EGINNNRUV**	unnerving
	signories	**EGILMNOPY**	employing	**EGINNOORT**	enrooting
EGIINORST	sortieing	**EGILMNOST**	molesting	**EGINNORRT**	Tengri Nor
EGIINORSY	seigniory	**EGILMOORS**	oligomers	**EGINNORSV**	vignerons
EGIINPPQU	equipping	**EGILM00ST**	gloomiest	**EGINNORSW**	worsening
EGIINPPST	peptising	**EGILM00SY**	myologies	**EGINNOSUU**	ingenuous
EGIINPPTT	pipetting		semiology	**EGINNRRTU**	returning
EGIINPPTZ	peptizing	**EGILMOSUU**	eulogiums	**EGINNRSTT**	stringent
EGIINPQRU	repiquing	**EGILMPRSS**	glimpsers	**EGINNRSTU**	insurgent
EGIINPRRS	reprising	**EGILNNNTU**	tunneling	**EGINNRTUV**	venturing
	respiring	**EGILNN00S**	loosening	**EGIN00SSS**	goosiness
	springier	**EGILNN0SS**	lessoning	**EGIN00SSU**	isogenous
EGIINPRST	priesting	**EGILNNOST**	singleton	**EGINOPPST**	estopping
	respiting	**EGILNNOSU**	ensouling	**EGINOPRRR**	porringer
EGIINPRSV	prevising	**EGILNNOSW**	lowsening	**EGINOPRRT**	reporting
EGIINQRRU	requiring	**EGILNNOTX**	Lexington	**EGINOPRRV**	reproving
EGIINQRSU	esquiring	**EGILNNRSU**	nurseling	**EGINOPRST**	progestin
EGIINQRTU	requiting	**EGILNNSST**	nestlings	**EGINOPRTT**	pottering
EGIINQRUV	quivering	**EGILNNVYY**	envyingly		repotting
EGIINRRST	stringier	**EGILNOORT**	retooling	**EGINOPRTX**	exporting
EGIINRRTU	intriguer	**EGILN00ST**	enologist	**EGINOPSST**	spongiest
EGIINRRTW	rewriting		neologist	**EGINOPSSU**	espousing
EGIINRRST	resisting	**EGILN00SU**	sinologue	**EGINOPSUY**	epigynous
EGIINRSTT	resitting	**EGILNOPRX**	exploring	**EGINOQRTU**	roqueting
EGIINRSTU	intrigues	**EGILNORSV**	resolving	**EGINORRST**	resorting
EGIINRTTT	tittering	**EGILNORTV**	revolting		restoring
EGIINRTTW	wittering	**EGILNORTW**	troweling		rostering
EGIINRTTY	integrity	**EGILNORVV**	revolving	**EGINORRTT**	retorting
EGIINSSTT	stingiest	**EGILNORVY**	overlying	**EGINORRTU**	rerouting
EGIINSSTW	swingiest	**EGILNOTVY**	longevity	**EGINORSTT**	gritstone
EGIIRSTTT	grittiest	**EGILNPRST**	springlet	**EGINORSTY**	oystering
EGIJKNNTU	junketing	**EGILNPRSU**	repulsing	**EGINORSUV**	overusing
EGIJLNSTU	jungliest	**EGILNRSSW**	newsgirls	**EGINORSVW**	wingovers

EGINORTTT	tottering	**EGNNNRRUU**	gunrunner	**EHIIRSTTT**	tritheist
EGINORTTX	extorting	**EGNNOOPRT**	Negropont	**EHIIRSTTZ**	zitherist
EGINOSSTU	goutiness	**EGNNORSSW**	wrongness	**EHIISSTTT**	shittiest
EGINPPRSU	suppering	**EGNOOPORS**	gonopores	**EHIISSTTX**	sixtieths
EGINPRRSS	springers	**EGNOOPRSS**	prognoses	**EHIISTWZZ**	whizziest
EGINPRSSS	pressings	**EGNOORRSV**	governors	**EHIJMNOTU**	Jotunheim
EGINPRTTU	puttering	**EGNOORRVW**	overgrown	**EHIKLLPSY**	sylphlike
EGINPRTTY	prettying	**EGNOORSUU**	urogenous	**EHIKLMNPY**	nymphlike
EGINPRUVY	purveying	**EGNOOSTUX**	oxtongues	**EHIKLNOSS**	sinkholes
EGINPSTTU	upsetting	**EGNOOSUXY**	oxygenous	**EHIKLNPRY**	hyperlink
EGINPSTWW	sweptwing	**EGNOPPRSU**	oppugners	**EHIKLOOST**	tikoloshe
EGINRRSST	restrings	**EGNOPRSUW**	newsgroup	**EHIKLOOTT**	toothlike
	ringsters	**EGNORSSSS**	grossness	**EHIKLORTZ**	kilohertz
	stringers	**EGNORSSST**	songsters	**EHIKNOSST**	shonkiest
EGINRSSST	stressing	**EGNORSSTT**	strongest	**EHIKNPRRS**	preshrink
EGINRSSTY	synergist	**EGNORSSTU**	sturgeons	**EHIKNRRSS**	shrinkers
EGINRSTUV	vesturing	**EGNORSTUY**	youngster	**EHIKNSSSU**	huskiness
EGINRSUVY	surveying	**EGOOPPRSU**	prorogues	**EHIKORRSY**	Yorkshire
EGINRTTUX	texturing	**EGOOPRSYZ**	zygospore	**EHILLLMOS**	molehills
EGINSSSTU	gustiness	**EGOORRSVW**	overgrows	**EHILLMOPS**	philomels
EGINSTTTU	tungstite	**EGOPPRTTU**	gruppetto	**EHILLOSTY**	hostilely
EGIOORSTV	grooviest	**EHHIIPRSS**	heirships	**EHILLOSWY**	yellowish
EGIOORSUV	ovigerous	**EHHIIRTTT**	thirtieth	**EHILLRRST**	thrillers
EGIOPRSSS	gossipers	**EHHILLLSY**	hellishly	**EHILLRSST**	shrillest
EGIORSTTT	grottiest	**EHHILMNST**	helminths	**EHILMNOST**	monthlies
EGIORSTTU	groutiest	**EHHILMOOP**	homophile	**EHILMNOSY**	hemolysin
EGIPPRRTU	gruppetti	**EHHIMPRSU**	Humphries	**EHILMOORS**	heirlooms
EGIPSTUZZ	Zugspitze	**EHHINOPPS**	phosphine	**EHILMOSSY**	hemolysis
EGJLNORSU	jongleurs	**EHHINORTW**	nowhither	**EHILMPPRY**	perilymph
EGJLNOSTU	jelutongs	**EHHIOPPST**	phosphite	**EHILMPSSY**	symphiles
EGKORSSUW	guesswork	**EHHIOPRSW**	horsewhip	**EHILMRSST**	mirthless
EGLLLOORR	logroller	**EHHIORSST**	horseshit	**EHILMRSTU**	Lutherism
EGLLMNORY	mongrelly	**EHHIORTTT**	thitherto	**EHILMRSUV**	Hilversum
EGLLMOOSS	gloomless	**EHHIOSTVY**	yeshivoth	**EHILNOOPT**	lithopone
EGLLMORSW	gromwells	**EHHLLMOTZ**	Helmholtz		phonolite
EGLLOOPRS	gollopers	**EHHLOOPTY**	holophyte	**EHILNOPST**	tholepins
EGLLOSSSS	glossless	**EHHMMNNOPP**	Phnom Penh	**EHILNOSST**	holsteins
EGLMNOOOU	monologue	**EHHMMNOOP**	homophone	**EHILNOSTU**	unholiest
EGLMOORTY	metrology	**EHHMRTUYY**	eurhythmy	**EHILNOSTX**	xenoliths
EGLMOOSUY	museology	**EHHNOORSS**	shoehorns	**EHILNOSUY**	heinously
EGLMOOTYY	etymology	**EHHOOPSTY**	theosophy	**EHILOOPSZ**	zoophiles
EGLMOPRSU	promulges	**EHHOOSSTU**	hothouses	**EHILOPRSS**	polishers
EGLNNOORS	longerons	**EHIIILLMW**	Wilhelm II	**EHILOPRST**	heliports
EGLNNPTUY	pungently	**EHIIINRVY**	Henry VIII	**EHILOPRXY**	xerophily
EGLNOOOPY	poenology	**EHIIKNSTT**	kittenish	**EHILOPSST**	isopleths
EGLNOOPRR	prolonger	**EHIILNTTW**	lintwhite	**EHILOPTYY**	heliotypy
EGLNOOPRS	prolonges	**EHIILRSTW**	Wiltshire	**EHILPSSTU**	sulphites
EGLNOORUY	neurology	**EHIIMRSTT**	tritheism	**EHILPSTTY**	pettishly
EGLNOOSUV	longevous	**EHIIMSSTW**	whimsiest	**EHILRSSTW**	whistlers
EGLNORSTY	strongyle	**EHIINNORT**	ornithine	**EHILRSTTW**	whittlers
EGLNORSUU	longueurs	**EHIINNRSS**	inshrines	**EHILSSSTU**	slushiest
EGLNOSTUU	glutenous	**EHIINNSSS**	shininess	**EHIMMNSUY**	hymeniums
EGLNRTTUY	turgently	**EHIINOPST**	Tisiphone	**EHIMNNOOS**	moonshine
EGLOOORTY	erotology	**EHIINORRT**	inheritor	**EHIMNOPRS**	premonish
EGLOOOSTY	osteology	**EHIINPRST**	nephritis	**EHIMNOPUU**	euphonium
EGLOOPRSU	prologues		phrenitis	**EHIMNORST**	horsemint
EGLOOPRTY	petrology	**EHIINPSST**	pithiness		thermions
EGLOOPSTY	logotypes	**EHIINRSTW**	winterish	**EHIMNOSTT**	monteiths
EGMMNOORS	groomsmen	**EHIIORSST**	histories	**EHIMNPSST**	shipments
EGMNNORST	strongmen	**EHIIPPSSY**	epiphysis	**EHIMNPSSU**	humpiness
EGMNOOOSS	gonosomes	**EHIIRRSTT**	thirstier	**EHIMNRTUU**	ruthenium
	mongooses	**EHIIRSSTT**	shirtiest	**EHIMNSSSU**	mushiness

EHIMNSTTU	tunesmith
EHIMOOSST	smoothies
EHIMOPPRR	perimorph
EHIMOPRTY	hemitropy
EHIMORSST	isotherms
EHIMOSTTU	mouthiest
	Thutmose I
EHIMPRRSS	shrimpers
EHIMPRRTU	triumpher
EHIMPSSUU	euphuisms
EHIMRRSTY	erythrism
EHIMSSSTU	isthmuses
EHINNOPSS	phoniness
EHINNOPTY	phenytoin
EHINNORSS	horniness
EHINNOSTW	whinstone
EHINNSSSU	sunshines
EHINOOOPR	ionophore
EHINOOPSS	isophones
EHINOPPRS	hornpipes
EHINOPRSS	nephrosis
EHINOPRSW	ownership
	shipowner
EHINOPSTT	phonetist
EHINOPSTY	hypnotise
EHINOPSVY	envoyship
EHINOPTYZ	hypnotize
EHINORRSU	nourisher
EHINORSSS	horsiness
EHINORSSU	nourishes
EHINORSSW	Weisshorn
EHINORSTT	thorniest
EHINORTXY	thyroxine
EHINOSSSW	showiness
EHINOSSTU	outshines
EHINPPSTU	unhippest
EHINPRRTY	pyrethrin
EHINPRSSU	punishers
EHINPSSSU	pushiness
EHINRSSSU	rushiness
EHINSSSTY	synthesis
EHIOOPRTW	wirephoto
EHIOOSTTT	toothiest
EHIOPRSST	prothesis
	sophister
EHIORSSTT	theorists
EHIORSTTW	worthiest
EHIORSTWZ	howitzers
EHIOSSSTU	stoushies
EHIOSSTTU	shoutiest
EHIOSTTUW	whiteouts
EHIPQSSUY	physiques
EHIPRSSTW	whipsters
EHIPSSTUU	euphuists
EHIRRSSTT	thirsters
EHIRSTTTW	whittrets
EHJOOSSSU	joss house
EHKKLOOSS	kolkhoses
EHKKLOOSZ	kolkhozes
EHKLNOOST	knotholes
EHKLOOOST	tokoloshe
EHKNNOORS	nonkosher

EHKNOOOSS	hooknoses
EHKNPRRSU	preshrunk
EHKOORRSW	workhorse
EHKOORSUW	housework
	workhouse
EHLLMOPSY	mesophyll
	phyllomes
EHLLNSSTU	nutshells
EHLLOOOPS	loopholes
EHLLOOSTU	tollhouse
EHLLOSTUW	Southwell
EHLMOORSW	wormholes
EHLMORSSU	humorless
EHLNOOPPY	polyphone
EHLNOOPXY	xylophone
EHLNOORSS	honorless
EHLNOOSTY	holystone
EHLNOPSSU	sulphones
EHLNORRTY	northerly
EHLNORSST	thornless
EHLNPSSSU	plushness
EHLOOPRST	portholes
	potholers
EHLOOPSSS	sploooshes
EHLOOPSTU	South Pole
EHLOOPSTY	holotypes
EHLOOSSTT	toothless
EHLOPRSTU	upholster
EHLOPSTYY	hypostyle
EHLORRTTT	throttler
EHLORSSTT	throstles
EHLORSSTW	worthless
EHLORSTTT	throttles
EHLORSTUY	southerly
EHLORTTUW	Lower Hutt
EHLOSSTUY	youthless
EHLPRSTUU	sulphuret
EHLRSSTTU	truthless
EHMMOOPRS	mesomorph
EHMMOORSU	humorsome
EHMMRRSTU	thrummers
EHMNNOOOY	honeymoon
EHMNOOSST	smoothens
EHMNOTTUY	Tynemouth
EHMOOOPRS	sophomore
EHMOOORSU	houseroom
EHMOOOSTT	toothsome
EHMOOPRSS	morphoses
EHMOORSST	smoothers
EHMOOSSTT	smoothest
EHMOOSSUU	houmouses
EHMORSTUV	vermouths
EHMPRRTUY	pyrethrum
EHMPSSSYY	symphyses
EHNNOORST	hornstone
EHNNORSTU	unthrones
EHNNPRTUY	thrupenny
EHNOOOPPT	optophone
EHNOOORTT	orthotone
EHNOOPPTY	phonotype
EHNOORRSU	honourers
EHNOORSSW	snowshoer

	whoresons
EHNOORSTW	honeworts
EHNOOSSSW	snowshoes
EHNOOSSUY	Syon House
EHNOOSTUW	townhouse
EHNOOTTTT	hottentot
EHNOPRTTU	pothunter
EHNOPSSTY	pythoness
EHNORSSST	shortness
EHNORSTTW	northwest
	North West
EHNORTTWW	Wentworth
EHNOSSTUU	nuthouses
EHOOOPRSU	poorhouse
EHOOORSTV	overshoot
EHOOPPTTY	phototype
EHOOPRRTT	orthopter
EHOOPRRTV	hoverport
EHOOPRSST	posthorse
EHOOPSSTT	photosets
EHOOPSSTU	housetops
	posthouse
	pothouses
EHOOPSTYZ	zoophytes
EHOORRTVW	overthrow
EHOOSSTUU	outhouses
EHOPRSSUV	pushovers
EHOPRSTXY	exstrophy
EHORRSTTW	throwster
EHORSSTUU	outrushes
EHOSSTTUW	southwest
EHRRSSTTU	thrusters
EIIILNNQU	inquiline
EIIILPPRS	liripipes
EIIILSTTU	utilities
EIIIMMNRS	minimiser
EIIIMMNRZ	minimizer
EIIIMMNSS	minimises
EIIIMMNSZ	minimizes
EIIIMPRTV	primitive
EIIINNPST	insipient
EIIINNRTU	Niu Tireni
EIIINQRSU	inquiries
EIIINRSTT	retinitis
	trinities
EIIINTTUV	intuitive
EIIIPRSTV	privities
EIIJLLNOV	Joinville
EIIJLLOST	jollities
EIIJMSSTU	jesuitism
EIIJQRTUV	jequirity
EIIKKNNSS	kinkiness
EIIKLLMNS	limekilns
EIIKLMNSS	milkiness
EIIKLMRSS	mislikers
EIIKLNNRT	interlink
EIIKLNRRW	wrinklier
EIIKLNRSW	wrinklies
EIIKLNSSS	silkiness
EIIKLNSST	slinkiest
EIIKMNRSS	mirkiness
EIIKMPSST	skimpiest

EIIKNNOSS	noiseniks	EIIMMNSUZ	immunizes	EIINRSSST	insisters
EIIKNNRTT	interknit	EIIMMORSS	isomerism	EIINRSSTZ	ritziness
EIIKNNSST	skinniest	EIIMMORST	memoirist	EIINRSTTW	wintriest
EIIKNNSSW	wineskins	EIIMMOSTV	emotivism	EIINRSTUV	intrusive
EIIKNPSSS	spikiness	EIIMMPSSS	pessimism	EIINRTTUV	nutritive
EIIKNRSSS	riskiness	EIIMMPSUY	epimysium	EIINSSSYZ	synizesis
EIIKQRSTU	quirkiest	EIIMMRTUX	immixture	EIINSSTTW	wittiness
EIILLMNRS	milliners	EIIMNNRTU	triennium	EIINSTTTU	institute
EIILLMNRY	millinery	EIIMNOPST	pimientos	EIIOOPSST	isotopies
EIILLMNSU	illumines	EIIMNORSS	missioner	EIIOPSSTV	positives
EIILLMSST	limitless		remission	EIIOQRSSU	Siqueiros
EIILLNNOP	penillion	EIIMNOSSS	emissions	EIIOSSTTV	sovietist
EIILLNRST	instiller	EIIMNOSST	misoneist	EIIPRRSTW	tripwires
EIILLNSSS	silliness	EIIMNOSUV	vimineous	EIIPRRTUV	irruptive
EIILLNSST	niellists	EIIMNPRRT	imprinter	EIIPRSSST	prissiest
EIILLNSTU	nullities	EIIMNPRSU	supermini	EIIPRSSTT	stripiest
EIILLNSTV	vitellins	EIIMNRSST	ministers	EIIQSSTTU	quietists
EIILLNTUY	inutilely	EIIMNRSTT	intermits	EIIRSSTTW	wristiest
EIILLOPRS	pillories	EIIMNSSST	mistiness	EIJKORRSS	skijorers
EIILLMMORS	meliorism	EIIMOPRSU	imperious	EIJLLNOSS	jolliness
EIILLMNNST	liniments	EIIMOPRSV	improvise	EIJMNPSSU	jumpiness
EIILLMNORV	vermilion	EIIMOPSST	optimises	EIJNORSST	jointress
EIILMNOST	limonites	EIIMOPSTT	epitomist	EIJNORSTU	jointures
EIILMNOSU	limousine	EIIMOPSTZ	optimizes	EIJNOSSTT	jettisons
EIILMNSSS	sliminess	EIIMOSSTV	sovietism	EIKLLNOVX	Knoxville
EIILMOPSV	implosive	EIIMOSTVV	vomitives	EIKLMNOSS	moleskins
EIILMOPTY	Ptolemy II	EIIMOTTVY	emotivity	EIKLMNSYZ	Zemlinsky
EIILMORST	meliorist	EIIMPRSSS	misprises	EIKLMORST	stormlike
EIILMOTTV	leitmotiv	EIIMPRSSZ	misprizes	EIKLMORSY	irksomely
EIILMPRSU	puerilism	EIIMPSSST	pessimist	EIKLNOSTU	snoutlike
EIILMPSUV	impulsive	EIIMSSSTT	semitists	EIKLNPRRS	sprinkler
EIILMRSSY	missilery	EIINNNOST	intension	EIKLNPRSS	sprinkles
EIILMSSST	slimsiest	EIINNNOTT	intention	EIKLNRSTU	knurliest
EIILMSSTT	mistitles	EIINNNOTV	invention	EIKLNRSTW	twinklers
EIILNNOQU	quinoline	EIINNNSST	tinniness	EIKLNSSSU	sulkiness
EIILNORSS	lionisers	EIINNORST	insertion	EIKLSTTUZ	klutziest
EIILNORSZ	lionizers	EIINNORSV	inversion	EIKMNNOSW	kinswomen
EIILNPSST	splenitis	EIINNOSSS	noisiness	EIKMNOORS	monoskier
EIILNPSTY	pensility	EIINNOSSU	unionises	EIKMNOSSS	smokiness
EIILNQSTU	quintiles	EIINNOSSV	envisions	EIKMNRRSU	murkiness
EIILNQTUY	inquietly	EIINNOSUZ	unionizes	EIKMNSSSU	muskiness
EIILNSTTU	intitules	EIINNPPSS	nippiness	EIKNNOPRT	pinkerton
EIILNSTTY	tensility	EIINNPSSS	spininess	EIKNOPRSS	porkiness
EIILNTUVY	unitively	EIINNRSTT	internist	EIKNORRTW	interwork
EIILOPSST	pisolites	EIINNSSTT	insistent	EIKNOSTTT	knottiest
EIILOQSSU	siliquose	EIINNSTTY	intensity	EIKNPRSTU	turnpikes
EIILORRSV	Oil Rivers	EIINOPRST	poitrines	EIKNPSSTU	spunkiest
EIILPPSST	slippiest	EIINOPRSV	prevision	EIKNRRTTY	trinketry
EIILPRSTU	spirituel	EIINOPSTT	petitions	EIKOOPSST	spookiest
EIILPRTUY	puerility		pointiest	EIKORRSTV	overskirt
EIILRSSTU	utilisers	EIINOPTVW	viewpoint	EIKORRSWW	wireworks
EIILRSTTY	sterility	EIINORRST	interiors	EIKORSTTU	strikeout
EIILRSTUZ	utilizers	EIINORSSS	sironises	EIKOSSTYZ	Ossietzky
EIILRSTVY	servility	EIINORSSV	revisions	EIKPRRSSU	spruikers
EIILSSSTY	sessility	EIINORSSZ	sironizes	EIKRRSTWY	skywriter
EIIMMNNOS	menominis	EIINORSTY	seniority	EILLMNOST	millstone
EIIMMNORS	immersion	EIINPPRST	pinstripe	EILLMNSSU	sensillum
EIIMMNOSS	misoneism	EIINPPSST	snippiest	EILLMOOPT	Melitopol
EIIMMNRSU	immuniser	EIINPRRSS	inspirers	EILLMOPSS	plimsoles
EIIMMNRUZ	immunizer	EIINPSSST	tipsiness	EILLMORTU	multirole
EIIMMNSSU	immunises	EIINPSSSW	wispiness	EILLMOSSY	lissomely
EIIMMNSTY	immensity	EIINQRRSU	inquirers	EILLMPSSS	misspells

EILLMPSTU	multiples	EILNOSSSU	lousiness	EIMNOORRT	remontoir
EILLMPTTU	multiplet	EILNOSSSW	lewissons	EIMNOORSS	roominess
EILLMPTUX	multiplex	EILNOSSTT	siltstone	EIMNOORSV	omnivores
EILLMRTUU	tellurium	EILNOSSTV	novelists	EIMNOPRTU	importune
EILLNOPRU	nullipore	EILNOSSUV	evulsions	EIMNOPSST	nepotisms
EILLNORTU	tellurion	EILNOSTUV	involutes	EIMNORRTW	worriment
EILLNOSSW	lowliness	EILNOSUVY	enviously	EIMNORSST	monitress
EILLNOTVY	violently	EILNPPSSU	pulpiness	EIMNORSSU	sensorium
EILLNPSSW	pinswells	EILNPQTUU	quintuple	EIMNORSSW	worminess
EILLNSSST	stillness	EILNPRSST	splinters	EIMNORSUV	verminous
EILLNSSSY	sinlessly	EILNPRSTU	Nelspruit	EIMNOSSSS	mossiness
EILLOOPRV	Liverpool	EILNPRSTY	splintery	EIMNOSSST	moistness
EILLOOSTW	woolliest	EILNQTUUY	unquietly	EIMNOSSSU	mousiness
EILLOPRSV	overspill	EILNRSSSU	surliness	EIMNOSTTY	testimony
	spillover	EILNRSSTU	insulters	EIMNOTTZZ	mezzotint
EILLOPRTY	pellitory	EILNRSTTU	turnstile	EIMNSSSSU	mussiness
EILLOPRWW	willpower	EILNRSTUU	unruliest	EIMNSSSTU	mustiness
EILLOSTTY	stylolite	EILNRTUUV	vulturine	EIMNSSUZZ	muzziness
EILLPSSSY	syllepsis	EILNSSSTU	lustiness	EIMOOPRTV	promotive
EILLSSTWY	witlessly	EILNSSTTU	lutenists	EIMOORRSW	worrisome
EILMMNTUU	nummulite	EILOPPRSS	prolepsis	EIMOORSST	motorises
EILMMOPSY	misemploy	EILOPPRTY	propylite	EIMOORSSU	isomerous
EILMMPSTU	plummiest	EILOPPSST	sloppiest	EIMOORSTZ	motorizes
EILMNOOSY	noisomely	EILOPRSSV	slipovers	EIMOOSSSX	exosmosis
EILMNOPSS	spoilsmen	EILOPRSTT	portliest	EIMOPRRSS	primroses
EILMNOPST	simpleton	EILOPRSTV	overspilt		promisers
EILMNORTT	tormentil	EILOPRSTW	pileworts	EIMOPRRST	importers
EILMNORTU	Montreuil	EILOPSSTY	stylopise		misreport
EILMNOSSU	emulsions	EILOPSTUY	piteously		reimports
EILMNOSTY	solemnity	EILOPSTYZ	stylopize	EIMOPRRSV	improvers
EILMNOSWY	winsomely	EILORRTVW	liverwort	EIMOPRSST	imposters
EILMNPSSU	lumpiness	EILORSSSV	visorless	EIMOPRSTU	imposture
EILMNPSTU	tumplines	EILORSSUY	seriously	EIMOPSTUU	impetuous
EILMNRSST	minstrels	EILORSSVZ	vizorless	EIMOQSSTU	misquotes
EILMOOPSS	liposomes	EILOSSTTT	stilettos	EIMORRRST	terrorism
EILMOOSTY	ileostomy	EILPPRSST	stipplers	EIMORRSST	mortisers
EILMOPRRS	implorers	EILPPRSSU	suppliers	EIMORRSTT	remittors
EILMOPSST	mileposts	EILPRSSTT	splitters	EIMORRSTU	trimerous
	polemists	EILQRRSSU	squirrels	EIMORRSWW	wireworms
EILMOSSSU	semisolus	EILRSSSTY	stylisers	EIMORRTTW	miterwort
EILMOSTUY	timeously	EILRSSTTU	sultriest		mitrewort
EILMRSTUU	multiuser		surtitles	EIMORSSTT	stormiest
EILNNOOQU	quinolone	EILRSSTTW	wristlets	EIMORSUVY	voyeurism
EILNNOOSS	looniness	EILRSSTYZ	stylizers	EIMOSSTTT	totemists
EILNNOSTV	insolvent	EIMMNNSTU	muniments	EIMOSSTUV	vomituses
EILNOOPSS	slipnoose	EIMMNOPRS	persimmon	EIMPSSTTU	stumpiest
EILNOOPSX	explosion	EIMMNORRT	minor term	EIMQRRSSU	squirmers
EILNOOSST	oilstones	EIMMNORSS	misnomers	EIMQSSTUY	mystiques
EILNOOTUV	evolution	EIMMOPRSU	emporiums	EIMRRSSSU	surmisers
EILNOPRRU	purloiner	EIMMOPSTU	impostume	EIMSSTTTU	smuttiest
EILNOPRSU	neuropils	EIMNNNRTU	inurnment	EINNNOTTY	nonentity
	prelusion	EIMNNOOSS	mooniness	EINNNSSSU	sunniness
	repulsion	EIMNNOOST	noontimes	EINNOOPRT	pontonier
EILNOPSST	pointless	EIMNNOOTZ	monzonite		prenotion
EILNOPSSU	spinulose	EIMNNOPRT	prominent	EINNOORST	ironstone
EILNOPSSY	spinosely	EIMNNOPST	imponents		serotonin
EILNOPSUX	expulsion		pointsmen	EINNORSTU	neutrinos
EILNORSTT	trotlines	EIMNNORST	innermost	EINNORSTV	inventors
EILNORSTY	storyline	EIMNNOSTT	ointments	EINNORSWW	winnowers
EILNORSUV	revulsion	EIMNNPTUU	neptunium	EINNORTVY	inventory
EILNORSVV	involvers	EIMNNRTTU	nutriment	EINNOSSST	stoniness
EILNORTUY	routinely	EIMNOOPSS	empoisons	EINNOSSSW	snowiness

EINNOSSTX	nonsexist	EIOPPRRST	stroppier	ELLNOTTTY	Lyttelton
EINNPRSTW	newsprint	EIOPPRRTY	propriety	ELLNSSSUY	sunlessly
EINNRSSTU	runtiness	EIOPPRSUV	purposive	ELLOORRSV	rollovers
EINNRSTTU	nutrients	EIOPRRSSU	superiors	ELLOPRSST	pollsters
EINNRTTUW	unwritten	EIOPRRSTU	Pretorius	ELLOPRSTU	polluters
EINNSSTTU	nuttiness	EIOPRSSTT	sportiest	ELLOPRSUV	pullovers
EINOOPRSS	poisoners	EIOPRSSTU	posturise	ELLOPRSUY	leprously
EINOOPSSS	opsonises	EIOPRSTTU	proustite	ELLORRSST	strollers
EINOOPSST	spooniest	EIOPRSTTY	posterity	ELLORSTUU	tellurous
EINOOPSSZ	opsonizes	EIOPRSTUZ	posturize	ELMNNOOST	somnolent
EINOORRST	retorsion	EIOPSSTTT	spottiest	ELMNOOOPS	monopoles
EINOORRTT	retortion	EIOQRSTUU	turquoise	ELMNOORTV	Lermontov
EINOORSST	rootiness	EIORRRSTT	terrorist	ELMNPPSSU	plumpness
EINOORSSZ	ozonisers	EIORRRTTY	territory	ELMNSUUZZ	unmuzzles
EINOORSZZ	ozonizers	EIORRSSST	resistors	ELMOOPSSY	polysomes
EINOORTTX	extortion	EIORRSSTU	Sertorius	ELMOORSTW	lowermost
EINOORTTY	notoriety	EIORRSSTV	servitors	ELMOOSSSY	lysosomes
EINOOSSST	sootiness	EIORSSTTU	out sister	ELMORSTUU	tremulous
EINOOSSTT	snootiest	EIOSSTTTW	swottiest	ELMORTUVY	volumetry
EINOOSSWZ	wooziness	EIPPRRSST	strippers	ELMPRSSTU	trumpless
EINOOSTXX	exotoxins	EIPQRSSTU	quipsters	ELNNOOSSU	unloosens
EINOPPSSS	soppiness	EIPQRTTUY	triptyque	ELNNOPSSU	nonpluses
EINOPRRSS	prisoners	EIPRRRSSU	spurriers	ELNOOOPRV	provolone
EINOPRRTV	overprint		surpriser	ELNOORSUY	onerously
EINOPRSSS	prosiness	EIPRRSSSU	surprises	ELNORSSTU	turnsoles
EINOPRSTU	eruptions	EIPRRSSTZ	spritzers	ELNORSUVY	nervously
	Petronius	EIPRSSSTU	pertussis	ELNOSSSTU	snoutless
EINOPRSUU	penurious	EIQRRSSTU	squirters	ELNOSTUUY	tenuously
EINOPSSSU	piousness	EIRSSTTTU	trustiest	ELOOORSTZ	zoosterol
EINOPSSSY	synopsise	EJLLOSSYY	joylessly	ELOORSTUW	lousewort
EINOPSSTT	nepotists	EJLOPSSTU	pulsojets	ELOOSSSUV	osseously
	pottiness	EJMNORUWY	jurywomen	ELOPPRSUY	purposely
EINOPSSYZ	synopsize	EJNOORRSU	sojourner	ELOPRRSUY	prelusory
EINOQSSTU	questions	EKKOOPRRW	pokerwork	ELOPRRSYY	pyrolyser
EINOQSTTU	quotients	EKLMMNOSU	muskmelon	ELOPRRYYZ	pyrolyzer
EINORRSSS	sorriness	EKLMNPTUY	unkemptly	ELOPRSSTY	prostyles
EINORRSTV	invertors	EKLNOOORS	onlookers	ELOPRSSYY	pyrolyses
EINORRTTV	introvert	EKLNRSSTU	trunkless	ELOPRSYYZ	pyrolyzes
EINORRUWZ	Ruwenzori	EKLOOORSV	lookovers	ELOQRSUUU	querulous
EINORSSTU	Nestorius		overlooks	ELORSSTUY	urostyles
EINORSSTV	investors	EKLOOPSSW	slowpokes	ELPRSSSUU	surpluses
EINORSSUV	souvenirs	EKMNNOORS	nonsmoker	ELPRSSTTU	splutters
EINORSTUX	extrusion	EKMNOOPTY	monkeypot	ELRSSSTTU	trustless
EINOSSTTT	snottiest	EKMOOPRRS	moreporks	EMMMNOSTU	momentums
EINOSSTUU	Suetonius	EKNOOPSTU	outspoken	EMMNNOSTU	monuments
EINPRRSST	sprinters	EKNOORSTW	stonework	EMMNOOOSS	monosomes
EINPRRTTU	interrupt	EKNORSSTU	sunstroke	EMMNOOOST	monostome
EINPRSSST	spinsters	EKOORRSVW	overworks	EMMNOOSTU	momentous
EINQRSSTU	squinters	EKOORRTUW	outworker	EMMNORSSU	resummons
EINQRSTTU	quitrents	EKOORSTTW	twostroke	EMMNOSSSU	summonses
EINRSSSTU	rustiness	EKOORSTWW	kowtowers	EMMNRSTUU	menstruum
EINRSSTTU	ruttiness	EKOPRRSSW	presswork	EMMOORSTY	osmometry
EINRSSTTY	entryists	EKOPRSSTU	upstrokes	EMMRRRSUU	murmurers
EIOOPPRSS	porpoises	ELLLNOSWY	swollenly	EMMRRSSTU	strummers
EIOOPPSST	opposites	ELLMOOSUV	Sullom Voe	EMNNOOOST	monotones
EIOOPRRST	posterior	ELLMOPSUY	plumosely		moonstone
EIOOPRSSV	provisoes	ELLMORSTU	rostellum	EMNOOPSTW	postwomen
EIOOPRSTX	expositor	ELLMOSUUY	emulously	EMNOOPSTY	monotypes
EIOORSSTT	tortoises	ELLMRSTUU	surmullet	EMNOOPSUY	eponymous
EIOORSTTT	troostite	ELLNOPSUW	upswollen	EMNOORRTT	tormentor
EIOOSSSTX	exostosis	ELLNOPTUY	opulently	EMNOORSST	mesotrons
EIOOSSTTV	ovotestis	ELLNOSTVY	solvently	EMNOORSSW	newsrooms

EMNOORTTY	tonometry
EMNOORTUY	neurotomy
EMNOORTWY	moneywort
EMNOPRSST	sportsmen
EMNOPRSSU	responsum
EMNORSSTT	sternmost
EMNRSTUUV	Vertumnus
EMOOORRST	storeroom
EMOOOSTTY	osteotomy
EMOOPRRSS	pressroom
EMOOPRRST	promoters
EMOOPRSSZ	zoosperms
EMOOPRTTY	optometry
EMOORRSTU	tremorous
EMOORSTTU	outermost
EMOPPRRST	prompters
EMOPPRSTU	uppermost
EMOPRRTUV	overtrump
EMOPRRTYY	pyrometry
EMORSTTTU	uttermost
EMPRSSTTU	strumpets
ENNNOOPRS	nonperson
ENNNORRTU	nonreturn
ENNOOPPRT	proponent
ENNOOPPST	opponents
ENNOORSTV	nonvoters
ENNOPRSSU	unpersons
ENNOPRTWY	pennywort
ENNORRTUU	outrunner
ENNORSSST	sternsons
ENNORSTTU	turnstone
ENOOPPRST	postponer
ENOOPPRTU	opportune
ENOOPPSST	postpones
ENOOPRRSS	responsor
ENOORSSTY	ostensory
ENOORSTTW	stonewort
ENOOSSTTU	sostenuto
ENOPRSSSU	suspensor
ENOPRSSTT	sternpost
ENOPRSTUW	uptowners
ENOPSTTYY	stenotypy
ENORRSTUV	overturns
	turnovers
ENORSSTUU	strenuous
ENORSTUUV	venturous
ENOSSSTTU	stoutness
ENRRSTUU	nurturers
ENRSSSTUU	untrusses
EOOOPRRTU	Europoort
EOOOPRSSZ	zoospores
EOOORRSST	roseroots
EOOPRRRT	propretor
EOOPRRRSS	oppressor
	proposers
EOOPRRSST	prepostor
EOOPRSSST	proptoses
EOOPPRTTY	prototype
EOOPPSTTY	topotypes
EOOPRRSTT	protestor
EOOPRRSTU	uprooters
EOOPRRTTU	outporter

EOOPRSSSS	possessor
EOOPRSSTV	stopovers
EOOPSSTTV	stovetops
EOORRRSSW	sorrowers
EOPPRRSTU	supporter
EOPPRSSSU	supposers
EOPRRSSTU	posturers
	proestrus
EOPRRSUVY	purveyors
EORRRSTTU	torturers
EORRSSSST	stressors
EORRSSUVY	surveyors
EORRSTUUV	trouveurs
ERRSSTTTU	strutters
FFGHIILNW	whiffling
FFGHILNSU	shuffling
FFGHILRTU	frightful
FFGHINORS	shroffing
FFGIILNNS	sniffling
FFGIINSUX	suffixing
FFGILNNSU	snuffling
FFGIMNORU	fungiform
FFGINOPRS	offspring
FFGINSSTU	stuffings
FFGINSSUU	suffusing
FFHHILSUY	huffishly
FFHOOOSST	offshoots
FFIINOSUX	suffixion
FFIKLORST	forklifts
FFINOPRST	offprints
FFINOSSUU	suffusion
FFLMNOOSU	moufflons
FFLOOOOPR	foolproof
FGGHIILNT	flighting
FGGHIINRT	frighting
FGGHINSTU	gunfights
FGGIILNNU	ingulfing
FGGIILNUY	uglifying
FGGIINORV	forgiving
FGHIIINNS	finishing
FGHIILLTY	flightily
FGHIIMNUY	humifying
FGHILNSSU	flushings
FGHILOPTT	topflight
FGHINORTT	fortnight
FGHIOSTTU	outfights
FGHLORSUU	furloughs
FGHMOORTU	frogmouth
FGHOOTTUU	outfought
FGIIILLNN	infilling
FGIIILLNP	filliping
FGIIILMNS	misfiling
FGIIILNVY	vilifying
FGIIIMNNY	minifying
FGIIIMNRS	misfiring
FGIIINVVY	vivifying
FGIILMNOR	ligniform
FGIILNNOW	inflowing
FGIILNOPR	profiling
FGIILNORV	frivoling
FGIILNPTU	uplifting
FGIILNRST	firstling

FGIILNRZZ	frizzling
FGIILNTTY	fittingly
FGIIMNNOR	informing
FGIINNOTY	notifying
FGIINNTTU	unfitting
FGIINOPRT	profiting
FGIINOSSY	ossifying
FGIINPRUY	purifying
FGIINPTYY	typifying
FGIINRSSU	fissuring
FGILLNOOW	following
FGILNNRUU	unfurling
FGILNNSTU	gunflints
FGILNOTUY	outflying
FGILNPRSU	purflings
FGILNRRUY	flurrying
FGILOOSTU	ufologist
FGINNORTU	fortuning
FGINOOTUX	outfoxing
FGINORRUW	furrowing
FGINORSST	frostings
FGLLNOSUY	songfully
FGLOOOSST	footslogs
FGLORSUUU	fulgurous
FHHIKOOSS	fishhooks
FHHIORTTW	forthwith
FHIIIKLLS	killifish
FHIILRTTY	thriftily
FHIKNRSTU	trunkfish
FHIKORSTW	shiftwork
FHILLOOST	foothills
FHILLOOSY	foolishly
FHILLORST	hillforts
FHILLSUWY	wishfully
FHILOPPSY	foppishly
FHKLORSUW	flushwork
FHLLRTUUY	hurtfully
	ruthfully
FHLMORUUU	humourful
FHLMOSTUU	mouthfuls
FHMOOOPRT	mothproof
FHOORRTTW	Fort Worth
FIIIKRTUW	kiwifruit
FIIILSSTY	fissility
FIIIMNRTY	infirmity
FIIINNOSX	infixions
FIIKLNNST	skinflint
FIILLMORV	villiform
FIILLMOTU	multifoil
FIILLPTUY	pitifully
FIILMORTU	trifolium
FIILMPRST	filmstrip
FIILOPRST	profilist
FIILORSUV	filovirus
FIILORTVY	frivolity
FIIMMNORS	misinform
FIIMNOSSU	fusionism
FIIMOPRSS	pisiforms
FIIMOPRST	stipiform
FIIMORRTU	triforium
FIIMORRTV	vitriform
FIINNOSSU	infusions

FIINOSSTU	fusionist	GGHINNOTW	nightgown	GHIINNSUW	unwishing
FIKLLLSUY	skilfully	GGHOOPRSS	grogshops	GHIINPPSW	whippings
FIKLLNSUU	unskilful	GGIIIMNNP	impinging	GHIINQSSU	squishing
FILLLLUWY	willfully	GGIIILMNSV	misgiving	GHIINRRSS	shirrings
FILLSTUWY	wistfully	GGIILMNPS	glimpsing	GHIINRSST	shirtings
FILMMORSU	formulism	GGIILNNSW	swingling	GHIINRSTT	thirsting
FILMMORTU	multiform	GGIILNPRY	gripingly	GHIINSTTY	stithying
FILMNORUV	uniformly	GGIILNRZZ	grizzling	GHIIRRSSTT	rightists
FILMNOSUU	fulminous	GGIIMNNPU	impugning	GHIKLSSTY	skylights
FILMORSTU	formulist	GGIIMPRSS	priggisms	GHIKNNOOU	unhooking
FILMORSTY	styliform	GGIINNORW	ingrowing	GHILLNOOW	hollowing
FILMORUVV	vulviform	GGIINNPRS	springing	GHILLNOWY	howlingly
FILOOOPRT	portfolio	GGIINNRST	stringing	GHILLOOPY	philology
FILOORSSU	fluorosis	GGIINNRSY	syringing	GHILLOOTY	lithology
FILOORSUV	frivolous	GGIINOPSS	gossiping	GHILLOSTW	lowlights
FILORSUUY	furiously	GGILLNNOY	longingly	GHILMNOOT	moonlight
FILOSSTUU	fistulous	GGILLNOOP	golloping	GHILNOOPT	potholing
FINNOOPRT	nonprofit	GGILLNOWY	glowingly	GHILNOORY	rhinology
FINOOPRSU	profusion	GGILLNPUY	gulpingly	GHILNOPSS	longships
FINOOPRTT	footprint	GGILLOOSW	golliwogs		
FIRSSTTUU	futurists	GGILMNSUY	ginglymus	GHILNOPYY	philogyny
FKKLOORSW	workfolks	GGILNNOUY	youngling	GHILNOSST	slingshot
FKLMOOOST	folkmoots	GGILNOOPR	prologing	GHILNPSUY	pushingly
FKLNOOSTW	townsfolk	GGILNOOPY	gropingly	GHILNSTTU	shuttling
FKLNRSTUU	trunkfuls	GGILNPRSU	splurging	GHILNSTUY	unsightly
FKMOORRSW	formworks	GGIMNOORS	groomings	GHILOOOPY	ophiology
FKOORRSTW	frostwork	GGINNOOPU	oppugning	GHILOOSTY	histology
FLLLOSUUY	soulfully	GGINNOSSS	singsongs	GHILOPRTW	Plowright
FLLLSTUUY	lustfully	GGINOOSTU	outgoings	GHILOPSTT	spotlight
FLLNOORRY	forlornly	GGINOPRSU	groupings		stoplight
FLNOOPSSU	spoonfuls	GGINPRSUU	upsurging	GHILORSSW	showgirls
FLOOOSTT	footstool	GGKNNOOSY	Kyongsong	GHILORSUY	roguishly
FLOORRSUW	sorrowful	GHHHIIMST	Highsmith	GHILPRSTY	sprightly
FOOPRRSTU	rustproof	GHHIILPST	lightship		triglyphs
FOOPSSTUY	pussyfoot	GHHIINSTW	whishting	GHILPRTUY	uprightly
GGGGIILNS	gigglings	GHHILRSTU	rushlight	GHIMMNRTU	thrumming
GGGHINRSU	shrugging	GHHINOOSW	whooshing	GHIMMNTUY	thingummy
GGGIILNNS	nigglings	GHHLOOSTY	Holy Ghost	GHIMNOOST	smoothing
	sniggling	GHHLORTUY	throughly	GHIMNORUU	humouring
GGGIILNRW	wriggling	GHHNOTTUU	unthought	GHIMNOSST	songsmith
GGGIINNRU	unrigging	GHIIKMNST	King-Smith	GHIMNSSTU	gunsmiths
GGGIINPRS	sprigging	GHIIKNNRS	shrinking	GHIMOOPSS	gomphosis
GGGILLOOW	golliwogg	GHIIKNPSS	kingships	GHINNOORU	honouring
GGGILMNSU	smuggling	GHIIKNSTT	skintight	GHINNOPSY	syphoning
GGGILNNSU	snuggling	GHIIKNTTT	tightknit	GHINNORST	northings
GGHHHIILT	highlight	GHIILLNRS	shrilling	GHINNORSU	unhorsing
GGHHILOSY	hoggishly	GHIILLNRT	thrilling	GHINOOSSW	swooshing
GGHIIILRW	whirligig	GHIILLNSS	shillings	GHINOPSTT	nightspot
GGHIIKNNT	knighting	GHIILLRSY	girlishly	GHINORSST	strongish
GGHIILLNS	shingling	GHIILNNTY	hintingly	GHINORSTW	ingrowths
GGHIILNNT	lightning	GHIILNNWY	whiningly	GHINORTUW	inwrought
GGHIILNPT	plighting	GHIILNOPS	polishing	GHINOSSTU	southings
GGHIILNST	slighting	GHIILNSTW	whistling		stoushing
GGHIILPSY	piggishly	GHIILNTTW	whittling	GHINRSTTU	thrusting
GGHIINNNU	unhinging	GHIIMMNSY	shimmying	GHIORRSTY	hygristor
GGHILNNOT	nightlong	GHIIMNPRS	shrimping	GHLLOOOPY	hoplology
GGHILNOOS	shoogling	GHIINNNSY	shinnying	GHLMNOOVY	hymnology
GGHILNOPU	ploughing	GHIINNNWY	whinnying	GHLMOOTYY	mythology
GGHILNOSU	sloughing	GHIINNOPS	siphoning	GHLNNOORS	longhorns
GGHILNSUY	gushingly	GHIINNPSU	punishing	GHLNOOOPY	phonology
GGHILOOPR	logogriph	GHIINNRSU	inrushing	GHLNOOPYY	hypnology
GGHINNORT	thronging	GHIINNSTY	shintying	GHLNOSSTU	slungshot

GHLOOPTYY	phytology
GHLORSTUU	turloughs
GHMNOOSUU	humongous
GHMNOSUUU	humungous
GHNNOOOSZ	gohonzons
GHNNOOPRR	pronghorn
GHOORSTUY	yoghourts
GHOORTTUW	outgrowth
GHOPRSTUW	upgrowths
GIIIKLMNS	misliking
GIIILNNOS	lionising
GIIILNNOZ	lionizing
GIIILNSTU	utilising
GIIILNTUZ	utilizing
GIIILOSTU	litigious
GIIIMMNST	mistiming
GIIIMNRUV	virginium
GIIIMRSST	mistigris
GIIINNNOP	pinioning
GIIINNNTW	intwining
GIIINNORS	ironising
GIIINNORZ	ironizing
GIIINNOST	ignitions
GIIINNOSV	visioning
GIIINNPRS	inspiring
GIIINNPSS	Nipissing
GIIINNQRU	inquiring
GIIINNSST	insisting
GIIINNSTU	unitising
GIIINNTTU	intuiting
GIIINNTUZ	unitizing
GIIINOSSS	Issigonis
GIIINPRST	spiriting
GIIINRTVY	virginity
GIIJKLMNO	Kim Jong Il
GIIJKNORS	skijoring
GIIJNOSST	jingoists
GIIKKLNPS	kingklips
GIIKLLLNY	killingly
GIIKLLNSS	skillings
GIIKLMNSU	Kim Il Sung
GIIKLNNNU	unlinking
GIIKLNNOP	Linköping
GIIKLNNRW	wrinkling
GIIKLNNST	tinklings
GIIKLNNTW	twinkling
GIIKMMNSS	skimmings
GIIKNNNUW	unwinking
GIIKNPRSU	prusiking
	spruiking
GIIKNRSST	skirtings
GIIKNSVVY	skivvying
GIILLLNWY	willingly
GIILLMNPY	limpingly
GIILLMNSY	smilingly
GIILLMRST	gristmill
GIILLNNUW	unwilling
GIILLNOPW	pillowing
GIILLNORS	grillions
GIILLNPSY	lispingly
GIILMNNSU	unsmiling
GIILMNOPR	imploring

GIILMNRSU	misruling
GIILMRSTU	liturgism
GIILNNNWY	winningly
GIILNNOST	Islington
GIILNNOSU	insouling
GIILNNOTU	outlining
GIILNNOVV	involving
GIILNNPPY	nippingly
GIILNNPST	splinting
GIILNNSTU	insulting
GIILNOPST	pistoling
	postiling
GIILNOQRU	liquoring
GIILNOTUV	outliving
GIILNPPRY	rippingly
GIILNPPST	stippling
GIILNPRST	stripling
GIILNPRSY	springily
GIILNPSTT	splitting
GIILNPTTU	uptilting
	uptitling
GIILNPTYY	pityingly
GIILNQSSU	quislings
GIILNQSTU	quiltings
GIILNRSTY	stringily
GIILNSSTU	linguists
GIILNSSTY	stylising
GIILNSTYZ	stylizing
GIILNSWZZ	swizzling
GIILNTTWY	wittingly
GIILOSSST	glossitis
GIILPSSTU	pugilists
GIILRSTTU	liturgist
GIIMMNRST	trimmings
GIIMMNOOT	motioning
GIIMMNNTUY	mutinying
GIIMNOPRS	promising
GIIMNOPRT	importing
GIIMNOPRV	improving
GIIMNOPST	imposting
GIIMNORRR	mirroring
GIIMNORST	mortising
GIIMNPSTY	mistyping
GIIMNQRSU	squirming
GIIMNRSSU	surmising
GIINNNNPU	unpinning
GIINNNOWW	winnowing
GIINNNTUW	untwining
GIINNOOPS	poisoning
GIINNOOPT	optioning
GIINNOOSZ	ozonising
GIINNOOZZ	ozonizing
GIINNORSS	nigrosins
GIINNORST	ignitrons
GIINNPPRU	unripping
GIINNPPSS	snippings
GIINNPPUZ	unzipping
GIINNPRST	printings
	sprinting
GIINNPTTU	inputting
GIINNPTUY	unpitying
GIINNQSTU	squinting

GIINNTTUW	unwitting
GIINOPRST	riposting
GIINORRTW	worriting
GIINPPRST	stripping
GIINPRRTU	irrupting
GIINPRSSU	suspiring
	uprisings
GIINQRSTU	squirting
GIINRSUVV	surviving
GIIORRSST	rigorists
GIIORRSUU	irriguous
GIJKNNOOP	Jönköping
GIJLLNOTY	joltingly
GIJLMNPUY	jumpingly
GIKLLORRW	grillwork
GIKLNNNSY	King's Lynn
GIKLNNOOO	onlooking
GIKLNNOWY	knowingly
GIKLNOOOY	koniology
GIKNNNOUW	unknowing
GIKNNOSTW	Kingstown
GIKNOOPRV	provoking
GIKNOOTWW	kowtowing
GIKOORRVY	Krivoy Rog
GILLLNOOP	lolloping
GILLMNOOY	limnology
GILLMOORR	grillroom
GILLMOSSY	syllogism
GILLNNORU	unrolling
GILLNOPSY	slopingly
GILLNOPTU	polluting
GILLNORST	strolling
GILLNORUY	louringly
GILLOOOPY	oligopoly
GILLOOPSW	polliwogs
GILMMNOOS	mongolism
GILMMSTUY	multigyms
GILMNNOTY	Lymington
GILMOOSTY	myologist
GILNNOOSU	unloosing
GILNNRSSU	nurslings
GILNOPPST	stoppling
GILNOPTUY	poutingly
GILNORSUY	rousingly
GILNOSTUU	glutinous
GILNPPSUY	supplying
GILNRSSTU	lustrings
	rustlings
GILNSSTUU	singultus
GILOOORST	orologist
GILOOOSST	oologists
GILOOOSSU	isologous
GILOOOSTT	otologist
GILOOOSTZ	zoologist
GILOORSTU	urologist
GILOSSSST	glossists
GIMMNNOSU	summoning
GIMMNRRUU	murmuring
GIMMNRSTU	strumming
GIMNNOORS	monsignor
GIMNNOORU	unmooring
GIMNNOSTU	mountings

GIMNOOOSU	oogoniums	**HHMNOOOPY**	homophony	**HKLMMORUZ**	krummholz
GIMNOOPRT	promoting	**HHNOORRST**	shorthorn	**HKMMNORRU**	krummhorn
GIMNOORSU	ginormous	**HHOOPPRSS**	phosphors	**HKMOOORSW**	hookworms
GIMNOPPRT	prompting	**HIIIJNOXX**	John XXIII	**HKOOPRSSW**	workshops
GIMNORRSW	ringworms	**HIIILNSST**	nihilists	**HLLMNOOSU**	monohulls
GIMNORRUU	rumouring	**HIIIJLLNOT**	jillionth	**HLLNOPSUY**	sulphonyl
GIMOPRUUY	uropygium	**HIIKNSSVY**	Vishinsky	**HLLPRSUUY**	sulphuryl
GINNNOOTV	nonvoting	**HIILLMNOT**	millionth	**HLMOOPPRY**	polymorph
GINNOOPPR	proponing	**HIILLOSWW**	willowish	**HLNOOPPYY**	polyphony
GINNOOPRT	Orpington	**HIILMOPYY**	myiophily	**HLNOORSTU**	Solothurn
GINNOORTU	unrooting	**HIILMOSST**	homilists	**HLOOORTWW**	Woolworth
GINNOQTUU	unquoting	**HIILNORTT**	trilithon	**HLOOPPRSY**	sporophyl
GINNORSTU	tonsuring	**HIILNSSWY**	swinishly	**HMMOORSSU**	mushrooms
GINNOSUUU	unguinous	**HIILOPSST**	pisoliths	**HMNNOOOPY**	monophony
GINNPRTUU	upturning	**HIILOQRSU**	liquorish	**HMNOOOSST**	moonshots
GINNRRTUU	nurturing	**HIILOSTTY**	hostility	**HMOOOPRSY**	homospory
GINNRSSTU	unstrings	**HIILPSTTY**	typhlitis	**HMOOORSSW**	showrooms
GINOOPPRS	proposing	**HIILRSTTY**	thirstily	**HNOOOSTTU**	Sutton Hoo
GINOOPRSS	prognosis	**HIIMNSSTT**	tinsmiths	**HNOOPPTYY**	phonotypy
GINOOPRTU	uprooting	**HIIMOPSTU**	hospitium	**HNOOPRTTY**	phytotron
GINOOPWWW	powwowing	**HIIOPRSTU**	Pirithoüs	**HNOORRSTW**	hornworts
GINOORRSW	sorrowing	**HIKKNSSUU**	inukshuks	**HNOORSSTU**	southrons
GINOORSTU	trigonous	**HIKLMNOSY**	monkishly	**HOOORTTTW**	toothwort
GINOOTTUV	outvoting	**HIKNNORST**	stinkhorn	**HOOOSSTTU**	outshoots
GINOPPRST	stropping	**HIKNNORWY**	hornywink		shootouts
GINOPPRSU	purposing	**HIKNOORST**	Kórinthos		
GINOPPSST	stoppings	**HIKNOSTTU**	outthinks	**HOOPRSSTT**	shortstop
GINOPPSSU	supposing	**HIKNSSVVY**	Vyshinsky	**HOOPRSTTU**	Southport
GINOPRSTU	posturing	**HILLLLMTUU**	multihull	**HPRSSTTUU**	upthrusts
	sprouting	**HILLMPSUY**	lumpishly	**IIIILOSUV**	Louis VIII
GINOPRSUU	uprousing	**HILLNPSUY**	sulphinyl	**IIIILOSUX**	Louis XIII
GINOPSSST	signposts	**HILLOOPRW**	whirlpool	**IIIKLLNPS**	spillikin
GINORRTTU	torturing	**HILLOOPST**	lopoliths	**IIIKLNPSS**	spilikins
GINPPRSSU	upsprings	**HILLOSTUY**	loutishly	**IIIKMNRST**	miniskirt
GINPRRTUU	rupturing	**HILLSSTYY**	stylishly	**IIIILLMNPS**	minipills
GINRSTTTU	strutting	**HILMNOOST**	monoliths	**IIILMSUVX**	lixiviums
GIOPRSTWY	gipsywort	**HILMOOSSY**	homolysis	**IIILNOSTV**	violinist
GLLNOOOOS	songololo	**HILMOOSYZ**	hylozoism	**IIILNTTUY**	inutility
GLLOOPSTY	polyglots	**HILMOOTTY**	lithotomy	**IIILOSUVX**	Louis XVII
GLLOOPSWY	pollywogs	**HILOOPTXY**	toxophily	**IIIMPRSST**	spiritism
GLMNOOPUY	polygonum	**HILOOSTYZ**	hylozoist	**IIIMRRTUV**	triumviri
GLMNORSUW	lungworms	**HILORSSTT**	shortlist	**IIINNOTTU**	intuition
GLMNRSTUU	ngultrums	**HILRSTTUY**	ruttishly	**IIINPRSST**	inspirits
GLMOORSWW	glowworms	**HIMMOPRSU**	phormiums	**IIINSSSTU**	sinusitis
GLNOOOSTY	nostology	**HIMNOPSTY**	hypnotism	**IIIPRSSTT**	spiritist
GLNOPRSSU	longspurs	**HIMOOPRSS**	isomorphs	**IIJNORSUU**	injurious
GLNORSSTY	strongyls		morphosis	**IIKKMNOSW**	Minkowski
GLNORSTUW	lungworts	**HIMOORTYZ**	rhizotomy	**IIKLLNOSS**	skillions
GLOOOPRTY	tropology	**HIMOPRRST**	trimorphs	**IIKLNNOSW**	Wilkinson
GNOOOPRSY	sporogony	**HIMOPRSSW**	shipworms	**IIKNNNOOS**	onionskin
GNOOPRTYY	protogyny	**HIMOPRSWW**	whipworms	**IILLMNOPU**	pollinium
GNOSSTTUU	tungstous	**HIMORSSTU**	humorists	**IILLMPRSU**	spirillum
GOOPRSTUU	outgroups	**HIMOSTTUU**	Mutsuhito	**IILLMRSTU**	trilliums
GORRSTUWY	worryguts	**HIMPSSSYY**	symphysis	**IILLNNNOO**	nonillion
HHHOOPRST	shophroth	**HINOPPRRY**	porphyrin	**IILLNOQSU**	squillion
HHIIOOSTY	Yoshihito	**HINOPSSTW**	townships	**IILLNORST**	trillions
HHILLNORT	Thornhill	**HINOPSTTY**	hypnotist	**IILLNOSSU**	illusions
HHILMOSSS	shloshims	**HIOOPPRST**	troopship	**IILLOPSSY**	lipolysis
HHILORSWY	whorishly	**HIOORSTTT**	orthotist	**IILLOSTVY**	villosity
HHIMRSTTY	rhythmist	**HIOPRSSTY**	sophistry	**IILMNOOPS**	implosion
HHKLOOOSV	Sholokhov	**HIOPRSTTU**	tutorship	**IILMNOPSU**	impulsion
HHLMOOPYY	homophyly	**HIORRSTTY**	thyristor	**IILMNOSSU**	Mussolini
				IILMOPSSS	solipsism

IILMOPSUY	impiously	**IKNOOPRST**	pinkroots	**INOOOPSSU**	poisonous
IILNOOPST	postilion	**IKNOORRSW**	ironworks	**INOOORSTU**	notorious
IILNOOSTV	volitions	**IKNOPSSTT**	stinkpots	**INOOOSTXZ**	zootoxins
IILOOPPRS	liripoops	**IKORSSTTU**	outskirts	**INOOPPRST**	Propontis
IILOPRTXY	prolixity	**ILLLMOPSS**	plimsolls	**INOOPPRTU**	pourpoint
IILOPSSST	solipsist	**ILLLOOPPS**	lollipops	**INOOPRSST**	positrons
IILOQSSUU	siliquous	**ILLLOSUVY**	villously	**INOOPSSTT**	spittoons
IILORSSTT	troilists	**ILLLPSUUV**	pulvillus	**INOOPSTTU**	outpoints
IILORTTTY	tortility	**ILLMOORST**	stillroom	**INOPRSTTU**	outsprint
IILOSTVVZ	slivovitz	**ILLNOOPTU**	pollution		printouts
IIMNNOOST	monitions	**ILLNOORTT**	tortillon	**INOPSSTTY**	synoptist
IIMNNOSTU	munitions	**ILLNOPVYY**	polyvinyl	**INPRSSTTU**	surprints
IIMNOOSSS	omissions	**ILLOOQSUY**	soliloquy	**INPRSSTTU**	turnspits
IIMNOPRSS	imprisons	**ILLOPPSSS**	slipslops	**IOOORRRST**	orrisroot
IIMNOPSSZ	Spinozism	**ILLOQRTUW**	quillwort	**IOOPPRRTU**	potpourri
IIMNORSTT	intromits	**ILMNOOSUY**	ominously	**IOOPPRSST**	proptosis
IIMNOSSST	simonists	**ILMNOPTUU**	plutonium	**IOOPRRSVY**	provisory
IIMNPRSST	misprints	**ILMNOPXYY**	polymyxin	**IOORSSSUV**	voussoirs
IIMOPRTXY	proximity	**ILMOOOPRT**	pilomotor	**IOORSSTUV**	virtuosos
IIMOPSSTT	optimists	**ILMOPSTUY**	plumosity	**IOPRSSTTU**	outstrips
IIMOQSTUX	quixotism	**ILMOSSYYZ**	zymolysis	**IORRSSUVV**	survivors
IIMORSTTU	tutiorism	**ILNOOPRSU**	prolusion	**JNNOORRSU**	nonjurors
IIMRRSTUV	triumvirs	**ILNOOSSTU**	solutions	**KLLMNSSUU**	numskulls
IIMSSSTUW	swimsuits	**ILNOOSTUV**	volutions	**KLNORSSTY**	klystrons
IINNOORST	intorsion	**ILNOOSUXY**	noxiously	**KMOOORRSW**	workrooms
IINNOOSUX	innoxious	**ILNOPRXYY**	pyroxylin	**KMOPRSTUW**	stumpwork
IINNOPPST	pinpoints	**ILNORSUUY**	ruinously	**KOOORSSTV**	voorskots
IINNORSTU	intrusion	**ILNOSSUUY**	sinuously	**KOORSSTVY**	Ostrovsky
IINNORTTU	nutrition	**ILOOPPRSY**	isopropyl	**LMOOOOPRS**	poolrooms
IINNOSSTU	unionists	**ILOOPRSTU**	Port Louis	**LMOOOORST**	toolrooms
IINOOPRSV	provision	**ILOORSTUY**	riotously	**LMOOPPSUY**	pompously
IINOOPSST	positions	**ILOPPRSTY**	stroppily	**LMOOPRSTU**	pulmotors
IINOORSTT	sortition	**ILOPPSSTU**	populists	**LMOORSSWW**	slowworms
IINOPRRTU	irruption	**ILOPRSSYY**	pyrolysis	**LNOOOPPTY**	Pontypool
IINOPSSTY	spinosity	**ILORSUUUX**	luxurious	**LNOOOPRST**	poltroons
IINOSSTUY	sinuosity	**IMMOPPRTU**	impromptu	**LNOOPPRSY**	propylons
IINOSSTVY	synovitis	**IMMOPSSUY**	symposium	**LOOPRRSUY**	prolusory
IIOOPPRST	propositi	**IMNNOOPTW**	topminnow	**LORSTUUUV**	vulturous
IIOOPRSST	spiritoso	**IMNNOOSTT**	monotints	**MMORRSUUU**	murmurous
IIOOPSSTV	oviposits	**IMNOOOPRT**	promotion	**MNNOOOPSY**	monopsony
IIOORRRRS	riroriros	**IMNOOOSSU**	isonomous	**MNOORSSTU**	monstrous
IIOPRSSTU	spiritous	**IMNORSTTU**	strontium	**MNOORSSTW**	snowstorm
IIORSTTTU	tutiorist	**IMOOOSTTZ**	zootomist	**MNORSSTUU**	surmounts
IJMNOORTW	jointworm	**IMOOPPSTY**	pomposity	**MNORSTUUV**	Vortumnus
IKKKMOSUW	Kuskokwim	**IMOOPRRSS**	promisors	**MOOORRSTW**	tomorrows
IKKLNORSW	linkworks	**IMOOPRSST**	impostors	**MOPSSTUUU**	sumptuous
IKKNOOPRT	Kropotkin	**IMOOQSSŚU**	mosquitos	**NNOOOPRSU**	nonporous
IKKOOSSTW	Stokowski	**IMOORSSTT**	motorists	**NNOOOPSST**	spontoons
IKLLOOSTV	kilovolts	**IMORSUVXY**	myxovirus	**NOOOOPRTV**	Porto Novo
IKLMOPPSY	milksoppy	**IMRSSSTTU**	mistrusts	**NOOOOPRTZ**	protozoon
IKLMORSSW	silkworms	**INNNNOOSU**	nonunions	**OOOOPRSSU**	oosporous
IKLMORSTW	milkworts	**INNNORSTU**	trunnions	**OOPRSSTUU**	stuporous
IKLNOPSST	slipknots	**INNOOPSSS**	sponsions	**OOPRTTTUY**	puttyroot
IKMNOOPTY	Potyomkin	**INNOOSSUU**	unisonous	**OORRSTTUU**	torturous
IKMOPPRUY	Yom Kippur	**INOOOPRTY**	ionotropy		

459

Ten Letters

AAAAABCCRS	asarabacca	AAAAHINNST	Athanasian	AAABDMNRRU	barramunda
AAAABBDDIS	Addis Ababa	AAAAHIPPRS	paraphasia	AAABDMORSS	ambassador
AAAABCCLNP	Capablanca	AAAAHKPPSW	whakapapas	AAABEEGLMN	manageable
AAAABCCLNS	Casablanca	AAAAILLPRS	paralalias	AAABEELLPP	appealable
AAAABCENRS	scarabaean	AAAAIMNNNP	Panamanian	AAABEELPPS	appeasable
AAAABCLLSV	balaclavas	AAAAIMNRST	Santa Maria	AAABEGLLSU	Elagabalus
AAAABCLMNS	balmacaans	AAAAKMNORV	Arakan Yoma	AAABEGLMNY	manageably
AAAABDFILS	Faisalabad	AAAALMNRSZ	salmanazar	AAABEIJNRZ	Azerbaijan
AAAABEINRS	Arabian Sea	AAAALPRSTT	parastatal	AAABEILLSS	assailable
AAAABGKORY	kabaragoya	AAAAMNRSTT	Santa Marta	AAABEILNTT	attainable
AAAABIKLLS	balalaikas	AAAAMNRSTU	Santa Maura	AAABEKPRRS	parabrakes
AAAABJLMSY	jambalayas	AAAAMPRRTT	parramatta	AAABEKRSWY	breakaways
AAAABLRSTU	tabula rasa	AAABBCCHMO	Cochabamba	AAABELLNSY	analysable
AAAACCHMST	tacamahacs	AAABBCILST	sabbatical	AAABELLNYZ	analyzable
AAAACCINRT	Tacna-Arica	AAABBEILMT	baalebatim	AAABELMSTT	blastemata
AAAACDGMNS	Madagascan	AAABBEIRSS	Bessarabia	AAABELNRRT	narratable
AAAACDGMRS	Madagascar	AAABBIILNR	ibn-al-Arabi	AAABELRSTW	basaltware
AAAACDIMMS	macadamias	AAABBINRRS	barbarians	AAABFHHIIT	Baha'í Faith
AAAACDJNRS	jacarandas	AAABBORRSS	Barbarossa	AAABFHHINU	Abu Hanifah
AAAACDMMRT	tarmacadam	AAABCCHLNS	bacchanals	AAABGLORRS	algarrobas
AAAACHILPP	Appalachia	AAABCCHNRS	charabancs	AAABHIOPQU	aquaphobia
AAAACHKKLS	chakalakas	AAABCCKNSV	canvasback	AAABHLMQTU	Quathlamba
AAAACHSSUY	ayahuascas	AAABCDEIRS	scarabaeid	AAABHLPRUW	Bahawalpur
AAAACILPST	cataplasia	AAABCDELNR	candelabra	AAABHLRSTZ	balthazars
AAAACIRRSS	araucarias	AAABCDIIST	adiabatics	AAABHNRSSU	sub-Saharan
AAAACLMNRT	almacantar	AAABCDRRSU	barracudas	AAABIILRRT	atrabiliar
AAAACLNRST	Santa Clara	AAABCEGILN	Balenciaga	AAABIINRRT	Irian Barat
AAAACMNRST	catamarans	AAABCEHLSS	calabashes	AAABIKLNPP	Balikpapan
AAAADDLMNR	Damaraland	AAABCEHLTT	attachable	AAABILLNOS	labionasal
AAAADEGPRS	Pasargadae	AAABCEKLTT	attackable	AAABILRSTV	Bratislava
AAAADELLLN	Allan-a-Dale	AAABCELLLR	clarabella	AAABIMNPST	anabaptism
AAAADELMMT	Alma-Tadema	AAABCEMRST	carbamates	AAABIMOPRR	Paramaribo
AAAADEMNNS	Andaman Sea	AAABCERSSU	scarabaeus	AAABINPSTT	anabaptist
AAAADHMNRV	Vardhamana	AAABCHILNR	abranchial	AAABLMOSTT	blastomata
AAAADHMRUZ	Ahura Mazda	AAABCHINRT	batrachian	AAABLPRSST	parablasts
AAAADIJVWY	Vijayawada	AAABCIILST	Basilicata	AAABMNRSTU	marabuntas
AAAAEFRRSU	Arafura Sea	AAABCLLMRU	ambulacral	AAACCCIORT	cacciatora
AAAAEGLMMT	amalgamate	AAABCLMORS	carambolas	AAACCCRSTU	Caractacus
AAAAEHMNNV	Ahvenanmaa	AAABCORRTU	barracouta	AAACCDELSV	cavalcades
AAAAELMMNT	analemmata	AAABCORSTV	Costa Brava	AAACCDIOPP	Cappadocia
AAAAGGGGWW	Wagga Wagga	AAABDEEGLM	damageable	AAACCEHNNT	catananche
AAAAGHMRST	Sagarmatha	AAABDEEHHY	dahabeeyah	AAACCEHRSS	saccharase
AAAAGHRSTY	satyagraha	AAABDEGLOY	Delagoa Bay	AAACCEHRST	saccharate
AAAAGMSSSU	massasauga	AAABDEHLRZ	hazardable	AAACCEIPTT	capacitate
AAAAGNORSX	Anaxagoras	AAABDENRSS	sarabandes	AAACCELSST	cataclases
AAAAGNPRUY	Paraguayan	AAABDILNST	Stalinabad	AAACCENRUV	Cuernavaca
AAAAHHJMRS	maharajahs	AAABDINNST	anabantids	AAACCHILNR	anarchical

AAACCHKMST	tacmahacks
AAACCILLNT	cataclinal
AAACCILLRS	cascarilla
AAACCILNTV	Cavalcanti
AAACCILSST	cataclasis
AAACCINRTT	Antarctica
AAACCIPRTT	paratactic
AAACCIRSTT	ataractics
AAACCMOPRR	macrocarpa
AAACDDELRW	Cadwalader
AAACDEHLNV	avalanched
AAACDEHRSZ	azedarachs
AAACDEIMMS	macadamise
AAACDEIMMZ	macadamize
AAACDEKNPY	Pancake Day
AAACDELMNR	calamander
AAACDENNRV	caravanned
AAACDGGHIL	haggadical
AAACDGIILR	cardialgia
AAACDGLNNR	Grand Canal
AAACDHIKST	kadaitchas
AAACDHINNR	arachnidan
AAACDHNRSS	sandarachs
AAACDIIPRS	paradisiac
AAACDILNRS	calandrias
AAACDILRTY	caryatidal
AAACEEGNNR	carageenan
AAACEENPPR	appearance
AAACEFIRST	East Africa
AAACEFLQTU	catafalque
AAACEGNORT	Arctogaean
AAACEHIMNN	Manichaean
AAACEHIMNU	naumachiae
AAACEHLNSV	avalanches
AAACEIINRS	Icarian Sea
AAACEILMNT	catamenial
AAACEINNRT	catenarian
AAACEINPRS	paracasein
AAACEINPSS	Caspian Sea
AAACEINPST	anapaestic
AAACEINRRS	sarracenia
AAACEJKNPS	jackanapes
AAACELLMNP	Campanella
AAACELLNPT	aplacental
AAACELMPRT	metacarpal
AAACGGILNO	anagogical
AAACGGIORV	Caravaggio
AAACGHNRTT	tragacanth
AAACGILLMY	agamically
AAACGILLNO	analogical
AAACGILLNV	galvanical
AAACGINNRU	Nicaraguan
AAACGLLSSW	scallawags
AAACHHOPRY	Chao Phraya
AAACHILLNW	Wallachian
AAACHIMNSU	naumachias
AAACHJOPRS	chaparajos
AAACHKKMNT	Kamchatkan
AAACHKPRRS	pracharaks
AAACHLMOST	chloasmata
AAACHLNOTU	anacolutha
	Talcahuano

AAACHLNRST	charlatans
AAACHLPRRS	chaparrals
AAACHNPRTY	pyracantha
AAACHNPSTY	panchayats
AAACHOPRST	cataphoras
AAACHQTUUU	chautauqua
AAACIIRSSS	ascariasis
AAACILLMNU	animalcula
AAACILLMNY	maniacally
AAACILLMRS	camarillas
AAACILLNTY	analytical
AAACILMMNO	ammoniacal
AAACILMNOT	anatomical
AAACILNPST	anaplastic
AAACILNRSS	carnassial
AAACILNRST	scarlatina
AAACIMNPTY	Panama City
AAACINOPRS	paranoiacs
AAACINRRTT	tractarian
AAACINRSSU	casuarinas
AAACLMNPSU	campanulas
AAACLMNRTU	almucantar
AAACLMNRVY	cavalryman
AAACLMPSST	cataplasms
AAACLNSSTU	Santa Claus
AAACMRSTUX	taraxacums
AAACNORSSU	anasarcous
AAACNRTTTT	attractant
AAADDEGNTV	advantaged
AAADDELMPT	maladapted
AAADDELPSY	dasypaedal
AAADDHMRSY	hamadryads
AAADEEGHNP	phagedaena
AAADEELLNV	Avellaneda
AAADEELNRW	Delawarean
AAADEFIOST	asafoetida
AAADEGGRTV	aggravated
AAADEGHMNR	Ahmednagar
AAADEGINRV	devanagari
AAADEGLMTY	amygdalate
AAADEGLNTV	galavanted
AAADEGNNRW	New Granada
AAADEGNSTV	advantages
AAADEHLNPR	aphelandra
AAADEILNRX	Alexandria
AAADEIMNNT	adamantine
AAADEIMSTT	diastemata
AAADELMMRS	marmalades
AAADELMNRS	salamander
AAADELNPQU	aquaplaned
AAADEOPSTZ	zapateados
AAADGHLMNR	Graham Land
AAADGHNQRY	Qaraghandy
AAADGIILLR	gaillardia
AAADGILLNR	granadilla
AAADGLLNOR	allargando
AAADGMMMNR	grandmamma
AAADGMMNRS	grandmamas
AAADGMNNNR	Grand Manan
AAADGMNORR	mandragora
AAADGNOPPR	propaganda
AAADGNPPRS	grandpapas

AAADHHIMYY	Ahmadiyyah
AAADHHMRTU	Hadhramaut
AAADHMMMNU	Muhammadan
AAADIILNPR	lapidarian
AAADIIMMNR	Maid Marian
AAADILMNST	dalmatians
AAADILNOPS	diapasonal
AAADINOPTT	adaptation
AAADKLRSSU	Ruda Śląska
AAADLMMNNN	landammann
AAADLNNSSY	analysands
AAADLNQRTU	quadrantal
AAADORSTTU	autostrada
AAAEEHMNRS	maharanees
AAAEEKLPRY	parakeelya
AAAEELPRST	palaestrae
AAAEFLMNST	malfeasant
AAAEGGIMNT	gametangia
AAAEGGRSTV	aggravates
AAAEGHIOPR	aerophagia
AAAEGHLLNP	phalangeal
AAAEGILMNR	managerial
AAAEGILNST	East Anglia
AAAEGILPPR	paraplegia
AAAEGINPRS	asparagine
AAAEGLLMNS	Magallanes
AAAEGLMNSU	malaguenas
AAAEGLMNTU	Guatemalan
AAAEGLMTXY	metagalaxy
AAAEGMMNRR	anagrammer
AAAEGMNNST	manganates
AAAEGMRRTV	margravate
AAAEGPSSWY	passageway
AAAEHHSSTT	tatahashes
AAAEHIKKST	kahikateas
AAAEHIMRTU	haematuria
AAAEHINSTU	euthanasia
AAAEHMMOST	haematomas
AAAEHMMOTT	hematomata
AAAEHMOOTZ	haematozoa
AAAEHMORTT	atheromata
AAAEHNOPPR	epanaphora
AAAEHPPRRS	paraphrase
AAAEIILNTT	italianate
AAAEIKLPRS	parakelias
AAAEILLPST	palatalise
AAAEILLPTZ	palatalize
AAAEILMPST	metaplasia
AAAEILMRTU	tularaemia
AAAEILNPRT	planetaria
AAAEILNPTT	palatinate
AAAEIMNPRS	paramnesia
AAAEIMNQRU	aquamarine
AAAEIMNRTU	Mauretania
AAAEINNRTV	Tananarive
AAAELLNPST	panatellas
AAAELLNRTT	tarantella
AAAELLPRSX	parallaxes
AAAELMMNOT	melanomata
AAAELMRSTT	metatarsal
AAAELNNSTT	antenatals
AAAELNPQSU	aquaplanes

AAAELNRTTU tarantulae	**AAAILNORTT** natatorial	**AABBEIRRSS** barbarises
AAAELNSTTT tantalates	**AAAILNOTTX** taxational	**AABBEIRRSZ** barbarizes
AAAELPRSST palaestras	**AAAILNRSTU** Australian	**AABBEKLLST** basketball
AAAEMORTTT teratomata	saturnalia	**AABBELLOSV** absolvable
AAAEPPRRSX parapraxes	**AAAILNSSST** assailants	**AABBELNRUY** unbearably
AAAFFIKNRR Kaffrarian	**AAAILOPRSV** Valparaíso	**AABBGGILNR** balbriggan
AAAFIILLRS alfilarias	**AAAILPPRSS** appraisals	**AABBIKLSST** kabbalists
AAAFIJNNRS Rafsanjani	**AAAIMNORST** inamoratas	**AABBIKORUV** Aboukir Bay
AAAFLORSST solfataras	**AAAIMNRSST** samaritans	**AABBILLNTU** balibuntal
AAAGGILLNO algolagnia	**AAAINNPRSS** Parnassian	**AABBILLOOS** boobiallas
AAAGGILRST gastralgia	**AAAINOPRSS** saponarias	**AABBILMNOY** abominably
AAAGGNNRTU gargantuan	**AAAINPSSTV** vanaspatis	**AABBIMRRSS** barbarisms
AAAGHILRRT arthralgia	**AAAIPPRRSX** parapraxis	**AABBLLMTTU** albumblatt
AAAGHIMNOP phagomania	**AAAJJKKORT** Jokjakarta	**AABCCDEKKP** backpacked
AAAGHIRSTY satyagrahi	**AAALLNRTUW** natural law	**AABCCDEKPS** backspaced
AAAGHNPSTU agapanthus	**AAALMNOPRR** paranormal	**AABCCDELOR** accordable
AAAGHPPRRS paragraphs	**AAALNNOSST** assonantal	**AABCCEELPT** acceptable
AAAGIILMNR marginalia	**AAALNOORSV** Savonarola	**AABCCEFKLS** blackfaces
AAAGIILMST galimatias	**AAALNRSTTU** tarantulas	**AABCCEHNST** bacchantes
AAAGIKNNTY Tanganyika	**AAAMNNORTT** tramontana	**AABCCEKKPR** backpacker
AAAGILMNNO anglomania	**AAAMNPSSTU** Maupassant	**AABCCEKPSS** backspaces
AAAGILNPRS Graian Alps	**AAAMRTZZZZ** razzmatazz	**AABCCELLLU** calculable
AAAGIMMNRR grammarian	**AABBBEJNOS** bobbejaans	**AABCCELOST** accostable
AAAGIMNSTT anastigmat	**AABBBELORS** absorbable	**AABCCELPTY** acceptably
AAAGIMRRST margaritas	**AABBCDEEKR** barebacked	**AABCCGIKLM** black magic
AAAGINNOPT Patagonian	**AABBCDEKLR** Blackbeard	**AABCCHHKST** hatchbacks
AAAGINNRST rangatiras	**AABBCDKLOR** blackboard	**AABCCIILOU** coulibiaca
AAAGJJKORT Jogjakarta	**AABBCDKORS** backboards	**AABCCIILST** cabalistic
AAAGJLNRUW Gujranwala	**AABBCEEHLL** bleachable	**AABCCIINRT** bacitracin
AAAGJNOTUU Guanajuato	**AABBCEILRS** ascribable	**AABCCIKKPS** pickabacks
AAAGKORTYY Yogyakarta	**AABBCELMOT** combatable	**AABCCIKNRR** crackbrain
AAAGLMMNPU Mpumalanga	**AABBCENORS** absorbance	**AABCCIORST** acrobatics
AAAGLRSSTU astragalus	**AABBCIILNR** rabbinical	**AABCCJKKLS** blackjacks
AAAGMNNOTU Guantánamo	**AABBCIJKRT** jackrabbit	**AABCCKKRST** backtracks
AAAGMNSTTY syntagmata	**AABBCILSST** cabbalists	**AABCCKRRSY** carrybacks
AAAHIILPPR paraphilia	**AABBCKLLLS** blackballs	**AABCCLLLUY** calculably
AAAHIKKLST kathakalis	**AABBCKMRRS** barmbracks	**AABCDDEELU** adduceable
AAAHIMMMST mahatmaism	**AABBCKNRRS** barnbracks	**AABCDDEHKN** backhanded
AAAHINSSTU Athanasius	**AABBDDEENN** Baden-Baden	**AABCDDEIRR** barricaded
AAAHKKNSTZ Kazakhstan	**AABBDDEORR** breadboard	**AABCDDEKLS** saddleback
AAAHKNRSST astrakhans	**AABBDEEELT** debateable	**AABCDDEMSU** ambuscaded
AAAHLLOSTY ayatollahs	**AABBDEGILR** abridgable	**AABCDDORRY** cardboardy
AAAHLMNPST phantasmal	**AABBDEGORR** bargeboard	**AABCDEEEFL** defaceable
AAAHLMNRSU Al Mansûrah	**AABBDEIRRS** barbarised	**AABCDEEHHS** beachheads
AAAIIMNRTU Mauritania	**AABBDEIRRZ** barbarized	**AABCDEEHHY** Beachy Head
AAAIINNRST sanitarian	**AABBDELORS** adsorbable	**AABCDEEHLT** detachable
AAAIINOPRS Pasionaria	**AABBDELSST** beadblasts	**AABCDEEILR** eradicable
AAAIKLLNST antalkalis	**AABBDEOORV** aboveboard	**AABCDEEKNR** breakdance
AAAIKLMNNT Kalimantan	**AABBDEORSS** baseboards	**AABCDEELLR** declarable
AAAIKLMNRS Karamanlis		bosberaads	**AABCDEELTU** educatable
AAAIKMMRSW Wasim Akram	**AABBEEELRT** rebateable	**AABCDEFIRT** fabricated
AAAIKRRTTU titarakura	**AABBEEHLRT** breathable	**AABCDEHIRT** brachiated
AAAIKSSTVY Savitskaya	**AABBEEIRTV** abbreviate	**AABCDEHKLS** blackheads
AAAILLLPTY palatially	**AABBEEKLRS** breakables	**AABCDEHKNR** backhander
AAAILLMNNZ manzanilla	**AABBEELLRT** barbellate	**AABCDEHKSW** backwashed
AAAILLNOTV lavational	**AABBEELNRU** unbearable	**AABCDEIILS** Alcibiades
AAAILLORTV lavatorial	**AABBEELNTU** unbeatable	**AABCDEIITV** abdicative
AAAILMMMNS mammalians	**AABBEILMNO** abominable	**AABCDEILRT** calibrated
AAAILMNRWY railwayman	**AABBEILNOT** obtainable	**AABCDEILRY** eradicably
AAAILMPSTU Tamaulipas	**AABBEILRRT** arbitrable	**AABCDEIRRR** barricader
AAAILNNOTT natational	**AABBEIMNWZ** Zimbabwean	**AABCDEIRRS** barricades
AAAILNNPRS planarians	**AABBEINRST** rabbinates	**AABCDEKLPS** backpedals

AABCDEKSWY	swaybacked		acerbating	**AABCENORST**	carbonates
AABCDELNNU	unbalanced	**AABCEGLLOU**	coagulable	**AABCERRTUU**	bureaucrat
AABCDELORS	scaleboard	**AABCEGLMNN**	blancmange	**AABCFHKLSS**	flashbacks
AABCDELORT	carbolated	**AABCEGLMRS**	cablegrams	**AABCFIKLRR**	Black Friar
AABCDEMSSU	ambuscades	**AABCEGPRST**	carpetbags	**AABCFINRST**	fabricants
AABCDENNOS	abondances	**AABCEHHKLT**	Blackheath	**AABCFIORRT**	fabricator
AABCDENNSU	abundances	**AABCEHIIMM**	Miami Beach	**AABCGIILLM**	galliambic
AABCDENORS	carbonades	**AABCEHILMN**	machinable	**AABCGIKNRR**	barracking
AABCDENORT	carbonated	**AABCEHILNN**	Balanchine	**AABCGILLSU**	subglacial
AABCDENPSS	spacebands	**AABCEHILPT**	alphabetic	**AABCGKMMNO**	backgammon
AABCDERSTT	abstracted	**AABCEHILRT**	charitable	**AABCHHIMPR**	amphibrach
AABCDGIINT	abdicating	**AABCEHINRT**	branchiate	**AABCHHPSTY**	bathyscaph
AABCDGIKNT	backdating	**AABCEHIRST**	brachiates	**AABCHIKRSY**	hairybacks
AABCDGKLRU	blackguard	**AABCEHKLRT**	blackheart	**AABCHILRTY**	charitably
AABCDHILNO	baldachino	**AABCEHKLSS**	backlashes	**AABCHINOTT**	cohabitant
AABCDHILNS	baldachins	**AABCEHKLSW**	whalebacks	**AABCHIOOPR**	acrophobia
AABCDHKLOR	chalkboard	**AABCEHKSSW**	backwashes	**AABCHKLPSS**	splashback
AABCDHMORT	matchboard	**AABCEHLNST**	stanchable	**AABCHNRRUY**	brachyuran
AABCDHNSTW	watchbands	**AABCEHPSTY**	bathyscape	**AABCIIKLOU**	koulibiaca
AABCDHOPRT	patchboard	**AABCEHRRTT**	tetrabrach	**AABCIIKLST**	kabalistic
AABCDIILLO	diabolical	**AABCEIILLM**	bacillemia	**AABCIILLMY**	iambically
AABCDIINOT	abdication	**AABCEIINRR**	carabinier	**AABCIILLRU**	bacilluria
AABCDILMMS	lambdacism	**AABCEIINTU**	beautician	**AABCIILLRY**	biracially
AABCDIORST	abdicators	**AABCEIILLR**	claribella	**AABCIILNOT**	anabolitic
AABCDKLMPS	blackdamps	**AABCEILLMP**	implacable	**AABCIILPTY**	capability
AABCDKLRWY	backwardly	**AABCEILLPP**	applicable	**AABCIILTTY**	actability
AABCDLOPRS	clapboards	**AABCEILMNS**	imbalances	**AABCIIOPRT**	parabiotic
AABCDNNORT	contraband	**AABCEILMOT**	ametabolic	**AABCIKLLMS**	blackmails
AABCDNOORS	carbonados	**AABCEILMST**	masticable	**AABCIKLLST**	blacktails
AABCDORSST	broadcasts	**AABCEILNOT**	actionable	**AABCIKRSST**	backstairs
AABCEEEFFL	effaceable	**AABCEILNST**	cantabiles	**AABCILLMPY**	implacably
AABCEEELMR	amerceable	**AABCEILOSS**	associable	**AABCILLPPY**	applicably
AABCEEEMRR	macebearer	**AABCEILOTT**	catabolite	**AABCILMOPR**	procambial
AABCEEERTT	ebracteate	**AABCEILQRU**	acquirable	**AABCILMORU**	columbaria
AABCEEERTX	exacerbate	**AABCEILRRT**	calibrater	**AABCILMOST**	catabolism
AABCEEFNRR	Benacerraf	**AABCEILRST**	calibrates	**AABCILNNUU**	incunabula
AABCEEGHLN	changeable	**AABCEIMNRS**	mainbraces	**AABCILNOST**	botanicals
AABCEEGHLR	chargeable	**AABCEINNTY**	betacyanin	**AABCILNOTY**	actionably
AABCEEHILV	achievable	**AABCEINORT**	abreaction	**AABCILNRSU**	subcranial
AABCEEHLNS	encashable	**AABCEINRRS**	carabiners	**AABCILNSUV**	subclavian
AABCEEHLPR	preachable	**AABCEIORST**	aerobatics	**AABCILORRT**	calibrator
AABCEEHLRS	searchable	**AABCEIRRTU**	bacteruria	**AABCILPRSU**	bicapsular
AABCEEHLTY	chalybeate	**AABCEIRSTT**	tetrabasic	**AABCILRRUV**	vibracular
AABCEEHRST	sabretache	**AABCEJKMRS**	amberjacks	**AABCILRSTU**	ultrabasic
AABCEEIMRT	bacteremia	**AABCEKKLNS**	blacksnake	**AABCIMMNOZ**	Mozambican
AABCEEINRR	carabineer	**AABCEKKMRR**	backmarker	**AABCINNORS**	carbanions
AABCEEIRTU	eubacteria	**AABCEKLRTW**	blackwater	**AABCIOQRSU**	aquarobics
AABCEEKLSS	leasebacks	**AABCEKPPRS**	paperbacks	**AABCIQSTUU**	subaquatic
AABCEEKNRS	canebrakes	**AABCEKPRRT**	bratpacker	**AABCKLLOTV**	Black Volta
AABCEELLLR	recallable	**AABCEKRRRS**	barrackers	**AABCKLLRST**	trackballs
AABCEELLNS	cleansable	**AABCEKRSTW**	backwaters	**AABCKLMOOR**	blackamoor
AABCEELNRT	tabernacle	**AABCELLNSU**	unscalable	**AABCKLPRST**	blackstrap
AABCEELPPR	recappable	**AABCELLORR**	barcarolle	**AABCKORRSZ**	razorbacks
AABCEELRTU	trabeculae	**AABCELLORS**	caballeros	**AABCLLNNOU**	cannonball
AABCEERSTT	bracteates	**AABCELMNSU**	ambulances	**AABCLMMRUU**	ambulacrum
AABCEESTTU	subacetate	**AABCELMOPR**	comparable	**AABCLMOPRY**	comparably
AABCEFIILP	pacifiable	**AABCELMTUU**	acetabulum	**AABCLORUVY**	vocabulary
AABCEFIRST	fabricates	**AABCELNNSU**	unbalances	**AABCMNOSTT**	combatants
AABCEFLORT	factorable	**AABCELNOTU**	outbalance	**AABCNOORRS**	barracoons
AABCEGHLNY	changeably	**AABCELOOSS**	calabooses	**AABCNORSST**	contrabass
AABCEGHLRY	chargeably	**AABCELORRS**	barcaroles	**AABDDDEEHL**	baldheaded
AABCEGINRT	abreacting	**AABCELRRTU**	trabecular	**AABDDEEEHR**	bareheaded

AABDDEEGHN	headbanged	**AABDEIQRTU**	biquadrate	**AABEEFNSST**	beanfeasts
AABDDEEGLR	degradable	**AABDEIRRTT**	arbitrated	**AABEEGHLRT**	gatherable
AABDDEEHNR	barehanded	**AABDEIRSST**	bastardise	**AABEEGILNR**	regainable
AABDDEEKLR	Abdelkader	**AABDEIRSTZ**	bastardize	**AABEEGIMNS**	Senegambia
AABDDEELMN	demandable	**AABDEJLSTU**	adjustable	**AABEEGLLST**	bagatelles
AABDDEGGNS	sandbagged	**AABDEKORST**	skateboard	**AABEEGLMSS**	assemblage
AABDDEGLSS	saddlebags	**AABDELLNNO**	belladonna	**AABEEGLNST**	East Bengal
AABDDEHLLN	handballed	**AABDELLNST**	tablelands	**AABEEGNORT**	baronetage
AABDDEHLMO	hebdomadal	**AABDELNOPR**	pardonable	**AABEEGRSUV**	subaverage
AABDDEHLRS	balderdash	**AABDELNRUV**	unreadably	**AABEEHKRRT**	heartbreak
AABDDEHORS	headboards	**AABDELNTUY**	unabatedly	**AABEEHLSTW**	swatheable
AABDDEMRTU	adumbrated	**AABDELRTSU**	balustrade	**AABEEHRRSS**	earbashers
AABDDHORSS	dashboards	**AABDELSTWY**	twayblades	**AABEEHRSTT**	heartbeats
AABDDILLMO	lambdoidal	**AABDEMNRST**	bandmaster	**AABEEILLRS**	realisable
AABDDLNORS	Broadlands	**AABDEMORST**	dreamboats	**AABEEILLRZ**	realizable
AABDDNNSST	bandstands	**AABDEMRSTU**	adumbrates	**AABEEILMNX**	examinable
AABDDORRST	dartboards	**AABDENSSTW**	sweatbands	**AABEEILNRT**	retainable
AABDEEEMNO	endamoebae	**AABDEOPPRR**	paperboard	**AABEEILPRR**	repairable
AABDEEFLRV	defrayable	**AABDEOPPRT**	approbated	**AABEEIMOSS**	amoebiases
AABDEEGLRR	regardable	**AABDEOPRST**	pasteboard	**AABEEJKRRW**	jawbreaker
AABDEEHLLN	handleable	**AABDEORSST**	adsorbates	**AABEEKLMRR**	remarkable
AABDEEHRRT	threadbare	**AABDFHLORS**	flashboard	**AABEEKLMRT**	marketable
AABDEEILNT	detainable	**AABDGIILRS**	garibaldis	**AABEEKLPPS**	bakeapples
AABDEEILRU	Baudelaire	**AABDGINNNO**	abandoning	**AABEEKLRRW**	lawbreaker
AABDEELLRS	balladeers	**AABDGKNNRS**	Grand Banks	**AABEEKRRTW**	breakwater
AABDEELNPX	expandable	**AABDGNNOSW**	bandwagons	**AABEELLLSZ**	sleazeball
AABDEELNRU	unreadable	**AABDHIILLU**	Abdullah II	**AABEELLMNT**	lamentable
AABDEELORT	elaborated	**AABDHIORSZ**	biohazards	**AABEELLNSU**	unsaleable
AABDEELPRS	spreadable	**AABDHMMNSU**	husbandman		unsealable
AABDEELPTU	updateable	**AABDHNORRW**	handbarrow	**AABEELLPRR**	pallbearer
AABDEELRRV	laverbread	**AABDHORSSW**	washboards	**AABEELMNNU**	unnameable
AABDEELRRW	rewardable	**AABDIIKRRY**	Diyarbakir	**AABEELMNTU**	untameable
AABDEEMNOS	endamoebas	**AABDIJNORS**	jaborandis	**AABEELMRSU**	measurable
AABDEENNOS	abandonees	**AABDIJOORU**	Ouija board	**AABEELMSTT**	metastable
AABDEFFLOR	affordable	**AABDILMNRU**	mandibular	**AABEELNNTT**	tenantable
AABDEFLRST	flatbreads	**AABDILNQSU**	baldaquins	**AABEELNORS**	reasonable
AABDEGGGNN	gangbanged	**AABDILOOPR**	paraboloid	**AABEELNOSS**	seasonable
AABDEGGINR	brigandage	**AABDILORSS**	sailboards	**AABEELNPTT**	patentable
AABDEGGNRS	sandbagger	**AABDILORST**	broadtails	**AABEELNRSW**	answerable
AABDEGHLNS	Bangladesh		tailboards	**AABEELOPRV**	evaporable
AABDEGINNO	gabionnade	**AABDILSSSU**	disabusals	**AABEELORST**	elaborates
AABDEGINOS	gabionades	**AABDIMNRRU**	barramundi	**AABEELPPRT**	palpebrate
AABDEGINRS	gabardines	**AABDINNRST**	trainbands	**AABEELPPRY**	prepayable
AABDEGORST	goatsbeard	**AABDINSSTW**	waistbands	**AABEELRRST**	arrestable
AABDEGRRSY	graybeards	**AABDJLSTUY**	adjustably	**AABEELSSSS**	assessable
AABDEHITTU	habituated	**AABDKLORSW**	boardwalks	**AABEELSTTT**	attestable
AABDEHKNRS	handbrakes	**AABDLNNTUY**	abundantly	**AABEEMNOST**	entamoebas
AABDEHKRSW	hawksbeard	**AABDLNOPRY**	pardonably	**AABEEMNSTT**	abatements
AABDEHLLNR	handballer	**AABDLNOSTU**	Basutoland	**AABEENRSST**	Barents Sea
AABDEHLNRS	handlebars	**AABDLNSSST**	sandblasts	**AABEEQRSSU**	arabesques
AABDEIILLS	labialised	**AABDLORRTY**	bardolatry	**AABEFGIILS**	gasifiable
AABDEIILLZ	labialized	**AABDORRSST**	starboards	**AABEFGKLNR**	klangfarbe
AABDEIKLNS	balkanised	**AABDORRSTW**	strawboard	**AABEFHLMOT**	fathomable
AABDEIKLNZ	balkanized	**AABEEEILLPR**	repealable	**AABEFIILLS**	salifiable
AABDEILLNR	banderilla	**AABEEEELLRS**	resaleable	**AABEFIILRT**	ratifiable
AABDEILLSY	dialysable		resealable	**AABEFILLNT**	inflatable
AABDEILLYZ	dialyzable	**AABEEELLRV**	revealable	**AABEFIMORS**	framboesia
AABDEILRSV	adverbials	**AABEEELPRT**	repeatable	**AABEFINRRT**	afterbrain
AABDEIMNOT	abominated	**AABEEEMNOT**	entamoebae	**AABEFKRSST**	breakfasts
AABDEINNOR	Aberdonian	**AABEEFILRR**	rarefiable	**AABEFLORUV**	favourable
AABDEINRTZ	bartizaned	**AABEEFLLLT**	flabellate	**AABEGGGNNR**	gangbanger
AABDEIOSSY	bioassayed	**AABEEFLNTT**	fattenable	**AABEGGINNT**	abnegating

AABEGGRRTY	ratbaggery	AABEILNNTU	biannulate	AABGIINNST	abstaining
AABEGHINRS	earbashing	AABEILNOST	anabolites	AABGILLNST	ballasting
AABEGHORRS	harborages	AABEILOPRS	parabolise	AABGILMNST	lambasting
AABEGHORRU	harbourage	AABEILOPRZ	parabolize	AABGILMNTU	ambulating
AABEGIILMN	imaginable	AABEILRSTU	tabularise	AABGILNSSY	assignably
AABEGILNOZ	zabaglione	AABEILRTTT	titratable	AABGILNTTU	tabulating
AABEGILNSS	assignable	AABEILRTUZ	tabularize	AABGIMNRSU	brugmansia
AABEGILRST	algebraist	AABEIMNORU	anaerobium	AABGINNOOT	Tobagonian
AABEGINNOT	abnegation	AABEIMNOST	abominates	AABGINNOTW	angwantibo
AABEGINNPT	gabapentin	AABEINORRT	aberration	AABGINOORT	abrogation
AABEGINNRT	interabang	AABEINORTT	trabeation	AABGINORTU	outbargain
AABEGINNRS	bargainers	AABEINRRTW	waterbrain	AABGIOSSSS	bagassosis
AABEGINRST	Great Basin	AABEINRSST	abstainers	AABGLNRUUY	unarguably
AABEGIRRST	arbitrages	AABEINRSVW	brainwaves	AABGNRRSUW	burrawangs
AABEGIRRSU	bigarreaus	AABEINSSTT	bastnasite	AABGOORRST	abrogators
AABEGKLORS	gaolbreaks	AABEINSTUV	Buena Vista	AABHHIKSSU	hibakushas
AABEGLNRUU	unarguable	AABEIORRTV	arborvitae	AABHIILOPS	basophilia
AABEGLOPPR	propagable	AABEIRRRST	barratries	AABHIILRSZ	bilharzias
AABEGMNRSU	submanager	AABEIRRSTT	arbitrates	AABHIIMNPS	amphibians
AABEGMNRTU	Baumgarten	AABEIRRTTT	bitartrate	AABHIINNTT	inhabitant
AABEGNORST	abnegators	AABEKLMRRY	remarkably	AABHIINOTT	habitation
AABEHIILTT	habilitate	AABEKLMRTY	marketably	AABHIKKLNU	Kublai Khan
AABEHILORV	behavioral	AABEKLNOOR	Alanbrooke	AABHIKLLRU	Rub' al Khali
AABEHIOOPR	aerophobia	AABEKLNSST	beanstalks	AABHILLTUY	habitually
AABEHISTTU	habituates	AABEKPPRRS	paperbarks	AABHIMMNRS	Brahmanism
AABEHKLNSU	unshakable	AABELLLNNU	annullable	AABHIMRTVZ	Bar Mitzvah
AABEHKNRSU	Barkhausen	AABELLLPRY	ballplayer	AABHIMSTVZ	Bas Mitzvah
AABEHLOSTW	whaleboats	AABELLMNTY	lamentably	AABHIMTTVZ	Bat Mitzvah
AABEHLQSSU	squashable	AABELLMOST	ameloblast	AABHINSSSW	washbasins
AABEHLRSZZ	belshazzar	AABELLNNTY	Ballantyne	AABHIPRRSV	vibraharps
AABEIIILLS	Isabella II	AABELLNPUY	unplayable	AABHKKORSV	Khabarovsk
AABEIILLSS	labialises	AABELMOSUX	ambosexual	AABHKLNSUY	unshakably
AABEIILLSZ	labializes	AABELMRSUY	measurably	AABHLLLOOU	hullabaloo
AABEIILMPR	impairable	AABELNNOTX	nontaxable	AABHLPSSYY	hypabyssal
AABEIILNRV	invariable	AABELNORSY	reasonably	AABIIILMTY	amiability
AABEIILNST	banalities	AABELNOSSY	seasonably	AABIILLNOT	libational
	insatiable	AABELNPRST	Barnstaple	AABIILLSTY	salability
AABEIILPRT	biparietal	AABELNRSWY	answerably	AABIILMTTY	tamability
AABEIILRSV	braaivleis	AABELOORRT	elaborator	AABIILNRRS	librarians
AABEIILSST	assibilate	AABELOPRRT	proratable	AABIILNRVY	invariably
AABEIIMOSS	amoebiasis	AABELOPRUV	vapourable	AABIILNSTY	insatiably
AABEIIRRTT	abirritate	AABELORSST	astrolabes	AABIILRTTY	ratability
AABEIIRSTU	aubrietias	AABELRSTTU	tablatures	AABIILTTXY	taxability
AABEIJKLRS	jailbreaks	AABELSTTTU	statutable	AABIIMNNSS	Minas Basin
AABEIJLOSU	beaujolais	AABEMOSSTT	steamboats	AABIINNSSY	Abyssinian
AABEIKLMST	mistakable	AABEMRSTTU	masturbate	AABIINNPRST	bipartisan
AABEIKLNSS	balkanises	AABENOPRTU	Buonaparte	AABIINRRTT	abirritant
AABEIKLNSZ	balkanizes	AABEOPPRST	approbates	AABIIOPRSS	parabiosis
AABEIKNNRT	barkantine	AABEPRRSUZ	superbazar	AABIJNORTU	abjuration
AABEIKNRRS	karabiners	AABEQRRSTU	Quatre Bras	AABIKLMOST	katabolism
AABEILLMPP	impalpable	AABFFIILTY	affability	AABIKLMSTY	mistakably
AABEILLNRS	ballerinas	AABFHILSWY	Walfish Bay	AABILLMNUY	bimanually
AABEILLNUV	invaluable	AABFLMNOTY	flamboyant	AABILLMPPY	impalpably
AABEILLORV	labiovelar	AABFLORUVY	favourably	AABILLNNUY	biannually
AABEILLRSY	realisably	AABGGGGINS	gasbagging	AABILLNOOT	oblational
AABEILLRYZ	realizably	AABGGIINNR	bargaining	AABILLNRUY	binaurally
AABEILMNRS	lamebrains	AABGGINORT	abrogating	AABILLNUVY	invaluably
AABEILMNTU	albuminate	AABGGINOST	sabotaging	AABILLORSS	isallobars
AABEILMNTV	ambivalent	AABGHILOOP	algophobia	AABILLRUVV	bivalvular
AABEILMPRT	impartable	AABGHOPRRS	barographs	AABILMNOSS	anabolisms
AABEILMPSS	impassable	AABGIILMNY	imaginably	AABILMNOTU	ambulation
AABEILMSUX	ambisexual	AABGIILNOR	aboriginal	AABILMPSSY	impassably

AABILMRSST	strabismal	**AACCEELLOT**	calceolate	**AACCGILNOR**	caracoling
AABILNOORT	abortional	**AACCEELNRS**	clearances	**AACCHIIRST**	archaistic
AABILNOOSV	Nova Lisboa	**AACCEELNRT**	accelerant	**AACCHILNPY**	chaplaincy
AABILNOSTT	battalions	**AACCEENTTU**	accentuate	**AACCHIMORT**	achromatic
AABILNOTTU	tabulation	**AACCEEORTV**	coacervate	**AACCHINNOR**	anachronic
AABILOPRST	parabolist	**AACCEFHKLS**	chalkfaces	**AACCHINRRS**	saccharins
AABIMNOORT	abominator	**AACCEFPRST**	spacecraft	**AACCHIOPRT**	cataphoric
AABINNORTY	antibaryon	**AACCEGHOST**	stagecoach	**AACCHIPRRS**	archicarps
AABINOSSTW	boatswains	**AACCEHILLM**	alchemical	**AACCHIQSUU**	Chuquisaca
AABIORRRTT	arbitrator	**AACCEHILLS**	cailleachs	**AACCHIRSTT**	cathartics
AABIRSSSTT	Bass Strait	**AACCEHILMN**	mechanical	**AACCHKLLUW**	chuckwalla
AABKKOORRU	kookaburra	**AACCEHILMR**	Carmichael	**AACCHLNORY**	acronychal
AABKLOSTUW	walkabouts	**AACCEHINNT**	cachinnate	**AACCHMORSU**	scaramouch
AABLLMNORY	abnormally	**AACCEHINRS**	saccharine	**AACCHNOTVY**	chatoyancy
AABLMNORSY	myrobalans	**AACCEHIRSS**	saccharise	**AACCIILLMT**	climatical
AABLMORTUY	ambulatory	**AACCEHIRSZ**	saccharize	**AACCIILLNU**	canaliculi
AABLOORRTY	laboratory	**AACCEHJKPS**	cheapjacks	**AACCIILORS**	sacroiliac
AABLORSTTU	tabulators	**AACCEHLNOT**	coelacanth	**AACCIILPRT**	accipitral
AABLOSSTTT	statoblast	**AACCEHORSS**	saccharose	**AACCIINPTY**	incapacity
AABLRSSTTU	substratal	**AACCEHRRST**	characters	**AACCIINRSS**	circassian
AABLSTTTUY	statutably	**AACCEHRRTY**	charactery	**AACCIINSTT**	tacticians
AABORRRSTU	barratrous	**AACCEHRTTW**	catchwater	**AACCILLRUV**	clavicular
AACCCDENOR	accordance	**AACCEHSSTW**	watchcases	**AACCILLTTY**	tactically
AACCCEENPT	acceptance	**AACCEIILNS**	caecilians	**AACCILMMUY**	immaculacy
AACCCEILTT	catalectic	**AACCEIINRV**	vicariance	**AACCILMNSU**	cacuminals
AACCCEINOT	catenaccio	**AACCEIIPST**	capacities	**AACCILNNOS**	canonicals
AACCCEIORT	cacciatore	**AACCEIIPTV**	capacitive	**AACCILNOOS**	occasional
AACCCEIRSU	accuracies	**AACCEIKMMO**	cockamamie	**AACCILOSTU**	acoustical
AACCCEOSTU	cactaceous	**AACCEILMRS**	acclaimers	**AACCILPRST**	practicals
AACCCINRUY	inaccuracy	**AACCEILMST**	acclimates	**AACCILRTUY**	articulacy
AACCDEENRS	ascendance	**AACCEILPTT**	cataleptic	**AACCIMNORS**	carcinomas
AACCDEENSU	succedanea	**AACCEINNOT**	canonicate		macaronics
AACCDEHIRS	saccharide	**AACCEINORV**	covariance		maccaronis
AACCDEHKRS	crackheads	**AACCEINPRT**	pancreatic	**AACCINNRSZ**	cancrizans
AACCDEHLOR	charcoaled	**AACCEINRRS**	cercarians	**AACCINORST**	Costa Rican
AACCDEHNOR	archdeacon	**AACCEINRTT**	cantatrice	**AACCINORTV**	vaccinator
AACCDEIIPR	epicardiac	**AACCEINRTU**	inaccurate	**AACCINOSTU**	accusation
AACCDEIIRS	acaricides	**AACCEINSTV**	vaccinates		anacoustic
AACCDEILMT	acclimated	**AACCEIRRTU**	caricature	**AACCINPTTY**	anaptyctic
AACCDEILNT	accidental	**AACCEISTUV**	accusative	**AACCINRSTU**	anacrustic
AACCDEILTU	aciculated	**AACCEJKLNS**	lancejacks	**AACCIOPRST**	capacitors
AACCDEIMNU	unacademic	**AACCEJKRRS**	carjackers	**AACCIORTTU**	autocratic
AACCDEINTV	vaccinated	**AACCEKNRSS**	crankcases	**AACCLLORTU**	calculator
AACCDEIOSV	advocacies	**AACCEKRRST**	racetracks	**AACCLMORSY**	cycloramas
AACCDELLTU	calculated	**AACCELLRST**	catcallers	**AACCLMSSTY**	cataclysms
AACCDELNOR	cladoceran	**AACCELLSTU**	calculates	**AACCLNOTTU**	contactual
AACCDELSTU	sacculated	**AACCELMSTY**	cyclamates	**AACCLNRRUU**	caruncular
AACCDEMNOO	cacodaemon	**AACCELMTUU**	accumulate	**AACCLORSVY**	slavocracy
AACCDENNSY	ascendancy	**AACCELORSU**	calcareous	**AACCMNORTY**	cartomancy
AACCDEORTT	coarctated	**AACCELRTUY**	accurately	**AACCNNOTTU**	accountant
AACCDGIILR	cardialgic	**AACCENRSTU**	crustacean	**AACCNORSST**	sacrosanct
AACCDHIILR	diarchical	**AACCEORSTT**	coarctates	**AACCOPRRSS**	sarcocarps
AACCDHILOT	cathodical	**AACCFGILLU**	calcifugal	**AACCORSTUY**	accusatory
AACCDHILRY	dyarchical	**AACCFHIRSY**	saccharify	**AACDDEEEFT**	defaecated
AACCDHIORS	saccharoid	**AACCFILLRY**	farcically	**AACDDEEEFLT**	defalcated
AACCDIIINT	adiactinic	**AACCFILRSU**	fascicular	**AACDDEEHLR**	decahedral
AACCDIIRTY	caryatidic	**AACCFINNRS**	Franciscan	**AACDDEEIRT**	eradicated
AACCDIISTU	diacaustic	**AACCGHIORY**	hagiocracy	**AACDDEELLR**	Calderdale
AACCDIORST	Caird Coast	**AACCGHIPRY**	graphicacy	**AACDDEELNR**	calendared
AACCEEELRT	accelerate	**AACCGHOPRY**	cacography	**AACDDEEMNS**	damascened
AACCEEGPRS	scapegrace	**AACCGIILMN**	acclaiming	**AACDDEEMRT**	demarcated
AACCEELLNT	cancellate	**AACCGILLNT**	catcalling	**AACDDEGNOS**	gasconaded

AACDDEEIJTU	adjudicate	**AACDEHKPRT**	packthread	**AACDELPSTU**	capsulated
AACDDEEILRU	Ciudad Real	**AACDEHLLNS**	dancehalls	**AACDELPTTU**	catapulted
AACDDEEILTU	acidulated	**AACDEHLMTY**	chlamydate	**AACDEMNSTU**	manducates
AACDDEEINOR	endocardia	**AACDEHLORT**	octahedral	**AACDEMORRT**	demarcator
AACDDEEINST	candidates	**AACDEHLRST**	cathedrals	**AACDENNNOS**	cannonades
AACDDEKLPS	packsaddle		clartheads	**AACDENNSST**	ascendants
AACDDEELNPS	landscaped	**AACDEHMNOR**	Andromache	**AACDENORRS**	carronades
AACDDEMNTU	manducated	**AACDEHNTTU**	unattached	**AACDENRSTT**	Tradescant
AACDDENNNO	cannonaded	**AACDEHOPPR**	approached		transacted
AACDDHKPWY	paddywhack	**AACDEHPRTU**	parachuted	**AACDENTTUU**	unactuated
AACDDIIMMR	MacDiarmid	**AACDEIILNT**	acetanilid	**AACDEOOPPT**	apocopated
AACDDIOTTU	autodidact		laciniated	**AACDEOPRRS**	radarscope
AACDDKPSWY	paddywacks	**AACDEIILPR**	epicardial	**AACDEORSUV**	cadaverous
AACDDMORSU	docudramas	**AACDEIINRR**	irradiance	**AACDFHINRT**	handicraft
AACDEEEFNS	defeasance	**AACDEIINRS**	radiancies	**AACDFHNRST**	handcrafts
AACDEEEFST	defaecates	**AACDEIIPRR**	pericardia	**AACDFIINOO**	aficionado
AACDEEEHNX	hexadecane	**AACDEIIPRT**	paediatric	**AACDFIMORR**	microfarad
AACDEEFHMS	shamefaced	**AACDEIIRTV**	divaricate	**AACDFIOPRS**	picofarads
AACDEEFLST	defalcates	**AACDEIISTU**	audacities	**AACDGHHINR**	Chandigarh
AACDEEFORT	defaecator	**AACDEIJLTV**	adjectival	**AACDGILMOT**	dogmatical
AACDEEGKPR	repackaged	**AACDEILLNS**	dalliances	**AACDGILNNS**	scandaling
AACDEEGNOT	anecdotage	**AACDEILLTV**	vacillated	**AACDGILNPR**	placarding
AACDEEHRTT	reattached	**AACDEILMNO**	demoniacal	**AACDGILOPR**	podagrical
AACDEEHRTX	ex cathedra	**AACDEILMNR**	aldermanic	**AACDGIMORR**	cardiogram
AACDEEIINT	taeniacide	**AACDEILNOR**	androecial	**AACDGINORS**	carangoids
AACDEEINRT	deracinate	**AACDEILNOS**	laodiceans	**AACDGINOTV**	advocating
AACDEEINRV	cadaverine	**AACDEILNSS**	scandalise	**AACDGLMORS**	cladograms
AACDEEIPTT	decapitate	**AACDEILNSZ**	scandalize	**AACDGORSTU**	coastguard
AACDEEIRST	eradicates	**AACDEILPSS**	asclepiads	**AACDHHIILR**	rhachidial
AACDEEITTV	deactivate	**AACDEILSTU**	acidulates	**AACDHHIMNS**	shadchanim
AACDEEJLTU	ejaculated		actualised	**AACDHIKRTU**	kurdaitcha
AACDEEJNNR	Jeanne d'Arc	**AACDEILTUZ**	actualized	**AACDHILMSY**	chlamydias
AACDEEKKLW	cakewalked	**AACDEIMNNO**	Macedonian	**AACDHINORS**	arachnoids
AACDEELMNO	Lacedaemon	**AACDEIMNTT**	admittance	**AACDHINORT**	anthracoid
AACDEELRSS	escaladers	**AACDEIMNTU**	acuminated	**AACDHINRST**	cantharids
AACDEELRTT	altercated	**AACDEIMPRS**	paramedics	**AACDHLMNRS**	marchlands
AACDEELTTY	acetylated	**AACDEIMSST**	steadicams	**AACDHLNPSS**	handclasps
AACDEEMNSS	damascenes	**AACDEIMSTT**	masticated	**AACDHLNRSS**	crashlands
AACDEEMRST	demarcates	**AACDEINNOR**	endocrania	**AACDHMNORR**	orchardman
AACDEENNTT	attendance	**AACDEINNRT**	incarnated	**AACDHNNORY**	chardonnay
AACDEENORU	Ecuadorean	**AACDEINOST**	diaconates	**AACDHPRRSS**	cardsharps
AACDEFINRU	fricandeau	**AACDEINOTV**	vacationed	**AACDIIILMR**	miracidial
AACDEFINST	fascinated	**AACDEINOTU**	acquainted	**AACDIILLRV**	larvicidal
AACDEFJNUU	Juan de Fuca	**AACDEINQUY**	inadequacy	**AACDIILMRS**	radicalism
AACDEFLORT	defalcator	**AACDEIORRT**	eradicator	**AACDIILMRT**	matricidal
AACDEGHHMU	gamahuched	**AACDEIOSST**	associated	**AACDIILNNR**	clinandria
AACDEGHHNR	chargehand	**AACDEIPSTU**	auspicated	**AACDIILPRR**	parricidal
AACDEGHMRU	gamaruched	**AACDEIPTTV**	captivated	**AACDIILPRT**	patricidal
AACDEGILNS	escalading	**AACDEIRSTY**	caryatides	**AACDIILSTT**	diastaltic
AACDEGIMNP	campaigned	**AACDEJLNTY**	adjacently	**AACDIINNRS**	cnidarians
AACDEGISTT	castigated	**AACDELLNOW**	allowanced	**AACDIINOPS**	diapasonic
AACDEGLOTU	catalogued	**AACDELLNSU**	calendulas	**AACDILLNRY**	cardinally
	coagulated	**AACDELMOPR**	camelopard	**AACDILMNNO**	calamondin
AACDEGNORS	gasconader	**AACDELNNTU**	cannulated	**AACDILMORY**	myocardial
AACDEGNOSS	gasconades	**AACDELNOPR**	endocarpal	**AACDILNSTY**	dynastical
AACDEHHTTW	deathwatch	**AACDELNPSS**	landscapes	**AACDIMNRTU**	undramatic
AACDEHILNS	enchiladas	**AACDELNRST**	declarants	**AACDINOOTV**	advocation
AACDEHILRS	charladies	**AACDELNSST**	sandcastle	**AACDINOSTU**	caudations
AACDEHILRT	tracheidal	**AACDELOPSS**	loadspaces	**AACDINRSTU**	traducians
AACDEHIMNT	machinated	**AACDELORRT**	declarator	**AACDIQRSTU**	quadratics
AACDEHIORS	icosahedra	**AACDELORST**	sacerdotal	**AACDJNOTTU**	coadjutant
AACDEHKMSS	smackheads	**AACDELOTUV**	autoclaved	**AACDLNOSSU**	scandalous

AACDLOSTUY	adactylous	**AACEELRTVY**	acervately
AACDMMNNOT	commandant	**AACEELSTTY**	acetylates
AACDMOSSUV	muscavados	**AACEEMPSST**	meatspaces
AACDNOORST	ostracodan	**AACEEMRRST**	maceraters
AACDNORRSS	crossandra	**AACEENNRSS**	arcaneness
AACDOORTVY	advocatory	**AACEENORSU**	arenaceous
AACEEEGHST	escheatage	**AACEENPRSS**	pancreases
AACEEEGNRS	careenages	**AACEENRSTU**	centaureas
AACEEEKMPR	peacemaker	**AACEEPRSTW**	waterscape
AACEEEELMNP	elecampane	**AACEERSSTV**	stavesacre
AACEEFIRST	cafeterias	**AACEFFIRST**	affricates
AACEEFLPST	faceplates	**AACEFGLMOU**	camouflage
AACEEFMRST	farcemeats	**AACEFGNRRS**	fragrances
AACEEGHNNR	carragheen	**AACEFGRSTT**	stagecraft
AACEEGHRUV	Che Guevara	**AACEFHLLNP**	chapfallen
AACEEGILLN	allegiance	**AACEFIILTT**	facilitate
AACEEGKPPR	prepackage	**AACEFIINST**	fanaticise
AACEEGKPRS	repackages	**AACEFIINTZ**	fanaticize
AACEEHHRST	heartaches	**AACEFILNSU**	final cause
AACEEHILNT	chatelaine	**AACEFILSTY**	fasciately
AACEEHINNP	phenacaine	**AACEFINSST**	fascinates
AACEEHIPRT	aphaeretic	**AACEFKMPRS**	packframes
AACEEHKPST	cheapskate	**AACEFLMORT**	malefactor
AACEEHLMNO	chamaeleon	**AACEFNNOOR**	Caernarfon
AACEEHLMNR	menarcheal	**AACEFRRTTW**	watercraft
AACEEHMNRV	aerenchyma	**AACEFRSTTT**	statecraft
AACEEHNNRT	anthracene	**AACEGHHMSU**	gamahuches
AACEEHPRST	eparchates	**AACEGHILNR**	alcheringa
AACEEHRSTT	reattaches	**AACEGHIMNP**	Champaigne
AACEEHRSTX	exarchates	**AACEGHIMRS**	archimages
AACEEILMRS	caramelise	**AACEGHINOR**	archegonia
AACEEILMRZ	caramelize	**AACEGHLMOU**	guachamole
AACEEILPRT	altarpiece	**AACEGHLNRS**	archangels
AACEEILRTV	calaverite	**AACEGHLOPS**	phascogale
	lacerative	**AACEGHMNPS**	champagnes
AACEEILSTT	elasticate	**AACEGHMOPR**	macrophage
AACEEIMNOT	acetonemia	**AACEGHMRSU**	gamaruches
AACEEIMNPT	emancipate	**AACEGHNORS**	anchorages
AACEEIMRTV	macerative	**AACEGIIMNT**	emaciating
AACEEINRST	catenaries	**AACEGIINRT**	acierating
AACEEIPPRT	appreciate	**AACEGIKNRT**	caretaking
AACEEIRTTV	reactivate	**AACEGILLNS**	galenicals
AACEEITUVV	evacuative	**AACEGILLPR**	preglacial
AACEEJLSTU	ejaculates	**AACEGILNRT**	lacerating
AACEEKKLRW	cakewalker	**AACEGILNSS**	analgesics
AACEEKMPRS	pacemakers	**AACEGILNST**	escalating
AACEEKRRST	caretakers	**AACEGILORT**	categorial
AACEELLLUV	valleculae	**AACEGILPPR**	paraplegic
AACEELLMSU	melaleucas	**AACEGILTUV**	victualage
AACEELLNOT	lanceolate	**AACEGIMNOS**	egomaniacs
AACEELLORT	reallocate	**AACEGIMNPR**	campaigner
AACEELLPRT	carpellate	**AACEGIMNRT**	macerating
AACEELMSTU	emasculate	**AACEGINNTT**	catenating
AACEELNPSS	pleasances	**AACEGINRSV**	vagrancies
AACEELNPTT	placentate	**AACEGINTUV**	evacuating
AACEELNSST	elastances	**AACEGINTVX**	excavating
AACEELNTTU	catenulate	**AACEGISSTT**	castigates
AACEELOPRT	capreolate	**AACEGJKRUV**	Kragujevac
AACEELOPSU	paleaceous	**AACEGKRSWV**	graywackes
AACEELPPSU	applesauce	**AACEGLMNOR**	carmagnole
AACEELPRST	paracletes	**AACEGLMORY**	acromegaly
AACEELRSTT	altercates	**AACEGLMOSU**	guacamoles

AACEGLORTU	cataloguer
AACEGLOSSU	coagulases
AACEGLOSTU	catalogues
	coagulates
AACEGMNRTY	termagancy
AACEGOPSST	scapegoats
AACEGORSTT	greatcoats
AACEHHILRR	hierarchal
AACEHHKLMS	hamshackle
AACEHHLPRT	heptarchal
AACEHIILRT	hieratical
AACEHIIMNT	haematinic
AACEHIIMSS	ischaemias
AACEHIIMTT	haematitic
AACEHIINPT	Cap-Haitien
AACEHILMNR	menarchial
AACEHILMPR	alphameric
AACEHILNOP	Cephalonia
AACEHILNPT	chainplate
AACEHILNRS	Lancashire
AACEHILNSS	selachians
AACEHILNST	chatelains
AACEHILOPT	apothecial
AACEHILPRS	seraphical
AACEHILPRX	hexaplaric
AACEHILPST	caliphates
	chaptalise
AACEHILPTZ	chaptalize
AACEHILRTT	theatrical
AACEHIMMPR	amphimacer
AACEHIMMTT	mathematic
AACEHIMNOT	theomaniac
AACEHIMNST	machinates
AACEHIMNSU	Manichaeus
	naumachies
AACEHIMPRS	pharmacies
AACEHIMRTU	haematuric
AACEHINNOU	ouananiche
AACEHINNRT	catarrhine
AACEHINRTT	anthracite
AACEHIOPRX	echopraxia
AACEHIPSTT	chapatties
AACEHIRRSS	archaisers
AACEHIRRSZ	archaizers
AACEHIRRTV	architrave
AACEHIRSTU	autarchies
AACEHIRTTT	chatterati
AACEHJKMMR	jackhammer
AACEHJOPRS	chaparejos
AACEHKLMRS	ramshackle
AACEHKLNOS	kalanchoes
AACEHKMMRT	matchmaker
AACEHKMNPU	Kampuchean
AACEHKMORS	hackamores
AACEHKMRTW	watchmaker
AACEHKRSSV	haversacks
AACEHLMMRW	clawhammer
AACEHLNPTY	phlyctaena
AACEHLOPSU	acephalous
AACEHLPRTY	archetypal
AACEHLRSTT	clathrates
	scarlet hat

AACEHMNPRY parenchyma	**AACEILPRRS** perisarcal	**AACELNNSTU** cannulates
AACEHMNRRT Carmarthen	**AACEILPTTU** capitulate	**AACELNOPTU** cantaloupe
AACEHMNRTY athermancy	**AACEILRTTU** articulate	**AACELNOTTV** octavalent
AACEHMNTTT attachment	**AACEILRTUU** auriculate	**AACELNRRUV** vernacular
AACEHMOPRT camphorate	**AACEILSSTU** actualises	**AACELNRTTU** tentacular
AACEHMORST Samothrace	casualties	**AACELNSSSU** casualness
AACEHNOPTY tachypnoea	**AACEILSTTT** stalactite	**AACELNTUUV** avunculate
AACEHNOSTV anchovetas	**AACEILSTUZ** actualizes	**AACELOPPSY** apocalypse
AACEHNPRSS sarpanches	**AACEIMMPRU** paramecium	**AACELOPRST** cleopatras
AACEHNSSTU acanthuses	**AACEIMNNOR** necromania	**AACELOPRSU** acarpelous
AACEHOPPRS approaches	**AACEIMNNST** anamnestic	**AACELORSST** escalators
AACEHOPRTY apothecary	**AACEIMNORS** macaronies	**AACELORSUU** lauraceous
AACEHPPRSS scrapheaps	**AACEIMNORT** maceration	**AACELOSSTV** Slave Coast
AACEHPRSTU parachutes	**AACEIMNORU** oceanarium	**AACELOSTUV** autoclaves
AACEIILMST calamities	**AACEIMNSTU** acuminates	**AACELPPRST** applecarts
AACEIILMTU maieutical	**AACEIMOPST** aposematic	**AACELPRSSU** Paracelsus
AACEIILPST capitalise	**AACEIMORRT** crematoria	**AACELPRTTY** calyptrate
AACEIILPTZ capitalize	**AACEIMPRRT** parametric	**AACELRSSTY** catalysers
AACEIIMNOT emaciation	**AACEIMSSTT** masticates	**AACELRSTUW** caterwauls
AACEIINNRV invariance	**AACEIMSTTT** metastatic	**AACELRSTYZ** catalyzers
AACEIINORT acieration	**AACEINNNTU** annunciate	**AACELSTTUU** auscultate
AACEIINPRR pericrania	**AACEINNOTT** catenation	**AACEMMOTTY** mycetomata
AACEIINPTT anticipate	**AACEINNPRT** pancreatin	**AACEMNOPRS** mascarpone
AACEIINRRS cinerarias	**AACEINNRST** incarnates	**AACEMNOPSW** spacewoman
AACEIINRST insectaria	**AACEINORTU** acetonuria	**AACEMNORST** Sacramento
AACEIINTTV inactivate	**AACEINORTV** vacationer	**AACEMNRSST** sacraments
vaticinate	**AACEINOTUV** evacuation	**AACEMORRST** macerators
AACEIIOPSS Cassiopeia	**AACEINOTVX** excavation	**AACEMPRSTU** metacarpus
AACEIIPRRS persicaria	**AACEINQRTU** reacquaint	**AACEMRRSSS** massacrers
AACEIIPRTT patriciate	**AACEINRRST** tarriances	**AACENNNOSY** annoyances
AACEIIPTTV capitative	**AACEINRSST** ascertains	**AACENNOTTZ** canzonetta
AACEIIRSTV vicariates	incrassate	**AACENNSSTV** vacantness
AACEIJLMST majestical	sectarians	**AACENORRTV** Travancore
AACEILLMNU animalcule	**AACEINSSST** assistance	**AACENRSSSU** assurances
AACEILLNOS escallonia	**AACEIORSTT** aerostatic	**AACENRSSSV** canvassers
AACEILLNRT carnallite	**AACEIOSSST** associates	**AACENRSTTU** cauterants
AACEILLNTT cantillate	**AACEIOSTVV** vasoactive	**AACEOOPPST** apocopates
AACEILLOSU alliaceous	**AACEIPSSTU** auspicates	**AACEORRTTT** terracotta
AACEILLPRT prelatical	**AACEIPSTTV** captivates	**AACEORSTUV** evacuators
AACEILLRRV varicellar	**AACEIRSSST** staircases	**AACEORSTVX** excavators
AACEILLRVY cavalierly	**AACEIRTTTV** attractive	**AACERRSTTT** attracters
AACEILLSTV vacillates	**AACEISSTUV** causatives	**AACFFGIINN** affiancing
AACEILLSTY salicylate	**AACEJKNRRT** natterjack	**AACFFHIOTT** act of faith
AACEILMMTU immaculate	**AACEJLORTU** ejaculator	**AACFGIILMN** magnifical
AACEILMNPS campaniles	**AACEKLPSSW** spacewalks	**AACFGIIMNT** magnificat
AACEILMNRT reclaimant	**AACEKNRRSS** ransackers	**AACFHIMNRS** chamfrains
AACEILMNRU unicameral	**AACELLLORT** collateral	**AACFHJKSST** jackshafts
AACEILMNTU calumniate	**AACELLLRST** saltcellar	**AACFHKNRST** crankshaft
AACEILMRTU tularaemic	**AACELLLRUV** vallecular	**AACFIIILRT** artificial
AACEILMSTV calmatives	**AACELLNOSW** allowances	**AACFIILNOR** California
AACEILNNRS carnelians	**AACELLNSST** castellans	**AACFIILSTT** fatalistic
AACEILNORT creational	**AACELLPRRY** carpellary	**AACFIIMNST** fanaticism
laceration	**AACELMMORS** sarcolemma	**AACFIIMORR** formicaria
reactional	**AACELMNOPT** complanate	**AACFIINOST** fasciation
AACEILNOST escalation	**AACELMNRVY** cavalrymen	**AACFILLOSU** fallacious
AACEILNPPS appliances	**AACELMOPSU** palmaceous	**AACFILMSTU** factualism
AACEILNPST analeptics	**AACELMORST** scleromata	**AACFILNORT** fractional
AACEILNPTU paniculate	**AACELMOSUV** malvaceous	**AACFILORST** solfataric
AACEILNRSS arsenicals	**AACELMOSUY** amylaceous	**AACFILORSV** varifocals
AACEILNRST lacertians	**AACELMPRST** campestral	**AACFILSTTU** factualist
AACEILNRTU retinacula	**AACELMSSST** classmates	**AACFILTTUY** factuality
AACEILNRUV naviculare	**AACELNNOTV** covenantal	**AACFINNNOR** Franconian

AACFINORST fascinator	**AACGLNORTU** octangular	**AACIILNNST** annalistic
AACFINSSTT fantastics	**AACGLNOSTU** coagulants	**AACIILNORS** salicornia
AACFLNNOTU nonfactual	**AACGLOORTU** coagulator	**AACIILNOST** antisocial
AACFNRSTTU surfactant	**AACGMORRST** cartograms	**AACIILNRST** Saint Clair
AACGGGGIMN cagmagging	**AACGORSSTU** sugarcoats	**AACIILNSTU** Saint Lucia
AACGGIILNT glaciating	**AACHHHISUU** chihuahuas	**AACIILPPST** papistical
AACGGIILOS sialagogic	**AACHHHILLRS** rhachillas	**AACIILPSTT** capitalist
AACGGIKNPS packagings	**AACHHILNPT** naphthalic	**AACIILRRTU** urticarial
AACGGILLNO algolagnic	**AACHIIRRSV** charivaris	**AACIILRSST** racialists
AACGGILNOT cataloging	**AACHILLOPT** allopathic	**AACIIMNNOT** anamniotic
AACGGILRST gastralgic	**AACHILMNOR** monarchial	**AACIIMNNRT** Martinican
AACGGLLMNO McGonagall	**AACHILMNRT** Altrincham	**AACIIMNRST** antiracism
AACGHHOPRT tachograph	**AACHILNNOV** halcyonian	**AACIIMNSTV** Vaticanism
AACGHIINRS archaising	**AACHILNNPT** plainchant	**AACIIMSSTT** astaticism
AACGHIINRZ archaizing	**AACHILNOSZ** chalazions	**AACIINNOPS** poincianas
AACGHIKNSW hacksawing	**AACHILNPRY** chaplainry	**AACIINNPTT** anticipant
AACGHILNPY anaglyphic	**AACHILOPST** chipolatas	**AACIINNRRT** trinacrian
AACGHILRRT arthralgic	**AACHILOPSY** polychasia	**AACIINNRVV** invariancy
AACGHIMNPS champaigns	**AACHILPRSU** haruspical	**AACIINOPTT** capitation
AACGHIOPRS sarcophagi	**AACHIMNNOR** anharmonic	**AACIINORTV** victoriana
AACGHISSTT shagtastic	**AACHIMNNRU** Manchurian	**AACIINOTTV** activation
AACGHLSSTW watchglass	**AACHIMNOOS** monochasia	cavitation
AACGHMMOSY chasmogamy	**AACHIMNOPR** anamorphic	**AACIINPRST** patricians
AACGHMOPRR macrograph	**AACHIMNORS** anachorism	**AACIINRSTT** antiracist
AACGHMORST tachograms	harmonicas	**AACIINSTTT** antistatic
AACGHOPRRS arcographs	maraschino	**AACIIORSUV** avaricious
AACGIILLST glacialist	**AACHIMNORT** achromatin	**AACIJNOSTT** jactations
AACGIILNNS canalising	machinator	**AACIKNSSTY** Kansas City
AACGIILNNZ canalizing	**AACHIMNORW** chairwoman	**AACILLMNTY** mantically
AACGIILNOT glaciation	**AACHIMNPST** phantasmic	**AACILLMORT** matrilocal
AACGIIMRRT margaritic	**AACHIMPRST** pharmacist	**AACILLMOTY** atomically
AACGIIMSTT astigmatic	**AACHIMRRST** matriarchs	**AACILLNOOT** allocation
AACGIINNPT captaining	**AACHIMRRTY** matriarchy	**AACILLNTUY** nautically
AACGIINPST paganistic	**AACHIMRSTT** Maastricht	**AACILLOOPR** coprolalia
AACGIINTTV activating	**AACHIMSSTT** asthmatics	**AACILLOPRT** allopatric
AACGIKMNRT tarmacking	**AACHINRSST** anarchists	patrilocal
AACGIKMORY karyogamic	**AACHINRSTU** Carthusian	**AACILLORTV** vacillator
AACGIKNNRS ransacking	**AACHIPRRST** patriarchs	**AACILLPTYV** atypically
AACGILLNOT allocating	**AACHIPRRTY** patriarchy	**AACILLSTTY** statically
AACGILLOSS scagliolas	**AACHIPRSTY** parastichy	**AACILMNOST** monastical
AACGILLRTY tragically	**AACHKMMRST** matchmarks	**AACILMNOTU** maculation
AACGILMNNY malignancy	**AACHLLORTT** altar cloth	**AACILMNOTY** claymation
AACGILMNTU maculating	**AACHLLPSTY** cataphylls	**AACILMORRT** lacrimator
AACGILNNTU canulating	**AACHLNNNOT** nonchalant	**AACILMORSU** marlacious
AACGILNPTY anaglyptic	**AACHLOPPRY** apocryphal	**AACILMOSTU** calamitous
playacting	**AACHLRRTUV** chartulary	**AACILMPPRY** paralympic
AACGILNSTY catalysing	**AACHMOOPRT** apochromat	**AACILNNOOT** conational
AACGILNTYZ catalyzing	**AACHMORTUY** tauromachy	**AACILNNOTU** canulation
AACGILPRSY spagyrical	**AACHNOOPST** Pocahontas	**AACILNNRTY** tyrannical
AACGIMNORT morganatic	**AACHNOSTTY** chatoyants	**AACILNOOTV** vocational
AACGIMNRSS massacring	**AACHORRSTU** catarrhous	**AACILNOPPT** panoptical
AACGIMPRST pragmatics	**AACHPRSTTW** watchstrap	**AACILNOPRS** parsonical
AACGIMRSTY magistracy	**AACIILLNNT** anticlinal	**AACILNOPST** placations
AACGINNPPT catnapping	**AACIILLNOS** salicional	**AACILNOPTY** nyctalopia
AACGINNSSV canvassing	**AACIILLOPT** apolitical	**AACILNORSS** scansorial
AACGINOOPR carpogonia	**AACIILLRST** altricials	**AACILNORTT** tractional
AACGINORTU argonautic	**AACIILMNOS** simoniacal	**AACILNOSTY** claytonias
AACGINRSTT castrating	**AACIILMNST** talismanic	**AACILNPPST** applicants
AACGINRTTT attracting	**AACIILMNTX** anticlimax	**AACILNPSTY** synaptical
AACGIORSTT castigator	**AACIILMPST** capitalism	**AACILNRSST** carnalists
AACGLLMOOY malacology	**AACIILMRSS** racialisms	**AACILNRSUV** naviculars
AACGLLSSWY scallywags	**AACIILNNOR** Carolinian	**AACILOORRT** oratorical

AACILOPPRT	applicator
AACILORRTU	curatorial
AACILORSTU	alacritous
	lactosuria
AACILPRRSU	spiracular
AACILPRRTU	particular
AACILPRSTY	paralytics
AACILPRTUY	capitulary
AACILQSTTU	acquittals
AACILRRSUU	auriculars
AACIMMNNOO	monomaniac
AACIMNOPRY	pyromaniac
AACIMNPRTU	pancratium
AACIMORSTT	masticator
AACIMOSTTU	automatics
AACINNOOTZ	actinozoan
AACINNORRT	contrarian
AACINNORST	carnations
AACINNOSTT	Constantia
AACINOOPTT	coaptation
AACINOOSTV	avocations
	Nova Scotia
AACINOPRSS	caparisons
AACINORSTT	castration
AACINORSTU	arcuations
AACINORTTT	attraction
AACINORTUY	cautionary
AACINOSSST	cassations
AACINOSSTU	causations
AACINOSTTU	actuations
AACINRSSST	sacristans
AACIOOPPRT	apotropaic
AACIOORSST	associator
AACIOPRTTV	captivator
AACIORRSTT	aristocrat
AACIORSTTV	activators
AACIOSSTTW	waistcoats
AACJKRSSTW	jackstraws
AACJLMRSUU	majuscular
AACJLNORSU	Juan Carlos
AACLLOPRSS	collapsars
AACLLORRUY	oracularly
AACLLRSUVY	vascularly
AACLMMOPSY	mycoplasma
AACLMNNOSW	clanswoman
AACLMOPRSS	sarcoplasm
AACLMORRTY	lacrymator
AACLNNORTU	connatural
AACLNOPSTU	cantaloups
AACLOORRTU	coloratura
AACLOPPRSS	papal cross
AACLOPRSTU	portulacas
AACMNOSTTU	catamounts
AACMOOPRRT	comparator
AACNNNOSTT	constantan
AACNORRSTT	transactor
AACNORRSTW	narrowcast
AACOOPPRSU	apocarpous
AACOOPSSTT	capotastos
AACORRSSTT	castrators
AACORRSTTT	attractors
	stratocrat

AADDDDEEEH	deadheaded
AADDDDGNRV	granddaddy
AADDDEEHHR	hardheaded
AADDDEEMRY	daydreamed
AADDDEILPR	paradiddle
AADDDEILRT	taradiddle
AADDEEHIMN	maidenhead
AADDEEHMST	mastheaded
AADDEEHNRV	verandahed
AADDEEILLN	Adélie Land
AADDEEIMNT	deaminated
AADDEEIRST	desiderata
AADDEELTUV	devaluated
AADDEEMRRY	daydreamer
AADDEEMRSU	admeasured
AADDEEMRSY	readymades
AADDEEPPRT	preadapted
AADDEESTTV	devastated
AADDEFHNST	handfasted
AADDEGHNOR	dragonhead
AADDEGIMMR	diagrammed
AADDEGIMNV	Magen David
AADDEGINRR	darraigned
AADDEGIPRS	disparaged
AADDEGIRRT	tardigrade
AADDEGMNOR	Armageddon
AADDEGNNOR	dragonnade
AADDEHIMNN	handmaiden
AADDEHLMNN	manhandled
AADDEHLNNP	panhandled
AADDEHNSST	headstands
AADDEIILPT	dilapidate
AADDEIIRRT	irradiated
AADDEILLNS	landladies
AADDEILNSV	vandalised
AADDEILNVZ	vandalized
AADDEILORR	railroaded
AADDEIMPST	misadapted
AADDEIMRST	dramatised
AADDEIMRTZ	dramatized
AADDEIRRSY	disarrayed
AADDELMRSS	maladdress
AADDEMNNST	demandants
AADDEORSST	roadsteads
AADDGILMOY	amygdaloid
AADDGNNRST	grandstand
AADDHHIRST	Siddhartha
AADDHNNRSY	shandrydan
AADDHNNSST	handstands
AADDIILNOT	additional
AADDIIMRSY	dairymaids
AADDILLLOV	Valladolid
AADDINORRT	ritardando
AADDINPRST	dandiprats
AADDLNOOSW	sandalwood
AADEEEHNNR	enneahedra
AADEEEKNRW	reawakened
AADEEEPPRR	reappeared
AADEEFGLRT	deflagrate
AADEEFHRST	fatshedera
AADEEFILRR	fairleader
AADEEGGGRT	aggregated

AADEEGHMST	megadeaths
AADEEGHNPS	phagedenas
AADEEGINTV	evaginated
AADEEGIRTV	variegated
AADEEGLMNS	magdalenes
AADEEGNORS	orangeades
AADEEGNPPS	appendages
AADEEGNRRR	rearranged
AADEEGNRTU	guaranteed
AADEEHHLRX	hexahedral
AADEEHHMMR	hammerhead
AADEEHHPRT	heptahedra
AADEEHIRTW	headwaiter
AADEEHKNSS	snakeheads
AADEEHMRST	headmaster
	headstream
AADEEHNPRT	pentahedra
AADEEHNRVW	heavenward
AADEEHPRSS	spearheads
AADEEHQRSU	headsquare
AADEEHRRTT	tetrahedra
AADEEHRSTW	headwaters
AADEEIKSWW	wideawakes
AADEEILLTV	alleviated
AADEEILMNT	delaminate
AADEEILNNR	adrenaline
AADEEILNRX	Aleixandre
	Alexander I
AADEEILNST	desalinate
AADEEILRTT	retaliated
AADEEIMNOU	eudaemonia
AADEEIMNRT	reanimated
AADEEIMNST	deaminates
AADEEIMPRT	preadamite
AADEEINNPT	antependia
AADEEINQTU	inadequate
AADEEINRTT	reattained
AADEEIPRTU	eupatridae
AADEEIPTTX	expatiated
AADEEIRSTT	asteriated
AADEEISTTV	aestivated
AADEELLLMT	lamellated
AADEELLLPR	paralleled
AADEELLMNS	allemandes
AADEELLPPR	apparelled
AADEELMNRV	Val-de-Marne
AADEELMRTT	maltreated
AADEELMSTT	stalemated
AADEELNNWZ	New Zealand
AADEELNPSS	esplanades
AADEELNRSX	alexanders
AADEELNRTT	alternated
AADEELQTUY	adequately
AADEELRTTU	adulterate
AADEELRTUV	revaluated
AADEELSTUV	devaluates
AADEEMQRSU	masquerade
AADEEMQSTU	desquamate
AADEEMRSSU	admeasures
AADEENSTVZ	Zend-Avesta
AADEENTTTU	attenuated
AADEEOPRTV	evaporated

471

AADEEEORSTT	toadeaters	**AADEGLNRSV**	landgraves	**AADEILNPPR**	appledrain
AADEEPRSST	paederasts	**AADEGLNRTU**	granulated	**AADEILNRRY**	drainlayer
AADEEPRSTY	paederasty	**AADEGLRSVW**	waldgraves	**AADEILNRSU**	unsalaried
AADEEERRSTT	retardates	**AADEGLRTTU**	gratulated	**AADEILNRTW**	landwaiter
AADEESSTTV	devastates	**AADEGMRRTU**	dramaturge	**AADEILNSSS**	Sea Islands
AADEFFIILT	affiliated	**AADEGOPPRT**	propagated	**AADEILNSSU**	unassailed
AADEFGLNNS	fandangles	**AADEGRRRSU**	rearguards	**AADEILNSSV**	vandalises
AADEFGRSSU	safeguards	**AADEGRRSVY**	graveyards	**AADEILNSTT**	tantalised
AADEFHLNRT	fatherland	**AADEHHKNSS**	handshakes	**AADEILNSTU**	andalusite
AADEFIIKLL	alkalified	**AADEHIIMNR**	maidenhair	**AADEILNSVZ**	vandalizes
AADEFIMNOT	defamation	**AADEHIIMRT**	diathermia	**AADEILNTTZ**	tantalized
AADEFINSST	fantasised	**AADEHIINRT**	antheridia	**AADEILNTZZ**	antidazzle
AADEFINSTZ	fantasized	**AADEHIKMNO**	Makedhonia	**AADEILORST**	asteroidal
AADEFINTTU	infatuated	**AADEHILNNT**	lanthanide	**AADEILORTV**	variolated
AADEFIRRSS	faradisers	**AADEHILORR**	diarrhoeal	**AADEILPPTT**	palpitated
AADEFIRRSZ	faradizers	**AADEHIORRT**	arthrodiae	**AADEILSSST**	diastalses
AADEFLNORS	farandoles	**AADEHIRSST**	stairheads	**AADEILSSSV**	vassalises
AADEFLOSTX	toadflaxes	**AADEHKLLMR**	hallmarked	**AADEILSSVZ**	vassalized
AADEFMORTY	defamatory	**AADEHKMOTW**	tomahawked	**AADEIMMNOT**	ammoniated
AADEFMRSST	farmsteads	**AADEHLLMRS**	marshalled	**AADEIMNNSW**	swan maiden
AADEFRRSTW	afterwards	**AADEHLLSST**	headstalls	**AADEIMNNTU**	unanimated
AADEGGILNT	gangliated	**AADEHLMNNR**	Arnhem Land	**AADEIMNOST**	anatomised
AADEGGIMNN	endamaging	**AADEHLMNNS**	manhandles	**AADEIMNOTZ**	anatomized
AADEGGINRS	aggrandise	**AADEHLNNPR**	panhandler	**AADEIMNRTV**	animadvert
AADEGGINRZ	aggrandize	**AADEHLNNPS**	panhandles	**AADEIMORST**	aromatised
AADEGGNOOR	dragoonage	**AADEHLNRST**	heartlands	**AADEIMORTZ**	aromatized
AADEGHHINS	shanghaied	**AADEHMMNOR**	Mohammedan	**AADEIMRRST**	dramatiser
AADEGHLNNR	handlanger	**AADEHMRSST**	stramashed	**AADEIMRRTZ**	dramatizer
AADEGHNRSY	hydrangeas	**AADEHNOPTY**	adenopathy	**AADEIMRSST**	dramatises
AADEGHNSST	stagehands	**AADEHORRSW**	arrowheads	**AADEIMRSTZ**	dramatizes
AADEGIINRT	eradiating	**AADEHNPRST**	deathtraps	**AADEINNOPT**	antipodean
AADEGILMNY	amygdaline	**AADEHRRSTW**	earthwards	**AADEINNQRU**	quadrennia
AADEGILNOS	analogised	**AADEHRRSSVW**	drawshaves	**AADEINORTY**	arytaenoid
AADEGILNOZ	analogized	**AADEIILMNS**	animalised	**AADEINPQSU**	pasquinade
AADEGILNSV	galvanised	**AADEIILMNZ**	animalized	**AADEINPRST**	pintaderas
AADEGILNTV	galivanted	**AADEIILMRW**	Waldemar II	**AADEINQRSU**	quandaries
AADEGILNVZ	galvanized	**AADEIILNTV**	invalidate	**AADEINQTTU**	antiquated
AADEGILPRR	paraglider	**AADEIILPRS**	lapidaries		aquatinted
AADEGILRST	saltigrade	**AADEIIMNNT**	diamantine	**AADEINRSST**	steradians
AADEGILTTY	agitatedly		maintained	**AADEINRSTT**	antitrades
AADEGIMMNS	mismanaged	**AADEIIMNST**	mediastina		attainders
AADEGIMNRS	smaragdine	**AADEIIMPRS**	imparadise	**AADEIOPQRU**	radiopaque
AADEGIMNRT	marginated	**AADEIINNTV**	vanadinite	**AADEIPPRSS**	disappears
AADEGIMNST	diamagnets	**AADEIINORT**	eradiation	**AADEIPPTTT**	pitapatted
AADEGIMRST	smaragdite	**AADEIINTTV**	adventitia	**AADEIPRSST**	disparates
AADEGINNTT	antedating	**AADEIIRRST**	irradiates	**AADEIPSSTV**	passivated
AADEGINPRT	readapting	**AADEIIRRTT**	triradiate	**AADEIRRSTT**	tartarised
AADEGINRRS	disarrange	**AADEIKLNSW**	Wake Island	**AADEIRRTTZ**	tartarized
AADEGINRST	tragedians	**AADEILLMMT**	mamillated	**AADEKLMORW**	meadowlark
AADEGINRTU	quarantied	**AADEILLMST**	Lammastide	**AADEKMRRST**	trademarks
AADEGIOPRR	radiopager	**AADEILMNNR**	mainlander	**AADELLMNPR**	Palmer Land
AADEGIORST	Deo gratias	**AADEILMNNS**	almandines	**AADELLMNRS**	mallanders
AADEGIPRRS	disparager	**AADEILMNRV**	Viña del Mar	**AADELLNPTT**	platteland
AADEGIPRSS	disparages	**AADEILMNTY**	animatedly	**AADELLNSTU**	landaulets
AADEGIRSTV	stravaiged	**AADEILMORT**	tailormade	**AADELLORSV**	El Salvador
AADEGIRTTV	gravitated	**AADEILMRTX**	taxidermal	**AADELLQRSU**	quadrellas
AADEGKNOOR	kangarooed	**AADEILMRVW**	Waldemar IV	**AADELMMNST**	Mandelstam
AADEGLLNRU	eglandular	**AADEILNNNS**	annelidans	**AADELMMORS**	melodramas
AADEGLLOPS	gallopades	**AADEILNNSU**	annualised	**AADELMNRRY**	aldermanry
AADEGLMNTU	mangulated	**AADEILNNUZ**	annualized	**AADELMNSSS**	landmasses
AADEGLNNRS	rangelands	**AADEILNOPR**	Adrianople	**AADELMOOST**	stomodaeal
AADEGLNQRU	quadrangle	**AADEILNOST**	dealations	**AADELMOPRR**	madreporal

AADELNRSTT translated	**AADGILRSTU** gradualist	**AADILORTVY** validatory
AADELNRTTU adulterant	**AADGIMORRS** radiograms	**AADILOSSVW** disavowals
AADELNSSTW wastelands	**AADGIMORSU** audiograms	**AADIMNNOST** damnations
AADELOPRST pardalotes	**AADGINNNVY** Yin and Yang	**AADIMNOPRY** myriapodan
AADELORSVW aardwolves	**AADGINORST** gradations	**AADIMNSUVZ** avizandums
AADELPPRSU applauders	**AADGINORTU** graduation	**AADIMOPPRU** parapodium
AADELPRSTW drawplates	**AADGINQRTU** quadrating	**AADIMRSSTT** dramatists
AADELRRTUX extradural	**AADGLMNSUY** salmagundy	**AADINNNOST** andantinos
AADELRSTWY eastwardly	**AADGLNOOSW** wagonloads	**AADINOORST** adorations
AADEMMNSSU mandamuses	**AADGLNRSSS** grasslands	**AADIOQRSUV** Quai d'Orsay
AADEMNORTY amendatory	**AADGMNNORT** montagnard	**AADJMNNPRU** panjandrum
AADEMNPRSS ampersands	**AADGMRRSTU** dramaturgs	**AADJORRTUY** adjuratory
AADEMOQRTU Torquemada	**AADGMRRTUY** dramaturgy	**AADLMNNRUY** laundryman
AADEMRRSST smartarsed	**AADGNNOPRS** snapdragon	**AADLMNPSSW** swamplands
AADENNPPST appendants	**AADGNNRSTU** grandaunts	**AADLMNPSUY** Palm Sunday
AADENNPSSU pandanuses	**AADGORRSTU** graduators	**AADMMNOORS** monodramas
AADENNRTTU denaturant	**AADHIILPSY** diaphysial	**AADMNOORSU** anadromous
AADENNSTTT attendants	**AADHIIMNOT** amianthoid	**AADNOOPPSW** sappanwood
AADENOPPRU Papandreou	**AADHILORRT** arthrodial	**AADNOPRRUW** wraparound
AADENOPRSU andropause	**AADHILRSST** tahsildars	**AAEEEFLMMT** metafemale
AADENOSWWX woadwaxens	**AADHILRTWW** withdrawal	**AAEEEGGMMT** megagamete
AADENPPRSS sandpapers	**AADHINNOST** danthonias	**AAEEEGGRTX** exaggerate
AADENRRSTT retardants	**AADHINOPSU** diaphanous	**AAEEEHNNST** Asantehene
AADENRSTTU transudate	**AADHIRRRSY** dysarthria	**AAEEEHRSST** heartsease
AADEORSTTV devastator	**AADHKLNRSS** landsharks	**AAEEELNPRS** paraselene
AADEQRRTUU quadrature	**AADHLMNRSS** marshlands	**AAEEELRTUV** reevaluate
AADFFGHNSY shandygaff	**AADHNSSSTW** washstands	**AAEEEPRSTX** exasperate
AADFFIISTV affidavits	**AADHORRSSU** hadrosaurs	**AAEEERSSTV** asseverate
AADFGIINRS faradising	**AADIIKLNST** Saint Kilda	**AAEEFGIMRT** afterimage
AADFGIINRZ faradizing	**AADIILLNST** tillandsia	**AAEEFGINTU** taeniafuge
AADFGLLNRS Grand Falls	**AADIILLSSU** Ladislaus I	**AAEEFGLLLT** flagellate
AADFIILNTU latifundia	**AADIILMMOT** ommatidial	**AAEEFHRSTV** aftershave
AADGGHISST haggadists	**AADIILNOPT** lapidation	**AAEEFKLMRT** fleamarket
AADGGIIMNR diagraming	**AADIILNOTV** validation	**AAEEFKPRST** afterpeaks
AADGGIINTV divagating	**AADIILNPRW** Rawalpindi	**AAEEFNRRST** Far Eastern
AADGGILMNY damagingly	**AADIILORTU** auditorial	**AAEEFRSTTT** aftertaste
AADGGILNNR garlanding	**AADIILQRUV** quadrivial	**AAEEGGGRST** aggregates
AADGGINRTU graduating	**AADIILSSST** diastalsis	**AAEEGGHMOU** haemagogue
AADGGLNOOW waggonload	**AADIILSSST** diastalsis	**AAEEGGHNRV** Gravenhage
AADGHHLNSU Lughnasadh	**AADIIMNOPS** dipsomania	**AAEEGHLNOT** halogenate
AADGHIILRU Dhaulagiri	**AADIIMNORT** admiration	**AAEEGHLOPS** esophageal
AADGHIMPRS diaphragms	**AADIIMNOST** staminodia	**AAEEGHRRSV** Hargreaves
AADGHIOPRR radiograph	**AADIIMNRSZ** zamindaris	**AAEEGILMNN** emalangeni
AADGHIPRSY dysgraphia	**AADIINORST** radiations	**AAEEGIMNRT** emarginate
AADGIIIRSS giardiasis	**AADIINRSSU** Nuri as-Said	**AAEEGIMRRR** remarriage
AADGIILNPS palisading	**AADIIOPRST** parasitoid	**AAEEGIMSSX** Sexagesima
AADGIILNPT lapidating	**AADIIORRRT** irradiator	**AAEEGINRTV** vegetarian
AADGIILNTV validating	**AADIIPRSST** aspidistra	**AAEEGINSTV** evaginates
AADGIIMNNR marinading	**AADIIRRSTV** Stradivari	**AAEEGIRSSV** savageries
AADGIINOTV divagation	**AADIJNORTU** adjuration	**AAEEGIRSTV** variegates
AADGIJNORU jaguarondi	**AADILLMNOS** Somaliland	**AAEEGKLRST** Great Lakes
AADGIJNRUU jaguarundi	**AADILLMOPS** plasmodial	**AAEEGLLSSS** galleasses
AADGILLNOY diagonally	**AADILLMORS** armadillos	**AAEEGLMNPS** plasmagene
AADGILLMNSU salmagundi	**AADILLMPSU** palladiums	**AAEEGMMNNT** management
AADGILMRSU gradualism	**AADILLNOST** allantoids	**AAEEGMMORR** aerogramme
AADGILNOOT odontalgia	**AADILLNPRY** prandially	**AAEEGMNORV** overmanage
AADGILNORS girandolas	**AADILLOPSS** sapodillas	**AAEEGMNRSS** manageress
AADGILNPPU applauding	**AADILMNNOS** adnominals	**AAEEGMNRST** East German
AADGILNRST Stalingrad	**AADILNORTU** durational	**AAEEGMNRTV** ravagement
AADGILORST gladiators	**AADILNRSSU** Aru Islands	**AAEEGNPRRR** prearrange
AADGILPSUV Daugavpils	**AADILNSSUW** duniwassal	**AAEEGNRRRR** rearranger
AADGILRRSU guardrails	**AADILORSTT** dilatators	**AAEEGNRRRS** rearranges

AAEEGNRSTU	guarantees	**AAEEELNOPRS**	aeroplanes	**AAEGHIMMNO**	hemangioma
AAEEGNRSXY	sexagenary	**AAEEELNPRRT**	parenteral	**AAEGHIMNOS**	mahoganies
AAEEGNSSSV	savageness	**AAEEELNRSTT**	alternates	**AAEGHINNNS**	shenanigan
AAEEGQRRTU	quarterage	**AAEEELNSTVX**	sexavalent	**AAEGHLNOPT**	heptagonal
AAEEHILRTX	exhilarate	**AAEEELPRSTY**	separately	**AAEGHLNPRS**	phalangers
AAEEHIMNST	haemateins	**AAEEELRSTTZ**	lazarettes	**AAEGHLNPRY**	pharyngeal
AAEEHIMPRY	hyperaemia	**AAEEELRSTUV**	revaluates	**AAEGHLNRUX**	hexangular
AAEEHINSST	anesthesia	**AAEEEMMNRRT**	rearmament	**AAEGHMNOPR**	anemograph
AAEEHIPRSS	aphaeresis	**AAEEEMPPRSS**	parameters		phanerogam
AAEEHKNPRY	Harney Peak	**AAEEEMSSSTT**	metastases	**AAEGHNOPRS**	orphanages
AAEEHKQRTU	earthquake	**AAEEENPPRST**	parapentes	**AAEGHNORSS**	angashores
AAEEHLMRTX	hexametral	**AAEEENRRSTW**	warrantees	**AAEGHNRRSU**	haranguers
AAEEHLNTTVX	hexavalent	**AAEEENSTTTU**	attenuates	**AAEGHOPRRY**	aerography
AAEEHLRRSS	rehearsals	**AAEEEOPRSSU**	aeropauses		areography
AAEEHMNORR	amenorrhea	**AAEEEOPRSTV**	evaporates	**AAEGHRSSTW**	wheatgrass
AAEEHMNRTU	Haute-Marne	**AAEEEPPRSTW**	wastepaper	**AAEGIILLNV**	villainage
AAEEHMNRTW	weatherman	**AAEEEPPRSTY**	ratepayers	**AAEGIILNNT**	alienating
AAEEHMNSTU	athenaeums	**AAEFFHRSTT**	aftershaft	**AAEGIILPRS**	plagiaries
AAEEHMNSTX	exanthemas	**AAEFFIILST**	affiliates		plagiarise
AAEEHMPRST	metaphrase	**AAEFFILRSS**	rafflesias	**AAEGIILPRZ**	plagiarize
AAEEHNOSTU	Haute-Saône	**AAEFFINPRS**	paraffines	**AAEGIINNTV**	invaginate
AAEEHNPRSV	Enver Pasha	**AAEFFINRST**	raffinates	**AAEGIINRTT**	ingratiate
AAEEHRRSTW	shearwater	**AAEFGHNRTU**	fearnaught	**AAEGIIPRST**	epigastria
AAEEHRRTTW	heartwater	**AAEFGISTST**	fastigiate	**AAEGIKMNRR**	earmarking
AAEEHRSTWW	Hawes Water	**AAEFGINNPR**	frangipane	**AAEGILLMNT**	ligamental
AAEEIILNRS	Eilean Siar	**AAEFGIRSSX**	saxifrages	**AAEGILLMOS**	allogamies
AAEEIKLMNS	seamanlike	**AAEFGLLLNS**	Angel Falls	**AAEGILLMQU**	maquillage
AAEEIKMNOT	ketonaemia	**AAEFGLLLNT**	flagellant	**AAEGILLNOT**	allegation
AAEEILLMMT	Tamil Eelam	**AAEFGLLNRU**	langlaufer	**AAEGILLORT**	legatorial
AAEEILLRTT	alliterate	**AAEFGLMNRT**	fragmental	**AAEGILLPRS**	aspergilla
AAEEILLSTV	alleviates	**AAEFGLSSTV**	flagstaves	**AAEGILLRSU**	sugarallie
AAEEILMORT	ameliorate	**AAEFHNRSUU**	hausfrauen	**AAEGILLSSS**	galliasses
AAEEILMRSS	lamaseries	**AAEFIIKLLS**	alkalifies	**AAEGILMNRT**	martingale
AAEEILNPRT	penetralia	**AAEFIILLRS**	alfilerias	**AAEGILMORR**	rigamarole
AAEEILRSTT	aliterates	**AAEFIILSTT**	fatalities	**AAEGILMSTT**	stalagmite
	retaliates	**AAEFILLNRX**	fraxinella	**AAEGILNNST**	galantines
AAEEILRTTV	alterative	**AAEFILMNOU**	meiofaunal	**AAEGILNNTT**	tangential
AAEEILTUVV	evaluative	**AAEFILNNOT**	La Fontaine	**AAEGILNOSS**	analogises
AAEEIMNNSX	Anaximenes	**AAEFIMMNRS**	mainframes	**AAEGILNOSZ**	analogizes
AAEEIMNRRW	weimaraner	**AAEFINNRSS**	safranines	**AAEGILNPPR**	appareling
AAEEIMNRST	reanimates	**AAEFINPRST**	afterpains	**AAEGILNPPS**	lagniappes
AAEEINPPRV	papaverine	**AAEFINSSST**	fantasises	**AAEGILNPRV**	palavering
AAEEIPPRRS	reappraise	**AAEFINSSTZ**	fantasizes	**AAEGILNRSV**	galvaniser
AAEEIPRRTT	repatriate	**AAEFINSTTU**	infatuates	**AAEGILNRVZ**	galvanizer
AAEEIPRRTV	reparative	**AAEFKLLSST**	leafstalks	**AAEGILNSSV**	galvanises
AAEEIPRSTV	separative	**AAEFKLNRRS**	farnarkels	**AAEGILNSVZ**	galvanizes
AAEEIPRTTX	expatriate	**AAEFLLNSTU**	fustanella	**AAEGILNTUV**	evaluating
AAEEIPSTTX	expatiates	**AAEFLLRSTW**	waterfalls	**AAEGILPRTY**	apterygial
AAEEISSTTV	aestivates	**AAEFLNRRST**	transferal	**AAEGILRSTT**	tailgaters
AAEEJPRRSW	jasperware	**AAEFNNOSST**	San Stefano	**AAEGIMMNRS**	mismanager
AAEEKLNNPS	palankeens	**AAEGGGORRT**	aggregator	**AAEGIMMNSS**	mismanages
AAEEKLNPSS	Lassen Peak	**AAEGGILLNS**	galingales	**AAEGIMNRRS**	margarines
AAEEKMRSTT	tastemaker	**AAEGGILNSW**	Glaswegian		misarrange
AAEEKNPSTW	wapentakes	**AAEGGILOSU**	sialagogue	**AAEGIMNRRV**	margravine
AAEEKPRRST	parrakeets	**AAEGGLLNOS**	gallonages	**AAEGIMNRST**	marginates
AAEELLPRTY	platelayer	**AAEGGLMOSU**	magalogues	**AAEGIMRSTT**	magistrate
AAEELLQRSU	aquarelles	**AAEGGOPRSU**	paragogues	**AAEGINNOST**	antagonise
AAEELLTTTT	tattletale	**AAEGHILLSS**	Galashiels	**AAEGINNOTZ**	antagonize
AAEELMNPST	nameplates	**AAEGHILNPR**	nephralgia	**AAEGINNSTU**	nauseating
AAEELMPRRT	marprelate	**AAEGHILORT**	hagiolater	**AAEGINPRSS**	paganisers
AAEELMRRTT	maltreater	**AAEGHILPSY**	hypalgesia	**AAEGINPRST**	separating
AAEELMSSTT	stalemates	**AAEGHILRTU**	gaultheria	**AAEGINPRSZ**	paganizers

AAEGINRRRS	arraigners	**AAEHINOPST**	asthenopia
AAEGINRSSY	gainsayers	**AAEHINPSST**	phantasies
AAEGINRSTU	guaranties	**AAEHIPSTXY**	asphyxiate
AAEGINRTUU	inaugurate	**AAEHLLMRRS**	marshaller
AAEGIORRTV	arrogative	**AAEHLMRRSS**	marshalers
AAEGIRRTTV	gravitater	**AAEHLNOPSY**	synaloepha
AAEGIRSTTV	gravitates	**AAEHLNPSSY**	synalephas
AAEGKLMNOS	maskalonge	**AAEHLOPPRS**	phalaropes
AAEGKLMRSS	glassmaker	**AAEHLPSTTU**	spathulate
AAEGKLNOPY	Poyang Lake	**AAEHMNRSST**	harassment
AAEGKMNNOS	maskanonge	**AAEHMNRSTV**	harvestman
AAEGLLPSST	plateglass	**AAEHMORTTX**	metathorax
AAEGLLRRTU	ultralarge	**AAEHMOSSTT**	haemostats
AAEGLMNSTU	mangulates	**AAEHMPRSTT**	metaphrast
AAEGLMORSU	megalosaur	**AAEHMRSSST**	stramashes
AAEGLMSTTU	glutamates	**AAEHMRSSTU**	shamateurs
AAEGLNNOPT	pentagonal	**AAEHNNRSTU**	Tannhäuser
AAEGLNORTT	tetragonal	**AAEHNOPRST**	anastrophe
AAEGLNRRTU	granulater	**AAEHNPPSWW**	wappenshaw
AAEGLNRSTU	granulates	**AAEHOPPSTY**	apophysate
AAEGLNRSUX	sexangular	**AAEHPPRSSY**	paraphyses
AAEGLPPRSS	glasspaper	**AAEIIILNST**	italianise
AAEGLPRSSV	palsgraves	**AAEIIILNTZ**	italianize
AAEGLRSSTW	waterglass	**AAEIIJNRSZ**	janizaries
AAEGLRSTTU	gratulates	**AAEIIKNOST**	Seto Naikai
AAEGMMNOST	Mostaganem	**AAEIILLPTV**	palliative
AAEGMMORST	agrostemma	**AAEIILLRSX**	axillaries
AAEGMNPRST	pentagrams	**AAEIILMMRT**	immaterial
AAEGMNRSTT	termagants	**AAEIILMNRS**	animaliers
AAEGMOPRSU	rampageous		seminarial
AAEGMRRSTT	tetragrams	**AAEIILMNSS**	animalises
AAEGMRSSTT	stratagems	**AAEIILMNSZ**	animalizes
AAEGNOPRSS	parsonages	**AAEIILMRST**	latimerias
AAEGOPPRST	propagates	**AAEIILMSST**	assimilate
AAEGOPSTTY	steatopyga	**AAEIILNNOT**	alienation
AAEGRRSSTZ	stargazers	**AAEIILNNST**	salientian
AAEHHHILLLU	halleluiah	**AAEIILNPST**	sapiential
AAEHHJLLLU	hallelujah	**AAEIILNSST**	nasalities
AAEHHKMNRS	Kermanshah	**AAEIILNSTT**	natalities
AAEHHLPRTY	hypaethral	**AAEIILNSTV**	insalivate
AAEHHMNRSV	Marheshvan	**AAEIILRSST**	aerialists
AAEHIILMNS	leishmania	**AAEIIMNNRS**	seminarian
AAEHIILNNT	annihilate	**AAEIIMNNRT**	maintainer
AAEHIILRSV	Rhea Silvia	**AAEIIMPPRR**	primiparae
AAEHIIMNNT	amianthine	**AAEIIMRRTT**	termitaria
AAEHIIMNOP	hemianopia	**AAEIIPPRSV**	appraisive
AAEHIKRRST	hairstreak	**AAEIIPRSST**	parasitise
AAEHILLOPT	palaeolith	**AAEIIPRSTZ**	parasitize
AAEHILNOTX	exhalation	**AAEIIRSTVX**	aviatrixes
AAEHILNRTX	exhilarant	**AAEIKLNPST**	Stalin Peak
AAEHILNSST	Thessalian	**AAEIKMNNRS**	rainmakers
AAEHILNSTV	leviathans	**AAEIKMRSST**	samarskite
AAEHILPSTT	asphaltite	**AAEIKNNRST**	Transkeian
AAEHILPSTW	Westphalia	**AAEIKOSSTU**	Sato Eisaku
AAEHILRSST	harestails	**AAEILLLLNV**	villanella
AAEHIMNPRY	hypermania	**AAEILLLRST**	saltarelli
AAEHIMNPSS	seamanship	**AAEILLMMMT**	mammillate
AAEHIMNSTY	myasthenia	**AAEILLMPRX**	premaxilla
AAEHIMOSST	haematosis	**AAEILLMRTY**	materially
	hemostasia	**AAEILLNORT**	relational
AAEHIMRSTU	amateurish	**AAEILLNPRS**	enalaprils
AAEHINNORV	Hanoverian	**AAEILLNPRU**	nulliparae

AAEILLNPSS	sailplanes
AAEILLNPST	tailplanes
AAEILLNRTU	unilateral
AAEILLORTV	alleviator
AAEILLPRXY	preaxially
AAEILLPSSS	paillasses
	palliasses
AAEILLRRTT	trilateral
AAEILLRRTY	arterially
AAEILLRTTY	laterality
AAEILLRTVY	varietally
AAEILMNNSU	semiannual
AAEILMNORT	ameliorant
AAEILMNPRT	parliament
AAEILMNPTU	manipulate
AAEILMNRSU	aneurismal
AAEILMNRTY	alimentary
AAEILMNRWY	railwaymen
AAEILMNSST	assailment
AAEILMNSTU	aluminates
AAEILMPRRT	premarital
AAEILMPRTU	multiparae
AAEILMPSTT	palmitates
AAEILNNOPT	neapolitan
AAEILNNOTV	venational
AAEILNNRTU	Laurentien
AAEILNNSSU	annualises
AAEILNNSUZ	annualizes
AAEILNOORT	areolation
AAEILNOQTU	equational
AAEILNORST	alienators
	rationales
	senatorial
AAEILNORTT	alteration
AAEILNORTU	laureation
AAEILNORTX	relaxation
AAEILNOTTX	exaltation
AAEILNOTUV	evaluation
AAEILNPRST	Palestrina
AAEILNPSTX	taxiplanes
AAEILNRSSY	reanalysis
AAEILNRSTT	tantaliser
AAEILNRSTU	naturalise
AAEILNRTTZ	tantalizer
AAEILNRTUZ	naturalize
AAEILNSSTT	tantalises
AAEILNSTTZ	tantalizes
AAEILOPRRS	leprosaria
AAEILOPRRT	praetorial
AAEILOQRTU	equatorial
AAEILORRTT	retaliator
AAEILORSTV	lavatories
	variolates
AAEILPPRSS	paralipses
AAEILPPSTT	palpitates
AAEILRSSSW	wassailers
AAEILSSSSV	vassalises
AAEILSSSVZ	vassalizes
AAEILSSTUV	assaultive
AAEILSTUXY	asexuality
AAEIMMNOST	ammoniates
AAEIMMNRST	mainstream

AAEIMMRSTU	amateurism	AAEKLMPRSV	playmakers	AAEMPRSSTY	paymasters
AAEIMNNOPR	praenomina	AAEKLPRSST	lapstrakes	AAEMRRSSST	smartarses
AAEIMNNOST	anamniotes		lapstreaks	AAEMRSSSTT	mattrasses
	emanations	AAEKMRRSTW	watermarks	AAEMRSSTTU	metatarsus
AAEIMNNOSV	mayonnaise	AAEKMRSSTT	taskmaster	AAENNPPRTU	unapparent
AAEIMNNSSU	amanuensis	AAEKNORTTZ	Kazan Retto	AAENNPRRST	trapanners
AAEIMNNTTT	attainment	AAEKRRSTUU	sauerkraut	AAENNSTTTU	attenuants
AAEIMNOORT	erotomania	AAELLLLMRY	lamellarly	AAENORTTTU	attenuator
AAEIMNORST	anatomiser	AAELLLMNOS	salmonella	AAENPSSTTW	sweatpants
AAEIMNORTZ	anatomizer	AAELLLORST	saltarello	AAENQRRTUV	quaternary
AAEIMNOSST	anatomises	AAELLMNRTY	maternally	AAENRRRSTW	warranters
AAEIMNOSTZ	anatomizes	AAELLMORTT	martellato	AAENRRSTTU	restaurant
AAEIMNPRTZ	nitrazepam	AAELLMORZZ	mozzarella	AAENSSTTTT	attestants
AAEIMNQSTU	antimasque	AAELLMPRTY	malapertly	AAEOOPRRTV	evaporator
AAEIMNRTTT	antimatter	AAELLNNOTY	neonatally	AAEOPRRRTY	reparatory
AAEIMORSST	aromatises	AAELLNOSSY	seasonally	AAEOPRRSST	separators
AAEIMORSTZ	aromatizes	AAELLNPPST	appellants	AAEOPRRSTY	separatory
AAEIMOSSTT	Metastasio	AAELLNPRTY	parentally	AAEOPRSSTT	pastorates
AAEIMOSTTU	automatise		paternally	AAEORSTTTT	attestator
AAEIMOTTUZ	automatize		prenatally	AAEQRRSTUW	quartersaw
AAEIMPRSST	separatism	AAELLNPSTY	pleasantly	AAERRSSTTU	saturaters
AAEIMQRSTU	marquisate	AAELLPPRSW	wallpapers	AAFFFGLSST	flagstaffs
AAEIMRRSST	airstreams	AAELLRSTTT	tattersall	AAFFGIMNRU	ragamuffin
AAEIMRSTTU	traumatise	AAELMMPSST	metaplasms	AAFFGNRSSU	suffragans
AAEIMRTTUV	maturative	AAELMNNORT	ornamental	AAFFIINOTX	affixation
AAEIMRTTUZ	traumatize	AAELMNNOPSU	menopausal	AAFFIMNRST	affirmants
AAEIMSSSTT	metastasis	AAELMNOSSW	saleswoman	AAFGIINNPR	frangipani
AAEINNNOTX	annexation	AAELMNRSUV	aneurysmal	AAFGILNNTU	antifungal
AAEINNOSTU	nauseation	AAELMORSSU	elasmosaur	AAFGILNSST	falangists
AAEINNOTTV	annotative	AAELMRRTUX	extramural	AAFGINNSTY	fantasying
AAEINNQRTU	quarantine	AAELNNNPRU	penannular	AAFGINRSWY	wayfarings
AAEINNRSST	stannaries	AAELNNPSTU	unpleasant	AAFGLLNRTY	flagrantly
AAEINNRTUV	avanturine	AAELNOPRST	rotaplanes	AAFGLLORST	allografts
AAEINNSSST	Saint-Saëns	AAELNORRTT	alternator	AAFGLNRRTY	fragrantly
AAEINOPRRT	praetorian	AAELNPPRTY	apparently	AAFGORSTTU	autografts
	reparation	AAELNPRRSU	suprarenal	AAFHHINORS	Shah of Iran
AAEINOPRST	separation	AAELNPRSTT	transeptal	AAFIIILRSS	filariasis
AAEINOPSST	passionate	AAELNPRSTY	pleasantry	AAFIIKNRST	Kafiristan
AAEINPPRST	appertains	AAELNRSSTT	translates	AAFIILLMRY	familiarly
AAEINQSTTU	antiquates	AAELNRSSUY	uranalyses	AAFIILMNRU	unfamiliar
AAEINRRSTV	narratives	AAELNRSTUV	transvalue	AAFIINRRTU	fruitarian
AAEINRRSTW	warranties	AAELNRSTUX	transexual	AAFILNOOTT	floatation
AAEINRRTTZ	tartrazine	AAELNSSTTU	sultanates	AAFILNOSTX	aflatoxins
AAEINRSTTT	intrastate		tantaluses	AAFILORSUW	rauwolfias
AAEINRTTTU	attainture	AAELOOPSTT	apostolate	AAFIMMORRS	samariform
AAEIOPRRSS	aspersoria	AAELOPRSST	pastorales	AAFIMOORRS	afrormosia
AAEIOPRTTX	expatiator	AAELORRSSU	rearousals	AAFIOQRSTU	aquafortis
AAEIOPSSST	apostasies	AAELORRSTX	extrasolar	AAGGHINNRU	haranguing
AAEIOPSSTT	apostatise	AAELORRTTV	travelator	AAGGIILNTT	tailgating
AAEIOPSTTZ	apostatize	AAELORSSTT	attolasers	AAGGIINNPS	paganising
AAEIORSTTV	aestivator	AAELORSTTZ	lazarettos	AAGGIINNPT	paginating
AAEIPPRRSS	appraisers	AAELORSTUV	evaluators	AAGGIINNPZ	paganizing
AAEIPPRRSTX	separatrix	AAELPRRSTU	superaltar	AAGGIINNRR	arraigning
AAEIPRSSTT	separatist	AAELPRRTTT	rattletrap	AAGGIINNSY	gainsaying
AAEIPSSSTV	passivates	AAELRRSSTV	traversals	AAGGIINNTV	navigating
AAEIRRRRVY	Yarra River	AAELRSSSTU	assaulters	AAGGILLNNT	gallanting
AAEIRRSSTT	tartarises	AAEMMORSTT	mattamores	AAGGILNNTU	angulating
AAEIRRSTTZ	tartarizes	AAEMMNNORTT	tramontane	AAGGIMMNUY	mamaguying
AAEJKLRSWY	jaywalkers	AAEMMNNRSV	manservant	AAGGIMNORS	angiograms
AAEJNNORTU	Juantorena	AAEMMNOOSST	anastomose	AAGGINNOPR	paragoning
AAEJOOOPSS	João Pessoa	AAEMNPRSTT	apartments	AAGGINNSTT	stagnating
AAEKLMPRST	platemarks	AAEMPRSSTT	pastmaster	AAGGINORRT	arrogating

AAGGINRSTZ	stargazing
AAGGKLNNPS	gangplanks
AAGGLLLOSS	galloglass
AAGGNNOOPP	Pango Pango
AAGHHIMNWY	highwayman
AAGHILLLLN	hallalling
AAGHILMNRS	marshaling
AAGHILMNSW	Walsingham
AAGHILNPST	asphalting
	phalangist
AAGHILOPPY	polyphagia
AAGHILORTY	hagiolatry
AAGHILPSSU	ispaghulas
AAGHIMPRRS	marigraphs
AAGHINPRSS	springhaas
AAGHINRSSS	harassings
AAGHLLOPRS	allographs
AAGHMMMOPR	mammograph
AAGHNNSSTU	Hsüan-tsang
AAGHNOPPRT	pantograph
AAGHOPRSTU	autographs
AAGHOPRSTY	Pythagoras
AAGHOPRTUY	autography
AAGIIILMNR	airmailing
AAGIIKLLNS	alkalising
AAGIIKLLNZ	alkalizing
AAGIIKMNNR	rainmaking
AAGIIKNPRS	paraskiing
AAGIILLNPT	palliating
AAGIILLNVY	availingly
AAGIILMNNT	laminating
AAGIILMPRS	plagiarism
AAGIILNNPS	salpingian
AAGIILNNSS	nasalising
AAGIILNNSZ	nasalizing
AAGIILNNUV	unavailing
AAGIILNRTV	travailing
AAGIILNSSW	wassailing
AAGIILNSTV	salivating
AAGIILPRST	plagiarist
AAGIIMNNRT	marinating
AAGIIMNOPR	parmigiano
AAGIINNOPT	pagination
AAGIINNOTV	navigation
AAGIINNTTT	attainting
AAGIINOSTT	agitations
AAGIINPPRS	appraising
AAGIINPRST	aspirating
AAGIINRSTV	Tsvangirai
AAGIJKLNWY	jaywalking
AAGIJLOSUV	Jugoslavia
AAGIKLLNTY	alkylating
AAGIKMRSSS	kissagrams
AAGILLMNRY	alarmingly
	marginally
AAGILLNSTV	gallivants
AAGILLORSS	glossarial
AAGILLORST	alligators
AAGILLPSSW	galliwasps
AAGILLSTTY	sagittally
AAGILMNNST	malignants
AAGILMNORS	organismal
AAGILMOPRS	paralogism
AAGILMRSST	magistrals
AAGILNNOTU	angulation
AAGILNOPRS	sporangial
AAGILNOSST	analogists
AAGILNPRSY	paralysing
AAGILNPRYZ	paralyzing
AAGILNRRTU	triangular
AAGILNRSUU	inaugurals
AAGILNRSUV	vulgarians
AAGILNRTUY	angularity
AAGILNSSTU	assaulting
AAGILOPRST	paralogist
AAGILOSUVY	Yugoslavia
AAGIMMPRST	pragmatism
AAGIMMNNOST	antagonism
AAGIMNOTTU	automating
AAGIMNPRRT	ramparting
AAGIMNPRST	ptarmigans
AAGIMNPTTU	amputating
AAGIMNRTTU	maturating
AAGIMNSSTY	gymnasiast
AAGIMORSTU	matagouris
AAGIMPRSST	pragmatist
AAGIMSSSST	massagists
AAGINNNOTT	annotating
AAGINNNPRT	trapanning
AAGINNOSTT	antagonist
	stagnation
AAGINNRRTW	warranting
AAGINNRSUY	sanguinary
AAGINOOPST	topagnosia
AAGINOORRT	arrogation
AAGINOOSTV	vagotonias
AAGINORSTV	navigators
AAGINORTTV	rotavating
AAGINRSTTU	antitragus
	saturating
AAGINSSTTU	sitatungas
AAGKMORRSY	karyograms
AAGLLMOOSU	allogamous
AAGLLNOPTT	topgallant
AAGLLNRRUY	granularly
AAGLMMNOOQ	Qomolangma
AAGLMNORSU	granulomas
AAGLMOOPRR	polarogram
AAGLNNSTTY	stagnantly
AAGLNORRTU	granulator
AAGLNORRTY	arrogantly
AAGMMMMORS	mammograms
AAGMOOSTUU	autogamous
AAGNNORSTU	orangutans
AAGNORRSTU	guarantors
AAGOOPPRRT	propagator
AAGOOPRRST	Protagoras
AAGOORRRST	arrogators
AAGORRRSSW	arrowgrass
AAHHHOPRTT	haphtaroth
AAHHIIMRSS	maharishis
AAHHILMOPT	ophthalmia
AAHHILNNPT	naphthalin
AAHHILNPTY	hypanthial
AAHHIMMMSS	shammashim
AAHHIMRRTY	arrhythmia
AAHHLORSTT	throatlash
AAHIIKMNRS	Kashmirian
AAHIIKNSUY	Yuan Shi Kai
AAHIILNNOT	inhalation
AAHIILNOPS	Hispaniola
AAHIIMPRSS	pharisaism
AAHIKMORST	matrioshka
AAHIKPPSSS	Shipka Pass
AAHILLOPRT	prothallia
AAHILMOOTX	homotaxial
AAHILMTTUZ	altazimuth
AAHILNNOPT	antiphonal
AAHILNORST	inhalators
AAHILOPPSY	apophysial
	hypoplasia
AAHILORSTU	haustorial
AAHIMMNOTY	mythomania
AAHIMNSSST	shamanists
AAHINNOTTX	xanthation
AAHINPSTXY	asphyxiant
AAHINRSTUV	hantavirus
AAHIPPRSSY	paraphysis
AAHIPRRSSY	hairsprays
AAHKLOORSY	Yoshkar-Ola
AAHKMORSTY	matryoshka
AAHKOPTUUW	pohutukawa
AAHLLLLOSW	Allhallows
AAHLLMOPSY	hyaloplasm
AAHLLMMOPTY	lymphomata
AAHLNNNOST	lanthanons
AAHMNPPRSY	paranymphs
AAHMOPPRRS	paramorphs
AAHNNOOSTZ	anthozoans
AAHNNRSTUY	thysanuran
AAHNOPRTTU	naturopath
AAHNORRSTU	anarthrous
AAHORSTWWY	throwaways
AAIIIKNRST	Kristiania
AAIIILMMNT	militiaman
AAIIILMMNX	Maximilian
AAIIILMNRT	limitarian
AAIIJKNSTT	Tajikistan
AAIIJLNORT	janitorial
AAIIKLLNTY	alkalinity
AAIIILLNOPT	palliation
AAIIILLNUXY	uniaxially
AAIIILMMNSS	animalisms
AAIIILMMRST	martialism
AAIIILMMSTX	maximalist
AAIIILMNNOT	antimonial
	lamination
AAIIILMNORT	minatorial
AAIIILMNSST	animalists
AAIIILMRSTT	martialist
AAIIILNNSTU	Lusitanian
AAIIILNOPSS	palinopsia
AAIIILNORRT	irrational
AAIIILNOSTV	salivation
AAIIILNRSTY	sanitarily
AAIIILPPRSS	paralipsis

AAIILPRTTY	partiality	
AAIILPSTTY	spatiality	
AAIIMMNOTX	maximation	
AAIIMNNNOT	antinomian	
AAIIMNNOPT	impanation	
AAIIMNNORT	marination	
AAIIMNNOST	animations	
AAIIMNRSTU	sanitarium	
AAIIMNSSSS	Massinissa	
AAIIMPPRRS	primiparas	
AAIIMPRSST	parasitism	
AAIINNOSTT	sanitation	
AAIINNRRTU	Ruritanian	
AAIINNRSTU	unitarians	
AAIINNRSTV	invariants	
AAIINNRSTY	insanitary	
AAIINOPPRT	apparition	
AAIINOPRST	aspiration	
AAIINOPRTT	patriation	
	tritanopia	
AAIINORSTV	variations	
AAIINRSTWZ	Waziristan	
AAIIRSSSTY	satyriasis	
AAIJLLNPSU	Julian Alps	
AAIJRSSSTW	swarajists	
AAIKKMOSVY	Mayakovski	
AAIKLLNOTY	alkylation	
AAIKLPRSTT	Palk Strait	
AAIKNNOPST	pontianaks	
AAIKNOSTTU	taikonauts	
AAIKNQRSTU	antiquarks	
AAIKRSSTTU	autarkists	
AAILLLPSTU	pulsatilla	
AAILLMMMRY	mammillary	
AAILLMOPPS	papillomas	
AAILLMORST	tamarillos	
AAILLNNOOP	Apollonian	
AAILLNNOTY	nationally	
AAILLNNSTT	installant	
AAILLNOPST	spallation	
AAILLNORSY	orinasally	
AAILLNORTY	notarially	
	rationally	
AAILLNOSTV	vallations	
AAILLOPRST	palliators	
AAILLRSTUY	salutarily	
AAILMNOPST	palmations	
AAILMNORST	laminators	
AAILMNOTTU	mutational	
AAILMNRRTU	intramural	
AAILMNRSTU	naturalism	
AAILMOPPRX	approximal	
AAILMORRTY	Mariolatry	
AAILMPRSSU	marsupials	
AAILNNNOTU	annulation	
AAILNNOOTT	notational	
AAILNNOPTT	plantation	
AAILNNORTZ	intrazonal	
AAILNNOTTU	nutational	
AAILNNPQSU	palanquins	
AAILNNRTUY	annularity	
AAILNOORTT	rotational	

AAILNOPPST	palpations	
AAILNOPSSS	passionals	
AAILNOPSUW	paulownias	
AAILNOSSTT	saltations	
AAILNOSSTV	salvations	
AAILNOSTTU	salutation	
AAILNOSTUV	valuations	
AAILNPRSTU	tarpaulins	
AAILNPSSTU	Saint Paul's	
AAILNRSSUY	uranalysis	
AAILNRSTTU	naturalist	
AAILOOPRYZ	polyzoaria	
AAILORSTTT	altostrati	
AAILOSSTTT	tsotsitaal	
AAIMMOSTTU	automatism	
AAIMMRSTTU	traumatism	
AAIMNOORST	inamoratos	
AAIMNOOTTU	automation	
AAIMNOPTTU	amputation	
AAIMNOQSTU	squamation	
AAIMNORSTU	sanatorium	
AAIMNORTTU	maturation	
	natatorium	
AAIMNOSSTT	anatomists	
AAIMNPRSSU	marsupians	
AAIMOSTTTU	automatist	
AAINNNOOST	San Antonio	
AAINNNOOTT	annotation	
AAINNNSSSY	sannyasins	
AAINNNSTTU	annuitants	
AAINNORRST	narrations	
AAINNRSTUY	unsanitary	
AAINOOPPRT	protanopia	
AAINOORRST	oratorians	
AAINOPSSTT	antipastos	
AAINORSTTU	saturation	
	titanosaur	
AAINORSTTV	starvation	
AAINORSTTY	stationary	
AAINPRSTTWY	pantywaist	
AAINRSTTTV	Vansittart	
AAINSSSSTT	assistants	
AAIOPPRRST	apparitors	
AAIOPRRSST	aspirators	
AAIOPRRSTY	aspiratory	
AAIOPSSTTU	autopistas	
AAIORRSTTT	trattorias	
AAKKLNORRS	Karlskrona	
AAKKMORRST	Kramatorsk	
AAKLMOPRSY	karyoplasm	
AAKLNORSUY	ankylosaur	
AAKMMNORSW	markswoman	
AAKMNNORTY	Mark Antony	
AAKNOOSSST	saskatoons	
AALLMNORUY	monaurally	
AALLMNOTWY	tallywoman	
AALLMNTUUY	autumnally	
AALLNNOPSY	pollyannas	
AALLOPRSTY	pastorally	
AALLORSSUU	allosaurus	
AALLRSTTWY	stalwartly	
AALMOOPPRS	malapropos	

AALMOOPRTY	laparotomy	
AALMOPRSXY	paroxysmal	
AALMOQSSSU	squamosals	
AALMORRTYY	Maryolatry	
AALNNNORTU	nonnatural	
AALNNOOPST	pantaloons	
AALNNPRSTT	transplant	
AALNNRRSTU	translunar	
AALNOOPSZZ	pozzolanas	
AALNOOPUZZ	pozzuolana	
AALNOPRRST	transpolar	
AALNOPRSST	transposal	
AALNOPSUZZ	puzzolanas	
AALNORRSTT	translator	
AALOORRTTV	travolator	
AALOPRRSTY	portrayals	
AALOPSTTUY	autoplasty	
AALORSTTTY	statolatry	
AALORSTTUY	salutatory	
AAMNNOTTTU	tantamount	
AAMNOOSTTU	automatons	
AAMNOPRSTU	paramounts	
AAMOOPPTTX	Appomattox	
AAMOOSSTTU	astomatous	
AAMOOSTTUU	automatous	
AAMOOPRSTTU	amputators	
AAMORSSSUU	mosasaurus	
AANNOORSTT	annotators	
AANOOPRSTU	anatropous	
AANORRRSTW	warrantors	
AANORSSTTU	astronauts	
AANOSTTTWW	Watson-Watt	
AAOOPPRRST	paratroops	
AAOORRSTTV	rotavators	
AAORRSSTTU	saturators	
ABBBEELMNT	babblement	
ABBBEGILNR	blabbering	
ABBBEHISSU	bushbabies	
ABBBEILNRU	unbribable	
ABBBGIINTT	babbitting	
ABBCCDEKMO	backcombed	
ABBCCKKLOS	backblocks	
ABBCCKKLSU	blackbucks	
ABBCDEEHMR	bedchamber	
ABBCDEHINO	Bondi Beach	
ABBCDEKNRU	backburned	
ABBCDEMRRU	breadcrumb	
ABBCDIKLRS	blackbirds	
ABBCDKLOOR	blockboard	
ABBCDKORSU	buckboards	
ABBCEFHIIR	Chief Rabbi	
ABBCEGINRU	barbecuing	
ABBCEIKNTT	backbitten	
ABBCEIKRST	backbiters	
ABBCEILMNO	combinable	
ABBCEILRSU	subcaliber	
	subcalibre	
ABBCEINSSS	scabbiness	
ABBCEKLRRY	blackberry	
ABBCELRRSS	scrabblers	
ABBCENORSY	absorbency	
ABBCFGINNO	confabbing	

ABBCGIIKNT backbiting	**ABBEILNOTU** obnubilate	**ABCCHIIMOR** choriambic
ABBCGIIORT gabbroitic	**ABBEIMNOST** bombinates	**ABCCHIIRRT** tribrachic
ABBCGILNRS scrabbling	**ABBEINORSX** brainboxes	**ABCCHIKSTT** backstitch
ABBCIILLLY biblically	**ABBELLRTTU** butterball	**ABCCHIKSTW** switchback
ABBCIIRRTU barbituric	**ABBELMOORZ** bamboozler	**ABCCHILOTU** coachbuilt
ABBCKLLSUY buckyballs	**ABBELMOOSZ** bamboozles	**ABCCHIOOPR** acrophobic
ABBCKLOOST bootblacks	**ABBELMSSUU** subsumable	**ABCCHKLOST** backcloths
ABBCKLSTTU blackbutts	**ABBELORSVY** observably	**ABCCHKOSTU** touchbacks
ABBCLMOOSU abcoulombs	**ABBELOSSTY** stableboys	**ABCCIILOST** bioclastic
ABBDDOORSY bodyboards	**ABBELQRSSU** squabblers	**ABCCIKRSST** crabsticks
ABBDEEGILR bridgeable	**ABBENORSST** absorbents	**ABCCILNORY** carbonylic
ABBDEEHLPS pebbledash	**ABBERSSUUU** subbureaus	**ABCCILORXY** carboxylic
ABBDEELNNU unbendable	**ABBERSUUUX** subbureaux	**ABCCILOTUU** Boucicault
ABBDEELORU belaboured	**ABBFFIILMU** bumbailiff	**ABCCIMOORT** mobocratic
ABBDEELRSU bluebeards	**ABBFHIIRST** rabbitfish	**ABCCINORTU** buccinator
ABBDEEORRS reabsorbed	**ABBFHLLSSU** flashbulbs	**ABCCINORTY** corybantic
ABBDEFIORR fiberboard	**ABBFILORST** fibroblast	**ABCCIOOPRS** baroscopic
fibreboard	**ABBGHINRRU** rhubarbing	**ABCCKKOORS** crookbacks
ABBDEGIINR Bainbridge	**ABBGIILNOR** ibn-Gabirol	**ABCCKLLOUY** cockabully
ABBDEILMOT bombilated	**ABBGIILNOT** bobtailing	**ABCCKNOSTU** countbacks
ABBDEILOUY Douay Bible	**ABBGILLNOS** billabongs	**ABCCKORSTU** backcourts
ABBDEIMNOT bombinated	**ABBGILMNRS** bramblings	**ABCDDEFIKL** fiddleback
ABBDEIMORR bombardier	**ABBGILNQSU** squabbling	fiddle-back
ABBDELLNRU landlubber	**ABBGILOOST** obbligatos	**ABCDDKORSU** duckboards
ABBDELLNSY bellybands	**ABBHILMSUU** Lubumbashi	**ABCDEEEELR** decreeable
ABBDELMOOZ bamboozled	**ABBHIOPSST** abbotships	**ABCDEEEELX** exceedable
ABBDELORSY absorbedly	**ABBIILLORR** Barbirolli	**ABCDEEEHSU** debauchees
ABBDENORSU unabsorbed	**ABBIINRSST** rabbinists	**ABCDEEEILV** deceivable
ABBDGIMNOR bombarding	**ABBILMOPRY** improbably	**ABCDEEELLT** delectable
ABBDHORRSU broadbrush	**ABBILORSTU** suborbital	**ABCDEEELRT** celebrated
ABBDILLORS billboards	**ABBLLNOTTU** buttonball	**ABCDEEELSU** seduceable
broadbills	**ABCCCEFIOS** beccaficos	**ABCDEEELTT** detectable
ABBDIMORRS broadbrims	**ABCCCEMNUY** accumbency	**ABCDEEERRT** cerebrated
ABBDMNOORS bombardons	**ABCCCIILLY** bicyclical	**ABCDEEGNRS** Scanderbeg
ABBDNORSSU brassbound	**ABCCCKKLOS** blackcocks	**ABCDEEHLLY** bellyached
ABBDNOSSTU bandobusts	**ABCCDEEIRT** brecciated	**ABCDEEHLNU** unbleached
ABBEEEILLV believable	**ABCCDELNRU** carbuncled	**ABCDEEHRSU** debauchers
ABBEEILLVY believably	**ABCCEEELNS** albescence	**ABCDEEHRUY** debauchery
ABBEEIRRNS barberries	**ABCCEEENST** tabescence	**ABCDEEILLN** declinable
ABBEEIRRSY bayberries	**ABCCEEFRSY** cybercafes	**ABCDEEILNU** ineducable
ABBEELLMSS semblables	**ABCCEEILMP** impeccable	**ABCDEEILPR** predicable
ABBEELORSV observable	**ABCCEEILSS** accessible	**ABCDEEILPS** despicable
ABBEELRRSS slabberers	**ABCCEELLRY** recyclable	**ABCDEEILRT** creditable
ABBEELRTTU rebuttable	**ABCCEENRSU** buccaneers	**ABCDEEILVY** deceivably
ABBEENORST breastbone	**ABCCEEPRSY** cyberspace	**ABCDEEKKSW** skewbacked
ABBEENORTW browbeaten	**ABCCEGHINN** bechancing	**ABCDEEKLRV** backvelder
ABBEENRRSU baseburner	**ABCCEHHOOR** Cooch Behar	**ABCDEELLTY** delectably
ABBEEORRTW browbeater	**ABCCEHILRU** cherubical	**ABCDEELLUX** excludable
ABBEFILNSS flabbiness	**ABCCEHLNRU** crunchable	**ABCDEELMRS** descramble
ABBEGHINSU Ebbinghaus	**ABCCEILMPY** impeccably	**ABCDEELNUU** uneducable
ABBEGILNOR belaboring	**ABCCEILORU** corbiculae	**ABCDEELORR** recordable
ABBEGILNRS slabbering	**ABCCEILSSY** accessibly	**ABCDEEMORT** embrocated
ABBEGJLSUU subjugable	**ABCCEINOSU** suboceanic	**ABCDEENRTY** cybernated
ABBEHINSSS shabbiness	**ABCCEJNSUY** subjacency	**ABCDEENSTU** abducentes
ABBEHOPRRS barbershop	**ABCCEKLOOT** cockleboat	**ABCDEEORST** obsecrated
ABBEIIOSSS babesiosis	**ABCCEKNORR** cornerback	**ABCDEFIKLL** backfilled
ABBEIIRRST rabbitries	**ABCCELNRSU** carbuncles	**ABCDEFIKLS** backfields
ABBEIKRRTT bitterbark	**ABCCELORSU** succorable	**ABCDEFIRTU** bifurcated
ABBEILLMSU sublimable	**ABCCELORSY** cryocables	**ABCDEFOSTU** obfuscated
ABBEILMOPR improbable	**ABCCELRTUU** Culebra Cut	**ABCDEGHINU** debauching
ABBEILMOST bombilates	**ABCCEMNRSU** cumbrances	**ABCDEGIKRS** ridgebacks
ABBEILMRST brambliest	**ABCCHHKNSU** hunchbacks	**ABCDEGIORT** Coatbridge

ABCDEGKMOS	gobsmacked	
ABCDEHIILR	herbicidal	
ABCDEHKLOS	blockheads	
ABCDEHKMPU	humpbacked	
ABCDEHLLUU	clubhauled	
ABCDEHLNUW	Buchenwald	
ABCDEHORSS	chessboard	
ABCDEIILMO	biomedical	
ABCDEIILNT	indictable	
ABCDEIILNV	vindicable	
ABCDEIIMRT	imbricated	
ABCDEIKLRS	backslider	
ABCDEIKLSS	backslides	
ABCDEIKOUV	bivouacked	
ABCDEIKRSU	rudbeckias	
ABCDEILLNU	includable	
ABCDEILLPU	duplicable	
ABCDEILORS	carbolised	
ABCDEILORZ	carbolized	
ABCDEILPSY	despicably	
ABCDEILRTU	lubricated	
	traducible	
ABCDEILRTY	creditably	
ABCDEILSTU	subdialect	
ABCDEINORS	carbonised	
ABCDEINORZ	carbonized	
ABCDEIORST	bacteroids	
ABCDEIPRRS	crispbread	
ABCDEIRRSU	carburised	
ABCDEIRRTU	rubricated	
ABCDEIRRUZ	carburized	
ABCDEJKOOT	jackbooted	
ABCDEKLLOS	ballocksed	
ABCDEKLORS	blockaders	
ABCDEKLPRU	parbuckled	
ABCDEKMOSS	mossbacked	
ABCDELMNRU	Cumberland	
ABCDELNNOO	condonable	
ABCDELRTUU	lucubrated	
ABCDELSSSU	subclassed	
ABCDENORSS	absconders	
ABCDENOSSU	subdeacons	
ABCDEOORRS	scoreboard	
ABCDERSTTU	subtracted	
ABCDGIKLNO	blockading	
ABCDGINNOS	absconding	
ABCDGKNORU	background	
ABCDHIILNR	brainchild	
ABCDHINNRU	nudibranch	
ABCDHINORU	chairbound	
ABCDHIOOPR	brachiopod	
ABCDHKRRTU	Burckhardt	
ABCDHLOORT	broadcloth	
ABCDHNOPRU	punchboard	
ABCDIIISTY	dibasicity	
ABCDIILLSY	disyllabic	
ABCDIILNTY	indictably	
ABCDIIMNOY	biodynamic	
ABCDIIRSTY	scabridity	
ABCDIISTUY	subacidity	
ABCDIKRRSY	brickyards	
ABCDILMOOR	Arcimboldo	

ABCDILNOST	cnidoblast	
ABCDILOPRS	clipboards	
ABCDILOSST	blastodisc	
ABCDINOOST	bandicoots	
ABCDINOSTU	abductions	
ABCDKLOORS	roadblocks	
ABCDKLOOSW	blackwoods	
ABCDKORSSW	backswords	
ABCDLNRSSU	scrublands	
ABCEEEELSS	Celebes Sea	
ABCEEEHKRS	Schaerbeek	
ABCEEEIKRR	icebreaker	
ABCEEEILPR	pierceable	
ABCEEEILRV	receivable	
ABCEEEJLRT	rejectable	
ABCEEELLRR	cerebellar	
ABCEEELNRS	screenable	
ABCEEELPTX	expectable	
ABCEEELRST	celebrates	
ABCEEELTUX	executable	
ABCEEENRUX	exuberance	
ABCEEERRST	cerebrates	
ABCEEFIILN	beneficial	
ABCEEFIRSS	briefcases	
ABCEEFNORT	benefactor	
ABCEEGKNRS	greenbacks	
ABCEEHHKSS	backsheesh	
ABCEEHILNR	hibernacle	
ABCEEHIOST	cohabitees	
ABCEEHKLST	sketchable	
ABCEEHKRTU	hackbuteer	
ABCEEHLLRY	bellyacher	
ABCEEHLLSY	bellyaches	
ABCEEHLNQU	quenchable	
ABCEEHNORR	abhorrence	
ABCEEHORSU	herbaceous	
ABCEEIILLT	elicitable	
ABCEEIIRST	acerbities	
ABCEEIJLNT	injectable	
ABCEEIKLNR	linebacker	
ABCEEILLNR	reclinable	
ABCEEILLNS	licensable	
ABCEEILLOT	biocellate	
ABCEEILLPX	explicable	
ABCEEILMMT	emblematic	
ABCEEILMNS	lambencies	
ABCEEILNNU	enunciable	
ABCEEILNOT	noticeable	
ABCEEILNSV	bivalences	
ABCEEILNTU	binucleate	
ABCEEILPST	pectisable	
ABCEEILRTX	extricable	
ABCEEINNOZ	benzocaine	
ABCEEINNST	abstinence	
ABCEEINOSS	obeisances	
ABCEEINRRS	carbineers	
ABCEEJKLTU	bluejacket	
ABCEEJNSST	abjectness	
ABCEEKLOPT	pocketable	
ABCEEKRSTT	backstreet	
ABCEELLNOS	enclosable	
ABCEELLOPR	percolable	

ABCEELLORT	brocatelle	
ABCEELLPUX	exculpable	
ABCEELLRRY	cerebrally	
ABCEELMNSS	semblances	
ABCEELMRRS	clamberers	
ABCEELMRSY	cymbaleers	
ABCEELNORS	censorable	
ABCEELNOTT	balconette	
ABCEELNOTU	Canteloube	
ABCEELNOVY	conveyable	
ABCEELNRST	celebrants	
ABCEELNRSU	censurable	
ABCEELOPRU	recoupable	
ABCEELORRT	celebrator	
ABCEELORST	bracteoles	
ABCEELPTXY	expectably	
ABCEEMOOTY	amoebocyte	
ABCEEMORRS	embraceors	
ABCEEMORST	embrocates	
ABCEEMOSTY	amebocytes	
ABCEENORSV	observance	
ABCEENORTT	carbonette	
ABCEENRRTY	barycentre	
ABCEENRSTY	cybernates	
ABCEEORSST	obsecrates	
ABCEEOSSUX	sauceboxes	
ABCEEPRRSU	cupbearers	
ABCEFHLSSU	flashcubes	
ABCEFIKLLS	blackflies	
ABCEFILNNO	confinable	
ABCEFIRSTU	bifurcates	
ABCEFLNOSU	confusable	
ABCEFLNOTU	confutable	
ABCEFOSSTU	obfuscates	
ABCEFRSSUU	subsurface	
ABCEGHIMNR	chambering	
ABCEGIKLNN	blackening	
ABCEGIKNRT	bracketing	
ABCEGILMNR	clambering	
ABCEGILNOS	cognisable	
ABCEGILNOZ	cognizable	
ABCEGILORS	bricolages	
ABCEGINNNY	benignancy	
ABCEGINSSS	abscessing	
ABCEGJLNOU	conjugable	
ABCEGKRSTU	tuckerbags	
ABCEGLNOOT	conglobate	
ABCEHIILOT	bioethical	
ABCEHIKLNR	branchlike	
ABCEHIKRRT	brickearth	
ABCEHILNNR	branchline	
ABCEHILPRT	birthplace	
ABCEHIMORT	bichromate	
ABCEHINORR	chairborne	
ABCEHINOST	aitchbones	
ABCEHINRRY	chinaberry	
ABCEHIOOPR	aerophobic	
ABCEHIORST	cohabiters	
ABCEHIPRRY	hyperbaric	
ABCEHKLLSS	shellbacks	
ABCEHKLOSS	shoeblacks	
ABCEHKMNRS	benchmarks	

ABCEHKORSY Cheboksary	**ABCEJKLMRU** lumberjack	**ABCGIKMNRU** buckraming
ABCEHKRTTU hackbutter	**ABCEKKORST** backstroke	**ABCGILMNRS** scrambling
ABCEHLLOTT tablecloth	**ABCEKLLNOU** unlockable	**ABCGILNOSY** cognisably
ABCEHLNRSS branchless	**ABCEKLLOSS** ballockses	**ABCGILNOYZ** cognizably
ABCEHMOPRT chamberpot	**ABCEKLNOST** Blackstone	**ABCHHIOPRS** archbishop
ABCEHMOSTX matchboxes	**ABCEKLPRSU** parbuckles	**ABCHHKSSUW** bushwhacks
ABCEHNNOOR Baron-Cohen	**ABCEKLRTTU** turtleback	**ABCHIILLNS** chilblains
ABCEHOQRSU quebrachos	**ABCEKRSTUW** waterbucks	**ABCHIILMOP** amphibolic
ABCEHORSTU tarbouches	**ABCELLMOOP** Campobello	**ABCHIILOPR** barophilic
ABCEHORTTX chatterbox	**ABCELLNOOR** collarbone	**ABCHIILOPS** basophilic
ABCEHPRSTU subchapter	**ABCELLNOOS** consolable	**ABCHIILOTT** batholitic
ABCEHRSTTU bruschetta	**ABCELLOORU** colourable	**ABCHIKLLLS** Black Hills
ABCEIIISST basicities	**ABCELLOOST** blastocoel	**ABCHIKLLSY** blackishly
ABCEIILLMT bimetallic	**ABCELLOSTU** leucoblast	**ABCHIKLMST** blacksmith
ABCEIILLNN inclinable	**ABCELLRSSU** subcellars	**ABCHIMMNSU** Buchmanism
ABCEIILLNR brilliance	**ABCELLRSSW** screwballs	**ABCHIMOORZ** Chimborazo
ABCEIILMTU umbilicate	**ABCELMMNOO** commonable	**ABCHIMORSU** choriambus
ABCEIILPST epiblastic	**ABCELMMOTU** commutable	**ABCHINOOPY** cynophobia
ABCEIIMRST imbricates	**ABCELMNOSU** consumable	**ABCHKLNORT** blackthorn
ABCEIINRSV vibrancies	**ABCELMNRSU** unscramble	**ABCHKMRSSU** marshbucks
ABCEIINTUV incubative	**ABCELMOPTU** computable	**ABCHKMSTTU** thumbtacks
ABCEIIOORT aerobiotic	**ABCELMOSTU** customable	**ABCHKNORST** thornbacks
ABCEIIORST aerobicist	**ABCELMRRSS** scramblers	**ABCHKORSSV** boschvarks
ABCEIJLOTV objectival	**ABCELNORRY** barleycorn	**ABCHKORSTW** throwbacks
ABCEIKKSTY stickybeak	**ABCELNOSST** constables	**ABCHLLNPSU** punchballs
ABCEIKLRRY bricklayer	**ABCELNRSUU** subnuclear	**ABCIIKLSW** bailiwicks
ABCEIKLRSV silverback	**ABCELNRSUY** censurably	**ABCIIILNST** albinistic
ABCEILLMOP compliable	**ABCELOPRRU** procurable	**ABCIIINOTT** antibiotic
ABCEILLNOS inclosable	**ABCELOSSTT** ectoblasts	**ABCIILLMSU** umbilicals
ABCEILLNOU inoculable	**ABCELRRTUU** tubercular	**ABCIILLNRV** brilliancy
ABCEILLNPU inculpable	**ABCELRSTUU** lucubrates	**ABCIILLSST** ballistics
ABCEILLNRS cranesbill	**ABCELSSSSU** subclasses	**ABCIILMOPS** bioplasmic
ABCEILLTUV cultivable	**ABCELSSSSU** subclauses	**ABCIILRTUY** curability
ABCEILMOPT compatible	**ABCEMNOPRU** Pernambuco	**ABCIIMNOSS** ambisonics
ABCEILMSST cembalists	**ABCEMOOPRT** amboceptor	**ABCIIMRSST** strabismic
ABCEILNOSU unsociable	**ABCEMORSSS** crossbeams	**ABCIINNOTU** incubation
ABCEILNOTY noticeably	**ABCEMOSSUU** submucosae	**ABCIINOSSS** abscission
ABCEILNPRU republican	**ABCEMRSSUV** verbascums	**ABCIINRRSU** rubricians
ABCEILNRRU incurrable	**ABCENNSTUY** subtenancy	**ABCIIOSSTT** biostatics
ABCEILNRSU incurables	**ABCENORSTY** corybantes	**ABCIKLLORY** rockabilly
ABCEILORSS carbolises	**ABCENRRTUY** canterbury	**ABCIKLLSST** blacklists
ABCEILORST cabriolets	**ABCENRSTUU** bucentaurs	**ABCILLMOPY** compliably
ABCEILORSZ carbolizes	**ABCENSSSTU** substances	**ABCILLMOSY** symbolical
ABCEILORTU orbiculate	**ABCEOOPRRT** baroceptor	**ABCILLNPUY** inculpably
ABCEILRSTU lubricates	**ABCEOOPRSS** baroscopes	**ABCILLRRUY** rubrically
	subarticle	**ABCEORRRTU** carburetor	**ABCILMOPTY** compatibly
ABCEIMMOQU Moçambique	**ABCERRSTTU** subtracter	**ABCILMRUUV** vibraculum
ABCEIMOORT Coimbatore	**ABCFGHIKST** fightbacks	**ABCILMSSTY** cymbalists
ABCEIMORRT barometric	**ABCFGIIKNR** backfiring	**ABCILNORSU** binoculars
ABCEINORRS carboniser	**ABCFILMORU** baculiform	**ABCILNOSUY** unsociably
ABCEINORRZ carbonizer	**ABCGGIKPSY** piggybacks	**ABCILNRSTU** lubricants
ABCEINORSS carbonises	**ABCGHIINOT** cohabiting	**ABCILORRSU** courbarils
ABCEINORSZ carbonizes	**ABCGHIIOPR** biographic	**ABCILORRTU** lubricator
ABCEINORTU bicornuate	**ABCGHIKMNU** Buckingham	**ABCILPSTUY** subtypical
ABCEINOSUY buoyancies	**ABCGHIKSST** backsights	**ABCIMMOPRU** procambium
ABCEINRRST transcribe	**ABCGHINNRS** branchings	**ABCINORSTU** incubators
ABCEIORSUU rubiaceous	**ABCGHINOOT** cohobating	**ABCINORTUY** incubatory
ABCEIOSSSU scabiouses	**ABCGHLORYY** brachylogy	**ABCIORRRTU** rubricator
ABCEIRRRSU subcarrier	**ABCGIILLOO** biological	**ABCKKNOOTU** knockabout
ABCEIRRSSU carburises	**ABCGIINNTU** incubating	**ABCKLLLOPS** blackpolls
ABCEIRRSTU rubricates	**ABCGIINRTT** bratticing	**ABCKNPRTUY** bankruptcy
ABCEIRRSUZ carburizes	**ABCGIKLNSS** slingbacks	**ABCKOOPRSS** scrapbooks

ABCLLOORUY	colourably	**ABDEEERSTW**	sweetbread
ABCLORRTUU	lucubrator	**ABDEEERTXZ**	exuberated
ABCLORSSUY	scabrously	**ABDEEFFHLU**	bufflehead
ABCLOSSTTY	blastocyst	**ABDEEFHNOR**	beforehand
ABCNORSSTU	obscurants	**ABDEEFIITU**	beautified
ABDDEEEFLN	defendable	**ABDEEFLMOR**	deformable
ABDDEEEHNO	boneheaded	**ABDEEFLNRU**	refundable
ABDDEEEGLNP	dependable	**ABDEEFOORT**	barefooted
ABDDEEGGLR	bedraggled	**ABDEEGGLRS**	bedraggles
ABDDEEGHIR	bridgehead	**ABDEEGHIRT**	bighearted
ABDDEEHLLU	bullheaded	**ABDEEGHNNR**	Hardenberg
ABDDEEILNS	disenabled	**ABDEEGILNS**	designable
ABDDEEKORY	keyboarded	**ABDEEGINRS**	gaberdines
ABDDEELNPY	dependably	**ABDEEGINST**	besteading
ABDDEEENNOS	nosebanded	**ABDEEGLMNR**	embrangled
ABDDEEPRSS	bedspreads	**ABDEEGLNPS**	bespangled
ABDDEGINRU	unabridged	**ABDEEGORRS**	garderobes
ABDDEGIRRW	drawbridge	**ABDEEGORRV**	vergeboard
ABDDEHHINN	behindhand	**ABDEEGRRSY**	greybeards
ABDDEHILNR	Hildebrand	**ABDEEHIKNR**	Birkenhead
ABDDEHILLS	blandished	**ABDEEHILLS**	deshabille
ABDDEHINRS	brandished	**ABDEEHILPS**	beadleship
ABDDEHMOTU	badmouthed	**ABDEEHILRR**	halberdier
ABDDEIILOS	diabolised	**ABDEEHIMRT**	timberhead
ABDDEIILOZ	diabolized	**ABDEEHIMSV**	misbehaved
ABDDEIIMRS	bridesmaid	**ABDEEHINRT**	hibernated
ABDDEILLLS	saddlebill		inbreathed
ABDDEILLUW	bullwaddie	**ABDEEHLMPS**	blasphemed
ABDDEIORSS	broadsides	**ABDEEHORST**	broadsheet
	sideboards	**ABDEEIILTT**	debilitate
ABDDELMORU	Boulder Dam	**ABDEEIINRS**	badineries
ABDDELNORR	borderland	**ABDEEIINRT**	inebriated
ABDDELNRTU	bladdernut	**ABDEEILMRV**	remediably
ABDDELOSSW	saddlebows	**ABDEEILMST**	bedlamites
ABDDGIINNS	disbanding	**ABDEEILMTT**	timetabled
ABDDGORSUY	bodyguards	**ABDEEILNNU**	undeniable
ABDDHINSTW	bandwidths	**ABDEEILNRS**	breadlines
ABDDILLORR	dollarbird	**ABDEEILNSS**	disenables
ABDDLMOORS	moldboards	**ABDEEILPRU**	repudiable
ABDDLMOORU	mouldboard	**ABDEEILPRV**	deprivable
ABDDNOORSU	soundboard	**ABDEEILRSS**	desirables
ABDDOOORRSW	broadsword	**ABDEEILRSV**	verbalised
ABDEEEELMR	redeemable	**ABDEEILRVZ**	verbalized
ABDEEEFHRT	featherbed	**ABDEEINNOR**	debonnaire
ABDEEEFILS	defeasible	**ABDEEINNRR**	Bernardine
ABDEEEFLRR	deferrable	**ABDEEIORUV**	de Beauvoir
ABDEEEGGRW	beggarweed	**ABDEEIPRST**	rebaptised
ABDEEEHQTU	bequeathed	**ABDEEIPRTZ**	rebaptized
ABDEEEILLN	delineable	**ABDEEIRRVW**	weaverbird
ABDEEEILMR	remediable	**ABDEEISTTU**	beatitudes
ABDEEEILRT	deliberate	**ABDEEKORRY**	keyboarder
ABDEEEINRV	aberdevine		rekeyboard
ABDEEEKMRR	reembarked	**ABDEELLLNU**	unlabelled
ABDEEELLLR	relabelled	**ABDEELLMTU**	umbellated
ABDEEELLPT	depletable	**ABDEELLOPR**	deplorable
ABDEEEELMRY	redeemably	**ABDEELLORS**	solderable
ABDEEELNPX	expendable	**ABDEELLPSS**	speedballs
ABDEEELNRR	renderable	**ABDEELMNOZ**	emblazoned
ABDEEELNRT	tenderable	**ABDEELMNRU**	demurrable
ABDEEELNTX	extendable	**ABDEELNOPR**	ponderable
ABDEEELSTT	detestable	**ABDEELNORS**	banderoles
ABDEEEMNST	debasement		bandoleers
			endorsable
		ABDEELNRSU	sunderable
		ABDEELOPRT	deportable
		ABDEELORTT	battledore
		ABDEELPRRU	perdurable
		ABDEELSTTY	detestably
		ABDEEMNRST	debarments
		ABDEEMRRSU	embrasured
		ABDEEMRRSW	bedwarmers
		ABDEENOPSU	subpoenaed
		ABDEENORTT	Bernadotte
		ABDEENOTTY	bayonetted
		ABDEENPRRY	prebendary
		ABDEENRRST	bartenders
		ABDEENSTTU	debutantes
		ABDEEOPRRT	reprobated
		ABDEEOPSST	speedboats
		ABDEEORRUX	bordereaux
		ABDEERRSST	redbreasts
		ABDEERRSTT	Bradstreet
		ABDEFIILMO	modifiable
		ABDEFIIMRT	fimbriated
		ABDEFILMOR	formidable
		ABDEFINRRS	firebrands
		ABDEFINRSS	Fassbinder
		ABDEFIRRTU	breadfruit
		ABDEFORRST	fretboards
		ABDEGGHOOR	beggarhood
		ABDEGGIRRU	budgerigar
		ABDEGGKNOR	Dogger Bank
		ABDEGGNOOT	tobogganed
		ABDEGHHILL	highballed
		ABDEGHINSU	subheading
		ABDEGHNRRU	Hardenburg
		ABDEGIINNR	brigandine
		ABDEGIINSU	biguanides
		ABDEGIIRRS	brigadiers
		ABDEGIKNRR	ringbarked
		ABDEGILLOS	globalised
		ABDEGILLNSY	debasingly
		ABDEGILNZZ	bedazzling
		ABDEGIMNRT	abridgment
		ABDEGINNOR	broadening
		ABDEGINNRR	rebranding
		ABDEGIRRTW	Bridgwater
		ABDEGJORTU	objurgated
		ABDEGJSTUU	subjugated
		ABDEGKRSTU	grubstaked
		ABDEGLNNRU	Burgenland
		ABDEGLNRUW	Waldenburg
		ABDEGNNRUU	Graubünden
		ABDEGORSTU	subrogated
		ABDEHHSSSU	shadbushes
		ABDEHIILLS	dishabille
		ABDEHILNSS	blandishes
		ABDEHILSST	stablished
		ABDEHINRRS	brandisher
		ABDEHINRSS	brandishes
		ABDEHIORTW	whiteboard
		ABDEHIRRSU	airbrushed
		ABDEHLLMOT	mothballed
		ABDEHLLOOY	ballyhooed

ABDEHLOSTW	deathblows
ABDEHMNNSU	husbandmen
ABDEHNORTU	earthbound
ABDEHNRSSU	husbanders
ABDEHNRSTU	subtrahend
ABDEHNRTUY	Thunder Bay
ABDEHORRST	shortbread
ABDEHOSUWY	bawdyhouse
ABDEIIKLLS	dislikable
ABDEIILMSS	admissible
ABDEIILOSS	diabolises
ABDEIILOSZ	diabolizes
ABDEIILRRS	ribaldries
ABDEIILRSU	subdeliria
ABDEIILSST	stabilised
ABDEIILSTZ	stabilized
ABDEIINOST	antibodies
ABDEIKMRSS	disembarks
ABDEIKNRSS	snakebirds
ABDEIKNRSW	windbreaks
ABDEILLLSY	disyllable
ABDEILMNRT	timberland
ABDEILMORS	bromeliads
ABDEILMSTU	sublimated
ABDEILNNUW	unwindable
ABDEILNNUY	undeniably
ABDEILNORS	bandoliers
	indorsable
ABDEILNORY	debonairly
ABDEILNRTV	Vanderbilt
ABDEILNSUY	unbiasedly
ABDEILOPSS	disposable
ABDEILPSTU	disputable
ABDEILRSTU	brutalised
ABDEILRTTW	wattlebird
ABDEILRTUZ	brutalized
ABDEIMNORT	brominated
ABDEIMNRST	disbarment
ABDEIMNRSU	submediant
ABDEIMRRTY	timberyard
ABDEIMRTUW	dumbwaiter
ABDEINNOTU	unobtained
ABDEINORSU	boundaries
ABDEINPSTU	unbaptised
ABDEINPTUZ	unbaptized
ABDEINRTTU	turbinated
ABDEIPRRSU	upbraiders
ABDEIRTTTU	attributed
ABDEJKKMOS	sjambokked
ABDEKLLNOR	bankrolled
ABDEKNORSW	breakdowns
ABDEKNPRTU	bankrupted
ABDEKORRSW	wordbreaks
ABDELLNOSW	snowballed
ABDELLOPRY	deplorably
ABDELLORST	Lord's table
ABDELLORUY	labouredly
ABDELMOORW	marblewood
ABDELMORST	blastoderm
ABDELMOSTY	molybdates
ABDELMRRUY	lumberyard
ABDELNNORU	nondurable

ABDELNOPRY	ponderably
ABDELNORTU	roundtable
	Round Table
ABDELNORUU	unlaboured
ABDELNOSST	endoblasts
ABDELOOORT	bootloader
ABDELORSUV	boulevards
ABDELORTUY	obdurately
ABDELOSTTU	subtotaled
ABDELPRRUY	perdurably
ABDELSTUUX	subluxated
ABDENOORUV	overabound
ABDENOPPRU	paperbound
ABDENORSST	adsorbents
ABDENRSSSU	absurdness
ABDENRSSTY	bystanders
ABDEOORRST	breadroots
ABDEOORSWZ	zebrawoods
ABDEOOSTTU	outboasted
ABDFIIRRRS	friarbirds
ABDFILMORY	formidably
ABDFILNORU	floribunda
ABDFLOOORR	floorboard
ABDFOOORST	footboards
ABDFORRSSU	surfboards
ABDGHIIINT	adhibiting
ABDGHINNSU	husbanding
ABDGIINPRU	upbraiding
ABDGIINRRS	disbarring
ABDGIINSSU	disabusing
ABDGILNNRS	brandlings
ABDGINNRUU	Burgundian
ABDGINORSS	signboards
ABDGINORTU	groundbait
ABDGLOPRSU	plugboards
ABDHIIINOT	adhibition
ABDHIKLNNU	ibn-Khaldun
ABDHILMOOR	rhomboidal
ABDHIMORSY	hybridomas
ABDHIMRSTY	dithyrambs
ABDHINRTUV	unbirthday
ABDHKNOSYZ	Dobzhansky
ABDIIILSTV	disability
ABDIIILTUV	audibility
ABDIIKNNRY	bradykinin
ABDIILMNOU	albuminoid
ABDIILORRT	tailorbird
ABDIILOSST	diabolists
	idioblasts
ABDIILPTUY	dupability
ABDIILRTUY	durability
ABDIIMPRSY	bipyramids
ABDIINOTTU	dubitation
ABDIIRSSUY	subsidiary
ABDIKMORSS	skimboards
ABDILNOOST	bloodstain
ABDILNORSU	subordinal
ABDILOORTY	botryoidal
ABDILOORWZ	brazilwood
ABDILPSTUY	disputably
ABDIMNNOST	badmintons
ABDIMNOOSU	abdominous

ABDINRSSTW	wristbands
ABDLMOOORS	broadlooms
ABDMOOORRS	boardrooms
ABDNOORSSW	snowboards
ABDNOORTUU	roundabout
ABDOORRSTY	storyboard
ABDOORRTUU	troubadour
ABEEEEFRST	beefeaters
ABEEEFKSST	beefsteaks
ABEEEFLPRR	preferable
ABEEEFLRRR	referrable
ABEEEGGLRS	segregable
ABEEEGGRST	eggbeaters
ABEEEGHLLO	Beaglehole
ABEEEGLRSU	beleaguers
ABEEEGLSTV	vegetables
ABEEEHITTV	hebetative
ABEEEHLSSW	wheelbases
ABEEEHQRTU	bequeather
ABEEEHRSTT	hartebeest
ABEEEIKLNR	Berkeleian
ABEEEIKRRT	tiebreaker
ABEEEILLRV	relievable
ABEEEILMRR	irremeable
ABEEEILRVW	reviewable
ABEEEIRRST	teaberries
ABEEEKPRRS	barkeepers
ABEEELLLPX	expellable
ABEEELLSTT	settleable
ABEEELMNNT	enablement
ABEEELMNRU	enumerable
ABEEELMPRT	temperable
ABEEELMRSS	reassemble
ABEEELNPRT	penetrable
ABEEELNRSW	renewables
ABEEELQSUZ	squeezable
ABEEELRRSV	reservable
ABEEENNOZZ	azobenzene
ABEEENNRTT	bannerette
ABEEEORSTT	stereobate
ABEEERRSST	Basseterre
	Basse-Terre
ABEEERRTTV	vertebrate
ABEEERSTUX	exuberates
ABEEERSWYZ	breezeways
ABEEFFLMNT	bafflement
ABEEFFLRSU	sufferable
ABEEFGILMN	flambeeing
ABEEFGINRS	freebasing
ABEEFGKNPR	Kapfenberg
ABEEFIILNS	infeasible
ABEEFIILRV	verifiable
ABEEFIIRTU	beautifier
ABEEFIISTU	beautifies
ABEEFIKRRS	firebreaks
ABEEFILLLR	refillable
ABEEFILLRT	filterable
ABEEFILNRR	inferrable
ABEEFILNSU	unfeasible
ABEEFLMORR	reformable
ABEEFLOPRR	perforable
ABEEFLPRRY	preferably

ABEEFORRRS	forbearers	**ABEEIINRST**	inebriates	**ABEEJMMNNT**	enjambment
ABEEGHINTT	hebetating	**ABEEIIRRRZ**	bizarrerie	**ABEEKLNNOS**	anklebones
ABEEGHNORS	habergeons	**ABEEIIRRSV**	breviaries	**ABEEKMMNNT**	embankment
ABEEGHNORU	haubergeon	**ABEEIIRRSZ**	brazieries	**ABEEKMMNRT**	embarkment
ABEEGHRSTU	hagbuteers	**ABEEIIRSST**	bestiaries	**ABEELLMNTU**	antebellum
ABEEGIKNPS	bespeaking	**ABEEIKLLNU**	unlikeable	**ABEELLMOPY**	employable
ABEEGILLNR	relabeling	**ABEEIKLMRT**	Timberlake	**ABEELLNOUV**	unloveable
ABEEGILMNR	germinable	**ABEEIKNNRT**	barkentine	**ABEELLNRST**	netballers
ABEEGILNOT	negotiable	**ABEEIKNSST**	snakebites	**ABEELLNRUV**	vulnerable
ABEEGILNRT	integrable	**ABEEILLLLT**	Lille Bælt	**ABEELLORSV**	resolvable
ABEEGILNSS	Albigenses	**ABEEILLMNR**	bellarmine	**ABEELLORVV**	revolvable
ABEEGILRTW	bilgewater	**ABEEILLMOR**	meliorable	**ABEELLPRUV**	pulverable
ABEEGIMNRS	besmearing	**ABEEILLNOR**	neoliberal	**ABEELLSSSY**	baselessly
ABEEGINORT	bioreagent	**ABEEILLNRU**	unreliable	**ABEELMMMNT**	embalmment
ABEEGINRSU	aubergines	**ABEEILLNSS**	liableness	**ABEELMMOOT**	metabolome
ABEEGINSWX	beeswaxing	**ABEEILLNST**	listenable	**ABEELMNOUV**	unmoveable
ABEEGKORRS	brokerages	**ABEEILLNTV**	ventilable	**ABEELMNRST**	resemblant
ABEEGLLNRW	Wallenberg	**ABEEILLNUV**	unliveable	**ABEELMNRSU**	lebensraum
ABEEGLMNRS	embrangles	**ABEEILLMMOR**	memorabile		mensurable
ABEEGLNORV	governable	**ABEEILMMOV**	immoveable	**ABEELMNTTT**	battlement
ABEEGLNPSS	bespangles	**ABEEILMNRT**	terminable	**ABEELMORST**	astrobleme
ABEEGLNSTW	West Bengal	**ABEEILMNSU**	albumenise		blastomere
ABEEGLOPRS	bargepoles	**ABEEILMNUZ**	albumenize	**ABEELMPRSU**	presumable
	porbeagles	**ABEEILMOST**	metabolise	**ABEELMPRTU**	permutable
ABEEGMNRSW	wambengers	**ABEEILMOTT**	metabolite	**ABEELMRSSS**	assemblers
ABEEGNNNRT	Tannenberg	**ABEEILMOTZ**	metabolize	**ABEELMRSSY**	reassembly
ABEEGNNSYZ	Nagyszeben	**ABEEILMRRY**	irremeably	**ABEELNNNOY**	Anne Boleyn
ABEEGNRSTT	abstergent	**ABEEILMRTT**	remittable	**ABEELNPRSS**	personable
ABEEHHRRTY	heathberry	**ABEEILMSSS**	assemblies	**ABEELNPRTY**	penetrably
ABEEHIILTZ	Elizabeth I	**ABEEILMSTT**	timetables	**ABEELNQTTU**	blanquette
ABEEHILLRS	relishable	**ABEEILNNTV**	inventable	**ABEELNRRTU**	returnable
ABEEHILPRS	perishable	**ABEEILNNUV**	unenviable	**ABEELNSSST**	stableness
ABEEHIMRSV	misbehaver	**ABEEILNOPR**	inoperable	**ABEELNSSSU**	usableness
ABEEHIMSSV	misbehaves	**ABEEILNORX**	inexorable	**ABEELOPRRT**	reportable
ABEEHIMSTW	whitebeams	**ABEEILNPSX**	expansible	**ABEELOPRRV**	reprovable
ABEEHINOTT	hebetation	**ABEEILNRSS**	bleariness	**ABEELOPRTX**	exportable
ABEEHINRST	hibernates	**ABEEILNRST**	East Berlin	**ABEELORRST**	restorable
	inbreathes		insertable	**ABEELORSTT**	Store Bælt
ABEEHIRSTT	breathiest	**ABEEILNRTU**	reunitable	**ABEELPSTTU**	upsettable
ABEEHKNORS	boneshaker	**ABEEILNSTV**	investable	**ABEELRSUVY**	surveyable
ABEEHKOSSU	bakehouses	**ABEEILORTT**	obliterate	**ABEEMMNSTY**	embayments
ABEEHLMPRS	blasphemer	**ABEEILPPST**	peptisable	**ABEEMNSTTT**	battements
ABEEHLMPSS	blasphemes	**ABEEILPPTZ**	peptizable	**ABEEMORRST**	barometers
ABEEHLNOSW	whalebones	**ABEEILPRRS**	respirable	**ABEEMRRSSU**	embrasures
ABEEHLORRS	seborrheal	**ABEEILQRRU**	requirable	**ABEEMRSSTW**	webmasters
ABEEHLRSST	breathless	**ABEEILQRTU**	requitable	**ABEENNRRSS**	barrenness
ABEEHMORTT	bathometer	**ABEEILRRSV**	verbaliser	**ABEENNRSSU**	urbaneness
ABEEHNORSU	Oberhausen	**ABEEILRRTX**	Liber Extra	**ABEENNRSSZ**	brazenness
ABEEHOORRS	seborrhoea	**ABEEILRRVZ**	verbalizer	**ABEENORRTW**	waterborne
ABEEHORSTU	hereabouts	**ABEEILRSST**	assertible	**ABEENORSSS**	baronesses
ABEEHORTTU	thereabout	**ABEEILRSSV**	verbalises	**ABEENORSTU**	Eastbourne
ABEEHORTUW	whereabout	**ABEEILRSVZ**	verbalizes	**ABEENOSSSW**	sawboneses
ABEEHPRRSY	barysphere	**ABEEILSSTT**	beastliest	**ABEENQRSTU**	banqueters
ABEEHRSSTT	hartbeests	**ABEEIOORSS**	aerobioses	**ABEENQSTTU**	banquettes
ABEEIIILLMN	eliminable	**ABEEIPRSST**	rebaptises	**ABEEOPRRRT**	reprobater
ABEEIIILLNS	isabelline	**ABEEIPRSTZ**	rebaptizes	**ABEEOPRRST**	perborates
ABEEIIILLRS	liberalise	**ABEEIRRRST**	barretries		reprobates
ABEEIILLRZ	liberalize	**ABEEIRRSSS**	brasseries	**ABEEOSSTWX**	sweatboxes
ABEEIILNPX	inexpiable		brassieres	**ABEEPRSSTT**	bespatters
ABEEIILNTV	inevitable	**ABEEIRRSTY**	tayberries	**ABEEQRSSUU**	arquebuses
ABEEIILSST	bestialise	**ABEEIRRSWX**	waxberries	**ABEFFGILRU**	febrifugal
ABEEIILSTZ	bestialize	**ABEEJLLNSY**	jellybeans	**ABEFFHINRS**	Banffshire

ABEFFLRSUY	sufferably
ABEFGIINTY	beatifying
ABEFGILORV	forgivable
ABEFGILRSS	fiberglass
	fibreglass
ABEFGINORR	forbearing
ABEFHIORSS	boarfishes
ABEFHIRRTT	afterbirth
ABEFIILLLN	infallible
ABEFIILNOT	notifiable
ABEFIILNTU	infibulate
ABEFIILRVV	verifiably
ABEFILMNOR	informable
ABEFILOPRT	profitable
ABEFINORRS	forebrains
ABEFKLSSTU	basketfuls
ABEFKNORRT	breakfront
ABEFLLLMUY	blamefully
ABEFLLLOOW	followable
ABEFLLLORW	ballflower
ABEFLLOORT	footballer
ABEFLLRRSU	barrelfuls
ABEFLORSTW	batfowlers
ABEFNNORUZ	benzofuran
ABEFNORSTY	Fray Bentos
ABEFORRSTY	ferryboats
ABEGGIMNOR	embargoing
ABEGGINRSW	bagswinger
ABEGGKLOUZ	Gülek Bogaz
ABEGGNOORT	tobogganer
ABEGHIINRZ	hebraizing
ABEGHILNRT	blathering
ABEGHINRRS	harbingers
ABEGHINRST	breathings
ABEGHINRTU	thunbergia
ABEGHIOPRR	biographer
ABEGHLNOOP	anglophobe
ABEGHMRRSU	hamburgers
ABEGHNRRSU	bushranger
ABEGHQSUUU	usquebaugh
ABEGHRSTTU	hagbutters
ABEGIILNNT	intangible
ABEGIILNRT	liberating
ABEGIILNSW	bewailings
ABEGIILOTV	obligative
ABEGIINNRT	brigantine
ABEGIINORS	aborigines
ABEGIINOST	abiogenist
ABEGIKLNNU	Gulbenkian
ABEGILLNRR	barrelling
ABEGILLNRV	verballing
ABEGILLOSS	globalises
ABEGILMNPU	impugnable
ABEGILMNSS	assembling
ABEGILMNTT	embattling
ABEGILNNRY	blarneying
ABEGILNSSU	subleasing
ABEGILRRSU	burglaries
	burglarise
ABEGILRRUZ	burglarize
ABEGIMORSU	seaborgium
ABEGIMOSSU	subimagoes

ABEGINNORS	Bergsonian
ABEGINNOTY	bayoneting
ABEGINNQTU	banqueting
ABEGINNSTT	battenings
ABEGINOORS	boongaries
ABEGINRSTT	batterings
ABEGINRSUY	guberniyas
ABEGJORSTU	objurgates
ABEGJSSTUU	subjugates
ABEGKRRSTU	grubstaker
ABEGKRSSTU	grubstakes
ABEGLLNOOY	balneology
ABEGLNORRY	loganberry
ABEGLORRRV	Vorarlberg
ABEGMNOORS	boomerangs
ABEGMNOOTY	Montego Bay
ABEGMORRSS	bromegrass
ABEGMORSUU	umbrageous
ABEGNNSTTU	subtangent
ABEGNOORTU	Baton Rouge
ABEGORSSTU	subrogates
ABEHHILLST	sheathbill
ABEHHIOOPT	theophobia
ABEHHMMRSU	bushhammer
ABEHHORRTT	heartthrob
ABEHHOSSTU	bathhouses
ABEHIILMNT	habiliment
ABEHIKLNRS	shrinkable
ABEHIKLORS	kohlrabies
ABEHILLOPS	polishable
ABEHILMOPS	amphiboles
ABEHILMPRS	blepharism
ABEHILNPSU	punishable
ABEHILOPRS	barophiles
ABEHILOPSS	basophiles
ABEHILOPST	hospitable
ABEHILORSS	abolishers
ABEHILOSTT	batholites
ABEHILPRSY	perishably
ABEHILPSTT	battleship
ABEHILPSTU	bisulphate
ABEHILRSST	herbalists
ABEHILSSST	stablishes
ABEHILTWYY	Whitley Bay
ABEHIMMNST	Benthamism
ABEHIMNNST	banishment
ABEHIMRRSU	herbariums
ABEHINOOPX	xenophobia
ABEHINOPRV	vibraphone
ABEHINORRT	hibernator
ABEHINRSSS	brashiness
ABEHIOPRSU	euphorbias
ABEHIORSUV	behaviours
ABEHIRRSSU	airbrushes
ABEHKLLRSS	shellbarks
ABEHKPRSSY	Khyber Pass
ABEHLMOOST	smoothable
ABEHLMOTTU	ethambutol
ABEHLNOORU	honourable
ABEHLOPRSY	hyperbolas
ABEHLORRSS	harborless
ABEHLORRTY	lay brother

ABEHLORSTT	betrothals
ABEHLORTTU	bluethroat
ABEHLRTTTU	truth table
ABEHLSSSTU	saltbushes
ABEHMMRRSU	Masherbrum
ABEHMORTTY	bathometry
ABEHMRSSTU	bushmaster
ABEHMRTTVY	bathymetry
ABEHNOPRTY	hyperbaton
ABEHNRSSTU	sunbathers
ABEHOORSST	tarbooshes
ABEHOOSSTU	boathouses
	houseboats
ABEHORRRSU	harbourers
ABEIIILMNT	inimitable
ABEIIILNNZ	Leibnizian
ABEIIILNSS	sensibilia
ABEIIILQRU	equilibria
ABEIILLMRS	liberalism
ABEIILLNNY	biennially
ABEIILLNOV	inviolable
ABEIILLNRT	brilliante
ABEIILLRST	liberalist
ABEIILLRTY	liberality
ABEIILLSTU	utilisable
ABEIILLTUZ	utilizable
ABEIILMNSS	lesbianism
ABEIILMPRT	impartible
ABEIILMPSS	impassible
ABEIILMRST	bimestrial
ABEIILNORT	liberation
ABEIILNPRS	inspirable
ABEIILNPXY	inexpiably
ABEIILNRST	nailbiters
ABEIILNTTU	intuitable
ABEIILNTTY	tenability
ABEIILNTVY	inevitably
ABEIILQTUV	equability
ABEIILRSST	stabiliser
ABEIILRSSU	Belisarius
ABEIILRSTZ	stabilizer
ABEIILSSST	stabilises
ABEIILSSTZ	stabilizes
ABEIILSTTY	bestiality
ABEIILSTUY	useability
ABEIINNRRT	interbrain
ABEIINNRSS	braininess
ABEIINNRST	inebriants
ABEIINNRTW	New Britain
ABEIINRSTU	urbanities
ABEIIOORSS	aerobiosis
ABEIIORSTU	obituaries
ABEIKLNNSU	unsinkable
ABEIKLNSSU	baulkiness
ABEIKMORRS	biomarkers
ABEIKNOPRT	breakpoint
ABEIKNSTUZ	Uzbekistan
ABEILLLNST	libellants
ABEILLLNTU	untillable
ABEILLMSTU	stimulable
ABEILLNNOZ	Bellinzona
ABEILLNOSV	insolvable

ABEILLPPSU	suppliable
ABEILLPSTU	stipulable
ABEILLSUXY	bisexually
ABEILMMOST	metabolism
ABEILMMOVY	immoveably
ABEILMNNRU	Melburnian
ABEILMNQRU	lambrequin
ABEILMNRTY	terminably
ABEILMNSSU	unmissable
ABEILMNSSW	wambliness
ABEILMOOTU	automobile
ABEILMOPRT	importable
ABEILMOPRV	improvable
ABEILMORTY	traymobile
ABEILMRSSU	surmisable
ABEILMRSSV	verbalisms
ABEILMSSTU	sublimates
ABEILNNNUW	unwinnable
ABEILNNRUY	inurbanely
ABEILNOPRY	inoperably
ABEILNORSZ	blazonries
ABEILNORXY	inexorably
ABEILNOSTY	obeisantly
ABEILNSTUU	unsuitable
ABEILOPRRV	proverbial
ABEILOPSTU	bipetalous
ABEILOPSTY	polybasite
ABEILORRST	liberators
ABEILORSSU	Belorussia
ABEILRRTTU	triturable
ABEILRSSTU	brutalises
ABEILRSSTV	verbalists
ABEILRSTUV	vestibular
ABEILRSTUZ	brutalizes
ABEILRSUVV	survivable
ABEIMMOQUZ	Mozambique
ABEIMNNOTT	obtainment
ABEIMNORST	brominates
ABEIMNORTT	montbretia
ABEIMNORTU	tambourine
ABEIMNRRSU	submariner
ABEIMNRSST	brainstems
ABEIMNRSSU	submarines
ABEIMOSSTU	abstemious
ABEIMPRSST	rebaptisms
ABEINNORTU	eburnation
ABEINNOSST	sanbenitos
ABEINNOSTT	abstention
ABEINNRRTU	interurban
ABEINNRSST	bannisters
ABEINNRSSW	brawniness
ABEINOOPSW	bioweapons
ABEINOPRRW	brainpower
ABEINOPSTX	paintboxes
ABEINORTTX	exorbitant
ABEINPRSST	breastpins
ABEINRSSSS	brassiness
ABEINRSTTU	turbinates
ABEIOPPRSY	presbyopia
ABEIOPRSTV	absorptive
ABEIOSSSST	asbestosis
ABEIPRSTTY	baptistery

ABEIRRRSST	barristers
ABEIRRTTTU	attributer
ABEIRSTTTU	attributes
ABEIRSTUVY	subvariety
ABEJLMOTUU	autojumble
ABEKKMOORR	bookmarker
ABEKKMOORS	bookmakers
ABEKKORSTW	basketwork
	workbasket
ABEKLLNORR	bankroller
ABEKLLORWY	yellowbark
ABEKLLOSTU	leukoblast
ABEKLNNOUW	unknowable
ABEKLNORUW	unworkable
ABEKLOOPST	bookplates
ABEKLORSTW	worktables
ABEKMNNOTU	mountebank
ABEKNOPRRW	pawnbroker
ABEKNORWYY	New York Bay
ABEKOOPRRY	prayer book
ABEKORRSTW	breastwork
ABELLLLORR	rollerball
ABELLLLOVY	volleyball
ABELLMNOVY	Ballymoney
ABELLMOOOP	Pool Malebo
ABELLMOSTY	myeloblast
ABELLNOSUV	unsolvable
ABELLNRUVY	vulnerably
ABELLORRRU	bullroarer
ABELLORVVY	revolvably
ABELLOSTUY	absolutely
ABELLSSSUY	syllabuses
ABELMMNOSU	summonable
ABELMNNOOW	noblewoman
ABELMNOOST	monostable
ABELMNORYZ	emblazonry
ABELMOOPRT	promotable
ABELMOSSST	mesoblasts
ABELMPRSUY	presumably
ABELMPRTUY	permutably
ABELNOOPST	tablespoon
ABELNOPRSY	personably
ABELNOQTUU	unquotable
ABELNORSTU	neuroblast
ABELNOSSTT	entoblasts
ABELNRRTUU	nurturable
ABELNRSSTU	subalterns
ABELNRSTTU	turntables
ABELOOPPRS	proposable
ABELOOPRST	blastopore
ABELOOPSST	Sebastopol
ABELOOSSTT	osteoblast
ABELOPPSSU	supposable
ABELOSSTTY	stylobates
ABELPRRTUU	rupturable
ABELPRSTTU	prebuttals
ABELRSSTUY	abstrusely
ABELSSTUUX	subluxates
ABEMMNORSU	membranous
ABEMNNOSTU	submontane
ABEMNOORRW	marrowbone
ABEMOPRSTY	ambrotypes

ABEMORRSTU	arboretums
ABEMRRSSUY	burramyses
ABENNSSTTU	subtenants
ABENOOSSTT	stoneboats
ABENOPRRSS	barpersons
ABENORRRTW	barrenwort
ABENPRSSTU	abruptness
ABEOOPRSTW	powerboats
ABEOORSTUU	rouseabout
ABEOQSSUUU	subaqueous
ABEORRRSTU	barretrous
ABERRRSTWY	strawberry
ABERSSSTTU	substrates
ABFFGILLNY	bafflingly
ABFFGILNOU	buffaloing
ABFFIKMOOR	kaffirboom
ABFGILNOTW	batfowling
ABFGILORVY	forgivably
ABFIIILRTY	friability
ABFIILLLNY	infallibly
ABFIILNORV	riboflavin
ABFILOPRTY	profitably
ABFLLOSTUY	boastfully
ABFLLOSUUY	fabulously
ABFLORRSUW	barrowfuls
ABGGGILNRY	braggingly
ABGGIILNOT	obligating
ABGGILLMNO	gambolling
ABGHIIINNT	inhabiting
ABGHIILNOS	abolishing
ABGHIIMMNR	Birmingham
ABGHILMNSS	shamblings
ABGHILNOUX	boxhauling
ABGHINNSTU	sunbathing
ABGHINORNU	harbouring
ABGHINSWZZ	whizzbangs
ABGHIRRRSU	Harrisburg
ABGHOORRUY	yarborough
ABGIIILNST	sibilating
ABGIIJLNTU	jubilating
ABGIILLNSU	bilinguals
ABGIILNNTY	intangibly
ABGIILNOOT	obligation
ABGIILNOPR	parboiling
ABGIIMNNOO	Mabinogion
ABGIINNOST	botanising
ABGIINNOTZ	botanizing
ABGIINNRSU	urbanising
ABGIINNRUZ	urbanizing
ABGIINNTTU	intubating
ABGIKKMNOO	bookmaking
ABGIKLNRUW	bulwarking
ABGILLLNSY	syllabling
ABGILLLNUY	lullabying
ABGILLNNOO	ballooning
ABGILLNORY	laboringly
ABGILLNSUU	sublingual
ABGILMOSUY	bigamously
ABGILNOSTY	boastingly
ABGILNTTUU	tubulating
ABGILOORST	obligators
ABGILOORTY	obligatory

ABGIMNORTU	tambouring
ABGINNORRT	Barrington
ABGINOORSS	barognosis
ABGINORTTU	obturating
ABGINORTUV	outbraving
ABGINOSSTW	swingboats
ABGJOORRTU	objurgator
ABGJORSTUU	subjugator
ABGLLLORUY	globularly
ABGLLORUUU	Luluabourg
ABGLMNOOSS	boomslangs
ABGMOPRRSU	subprogram
ABGORRSSTU	Strasbourg
ABHHIIRSUV	bahuvrihis
ABHHILOSTT	batholiths
ABHHIMOOOP	homophobia
ABHIIMNSST	absinthism
ABHIIMOPSU	amphibious
ABHIKLLSSW	hawksbills
ABHIKMRRST	birthmarks
ABHILMNSTU	thumbnails
ABHILNOOPT	haplobiont
ABHILNOOST	halobionts
ABHILNRSTY	labyrinths
ABHILOPSTY	hospitably
ABHILORTUW	whirlabout
ABHIMNOOOP	monophobia
ABHIMNOOPY	ambiophony
ABHINOOOPS	nosophobia
ABHINPRSTU	paintbrush
ABHIPRRSSU	bursarship
ABHKMRRSSU	brushmarks
ABHLLMSTTU	thumbstall
ABHLNOORUY	honourably
ABHLOPSSTY	hypoblasts
ABHMNORRTU	rhumbatron
ABIIILLPTY	pliability
ABIIILLTVY	livability
ABIIILMNTY	inimitably
ABIIILMTXY	mixability
ABIIILNOST	sibilation
ABIIINOSST	antibiosis
ABIIJLNOTU	jubilation
ABIILLMNOY	binomially
ABIILLMNSU	subliminal
ABIILLNOVV	inviolably
ABIILLNRST	brilliants
ABIILLNSTY	sibilantly
ABIILLOTVY	lovability
ABIILMNNOS	binominals
ABIILMOTVY	movability
ABIILMPRTY	impartibly
ABIILMPSSY	impassibly
ABIILMTTUY	mutability
ABIILNOOSV	bolivianos
ABIILNORST	librations
ABIILNOTTY	notability
ABIILOPRTY	bipolarity
ABIILOPTTY	potability
ABIILORRTU	lubritoria
ABIILRSSTT	tribalists
ABIIMORSSV	bravissimo
ABIIMRSSTY	sybaritism
ABIINNOTTU	intubation
ABIINNRTUY	inurbanity
ABIINOOSTV	obviations
ABIINORSTV	vibrations
ABIINOTTTU	titubation
ABIIORSTTU	obituarist
ABIJLLNTUY	jubilantly
ABIJNOORTU	objuration
ABIKKNSTUY	Aktyubinsk
ABILLLOOSV	Villa-Lobos
ABILLNOOST	balloonist
ABILLNOSUU	lobulation
ABILLNOPST	ballpoints
ABILLNOSVY	insolvably
ABILLORRSZ	razorbills
ABILMNOSUU	albuminous
ABILMNOTUX	toxalbumin
ABILMOPRVY	improvably
ABILMORSXY	xylorimbas
ABILMOSSTU	absolutism
ABILMSSTTU	submittals
ABILNOOSTU	absolution
ABILNOTTUU	tubulation
ABILORSSTU	labourists
ABILORSSUU	salubrious
ABILOSSTTU	absolutist
ABILOSSTUY	sabulosity
ABILRSSTTU	brutalists
ABILRSTTUU	subtitular
ABILRTTUUY	tubularity
ABIMMNRSUU	manubriums
ABIMNORRST	brainstorm
ABIMNORSTU	tambourins
ABIMRSSSTU	strabismus
ABINOOPRST	absorption
	probations
	saprobiont
ABINOOPSST	spoonbaits
ABINOORRTU	Buonarroti
ABINOORTTU	obturation
ABINOOSSST	bassoonist
ABINOSSTTU	substation
ABINRSSTUY	Saintsbury
ABIORRTTTU	attributor
ABKLLOOSST	bookstalls
ABKLNNOUWY	unknowably
ABKMORSSYZ	Szymborska
ABLMNORSSU	subnormals
ABLOOPRSST	blastopors
ABLOOPRTTT	Port Talbot
ABLOORSTUY	absolutory
ABLORSTTUU	tubulators
ABMNORRSST	barnstorms
ABMOOORSTT	motorboats
ABMOORSTTY	strabotomy
ABMRSSTTUU	substratum
ABNOORRSTU	brontosaur
ABNOORSTUZ	zorbonauts
ABNORSTTUU	turnabouts
ABOOPRSSTT	bootstraps
ABOORRSTTU	obturators
ABOORSTTUU	roustabout
ABRRSSSTTU	starbursts
ABRRSSTTUW	bratwursts
ACCCDEHIIL	Chalcidice
ACCCEEENNS	canescence
ACCCEEHITT	catechetic
ACCCEENRST	accrescent
ACCCEFHKOR	cockchafer
ACCCEGINOS	cacogenics
ACCCEHILOT	chalcocite
ACCCEHORTW	cowcatcher
ACCCEHORUU	accoucheur
ACCCEIILRT	cicatricle
ACCCEIIRST	cicatrices
ACCCEIKORT	cockatrice
ACCCEILLNY	encyclical
ACCCEILLOS	calcicoles
ACCCEILMOP	accomplice
ACCCEIMNPY	impeccancy
ACCCGLNOOO	gonococcal
ACCCHHILOO	chocaholic
ACCCHINOOP	cacophonic
ACCCHKOPST	spatchcock
ACCCHLOORY	ochlocracy
ACCCHOOTUU	caoutchouc
ACCCIILLOT	laccolitic
ACCCIIOPRS	capriccios
ACCCILLLYY	cyclically
ACCCILLNOV	cyclonical
ACCCILMOPY	complicacy
ACCCILMORY	cycloramic
ACCCIMORTY	macrocytic
ACCCINOPPU	cappuccino
ACCDDEEENS	decadences
ACCDDEEIRT	accredited
ACCDDEEIST	desiccated
ACCDDEINOO	dodecanoic
ACCDDIORSS	disaccords
ACCDEEEELRS	recalesced
ACCDEEENNS	ascendence
ACCDEEENRT	reaccented
ACCDEEEPRT	reaccepted
ACCDEEGINR	reacceding
ACCDEEHIKS	chickadees
ACCDEEHIST	catechised
ACCDEEHITZ	catechized
ACCDEEHKMT	checkmated
ACCDEEHLOT	cochleated
ACCDEEHNOR	encroached
ACCDEEIILS	delicacies
ACCDEEINNS	incandesce
ACCDEEIQSU	acquiesced
ACCDEEIRRT	reaccredit
ACCDEEISST	desiccates
ACCDEEISTX	exsiccated
ACCDEELLOR	clearcoled
ACCDEELPST	spectacled
ACCDEELPTY	acceptedly
ACCDEENNST	candescent
ACCDEENNSY	ascendency
ACCDEENNTU	unaccented
ACCDEEORTU	accoutered

ACCDEFIIRS	sacrificed	**ACCEEHIKRS**	chickarees	**ACCEGHLNOS**	chalcogens
ACCDEGHORT	dogcatcher	**ACCEEHILLR**	cheliceral	**ACCEGIINOR**	cariogenic
ACCDEHLNOV	chalcedony	**ACCEEHILNP**	encephalic	**ACCEGIKNOP**	peacocking
ACCDEIILMN	calcimined	**ACCEEHINRS**	chanceries	**ACCEGILLNN**	cancelling
ACCDEIILNY	indelicacy	**ACCEEHIRST**	catechiser	**ACCEGILLNO**	collagenic
ACCDEIILST	dialectics	**ACCEEHIRTZ**	catechizer	**ACCEGILLOO**	ecological
ACCDEIINOS	cocainised	**ACCEEHISST**	catechises	**ACCEGILNNO**	concealing
ACCDEIINOZ	cocainized	**ACCEEHISTZ**	catechizes	**ACCEGILNOS**	coalescing
ACCDEIIOPT	apodeictic	**ACCEEHKMNS**	namechecks	**ACCEGILNOT**	lactogenic
ACCDEIIRST	cicatrised	**ACCEEHKMST**	checkmates	**ACCEGILOOS**	cacologies
ACCDEIIRTZ	cicatrized	**ACCEEHLNRT**	chantecler	**ACCEGIMOPS**	megascopic
ACCDEIKLNW	candlewick	**ACCEEHLNSS**	chanceless	**ACCEGINNOR**	carcinogen
ACCDEILLOP	peccadillo	**ACCEEHMNTU**	catechumen	**ACCEGINNOS**	cognisance
ACCDEILNOT	occidental	**ACCEEHNORR**	encroacher	**ACCEGINNOZ**	cognizance
ACCDEILNTU	inculcated	**ACCEEHNORS**	encroaches	**ACCEHHIIRR**	hierarchic
ACCDEILOPY	cyclopedia	**ACCEEILLRT**	electrical	**ACCEHHIKSU**	Chukchi Sea
ACCDEILRTU	circulated	**ACCEEILMNU**	ecumenical	**ACCEHHIMRS**	Carchemish
ACCDEIMNNY	mendicancy	**ACCEEILNTY**	acetylenic	**ACCEHHIPRT**	heptarchic
ACCDEIMORT	democratic	**ACCEEILORV**	varicocele	**ACCEHHMRSU**	Schumacher
ACCDEINNTU	inductance	**ACCEEILPSY**	epicalyces	**ACCEHIILMR**	chimerical
ACCDEINOOS	occasioned	**ACCEEIMNRS**	miscreance	**ACCEHIINNT**	technician
ACCDEINOPR	endocarpic	**ACCEEINNSS**	nascencies	**ACCEHIINPT**	epicanthic
ACCDEINSST	desiccants	**ACCEEIORSU**	ericaceous	**ACCEHIKLRS**	checkrails
ACCDEIORST	desiccator	**ACCEEIQSSU**	acquiesces	**ACCEHIKOPS**	peacockish
ACCDEIORTT	corticated	**ACCEEIRTUX**	excruciate	**ACCEHILLMV**	chemically
ACCDELLOOT	collocated	**ACCEEISSTX**	exsiccates	**ACCEHILLRU**	cleruchial
ACCDELOPSU	cloudscape	**ACCEEKLOST**	cockateels	**ACCEHILLTY**	hectically
ACCDELRSUY	accursedly	**ACCEELLNRS**	cancellers	**ACCEHILNOS**	cochineals
ACCDEMNOOS	cacodemons	**ACCEELLORS**	clearcoles	**ACCEHILOST**	chicalotes
ACCDEMORRS	camcorders	**ACCEELNORS**	concealers	**ACCEHIMSST**	schematics
ACCDEMOSTU	accustomed	**ACCEELNOST**	coalescent	**ACCEHINNSS**	chanciness
ACCDENORTT	contracted	**ACCEELNOSV**	convalesce	**ACCEHINOPT**	cenotaphic
ACCDEORRSS	scorecards		covalences	**ACCEHINRRU**	craunchier
ACCDEORSTU	coruscated	**ACCEELNPRS**	precancels	**ACCEHINSST**	catchiness
ACCDFIILTY	flaccidity	**ACCEELNPRU**	crapulence	**ACCEHIORRY**	hierocracy
ACCDGHIIMO	dichogamic	**ACCEELNRTU**	reluctance	**ACCEHIORST**	escharotic
ACCDHHRRUY	churchyard	**ACCEELNSTT**	lactescent		octarchies
ACCDHIINOR	diachronic	**ACCEELNSTU**	caulescent	**ACCEHIORTT**	rheotactic
ACCDHIIORS	radicchios	**ACCEELPSST**	spectacles		theocratic
ACCDHILNOO	conchoidal	**ACCEEMNRST**	marcescent	**ACCEHIRRTT**	tetrarchic
ACCDHILORV	clavichord		scarcement	**ACCEHIRSST**	scratchies
ACCDHINORS	chancroids	**ACCEEMOSTY**	ascomycete	**ACCEHIRSTT**	architects
ACCDHOOOSW	coachwoods	**ACCEENNNOV**	convenance	**ACCEHIRTVZ**	czarevitch
ACCDHOORST	octachords	**ACCEENNOVY**	conveyance	**ACCEHISSTT**	catechists
ACCDHORSTW	catchwords	**ACCEENOPRR**	coparcener	**ACCEHLLNOR**	chancellor
ACCDIIIRST	diacritics	**ACCEENORST**	consecrate	**ACCEHLMOOR**	homocercal
ACCDIILLPY	piccadilly	**ACCEENPTXY**	expectancy	**ACCEHLOOST**	chocolates
ACCDIILSST	cladistics	**ACCEENRSSS**	scarceness	**ACCEHLOPST**	catchpoles
ACCDIIMNOO	monoacidic	**ACCEEORRSU**	racecourse	**ACCEHLOSUY**	chylaceous
ACCDINOORS	accordions	**ACCEEORSTU**	cretaceous	**ACCEHMNSTT**	catchments
ACCDINORTT	contradict	**ACCEFFIINY**	inefficacy	**ACCEHNNPTY**	catchpenny
ACCDKNORSW	crackdowns	**ACCEFGILSU**	calcifuges	**ACCEHNNRTY**	trenchancy
ACCDNNOORT	concordant	**ACCEFHILST**	catchflies	**ACCEHNOOTY**	choanocyte
ACCDNOORST	concordats	**ACCEFHLRTY**	flycatcher	**ACCEHNORTT**	technocrat
ACCEEEEHKS	cheesecake	**ACCEFIILPS**	specifical	**ACCEHORSTU**	cartouches
ACCEEEHILR	chelicerae	**ACCEFIIRRS**	sacrificer	**ACCEHRRSST**	scratchers
ACCEEELMNU	Clemenceau	**ACCEFIIRSS**	sacrifices	**ACCEIILMNS**	calcimines
ACCEEELPRT	receptacle	**ACCEFILLOR**	calciferol	**ACCEIILNOT**	conciliate
ACCEEELRSS	recalesces	**ACCEFILMOR**	calceiform	**ACCEIILRRT**	rectricial
ACCEEENNRS	renascence	**ACCEFILSSU**	fascicules	**ACCEIILRTT**	tectricial
ACCEEENPTX	expectance	**ACCEFINOST**	confiscate	**ACCEIILSSS**	classicise
ACCEEGLMSY	megacycles	**ACCEFLLOTU**	flocculate	**ACCEIILSSZ**	classicize

ACCEIIMRST	ceramicist	ACCEKNORRS	corncrakes	ACCHIKPSST	chapsticks
ACCEIIMSST	asceticism	ACCEKNRRTU	nutcracker	ACCHILLOOS	alcoholics
ACCEIINOSS	cocainises	ACCELLNOSU	cancellous	ACCHILLOST	laccoliths
ACCEIINOSZ	cocainizes	ACCELLOORT	colorectal	ACCHILLOTY	catholicly
ACCEIINRST	Cistercian	ACCELLOOST	collocates	ACCHILMOPS	accomplish
ACCEIIORSS	accessorii	ACCELLSSUU	calculuses	ACCHILNNPS	splanchnic
	isocracies	ACCELMNOPT	complacent	ACCHILNOOT	catholicon
ACCEIIPPRR	pericarpic	ACCELNOOPY	Cape Colony	ACCHILNOTY	anchylotic
ACCEIIPRST	accipiters	ACCELNOPTU	conceptual	ACCHILOOST	Catholicos
ACCEIIRRST	cicatriser	ACCELNRTUY	reluctancy	ACCHILOSST	scholastic
ACCEIIRRTZ	cicatrizer	ACCELOOPST	lactoscope	ACCHILRSTY	scratchily
ACCEIIRSST	cicatrises	ACCELOSTUY	autocycles	ACCHILTTVY	tachylytic
	scarcities	ACCEMNNORY	necromancy	ACCHIMNORY	chiromancy
ACCEIIRSTZ	cicatrizes	ACCEMOPRST	compacters	ACCHIMORST	chromatics
ACCEIISSTV	siccatives	ACCEMORSTU	reaccustom	ACCHIMOSST	stomachics
ACCEIKKLPS	placekicks	ACCEMORSTY	macrocytes	ACCHIOPRSZ	schizocarp
ACCEIKLOST	cockatiels	ACCENNNOOS	consonance	ACCHIOPTTY	hypotactic
ACCEIKRSSW	wisecracks	ACCENOORSS	coenosarcs	ACCHIOSSTT	stochastic
ACCEILLLPS	scalpellic	ACCENOORSU	cornaceous	ACCHKLMOST	matchlocks
ACCEILLLRV	clerically	ACCENOPRRU	procurance	ACCHKLSSTU	saltchucks
ACCEILLNSY	scenically	ACCENORTTU	counteract	ACCHKOORSW	coachworks
ACCEILLOST	laccolites	ACCEORRSSW	scarecrows	ACCHLLOPST	catchpolls
ACCEILMMOR	commercial	ACCEORRSTU	securocrat	ACCHLOORST	ochlocrats
ACCEILMNOO	economical	ACCEORSSTU	coruscates	ACCHMOOORT	motorcoach
ACCEILMNOP	compliance	ACCEORSUUV	curvaceous	ACCHNOPSYY	sycophancy
ACCEILMOPT	complicate	ACCFFFFHHI	chiffchaff	ACCHNORRST	cornstarch
ACCEILMOST	cacomistle	ACCFGIILNY	calcifying	ACCHOPRSST	crosspatch
ACCEILMOSX	cacomixles	ACCFHIRTTW	witchcraft	ACCIIILLLP	piccalilli
ACCEILNOSS	neoclassic	ACCFIINNOT	fantoccini	ACCIIILNNS	clinicians
ACCEILNOTU	noctilucae	ACCFILSSUU	fasciculus	ACCIIINNNT	Cincinnati
ACCEILNRST	calcsinter	ACCFIMOPTY	compactify	ACCIIKKMNS	camiknicks
ACCEILNSTU	inculcates	ACCFLLNOTU	flocculant	ACCIILLLNY	clinically
ACCEILOPPT	apoplectic	ACCGGHILOO	cholagogic	ACCIILLOST	localistic
ACCEILOPRR	reciprocal	ACCGHHIIRT	High Arctic	ACCIILLRTY	critically
ACCEILOPRS	precocials	ACCGHIILOR	oligarchic	ACCIILMNOS	laconicism
ACCEILOPRV	prevocalic	ACCGHINNRU	craunching	ACCIILMSSS	classicism
ACCEILOTVY	coactively	ACCGHINRST	scratching	ACCIILNNOT	calcitonin
ACCEILRSTU	circulates	ACCGHIOPTY	phagocytic	ACCIILNOSS	calcinosis
ACCEILRTUY	cruciately	ACCGHOPRRY	cyclograph	ACCIILNRTU	uncritical
ACCEIMNORS	sciomancer	ACCGIIMORT	tragicomic	ACCIILOPST	occipitals
ACCEIMNRSY	miscreancy	ACCGIINPRT	practicing	ACCIILORTY	caloricity
ACCEIMORST	mesocratic	ACCGIKLNRS	cracklings	ACCIILSSST	classicist
ACCEINNNOV	connivance	ACCGILNSUY	accusingly	ACCIIMNNNO	cinnamonic
ACCEINNORT	concertina	ACCGILOOST	scatologic	ACCIIMNOOT	iconomatic
ACCEINNSSY	incessancy	ACCGIMNOPT	compacting	ACCIIMNOST	sciomantic
ACCEINOOST	consociate	ACCGINNORT	Accrington	ACCIIMORTT	timocratic
ACCEINORST	accretions	ACCGINNOTT	contacting	ACCIINNNPY	piccaninny
	anorectics	ACCGINNOTU	accounting	ACCIINNOTY	canonicity
ACCEINOSSS	accessions	ACCGINORTU	accoutring	ACCIINORSS	carcinosis
ACCEINOSST	oscitances	ACCHHIILLN	chinchilla	ACCIIOPRSU	auriscopic
ACCEINSSTU	encaustics	ACCHHIIPUU	Ch'ü Ch'iu-		capricious
	succinates		pai	ACCIIOPSST	pasticcios
ACCEINTTUV	cunctative	ACCHHINRTU	antichurch	ACCIIOTTVY	coactivity
ACCEIOORSU	coriaceous	ACCHHMRRUY	Church Army	ACCIISTTUY	causticity
ACCEIOPPSY	episcopacy	ACCHHORSST	crosshatch	ACCIKKKKNN	knickknack
ACCEIORSTX	exsiccator	ACCHIIILST	chiliastic	ACCIKKRRTT	tricktrack
ACCEIORTUY	eucaryotic	ACCHIILORT	acrolithic	ACCIKNOSSW	cockswains
ACCEIOSSTU	cistaceous	ACCHIILTTY	tachylitic	ACCILLMOSY	cosmically
ACCEIPSSTY	cityscapes	ACCHIIMSST	schismatic	ACCILLORTY	cortically
ACCEJKRSSW	jackscrews	ACCHIINNPS	chincapins	ACCILLRRUY	circularly
ACCEJNOSUU	juncaceous	ACCHIINOTY	thiocyanic	ACCILMNNOU	councilman
ACCEKKLMOR	clockmaker	ACCHIKMSTT	matchstick	ACCILMNOOS	iconoclasm

ACCILMNOPY compliancy	**ACDDEESSTU** decussated	**ACDEEENRTV** advertence
ACCILNOOST iconoclast	**ACDDEFFHNU** handcuffed	**ACDEEEORRT** redecorate
ACCILNORSV clavicorns	**ACDDEFFIRT** diffracted	**ACDEEEPRST** deprecates
ACCILNORTU inculcator	**ACDDEFFLOS** scaffolded	**ACDEEERRST** desecrater
ACCILNOSTV conclavist	**ACDDEGHIRS** discharged	**ACDEEERSST** desecrates
ACCILNSSTY synclastic	**ACDDEGHNNY** cynghanedd	**ACDEEERSTU** reeducates
ACCILOPPRY polycarpic	**ACDDEGIINT** dedicating	**ACDEEFFLTY** affectedly
ACCILORRTU circulator	**ACDDEGNOOS** dodecagons	**ACDEEFFNTU** unaffected
ACCILRRRUU curricular	**ACDDEHIIOS** diadochies	**ACDEEFGINT** defecating
ACCIMNNOVY vancomycin	**ACDDEHIKNP** handpicked	**ACDEEFIIRR** Fredericia
ACCIMNOOPR monocarpic	**ACDDEHINSW** sandwiched	**ACDEEFINOT** defecation
ACCIMNOOPT compaction	**ACDDEHIPST** dispatched	**ACDEEFINRT** interfaced
ACCIMNOORT monocratic	**ACDDEHNNOS** secondhand	**ACDEEFIRSS** fricasseed
ACCIMOORSS crocosmias	**ACDDEHNORT** Chadderton	**ACDEEFKRST** afterdecks
ACCINNOTTU cunctation	**ACDDEIILMS** disclaimed	**ACDEEFLNOR** confederal
ACCINOOPRU cornucopia	**ACDDEIINOT** dedication	**ACDEEFNSTU** fecundates
ACCINOOPTU occupation	**ACDDEIINTV** vindicated	**ACDEEFORST** defecators
ACCINOPRSY conspiracy	**ACDDEILMOU** duodecimal	forecasted
ACCINORSTY Carson City	**ACDDEILOST** dislocated	**ACDEEFRRSU** resurfaced
ACCINSSTTY syntactics	**ACDDEILPTU** duplicated	**ACDEEGHLLN** challenged
ACCIOPRSTT catoptrics	**ACDDEILTTW** wildcatted	**ACDEEGHNNO** hendecagon
ACCJKORSSS crossjacks	**ACDDEINNSS** candidness	**ACDEEGIIMN** mediagenic
ACCKKMMSUU muckamucks	**ACDDEINSTY** syndicated	**ACDEEGIINT** diagenetic
ACCKLMOORU cockalorum	**ACDDEIORST** dedicators	**ACDEEGIKLR** girdlecake
ACCLOPRTUY plutocracy	**ACDDEIORTY** dedicatory	**ACDEEGILOS** geodesical
ACCLRSSSUU succursals	**ACDDEIPSTU** cuspidated	**ACDEEGINNR** grandniece
ACCMMOORSS macrocosms	**ACDDEIRRSS** discarders	**ACDEEGINNT** anteceding
ACCMORSSTY macrocysts	**ACDDEIRSTT** distracted	**ACDEEGINOP** paedogenic
ACCNNNOOSY consonancy	**ACDDEKLLNO** landlocked	**ACDEEGINRR** adrenergic
ACCNOOORTV convocator	**ACDDEKLORS** dreadlocks	**ACDEEGINRS** decreasing
ACCNOOPRRY pornocracy	**ACDDELNNOO** colonnaded	**ACDEEGINRT** centigrade
ACCNOORRTT contractor	**ACDDELNOOW** candlewood	**ACDEEGNORU** encouraged
ACCNOORSTT contactors	**ACDDENNRUY** redundancy	**ACDEEHHLLT** hatchelled
ACCNORSTTU cunctators	**ACDDEOOPSU** decapodous	**ACDEEHILMS** alchemised
ACCOPRSSTY cystocarps	**ACDDFHIORU** chaudfroid	**ACDEEHILMZ** alchemized
ACDDDEEKLO deadlocked	**ACDDGHILNR** grandchild	**ACDEEHILNR** chandelier
ACDDEEEIRT rededicate	**ACDDGIINRS** discarding	**ACDEEHIMNS** mechanised
ACDDEEEIST dedicatees	**ACDDGIKNOP** paddocking	**ACDEEHIMNZ** mechanized
ACDDEEELNR calendered	**ACDDHHNSSU** dachshunds	**ACDEEHIMRS** Archimedes
ACDDEEENNP dependance	**ACDDIINOST** addictions	**ACDEEHINOT** endothecia
ACDDEEENOS Dodecanese	**ACDDIMORSW** caddisworm	theodicean
ACDDEEENRS reascended	**ACDDINORST** discordant	**ACDEEHIRST** tracheides
ACDDEEEPRT deprecated	**ACDEEEEHHS** headcheese	**ACDEEHKLLS** shellacked
ACDDEEERST desecrated	**ACDEEEELRT** decelerate	**ACDEEHLLNN** channelled
ACDDEEERTU reeducated	**ACDEEEEPRS** predecease	**ACDEEHLLNS** chandelles
ACDDEEFLNU fecundated	**ACDEEEFLNR** freelanced	**ACDEEHLLST** satchelled
ACDDEEHLLN chandelled	**ACDEEEFMNT** defacement	**ACDEEHLNRT** Anderlecht
ACDDEEHNOR decahedron	**ACDEEEGILS** delegacies	**ACDEEHMNRT** merchanted
ACDDEEHPST despatched	**ACDEEEGNRY** degeneracy	**ACDEEHMNTT** detachment
ACDDEEIIPT diapedetic	**ACDEEEHIPS** headpieces	**ACDEEHNOPR** chaperoned
ACDDEEIITV dedicative	**ACDEEEHLTT** decathlete	**ACDEEHOPPR** copperhead
ACDDEEIKMV medivacked	**ACDEEEHNRS** adherences	**ACDEEHOPRR** reproached
ACDDEEILMT maledicted	**ACDEEEHRRS** researched	**ACDEEHORRV** overarched
ACDDEEILTU elucidated	**ACDEEEIPRT** depreciate	**ACDEEHORTU** outreached
ACDDEEIPRT predicated	**ACDEEEKNPP** kneecapped	**ACDEEHPRST** despatcher
ACDDEELLOT decollated	**ACDEEELNPR** precleaned	**ACDEEHPSST** despatches
ACDDEELNRU undeclared	**ACDEEELNRT** crenelated	**ACDEEIILMS** decimalise
ACDDEELNTY decadently	**ACDEEELNTU** enucleated	**ACDEEIILMZ** decimalize
ACDDEENNPY dependancy	**ACDEEELSTT** telecasted	**ACDEEIILNT** indelicate
ACDDEENNST descendant	**ACDEEEMRST** decameters	**ACDEEIILTT** dietetical
ACDDEENRTU underacted		decametres	**ACDEEIIMRT** acidimeter
ACDDEENTUU uneducated	**ACDEEENNTT** antecedent	**ACDEEIIMTV** medicative

ACDEEIINST	teniacides	**ACDEELLMSU**	muscadelle	**ACDEFIIINT**	nidificate
ACDEEIINSV	deviancies	**ACDEELLNPS**	spancelled	**ACDEFIIIRS**	acidifiers
ACDEEIJSTV	adjectives	**ACDEELLORV**	overcalled	**ACDEFIILMS**	facsimiled
ACDEEILLOS	delocalise	**ACDEELLOST**	decollates	**ACDEFIILOT**	foeticidal
ACDEEILLOZ	delocalize	**ACDEELLOTT**	dolcelatte	**ACDEFIILSS**	classified
ACDEEILLPR	callipered	**ACDEELMORT**	ectodermal	**ACDEFIINPU**	unpacified
ACDEEILLPS	specialled	**ACDEELMORU**	leucoderma	**ACDEFIINST**	sanctified
ACDEEILLRS	escadrille	**ACDEELNOST**	adolescent	**ACDEFIIRRT**	fratricide
ACDEEILLTV	vellicated	**ACDEELNRTU**	crenulated	**ACDEFIISST**	satisficed
ACDEEILLTY	delicately	**ACDEELOPRT**	percolated	**ACDEFIJKKN**	jackknifed
ACDEEILMPR	premedical	**ACDEELORRT**	correlated	**ACDEFIKRTU**	fruitcaked
ACDEEILMRS	declaimers	**ACDEELORSS**	casseroled	**ACDEFILLOS**	coalfields
ACDEEILMRV	decemviral	**ACDEELORSW**	lowercased	**ACDEFILSSY**	declassify
ACDEEILNNS	celandines	**ACDEELORTU**	edulcorate	**ACDEFIMORT**	formicated
	decennials	**ACDEELPRSY**	clepsydrae	**ACDEFINNOT**	confidante
ACDEEILNPP	appendicle	**ACDEELPSTU**	speculated	**ACDEFINORS**	fricandoes
ACDEEILNRT	credential	**ACDEELPTUX**	exculpated	**ACDEFINORT**	fornicated
	interlaced	**ACDEELSSTY**	decastyles		fractioned
ACDEEILOSV	devocalise	**ACDEEMMNOR**	commandeer	**ACDEFINSTU**	infuscated
ACDEEILOVZ	devocalize	**ACDEEMMNPT**	decampment	**ACDEFIORST**	factorised
ACDEEILPPY	pipeclayed	**ACDEEMNOTY**	adenectomy	**ACDEFIORTZ**	factorized
ACDEEILPRT	replicated	**ACDEEMRRTU**	mercurated	**ACDEFLNORS**	landforces
ACDEEILPTU	pediculate	**ACDEENNOST**	condensate	**ACDEFLORST**	Castleford
ACDEEILPTX	explicated	**ACDEENNOTV**	covenanted	**ACDEFLTTUU**	fluctuated
ACDEEILRST	cartelised	**ACDEENNRSU**	sunderance	**ACDEFNORTU**	fecundator
	decaliters	**ACDEENNSST**	ascendents	**ACDEGGIOPS**	pedagogics
	decalitres	**ACDEENOPRR**	ropedancer	**ACDEGHHIJK**	highjacked
ACDEEILRTZ	cartelized	**ACDEENRSSS**	sacredness	**ACDEGHIRRS**	discharger
ACDEEILSTU	elucidates	**ACDEENRSST**	descanters	**ACDEGHIRSS**	discharges
ACDEEILSTY	acetylides	**ACDEENRSSU**	ascendeurs	**ACDEGHLLOR**	gralloched
ACDEEIMMNT	medicament	**ACDEENRSTT**	transected	**ACDEGHOSTW**	dogwatches
ACDEEIMNOS	macedoines	**ACDEENRSTY**	daycentres	**ACDEGHRRSU**	surcharged
ACDEEIMNOU	eudaemonic	**ACDEENRTTU**	detruncate	**ACDEGIILLS**	gallicised
ACDEEIMNPS	impedances	**ACDEENRTVY**	advertency	**ACDEGIILLZ**	gallicized
ACDEEIMORT	acidometer	**ACDEEOOPRT**	cooperated	**ACDEGIILMN**	declaiming
ACDEEIMPRT	imprecated	**ACDEEOPRRT**	deprecator	**ACDEGIILMR**	germicidal
	mercaptide		procreated	**ACDEGIILNS**	anglicised
ACDEEIMRSS	semisacred	**ACDEEOPRRY**	copyreader	**ACDEGIILNZ**	anglicized
ACDEEIMRST	miscreated	**ACDEEOPRSS**	Pescadores	**ACDEGIIMNT**	decimating
ACDEEIMRTT	metricated	**ACDEEOPRSU**	predaceous		medicating
ACDEEIMSTU	miseducate	**ACDEEORRST**	desecrator	**ACDEGIINOR**	radiogenic
ACDEEINNNT	intendance	**ACDEEORRTT**	retroacted	**ACDEGIINOU**	audiogenic
ACDEEINNTU	denunciate	**ACDEEPPRSU**	uppercased	**ACDEGILLOT**	colligated
	enunciated	**ACDEEPRRTU**	recaptured	**ACDEGILNSS**	declassing
ACDEEINOPR	percoidean	**ACDEERSSTU**	reductases	**ACDEGILNTU**	cingulated
ACDEEINORS	deaconries	**ACDEESSSTU**	decussates	**ACDEGILOOP**	logopaedic
ACDEEINPPS	appendices	**ACDEFFFLRU**	carfuffled	**ACDEGILOOS**	logaoedics
ACDEEINPTT	pectinated	**ACDEFFHINO**	chiffonade	**ACDEGIMMRS**	scrimmaged
ACDEEINRTT	interacted	**ACDEFFIIOT**	officiated	**ACDEGIMNOY**	geodynamic
ACDEEINSST	desistance	**ACDEFFIKRT**	trafficked	**ACDEGINNOR**	androgenic
ACDEEIORTV	decorative	**ACDEFFILRT**	fieldcraft	**ACDEGINORR**	corrigenda
ACDEEIORTX	excoriated	**ACDEFFISST**	disaffects	**ACDEGINORT**	decorating
ACDEEIOTTX	detoxicate	**ACDEFFLORS**	scaffolder	**ACDEGINRTT**	detracting
ACDEEIPRST	pederastic	**ACDEFFMORS**	cofferdams	**ACDEGIORSU**	discourage
	predicates	**ACDEFFOSTU**	suffocated	**ACDEGIRRSS**	disgracers
ACDEEIPRTT	crepitated	**ACDEFGHILT**	lightfaced	**ACDEGIRRST**	cartridges
ACDEEIQRRU	reacquired	**ACDEFGLLNO**	golden calf	**ACDEGJNOTU**	conjugated
ACDEEIRSTU	cauterised	**ACDEFHILNS**	candlefish	**ACDEGLNNRU**	granduncle
ACDEEIRTTV	detractive	**ACDEFHINRS**	archfiends	**ACDEGLNORS**	cradlesong
ACDEEIRTTX	extricated		franchised	**ACDEGLNORU**	clangoured
ACDEEIRTUZ	cauterized	**ACDEFHLRSS**	feldschars	**ACDEGMMRSU**	scrummaged
ACDEEITTUX	exactitude	**ACDEFHOSUV**	vouchsafed	**ACDEGNNOOT**	contangoed

ACDEGNNNOSU	undecagons
ACDEGORRTU	corrugated
ACDEHHIKST	thickheads
ACDEHHILRT	Leichhardt
ACDEHHLMOO	Chol Hamoed
ACDEHHORSX	hexachords
ACDEHIIINR	enchiridia
ACDEHIILLO	helicoidal
ACDEHIILOP	acidophile
ACDEHIIMRT	diathermic
ACDEHIIORR	diarrhoeic
ACDEHILMOT	methodical
ACDEHILMRS	childermas
ACDEHIMMST	mismatched
ACDEHIMNOP	championed
ACDEHIMORT	dichromate
ACDEHINNRS	hindrances
ACDEHINNST	disenchant
ACDEHINOPS	deaconship
ACDEHINORT	achondrite
ACDEHINRSZ	scherzandi
ACDEHINSSW	sandwiches
ACDEHIPRST	dispatcher
ACDEHIPSST	cadetships
	dispatches
ACDEHIRTTW	ditchwater
ACDEHKMPSU	chempaduks
ACDEHKOSST	headstocks
ACDEHLNOST	decathlons
ACDEHLNOSY	anchylosed
ACDEHLOOPP	cephalopod
ACDEHMNORR	orchardmen
ACDEHMOSTU	moustached
ACDEHMOTTU	outmatched
ACDEHMPRSY	pachyderms
ACDEHNNORT	Chardonnet
ACDEHNOORT	octahedron
ACDEHNOPRS	cardphones
	phonecards
ACDEHNORSZ	scherzando
ACDEHOOPST	chaetopods
ACDEHOORTU	coauthored
ACDEHORRSW	wordsearch
ACDEHORRTT	tetrachord
ACDEHORSSS	crossheads
ACDEIIILST	idealistic
	italicised
ACDEIIILTZ	italicized
ACDEIIINST	dieticians
ACDEIIINTV	indicative
ACDEIIJTUV	judicative
ACDEIIILLOT	idiolectal
ACDEIIILMMT	dilemmatic
ACDEIIILMNS	adminicles
	medicinals
ACDEIIILMPT	implicated
ACDEIIILMRS	disclaimer
ACDEIIILMRV	vermicidal
ACDEIIILNNT	incidental
ACDEIIILNOS	decisional
ACDEIIILNOT	Diocletian
ACDEIIILNSX	indexicals

ACDEIIILOPR	periodical
ACDEIIILOPS	episodical
ACDEIIILOSS	socialised
ACDEIIILOSZ	socialized
ACDEIIILPST	pesticidal
	septicidal
ACDEIIILRSV	larvicides
ACDEIIMNOT	decimation
	medication
ACDEIIMNRT	criminated
ACDEIIMPRU	epicardium
ACDEIIMRRS	miscarried
ACDEIIMRST	matricides
ACDEIIMRTX	taxidermic
ACDEIIMRTY	acidimetry
ACDEIINNRY	incendiary
ACDEIINOSS	sciaenoids
ACDEIINOSY	isocyanide
ACDEIINSTV	vindicates
ACDEIINTTT	nictitated
ACDEIIORSU	iridaceous
ACDEIIOSST	dissociate
ACDEIIPRRS	parricides
ACDEIIPRST	patricides
	pediatrics
ACDEIIPRTY	peracidity
ACDEIJNTUV	adjunctive
ACDEIJRTUU	judicature
ACDEIKRSST	sidetracks
ACDEILLMOT	collimated
ACDEILLORR	cordillera
ACDEILLOST	Old Castile
	oscillated
ACDEILLTUV	victualled
ACDEILMNNO	nonmedical
ACDEILMNOP	complained
ACDEILMNTU	culminated
ACDEILMOPR	proclaimed
ACDEILNNOR	endocrinal
ACDEILNNPS	candlepins
ACDEILNOSV	volcanised
ACDEILNOTU	inoculated
ACDEILNOVZ	volcanized
ACDEILNPSS	placidness
ACDEILNPTU	inculpated
ACDEILNSUV	vulcanised
ACDEILNUVZ	vulcanized
ACDEILOPST	despotical
ACDEILORTU	elucidator
ACDEILOSST	dislocates
ACDEILOSUY	edaciously
ACDEILOTTU	colatitude
ACDEILPRSS	displacers
ACDEILPSSU	capsulised
ACDEILPSTU	duplicates
ACDEILPSUZ	capsulized
ACDEILRSSS	laserdiscs
ACDEILRTTW	wildcatter
ACDEILTTUV	cultivated
ACDEIMMORT	dermatomic
ACDEIMNNOP	pandemonic
ACDEIMNNOT	demicanton

ACDEIMNNST	mendicants
ACDEIMNORU	androecium
ACDEIMNOSU	mendacious
ACDEIMNSSU	muscadines
ACDEIMOPRR	madreporic
ACDEIMORST	decimators
ACDEIMORVW	microwaved
ACDEIMRTTU	micturated
ACDEINNNTY	intendancy
ACDEINNORS	ordinances
ACDEINNOSS	dissonance
ACDEINNOST	sanctioned
ACDEINNRSS	rancidness
ACDEINOORT	carotenoid
	coordinate
	decoration
ACDEINOPRS	scorpaenid
ACDEINORRW	cordwainer
ACDEINORST	narcotised
	redactions
ACDEINORTT	detraction
ACDEINORTZ	narcotized
ACDEINOSTT	anecdotist
ACDEINOSTU	educations
ACDEINOSTV	advections
ACDEINOSTW	wainscoted
ACDEINOTTX	detoxicant
ACDEINPRST	discrepant
	predicants
ACDEINRSST	discanters
ACDEINRTUV	incurvated
ACDEINSSTY	syndicates
ACDEINSTTU	sanctitude
ACDEIOOPRS	radioscope
ACDEIOPRRT	predicator
ACDEIOPRSU	predacious
ACDEIOPRTT	tetrapodic
ACDEIOPSSU	spadiceous
ACDEIOPSTY	adipocytes
ACDEIORSST	ostracised
ACDEIORSTZ	ostracized
ACDEIPQRSU	quadriceps
ACDEIQRSTU	quadrisect
ACDEIRRSTT	distracter
ACDEIRSSTT	dictatress
ACDEIRSSTU	crassitude
ACDEIRSTTU	rusticated
ACDEISSSTY	ecdysiasts
ACDEKKMOPR	pockmarked
ACDEKORSTY	rocksteady
ACDELLOORT	decollator
ACDELMNOOR	coromandel
ACDELMNOTU	columnated
	documental
ACDELMOPRR	palmcorder
ACDELMOPRS	placoderms
ACDELMORST	Coldstream
ACDELNNOOS	colonnades
ACDELNNOOY	Conan Doyle
ACDELNNSTU	candlenuts
ACDELNOORS	canoodlers
ACDELNOORT	decolorant

ACDELNOOSW lancewoods	**ACDGILOORY** cardiology	**ACDIKRSSTY** yardsticks
ACDELNOOTY acotyledon	**ACDGIMMNNO** commanding	**ACDILLMNOU** calmodulin
ACDELNPRUU peduncular	**ACDGINNOTU** outdancing	**ACDILLNOOV** conoidally
ACDELNRSSU underclass	**ACDGLOTYYZ** zygodactyl	**ACDILLOOTY** cotyloidal
ACDELOPRRU procedural	**ACDHIIIIRR** Richard III	**ACDILMOSTU** comatulids
ACDELORTYY D'Oyly Carte	**ACDHIIIOPT** idiopathic	**ACDILNOSTU** Saint-Cloud
ACDELOSSTU outclassed	**ACDHIINORT** anhidrotic	**ACDILOPRTU** duplicator
ACDELPRSSY clepsydras	**ACDHILMNOY** hymnodical	**ACDILPSSTY** dysplastic
ACDEMMMNOS commendams	**ACDHILMOOR** harmolodic	**ACDIMMORUY** myocardium
ACDEMMNOOS commandoes	**ACDHILNOOP** chilopodan	**ACDIMNNOOT** codominant
ACDEMMNORS commanders	**ACDHILOORT** trochoidal	**ACDIMOORSU** mordacious
ACDEMMOTTU commutated	**ACDHILRSSY** chrysalids	**ACDINNOSSY** dissonancy
ACDEMNOPRS companders	**ACDHILRSUY** hydraulics	**ACDINOOPST** actinopods
ACDEMNORTU mucronated	**ACDHIMOORT** chromatoid	**ACDINOSSTU** custodians
ACDEMOOPRR compradore	**ACDHIMORST** chromatids	**ACDINPSSSU** scindapsus
ACDEMOORST motorcades	**ACDHINOOOX** chionodoxa	**ACDINSSSTU** discussant
ACDEMOPRSU dampcourse	**ACDHINORRS** Richardson	**ACDIOOPRSY** radioscopy
ACDENNNOOR ordonnance	**ACDHIORTTY** trachytoid	**ACDJOORSTU** coadjutors
ACDENNNOOS nanosecond	**ACDHIRSTWY** switchyard	**ACDKLORSTU** truckloads
ACDENNRSST transcends	**ACDHLLLOPY** cladophyll	**ACDKMNNOOS** monadnocks
ACDENOOOSW canoewoods	phylloclad	**ACDKNORSTU** soundtrack
ACDENOPPSW snowcapped	**ACDHLOORRU** urochordal	**ACDKORSSTY** stockyards
ACDENOPSTY syncopated	**ACDHLOORRY** hydrocoral	**ACDLLOOPSW** codswallop
ACDENORSTT contrasted	**ACDHMMNOORS** chondromas	**ACDLLOPTYY** polydactyl
ACDENORSTU undercoats	**ACDHMNORVY** hydromancy	**ACDLMNOOSY** condylomas
ACDENPSUYY Puy de Sancy	**ACDHOOPPSS** scaphopods	**ACDLMNOPSW** clampdowns
ACDENPTTUU punctuated	**ACDHORSTWW** watchwords	**ACDLNSSTYY** syndactyls
ACDENRRRTU redcurrant	**ACDIIILSUU** Claudius II	**ACDMMNORSU** communards
ACDENRRSTU transducer	**ACDIIIMMRU** miracidium	**ACDMOOPRRS** compradors
undercarts	**ACDIIIMNST** diactinism	**ACDNOORRST** corrodants
ACDEOOORST decorators	**ACDIIINNOT** indication	**ACDOORRSSS** crossroads
ACDEOOORVW woodcarver	**ACDIIJLLUY** judicially	**ACDORRSTUY** courtyards
ACDEOORSTT doctorates	**ACDIILLSUY** suicidally	**ACEEEFFMNT** effacement
ACDEOPPRSU pseudocarp	**ACDIILMOPT** diplomatic	**ACEEEFFTTU** effectuate
ACDEOPRRTT protracted	**ACDIILOPRT** dioptrical	**ACEEEFIPRT** afterpiece
ACDEOPRSUU drupaceous	**ACDIILORST** clostridia	**ACEEEFIRST** cafetieres
ACDEORRSTT detractors	**ACDIILORTY** cordiality	**ACEEEFLNRR** freelancer
ACDEORRTTY detractory	radiolytic	**ACEEEFLNRS** freelances
ACDFGIIINY acidifying	**ACDIILORUX** uxoricidal	**ACEEEFMNNT** enfacement
ACDFGIILNU fungicidal	**ACDIILPRSU** discipular	**ACEEEGHPRS** repechages
ACDFIILLUV fiducially	**ACDIIMNORT** antidromic	**ACEEEGILNN** inelegance
ACDFIMNNOR confirmand	**ACDIIMNOST** monadistic	**ACEEEGILNS** elegancies
ACDFINNOST confidants	**ACDIIMNOSY** isodynamic	**ACEEEGILTX** exegetical
ACDFLNOSSY candyfloss	**ACDIIMNOTU** coatimundi	**ACEEEGNPRT** percentage
ACDFNSTTUY candytufts	**ACDIIMNSTY** dynamistic	**ACEEEGNRRS** screenager
ACDFORRSTW swordcraft	**ACDIIMRSTY** mydriatics	**ACEEEGNRRY** regeneracy
ACDGGIINRS disgracing	**ACDIINNORY** inordinacy	**ACEEEHIMRX** hexaemeric
ACDGHIINNS Ding an sich	**ACDIINOORT** carotinoid	**ACEEEHIRSV** echeverias
ACDGIIIMNR gramicidin	**ACDIINORST** indicators	**ACEEEHLMOT** hematocele
ACDGIIINNT indicating	**ACDIINORTV** vindicator	**ACEEEHLPSW** scapewheel
ACDGIIJNNU jaundicing	**ACDIINORTY** dictionary	**ACEEEHNPRS** cheapeners
ACDGIILNPS displacing	indicatory	**ACEEEHRRRS** researcher
ACDGIINNST discanting	**ACDIINOSTT** dictations	**ACEEEHRRSS** researches
distancing	**ACDIINRTUY** iracundity	**ACEEEIMRRS** creameries
ACDGIINOST diagnostic	**ACDIIOORTX** radiotoxic	**ACEEEIOPRV** apperceive
ACDGIIRSST digastrics	**ACDIIOSSSU** Dio Cassius	**ACEEEIPRRV** Peace River
ACDGIKLNOP padlocking	**ACDIJNNOTU** adjunction	**ACEEEIRRST** secretaire
ACDGIKNOST stockading	**ACDIJORSTU** judicators	**ACEEEIRRTV** recreative
ACDGILLMOO modal logic	**ACDIJORTUX** coadjutrix	**ACEEEIRSTV** eviscerate
ACDGILLOSU glucosidal	**ACDIJORTUY** judicatory	**ACEEEIRTVX** execrative
ACDGILNNOO canoodling	**ACDIKKNSST** kickstands	**ACEEEKNQSU** queencakes
ACDGILNOOT odontalgic	**ACDIKNQSSU** quicksands	**ACEEEKRRST** racketeers

493

ACEEELLNRT	crenellate	**ACEEGHINST**	escheating	**ACEEHILMNN**	manchineel
ACEEEELMNNT	enlacement	**ACEEGHIRSU**	gaucheries	**ACEEHILMRT**	hermetical
ACEEEELNORT	coelentera	**ACEEGHLLNR**	challenger	**ACEEHILMSS**	alchemises
ACEEEELNPRV	prevalence	**ACEEGHLLNS**	challenges	**ACEEHILMSZ**	alchemizes
ACEEELNRST	crenelates	**ACEEGHLNSS**	changeless	**ACEEHILNNP**	encephalin
ACEEELNSTU	enucleates	**ACEEGHNNOP**	Copenhagen	**ACEEHILNNS**	channelise
ACEEELORTT	electorate	**ACEEGHNORV**	changeover	**ACEEHILNNZ**	channelize
ACEEELPRVY	everyplace	**ACEEGHNRSX**	exchangers	**ACEEHILNST**	anthelices
ACEEELRSSS	creaseless	**ACEEGHNSSU**	gaucheness	**ACEEHILPTT**	telepathic
ACEEELRSTT	telecaster	**ACEEGHORRV**	overcharge	**ACEEHILRSV**	chevaliers
ACEEEMMNRT	amercement	**ACEEGIILPP**	epipelagic	**ACEEHILSTT**	esthetical
ACEEEMNNPR	permanence	**ACEEGILLNR**	allergenic	**ACEEHIMNPZ**	chimpanzee
ACEEEMNNST	encasement	**ACEEGILLOT**	collegiate	**ACEEHIMNRS**	mechaniser
ACEEEMNPRT	temperance	**ACEEGILNNY**	inelegancy	**ACEEHIMNRZ**	mechanizer
ACEEEMNPST	escapement	**ACEEGILNTU**	geniculate	**ACEEHIMNSS**	mechanises
ACEEEMNRTT	metacenter	**ACEEGILSTU**	sluicegate	**ACEEHIMNSZ**	mechanizes
	metacentre	**ACEEGIMNOS**	geomancies	**ACEEHIMPRS**	impeachers
ACEEEMORTT	acetometer	**ACEEGINNOS**	caseinogen	**ACEEHIMPRY**	hyperaemic
ACEEENNOTV	covenantee	**ACEEGINNPT**	pangenetic	**ACEEHIMPTT**	empathetic
ACEEENNPRT	penetrance	**ACEEGINNRT**	reenacting	**ACEEHIMRTX**	hexametric
	repentance	**ACEEGINNST**	tangencies	**ACEEHIMSST**	misteaches
ACEEENNRRT	reentrance	**ACEEGINNSV**	evanescing		schematise
ACEEENNSTV	evanescent	**ACEEGINRRT**	recreating	**ACEEHIMSTT**	metaethics
ACEEENPPST	appetences	**ACEEGINRSV**	grievances		meta-ethics
ACEEENPRSS	esperances	**ACEEGINRTX**	execrating	**ACEEHIMSTZ**	schematize
ACEEENRSSV	severances	**ACEEGIOPRS**	geocarpies	**ACEEHIMTTT**	metathetic
ACEEEPRRTU	recuperate	**ACEEGIORST**	categories	**ACEEHINNPT**	phenacetin
ACEEEPRSTT	pacesetter		categorise	**ACEEHINPSS**	peachiness
ACEEFFHRRS	chafferers	**ACEEGIORTZ**	categorize	**ACEEHINRRS**	rancheries
ACEEFFHSUU	chauffeuse	**ACEEGIOTTX**	excogitate	**ACEEHINSTT**	anesthetic
ACEEFFIMNY	effeminacy	**ACEEGIRRSV**	caregivers	**ACEEHIORRT**	charioteer
ACEEFFLSST	affectless	**ACEEGIRSTT**	cigarettes	**ACEEHIPRST**	preachiest
ACEEFFNRSU	sufferance	**ACEEGKRSWY**	greywackes	**ACEEHIRSSU**	eucharises
ACEEFHISSV	cavefishes	**ACEEGLLOSU**	colleagues	**ACEEHISSTT**	aesthetics
ACEEFHLPRS	parfleches	**ACEEGLMNOR**	camerlengo	**ACEEHKLLRS**	shellacker
ACEEFHMRRS	chamferers	**ACEEGLNORS**	congealers	**ACEEHKLNRT**	halterneck
ACEEFHNORT	technofear	**ACEEGLNRST**	rectangles	**ACEEHLLLOR**	La Rochelle
ACEEFHSSTT	factsheets	**ACEEGMMOSU**	gemmaceous	**ACEEHLLNNR**	channeller
ACEEFIILTT	felicitate	**ACEEGMNORS**	geomancers	**ACEEHLLNOP**	cellophane
ACEEFIIRST	acetifiers	**ACEEGMOTTY**	gametocyte	**ACEEHLMNOS**	chameleons
ACEEFILMNT	maleficent	**ACEEGNNORV**	governance	**ACEEHLMOOS**	haemocoels
ACEEFILNSS	facileness	**ACEEGNNPRU**	repugnance	**ACEEHLMSTU**	Telemachus
ACEEFILORV	overfacile	**ACEEGNNSWY**	newsagency	**ACEEHLNNOP**	encephalon
ACEEFILPRS	fireplaces	**ACEEGNORRU**	encourager	**ACEEHLNPRU**	leprechaun
ACEEFINRST	interfaces	**ACEEGNORSU**	encourages	**ACEEHLNPTT**	planchette
ACEEFIORTV	vociferate	**ACEEGNRSSV**	scavengers	**ACEEHLNPTY**	phlyctenae
ACEEFIORTW	cowfeteria	**ACEEGNRSVY**	scavengery	**ACEEHLNSSS**	seneschals
ACEEFIRRTV	refractive	**ACEEGOOPRS**	cooperages	**ACEEHLOPTY**	polychaete
ACEEFIRSSS	fricassees	**ACEEHHILNW**	chainwheel	**ACEEHLRSTW**	cartwheels
ACEEFLLNTU	flatulence	**ACEEHHILRW**	wheelchair	**ACEEHLSSST**	scatheless
ACEEFLLORV	cloverleaf	**ACEEHHIRRS**	heresiarch	**ACEEHMMRST**	machmeters
ACEEFLLPUY	peacefully	**ACEEHHIRST**	hatcheries	**ACEEHMMRSU**	meerschaum
ACEEFLNPUU	unpeaceful		thearchies	**ACEEHMNNST**	encashment
ACEEFLNSTV	flavescent	**ACEEHHLLRT**	hatcheller	**ACEEHMNOOR**	anemochore
ACEEFLORST	forecastle	**ACEEHHLMNT**	Cheltenham	**ACEEHMNPRT**	preachment
ACEEFLRTTU	leafcutter	**ACEEHHMMOR**	hemachrome	**ACEEHMNRST**	manchester
ACEEFORRST	forecaster	**ACEEHHOPTY**	hypothecae	**ACEEHMORTT**	tachometer
ACEEFRRPTU	resurfaces	**ACEEHHOPTU**	Heptateuch	**ACEEHMOSTY**	haemocytes
ACEEGGILNO	genealogic	**ACEEHHRRTY**	heterarchy	**ACEEHMRTTY**	tachymeter
ACEEGGNORT	congregate	**ACEEHIINRT**	Catherine I	**ACEEHNNRST**	enchanters
ACEEGHINNP	cheapening	**ACEEHIIPRS**	hairpieces	**ACEEHNOPRS**	chaperones
ACEEGHINRT	reteaching	**ACEEHIIPRT**	perithecia	**ACEEHNORTT**	anchorette

ACEEHNPTTU	Pentateuch
ACEEHNRSST	chasteners
ACEEHNRSTT	entrechats
ACEEHNSSST	chasteness
ACEEHNSSTU	chanteuses
ACEEHOPRRR	reproacher
ACEEHOPRRS	archespore
	reproaches
ACEEHORRSS	racehorses
ACEEHORRSV	overarches
ACEEHORSTU	outreaches
ACEEHPPRSY	hyperspace
ACEEHPPRSU	repurchase
ACEEHPRSTY	archetypes
ACEEHPRTUY	hyperacute
ACEEHRRRST	charterers
	recharters
ACEEHRRSTT	chatterers
ACEEHRRSTU	chartreuse
ACEEIILLSX	lexicalise
ACEEIILLXZ	lexicalize
ACEEIILMRT	eremitical
ACEEIILNTT	licentiate
ACEEIILPSS	specialise
ACEEIILPST	tailpieces
ACEEIILPSZ	specialize
ACEEIILSST	elasticise
ACEEIILSTZ	elasticize
ACEEIIMNPT	impatience
ACEEIIMNTT	antiemetic
ACEEIIMPST	episematic
	septicemia
ACEEIINNRT	creatinine
	incinerate
ACEEIIRSTV	veracities
ACEEIIRTTV	recitative
ACEEIITTVX	excitative
ACEEIJLORS	cajoleries
ACEEIJLRTT	trajectile
ACEEIKKNRS	knackeries
ACEEIKLNRT	trancelike
ACEEIKLRRT	craterlike
ACEEIKNRSS	creakiness
ACEEIKQRSU	quackeries
ACEEILLMTY	emetically
ACEEILLNNT	cellentani
ACEEILLNST	cleanliest
ACEEILLPRX	prelexical
ACEEILLPSY	especially
ACEEILLSTV	vellicates
ACEEILMNOR	ceremonial
ACEEILMNOT	colemanite
ACEEILMNOU	leucomaine
ACEEILMNRT	mercantile
ACEEILMNST	centesimal
	lemniscate
ACEEILMOSU	meliaceous
ACEEILMRRS	reclaimers
ACEEILMRST	carmelites
ACEEILMRSX	exclaimers
ACEEILMSST	timescales
ACEEILMSTT	telematics

ACEEILNNNT	centennial
ACEEILNOPU	leucopenia
ACEEILNOTV	evectional
ACEEILNPRT	epicentral
ACEEILNRST	centralise
	interlaces
	linecaster
ACEEILNRTV	cantilever
ACEEILNRTY	increately
ACEEILNRTZ	centralize
ACEEILNSTW	New Castile
ACEEILPRST	replicates
ACEEILPSTX	explicates
ACEEILPSXY	epicalyxes
ACEEILRRTT	retractile
ACEEILRSST	cartelises
ACEEILRSSU	secularise
ACEEILRSTZ	cartelizes
ACEEILRSUZ	secularize
ACEEILRTTU	reticulate
ACEEILRTUV	ulcerative
ACEEILRTVY	creatively
	reactively
ACEEILSTUV	vesiculate
ACEEIMNNST	incasement
ACEEIMNNWX	New Mexican
ACEEIMNORT	actinomere
ACEEIMNRSS	creaminess
ACEEIMNRSV	serviceman
ACEEIMNRTT	remittance
ACEEIMORRT	aerometric
ACEEIMPRST	imprecates
	spermaceti
ACEEIMRSST	masseteric
	miscreates
ACEEIMRSTT	metricates
ACEEIMRSVW	crimewaves
ACEEINNRST	nectarines
	transience
ACEEINNRTU	renunciate
ACEEINNSTU	enunciates
ACEEINORRT	recreation
ACEEINORSU	erinaceous
ACEEINORTU	auctioneer
ACEEINORTX	execration
ACEEINPPRT	apprentice
ACEEINPRRT	Carpentier
ACEEINPRST	interspace
ACEEINPRSU	epicureans
ACEEINRRSS	increasers
ACEEINRSST	ancestries
	resistance
ACEEINRSTT	intercaste
ACEEINRSTU	centauries
ACEEINRTUV	uncreative
	unreactive
ACEEINRTVY	inveteracy
ACEEINSSTV	activeness
ACEEIOOPRS	aeciospore
ACEEIOPPST	episcopate
ACEEIOPSST	caespitose
ACEEIOQTUV	equivocate

ACEEIORSTX	excoriates
ACEEIORTVV	overactive
ACEEIPQRSU	picaresque
ACEEIPRSTT	crepitates
ACEEIQRRSU	reacquires
ACEEIQRSTU	requiescat
ACEEIRRSST	careerists
ACEEIRRSTX	creatrixes
ACEEIRRTTV	retractive
ACEEIRSSTU	cauterises
ACEEIRSTTX	extricates
ACEEIRSTUZ	cauterizes
ACEEIRTTUV	eructative
ACEEIRTTVX	extractive
ACEEJLMNOT	cajolement
ACEEKLLOWY	yellowcake
ACEEKLLRSS	salesclerk
ACEEKNSSTT	snackettes
ACEEKORRSW	caseworker
ACEELLLMOU	columellae
ACEELLMRRS	marcellers
ACEELLNOTU	nucleolate
ACEELLNPST	pallescent
ACEELLORTT	collarette
ACEELLRSSY	carelessly
ACEELLSTTU	scutellate
ACEELMNOTY	melanocyte
ACEELMNPST	placements
ACEELMOPRT	clapometer
ACEELMORST	latecomers
ACEELMORSY	racemosely
ACEELMORTT	lactometer
ACEELNNRSU	cannelures
ACEELNOPST	opalescent
ACEELNORST	tolerances
ACEELNPRSY	screenplay
ACEELNRRTY	recreantly
ACEELNRTVY	tervalency
ACEELNSSUW	Wenceslaus
ACEELOPRST	percolates
ACEELOPRTU	operculate
ACEELORRST	correlates
ACEELORSSS	casseroles
ACEELORSSW	lowercases
ACEELORSTT	lectorates
ACEELPPRTU	perceptual
ACEELPSSTU	speculates
ACEELPSTUX	exculpates
ACEELQRRSU	lacquerers
ACEELQRRUU	craquelure
ACEELRRSST	craterless
ACEELRRSTT	clatterers
ACEELRRTUY	creaturely
ACEELRSSSU	saucerless
ACEEMMNNPT	encampment
ACEEMMNOTT	commentate
ACEEMMORRS	macromeres
ACEEMMORSU	commeasure
ACEEMMNORR	amen corner
ACEEMMNPRY	permanency
ACEEMNNSTT	enactments
ACEEMNOOPS	anemoscope

495

ACEEMNOPST compensate	**ACEFHHINSW** hawfinches	**ACEFNRSSTT** transfects
ACEEMNOPSW spacewomen	**ACEFHHIRRS** archerfish	**ACEFORRRST** refractors
ACEEMNPRST escarpment	**ACEFHIINST** chieftains	**ACEFORRRSU** carrefours
ACEEMOPRSS capsomeres	**ACEFHIINTT** fianchetti	**ACEFORRRTY** refractory
ACEEMORRSS sarcomeres	**ACEFHIJKSS** jackfishes	**ACEFRRSSTU** surfcaster
ACEEMORSTT octameters	**ACEFHILOSS** coalfishes	**ACEGGHILNN** changeling
ACEEMOSTUZ eczematous	**ACEFHILPST** felspathic	**ACEGGHINNX** exchanging
ACEEMPRRSS scamperers	**ACEFHILRTU** ultrafiche	**ACEGGHINRR** recharging
ACEEMRRSTU mercurates	**ACEFHINOTT** fianchetto	**ACEGGHIOPR** geographic
ACEENNNORS cannoneers	**ACEFHINRSS** franchises	**ACEGGHLOOU** cholagogue
ACEENNOPRV provenance	**ACEFHIRSSW** crawfishes	**ACEGGIINRZ** graecizing
ACEENNOPSU pennaceous	**ACEFHIRSSY** crayfishes	**ACEGGILLOO** geological
ACEENNORSS resonances	**ACEFHIRSTT** fratchiest	**ACEGGILNNO** congealing
ACEENNORTV contravene	**ACEFHKORST** aftershock	**ACEGGILRRS** scragglier
covenanter	**ACEFHLLNOP** chopfallen	**ACEGGINNOO** oceangoing
ACEENNOSSS canonesses	**ACEFHLOPRY** hyperfocal	**ACEGGINNSV** scavenging
ACEENNPRTU purtenance	**ACEFHORRTV** hovercraft	**ACEGGINRSS** cragginess
ACEENNRSSV cravenness	**ACEFHORSTU** housecraft	**ACEGGIRSST** scraggiest
ACEENNSSTU sustenance	**ACEFHOSSUV** vouchsafes	**ACEGGNNORT** congregant
ACEENOOSTU coetaneous	**ACEFIIILST** facilities	**ACEGHHIJKR** highjacker
ACEENORSSS coarseness	**ACEFIILMSS** facsimiles	**ACEGHHILNT** hatcheling
ACEENORSTU nectareous	**ACEFIILPST** spiflicate	**ACEGHHOPRT** hectograph
ACEENORSTX Xenocrates	**ACEFIILRRS** clarifiers	**ACEGHHOPRY** echography
ACEENPRRST carpenters	**ACEFIILRSS** classifier	**ACEGHIILMT** megalithic
ACEENPRUVY purveyance	**ACEFIILRST** laticifers	**ACEGHIIMNP** impeaching
ACEENPSTTX expectants	**ACEFIILSSS** classifies	**ACEGHIINNN** enchaining
ACEENRRSTU crenatures	**ACEFIINNRS** financiers	**ACEGHIINRS** cashiering
ACEENRSSST ancestress	**ACEFIINRST** sanctifier	**ACEGHIINTU** authigenic
ACEENRSSTW newscaster	**ACEFIINSST** sanctifies	**ACEGHIIPPR** epigraphic
ACEENRSTTU utterances	**ACEFIIRRSS** scarifiers	**ACEGHIKNNY** hackneying
ACEENSTTUX executants	**ACEFIIRRST** artificers	**ACEGHILMPT** phlegmatic
ACEEOOPRST cooperates	**ACEFIIRSST** satisficer	**ACEGHILNNN** channeling
ACEEOPRRST procreates	**ACEFIIRSTV** fricatives	**ACEGHILNPR** nephralgic
ACEEORRRST recreators	**ACEFIISSST** satisfices	**ACEGHILNTY** cheatingly
ACEEORRSTT rectorates	**ACEFIJKKNS** jackknifes	**ACEGHILPSY** hypalgesic
ACEEORRSTV overreacts	**ACEFIKRSTU** fruitcakes	**ACEGHILRTU** theurgical
ACEEORRTXY execratory	**ACEFILLNOT** flectional	**ACEGHIMNNU** machinegun
ACEEORSTUY eucaryotes	**ACEFILNTUU** funiculate	**ACEGHIMNOP** megaphonic
ACEEOSSTTU testaceous	**ACEFILOOSU** foliaceous	**ACEGHIMNRT** rematching
ACEEPPRSSU uppercases	**ACEFILORST** fortalices	**ACEGHINNNT** enchanting
ACEEPRRSTU recaptures	**ACEFILRSSY** reclassify	**ACEGHINNST** chastening
ACEEPRSTTY typecaster	**ACEFIMORST** formicates	**ACEGHINNTU** unteaching
ACEERRSSTT scatterers	**ACEFINORRT** refraction	**ACEGHINOPT** pathogenic
streetcars	**ACEFINORST** fornicates	**ACEGHINRRT** chartering
ACEERRSSTW watercress	**ACEFINORTV** vociferant	recharting
ACEFFFLRSU carfuffles	**ACEFINPRST** faceprints	**ACEGHINRSY** gynarchies
ACEFFGHINR chaffering	**ACEFINRSST** craftiness	**ACEGHINRTT** chattering
ACEFFHRSUU chauffeurs	**ACEFINSTTV** ventifacts	**ACEGHIOOPS** hagioscope
ACEFFIILTV afflictive	**ACEFIORSST** factorises	**ACEGHIRSTW** switchgear
ACEFFIIOST officiates	**ACEFIORSTZ** factorizes	**ACEGHLOORY** archeology
ACEFFIKMRS maffickers	**ACEFIRRTTU** trifurcate	**ACEGHMNOSS** cheongsams
ACEFFIKRRT trafficker	**ACEFIRSSTU** first cause	**ACEGHMORST** hectograms
ACEFFILOOV Oval Office	**ACEFKLNORS** cornflakes	**ACEGHNORSU** Schongauer
ACEFFINOST affections	**ACEFKRRSTU** starfucker	**ACEGHOPRRY** cerography
ACEFFOSSTU suffocates	**ACEFLLNTUY** flatulency	**ACEGHOPSTY** phagocytes
ACEFFOSTUU tuffaceous	**ACEFLNORRS** conferrals	**ACEGHORSSU** choraguses
ACEFGHIMNR chamfering	**ACEFLPSTUU** teacupfuls	**ACEGHRRRSU** surcharger
ACEFGIINTY acetifying	**ACEFLRSSUU** saucerfuls	**ACEGHRRSSU** surcharges
ACEFGINRRT refracting	**ACEFLSTTUU** fluctuates	**ACEGIILLSS** gallicises
ACEFGLLRUY gracefully	**ACEFMNOORT** canto fermo	**ACEGIILLST** legalistic
ACEFGLNORS gerfalcons	**ACEFNNOSST** confessant	**ACEGIILLSZ** gallicizes
ACEFGLNRUU ungraceful	**ACEFNOPRTT** Pontefract	**ACEGIILMNR** reclaiming

ACEGIILMNX	exclaiming	ACEGINNRST	transgenic	ACEHIINOTV	inchoative
ACEGIILMTY	legitimacy	ACEGINOPRS	saprogenic	ACEHIINTTT	antithetic
ACEGIILNNO	lignocaine	ACEGINORTV	overacting	ACEHIIPRRT	peritricha
ACEGIILNPR	calipering	ACEGINOSTU	autogenics	ACEHIIRRST	triarchies
ACEGIILNSS	anglicises	ACEGINPRRS	scarpering	ACEHIIRSTT	tracheitis
ACEGIILNSZ	anglicizes	ACEGINPRST	precasting	ACEHIKLNSS	chalkiness
ACEGIILOST	egoistical	ACEGINPRSY	panegyrics	ACEHIKLRST	starchlike
ACEGIIMNRS	racemising	ACEGINPSTT	spectating	ACEHIKMNSY	hackneyism
ACEGIIMNRZ	racemizing	ACEGINQRTU	racqueting	ACEHIKMNTW	Twickenham
ACEGIIMNTT	magnetitic	ACEGINRRST	terracings	ACEHIKMRRS	reichsmark
ACEGIIMOST	isogametic	ACEGINRRTT	retracting	ACEHIKNOPR	Archipenko
ACEGIIMOTT	Giacometti	ACEGINRSSU	surceasing	ACEHIKORST	artichokes
ACEGIIMPTT	pegmatitic	ACEGINRSSV	crevassing	ACEHILLNTY	ethnically
ACEGIINNRS	increasing	ACEGINRSTT	scattering	ACEHILLOOS	alcoholise
ACEGIINORT	iatrogenic	ACEGINRTTU	eructating	ACEHILLOOZ	alcoholize
ACEGIINPST	speciating	ACEGINRTTX	extracting	ACEHILLORY	heroically
ACEGIINSTV	vesicating	ACEGIOSSTT	geostatics	ACEHILLOSU	hellacious
ACEGIIOTTV	cogitative	ACEGIRSSTT	strategics	ACEHILLPRY	Caerphilly
ACEGIIPRST	epigastric	ACEGJNOSTU	conjugates	ACEHILLTTY	thetically
ACEGIIRRST	geriatrics	ACEGKORSTU	goatsucker	ACEHILMMOS	chamomiles
ACEGIIJNRTT	trajecting	ACEGLMOSUU	glumaceous	ACEHILMMST	mischmetal
ACEGIKKNNR	knackering	ACEGLNOOOY	oceanology	ACEHILMNNS	Schliemann
ACEGIKLNNS	slackening	ACEGLOOPRT	colportage	ACEHILMNOR	chloramine
ACEGIKLNRY	creakingly	ACEGLOOPSY	escapology	ACEHILMOOP	phocomelia
ACEGIKNPPR	prepacking	ACEGLOOTUY	autecology	ACEHILMOTV	haemolytic
ACEGIKNRST	restacking	ACEGMMRRSU	scrummager	ACEHILMSST	alchemists
ACEGIKPRRS	ragpickers	ACEGMMRSSU	scrummages	ACEHILNNOS	chelonians
ACEGILLMNR	marcelling	ACEGNNOOST	contangoes	ACEHILNNOT	nonethical
ACEGILLNOO	enological	ACEGNNOSTT	cotangents	ACEHILNORT	chlorinate
	neological	ACEGNNPRUY	repugnancy	ACEHILNOST	chelations
ACEGILLNOS	collegians	ACEGNOORVU	acrogenous	ACEHILNOTY	inchoately
ACEGILLNPR	parcelling	ACEGNOORTY	octogenary	ACEHILNSTY	thylacines
ACEGILLOOS	oligoclase	ACEGNRSSUY	assurgency	ACEHILOORZ	coleorhiza
ACEGILLOST	colligates	ACEGNRSTTU	scattergun	ACEHILOPRT	arctophile
ACEGILMNNY	menacingly	ACEGOORSSU	courageous	ACEHILOPST	telophasic
ACEGILMNOR	camerlingo	ACEGOPRRSU	supercargo	ACEHILORRT	rhetorical
ACEGILNNOT	congenital	ACEGORRSTU	corrugates	ACEHILPRSS	clipshears
ACEGILNNPS	enclasping	ACEHHILOPT	Achitophel	ACEHILRSTU	Heraclitus
	spanceling	ACEHHILORS	holarchies	ACEHILRSTY	hysterical
ACEGILNNTU	nucleating	ACEHHILPSS	chelaships	ACEHILRSVX	Charles XIV
ACEGILNOPR	pelargonic	ACEHHINOPT	theophanic	ACEHIMMNSS	mechanisms
ACEGILNOPS	opalescing	ACEHHIOPTT	theopathic	ACEHIMMSST	mismatches
ACEGILNORT	relocating	ACEHHIPSTT	heptastich		schematism
ACEGILNOTU	glauconite	ACEHHISSTX	hexastichs	ACEHIMNNOR	enharmonic
ACEGILNPRY	caperingly	ACEHHLSSTT	thatchless	ACEHIMNNOV	hemocyanin
ACEGILNPTU	peculating	ACEHHMNSTT	hatchments	ACEHIMNORS	monarchies
ACEGILNQRU	lacquering	ACEHHNSTTU	nuthatches		nomarchies
ACEGILNRSW	clearwings	ACEHHOOSTT	toothaches	ACEHIMNORW	chairwomen
ACEGILNRTT	clattering	ACEHIIILRS	Charles III	ACEHIMNPTU	unemphatic
ACEGILNRTU	ulcerating	ACEHIILLPT	philatelic	ACEHIMNRSV	revanchism
ACEGILNTXY	exactingly	ACEHIILMNS	Sanmicheli	ACEHIMNSST	mechanists
ACEGILOOPT	apologetic	ACEHIILMOS	isocheimal	ACEHIMNSSU	Ssu-ma Ch'ien
ACEGILRSTU	graticules	ACEHIILMPT	mephitical	ACEHIMNSTY	myasthenic
ACEGIMMRRS	scrimmager	ACEHIILMRT	hermitical	ACEHIMOPRS	semaphoric
ACEGIMMRSS	scrimmages	ACEHIILNOP	neophiliac	ACEHIMOPRT	amphoteric
ACEGIMNPRS	scampering	ACEHIILRSV	Charles VII		metaphoric
ACEGIMNRST	centigrams		chivalries	ACEHIMOPTU	apothecium
ACEGIMOPRS	megasporic	ACEHIILRSX	Charles XII	ACEHIMORTT	hematocrit
ACEGIMORST	gasometric	ACEHIILSTT	theistical	ACEHIMOSTT	hemostatic
ACEGINNNRT	entrancing	ACEHIILTTY	ethicality	ACEHIMOSTX	chemotaxis
ACEGINNORS	coarsening	ACEHIIMNST	hematinics	ACEHIMPSTY	metaphysic
	ignorances	ACEHIIMRTT	arithmetic	ACEHIMRSTT	Maestricht

ACEHIMRSTU	rheumatics
ACEHINOPST	asthenopic
ACEHINORRT	chitarrone
ACEHINORST	anchorites
	antechoirs
ACEHINORSX	chronaxies
ACEHINORTV	chevrotain
ACEHINPSST	patchiness
ACEHINPSTT	pentastich
ACEHINPSTU	epicanthus
ACEHINRRSU	hurricanes
ACEHINRSSY	synarchies
ACEHINRSTU	raunchiest
ACEHINRSTV	revanchist
ACEHINSSTT	chattiness
	snatchiest
ACEHIOPRST	toparchies
ACEHIOPRSX	echopraxis
ACEHIOPSTY	isopachyte
ACEHIORSTT	rheostatic
ACEHIORSTV	tovariches
ACEHIPPSSS	spaceships
ACEHIPRRST	archpriest
ACEHIPRSSU	haruspices
ACEHIPRSTU	pasticheur
ACEHIPRSUY	eucryphias
ACEHIPSTTU	chupatties
ACEHIRRRST	trierarchs
ACEHIRRRTY	trierarchy
ACEHIRSSST	chastisers
ACEHIRSSTT	starchiest
ACEHIRSTTT	tetrastich
ACEHIRSTTV	tsarevitch
ACEHIRTTWW	water witch
ACEHJKNNOY	johnnycake
ACEHJRRSUW	jawcrusher
ACEHKLMMOR	hammerlock
ACEHKLNOST	chalkstone
	Shackleton
ACEHKMORSY	chromakeys
ACEHKOPRSS	packhorses
ACEHKORSST	shortcakes
ACEHLLLMSS	clamshells
ACEHLLLORS	chlorellas
ACEHLLMNOY	melancholy
ACEHLLPRSU	sepulchral
ACEHLMOOST	schoolmate
ACEHLMORSY	lachrymose
ACEHLMOSST	moschatels
ACEHLNORST	charleston
ACEHLNOSSY	anchyloses
ACEHLOORST	orthoclase
ACEHLOPSSW	showplaces
ACEHLOPSTT	potlatches
ACEHLOPXYY	oxycephaly
ACEHLORRST	orchestral
	trochlears
ACEHLORSSU	housecarls
ACEHLORSTT	charlottes
ACEHLOSTTY	catholytes
ACEHLPRTYY	phylactery
ACEHMMNOOR	chromonema

ACEHMNOPRS	Macpherson
ACEHMNORST	metarchons
ACEHMNOSTY	chemonasty
ACEHMNOTUV	avouchment
ACEHMNPRST	parchments
ACEHMNPRTY	parchmenty
ACEHMNSTTU	humectants
ACEHMOORUX	auxochrome
ACEHMORRTU	routemarch
ACEHMORSST	stomachers
ACEHMORTTY	tachometry
ACEHMOSSTT	chemostats
ACEHMOSSTU	moustaches
ACEHMOSTTU	outmatches
ACEHMRTTVY	tachymetry
ACEHNOPTVY	cyanophyte
ACEHNORRTT	trochanter
ACEHNORTTT	Chatterton
ACEHNOSSTT	stonechats
ACEHNPPRSS	schnappers
ACEHNRSSTU	staunchers
ACEHNRSSUZ	schnauzers
ACEHNSSTTU	staunchest
ACEHOOPPRR	carpophore
ACEHOOPSTU	tophaceous
ACEHOOSSTU	housecoats
ACEHOPPRRS	hoppercars
ACEHOPPRTU	touchpaper
ACEHOPRRSS	sharecrops
ACEHOPRSUY	coryphaeus
ACEHOPRSST	chassepots
ACEHORRSST	carthorses
	orchestras
ACEHORRSYZ	Crazy Horse
ACEHORSTTU	rotachutes
ACEHORTTWW	watchtower
ACEHPRRSSU	purchasers
ACEIIIKNST	ekistician
ACEIIILLNP	penicillia
ACEIIILSST	italicises
ACEIIILSTZ	italicizes
ACEIIIMNST	intimacies
ACEIIISTTV	activities
ACEIIISTVV	vivacities
ACEIIJLSTU	jesuitical
ACEIIKMNST	kinematics
ACEIIKMRWZ	Markiewicz
ACEIIKRSTT	rickettsia
ACEIILLLPT	elliptical
ACEIILLNPR	periclinal
ACEIILLNRV	irenically
ACEIILLOST	localities
ACEIILLOSU	liliaceous
ACEIILLRTY	illiteracy
ACEIILLTXY	lexicality
ACEIILMMST	melismatic
ACEIILMNST	melanistic
ACEIILMOPT	epitomical
ACEIILMPSS	specialism
ACEIILMPST	implicates
ACEIILMRST	salimetric
ACEIILNNST	anticlines

ACEIILNOPT	capitoline
ACEIILNOTT	actinolite
ACEIILNPST	plasticine
ACEIILNTVY	inactively
ACEIILORSS	socialiser
ACEIILORSZ	socializer
ACEIILOSSS	socialises
ACEIILOSST	socialites
ACEIILOSSZ	socializes
ACEIILOSTU	tiliaceous
ACEIILOSTV	vocalities
ACEIILPPRT	participle
ACEIILPRTT	triplicate
ACEIILPSST	plasticise
	specialist
ACEIILPSTY	speciality
ACEIILPSTZ	plasticize
ACEIILRSSS	scleriasis
ACEIILRSTT	recitalist
ACEIILSTTY	elasticity
ACEIIMNORS	acrimonies
	anisomeric
	Micronesia
ACEIIMNORT	romanicite
ACEIIMNPST	emancipist
ACEIIMNRRU	cinerarium
ACEIIMNRST	criminates
ACEIIMRRSS	miscarries
ACEIIMRSST	armistices
ACEIIMRSTT	tasimetric
ACEIINNORT	cineration
ACEIINNORU	quinacrine
ACEIINNRTY	itinerancy
ACEIINOPST	speciation
ACEIINORTT	recitation
ACEIINOSTV	noviciates
	vesication
ACEIINOTTX	excitation
	intoxicate
ACEIINOTVV	invocative
ACEIINPPRT	principate
ACEIINPRSS	precisians
ACEIINPSTT	antiseptic
	psittacine
ACEIINRTVY	inveracity
ACEIINSSTT	sanctities
ACEIINSTTT	nictitates
ACEIINSTTU	austenitic
ACEIIORRRT	certiorari
ACEIIORSTT	atrocities
ACEIIPPSST	epispastic
ACEIIRRSSU	cuirassier
ACEIIRSSST	sacristies
ACEIIRSTTV	astrictive
ACEIIRTTVY	creativity
	reactivity
ACEIJKKNSV	jackknives
ACEIJKNPSS	jacksnipes
ACEIJNORTT	trajection
ACEIKKNNTU	Kentuckian
ACEIKLNNSS	cleanskins
ACEIKNNRSS	crankiness

ACEIKNORSS	croakiness	**ACEILNOPTU**	peculation	**ACEIMNOPRT**	importance
ACEIKNPTTW	pawnticket	**ACEILNORRS**	resorcinal	**ACEIMNOPSU**	menopausic
ACEIKOPSSS	skiascopes	**ACEILNORST**	clarionets	**ACEIMNOPTT**	pentatomic
ACEIKORTUY	eukaryotic	**ACEILNORTU**	ulceration	**ACEIMNORST**	cremations
ACEIKPRRST	peritracks	**ACEILNORTY**	lectionary	**ACEIMNOSST**	encomiasts
ACEILLLPRU	pellicular	**ACEILNOSSS**	socialness	**ACEIMNPSTU**	pneumatics
ACEILLLTUV	luetically	**ACEILNOSST**	coastlines	**ACEIMNRSST**	miscreants
ACEILLMNSY	miscellany	**ACEILNOSSV**	volcanises	**ACEIMOPPPT**	apopemptic
ACEILLMORT	allometric	**ACEILNOSTU**	inoculates	**ACEIMORRTT**	meritocrat
ACEILLMOST	collimates		inosculate	**ACEIMORSST**	costmaries
ACEILLMPTU	capitellum	**ACEILNOSVZ**	volcanizes	**ACEIMORSVW**	microwaves
ACEILLMRSS	miscallers	**ACEILNOTUV**	novaculite	**ACEIMORTTT**	tetratomic
ACEILLMRTY	metrically	**ACEILNPPSU**	suppliance	**ACEIMORTTU**	tautomeric
ACEILLNNNO	cannelloni	**ACEILNPSTU**	inculpates	**ACEIMRSTTU**	micturates
ACEILLNOOT	ocellation	**ACEILNRSST**	interclass	**ACEIMSSTTY**	systematic
ACEILLNORS	corallines		larcenists	**ACEINNNORS**	cannonries
ACEILLNORT	citronella	**ACEILNRSTT**	centralist	**ACEINNNSTU**	uncanniest
ACEILLNPSS	spellicans	**ACEILNRSTU**	lacustrine	**ACEINNOPTT**	pentatonic
ACEILLNRTU	lenticular	**ACEILNRSUV**	vulcaniser	**ACEINNORST**	containers
ACEILLOPSW	pillowcase	**ACEILNRTTY**	centrality		creations
ACEILLOPTY	poetically	**ACEILNRTVY**	trivalency		sanctioner
ACEILLORSS	localisers	**ACEILNRUUX**	luxuriance	**ACEINNORTU**	enunciator
ACEILLORST	allosteric	**ACEILNRUVZ**	vulcanizer	**ACEINNOSSS**	ascensions
	corallites	**ACEILNSSSS**	classiness	**ACEINNRSSU**	insurances
	sclerotial	**ACEILNSSUV**	vulcanises	**ACEINNRSTY**	transiency
ACEILLORSZ	localizers	**ACEILNSUVZ**	vulcanizes	**ACEINNRTUU**	nunciature
ACEILLORTV	vorticella	**ACEILOOSUV**	olivaceous	**ACEINNSSST**	scantiness
ACEILLORTY	erotically		violaceous	**ACEINNSSTT**	intactness
ACEILLOSST	oscillates	**ACEILOPPRS**	sapropelic	**ACEINOORRS**	coronaries
ACEILLOSTY	societally	**ACEILOPRTX**	explicator	**ACEINOORST**	octonaries
ACEILLOTXY	exotically	**ACEILOPSST**	scapolites	**ACEINOORTV**	revocation
ACEILLPRUY	peculiarly	**ACEILOPTUV**	copulative	**ACEINOOSST**	isooctanes
ACEILLPSTY	septically	**ACEILOQTUY**	coequality	**ACEINOOSTV**	evocations
ACEILLRSTY	sterically	**ACEILORSSV**	vocalisers	**ACEINOPRTU**	precaution
ACEILLRSVY	viscerally	**ACEILORSVZ**	vocalizers	**ACEINOPSTT**	constipate
ACEILLRTUV	victualler	**ACEILOTVVY**	vocatively	**ACEINORRST**	cinerators
ACEILLRTVY	vertically	**ACEILPPPRS**	paperclips		contraries
ACEILMMNSS	clamminess	**ACEILPPSTU**	supplicate	**ACEINORRSV**	carnivores
ACEILMNOPR	complainer	**ACEILPRSTU**	plicatures	**ACEINORRTT**	retraction
ACEILMNORS	normalcies	**ACEILPRTUU**	apiculture	**ACEINORSST**	narcotises
	sermonical	**ACEILPSSSU**	capsulises	**ACEINORSSY**	cessionary
ACEILMNRST	centralism	**ACEILPSSUZ**	capsulizes	**ACEINORSTU**	cautioners
ACEILMNRTU	unmetrical	**ACEILRRSTU**	curtailers	**ACEINORSTZ**	narcotizes
ACEILMNRUW	lawrencium	**ACEILRRSUV**	versicular	**ACEINORTTU**	eructation
ACEILMNSTU	culminates	**ACEILRSSTU**	secularist	**ACEINORTTX**	extraction
ACEILMOPRR	proclaimer	**ACEILRSSTY**	crystalise	**ACEINOSSST**	cessations
ACEILMOPRY	promycelia	**ACEILRSTTU**	testicular	**ACEINOSTTU**	unicostate
ACEILMOSSS	coseismals	**ACEILRSTUV**	revictuals	**ACEINQSTTU**	quittances
ACEILMRRSU	mercurials	**ACEILRSTUY**	secularity	**ACEINRSSST**	scenarists
ACEILMRRUV	vermicular	**ACEILRSTYZ**	crystalize	**ACEINRSSTW**	scrawniest
ACEILMRSSU	secularism	**ACEILRTTUU**	utriculate	**ACEINRSTUV**	incurvates
ACEILMTUUV	cumulative	**ACEILRTUUV**	aviculture	**ACEINSSSTT**	scattiness
ACEILNNORS	cornelians	**ACEILRTUVY**	curatively	**ACEIOOPRSU**	paroecious
ACEILNNOST	nonelastic	**ACEILSSUWY**	sluiceways	**ACEIOOPRTZ**	azeotropic
ACEILNNOTU	nucleation	**ACEILSTTUV**	cultivates	**ACEIOOPTTV**	cooptative
ACEILNNUVY	univalency	**ACEILSTUWZ**	Clausewitz	**ACEIOORTTU**	autoerotic
ACEILNOORT	iconolater	**ACEIMMNORT**	manometric	**ACEIOOSTUU**	autoecious
	relocation	**ACEIMMNOSS**	scammonies	**ACEIOPRRSS**	acrospires
ACEILNOPPS	scaloppine	**ACEIMMPRTY**	campimetry	**ACEIOPRRSU**	precarious
ACEILNOPRT	pratincole	**ACEIMMRSTY**	asymmetric	**ACEIOPSSTV**	vitascopes
ACEILNOPST	neoplastic	**ACEIMMNOST**	cismontane	**ACEIOPSTTT**	petticoats
	pleonastic	**ACEIMNNRUY**	innumeracy	**ACEIOQSSUU**	sequacious

ACEIORRSST	assertoric	ACELNOPRRU	pronuclear	ACEOPRSSTT	spectators
	ostraciser	ACELNOPRSY	narcolepsy	ACEORRRSTT	retractors
ACEIORRSTZ	ostracizer	ACELNORRTY	necrolatry	ACEORRRSVY	carryovers
ACEIORSSST	ostracises	ACELNORSTU	nucleators	ACEORRSSTTX	extractors
ACEIORSSTZ	ostracizes		recountals	ACEORSSTTY	astrocytes
ACEIORSTTT	tricostate	ACELNOSSTU	consulates	ACEORSTUXY	excusatory
ACEIORSTVY	vesicatory	ACELNOSSTY	claystones	ACERRSTUUV	curvatures
ACEIORTTXY	excitatory	ACELNOTTUX	contextual	ACFFGIIKMN	mafficking
ACEIOSTTUU	autocuties	ACELNRTTUY	truncately	ACFFGIILNT	afflicting
ACEIPPRSST	scrappiest	ACELOOPRRS	corporales	ACFFIILLOY	officially
ACEIPSSSTU	spacesuits	ACELOOPRRT	percolator	ACFFIILNOS	officinals
ACEIQRSTTU	acquitters	ACELOORRTU	colorature	ACFFIILNOT	affliction
ACEIRSSTTU	rusticates	ACELOORRTW	watercolor	ACFFIILNOU	unofficial
ACEIRSSUWY	cruiseways	ACELOOSSTT	coelostats	ACFFIINOST	officiants
ACEJKKMOSS	smokejacks		osteoclast	ACFFIIOORT	officiator
ACEJKKRSSY	skyjackers	ACELOPRSTU	peculators	ACFFILLNUY	fancifully
ACEJKLMSST	jacksmelts		speculator	ACFGHILNNU	flaunching
ACEJKLPPSU	supplejack	ACELOPRSTY	Polycrates	ACFGHINRSS	grassfinch
ACEJKNOSST	jackstones	ACELOPRSUY	pelycosaur	ACFGIILNOS	focalising
ACEJLMSSUU	majuscules	ACELORRSSU	carrousels	ACFGIILNOZ	focalizing
ACEJORRTTY	trajectory	ACELORRSTY	clearstory	ACFGIILNRY	clarifying
ACEKKMOSST	smokestack	ACELOSSSTU	cassoulets	ACFGIINNRT	infracting
ACEKKMRRSU	muckrakers		outclasses	ACFGIINNRY	carnifying
ACEKLLMMSU	mallemucks	ACELPPRRSU	curlpapers	ACFGIINRSY	scarifying
ACEKLLRSTU	lackluster	ACELPRSSSU	superclass	ACFGILNNOT	conflating
	lacklustre	ACELPSTUUY	eucalyptus	ACFGILOPRY	profligacy
ACEKLNOPST	alpenstock	ACEMMNORTY	commentary	ACFGINORST	factorings
ACEKLOPRSW	workplaces	ACEMMNOSTU	consummate	ACFGINRRTU	fracturing
ACEKMNORRW	cankerworm	ACEMMOSTTU	commutates	ACFGLNORSY	gyrfalcons
ACEKMSSTUW	mucksweats	ACEMMOSTTY	mastectomy	ACFHIILRST	chairlifts
ACEKOPRRST	retropacks	ACEMNNNOTT	cantonment	ACFHILNOPR	francophil
ACEKOPRSTY	copytakers	ACEMNNORST	monstrance	ACFHIOPRST	factorship
ACEKPRRSSY	skyscraper	ACEMNOOPSS	moonscapes	ACFHKORSST	rockshafts
ACEKPRSSSU	sapsuckers	ACEMNOOTYZ	mycetozoan	ACFHLLTUWY	watchfully
ACELLLMORU	columellar	ACEMNOPRRY	pyromancer	ACFIIILNST	finalistic
ACELLMTUUY	cumulately	ACEMNOSTTY	nematocyst	ACFIIILNTY	finicality
ACELLNOSSW	callowness	ACEMOOPRRS	macrospore	ACFIIIMNPR	rifampicin
ACELLNOTVV	covalently	ACEMOORSTU	octamerous	ACFIILLLMY	filmically
ACELLOPRSS	scallopers	ACEMORSTUY	myrtaceous	ACFIILMMOR	limaciform
ACELLOPRTY	pectorally	ACENNNORSU	announcers	ACFIILNOPT	pontifical
ACELLOPSTU	leucoplast	ACENNOORTV	covenantor	ACFIILNORT	frictional
ACELLOPTUY	eucalyptol	ACENNORSTV	conversant	ACFIIMNORT	actiniform
ACELLPRSTY	spectrally	ACENNORTUY	Courantyne	ACFIINNORS	infrasonic
ACELLPRSUY	specularly	ACENNOSTTT	contestant	ACFIINNORT	infarction
ACELLPRUUV	vulpecular	ACENOPRRST	copartners		infraction
ACELLSSTTY	tactlessly	ACENOPRTTT	protectant	ACFIIOSTTU	factitious
ACELMMNOOW	commonweal	ACENOPSSTW	townscapes	ACFIJKRSTU	jackfruits
ACELMMNOSS	commensals	ACENOPSSTY	syncopates	ACFIKNRSSS	scarfskins
ACELMNNOSW	clanswomen	ACENOPSTYY	cyanotypes	ACFILLLORU	follicular
ACELMNNOTT	malcontent	ACENORRSTU	raconteurs	ACFILLORUY	cauliflory
ACELMNORTU	Monte Carlo	ACENORRSWY	cornerways	ACFILLNNOT	conflation
ACELMNOOSV	mooncalves	ACENORSSTU	courtesans	ACFILNNORS	francolins
ACELMOOPST	Compostela	ACENORSTUZ	courtezans	ACFILNNOTU	functional
ACELMOOSTY	comatosely	ACENPSTTUU	punctuates	ACFILNRSUU	funiculars
ACELMORRSU	clamourers	ACEOOOPRRT	cooperator	ACFILOSTUY	factiously
ACELMORSUY	racemously	ACEOOPPRRS	carpospore	ACFINOORRT	fornicator
ACELNNNORT	noncentral	ACEOOPRRRT	procreator	ACFINORRST	infractors
ACELNNNORU	nonnuclear	ACEOOPPRRTY	procaryote	ACFINORSTU	furcations
ACELNNOORS	olecranons	ACEOOPRSSS	ascospores	ACFIOPRSST	profascist
ACELNNOSSU	consensual	ACEOOPSSTT	statoscope	ACFLNOORTW	contraflow
ACELNNOSTU	Launceston	ACEOORRTVY	revocatory	ACFLNRRUUU	furuncular
ACELNNOTUV	conventual	ACEOPPRSST	spaceports	ACFLOORSTU	colourfast

ACGGHIILOO	hagiologic	**ACGIILLOTY**	logicality	**ACGILLNRWY**	crawlingly
ACGGHIINNR	chagrining	**ACGIILLPRS**	pilgarlics	**ACGILLOOOR**	orological
ACGGHINNNU	unchanging	**ACGIILLRTU**	liturgical	**ACGILLOOOT**	otological
ACGGHINNRU	graunching	**ACGIILMNPS**	misplacing	**ACGILLOOOZ**	zoological
ACGGHINOPY	hypnagogic	**ACGIILMNSS**	anglicisms	**ACGILLOORU**	urological
ACGGHINOTT	chittagong	**ACGIILMNTU**	glutaminic	**ACGILLOPRY**	pyrogallic
ACGGIILNNO	ganglionic	**ACGIILMORS**	algorismic	**ACGILLOSST**	collagists
ACGGIILOOS	sialogogic		microglias	**ACGILLRSUY**	surgically
ACGGIINOTT	cogitating	**ACGIILNNNP**	pinnacling	**ACGILMNNOO**	cognominal
ACGGILLNNY	glancingly	**ACGIILNNOR**	clarioning	**ACGILMNORU**	clamouring
ACGGILLOOY	glaciology	**ACGIILNOPR**	caprioling	**ACGILMNTUU**	cumulating
ACGGILNNOR	clangoring	**ACGIILNORZ**	calorizing	**ACGILNNPRY**	prancingly
ACGGIMOSTY	mystagogic	**ACGIILNOSU**	caliginous	**ACGILNNPSU**	unclasping
ACGHHHIIRS	highchairs	**ACGIILNOSV**	vocalising	**ACGILNNSST**	scantlings
ACGHHILNST	hatchlings	**ACGIILNOVZ**	vocalizing	**ACGILNOORY**	craniology
ACGHHINTTW	watch night	**ACGIILNRTU**	curtailing	**ACGILNOPTU**	copulating
ACGHIIMOPR	amphigoric		granulitic	**ACGILNOSTU**	osculating
ACGHIINNNU	unchaining	**ACGIILNRTY**	laryngitic	**ACGILOORST**	Cagliostro
ACGHIINNOT	inchoating	**ACGIILNSST**	anglicists	**ACGILOOTTU**	tautologic
ACGHIINSST	chastising	**ACGIILNTUV**	victualing	**ACGILORSSU**	glucosuria
ACGHIIPRRT	trigraphic	**ACGIIMNNRU**	manicuring	**ACGILORSUY**	glycosuria
ACGHIJKLST	jacklights	**ACGIIMNORS**	organicism		graciously
ACGHIKMNOR	Rockingham		organismic	**ACGIMNNOPR**	cramponing
ACGHIKNOPS	hopsacking	**ACGIIMNSST**	miscasting	**ACGIMNNOPY**	companying
ACGHILLNSY	clashingly	**ACGIIMSSTT**	stigmatics	**ACGIMNOORS**	agronomics
ACGHILLOOP	haplologic	**ACGIINNNOS**	canonising	**ACGIMNOOSU**	ascogonium
ACGHILLOTY	gothically	**ACGIINNNOT**	containing	**ACGIMNOPSS**	compassing
ACGHILMNRY	charmingly	**ACGIINNNOZ**	canonizing	**ACGIMNORRS**	cairngorms
ACGHILNNTU	unlatching	**ACGIINNNST**	instancing	**ACGIMNSSTY**	gymnastics
ACGHILNNTY	chantingly	**ACGIINNOPS**	caponising	**ACGIMOPRST**	pictograms
ACGHILNSTY	scathingly	**ACGIINNOPT**	captioning	**ACGINNNNOU**	announcing
ACGHILOOPT	pathologic	**ACGIINNOPZ**	caponizing	**ACGINNNOOR**	nonorganic
ACGHILOOST	chaologist	**ACGIINNOST**	incognitas	**ACGINNOOST**	cognations
ACGHIMNNNU	Cunningham	**ACGIINNOTT**	incogitant		contagions
ACGHIMNNOP	champignon	**ACGIINNOTU**	auctioning	**ACGINNORRT**	Carrington
ACGHIMNOOR	homorganic		cautioning	**ACGINNRTTU**	truncating
ACGHIMNOST	stomaching	**ACGIINNOTV**	invocating	**ACGINOOSTU**	contagious
ACGHIMOPRR	micrograph	**ACGIINNRTU**	curtaining	**ACGINOPRTY**	agrypnotic
ACGHIMOPRY	myographic	**ACGIINOOTT**	cogitation	**ACGINOPSUU**	pugnacious
ACGHINNSTU	staunching	**ACGIINORST**	organicist	**ACGINORRST**	costarring
ACGHINOPRT	prognathic	**ACGIINPRST**	practising	**ACGINORSUU**	ungracious
ACGHINOPRZ	zincograph	**ACGIINQTTU**	acquitting	**ACGINOSTTU**	outcasting
ACGHINOSSW	showcasing	**ACGIINRRSU**	curarising	**ACGIOOPRTV**	vagotropic
ACGHINPRSU	purchasing	**ACGIINRRUZ**	curarizing	**ACGIOORSTT**	cogitators
ACGHIOOPRR	orographic	**ACGIINRSSU**	cuirassing	**ACGIORSTTY**	gyrostatic
ACGHIOOPRZ	zoographic	**ACGIINRSTT**	astricting	**ACGJLLNOUY**	conjugally
ACGHIOPPRT	pictograph	**ACGIINRSTY**	gyniatrics	**ACGJNNOSTU**	conjugants
ACGHIRRTTW	cartwright	**ACGIINRTTU**	urticating	**ACGJNOORTU**	conjugator
ACGHMNOORR	chronogram	**ACGIJKKNSY**	skyjacking	**ACGJNORRSU**	currajongs
ACGHMOPRSY	cymographs	**ACGIJLLNOY**	cajolingly	**ACGLLOSUUY**	glaucously
ACGHOOPPRY	coprophagy	**ACGIKKMNRU**	muckraking	**ACGLMNOOOS**	cosmogonal
ACGHOPPRSY	copygraphs	**ACGIKLLNNY**	clankingly	**ACGLNOORSU**	clangorous
ACGHORSSTU	roughcasts	**ACGIKMMMNO**	mammocking	**ACGMOPRSTY**	cryptogams
ACGIIILLRT	argillitic	**ACGILLMNOY**	gnomically	**ACGNNOPPUY**	oppugnancy
ACGIIKLNNN	calkinning	**ACGILLMOOY**	myological	**ACGNORRSUW**	currawongs
ACGIIKMNNN	nicknaming	**ACGILLMOSU**	logical sum	**ACGOORRRTU**	corrugator
ACGIILLMNS	miscalling	**ACGILLNNOO**	nonlogical	**ACHHIILLOP**	halophilic
ACGIILLMSS	gallicisms	**ACGILLNOPS**	collapsing	**ACHHIILPST**	phthisical
ACGIILLNOS	localising		scalloping	**ACHHIKLSSS**	shashlicks
ACGIILLNOZ	localizing	**ACGILLNORR**	corralling	**ACHHILMOPT**	ophthalmic
ACGIILLORS	cigarillos	**ACGILLNORS**	carollings	**ACHHILMRTY**	rhythmical
ACGIILLOST	logistical	**ACGILLNOSU**	callousing	**ACHHILOOPS**	shopaholic

ACHHILOPTY	halophytic	
ACHHINOPRS	archonship	
ACHHINSTUY	Hyacinthus	
ACHHIOPPST	phosphatic	
ACHHIPPRSU	Hipparchus	
ACHHIPRSSU	pushchairs	
ACHHLOSSTW	washcloths	
ACHHNOOTTU	autochthon	
ACHHOPPSTY	psychopath	
ACHIIILNOS	Nicholas II	
ACHIIIMNST	histaminic	
ACHIIIRSST	trichiasis	
ACHIIJKNRS	jinricksha	
ACHIIKNNPS	chinkapins	
ACHIILLMPS	phallicism	
ACHIILLPST	phallicist	
ACHIILORST	historical	
ACHIILORTU	thiouracil	
ACHIIMNNOR	inharmonic	
ACHIIMNSST	machinists	
ACHIIMNSTU	humanistic	
ACHIIMNSUV	chauvinism	
ACHIIMOPPP	hippocampi	
ACHIINNOOT	inchoation	
ACHIINNORT	Corinthian	
ACHIINNPQU	chinquapin	
ACHIINORRT	chitarroni	
ACHIINORTT	anorthitic	
ACHIINPSSY	physicians	
ACHIINPSUY	picayunish	
ACHIINRSTT	Antichrist	
ACHIINRSTX	Christian X	
ACHIINSTUV	chauvinist	
ACHIIOPRST	aphoristic	
ACHIIOPSST	pistachios	
ACHIIPRSSV	vicarships	
ACHIIPRSTY	physiatric	
ACHIIRRSTT	arthritics	
ACHIIRSSTV	archivists	
ACHIKKNRSU	Cruikshank	
ACHIKLMSST	mahlsticks	
ACHIKLOORW	workaholic	
ACHIKMNOST	mackintosh	
ACHIKMNRSS	scrimshank	
ACHILLMOOS	alcoholism	
ACHILLMTVY	mythically	
ACHILLNNSY	clannishly	
ACHILLNOOP	allophonic	
ACHILLNOPY	phonically	
ACHILLOPRT	prothallic	
ACHILLOPRY	orphically	
ACHILLPSVY	physically	
ACHILMOOOS	homosocial	
ACHILMOPTY	polymathic	
ACHILMORVZ	mycorhizal	
ACHILMPSTY	lymphatics	
ACHILMSSUY	Lysimachus	
ACHILNOORS	isochronal	
ACHILNORUY	hyaluronic	
ACHILNOSSY	anchylosis	
ACHILOPRST	strophical	
ACHILOPRTY	cartophily	
ACHILORSTV	archivolts	
ACHILORSUV	chivalrous	
ACHILOSSST	scholiasts	
ACHILOSTTW	waistcloth	
ACHIMMNORS	monarchism	
ACHIMMNORS	Cornishman	
ACHIMNOOPT	taphonomic	
ACHIMNOPTY	amphictyon	
ACHIMNORST	chromatins	
	monarchist	
ACHIMNOSST	monachists	
ACHIMNSSTU	miscanthus	
ACHIMOORTY	rachiotomy	
ACHIMORRTT	trichromat	
ACHIMORRYZ	mycorrhiza	
ACHIMORSTT	chromatist	
ACHIMORSYZ	mycorhizas	
ACHIMOSSST	masochists	
ACHIMOSSTU	mustachios	
ACHIMRSSSW	scrimshaws	
ACHINNOSST	stanchions	
ACHINOOPSX	saxophonic	
ACHINOORST	cartoonish	
ACHINOPSST	cashpoints	
ACHINOPSTY	hyponastic	
ACHIOOPSST	sociopaths	
ACHIOOPSTY	sociopathy	
ACHIOPRSTY	physiocrat	
ACHIOPSTTY	hypostatic	
ACHIOPTTUY	autophytic	
ACHIORRSSS	crosshairs	
ACHIORSSTT	rhotacists	
ACHIPRSTYY	psychiatry	
ACHIQRRSUY	squirarchy	
ACHIRSTTWW	wristwatch	
ACHKLLOSST	shockstall	
ACHKLMNOOT	klootchman	
ACHKMORSTU	touchmarks	
ACHKNOOTTU	Nouakchott	
ACHLLOOPSY	playschool	
ACHLMMOORS	schoolmarm	
ACHLMNORUU	homuncular	
ACHLOORSUW	colourwash	
ACHLOOSSTU	holocausts	
ACHMOSSUVY	hyoscyamus	
ACHNOOPSYZ	scyphozoan	
ACHNOPSSTY	sycophants	
ACHOPSSTUY	hypocausts	
ACHORSTTTU	cutthroats	
ACIIIIMPRS	Casimir III	
ACIIILLMMO	Malcolm III	
ACIIILLMNP	ampicillin	
ACIIILLMNY	inimically	
ACIIILNOPT	politician	
ACIIILNOSS	sicilianos	
ACIIILNOST	ciliations	
ACIIILNPST	sincipital	
ACIIILORTV	variolitic	
ACIIILSTTV	vitalistic	
ACIIINNOTT	incitation	
ACIIINRSTT	inartistic	
ACIIINSTTV	nativistic	
ACIIINTTVY	inactivity	
ACIIJLRSTU	juristical	
ACIIJRSSTU	justiciars	
ACIIJRSTUY	justiciary	
ACIIKNNNPV	pickaninny	
ACIILLMNRY	criminally	
ACIILLNNOS	Scillonian	
ACIILLNORY	ironically	
ACIILLNOSS	isoclinals	
ACIILLNRUY	culinarily	
ACIILLNSST	scintillas	
ACIILLOPSS	calliopsis	
ACIILMNSUY	musicianly	
ACIILMORST	moralistic	
ACIILMQSTU	quitclaims	
ACIILMSTUY	musicality	
ACIILNNOST	clintonias	
ACIILNOOST	coalitions	
ACIILNOPPR	pilocarpin	
ACIILNOPPS	scaloppini	
ACIILNOPRV	provincial	
ACIILNOPST	plications	
ACIILNORTT	tinctorial	
ACIILNOTXY	anxiolytic	
ACIILNPPRS	principals	
ACIILOPRST	pictorials	
	saprolitic	
ACIILOPTTY	topicality	
ACIILORSTY	royalistic	
ACIILOSSST	socialists	
ACIILOSSUV	lascivious	
ACIILPSTTY	plasticity	
ACIILPTTYY	typicality	
ACIILRSTTU	altruistic	
	ultraistic	
ACIILRTTTY	tractility	
ACIILSSTUV	vasculitis	
ACIIMMNOPT	pantomimic	
ACIIMMNORS	Marcionism	
ACIIMMNSTU	numismatic	
ACIIMNNOSS	insomniacs	
ACIIMNORRT	criminator	
ACIIMNORST	morticians	
ACIIMNPTTY	tympanitic	
ACIIMNRSSS	narcissism	
ACIIMNRSTU	manicurist	
ACIIMOPRSS	prosaicism	
ACIIMOPRST	porismatic	
ACIIMOSSST	mosaicists	
ACIIMOSTTT	stomatitic	
ACIINNOOTV	invocation	
ACIINNOSTT	nictations	
ACIINNOSTU	incautions	
	insouciant	
ACIINNOTTX	intoxicant	
ACIINOOSTT	oscitation	
ACIINOPRST	ascription	
	crispation	
ACIINOPRTT	tritanopic	
ACIINOPSTU	ancipitous	
ACIINORSTT	astriction	
ACIINORSTX	Saint Croix	

ACIINORTTU	urtication
ACIINOSTUU	incautious
ACIINRSSST	narcissist
ACIINRSTTU	unartistic
ACIIOPRRST	scriptoria
ACIIOPSSUU	auspicious
ACIIORSTVY	varicosity
ACIIPRSSTT	patristics
ACIIPSSTTY	spasticity
ACIISSSTTT	statistics
ACIJLNNOTU	junctional
ACIJLORTUY	jocularity
ACIKKLMNOR	Kilmarnock
ACIKKNNOST	antiknocks
ACIKLMPSTU	multipacks
ACIKLMRTTU	multitrack
ACIKLMSSTU	maulsticks
ACIKLNNOPT	planktonic
ACIKLORTYY	karyolytic
ACIKLOSSTT	tailstocks
ACIKLPSSST	slapsticks
ACIKNOOPRS	pickaroons
ACIKOORSTT	Cook Strait
ACIKOPRTYY	karyotypic
ACIKRSSTTU	tracksuits
ACILLLNOOY	colonially
ACILLLOOQU	colloquial
ACILLMNNOO	monoclinal
ACILLMOORT	collimator
ACILLMOPYY	myopically
ACILLMOTUU	altocumuli
ACILLMOTUV	multivocal
ACILLMOTYY	amylolytic
ACILLMSTYY	mystically
ACILLNOOST	collations
ACILLNOOTU	allocution
	loculation
ACILLNORSW	Cornwallis
ACILLNORUU	unilocular
ACILLNORUV	involucral
ACILLNOUVY	univocally
ACILLOOPRT	allotropic
ACILLOORST	oscillator
ACILLOPRTY	tropically
ACILLOPSTY	postically
ACILLORRTU	trilocular
ACILLORSYZ	zircalloys
ACILLORTVY	vortically
ACILLRSTUY	rustically
ACILMMOORS	microsomal
ACILMMOSTT	committals
ACILMMRSUU	simulacrum
ACILMNOOOS	nosocomial
ACILMNOORT	microtonal
ACILMNOPST	complaints
ACILMNOSUU	calumnious
ACILMNOTUU	cumulation
ACILMNRSUU	minuscular
ACILMOOOTZ	zootomical
ACILMOOPTY	polyatomic
ACILMOPRRY	micropylar
ACILMOPRSS	comprisals

ACILMORSUU	miraculous
ACILMPSSTY	symplastic
ACILMSSSTU	masculists
	simulcasts
ACILNNOPTY	nontypical
ACILNNOSTU	inoculants
ACILNOOORT	coloration
ACILNOOPTU	copulation
ACILNOORST	consortial
ACILNOORSU	Coriolanus
ACILNOORTU	inoculator
ACILNOORVY	iconolatry
ACILNOOSSS	Colossians
ACILNOOSTU	osculation
ACILNOOTTT	cottontail
ACILNORRTU	trinocular
ACILNORRTY	contrarily
ACILNORSTU	ultrasonic
ACILNOSSTT	clinostats
ACILNOSSTU	sulcations
ACILNOSTUY	lacunosity
ACILNPPSTU	supplicant
ACILNRTTUY	taciturnly
ACILOOPRRT	proctorial
ACILOOPSTT	postcoital
ACILOOPSTZ	zooplastic
ACILOOQSUU	loquacious
ACILOOSSUX	saxicolous
ACILOPPRST	captoprils
ACILOPSSUY	spaciously
ACILOPSTUY	captiously
ACILORRRVY	corrivalry
ACILORSSTU	ocularists
ACILORTTUV	cultivator
ACILOSTUUY	cautiously
ACILPRRSTU	scriptural
ACIMMNOOOT	monoatomic
ACIMMNOPSS	pancosmism
ACIMMNORYU	matronymic
ACIMMORSSS	commissars
ACIMMORSSY	commissary
ACIMNNNOOR	minor canon
ACIMMNOOPS	companions
ACIMMNORTU	unromantic
ACIMMNOSTY	sanctimony
ACIMMNOPRS	comparison
ACIMNOOPSS	compassion
ACIMNOORST	astronomic
ACIMNOORTY	craniotomy
ACIMNOOSST	onomastics
ACIMNOOSTU	autonomics
ACIMNOOSTY	actomyosin
ACIMNOPRTY	patronymic
	pyromantic
ACIMNOTTUV	tautonymic
ACIMNPRSTU	manuscript
ACIMOOPRTT	compatriot
ACIMOORTVY	varicotomy
ACIMOPRSXY	paroxysmic
ACIMOPSSSY	symposiacs
ACIMOPSTTY	asymptotic
ACIMORSSST	ostracisms

ACINNNOSTT	inconstant
ACINNNOTTU	continuant
ACINNOOORT	coronation
ACINNOPTTU	punctation
ACINNORSST	constrains
ACINNORSTT	constraint
ACINNORTTU	truncation
ACINNRSTTU	incrustant
ACINNSTTVY	nyctinasty
ACINOOOPTT	cooptation
ACINOOPPRT	protanopic
ACINOOPPRT	Porto Rican
ACINOORRSS	corrasions
ACINOORSTT	cartoonist
ACINOORSTV	invocators
ACINOORTVY	invocatory
ACINORSSST	croissants
ACINORSSTY	crayonists
ACINPRRSTT	transcript
ACIOORSTVY	Ivory Coast
ACIOPRSTTY	pyrostatic
ACIORRSTTU	rusticator
ACJKOPRSST	jockstraps
ACKKNRSTUW	knackwurst
ACKLMOOORS	cloakrooms
ACKLNORSST	cornstalks
ACKLORSSSW	crosswalks
ACKRRSSTTU	starstruck
ACLLLOOSSY	colossally
ACLLLRTUUY	culturally
ACLLMMNOUY	communally
ACLLMNNOOO	monoclonal
ACLLMRSUUY	muscularly
ACLLNPTUUY	punctually
ACLLOOPRRY	corporally
ACLLORRSSY	rallycross
ACLLPRSTUU	sculptural
ACLMMNOOTY	commonalty
ACLMNOORSU	monoculars
ACLMOORSSS	classrooms
ACLNNOSTTU	consultant
ACLNNOSTTY	constantly
ACLNNOSTUV	convulsant
ACLNNPTUUU	unpunctual
ACLNNRSUUU	ranunculus
ACLNOORSTT	contraltos
ACLNOORSUY	canorously
ACLNOPSTUY	postulancy
ACLOOOORRST	coralroots
ACLOOPRTUY	copulatory
ACLOORSTUY	osculatory
ACLOORSUWY	colourways
ACLOPRSTTU	plutocrats
ACLRRSTTUU	structural
ACMMOORTTU	commutator
ACMNNORTUY	countryman
ACMNOORRST	cormorants
ACMNOORSUY	acronymous
ACMNOOSSTU	cosmonauts
ACMOOOPRTT	compotator
ACNNNOOSST	consonants
ACNOOPRSST	corposants

ACNOOPRSTY	syncopator
ACNOPRSSUY	syncarpous
ACNOPRTTUU	punctuator
ACOOOPRRRT	corporator
ACOOPPRRSS	sporocarps
ACOOPRRRTT	protractor
ACOOPRRRTU	procurator
ACOPRSSSTT	sportscast
ACORRSSTTU	scrutators
ACOSSSTTTY	statocysts
ADDDDEEKLS	skedaddled
ADDDEEEMNR	redemanded
ADDDEEEPRT	depredated
ADDDEEFHIL	fiddlehead
ADDDEEHNRU	dunderhead
ADDDEEHRRU	rudderhead
ADDDEEHRTY	dehydrated
ADDDEEILSS	sidesaddle
ADDDEEKLSS	skedaddles
ADDDEEPRSU	superadded
ADDDEGNORW	downgraded
ADDDEIIIMT	dimidiated
ADDDEILNOR	dendroidal
ADDDELNOOW	downloaded
ADDEEEFHNR	freehanded
ADDEEEFLOR	freeloaded
ADDEEEFNTU	undefeated
ADDEEEGNNR	endangered
ADDEEEHNNV	evenhanded
ADDEEEHNRR	rehardened
ADDEEEHRRT	rethreaded
ADDEEEILNT	delineated
ADDEEEIRST	desiderate
ADDEEEKMRT	demarketed
ADDEEELLSW	Weddell Sea
ADDEEELNVV	van de Velde
ADDEEELRST	saddletree
ADDEEEENORV	endeavored
ADDEEENRTV	denervated
ADDEEEPRST	depredates
ADDEEERSSS	addressees
ADDEEERTTU	deuterated
ADDEEFHNOR	forehanded
ADDEEFHOST	softheaded
ADDEEFIINN	definienda
ADDEEFIINZ	denazified
ADDEEFILOT	defoliated
ADDEEFILSU	feudalised
ADDEEFILUZ	feudalized
ADDEEFNNST	defendants
ADDEEFRRSU	defrauders
ADDEEGGINS	disengaged
ADDEEGHITW	deadweight
ADDEEGHLNO	longheaded
ADDEEGINRT	denigrated
ADDEEGINST	designated
ADDEEGLLNR	Gelderland
ADDEEGLLNRS	gladdeners
ADDEEGNRUZ	gazundered
ADDEEGSTTU	degustated
ADDEEHLLNS	handselled
ADDEEHLMMU	dummelhead

ADDEEHLNRU	unheralded
ADDEEHNNOP	openhanded
ADDEEHNNRU	unhardened
ADDEEHNNSS	handedness
ADDEEHNOOW	woodenhead
ADDEEHNORV	overhanded
ADDEEHNRTU	unthreaded
ADDEEHRSTY	dehydrates
ADDEEIIMNS	deaminised
ADDEEIIMNZ	deaminized
ADDEEIIMST	mediatised
ADDEEIIMTZ	mediatized
ADDEEIIPSS	diapedesis
ADDEEIILMPS	mispleaded
ADDEEIILMST	Middle East
ADDEEIILNSS	deadliness
ADDEEIILPSS	displeased
ADDEEIILRSS	saddleries
ADDEEIILRSV	daredevils
ADDEEIMRTT	readmitted
ADDEEINORT	derationed
ADDEEINRTT	denitrated
ADDEEINSTU	unsteadied
ADDEEIOPTV	videotaped
ADDEEIPRSW	widespread
ADDEEIPRTU	repudiated
ADDEEIRSTV	advertised
ADDEEIRTTX	extradited
ADDEEIRTVZ	advertized
ADDEEJRSTU	readjusted
ADDEELLMTU	medullated
ADDEELLSSS	saddleless
ADDEELMNOR	endodermal
ADDEELMOTU	demodulate
ADDEELNORV	overlanded
ADDEELOORV	overloaded
ADDEELPRST	stepladder
ADDEEMNNRU	undernamed
ADDEEMNOPR	promenaded
ADDEEMPSTU	despumated
ADDEENNPST	dependants
ADDEENNTTU	unattended
ADDEENPRTU	dunderpate
ADDEENQRSU	squandered
ADDEENRRTU	underrated
ADDEENRRUW	unrewarded
ADDEENRTUV	adventured
ADDEEOPRRT	depredator
ADDEEOPRSS	desperados
ADDEEORRTV	overtraded
ADDEEPRSTU	depastured
ADDEERRSSS	addressers
ADDEFGIILN	defilading
ADDEFGINRU	defrauding
ADDEFGLLNO	oldfangled
ADDEFHILPS	paddlefish
ADDEFIIILP	lapidified
ADDEFIINNR	Ferdinand I
ADDEFILLSU	fusilladed
ADDEFILMNO	manifolded
ADDEFINNRV	Ferdinand V
ADDEFINRSU	fundraised

ADDEFIORSV	disfavored
ADDEFLLOOP	flapdoodle
ADDEFLLRUY	dreadfully
ADDEGGILNN	gladdening
ADDEGHILST	deadlights
ADDEGHLORT	goldthread
ADDEGIILOS	dialogised
ADDEGIILOZ	dialogized
ADDEGILLNW	windgalled
ADDEGILTUV	divulgated
ADDEGIMNOV	Mogen David
ADDEGIMOST	dogmatised
ADDEGIMOTZ	dogmatized
ADDEGINNTU	denudating
ADDEGINRSS	addressing
ADDEGINUUV	Du Vigneaud
ADDEGIORRS	dorsigrade
ADDEGIRRSS	disregards
ADDEGMNORR	dendrogram
ADDEGNORSW	downgrades
ADDEGNRRSU	undergrads
ADDEHHOSTY	hydathodes
ADDEHIJMNU	mujaheddin
ADDEHILMNS	mishandled
ADDEHIMNOO	maidenhood
ADDEHIMNOS	admonished
ADDEHINRSY	anhydrides
ADDEHIRSYZ	hydrazides
ADDEHKNORW	handworked
ADDEHLLNOR	landholder
ADDEHLORST	stadholder
ADDEHNOSUW	unshadowed
ADDEHORRTY	dehydrator
ADDEIIIMST	dimidiates
ADDEIIIRVW	Edward VIII
ADDEIILMPY	epididymal
ADDEIILQTU	liquidated
ADDEIINOTU	auditioned
ADDEIINRST	distrained
ADDEIIOSTZ	diazotised
ADDEIIOTZZ	diazotized
ADDEIIPRSS	dispraised
ADDEIIPSST	dissipated
ADDEILLNSS	landslides
ADDEILLOSW	disallowed
ADDEILMNST	dismantled
ADDEILMTTY	admittedly
ADDEILNNOS	dandelions
ADDEILNNSY	Disneyland
ADDEILNPST	displanted
ADDEILNSSW	windlassed
ADDEILNSSY	deadly sins
ADDEIMNORS	randomised
ADDEIMNORZ	randomized
ADDEIMNOST	demantoids
ADDEIMNSUY	undismayed
ADDEIMRSSS	misaddress
ADDEINNORU	unordained
ADDEINNOTU	denudation
ADDEINNRRU	underdrain
ADDEINOORS	radiosonde
ADDEINOPSW	pandowdies

ADDEINRSTT	dittanders	ADEEEHORTV	overheated	ADEEFILRST	federalist
ADDEIOPPRR	airdropped	ADEEEIKLRU	Auld Reekie	ADEEFILSSU	feudalises
ADDEIRSSSU	dissuaders	ADEEEILMNS	madeleines	ADEEFILSUZ	feudalizes
ADDELMNOPY	paddymelon	ADEEEILNST	delineates	ADEEFIMNST	manifested
ADDELNNOOT	endodontal	ADEEEILPRS	espaliered	ADEEFINORT	federation
ADDELNNORW	wonderland	ADEEEIMNRX	reexamined	ADEEFINRRW	firewarden
ADDELNNRSU	Sunderland	ADEEEIRRTT	reiterated	ADEEFIRSTU	disfeature
ADDELNOORW	woodlander	ADEEEKNSSW	snakeweeds	ADEEFISSTT	defeatists
ADDELNOPWY	downplayed	ADEEELLMNP	empanelled	ADEEFKNPRR	prefranked
ADDELPQRUU	quadrupled	ADEEELLRSS	leaderless	ADEEFLLLNN	flannelled
ADDELRRSST	straddlers	ADEEELNNSS	leadenness	ADEEFLNNOR	nonfederal
ADDENNRSTU	understand	ADEEELNNUV	unleavened	ADEEFLOOTV	foveolated
ADDENOORST	deodorants	ADEEELNPRU	unrepealed	ADEEFLRSTU	defaulters
ADDEORRSSS	addressors	ADEEELNRSW	newsdealer	ADEEFMNORW	freedwoman
ADDEPQRSUU	quadrupeds	ADEEELNRUV	unrevealed	ADEEFMNRTY	defrayment
ADDFGIINNY	dandifying	ADEEELNNRUW	Leeuwarden	ADEEFMORST	fadometers
ADDFGIOORY	Good Friday	ADEEELNSST	elatedness	ADEEFNNSTU	unfastened
ADDFIILNSU	disdainful	ADEEELNTTU	edentulate	ADEEFNORRW	forewarned
ADDGHNORSU	draghounds	ADEEELOPRV	overleaped	ADEEFNRTUU	unfeatured
ADDGIIINNS	disdaining	ADEEELPRTY	repeatedly	ADEEFOOPRRT	perforated
ADDGIIMNNO	diamonding	ADEEEMNNRT	endearment	ADEEFORSTT	foretasted
ADDGIINSSU	dissuading	ADEEEMNRRS	meanderers	ADEEGGHLOR	loggerhead
ADDGILLNWY	dawdlingly	ADEEEMNRTU	enumerated	ADEEGGILNT	delegating
ADDGILNNSU	unsaddling	ADEEEMNRUV	maneuvered	ADEEGGIMOS	demagogies
ADDGILNRST	straddling	ADEEEMOOST	oedematose	ADEEGGINRS	degreasing
ADDGINNOTW	Waddington	ADEEEMPRTT	attempered	ADEEGGINSS	disengages
ADDHLOOSTU	adulthoods	ADEEEMRRST	remastered	ADEEGGJNSS	jaggedness
ADDIIILNUV	individual	ADEEEMRRSU	remeasured	ADEEGGLNOT	Golden Gate
ADDILLLLYY	dillydally	ADEEENNPRT	perennated	ADEEGGMOSU	demagogues
ADDILNPSSU	Spud Island	ADEEENNRTU	undereaten	ADEEGGNRSS	raggedness
ADDIMNOSUY	didynamous	ADEEENORRV	endeavorer	ADEEGGOPSU	pedagogues
ADDIMOORSU	diadromous	ADEEENORTX	exonerated	ADEEGHINRS	garnisheed
ADDLNORSST	landdrosts	ADEEENPRTT	penetrated	ADEEGHINRT	ingathered
ADDLNORWWY	downwardly	ADEEENRRSS	serenaders	ADEEGHNRTU	ungathered
ADEEEEGNRT	degenerate	ADEEENRRSW	newsreader	ADEEGIINSS	diagenesis
ADEEEFILRS	federalise	ADEEENRRSTV	denervates	ADEEGIJLNR	Darjeeling
ADEEEFILRZ	federalize	ADEEENRTTV	anteverted	ADEEGILLST	legislated
ADEEEFIRTV	federative	ADEEENSSST	sedateness	ADEEGILMNR	malingered
ADEEEFKPRS	speedfreak	ADEEENTTUV	eventuated	ADEEGILNOT	delegation
ADEEEFLLRW	farewelled	ADEEENTTUX	extenuated	ADEEGILNRR	ringleader
ADEEEFLORR	freeloader	ADEEERRRST	rearrested	ADEEGILNRV	delayering
ADEEEFNRST	refastened	ADEEERRSST	reasserted	ADEEGILRST	gradeliest
ADEEEGGRST	gadgeteers	ADEEERSSSS	reassessed	ADEEGIMNNR	meandering
	segregated	ADEEERSTTU	deuterates	ADEEGIMNOS	endogamies
ADEEEGHNRS	greenheads	ADEEERSTWW	waterweeds	ADEEGIMNRT	germinated
ADEEEGHRRT	regathered	ADEEFFILRS	fieldfares	ADEEGIMNRZ	germanized
ADEEEGLNTW	tangleweed	ADEEFFIMRR	reaffirmed	ADEEGIMNST	magnetised
ADEEEGLOPV	Lope de Vega	ADEEFFLNRU	Frauenfeld	ADEEGIMNTZ	magnetized
ADEEEGLRSV	everglades	ADEEFFORST	afforested	ADEEGIMRRT	remigrated
ADEEEGLRTU	deregulate	ADEEFGHIRU	figurehead	ADEEGINNOT	denegation
ADEEEGORRV	overgeared	ADEEFGILLR	fillagreed	ADEEGINPRR	prereading
ADEEEHHPSS	sheepshead	ADEEFGINRT	federating	ADEEGINPRT	interpaged
ADEEEHJMNU	mujahedeen	ADEEFGLNNW	newfangled	ADEEGINRRS	grenadiers
ADEEEHKLLU	keelhauled	ADEEFGMNRT	fragmented	ADEEGINRRT	intergrade
ADEEEHLPSY	sleepyhead	ADEEFHILSS	dealfishes		retreading
ADEEEHLPTT	telepathed	ADEEFHNRTU	unfathered	ADEEGINRSS	reassigned
ADEEEHLRTT	letterhead	ADEEFIINSZ	denazifies	ADEEGINRST	denigrates
ADEEEHLRTW	treadwheel	ADEEFIKRRS	firedrakes	ADEEGINRTT	integrated
ADEEEHLSST	steelheads	ADEEFILLLS	Sellafield	ADEEGINSST	designates
ADEEEHNRTT	threatened	ADEEFILMRS	federalism		
ADEEEHNRTW	enwreathed	ADEEFILOST	defoliates		
ADEEEHNSST	heatedness	ADEEFILOTX	exfoliated		

ADEEGIORTV	derogative	ADEEHIRSTT	threadiest	ADEEILLPRS	espadrille
ADEEGISUVW	waveguides	ADEEHKLRSS	sheldrakes	ADEEILLPST	palletised
ADEEGLLNOS	goldenseal	ADEEHKORRW	headworker	ADEEILLPTZ	palletized
ADEEGLNNNW	New England	ADEEHLLNRT	enthralled	ADEEILLRRU	derailleur
ADEEGLNPRU	plunderage	ADEEHLLNSS	handleless	ADEEILLRSV	sidereally
ADEEGLNRSS	dangerless	ADEEHLLOSS	leaseholds	ADEEILLSTT	satellited
	gardenless	ADEEHLLOSW	wholesaled	ADEEILLUVV	vaudeville
ADEEGLNRUZ	underglaze	ADEEHLLOWY	yellowhead	ADEEILMMST	lemmatised
ADEEGLOOSW	eaglewoods	ADEEHLMTTY	methylated	ADEEILMMTZ	lemmatized
ADEEGLOPUU	Guadeloupe	ADEEHLNOPT	phenolated	ADEEILMNPT	pedimental
ADEEGLORTY	derogately	ADEEHLOOSX	aldohexose	ADEEILMNRS	madrilenes
ADEEGLRRSS	regardless	ADEEHLOPRT	petrolhead	ADEEILMNRT	derailment
ADEEGMNORT	dermatogen	ADEEHLORUV	overhauled	ADEEILMNTY	myelinated
ADEEGMNRRS	germanders	ADEEHLRSST	threadless	ADEEILMORS	demoralise
ADEEGMNRRY	gendarmery	ADEEHMNPRU	unhampered	ADEEILMORT	meliorated
ADEEGMRRSU	demurrages	ADEEHMOPRS	semaphored	ADEEILMORZ	demoralize
ADEEGNOTXY	oxygenated	ADEEHMOSST	homesteads	ADEEILMPRR	peridermal
ADEEGNRRSW	greensward	ADEEHNNRTU	underneath	ADEEILMPRS	impleaders
ADEEGNRRUZ	gazunderer	ADEEHNOSST	headstones	ADEEILMRSS	misdealers
ADEEGOORSV	overdosage	ADEEHNNPPRS	apprehends		misleaders
ADEEGOORSW	greasewood	ADEEHORSUW	warehoused	ADEEILMRST	misrelated
ADEEGORRRT	retrograde	ADEEHRRSTT	Thar Desert	ADEEILNNRW	New Ireland
ADEEGORRVZ	overgrazed	ADEEHRSSTW	watersheds	ADEEILNORT	delineator
ADEEGPRTUX	expurgated	ADEEIIILST	idealities	ADEEILNPRT	interplead
ADEEGSSTTU	degustates	ADEEIIJNRR	jardiniere	ADEEILNRSU	unrealised
ADEEHHILMR	hemihedral	ADEEIIKLMN	maidenlike	ADEEILNRSV	vernalised
ADEEHHLOSV	shovelhead	ADEEIILMNT	eliminated	ADEEILNRTU	adulterine
ADEEHHMNOT	heathendom	ADEEIILMNT	delimitate	ADEEILNRUZ	unrealized
ADEEHHNOPS	headphones	ADEEIILNSS	desalinise	ADEEILNRVZ	vernalized
ADEEHHNORX	hexahedron	ADEEIILNSZ	desalinize	ADEEILNSSS	Dessalines
ADEEHHNPTY	hyphenated	ADEEIILNTV	evidential	ADEEILNTTT	dilettante
ADEEHHNRTU	headhunter	ADEEIILRSS	idealisers	ADEEILNTTV	ventilated
ADEEHHNSTU	unsheathed		serialised	ADEEILOPRS	depolarise
ADEEHIIKTV	khediviate	ADEEIILRSZ	idealizers	ADEEILOPRZ	depolarize
ADEEHIIRRW	wirehaired		serialized	ADEEILOPTT	petiolated
ADEEHIJMNU	mujahideen	ADEEIILSTV	devitalise	ADEEILPRST	pilastered
ADEEHIKLRT	threadlike	ADEEIILTVZ	devitalize	ADEEILPSSS	displeases
ADEEHILNOT	endothelia	ADEEIIMNSS	deaminises	ADEEILRSST	slaistered
	ethanediol	ADEEIIMNSZ	deaminizes	ADEEILRSTU	adulteries
ADEEHILNRS	headliners	ADEEIIMSST	mediatises	ADEEILRTTU	elutriated
ADEEHILNTU	heulandite	ADEEIIMSTZ	mediatizes	ADEEILSSUX	sexualised
ADEEHILOPP	paedophile	ADEEIIMTTV	meditative	ADEEILSUXZ	sexualized
ADEEHILPPR	harelipped	ADEEIINRST	distrainee	ADEEIMMNSS	maimedness
ADEEHILPRS	dealership	ADEEIINRTT	itinerated		misdemeans
	leadership	ADEEIINRVV	vivandiere	ADEEIMMORT	immoderate
ADEEHILRRS	heraldries	ADEEIINSST	dessiatine	ADEEIMNNOT	denominate
ADEEHILSVY	adhesively		East Indies		emendation
ADEEHILSWY	daisywheel	ADEEIIRTTW	tidewaiter	ADEEIMNNTT	detainment
ADEEHIMNSU	dehumanise	ADEEIIRTVV	derivative	ADEEIMNORT	endometria
ADEEHIMNUZ	dehumanize	ADEEIJOPRS	jeopardise	ADEEIMNPRS	Parmenides
ADEEHIMPRY	hypermedia	ADEEIJOPRZ	jeopardize	ADEEIMNRRS	remainders
ADEEHIMPSS	emphasised	ADEEIKNRRT	dreikanter	ADEEIMNRSS	dreaminess
ADEEHIMPST	empathised	ADEEIKPRSW	Paderewski	ADEEIMNRTT	terminated
ADEEHIMPSZ	emphasized	ADEEIKRSST	asterisked	ADEEIMNSTV	advisement
ADEEHIMPTZ	empathized	ADEEILLMNP	impanelled	ADEEIMORRT	radiometer
ADEEHINRST	dishearten	ADEEILLMNV	Mandeville	ADEEIMORRX	xerodermia
ADEEHINRTT	thenardite	ADEEILLMOS	damoiselle	ADEEIMORTU	audiometer
ADEEHIOPSX	hexapodies	ADEEILLMRY	remedially	ADEEIMPRTT	impetrated
ADEEHIPRRS	readership	ADEEILLMST	metallised	ADEEIMRSTT	mistreated
ADEEHIRRSS	sherardise	ADEEILLMTZ	metallized	ADEEIMSSST	demitasses
ADEEHIRRSZ	sherardize	ADEEILLMVY	medievally	ADEEINNRTV	innervated
ADEEHIRRTV	hereditary	ADEEILLNOT	lineolated	ADEEINOPSW	weaponised

ADEEEINOPWZ	weaponized	**ADEELLORTT**	reallotted	**ADEEMPSSTU**	despumates
ADEEEINORTT	orientated	**ADEELLOSTY**	desolately	**ADEENNNTTU**	untenanted
ADEEEINOTTV	denotative	**ADEELLQRRU**	quarrelled	**ADEENNORRS**	nonreaders
	detonative	**ADEELMMORS**	mesodermal	**ADEENNORSU**	unreasoned
ADEEEINPPST	pepsinated	**ADEELMNNTU**	unlamented	**ADEENNOSSU**	unseasoned
ADEEEINPPSX	appendixes	**ADEELMNOPS**	pademelons	**ADEENNPRSU**	depanneurs
ADEEEINPRRU	unrepaired	**ADEELMNORT**	entodermal	**ADEENNPTTU**	unpatented
ADEEEINPRST	pedantries	**ADEELMNPUX**	unexampled	**ADEENNRSUW**	unanswered
	pedestrian	**ADEELMORTY**	moderately	**ADEENOPRST**	personated
ADEEEINPTUX	unexpiated	**ADEELMRSUY**	measuredly	**ADEENOPRTV**	Pontevedra
ADEEEINRRSS	dreariness	**ADEELNNPPR**	preplanned	**ADEENOPRVX**	overexpand
ADEEEINRRST	restrained	**ADEELNNQSU**	Queensland	**ADEENORSUV**	endeavours
ADEEEINRSSV	variedness	**ADEELNNTTU**	untalented	**ADEENPPRRU**	unprepared
ADEEEINRSTT	denitrates	**ADEELNORRV**	overlander	**ADEENPPRSS**	dapperness
	reinstated	**ADEELNORSY**	reasonedly	**ADEENPRRTU**	enraptured
	straitened	**ADEELNRRSS**	slanderers	**ADEENPRSST**	depressant
ADEEEINRSTU	denaturise	**ADEELNRRSU**	launderers	**ADEENQRRSU**	squanderer
ADEEEINRTTT	tridentate	**ADEELNRRUY**	underlayer	**ADEENRRSTU**	underrates
ADEEEINRTUZ	denaturize	**ADEELNRSSU**	underseals	**ADEENRRTUV**	adventurer
ADEEEINSSST	steadiness	**ADEELNRTTU**	laundrette	**ADEENRRTUW**	underwater
ADEEEINSSTT	Eisenstadt	**ADEELNRTUV**	untraveled	**ADEENRSTTU**	understate
ADEEEINSSTU	unsteadies	**ADEELNRUUV**	undervalue	**ADEENRSTUV**	adventures
ADEEEINSTVV	adventives	**ADEELOPPRV**	overlapped	**ADEENSTTTU**	unattested
ADEEEIOPRST	operatised	**ADEELOPPTU**	depopulate	**ADEEOPRRSV**	overspread
	periodates	**ADEELOPRSS**	leopardess	**ADEEOPRRTV**	overparted
ADEEEIOPRSX	peroxidase	**ADEELOPRVY**	overplayed	**ADEEOPRSSV**	eavesdrops
ADEEEIOPRTZ	operatized	**ADEELORSST**	desolaters		overpassed
ADEEEIOPSTV	videotapes	**ADEELORUVV**	overvalued	**ADEEORRSTV**	overtrades
ADEEEIPPRSU	pauperised	**ADEELPPRRY**	preparedly	**ADEEORSSTX**	extradoses
ADEEEIPPRTW	wiretapped	**ADEELPRSTT**	splattered	**ADEEORSTTV**	overstated
ADEEEIPPRUZ	pauperized	**ADEELRRSSW**	rewardless	**ADEEORSTVY**	overstayed
ADEEEIPPSSS	passepieds	**ADEELRRSTU**	adulterers	**ADEEPRRSSU**	persuaders
ADEEEIPPSST	peptidases		serrulated	**ADEEPRRSTU**	departures
ADEEEIPRSTT	tapestried	**ADEELRSSTU**	adulteress	**ADEEPRSSST**	trespassed
ADEEEIPRSTU	repudiates	**ADEELRSSTY**	steelyards	**ADEEPRSSTU**	depastures
ADEEEIPRTTX	extirpated	**ADEEMMNNRT**	remandment	**ADEERRSSSW**	wardresses
ADEEEIPRTUV	depurative	**ADEEMMNNST**	amendments	**ADEERRSSTW**	stewardess
ADEEEIRRSTV	advertiser	**ADEEMMORST**	dermatomes	**ADEERSSTVY**	yesterdays
ADEEEIRRSTW	watersider	**ADEEMNNNRU**	unmannered	**ADEFFGHIRT**	affrighted
ADEEEIRRTVZ	advertizer	**ADEEMNNORT**	ornamented	**ADEFFLOOTT**	flatfooted
ADEEEIRSSTT	dissertate	**ADEEMNNORV**	overmanned	**ADEFGHIRST**	farsighted
ADEEEIRSSTV	advertises	**ADEEMNOPRR**	promenader	**ADEFGHORST**	godfathers
ADEEEIRSSTW	waitressed	**ADEEMNOPRS**	promenades	**ADEFGIILNN**	enfilading
ADEEEIRSTTV	travestied	**ADEEMNORST**	emendators	**ADEFGILNRY**	ladyfinger
ADEEEIRSTTW	tidewaters	**ADEEMNORSU**	demeanours	**ADEFGILNTU**	defaulting
ADEEEIRSTTX	extradites	**ADEEMNORTY**	emendatory	**ADEFGILRSU**	lifeguards
ADEEEIRSTVZ	advertizes	**ADEEMNORUV**	manoeuvred	**ADEFGILRTZ**	Fitzgerald
ADEEEJRRSTU	readjuster	**ADEEMNPRTT**	department	**ADEFGINORR**	firedragon
ADEEEKLMORU	leukoderma	**ADEEMNRRSU**	maunderers	**ADEFGINRRT**	redrafting
ADEEEKMNRSS	markedness	**ADEEMNRRTT**	retardment	**ADEFGIRRSU**	fireguards
ADEEEKMRRSS	dressmaker	**ADEEMNRSTU**	unmastered	**ADEFGISTTU**	fustigated
ADEEEKNNRTU	undertaken		unstreamed	**ADEFGLOOST**	floodgates
ADEEEKNRRTU	undertaker	**ADEEMNRSTY**	dynameters	**ADEFGLRTUU**	fulgurated
ADEEEKNRSTU	undertakes	**ADEEMNNRSUU**	unmeasured	**ADEFHHOORT**	fatherhood
ADEEEKORSTT	overtasked	**ADEEMNSTUU**	mansuetude	**ADEFHIILST**	fishtailed
ADEEELLMMRT	trammelled	**ADEEMOORRS**	aerodromes	**ADEFHILMSS**	damselfish
ADEEELLMNRS	mallenders	**ADEEMOOSTU**	oedematous	**ADEFHILTTW**	halfwitted
ADEEELLMNTY	lamentedly	**ADEEMOPRRS**	madrepores	**ADEFHINPRT**	pathfinder
ADEEELLNQUU	unequalled	**ADEEMORSST**	dermatoses	**ADEFHINRST**	threadfins
ADEEELLNRSS	sallenders	**ADEEMORSTT**	trematodes	**ADEFHIOSST**	toadfishes
ADEEELLNRUV	unravelled	**ADEEMPRSST**	stampeders	**ADEFHIRSST**	starfished
ADEEELLOPST	sellotaped	**ADEEMPRTTU**	permutated	**ADEFHIRSTV**	driveshaft

ADEFHLOOSS falsehoods	**ADEGHHILST** headlights	**ADEGILNNRU** laundering
ADEFHLTTWY Twelfth Day	**ADEGHHINST** nightshade	**ADEGILNORS** girandoles
ADEFHMNOTU unfathomed	**ADEGHILLNO** Heligoland	**ADEGILNOST** desolating
ADEFHOORSW foreshadow	**ADEGHILNNR** rehandling	**ADEGILNOTT** glottidean
ADEFIIILPS lapidifies	**ADEGHILNNS** handseling	**ADEGILNRUV** gerundival
ADEFIILPSS fissipedal	**ADEGHILNOO** halogenoid	**ADEGILOOPS** apologised
ADEFIIMMNO ammonified	**ADEGHILNSU** languished	**ADEGILOOPZ** apologized
ADEFIINOPS saponified	**ADEGHINNNS** hardenings	**ADEGILORRY** goliardery
ADEFIINQTU quantified	**ADEGHINNPRS** headspring	**ADEGILORSU** dialoguers
ADEFIINRTU infuriated		**ADEGILRRSS** rigsdalers
ADEFIIRSTT stratified	springhead	**ADEGILRSSS** glissaders
ADEFIJORUZ Juiz de Fora	**ADEGHIOPRS** ideographs	**ADEGILRSUV** vulgarised
ADEFILLNTY inflatedly	**ADEGHIOPRY** ideography	**ADEGILRSUV** vulgarised
ADEFILLSSU fusillades	**ADEGHIRRTU** draughtier	**ADEGILRTUV** divulgater
ADEFILMNOR manifolder	**ADEGHISSTT** tightassed	**ADEGILRUVZ** vulgarized
ADEFILMNTU fulminated	**ADEGHLORSS** gasholders	**ADEGILSTUV** divulgates
ADEFILMORS formalised	**ADEGHLOTUU** outlaughed	**ADEGIMNNRU** maundering
ADEFILMORZ formalized	**ADEGHLRTUY** daughterly	**ADEGIMNOPU** impoundage
ADEFILNNSZ zinfandels	**ADEGHMOPRY** demography	**ADEGIMNORS** gormandise
ADEFILNOST deflations	**ADEGHNNORST** headstrong	**ADEGIMNORT** moderating
	defoliants	**ADEGHNOSUZ** gazehounds	**ADEGIMNORZ** gormandize
ADEFILOORT defoliator	**ADEGHORSUU** guardhouse	**ADEGIMNPST** stampeding
ADEFILORTU fluoridate	**ADEGHRRSTU** draughters	**ADEGIMORST** dogmatiser
ADEFILSSTU feudalists	**ADEGIIILNS** idealising	**ADEGIMORTZ** dogmatizer
ADEFINNOTU fountained	**ADEGIIILNZ** idealizing	**ADEGIMOSST** dogmatises
ADEFINOORR foreordain	**ADEGIIILST** digitalise	**ADEGIMOSTZ** dogmatizes
ADEFINRRSU fundraiser	**ADEGIIILTZ** digitalize	**ADEGINNOTT** detonating
ADEFINRSST draftiness	**ADEGIIILLNR** redialling	**ADEGINNRST** integrands
ADEFINRSSU fundraises	**ADEGIIILLSU** seguidilla	**ADEGINNRSW** wanderings
ADEFINRSTX transfixed	**ADEGIIILMNP** impleading	**ADEGINNRTU** denaturing
ADEFKLNOTU outflanked	**ADEGIIILMNS** misaligned	
ADEFKLORST tradesfolk		misdealing	untreading
	misleading	**ADEGINNSSU** unassigned
ADEFLLMRUY dreamfully	**ADEGIIILNOT** gadolinite	**ADEGINOORT** derogation
ADEFLLNNOW downfallen	gelatinoid	**ADEGINOPRT** readopting
ADEFLMMOOR formal mode	**ADEGIIILNPR** lipreading	**ADEGINORRS** garrisoned
ADEFLMORTU formulated	**ADEGIIILNPT** depilating	**ADEGINORRT** denigrator
ADEFLNRTUU fraudulent	**ADEGIIILNRS** grindelias	**ADEGINORST** designator
ADEFLORRTW afterworld	**ADEGIIILNSS** signalised	**ADEGINPRSU** persuading
ADEFLORSWY dayflowers	**ADEGIIILNSZ** signalized	**ADEGINPRSW** wingspread
ADEFLSSTTY stedfastly	**ADEGIIILOSS** dialogises	**ADEGINPRTU** depurating
ADEFMNNSTU fundaments	**ADEGIIILOSZ** dialogizes	**ADEGINRRSS** grandsires
ADEFMOORRS doorframes	**ADEGIIILTTY** digitately	**ADEGINRRSV** gravidness
ADEFNNOOPR Fernando Po	**ADEGIIMMRT** immigrated	**ADEGINRSTW** stewarding
ADEFNORUUV unfavoured	**ADEGIIMNNU** unimagined	**ADEGINSSTT** digestants
ADEFNRSSTU transfused	**ADEGIIMNRS** misreading	**ADEGINSTTW** wadsetting
ADEFOOPRRS proofreads	**ADEGIIMNTT** meditating	**ADEGIPPRRST** partridges
ADEFORRRSW forwarders	**ADEGIINNRT** detraining	**ADEGJLMNTU** judgmental
ADEFORRSTV overdrafts	**ADEGIINNRV** reinvading	**ADEGKNRRRU** krugerrand
ADEFORRSTW afterwords	**ADEGIINORT** originated	**ADEGLLMOSY** gladsomely
ADEFRRSSTU fraudsters	**ADEGIINPRS** despairing	**ADEGLNOORT** Togolander
ADEFRRSTTU frustrated	**ADEGIINSTT** instigated	**ADEGLNORSU** glanderous
ADEGGHORUY hydragogue	**ADEGIJNORS** jargonised	**ADEGLNOSST** gladstones
ADEGGIINNR deraigning	**ADEGIJNORZ** jargonized	**ADEGMMOPRR** programmed
ADEGGIISTZ dziggetais	**ADEGIKLNSV** gavelkinds	**ADEGMNOOSU** endogamous
ADEGGIMOPS pedagogism	**ADEGILLNTU** lingulated	**ADEGMOPRRS** deprograms
ADEGGINORT derogating	**ADEGILMNRY** dreamingly	**ADEGNNOOPRS** pendragons
ADEGGINNSU degaussing	**ADEGILMORS** glamorised	**ADEGNNORSY** androgynes
ADEGGNORSU groundages	**ADEGILMORZ** glamorized	**ADEGNOOORW** orangewood
ADEGGNUWZZ zugzwanged	**ADEGILNNNO** nonaligned	**ADEGNOORSS** goosanders
ADEGHHIILT hightailed	**ADEGILNNPY** endplaying	**ADEGNOPRST** godparents
ADEGHHIKNT knighthead	**ADEGILNNRS** sanderling	**ADEGNORSSU** sandgrouse
ADEGHHILNR highlander	slandering	**ADEGNOSSTU** soundstage

ADEGOOPRST	gasteropod
ADEGOORRTY	derogatory
ADEGORRSTU	surrogated
ADEHHIIPRT	diphtheria
ADEHHIRRTW	hitherward
ADEHHIRSSW	dishwasher
ADEHHLLOOR	holohedral
ADEHHMPRRU	harrumphed
ADEHHNOPRY	hydrophane
ADEHIILMTU	humiliated
ADEHIILNPR	nephridial
ADEHIILOPP	pedophilia
ADEHIILOPU	audiophile
ADEHIIMMMO	Mohammed II
ADEHIIMRTT	mithridate
ADEHIINOPR	heparinoid
ADEHIIPSUU	euphausiid
ADEHIIRRRS	hairdriers
ADEHIJNSSS	jadishness
ADEHIKNPSS	handspikes
ADEHILLORU	loudhailer
ADEHILMNSS	mishandles
ADEHILNNRT	hinterland
ADEHILNOPS	sphenoidal
ADEHILNORT	threnodial
ADEHILNPRS	philanders
ADEHILNRRS	hardliners
ADEHILNRST	disenthral
ADEHILOPRS	spheroidal
ADEHILPRUY	hyperdulia
ADEHILPSTU	disulphate
ADEHILRRST	trihedrals
ADEHILRSST	heraldists
ADEHIMNORS	admonisher
	harmonised
	rhodamines
ADEHIMNORZ	harmonized
ADEHIMNOSS	admonishes
ADEHIMNRSS	mindshares
ADEHIMORTU	rheumatoid
ADEHIMOSSU	housemaids
ADEHINOOPR	radiophone
ADEHINOPSU	audiophones
ADEHINOSST	astonished
ADEHINPRST	printheads
ADEHINPSSU	dauphiness
ADEHINQSUV	vanquished
ADEHINRSTY	anhydrites
	hydrastine
ADEHINSSTU	dianthuses
ADEHIOPRSS	rhapsodies
	rhapsodise
ADEHIOPRSZ	rhapsodize
ADEHIORSTU	authorised
ADEHIORTUZ	authorized
ADEHIPRRST	tradership
ADEHIPRRSW	wardership
ADEHIPRSST	therapsids
ADEHIRRRSY	hairdryers
ADEHIRRTTY	trihydrate
ADEHIRRTWW	withdrawer
ADEHJMPRSU	Jamshedpur

ADEHKNORST	handstroke
ADEHKNOSSW	shakedowns
ADEHLLNOUW	unhallowed
ADEHLLOPRY	polyhedral
ADEHLMNORT	motherland
ADEHLMNOSY	handsomely
ADEHLMOPRY	hypodermal
ADEHLMOPTY	methyldopa
ADEHLNOPRY	hydroplane
ADEHLNRSTU	Sutherland
ADEHLORSSY	hydrolases
ADEHLOSSSW	shadowless
ADEHLRTTWY	thwartedly
ADEHMNOSST	handsomest
ADEHMNOTTU	muttonhead
ADEHMOORST	masterhood
ADEHMORRTW	threadworm
ADEHMORSTY	Mother's Day
ADEHNOOPRR	androphore
ADEHNOOPRT	parenthood
	theropodan
ADEHNORSVY	hydrovanes
ADEHNOSSWW	downwashes
ADEHOORSSU	roadhouses
ADEHOORSVW	overshadow
ADEHOPPPSY	poppyheads
ADEHORRSSW	shorewards
ADEHORRSSY	drayhorses
ADEIIIKNSS	diakinesis
ADEIIILLNT	initialled
ADEIIILTVX	lixiviated
ADEIIIMNTT	intimidate
ADEIIINSTT	dietitians
ADEIIIPSTV	vapidities
ADEIIKLNOZ	kaolinized
ADEIIKNSSY	dyskinesia
ADEIILLMPX	maxilliped
ADEIILLPTX	pixillated
ADEIILLSTT	distillate
ADEIILLTTT	titillated
ADEIILMMTU	multimedia
ADEIILMNOR	meridional
ADEIILMNSU	aluminised
ADEIILMNUZ	aluminized
ADEIILMOST	modalities
ADEIILMOSZ	imidazoles
ADEIILMPPS	misapplied
ADEIILNOPT	depilation
ADEIILNOPV	pavilioned
ADEIILNPST	platinised
ADEIILNPTZ	platinized
ADEIILNRTT	intertidal
ADEIILNSST	disentails
ADEIILNTTT	dilettanti
ADEIILORST	editorials
	idolatries
	idolatrise
ADEIILORTZ	idolatrize
ADEIILOSST	sodalities
ADEIILPRTY	prediality
ADEIILQSTU	liquidates
ADEIILRSTU	ritualised

ADEIILRTUZ	ritualized
ADEIILSSUV	visualised
ADEIILSUVZ	visualized
ADEIIMMNOS	Maimonides
ADEIIMNOST	mediations
ADEIIMNOTT	meditation
ADEIIMNOTV	dominative
ADEIIMNPRU	unimpaired
ADEIIMNRST	administer
ADEIIMNRSZ	zemindaris
ADEIIMOSTT	diatomites
ADEIIMPRSU	praesidium
ADEIIMRSTT	dermatitis
ADEIINNNOS	Indonesian
ADEIINNORT	inordinate
ADEIINNOTW	nationwide
ADEIINNOTX	indexation
ADEIINNPPT	pinnatiped
ADEIINNSST	daintiness
	Saint-Denis
ADEIINNSTU	insinuated
ADEIINNSTW	West Indian
ADEIINORRS	ordinaries
ADEIINORTU	auditioner
ADEIINORTV	derivation
ADEIINOSTV	deviations
ADEIINPPRS	drainpipes
ADEIINPTTU	inaptitude
ADEIINRRST	distrainer
ADEIINRTUV	indurative
ADEIIORSSV	advisories
ADEIIORSTU	auditories
ADEIIOSSTZ	diazotises
ADEIIOSTZZ	diazotizes
ADEIIPRRSS	dispraiser
ADEIIPRSSS	dispraises
ADEIIPRSST	dissipater
ADEIIPRSTV	privatised
ADEIIPRTVZ	privatized
ADEIIPSSST	dissipates
ADEIISSSUV	dissuasive
ADEIITTTTV	tittivated
ADEIJLLOTV	Jadotville
ADEIJMMNRW	windjammer
ADEIKLLNSW	Wilkes Land
ADEIKLLNUY	unladylike
ADEIKLMNOS	kalsomined
ADEIKLNOSU	soundalike
ADEIKLRSSS	laserdisks
ADEIKNPPRS	kidnappers
ADEIKNPRST	predikants
ADEIKNRRTW	Drinkwater
ADEIKNRSVW	drawknives
ADEILLMNOS	medaillons
	medallions
ADEILLMOST	metalloids
ADEILLMRST	treadmills
ADEILLMSST	medallists
ADEILLMSTW	Willemstad
ADEILLNOOS	solenoidal
ADEILLNOPR	Pirandello
ADEILLNOPT	pollinated

ADEILLLNOSU	delusional	ADEIMMRSUZ	summarized	ADEIRRTTTU	triturated
ADEILLNPSS	pallidness	ADEIMNNORT	ordainment	ADEJMNSTTU	adjustment
ADEILLNRRT	tendrillar	ADEIMNNOORT	moderation	ADEJOPSTUX	juxtaposed
ADEILLNRUV	unrivalled	ADEIMNNORRS	randomiser	ADEKMOPRST	postmarked
ADEILLPQSU	pasquilled	ADEIMNNORRZ	randomizer	ADEKOPRTVY	karyotyped
ADEILLPRSU	pluralised	ADEIMNNORSS	randomises	ADELLLPTUU	pullulated
ADEILLPRUZ	pluralized	ADEIMNNORSZ	randomizes	ADELLNNSUY	Lundy's Lane
ADEILLQRSU	quadrilles	ADEIMNNOSST	staminodes	ADELLNOPRS	landlopers
ADEILLRSUY	residually	ADEIMNPRRS	reprimands	ADELLNORSW	lowlanders
ADEILMNNOS	mandolines	ADEIMNQRUU	Marinduque	ADELLOORRR	roadroller
ADEILMNOPR	palindrome	ADEIMNRRTT	Mitterrand	ADELLOORRU	eurodollar
ADEILMNORS	normalised	ADEIMNRSSU	nursemaids	ADELMMOPSS	plasmodesm
ADEILMNORT	intermodal	ADEIMNRSTY	dynamiters	ADELMNNRUY	laundrymen
ADEILMNORZ	normalized	ADEIMORRTY	radiometry	ADELMOPSTU	deutoplasm
ADEILMNRST	dismantler	ADEIMORSST	dermatosis	ADELNNNOOR	nandrolone
ADEILMNRTU	rudimental	ADEIMORSTT	meditators	ADELNNOOST	East London
ADEILMNSSS	dismalness	ADEIMORTUY	audiometry	ADELNNORSW	landowners
ADEILMNSST	dismantles	ADEIMORTWW	mowdiewart	ADELNOOSST	loadstones
ADEILMNSTU	dentaliums	ADEIMPRSST	spermatids	ADELNOPRSS	pardonless
ADEILMOPSS	psalmodies	ADEIMRRSTY	martyrised	ADELNORSSU	slanderous
ADEILMOPST	diplomates	ADEIMRRTYZ	martyrized	ADELNORSTU	outlanders
ADEILMOPSY	polyamides	ADEIMRSTUX	admixtures	ADELNORSUY	roundelays
ADEILMOTUV	modulative	ADEIMRTUUV	duumvirate	ADELNPPSTU	supplanted
ADEILMPSTU	amplitudes	ADEINNNOTT	intendants	ADELNPRSUY	underplays
ADEILMSTTU	stimulated	ADEINNOOTT	denotation	ADELNRSTUW	wanderlust
ADEILMSTUU	mutualised		detonation	ADELOORSST	desolators
ADEILMTUUZ	mutualized	ADEINNOPWW	windowpane	ADELOPQRUU	quadrupole
ADEILNNORT	internodal	ADEINNORSW	rawinsonde	ADELOPRSSU	superloads
ADEILNOOST	desolation	ADEINNOSTT	dentations	ADELOPRSTU	sporulated
ADEILNOOTV	devotional	ADEINNRSSW	inwardness	ADELOPSTTU	postulated
ADEILNOPST	planetoids	ADEINNRSTU	unstrained	ADELORRSTX	dextrorsal
ADEILNOPSU	aneuploids	ADEINNRSTY	tyrannised	ADELORSTUU	adulterous
ADEILNOPUY	aneuploidy	ADEINNRTYZ	tyrannized	ADELPQRSUU	quadruples
ADEILNPRTU	prudential	ADEINOPRRS	preordains	ADELPQRTUU	quadruplet
ADEILNPTUV	pulvinated	ADEINOPRST	patronised	ADELPQRUUX	quadruplex
ADEILNRRST	interlards		predations	ADELPSTTUU	pustulated
ADEILNRSTU	uitlanders	ADEINOPRTU	depuration	ADELRRSSTY	drysalters
ADEILNSSSW	windlasses	ADEINOPRTZ	patronized	ADELRSTWWY	westwardly
ADEILNSTTU	testudinal	ADEINOPTUU	deputation	ADEMMMNORU	memorandum
ADEILNSTUY	unsteadily	ADEINORRSS	serranoids	ADEMMOOSTU	stomodaeum
ADEILOORST	oestradiol	ADEINORSST	adroitness	ADEMMNORSS	randomness
ADEILOPQRU	quadripole		intradoses	ADEMMNORST	adornments
ADEILOPRST	depilators	ADEINORSTY	arytenoids	ADEMNORSTW	downstream
ADEILOPRTT	tetraploid	ADEINORSUV	adenovirus	ADEMNRRTTU	Dürrenmatt
ADEILOPRTY	depilatory	ADEINORTUW	autowinder	ADEMNRSTTU	transmuted
ADEILOPSSU	disepalous	ADEINOSTUX	exudations	ADEMOORRST	moderators
ADEILOPSTU	dipetalous	ADEINPPRSS	sandpipers	ADEMOORSST	astrodomes
ADEILOQSSU	odalisques	ADEINPPSST	standpipes	ADEMOORSTT	outsmarted
ADEILORSST	idolatress	ADEINPRRST	transpired	ADENNOPSTU	outspanned
ADEILORTUV	outrivaled	ADEINPRSST	dispersant	ADENNORRRU	roadrunner
ADEILPRSSS	dispersals	ADEINPRSSY	dispensary	ADENNOSSST	sandstones
ADEILPRSSY	displayers	ADEINRSSTW	tawdriness	ADENNPRSTU	underpants
ADEILPSTTU	platitudes	ADEINRSTTU	unstriated	ADENNSSSTW	newsstands
	stipulated	ADEINSSSTU	unassisted	ADENOORSTT	detonators
ADEILRSTTU	stridulate	ADEIOPPRSV	disapprove	ADENOOSWWX	woodwaxens
ADEILRTTXY	dextrality	ADEIOPRRTU	repudiator	ADENOPPRUV	unapproved
ADEILRTUUX	luxuriated	ADEIOPRSTY	depositary	ADENOPPRST	transposed
ADEIMMNOPT	pantomimed	ADEIOPRSTZ	trapezoids	ADENOPRSTV	davenports
ADEIMMNRST	mastermind	ADEIORRSTT	traditores		Van der Post
ADEIMMNTTU	manumitted	ADEIORSSTT	siderostat	ADENORSSTV	standovers
ADEIMMORST	moderatism	ADEIORSSTU	sudatories	ADENORSSTW	towardness
ADEIMMRSSU	summarised	ADEIORSSVW	disavowers	ADENOSSTTW	downstates

ADENOSTTWY wyandottes	**ADGIIINOTT** digitation	**ADHIINNSTU** Hindustani
ADENPPRSTU unstrapped	**ADGIIKNNPP** kidnapping	**ADHIINORSS** anhidrosis
ADENPRRSTU underparts	**ADGIIKNNPS** kidnapings	**ADHILLLOPY** phyllodial
ADENPRSSUW upwardness	**ADGIILMNOU** gadolinium	**ADHILLNOSY** Holy Island
ADENRRSSTW sternwards	**ADGIILMNRV** admiringly	**ADHILMNPSY** nymphalids
ADEOPRRSTT prostrated	**ADGIILNPSY** displaying	**ADHILNOPSY** hypolydian
ADEOPRRSTU depurators	**ADGIILOSST** dialogists	**ADHILNOSTU** outlandish
ADEOPRSSTU outspreads	**ADGIIMNNOS** nomadising	**ADHILOOPRS** drosophila
ADEORRSSWW swearwords	**ADGIIMNNOT** dominating	**ADHIMNORSY** disharmony
ADEPPRSTUU suppurated	**ADGIIMNNOZ** nomadizing	**ADHIMNOTWY** Whit Monday
ADERRSSTUU susurrated	**ADGIIMNNTY** dynamiting	**ADHINNOOOT** nationhood
ADFFGILNOO offloading	**ADGIIMNPRY** pyramiding	**ADHINNOSTY** hydantoins
ADFFIIMRSS disaffirms	**ADGIIMNSST** dismasting	**ADHINOOPRT** anthropoid
ADFGIIMNNY damnifying	**ADGIINNNTU** inundating	**ADHINOOPRY** hypodorian
ADFGIMNRTU Grand Mufti	**ADGIINNNOPR** poniarding	radiophony
ADFGINORRU fairground	**ADGIINNRTU** indurating	**ADHINOOPRZ** rhizopodan
ADFGINORRW forwarding	**ADGIINOSVW** disavowing	**ADHINOPSTU** Diophantus
ADFHILLORS dollarfish	**ADGIINRSST** distringas	**ADHINORSTY** hydrations
ADFHILRSWY dwarfishly	**ADGIINSSTT** distasting	**ADHINSSTTW** withstands
ADFHINNOOT infanthood	**ADGIJNNORU** adjourning	**ADHINSTUWY** Whitsunday
ADFIIILNOS solifidian	**ADGIKLORTU** Utgard-Loki	Whit Sunday
ADFIIILPTT Fittipaldi	**ADGIKOORRV** Kirovograd	**ADHIOPRSST** rhapsodist
ADFIIINNPT pinnatifid	**ADGILLNNOS** Long Island	**ADHIOPRSTY** dystrophia
ADFIILMRSU disulfiram	**ADGILLNOPR** pollarding	**ADHIORSTXY** hydrotaxis
ADFIILQSUY disqualify	**ADGILLNYZZ** dazzlingly	**ADHKNNORTU** drunkathon
ADFIIOSSTU fastidious	**ADGILLOPRY** prodigally	**ADHLNOPSSW** splashdown
ADFIISSSTY dissatisfy	**ADGILMNOSW** gildswoman	**ADHMNOOORT** matronhood
ADFILLMNOY manifoldly	**ADGILMNOTU** modulating	**ADHNOORSYZ** hydrozoans
ADFILLNOOP floodplain	**ADGILNNNOW** landowning	**ADHNORRSTW** northwards
ADFILNOOSV flavonoids	**ADGILNNORT** Darlington	**ADHNORSTUY** hydronauts
ADFINNOOTU foundation	**ADGILNNNTUU** undulating	**ADHNORSTWW** Wandsworth
ADFINNORSU infrasound	**ADGILNNTUY** dauntingly	**ADHOOPRRST** arthropods
ADFINRSSTT standfirst	**ADGILNOSSS** glissandos	**ADHOORRTWY** roadworthy
ADFIORSSUV disfavours	**ADGILNOSTT** Ingolstadt	**ADHORSSTTY** hydrostats
ADFLLOOSST faldstools	**ADGILORTUV** divulgator	**ADHORSSTUW** southwards
ADFLNORSTW strandwolf	**ADGIMNNORT** mordanting	**ADIIILMNSV** invalidism
ADFNOORSSZ sforzandos	**ADGIMNNRSY** gynandrism	**ADIIILMRSS** dissimilar
ADFNOORTUY foudroyant	**ADGIMOSSTT** dogmatists	**ADIIILNOSV** divisional
ADFNORRSTW frontwards	**ADGINNOOSU** iguanodons	**ADIIILNTVY** invalidity
ADGGIILNOU dialoguing	**ADGINNOSTU** astounding	**ADIIINNOTV** divination
ADGGIILNSS glissading	**ADGINNPSTU** upstanding	**ADIIINOOST** iodisation
ADGGIINNOS diagnosing	**ADGINNRSTU** transuding	**ADIIINOOTZ** iodization
ADGGILLNNY danglingly	**ADGINOPSTT** postdating	**ADIILLORTY** dilatorily
ADGGINNOOR dragooning	**ADGINRRSTW** drawstring	**ADIILMMNSU** maudlinism
ADGGINNOPP dognapping	**ADGLLNOSUU** glandulous	**ADIILMNOXY** mixolydian
ADGGLLRSUY sluggardly	**ADGLMNOOOY** monadology	**ADIILMOPRR** primordial
ADGHHOOPRS hodographs	**ADGLNOPRUY** playground	**ADIILMOPRS** prismoidal
ADGHHOPRRY hydrograph	**ADGMNNORSU** groundsman	**ADIILMSSSS** dismissals
ADGHIILNOY holidaying	**ADGMNORSSU** groundmass	**ADIILNORRY** ordinarily
ADGHILLLSU guildhalls	**ADGMOORRSU** guardrooms	**ADIILNOSSU** sinusoidal
ADGHILRTUY draughtily	**ADGNNORSUY** gynandrous	**ADIILNOSTU** nautiloids
ADGHINNPRS handspring	**ADGNOOORRT** dragonroot	**ADIILNRSTU** industrial
ADGHINRSTU indraughts	**ADGOOPRSST** gastropods	**ADIILOPPSY** polydipsia
ADGHIRRSTW rightwards	**ADHHNOORSU** hoarhounds	**ADIILOQRTU** liquidator
ADGHIRSTTU distraught	**ADHHNOSTTU** thousandth	**ADIILORSYY** radiolysis
ADGHNOOPRS ondographs	**ADHHOPRSTY** hydropaths	**ADIILORSTY** solidarity
ADGHNOSSTU staghounds	**ADHHOPRTYY** hydropathy	**ADIILQSTUY** squalidity
ADGHOOPRXY doxography	**ADHIIIKKKL** Khalkidíki	**ADIIMMMOTU** ommatidium
ADGHPRSTUU updraughts	**ADHIILLNOP** phalloidin	**ADIIMNNOOT** admonition
ADGIIILMNO Modigliani	**ADHIILMNOT** Midlothian	domination
ADGIIILMST digitalism	**ADHIIMMNPS** midshipman	**ADIIMNORTX** dominatrix
ADGIIILNNV invaliding	**ADHIIMSTTU** humidistat	**ADIIMNOSSS** admissions

ADIIMNRSST	misandrist
ADIIMOPRST	diatropism
	prismatoid
ADIIMORTUU	auditorium
ADIIMQRUUV	quadrivium
ADIINNNOTU	inundation
ADIINNOORT	ordination
ADIINNORTU	induration
ADIINOPPST	disappoint
ADIINOPSSS	dispassion
ADIINOQSTU	quotidians
ADIINORRST	distrainor
ADIINORSTT	traditions
ADIINORTVY	divinatory
ADIINOSSSU	dissuasion
ADIINRSSTT	distraints
ADIINRSSTU	saturniids
ADIIOPRSST	dissipator
ADIIOPRSTT	podiatrist
ADILLLOSYY	disloyally
ADILLNSSTT	standstill
ADILLOSTYY	disloyalty
ADILMMOPSU	plasmodium
ADILMNNOTY	dominantly
ADILMNOOOP	monopodial
ADILMNOOSS	salmonoids
ADILMNOOTU	modulation
ADILMOPSST	psalmodist
ADILMORTUY	modularity
ADILNNOTUU	undulation
ADILNORSSS	Ross Island
ADILNORSTW	antiworlds
ADILNRSTTU	stridulant
ADILOOPSTY	stylopodia
ADILOORSTU	idolatrous
ADILORSSTW	swordtails
ADIMNOORST	admonitors
	dominators
ADIMNOORTY	admonitory
ADIMNORSSU	misandrous
ADIMNRRTUV	Trivandrum
ADIMORSTUU	sudatorium
ADINNOPSTT	standpoint
ADINNORSTU	inundators
ADINNORTUY	inundatory
ADINOOPRST	adsorption
ADINOPSSTY	dystopians
ADINORSSTW	downstairs
ADINPSSTTU	disputants
ADIORSSSTU	disastrous
ADJMMOOORS	majordomos
ADKNOORRUW	workaround
ADLLMORSSW	smallsword
ADLMOOORSU	malodorous
ADLMOORSTU	modulators
ADLMOORTUY	modulatory
ADLMOPRSUW	mouldwarps
ADLMOPRUWY	mouldwarp
ADLNNOORSW	nanoworlds
	Rowlandson
ADLNORSTUU	ultrasound
	undulators

ADLNORTUUY	undulatory
ADLNORTUWY	untowardly
ADLOOOSSTT	toadstools
ADMNNOORSU	monandrous
ADMNOORSTY	dynamotors
ADMNORSSST	sandstorms
ADMOOOPSTT	stomatopod
ADMOOPPRSU	pompadours
ADNNORRTUU	turnaround
ADNOPRRSUW	wraprounds
ADOOORRSWW	arrowwoods
AEEEEGRSTTZ	gazetteers
AEEEEHHINST	heathenise
AEEEEHHINTZ	heathenize
AEEEEHILMMT	Mehemet Ali
AEEEEHKNRRS	hearkeners
AEEEEHLLRTY	ethereally
AEEEEHLMPRS	ephemerals
AEEEEHLRTWW	waterwheel
AEEEEHMNORX	hexaemeron
AEEEEHMNRTW	weathermen
AEEEEHMPRTT	heptameter
AEEEEHMRSTX	hexameters
AEEEEHMSSTT	metatheses
AEEEEHNNNPT	nepenthean
AEEEEHNORTY	honeyeater
AEEEEHNRRTT	threatener
AEEEEHOPRRS	aerosphere
AEEEEHRRRSS	rehearsers
AEEEEHRRSTW	weatherers
AEEEEHRSTTW	sweetheart
AEEEEIIPPRT	peripeteia
AEEEEILNRST	eternalise
AEEEEILNRTV	interleave
AEEEEILNRTZ	eternalize
AEEEEILRSST	easterlies
AEEEEIMNRSX	reexamines
AEEEEIMNRTT	intemerate
AEEEEIMNSTV	Vietnamese
AEEEEIMPRTV	permeative
AEEEEINNNTV	antivenene
AEEEEINNRTT	intenerate
AEEEEINRSTT	entreaties
AEEEEINRTTV	inveterate
AEEEEINRTVV	enervative
AEEEEINRTVW	interweave
AEEEEIPPRST	papeteries
AEEEEIRRSTT	reiterates
AEEEEJKRRRT	tearjerker
AEEEEJNRTUV	rejuvenate
AEEEEKLSTTT	teakettles
AEEEEKNSSSW	weaknesses
AEEEEKPSSTW	sweepstake
AEEEELLMNRS	enamellers
AEEEELLRSST	teasellers
AEEEELLSSTT	tessellate
AEEEELMMNPT	empalement
AEEEELMNNTT	lentamente
	tenemental
AEEEELMNRTT	manteltree
	mantletree
AEEEELMNRTV	revealment
AEEEELMNRTY	elementary
AEEEELNNPPS	peneplanes
AEEEELNNUVZ	Venezuelan
AEEEELNPRTT	terneplate
AEEEELPSTTU	epaulettes
AEEEEMMNORT	anemometer
AEEEEMMNSST	semantemes
AEEEEMNNRST	nemerteans
AEEEEMNPRTT	pentameter
AEEEEMNRRTU	remunerate
AEEEEMNRRUV	maneuverer

ADIIMNRSST	misandrist
ADLNORTUUY	undulatory
ADLNORTUWY	untowardly
ADLOOOSSTT	toadstools
ADMNNOORSU	monandrous

ADLNORTUUY	undulatory
AEEEEGKMPR	gamekeeper
AEEEEGKPRT	gatekeeper
AEEEEGLNSS	Senegalese
AEEEEGNRRT	regenerate
AEEEEGRRTTV	revegetate
AEEEEELNOPT	elaeoptene
AEEEEENRTTX	exenterate
AEEEEFFGLRU	effleurage
AEEEEFFIMNT	effeminate
AEEEEFGLNRU	enfleurage
AEEEEFHRRTT	thereafter
AEEEEFHRRTW	whereafter
AEEEEFINRTZ	antifreeze
AEEEEFLLNST	fenestella
AEEEEFLLRST	leafleters
AEEEEFLMNSS	femaleness
AEEEEFLNOOZ	Zeno of Elea
AEEEEFNRRST	transferee
AEEEEFNRSTT	fenestrate
AEEEEGGGNRS	greengages
AEEEEGGMNNT	engagement
AEEEEGGRSST	segregates
AEEEEGHLPRT	telpherage
AEEEEGHLRSW	gearwheels
AEEEEGHMNST	Gethsemane
AEEEEGHMRST	megatheres
AEEEEGHNRRT	greenheart
AEEEEGILNRS	generalise
AEEEEGILNRZ	generalize
AEEEEGILNSV	evangelise
AEEEEGILNUV	eigenvalue
AEEEEGILNVZ	evangelize
AEEEEGIMNRS	menageries
AEEEEGINNRT	ingenerate
AEEEEGINRTV	generative
AEEEEGITTVV	vegetative
AEEEEGKLOPR	goalkeeper
AEEEEGLMNRT	regalement
AEEEEGLMPSX	megaplexes
AEEEEGLNOST	eaglestone
AEEEEGLRSSS	eelgrasses
	greaseless
AEEEEGLSSSY	eyeglasses
AEEEEGMNNPS	empennages
AEEEEGMNNRT	enragement
AEEEEGMNRSS	meagerness
	meagreness
AEEEEGMNRST	agreements
AEEEEGNRSTW	tweenagers
AEEEEGPRSSX	expressage
AEEEEGQSTUU	squeteague

AEEEMNRSTU enumerates	**AEEFLMORSY** fearsomely	**AEEGIILLST** legalities
AEEEMORRST aerometers	**AEEFLNRSTT** flatteners	**AEEGIILMTT** legitimate
AEEEMRRSSU remeasures	**AEEFLRRSTT** flatterers	**AEEGIILNST** gelatinise
AEEEMRRTTT tetrameter	**AEEFMNORSS** freemasons	**AEEGIILNTZ** gelatinize
AEEEMRSTVW wavemeters	**AEEFNORRRW** forewarner	**AEEGIILRST** regalities
AEEEMSSTTW sweetmeats	**AEEFNRRRST** retransfer	**AEEGIILRSZ** glazieries
AEEENNNSST Tennessean	**AEEFOPRRST** perforates	**AEEGIIMNNT** ingeminate
AEEENNPRST perennates	**AEEFORRRSW** forswearer	**AEEGIIMNST** enigmatise
AEEENOPRSW weaponeers	**AEEFORSSTT** foretastes	**AEEGIIMNTZ** enigmatize
AEEENORSTX exonerates	**AEEGGGINNR** reengaging	**AEEGIINRRT** garnierite
AEEENPRSST sea serpent	**AEEGGHILRT** lighterage	**AEEGIKNNRW** rewakening
AEEENPRSTT penetrates	**AEEGGHMOSU** hemagogues	**AEEGILLMNN** enamelling
AEEENRRSST easterners	**AEEGGHOPRR** geographer	**AEEGILLNST** teaselling
AEEENRSSSV averseness	**AEEGGILNRT** regelating	**AEEGILLNSW** weaselling
AEEENSTTUV eventuates		relegating	**AEEGILLNTZ** teazelling
AEEENSTTUX extenuates	**AEEGGINNRT** generating	**AEEGILLORS** allegories
AEEEPPRRTT perpetrate		greatening		allegorise
AEEEPPRTTU perpetuate	**AEEGGINORW** New Georgia	**AEEGILLORZ** allegorize
AEEERRSTTW streetwear	**AEEGGINRRS** grangerise	**AEEGILLRSV** grevilleas
AEEERRSTYY yesteryear		gregarines	**AEEGILLSST** legislates
AEEERSSSSS reassesses	**AEEGGINRRZ** grangerize	**AEEGILMNNP** empaneling
AEEFFHORRT forefather	**AEEGGINTTV** vegetating	**AEEGILMNRR** malingerer
AEEFFORRST reafforest	**AEEGGIRSSV** aggressive	**AEEGILMNRT** regimental
AEEFGGHIRT freightage	**AEEGGMNOTY** gametogeny	**AEEGILMNSV** evangelism
AEEFGHINRT feathering	**AEEGGMORRT** remortgage	**AEEGILMNTY** geminately
AEEFGHORRT foregather	**AEEGGMORST** mortgagees	**AEEGILNNRR** relearning
AEEFGILLNT leafleting	**AEEGGNNRTU** Terengganu	**AEEGILNNSS** genialness
AEEFGILLRS fillagrees	**AEEGGNOTTW** waggonette	**AEEGILNNST** eglantines
AEEFGILPRS persiflage	**AEEGGORRST** segregator	**AEEGILNNSV** leavenings
AEEFGINSTU teniafuges	**AEEGGRRSST** staggerers	**AEEGILNORT** regelation
AEEFGLLNSS flangeless	**AEEGGRRSSW** swaggerers		relegation
AEEFGLLOST flageolets	**AEEGHHMORR** hemorrhage	**AEEGILNRRT** realtering
AEEFGLPRSU presageful	**AEEGHIILMP** hemiplegia	**AEEGILNRST** generalist
AEEFGORRRU fourragere	**AEEGHIKMTW** makeweight	**AEEGILNRTU** Argenteuil
AEEFHHINRT Fahrenheit	**AEEGHIKNNR** hearkening	**AEEGILNRTY** generality
AEEFHIKLRT fatherlike	**AEEGHILNRT** leathering	**AEEGILNSTV** evangelist
AEEFHIKSSW weakfishes	**AEEGHILPST** legateship	**AEEGILNTVY** negatively
AEEFHINPRT pinfeather	**AEEGHILRST** lethargies	**AEEGILRRSU** regularise
AEEFHLOPPR leafhopper	**AEEGHIMRST** hermitages	**AEEGILRRUZ** regularize
AEEFHLRSST fatherless	**AEEGHINNRT** heartening	**AEEGILRSST** gaiterless
AEEFHMMRST Hammerfest	**AEEGHINPRT** preheating	**AEEGILRSTU** gauleiters
AEEFHMORTT fathometer	**AEEGHINRRS** rehearsing	**AEEGILRTUV** regulative
AEEFHPRSTT stepfather	**AEEGHINRRT** ingatherer	**AEEGIMNOSX** xenogamies
AEEFHRRSTW freshwater	**AEEGHINRSS** garnishees	**AEEGIMNPRT** impregnate
AEEFIIRRRS farrieries	**AEEGHINRST** reheatings		permeating
AEEFIKNPPR paperknife	**AEEGHINRTW** weathering	**AEEGIMNRST** germanites
AEEFIKNPRS freakiness	**AEEGHIPPRR** epigrapher		germinates
AEEFILNSST featliness	**AEEGHKNNRS** greenshank		magnetiser
AEEFILOPRT perfoliate	**AEEGHLMORT** geothermal	**AEEGIMNRSZ** germanizes
AEEFILOSTX exfoliates	**AEEGHLNTVW** wavelength	**AEEGIMNRTZ** magnetizer
AEEFILRSSV lifesavers	**AEEGHLORTT** altogether	**AEEGIMNSST** magnetises
AEEFILRSTT flatteries	**AEEGHLPRST** telegraphs	**AEEGIMNSTU** mutagenise
AEEFILRSTV afterlives	**AEEGHLPRTY** telegraphy	**AEEGIMNSTZ** magnetizes
AEEFIMNRRT freemartin	**AEEGHMNOOT** homogenate	**AEEGIMNTUZ** mutagenize
AEEFINRRRS refrainers	**AEEGHMNOPS** megaphones	**AEEGIMOSST** isogametes
AEEFINRRST fraternise	**AEEGHMORTY** heterogamy	**AEEGIMPSTT** pegmatites
AEEFINRRTZ fraternize	**AEEGHNOPST** pathogenes	**AEEGIMRRST** remigrates
AEEFKOPRSS forespeaks	**AEEGHORSTT** othergates	**AEEGIMRRTU** marguerite
AEEFLLNNOT fontanelle	**AEEGHOSSTU** gatehouses	**AEEGIMRRTV** gravimeter
AEEFLLNRUY funereally	**AEEGIILLLS** illegalise	**AEEGIMSTTU** guestimate
AEEFLLNSTU fustanelle	**AEEGIILLLZ** illegalize	**AEEGINNNSU** ensanguine
AEEFLLRSSY fearlessly	**AEEGIILLNV** villeinage	**AEEGINNORT** generation

AEEGINNPSS	pangenesis
AEEGINNRRT	interregna
AEEGINNRST	argentines
	tangerines
AEEGINNRTT	entreating
AEEGINNRTV	enervating
	venerating
AEEGINNSUX	exsanguine
AEEGINORRS	orangeries
	reorganise
AEEGINORRZ	reorganize
AEEGINORTV	overeating
AEEGINOSTT	negotiates
AEEGINOTTV	vegetation
AEEGINPPRR	repapering
AEEGINPRST	interpages
AEEGINPRSV	grapevines
AEEGINPRSY	panegyrise
AEEGINPRYZ	panegyrize
AEEGINRRTT	retreating
AEEGINRRTX	generatrix
AEEGINRSSS	greasiness
AEEGINRSST	stingarees
AEEGINRSSV	vernissage
AEEGINRSTT	estreating
	integrates
AEEGINSSST	giantesses
AEEGIRSSTT	strategies
AEEGKORRWW	wageworker
AEEGLLNORS	organelles
AEEGLLNOSS	los Angeles
AEEGLLORTT	allegretto
AEEGLMMOSY	gamesomely
AEEGLMNNTT	tanglement
AEEGLMNNTTU	tegumental
AEEGLMORST	algometers
AEEGLMRRSW	legwarmers
AEEGLNNPST	pentangles
AEEGLNNRST	entanglers
AEEGLNORSS	sloganeers
AEEGLNORTU	outgeneral
AEEGLNORTV	graveolent
AEEGLORTUV	travelogue
AEEGLRSSTT	targetless
AEEGMNNOST	mangosteen
AEEGMNNOQSU	Monegasque
AEEGMNNRRS	mergansers
AEEGMNRSTU	augmenters
AEEGMNRSTW	West German
AEEGMNRSTY	segmentary
AEEGMOPRSS	megaspores
AEEGMORRST	stereogram
AEEGMORSST	gasometers
AEEGMRSSTU	gaussmeter
AEEGNNORTT	Teton Range
AEEGNNSSTW	newsagents
AEEGNOPRSS	personages
AEEGNORRST	generators
AEEGNORSTT	teratogens
AEEGNORSTU	entourages
AEEGNORSTV	gravestone
AEEGNOSTTW	wagonettes

AEEGNOSTXY	oxygenates
AEEGNPRSSS	passengers
AEEGNRRSST	estrangers
AEEGOPRRST	reportages
AEEGORRSVZ	overgrazes
AEEGPRSTUX	expurgates
AEEGRRSSSY	ryegrasses
AEEHHHINST	heathenish
AEEHHILMOP	haemophile
AEEHHILSTT	healthiest
AEEHHIMNST	heathenism
AEEHHINRST	earthshine
AEEHHKNPSS	sheepshank
AEEHHLMSTU	Methuselah
AEEHHLOSSW	hawseholes
AEEHHLOTWW	wholewheat
AEEHHNNPST	naphthenes
AEEHHNPSTY	hyphenates
AEEHHNSSTU	unsheathes
AEEHHPSSTU	Hephaestus
AEEHIILLPT	epithelial
AEEHIILMST	Ishmaelite
AEEHIIMPRT	Ephraimite
AEEHIINPPS	epiphanies
AEEHIISTTV	hesitative
AEEHIKLNNP	enkephalin
AEEHIKLNOR	Herakleion
AEEHIKLRTW	wreathlike
AEEHILLORT	heliolater
AEEHILMOST	mesothelia
AEEHILMRST	thermalise
AEEHILMRTY	hemielytra
AEEHILMRTZ	thermalize
AEEHILNRUV	euryhaline
AEEHILNSSV	shinleaves
AEEHILNSTW	Wiesenthal
AEEHILNSTX	anthelixes
AEEHILOPSU	heliopause
AEEHILORTU	Haute-Loire
AEEHILPPRR	peripheral
AEEHILPPSY	epiphyseal
AEEHILPRST	sphalerite
AEEHILPSST	shapeliest
AEEHILRSTT	earthliest
	stealthier
AEEHILRTTT	triathlete
AEEHILSTTW	wealthiest
AEEHIMMNNR	Mannerheim
AEEHIMMRSX	hexamerism
AEEHIMNPRT	hemipteran
AEEHIMNRUZ	rehumanize
AEEHIMNSST	mainsheets
AEEHIMPSSS	emphasises
AEEHIMPSST	empathises
AEEHIMPSSZ	emphasizes
AEEHIMPSTZ	empathizes
AEEHIMRRTY	erythremia
AEEHIMRRST	hetaerisms
AEEHIMSSTT	metathesis
AEEHINORST	antiheroes
AEEHINPRST	interphase
AEEHINRSST	earthiness

	heartiness
AEEHINRSSV	haversines
AEEHINRSTU	eutherians
AEEHINRTTU	uintathere
AEEHINSSTT	antitheses
AEEHIPPSSW	hawsepipes
AEEHIPRSSU	euphrasies
AEEHIRRSST	earthrises
	trasheries
AEEHIRSSTT	hesitaters
	hetaerists
AEEHISTUVX	exhaustive
AEEHKLORRU	leukorrhea
AEEHKLPSSW	sheepwalks
AEEHKMMORS	homemakers
AEEHKMORSS	shoemakers
AEEHKOPSSV	spokeshave
AEEHKORSTT	heatstroke
AEEHKORSTV	Tereshkova
AEEHKOSSTU	steakhouse
AEEHLLMRTY	hemelytral
AEEHLLNRRT	enthraller
AEEHLLORSW	wholesaler
AEEHLLOSSW	wholesales
AEEHLLSSTW	wealthless
AEEHLMMRSS	hammerless
AEEHLMNNOP	phenomenal
AEEHLMORTX	exothermal
AEEHLMOSSY	haemolyses
AEEHLMSTTY	methylates
AEEHLNOPRS	Rhône-Alpes
AEEHLNOPST	phenolates
AEEHLNPPRY	hyperplane
AEEHLRSSTW	wreathless
AEEHLRSTTY	Hattersley
AEEHLRTTTY	tetraethyl
AEEHLSSTXY	hexastyles
AEEHMMORST	hammertoes
AEEHMMNNSSU	humaneness
AEEHMNNOORR	menorrhoea
AEEHMNOPRT	Promethean
AEEHMNRSTV	harvestmen
AEEHMOPRSS	semaphores
AEEHMOPRST	atmosphere
AEEHMORRRT	arthromere
AEEHMORRTV	earthmover
AEEHMORSUX	hexamerous
AEEHMORTTY	metatheory
AEEHMPRSST	petershams
AEEHNNOPSX	Xenophanes
AEEHNOOPRR	harpooneer
AEEHNOORST	oenotheras
AEEHNOPPRT	Parthenope
AEEHNOPPRY	hyperpnoea
AEEHNORSSS	hoarseness
AEEHNPRRSS	sharpeners
AEEHNRRSSS	harnessers
AEEHOOPRST	peashooter
AEEHOOPSST	apotheoses
AEEHOPRSTY	aerophytes
AEEHOPTTTY	typothetae
AEEHORSSUW	warehouses

AEEHORSTUW	Waterhouse	AEEIKNRRSV	Snake River	AEEILNRSTU	neutralise
AEEHORSTVW	whatsoever	AEEIKQSSTU	squeakiest	AEEILNRSVZ	vernalizes
AEEHORTTXY	heterotaxy	AEEIKRSSTT	streakiest	AEEILNRTTY	eternality
AEEHOSSTTU	statehouse	AEEILLLLNV	villanelle	AEEILNRTUZ	neutralize
AEEHPRSSTU	superheats	AEEILLMNST	enamellist	AEEILNSSST	essentials
AEEHPRSUVY	superheavy	AEEILLMRSS	marseilles	AEEILNSSSZ	sleaziness
AEEHRRSSTT	shatterers	AEEILLMSST	metallises	AEEILNSTTV	ventilates
AEEHRRSSTV	harvesters	AEEILLMSTZ	metallizes	AEEILNSTVX	sexivalent
AEEHRSSTUX	exhausters	AEEILLNOST	linoleates	AEEILOPRST	periosteal
AEEIIKNRST	keratinise	AEEILLNSVV	Evansville	AEEILORRST	arterioles
AEEIIKNRTZ	keratinize	AEEILLORSY	Isle Royale	AEEILORRSV	revalorise
AEEIILLOPS	aeolipiles	AEEILLPSST	palletises	AEEILORRVZ	revalorize
AEEIILLRRS	railleries	AEEILLPSTT	paillettes	AEEILORTTV	tolerative
AEEIILLRTT	illiterate		stipellate	AEEILPPRRT	peripteral
AEEIILMNRS	mineralise	AEEILLPSTZ	palletizes	AEEILPRRRV	Pearl River
AEEIILMNRZ	mineralize	AEEILLRSSV	Versailles	AEEILPRRSV	prevailers
AEEIILMNST	eliminates	AEEILLRSTV	trevallies	AEEILPRSST	psalteries
AEEIILNPRU	epineurial	AEEILLRTTY	literately	AEEILPRSSY	erysipelas
AEEIILNPRX	pre-exilian	AEEILLRTVY	relatively	AEEILPRSTX	Praxiteles
AEEIILNSTV	venalities	AEEILLSSTT	satellites	AEEILPSTTU	estipulate
AEEIILQSTU	equalities	AEEILLSTUV	televisual	AEEILQRSSU	equalisers
AEEIILRRTV	irrelative	AEEILMMNPT	impalement	AEEILQRSUZ	equalizers
AEEIILRSSS	serialises	AEEILMMNRU	neurilemma	AEEILRRSTV	retrievals
AEEIILRSSZ	serializes	AEEILMMSST	lemmatises	AEEILRRSVV	Slave River
AEEIILRSTV	relativise	AEEILMMSTZ	lemmatizes	AEEILRRSVW	silverware
	revitalise	AEEILMNNNO	Nemean lion	AEEILRRTTU	literature
AEEIILRTVZ	relativize	AEEILMNNST	alinements	AEEILRSTTU	elutriates
	revitalize		lineaments		tutelaries
AEEIIMNNST	inseminate	AEEILMNNTT	entailment	AEEILRSVVY	aversively
AEEIIMNNTT	tiemannite	AEEILMNORS	neorealism	AEEILSSSUX	sexualises
AEEIIMNRSS	seminaries	AEEILMNPRT	planimeter	AEEILSSTTT	stateliest
AEEIIMPRTV	imperative	AEEILMNRST	streamline	AEEILSSUXZ	sexualizes
AEEIIMRSSS	emissaries	AEEILMNRSY	minelayers	AEEIMMMRST	metamerism
AEEIIMSTTV	estimative	AEEILMNSST	enamelists	AEEIMMOPRT	emmetropia
AEEIINPPRT	peripetian		mesnalties	AEEIMMRSSU	mismeasure
AEEIINPPRZ	piperazine	AEEILMOOSS	elaiosomes	AEEIMNNORT	enantiomer
AEEIINPSST	epinasties	AEEILMORST	meliorates		renominate
AEEIINRSTT	itinerates	AEEILMRSST	misrelates	AEEIMNNRTT	retainment
AEEIINRSTU	uniseriate		salimeters	AEEIMNNRTU	innumerate
AEEIINTTTV	entitative	AEEILMRSTT	altimeters	AEEIMNNSZZ	mezzanines
AEEIIPPRST	peripetias	AEEILMRSVY	semiyearly	AEEIMNOPRT	permeation
AEEIIPPTTV	appetitive	AEEILNNPPS	peneplains	AEEIMNORTT	marionette
AEEIIPRSST	asperities	AEEILNNPRS	perennials	AEEIMNOSTT	maisonette
	patisserie	AEEILNNPST	septennial	AEEIMNPRRU	praemunire
AEEIIPRSSV	vespiaries	AEEILNNSSX	sexennials	AEEIMNRSSS	smeariness
AEEIIRRSTT	tertiaries	AEEILNNSTT	sentential	AEEIMNRSTT	martensite
AEEIIRSSTV	vestiaries	AEEILNNSTV	levantines		terminates
AEEIIRSTVZ	vizierates		valentines	AEEIMNRTUV	numerative
AEEIJLOSSU	jealousies	AEEILNNTTU	lieutenant	AEEIMNSSST	steaminess
AEEIJMNSSS	jessamines	AEEILNOPRT	peritoneal	AEEIMNSSTT	estaminets
AEEIJOPRTV	pejorative	AEEILNORST	neorealist	AEEIMOPPRS	peperomias
AEEIKKLRST	streaklike	AEEILNORTV	revelation	AEEIMOPQSU	semiopaque
AEEIKLLNSS	silkalenes	AEEILNOSTV	elevations	AEEIMORRSS	rosemaries
AEEIKLMRST	streamlike	AEEILNPPPS	pineapples	AEEIMORRTV	variometer
AEEIKLNNRT	Interlaken	AEEILNPRSS	pearliness	AEEIMORSSS	isomerases
AEEIKLNOPU	leukopenia	AEEILNPRST	alpestrine	AEEIMPRRSS	spermaries
AEEIKLNSSW	weakliness		episternal	AEEIMPRSTT	impetrates
AEEIKLPRSS	sprekelias	AEEILNPRSX	explainers	AEEIMQRSUV	semiquaver
AEEIKLRRWW	wirewalker	AEEILNQSTU	sequential	AEEIMRSSTT	streamiest
AEEIKMNORS	noisemaker	AEEILNQTUV	equivalent		tasimeters
AEEIKMRRST	Steiermark	AEEILNRRTV	irrelevant	AEEIMRSTTX	taximeters
AEEIKNNSSS	sneakiness	AEEILNRSSV	vernalises	AEEINNNPWY	Pennine Way

AEEINNNSSS	insaneness	**AEEIRSSSTW**	waitresses	**AEELNOPSSW**	weaponless
AEEINNNSST	innateness	**AEEIRSSTTV**	travesties	**AEELNOPSTX**	exoplanets
AEEINNORTV	enervation	**AEEIRSSTWW**	wasteweirs	**AEELNOSSSS**	seasonless
	veneration	**AEEIRSTTUX**	textuaries	**AEELNPRSST**	parentless
AEEINNOTTT	Antoinette	**AEEJLNORSU**	journalese	**AEELNPRTTW**	wentletrap
AEEINNPPTT	inappetent	**AEEJMORSTT**	majorettes	**AEELOPPRTU**	repopulate
AEEINNRSSW	swanneries	**AEEKLLLSTY**	skeletally	**AEELOPSSTT**	salopettes
AEEINNRSTT	entertains	**AEEKLLORSW**	Lower Lakes	**AEELOQRRUU**	roquelaure
	tenantries	**AEEKLLPSSW**	sleepwalks	**AEELORSTTU**	lotus-eater
AEEINNRSTV	innervates	**AEEKLMNNRT**	kernmantel	**AEELORSUVV**	overvalues
AEEINNRTUV	aventurine	**AEEKLMNORW**	enamelwork	**AEELPPRSTU**	perpetuals
AEEINNSSSU	uneasiness	**AEEKMMNORY**	moneymaker	**AEELPRRSST**	plasterers
AEEINNSSTT	assentient	**AEEKMMRRRY**	merrymaker	**AEELPRRSSY**	prayerless
AEEINNSSTV	nativeness	**AEEKMNRSTW**	newmarkets	**AEELPRRSTU**	prelatures
AEEINOPPST	appointees	**AEEKMORRTU**	euromarket	**AEELQRRRSU**	quarrelers
AEEINOPRST	proteinase	**AEEKMPRRTV**	verkrampte	**AEELQRSSTU**	sequestral
AEEINOPRTX	paroxetine	**AEEKORSTUY**	eukaryotes	**AEELRRSTUW**	lusterware
AEEINOPSSW	weaponises	**AEELLLSTTY**	stellately		lustreware
AEEINOPSWZ	weaponizes	**AEELLMMRRT**	trammeller	**AEELRSSTTY**	treatyless
AEEINOPTTT	potentiate	**AEELLMNOTV**	malevolent	**AEEMMNNORST**	manometers
AEEINORSTT	orientates	**AEELLMNRTU**	allurement	**AEEMMNNORTT**	antemortem
AEEINORTVV	renovative	**AEELLMNSSY**	namelessly	**AEEMMNNORTY**	anemometry
AEEINPPRSS	paperiness	**AEELLNPRST**	repellants	**AEEMMNSSTU**	amusements
AEEINPPSST	pepsinates	**AEELLNPSTX**	expellants	**AEEMMORSTT**	atmometers
AEEINPRSSS	passerines	**AEELLNRRUV**	unraveller	**AEEMMRRSST**	stammerers
AEEINPRSST	pistareens	**AEELLNRTVY**	relevantly	**AEEMNNOPRS**	praenomens
AEEINPRSTU	resupinate	**AEELLNRTXY**	externally	**AEEMMNNORST**	nanometres
AEEINPSTTU	uniseptate	**AEELLNTUVY**	eventually	**AEEMNNORUV**	mavourneen
AEEINQRSTU	equestrian	**AEELLOPSST**	sellotapes	**AEEMNNOSTT**	atonements
AEEINQSSSU	queasiness		soleplates	**AEEMNNPRTT**	entrapment
AEEINRRRST	errantries	**AEELLORSTT**	rostellate	**AEEMMNNRSST**	Stresemann
	restrainer	**AEELLOTTTY**	teetotally	**AEEMNOPRST**	treponemas
AEEINRRTTV	travertine	**AEELLQRRRU**	quarreller	**AEEMNOPSYZ**	apoenzymes
AEEINRRTVY	veterinary	**AEELLRRSTV**	travellers	**AEEMNORRTU**	enumerator
AEEINRSSSY	synaeresis	**AEELLRSTTU**	tellurates	**AEEMNORRUV**	manoeuvrer
AEEINRSSTT	reinstates	**AEELLRSTTW**	Wall Street	**AEEMNORSST**	sarmentose
AEEINRSSTW	wateriness	**AEELMMNORU**	neurolemma	**AEEMNORSUV**	manoeuvres
AEEINRSTTT	interstate	**AEELMMNRST**	entrammels	**AEEMNPPRTY**	prepayment
AEEINSSSTT	titanesses	**AEELMMNRST**	trammelers	**AEEMNPRSTY**	repayments
AEEINSSSTW	sweatiness	**AEELMNNRSS**	mannerless	**AEEMNRRSTT**	arrestment
AEEINSSSTY	yeastiness	**AEELMNOPRT**	planometer	**AEEMNRSSTU**	matureness
AEEINSSTTT	intestates	**AEELMNORTV**	overmantel	**AEEMNRSTTT**	treatments
AEEIOPRRSV	overpraise	**AEELMNORTW**	watermelon	**AEEMNRSTTU**	menstruate
AEEIOPRSST	operatises	**AEELMNOSSW**	saleswomen	**AEEMNSSSST**	assessment
AEEIOPRSTV	evaporites	**AEELMNPRST**	parlements	**AEEMNSSTTT**	statements
	operatives	**AEELMNRSTV**	ravelments		testaments
AEEIOPRSTZ	operatizes	**AEELMNRSTV**	vestmental	**AEEMORRSTT**	rotameters
AEEIPPRRTW	wiretapper	**AEELMOPRSY**	polymerase	**AEEMORRSTV**	overmaster
AEEIPPRSST	appetisers	**AEELMOPSTT**	palmettoes	**AEEMORRTTV**	overmatter
AEEIPPRSSU	pauperises	**AEELMORSST**	elastomers	**AEEMORSSSY**	mayoresses
AEEIPPRSTZ	appetizers	**AEELMORTTV**	voltameter	**AEEMORSTTU**	autometers
AEEIPPRSUZ	pauperizes	**AEELMOSTTT**	matelottes	**AEEMPRSTTT**	attempters
AEEIPRRSTV	privateers	**AEELMPRSSU**	supermales		reattempts
AEEIPRSSTT	striptease	**AEELMPRSTT**	streetlamp	**AEEMPRSTTU**	permutates
	tapestries	**AEELMRSSST**	masterless	**AEEMQRSSSU**	marquesses
AEEIPRSSTU	pasteurise	**AEELMRSSTT**	streamlets	**AEEMRRSSTT**	smatterers
AEEIPRSSUV	persuasive	**AEELNNNSTU**	antennules	**AEEMRSSSST**	seamstress
AEEIPRSTTX	extirpates	**AEELNNORSW**	New Orleans	**AEEMRSSSTT**	mattresses
	sexpartite	**AEELNNPSTW**	new planets	**AEEMRSTTTW**	wattmeters
AEEIPRSTUZ	pasteurize	**AEELNNPTTU**	antepenult	**AEENNOPSTT**	panettones
AEEIPRTTUV	vituperate	**AEELNNQSTU**	lansquenet	**AEENNORSST**	ornateness
AEEIRRSSTU	treasuries	**AEELNNSSTT**	tenantless	**AEENNPRRST**	trepanners

AEENNPRSTT	penetrants	AEFFIRSTUX	affixtures	AEFHKNORSS	foreshanks
AEENNRRSTT	reentrants	AEFFLMOOPR	flameproof	AEFHLLMSUV	shamefully
AEENOORRTX	exonerator	AEFFLMOORW	foamflower	AEFHLLSTTU	stealthful
AEENOPPRST	notepapers	AEFFLNOPST	pantoffles	AEFHLLSTUY	hastefully
AEENOPPQSSU	opaqueness	AEFFOOSTTU	affettuoso	AEFHLMOSST	fathomless
AEENOPPRTT	penetrator	AEFFORSSTV	overstaffs	AEFHLORSSV	flashovers
AEENOPRRTU	neuroptera	AEFGGHNOUU	Hua Guo Feng	AEFHMORSSU	farmhouses
AEENOPRSST	personates	AEFGGINNRT	engrafting	AEFHORSSTW	aftershows
AEENOPRSUV	supernovae	AEFGHIIRRT	airfright	AEFIIILNST	finalities
AEENOPSTTT	potentates	AEFGHILNRS	anglerfish	AEFIILLNSS	filialness
AEENORRSTV	enervators	AEFGHILSST	safelights	AEFIILLTUV	fluviatile
	venerators	AEFGHINRRW	wharfinger	AEFIILMNSS	semifinals
AEENORSTUX	extraneous	AEFGHIOSST	goatfishes	AEFIILMPRS	amplifiers
AEENORTTUX	extenuator	AEFGHIRSST	gearshifts	AEFIILNOTU	unifoliate
AEENPPRRST	entrappers	AEFGHNORTU	fearnought	AEFIILNRTT	infiltrate
AEENPPRSSW	newspapers	AEFGHORRST	forgathers	AEFIILORTT	trifoliate
AEENPPRSTT	stepparent	AEFGIILLOR	florilegia	AEFIILQRSU	qualifiers
AEENPRRSTU	enraptures	AEFGIILNNR	fingernail	AEFIIMMNOS	ammonifies
AEENPRSSSS	sparseness	AEFGIILNSV	lifesaving	AEFIINNRST	infantries
AEENQRSSSU	squareness	AEFGIIMNRS	magnifiers	AEFIINOPRS	saponifier
AEENRRSSTU	saunterers	AEFGIINMNR	refraining	AEFIINOPSS	saponifies
AEENRRSSTV	transverse	AEFGIIRRST	gratifiers	AEFIINQRTU	quantifier
AEENRRSTUV	nervatures	AEFGIIRTUV	figurative	AEFIINQSTU	quantifies
AEENSSSTTU	astuteness	AEFGIKMNRR	fingermark	AEFIINRSTU	infuriates
AEEOOPRSTZ	azeotropes	AEFGILLNNN	flanneling	AEFIIRSSST	satisfiers
AEEOOPPRSSU	peasoupers	AEFGILMNNU	meaningful	AEFIIRSSTT	stratifies
AEEOOPRRSTT	tetraspore	AEFGILMNOS	flamingoes	AEFIJLRSTT	rijsttafel
AEEOPRRTWW	waterpower	AEFGILMRUV	vermifugal	AEFILLNNRY	infernally
AEEOOPRSSV	overpasses	AEFGILNNTT	flattening	AEFILLNNUZ	influenzal
AEEOPRSSTT	poetasters	AEFGILNORT	refloating	AEFILLNOST	fellations
AEEOORRSSTV	overassert	AEFGILNRTT	flattering	AEFILLPRXY	prefixally
AEEOORRSTVW	overwaters	AEFGILOPRT	profligate	AEFILLRUWY	wearifully
AEEOORRSTVY	overstayer	AEFGILRTUY	figurately	AEFILMNSTU	fulminates
AEEORSSSTV	votaresses	AEFGIMNORR	forearming	AEFILMNSTY	manifestly
AEEORSSTTV	overstates	AEFGINNSST	fastenings	AEFILMORRS	formaliser
AEEORSSTTW	twoseaters	AEFGINNRTU	figurantes		Miraflores
AEEPPRRSSST	trespasser	AEFGIORSSS	ossifrages	AEFILMORRZ	formalizer
AEEPRSSSST	trespasses	AEFGIPRRTU	grapefruit	AEFILMORSS	formalises
AEEPRSSTTU	superstate	AEFGISSTTU	fustigates	AEFILMORSZ	formalizes
AEEPRSSTUX	supertaxes	AEFGKLNRTU	Klagenfurt	AEFILMORTW	wolframite
AEEPRSSWXY	expressway	AEFGLLLMSU	flagellums	AEFILNNSUZ	influenzas
AEEQRSTTTU	quartettes	AEFGLLRTUY	gratefully	AEFILNORST	reflations
AEEQRSTUUX	exequaturs	AEFGLNOSST	flagstones	AEFILNORSU	laniferous
AEEQSSTTUU	statuesque	AEFGLNRSSU	frugalness	AEFILNORSY	farinosely
AEERRRSSSU	reassurers	AEFGLNRTUU	ungrateful	AEFILNORTU	fluorinate
AEERRRSSTU	serratures	AEFGLRSTUU	fulgurates	AEFILNSSTU	faultiness
	treasurers	AEFGLSSTTU	Gulf States	AEFILNSTTU	flauntiest
AEERRRSSTV	traversers	AEFGNORSTX	xenografts	AEFILOQRTU	quatrefoil
AEERRSTTVX	extraverts	AEFHHLORTY	Holy Father	AEFILORSSU	saliferous
AEESSSSTUX	East Sussex	AEFHHLOSTW	heathfowls	AEFILRSSTW	welfarists
AEESSTTTTU	statuettes	AEFHIILSSS	sailfishes	AEFIMMNOST	manifestos
AEFFGGINRU	gauffering	AEFHIINRTT	interfaith	AEFIMMORSSS	misfeasors
AEFFGINRST	restaffing	AEFHIIRRTW	white friar	AEFIMORSTU	fumatories
AEFFHILLSS	fallfishes	AEFHIKLRSY	freakishly	AEFINNRSSU	unfairness
AEFFHILSST	flatfishes	AEFHIKMSST	makeshifts	AEFINOOPRT	fortepiano
AEFFHNORRU	Fraunhofer	AEFHILNSSS	flashiness		pianoforte
AEFFIIINST	affinities	AEFHILPSST	fishplates	AEFINOPRRS	poriferans
AEFFIIINTV	affinitive	AEFHIMMNST	famishment	AEFINORRST	rainforest
AEFFIILRSS	falsifiers	AEFHINORSS	fashioners	AEFINORTTU	refutation
AEFFIKPSST	pikestaffs		refashions	AEFINRRTTY	fraternity
AEFFILNSTU	insufflate	AEFHINOSSS	oafishness	AEFINRSSTX	transfixes
AEFFILRSST	tariffless	AEFHIRSSST	starfishes	AEFIOPRSTU	fetiparous

AEFIORRSUU auriferous	**AEGGIILLNZ** legalizing	**AEGHILLNRT** allnighter
AEFIORSTUV favourites	**AEGGIILMPR** pilgrimage	**AEGHILMORT** lithomarge
AEFKLNORSY forsakenly	**AEGGIILNNR** engrailing	**AEGHILNNSU** unleashing
AEFKLNOSSW snowflakes	realigning	**AEGHILNOOT** theologian
AEFKLORSSW falseworks	**AEGGIILNTV** levigating	**AEGHILNRSS** ringhalses
AEFKMORRSW frameworks	**AEGGIIMNNT** geminating	shearlings
AEFKNNORSU unforsaken	**AEGGIIMNRT** emigrating	**AEGHILNRST** earthlings
AEFLLLOPWY playfellow	**AEGGIINNNR** engraining	slathering
AEFLLLORWW wallflower	**AEGGIINNSV** envisaging	**AEGHILNSSU** languishes
AEFLLLSSWY flawlessly	**AEGGIINNTV** negativing	**AEGHILNSSV** shavelings
AEFLLNOSSW fallowness	**AEGGIJMRST** jiggermast	**AEGHILNTTY** ethylating
AEFLLNSSUW lawfulness	**AEGGILLNRV** gravelling	**AEGHILPRXY** lexigraphy
AEFLLORSST forestalls	**AEGGILLNNT** entangling	**AEGHILSSTT** ghastliest
AEFLLORSSV flavorless	**AEGGILNNOT** elongating	**AEGHIMMOPR** mimeograph
AEFLLSTTUV tastefully	**AEGGILNRTU** regulating	**AEGHIMNRST** nightmares
AEFLLSTUWY wastefully	**AEGGILOOSU** sialogogue	**AEGHIMORRS** hierograms
AEFLMNNSSU manfulness	**AEGGIMNNRT** garmenting	**AEGHIMPPRS** epiphragms
AEFLMNORSS formalness	margenting	**AEGHIMSTTT** steamtight
AEFLMOORSV flavorsome	**AEGGIMNNTU** augmenting	**AEGHINNORS** hoarsening
AEFLMOOSSW Law of Moses	**AEGGIMNRRS** grangerism	**AEGHINNPPS** happenings
AEFLMORRSV salverform	**AEGGIMNRRT** triggerman	**AEGHINNPRS** sharpening
AEFLMORSTU formulates	**AEGGINNRST** estranging	**AEGHINNRSS** harnessing
AEFLMORSWY mayflowers	**AEGGINNRSV** engravings	**AEGHINNRTU** unearthing
AEFLNOPRRT prefrontal	**AEGGINORSS** aggression	**AEGHINNSTW** enswathing
AEFLNOPSTU pantoufles	**AEGGINQSSU** quagginess	**AEGHINPPRS** preshaping
AEFLNRSSTU artfulness	**AEGGIORRSU** gregarious	**AEGHINPRRS** rephrasing
AEFLOOPSTT footplates	**AEGGJNRTUU** juggernaut	**AEGHINPRSS** springhase
AEFLORRSTW starflower	**AEGGLLNOOY** angelology	**AEGHINPRSW** prewashing
AEFLORRSUV flavourers	**AEGGLNOSSW** waggonless	**AEGHINRRSS** garnishers
AEFLORSTWW waterfowls	**AEGGLOORTY** geratology	**AEGHINRSSS** garishness
AEFMMORRST Tammerfors	**AEGGLRRSST** stragglers	**AEGHINRSTT** shattering
AEFMNOSSSU famousness	**AEGGMORRST** mortgagers	straighten
AEFMOORRST Amersfoort	**AEGGMOSTUY** mystagogue	**AEGHINRSTV** harvesting
AEFMOPRRST permafrost	**AEGGNNOORY** organogeny	**AEGHINSTTU** naughtiest
AEFNNOORST afternoons	**AEGGNNORSU** gangrenous	**AEGHINSTUX** exhausting
AEFNNOSSST Stefansson	**AEGGNOSSUY** synagogues	**AEGHIPRRSS** serigraphs
AEFNORRRST transferor	**AEGGOORSSS** goosegrass	**AEGHIPRRSY** serigraphy
AEFNORRTTW waterfront	**AEGGORRSSS** aggressors	**AEGHIRRSTT** straighter
AEFNORSTVW wavefronts	**AEGHHILLLS** shillelagh	**AEGHIRTTTW** watertight
AEFNRRSSTU transfuser	**AEGHHILOPR** heliograph	**AEGHISSSTT** tightasses
AEFNRSSSTU transfuses	**AEGHHILRTT** earthlight	**AEGHLLMPSY** megaphylls
AEFOOPRRRT perforator	**AEGHHIMNWY** highwaymen	**AEGHLMOOOT** homologate
AEFOOPRRTW waterproof	**AEGHHINSST** sheathings	**AEGHLMOOTY** hematology
AEFOORRSTT tortfeasor	**AEGHHISTTU** haughtiest	**AEGHLMORTU** largemouth
AEFOQRRSUU foursquare	**AEGHHLORSU** horselaugh	**AEGHLNNOOP** anglophone
AEFRRRSTTU frustrater	**AEGHHMOPPT** apophthegm	**AEGHLNOORR** gonorrheal
AEFRRSSTTU frustrates	**AEGHHNOPPR** nephograph	**AEGHLNOORS** alongshore
AEGGGIINRV aggrieving	**AEGHHOPRTY** hyetograph	**AEGHLNOOSU** halogenous
AEGGGIINRW earwigging	**AEGHIIMNRS** mishearing	**AEGHLNSTWY** lengthways
AEGGGILNNY engagingly	**AEGHIINNRT** inearthing	**AEGHLOOORR** logorrhoea
AEGGGINNNR gangrening	**AEGHIINNSV** evanishing	**AEGHLOOPRS** oleographs
AEGGGINRSS aggressing	**AEGHIINRSV** vinegarish	**AEGHLOOPRY** oleography
AEGGGINRST staggering	**AEGHIINSTT** hesitating	**AEGHLOOPST** gospel oath
AEGGGINRSW swaggering	**AEGHIIPRST** graphitise	**AEGHLORSTT** larghettos
AEGGGIRSWW wigwaggers	**AEGHIIPRTZ** graphitize	**AEGHLORSUV** overslaugh
AEGGHIMOPS geophagism	**AEGHIKMMNO** homemaking	**AEGHLOSSSU** glasshouse
AEGGHINRST gatherings	**AEGHIKMNOS** shoemaking	**AEGHLRSSTU** slaughters
AEGGHINNSS shagginess	**AEGHIKNNRS** hankerings	**AEGHMMORRT** thermogram
AEGGHIOPST geophagist	**AEGHIKNNRT** Tengri Khan	**AEGHMNOOPR** gramophone
AEGGHOOPSU geophagous	**AEGHIKNRSS** shrinkages	**AEGHMNOOPR** nephograms
AEGGHOPRRS ergographs	**AEGHILLNNS** hanselling	sphenogram
AEGGIILLNS legalising	**AEGHILLNOP** anglophile	**AEGHMNOSTY** mesognathy

AEGHNOOORR	gonorrhoea	
AEGHNOPRRY	granophyre	
AEGHNOPRST	stenograph	
AEGHNOPRVY	venography	
AEGHNOSSTU	shogunates	
AEGHOOPRRR	orographer	
AEGHOOPRRZ	zoographer	
AEGHOOPSSU	oesophagus	
AEGHOPRRXY	xerography	
AEGIIILNTV	invigilate	
AEGIIIMTTV	mitigative	
AEGIIIRRTV	irrigative	
AEGIIJMNNZ	Jiang Zemin	
AEGIILLLTY	illegality	
AEGIILLPRS	aspergilli	
AEGIILLRSS	grisailles	
AEGIILLRST	argillites	
AEGIILMNNP	impaneling	
AEGIILMNNT	alimenting	
AEGIILMNPR	impearling	
AEGIILMNRT	trigeminal	
AEGIILMNTZ	metalizing	
AEGIILNNOT	toenailing	
AEGIILNNPS	penalising	
AEGIILNNPX	explaining	
AEGIILNNPZ	penalizing	
AEGIILNNRU	ungainlier	
AEGIILNNSS	gainliness	
AEGIILNOST	antilogies	
AEGIILNOTT	etiolating	
AEGIILNOTV	levigation	
AEGIILNPRV	prevailing	
AEGIILNQSU	equalising	
AEGIILNQUZ	equalizing	
AEGIILNRSS	glairiness	
AEGIILNRSV	velarising	
AEGIILNRVZ	velarizing	
AEGIILNSSS	signalises	
AEGIILNSSZ	signalizes	
AEGIILNSTV	vigilantes	
AEGIILNTTV	levitating	
AEGIILRTTT	glitterati	
AEGIIMMRST	immigrates	
AEGIIMMSTT	migmatites	
AEGIIMNNOT	gemination	
AEGIIMNORS	agrimonies	
AEGIIMNORT	emigration	
AEGIIMNSTT	estimating	
AEGIIMNSTV	negativism	
	timesaving	
AEGIIMSSTT	stigmatise	
AEGIIMSTTZ	stigmatize	
AEGIINNNRT	entraining	
AEGIINNOST	isoantigen	
AEGIINNPRT	pertaining	
	repainting	
AEGIINNRRT	retraining	
AEGIINNRSS	graininess	
AEGIINNRST	resinating	
AEGIINNRTT	intreating	
	intrigante	
AEGIINNSST	tetanising	
AEGIINNTTZ	tetanizing	
AEGIINORST	originates	
AEGIINORTV	invigorate	
AEGIINOSTT	goniatites	
AEGIINPPST	appetising	
AEGIINPPTZ	appetizing	
AEGIINSSTT	instigates	
AEGIINSTTV	estivating	
	negativist	
AEGIINTTVY	negativity	
AEGIINTUVX	exuviating	
AEGIIRRSTT	geriatrist	
AEGIIRSTTT	targetitis	
AEGIIRSTTU	gratuities	
AEGIISSSTV	visagistes	
AEGIJNORSS	jargonises	
AEGIJNORSZ	jargonizes	
AEGIKKMNRS	kingmakers	
AEGIKLLOOR	Kalgoorlie	
AEGIKLMMOR	kilogramme	
AEGIKLMNOV	lovemaking	
AEGIKLNNSY	sneakingly	
AEGIKLRSTV	Lagerkvist	
AEGIKMNNOS	maskinonge	
AEGIKNNPSU	unspeaking	
AEGIKNNSST	takingness	
AEGIKNOPRS	presoaking	
AEGIKNORTV	overtaking	
AEGILLLNRU	laurelling	
AEGILLLNSU	gallinules	
AEGILLMNRV	marvelling	
AEGILLMNRY	germinally	
AEGILLNORY	regionally	
AEGILLNOXY	glyoxaline	
AEGILLNPPR	rappelling	
AEGILLNPSY	pleasingly	
AEGILLNRSS	signallers	
AEGILLNRTV	travelling	
AEGILLNRTY	integrally	
AEGILLNSST	tasselling	
AEGILLOPTT	epiglottal	
AEGILLORST	allegorist	
	legislator	
AEGILLPRSS	aspergills	
AEGILLRRSU	guerrillas	
AEGILLRSSS	salesgirls	
AEGILLRSST	allergists	
	gallerists	
AEGILMMNRT	trammeling	
AEGILMNNST	alignments	
	signalment	
AEGILMNOOP	monoplegia	
AEGILMNORS	rosemaling	
AEGILMNORY	mineralogy	
AEGILMORRS	glamoriser	
	rigmaroles	
AEGILMORRZ	glamorizer	
AEGILMORSS	glamorises	
AEGILMORSZ	glamorizes	
AEGILMORUZ	glamourize	
AEGILMSTTU	multistage	
AEGILNNNPR	replanning	
AEGILNNNRU	unlearning	
AEGILNNOOT	elongation	
AEGILNNOSU	lanuginose	
AEGILNNPRT	replanting	
AEGILNNPSU	unpleasing	
AEGILNNPTX	explanting	
AEGILNNRUV	unraveling	
AEGILNNRVY	raveningly	
AEGILNNRYY	yearningly	
AEGILNNSSS	slanginess	
AEGILNNSUY	sanguinely	
AEGILNOOSU	oleaginous	
AEGILNOPTU	outleaping	
AEGILNORSU	lanigerous	
	neuroglias	
AEGILNORTT	tolerating	
AEGILNORTU	regulation	
	urogenital	
AEGILNORVY	overlaying	
AEGILNOSTU	gelatinous	
AEGILNPPRY	reapplying	
AEGILNPRST	plastering	
AEGILNPRSU	pleasuring	
AEGILNPRTY	taperingly	
AEGILNQRRU	quarreling	
AEGILNRSTU	granulites	
AEGILNRSTV	starveling	
AEGILNRVWY	waveringly	
AEGILNRWYY	wearyingly	
AEGILNSSSS	glassiness	
AEGILOOPRS	apologiser	
AEGILOOPRZ	apologizer	
AEGILOOPSS	apologises	
AEGILOOPSZ	apologizes	
AEGILOORST	aerologist	
AEGILOPRTT	graptolite	
AEGILORRSS	gressorial	
AEGILORRSS	glossaries	
AEGILORSTV	levigators	
AEGILPPRRS	papergirls	
AEGILRRRSU	irregulars	
AEGILRRSUV	vulgariser	
AEGILRRTUY	regularity	
AEGILRRUVZ	vulgarizer	
AEGILRSSUV	vulgarises	
AEGILRSTTZ	Salzgitter	
AEGILRSUVZ	vulgarizes	
AEGIMMNOST	gemmations	
AEGIMMNRST	stammering	
AEGIMMNNORS	omniranges	
AEGIMMNNORU	enamouring	
AEGIMNNRST	smartening	
AEGIMNNRTU	numerating	
AEGIMNNSST	assignment	
AEGIMNNSTY	amnestying	
AEGIMNOPRS	angiosperm	
AEGIMNORRT	germinator	
AEGIMNORSU	gramineous	
AEGIMNPRRW	prewarming	
AEGIMNPRSV	revampings	
AEGIMNPRTY	pigmentary	
AEGIMNPTTT	attempting	

AEGIMNRRRY	remarrying	**AEGIRSSTTT**	strategist	**AEHHIMNNOPV**	Phomvihane
AEGIMNRRST	ringmaster	**AEGKLNOOPS**	pokelogans	**AEHHINOPRT**	hierophant
AEGIMNRSSU	reassuming	**AEGKORSSTT**	agterskots	**AEHHLMNSUU**	Mühlhausen
AEGIMNRSTT	smattering	**AEGLLLLNNO**	Llangollen	**AEHHLNOPTT**	heptathlon
AEGIMNSSTT	magnetists	**AEGLLMORRU**	glomerular	**AEHHLOPSTY**	halophytes
AEGIMOOSTV	vagotomies	**AEGLLMRTUY**	metallurgy	**AEHHMOOOPT**	homoeopath
AEGIMORRSU	armigerous	**AEGLLNNPTY**	plangently	**AEHHMOOPST**	homeopaths
AEGIMORRTY	emigratory	**AEGLLNOPSW**	alpenglows	**AEHHMOOPTY**	homeopathy
AEGIMOSSTY	stegomyias	**AEGLLNOSST**	gallstones	**AEHHNNOOPRT**	anthophore
AEGIMRRTVY	gravimetry	**AEGLLOPRSU**	pellagrous	**AEHHOPPSST**	phosphates
AEGINNNNOR	nonearning	**AEGLMMORSY**	myelograms	**AEHHPSSTTU**	Hatshepsut
AEGINNNOTV	nonvintage	**AEGLMNOOOV**	avgolemono	**AEHIIILNNS**	Sinhailien
AEGINNNPRT	trepanning	**AEGLMNORSS**	lemongrass	**AEHIIKLRTW**	wraithlike
AEGINNORST	resonating	**AEGLMNORSW**	angleworms	**AEHIILLLNT**	Lilienthal
AEGINNORSZ	organzines	**AEGLMOOSTY**	sematology	**AEHIILMSTU**	humiliates
AEGINNORTV	renovating	**AEGLMOPRTU**	promulgate	**AEHIILOSTX**	heliotaxis
AEGINNOSSS	seasonings	**AEGLNOPRSY**	gyroplanes	**AEHIILPPSY**	epiphysial
AEGINNOSTT	negotiants	**AEGLNOSSTU**	langoustes	**AEHIIMMPSX**	amphimixes
AEGINNPPRT	entrapping	**AEGLNRRSST**	stranglers	**AEHIIMNSTT**	antitheism
AEGINNPPRW	enwrapping	**AEGLNSSSSU**	sunglasses	**AEHIIMNSTU**	humanities
AEGINNPRRT	partnering	**AEGLOOORRST**	astrologer	**AEHIIMPRTT**	Amphitrite
AEGINNPRTT	patterning	**AEGLOORTTY**	teratology	**AEHIIMRSST**	hetairisms
AEGINNRSTT	astringent	**AEGLOPPRSU**	propagules	**AEHIINNRRS**	Nairnshire
	integrants	**AEGLORRSTU**	regulators	**AEHIINORTT**	thorianite
AEGINNRRSTU	sauntering	**AEGLORRTUY**	regulatory	**AEHIINOSTT**	hesitation
AEGINNRSUW	unswearing	**AEGLPRSSUU**	surplusage	**AEHIINPPRS**	sapphirine
AEGINNRUVW	unwavering	**AEGLPSSSSY**	spyglasses	**AEHIINSSTT**	antithesis
AEGINNRUWY	unwearying	**AEGMMNOPRU**	pneumogram	**AEHIINSTTT**	antitheist
AEGINOORTT	negotiator	**AEGMMOPRRR**	programmer	**AEHIIPPSTT**	epitaphist
AEGINOPRRT	perorating	**AEGMMOPRRS**	programmes	**AEHIIRSSTT**	hetairists
AEGINOPRVY	overpaying	**AEGMNNORST**	magnetrons	**AEHIJLOSSU**	jailhouses
AEGINORRSS	organisers	**AEGMNOORST**	gastronome	**AEHIKLNRSS**	rinkhalses
AEGINORRSU	rearousing	**AEGMNOOSUX**	xenogamous	**AEHIKNRSSS**	rakishness
AEGINORRSV	granivores	**AEGMNORRSW**	warmongers	**AEHILLMOPS**	philomelas
AEGINORRSZ	organizers	**AEGMNORSTU**	augmentors	**AEHILLORTY**	heliolatry
AEGINORRTT	integrator	**AEGMNOSTTU**	mangetouts	**AEHILLSTTY**	stealthily
AEGINORRTV	overrating		Mao Tse-tung	**AEHILLSTWW**	whitewalls
AEGINORSTT	gittarones	**AEGNNOOSSU**	nongaseous	**AEHILMNNUY**	inhumanely
AEGINORSUU	aeruginous	**AEGNNRTUUY**	unguentary	**AEHILMNOPY**	anemophily
AEGINORTUW	outwearing	**AEGNOORTXY**	oxygenator	**AEHILMNOSY**	haemolysin
AEGINORTVX	overtaxing	**AEGNOOSTUU**	autogenous	**AEHILMNSTV**	lavishment
AEGINOSSTT	gestations	**AEGNORRSWY**	garryowens	**AEHILMORST**	isothermal
AEGINPPRRW	rewrapping	**AEGNRRSSST**	transgress		thimerosal
AEGINPQRTU	parqueting	**AEGNSSSTUU**	augustness	**AEHILMOSSY**	haemolysis
AEGINPRRSY	respraying	**AEGOOPRSYZ**	azygospore	**AEHILMPSTU**	multiphase
AEGINPRSSS	preassigns	**AEGOORSTUU**	outrageous	**AEHILNOOSZ**	heliozoans
AEGINPRSTT	spattering	**AEGOOSSWYZ**	wayzgooses	**AEHILNOPTT**	thiopental
AEGINPRSTU	supergiant	**AEGOPRRSUW**	groupwares	**AEHILNOSSS**	shoaliness
AEGINPRSTY	panegyrist	**AEGOPRRTUX**	expurgator	**AEHILNOSST**	hailstones
AEGINPSTTU	Septuagint	**AEGORRRSTT**	garrotters	**AEHILNOTTY**	ethylation
AEGINQRRTU	quartering	**AEGORRSSTU**	surrogates	**AEHILNPRSS**	planishers
AEGINRRSSU	reassuring	**AEGORRSTTU**	Great Stour	**AEHILNQRSU**	harlequins
AEGINRRSTT	registrant	**AEGORSSSTU**	stegosaurs	**AEHILNSSSV**	lavishness
	restarting	**AEGPRRSSSU**	supergrass	**AEHILNSTTY**	hesitantly
AEGINRRSTU	garnitures	**AEHHHHILOPT**	Ahithophel	**AEHILOPRST**	hospitaler
	treasuring	**AEHHIILMOP**	hemophilia	**AEHILOPSTT**	Hospitalet
AEGINRRSTV	traversing	**AEHHILLOPS**	halophiles	**AEHILORSST**	horsetails
AEGINRSSSS	grassiness	**AEHHILNPST**	phthaleins	**AEHILORSVV**	overlavish
AEGINRSSSU	sugariness	**AEHHILNSTU**	helianthus	**AEHILOSSTT**	heliostats
AEGINRSSTU	signatures	**AEHHILPSSW**	whiplashes	**AEHILOTTVW**	White Volta
AEGIPRSTUV	purgatives	**AEHHIMMSSS**	mishmashes	**AEHILPSSST**	splashiest
AEGIRRRSST	registrars			**AEHILRSSTY**	hairstyles

AEHILRSTVY	shrievalty
AEHIMMPRRT	triphammer
AEHIMMRSTU	rheumatism
AEHIMNNPPS	penmanship
AEHIMNORRS	harmoniser
AEHIMNORRZ	harmonizer
AEHIMNORSS	harmonises
AEHIMNORSZ	harmonizes
AEHIMNOTUX	exhumation
AEHIMNRSSS	marshiness
AEHIMNRSSU	humanisers
AEHIMNRSTV	ravishment
AEHIMNRSUZ	humanizers
AEHIMNSSTU	enthusiasm
AEHIMOOPTY	mythopoeia
AEHIMOPRSY	hyperosmia
AEHIMOPSTY	myopathies
AEHIMOSSST	hemostasis
AEHIMPRSST	mastership
	shipmaster
AEHIMPSSST	steamships
AEHIMPSSTT	empathists
AEHIMPSSTY	sympathies
	sympathise
AEHIMPSTYZ	sympathize
AEHINOPRTU	euphoriant
AEHINORRTV	hovertrain
AEHINOSSST	astonishes
AEHINOSTUX	exhaustion
AEHINPPSTU	unhappiest
AEHINPRSUW	wharepunis
AEHINPSSTT	pantheists
AEHINQRSUV	vanquisher
AEHINQSSUV	vanquishes
AEHINRRSST	tarnishers
AEHINRRSSU	varnishers
AEHINRRSST	trashiness
AEHINSSTTU	enthusiast
AEHIOOPSST	apotheosis
AEHIORRSTU	authoriser
AEHIORRTUZ	authorizer
AEHIORSSTT	hesitators
AEHIORSSTU	authorises
AEHIORSSTV	tovarishes
AEHIORSTTT	throatiest
AEHIORSTUZ	authorizes
AEHIPRSSTT	therapists
AEHIQSSSTU	squashiest
AEHIRSSTTW	swarthiest
	sweatshirt
AEHKLOPRSW	shopwalker
AEHKMNOSTU	snakemouth
AEHKNOORRT	North Korea
AEHKOORSTU	South Korea
AEHKORRSTW	earthworks
AEHLLMRSSY	harmlessly
AEHLLMSTUU	haustellum
AEHLLNOOPS	allophones
AEHLLOOPRT	Hartlepool
AEHLLOORWW	hollowware
AEHLLOPRXY	phylloxera
AEHLLOSSTW	shallowest

AEHLMOOSUX	homosexual
AEHLMORTTY	methylator
AEHLMOSSSU	almshouses
AEHLMPSSYY	symphyseal
AEHLNNOPRS	alpenhorns
AEHLNNOPTT	pentathlon
AEHLNOPSTU	houseplant
	sulphonate
AEHLOOPRRY	pyorrhoeal
AEHLOPRSSW	plowshares
AEHLOPSSUY	playhouses
AEHLORSTUU	outhaulers
AEHLPRSTUU	sulphurate
AEHLRTTUUV	truth-value
AEHMNNORWY	New Harmony
AEHMNNRSTU	manhunters
AEHMNOOOTZ	hematozoon
AEHMNOOPRT	homopteran
AEHMNOORSW	horsewoman
AEHMNORRTT	Matterhorn
AEHMNORRTW	harrowment
AEHMNPRSUU	superhuman
AEHMNPRTWY	water nymph
AEHMNRSTUY	Erymanthus
AEHMOOPRSS	shampooers
AEHMOORSTX	mesothorax
AEHMORRSTW	earthworms
	heartworms
AEHMORSTTT	thermostat
AEHMORSTWW	wheatworms
AEHMQSSSUU	musquashes
AEHNNNOOTY	hootenanny
AEHNOOPRRS	harpooners
AEHNOOPSSU	sousaphone
AEHNOOPSSX	saxophones
AEHNOPRSTU	neuropaths
AEHNOPRSTY	honeytraps
AEHNOPRTUY	neuropathy
AEHNORRSTW	Rawsthorne
AEHNRSSSTW	swarthness
AEHOOPPRST	apostrophe
AEHOOPRRTT	orthoptera
AEHOOPRYZZ	Zaporozhye
AEHOOPSSTT	osteopaths
AEHOOPSTTT	toothpaste
AEHOOPSTTY	osteopathy
AEHOORSSTY	soothsayer
AEHOPPRSTY	saprophyte
AEHOPSSSTW	sweatshops
AEHOPSSSTY	hypostases
AEHOPSTTUY	autophytes
AEHORRRSTW	restharrow
AEHPRSSTTY	strathspey
AEIIIIINRR	Rainier III
AEIIIILNST	initialise
AEIIIILNTZ	initialize
AEIIIINTTV	initiative
AEIIILLNRT	initialler
AEIIILLNSV	villainies
AEIIILMMNT	militiamen
AEIIILMRST	militaries
	militarise

AEIIILMRTZ	militarize
AEIIILNRST	initialers
AEIIILRSTV	trivialise
AEIIILRTVZ	trivialize
AEIIILSTTV	vitalities
AEIIILSTVX	lixiviates
AEIIIMMNPR	imipramine
AEIIIMNRST	ministeria
AEIIIMPRST	imparities
AEIIINNSST	insanities
AEIIINSTTV	nativities
AEIIIPRSVV	viviparies
AEIIIRRTTV	irritative
AEIIJMORST	majorities
AEIIKKSTTW	kittiwakes
AEIIKLLNPR	painkiller
AEIIKLMRSY	Yeşil Irmak
AEIIKLNOSZ	kaolinizes
AEIILLLMMS	millesimal
AEIILLLMNN	millennial
AEIILLLTVY	illatively
AEIILLMNSS	sinsemilla
AEIILLMNTU	illuminate
AEIILLMOST	molalities
AEIILLMPRY	imperially
AEIILLMRST	literalism
AEIILLNRTU	uniliteral
AEIILLNSSV	villainess
AEIILLOSTV	volatilise
AEIILLOTVZ	volatilize
AEIILLPRTT	tripletail
AEIILLPSTT	pistillate
AEIILLRRTT	triliteral
AEIILLRRTY	literarily
AEIILLRSTT	literalist
AEIILLRSTV	silvertail
AEIILLRTTY	literality
AEIILLSTTT	titillates
AEIILMMMOR	immemorial
AEIILMNNRS	mainliners
AEIILMNNST	eliminants
AEIILMNORT	eliminator
AEIILMNOSZ	iminazoles
AEIILMNRSU	luminaries
AEIILMNSSU	aluminises
AEIILMNSTY	seminality
AEIILMNSUZ	aluminizes
AEIILMNTTY	intimately
AEIILMORST	molarities
	moralities
AEIILMOSSS	isoseismal
AEIILMPPSS	misapplies
AEIILMRSTV	relativism
AEIILMRSVV	revivalism
AEIILMSTUV	simulative
AEIILMTTUV	mutilative
AEIILMTTUZ	Mutazilite
AEIILNNOOP	Napoleon II
AEIILNNORS	rosaniline
AEIILNNOST	lineations
AEIILNNRST	triennials
AEIILNNSTT	intestinal

AEIILNOOTT	etiolation	AEIINOPPTV	appointive	AEILLNRSTU	tellurians
AEIILNOPST	epilations	AEIINOPRTX	expiration	AEILLNRTTU	Tertullian
AEIILNOPTX	pixelation	AEIINOPSTT	poinsettia	AEILLNRTUY	tenurially
AEIILNORTT	literation	AEIINOPSTX	expiations	AEILLOPPST	papillotes
AEIILNOSTT	tonalities	AEIINOQTTU	equitation	AEILLPRRSU	pluraliser
AEIILNOTTV	levitation	AEIINORSTT	iterations	AEILLPRRUZ	pluralizer
AEIILNOTUV	eluviation	AEIINOSTTV	estivation	AEILLPRSSU	pluralises
AEIILNPRST	reptilians		novitiates	AEILLPRSUZ	pluralizes
AEIILNPSST	platinises	AEIINOTUVX	exuviation	AEILLPSSTT	pastellist
AEIILNPSTZ	platinizes	AEIINPSSST	antisepsis	AEILLRSSTW	stairwells
AEIILNQTUY	inequality		inspissate	AEILLRSTTU	illustrate
AEIILNSSTT	saintliest	AEIINQSTTU	quantities	AEILMMNNTY	immanently
AEIILNSSTW	waistlines	AEIINQTTUV	quantitive	AEILMMRTUY	immaturely
AEIILOPRST	polarities	AEIINRRSTT	tristearin	AEILMMRUUV	Verulamium
AEIILORSST	solitaires	AEIINRSTTV	transitive	AEILMNNOPR	prenominal
	solitaries	AEIINRTTZZ	tetrazzini	AEILMNNSTT	instalment
AEIILORSTV	variolites	AEIIOPPRTT	propitiate	AEILMNOPRS	impersonal
AEIILOSTTT	totalities	AEIIOPPSTV	appositive		prolamines
AEIILRSSTU	ritualises	AEIIPPSSSW	pipsissewa	AEILMNOPRT	trampoline
AEIILRSSTV	vitalisers	AEIIPRRTTT	tripartite	AEILMNORSS	normalises
AEIILRSSUV	visualiser	AEIIPRSSTV	privatises	AEILMNORSZ	normalizes
AEIILRSTTU	titularies	AEIIPRSTTV	partitives	AEILMNORTU	tourmaline
AEIILRSTTV	relativist	AEIIPRSTVZ	privatizes	AEILMNORTY	monetarily
AEIILRSTTZ	strelitzia	AEIIRRSSST	satirisers	AEILMNOSTU	emulations
AEIILRSTUZ	ritualizes	AEIIRRSSTV	arrivistes	AEILMNOSTY	melanosity
AEIILRSTVV	revivalist	AEIIRRSSTZ	satirizers	AEILMNPRST	implanters
AEIILRSTVZ	vitalizers	AEIISTTTTV	tittivates	AEILMNPRTY	planimetry
AEIILRSUVZ	visualizer	AEIJKLRSUZ	Jaruzelski	AEILMNPSSU	aspleniums
AEIILRTTVY	relativity	AEIJLNORSU	journalise	AEILMNPSTU	penultimas
AEIILSSSUV	visualises	AEIJLNORUZ	journalize	AEILMNRSTU	neutralism
AEIILSSUVZ	visualizes	AEIJLNOSSV	jovialness	AEILMNSSSU	sensualism
AEIIMMNPRT	impairment	AEIJNNSSTU	jauntiness	AEILMNSSTT	mentalists
AEIIMMNRST	antimerism	AEIJNOOPRT	pejoration	AEILMOORRT	meliorator
AEIIMMNSSS	messianism	AEIKKLLOOS	lookalikes	AEILMOPPSS	ampelopsis
AEIIMMRSSX	maximisers	AEIKKNNSSS	snakeskins	AEILMOPRST	peristomal
AEIIMMRSXZ	maximizers	AEIKLMNOSS	kalsomines	AEILMOPSST	semipostal
AEIIMNNNOT	innominate	AEIKLMNSTY	mistakenly	AEILMORRSS	moralisers
AEIIMNNOST	antinomies	AEIKLNSSST	stalkiness	AEILMORRSZ	moralizers
	semination	AEIKLNSSTU	Eskilstuna	AEILMORSTV	removalist
AEIIMNNOTV	nominative	AEIKMNPRRT	printmaker	AEILMOSSTU	mousetails
AEIIMNORSU	iminoureas	AEIKNNPRSS	spinnakers	AEILMPPSST	palimpsest
AEIIMNOSTT	estimation	AEIKNNSSSW	swankiness	AEILMPRSST	slipstream
AEIIMNPQRU	primaquine	AEIKNRSTTU	Turkestani	AEILMPRSTU	psalterium
AEIIMNQRTU	Martinique	AEIKPPQSSU	pipsqueaks	AEILMRRSSU	surrealism
AEIIMNQTUY	equanimity	AEILLLOTWY	yellowtail	AEILMRRSTT	trimestral
AEIIMNRSTT	intimaters	AEILLLSSTY	taillessly	AEILMRSTTU	stimulater
AEIIMNRSTU	miniatures	AEILLLSUVY	allusively	AEILMSSTTU	stimulates
AEIIMNRTUV	ruminative	AEILLLMMORS	allomerism	AEILMSSTUU	mutualises
AEIIMOPRRS	impresario	AEILLMMORY	memorially	AEILMSTTUX	textualism
AEIIMOTTVV	motivative	AEILLMMRST	millstream	AEILMSTUUZ	mutualizes
AEIIMPTTUV	imputative	AEILLMNPTU	multiplane	AEILNNOPRS	nonpareils
AEIIMRSTTU	maturities	AEILLMNRTY	terminally	AEILNNOPTT	antilepton
AEIINNNSTV	antivenins	AEILLMPRVY	primevally	AEILNNORTT	intolerant
AEIINNORSV	reinvasion	AEILLMSSTT	metallists	AEILNNOSST	nationless
AEIINNOTVV	innovative	AEILLMTTUY	ultimately	AEILNNOSTV	antinovels
AEIINNPRTT	tripinnate	AEILLNNRTY	internally	AEILNNPRSU	peninsular
AEIINNPRTY	antipyrine	AEILLNOPST	pollinates	AEILNNPSST	pliantness
AEIINNPSTT	inpatients	AEILLNOPTT	potentilla	AEILNNPSSU	peninsulas
AEIINNRSTT	itinerants	AEILLNPSST	panellists	AEILNNRTUU	interlunar
AEIINNRSTU	uraninites	AEILLNPSSY	painlessly	AEILNNSTWY	Winstanley
AEIINNSSTU	insinuates	AEILLNRSST	installers	AEILNOOPRT	tropaeolin
AEIINOPPST	inapposite		reinstalls	AEILNOOPSS	polonaises

AEILNOORTT	toleration	**AEIMMNRSSS**	smarminess	**AEINNOSTTV**	nonstative
AEILNOPRRT	interpolar	**AEIMMNRRTTU**	manumitter	**AEINNPPSSS**	snappiness
AEILNOPRST	interposal	**AEIMMNSSTZ**	mizenmasts	**AEINNQSSTU**	quaintness
AEILNOPSST	sealpoints	**AEIMMNSTZZ**	mizzenmast	**AEINNRRSTY**	tyranniser
AEILNOPSTT	peltations	**AEIMMPRSTU**	spermatium	**AEINNRRTYZ**	tyrannizer
	potentials	**AEIMMRRSSU**	summariser	**AEINNRSSTT**	transients
AEILNORRTT	torrential	**AEIMMRRSUZ**	summarizer	**AEINNRSSTY**	tyrannises
AEILNORTTV	ventilator	**AEIMMRSSSU**	summarises	**AEINNRSSUW**	unwariness
AEILNOTTUX	exultation	**AEIMMRSSUZ**	summarizes	**AEINNRSTUV**	aventurins
AEILNPPRTU	prenuptial	**AEIMNNNOST**	Minnesotan	**AEINNRSTYZ**	tyrannizes
AEILNPRSST	paltriness	**AEIMNNNOTT**	anointment	**AEINNSSSZZ**	snazziness
	straplines	**AEIMNNNQSU**	mannequins	**AEINOOPPRT**	apoprotein
AEILNPRSTY	interplays	**AEIMNNNORTU**	numeration		propionate
AEILNRSSTT	sterilants	**AEIMNNNOSTT**	mentations	**AEINOOPRRT**	peroration
AEILNRSSUV	universals	**AEIMNNNRSST**	mannerists	**AEINOOPRST**	operations
AEILNRSSUY	urinalyses	**AEIMNOOSTU**	autonomies	**AEINOPPPRT**	preappoint
AEILNRSTTU	neutralist	**AEIMNOOSTX**	taxonomies	**AEINOPPRRS**	Proserpina
AEILNRTTUY	neutrality	**AEIMNOPRST**	protamines	**AEINOPPRST**	appointers
AEILNRTTWW	Written Law	**AEIMNOPRTT**	armipotent		reappoints
AEILNSSSTU	sensualist		portamenti	**AEINOPRRST**	patroniser
AEILNSSTUU	nautiluses	**AEIMNOPTTT**	temptation		periastron
AEILNSSTUY	sensuality	**AEIMNOQSUU**	equanimous	**AEINOPRRTZ**	patronizer
AEILOOPRST	Portlaoise	**AEIMNORRST**	ironmaster	**AEINOPRSSS**	aspersions
AEILOOPTTZ	topazolite	**AEIMNORRTT**	terminator	**AEINOPRSST**	patronises
AEILOPPRSU	popularise	**AEIMNORSSW**	womanisers	**AEINOPRSSU**	persuasion
AEILOPPRSY	polyparies	**AEIMNORSTT**	monetarist	**AEINOPRSSV**	pervasions
AEILOPPRUZ	popularize	**AEIMNORSWZ**	womanizers	**AEINOPRSTZ**	patronizes
AEILOPPSTY	appositely	**AEIMNPPRST**	pentaprism	**AEINOPRTTU**	reputation
AEILOPRRSS	polarisers	**AEIMNPSTTY**	tympanites	**AEINOPTTTU**	outpatient
AEILOPRRSZ	polarizers	**AEIMNRRRTY**	intermarry	**AEINOQRSTU**	ortaniques
AEILOPRSST	saprolites	**AEIMNRRSTT**	retransmit	**AEINORRSST**	serrations
AEILOPRSSU	plesiosaur	**AEIMNRSSTU**	antiserums	**AEINORRSTT**	reinstator
AEILOPRSTY	epistolary	**AEIMOOPPST**	pampooties	**AEINORRSTU**	souterrain
AEILOPSTZZ	Pestalozzi	**AEIMOORSTX**	xerostomia	**AEINORRSTV**	overstrain
AEILOQRSTU	questorial	**AEIMOOSTTU**	autotomies		overtrains
AEILORRRTV	retroviral		autotomise	**AEINORSSST**	assertions
AEILORRSTT	literators	**AEIMOOTTUV**	automotive	**AEINORSSSV**	savoriness
AEILORRTTU	elutriator	**AEIMOOTTUZ**	autotomize	**AEINORSSTT**	stationers
AEILORSSTT	aristotles	**AEIMOPRRST**	imperators	**AEINORSSTV**	sovranties
	totalisers	**AEIMOPRRTT**	impetrator	**AEINORSSTY**	tyrosinase
AEILORSTTU	staurolite	**AEIMOPRTUU**	eupatorium	**AEINORSTTY**	stationery
AEILORSTTV	levitators	**AEIMORRSTU**	mortuaries	**AEINPRRSST**	transpires
AEILORSTTZ	totalizers	**AEIMORSSTT**	estimators	**AEINPRRTTU**	parturient
AEILORSTUW	outlawries	**AEIMORSTTU**	autotimers	**AEINPRSTTT**	strepitant
AEILORTTVY	rotatively	**AEIMPRSSTU**	pasteurism	**AEINQRTTUY**	quaternity
AEILPRRSTY	peristylar	**AEIMPRSTUU**	Maupertuis	**AEINRRSSST**	starriness
AEILPRSSTT	prelatists	**AEIMPRSTUZ**	trapeziums	**AEINRRSSTT**	restraints
AEILPSSSTT	pastelists	**AEIMPSSTUV**	assumptive	**AEINRSSSTT**	resistants
AEILPSSTTU	stipulates	**AEIMQRSTUZ**	quizmaster		straitness
AEILPTTUVY	putatively	**AEIMRRRSTU**	terrariums	**AEINRSSSTU**	sustainers
AEILRRSSTU	surrealist	**AEIMRRSSTY**	martyrises	**AEINRSTUYZ**	suzerainty
AEILRSTTUV	lustrative	**AEIMRRSTYZ**	martyrizes	**AEIOOPPRST**	propositae
AEILRSTTUZ	Austerlitz	**AEINNOORST**	resonation	**AEIOPRRRST**	respirator
AEILRSTUUX	luxuriates	**AEINNOORTV**	renovation	**AEIOPRRSSV**	vaporisers
AEILSTTTUX	textualist	**AEINNOPRSY**	pensionary	**AEIOPRRSTU**	Praetorius
AEIMMMNOST	mammonites	**AEINNOPSSX**	expansions	**AEIOPRRSVZ**	vaporizers
AEIMMNNOOS	monoamines	**AEINNOQRTU**	quaternion	**AEIOPRRTTX**	extirpator
AEIMMNNRSS	mannerisms	**AEINNORSTT**	stentorian	**AEIOPRRTXY**	expiratory
AEIMMNOPST	pantomimes	**AEINNORSTV**	nervations	**AEIORSSTTV**	estivators
AEIMMNORST	monetarism		vernations	**AEIORSTUVV**	uvarovites
AEIMMNOTUU	autoimmune	**AEINNOSSST**	sensations	**AEIPRSSSTU**	prussiates
AEIMMNPRTT	impartment	**AEINNOSTTT**	attentions	**AEIPRSSTTU**	petaurists

AEIPRSTUUV	usurpative		protonemal	**AEMOPRSSTT**	postmaster
AEIQRSTTUZ	quartzites	**AELMNOOPRY**	lampoonery	**AEMOPRSSTU**	mousetraps
AEIRRSTTTU	triturates	**AELMNOORST**	monolaters	**AEMOPSSTTY**	asymptotes
AEJMNNORUY	journeyman	**AELMNOORSY**	monolayers	**AEMORRSTTY**	astrometry
AEJOPSSTUX	juxtaposes	**AELMNOPRST**	Palmerston	**AENNNOSSTW**	wantonness
AEKKLRRSSY	skylarkers	**AELMNOPRTY**	planometry	**AENNORRSST**	resnatrons
AEKLLMRUWY	lukewarmly	**AELMNOPSTU**	pulmonates	**AENNORRSSW**	narrowness
AEKLMOORST	toolmakers	**AELMNRSTTU**	tremulants	**AENNORRSTT**	nonstarter
AEKLMORSSS	lossmakers	**AELMNSSTUU**	mutualness	**AENOOPRRST**	personator
AEKMMNORSW	markswomen	**AELMOOPRTU**	tropaeolum	**AENOOPRTXY**	paroxytone
AEKMNOOQSU	moonquakes	**AELMOORSSS**	salesrooms	**AENOOPSSST**	postseason
AEKMNOORRS	moonrakers	**AELMOPPRUY**	propylaeum	**AENOORRSST**	resonators
AEKMOORRSV	voorkamers	**AELMOPRTTU**	petrolatum	**AENOORRSTV**	renovators
AEKMOORSSY	karyosomes	**AELMOQSSUU**	squamulose	**AENOORSSTU**	anoestrous
AEKMOORTTY	keratotomy	**AELMOQSSUY**	squamosely		treasonous
AEKMORRSTW	masterwork	**AELMORSSTU**	somersault	**AENOPRRSST**	transposer
AEKMPRRSSS	pressmarks	**AELMORSTTT**	lattermost	**AENOPRSSST**	transposes
AEKNOORSST	snakeroots	**AELNNOPRYY**	pennyroyal	**AENOPRSSUV**	supernovas
AEKNPRRSST	pranksters	**AELNNORSTY**	resonantly	**AENOPRSTTT**	protestant
AEKOOPRRTY	prokaryote	**AELNOPRSTY**	personalty	**AENPRRSTTU**	transputer
AEKOPRSTYY	karyotypes	**AELNORRSTY**	antrorsely	**AENSSTTUVY**	Stuyvesant
AEKORRSTWW	waterworks	**AELNORSTVW**	navelworts	**AEOOPPRRRT**	propraetor
AEKORRSWWX	waxworkers	**AELNORSUVY**	ravenously	**AEOOPPRSTU**	tropopause
AELLLPSTUU	pullulates	**AELNOSSUUY**	nauseously	**AEOOPRSSTU**	autospores
AELLMNNOUY	noumenally	**AELNPPRSTU**	supplanter	**AEOOPRSSUX**	auxospores
AELLMNOSTT	allotments	**AELNPRRSUU**	superlunar	**AEOOPRSTTV**	vaporettos
AELLMNOTWY	tallywomen	**AELNRSSTTU**	resultants	**AEOORRSSTV**	overroasts
AELLMOORSU	allomerous	**AELOOPRSVV**	parleyvoos	**AEOORSTTUU**	autoroutes
AELLMOPRSY	permalloys	**AELOOPSSTV**	Sevastopol	**AEOPPRRRTU**	rapporteur
AELLMOPRTY	temporally	**AELOORRSTT**	tolerators	**AEOPRRRSTY**	portrayers
AELLMOPSSY	plasmolyse	**AELOPPRRRU**	pourparler	**AEOPRRSSTT**	prostrates
AELLMOPSYZ	plasmolyze	**AELOPPRTUV**	Upper Volta	**AEOPRRSSTU**	pterosaurs
AELLMORSUV	marvellous	**AELOPRRSTW**	pearlworts	**AEOPRRSSTW**	spearworts
AELLMOSSVY	amylolyses	**AELOPRRSVY**	proslavery		sportswear
AELLNOPPRT	propellant	**AELOPRSSTU**	sporulates	**AEOPRSTTUW**	waterspout
AELLNOPRSY	personally	**AELOPRSSUV**	vapourless	**AEORSSSTUU**	trousseaus
AELLNOPTVY	polyvalent	**AELOPSSTTU**	postulates	**AEORSSTUUX**	trousseaux
AELLNORTTY	tolerantly	**AELORSSSUV**	savourless	**AEPPRSSTUU**	suppurates
AELLNOSSSW	sallowness	**AELPPRSSTU**	Last Supper	**AEPRRSSSTU**	superstars
AELLNOSSTW	stonewalls	**AELPPSSTUY**	platypuses	**AERRSSSTUU**	susurrates
AELLNPRSUY	supernally	**AELPSSTTUU**	pustulates	**AFFGIILNSY**	falsifying
AELLNPTTUY	petulantly	**AEMMNNORRTT**	Montmartre	**AFFGIINORT**	forfaiting
AELLNRSTTY	slatternly	**AEMNNNNOUV**	von Neumann	**AFFGIIRSTT**	graffitist
AELLNTTUXY	exultantly	**AEMNNNOPTY**	nonpayment	**AFFGILNSTU**	sufflating
AELLOOPRST	allotropes	**AEMNNOOSST**	stonemason	**AFFGIMRSSU**	suffragism
AELLOPRRST	patrollers	**AEMNNORSTT**	remontants	**AFFGINNORT**	affronting
AELLOPRSTW	potwallers	**AEMNNORTTT**	attornment	**AFFGIRSSTU**	suffragist
	wallposter	**AEMNNORTTU**	tournament	**AFFGNOORST**	stroganoff
AELLORSSWW	swallowers	**AEMNNRRSUY**	nurseryman	**AFFHILLTUY**	faithfully
AELLRSSTVY	sylvestral	**AEMNOOPRTT**	portamento	**AFFHILNTUU**	unfaithful
AELLRTTUXY	texturally	**AEMNOORRST**	astronomer	**AFFIILNPST**	plaintiffs
AELMMNNOTU	monumental	**AEMNOORSTX**	taxonomers	**AFFIIMNRSU**	ruffianism
AELMMOOPSS	plasmosome	**AEMNOORTXY**	axonometry	**AFFILNOSTU**	sufflation
AELMMOPRRW	palmerworm	**AEMNOPRSUW**	superwoman	**AFFILORSSY**	fairyfloss
AELMMORSST	maelstroms	**AEMNORRSTT**	Montserrat	**AFFLLMOPUW**	mallowpuff
AELMMOSSUU	mausoleums	**AEMNORRSTU**	numerators	**AFFLLORUUV**	flavourful
AELMMNNRUY	unmannerly	**AEMNORSSTT**	assortment	**AFFLOPSSTW**	plowstaffs
AELMMNNSTU	annulments	**AEMNORSSTU**	sarmentous	**AFGGGILNNU**	unflagging
AELMNNOOPS	monoplanes	**AEMNRRSTTU**	transmuter	**AFGGIILNNY**	anglifying
AELMNNOOTV	monovalent	**AEMNRSSTTU**	transmutes	**AFGGIIMNNY**	magnifying
AELMNNOOPRS	lampooners	**AEMOOPSTTY**	somatotype	**AFGGIIMNTU**	fumigating
AELMNNOOPRT	monopteral	**AEMOORSSTT**	staterooms	**AFGGIINNRT**	ingrafting

AFGGIINRTY	gratifying
AFGHHILLST	flashlight
AFGHIINNOS	fashioning
AFGHIIRSTU	guitarfish
AFGHILLNST	nightfalls
AFGHMOORST	homografts
AFGIIILNNS	finalising
AFGIIILNNZ	finalizing
AFGIIILNRT	airlifting
AFGIIIMNNS	infamising
AFGIIIMNNZ	infamizing
AFGIILLNNT	flatlining
AFGIILMNPY	amplifying
AFGIILNNTY	faintingly
AFGIILNQUY	qualifying
AFGIILNRTT	filtrating
AFGIILOSTU	flagitious
AFGIIMNOTU	fumigation
AFGIIMNTTY	mattifying
AFGIINORTU	figuration
AFGIINSSTY	satisfying
AFGILLNOTY	floatingly
AFGILNORSV	flavorings
AFGILNORUV	flavouring
AFGILNORVY	favoringly
AFGIMNORSU	ausforming
AFGIMNORTT	formatting
AFGIMORSTU	fumigators
AFGINSSTTU	fungistats
AFGIORSTTU	fustigator
AFGNOPRSSW	frogspawns
AFHHLOOPST	photoflash
AFHIIKNOPS	kniphofias
AFHIKNRSST	rankshifts
AFHILLMOYY	Holy Family
AFHIMORRTY	Moray Firth
AFHIOPRRST	parrotfish
AFHIORSSTY	forsythias
AFHKLLNTUY	thankfully
AFHKLNNTUU	unthankful
AFHLLORSST	shortfalls
AFHLLRTUWY	wrathfully
AFIIILNOST	filiations
AFIIINNOTX	infixation
AFIILLRRTY	fritillary
AFIILMNNSU	Flamininus
AFIILNNOST	inflations
AFIILNOOST	foliations
AFIILNORSU	infusorial
AFIILNORTT	filtration
	flirtation
AFIILRSUVV	flavivirus
AFIIMNORRR	Friar Minor
AFIIMORSTV	favoritism
AFIINNORSU	infusorian
AFILLMNORY	informally
AFILLMORTU	multiflora
AFILLNPPTY	flippantly
AFILMNORTU	fulminator
AFILMNOSUY	infamously
AFILMORRVY	variformly
AFILMORSST	formalists

AFILNOOSTT	flotations
AFILNORTTY	frontality
AFILNORUXY	fluxionary
AFIMMOQRSU	squamiform
AFIMMORTUU	fumatorium
AFIMNNORST	informants
AFIMNOORST	formations
AFIMORRSTT	stratiform
AFINOOPRRS	rainproofs
AFKLOOSSTT	footstalks
AFLLLNUUWY	unlawfully
AFLLOOSSTT	footstalls
AFLMOORRTU	formulator
AFMNORRSST	transforms
AGGGGIINWW	wigwagging
AGGGGIINZZ	zigzagging
AGGGIIMNSU	misgauging
AGGGILLNWY	wagglingly
AGGGILNRST	straggling
AGGGIMNORT	mortgaging
AGGHHOPRRY	hygrograph
AGGHIILLMN	Gillingham
AGGHIINNRS	garnishing
AGGHIINNSU	anguishing
AGGHILLNUY	laughingly
AGGHILMNPU	galumphing
AGGHILNNSY	gnashingly
AGGHLOOPRS	logographs
AGGHLOOPRY	graphology
	logography
AGGHNNRRTUU	Guru Granth
AGGIIILLNTT	litigating
AGGIIIMNTT	mitigating
AGGIIINNNR	ingraining
AGGIIINRRT	irrigating
AGGIILLNNS	signalling
AGGIILNNTU	agglutinin
AGGIILNRTU	ligaturing
AGGIINNORS	organising
AGGIINNORZ	organizing
AGGIJLNTUU	jugulating
AGGIKNORTZ	Königgrätz
AGGILLNOTY	gloatingly
AGGILLOOST	algologist
AGGILNNNTU	untangling
AGGILNNOOO	ologoaning
AGGILNNORY	groaningly
AGGILNNOSS	singalongs
AGGILNNRST	strangling
AGGILNOOOY	agnoiology
AGGILNPPRS	grapplings
AGGILNPRSY	graspingly
AGGINNOORS	gorgonians
AGGINNORTU	outranging
AGGINORRSS	grosgrains
AGGINORRTT	garrotting
AGGINOSSTU	outgassing
AGGLNOOORY	organology
AGGLOORSTY	gastrology
AGGMOORRST	mortgagors
AGGHHIKNSTW	nighthawks
AGGHHILOPRT	lithograph

AGHHIMRRTT	Mithgarthr
AGHHINRSST	thrashings
AGHHLOOPRS	holographs
AGHHLOOPRY	holography
AGHHMOOPRS	homographs
AGHHNOOPPR	phonograph
AGHHOOPPRT	photograph
AGHHOPPTYY	phytophagy
AGHHORTUWY	throughway
AGHIIKNRRS	shikarring
AGHIILLMTY	almightily
AGHIILLSTT	taillights
AGHIILNNPS	planishing
AGHIIMNNSU	humanising
AGHIIMNNUZ	humanizing
AGHIIMNPSS	misshaping
AGHIIMOPRU	amphigouri
AGHIINNRST	tarnishing
AGHIINNRSV	varnishing
AGHIINNRTU	Thuringian
AGHIINOPRS	aphorising
AGHIINOPRZ	aphorizing
AGHIINPRRS	hairspring
AGHIINPRST	thraipings
AGHIINPSWW	whipsawing
AGHIINRTWW	wainwright
AGHILLNOPS	anglophils
AGHILLNOSW	shallowing
AGHILLNOTY	loathingly
	tallyhoing
AGHILLNSSY	slashingly
AGHILMORST	algorithms
	logarithms
AGHILNNTUY	hauntingly
AGHILNPPRT	thrappling
AGHILNPRST	springhalt
AGHILNPSTU	sulphating
AGHILNPSTY	playthings
AGHILNRSTT	stringhalt
AGHILOPPRY	lipography
AGHILOPPSY	gypsophila
AGHILORSTT	gastrolith
AGHILPRTWY	playwright
AGHILRSTTY	straightly
AGHIMNNOTT	Nottingham
AGHIMNNPSU	gunmanship
AGHIMNOOPS	shampooing
AGHIMNRSST	hamstrings
AGHIMORSST	histograms
AGHINNOOPR	harpooning
AGHINNORRT	Harrington
AGHINNORTT	Hartington
AGHINNOSTW	Washington
AGHINNSTUW	unswathing
AGHINOPRTY	atrophying
AGHIOPPRRS	spirograph
AGHKMOPRSY	kymographs
AGHKNNORSU	Kongur Shan
AGHKOORSSS	grasshooks
AGHLMNOOVY	Moholy-Nagy
AGHLMOOPRS	lagomorphs
AGHLMOOSTU	goalmouths

AGHLNOOORT	orthogonal	
AGHLNOSSTU	onslaughts	
AGHLOPPRSY	polygraphs	
AGHLOPRSTY	stylograph	
AGHLOPRSXY	xylographs	
AGHLOPRXYY	xylography	
AGHLORSTWY	Galsworthy	
AGHMMOOOSU	homogamous	
AGHMNOOPRS	monographs	
	nomographs	
	phonograms	
AGHMNOOPRY	nomography	
AGHMNOOPTY	pathognomy	
AGHMOOOPSU	omophagous	
AGHMOOPRST	photograms	
AGHMOOPRTY	tomography	
AGHNNSSTUU	Hsüan-tsung	
AGHNOOPRSY	nosography	
AGHOOOPSUZ	zoophagous	
AGHOOPPRTY	topography	
AGHOPPRRYY	pyrography	
AGHOPPRTYY	typography	
AGHORSSTTY	hygrostats	
AGIIIILNNT	initialing	
AGIIIINNTT	initiating	
AGIIILMNNN	mainlining	
AGIIILMNTT	militating	
AGIIILNNTZ	latinizing	
AGIIILNOTT	litigation	
AGIIILNSTV	vitalising	
AGIIILNTVZ	vitalizing	
AGIIIMMNSX	maximising	
AGIIIMMNXZ	maximizing	
AGIIIMNNTT	intimating	
AGIIIMNOTT	mitigation	
AGIIINNSST	sanitising	
AGIIINNSTZ	sanitizing	
AGIIINORRT	irrigation	
AGIIINRRTT	irritating	
AGIIINRSST	satirising	
AGIIINRSTZ	satirizing	
AGIIINRTTT	tritiating	
AGIIINTTTV	titivating	
AGIIKLMNRS	grimalkins	
AGIILLMMRS	milligrams	
AGIILLNNST	installing	
AGIILLNNUU	unilingual	
AGIILLNORY	originally	
AGIILLNPRS	spiralling	
AGIILLNRTU	trilingual	
AGIILLNRTY	trailingly	
AGIILLNRVY	virginally	
AGIILLLNTVY	vigilantly	
AGIILMMNOT	immolating	
AGIILMNNPT	implanting	
AGIILMNORS	moralising	
AGIILMNORZ	moralizing	
AGIILMNPSY	misplaying	
AGIILMNSTU	simulating	
AGIILMNSUV	misvaluing	
AGIILMNTTU	mutilating	
AGIILNNORU	unoriginal	
AGIILNNOST	insolating	
AGIILNNPTT	tinplating	
AGIILNNSTU	insulating	
AGIILNOPPT	oppilating	
AGIILNOPRS	polarising	
AGIILNOPRZ	polarizing	
AGIILNOPST	spoliating	
AGIILNORSS	solarising	
AGIILNORSV	valorising	
AGIILNORSZ	solarizing	
AGIILNORVZ	valorizing	
AGIILNOSTT	totalising	
AGIILNOTTZ	totalizing	
AGIILNPRST	springtail	
AGIILNRRSU	ruralising	
AGIILNRRUZ	ruralizing	
AGIILNRSTY	laryngitis	
AGIILOOSTX	axiologist	
AGIILORSTT	litigators	
AGIIMMNRST	immigrants	
AGIIMMORRT	immigrator	
AGIIMMOSST	misogamist	
AGIIMMSSTT	stigmatism	
AGIIMNNNOT	nominating	
AGIIMNNORS	romanising	
AGIIMNNORZ	romanizing	
AGIIMNNOSW	womanising	
AGIIMNNOWZ	womanizing	
AGIIMNNPRS	mainspring	
AGIIMNNRST	inmigrants	
AGIIMNNRTU	ruminating	
AGIIMNORST	amortising	
	migrations	
AGIIMNORSU	migrainous	
AGIIMNORTZ	amortizing	
AGIIMNOTTV	motivating	
AGIIMNRRVY	Virgin Mary	
AGIIMNSSTT	misstating	
AGIIMNSSUV	vaginismus	
AGIIMORSTT	mitigators	
AGIIMORTTY	mitigatory	
AGIIMSSTTT	stigmatist	
AGIIINNNPS	inspanning	
AGIINNNOTT	intonating	
AGIINNNOTV	innovating	
AGIINNOPPT	appointing	
AGIINNORSS	signorinas	
AGIINNORST	notarising	
AGIINNORTZ	notarizing	
AGIINNOSST	stationing	
AGIINNOSTU	Antigonus I	
AGIINNPPRW	inwrapping	
AGIINNPRSU	unaspiring	
AGIINNPSTU	supinating	
AGIINNQSTU	quantising	
AGIINNQTUZ	quantizing	
AGIINNRSTT	intrigants	
	transiting	
AGIINNRTTU	intriguant	
AGIINNSSTU	sustaining	
AGIINNSTUY	sanguinity	
AGIINOORRT	originator	
AGIINOPRSV	vaporising	
AGIINOPRVZ	vaporizing	
AGIINORSTT	instigator	
AGIINORSTV	grivations	
AGIINORSUV	viraginous	
AGIINPRTVY	varityping	
AGIINRTTTT	attritting	
AGIIORRRST	irrigators	
AGIIRSSTTU	guitarists	
AGIISSTUUV	Gustavus II	
AGIJLNNTUY	jauntingly	
AGIJLNOTUU	jugulation	
AGIKKLNRSY	skylarking	
AGIKLMNOOT	toolmaking	
AGIKLMNOSS	lossmaking	
AGIKLNNOSY	ankylosing	
AGIKLNOTTU	outtalking	
AGIKLNOTUW	outwalking	
AGIKNNORTT	Tarkington	
AGIKNNORTU	outranking	
AGILLLNRUY	alluringly	
AGILLNNRSY	snarlingly	
AGILLNNSTY	slantingly	
AGILLNOPRT	patrolling	
AGILLNOPSW	wallopings	
AGILLNOSHW	swallowing	
AGILLNRSUY	singularly	
AGILLOOSSS	isoglossal	
AGILMNNOOP	lampooning	
AGILMNNOST	lamingtons	
AGILMOOSTU	gliomatous	
AGILMOPSTY	polygamist	
AGILMRSSUV	vulgarisms	
AGILNNNOPY	nonplaying	
AGILNNNOVY	annoyingly	
AGILNNNRSU	unsnarling	
AGILNNOPTY	poignantly	
AGILNNORTY	ignorantly	
AGILNNOSUU	lanuginous	
AGILNNTTUY	tauntingly	
AGILNOPPRS	prolapsing	
AGILNOPPTU	populating	
AGILNOPTUY	outplaying	
AGILNOSSTT	nostalgist	
AGILNOSTTU	outlasting	
AGILNOSTUY	autolysing	
AGILNOTUUV	outvaluing	
AGILNOTUYZ	autolyzing	
AGILNPPRRU	larrupping	
AGILNRSTTU	lustrating	
AGILOOPSST	apologists	
AGILORSSST	glossarist	
AGIMMNOOST	monogamist	
AGIMMNOSSU	Simon Magus	
AGIMMNSSUY	gymnasiums	
AGIMNNNOTU	outmanning	
AGIMNNSSUU	unassuming	
AGIMNOORST	agronomist	
AGIMNOPRSU	sporangium	
AGINNNPPSU	unsnapping	
AGINNOORTT	rattooning	
AGINNORRTW	Warrington	

AGINNPPRUW	unwrapping	
AGINOOOPRS	sporogonia	
AGINOOPSST	topagnosis	
AGINOORRTTV	rotovating	
AGINOPRRTY	portraying	
AGINORSTTU	outstaring	
AGINOSSTTU	gustations	
AGINOSTTUY	outstaying	
AGINPRSSSU	surpassing	
AGINPRSTTU	upstarting	
AGIORSTTUU	gratuitous	
AGIQRSSSTU	grassquits	
AGISSTUUVV	Gustavus VI	
AGJKNORRSU	kurrajongs	
AGKLORSSSW	glassworks	
AGKNRSTYYZ	Kyrgyzstan	
AGLLLOOPRY	pyrogallol	
AGLLNOOPVY	palynology	
AGLLRTTUUY	gutturally	
AGLMOOOPTY	potamology	
AGLMOOOSTY	somatology	
AGLMOOPSUY	polygamous	
AGLMOORSUU	glamourous	
AGLMOPPRUU	propagulum	
AGLMPRSSUU	sugarplums	
AGLNOORSUU	languorous	
AGLOOOSTUU	autologous	
AGLOOPPRVY	papyrology	
AGLOORSSST	glossators	
AGLOPPRSUY	playgroups	
AGLORSSSTW	glassworts	
AGMMNOOOSU	monogamous	
AGMNOORSTY	gastronomy	
AGMNORRSST	strongarms	
AGMOOORSST	Mato Grosso	
AGMOORSTTY	gastrotomy	
AGOORRSSST	grassroots	
AHHIMNPTUY	hypanthium	
AHHIMOPTYY	hypothymia	
AHHIOPRSTU	authorship	
AHHLNOPTXY	xanthophyl	
AHHMORRSTW	Harmsworth	
AHIIIJKNRS	jinrikisha	
AHIIILNPPP	Philippian	
AHIIILNPST	Philistian	
AHIIIMMPSX	amphimixis	
AHIIJKNRSS	jinrikshas	
AHIIJLNOPU	John Paul II	
AHIIKLNSTV	Tskhinvali	
AHIILMORTU	humiliator	
AHIILRSSTT	shirttails	
AHIIMNNOTU	inhumation	
AHIIMNNTUY	inhumanity	
AHIINORSST	historians	
AHIIPRSSSZ	sizarships	
AHIIRSSTTW	shirtwaist	
AHIJNNOSST	Saint John's	
AHIKKSTUUY	Kitakyushu	
AHILLMQSUY	qualmishly	
AHILLPSSTW	whipstalls	
AHILMNOPYY	Polyhymnia	
AHILMNOSWY	womanishly	

AHILMOPSSY	syphilomas	
AHILMORSST	hailstorms	
AHILMPSSVY	symphysial	
AHILNOORTZ	horizontal	
AHILNOPSTU	sulphation	
AHILNORSTT	triathlons	
AHILNPSSTU	sultanship	
AHILOSSTTT	statoliths	
AHIMMNNOSU	harmoniums	
AHIMMOPRSS	amorphisms	
AHIMNOOOSU	homoousian	
AHIMNOORRU	honorarium	
AHIMNOORSU	harmonious	
AHIMNOOSST	Matosinhos	
AHIMNOPRST	matronship	
AHIMNOPRTY	Amphitryon	
AHIMNORSST	harmonists	
AHIMNPRTTU	triumphant	
AHIMORSTUU	haustorium	
AHINOOPRRS	orpharions	
AHINOORSTT	hortations	
AHINOOSSTU	houstonias	
AHINOPRSTY	notaryship	
AHINOPRSUX	xiphosuran	
AHINPRSSST	transships	
AHIOOPSTTX	phototaxis	
AHIOPPRSST	pastorship	
AHIOPSSSTY	hypostasis	
AHKLLMOSWY	mollyhawks	
AHKLMOPRVY	karyolymph	
AHKLORSSTW	walkshorts	
AHLLMMOSTU	smallmouth	
AHLLMOOPRS	allomorphs	
AHLLOPRSTU	prothallus	
AHLLOPTXYY	phyllotaxy	
AHLMOOPRTU	photomural	
AHLMOOPSTY	homoplasty	
AHLNOPSTUY	polyanthus	
AHLOPPSTYY	hypoplasty	
AHLORRSSTU	ultrashort	
AHMMORSTTU	smartmouth	
AHMNNOOSTU	monanthous	
AHMNOOPRTU	protohuman	
AHMOOPRTYY	amyotrophy	
AHMOPRSTTU	mouthparts	
AHNNOSTTWY	shantytown	
AHNOOPSTTY	photonasty	
AHNOPPRTTY	tryptophan	
AHNORRSTTY	thyratrons	
AHOOPPRRST	saprotroph	
AHOOPPRTTY	protopathy	
AHOOPRRTXY	orthopraxy	
AHOOPRSTTU	autotrophs	
AHOOPRSTUX	auxotrophs	
AHOOPSSTTT	photostats	
AHOPRRRTTU	Port Arthur	
AIIIIILLMW	William III	
AIIIIKKPRR	pakirikiri	
AIIIIKMRTT	Kiritimati	
AIIIINNOTT	initiation	
AIIIINRTTX	initiatrix	
AIIIJNNSTU	Justinian I	

AIIIKKLMRZ	Kizil Irmak
AIIILLMNTU	illuminati
AIIILLMRTY	militarily
AIIILLNNOS	Illinoisan
AIIILMMMNS	minimalism
AIIILMMNST	minimalist
AIIILMMNST	minimalist
AIIILMMRST	militarism
AIIILMNOTT	limitation
	militation
AIIILMRSTT	militarist
AIIILMRSTV	trivialism
AIIILMRSTY	similarity
AIIILNNQTU	Quintilian
AIIILNOPTX	pixilation
AIIILORSTV	visitorial
AIIILRTTVY	triviality
AIIIMMNOTT	intimation
AIIIMNOPSS	pianissimo
AIIIMNOSTT	imitations
AIIIMNSSST	Mistassini
AIIIMPRSVV	viviparism
AIIINNOOST	ionisation
AIIINNOOTZ	ionization
AIIINNOTTV	invitation
AIIINORRTT	irritation
AIIINORSTT	initiators
AIIINORTTT	tritiation
AIIINORTTY	initiatory
AIIINOSTTV	visitation
	vitiations
AIIINOTTTV	titivation
AIIIPRSSTY	pityriasis
AIIIPRTVVY	viviparity
AIIKLMNOSW	Malinowski
AIIKNSSTTT	Saint Kitts
AIILLLNOSU	illusional
AIILLMNNTU	illuminant
AIILLMNOSW	Williamson
AIILLMNOTU	illuminato
AIILLMNTTY	militantly
AIILLNOOTV	volitional
AIILLNOSUV	villainous
AIILLNOSVY	visionally
AIILLORSTY	solitarily
AIILLOSSTT	solstitial
AIILLOTTVY	volatility
AIILLRSSTT	triallists
AIILLSTUVV	valvulitis
AIILMMNNOS	nominalism
AIILMMNOOT	immolation
AIILMMORST	immoralist
AIILMMORTY	immorality
AIILMNNOST	nominalist
AIILMNOORT	monitorial
AIILMNORST	trinomials
AIILMNORTY	minatorily
AIILMNOSTU	simulation
AIILMNOTTU	mutilation
AIILMNRSSU	insularism
AIILMNRTUY	unmilitary
AIILMOPTTY	optimality
AIILMRRTUV	triumviral

AIILLNNOOST	insolation	**AIIOPRSUVV**	viviparous
AIILNNOSTU	insulation	**AIIOPSSSTT**	pastitsios
AIILNOOPPT	oppilation	**AIIORRRSTT**	irritators
AIILNOOPST	positional	**AIIORSTTTV**	titivators
	spoliation	**AIIORTTTTV**	tittivator
AIILNOOSTV	violations	**AIIPPRSSTU**	Aristippus
AIILNOQSTU	liquations	**AIIPRSTTVY**	varitypist
AIILNORSSV	livraisons	**AIIPSSSSTV**	passivists
AIILNOSSTU	Saint Louis	**AIJLMNORSU**	journalism
	Saint-Louis	**AIJLNORSTU**	journalist
AIILNPRSSU	spirulinas	**AIKLMOSSTT**	milktoasts
AIILNRSSUY	urinalysis	**AIKLMSSTTU**	multitasks
AIILNRSTUY	insularity	**AIKLORSSYY**	karyolysis
AIILPPRTUY	pupilarity	**AIKNRSSTVY**	Stravinsky
AIILPRSSST	spritsails	**AILLLOOOPU**	Pollaiuolo
AIILPRSSTU	spirituals	**AILLMMORTY**	immortally
AIILRSSTTU	ritualists	**AILLMNOOPY**	polynomial
AIILRTTUVY	virtuality	**AILLMOPRXY**	proximally
AIIMMNNOTU	ammunition	**AILLMOSSYY**	amylolysis
AIIMMPRRTU	imprimatur	**AILLNNOOTY**	notionally
AIIMMRTTUY	immaturity	**AILLNOOPRT**	pollinator
AIIMNNNOOT	nomination	**AILLNOOPTY**	optionally
AIIMNNORTU	rumination	**AILLNORSTY**	tonsillary
AIIMNNOSST	Saint-Simon	**AILLNOSTUU**	ululations
AIIMNNRSTT	ministrant	**AILLNOSVVY**	synovially
AIIMNOOTTV	motivation	**AILLNQRTUY**	tranquilly
AIIMNOPRSS	prosimians	**AILLOPPSST**	lipoplasts
AIIMNOPRTV	provitamin	**AILLPRSSTU**	pluralists
AIIMNOPSSS	impassions	**AILMMOORST**	immolators
AIIMNOPSTU	utopianism	**AILMMSTTUU**	ultimatums
AIIMNOPTTU	imputation	**AILMNNOOPR**	pronominal
AIIMNORSSU	Missourian	**AILMNNOSTY**	antimonyls
AIIMNORSSY	missionary	**AILMNOOPST**	lampoonist
AIIMNPRSTU	puritanism	**AILMNORTUY**	unmorality
AIIMNPSSTT	timpanists	**AILMNSSTTU**	stimulants
AIIMNPSSTU	impuissant	**AILMOOPRST**	prostomial
AIIMNPSTTY	tympanitis	**AILMOOPSTU**	lipomatous
AIIMNQRSSU	sinarquism	**AILMOPPRUY**	polyparium
AIIMOPRSTT	patriotism	**AILMORSSTU**	simulators
AIIMOSSTTT	stomatitis	**AILMORSTTU**	mutilators
AIINNNOOTT	intonation		stimulator
AIINNNOOTV	innovation	**AILMPRTTUY**	multiparty
AIINNNOPST	pinnations	**AILMSSTTUU**	mutualists
AIINNOPSTU	supination	**AILNOOPPTU**	population
AIINNORSTT	nitrations	**AILNOOPRSS**	sponsorial
	transition	**AILNOOSTUV**	ovulations
AIINNORSTU	insinuator	**AILNOPSSTU**	pulsations
	ruinations	**AILNORSSTU**	insulators
	urinations	**AILNORSTTU**	lustration
AIINNOSSTU	sinuations	**AILNORSUVY**	unsavorily
AIINNOSSTX	Six Nations	**AILNOSSTUY**	autolysins
AIINNOSTTX	antitoxins	**AILNOSTTUU**	ustulation
AIINOOPPST	apposition	**AILNPPSSTU**	suppliants
AIINOPRRST	inspirator	**AILNPSSTUY**	puissantly
AIINOPRSTT	partitions	**AILOOPRSTY**	spoliatory
AIINOPRSTV	privations	**AILOOPSTTU**	autopilots
AIINORSSTT	striations	**AILOPPRTUY**	popularity
AIINORSTTT	titrations	**AILOPRSTTU**	stipulator
AIINORTTVY	invitatory	**AILRRSTUUV**	ultravirus
AIINOSSTTU	situations	**AIMMMNOSST**	mammonists
AIINQRSSTU	sinarquist	**AIMMNORSTU**	stramonium
AIIOPRSSTT	topiarists	**AIMMNOSSTU**	summations
AIMMOORRTU	moratorium		
AIMMRSSSTU	summarists		
AIMNNOORST	nominators		
AIMNNOOSTU	antimonous		
AIMNOOSTTU	autonomist		
AIMNOOSTTX	taxonomist		
AIMNOPSSTU	assumption		
AIMNORRSST	rainstorms		
AIMNORRSTU	ruminators		
AIMNPSSTTY	tympanists		
AIMNRSTTUU	nasturtium		
AIMOOORTVY	ovariotomy		
AIMOPSSSTY	symposiast		
AIMPSSSSTU	assumpsits		
AINNOOPRSS	sopraninos		
AINNOOPRTT	antiproton		
AINNOORSTV	innovators		
AINNOORTVY	innovatory		
AINOOPPRST	appointors		
	apportions		
AINOOPRRST	prorations		
AINOOPRSTY	anisotropy		
AINOOQSTTU	quotations		
AINOOSTTTU	outstation		
AINOOSTTUX	autotoxins		
AINOPRSSTU	supinators		
AINOPRSTUU	usurpation		
AINORRSSTT	transistor		
AINORRSTTY	transitory		
AINPRSTUUV	pursuivant		
AIOOPRRSUU	uproarious		
AIOOPRSTVY	vaporosity		
AIOORRSTTU	traitorous		
AIOOSSTTTT	tattooists		
AIOPPPRSUU	pupiparous		
AIOPRRSUUV	parvovirus		
AIOPRSTTTY	tyropittas		
AIORRRTTTU	triturator		
AKKMMNORSU	Kommunarsk		
AKLLMMOSWY	mollymawks		
AKLOORSSTT	rootstalks		
AKNNORSSYY	synkaryons		
AKNOOPRRSY	prokaryons		
ALLNNOPSTU	pollutants		
ALLOORSUVY	valorously		
ALLOPRSSTY	sallyports		
ALLOPSTUUY	patulously		
ALMNOPRTUY	poultryman		
ALMOOPPRST	protoplasm		
ALMOQSSUUY	squamously		
ALNOOPSSTT	tonoplasts		
ALNOPSSTTU	postulants		
ALNPRSTUUY	pursuantly		
ALNPSSTTUU	pustulants		
ALOOORSTUZ	zoolatrous		
ALOOPPRSTT	protoplast		
ALOOPPRTTY	prototypal		
ALOOPRSTTU	postulator		
ALOOPRSUVY	vaporously		
ALOPRTUUVY	voluptuary		
ALORSSTTUU	Lotus Sutra		
AMMOOSTUXY	myxomatous		

AMNNOOSTUY	antonymous
AMNNOOSTWW	townswoman
AMNNOSTTUW	stuntwoman
AMNOOOSTUU	autonomous
AMNOOPRSUY	paronymous
AMOORRRSWW	arrowworms
AMOORSSTTU	stromatous
AMOPPRSTTU	postpartum
AMORRSSTWW	strawworms
ANNOOPRSST	transposon
ANOOOPRSSZ	sporozoans
ANOOOPRSTZ	protozoans
ANOPRRSSTT	transports
AOOORRSTTV	rotovators
AOOPRRSSTT	protostars
AOPRRSTUUY	usurpatory
AORRRSTWWY	worrywarts
BBBCKOOSSY	bobbysocks
BBBEEEELMSU	bumblebees
BBBEEIINRW	winebibber
BBBEELRRSU	blubberers
BBBEGILNRU	blubbering
BBBEIKORSS	skibobbers
BBBEOORSXY	bobbysoxer
BBBGHINNOO	hobnobbing
BBBGIIKNOS	skibobbing
BBBHRSSUUY	subshrubby
BBCDEIRSSU	subscribed
BBCEEKNRRU	rubberneck
BBCEELNOOU	bubonocele
BBCEGILNOR	clobbering
BBCEHINSSU	chubbiness
BBCEHLOSUY	cubbyholes
BBCEHNRRUY	bunchberry
BBCEILRRSS	scribblers
BBCEIRRSSU	subscriber
BBCEIRSSSU	subscribes
BBCEIRSSTU	scrubbiest
BBCEKSTUUY	buckytubes
BBCGIILNRS	scribbling
BBCIIILSST	biblicists
BBDDDEEELOS	bobsledded
BBDDEEIMOV	divebombed
BBDDEEORUV	overdubbed
BBDEEIRRSU	rubberised
BBDEEIRRUZ	rubberized
BBDEIKNOOR	bookbinder
BBDEIORRSW	bowerbirds
BBDEIOSSUY	busybodies
BBDHIIOPRS	bishopbird
BBDINOOORW	ribbonwood
BBDNOSSTUU	bundobusts
BBEEEFGRRU	beefburger
BBEEEHLMSU	humblebees
BBEEHLSSUU	bluebushes
BBEEIILRRS	bilberries
BBEEINRSTZ	rebbetzins
BBEEIORRSX	boxberries
BBEEIRRNSSU	rubberises
BBEEIRRSUZ	rubberizes
BBEELLOTTU	bluebottle
BBEELNNOTU	bluebonnet

BBEELORRSS	slobberers
BBEGGNOOSW	wobbegongs
BBEGHILOSS	bobsleighs
BBEGHIOSTW	bobweights
BBEGILNORS	slobbering
BBEGINRSSU	grubbiness
BBEGJNOORR	Björneborg
BBEHHILOST	shibboleth
BBEHHOORSY	hobbyhorse
BBEHIRSSTU	shrubbiest
BBEHLLMOSS	bombshells
BBEIIKLNOR	ribbonlike
BBEIILLOOP	bibliopole
BBEIIORRTU	urbi et orbi
BBEIKLMOOO	bookmobile
BBEIKLNOST	knobbliest
BBEILNOSSW	wobbliness
BBEINOPRRT	Ribbentrop
BBEINSSSTU	stubbiness
BBEJLOPRUU	Jubbulpore
BBEKLORRUW	rubblework
BBEKNORSTU	bonkbuster
BBERRSTTUU	butterburs
BBFHIINORS	ribbonfish
BBGHIINRSU	rubbishing
BBGHILNOOS	hobgoblins
BBGHIMOSST	bombsights
BBGIILNQSU	quibblings
BBGIMOORRY	borborygmi
BBHIIILLOP	bibliophil
BBHILNOSSY	snobbishly
BBIIIIMNOT	imbibition
BBIILLOOPY	bibliopoly
BBILLOSUUY	bibulously
BBIMNOORSU	bourbonism
BBJMMMOOUU	mumbo jumbo
BBLMOORSUY	Bloomsbury
BBLNORSTUY	stubbornly
BCCCKMOOSS	cockscombs
BCCDEEEMNU	decumbence
BCCDEEMNUY	decumbency
BCCDEHKOSY	bodychecks
BCCDEILNOU	conducible
BCCEEEMNRU	recumbence
BCCEEENPSU	pubescence
BCCEEENRSU	rubescence
BCCEEIINOS	bioscience
BCCEEIMNRY	cybercrime
BCCEEINRTY	cybernetic
BCCEEMNRUY	recumbency
BCCEHIINOR	Boccherini
BCCEHIKNPS	pinchbecks
BCCEHKKOOS	checkbooks
BCCEHNORSS	crossbench
BCCEIINOOT	biocenotic
	coenobitic
BCCEILORTU	Bertolucci
BCCEIMNNUY	incumbency
BCCEINNOSU	concubines
BCCEKLORSU	cockleburs
BCCEMRSSUU	succumbers
BCCGIMNSUU	succumbing

BCCHIINORT	bronchitic
BCCIILSSTY	bicyclists
BCCIKLLOSY	billycocks
BCCMORRSUY	currycombs
BCDDEEILTU	deductible
BCDDEIIKRY	dickeybird
BCDDIIKRSY	dickybirds
BCDEEEIINT	benedicite
BCDEEEILTT	detectible
BCDEEEIRRS	redescribe
BCDEEEMNRU	encumbered
BCDEEHIIRS	herbicides
BCDEEHIMRS	besmirched
BCDEEHLNNU	unblenched
BCDEEHLOST	bedclothes
BCDEEHORUU	debouchure
BCDEEIILNR	incredible
BCDEEILLUX	excludible
BCDEEIMNOR	recombined
BCDEEIMNRU	incumbered
BCDEEINSSU	subsidence
BCDEEINSTU	Benedictus
BCDEEINTVX	Benedict XV
BCDEEIPRRS	prescribed
BCDEEIRRSS	describers
BCDEEKLLNU	bullnecked
BCDEELOOSS	obsolesced
BCDEEORRSS	crossbreed
BCDEEOSTWY	Betws-y-Coed
BCDEFLOOTU	clubfooted
BCDEGHINOU	debouching
BCDEGIINRS	describing
BCDEGILNOU	beclouding
BCDEHIILOR	bichloride
BCDEHINPST	pitchbends
BCDEIILLNU	includible
BCDEIILNRY	incredibly
BCDEIILPSU	publicised
BCDEIILPUZ	publicized
BCDEIINOOT	endobiotic
BCDEIINSSU	subindices
BCDEIKLOOT	bootlicked
BCDEILOORR	corrodible
BCDEILOORU	bicoloured
BCDEILOPRU	producible
BCDEIMNNOU	uncombined
BCDEIOPRRS	proscribed
BCDEKLLOOS	bollocksed
BCDELORRUY	cloudberry
BCDEMMNRUU	cummerbund
BCDENORSUU	unobscured
BCDEORRSSS	crossbreds
BCDEORSTTU	obstructed
BCDGINSTUU	subducting
BCDHHIILRT	childbirth
BCDHKNOSUU	buckhounds
BCDHLNOOTU	clothbound
BCDIILMORU	lumbricoid
BCDIIOPRRT	tropicbird
BCDILOOOSS	discobolos
BCDILOOSSU	discobolus
BCDIMOORSS	scombroids

BCDINOSTUU	subduction	**BCEELRSUUY**	burleycues	**BCEIJNOSTU**	subjection
BCDKLOOOST	bloodstock	**BCEEMMORSU**	cumbersome	**BCEIKLLOSU**	bullockies
BCDKMRSTUU	dumbstruck	**BCEEOOORRR**	corroboree	**BCEIKLOORT**	bootlicker
BCDLORSTUU	cloudburst	**BCEFFIORSU**	subofficer	**BCEIKNOSST**	steinbocks
BCEEEEHKOO	Okeechobee	**BCEFFIOSSU**	suboffices	**BCEILMNOSU**	columbines
BCEEEEHRSS	beseechers	**BCEFHISSTT**	bitchfests	**BCEILMOORT**	bolometric
BCEEEEFFILT	effectible	**BCEFIIKRRS**	firebricks	**BCEILMRSTU**	crumbliest
BCEEEFINNT	beneficent	**BCEFIIMORR**	microfiber	**BCEILNOOST**	bolections
BCEEEGHINS	beseeching		microfibre	**BCEILNORSU**	Berlusconi
BCEEEEHKNOS	cheekbones	**BCEFIIOPRT**	fibreoptic	**BCEILNRTUU**	tuberculin
BCEEEILLNU	ebullience	**BCEFIJSTUY**	subjectify	**BCEIMNNSTU**	incumbents
BCEEEIRSTV	brevetcies	**BCEFKLSTUU**	bucketfuls	**BCEIMOSTUV**	combustive
BCEEELLMRU	cerebellum	**BCEGHIINTW**	bewitching	**BCEINNOSSU**	bounciness
BCEEELQRSU	becquerels	**BCEGHINRTU**	butchering	**BCEINOPSTU**	subception
BCEEEENRSTU	erubescent	**BCEGIIKNRS**	bickerings	**BCEINORTTU**	contribute
BCEEFGIINN	beneficing	**BCEGIILORR**	corrigible	**BCEINOSSTU**	subsection
BCEEFIOPRS	fiberscope	**BCEGIJNSTU**	subjecting	**BCEIOPPRSY**	presbyopic
	fibrescope	**BCEGIKLLNO**	bellocking	**BCEIOPRRRS**	proscriber
BCEEGHINRS	breechings	**BCEGIKLNRU**	bucklering	**BCEIOPRRSS**	proscribes
BCEEGHNORS	Schoenberg	**BCEGILLNOR**	corbelling	**BCEIORSSTT**	obstetrics
BCEEGIINOT	biogenetic	**BCEGILMNOY**	becomingly	**BCEJKMPRUU**	buckjumper
BCEEGINRSU	subgeneric	**BCEGILOOOY**	bioecology	**BCEKKOOOPT**	pocketbook
BCEEHIKLNT	Liebknecht	**BCEGIMNNOU**	unbecoming	**BCEKLLOOSS**	bollockses
BCEEHIMRSS	besmirches	**BCEHHNNOUY**	honeybunch	**BCEKLNRTUU**	turnbuckle
BCEEHIORRS	seborrheic	**BCEHIIMOST**	biochemist	**BCEKMRSSUU**	bumsuckers
BCEEHIRSTU	butcheries	**BCEHIINSST**	bitchiness	**BCEKNPRSUY**	cyberpunks
BCEEHKLNOU	hucklebone	**BCEHIISSSU**	hibiscuses	**BCEKRSTTUU**	rustbucket
BCEEHKOOQU	chequebook	**BCEHILNOOR**	bronchiole	**BCELNORSTU**	Culbertson
BCEEHKOORS	chokebores	**BCEHILOPRY**	hyperbolic	**BCELNRTUUY**	turbulency
BCEEHKORRY	chokeberry	**BCEHILOSTT**	blotchiest	**BCELRSTUUU**	subculture
BCEEHMNRSU	Übermensch	**BCEHIMORSS**	chemisorbs	**BCEMNOPRTU**	procumbent
BCEEHMORUU	embouchure	**BCEHINNSSU**	bunchiness	**BCENOORSSS**	crossbones
BCEEHNOOPR	necrophobe	**BCEHINOOPX**	xenophobic	**BCENORSSTU**	curbstones
BCEEHORSTT	brochettes	**BCEHINOSST**	botchiness	**BCEPRSTTUU**	buttercups
BCEEHPRSUY	hypercubes	**BCEHIOQSUU**	chibouques	**BCFIIMORRR**	cribriform
BCEEHRSTTU	trebuchets	**BCEHKKOOST**	sketchbook	**BCGHILNSTU**	nightclubs
BCEEIILLMV	imbecilely	**BCEHKLOOSU**	blockhouse	**BCGIIINNRS**	inscribing
BCEEIILPST	plebiscite	**BCEHKMRSUU**	humbuckers	**BCGIIKKNOX**	kickboxing
BCEEIILTYZ	Belize City	**BCEHLNOSUX**	lunchboxes	**BCGIILORRY**	corrigibly
BCEEIJOSTV	objectives	**BCEHLOSSUU**	clubhouses	**BCGIKLLNOO**	bollocking
BCEEIJSTUV	subjective	**BCEHMNOOSY**	honeycombs	**BCGIKLLNOU**	bullocking
BCEEILLNUY	ebulliency	**BCEHMOORSS**	chemosorbs	**BCGIKLNNOU**	unblocking
BCEEILLOOS	cellobiose	**BCEHMRSTUW**	thumbscrew	**BCGIKLNNUU**	unbuckling
BCEEILLORS	corbeilles	**BCEIIILLMS**	immiscible	**BCGIKMNSUU**	bumsucking
BCEEILMOST	comestible	**BCEIIILMTY**	imbecility	**BCGIKNPRSU**	springbuck
BCEEIMMOSS	misbecomes	**BCEIIILNNV**	invincible	**BCGIMNOSTU**	combusting
BCEEIMNORS	recombines	**BCEIIIMMOT**	biomimetic	**BCGINOOTTY**	boycotting
BCEEINOOST	coenobites	**BCEIIJNOST**	bijections	**BCHHIMOOOP**	homophobic
BCEEIOORUV	Courbevoie	**BCEIIKLLLS**	sicklebill	**BCHIILNOPY**	phycobilin
BCEEIORRSW	cowberries	**BCEIILLOTT**	Botticelli	**BCHIINORST**	bronchitis
BCEEIPRRRS	prescriber	**BCEIILMMOS**	embolismic	**BCHIIOPRSS**	bishoprics
BCEEIPRRSS	prescribes	**BCEIILMPSU**	semipublic	**BCHIIOPSSY**	biophysics
BCEEIPRRSY	spiceberry	**BCEIILNOST**	bilections	**BCHIKLLOSY**	blockishly
BCEEIPSSSU	subspecies	**BCEIILPSSU**	publicises	**BCHIMNOOOP**	monophobic
BCEEJNORST	jobcentres	**BCEIILPSUZ**	publicizes	**BCHIMOORTT**	thrombotic
BCEEKLNOTT	bottleneck	**BCEIIMOQTU**	coquimbite	**BCHIMOORTW**	witchbroom
BCEEKRSTTU	trebuckets	**BCEIIMORST**	biometrics	**BCHINOOPTY**	phycobiont
BCEELNOTTU	cuttlebone	**BCEIINOOSS**	biocenosis	**BCHIOOORRT**	orthoboric
BCEELNRTUU	turbulence	**BCEIINOSST**	bisections	**BCHIOPRTYY**	bryophytic
BCEELOOSSS	obsolesces	**BCEIINRRSS**	inscribers	**BCHKNORSTU**	buckthorns
BCEELOPPRT	Copper Belt	**BCEIIOOPSS**	bioscopies	**BCHLNOPSUW**	punchbowls
BCEELORSTU	beltcourse	**BCEIJNOOST**	objections	**BCHLOOOSSY**	schoolboys

BCIIILMMSY	immiscibly	BDDGIINOTU	outbidding	BDEEIILMOZ	demobilize
BCIIILNNVY	invincibly	BDDHLNOOOU	bloodhound	BDEEIILOSS	biodiesels
BCIIILORTT	trilobitic	BDDLOOOOSW	bloodwoods	BDEEIILRSW	bridlewise
BCIIIMMORY	biomimicry	BDEEEEJLLW	bejewelled	BDEEIILRTV	divertible
BCIILNOPSY	psilocybin	BDEEEELRSV	belvederes	BDEEIILSTV	divestible
BCIILORSUU	lubricious	BDEEEEMMRR	remembered	BDEEIILLNTU	bulletined
BCIILPSSTU	publicists	BDEEEFILNS	defensible	BDEEIILLOPT	potbellied
BCIIMNOSTY	symbiontic	BDEEEFINTT	benefitted	BDEEIILLRSW	bridewells
BCIKKNOSST	knobsticks	BDEEEFOORT	freebooted	BDEEILMNRU	unlimbered
BCIKKORRSW	brickworks	BDEEEGHILR	Heidelberg	BDEEILMOSW	disembowel
BCIKMOORST	broomstick	BDEEEHLLNR	hellbender	BDEEILMRSS	dissembler
BCILLORSSS	crossbills	BDEEEIILSV	disbelieve	BDEEILMSSS	dissembles
BCILOOSTUU	tubicolous	BDEEEILMMS	emblemised	BDEEEILNORR	borderline
BCIMNOOSTU	combustion	BDEEEILMMZ	emblemized	BDEEILNOTY	obediently
BCIMNOOSTY	mycobionts	BDEEEILNSS	edibleness	BDEEILORSW	bowdlerise
BCIMORRSTU	microburst	BDEEEILNTX	extendible	BDEEILORWZ	bowdlerize
BCIOPRSSTU	subtropics	BDEEEILSTW	wildebeest	BDEEIMMNOT	embodiment
BCIPRSSSTU	subscripts	BDEEEIMRTT	embittered	BDEEIMMRSS	dismembers
BCLMORSUUY	cumbrously	BDEEEINRRT	interbreed	BDEEIMOOSS	somebodies
BCMOOOTTUU	Tombouctou	BDEEEIRRSW	dewberries	BDEEIMORRS	embroiders
BCMOORSSTU	combustors	BDEEEIRTTW	bitterweed	BDEEIMORRY	embroidery
BCOORRSTTU	obstructor	BDEEEELLMOW	embowelled	BDEEIMRRSU	reimbursed
BDDDEGIOOS	dogsbodied	BDEEEELLORW	rebellowed	BDEEINSSUX	subindexes
BDDDEIISUV	subdivided	BDEEEELMTUW	tumbleweed	BDEEIORSSS	sobersides
BDDDGIINSU	disbudding	BDEEEELNOSS	nosebleeds	BDEEIORSSY	disobeyers
BDDEEEFINR	befriended	BDEEEELORTU	doubletree	BDEEIQRTTU	briquetted
BDDEEEILLV	bedevilled	BDEEEELRRRY	elderberry	BDEEIRSSTT	bedsitters
BDDEEEILRW	bewildered	BDEEEMMNST	embedments	BDEEKOOORV	overbooked
BDDEEEELMNO	emboldened	BDEEEEMNRRU	renumbered	BDEEKOORSW	brookweeds
BDDEEENRTU	debentured	BDEEEMOPRT	obtempered	BDEELLNRUY	underbelly
BDDEEFNORW	New Bedford	BDEEENRSTU	debentures	BDEELNNOSS	blondeness
BDDEEGLNOU	bludgeoned	BDEEFGIINR	debriefing	BDEELNOSSU	doubleness
BDDEEGNTUU	unbudgeted	BDEEFIILSS	disbeliefs	BDEELNRRSU	blunderers
BDDEEILMSS	dissembled	BDEEFILNSY	defensibly	BDEELQRSUU	burlesqued
BDDEEINORV	overbidden	BDEEFLLOSW	bedfellows	BDEEMNNRUU	unnumbered
BDDEEINRST	bestridden	BDEEFLORSW	flowerbeds	BDEEMNORSU	burdensome
BDDEEIORSS	sobersided	BDEEFLORUW	furbelowed	BDEENNNOTU	unbonneted
BDDEELMORU	dumbledore	BDEEFOORRS	foreboders	BDEENORRUV	overburden
BDDEENNRUU	unburdened	BDEEGGLOOT	bootlegged	BDEENORSUV	unobserved
BDDEFGILNU	befuddling	BDEEGHILRT	Lethbridge	BDEENORTTU	rebuttoned
BDDEFIORRS	forbidders	BDEEGHINOR	neighbored	BDEERSSTTU	buttressed
BDDEFORSUY	bodysurfed	BDEEGHINRT	brightened	BDEFFIILSU	diffusible
BDDEGIILOS	disobliged	BDEEGIILNV	bedeviling	BDEFFLOTUU	outbluffed
BDDEGILMRU	Middelburg	BDEEGIILST	digestible	BDEFGINOOR	foreboding
BDDEGIOOSS	dogsbodies	BDEEGIINNR	inbreeding	BDEFGIOORT	footbridge
BDDEGLOOSU	doodlebugs	BDEEGIINNZ	bedizening	BDEFGSSTUU	fussbudget
BDDEHIIRSY	hybridised	BDEEGILRSS	bridgeless	BDEFIILRRS	riflebirds
BDDEHIIRYZ	hybridized	BDEEGIMOSU	disembogue	BDEFILLMOO	Bloomfield
BDDEHLNOOR	bondholder	BDEEGINRSU	Duisenberg	BDEFILNORW	brownfield
BDDEIIMORS	dibromides	BDEEGINRSU	Duisenberg	BDEFINORSY	boyfriends
BDDEIIRSUV	subdivider	BDEEGINRSU	bludgeoner	BDEFORRSUY	bodysurfer
BDDEIISSSU	subsidised	BDEEGNOORU	bourgeoned	BDEGGGINRU	begrudging
BDDEIISSUV	subdivides	BDEEGNORSW	Swedenborg	BDEGGHIINT	bedighting
BDDEIISSUZ	subsidized	BDEEHILLRS	Breed's Hill	BDEGGLNOOO	boondoggle
BDDEILMORW	middlebrow	BDEEHIMOOS	homebodies	BDEGHHIINR	highbinder
BDDEIMOSTU	misdoubted	BDEEHIMRSU	Humberside	BDEGHHIORW	highbrowed
BDDEINNRUW	windburned	BDEEHIRRSY	Derbyshire	BDEGHIMOTU	bigmouthed
BDDEINRSSU	disburdens	BDEEHLNNOR	hornblende	BDEGHINNRU	Hindenburg
BDDELOOORW	Boldrewood	BDEEHLNNOU	unbeholden	BDEGIIILRS	dirigibles
BDDFGIINOR	forbidding	BDEEIIILST	debilities	BDEGIILNRU	rebuilding
BDDFILLNOS	blindfolds	BDEEIIILLNU	ineludible	BDEGIILOSS	disobliges
BDDFMNOSUU	dumbfounds	BDEEIILMOS	demobilise	BDEGIILSTY	digestibly

BDEGIINORR	broidering	**BDEINOORSS**	broodiness	**BEEEFIMORT**	beforetime
BDEGIINOSY	disobeying	**BDEINRSSTU**	turbidness	**BEEEFMRRUZ**	bumfreezer
BDEGIINRST	bestriding	**BDEIOORTTW**	bitterwood	**BEEEFOORRT**	freebooter
BDEGIINSTT	bedsitting	**BDEIORSSTU**	subeditors	**BEEEGGIRRZ**	Erzgebirge
BDEGIINSTU	subediting	**BDEIPRSSTU**	buprestids	**BEEEGGLMNR**	Mengelberg
BDEGIKOOSU	guidebooks	**BDEIRRSSSU**	disbursers	**BEEEGGRRUV**	vegeburger
BDEGIKORRW	bridgework	**BDEIRRSSTU**	disturbers	**BEEEGHINRS**	Heisenberg
BDEGILNNRU	blundering	**BDEKMMNRUU**	kummerbund	**BEEEGIILLR**	reeligible
BDEGILNORU	bouldering	**BDELLNOPSU**	spellbound	**BEEEGIJLNW**	bejeweling
	redoubling	**BDELLOOTUW**	bulletwood	**BEEEGINRRR**	greenbrier
BDEGIMOORR	bridegroom	**BDELLORSUZ**	bulldozers	**BEEEGNNORS**	greenbones
BDEGINNORU	rebounding	**BDELMMNOUY**	molybdenum	**BEEEHLLORS**	hellebores
BDEGINNSTU	subtending	**BDELMNOTUW**	tumbledown	**BEEEHLLRTW**	bellwether
BDEGINOORY	gooneybird	**BDELNOOOST**	bloodstone	**BEEEIIKLSW**	biweeklies
BDEGINORTW	Bridgetown	**BDELNOOSTU**	doubletons	**BEEEIKLLRR**	bierkeller
BDEGINRRST	Strindberg	**BDELNORTUU**	untroubled	**BEEEILMMSS**	emblemises
BDEGINRSUU	burgundies	**BDEMOORRRS**	smorrebrod	**BEEEILMMSZ**	emblemizes
BDEGIOPRRT	Bridgeport	**BDENNOORSW**	brownnosed	**BEEEILMNST**	belemnites
BDEGIORRTW	Trowbridge	**BDENNOOSST**	bondstones	**BEEEILNRUV**	unbeliever
BDEHIILPSU	bisulphide	**BDENNOTTUU**	unbuttoned	**BEEEILNSTX**	extensible
BDEHIIMOOR	rhomboidei	**BDENOOSSUX**	soundboxes	**BEEEILRRSV**	reversible
BDEHIIOPRT	prohibited	**BDEOOORRSW**	woodborers	**BEEEILRRTV**	revertible
BDEHIIRRSY	hybridiser	**BDFLLOTUUY**	doubtfully	**BEEEIMRRTT**	embitterer
BDEHIIRRYZ	hybridizer	**BDGHIILNNT**	nightblind	**BEEEIMRSSV**	semibreves
BDEHIIRSSY	hybridises	**BDGHIILNST**	blindsight	**BEEEINRSSZ**	breeziness
BDEHIIRSYZ	hybridizes	**BDGIIILMNR**	birdliming	**BEEEIRRSTW**	sweetbrier
BDEHIORSSU	birdhouses	**BDGIILLNNY**	blindingly	**BEEEKKOOPR**	bookkeeper
BDEHMOORST	thrombosed	**BDGIILNNRU**	unbridling	**BEEEKRRRSS**	berserkers
BDEHNOOSUU	housebound	**BDGIILNPUU**	upbuilding	**BEEELLRSST**	bestseller
BDEHNORTUX	thunderbox	**BDGIINRSSU**	disbursing	**BEEELMMNST**	emblements
BDEHNRRSUU	underbrush	**BDGIINRSTU**	disturbing	**BEEELMMRSS**	memberless
	undershrub	**BDGIKMNNOSU**	subkingdom	**BEEELMRRSS**	resemblers
BDEIIILNRV	biliverdin	**BDGILLNOUZ**	bulldozing	**BEEELMRSZZ**	embezzlers
BDEIIKLOOS	obeliskoid	**BDGILLOOTU**	bloodguilt	**BEEELNNOTV**	benevolent
BDEIILLNNUY	ineludibly	**BDGILNNNOU**	unbundling	**BEEELNRSST**	trebleness
BDEIILMORS	disembroil	**BDGILNOORY**	broodingly	**BEEELSSSSU**	sublessees
BDEIILNNOS	blennioids	**BDGILNOTUY**	doubtingly	**BEEEMMNRTU**	embruement
BDEIILSSTU	subtilised	**BDHIILRRWY**	whirlybird	**BEEEMMNSTU**	bemusement
BDEIILSTUZ	subtilized	**BDHIMNOORY**	monohybrid	**BEEEMNRTTT**	betterment
BDEIIRSSSU	subsidiser	**BDHNNOORTU**	northbound	**BEEEMRRTTU**	Buttermere
BDEIIRSSUZ	subsidizer	**BDHNOOSTUU**	southbound	**BEEENORSTT**	bonesetter
BDEIIRSTTU	distribute	**BDIIILNOSU**	libidinous	**BEEFFGIRSU**	febrifuges
	turbidites	**BDIILLNOOPT**	diplobiont	**BEEFFHNOOR**	Bonhoeffer
BDEIISSSSU	subsidises	**BDIIMNRSUU**	Brundisium	**BEEFGIINNT**	benefiting
BDEIISSSUZ	subsidizes	**BDILLORSSW**	swordbills	**BEEFGRSTUU**	subterfuge
BDEIJNORSU	subjoinder	**BDILMNORSW**	blindworms	**BEEFHILSSU**	bluefishes
BDEIKKORSU	duikerboks	**BDILMNORUY**	moribundly	**BEEFHINOSS**	bonefishes
BDEILLNOOS	bloodlines	**BDILNORSTY**	blindstory	**BEEFIILMNX**	inflexible
BDEILLNPSS	spellbinds	**BDKNNOOORY**	donnybrook	**BEEFIILMSS**	misbeliefs
BDEILLORWY	yellowbird	**BDLMOOORSW**	bloodworms	**BEEFIILNRR**	inferrible
BDEILLOSSU	dissoluble	**BDLOOOORST**	bloodroots	**BEEFILLMRU**	umbellifer
BDEILMOOSS	disselboom	**BDMNOORSTU**	stormbound	**BEEFILRSTU**	subfertile
BDEILMORSW	bowdlerism	**BDNOOOTTUW**	buttonwood	**BEEFIORSSU**	sebiferous
BDEILMOSSY	symbolised	**BDNORSSTUW**	downbursts	**BEEFLLLORW**	bellflower
BDEILMOSYZ	symbolized	**BEEEEEKPRS**	beekeepers	**BEEFLMNOTU**	befoulment
BDEILNOOSS	bloodiness	**BEEEEFLNRS**	enfeeblers	**BEEGGIILLN**	negligible
BDEILOQSTU	quodlibets	**BEEEEFLNSS**	feebleness	**BEEGGLOORT**	bootlegger
BDEILORSUV	overbuilds	**BEEEEGIKNP**	beekeeping	**BEEGGNRRSU**	Regensburg
BDEILPRSUU	upbuilders	**BEEEELNRRS**	Berners-Lee	**BEEGHILNRT**	blethering
BDEIMNORSS	morbidness	**BEEEEMMRRR**	rememberer	**BEEGHINRRT**	brightener
BDEIMNOSST	disentombs	**BEEEEFGILNN**	enfeebling	**BEEGHINRSW**	beshrewing
BDEIMORSSU	mousebirds	**BEEEEFILLRX**	reflexible	**BEEGHIRSTY**	eyebrights

BEEGHNOOPR	negrophobe	
BEEGIIILLN	ineligible	
BEEGIILNRT	Gilbertine	
BEEGIILNST	ingestible	
BEEGIINOSS	biogenesis	
BEEGIKNNOT	betokening	
BEEGILMNOT	obligement	
BEEGILMNRS	resembling	
BEEGILMNZZ	embezzling	
BEEGILNRSS	inselbergs	
BEEGIMMNOS	gombeenism	
BEEGIMNORW	embowering	
BEEGINRSTW	bestrewing	
BEEGINRTTV	brevetting	
BEEGINRTTW	Wittenberg	
BEEGIOORSU	bourgeoise	
BEEGLNOTUU	bluetongue	
BEEGMNORYY	embryogeny	
BEEGMNSSTU	subsegment	
BEEGNNOTTU	unbegotten	
BEEGNOORRS	Greensboro	
BEEGNSSSUU	subgenuses	
BEEGOORRSY	gooseberry	
BEEGPRRSTU	Petersburg	
BEEHIIITVX	exhibitive	
BEEHILMOST	blithesome	
BEEHILNSST	blitheness	
BEEHIMMPRS	membership	
BEEHINRSTT	terebinths	
BEEHIORRSV	herbivores	
BEEHKOORRS	Sherbrooke	
BEEHLLRSSU	bushellers	
BEEHLMMOTU	tumblehome	
BEEHLMNSSU	humbleness	
BEEHMOORST	bothersome	
BEEHNOOPSX	xenophobes	
BEEHOORSSX	horseboxes	
BEEIIJORTU	bijouterie	
BEEIIKLMRT	kimberlite	
BEEIIKNRRS	inkberries	
BEEIILLLRV	Libreville	
BEEIILMMRS	immersible	
BEEIILMNRT	timberline	
BEEIILMRSS	remissible	
BEEIILNNSS	insensible	
BEEIILNNTV	inventible	
BEEIILNRST	libertines	
BEEIILNRTV	invertible	
BEEIILNSTV	investible	
BEEIILRSST	resistible	
BEEIILSSTX	bissextile	
BEEIKKNORR	knobkerrie	
BEEIKLNPRS	besprinkle	
BEEIKPRSSU	superbikes	
BEEILLLTTT	Little Belt	
BEEILLMRST	belletrism	
BEEILLNORS	rebellions	
BEEILLOPST	potbellies	
BEEILLORSU	rebellious	
BEEILLRSTT	belittlers	
	belletrist	
BEEILMNNSS	nimbleness	
BEEILMNRSS	limberness	
BEEILMOORS	bloomeries	
BEEILMORRS	embroilers	
BEEILMPRSU	plumberies	
BEEILMRRSU	mulberries	
BEEILNOSST	bilestones	
	ostensible	
BEEILNRSSU	nebulisers	
BEEILNRSTW	West Berlin	
BEEILNRSUZ	nebulizers	
BEEILORSTT	briolettes	
BEEILOSTTU	oubliettes	
BEEILRRSVY	reversibly	
BEEILRSTUX	extrusible	
BEEILSSTTU	subtleties	
BEEILSSTUV	vestibules	
BEEIMMNRTU	imbruement	
BEEIMRRRSU	reimburser	
BEEIMRRSSU	reimburses	
BEEINORRTT	torbernite	
BEEINORSTU	tenebrious	
BEEINRSSTT	bitterness	
	tenebrists	
BEEINRSRTU	subentries	
BEEINSSSSU	businesses	
BEEIQRRSSU	brusquerie	
BEEIQRSTTU	briquettes	
BEEIRSSUVV	subversive	
BEEJNNORSU	Burne-Jones	
BEEKNORSST	kerbstones	
BEEKRSTUWY	Tewkesbury	
BEELLLMSUU	umbellules	
BEELLOOSTY	obsoletely	
BEELMNNOOW	noblewomen	
BEELMNRSSU	numberless	
BEELMOORST	bolometers	
BEELMRRSSU	slumberers	
BEELNOOSTT	bottlenose	
BEELNOSSTU	bluestones	
BEELNPRTUU	puberulent	
BEELNSSSTU	subtleness	
BEELOOOSSX	looseboxes	
BEELOORSUV	overblouse	
BEELORRSST	bolsterers	
BEELORSTUV	oversubtle	
BEELQRRSUU	burlesquer	
BEELQRSSUU	burlesques	
BEELRRSSTU	blusterers	
BEEMMNNORS	nonmembers	
BEEMMNNOTT	entombment	
BEEMMNOSST	embossment	
BEEMMNOSTW	embowments	
BEEMNORSSS	somberness	
	sombreness	
BEEMNOSTTW	bestowment	
BEENOSSSTU	obtuseness	
BEENPRSSSU	superbness	
BEENQSSTUU	subsequent	
BEEORSSTTU	soubrettes	
BEEPRRSSTY	presbyters	
BEEPRRSTYY	presbytery	
BEERRSSTUV	subverters	
BEERSSSTTU	buttresses	
BEFFGINSTU	buffetings	
BEFFNOORUY	buffoonery	
BEFFNOSSUX	snuffboxes	
BEFGIINNOR	fibrinogen	
BEFGIINRVY	verbifying	
BEFGILNORW	fingerbowl	
BEFHIILLSS	billfishes	
BEFHILLMTU	thimbleful	
BEFHILOSSW	blowfishes	
BEFHIMNSSU	numbfishes	
BEFHIRRSSU	furbishers	
BEFHIRSTTU	butterfish	
BEFIILLNXY	inflexibly	
BEFIILLORS	fibrillose	
BEFIILRSTU	filibuster	
BEFIORSSTT	frostbites	
BEFLLMRTUU	tumblerful	
BEFLLOSTTU	bottlefuls	
BEGGHILORT	Toghril Beg	
BEGGHMRSUU	humbuggers	
BEGGHMRUUY	humbuggery	
BEGGHNORTU	Gothenburg	
BEGGIILLNY	negligibly	
BEGGIINNNS	beginnings	
BEGGIKNORS	Königsberg	
BEGGILNNOS	belongings	
BEGGIMNRSU	submerging	
BEGGINNORU	burgeoning	
BEGGRSTTUY	Gettysburg	
BEGHHINOST	thighbones	
BEGHIIINTX	exhibiting	
BEGHIIKNNT	bethinking	
BEGHIILMNS	blemishing	
BEGHIILMRT	thimblerig	
BEGHIILNRT	blithering	
BEGHIINRRT	rebirthing	
BEGHILLNSU	bushelling	
BEGHILMNOO	hemoglobin	
BEGHILNNOO	hemoglobin	
BEGHILNORY	neighborly	
BEGHINORSU	neighbours	
BEGHINORTT	betrothing	
BEGHINRSST	brightness	
BEGHMNOORT	thrombogen	
BEGHOORRTU	Borgerhout	
BEGHOORTUV	overbought	
BEGIIILLNY	ineligibly	
BEGIIILLTY	legibility	
BEGIIIMNRT	ignimbrite	
BEGIIKLNNR	blinkering	
BEGIIKLRTZ	blitzkrieg	
BEGIIKNNRS	briskening	
BEGIILLNNR	brinelling	
BEGIILLNTT	belittling	
BEGIILMNOR	embroiling	
BEGIILMNOS	embolising	
BEGIILMNOZ	embolizing	
BEGIILNNSU	nebulising	
BEGIILNNUZ	nebulizing	
BEGIILNOPR	preboiling	
BEGIILNRST	blistering	
BEGIILNRTT	bitterling	

BEGIINQRTU	briqueting	**BEHNORSSTU**	buhrstones	**BEIMRSSTTU**	submitters
BEGIINRRST	bestirring	**BEHOOPSTTU**	phototubes	**BEINNOSTUV**	subvention
BEGIINRSSU	suberising	**BEHOPRSTYY**	bryophytes	**BEINOOPRST**	obreptions
BEGIINRSUZ	suberizing	**BEHRRSSUWY**	Shrewsbury	**BEINOORSSV**	obversions
BEGIJRSTTU	jitterbugs	**BEIIILMMOS**	immobilise	**BEINOOSSSS**	obsessions
BEGILMNRSU	lumberings	**BEIIILMMOZ**	immobilize	**BEINOPRSTU**	subreption
	slumbering	**BEIIILNOST**	nobilities	**BEINORSSUV**	subversion
BEGILNORST	bolstering	**BEIIILNSSV**	invisibles	**BEINORSTUU**	subroutine
BEGILNORSY	soberingly	**BEIIIMNSTU**	bituminise	**BEINRSTTTU**	bitternuts
BEGILNRSTU	blustering	**BEIIIMNTUZ**	bituminize	**BEINSSSTTU**	subsistent
BEGILNSTTU	subletting	**BEIIIOOPSS**	biopoiesis	**BEIOOPRRSU**	pourboires
BEGILOOOXY	exobiology	**BEIILLNOTU**	ebullition	**BEIOOQSSUU**	obsequious
BEGILPSTTU	spittlebug	**BEIILLOSSU**	solubilise	**BEIOORSSTU**	boisterous
BEGILRSTTU	litterbugs	**BEIILLOSUZ**	solubilize	**BEIOQRSSTU**	sobriquets
BEGIMMNOOS	embosoming	**BEIILMNSTW**	nimblewits	**BEIOQRSTUU**	soubriquet
BEGIMNORSS	Bergsonism	**BEIILMOPSS**	impossible	**BEIORSTTUY**	tuberosity
BEGIMNRSSU	submersing	**BEIILMRTUY**	muliebrity	**BEIRSSSSTU**	subsisters
BEGINNNNOT	Bennington	**BEIILNNSSY**	insensibly	**BEISSTTTUU**	substitute
BEGINOPRRV	proverbing	**BEIILORSTT**	trilobites	**BEKLLOORUW**	boullework
BEGINORSSU	subregions	**BEIILORSTU**	boilersuit	**BEKLNNORUY**	unbrokenly
BEGINORTUZ	Buitenzorg	**BEIILRSSTT**	bristliest	**BEKLOOSSTY**	stylebooks
BEGINORUVY	overbuying	**BEIILRSSTU**	subtiliser	**BEKMNORSSU**	mossbunker
BEGINPRRTU	perturbing	**BEIILRSSTY**	resistibly	**BELLMOPSTU**	postbellum
BEGINRSSUV	subserving	**BEIILRSTTT**	librettist	**BELLNOSUUY**	nebulously
BEGINRSTUV	subverting	**BEIILRSTTW**	Birtwistle	**BELLOOOPRT**	portobello
BEGIORRSUY	biosurgery	**BEIILRSTUZ**	subtilizer	**BELLOOSSTY**	bootlessly
BEGLMOORYY	embryology	**BEIILSSSTU**	subtilises	**BELLORSTUY**	trolleybus
BEGLMORUUX	Luxembourg	**BEIILSSTTU**	subtilties	**BELMOOSSTT**	bottomless
BEGLNNNOOT	Longbenton	**BEIILSSTUZ**	subtilizes	**BELMORSSUU**	slumberous
BEGMOORRSV	Bromsgrove	**BEIIMSSSUV**	submissive	**BELNOORSWW**	snowblower
BEGNORRUYY	youngberry	**BEIINNOQUU**	ubiquinone	**BELNOSSTTU**	buttonless
BEGOOPPRST	gobstopper	**BEIINNRSTU**	Rubinstein	**BELORSSSSU**	sublessors
BEGOORRTTT	bogtrotter	**BEIINORSTY**	insobriety	**BELORSSTUU**	blusterous
BEHHMOOOPS	homophobes	**BEIIORSSTU**	bistouries	**BEMNOORSSU**	unbosomers
BEHIIIINTV	inhibitive	**BEIKLMOORS**	brooklimes	**BEMNOOSSTT**	tombstones
BEHIIINOTX	exhibition	**BEIKLMRTTU**	buttermilk	**BEMNOPRSUU**	penumbrous
BEHIIINRST	inhibiters	**BEIKMOORST**	motorbikes	**BEMNORSTUU**	outnumbers
BEHIILMTTW	thimblewit	**BEIKMORRTW**	timberwork	**BEMOORSSTU**	motorbuses
BEHIILPSTU	bisulphite	**BEILLLLOOS**	loblollies	**BEMSSSSTUY**	subsystems
BEHIIOPRRT	prohibiter	**BEILLMSSUU**	subsellium	**BENNNOSSTU**	sunbonnets
BEHIIORSTX	exhibitors	**BEILLOPRST**	billposter	**BENNOORSSW**	brownnoses
BEHIIORTXY	exhibitory	**BEILMNOOSW**	snowmobile	**BENNOORSTW**	brownstone
BEHIKLLNOR	Broken Hill	**BEILMOOSTT**	lobotomies	**BENORRSSTU**	burrstones
BEHIKLOSSV	bolsheviks	**BEILMOSSSY**	symbolises	**BENORSSSTU**	robustness
BEHIKOPRRS	shipbroker	**BEILMOSSYZ**	symbolizes	**BENORSSTTU**	obstruents
BEHILLORWW	willowherb	**BEILNOSSSW**	blowsiness	**BENRSTTTUU**	butternuts
BEHILMOSSV	bolshevism	**BEILNOSSTY**	ostensibly	**BEORRTTTUW**	butterwort
BEHILNSSSU	bluishness	**BEILNOSSWZ**	blowziness	**BFGHIINRSU**	furbishing
BEHILOSSTV	bolshevist	**BEILNOSTUY**	nebulosity	**BFGHILLSTU**	bullfights
BEHILPRSSU	publishers	**BEILNPRSTU**	blueprints	**BFGIINRTUY**	brutifying
BEHIMMORTU	embothrium	**BEILNRRSSU**	blurriness	**BFGILLMNUY**	fumblingly
BEHINORSTT	birthstone	**BEILOOPRST**	potboilers	**BFGILLNOWY**	flyblowing
BEHINOSSSY	boyishness	**BEILOOTUVV**	obvolutive	**BFIIILSTUY**	fusibility
BEHINRRSSU	burnishers	**BEILORSSSU**	subsoilers	**BFIIIORSST**	fibrositis
BEHIOORSST	boosterish	**BEILORSSTT**	lost tribes	**BFIILMMORU**	umbiliform
BEHIORSSTT	theorbists	**BEIMMRSTYY**	bisymmetry	**BFILLLSSUY**	blissfully
BEHKNOSSUU	bunkhouses	**BEIMNNOOPT**	embonpoint	**BFINORRSST**	firstborns
BEHLMOOPTY	phlebotomy	**BEIMNNORSST**	brimstones	**BGGGHIMNUU**	humbugging
BEHLNOOTTU	buttonhole	**BEIMNNORSSU**	submersion	**BGGIILLNOY**	obligingly
BEHMOOORST	smoothbore	**BEIMOORSST**	biostromes	**BGGIINNPRU**	upbringing
BEHMOORSST	thromboses		boosterism	**BGHHIIRRTT**	birthright
BEHNNRSTUU	unburthens	**BEIMOORSTT**	bottomries	**BGHIIIINNT**	inhibiting

BGHIILNPSU publishing	**BIILLOSTUY** solubility	**CCCIIMORTY** microcytic
BGHIINNRSU burnishing	**BIILLOTUVY** volubility	**CCCILLOPYY** polycyclic
BGHIKLOOST booklights	**BIILMOPSSY** impossibly	**CCCILMNOOV** monocyclic
BGHIKORRTW brightwork	**BIIMNOOSST** bionomists	**CCCILNSTUY** succinctly
BGHILLMNUY humblingly	**BIIMNOSSSU** submission	**CCCINNOOOT** concoction
BGHILLNSUY blushingly	**BIIMNOSTUU** bituminous	**CCCIOOPRSY** cryoscopic
BGHILNNSUU unblushing	**BIINOSSSSY** byssinosis	**CCCNOOORST** concoctors
BGHIPRSTTU Pittsburgh	**BIIOQSTUUU** ubiquitous	**CCDDEEHLTU** declutched
BGHLOOPSUY ploughboys	**BIKLLORSST** storksbill	**CCDDEELNOV** concededly
BGIIILMNOS mobilising	**BILLNOOPSS** spoonbills	**CCDDEENNOS** condescend
BGIIILMNOZ mobilizing	**BILLNORSST** stillborns	**CCDEEEENPR** precedence
BGIIILNOTY ignobility	**BILMMOSSSY** symbolisms	**CCDEEEHINS** dehiscence
BGIIINSSTU subitising	**BILMOORSWW** lowbrowism	**CCDEEEHKPR** prechecked
BGIIINSTUZ subitizing	**BILMOSSSTY** symbolists	**CCDEEEENPRY** precedency
BGIIJMNOSU jumboising	**BILNOOOTUV** obvolution	**CCDEEEENRST** decrescent
BGIIJMNOUZ jumboizing	**BILOOPRSTU** politburos	**CCDEEERRSU** recrudesce
BGIIJNNOSU subjoining	**BIMNOORSTT** trombonist	**CCDEEERSSU** succeeders
BGIIKLNNNU unblinking	**BIMOOPPRRU** opprobrium	**CCDEEFIINY** deficiency
BGIILMOORS imbroglios	**BINOORSSTU** obtrusions	**CCDEEFINNO** confidence
BGIILNOSSU subsoiling	**BIOORSSTUU** robustious	**CCDEEGINSU** succeeding
BGIILNSTTU subtitling	**BKLLMNSSUU** numbskulls	**CCDEEHIKSW** chickweeds
BGIILOOSST biologists	**BKMOOOPPRT** promptbook	**CCDEEHIORT** ricocheted
BGIIMNSTTU submitting	**BKOOORSSTY** storybooks	**CCDEEHKORW** checkrowed
BGIINOORST robotising	**BLLOOTTUWY** woollybutt	**CCDEEHLSTU** declutches
BGIINOORTZ robotizing	**BLLOSTUUUY** tubulously	**CCDEEHMOSY** ecchymosed
BGIINORSUU rubiginous	**BMMOOOSTTT** bottommost	**CCDEEHNOSY** synecdoche
BGIINSSSTU subsisting	**BOOPPRRSTU** turboprops	**CCDEEIIIPT** epideictic
BGIKNOPRSS springboks	**CCCCGINOOO** gonococcic	**CCDEEIILRT** dielectric
BGILLMMNUY mumblingly	**CCCIIMOOR** micrococci	**CCDEEIIMRT** decimetric
BGILLMNOSY symbolling	**CCCDEILOPY** cyclopedic	**CCDEEIINNS** incidences
BGILLMNRUY rumblingly	**CCCDIILOOP** diplococci	**CCDEEIIPPR** precipiced
BGILMNOOSS blossoming	**CCCEEINNOS** conscience	**CCDEEIKLRV** cleverdick
BGILNNORTU Burlington	**CCCEEINORT** ecocentric	**CCDEEILNOR** reconciled
BGILOORSTY bryologist	**CCCEEINRST** crescentic	**CCDEEILOSW** colicweeds
BGILOORSUU Louisbourg		**CCDEEIMORT** ectodermic
BGILORSUUU lugubrious	eccentrics	**CCDEEIOPRU** reoccupied
BGIMNNOOSU unbosoming	**CCCEELNSUU** succulence	**CCDEELMOPT** complected
BGINNORSTU binturongs	**CCCEENORRU** occurrence	**CCDEELNNOO** condolence
BGINNOSTUW snowtubing	**CCCEHIILMV** hemicyclic	**CCDEENNORT** concentred
BGINORSSTW bowstrings	**CCCEHIILNO** colchicine	**CCDEENORSS** crescendos
BHHIMORSTY biorhythms	**CCCEHIIORS** chiccories	**CCDEEORRRU** reoccurred
BHHOORSTTU toothbrush	**CCCEHIMOTY** ecchymotic	**CCDEFIIKNO** cocknified
BHIIIINNOT inhibition	**CCCEHKORSS** crosscheck	**CCDEFILNOT** conflicted
BHIIINORST inhibitors	**CCCEIILPRY** pericyclic	**CCDEGHHIOU** hiccoughed
BHIIINORTY inhibitory	**CCCEIIMRSU** circumcise	**CCDEHHNRUU** unchurched
BHIILLNOST billionths	**CCCEIIRSTY** cysticerci	**CCDEHILNOR** chronicled
BHIILLRSTT stillbirth	**CCCEILOTUY** leucocytic	**CCDEIIILOT** idiolectic
BHIIOOPRRT prohibitor	**CCCEINNOOP** Concepción	**CCDEIIIRST** criticised
BHILLNORST thornbills	**CCCEINNORT** concentric	**CCDEIIIRTZ** criticized
BHIMNPRTTU thumbprint	**CCCEINOOTV** concoctive	**CCDEIILOPY** epicycloid
BHIMOORSST thrombosis	**CCCEINOOTY** coenocytic	**CCDEIINNOR** endocrinic
BHIMOSSTUU bismuthous	**CCCEKLNOOR** corncockle	**CCDEIINNOT** coincident
BHIOORRSTT birthroots	**CCCELNSUUY** succulency	**CCDEIKKOTT** ticktocked
BHIORRSTTW birthworts	**CCCENOORST** concocters	**CCDEILOORS** crocodiles
BHJOORSSTW jobsworths	**CCCGINNOOT** concocting	**CCDEIMOOOT** octodecimo
BHKNOOOTTU buttonhook	**CCCGNOOOSU** gonococcus	**CCDEINNOST** disconnect
BHLLOOOSTT tollbooths	**CCCHHILOOO** chocoholic	**CCDEINOOPS** endoscopic
BHOOOOPSUZ zoophobous	**CCCHIKNOPS** pinchcocks	picosecond
BIIIILRSTY risibility	**CCCHIKOPST** spitchcock	**CCDEINOOST** decoctions
BIIIILSTVY visibility	**CCCHILMOOY** homocyclic	**CCDEINOPUU** unoccupied
BIIILMMMOS immobilism	**CCCHILMOSU** colchicums	**CCDEINORST** disconcert
BIIILMMOTY immobility	**CCCHILOOST** coccoliths	**CCDEINOTUV** conductive
	CCCIILRSTY tricyclics	

CCDELNORSU concluders	**CCEEHMOSSY** ecchymoses	**CCEENOPRRT** preconcert
CCDGIIINNO coinciding	**CCEEHNOSTU** escutcheon	**CCEEOORTUX** coexecutor
CCDGIILOSU glucosidic	**CCEEHORRST** crocheters	**CCEFGINNOT** confecting
CCDGIILOSY glycosidic	**CCEEHOSTTU** couchettes	**CCEFHIIMOR** microfiche
CCDGIKLNOU cuckolding	**CCEEIIINNP** incipience	**CCEFIIINST** scientific
CCDGILNNOU concluding	**CCEEIILMRS** semicircle	**CCEFIIKNOS** cocknifies
CCDGILOOOY codicology	**CCEEIILPTU** epicuticle	**CCEFIINPSU** unspecific
CCDGINNOTU conducting	**CCEEIIMPST** septicemic	**CCEFIIRRSU** crucifiers
CCDHIIIORT dichroitic	**CCEEIIPPRS** precipices	**CCEFIIRSUX** crucifixes
CCDHIIMOOT dichotomic	**CCEEIKRRST** cricketers	**CCEFILMRUX** circumflex
CCDHIINORT chondritic	**CCEEILLOTV** collective	**CCEFIMRSUU** circumfuse
CCDHKOOSUW woodchucks	**CCEEILMNNY** inclemency	**CCEFINNOOT** confection
CCDIIOORST corticoids	**CCEEILNOPU** leucopenic	**CCEFLLNOTU** flocculent
CCDIMNOSTU misconduct	**CCEEILNORR** reconciler	**CCEFLSSSUU** successful
CCDINNOOTU conduction	**CCEEILNORS** reconciles	**CCEGGILNOY** glycogenic
CCDNOORSTU conductors	**CCEEILNORT** electronic	**CCEGHHORRU** churchgoer
CCDOOOSSUW cocuswoods	**CCEEILOPST** telescopic	**CCEGHIIIOP** pichiciego
CCEEEEHIKP cheekpiece	**CCEEILORVY** coercively	**CCEGHIILNO** conchiglie
CCEEEEELLNX excellence	**CCEEILOTUX** exocuticle	**CCEGHIIRNS** screiching
CCEEEEENNSS senescence	**CCEEILPRSY** pericycles	**CCEGHINORT** crocheting
CCEEEFNNOR conference	**CCEEINNNOT** continence	**CCEGIIKNRT** cricketing
CCEEEFNRSU rufescence	**CCEEINNOTV** connective	**CCEGIILNNR** encircling
CCEEEGINOS geoscience	**CCEEINNRRU** incurrence	**CCEGIINNOT** conceiting
CCEEEHIPSS chesspiece	**CCEEINNRST** increscent	**CCEGIINNOV** conceiving
CCEEEHRRSS screechers	**CCEEINOPRT** encopretic	**CCEGILLNOT** collecting
CCEEEIINPR recipience	**CCEEINOPRW** crownpiece	**CCEGIMMNNO** commencing
CCEEEIKNPS neckpieces	**CCEEINOPTV** conceptive	**CCEGINNNOR** concerning
CCEEEILMNS clemencies	**CCEEINORST** concertise	**CCEGINNNOS** ensconcing
CCEEEINPRS prescience		concretise	**CCEGINNNOT** connecting
CCEEEINQSU quiescence		cornetcies	**CCEGINNORT** concerting
CCEEEINRSV virescence		ectocrines		concreting
CCEEEIOPSS ecospecies	**CCEEINORSV** conceivers	**CCEGINORRT** correcting
CCEEEELLNXY excellency	**CCEEINORTV** concretive	**CCEGINORSY** cryogenics
CCEEEELNOST Ecclestone	**CCEEINORTX** exocentric	**CCEGNNORUY** congruency
CCEEEELORST rectoceles	**CCEEINORTZ** concertize	**CCEHHIRSTU** churchiest
CCEEEMMNOR recommence		concretize	**CCEHHNRSUU** unchurches
CCEEEMNOPT competence	**CCEEINNOSSV** concessive	**CCEHIINNNO** cinchonine
CCEEEMNSTU tumescence	**CCEEINOTVV** convective	**CCEHIINNOS** cinchonise
CCEEENRRRU recurrence	**CCEEINQSUY** quiescency	**CCEHIINNOZ** cinchonize
CCEEENRSTX excrescent	**CCEEINRRSU** currencies	**CCEHIKNOPT** checkpoint
CCEEFFIINY efficiency	**CCEEIOPRSS** crosspiece	**CCEHIKNOPX** chickenpox
CCEEFHHRRU Free Church	**CCEEIOPRSU** reoccupies	**CCEHIKNOSY** cockneyish
CCEEFINTTU fettuccine	**CCEEIOPSTT** copesettic	**CCEHILLORY** cholericly
CCEEFLNNOU confluence	**CCEEIORRTV** corrective	**CCEHILMOOP** phocomelic
CCEEGHIKNR checkering	**CCEEISSSUV** successive	**CCEHILNORR** chronicler
	rechecking	**CCEEJNORTU** conjecture	**CCEHILNORS** chronicles
CCEEGHINRS screeching	**CCEEKKLOYY** cockyleeky	**CCEHILOPPR** pleochroic
CCEEGINNOR congeneric	**CCEEKLORST** cockleerts	**CCEHILOPRR** perchloric
CCEEGINORS concierges	**CCEELLORST** recollects	**CCEHIMOSSY** ecchymosis
CCEEGINORT egocentric	**CCEELMORTY** cyclometer	**CCEHINRSSU** scrunchies
	geocentric	**CCEELNOPRU** corpulence	**CCEHINRSTU** crunchiest
CCEEGNNORU congruence	**CCEELNORTY** concretely	**CCEHIOORRV** Verrocchio
CCEEHHIRST Chichester	**CCEELNRTUU** truculence	**CCEHIOPTTY** ectophytic
CCEEHHKOPU cheekpouch	**CCEELOSSTY** cystoceles	**CCEHKLNOST** neckcloths
CCEEHIKNRS checkreins	**CCEELOSTUY** leucocytes	**CCEHKMOORS** checkrooms
CCEEHILMSY hemicycles	**CCEEMMNORS** commencers	**CCEHKNOOST** chockstone
CCEEHILRSU cleruchies	**CCEEMNOPTY** competency	**CCEHKOORSS** cockhorses
CCEEHINOSS choiceness	**CCEENNOOST** conoscente	**CCEHLOSSTY** cholecysts
CCEEHIRSTU cutcheries	**CCEENNORST** concentres	**CCEHMOORTY** cytochrome
CCEEHKORSV overchecks		connecters	**CCEHNNORSU** scruncheon
CCEEHLORST cerecloths		reconnects	**CCEHNNOSSU** scruncheons
	Colchester	**CCEENOOSTY** coenocytes	**CCEHNOPRUW** cowpuncher

CCEHNOSSTU	scutcheons
CCEHOSTTUZ	zucchettos
CCEIIIKMWZ	Mickiewicz
CCEIIILNOR	ricinoleic
CCEIIINNPV	incipiency
CCEIIIRRST	criticiser
CCEIIIRRTZ	criticizer
CCEIIIRSST	criticises
CCEIIIRSTU	circuities
CCEIIIRSTV	cervicitis
CCEIIIRSTZ	criticizes
CCEIIKNPRS	picnickers
CCEIILMNOR	microcline
CCEIIILMORT	cliometric
CCEIILNOST	niccolites
CCEIIILOSST	solecistic
CCEIIMOORS	seriocomic
CCEIIMOSSS	coseismics
CCEIIMOTXY	Mexico City
CCEIIMPSST	scepticism
CCEIINNORT	concertini
CCEIINOTVV	convictive
CCEIINRTTY	centricity
CCEIIOORST	crocoisite
CCEIIOPPRS	periscopic
CCEIIORTVY	coercivity
CCEIIKKOPPT	pickpocket
CCEIKLLOSY	kilocycles
CCEIKLOTUY	leukocytic
CCEIKMNOSY	cockneyism
CCEIILLLOSU	cellulosic
CCEIILLNOOT	collection
CCEIILMNNOU	councilmen
CCEIILMOTYY	myelocytic
CCEIILNNOSU	nucleonics
CCEIILNOSUV	conclusive
CCEIILOOQTU	coquelicot
CCEIILORSST	sclerotics
CCEIILOSSUV	occlusives
CCEIMNNOOU	uneconomic
CCEIMNRTUV	circumvent
CCEIMOOPRS	microscope
CCEIMORSTY	microcytes
CCEINNNOOT	connection
CCEINNNOTY	continency
CCEINNOOPT	conception
CCEINNOORT	concertino
	concretion
CCEINNOOSS	concession
CCEINNOOST	conoscenti
CCEINNOOTV	convection
CCEINNORSV	convincers
CCEINOOOPS	iconoscope
CCEINOOPRT	nociceptor
CCEINOORRT	correction
CCEINOPRSU	Copernicus
CCEINORSTV	reconvicts
CCEINOSSSU	succession
CCEINOSSUV	concussive
CCEIOOPRSU	precocious
CCEISSSUUV	successive
CCEKLORSUY	cocksurely

CCEKORRSSW	corkscrews
CCELLOORST	collectors
CCELLOSTYY	cyclostyle
CCELMNOOSY	monocycles
CCELMOORTY	motorcycle
CCELMOOSTY	cyclostome
CCELMORTYY	cyclometry
CCELNOPRUY	corpulency
CCELNOSSTU	occultness
CCELNRTUUY	truculency
CCELNSSTUU	succulents
CCELOOOPPS	colposcope
CCELOOPRSU	corpuscles
CCELOPRSUU	corpuscule
CCELORSSSU	succorless
CCEMOSTTYY	cystectomy
CCENNOORST	connectors
CCENNORRTU	concurrent
CCENOOPRSY	necroscopy
CCENOORSSU	concourses
CCENOORSTV	convectors
CCENOPSSTU	conspectus
CCENORSSTU	succentors
CCEOOPRSSY	cryoscopes
CCEOOPRSTT	ectoprocts
CCEOOPSSTY	cystoscope
CCEOOORRST	correctors
CCEORRSSUU	succourers
CCEORSSSSU	successors
CCFGHIKOST	cockfights
CCFGIINRUY	crucifying
CCFILMORUU	cuculiform
CCFIMORRSU	cruciforms
CCFKOOOSST	cocksfoots
CCGHHHHIRU	High Church
CCGHIINPPU	hiccupping
CCGHINNRSU	scrunching
CCGHINRSTU	crutchings
CCGHLNOOOY	conchology
CCGIIIKNNP	picnicking
CCGIIINRTU	circuiting
CCGIILNRTY	tricycling
CCGIINNNOV	convincing
CCGIINNOTV	convicting
CCGILMOOOS	cosmologic
CCGILOORSY	cyclogiros
CCGILORSUU	glucosuric
CCGILORSUY	glycosuric
CCGIMNOOOS	cosmogonic
CCGINNORRU	concurring
CCGINNOSSU	concussing
CCGINORSUU	succouring
CCGINSSSUU	succussing
CCGIOOPRSY	gyroscopic
CCHHHOOPTT	hotchpotch
CCHHIIOTTY	ichthyotic
CCHHIIRSTT	tristichic
CCHIILMOOX	Xochimilco
CCHIILNNOO	conchiolin
CCHIILOPRY	cryophilic
CCHIIMNNOS	cinchonism
CCHIIMOPRS	microchips

CCHIIMORRT	trichromic
CCHIINORTY	chronicity
CCHIIOPSTY	sciophytic
CCHIKLOSTT	lockstitch
CCHIKOPSST	chopsticks
CCHIMNOOOR	monochroic
CCHINNOORS	cornichons
CCHINNORSU	scrunchion
CCHINNORSY	synchronic
CCHIOOOPRS	horoscopic
CCHIOPSSTY	psychotics
CCHIORSTTY	trichocyst
CCHLNOOSTY	colocynths
CCIIILNOSS	isoclinics
CCIIILOSST	sciolistic
CCIIIMRSST	criticisms
CCIILLNOPY	polyclinic
CCIILMNNOO	monoclinic
CCIILMOPTY	complicity
CCIILNSTUV	unicyclist
CCIILOOPRT	coprolitic
CCIILOPRST	proclitics
CCIILRSTTY	tricyclist
CCIIMMOORT	microtomic
CCIINNNOTY	concinnity
CCIINNOOSS	concisions
CCIINNOOTV	conviction
CCIINOOPRS	scorpionic
CCIINOPSSY	isopycnics
CCIIORSTUU	circuitous
CCIKNOOPTU	cuckoopint
CCILLLOSUU	colliculus
CCILLNOORU	councillor
CCILLOOPTY	collotypic
CCILMRRUUU	curriculum
CCILNNOOSU	conclusion
CCILNOORSU	councilors
CCILNOOSSU	occlusions
CCILOOORST	colicroots
CCILOPSTYY	polycystic
CCILOSSTTU	occultists
CCIMMOORSS	microcosms
CCIMOOPRSY	microscopy
CCINNNOOSU	concinnous
CCINNOOSSU	concussion
CCINOPRSST	conscripts
CCINORSSTT	constricts
CCINOSSSUU	succussion
CCINOSTUVY	viscountcy
CCIOOPRTYZ	cryptozoic
CCIOPPRRTY	procryptic
CCIORRSSSS	crisscross
CCJLNNOTUY	conjunctly
CCKKLOORSW	clockworks
CCKOORSTUW	stuccowork
CCLLOOORTU	collocutor
CCLNOORSTY	cyclotrons
CCNORSSTTU	constructs
CCOOPSSTYY	cystoscopy
CDDEEEELST	deselected
CDDEEEENNP	dependence
CDDEEEHIPR	deciphered

CDDEEEEINRT	interceded	**CDDILOOPSU**	diplodocus	**CDEEEOPRRS**	proceeders
CDDEEEEINUV	undeceived	**CDDINNOOTY**	dicynodont	**CDEEEORRST**	retrocedes
CDDEEEEIRRT	redirected	**CDEEEEEFNRR**	referenced	**CDEEEPRSTU**	persecuted
CDDEEEEJLTY	dejectedly	**CDEEEEGNRT**	detergence	**CDEEFGILNT**	deflecting
CDDEEEELNOR	needlecord	**CDEEEEEINPX**	expedience	**CDEEFHLRSS**	feldschers
CDDEEEENNPY	dependency	**CDEEEEELPRT**	preelected	**CDEEFIIKRR**	Frederick I
CDDEEEENNST	descendent	**CDEEEEELRST**	reselected	**CDEEFIINRT**	dentifrice
CDDEEEENOTX	coextended	**CDEEEEENRRT**	deterrence	**CDEEFIIORS**	recodifies
CDDEEEENRSS	descenders	**CDEEEEENRRV**	reverenced	**CDEEFIIOST**	foeticides
	redescends	**CDEEEEFFINR**	difference	**CDEEFIKRRV**	Frederick V
CDDEEEENRSU	descendeur	**CDEEEEFHIKR**	kerchiefed	**CDEEFILNNU**	influenced
CDDEEEENTTU	undetected	**CDEEEEFIILP**	fieldpiece	**CDEEFILNOT**	deflection
CDDEEEORRR	rerecorded	**CDEEEEFILTV**	deflective	**CDEEFINNTU**	uninfected
CDDEEEORRT	retroceded	**CDEEEEFINRT**	reinfected	**CDEEFINORR**	reinforced
CDDEEFFIIN	diffidence	**CDEEEEFNORR**	reenforced	**CDEEFINOST**	defections
CDDEEFIIOR	recodified	**CDEEEEGINRV**	divergence	**CDEEFINTUV**	defunctive
CDDEEFIKLN	fiddleneck	**CDEEEEGNRTY**	detergency	**CDEEFKLOOR**	forelocked
CDDEEGINNS	descending	**CDEEEEHINPR**	enciphered	**CDEEFKLPSY**	flyspecked
CDDEEHLOOS	deschooled	**CDEEEEHIPRR**	decipherer	**CDEEFKOSST**	feedstocks
CDDEEIINSS	dissidence	**CDEEEEHIRRT**	Eric the Red	**CDEEFLNORT**	centerfold
CDDEEIIJPRU	prejudiced	**CDEEEEHLRSU**	reschedule		centrefold
CDDEEIILNRY	cylindered	**CDEEEEHNNRT**	entrenched	**CDEEFLNORY**	enforcedly
CDDEEIMNOR	endodermic	**CDEEEEHNRRT**	retrenched	**CDEEFLOORS**	foreclosed
CDDEEINORS	considered	**CDEEEEHOOSW**	cheesewood	**CDEEFLORST**	deflectors
CDDEEINPRS	prescinded	**CDEEEIKNPR**	Penderecki	**CDEEFLORSU**	fluoresced
CDDEEINRTU	undirected	**CDEEEEILNRS**	relicensed	**CDEEFNNORU**	unenforced
CDDEEIOPTY	copyedited	**CDEEEEILOPV**	velocipede	**CDEEFNORSS**	forcedness
CDDEEIORSV	discovered	**CDEEEEILQSU**	deliquesce	**CDEEFORSSU**	refocussed
CDDEEIPRTU	depictured	**CDEEEIMNNO**	comedienne	**CDEEGIILNS**	diligences
CDDEELLSUY	secludedly	**CDEEEEIMNNP**	impendence	**CDEEGIIMRS**	germicides
CDDEELMOSU	cuddlesome	**CDEEEIMRRS**	mercerised	**CDEEGIINNV**	evidencing
CDDEELOORU	decoloured	**CDEEEIMRRZ**	mercerized	**CDEEGIINOR**	Ceredigion
CDDEEMNOTU	documented	**CDEEEIMRST**	decimeters	**CDEEGILNNU**	indulgence
CDDEEMOOPS	decomposed		decimetres	**CDEEGILNUV**	divulgence
CDDEENNOSU	unseconded	**CDEEEINNSS**	desinences	**CDEEGILRSY**	glycerides
CDDEENORRU	unrecorded	**CDEEEINNST**	tendencies	**CDEEGIMNNO**	endergonic
CDDEEOPRRU	reproduced	**CDEEEINPST**	centipedes	**CDEEGINOPR**	proceeding
CDDEERSTTU	destructed	**CDEEEINPXY**	expediency	**CDEEGINORS**	recognised
CDDEFIKORS	disfrocked	**CDEEEINRRT**	interceder	**CDEEGINORZ**	recognized
CDDEFNNOOU	confounded	**CDEEEINRSS**	residences	**CDEEGINRVY**	divergency
CDDEGIKLOR	gridlocked	**CDEEEINRST**	intercedes	**CDEEGLLRSU**	cudgellers
CDDEHIILOR	dichloride	**CDEEEINRSW**	widescreen	**CDEEHIILOP**	ophicleide
CDDEHISTUY	Thucydides	**CDEEEINRUV**	undeceiver	**CDEEHIIOST**	theodicies
CDDEIIRSST	discredits	**CDEEEINSST**	desistence	**CDEEHILLPR**	prechilled
CDDEIIRSTT	districted	**CDEEEINSUV**	undeceives	**CDEEHIMNOR**	echinoderm
CDDEILOORS	discolored	**CDEEEISTTV**	detectives	**CDEEHINNRT**	intrenched
CDDEIMMNOO	incommoded	**CDEEELLNUX**	unexcelled	**CDEEHINRST**	christened
CDDEIMMNOS	discommend	**CDEEELMOPS**	Empedocles	**CDEEHKNPUY**	keypunched
CDDEIMMOOS	discommode	**CDEEEELNSTU**	unselected	**CDEEHKOSSU**	deckhouses
CDDEIMOOSU	duodecimos	**CDEEEELOPST**	telescoped	**CDEEHKRSTU**	huckstered
CDDEINNOOT	endodontic	**CDEEEELORST**	electrodes	**CDEEHLORSY**	hydroceles
CDDEINORTU	introduced	**CDEEEMNNOT**	encodement	**CDEEHLPRSU**	sepulchred
CDDEINOSTU	deductions	**CDEEEMNRST**	decrements	**CDEEHLRTWY**	wretchedly
	discounted	**CDEEEMSSTY**	metecdyses	**CDEEHMNOPR**	comprehend
CDDEIORSSU	discoursed	**CDEEENNORS**	recondense	**CDEEHNNQUU**	unquenched
CDDEMNOOPU	compounded	**CDEEENNORV**	reconvened	**CDEEHORRST**	Dorchester
	decompound	**CDEEENNRSU**	unscreened	**CDEEIIIMNT**	cimetidine
CDDGIINORS	discording	**CDEEENNSST**	decentness	**CDEEIIINSV**	indecisive
CDDHHIIMSU	shidduchim	**CDEEENORVY**	reconveyed	**CDEEIIILRST**	deciliters
CDDHHILOOS	childhoods	**CDEEENPRST**	precedents		decilitres
CDDHILLOSY	cloddishly	**CDEEENPTUX**	unexpected	**CDEEIILSVY**	decisively
CDDIILNORY	cylindroid	**CDEEENTUUX**	unexecuted	**CDEEIIMNRS**	reminisced

CDEEIIMNTV	endemicity	CDEEINRRSS	discerners	CDEFIIIILS	silicified
CDEEIIMPRR	peridermic		rescinders	CDEFIINSST	disinfects
CDEEIIMPRS	spermicide	CDEEINRSST	directness	CDEFILNNOV	confinedly
CDEEIIMRSV	vermicides	CDEEINRSTY	dysenteric	CDEFILNORS	cornfields
CDEEIINRST	indiscreet	CDEEIOPRRV	overpriced	CDEFINNNOU	unconfined
	indiscrete	CDEEIORRSV	discoverer	CDEFINNOTU	functioned
	iridescent		rediscover	CDEFINOORV	confervoid
CDEEIIOPST	poeticised	CDEEIOSTTU	eutectoids	CDEFLNOSUY	confusedly
CDEEIIOPTZ	poeticized	CDEEIPRSST	disrespect	CDEFNNOORT	confronted
CDEEIIORRT	cordierite	CDEEIPRSTU	depictures	CDEFNNOORU	confounder
CDEEIIORST	eroticised	CDEEIRRSST	directress	CDEFNNOSUU	unconfused
CDEEIIORTZ	eroticized	CDEEIRRSTT	derestrict	CDEFNORRTU	undercroft
CDEEIIPRRS	cirripedes		restricted	CDEGGILLNU	cudgelling
CDEEIIPRTV	predictive	CDEEIRSTTU	certitudes	CDEGHIIOST	gothicised
CDEEIIPSST	pesticides	CDEEKNNORU	unreckoned	CDEGHIIOTZ	gothicized
CDEEIIRSSV	disservice	CDEEKOOORV	overcooked	CDEGHILNSU	scheduling
CDEEIIRSTV	directives	CDEEKOOPRW	woodpecker	CDEGHINNRS	drenchings
CDEEIISTVV	vivisected	CDEELLNOSU	counselled	CDEGHINNRU	chundering
CDEEIJPRSU	prejudices	CDEELLNRSU	cullenders	CDEGHINSSU	duchessing
CDEEIKNSSW	wickedness	CDEELMNSTU	demulcents	CDEGIIJNST	disjecting
CDEEILLNST	stencilled	CDEELNNOSU	unenclosed	CDEGIIKNRR	derricking
CDEEILMNSU	luminesced	CDEELNSSTU	dulcetness	CDEGIINNRS	discerning
CDEEILNNOS	declension	CDEELOOORV	overcooled		rescinding
CDEEILNNSU	unlicensed	CDEELOPPSY	pelecypods	CDEGIINNRU	reinducing
CDEEILNNTY	indecently	CDEELOPSUY	Polydeuces	CDEGIINNSX	exscinding
CDEEILNOOS	decolonise	CDEELRSTTU	declutters	CDEGIINOTU	digoneutic
CDEEILNOOZ	decolonize	CDEEMMNORS	recommends	CDEGIINPRT	predicting
CDEEILNOSU	nucleoside	CDEEMMNOPR	precondemn	CDEGIINSST	dissecting
CDEEILNOTU	nucleotide	CDEEMMNORS	condemners	CDEGIKNOST	destocking
CDEEILNRVY	Inverclyde	CDEEMMNOST	secondment		stockinged
CDEEILOORS	decolorise	CDEEMOOPRS	decomposer	CDEGILMMNO	commingled
CDEEILOORZ	decolorize		recomposed	CDEGILNOPU	decoupling
CDEEILORST	cloistered	CDEEMOOPSS	decomposes	CDEGILNPRU	precluding
CDEEILPRTY	decrepitly	CDEEMOPRSS	compressed	CDEGILNRSU	surcingled
CDEEILRSST	creditless		decompress	CDEGILNSUU	Du Guesclin
CDEEILRSTY	discreetly	CDEENNORSS	condensers	CDEGILOOPS	logopedics
	discretely	CDEENNORST	contenders	CDEGILOSSU	glucosides
CDEEIMMORS	mesodermic	CDEENNORSU	denouncers	CDEGILOSSY	glycosides
CDEEIMMOXY	myxoedemic		uncensored	CDEGIMMNNO	commending
CDEEIMNNPY	impendency	CDEENNRSUU	uncensured	CDEGIMNNNO	condemning
CDEEIMNNSU	decenniums	CDEENOOPSS	endoscopes	CDEGINNNOS	condensing
CDEEIMNNTU	inducement	CDEENOOSTT	cottonseed	CDEGINNNOT	contending
CDEEIMNOSW	economised	CDEENOOTTW	cottonweed	CDEGINNNOU	denouncing
CDEEIMNOOZ	economized	CDEENORRSU	underscore	CDEGINORRS	recordings
CDEEIMNORT	entodermic	CDEENORRUV	undercover	CDEGINPRTY	decrypting
CDEEIMNOSU	eudemonics	CDEENORSTU	unescorted	CDEGIOORRR	corregidor
CDEEIMNPRU	imprudence	CDEENOSTUU	consuetude	CDEGLORSST	goldcrests
CDEEIMNPSU	impudences	CDEENRSSSU	cursedness	CDEGMNORUU	curmudgeon
CDEEIMNSTU	intumesced	CDEENRSSUV	curvedness	CDEGOOORRR	Cerro Gordo
CDEEIMSSTY	metecdysis	CDEENSSSSU	cussedness	CDEHHHIIKT	hitchhiked
CDEEINNORS	endocrines	CDEEOOORSV	overscored	CDEHHIIPRT	diphtheric
CDEEINNRSW	windscreen	CDEEOOPRSV	overscored	CDEHIIISTT	ditheistic
CDEEINNSSU	secundines	CDEEOPPRST	prospected	CDEHIIKOOS	doohickies
CDEEINOPRS	preconised	CDEEOPRRRS	prerecords	CDEHIILNOT	endolithic
CDEEINOPRV	providence	CDEEOPRRRU	reproducer	CDEHIILOPS	discophile
CDEEINOPRZ	preconized	CDEEOPRRSU	procedures	CDEHIILORU	hierodulic
CDEEINOPST	deceptions		reproduces	CDEHIILPTY	diphyletic
CDEEINORRS	considerer	CDEEOPRSTU	prosecuted	CDEHIIMSST	mythicised
	reconsider	CDEERSSSTU	seductress	CDEHIIMTYZ	mythicized
CDEEINPRRU	underprice	CDEFFIIRTU	fructified	CDEHIINOST	hedonistic
CDEEINPRSY	presidency	CDEFGIINSU	fungicides	CDEHILPRUY	hyperdulic
CDEEINRRRU	reincurred	CDEFGIKNOR	defrocking	CDEHIMOPRV	hypodermic
		CDEFHLMORS	Chelmsford		

CDEHINOPST	docentship	**CDEILNNOSU**	uninclosed	**CDELPRSTUU**	sculptured
CDEHINOPTY	endophytic	**CDEILNOSSU**	cloudiness	**CDEMMOOORS**	commodores
CDEHINORST	chondrites	**CDEILOORRT**	tricolored		cosmodrome
CDEHINPRTU	underpitch	**CDEILOORSU**	colourised	**CDEMNOOPRU**	compounder
CDEHIOOPRT	orthopedic	**CDEILOORUZ**	colourized	**CDEMNOORSW**	downcomers
CDEHIORSTW	dowitchers	**CDEILOPSUU**	pediculous	**CDENNOOPRU**	pronounced
CDEHIPPRRU	chirrupped	**CDEILORSSS**	disclosers	**CDENOOPRRS**	correspond
CDEHKORSUV	duckshover	**CDEILORSSU**	disclosure	**CDENOORRST**	corrodents
CDEHLNOOSU	unschooled	**CDEIMMNOOS**	incommodes	**CDEOOPPRTU**	outcropped
CDEHLNORSU	chondrules	**CDEIMMNOPU**	compendium	**CDEOOPRTRU**	outproduce
CDEHLOOPPR	clodhopper	**CDEIMMNOSU**	communised	**CDEOORRSVW**	overcrowds
CDEHLOOPRY	copyholder	**CDEIMMNOTU**	comminuted	**CDEOORSSTU**	outcrossed
CDEHNOOSTT	thecodonts	**CDEIMMNOUZ**	communized	**CDEOORSSWW**	woodscrews
CDEHNORSUU	chunderous	**CDEIMMNOST**	condiments	**CDEOORSTUU**	outsourced
CDEHOOOPSS	hodoscopes	**CDEIMNOOST**	endosmotic	**CDEOORTTUW**	woodcutter
CDEHOOPRSY	hydroscope	**CDEIMNOOSY**	diseconomy	**CDEORRSTTU**	destructor
CDEIIILLST	stillicide	**CDEIMNOPRS**	princedoms	**CDEORSSTTU**	destructos
CDEIIILNNS	disincline	**CDEIMNOSTU**	miscounted	**CDERRSTTUU**	structured
CDEIIILNOT	indicolite	**CDEIMOOPSS**	discompose	**CDFFIILTUY**	difficulty
CDEIIILNPS	discipline	**CDEIMOOPST**	composited	**CDFGIILNUY**	dulcifying
CDEIIIMRSV	recidivism	**CDEIMORSTU**	Democritus	**CDFIIMNORS**	disconfirm
CDEIIIMSTV	victimised	**CDEIMOSSTU**	customised	**CDFIIMOSST**	discomfits
CDEIIIMTVZ	victimized	**CDEIMOSTUZ**	customized	**CDFIIORSSU**	sudorifics
CDEIIINNOS	indecision	**CDEINNOSTT**	discontent	**CDFIMOORST**	discomfort
CDEIIINTVV	vindictive	**CDEINOORSU**	indecorous	**CDGHIILMOU**	glochidium
CDEIIIRSTV	recidivist	**CDEINOOSTX**	exodontics	**CDGHILOORY**	hydrologic
CDEIIKNPPR	pinpricked	**CDEINOPRTY**	decryption	**CDGIIILMNO**	domiciling
CDEIILLNOS	decillions	**CDEINORRTU**	introducer	**CDGIIILNNU**	ridiculing
CDEIILMSTU	multicides	**CDEINORSTU**	discounter	**CDGIILLOPY**	glycolipid
CDEIILNPPR	principled		introduces	**CDGIILNOSS**	disclosing
CDEIILNRTY	indirectly		rediscount	**CDGIINSSSU**	discussing
CDEIILOSTU	solicitude		reductions	**CDGIKLLOOS**	goldilocks
CDEIILOSUY	dieciously	**CDEINOSSTU**	seductions	**CDGILLNOSY**	scoldingly
CDEIILRRSU	ridiculers	**CDEINPRSTU**	unscripted	**CDHHIILLSY**	childishly
CDEIIMNNTT	indictment	**CDEINRSTTU**	instructed	**CDHHIIOSTY**	ichthyoids
CDEIIMNOST	midsection	**CDEIOPRRST**	predictors	**CDHHILORST**	Rothschild
CDEIIMOORT	iodometric	**CDEIOPRTUV**	productive	**CDHHILOSST**	dishcloths
CDEIIMORRS	misericord	**CDEIORRSSU**	discourser	**CDHHIOORST**	Christhood
CDEIIMORST	dosimetric	**CDEIORSSST**	dissectors	**CDHIIINOOP**	idiophonic
CDEIIMORTY	iridectomy	**CDEIORSSSU**	discourses	**CDHIILMTYY**	thymidylic
	mediocrity	**CDEIPPSSTY**	dyspeptics	**CDHIIMNOOR**	chironomid
CDEIIMRSST	misdirects	**CDEIRRSTTU**	strictured	**CDHIIINPSSY**	syndicship
CDEIINOPRT	prediction	**CDEIRSSSSU**	discussers	**CDHIIOSSTU**	distichous
CDEIINOPST	depictions	**CDEJNNOSSU**	jocundness	**CDHILOPRYY**	polyhydric
CDEIINORST	directions	**CDEKLMMOOS**	slommocked	**CDHILORTYY**	hydrolytic
	discretion	**CDEKNOORSU**	undercooks	**CDHILORXYY**	hydroxylic
CDEIINORTY	tyrocidine	**CDELLNOORT**	controlled	**CDHILOSSTU**	dishclouts
CDEIINOSST	dissection	**CDELMNOSUY**	consumedly	**CDHIMNOORY**	monohydric
CDEIINRSTT	interdicts	**CDELMOOPSY**	composedly	**CDHINOOOSU**	cousinhood
CDEIINSSSV	viscidness	**CDELMOOPTT**	complotted	**CDHINOOPRY**	hydroponic
CDEIIOORRS	sororicide	**CDELNNOOSU**	unconsoled	**CDHIOOPSSZ**	schizopods
CDEIIORSTY	iridocytes	**CDELNOORST**	decontrols	**CDHIOPRSTY**	dystrophic
CDEIIORSUV	recidivous	**CDELNOORSU**	undercools	**CDHLMMNOOO**	commonhold
CDEIIORSUX	uxoricides	**CDELNOORUU**	uncoloured	**CDHMMNOORS**	monochords
CDEIIRRSSUV	discursive	**CDELNOORUY**	Euroclydon	**CDHNNOOOSU**	coonhounds
CDEIKLLRSS	drecksills	**CDELNOOSSW**	closedowns	**CDHNOOORST**	notochords
CDEIKLOPST	stockpiled	**CDELNOOSTY**	cotyledons	**CDHNOOSTUW**	touchdowns
CDEIKLOPSU	liposucked	**CDELNOOTUV**	convoluted	**CDIIILNOTY**	indocility
CDEIKNRRTU	undertrick	**CDELNORSSU**	scoundrels	**CDIIIMPTUY**	impudicity
CDEIKNRSUW	windsucker	**CDELNRTUUU**	uncultured	**CDIIINNOST**	indictions
CDEILLLOSU	celluloids	**CDELOORSUV**	overclouds	**CDIIINNSTT**	indistinct
CDEILLLPUY	pellucidly	**CDELOORSUY**	decorously	**CDIIINOSSS**	discission

CDIILNOOSU	nidicolous	
CDIILNSTTY	distinctly	
CDIILOOSUY	dioicously	
CDIILOPPSY	polydipsic	
CDIILORSUU	ridiculous	
CDIIMNORST	doctrinism	
CDIINNOOST	conditions	
CDIINNOSTU	inductions	
CDIINOPRSY	cyprinoids	
CDIINORSTT	doctrinist	
CDIINOSSSU	discussion	
CDIIORRSTT	tortricids	
CDIIPRSSTU	tricuspids	
CDIKLLORST	drillstock	
CDIKMRSSTU	drumsticks	
CDIKORSSTW	swordstick	
CDILLMOOSU	molluscoid	
CDILMOOORX	loxodromic	
CDILMOOPUY	lycopodium	
CDILOORSSU	discolours	
CDIMMNOOSS	discommons	
CDIMMOOOSU	commodious	
CDIMNOOOTY	monocytoid	
CDINOOPRTU	production	
CDINORSSSW	crosswinds	
CDIRRSSTUU	duricrusts	
CDKKNNOOSW	knockdowns	
CDKKNOOORS	doorknocks	
CDMNNORSUU	conundrums	
CDNNOOSTUW	countdowns	
CDNOOOOTTW	cottonwood	
CDNOOOPSUY	cynopodous	
CDNOSSSTUU	Duns Scotus	
CDOORRSSSW	crosswords	
CEEEEFFRSV	effervesce	
CEEEEFNPRR	preference	
CEEEEFNRRR	referencer	
CEEEEFNRRS	references	
CEEEEGIPTX	epexegetic	
CEEEEGMNRS	emergences	
CEEEEHILPS	heelpieces	
CEEEEHIMST	cheesemite	
CEEEEIMRST	cemeteries	
CEEEEINPRX	experience	
CEEEELLNPR	repellence	
CEEEENRRRV	reverencer	
CEEEENRRSV	reverences	
CEEEEFFGLNU	effulgence	
CEEEFFLNSU	effluences	
CEEEEFFLORS	effloresce	
CEEEFGLNRU	refulgence	
CEEEFHLSTT	flechettes	
CEEEFILNSS	fleeciness	
CEEEFILRTV	reflective	
CEEEFINNNS	fescennine	
CEEEFINNRS	inferences	
CEEEFINRRS	firescreen	
CEEEFINRSS	fierceness	
CEEEFINRSY	fervencies	
CEEEFIPRTV	perfective	
CEEEFNORRS	conferrees	
	reenforces	

CEEEEFNQRSU	frequences	
CEEEEFPRRST	perfecters	
CEEEEFPRRTU	prefecture	
CEEEEGGILNN	negligence	
CEEEEGIINPT	epigenetic	
CEEEEGIINSX	exigencies	
CEEEEGILNRT	reelecting	
CEEEEGIMMNR	immergence	
CEEEEGINNOX	xenogeneic	
CEEEEGINORS	recognisee	
CEEEEGINORZ	recognizee	
CEEEEGINRRT	reerecting	
CEEEEGINRST	energetics	
CEEEEGINRTV	vicegerent	
	viceregent	
CEEEEGLLOPR	precollege	
CEEEEGLNORT	electrogen	
CEEEEGLNRST	neglecters	
CEEEEGNRRSU	resurgence	
CEEEEHHLORS	horseleech	
CEEEEHHMRTU	Erechtheum	
CEEEEHHRSTU	Erechtheus	
CEEEEHIKNSS	cheekiness	
CEEEEHIMSTT	chemisette	
CEEEEHINPRR	encipherer	
CEEEEHINPTT	epenthetic	
CEEEEHINRSS	cheeriness	
CEEEEHINSSS	cheesiness	
CEEEEHIPRRS	percheries	
CEEEEHLLSSY	Seychelles	
CEEEEHLPSSS	speechless	
CEEEEHMMNSY	mesenchyme	
CEEEEHMORTT	hectometer	
	hectometre	
CEEEEHNNRRT	entrencher	
CEEEEHNNRST	entrenches	
CEEEEHNORSS	chersonese	
CEEEEHNRRST	retrenches	
CEEEEHOPSST	sheepcotes	
CEEEEHOQRUU	eurocheque	
CEEEEHORRST	threescore	
CEEEEHQRSUX	exchequers	
CEEEEHRSTTV	chevrettes	
CEEEEIILNRS	resilience	
CEEEEIIMNNS	eminencies	
CEEEEIIMPST	timepieces	
CEEEEIINRSV	vicereines	
CEEEEIJLTVY	ejectively	
CEEEEIKLNRS	screenlike	
CEEEEILLMNO	emollience	
CEEEEILLTVY	electively	
CEEEEILMNNT	clementine	
CEEEEILMORT	ceilometer	
CEEEEILMRTT	telemetric	
CEEEEILNORT	reelection	
CEEEEILNPRT	percentile	
CEEEEILNPST	pestilence	
CEEEEILNRSS	relicenses	
CEEEEIMNNTT	enticement	
CEEEEIMNORS	ceremonies	
CEEEEIMNRST	mesenteric	
CEEEEIMNRSV	servicemen	

CEEEEIMNRTT	centimeter	
	centimetre	
	remittence	
CEEEEIMNTTX	excitement	
CEEEEIMRRSS	mercerises	
CEEEEIMRRSZ	mercerizes	
CEEEEINNPRT	pertinence	
CEEEEINOPSS	nosepieces	
CEEEEINPRRT	pericenter	
	pericentre	
CEEEEINPRSS	creepiness	
CEEEEINPRST	epicenters	
	epicentres	
CEEEEINSSTX	existences	
CEEEEINTTWY	winceyette	
CEEEEIORRST	corsetiere	
CEEEEIORRSV	recoveries	
CEEEEIORTVX	overexcite	
CEEEEIPPRTV	perceptive	
	preceptive	
CEEEEIPRRSV	perceivers	
CEEEEIPRSTV	respective	
CEEEEIRRSSX	exercisers	
CEEEEIRSSSV	recessives	
CEEEEISTUVX	executives	
CEEEEJLORTT	electrojet	
CEEEEJMNSTT	ejectments	
CEEEEKKLNPS	kenspeckle	
CEEEEKLRSSS	clerkesses	
CEEEEKORRST	rocketeers	
CEEEEKRRSSU	seersucker	
CEEEELLNPRY	repellency	
CEEEELMORRT	electromer	
CEEEELNOORU	neurocoele	
CEEEELNRSSV	cleverness	
CEEEELNSSST	selectness	
CEEEELOPSST	telescopes	
CEEEELPRSST	preselects	
CEEEEMNNRST	secernment	
CEEEEMNOPRS	recompense	
CEEEEMNORRT	centromere	
CEEEEMNOTYZ	ectoenzyme	
CEEEEMNRSTU	securement	
CEEEENNORSV	reconvenes	
CEEEENNRSST	recentness	
CEEEENOPRSS	encopreses	
CEEEENORSTT	entrecotes	
CEEEENOSSTY	synoecetes	
CEEEENQRSSU	sequencers	
CEEEENRSSSU	secureness	
CEEEEORRRSV	recoverers	
CEEEEPRRSST	respecters	
CEEEEPRSSTU	persecutes	
CEEEFFHILNS	Schlieffen	
CEEEFFIOSSU	coiffeuses	
CEEEFFOOPST	coffeepots	
CEEEFGHINNR	greenfinch	
CEEEFGILNRT	reflecting	
CEEEFGINOSU	Cienfuegos	
CEEEFGINPRT	perfecting	
CEEEFGINRTU	centrifuge	
CEEEFGLLNTU	neglectful	

CEEFGLNRUY	refulgency	**CEEGINNORU**	neurogenic	**CEEHIMNNRT**	enrichment
CEEFGLNSTU	genuflects	**CEEGINNOSS**	consignees	**CEEHIMNRTT**	Metternich
CEEFHHNORT	henceforth	**CEEGINNNQSU**	sequencing	**CEEHIMNTTU**	technetium
CEEFHLLRUY	cheerfully	**CEEGINNRSS**	screenings	**CEEHIMOPTU**	mouthpiece
CEEFHORTTU	fourchette	**CEEGINNRST**	centerings	**CEEHIMORRT**	rheometric
CEEFIIILST	felicities		nigrescent	**CEEHIMORTX**	exothermic
CEEFIILNTV	inflective	**CEEGINNRSU**	insurgence	**CEEHINNORT**	incoherent
CEEFIINORT	fictioneer	**CEEGINNSST**	ignescents	**CEEHINNRRT**	intrencher
CEEFIIPRSS	specifiers	**CEEGINOORS**	ecoregions	**CEEHINNRST**	intrenches
CEEFIIRRST	certifiers	**CEEGINOORT**	erotogenic	**CEEHINOPPR**	Hippocrene
	rectifiers		orogenetic	**CEEHINORSS**	heroicness
CEEFIKLNSS	fickleness	**CEEGINOOST**	osteogenic	**CEEHINQSTU**	techniques
CEEFILNNRU	influencer	**CEEGINORRS**	recogniser	**CEEHINRRST**	christener
CEEFILNNSU	influences	**CEEGINORRV**	recovering		rechristen
CEEFILNORT	reflection	**CEEGINORRZ**	recognizer	**CEEHINRSTW**	winchester
CEEFIMPRST	imperfects	**CEEGINORSS**	recognises	**CEEHINSSST**	chestiness
CEEFINOPRT	perfection	**CEEGINORST**	estrogenic	**CEEHINSSTT**	tetchiness
CEEFINORRS	reinforces	**CEEGINORSZ**	recognizes	**CEEHIOPPRS**	prophecies
CEEFIORRSU	ceriferous	**CEEGINOSTV**	congestive	**CEEHIOPRST**	spirochete
CEEFIRRSST	firecrests	**CEEGINPRSS**	precessing	**CEEHIOPSSW**	showpieces
CEEFKLLSSY	fecklessly	**CEEGINPRST**	respecting	**CEEHIORRST**	Österreich
CEEFKLORTT	fetterlock		sceptering		torchieres
CEEFLNOORW	coneflower	**CEEGINPRTX**	excerpting	**CEEHIORSTT**	theoretics
CEEFLNRSSU	screenfuls	**CEEGINRSTY**	synergetic	**CEEHIRRSTT**	stretchier
CEEFLNRSSY	flyscreens	**CEEGKNOOSS**	goosenecks	**CEEHIRSTTY**	hysteretic
CEEFLOORSS	forecloses	**CEEGLNORST**	neglectors	**CEEHIRSTWZ**	Schweitzer
CEEFLORRST	reflectors	**CEEGLORSTU**	Gloucester	**CEEHKNPSUY**	keypunches
CEEFLORSSU	fluoresces	**CEEGMOTYYZ**	zygomycete	**CEEHLLNOPS**	cellphones
CEEFLPPRTU	pluperfect	**CEEGNNORTV**	convergent	**CEEHLNORTY**	coherently
CEEFLPRSTU	respectful	**CEEGNOOSTU**	ectogenous	**CEEHLNQSSU**	quenchless
CEEFMNNORT	conferment	**CEEGNORSSS**	congresses	**CEEHLPRSSU**	sepulchers
CEEFMOORST	focometers	**CEEGNRSTTU**	turgescent		sepulchres
CEEFNOPRSU	fourpences	**CEEGORSTTU**	courgettes	**CEEHLQRSSU**	squelchers
CEEFNORRRS	conferrers	**CEEHHIRRSS**	cherishers	**CEEHMMOORR**	chromomere
CEEFNRSTTU	frutescent	**CEEHHMMOOR**	hemochrome	**CEEHNOOPPS**	nephoscope
CEEFOOPSST	fetoscopes	**CEEHIIILST**	helicities	**CEEHNOOPRT**	ctenophore
CEEFOORRSU	forecourse	**CEEHIIKNPT**	thinkpiece	**CEEHNOPRRS**	percherons
CEEFOPRRST	perfectors	**CEEHIILLNS**	heliclines	**CEEHNOPRTY**	hypocentre
CEEFORSSSU	refocusses	**CEEHIIMRST**	erethismic	**CEEHNORSTT**	Chesterton
CEEGGILNNT	neglecting	**CEEHIIRRST**	heritrices	**CEEHNORSTV**	chervonets
CEEGGLNOOY	genecology	**CEEHIIRSTT**	erethistic	**CEEHOPSTTY**	ectophytes
CEEGHIILMP	hemiplegic	**CEEHIIRSTW**	witcheries	**CEEHORRSTU**	retouchers
CEEGHIKNNP	henpecking	**CEEHIKLRRY**	cherrylike	**CEEHRRSSTT**	stretchers
CEEGHILNNO	echeloning	**CEEHIKLSTY**	scythelike	**CEEIIINNPS**	insipience
CEEGHILNRY	cheeringly	**CEEHIKNRST**	thickeners	**CEEIIKLLSU**	sluicelike
CEEGHIMORT	geothermic	**CEEHIKNSTT**	kitchenets	**CEEIIKLNPR**	princelike
CEEGHIMOST	geochemist	**CEEHIKPPRS**	schipperke	**CEEIIKNNTZ**	zinckenite
CEEGHINNOT	ethnogenic	**CEEHIKRSTT**	Treitschke	**CEEIIKRRST**	trickeries
CEEGHINQRU	chequering	**CEEHIKSSTT**	sketchiest	**CEEIILLMRV**	vermicelli
CEEGHKMNRU	Kremenchug	**CEEHILLMSS**	schlemiels	**CEEIILLORS**	collieries
CEEGIINNSS	ensigncies	**CEEHILLRSS**	chisellers	**CEEIILMNTV**	Clement VII
CEEGIINOPR	epirogenic	**CEEHILMNOP**	clomiphene	**CEEIILNOSU**	isoleucine
CEEGIINPRT	receipting	**CEEHILNOPR**	necrophile	**CEEIILNPRR**	princelier
CEEGIINPRV	perceiving	**CEEHILNOPT**	telephonic	**CEEIILNPRS**	periclines
CEEGIINRSX	exercising	**CEEHILNORU**	euchlorine	**CEEIILNRSY**	resiliency
CEEGIINSTT	geneticist	**CEEHILNSST**	Clisthenes	**CEEIILNRTT**	centiliter
CEEGIINSTU	eugenicist	**CEEHILOPRT**	helicopter		centilitre
CEEGIKNRST	greenstick	**CEEHILORRT**	Loir-et-Cher	**CEEIILOSTV**	velocities
CEEGILLOOT	teleologic	**CEEHILORTT**	hectoliter	**CEEIILPPST**	epileptics
CEEGILNOST	tense logic		hectolitre	**CEEIILRTTY**	erectility
CEEGILNPRT	prelecting	**CEEHILOSVY**	cohesively	**CEEIILTTVY**	electivity
CEEGINNNST	sentencing	**CEEHILSSTT**	telestichs	**CEEIIMMPRT**	metempiric

CEEIIMMNNTT	incitement	CEEILNPSST	splenetics	CEEINRSTYZ	syncretize
CEEIIMNRSS	reminisces	CEEILNQSTU	liquescent	CEEIOPPRSS	periscopes
CEEIIMNRTV	ivermectin	CEEILNRSTV	ventricles	CEEIOPRRST	receiptors
CEEIIMORTT	meteoritic	CEEILNRSUY	insecurely	CEEIOPRRSV	overprices
CEEIIMOSST	semeiotics	CEEILNRTTY	reticently	CEEIOPRTTV	protective
CEEIIMPRRT	perimetric	CEEILORSST	sclerotise	CEEIOQRSTU	coquetries
CEEIIMPSSS	speciesism	CEEILORSTZ	sclerotize	CEEIORRSST	corsetiers
CEEIIMPSST	epistemics	CEEILPRSUV	preclusive	CEEIORRSSX	exorcisers
CEEIINNORS	eirenicons	CEEILRSSTW	crewelists	CEEIORRSXZ	exorcizers
CEEIINNRST	encrinites	CEEILSSUVX	exclusives	CEEIORRTUU	couturiere
CEEIINNSST	insistence	CEEIMMOPRT	emmetropic	CEEIORSSTU	courtesies
CEEIINNSTV	incentives	CEEIMMORRS	micromeres	CEEIPRRSUV	precursive
CEEIINOPST	centipoise	CEEIMMORRT	micrometer	CEEIPRSSUV	percussive
CEEIINPPRT	percipient		micrometre	CEEIPSSTUV	susceptive
CEEIINPRST	recipients	CEEIMMOSTT	committees	CEEIRRRSTU	recruiters
CEEIINPSTV	inceptives	CEEIMNNOPR	prominence	CEEJNOOSSS	jocoseness
	inspective	CEEIMNNRST	increments	CEEJORRSTT	retrojects
CEEIINPSTX	excipients	CEEIMNOORS	economiser	CEEKLLRSSY	recklessly
CEEIINRSTT	interstice	CEEIMNOORZ	economizer	CEEKLNRTTU	turtleneck
CEEIINSSTZ	citizeness	CEEIMNOOSS	economises	CEEKLOPSST	pocketless
CEEIINSTVV	invectives	CEEIMNOOSZ	economizes	CEEKLORRWW	crewelwork
CEEIINTTVX	extinctive	CEEIMNOSST	centesimos	CEEKLOSTUY	leukocytes
CEEIIOPSST	poeticises	CEEIMNRTTY	remittency	CEELLMOPRS	compellers
CEEIIOPSTZ	poeticizes	CEEIMNSSSU	meniscuses	CEELLMOPTY	completely
CEEIIORRST	escritoire	CEEIMNSSTU	intumesces	CEELMMNOPT	complement
CEEIIORSST	eroticises	CEEIMORSTV	viscometer	CEELMNNOOS	somnolence
CEEIIORSTZ	eroticizes	CEEIMOSSTV	vicomtesse	CEELMNOOPX	complexone
CEEIIPSSST	speciesist	CEEINNNOTV	convenient	CEELMNOOSU	nucleosome
CEEIIRRRSU	currieries	CEEINNORSS	recensions	CEELMOORTU	coulometer
CEEIIRSSTU	securities	CEEINNPSST	spinescent	CEELMOPRST	completers
CEEIJLOPRT	projectile	CEEINOPPRT	perception	CEELMOSTYY	myelocytes
CEEIJNORST	rejections	CEEINOPRSS	encopresis	CEELNORSSU	enclosures
CEEIJNRSTT	interjects		necropsies	CEELNORSVY	conversely
CEEIJOPRTV	projective		precession	CEELOOPRST	coleopters
CEEIJRSTUV	surjective		preconises	CEELOPRRST	prelectors
CEEIJRSTYY	Jersey City	CEEINOPRST	receptions	CEELORRSTY	clerestory
CEEIKLLRST	clerkliest	CEEINOPRSZ	preconizes	CEELORSSUX	exclosures
CEEIKLNOPU	leukopenic	CEEINOPRTX	excerption	CEEMMNORST	commenters
CEEIKLNRSS	silkscreen	CEEINOPSTX	exceptions	CEEMMOTXYY	myxomycete
CEEIKNOPSS	kinescopes	CEEINORRST	Corrientes	CEEMMNORST	contemners
CEEIKNPRTY	pernickety	CEEINORRSW	cornerwise	CEEMMNSTTY	encystment
CEEIKNQRSU	requickens	CEEINORSSS	recessions	CEEMNOORST	centrosome
CEEIKNSSSS	sicknesses	CEEINORSST	resections	CEEMNOOSTU	coenosteum
CEEIKOPRSW	workpieces		secretions	CEEMNOPRTU	recoupment
CEEILLNPRS	pencillers	CEEINORSTV	ventricose	CEEMNOPRTY	pycnometer
CEEILLNRST	stenciller	CEEINORTTV	convertite	CEEMNORTUY	neurectomy
CEEILLNSTT	intellects	CEEINORTTY	coeternity	CEEMNPSSTU	spumescent
CEEILLOOPT	coleoptile	CEEINORTVV	convertive	CEEMOOPRSS	recomposes
CEEILLORSS	recoilless	CEEINOSSSS	secessions	CEEMOPRSSS	compresses
CEEILLRSSU	sculleries	CEEINOSSTX	exoticness	CEEMORRSTY	cryometers
CEEILMNOPT	incomplete	CEEINOSTTX	coexistent	CEEMOSSSTY	ecosystems
CEEILMNORT	clinometer	CEEINOSTUX	executions	CEENNOQSTU	consequent
CEEILMNOSS	comeliness	CEEINPRSSS	princesses	CEENNORRST	rencontres
CEEILMNSSU	luminesces	CEEINPRSST	reinspects	CEENNORRSU	renouncers
CEEILMOPRS	microsleep	CEEINPRSTT	intercepts	CEENNORRTU	rencounter
CEEILMOPTV	completive	CEEINPRSTU	putrescine	CEENNORSST	consenters
CEEILNOORS	recolonise	CEEINRRSSV	scriveners	CEENNORSTU	encounters
CEEILNOORZ	recolonize	CEEINRRSTU	scrutineer	CEENNPRSSY	pennycress
CEEILNOPRT	prelection	CEEINRSSTT	intersects	CEENOOPSST	copestones
CEEILNORST	centrioles	CEEINRSSTY	syncretise	CEENOPPPRR	peppercorn
CEEILNOSST	selections	CEEINRSTTT	trecentist	CEENOPPRTY	prepotency
CEEILNPRST	princelets	CEEINRSTTV	vitrescent	CEENOPRRSS	precensors

CEENOPRRST	precentors
CEENOQRRSU	reconquers
CEENOQRSTU	reconquest
CEENORRSSV	conservers
	conversers
CEENORRSTV	converters
	reconverts
CEENORSSTT	contesters
CEENORSSTV	covertness
CEENORTTUX	contexture
CEENOSSSTU	countesses
CEENPRSSSU	spruceness
CEENPRSTTU	putrescent
CEEOORRSSV	overscores
CEEOPPRRST	preceptors
CEEOPPRRTY	preceptory
CEEOPRRSTT	retrospect
CEEOPRRSTU	persecutor
CEEOPRRSTX	excerptors
CEEOPRSSTU	prosecutes
CEEOQRSTTU	croquettes
CEEORRSSST	crosstrees
CEEPRSSSTU	suspecters
CEERRRSSSU	resurrects
CEERSSSUUX	excursuses
CEFFGIINOR	officering
CEFFHIINOR	chiffonier
CEFFHILOOY	Holy Office
CEFFIINSTU	sufficient
CEFFIIRRTU	fructifier
CEFFIIRSTU	fructifies
CEFFIRSSTU	scruffiest
CEFFLLORUY	forcefully
CEFGHILNST	fletchings
CEFGHILNTY	fetchingly
CEFGIIKLNR	flickering
CEFGIILNNT	inflecting
CEFGIINPSY	specifying
CEFGIINRTY	certifying
	rectifying
CEFGINNORR	conferring
CEFGINNOSS	confessing
CEFGINORSU	refocusing
CEFHHINORT	Richthofen
CEFHIISSTT	fetichists
CEFHIKORSS	rockfishes
CEFHIKORSS	suckerfish
CEFHIKSSSU	suckfishes
CEFHILSTTU	cuttlefish
CEFHKOORSS	foreshocks
CEFIIIILSS	silicifies
CEFIIILNTV	inflictive
CEFIIILNTY	infelicity
CEFIILNNOT	inflection
CEFIILNOQU	cinquefoil
CEFIILNRST	inflicters
CEFIILOSTU	felicitous
CEFIIMNNOT	omnificent
CEFIIMNNTU	munificent
CEFIINNOST	infections
CEFIINOPRT	proficient
CEFIINOPST	pontifices

CEFIINOSTU	infectious
CEFIIORRSS	scorifiers
CEFIKLORRS	frolickers
CEFIKORSSS	fossickers
CEFILLMRUY	mercifully
CEFILMNRUU	unmerciful
CEFILMOORS	frolicsome
CEFILNORST	inflectors
CEFILORSUU	luciferous
CEFIMNORRS	confirmers
	reconfirms
CEFIMORSUY	cymiferous
CEFINNOOSS	confession
CEFINNORSU	coniferous
CEFINORSTU	confitures
CEFIOORSUV	vociferous
CEFKLOPSTU	pocketfuls
CEFKOORRSW	workforces
CEFLNNOSTU	confluents
CEFLNOORRW	cornflower
CEFMNOORRS	conformers
CEFMOORRST	comforters
CEFNNOORRT	confronter
CEFNOORSSS	confessors
CEFOORRSTU	forecourts
CEGGHIINRS	screighing
CEGGILNOSS	clogginess
CEGGINNORV	converging
CEGGINNOST	congesting
CEGGINOOST	geognostic
CEGGLNOOYY	gynecology
CEGHHIINRS	cherishing
CEGHIIINST	ethicising
CEGHIIINTZ	ethicizing
CEGHIIKNNT	thickening
CEGHIIKNRW	whickering
CEGHIILLNS	chiselling
CEGHIILOOR	hierologic
CEGHIINNUY	unhygienic
CEGHIINORZ	rhizogenic
CEGHIINOST	histogenic
CEGHIINRTT	chittering
CEGHIIOSST	gothicises
CEGHIIOSTZ	gothicizes
CEGHILLOSU	guilloches
CEGHILMNSY	schemingly
CEGHILNOOT	ethnologic
CEGHILNOPY	phylogenic
CEGHILNOPR	reclothing
CEGHILNPPS	schlepping
CEGHILNQSU	squelching
CEGHILNSTV	vetchlings
CEGHILOPRY	hypergolic
CEGHIMMNOO	homecoming
CEGHIMOOPR	geomorphic
CEGHINNRTU	chuntering
CEGHINOOPT	photogenic
CEGHINOORR	gonorrheic
CEGHINOORT	orthogenic
CEGHINOPTY	phytogenic
	typhogenic
CEGHINORRU	chirurgeon

CEGHINORTU	retouching
CEGHINORTY	trichogyne
CEGHINRSTT	stretching
CEGHIOPSSY	geophysics
CEGHIORSTU	grouchiest
CEGHIRRRUY	chirurgery
CEGHKNORSU	roughnecks
CEGHLNOOTY	technology
CEGHLOOPRU	glucophore
CEGHLOPTYY	glycophyte
CEGHMNOORS	chromogens
CEGHOOPRSY	hygroscope
CEGIIIMNNT	meningitic
CEGIIJNRUV	verjuicing
CEGIIKLLNN	nickelling
CEGIIKLNNR	clinkering
CEGIIKNNQU	quickening
CEGIIKNNRS	snickering
CEGIIKPRST	pigsticker
CEGIILLNNP	pencilling
CEGIILMOOS	semiologic
CEGIILNNPR	princeling
CEGIILNNSS	clinginess
CEGIILNNST	stenciling
CEGIILNNTY	enticingly
CEGIILNPRY	piercingly
CEGIILNQSU	liquescing
CEGIILNTXY	excitingly
CEGIILOPTT	epiglottic
CEGIILORTU	oliguretic
CEGIILOSTU	eulogistic
CEGIINNOST	sectioning
CEGIINNPST	inspecting
CEGIINNTUX	unexciting
CEGIINORSX	exorcising
CEGIINORXZ	exorcizing
CEGIINOSTX	coexisting
CEGIINOSTZ	Gnosticize
CEGIINRRTU	recruiting
CEGIINRSTT	trisecting
CEGIJNOPRT	projecting
CEGIKNNORS	reckonings
CEGIKNOOPR	precooking
CEGIKNORST	restocking
	stockinger
CEGILLMNOP	compelling
CEGILLMOSU	collegiums
CEGILLOOXY	lexicology
CEGILMMNOS	commingles
CEGILMNOOP	monoplegic
CEGILMNOPT	completing
CEGILMOOSY	mycologies
CEGILNNOST	clingstone
CEGILNNOSU	counseling
CEGILNNPTU	centupling
CEGILNRSSU	surcingles
CEGILNRSTU	clustering
CEGILNRTTU	cluttering
CEGILOOOST	oecologist
CEGILOOSST	ecologists
CEGILOOSTT	cetologist
CEGILOOSTY	cytologies

CEGIMMNNOT	commenting
CEGIMNNNOT	contemning
CEGIMNOORS	ergonomics
CEGIMNOORV	overcoming
CEGINNNORU	renouncing
CEGINNNOST	consenting
CEGINNNOTT	contenting
	contingent
CEGINNNRSU	scunnering
CEGINNOOST	congestion
CEGINNOQRU	conquering
CEGINNORRW	recrowning
CEGINNORSS	consigners
CEGINNORST	constringe
CEGINNORSV	conserving
	conversing
CEGINNORTU	countering
	recounting
CEGINNORTV	converting
CEGINNORUV	uncovering
CEGINNOSTT	contesting
CEGINNPRTY	encrypting
CEGINNRSTU	encrusting
CEGINNRSTY	stringency
CEGINNRSUW	unscrewing
CEGINNRSUY	insurgency
CEGINOOOPS	gonioscope
CEGINOOPRT	protogenic
CEGINOORRS	recognisor
CEGINOORRZ	recognizor
CEGINOORST	creosoting
CEGINOPRSS	processing
CEGINOPRTT	protecting
CEGINOQRTU	croqueting
CEGINOQTTU	coquetting
CEGINORRSS	recrossing
CEGINPPRSU	scuppering
CEGINPRSSU	percussing
CEGINPSSTU	suspecting
CEGINRSTTU	scuttering
CEGINRSTUY	curtseying
CEGINRTTUV	curvetting
CEGKMRSSUU	gumsuckers
CEGLNOOSYY	synecology
CEGNNOOOSU	oncogenous
CEGNORRSSU	scroungers
CEGOOPRSSY	gyroscopes
CEHHHIIKRT	hitchhiker
CEHHHIIKST	hitchhikes
CEHHHKRSUV	Khrushchev
CEHHIILMNT	helminthic
CEHHIILMOP	hemophilic
CEHHIIMSST	hemistichs
CEHHILLMSS	schlemihls
CEHHIMRTUY	eurhythmic
CEHHIOOPST	theosophic
CEHHIOPRST	Christophe
CEHHIOPTTY	hypothetic
CEHHKLLOSS	shellshock
CEHHLMOOOS	homeschool
CEHHLOOPRT	choropleth
CEHHLOOSTU	touchholes

CEHHLORTTW	Letchworth
CEHHMOOPTY	chomophyte
CEHHOOPSSU	chophouses
CEHIIINRST	trichinise
CEHIIINRTZ	trichinize
CEHIIKLPTY	kelyphitic
CEHIIKLRST	Christlike
CEHIIKLSTW	switchlike
CEHIIKRTTV	Trevithick
CEHIILLNSS	chilliness
CEHIILMOPS	mesophilic
CEHIILMOST	homiletics
CEHIILNOST	ichnolites
CEHIILNOTX	xenolithic
CEHIILOPTY	heliotypic
CEHIIMNORT	thermionic
CEHIIMOPPR	epimorphic
CEHIIMOPRT	hemitropic
CEHIIMRSTY	mythiciser
CEHIIMRTYZ	mythicizer
CEHIIMSSTY	mythicises
CEHIIMSTYZ	mythicizes
CEHIINPRSS	chirpiness
CEHIINPSST	pitchiness
CEHIINSSTT	snitchiest
CEHIINSTTZ	chintziest
CEHIIOSTTY	histiocyte
CEHIIPRSTY	sphericity
CEHIIPSTUU	euphuistic
CEHIIRRTTU	urethritic
CEHIIRSSTU	heuristics
CEHIKLNSUY	Chelyuskin
CEHIKLPRSS	clerkships
CEHIKNNOST	technikons
CEHIKNNSSU	chunkiness
CEHIKNSSST	kitschness
CEHIKPRSSW	shipwrecks
CEHILMOOZZ	Michelozzo
CEHILNOPST	clothespin
CEHILNOSTU	touchlines
CEHILNRSTZ	Schnitzler
CEHILNSSTZ	schnitzels
CEHILOPRST	lectorship
CEHILORSTY	chrysolite
	chrysotile
CEHILSSTTU	slutchiest
CEHIMMNSSU	chumminess
CEHIMNNOSU	ichneumons
CEHIMNOOPR	microphone
CEHIMNOOTT	nomothetic
CEHIMNOPTY	chimneypot
CEHIMOOORT	homoerotic
CEHIMOOPTY	homeotypic
	mythopoeic
CEHIMOPRTY	microphyte
CEHIMOPSTY	mesophytic
CEHIMPRSUY	hypericums
CEHIMRSTUY	eurythmics
CEHINNNPPY	pinchpenny
CEHINNPSSU	punchiness
CEHINNRSTY	strychnine
CEHINOORRS	rhinoceros

CEHINOORSS	isochrones
CEHINOPPRR	pronephric
CEHINOPPSS	choppiness
CEHINOPPTY	phenotypic
CEHINOPRSS	censorship
CEHINOPRSU	neurochips
CEHINOPRSY	hypersonic
CEHINOPRTY	hypertonic
CEHINOPSTT	pitchstone
CEHINOPTTY	enphytotic
	entophytic
CEHINOSSTU	touchiness
CEHINPRSST	sphincters
CEHINSSTTY	synthetics
CEHIOOPRRT	rheotropic
CEHIOOPRRY	pyorrhoeic
CEHIOORRRT	retrochoir
CEHIOORSTW	switcheroo
CEHIOPRRST	chiropters
	rectorship
CEHIOPRSTT	prosthetic
CEHIOPRSTY	hypocrites
CEHIOPRTXY	xerophytic
CEHIOPSSTY	sciophytes
CEHIOQSTTU	coquettish
CEHIORRSST	choristers
CEHIORSTTU	Theocritus
CEHIPRRRSU	chirrupers
CEHIRRSSSU	scirrhuses
CEHIRSSTTW	Schwitters
CEHKLMNOOT	klootchmen
CEHKLNORSS	schnorkels
CEHKOOOSSU	cookhouses
CEHKOOPPRR	rockhopper
CEHKOORSST	stockhorse
CEHLLOOPST	photocells
CEHLMNOSUU	homuncules
CEHLMOOPRV	polychrome
CEHLMOPTYY	lymphocyte
CEHLNOSSZZ	schnozzles
CEHLOOOPRT	tocopherol
CEHMMNOOOR	monochrome
CEHMMOOORS	chromosome
CEHMMOTTYY	thymectomy
CEHMOOPRST	ectomorphs
CEHMOOPRTY	cormophyte
	ectomorphy
CEHMOSTTYY	thymocytes
CEHNNORSTU	truncheons
CEHNOOOPPS	phonoscope
CEHNOOPRRT	necrotroph
CEHNOOPRTT	topnotcher
CEHNOOSTTU	touchstone
CEHNOPRSTU	Scunthorpe
CEHNOPRSTY	phenocryst
CEHNOPRTYY	pyrotechny
CEHNORRRSS	schnorrers
CEHNORSTVY	Chernovtsy
CEHOOOPRSS	horoscopes
CEHOOOPRST	orthoscope
CEHOORSTUU	courthouse
CEHOPRSTYY	cryophytes

CEHORSTTTU	outstretch
CEIIIILSTV	civilities
CEIIIINSTV	vicinities
CEIIIILLMNO	limicoline
CEIIILLNNP	penicillin
CEIIILMOPS	impolicies
CEIIILNPTX	inexplicit
CEIIILNSVY	incisively
CEIIILOPST	politicise
CEIIILOPTZ	politicize
CEIIILRSSV	civilisers
CEIIILRSVZ	civilizers
CEIIIMMPRS	empiricism
CEIIIMOSSS	isoseismic
CEIIIMPRST	empiricist
CEIIIMRSTV	victimiser
CEIIIMRTVZ	victimizer
CEIIIMSSTV	victimises
CEIIIMSSTY	seismicity
CEIIIMSTVZ	victimizes
CEIIINNNOT	Innocent II
CEIIINNORT	interionic
CEIIINOSTT	tonicities
CEIIINPPRT	precipitin
CEIIIOPSST	isopiestic
CEIIIOSTTX	toxicities
CEIIJNNOST	injections
CEIIJNNTUV	injunctive
CEIIJNSSTU	injustices
CEIIJOOSST	jocosities
CEIIKLMORT	kilometric
CEIIKLNSSS	sickliness
CEIIKLOPRT	politicker
CEIIKLPRST	prickliest
CEIIKMPSST	skepticism
CEIIKNNPRS	princekins
CEIIKNOSTT	tokenistic
CEIIKNPRST	nitpickers
CEIIKNRSST	trickiness
CEIIKNSSST	stickiness
CEIIKRSSTT	tricksiest
CEIILLLSTU	cellulitis
CEIILLNNOT	centillion
CEIILLNRTU	citrulline
CEIILLORRT	Torricelli
CEIILLOSSU	siliculose
CEIILLPTXY	explicitly
CEIILMOPST	polemicist
CEIILMORST	microlites
CEIILNNORS	crinolines
CEIILNOSTU	licentious
CEIILNOSTV	novelistic
CEIILNPPRS	principles
CEIILNRTUV	ventriculi
CEIILOPSTX	postexilic
CEIILORSST	clitorises
CEIIMMORSS	microseism
CEIIMMNNOST	omniscient
CEIIMNOSYZ	isoenzymic
CEIIMNRSSU	sinecurism
CEIIMORSST	isometrics
	microsites

CEIIMOSSTX	exoticisms
CEIIMOSTTT	totemistic
CEIIMPRSSU	epicurisms
CEIINNNOTV	Innocent IV
CEIINNOPST	inceptions
	inspection
CEIINNORST	incretions
CEIINNOTTX	extinction
CEIINNSSTY	insistency
CEIINOPRST	isentropic
CEIINOPRSU	pernicious
CEIINOPRTV	voiceprint
CEIINOPSTT	nepotistic
CEIINORRST	criterions
CEIINORSSS	rescission
CEIINORSTT	trisection
CEIINPRSSS	crispiness
CEIINRSSTU	scrutinies
	scrutinise
	sinecurist
CEIINRSTUV	insecurity
CEIINRSTUZ	scrutinize
CEIINSSSTT	scientists
CEIIOOPSTZ	epizootics
CEIIOORSTU	trioecious
CEIIOPRSTY	preciosity
CEIIOPSSTY	speciosity
CEIIORSTUV	vivisector
CEIJNNOORS	conjoiners
CEIJNOOPRT	projection
CEIJNORSTT	introjects
CEIJNORSTU	surjection
CEIKKLNSTU	knuckliest
CEIKKORRST	kicksorter
CEIKKORRWW	wickerwork
CEIKLLORSS	sollickers
CEIKLLORTT	Little Rock
CEIKLNNOST	clinkstone
CEIKLNORST	interlocks
CEIKLNPSSU	pluckiness
CEIKLNRSTY	strickenly
CEIKLNSTUU	unluckiest
CEIKLOPRST	stockpiler
CEIKLOPSST	stockpiles
CEIKLPRSSU	superslick
CEIKMORSTU	mesokurtic
CEIKNOSSST	stockiness
CEIKNOSSTT	stockinets
CEIKORRSTV	overtricks
CEIKPQSSTU	quicksteps
CEIKRRSSTT	tricksters
CEILLNOSUV	involucels
CEILLOOPST	colestipol
CEILLOOQSU	colloquies
CEILMMNOPT	compliment
CEILMNNOOS	monoclines
CEILMNOOPT	completion
CEILMNOOPX	complexion
CEILMNOOSS	semicolons
CEILMNORTY	clinometry
CEILMNOSTU	monticules
CEILMNPSSU	clumpiness

CEILMNSSSU	clumsiness
CEILMNSSUU	minuscules
CEILMOOOST	colotomies
CEILMOOOTV	locomotive
CEILMOOPST	leptosomic
CEILMOPRSY	micropyles
CEILMOPSTT	completist
CEILMOPSUV	compulsive
CEILMOPTXY	complexity
CEILMORSTU	sclerotium
CEILMORTUV	volumetric
CEILMOSTUU	meticulous
CEILNNNOTY	innocently
CEILNOOSS	cloisonnes
CEILNNOSVY	insolvency
CEILNOOPRS	necropolis
CEILNOORRS	resorcinol
CEILNOORSS	colonisers
CEILNOORSZ	colonizers
CEILNOPRSU	preclusion
CEILNOPSTU	pleustonic
CEILNORSSU	inclosures
CEILNORSUV	involucres
CEILNORTTY	contritely
CEILNOSSST	costliness
CEILNOSSUX	exclusions
CEILNOSTUV	consultive
CEILNOSUVV	convulsive
CEILOOPRST	coprolites
CEILOORRSV	versicolor
CEILOORSSU	colourises
CEILOORSUZ	colourizes
CEILOPRSSV	slipcovers
CEILOPRSTY	proselytic
CEILOPRSUY	preciously
CEILOPSSUY	speciously
CEILORSTTU	courtliest
CEIMMMNOTT	commitment
CEIMMNOORT	metronomic
	monometric
CEIMMNOQUU	communique
CEIMMNORTY	metronymic
CEIMMNOSSU	communises
CEIMMNOSTU	comminutes
CEIMMNOSUZ	communizes
CEIMMOOPRS	compromise
CEIMMOORSS	microsomes
CEIMMOORST	microtomes
	osmometric
CEIMMOORTV	overcommit
CEIMMORRTY	micrometry
CEIMMORSSU	commissure
CEIMMORSTT	committers
CEIMMORTUX	commixture
CEIMNNORTV	Mont Cervin
CEIMNOOOSU	monoecious
CEIMNOOPSS	meconopsis
CEIMNOOPST	coemptions
CEIMNOORST	microtones
CEIMNOORTT	tonometric
CEIMNOOSST	economists
CEIMNOPRSU	proscenium

CEIMNORSUU	ceruminous	CEIOORSSTT	scooterist	CENOORRTTV	controvert
CEIMNRSSTY	syncretism	CEIOORSTTU	ecotourist	CENOPRRTUY	counterspy
CEIMOOPRRS	microspore	CEIOOSSTXY	exocytosis	CENORRSSTU	construers
	poromerics	CEIOPRRTUV	corruptive	CENORSSTXY	xenocrysts
CEIMOOPRRW	micropower	CEIOPRRTWY	copywriter	CENPRRSTUU	puncturers
CEIMOOPRST	proteomics	CEIORRRSSV	Cross River	CEOOPPRRST	prospector
CEIMOOPRTT	competitor	CEIORRSSSY	rescissory	CEOOPRRSSS	processors
	optometric	CEIORRSSTT	trisectors	CEOOPRRSST	prosectors
CEIMOOPSST	composites	CEIORRSTUU	couturiers	CEOOPRRSTT	protectors
CEIMOORSTU	ecotourism	CEIPPRRSST	prescripts	CEOOPRRSTU	prosecutor
CEIMOORSTY	sociometry	CEIPPRSTTY	typescript	CEOOPRRTTY	protectory
CEIMOPRRTY	pyrometric	CEIPRRSSTU	scriptures	CEOOPRSSTY	sporocytes
CEIMORSSTU	costumiers	CEIRRSSTTU	strictures	CEOORRSSSV	crossovers
CEIMORSTVY	viscometry	CEJKOOSTUY	outjockeys	CEOORSSSTU	outcrosses
CEIMOSSSTU	customises	CEJOOPRRST	projectors	CEOORSSTUU	outsources
CEIMOSSTUV	muscovites	CEKKORSSTY	skyrockets	CEOPPRSSTU	prospectus
CEIMOSSTUZ	customizes	CEKLLLSSUY	lucklessly	CEOPRRRSSU	precursors
CEINNNOOSX	connexions	CEKLMPRSUU	lumpsucker	CEOPRRRSTU	corrupters
CEINNNOOTT	contention	CEKOORRSUW	coursework	CEOPRRRSUY	precursory
CEINNNOOTV	convention	CEKOORRSTV	overstocks	CEOPRRSSSU	percussors
CEINNNOSTT	continents	CEKOORSTTU	stockroute	CEOPRRSSTU	Procrustes
CEINNOORSV	conversion	CELLLNTUUY	luculently	CERRSSTTUU	structures
CEINNOPRTY	encryption	CELLNOORRT	controller	CFFFIISSTU	fisticuffs
CEINNOPTUX	expunction	CELLNOORSU	counsellor	CFFGIIIORR	frigorific
CEINNORSTU	centurions	CELLOOOSST	closestool	CFFGIINORU	coiffuring
	continuers	CELLOOPSTY	collotypes	CFFGILNOSY	scoffingly
CEINNOSSTT	consistent	CELLOORSSU	colourless	CFFORRSSSU	crossruffs
CEINNQSUUX	quincunxes	CELLORRSUY	ulcerously	CFGIIILNNT	inflicting
CEINOOPRSS	procession	CELMMOPTUY	lumpectomy	CFGIIKLNOR	frolicking
CEINOOPRTT	protection	CELMNNOOSY	somnolency	CFGIIKNOSS	fossicking
CEINOOPSTT	stenotopic	CELMOOPRSY	copolymers	CFGIIMNNOR	confirming
CEINOORSSU	censorious	CELMOOPRTT	complotter	CFGIINORSY	scorifying
CEINOORTTV	contortive	CELMOORSTY	sclerotomy	CFGIKNNORU	unfrocking
CEINOORTUX	neurotoxic	CELMOORTUY	coulometry	CFGILOSUUU	lucifugous
CEINOOSSUY	synoecious	CELMOOSSSU	colosseums	CFGILOUYZZ	fuzzy logic
CEINOOPPRSU	porcupines	CELMOPRSUU	operculums	CFGIMNNOOR	conforming
CEINOOPRRSS	conspirers	CELNOORSSU	counselors	CFGIMNOORT	comforting
CEINOOPRRST	intercrops	CELNOOSTUV	convolutes	CFHIKOPRST	pitchforks
CEINOOPRSST	inspectors	CELNOPRSUU	pronucleus	CFHIMOPRSY	scyphiform
CEINOOPRSSU	percussion	CELNORSSTU	consulters	CFHKOOOPRS	shockproof
	supersonic	CELOOPRRTU	colporteur	CFHLMOOORR	chloroform
CEINOOPRSTT	introspect	CELOOPRSSU	supercools	CFHLOOOSTT	footcloths
CEINOOPRSTU	supertonic	CELOOSSSSU	colossuses	CFIIILNNOT	infliction
CEINOOPSTTY	stenotypic	CELOOSTUVY	covetously	CFIIIMNORS	incisiform
CEINOQTUYZ	Quezon City	CELPRSSSTU	sculptress	CFIIINOSTT	fictionist
CEINORRRSST	intercross	CELPRSSTUU	sculptures	CFIIIOSTTU	fictitious
CEINORRSSU	coinsurers	CEMMMOOTYY	myomectomy	CFIILLLNOU	folliculin
	recursions	CEMMNNOOSS	commonness	CFIILMMORS	microfilms
CEINORRSTV	contrivers	CEMMNOOORT	Monte Corno	CFIILMOOSU	fimicolous
CEINORSSTT	cornetists	CEMMNOOPST	components	CFIILNORST	inflictors
CEINORSSUX	excursions	CEMMNNORTUY	countrymen	CFIILORSST	floristics
CEINORSTTT	cornettist	CEMNOOOQSU	monocoques	CFIINNNOOT	nonfiction
CEINORTWZZ	Czernowitz	CEMNORTUUV	covermount	CFIIOOPRRT	torporific
CEINOSSTUU	incestuous	CEMOOPRRSS	compressor	CFIIOOPRSS	soporifics
CEINOSTTTU	constitute	CEMORRSSWW	screwworms	CFIIRSTTUU	futuristic
CEINRSSSTT	strictness	CENNNORRTU	noncurrent	CFIKLLNOST	flintlocks
CEINRSSSTU	crustiness	CENNOOPRRU	pronouncer	CFILMMORUU	cumuliform
CEINRSSSUV	scurviness	CENNOOPRSU	pronounces	CFIMNOORST	conformist
CEINRSSTTY	syncretist	CENOOPRSST	stonecrops	CFIMNOORTY	conformity
CEIOOPRRTU	Puerto Rico	CENOOQRRSU	conquerors	CFINNOOSSU	confusions
CEIOOPRRTY	corporeity	CENOORRSST	consorters	CFIOORSUUV	fucivorous
CEIOORRSSV	corrosives	CENOORRSTV	convertors	CFKOOOSSTT	footstocks

CFLLNORSUV scornfully	**CGIIMMNOTT** committing	**CHHLLOOPRY** chlorophyl
CFLOOOSSTT coltsfoots	**CGIIMMNNORS** crimsoning	**CHIIIILNST** nihilistic
CFLOORSSUU scrofulous	**CGIIMNOPRS** comprising	**CHIIILLOPP** lipophilic
CFNOORRTTU frontcourt	**CGIIMNOPSY** miscopying	**CHIIILPPPS** philippics
CGGGILNNOU unclogging	**CGIIMNOSST** gnosticism	**CHIIILPSTY** syphilitic
CGGHINOOPY hypnogogic	**CGIINNNOTU** continuing	**CHIIINORST** histrionic
CGGIILLNNY clingingly	**CGIINNOOST** cognitions	**CHIIKLLSTY** ticklishly
CGGIILNNRY cringingly	incognitos	**CHIILLQSUY** cliquishly
CGGIINNNOS consigning	**CGIINNOPRS** conspiring	**CHIILMNOOT** monolithic
CGGILLNOOU colloguing	**CGIINNORSS** incrossing	**CHIILMOOTT** lithotomic
CGGINNORSU scrounging	**CGIINNORSU** coinsuring	**CHIILMORST** microliths
CGHHIINNTU unhitching	**CGIINNORTV** contriving	**CHIILNOOPT** phonolitic
CGHIIKNPSY physicking	**CGIINNOSST** consisting	**CHIILOSTTY** histolytic
CGHIIKNSTT nightstick	**CGIINNRSTU** incrusting	**CHIIMOOPRS** isomorphic
CGHIIKNSTW wickthings	**CGIINNRTTU** tincturing	**CHIIMOPRRT** trimorphic
CGHIIKSTTT sticktight	**CGIINORSSS** scissoring	**CHIIMORRST** trichroism
CGHIILLLNY chillingly	**CGIINOTTUY** contiguity	**CHIIMORSTU** humoristic
CGHIILLNSS schillings	**CGIJNNORSU** conjurings	**CHIIMSSTTY** mythicists
CGHIILLOOT lithologic	**CGIKLOSSTW** glowsticks	**CHIINNOPPT** pinchpoint
CGHIILMORT microlight	**CGILLNOOPS** scolloping	**CHIINNOPSU** pincushion
CGHIILNTWY witchingly	**CGILLOSSVY** glycolysis	**CHIINOPSSU** cousinship
CGHIILOOST histologic	**CGILMNPRSU** scrumpling	**CHIINORSTU** trichinous
CGHIILOPST phlogistic	**CGILMOOSTY** mycologist	**CHIIOOOPRT** oophoritic
CGHIILPRTY triglyphic	**CGILMOOSUY** musicology	**CHIIORSSSU** rhoicissus
CGHIILRSTW switchgirl	**CGILNNORSU** longicorns	**CHIIPSSSTY** physicists
CGHIINNOSU cushioning	**CGILNNOOVV** convolving	**CHIKLMOSST** locksmiths
CGHIKLNOSY shockingly	**CGILNNOPUU** uncoupling	**CHIKLOSSTY** stockishly
CGHILLOORS schoolgirl	**CGILNNOSTU** consulting	**CHIKNOQRTU** quickthorn
CGHILMNOOY hymnologic	**CGILNNOSUV** convulsing	**CHIKOOPSTT** toothpicks
CGHILNNOTU unclothing	**CGILNOOOST** nostologic	**CHIKOPSSTW** whipstocks
CGHILNOOPY hypnologic	oncologist	**CHILLMOPRY** microphyll
CGHILNOOSS schoolings	**CGILNOORSU** colourings	**CHILLNOOST** loincloths
CGHILNOTUY touchingly	**CGILOOOPRT** tropologic	**CHILLNOSWY** clownishly
CGHILOORTY trichology	**CGILOOOTXY** toxicology	**CHILMOOSUU** humicolous
CGHIMNOOSZ schmoozing	**CGILOOPRTT** proglottic	**CHILNOOPPY** polyphonic
CGHINOOOPR gonophoric	**CGILOOSTTY** cytologist	**CHILNOOPXY** xylophonic
CGHINOOPRY gynophoric	**CGIMNOOPRT** comporting	**CHILNOPSSU** consulship
CGHINOOSYZ schizogony	**CGIMNOOPST** composting	**CHILOOPTTY** photolytic
CGHIOPRSTY copyrights	**CGINNNORUW** uncrowning	**CHILOSSTTY** cystoliths
CGHLNOOORY chronology	**CGINNOORSS** consignors	**CHIMNNOOOP** monophonic
CGHLOOPSYY psychology	**CGINNOORST** consorting	**CHIMNOOSST** monostichs
CGIIIILNSV civilising	**CGINNOORTT** contorting	**CHIMOOOPRZ** zoomorphic
CGIIIILNVZ civilizing	**CGINNOORTU** contouring	**CHIMOOPRSY** hypocorism
CGIIIJNOST jingoistic	**CGINNORSSU** uncrossing	**CHIMOORTTY** trichotomy
CGIIIKNNPT nitpicking	**CGINNORSTU** construing	**CHIMPSSTYY** symphystic
CGIIILNNTY incitingly	**CGINNPRTUU** puncturing	**CHINOOOPTT** phototonic
CGIIILNOST soliciting	**CGINOOPRRT** proctoring	**CHINOOPPTY** phonotypic
CGIIILNSTU linguistic	**CGINOOPRST** prognostic	**CHINOOPRSY** rhinoscopy
CGIIILPSTU pugilistic	**CGINOOSTUU** contiguous	**CHINOPSSTU** countships
CGIIINNSTU cutinising	**CGINOPRRTU** corrupting	**CHIOOOPTTX** phototoxic
CGIIINNTUZ cutinizing	**CGIOOPRSYZ** zygosporic	**CHIOOORSSU** isochorous
CGIIIORRST rigoristic	**CGLOOOPRTY** proctology	**CHIOOPPRRY** pyrophoric
CGIIJNNNOO conjoining	**CGLOOPRTVY** cryptology	**CHIOOPPTTY** phototypic
CGIIKLLNOR rollicking	**CHHIIOSSTY** ichthyosis	**CHIOOPRSTT** orthoptics
CGIIKLNRST strickling	**CHHIIPSTTW** whipstitch	**CHIOOPTTXY** phytotoxic
CGIIKNNSTU unsticking	**CHHILLRSUY** churlishly	**CHIOPRSSTU** courtships
CGIILLMNOO limnologic	**CHHILOOPTY** holophytic	**CHIORSTTTW** stitchwort
CGIILNNOOS colonising	**CHHIMNOOOP** homophonic	**CHLMNOORSU** lunchrooms
CGIILNNOOZ colonizing	**CHHIMNRTUY** unrhythmic	**CHLMNOSUUU** homunculus
CGIILNOORZ colorizing	**CHHINOOPPS** phosphonic	**CHLMOOPRYY** polychromy
CGIILNOPRY pyrolignic	**CHHIOOPPRS** phosphoric	**CHLOOPSTYY** hypocotyls
CGIILOOSTT isoglottic	**CHHKLLOOSY** hollyhocks	**CHLOPPSTYY** polyptychs

CHMOORSSTY	Chrysostom	CILLNOOSSU	collusions	DDDEEIIOSX	deoxidised
CHOOOORSUZ	zoochorous	CILLNOOUVV	convolvuli	DDDEEIIOXZ	deoxidized
CHORRSSTTU	shortcrust	CILLOOOSTY	coyotillos	DDDEEINOSW	disendowed
CIIIIKKNNN	kinnikinic	CILLOOQSTU	colloquist	DDDEEIOORS	deodorised
CIIIILNTVY	incivility	CILLOPRSTU	portcullis	DDDEEIOORZ	deodorized
CIIIILLMORV	microvilli	CILLOPSTUY	Polyclitus	DDDEEIORRS	disordered
CIIIILLMPTY	implicitly	CILLOSSUUY	lusciously	DDDEFILOOW	fiddlewood
CIIIILMNRTU	triclinium	CILMNOOOOT	locomotion	DDDEFMNOUU	dumfounded
CIIIILMPSST	simplistic	CILMNOOPSU	compulsion	DDDEGIIOOR	didgeridoo
CIIIILMPSTY	simplicity	CILMNORUUV	involucrum	DDEEEEELTW	tweedledee
CIIIILNTUVY	uncivility	CILMNOSSTU	columnists	DDEEEEGNNR	engendered
CIIIILPRTTY	triplicity	CILMOOOPSS	cosmopolis	DDEEEEMNRU	unredeemed
CIIIMNNOST	nicotinism	CILNNOOSUV	convulsion	DDEEEEFFNOR	forefended
CIIIMNPPRU	principium	CILNOSSTYY	cytolysins	DDEEEEFLORW	deflowered
CIIIMOPSTT	optimistic	CILOOPRSUU	rupicolous	DDEEEEFNRSU	underfeeds
CIIIMSSTTW	witticisms	CILOORRSTU	tricolours	DDEEEEFORST	deforested
CIIINNNOTT	intinction	CILOORSSTU	colourists	DDEEEEGINRS	redesigned
CIIINNOSTU	unionistic	CILORRSSUU	scurrilous	DDEEEEGIRST	redigested
CIIJNNNOTU	injunction	CILRSSTTUU	culturists	DDEEEEHHPRS	shepherded
CIIKKNNOPT	knickpoint	CIMMNNOOSU	communions	DDEEEEHILSV	disheveled
CIIKNNOPST	nickpoints	CIMMNOOOST	commotions	DDEEEEHLNUY	unheededly
CIIKNNOSTY	cytokinins	CIMMNOSSTU	communists	DDEEEEHNOWY	honeydewed
CIIILLMOOSU	limicolous	CIMNNOOOPP	nincompoop	DDEEEEIMNOR	domineered
CIIILLNNOST	scintillon	CIMNNOSTUU	continuums	DDEEEEIMNRT	determined
CIIILLNOOSS	collisions	CIMNOORSTU	consortium	DDEEEEIMNRU	unremedied
CIIILLNOOST	cotillions	CIMNOOSTXY	mycotoxins	DDEEEEINRST	tenderised
	octillions	CIMOOOPRST	compositor	DDEEEEINRTZ	tenderized
CIIILLNOOTU	illocution	CINNOOORTT	contortion	DDEEEEIRSSV	dissevered
CIIILLOSTTY	stylolitic	CINNOOSSTU	contusions	DDEEEEIRSTU	deuterides
CIIILMMNTUU	nummulitic	CINNOOSTUU	continuous	DDEEEELLMOR	remodelled
CIIILNNOSSU	inclusions	CINOOPRRTU	corruption	DDEEEELMMOS	meddlesome
CIIILNOPSTU	punctilios	CINOORSSTY	consistory	DDEEEELMNTY	dementedly
CIIILOOPPRT	lipotropic	CINOORSUUV	nucivorous	DDEEEELMOPR	empoldered
CIIILOORSST	solicitors	CINOOSTTXY	cytotoxins	DDEEEELNTXY	extendedly
CIIILOOSSTU	solicitous	CINORRSTTU	instructor	DDEEEELOPRY	redeployed
CIIILOPPSTU	populistic	CINOSTTUUY	unctuosity	DDEEEELRSVY	deservedly
CIIILOPRTVY	proclivity	CIOOPPRTTY	prototypic	DDEEEENNPST	dependents
CIIILRRSTUY	scurrility	CIOOPRSSTU	uroscopist	DDEEEENNRRU	unrendered
CIIILSSSTTY	stylistics	CIOOPRSTTT	protoctist	DDEEEENNTUX	unextended
CIIMMNNOOSS	commission	CIOOPRSTTU	prosciutto	DDEEEENRRTU	undeterred
CIIMMOPRRS	microprism	CIOPPRSSTT	postscript	DDEEEENRSUV	undeserved
CIIMNNOOTZ	monzonitic	CKKNORSTUW	knockwurst	DDEEEENRSUX	undersexed
CIIMNOPRRT	microprint	CKLLOORRSW	scrollwork	DDEEEORRST	ordered set
CIIMORRSTT	tricrotism	CKMNOORSTU	moonstruck	DDEEEORSTV	stevedored
CIIINNNOOPT	conniption	CKMOOORSST	stockrooms	DDEEEPRSSU	superseded
CIIINNNOSTU	inunctions	CKOOORSSTT	rootstocks	DDEEFFNNOU	unoffended
CIIINNOORTT	contrition	CLMMNNOOUY	uncommonly	DDEEFGJORU	forejudged
CIIINNORSSU	incursions	CLMOOOORTU	oculomotor	DDEEFIIINT	identified
CIIINNOTTUY	continuity	CLMOOPRSUY	compulsory	DDEEFIIMNS	misdefined
CIIINOOPRTX	picrotoxin	CLNOOOPTTY	polycotton	DDEEFIIMOR	remodified
CIIINOPSSSU	suspicions	CLNOOPRSSU	proconsuls	DDEEFIINRT	trendified
CIIOORSTUV	victorious	CLNOORSSTU	consultors	DDEEFIINTU	definitude
CIIOPSSSUU	suspicious	CLNOSTUUUY	unctuously	DDEEFIIOTX	detoxified
CIIORSSRTTV	vorticists	CLOOOPRRTU	prolocutor	DDEEFIMORS	semifreddo
CIIPSTTTYV	stypticity	CLOPRSSUUU	scrupulous	DDEEFINNRU	unfriended
CIJLNNOOTY	conjointly	CMNOOOOSTU	monotocous	DDEEFLMORY	deformedly
CIKKOOSSUZ	Kosciuszko	CMNOOORSST	cosmotrons	DDEEFLNORU	floundered
CIKLORSSTW	wristlocks	CMOOORRSTU	courtrooms	DDEEFMOOOR	foredoomed
CIKORRSTUW	rusticwork	COOPRRRSTU	corruptors	DDEEGGHOOP	hodgepodge
CILLMOOQUU	colloquium	COOPRSSSTY	sporocysts	DDEEGGIRSU	ruggedised
CILLMORSUY	collyriums	DDDEEEEFNNU	undefended	DDEEGGIRUZ	ruggedized
CILLMOSUUV	colluviums	DDDEEFIOST	eisteddfod	DDEEGGNOSS	doggedness

549

DDEEGIINNX	deindexing	DDEFIIMNOU	unmodified	DDEINPSTUU	undisputed
DDEEGIINST	indigested	DDEFIMNORR	dendriform	DDEIRSSTTU	distrusted
DDEEGILNSY	designedly	DDEFINRSUW	windsurfed	DDELMOOTUY	outmodedly
DDEEGINNSU	undesigned	DDEFLORSSU	Düsseldorf	DDELNORRUW	underworld
DDEEGINSTU	undigested	DDEGHINRSU	shuddering	DDENOOPPRU	propounded
DDEEGIRRSU	drudgeries	DDEGHIORRU	roughdried	DDENOOPRSS	dropsondes
DDEEHIINST	hiddenites	DDEGIIINRV	redividing	DDENOORSTU	understood
DDEEHILMOS	demolished	DDEGIILNRY	deridingly	DDENORRSUU	surrounded
DDEEHILNSU	unshielded	DDEGIINNPS	dispending	DDENRSTUUY	understudy
DDEEHIMOST	methodised	DDEGIINNRS	nidderings	DDEOPRRSTU	rudderpost
DDEEHIMOTZ	methodized	DDEGIINNST	distending	DDGGIILNOS	dislodging
DDEEHINNRU	unhindered	DDEGILLMNY	meddlingly	DDGGILNRUY	drudgingly
DDEEHINNSS	hiddenness	DDEGILLNUY	deludingly	DDGGINOOTU	outdodging
DDEEHLORSU	shouldered	DDEGINNOOS	desnooding	DDGIILLMNY	middlingly
DDEEHNORSU	deerhounds	DDEGINNOPS	desponding	DDGIILLNPY	piddlingly
	enshrouded	DDEGINNORU	redounding	DDGIILLNNU	unriddling
DDEEIILNPV	vilipended		underdoing	DDGIILNOPS	disploding
DDEEIIMOPR	epidermoid	DDEGINRRSU	undergirds	DDGILLMNUY	muddlingly
DDEEIINRSW	sidewinder	DDEGLNOORS	goldenrods	DDGILLNOPY	ploddingly
DDEEIIORSX	deoxidiser	DDEGLNOORY	dendrology	DDHINOOPTY	diphyodont
DDEEIIORXZ	deoxidizer	DDEGNNORUU	ungrounded	DDIIKLNTWY	tiddlywink
DDEEIIOSSX	deoxidises	DDEHHNRSTU	hundredths	DDINOOOPRT	diprotodon
DDEEIIOSXZ	deoxidizes	DDEHIIIMNS	diminished	DDINOPPRTY	Pontypridd
DDEEIIPPST	dipeptides	DDEHIILNSW	windshield	DEEEEEFPRZ	deepfreeze
DDEEIIPSSW	sideswiped	DDEHIILPSU	disulphide	DEEEEFLNRS	Senefelder
DDEEIIQSTU	disquieted	DDEHIKNOOW	hoodwinked	DEEEEFNRTT	tenderfeet
DDEEILMMRT	middle term	DDEHINNORS	dishonored	DEEEEGINNR	engineered
DDEEILMOPR	impoldered	DDEHINOSSS	shoddiness	DEEEEGLRSS	degreeless
DDEEILMSTW	Middle West	DDEHIOOOPT	photodiode	DEEEEGNNRR	engenderer
DDEEILNNRU	underlined	DDEHIORRRT	Third Order	DEEEEKNRSW	weekenders
DDEEIMMNRU	undermined	DDEHIORSXY	hydroxides	DEEEELMNVY	Mendeleyev
DDEEIMNORS	endodermis	DDEHLNOSTU	Huddleston	DEEEEMNNPU	Peenemünde
	modernised	DDEHLORSVY	hydrolysed	DEEEEMNNTT	tenemented
DDEEIMNORZ	modernized	DDEHLORVYZ	hydrolyzed	DEEEEPRRSV	persevered
DDEEINNNTU	unintended	DDEIIILQSU	liquidised	DEEEFGILNR	greenfield
DDEEINNRTU	indentured	DDEIIILQUZ	liquidized	DEEEFHIIRT	etherified
DDEEINORRV	overridden	DDEIIIMPSY	epididymis	DEEEFHILNS	needlefish
DDEEINORSW	disendower	DDEIIIPRST	dispirited	DEEEFHLORR	freeholder
	eiderdowns	DDEIIIQSTU	quiddities	DEEEFIILMR	demirelief
DDEEINRSST	distenders	DDEIIJNOST	disjointed	DEEEFIIRRV	reverified
DDEEINRSSU	undersides	DDEIIKOSSV	videodisks	DEEEFIIRST	esterified
DDEEINRSUZ	undersized	DDEIILLMNW	windmilled	DEEEFILMNT	defilement
DDEEIOORRS	deodoriser	DDEIIMMNOU	diminuendo	DEEEFILRRT	refiltered
DDEEIOORRZ	deodorizer	DDEIINOPSS	indisposed	DEEEFIMRSW	swimfeeder
DDEEIOORSS	deodorises	DDEIINOSTU	duodenitis	DEEEFINRRT	interfered
DDEEIOORSZ	deodorizes	DDEIINOUVZ	zidovudine	DEEEFINRTW	winterfeed
DDEEIRSSST	distressed	DDEIINSSST	dissidents	DEEEFLLNSU	needlefuls
DDEEIRSSSU	druidesses	DDEIIOPRSS	dispersoid	DEEEFLORRW	deflowerer
DDEELMMNTU	muddlement	DDEIKNNRUW	wunderkind		reflowered
DDEELMORSU	smouldered	DDEILLNPSY	splendidly	DEEEFMNRRU	referendum
DDEELRRSSU	rudderless	DDEILLOPSY	lopsidedly	DEEEFMNRST	deferments
DDEENNOPST	despondent	DDEILMMOST	middlemost	DEEEFNQRTU	frequented
DDEENNOSSS	soddenness	DDEILNRRSU	unriddlers	DEEEFNRTTU	unfettered
DDEENNPRSU	underspend	DDEILOOPSS	podsolised	DEEEFORRST	deforester
DDEENNSSSU	suddenness	DDEILOOPSZ	podsolized		reforested
DDEFFLNORU	Ludendorff		podzolised	DEEEGHHINT	heightened
DDEFGIIIIR	rigidified	DDEILOOPZZ	podzolized	DEEEGHLNNT	lengthened
DDEFGIIRSU	disfigured	DDEILORRSY	disorderly	DEEEGIIMRV	demivierge
DDEFHIIIMU	humidified	DDEIMNOSTU	dismounted	DEEEGIKNNW	weekending
DDEFHIIMUV	dehumidify	DDEINOPRUV	unprovided	DEEEGILNRS	legendries
DDEFHLNORU	fundholder	DDEINOPSSU	undisposed	DEEEGILOVW	Vogelweide
DDEFIIILOS	solidified	DDEINORSSS	sordidness	DEEEGIMNRT	regimented

DEEEGINRSS	greediness	DEEEINRRST	reinserted	DEEFFHLRSU	reshuffled
DEEEGIRRST	deregister		tenderiser	DEEFGGILLN	fledgeling
	registered	DEEEINRRTZ	tenderizer	DEEFGHINRT	frightened
	ridgetrees	DEEEINRSST	tenderises	DEEFGIINNR	redefining
DEEEGLNOSY	goldeneyes	DEEEINRSTT	interested	DEEFGINSST	giftedness
DEEEGLNRSS	genderless	DEEEINRSTZ	tenderizes	DEEFGIPRRU	prefigured
DEEEGMNNOR	mondegreen	DEEEINSSTW	tweediness	DEEFGJORSU	forejudges
DEEEGNRSTT	detergents	DEEEIPPQRU	reequipped	DEEFHIILTW	Whitefield
DEEEHIILRT	Ethelred II	DEEEIPRSSV	depressive	DEEFHIINRS	refinished
DEEEHIIRST	heredities	DEEEIPRSTX	expediters	DEEFHIORSV	overfished
DEEEHILLNS	hellenised		expertised	DEEFHLOPSS	sheepfolds
DEEEHILLNZ	hellenized		preexisted	DEEFHOORSW	foreshowed
DEEEHILNTY	diethylene	DEEEIPRTXZ	expertized	DEEFIIILST	fidelities
DEEEHILSSW	sidewheels	DEEEIRSSTT	sidestreet	DEEFIIINNP	nifedipine
DEEEHIMPRS	ephemerids	DEEEKLNNNU	unkenneled	DEEFIIINNT	indefinite
DEEEHIMPSU	euphemised	DEEEKLNORW	needlework	DEEFIIINRT	identifier
DEEEHIMPUZ	euphemized	DEEEKOOPRR	doorkeeper	DEEFIIINST	identifies
DEEEHIPRSS	Hesperides	DEEEELLNSSY	needlessly	DEEFIIINTV	definitive
DEEEHKNNOS	keeshonden	DEEELLOWWY	yellowweed	DEEFIIIRVV	revivified
DEEEHLLSSY	heedlessly	DEEELLPSSW	speedwells	DEEFIILLST	stellified
DEEEHLNOPT	telephoned	DEEELMOPRY	reemployed	DEEFIILMNS	minefields
DEEEHLNORS	lederhosen	DEEELNOOTV	Deo volente	DEEFIILMSU	emulsified
DEEEHNORTY	heterodyne	DEEELNORSS	nesselrode	DEEFIILNRR	friendlier
DEEEHNPRRS	reprehends	DEEELNRTTU	unlettered	DEEFIILNRS	friendlies
DEEEHNRRTU	thereunder	DEEELOPRSV	developers		infielders
DEEEHNRTTU	untethered		redevelops	DEEFIILNRT	interfiled
DEEEIILRSV	deliveries	DEEELOPRTT	teleported	DEEFIILNTY	definitely
DEEEIIMNPR	meperidine	DEEELRRSVY	reservedly	DEEFIILRST	fertilised
DEEEIKLLRW	weedkiller	DEEEMNNOTT	denotement	DEEFIILRTZ	fertilized
DEEEILLMOS	demoiselle	DEEEMNNOTU	denouement	DEEFIIMNSS	misdefines
DEEEILLMPS	millepedes	DEEEMNNOVZ	endoenzyme	DEEFIIMORS	remodifies
DEEEILMRSS	remediless	DEEEMNOTTV	devotement	DEEFIINORT	renotified
DEEEILNNST	sentineled	DEEEMNPRTU	untempered	DEEFIINRST	trendifies
DEEEILNPRV	replevined	DEEEMNRSSU	demureness	DEEFIINRUV	unverified
DEEEILNRSS	slenderise	DEEEMNRSTT	determents	DEEFIINRVW	viewfinder
DEEEILNRSZ	slenderize	DEEEMNRSUW	Wesermünde	DEEFIIOSTX	detoxifies
DEEEILNRUV	unrelieved	DEEEMNSTTV	vestmented	DEEFIIPRRU	repurified
DEEEILRRSV	deliverers	DEEEMOORST	oedometers	DEEFIIPRTT	prettified
	redelivers	DEEEMOPRST	pedometers	DEEFILLORV	overfilled
DEEEILRRVY	redelivery	DEEEMORSST	dosemeters	DEEFILLRSU	fullerides
DEEEILRSSW	wirelessed	DEEENNRSST	tenderness	DEEFILMOSU	fieldmouse
DEEEILRSVW	silverweed	DEEENNRSSU	enuredness	DEEFILNOST	fieldstone
DEEEIMMRSS	mesmerised	DEEENOOSWZ	sneezewood	DEEFILNOSX	deflexions
DEEEIMMRSZ	mesmerized	DEEENORTVX	overextend	DEEFILNRSS	friendless
DEEEIMNOST	demonetise	DEEENPPPRU	unpeppered	DEEFILNRTU	unfiltered
DEEEIMNOTZ	demonetize	DEEENPRRST	pretenders	DEEFILNRYZ	frenziedly
DEEEIMNRRT	determiner	DEEENPRSSU	superdense	DEEFILORTU	outfielder
DEEEIMNRRW	Windermere	DEEENPRSUV	supervened	DEEFILPSTU	despiteful
DEEEIMNRST	densimeter	DEEENRRSTT	deterrents	DEEFIMNORR	reinformed
	determines	DEEENRRSTU	understeer	DEEFIMORSU	furosemide
DEEEIMORTU	eudiometer	DEEENRRSUV	unreserved	DEEFINORRX	ferredoxin
DEEEIMPRTV	redemptive	DEEEOPRRTX	reexported	DEEFINOSST	foetidness
DEEEIMRSSY	Merseyside	DEEEORRRRT	reredorter	DEEFINRSSV	fervidness
DEEEIMSSST	disesteems	DEEEORSSTV	stevedores	DEEFINRSTU	interfused
DEEEINNPTV	pendentive	DEEEPRRSSU	superseder	DEEFKNORSS	forkedness
DEEEINNRTV	intervened	DEEEPRSSST	speedsters	DEEFLLMORW	well-formed
	reinvented	DEEEPRSSSU	supersedes	DEEFLMNNOT	enfoldment
DEEEINORRT	reoriented	DEEEPRSSUW	superweeds	DEEFLNRSTU	underfelts
DEEEINPRST	predestine	DEEERRRSSS	redressers	DEEFLOORVW	overflowed
DEEEINPSSS	speediness	DEEERRSUVY	resurveyed	DEEFNOORTT	tenderfoot
DEEEINPSTX	expedients	DEEERSSUVX	Deux-Sèvres	DEEFNORSTU	unforested
DEEEINRRRT	reinterred	DEEFFFKLRU	kerfuffled	DEEFOORSTU	surefooted

DEEFORRSST	defrosters	
	fortressed	
DEEFPRSSUU	superfused	
DEEGGILOOS	geologised	
DEEGGILOOZ	geologized	
DEEGGIRSSU	ruggedises	
DEEGGIRSUZ	ruggedizes	
DEEGGLRSSU	grudgeless	
DEEGGNRSSU	ruggedness	
DEEGHHORUW	roughhewed	
DEEGHIJNNZ	Jingdezhen	
DEEGHILRST	delighters	
DEEGHINOPS	diphosgene	
DEEGHINOUY	honeyguide	
DEEGHINSTU	gesundheit	
DEEGHIOSTT	ghettoised	
DEEGHIOTTZ	ghettoized	
DEEGHIOTUW	outweighed	
DEEGIILNRV	delivering	
DEEGIILNSU	guidelines	
DEEGIILOOS	ideologies	
DEEGIILPRV	privileged	
DEEGIINNRT	ingredient	
DEEGIINNRW	rewidening	
DEEGIINPTX	expediting	
DEEGIINRRS	grinderies	
DEEGIIRSSV	digressive	
DEEGIISSTV	digestives	
DEEGILNOOS	neologised	
DEEGILNOOZ	neologized	
DEEGILNOPV	developing	
DEEGILNRSY	resignedly	
DEEGILOOSU	ideologues	
DEEGILOPRS	ridgepoles	
DEEGILRSTY	greylisted	
DEEGIMORST	geometrids	
DEEGINNORW	reendowing	
DEEGINNPPR	perpending	
DEEGINNPRT	pretending	
DEEGINNRRS	renderings	
DEEGINORRR	reordering	
DEEGINORSS	degression	
DEEGINOOST	redingotes	
DEEGINORVY	overdyeing	
DEEGINOSXY	oxygenised	
DEEGINOXYZ	oxygenized	
DEEGINPRSS	depressing	
	predesigns	
DEEGINRRRS	derringers	
DEEGINRRSS	redressing	
DEEGINRSUV	gerundives	
DEEGIOSSST	geodesists	
DEEGIPRSST	predigests	
DEEGIRRSSS	digressers	
DEEGJMNSTU	judgements	
DEEGJPRRSU	prejudgers	
DEEGLLNORU	golden rule	
DEEGLMNOST	lodgements	
DEEGLMSSSU	smudgeless	
DEEGLNNOSS	goldenness	
DEEGLOOOPP	good people	
DEEGNNOOSU	endogenous	

DEEGNNORUV	ungoverned
DEEGNOORSW	greenwoods
DEEGNORRSU	guerdoners
	undergoers
DEEGOPRRSS	progressed
DEEGORRTXY	dextrogyre
DEEGOSSTUU	outguessed
DEEHHIILMS	Hildesheim
DEEHHIORSS	horsehides
DEEHHOORSS	horseshoed
DEEHIIKLLS	shieldlike
DEEHIINPRS	hesperidin
DEEHIIRSTT	hereditist
DEEHILLRSV	helldivers
	shrivelled
DEEHILMORS	demolisher
DEEHILMOSS	demolishes
DEEHILOOTT	theodolite
DEEHILOPPS	pedophiles
DEEHILOPRS	repolished
DEEHILORSU	hierodules
DEEHILPRSS	elderships
DEEHIMORST	methodiser
DEEHIMORTZ	methodizer
DEEHIMOSST	methodises
DEEHIMOSTX	methoxides
DEEHIMOSTZ	methodizes
DEEHINOOPV	videophone
DEEHINOPSU	euphonised
DEEHINOPSX	phenoxides
DEEHINOPUZ	euphonized
DEEHINORST	dinotheres
	threnodies
DEEHINORSV	Devonshire
DEEHINRSSW	swineherds
DEEHINRTUW	unwithered
DEEHIOPPRS	prophesied
DEEHIORSTV	Shrovetide
DEEHKNOOSS	hookedness
DEEHLLMOPR	phelloderm
DEEHLMNRUW	underwhelm
DEEHLNOSUU	unhouseled
DEEHMNOOST	smoothened
DEEHMOORST	hodometers
DEEHMORRTY	hydrometer
DEEHNNORSS	hornedness
DEEHNOORTT	heterodont
DEEHNOPSTY	endophytes
DEEHNORRST	dethroners
DEEHNRRSTU	thunderers
DEEHNRSSSW	shrewdness
DEEHOORTXY	heterodoxy
DEEHOPRSST	hotpressed
DEEHOORRSY	hydroseres
DEEHSSSTTU	dustsheets
DEEIIIMNSV	semidivine
DEEIIINPPR	piperidine
DEEIIINSTT	identities
DEEIIKKLNV	kidneylike
DEEIIKLNRW	Winkelried
DEEIILLMPR	imperilled
DEEIIILLMPS	millipedes

DEEIILLOPT	lepidolite
DEEIILNNRT	interlined
DEEIILNNVY	vinylidene
DEEIILNPRV	vilipender
DEEIILNSTT	disentitle
DEEIILOPPT	epileptoid
DEEIILORSS	soldieries
DEEIILORST	siderolite
DEEIILRSST	sterilised
DEEIILRSSV	silverside
DEEIILRSTV	deviltries
DEEIILRSTZ	sterilized
DEEIILRSVY	derisively
DEEIILRTUZ	reutilized
DEEIIMMNPT	impediment
DEEIIMNNTT	inditement
DEEIIMNRST	ministered
DEEIIMNRTX	intermixed
DEEIIMNSTT	midinettes
DEEIIMOPST	epitomised
DEEIIMOPTZ	epitomized
DEEIIMORSS	isomerised
DEEIIMORSZ	isomerized
DEEIINNOSV	envisioned
DEEIINNRTT	Tridentine
DEEIINNSSV	divineness
DEEIINNSTW	disentwine
DEEIINOPPT	petitioned
DEEIINOPTX	expedition
DEEIINPTTU	ineptitude
DEEIINQTUU	inquietude
DEEIINRSTW	winterised
DEEIINRTTW	wintertide
DEEIINRTWZ	winterized
DEEIINSSST	sensitised
DEEIINSSTW	West Indies
DEEIINSSTZ	sensitized
DEEIIOPQSU	equipoised
DEEIIOPRTT	peridotite
DEEIIOSSTV	sovietised
DEEIIOSTVZ	sovietized
DEEIIPRSSV	dispersive
DEEIIPRSSW	sideswiper
DEEIIPSSSW	sideswipes
DEEIJMNOSW	jimsonweed
DEEIJNORRS	rejoinders
DEEIJNOSTT	jettisoned
DEEIKLNNRS	enkindlers
DEEIKNNRSU	Iskenderun
DEEIKNNSSS	kindnesses
DEEIKORSST	sidestroke
DEEILLMPSS	misspelled
DEEILLNRSW	indwellers
DEEILLORRS	drolleries
DEEILLPRSS	dispellers
DEEILLRRSV	drivellers
DEEILLRSTU	tellurides
	tellurised
DEEILLRTUZ	tellurized
DEEILLSUVY	delusively
DEEILMNOSS	solemnised
DEEILMNOSZ	solemnized

DEEEILMNRTW	wilderment	DEEEINNRSST	trendiness	DEELNNOOST	selenodont
DEEEILMNSTV	devilments	DEEEINNRSSU	inuredness	DEELNNOOSU	unloosened
DEEEILMORSS	melodisers	DEEEINNRSTU	indentures	DEELNOOSST	lodestones
DEEEILMORSZ	melodizers	DEEEINNSSTU	unitedness	DEELNOPRUX	unexplored
DEEEILMOSTV	demivoltes	DEEEINNSTUV	uninvested	DEELNORSSW	wonderless
DEEEILMPSTU	multipedes	DEEEINOPPST	peptonised	DEELNORSUV	unresolved
DEEEILNNNRU	underlinen	DEEEINOPPTZ	peptonized	DEELNOSTUU	edentulous
DEEEILNNORT	tenderloin	DEEEINOPRSS	depression	DEELNPRRSU	plunderers
DEEEILNNQTU	delinquent	DEEEINOPRST	interposed	DEELOPRRTY	reportedly
DEEEILNNRSU	underlines	DEEEINOPSTX	pentoxides	DEELOPRSTY	proselyted
DEEEILNOPST	depletions	DEEEINOQSTU	questioned	DEELORTTUV	turtledove
DEEEILNORVV	reinvolved	DEEEINORRVV	overdriven	DEELPRSTTU	spluttered
DEEEILNPRST	splintered	DEEEINORSST	desertions	DEEMMNORSU	resummoned
DEEEILNRRSU	underliers	DEEEINORSSW	rosinweeds	DEEMMOOSSS	desmosomes
DEEEILNRSSW	wilderness	DEEEINORSUV	souvenired	DEEMMNORSS	modernness
DEEEILNRSTU	interludes	DEEEINOTTUZ	teutonized	DEEMMNNORTW	wonderment
DEEEILOPRSS	despoilers	DEEEINPPQUU	unequipped	DEEMMNNOSTW	endowments
DEEEILORSSV	redissolve	DEEEINPRRST	rinderpest	DEEMMNOPRTT	deportment
DEEEILOSTTT	stilettoed	DEEEINPRSSS	dispensers	DEEMMNORSTU	tremendous
DEEEILPPRSU	resupplied	DEEEINPRSST	presidents	DEEMOOORRST	drosometer
DEEEILPRSUV	pulverised	DEEEINQRTUU	unrequited	DEEMOOORSTV	overmodest
DEEEILPRUVZ	pulverized	DEEEINRRTUW	underwrite	DEEMOOPRRTY	redemptory
DEEEILQRRSU	squirreled	DEEEINRSSSS	dressiness	DEENNOOSSW	woodenness
DEEEILRRSSV	driverless	DEEEINRSSST	dissenters	DEENNOPRST	respondent
DEEEIMMNOSU	eudemonism	DEEEINRSSTU	unresisted	DEENNORSTU	undertones
DEEEIMNNNTT	intendment	DEEEINSSTTU	testudines	DEENNPRSTU	underspent
DEEEIMNNRRU	underminer	DEEEINSTTTV	vendettist	DEENNRRTUU	unreturned
DEEEIMNNRSU	undermines	DEEEIOPPRRT	propertied	DEENOOPRSS	endospores
DEEEIMNNSTZ	dizenments	DEEEIOPPRSS	predispose	DEENOOSSST	endostoses
DEEEIMNOOPS	empoisoned	DEEEIOPPRST	predeposit	DEENOOPRRSS	responders
DEEEIMNOOTV	Montevideo	DEEEIOPRSST	redeposits	DEENOPRRTU	unreported
DEEEIMNOPRT	redemption	DEEEIOPRSTX	expeditors	DEENOPRRUV	unreproved
DEEEIMNOPTT	idempotent	DEEEIOPRSUX	superoxide	DEENOPRSSV	overspends
DEEEIMNORRS	moderniser	DEEEIOPRTTU	pirouetted	DEENOPRSUX	expounders
DEEEIMNORRZ	modernizer	DEEEIOPSSTU	despiteous	DEENOQRTUU	underquote
DEEEIMNORSS	modernises	DEEEIORRRST	terrorised	DEENORRTUV	overturned
	sermonised	DEEEIORRRSV	overriders	DEENORRTUW	underwrote
DEEEIMNORSZ	modernizes	DEEEIORRRTZ	terrorized	DEENORSSSU	rousedness
	sermonized	DEEEIORRSTV	overstride	DEENORSUVZ	rendezvous
DEEEIMNORTV	Monteverdi	DEEEIORRSVV	overdrives	DEENOSSTUV	devoutness
DEEEIMNOSTU	eudemonist	DEEEIORSSUV	overissued	DEENPRSSSU	suspenders
DEEEIMNPRSS	misspender	DEEEIORSTTX	tetroxides	DEENRRRSSU	surrenders
DEEEIMNRSTW	Midwestern	DEEEIPRRSSS	dispersers	DEENRSSSSU	sundresses
	stemwinder	DEEEIPRRTUY	eurypterid	DEENRSSSTU	unstressed
DEEEIMNRSTY	densimetry	DEEEIPRSSUV	supervised	DEENRSSTUV	undervests
DEEEIMNRTTU	unremitted	DEEEIRSSSST	distresses	DEEOOPPRTV	overtopped
DEEEIMNSSTV	divestment	DEEEIRSSTUV	divestures	DEEOOPRRSU	uredospore
DEEEIMOORST	meteoroids	DEEEKKNSSUW	skunkweeds	DEEOOORRSTV	overstrode
DEEEIMOPRRT	reimported	DEEEKLLNORS	snorkelled	DEEOOPRRSU	superposed
DEEEIMOPRST	temporised	DEEEKLMRTTU	kettledrum	DEEOOPSTTU	outstepped
DEEEIMOPRSW	disempower	DEEEKLNOSSV	veldskoens	DEEOOPRRSU	superorder
DEEEIMOPRTZ	temporized	DEEEKLOOORV	overlooked	DEEOOPRRSSS	depressors
DEEEIMORSST	dosimeters	DEEEKOORRVW	overworked	DEEOOPSSTTU	poussetted
DEEEIMORTUY	eudiometry	DEEELLNORTY	redolently	DEEOORRRSSS	redressors
DEEEIMPRSST	distempers	DEEELLNRSSU	undersells	DEEOORRSSTY	destroyers
DEEEIMRSTUW	Tweedsmuir	DEEELLORSVY	resolvedly	DEEPPRSSSU	suppressed
DEEEIMSSSTY	systemised	DEEELMNOPTY	deployment	DEEFFFKLRUU	kurfuffled
DEEEIMSSTYZ	systemized	DEEELMNOPUY	unemployed	DEEFFGINNOR	forfending
DEEEINNNOSU	innuendoes	DEEELMNOSTU	unmolested	DEEFFHIMORS	sheriffdom
DEEEINNOPRS	prednisone	DEEELMOORSV	velodromes	DEEFFINOPRT	offprinted
DEEEINNORST	internodes	DEEELMOPRSU	supermodel	DEEFGGILLNS	fledglings
DEEEINNOSTT	detentions	DEEELMPRSUY	presumedly	DEEFGHILLTU	delightful

DEFGHILOSS	goldfishes
DEFGHLORUU	furloughed
DEFGHOOOSU	house of God
DEFGIIIIRS	rigidifies
DEFGIILNRR	girlfriend
DEFGIILNYY	edifyingly
DEFGIINNUY	unedifying
DEFGIINRSS	frigidness
DEFGIIRRSU	disfigurer
DEFGIIRSSU	disfigures
DEFGILNOOR	reflooding
DEFGILOOSS	Isle of Dogs
DEFGINNORU	foundering
DEFGINORST	defrosting
DEFGNOORRU	foreground
DEFHIIIMRU	humidifier
DEFHIIIMSU	humidifies
DEFHIILNSY	fiendishly
DEFHIINNSU	unfinished
DEFHIINPRS	friendship
DEFHILORSU	flourished
DEFHIMRSSU	drumfishes
DEFHLOOOSW	wholefoods
DEFHORRRTU	rutherford
DEFIIIILMPS	simplified
DEFIIILNTY	infidelity
DEFIIILORS	solidifier
DEFIIILOSS	solidifies
DEFIIINNOT	definition
DEFIIINNTU	infinitude
DEFIIILLNRY	friendlily
DEFIILMSSU	semifluids
DEFIILOSSS	fossilised
DEFIILOSSZ	fossilized
DEFIILRSSU	fluidisers
DEFIILRSUZ	fluidizers
DEFIILSTTU	stultified
DEFIINOOPS	opsonified
DEFIINPRUU	unpurified
DEFIINSSST	disinfests
DEFIIOPRSU	perfidious
DEFIKLORSW	fieldworks
DEFILLORWW	wildflower
	wildfowler
DEFILLPRUY	pridefully
DEFILMNNOT	infoldment
DEFILMNORY	informedly
DEFILNNRUY	unfriendly
DEFILNORSS	floridness
DEFILNORST	interfolds
DEFILNORWW	windflower
DEFILNOSSW	snowfields
DEFILPRSUU	superfluid
DEFIMNNORU	uninformed
DEFINNORZZ	Zinzendorf
DEFINRRSUW	windsurfer
DEFIORRRST	first-order
DEFIORSSST	disforests
DEFLNOORRU	underfloor
DEFLNOORTU	unforetold
DEFLNORSUW	underflows
DEFNOOPRRU	underproof

DEFNORRRUUW	unfurrowed
DEFOORTTTX	foxtrotted
DEGGGGILNO	doglegging
DEGGGINNOU	gudgeoning
DEGGHIILNT	delighting
DEGGIILNRS	ridgelings
DEGGIINRSS	digressing
DEGGIJNPRU	prejudging
DEGGINNORU	guerdoning
	undergoing
DEGGIORRSS	disgorgers
DEGGMNOOOR	Demogorgon
DEGHIILSST	sidelights
DEGHIINRRT	nightrider
DEGHIIRSTZ	rightsized
DEGHIJPSSU	judgeships
DEGHILMSSU	gumshields
DEGHIMNRSU	humdingers
DEGHINNORT	dethroning
DEGHINNRTU	thundering
DEGHINRSST	nightdress
DEGHIORRRU	roughrider
DEGHIORRSU	roughdries
DEGHIOSTTU	doughtiest
DEGHLNNOOR	Golden Horn
DEGHLNOPUU	unploughed
DEGHMOORST	godmothers
DEGHNNOSTU	shotgunned
DEGHNOORSU	gorehounds
DEGHNORSUV	greyhounds
DEGHOOOPRW	gopher wood
	gopherwood
DEGIIILMNT	delimiting
DEGIIILNNS	sidelining
DEGIIILNOT	indigolite
DEGIIIMNRS	dimerising
DEGIIIMNRZ	dimerizing
DEGIIINNOZ	deionizing
DEGIIINNTY	indigenity
DEGIIINSSS	disseising
DEGIIINSSZ	disseizing
DEGIIIRSST	digitisers
DEGIIIRSTZ	digitizers
DEGIIKLLNS	deskilling
DEGIIKLNNN	enkindling
DEGIIKLNNR	rekindling
DEGIILLNNW	indwelling
DEGIILLNPS	dispelling
DEGIILLNRR	redrilling
DEGIILLNRV	drivelling
DEGIILLNTY	diligently
DEGIILLNVY	yieldingly
DEGIILMNOS	melodising
DEGIILMNOZ	melodizing
DEGIILMNPY	impedingly
DEGIILNNTY	indigently
DEGIILNNUY	unyielding
DEGIILNOPS	despoiling
DEGIILNORS	soldiering
DEGIILNOSV	evildoings
DEGIILOOST	ideologist
DEGIIMNNOS	demonising

DEGIIMNNOZ	demonizing
DEGIIMRSSU	misguiders
DEGIINNORT	dinitrogen
DEGIINNOSU	indigenous
DEGIINNOSV	nosediving
DEGIINNPSS	dispensing
DEGIINNSST	dissenting
DEGIINOPRX	peroxiding
DEGIINOPST	depositing
DEGIINORRV	overriding
DEGIINORSS	digression
DEGIINPRSS	dispersing
DEGIINPRST	springtide
DEGIINPSTU	deputising
DEGIINPTUZ	deputizing
DEGIINRSSV	disserving
DEGIINRSTU	nigritudes
DEGIINRSTW	West Riding
DEGIIQSSTU	squidgiest
DEGIIRSSSU	disguisers
DEGIJMRSSU	misjudgers
DEGILLOOTY	deltiology
DEGILLOSSY	syllogised
DEGILLOSYZ	syllogized
DEGILMNORS	goldminers
	smoldering
DEGILMNORU	mouldering
	remoulding
DEGILMNOSW	gildswomen
DEGILMNRSU	mudslinger
DEGILNNPRU	plundering
DEGILNNRSU	underlings
DEGILNNRUY	enduringly
	underlying
DEGILNOORS	gondoliers
DEGILNOOSS	goodliness
DEGILNOSTU	longitudes
	ungodliest
DEGILNRSTU	disgruntle
DEGILOOOSX	doxologies
DEGILOOPST	pedologist
DEGIMNNOTU	demounting
DEGIMNOOPR	predooming
DEGIMNSSSU	smudginess
DEGINNOPPR	propending
DEGINNOPRS	responding
DEGINNOPRT	portending
DEGINNOPUX	expounding
DEGINNORST	grindstone
	stringendo
DEGINNORSU	resounding
DEGINNPSSU	suspending
DEGINNRSSU	undressing
DEGINNRSUW	underwings
DEGINOOOPW	woodpigeon
DEGINOOPRT	torpedoing
DEGINOORSV	overdosing
DEGINOPSST	signposted
DEGINORSTY	destroying
DEGINOSSST	stodginess
DEGINRSSTU	turgidness
DEGIOPSSTU	guideposts

DEGLMNOOOY	demonology	DEHINORRST	trihedrons	DEIILLNOSU	illusioned
DEGLNNRSUU	underslung	DEHINORSTT	threnodist	DEIILLNUWY	unwieldily
DEGLNOOOTY	deontology	DEHINORSVW	windhovers	DEIILLOPSS	ellipsoids
DEGLNORSSU	groundsels	DEHINOSSTY	dishonesty	DEIILLORTV	vitriolled
	groundsels	DEHINRRSTU	undershirt	DEIILLRSST	distillers
DEGLOORTTY	troglodyte	DEHIOOOPRR	odoriphore	DEIILLRSTY	distillery
DEGMNNORSU	groundsmen	DEHIOOPRST	priesthood	DEIILMNOOT	demolition
DEGNNORRUW	undergrown	DEHIOORSST	sisterhood	DEIILMNPSS	limpidness
DEGNOORRSW	wrongdoers	DEHIOOSTWW	whitewoods	DEIILMOSSS	semisolids
DEGNOORRUV	overground	DEHIOPPRSW	worshipped	DEIILNPRTY	intrepidly
DEGNOORRUZ	ground zero	DEHIOPRRTY	pyrethroid	DEIILNPSST	spindliest
DEGNOOSSTT	stegodonts	DEHIRRSSST	shirtdress	DEIILNQSSU	liquidness
DEGNOPRSUW	gunpowders	DEHKLOOSST	stokeholds	DEIILPRSTY	spiritedly
DEGNOPRUWY	gunpowdery	DEHLNOOPRY	polyhedron	DEIILQSTUY	disquietly
DEGNOPSTUU	Puget Sound	DEHLNOOSTY	holystoned	DEIILRSTZZ	drizzliest
DEGOOORSUW	woodgrouse	DEHLOORRSY	holy orders	DEIIMNNOSS	dimensions
DEGORRSSTU	drugstores	DEHLOORRTW	otherworld	DEIIMNNOTU	munitioned
DEHHIKMOSS	sheikhdoms	DEHLORRSYY	hydrolyser	DEIIMNOPRS	imprisoned
DEHHILOPRS	holdership	DEHLORRYYZ	hydrolyzer	DEIIMNOSSS	demissions
DEHHILOPRY	hydrophile	DEHLORSSSU	shroudless	DEIIMNPRST	misprinted
DEHHILORTW	withholder	DEHLORSSYY	hydrolyses	DEIIMNRSTW	midwinters
DEHHIOPPSS	phosphides	DEHLORSTYY	hydrolytes	DEIIMNSTUY	seminudity
DEHHLLNOSU	hellhounds	DEHLORSYYZ	hydrolyzes	DEIIMOPRSV	improvised
DEHHLOOSSU	households	DEHMMOORSU	mushroomed	DEIIMORTXY	oxidimetry
DEHHLORSST	thresholds	DEHMNOOPRS	endomorphs	DEIIMPRSSU	presidiums
DEHHMOOORT	motherhood	DEHMNOOPRY	endomorphy	DEIINNNOST	indentions
DEHHNOOPRY	hydrophone	DEHMORRTYY	hydrometry	DEIINNOPPT	pinpointed
DEHHNOORSU	horehounds	DEHNNOOPSS	sphenodons	DEIINNORST	renditions
DEHHOPRTYY	hydrophyte	DEHNNOORUU	unhonoured	DEIINNOSSS	dissension
DEHIIIMNSS	diminishes	DEHNNORSUU	nursehound	DEIINNOSST	distension
	minidishes	DEHNNOSSUW	newshounds	DEIINNOSTT	dentitions
DEHIIINOTT	dithionite	DEHNOORRSU	horrendous		distention
DEHIIINRST	disinherit	DEHNOORSTU	undershoot	DEIINNOSTV	venditions
DEHIIKLLOO	likelihood	DEHNOORSUU	roundhouse	DEIINNPRSU	uninspired
DEHIIKMRSS	skirmished	DEHNORSTUU	thunderous	DEIINNRSTW	interwinds
DEHIILLOOV	livelihood	DEHOOPPTTY	phototyped	DEIINNSSTU	untidiness
DEHIILLSVY	devilishly	DEHOOPRRWY	hydropower	DEIINOOPST	deposition
DEHIILMNPU	delphinium	DEHOORRSUW	woodrushes		positioned
DEHIIMMNPS	midshipmen	DEHOOSSSUW	dosshouses	DEIINOPRSS	dispersion
DEHIIMNOPR	prehominid	DEHORSSSTU	studhorses	DEIINOPRXY	pyridoxine
DEHIIMNPRU	nephridium	DEIIIINSTV	divinities	DEIINOPSSS	indisposes
DEHIINOOPS	idiophones	DEIIILLOOP	Leopold III	DEIINORSST	disorients
DEHIIOPRST	editorship	DEIIILMQSU	semiliquid	DEIINORSSV	diversions
DEHIKNOORW	hoodwinker	DEIIILMSTU	similitude	DEIINORSTT	detritions
DEHIKNRSZZ	Dzerzhinsk	DEIIILQRSU	liquidiser	DEIINRSSTU	disuniters
DEHILNNOOP	indophenol	DEIIILQRUZ	liquidizer		industries
DEHILNOPSU	unpolished	DEIIILQSSU	liquidises	DEIINSSSTV	disinvests
DEHILOOPSS	shopsoiled	DEIIILQSUZ	liquidizes	DEIINSTTTU	instituted
DEHILOPPRY	hyperploid	DEIIILSVVY	divisively	DEIIOOPSTV	oviposited
DEHILOSSTW	dishtowels	DEIIIMNORS	iridosmine	DEIIORSSSS	disseisors
DEHIMMPSSY	dysphemism	DEIIIMNPRY	pyrimidine	DEIIORSSSZ	disseizors
DEHIMNORST	hindermost	DEIIIMNTUV	diminutive	DEIIORSTTV	distortive
DEHIMNOSSS	modishness	DEIIIMSSSV	dismissive	DEIIPRSTUV	disruptive
DEHIMOOPPR	hippodrome	DEIIINORSV	redivision	DEIJNNNOOR	nonjoinder
DEHIMOPRSY	hypodermis	DEIIINPRST	inspirited	DEIKKLNORS	klondikers
DEHIMOSSTT	methodists	DEIIINSSSS	disseisins	DEIKKNOOPS	pondokkies
DEHINNOPRS	endorphins	DEIIINSSSZ	disseizins	DEIKLLNSSY	kindlessly
DEHINNPSUU	unpunished	DEIIINSSTU	disunities	DEIKMPPRSU	mudskipper
DEHINOORRS	dishonorer	DEIIJMNORS	misjoinder	DEIKNNNORR	nondrinker
DEHINOPSTY	hypnotised	DEIIKKLNRS	kilderkins	DEIKNNNSSU	unkindness
DEHINOPTYZ	hypnotized	DEIIKLNNSS	kindliness	DEIKNORRSV	overdrinks
DEHINORRSS	horridness	DEIILLMPTU	multiplied	DEIKNRRSTU	underskirt

DEILLLLSUV	dullsville	DEINORSSTU	detrusions	DFFFOOSSTU	foodstuffs
DEILLMNSSY	mindlessly	DEINPRRSTU	surprinted	DFFIINOSSU	diffusions
DEILLNNOTY	indolently	DEINPRSSTU	putridness	DFGGIIINNY	dignifying
DEILLNORSS	lordliness	DEINPRSTUU	Prudentius	DFGGIJNORU	forjudging
DEILLNSSWY	windlessly	DEINPSSSTU	stupidness	DFGHILLOOT	floodlight
DEILLOOTTW	Littlewood	DEINRSSSTU	sturdiness	DFGIIILLNR	fringillid
DEILLORSTW	worldliest	DEIOOPRSST	depositors	DFGIIILNSU	fluidising
DEILMMOSTY	immodestly	DEIOOPRSTX	protoxides	DFGIIILNUZ	fluidizing
DEILMNOSSU	Desmoulins	DEIOOPRSTY	depository	DFGIIIMORT	digitiform
	mouldiness	DEIOPRRSST	postriders	DFGIILNNOP	pinfolding
DEILMNPTUY	impudently	DEIOPRRSTW	spiderwort	DFGIINOSUU	nidifugous
DEILMSTTUU	multitudes	DEIOPRSSSU	disposures	DFGILLNNOY	fondlingly
DEILNNOUVV	uninvolved	DEIOPRSSTU	posturised	DFGILNNOSU	foundlings
DEILNOOOTT	odontolite	DEIOPRSTUZ	posturized	DFGILSSTUU	disgustful
DEILNOOTUV	devolution	DEIOPSSSSS	dispossess	DFHILOORSY	hydrofoils
DEILNORSTU	tendrilous	DEIORRSSTT	distorters	DFHLNOOSUW	wolfhounds
DEILNOSSST	stolidness	DEIPRRSSTU	disrupters	DFHLOOOOPT	photoflood
DEILNOSSTV	dissolvent	DEIRRSSTTU	distruster	DFIILLMTUY	multifidly
DEILNPQTUU	quintupled	DEKKLNORSY	klondykers	DFINOOPRST	spoondrift
DEILNRSTTY	stridently	DEKKNOORWY	donkeywork	DFINOPRTUY	profundity
DEILOOPPSY	polypodies	DEKLORSSVV	Sverdlovsk	DFINORSSTW	snowdrifts
DEILOOPSSS	podsolises	DEKNOOPRUV	unprovoked	DFLNOOPRUY	profoundly
DEILOOPSSZ	podsolizes	DEKNOORRWW	wonderwork	DFNOOOPRSU	soundproof
	podzolises	DEKOOORRWW	woodworker	DGGGHINOOT	hotdogging
DEILOOPSZZ	podzolizes	DEKOOSSTVY	Dostoevsky	DGGGIINORS	disgorging
DEILOPSSTY	stylopised	DELLNOPTUU	unpolluted	DGGGILNRUY	grudgingly
DEILOPSTYZ	stylopized	DELLOOOWWY	yellowwood	DGGGINNRUU	ungrudging
DEILORSSSV	dissolvers	DELLOORRWW	lower world	DGGHNOORSU	groundhogs
DEILORSSUY	desirously	DELLORSSWY	wordlessly	DGGIIIINST	digitising
DEILORSVWW	worldviews	DELLOSSUUY	sedulously	DGGIIIINTZ	digitizing
DEIMMMRSSU	midsummers	DELMNOOOSW	lemonwoods	DGGIIIMNSU	misguiding
DEIMMNNTUU	indumentum	DELNNOOOSS	solenodons	DGGIIINNSU	disguising
DEIMNNOSTW	disownment	DELNNOPSSU	nonplussed	DGGIIJMNSU	misjudging
DEIMNNSTYZ	Mindszenty	DELNNOTUWY	unwontedly	DGGIILNNRY	grindingly
DEIMNOOSSS	endosmosis	DELNOOOSST	dolostones	DGGIINSSTU	disgusting
DEIMNOPRSU	impounders	DELNOOPRTU	pleurodont	DGGILNNORU	groundling
DEIMNOPRTU	importuned	DELNOPRSSU	splendours	DGGINNOORW	wrongdoing
DEIMNOPRUV	unimproved		splendrous	DGGINNORSU	groundings
DEIMNORSST	modernists	DELNOPRSTU	underplots	DGHHIINSST	hindsights
DEIMOORRTY	odorimetry	DELNOPRSUU	plunderous	DGHHIKNOOT	knighthood
DEIMOPRSSU	dispermous	DELOPPSSUY	supposedly	DGHHINOPST	diphthongs
DEIMRSSTTU	mistrusted	DELORRTTUY	torturedly	DGHIILLNNO	Hillingdon
DEINNNORTU	trunnioned	DELORSTUXY	dextrously	DGHIILMNTY	midnightly
DEINNOOSTX	endotoxins	DEMMOORSUW	summerwood	DGHILMOSST	goldsmiths
DEINNORRSV	nondrivers	DEMNOOPRST	postmodern	DGHILOPRST	droplights
DEINNORSWW	New Windsor	DEMNOPPRTU	unprompted	DGHINNNOTU	Huntingdon
DEINNORTUW	interwound	DEMNOPSSUY	pseudonyms	DGHLNOORST	stronghold
DEINNRSTTU	undertints	DEMNORSTUU	surmounted	DGHNOORSUW	showground
DEINOOPRSS	droopiness	DEMNPRRTUU	undertrump	DGHOORSSUU	sourdoughs
DEINOOPRST	desorption	DENNOOPRSS	nonpressed	DGIIIINNSV	divinising
DEINOOPTTU	outpointed	DENNOORTWW	downtowner	DGIIIINNVZ	divinizing
DEINOOSSST	endostosis	DENNORSSTU	rotundness	DGIIIJNNOS	disjoining
DEINOOSSSU	odiousness	DENNORSSUW	sundowners	DGIIILLNST	distilling
DEINOOSTTX	exodontist	DENNRRTUUU	unnurtured	DGIIILMNNS	dislimning
DEINOPRSST	dripstones	DENOOPPRRU	propounder	DGIIIMNSSS	dismissing
DEINOPSSSU	suspensoid	DENOOPPRSU	unproposed	DGIIINNSTU	disuniting
DEINOPSSSY	synopsised	DENOPPRRSU	underprops	DGIIINOSTX	digitoxins
DEINOPSSYZ	synopsized	DENOPRRTTU	protrudent	DGIIINPRZZ	disprizing
DEINORRSST	torridness	DENOPSSTTU	sunspotted	DGIIINPTUY	pinguidity
DEINORRSWW	windrowers	DENOPSSTUU	stupendous	DGIILLNPSS	spindlings
DEINORSSSS	drossiness	DEOOOOPRRT	Roodepoort	DGIILNOSSV	dissolving
DEINORSSSW	drowsiness	DEOORRSSUU	uredosorus	DGIIMNNOPU	impounding

DGIIMNOOSS	sodomising
DGIIMNOOSZ	sodomizing
DGIINNORWW	windrowing
DGIINNOSWZ	downsizing
DGIINOPRST	disporting
DGIINOPRSV	disproving
DGIINORSTT	distorting
DGIINPRSTU	disrupting
DGIIOOPRSU	prodigious
DGILLNORSU	groundsill
DGILLNORSW	worldlings
DGILMNOOOS	mongoloids
DGILNNOSUY	soundingly
DGILNNOUWY	woundingly
DGILNOOPRY	droopingly
DGILOOPRTT	proglottid
DGINNOSSWW	downswings
DGINOOPRSW	springwood
DGINOPRRTU	protruding
DGKNOOORUW	groundwork
DGLNOOOOTY	odontology
DGLNOOPTTY	glyptodont
DGNNORSTUU	groundnuts
DHHILOPRYY	hydrophily
DHIILNRSWW	whirlwinds
DHIIMMOPRS	dimorphism
DHIINNNRSY	ninhydrins
DHIINOOSTU	dithionous
DHILLOPSUY	diphyllous
DHILMMOOSU	hoodlumism
DHILNOOPPY	podophylin
DHILOOPPYY	hypoploidy
DHILORSSYY	hydrolysis
DHIMMNNOST	month's mind
DHIMNOSSTY	hymnodists
DHIMOOPRSU	dimorphous
DHIMORSSTW	wordsmiths
DHINNOSTUW	whodunnits
DHINNSTUWY	whydunnits
DHINOOOPRT	ornithopod
DHINOOPRSS	donorships
DHINOORSSU	dishonours
DHINOPRSTY	dystrophin
DHIOOPPRRY	porphyroid
DHIORRTXYY	trihydroxy
DHLMOOSTUU	loudmouths
DHLNOORSUW	howlrounds
DHLOOORTXY	orthodoxly
DHNOOORTUX	unorthodox
DHNOORSTWW	downthrows
DHNOOSSTUW	South Downs
DHOORRSTWW	Wordsworth
DIIIINPSTY	insipidity
DIIIILSTTUY	disutility
DIIIMMORSU	iridosmium
	osmiridium
DIIIMNNOTU	diminution
DIILLMNOOS	modillions
DIILLNOSWW	windowsill
DIILNOSSUV	divulsions
DIIMMOPRRU	primordium
DIINOORSTT	distortion

DIINOPRSTU	disruption
DILLOOPPSY	polyploids
DILLOOPPYY	polyploidy
DILMNPSUUU	impundulus
DILORSSTUU	stridulous
DILOSSTUUY	studiously
DIMMNOOOPU	monopodium
DIMMNOOOSU	monosodium
DIMNOPRSUU	purdoniums
DIMNORSSTW	windstorms
DIMOPRSSUY	dysprosium
DINOOPRSTW	woodprints
DIOOOOSSTV	voodooists
DIOOORSVWY	ivorywoods
DIOOPRSSST	prosodists
DIOPRRSSTU	disruptors
DLLOOORSUY	dolorously
DLNOORSUWY	wondrously
DLOOOPPSUY	polypodous
DMNOORRSUW	roundworms
DNNORRSTUU	turnrounds
DNOOPSSSTU	soundposts
DNOOPSSTUW	downspouts
DNOORSTUWW	woundworts
EEEEEGPSSS	epexegeses
EEEEELRSTY	eyeleteers
EEEEFFNSST	effeteness
EEEEFGINRR	refereeing
EEEEFHLRSW	freewheels
EEEEFHRSST	freesheets
EEEEFPRRSZ	prefreezes
EEEEGINRRS	greeneries
EEEEGIPSSX	epexegesis
EEEEGLNSTT	genteelest
EEEEGNRRSV	evergreens
EEEEHIMRSU	euhemerise
EEEEHIMRUZ	euhemerize
EEEEHNPSST	epentheses
EEEEHRRVWY	everywhere
EEEEIJLRTZ	Jezreelite
EEEEIKLLSV	sleevelike
EEEEIKMPRT	timekeeper
EEEEKLPRSS	keeperless
EEEEKMRRSY	kerseymere
EEEELLSSSV	sleeveless
EEEELMRSTT	telemeters
EEEELNOPST	eleoptenes
EEEELNSSSZ	sneezeless
EEEELNSTVV	velveteens
EEEELORSVV	oversleeve
EEEENNRSSS	sereneness
EEEENNSSTV	seventeens
EEEENPRSST	presentees
EEEENRSSSV	severeness
EEEENRSSTW	sweeteners
EEEEPPPRRT	peppertree
EEEEPRRSSV	perseveres
EEEFFILORT	tree of life
EEEFFLNRTY	efferently
EEEFGILNRS	greenflies
EEEFGIMRSU	refugeeism
EEEFGINORS	foreseeing

EEEFGINRRZ	refreezing
EEEFGLNRUV	revengeful
EEEFHIIRST	etherifies
EEEFHNRRSS	fresheners
EEEFHOORRT	heretofore
EEEFHORRSW	wherefores
EEEFHORSST	foresheets
EEEFHRRRSS	refreshers
EEEFIINRRS	refineries
EEEFIIRRSV	reverifies
EEEFIIRSST	esterifies
EEEFILNNSS	felineness
EEEFILRSVX	reflexives
EEEFIMNNRT	refinement
EEEFINORRV	overrefine
EEEFINRRRT	interferer
EEEFINRRST	interferes
EEEFIORRST	feretories
EEEFLLNNOT	Fontenelle
EEEFLLNRSU	fullerenes
EEEFLLORRT	foreteller
EEEFLRSSTT	fetterless
EEEFLRSTTU	fleurettes
EEEFMNPRRT	preferment
EEEFMNRRST	fermenters
EEEFNNORSU	unforeseen
EEEFNORSST	freestones
EEEFNQRRTU	frequenter
EEEFPRRRRS	preferrers
EEEGGIMNRR	reemerging
EEEGHHINRT	heightener
EEEGHHINTT	eighteenth
EEEGHILNST	gehlenites
EEEGHIMNOS	hegemonies
EEEGHIMNOT	eighteenmo
EEEGHLMNRT	lengthener
EEEGHNNOST	Stonehenge
EEEGHNORSU	greenhouse
EEEGHRRTWY	greywether
EEEGIILRSU	religieuse
EEEGIINNRS	engineries
EEEGIINPSS	epigenesis
EEEGILMNST	genteelism
EEEGILNOST	telegonies
EEEGILNRST	singletree
EEEGILNSST	gentilesse
EEEGILOTTX	geotextile
EEEGIMORST	geometries
	geometrise
EEEGIMORTZ	geometrize
EEEGINNOST	eigentones
EEEGINNPST	steepening
EEEGINNRRT	reentering
EEEGINNSTW	sweetening
EEEGINOPRY	epeirogeny
EEEGINORSV	overseeing
EEEGINORTY	erogeneity
EEEGINRRRV	Green River
EEEGINRRSS	energisers
EEEGINRRST	interreges
EEEGINRRSZ	energizers
EEEGIRRRST	registerer

EEEGIRRSSV	regressive	EEEIIPRTTV	repetitive	EEEIPRRRSV	reprievers
EEEGISSTTX	exegetists	EEEIIRSSTV	severities	EEEIPRRSSV	repressive
EEEGLMNRTY	emergently	EEEIJLMRSS	IJsselmeer	EEEIPRRSTT	preterites
EEEGLNNSST	gentleness	EEEIKLLNTT	nettlelike	EEEIPRRSVV	perversive
EEEGMNNRSU	energumens	EEEIKLLTVV	velvetlike	EEEIPRRTTU	repetiteur
EEEGMNORSS	greensomes	EEEIKLMSWY	semiweekly	EEEIPRSSTX	expertises
EEEGMNRSSS	messengers	EEEIKLNSSS	likenesses	EEEIPRSSVX	expressive
EEEGMORRST	ergometers	EEEIKNNPRS	innkeepers	EEEIPRSTXZ	expertizes
EEEGNNORST	greenstone	EEEILLNUVV	Villeneuve	EEEIQSTTTU	etiquettes
EEEGRRRSTT	regretters	EEEILMMORT	mileometer	EEEIRRRSTV	retrievers
EEEHHIMPRS	hemisphere	EEEILMMSSW	Semmelweis	EEEIRSSTTV	serviettes
EEEHHLORSW	wheelhorse	EEEILMNRST	resilement	EEEIRSSTTW	streetwise
EEEHHLOSUW	wheelhouse	EEEILMNRTV	revilement	EEEJJNNSSU	jejuneness
EEEHHORRTW	otherwhere	EEEILMNSSS	seemliness	EEEJKNRSTU	junketeers
EEEHIKPPRS	keepership	EEEILMNSTY	mesitylene	EEEKLNRSUV	Leverkusen
EEEHILLNSS	hellenises	EEEILMRSST	smelteries	EEEKLORRTW	teleworker
EEEHILLNSZ	hellenizes	EEEILNNRSV	enliveners	EEEKMRSSTU	musketeers
EEEHILMORT	heliometer	EEEILNPRRT	terreplein	EEEKNOSSTY	synoeketes
EEEHILNPRS	prehensile	EEEILNPSSS	sleepiness	EEELLNPRST	repellents
EEEHILPSSS	lesseeship	EEEILNQSTU	queenliest	EEELLNPSTX	expellents
EEEHIMMRSU	euhemerism	EEEILNSSST	steeliness	EEELLNRSST	relentless
EEEHIMPRSU	euphemiser	EEEILORRTU	Eure-et-Loir	EEELLNSSTU	entelluses
EEEHIMPRUZ	euphemizer	EEEILPSTVX	expletives	EEELMMOSTT	mettlesome
EEEHIMPSSU	euphemises	EEEILRRTTW	telewriter	EEELMNOPRS	perlemoens
EEEHIMPSUZ	euphemizes	EEEILRSSSW	wirelesses	EEELMNOPST	elopements
EEEHIMRSTU	euhemerist	EEEILRSSTW	westerlies	EEELMNOSTT	nettlesome
EEEHINNNTT	nineteenth	EEEIMMNNOS	menominees	EEELMNOTVV	evolvement
EEEHINNORSW	Eisenhower	EEEIMMNORS	mesmeriser	EEELMNRSTV	revelments
EEEHINPSST	epenthesis	EEEIMMRRSZ	mesmerizer	EEELMNSTTT	settlement
EEEHINSSWZ	wheeziness	EEEIMMRSSS	mesmerises	EEELNOSSTT	solenettes
EEEHINSTTV	seventieth	EEEIMMRSSZ	mesmerizes	EEELNOSTTV	novelettes
EEEHIRRSST	etherisers	EEEIMNNPRT	preeminent	EEELNRRTVY	reverently
EEEHIRRSTZ	etherizers	EEEIMNNRST	nemertines	EEELNRSTTW	newsletter
EEEHKLOSSU	houseleeks	EEEIMNORST	remonetise	EEELOPRSSV	oversleeps
EEEHKOPPRS	shopkeeper	EEEIMNORTZ	remonetize	EEELORSVWW	werewolves
EEEHLLMRUV	Leverhulme	EEEIMNPRTX	experiment	EEELPRRSVY	perversely
EEEHLMNTVY	vehemently	EEEIMNRRTT	retirement	EEEMNNORST	mesenteron
EEEHLMSSTV	themselves	EEEIMNRSTT	tensimeter	EEEMNNRSTT	resentment
EEEHLNOPRT	telephoner	EEEIMOPRTZ	piezometer	EEEMNNRSTU	enurements
EEEHLNOPST	telephones	EEEIMORSTT	meteorites	EEEMNNSSTU	unmeetness
EEEHLNOPTY	polyethene	EEEIMPPRTV	preemptive	EEEMNOPRST	treponemes
EEEHLRRSST	shelterers	EEEIMPRRST	perimeters	EEEMNORSST	remoteness
EEEHMMMNST	enmeshment	EEEIMRRSTV	timeserver	EEEMNOSXYZ	exoenzymes
EEEHMMNSTY	enthymemes	EEEINNOPRS	pensioneer	EEEMNRSTTV	revetments
EEEHMNOPRS	ephemerons	EEEINNPRSS	persiennes	EEENNNSSUV	unevenness
EEEHMOPRSS	mesosphere	EEEINNPRST	serpentine	EEENNORSST	sonneteers
EEEHMORRRT	Rothermere	EEEINNPRTV	prevenient	EEENORSTWZ	sneezewort
EEEHMORRST	rheometers	EEEINNRRTV	intervener	EEENPRRSST	presenters
EEEHMORSST	threesomes	EEEINNRSST	entireness		represents
EEEHMPRRTY	hypermeter	EEEINNRSTV	intervenes	EEENPRRSTV	preventers
EEEHMRSTTT	thermettes	EEEINOORST	orienteers	EEENPRSSTX	expertness
EEEHNNPRTY	threepenny	EEEINPRRST	enterprise	EEENPRSSUV	supervenes
EEEHNOPPRS	Persephone	EEEINPRSTV	pretensive	EEENRRSSTW	westerners
EEEHNORSVW	whensoever		vespertine	EEEOOPRSVX	overexpose
EEEHOPPRRT	treehopper	EEEINPRTVV	preventive	EEEOPRSTTY	stereotype
EEEHRSSTTU	usherettes	EEEINQTTTU	netiquette	EEEORRRSTV	retroverse
EEEIILLSTV	velleities	EEEINRRRTV	irreverent	EEEORRSSTV	oversteers
EEEIINNSST	Eisenstein	EEEINRSSTW	westernise	EEEORRSTVX	overexerts
EEEIINNRSS	serenities	EEEINRSSTX	intersexes	EEEPPPRSTU	puppeteers
EEEIINRSTT	entireties	EEEINRSTWZ	westernize	EEEPRRRSSS	repressers
	eternities	EEEINSSTWY	eyewitness	EEEPRRRSSV	preservers
EEEIIPPRST	peripeties	EEEIOPRRRT	repertoire	EEEPRRRSTV	perverters

EEEPRRSSSX	expressers	**EEFHILOSSU**	houseflies	**EEFIMNRSTT**	refitments
EEEPRSSSUX	supersexes	**EEFHILRSVY**	feverishly	**EEFIMNRSTU**	frumenties
EEEPRSSTTU	superettes	**EEFHIORSSS**	rosefishes		furmenties
EEEPRSSTUW	supersweet	**EEFHIORSSU**	firehouses	**EEFIMPRRSU**	perfumiers
EEEPRSTTTY	typesetter	**EEFHIORSSV**	overfishes	**EEFINNORRT**	interferon
EEEQRRSSTU	requesters	**EEFHIOSUWY**	housewifey	**EEFINNQRTU**	infrequent
EEEQRSSSTU	sequesters	**EEFHLNOORS**	Holofernes	**EEFINORSST**	firestones
EEFFFGINNO	enfeoffing	**EEFHMOORRT**	foremother	**EEFINRSSTU**	interfuses
EEFFFKLRSU	kerfuffles	**EEFHNORTTU**	fourteenth	**EEFIOPRRST**	profiteers
EEFFFMNOST	feoffments	**EEFHOORRSS**	foreshores	**EEFIORRRST**	retrofires
EEFFGIINRV	fivefinger	**EEFHRRRSTU**	furtherers	**EEFIORRRST**	forestries
EEFFGINORR	forefinger	**EEFIIIRSVV**	revivifies	**EEFIORRSTT**	forsterite
EEFFGNRSTU	greenstuff	**EEFIIKLLNU**	unlifelike	**EEFIORSSTU**	setiferous
EEFFHIILSS	filefishes	**EEFIILLSST**	stellifies	**EEFIPRRSTU**	putrefiers
EEFFHINSTT	fifteenths	**EEFIILMNNY**	femininely	**EEFIPRSSTU**	stupefiers
EEFFHLRRSU	refreshful	**EEFIILMRSU**	emulsifier	**EEFIPRSSUX**	superfixes
EEFFHLRSSU	reshuffles	**EEFIILMSSU**	emulsifies	**EEFIRRRSTT**	fritterers
EEFFIILLRZ	Zeffirelli	**EEFIILNRST**	interfiles	**EEFIRRRSTU**	fruiterers
EEFFILSUVY	effusively	**EEFIILNSSW**	wifeliness	**EEFIRRSSTU**	surfeiters
EEFFINOSSV	offensives	**EEFIILQRSU**	liquefiers	**EEFKLLOOWY**	yokefellow
EEFFINRRST	stiffeners	**EEFIILRRST**	fertiliser	**EEFKLNOOST**	Folkestone
EEFFIORRST	forfeiters	**EEFIILRRTZ**	fertilizer	**EEFKNOOPRS**	forespoken
EEFFIORRTU	forfeiture	**EEFIILRSST**	fertilises	**EEFKNOORST**	foretokens
EEFFLOORTT	left-footer	**EEFIILRSTZ**	fertilizes	**EEFLLLSSSY**	selflessly
EEFFLORSST	effortless	**EEFIIMNNNU**	unfeminine	**EEFLLNTUVY**	eventfully
EEFFNORRTY	effrontery	**EEFIIMRRST**	metrifiers	**EEFLLORSSW**	flowerless
EEFFOPRRRS	profferers	**EEFIINNSST**	finiteness	**EEFLMORRSU**	remorseful
EEFGHHILRS	higher self	**EEFIINORST**	renotifies	**EEFLMORSTW**	flowmeters
EEFGHINNRS	freshening	**EEFIINORST**	Finisterre	**EEFLMRSTUX**	fluxmeters
EEFGHINNRS	refreshing	**EEFIIPPRRS**	fripperies	**EEFLNNTUUV**	uneventful
EEFGHINNRT	frightener	**EEFIIPPRTT**	pipefitter	**EEFLNOSSUW**	woefulness
EEFGHIRRST	freighters	**EEFIIPRRST**	petrifiers	**EEFLNQRTUY**	frequently
EEFGHLOOSS	gooseflesh	**EEFIIPRRSU**	repurifies	**EEFLNRSSUU**	ruefulness
EEFGIINRRT	gentrifier	**EEFIIPRRTT**	prettifier	**EEFLNSSSUU**	usefulness
EEFGILLNRU	refuelling	**EEFIIPRSTT**	prettifies	**EEFLORSSST**	forestless
EEFGILLNRY	fleeringly	**EEFIIRRRST**	terrifiers	**EEFLORSUVY**	feverously
EEFGILLNTY	fleetingly	**EEFIIRRRTU**	furrieries	**EEFLRRSTTU**	flutterers
EEFGILNRSS	fingerless	**EEFIIRRSSV**	versifiers	**EEFLRSSTUU**	futureless
	fringeless	**EEFIIRSSTT**	testifiers	**EEFMOPRRRS**	performers
EEFGILRSSU	figureless	**EEFIKLLORW**	flowerlike	**EEFNNORRRU**	forerunner
EEFGIMNNRT	fermenting	**EEFIKNRRST**	kniferests	**EEFNNORSSZ**	frozenness
EEFGIMRSUV	vermifuges	**EEFIKNRSSU**	refuseniks	**EEFNOORSTY**	festoonery
EEFGINNRRT	refringent	**EEFILLLOSS**	filoselles	**EEFOPRRSTY**	ferrotypes
EEFGINNRUZ	unfreezing	**EEFILLLSSY**	lifelessly	**EEFORRSSTT**	fortresses
EEFGINORRS	foreigners	**EEFILLNOTU**	feuilleton	**EEFPRSSSUU**	superfuses
EEFGINPRRR	preferring	**EEFILLRSST**	fillesters	**EEGGHIINRW**	reweighing
EEFGIPRRSU	prefigures	**EEFILLRSTU**	fullerites	**EEGGHILNRT**	greenlight
EEFGKLLNOT	gentlefolk	**EEFILLRSTY**	lifestyler	**EEGGIINNRS**	energising
EEFGLLMNOR	fellmonger	**EEFILLSSTY**	lifestyles	**EEGGIINNRZ**	energizing
EEFGLLNUVY	vengefully	**EEFILMMRSU**	flummeries	**EEGGILNNRS**	greenlings
EEFGLMNNTU	engulfment	**EEFILMNOQU**	mefloquine	**EEGGILOOSS**	geologises
EEFGORRSTT	forgetters	**EEFILMRSTT**	filmsetter	**EEGGILOOSZ**	geologizes
EEFHHLORSS	horseflesh	**EEFILNNORT**	florentine	**EEGGIMNNST**	segmenting
EEFHIILSST	tilefishes	**EEFILNORSX**	reflexions	**EEGGINNRSS**	regressing
EEFHIILSTW	whiteflies	**EEFILNOSST**	stoneflies	**EEGGINRRTT**	regretting
EEFHIINRRS	refinisher	**EEFILNOTUX**	fluoxetine	**EEGGINRSSU**	snuggeries
EEFHIINRSS	refinishes	**EEFILNRSSU**	irefulness	**EEGGISSTUV**	suggestive
EEFHIIPPSS	pipefishes	**EEFILNRTUV**	interfluve	**EEGGNOORTW**	Georgetown
EEFHILLSST	fleshliest	**EEFILNSSTU**	futileness		George Town
EEFHILNSSS	elfishness	**EEFILOSTWX**	Felixstowe	**EEGGRSSSTU**	suggesters
	fleshiness	**EEFIMNORST**	fromenties	**EEGHHIISTT**	eightieths
EEFHILORSS	horseflies	**EEFIMNOSTT**	oftentimes	**EEGHHINSSS**	highnesses

EEGHHINSTW wheeshting	**EEGIINNNRST** eternising	**EEGINORSVW** oversewing
EEGHHIRSTT High Street	**EEGIINNNRTZ** eternizing	**EEGINORSXY** oxygeniser
EEGHHLNOPT Phlegethon	**EEGIINPRRV** reprieving	**EEGINORXYZ** oxygenizer
EEGHIINRST etherising	**EEGIINPRVW** previewing	**EEGINOSSXY** oxygenises
EEGHIINRSV inveighers	**EEGIINPSST** epigenists	**EEGINOSXYZ** oxygenizes
EEGHIINRTZ etherizing	**EEGIINRRTV** retrieving	**EEGINPPSUW** upsweeping
EEGHIISTTW weightiest	**EEGIINRSSV** ingressive	**EEGINPRRSS** repressing
EEGHIKLRSU kieselguhr	**EEGIINRSTV** vertigines	**EEGINPRRSV** preserving
EEGHIKNSTW weeknights	**EEGIIRRSST** registries	**EEGINPRRTV** perverting
EEGHILNNST enlightens	**EEGIISSTTZ** zeitgeists	**EEGINPRSSX** expressing
EEGHILNOOP pigeonhole	**EEGIKLLNNN** kennelling	**EEGINPRSTT** presetting
EEGHILNOPR negrophile	**EEGIKLLNNR** kernelling	**EEGINPRSTT** pretesting
EEGHILNPRT telphering	**EEGIKLNOPS** spongelike	**EEGINQRSTU** requesting
EEGHILNRST sheltering	**EEGIKLNOTU** tonguelike	**EEGIORSSTU** setigerous
EEGHILNSTT lengthiest	**EEGIKLNRSS** Kesselring	**EEGIRRSSSU** regisseurs
EEGHILNSTW lengthwise	**EEGIKLOORV** groovelike	**EEGLLLOSWY** yellowlegs
EEGHILNSTY seethingly	**EEGIKLORSU** grouselike	**EEGLLMORSU** glomerules
EEGHILOOST theologies	**EEGIKNNNTT** kennetting	**EEGLLNOOSY** selenology
	theologise	**EEGILLMSTU** guillemets	**EEGLLOOPSY** speleology
EEGHILOOTZ theologize	**EEGILLNPRS** preselling	**EEGLLOPRSS** gospellers
EEGHILSSTW weightless	**EEGILLMORSU** gelsemiums	**EEGLLORRSV** grovellers
EEGHIMNOOS homogenise	**EEGILMNNOT** eloignment	**EEGLMNNOSU** melungeons
EEGHIMNOOZ homogenize	**EEGILMNOOS** menologies	**EEGLMORSUY** gruesomely
EEGHIMOSST eightsomes	**EEGILMNORS** mongrelise	**EEGLNOOSTU** telegonous
EEGHINNPRS ensphering	**EEGILMNORZ** mongrelize	**EEGLNORSTT** lorgnettes
EEGHINOOST theogonies	**EEGILMOOSY** semeiology	**EEGLNORSUY** generously
EEGHINOPST phosgenite	**EEGILNNOPV** enveloping	**EEGLNOSSTU** tongueless
EEGHINPRST regentship	**EEGILNNRSY** sneeringly	**EEGLOORRST** ergosterol
EEGHINRSTT tighteners	**EEGILNNRTU** Reutlingen	**EEGLOORSSV** grooveless
EEGHINRTVY everything	**EEGILNNSSS** singleness	**EEGLOPRTWY** Lower Egypt
EEGHIORSVW overweighs	**EEGILNNSTU** unsteeling	**EEGMNNOORT** Montenegro
EEGHIORTVW overweight	**EEGILNOOSS** neologises	**EEGMNNORSW** newsmonger
EEGHIOSSTT ghettoises	**EEGILNOOSZ** neologizes	**EEGMNNORTV** government
EEGHIOSTTZ ghettoizes	**EEGILNOPPR** repeopling	**EEGMNOORRS** greenrooms
EEGHIRSSST sightseers	**EEGILNOSST** telegnosis	**EEGNNORSUU** ungenerous
EEGHLLNOPS phellogens	**EEGILNOPRX** perplexing	**EEGNOORSST** oestrogens
EEGHLNORST Glenrothes	**EEGILNPRVY** replevying	**EEGNORRSSS** engrossers
EEGHLOOPRT Oglethorpe	**EEGILNPSWY** sweepingly	**EEGOPRRSSS** progresses
EEGHLOORTY heterology	**EEGILNRSTT** resettling	**EEGOQRSSTU** grotesques
EEGHMORRTY hygrometer	**EEGILNRSTW** sweltering	**EEGORRRSSS** regressors
EEGHNNORRS greenhorns	**EEGILORSST** sortileges	**EEGORRRSST** retrogress
EEGHNNRSTT strengthen	**EEGILORSSU** eulogisers	**EEGOSSSTUU** outguesses
EEGHNOOPST photogenes	**EEGILORSUZ** eulogizers	**EEGPPPRTUY** Upper Egypt
EEGHNOORTY heterogony	**EEGIMNNNOV** envenoming	**EEHHIKMORR** Horkheimer
EEGHNOPTTY gnetophyte	**EEGIMNNOTT** mignonette	**EEHHILMOPS** hemophiles
EEGHNORTTU untogether	**EEGIMNNTTU** integument	**EEHHILOPTY** heliophyte
EEGHORSSTU otherguess	**EEGIMNOORT** goniometer	**EEHHILPSSY** sheepishly
EEGHOSSTUU guesthouse	**EEGIMNOPRW** empowering	**EEHHIMNOST** henotheism
	houseguest	**EEGIMNPPRT** preempting	**EEHHINOSTT** henotheist
EEGIIILMST legitimise	**EEGIMNPSTT** tempesting	**EEHHINRTTT** thirteenth
EEGIIILMTZ legitimize	**EEGINNOPPS** pepsinogen	**EEHHIORSTW** Whitehorse
EEGIIKLPRS kriegspiel	**EEGINNORST** rontgenise	**EEHHIPRRST** Perthshire
EEGIILNNNV enlivening	**EEGINNORTZ** rontgenize	**EEHHLOPSTY** helophytes
EEGIILNNST lentigines	**EEGINNPRST** presenting	**EEHHNOPPSS** phosphenes
EEGIILNRST leistering	**EEGINNPRTV** preventing	**EEHHOORSSS** horseshoes
EEGIILNRSV inveiglers	**EEGINNSSSY** syngenesis	**EEHHOORSUW** whorehouse
EEGIILNSTV televising	**EEGINOORSS** orogenesis	**EEHHOPRTTY** therophyte
EEGIILOOST etiologies	**EEGINOPSSY** pyogenesis	**EEHHOPSSTY** hypotheses
EEGIILPRSV privileges	**EEGINORRSS** regression	**EEHHIIKLNRS** shrinelike
EEGIIMNPRR premiering	**EEGINORRWW** winegrower	**EEHIILMPTU** epithelium
EEGIINNOPR pioneering	**EEGINORSSV** sovereigns	**EEHIILNOPR** perihelion
EEGIINNQTU quietening	**EEGINORSTY** generosity	**EEHIIMNNOT** methionine

EEHIIMRSST	smitheries
EEHIINNPPR	epinephrin
EEHIINNSTT	ninetieths
EEHIIPRSVW	viewership
EEHIIRRSTX	heritrixes
EEHIKNPSSS	sheepskins
EEHILLLMSW	millwheels
EEHILLPRST	tellership
EEHILMNOSS	homeliness
EEHILMOPRT	thermopile
EEHILMOPSS	mesophiles
EEHILMORTY	heliometry
EEHILNNRTY	inherently
EEHILNOOPS	oenophiles
EEHILNOPSX	xenophiles
EEHILNORSS	shorelines
EEHILNOSSS	holinesses
EEHILNOSSU	houselines
EEHILNPRSS	plenishers
EEHILNPRTW	printwheel
EEHILNSSSV	elvishness
EEHILOOPRT	heliotrope
EEHILOPRSS	repolishes
EEHILOPRSX	xerophiles
EEHILOPSTY	heliotypes
EEHILORSST	hostelries
EEHILOSTTU	silhouette
EEHILPPRSY	Lippershey
EEHILPRSTU	spherulite
EEHILPSSST	slipsheets
EEHIMPPSSU	euphemisms
EEHIMNNRTU	minehunter
EEHIMNOPPS	Hippomenes
EEHIMNOPRT	hemipteron
EEHIMOPRST	hemitropes
EEHIMOPRSV	empoverish
EEHIMPRRSW	whimperers
EEHINNOPRS	prehension
EEHINNOPRT	interphone
EEHINNORST	rhinestone
EEHINNSSSW	newishness
EEHINOOPRS	ionosphere
EEHINOPSSU	euphonises
EEHINOPSUZ	euphonizes
EEHINSSSTX	sixth sense
EEHINSSSTY	synthesise
EEHINSSTTU	euthenists
EEHINSSTTX	sixteenths
EEHINSSTTY	synthetise
EEHINSSTYZ	synthesize
EEHINSTTTW	twentieths
EEHINSTTYZ	synthetize
EEHIOPPRRS	prophesier
EEHIOPPRSS	prophesies
EEHIOPPRST	epistrophe
EEHIOPPSSU	eohippuses
EEHIORRSST	theorisers
EEHIORRSTZ	theorizers
EEHIOSSUVW	housewives
EEHIPRRSSW	whisperers
EEHIRSSSTY	hysteresis
EEHKKOOPYY	hokeypokey

EEHKLLORRW	Hellerwork
EEHKLNORRV	herrenvolk
EEHKLOOOWY	Wookey Hole
EEHKLOOSST	stokeholes
EEHKLORSWW	wheelworks
EEHKMOORRW	homeworker
EEHKMOOSSU	smokehouse
EEHKNOORTT	heterokont
	tenterhook
EEHKORSSTW	worksheets
EEHLLLPSSY	helplessly
EEHLLMNOOP	mellophone
EEHLLMORTW	Motherwell
EEHLLNOPST	Hellespont
EEHLLOPSSY	hopelessly
EEHLLORSST	hostellers
EEHLLORSSV	shovellers
EEHLMNOOYZ	holoenzyme
EEHLMNORTY	hemelytron
EEHLMORSST	motherless
EEHLMORSWV	overwhelms
EEHLNOOSSV	shovelnose
EEHLNOPSTY	polythenes
EEHLNORSST	throneless
EEHMNNNOOP	phenomenon
EEHMNNORTY	North Yemen
EEHMNOOPRS	pheromones
EEHMNOOPRT	phonometer
EEHMNOORSW	homeowners
	horsewomen
EEHMNOORTY	heteronomy
EEHMNORSTT	nethermost
EEHMNORSTY	heteronyms
EEHMNOSTUY	South Yemen
EEHMOOPRTT	photometer
EEHMOORSVW	whomsoever
EEHMOPRSTT	stepmother
EEHMOPRSTU	Prometheus
EEHMOPRSTY	hypsometer
EEHMOPSSTY	hemoptyses
	mesophytes
EEHMOQRSUU	humoresque
EEHMORSSUW	shrewmouse
EEHMRRRSTU	murtherers
EEHMRRSSTY	rhymesters
EEHNNOPSST	Stephenson
EEHNNOPSSY	phoneyness
EEHNNORRRT	northerner
EEHNNOSSST	honestness
EEHNOPPSTY	phenotypes
EEHNOPRSUY	Euphrosyne
EEHNOPSSTU	penthouses
EEHNOPSTTY	entophytes
EEHNOPSTUY	hypotenuse
EEHNORRSST	shorteners
EEHNORRSTU	southerner
EEHNORRTTW	Wetterhorn
EEHNOSSTTW	whetstones
EEHNPPSSUU	penpushers
EEHNRSSSTU	huntresses
EEHOOPRRSW	horsepower
EEHOOPRSUW	powerhouse

EEHOOPRTTY	heterotopy
EEHOOPSSTY	osteophyte
EEHOORSSTU	storehouse
EEHOPPRRWY	hyperpower
EEHOPPRSST	prophetess
EEHOPRRSTV	Shreveport
EEHOPRSSST	hotpresses
	prostheses
EEHOPRSTXY	xerophytes
EEHOPSSSTU	pesthouses
EEHPRSTTXY	hypertexts
EEHRSSTUUY	Eurystheus
EEIIIMNRSS	miniseries
EEIIINQSTU	inequities
EEIIKLLNRU	unlikelier
EEIIKLLNSS	likeliness
EEIIKLNPRW	periwinkle
EEIIKLPRST	priestlike
EEIIKNNSTZ	zinkenites
EEIIILLLNWY	Llewelyn II
EEIIILLMMRT	millimeter
	millimetre
EEIIILLNSSV	liveliness
EEIIILMNSST	timeliness
EEIIILNNRRT	interliner
EEIIILNNRST	interlines
EEIIILNOSTV	olivenites
	television
EEIIILNSSSW	wiliness
EEIIILOPSST	sepiolites
EEIIILOPTVX	exploitive
EEIIILORSTT	toiletries
EEIIILPRRST	priestlier
EEIIILRRSST	steriliser
EEIIILRRSTZ	sterilizer
EEIIILRSSST	sterilises
EEIIILRSSTZ	sterilizes
EEIIILRSTUZ	reutilizes
EEIIMMNRTU	meitnerium
EEIIMMNPTT	impenitent
	pentimenti
EEIIMNORST	enormities
EEIIMNPRUU	epineurium
EEIIMNRSTX	intermixes
EEIIMNRTTW	wintertime
EEIIMNRTZZ	intermezzi
EEIIMOPRST	epitomiser
EEIIMOPRTZ	epitomizer
EEIIMOPSST	epitomises
EEIIMOPSTZ	epitomizes
EEIIMORSSS	isomerises
EEIIMORSSZ	isomerizes
EEIIMPRSSV	impressive
	permissive
EEIIINNNSTT	insentient
EEIIINNRTTW	intertwine
EEIINNSSSW	sineweness
EEIINNSSTT	intestines
EEIINNSSTV	intensives
EEIINNSTTX	inexistent
EEIINOPRTT	petitioner
	repetition

EEIINPRRST printeries	**EEILMNOSSZ** solemnizes	**EEIMNNOPTT** pentimento
EEIINRRSVV viverrines	**EEILMNPPRS** pimpernels	**EEIMNNORST** mentioners
EEIINRSSST sensitiser	**EEILMNPSSS** simpleness	minestrone
EEIINRSSTW winterises	**EEILMNSSTU** mustelines	**EEIMNNPSTU** septennium
EEIINRSSTZ sensitizer	**EEILMOPRSY** polymerise	**EEIMNNRSTT** interments
EEIINRSTVW interviews	**EEILMOPRYZ** polymerize	**EEIMNNRSTU** inurements
EEIINRSTWZ winterizes	**EEILMORSTT** Timor-Leste	**EEIMNNSSTT** sentiments
EEIINSSSST sensitises	**EEILMORSTY** tiresomely	**EEIMNNSSTU** minuteness
EEIINSSSTZ sensitizes	**EEILMOSSTV** motiveless	**EEIMNNSTTV** investment
EEIIOPQSSU equipoises	**EEILMOSSVW** semivowels	**EEIMNOORRT** remontoire
EEIIOPSTVX expositive	**EEILMPRSTU** pulsimeter	**EEIMNOORST** eriostemon
EEIIORRSST rotisserie	**EEILMPRTVY** pelvimetry	**EEIMNOOSTT** tenotomies
EEIIOSSSTV sovieties	**EEILMRSSTY** lysimeters	**EEIMNOPPRT** preemption
EEIIOSSTVZ sovietizes	**EEILNNOQTU** ineloquent	**EEIMNOPRST** Simon Peter
EEIIPQRSTU perquisite	**EEILNNPTTY** penitently	**EEIMNOPRTU** peritoneum
EEIIQRSSTU requisites	**EEILNNSSST** silentness	**EEIMNOPSTX** exemptions
EEIIQSSTUX exquisites	**EEILNNSTTY** sentiently	**EEIMNORRSS** sermoniser
EEIJLLNUVY juvenilely	**EEILNOORSS** oleoresins	**EEIMNORRSZ** sermonizer
EEIJLORSSV Overijssel	**EEILNOPRRT** interloper	**EEIMNORRTT** nitrometer
EEIJMNNNOT enjoinment	**EEILNOPSST** politeness	**EEIMNORRTU** urinometer
EEIKKMORSS kromeskies	**EEILNORSVV** reinvolves	**EEIMNORSSS** sermonises
EEIKKORSST koeksister	**EEILNORSVW** wolverines	**EEIMNORSST** moisteners
EEIKLMMRSU summerlike	**EEILNORTVV** intervolve	**EEIMNORSSZ** sermonizes
EEIKLMORST kilometers	**EEILNPRTXY** inexpertly	**EEIMNORTTT** tintometer
kilometres	**EEILNRSSTW** winterless	**EEIMNORTZZ** intermezzo
EEIKLNNOPT Pentelikon	**EEILNRSTUY** esuriently	**EEIMNOSSTX** sixteenmos
EEIKLNNSSU unlikeness	**EEILOOPRST** teliospore	**EEIMNOSSYZ** isoenzymes
EEIKLRSSST strikeless	**EEILOPPRSS** Persepolis	**EEIMNPPPRT** peppermint
EEIKMNORST konimeters	**EEILOPRSST** epistolers	**EEIMNPRSSU** impureness
EEIKMORRTW timeworker	pistoleers	**EEIMNPRSTU** episternum
EEIKOPRSTV perovskite	**EEILOPSSVX** explosives	**EEIMNRSSSS** remissness
EEILLLRSST tillerless	**EEILORRSTU** irresolute	**EEIMNRSSTU** terminuses
EEILLMMORT immortelle	**EEILORRTTW** rottweiler	**EEIMNRSSTW** westernism
EEILLMNOST emollients	**EEILORRTXY** exteriorly	**EEIMOOPRSS** meiospores
EEILLMNPST impellents	**EEILORSTUV** resolutive	**EEIMOOPRSX** peroxisome
EEILLMNSSS smelliness	**EEILOSSTTT** stilettoes	**EEIMOORSSZ** merozoites
EEILLMOPRS millepores	**EEILPPRSSU** resupplies	**EEIMOPRRRT** reimporter
EEILLMORSV Somerville	**EEILPPRTXY** perplexity	**EEIMOPRRST** spirometer
EEILLMPPPR peppermill	**EEILPPSTUV** suppletive	temporiser
EEILLMSSTY timelessly	**EEILPRRSTY** sperrylite	**EEIMOPRRTZ** temporizer
EEILLNNOSS loneliness	**EEILPRRSUV** pulveriser	**EEIMOPRSST** peristomes
EEILLNOSSV loveliness	**EEILPRRUVZ** pulverizer	temporises
EEILLNRSSV snivellers	**EEILPRSSTY** peristyles	**EEIMOPRSTU** periosteum
EEILLOPSTU petiolules	**EEILPRSSUV** pulverises	**EEIMOPRSTZ** temporizes
EEILLPRRUW wirepuller	**EEILPRSUVZ** pulverizes	**EEIMOPRTYZ** piezometry
EEILLRSSTU tellurises	**EEILPRTUVY** eruptively	**EEIMPPRRUU** puerperium
EEILLRSSTY tirelessly	**EEILRSSSST** resistless	**EEIMPPRRSS** impressers
EEILLRSTTU tellurites	**EEILRSSTUV** virtueless	**EEIMPRRSSU** impressure
EEILLRSTUZ tellurizes	**EEILRSSUVV** revulsives	**EEIMPRRSTT** permitters
EEILLSSTUV vitelluses	**EEIMMMNRTU** immurement	pretermits
EEILMMNPST implements	**EEIMMMRSTU** summertime	**EEIMPRRSTU** trumperies
EEILMMORSS sommeliers	**EEIMMNOSTY** metonymies	**EEIMPRSTUV** resumptive
EEILMMORST milometers	**EEIMMOPRRV** prime mover	**EEIMQSSTUU** equisetums
EEILMMRTTU multimeter	Prime Mover	**EEIMRRSSTT** trimesters
EEILMNNOTT entoilment	**EEIMMORRSS** memorisers	**EEIMRSSSST** mistresses
EEILMNNSST enlistment	**EEIMMORRSZ** memorizers	**EEIMRSSSTY** systemiser
EEILMNOPRT Montpelier	**EEIMMRSSST** mesmerists	**EEIMRSSTTU** sestertium
EEILMNORSS solemniser	**EEIMMRSSTW** swimmerets	**EEIMRSSTTX** extremists
EEILMNORSZ solemnizer	**EEIMMRSSTY** symmetries	**EEIMRSSTYZ** systemizer
EEILMNOSSS solemnises	symmetrise	**EEIMSSSSTY** systemises
EEILMNOSST milestones	**EEIMMRSTYZ** symmetrize	**EEIMSSSTYZ** systemizes
EEILMNOSSU mousseline	**EEIMNNNRTT** internment	**EEINNNSSTT** intentness

EEINNOPRSS	pensioners	
EEINNOPRST	pretension	
EEINNOPRTV	prevention	
EEINNORRSS	orneriness	
EEINNORRTV	intervenor	
EEINNORSTT	retentions	
EEINNORTVW	interwoven	
EEINNOSSTV	veinstones	
EEINNOSSTX	extensions	
EEINNPRSST	spinnerets	
EEINNPRSSU	unripeness	
EEINNPRTTU	turpentine	
EEINNPSSSU	supineness	
EEINNQSSUU	uniqueness	
EEINNRSSTV	inventress	
EEINNSSSUW	unwiseness	
EEINOOSSST	otioseness	
EEINOOSTVZ	Soviet Zone	
EEINOPPRST	peptoniser	
EEINOPPRTZ	peptonizer	
EEINOPPSSU	peptonises	
EEINOPPSTZ	peptonizes	
EEINOPQTTU	equipotent	
EEINOPRRSS	repression	
EEINOPRRST	interposer	
EEINOPRRSV	perversion	
EEINOPRSST	interposes	
EEINOPRSSV	responsive	
EEINOPRSSX	expression	
EEINOPRTXY	pyroxenite	
EEINOQRSTU	questioner	
EEINORRSSV	reversions	
EEINORRSUV	overinsure	
EEINORRTVW	overwinter	
EEINOSSTVV	votiveness	
EEINOSTTUZ	teutonizes	
EEINPRRRST	reprinters	
EEINPRRSTT	interprets	
EEINPRSSTT	persistent	
	prettiness	
EEINPSSSUV	suspensive	
EEINQSTTTU	quintettes	
EEINRRRSSU	reinsurers	
EEINRSSSTW	witnessers	
EEIOPPRRST	properties	
EEIOPPRSSV	oppressive	
EEIOPPSSTV	stovepipes	
EEIOPRRSSS	prioresses	
EEIOPRRSTV	resorptive	
EEIOPRSSST	stereopsis	
EEIOPRSSSV	espressivo	
EEIOPRSTTT	operettist	
EEIOPRSTTU	pirouettes	
EEIOPSSSSV	possessive	
EEIOQQSUUV	equivoques	
EEIORRRRST	terroriser	
EEIORRRRTZ	terrorizer	
EEIORRRSST	roisterers	
	terrorises	
EEIORRRSSV	reservoirs	
EEIORRRSTZ	terrorizes	
EEIORRSTTU	tourtieres	

EEIORRSTVW	overwrites	
EEIORSSSUV	overissues	
EEIPPRRTUY	perpetuity	
EEIPRRSSST	persisters	
EEIPRRSSSU	pressurise	
EEIPRRSSUZ	pressurize	
EEIPRRSTVY	perversity	
EEIPRRTTWY	typewriter	
EEIPRSSSTT	stepsister	
EEIPRSSSUV	supervises	
EEIPRSTTWY	typewrites	
EEIRRSSSTV	reservists	
EEIRRSTTTW	twitterers	
EEIRSSSTTU	sestertius	
EEJKNRSTTU	junketters	
EEJLMNOSTT	jostlement	
EEJMNNORUY	journeymen	
EEJMNNOSTY	enjoyments	
EEJNORRSUY	journeyers	
EEKKORRSSTY	keystrokes	
EEKLNPRSSU	spelunkers	
EEKLOOORRV	overlooker	
EEKLOOPPRW	workpeople	
EEKLORRSSW	workerless	
EEKLORSSTW	steelworks	
EEKNORRSTW	networkers	
EELLLOSSVY	lovelessly	
EELLMNNORT	enrollment	
EELLMNOOSY	lonesomely	
EELLMNOSSW	mellowness	
EELLNNRSTU	tunnellers	
EELLNNSSSU	sullenness	
EELLNOPPRT	propellent	
EELLNOQTUY	eloquently	
EELLNOSSTY	tonelessly	
EELLNOSSWY	yellowness	
EELLNSSTUY	tunelessly	
EELLOPPRRS	propellers	
EELLORRSTW	trowellers	
EELLORSTUY	resolutely	
EELLRSSSTU	lusterless	
	lustreless	
EELLRSSSTY	restlessly	
EELMMNOPTY	employment	
EELMMNOSTU	emoluments	
EELMMRSSSU	summerless	
EELMNNORST	enrolments	
EELMNNOSSU	solemnness	
EELMNNOSTU	ensoulment	
EELMNOSTTX	extolments	
EELMNPPSTU	supplement	
EELMNPTUZZ	puzzlement	
EELMOOPSST	leptosomes	
EELMOPRSTU	pulsometer	
EELMORRSST	tremorless	
EELMORSTTV	voltmeters	
EELMORSTUV	volumeters	
EELMSSSSTY	systemless	
EELNOPRSTW	spleenwort	
EELNORSSTV	resolvents	
EELNORSTUV	volunteers	
EELNPPRSSU	purpleness	

EELNPPSSSU	suppleness	
EELOOPRSTT	protostele	
EELOOPRRSTU	poulterers	
EELOPRSSTY	polyesters	
	proselytes	
EELORRRSST	terrorless	
EELORRRSTY	retrorsely	
EELORSSUVY	yourselves	
EELPPRSSSU	supperless	
EELPPSSTTU	septuplets	
EELPRRSTTU	splutterer	
EELPRSSTUU	sepultures	
EELPSSTTUX	sextuplets	
EEMMNOORST	metronomes	
	monometers	
	monotremes	
EEMMOORSST	osmometers	
EEMMORSTYZ	zymometers	
EEMMNOPSST	penstemons	
EEMMNOPSTT	pentstemon	
EEMMNRSUYR	nurserymen	
EEMMNNRSTUU	Neumünster	
EEMNOORSSS	moroseness	
EEMNOORSTT	tonometers	
EEMNOORTTY	enterotomy	
EEMNOPRSUW	superwomen	
EEMNOPRSYZ	proenzymes	
EEMNORRSTT	tormenters	
EEMNOSSUUY	euonymuses	
EEMNOSSUVY	evonymuses	
EEMOOOSSTT	osteotomes	
EEMOOPRSTT	optometers	
	potometers	
EEMOORSTTY	stereotomy	
EEMOPPRRST	preemptors	
EEMOPPRRTY	peremptory	
EEMOPPRRTY	pyrometers	
EEMORSSTTU	metestrous	
	metoestrus	
EEMPRRSTTU	trumpeters	
EEMPRSSSST	sempstress	
EEMQRSSTUU	sequestrum	
EENNOPSSTT	potentness	
EENNOQRSTU	quernstone	
EENNOQSTUW	Queenstown	
EENNORSTT	rottenness	
EENNOSSSUV	venousness	
EENNRSSTUU	untrueness	
EENOPPRRSS	properness	
EENOPRRSSS	responsers	
EENOPSSTTY	stenotypes	
EENORRSSST	Stroessner	
EENORRSTUY	tourneyers	
EENORSSSSU	serousness	
EENORSTTTU	neutrettos	
EENPRRSSUU	supernurse	
EEOOPRRSVW	overpowers	
EEOORRRSTV	rootserver	
EEOOSSTTTV	voetstoets	
EEOPPPRRTW	pepperwort	
EEOPPPRSSU	presuppose	
EEOPPRRSUW	superpower	

EEOPPRSSSS	prepossess	**EFGIIIMMNZ**	feminizing
EEOPPRSSSU	superposes	**EFGIIINRSS**	signifiers
EEOPRRRSSS	repressors	**EFGIIJLLNY**	jellifying
EEOPRRSSST	portresses	**EFGIILNQUY**	liquefying
EEOPRRSSTT	protesters	**EFGIILNRTT**	flittering
EEOPRRSSTU	superstore	**EFGIILORRS**	glorifiers
EEOPRSTTYY	stereotypy	**EFGIILTUVY**	fugitively
EEOPSSSTTU	poussettes	**EFGIIMNORS**	foreignism
EEORRSTTVX	extroverts	**EFGIIMNRTY**	metrifying
EEPPRRSSSU	suppresser	**EFGIINNRRS**	infringers
EEPPRSSSSU	suppresses	**EFGIINNRSU**	reinfusing
EEPRRSSTTU	sputterers	**EFGIINNRUY**	reunifying
EERRSSTTTU	stutterers	**EFGIINPRST**	fingertips
EESSSSTUWX	West Sussex		presifting
EFFFILNSSU	fluffiness	**EFGIINPRSY**	presignify
EFFFKLRSUU	kurfuffles	**EFGIINPRTY**	petrifying
EFFGHIINRS	fishfinger	**EFGIINRRTT**	frittering
EFFGHIIRST	firefights	**EFGIINRRTY**	terrifying
EFFGHIORSS	frogfishes	**EFGIINRSTU**	surfeiting
EFFGIINNST	stiffening	**EFGIINRSVY**	versifying
EFFGIINORT	forfeiting	**EFGIINSTTY**	testifying
EFFGIINOST	Ffestiniog	**EFGIKLNORS**	folksinger
EFFGINOPRR	proffering	**EFGILLLUUY**	guilefully
EFFGINOSTT	offsetting	**EFGILLNNNU**	funnelling
EFFGINRSSU	sufferings	**EFGILMNNTU**	ingulfment
EFFHILOSSW	wolffishes	**EFGILNORST**	fosterling
EFFHINOSSS	offishness	**EFGILNORVY**	overflying
EFFIINNSSS	sniffiness	**EFGILNRSTU**	flustering
EFFIINPSSS	spiffiness	**EFGILNRTTU**	fluttering
EFFIIORRST	fortifiers	**EFGILRSTUU**	fulgurites
EFFIIQSSTU	squiffiest	**EFGIMNOPRR**	performing
EFFILLLRSU	fulfillers		preforming
EFFILLMNTU	fulfilment	**EFGINNOOST**	festooning
EFFILMSUUV	effluviums	**EFGINNORUV**	unforgiven
EFFILNSSTU	fitfulness	**EFGINOOPRR**	reproofing
EFFINNSSSU	snuffiness	**EFGINOPRSS**	professing
EFFINSSSTU	stuffiness	**EFGINOPRST**	fingerpost
EFFIOOPRRS	fireproofs	**EFGINORRTY**	torrefying
EFFORSSTUV	overstuffs	**EFGINPRTUY**	putrefying
EFGGHIINRT	freighting	**EFGINPSTUY**	stupefying
EFGGHINRTU	gunfighter	**EFGLLLNOOW**	Longfellow
EFGGIILLNR	fingerling	**EFGOOOOSST**	goosefoots
EFGGIILNNY	feigningly	**EFHIIKLMSS**	milkfishes
EFGGILOOSS	solfeggios	**EFHIILNOSS**	lionfishes
EFGGINORTT	forgetting	**EFHIILNRST**	Flintshire
EFGHHIILRS	highfliers	**EFHIILNSST**	filthiness
EFGHHILRSY	highflyers	**EFHIILRSSV**	silverfish
EFGHIIKNRS	kingfisher	**EFHIINSSST**	shiftiness
EFGHIIKNSS	kingfishes	**EFHIIRSTTT**	thriftiest
EFGHIILNST	nightlifes	**EFHIISSSTT**	fetishists
EFGHIILSTT	flightiest	**EFHIKMNOSS**	monkfishes
EFGHIINRST	infighters	**EFHILLOPSW**	fellowship
EFGHIIPRTZ	prizefight	**EFHILMPSSU**	lumpfishes
EFGHILLSST	flightless	**EFHILOPRST**	shoplifter
EFGHILNSSU	lungfishes	**EFHILORRSU**	flourisher
EFGHILORTV	overflight	**EFHILORSSU**	flourishes
EFGHILSTWY	flyweights	**EFHILRSSTT**	thriftless
EFGHIMNNRS	fishmonger	**EFHIMNNOPR**	phenformin
EFGHINRRTU	furthering	**EFHIMNOOSS**	moonfishes
EFGHLLNORU	flugelhorn	**EFHINORRST**	firethorns
EFGHOOPPRR	froghopper	**EFHINORSST**	frothiness
EFGIIIMMNS	feminising	**EFHINRRSSU**	furnishers

EFHLLOOPRS	shellproof
EFHLLOSSUV	shovelfuls
	shovelsful
EFHLNNOOSW	Wolfensohn
EFHLOOPSSU	flophouses
EFHNORSTUX	foxhunters
EFIIIINNST	infinities
EFIIIINNTV	infinitive
EFIIILLMOR	millefiori
EFIIILMPRS	simplifier
EFIIILMPSS	simplifies
EFIIILNNTY	infinitely
EFIIILSTTU	futilities
EFIIIMMNNTY	femininity
EFIIJRSSTU	justifiers
EFIIKNNOPT	knifepoint
EFIIKNRSSS	friskiness
EFIILLMORS	mollifiers
EFIILLNRSS	frilliness
EFIILLNRSU	nullifiers
EFIILLRSST	fillisters
EFIILMNSSS	flimsiness
EFIILMOSTT	leitmotifs
EFIILNNOSX	inflexions
EFIILNNSST	flintiness
EFIILNORRV	inferiorly
EFIILOPRSU	piliferous
EFIILOSSSS	fossilises
EFIILOSSSZ	fossilizes
EFIILRSTTU	stultifier
EFIILRSTZZ	frizzliest
EFIILSSTTU	stultifies
EFIIMNNRSS	infirmness
EFIIMORRST	mortifiers
EFIIMORSTU	fumitories
EFIIMRSSTY	mystifiers
EFIINOOPSS	opsonifies
EFIINORSUV	viniferous
EFIINRSSTU	fruitiness
EFIINRSSZZ	frizziness
EFIIORSTTU	fortuities
EFIIRSTTUU	futurities
EFIKLNOSSS	folksiness
EFIKLRSSTY	flystrikes
EFILLMOPSU	filoplumes
EFILLMORST	stelliform
EFILLNSSUW	wilfulness
EFILLORRSV	frivollers
EFILLPSTUY	spitefully
EFILMOOPRS	Simferopol
EFILNNSSSU	sinfulness
EFILNOPPSS	floppiness
EFILNORSTW	interflows
EFILNORTWW	twinflower
EFILOPRSST	profitless
EFILQRSUUV	quiverfuls
EFIMMORRSS	reformisms
EFIMNORSTU	misfortune
EFIMNPRSSU	frumpiness
EFIMOOPRSU	pomiferous
EFIMORRSST	firestorms
	reformists

EFIMORRSTV	First Mover	**EGGILNNTTU**	englutting	**EGHILOOSTT**	ethologist
EFINOOPRSS	profession	**EGGILNSSUY**	guessingly		theologist
EFINOORSSU	soniferous	**EGGILQRSSU**	squigglers	**EGHILOSSTT**	ghostliest
EFINOPRSSU	perfusions	**EGGINNOOOR**	gorgoneion	**EGHILPRSTU**	uplighters
EFINORSSST	frostiness	**EGGINNORSS**	engrossing	**EGHIMNORST**	smothering
EFINORSSSW	frowsiness	**EGGINOPRRU**	regrouping	**EGHIMNRRTU**	murthering
EFINORSSUZ	frouziness	**EGGINOSSTU**	suggestion	**EGHIMOSUYZ**	hemizygous
EFINORSSWZ	frowziness	**EGGIORRSTU**	outriggers	**EGHINNNORT**	enthroning
EFINSSSTUU	unfussiest	**EGGLLOOOPX**	googolplex	**EGHINNORST**	shortening
EFIOOPRRSU	poriferous	**EGGLOORSUY**	gorgeously	**EGHINNOSUZ**	Ingenhousz
EFIOORRSTU	rotiferous	**EGGLRRSSTU**	strugglers	**EGHINNPPSU**	penpushing
EFIOORSSSU	ossiferous	**EGHHIIPRST**	high priest	**EGHINNPRSU**	gunnership
EFIORSSTTW	frowstiest	**EGHHILOPRY**	hieroglyph		unsphering
EFIORSTTTU	outfitters		hygrophile	**EGHINNPRSY**	phrensying
EFJLNOSSUY	joyfulness	**EGHHILOSTU**	lighthouse	**EGHINNRSSU**	hungriness
EFKLMNOOSW	womenfolks	**EGHHNOTTUW**	New Thought	**EGHINOOSTT**	theogonist
EFLLMORSSY	formlessly	**EGHHOORSUU**	roughhouse	**EGHINORSST**	shoestring
EFLLOPRUWY	powerfully	**EGHHOPPSYY**	hypophyges	**EGHINORSTV**	overnights
EFLLOSUUXY	flexuously	**EGHHOPRTYY**	hygrophyte	**EGHINRSTTU**	shuttering
EFLMNOOORW	moonflower	**EGHIIINNRT**	inheriting	**EGHIOPRSTT**	tightropes
EFLMOOORTY	tomfoolery	**EGHIIKNNRT**	rethinking	**EGHIORSSTV**	oversights
EFLNORSSUW	sunflowers	**EGHIILNNPS**	plenishing	**EGHIORSTTW**	ghostwrite
EFLOOPRSTW	flowerpots	**EGHIILNNRT**	Inner Light	**EGHIRSSTTU**	theurgists
EFLOPPRSUU	purposeful	**EGHIILNRST**	slithering	**EGHLMOOOSU**	homologues
EFLORRSSUW	furrowless	**EGHIILNRSV**	shrivelling	**EGHLMOORTY**	mythologer
EFMOOPRRTU	outperform	**EGHIILNSST**	sightlines	**EGHLNOOPRY**	nephrology
EFMORRSTTU	Fort Sumter	**EGHIILRSTY**	tigerishly		phrenology
EFNNOORRSU	nonferrous	**EGHIILSSTT**	sightliest	**EGHLOOORRS**	horologers
EFOOPRRSSS	professors	**EGHIIMMNRS**	shimmering	**EGHLOOPPSY**	psephology
EGGGIINNRS	sniggering	**EGHIIMNORT**	moithering	**EGHLOPPRTY**	petroglyph
EGGGIINRRT	triggering	**EGHIIMNPRW**	whimpering	**EGHMNOOOSU**	homogenous
EGGGIMNNTU	nutmegging	**EGHIIMNSST**	mightiness	**EGHMOOOTYZ**	homozygote
EGGGINNTTU	nuggetting	**EGHIIMNSTT**	nighttimes	**EGHMORRTVY**	hygrometry
EGGGINORSS	grogginess	**EGHIINNNRS**	enshrining	**EGHNOOOPRS**	gonophores
EGGGINSSTU	suggesting	**EGHIINNPRS**	insphering	**EGHNOOPRSY**	gynophores
EGGHIIINNV	inveighing	**EGHIINNPRT**	trephining	**EGHNOOPSUY**	hypogenous
EGGHIILNNT	lightening	**EGHIINNPSS**	ensignship	**EGHOOPRSUU**	house group
EGGHIILNRT	relighting	**EGHIINORST**	theorising	**EGHOORRTVW**	overgrowth
EGGHIINNRT	rightening	**EGHIINORTZ**	theorizing	**EGHOORSTTW**	ghostwrote
EGGHIINNSW	whingeings	**EGHIINPPRS**	reshipping	**EGHOPSTYYZ**	zygophytes
EGGHIINNTT	tightening	**EGHIINPRSW**	whispering	**EGIIILMMST**	legitimism
EGGHIINSTW	weightings	**EGHIINRSTW**	swithering	**EGIIILMNPR**	imperiling
EGGHIMNOSU	gumshoeing	**EGHIINRTTW**	whittering	**EGIIILMSTT**	legitimist
EGGHINNORU	roughening	**EGHIINSSTY**	hygienists	**EGIIILNNPP**	pipelining
EGGHINNOTU	toughening	**EGHIINSTUX**	extinguish	**EGIIILNORR**	irreligion
EGGIIILNNV	inveigling	**EGHIIRSSTZ**	rightsizes	**EGIIIMNNOS**	ignominies
EGGIIINNRT	reigniting	**EGHIKLORTU**	troughlike	**EGIIIMNNST**	meningitis
EGGIILMMNR	glimmering	**EGHILLNOST**	hostelling	**EGIIINNRTV**	reinviting
EGGIILNNST	glistening	**EGHILLNOSU**	houselling	**EGIIINRSTV**	revisiting
EGGIILNOSU	eulogising	**EGHILLNOSV**	shovelling	**EGIIKLLNRS**	reskilling
EGGIILNOUZ	eulogizing	**EGHILLOOPR**	philologer	**EGIIKLNNSS**	kingliness
EGGIILNRST	glistering	**EGHILMNOOS**	Mesolonghi	**EGIIKLNPRS**	springlike
EGGIILNRTT	glittering	**EGHILMOOOS**	homologies	**EGIIKLNRST**	stringlike
EGGIILNRVY	grievingly		homologise	**EGIIKNNORV**	reinvoking
EGGIINNNOPW	pigeonwing	**EGHILMOOOZ**	homologize	**EGIIKNPPRS**	skippering
EGGIINNTTV	vignetting	**EGHILNNORT**	Lothringen	**EGIIKNRSTT**	skittering
EGGIIORRVY	Gregory VII	**EGHILNOPRS**	negrophils	**EGIIKRSSTZ**	sitzkriegs
EGGILLNORV	grovelling	**EGHILNORVY**	hoveringly	**EGIILLNNST**	tinselling
EGGILLNRSU	gruellings	**EGHILNSSST**	slightness	**EGIILLNNSV**	snivelling
EGGILLPSUU	pluguglies	**EGHILOOPPT**	phlogopite	**EGIILLNORS**	Signorelli
EGGILMOOST	gemologist	**EGHILOORST**	rheologist	**EGIILLNOTU**	guillotine
EGGILNNNRSU	gunslinger	**EGHILOOSST**	shoogliest	**EGIILLNRST**	trellising

EGIILLNSVW	swivelling	EGIINRTTTW	twittering	EGILOOSSSS	isoglosses
EGIILMNNRU	relumining	EGIINSTTTV	vignettist	EGILOOSSTX	sexologist
EGIILNNOSV	novelising	EGIJKNNTTU	junketting	EGILORSUVY	grievously
EGIILNNOVZ	novelizing	EGIJNNORUY	journeying	EGILOSUUXY	exiguously
EGIILNNSSV	Vlissingen	EGIJNOORVY	overjoying	EGIMMNNOSU	immunogens
EGIILNNSUV	unveilings	EGIKLNNOOS	inglenooks	EGIMMNNPTU	impugnment
EGIILNOPTX	exploiting	EGIKLNNORS	snorkeling	EGIMNNOORR	ironmonger
EGIILNORST	loiterings	EGIKLNNPSU	spelunking	EGIMNNORST	monstering
EGIILNORVV	overliving	EGIKNNOORS	snookering	EGIMNNORTT	tormenting
EGIILNOSVW	vowelising	EGIKNNORTW	networking	EGIMNNORTU	remounting
EGIILNOVWZ	vowelizing	EGILLMMNOP	pommelling	EGIMNOORST	ergonomist
EGIILNPPRS	slippering	EGILLMMNPU	pummelling	EGIMNOORTY	goniometry
EGIILNPSSS	singspiels	EGILLMOSTU	guillemots	EGIMNORSSU	misgoverns
EGIILNQRSU	squireling	EGILLNNNTU	tunnelling	EGIMNPRSSU	grumpiness
EGIILNRRTY	retiringly	EGILLNNOTW	wellington	EGIMNPRTTU	trumpeting
EGIILNRSSS	grisliness	EGILLNOPPR	propelling	EGIMNRSSSY	synergisms
EGIILNRVVY	revivingly	EGILLNORTW	trowelling	EGIMNRSTTU	mutterings
EGIILNSSTU	guiltiness	EGILLNORWY	loweringly	EGIMOOPRST	geotropism
EGIILOORSV	virologies	EGILLNOSTU	outselling	EGIMRRSTUU	Tîrgu Mureş
EGIILOOSTT	etiologist	EGILLNPRSW	wellspring	EGINNOPSSS	sponginess
EGIILOPSST	epilogists	EGILLNPSUW	upswelling	EGINNORSTT	snottering
EGIILOPSTT	epiglottis	EGILLNTUXY	exultingly	EGINNORTUY	tourneying
EGIILORSSU	oliguresis	EGILLORSSY	syllogiser	EGINNPPSTU	unstepping
EGIILRSSTT	gristliest	EGILLORSYZ	syllogizer	EGINNRSSTU	insurgents
EGIILRSTZZ	grizzliest	EGILLOSSSY	syllogises	EGINNRSSTY	tryingness
EGIIMMNORS	memorising	EGILLOSSYZ	syllogizes	EGINNRSTTU	entrusting
EGIIMMNORZ	memorizing	EGILMMNORS	mongrelism	EGINNRSUVW	unswerving
EGIIMMNRRT	retrimming	EGILMMNPTU	plummeting	EGINOOPRRT	progenitor
EGIIMMNRST	misterming	EGILMNOOSS	gloominess	EGINOOPPRS	prospering
EGIIMNNNOT	mentioning		neologisms	EGINOOPPRS	oppressing
EGIIMNNOST	moistening	EGILMNOPRR	longprimer	EGINOOPPRS	stoppering
	monetising	EGILMNOSUU	leguminous	EGINOOPRRS	porringers
EGIIMNNOTZ	monetizing	EGILMNPTTY	temptingly	EGINOOPRRTU	intergroup
EGIIMNOPRS	reimposing	EGILMOOSSY	seismology	EGINOOPRST	progestins
EGIIMNOPRW	impowering	EGILNNOPPU	unpeopling	EGINOOPRST	protesting
EGIIMNORTV	overtiming	EGILNNOSST	singletons	EGINOOPRSY	perigynous
EGIIMNOTWY	Wyomingite	EGILNNOSSV	lovingness	EGINOOPSSS	possessing
EGIIMNPRSS	impressing	EGILNNOSSW	lowsenings	EGINOORRSW	songwriter
EGIIMNPRST	springtime	EGILNNRRUY	unerringly	EGINOORRTUV	overturing
EGIIMNPRTT	permitting	EGILNNRSSU	nurselings	EGINORRSTT	stottering
EGIINNNOPS	pensioning	EGILNNSTTU	unsettling	EGINOORSTUW	outswinger
EGIINNNORV	environing	EGILNOOOST	oenologist	EGINPRRSSU	pressuring
EGIINNOPRT	repointing		ontologies	EGINPRSTTU	sputtering
EGIINNORSS	ingression	EGILNOOPST	penologist	EGINRSSSTY	synergists
	nigrosines	EGILNOOSST	neologists	EGINRSTTTU	stuttering
EGIINNORSV	versioning	EGILNOOSSU	sinologues		Turing test
EGIINNPRRT	reprinting	EGILNOPRTT	Port-Gentil	EGKORSSSUW	guessworks
EGIINNRRTU	reinsuring	EGILNOPRTU	ploutering	EGLLLOORRS	logrollers
EGIINNRSSW	inswingers	EGILNOPRTW	plowtering	EGLLMORSUU	glomerulus
EGIINNSSST	stinginess	EGILNORRUV	overruling	EGLMNOOOSU	monologues
EGIINNSSTW	witnessing	EGILNORTTU	rouletting	EGLMNOOOTY	entomology
EGIINOPRST	repositing	EGILNORTWY	toweringly	EGLMNOORUY	numerology
EGIINORRST	roistering	EGILNOSSSS	glossiness	EGLMNOOYYZ	enzymology
EGIINORRTT	intertrigo	EGILNPPSTU	septupling	EGLNOOPRRS	prolongers
EGIINORRTV	overtiring	EGILNPRSSS	springless	EGLNOOSSXY	xenoglossy
EGIINPPRRS	perspiring	EGILNPRSST	springlets	EGLNOOSUXY	xylogenous
EGIINPRSST	persisting	EGILNPRSSY	pressingly	EGLNORSSTY	strongyles
	springiest	EGILNQSTUY	questingly	EGLOOORRWW	woolgrower
EGIINRRSTU	intriguers	EGILNRSTTU	lutestring	EGMMNOORTY	Montgomery
EGIINRSSTT	grittiness	EGILOOOPST	topologies	EGMMNOOPRS	gymnosperm
	stringiest	EGILOOPSTY	typologies	EGMMPRUUWY	mugwumpery
EGIINRSTTW	retwisting	EGILOORSST	serologist	EGMNNOOOSU	monogenous

EGNNNRRSUU	gunrunners	
EGNNORSSST	strongness	
EGNOOPRSUV	pyrogenous	
EGNORRSTUV	overstrung	
EGNORSSSST	songstress	
EGNORSSUVY	youngsters	
EGOOPRSSYZ	zygospores	
EGOPPRRSUU	supergroup	
EHHIILSTVY	thievishly	
EHHIIMSTTW	whitesmith	
EHHIIRSTTT	thirtieths	
EHHILMOOPS	homophiles	
EHHILMOPRT	thermophil	
EHHILMOSTY	hylotheism	
EHHILOPRSU	Herophilus	
EHHILOPSTU	Theophilus	
EHHILOPTTY	lithophyte	
EHHILORTWW	worthwhile	
EHHILRSSWY	shrewishly	
EHHIMMOPRV	hemimorphy	
EHHIMORSTT	hithermost	
EHHINORTTW	whitethorn	
EHHIOPPSST	phosphites	
EHHIOPRRSS	Shropshire	
EHHIOPRSSW	horsewhips	
EHHIOPSSTY	hypothesis	
EHHLLOOSTT	toothshell	
EHHLMRSSTY	rhythmless	
EHHLOOOPPR	lophophore	
EHHLOOPSTY	holophytes	
EHHMMOORTY	homothermy	
EHHMNOOOPS	homophones	
EHHOOOPPRT	photophore	
EHHOPPSSYY	hypophyses	
EHIIILMSTU	humilities	
EHIIILNPPP	philippine	
EHIIILNPST	philistine	
EHIIINRRTX	inheritrix	
EHIIIPRSVZ	viziership	
EHIIKLNPSX	sphinxlike	
EHIIKMRRSS	skirmisher	
EHIIKMRSSS	skirmishes	
EHIILLOOPS	Heliopolis	
EHIILLOPSY	lyophilise	
EHIILLOPYZ	lyophilize	
EHIILMOPRT	limitrophe	
EHIILNOOPS	eosinophil	
EHIILNQRSU	relinquish	
EHIILNSTTW	lintwhites	
EHIILNSVXY	vixenishly	
EHIILORTTT	lithotrite	
EHIILPRSVY	viperishly	
EHIILPRTTY	triphylite	
EHIIMNPSSS	impishness	
EHIIMOPRSV	impoverish	
EHIIMPPRSU	umpireship	
EHIINNPRST	internship	
EHIINORRST	inheritors	
EHIINRSSST	shirtiness	
EHIINSSSTT	shittiness	
EHIIRRSTTU	urethritis	
EHIIRSSTTT	thirstiest	
	tritheists	
EHIIRSSTTZ	zitherists	
EHIJLLNOTT	Little John	
EHIKLMNOPY	lymphokine	
EHIKLNORTW	Kenilworth	
EHIKLOOSST	tikoloshes	
EHIKMNOOST	Timoshenko	
EHIKNPRRSS	preshrinks	
EHILLMNPUY	phillumeny	
EHILLMOORS	Hermosillo	
EHILLNRSSS	shrillness	
EHILLNSTUV	Huntsville	
EHILMNOOOS	homolosine	
EHILMNOSSY	hemolysins	
EHILMNSSSU	mulishness	
EHILMOPSTY	polytheism	
EHILNNOSSU	unholiness	
EHILNOOPST	lithopones	
EHILNOPRTU	neutrophil	
EHILNORRSV	silverhorn	
EHILNOSSSW	owlishness	
EHILNSSSSU	slushiness	
EHILOOPSTU	pilothouse	
EHILOPSTTY	polytheist	
EHILORRTTY	erythritol	
EHILPRSSTU	sutlership	
EHILPRSSUU	sulphurise	
EHILPRSUUZ	sulphurize	
EHIMMNOOST	monotheism	
EHIMMOPRTU	promethium	
EHIMMOPSTU	imposthume	
EHIMNNOORS	moonshiner	
EHIMNNPSTU	punishment	
EHIMNOOSTT	monotheist	
EHIMNOPSSY	symphonies	
EHIMNOPSUU	euphoniums	
EHIMNORSST	horsemints	
EHIMNORSUY	Hieronymus	
EHIMNSSTTU	tunesmiths	
EHIMNSSTTY	synthetism	
EHIMOPPRRS	perimorphs	
EHIMOPSSTY	hemoptysis	
EHIMORRSTT	thermistor	
EHIMPRRSTU	triumphers	
EHINNNORSST	thorniness	
EHINOOOPRS	ionophores	
EHINOOPPRR	pronephroi	
EHINOOPSUU	euphonious	
EHINOOSSTT	toothiness	
EHINOPPRTY	periphyton	
EHINOPRRTY	pyrrhotine	
EHINOPRSSW	shipowners	
EHINOPRSTY	hypnotiser	
EHINOPRTYZ	hypnotizer	
EHINOPSSTT	phonetists	
EHINOPSSTY	hypnotises	
EHINOPSSVY	envoyships	
EHINOPSTYZ	hypnotizes	
EHINORRSSU	nourishers	
EHINORSSTW	worthiness	
EHINORSTUU	ruthenious	
EHINPPSSSU	uppishness	
EHINRRTTUW	Winterthur	
EHINSSSTTY	synthesist	
EHINSSTTTY	synthetist	
EHIOOPRSTW	wirephotos	
EHIOOPRTTX	thixotrope	
EHIOPPRRST	pretorship	
EHIOPPRRSW	worshipper	
EHIOPPRRSY	porphyries	
EHIOPRRSTY	prehistory	
EHIOPRRTTY	pyrrhotite	
EHIOPRSSST	prosthesis	
	sophisters	
EHIOPRSSUZ	rhizopuses	
EHIPRSSTUY	suretyship	
EHJMOPRSUW	showjumper	
EHKLOOOSST	tokoloshes	
EHKNORRSUV	Krušné Hory	
EHKOORRSSW	workhorses	
EHKOORSSUW	workhouses	
EHLLLOORRY	Holy Roller	
EHLLMOPSSY	mesophylls	
EHLLNOOSSW	hollowness	
EHLLOOSSTU	tollhouses	
EHLLRSSTUY	ruthlessly	
EHLMNOPPTY	nympholept	
EHLMOOPPRY	pleomorphy	
EHLMOPPSUY	Polyphemus	
EHLMORSSUU	humourless	
EHLNOOPPSY	polyphones	
EHLNOOPSTY	stylophone	
EHLNOOPSXY	xylophones	
EHLNOORSSU	honourless	
EHLNOOSSTY	holystones	
EHLNORSTUY	southernly	
EHLOOOPRTV	Porto Velho	
EHLOOPRSTU	toolpusher	
EHLOPRSSTU	upholsters	
EHLOPRSTUY	upholstery	
EHLOPSSTYY	hypostyles	
EHLORRSTTT	throttlers	
EHLPRSSTUU	sulphurets	
EHMMOOPRSS	mesomorphs	
EHMMOOPRSY	mesomorphy	
EHMMOORSUU	humoursome	
EHMMNOOOSY	honeymoons	
EHMNOOPRTY	nephrotomy	
EHMMNOOSSST	smoothness	
EHMOOOPRSS	sophomores	
EHMOOPRTTY	photometry	
EHMOORRTTW	motherwort	
EHMOPRSTYY	hypsometry	
EHMPRRSTUY	pyrethrums	
EHNNOPRTWY	pennyworth	
EHNOOOPPST	optophones	
EHNOOORSTT	orthotones	
EHNOOPPRRS	pronephros	
EHNOOPPRTY	phonotyper	
EHNOOPPSTY	phonotypes	
EHNOORRTWW	overthrown	
EHNOORSSSW	snowshoers	
EHNOORTTWY	noteworthy	
EHNOOSTTTT	hottentots	

EHNOPRSTTU	pothunters
EHNORSTWWY	newsworthy
EHOOOPPRRS	sporophore
EHOOOPRSSU	poorhouses
EHOOORSSTV	overshoots
EHOOPPRSTY	sporophyte
EHOOPPRTTY	tropophyte
EHOOPPSTTY	phototypes
EHOOPRRSTT	orthopters
EHOOPRRSTV	hoverports
EHOORRSTVW	overthrows
EHORRSSTTW	throwsters
EHORRSTTUV	overthrust
EIIIINQSTU	iniquities
EIIIILLLMRT	milliliter
	millilitre
EIIILMNNOP	epilimnion
EIIILNNQSU	inquilines
EIIILORSTV	vitriolise
EIIILORTVZ	vitriolize
EIIIMMNRSS	minimisers
EIIIMMNRSZ	minimizers
EIIIMMNSTU	immunities
EIIIMNORST	minorities
EIIIMNPSTU	impunities
EIIIMNRSST	ministries
EIIIMPRSTU	impurities
EIIIMPRSTV	primitives
EIIIMSSTVY	emissivity
EIIINPRRST	inspiriter
EIIIOPRRST	priorities
	prioritise
EIIIOPRRTZ	prioritize
EIIJLNTUVY	juvenility
EIIKKLNOSS	kolinskies
EIIKKLOSSW	Kieślowski
EIIKLLLOWW	willowlike
EIIKLLNPST	splintlike
EIIKLLNRTW	winterkill
EIIKLMORRR	mirrorlike
EIIKLNNRST	interlinks
EIIKLNNSSS	slinkiness
EIIKLNORST	triskelion
EIIKLNRSTW	wrinkliest
EIIKMNORST	ministroke
EIIKMNPSSS	skimpiness
EIIKNNNSSS	skinniness
EIIKNNRSTT	interknits
EIIKNOSVVZ	Zinovievsk
EIIKNQRSSU	quirkiness
EIIILLLOSUV	Louisville
EIIILLLSUVY	illusively
EIIILLMMNNU	millennium
EIIILLMNORV	vermillion
EIIILLMOPTY	impolitely
EIIILLMPRTU	multiplier
EIIILLMPSTU	multiplies
EIIILLNNNOP	pennillion
EIIILLNOPST	septillion
EIIILLNORRT	ritornelli
EIIILLNORSS	Rossellini
EIIILLNORTT	tortellini

EIIILLNOSTX	sextillion
EIIILLNRSST	instillers
EIIILLPPRSY	slipperily
EIIILLPSSTY	pitilessly
EIIILMMNNTY	imminently
EIIILMNNSTT	instilment
EIIILMNORSV	vermilions
EIIILMNOSST	lentissimo
EIIILMNOSSU	limousines
EIIILMNPPSS	pimpliness
EIIILMOPSSV	implosives
EIIILMORSST	meliorists
EIIILMOSTTV	leitmotivs
EIIILMOSUXY	eximiously
EIIILNNOQSU	quinolines
EIIILNORRTY	interiorly
EIIILNOSSSV	visionless
EIIILNPPSSS	slippiness
EIIILNPTUVY	punitively
EIIILNRSSTY	sinisterly
EIIILNRSTUV	lentivirus
EIIILOPSTVY	positively
EIIILPRSSST	spiritless
EIIIMMNORSS	immersions
EIIIMMNNRSU	immunisers
EIIIMMNRSUZ	immunizers
EIIIMMORSSS	isomerisms
EIIIMMORSST	memoirists
EIIIMMPRSUY	perimysium
EIIIMMSSTTU	mittimuses
EIIIMNNORSU	reunionism
EIIIMNNORTU	munitioner
EIIIMNNRSTU	trienniums
EIIIMNOORST	monitories
EIIIMNOPRRS	imprisoner
EIIIMNOPRSS	impression
	permission
EIIIMNORSSS	missioners
	remissions
EIIIMNOSSST	misoneists
EIIIMNPRRST	imprinters
EIIIMOOPSTY	episiotomy
EIIIMOORSTV	vomitories
EIIIMOPRRSV	improviser
EIIIMOPRSSV	improvises
EIIIMOPRSUV	impervious
EIIIMOPSSTT	epitomists
EIIIMORSSTU	moisturise
EIIIMORSTUZ	moisturize
EIIIMOSSSTV	sovietisms
EIIIMPSSSST	pessimists
EIIINNNOSST	intensions
EIIINNNOSTT	intentions
EIIINNNOSTV	inventions
EIIINNORSST	insertions
EIIINNORSSV	inversions
EIIINNORSTU	reunionist
EIIINNPPSSS	snippiness
EIIINNRSTST	internists
EIIINNRSSTW	wintriness
EIIINOOPRST	reposition
EIIINOOPSTX	exposition

EIIINOORSST	sonorities
EIIINOPRSSV	previsions
EIIINOPSTVW	viewpoints
EIIINORTTWZ	zwitterion
EIIINPPRSST	pinstripes
EIIINPRSSSS	prissiness
EIIINRSTTTU	instituter
EIIINRSTTTW	intertwist
EIIINRSTTUV	nutritives
EIIINRSTUVY	university
EIIINSSTTTU	institutes
EIIIOOPPSTV	oppositive
EIIIOOPRSST	porosities
EIIIOOORRSST	sororities
EIIIOORSSTT	torosities
EIIIORSSSST	Sesostris I
EIIIORSTTVY	vitreosity
EIIIOSSSTTV	sovietists
EIIIPRRSTTV	Pitt-Rivers
EIIIPRTTUVY	eruptivity
EIIJOPRRSUU	perjurious
EIIKLNPRRSS	sprinklers
EIIKMNOORSS	monoskiers
EIIKNNOSSTT	knottiness
	stinkstone
EIIKNOOPSSS	spookiness
EIIKNOORRRW	ironworker
EIIKNORRSTW	interworks
EIIKNORRUVY	Yukon River
EIIKORRSSTV	overskirts
EIIKRRSSTWY	skywriters
EIIILLLSSSTY	listlessly
EIIILLMNOSST	millstones
EIIILLMOOSTY	toilsomely
EIIILLMORSTU	lumisterol
EIIILLMPSTTU	multiplets
EIIILLNNOSTY	insolently
EIIILLNOOPSS	pollenosis
EIIILLNOORRT	ritornello
EIIILLNOOSSW	woolliness
EIIILLNOPRSU	nullipores
EIIILLNORSTU	tellurions
EIIILLNOSTVW	Townsville
EIIILLNOTUVY	involutely
EIIILLNRTUVY	virulently
EIIILLOPRSSV	overspills
	spillovers
EIIILLOPRSUY	perilously
EIIILLORRTUY	ulteriorly
EIIILLORSSTU	trolliuses
EIIILLOSSTTY	stylolites
EIIILMMNSTUU	nummulites
EIIILMMOPRSY	polymerism
EIIILMMOPSSY	misemploys
EIIILMMSSSTU	summitless
EIIILMNNOSTU	insoulment
EIIILMNOOOPS	monopolies
	monopolise
EIIILMNOOOPZ	monopolize
EIIILMNOOSST	motionless
EIIILMNOPSST	simpletons
EIIILMNOPTTY	impotently

EILMNORSTT	tormentils	EIMNOOPRSS	spoonerism	EIOORRSSTU	roisterous
EILMNOSSSS	lissomness	EIMNOORRST	remontoirs	EIOORSTTUZ	zootsuiter
EILMNRSSTY	minstrelsy	EIMNOORSST	Montessori	EIOPPRRSTU	Propertius
EILMOOPRST	metropolis	EIMNOOSTTT	tenotomist	EIOPPRRSTY	prosperity
EILMOPPRRY	improperly	EIMNOPRRTU	importuner	EIOPPRSSTT	stroppiest
EILNNNOOTV	nonviolent	EIMNOPRSTU	importunes	EIOPPRSTUV	supportive
EILNNOSSTV	insolvents		resumption	EIOPRRSSUV	proviruses
EILNNOSTTW	Tinseltown	EIMNORRSTW	worriments		supervisor
EILNNRSSUU	unruliness	EIMNORSSST	storminess	EIOPRRSTTU	tripterous
EILNOOPSSS	slipnooses	EIMNORSSSU	sensoriums	EIOPRRSTUV	protrusive
EILNOOPSSX	explosions	EIMNOSTTZZ	mezzotints	EIOPRSSSTU	posturises
EILNOORSTU	resolution	EIMNPSSSTU	stumpiness	EIOPRSSTTU	strepitous
EILNOORTUV	revolution	EIMNSSSTTU	smuttiness	EIOPRSSTUZ	posturizes
EILNOOSTUV	evolutions	EIMOOQSSTU	mosquitoes	EIOPRSTTTU	prostitute
EILNOPPRTW	nipplewort	EIMOPRRSST	misreports	EIORRRSSTT	terrorists
EILNOPPSSS	sloppiness	EIMOPRRSTY	spirometry	EIORRRSTUV	retrovirus
EILNOPPSTU	suppletion	EIMOPRSSTU	impostures	EIPQRSTTUV	triptyques
EILNOPRRSU	purloiners	EIMORRSTTW	miterworts	EIPRRRSSSU	surprisers
EILNOPRSST	portliness		mitreworts	EJNNSSSTUU	unjustness
EILNOPRSSU	repulsions	EIMORSSTUY	mysterious	EJNOORRSSU	sojourners
EILNOPRSSX	prolixness	EIMRRSSTTU	mistruster	EJNOOSSSUY	joyousness
EILNOPSSUX	expulsions	EINNNOORTU	nonroutine	EKLMMNOSSU	muskmelons
EILNORRSTY	introrsely	EINNOOPRST	pontoniers	EKLOOPRRSW	slopworker
EILNORSSUV	revulsions		prenotions	EKMNNOORSS	nonsmokers
EILNORSSUY	resinously	EINNOORSST	ironstones	EKMNOOPSTY	monkeypots
EILNOSTUUV	velutinous		notornises	EKOORRSTUW	outworkers
EILNPQSTUU	quintuples	EINNOORTUX	neurotoxin	EKOPPRRSUW	upperworks
EILNPQTTUU	quintuplet	EINNOOSSST	snootiness	ELLLOSSSUY	soullessly
EILNPRRTUY	pruriently	EINNOPSSSU	suspension	ELLMRSSTUU	surmullets
EILNRSSSTU	sultriness	EINNOSSSTT	snottiness	ELLNNOPTUY	polytunnel
EILNRSSTTU	turnstiles	EINNOSSTTU	sustention	ELLNPRTUUY	purulently
EILOOPPRST	Petrópolis	EINOOPPRSS	oppression	ELLOORTWWY	yellowwort
EILOOPPSTY	oppositely	EINOOPPRST	resorption	ELLOPSSSTY	spotlessly
EILOORSSTT	sitosterol	EINOOPRSTU	proteinous	ELLOSSUUVV	volvuluses
EILOPPRSTY	propylites	EINOOPSSSS	possession	ELMNOORSUY	enormously
EILOPPRSUV	propulsive	EINOOPTTTT	totipotent	ELMNOOSUVY	venomously
EILOPRRSTU	protrusile	EINOORRSST	retorsions	ELMNOPRTUY	poultrymen
EILOPRRSUY	superiorly	EINOORRSTT	retortions	ELMNORSUUY	numerously
EILOPRSTUY	pyrolusite	EINOORSSTU	serotinous	ELMOOPRSUY	polymerous
EILOPRSTVY	sportively	EINOORSSTX	extortions	ELMOOPRTUY	pleurotomy
EILOPRSUVY	perviously	EINOORTTTT	Tintoretto	ELMOOPRTXY	protoxylem
	previously	EINOPPRSTY	propensity	ELMOOPSSUY	polysemous
	viperously	EINOPRRRST	ripsnorter	ELNNOPSSSU	nonplusses
EILOPSSSTY	stylopises	EINOPRRSTV	overprints	ELNOSSSUUY	sensuously
EILOPSSTYZ	stylopizes	EINOPRSSST	sportiness	ELOOORRSTW	woolsorter
EILORRSTVW	liverworts	EINOPRSSSY	synopsises	ELOOORSSTZ	zoosterols
EILORSTUVY	vitreously	EINOPSSSTT	spottiness	ELOORSSTUW	louseworts
EILRRSTUVW	liverwurst	EINOPSSSYZ	synopsizes	ELOPPRSTUY	suppletory
EIMMNNORSW	nonswimmer	EINOQRTTUU	tourniquet	ELOPPRSUVY	oversupply
EIMMOPSSTU	impostumes	EINORRSTTV	introverts	ELOPRRSSYY	pyrolysers
EIMNNNRSTU	inurnments	EINORRSVWY	Snowy River	ELOPRRSYYZ	pyrolyzers
EIMNNOOOST	monotonies	EINORSSTUX	extrusions	EMMNOOORSU	monomerous
	monotonise	EINPRRSTTU	interrupts	EMMNRSSTUU	menstruums
EIMNNOOOTZ	monotonize	EINRSSSTTU	trustiness	EMMOOPRSTT	postmortem
EIMNNOOPTT	omnipotent	EIOOOPRSTZ	sporozoite	EMMNOOOPRT	monopteron
EIMNNORSUU	innumerous	EIOOPPRRRT	proprietor	EMMNOOORTU	motoneuron
EIMNNOSSYY	synonymies	EIOOPPRRST	prepositor	EMMNOOOSST	moonstones
	synonymise	EIOOPRRSST	posteriors	EMMNOOSTWW	townswomen
EIMNNOSYYZ	synonymize	EIOOPRRSTY	repository	EMMNNOSTTUW	stuntwomen
EIMNNRSTTU	instrument	EIOOPRSSTT	strepitoso	EMNOOOPRST	monopteros
	nutriments	EIOOPRSSTX	expositors	EMNOOORSST	sensomotor
EIMNOOOPRT	monopteroi	EIOOPRSTXY	expository	EMNOORRSTT	tormentors

EMNOPPRSST	promptness	FGHMOORSTU	frogmouths	FIINOSSSTU	fusionists
EMNOPRRSTU	prosternum	FGIIILLNNS	infillings	FIIORSTTTU	fortuitist
EMNORRSTUU	surmounter	FGIIIMNSTT	misfitting	FIKLLLLSUY	skillfully
EMNORSSTUU	menstruous	FGIIINNRTY	nitrifying	FIKLLLNSUU	unskillful
EMOOORRSST	storerooms	FGIIINRTVY	vitrifying	FIKLLOORST	folklorist
EMOOORRSTV	servomotor	FGIIJLLNOY	jollifying	FILLOOPTTY	toploftily
EMOOPRRSSS	pressrooms	FGIIJNSTUY	justifying	FILLRSTTUY	tristfully
EMOPRRSTUV	overtrumps	FGIIKLNRSY	friskingly	FILMORSSTU	formulists
ENNNOOPRSS	nonpersons	FGIILLMNOY	mollifying	FILOOOPRST	portfolios
ENNOOPPRST	proponents	FGIILLNNUY	nullifying	FIMNNNOORU	nonuniform
ENNOOPRSSS	nonprosses	FGIILLNORV	frivolling	FINOOPRSSU	profusions
ENNOPRSTWY	pennyworts	FGIILLNRTY	flirtingly	FINOOPRSTT	footprints
ENNORRSTUU	outrunners		triflingly	FIOORSTTUU	fortuitous
ENNORSSTTU	turnstones	FGIILLNSTY	stiflingly	FLLMNORUUY	mournfully
ENOOOPPRSST	postponers	FGIILMNORU	linguiform	FLLOOPRSTUY	sportfully
ENOOOPRRSSS	responsors	FGIILNNOSW	inflowings	FLLRSTTUUY	trustfully
ENOOPRRSSY	responsory	FGIILNOSUU	fuliginous	FLOOOOSSTT	footstools
ENOOPRSSSU	porousness	FGIILNRSST	firstlings	FMOOOPRRST	stormproof
ENOOPRSTTU	portentous	FGIIMMMNUY	mummifying	FOOPSSSTUY	pussyfoots
ENOORSSTTW	stoneworts	FGIIMMNORU	uniforming	GGGGIILLNY	gigglingly
ENOPRSSSSU	suspensors	FGIIMNORTY	mortifying	GGGIILLNNY	nigglingly
ENOPRSSSTT	sternposts	FGIIMNSTYY	mystifying	GGGIILNQSU	squiggling
ENOPRSSSUY	suspensory	FGIIMORRST	strigiform	GGGILLOOSW	golliwoggs
EOOOPRSSUX	exosporous	FGIINNOPTY	pontifying	GGGILNNPUU	unplugging
EOOOSSTTTV	voetstoots	FGIINNOPSTX	postfixing	GGGILNRSTU	struggling
EOOPPRRRST	propretors	FGIINOTTTU	outfitting	GGHHHIILST	highlights
EOOPPRRSSS	oppressors	FGIINPPUYY	yuppifying	GGHIIILLTV	vigil light
EOOPPRRSST	prepostors	FGIINRSSUY	russifying	GGHIIILRSW	whirligigs
EOOPPRRSSU	prosperous	FGILLNOOSW	followings	GGHIILPRSY	priggishly
EOOPPRSTTY	prototypes	FGILLNOTUY	floutingly	GGHIINPRTU	uprighting
EOOPRRSSTT	protestors	FGILMMNOUX	flummoxing	GGHILLSSUY	sluggishly
EOOPRRSTTU	outporters	FGILNNORWY	frowningly	GGHILOOPRS	logogriphs
EOOPRSSSSS	possessors	FGILNOPSTY	flyposting	GGHINNOSTW	nightgowns
EOOPRSSSSY	possessory	FGILOOSSTU	ufologists	GGIIIINSTV	gingivitis
EOORRSSTTU	stertorous	FGIMNOOPRS	spongiform	GGIIILMMNN	immingling
EOPPRRSSSU	suppressor	FGINNOOOTT	footnoting	GGIIIMNSSV	misgivings
EOPPRRSSTU	supporters	FGINOOOTTU	outfooting	GGIIINNRTU	intriguing
EOPRSSSSUU	sourpusses	FGLLLMOOUY	gloomfully	GGIILLNNTY	tinglingly
FFGHIIOPPR	hippogriff	FGLLNORUWY	wrongfully	GGIILNNNSU	unslinging
FFGIILLLNU	fulfilling	FGLOORTUUY	futurology	GGIILNNSTY	stingingly
FFGIINORTY	fortifying	FHILLMRTUY	mirthfully	GGIILNNSWY	swingingly
FFGILMNNUU	unmuffling	FHILLNOOWW	Howlin' Wolf	GGIILNPPRY	grippingly
FFGINNOOTW	Woffington	FHILLOOPSW	followship	GGIINNOSTU	outsinging
FFGINOPRSS	offsprings	FHILMOOOST	tomfoolish	GGIINNPRSS	springings
FFILLRTUUY	fruitfully	FHILMPRSUY	frumpishly	GGIINNPSUW	upswinging
FFILNRTUUU	unfruitful	FHILOPRSUW	worshipful	GGILLLNOOR	logrolling
FFINOSSSTU	suffusions	FHLLLOSTUY	slothfully	GGILLNORWY	growlingly
FGGHIIINNT	infighting	FHLLOTUUYY	youthfully	GGILLNOSSY	glossingly
FGGIIILLNY	lignifying	FHLLRTTUUY	truthfully	GGILLNTTUY	gluttingly
FGGIIINNNR	infringing	FHLNRTTUUU	untruthful	GGILMNOPRU	promulging
FGGIIINNSY	signifying	FHMOOOPRST	mothproofs	GGILNNOOPR	prolonging
FGGIILNORY	glorifying	FIIKLNNSST	skinflints	GGILNNOSUY	younglings
FGHHIORRTT	forthright	FIIKLNNSTY	skinflinty	GGILNNRTUY	gruntingly
FGHHLOTTUU	thoughtful	FIILLMORST	stilliform	GGILNOOPRU	prologuing
FGHIILNSTU	insightful	FIILLMOSTU	multifoils	GGINNNNRUU	gunrunning
FGHIINNRSU	furnishing	FIILMMNOOR	moniliform	GGINNNOTUU	outgunning
FGHIINORRY	horrifying	FIILMORSTU	trifoliums	GGINOOPRRU	proroguing
FGHILLRTUY	rightfully	FIILOPRSST	profilists	GGINOORTUW	outgrowing
FGHILOOSTT	footlights	FIIMMNORSS	misinforms	GGLLNOOOW	Wollongong
FGHINNOTUX	foxhunting	FIIMNORTUY	uniformity	GGLLOOOSSY	glossology
FGHINOOOTT	hotfooting	FIIMOORSST	fortissimo	GHHIILPSST	lightships
FGHINORSTT	fortnights	FIIMORSTTU	fortuitism	GHHIINRSTT	nightshirt

GHHIIPRSTW shipwright	**GIIILLMNNU** illumining	**GIINNOOPRT** portioning
GHHILLOSUY ghoulishly	**GIIILLNNST** instilling	**GIINNOOPSS** opsonising
GHHINOPRTT triphthong	**GIIILMNSTT** mistitling	**GIINNOOPSZ** opsonizing
GHHIOPPPRY hippogryph	**GIIILNNTTU** intituling	**GIINNRSTTU** intrusting
GHHLOORTUY thoroughly	**GIIILNNTVY** invitingly	**GIINNSTTUW** untwisting
GHHOORTTUU throughout	**GIIILNORTV** vitrioling	**GIINOSTTTU** outsitting
GHHOOTTTUU outthought	**GIIIMMNNSU** immunising	**GIINOTTTUW** outwitting
GHHOPRTTUU throughput	**GIIIMMNNUZ** immunizing	**GIINPPTTTU** tittupping
GHIIIMNSTT mishitting	**GIIIMNNOSS** missioning	**GIINPRRSSU** surprising
GHIIINNNRS inshrining	**GIIIMNNPRT** imprinting	**GIJMNOPTUU** outjumping
GHIIKNNNTU unthinking	**GIIIMNOPST** optimising	**GIJNNOORSU** sojourning
GHIILLMRTW millwright	**GIIIMNOPTZ** optimizing	**GIJNOOPPPY** joypopping
GHIILLNOTW Linlithgow	**GIIIMNPRSS** misprising	**GIKLLORRSW** grillworks
GHIILLNRWY whirlingly	**GIIIMNPRSZ** misprizing	**GIKMNNNOOS** nonsmoking
GHIILNRTVY thrivingly	**GIIINNNOSU** unionising	**GIKNNNOORW** nonworking
GHIILNSSWY swishingly	**GIIINNNOUZ** unionizing	**GIKNNNOTTU** unknotting
GHIILNSTTW whittlings	**GIIINNNTUV** uninviting	**GIKNNOOPRR** Norrköping
GHIIMNPRTU triumphing	**GIIINNORSS** sironising	**GIKNOORTUW** outworking
GHIINNORSU nourishing	**GIIINNORSZ** sironizing	**GILLMOORRS** grillrooms
GHIINNOSTU outshining	**GIIKLLNPSU** upskilling	**GILLMOSSSY** syllogisms
GHIINNPPSU unshipping	**GIIKLMNRSY** smirkingly	**GILLNRSTUY** rustlingly
GHIINNRSSU inrushings	**GIIKLNNPRS** sprinkling	**GILLOORSUY** gloriously
GHIINOPRSW worshiping	**GIIKLNNSTW** twinklings	**GILMMNOOUV** immunology
GHIINOTTTU outhitting	**GIIKLNNSTY** stinkingly	**GILMNNORUY** mourningly
GHIKNOPRTU groupthink	**GIIKLNRSTY** strikingly	**GILMNNUUZZ** unmuzzling
GHILLNOOOP loopholing	**GIIKMNNOOS** monoskiing	**GILMNOOOST** monologist
GHILMNOOST moonlights	**GIIKNNNTTU** unknitting	nomologist
GHILMNPTUY thumpingly	**GIIKNNRSTY** skywriting	**GILMOOOPST** pomologist
GHILMOOORU horologium	**GIILLMNNOU** mullioning	**GILMOOSSTY** myologists
GHILMPRSUY grumpishly	**GIILLMRSST** gristmills	**GILMOOSTYZ** zymologist
GHILNOOOOR horologion	**GIILLNOPRY** pillorying	**GILNNNOPSU** nonplusing
GHILNOOPSS splooshing	**GIILLNOPST** pistolling	**GILNNNSTUY** stunningly
GHILNOOPST phlogiston	postilling	**GILNNOOSWY** swooningly
GHILNOOSTY soothingly	**GIILLNPPRY** ripplingly	**GILNNORSTY** snortingly
GHILNORTTT throttling	**GIILLNRSWY** swirlingly	**GILNOOOPSY** oligopsony
GHILNOSSST slingshots	**GIILMMNSWY** swimmingly	**GILNOOOSST** nosologist
GHILNRRUYY hurryingly	**GIILMNNOTW** Wilmington	**GILNOOPPSY** opposingly
GHILOOORST horologist	**GIILMNOPSY** imposingly	**GILNOOPSTY** stoopingly
GHILOOPSYY physiology	**GIILMNORTU** turmoiling	**GILNOPRSTY** sportingly
GHILOPSSTT spotlights	**GIILMOOSST** misologist	**GILNOPRSYY** pyrolysing
stoplights	**GIILMOOSSY** missiology	**GILNOPRYYZ** pyrolyzing
GHIMMPSUUW mugwumpish	**GIILMOOSTX** mixologist	**GILNOPSTYY** polygynist
GHIMNOSSST songsmiths	**GIILNNOPRU** purloining	**GILNORRWYY** worryingly
GHINNNORTU unthroning	**GIILNNOSTV** Livingston	**GILNRSTTUY** trustingly
GHINNOPTTU pothunting	**GIILNNOTUV** involuting	**GILOOOPSTT** topologist
GHINOPSSTT nightspots	**GIILNOOPST** topsoiling	**GILOOORSST** orologists
GHIORRSSTY hygristors	**GIILNOORSU** inglorious	**GILOOOSSTT** otologists
GHLLOOPTYY typhlology	**GIILNOOSST** sinologist	**GILOOOSSTZ** zoologists
GHLMOOOOSU homologous	**GIILNPPRTY** trippingly	**GILOOPRSTT** proglottis
GHLMOOOPRY morphology	**GIILNPRSST** striplings	**GILOOPSTTY** typologist
GHLNOOPSUW snowplough	**GIILNRRSTY** stirringly	**GILOORRSUY** rigorously
GHMNOOOOSU homogonous	**GIILOORSTV** virologist	**GILOORSSTU** urologists
GHMNOOPSYY gymnosophy	**GIILRSSTTU** liturgists	**GILOORSUVY** vigorously
GHMOOOSUYZ homozygous	**GIIMMNNOOS** monsignori	**GIMMMPSUUW** mugwumpism
GHMOOPRYYZ zygomorphy	**GIIMMNNORT** monitoring	**GIMMNNOSSU** summonsing
GHNNOOPRRS pronghorns	**GIIMMNNOPSU** unimposing	**GIMMNRRSUU** murmurings
GHNOOPSUYY hypogynous	**GIIMNOORST** motorising	**GIMNNOORSS** monsignors
GHOORSTTUW outgrowths	**GIIMNOORTZ** motorizing	**GIMNNOOSTY** monogynist
GHOORTTUUW outwrought	**GIIMNOQSTU** misquoting	**GIMNOOSSUY** misogynous
GIIIIMMNNS minimising	**GIIMNOSSTY** misogynist	**GIMOPRSUUY** uropygiums
GIIIIMMNNZ minimizing	**GIINNNOSTU** nonsuiting	**GINNNOORRT** Norrington
GIIIKLMNSS mislikings	**GIINNNSTTU** unstinting	**GINNNORTUU** outrunning

GINNOOPPST	postponing		symphonist	**IINNOORSST**	intorsions
GINNOOPRSS	sponsoring	**HINOOPTTXY**	phytotoxin	**IINNORSSTU**	intrusions
GINNOPPSTU	unstopping	**HINOPPRRSY**	porphyrins	**IINOOOPPST**	opposition
GINNOPRSTU	unsporting	**HINOPSSTTY**	hypnotists	**IINOOPRSSV**	provisions
GINNRSSTUU	untrussing	**HIOOPPRSST**	troopships	**IINOORSSTT**	sortitions
GINOOORTTU	outrooting	**HIOOPRSTTT**	orthoptist	**IINOPRRSTU**	irruptions
GINOOPRTUU	outpouring	**HIOOPRTTXY**	thixotropy	**IINORSSSTU**	sinistrous
GINOPPRRTU	purporting	**HIOORSSTTT**	orthotists	**IINORSTTTU**	institutor
GINOPPRSTU	supporting	**HIORRSSTTY**	thyristors	**IINORSTTUU**	nutritious
GINOPTTTUU	outputting	**HIORSSTTUU**	struthious	**IIOOOPRSTV**	ovipositor
GIOPRSSTWY	gipsyworts	**HKMMNORRSU**	krummhorns	**IIOOPPRSTU**	propitious
GKLMOOOORV	Kolmogorov	**HLLOOPPRSY**	sporophyll	**IIOPRSSTUU**	spirituous
GKMORSSSUY	Mussorgsky	**HLMOOPPRSY**	polymorphs	**IIORSSTTTU**	tutiorists
GLLNOOOOSS	songololos	**HLMOORSUUY**	humorously	**IIORSTTUVY**	virtuosity
GLMNOOPSUY	polygonums	**HLOOPPRSSY**	sporophyls	**IJMNOORSTW**	jointworms
GLNOOPSTUY	Polygnotus	**HLOORSTTUY**	South Tyrol	**ILLMNOSUUY**	luminously
GLNOOPSUYY	polygynous	**HLOPRSSUUU**	sulphurous	**ILLNOOPSTU**	pollutions
GLNOOSTTUU	gluttonous	**HMMNOOOSUY**	homonymous	**ILLNOORSSU**	Roussillon
GMNNOOOSUY	monogynous	**HMOOPRSTTU**	Portsmouth	**ILLNOORSTT**	tortillons
GMNOOORRST	strongroom	**HMOOPSSTUU**	posthumous	**ILLOOSSSVY**	solvolysis
GNNOOSTUWY	Youngstown	**HMOOPTTTUY**	pottymouth	**ILLOQRSTUW**	quillworts
HHILOOOPTT	photolitho	**HNOOOPSTTU**	phototonus	**ILMMNOOOPS**	monopolism
HHILOOPPSY	philosophy	**HNOOPRSTTY**	phytotrons	**ILMNOOOPST**	monopolist
HHILOOPPTY	photophily	**HOOOPPRTTY**	phototropy	**ILMNOOQSUY**	somniloquy
HHIMOOPRRZ	rhizomorph	**HOOORSTTTW**	toothworts	**ILMNOOSUUV**	voluminous
HHIMRSSTTY	rhythmists	**HOOPRSSSTT**	shortstops	**ILMNOPSXYY**	polymyxins
HHIOPPSSYY	hypophysis	**IIIILOSUVX**	Louis XVIII	**ILMNOSTUUV**	mutinously
HHLMOPRTVY	polyrhythm	**IIIKLLNPSS**	spillikins	**ILMOORSTUV**	timorously
HHMMOOOPRY	homomorphy	**IIIKLLNPSW**	pilliwinks	**ILMOOSTTXY**	xylotomist
HHNOORRSST	shorthorns	**IIIKMNRSST**	miniskirts	**ILMOSTTUUY**	tumulosity
HHOOOPPRTT	phototroph	**IIILLMMNSU**	illuminism	**ILNOOOSSYZ**	ozonolysis
HHOOPPRSSU	phosphorus	**IIILLMNSTU**	illuminist	**ILNOOPPRSU**	propulsion
HIIKLSSTTY	skittishly	**IIILMMOTTY**	immotility	**ILNOOPRSSU**	prolusions
HIILLMNOST	millionths	**IIILNOSSTV**	violinists	**ILOOPPRSST**	spoilsport
HIILLNORTT	trillionth	**IIIMNOOPST**	imposition	**ILOORSTTUY**	tortiously
HIILMOOPSZ	zoophilism	**IIIMNOPRSS**	misprision	**ILOORSUUXY**	uxoriously
HIILNORSTT	trilithons	**IIIMOPSSTV**	positivism	**ILOPRSSUUY**	spuriously
HIILOPRSTY	Holy Spirit	**IIINNOSTTU**	intuitions	**ILORSTUUVY**	virtuously
HIILORTTTY	lithotrity	**IIINOQRSTU**	inquisitor	**IMMOOPRSTU**	prostomium
HIILOSSSTY	histolysis	**IIINOQSTUU**	iniquitous	**IMMOPPRSTU**	impromptus
HIIMMNOPRS	morphinism	**IIIOPSSTTV**	positivist	**IMMOPSSSUY**	symposiums
HIINOORSST	ornithosis	**IIIOPSTTVY**	positivity	**IMNNOOPSTW**	topminnows
HIIOOOPRST	oophoritis	**IIIPRSSSTT**	spiritists	**IMNNOSTYVY**	synonymity
HIKNNORSST	stinkhorns	**IIKLMMOPSS**	milksopism	**IMNOOOPRST**	promotions
HIKNNORSWY	hornywinks	**IIKNNNOOSS**	onionskins	**IMNOOORSUV**	omnivorous
HILLLMSTUU	multihulls	**IIKOPRSSTW**	kiwisports	**IMOOOSSTTZ**	zootomists
HILLNPSSUY	sulphinyls	**IILLLOPPSW**	pillowslip	**IMOOPRRSSY**	promissory
HILLOOPRSW	whirlpools	**IILLLORSUY**	illusorily	**IMOOPRSSTU**	impostrous
HILLSSTTUY	sluttishly	**IILLNNNOOS**	nonillions	**INOOOPPRRT**	proportion
HILMNOPSUU	sulphonium	**IILLNOOPSS**	pollinosis	**INOOPPRSTU**	pourpoints
HILMNORTTY	trimonthly	**IILLNOOPST**	postillion	**INOOPPRSTU**	protrusion
HILMOOPSUY	myophilous	**IILLNOQSSU**	squillions	**INOPRSSTTU**	outsprints
HILNORTUWY	unworthily	**IILMNOOPSS**	implosions	**INOPSSSTTY**	synoptists
HILOOOPSUZ	zoophilous	**IILMNOPSSU**	impulsions	**IOOOPRSSTU**	isotropous
HILOOORSVV	Voroshilov	**IILMNOPSTY**	postliminy	**IOOPPRRSTU**	potpourris
HILOOPSSTY	photolysis	**IILMNOSTUY**	luminosity	**IOOPPRSSTU**	propositus
HILOOSSTYZ	hylozoists	**IILMOORSUV**	limivorous	**IOORSTTTUV**	tortuosity
HILOPPSTUV	Hippolytus	**IILNNOOTUV**	involution	**KKLMMOOOSS**	Komsomolsk
HILORSSSTT	shortlists	**IILNOOPSST**	postilions	**LLOOPPSUUY**	populously
HIMMNOOTVY	homonymity	**IILOPSSSST**	solipsists	**LMOOOSTUXY**	xylotomous
HIMNOPRRSY	Pyrrhonism	**IIMMOORTUV**	vomitorium	**LMOSTTUUUU**	tumultuous
HIMNOPSSTY	hypnotisms	**IIMNNOOSSU**	insomnious	**LNOOORSSUY**	sonorously

LOOPPRRSUY propulsory
LOOPSTUUUV voluptuous
LOORSTTUUY tortuously

MNNOOOOSTU monotonous
MNNOOSSUYY synonymous
MNOOOPRRTY promontory

MNOORSSSTW snowstorms
OOOOPRSSUZ zoosporous

Eleven Letters

AAAAABBCDRR	abracadabra	AAAAHHMRRST	Maharashtra	AAABEILPPRS	appraisable
AAAAABHHMRT	Mahabharata	AAAAILRSSTU	Australasia	AAABEJLOTUV	Vuelta Abajo
AAAAACLMNNP	Panama Canal	AAAALLLOOPZ	lalapalooza	AAABELLNPTU	unpalatable
AAAAADGJLRU	Guadalajara	AAAALPRSSTT	parastatals	AAABELNNOTT	annotatable
AAAABBCHILN	Bahía Blanca	AAABBCEELLN	balanceable	AAABELNRRTW	warrantable
AAAABBCORSS	Cabora Bassa	AAABBCILSST	sabbaticals	AAABEMRSTTT	Stabat Mater
AAAABBINRST	sabbatarian	AAABCCKNSSV	canvasbacks	AAABEPRRSUZ	superbazaar
AAAABCCHILN	bacchanalia	AAABCDDIRRY	bradycardia	AAABGHIOOPR	agoraphobia
AAAABCEELTT	Cetatea Albă	AAABCDEEINR	abecedarian	AAABHIOPRST	astraphobia
AAAABCENRSS	scarabaeans	AAABCDEIORS	scarabaeoid	AAABHIORSTU	South Arabia
AAAABCGMNRU	Bucaramanga	AAABCDEIRSS	scarabaeids	AAABHMPRRTU	Brahmaputra
AAAABDGHMNR	Grand Bahama	AAABCDELNRS	candelabras	AAABIJMNNRS	Banjarmasin
AAAABDIIRSU	Saudi Arabia	AAABCDGINRY	Cardigan Bay	AAABILLNOSS	labionasals
AAAABGKORSY	kabaragoyas	AAABCEEIMRT	bacteraemia	AAABILNNSST	Saint Albans
AAAABGNNPRT	Nanga Parbat	AAABCEGILLR	algebraical	AAABINPSSTT	anabaptists
AAAABHKLLRU	Allahu Akbar	AAABCEHINRT	abranchiate	AAABLNRRTWY	warrantably
AAAABHLRSTT	Shatt-al-	AAABCEHNNRS	anabranches	AAACCCEILTT	acatalectic
	Arab	AAABCEIILLM	bacillaemia	AAACCCEINPT	capacitance
AAAACDGLLNU	Guadalcanal	AAABCELLLOT	allocatable	AAACCCIISSU	Ciscaucasia
AAAACDGMOSV	Vasco da	AAABCELLLRS	clarabellas	AAACCCILSTT	cataclastic
	Gama	AAABCELRTTT	attractable	AAACCCISTTU	catacaustic
AAAACDHMNRR	Ramachandra	AAABCHINRST	batrachians	AAACCDEIIMN	academician
AAAACGILPSS	passacaglia	AAABCHLLMPS	Paschal Lamb	AAACCDEILMS	academicals
AAAACGINNRR	Gran Canaria	AAABCIILNRS	basicranial	AAACCDEIPTT	capacitated
AAAACHHKKLM	Makhachkala	AAABCILLNTY	abactinally	AAACCDEOPRU	Pão de
AAAACHILNPP	Appalachian	AAABCILLOPR	parabolical		Açúcar
AAAACLMNRST	almacantars	AAABCILNOTT	ablactation	AAACCDHIRTY	tachycardia
AAAACNRRSVY	caravansary	AAABCILPRST	parablastic	AAACCDINOPP	Cappadocian
AAAADEGLMMT	amalgamated	AAABCORRSTU	barracoutas	AAACCEHINPU	ipecacuanha
AAAADEHRTVV	Atharva-Veda	AAABDEEHHSY	dahabeeyahs	AAACCEHNNST	catananches
AAAADELMRSS	Dar es	AAABDEGGNOV	vagabondage	AAACCEHRSST	saccharates
	Salaam	AAABDELNPTU	unadaptable	AAACCEILLOR	calceolaria
AAAADLMNNQU	Namaqualand	AAABDGNNOOU	Oda Nobunaga	AAACCEIPSTT	capacitates
AAAAEGKLNRS	Alaska Range	AAABDHLMNRU	Abdul Rahman	AAACCGILORR	García Lorca
AAAAEGLMMST	amalgamates	AAABDMNRRSU	barramundas	AAACCHILLRV	archaically
AAAAEHHMMOTT	haematomata	AAABDMORSSS	ambassadors	AAACCHILRTU	autarchical
AAAAEJKLSTT	Jataka Tales	AAABEEGLLSV	salvageable	AAACCILLNRU	canalicular
AAAAENNNRST	Antseranana	AAABEEGLNRR	arrangeable	AAACCILLPRT	parallactic
AAAAFGNOSTT	Antofagasta	AAABEHIMNPS	amphisbaena	AAACCILLRSS	cascarillas
AAAAFINRRST	rastafarian	AAABEHINRRT	breatharian	AAACCILMNOT	acclamation
AAAAGGNOSTY	Astanga yoga	AAABEHINRSU	Beauharnais	AAACCILOSVV	Cavaco Silva
AAAAGHIPPRR	paragraphia	AAABEIKLLLS	alkalisable	AAACCILPSTT	cataplastic
AAAAGIMPTVZ	Vizagapatam	AAABEIKLLLZ	alkalizable	AAACCILRRTU	caricatural
AAAAGJNNNRY	Narayanganj	AAABEILLNUV	unavailable	AAACCILSSTU	accusatival
AAAAGMSSSSU	massasaugas	AAABEILNRST	alabastrine	AAACCIMNORT	carcinomata
AAAAGORRSTZ	Stara Zagora	AAABEILNSST	Santa Isabel	AAACCKLMNNN	Clackmannan

AAACCLLMSTY	cataclysmal
AAACCLMOPRT	caprolactam
AAACCLMORTY	acclamatory
AAACDDEIMMS	macadamised
AAACDDEIMMZ	macadamized
AAACDEEIMRR	camaraderie
AAACDEHINRT	acidanthera
AAACDEIIRST	Adriatic Sea
AAACDEILMPR	paramedical
AAACDEILNRT	cardinalate
AAACDEILPSS	Pas-de-Calais
AAACDEIMMRS	macadamiser
AAACDEIMMRZ	macadamizer
AAACDEIMMSS	macadamises
AAACDEIMMSZ	macadamizes
AAACDEINRTY	caryatidean
AAACDELNORW	Lower Canada
AAACDENPPRU	Upper Canada
AAACDGIILRS	cardialgias
AAACDGNNRRY	Grand Canary
AAACDHINNRS	arachnidans
AAACDIINNSV	Scandinavia
AAACDILOPRX	paradoxical
AAACEEFLMNS	malfeasance
AAACEEGNNRR	carrageenan
AAACEEGNNRS	carageenans
AAACEEIMNOT	acetonaemia
AAACEENPPRS	appearances
AAACEFINRST	East African
AAACEFLQSTU	catafalques
AAACEGHILLP	cephalalgia
AAACEGILLNN	gallinacean
AAACEGILMNO	egomaniacal
AAACEGIRRWV	carriageway
AAACEHILLPR	parheliacal
AAACEHLMNNP	Panchen Lama
AAACEILMMNT	analemmatic
AAACEILORSU	araliaceous
AAACEINPRRT	carpentaria
AAACEINRRSS	sarracenias
AAACEIPPRRT	paraparetic
AAACELLLMPU	ampullaceal
AAACELMNPTU	campanulate
AAACELMNRST	sacramental
AAACELMOPRT	paracetamol
AAACELMPRST	metacarpals
AAACFILLNTY	fanatically
AAACFILNSTT	fantastical
AAACFIMNRRT	aircraftman
AAACGGILOPR	paragogical
AAACGHILNNV	avalanching
AAACGHIMNOP	phagomaniac
AAACGHIPPRR	paragraphic
AAACGHNOOTT	Chattanooga
AAACGHNRSTT	tragacanths
AAACGILMMRT	grammatical
AAACGILMNNO	anglomaniac
AAACGILMPRT	pragmatical
AAACGINNNRV	caravanning
AAACHHINPTX	hapaxanthic
AAACHIILPRS	pharisaical
AAACHIKPPRT	apparatchik
AAACHILMRRT	matriarchal
AAACHILNOTU	anacoluthia
AAACHILPRRT	patriarchal
AAACHLNNRTY	charlatanry
AAACHLNRTTU	Uttaranchal
AAACHNPRSTY	pyracanthas
AAACHQSTUUU	chautauquas
AAACIILMMST	miasmatical
AAACIILMOTX	axiomatical
AAACIILPRST	parasitical
AAACILLMNRU	animalcular
AAACILLMORT	clamatorial
AAACILLNOTT	lactational
AAACILLNRST	scarlatinal
AAACILLNSSY	satanically
AAACILLSTTY	astatically
AAACILNNRST	Lancastrian
AAACILNOSTU	causational
AAACILNRSSS	carnassials
AAACILOPSTT	apostatical
AAACINRRSTT	tractarians
AAACLMNRSTU	almucantars
AAACNORSUXY	Roxas y Acuña
AAACNRSTTTT	attractants
AAADDDIMNNU	Daman and Diu
AAADEEGHNPS	phagedaenas
AAADEEJNRWY	Jayawardene
AAADEFFNNOR	fanfaronade
AAADEGHPPRR	paragraphed
AAADEGLNRTV	landgravate
AAADEHLNPRS	aphelandras
AAADEHMRSSY	hamadryases
AAADEHPPRRS	paraphrased
AAADEIKNNVV	Vivekananda
AAADEILLPST	palatalised
AAADEILLPTZ	palatalized
AAADEILMPTV	maladaptive
AAADEILNNRX	Alexandrian
AAADEILNRSS	Alessandria
AAADEILRRSV	adversarial
AAADEIMNNRT	mandarinate
AAADEIMNNRX	Anaximander
AAADEIMNRST	mandataries
AAADELLMPRT	Mar del Plata
AAADELLOSTV	Valle d'Aosta
AAADELMNRSS	salamanders
AAADELNRSVW	van der Waals
AAADENNPRST	transpadane
AAADGGINNTV	advantaging
AAADGGINORT	aggradation
AAADGIILLRS	gaillardias
AAADGIILMNR	madrigalian
AAADGILLNRS	granadillas
AAADGILNORT	gradational
AAADGMMMNRS	grandmammas
AAADGMNORRS	mandragoras
AAADGNOPPRS	propagandas
AAADHHIJNSU	Judah ha-Nasi
AAADHHLPRYZ	haphazardly
AAADHILMMMU	Muhammad Ali
AAADIILNORR	radiolarian
AAADIILNORT	radiational
AAADIKKLVVZ	Vladikavkaz
AAADILLLNOT	allantoidal
AAADILNNRSS	Aran Islands
AAADILNORSV	Salvadorian
AAADILOPRRX	liar paradox
AAADINOPSTT	adaptations
AAADLMMNNNS	landammanns
AAADLNORSSV	San Salvador
AAADLOORSSV	São Salvador
AAADORSSTTU	autostradas
AAAEEELNPRS	paraselenae
AAAEEGINPRS	paragenesia
AAAEEGRTTVX	extravagate
AAAEEHINSST	anaesthesia
AAAEEHLLSST	Tallahassee
AAAEEHMNTTX	exanthemata
AAAEEKLPRSY	parakeelyas
AAAEERSTTVX	extravasate
AAAEFLMNSST	malfeasants
AAAEFRSSSSS	sassafrases
AAAEGGILMNT	gametangial
AAAEGHIMMNO	haemangioma
AAAEGIILNRT	egalitarian
AAAEGILMMNO	megalomania
AAAEGILMNNT	galantamine
AAAEGILNNST	East Anglian
AAAEGIMRRTV	margraviate
AAAEGMMNRRS	anagrammers
AAAEGMNOPSS	Mona Passage
AAAEGMRRSTV	margravates
AAAEGNRTTVX	extravagant
AAAEGORSSSS	Sargasso Sea
AAAEGPSSSWY	passageways
AAAEHIILMPT	epithalamia
AAAEHILMSST	thalassemia
AAAEHILNPRX	hexaplarian
AAAEHIMNNRT	amaranthine
AAAEHIMOSST	haemostasia
AAAEHLNOPPR	epanaphoral
AAAEHPPRRSS	paraphrases
AAAEHPPRSTY	paraphysate
AAAEIKLLNNT	antalkaline
AAAEIKLLNST	antalkalies
AAAEILLPSST	palatalises
AAAEILLPSTZ	palatalizes
AAAEILMNNOT	emanational
AAAEILNPRTU	Telanaipura
AAAEILNPSST	anaplasties
AAAEILNPSTT	palatinates
AAAEILPPRRS	reappraisal
AAAEIMNNRTU	Mauretanian
AAAEIMNQRSU	aquamarines
AAAEINSSSST	assassinate
AAAEIPPRRSS	paraparesis
AAAELLMMMPS	plasmalemma

AAAAELLNNTTY	antenatally
AAAAELLNRSTT	tarantellas
AAAAELMRSSTT	metatarsals
AAAAELMSSTTY	Malay States
AAAAENNPRSTU	Punta Arenas
AAAAENRSSSTT	tarantasses
AAAAEPPRSSTU	apparatuses
AAAAFGHINNST	Afghanistan
AAAFLLMNSTY	fantasmally
AAAGGGINRTV	aggravating
AAAGGHHIOPR	Hagiographa
AAAGGHILOPR	logagraphia
AAAGGILNNTV	galavanting
AAAGGILRSST	gastralgias
AAAGGINORTV	aggravation
AAAGHILNOPP	Paphlagonia
AAAGHIRSSTY	satyagrahis
AAAGIILNOTT	agitational
AAAGIILNPRS	parasailing
AAAGIIMNNRS	agrarianism
AAAGIINNRSU	sanguinaria
AAAGIINRSTT	sagittarian
AAAGIKNNNTY	Tanganyikan
AAAGILNNPQU	aquaplaning
AAAGIMMNNRS	grammarians
AAAGIMNSSTT	anastigmats
AAAGLLORSSV	Vargas Llosa
AAAGLMNORTU	granulomata
AAAHIILMPSS	Ismail Pasha
AAAHIILPPRS	paraphilias
AAAHIKMNNRS	Ramakrishna
AAAHILMOPRT	prothalamia
AAAHILNPSXY	anaphylaxis
AAAHIMMMSST	mahatmaisms
AAAHKMMORYY	Omar Khayyám
AAAHRRSTTUZ	Zarathustra
AAAIILNORTV	variational
AAAIILNPSTU	saintpaulia
AAAIIMNNRTU	Mauritanian
AAAIINNQRTU	antiquarian
AAAIINNRSST	sanitarians
AAAIKKNSTZZ	Kazantzakis
AAAIKRRSTTU	titarakuras
AAAILLMNNSZ	manzanillas
AAAILLMOPPT	papillomata
AAAILLNNPSZ	Spallanzani
AAAILLNOSTV	salvational
AAAILLNOTUV	valuational
AAAILLORSTT	saltatorial
AAAILMNOPPR	malapropian
AAAILNNOSTY	analysation
AAAILNNOTYZ	analyzation
AAAILNNRSTU	saturnalian
AAAILNORTVV	Navratilova
AAAILNRSSTU	saturnalias
AAAIMNNOOST	antonomasia
AAAIMNOOPRS	paronomasia
AAAINNNNOST	San Antonian
AAAIRRSTTTT	Tatar Strait
AAAKNPRRSUU	Sukarnapura
AABBBDEELMN	Bab el Mandeb

AABBCCIILST	cabbalistic
AABBCDEKLLL	blackballed
AABBCDKLORS	blackboards
AABBCEEELMR	embraceable
AABBCEEKKRR	backbreaker
AABBCEGMORW	cabbageworm
AABBCEGNOTW	cabbagetown
AABBCEINORT	bicarbonate
AABBCIIKLST	kabbalistic
AABBDDEELST	beadblasted
AABBDDEORRS	breadboards
AABBDEEGILR	abridgeable
AABBDEEIRTV	abbreviated
AABBDEEKRST	breadbasket
AABBDEELNTU	undebatable
AABBDEELRST	beadblaster
AABBDEEORRV	beaverboard
AABBDEGORRS	bargeboards
AABBDEILLOR	della Robbia
AABBEEIRRTV	rebarbative
AABBEEIRSTV	abbreviates
AABBEEKLLRR	ballbreaker
AABBEEKLNRU	unbreakable
AABBEELLRST	barbastelle
AABBEFGLRST	flabbergast
AABBEGIINRT	bearbaiting
AABBEHIILNT	inhabitable
AABBEHILLOS	abolishable
AABBEHNRSUW	Bhubaneswar
AABBEIIRRST	barbarities
AABBEIORRTV	abbreviator
AABBEIRRTTU	barbiturate
AABBEKLLSST	basketballs
AABBGGILNRS	balbriggans
AABBGHIMNOT	thingamabob
AABBGIINNRS	barbarising
AABBGIINRRZ	barbarizing
AABBHIKOSUZ	bashibazouk
AABBIIILMNO	bibliomania
AABBIIKLNTY	bankability
AABBILLNSTU	balibuntals
AABBKKMOOOO	amabokoboko
AABBLLMSTTU	albumblatts
AABBLORRSUY	barbarously
AABCCDEIKKP	pickabacked
AABCCDEJKKL	blackjacked
AABCCDEKKRT	backtracked
AABCCEEEELLR	accelerable
AABCCEELLNO	concealable
AABCCEHLNRU	craunchable
AABCCEILPRT	practicable
AABCCEKKPRS	backpackers
AABCCEKRSTT	backscatter
AABCCELLMUU	accumulable
AABCCELNOTT	contactable
AABCCELNOTU	accountable
AABCCERRUUY	bureaucracy
AABCCGIKKNP	backpacking
AABCCGIKNPS	backspacing
AABCCIILOSU	coulibiacas
AABCCIKNRRS	crackbrains
AABCCILPRTY	practicably

AABCCLNOTUY	accountably
AABCCLNRRUU	carbuncular
AABCDDEEKLP	backpedaled
AABCDDEEKNR	breakdanced
AABCDDEKLSS	saddlebacks
AABCDDELOPR	clapboarded
AABCDDENOOR	carbonadoed
AABCDDEORST	broadcasted
AABCDDIKMNO	diamondback
AABCDEEEERTX	exacerbated
AABCDEEFLRY	barefacedly
AABCDEEILMT	alembicated
AABCDEEKNRR	breakdancer
AABCDEEKNRS	breakdances
AABCDEEKPPR	paperbacked
AABCDEENORT	decarbonate
AABCDEFIIIL	acidifiable
AABCDEHHMNR	chamberhand
AABCDEHIMMR	chambermaid
AABCDEHKNRS	backhanders
AABCDEIILNT	indicatable
AABCDEIIMNR	carbamidine
AABCDEIKLLM	blackmailed
AABCDEIRRRS	barricaders
AABCDELMNRU	candelabrum
AABCDELNOTU	outbalanced
AABCDELORSS	scaleboards
AABCDENOORS	carbonadoes
AABCDEORRST	broadcaster rebroadcast
AABCDGGIOOR	braggadocio
AABCDGHIKNN	backhanding
AABCDGIINRR	barricading
AABCDGIMNSU	ambuscading
AABCDGKLRSU	blackguards
AABCDHILNOS	baldachinos
AABCDHKLORS	chalkboards
AABCDHMNORY	rhabdomancy
AABCDHMORST	matchboards
AABCDIINNNO	cannabinoid
AABCDIINOST	abdications
AABCDIIOPRS	basidiocarp
AABCDIIQRTU	biquadratic
AABCDILNOSU	subdiaconal
AABCDINOORR	radiocarbon
AABCEEEHLST	escheatable
AABCEEELLPR	replaceable
AABCEEELRRT	retraceable
AABCEEEMRRS	macebearers
AABCEEERSTX	exacerbates
AABCEEFLRRT	refractable
AABCEEFNORR	forbearance
AABCEEGLLNO	congealable
AABCEEHILMP	machineable
AABCEEHILMP	impeachable
AABCEEHKLRT	leatherback
AABCEEHLMNR	Malebranche
AABCEEHLNTU	unteachable
AABCEEHLSTY	chalybeates
AABCEEHMNRT	antechamber
AABCEEHRSST	sabretaches
AABCEEIINRR	carabiniere

AABCEEILLMR	reclaimable
AABCEEILMNV	ambivalence
AABCEEILNPS	inescapable
AABCEEILNRS	increasable
AABCEEILPPR	appreciable
AABCEEINRRS	aberrancies
	carabineers
AABCEEKPPRR	paperbacker
AABCEELNORV	overbalance
AABCEELNPSS	capableness
AABCEELNPSU	unescapable
AABCEELNRST	tabernacles
AABCEELNRTU	untraceable
AABCEELORTT	bracteolate
AABCEELRRTT	retractable
AABCEELRSTT	scatterable
AABCEELRTTU	trabeculate
AABCEELRTTX	extractable
AABCEESSTTU	subacetates
AABCEFIIRTV	fabricative
AABCEFILNOT	labefaction
AABCEFLMNOY	flamboyance
AABCEFLNOTU	confabulate
AABCEFLRRTU	fracturable
AABCEGLMNNS	blancmanges
AABCEHHPSTY	bathyscaphe
AABCEHIINNT	inhabitance
AABCEHILMNR	chamberlain
AABCEHILNRU	hibernacula
AABCEHILSST	chastisable
AABCEHIPRRY	hypercarbia
AABCEHKLRST	blackhearts
AABCEHLNSTU	staunchable
AABCEHLPRSU	purchasable
AABCEHPSSTY	bathyscapes
AABCEHRRSTT	tetrabrachs
AABCEIIINRR	carabinieri
AABCEIILNNS	cannibalise
AABCEIILNNZ	cannibalize
AABCEIINPUV	bupivacaine
AABCEIINRRS	carabiniers
AABCEIINSTU	beauticians
AABCEIIRRTU	bacteriuria
AABCEIKLLMR	blackmailer
AABCEILLLOS	localisable
AABCEILLLOZ	localizable
AABCEILLLTY	claribellas
AABCEILLMNU	calumniable
AABCEILLNSU	suballiance
AABCEILLRTT	ballicatter
AABCEILLRTY	bacterially
AABCEILLSTY	syllabicate
AABCEILMNRY	carbylamine
AABCEILMNVY	ambivalency
AABCEILMORZ	carbimazole
AABCEILNNOT	containable
AABCEILNPSY	inescapably
AABCEILNRTT	intractable
AABCEILPPRY	appreciably
AABCEILRRST	calibraters
AABCEINNSTY	betacyanins
AABCEINORST	abreactions

AABCEIOQRSU	aquaerobics
AABCEIRSTTV	abstractive
AABCEKKLNSS	blacksnakes
AABCEKLLRRT	trackerball
AABCEKNRRSU	Saarbrücken
AABCEKPRRST	bratpackers
AABCEKQRRTU	quarterback
AABCELLLOPS	collapsable
AABCELLOORT	collaborate
AABCELLORRS	barcarolles
AABCELMOPSS	compassable
AABCELNOSTU	outbalances
AABCELNRTTU	untractable
AABCELORSXY	carboxylase
AABCELORTXY	carboxylate
AABCENOPRST	absorptance
AABCEOORRSU	arboraceous
AABCEOORTTZ	azotobacter
AABCERRSTUU	bureaucrats
AABCFGIINRT	fabricating
AABCFIINORT	fabrication
AABCFIORRST	fabricators
AABCFIORRVY	Vicar of
	Bray
AABCFLMNOYY	flamboyancy
AABCGHIINRT	brachiating
AABCGHIKNSW	backwashing
AABCGHIOOPR	agoraphobic
AABCGHIOPRR	barographic
AABCGIILLMS	galliambics
AABCGIILNRT	calibrating
AABCGILNNNU	unbalancing
AABCGINNORT	carbonating
AABCGINRSTT	abstracting
AABCGKMMNOS	backgammons
AABCHHIMPRS	amphibrachs
AABCHHPSSTY	bathyscaphs
AABCHIILRRT	tribrachial
AABCHIINNTY	inhabitancy
AABCHIINORT	brachiation
AABCHILNSTU	Baluchistan
AABCHINOSTT	cohabitants
AABCHIOPRST	astraphobic
AABCHKLPSSS	splashbacks
AABCHNRRSUY	brachyurans
AABCIIILMRS	biracialism
AABCIIILMTY	amicability
AABCIIKLOSU	koulibiacas
AABCIILLPTY	placability
AABCIILMNNS	cannibalism
AABCIILNORT	calibration
AABCIILRRUU	biauricular
AABCIILRSTY	sybaritical
AABCIILSTUY	causability
AABCILLMNTU	lactalbumin
AABCILLNOTY	botanically
AABCILMOSST	catabolisms
AABCILNNRUU	incunabular
AABCILNRTTY	intractably
AABCILORRST	calibrators
AABCILOSTTY	biocatalyst
AABCINNOORT	carbonation

AABCINORRTU	carburation
AABCINORSTT	abstraction
AABCKLMOORS	blackamoors
AABCLLLRSTY	crystal ball
AABCLLNNNOS	cannonballs
AABCLPRSSUU	subscapular
AABDDEEGRRY	graybearded
AABDDEELORR	leaderboard
AABDDEELRSS	addressable
AABDDEGGORR	daggerboard
AABDDEGLLLR	gallbladder
AABDDEHHMRY	handbreadth
AABDDEHMORY	hebdomadary
AABDDEILSSU	dissuadable
AABDDEINOST	bastinadoed
AABDDEIRSST	bastardised
AABDDEIRSTZ	bastardized
AABDDELNSST	sandblasted
AABDDEORRST	starboarded
AABDDHHIMOR	Bodhidharma
AABDDILLRRU	Baudrillard
AABDDNRSSTU	substandard
AABDEEFKRST	breakfasted
AABDEEHHRRS	haberdasher
AABDEEHINRR	harebrained
AABDEEIILLMP	impleadable
AABDEEIMNTT	ambidentate
AABDEEELORSV	broadleaves
AABDEEELPPRT	palpebrated
AABDEEELPRSU	persuadable
AABDEEMRRSS	embarrassed
AABDEEPRRSY	prayer beads
AABDEGGHINN	headbanging
AABDEGGINRS	brigandages
AABDEGGLLRY	ballyragged
AABDEGGNRSS	sandbaggers
AABDEGHILNS	Bangladeshi
AABDEGILNOS	diagnosable
AABDEGINNOS	gabionnades
AABDEGORSST	goatsbeards
AABDEHIILTT	habilitated
AABDEHIINRR	hairbrained
AABDEHINRSW	brainwashed
AABDEHLLNRS	handballers
AABDEHLRSTT	Halberstadt
AABDEHRSTWV	breadthways
AABDEIILLNT	dentilabial
AABDEIILLNSV	inadvisable
AABDEIILRTY	readability
AABDEIILSST	assibilated
AABDEIIRRTT	abirritated
AABDEIKNORT	debarkation
AABDEILLNOT	labiodental
AABDEILLNRS	banderillas
AABDEILLRVY	adverbially
AABDEILMNTU	mandibulate
AABDEILNOUV	unavoidable
AABDEILNSUV	unadvisable
AABDEILOPRS	parabolised
AABDEILOPRZ	parabolized
AABDEILORRT	labradorite
AABDEILRSTU	tabularised

AABDEILRTUZ	tabularized	**AABEEILLNNU**	unalienable	**AABEGILNOSZ**	zabagliones
AABDEIMRTUV	adumbrative	**AABEEILLNPX**	explainable	**AABEGILRSST**	algebraists
AABDEINOSST	bastinadoes	**AABEEILLNRT**	inalterable	**AABEGINNPST**	gabapentins
AABDEIQRSTU	biquadrates	**AABEEILMNSS**	amiableness	**AABEGINNRST**	interabangs
AABDEIRSSST	bastardises	**AABEEILNPRS**	inseparable	**AABEGIRRRTU**	arbitrageur
AABDEIRSSTZ	bastardizes	**AABEEILORTV**	elaborative	**AABEGLLMOST**	megaloblast
AABDEKORSST	skateboards	**AABEEILPRRR**	irreparable	**AABEGLMOPRR**	programable
AABDELLNNOS	belladonnas	**AABEEINRRRT**	trainbearer	**AABEGMNRSSU**	submanagers
AABDELNNRRS	Barren Lands	**AABEEINRRST**	brainteaser	**AABEHHIOPPT**	taphephobia
AABDELNRSST	sandblaster	**AABEEINSSTT**	bastnaesite	**AABEHIILLNN**	annihilable
AABDELRSSTU	balustrades	**AABEEJKRRSW**	jawbreakers	**AABEHIILSTT**	habilitates
AABDEMNNNOT	abandonment	**AABEEKLNPSU**	unspeakable	**AABEHILNRST**	tarnishable
AABDEMNRSST	bandmasters	**AABEEKKLRRSW**	lawbreakers	**AABEHILORUV**	behavioural
AABDEMRSTTU	masturbated	**AABEEKRRSTW**	breakwaters	**AABEHINRRSW**	brainwasher
AABDEOPRSST	pasteboards	**AABEEKSSTTW**	wastebasket	**AABEHINRSSW**	brainwashes
AABDFFHLORSS	flashboards	**AABEELLLSSZ**	sleazeballs	**AABEHKLNSUY**	unshakeably
AABDGGGINNS	sandbagging	**AABEELLMNNOT**	balletomane	**AABEHLMOSTT**	hematoblast
AABDGHILLNN	handballing	**AABEELLNPTT**	battleplane	**AABEHLMOSTV**	Baal Shem
AABDGHINOSV	vagabondish	**AABEELLNRTU**	unalterable		Tov
AABDGIILRTY	gradability	**AABEELLNSSS**	salableness	**AABEHLOPRRR**	Pearl Harbor
AABDGIMNOSV	vagabondism	**AABEELLORTY**	elaborately	**AABEIILLMSS**	assimilable
AABDGIMNRTU	adumbrating	**AABEELLPRRS**	pallbearers	**AABEIILLNNY**	inalienably
AABDHIILNTU	habitudinal	**AABEELLPRSU**	pleasurable	**AABEIILLSTY**	saleability
AABDHIOSTTV	bodhisattva	**AABEELMNSST**	tamableness	**AABEIILMMOR**	memorabilia
AABDHLOPRSS	splashboard	**AABEELMPRTU**	perambulate	**AABEIILMNTY**	amenability
AABDHMMOORY	rhabdomyoma	**AABEELMPTTT**	attemptable	**AABEIILMTTY**	tameability
AABDHNORRSW	handbarrows	**AABEELMSSTT**	metastables	**AABEIILNRRT**	libertarian
AABDIILLTUY	laudability	**AABEELNORST**	treasonable	**AABEIILNRSV**	invariables
AABDIILMNTY	damnability	**AABEELNRSST**	ratableness	**AABEIILNSSX**	Aix-les-
AABDIILMQRU	liquidambar	**AABEELNRTTU**	entablature		Bains
AABDIILNSVY	inadvisably	**AABEELNSSSV**	savableness	**AABEIILRTTY**	rateability
AABDIKLNNSS	Banks Island	**AABEELNSSTX**	taxableness	**AABEIILRTWY**	wearability
AABDILLMNOY	abdominally	**AABEELPPRST**	palpebrates	**AABEIILSSST**	assibilates
AABDILNOUVY	unavoidably	**AABEELPRSTT**	breastplate	**AABEIINOORT**	bioaeration
AABDILOOPRS	paraboloids	**AABEELPSSSS**	Basses-Alpes	**AABEIIRRSTT**	abirritates
AABDILOORRS	boardsailor	**AABEELRRSTU**	treasurable	**AABEIKLMSTY**	mistakeably
AABDIMNORTU	adumbration	**AABEELRRSTV**	traversable	**AABEIKMNORT**	embarkation
AABDIMNRRSU	barramundis	**AABEEMMOPRT**	meprobamate	**AABEIKNNRST**	barkantines
AABDINRSSSU	Buridan's	**AABEEMRRSSS**	embarrasses	**AABEILLLRTY**	bilaterally
	ass	**AABEENRRSTU**	sauerbraten	**AABEILLMNPU**	manipulable
AABDMOORRRT	mortarboard	**AABEFFIILLS**	falsifiable	**AABEILLNRTY**	inalterably
AABEEEEGKMRR	gamebreaker	**AABEFGIILMN**	magnifiable	**AABEILLOPRS**	polarisable
AABEEEGLLNR	enlargeable	**AABEFHILNOS**	fashionable	**AABEILLOPRZ**	polarizable
AABEEEGLLRT	relegatable	**AABEFIILLMP**	amplifiable	**AABEILLORSV**	labiovelars
AABEEEKSTVW	basketweave	**AABEFIILLQU**	qualifiable	**AABEILLRRTZ**	trailblazer
AABEEFKRRST	breakfaster	**AABEFIILSST**	satisfiable	**AABEILLRSSY**	syllabaries
AABEEFLLRTT	flatterable	**AABEFILLMMN**	inflammable	**AABEILLRVZZ**	Brazzaville
AABEEFORSTU	Beaufort Sea	**AABEFILLNST**	inflatables	**AABEILMNRTU**	Tamburlaine
AABEEGILNST	East Bengali	**AABEFILLRTT**	filtratable	**AABEILMNSTU**	albuminates
AABEEGINNRT	annabergite	**AABEFINRRST**	afterbrains	**AABEILMORST**	amortisable
AABEEGLMNTU	augmentable	**AABEFLLNPPU**	unflappable	**AABEILMORTZ**	amortizable
AABEEGLMSSS	assemblages	**AABEFLNORUV**	unfavorable	**AABEILNNNOT**	Anti-Lebanon
AABEEGNORST	baronetages	**AABEGGGNNRS**	gangbangers	**AABEILNOORT**	elaboration
AABEEHILPST	alphabetise	**AABEGGINORY**	Georgian Bay	**AABEILNPRSY**	inseparably
AABEEHILPTZ	alphabetize	**AABEGHINRSS**	earbashings	**AABEILNRRTT**	rattlebrain
AABEEHIRSST	baresthesia	**AABEGHORRSU**	harbourages	**AABEILNRSSU**	Belarussian
AABEEHKLNSU	unshakeable	**AABEGIILNNV**	invaginable	**AABEILNRSTT**	transitable
AABEEHLRSTY	breathalyse	**AABEGIJKNRW**	jawbreaking	**AABEILNSSTU**	sustainable
AABEEHLRTYZ	breathalyze	**AABEGIKLNRW**	lawbreaking	**AABEILOPRSS**	parabolises
AABEEIILLNN	inalienable	**AABEGIKNORR**	aerobraking	**AABEILOPRSV**	vaporisable
AABEEIKLMST	mistakeable	**AABEGILNNUV**	unnavigable	**AABEILOPRSZ**	parabolizes
AABEEILLMOR	ameliorable	**AABEGILNORT**	elaborating	**AABEILOPRVZ**	vaporizable

AABEEILPRRRY	irreparably	**AABIIKLLTTY**	talkability	**AACCDEIILLT**	dialectical
AABEIMNRRTT	arbitrament	**AABIILLMSSY**	assimilably	**AACCDEIIMMS**	academicism
AABEINNPRSS	Bernina Pass	**AABIILLNORT**	librational	**AACCDEIIPRR**	pericardiac
AABEINNQRTU	barquantine	**AABIILLPPTY**	palpability	**AACCDEILLNR**	calendrical
AABEINORRST	aberrations	**AABIILLPTVY**	playability	**AACCDEILLNY**	decanically
AABEINRRSTW	waterbrains	**AABIILLSTVY**	salvability	**AACCDEILNST**	accidentals
AABEIOPPRTV	approbative	**AABIILMNRUU**	albuminuria	**AACCDEILOPY**	cyclopaedia
AABEIRRSTTT	bitartrates	**AABIILMOOTU**	automobilia	**AACCDEIMNNO**	nonacademic
AABEKLNPSUY	unspeakably	**AABIILNORTV**	vibrational	**AACCDEIMNOP**	accompanied
AABELLLNOUW	unallowable	**AABIILNORTY**	libationary	**AACCDEIRRTU**	caricatured
AABELLLOSWW	swallowable	**AABIILORSTU**	atrabilious	**AACCDELMTUU**	accumulated
AABELLLPRSY	ballplayers	**AABIILRRRTY**	arbitrarily	**AACCDELNORS**	cladocerans
AABELLMOSST	ameloblasts	**AABIIMNNOOT**	abomination	**AACCDEMMOOT**	accommodate
AABELLPRSUY	pleasurably	**AABIINORRTT**	arbitration	**AACCDEMNOOS**	cacodaemons
AABELMMNSSY	assemblyman	**AABIINRRSTT**	abirritants	**AACCDENNORT**	contradance
AABELNORSTY	treasonably	**AABIKLMOSST**	katabolisms	**AACCDHIINOR**	arachidonic
AABELOORRST	elaborators	**AABILLMORSY**	ambrosially	**AACCDHILNOR**	chancroidal
AABELOPRRTY	portrayable	**AABILLMPSTY**	baptismally	**AACCDHIORSS**	saccharoids
AABELORSSST	albatrosses	**AABILLRSUXY**	subaxillary	**AACCDIIILRT**	diacritical
AABELPRSSSU	surpassable	**AABILMNORSY**	abnormality	**AACCDIISSTU**	diacaustics
AABEMRSSTTU	masturbates	**AABILMNOSTU**	ambulations	**AACCDILLSUY**	dyscalculia
AABENNORTUV	Bonaventura	**AABILNOOPRT**	probational	**AACCDLNORTY**	accordantly
AABEPRRSSUZ	superbazars	**AABILNORTUV**	ablutionary	**AACCEEELRST**	accelerates
AABFHILNOSY	fashionably	**AABILNOSTTU**	tabulations	**AACCEEFILNT**	calefacient
AABFIKNORSU	Burkina-Faso	**AABILNSSTTU**	substantial	**AACCEEFKRRS**	safecracker
AABFILLMMNY	inflammably	**AABILOPRSST**	parabolists	**AACCEEGPRSS**	scapegraces
AABFLLMOOSY	Boyoma Falls	**AABIMMNOQUZ**	Mozambiquan	**AACCEEINPRS**	parascience
AABFLLNPPUV	unflappably	**AABIMNOORST**	abominators	**AACCEEINRRT**	incarcerate
AABFLMNOSTY	flamboyants	**AABINNORSTY**	antibaryons	**AACCEEINRTV**	revaccinate
AABFLNORUVY	unfavorably	**AABINOOPPRT**	approbation	**AACCEEIRSSS**	accessaries
AABGGGGINNN	gangbanging	**AABIORRRSTT**	arbitrators	**AACCEEKLRRW**	crackleware
AABGGIINNRS	bargainings	**AABKKOORRSU**	kookaburras	**AACCEELLNOT**	collectanea
AABGGILMNOO	Giambologna	**AABLLMOORSV**	Vallombrosa	**AACCEELLRTU**	recalculate
AABGHIINRSU	Ubangi-Shari	**AABLLOOPRST**	blastoporal	**AACCEELNRST**	accelerants
AABGHIINTTU	habituating	**AABLOSSSTTT**	statoblasts	**AACCEELNSTU**	acaulescent
AABGHILNOOP	anglophobia	**AABMORRSTTU**	masturbator	**AACCEELORRT**	accelerator
AABGIIILLNS	labialising	**AABNOORSTTY**	astrobotany	**AACCEENNOTT**	concatenate
AABGIIILLNZ	labializing	**AABOOPPRRTY**	approbatory	**AACCEENSTTU**	accentuates
AABGIIKLNNS	balkanising	**AACCCDEOSUY**	cycadaceous	**AACCEEORSTV**	coacervates
AABGIIKLNNZ	balkanizing	**AACCCDHRRST**	scratchcard	**AACCEFILNOT**	calefaction
AABGIILNORS	aboriginals	**AACCCEENPST**	acceptances	**AACCEFILSTU**	fasciculate
AABGIIMNNOT	abominating	**AACCCEILPTT**	cataplectic	**AACCEFLORTY**	calefactory
AABGIINOSSY	bioassaying	**AACCCEINORT**	Arctic Ocean	**AACCEFPRSST**	spacecrafts
AABGIINRRTT	arbitrating	**AACCCEJKKRR**	crackerjack	**AACCEGHILNR**	archangelic
AABGILMNRSU	submarginal	**AACCCGHIOPR**	cacographic	**AACCEGHNRTT**	gnatcatcher
AABGINNOSTW	angwantibos	**AACCCIIILRT**	cicatricial	**AACCEGHOPRR**	cacographer
AABGINOPPRT	approbating	**AACCCIILLMT**	climactical	**AACCEGILMOR**	acromegalic
AABGINORSTU	outbargains	**AACCCILMSTY**	cataclysmic	**AACCEGILORT**	categorical
AABGLLMORSY	syllabogram	**AACCCNNOTUY**	accountancy	**AACCEGORRTY**	ergatocracy
AABHIILORTT	habilitator	**AACCDDEIINS**	candidacies	**AACCEHHMOST**	stomachache
AABHIILSTWY	washability	**AACCDDEINOR**	endocardiac	**AACCEHHPRST**	catchphrase
AABHIINNSTT	inhabitants	**AACCDDHIIRS**	disaccharid	**AACCEHIIMNN**	mechanician
AABHIINOSTT	habitations	**AACCDEEELRT**	accelerated	**AACCEHIIMSS**	sciamachies
AABHIINOTTU	habituation	**AACCDEELLNT**	cancellated	**AACCEHILMNS**	mechanicals
AABHIMNPSST	batsmanship	**AACCDEELNOR**	accelerando	**AACCEHILMOS**	mailcoaches
AABHIOOPRST	astrophobia	**AACCDEENTTU**	accentuated	**AACCEHILMOT**	machicolate
AABHLLLLOOU	hullaballoo	**AACCDEHINNT**	cachinnated	**AACCEHILMST**	catechismal
AABHLLLOOSU	hullabaloos	**AACCDEHIORS**	adhocracies	**AACCEHINNST**	cachinnates
AABHMOOSSTU	Matsuo Basho	**AACCDEHIRSS**	saccharides	**AACCEHIRSSS**	saccharises
AABIIILLMTY	mailability		saccharised	**AACCEHIRSST**	catachresis
AABIIILRTVY	variability	**AACCDEHIRSZ**	saccharized	**AACCEHIRSSZ**	saccharizes
AABIIILSTTY	satiability	**AACCDEHNORS**	archdeacons	**AACCEHLNNNO**	nonchalance

AACCEHLNOST	coelacanths	
AACCEHMORSU	scaramouche	
AACCEHRSTTW	catchwaters	
AACCEIILMST	acclimatise	
AACCEIILMTZ	acclimatize	
AACCEIINPST	captaincies	
AACCEILLRST	Callicrates	
AACCEILLSTY	ascetically	
AACCEILLTUV	calculative	
	claviculate	
AACCEILMPRT	malpractice	
AACCEILNORS	anisocercal	
AACCEILNOSS	accessional	
AACCEILORSS	accessorial	
AACCEILOSSU	salicaceous	
AACCEILRSSY	accessarily	
AACCEIMNNOR	necromaniac	
AACCEIMNOPR	accompanier	
AACCEIMNOPS	accompanies	
AACCEIMNORS	maccaronies	
AACCEINNORT	anacreontic	
AACCEINNOST	canonicates	
AACCEINOPTT	acceptation	
AACCEINQTTU	acquittance	
AACCEINRSTT	cantatrices	
AACCEIORSTU	autocracies	
AACCEIRRSTU	caricatures	
AACCEISSTUV	accusatives	
AACCEKLLNOV	cycloalkane	
AACCELLNTUY	accentually	
AACCELLPPRW	clapperclaw	
AACCELMSTUU	accumulates	
AACCELNRTUU	carunculate	
AACCELPRSTU	spectacular	
AACCELRTTUU	acculturate	
AACCENNORSS	Carcassonne	
AACCENOPRRY	coparcenary	
AACCENRSSTU	crustaceans	
AACCFIIILRS	sacrificial	
AACCFIILLPY	pacifically	
AACCFIILRTY	farcicality	
AACCFIIMNOR	acinaciform	
AACCGHILNOR	charcoaling	
AACCGHIMOPR	macrophagic	
AACCGIILMNT	acclimating	
AACCGIINNTV	vaccinating	
AACCGILLNTU	calculating	
AACCGINORTT	coarctating	
AACCGNOQRUY	quangocracy	
AACCHIIMRRT	matriarchic	
AACCHIIMRST	charismatic	
AACCHIINRST	anarchistic	
AACCHIINRTT	anthracitic	
AACCHILLMSU	Callimachus	
AACCHILLOTY	chaotically	
AACCHILMNOR	monarchical	
AACCHILMOST	stomachical	
AACCHILNNPS	asplanchnic	
AACCHILNOTU	anacoluthic	
AACCHKLLSUW	chuckwallas	
AACCIIILLNTY	actinically	
AACCIIILMNOT	acclimation	
AACCIILMPRT	impractical	
AACCIILNNOT	calcination	
AACCIILNSTT	anticlastic	
AACCIILSSTU	casuistical	
AACCIILSTTT	stalactitic	
AACCIINNOTV	vaccination	
AACCIINOPRR	Capricornia	
AACCIINOSTU	acoustician	
AACCIINRSSS	circassians	
AACCIINRSTT	cicatrisant	
AACCIINRTTZ	cicatrizant	
AACCIINTTVY	Vatican City	
AACCILLLNOY	laconically	
AACCILLLSSY	classically	
AACCILLNNOY	canonically	
AACCILLNORY	acronically	
AACCILLNOTU	calculation	
AACCILLNSUU	canaliculus	
AACCILLPRTY	practically	
AACCILLSTUY	caustically	
AACCILNOSTU	sacculation	
AACCILNPRTU	unpractical	
AACCILNSTTY	syntactical	
AACCILOPPTY	apocalyptic	
AACCILOPRTT	catoptrical	
AACCILOPSUY	capaciously	
AACCIMNOPST	accompanist	
AACCINNOORT	coarctation	
AACCINORSTV	vaccinators	
AACCINOSSTU	accusations	
AACCIORRSTY	aristocracy	
AACCLLNORVY	acronycally	
AACCLLORSTU	calculators	
AACCLMORTUU	accumulator	
AACCLNOPRTY	plantocracy	
AACCLNORTTU	contractual	
AACCMOORRSZ	Occam's razor	
AACCNNOSSTU	accountants	
AACCOOPRRSU	acrocarpous	
AACCORRSTTY	stratocracy	
AACDDDEIJTU	adjudicated	
AACDDEEEHHR	headreached	
AACDDEEEHLR	clearheaded	
AACDDEEINRT	deracinated	
AACDDEEIPTT	decapitated	
AACDDEEITTV	deactivated	
AACDDEFHNRT	handcrafted	
AACDDEGLNOO	dodecagonal	
AACDDEHINPP	handicapped	
AACDDEHLNRS	crashlanded	
AACDDEIIRTV	divaricated	
AACDDEIJSTU	adjudicates	
AACDDEILNOR	endocardial	
AACDDEILNSS	scandalised	
AACDDEILNSZ	scandalized	
AACDDEINRTU	candidature	
AACDDEINTUU	nudicaudate	
AACDDEIPRRS	Cedar Rapids	
AACDDEKLPSS	packsaddles	
AACDDHKPSWY	paddywhacks	
AACDDIIINSS	candidiasis	
AACDDIJORTU	adjudicator	
AACDDIOSTTU	autodidacts	
AACDEEEFNSS	defeasances	
AACDEEEHHRS	headreaches	
AACDEEENPRV	Cape Verdean	
AACDEEFFINT	caffeinated	
AACDEEFGINT	defaecating	
AACDEEFINOT	defaecation	
AACDEEFORST	defaecators	
AACDEEGHRST	gatecrashed	
AACDEEGKPPR	prepackaged	
AACDEEGORTT	greatcoated	
AACDEEHHILMX	hexadecimal	
AACDEEHNRTU	Hardecanute	
AACDEEHRRST	Sacred Heart	
AACDEEHRSSV	headscarves	
AACDEEIILNT	acetanilide	
AACDEEIINST	taeniacides	
AACDEEIIRTV	eradicative	
AACDEEILMRS	caramelised	
AACDEEILMRZ	caramelized	
AACDEEILRTV	declarative	
AACDEEILSTT	elasticated	
AACDEEIMNPT	emancipated	
AACDEEINRST	ascertained	
	deracinates	
AACDEEIPPRT	appreciated	
AACDEEIPPRST	paederastic	
AACDEEIPSTT	decapitates	
AACDEEIRTTV	reactivated	
AACDEEISTTV	deactivates	
AACDEEKLPSW	spacewalked	
AACDEELLORT	reallocated	
AACDEELLSTT	castellated	
AACDEELMSTU	emasculated	
AACDEELPSTU	decapsulate	
AACDEELRTUW	caterwauled	
AACDEEMNNTV	advancement	
AACDEENNSTT	attendances	
AACDEFGILNT	defalcating	
AACDEFGLMOU	camouflaged	
AACDEFIILTT	facilitated	
AACDEFIINST	fanaticised	
AACDEFIINTZ	fanaticized	
AACDEFILNOT	defalcation	
AACDEFINRSU	fricandeaus	
AACDEFINRUX	fricandeaux	
AACDEFLORST	defalcators	
AACDEGGILMO	demagogical	
AACDEGGILOP	pedagogical	
AACDEGIIMNT	diamagnetic	
AACDEGIINRT	eradicating	
AACDEGIIRSY	Erciyas Daği	
AACDEGILNNR	calendaring	
AACDEGIMNNS	damascening	
AACDEGIMNRT	demarcating	
AACDEGLLNOY	decagonally	
AACDEGMNOPR	Campo Grande	
AACDEGNORSS	gasconaders	
AACDEGORSTU	sugarcoated	
AACDEHHKLMS	hamshackled	
AACDEHILLPY	edaphically	

AACDEHILORS	icosahedral
AACDEHILPST	chaptalised
AACDEHILPTZ	chaptalized
AACDEHINORV	hyracoidean
AACDEHINOTT	anticathode
AACDEHINPPR	handicapper
AACDEHINRST	cantharides
AACDEHINRTU	Hardicanute
AACDEHKLNNR	crankhandle
AACDEHKMMRT	matchmarked
AACDEHMOORR	choreodrama
AACDEHMOPRT	camphorated
AACDEHPRRRS	cardsharper
AACDEIILMRT	diametrical
AACDEIILPRR	pericardial
AACDEIILPST	capitalised
AACDEIILPTZ	capitalized
AACDEIINNNO	Indian Ocean
AACDEIINNNR	incarnadine
AACDEIINNRT	incardinate
AACDEIINORT	eradication
AACDEIINPTT	anticipated
AACDEIINRRS	irradiances
AACDEIINTTV	inactivated
	vaticinated
AACDEIIORTV	radioactive
AACDEIIPRST	paediatrics
AACDEIIPRSU	parasuicide
AACDEIIRSTV	divaricates
AACDEIJNSTU	adjutancies
AACDEILLNTT	cantillated
AACDEILMNOT	declamation
AACDEILMNTU	calumniated
AACDEILNNOR	endocranial
AACDEILNORT	declaration
	redactional
AACDEILNOTU	educational
AACDEILNPTU	paniculated
AACDEILNRSS	radicalness
	scandaliser
AACDEILNRSZ	scandalizer
AACDEILNSSS	scandalises
AACDEILNSSZ	scandalizes
AACDEILPTTU	capitulated
AACDEILRSTT	straitlaced
AACDEILRTTU	articulated
AACDEILRTUU	auriculated
AACDEIMNNOP	pandemoniac
AACDEIMNORT	demarcation
AACDEIMNORV	aerodynamic
AACDEINNNTU	annunciated
AACDEINOPRS	caparisoned
AACDEINOTUV	coadunative
AACDEINRSST	incrassated
AACDEIOPRTT	decapitator
AACDEIORRST	eradicators
AACDEIORTTV	deactivator
AACDEIOSTTW	waistcoated
AACDELMOPRS	camelopards
AACDELMORTY	declamatory
AACDELNPTTY	pentadactyl
AACDELORRST	declarators

AACDELORRTY	declaratory
AACDELRTTTY	tetradactyl
AACDELSTTUU	auscultated
AACDEMORRST	demarcators
AACDEOPRRSS	radarscopes
AACDFHINRST	handicrafts
AACDFIILLTY	fatidically
AACDFIILRRT	fratricidal
AACDFIINOOS	aficionados
AACDFIMORRS	microfarads
AACDGGHIIST	haggadistic
AACDGGINNOS	gasconading
AACDGHHMNOY	hochmagandy
AACDGHINTUU	Dutch Guiana
AACDGHIOPRR	cardiograph
AACDGIILNTU	acidulating
AACDGILLRTU	Gaillard Cut
AACDGILNNPS	landscaping
AACDGILNNVY	advancingly
AACDGIMNNTU	manducating
AACDGIMORRS	cardiograms
AACDGIMRRTU	dramaturgic
AACDGINNNNO	cannonading
AACDGLMORTY	dactylogram
AACDGNNNORY	Grand Canyon
AACDGORSSTU	coastguards
AACDHIILLSV	dichasially
AACDHIIOPRS	aphrodisiac
AACDHIKRSTU	kurdaitchas
AACDHILLRSY	chrysalidal
AACDHLRSWWZ	Schwarzwald
AACDHMHNOORT	chondromata
AACDHMOPRSY	psychodrama
AACDHNNORSY	chardonnays
AACDIIILMOT	idiomatical
AACDIILMPRY	pyramidical
AACDIILMRSS	radicalisms
AACDIILNNOR	androclinia
AACDIILNOTT	dictational
AACDIILNOTU	acidulation
AACDIILNPRS	Dinaric Alps
AACDIILNRTY	cardinality
AACDIILNSTV	vandalistic
AACDIILORTT	dictatorial
AACDIIMNOPS	dipsomaniac
AACDIINNOTY	cyanidation
AACDIIOPRTY	radiopacity
AACDIIORRTV	divaricator
AACDILLMNOV	monadically
	nomadically
AACDILLMNVY	dynamically
AACDILLRSTY	drastically
AACDILMNNOS	calamondins
AACDILMOPSS	spasmodical
AACDILNOSTY	anisodactyl
AACDILNPSST	landscapist
AACDILORTTY	artiodactyl
AACDILOSUUV	audaciously
AACDIMNNORT	nondramatic
AACDIMNNOTU	manduction
AACDIMOORST	sarcomatoid
AACDINNOOTU	coadunation

AACDINOOSTV	advocations
AACDJNOSTTU	coadjutants
AACDLMNOOTY	condylomata
AACDMMNNOST	commandants
AACDMNORTUY	manducatory
AACDMOORSTU	catadromous
AACDNORRSSS	crossandras
AACEEEHLMOT	haematocele
AACEEEHLNPP	epencephala
AACEEEKMPRS	peacemakers
AACEEEENPRST	Eastern Cape
AACEEFGORRY	year of
	grace
AACEEFIMNSS	misfeasance
AACEEFIRRTV	rarefactive
AACEEFNNNOS	nonfeasance
AACEEGHLMNR	Charlemagne
AACEEGHLMPY	megacephaly
AACEEGHLRST	Castlereagh
AACEEGHNOPR	chaperonage
AACEEGHRRST	gatecrasher
AACEEGHRSST	gatecrashes
AACEEGIKMNP	peacemaking
AACEEGILLLY	elegiacally
AACEEGILLNS	allegiances
AACEEGILLNV	evangelical
AACEEGINPRT	paragenetic
AACEEGKPRPS	prepackages
AACEEGMMORT	macrogamete
AACEEGMNNOR	German Ocean
AACEEHHLTUX	hexateuchal
AACEEHHMMOR	haemachrome
AACEEHHMPTY	chamaephyte
AACEEHILMTT	metaethical
AACEEHILNST	chatelaines
AACEEHILSTT	aesthetical
AACEEHINSTT	anaesthetic
AACEEHKPSST	cheapskates
AACEEHLMNOP	encephaloma
AACEEHLNNPY	anencephaly
AACEEHLNPTY	phlyctaenae
AACEEHMPRST	spermatheca
AACEEHRRTTT	tetrarchate
AACEEIIMPST	septicaemia
AACEEIJLTUV	ejaculative
AACEEILLMNS	mesalliance
	miscellanea
AACEEIILLRTV	varicellate
AACEEILMRSS	caramelises
AACEEILMRSZ	caramelizes
AACEEILNNRS	encarnalise
AACEEILNNRZ	encarnalize
AACEEILNPPT	epanaleptic
AACEEILNPRS	paraselenic
AACEEILNRTT	intercalate
AACEEILPRST	altarpieces
AACEEILRRST	secretarial
AACEEILSSTT	atelectasis
	elasticates
AACEEIMMORS	Mesoamerica
AACEEIMNNNT	maintenance
AACEEIMNPST	emancipates

AACEEINNNRT	centenarian
AACEEINNRRT	reincarnate
AACEEINNRSS	necessarian
	renaissance
AACEEIPPRST	appreciates
AACEEIPRRTV	prevaricate
AACEEIRRSST	tracasserie
AACEEIRRSTT	secretariat
AACEEIRSTTV	reactivates
AACEEKKLRSW	cakewalkers
AACEEKLMPRT	marketplace
AACEELLLTUV	valleculate
AACEELLORST	reallocates
AACEELMSSTU	emasculates
AACEELNPSTU	encapsulate
AACEELRRTUW	caterwauler
AACEEMNOSTU	amentaceous
AACEENRRSSU	reassurance
AACEEPRSSTW	waterscapes
AACEERSSSTV	stavesacres
AACEFFHINRS	affranchise
AACEFFIIRTV	affricative
AACEFFILNOT	affectional
AACEFFINOTT	affectation
AACEFGILNSV	Fingal's
	Cave
AACEFGINRRS	fragrancies
AACEFGLMOSU	camouflages
AACEFIILNRT	interfacial
AACEFIILNRV	acriflavine
AACEFIILSTT	facilitates
AACEFIINSST	fanaticises
AACEFIINSTV	fascinative
AACEFIINSTZ	fanaticizes
AACEFILMNOT	malefaction
AACEFILTTUV	facultative
AACEFIMNRRT	aircraftmen
AACEFINORRT	rarefaction
AACEFINORRV	vicar forane
AACEFINORSU	farinaceous
AACEFINORTT	fractionate
AACEFLMORST	malefactors
AACEFLNSSTU	factualness
AACEFMNRTUU	manufacture
AACEGGIKNPR	repackaging
AACEGGILPTU	Tegucigalpa
AACEGHHIIRS	hagiarchies
AACEGHHNOTT	chaetognath
AACEGHILLRT	lethargical
AACEGHILOPR	archipelago
AACEGHINRTT	reattaching
AACEGHKLORV	Gerlachovka
AACEGHLMOSU	guachamoles
AACEGHLOORY	archaeology
AACEGHLOPSS	phascogales
AACEGHMOPRS	macrophages
AACEGHNORTU	autochanger
AACEGIILLPR	periglacial
AACEGIILMNT	enigmatical
AACEGIIMRRS	miscarriage
AACEGIJLNTU	ejaculating
AACEGIKKLNW	cakewalking

AACEGILLLNY	angelically
	englacially
AACEGILLLOR	allegorical
AACEGILLOOR	aerological
AACEGILLOPS	plagioclase
AACEGILMNPS	plasmagenic
AACEGILNPRV	panegyrical
AACEGILNRTT	altercating
AACEGILNTTY	acetylating
AACEGILOTUV	coagulative
AACEGILPPRS	paraplegics
AACEGILRSTT	strategical
AACEGIMMNOR	micromanage
AACEGIMMNRT	engrammatic
AACEGIMNNPR	permanganic
AACEGIMNPRS	campaigners
AACEGLMNORS	carmagnoles
AACEGLNRRTU	rectangular
AACEGLORSTU	cataloguers
AACEGNOORSU	onagraceous
AACEHHIIMPT	amphithecia
AACEHHIKNNV	Nakhichevan
AACEHHKLMSS	hamshackles
AACEHHMNRSV	Marcheshvan
AACEHIIKLNT	kitchenalia
AACEHIIKMSS	skiamachies
AACEHIILLMV	Machiavelli
AACEHIILMPT	epithalamic
AACEHIILSTT	atheistical
AACEHIIMMNS	Manichaeism
AACEHIIMNST	haematinics
AACEHILLMNO	melancholia
AACEHILLNTU	hallucinate
AACEHILLPSS	callipashes
AACEHILLPTY	aphetically
AACEHILNPST	chainplates
AACEHILPSST	chaptalises
AACEHILPSTZ	chaptalizes
AACEHILRSTT	theatricals
AACEHIMMPRS	amphimacers
AACEHIMMSTT	mathematics
AACEHIMNNOY	haemocyanin
AACEHIMNOST	theomaniacs
AACEHIMORST	achromatise
AACEHIMORTT	haematocrit
AACEHIMORTZ	achromatize
AACEHIMOSTT	haemostatic
AACEHINNOSU	ouananiches
AACEHINORRS	archaeornis
AACEHINOTTY	thiocyanate
AACEHINPPRY	hypercapnia
AACEHINRRST	catarrhines
AACEHIOPRRS	archesporia
AACEHIRRSTV	architraves
AACEHJKMMRS	jackhammers
AACEHKMMRST	matchmakers
AACEHKMRSTW	watchmakers
AACEHLMORTY	hematocryal
AACEHLOPTUY	autocephaly
AACEHMMNNRT	merchantman
AACEHMNORSU	rhamnaceous
AACEHMNSTTT	attachments

AACEHMMOPRST	camphorates
AACEHNNORST	anthracnose
AACEHOPRSTT	catastrophe
AACEHOPSSTU	spathaceous
AACEHORTUUX	Châteauroux
AACEIILLMNS	misalliance
AACEIILLNRS	ancillaries
AACEIILLNRT	lacertilian
AACEIILLNNV	incarvillea
AACEIILLPRS	capillaries
AACEIILLRTV	leviratical
AACEIILNPRR	pericranial
AACEIILNNRT	interracial
AACEIILNRST	carnalities
AACEIILPPRR	pericarpial
AACEIILPPTV	applicative
AACEIILPSST	capitalises
AACEIILPSTZ	capitalizes
AACEIILRSST	rascalities
AACEIILSSTU	causalities
AACEIILSTTU	actualities
AACEIIMNRTV	carminative
AACEIIMQSTU	semiaquatic
AACEIINORTT	ratiocinate
AACEIINPSTT	anticipates
AACEIINSTTV	inactivates
	vaticinates
AACEIIOSSTV	associative
AACEIIPPRTT	participate
AACEIJLNOTU	ejaculation
AACEILLLNNV	Valle-Inclán
AACEILLLSTY	elastically
AACEILLMNPT	implacental
AACEILLMNSU	animalcules
AACEILLMPUX	amplexicaul
AACEILLNOSS	escallonias
AACEILLNSTT	cantillates
AACEILLNTTY	tetanically
AACEILLNTVY	venatically
AACEILLPRRT	caterpillar
AACEILLRRTY	erratically
AACEILLSSTY	salicylates
AACEILMMPST	metaplasmic
AACEILMNOPT	cleptomania
AACEILMNORT	reclamation
AACEILMNOTX	exclamation
AACEILMNRST	reclaimants
AACEILMNSTU	calumniates
AACEILMRTTU	matriculate
AACEILNNOSS	ascensional
AACEILNNRTU	antinuclear
AACEILNORST	lacerations
AACEILNORTT	altercation
AACEILNOSST	escalations
AACEILNOTTY	acetylation
AACEILNPSTU	incapsulate
AACEILNRRTU	retinacular
AACEILNRRTY	intercalary
AACEILNRSUV	naviculares
AACEILPRSSU	scapularies
AACEILPRSTU	spiraculate
AACEILPRTTU	particulate

AACEILPSSUU	Aesculapius
AACEILPSTTU	capitulates
AACEILRRSTU	cartularies
AACEILRSTTU	articulates
AACEILSSTTT	stalactites
AACEILSTUVY	causatively
AACEIMMNOST	scammoniate
AACEIMMNOTT	contaminate
AACEIMNOORT	erotomaniac
AACEIMNOPRT	emancipator
AACEIMNORST	macerations
AACEIMNORSU	oceanariums
AACEIMOPRTV	comparative
AACEINNNSTU	annunciates
AACEINNORTT	recantation
AACEINNOSTT	catenations
AACEINORRTY	reactionary
AACEINORSTU	aeronautics
AACEINORSTV	vacationers
AACEINOSTUV	evacuations
AACEINOSTVX	excavations
AACEINPQRTU	preacquaint
AACEINQRSTU	reacquaints
AACEINRSSST	incrassates
AACEINRSSTU	sanctuaries
AACEIOPPRRT	appreciator
AACEIORSSSW	cassowaries
AACEIORSSTT	aerostatics
AACEJKNRSTT	natterjacks
AACEJLORSTU	ejaculators
AACEJLORTUY	ejaculatory
AACEKLQRSUV	quacksalver
AACELLLNOOV	Leoncavallo
AACELLLORST	collaterals
AACELLLRSST	saltcellars
AACELLNRSTY	ancestrally
AACELLOPRSU	acarpellous
AACELMMORSS	sarcolemmas
AACELMORSTU	emasculator
AACELMORTXY	exclamatory
AACELMRSSST	masterclass
AACELNNRSTT	transcalent
AACELNOOSSU	solanaceous
AACELNOPSTU	cantaloupes
AACELNORSTT	translocate
AACELNRRSUV	vernaculars
AACELOOPPRS	laparoscope
AACELOPPRSSY	apocalypses
AACELQRTUUU	aquaculture
AACELSSTTUU	auscultates
AACENNOSTTZ	canzonettas
AACENOOPSSU	saponaceous
AACENORRTVY	contrayerva
AACEOOPSSTU	sapotaceous
AACEOPPRSUY	papyraceous
AACEORRSTTT	terracottas
AACFFIORRTT	trafficator
AACFGIIMNST	magnificats
AACFGIINNST	fascinating
AACFGILLSUU	Iguaçú Falls
AACFGLNNORT	conflagrant
AACFHINORRT	North Africa

AACFHIORSTU	South Africa
AACFHKNRSST	crankshafts
AACFIILLNNY	financially
AACFIILNNOR	Californian
AACFIILORTT	facilitator
AACFIINNOST	fascination
AACFIINSSTT	antifascist
AACFILLNOTV	lactoflavin
AACFILLNRTY	frantically
AACFILLORTY	factorially
AACFILMORRS	scalariform
AACFILNORST	infracostal
AACFILSSTTU	factualists
AACFINORRTY	fractionary
AACFINORSST	fascinators
AACFLMNRSTY	craftsmanly
AACFMNORSTW	craftswoman
AACFMNORTUY	manufactory
AACFNORSTUU	anfractuous
AACFNRSSTTU	surfactants
AACGGHHIMNU	gamahuching
AACGGHIMNRU	gamaruching
AACGGIIMNNP	campaigning
AACGGIIINST	castigating
AACGGILLLOO	algological
AACGGILLOOR	agrological
AACGGILNOSY	synagogical
AACGGILNOTU	cataloguing
	coagulating
AACGHHOPRST	tachographs
AACGHHPRTYY	tachygraphy
AACGHIIMNNT	machinating
AACGHIKLNRW	warchalking
AACGHIKMMNT	matchmaking
AACGHIKMNTW	watchmaking
AACGHILLOPR	allographic
AACGHILLPRY	calligraphy
	graphically
AACGHIMNRSY	gymnasiarch
AACGHINOPPR	approaching
AACGHINPRTU	parachuting
AACGHIOPRTU	autographic
AACGHKNNOWW	Kwangchowan
AACGHLMMNOO	Chomolangma
AACGHLMOORU	chaulmoogra
AACGHLNOORY	arachnology
AACGHMOPRRS	macrographs
AACGHNOOPRR	coronagraph
AACGHNOPRTU	Chota Nagpur
AACGHOPRRTY	cartography
AACGHOPRSSU	sarcophagus
AACGIILLMNS	Gallicanism
AACGIILLNPY	callipygian
AACGIILLNTV	vacillating
AACGIILLOOX	axiological
AACGIILLSST	glacialists
AACGIILMNNS	Anglicanism
AACGIILMSTT	stalagmitic
AACGIILNSTU	actualising
AACGIILNTUZ	actualizing
AACGIIMNNTU	acuminating
AACGIIMNSTT	masticating

AACGIIMSSTT	astigmatics
AACGIINNNRT	incarnating
AACGIINNOTV	vacationing
AACGIINNQTU	acquainting
AACGIINOSST	associating
AACGIINOSTT	castigation
AACGIINPSTU	auspicating
AACGIINPTTV	captivating
AACGIKLNRTY	tracklaying
AACGILLNNOW	allowancing
AACGILLNORY	organically
AACGILLOPST	postglacial
AACGILMNOOR	agronomical
AACGILNNNTU	cannulating
AACGILNOOPR	carpogonial
AACGILNOOTU	coagulation
AACGILNOTUV	autoclaving
AACGILNPTTU	catapulting
AACGILOSSUY	sagaciously
AACGILOSTTU	cataloguist
AACGIMNSTTY	syntagmatic
AACGINNRSTT	transacting
AACGINOOPPT	apocopating
AACGINOPRSU	craniopagus
AACGINORSST	nasogastric
AACGIORSSTT	castigators
AACGIORSTTY	castigatory
AACGLLNOOTY	octagonally
AACGLMNOOPY	campanology
AACGLOORSTU	coagulators
AACHHIIMPPT	amphipathic
AACHHIIMPRT	amphitricha
AACHHIMNPPS	chapmanship
AACHHLORTTT	throatlatch
AACHIIINRST	christiania
AACHIILORST	ahistorical
AACHIIMNNOT	machination
AACHIIMNSST	shamanistic
AACHIINNPPST	captainship
AACHIINRSSU	saurischian
AACHIKMNPRU	Kanchipuram
AACHILLMOPY	malacophily
AACHILLOPRY	parochially
AACHILMNOOS	monochasial
AACHILMOPPP	hippocampal
AACHILNOPPS	pansophical
AACHILNORST	thrasonical
AACHILQRRSU	squirarchal
AACHIMMNOTY	mythomaniac
AACHIMMORST	achromatism
AACHIMNNORS	anachronism
AACHIMNORSS	anachorisms
	maraschinos
AACHIMNORST	machinators
AACHIMNOTTY	Titanomachy
AACHIMOPPRR	paramorphic
AACHIMPRSST	pharmacists
AACHINNNOTY	anthocyanin
AACHINORSST	anthracosis
AACHIPRSTTU	parachutist
AACHLLMNORY	monarchally
AACHLLOOSTU	holocaustal

AACHLMORRTY	lachrymator	**AACILLPSSTY**	spastically	**AACORRSSTTT**	stratocrats
AACHLNNOOTU	anacoluthon	**AACILLRRUUY**	auricularly	**AADDDEEGHIN**	deadheading
AACHLPPPPYY	happy-clappy	**AACILMNNOPT**	complainant	**AADDDEGINRS**	grandaddies
AACHMNNOORW	anchorwoman	**AACILMNOOTX**	taxonomical	**AADDDEGNNOR**	dragonnaded
AACHMNNOSTWY	yachtswoman	**AACILMNOPST**	complaisant	**AADDDEIILPT**	dilapidated
AACHMOOPRST	apochromats	**AACILMNORTU**	calumniator	**AADDDEILPRS**	paradiddles
AACHMOORSTU	achromatous	**AACILMNOSTU**	maculations	**AADDDEILRRT**	tarradiddle
AACHPRSSTTW	watchstraps	**AACILMNRTTU**	matriculant	**AADDDEILRST**	taradiddles
AACIIILNNOT	lacination	**AACILMORRST**	lacrimators	**AADDEEEHPRS**	spearheaded
AACIIILNOST	laicisation	**AACILMORRTY**	lacrimatory	**AADDEEFGLRT**	deflagrated
AACIIILNOTZ	laicization	**AACILMPPRSY**	paralympics	**AADDEEFGRSU**	safeguarded
AACIIILPPRT	participial	**AACILNNNOTU**	cannulation	**AADDEEHHRRT**	hardhearted
AACIIJNOTTT	jactitation	**AACILNNNOPSY**	calypsonian	**AADDEEHIMNS**	maidenheads
AACIILLMRTU	multiracial	**AACILNNNOSTU**	canulations	**AADDEEHLPRY**	paraldehyde
AACIILLNOOT	coalitional	**AACILNOOTUV**	vacuolation	**AADDEEILMNT**	delaminated
AACIILLNOSS	salicionals	**AACILNOPRTY**	coplanarity	**AADDEEILNRS**	adrenalised
AACIILLNOTV	vacillation	**AACILNOPSTT**	Cottian Alps	**AADDEEILNRZ**	adrenalized
AACIILLNTTY	titanically	**AACILNOPSTU**	capsulation	**AADDEEILNST**	desalinated
AACIILLPRTY	capillarity	**AACILNORRTU**	intraocular	**AADDEEIPPRS**	disappeared
	piratically	**AACILNORTVY**	clairvoyant	**AADDEEKMRRT**	trademarked
AACIILLRSTY	satirically	**AACILOPPRST**	applicators	**AADDEELLNRS**	Dardanelles
AACIILMNORT	lacrimation	**AACILOPPRTY**	applicatory	**AADDEELRTTU**	adulterated
AACIILMNOST	anomalistic	**AACILOPRSUY**	rapaciously	**AADDEEMQRSU**	masqueraded
AACIILMOSTT	atomistical	**AACILOPRTTU**	capitulator	**AADDEEMQSTU**	desquamated
AACIILNNNOT	lancination	**AACILOPSTTU**	autoplastic	**AADDEEMRRSY**	daydreamers
AACIILNOPPT	application	**AACILORRTTU**	articulator	**AADDEENPPRS**	sandpapered
AACIILNPRTU	puritanical	**AACILPRRSTU**	particulars	**AADDEGGINRS**	aggrandised
AACIILNPTTY	antitypical	**AACILRSTUVY**	vascularity	**AADDEGGINRZ**	aggrandized
AACIILOPRST	piscatorial	**AACIMMNNOOS**	monomaniacs	**AADDEGHNORS**	dragonheads
AACIILPRSTT	patristical	**AACIMNNNOTT**	contaminant	**AADDEGHNRTU**	dreadnaught
AACIILPSSTT	capitalists	**AACIMNOOSTT**	anastomotic	**AADDEGIMNRY**	daydreaming
AACIILSSTTT	statistical	**AACIMNOPRSY**	pyromaniacs	**AADDEGINORT**	degradation
AACIIMNNORT	animatronic	**AACIMORSSTT**	masticators	**AADDEGINRRS**	disarranged
AACIIMNNOTU	acumination	**AACIMORSTTY**	masticatory	**AADDEGIRRST**	tardigrades
AACIIMNOSTT	mastication	**AACINNNOOTU**	annunciator	**AADDEGNNORS**	dragonnades
AACIIMORTTY	aromaticity	**AACINNNOOSTV**	Nova Scotian	**AADDEHILLNV**	de Havilland
AACIINNNORT	incarnation	**AACINNOOSTZ**	actinozoans	**AADDEHIMNNS**	handmaidens
AACIINNNOTT	incantation	**AACINNORSTT**	transaction	**AADDEIILNTV**	invalidated
AACIINNPSTT	anticipants	**AACINNORTTY**	incantatory	**AADDEIILPST**	dilapidates
AACIINOOSST	association	**AACINNRRSTU**	transuranic	**AADDEIIMPRS**	imparadised
AACIINOPRTT	anticipator	**AACINOOOPPT**	apocopation	**AADDEIIRVVZ**	Díaz de
AACIINOPSTT	capitations	**AACINOOPSTT**	coaptations		Vivar
AACIINOPTTV	captivation	**AACINORSSTT**	castrations	**AADDEINPQSU**	pasquinaded
AACIINORTTV	vaticinator	**AACINORSTTT**	attractions	**AADDEINRSST**	standardise
AACIINOSTTV	activations	**AACINORSTTU**	astronautic	**AADDEINRSTZ**	standardize
	vacationist	**AACIOORSSST**	associators	**AADDEJLMSTU**	maladjusted
AACIINPPRTT	participant	**AACIOORSSTY**	associatory	**AADDELPQRUU**	quadrupedal
AACIINRSSTT	antiracists	**AACIOPPPRRY**	appropriacy	**AADDFIORSTV**	Star of
AACILLLNTUV	lunatically	**AACIOPRSTTV**	captivators		David
AACILLLPSTY	plastically	**AACIORRSSTT**	aristocrats	**AADDGILMOSY**	amygdaloids
AACILLMMNUU	animalculum	**AACLMORRSTY**	lacrymators	**AADDGINPRRS**	Grand Rapids
AACILLMNORT	matroclinal	**AACLMORRTVY**	lacrymatory	**AADDGNNRSST**	grandstands
AACILLMNOSY	masonically	**AACLNNNOOST**	consonantal	**AADDHIKUUZZ**	Dzaudzhikau
AACILLMOSTY	somatically	**AACLOOPPRSY**	laparoscopy	**AADDHNNRSSY**	shandrydans
AACILLNOOST	allocations	**AACLOORRSTU**	coloraturas	**AADDIIINNRT**	Trinidadian
AACILLNOPRS	rapscallion	**AACLORSTTUU**	auscultator	**AADDIILOPRT**	dilapidator
AACILLOOPST	apostolical	**AACMMNORSTU**	Murman Coast	**AADDIINSSTV**	Saint
AACILLOPRSY	prosaically	**AACMNOPRTUY**	paramountcy		David's
AACILLORSTV	vacillators	**AACMOOPRRST**	comparators	**AADDNNNORST**	nonstandard
AACILLOSSUY	salaciously	**AACMOORSSTU**	sarcomatous	**AADEEEFHHRT**	featherhead
AACILLPRTUU	apicultural	**AACNORRSSTT**	transactors	**AADEEEGGRTX**	exaggerated
AACILLPRTUY	capitularly	**AACNORRSSTW**	narrowcasts	**AADEEEHHLRT**	leatherhead

AADEEEEHLNNR	enneahedral	
AADEEEELRTUV	reevaluated	
AADEEEEPRSTX	exasperated	
AADEEEERSSTV	asseverated	
AADEEFGLLLT	flagellated	
AADEEFGLRST	deflagrates	
AADEEFHHLRT	halfhearted	
AADEEFHRSST	fatshederas	
AADEEFILRRS	fairleaders	
AADEEFKLNRR	farnarkeled	
AADEEGHLNOT	halogenated	
AADEEGHLNPY	Handley Page	
AADEEGIKKRR	Kierkegaard	
AADEEGILRRT	lateorigrade	
AADEEGIMNRT	emarginated	
AADEEGINRTU	aguardiente	
AADEEGMNORV	overmanaged	
AADEEGNORRT	anterograde	
AADEEGNPRRR	prearranged	
AADEEHHLPRT	heptahedral	
AADEEHHMMRS	hammerheads	
AADEEHHRTXY	hexahydrate	
AADEEHILRTX	exhilarated	
AADEEHLLTVY	Death Valley	
AADEEHLNNRT	neanderthal	
AADEEHLNPRT	pentahedral	
AADEEHLRRTT	tetrahedral	
AADEEHMPRST	metaphrased	
AADEEHMRRTW	warmhearted	
AADEEHMRSST	headmasters	
	headstreams	
AADEEHNRSVW	heavenwards	
AADEEHQRRTU	headquarter	
AADEEHQRSSU	headsquares	
AADEEIILNRX	Alexander II	
AADEEILLMVY	mediaevally	
AADEEILLRTT	alliterated	
AADEEILLSSS	salesladies	
AADEEILMNST	delaminates	
AADEEILMORT	ameliorated	
AADEEILNNRX	alexandrine	
AADEEILNRTX	alexandrite	
AADEEILNRVX	Alexander VI	
AADEEILNSST	desalinates	
AADEEIMPRST	preadamites	
AADEEIMRRRS	Sierra Madre	
AADEEINORST	asteroidean	
AADEEINPPRT	appertained	
AADEEIPPRRS	reappraised	
AADEEIPRRTT	repatriated	
AADEEIPRTTX	expatriated	
AADEEIRRSSV	adversaries	
AADEEIRRTTV	retardative	
AADEEIRSRTV	adversative	
AADEEISTTVV	devastative	
AADEEKMRRTW	watermarked	
AADEELLNTTU	landaulette	
AADEELLPPRW	wallpapered	
AADEELRSTTU	adulterates	
AADEEMNNSSU	Amundsen Sea	
AADEEMNPRRT	dermapteran	
AADEEMQRRSU	masquerader	

AADEEMQRSSU	masquerades	
AADEEMQSSTU	desquamates	
AADEEMRRSTU	Estremadura	
AADEEMRRTUX	Extremadura	
AADEENNRTWY	Tyne and	
	Wear	
AADEENPRSTU	unseparated	
AADEFGHNRRT	grandfather	
AADEFGIISTT	fastigiated	
AADEFHLNRST	fatherlands	
AADEFIMNOST	defamations	
AADEFLMNNTU	fundamental	
AADEFLSSTTY	steadfastly	
AADEFNNNORS	San Fernando	
AADEFNNSSTU	Stefan Dušan	
AADEGGGLLLY	lallygagged	
AADEGGHNRSS	haggardness	
AADEGGINRRS	aggrandiser	
AADEGGINRRZ	aggrandizer	
AADEGGINRSS	aggrandises	
AADEGGINRSZ	aggrandizes	
AADEGGLNRSS	laggardness	
AADEGHIMNST	mastheading	
AADEGHLNNRS	handlangers	
AADEGHOPRTU	autographed	
AADEGIILNTT	intagliated	
AADEGIILPRS	plagiarised	
AADEGIILPRZ	plagiarized	
AADEGIIMNNT	deaminating	
AADEGIINNTV	invaginated	
AADEGIINRTT	ingratiated	
AADEGILLNTV	gallivanted	
AADEGILNNRV	landgravine	
	Vlaardingen	
AADEGILNPRT	plantigrade	
AADEGILNTUV	devaluating	
AADEGILPRRS	paragliders	
AADEGIMNNRV	Venn diagram	
AADEGIMNNRS	misarranged	
AADEGIMNRSU	admeasuring	
AADEGINNOST	antagonised	
AADEGINNOTZ	antagonized	
AADEGINNTUV	unnavigated	
AADEGINPPRT	preadapting	
AADEGINRRSS	disarranges	
AADEGINRTUU	inaugurated	
AADEGINSTTV	devastating	
AADEGIOPRRS	radiopagers	
AADEGIPRRSS	disparagers	
AADEGLNQRSU	quadrangles	
AADEGLNRSSU	gradualness	
AADEGLNSSSS	sandglasses	
AADEGMNRRST	grandmaster	
AADEGMRRSTU	dramaturges	
AADEGNNPRRT	grandparent	
AADEHHIJLUV	Judah ha-	
	Levi	
AADEHIILNNT	annihilated	
AADEHIILNRT	antheridial	
AADEHIILOPP	paedophilia	
AADEHIINPTY	diaphaneity	
AADEHILLNOS	hollandaise	

AADEHILMMMO	Mohammed Ali	
AADEHILNNST	lanthanides	
AADEHILNOSW	Noahide Laws	
AADEHINOPPY	hypnopaedia	
AADEHIPSTXY	asphyxiated	
AADEHLMNSUY	unashamedly	
AADEHLNNPRS	panhandlers	
AADEHPRSSTT	spatterdash	
AADEIIILNST	italianised	
AADEIIILNTZ	italianized	
AADEIIILNTZ	italianized	
AADEIIIRRTV	irradiative	
AADEIIILMNST	mediastinal	
AADEIIILMORT	mediatorial	
AADEIIILMRST	admiralties	
AADEIIILMSST	assimilated	
AADEIIILNRRT	interradial	
AADEIIILNSTV	insalivated	
	invalidates	
AADEIIILPRTY	praediality	
AADEIIIMNNOT	deamination	
AADEIIIMPRSS	imparadises	
AADEIIINORRT	reradiation	
AADEIIINORST	eradiations	
AADEIIINSTTV	adventitias	
AADEIIIPRSST	parasitised	
AADEIIIPRSTZ	parasitized	
AADEIIJKLRRS	rijksdaaler	
AADEIIKLNPST	Staked Plain	
AADEIIKMNORT	demarkation	
AADEIILLLMOT	metalloidal	
AADEIILLMMMT	mammillated	
AADEIILLMRTY	diametrally	
AADEIILLNOPT	planetoidal	
AADEIILLNOST	allantoides	
AADEIILMNNRS	mainlanders	
AADEIILMNORR	Māorilander	
AADEIILMNPTU	manipulated	
AADEIILMNRRT	intradermal	
AADEIILNNQRU	quadrennial	
AADEIILNOPSS	anadiploses	
AADEIILNORTY	arytenoidal	
AADEIILNOTUV	devaluation	
AADEIILNPPRR	preprandial	
AADEIILNPPRS	appledrains	
AADEIILNRRSY	drainlayers	
AADEIILNRSTU	naturalised	
AADEIILNRSTW	landwaiters	
AADEIILNRTUZ	naturalized	
AADEIILORRTV	advertorial	
AADEIILPRSTY	disparately	
AADEIIMMNRST	disarmament	
AADEIIMNNNOV	Vandemonian	
AADEIIMNNOPS	Epaminondas	
AADEIIMNOPRR	madreporian	
AADEIIMNORST	mandatories	
AADEIIMNRSTV	animadverts	
	maidservant	
AADEIIMOSTTU	automatised	
AADEIIMOTTUZ	automatized	
AADEIIMRRSST	dramatisers	
AADEIIMRRSTZ	dramatizers	
AADEIIMRSTTU	traumatised	

AADEIMRTTUZ	traumatized	**AADGIILNNSV**	vandalising	**AADILMMPSSW**	Dismal Swamp
AADEINNQRTU	quarantined	**AADGIILNNVZ**	vandalizing	**AADILMNORTY**	mandatorily
AADEINOPRTV	depravation	**AADGIILNORR**	railroading	**AADILNRRSSU**	Arru Islands
AADEINORRTT	retardation	**AADGIIMNPST**	misadapting	**AADILNSSSUW**	duniwassals
AADEINORSST	diatessaron	**AADGIIMNRST**	dramatising	**AADILOOORSV**	Via Dolorosa
AADEINORSTY	arytaenoids	**AADGIIMNRTZ**	dramatizing	**AADILOORSTV**	vasodilator
AADEINOSTTV	devastation	**AADGIINOSTV**	divagations	**AADILOPPRSV**	disapproval
AADEINPQRSU	pasquinader	**AADGIINRRSY**	disarraying	**AADINRSSTTU**	Sunda Strait
AADEINPQSSU	pasquinades	**AADGIJNORSU**	jaguarondis	**AADJMNNPRSU**	panjandrums
AADEINPRSTU	unaspirated	**AADGIJNRSUU**	jaguarundis	**AADJNNORRST**	Trans-Jordan
AADEIOPSSTT	apostatised	**AADGILMNSSU**	salmagundis	**AADLLLOSSUY**	All Souls'
AADEIOPSTTZ	apostatized	**AADGILNOOTU**	autoloading		Day
AADEKLMORSW	meadowlarks	**AADGILRSSTU**	gradualists	**AADMNORSSTU**	Nostradamus
AADEKNRSSWW	awkwardness	**AADGINORSTU**	graduations	**AADNOPRRSUW**	wraparounds
AADELLMNORT	martellando	**AADGLLLNRUY**	glandularly	**AAEEEFLMMST**	metafemales
AADELLNNORT	rallentando	**AADGMNNORST**	montagnards	**AAEEEGGMMST**	megagametes
AADELMMOPSS	plasmodesma	**AADGNNOPRSS**	snapdragons	**AAEEEGGRSTX**	exaggerates
AADELMNORST	Aldermaston	**AADGNOOPRST**	gastropodan	**AAEEEGRSTWY**	steerageway
AADELMNNRST	transdermal	**AADHIIKRSTV**	Dasht-i-	**AAEEEHKPRSS**	Shakespeare
AADELNRSTTU	adulterants		Kavir	**AAEEEHLLRTY**	aethereally
AADELNRSTUV	transvalued	**AADHIILLLSV**	Valdai Hills	**AAEEEHNRRTW**	earthenware
AADELORRTTU	adulterator	**AADHIILMPRS**	admiralship	**AAEEEIKPSSS**	speakeasies
AADEMNOOSST	anastomosed	**AADHIIMOPRS**	adiaphorism	**AAEEELRSTUV**	reevaluates
AADEMNORSTW	tradeswoman	**AADHIIOPRST**	adiaphorist	**AAEEEMNPPST**	appeasement
AADENNNRRTUW	unwarranted	**AADHILRSTWW**	withdrawals	**AAEEENRSSTU**	aureateness
AADENNRSTTU	denaturants	**AADHIOOPRSU**	adiaphorous	**AAEEEPRRSTX**	exasperater
AADENOPRSSU	andropauses	**AADHIOPPRTY**	paratyphoid	**AAEEEPRSSTX**	exasperates
AADENPRSTTT	standpatter	**AADHIOPPSSY**	hypospadias	**AAEEERSSSTV**	asseverates
AADENRSSTTU	transudates	**AADHIOPRRTY**	parathyroid	**AAEEFGHLMRT**	Magherafelt
AADENRSSWWY	waywardness	**AADHKNOORTT**	North Dakota	**AAEEFGIMRST**	afterimages
AADENRSTTUU	unsaturated	**AADHKOOSTTU**	South Dakota	**AAEEFGINSTU**	taeniafuges
AADEOPPRSST	strappadoes	**AADHLOOPRRT**	arthropodal	**AAEEFGLLLST**	flagellates
AADEORRRTTY	retardatory	**AADHLORSUYZ**	hazardously	**AAEEFHIRRTW**	Fairweather
AADEORSSTTV	devastators	**AADHNOPQRUY**	quadraphony	**AAEEFHMRRRS**	sharefarmer
AADEQRRSSUU	quadratures	**AADHORRSSUU**	hadrosaurus	**AAEEFHRSSTW**	aftershows
AADFFGHNSSY	shandygaffs	**AADIIINORRT**	irradiation	**AAEEFNRRSST**	transferase
AADFGHINNST	handfasting	**AADIILLNTTU**	altitudinal	**AAEEFRSSTTT**	aftertastes
AADFIKNNOOR	Kordofanian		latitudinal	**AAEEGGGIRTV**	aggregative
AADFMNORSTW	draftswoman	**AADIILLSWWY**	Władysław II	**AAEEGGGLRTY**	aggregately
AADGGGGMNOO	Gog and	**AADIILNOOTX**	oxidational	**AAEEGGHMOSU**	haemagogues
	Magog	**AADIILNOPSS**	anadiplosis	**AAEEGGIMNRV**	graven image
AADGGIILNPR	paragliding	**AADIILNOPST**	lapidations	**AAEEGGLMORT**	agglomerate
AADGGIIMMNR	diagramming	**AADIILNORTT**	traditional	**AAEEGGORRTX**	exaggerator
AADGGIINNRR	darraigning	**AADIILNORTV**	invalidator	**AAEEGHHMORR**	haemorrhage
AADGGIINOPR	radiopaging	**AADIILNOSTT**	dilatations	**AAEEGHIMNRT**	megatherian
AADGGIINPRS	disparaging	**AADIILNOSTV**	validations	**AAEEGHLNOST**	halogenates
AADGGLNOOSW	waggonloads	**AADIILNOSTY**	dialysation	**AAEEGHLOOPS**	oesophageal
AADGGOOOUUU	Ouagadougou	**AADIILNOTYZ**	dialyzation	**AAEEGHNPPRR**	paperhanger
AADGHHIKNNS	handshaking	**AADIILNTTTU**	attitudinal	**AAEEGIKNNRW**	reawakening
AADGHHOPRSW	shadowgraph	**AADIILOSUVV**	audiovisual	**AAEEGILLLNS**	selaginella
AADGHIILNOR	Ghirlandaio	**AADIIMNORST**	admirations	**AAEEGILLLTT**	tagliatelle
AADGHILMNNN	manhandling	**AADIINNORSU**	dinosaurian	**AAEEGILLNNT**	gentianella
AADGHILNNNP	panhandling	**AADIINNOTTX**	antioxidant	**AAEEGILMSSX**	sexagesimal
AADGHIMNNRS	Sandringham	**AADIIOPRSST**	parasitoids	**AAEEGILPRTT**	tetraplegia
AADGHIOPRRS	radiographs	**AADIIORRRST**	irradiators	**AAEEGIMRRRS**	remarriages
AADGHIOPRRY	radiography	**AADIIPRSSST**	aspidistras	**AAEEGINPPRR**	reappearing
AADGHIRRRVY	hydrargyria	**AADIIRSSTTV**	Davis Strait	**AAEEGINPRSS**	paragenesis
AADGHMNRSTU	draughtsman	**AADIJNORSTU**	adjurations	**AAEEGINPRST**	greasepaint
AADGIIINNRT	irradiating	**AADILLMNOOT**	amontillado		pageantries
AADGIIKLNNR	Kaliningrad	**AADILLMORTY**	maladroitly	**AAEEGINRRTW**	graniteware
AADGIILLNOV	Gallovidian	**AADILLMPRYV**	pyramidally	**AAEEGINRSTV**	vegetarians
AADGIILMRST	madrigalist	**AADILLSVWWY**	Władysław IV	**AAEEGLMNOPT**	planogamete

AAEEGLMNPSS	plasmagenes	AAEEEIMNNRSS	San Marinese	AAEGGIINNRR	gregarinian
AAEEGLNNPTT	Plantagenet	AAEEEIMNRRSW	weimaraners	AAEGGIINNTV	evaginating
AAEEGLNSSTV	vantageless	AAEEEIMNSSTV	amativeness	AAEGGIINRTV	variegating
AAEEGLORTVY	laevogyrate	AAEEEIMSSSTT	metastasise	AAEGGILNTTU	agglutinate
AAEEGMMNNST	managements	AAEEEIMSSTTZ	metastasize	AAEGGILOSSU	sialagogues
AAEEGMMORRS	aerogrammes	AAEEEIOPRSTX	exoparasite	AAEGGIMMNTU	gametangium
AAEEGMNNNRT	arrangement	AAEEEIOPRTVV	evaporative	AAEGGIMNOOS	agamogonies
AAEEGMNOPRT	pomegranate	AAEEEIPPRRSS	reappraises	AAEGGINNRRR	rearranging
AAEEGMNORSV	overmanages	AAEEEIPPRRTV	preparative	AAEGGLMMORU	grammalogue
AAEEGMNRSTV	ravagements	AAEEEIPRRSTT	repatriates	AAEGHHIPPRY	hyperphagia
AAEEGMNRSTY	East Germany	AAEEEIPRSTTX	expatriates	AAEGHIINRVW	hairweaving
AAEEGMNSSTU	assuagement	AAEEEIRRSTXX	Artaxerxes I	AAEGHILNPRS	nephralgias
AAEEGNPRRRS	prearranges	AAEEEIRSSSTV	aviatresses	AAEGHILORST	hagiolaters
AAEEGNRRRRS	rearrangers	AAEEEKLNRSTT	rattlesnake	AAEGHILRSTU	gaultherias
AAEEGQRRSTU	quarterages	AAEEELLLLMTY	lamellately	AAEGHIMMNOS	hemangiomas
AAEEHHKRRST	earthshaker	AAEEELLLMNOS	salmonellae	AAEGHIMNORR	menorrhagia
AAEEHHLNNPT	naphthalene	AAEELLLMNTTT	mantelletta	AAEGHIMNPRS	managership
AAEEHILMOPR	hemeralopia	AAEEELLNRTTY	alternately	AAEGHINNNSS	shenanigans
AAEEHILNNST	Saint Helena	AAEEELLPRSTY	platelayers	AAEGHINRYYZ	Nyíregyháza
AAEEHILRSTX	exhilarates	AAEEELLSTTTT	tattletales	AAEGHKKLNRS	Arkhangelsk
AAEEHIMMNPT	amphetamine	AAEEELMNSTTT	testamental	AAEGHLLNOXY	hexagonally
AAEEHIMNRTT	metatherian	AAEEELMRRSTT	maltreaters	AAEGHLMMNOO	Monongahela
AAEEHIMRRTY	erythraemia	AAEEELNNPTTV	pentavalent	AAEGHLMOOTY	haematology
AAEEHIORTTX	heterotaxia	AAEELNPSTTT	pantalettes	AAEGHLNPRTU	heptangular
AAEEHIOSTUV	Haute-Savoie	AAEEELNPSTTV	septavalent	AAEGHMNOPRS	anemographs
AAEEHIPRSST	paresthesia	AAEELNRRSTT	retranslate		phanerogams
AAEEHKQRSTU	earthquakes	AAEEELNRTTTV	tetravalent	AAEGHMNOPRY	anemography
AAEEHLLSTTU	haustellate	AAEELOPRTTX	extrapolate	AAEGHMOPRRS	phraseogram
AAEEHLNPTTV	heptavalent	AAEEMMNRRST	rearmaments	AAEGHMRTTUU	thaumaturge
AAEEHLPSSTU	Hautes-Alpes	AAEEMMPRTUY	empyreumata	AAEGHNPRRST	straphanger
AAEEHMNOORR	amenorrhoea	AAEEMNOPRTT	treponemata	AAEGIIIMNTV	imaginative
AAEEHMPRSST	metaphrases	AAEEMNORTUX	auxanometer	AAEGIILLNTV	alleviating
AAEEHNOPRSS	anaphoreses	AAEEMQRSSTU	marquessate	AAEGIILMNPS	Pelagianism
AAEEHNSSSSU	Hesse-Nassau	AAEENNRSSUW	unawareness	AAEGIILMNRS	marginalise
AAEEHORRSTT	steatorrhea	AAEFFHRSSTT	aftershafts	AAEGIILMNRZ	marginalize
AAEEHRRSSTW	shearwaters	AAEFFIIMRTV	affirmative	AAEGIILMRST	magisterial
AAEEIILLTVV	alleviative	AAEFFILLNTU	affluential	AAEGIILNRTT	retaliating
AAEEIILMRST	materialise	AAEFGHILNRT	farthingale	AAEGIILPRRS	plagiariser
AAEEIILMRTZ	materialize	AAEFGHNRSTU	fearnaughts	AAEGIILPRRZ	plagiarizer
AAEEIILRRST	arterialise	AAEFGILPRST	septifragal	AAEGIILPRSS	plagiarises
AAEEIILRRTZ	arterialize	AAEFGINNPRS	frangipanes	AAEGIILPRST	epigastrial
AAEEIILRTTV	retaliative	AAEFGLLLNST	flagellants	AAEGIILPRSZ	plagiarizes
AAEEIINRSSV	sansevieria	AAEFGILLORT	flagellator	AAEGIIMMRRS	mismarriage
AAEEIKLLMRT	alkalimeter	AAEFGLLNRSU	langlaufers	AAEGIIMNNRT	reanimating
AAEEIKLMNUW	Milwaukeean	AAEFGLMNORY	Morgan le	AAEGIIMNRSS	Minas Gerais
AAEEILLMNNT	lineamental		Fay	AAEGIINNOTV	evagination
AAEEILLMPRX	premaxillae	AAEFGMNRRTY	fragmentary	AAEGIINNRTT	reattaining
AAEEILLNOTV	elevational	AAEFIIILMRS	familiarise	AAEGIINNSTV	invaginates
AAEEILLNPRT	Pantelleria	AAEFIIILMRZ	familiarize	AAEGIINORTV	variegation
AAEEILLPPTV	appellative	AAEFIIMOSUV	mauvaise foi	AAEGIINPTTX	expatiating
AAEEILLQRTU	equilateral	AAEFILMMNRT	firmamental	AAEGIINRSTT	ingratiates
AAEEILLRSTT	alliterates	AAEFILMNRTY	filamentary	AAEGIINSTTV	aestivating
AAEEILMMPST	semipalmate	AAEFILOPRRT	prefatorial	AAEGIIRRTVV	gravitative
AAEEILMORST	ameliorates	AAEFLLNRRTY	fraternally	AAEGILLNPRR	paralleling
AAEEILNNPRT	penetralian	AAEFLLNSSTU	fustanellas	AAEGILLNOST	allegations
AAEEILNPPSS	epanalepsis	AAEFLLORRTX	extrafloral	AAEGILLNPPR	apparelling
AAEEILNPRST	planetaries	AAEFLNORTUW	law of	AAEGILLNPPY	appealingly
AAEEILNPTVX	explanative		nature	AAEGILLNRST	gallantries
AAEEILNRTTV	alternative	AAEFLNRRRST	transferral	AAEGILMNRST	martingales
AAEEILPPRSS	paraleipses	AAEGGGGINRT	aggregating	AAEGILMNRTT	maltreating
AAEEILRSTTV	alteratives	AAEGGGINORT	aggregation	AAEGILMNRTY	ligamentary
AAEEIMMNRSS	Sammarinese	AAEGGGORRST	aggregators	AAEGILMNSTT	stalemating

587

AAEGILMORRS	rigamaroles	AAEHIILMNSS	leishmanias	AAEIILNNSST	salientians
AAEGILMSSTT	stalagmites	AAEHIILNNST	annihilates	AAEIILNORST	rationalise
AAEGILNNPPU	unappealing	AAEHIIMNOPS	hemianopsia		realisation
AAEGILNNRTT	alternating	AAEHIIMNSST	histaminase	AAEIILNORTT	retaliation
AAEGILNORTY	legationary	AAEHIINPSTT	antipathies	AAEIILNORTZ	rationalize
AAEGILNOSTT	gestational	AAEHIKLNRRS	Lanarkshire		realization
AAEGILNPRST	Great Plains	AAEHIKRRSST	hairstreaks	AAEIILNPRRT	patrilinear
AAEGILNPRSV	palsgravine	AAEHILLOPST	palaeoliths	AAEIILNSSTV	insalivates
AAEGILNQRUU	equiangular	AAEHILLNOSTT	East Lothian	AAEIILNSTTY	insatiately
AAEGILNRSSV	galvanisers	AAEHILNOSTX	exhalations	AAEIILPPRSS	paraleipsis
AAEGILNRSVZ	galvanizers	AAEHILNPSTW	Westphalian	AAEIILQTTUV	qualitative
AAEGILNRTTU	triangulate	AAEHILNRSTX	exhilarants	AAEIIMNNORT	reanimation
AAEGILNRTUV	granulative	AAEHILNSSTU	ailanthuses	AAEIIMNNOTX	examination
	revaluating	AAEHILORRTX	exhilarator		examination
AAEGILORSTT	gestatorial	AAEHILPPPRS	slaphappier	AAEIIMNNRSS	seminarians
AAEGIMMNRSS	mismanagers	AAEHILPPRSY	hyperplasia	AAEIIMNNRST	maintainers
AAEGIMNNRRT	arraignment	AAEHILPSSTT	asphaltites	AAEIIMNRSTT	Menai Strait
AAEGIMNNTTU	antimutagen	AAEHIMNPRSY	hypermanias	AAEIINNPPRT	paripinnate
AAEGIMNRRSS	misarranges	AAEHIMNSSTU	amianthuses	AAEIINNSTTT	instantiate
AAEGIMNNRSV	margravines	AAEHIMNSSTY	myasthenias	AAEIINOPTTX	expatiation
AAEGIMOOPST	Aegospotami	AAEHIMOSSST	haemostasis	AAEIINOSTTV	aestivation
AAEGIMRSSTT	magistrates	AAEHINOPRSS	anaphoresis	AAEIINQRSTU	antiquaries
AAEGINNOPRS	Singaporean	AAEHIPSSTXY	asphyxiates	AAEIIPRSSST	parasitises
AAEGINNORSS	anagnorises	AAEHKLORSTT	Holkar State	AAEIIPRSSTZ	parasitizes
AAEGINNOSST	antagonises	AAEHKMNNTTU	Tutankhamen	AAEIKLLMRTY	alkalimetry
AAEGINNOSTZ	antagonizes	AAEHLLLOPTY	allelopathy	AAEIKLLTTVY	talkatively
AAEGINNTTTU	attenuating	AAEHLLMRRSS	marshallers	AAEIKLMNOPT	kleptomania
AAEGINOPRTV	evaporating	AAEHLNOPSSY	synaloephas	AAEIKLMRSTT	Sterlitamak
AAEGINRSTUU	inaugurates	AAEHLNPRSTY	phalanstery	AAEIKORRSTT	Korea Strait
AAEGIOPPRTV	propagative	AAEHLPRRSWY	prayer shawl	AAEILLLLNSV	villanellas
AAEGIOPSTTY	steatopygia	AAEHMNOOOTZ	haematozoon	AAEILLLMNOT	lamellation
AAEGIRRSTTV	gravitaters	AAEHMMNORSTU	athermanous	AAEILLLMPRS	parallelism
AAEGKLMNORY	Kolyma Range	AAEHMNORSWW	washerwoman	AAEILLLOOPS	soapolallie
AAEGKLMNOSS	maskalonges	AAEHMNRSSST	harassments	AAEILLLPRST	parallelist
AAEGKLMRSSS	glassmakers	AAEHMOPRTTU	thaumatrope	AAEILLMPRVY	primaevally
AAEGKMNNOSS	maskanonges	AAEHMPRSSTT	metaphrasts	AAEILLMRSSY	amaryllises
AAEGKMNRTUU	Kumaratunge	AAEHNNQSSUU	Susquehanna	AAEILLNOOTV	alveolation
AAEGKOPRSSW	passagework	AAEHNOPRSST	anastrophes	AAEILLNOPPT	appellation
AAEGLLLNRVY	laryngeally	AAEHNOPSSTT	thanatopses	AAEILLORSTV	alleviators
AAEGLLNNSST	gallantness	AAEHNPPSSWW	wappenshaws	AAEILLORTTU	ratatouille
AAEGLLNNTTY	tangentally	AAEIIIKNNOS	aniseikonia	AAEILLQRSTU	aquarellist
AAEGLLOPRTY	pyrogallate	AAEIIILNSST	italianises	AAEILMMNRST	maternalism
AAEGLMMRRSS	grammarless	AAEIIILNSTZ	italianizes	AAEILMNNOPR	praenominal
AAEGLMNRTTY	termagantly	AAEIIILRSUX	auxiliaries	AAEILMNNOTT	lamentation
AAEGLMORSSU	megalosaurs	AAEIIJNRSSS	janissaries	AAEILMNORST	ameliorants
AAEGLNNPRTU	pentangular	AAEIILLMNNR	millenarian		monasterial
AAEGLNNRSSU	angularness	AAEIILLMNRT	matrilineal	AAEILMNPRST	parliaments
AAEGLNRRSTU	granulaters	AAEIILLNOPR	Apollinaire		paternalism
AAEGLNRSTTU	strangulate	AAEIILLNOTV	alleviation	AAEILMNPRTU	planetarium
AAEGLPPRSSS	glasspapers	AAEIILLNPRT	patrilineal	AAEILMNPSTU	manipulates
AAEGMMOPRSY	agamospermy	AAEIILLPRST	ipsilateral	AAEILMNRRTU	ultramarine
AAEGMMORSST	agrostemmas	AAEIILLPSTV	palliatives	AAEILMNRSST	martialness
AAEGNNRSSTV	vagrantness	AAEIILMMRST	materialism	AAEILMOORRT	ameliorator
AAEGOPSSTTY	steatopygas	AAEIILMNNTY	inanimately	AAEILMOPTTT	totipalmate
AAEHHHJOPST	Jehoshaphat	AAEIILMPRTV	imperatival	AAEILMORSTY	mayoralties
AAEHHIILMOP	haemophilia	AAEIILMRSTT	materialist	AAEILNNOPST	neapolitans
AAEHHIKNRRS	Hare Krishna	AAEIILMRTTY	materiality	AAEILNNOPTX	explanation
AAEHHILLLSU	halleluiahs	AAEIILMSSST	assimilates	AAEILNNORTT	alternation
AAEHHILNNPT	naphthaline	AAEIILNNOST	alienations	AAEILNNOSST	sensational
AAEHHJLLLSU	hallelujahs		nationalise	AAEILNPRST	transalpine
AAEHHOPPSST	phosphatase	AAEIILNNOTZ	nationalize	AAEILNNPTTU	antenuptial
AAEHIIKLLNP	Kephallinía	AAEIILNNPST	Palestinian	AAEILNOOPRT	operational

AAEILNOPRRT	proletarian	
AAEILNORSTT	alterations	
AAEILNORSTU	laureations	
AAEILNORSTX	relaxations	
AAEILNORTUV	revaluation	
AAEILNOSTTX	exaltations	
AAEILNOSTUV	evaluations	
AAEILNPRSST	partialness	
AAEILNPRSTT	paternalist	
AAEILNRRSTU	sertularian	
AAEILNRRTVY	narratively	
AAEILNRSSTT	tantalisers	
AAEILNRSSTU	naturalises	
AAEILNRSTTZ	tantalizers	
AAEILNRSTUZ	naturalizes	
AAEILNRSTVY	antislavery	
AAEILOPRRTT	proletariat	
AAEILOQRSTU	quaestorial	
AAEILORRSTT	retaliators	
AAEILORRTTY	retaliatory	
AAEILORSSSS	assessorial	
AAEIMMOOPST	Mesopotamia	
AAEIMNNOSSY	mayonnaises	
AAEIMNNRSTU	transmarine	
AAEIMNNRSTT	Sint Maarten	
AAEIMNNSTTT	attainments	
AAEIMNORSST	anatomisers	
AAEIMNORSTZ	anatomizers	
AAEIMNQSSTU	antimasques	
AAEIMOOPRSZ	azoospermia	
AAEIMOOTTUX	autotoxemia	
AAEIMOPPRTX	approximate	
AAEIMOSSTTU	automatises	
AAEIMOSTTUZ	automatizes	
AAEIMQRSSTU	marquisates	
AAEIMRSSTTU	traumatises	
AAEIMRSTTUZ	traumatizes	
AAEINNNOSTX	annexations	
AAEINNOPRTT	trepanation	
AAEINNOSSTT	assentation	
AAEINNOTTTU	attenuation	
AAEINNQRSTU	quarantines	
AAEINNRRSVY	anniversary	
AAEINOOPRTV	evaporation	
AAEINOORSTT	aerostation	
AAEINOPPRRT	preparation	
AAEINOPRRST	praetorians	
	reparations	
AAEINOPRSST	separations	
AAEINORRSTT	arrestation	
AAEINORSSTU	Austronesia	
AAEINOSTTTT	attestation	
AAEIOPPPRRT	appropriate	
AAEIOPPRRSS	appressoria	
AAEIOPRRSST	raspatories	
AAEIOPRSTTX	expatiators	
AAEIOPSSSTT	apostasises	
AAEIOPSSTTZ	apostazizes	
AAEIORSSTTV	aestivators	
	assortative	
AAEIPRSSSTT	separatists	
AAEIPRSSSTU	East Prussia	

AAEKKNOPRSU	Sukarno Peak	
AAEKMRSSSTT	taskmasters	
AAELLLNNOPR	nonparallel	
AAELLLORSST	saltarellos	
AAELLMMORRY	marmoreally	
AAELLMNORUY	malonylurea	
AAELLORRSTT	stellarator	
AAELLRSSTTT	Tattersall's	
AAELMNNORST	ornamentals	
AAELMNSSTTY	statesmanly	
AAELMORSSSU	elasmosaurs	
AAELNNNOOSS	nonseasonal	
AAELNNRSSTU	naturalness	
AAELNOOPPRS	aplanospore	
AAELNOPRTXY	explanatory	
AAELNORRSST	alternators	
AAELNRRSSTV	transversal	
AAELNRRSSTW	warrantless	
AAELNRRSSTU	transvaluer	
AAELNRSSTUV	transvalues	
AAELNRSSTUX	transexuals	
	transsexual	
AAELOOPSSTT	apostolates	
AAELOORRTVY	laevorotary	
AAELORRSTTV	travelators	
AAELPRRSSTU	superaltars	
AAELPRRSTTT	rattletraps	
AAEMNNORSTT	tramontanes	
AAEMNOOPRTT	protonemata	
AAEMNOOSSST	anastomoses	
AAEMNOPRTTU	portmanteau	
AAEMNOSSTTW	stateswoman	
AAEMOOPRSTZ	spermatozoa	
AAEMORSSTTT	toastmaster	
AAENNPPRTTU	appurtenant	
AAENNPRRSTT	transparent	
AAENNPRSTTU	supernatant	
AAENORSTTTU	attenuators	
AAENOQRRSTUW	quartersawn	
AAENRRSSTTU	restaurants	
AAEOOPRRSTV	evaporators	
AAEOPPRRRTY	preparatory	
AAEOPRSSTTU	stratopause	
AAEORSSTTTT	attestators	
AAEPRRSSTTU	superstrata	
AAEQRRSSTUW	quartersaws	
AAFFGIIILNT	affiliating	
AAFFGIMNRSU	ragamuffins	
AAFFIIILNOT	affiliation	
AAFFIIMNORT	affirmation	
AAFFIINOSTX	affixations	
AAFGHIKLRUU	Hauraki Gulf	
AAFGIIKLLNY	alkalifying	
AAFGIINNPRS	frangipanis	
AAFGIINNSST	fantasising	
AAFGIINNSTZ	fantasizing	
AAFGIINNTTU	infatuating	
AAFGILLMRUV	gallimaufry	
AAFGILNOSTT	stagflation	
AAFGINORRSU	farraginous	
AAFHIINOSST	fashionista	
AAFIIILMRTY	familiarity	

AAFIINNOTTU	infatuation	
AAFIINRRSTU	fruitarians	
AAFILMNOORT	formational	
AAFILNOOSTT	floatations	
AAFIMNNORTY	infantryman	
AAFINNOOPRT	profanation	
AAFLNNOORST	nasofrontal	
AAFNOOPRRTY	profanatory	
AAFOPRRRSTW	sparrowfart	
AAGGHHIINNS	shanghaiing	
AAGGHHIOPRV	hagiography	
AAGGHIIJMNT	thingamajig	
AAGGHINOPRY	angiography	
AAGGIIJNNOX	Gao Xingjian	
AAGGIILNNOS	analogising	
AAGGIILNNOZ	analogizing	
AAGGIILNNSV	galvanising	
AAGGIILNNTV	galivanting	
AAGGIILNNVZ	galvanizing	
AAGGIIMMNNS	mismanaging	
AAGGIIMNNRT	marginating	
AAGGIINRSTV	stravaiging	
AAGGIINRTTV	gravitating	
AAGGIKLMNSS	glassmaking	
AAGGIKNNOOR	kangarooing	
AAGGILLMORR	gorillagram	
AAGGILLNOST	algolagnist	
AAGGILMNNUL	mangulating	
AAGGILNNNUY	Lianyungang	
AAGGILNNRTU	granulating	
AAGGILNNTTU	agglutinant	
AAGGILNRTTU	gratulating	
AAGGINNRTUY	guarantying	
AAGGINOPPRT	propagating	
AAGGLLLOSSW	gallowglass	
AAGHHLOPPRY	haplography	
AAGHIILLNOP	anglophilia	
AAGHIJKNOUZ	Zhangjiakou	
AAGHIKLLMNR	hallmarking	
AAGHIKMNOTW	tomahawking	
AAGHILLMNPY	lymphangial	
AAGHILLMNRS	marshalling	
AAGHILNPSST	phalangists	
AAGHIMNRSST	stramashing	
AAGHIOPRSTY	hypogastria	
AAGHIRSTTWY	straightway	
AAGHLNOOTTY	thanatology	
AAGHLNOPPRY	planography	
AAGHLOOPPRR	polarograph	
AAGHMMMOPRS	mammographs	
AAGHMMMOPRY	mammography	
AAGHMRTTUUY	thaumaturgy	
AAGHNOPPRST	pantographs	
AAGHNOPPRTY	pantography	
AAGHNOPRRUY	uranography	
AAGIIILMNNS	animalising	
AAGIIILMNNZ	animalizing	
AAGIIILMNRY	imaginarily	
AAGIIIMNNNT	maintaining	
AAGIIIMNNOT	imagination	
AAGIIKNNPST	painstaking	
AAGIILLLNWW	Wailing Wall	

AAGIILMNORT	migrational
AAGIILMNRTY	marginality
AAGIILMPRSS	plagiarisms
AAGIILNNNSU	annualising
AAGIILNNNUZ	annualizing
AAGIILNNSTT	tantalising
AAGIILNNTTZ	tantalizing
AAGIILNORTV	variolating
AAGIILNPPTT	palpitating
AAGIILNSSSV	vassalising
AAGIILNSSVZ	vassalizing
AAGIILOPRRT	Gloria Patri
AAGIILPRSST	plagiarists
AAGIIMMNNOT	ammoniating
AAGIIMMNNTY	magnanimity
AAGIIMMSSTT	astigmatism
AAGIIMNNORT	margination
AAGIIMNNOST	anatomising
AAGIIMNNOTZ	anatomizing
AAGIIMNORST	aromatising
AAGIIMNORTZ	aromatizing
AAGIIMSSSSU	Mississauga
AAGIINNOPST	paginations
AAGIINNORSS	anagnorisis
AAGIINNOSST	assignation
AAGIINNOSTV	navigations
AAGIINNQTTU	antiquating
	aquatinting
AAGIINNSTUU	Augustinian
AAGIINORTTV	gravitation
AAGIINPPTTT	pitapatting
AAGIINPSSTV	passivating
AAGIINRRSTT	tartarising
AAGIINRRTTZ	tartarizing
AAGIIRSSTTU	Sagittarius
AAGILLLNPPY	appallingly
AAGILLLOOSS	glossolalia
AAGILLMNNTY	malignantly
AAGILLMOORY	malariology
AAGILMMMOST	mammalogist
AAGILMOPRSS	paralogisms
AAGILNNORTU	granulation
AAGILNNOSTU	angulations
AAGILNNPPUU	Pulau Pinang
AAGILNNRSTT	translating
AAGILNOPSTY	angioplasty
AAGILNORTTU	gratulation
AAGILNOSUVY	Yugoslavian
AAGILNRRTUY	granularity
AAGILOPRRTU	purgatorial
AAGILOPRSST	paralogists
AAGILORSUVY	vagariously
AAGIMMNNOSU	magnanimous
AAGIMMNNOST	antagonisms
AAGIMNOOSSU	anisogamous
AAGIMNOOSTU	angiomatous
AAGIMNSSSTY	gymnasiasts
AAGIMPRSSTT	pragmatists
AAGINNOSSTT	antagonists
AAGINOOPPRT	propagation
AAGINOOORRST	arrogations
AAGINORRTUU	inaugurator

AAGLLMNRTUU	multangular
AAGLLNOOSUY	analogously
AAGLLNOPSTT	topgallants
AAGLMOOPRRS	polarograms
AAGLNORRSTU	granulators
AAGLOOPRTXY	protogalaxy
AAGLORRTTUY	gratulatory
AAGOOPPRRST	propagators
AAHHHKLLLMO	Holkham Hall
AAHHIIKOSWW	kowhaiwhais
AAHHILMOPTY	hypothalami
AAHHILMPRSS	marshalship
AAHIIJNNOOU	Haji-Ioannou
AAHIILNNORT	annihilator
AAHIILNNOST	inhalations
AAHIINPRSST	antiphrasis
AAHIKKLNOSV	kalashnikov
AAHILLLOPRT	prothallial
AAHILLMTUVZ	azimuthally
AAHILLOPSTT	allopathist
AAHILMOPSTY	syphilomata
AAHILMPRSTY	amphistylar
AAHILMSTTUZ	altazimuths
AAHILNNOPST	antiphonals
AAHIMMNNOPY	nymphomania
AAHIMMNNOPRS	anamorphism
AAHIMNOPRSS	oarsmanship
AAHIMNOSSTT	Saint Thomas
AAHINNOPRTY	antiphonary
AAHINNOSTTX	xanthations
AAHINOPSSTT	thanatopsis
AAHINPSSTXY	asphyxiants
AAHIOPRSTXY	asphyxiator
AAHKOPRRSWW	sparrowhawk
AAHKOPSTUUW	pohutukawas
AAHLLMMORSW	marshmallow
AAHMNNRSTTU	transhumant
AAHNNOPRSXY	nasopharynx
AAHNNRSSTUY	thysanurans
AAHNOPRSTTU	naturopaths
AAHNOPRTTUY	naturopathy
AAIIIIKMORS	Makarios III
AAIIIILMMNX	Maximilian I
AAIIILMNOTT	imitational
AAIIILMNRST	limitarians
AAIIILNRTTU	utilitarian
AAIIILNSSTW	Stanisław II
AAIIIMNNNOT	inanimation
AAIIINNRRTT	trinitarian
AAIIJKLMNOR	Kilimanjaro
AAIIKNNOSTY	kyanisation
AAIIKNNOTYZ	kyanization
AAIILLMPRTY	impartially
AAIILLNOPST	palliations
AAIILMMNORT	matrimonial
AAIILMNSSTX	maximalists
AAIILMNNOPR	paralimnion
AAIILMNNOST	antimonials
	laminations
	nationalism
AAIILMNNOTV	nominatival
AAIILMNOPRT	patrimonial

AAIILMNOPST	maintopsail
AAIILMNORST	rationalism
AAIILMORSST	assimilator
AAIILMRSSTT	martialists
AAIILNNOSTT	nationalist
AAIILNNOTTY	nationality
AAIILNOORTV	variolation
AAIILNOPPTT	palpitation
AAIILNORSTT	rationalist
AAIILNORTTT	attritional
AAIILNORTTY	rationality
AAIILNOSTTU	situational
AAIIMMMNORY	Yamim
	Nora'im
AAIIMMNNOOT	ammoniation
AAIIMMNNOSTX	maximations
AAIIMMNNOST	antinomians
AAIIMNNORST	marinations
	Mastroianni
AAIIMNNRSTT	Saint Martin
AAIIMNOOSTT	atomisation
AAIIMNOOTTZ	atomization
AAIIMNOPRTT	impartation
AAIIMNOPSTT	impastation
AAIIMNRSSTU	sanitariums
AAIINOPPRST	apparitions
AAIINOPRSST	aspirations
AAIKLLMMNUZ	Nizam al-Mulk
AAIKLLNOSTY	alkylations
AAILLLOSTWW	swallowtail
AAILLLPSSTU	pulsatillas
AAILLMNTTUY	matutinally
AAILLNNSSTT	installants
AAILLNOPSST	spallations
AAILLOOPRYZ	polyzoarial
AAILLORRSTY	sartorially
AAILMMNOSTU	summational
AAILMMOPPRS	malapropism
AAILMNOPRTU	manipulator
AAILMNRSTTT	transmittal
AAILMOPRSST	pastoralism
AAILNNNOOOT	nonnational
AAILNNNOORT	nonrational
AAILNNNOSTU	annulations
AAILNNOPSTT	plantations
AAILNNORSTT	translation
AAILNOSSTTU	salutations
AAILNRSSTTU	naturalists
AAILOORSTTT	totalisator
AAILOORTTTZ	totalizator
AAILOPRSSTT	pastoralist
AAIMMNOPSTT	maintopmast
AAIMMNOSSUY	immunoassay
AAIMMRSSTTU	traumatisms
AAIMNOOOSTT	somatotonia
AAIMNOOSSST	anastomosis
AAIMNOPSTTU	amputations
AAIMNOQSSTU	squamations
AAIMNORSSTU	sanatoriums
AAIMNORSTTU	maturations
	natatoriums

AAIMNPRRTTU	intrapartum
AAIMOSSTTTU	automatists
AAINNNNOOSTT	annotations
AAINNNNOPRST	nonpartisan
AAINNNOPRTZ	nonpartizan
AAINNOOQRTU	Quintana Roo
AAINNOPRSTT	patron saint
AAINOORRSTZ	Zoroastrian
AAINORRSTTU	instaurator
AAINORSSTTU	titanosaurs
AAINPSSTTWY	pantywaists
AAKKNORRSSY	Krasnoyarsk
AAKLLMPRUUU	Kuala Lumpur
AAKLNORSSUV	ankylosaurs
AAKLORRVVVY	Karlovy Vary
AALLMNOOSUV	anomalously
AALLNNRTUUV	unnaturally
AALMMOOPSST	somatoplasm
AALMNNOPSTW	plantswoman
AALMNOPRTUV	paramountly
AALNNPRSSTT	transplants
AALNNRRSTUV	translunary
AALNOOPSUZZ	pozzuolanas
AALNOPRSSST	transposals
AALNORRSSTT	translators
AALOORRSTTV	travolators
AALORSSTTTU	altostratus
AAMNPRSSTTY	smartypants
AANNORRSTUV	tyrannosaur
ABBBEELMNST	babblements
ABBBENORUWY	Woburn Abbey
ABBCCEEHKNR	backbencher
ABBCCEEHMOR	beachcomber
ABBCCEKKLOR	backblocker
ABBCCGIKMNO	backcombing
ABBCDDEIKLR	blackbirded
ABBCDEEFIKO	biofeedback
ABBCDEEHMRS	bedchambers
ABBCDEEILRS	describable
ABBCDEENRSS	crabbedness
ABBCDEMRRSU	breadcrumbs
ABBCDKLOORS	blockboards
ABBCEEEKNRU	Beckenbauer
ABBCEEIMORR	Abercrombie
ABBCEEJLSTU	subjectable
ABBCEHIILOT	bibliotheca
ABBCEHIOPRY	cyberphobia
ABBCEHNRSSU	subbranches
ABBCEIILNRS	inscribable
ABBCEJKORWY	jabberwocky
ABBCGIKNNRU	backburning
ABBCIIINRST	rabbinistic
ABBCIILLTUY	clubability
ABBCIILMNOY	bibliomancy
ABBCKNNNORU	Bannockburn
ABBDDEGIORR	bridgeboard
ABBDDEIINRR	birdbrained
ABBDEELORTU	redoubtable
ABBDEGNNRRU	Brandenburg
ABBDEIILNTU	indubitable
ABBDEILRSSU	disbursable

ABBDEIMORRS	bombardiers
ABBDELLNRSU	landlubbers
ABBDELNOTUU	undoubtable
ABBDELORTUY	redoubtably
ABBDEMMNORT	bombardment
ABBDHIINORZ	Birobidzhan
ABBDIILNTUY	indubitably
ABBEEEILRRS	blaeberries
ABBEEEINRRS	baneberries
ABBEEEIRRRS	bearberries
ABBEEKOORRV	Beaverbrook
ABBEELPRRTU	perturbable
ABBEELSSTTU	battlebuses
ABBEEMNSSTU	subbasement
ABBEENORSST	breastbones
ABBEENRRSSU	baseburners
ABBEEORRSTW	browbeaters
ABBEGILNORU	belabouring
ABBEGINORRS	reabsorbing
ABBEGINORTW	browbeating
ABBEHIIILNT	inhibitable
ABBEHILLPSU	publishable
ABBEHILNRSU	burnishable
ABBEHOPRRSS	barbershops
ABBEIILLMOS	mobilisable
ABBEIILLMOZ	mobilizable
ABBEIKRRSTT	bitterbarks
ABBEILMSTTU	submittable
ABBEILNOSTU	obnubilates
ABBEINRSSUU	suburbanise
ABBEINRSSUU	suburbanist
ABBEINRSUUZ	suburbanize
ABBELLRSTTU	butterballs
ABBELMOORSZ	bamboozlers
ABBELMSSSUY	subassembly
ABBELPRRTUY	perturbably
ABBFFIILMSU	bumbailiffs
ABBFFILLLOU	Buffalo Bill
ABBFILORSST	fibroblasts
ABBGHHINSSU	bushbashing
ABBGHIMNOTU	thingumabob
ABBGIILMNOT	bombilating
ABBGIIMNNOT	bombinating
ABBGILMNOOZ	bamboozling
ABBGILNORSY	absorbingly
ABBGLMOORRY	borborygmal
ABBHILLMOSY	Bombay Hills
ABBIILLORTY	bibliolatry
ABBIILMOPRS	probabilism
ABBIILOPRST	probabilist
ABBIILOPRTY	probability
ABBIIMNNOOT	bombination
ABBLLNOSTTU	buttonballs
ABCCCCILORY	carbocyclic
ABCCCHKKLOO	chockablock
ABCCDDHIIKY	chickabiddy
ABCCDEEELSU	succeedable
ABCCDEEENRU	buccaneered
ABCCDEEIIRT	bactericide
ABCCDEHHKNU	hunchbacked
ABCCDEKKOOR	crookbacked
ABCCDEKORSS	backcrossed

ABCCDHHORRU	Broad Church
ABCCEEEELLRY	recycleable
ABCCEEEILNOV	conceivable
ABCCEEELLLOT	collectable
ABCCEELNNOT	connectable
ABCCEELORRT	correctable
ABCCEEMNNRU	encumbrance
ABCCEFILNOS	confiscable
ABCCEFIORSU	bacciferous
ABCCEGINNOU	concubinage
ABCCEHIILMO	biochemical
ABCCEHINRTT	tectibranch
ABCCEHKRSTT	backstretch
ABCCEIILLNO	conciliable
ABCCEIILNOT	cenobitical
ABCCEIILPTY	peccability
ABCCEIKKLST	stickleback
ABCCEIKLNPR	Black Prince
ABCCEILNOTV	convictable
ABCCEILNOVY	conceivably
ABCCEILNSSU	cubicalness
ABCCEILOSTT	ectoblastic
ABCCEIMNNRU	incumbrance
ABCCEIMOORS	mobocracies
ABCCEINORRT	centrobaric
ABCCEINRRTY	barycentric
ABCCEKLOOST	cockleboats
ABCCEKNORRS	cornerbacks
ABCCEKORSSS	backcrosses
ABCCELOOSST	tobaccoless
ABCCELORSUU	succourable
ABCCHIKSSTW	switchbacks
ABCCIILLNSU	subclinical
ABCCIILRSTU	subcritical
ABCCIIMOORT	macrobiotic
ABCCIINOTVY	biconcavity
ABCCILLLOUY	bucolically
ABCCILORSTU	subcortical
ABCCINNORUY	concubinary
ABCCINOOSTT	tobacconist
ABCCINORSTU	buccinators
ABCCIOORSUV	baccivorous
ABCCKNORTUY	backcountry
ABCCNORSTTU	subcontract
ABCDDEEELNS	descendable
ABCDDEEHHKLO	blockheaded
ABCDDEEHLUY	debauchedly
ABCDDEELMRS	descrambled
ABCDDEFIKLS	fiddlebacks
ABCDDEFINOR	forbiddance
ABCDDEHINRS	disbranched
ABCDDEIKLNS	backslidden
ABCDDEINOOT	bandicooted
ABCDDEKLORS	badderlocks
ABCDEEEERRT	decerebrate
ABCDEEEHORS	cheeseboard
ABCDEEEILPR	depreciable
ABCDEEGGKLL	blacklegged
ABCDEEHMNTU	debauchment
ABCDEEIILMM	immedicable
ABCDEEEILNRS	discernable
	rescindable

ABCDEEILNTU binucleated	**ABCDIILLSSY** dissyllabic	**ABCEEINORST** baronetcies
ABCDEEILORV divorceable	**ABCDIILORUV** vibraculoid	**ABCEEINORTX** exorbitance
ABCDEEILPRS predicables	**ABCDIILOSSY** dissociably	**ABCEEINRRRS** cranberries
ABCDEEILPRT predictable	**ABCDIIMNOSY** biodynamics	**ABCEEJKLSTU** bluejackets
ABCDEEINORS decarbonise	**ABCDILNOSST** cnidoblasts	**ABCEEKRSSTT** backstreets
ABCDEEINORZ decarbonize	**ABCEEEFLNOR** enforceable	**ABCEELLLMOP** compellable
ABCDEEIRRSU decarburise	**ABCEEEGKNRR** greenbacker	**ABCEELLNOSU** counselable
ABCDEEIRRUZ decarburize	**ABCEEEIKRRS** icebreakers	**ABCEELLOOST** blastocoele
ABCDEEKLRSV backvelders	**ABCEEEILPRV** perceivable	**ABCEELMNOPS** compensable
ABCDEELLPRU precludable	**ABCEEEILPTT** battlepiece	**ABCEELNOQRU** conquerable
ABCDEELMMNO commendable	**ABCEEEILRSV** receivables	**ABCEELNORSV** conservable
ABCDEELMMNO condemnable	serviceable	conversable
ABCDEELMRRS descrambler	**ABCEEEILRSX** exercisable	**ABCEELNOSTT** contestable
ABCDEELMRSS descrambles	**ABCEEEILRTV** celebrative	**ABCEELNRSSU** curableness
ABCDEELNNOS condensable	**ABCEEEIMRRS** embraceries	**ABCEELORRST** celebrators
ABCDEELNRRY candleberry	**ABCEEELLNTU** unelectable	**ABCEELORRTY** celebratory
ABCDEENORRT centreboard	**ABCEEELMNRS** resemblance	**ABCEELOSTUU** betulaceous
ABCDEERRTTU carburetted	**ABCEEELORRV** recoverable	**ABCEELPRSTY** respectably
ABCDEFILORS Frescobaldi	**ABCEEELPRST** respectable	**ABCEELRTTUU** tuberculate
ABCDEGGIKPY piggybacked	**ABCEEEMMNRR** remembrance	**ABCEEMOOSTY** amoebocytes
ABCDEGLNOOT conglobated	**ABCEEEMMNRT** embracement	**ABCEENORRST** arborescent
ABCDEHHKSUW bushwhacked	**ABCEEENRSUX** exuberances	**ABCEENORSSV** observances
ABCDEHIILLN chilblained	**ABCEEFIILPS** specifiable	**ABCEENORSTT** carbonettes
ABCDEHILSTW switchblade	**ABCEEFIILRT** certifiable	**ABCEENRRSTY** barycentres
ABCDEHINRSS disbranches	rectifiable	**ABCEERRRTTU** carburetter
ABCDEHIRRTW birdwatcher	**ABCEEFIINRY** beneficiary	**ABCEFHIKLSS** blackfishes
ABCDEHORSSS chessboards	**ABCEEFILNNO** confineable	**ABCEFHNOOPR** francophobe
ABCDEIILMMY immedicably	**ABCEEFINNOT** benefaction	**ABCEFIILLNT** inflictable
ABCDEIILOSS dissociable	**ABCEEFINRTU** rubefacient	**ABCEFIILRTY** certifiably
ABCDEIILTUV educability	**ABCEEFLNORR** conferrable	**ABCEFILMNOR** confirmable
ABCDEIIPSTU bicuspidate	**ABCEEFLNOSS** confessable	**ABCEFINORTU** rubefaction
ABCDEIKLLST blacklisted	**ABCEEFNORST** benefactors	**ABCEFKLORST** Black Forest
ABCDEIKLRSS backsliders	**ABCEEGIINOT** abiogenetic	**ABCEFLMNOOR** conformable
ABCDEILNOST endoblastic	**ABCEEGILNRT** celebrating	**ABCEFLMOORT** comfortable
ABCDEILNRSY discernably	**ABCEEGILOTX** excogitable	**ABCEGHILLNY** bellyaching
ABCDEILORTU orbiculated	**ABCEEGINRRT** cerebrating	**ABCEGIILNOT** incogitable
ABCDEILPRTY predictably	**ABCEEGLNRST** glabrescent	**ABCEGIKNRST** bracketings
ABCDEILSSSU discussable	**ABCEEHHILRS** cherishable	**ABCEGILLNRS** sacring bell
ABCDEILSSTU subdialects	**ABCEEHIKRRS** hackberries	**ABCEGILNNOS** consignable
ABCDEINRRST transcribed	**ABCEEHILNRS** hibernacles	**ABCEGILNOST** blastogenic
ABCDEINRSTU disturbance	**ABCEEHINNRS** Sennacherib	**ABCEGIMNORT** embrocating
ABCDEINSSSU subacidness	**ABCEEHKRSTU** hackbuteers	**ABCEGINNRTY** cybernating
ABCDEIPRRSS crispbreads	**ABCEEHLLRSY** bellyachers	**ABCEGINORST** obsecrating
ABCDEKOPPST backstopped	**ABCEEHLORTU** retouchable	**ABCEGLNOOST** conglobates
ABCDELMMNOY commendably	**ABCEEHLRSTT** stretchable	**ABCEGORSTUY** subcategory
ABCDELMNNOY condemnably	**ABCEEHNORRS** abhorrences	**ABCEHHIOOPT** theophobiac
ABCDELMNRSU unscrambled	**ABCEEHORRRT** torchbearer	**ABCEHHIOPPT** taphephobic
ABCDELMNRUU Cumbernauld	**ABCEEIILNSV** bivalencies	**ABCEHHKORSV** Shcherbakov
ABCDEOORRSS scoreboards	**ABCEEIKLNRS** linebackers	**ABCEHHKRSUW** bushwhacker
ABCDGIIKLNS backsliding	**ABCEEILLNRT** ineluctable	**ABCEHHMOORT** bathochrome
ABCDGKNORSU backgrounds	**ABCEEILNORT** celebration	**ABCEHIILPRT** blepharitic
ABCDHIIMRTY dithyrambic	**ABCEEILNPST** inspectable	**ABCEHIKLNSY** Chelyabinsk
ABCDHIIRSTU hudibrastic	**ABCEEILNSUX** inexcusable	**ABCEHIKRRST** brickearths
ABCDHINNRSU nudibranchs	**ABCEEILORRV** irrevocable	**ABCEHILOPSU** bicephalous
ABCDHINOOPR branchiopod	**ABCEEILPRVY** perceivably	**ABCEHILPRST** birthplaces
ABCDHIOOPRS brachiopods	**ABCEEILRRSU** irrecusable	**ABCEHIMORST** bichromates
ABCDHIORSTW switchboard	**ABCEEILRRTT** retractible	**ABCEHIMORTT** bathometric
ABCDHLOORST broadcloths	**ABCEEILRRTU** recruitable	**ABCEHIMRTTY** bathymetric
ABCDHNOORRY hydrocarbon	**ABCEEILRSVY** serviceably	**ABCEHINNRRT** interbranch
ABCDHNOORTY brachyodont	**ABCEEIMRTUU** eubacterium	**ABCEHINOOPR** necrophobia
ABCDHNOPRSU punchboards	**ABCEEINNRTY** bicentenary	**ABCEHKLNOSU** unshockable
ABCDIIILOST idioblastic	**ABCEEINORRT** cerebration	**ABCEHKLOSVY** Lobachevsky

ABCEHKRSTTU	hackbutters	**ABCELLNOSTU**	consultable	**ABCHIILOPSY**	biophysical
ABCEHLLOSTT	tablecloths	**ABCELLNSSTU**	Sanctus bell	**ABCHIKLMSST**	blacksmiths
ABCEHLNOTUU	untouchable	**ABCELLOOSST**	blastocoels	**ABCHILLNORY**	bronchially
ABCEHPRSSTU	subchapters	**ABCELLOOSTU**	leucoblasts	**ABCHILLOOST**	holoblastic
ABCEHRSSTTU	bruschettas	**ABCELMNOSSU**	consumables	**ABCHILMOOST**	homoblastic
ABCEIIILLSV	civilisable	**ABCELMNRRSU**	unscrambler	**ABCHILNOORR**	bronchiolar
ABCEIIILLVZ	civilizable	**ABCELMNRSSU**	unscrambles	**ABCHILOPSTY**	hypoblastic
ABCEIIJLSTU	justiciable	**ABCELMOOPST**	compostable	**ABCHIMNORSU**	subharmonic
ABCEIILMRTY	imbricately	**ABCELNNOTUU**	uncountable	**ABCHINOOPTY**	nyctophobia
ABCEIILNOTX	intoxicable	**ABCELNOORST**	consortable	**ABCHINORRSY**	chrysarobin
ABCEIILRTUV	lubricative	**ABCELNORRSY**	barleycorns	**ABCHIOOPRST**	astrophobic
ABCEIIMNOTV	combinative	**ABCELNORSTU**	construable	**ABCHKLNORST**	blackthorns
ABCEIINOSST	obstinacies	**ABCELNORSVY**	conversably	**ABCIIILOSTY**	sociability
ABCEIINRSTU	Saint-Brieuc	**ABCELNOSTTY**	contestably	**ABCIIILRSTT**	tribalistic
ABCEIIORSST	aerobicists	**ABCELNPRTUU**	puncturable	**ABCIIIMNORT**	imbrication
ABCEIKKSSTY	stickybeaks	**ABCELRRSTUU**	tuberculars	**ABCIIINOSTT**	antibiotics
ABCEIKLRRSY	bricklayers	**ABCEMOOPRST**	amboceptors	**ABCIIKLNRSY**	brainsickly
ABCEIKLRSSV	silverbacks	**ABCEOOORRRT**	corroborate	**ABCIILLLMUY**	umbilically
ABCEIKNORTW	cabinetwork	**ABCEOOPRRST**	baroceptors	**ABCIILLMRSU**	lumbricalis
ABCEILLLOPS	collapsible	**ABCEORRRSTU**	carburetors	**ABCIILLPTUY**	culpability
ABCEILLMORU	bimolecular	**ABCEORRRTTU**	carburettor	**ABCIILLRSTY**	trisyllabic
ABCEILLMRSU	lumbricales	**ABCEORSTUUY**	butyraceous	**ABCIILMOSTY**	symbiotical
ABCEILLNOOS	colonisable	**ABCERRSSTTU**	subtracters	**ABCIILNOPTU**	publication
ABCEILLNOOZ	colonizable	**ABCFGIIKLLN**	backfilling	**ABCIILNORTU**	lubrication
ABCEILLNRSS	cranesbills	**ABCFGIINRTU**	bifurcating	**ABCIIMNNOOT**	combination
ABCEILLNTUY	ineluctably	**ABCFGINOSTU**	obfuscating	**ABCIINNOSTU**	incubations
ABCEILMMOTT	committable	**ABCFHINOOST**	sonofabitch	**ABCIINORRTU**	rubrication
ABCEILMOPRS	comprisable	**ABCFIILLMOR**	bacilliform	**ABCIINORSTT**	abstriction
ABCEILMOPRT	problematic	**ABCFIINORTU**	bifurcation	**ABCIKLLMMSU**	Black Muslim
ABCEILMORST	blastomeric	**ABCFILSSSUY**	subclassify	**ABCILLNNOUY**	connubially
	meroblastic	**ABCFINOOSTU**	obfuscation	**ABCILLORRUY**	orbicularly
ABCEILMOSST	mesoblastic	**ABCFLMNOORY**	conformably	**ABCILLOSSUY**	subsocially
ABCEILMOTVY	combatively	**ABCFLMOORTY**	comfortably	**ABCILMMORUU**	columbarium
ABCEILMSSUX	subclimaxes	**ABCFOORSTUY**	obfuscatory	**ABCILMNNUUU**	incunabulum
ABCEILNNOTU	continuable	**ABCGHILLNUU**	clubhauling	**ABCILNORTUU**	lucubration
ABCEILNORTV	contrivable	**ABCGHOORRSU**	Scarborough	**ABCILNRSTUY**	inscrutably
ABCEILNOSTT	entoblastic	**ABCGIIIMNRT**	imbricating	**ABCILOOPRST**	blastoporic
ABCEILNPRSU	republicans	**ABCGIIKLNRY**	bricklaying	**ABCILOPRSTU**	subtropical
ABCEILNRSTU	inscrutable	**ABCGIIKNOUV**	bivouacking	**ABCILORRSTU**	lubricators
ABCEILNSUXY	inexcusably	**ABCGIILLOOS**	biologicals	**ABCIMNOORTY**	combinatory
ABCEILORRVY	irrevocably	**ABCGIILNORS**	carbolising	**ABCIMOPSUVX**	pax vobiscum
ABCEILORSTT	obstetrical	**ABCGIILNORZ**	carbolizing	**ABCINNOORTU**	conurbation
ABCEILRRSUY	irrecusably	**ABCGIILNRTU**	lubricating	**ABCINOORSTU**	obscuration
ABCEILRSSTU	subarticles	**ABCGIINNORS**	carbonising	**ABCINORSTTU**	subtraction
ABCEIMNNORT	recombinant	**ABCGIINNORZ**	carbonizing	**ABCIORRRSTU**	rubricators
ABCEIMNOORT	embrocation	**ABCGIINNRSU**	carburising	**ABCKKNOOSTU**	knockabouts
ABCEINNORTY	cybernation	**ABCGIINNRTU**	rubricating	**ABCLLRSTUUU**	subcultural
ABCEINOORST	obsecration	**ABCGIINNRRU**	carburizing	**ABCLORRSTUU**	lucubrators
ABCEINORRSS	carbonisers	**ABCGIKLLNOS**	ballocksing	**ABCLOSSSTTY**	blastocysts
ABCEINORRSZ	carbonizers	**ABCGIKLNPRU**	parbuckling	**ABCMNOORSSW**	crossbowman
ABCEINRRRST	transcriber	**ABCGILLOORY**	bryological	**ABCNOOORRRT**	corroborant
ABCEINRRSST	transcribes	**ABCGILNRTUU**	lucubrating	**ABCNORRSTUY**	subcontrary
ABCEIOORRRV	Barcoo River	**ABCGILNSSSU**	subclassing	**ABDDDEIMNOR**	broadminded
ABCEIRRRSSU	subcarriers	**ABCGINRSTTU**	subtracting	**ABDDEEEGRRY**	greybearded
ABCEIRSTTUV	subtractive	**ABCHHIILOTT**	batholithic	**ABDDEEEILRT**	deliberated
ABCEJKLMRSU	lumberjacks	**ABCHHILOOOP**	ochlophobia	**ABDDEEEILTY**	baddeleyite
ABCEJLNSTUY	subjacently	**ABCHHIOOPTT**	photobathic	**ABDDEEENSSS**	debasedness
ABCEKKORSST	backstrokes	**ABCHHIOPRSS**	archbishops	**ABDDEEGHILY**	bigheadedly
ABCEKLRSTTU	turtlebacks	**ABCHHLNOOPR**	lophobranch	**ABDDEEGHIRS**	bridgeheads
ABCELLLMNOO	collembolan	**ABCHIIIMOPT**	amphibiotic	**ABDDEEIILLU**	Île du
ABCELLLMOPY	compellably	**ABCHIILNOOT**	halobiontic		Diable
ABCELLNOORS	collarbones	**ABCHIILNRTY**	labyrinthic	**ABDDEEIILTT**	debilitated

ABDDEEEIKMRS	disembarked	
ABDDEELNNRY	Enderby Land	
ABDDEELNORS	bladdernose	
ABDDEGIRRSW	drawbridges	
ABDDEHKLNNU	Bundelkhand	
ABDDEHOOSWX	shadowboxed	
ABDDEIIMRSS	bridesmaids	
ABDDEILLLSS	saddlebills	
ABDDEIMNNST	disbandment	
ABDDELNORRS	borderlands	
ABDDELNRSTU	bladdernuts	
ABDDELORRTW	bladderwort	
ABDDILLORRS	dollarbirds	
ABDDLMOORSU	mouldboards	
ABDDOORRSSW	broadswords	
ABDEEEEGLRU	beleaguered	
ABDEEEFHRST	featherbeds	
ABDEEEFIKNR	Diefenbaker	
ABDEEEGGRSW	beggarweeds	
ABDEEEHHKSS	baksheeshed	
ABDEEEHILRT	hereditable	
ABDEEEILLRV	deliverable	
ABDEEEILRST	deliberates	
ABDEEEINNRSV	aberdevines	
ABDEEELLOPV	developable	
ABDEEELMNRU	denumerable	
ABDEEELMRSS	reassembled	
ABDEEELNPSX	expendables	
ABDEEELNSST	belatedness	
ABDEEELRRSS	redressable	
ABDEEEMNSST	debasements	
ABDEEEPRSTT	bespattered	
ABDEEERSSTW	sweetbreads	
ABDEEFFHLSU	buffleheads	
ABDEEFIILNN	indefinable	
ABDEEFILLTT	battlefield	
ABDEEFILNNU	undefinable	
ABDEEFIORST	afterbodies	
ABDEEGGINRR	gingerbread	
ABDEEGHINRR	harbingered	
ABDEEGIMNRT	abridgement	
ABDEEGINPRS	bespreading	
ABDEEGKNRRS	Drakensberg	
ABDEEGMNOOR	boomeranged	
ABDEEGORRSV	vergeboards	
ABDEEHILLSS	deshabilles	
ABDEEHILPSS	beadleships	
ABDEEHILRRS	halberdiers	
ABDEEHILRTY	hereditably	
ABDEEHILSST	established	
ABDEEHIMRST	timberheads	
ABDEEHIRRSS	shadberries	
ABDEEHIRSTW	breadthwise	
ABDEEHNPRRS	sharpbender	
ABDEEHORSST	broadsheets	
ABDEEIIKLLS	dislikeable	
ABDEEIIILLRS	liberalised	
ABDEEIIILRZ	liberalized	
ABDEEIILRST	detribalise	
ABDEEIILRTZ	detribalize	
ABDEEIILSST	bestialised	
	destabilise	
ABDEEIILSTT	debilitates	
ABDEEIILSTZ	bestialized	
	destabilize	
ABDEEIKNRRW	windbreaker	
ABDEEIKNRSY	Iskander Bey	
ABDEEILLLMS	mislabelled	
ABDEEILMNNO	denominable	
ABDEEILMNST	disablement	
ABDEEILMNSU	albumenised	
ABDEEILMNUZ	albumenized	
ABDEEILMOST	metabolised	
ABDEEILMOTZ	metabolized	
ABDEEILMSSS	disassemble	
ABDEEILNPSS	dispensable	
ABDEEILNRSU	undesirable	
ABDEEILNRTU	unliberated	
ABDEEILNSSU	audibleness	
ABDEEILORRT	deliberator	
ABDEEILORTT	obliterated	
ABDEEINNRRW	breadwinner	
ABDEEIRRSVW	weaverbirds	
ABDEEKORRSY	keyboarders	
	rekeyboards	
ABDEELLLORR	rollerblade	
ABDEELLNOPW	Baden-Powell	
ABDEELLNPRU	plunderable	
ABDEELLOOUW	Belleau Wood	
ABDEELMNOTU	demountable	
ABDEELMNRUY	denumerably	
ABDEELNNRUU	unendurable	
ABDEELNOPRS	ponderables	
ABDEELNORSS	laboredness	
ABDEELNRSSU	durableness	
ABDEELNRSTW	waldsterben	
ABDEELORSTT	battledores	
ABDEELORSTY	destroyable	
ABDEELRSSTT	battledress	
ABDEEOORRSW	swordbearer	
ABDEFGINORR	fingerboard	
ABDEFIILLSY	syllabified	
ABDEFIILLNNY	indefinably	
ABDEFIILNTU	infibulated	
ABDEFIRRSTU	breadfruits	
ABDEGGGILNR	bedraggling	
ABDEGGINRWY	windbaggery	
ABDEGGIRRSU	budgerigars	
ABDEGGLLRUY	bullyragged	
ABDEGHINSSU	subheadings	
ABDEGIILNNS	disenabling	
ABDEGIILSSU	disguisable	
ABDEGIINNRS	brigandines	
ABDEGIINRRS	brigandries	
ABDEGIKNORY	keyboarding	
ABDEGILRRSU	burglarised	
ABDEGILRRUZ	burglarized	
ABDEGIMNRST	abridgments	
ABDEHHMOORR	rhombohedra	
ABDEHIILLSS	dishabilles	
ABDEHIINNTU	uninhabited	
ABDEHINRRSS	brandishers	
ABDEHIORSTW	whiteboards	
ABDEHLNSSSU	husbandless	
ABDEHMOORRT	motherboard	
ABDEHNNRSSTU	subtrahends	
ABDEHOOSSWX	shadowboxes	
ABDEHORRSST	shortbreads	
ABDEHOSSUWY	bawdyhouses	
ABDEIIJLNOS	disjoinable	
ABDEIIILLLST	distillable	
ABDEIIILLTWY	weldability	
ABDEIIILMNOT	indomitable	
ABDEIIMNOST	demibastion	
ABDEIIRSSTU	absurdities	
ABDEIKLNNRU	undrinkable	
ABDEIKORSTY	keyboardist	
ABDEILLLSSY	dissyllable	
	disyllables	
ABDEILLOSSV	dissolvable	
ABDEILMNOPU	impoundable	
ABDEILMNORT	Montbéliard	
ABDEILMNRST	timberlands	
ABDEILMOTTU	tolbutamide	
ABDEILMSSSY	disassembly	
ABDEILNRSUY	undesirably	
ABDEILNSSUY	unbiassedly	
ABDEILOPRSV	disprovable	
ABDEILOPSSS	disposables	
ABDEILRSTTW	wattlebirds	
ABDEIMNRSST	disbarments	
ABDEIMNSSTU	submediants	
ABDEIMRRSTY	timberyards	
ABDEIMRSTUW	dumbwaiters	
ABDEINNOSST	Donets Basin	
ABDEINORSTU	subordinate	
ABDEJKLLNOR	Jodrell Bank	
ABDELLOSTTU	subtotalled	
ABDELMOORST	bloodstream	
ABDELMOORSW	marblewoods	
ABDELMOORSST	blastoderms	
ABDELMRRSUY	lumberyards	
ABDELOOORST	bootloaders	
ABDELOPRRTU	protrudable	
ABDEMNORRST	barnstormed	
ABDENNORSTV	bondservant	
ABDENOORSUV	overabounds	
ABDENOPRSUU	superabound	
ABDFIILNNUU	infundibula	
ABDFILMOORR	dolabriform	
ABDFILNORSU	floribundas	
ABDFLOOORRS	floorboards	
ABDGHIILNNS	blandishing	
ABDGHIINNRS	brandishing	
ABDGHIMNOTU	badmouthing	
ABDGIIILNOS	diabolising	
ABDGIIILNOZ	diabolizing	
ABDGIINPRSU	upbraidings	
ABDGINOPRRS	springboard	
ABDGINORRST	stringboard	
ABDGINORSTU	groundbaits	
ABDGMOORRSS	smorgasbord	
ABDHHIOOPRY	hydrophobia	
ABDHIIINOST	adhibitions	
ABDHINRSTUY	unbirthdays	
ABDIIIILLLNY	libidinally	

ABDIIILRTVY	drivability	
ABDIIILTTUY	dutiability	
ABDIILLMOTY	moldability	
ABDIILMNOSU	albuminoids	
ABDIILMNOTY	indomitably	
ABDIILORRST	tailorbirds	
ABDIINOSTUU	subaudition	
ABDILNOOSST	bloodstains	
ABDIMNNOSTU	subdominant	
ABDINORRSUY	subordinary	
ABDLNOOOSTT	odontoblast	
ABDNOORSTUU	roundabouts	
ABDOORRSSTY	storyboards	
ABDOORRSTUU	troubadours	
ABEEEEFLORS	foreseeable	
ABEEEEGLNRR	regenerable	
ABEEEEMNRTV	bereavement	
ABEEEEERRRTV	reverberate	
ABEEEGILRRS	bersagliere	
ABEEEGLRRTT	regrettable	
ABEEEEHHINPR	hebephrenia	
ABEEEHHKSSS	baksheeshes	
ABEEEEHINRST	abernethies	
ABEEEHMNRRV	Bremerhaven	
ABEEEHQRSTU	bequeathers	
ABEEEHRSSTT	hartebeests	
ABEEEIKRRST	tiebreakers	
ABEEEEILLPRV	repleviable	
ABEEEEILMMPR	impermeable	
ABEEEILMMST	emblematise	
ABEEEEILMMTZ	emblematize	
ABEEEEILPRRV	reprievable	
ABEEEEILRRTV	retrievable	
ABEEEIMNSST	absenteeism	
ABEEEINRRSS	naseberries	
ABEEEINSTUV	Sainte-Beuve	
ABEEEJMNNNT	enjambement	
ABEEELMNNSU	enableness	
ABEEELMNNTT	entablement	
ABEEELMNRRU	remunerable	
ABEEELMRSSS	reassembles	
ABEEELNNSST	tenableness	
ABEEELNPRSS	Bernese Alps	
ABEEELNPRST	presentable	
ABEEELNPRTV	preventable	
ABEEELNQSSU	equableness	
ABEEELNSSSU	useableness	
ABEEELPRRSV	preservable	
ABEEENNRSTT	bannerettes	
ABEEENRRRTV	reverberant	
ABEEEORSSTT	stereobates	
ABEEERRSTTV	vertebrates	
ABEEFFILORT	forfeitable	
ABEEFGILNRR	refrangible	
ABEEFGLORTT	forgettable	
ABEEFIILLQU	liquefiable	
ABEEFIILNRT	antifebrile	
ABEEFIIRSTU	beautifiers	
ABEEFILNNSS	finableness	
ABEEFILNRSS	friableness	
ABEEFILPRTU	putrefiable	

ABEEFILRRTU	irrefutable	
ABEEFLLNSSU	balefulness	
ABEEFLMOPRR	performable	
ABEEFLNNSSU	banefulness	
ABEEFNRRRTU	afterburner	
ABEEGHINQTU	bequeathing	
ABEEGHNORSU	haubergeons	
ABEEGIILLRT	belligerati	
ABEEGIILNRT	libertinage	
ABEEGIILRRS	bersaglieri	
ABEEGIINOSS	abiogenesis	
ABEEGIKMNRR	reembarking	
ABEEGILLLNR	relabelling	
ABEEGILMNPR	impregnable	
ABEEGILNRUZ	gaberlunzie	
ABEEGIILRRST	registrable	
ABEEGINORRV	overbearing	
ABEEGINORST	bioreagents	
ABEEGINRTUX	exuberating	
ABEEGLRRTTY	regrettably	
ABEEGLRSSSU	bluegrasses	
ABEEHHPRSTY	bathysphere	
ABEEHIIILTZ	Elizabeth II	
ABEEHIIILNRT	inheritable	
ABEEHILMPSS	blasphemies	
ABEEHILPRSS	perishables	
ABEEHILRSST	establisher	
	reestablish	
ABEEHILSSST	establishes	
ABEEHILSTUX	exhaustible	
ABEEHIMRSSV	misbehavers	
ABEEHINRSSS	bearishness	
ABEEHINRSST	breathiness	
ABEEHKNORRT	heartbroken	
ABEEHKNORSS	boneshakers	
ABEEHLMPRSS	blasphemers	
ABEEHLNNORR	blennorrhea	
ABEEHLOORRS	seborrhoeal	
ABEEHLORRSU	barrelhouse	
ABEEHLORRWW	wheelbarrow	
ABEEHMORSTT	bathometers	
ABEEHNOPRRY	hyperborean	
ABEEHORSTTU	thereabouts	
ABEEHORSTUW	whereabouts	
ABEEHPRRSSY	baryspheres	
ABEEHQRSSUU	harquebuses	
ABEEIIKKMOR	bokmakierie	
ABEEIILLRRS	liberaliser	
ABEEIILLRRZ	liberalizer	
ABEEIILLRSS	liberalises	
ABEEIILLRSZ	liberalizes	
ABEEIILMNPS	plebeianism	
ABEEIILMNST	inestimable	
ABEEIILMPRV	imperviable	
ABEEIILNQTU	inequitable	
ABEEIILQRTU	equilibrate	
ABEEIILSSST	bestialises	
ABEEIILSSTZ	bestializes	
ABEEIIRRRSZ	bizarreries	
ABEEIKLLNSS	likableness	
ABEEIKLMORR	boilermaker	
ABEEIKLRSTT	Bitter Lakes	

ABEEIKNNRST	barkentines	
ABEEILLMNRS	bellarmines	
ABEEILLMOPT	tempolabile	
ABEEILLNORT	intolerable	
ABEEILLNPSS	pliableness	
ABEEILLNRSS	liberalness	
ABEEILLNSSV	livableness	
ABEEILLOPRT	boilerplate	
ABEEILLOPTX	exploitable	
ABEEILMMORS	memorisable	
ABEEILMMORZ	memorizable	
ABEEILMMOSV	immoveables	
ABEEILMMPRY	impermeably	
ABEEILMNNOT	mentionable	
ABEEILMNNRU	innumerable	
ABEEILLMNSSU	albumenises	
ABEEILMNSUZ	albumenizes	
ABEEILMORRV	irremovable	
ABEEILMOSST	metabolises	
ABEEILMOSTT	metabolites	
ABEEILMOSTZ	metabolizes	
ABEEILNNOPS	pensionable	
ABEEILNPRSU	insuperable	
ABEEILNRRTV	invertebral	
ABEEILNRRST	triableness	
ABEEILNSSST	beastliness	
ABEEILNSSSZ	sizableness	
ABEEILNSSTW	witnessable	
ABEEILORSTT	obliterates	
ABEEILPRSSU	persuasible	
ABEEILRRSSV	verbalisers	
ABEEILRRSVZ	verbalizers	
ABEEILRRTVY	retrievably	
ABEEINNQRTU	barquentine	
ABEEINORSSU	Buenos Aires	
ABEEINRRSSZ	bizarreness	
ABEEINRSTUX	exurbanites	
ABEEINSSSUV	abusiveness	
ABEEIOPPRSS	soapberries	
ABEEIOPPRRTV	reprobative	
ABEEIPRRRSS	raspberries	
ABEEIQRRSUU	arquebusier	
ABEEIRRRSST	arbitresses	
ABEEJLNNOUY	unenjoyable	
ABEEJMMNNST	enjambments	
ABEEKMMNNST	embankments	
ABEEKMMNRST	embarkments	
ABEELLLMSSY	blamelessly	
ABEELLLMTUU	umbellulate	
ABEELLLMTUY	umbellately	
ABEELLNOSSS	losableness	
ABEELLNOSSV	lovableness	
ABEELLORSST	Ballesteros	
ABEELLRRTVY	vertebrally	
ABEELMMNORU	unmemorable	
ABEELMMNSSY	assemblymen	
ABEELMNOSSV	movableness	
ABEELMNPRTU	numberplate	
ABEELMNRSUS	lebensraums	
ABEELMNSSTU	mutableness	
ABEELMNSTTT	battlements	
ABEELMORSST	astroblemes	

	blastomeres	**ABEGHNRRSSU**	bushrangers	**ABEHINORRST**	hibernators
ABEELNNOSST	notableness	**ABEGHORSSTU**	broughtases	**ABEHINORSSS**	boarishness
ABEELNPRSTY	presentably	**ABEGHQSSUUU**	usquebaughs	**ABEHLMOORTW**	Bartholomew
ABEELNPRTVY	preventably	**ABEGIIILMMT**	immitigable	**ABEHLMOPSSU**	blasphemous
ABEELNQSTTU	blanquettes	**ABEGIIIMSTU**	ambiguities	**ABEHLMORTWY**	blameworthy
ABEELNRTTUU	unutterable	**ABEGIIINNRT**	inebriating	**ABEHLMOSTYZ**	Szombathely
ABEELNRTUXY	exuberantly	**ABEGIILLNWY**	bewailingly	**ABEHLNORRTY**	abhorrently
ABEELORSTTX	rattleboxes	**ABEGIILMNTT**	timetabling	**ABEHLORRSSU**	harbourless
ABEELOSTUUY	beauteously	**ABEGIILMNST**	intangibles	**ABEHLORSTTU**	bluethroats
ABEELPRRSTY	presbyteral	**ABEGIILNRSV**	verbalising	**ABEHMRSSSTU**	bushmasters
ABEELPRRSVY	preservably	**ABEGIILNRVZ**	verbalizing	**ABEHNNOOTTY**	ethnobotany
ABEELQQRUUU	Albuquerque	**ABEGIIMNSSU**	subimagines	**ABEHRSTTWYY**	Aberystwyth
ABEEMMNORSU	membraneous	**ABEGIINNRST**	brigantines	**ABEIIIILLST**	liabilities
ABEEMNRSSTU	surbasement	**ABEGIINOSST**	abiogenists	**ABEIIIILNST**	inabilities
ABEENNPRRSS	Brenner Pass	**ABEGIINPRST**	rebaptising	**ABEIIIILSTV**	viabilities
ABEEOPRRRST	reprobaters	**ABEGIINPRTZ**	rebaptizing	**ABEIIILLLMT**	illimitable
ABEEOPRRTTU	protuberate	**ABEGIIRRSTU**	subirrigate	**ABEIIILLNOR**	billionaire
ABEFFGIKNRT	Krafft-Ebing	**ABEGIJORTUV**	objurgative	**ABEIIILLRTY**	reliability
ABEFFIILORT	fortifiable	**ABEGIKNOSST**	Basingstoke	**ABEIIILLTVY**	liveability
ABEFGIIILNS	signifiable	**ABEGILMNNOZ**	emblazoning	**ABEIIILSSTT**	stabilities
ABEFGIILLOR	glorifiable	**ABEGILMNOTY**	amblygonite	**ABEIIINNORT**	inebriation
ABEFGIILNNR	infrangible	**ABEGILMNPRY**	impregnably	**ABEIIINNOSS**	Assiniboine
ABEFGIINTUY	beautifying	**ABEGILNNNTY**	benignantly	**ABEIIILLLRY**	illiberally
ABEFHIRRSTT	afterbirths	**ABEGILNNOSU**	subregional	**ABEIIILLLMNU**	illuminable
ABEFHLNSSSU	bashfulness	**ABEGILOOORY**	aerobiology	**ABEIIILLMMST**	bimetallism
ABEFHRSSTUY	Shaftesbury	**ABEGILRRSSU**	burglarises	**ABEIIILLMNRY**	bimillenary
ABEFIIILNRT	nitrifiable	**ABEGILRRSUZ**	burglarizes	**ABEIIILLMPSU**	implausible
ABEFIIILRTV	vitrifiable	**ABEGINNOPSU**	subpoenaing	**ABEIIILLMSTT**	bimetallist
ABEFIIILSTY	feasibility	**ABEGINNORRT**	interrobang	**ABEIIILLMTTY**	meltability
ABEFIIJLSTU	justifiable	**ABEGINNOTTY**	bayonetting	**ABEIIILLNSWZ**	Leibniz's
ABEFIILLLMO	mollifiable	**ABEGINOPRRT**	reprobating		law
ABEFIILLLNS	infallibles	**ABEGKLNRSUU**	Klausenburg	**ABEIIILLOTVY**	loveability
ABEFIILLMRT	fimbrillate	**ABEGKNOORRS**	Brooks Range	**ABEIIILLRSST**	liberalists
ABEFIILLOOT	bifoliolate	**ABEGKRRSSTU**	grubstakers	**ABEIIILLRSTT**	bristletail
ABEFIILLSSY	syllabifies	**ABEGLLORSSW**	glassblower	**ABEIIILMMRSS**	miserablism
ABEFIILMSSU	subfamilies	**ABEGMORRSTU**	burgomaster	**ABEIIILMNSTY**	inestimably
ABEFIILNORV	riboflavine	**ABEGNNSSTTU**	subtangents	**ABEIIILMSSUX**	bisexualism
ABEFIILNOSS	fissionable	**ABEHHILLSST**	sheathbills	**ABEIIILNNPTY**	bipinnately
ABEFIILNSTU	infibulates	**ABEHHIRRSSU**	hairbrushes	**ABEIIILNNSTV**	vinblastine
ABEFILLTUUY	beautifully	**ABEHHJOORRU**	Johore Bahru	**ABEIIILNOPRT**	prelibation
ABEFILRRTUY	irrefutably	**ABEHHMMRSSU**	bushhammers	**ABEIIILNQRTU**	equilibrant
ABEFLLLORSW	ballflowers	**ABEHHORRSTT**	heartthrobs	**ABEIIILNQTUY**	inequitably
ABEFLLOORST	footballers	**ABEHIILMOPS**	habiliments	**ABEIIILNRRTT**	intertribal
ABEFLMOORTT	footlambert	**ABEHIILMOPS**	amphibolies	**ABEIIILNRTTY**	rentability
ABEGGHRSSTU	staggerbush	**ABEHIILMOPT**	amphibolite	**ABEIIILOPPRT**	propitiable
ABEGGIILNOR	globigerina	**ABEHIILNRTY**	inheritably	**ABEIIILOPRTY**	operability
ABEGGILMNNR	embrangling	**ABEHIILPRST**	blepharitis	**ABEIIILORTXY**	exorability
ABEGGILNNPS	bespangling	**ABEHIIMMNOS**	bohemianism	**ABEIIILPRTTY**	bipartitely
ABEGGINRSSW	bagswingers	**ABEHIIMORSV**	behaviorism	**ABEIIILRSSST**	stabilisers
ABEGGNOORST	tobogganers	**ABEHIINNORT**	hibernation	**ABEIIILRSSTZ**	stabilizers
ABEGHIIMNSV	misbehaving	**ABEHIIORSTV**	behaviorist	**ABEIIILRSTTU**	brutalities
ABEGHIINNRT	hibernating	**ABEHIKLNNTU**	unthinkable	**ABEIIILRSTUY**	reusability
	inbreathing	**ABEHILMNOST**	abolishment	**ABEIIILSTTTY**	testability
ABEGHIIOPRS	biographies	**ABEHILMPRSS**	blepharisms	**ABEIIILSTUXY**	bisexuality
	biographise	**ABEHILNRSSU**	nailbrushes	**ABEIIILTTTWY**	wettability
ABEGHIIOPRZ	biographize	**ABEHILOOPRU**	ailurophobe	**ABEIIMNORSV**	ambiversion
ABEGHILMNOO	haemoglobin	**ABEHILOPRSW**	worshipable	**ABEIINNRRST**	interbrains
ABEGHILMNPS	blaspheming	**ABEHILPSSTT**	battleships	**ABEIIPRSSTT**	baptistries
ABEGHINOOPR	negrophobia	**ABEHILPSSTU**	bisulphates	**ABEIIRRSTTU**	tributaries
ABEGHINRSTU	thunbergias	**ABEHIMNNSST**	banishments	**ABEIIRTTTUV**	attributive
ABEGHIOPRRS	biographers	**ABEHINOORTT**	botheration	**ABEIKLNNNOS**	nonsinkable
ABEGHLNOOPS	anglophobes	**ABEHINOPRSV**	vibraphones	**ABEIKNOPRST**	breakpoints

ABEILLLRSTY	trisyllable	**ABEMNNOTTTU**	Mountbatten	**ABGILLNORUY**	labouringly
ABEILLMORTU	rambouillet	**ABEMNOORRSW**	marrowbones	**ABGILLORTUY**	globularity
ABEILLNORTY	intolerably	**ABEMNORRRST**	barnstormer	**ABGILMOSUUY**	ambiguously
ABEILLNRSSY	brainlessly	**ABENNORSTUV**	unobservant	**ABGILNOSTTU**	subtotaling
ABEILMMOSST	metabolisms	**ABENOPRRTTU**	protuberant	**ABGILNSTUUX**	subluxating
ABEILMNNRUY	innumerably	**ABEOORRSTVY**	observatory	**ABGILORRSUU**	burglarious
ABEILMNQRSU	lambrequins	**ABEOORSSTUU**	rouseabouts	**ABGIMNOSUUU**	unambiguous
ABEILMNRSTU	subterminal	**ABERRSSTUUY**	subtreasury	**ABGINOORSTU**	subrogation
ABEILMOOSTU	automobiles	**ABFFFHILOSU**	buffalofish	**ABGINOOSTTU**	outboasting
ABEILMORRVY	irremovably	**ABFFIKMOORS**	kaffirbooms	**ABGJOORRSTU**	objurgators
ABEILMORSTY	traymobiles	**ABFFILLMSTU**	bullmastiff	**ABGJOORRTUY**	objurgatory
ABEILNNPRTU	unprintable	**ABFGHNOORRU**	Farnborough	**ABGJORSSTUU**	subjugators
ABEILNNRSUU	uninsurable	**ABFGIILNNRY**	infrangibly	**ABGLNORSTUY**	Glastonbury
ABEILNOOSSS	obsessional	**ABFIIILLLTY**	fallibility	**ABGMOPRRSSU**	subprograms
ABEILNORSSU	Belorussian	**ABFIIIMNORT**	fimbriation	**ABHHIOOOPPT**	photophobia
ABEILNOSTTY	obstinately	**ABFIIJLSTUY**	justifiably	**ABHIILNOSTT**	nihil obstat
ABEILNPRSUY	insuperably	**ABFIILORSUY**	bifariously	**ABHIKLNNTUY**	unthinkably
ABEILOORRTT	obliterator	**ABFILMMNSUU**	funambulism	**ABHIKNORSVY**	Baryshnikov
ABEILOPRTVY	probatively	**ABFILMNSTUU**	funambulist	**ABHILMOOPSU**	amphibolous
ABEILORSSTW	belowstairs	**ABFIMOORSTU**	fibromatous	**ABHILNOOPST**	haplobionts
ABEILORSSUY	Byelorussia	**ABGGGINNOOT**	tobogganing	**ABHILORSTUW**	whirlabouts
ABEILQRRTUY	biquarterly	**ABGGHHIILLN**	highballing	**ABHIMNORRTU**	Northumbria
ABEIMNNSSSU	businessman	**ABGGHILNORS**	Hälsingborg	**ABHIPRRSSSU**	bursarships
ABEIMNORSTT	montbretias	**ABGGIIKNNRR**	ringbarking	**ABHLLMOPSTY**	lymphoblast
ABEIMNORSTU	tambourines	**ABGGIILLNOS**	globalising	**ABHLLMSSTTU**	thumbstalls
ABEIMNRRSSU	submariners	**ABGGIJNORTU**	objurgating	**ABHLOOPRSTT**	trophoblast
ABEINNORSTV	inobservant	**ABGGIJNSTUU**	subjugating	**ABHMNORRSTU**	rhumbatrons
ABEINNSSSTT	abstentions	**ABGGIKNRSTU**	grubstaking	**ABIIIILMTTY**	imitability
ABEINOOPRRT	probationer	**ABGGILOOORY**	agrobiology	**ABIIIILNTVY**	inviability
	reprobation	**ABGGILOORST**	garbologist	**ABIIILLLMTY**	illimitably
ABEINOORSTV	observation	**ABGGINOOSTT**	tobogganist	**ABIIILLOSTY**	isolability
ABEINOOSTTT	obtestation	**ABGGINORSTU**	subrogating	**ABIIILLOTVY**	violability
ABEINORSTUV	subornative	**ABGHIILNSST**	stablishing	**ABIIILNOSST**	sibilations
ABEINOSSTTU	abstentious	**ABGHIINRRSU**	airbrushing	**ABIIILNRSTY**	rinsability
ABEINSSTTUV	substantive	**ABGHIINRSTT**	brattishing	**ABIIILNSTTY**	instability
ABEIORRSSUV	arboviruses	**ABGHIKLNSUW**	bushwalking	**ABIIILPSSTY**	passibility
ABEIRRSTTTU	attributers	**ABGHILLMNOT**	mothballing	**ABIIILRTTVY**	vibratility
ABEIRSSTTUV	substrative	**ABGHILLNOOY**	ballyhooing	**ABIIILSTTUY**	suitability
ABEJLMOSTUU	autojumbles	**ABGHILMOOPY**	amphibology	**ABIIINOPRTT**	bipartition
ABEKKMOORRS	bookmarkers	**ABGHLMOORRU**	Marlborough	**ABIIJLNOSTU**	jubilations
ABEKLLORSWY	yellowbarks	**ABGHOORRSUY**	yarboroughs	**ABIIKLORTWY**	workability
ABEKLLOSSTU	leukoblasts	**ABGIIILMMTY**	immitigably	**ABIILLLNRTY**	brilliantly
ABEKMNNOSTU	mountebanks	**ABGIIILNSST**	stabilising	**ABIILLMPSUY**	implausibly
ABEKNOPRRSW	pawnbrokers	**ABGIIILNSTZ**	stabilizing	**ABIILLOSTVY**	solvability
ABEKORRSSTW	breastworks	**ABGIIILNTTY**	tangibility	**ABIILMNOSTU**	sublimation
ABELLLLORRS	rollerballs	**ABGIILLLNUY**	bilingually	**ABIILMOSTUY**	ambitiously
ABELLLLOSVY	volleyballs	**ABGIILMNSTU**	sublimating	**ABIILNORTTU**	tribulation
ABELLMOSSTY	myeloblasts	**ABGIILNOOST**	obligations	**ABIILNRSTUY**	insalubrity
ABELLORRRSU	bullroarers	**ABGIILNRSTU**	brutalising	**ABIILOPRTTY**	portability
ABELMMOOORT	Bartolommeo	**ABGIILNRTUZ**	brutalizing	**ABIILOQTTUY**	quotability
ABELMNORRSY	salmonberry	**ABGIILNRTVY**	vibratingly	**ABIILRRTTUY**	tributarily
ABELNOOPPST	postponable	**ABGIIMNNORT**	brominating	**ABIIMNNOORT**	bromination
ABELNOOPSST	tablespoons	**ABGIINRTTTU**	attributing	**ABIIMNORSTT**	nimbostrati
ABELNOPPSTU	unstoppable	**ABGIJKKMNOS**	sjambokking	**ABIIMNOSTUU**	unambitious
ABELNORSSTU	neuroblasts	**ABGIJNOORTU**	objurgation	**ABIINNORTTU**	turbination
ABELNORSTVY	observantly	**ABGIJNOSTUU**	subjugation	**ABIINNOSTTU**	intubations
ABELNRTTUUY	unutterably	**ABGIKLLNNOR**	bankrolling	**ABIINOOPSTT**	obstipation
ABELOOPRSST	blastopores	**ABGIKNNOPRW**	pawnbroking	**ABIINOORSTT**	abortionist
	blastospore	**ABGIKNNPRTU**	bankrupting	**ABIINORTTTU**	attribution
ABELOOSSSTT	osteoblasts	**ABGIKNRRSTY**	stringybark	**ABIIORSSTTU**	obituarists
ABELOPPRSTU	supportable	**ABGILLNNOOS**	balloonings		tibiotarsus
ABELRRSTTUU	surrebuttal	**ABGILLNNOSW**	snowballing	**ABIJNOORSTU**	objurations

ABILLNOOSST	balloonists	ACCCHILOORT	ochlocratic	ACCDEILLOPS	peccadillos
ABILLOORSUY	laboriously	ACCCHKOPSST	spatchcocks	ACCDEILMOPT	complicated
ABILLORSTTU	sublittoral	ACCCHOOPRTY	ptochocracy	ACCDEILNOST	occidentals
ABILMNOSTUX	toxalbumins	ACCCIIOOPRS	capriccioso	ACCDEILOPSY	cyclopedias
ABILNNPRTUY	unprintably	ACCCILLOOSU	calcicolous	ACCDEIMNNOO	codominance
ABILNOOSSTU	absolutions	ACCCIMMOORS	macrocosmic	ACCDEINNSTU	inductances
ABILNOSTTUU	tubulations	ACCCIMOOPRS	macroscopic	ACCDEINOOST	consociated
ABILNOSTUUX	subluxation	ACCCINOPPSU	cappuccinos	ACCDEINOOTU	coeducation
ABILOOPRSTT	postorbital	ACCCIOOPRSY	cystocarpic	ACCDEINPRSY	discrepancy
ABILOSSSTTU	absolutists	ACCDDDEIORS	disaccorded	ACCDEINPRTU	unpracticed
ABIMNORRSST	brainstorms	ACCDDEEEINS	decadencies	ACCDEIORSST	desiccators
ABINNOORSTU	subornation	ACCDDEEFIIL	decalcified	ACCDEKKMMUU	muckamucked
ABINOOOPRRT	proabortion	ACCDDEEIOIO	decanedioic	ACCDELOPSSU	cloudscapes
ABINOOPRRTW	Barrow Point	ACCDDEEINNS	incandensed	ACCDENNOTUU	unaccounted
ABINOOPRSST	saprobionts	ACCDDEEIIRST	disaccredit	ACCDGILNORY	accordingly
ABINOORSTTU	obturations	ACCDDEEINORS	discordance	ACCDHHRRSUY	churchyards
ABINOOSSSST	bassoonists	ACCDDELLMOU	maloccluded	ACCDHIIILOP	acidophilic
ABINOSSSTTU	substations	ACCDDIIIMST	didacticism	ACCDHIIMORT	dichromatic
ABIORRSTTTU	attributors	ACCDDIINORSY	discordancy	ACCDHIINORT	achondritic
ABLLMNORSUY	subnormally	ACCDEEEEENNT	antecedence	ACCDHILLOOT	Old Catholic
ABLNOPPSTUY	unstoppably	ACCDEEEHKMN	namechecked	ACCDHILORSV	clavichords
ABLOPPRSTUY	supportably	ACCDEEELNOS	adolescence	ACCDHINOPRY	hydnocarpic
ABNOORRSSTU	brontosaurs	ACCDEEELNPR	precanceled	ACCDHINORYY	hydrocyanic
ABOORSSTTUU	roustabouts	ACCDEEELNST	decalescent	ACCDHIORTTY	hydrotactic
ACCCDEEENNS	candescence	ACCDEEFIILR	decalcifier	ACCDIIINNOS	scincoidian
ACCCDEHILNO	chalcedonic	ACCDEEFIILS	decalcifies	ACCDIILLNRY	cylindrical
ACCCDEILOPY	cyclopaedic	ACCDEEFNORY	confederacy	ACCDIILLORY	codicillary
ACCCDENNOOR	concordance	ACCDEEHHKLU	chucklehead	ACCDIILNOOR	crocodilian
ACCCDENNOTU	conductance	ACCDEEHIORS	archdiocese	ACCDIIOOPRS	radioscopic
ACCCDILLOOP	diplococcal	ACCDEEIISTV	desiccative	ACCDILLLOVY	cycloidally
ACCCEEEELNOS	coalescence	ACCDEEIKKLP	placekicked	ACCDIMOSSTU	disaccustom
ACCCEEELNST	lactescence	ACCDEEIKRSW	wisecracked	ACCDINORSTT	contradicts
ACCCEEEMNRS	marcescence	ACCDEEIMORS	democracies	ACCEEEEHKSS	cheesecakes
ACCCEEHOSUU	accoucheuse	ACCDEEINNSS	incandesces	ACCEEEENNSV	evanescence
ACCCEELMNOP	complacence	ACCDEEIORTT	decorticate	ACCEEEFILMN	maleficence
ACCCEELNOPT	conceptacle	ACCDEEIRRST	reaccredits	ACCEEEFLNRT	reflectance
ACCCEFHKORS	cockchafers	ACCDEEIRTUX	excruciated	ACCEEEHIIST	haecceities
ACCCEGNORYY	gynecocracy	ACCDEELNNOU	unconcealed	ACCEEEHILRT	chelicerate
ACCCEHIISTT	catechistic	ACCDEELNOSV	convalesced	ACCEEEIKKLO	cockaleekie
ACCCEHILORT	chloracetic	ACCDEEMNSUU	succedaneum	ACCEEEELNOPS	opalescence
ACCCEHIMOTT	chemotactic	ACCDEENORST	consecrated	ACCEEELNRST	recalescent
ACCCEHKOORS	cockroaches	ACCDEFILNSS	flaccidness	ACCEEELPRST	receptacles
ACCCEHNORTY	technocracy	ACCDEFINOST	confiscated	ACCEEENNRSS	renascences
ACCCEHORSTW	cowcatchers	ACCDEFLLOTU	flocculated	ACCEEENPSTX	expectances
ACCCEHORSUU	accoucheurs	ACCDEGHORST	dogcatchers	ACCEEFIIRTT	certificate
ACCCEIIILPY	epicyclical	ACCDEGIINRT	accrediting	ACCEEFIKRRR	firecracker
ACCCEIILMRT	climacteric	ACCDEGIINST	desiccating	ACCEEFINORV	vociferance
ACCCEIILRST	cicatricles	ACCDEHHIRSU	archduchies	ACCEEGHILMO	geochemical
ACCCEIIOPST	cacoepistic	ACCDEHHITTT	chitchatted	ACCEEGILNRS	recalescing
ACCCEIIORST	cicatricose	ACCDEHHRSSU	archduchess	ACCEEGINNRT	reaccenting
ACCCEIKORST	cockatrices	ACCDEHILPRY	diphycercal	ACCEEGINPRT	reaccepting
ACCCEILLNSY	encyclicals	ACCDEHNRSTU	unscratched	ACCEEHIINRS	chicaneries
ACCCEILMOPS	accomplices	ACCDEIIIMRT	acidimetric	ACCEEHILMNO	chameleonic
ACCCEILORTU	leucocratic	ACCDEIILLTY	deictically	ACCEEHILNRT	chanticleer
ACCCEILRTTY	tetracyclic	ACCDEIILNOT	conciliated	ACCEEHINRRT	archenteric
ACCCEINOPSU	occupancies	ACCDEIILSSS	classicised	ACCEEHIORST	theocracies
ACCCEINORRT	acrocentric	ACCDEIILSSZ	classicized	ACCEEHIRRTU	charcuterie
ACCCELMNOPY	complacency	ACCDEIINOOT	octanedioic	ACCEEHIRSST	catechisers
ACCCHHIINNO	Cochin China	ACCDEIINOST	desiccation	ACCEEHIRSTZ	catechizers
ACCCHHILOOS	chocaholics	ACCDEIIRSTT	dictatrices	ACCEEHKORTW	weathercock
ACCCHHIMPUU	Machu Picchu	ACCDEIKLNST	candlestick	ACCEEHLLNRY	chancellery
ACCCHIILLOT	laccolithic	ACCDEIKLNSW	candlewicks	ACCEEHLNOXY	cyclohexane

ACCEEHLNRST	chanteclers
ACCEEHMNSTU	catechumens
ACCEEHNORRS	encroachers
ACCEEIILNRT	electrician
ACCEEIIMPST	septicaemic
ACCEEIISTVX	exsiccative
ACCEEIKRRSW	wisecracker
ACCEEILMNOU	oecumenical
ACCEEILNNST	incalescent
ACCEEILNORT	electronica
ACCEEILNOSV	covalencies
ACCEEILRRTU	recirculate
ACCEEIMNRTT	metacentric
ACCEEINNOST	cotenancies
ACCEEINQSTU	acquiescent
ACCEEIOPRRT	reciprocate
ACCEEIORSSS	accessories
	accessorise
ACCEEIORSSZ	accessorize
ACCEEIRSTUX	excruciates
ACCEEKLSSSU	Lake Success
ACCEELLOPRT	leptocercal
ACCEELMNNOT	concealment
ACCEELNORST	calorescent
ACCEELNOSSV	convalesces
ACCEEMNNORR	necromancer
ACCEEMNOPPU	comeuppance
ACCEEMOSSTY	ascomycetes
ACCEENNNOTU	countenance
ACCEENNORSV	conversance
ACCEENNORTT	concentrate
	concertante
ACCEENNORVY	conveyancer
ACCEENNOSSV	concaveness
ACCEENNOSVY	conveyances
ACCEENOPRRS	coparceners
ACCEENORSST	consecrates
ACCEENPSSTU	susceptance
ACCEEOPRSUY	cyperaceous
ACCEEORRSSU	racecourses
ACCEFFHHINS	chaffinches
ACCEFFIIOSU	efficacious
ACCEFHIINTY	chieftaincy
ACCEFHLRSTY	flycatchers
ACCEFIINRRY	ferricyanic
ACCEFIIRRSS	sacrificers
ACCEFILORSU	calciferous
ACCEFINORRY	ferrocyanic
ACCEFINOSST	confiscates
ACCEFLLOSTU	flocculates
ACCEFMNNOOR	conformance
ACCEGGHHINN	Cheng-chiang
ACCEGHHITTW	catchweight
ACCEGHIINST	catechising
ACCEGHIINTZ	catechizing
ACCEGHIKMNT	checkmating
ACCEGHILMRU	chemurgical
ACCEGHINNOR	encroaching
ACCEGHIOPRR	cerographic
ACCEGIINQSU	acquiescing
ACCEGIINSTX	exsiccating
ACCEGIKMRRY	gimcrackery

ACCEGILLNOR	clearcoling
ACCEGILLOOO	oecological
ACCEGILLOOT	cetological
ACCEGILLOPY	cycloplegia
ACCEGINNORS	carcinogens
ACCEGINORTU	accoutering
ACCEHHHHIIR	Chichihaerh
ACCEHHIINTZ	Chichen Itzá
ACCEHHIISTX	hexastichic
ACCEHIILMST	alchemistic
ACCEHIILNST	calisthenic
ACCEHIILOST	catholicise
ACCEHIILOTT	heliotactic
ACCEHIILOTZ	catholicize
ACCEHIIMNST	mechanistic
ACCEHIIMOSS	sciomachies
ACCEHIINNST	technicians
ACCEHIIORRT	hierocratic
ACCEHIIRSTU	eucharistic
ACCEHILLMNO	melancholic
ACCEHILLNTY	technically
ACCEHILMOOZ	zoochemical
ACCEHILMRTY	methacrylic
ACCEHILOORT	chocolatier
ACCEHILOPPR	procephalic
ACCEHILOPXY	oxycephalic
ACCEHIMNNOR	chrominance
ACCEHIMNORR	chiromancer
ACCEHIMORTT	tachometric
ACCEHIMORTU	euchromatic
ACCEHIMRTTY	tachymetric
ACCEHINOOPS	cacophonies
ACCEHINPPRY	hypercapnic
ACCEHINRSTU	craunchiest
ACCEHIORSST	escharotics
ACCEHKLRSTU	saltchucker
ACCEHLLMNOY	collenchyma
ACCEHLLNORS	chancellors
ACCEHLLNORY	chancellory
ACCEHLOOSSW	slowcoaches
ACCEHNOOSTY	choanocytes
ACCEHNNORST	technocrats
ACCEHOOSTWZ	Częstochowa
ACCEIIILSTV	acclivities
ACCEIIINPRT	accipitrine
ACCEIIINRST	intricacies
ACCEIILLMRS	clericalism
ACCEIILLNPR	preclinical
ACCEIILLRST	clericalist
ACCEIILMOSV	semivocalic
ACCEIILNOST	conciliates
ACCEIILNRTY	circinately
ACCEIILPRRT	precritical
ACCEIILPRST	periclastic
ACCEIILRRSU	circularise
ACCEIILRRUZ	circularize
ACCEIILRTUV	circulative
ACCEIILSSSS	classicises
ACCEIILSSSZ	classicizes
ACCEIIMNOST	cosmetician
	encomiastic
ACCEIIMORST	timocracies

ACCEIIMRSST	ceramicists
ACCEIINNOSU	insouciance
ACCEIINOSST	oscitancies
ACCEIINOSTV	concavities
ACCEIINOSTX	exsiccation
ACCEIIRRSST	cicatrisers
ACCEIIRRSTZ	cicatrizers
ACCEIKKOTTT	ticktacktoe
ACCEIKLMRST	clickstream
ACCEIKNRSSS	carsickness
ACCEILLNNOR	nonclerical
ACCEILLNRTY	centrically
ACCEILLPSTY	sceptically
ACCEILMMORS	commercials
ACCEILMNOPS	compliances
ACCEILMNORU	macronuclei
ACCEILMNOSS	comicalness
ACCEILMOPST	complicates
	ectoplasmic
ACCEILMOSST	cacomistles
ACCEILMSSTU	multiaccess
ACCEILNNOTY	anticyclone
ACCEILNNSSY	cynicalness
ACCEILNOPRT	narcoleptic
ACCEILNORTT	contractile
ACCEILNORTU	corniculate
ACCEILOPPST	apoplectics
ACCEILOPRRS	reciprocals
ACCEILOPRST	ceroplastic
ACCEILORSSY	accessorily
ACCEIMMNOTU	communicate
ACCEIMNNORT	necromantic
ACCEIMNOORS	monocracies
	nomocracies
ACCEIMNORSS	sciomancers
ACCEIMNOSTU	contumacies
ACCEIMORRTY	meritocracy
ACCEINNNOSV	connivances
ACCEINNNOTU	continuance
ACCEINNORST	concertinas
ACCEINNORSU	coinsurance
ACCEINNORTT	concertanti
ACCEINNORTV	contrivance
ACCEINOOSST	consociates
ACCEINOOTVV	convocative
ACCEINORTTV	contractive
ACCEINSSSTU	causticness
ACCEIOORSSU	scoriaceous
ACCEIOPRRSU	procuracies
ACCEIORSSSU	accessorius
ACCEIORSSTX	exsiccators
ACCEIORSTUU	urticaceous
ACCEJLNORTU	conjectural
ACCEKKLMORS	clockmakers
ACCEKNRRSTU	nutcrackers
ACCELLLTUUY	cucullately
ACCELMMNOOP	commonplace
ACCELNORSUY	cancerously
ACCELOOPSST	lactoscopes
ACCELORSSSU	successoral
ACCELPRRSUU	crepuscular
ACCEMNOPSST	compactness

ACCEMORSSTU	reaccustoms	
ACCENNNOOSS	consonances	
ACCENNORSVY	conservancy	
	conversancy	
ACCENOOPRTU	pococurante	
ACCENOORRST	consecrator	
ACCENOPRRSU	procurances	
ACCENOPRRTT	precontract	
ACCENORRTTU	contracture	
ACCENORSTTU	counteracts	
ACCENPRTUUU	acupuncture	
ACCEOOORSSU	ectosarcous	
ACCEORRSSTU	securocrats	
ACCEORSSTUU	crustaceous	
ACCFFFFHHIS	chiffchaffs	
ACCFGIIINRS	sacrificing	
ACCFGILOSUU	calcifugous	
ACCFIILOPRY	prolificacy	
ACCFIIMOORR	coraciiform	
ACCFILMORSU	sacculiform	
ACCFINOORST	confiscator	
ACCGGHHIINN	Chiang	
	Ch'ing	
ACCGGIILLOO	glaciologic	
ACCGHIIOOPS	hagioscopic	
ACCGHIMOPRY	cymographic	
ACCGHINRSST	scratchings	
ACCGHLOPRSY	cyclographs	
ACCGIIIILMNN	calcimining	
ACCGIIINNOS	cocainising	
ACCGIIINNOZ	cocainizing	
ACCGIIINRST	cicatrising	
ACCGIIINRTZ	cicatrizing	
ACCGIILNNTU	inculcating	
ACCGIILNOTU	glauconitic	
ACCGIILNRTU	circulating	
ACCGIINNOOS	occasioning	
ACCGILLMOOY	mycological	
ACCGILLNOOO	oncological	
ACCGILLNOOT	collocating	
ACCGILLOOTY	cytological	
ACCGILOORST	gastrocolic	
ACCGIMNOSTU	accustoming	
ACCGIMOPRTY	cryptogamic	
ACCGINNORTT	contracting	
ACCGINORSTU	coruscating	
ACCHHIILLNS	chinchillas	
ACCHHIIMOPR	amphichroic	
ACCHHIINSTT	chainstitch	
ACCHHILNRTU	Latin Church	
ACCHHILORSU	Archilochus	
ACCHHLMNRUY	churchmanly	
ACCHHMNORUW	churchwoman	
ACCHHMOPSYY	psychomachy	
ACCHIIIMMPT	amphimictic	
ACCHIILLSTY	stichically	
ACCHIILMOST	catholicism	
ACCHIILOSST	scholiastic	
ACCHIILOTTY	catholicity	
ACCHIIMNORT	chromatinic	
ACCHIIMOSST	masochistic	
ACCHIIMSSST	schismatics	

ACCHIIOOPST	sociopathic	
ACCHIIORSTT	rhotacistic	
ACCHIIPRSTY	psychiatric	
ACCHIKMSSTT	matchsticks	
ACCHILLNORY	chronically	
ACCHILLPSYY	psychically	
ACCHILMOTYY	cyclothymia	
ACCHILNNOOT	non-Catholic	
ACCHILNOOST	catholicons	
ACCHILOOSTU	holocaustic	
ACCHINOPSTY	sycophantic	
ACCHIOOPTTT	phototactic	
ACCHIOORRSU	chiaroscuro	
ACCHIOPRSSZ	schizocarps	
ACCHIOPRSYY	physiocracy	
ACCHNNOOPSU	cacophonous	
ACCIIILOSST	socialistic	
ACCIIILRTTY	criticality	
ACCIILLLNOX	cloxacillin	
ACCIILLNNNO	nonclinical	
ACCIILLNORY	conciliarly	
ACCIILMNOSS	laconicisms	
ACCIILMSSSS	classicisms	
ACCIILNNORT	noncritical	
ACCIILNNOTU	inculcation	
ACCIILNNQUU	quincuncial	
ACCIILNOORT	conciliator	
ACCIILNORTU	circulation	
ACCIILNOTVY	volcanicity	
ACCIILOSTUV	acclivitous	
ACCIILRRTUY	circularity	
ACCIILSSSST	classicists	
ACCIIMMORST	microsmatic	
ACCIIMNNOTY	actinomycin	
ACCIIMNNOTTY	antimycotic	
ACCIINNNSTU	Cincinnatus	
ACCIINNSTTY	nyctinastic	
ACCIINOORTT	cortication	
ACCIINORRSU	Rosicrucian	
ACCIJNNOTUV	conjunctiva	
ACCIKKKKNNS	knickknacks	
ACCILLNOOOT	collocation	
ACCILLPRTYY	cryptically	
ACCILMNRRUU	circumlunar	
ACCILMOPRRU	circumpolar	
ACCILMOPSTY	cytoplasmic	
ACCILMORRSU	circumsolar	
ACCILNOOSST	iconoclasts	
ACCILNOOTTU	occultation	
ACCILNORSTU	inculcators	
ACCILNOSSTV	conclavists	
ACCILOOPSTV	postvocalic	
ACCILOPRSTY	pyroclastic	
ACCILOPRTTU	plutocratic	
ACCILORRSTU	circulators	
ACCILORRTUY	circulatory	
ACCIMMNNOTU	communicant	
ACCIMMNOOTT	concomitant	
ACCINNNOSTY	inconstancy	
ACCINNOOOTV	convocation	
ACCINNOOPRU	cornucopian	
ACCINNOORTT	contraction	

ACCINNOSTTU	cunctations	
ACCINOOPRSU	cornucopias	
ACCINOOPSTU	occupations	
ACCINOORSTU	coruscation	
ACCIOOPRRTY	procaryotic	
ACCIORSSSTY	syssarcotic	
ACCKLMOORSU	cockalorums	
ACCLNNOSTUY	consultancy	
ACCLNORSUUU	carunculous	
ACCLOPRRSUU	corpuscular	
ACCNOOORSTV	convocators	
ACCNOORRSTT	contractors	
ACDDDEEEIRT	rededicated	
ACDDEEEELRT	decelerated	
ACDDEEEEPRS	predeceased	
ACDDEEEIPRT	depreciated	
ACDDEEEIRST	rededicates	
ACDDEEEORRT	redecorated	
ACDDEEFFIST	disaffected	
ACDDEEGIKLR	griddlecake	
ACDDEEHHIKT	thickheaded	
ACDDEEHHKOS	shockheaded	
ACDDEEHLORT	coldhearted	
ACDDEEHNORS	decahedrons	
ACDDEEIIILMS	decimalised	
ACDDEEIIILMZ	decimalized	
ACDDEEIKRST	sidetracked	
ACDDEEIILLOS	delocalised	
ACDDEEIILLOZ	delocalized	
ACDDEEIILOSV	devocalised	
ACDDEEIILOVZ	devocalized	
ACDDEEIMNTU	unmedicated	
ACDDEEIMSTU	miseducated	
ACDDEEINNTU	denunciated	
ACDDEEIOTTX	detoxicated	
ACDDEELORTU	edulcorated	
ACDDEENNRST	transcended	
ACDDEENNSST	descendants	
ACDDEENORTU	undecorated	
	undercoated	
ACDDEENRTTU	detruncated	
ACDDEFIIINT	nidificated	
ACDDEGIKLNO	deadlocking	
ACDDEGIORSU	discouraged	
ACDDEHLLOST	saddlecloth	
ACDDEHLNSTU	Deutschland	
ACDDEHNOOPY	dodecaphony	
ACDDEIILNRT	dendritical	
ACDDEIINOST	dedications	
ACDDEIIOSST	dissociated	
ACDDEILMOSU	duodecimals	
ACDDEIMNORU	endocardium	
ACDDEINOORT	coordinated	
ACDDELNOOSW	candlewoods	
ACDDFHIORSU	chaudfroids	
ACDDIILMSTY	didactylism	
ACDEEEEHLRR	cheerleader	
ACDEEEEKRRT	racketeered	
ACDEEEELRST	decelerates	
ACDEEEEPRSS	predeceases	
ACDEEEFFTTU	effectuated	
ACDEEEFHORR	forereached	

ACDEEEFILNR	Île-de-France	
ACDEEEFLNRT	needlecraft	
ACDEEEFMNST	defacements	
ACDEEEFNORT	confederate	
ACDEEEGLLOT	decolletage	
ACDEEEHILRS	Heracleides	
ACDEEEHLSTT	decathletes	
ACDEEEHORRV	overreached	
ACDEEEHRRRT	rechartered	
ACDEEEILLPT	pedicellate	
ACDEEEILNRV	deliverance	
ACDEEEIMRTV	decemvirate	
ACDEEEINNRS	decennaries	
ACDEEEIPPRV	apperceived	
ACDEEEIPRST	depreciates	
ACDEEEIPRTT	decrepitate	
ACDEEEIPRTV	deprecative	
ACDEEEIRSTV	eviscerated	
ACDEEELLNRT	crenellated	
ACDEEELLSST	Leeds Castle	
ACDEEELORRT	decelerator	
ACDEEENNSTT	antecedents	
ACDEEENOSSS	deaconesses	
ACDEEENPRRT	carpentered	
ACDEEENRSTV	advertences	
ACDEEEOORRST	redecorates	
ACDEEEOORRTV	overreacted	
ACDEEEORTUV	overeducate	
ACDEEEPRRTU	recuperated	
ACDEEERRSST	desecraters	
ACDEEFFHRUU	chauffeured	
ACDEEFHIIPR	preachified	
ACDEEFIILLT	felicitated	
ACDEEFINOST	defecations	
ACDEEFIORTV	vociferated	
ACDEEFLNRUU	fraudulence	
ACDEEFNRSTT	transfected	
ACDEEFORRTT	tractorfeed	
ACDEEGGNORT	congregated	
ACDEEGHNNOS	hendecagons	
ACDEEGHNRRU	undercharge	
ACDEEGHORRV	overcharged	
ACDEEGIKLRS	girdlecakes	
ACDEEGILNNR	calendering	
	Greenlandic	
ACDEEGINNRS	grandnieces	
	reascending	
ACDEEGINPRT	deprecating	
ACDEEGINRST	desecrating	
ACDEEGINRTU	reeducating	
ACDEEGIORST	categorised	
ACDEEGIORTZ	categorized	
ACDEEGIOTTX	excogitated	
ACDEEGKLNOW	acknowledge	
ACDEEGLNORU	Grand Coulee	
ACDEEHIINOT	ethanedioic	
ACDEEHILNNS	channelised	
ACDEEHILNNZ	channelized	
ACDEEHILNOT	endothecial	
ACDEEHILNPP	Chippendale	
ACDEEHILNRS	chandeliers	

	chandleries	
ACDEEHILPSY	psychedelia	
ACDEEHIMNRS	merchandise	
ACDEEHIMSST	schematised	
ACDEEHIMSTZ	schematized	
ACDEEHINRTW	windcheater	
ACDEEHIORTT	octahedrite	
ACDEEHKKLNU	knucklehead	
ACDEEHKNNUY	unhackneyed	
ACDEEHMNSTT	detachments	
ACDEEHMORTV	overmatched	
ACDEEHNRRTU	unchartered	
ACDEEHOPPRS	copperheads	
ACDEEHORTVW	overwatched	
ACDEEHPRRSU	repurchased	
ACDEEHPRRST	despatchers	
ACDEEIILLSX	lexicalised	
ACDEEIILLTV	eidetically	
ACDEEIILLXZ	lexicalized	
ACDEEIILMSS	decimalises	
ACDEEIILMSZ	decimalizes	
ACDEEIILMTV	maledictive	
ACDEEIILNSV	divalencies	
ACDEEIILPSS	specialised	
ACDEEIILPSZ	specialized	
ACDEEIILSST	elasticised	
ACDEEIILSTZ	elasticized	
ACDEEIILTUV	elucidative	
ACDEEIIMNST	mendacities	
ACDEEIIMRST	acidimeters	
ACDEEIINNOT	neonaticide	
ACDEEIINNRT	incinerated	
ACDEEIIOPPS	epidiascope	
ACDEEIIPRTV	predicative	
ACDEEIIRRRV	arrivederci	
ACDEEIILLMNY	endemically	
ACDEEIILLNNY	decennially	
ACDEEIILLOSS	delocalises	
ACDEEIILLOSZ	delocalizes	
ACDEEIILLRSS	escadrilles	
ACDEEIILNNST	clandestine	
ACDEEIILNOTT	delectation	
ACDEEIILNPPS	appendicles	
ACDEEIILNRST	centralised	
	credentials	
ACDEEIILNRSY	increasedly	
ACDEEIILNRTZ	centralized	
ACDEEIILNTTU	denticulate	
ACDEEIILOSSV	devocalises	
ACDEEIILOSVZ	devocalizes	
ACDEEIILPRTU	reduplicate	
ACDEEIILPSTU	pediculates	
ACDEEIILRSSU	secularised	
ACDEEIILRSTT	decretalist	
ACDEEIILRSUZ	secularized	
ACDEEIILRTTU	reticulated	
ACDEEIILSTUV	vesiculated	
ACDEEIIMMNST	medicaments	
ACDEEIMNOSU	eudaemonics	
ACDEEIMNPRT	predicament	
ACDEEIMORRR	microreader	
ACDEEIMORST	acidometers	

	democratise	
ACDEEIMORTZ	democratize	
ACDEEIMOSTT	domesticate	
ACDEEIMPRST	mercaptides	
ACDEEIMSSTU	miseducates	
ACDEEINNNST	intendances	
ACDEEINNSTU	denunciates	
ACDEEINOOPT	Pico de Aneto	
ACDEEINOPRS	percoideans	
ACDEEINOPRT	deprecation	
ACDEEINORSS	dinocerases	
	secondaries	
ACDEEINORST	considerate	
	desecration	
ACDEEINORTU	reeducation	
ACDEEINPPRT	apprenticed	
ACDEEINPRST	interspaced	
ACDEEINRTUV	underactive	
ACDEEIOOPRS	aecidospore	
ACDEEIOPRRT	depreciator	
ACDEEIOQTUV	equivocated	
ACDEEIORRTT	directorate	
ACDEEIOSTTX	detoxicates	
ACDEEKNORSW	Dawson Creek	
ACDEEKQRRTU	quarterdeck	
ACDEELLMORU	leucodermal	
ACDEELLMSSU	muscadelles	
ACDEELLNOTU	nucleolated	
ACDEELMORRS	scleroderma	
ACDEELMORSU	leucodermas	
ACDEELNOPRW	candlepower	
ACDEELNOSST	adolescents	
ACDEELNPTUU	pedunculate	
ACDEELORSTU	edulcorates	
ACDEELSSTUY	decussately	
ACDEEMMNORS	commandeers	
ACDEEMMNOTT	commentated	
ACDEEMMNPRST	decampments	
ACDEEMMORSU	commeasured	
ACDEEMNOPSS	encompassed	
ACDEEMNOPST	compensated	
ACDEEMNRTTU	traducement	
ACDEENNORST	contredanse	
ACDEENNORTV	contravened	
ACDEENNOSST	condensates	
ACDEENRSTTU	detruncates	
ACDEEOPRRST	deprecators	
ACDEEOPRRSY	copyreaders	
ACDEEOPRRTY	deprecatory	
ACDEEORRSST	desecrators	
ACDEEORSSTU	ceratoduses	
ACDEFFIIRTV	diffractive	
ACDEFFLORSS	scaffolders	
ACDEFGHMORR	frogmarched	
ACDEFGILRSU	disgraceful	
ACDEFGINNTU	fecundating	
ACDEFHIINNR	French India	
ACDEFHILPST	feldspathic	
ACDEFHILSSS	scaldfishes	
ACDEFHNNRSU	French Sudan	
ACDEFIIINNT	infanticide	

ACDEFIIINOT	deification	
	edification	
ACDEFIIINST	nidificates	
ACDEFIIIRSU	fiduciaries	
ACDEFIILNRU	unclarified	
ACDEFIILPST	spiflicated	
ACDEFIILSTU	feudalistic	
ACDEFIIORTY	edificatory	
ACDEFIIRRST	fratricides	
ACDEFINNOST	confidantes	
ACDEFINNOTU	fecundation	
ACDEFIRRTTU	trifurcated	
ACDEFLNRUUY	fraudulency	
ACDEFNORSTU	fecundators	
ACDEFNORTUY	fecundatory	
ACDEGHIILOT	glochidiate	
ACDEGHIIMNR	Michigander	
ACDEGHILLNN	chandelling	
ACDEGHILLNT	candlelight	
ACDEGHILLRR	chargrilled	
ACDEGHIMOPR	demographic	
ACDEGHINNRT	night dancer	
ACDEGHINPST	despatching	
ACDEGHIRRSS	dischargers	
ACDEGHNNORU	changeround	
ACDEGIILLOO	ideological	
ACDEGIILMNT	maledicting	
ACDEGIILMRU	demiurgical	
ACDEGIILNTU	elucidating	
ACDEGIIMNSU	misguidance	
ACDEGIINPRT	predicating	
ACDEGILLNOT	decollating	
ACDEGILLOOP	pedological	
ACDEGILOOPS	logopaedics	
ACDEGIMNOSY	geodynamics	
ACDEGIMORTY	tragicomedy	
ACDEGINNOQU	quindecagon	
ACDEGINNRTU	underacting	
ACDEGINOORT	Ticonderoga	
ACDEGINOPRY	copyreading	
ACDEGINSSTU	decussating	
ACDEGIORRSU	discourager	
ACDEGIORSSU	discourages	
ACDEGKLOORS	sockdolager	
ACDEGLNNRSU	granduncles	
ACDEGLNORSS	cradlesongs	
ACDEHIILMPS	dicephalism	
ACDEHIILOPP	pedophiliac	
ACDEHIIOPRT	diaphoretic	
ACDEHIKLNST	stickhandle	
ACDEHILLOOS	alcoholised	
ACDEHILLOOZ	alcoholized	
ACDEHILNORT	chlorinated	
ACDEHILOPSU	dicephalous	
ACDEHILRSSY	chrysalides	
ACDEHIMOPRS	comradeship	
ACDEHIMORST	dichromates	
ACDEHIMOSTU	mustachioed	
ACDEHIMRSSW	scrimshawed	
ACDEHINNOST	stanchioned	
ACDEHINNSST	disenchants	
ACDEHINOORS	icosahedron	

ACDEHINOPSS	deaconships	
ACDEHINORST	achondrites	
ACDEHIOOPRT	orthopaedic	
ACDEHIPRSST	dispatchers	
ACDEHKLNNST	landsknecht	
ACDEHLLLOPY	phylloclade	
ACDEHLMOSUV	chlamydeous	
ACDEHLNPRTU	thunderclap	
ACDEHLOOPPS	cephalopods	
ACDEHMNNOOR	enchondroma	
ACDEHMNORRY	hydromancer	
ACDEHMOORTW	doomwatcher	
ACDEHNOORST	octahedrons	
ACDEHNOORSSZ	scherzandos	
ACDEHOORRTU	urochordate	
ACDEHORRSTT	tetrachords	
ACDEHORRTYY	cryohydrate	
ACDEIIIJRSU	judiciaries	
ACDEIIILMOT	domiciliate	
ACDEIIINSTV	indicatives	
ACDEIIJLPRU	prejudicial	
ACDEIIILLMNY	medicinally	
ACDEIIILLNTY	identically	
ACDEIILLORV	varicelloid	
ACDEIIILLRVY	veridically	
ACDEIIILLSTY	deistically	
ACDEIIILMNOT	malediction	
ACDEIIILMOPS	diplomacies	
ACDEIIILMPRS	spermicidal	
ACDEIIILMQTU	quitclaimed	
ACDEIIILMRSS	disclaimers	
ACDEIIILMSSX	disclimaxes	
ACDEIIILLNNOT	declination	
ACDEIILNNST	incidentals	
ACDEIILNORT	directional	
ACDEIILNOTU	elucidation	
ACDEIILNOTV	valediction	
ACDEIILNPTU	induplicate	
ACDEIILOPRS	periodicals	
ACDEIILORRT	directorial	
ACDEIILPRTT	triplicated	
ACDEIILPSST	plasticised	
ACDEIILPSTZ	plasticized	
ACDEIILPTUV	duplicative	
ACDEIILRTUV	diverticula	
ACDEIIMNOST	medications	
ACDEIIMNRRT	intradermic	
ACDEIIMORRT	radiometric	
ACDEIIMORTU	audiometric	
ACDEIIMPRRU	pericardium	
ACDEIINNRTY	tyrannicide	
ACDEIINOPRT	predication	
ACDEIINORRT	doctrinaire	
ACDEIINOSSY	isocyanides	
ACDEIINOTTX	intoxicated	
ACDEIIOSSST	dissociates	
ACDEIIRSTTV	distractive	
ACDEIJRSTUU	judicatures	
ACDEILLLMOY	melodically	
ACDEILLMNOY	demonically	
ACDEILLNNOR	carillonned	
ACDEILLNOOT	decollation	

ACDEILLNORR	cordilleran	
ACDEILLORRS	cordilleras	
ACDEILLPTUY	duplicately	
ACDEILMNOPS	endoplasmic	
ACDEILMOPRR	dimercaprol	
ACDEILMORTY	maledictory	
ACDEILMSSTU	simulcasted	
ACDEILNNOSY	Coney Island	
ACDEILNOOST	consolidate	
ACDEILNORSS	cordialness	
ACDEILNORSY	secondarily	
ACDEILNORTU	radiolucent	
ACDEILNOSTU	inosculated	
ACDEILNOTTU	tentaculoid	
ACDEILNRSTU	stridulance	
ACDEILOORRV	varicolored	
ACDEILORSTU	elucidators	
ACDEILORTUY	elucidatory	
ACDEILORTVY	valedictory	
ACDEILPPSTU	supplicated	
ACDEILPPSTY	dyspeptical	
ACDEILRSSTY	crystalised	
ACDEILRSTTW	wildcatters	
ACDEILRSTYZ	crystalized	
ACDEIMNNOOP	companioned	
ACDEIMNNORU	endocranium	
ACDEIMNNOST	demicantons	
ACDEINNORST	constrained	
ACDEINNORTU	denunciator	
ACDEINOOPRS	scorpaenoid	
ACDEINOORST	carotenoids	
	coordinates	
	decorations	
ACDEINOPRSS	scorpaenids	
ACDEINOPSTT	constipated	
ACDEINORRSW	cordwainers	
ACDEINORRWY	cordwainery	
ACDEINORSTT	detractions	
ACDEINOSSTU	decussation	
ACDEINOSTTU	outdistance	
ACDEINOSTTW	wainscotted	
ACDEINOSTTX	detoxicants	
ACDEINPRSTU	unpractised	
ACDEINPRSTY	predynastic	
ACDEIOOPRSS	radioscopes	
ACDEIOOPRSU	adipocerous	
ACDEIOPRRST	predicators	
ACDEIOPRRTY	predicatory	
ACDEIOPRSSY	caryopsides	
ACDEIQRSSTU	quadrisects	
ACDEIRRSSTT	distracters	
ACDEJORSSTU	coadjutress	
ACDEKNNOPRY	Nordkyn Cape	
ACDELLNOOTY	cotyledonal	
ACDELLOORST	decollators	
ACDELMOPRRS	palmcorders	
ACDELNOORST	decolorants	
ACDELNOOSTY	acotyledons	
ACDELOPRTTY	pterodactyl	
ACDEMMMNNOT	commandment	
ACDEMMNOSTU	consummated	
ACDEMNNORTU	countermand	

ACDEMNORTUY	documentary	ACDHINOORSU	diachronous	ACDOOORSSTU	ostracodous
ACDEMOOPRRS	compradores	ACDHIORSTTY	hydrostatic	ACEEEEEKPPR	peacekeeper
ACDEMOORRST	Côtes-d'Armor	ACDHLLLOPSY	cladophylls	ACEEEFFFRTT	aftereffect
			phylloclads	ACEEEFFMNST	effacements
	ostracoderm	ACDHLNOOORT	notochordal	ACEEEFFSTTU	effectuates
ACDEMOPRSSU	dampcourses	ACDHLOORRSY	hydrocorals	ACEEEFHORRS	forereaches
ACDENNNNOUU	unannounced	ACDIIILLNPS	disciplinal	ACEEEFIPRST	afterpieces
ACDENNNOORS	ordonnances	ACDIIILLOTY	idiotically	ACEEEFLNRRS	freelancers
ACDENNNOOSS	nanoseconds	ACDIIILMOPS	idioplasmic	ACEEEFMNNST	enfacements
ACDENRRRSTU	redcurrants	ACDIIILMORY	domiciliary	ACEEEGHHRST	chargesheet
ACDENRRRSSTU	transducers	ACDIIILNNOT	indictional	ACEEEGHLLNR	rechallenge
ACDEOORRSVW	woodcarvers	ACDIIIMNOST	diatonicism	ACEEEGIMNNT	metagenetic
ACDEOPPRSSU	pseudocarps	ACDIIIMNOTU	unidiomatic	ACEEEGLOTTT	telecottage
ACDFFGHINNU	handcuffing	ACDIIIMOTTY	diatomicity	ACEEEGNPRST	percentages
ACDFFGIINRT	diffracting	ACDIIINNOST	indications	ACEEEGNRRSS	screenagers
ACDFFGILNOS	scaffolding	ACDIIINNOTV	vindication	ACEEEHHIMRX	hexahemeric
ACDFFIILMOO	officialdom	ACDIIIOPRTT	parotiditic	ACEEEHIMNRS	archenemies
ACDFFIINORT	diffraction	ACDIIJLLRUV	juridically	ACEEEHIMNTV	achievement
ACDFIIILRUY	fiduciarily	ACDIILLLLYV	idyllically	ACEEEHINSST	cenesthesia
ACDFIMNNORS	confirmands	ACDIILLORST	clostridial	ACEEEHIORVV	overachieve
ACDGGHIINRS	discharging	ACDIILMNNRU	clinandrium	ACEEEHIRRST	treacheries
ACDGHHIOOPR	hodographic	ACDIILMNOPR	palindromic	ACEEEHIRSTT	catheterise
ACDGHIIIOPR	idiographic	ACDIILMNSSY	syndicalism	ACEEEHIRTTZ	catheterize
ACDGHIIKNNP	handpicking	ACDIILMOPST	diplomatics	ACEEEHKLNRT	leatherneck
ACDGHIINNSW	sandwiching	ACDIILNNOOT	conditional	ACEEEHLLNRT	chanterelle
ACDGHIINPST	dispatching	ACDIILNNOTU	inductional	ACEEEHLMOST	hematoceles
ACDGHIMOOSU	dichogamous	ACDIILNOOST	dislocation	ACEEEHLPSSW	scapewheels
ACDGHIOOPRX	doxographic	ACDIILNOPTU	duplication	ACEEEHLRSST	teacherless
ACDGHIOPRSY	discography	ACDIILNORST	clostridian	ACEEEHLRSTV	Hever Castle
ACDGHIRRRVY	hydrargyric	ACDIILNSSTY	syndicalist	ACEEEHMNNNT	enhancement
ACDGIIILMNS	disclaiming	ACDIILOORRS	sororicidal	ACEEEHMORTT	tacheometer
ACDGIIILOST	dialogistic	ACDIILPRSTU	tricuspidal	ACEEEHNPTTU	Tehuantepec
ACDGIIINNTV	vindicating	ACDIIMNORSS	sardonicism	ACEEEHORRSV	overreaches
ACDGIILNOST	dislocating	ACDIIMNOSTU	coatimundis	ACEEEHRRRSS	researchers
ACDGIILNPTU	duplicating	ACDIIMORSTY	myocarditis	ACEEEIKLNNW	Wanne-Eickel
ACDGIILNTTW	wildcatting	ACDIINNOSTY	syndication	ACEEEILMNPT	mantelpiece
ACDGIINNSTY	syndicating	ACDIINOORST	carotinoids	ACEEEILNQUV	equivalence
ACDGIINOSST	diagnostics	ACDIINOPRST	adscription	ACEEEILNRRV	irrelevance
ACDGIINRSTT	distracting	ACDIINOPSTU	cuspidation	ACEEEILRSTU	electuaries
ACDGILLOOOX	doxological	ACDIINORSTT	distraction	ACEEEIMNRRS	mercenaries
ACDGIMNNOOT	nondogmatic	ACDIINORSTV	vindicators	ACEEEIMPRST	masterpiece
ACDGINOORVW	woodcarving	ACDIINORTVY	vindicatory	ACEEEINNPPT	inappetence
ACDGLLOOTYY	dactylology	ACDIJNNOSTU	adjunctions	ACEEEINNRST	centenaries
ACDGLOSTYYZ	zygodactyls	ACDIKLNOOSS	Cook Islands	ACEEEINNPPS	appetencies
ACDHHIILOTY	ichthyoidal	ACDIKNOPRTW	Downpatrick	ACEEEINRSSS	necessaries
ACDHHIOPRRS	harpsichord	ACDILLMNOOY	monodically	ACEEEINSSTT	necessitate
ACDHHIOPRTY	hydropathic	ACDILLNORTY	doctrinally	ACEEEIPPRSV	apperceives
ACDHIIIMRTT	mithridatic	ACDILLOOSTY	cotyloidals	ACEEEIPTTVX	expectative
ACDHIILLMOY	homicidally	ACDILLOPRSY	dropsically	ACEEEIRRSST	secretaires
ACDHIILOOPR	chiropodial	ACDILLORSTY	crystalloid		secretaries
ACDHIILMNRS	diachronism	ACDILNOSUUU	nudicaulous	ACEEEIRSSTV	eviscerates
ACDHIINOOPR	radiophonic	ACDILOPRSTU	duplicators	ACEEEJKLPST	steeplejack
ACDHIINORST	anhidrotics	ACDIMNOOSTT	mastodontic	ACEEEKLORTW	electroweak
ACDHIIOPRST	diastrophic	ACDIMNORSUY	urodynamics	ACEEELLMNOT	metallocene
ACDHIIOPTVY	hypoacidity	ACDINNNOOOT	condonation	ACEEELLMNOV	malevolence
ACDHILMOORS	harmolodics	ACDINOOORRT	coordinator	ACEEELLNRST	crenellates
ACDHILNOOPS	chilopodans	ACDIOORSSSU	Cassiodorus	ACEEELLSSSY	ceaselessly
ACDHIMNNSTU	Duncan Smith	ACDKNORSSTU	soundtracks	ACEEELMMNPT	emplacement
ACDHIMNOORT	trichomonad	ACDLLOPSTYY	polydactyls	ACEEELMNNST	enlacements
ACDHIMNORTY	hydromantic	ACDLNOOORTY	condolatory	ACEEELMNPRT	replacement
ACDHINNORYY	cyanohydrin	ACDMOOORRSU	acrodromous	ACEEELMNRRT	recremental
ACDHINOOOSX	chionodoxas	ACDMORRSSUU	sursum corda	ACEEELMNRTX	excremental

ACEEEELNOSUX	exonuclease	
ACEEEELORSTT	electorates	
	selectorate	
ACEEEELRRSST	terraceless	
ACEEEELRSSTT	telecasters	
ACEEEEMMNRST	amercements	
ACEEEEMNNRTT	reenactment	
ACEEEEMNNSST	encasements	
ACEEEEMNPSST	escapements	
ACEEEEMNRRTT	retracement	
ACEEEEMNRSTT	metacenters	
	metacentres	
ACEEEEMORSTT	acetometers	
ACEEEENNOSTV	covenantees	
ACEEEENNPRST	repentances	
ACEEEENNRRST	reentrances	
ACEEEENPRSTW	Western Cape	
ACEEEENRRSSV	screensaver	
ACEEEEOPRTTX	expectorate	
ACEEEEPRRSTU	recuperates	
ACEEEEPRSSTT	pacesetters	
ACEEEERRSSST	creatresses	
ACEEEERRSTTY	Carey Street	
ACEEFFHSSUU	chauffeuses	
ACEEFFIILOS	officialese	
ACEEFFILNTU	ineffectual	
ACEEFFLLTUY	effectually	
ACEEFGILNNR	freelancing	
ACEEFHIIPRS	preachifies	
ACEEFHINNRS	enfranchise	
ACEEFHNNRRTU	furtherance	
ACEEFIILSTT	felicitates	
ACEEFIKLLLPS	Scafell Pike	
ACEEFILLRST	fellatrices	
ACEEFIMNORS	freemasonic	
ACEEFIMNTTU	tumefacient	
ACEEFINOPTT	tepefaction	
ACEEFIORSTV	vociferates	
ACEEFIORSTW	cowfeterias	
ACEEFLLNRST	crestfallen	
ACEEFLNRSSU	carefulness	
ACEEFLORRUV	overcareful	
ACEEFLORSST	forecastles	
ACEEFLORSUU	ferulaceous	
ACEEFLPRRTU	prefectural	
ACEEFLRSSSU	surfaceless	
ACEEFLRSTTU	leafcutters	
ACEEFMNOPRR	performance	
ACEEFORRSST	forecasters	
ACEEGGIMMNO	emmenagogic	
ACEEGGIMNOT	gametogenic	
	gamogenetic	
	geomagnetic	
ACEEGGNORST	congregates	
ACEEGHHPRRY	hypercharge	
ACEEGHILOOT	oligochaete	
ACEEGHILPRT	telegraphic	
ACEEGHIMNOT	hematogenic	
ACEEGHINNR	interchange	
ACEEGHINORT	atherogenic	
ACEEGHINORV	Hercegovina	
ACEEGHINRRS	researching	

ACEEGHLLNRS	challengers
ACEEGHMMORT	hectogramme
ACEEGHNORSV	changeovers
ACEEGHNRRSU	chargenurse
ACEEGHORRSV	overcharges
ACEEGHPRRSU	supercharge
ACEEGIILNNT	geanticline
ACEEGIKNNPP	kneecapping
ACEEGILLNRY	generically
ACEEGILLNTY	genetically
ACEEGILLNUY	eugenically
ACEEGILLRVY	viceregally
ACEEGILLMMRT	telegrammic
ACEEGILMOPS	mesopelagic
ACEEGILMORT	geometrical
ACEEGILNNPR	precleaning
ACEEGILNLNRT	crenelating
ACEEGILNNTU	enucleating
ACEEGILNRSS	gracileness
ACEEGILNSTT	telecasting
ACEEGILPRTT	tetraplegic
ACEEGILSSTU	sluicegates
ACEEGILSTTU	gesticulate
ACEEGIMMNPT	camp meeting
ACEEGIMMNRT	centigramme
ACEEGIMMORT	microgamete
ACEEGINNPRS	pregnancies
ACEEGINNRST	astringence
ACEEGINORTT	teratogenic
ACEEGINOTTU	autogenetic
ACEEGIORSST	categorises
ACEEGIORSTZ	categorizes
ACEEGIOSTTX	excogitates
ACEEGIRRRTY	cerargyrite
ACEEGLLRSSY	gracelessly
ACEEGLMNNOT	congealment
ACEEGLMNORS	camerlengos
ACEEGMNORRS	scaremonger
ACEEGMOSTTY	gametocytes
ACEEGNNOSST	cognateness
ACEEGNORRSU	encouragers
ACEEHHIIRRS	hierarchies
ACEEHHILRSW	wheelchairs
ACEEHHIMOST	theomachies
ACEEHHINRST	ethnarchies
ACEEHHIPRST	heptarchies
ACEEHHIRRSS	heresiarchs
ACEEHHLLRST	hatchellers
ACEEHHMMOOR	haemochrome
ACEEHHMMORS	hemachromes
ACEEHHOPTTY	hypothecate
ACEEHIIINRT	Catherine II
ACEEHIIKLMN	machinelike
ACEEHIILNST	antihelices
	lecithinase
ACEEHIILPTT	epithetical
ACEEHIIMNRS	machineries
ACEEHIINNRT	inheritance
ACEEHIINSTT	esthetician
ACEEHIIRSTT	hetaeristic
ACEEHIKLSTV	thickleaves
ACEEHIKNRTW	kitchenware

ACEEHILLNNP	panhellenic
ACEEHILLRTY	heretically
ACEEHILMNNS	manchineels
ACEEHILMNSS	machineless
ACEEHILMOPR	hemeralopic
ACEEHILNNSS	channelises
ACEEHILNNSZ	channelizes
ACEEHILNSST	ethicalness
ACEEHILOORZ	coleorhizae
ACEEHILORTT	theoretical
ACEEHIMMNPT	impeachment
ACEEHIMNNNT	enchainment
ACEEHIMNPSZ	chimpanzees
ACEEHIMNRSS	mechanisers
ACEEHIMNRSZ	mechanizers
ACEEHIMORTT	theorematic
ACEEHIMPRST	champerties
ACEEHIMRTTY	erythematic
ACEEHIMSSST	schematises
ACEEHIMSSTZ	schematizes
ACEEHINNSTZ	Nietzschean
ACEEHINPRRT	Charpentier
ACEEHINPRST	pentarchies
ACEEHINPRTT	parenthetic
ACEEHINSSTT	anesthetics
ACEEHIOPRST	pothecaries
	spirochaete
ACEEHIORRST	charioteers
ACEEHIORSST	theocrasies
ACEEHIORTTX	heterotaxic
ACEEHIPRSTT	paresthetic
ACEEHIPRTTU	therapeutic
ACEEHIPRTVY	hyperactive
ACEEHIRRSTT	tetrarchies
ACEEHKLLRSS	shellackers
ACEEHKLNRST	halternecks
ACEEHLLNNRS	channellers
ACEEHLMMNSY	mesenchymal
ACEEHLMNRUU	Herculaneum
ACEEHLMOPRS	polemarches
ACEEHLMOPSY	mesocephaly
ACEEHLNOPSU	encephalous
ACEEHLNPRSU	leprechauns
ACEEHLNPSTT	planchettes
ACEEHLOORRU	leucorrhoea
ACEEHLOPRRT	perchlorate
ACEEHLOPSTY	polychaetes
ACEEHMMNNRT	merchantmen
ACEEHMMRSSU	meerschaums
ACEEHMNNNTT	enchantment
ACEEHMNNRRT	trencherman
ACEEHMNNSST	encashments
ACEEHMNOORS	anemochores
ACEEHMNOSTU	menthaceous
ACEEHMNPRST	preachments
ACEEHMNRSST	manchesters
ACEEHMORSTT	tachometers
ACEEHMORSTV	overmatches
ACEEHMORTTY	tacheometry
ACEEHMRSTTY	tachymeters
ACEEHNNORRT	archenteron
ACEEHNNRSST	enchantress

ACEEHNORSSS anchoresses	**ACEEILNNRST** intercensal	**ACEEIOOPRSS** aeciospores
ACEEHNORSTT anchorettes	**ACEEILMNNTUV** lieutenancy	**ACEEIOOPPRTV** cooperative
ACEEHOPRRRS reproachers	**ACEEILNOPTX** exceptional	**ACEEIOPPRSU** piperaceous
ACEEHOPRRSS archespores	**ACEEILNORSS** recessional	**ACEEIOPPSST** episcopates
ACEEHORRSTT orchestrate	**ACEEILNORST** resectional	**ACEEIOPRRTV** procreative
ACEEHORRSTU treacherous	**ACEEILNORTU** reinoculate	**ACEEIOQSTUV** equivocates
ACEEHORSTVW overwatches	**ACEEILNOSSS** secessional	**ACEEIORRSTV** eviscerator
ACEEHPRRSSU repurchases	**ACEEILNOSST** coessential	**ACEEIORRTTV** retroactive
ACEEIIINRST itineracies	**ACEEILNPRTT** centripetal	**ACEEIPRSTUV** superactive
ACEEIIKRSTT rickettsiae	**ACEEILNPSSS** specialness	**ACEEIQRSSTU** requiescats
ACEEIILLNPT penicillate	**ACEEILNPSST** plicateness	**ACEEIRSSTTU** resuscitate
ACEEIILLNRT rectilineal	**ACEEILNQUVY** equivalency	**ACEEJLMNOST** cajolements
ACEEIILLNRY eirenically	**ACEEILNNRST** centraliser	**ACEEJNPRSTU** superjacent
ACEEIILLSSX lexicalises	**ACEEILNRTSZ** centralizer	**ACEEKLLRSSS** salesclerks
ACEEIILLSXZ lexicalizes	**ACEEILNRRTZ** irrelevancy	**ACEEKORRSSW** caseworkers
ACEEIILLTVV vellicative	**ACEEILNRSST** centralises	**ACEELLLORTY** electorally
ACEEIILNRRT rectilinear		linecasters	**ACEELLNORTY** coeternally
ACEEIILNSTT licentiates		treacliness	**ACEELLNOSTT** constellate
ACEEIILPRTV replicative	**ACEEILNRSSY** necessarily	**ACEELLOPTUY** eucalyptole
ACEEIILPSSS specialises	**ACEEILNRSTV** cantilevers	**ACEELLORSTT** collarettes
ACEEIILPSST specialties	**ACEEILNRSTZ** centralizes	**ACEELLRSSTY** tracelessly
ACEEIILPSSZ specializes	**ACEEILNRTTY** Eternal City	**ACEELMNNOOV** monovalence
ACEEIILPTVX explicative	**ACEEILOPRTV** percolative	**ACEELMNOPTT** contemplate
ACEEIILSSST elasticises	**ACEEILORRTV** correlative	**ACEELMNOSTY** melanocytes
ACEEIILSSTZ elasticizes	**ACEEILORTUX** executorial	**ACEELMORSTT** lactometers
ACEEIIMNRRT recriminate	**ACEEILOTVVY** evocatively	**ACEELNNNSSU** uncleanness
ACEEIIMNSTT antiemetics	**ACEEILPRRTY** preliteracy	**ACEELNNRSSU** unclearness
ACEEIINNRST incinerates	**ACEEILPSTUV** speculative	**ACEELNOOPRT** coleopteran
ACEEIINNTUV enunciative	**ACEEILRRSSU** seculariser	**ACEELNOPSTT** Pentecostal
ACEEIINRSST insectaries	**ACEEILRRSUZ** secularizer	**ACEELNOQSSU** coequalness
	Resistencia	**ACEEILRSSSU** secularises	**ACEELNPRSSY** screenplays
ACEEIINRSTT certainties	**ACEEILRSSUZ** secularizes	**ACEELNPTTXY** expectantly
ACEEIINRTTV interactive	**ACEEILRSTTU** reticulates	**ACEELOORRTW** watercooler
ACEEIINSSTT intestacies	**ACEEILSSTUV** vesiculates	**ACEELOPPPRT** copperplate
ACEEIIPPRTT peripatetic	**ACEEILSTTTU** testiculate	**ACEELOPPRRT** preceptoral
	precipitate	**ACEEIMMNNORT** anemometric	**ACEELOSSTUY** setaceously
ACEEIIRSSTT cassiterite	**ACEEIMMORST** commiserate	**ACEEMMMOORT** commemorate
ACEEIIRSTTV recitatives	**ACEEIMMNOTT** cementation	**ACEEMMNNPST** encampments
ACEEIJNNRTT interjacent	**ACEEIMMNNSST** incasements	**ACEEMMNOSTT** commentates
ACEEIKLMNRT Maeterlinck	**ACEEIMMNOPRT** armipotence	**ACEEMMORSSU** commeasures
ACEEIKNRSTW awestricken	**ACEEIMMNORRT** craniometer	**ACEEMNOOPSS** anemoscopes
ACEEIKNSSSS seasickness	**ACEEIMNORST** actinomeres	**ACEEMNOPSSS** encompasses
ACEEIILLLORT colleterial	**ACEEIMNORTT** actinometer	**ACEEMNOPSST** compensates
ACEEIILLSTY celestially	**ACEEIMNQRTU** acquirement	**ACEEMNPRSST** escarpments
ACEEIILLNNSS cleanliness	**ACEEIMNRSTT** remittances	**ACEEMOPRTTU** computerate
ACEEIILLORTV vorticellae	**ACEEIMORRST** crematories	**ACEENNNOPRU** preannounce
ACEEIILLPPTT cappelletti	**ACEEIMOSSTV** vasectomies	**ACEENNNOSST** connateness
ACEEIILMNNRT incremental	**ACEEINNNSST** ancientness	**ACEENNOPRTU** counterpane
ACEEIILMNORS ceremonials	**ACEEINNOPTZ** pentazocine	**ACEENNORRTV** contravener
ACEEIILMNORT Trincomalee	**ACEEINNORTV** noncreative	**ACEENNORSTT** consternate
ACEEIILMNOSU leucomaines	**ACEEINNPPTY** inappetency	**ACEENNORSTV** contravenes
ACEEIILMNRRY mercenarily	**ACEEINNRRSU** reinsurance		covenanters
ACEEIILMNSST centesimals	**ACEEINNSSTX** inexactness	**ACEENNPRSTU** purtenances
	lemniscates	**ACEEINOPTTX** expectation	**ACEENNRSSUY** unnecessary
ACEEIILMORRT calorimeter	**ACEEINORRST** recreations	**ACEENOORSTT** cotoneaster
ACEEIILMORST elastomeric	**ACEEINORSTU** auctioneers	**ACEENOPRSTV** vaporescent
ACEEIILMPSST esemplastic	**ACEEINORSTX** execrations	**ACEENOPRTTX** expectorant
ACEEIILMRTUV vermiculate	**ACEEINPPRST** apprentices	**ACEENRSSSTW** newscasters
ACEEIILNNNST centennials	**ACEEINPRRST** transpierce	**ACEEOOPRSTU** proteaceous
ACEEIILNNORT crenelation	**ACEEINPRSST** interspaces	**ACEEOPRRRTU** recuperator
	intolerance	**ACEEINRRSTV** transceiver	**ACEEORRSTUW** watercourse
ACEEIILNNOTU enucleation	**ACEEINRSSST** resistances	**ACEEPRRSSUU** acupressure

ACEEPRSSTTY	typecasters	
ACEFFGHILNR	cliffhanger	
ACEFFGILNTY	affectingly	
ACEFFIIIORS	officiaries	
ACEFFIILPST	spifflicate	
ACEFFIITTVY	affectivity	
ACEFFIKRRST	traffickers	
ACEFFILRSST	trafficless	
ACEFFIOSTUV	suffocative	
ACEFGHLLNUY	changefully	
ACEFGHMORRS	frogmarches	
ACEFGIIMNNT	magnificent	
ACEFGIIMNOS	magnificoes	
ACEFGIINNNR	refinancing	
ACEFGIINNRT	interfacing	
ACEFGILNRTU	centrifugal	
ACEFGINORST	forecasting	
ACEFGINRRSU	resurfacing	
ACEFHILNOPR	francophile	
ACEFHILRSTU	ultrafiches	
ACEFHINOSTT	fianchettos	
ACEFHKORSST	aftershocks	
ACEFHLOPRRU	reproachful	
ACEFHNNOOPR	francophone	
ACEFHORRSTV	hovercrafts	
ACEFIIINORT	reification	
ACEFIILMNOR	infomercial	
ACEFIILNNSS	finicalness	
ACEFIILORTT	felicitator	
ACEFIILPRSU	superficial	
ACEFIILPSST	spifflicates	
ACEFIILRSSS	classifiers	
ACEFIILTTVY	factitively	
ACEFIIMORRS	formicaries	
ACEFIINOPTT	pontificate	
ACEFIINORST	fractionise	
ACEFIINORTZ	fractionize	
ACEFIINRSST	sanctifiers	
ACEFIIORRTY	reificatory	
ACEFIIRSSST	satisficers	
ACEFIKLORTY	factorylike	
ACEFILLLOTU	folliculate	
ACEFILLORUW	cauliflower	
ACEFILOORST	olfactories	
ACEFILORSTU	lactiferous	
ACEFILOSTUY	facetiously	
ACEFIMNOTTU	tumefaction	
ACEFINNRSST	franticness	
ACEFINORRST	refractions	
ACEFINORSTV	vociferants	
ACEFINOTTUV	confutative	
ACEFIOORRTV	vociferator	
ACEFIPRRSTT	priestcraft	
ACEFKRRRSSU	starfuckers	
ACEFLNSSTTU	tactfulness	
ACEFMNORSTW	craftswomen	
ACEFNNOSSST	confessants	
ACEFRRSSSTU	surfcasters	
ACEGGHILLNN	challenging	
ACEGGHILNNS	changelings	
ACEGGHLOOSU	cholagogues	
ACEGGILLMOO	gemological	

ACEGGILRSST	scraggliest	
ACEGGINNNORU	encouraging	
ACEGGINRSSS	scragginess	
ACEGGLNOOYY	gynaecology	
ACEGGNNORST	congregants	
ACEGGNOORRT	congregator	
ACEGHHIJKRS	highjackers	
ACEGHHILLNT	hatchelling	
ACEGHHILOPR	helicograph	
ACEGHHILRST	searchlight	
ACEGHHIMORR	hemorrhagic	
ACEGHHNORST	shortchange	
ACEGHHOOPRR	choreograph	
ACEGHHOPRRY	choregraphy	
ACEGHHOPRST	hectographs	
ACEGHHOPRTY	hectography	
ACEGHIIIMNT	Michiganite	
ACEGHIILMNS	alchemising	
ACEGHIILMNZ	alchemizing	
ACEGHIILORS	oligarchies	
ACEGHIIMNNS	mechanising	
ACEGHIIMNNZ	mechanizing	
ACEGHIIMNST	misteaching	
ACEGHIKLLNS	shellacking	
ACEGHILLNNN	channelling	
ACEGHILLOOR	rheological	
ACEGHILLOOT	ethological	
	theological	
ACEGHILMOOS	logomachies	
ACEGHILMOOT	hematologic	
ACEGHILNRSY	searchingly	
ACEGHILNTTW	angletwitch	
ACEGHILOOPR	oleographic	
ACEGHILOPSY	geophysical	
ACEGHIMMOOT	homogametic	
ACEGHIMNNRT	merchanting	
ACEGHIMNNSU	machineguns	
ACEGHIMNORR	menorrhagic	
ACEGHIMNORU	archegonium	
ACEGHIMRSST	Great Schism	
ACEGHINNNOT	nonteaching	
ACEGHINNOPR	chaperoning	
ACEGHINOPRR	reproaching	
ACEGHINORRV	overarching	
ACEGHINORTU	outreaching	
ACEGHINPRSS	graphicness	
ACEGHINRRST	chatterings	
ACEGHIOOPSS	hagioscopes	
ACEGHIOPRRX	xerographic	
ACEGHIRSSTW	switchgears	
ACEGHLNOPTT	plectognath	
ACEGHLOOSTY	eschatology	
ACEGHNOPRSY	scenography	
ACEGHOOPRSU	creophagous	
ACEGHORRSTU	roughcaster	
ACEGHRRRSSU	surchargers	
ACEGIILLNPR	callipering	
ACEGIILLNPS	specialling	
ACEGIILLNTV	vellicating	
ACEGIILLOOT	etiological	
ACEGIILLOTV	colligative	
ACEGIILMNOR	mineralogic	

ACEGIILMRRU	Muir Glacier	
ACEGIILNNRT	interlacing	
ACEGIILNOST	Castiglione	
ACEGIILNPPY	pipeclaying	
ACEGIILNPRT	replicating	
ACEGIILNPTX	explicating	
ACEGIILNRST	cartelising	
ACEGIILNRTZ	cartelizing	
ACEGIILOSTT	egotistical	
ACEGIILRSST	sacrilegist	
ACEGIIMNOST	isomagnetic	
ACEGIIMNPRT	imprecating	
ACEGIIMNRST	miscreating	
ACEGIIMNRTT	metricating	
ACEGIIMRRTV	gravimetric	
ACEGIINNNTU	enunciating	
ACEGIINNRTT	interacting	
ACEGIINORTX	excoriating	
ACEGIINPRTT	crepitating	
ACEGIINQRRU	reacquiring	
ACEGIINRSTU	cauterising	
ACEGIINRTTX	extricating	
ACEGIINRTUZ	cauterizing	
ACEGIJNOTUV	conjugative	
ACEGILLLLOY	collegially	
ACEGILLMRTU	metallurgic	
ACEGILLNNOY	congenially	
ACEGILLNNPS	spancelling	
ACEGILLNOOO	oenological	
ACEGILLNOOP	penological	
ACEGILLNORV	overcalling	
ACEGILLNOSS	logicalness	
ACEGILLOORS	serological	
ACEGILLOOSS	oligoclases	
ACEGILLOOSX	sexological	
ACEGILMNORS	camerlingos	
ACEGILMNOSU	glucosamine	
ACEGILMOSTY	cleistogamy	
ACEGILNNNOU	uncongenial	
ACEGILNNOOT	congelation	
ACEGILNNSUY	unceasingly	
ACEGILNOPRT	percolating	
ACEGILNOPTY	genotypical	
ACEGILNORRT	correlating	
ACEGILNORSS	casseroling	
ACEGILNORSW	lowercasing	
ACEGILNPSTU	speculating	
ACEGILNPTUX	exculpating	
ACEGILNRSSY	caressingly	
ACEGILNTUUU	unguiculate	
ACEGILOOPST	apologetics	
ACEGILOORTT	teratologic	
ACEGILRRTUU	agriculture	
ACEGIMMRRSS	scrimmagers	
ACEGIMNNNOT	nonmagnetic	
ACEGIMNNOPR	panicmonger	
ACEGIMNNORT	centimorgan	
ACEGIMNOOST	somatogenic	
ACEGIMNOTVY	vaginectomy	
ACEGIMNRRTU	mercurating	
ACEGIMORSST	mesogastric	
ACEGINNNOSU	consanguine	

ACEGINNNOTV	covenanting	ACEHILLPRSY	spherically
ACEGINNORST	recognisant	ACEHILMNOOR	melanochroi
ACEGINNORTZ	recognizant	ACEHILMNORS	chloramines
ACEGINNRSTT	transecting	ACEHILMOPSU	mailpouches
ACEGINNRSTY	astringency	ACEHILMRTUV	eurythmical
ACEGINOOPRT	cooperating	ACEHILNORST	chlorinates
ACEGINOOPRRT	procreating	ACEHILNPRST	sphincteral
ACEGINORRTT	retroacting	ACEHILNSSTU	clianthuses
ACEGINORSTV	overcasting	ACEHILNSTTY	synthetical
ACEGINPPRSU	uppercasing	ACEHILOPRST	arctophiles
ACEGINPRRTU	recapturing	ACEHILOPRSY	polyarchies
ACEGINPSTTY	typecasting	ACEHILRSSSY	chrysalises
ACEGINRSSTT	scatterings	ACEHIMMOPRT	metamorphic
ACEGIOORTTX	excogitator	ACEHIMNORSS	marchioness
ACEGIOPSTTY	steatopygic	ACEHIMNORTU	euchromatin
ACEGJLNOTUY	conjugately	ACEHIMNOSST	macintoshes
ACEGKORSSTU	goatsuckers	ACEHIMNOSVY	hyoscyamine
ACEGKRSSTTU	stagestruck	ACEHIMNRSSV	revanchisms
ACEGLLNOOSU	collagenous	ACEHIMOOSTT	homeostatic
ACEGLNOPRTY	calyptrogen	ACEHIMOPRST	atmospheric
ACEGLNORTUY	granulocyte	ACEHIMORRRT	arthromeric
ACEGMMRRSSU	scrummagers	ACEHIMORRST	choirmaster
ACEGMNNORSS	congressman	ACEHIMORRYZ	mycorrhizae
ACEGMOPRRST	spectrogram	ACEHIMORSST	metachrosis
ACEGNOORRTT	gerontocrat	ACEHIMORSTT	hematocrits
ACEGNORRSTT	congratters	ACEHIMORTTX	thermotaxic
ACEGNRSSTTU	scatterguns	ACEHIMOSSTT	hemostatics
ACEGOOPRSST	gastroscope	ACEHIMPSSTY	metaphysics
ACEHHIILMOP	haemophilic	ACEHIMPSTTY	sympathetic
	hemophiliac	ACEHINNOPTT	pantothenic
ACEHHIIMRRS	hierarchism	ACEHINNPSSU	paunchiness
ACEHHIINNTY	hyacinthine	ACEHINNRSSU	raunchiness
ACEHHILNOTT	chloanthite	ACEHINNTTUU	unauthentic
ACEHHIMOOPT	homeopathic	ACEHINOPRRS	chairperson
ACEHHINOSTX	hexastichon	ACEHINOPRRT	chiropteran
ACEHHIPSSTT	heptastichs	ACEHINOPRTU	neuropathic
ACEHHIRSTUV	Turishcheva	ACEHINOPRTY	hyperaction
ACEHHLMNNOT	Melanchthon	ACEHINORRST	orchestrina
ACEHIIILMLV	Michael VIII	ACEHINORSTV	chevrotains
ACEHIIINPSS	hispanicise	ACEHINRSSST	starchiness
ACEHIIINPSZ	hispanicize	ACEHINRSSTV	revanchists
ACEHIIIRSTT	hetairistic	ACEHINSSSTT	cattishness
ACEHIILLMOT	homiletical	ACEHIOOPRST	osteopathic
ACEHIILLOST	isolecithal	ACEHIOOPTTV	photoactive
ACEHIILMSTT	athleticism	ACEHIOPPRST	Hippocrates
ACEHIILNOPR	necrophilia	ACEHIOPRRST	creatorship
ACEHIILNOPS	neophiliacs	ACEHIOPSSTY	isopachytes
ACEHIILOSTT	chiastolite	ACEHIORSSTV	tovarisches
	heliostatic	ACEHIPRRSST	archpriests
ACEHIILPPTY	epiphytical	ACEHIQRRSUY	squirearchy
ACEHIILRSTT	thersitical	ACEHIRSSTTT	tetrastichs
ACEHIILSTWW	welwitschia	ACEHJKNNOSY	johnnycakes
ACEHIINNOPT	phonetician	ACEHJRRSSUW	jawcrushers
ACEHIINOPRY	perionychia	ACEHKKRRSSU	sharksucker
ACEHIINORRT	rhetorician	ACEHKLMMORS	hammerlocks
ACEHIINPSTT	pantheistic	ACEHKLNOSST	chalkstones
ACEHIIPRSSU	haruspicies	ACEHKNOSSTU	Stockhausen
ACEHIKLPRRS	parish clerk	ACEHLLMSSTY	matchlessly
ACEHIKMRRSS	reichsmarks	ACEHLMMNOOR	chromonemal
ACEHILLOOSS	alcoholises	ACEHLMOOSST	schoolmates
ACEHILLOOSZ	alcoholizes	ACEHLNNRTTY	trenchantly
		ACEHLNOPRTY	lycanthrope

ACEHLNORSST	charlestons
ACEHLORSTUY	lythraceous
ACEHMNNOORW	anchorwomen
ACEHMNOPRSY	prosenchyma
ACEHMNOSTWY	yachtswomen
ACEHMOORSUX	auxochromes
ACEHMOORTTY	tracheotomy
ACEHMOPRSTU	champertous
ACEHMORRTTY	arthrectomy
ACEHNNOOPRT	ctenophoran
ACEHNNSSSTU	staunchness
ACEHNOPSTYY	cyanophytes
ACEHNORRSTT	trochanters
ACEHOOPPRRS	carpophores
ACEHOOPPRST	arthroscope
	crapshooter
	prothoraces
ACEHOPPRSTU	touchpapers
ACEHOPRRSSY	chrysoprase
ACEHOPRRTYY	cryotherapy
ACEHOPSSTTW	stopwatches
ACEHORSTTWW	watchtowers
ACEIIIILNSV	civilianise
ACEIIIILNVZ	civilianize
ACEIIIKNNOS	aniseikonic
ACEIIIKNSST	ekisticians
ACEIIILMNRS	criminalise
ACEIIILMNRZ	criminalize
ACEIIILMPTV	implicative
ACEIIILNOTT	elicitation
ACEIIILOSST	socialities
ACEIIILPSTT	pietistical
ACEIIIMNNRT	incriminate
ACEIIIMNOST	semiotician
ACEIIIMNRTV	criminative
ACEIIIPSTTV	captivities
ACEIIIQSTUV	acquisitive
ACEIIKLLNTY	kinetically
ACEIIKLLOOR	kilocalorie
ACEIIKLRSTT	rickettsial
ACEIIKNOTTU	autokinetic
ACEIIKNRSSS	airsickness
ACEIIKRSSTT	rickettsias
ACEIILLLTVY	levitically
ACEIILLMMTY	mimetically
ACEIILLMNNU	illuminance
ACEIILLMOTY	meiotically
ACEIILLMPRY	empirically
ACEIILLMSSY	seismically
ACEIILLNOTV	vellication
ACEIILLNRTV	intervallic
ACEIILLNRUV	curvilineal
ACEIILLNSTT	scintillate
ACEIILLOSST	callosities
ACEIILMNPRT	planimetric
ACEIILMNSSU	masculinise
ACEIILMNSTT	mentalistic
ACEIILMNSUZ	masculinize
ACEIILMORST	isometrical
ACEIILMOTTU	itacolumite
ACEIILMPRTU	implicature
ACEIILMRRTT	trimetrical

ACEIILLNNORT	reclination		intoxicates
ACEIILNOORT	coalitioner	ACEIINPPRST	principates
ACEIILNOPPR	pilocarpine	ACEIINPPRTT	precipitant
ACEIILNOPRT	replication	ACEIINPRTTY	antipyretic
ACEIILNOPTX	explication		pertinacity
ACEIILNOQTU	equinoctial	ACEIINPSSTT	antiseptics
ACEIILNOTUV	inoculative	ACEIIOOPPST	aposiopetic
ACEIILNPRUY	pecuniarily	ACEIIORRRST	certioraris
ACEIILNPTUV	inculpative	ACEIIPPSSST	epispastics
ACEIILNRRUV	curvilinear	ACEIIRRSSSU	cuirassiers
ACEIILNRSTT	clarinetist	ACEIIRRSSSTU	casuistries
ACEIILNRSTU	unrealistic	ACEIJNORSTT	trajections
ACEIILNRTTY	intricately	ACEIKLLPSTY	skeptically
ACEIILOPRST	tropicalise	ACEIKLMNNNW	Winckelmann
ACEIILOPRTZ	tropicalize	ACEIKLORTTW	latticework
ACEIILORSSS	socialisers	ACEILLLMNOR	lamellicorn
ACEIILORSSZ	socializers	ACEILLLMOPY	polemically
ACEIILPPRST	participles	ACEILLLNORT	citronellal
ACEIILPRSST	plasticiser	ACEILLLNORY	collinearly
ACEIILPRSTT	peristaltic	ACEILLLNOUV	involucella
	triplicates	ACEILLLNRUU	unicellular
ACEIILPRSTZ	plasticizer	ACEILLLRTUV	cellularity
ACEIILPRTUY	peculiarity	ACEILLMMSTY	symmetallic
ACEIILPSSST	plasticises	ACEILLMMNOT	nonmetallic
	specialists	ACEILLMNOST	callistemon
ACEIILPSSTZ	plasticizes	ACEILLMNRUY	numerically
ACEIILRSSTT	recitalists	ACEILLMNSUV	masculinely
ACEIILRTTVV	verticality	ACEILLMOPRY	promycelial
ACEIIMMORSS	commissaire	ACEILLMOTTY	totemically
ACEIIMNNRST	manneristic	ACEILLMRRUY	mercurially
ACEIIMNOPRT	imprecation	ACEILLNNOOO	neocolonial
ACEIIMNORST	anisometric	ACEILLNNOTY	octennially
	creationism	ACEILLNOOST	ocellations
	miscreation	ACEILLNOPTU	cupellation
	reactionism	ACEILLNOSTY	sectionally
	romanticise	ACEILLNOTTY	tonetically
ACEIIMNORTT	interatomic	ACEILLNRSSY	lyricalness
	metrication	ACEILLNRSTY	crystalline
ACEIIMNORTZ	romanticize	ACEILLOORRS	corollaries
ACEIIMNPRRU	pericranium	ACEILLOPPSY	episcopally
ACEIIMNPSST	emancipists	ACEILLOPSSW	pillowcases
ACEIIMNPSSU	impuissance	ACEILLOQUVY	equivocally
ACEIIMNRSTT	martensitic	ACEILLORTVY	vectorially
ACEIIMNRSTU	insectarium	ACEILLRSSTY	crystallise
ACEIIMNSSTT	semanticist	ACEILLRSTTY	crystallite
ACEIINNNOST	incensation	ACEILLRSTUV	victuallers
ACEIINNNOTU	enunciation	ACEILLRSTYZ	crystallize
ACEIINNOPTT	pectination	ACEILLRSUVY	vesicularly
ACEIINNORRT	incinerator	ACEILLRTUVY	lucratively
ACEIINNORST	cinerations	ACEILLSSTUV	victualless
ACEIINNORTT	interaction	ACEILMMNNOSU	communalise
ACEIINNPSTT	pinnatisect	ACEILMMNOTY	laminectomy
ACEIINOORTX	excoriation		metonymical
ACEIINOPRTT	crepitation	ACEILMMNOUZ	communalize
ACEIINOPSTT	pectisation	ACEILMMORTT	recommittal
ACEIINOPTTZ	pectization	ACEILMMRSTY	symmetrical
ACEIINORSTT	creationist	ACEILMNNORT	conterminal
	reactionist	ACEILMNNOOPS	scopolamine
	recitations	ACEILMNOOPW	policewoman
ACEIINORTTX	extrication	ACEILMNOPRS	complainers
ACEIINOSSTV	vesications	ACEILMNOPRT	planometric
ACEIINOSTTX	excitations	ACEILMNOPTY	amylopectin

ACEILMNRTTU	curtailment
ACEILMNRTUU	retinaculum
ACEILMNSSSU	musicalness
ACEILMOORTZ	zoometrical
ACEILMOPRRS	proclaimers
ACEILMORRTY	calorimetry
ACEILMORTTV	voltametric
ACEILMRRTUU	mariculture
ACEILNNNOOX	connexional
ACEILNNNOSS	nonsensical
ACEILNNNOTT	continental
ACEILNNNOTU	antinucleon
ACEILNNNORTU	crenulation
ACEILNNOSTU	nucleations
ACEILNNRTUY	uncertainly
ACEILNNNSSY	incessantly
ACEILNOOPRR	incorporeal
ACEILNOOPRT	percolation
ACEILNOORRT	correlation
ACEILNOORST	iconolaters
	relocations
ACEILNOORSU	arenicolous
ACEILNOPRST	inspectoral
	pratincoles
ACEILNOPSTU	peculations
	speculation
ACEILNOPTUX	exculpation
ACEILNOQUUV	unequivocal
ACEILNORSTT	intercostal
ACEILNORSTU	ulcerations
ACEILNORTUV	countervail
	involucrate
ACEILNOSSST	stoicalness
ACEILNOSSTU	inosculates
ACEILNOSTUV	novaculites
ACEILNOSTUY	tenaciously
ACEILNPSSTY	typicalness
ACEILNRRRTU	intercrural
ACEILNRRTUV	ventricular
ACEILNRSSTT	centralists
ACEILNRSSSUV	vulcanisers
ACEILNRSUUX	luxuriances
ACEILNRSUVZ	vulcanizers
ACEILOOOPRT	aeolotropic
ACEILOOPPRS	polariscope
ACEILOOPRSS	acropolises
ACEILOOSSST	osteoclasis
ACEILOPRRTT	protractile
ACEILOPRSTX	explicators
ACEILOPRTXY	explicatory
ACEILORSUVY	veraciously
ACEILORTVYY	viceroyalty
ACEILPPSSTU	supplicates
ACEILPRSTTY	spectrality
ACEILQRTUUU	aquiculture
ACEILRRSSTY	crystaliser
ACEILRRSTYZ	crystalizer
ACEILRRTTUU	turriculate
ACEILRSSSTU	secularists
ACEILRSSSTY	crystalises
ACEILRSSTYZ	crystalizes
ACEIMMOOSSU	mimosaceous

ACEIMMORRTU	crematorium	ACEIOPRRTTV	protractive	ACENOPRRTTU	counterpart
ACEIMMOTTUV	commutative	ACEIOPRSTUU	precautious	ACENOPRSTTT	protectants
ACEIMMPRSSU	supremacism	ACEIORRSSST	ostracisers	ACENORSSSUU	raucousness
ACEIMNNNOTT	containment	ACEIORRSSTZ	ostracizers	ACENORSTTUY	countryseat
ACEIMNNOORY	oneiromancy	ACEJKLPPSSU	supplejacks	ACENOSSSUUV	vacuousness
ACEIMNNOORTX	axonometric	ACEKKMOSSST	smokestacks	ACEOOOPRRST	cooperators
ACEIMNOPRST	importances	ACEKLLRSSTY	tracklessly	ACEOOPPRRSS	carpospores
ACEIMNORRTU	mercuration	ACEKLNOPSST	alpenstocks	ACEOOPRRRST	procreators
ACEIMNORRTY	craniometry	ACEKMNNORRSW	cankerworms	ACEOOPRRSTY	procaryotes
ACEIMNORTTY	actinometry	ACEKNNORSTU	countersank	ACEOOPRSSTU	stauroscope
ACEIMOOPRSZ	azoospermic	ACEKPRRSSSY	skyscrapers	ACEOOPSSSTT	statoscopes
ACEIMOORTVY	ovariectomy	ACELLLLMORUY	molecularly	ACEORSSSSSY	syssarcoses
ACEIMOPRRTY	cryptomeria	ACELLLNNORU	noncellular	ACFFFGILNRU	carfuffling
	imprecatory	ACELLLMMNOSY	commensally	ACFFGIIINOT	officiating
ACEIMORRSTT	astrometric	ACELLMNOPSU	nucleoplasm	ACFFGIIKNRT	trafficking
	meritocrats	ACELLNOPRUV	polynuclear	ACFFGINOSTU	suffocating
ACEIMORSSTU	customaries	ACELLNOPVYY	polyvalency	ACFFIIINOOT	officiation
ACEIMPRSSTU	supremacist	ACELLNORSUY	larcenously	ACFFIILLNOY	officinally
ACEIMSSSTTY	systematics	ACELLNOSSSU	callousness	ACFFIILNOST	nonofficial
ACEINNNNSSU	uncanniness	ACELLNPRTUY	crapulently	ACFFIILNOST	afflictions
ACEINNNOSTT	Constantine	ACELLNRTTUY	reluctantly	ACFFIIOORST	officiators
ACEINNOOTTV	connotative	ACELLOOPRRY	corporeally	ACFFILMNOOR	falconiform
ACEINNORRST	constrainer	ACELLOPSSTU	leucoplasts	ACFFINOOSTU	suffocation
ACEINNORRTV	Canton River	ACELMMNNOORT	nomenclator	ACFGHIINNRS	franchising
ACEINNORSST	sanctioners	ACELMMNNOORU	mononuclear	ACFGHILNNSU	flaunchings
ACEINNORSTT	transection	ACELMMNNOOVY	monovalency	ACFGHINOSUV	vouchsafing
ACEINNORSTU	enunciators	ACELMMNNOSTT	malcontents	ACFGIIINNST	significant
ACEINNORTUY	enunciatory	ACELMMRSTUU	musculature	ACFGIIINSST	satisficing
ACEINNOSTTY	encystation	ACELNNOPRSU	nonspecular	ACFGIIJKKNN	jackknifing
ACEINNPTUUV	nuncupative	ACELNNOSTUV	conventuals	ACFGIILNSSY	classifying
ACEINNRSSSW	scrawniness	ACELNNRSTTU	translucent	ACFGIIMNORT	formicating
ACEINNRSTUU	nunciatures	ACELNORSUVY	cavernously	ACFGIINNORT	fornicating
ACEINNRTTUY	uncertainty	ACELNORTTUX	contextural		fractioning
ACEINOOOPRT	cooperation	ACELNOSSTTU	sansculotte	ACFGIINNSTY	sanctifying
ACEINOOPRRT	incorporate	ACELNOSTUUY	cutaneously	ACFGIINORST	factorising
	procreation	ACELOOPRRST	percolators	ACFGIINORTZ	factorizing
ACEINOOPRTU	aponeurotic	ACELOOPRRTT	protectoral	ACFGIINSTTU	fungistatic
ACEINOORRTT	retroaction	ACELOOPRRTY	corporately	ACFGIKNRSTU	starfucking
ACEINOORSTV	revocations	ACELOORRSTU	coloratures	ACFGILLMOOR	formal logic
ACEINOOSSST	iconostases	ACELOORRSTW	watercolors		logical form
ACEINOPRRTU	Puerto Rican	ACELOORRSSU	coelurosaur	ACFGILNORSU	Saronic Gulf
ACEINOPRSSS	prosaicness	ACELOORRTUW	watercolour	ACFGILNTTUU	fluctuating
ACEINOPRSTU	precautions	ACELOOSSSTT	osteoclasts	ACFGILOSUUY	fugaciously
ACEINOPSSTT	constipates	ACELOPRSSTU	speculators	ACFGINRSSTU	surfcasting
ACEINORRSTT	retractions	ACELOPRSSUY	pelycosaurs	ACFHILNOPRS	francophils
ACEINORRTTY	contrariety	ACELOPRTUXY	exculpatory	ACFHINNOTUX	fucoxanthin
ACEINORSSSU	cariousness	ACEMMNNOORT	commentator	ACFHKOPRSWZ	Schwarzkopf
ACEINORSTTU	eructations	ACEMMNOPRTT	compartment	ACFIIINNOTU	unification
ACEINORSTTV	contrastive	ACEMMNOSSTU	consummates	ACFIIINORTV	vinificator
ACEINORSTTX	extractions	ACEMMNNNOSTT	cantonments	ACFIIKPRTTZ	Fitzpatrick
ACEINPPRSSS	scrappiness	ACEMMNNORSST	monstrances	ACFIILLNOTY	fictionally
ACEINPRRTUY	parturiency	ACEMMNOOPRST	compensator	ACFIILMNORU	californium
ACEINRRTUUV	incurvature	ACEMNOOSTYZ	mycetozoans	ACFIILMORST	formalistic
ACEINRSSSSU	narcissuses	ACEMNOPRRSY	pyromancers	ACFIILMSSSY	misclassify
ACEIOOPRRST	corporatise	ACEMNOSSTTY	nematocysts	ACFIILNOPST	pontificals
ACEIOOPRRTV	corporative	ACEMOOPRRSS	macrospores	ACFIIMMORRU	formicarium
ACEIOOPRRTZ	corporatize	ACEMOOPRRTY	cotemporary	ACFIIMNOORT	formication
ACEIOOPRSTVV	provocative	ACEMORSSTTU	scoutmaster	ACFIIMNORST	informatics
ACEIOOQRTUV	equivocator	ACENNOORSTV	covenantors	ACFIINNOORT	fornication
ACEIOPRRSSU	perisarcous	ACENNOSSTTT	contestants	ACFIINNORST	infarctions
ACEIOPRRSTT	tetrasporic	ACENOORRSTV	conservator		infractions
	triceratops	ACENOPRRSTU	procrustean	ACFIIOPRRTU	purificator

ACFILMNNOTU	malfunction
ACFILNNOOST	conflations
ACFILNNOOSU	confusional
ACFILNNOSTU	functionals
ACFILNOTTUU	fluctuation
ACFILORSTUY	fractiously
ACFIMMOOOPR	Campo Formio
ACFINNOOTTU	confutation
ACFINNORTUY	functionary
ACFINOORRST	fornicators
ACFLNOORSTW	contraflows
ACGGHHIIJKN	highjacking
ACGGHILLNOR	gralloching
ACGGHILOOPR	graphologic
	logographic
ACGGHINRRSU	surcharging
ACGGIIILLNS	gallicising
ACGGIIILLNZ	gallicizing
ACGGIIILLNNS	anglicising
ACGGIIILNNZ	anglicizing
ACGGIIILLNOT	colligating
ACGGIILMNRY	grimacingly
ACGGIIMMNRS	scrimmaging
ACGGIJNNOTU	conjugating
ACGGILNNORU	clangouring
ACGGIMMNRSU	scrummaging
ACGGINNNOOT	contangoing
ACGGINORRTU	corrugating
ACGHHILOOPR	holographic
ACGHHIMOOPR	homographic
ACGHHINOPRY	ichnography
ACGHHIOPRRY	chirography
ACGHHNOOOPR	chronograph
ACGHHOOPRRY	chorography
ACGHIILLNOP	anglophilic
ACGHIILMORT	algorithmic
	logarithmic
ACGHIILNORT	granolithic
ACGHIIMMNST	mismatching
ACGHIIMNNOP	championing
ACGHIIPRSST	sphragistic
ACGHIKMOPRY	kymographic
ACGHILLMOOO	homological
ACGHILLOOOR	horological
ACGHILMOOPR	lagomorphic
ACGHILMOORT	cologarithm
ACGHILMOOST	logomachist
ACGHILNNOSY	anchylosing
ACGHILNRSTT	latchstring
ACGHILOOSST	chaologists
ACGHILOPPRY	polygraphic
ACGHILOPRXY	xylographic
ACGHIMNNOPS	champignons
ACGHIMNOOPR	gramophonic
	monographic
	nomographic
	phonogramic
ACGHIMNOTTU	outmatching
ACGHIMOPRRS	micrographs
ACGHIMOPRRY	micrography
ACGHINOOPRS	nosographic
ACGHINOOPRY	iconography
ACGHINOORTU	coauthoring
ACGHINOPRRY	granophyric
ACGHINOPRSZ	zincographs
ACGHINOPRYZ	zincography
ACGHIOOPPRT	topographic
ACGHIOOPPRY	pyrographic
ACGHIOPPRST	pictographs
ACGHIOPPRTY	pictography
	typographic
ACGHIOPRSTY	hypogastric
ACGHIORRSTT	gastrotrich
ACGHIRRSTTW	cartwrights
ACGHMNOORRS	chronograms
ACGHMOOPRSY	cosmography
ACGHNOOOPRR	coronograph
ACGHOPPRRTY	cryptograph
ACGHOPRSTYY	cystography
ACGIIIILNST	italicising
ACGIIIILNTZ	italicizing
ACGIIILMNPT	implicating
ACGIIILNOSS	socialising
ACGIIILNOST	logistician
ACGIIILNOSZ	socializing
ACGIIILNPST	salpingitic
ACGIIIMNNRT	criminating
ACGIIINNTTT	nictitating
ACGIILLLLOY	illogically
ACGIILLMNOT	collimating
ACGIILLNOOS	sinological
ACGIILLNOOT	colligation
ACGIILLNOST	oscillating
ACGIILLNTUV	victualling
ACGIILLOORV	virological
ACGIILMNNOP	complaining
ACGIILMNNTU	culminating
ACGIILMNOPR	proclaiming
ACGIILNNOOT	cognitional
ACGIILNNOSV	volcanising
ACGIILNNOTU	inoculating
ACGIILNNOVZ	volcanizing
ACGIILNNPTU	inculpating
ACGIILNNSUV	vulcanising
ACGIILNNUVZ	vulcanizing
ACGIILNPSSU	capsulising
ACGIILNPSUZ	capsulizing
ACGIILNTTUV	cultivating
ACGIIMNORVW	microwaving
ACGIIMNOSST	agnosticism
ACGIIMNRRSY	miscarrying
ACGIIMNRSTT	scintigrams
ACGIIMNRTTU	micturating
ACGIINNNOST	sanctioning
ACGIINNNOTZ	incognizant
ACGIINNORST	narcotising
ACGIINNORTZ	narcotizing
ACGIINNOSTW	wainscoting
ACGIINNRTUV	incurvating
ACGIINOOSTT	cogitations
ACGIINORSST	organicists
	ostracising
ACGIINORSTZ	ostracizing
ACGIINRSTTU	rusticating
ACGIJLNOTUY	conjugality
ACGIJNNOOTU	conjugation
ACGIKKMNOPR	pockmarking
ACGIKKNOSTT	stocktaking
ACGILLMNOOO	monological
	nomological
ACGILLMOOOP	pomological
ACGILLMOORS	oscillogram
ACGILLMOOTY	climatology
ACGILLMOOYZ	zymological
ACGILLNOOOS	nosological
ACGILLNOOOT	ontological
ACGILLNOSTY	gnostically
ACGILLOOOPS	posological
ACGILLOOOPT	topological
ACGILLOOPTY	typological
ACGILLOPSUY	callipygous
ACGILLOPSUV	callipygous
ACGILLOPSUV	
ACGILLOTYYZ	zygotically
ACGILMOOOST	somatologic
ACGILNNORSU	nonsurgical
ACGILNOSSTU	outclassing
ACGILOOPRST	carpologist
ACGILOOSSTT	scatologist
ACGIMMNNOTU	commutating
ACGIMNOOPRU	carpogonium
ACGIMNOORST	gastronomic
ACGINNOPSTY	syncopating
ACGINNORSTT	contrasting
ACGINNPTTUU	punctuating
ACGINOORRTU	corrugation
ACGINOORSTY	cosignatory
ACGINOPRRTT	protracting
ACGINOPRSTY	agrypnotics
ACGIORSSTTY	gyrostatics
ACGJNOORSTU	conjugators
ACGLLNOOOVY	volcanology
ACGLLNOOUVY	vulcanology
ACGMOOPRRTU	compurgator
ACGMOOPRSSY	gyrocompass
ACGMOPRRSSY	cryptograms
ACGOOPRSSTY	gastroscopy
ACGOORRRSTU	corrugators
ACHHIILLPTY	ithyphallic
ACHHILLMOOT	homothallic
ACHHILLOOOT	thioalcohol
ACHHILOOPSS	shopaholics
ACHHILOPRSS	scholarship
ACHHINOPRSS	archonships
ACHHINSSTUZ	schizanthus
ACHHIORSTUY	ichthyosaur
ACHHNOOSTTU	autochthons
ACHHNOOTTUY	autochthony
ACHHOPPSSTY	psychopaths
ACHHOPPSTYY	psychopathy
ACHHORRSTWY	crashworthy
ACHIIIHMNPSS	hispanicism
ACHIIINRSTV	Christian IV
ACHIIJKNRSS	jinrickshas
ACHIIJKNRSW	jinrickshaw
ACHIILLMSWY	whimsically
ACHIILLPSST	phallicists
ACHIILMPSSY	physicalism

ACHIILNRSTY christianly	**ACHLMMOORSS** schoolmarms	**ACIIMNORRTY** criminatory
ACHIILOOPPR coprophilia	**ACHLMOOPRST** chromoplast	**ACIIMNORSTT** romanticist
ACHIILOPSST sophistical	**ACHLNOPRTYY** lycanthropy	**ACIIMNRSSTU** manicurists
ACHIILOSTTT lithostatic	**ACHMMNOOORT** monochromat	**ACIIMOPRSSS** prosaicisms
statolithic	**ACHMOOORTTY** thoracotomy	**ACIIMOPRSTT** tropismatic
ACHIILPSSTY physicalist	**ACHNNOORRTU** Harnoncourt	**ACIINNOOSTV** invocations
ACHIILPSTYY physicality	**ACHNNOSTTUY** nyctanthous	**ACIINNORTUV** incurvation
ACHIIMNORST chrismation	**ACHNOOPSSYZ** scyphozoans	**ACIINNOSTTX** intoxicants
harmonistic	**ACHOOPRRSTY** arthroscopy	**ACIINOOPRST** anisotropic
ACHIIMNSSUV chauvinisms	**ACIIIILMNTY** inimicality	**ACIINOORTTX** intoxicator
ACHIIMOPPRT amphiprotic	**ACIIILMNOPT** implication	**ACIINOOSSST** iconostasis
ACHIINNORST Corinthians	**ACIIILMNRTY** criminality	**ACIINOOSSTT** oscitations
ACHIINNPQSU chinquapins	**ACIIILMNNOT** inclination	**ACIINOPRSST** ascriptions
ACHIINNRSTU unchristian	**ACIIILNNRST** intrinsical	crispations
ACHIINOSTUV Antiochus IV	**ACIIILNOPST** politicians	**ACIINOPRTTU** unpatriotic
ACHIINSSTUV chauvinists	**ACIIILRSTTU** ritualistic	**ACIINORSSTT** astrictions
ACHIIPRSSTY physiatrics	**ACIIIMMNORT** crimination	**ACIINORSTTU** rustication
ACHIKKOSTVY Tchaikovsky	**ACIIINNOTTT** nictitation	urtications
ACHIKLOORSW workaholics	**ACIIINOQSTU** acquisition	**ACIINRSSSST** narcissists
ACHIKMNRSSS scrimshanks	**ACIIKKKPRRT** Kirkpatrick	**ACIINRTTTUY** taciturnity
ACHILLMNOOP Champollion	**ACIILLLOPTY** politically	**ACIIOPSSSTT** psittacosis
ACHILLMOOPR allomorphic	**ACIILLMNOOS** colonialism	**ACIIORRRSTT** cirrostrati
ACHILLOPRTY trophically	**ACIILLMNOOT** collimation	**ACIIORRSTUU** urticarious
ACHILMNOORT trichomonal	**ACIILLMNPUY** municipally	**ACIJNNOORTU** conjuration
ACHILMOOPST homoplastic	**ACIILLMOSUY** maliciously	**ACIKLPRTTUY** platykurtic
ACHILMOPSUY polychasium	**ACIILLMOTTY** mitotically	**ACIKNNORSYY** synkaryonic
ACHILMORRYZ mycorrhizal	**ACIILLNNSTT** scintillant	**ACIKOOPRRTY** prokaryotic
ACHILNNOPSY nonphysical	**ACIILLNOOST** colonialist	**ACILLMNOORY** moronically
ACHILNOORRT chlorinator	oscillation	**ACILLMNOPTY** compliantly
ACHILOOPTYZ zoophytical	**ACIILLNOVVY** convivially	**ACILLMNSUUY** unmusically
ACHILOPPSTY hypoplastic	**ACIILLNPPRY** principally	**ACILLMOORST** collimators
ACHILOSSTTW waistcloths	**ACIILLOPRTY** pictorially	**ACILLMOOSTY** osmotically
ACHIMMNOOSU monochasium	**ACIILLPRSTU** pluralistic	**ACILLMOPSTY** plasmolytic
ACHIMNNNOOR nonharmonic	**ACIILLQUYZZ** quizzically	**ACILLMOTVYZ** zymotically
ACHIMNOPSTY amphictyons	**ACIILMNNNOR** noncriminal	**ACILLNNOTUY** continually
ACHIMNOPTYY amphictyony	**ACIILMNNOPT** incompliant	**ACILLNOOSTU** allocutions
ACHIMNORSST monarchists	**ACIILMNNOTU** culmination	**ACILLOORRTT** torticollar
ACHIMOOOPST photomosaic	**ACIILMNOOPT** compilation	**ACILLOORSST** oscillators
ACHIMOPPPSU hippocampus	**ACIILMNORTU** tourmalinic	**ACILLOORSTY** oscillatory
ACHIMOPRSSY symposiarch	**ACIILMNOSUV** minaciously	**ACILLOPPTYY** polytypical
ACHIMOPSSTY scyphistoma	**ACIILMNSSTU** masculinist	**ACILMMMNOSU** communalism
ACHIMORRSTT trichromats	**ACIILMNSTUY** masculinity	**ACILMMNNOOU** communional
ACHIMORRSTY chrismatory	**ACIILMSTTUU** mutualistic	**ACILMMNOOOT** commotional
ACHIMORSSTT chromatists	**ACIILNNOOTU** inoculation	**ACILMMNOOTY** commonality
ACHINNOOPTY apocynthion	**ACIILNNOPTU** inculpation	**ACILMMNOSTU** communalist
ACHINNOPSSY nanophysics	**ACIILNNORSY** synclinoria	**ACILMMNOTUY** communality
ACHINOOPSTT photonastic	**ACIILNNSSTU** instinctual	**ACILMMORSSU** commissural
ACHIOOPPRST apostrophic	**ACIILNOPRSV** provincials	**ACILMNNOPTU** uncompliant
ACHIOOPPRTT protopathic	**ACIILNOPSSU** suspicional	**ACILMNNOSTY** nonmystical
ACHIOOPRTTU autotrophic	**ACIILNOSTXY** anxiolytics	**ACILMNNOSYY** synonymical
ACHIOOPRTUX auxotrophic	**ACIILNOTTUV** cultivation	**ACILMNOOPTY** toponymical
ACHIOOPSTTT photostatic	**ACIILOPRTTY** tropicality	**ACILMNOSTUU** cumulations
ACHIOPPRSTY saprophytic	**ACIILORSTTU** staurolitic	**ACILMOOPSTX** toxoplasmic
ACHIOPRRSTU curatorship	**ACIILOSRTUV** vicariously	**ACILMORSTUY** customarily
ACHIOPRSSTY physiocrats	**ACIILOSUVVY** vivaciously	**ACILMRSTUUY** muscularity
ACHIOPSSTTY attophysics	**ACIIMMMNOST** mammonistic	**ACILNNOOOST** consolation
ACHKLMNOOST kloothmans	**ACIIMMNNOOT** commination	**ACILNNOOPRT** nontropical
ACHKMNOOPRT Rockhampton	**ACIIMMNORST** romanticism	**ACILNOOORST** colorations
ACHLLNORSUY unscholarly	**ACIIMMNOSST** monasticism	**ACILNOOORTU** colouration
ACHLLOOPRST chloroplast	**ACIIMMNSSTU** numismatics	**ACILNOOPSTU** copulations
ACHLLOOPSSY playschools	**ACIIMNOORSU** acrimonious	**ACILNOORSTU** inoculators
ACHLMMOOORS chromosomal	**ACIIMNORRST** criminators	**ACILNOORTUY** locutionary

611

ACILNOOSSTU	osculations	**ACLOOPPRSUY**	polycarpous	**ADDEEHIMNSU**	dehumanised
ACILNOOSTTT	cottontails	**ACLOOPRSUXY**	xylocarpous	**ADDEEHIMNUZ**	dehumanized
ACILNOPRTUY	inculpatory	**ACMMNOORSTU**	consummator	**ADDEEHIRRSS**	sherardised
ACILNORSSTU	ultrasonics	**ACMMOORSTTU**	commutators	**ADDEEHIRRSZ**	sherardized
ACILNPPSSTU	supplicants	**ACMNOOOPRSU**	monocarpous	**ADDEEHLMMSU**	dummelheads
ACILNPTTUUY	punctuality	**ACMNORSTUUY**	uncustomary	**ADDEEHNOOSW**	woodenheads
ACILOOPRRTY	corporality	**ACMOOOPRSTT**	compotators	**ADDEEHNORTW**	downhearted
ACILOORSTUY	atrociously	**ACMOOOSSTTU**	scotomatous	**ADDEEIILMTT**	delimitated
ACILOORSUVY	voraciously	**ACNOOPRRSTT**	cotransport	**ADDEEIILNSS**	desalinised
ACILORSTTUV	cultivators	**ACNOOPRSSTY**	syncopators	**ADDEEIILNST**	disentailed
ACIMMNOORTY	comminatory	**ACNOPRSTTUU**	punctuators	**ADDEEIILNSZ**	desalinized
ACIMMNOOTTU	commutation	**ACOOOPRRRST**	corporators	**ADDEEIILSTV**	devitalised
ACIMMOPSTTY	symptomatic	**ACOOPRRRSTT**	protractors	**ADDEEIILTVZ**	devitalized
ACIMNNNOORTU	mucronation	**ACOOPRRRSTU**	procurators	**ADDEEIJOPRS**	jeopardised
ACIMNOOOPTT	compotation	**ACOOPRRRTUY**	procuratory	**ADDEEIJOPRZ**	jeopardized
ACIMNOOPRSS	comparisons	**ACOPRSSSSTT**	sportscasts	**ADDEEIILMORS**	demoralised
ACIMNOOPTTU	computation	**ADDDEEEIRST**	desiderated	**ADDEEIILMORZ**	demoralized
ACIMNOPRSTY	patronymics	**ADDDEEEERSS**	readdressed	**ADDEEIILNRRT**	interlarded
ACIMNOPRTUY	importunacy	**ADDDEEFHILS**	fiddleheads	**ADDEEIILOPRS**	depolarised
ACIMNPRSSTU	manuscripts	**ADDDEEGIRRS**	disregarded	**ADDEEIILOPRZ**	depolarized
ACIMOOPRRST	corporatism	**ADDDEEHNNRU**	underhanded	**ADDEEIILRRVY**	daredevilry
ACIMOOPRSTT	compatriots	**ADDDEEHNRSU**	dunderheads	**ADDEEIIMNNOT**	denominated
ACINNNNOOST	inconsonant	**ADDDEEHRRSU**	rudderheads	**ADDEEIIMNPRR**	reprimanded
ACINNNOOOTT	connotation	**ADDDEEILSSS**	sidesaddles	**ADDEEIIMORRS**	dromedaries
ACINNNOSTTU	continuants	**ADDDEEIMORS**	Madre de	**ADDEEIIMRSTU**	desideratum
ACINNOOORST	coronations		Dios	**ADDEEIINOPRR**	preordained
ACINNOOPRTT	contraption	**ADDDEELMOTU**	demodulated	**ADDEEIINOPRT**	depredation
ACINNOOPSTY	syncopation	**ADDDEENRSSU**	unaddressed	**ADDEEIINRSTU**	denaturised
ACINNOORTTU	continuator	**ADDDEGIKLNS**	skedaddling	**ADDEEIINRTUZ**	denaturized
ACINNOPSTTU	punctations	**ADDEEEEGNRT**	degenerated	**ADDEEIIRSSTT**	dissertated
ACINNOPTTUU	punctuation	**ADDEEEEHLLV**	levelheaded	**ADDEEILMOSTU**	demodulates
ACINNORSSTT	constraints	**ADDEEEFILRS**	federalised	**ADDEEELNNSTU**	Sudetenland
ACINNORSTTU	truncations	**ADDEEEFILRZ**	federalized	**ADDEEELNPRUY**	underplayed
ACINNRSSTTU	incrustants	**ADDEEEFNRTU**	unfederated	**ADDEEELNRUUV**	undervalued
ACINOOOPRRT	corporation	**ADDEEEGLRTU**	deregulated	**ADDEEELOPPTU**	depopulated
ACINOOOPRTV	provocation	**ADDEEEHLLSW**	swellheaded	**ADDEEELPRSST**	stepladders
ACINOOOPSTT	cooptations	**ADDEEEHNPPR**	apprehended	**ADDEEEMNNNRU**	undermanned
ACINOOPRRST	conspirator	**ADDEEEHRSSS**	headdresses	**ADDEEENPRSTU**	dunderpates
ACINOOPRRTT	protraction	**ADDEEEIMMNS**	misdemeaned	**ADDEEENPRSUU**	unpersuaded
ACINOOPRRTU	procuration	**ADDEEEIMNRR**	remaindered	**ADDEEENRSTTU**	understated
ACINOOPRTXY	paroxytonic	**ADDEEEIRSST**	desiderates	**ADDEEEOPRRST**	depredators
ACINOORRSTU	contrarious	**ADDEEEELNRSU**	undersealed	**ADDEEEOPRRTY**	depredatory
ACINOOORSUV	carnivorous	**ADDEEELRSST**	saddletrees	**ADDEFFHLNOY**	offhandedly
ACINOORSSTT	cartoonists	**ADDEEENORUV**	endeavoured	**ADDEFFIIMRS**	disaffirmed
ACINPRRSSTT	transcripts	**ADDEEEOPRSS**	desperadoes	**ADDEFFHINSSS**	faddishness
ACIOOPRRSTT	corporatist	**ADDEEERRSSS**	readdresses	**ADDEFIIINNR**	Ferdinand II
ACIORRSSTTU	rusticators	**ADDEEFGHINN**	handfeeding	**ADDEFIKRRST**	Fredrikstad
ACIORSSSSSY	syssarcosis	**ADDEEFHLRUY**	furaldehyde	**ADDEFILORTU**	fluoridated
ACJKNOOPRST	Port Jackson	**ADDEEFIRSTU**	disfeatured	**ADDEFIORSUV**	disfavoured
ACKKNRSSTUW	knackwursts	**ADDEEFMNRTU**	defraudment	**ADDEGGHORTU**	goddaughter
ACLLMNOORUY	monocularly	**ADDEEGHILPY**	pigheadedly	**ADDEGGIIIRT**	digitigrade
ACLLMOORSUY	clamorously	**ADDEEGHNNORW**	wrongheaded	**ADDEGGILNRY**	degradingly
ACLLMOSTUUU	altocumulus	**ADDEEGIMNNR**	redemanding	**ADDEGHINRTY**	dehydrating
ACLLNNORTUY	nocturnally	**ADDEEGINPRT**	depredating	**ADDEGHLORST**	goldthreads
ACLLOPRSTYY	polycrystal	**ADDEEGINRRT**	intergraded	**ADDEGHNORTU**	dreadnought
ACLLOPRSUUY	crapulously	**ADDEEGIRRRS**	disregarder	**ADDEGIIILST**	digitalised
ACLNNNOOSTY	consonantly	**ADDEEGNRSSU**	guardedness	**ADDEGIIILTZ**	digitalized
ACLNNOSSTTU	consultants	**ADDEEGORRRT**	retrograded	**ADDEGILLNRW**	Grindelwald
ACLNNOSSTUV	convulsants	**ADDEEHHLOTY**	hotheadedly	**ADDEGILMNNY**	demandingly
ACLNOOORSTY	consolatory	**ADDEEHHNRTU**	thunderhead		maddeningly
ACLNOOPRRSU	proconsular	**ADDEEHIKNRT**	kindhearted	**ADDEGIMNNNU**	undemanding
ACLNOORRSUY	rancorously	**ADDEEHILNPR**	philandered	**ADDEGIMNORS**	gormandised

ADDEGIMNORZ	gormandized
ADDEGINNOSU	undiagnosed
ADDEGINPRSU	superadding
ADDEGJMNTUY	Judgment Day
ADDEGLNRUUY	unguardedly
ADDEGMNORRS	dendrograms
ADDEHHMORTU	hardmouthed
ADDEHHNORST	shorthanded
ADDEHIILMOT	thalidomide
ADDEHILLLRT	Liddell Hart
ADDEHILNOPR	philodendra
ADDEHILNORS	Rhode Island
ADDEHILNSSS	laddishness
ADDEHILOPSU	diadelphous
ADDEHINORTY	dehydration
ADDEHIOPRSS	rhapsodised
ADDEHIOPRSZ	rhapsodized
ADDEHIRRTTY	trihydrated
ADDEHLLNORS	landholders
ADDEHLNOPRY	hydroplaned
ADDEHLORSST	stadholders
ADDEHLORSTT	stadtholder
ADDEHMORSUY	hydromedusa
ADDEHORRSTY	dehydrators
ADDEIIIMNTT	intimidated
ADDEIIINTUV	individuate
ADDEIILNORR	liriodendra
ADDEIILORST	idolatrised
ADDEIILORTZ	idolatrized
ADDEILLNNSU	disannulled
ADDEILNSUVY	unadvisedly
ADDEILOSVWY	disavowedly
ADDEILRSTTU	stridulated
ADDEINNOSTU	denudations
ADDEINNRRSU	underdrains
ADDEINOORSS	radiosondes
ADDEIOOPPSU	pseudopodia
ADDEIOPPRSV	disapproved
ADDELMNOPSY	paddymelons
ADDELMNOTUU	unmodulated
ADDELMOORTU	demodulator
ADDELNNORSW	wonderlands
ADDELNNRTUV	redundantly
ADDELNNTUUY	undauntedly
ADDELNOORSW	woodlanders
ADDEMNOOORT	rodomontade
ADDENNRSSTU	understands
ADDGGINNORW	downgrading
ADDGHILLNNO	landholding
ADDGHILNOOR	roadholding
ADDGHNORTUW	downdraught
ADDGIIIIMNT	dimidiating
ADDGILNNOOW	downloading
ADDHILLNOUZ	Zuidholland
ADDIIIIMNOT	dimidiation
ADDIIILNSUV	individuals
ADDILLMNORS	landlordism
ADEEEEEFGHRT	featheredge
ADEEEEEFHRRT	freehearted
ADEEEEEGGRST	desegregate
ADEEEEEGNRRT	regenerated
ADEEEEEGNRST	degenerates

ADEEEEGRTTV	revegetated
ADEEEEILRRT	Terre Adélie
ADEEEENRTTX	exenterated
ADEEEFILNRT	deferential
ADEEEFILRSS	federalises
ADEEEFILRSZ	federalizes
ADEEEFKPRSS	speedfreaks
ADEEEFLORRS	freeloaders
ADEEEFNRSTT	fenestrated
ADEEEGHLPRT	telegraphed
ADEEEGILMNR	legerdemain
ADEEEGILNRS	generalised
ADEEEGILNRZ	generalized
ADEEEGILNSV	evangelised
ADEEEGILNVZ	evangelized
ADEEEGIMNRR	gendarmerie
ADEEEGIMNST	demagnetise
ADEEEGIMNTZ	demagnetize
ADEEEGINNRT	ingenerated
	tragedienne
ADEEEGJMNNU	Jean de
	Meung
ADEEEGLNNRR	Greenlander
ADEEEGLNORS	sloganeered
ADEEEGLRSTU	deregulates
ADEEEGMNNRT	derangement
ADEEEGNOTXY	deoxygenate
ADEEEGNRRRT	Grande-Terre
ADEEEGRRSSS	deergrasses
ADEEEHHINST	heathenised
ADEEEHHINTZ	heathenized
ADEEEHHPSSS	sheepsheads
ADEEEHLLORS	leaseholder
ADEEEHLPSSY	sleepyheads
ADEEEHLRSTT	letterheads
ADEEEHLRSTW	treadwheels
ADEEEHMORST	homesteader
ADEEEHNNNOR	enneahedron
ADEEEHNOPRT	openhearted
ADEEEHNRRSU	unrehearsed
ADEEEHPRSST	spreadsheet
ADEEEHPRSTU	superheated
ADEEEILNTTV	delineative
ADEEEILLMRS	Emerald Isle
ADEEEILNRST	eternalised
ADEEEILNRTV	interleaved
ADEEEILNRTZ	eternalized
ADEEEILSSUX	desexualise
ADEEEILSUXZ	desexualize
ADEEEIMNRTT	determinate
ADEEEIMNSST	mediateness
ADEEEIMPRTT	premeditate
ADEEEINNRTT	entertained
	intenerated
ADEEEINRTVW	interweaved
ADEEEINSSTT	Eisenstaedt
ADEEEIORRTT	deteriorate
ADEEEIORTVV	overdeviate
ADEEEIPRRTV	privateered
ADEEEJNRTUV	rejuvenated
ADEEEKLLPSW	sleepwalked
ADEEEKLRRST	deerstalker

ADEEEELLNSWY	wensleydale
ADEEELLSSTT	tessellated
ADEEEELMNNOW	needlewoman
ADEEEELNNRSS	learnedness
ADEEEELNRSST	relatedness
ADEEEELNRSSW	newsdealers
ADEEEELNRSUV	underleaves
ADEEEELNRTTU	launderette
ADEEEELNSSTX	exaltedness
ADEEEELPRSTY	desperately
ADEEEEMNNRST	endearments
ADEEEEMNPRTT	departement
ADEEEEMNRRTU	remunerated
ADEEEEMOSTWW	meadowsweet
ADEEEEMPRTTT	reattempted
ADEEEENORRSV	endeavorers
ADEEEENORRUV	endeavourer
ADEEEENRRSSW	newsreaders
ADEEEENRSSSV	adverseness
ADEEEEORRTVW	overwatered
ADEEEEPPRRTT	perpetrated
ADEEEEPPRRTTU	perpetuated
ADEEEERRTTVX	extraverted
ADEEFFIINRT	differentia
ADEEFFORSTV	overstaffed
ADEEFGGLOPR	leapfrogged
ADEEFGHIRSU	figureheads
ADEEFGHORRT	forgathered
ADEEFGILNNY	deafeningly
ADEEFGILNOR	freeloading
ADEEFGINNRR	rangefinder
ADEEFGKLNPR	frankpledge
ADEEFHINORS	refashioned
ADEEFHORSTT	softhearted
ADEEFIIINNT	definientia
ADEEFIILSTU	feudalities
ADEEFILLMSS	damselflies
ADEEFILRSST	federalists
ADEEFINORST	federations
ADEEFINRRST	fraternised
ADEEFINRRSW	firewardens
ADEEFINRRTZ	fraternized
ADEEFIORSTU	feudatories
ADEEFIRSSTU	disfeatures
ADEEFLLORST	forestalled
ADEEFMNRSTY	defrayments
ADEEFNRRRST	transferred
ADEEFOOPRRR	proofreader
ADEEGGHLORS	loggerheads
ADEEGGIINRS	disagreeing
ADEEGGILRVY	aggrievedly
ADEEGGINNNR	endangering
ADEEGGINRRS	grangerised
ADEEGGINRRZ	grangerized
ADEEGGLORTW	waterlogged
ADEEGGMORRT	remortgaged
ADEEGGMORUY	demagoguery
ADEEGHHMORR	hemorrhaged
ADEEGHHNNRR	rehardening
ADEEGHINPRS	grandeeship
ADEEGHINRRT	rethreading

ADEEGHINRST	nearsighted	**ADEEHHLOSSV**	shovelheads
ADEEGHLRSTU	slaughtered	**ADEEHHNOPRT**	heptahedron
ADEEGHMOPRR	demographer	**ADEEHHNORSX**	hexahedrons
ADEEGHNNPRW	grandnephew	**ADEEHHNRSTU**	headhunters
ADEEGHNORTY	hydrogenate	**ADEEHIIOPRS**	isodiaphere
ADEEGIILLLS	illegalised	**ADEEHILLNOT**	endothelial
ADEEGIILLLZ	illegalized	**ADEEHILMRST**	thermalised
ADEEGIILMTT	legitimated	**ADEEHILMRTZ**	thermalized
ADEEGIILNNT	delineating	**ADEEHILNOPT**	elephantoid
ADEEGIILNST	gelatinised	**ADEEHILNORT**	lionhearted
ADEEGIILNTZ	gelatinized	**ADEEHILNPRR**	philanderer
ADEEGIIMNNT	ingeminated	**ADEEHILNSST**	deathliness
ADEEGIIMNST	enigmatised	**ADEEHILOPPS**	paedophiles
ADEEGIIMNTZ	enigmatized	**ADEEHILSSWY**	daisywheels
ADEEGIINSTV	designative	**ADEEHIMNRUZ**	rehumanized
ADEEGIKMNRT	demarketing	**ADEEHIMNSSU**	dehumanises
ADEEGILLORS	allegorised	**ADEEHIMNSUZ**	dehumanizes
ADEEGILLORZ	allegorized	**ADEEHINRSST**	disheartens
ADEEGILNNRY	endearingly		threadiness
	engrainedly	**ADEEHIPRRSS**	readerships
ADEEGILNNST	disentangle	**ADEEHIRRRSS**	hairdresser
ADEEGILNOST	delegations	**ADEEHIRRRSS**	sherardises
ADEEGILNRRS	ringleaders	**ADEEHIRRSSZ**	sherardizes
ADEEGILNRSY	delayerings	**ADEEHKLORST**	stakeholder
ADEEGILNTTU	deglutinate	**ADEEHKORRSW**	headworkers
ADEEGILRRSU	regularised	**ADEEHLLORSV**	slaveholder
ADEEGILRRUZ	regularized	**ADEEHLLOSWY**	yellowheads
ADEEGIMNNRT	deraignment	**ADEEHLLSSTY**	deathlessly
ADEEGIMNPRT	impregnated	**ADEEHLMNORT**	endothermal
ADEEGIMORRT	gradiometer	**ADEEHLMNOTT**	mentholated
ADEEGIMSTTU	guestimated	**ADEEHLNNRST**	Netherlands
ADEEGINNNSU	ensanguined	**ADEEHLNORTY**	theory-laden
ADEEGINNORV	endeavoring	**ADEEHLOORTW**	leatherwood
ADEEGINNOST	denegations	**ADEEHLOOSSX**	aldohexoses
ADEEGINNRTU	undereating	**ADEEHLOPRST**	petrolheads
ADEEGINNRTV	denervating	**ADEEHNNOPRT**	pentahedron
ADEEGINORRS	reorganised	**ADEEHNNRSSU**	unharnessed
ADEEGINORRZ	reorganized	**ADEEHNORRTT**	tetrahedron
ADEEGINPRSS	preassigned	**ADEEHNOSSTW**	stonewashed
ADEEGINPRSY	panegyrised	**ADEEHNRSTUV**	unharvested
ADEEGINPRYZ	panegyrized	**ADEEIIJNRRS**	jardinieres
ADEEGINRRST	intergrades	**ADEEIIKNRST**	keratinised
ADEEGINRTTU	deuterating	**ADEEIIKNRTZ**	keratinized
ADEEGIORSUZ	Diégo-Suarez	**ADEEIILLNRT**	interallied
ADEEGJLMNTU	judgemental	**ADEEIILMMSV**	medievalism
ADEEGLLNOSS	goldenseals	**ADEEIILMMTY**	immediately
ADEEGLNRSUZ	underglazes	**ADEEIILMNRS**	mineralised
ADEEGLNRTUU	unregulated	**ADEEIILMNRZ**	mineralized
ADEEGLOPRSZ	Pérez Galdós	**ADEEIILMSTT**	delimitates
ADEEGLORRTU	deregulator	**ADEEIILMSTV**	medievalist
ADEEGMMOPRR	deprogramme	**ADEEIILNNOT**	delineation
ADEEGMNRRRY	gerrymander	**ADEEIILNNST**	desinential
ADEEGMORTUY	deuterogamy	**ADEEIILNRST**	residential
ADEEGNNRRST	transgender	**ADEEIILNSSS**	desalinises
ADEEGNORSSS	dragonesses	**ADEEIILNSSZ**	desalinizes
ADEEGNRRSUZ	gazunderers	**ADEEIILRSTV**	relativised
ADEEGOORSSV	overdosages		revitalised
ADEEGOORSSW	greasewoods	**ADEEIILRTVZ**	relativized
ADEEGORRRST	retrogrades		revitalized
ADEEHHIMRTY	hemihydrate	**ADEEIILSSTV**	devitalises
ADEEHHISTWW	whitewashed	**ADEEIILSTVZ**	devitalizes
ADEEHHLORRS	shareholder	**ADEEIIMMNPT**	impedimenta

ADEEIIMNNPT	pentamidine
ADEEIIMNNST	inseminated
ADEEIIMNORT	remediation
ADEEIIMNSST	disseminate
ADEEIINRRTV	veratridine
ADEEIINRSST	distrainees
ADEEIINRSVV	vivandieres
ADEEIINSSST	dessiatines
ADEEIIPRSTV	depravities
ADEEIIPRTUV	repudiative
ADEEIIRSSTV	adversities
ADEEIIRSTTW	tidewaiters
ADEEIIRSTVV	derivatives
ADEEIJOPRSS	jeopardises
ADEEIJOPRSZ	jeopardizes
ADEEIKNRRST	dreikanters
ADEEIKRRSTV	Kavir Desert
ADEEILLMOSS	damoiselles
ADEEILLNRST	reinstalled
ADEEILLPRSS	espadrilles
ADEEILLRRSU	derailleurs
ADEEILLSUVV	vaudevilles
ADEEILMNORT	endometrial
ADEEILMNRST	derailments
	streamlined
ADEEILMNRTT	detrimental
ADEEILMOORT	meteoroidal
ADEEILMORRS	demoraliser
ADEEILMORRZ	demoralizer
ADEEILMORSS	demoralises
ADEEILMORSZ	demoralizes
ADEEILMORTT	dilatometer
ADEEILMSTUU	demutualise
ADEEILMTUUZ	demutualize
ADEEILNNPPT	pentlandite
ADEEILNNPUX	unexplained
ADEEILNNRST	Landsteiner
ADEEILNNRTT	interdental
ADEEILNORST	delineators
ADEEILNPPRT	interlapped
ADEEILNPRST	interpleads
ADEEILNRSTU	neutralised
ADEEILNRSTY	sedentarily
ADEEILNRTUZ	neutralized
ADEEILNRUWY	unweariedly
ADEEILNSTTT	dilettantes
ADEEILOPPRT	lepidoptera
ADEEILOPRRS	depolariser
ADEEILOPRRZ	depolarizer
ADEEILOPRSS	depolarises
ADEEILOPRSZ	depolarizes
ADEEILORRSV	revalorised
ADEEILORRVZ	revalorized
ADEEILPPRTV	livetrapped
ADEEILPQSSU	sesquipedal
ADEEILPRSSU	displeasure
ADEEIMMNORS	misdemeanor
ADEEIMMNOSU	eudaemonism
ADEEIMMRSSU	mismeasured
ADEEIMNNORT	renominated
ADEEIMNNOST	denominates
	emendations

ADEEIMNNPTU	antependium	
ADEEIMNNRTT	determinant	
	detrainment	
ADEEIMNNTTU	edutainment	
ADEEIMNOPRT	predominate	
ADEEIMNOSTU	eudaemonist	
ADEEIMNRSTY	sedimentary	
ADEEIMORRST	radiometers	
ADEEIMORSTT	stadiometer	
ADEEIMORSTU	audiometers	
ADEEIMRTTTY	tetradymite	
ADEEINNORTV	denervation	
ADEEINNRSSU	unreadiness	
ADEEINNRRTV	inadvertent	
ADEEINOPPRT	reappointed	
ADEEINOPRST	desperation	
ADEEINOPTTT	potentiated	
ADEEINORRTV	overtrained	
ADEEINOSTTT	detestation	
ADEEINPRRSU	underpraise	
ADEEINPRSST	pedestrians	
ADEEINRSSTU	denaturises	
ADEEINRSTUZ	denaturizes	
ADEEIOPRRSV	overpraised	
ADEEIOPRSSX	peroxidases	
ADEEIOPRSTT	tetrapodies	
ADEEIPRSSTU	pasteurised	
ADEEIPRSTUV	depuratives	
ADEEIPRSTUZ	pasteurized	
ADEEIPRTTUV	vituperated	
ADEEIRRSSTV	advertisers	
ADEEIRRSSTW	watersiders	
ADEEIRRSTVZ	advertizers	
ADEEIRSSSTT	dissertates	
ADEEJRRSSTU	readjusters	
ADEEKLLMORU	leukodermal	
ADEEKLMORSU	leukodermas	
ADEEKLOPRSU	loudspeaker	
ADEEKMRRSSS	dressmakers	
ADEEKNRRSTU	undertakers	
ADEELLMRSSY	dreamlessly	
ADEELLNNRUY	unlearnedly	
ADEELLNOSTW	stonewalled	
ADEELLNRTUV	untravelled	
ADEELLOPRTT	preallotted	
ADEELMMNRTU	untrammeled	
ADEELMNOOST	demonolater	
ADEELNNRTUW	Unterwalden	
ADEELNOORST	aldosterone	
ADEELNOORUV	Nuevo Laredo	
ADEELNORRSV	overlanders	
ADEELNRRSUY	underlayers	
ADEELNRRUUV	undervaluer	
ADEELNRSSSU	laundresses	
ADEELNRSTTU	laundrettes	
ADEELNRSUUV	undervalues	
ADEELNRTTVY	advertently	
ADEELOOPRUV	parleyvooed	
ADEELOPPRTU	repopulated	
ADEELOPPSTU	depopulates	
ADEEMMNNRST	remandments	
ADEEMMNORTY	dynamometer	
ADEEMNNNSSU	mundaneness	
ADEEMNOPRRS	promenaders	
ADEEMNORSTT	demonstrate	
ADEEMNORSTW	tradeswomen	
ADEEMNPRSTT	departments	
ADEEMNPTTTU	unattempted	
ADEEMNRRSTT	retardments	
ADEEMNRSTTU	menstruated	
ADEENOPRSVX	overexpands	
ADEENPRSSST	depressants	
ADEENPRSSSU	underpasses	
ADEENQRRSSU	squanderers	
ADEENRRSSTU	adventurers	
ADEENRSSSSU	assuredness	
ADEENRSSTTU	understates	
ADEENRSSTUU	adventuress	
ADEEOORRSTV	overroasted	
ADEEOPRRSSV	overspreads	
ADEFFILLMMM	flimflammed	
ADEFFILNRTU	faultfinder	
ADEFFILNSTU	insufflated	
ADEFFIORSST	disafforest	
ADEFGHINNOR	forehanding	
ADEFGIILNOT	defoliating	
ADEFGIILNSU	feudalising	
ADEFGIILNUZ	feudalizing	
ADEFGIIMNNU	unmagnified	
ADEFGIINNYZ	denazifying	
ADEFGILNORS	dragonflies	
ADEFGILNRSY	ladyfingers	
ADEFGINORRS	firedragons	
ADEFGIPPRTW	giftwrapped	
ADEFGKNOORS	godforsaken	
ADEFGLLRRUY	regardfully	
ADEFHIKNRST	rankshifted	
ADEFHILOORR	foolhardier	
ADEFHINPRST	pathfinders	
ADEFHOORSSW	foreshadows	
ADEFIILMNNS	infieldsman	
ADEFIILMNPU	unamplified	
ADEFIILNNRS	Lindisfarne	
ADEFIILNOOT	defoliation	
ADEFIILNQUU	unqualified	
ADEFIILNRTT	infiltrated	
ADEFIILORTT	trifoliated	
ADEFIINNOTU	infeudation	
ADEFIINSSTU	unsatisfied	
ADEFILMNORS	manifolders	
ADEFILNOORT	defloration	
ADEFILNORTU	fluorinated	
ADEFILOORST	defoliators	
ADEFILORSTU	fluoridates	
ADEFILSSTTU	distasteful	
ADEFIMNOORT	deformation	
ADEFINOOPRR	rainproofed	
ADEFINOORRS	foreordains	
ADEFINRRSSU	fundraisers	
ADEFLNORUUV	unflavoured	
ADEFLOOPSTY	splayfooted	
ADEFLORRSTW	afterworlds	
ADEFMNORRST	transformed	
ADEFMNORSTW	draftswomen	
ADEFNORRSSW	forwardness	
	frowardness	
ADEGGGIINNS	disengaging	
ADEGGGLLLOY	lollygagged	
ADEGGHORSUY	hydragogues	
ADEGGIILMPR	pilgrimaged	
ADEGGIINNRT	denigrating	
ADEGGIINNST	designating	
ADEGGILNRUU	unguligrade	
ADEGGIMMOSU	demagoguism	
ADEGGIMOPSU	pedagoguism	
ADEGGINNRUZ	gazundering	
ADEGGINSTTU	degustating	
ADEGHHIKNST	knightheads	
ADEGHHILNRS	highlanders	
ADEGHHINNTU	headhunting	
ADEGHIIPRST	graphitised	
ADEGHIIPRTZ	graphitized	
ADEGHILLNNS	handselling	
ADEGHILRSTT	starlighted	
ADEGHINNORV	overhanding	
ADEGHINNRTU	unthreading	
ADEGHINPRSS	headsprings	
	springheads	
ADEGHIOPRVY	videography	
ADEGHIRSTTU	draughtiest	
ADEGHLMOOOT	homologated	
ADEGHLMOOSU	Douglas-Home	
ADEGHLOPRXY	xylographed	
ADEGHMNOOPR	monographed	
ADEGHMNORRT	grandmother	
ADEGHMNRSTU	draughtsmen	
ADEGHOOPRRX	doxographer	
ADEGHORRSSU	Horse Guards	
ADEGHORRTUV	overdraught	
ADEGHORSSUU	guardhouses	
ADEGIIILNTV	invigilated	
ADEGIIILSST	digitalises	
ADEGIIILSTZ	digitalizes	
ADEGIIIMNNS	deaminising	
ADEGIIIMNNZ	deaminizing	
ADEGIIIMNST	mediatising	
ADEGIIIMNTZ	mediatizing	
ADEGIIINRST	dignitaries	
ADEGIIILLSSU	seguidillas	
ADEGIILMNPS	mispleading	
ADEGIILNNRY	ingrainedly	
ADEGIILNOST	digestional	
	gelatinoids	
ADEGIILNPSS	displeasing	
ADEGIIMNOSS	misdiagnose	
ADEGIIMNRTT	readmitting	
ADEGIIMNTTU	unmitigated	
ADEGIIMSSTT	stigmatised	
ADEGIIMSTTZ	stigmatized	
ADEGIINNORT	denigration	
	derationing	
ADEGIINNOST	designation	
ADEGIINNRTT	denitrating	
ADEGIINOPTV	videotaping	
ADEGIINORSS	disorganise	
ADEGIINORSZ	disorganize	

ADEGIINORTV	invigorated	ADEHHIRRTWW	whitherward	ADEHOOPSTTT	photostated
ADEGIINPRTU	repudiating	ADEHHIRSSSW	dishwashers	ADEHOORSSVW	overshadows
ADEGIINRRWW	wiredrawing	ADEHIIIOPST	idiopathies	ADEIIIILNST	initialised
ADEGIINRSTV	advertising	ADEHIILOPSU	audiophiles	ADEIIIILNTZ	initialized
ADEGIINRTTU	ingratitude	ADEHIIMNOPR	diamorphine	ADEIIILMRST	militarised
ADEGIINRTTX	extraditing	ADEHIIMNRTU	antheridium	ADEIIILMRTZ	militarized
ADEGIINRTVZ	advertizing	ADEHIIMNSSS	maidishness	ADEIIILMSST	dissimilate
ADEGIJNRSTU	readjusting	ADEHIIMRSTT	mithridates	ADEIIILRSTV	trivialised
ADEGIKMNRSS	dressmaking	ADEHIIOPRSS	diaphoresis	ADEIIILRTVZ	trivialized
ADEGIKNNRTU	undertaking	ADEHIIORSTT	historiated	ADEIIIMNSTT	intimidates
ADEGILLOSSU	gladioluses	ADEHIIPSSUU	euphausiids	ADEIIIMRSTY	semiaridity
ADEGILMORUZ	glamourized	ADEHIKOORST	Theodorakis	ADEIIINNNPP	pinnipedian
ADEGILNNORV	overlanding	ADEHILLNRST	disenthrall	ADEIIINNTTU	uninitiated
ADEGILNNRSS	sanderlings	ADEHILLORSU	loudhailers	ADEIIIOPSTV	diapositive
ADEGILNNRUY	underlaying	ADEHILNNRST	hinterlands	ADEIIIPRSST	disparities
ADEGILNNRWY	wanderingly	ADEHILNRSST	disenthrals	ADEIIIPSSTV	dissipative
ADEGILNNSSU	languidness	ADEHILOOPRS	drosophilae	ADEIIISSSTU	assiduities
ADEGILNOORV	overloading	ADEHILORSTY	hysteroidal	ADEIILLLOPS	ellipsoidal
ADEGILNORST	Tselinograd	ADEHILPSSTU	disulphates	ADEIILLMNTU	illuminated
ADEGILNORSY	grandiosely	ADEHIMMNRSS	admonishers	ADEIILLMPSX	maxillipeds
ADEGILOOPST	paedologist	ADEHIMORRTY	radiothermy	ADEIILLNNSS	Line Islands
ADEGILRSTUV	divulgaters	ADEHIMPSSTY	sympathised	ADEIILLORTY	editorially
ADEGIMNNOPR	promenading	ADEHIMPSTYZ	sympathized	ADEIILLOSTV	volatilised
ADEGIMNORRS	gormandiser	ADEHIMRRSTT	thirdstream	ADEIILLOTVZ	volatilized
ADEGIMNORRZ	gormandizer	ADEHINNRSTU	untarnished	ADEIILLSSTT	distillates
ADEGIMNORSS	gormandises	ADEHINNRSUV	unvarnished	ADEIILMNNOS	dimensional
ADEGIMNORSU	gourmandise	ADEHINNRTTW	handwritten	ADEIILMNORS	meridionals
ADEGIMNORSZ	gormandizes	ADEHINOOPRS	radiophones	ADEIILMNRSU	semidiurnal
ADEGIMNPSTU	despumating	ADEHINOORTZ	antherozoid	ADEIILMSSTU	dissimulate
ADEGIMORSST	dogmatisers	ADEHINORRRS	Radnorshire	ADEIILNNSSV	invalidness
ADEGIMORSTZ	dogmatizers	ADEHINOSSSW	shadowiness	ADEIILNOPRR	Pinar del
ADEGINNORSU	unorganised	ADEHINPPRST	transhipped		Río
ADEGINNORUZ	unorganized	ADEHINQRRTU	hindquarter	ADEIILNOPST	depilations
ADEGINNPRUY	underpaying	ADEHINRSSTY	hydrastines	ADEIILNORSV	diversional
ADEGINNQRSU	squandering	ADEHINRSTTW	withstander	ADEIILORRST	idolatriser
ADEGINNRRTU	underrating	ADEHIOPPSSY	diapophyses	ADEIILORRTZ	idolatrizer
ADEGINNRRUW	unrewarding	ADEHIOPRSSS	rhapsodises	ADEIILORSST	idolatrises
ADEGINNRTUV	adventuring	ADEHIOPRSSZ	rhapsodizes	ADEIILORSTZ	idolatrizes
ADEGINNSTUY	unsteadying	ADEHIORRSST	diarthroses	ADEIIMMNSTU	mediastinum
ADEGINORRST	denigrators	ADEHIPRRSST	traderships	ADEIIMNNSTU	mundanities
ADEGINORRTV	overtrading	ADEHIPRRSSW	warderships	ADEIIMNOPSS	impassioned
ADEGINORRVW	overdrawing	ADEHIPRSSTW	stewardship	ADEIIMNORSS	readmission
ADEGINORSST	designators	ADEHIRRSTTY	trihydrates	ADEIIMNOSST	staminodies
ADEGINORSTY	designatory	ADEHIRRSTWW	withdrawers	ADEIIMNOSTT	meditations
ADEGINOSTTU	degustation	ADEHIRSSSTY	hydrastises	ADEIIMNRSST	administers
ADEGINPRSSW	wingspreads	ADEHJMNOOOR	Mohenjo-Daro	ADEIIMPRSSU	praesidiums
ADEGINPRSTU	depasturing	ADEHKNORSST	handstrokes	ADEIIMRSTTX	taxidermist
ADEGINRSSYY	dyssynergia	ADEHLLLMORS	smallholder	ADEIINNNOTT	indentation
ADEGKNRRRSU	krugerrands	ADEHLLLORST	stallholder	ADEIINNOOPT	opinionated
ADEGLMOORTY	dermatology	ADEHLMNORST	motherlands	ADEIINNORTT	denitration
ADEGLMOPRTU	promulgated	ADEHLNNORRT	Northlander	ADEIINNOSTT	destination
ADEGLNORSUY	dangerously	ADEHLNOPRSY	hydroplanes	ADEIINNOSTX	indexations
ADEGMMMNOOR	monogrammed	ADEHLNOPSTU	sulphonated	ADEIINOPRTT	partitioned
ADEGMNORRST	strongarmed	ADEHLNORSTV	Thorvaldsen		trepidation
ADEGNNOORSU	androgenous	ADEHLORSTVY	hydrolysate	ADEIINOPRTU	repudiation
ADEGNORRTUW	groundwater	ADEHLPRSTUU	sulphurated	ADEIINOPRTV	deprivation
ADEGOOPRSST	gasteropods	ADEHMNOORTY	monohydrate	ADEIINOPSST	Passiontide
ADEHHIILPRT	diphtherial	ADEHMNOSTTU	muttonheads	ADEIINORSTU	auditioners
ADEHHIOPPST	phosphatide	ADEHMOOPPPT	photomapped	ADEIINORSTV	derivations
ADEHHIORRSS	horseradish	ADEHMORRSTW	threadworms	ADEIINORSTY	seditionary
ADEHHIRRSTW	hitherwards	ADEHNOOPRRS	androphores	ADEIINORTTX	extradition
ADEHHIRRTTW	thitherward	ADEHNOOPRST	theropodans	ADEIINPRSTY	stipendiary

ADEIINPSSST	inspissated	**ADEIMRSTUUV**	duumvirates	**ADFHINNOOST**	infanthoods
ADEIINQSTTU	equidistant	**ADEINNOOSTT**	denotations	**ADFIIILLNNU**	nullifidian
ADEIINRRSST	distrainers		detonations	**ADFIIILNOSS**	solifidians
ADEIINRSTVY	vineyardist	**ADEINNOPPTU**	unappointed	**ADFIILMNTUU**	latifundium
ADEIIOPPRTT	propitiated	**ADEINNOPSWW**	windowpanes	**ADFIMNOPRRU**	panduriform
ADEIIPRRSSS	dispraisers	**ADEINNORSSW**	rawinsondes	**ADFINNOORRZ**	rinforzando
ADEIIPRSSST	dissipaters	**ADEINNORSTT**	nonstriated	**ADFINNOOSTU**	foundations
ADEIIPSTTUV	disputative	**ADEINNSSSTT**	distantness	**ADFINRSSSTT**	standfirsts
ADEIJLNORSU	journalised	**ADEINNSSTUU**	unsustained	**ADGGIIILNOS**	dialogising
ADEIJLNORUZ	journalized	**ADEINOOPPRT**	apportioned	**ADGGIIILNOZ**	dialogizing
ADEIJMMNRSW	windjammers	**ADEINOOPRTT**	deportation	**ADGGIILNTUV**	divulgating
ADEIKLMSTTU	multitasked	**ADEINOPRSTU**	depurations	**ADGGIIMNOST**	dogmatising
ADEIKLNOSSU	soundalikes	**ADEINOPSTTU**	deputations	**ADGGIIMNOTZ**	dogmatizing
ADEILLMRRST	drillmaster	**ADEINORSTUW**	autowinders	**ADGHHILNOPT**	diphthongal
ADEILLORTUV	outrivalled	**ADEINPRSSST**	dispersants	**ADGHHOPRRSY**	hydrographs
ADEILLRSTTU	illustrated	**ADEINRSTTUV**	adventurist	**ADGHHOPRRYY**	hydrography
ADEILLSSTUU	Îles du	**ADEINRSTTUY**	testudinary	**ADGHIILMNNS**	mishandling
	Salut	**ADEIOPPRSSV**	disapproves	**ADGHIIMNNOS**	admonishing
ADEILMMOOTY	myelomatoid	**ADEIOPRRSTU**	repudiators	**ADGHIINNRTW**	handwriting
ADEILMNNSSU	maudlinness	**ADEIORRSSTT**	dissertator	**ADGHIINRTWW**	withdrawing
ADEILMNOPRS	palindromes	**ADEIORSSSTT**	siderostats	**ADGHIKNORRW**	hardworking
ADEILMNOPRT	trampolined	**ADEJMNNORTU**	adjournment	**ADGHINNPRSS**	handsprings
ADEILMNOPTU	deplumation	**ADEJMNSSTTU**	adjustments	**ADGHIOPRTTY**	dittography
ADEILMNRRST	dismantlers	**ADEJMOORRRS**	major orders	**ADGHMRRRUYY**	hydrargyrum
ADEILMOOSSY	amyloidoses	**ADELLMOPSSY**	plasmolysed	**ADGIIILNQTU**	liquidating
ADEILMORTTY	dilatometry	**ADELLMOPSYZ**	plasmolyzed	**ADGIIILOOSS**	idioglossia
ADEILNOOPRT	periodontal	**ADELLNSSTUY**	dauntlessly	**ADGIIINNNOT**	indignation
ADEILNOOSTV	devotionals	**ADELLOOPRRT**	petrodollar	**ADGIIINNOTU**	auditioning
ADEILNOPRSU	unpolarised	**ADELLOORRRS**	roadrollers	**ADGIIINNRST**	distraining
ADEILNOPRUY	pleurodynia	**ADELLOORRSU**	eurodollars	**ADGIIINNOSTZ**	diazotising
ADEILNOPRUZ	unpolarized	**ADELMMOPSSS**	plasmodesms	**ADGIIINOTZZ**	diazotizing
ADEILNQSSSU	squalidness	**ADELMNOORTY**	demonolatry	**ADGIIINPRSS**	dispraising
ADEILNRSTWW	windlestraw	**ADELMNORRTU**	ultramodern	**ADGIIINPSST**	dissipating
ADEILNRSTWZ	Switzerland	**ADELMNORSTW**	Westmorland	**ADGIIKNNPPS**	kidnappings
ADEILNSSTUY	sustainedly	**ADELMOPSSTU**	deutoplasms	**ADGIILLNOSW**	disallowing
ADEILOPPRSS	predisposal	**ADELNOPPTUU**	unpopulated	**ADGIILMNNST**	dismantling
ADEILOPPRSU	popularised	**ADELNPRRSTU**	Rupert's	**ADGIILMNNRSY**	disarmingly
ADEILOPPRUZ	popularized		Land	**ADGIILNNNTY**	indignantly
ADEILOPQRSU	quadripoles	**ADELOPOQRSUU**	quadrupoles	**ADGIILNNPST**	displanting
ADEILOPRRTY	predatorily	**ADELOPRRRSY**	Lord's	**ADGIILNNSSW**	windlassing
ADEILOPRSTT	tetraploids		Prayer	**ADGIILNOTUV**	divulgation
ADEILRSSTTU	stridulates	**ADELOPRRSWY**	swordplayer	**ADGIILOORST**	radiologist
ADEIMMNNOPU	pandemonium	**ADELPPQRSTU**	quadruplets	**ADGIILOOSTU**	audiologist
ADEIMMNOOST	somatomedin	**ADEMMMNORSU**	memorandums	**ADGIILOPRTY**	prodigality
ADEIMMNRSST	masterminds	**ADEMMNNOUVY**	Maundy money	**ADGIIMMNNORS**	randomising
ADEIMMNSSTT	dismastment	**ADEMMNNORTYY**	dynamometry	**ADGIIMMNORZ**	randomizing
ADEIMMNNOORT	denominator	**ADEMNOOPSSU**	pseudomonas	**ADGIINOPPRR**	airdropping
ADEIMMNNOPRT	predominant	**ADENNOPPRST**	transponder	**ADGIINOPTUY**	audiotyping
ADEIMMNNORST	ordainments	**ADENNORRRSU**	roadrunners	**ADGIINORSTY**	grandiosity
ADEIMMNNQRUU	quadrennium	**ADENOPPRRSTT**	transported	**ADGIKNNOORT**	Gordian knot
ADEIMMNOORST	moderations	**ADENORSSSUU**	arduousness	**ADGILMNOSUW**	guildswoman
ADEIMMNOPSTU	despumation	**ADENORSSTUW**	outwardness	**ADGILNNOPWY**	downplaying
ADEIMMNORSS	randomisers	**ADENORSTUUV**	adventurous	**ADGILNOORST**	andrologist
ADEIMMNORRSZ	randomizers	**ADENPRSSSUU**	unsurpassed		Stalingrod
ADEIMNOTTUV	unmotivated	**ADFFHINOSST**	standoffish	**ADGILNPQRUU**	quadrupling
ADEIMNRRSUY	nurserymaid	**ADFGHIINNPT**	pathfinding	**ADGILORSTUV**	divulgators
ADEIMNRRTUY	rudimentary	**ADFGIIILNPY**	lapidifying	**ADGIMMNORSU**	gourmandism
ADEIMNRSTTT	transmitted	**ADFGIILLNSU**	fusillading	**ADGINNOSTTU**	outstanding
ADEIMNRSTUV	adventurism	**ADFGIILMNNO**	manifolding	**ADGINRRSSTW**	drawstrings
ADEIMOOSSTTU	autotomised	**ADFGIINORSV**	disfavoring	**ADGLNOPRSUY**	playgrounds
ADEIMOOTTUZ	autotomized	**ADFGINORRSU**	fairgrounds	**ADGNNOORSUY**	androgynous
ADEIMORSTWW	mowdiewarts	**ADFHILLOORY**	foolhardily	**ADGNOOORRST**	dragonroots

ADGORRSTTUY	Dry Tortugas	
ADHHNOSSTTU	thousandths	
ADHHOORRTXY	hydrothorax	
ADHIIMSSTTU	humidistats	
ADHIIOPPSSY	diapophysis	
ADHIIORRSST	diarthrosis	
ADHILNNORST	North Island	
ADHILNOSSTU	South Island	
ADHILOOPRSS	drosophilas	
ADHIMOOPPSU	amphipodous	
ADHINNOOOST	nationhoods	
ADHINNOPRSX	androsphinx	
ADHINOOORTT	orthodontia	
ADHINOOPRST	anthropoids	
ADHINOOPRSZ	rhizopodans	
ADHIOPRSSST	rhapsodists	
ADHKNNORSTU	drunkathons	
ADHLNOPSSSW	splashdowns	
ADHLNORRTWY	northwardly	
ADHLORSTUWY	southwardly	
ADHNOOPQRUY	quadrophony	
ADIIILLMSUV	diluvialism	
ADIIILMNTUV	diminutival	
ADIIILNOOST	idolisation	
ADIIILNOOTZ	idolization	
ADIIILNOQTU	liquidation	
ADIIIMNORTT	intimidator	
ADIIIMOSSTT	mastoiditis	
ADIIINNOSTV	divinations	
ADIIINOOSST	iodisations	
ADIIINOOSTX	oxidisation	
ADIIINOOSTZ	iodizations	
ADIIINOOTXZ	oxidization	
ADIIINOPSST	dissipation	
ADIIINORSVY	divisionary	
ADIIIOPRSTT	parotiditis	
ADIILLNOQRU	quadrillion	
ADIILLOPPST	lipidoplast	
ADIILMLNNOT	mandolinist	
ADIILMOOSSY	amyloidosis	
ADIILMOPRRS	primordials	
ADIILMOPSTT	diplomatist	
ADIILNRSSTU	industrials	
ADIILOQRSTU	liquidators	
ADIIMMNOSTU	staminodium	
ADIIMNNOOST	admonitions	
	dominations	
ADIIMNRSSST	misandrists	
ADIIMOPRSST	prismatoids	
ADIIMORSTUU	auditoriums	
ADIINNNOSTU	inundations	
ADIINNOORST	ordinations	
ADIINNORSTU	indurations	
ADIINOPPSST	disappoints	
ADIINOPSTTU	disputation	
ADIINORRSST	distrainors	
ADIINOSSSSU	dissuasions	
ADIIOOPRSUV	avoirdupois	
ADIIOPRSSST	dissipators	
ADIIOPRSSTT	podiatrists	
ADIIOPSTTUY	audiotypist	
ADIKLNRSSTU	Truk Islands	

ADIKLOOSTVV	Vladivostok
ADILLLOOPPY	polyploidal
ADILLMOPSYY	sympodially
ADILLNSSSTT	standstills
ADILMNNOOSTU	modulations
ADILMOPSSST	psalmodists
ADILNNOSSTY	dissonantly
ADILNNOSTUU	undulations
ADILORRSTTU	stridulator
ADILOSSSUUY	assiduously
ADIMOOPRSUY	myriapodous
ADINNOOPPPT	Pontoppidan
ADINNNOPSST	standpoints
ADLLMORSSSW	smallswords
ADLLOOOSWWW	woodswallow
ADLMOPRSUWY	mouldywarps
ADLNOOPRSUY	polyandrous
ADMOOOPSSTT	stomatopods
ADNNOOPRRST	transpondor
ADNNORRSTUU	turnarounds
ADNOOPRRSTU	protandrous
ADOOOPRSSUU	sauropodous
AEEEEFLLNST	fenestellae
AEEEEGKMPRS	gamekeepers
AEEEEGKPRST	gatekeepers
AEEEEGNRRST	regenerates
AEEEEGRSTTV	revegetates
AEEEEHILRST	etherealise
AEEEEHILRTZ	etherealize
AEEEEHLRTTT	leatherette
AEEEEELNOPST	elaeoptenes
AEEEENRSTTX	exenterates
AEEEEFGIKNPS	safekeeping
AEEEFGIRRRT	refrigerate
AEEEFGLNRSU	enfleurages
AEEEFHINRRT	hereinafter
AEEEFHLRSST	featherless
AEEEFILNRRT	referential
AEEEFLLNNTT	flannelette
AEEEFLMPRSU	superfemale
AEEEFLNSSSU	easefulness
AEEEFLRSSTU	featureless
AEEEFNRRSST	transferees
AEEEFPRSTTU	superfetate
AEEEGGIKMNP	gamekeeping
AEEEGGILNOS	genealogies
AEEEGGIRSTV	segregative
AEEEGGMMNOU	emmenagogue
AEEEGGMNNST	engagements
AEEEGGNNRRT	Gretna Green
AEEEGHLPRRT	telegrapher
AEEEGHNRRST	greenhearts
AEEEGILMMRR	lammergeier
AEEEGILNRRS	generaliser
AEEEGILNRRZ	generalizer
AEEEGILNRSS	generalises
AEEEGILNRSV	evangeliser
AEEEGILNRSZ	generalizes
AEEEGILNRVZ	evangelizer
AEEEGILNSSV	evangelises
AEEEGILNSUV	eigenvalues
AEEEGILNSVZ	evangelizes

AEEEGIMNNSST	metagenesis
AEEEGINNRST	ingenerates
AEEEGINORTT	renegotiate
AEEEGINPRRT	peregrinate
AEEEGINRNTT	reintegrate
AEEEGINRTTV	vinegarette
AEEEGKLOPRS	goalkeepers
AEEEGLMMRRY	lammergeyer
AEEEGLMNNRT	enlargement
AEEEGLMNRST	regalements
AEEEGLNNRSS	generalness
AEEEGLNOSST	eaglestones
AEEEGLNSSSS	agelessness
AEEEGMNNRSS	germaneness
AEEEGMNNRST	enragements
AEEEGNORRRT	regenerator
AEEEGPRSSSX	expressages
AEEEGQSSTUU	squeteagues
AEEEHHINSST	heathenises
AEEEHHINSTZ	heathenizes
AEEEHHLPSTT	heptathlete
AEEEHHMMNORX	hexahemeron
AEEEHHNNSST	heathenness
AEEEHILNNPT	elephantine
AEEEHILPSTT	telepathise
AEEEHILPTTZ	telepathize
AEEEHILRTTY	ethereality
AEEEHILSSTT	telesthesia
AEEEHIMMNNT	methenamine
AEEEHIMMSST	hematemesis
AEEEHIMPRSZ	reemphasize
AEEEHIMSSTT	metathesise
AEEEHIMSTTZ	metathesize
AEEEHINNTUV	Haute-Vienne
AEEEHINSTTZ	anesthetize
AEEEHLLMPRY	ephemerally
AEEEHLMPPRT	pamphleteer
AEEEHLNPTTT	pentathlete
AEEEHLPRRWY	prayer wheel
AEEEHMPRSTT	heptameters
AEEEHNORSTY	honeyeaters
AEEEHNPRSST	parentheses
AEEEHNRRSTT	threateners
AEEEHOPRRSS	aerospheres
AEEEHPRRSTU	superheater
AEEEHRSSTTW	sweethearts
AEEEIINPPRT	peripeteian
AEEEIIPPRST	peripeteias
AEEEIIRRTTV	reiterative
AEEEILNORRS	Sierra Leone
AEEEILNRRTT	interrelate
AEEEILNRRTV	reverential
AEEEILNRSST	eternalises
AEEEILNRSTV	interleaves
AEEEILNRSTX	externalise
AEEEILNRSTZ	eternalizes
AEEEILNRTXZ	externalize
AEEEILPRRTT	preliterate
AEEEILRSSTV	severalties
AEEEIMNPRTT	intemperate
AEEEIMNRRST	Armentières
AEEEIMNRTTX	exterminate

AEEEIMNRTUV	enumerative	AEEFGHORRST	foregathers	AEEGGINORRV	overgearing
AEEEIMPRSTT	Empire State	AEEFGHORRTT	heterograft	AEEGGINORST	segregation
AEEEIMQRRTU	marqueterie	AEEFGILLNRW	farewelling	AEEGGINQSTU	gigantesque
AEEEINNNSTV	antivenenes	AEEFGILNRSS	fragileness	AEEGGINRRRS	grangeriser
AEEEINNRRTT	entertainer	AEEFGILSSTU	fatigueless	AEEGGINRRRZ	grangerizer
AEEEINNRSTT	intenerates	AEEFGIMNRTZ	fragmentize	AEEGGINRRSS	grangerises
AEEEINOPRSU	europeanise	AEEFGINNRST	refastening	AEEGGINRRSZ	grangerizes
AEEEINOPRUZ	europeanize	AEEFGINRRRT	refrigerant	AEEGGIRRRTU	regurgitate
AEEEINORTVX	exonerative	AEEFGLLORVY	Valley Forge	AEEGGMORRST	remortgages
AEEEINPRSST	septenaries	AEEFGMNNRTT	engraftment	AEEGGNOSTTW	waggonettes
AEEEINPRTTV	penetrative	AEEFGORRRSU	fourrageres	AEEGGORRSST	segregators
AEEEINRRSTT	Eastern rite	AEEFHHISSST	sheatfishes	AEEGGORSTTY	geostrategy
AEEEINRRTVW	interweaver	AEEFHHORSTU	housefather	AEEGHHIOPST	theophagies
AEEEINRSTVW	interweaves	AEEFHILNNPS	halfpennies	AEEGHHITVWY	heavyweight
AEEEINSSSVV	evasiveness	AEEFHILNRST	Riefenstahl	AEEGHHMORRS	hemorrhages
AEEEJKRRRST	tearjerkers	AEEFHINPRST	pinfeathers	AEEGHIIMRRT	Margrethe II
AEEEJNRSTUV	rejuvenates	AEEFHIPRSSS	spearfishes	AEEGHIKLLNU	keelhauling
AEEEKLLOSTX	exoskeletal	AEEFHLLMNST	mantelshelf	AEEGHIKMSTW	makeweights
AEEEKLLPRSW	sleepwalker	AEEFHLNSSSW	newsflashes	AEEGHILNPRS	generalship
AEEEKPSSSTW	sweepstakes	AEEFHLNSSTU	hatefulness	AEEGHILNPTT	telepathing
AEEELLLMNTY	elementally	AEEFHLOPPRS	leafhoppers	AEEGHILPSST	legateships
AEEELLORTTT	teetotaller	AEEFHLOPSST	felspathose	AEEGHIMPRSY	hypergamies
AEEELLSSSTT	tessellates	AEEFHMORSTT	fathometers	AEEGHINNRTT	threatening
AEEELMMNNPT	empanelment	AEEFHMPRSST	stepfathers	AEEGHINNRTW	enwreathing
AEEELMMNPST	empalements	AEEFIILNNRT	inferential	AEEGHINORRV	overhearing
AEEELMNNSTV	enslavement	AEEFIILOTVX	exfoliative	AEEGHINORTV	overheating
AEEELMNRSTT	manteltrees	AEEFILLNORX	reflexional	AEEGHINORVZ	Herzegovina
	mantletrees	AEEFILNORTV	overinflate	AEEGHINRRST	ingatherers
AEEELMPRTTY	temperately	AEEFILOPRRT	proliferate	AEEGHIPPRRS	epigraphers
AEEELMRSSSU	measureless	AEEFIMNNRRT	refrainment	AEEGHIPPRTW	paperweight
AEEELNNRSST	eternalness	AEEFIMNOSST	manifestoes	AEEGHKNNRSS	greenshanks
AEEEMMNORST	anemometers	AEEFIMNRRST	freemartins	AEEGHLNOPRS	selenograph
AEEEMMNPRTT	temperament	AEEFIMOPRRT	imperforate	AEEGHLNSTVW	wavelengths
AEEEMMNRSTU	measurement	AEEFIMORRTV	reformative	AEEGHLRRSTU	slaughterer
AEEEMNNNRST	ensnarement	AEEFINRRRST	fraterniser	AEEGHMNOOST	homogenates
AEEEMNNRTTT	entreatment	AEEFINRRRTZ	fraternizer	AEEGHMOOPRT	gametophore
AEEEMNNRTTY	tenementary	AEEFINRRSST	fraternises	AEEGHMOPTTY	gametophyte
AEEEMNOSSSW	awesomeness	AEEFINRRSTZ	fraternizes	AEEGHNPRSTV	stevengraph
AEEEMNPRSTT	pentameters	AEEFIOPRRTV	perforative	AEEGHOPRRRX	xerographer
AEEEMNRRSTU	remunerates	AEEFKLNSSUW	wakefulness	AEEGHOPRRST	stereograph
AEEEMNRRSUV	maneuverers	AEEFLLNNOST	fontanelles	AEEGHOPSSSU	esophaguses
AEEEMNRSTTT	restatement	AEEFLLNSSTU	fustanelles	AEEGIIKLNRT	granitelike
AEEEMORRSUV	overmeasure	AEEFLLORRST	forestaller	AEEGIILLLSS	illegalises
AEEEMPRRTTU	temperature	AEEFLLPRSUU	pleasureful	AEEGIILLLSZ	illegalizes
AEEEMRRSTTT	tetrameters	AEEFLMORRTU	reformulate	AEEGIILLSTV	legislative
AEEENNRSSST	earnestness	AEEFLNRSSTU	tearfulness	AEEGIILLTTU	aiguillette
AEEENOPRSTT	stearoptene	AEEFMMNORSY	freemasonry	AEEGIILMSTT	legitimates
AEEENORRSTV	overearnest	AEEFNNOPRSS	profaneness	AEEGIILNNOR	legionnaire
AEEENPRRSTV	perseverant	AEEFNORRRSW	forewarners	AEEGIILNORS	legionaries
AEEENRSSSTU	austereness	AEEFNRRRRST	transferrer	AEEGIILNPRS	espaliering
AEEEPPRRRST	perpetrates	AEEFNRRRSST	retransfers	AEEGIILNRST	gelatiniser
AEEEPPRSTTU	perpetuates	AEEFOQRRRTU	forequarter	AEEGIILNRTZ	gelatinizer
AEEEQRSSTTU	sequestrate	AEEFORRRSSW	forswearers	AEEGIILNSST	gelatinises
AEEERRSSTYY	yesteryears	AEEGGGGINRST	segregating	AEEGIILNSTZ	gelatinizes
AEEFFGRSTTU	suffragette	AEEGGHINNRT	regathering	AEEGIILOOST	aetiologies
AEEFFHORRST	forefathers	AEEGGHIOPRS	geographies	AEEGIIMNNRX	reexamining
AEEFFLNRSSU	fearfulness	AEEGGHOPRRS	geographers	AEEGIIMNNST	ingeminates
AEEFFLNSSTU	fatefulness	AEEGGIINORS	seigniorage	AEEGIIMNRTV	germinative
AEEFFORRSST	reafforests	AEEGGIKLNOP	goalkeeping	AEEGIIMNSST	enigmatises
AEEFGGIILNR	filagreeing	AEEGGILNOST	genealogist	AEEGIIMNSTZ	enigmatizes
AEEFGHILNSS	angelfishes	AEEGGILNRRS	glengarries	AEEGIIMRSST	magisteries
AEEFGHINRST	featherings	AEEGGIMNOSS	gamogenesis		

AEEGIINRRTT	reiterating	AEEGINRSSSV	vernissages	AEEHILNPPPRS	planisphere
AEEGIINRTTV	integrative	AEEGIOPRRTV	prerogative	AEEHILNPSSS	shapeliness
	vinaigrette	AEEGIOSTTUV	vegetatious	AEEHILNRSST	earthliness
AEEGIINSTTV	investigate	AEEGKNPRRST	Regent's	AEEHILNSSTW	wealthiness
AEEGIKLNSST	glaiketness		Park	AEEHILPSTTT	telepathist
AEEGILLLNRW	general will	AEEGLLMNNTY	gentlemanly	AEEHILRSTTT	triathletes
AEEGILLMNNP	empanelling	AEEGLLMNSTY	segmentally	AEEHILSTTTT	stealthiest
AEEGILLNNTY	inelegantly	AEEGLLMORTU	glomerulate	AEEHIMNNSTV	evanishment
AEEGILLNRVY	revealingly	AEEGLLOOPSY	spelaeology	AEEHIMNOPRT	metanephroi
AEEGILLORSS	allegorises	AEEGLLORSTT	allegrettos	AEEHIMNOPTV	Amenhotep IV
AEEGILLORSZ	allegorizes	AEEGLMNNOTW	gentlewoman	AEEHIMNPRST	hemipterans
AEEGILLRSTU	legislature	AEEGLMNNSTT	tanglements	AEEHIMNPRSY	hypermnesia
AEEGILMNNRT	engrailment	AEEGLMNOOPR	prolegomena	AEEHIMNRSUZ	rehumanizes
	realignment	AEEGLMNRSST	garmentless	AEEHIMNSTTY	amethystine
AEEGILMNNSS	meaningless	AEEGLNORSTU	outgenerals	AEEHIMOSSST	somesthesia
AEEGILMNRRS	malingerers	AEEGLOORPRT	Porto Alegre	AEEHINNSSTT	Antisthenes
AEEGILMNRST	regimentals	AEEGLOORTVV	overvoltage	AEEHINORTTT	titanothere
AEEGILNNRRT	interregnal	AEEGLORSTUV	travelogues	AEEHINPRSST	interphases
AEEGILNNRUV	unrevealing	AEEGMNNOSST	mangosteens		parenthesis
AEEGILNOPRV	overleaping	AEEGMNORRTV	overgarment	AEEHINRSTTU	uintatheres
AEEGILNORRTV	regelations	AEEGMNRSTWY	West Germany	AEEHINSSSTY	synesthesia
AEEGILNORST	regelations	AEEGMNRTTUY	tegumentary	AEEHINSSTTT	anesthetist
	relegations	AEEGMORRSST	stereograms	AEEHIOOPRTT	heterotopia
AEEGILNRSST	generalists	AEEGMRSSSTU	gaussmeters	AEEHIOOPSST	apotheosise
AEEGILNRSTV	everlasting	AEEGNNRRSST	strangeness	AEEHIOOPSTZ	apotheosize
AEEGILNSSSW	wineglasses	AEEGNORSSTV	gravestones	AEEHIOPRRXY	hyperorexia
AEEGILNSSTV	evangelists	AEEGNOSSSSU	gaseousness	AEEHIORSTTX	heterotaxis
AEEGILORSTT	tetralogies	AEEGPPPRRSS	peppergrass	AEEHIORTTVX	exhortative
AEEGILRRSSU	regularises	AEEHHILMOPS	haemophiles	AEEHIPPRRSS	periphrases
AEEGILRRSUZ	regularizes	AEEHHILNRTU	unhealthier	AEEHKLLORRU	leukorrheal
AEEGIMNNRTU	enumerating	AEEHHILNSST	healthiness	AEEHKMPRRTY	hypermarket
AEEGIMNNRUV	maneuvering	AEEHHILRTTW	therewithal	AEEHKOPSSSV	spokeshaves
AEEGIMNOTTW	witenagemot		whitleather	AEEHKOSSSTU	steakhouses
AEEGIMNPRST	impregnates	AEEHHILRTWW	wherewithal	AEEHLLMSSSY	shamelessly
AEEGIMNPRTT	attempering	AEEHHINOPST	theophanies	AEEHLLNRRST	enthrallers
AEEGIMNRRST	remastering	AEEHHIPSSTY	hypesthesia	AEEHLLNPRXY	phylloxerae
AEEGIMNRRSU	remeasuring	AEEHHIRSTWW	whitewasher	AEEHLLORSSW	wholesalers
AEEGIMNRSTS	magnetisers	AEEHHISSTWW	whitewashes	AEEHLLPSSSY	shapelessly
AEEGIMNRSTZ	magnetizers	AEEHHKNPSSS	sheepshanks	AEEHLLRSSTY	heartlessly
AEEGIMNSSTU	mutagenesis	AEEHHMMORRT	earth mother	AEEHLMNNRTT	enthralment
AEEGIMRRSTU	marguerites	AEEHHMNORST	hearthstone	AEEHLMOPRTY	Thermopylae
AEEGIMRRSTV	gravimeters	AEEHIIKNSST	kinesthesia	AEEHLMORSTY	heartsomely
AEEGIMSSTTU	guesstimate	AEEHIILLSTT	lethalities	AEEHLMOSSTY	hematolyses
	guestimates	AEEHIILMOPT	epithelioma	AEEHLMRRTUY	eurythermal
AEEGINNNPRT	perennating	AEEHIILNRST	Saint Helier	AEEHLNORTVW	Leavenworth
AEEGINNNSSU	ensanguines	AEEHIILNSTX	antihelixes	AEEHLNPPRSY	hyperplanes
AEEGINNORST	generations	AEEHIIMPRSS	phariseeism	AEEHLNPSSSS	haplessness
AEEGINNORTX	exonerating	AEEHIINPPRR	perinephria	AEEHLNRSSSS	harnessless
AEEGINNPRTT	penetrating	AEEHIKLMRRS	sharemilker	AEEHLOOPRRT	heteropolar
AEEGINNRTTV	anteverting	AEEHIKNSSSW	weakishness	AEEHLPPRRTU	purpleheart
AEEGINNTTUV	eventuating	AEEHIKPPRSS	speakership	AEEHLRSSSTV	harvestless
AEEGINNTTUX	extenuating	AEEHILLMOST	mesothelial	AEEHMMNORST	hammerstone
AEEGINORRRZ	reorganizer	AEEHILLMRTY	hemielytral	AEEHMMNRTUX	xeranthemum
AEEGINORRSS	reorganises	AEEHILLMRUV	humeral veil	AEEHMNOPRST	metanephros
AEEGINORRSZ	reorganizes	AEEHILLORST	heliolaters	AEEHMNOPRTY	hymenoptera
AEEGINORRTT	interrogate	AEEHILLPRSV	Sharpeville	AEEHMNORSWW	washerwomen
AEEGINOSSTU	autogenesis	AEEHILMMNTY	methylamine	AEEHMNPRRTU	preterhuman
AEEGINOSTTV	vegetations	AEEHILMNNPY	phenylamine	AEEHMOPRSST	atmospheres
AEEGINPRSSY	panegyrises	AEEHILMRSST	thermalises	AEEHMOPRSTU	heptamerous
AEEGINPRSYZ	panegyrizes	AEEHILMRSTZ	thermalizes	AEEHMOPSSTY	haemoptyses
AEEGINRRRST	rearresting	AEEHILNNOST	stenohaline	AEEHMORRRST	arthromeres
AEEGINRRSST	reasserting	AEEHILNNSST	Saint Helens	AEEHMORRSTW	whoremaster
AEEGINRSSSS	reassessing				

AEEHMORSSTU	housemaster	**AEEIIPRTTVX**	extirpative
AEEHNNOPRSW	answerphone	**AEEIIRSSTTU**	austerities
AEEHNNRSSSU	unharnesses	**AEEIJNRSSST**	janitresses
AEEHNOOPRRS	harpooneers	**AEEIJOPRSTV**	pejoratives
AEEHNORRSST	enarthroses	**AEEIKLRRSWW**	wirewalkers
	nearthroses	**AEEIKMNORSS**	noisemakers
AEEHNORRSTT	northeaster	**AEEIKNOPSSW**	Passion Week
AEEHNORRTWW	weatherworn	**AEEIKNPPRSV**	paperknives
AEEHOOPRSSS	peashooters	**AEEIKNQSSSU**	squeakiness
AEEHOPRRSTY	serotherapy	**AEEIKNRSSST**	streakiness
AEEHORSSSTU	authoresses	**AEEIKOPRRST**	perestroika
AEEHORSSTTU	southeaster	**AEEILLLLNSV**	villanelles
AEEHOSSSTTU	statehouses	**AEEILLMMNPT**	implemental
AEEHRSSSTUU	thesauruses	**AEEILLMMNOPS**	psilomelane
AEEIIILMNTV	eliminative	**AEEILLMMNSST**	enamellists
AEEIIILNSTV	venialities	**AEEILLMPRXY**	exemplarily
AEEIIINRRST	itineraries	**AEEILLMTUVY**	emulatively
AEEIIKNRSST	keratinises	**AEEILLNNPRY**	perennially
AEEIIKNRSTZ	keratinizes	**AEEILLNNSXY**	sexennially
AEEIILLMNRS	millenaries	**AEEILLNRSST**	literalness
AEEIILLNNRT	interlineal	**AEEILLNSSTY**	essentially
AEEIILLRSTT	illiterates	**AEEILLOPSTV**	Elisavetpol
AEEIILMMORS	memorialise	**AEEILLRSSWY**	wearilessly
AEEIILMMORZ	memorialize	**AEEILLRSTVY**	versatilely
AEEIILMNRRS	mineraliser	**AEEILMMNNPT**	impanelment
AEEIILMNRRZ	mineralizer	**AEEILMMNPST**	impalements
AEEIILMNRSS	mineralises	**AEEILMMNRSU**	neurilemmas
AEEIILMNRSZ	mineralizes	**AEEILMNNSTT**	entailments
AEEIILMNSTT	mentalities		sentimental
AEEIILMORSU	Marie Louise	**AEEILMNORST**	salinometer
AEEIILMORTV	meliorative	**AEEILMNPRST**	planimeters
AEEIILMRRST	semitrailer		sempiternal
AEEIILNNPTT	penitential	**AEEILMNPTTU**	penultimate
AEEIILNNRRT	interlinear	**AEEILMNRSST**	streamlines
AEEIILNNRST	internalise	**AEEILMNRSTX**	externalism
AEEIILNNRTZ	internalize	**AEEILMNSSSS**	aimlessness
AEEIILNNSST	inessential	**AEEILMOPRRT**	polarimeter
AEEIILNORST	orientalise	**AEEILMORRST**	solarimeter
AEEIILNORTZ	orientalize	**AEEILMORSWY**	wearisomely
AEEIILNPRRU	perineurial	**AEEILMOSTTT**	teetotalism
AEEIILNRSTU	unrealities	**AEEILMPPRRS**	perispermal
AEEIILNSTTX	existential	**AEEILMPPRSY**	semelpparity
AEEIILNTTVV	ventilative	**AEEILNNNPPS**	Pennine Alps
AEEIILQRRSU	reliquaries	**AEEILNNOPTX**	exponential
AEEIILRSSTV	relativises	**AEEILNNOSTX**	extensional
	revitalises	**AEEILNNPSTU**	peninsulate
AEEIILRSTVZ	relativizes	**AEEILNNSSTU**	unessential
	revitalizes	**AEEILNNSSTY**	insensately
AEEIILRTTVY	iteratively	**AEEILNNSTTU**	lieutenants
AEEIILSSTUX	sexualities	**AEEILNOPRSS**	personalise
AEEIIMMSSTT	misestimate	**AEEILNOPRSZ**	personalize
AEEIIMNNSST	inseminates	**AEEILNOPRTT**	interpolate
AEEIIMNRTTV	terminative	**AEEILNOPSST**	neoplasties
AEEIIMPRSTV	imperatives	**AEEILNORRSV**	reversional
	semiprivate	**AEEILNORSST**	neorealists
AEEIIMPRTTV	impetrative	**AEEILNORSTV**	revelations
AEEIINNTTTV	inattentive	**AEEILNPRSTT**	interseptal
AEEIINOPRTV	inoperative	**AEEILNPSTTV**	septivalent
AEEIINORRTT	reiteration	**AEEILNPSVXY**	expansively
AEEIINPRRST	Saint-Pierre	**AEEILNQSTUV**	equivalents
AEEIINSTUVV	vesuvianite	**AEEILNRRSTU**	neutraliser
AEEIIPRSSST	patisseries	**AEEILNRRSUV**	vulneraries
		AEEILNRRTUZ	neutralizer
		AEEILNRSSSS	airlessness
		AEEILNRSSTU	neutralises
		AEEILNRSTTX	externalist
		AEEILNRSTUX	intersexual
		AEEILNRSTUZ	neutralizes
		AEEILNRTTXY	externality
		AEEILNSSSTT	stateliness
		AEEILNTTTVY	attentively
			tentatively
		AEEILNTTUVY	eventuality
		AEEILOPPSTU	epipetalous
		AEEILOPRRRT	repertorial
		AEEILOPRRST	proletaries
		AEEILOPRTVX	explorative
		AEEILOPRTVY	operatively
		AEEILORRSSV	revalorises
		AEEILORRSVZ	revalorizes
		AEEILPRSSST	peristalses
		AEEILPRSSVY	aspersively
		AEEILPRSTUV	superlative
		AEEILPRSVVY	pervasively
		AEEILPSTTUX	exstipulate
		AEEILQRRSTU	quarterlies
		AEEILRRRSTT	terrestrial
		AEEILRRTTTU	litterateur
		AEEILRSSTVY	assertively
		AEEIMMNNPRT	impermanent
		AEEIMMNPRST	pentamerism
		AEEIMMRRSTT	tetramerism
		AEEIMMRSSSU	mismeasures
		AEEIMNNNOQU	menaquinone
		AEEIMNNNRST	insnarement
		AEEIMNNNRTT	entrainment
		AEEIMNNORST	enantiomers
			renominates
		AEEIMNNORTU	enumeration
			mountaineer
		AEEIMNNOSTT	maisonnette
		AEEIMNNRSTU	innumerates
		AEEIMNNRTTT	intreatment
		AEEIMNNSTTT	instatement
		AEEIMNOPRST	impersonate
		AEEIMNORSST	monasteries
		AEEIMNORSTT	marionettes
		AEEIMNOSSTT	maisonettes
		AEEIMNPRRSU	praemunires
		AEEIMNRSSST	streaminess
		AEEIMNRSTUV	mensurative
		AEEIMRSSSVV	massiveness
		AEEIMOPRRST	temporaries
		AEEIMOPRRTV	vaporimeter
		AEEIMORRSTU	temerarious
		AEEIMORRSTV	variometers
		AEEIMQRRSTU	marquetries
		AEEIMQRSSTU	Times Square
		AEEIMQRSSUV	semiquavers
		AEEIMQRSTTU	marquisette
		AEEIMSSSTTY	systematise
		AEEIMSSTTVZ	systematize
		AEEINNOORTX	exoneration

AEEINNOPRTT	penetration	**AEELMMNORSU**	neurolemmas	**AEENRRSSSTV**	transverses
AEEINNOPRTU	neutropenia	**AEELMMORTTV**	voltammeter	**AEEOPPRRRTT**	perpetrator
AEEINNORSTV	anteversion	**AEELMNNPRTY**	permanently	**AEEOPRRSSTT**	tetraspores
AEEINNORSTX	Oxenstierna	**AEELMNNRTUV**	unravelment	**AEEORRSSSTV**	overasserts
AEEINNORTTV	eventration	**AEELMNOPRST**	planometers	**AEEORRSSTVY**	overstayers
AEEINNOTTUV	eventuation	**AEELMNORSTV**	overmantels	**AEEPRRSSSST**	trespassers
AEEINNOTTUX	extenuation	**AEELMNORSTW**	watermelons	**AEEPRSSSSTT**	tapstresses
AEEINNSSSTT	assentients	**AEELMOPRSSU**	semelparous	**AEEPRSSSTTU**	superstates
AEEINOPRSST	proteinases	**AEELMOPRSSY**	polymerases	**AEEPRSSSWXY**	expressways
AEEINOPRSSY	aepyornises	**AEELMOPRSTT**	plastometer	**AEFFGIIMNRR**	reaffirming
AEEINOPRSTV	personative	**AEELMOQRRSU**	quarrelsome	**AEFFGIMSTUU**	suffumigate
AEEINOPRSTX	paroxetines	**AEELMORSTTV**	voltameters	**AEFFGINORST**	afforesting
AEEINOPSTTT	potentiates	**AEELMPRRTUY**	prematurely	**AEFFHINRSSS**	raffishness
AEEINORRSST	reassertion	**AEELMPRSSTT**	streetlamps	**AEFFIIMNORR**	foraminifer
AEEINORRSTV	reservation	**AEELNNPRTTY**	repentantly	**AEFFIJNORSZ**	Franz
AEEINPRSSST	spessartine	**AEELNNPSTTU**	antepenults		Josef I
AEEINPRSSTT	Saint	**AEELNNQSSTU**	lansquenets	**AEFFILLMMMR**	flimflammer
	Peter's	**AEELNNSSSSU**	sensualness	**AEFFILNSSTU**	insufflates
AEEINPRSSTY	antipyreses	**AEELNOPRSSS**	salesperson	**AEFFILORRRW**	Wolf-Ferrari
AEEINPSSSSV	passiveness	**AEELNOPRSST**	prolateness	**AEFFKNRRRTU**	frankfurter
AEEINQRSSTU	equestrians	**AEELNOSSSUZ**	zealousness	**AEFFLMOORSW**	foamflowers
AEEINRRRSST	restrainers	**AEELNPRRSST**	partnerless	**AEFGGIMNNRT**	fragmenting
AEEINRSSTUV	unassertive	**AEELNPRSTTW**	wentletraps	**AEFGHIIRRST**	airfreights
AEEIOOPPSSS	aposiopeses	**AEELNRSSSST**	artlessness	**AEFGHINRRSW**	wharfingers
AEEIOPPRRTX	expropriate	**AEELNRSSSSY**	raylessness	**AEFGHLOPRXY**	flexography
AEEIOPRRSSV	overpraises	**AEELNSSSSTU**	sultanesses	**AEFGHNORSTU**	fearnoughts
AEEIORRSTTV	restorative	**AEELOORSUVZ**	overzealous	**AEFGIIKLNRW**	fire walking
AEEIORSSTTX	stereotaxis	**AEELOPPRSTU**	repopulates	**AEFGIILLNNRS**	fingernails
AEEIPPRRSTW	wiretappers	**AEELOPSTTUX**	expostulate	**AEFGIILNOTX**	exfoliating
AEEIPRRSSTT	stripteaser	**AEELOQRRSUU**	roquelaures	**AEFGIIMNNST**	manifesting
AEEIPRRSSTU	pasteuriser	**AEEMMNNPRSTT**	entrapments	**AEFGIKMNRRS**	fingermarks
AEEIPRRSTUZ	pasteurizer	**AEEMMNNRSSTV**	menservants	**AEFGIKNOPRS**	forspeaking
AEEIPRSSSTT	spessartite	**AEEMMNOPRRTY**	pyranometer	**AEFGILLLNNN**	flannelling
AEEIPRSSSTU	pasteurises	**AEEMMNOPRSTU**	pentamerous	**AEFGILLNRST**	fingerstall
AEEIPRSSTUZ	pasteurizes	**AEEMMNOQRTTU**	quantometer	**AEFGILLNRTY**	falteringly
	trapeziuses	**AEEMMNORRRTU**	remunerator	**AEFGILNNOOR**	gonfalonier
AEEIPRSTTUV	vituperates	**AEEMMNORRSTT**	remonstrate	**AEFGILNNSSU**	gainfulness
AEEIRRSSSTT	traitresses	**AEEMMNORRSTU**	enumerators	**AEFGILNPRSU**	Persian Gulf
AEEIRSSTTTX	testatrixes	**AEEMMNORRSUV**	manoeuvrers	**AEFGILOPRST**	profligates
AEEJLNOSSSU	jealousness	**AEEMMNORSSTT**	easternmost	**AEFGIMNNRTT**	ingraftment
AEEJNORRTUV	rejuvenator	**AEEMMNORTUUV**	outmaneuver	**AEFGINNNSSW**	fawningness
AEEKLMNNRST	kernmantels	**AEEMNOSSTTW**	stateswomen	**AEFGINNNSTU**	unfastening
AEEKLMNORTT	metalworker	**AEEMNNPPRSTY**	prepayments	**AEFGINNORRW**	forewarning
AEEKMMNORSY	moneymakers	**AEEMNNRRSSTT**	arrestments	**AEFGINOPRRT**	perforating
AEEKMMRRRSY	merrymakers	**AEEMNNRSSTTU**	menstruates	**AEFGINORRSW**	forswearing
AEEKMORRSTU	euromarkets	**AEEMNSSSSST**	assessments	**AEFGINORSTT**	foretasting
AEEKMPRRSTU	supermarket	**AEEMOPRRTXY**	extemporary	**AEFGINRRSTU**	transfigure
AEEKMPRRSTV	verkramptes	**AEEMORRSSTV**	overmasters	**AEFGIPRRSTU**	grapefruits
AEEKNPRRSTU	supertanker	**AEEMORRSSTTU**	tetramerous	**AEFGLNRRTUW**	Furtwängler
AEELLMMRRST	trammellers	**AEEMRRSSTTT**	streetsmart	**AEFHHLLLTUY**	healthfully
AEELLMNORTT	reallotment	**AEENNNPRTTU**	unrepentant	**AEFHIILNSSS**	snailfishes
AEELLMNRSTU	allurements	**AEENNOPRRTU**	neuropteran	**AEFHILLSSTY**	faithlessly
AEELLMORRST	steamroller	**AEENOOPRSSU**	aponeuroses	**AEFHIMNOPRS**	foremanship
AEELLNORRTT	retrolental	**AEENOORRSTX**	exonerators	**AEFHLMNRSSU**	harmfulness
AEELLNORSTW	stonewaller	**AEENOPRRSTT**	paternoster	**AEFHMORRSTT**	farthermost
AEELLNPRTVY	prevalently		penetrators	**AEFIIIMNRRS**	infirmaries
AEELLNRRSUV	unravellers	**AEENOPRSSST**	patronesses	**AEFIIKLNRRT**	franklinite
AEELLNRSTTW	Western Wall	**AEENORSTTUX**	extenuators	**AEFIILLNNOX**	inflexional
AEELLNSSSSW	lawlessness	**AEENORTTUXY**	extenuatory	**AEFIILLNNTU**	influential
AEELLPPRTUY	perpetually	**AEENPPRSSTT**	stepparents	**AEFIILMORST**	formalities
AEELLQRRSU	quarrellers	**AEENQRSSTTU**	sequestrant	**AEFIILNNRTY**	infernality
AEELLSSSTTY	tastelessly	**AEENRRRSSTTV**	transverter	**AEFIILNOOTX**	exfoliation

AEFIILNRSTT	infiltrates	AEFNORRRSST	transferors	AEGHHOPRTVY	hyetography
AEFIILNRTUY	infuriately	AEFNORRSTTW	waterfronts	AEGHIIIJJNS	Jiang Jie
AEFIIMNORTV	informative	AEFNOSSSTUU	fatuousness		Shi
AEFIINNORTV	infantivore	AEFNRRSSSTU	transfusers	AEGHIIMNPSS	emphasising
AEFIINNOSTT	festination	AEFOOPRRRST	perforators	AEGHIIMNPST	empathising
	infestation	AEFOOPRRRTY	perforatory	AEGHIIMNPSZ	emphasizing
	sinfonietta	AEFOOPRRSTW	waterproofs	AEGHIIMNPTZ	empathizing
AEFIINNRSTT	transfinite	AEFOORRSSTT	tortfeasors	AEGHIIMNPRS	amphigories
AEFIINOPRSS	saponifiers	AEFRRRSSTTU	frustraters	AEGHIINPSTT	spaghettini
AEFIINOPRST	profanities	AEGGGIINRSW	earwiggings	AEGHIIPPRST	epigraphist
AEFIINQRSTU	quantifiers	AEGGHHIKNNS	Genghis Khan	AEGHIIPRSST	graphitises
AEFILLLMMOR	lamelliform	AEGGHHINSSS	haggishness	AEGHIIPRSTZ	graphitizes
AEFILLMOPRT	patelliform	AEGGHIILLNNT	nightingale	AEGHIKNSSSW	gawkishness
AEFILLRRTTU	ultrafilter	AEGGHIILOOS	hagiologies	AEGHILLMPRT	lamplighter
AEFILMNOSTU	filamentous	AEGGHIINNRT	ingathering	AEGHILLNNRT	enthralling
AEFILMNOUVX	fluvoxamine	AEGGHINNORV	overhanging	AEGHILLNOPS	anglophiles
AEFILMORRSS	formalisers	AEGGHINSSSW	waggishness	AEGHILLNOSW	wholesaling
AEFILMORRSU	formularies	AEGGHIOPSST	geophagists	AEGHILLNRST	allnighters
	formularise	AEGGHLOOPRR	logographer	AEGHILLRRSY	Argyllshire
AEFILMORRSZ	formalizers	AEGGHMNORTU	Grangemouth	AEGHILMNTTY	methylating
AEFILMORRUZ	formularize	AEGGIIJNNWW	Wang Jing	AEGHILNNOPT	phenolating
AEFILMORTVY	formatively		Wei	AEGHILNNSST	haltingness
AEFILMPRSUY	superfamily	AEGGIILLNST	legislating	AEGHILNOOST	anthologies
AEFILNNPSSU	painfulness	AEGGIILLMNNR	mailmerging		anthologise
AEFILNNSSTU	flauntiness	AEGGIILMNNR	malingering		theologians
AEFILNORSTU	fluorinates	AEGGIILMPRS	pilgrimages	AEGHILNOOTZ	anthologize
AEFILNORSTW	satinflower	AEGGIIMNNRT	germinating	AEGHILNORUV	overhauling
AEFILNORSUY	nefariously	AEGGIIMNNRZ	germanizing	AEGHILNOTTU	glutathione
AEFILOPRRTY	prefatorily	AEGGIIMNNST	magnetising	AEGHILNSSST	ghastliness
AEFILOQRSTU	quatrefoils	AEGGIIMNNTZ	magnetizing	AEGHILOOPST	pathologies
AEFIMMMORSU	mammiferous	AEGGIIMNRRT	remigrating		pathologise
AEFIMNNNRTY	infantrymen	AEGGIINNOTT	negotiating	AEGHILOOPTZ	pathologize
AEFIMNNOOTT	fomentation	AEGGIINNPRT	interpaging	AEGHIMMOPRS	mimeographs
AEFIMNOORRT	reformation	AEGGIINNRSS	reassigning	AEGHIMNNRST	garnishment
AEFIMOPRRTZ	trapeziform	AEGGIINNRTT	integrating	AEGHIMNOPRS	semaphoring
AEFINNRRRST	transferrin	AEGGIINRTTU	ingurgitate	AEGHIMOPRSS	seismograph
AEFINOOPRRT	perforation	AEGGIJMRSST	jiggermasts	AEGHINNSSTU	naughtiness
AEFINOOPRST	fortepianos	AEGGILNRSS	glaringness	AEGHINOPSTU	epignathous
	pianofortes	AEGGILOOSSU	sialogogues	AEGHINORSUW	warehousing
AEFINOORSTT	forestation	AEGGIMNOOTY	geitonogamy	AEGHINOSSST	goatishness
AEFINORRSST	rainforests	AEGGIMNRSS	grangerisms	AEGHINRSSTT	straightens
AEFINORSTTU	refutations	AEGGIMNRSST	gangsterism	AEGHINRSSTV	harvestings
AEFINRSSTUV	transfusive	AEGGINNOTXY	oxygenating	AEGHIRSSTTT	straightest
AEFIOOPRSTU	foetiparous	AEGGINORRVZ	overgrazing	AEGHIRSTTWW	strawweight
AEFKLLOORRW	floorwalker	AEGGINORSSS	aggressions	AEGHLMOOOST	homologates
AEFLLLNTTUY	flatulently	AEGGINPRTUX	expurgating	AEGHLMOPRVY	myelography
AEFLLLOPSWY	playfellows	AEGGINRRTTU	regurgitant	AEGHLNNOOPS	anglophones
AEFLLLORSWW	wallflowers	AEGGJNRSTUU	juggernauts	AEGHLNOOORR	gonorrhoeal
AEFLLLSSTUY	faultlessly	AEGGMOSSTUY	mystagogues	AEGHLOOPRSY	phraseology
AEFLLMRSTUY	masterfully	AEGHHIJKNNS	Jenghis Khan	AEGHLOPPRYY	pyelography
AEFLLNPSSUY	playfulness	AEGHHILLLSS	shillelaghs	AEGHLOPRRXY	xylographer
AEFLLORSSUV	flavourless	AEGHHILOPRS	heliographs	AEGHLORSSSU	hourglasses
AEFLLPRRUVY	prayerfully	AEGHHILOPRY	heliography	AEGHLORSSUV	overslaughs
AEFLMOORSUV	flavoursome	AEGHHINNPTY	hyphenating	AEGHLOSSSSU	glasshouses
AEFLNOOPSTU	teaspoonful	AEGHHINNSTU	unsheathing	AEGHMMORRST	thermograms
AEFLNORTTUY	fortunately	AEGHHINSSTU	haughtiness	AEGHMNOOPRR	monographer
AEFLORRSSTW	starflowers	AEGHHLOPRSU	ploughshare		nomographer
AEFLORRSTWW	strawflower	AEGHHMOPPST	apophthegms	AEGHMNOOPRS	gramophones
AEFMNORRRST	transformer	AEGHHMOPRRT	thermograph	AEGHMNOOSTT	gnathostome
AEFMOOPRSTT	foretopmast	AEGHHNOPPRS	nephographs	AEGHMNOPPRU	pneumograph
AEFMOORRRTY	reformatory	AEGHHNOPRTY	ethnography	AEGHMNOPRSS	sphenograms
AEFNNORTTUU	unfortunate	AEGHHOPRSTY	hyetographs	AEGHMOPRSUY	hypergamous

AEGHNOOPRRS	nosographer	**AEGIIMNRSTT**	mistreating	**AEGILMORRSZ**	glamorizers
AEGHNOPRSST	stenographs	**AEGIIMPRSTU**	epigastrium	**AEGILMORSUZ**	glamourizes
AEGHNOPRSTY	stenography	**AEGIIMRSSTT**	stigmatiser	**AEGILNNNPPR**	preplanning
AEGHOOPPRRT	topographer	**AEGIIMRSTTZ**	stigmatizer	**AEGILNNOOST**	elongations
AEGHOOPRRRS	orographers	**AEGIIMSSSTT**	stigmatises	**AEGILNNOSTU**	langoustine
AEGHOOPRRSZ	zoographers	**AEGIIMSSTTZ**	stigmatizes	**AEGILNNSSST**	lastingness
AEGHOPPRRRV	pyrographer	**AEGIINNNOST**	angiotensin	**AEGILNOORRT**	Oregon trail
	reprography	**AEGIINNNRTV**	innervating	**AEGILNOOSSX**	xenoglossia
AEGHOPPRRSS	grasshopper	**AEGIINNOOTT**	negotiation	**AEGILNOPPRV**	overlapping
AEGHOPPRRTY	petrography	**AEGIINNOPSW**	weaponising	**AEGILNOPRVY**	overplaying
	typographer	**AEGIINNOPWZ**	weaponizing	**AEGILNORSTU**	regulations
AEGIIILMNNT	eliminating	**AEGIINNORST**	resignation	**AEGILNORUVV**	overvaluing
AEGIIILMNST	malignities	**AEGIINNORTT**	integration	**AEGILNPRSST**	plasterings
AEGIIILNORS	seigniorial		orientating	**AEGILNPRSTT**	splattering
AEGIIILNRSS	serialising	**AEGIINNOSST**	isoantigens	**AEGILNQRUVY**	quaveringly
AEGIIILNRSZ	serializing	**AEGIINNPPST**	pepsinating	**AEGILNRRSTY**	arrestingly
AEGIIILNSTV	invigilates	**AEGIINNRRST**	restraining	**AEGILNRSSTV**	starvelings
AEGIIINNRRT	itinerating	**AEGIINNRSTT**	intrigantes	**AEGILOOPRSS**	apologisers
AEGIIINSTTV	instigative		reinstating	**AEGILOOPRSZ**	apologizers
AEGIIKLNSST	glaikitness		straitening	**AEGILOORSST**	aerologists
AEGIIKMNNOS	noisemaking	**AEGIINNRTTU**	intriguante	**AEGILOOSTTU**	tautologies
AEGIIKNRSST	asterisking	**AEGIINOPRST**	operatising		tautologise
AEGIIKNRSTW	waterskiing	**AEGIINOPRTZ**	operatizing	**AEGILOOTTUZ**	tautologize
AEGIILLMMMR	milligramme	**AEGIINORSST**	signatories	**AEGILOPRSTT**	graptolites
AEGIILLMNNP	impanelling	**AEGIINORSTV**	invigorates	**AEGILPRTUVY**	purgatively
AEGIILLMNST	metallising	**AEGIINPPRSU**	pauperising	**AEGILRRSSUV**	vulgarisers
AEGIILLMNTZ	metallizing	**AEGIINPPRTW**	wiretapping	**AEGILRRSUVZ**	vulgarizers
AEGIILLMRSU	guerillaism	**AEGIINPPRUZ**	pauperizing	**AEGILRSTTUU**	gutturalise
AEGIILLNOST	legislation	**AEGIINPRTTX**	extirpating	**AEGILRTTUUZ**	gutturalize
AEGIILLNPST	palletising	**AEGIINRSSTW**	waitressing	**AEGIMMNNRSS**	stammerings
AEGIILLNPTZ	palletizing	**AEGIINSSTTV**	negativists	**AEGIMMOPRSU**	gemmiparous
AEGIILLNSTT	satelliting	**AEGIIRRSSTT**	geriatrists	**AEGIMNNNORT**	ornamenting
AEGIILLNTVV	genitivally	**AEGIKLMMORS**	kilogrammes	**AEGIMNNNORV**	overmanning
AEGIILLSTVY	vestigially	**AEGIKMMNNOY**	moneymaking	**AEGIMNNORUV**	manoeuvring
AEGIILMMNST	lemmatising	**AEGIKMMNNRY**	merrymaking	**AEGIMNNSSST**	assignments
AEGIILMMNTZ	lemmatizing	**AEGIKMNNOSS**	maskinonges	**AEGIMNOOPRS**	spermogonia
AEGIILMNORS	regionalism	**AEGIKNNNOPS**	nonspeaking	**AEGIMNOPRRT**	impregnator
AEGIILMNORT	meliorating	**AEGIKNOPSTU**	outspeaking	**AEGIMNOPRSS**	angiosperms
AEGIILMNRST	misrelating	**AEGIKNORSTV**	overtasking	**AEGIMNORRST**	germinators
AEGIILNNRSV	vernalising	**AEGILLMMNRT**	trammelling	**AEGIMNORSSU**	ignoramuses
AEGIILNNRTU	interlingua	**AEGILLMNNTY**	lamentingly	**AEGIMNPRTTU**	permutating
AEGIILNNRTY	interlaying	**AEGILLMOOPS**	megalopolis	**AEGIMNRRSST**	ringmasters
AEGIILNNRVZ	vernalizing	**AEGILLMPRSU**	aspergillum	**AEGIMNRSSTT**	smatterings
AEGIILNNSTU	ungainliest	**AEGILLNNRUV**	unravelling	**AEGINNNORSU**	unreasoning
AEGIILNNTTV	ventilating	**AEGILLNOPST**	sellotaping	**AEGINNOORRV**	vinegarroon
AEGIILNORST	regionalist	**AEGILLNORTT**	reallotting	**AEGINNOOTXY**	oxygenation
AEGIILNORSV	vainglories	**AEGILLNQRRU**	quarrelling	**AEGINNOPRST**	personating
AEGIILNPPQU	appliqueing	**AEGILLORSST**	allegorists	**AEGINNOSSUU**	sanguineous
AEGIILNRSST	slaistering		legislators	**AEGINNPRRTU**	enrapturing
AEGIILNRSSU	singularise	**AEGILLPRRRZ**	Grillparzer	**AEGINNPRSSS**	sparingness
AEGIILNRSUZ	singularize	**AEGILLPRSSU**	aspergillus	**AEGINNRSSTT**	astringents
AEGIILNRTTU	elutriating	**AEGILLRRRUY**	irregularly	**AEGINOORSTT**	negotiators
AEGIILNRTTY	integrality	**AEGILMMNOTU**	gemmulation	**AEGINOPRSSV**	overpassing
AEGIILNSUXZ	sexualizing	**AEGILMMNNUY**	unmeaningly	**AEGINOPRTUX**	expurgation
AEGIILOOSTT	aetiologist	**AEGILMNNOPS**	plasminogen	**AEGINORRSTT**	integrators
AEGIILRSTUV	vulgarities	**AEGILMNNSST**	signalments	**AEGINORSTTV**	overstating
AEGIIMMRSTU	magisterium	**AEGILMNOORT**	glomeration	**AEGINORSTVY**	overstaying
AEGIIMNNORT	germination	**AEGILMNOPRU**	pelargonium	**AEGINPRSSST**	trespassing
AEGIIMNNOST	geminations	**AEGILMNORSS**	rosemalings	**AEGINPRSSTU**	supergiants
AEGIIMNNRTT	terminating	**AEGILMNOSTU**	ligamentous	**AEGINPRSSTY**	panegyrists
AEGIIMNORST	emigrations	**AEGILMOOSSY**	semasiology	**AEGINQRRSTU**	quarterings
AEGIIMNPRTT	impetrating	**AEGILMORRSS**	glamorisers	**AEGINRRSSTT**	registrants

AEGINRSTTVY travestying	**AEHIINSSTTT** antitheists	**nearthrosis**
AEGIOPRRSTU purgatories	**AEHIIORSTTU** authorities	**AEHINORRSTV** hovertrains
AEGIPRRRTYY pyrargyrite	**AEHIIPPRRSS** periphrasis	**AEHINORSSTT** throatiness
AEGIRSSSTTT strategists	**AEHIIPPSSTT** epitaphists	**AEHINPPRRST** partnership
AEGKKKNNOUVY Nguyen	**AEHIISRSSTUW** White Russia	**AEHINPSSSSW** waspishness
Kao Ky	**AEHIKLNRSSS** larkishness	**AEHINQRSSUV** vanquishers
AEGKLORRSSW glassworker	**AEHIKMNSSSW** mawkishness	**AEHINQSSSSU** squashiness
AEGLLNOOPTY planetology	**AEHIKNNSSSV** knavishness	**AEHINRSSSTW** swarthiness
AEGLMOPRSTU promulgates	**AEHILLMTTUU** ultima Thule	**AEHINSSSTTU** enthusiasts
AEGLNNOOOTY neonatology	**AEHILLOPPTY** apophyllite	**AEHIOPPRRST** praetorship
AEGLNNPRTUY repugnantly	**AEHILLOPRST** hospitaller	**AEHIOPRRSTY** erythropsia
AEGLOORRSST astrologers	**AEHILMNNOOP** aminophenol	**AEHIOPSSSTY** hypostasise
AEGLPRSSSUU surplusages	**AEHILMNOPPY** lymphopenia	**AEHIOPSSTTY** hypostatise
AEGMMNOPRSU pneumograms	**AEHILMNOSSY** haemolysins	**AEHIOPSSTYZ** hypostasize
AEGMMOPRRRS programmers	**AEHILMNOTTY** methylation	**AEHIOPSTTYZ** hypostatize
AEGMNOORRST gastronomer	**AEHILMNOTXY** hematoxylin	**AEHIORRSSTU** authorisers
AEGMNOORSST gastronomes	**AEHILMNPSSY** misshapenly	**AEHIORRSTUZ** authorizers
AEGMNSSSTUY nystagmuses	**AEHILMNSSTV** lavishments	**AEHIRSSSTTW** sweatshirts
AEGNOOPRSSU saprogenous	**AEHILMORSST** isothermals	**AEHJNOORRST** Trojan Horse
AEGNOORSTXY oxygenators	**AEHILMOSSTY** hematolysis	**AEHKLLNSSTY** thanklessly
AEGOOPRSSYZ azygospores	**AEHILMQSSUV** squeamishly	**AEHKLOPRSSW** shopwalkers
AEGOORRRTUV rotogravure	**AEHILMRRSTY** erythrismal	**AEHKMNOSSTU** snakemouths
AEGOPRRSTUX expurgators	**AEHILNOPTXY** phytoalexin	**AEHKNNOORRT** North Korean
AEGOPRRTUXY expurgatory	**AEHILNOSTTW** West Lothian	**AEHKNOORSTU** South Korean
AEGORSSSTUU stegosaurus	**AEHILNOSTTY** ethylations	**AEHLLLMOOPR** allelomorph
AEHHIIILLNNS Hsin-hai-	**AEHILNPRRTY** platyrrhine	**AEHLLLNOPPY** phylloplane
lien	**AEHILNPRSST** shinplaster	**AEHLLLMOOSTY** loathsomely
AEHHIIMPSSS messiahship	**AEHILNPSSSS** splashiness	**AEHLLNOSSSW** shallowness
AEHHILLNTUV unhealthily	**AEHILNSSSSV** slavishness	**AEHLLOPRSXY** phylloxeras
AEHHIMOPRTY hypothermia	**AEHILOPRSST** hospitalers	**AEHLLOPSTXY** phyllotaxes
AEHHIMPRTYY hyperthymia	**AEHILORSTVY** overhastily	**AEHLMNNORTT** Montherlant
AEHHINNNOPTY hyphenation	**AEHILORTTVY** hortatively	**AEHLMOOSSUX** homosexuals
AEHHINOPRST hierophants	**AEHIMMNRSSS** rammishness	**AEHLMOPPRRY** lamprophyre
AEHHINOPSTY hyposthenia	**AEHIMMPRRST** triphammers	**AEHLMORSTTY** methylators
AEHHIOPPSST phosphatise	**AEHIMMRSSTU** rheumatisms	**AEHLNNOPSTT** pentathlons
AEHHIOPPSTZ phosphatize	**AEHIMNNNSSS** mannishness	**AEHLNOPRTUY** polyurethan
AEHHIORTTTW whitethroat	**AEHIMNNNSSU** inhumanness	**AEHLNOPSSTU** sulphonates
AEHHLLOPTTY thallophyte	**AEHIMNOOPPR** apomorphine	**AEHLPRSSTUU** sulphurates
AEHHLMMOORT homothermal	**AEHIMMNOPRST** misanthrope	**AEHMMNORRSY** Romney Marsh
AEHHLMOPRTY hypothermal	**AEHIMNORSSS** harmonisers	**AEHMMOOOPRT** ommatophore
AEHHLNOPSTT heptathlons	**AEHIMNORRSZ** harmonizers	**AEHMNORRSTW** harrowments
AEHHLOPPSYY hypophyseal	**AEHIMNOSTUX** exhumations	**AEHMNORSTTY** thermonasty
AEHHMOOOPST homoeopaths	**AEHIMNRSSTV** ravishments	**AEHMORSSTTT** thermostats
AEHHMOOOPTY homoeopathy	**AEHIMNSSSTU** enthusiasms	**AEHNOOPRRTT** orthopteran
AEHHMOSSTUW mouthwashes	**AEHIMOOSSST** homeostasis	**AEHNOOPSSSU** sousaphones
AEHHNOOPRST anthophores	**AEHIMOPSSTY** haemoptysis	**AEHNORSTUWY** unseaworthy
AEHHNOOPSTU theophanous	**AEHIMORSTTX** thermotaxis	**AEHOOPPRSST** apostrophes
AEHHNOPRRTY tenorrhaphy	**AEHIMPPRSTU** hippeastrum	**AEHOOPRRRST** arthrospore
AEHHOOPPRST phosphorate	**AEHIMPRSSST** shipmasters	**AEHOOPRRSTT** trapshooter
AEHHRRSTTUW waterthrush	**AEHIMPRSSTY** sympathiser	**AEHOOPRRSTX** prothoraxes
AEHIIILLMNW Wilhelmina I	**AEHIMPRSTYZ** sympathizer	**AEHOOPSSTTT** toothpastes
AEHIIILMNST Saint-Mihiel	**AEHIMPSSTYS** sympathises	**AEHOORRTTXY** exhortatory
AEHIIILMTUV humiliative	**AEHIMPSSTYZ** sympathizes	**AEHOORSSSTY** soothsayers
AEHIILLOPRU ailurophile	**AEHINNNOOST** hootnannies	**AEHOPPRSSTY** saprophytes
AEHIILLPSTT philatelist	**AEHINNPPSSU** unhappiness	**AEHORRRSSTW** restharrows
AEHIILOPSST hospitalise	**AEHINNPSSTY** synthespian	**AEHPRSSSTTY** strathspeys
AEHIILOPSTZ hospitalize	**AEHINOORSTT** anorthosite	**AEIIIILNSST** initialises
AEHIIMNRTTX martinetish	**AEHINOORTTX** exhortation	**AEIIIILNSTZ** initializes
AEHIINNOPST antiphonies	**AEHINOPRSTT** antistrophe	**AEIIIINSTTV** initiatives
AEHIINOPRRS parishioner	**AEHINOPRSTU** euphoriants	**AEIIILLMNOR** millionaire
AEHIINOSSTT hesitations	**AEHINOPSSTT** stephanotis	**AEIIILLMNST** sillimanite
AEHIINPRSTX xiphisterna	**AEHINORRSST** enarthrosis	**AEIIILLNRST** initiallers

AEIIILLTTTV	titillative	AEIIILMSTTUV	stimulative	AEIINOPRSTX	expirations
AEIIILMMPRS	imperialism	AEIILNNNOST	intensional	AEIINOPRTTX	extirpation
AEIIILMNNOT	elimination	AEIILNNNOTT	intentional	AEIINOPRTTY	petitionary
AEIIILMNRST	ministerial	AEIILNNNOTV	inventional	AEIINOPSSTT	poinsettias
AEIIILMNSST	antimissile	AEIILNNORST	insertional	AEIINOQSTTU	equitations
AEIIILMPRST	imperialist	AEIILNNORTV	inventorial	AEIINORRSVY	revisionary
AEIIILMRRSV	verisimilar	AEIILNNOTTV	ventilation	AEIINORRTTY	anteriority
AEIIILMRSST	militarises	AEIILNNPRST	interspinal	AEIINPRSSSU	prussianise
AEIIILMRSTZ	militarizes	AEIILNNRRST	transilient	AEIINPRSSTY	antipyresis
AEIIILMTTVY	imitatively	AEIILNNRRTY	internality	AEIINPRSSUZ	prussianize
AEIIILNNOOP	Napoleon III		itinerantly	AEIINPSSSST	inspissates
AEIIILNPRST	pleinairist	AEIILNNSSST	saintliness	AEIINPSTVXY	expansivity
AEIIILRSSTV	trivialises	AEIILNOPSTX	pixelations	AEIINRSSTTV	transitives
AEIIILRSTVZ	trivializes		postexilian	AEIINSSTTUV	antitussive
AEIIIMNOSST	animosities	AEIILNORSSS	insessorial	AEIIOOPPSSS	aposiopesis
AEIIIMNOSTT	itemisation	AEIILNORSTT	orientalist	AEIIOOPRRST	a posteriori
AEIIIMNOTTZ	itemization	AEIILNORTTU	elutriation	AEIIOOPPRSTT	propitiates
AEIIIMNRSTU	miniaturise	AEIILNOSTTV	levitations	AEIIOPRTTVY	operativity
AEIIIMNRTUZ	miniaturize	AEIILNQRTUZ	tranquilize	AEIIPPSSSSW	pipsissewas
AEIIINNORTT	itineration	AEIILNRSSTV	trivialness	AEIJLNORRSU	journaliser
AEIIINNSSUV	insinuative	AEIILORRRTT	territorial	AEIJLNORRUZ	journalizer
AEIIINORSSV	visionaries	AEIILPRSSST	peristalsis	AEIJLNORSSU	journalises
AEIIINPRSTV	inspirative	AEIILPRTTVY	partitively	AEIJLNORSUZ	journalizes
AEIIINQSTTU	antiquities	AEIILPRTVVY	privatively	AEIKKLMNORW	workmanlike
AEIIINRSSTT	initiatress	AEIILRSSSUV	visualisers	AEIKLNNOPPS	plainspoken
AEIIIPRSTTU	pituitaries	AEIILRSSTTV	relativists	AEIKLNOPSTT	kinetoplast
AEIIKLLNPRS	painkillers	AEIILRSSTTZ	strelitzias	AEIKLOPRRSW	sparrowlike
AEIIKLLOPRT	realpolitik	AEIILRSSTVV	revivalists	AEIKMNPRRST	printmakers
AEIIKLMNPRS	marlinspike	AEIILRSSUVZ	visualizers	AEILLLMOSTY	lamellosity
AEIIKNNRSST	Kristiansen	AEIILRSTTVY	versatility	AEILLLOSTWY	yellowtails
AEIILLMNSTU	illuminates	AEIIMMMNNST	immanentism	AEILLMMORSS	allomerisms
AEIILLMSTTU	satellitium	AEIIMMNNSTT	immanentist	AEILLMMRSST	millstreams
AEIILLNNRTY	triennially	AEIIMMNNRST	matrimonies	AEILLMNNSTT	installment
AEIILLNOTVY	inviolately	AEIIMMNNOTUZ	Montezuma II	AEILLMNOOTY	emotionally
AEIILLNPTVY	plaintively	AEIIMMNRSTT	martinetism	AEILLMNOSTY	semitonally
AEIILLNTUUX	luxulianite	AEIIMMRRTTU	termitarium	AEILLMNPSTU	multiplanes
AEIILLOSSTV	volatilises	AEIIMNNOPRY	aminopyrine	AEILLMNTTUV	multivalent
AEIILLOSTVZ	volatilizes	AEIIMNNORST	inseminator	AEILLNNOOTV	nonvolatile
AEIILLPRSTT	tripletails		nitrosamine	AEILLNOOTUV	evolutional
AEIILLPRSTU	pluralities	AEIIMNNORTT	termination	AEILLNOPSTT	potentillas
AEIILLRRSTT	triliterals	AEIIMNNORTV	vermination	AEILLNOPTTY	potentially
AEIILLRSSTT	literalists	AEIIMNNOSST	seminations	AEILLNOSSSY	sessionally
AEIILLRSSTV	silvertails	AEIIMNNOSTV	nominatives	AEILLNRSTUV	surveillant
AEIILMMORST	immortalise	AEIIMNOPRST	patrimonies	AEILLNRSUVY	universally
	memorialist	AEIIMNOPRTT	impetration	AEILLNSSSTY	stainlessly
AEIILMMORTZ	immortalize	AEIIMNOSSTT	estimations	AEILLNSSUXY	unisexually
AEIILMNNOPS	Minneapolis	AEIIMOOPRST	isometropia	AEILLOOPRST	allotropies
AEIILMNOORT	melioration	AEIIMOPPRRT	impropriate	AEILLORTTUV	ultraviolet
AEIILMNORST	eliminators	AEIIMOPRRSS	impresarios	AEILLPPSUVY	appulsively
	misrelation	AEIIMRRTTUV	triumvirate	AEILLPRRSSU	pluralisers
	normalities	AEIINNNORTV	innervation	AEILLPRRSUZ	pluralizers
	orientalism	AEIINNOSVV	noninvasive	AEILLPSSSTT	pastellists
AEIILMNORTY	eliminatory	AEIINNNOTTT	inattention	AEILLPSTUVY	pulsatively
AEIILMNOSTT	testimonial	AEIINNNQQUU	quinquennia	AEILLRSSTTU	illustrates
AEIILMNPRRY	preliminary	AEIINNOORTT	orientation	AEILMMMSSTY	symmetalism
AEIILMNPTTY	impatiently	AEIINNORSSV	reinvasions	AEILMMNNOSU	noumenalism
AEIILMOPRST	peristomial	AEIINOPPSTT	peptisation	AEILMMNORTY	momentarily
AEIILMORSTT	mortalities	AEIINOPPTTZ	peptization	AEILMNNNSSU	unmanliness
AEIILMOSSSS	isoseismals	AEIINOPRRST	respiration	AEILMNNOOTU	unemotional
AEIILMPSSVY	impassively	AEIINOPRRTT	partitioner	AEILMNNOSSW	womanliness
AEIILMRRSTT	trimestrial		repartition	AEILMNNOSTU	noumenalist
AEIILMRSSVV	revivalisms	AEIINOPRRTU	proteinuria	AEILMNNOTUY	noumenality

AEILMNNRRTTU	nutrimental
AEILMNNSSTT	instalments
AEILMNOOSTT	molestation
AEILMNOPRRT	trampoliner
AEILMNOPRSS	personalism
AEILMNOPRST	trampolines
AEILMNORSTY	salinometry
AEILMNORTVY	normatively
AEILMOORRST	meliorators
AEILMOPRRSU	leprosarium
AEILMOPRRTY	polarimetry
	temporarily
AEILMOPRTTY	temporality
AEILMOPRTXY	proximately
AEILMOQSTTU	milquetoast
AEILMORSSTV	removalists
AEILMPPSSST	palimpsests
AEILMPRSSST	slipstreams
AEILMRSSTTU	stimulaters
AEILNNOPRSU	unipersonal
AEILNNOPSTT	antileptons
	Saint Pölten
AEILNNORRTY	nonliterary
AEILNNRSTTY	transiently
AEILNNRSTUY	saturninely
AEILNOOPRTX	exploration
AEILNOPPTTY	platinotype
AEILNOPRRST	tripersonal
AEILNOPRSST	interposals
	personalist
AEILNOPRSTY	personality
AEILNOPSSSS	passionless
AEILNORRSTU	serrulation
AEILNORSTTV	ventilators
AEILNORSTUV	voluntaries
AEILNORTTVY	ventilatory
AEILNOSTTUX	exultations
AEILNRSSTTU	neutralists
AEILNSSSTTU	sensualists
AEILOOPRRRT	reportorial
AEILOPPRRSU	populariser
AEILOPPRRUZ	popularizer
AEILOPPRRSS	popularises
AEILOPPRSUZ	popularizes
AEILOPRSSSU	plesiosaurs
AEILORRSTTU	elutriators
AEILOSSSTTY	steatolysis
AEILOSTUVXY	vexatiously
AEILRRSSSTU	surrealists
AEILRSSSTUV	Lévi-Strauss
AEILSSTTTUX	textualists
AEIMMNPRSTT	impartments
AEIMMNRSSSU	summariness
AEIMMNRSTTU	manumitters
AEIMMNSSTZZ	mizzenmasts
AEIMMORSTTU	tautomerism
AEIMMPRSSTU	suprematism
AEIMMRRSSSU	summarisers
AEIMMRRSSUZ	summarizers
AEIMMSSSTTY	systematism
AEIMNNNOSTT	anointments
AEIMNNOPPTT	appointment

AEIMNNORSTU	mensuration
	numerations
AEIMNNSSSTTU	sustainment
AEIMNOORSSU	anisomerous
AEIMNOPRTTU	importunate
	permutation
AEIMNOPSTTT	temptations
AEIMNORRSST	ironmasters
AEIMNORRSTT	terminators
AEIMNORRTTY	terminatory
AEIMNORSSTT	monetarists
AEIMNOSSSTY	seismonasty
AEIMNPPRSST	pentaprisms
AEIMNRRSSTT	retransmits
AEIMNRRSTTT	transmitter
AEIMOORSTTU	autoerotism
AEIMOOSSTTU	autotomises
AEIMOOSTTUZ	autotomizes
AEIMOPRRSSU	aspersorium
AEIMOPRRSTT	impetrators
AEIMOPRSTUU	eupatoriums
AEIMPRRTTUY	prematurity
AEIMPRSSTTU	suprematist
AEIMQRSSTUZ	quizmasters
AEIMSSSTTTY	systematist
AEINNNORTTU	antineutron
AEINNOOPRST	personation
AEINNOORSST	resonations
AEINNOORSTV	renovations
AEINNOOSTTT	ostentation
AEINNOPSTTY	spontaneity
AEINNOQRSTU	quaternions
AEINNORSSUZ	Russian Zone
AEINNORSTUV	intravenous
AEINNOSSSUX	anxiousness
AEINNOSSTTV	nonstatives
AEINNPQSSTU	piquantness
AEINNRRSSTY	tyrannisers
AEINNRRSTYZ	tyrannizers
AEINNRSSTTU	unresistant
AEINOOPPRRT	apportioner
	reapportion
AEINOOPPRST	apoproteins
	propionates
AEINOOPRRST	perorations
AEINOOPRSSU	aponeurosis
AEINOOPRRTTX	exportation
AEINOORRSTT	restoration
AEINOORSUVX	overanxious
AEINOPPPRST	preappoints
AEINOPRRSST	patronisers
	periastrons
AEINOPRRSTZ	patronizers
AEINOPRSSSU	persuasions
AEINOPRSSSV	vasopressin
AEINOPRSTTU	reputations
AEINOPSTTTU	outpatients
AEINORRSSTT	reinstators
AEINORRSSTU	souterrains
AEINORRSSTV	overstrains
AEINORSSSUV	savouriness
	variousness

AEIOOOPPPRS	prosopopeia
AEIOOPRRSTU	iteroparous
AEIOPPRRRTY	proprietary
AEIOPRRRSST	respirators
AEIOPRRRSTY	respiratory
AEIOPRRRTTU	portraiture
AEIOPRRSTTX	extirpators
AEIOPRRTTUV	vituperator
AEIPPRSTUUV	suppurative
AEIPRSSSTUW	West Prussia
AEKLNNOPSTT	Sankt Pölten
AEKMNOOPSSW	spokeswoman
AEKMORRSSTW	masterworks
AEKOOPRRSTY	prokaryotes
AELLLLRSTUY	stellularly
AELLMOPSSSY	plasmolyses
AELLMOPSSYZ	plasmolyzes
AELLMORSUVY	marvelously
AELLNOOPSTY	Stanley Pool
AELLNOPPRST	propellants
AELLOPRSSTW	wallposters
AELMMNOOPRS	monospermal
AELMMOOPSSS	plasmosomes
AELMMRSSTUU	summersault
AELMNNOOPRT	nontemporal
AELMNNOPSTW	plantswomen
AELMNOPRSU	supernormal
AELMOOPRSTU	tropaeolums
AELMOPRSTTY	plastometry
AELMOPSSTUY	sympetalous
AELMORSSSTU	somersaults
AELNNOPRSYY	pennyroyals
AELNNSSSUUU	unusualness
AELNOOPPRTT	protoplanet
AELNOORSTTW	Alton Towers
AELNOORSWXY	Lower Saxony
AELNOPRSSSU	parlousness
AELNOPSSSUY	synsepalous
AELNPPRSSTU	supplanters
AELNPRRSUUY	superlunary
AELOOPRRTXY	exploratory
AELOOPSSTTY	osteoplasty
AELOPPRRRSU	pourparlers
AELOPRTTUVY	Port Lyautey
AEMMNORRSTU	mare nostrum
AEMNNNOPSTY	nonpayments
AEMNNOOSSST	stonemasons
AEMNNORRSTT	remonstrant
AEMNNORSTTT	attornments
AEMNNORSTTU	tournaments
AEMNOOPRSTY	trypanosome
AEMNOORRSST	astronomers
AEMNOORSSSU	amorousness
AEMNOOORSTU	neuromatous
AEMNORSSSTT	assortments
AEMNRRSSTTU	transmuters
AEMOOPSSTTY	somatotypes
AEMOPRSSSTT	postmasters
AENNOOPSSTU	spontaneous
AENNOPPRSST	Prestonpans
AENNORRSSTT	nonstarters
AENOOPRRSST	personators

AENOOPRSTXY	paroxytones	**AFIILMNNOTU**	fulmination	**AGHHLOOPSUY**	hylophagous
AENOPRRRRST	transporter	**AFIILMNORTY**	informality	**AGHHNOOPPRS**	phonographs
AENOPRRSSST	transposers	**AFIILNORRTT**	infiltrator	**AGHHNOOPPRV**	phonography
AENOPRSSTTT	protestants	**AFIILNORSTT**	filtrations	**AGHHNOORTTY**	orthognathy
AENORRSTTTU	sternutator		flirtations	**AGHHOOPPRST**	photographs
AENPRRSSSTU	suppressant	**AFIILORSTTU**	flirtatious	**AGHHOOPPRTY**	photography
AENPRRSSTTU	transputers	**AFIIMNNOORT**	information	**AGHHOOPRRTY**	orthography
AEOOPPRRRST	propraetors	**AFIIMNOORSU**	omnifarious	**AGHHOPPRSYY**	hypsography
AEOOPRRSSSU	vasopressor	**AFIIMORSTTU**	favouritism	**AGHHOPPRTYY**	phytography
AEOPPRRRSTU	rapporteurs	**AFIINNORSSU**	infusorians	**AGHHORSTUWY**	throughways
AEOPRRSSSTW	sportswears	**AFIINNORSTX**	transfixion	**AGHIIILMNTU**	humiliating
AEOPRSSTTUW	waterspouts	**AFIIOPRSSSU**	fissiparous	**AGHIIILNNTZ**	Nizhni Tagil
AFFGHIIINRT	affrighting	**AFILLLNOUXY**	fluxionally	**AGHIIJNNRST**	Ranjit
AFFGHLOPSTU	ploughstaff	**AFILMNOORTU**	formulation		Singh
AFFGIIRSSTT	graffitists	**AFILMNORSTU**	fulminators	**AGHIILMNOOS**	hooliganism
AFFGIRSSSTU	suffragists	**AFILMNORTUY**	fulminatory	**AGHIILNNSVY**	vanishingly
AFFILNORSTU	insufflator	**AFIMMORSTUU**	fumatoriums	**AGHIILNRSVY**	ravishingly
AFFILNOSSTU	sufflations	**AFIMNOORRTY**	informatory	**AGHIIMNNORS**	harmonising
AFFLLLORUVY	flavorfully	**AFINNORSSTU**	transfusion	**AGHIIMNNORZ**	harmonizing
AFFLLMOPSUW	mallowpuffs	**AFINOOPPRST**	Port of	**AGHIIMOPRSU**	amphigouris
AFGGIINSTTU	fustigating		Spain	**AGHIIMOSTTX**	thigmotaxis
AFGGILNRTUU	fulgurating	**AFINORRSTTU**	frustration	**AGHIINNOSST**	astonishing
AFGHHIILNTU	highfalutin	**AFLMOORRSTU**	formulators	**AGHIINNQSUV**	vanquishing
AFGHHILLSST	flashlights	**AGGGINNUWZZ**	zugzwanging	**AGHIINORSTU**	authorising
AFGHIIILNST	fishtailing	**AGGHHIIILNT**	hightailing	**AGHIINORTUZ**	authorizing
AFGHILMOPRY	filmography	**AGGHHLOPPRY**	glyphograph	**AGHIINPRRSS**	hairsprings
AFGHJNNOOTU	John of	**AGGHHOPRRSY**	hygrographs	**AGHIINPRSTY**	pharyngitis
	Gaunt	**AGGHIIJMNTU**	thingumajig	**AGHIINRSTWW**	wainwrights
AFGIIINNRTU	infuriating	**AGGHIILNNSU**	languishing	**AGHILLNNOUW**	unhallowing
AFGIILLMNNY	inflamingly	**AGGHIILOOST**	hagiologist	**AGHILNOOSTT**	anthologist
AFGIILLNNUY	unfailingly	**AGGHILNOTUU**	outlaughing	**AGHILOOPSTT**	pathologist
AFGIILMNNTU	fulminating	**AGGHMMOPRSY**	sphygmogram	**AGHILOPPSSY**	gypsophilas
AFGIILMNORS	formalising	**AGGIIILMNNS**	misaligning	**AGHILORSSTT**	gastroliths
AFGIILMNORZ	formalizing	**AGGIIILNNSS**	signalising	**AGHILPRSTWY**	playwrights
AFGIILNNOTU	antifouling	**AGGIIILNNSZ**	signalizing	**AGHIMNOPRST**	prognathism
AFGIIMMNNOY	ammonifying	**AGGIIIMMNRT**	immigrating	**AGHINNOQUUX**	Hong Xiu
AFGIIMNNOST	fumigations	**AGGIIINNORT**	originating		Quan
AFGIIMORSTT	sagittiform	**AGGIIINNSTT**	instigating	**AGHINOOSSTY**	soothsaying
AFGIINNOPSY	saponifying	**AGGIIJNNORS**	jargonising	**AGHIOPPRRSS**	spirographs
AFGIINNQTUY	quantifying	**AGGIIJNNORZ**	jargonizing	**AGHJNOOORST**	John
AFGIINNRSTX	transfixing	**AGGIILMNORS**	glamorising		o'Groats
AFGIINORSTU	figurations	**AGGIILMNORZ**	glamorizing	**AGHLLOOPSSY**	hypoglossal
AFGIINOSTTU	fustigation	**AGGIILNNOSY**	agonisingly	**AGHLOOPPSUY**	polyphagous
AFGIINRSTTY	stratifying	**AGGIILNNOYZ**	agonizingly	**AGHLOOPSUXY**	xylophagous
AFGIKLNNOTU	outflanking	**AGGIILNNSTU**	agglutinins	**AGHLOPRSSTY**	stylographs
AFGILLNNTUY	flauntingly	**AGGIILNOOPS**	apologising	**AGHLOPRSTYY**	stylography
AFGILMNORTU	formulating	**AGGIILNOOPZ**	apologizing	**AGHMNNOOOPSU**	monophagous
AFGILNORSUV	flavourings	**AGGIILNRSUV**	vulgarising	**AGHMOOOPRRT**	graphomotor
AFGILNORTUU	fulguration	**AGGIILNRUVZ**	vulgarizing	**AGHNOOOPPRRY**	pornography
AFGILNORUVY	favouringly	**AGGIINNORRS**	garrisoning	**AGHNOOPRSTU**	prognathous
AFGINNRSSTU	transfusing	**AGGIINORTTU**	gurgitation	**AGIIIILLNNT**	initialling
AFGINRRSTTU	frustrating	**AGGILLOOSST**	algologists	**AGIIIILNTVX**	lixiviating
AFGIORSSTTU	fustigators	**AGGILMNNOORY**	graminology	**AGIIIJJKMOU**	Kigoma-Ujiji
AFGIORSTTUY	fustigatory	**AGGIMMNNOPR**	programming	**AGIIIKLNNOZ**	kaolinizing
AFHILORSTWY	Solway Firth	**AGGINORRSTU**	surrogating	**AGIIILLNTTT**	titillating
AFIIIILNNTV	infinitival	**AGGLLNOORYY**	laryngology	**AGIIILMNNSU**	aluminising
AFIIIILMNNST	infantilism	**AGGLOOORSTY**	agrostology	**AGIIILMNNUZ**	aluminizing
AFIIILNNTTY	infantility	**AGHHIIJKNNS**	Jinghis Khan	**AGIIILMNSTV**	vigilantism
AFIIILNOOSX	Alfonso XIII	**AGHHIIMNRST**	nightmarish	**AGIIILNNOPV**	pavilioning
AFIIINNORTU	infuriation	**AGHHILOPRST**	lithographs	**AGIIILNNORS**	original sin
AFIIINNOSTX	infixations	**AGHHILOPRTY**	lithography	**AGIIILNNPST**	platinising
AFIILLMORTW	Fort William	**AGHHIMNPRRU**	harrumphing	**AGIIILNNPTZ**	platinizing

AGIIIILNORTV	invigilator
AGIIILNORTY	originality
AGIIILNOSTT	litigations
AGIIILNPSST	salpingitis
AGIIILNRSTU	ritualising
AGIIILNRSTV	virginalist
AGIIILNRTUZ	ritualizing
AGIIILNSSUV	visualising
AGIIILNSUVZ	visualizing
AGIIIMMNORT	immigration
AGIIINNNSTU	insinuating
AGIIINNOORT	origination
AGIIINNOSTT	instigation
AGIIINORRST	irrigations
AGIIINPRSTV	privatising
AGIIINPRTVZ	privatizing
AGIIINTTTTV	tittivating
AGIIKLMNNOS	kalsomining
AGIILLNNOPT	pollinating
AGIILLNPQSU	pasquilling
AGIILLNPRSU	pluralising
AGIILLNPRUZ	pluralizing
AGIILMNNORS	normalising
AGIILMNNORZ	normalizing
AGIILMNNOTY	longanimity
AGIILMNPPSY	misapplying
AGIILMNSTTU	stimulating
AGIILMNSTUU	mutualising
AGIILMNTUUZ	mutualizing
AGIILNORTUV	outrivaling
AGIILNPRSST	springtails
AGIILNPSTTU	stipulating
AGIILNRSTUY	singularity
AGIILNRTUUX	luxuriating
AGIILOOSSTX	axiologists
AGIIMMNNOPT	pantomiming
AGIIMMNNTTU	manumitting
AGIIMMNRSSU	summarising
AGIIMMNRSUZ	summarizing
AGIIMMORRST	immigrators
AGIIMMORRTY	immigratory
AGIIMMOSSST	misogamists
AGIIMNNOPTU	impugnation
AGIIMNNPRSS	mainsprings
AGIIMNRRSTY	martyrising
AGIIMNRRTYZ	martyrizing
AGIIMSSSTTT	stigmatists
AGIINNNRSTY	tyrannising
AGIINNNRTYZ	tyrannizing
AGIINNOPRST	patronising
AGIINNOPRTZ	patronizing
AGIINNPRRST	transpiring
AGIINNRSTTU	intriguants
AGIINOORRST	originators
AGIINOORRTV	invigorator
AGIINORPSSTU	authorships
AGIINORSSTT	instigators
AGIINRRTTTU	triturating
AGIJLNOSTUU	jugulations
AGIJNOPSTUX	juxtaposing
AGIKLOORSTY	karyologist
AGIKMNOPRST	postmarking
AGIKNOPRTYY	karyotyping

AGILLLNPTUU	pullulating
AGILLMNNOOU	monolingual
AGILLNPRTTY	prattlingly
AGILLNRSTTY	startlingly
AGILMNNNOSU	longanimous
AGILMNPPRSS	Palm Springs
AGILMOOPRTY	primatology
AGILMOPSSTY	polygamists
AGILMRSTTUU	gutturalism
AGILNNNPPSTU	supplanting
AGILNNPRSUY	unsparingly
AGILNOOOPRS	sporogonial
AGILNOOPRRVY	approvingly
AGILNOPRSTU	sporulating
AGILNOPSTTU	postulating
AGILNPSTTUU	pustulating
AGILOOPRSTT	patrologist
AGILOORSSTT	astrologist
AGILOOSTTTU	tautologist
AGILORSSSST	glossarists
AGILRTTTUUY	gutturality
AGIMMNOOSST	monogamists
AGIMNNRSTTU	transmuting
AGIMNNOOPRST	protagonism
AGIMNOORSST	agronomists
AGIMNORSTTU	outsmarting
AGINNNOPSTU	outspanning
AGINNOPRSST	transposing
AGINNPPRSTU	unstrapping
AGINOOOPRRT	prorogation
AGINOOPRSTT	protagonist
AGINOORRSTU	surrogation
AGINOORRSVU	granivorous
AGINOPRRSTT	prostrating
AGINPPRSTUU	suppurating
AGINRRSSTUU	susurrating
AGLLLNOOPYV	polygonally
AGLLMOORSUV	glamorously
AGLLORRSSUY	garrulously
AGLMNOORSUU	unglamorous
AGLMNOORTYY	laryngotomy
AGLMOOOSTTY	stomatology
AGLMOOPRRTU	promulgator
AGLMOORRTYY	martyrology
AGLNNOPPTUY	oppugnantly
AGLOOOSTTUU	tautologous
AGMOOORSSTT	Matto Grosso
AGMOORSSTTY	gastrostomy
AHHIIIPRSST	phthiriasis
AHHILMOPSTY	halophytism
AHHILNOORTU	holothurian
AHHILOPPSYV	hypophysial
AHHIMNOPSSW	showmanship
AHHIMOPSTYY	hypothymias
AHHIOPRSSTU	authorships
AHHLLNOPTXY	xanthophyll
AHHLNOPSTXY	xanthophyls
AHIIIJKNRSS	jinrikishas
AHIIILMNOTU	humiliation
AHIIILNPPPS	Philippians
AHIIIMNNOSY	Nishinomiya
AHIILLORSUY	hilariously

AHIILMORSTU	humiliators
AHIILMORTUY	humiliatory
AHIILNPSSTY	Hypsilantis
AHIILOPSTTY	hospitality
AHIILRSSTTY	hairstylist
AHIIMNNOSTU	inhumations
AHIIMNNRRTU	antirrhinum
AHIIMNOOOSU	homoiousian
AHIIMOOPPPT	hippopotami
AHIIOPRRSTT	traitorship
AHIIRSSSTTW	shirtwaists
AHIKKOORRSW	kwashiorkor
AHIKMNOPRSW	workmanship
AHILLMOOPST	Matopo Hills
AHILLMOPRTU	prothallium
AHILLNOPSYY	anisophylly
AHILLOPSTXY	phyllotaxis
AHILMNOPPSW	plowmanship
AHILNOORSTZ	horizontals
AHILNOPRSTY	rhinoplasty
AHILOORRTTY	hortatorily
AHILOPPRSXY	prophylaxis
AHILOPRRUXY	pyrrhuloxia
AHIMNOOOSSU	homoousians
AHIMNOORRSU	honorariums
AHIMNOPRSTY	misanthropy
AHIMOOOPSST	opisthosoma
AHIMOORSTUZ	rhizomatous
AHINOOPPRST	patroonship
AHINOOPSSTX	saxophonist
AHINOPRSSUX	xiphosurans
AHIOPPRSSST	pastorships
AHLMNOTUXYZ	zanthoxylum
AHLMOOPPRST	trophoplasm
AHLMOOPRSTU	photomurals
AHLMOOPRSUY	amorphously
AHMMORSSTTU	smartmouths
AHMNNOOPRTT	Northampton
AHMNOOPRSTU	protohumans
AHMNOOPSTTU	Southampton
AHNNOSSTTWY	shantytowns
AHNORSSTUUY	thysanurous
AHOOPPRRSST	saprotrophs
AIIIIJNNSTU	Justinian II
AIIIILNOTVX	lixiviation
AIIIINNOSTT	initiations
AIIILLLNPTU	lilliputian
AIIILLNOPTX	pixillation
AIIILLNOTTT	titillation
AIIILLNOTUV	illuviation
AIIILMMNSST	minimalists
AIIILMNOPST	postliminia
AIIILMNOSTT	limitations
	militations
AIIILMNPRTT	tripalmitin
AIIILMRSSTT	militarists
AIIILNNOOST	lionisation
AIIILNNOOTZ	lionization
AIIILNNOTTU	intuitional
AIIILNOSTTU	utilisation
AIIILNOTTUZ	utilization
AIIIMNNOSTT	intimations

AIIIMNRSTTU	miniaturist	
AIIIMPPRRTY	primiparity	
AIIIMPSSTVY	impassivity	
AIIINNNOSTU	insinuation	
AIIINNOOSST	ionisations	
AIIINNOOSTZ	ionizations	
AIIINNOPRST	inspiration	
AIIINNOSTTU	unitisation	
AIIINNOSTTV	invitations	
AIIINNOTTUZ	unitization	
AIIINORRSTT	irritations	
AIIINOSSTTV	visitations	
AIIINOSTTTV	titivations	
AIIINOTTTTV	tittivation	
AIIILLMMNOTU	multinomial	
AIIILLMNNSTU	illuminants	
AIIILLMNORTU	illuminator	
AIIILLMNORTY	trinomially	
AIIILLNNOOPT	pollination	
AIIILLNORSUY	illusionary	
AIIILLNRSSTY	sinistrally	
AIIILLPPRTUY	pupillarity	
AIIILLPRSTUY	spiritually	
AIIILLPSTTUY	pulsatility	
AIIILMMNOOST	immolations	
AIIILMMORSST	immoralists	
AIIILMMORTTY	immortality	
AIIILMNNNOTT	nonmilitant	
AIIILMNNOSST	nominalists	
AIIILMNOOPRT	imploration	
AIIILMNOOPST	malposition	
AIIILMNOOSST	solmisation	
AIIILMNOOSTZ	solmization	
AIIILMNOSSTU	simulations	
AIIILMNOSTTU	mutilations	
	stimulation	
AIIILMNOSTUY	aluminosity	
AIIILMOPRRTY	promilitary	
AIIILMPRTTUY	multiparity	
AIIILMRSSUVV	survivalism	
AIIILNNOOSST	insolations	
AIIILNNORSTU	intrusional	
AIIILNNORTTU	nutritional	
AIIILNNOSSTU	insulations	
AIIILNOOPPST	oppilations	
AIIILNOOPRSV	provisional	
AIIILNOORTVV	volitionary	
AIIILNOPRTUY	unipolarity	
AIIILNOPSTTU	stipulation	
AIIILNORTUUX	luxuriation	
AIIILNOSSTTY	stylisation	
AIIILNOSTTYZ	stylization	
AIIILNPRSTUU	unspiritual	
AIIILNQRTTUY	tranquility	
AIIILPRSTTUY	spiritualty	
AIIILRSSTUVV	survivalist	
AIIMMMNNOSSU	manumission	
AIIMMNOOPST	pantomimist	
AIIMMNSSTTU	numismatist	
AIIMMPRRSTU	imprimaturs	
AIIMNNNOOST	nominations	
AIIMNNORSTU	ruminations	
AIIMNNRSSTT	ministrants	
AIIMNOOPRTT	importation	
AIIMNOOPRTX	proximation	
AIIMNOOSTTV	motivations	
AIIMNOPRSTV	provitamins	
AIIMNOPSTTU	imputations	
AIIMNORSTTZ	Saint Moritz	
AIIMOPPRRSU	primiparous	
AIINNNOOSTT	intonations	
AIINNNOOSTV	innovations	
AIINNNORRTT	nonirritant	
AIINNOOOSTZ	ozonisation	
AIINNOOOTZZ	ozonization	
AIINNORSSTT	transitions	
AIINNORSSTU	insinuators	
AIINNORSTUY	insinuatory	
AIINNRSTTUY	saturninity	
AIINOOPPSST	appositions	
AIINOPRRSST	inspirators	
AIINOPRRSTY	inspiratory	
AIINOPRRTTU	parturition	
AIINOPRSSST	inspissator	
AIINOPRSSTU	suspiration	
AIINORRTTTU	trituration	
AIINQRSSSTU	sinarquists	
AIIOOPPRRTT	propitiator	
AIIOPRRSTTT	portraitist	
AIIOPRSSTTT	prostatitis	
AIIORSTTTTV	tittivators	
AIIPRSSSTTU	Pisistratus	
AIIPRSSTTVY	varitypists	
AIJLNORSSTU	journalists	
AIKLLOSSTUW	Lutosławski	
AIKMNOSSWYZ	Szymanowski	
AIKNOORSTTW	workstation	
AILLLNOOPRU	allopurinol	
AILLLNOPTUU	pullulation	
AILLMNOOPSY	polynomials	
AILLMOOPRST	allotropism	
AILLMOPSSSY	plasmolysis	
AILLNOOPRST	pollinators	
AILLNOORSTY	torsionally	
AILLNOPRSSU	nulliparous	
AILLNORTUVY	voluntarily	
AILLNPPSTUY	suppliantly	
AILLNRTUUXY	luxuriantly	
AILLORRSSTU	illustrator	
AILMMNOOSSY	ammonolysis	
AILMNNOSUUY	unanimously	
AILMNOOOPRT	promotional	
AILMNOOPSST	lampoonists	
AILMNOORSTT	monolatrist	
AILMNOPPSSS	Simplon Pass	
AILMNOPRTTY	importantly	
AILMNORSTUV	voluntarism	
AILMOOPRRTY	imploratory	
AILMOOPRUYZ	polyzoarium	
AILMOPRSSTU	multiparous	
AILMORSSTTU	stimulators	
AILNNORTUVY	involuntary	
AILNOOPPSTU	populations	
AILNOOPRSTU	sporulation	
AILNOOPSTTU	postulation	
AILNOPPSTTU	postnuptial	
AILNOPSTTUU	pustulation	
AILNORSSTTU	lustrations	
AILNORSTTUV	voluntarist	
AILNORSUUVY	unsavourily	
AILNOSSTTUU	ustulations	
AILNRSSTUUU	laurustinus	
AILOOPRSUVY	oviparously	
AILOPRSSTTU	stipulators	
AILOPRSTTUY	stipulatory	
AILORSTTTUY	statutorily	
AIMMNNORSSTU	stramoniums	
AIMMOORRSTU	moratoriums	
AIMMOOSSTXY	myxomatosis	
AIMNNOOSTTU	mountainous	
AIMNNOPRTTU	unimportant	
AIMNOOSSTTU	autonomists	
AIMNOOSSTTX	taxonomists	
AIMNOPSSSTU	assumptions	
AIMNRSSTTUU	nasturtiums	
AIMOPSSSSTY	symposiasts	
AINNNOOORTT	Torontonian	
AINNOOPRSTT	antiprotons	
AINOOPRRSTT	prostration	
AINOOSSTTTU	outstations	
AINOPPRSTUU	suppuration	
AINOPRSSTUU	usurpations	
AINORRSSSTT	transistors	
AINORRSSTUU	susurration	
AINPRSSTUUV	pursuivants	
AIORRRSTTTU	triturators	
AKLNNOOOPTZ	zooplankton	
ALLLNOOPTYY	polytonally	
ALLNOOOPPRR	propranolol	
ALLNOPPRUUY	unpopularly	
ALLOOOPRSTU	allotropous	
ALLOORSTWWW	swallowwort	
ALMNNOOSUYY	anonymously	
ALMNOOORSTU	monolatrous	
ALMNOPRSSTY	sportsmanly	
ALNNORSTUYY	tyrannously	
ALOOPPRSSTT	protoplasts	
ALOOPRSSTTU	postulators	
ALOPRRSTUUY	rapturously	
AMMNOOOORRST	Marston Moor	
AMNOOPRSSTW	sportswoman	
AMNOOSTTUUY	tautonymous	
AMOOPRRRTTY	protomartyr	
ANNOOPRSSST	transposons	
ANOOOPRRTTY	protonotary	
BBBEEIINRSW	winebibbers	
BBBEGIIINNW	winebibbing	
BBBEOORSSXY	bobbysoxers	
BBCCEEHKLOR	breechblock	
BBCCEHIOPRY	cyberphobic	
BBCDEEEEIKR	Beiderbecke	
BBCDEHIRRTU	butcherbird	
BBCEEGIILLR	gibberellic	
BBCEEKNRRSU	rubbernecks	
BBCEELNOOST	cobblestone	
BBCEELNOOSU	bubonoceles	

BBCEILMOSTU	combustible
BBCEINRSSSU	scrubbiness
BBCEINRSSUU	unsubscribe
BBCEIRRSSSU	subscribers
BBCEJKOORST	stockjobber
BBCEKLORSTU	blockbuster
BBCGIINRSSU	subscribing
BBCGIMOORRY	borborygmic
BBCILMOSTUY	combustibly
BBDDEGILNOS	bobsledding
BBDEEGHILOS	bobsleighed
BBDEEGIILNO	Gideon Bible
BBDEEHHLOOY	hobbledehoy
BBDEELLORWY	Lloyd Webber
BBDEGIIMNOV	divebombing
BBDEGINORUV	overdubbing
BBDEHHOORSY	hobbyhorsed
BBDEIKNOORS	bookbinders
BBDEIKNOORY	bookbindery
BBDEILLMOOO	bloodmobile
BBDELNRSSUU	blunderbuss
BBDGIIKNNOO	bookbinding
BBDGINOSUVY	busybodying
BBDHIIOPRSS	bishopbirds
BBDINOOORSW	ribbonwoods
BBEEEFGRRSU	beefburgers
BBEEEILRRSU	blueberries
BBEEGIILLNR	gibberellin
BBEEGILMRSU	submergible
BBEEHIRRSSU	shrubberies
BBEEILMRSSU	submersible
BBEELLOSTTU	bluebottles
BBEELNNOSTU	bluebonnets
BBEENORRSYY	boysenberry
BBEFILORSUU	bulbiferous
BBEGIIIOSST	gibbosities
BBEGIINRRSU	rubberising
BBEGIINRRUZ	rubberizing
BBEGIKLNOOR	Bolingbroke
BBEGILMNNUY	benumbingly
BBEGINOSSSU	gibbousness
BBEHHILOSST	shibboleths
BBEHHOORSSY	hobbyhorses
BBEHIIILLOP	bibliophile
BBEHINRSSSU	shrubbiness
BBEHLORSTTU	bottlebrush
BBEIILLOOPS	bibliopoles
BBEIILMSSSU	submissible
BBEIKLMOOOS	bookmobiles
BBEKNORSSTU	bonkbusters
BBELLNOTTUY	bellybutton
BBGHILNORTY	throbbingly
BBGHINNRSUU	burning bush
BBGIILLNQUY	quibblingly
BBGMOORRSUY	borborygmus
BBHIIILLOPS	bibliophils
BBCCDDEEHKOY	bodychecked
BCCDEILNOTU	conductible
BCCEEEEFINN	beneficence
BCCEEEENRSU	erubescence
BCCEEHHLORT	breechcloth
BCCEEHLORTU	breechclout

BCCEEIILNOR	incoercible
BCCEEIILORT	bioelectric
BCCEEIINOSS	biosciences
BCCEEIIRSST	bisectrices
BCCEEILLLOT	collectible
BCCEEILNNOT	connectible
BCCEEILNOSS	concessible
BCCEEILORRT	correctible
BCCEEIMRRSY	cybercrimes
BCCEEINRSTY	cybernetics
BCCEFIIPSSU	subspecific
BCCEHINOOPR	necrophobic
BCCEIILNNOV	convincible
BCCEIILNORU	ribonucleic
BCCEIILNOTV	convictible
BCCEIINOOOT	biocoenotic
BCCEIINOORT	necrobiotic
BCCEIMOORSX	coxcombries
BCCEIORSSTU	subcortices
BCCHINOOPTY	nyctophobic
BCDDEEEEILNS	descendible
BCDDEEEIRRS	redescribed
BCDDEEILSTU	deductibles
BCDDEIIKRSY	dickeybirds
BCDEEEIINNT	Benedictine
BCDEEEIINST	benedicites
BCDEEEEIORRS	cerebroside
BCDEEEEIRRSS	redescribes
BCDEEFIIJOT	objectified
BCDEEHILNPT	pitchblende
BCDEEHIMORS	chemisorbed
BCDEEHMNOOY	honeycombed
BCDEEHMNOTU	debouchment
BCDEEHMOORS	chemosorbed
BCDEEHORSUU	debouchures
BCDEEIIILRT	liberticide
BCDEEIIIMNO	biomedicine
BCDEEIILNRS	discernible
BCDEEIILRRU	irreducible
BCDEEIILSST	dissectible
BCDEEIINNOT	benediction
BCDEEIINOTU	butenedioic
BCDEEILNNOS	condensible
BCDEEIMNRSU	disencumber
BCDEEINORTY	benedictory
BCDEEINSSSU	subsidences
BCDEELMNTUY	decumbently
BCDEEORRSSS	crossbreeds
BCDEGHNRRSU	bergschrund
BCDEHIILORS	bichlorides
BCDEHILNNOR	hornblendic
BCDEHILORSU	subchloride
BCDEHKOOTTU	bucktoothed
BCDEIIILRTY	credibility
BCDEIILNRSY	discernibly
BCDEIILRRUY	irreducibly
BCDEIILSSSU	discussible
BCDEINORTTU	contributed
BCDEIOOPRSS	proboscides
BCDEIORRSTU	subdirector
BCDEKLOORSU	bloodsucker
BCDELRSTUUU	subcultured

BCDEMMNRSUU	cummerbunds
BCDGIIKMNOR	mockingbird
BCDHHIOOPRV	hydrophobic
BCDHIMOORRY	hydrobromic
BCDIINRTUUY	rubicundity
BCDIIOPRRST	tropicbirds
BCDIIRSSTTU	subdistrict
BCDINOSSTUU	subductions
BCDLORSSTUU	cloudbursts
BCEEEELNNOV	benevolence
BCEEEFILPRT	perfectible
BCEEEGHINRR	Reichenberg
BCEEEGMNRSU	submergence
BCEEEHHINPR	hebephrenic
BCEEEIILRST	celebrities
BCEEEILPPRT	perceptible
BCEEEILPRTX	excerptible
BCEEELLMRSU	cerebellums
BCEEENQSSUU	subsequence
BCEEFIIJOST	objectifies
BCEEFILORRW	Wilberforce
BCEEFIMNORT	fibrocement
BCEEFIOPRSS	fiberscopes
	fibrescopes
BCEEGIIOTVZ	Izetbegović
BCEEGILNOST	congestible
BCEEGIMNNRU	encumbering
BCEEGIMNORY	embryogenic
BCEEGKLMNRU	Mecklenburg
BCEEHHNOOPT	technophobe
BCEEHINORRS	Breconshire
BCEEHIOORRS	seborrhoeic
BCEEHKLNOSU	hucklebones
BCEEHKLRRUY	huckleberry
BCEEHKNORSW	workbenches
BCEEHKOOQSU	chequebooks
BCEEHLMOPTY	phlebectomy
BCEEHMORSUU	embouchures
BCEEHNOOPRS	necrophobes
BCEEIILPSST	plebiscites
BCEEIILRSSS	rescissible
BCEEIINOSST	obscenities
BCEEIJLOTVY	objectively
BCEEIJSSTUV	subjectives
BCEEILLLOSY	bellicosely
BCEEILMNNOT	contemnible
BCEEILMOOST	lobectomies
BCEEILMOSTS	comestibles
BCEEILNORST	bristlecone
BCEEILNORTV	convertible
BCEEILORRSU	Le Corbusier
BCEEILPPRTY	perceptibly
BCEEILPRSTU	putrescible
BCEEILPSSTU	susceptible
BCEEINSSSTU	subsistence
BCEEIORRRSW	crowberries
BCEEIPRRRSS	prescribers
BCEEIPRRSSU	superscribe
BCEEIRRSSTT	bittercress
BCEEJLSSSTU	subjectless
BCEEKKLNNOU	knucklebone
BCEEKLNOSTT	bottlenecks

BCEEKORSTUX	tuckerboxes	**BCEIORSTTUV**	obstructive	**BDDEENSSSUU**	subduedness
BCEELMMOOTY	embolectomy	**BCEJKMPRSUU**	buckjumpers	**BDDEFINNORU**	unforbidden
BCEELMNRTUY	recumbently	**BCEKKOOOPST**	pocketbooks	**BDDEGGLNOOO**	boondoggled
BCEELNOOSST	obsolescent	**BCEKKOORRST**	stockbroker	**BDDEGIINORV**	overbidding
BCEELNOSTTU	cuttlebones	**BCEKLNRSTUU**	turnbuckles	**BDDEHINRRTU**	thunderbird
BCEELORSSTU	beltcourses	**BCELMOORSVY**	corymbosely	**BDDEHLNOORS**	bondholders
BCEEMMORTYY	embryectomy	**BCELORSTUUU**	tuberculous	**BDDEIIRSSUV**	subdividers
BCEEMNOSTTU	obmutescent	**BCELRSSTUUU**	subcultures	**BDDEIIRSTTU**	distributed
BCEENORSSSU	obscureness	**BCELSTTTTUU**	scuttlebutt	**BDDEILLNRUY**	unbridledly
BCEEOOORRRS	corroborees	**BCEMNOORSSW**	crossbowmen	**BDDEILMORSW**	middlebrows
BCEFFIORSSU	subofficers	**BCEOOOPRSST**	stroboscope	**BDDEINRSTUU**	undisturbed
BCEFHILLNSU	bullfinches	**BCFIIILORTY**	forcibility	**BDDELNNOUUY**	unboundedly
BCEFIIMORRS	microfibers	**BCGIIILNPSU**	publicising	**BDDELNOTUUY**	undoubtedly
BCEGHHIMOWY	High Wycombe	**BCGIIILNPUZ**	publicizing	**BDDGGINOOSY**	dogsbodying
BCEGHIIMNRS	besmirching	**BCGIIKLNOOT**	bootlicking	**BDDGIIINSUV**	subdividing
BCEGIIMMNOS	misbecoming	**BCGIINOOOTT**	gnotobiotic	**BDDHIIIMRSY**	dihybridism
BCEGIIMNNOR	recombining	**BCGIINOPRRS**	proscribing	**BDDHLNOOOSU**	bloodhounds
BCEGIIMNNRU	incumbering	**BCGIJKMNPUU**	buckjumping	**BDEEEEHIKRSW**	bewhiskered
BCEGIINPRRS	prescribing	**BCGIKLLNOOS**	bollockings	**BDEEEEHILLMS**	embellished
BCEGILMOORY	embryologic		bollockings	**BDEEEEHILMTW**	thimbleweed
BCEGILNOOOY	biocenology	**BCGIKNPRSSU**	springbucks	**BDEEEEHINRSW**	New Hebrides
BCEGILNOOSS	obsolescing	**BCGILOOORYV**	cryobiology	**BDEEEEHLLNRS**	hellbenders
BCEHHILNOOT	holobenthic	**BCGINORSTTU**	obstructing	**BDEEEEIILRSV**	disbeliever
BCEHIIIOSTT	bioethicist	**BCHHIIMORTY**	biorhythmic	**BDEEEEIILSSV**	disbelieves
BCEHIIMOSST	biochemists	**BCHHIOOOPPT**	photophobic	**BDEEEEILMNTV**	bedevilment
BCEHILMOOPT	phlebotomic	**BCHIILNOPSY**	phycobilins	**BDEEEEILMPRT**	redemptible
BCEHILNOORS	bronchioles	**BCHILLOPSYY**	psychobilly	**BDEEEEILPRSS**	depressible
BCEHILNOSST	blotchiness	**BCHIMOORSTW**	witchbrooms	**BDEEEEILRSSS**	redressible
BCEHKKOOSST	sketchbooks	**BCIIIILMSTY**	miscibility	**BDEEEEILSSTW**	wildebeests
BCEHKLOOSSU	blockhouses	**BCIIIILNTVY**	vincibility	**BDEEEEIMMRRS**	dismemberer
BCEHLOORSTW	blowtorches	**BCIILMMNOUU**	cumulonimbi		disremember
BCEHLORRSYY	chrysoberyl	**BCIILMOSSTY**	symbolistic	**BDEEEIMNNOU**	Boumédienne
BCEHMOORTTY	thrombocyte	**BCIJNNOSTUU**	subjunction	**BDEEEIMNNTZ**	bedizenment
BCEHMRSSTUW	thumbscrews	**BCIKMOORSST**	broomsticks	**BDEEEIMORRR**	embroiderer
BCEIIJMOSTV	objectivism	**BCILLORSUUY**	lubricously	**BDEEEINRRRT**	interbreeds
BCEIIJOSTTV	objectivist	**BCILMNNOOSY**	nonsymbolic	**BDEEEIRSTTW**	bitterweeds
BCEIIJOTTVY	objectivity	**BCILOPRRTUY**	corruptibly	**BDEEEELMSTUW**	tumbleweeds
BCEIIKLLLSS	sicklebills	**BCIMNOOSSTU**	combustions	**BDEEEELNSSSS**	blessedness
BCEIIKLLRST	billsticker	**BCIMORRSSTU**	microbursts	**BDEEEELORSST**	doubletrees
BCEIIILLOSTY	bellicosity	**BCINOOPRTTY**	cryptobiont	**BDEEEFGIINNR**	befriending
BCEIIMMRSTY	bisymmetric	**BCINOORRTTU**	contributor	**BDEEEFHIRRSU**	refurbished
BCEIINOOOSS	biocoenosis	**BCINOORSTTU**	obstruction	**BDEEEFILRTTU**	Butterfield
BCEIINOORSS	necrobiosis	**BCOOORRSSTTU**	obstructors	**BDEEEFLLNOUR**	bellfounder
BCEIIORSSTU	obscurities	**BDDDEEEEINRT**	interbedded	**BDEEEGGHIIRW**	weighbridge
BCEIJNOSSTU	subjections	**BDDDEEIIMOS**	disembodied	**BDEEEGHILNTY**	benightedly
BCEIJNSTUUV	subjunctive	**BDDDEEINRRU**	underbidder	**BDEEEGHINORU**	neighboured
BCEIKLOORST	bootlickers	**BDDDEEINRSU**	disburdened	**BDEEEGHOORRT**	God-botherer
BCEILLORSSU	brucellosis	**BDDDEFILLNO**	blindfolded	**BDEEEGIILLNV**	bedevilling
BCEILMNNOTY	contemnibly	**BDDDEFMNOUU**	dumbfounded	**BDEEEGIILNRW**	bewildering
BCEILMNNTUY	incumbently	**BDDEEEIILSV**	disbelieved	**BDEEEGIINNRS**	inbreedings
BCEILMNRSSU	crumbliness	**BDDEEEEIMMRS**	dismembered	**BDEEEGILMNNO**	emboldening
BCEILMOOPSS	compossible	**BDDEEEEIMNRT**	debridement	**BDEEEGIMOSSU**	disembogues
BCEILMORTUU	microtubule	**BDDEEEEIMORR**	embroidered	**BDEEEGINORTU**	outbreeding
BCEILNNOSUU	Cunobelinus	**BDDEEGIMOSU**	disembogued	**BDEEEGLNORSU**	bludgeoners
BCEILNORTVY	convertibly	**BDDEEIIILMOS**	demobilised	**BDEEEHIINNPU**	Dien Bien
BCEILOPRRTU	corruptible	**BDDEEIILMOZ**	demobilized		Phu
BCEILPSSTUY	susceptibly	**BDDEEIIMOSS**	disembodies	**BDEEEHILMNSU**	unblemished
BCEIMOSSTUU	combustious	**BDDEEIINOST**	disobedient	**BDEEEHILPRSU**	republished
BCEINORSTTU	contributes	**BDDEEILORSW**	bowdlerised	**BDEEEHNNRTUU**	unburthened
BCEINOSSSTU	subsections	**BDDEEILORWZ**	bowdlerized	**BDEEEIILMOSS**	demobilises
BCEIOOPRSSS	proboscises	**BDDEEIMNOST**	disentombed	**BDEEEIILMOSZ**	demobilizes
BCEIOPRRRSS	proscribers	**BDDEEINORSU**	underbodies	**BDEEEIILNSST**	distensible

BDEEIIRSTTU distributee	**BDEHNRRSSUU** undershrubs	**BEEEFMRRSUZ** bumfreezers
BDEEIKLNPRS besprinkled	**BDEIIIILNSV** indivisible	**BEEEFOORRST** freebooters
BDEEILLNPRS spellbinder	**BDEIIIILNTY** inedibility	**BEEEGGRRSUV** vegeburgers
BDEEILMNOTY molybdenite	**BDEIIILMMOS** immobilised	**BEEEGIINNOR** bioengineer
BDEEILMOSSW disembowels	**BDEIIILMMOZ** immobilized	**BEEEGIJLLNW** bejewelling
BDEEILMRSSS dissemblers	**BDEIIILMSSS** dismissible	**BEEEGILLNRT** belligerent
BDEEILNORRS borderlines	**BDEIIILNTVY** vendibility	**BEEEGILLNSS** legibleness
BDEEILNPRTU blueprinted	**BDEIIIMNSTU** bituminised	**BEEEGILMNTU** beguilement
BDEEILNPSSU suspendible	**BDEIIIMNTUZ** bituminized	**BEEEGILNRUV** Vigée-Lebrun
BDEEILORRSW bowdleriser	**BDEIIIMORST** morbidities	**BEEEGIMMNRR** remembering
BDEEILORRWZ bowdlerizer	**BDEIIIOSSTU** dubiosities	**BEEEGINRRRS** greenbriers
BDEEILORSSW bowdlerises	**BDEIIILLOSSU** solubilised	**BEEEGLNORTT** greenbottle
BDEEILORSWZ bowdlerizes	**BDEIIILLOSUZ** solubilized	**BEEEHILLMRS** embellisher
BDEEIMMNOST embodiments	**BDEIILMORSS** disembroils	**BEEEHILLMSS** embellishes
BDEEIMNORST disrobement	**BDEIILMRSUU** subdelirium	**BEEEHILLNOR** helleborine
BDEEIMRSTTU resubmitted	**BDEIIRRSTTU** distributer	**BEEEHILRSTT** shelterbelt
BDEEINORSTX tinderboxes	**BDEIIRSSSSU** subsidisers	**BEEEHLLRSTW** bellwethers
BDEEIOORSXY deoxyribose	**BDEIIRSSSUZ** subsidizers	**BEEEHLPSSTU** steeplebush
BDEELNRRSSU blurredness	**BDEIIRSSTTU** distributes	**BEEEIINRRSW** wineberries
BDEEMNORTUU outnumbered	**BDEIJNORSSU** subjoinders	**BEEEIKLLRRS** bierkellers
BDEENNNOSTU sunbonneted	**BDEIKNORSTU** strikebound	**BEEEIKMORSU** boeremusiek
BDEENORRSUV overburdens	**BDEILLORSWY** yellowbirds	**BEEEIKNSSTT** Beit Knesset
BDEENPRRTUU unperturbed	**BDEILMOOOST** lobotomised	**BEEEIKOPRRS** pokeberries
BDEFGINOORS forebodings	**BDEILMOOOTZ** lobotomized	**BEEEILNNORV** nonbeliever
BDEFGIOORST footbridges	**BDEILMOOSSS** disselbooms	**BEEEILNPRTV** preventible
BDEFGSSSTUU fussbudgets	**BDEILNORSTY** blindstorey	**BEEEILNRSUV** unbelievers
BDEFHIILNSS blindfishes	**BDEINOSSSUU** dubiousness	**BEEEILPRRSS** repressible
BDEFILNOOSS dobsonflies	**BDEIOOORSTTW** bitterwoods	**BEEEILPRRTV** pervertible
BDEFILNORSW brownfields	**BDEISSTTTUU** substituted	**BEEEILPRSSX** expressible
BDEFLLNORUY bellfoundry	**BDEKMMNRSUU** kummerbunds	**BEEEILRRSSV** reversibles
BDEFORRSSUY bodysurfers	**BDELLLOOSSY** bloodlessly	**BEEEIMMMRRS** misremember
BDEGGILNNOU bludgeoning	**BDELLNOSSUY** boundlessly	**BEEEIMRRSTT** embitterers
BDEGGLNOOOR boondoggler	**BDELLOSSTUY** doubtlessly	**BEEEINNRRTU** breunnerite
BDEGGLNOOOS boondoggles	**BDELMNOOSUY** molybdenous	**BEEEIOPRRRS** Robespierre
BDEGHHIINRS highbinders	**BDELNOOOSST** bloodstones	**BEEEIRRSSTW** sweetbriers
BDEGHNORTUU underbought	**BDFGINORSUY** bodysurfing	**BEEEIRSTTTW** bittersweet
BDEGIILMNSS dissembling	**BDGGHIINNOS** Gobind Singh	**BEEEKKOOPRS** bookkeepers
BDEGIKORRSW bridgeworks	**BDGGIIILNOS** disobliging	**BEEELLRSSST** bestsellers
BDEGILNNNUY unbendingly	**BDGGILRSUUW** Ludwigsburg	**BEEELMNNNOT** ennoblement
BDEGILNNRSU blunderings	**BDGHIIINRSY** hybridising	**BEEEMNRSTTT** betterments
BDEGIMOORRS bridegrooms	**BDGHIIINRYZ** hybridizing	**BEEENOPPRTY** teenybopper
BDEGIMORRSY dogberryism	**BDGHIILNSST** blindsights	**BEEENORSSSV** verboseness
BDEGINNNRUU unburdening	**BDGHIIMMNRU** hummingbird	**BEEENORSSTT** bonesetters
BDEGINNRUUY underbuying	**BDGIIINSSSU** subsidising	**BEEFFIORRSU** febriferous
BDEGIORRSTU Stourbridge	**BDGIIINSSUZ** subsidizing	**BEEFGHILOSS** globefishes
BDEHHOOOORRT brotherhood	**BDGIILNOTUU** outbuilding	**BEEFGIINNTT** benefitting
BDEHIIINNTU uninhibited	**BDGIIMNOSTU** misdoubting	**BEEFGINOOOT** freebooting
BDEHIIKLLTY Billy the	**BDGIKMNOSSU** subkingdoms	**BEEFGINRSUZ** subfreezing
Kid	**BDGILLOOTUY** bloodguilty	**BEEFGLLOORW** globeflower
BDEHIILPRSU shipbuilder	**BDGILNNNSUU** unbundlings	**BEEFGRSSTUU** subterfuges
BDEHIILPSSU bisulphides	**BDHIILRRSWY** whirlybirds	**BEEFHIRRSSU** refurbishes
BDEHIIRRSSY hybridisers	**BDHIMNOORSY** monohybrids	**BEEFIIILRST** febrilities
BDEHIIRRSYZ hybridizers	**BDIIIILNSVY** indivisibly	**BEEFILLMRSU** umbellifers
BDEHIKLNOTU doublethink	**BDIIINOSSUV** subdivision	**BEEFILNLSSU** fusibleness
BDEHILLPPUW bullwhipped	**BDIILNOOPST** diplobionts	**BEEFILRSTTU** butterflies
BDEHILLSTTU bullshitted	**BDIIMNORTUY** moribundity	**BEEFLLLORSW** bellflowers
BDEHILNPSUU unpublished	**BDIIORRSTTU** distributor	**BEEFLMNOSTU** befoulments
BDEHILOOPRY hyperboloid	**BDKNNOOORSY** donnybrooks	**BEEGGGLOOSX** goggleboxes
BDEHIMOORSU rhomboideus	**BDLMNOOTTUU** buttonmould	**BEEGGHNRRTU** Terbrugghen
BDEHLNOOTTU buttonholed	**BDNOOOSTTUW** buttonwoods	**BEEGGILSSTU** suggestible
BDEHLNORTTU thunderbolt	**BEEEEMMRRRS** rememberers	**BEEGGLOORST** bootleggers
BDEHMOOOORST smoothbored		**BEEGHINNORR** herringbone

BEEGHINRRST	brighteners	**BEEILOSSSVY**	obsessively	**BEGILPSSTTU**	spittlebugs
BEEGHNOOPRS	negrophobes	**BEEIMNNSSSU**	businessmen	**BEGINNNNOTU**	unbonneting
BEEGIIILLNS	ineligibles	**BEEIMRRRSSU**	reimbursers	**BEGINNORTTU**	rebuttoning
BEEGIIINNST	benignities	**BEEINNOORTU**	boutonniere	**BEGINRSSTTU**	buttressing
BEEGIILMMNS	emblemising	**BEEINORRSSW**	snowberries	**BEGMNOOORSU**	ombrogenous
BEEGIILMMNZ	emblemizing	**BEEINORSTTY**	tenebrosity	**BEGNOORSSTX**	strongboxes
BEEGIIILNNUV	unbelieving	**BEEINRSSTTU**	butteriness	**BEGOOPPRSST**	gobstoppers
BEEGIIMNRTT	embittering	**BEEINRSSTUV**	subservient	**BEGOORRSTTT**	bogtrotters
BEEGIIOORSU	bourgeoisie	**BEEIRSSSUVV**	subversives	**BEHIIILLLLS**	hillbillies
BEEGIKKNOOP	bookkeeping	**BEEJLNOSSSS**	joblessness	**BEHIIINOSTX**	exhibitions
BEEGILLMNOW	embowelling	**BEELLMRSSSU**	slumberless	**BEHIIIOPRTV**	prohibitive
BEEGILLNORW	rebellowing	**BEELLNOSSSU**	solubleness	**BEHIILMNOST**	bimonthlies
BEEGILLNSST	bestselling	**BEELLNOSSUV**	volubleness	**BEHIILMSTTW**	thimblewits
BEEGILMNOST	obligements	**BEELMOORSTU**	troublesome	**BEHIILPSSTU**	bisulphites
BEEGILNNOSS	ignobleness	**BEELNNSSSTU**	bluntnesses	**BEHIILMOPRSY**	hyperbolism
BEEGIMNNRRU	renumbering	**BEELNOOSSTT**	bottlenoses	**BEHILOSSSTV**	bolshevists
BEEGIMNOPRT	obtempering	**BEELOORSSUV**	overblouses	**BEHIMMORSTU**	embothriums
BEEGIMNOSTT	misbegotten	**BEELQRRSSUU**	burlesquers	**BEHINOORSSS**	boorishness
BEEGINPRSST	Spitsbergen	**BEEMMNNOSTT**	entombments	**BEHINORSSTT**	birthstones
BEEGIOORSSU	bourgeoises	**BEEMMNOSSST**	embossments	**BEHINRSSSTU**	brutishness
BEEGKLNTTUU	Telukbetung	**BEENQRSSSUU**	brusqueness	**BEHIOORRSUV**	herbivorous
BEEGLMMPTUY	mumbletypeg	**BEERRRSTTUU**	surrebutter	**BEHIORSSTTU**	soubrettish
BEEGLNOSTUU	bluetongues	**BEFGHILLRTU**	bullfighter	**BEHLNOOSTTU**	buttonholes
BEEGMNRRSTU	Münsterberg	**BEFGIILMORZ**	gemfibrozil	**BEHMNOORTUU**	Bournemouth
BEEGMNSSSTU	subsegments	**BEFGIILNTTY**	befittingly	**BEHMOOORSST**	smoothbores
BEEGMRRTTUW	Württemberg	**BEFGIINNTTU**	unbefitting	**BEHNNOOORRT**	North Borneo
BEEGPRRRSSU	Pressburger	**BEFGILNORUW**	furbelowing	**BEHORRTTTUW**	Butterworth
BEEHIKORTUW	Bourke-White	**BEFHILLMSTU**	thimblefuls	**BEIIILMMORS**	immobiliser
BEEHILNSSSU	blueishness	**BEFIIILLTXY**	flexibility	**BEIIILMMORZ**	immobilizer
BEEHILOPRSY	hyperbolise	**BEFIILNORRU**	neurofibril	**BEIIILMMOSS**	immobilises
BEEHILOPRYZ	hyperbolize	**BEFIILRSSTU**	filibusters	**BEIIILMMOSZ**	immobilizes
BEEHILPRSSU	republishes	**BEFINORSSSU**	fibrousness	**BEIIILMNRST**	libertinism
BEEHIMMPRSS	memberships	**BEFINORSTTT**	frostbitten	**BEIIILMQRUU**	equilibrium
BEEHIMNOORT	theobromine	**BEFKKLLOOOS**	Book of	**BEIIILNSSTY**	sensibility
BEEHKNOORSU	housebroken		Kells	**BEIIILNSTTY**	tensibility
BEEHLLNOOPR	Bellerophon	**BEFLLMRSTUU**	tumblerfuls	**BEIIILOQSTU**	obliquities
BEEHMNOOSST	mesobenthos	**BEFLLOOPRTU**	bulletproof	**BEIIILQRSTU**	equilibrist
BEEHMNORSTU	burthensome	**BEGGGILNOOT**	bootlegging	**BEIIILSSTTU**	subtilities
BEEHOPRRSTT	stepbrother	**BEGGHIINNOR**	neighboring	**BEIIIMNSSTU**	bituminises
BEEIIJORSTU	bijouterie	**BEGGHIINNRT**	brightening	**BEIIIMNSTUZ**	bituminizes
BEEIILMPRSS	impressible	**BEGGHILNORS**	Helsingborg	**BEIIIMOPRST**	improbities
	permissible	**BEGGIILLNUY**	beguilingly	**BEIILLNOSSW**	billowiness
BEEIILNSSSV	visibleness	**BEGGILSSTUY**	suggestibly	**BEIILLNOSTU**	ebullitions
BEEIILSSSTX	bissextiles	**BEGGINNOORU**	bourgeoning	**BEIILLOSSSU**	solubilises
BEEIINRRSTW	twinberries	**BEGGINOORRS**	Bognor Regis	**BEIILLOSSUZ**	solubilizes
BEEIIRRTTUV	retributive	**BEGHIILMRST**	thimblerigs	**BEIILMPRSSY**	permissibly
BEEIKKNORRS	knobkerries	**BEGHIINRRST**	rebirthings	**BEIILNOSSSU**	biliousness
BEEIKLNPRSS	besprinkles	**BEGHILNORUY**	neighbourly	**BEIILRSSSTU**	subtilisers
BEEIKNORRRT	interbroker	**BEGIIIILLTY**	eligibility	**BEIILRSSTTT**	librettists
BEEILLLNTUY	ebulliently	**BEGIIIMNRST**	ignimbrites	**BEIILRSSTUZ**	subtilizers
BEEILLMNOPT	Bontempelli	**BEGIIKLRSTZ**	blitzkriegs	**BEIINORRTTU**	retribution
BEEILLMRSST	belletrisms	**BEGIILLNNTU**	bulletining	**BEILLMPSTUU**	submultiple
BEEILLORRSU	irresoluble	**BEGIILMNNRU**	unlimbering		
BEEILLRRRTU	bullterrier	**BEGIILNRSTT**	bitterlings		
BEEILLRSSTT	belletrists	**BEGIIMNRRSU**	reimbursing		
BEEILMMNORT	embroilment	**BEGIINORTTU**	briquetting		
BEEILNOPRSS	responsible	**BEGIKNOOORV**	overbooking		
BEEILNOQSSU	obliqueness	**BEGILLMNRTY**	tremblingly		
BEEILNPRTVY	preventibly	**BEGILLMNRUY**	lumberingly		
BEEILNPSSSU	suspensible	**BEGILNOORVW**	overblowing		
BEEILNRSSTT	brittleness	**BEGILNQRSUU**	burlesquing		
BEEILNSSSTU	subtileness	**BEGILNRSSTU**	blusterings		

BEILLOPRSST	billposters
BEILLORRSUY	irresolubly
BEILLORSSTT	stilbestrol
BEILMNOOSSW	snowmobiles
BEILNOPRSSY	responsibly
BEILNOSSTUU	botulinuses
BEILORSSSTU	strobiluses
BEILORSTUVY	obtrusively
BEIMNORSSSU	submersions
BEIMPSSTUUV	subsumptive
BEINNOSSTUV	subventions
BEINOOSSSUV	obviousness
BEINOPRSSSU	probusiness
BEINOPRSSTU	subreptions
BEINORSSSSUV	subversions
BEINORSSTUU	subroutines
BEINORSTUUV	unobtrusive
BEINSSTTTUU	substituent
BEIOQRSSTUU	soubriquets
BEIORRRTTUY	retributory
BEISSSTTTUU	substitutes
BEKMNORSSSU	mossbunkers
BEKNNNOSTUW	unbeknownst
BELLMOOSSSS	blossomless
BELLNRTTUUY	turbulently
BELNOORSSWW	snowblowers
BELNOOSTUUY	bounteously
BEMOOPRRSTY	Port Moresby
BENNORSSSTW	brownstones
BEORRSTTTUW	butterworts
BERRSSTTTUU	trustbuster
BFFGILNOTUU	outbluffing
BFGIIILNTUY	fungibility
BFHKOOOORSU	book of
	hours
BFILLNOTUUY	bountifully
BGGIINNPRSU	upbringings
BGGILLMNRUY	grumblingly
BGGINNOORUU	bourguignon
BGHHIIRRSTT	birthrights
BGHIIINOPRT	prohibiting
BGHIIINRRTV	virgin birth
	Virgin Birth
BGHIMNOORST	thrombosing
BGIIILLLTUY	gullibility
BGIIILNSSTU	subtilising
BGIIILNSTUZ	subtilizing
BGIILLNOPST	billposting
BGIILLNSTTU	Sitting Bull
BGIILMNOSSY	symbolising
BGIILMNOSYZ	symbolizing
BGILLMNSTUY	stumblingly
BGILMNNOOOT	Bloomington
BGILMOOSSTY	symbologist
BGILOORSSTY	bryologists
BGINNNOORSW	brownnosing
BGINNNOTTUU	unbuttoning
BHIIINNOST	inhibitions
BHIIINOOPRT	prohibition
BHIIIOPRSTU	triphibious
BHIILLRSSTT	stillbirths
BHIIOOPRRST	prohibitors

BHIIOOPRRTY	prohibitory
BHILMOOSTYY	tomboyishly
BHIMNOOPRRT	prothrombin
BHIMNPRSTTU	thumbprints
BHINOORSTUY	Ryobu Shinto
BHKNOOOSTTU	buttonhooks
BIIIILNRSTY	rinsibility
BIIILOPSSTY	possibility
BIIILORSTTY	torsibility
BIIKNOORSSV	Novosibirsk
BIILLNOORTU	tourbillion
BIILLOOSUVY	obliviously
BIILMOOPPTY	popmobility
BIILMORRTUU	lubritorium
BIILOOQSTUU	obliquitous
BIIMNOOSTUX	moxibustion
BIIMNOSSSSU	submissions
BIKLLORSSST	storksbills
BILMOPSTUUY	bumptiously
BILNOOOSTUV	obvolutions
BILNOOOSUXY	obnoxiously
BIMNOORSSTT	trombonists
BIMNOPSSTUU	subsumption
BIMORRSSTUU	rumbustious
BIOOOPPRRSU	opprobrious
BKMOOOPPRST	promptbooks
BLLOORSTUUY	troublously
BLLOOSTTUWY	woollybutts
BMMMMNOSUUU	summum bonum
CCCCDIILOOP	diplococcic
CCCCIMOORSU	micrococcus
CCCDEEEENRS	decrescence
CCCDEEIINNO	coincidence
CCCDEHINOSY	synecdochic
CCCDEIIMRSU	circumcised
CCCDEIIOOSS	coccidioses
CCCDGINOOOO	gonococcoid
CCCDIIIOOSS	coccidiosis
CCCDILOOPSU	diplococcus
CCCEEEENRSX	excrescence
CCCEEENRSXY	excrescency
CCCEEFIIOPS	ecospecific
CCCEEFLLNOU	flocculence
CCCEEIILMST	eclecticism
CCCEEINNOSS	consciences
CCCEENNORRU	concurrence
CCCEENNORST	concrescent
CCCEENORRSU	occurrences
CCCEFIINOPS	conspecific
CCCEFIOORSU	cocciferous
CCCEFLLNOUY	flocculency
CCCEGILLOPY	cycloplegic
CCCEHKORSSS	crosschecks
CCCEIIMRRSU	circumciser
CCCEIIMRSSU	circumcises
CCCEILORSST	Celtic cross
CCCEIMNOOPU	pneumococci
CCCEIMPRSTU	circumspect
CCCEINNOTTU	Connecticut
CCCEIRSSTUY	cysticercus
CCCEKLNOORS	corncockles
CCCENNORRUY	concurrency

CCCGIKNOORW	cockcrowing
CCCHHILOOOS	chocoholics
CCCHIKOPSST	spitchcocks
CCCHILMOTYY	cyclothymic
CCCIIMMOORS	microcosmic
CCCIIMOOPRS	microscopic
CCCILLOPSYY	polycyclics
CCCINNOOOST	concoctions
CCCIOOPSSTY	cystoscopic
CCDDEEEENORS	crescendoed
	decrescendo
CCDDEEEERRSU	recrudesced
CCDDEENNOSS	condescends
CCDEEEEINNR	Nicene Creed
CCDEEEIINNS	indecencies
CCDEEEIINRS	iridescence
CCDEEEELLORT	recollected
CCDEEEMMNOR	recommenced
CCDEEEENNORT	reconnected
CCDEEEENORSS	crescendoes
CCDEEEERRSSU	recrudesces
CCDEEFIKNOY	cockneyfied
CCDEEFINNOS	confidences
CCDEEHILPSY	psychedelic
CCDEEHIORTT	ricochetted
CCDEEHNOSSY	synecdoches
CCDEEIIINST	insecticide
CCDEEIILRST	dielectrics
CCDEEIKLRSV	cleverdicks
CCDEEILMORU	leucodermic
CCDEEILNOTU	endocuticle
CCDEEILNOTY	conceitedly
CCDEEINNORT	endocentric
CCDEEINORST	concertised
	concretised
CCDEEINORTV	reconvicted
CCDEEINORTZ	concertized
	concretized
CCDEEIOPPRU	preoccupied
CCDEEJNORTU	conjectured
CCDEEKORRSW	corkscrewed
CCDEELLLOTY	collectedly
CCDEELLNOTU	uncollected
CCDEELNNOOS	condolences
CCDEELNNORY	concernedly
CCDEELNNOTY	connectedly
CCDEELNORTY	concertedly
CCDEENNNORU	unconcerned
CCDEENNNOTU	unconnected
CCDEENNORTU	unconcerted
CCDEENORRTU	unconcerted
CCDEFIMRSUU	circumfused
CCDEGHILNTU	declutching
CCDEHIINNOS	cinchonised
CCDEHIINNOZ	cinchonized
CCDEHILOPSY	psychodelic
CCDEHIOOPRS	dichroscope
CCDEIILOORT	crocidolite
CCDEIILOPSY	epicycloids
CCDEILNOXYY	doxycycline
CCDEILOPSTY	cyclopedist
CCDEIMNOORS	microsecond

CCDEIMOOOST octodecimos	**CCEEFLNNOSU** confluences	**CCEENORRSST** correctness
CCDEINNNOUV unconvinced	**CCEEGHHKRRU** Greek Church	**CCEEOORRRTV** overcorrect
CCDEINNOSST disconnects	**CCEEGHIKNPR** prechecking	**CCEEOORSTUX** coexecutors
CCDEINOOPSS picoseconds	**CCEEGINNNOT** contingence	**CCEFFIINSUY** sufficiency
CCDEINOPRST conscripted	**CCEEGINOOTT** geotectonic	**CCEFHIIISTT** fetichistic
CCDEINORSST disconcerts	**CCEEGINORST** egocentrics	**CCEFHIIMORS** microfiches
CCDEINORSTT constricted	**CCEEGINOTTY** cytogenetic	**CCEFIIIPSTY** specificity
CCDELLOSTYY cyclostyled	**CCEEGNNOOST** cognoscente	**CCEFIILNOTV** conflictive
CCDELMOORTY motorcycled	**CCEEGNNORSU** congruences	**CCEFIINNOPS** nonspecific
CCDENORSSTU conductress	**CCEEGNNORVY** convergency	**CCEFIINOPRY** proficiency
CCDENORSTTU constructed	**CCEEGNOORRT** concertgoer	**CCEFIMRSSUU** circumfuses
deconstruct	**CCEEGNRSTUY** turgescency	**CCEFINNOOST** confections
CCDGILNNOUY conducingly	**CCEEHHKORRY** chokecherry	**CCEFIORRSUU** cruciferous
CCDHILOOPYY hypocycloid	**CCEEHINNORY** incoherency	**CCEGGILNOOY** gynecologic
CCDHIOOPRSY hydroscopic	**CCEEHINORTT** theocentric	**CCEGHHORRSU** churchgoers
CCDHIOPRRTY cryptorchid	**CCEEHIRRRSTU** cutcherries	**CCEGHIIIOPS** pichiciegos
CCDIMNOSSTU misconducts	**CCEEHKLLLOS** cockleshell	**CCEGHIILNOR** cholinergic
CCDINNOOSTU conductions	**CCEEHMOOPRT** chemoceptor	**CCEGHIINORT** ricocheting
CCEEEEHIKPS cheekpieces	**CCEEHMOPTYY** phycomycete	**CCEGHIKNORW** checkrowing
CCEEEEILNST telescience	**CCEEHNNOSSTU** escutcheons	**CCEGHIMNOOR** chromogenic
CCEEEEINPRT centrepiece	**CCEEIILMRSS** semicircles	**CCEGHINOPSY** psychogenic
CCEEEEELLNSX excellences	**CCEEIILORST** isoelectric	**CCEGIILNNOR** reconciling
CCEEEFHIKNR neckerchief	**CCEEIILPSTU** epicuticles	**CCEGIINOOTX** toxicogenic
CCEEEFLNORS florescence	**CCEEIILRTTY** electricity	**CCEGILMNOPT** complecting
CCEEEFNNORS conferences	**CCEEIIMMNSU** ecumenicism	**CCEGILNOORY** eccrinology
CCEEEFNRSTU frutescence	**CCEEIIMMNOS** omniscience	**CCEGILNOOSY** synecologic
CCEEEGINNOT cenogenetic	**CCEEIIMNOSV** misconceive	**CCEGINNNORT** concentring
CCEEEGINNRS nigrescence	**CCEEIINOPTV** nociceptive	**CCEGINNNOTY** contingency
CCEEEGINOSS geosciences	**CCEEIILLNOOS** colonelcies	**CCEGINNOOST** cognoscenti
CCEEEGINOTT ectogenetic	**CCEEIILLOSTV** collectives	**CCEGINOPRTY** cryptogenic
CCEEEGINRVY vicegerency	**CCEEIILMOOST** colectomies	**CCEGINOPRUY** reoccupying
CCEEEGNNORV convergence	**CCEEIILMORTY** myoelectric	**CCEGINORRRU** reoccurring
CCEEEGNRSTU turgescence	**CCEEIILNNOTV** conventicle	**CCEHHHORSUU** house church
CCEEEHHLOST cheesecloth	**CCEEIILNORRS** reconcilers	**CCEHHIOSSTT** schottische
CCEEEHINNOR incoherence	**CCEEIILNORST** electronics	**CCEHHMMNORUW** churchwomen
CCEEEHINSTT cenesthetic	**CCEEIILNORTT** telocentric	**CCEHIILNOPR** necrophilic
CCEEEHIPSSS chesspieces	**CCEEIILNQSUY** liquescency	**CCEHIINNOSS** cinchonises
CCEEEIINPPR percipience	**CCEEIILOSTUX** exocuticles	**CCEHIINNOSZ** cinchonizes
CCEEEIILNORT coelenteric	**CCEEIIMNNORT** econometric	**CCEHIIPRRTY** hypercritic
CCEEEIILNQSU liquescence	**CCEEIMNORRT** centromeric	**CCEHIKNOPST** checkpoints
CCEEEIMORRT coercimeter	**CCEEIINNOQTU** cinquecento	**CCEHILNOPTY** polytechnic
CCEEEINNNOV convenience	**CCEEIINNOSSS** conciseness	**CCEHILNORRS** chroniclers
CCEEEINNPSS spinescence	**CCEEIINNOSST** consistence	**CCEHILOOTTY** hectocotyli
CCEEEINOPRV preconceive	**CCEEIINNOSTV** connectives	**CCEHIMMNOOR** chromonemic
CCEEEINOPSS cenospecies	**CCEEIINNRRSU** incurrences	**CCEHIMMOOST** chemosmotic
CCEEEIINOSTX coexistence	**CCEEIINOPRSW** crownpieces	**CCEHIMNOORT** homocentric
CCEEEIINRRST Cirencester	**CCEEIINORSST** concertises	**CCEHIMOOPRT** chemotropic
CCEEEIINRSSV virescences	concretises	ectomorphic
CCEEEIINRSTV vitrescence	**CCEEIINORSTZ** concertizes	**CCEHINNRSSU** crunchiness
CCEEEIIRSTUX executrices	concretizes	**CCEHINOOSTZ** zootechnics
CCEEEKOOPRR Cooper Creek	**CCEEIINOSTUV** consecutive	**CCEHINOPRTY** pyrotechnic
CCEEELORTTU electrocute	**CCEEIOPPRSU** preoccupies	**CCEHIOOPRTT** ectotrophic
CCEEELORTTY electrocyte	**CCEEIOPRSSS** crosspieces	**CCEHKLOSTTU** shuttlecock
CCEEEMMNORS recommences	**CCEEIORRSTV** correctives	**CCEHKNOOSST** chockstones
CCEEEMNPSSU spumescence	**CCEEIORTUXX** coexecutrix	**CCEHKOOPPRR** rock chopper
CCEEENNOQSU consequence	**CCEEJNORRTU** conjecturer	**CCEHMOORSTY** cytochromes
CCEEENPRSTU putrescence	**CCEEJNORSTU** conjectures	**CCEHNNORSSU** scruncheons
CCEEENRRRSU recurrences	**CCEELMORSTY** cyclometers	**CCEHNOOOPRS** chronoscope
CCEEFFIINOT coefficient	**CCEELSSSSSU** successless	**CCEHNOPRSUW** cowpunchers
CCEEFIIMNNO omnificence	**CCEEMNNNORT** concernment	**CCEIIINSSTT** scientistic
CCEEFIIMNNU munificence	**CCEENNOORRV** overconcern	**CCEIIIRRSST** criticisers
CCEEFIKNOSY cockneyfies	**CCEENOPRRST** preconcerts	**CCEIIIRRSTU** circuitries

CCEIIIRRSTZ	criticizers	CCGHIINORTY	trichogynic	CDDDEEEEENRS	redescended
CCEIIILMNORT	clinometric	CCGHIKLLNUY	chucklingly	CDDDEEEEINSS	decidedness
CCEIIILMNORU	micronuclei	CCGHILNOOOR	chronologic	CDDDEEEENNSU	undescended
CCEIIILMORST	cliometrics	CCGHILOPTYY	glycophytic	CDDDEEIIRST	discredited
CCEIIMMORRT	micrometric	CCGHIOOPRSY	hygroscopic	CDDDEEIILNUY	undecidedly
CCEIIMNOOST	economistic	CCGIIIINRST	criticising	CDDDEIMMOOS	discommoded
CCEIIMOOPRS	microcopies	CCGIIIINRTZ	criticizing	CDDEEEENPRT	precedented
CCEIIMOORST	sociometric	CCGIIKKNOTT	ticktocking	CDDEEEEFFINR	differenced
CCEIIMVORST	viscometric	CCGIILOOOTX	toxicologic	CDDEEEEHLRSU	rescheduled
CCEIINOORST	coercionist	CCGIOOPRSSY	gyroscopics	CDDEEEEIIOPT	Pico de
CCEIIOPRRTY	reciprocity	CCHIIILMORT	microlithic		Teide
CCEIJNNOTUV	conjunctive	CCHIIIOSTTY	histiocytic	CDDEEEEILQSU	deliquesced
CCEIKKOPPST	pickpockets	CCHIILNOPRR	chlorpicrin	CDDEEEIPRTU	decrepitude
CCEIKLNOPRU	cupronickel	CCHIILOOPPR	coprophilic	CDDEEEELNORS	needlecords
CCEIKMNOSSY	cockneyisms	CCHIILORSTY	chrysolitic	CDDEEEELRTTU	decluttered
CCEILLNOOST	collections	CCHIIMNOOPR	microphonic	CDDEEEEMMNOR	recommended
CCEILMOORTU	coulometric	CCHIIMNOORT	monotrichic	CDDEEEENNOPS	despondence
CCEILNNOTTU	noctilucent	CCHIIMNOOST	monostichic	CDDEEEENNOPT	codependent
CCEILNORRTY	incorrectly	CCHIIMOORTT	trichotomic	CDDEEEENNORS	recondensed
CCEILOOQSTU	coquelicots	CCHIIMOPRTY	microphytic	CDDEEEENRSSU	descendeurs
CCEIMNNNOOO	noneconomic	CCHIIMORSTW	microswitch	CDDEEEEOPRRR	prerecorded
CCEIMNOORST	centrosomic	CCHIINOOPRS	rhinoscopic	CDDEEFIINST	disinfected
CCEIMNOPRTY	pycnometric	CCHILMNOORY	chylomicron	CDDEEFIKLNS	fiddlenecks
CCEIMNRSTUV	circumvents	CCHILMOOPRY	polychromic	CDDEEGILNNU	indulgenced
CCEIMOOPRSS	microscopes	CCHILMOPTYY	lymphocytic	CDDEEHILNSU	Lüdenscheid
CCEINNNOOST	connections	CCHIMMNOOOR	monochromic	CDDEEHLNSUU	unscheduled
CCEINNOOPST	conceptions	CCHIMNOOORS	monochroics	CDDEEIIMRST	misdirected
CCEINNOORST	concretions	CCHIMOOPRTY	cormophytic	CDDEEIINORT	rodenticide
CCEINNOOSSS	concessions		mycotrophic	CDDEEIINRTT	interdicted
CCEINNOOSTU	consecution	CCHINNORSSU	scrunchions	CDDEEIILNOOS	decolonised
CCEINNOSSTY	consistency	CCHIOOOPRST	orthoscopic	CDDEEIILNOOZ	decolonized
CCEINOOOSSS	iconoscopes	CCHIORRSSST	christcross	CDDEEIILOORS	decolorised
CCEINOOPRST	nociceptors	CCHIORSSTTY	trichocysts	CDDEEIILOORZ	decolorized
CCEINOORRST	corrections	CCIILLNOPSY	polyclinics	CDDEEIILTUVY	deductively
CCEINOSSSSU	successions	CCIILMORRUU	cirrocumuli	CDDEEIINPRRU	underpriced
CCEIOOPRSSY	cryoscopies	CCIILNOOPRS	ciclosporin	CDDEEIINPRTU	unpredicted
CCEJNNORTUU	conjuncture	CCIILNSSTUY	unicyclists	CDDEEEKNOORU	undercooked
CCEKMOORSTY	comstockery	CCIILOORSTU	colouristic	CDDEELNOORU	undercooled
CCELLNSTUUY	succulently	CCIILRSSTTY	tricyclists	CDDEELOORUV	overclouded
CCELLOSSTYY	cyclostyles	CCIIMMNOSTU	communistic	CDDEENNOPSY	despondency
CCELMOORSTY	motorcycles	CCIIMOOPRRS	microsporic	CDDEENORRSU	underscored
CCELMOOSSTY	cyclostomes	CCIINNOOSTV	convictions	CDDEENORSSW	crowdedness
CCELNOOOOPS	colonoscope	CCIINOPRTTY	nyctitropic	CDDEEOORRVW	overcrowded
CCELOOOPPSS	colposcopes	CCIJNNNOOTU	conjunction	CDDEFHIINOR	chondrified
CCELOPRSSUU	corpuscules	CCIKNOOPSTU	cuckoopints	CDDEFIIKLST	fiddlestick
CCELORSSSUU	succourless	CCILLNOORSU	councillors	CDDEFIIMOST	discomfited
CCENNORRSTU	concurrents	CCILMRRSUUU	curriculums	CDDEGHILNOR	godchildren
CCENORRSTTU	constructer	CCILNNOOSSU	conclusions	CDDEGILMNOO	Middle Congo
	reconstruct	CCILNOOPRSY	cyclosporin	CDDEGILNOOR	dendrologic
CCEOOOPPRST	proctoscope	CCILNOOSSUY	consciously	CDDEHIILMNR	childminder
CCEOOOPRRSS	coprocessor	CCILOOORSTU	corticolous	CDDEHIILORS	dichlorides
CCEOOPSSSTY	cystoscopes	CCIMMOOORSS	microcosmos	CDDEIIILLNNS	disinclined
CCFGIIKNNOY	cocknifying	CCIMNNOOPTU	compunction	CDDEIIILNPS	disciplined
CCFGIIILNNOT	conflicting	CCINNOOSSSU	concussions	CDDEIIILNPTU	duplicident
CCFIIINORUX	crucifixion	CCINNOOSSUU	unconscious	CDDEIIINNOOT	conditioned
CCFIIILNNOOT	confliction	CCINOOPSSUU	conspicuous	CDDEIIINOSU	indeciduous
CCFILMORRUY	cruciformly	CCINOORRSTT	constrictor	CDDEILNOOTY	dicotyledon
CCFILNOORTY	conflictory	CCINOSSSSUU	succussions	CDDEILNOSSU	undisclosed
CCGGHHIINOU	hiccoughing	CCLLOOORSTU	collocutors	CDDEILOORSU	discoloured
CCGGHHINORU	churchgoing	CCLNOOOOPSY	colonoscopy	CDDEILOSUUY	deciduously
CCGHHINNRUU	unchurching	CCNOORRSTTU	constructor	CDDEIMMNOOS	discommoned
CCGHIILLNNOR	chronicling	CCOOOPPRSTY	proctoscopy	CDDEIMMNOSS	discommends

CDDEIMMOOSS	discommodes
CDDEIMOOPSS	discomposed
CDDEINNOOST	endodontics
CDDEKORRSTU	rudderstock
CDDELLLMOOY	mollycoddle
CDDEMNOOPSU	decompounds
CDDENOORSTU	Côtes-du-Nord
CDDEOOPRTUU	outproduced
CDDGHILMOST	Goldschmidt
CDDIILNORSY	cylindroids
CDDINNOOSTY	dicynodonts
CDEEEEFFRSV	effervesced
CDEEEEFLNSS	defenceless
CDEEEEGNRST	detergences
CDEEEEINPRX	experienced
CDEEEEINPSX	expediences
CDEEEEELPRST	preselected
CDEEEENRRST	deterrences
CDEEEFFINRS	differences
CDEEEFFLORS	effloresced
CDEEEFGLNTU	genuflected
CDEEEFHIIPS	speechified
CDEEEFIILPS	fieldpieces
CDEEEFIILRT	electrified
CDEEEFILTVY	defectively
CDEEEFLNRTU	unreflected
CDEEEFMNORT	deforcement
CDEEEGILNST	deselecting
CDEEEGILNXY	exceedingly
CDEEEGINORS	derecognise
CDEEEGINORZ	derecognize
CDEEEGINRSV	divergences
CDEEEGKNOOS	goosenecked
CDEEEHIKLMZ	Melchizedek
CDEEEHIPRRS	decipherers
CDEEEHLPRSU	sepulchered
CDEEEHLRSSU	reschedules
CDEEEHRRSTT	stretchered
CDEEEIINRSS	residencies
CDEEEIJNRTT	interjected
CDEEEIKLNST	needlestick
CDEEEIKNQRU	requickened
CDEEEILNOST	deselection
CDEEEILNSTT	delitescent
CDEEEILOPSV	velocipedes
CDEEEILPTVY	deceptively
CDEEEILQSSU	deliquesces
CDEEEIMNNOS	comediennes
CDEEEINPRST	reinspected
CDEEEINPRTT	intercepted
CDEEEINPRUV	unperceived
CDEEEINRRST	interceders
CDEEEINRSTT	intersected
CDEEEINRSUV	undeceivers
CDEEEINRSUX	unexercised
CDEEEINSSTX	excitedness
CDEEEIORTVX	overexcited
CDEEEJORRTT	retrojected
CDEEELNNOOP	Ponce de León
CDEEEMMNORR	recommender

CDEEEMNNOST	encodements
CDEEEMNOPRS	recompensed
CDEEENNOPRS	respondence
CDEEENNORSS	recondenses
CDEEENNORTU	encountered
CDEEENOPRRS	precensored
CDEEENOQRRU	reconquered
CDEEENORRTT	retrocedent
CDEEENORRTV	reconverted
CDEEEOPRRSS	predecessor reprocessed
CDEEERRRSTU	resurrected
CDEEFFHIINR	frenchified
CDEEFFHINOR	Eichendorff
CDEEFGINRTU	centrifuged
CDEEFIIIKRR	Frederick II
CDEEFIIKRRV	Frederick IV
CDEEFIIKRRX	Frederick IX
CDEEFIILNTY	deficiently
CDEEFIINPSU	unspecified
CDEEFIINRST	dentifrices
CDEEFIINRTU	uncertified unrectified
CDEEFILLTUY	deceitfully
CDEEFILNNTU	uninflected
CDEEFILNORY	ecofriendly
CDEEFILNOST	deflections
CDEEFILOSST	closefisted
CDEEFIMNORR	reconfirmed
CDEEFINORRT	Fredericton
CDEEFLNORST	centerfolds centrefolds
CDEEFLNOSSY	confessedly
CDEEFNNORST	frondescent
CDEEFNNSSTU	defunctness
CDEEGHIINPR	deciphering
CDEEGIILNVY	deceivingly
CDEEGIINNRT	interceding
CDEEGIINNUV	undeceiving
CDEEGIINRRT	redirecting
CDEEGILNNSU	indulgences
CDEEGILNORS	girdlescone
CDEEGILNSUV	divulgences
CDEEGINNOTX	coextending
CDEEGINOPRS	proceedings
CDEEGINORRT	retroceding
CDEEHHIMSTT	hemstitched
CDEEHIILOPS	ophicleides
CDEEHIINNOS	Indochinese
CDEEHIINNST	indehiscent
CDEEHIKPRSW	shipwrecked
CDEEHILOPRR	perchloride
CDEEHIMNORS	echinoderms
CDEEHIMNORT	endothermic
CDEEHIMNOTU	endothecium
CDEEHIOPRTV	overpitched
CDEEHIOQSTU	discotheque
CDEEHMNOPRS	comprehends
CDEEHNNORTU	truncheoned
CDEEHPRSTTU	upstretched
CDEEIIIILSTV	declivities
CDEEIIKLNSS	slickenside

CDEEIILNORT	dereliction
CDEEIIMNPSU	impudencies
CDEEIIMNRST	densimetric
CDEEIIMORRS	misericorde
CDEEIIMORTU	eudiometric
CDEEIIMOSTZ	domesticize
CDEEIIMPRSS	spermicides
CDEEIINORRT	redirection
CDEEIINRSTV	viridescent
CDEEIINRTTU	incertitude
CDEEIIOORTV	Côte d'Ivoire
CDEEIIORRST	directories
CDEEIIORSSV	discoveries
CDEEIIPRSTV	descriptive
CDEEIIRRSTX	directrixes
CDEEIIRSSSV	disservices
CDEEIJNORTT	introjected
CDEEIKLMORU	leukodermic
CDEEIKLNNOO	nickelodeon
CDEEIKLNORT	interlocked
CDEEILNNOSS	declensions
CDEEILNNQUY	delinquency
CDEEILNOORS	recolonise
CDEEILNOORZ	recolonized
CDEEILNOOSS	decolonises
CDEEILNOOSZ	decolonizes
CDEEILNORTY	reconditely
CDEEILNOSSU	nucleosides
CDEEILNOSTU	nucleotides
CDEEILNSSTU	ductileness
CDEEILOORSS	decolorises
CDEEILOORSZ	decolorizes
CDEEILORSST	sclerotised
CDEEILORSTZ	sclerotized
CDEEILSTUVY	seductively
CDEEIMMORTT	recommitted
CDEEIMNNRST	discernment rescindment
CDEEIMNNSTU	inducements
CDEEIMNOPRS	endospermic
CDEEIMNOVRT	divorcement
CDEEIMOOSTX	sextodecimo
CDEEINNOSTU	tendencious
CDEEINNRSSW	windscreens
CDEEINOOPSS	endoscopies
CDEEINOORTT	condottiere
CDEEINORRRT	tricornered
CDEEINORRSS	considerers reconsiders
CDEEINORRTU	reintroduce
CDEEINPRRSU	underprices
CDEEINPRSUU	superinduce
CDEEINRSSTY	syncretised
CDEEINRSTYZ	syncretized
CDEEIORRSSV	discoverers rediscovers
CDEEIORRSVY	rediscovery
CDEEIORSTTT	detectorist
CDEEIPRSSST	disrespects
CDEEIRRRSVW	screwdriver

CDEEIRRSSTT	derestricts
CDEEIRSTTUV	destructive
CDEEJKOOTUV	outjockeyed
CDEEKKORSTY	skyrocketed
CDEEKNOORSS	crookedness
CDEEKOOPRSW	woodpeckers
CDEEKOORSTV	overstocked
CDEELMNNOOT	condolement
CDEELMNOPTU	uncompleted
CDEELNNOTTY	contentedly
CDEELNRRTUY	decurrently
CDEELNRTTUU	uncluttered
CDEELOOPRSU	supercooled
CDEEMNNOPRS	precondemns
CDEEMOOPRSS	decomposers
CDEENNOPRSY	respondency
CDEENNOQRUU	unconquered
CDEENNORTUV	unconverted
CDEENNOSTTU	uncontested
CDEENOOSSTT	cottonseeds
CDEENOOSTTW	cottonweeds
CDEENOPRSSU	unprocessed
CDEENOPRTTU	unprotected
CDEENORRSSU	underscores
CDEENOSSTUU	consuetudes
CDEENPSSTUU	unsuspected
CDEEOOPPRRV	overcropped
CDEEOOPPRRV	overproduce
CDEEOPRRRSU	reproducers
CDEFFORRSSU	crossruffed
CDEFGHILNOS	goldfinches
CDEFGIINORY	recodifying
CDEFHIINORS	chondrifies
CDEFHIKOPRT	pitchforked
CDEFIIILMSU	semifluidic
CDEFIILMMOR	microfilmed
CDEFIIMORST	discomfiter
CDEFIINNTUY	infecundity
CDEFIINORST	disinfector
CDEFIINORTU	countrified
CDEFILMNORY	confirmedly
CDEFILNNOTY	confidently
CDEFIMNNORU	unconfirmed
CDEFINOORSV	confervoids
CDEFINORTUY	countryfied
CDEFNNOORSU	confounders
CDEFNORRSTU	undercrofts
CDEGHILNOOS	deschooling
CDEGHINORRS	Schrödinger
CDEGHIOPRTY	copyrighted
CDEGIIJNPRU	prejudicing
CDEGIILNNRY	cylindering
CDEGIINNORS	considering
CDEGIINNPRS	prescinding
CDEGIINOPTY	copyediting
CDEGIINORSV	discovering
CDEGIINPRTU	depicturing
CDEGILNOORU	decolouring
CDEGILNOPSU	decouplings
CDEGIMNNOTU	documenting
CDEGIMNOOPS	decomposing
CDEGIMNORRU	corrigendum

CDEGINNORST	constringed
CDEGINOPRRU	reproducing
CDEGINRSTTU	destructing
CDEGKLOOORS	sockdologer
CDEGMNORSUU	curmudgeons
CDEHHHOORSS	Rosh Chodesh
CDEHHNOOOPR	chordophone
CDEHIIINNOR	enchiridion
CDEHIIINRST	trichinised
CDEHIIINRTZ	trichinized
CDEHIILLNOT	decillionth
CDEHIILOTTT	theodolitic
CDEHIILOPSS	discophiles
CDEHIILORRT	trichloride
CDEHIIMNNOO	Domenichino
CDEHIIMOOST	dichotomies
	dichotomise
CDEHIIMOOTZ	dichotomize
CDEHIIMOSTT	methodistic
CDEHIINOOPV	videophonic
CDEHIKMNPRU	Humperdinck
CDEHILPRTUU	pulchritude
CDEHIMNOOPR	endomorphic
CDEHIMNORST	Christendom
CDEHIMOPRSY	hypodermics
CDEHIMORRTY	hydrometric
CDEHINOOPRT	endotrophic
CDEHINOPRRY	Pondicherry
CDEHINOPSST	docentships
CDEHIOOOPPT	photocopied
CDEHIOOPRST	orthopedics
CDEHKLOORST	stockholder
CDEHLOOPPRS	clodhoppers
CDEHLOOPRSY	copyholders
CDEHOOPRSSY	hydroscopes
CDEIIIILSST	stillicides
CDEIIILNNSS	disinclines
CDEIIILNPRS	discipliner
CDEIIILNPSS	disciplines
CDEIIILNSUV	uncivilised
CDEIIILNUVZ	uncivilized
CDEIIILOPST	politicised
CDEIIILOPTZ	politicized
CDEIIILPSTU	duplicities
CDEIIIMMSTU	mediumistic
CDEIIIMORTX	oxidimetric
CDEIIINNORT	indirection
CDEIIINSTTV	distinctive
CDEIIIOPRTT	peridotitic
CDEIIIOPRTY	periodicity
CDEIIIRSSTV	recidivists
CDEIIISSTUV	vicissitude
CDEIIJNOSTU	jocundities
CDEIIJNSTUV	disjunctive
CDEIILLMNOS	millisecond
CDEIILLOSUY	deliciously
CDEIILLPTUY	pellucidity
CDEIILNNROY	incondirely
CDEIILNOSTU	unsolicited
CDEIILNRTUY	incredulity
CDEIILNTUVY	inductively
CDEIILOORST	sclerotioid

CDEIILOOSUY	dioeciously
CDEIILOPSSU	pediculosis
CDEIILOSTUV	declivitous
CDEIIMMOOST	commodities
CDEIIMNNSTT	indictments
CDEIIMNORST	modernistic
CDEIIMNOSST	midsections
CDEIIMORRSS	misericords
CDEIIMOSTTY	domesticity
CDEIIMPPRUY	cypripedium
CDEIINNOORT	conditioner
	recondition
CDEIINNOSTU	discontinue
CDEIINOOPRT	periodontic
CDEIINOORTT	condottieri
CDEIINOPRST	description
	predictions
CDEIINORRTT	interdictor
CDEIINORSST	discretions
CDEIINOSSST	dissections
CDEIINRSSTU	scrutinised
CDEIINRSTUZ	scrutinized
CDEIIOOPRTX	dexiotropic
CDEIIOORRSS	sororicides
CDEIJNRRSTU	disjuncture
CDEIKNRRSTU	undertricks
CDEIKNRSSUW	windsuckers
CDEILNORSUU	incredulous
CDEILOORRTU	tricoloured
CDEILORSSSU	disclosures
CDEIMMNOPSU	compendiums
CDEIMMNOTTU	uncommitted
CDEIMMOOPRS	compromised
CDEIMNOOPSU	compendious
CDEIMNOSSTY	syndesmotic
CDEIMOOPSSS	discomposes
CDEINNOORSU	endocrinous
CDEINNOOSTU	contusioned
CDEINNOPRST	nondescript
CDEINNORTUV	uncontrived
CDEINNOSSTT	discontents
CDEINOOPSST	endoscopist
CDEINOOSSTY	endocytosis
CDEINORRSTU	introducers
CDEINORSSTU	discounters
	rediscounts
CDEINORSTTU	destruction
CDEINORSTUY	countryside
CDEINOSTTTU	constituted
CDEIORRSSSU	discoursers
CDEIORSSTUY	discourtesy
CDELLLOSSUY	cloudlessly
CDELLNORSUY	scoundrelly
CDELLORSUUY	credulously
CDELNOORTTY	contortedly
CDEMMOOORSS	cosmodromes
CDEMNOOPRSU	compounders
CDENOOPRRSS	corresponds
CDENOORRTUW	counterword
CDENOPRRTUU	uncorrupted
CDEOOPRSTUU	outproduces
CDEOORSTTUW	woodcutters

CDEORRSSTTU	destructors
CDFFIILLTUY	difficultly
CDFGIIKNORS	disfrocking
CDFGIILNNOY	confidingly
CDFGINNNOOU	confounding
CDFIIMNORSS	disconfirms
CDFIMOORSST	discomforts
CDFINNOSTUY	dysfunction
CDGGIIKLNOR	gridlocking
CDGHIKNOSUV	duckshoving
CDGHILNOOPP	clodhopping
CDGIIINRSTT	districting
CDGIILLOPSY	glycolipids
CDGIILNOORS	discoloring
CDGIILOOSST	discologist
CDGIILOSSTY	dyslogistic
CDGIIMMNNOO	incommoding
CDGIINNORTU	introducing
CDGIINNOSTU	discounting
CDGIINORSSU	discoursing
CDGILLNNOOY	condolingly
CDGILOORTTY	troglodytic
CDGIMNNOOPU	compounding
CDGINOOTTUW	woodcutting
CDHHIILOPRY	hydrophilic
CDHHIOPRTYY	hydrophytic
CDHIIIMOOPR	idiomorphic
CDHIIMNOORS	chironomids
CDHIIMOOSTT	dichotomist
CDHIIOOPRST	chiropodist
CDHILOOOPSU	chilopodous
CDHIMOOOSTU	dichotomous
CDHINOOORTT	orthodontic
CDHINOOPRSY	hydroponics
CDHIOOPRRTY	hydrotropic
CDIIIJNOSUU	injudicious
CDIIILNTTUY	inductility
CDIIINNOSTT	distinction
CDIIINOSSSS	discissions
CDIIIRSSTTX	District Six
CDIIJLOSUUY	judiciously
CDIIJNNOSTU	disjunction
CDIILLOOPPY	polyploidic
CDIILMORSTU	clostridium
CDIILOOPSTU	duopolistic
CDIILOPSTUU	duplicitous
CDIIMMNNOOU	condominium
CDIIMMNOOTY	incommodity
CDIINORSSTT	doctrinists
CDIINOSSSSU	discussions
CDIIOOOOSTV	voodooistic
CDIKLLORSST	drillstocks
CDIKLNOPSSU	spondulicks
CDIKORSSSTW	swordsticks
CDILLORSUUY	ludicrously
CDILMOOORSX	loxodromics
CDILMOOPSUY	lycopodiums
CDILOOORUUU	douroucouli
CDINNOOPRTY	cyprinodont
CDINOOPRSTU	productions
CDNOOOOSTTW	cottonwoods
CEEEEEGMNRR	reemergence

CEEEEEFFRSSV	effervesces
CEEEEEFNPRRS	preferences
CEEEEEFNRRRS	referencers
CEEEEEGIMNRS	emergencies
CEEEEHILNST	entelechies
CEEEEEILNORT	electioneer
CEEEEEIMNNPR	preeminence
CEEEEINPRSX	experiences
CEEEEINRRRV	irreverence
CEEEEJNRSUV	rejuvenesce
CEEEEENPPRST	Peter's
	pence
CEEEENRRRSV	reverencers
CEEEEFFHOOSU	coffeehouse
CEEEFFIINTV	ineffective
CEEEFFILTVY	effectively
CEEEFFLNOSS	offenceless
CEEEFFLORSS	effloresces
CEEEFGINNRR	referencing
	refringence
CEEEFHIIPRS	speechifier
CEEEFHIIPSS	speechifies
CEEEFIILRRT	electrifier
CEEEFIILRST	electrifies
CEEEFILTUVX	flexecutive
CEEEFINNQRU	infrequence
CEEEFINQRSU	frequencies
CEEEFIORRST	refectories
CEEEFKLLORR	Rockefeller
CEEEFMNNORT	enforcement
CEEEFNPRSST	perfectness
CEEEFPRRSTU	prefectures
CEEEGGHINNS	gegenschein
CEEEGGILNNS	negligences
CEEEGGNORRR	greengrocer
CEEEGHINORT	heterogenic
CEEEGIINOPR	epeirogenic
CEEEGIKNNOT	kenogenetic
CEEEGIKNORT	greenockite
CEEEGILMNNO	meningocele
CEEEGILNPRT	preelecting
CEEEGILNRST	reselecting
CEEEGINNNOS	cenogenesis
CEEEGINNOTX	xenogenetic
CEEEGINNRRV	reverencing
CEEEGINORSS	recognisees
CEEEGINORSZ	recognizees
CEEEGINORTV	eigenvector
CEEEGINOSST	ectogenesis
CEEEGINRSTV	vicegerents
	viceregents
CEEEGLNORST	electrogens
CEEEGNNOOSS	oncogeneses
CEEEGNRRSSU	resurgences
CEEEHHIRSTT	heresthetic
CEEEHHKLNOP	heckelphone
CEEEHHMOPRS	chemosphere
CEEEHIKNTTT	kitchenette
CEEEHIKPPRS	pikeperches
CEEEHILNSST	Cleisthenes
CEEEHILORTT	heteroclite
CEEEHILSTTT	telesthetic

CEEEHIMNRTU	hermeneutic
CEEEHIMORST	heteroecism
CEEEHIMSSTT	chemisettes
CEEEHINPRRS	encipherers
CEEEHINSSST	cenesthesis
CEEEHIORSSS	coheiresses
CEEEHLLRSSY	cheerlessly
CEEEHLOPRST	Cleethorpes
CEEEHMMNSSY	mesenchymes
CEEEHMNNRRT	trenchermen
CEEEHMORSTT	hectometers
	hectometres
CEEEHNNRRST	entrenchers
CEEEHNORSSS	chersoneses
CEEEHOQRSUU	eurocheques
CEEEIIKLNTT	telekinetic
CEEEIIMNNPT	impenitence
CEEEIINNNRT	internecine
CEEEIINNNST	insentience
CEEEIINNSTX	inexistence
CEEEIINNSST	necessities
CEEEIIKNNRSS	snickersnee
CEEEILLSTVY	selectively
CEEEILMNNST	clementines
CEEEILMORST	ceilometers
CEEEILNNOQU	ineloquence
CEEEILNNOTV	nonelective
CEEEILNOPRT	preelection
CEEEILNORST	reelections
	reselection
CEEEILNPRST	percentiles
CEEEILNPSST	pestilences
CEEEILNSTUV	unselective
CEEEILPRTVY	receptively
CEEEILRSSVY	recessively
CEEEILRSTVY	secretively
CEEEILSSVXY	excessively
CEEEILTUVXY	executively
CEEEIMNNNST	incensement
CEEEIMNNSTT	enticements
CEEEIMNRSTT	centimeters
	centimetres
CEEEIMNSTTX	excitements
CEEEINNOPRV	provenience
CEEEINNOSTV	venesection
CEEEINNRSSS	sincereness
CEEEINORTUX	executioner
CEEEINOSTVX	coextensive
CEEEINPRRST	pericenters
	pericentres
CEEEINPRRTT	intercepter
CEEEINPRSSS	preciseness
CEEEINPRSST	persistence
CEEEINPRTUV	unreceptive
CEEEIOPRRSV	overprecise
CEEEIORRSST	corsetieres
CEEEIORSTVX	overexcites
CEEEIPPRSTV	perspective
CEEEIPRSTUV	persecutive
CEEEIRSTUXX	executrixes
CEEEJNNSTUV	juvenescent
CEEEKMNORSS	smokescreen

CEEELLLNNTXY	excellently	CEEFLOORRSU	foreclosure	CEEHIISTTTW	witchetties
CEEELLORSTY	electrolyse	CEEFLORRSSUU	resourceful	CEEHIKNSSST	sketchiness
CEEELLORTTY	electrolyte	CEEFLPPRSTU	pluperfects	CEEHIKPPRSS	schipperkes
CEEELLORTYZ	electrolyze	CEEFMNNORST	conferments	CEEHILLNOST	clothesline
CEEELMNOSSW	welcomeness	CEEFOORRSSU	forecourses	CEEHILMNORT	thermocline
CEEELMORRST	electromers	CEEGHIINNPR	enciphering	CEEHILNOPRS	necrophiles
	sclerometer	CEEGHILLNOP	phellogenic	CEEHILNORST	cholesterin
CEEELNNOORT	coelenteron	CEEGHILNRSS	Schlesinger	CEEHILOPRST	electorship
CEEELNOORSU	neurocoeles	CEEGHIMNORT	thermogenic		helicopters
CEEELOPRTTY	electrotype	CEEGHIMOSST	geochemists	CEEHILOPSTT	Philoctetes
CEEEMNNNOTU	enouncement	CEEGHINNNRT	entrenching	CEEHILORSTT	hectoliters
CEEEMNOPRRS	recompenser	CEEGHINNNRT	retrenching		hectolitres
CEEEMNOPRSS	recompenses	CEEGHINRSST	sightscreen	CEEHILORTTY	heterolytic
CEEEMNORRST	centromeres	CEEGIILMOOS	semeiologic	CEEHILPRSTU	lectureship
CEEEMNORTTY	enterectomy	CEEGIILNNRS	relicensing	CEEHIMNNRST	enrichments
CEEEMNOSTYZ	ectoenzymes	CEEGIIMNNRS	mercerising	CEEHIMNOPRS	mesonephric
CEEEMNRTTTU	curettement	CEEGIIMNRRZ	mercerizing	CEEHIMOPRSS	mesospheric
CEEENNORRTU	encounterer	CEEGIINORTV	recognitive	CEEHIMOPRTT	pitchometer
CEEEOOPRSST	stereoscope	CEEGIINPRST	stringpiece	CEEHIMOPSTU	mouthpieces
CEEEOPRRSSS	reprocesses	CEEGIINSSTT	geneticists	CEEHIMOSSTT	somesthetic
CEEEORRSSSS	sorceresses	CEEGIINSSTU	eugenicists	CEEHIMPRRTY	hypermetric
CEEEPPRRSST	preceptress	CEEGILNNOSY	geosyncline	CEEHIMRRTUY	eurythermic
CEEEPRRSSTU	supersecret	CEEGILNOORS	necrologies	CEEHINNRRST	intrenchers
CEEFFHIINRS	frenchifies	CEEGILNOPST	telescoping	CEEHINOOPPS	phenocopies
CEEFFIIINNT	inefficient	CEEGILNOPTY	polygenetic	CEEHINRRSST	christeners
CEEFFIIILNTY	efficiently	CEEGILNOSTT	telegnostic		rechristens
CEEFFIINORT	interoffice	CEEGIMNNOOT	monogenetic	CEEHINRSSTW	winchesters
CEEFGIINNNR	inferencing	CEEGIMNNORST	egocentrism	CEEHINSSTTY	synesthetic
CEEFGIINNRT	reinfecting	CEEGIMNNORV	reconvening	CEEHIOOPRTT	heterotopic
CEEFGINNORR	reenforcing	CEEGINNNOSS	oncogenesis	CEEHIOPRRST	Terpsichore
CEEFGINNRRY	refringency	CEEGINNNOTT	ontogenetic	CEEHIOPRSST	spirochetes
CEEFGINRSTU	centrifuges	CEEGINNORVV	reconveying	CEEHIOPRSTV	overpitches
CEEFGLNORTU	genuflector	CEEGINNRSSU	insurgences	CEEHIOPRTTY	heterotypic
CEEFGLNPRSU	Spencer Gulf	CEEGINOORST	oestrogenic	CEEHIORSSUV	echoviruses
CEEFHHNNORT	thenceforth	CEEGINORRSS	recognisers	CEEHIRSSTTT	stretchiest
CEEFHIKRSSW	wreckfishes	CEEGINORRSZ	recognizers	CEEHKLNOSUY	honeysuckle
CEEFHILORSU	cheliferous	CEEGINORSSU	surgeoncies	CEEHKNORSUY	honeysucker
CEEFHMOORRR	ferrochrome	CEEGINOSSTY	cytogenesis	CEEHLLOORST	cholesterol
CEEFHORSTTU	fourchettes	CEEGINPRSTU	persecuting	CEEHLLORSUY	lecherously
CEEFHPRRSSU	surfperches	CEEGIOPRRTU	picturegoer	CEEHLMRSTWZ	weltschmerz
CEEFIILMRTT	flittermice	CEEGMNNORSS	congressmen	CEEHLNOOPRR	chloroprene
CEEFIILNORS	Leif Ericson	CEEGMOSTYYZ	zygomycetes	CEEHMMOORRS	chromomeres
CEEFIILNTVY	infectively	CEEGNNOORSU	congenerous	CEEHMNOORRT	chronometer
CEEFIINNORT	reinfection	CEEHHIIMPRS	hemispheric	CEEHMNOPRTY	nephrectomy
CEEFIINORST	fictioneers	CEEHHILMOOR	heliochrome	CEEHMNORSST	tschernosem
CEEFIIPRSSU	superficies	CEEHHILNOPT	technophile	CEEHMOOPRST	thermoscope
CEEFIKKNOPT	pocketknife	CEEHHIMRSTT	hemstitcher	CEEHNOOPPRS	nephroscope
CEEFIKLNORR	ferronickel	CEEHHIMSSTT	hemstitches	CEEHNOOPPSS	nephoscopes
CEEFIKLOPRS	forcepslike	CEEHHIORSVW	whichsoever	CEEHNOOPRST	ctenophores
CEEFILMPRTY	imperfectly	CEEHHIPSSTY	hypesthesic	CEEHNOORRTT	orthocenter
CEEFILNNOSS	confineless	CEEHHMMOORS	hemochromes		orthocentre
CEEFILNNRSU	influencers	CEEHHMORSTT	homestretch	CEEHNOPRSTY	hypocentres
CEEFILNORST	reflections	CEEHIIINORS	chinoiserie	CEEHOOPSSTT	stethoscope
CEEFILNORSU	fluorescein	CEEHIIKNPST	thinkpieces	CEEHORRSSTT	overstretch
CEEFIMNNNOT	confinement	CEEHIIKNSTT	kinesthetic	CEEHORRTTVY	erythrocyte
CEEFINNQRUY	infrequency	CEEHIILMORT	heliometric	CEEIIKNSWZ	Sienkiewicz
CEEFINORTTU	counterfeit	CEEHIIMOOPT	hemopoietic	CEEIIINNSTV	incentivise
CEEFIOOPSST	fetoscopies	CEEHIIMPRTU	perithecium	CEEIIINNTVZ	incentivize
CEEFKLORSTT	fetterlocks	CEEHIIMPSTU	euphemistic	CEEIIINRSTZ	citizenries
CEEFLMOORRT	electroform	CEEHIIMRSST	chemistries	CEEIIKNNSTZ	zinckenites
CEEFLNOORSW	coneflowers	CEEHIIMSSTT	estheticism	CEEIIKNRSST	ricketiness
CEEFLNORSTU	fluorescent	CEEHIINNPPRR	perinephric	CEEIILMPRSY	imprecisely

CEEIILMRTUV	vermiculite	CEEILNOPRTU	neuroleptic	CEELMNOOPSX	complexones
CEEIILNNNORV	overincline	CEEILNORTTT	electrotint	CEELMNOOSSU	nucleosomes
CEEIILNNNRSY	insincerely	CEEILNPRSTY	presciently	CEELMNOPSSX	complexness
CEEIILNNTVY	incentively	CEEILNQSTUY	quiescently	CEELMNOPSTY	splenectomy
CEEIILNPRST	princeliest	CEEILOPSSTY	cespitosely	CEELMNOPTTY	competently
CEEIILNPTVY	inceptively	CEEILORSSST	sclerotises	CEELMOOPRVX	overcomplex
CEEIILNRSTT	centiliters	CEEILORSSTZ	sclerotizes	CEELMOORSTU	coulometers
	centilitres	CEEILORSUVX	exclusive or	CEELNOOOPRT	coleopteron
CEEIILNTVVY	invectively	CEEILRRSTUU	sericulture	CEELNRRRTUY	recurrently
CEEIILSTTVY	selectivity	CEEILRSUVXY	excursively	CEELPSSSSTU	suspectless
CEEIIMMPRST	metempirics	CEEIMMORRST	micrometers	CEEMMNNOOSS	commonsense
CEEIIMMNNPTY	impenitency		micrometres	CEEMMNOPTUY	pneumectomy
CEEIIMMNNRST	reminiscent	CEEIMNNOOPT	omnipotence	CEEMMOSTXYY	myxomycetes
CEEIIMNNNSTT	incitements	CEEIMMNNOPRS	prominences	CEEMNNNOTTT	contentment
CEEIIMOPRTZ	piezometric	CEEIMMNNOPTT	incompetent	CEEMNOORSST	centrosomes
CEEIIMOPTTV	competitive	CEEIMMNNORTU	countermine	CEEMNOORSUV	overconsume
CEEIIMORSST	esotericism	CEEIMMNNSTTU	intumescent	CEEMNOORTUV	countermove
CEEIIMORSTT	meteoritics	CEEIMMNOORSS	economisers	CEEMNOOSSTU	coenosteums
CEEIIMORSTX	exotericism	CEEIMMNOORST	necrotomies	CEEMNOPRRTU	procurement
CEEIINNNSTY	insentiency	CEEIMMNOORSU	ceremonious	CEEMNOPRSTT	contretemps
CEEIINNNSTY	insentiency	CEEIMMNOORSZ	economizers	CEEMNOPRSTU	recoupments
CEEIINNORSS	incensories	CEEIMMNORSTU	emunctories	CEEMNOPRSTY	pycnometers
CEEIINNSTXY	inexistency	CEEIMMNRRTTU	recruitment	CEEMOPRRSSU	compressure
CEEIINOPSST	centipoises	CEEIMOOPSSS	seismoscope	CEEMOPRRTTY	cryptometer
CEEIINORSTV	insectivore	CEEIMOPRSSV	compressive	CEENNOORRST	cornerstone
CEEIINOSTVX	convexities	CEEIMOPRSTU	computerise	CEENNORRSTU	rencounters
CEEIINPPRST	percipients	CEEIMOPRTUZ	computerize	CEENNRRSSTU	currentness
CEEIINPRSST	resipiscent	CEEIMORSSTV	viscometers	CEENOORRSTV	seroconvert
CEEIINRSSTT	intersticies	CEEIMOSSSTV	vicomtesses	CEENOPPPRRS	peppercorns
CEEIINRSTVV	reviviscent	CEEINNNOSTT	consentient	CEENOPRTTUY	countertype
CEEIIORRSST	escritoires	CEEINNOORRT	reconnoiter	CEENOQRSSTU	reconquests
CEEIIPRTTVY	receptivity		reconnoitre	CEENORSTTUR	stonecutter
CEEIIRRSTTV	restrictive	CEEINNOOSTX	coextension	CEENORSTTUX	contextures
CEEIJLOPRST	projectiles	CEEINOOPRST	retinoscope	CEEOOPRRTTV	overprotect
CEEIJNORRTT	interjector	CEEINOPPRSS	sniperscope	CEEOOPRSSTY	stereoscopy
CEEIKLLNRSS	clerkliness	CEEINOPPRST	perceptions	CEEOOORRSTU	outercourse
CEEIKLLNRST	skillcentre	CEEINOPRRTT	interceptor	CEEOPRRSSSU	procuresses
CEEIKLNNPSU	luckpennies	CEEINOPRSSS	precessions	CEEOPRRSSTT	protectress
CEEIKLNORRT	interlocker	CEEINOPRSTU	persecution		retrospects
CEEIKNPRSTY	persnickety	CEEINOPRSTX	excerptions	CEEOPRRSSTU	persecutors
CEEILLMNNTY	inclemently	CEEINORRSST	intercessor	CEEOPRRSTUY	persecutory
CEEILLMRSSY	mercilessly	CEEINORRSTU	intercourse	CEEPRSSSSUU	cupressuses
CEEILLNRSST	stencillers	CEEINORSTTV	convertites	CEERRRSTTUU	restructure
CEEILLOOPST	coleoptiles	CEEINOSSSTU	necessitous	CEFFHIINNOR	chiffonnier
CEEILLOQTUV	Tocqueville	CEEINOSSSTV	costiveness	CEFFHIINORS	chiffoniers
CEEILLOSSVY	voicelessly	CEEINPRSSTY	persistency	CEFFHIKMNOT	Metchnikoff
CEEILLPRSSY	pricelessly	CEEINRRSSTU	scrutineers	CEFFHILNORT	Northcliffe
CEEILLSSUVY	seclusively	CEEINRRSSTW	wintercress	CEFFHIRSSTT	festschrift
CEEILLSUVXY	exclusively	CEEINRSSSTY	syncretises	CEFFIIRRSTU	fructifiers
CEEILMNNSTU	luminescent	CEEINRSSTTT	trecentists	CEFGHIILNSS	clingfishes
CEEILMNOOPW	policewomen	CEEINRSSTYZ	syncretizes	CEFGIILNNNU	influencing
CEEILMNORST	clinometers	CEEIOPPRSTV	prospective	CEFGIINNORR	reinforcing
CEEILMNOSTU	contumelies	CEEIOPRSTTV	protectives	CEFGIKLNOOR	forelocking
CEEILMOORRT	colorimeter	CEEIOPRSTTY	stereotypic	CEFGIKLNPSY	flyspecking
CEEILMOORSS	Îles Comores	CEEIORRSTUU	couturieres	CEFGILNOORS	foreclosing
CEEILMOOSTU	leucotomies	CEEIPQRSTUU	picturesque	CEFGILNORSU	fluorescing
CEEILMOPRSS	microsleeps	CEEKLNRSTTU	turtlenecks	CEFGINORSSU	refocussing
CEEILNNNOOT	nonelection	CEEKOORRRTT	retrorocket	CEFHIIISSTT	fetishistic
CEEILNNNOOV	nonviolence	CEELLMNOUWY	unwelcomely	CEFHIKOSSST	stockfishes
CEEILNOOPRS	necropoleis	CEELLPRSSSU	scrupleless	CEFHINRSTUW	Schweinfurt
CEEILNOORRT	intercooler	CEELLRSSTUU	cultureless	CEFIIINTTVY	infectivity
CEEILNOORSS	recolonises	CEELMMNOPST	complements	CEFIILNNOST	inflections
CEEILNOORSZ	recolonizes	CEELMMNOPST	complements		

CEFIILNOQSU	cinquefoils
CEFIINOPRST	proficients
CEFIINORSUZ	zinciferous
CEFILMORSUU	culmiferous
CEFILNOORTU	counterfoil
CEFILOORSUY	ferociously
CEFILPRRSUU	persulfuric
CEFINNOOSSS	confessions
CEFIOPRRSUU	cupriferous
CEFLMOORSST	comfortless
CEFLNOORRSW	cornflowers
CEFLOOOPRSU	fluoroscope
CEFNNOORRST	confronters
CEFNOORRTTU	counterfort
CEFNOPRRTUY	perfunctory
CEGGIINNORS	recognising
CEGGIINNORZ	recognizing
CEGHHKLOSSV	Shcheglovsk
CEGHIIKNNST	thickenings
CEGHIILLNPR	prechilling
CEGHIILNRST	Christingle
CEGHIINNNRT	intrenching
CEGHIINNRST	christening
CEGHIKNNPUV	keypunching
CEGHIKNRSTU	huckstering
CEGHILLNOOY	lichenology
CEGHILNPRSU	sepulchring
CEGHIMMNOOS	homecomings
CEGHIMNOOPR	morphogenic
CEGHIMORRTY	hygrometric
CEGHINOOORR	gonorrhoeic
CEGHINORRSU	chirurgeons
CEGHINORSSU	grouchiness
CEGHINORSTY	trichogynes
CEGHINSUWZZ	zwischenzug
CEGHIOOPRST	geostrophic
CEGHIOPRRTY	copyrighter
CEGHLOOPRSU	glucophores
CEGHLOPSTYY	glycophytes
CEGHOOPRSSY	hygroscopes
CEGIIIMNNRS	reminiscing
CEGIIINOPST	poeticising
CEGIIINOPTZ	poeticizing
CEGIIINORST	eroticising
CEGIIINORTZ	eroticizing
CEGIIINSTVV	vivisecting
CEGIIKLNNSY	sickeningly
CEGIIKLNSST	singlestick
CEGIIKPRSST	pigstickers
CEGIILLNNST	stencilling
CEGIILMNNSU	luminescing
CEGIILMOOSS	seismologic
CEGIILNNPRS	princelings
CEGIILNOOST	neologistic
CEGIILNORST	cloistering
CEGIILOOPST	geopolitics
CEGIIMMNNOU	immunogenic
CEGIIMNNOOS	economising
CEGIIMNNOOZ	economizing
CEGIIMNNSTU	intumescing
CEGIIMNOORT	goniometric
CEGIINNOORT	recognition

CEGIINNOPRS	preconising
CEGIINNOPRZ	preconizing
CEGIINNRRRU	reincurring
CEGIINOPRRV	overpricing
CEGIINORSTU	congruities
CEGIINRRSTT	restricting
CEGIINRSSTY	synergistic
CEGIKNOOORV	overcooking
CEGIKNORSST	stockingers
CEGILLNNOSU	counselling
CEGILMNOOOT	entomologic
CEGILNNOOSS	coolingness
CEGILNNOSST	clingstones
CEGILNOOORV	overcooling
CEGILNOORST	necrologist
CEGILNOOSTY	Scientology
CEGILNRRRUY	recurringly
CEGILOOOSST	oecologists
CEGILOOSSTT	cetologists
CEGIMNNNOST	consignment
CEGIMNOOOSS	cosmogonies
CEGIMNOOPRS	recomposing
CEGIMNOPRSS	compressing
CEGIMOOORRV	microgroove
CEGINNNNSSU	cunningness
CEGINNNORTU	incongruent
CEGINNNOSTT	contingents
CEGINNOOPST	copingstone
CEGINNORSST	constringes
CEGINNORSTU	countersign
CEGINOOOPSS	gonioscopes
CEGINOORRSS	recognisors
CEGINOORRSV	overscoring
CEGINOORRSZ	recognizors
CEGINOORRTY	recognitory
CEGINOPPRST	prospecting
CEGINOPRSTU	prosecuting
CEGLMMOORYY	myrmecology
CEGLMOOSSTY	glossectomy
CEGLNNORTUY	congruently
CEGLNOORTUW	counterglow
CEGLOPRSUUU	groupuscule
CEGNNOPRSUU	scuppernong
CEGNOOSSTUY	cystogenous
CEGORRRSUYY	cryosurgery
CEHHHIIKRST	hitchhikers
CEHHIIILLOT	heliolithic
CEHHIILMNST	helminthics
CEHHIILOTTY	ichthyolite
CEHHIIMMOPR	hemimorphic
CEHHILMRSUY	helichrysum
CEHHIMOOPRR	rheomorphic
CEHHIMOOPRT	theomorphic
CEHHIMRSTUV	eurhythmics
CEHHINOPSTY	hyposthenic
CEHHIOPRRST	Christopher
CEHHIOPSTYZ	schizophyte
CEHHLOOOSSU	schoolhouse
CEHHLOOPRST	choropleths
CEHHMNORSSY	synchromesh
CEHHMOOOPRR	chromophore
CEHHMOOPRSY	hypsochrome

CEHHMOOPRTY	phytochrome
CEHHMOOPSTY	chomophytes
CEHHOOOPRRT	trochophore
CEHIIINPSTZ	citizenship
CEHIIINRSST	trichinises
CEHIIINRSTZ	trichinizes
CEHIIIRSTTT	tritheistic
CEHIIJPSSTU	justiceship
CEHIIKLLRSY	lickerishly
CEHIILMNTTU	multiethnic
CEHIILOOPRT	heliotropic
CEHIILOPPRS	scripophile
CEHIILPRSTU	spherulitic
CEHIIMNOPST	phonemicist
CEHIIMNORST	thermionics
CEHIIMOPPRR	perimorphic
CEHIIMOSSUV	mischievous
CEHIIMRSSTY	mythicisers
CEHIIMRSTYZ	mythicizers
CEHIINOOPRS	ionospheric
CEHIINOORSS	isochronise
CEHIINOORSZ	isochronize
CEHIIOPPTTY	epiphytotic
CEHIIOPRRST	prehistoric
CEHIIOPRSSY	hypocrisies
CEHIIOPRSVY	viceroyship
CEHIIOSSSVY	vichyssoise
CEHIKMRSSTU	hucksterism
CEHILLMOPSY	mesophyllic
CEHILLNNOPU	punchinello
CEHILLNOOPS	colonelship
CEHILMOOPPR	pleomorphic
CEHILMOOPRS	pleochroism
CEHILMORTTY	thermolytic
CEHILNOOQRU	chloroquine
CEHILNOORST	interschool
CEHILNOPSST	clothespins
CEHILNOSSST	coltishness
CEHILNOSSSU	slouchiness
CEHILOPRSST	lectorships
CEHILORSSTY	chrysolites
CEHIMMOOPRS	mesomorphic
CEHIMMOOSSS	chemosmosis
CEHIMNNNOOP	nonphonemic
CEHIMNOOPRS	microphones
CEHIMNOOPRT	phonometric
CEHIMNOOPRX	xenomorphic
CEHIMNOPSTY	chimneypots
CEHIMOOOPTY	homoeotypic
CEHIMOOPRRX	xeromorphic
CEHIMOOPRTT	photometric
CEHIMOOSSST	schistosome
CEHIMOPPRST	coppersmith
CEHIMOPRSTY	hypsometric
	microphytes
CEHIMORSTTY	stichometry
CEHINNORSSY	synchronise
CEHINNORSYZ	synchronize
CEHINOOPRRS	coronership
CEHINOORRST	orchestrion
CEHINOPRSSS	censorships
CEHINOPRSSY	hypersonics

CEHINRRSSSU	currishness	CEIIKLQRSUV	quicksilver	CEILMNOOSUY	moneciously
CEHIOOOPPRT	photocopier	CEIIKNOSSTY	cytokinesis	CEILMNOTYYZ	enzymolytic
CEHIOOOPPST	photocopies	CEIIKNRSSST	tricksiness	CEILMOOOPST	colpotomies
CEHIOOOPRSS	horoscopies	CEIIKPRSSTT	spitsticker		cosmopolite
CEHIOOPSTTY	osteophytic	CEIILLLSSSY	Scilly Isles	CEILMOOOSST	colostomies
CEHIOORRRST	retrochoirs	CEIILLNNOST	centillions	CEILMOOOSTV	locomotives
CEHIOORSSTW	switcheroos	CEIILLNSUVY	inclusively	CEILMOOPSTY	compositely
CEHIOPRRSST	rectorships	CEIILMOPSST	polemicists	CEILMOORRTY	colorimetry
CEHIOPRSSTT	prosthetics	CEIILNNSSUV	uncivilness	CEILMOPRTUU	pomiculture
CEHKOOPPRRS	rockhoppers	CEIILNORSUV	inclusive or	CEILMOPSSTT	completists
CEHKOORSSST	stockhorses	CEIILNRTUUV	viniculture	CEILMOPSSUV	compulsives
CEHLLLOPRSY	sclerophyll	CEIILORSSTT	sclerotitis	CEILNNNOTTY	continently
CEHLMOOPRSY	polychromes	CEIILRTTUUV	viticulture	CEILNNNOOTV	connivently
CEHLMOPSTYY	lymphocytes	CEIILRTTUVY	reluctivity	CEILNNOOTVY	connotively
CEHMMNOOORS	monochromes	CEIILSTUVXY	exclusivity	CEILNNOOSSTU	unctionless
CEHMMOOORSS	chromosomes	CEIIMMNOSTU	communities	CEILNOOOTUV	coevolution
CEHMNOORRTY	chronometry	CEIIMMOORST	microtomies	CEILNOOPRTU	perlocution
CEHMOOPRSTY	cormophytes	CEIIMMORSSS	microseisms	CEILNOPRRTW	triple crown
CEHMOOSSTUU	customhouse	CEIIMNOOPTT	competition	CEILNORSSTU	courtliness
CEHMOPRSTYY	psychometry	CEIIMNOPSUU	impecunious	CEILNRSTUUV	ventriculus
CEHNNOSSTUU	uncouthness	CEIIMNORRTT	nitrometric	CEILOOPRSTT	protostelic
CEHNOOOPPSS	phonoscopes	CEIIMNORSTU	neuroticism	CEILOOPRTTU	luteotropic
CEHNOOPPRSY	nephroscopy	CEIIMNPRSSS	scrimpiness	CEILOOPRTTY	proteolytic
CEHNOOPRRST	necrotrophs	CEIIMOPRRST	spirometric	CEILOORRSTU	terricolous
CEHNOOPRSTT	topnotchers	CEIIMOPRSST	semitropics	CEILOORRSUV	versicolour
CEHNOOSSTTU	touchstones	CEIIMORRRTW	microwriter	CEILOORRSVY	corrosively
CEHNOPRSSTY	phenocrysts	CEIIINNNOTT	incontinent	CEIMMMNOSTT	commitments
CEHOOOPRSST	orthoscopes	CEIINNNORTU	internuncio	CEIMMNOQSUU	communiques
CEHOOPSSTTY	stethoscopy	CEIINNOPSST	inspections	CEIMMNORSSU	consumerism
CEHOORSSTUU	courthouses	CEIINNOSTTX	extinctions	CEIMMNORSTY	metronymics
CEHOPPRTTYY	cryptophyte	CEIINOPRSTV	voiceprints	CEIMMOOPRRS	compromiser
CEIIIINNNOT	Innocent III	CEIINORRRST	restriction	CEIMMOOPRSS	compromises
CEIIILLMNPU	penicillium	CEIINORSSSS	rescissions	CEIMMOORSTV	overcommits
CEIIILLNSST	illicitness	CEIINORSSTT	trisections	CEIMMORSSSU	commissures
CEIIILLPTTY	ellipticity	CEIINOSSSUV	viciousness	CEIMMORSTUX	commixtures
CEIIILMORST	melioristic	CEIINOSSTUV	viscounties	CEIMNNORSSS	crimsonness
CEIIILNNPTY	incipiently	CEIINOSSTUX	Six Counties	CEIMNOOPRSS	compression
CEIIILOPSST	politicises	CEIINRRSSTU	scrutiniser	CEIMNOOPRTU	mucoprotein
CEIIILOPSTZ	politicizes	CEIINRRSTUZ	scrutinizer	CEIMNOORSTU	coterminous
CEIIILOSSTW	Two Sicilies	CEIINRSSSTU	scrutinises	CEIMNOPRSSU	prosceniums
CEIIIMNOPRS	imprecision		sinecurists	CEIMNOPSTUV	consumptive
CEIIIMNOSST	misoneistic	CEIINRSSSTUZ	scrutinizes	CEIMNORSSTU	consumerist
CEIIIMOSSSS	isoseismics	CEIINRSTTUV	instructive		misconstrue
CEIIIMPRSST	empiricists	CEIIOPPRSTU	precipitous	CEIMNRSSSTY	syncretisms
CEIIIMPSSST	pessimistic	CEIIORRRSTT	terroristic	CEIMOOOSSTT	costotomies
CEIIIMRSSTV	victimisers	CEIIORSSTVV	vivisectors	CEIMOOPRRSS	microspores
CEIIIMRSTVZ	victimizers	CEIIORSTUVY	voyeuristic	CEIMOOPRSTT	competitors
CEIIINNRSTV	vincristine	CEIIPPRSTUV	perspicuity	CEIMOOSSTTY	cystotomies
CEIIINNRSTY	insincerity	CEIJNOOPRST	projections	CEINNNOOSTT	contentions
CEIIINNSSTV	instinctive	CEIJNORSSTU	surjections	CEINNNOOSTV	conventions
CEIIINOPRTT	peritonitic	CEIKKORRSST	kicksorters	CEINNOORSSU	connoisseur
CEIIINORSTU	cineritious	CEIKLNNSSUU	unluckiness	CEINNOORSSV	conversions
CEIIINOSTVV	vivisection	CEIKLNOORRT	crinkleroot	CEINNOOSTTU	contentious
CEIIINPRSTV	inscriptive	CEIKLOORSSU	cokulorises	CEINNOPRSTY	encryptions
CEIIIOPRSTT	periostitic	CEIKLOPRSST	stockpilers	CEINNOPSTUX	expunctions
CEIIIORSSTU	curiosities	CEIKLOPRTTU	leptokurtic	CEINNORTTUY	intercounty
CEIIIOSSSTV	viscosities	CEIKNNORSTU	countersink	CEINNOSTTTU	constituent
CEIIIOSSTTV	sovietistic	CEILLLNOOOV	violoncello	CEINOOPRSSS	processions
CEIIJLOORTU	Joliot-Curie	CEILMMNOPST	compliments	CEINOOPRSTT	stenotropic
CEIIKLLPSTT	lickspittle	CEILMMOPRUY	promycelium	CEINOOPRSTU	prosecution
CEIIKLNPRSS	prickliness	CEILMNOOPST	completions	CEINOOPRSTY	retinoscopy
CEIIKLOOPTY	poikilocyte	CEILMNOOPSX	complexions	CEINOOPSSSU	copiousness

CEINOOPTTTY	totipotency
CEINOPRSSSU	percussions
	supersonics
CEINOPRSSTT	introspects
CEINOPRSSTU	supertonics
CEINORRSSSU	cursoriness
CEINORSSSUU	curiousness
CEINORSSTTT	cornettists
CEINORSTTTU	constituter
CEINOSSSSUV	viscousness
CEINOSSSTUV	viscountess
CEINOSSTTTU	constitutes
CEINRSSSTTY	syncretists
CEIOOPRTTYZ	cryptozoite
CEIOORSSSTT	scooterists
CEIOORSSTTU	ecotourists
CEIOPPRSSUU	perspicuous
CEIOPRRSTWY	copywriters
CEIORRSTUVY	verrucosity
CEIPPRRSSTU	superscript
CEIPPRSSTTY	typescripts
CEKLMPRSSUU	lumpsuckers
CEKNNORSTUU	countersunk
CEKNOORRTUW	counterwork
CEKOORSSTTU	stockroutes
CELLMOOPRRT	comptroller
CELLNOORRST	controllers
CELLNOORSSU	counsellors
CELLNOOTUVY	convolutely
CELLNOPRTUY	corpulently
CELLNRTTUUY	truculently
CELLOOOSSST	closestools
CELMNOORTUU	monoculture
CELMOOPRSTT	complotters
CELMOOPRTYY	pylorectomy
CELNOOPRTTU	counterplot
CELOOPRRSTU	colporteurs
CELOORSTUUY	courteously
CEMMNOOPRTT	comportment
CEMNOORSTUV	covermounts
CEMOOPRRSSS	compressors
CENNOOPRRSU	pronouncers
CENNOOSSSUU	nocuousness
CENOORRSTTV	controverts
CENOORRSTVY	controversy
CENOORSTUUU	uncourteous
CENOPRRSSTU	corruptness
CENORSTTUWY	West Country
CEOOPPRRSST	prospectors
CEOOPRRSSTU	prosecutors
CEPRRSSTTUU	superstruct
CFFGIINRTUY	fructifying
CFFIIINOOSU	inofficious
CFFIILOOSUY	officiously
CFFIINOOSUU	unofficious
CFGHIILLNNY	flinchingly
CFGHIILNNNU	unflinching
CFGHIMNOORT	forthcoming
CFGIIIILNSY	silicifying
CFGIINNNOTU	functioning
CFGILNNOSUY	confusingly
CFGINNNOORT	confronting

CFHIILNOOSS	ichnofossil
CFIIILLNNOST	inflictions
CFIIINOSSTT	fictionists
CFIILMOORSS	microfossil
CFIILMORSTU	formulistic
CFIMNOORSST	conformists
CFLLLOORUUY	colourfully
CFLNOORTUWY	Flow Country
CFLNORSUUUU	furunculous
CFLOOOPRSUY	fluoroscopy
CFLORSTUUUY	fructuously
CGGHIIINOST	gothicising
CGGHIIINOTZ	gothicizing
CGGHIILOOPR	logogriphic
CGGIIIKNPST	pigsticking
CGGIILMMNNO	commingling
CGGIILNNRSU	surcingling
CGGIINOORST	gongoristic
CGHHHIIIKNT	hitchhiking
CGHHILOOTYY	ichthyology
CGHHIOPRTYY	hygrophytic
CGHIIIMNSTY	mythicising
CGHIIIMNTYZ	mythicizing
CGHIILMORST	microlights
CGHIILRSSTW	switchgirls
CGHIINPPRRU	chirrupping
CGHILLNOSUY	slouchingly
CGHILLOORSS	schoolgirls
CGHILMOOOPR	morphologic
CGHILOOORST	chorologist
CGHILOOPSTY	phycologist
CGHILOORSTY	Christology
CGHIMNOORST	shortcoming
CGHIMOOOTYZ	homozygotic
CGHIMOOPRYZ	zygomorphic
CGIIIIMNSTV	victimising
CGIIIIMNTVZ	victimizing
CGIIIKLNOPT	politicking
CGIIIKNNPPR	pinpricking
CGIIILNSSTU	linguistics
CGIIILRSTTU	liturgistic
CGIIIMNOSTV	cognitivism
CGIIKLLNORS	rollickings
CGIIKLLNRTY	tricklingly
CGIIKLNOPST	stockpiling
CGIIKLNOPSU	liposucking
CGIILLNOOSU	lignicolous
CGIILLNPPRY	cripplingly
CGIILLOSSTY	syllogistic
CGIILMMNOOU	immunologic
CGIILMNOORY	criminology
CGIILMOOTVY	victimology
CGIILNNNOVY	connivingly
CGIILNNNSUU	cunnilingus
CGIILNOOOST	iconologist
CGIILNOORSU	colourising
CGIILNOORUZ	colourizing
CGIILOOOSST	sociologist
CGIIMMNNOSU	communising
CGIIMMNNOTU	comminuting
CGIIMMNNOUZ	communizing
CGIIMNNOSTU	miscounting

CGIIMNOOPST	compositing
CGIIMNOSSTU	customising
CGIIMNOSTUZ	customizing
CGIINNORTUY	incongruity
CGIINNRSTTU	instructing
CGIINOPRTWY	copywriting
CGIKLMMNOOS	slommocking
CGIKNNORTUY	King Country
CGILLNNOORT	controlling
CGILLNNOOSY	consolingly
CGILMNNOSUY	consumingly
CGILMNOOPTT	complotting
CGILMOOOSST	cosmologist
CGILMOOSSTY	mycologists
CGILNNOOTUV	convoluting
CGILNOOOSST	oncologists
CGILNPRSTUU	sculpturing
CGILOOSSTTY	cytologists
CGIMNOOOSST	cosmogonist
CGINNNOOPRU	pronouncing
CGINNOORSUU	incongruous
CGINOOPPRTU	outcropping
CGINOOPRSST	prognostics
CGINOORSSTU	outcrossing
CGINOORSTUU	outsourcing
CGINNRSTTUU	structuring
CGLNOORSUUY	congruously
CHHIILOOPPS	philosophic
CHHIILOPTTY	lithophytic
CHHIIMORSTY	isorhythmic
CHHIIMRTTYY	rhythmicity
CHHIINORSTY	ichthyornis
CHHILLMOOPY	homophyllic
CHHILMOOOPR	holomorphic
CHHIMMOOOPR	homomorphic
CHHIMOSTTYY	stichomythy
CHHIOORSTTY	orthostichy
CHHLLLOOPRY	chlorophyll
CHIIIMORSST	historicism
CHIIINORSST	histrionics
	trichinosis
CHIIIORSSTT	historicist
CHIIIORSTTY	historicity
CHIILLNOOTT	octillionth
CHIILOOPPRT	protophilic
CHIILOOPRTT	protolithic
CHIILOOSTYZ	hylozoistic
CHIILOPPRSY	scripophily
CHIIMNOORSS	isochronism
CHIIMNOSTWZ	Nimzowitsch
CHIINNOPSSU	pincushions
CHIINOPPRSU	porcupinish
CHIINORRTTY	tyrothricin
CHIIOOPRTTX	thixotropic
CHIIOPPRRTY	porphyritic
CHIIORRSSTY	scirrhosity
CHIIORSSTTU	tristichous
CHIIOSSSTTY	schistosity
CHIKNOQRSTU	quickthorns
CHILLMOPRSY	microphylls
CHILMOOPPRY	polymorphic
CHILNOPSSSU	consulships

CHILOOPPRRTY	polytrophic
CHILOORSTUU	ulotrichous
CHIMMNOOOOPR	monomorphic
CHIMNNORSSY	synchronism
CHIMNOOPPPY	hypnopompic
CHIMNOOPRRS	prochronism
CHIMOOPRSSY	hypocorisms
CHINOOORSSU	isochronous
CHIOOOPPRTT	phototropic
CHIOOOPRRTT	orthotropic
CHIOOPPRSTY	sporophytic
CHIOOPRRTTY	tropophytic
CHIORSSTTTW	stitchworts
CHMNOOOTTTU	cottonmouth
CHMNOOPSTTU	muttonchops
CHMOOOPRSTY	psychomotor
CHNNOORRSTY	synchrotron
CHNNOORSSUY	synchronous
CIIIIKKKLLN	killikinick
CIIIIKKNNNS	kinnikinics
CIIIIPRSSTT	spiritistic
CIIILLMMNOR	millimicron
CIIILLMOPTY	impoliticly
CIIILLNOSTT	tonsillitic
CIIILNSTUVY	inclusivity
CIIILOPSSST	solipsistic
CIIILRSTTUU	utriculitis
CIIIMNORTTU	micturition
CIIINNOPRST	inscription
CIIINOOSTTY	isotonicity
CIIINORSTUY	incuriosity
CIIJNNNOSTU	injunctions
CIIKKNNOPST	knickpoints
CIILLMORSUV	microvillus
CIILLNNOSST	scintillons
CIILLNOOSTU	illocutions
CIILLOORSTT	torticollis
CIILMMNNOOS	monoclinism
CIILNOOPSTU	liposuction
CIILNOPSTUU	punctilious
CIILNORSUUY	incuriously
CIIMMNNOOTU	comminution
CIIMMNOOSSS	commissions
CIIMMOORSTT	microtomist
CIIMMOPRRSS	microprisms
CIIMNOPRRST	microprints
CIIMNRSSTTU	misinstruct
CIIMOPRRSTU	scriptorium
CIIMOPRSTUY	promiscuity
CIIINNNOOPST	conniptions
CIIINNORSTTU	instruction
CIIOOPRSSUV	piscivorous
CILLMOOQSUU	colloquiums
CILLOOQSSTU	colloquists
CILMNNOOOSU	monoclinous
CILMNOOOSUY	monoicously
CILMNOOPSSU	compulsions
CILNNOOOTUV	convolution
CILNNOOSSUV	convulsions
CILNNOOSUUY	innocuously
CILNOOOPRTU	colourpoint

CILNOPRRTUY	incorruptly
CIMNNOOOOPPS	nincompoops
CIMNNOOPSTU	consumption
CIMOOOPRSST	compositors
CIMOOPRSSUU	promiscuous
CIMOPRSSTUU	scrumptious
CINNOOORSTT	contortions
CINOOPRRSTU	corruptions
CINOORSTTTU	constitutor
CINORRSSTTU	instructors
CIOOPRSSSTU	uroscopists
CIOOPRSSTTT	protoctists
CIOPPRSSSTT	postscripts
CKKNORSSTUW	knockwursts
CLLNOOSUUVV	convolvulus
CLOOOPPRRSTU	prolocutors
CNNOOOORRRY	Rory
	O'Connor
DDDDEEEEEFIL	fiddlededee
DDDEEFIOSST	eisteddfods
DDDEEFNNRUU	underfunded
DDDEEGIMOSS	demigoddess
DDDEEGINRRU	undergirded
DDDEEIINSSV	dividedness
DDDEELMNSSU	muddledness
DDDGEHOOOSS	goddesshood
DDDEGIIOORS	didgeridoos
DDDEHLOOORT	toddlerhood
DDDENNOORTW	downtrodden
DDEEEEFIRRZ	freeze-dried
DDEEEEHNPRR	reprehended
DDEEEEILRRV	redelivered
DDEEEEIMSST	disesteemed
DDEEEEELOPRV	redeveloped
DDEEEGHHOPP	hedgehopped
DDEEEGINPRS	predesigned
DDEEEGIPRST	predigested
DDEEEHILLSV	dishevelled
DDEEEHNORTY	heterodyned
DDEEEILMNRT	intermeddle
DDEEEILNRSS	slenderised
DDEEEILNRSZ	slenderized
DDEEEIMNNOST	demonetised
DDEEEIMNOTZ	demonetized
DDEEEIMPRST	distempered
DDEEEINNNPT	independent
DDEEEINNPRT	interdepend
DDEEEINPRST	predestined
DDEEEIOPRST	redeposited
DDEEEIPPSST	sidestepped
DDEEEIRSSSS	sidedresses
DDEEELLORRW	well-ordered
DDEEELNNPTY	dependently
DDEEELNOPUV	undeveloped
DDEEENOSSTV	devotedness
DDEEENRRRSU	surrendered
DDEEEORRSSV	overdressed
DDEEFIIIMNN	indemnified
DDEEFIIINRT	denitrified
DDEEFIIIRSV	diversified
DDEEFIIIRTV	devitrified
DDEEFIILMSU	demulsified

DDEEFIIMNNU	definiendum
DDEEFIIMSTY	demystified
DDEEFIINSST	disinfested
DDEEFILNORT	interfolded
DDEEFIMORSS	semifreddos
DDEEFIORSST	disforested
DDEEGGHOOPS	hodgepodges
DDEEGHILLTY	delightedly
DDEEGINNRSU	undersigned
DDEEGNOPRSU	groundspeed
DDEEHIILRSS	disrelished
DDEEHINRSSS	reddishness
DDEEIILNSTT	disentitled
DDEEIILPPSS	sideslipped
DDEEIIMNNOS	dimensioned
DDEEIINNSTW	disentwined
DDEEIINORST	disoriented
DDEEIINRRST	disinterred
DDEEIINRSSW	sidewinders
DDEEIINSSTV	disinvested
DDEEIIORSSX	deoxidisers
DDEEIIORSXZ	deoxidizers
DDEEIIQSTUU	disquietude
DDEEIKNNRSS	kindredness
DDEEILORSSV	redissolved
DDEEILPRSSY	dispersedly
DDEEINNNPRU	underpinned
DDEEINORSSW	disendowers
DDEEINSSSTU	studiedness
DDEEIOORRSS	deodorisers
DDEEIOORRSZ	deodorizers
DDEEIOPPRSS	predisposed
DDEENNORSSU	roundedness
DDEENNPRSSU	underspends
DDEENOQRTUU	underquoted
DDEENORSTUY	understroyed
DDEEOOPPRST	doorstepped
DDEFFIILNTY	diffidently
DDEFGIIILNY	dignifiedly
DDEFGIIINNU	undignified
DDEFHLNORSU	fundholders
DDEFINOPRSU	de profundis
DDEFLNNOUUY	unfoundedly
DDEGHNOTTUU	doughnutted
DDEGIIINOSX	deoxidising
DDEGIIINOXZ	deoxidizing
DDEGIILMSUY	misguidedly
DDEGIILSSUY	disguisedly
DDEGINNNOSW	disendowing
DDEGIINOORS	deodorising
DDEGINOORZ	deodorizing
DDEGIINORRS	disordering
DDEGINNSSUU	undisguised
DDEGILMNOST	dislodgment
DDEGILNRSTU	disgruntled
DDEGILSSTUY	disgustedly
DDEGNNORRUU	underground
DDEHHIIOPRT	diphtheroid
DDEHIIIPPPS	Phidippides
DDEHIIKNPRS	kindredship
DDEHIIKNSSS	kiddishness
DDEHIILNSSW	windshields

DDEHIILPSSU	disulphides	DEEEGHIORVW	overweighed	DEEEELMNOPTV	development
DDEHIINRSSW	widdershins	DEEEEGIIMRSV	demivierges	DEEEELMNOTVV	devolvement
DDEHINOORSU	dishonoured	DEEEEGIMORST	geometrised	DEEEELNNPRST	resplendent
DDEHIOOOPST	photodiodes	DEEEEGIMORTZ	geometrized	DEEEELNNRSSS	slenderness
DDEHLMOOTUU	loudmouthed	DEEEGINOSXY	deoxygenise	DEEEELNNSSSS	endlessness
DDEIILNSSTY	dissidently	DEEEGINOXYZ	deoxygenize	DEEEELNORSSS	nesselrodes
DDEIIMNNOSU	diminuendos	DEEEGIRRSST	deregisters	DEEEELNORTUV	volunteered
DDEIIOPRSSS	dispersoids	DEEEGMNNORS	mondegreens	DEEEELNPPRUX	unperplexed
DDEIKNNRSUW	wunderkinds	DEEEGMNNSTU	unsegmented	DEEEELNRRTTU	underletter
DDEILNOSSUV	undissolved	DEEEHHPRSSS	shepherdess	DEEEELOOPPRV	overpeopled
DDEILORSTTY	distortedly	DEEEHIINNPT	phenetidine	DEEEELOOPRVV	overdevelop
DDEINNOOSTT	endodontist	DEEEHILNPRS	replenished	DEEEELPRRTVY	pervertedly
DDELNNOORRY	Londonderry	DEEEHILPSST	slipsheeted	DEEEEMNNORST	endorsement
DDELNORRSUW	underworlds	DEEEHIMNRST	intermeshed	DEEEEMNNOSTT	denotements
DDEOPRRSSTU	rudderposts	DEEEHLMORVW	overwhelmed	DEEEEMNNOSTU	denouements
DDFGHILNNOU	fundholding	DEEEHLNNORT	heldentenor	DEEEEMNNOSYZ	endoenzymes
DDFGIMNNOUU	dumfounding	DEEEHLNRSTU	unsheltered	DEEEEMNORSSV	removedness
DDIIKLNSTWY	tiddlywinks	DEEEHMNOSST	Demosthenes	DEEEEMPRTTUW	trumpetweed
DEEEEEFHLRW	freewheeled	DEEEHNORSTY	heterodynes	DEEEEMRRSSSU	murderesses
DEEEEEFPRSZ	deepfreezes	DEEEIIMRRST	semiretired	DEEEENOOSSWZ	sneezewoods
DEEEEELMRTT	telemetered	DEEEIINNPTX	inexpedient	DEEEENOPRSUX	underexpose
DEEEEELNTVV	velveteened	DEEEIINRTVW	interviewed	DEEEENOPRSSSX	exposedness
DEEEEFLNSSS	defenseless	DEEEIINSSTS	desensitise	DEEEENORSTVX	overextends
DEEEEGNNRRS	engenderers	DEEEIINSSTZ	desensitize	DEEEENPRSSUX	unexpressed
DEEEEHILRSW	sidewheeler	DEEEIIRSTTX	dexterities	DEEEENRRRRSU	surrenderer
DEEEEHIMPRS	ephemerides	DEEEIKLLRSW	weedkillers	DEEEENRRSSTU	understeers
DEEEEHIMRSU	euhemerised	DEEEILLMOSS	demoiselles	DEEEENRRSTTT	trendsetter
DEEEEHIMRUZ	euhemerized	DEEEILLNNST	sentinelled	DEEEEOOPRRVW	overpowered
DEEEEHNPRRR	reprehender	DEEEILLNPPZ	Led Zeppelin	DEEEEOOPRSVX	overexposed
DEEEEIMNRRT	redetermine	DEEEILLNRSS	elderliness	DEEEEOPPRSTV	overstepped
DEEEEINORRT	orienteered	DEEEILMMNPT	implemented	DEEEEOPRSSSS	repossessed
DEEEELMNNOW	needlewomen	DEEEILMMNUV	mendelevium	DEEEEOPRSTTY	stereotyped
DEEEELOPRRV	redeveloper	DEEEILNNOPT	needlepoint	DEEEEORRRRST	reredorters
DEEEEMOPRST	speedometer	DEEEILNPTXY	expediently	DEEEEORRRTTV	retroverted
DEEEENNSTUW	unsweetened	DEEEILNRSSS	slenderises	DEEEEORRSSSV	overdresses
DEEEENPRRST	represented	DEEEILNRSSZ	slenderizes	DEEEEORRTTVX	extroverted
DEEEEORRSTV	oversteered	DEEEILORSTU	deleterious	DEEEEPRRSSST	prestressed
DEEEEORRTVX	overexerted	DEEEILRSSVW	silverweeds	DEEEEPRRSSSU	superseders
DEEEEQRSSTU	sequestered	DEEEIMNNORT	remonetised	DEEEEPRRSSUU	supersedure
DEEEFGINORV	overfeeding	DEEEIMNORTZ	remonetized	DEEEFFGINNOR	forefending
DEEEFHLNSSU	heedfulness	DEEEIMNOSST	demonetizes	DEEEFFIINNRT	indifferent
DEEEFHLORRS	freeholders	DEEEIMNOSTZ	demonetizes	DEEEFFIIORRT	refortified
DEEEFHNNRSU	unrefreshed	DEEEIMNNRRST	determiners	DEEEFFILNRTY	differently
DEEEFIILMPX	exemplified	DEEEIMNRSST	densimeters	DEEEFFINSSSU	diffuseness
DEEEFIILMRS	demireliefs	DEEEIMORSTU	eudiometers	DEEEFFIOOPRR	fireproofed
DEEEFILMNST	defilements	DEEEINNOPSTV	pendentives	DEEEFFORSTUV	overstuffed
DEEEFILNSVY	defensively	DEEEINPRRTT	interpreted	DEEEFGGILLNS	fledgelings
DEEEFIMRSSW	swimfeeders	DEEEINPRSST	predestines	DEEEFGGIOPTT	pettifogged
DEEEFINORRV	overrefined	DEEEINPRTUX	expenditure	DEEEFGHHORTU	feedthrough
DEEEFINRSTW	winterfeeds	DEEEINRRSST	tenderisers	DEEEFGHIORST	foresighted
DEEEFIOPRRT	profiteered	DEEEINRRSSV	vinedresser	DEEEFGILNORW	deflowering
DEEEFKNOORT	foretokened	DEEEINRRSTZ	tenderizers	DEEEFGINORST	deforesting
DEEEFLNNSSU	needfulness	DEEEINRSSSV	diverseness	DEEEFHIILSSV	devilfishes
DEEEFLORRSW	deflowerers	DEEEINRSSTU	eruditeness	DEEEFHILTTTW	Twelfthtide
DEEEFLORRTX	retroflexed	DEEEINRSSTW	westernised	DEEEFHINRRSU	refurnished
DEEEFMNNRTU	unfermented	DEEEINRSTWZ	westernized	DEEEFIIIMNNR	indemnifier
DEEEFMNRRSU	referendums	DEEEIPPRSST	sidestepper	DEEEFIIIMNNS	indemnifies
DEEEFORRSST	deforesters	DEEEKLLNNNU	unkennelled	DEEEFIIINNST	intensified
DEEEGGINNNR	engendering	DEEEKLNORSW	needleworks	DEEEFIIINRST	denitrifies
DEEEGHHOPPR	hedgehopper	DEEEKOOPRRS	doorkeepers		identifiers
DEEEGHILNNT	enlightened	DEEELLNRRSU	underseller	DEEEFIIINSTV	definitives
		DEEELMNNORY	moneylender	DEEEFIIIRRSV	diversifier

647

DEEFIIIRSSV	diversifies	
DEEFIIIRSTV	devitrifies	
DEEFIILMNNS	infieldsmen	
DEEFIILMNOS	solemnified	
DEEFIILMRSU	demulsifier	
DEEFIILMSSU	demulsifies	
DEEFIILNRST	friendliest	
DEEFIIMORST	deformities	
DEEFIIMSSTY	demystifies	
DEEFIINOPRS	personified	
DEEFIINRSVW	viewfinders	
DEEFIKLORRW	fieldworker	
DEEFILMNNRU	Dunfermline	
DEEFILNORTW	interflowed	
DEEFILNOSST	fieldstones	
DEEFILORSTU	outfielders	
DEEFILPRRVY	perfervidly	
DEEFINORRSX	ferredoxins	
DEEFIORRTTT	retrofitted	
DEEFLLNOSSU	dolefulness	
DEEFLMNNOST	enfoldments	
DEEFLOPRSSY	professedly	
DEEFMNOPRRU	unperformed	
DEEFNOORSTT	tenderfoots	
DEEFNOPRSSU	unprofessed	
DEEFNOPRTUY	typefounder	
DEEGGIINNRS	redesigning	
DEEGGIINRST	redigesting	
DEEGGLLOORY	Lloyd George	
DEEGGLNOOOS	golden goose	
DEEGHHINPRS	shepherding	
DEEGHIILNSV	disheveling	
DEEGHILLNWY	wheedlingly	
DEEGHILNOOP	pigeonholed	
DEEGHILOOST	theologised	
DEEGHILOOTZ	theologized	
DEEGHIMNOOS	homogenised	
DEEGHIMNOOZ	homogenized	
DEEGHINORSY	hydrogenise	
DEEGHINORTV	overnighted	
DEEGHINORYZ	hydrogenize	
DEEGHINRTUW	underweight	
DEEGHNORSTU	groundsheet	
DEEGIIILMST	legitimised	
DEEGIIILMTZ	legitimized	
DEEGIIINSTV	indigestive	
DEEGIILSTVY	digestively	
DEEGIIMNNOR	domineering	
DEEGIIMNNRT	determining	
DEEGIINNRST	ingredients	
	tenderising	
DEEGIINNRTZ	tenderizing	
DEEGIINORST	redigestion	
DEEGIINRSSV	dissevering	
DEEGILLMNOR	remodelling	
DEEGILLNPSS	spindlelegs	
DEEGILMNOPR	empoldering	
DEEGILMNORS	mongrelised	
DEEGILMNORZ	mongrelized	
DEEGILMNTUV	divulgement	
DEEGILNOPRY	redeploying	
DEEGILNORUV	overindulge	
DEEGILNRSVY	deservingly	
DEEGILNRTVY	divergently	
DEEGILNRUVY	gerundively	
DEEGIMNORSV	misgoverned	
DEEGIMORSUU	demiurgeous	
DEEGINNORST	rontgenised	
DEEGINNORTZ	rontgenized	
DEEGINNRSUV	undeserving	
DEEGINORSSS	degressions	
DEEGINORSTV	stevedoring	
DEEGINPRSSU	superseding	
DEEGJMNPRTU	prejudgment	
DEEGLNORSSY	engrossedly	
DEEGLNOSSSS	godlessness	
DEEHHILNNNO	Hohenlinden	
DEEHHLLOORSU	householder	
DEEHHOPRRSY	hydrosphere	
DEEHIILRSSS	disrelishes	
DEEHIIMPRSU	hesperidium	
DEEHIIRRSST	hereditists	
DEEHILLORTT	titleholder	
DEEHILMNOTU	endothelium	
DEEHILMORSS	demolishers	
DEEHILOOPRT	heteroploid	
DEEHILOOSTT	theodolites	
DEEHILOSTTU	silhouetted	
DEEHIMNOPRS	premonished	
DEEHIMNORST	methodisers	
DEEHIMORSTZ	methodizers	
DEEHINOOPSV	videophones	
DEEHINOPSTY	dehypnotise	
DEEHINOPTYZ	dehypnotize	
DEEHINOSSSU	hideousness	
DEEHINRRSSU	hurriedness	
DEEHINSSSTY	synthesised	
DEEHINSSTTY	synthetised	
DEEHINSSTYZ	synthesized	
DEEHINSTTYZ	synthetized	
DEEHLLMOPRS	phelloderms	
DEEHLMNNOSS	Mendelssohn	
DEEHLMNRSUW	underwhelms	
DEEHLMOORTY	model theory	
DEEHLNORRTW	netherworld	
DEEHLOPRSTU	upholstered	
DEEHLPRSTUU	sulphureted	
DEEHMNNOOOY	honeymooned	
DEEHMNOOPTU	openmouthed	
DEEHMNOPRRY	hypermodern	
DEEHMOORRTY	hydrometeor	
DEEHMORRSTY	hydrometers	
DEEHNOOORSW	Wooden Horse	
DEEIIIMNNST	indemnities	
DEEIIIRSSTV	diversities	
DEEIIKLLMSS	semiskilled	
DEEIIKLNNRT	interlinked	
DEEIILLOPST	lepidolites	
DEEIILMNSST	limitedness	
DEEIILMNSSU	disseminule	
DEEIILNOPRS	lepidosiren	
DEEIILNPRSV	vilipenders	
DEEIILNSSTT	disentitles	
DEEIILOPRSY	erysipeloid	

DEEIILORSST	siderolites	
DEEIILPSTUX	duplexities	
DEEIILRSSSV	silversides	
DEEIIMMNPST	impediments	
DEEIIMMNRST	determinism	
DEEIIMNNSTT	inditements	
DEEIIMNOPTT	piedmontite	
DEEIIMNORST	modernities	
DEEIIMNPSST	dissepiment	
DEEIIMNRRST	irredentism	
DEEIIMNRSSS	minidresses	
DEEIIMNRSTT	determinist	
DEEIIMNRTTT	intermitted	
DEEIINNORTV	inventoried	
DEEIINNRTTW	intertwined	
DEEIINNSSTT	dissentient	
DEEIINNSSTW	disentwines	
DEEIINOPSTX	expeditions	
DEEIINPRSTY	serendipity	
DEEIINRRSTT	irredentist	
DEEIINRRSTT	disinterest	
DEEIIOPSTUX	expeditious	
DEEIIOQSSUX	sesquioxide	
DEEIIPRSSSW	sideswipers	
DEEIIRSTTUV	divestiture	
DEEIJNNOSST	jointedness	
DEEIKLLORSV	volkslieder	
DEEIKMNPPSU	pumpkinseed	
DEEIKNORRTW	interworked	
DEEIKORSSST	sidestrokes	
DEEILLMPTUX	multiplexed	
DEEILLOPRSV	overspilled	
DEEILLQRRSU	squirrelled	
DEEILMMOPSY	misemployed	
DEEILMMNOPST	despoilment	
DEEILMNRSTW	wilderments	
DEEILMOPRSY	polymerised	
DEEILMOPRYZ	polymerized	
DEEILNNNRSU	underlinens	
DEEILNNORST	tenderloins	
DEEILNNORVY	nondelivery	
DEEILNNQSTU	delinquents	
DEEILNOPTUX	unexploited	
DEEILNORSS	orderliness	
DEEILNORTVV	intervolved	
DEEILNSSSTT	stiltedness	
DEEILOPPPTY	polypeptide	
DEEILORSSSV	redissolves	
DEEIMMNORTU	endometrium	
DEEIMMRSSTY	symmetrised	
DEEIMMRSTYZ	symmetrized	
DEEIMNNNOTU	unmentioned	
DEEIMNNNSTT	intendments	
DEEIMNNORST	indorsement	
DEEIMNNORUU	endoneurium	
DEEIMNNRRSU	underminers	
DEEIMNOPRST	redemptions	
DEEIMNNORSS	modernisers	
DEEIMNORRSZ	modernizers	
DEEIMNOSSTU	eudemonists	
	sedimentous	
DEEIMNOTTZZ	mezzotinted	

DEEIMNPRSSS	misspenders
DEEIMNPRSSU	unimpressed
DEEIMNRSSTW	stemwinders
DEEIMNSSTTV	divestments
DEEIMOOPRTT	dioptometer
DEEIMOPRRST	misreported
DEEIMOPRSSW	disempowers
DEEINNNOPSU	unpensioned
DEEINNNORST	nonresident
DEEINNOPSST	pointedness
DEEINNOSTTU	tendentious
DEEINNPRSTU	superintend
DEEINNSSTUW	unwitnessed
DEEINOPRRTV	overprinted
DEEINOPRSSS	depressions
DEEINORRSSU	overinsured
DEEINORRTTV	introverted
DEEINOSSSTU	tediousness
DEEINOSSSUV	deviousness
DEEINPRRTTU	interrupted
DEEINRRRTUW	underwriter
DEEINRRSTUW	underwrites
DEEINSSTTTV	vendettists
DEEIOOPRSTU	eurodeposit
DEEIOORRTTV	detritovore
DEEIOPPRSSS	predisposes
DEEIOPPRSST	predeposits
DEEIOPRSSUX	superoxides
DEEIORRSSTV	overstrides
DEEIPRRSSSU	pressurised
DEEIPRRSSUZ	pressurized
DEEIPRRSTUY	eurypterids
DEEKLMRSTTU	kettledrums
DEEKNNNRSSU	drunkenness
DEEKOORTTYU	deuterotoky
DEELMNOPSTY	deployments
DEELMNORTTY	tormentedly
DEELNNOOSST	selenodonts
DEELORRSTXY	dextrosely
DEELORSTTUV	turtledoves
DEELORSTUXY	dexterously
DEEMNNORSTW	wonderments
DEEMNOORTUY	Deuteronomy
DEEMNOSSSSY	syndesmoses
DEEMOORRSST	drosometers
DEEMOPRRTUV	overtrumped
DEENNOPRSST	respondents
DEENNSSSTTU	stuntedness
DEENOQRSTUU	underquotes
DEENORRSTUY	understorey
DEENOSSSTUU	duteousness
DEEOOPRRSSU	uredospores
DEEOPPPRSSU	presupposed
DEEOPRRRSSU	superorders
DEFFGINNNOU	unoffending
DEFFHIMORSS	sheriffdoms
DEFFIILSUVY	diffusively
DEFFIINORTU	unfortified
DEFFILLLNUU	unfulfilled
DEFGGIILNTY	fidgetingly
DEFGGIJNORU	forejudging
DEFGGLOOOST	footslogged

DEFGHIISTTT	tightfisted
DEFGHMOOORT	Mother of God
DEFGIIIMNNS	misdefining
DEFGIIINNTY	identifying
DEFGIILNNOS	goldfinnies
DEFGIILNPRS	Springfield
DEFGIILNRRS	girlfriends
DEFGIIMNORY	remodifying
DEFGIINNRTY	trendifying
DEFGIINOTXY	detoxifying
DEFGIIRRSSU	disfigurers
DEFGILNNORU	floundering
DEFGIMNOOOR	foredooming
DEFGINNORUV	overfunding
DEFGJMNORTU	forjudgment
DEFHHINOSSU	houndfishes
DEFHIIIMRSU	humidifiers
DEFHIINPRSS	friendships
DEFHINNNRSU	unfurnished
DEFHINPRSTT	spendthrift
DEFHIOORRSX	Oxfordshire
DEFHIORSSSW	swordfishes
DEFHLLMOPTU	fullmouthed
DEFHLMOOTUU	foulmouthed
DEFHMOOOPRT	mothproofed
DEFHORRRSTU	rutherfords
DEFIIILORSS	solidifiers
DEFIIIMNSTY	misidentify
DEFIIINNOST	definitions
DEFIIINNSTU	infinitudes
DEFIIJNSTUU	unjustified
DEFIIMMNORS	misinformed
DEFIIMORRSV	diversiform
DEFIINORRRU	fourdrinier
DEFILLORSWW	wildfowlers
DEFILMNNOST	infoldments
DEFILMNNSSU	mindfulness
DEFILNORSWW	windflowers
DEFILNSSTUU	dutifulness
DEFILPRSSUU	superfluids
DEFILRSSSTU	distressful
DEFINNRSSUW	windsurfers
DEFIOOORRSU	odoriferous
DEFIOORRSSU	dorsiferous
DEFLLNORUWY	wonderfully
DEFOOPSSTUY	pussyfooted
DEGGGIINRSU	ruggedising
DEGGGIINRUZ	ruggedizing
DEGGHHHIILT	highlighted
DEGGHILNOST	longsighted
DEGGHINOSSS	doggishness
DEGGIILNNSY	designingly
DEGGIINNRSU	undesigning
DEGGKLRSUUY	skulduggery
DEGHHOORSUU	roughhoused
DEGHIILMNOS	demolishing
DEGHIIMNOST	methodising
DEGHIIMNOTZ	methodizing
DEGHIINRRST	nightriders
DEGHILMNOOT	moonlighted
DEGHILMOOOS	homologised

DEGHILMOOOZ	homologized
DEGHILNORSU	shouldering
DEGHILNSTUY	unsightedly
DEGHILOPSTT	spotlighted
DEGHINNORSU	enshrouding
DEGHINNRSTU	underthings
DEGHINOSSTU	doughtiness
DEGHIORRRSU	roughriders
DEGHLMOOOTY	methodology
DEGHNOORSUY	hydrogenous
DEGHNOORXYY	oxyhydrogen
DEGHNORRTUW	undergrowth
DEGHOOOPRSW	gopherwoods
DEGIIIINNST	indignities
DEGIIILNNPV	vilipending
DEGIIINNOST	indigestion
DEGIIINPSSW	sideswiping
DEGIIINQSTU	disquieting
DEGIILLNOTU	guillotined
DEGIILMNOPR	impoldering
DEGIILNNNRU	underlining
DEGIILNNOSS	goldsinnies
DEGIILNOTTU	deglutition
DEGIILNRTVY	divertingly
DEGIILOOSST	ideologists
DEGIIMNNNRU	undermining
DEGIIMNNORS	modernising
DEGIIMNNORZ	modernizing
DEGIIMNNPSS	misspending
DEGIIMNOSTU	digoneutism
DEGIINNNRTU	indenturing
DEGIINNORVW	overwinding
DEGIINORRVV	overdriving
DEGIINORSSS	digressions
DEGIINRSSST	distressing
DEGIJMMNSTU	misjudgment
DEGIKLMNOSS	kingdomless
DEGILLNNTUY	indulgently
DEGILLNOPRY	deploringly
DEGILMNORSU	smouldering
DEGILMNOSUW	guildswomen
DEGILMNRSSU	mudslingers
DEGILNNOSSU	ungodliness
DEGILNORUVY	devouringly
DEGILNRSSTU	disgruntles
DEGILOOPRTY	pteridology
DEGILOOPSST	pedologists
DEGINNORSST	grindstones
DEGINOPRSST	topdressing
DEGKOPRRRSU	Krugersdorp
DEGLLNORSUW	groundswell
DEGLOORSTTY	troglodytes
DEGNNOORSTU	stoneground
DEGOOORSSUW	woodgrouses
DEHHIILMNOT	helminthoid
DEHHILMOORS	holohedrism
DEHHILNOOSW	Hinshelwood
DEHHILOPRSS	holderships
DEHHILOPRSY	hydrophiles
DEHHILORSTW	withholders
DEHHIMOORRS	hemorrhoids
DEHHLNOSTUU	sleuthhound

DEHHNOOPRSY	hydrophones	
DEHHOPRSTYY	hydrophytes	
DEHIIINOSTT	dithionites	
DEHIIINRSST	disinherits	
DEHIILLOOSV	livelihoods	
DEHIILLOPSY	lyophilised	
DEHIILLOPYZ	lyophilized	
DEHIILMNPSU	delphiniums	
DEHIILPRSTU	trisulphide	
DEHIIMNOPRS	prehominids	
DEHIINSTTUW	Whitsuntide	
DEHIIOOSSTU	Theodosius I	
DEHIIOPRSST	editorships	
DEHIKNOORSW	hoodwinkers	
DEHILLNOSSS	dollishness	
DEHILNNOOPS	indophenols	
DEHILNOSSST	doltishness	
DEHILNOSSTY	dishonestly	
DEHILNOSTTW	thistledown	
DEHILNRRUUY	unhurriedly	
DEHILOPPRVY	hyperploidy	
DEHILOPSUXY	oxysulphide	
DEHILPRSSUU	sulphurised	
DEHILPRSUUZ	sulphurized	
DEHIMMPSSSY	dysphemisms	
DEHIMOOPPRS	hippodromes	
DEHINNNOSSS	donnishness	
DEHINOORRSS	dishonorers	
DEHINOORRSU	dishonourer	
DEHINORRSUV	Hudson River	
DEHINORSSTT	threnodists	
DEHINPRSSSU	prudishness	
DEHINPSSTTU	studentship	
DEHINRRSSTU	undershirts	
DEHIOOOPPRT	photoperiod	
DEHIOOOPRRS	odoriphores	
DEHIOOORSTX	orthodoxies	
DEHIOOPRSTT	orthopedist	
DEHIOORSSST	sisterhoods	
DEHIOPRRSTY	pyrethroids	
DEHLNOOPRSY	polyhedrons	
DEHLORRSSYY	hydrolysers	
DEHLORRSYYZ	hydrolyzers	
DEHMMNRSSUU	humdrumness	
DEHMOOPPRSU	pseudomorph	
DEHNNORSSUU	nursehounds	
DEHNOOOOPRT	odontophore	
DEHNOOOORTX	neoorthodox	
DEHNOORSSTU	undershoots	
DEHNOORSSUU	roundhouses	
DEHNORRSSTU	undershorts	
DEHNRRSTTUU	underthrust	
DEIIIKMNRST	miniskirted	
DEIIILLSSUV	disillusive	
DEIIILMSSTU	similitudes	
DEIIILORSTV	vitriolised	
DEIIILORTVZ	vitriolized	
DEIIILQRSSU	liquidisers	
DEIIILQRSUZ	liquidizers	
DEIIIMNSTUV	diminutives	
DEIIIMOORST	iridotomies	
DEIIINNPSSS	insipidness	

DEIIINORSSV	redivisions	
DEIIINPRTTY	intrepidity	
DEIIIOPRRST	prioritised	
DEIIIOPRRTZ	prioritized	
DEIIIPSSTTU	stupidities	
DEIIJKNOORZ	Orjonikidze	
DEIILLLNUWY	unwieldlily	
DEIILLMNTUV	unlimitedly	
DEIILLORSUV	deliriously	
DEIILMNOOST	demolitions	
DEIILNOPRRY	pyrrolidine	
DEIILOSSTUV	dissolutive	
DEIILOSSTUY	seditiously	
DEIIMNOOSST	endomitosis	
DEIIMNOPRTV	improvident	
DEIIMNORTTT	intromitted	
DEIIMOORRST	dormitories	
DEIIMORSSTT	dosimetrist	
DEIIMORSSTU	moisturised	
DEIIMORSTUZ	moisturized	
DEIINNOSSSS	dissensions	
DEIINNOSSST	distensions	
DEIINNOSSTT	distentions	
DEIINOOPRSV	provisioned	
DEIINOOPSST	depositions	
DEIINOPRSSS	dispersions	
DEIINOSSSTU	dissentious	
DEIINOSTTTU	destitution	
DEIKMPPRSSU	mudskippers	
DEIKNNNORRS	nondrinkers	
DEIKNRRSSTU	underskirts	
DEILLMOOSUY	melodiously	
DEILLNORSSW	worldliness	
DEILLNOTUVY	involutedly	
DEILLORSTUY	desultorily	
DEILLOSSTUY	dissolutely	
DEILMNOOOPS	monopolised	
DEILMNOOOPZ	monopolized	
DEILMNOOSUU	unmelodious	
DEILMNPRTUY	imprudently	
DEILMOORRTY	dolorimetry	
DEILNOOSTUV	devolutions	
DEILNOPRTVY	providently	
DEILNOSSSTV	dissolvents	
DEILPRRSSUY	surprisedly	
DEIMMNNOPTU	impoundment	
DEIMMNNSTUU	indumentums	
DEIMMRSSTYY	dissymmetry	
DEIMNNOOOST	monotonised	
DEIMNNOOOTZ	monotonized	
DEIMNNOSSYY	synonymised	
DEIMNNOSYYZ	synonymized	
DEIMNOORRRS	minor orders	
DEIMNOSSSSY	syndesmosis	
DEIMOOPRTTY	dioptometry	
DEIMOPPRTTU	promptitude	
DEINOOPRSTY	ponderosity	
DEINOOSSTTX	exodontists	
DEINOPRSTTU	outsprinted	
DEINOPSSSSU	suspensoids	
DEINPRRSSUU	unsurprised	
DEIOPPRSTTU	outstripped	

DEIOPRSTTTU	prostituted	
DEIRRSSSTTU	distrusters	
DEKNOORRSWW	wonderworks	
DEKOOORRSWW	woodworkers	
DELLNOPSUUY	pendulously	
DELLNOSSSUY	soundlessly	
DELLOOOSWWY	yellowwoods	
DELMORRSUUY	murderously	
DELNOOPRSSU	splendorous	
DELNOOPRSTU	pleurodonts	
DELNOOPRSUY	ponderously	
DELNPPRSUUY	undersupply	
DELOPPRRSSU	Lord's Supper	
DELOPPRRTUY	purportedly	
DEMNNOOPSSU	modus ponens	
DEMNPRRSTUU	undertrumps	
DENNNOSSSUU	unsoundness	
DENNOORSTWW	downtowners	
DENOOOPRSSU	endosporous	
DENOOOORSSU	odorousness	
DENOOOPPRRS	propounders	
DENOPPRSTUU	unsupported	
DFFIIISTUVY	diffusivity	
DFGGIIIINRY	rigidifying	
DFGGIIINRSU	disfiguring	
DFGHIIIMNUY	humidifying	
DFGHILLOOST	floodlights	
DFGIIILNOSY	solidifying	
DFGIILLNOWW	wildfowling	
DFGIILNNOTW	downlifting	
DFGIINNRSUW	windsurfing	
DFGOOOPRRUX	Oxford Group	
DFHLOOOOPST	photofloods	
DFHLOOORSST	Lord of Hosts	
DFIILMOSTUU	multifidous	
DFILLMNNUUY	unmindfully	
DFILRSSTTUU	distrustful	
DFNOOOPRSSU	soundproofs	
DGGHIIINNRT	nightriding	
DGGHIINNOSV	Govind Singh	
DGGHINORRUY	roughdrying	
DGGIILLNNUY	indulgingly	
DGGIILMNNSU	mudslinging	
DGGILNNORSU	groundlings	
DGGINNOORSW	wrongdoings	
DGHHIILNOTW	withholding	
DGHHIKNOOST	knighthoods	
DGHIIIIMNNS	diminishing	
DGHIIINSSTU	distinguish	
DGHIIKNNOOW	hoodwinking	
DGHIINNOORS	dishonoring	
DGHIINNORRT	North Riding	
DGHILNORSYY	hydrolysing	
DGHILNORTWY	downrightly	
DGHILNORYYZ	hydrolyzing	
DGHILOORSTY	hydrologist	
DGHLNOORSST	strongholds	
DGHNOORSSUW	showgrounds	
DGIIIILNQSU	liquidising	
DGIIIILNQUZ	liquidizing	

DGIIIIMNSSU	Sigismund II	
DGIIIINPRST	dispiriting	
DGIIIJNNOST	disjointing	
DGIIILLMNNW	windmilling	
DGIIILOORST	iridologist	
DGIIINNOPSS	indisposing	
DGIIKNNORTU	outdrinking	
DGIILNNRTUY	intrudingly	
DGIILNOOPSS	podsolising	
DGIILNOOPSZ	podsolizing	
	podzolising	
DGIILNOOPZZ	podzolizing	
DGIIMNNOSTU	dismounting	
DGIINRSSTTU	distrusting	
DGIKNOOORWW	woodworking	
DGILLNORSSU	groundsills	
DGINNOOPPRU	propounding	
DGINNORRSUU	surrounding	
DGKNOORRSUW	groundworks	
DGLNOOPSTTY	glyptodonts	
DHHIOOPRTYY	hypothyroid	
DHIIIORSTTY	thyroiditis	
DHIIMMOPRSS	dimorphisms	
DHIIMOOSTTW	shittim wood	
	shittimwood	
DHIINOORSTW	withindoors	
DHILLNOOPPY	podophyllin	
DHILNOOQRUY	hydroquinol	
DHIMNOORUXY	hydroxonium	
DHINOOOPRST	ornithopods	
DHINOPRSSTY	dystrophins	
DHIOOOPRSUZ	rhizopodous	
DHIOOPPRRSY	porphyroids	
DHLOOPRXYYY	polyhydroxy	
DHMNOOORXYY	monohydroxy	
DHNNOOOORTX	nonorthodox	
DIIIIMNOSSV	divisionism	
DIIIINOSSTV	divisionist	
DIIILLNOSSU	disillusion	
DIIILNOSSUY	insidiously	
DIIILNOSUVY	invidiously	
DIIIMNNOSTU	diminutions	
DIIINOOPSST	disposition	
DIILLNOSSWW	windowsills	
DIILMNOTUWW	multiwindow	
DIILNOOSSTU	dissolution	
DIILNOPRSSY	spondylitis	
DIINOORSSTT	distortions	
DIINOPRSSTU	disruptions	
DIINORSSTUU	industrious	
DILMOOPSTUY	stylopodium	
EEEEEGKNPRR	greenkeeper	
EEEEFIISTWW	sweetiewife	
EEEEFILQRTU	teleferique	
EEEEFLRSTTT	Fleet Street	
EEEEGGINQSU	squeegeeing	
EEEEGLNNSST	genteelness	
EEEEGLNRSSV	revengeless	
EEEEHIMNPRT	hemiterpene	
EEEEHIMRSSU	euhemerises	
EEEEHIMRSUZ	euhemerizes	
EEEEHKLNOUW	Leeuwenhoek	

EEEEHKOPRSU	housekeeper	
EEEEHNNSTTV	seventeenth	
EEEEHORRSVW	wheresoever	
EEEEIINRTVW	interviewee	
EEEEIKMPRST	timekeepers	
EEEEIMNPRSW	minesweeper	
EEEEIMNRSST	mesenteries	
EEEEIPRSTTU	repetiteuse	
EEEEKOPRRST	storekeeper	
EEEELNPRSST	repleteness	
EEEELORSSVV	oversleeves	
EEEELRRSTTT	trestletree	
EEEEMNRSSTX	extremeness	
EEEENQRSSSU	queernesses	
EEEEPPPRRST	peppertrees	
EEEFFFMNNOT	enfeoffment	
EEEFFHILRTW	whiffletree	
EEEFFILORTW	Eiffel Tower	
EEEFFLNOSSS	offenseless	
EEEFGINPRRZ	prefreezing	
EEEFGLLNSSU	gleefulness	
EEEFHIJLSSW	jewelfishes	
EEEFHIKNRRT	freethinker	
EEEFHMNNRST	refreshment	
EEEFHOORRTT	theretofore	
EEEFIILMPRX	exemplifier	
EEEFIILMPSX	exemplifies	
EEEFIILRRVX	irreflexive	
EEEFILLRVXY	reflexively	
EEEFILNRSST	fertileness	
EEEFIMNNRST	refinements	
EEEFIMPRRSU	perfumeries	
EEEFINORRSV	overrefines	
EEEFINPRRSU	superrefine	
EEEFINRRRST	interferers	
EEEFINSSSTV	festiveness	
EEEFLLORRST	foretellers	
EEEFMNPRRST	preferments	
EEEFMOORRRV	forevermore	
EEEFNNRSSTV	ferventness	
EEEFNQRRSTU	frequenters	
EEEGGIINNNR	engineering	
EEEGGIINNRV	Vereeniging	
EEEGGMNNORT	engorgement	
EEEGHHINRST	heighteners	
EEEGHHINSTT	eighteenths	
EEEGHILNNRT	enlightener	
EEEGHIMNOST	eighteenmos	
EEEGHLNNRST	lengtheners	
EEEGHNORSSU	greenhouses	
EEEGHRRSTWY	greywethers	
EEEGIIKMNPT	timekeeping	
EEEGIILRSSU	religieuses	
EEEGIINPSST	epigenesist	
EEEGIINRSSU	seigneuries	
EEEGIKNNOSS	kenogenesis	
EEEGILLOOST	teleologies	
EEEGILMNSST	genteelisms	
EEEGILNRSST	singletrees	
EEEGILNRSTW	swingletree	
EEEGILOSTTX	geotextiles	
EEEGIMNNSSS	seemingness	

EEEGIMORSST	geometrises	
EEEGIMORSTZ	geometrizes	
EEEGINNNSSU	genuineness	
EEEGINNORST	roentgenise	
EEEGINNORTZ	roentgenize	
EEEGINNORVW	overweening	
EEEGINNOSSX	xenogenesis	
EEEGINNRRTW	wintergreen	
EEEGINNSSTW	sweetenings	
EEEGINPRRSV	persevering	
EEEGIPRRRST	preregister	
EEEGIRRRSST	registerers	
EEEGLMNNOTW	gentlewomen	
EEEGLNOORVY	venereology	
EEEGMOPRRTY	pyrgeometer	
EEEGNNORSST	greenstones	
EEEGNORSSSV	governesses	
EEEGORSSSTT	Grosseteste	
EEEHHILLLNP	philhellene	
EEEHHILOPRS	heliosphere	
EEEHHIMPRSS	hemispheres	
EEEHHLOSSUW	wheelhouses	
EEEHHNPRSTY	hypersthene	
EEEHIILNNPT	nephelinite	
EEEHIINNPPR	epinephrine	
EEEHIIPPRRS	peripheries	
EEEHILLNPRT	telpherline	
EEEHILMORST	heliometers	
EEEHILNPRRS	replenisher	
EEEHILNPRSS	replenishes	
EEEHILPPRTW	whippletree	
EEEHILPSSSS	lesseeships	
EEEHILRSSTV	shirtsleeve	
EEEHIMMRSSU	euhemerisms	
EEEHIMNOPPR	Oppenheimer	
EEEHIMNRSST	intermeshes	
	smithereens	
EEEHIMORRST	rheometries	
EEEHIMPRSSU	euphemisers	
EEEHIMPRSUZ	euphemizers	
EEEHIMRSSTU	euhemerists	
EEEHINNNSTT	nineteenths	
EEEHINPSSSV	peevishness	
EEEHINSSTTV	seventieths	
EEEHIRRRSTV	Three Rivers	
EEEHIRRSSST	heritresses	
EEEHKOPPRSS	shopkeepers	
EEEHLLRSSST	shelterless	
EEEHLNNOSST	nonetheless	
EEEHLNOPRST	telephoners	
EEEHLNOPSTY	polyethenes	
EEEHMMNNSST	enmeshments	
EEEHMMORRTT	thermometer	
EEEHMOPRRST	spherometer	
EEEHMPRRSTY	hypermeters	
EEEHNOQSSUU	Queen's	
	House	
EEEHNRSSSTT	sternsheets	
EEEHOPPRRST	treehoppers	
EEEHOPRRSSU	superheroes	
EEEIIJQRSTU	jequerities	
EEEIIKLNSST	telekinesis	

EEEIIKLRSTW	triweeklies	EEEINPRSSSW	winepresses	EEFGIINNRRT	interfering
EEEIIMRSTTX	extremities	EEEINPRSTVV	preventives	EEFGIINRRST	gentrifiers
EEEIINNPSVX	inexpensive	EEEINRSSSTV	restiveness	EEFGIINRRVY	reverifying
EEEIINRRTTV	irretentive	EEEINRSSSTW	westernises	EEFGIINRSTY	esterifying
EEEIINRRTVW	interviewer	EEEINRSSTWZ	westernizes	EEFGILLNNUY	unfeelingly
EEEIIORRSTX	exteriorise	EEEIOPRRRST	repertoires	EEFGILLNORT	foretelling
EEEIIORRTXZ	exteriorize		repertories	EEFGILNNOUX	genuflexion
EEEIIPRRTTV	preteritive	EEEIPRRSTTU	repetiteurs	EEFGILNORRW	reflowering
EEEIKLNORTU	leukotriene	EEEIPRSSSST	priestesses	EEFGILNRSTY	freestyling
EEEIKLNOSST	skeletonise	EEEKLNOOSTX	exoskeleton	EEFGIMMORSU	gemmiferous
EEEIKLNOSTZ	skeletonize	EEEKLORRSTW	steelworker	EEFGIMORTTU	fugitometer
EEEIILLPTVXY	expletively		teleworkers	EEFGINNNORZ	nonfreezing
EEEILMMNPRT	implementer	EEELLLNPRTY	repellently	EEFGINNNRSS	foreignness
EEEILMMORST	mileometers	EEELLLPSSSY	sleeplessly	EEFGINNQRTU	frequenting
EEEILMNNNTV	enlivenment	EEELLNRSSVY	nervelessly	EEFGINNRTTU	unfettering
EEEILMNNTTT	entitlement	EEELLNSSSSY	senselessly	EEFGINORRST	reforesting
EEEILNNPSSS	pensileness	EEELMNNOPTV	envelopment	EEFGINORSSV	forgiveness
EEEILNNQSSU	queenliness	EEELMNSSTTT	settlements	EEFGKLLNOST	gentlefolks
EEEILNNSSST	tensileness	EEELMORRSSS	remorseless	EEFGLLMNORS	fellmongers
EEEILNPRRST	terrepleins	EEELNNOOPPS	Peloponnese	EEFGLLMNORY	fellmongery
EEEILNPRRTT	teleprinter	EEELNRSSTTW	newsletters	EEFGLLNRTUY	refulgently
EEEILNPSVXY	expensively	EEELNSSSSSU	uselessness	EEFGLLOORXY	reflexology
EEEILNRSSSV	servileness	EEELNSSSSSX	sexlessness	EEFGLLRRTUY	regretfully
EEEILNRTTVY	retentively	EEELPRRSSTT	letterpress	EEFGLMNNSTU	engulfments
EEEILNSSSUV	elusiveness	EEELRSSTTUX	textureless	EEFHHIISSTW	whitefishes
EEEILNSTVXY	extensively	EEEMMNNOPRTW	empowerment	EEFHHILLSSS	shellfishes
EEEILPRSSST	respiteless	EEEMNNOOPPS	monoterpene	EEFHIINPSSS	snipefishes
EEEILRRSTTW	telewriters	EEEMNNPRSTT	presentment	EEFHIINRRSS	refinishers
EEEIMMNNSSS	immenseness	EEEMNNRSSTT	resentments	EEFHIJLLSSY	jellyfishes
EEEIMMORSST	seismometer	EEEMNORSTUV	venturesome	EEFHILLNSSS	fleshliness
EEEIMMRRSSS	mesmerisers	EEEMNPRSSSU	supremeness	EEFHILLSSSW	swellfishes
EEEIMMRRSSZ	mesmerizers	EEEMORRSSTY	stereometry	EEFHILNSSSS	selfishness
EEEIMNNNTTW	entwinement	EEEMPRSSSTT	temptresses	EEFHILOSUWY	housewifely
EEEIMNNRRTT	reinterment	EEENOOPRSSS	operoseness	EEFHINOSSST	stonefishes
EEEIMNORSST	remonetises	EEENOPRTTUX	open texture	EEFHINRRSSU	refurnishes
EEEIMNORSTT	tensiometer	EEENORSSTWZ	sneezeworts	EEFHIORSUWY	housewifery
EEEIMNORSTZ	remonetizes	EEEOOPRSSVX	overexposes	EEFHLLNPSSU	helpfulness
EEEIMNOSSTV	emotiveness	EEEOPRRSTTY	stereotyper	EEFHLNOPSSU	hopefulness
EEEIMNPRSTX	experiments	EEEOPRSSSSS	repossesses	EEFHMORRRTU	furthermore
EEEIMNQQRUU	quinquereme	EEEOPRSSTTY	stereotypes	EEFHNOORRST	foreshorten
EEEIMNQRRTU	requirement	EEEPRRSSSST	prestresses	EEFIIINNRST	intensifier
EEEIMNQRTTU	requitement	EEEPRSSTTTY	typesetters	EEFIIINNSST	intensifies
EEEIMNRRSTT	retirements	EEFFGHIIRRT	firefighter	EEFIIISSTTV	festivities
EEEIMNRSSTT	tensimeters	EEFFGIINRSV	fivefingers	EEFIILLNRTY	infertilely
EEEIMOPRSTX	extemporise	EEFFGINORRS	forefingers	EEFIILMNOSS	solemnifies
EEEIMOPRSTZ	piezometers	EEFFGLLNTUY	effulgently	EEFIILMRSSU	emulsifiers
EEEIMOPRTXZ	extemporize	EEFFIINNOSV	inoffensive	EEFIILNOPSS	Isle of
EEEIMRRSSTV	timeservers	EEFFIIORRST	refortifies		Pines
EEEINNNSSST	intenseness	EEFFILNOSVY	offensively	EEFIILRRSST	fertilisers
EEEINNOPRSS	pensioneers	EEFFINNOSUV	unoffensive	EEFIILRRSTZ	fertilizers
EEEINNORSTV	overintense	EEFFIOORRST	offertories	EEFIILRTVXY	reflexivity
EEEINNPRSST	serpentines	EEFFIORRRSU	ferriferous	EEFIINOPRRS	personifier
EEEINNPRSTT	presentient	EEFFIORRSTU	forfeitures	EEFIINOPRSS	personifies
EEEINNPSSSV	pensiveness	EEFFLNRSSTU	fretfulness	EEFIIPPRSTT	pipefitters
EEEINNRRSTV	interveners	EEFGGIIILNR	filigreeing	EEFIIPRRSTT	prettifiers
EEEINORRRSV	reversioner	EEFGGIOPRTT	pettifogger	EEFIKLLNOWY	Yellowknife
EEEINPPPRSS	pepperiness	EEFGHIINRTY	etherifying	EEFILLLMNTU	mellifluent
EEEINPRRRST	enterpriser	EEFGHILMORR	Leigh Fermor	EEFILLLMRSU	millefleurs
EEEINPRRRTT	interpreter	EEFGHILRSST	freightless	EEFILLMORSU	melliferous
	reinterpret	EEFGHINRRST	frighteners	EEFILLNOSSX	flexionless
EEEINPRRSST	enterprises	EEFGHIOOSSS	goosefishes	EEFILLNOSTU	feuilletons
	intersperse	EEFGIILNRRT	refiltering	EEFILLRSSTY	lifestylers

EEFILMORRTU	fluorimeter	EEGHIMNOOSZ	homogenizes	EEGILMNORSS	mongrelises
EEFILMRSSTT	filmsetters	EEGHIMNOOTY	homogeneity	EEGILMNORSZ	mongrelizes
EEFILNNORST	florentines	EEGHIMOORST	isogeotherm	EEGILMOORST	metrologies
EEFILNNRTTU	interfluent	EEGHINNOSTT	ethnogenist	EEGILMOOSTY	etymologies
EEFILNORSSW	floweriness	EEGHINNPTWY	pennyweight		etymologise
EEFILNRSTUV	interfluves	EEGHINPRSST	regentships	EEGILMOOTYZ	etymologize
EEFILOOPRRT	profiterole	EEGHIORSTVW	overweights	EEGILNNNRTU	unrelenting
EEFILOORSST	loosestrife	EEGHLOOPRTY	herpetology	EEGILNOORSU	neurologies
EEFILRSSTUX	fixtureless	EEGHMNOOOSU	homogeneous	EEGILNOPRTT	teleporting
EEFINNORRST	interferons	EEGHMNOORRW	whoremonger	EEGILNOPSSY	polygenesis
EEFINRSSTUV	furtiveness	EEGHMORRSTY	hygrometers	EEGILNORSVY	sovereignly
EEFIOPRSSTU	pestiferous	EEGHNNRSSTT	strengthens	EEGILNPRSTY	pesteringly
EEFKLLOOSWY	yokefellows	EEGHNOPSTTY	gnetophytes	EEGILOPRSTT	petrologies
EEFLLLNPSUY	spleenfully	EEGHNORSTYY	hysterogeny	EEGILOPRSTT	poltergeist
EEFLLNRSTUY	resentfully	EEGHOSSSTUU	guesthouses	EEGIMMNNNORT	Montenegrin
EEFLLOPRSUY	reposefully	EEGIIILMSST	legitimises	EEGIMNNOOSS	monogenesis
EEFLMNOORTT	Montefeltro	EEGIIILMSTZ	legitimizes	EEGIMNNORSU	monseigneur
EEFLMNOSSSU	fulsomeness	EEGIIILNSTT	gentilities	EEGIMNNOSTT	mignonettes
EEFLMOORRTU	fluorometer	EEGIIIMNPST	impetigines	EEGIMNNRRTU	interregnum
EEFLNNRSTUU	unresentful	EEGIIINNSTU	ingenuities	EEGIMNNRSTU	integuments
EEFLNNSSTUU	tunefulness	EEGIIINORSS	seigniories	EEGIMNOORST	goniometers
EEFLNORSSTU	fortuneless	EEGIIINRSTT	integrities	EEGIMNOORSTW	swingometer
EEFLNPSSSUU	suspenseful	EEGIIKLLMMN	lemminglike	EEGIMNOSSYZ	zymogenesis
EEFLNRSSSTU	restfulness	EEGIIKLPRSS	kriegspiels	EEGINNOOSST	ontogenesis
EEFLNSSSTUZ	zestfulness	EEGIILLNNTT	intelligent	EEGINNORSST	rontgenises
EEFNNORRRSU	forerunners	EEGIILLORSY	religiosely	EEGINNORSTZ	rontgenizes
EEFNOPRSSSU	profuseness	EEGIILMNNRT	intermingle	EEGINNPRSST	Springsteen
EEGGHHIINNT	heightening	EEGIILNNNST	sentineling	EEGINNPRSUV	supervening
EEGGHIINSST	sightseeing	EEGIILNNOST	lentiginose	EEGINOPRRTX	reexporting
EEGGHILNNNT	lengthening	EEGIILNNPRV	replevining	EEGINORRSSS	regressions
EEGGHILNRST	greenlights	EEGIILNOPSS	lipogenesis	EEGINORRSTU	terrigenous
EEGGIILNQSU	squilgeeing	EEGIILNRSSW	wirelessing	EEGINORSSXY	oxygenisers
EEGGIIMNNRT	regimenting	EEGIIMMNNPT	impingement	EEGINORSTTV	oversetting
EEGGIINNPRW	Winnipegger	EEGIIMMNRSS	mesmerising	EEGINORSTVY	sovereignty
EEGGIINNRRST	registering	EEGIIMMNRSZ	mesmerizing	EEGINORSXYZ	oxygenizers
EEGGILLNNTY	negligently	EEGIIMMNNSS	minnesinger	EEGINPRSTTU	guttersnipe
EEGGILNNRVY	revengingly	EEGIIMNRSTV	timeserving	EEGINPSTTTY	typesetting
EEGGILORSUY	egregiously	EEGIINNNRTV	intervening	EEGINRRSUVY	resurveying
EEGGILRRSST	triggerless		reinventing	EEGIOPRRSSV	progressive
EEGGNOOPRST	progestogen	EEGIINNORRT	reorienting	EEGKLLMNSUU	muskellunge
EEGGHHILRTWW	wheelwright	EEGIINNORST	nitrogenise	EEGLMOOORTY	meteorology
EEGHIILLMRT	limelighter	EEGIINNORTZ	nitrogenize	EEGLNOOSUXY	exogenously
EEGHIILLNNS	hellenising	EEGIINNQRUV	Virgin Queen	EEGLOQRSTUY	grotesquely
EEGHIILLNNZ	hellenizing	EEGIINNRRRT	reinterring	EEGMMNNORSST	engrossment
EEGHIILOORS	hierologies	EEGIINNRRST	reinserting	EEGMNNORSSW	newsmongers
EEGHIIMNPSU	euphemising	EEGIINNRSTT	interesting	EEGMNNORSTV	governments
EEGHIIMNPUZ	euphemizing	EEGIINOPRTV	progenitive	EEGOQRRSTUY	grotesquery
EEGHIINSSTW	weightiness	EEGIINPPQRU	reequipping	EEHHILLNSSS	hellishness
EEGHIKNOPPS	shopkeeping	EEGIINPRSTX	expertising	EEHHILMOPRT	thermophile
EEGHILNNOPT	telephoning		preexisting	EEHHILOPRST	lithosphere
EEGHILNNSST	lengthiness	EEGIINPRTXZ	expertizing	EEHHILOPSTY	heliophytes
EEGHILNOOPS	pigeonholes	EEGIINRSSSV	ingressives	EEHHINOSSTT	henotheists
EEGHILNOPRS	negrophiles	EEGIKLNNNNU	unkenneling	EEHHINRSTTT	thirteenths
EEGHILNOPSY	phylogenies	EEGIKLNORTW	teleworking	EEHHIOOPSST	theosophies
EEGHILOORST	theologiser	EEGILLLSSUV	guilelessly	EEHHIOPRRSZ	rhizosphere
EEGHILOORTZ	theologizer	EEGILLMOOST	teleologism	EEHHIOPSTTY	hypothesise
EEGHILOOSST	theologises	EEGILLNORSV	overselling	EEHHIOPSTYZ	hypothesize
EEGHILOOSTZ	theologizes	EEGILLOOSTT	teleologist	EEHHMNOOPRY	hymenophore
EEGHILRSTTT	streetlight	EEGILMNNSTT	meltingness	EEHHMOORSTU	housemother
EEGHIMNNOORS	homogeniser	EEGILMNOPRY	reemploying	EEHHMPRRTYY	hyperthermy
EEGHIMNNOORZ	homogenizer	EEGILMNORRS	mongreliser	EEHHNOOPRTY	heterophony
EEGHIMNNOOSS	homogenises	EEGILMNORRZ	mongrelizer	EEHHOOPPRST	photosphere

EEHHOOPRRTT	heterotroph	
EEHHOORSSUW	whorehouses	
EEHHOPRSTTY	therophytes	
EEHIIIKLNSU	kleinhuisie	
EEHIIKNSSST	kinesthesis	
EEHIILMPSTU	epitheliums	
EEHIILNOOPS	eosinophile	
EEHIIMOOPSS	hemopoiesis	
EEHIIMPPRRS	premiership	
EEHIINRRSST	inheritress	
EEHILMMOSTU	mesothelium	
EEHILMNNPST	plenishment	
EEHILMNNRTY	hemielytron	
EEHILMOORTT	lithometeor	
EEHILMOPPRS	spermophile	
EEHILMOPRST	thermopiles	
EEHILNOPPRS	nephrolepis	
EEHILNOPRRT	leptorrhine	
EEHILNOPRTU	neutrophile	
EEHILNOPSTT	telephonist	
EEHILNORRST	northerlies	
EEHILNOSTTV	novelettish	
EEHILNPRSTW	printwheels	
EEHILOOPRST	heliotropes	
EEHILORSSTU	southerlies	
EEHILORSSTY	heterolysis	
EEHILOSSTTU	silhouettes	
EEHIMNNRSTU	minehunters	
EEHIMNOPRSS	premonishes	
EEHIMNOPRST	hemipterons	
EEHIMNPSSSU	humpinesses	
EEHIMOPPRRS	emperorship	
EEHIMOPRSTU	hemipterous	
EEHIMOSSSST	somesthesis	
EEHINNOOPTT	thiopentone	
EEHINNOPRST	interphones	
EEHINNORSST	rhinestones	
EEHINNOSSSU	heinousness	
EEHINOPSTVY	hypotensive	
EEHINPSSSTT	pettishness	
EEHINRSSSTU	hirsuteness	
EEHINRSSSTY	synthesiser	
EEHINRSSTYZ	synthesizer	
EEHINSSSSTY	synthesises	
EEHINSSSTTY	synthetises	
EEHINSSSTYZ	synthesizes	
EEHINSSTTYZ	synthetizes	
EEHIOPPRRSS	prophesiers	
EEHIOPRSSTX	exstrophies	
EEHIPRRSSUV	herpesvirus	
EEHIPRSSTTU	trusteeship	
EEHJNOPRRST	Prester John	
EEHKMOORRSW	homeworkers	
EEHKMOOSSSU	smokehouses	
EEHKNOORSTT	tenterhooks	
EEHKNOSTUVY	Yevtushenko	
EEHKOORRSUW	houseworker	
EEHLLMNOOPS	mellophones	
EEHLLMOOSWY	wholesomely	
EEHLMNOOSUW	unwholesome	
EEHLMNOOSYZ	holoenzymes	
EEHLMNOTTVW	twelvemonth	

EEHLNOOSSSV	shovelnoses	
EEHLOPRRSTU	reupholster	
	upholsterer	
EEHLORSTTYY	heterostyly	
EEHMMORRTTY	thermometry	
EEHMMORSSUU	summerhouse	
EEHMMNNOOPS	phenomenons	
EEHMMNNOOORY	honeymooner	
EEHMMNOOPRS	mesonephros	
EEHMMNOOPRST	phonometers	
EEHMMOOPRSTT	photometers	
EEHMMOPPRSTY	spermophyte	
EEHMMOPRSSTT	stepmothers	
EEHMMOPRSSTY	hypsometers	
EEHMMOQRSSUU	humoresques	
EEHNNORRRST	northerners	
EEHNOOOOPRSZ	ozonosphere	
EEHNOOPRSTY	stereophony	
EEHNOPSSSSTY	pythonesses	
EEHNOPSSTUY	hypotenuses	
EEHNORRSSTU	southerners	
EEHNORRSTTW	northwester	
EEHOOPPRRST	troposphere	
EEHOOPPRRSTU	porterhouse	
EEHOOPRSSTY	heterospory	
EEHOOPRSSUW	powerhouses	
EEHOOPRSTTT	photosetter	
EEHOOPSSTTY	osteophytes	
EEHOORSSSTU	storehouses	
EEHOPPRRSWY	hyperpowers	
EEHORSSTTUW	southwester	
EEIIIJQRSTU	jequirities	
EEIIIMMNNST	immensities	
EEIIIMNNSTU	einsteinium	
EEIIINNSSTT	intensities	
EEIIINNSSTV	insensitive	
EEIIINORRST	interiorise	
EEIIINORRTZ	interiorize	
EEIIINORSST	seniorities	
EEIIINSTTVV	investitive	
EEIIJNRSSTT	jitteriness	
EEIIKLLNNNS	Enniskillen	
EEIIKLLNSTU	unlikeliest	
EEIIKLNNRTU	interleukin	
EEIIKLNPRSW	periwinkles	
EEIILLMMRST	millimeters	
	millimetres	
EEIILLNRSTY	resiliently	
EEIILLNRTUV	Tirunelveli	
EEIILLOPRST	pellitories	
EEIILLPPRST	pipistrelle	
EEIILLPRSTU	spirituelle	
EEIILMMNPRT	imperilment	
EEIILMNOSST	solemnities	
EEIILMNRSSS	miserliness	
EEIILMOOSST	ileostomies	
EEIILMRSSVY	remissively	
EEIILNNRRST	interliners	
EEIILNNSTTV	intensively	
EEIILNNTVVY	inventively	
EEIILNOSSTV	televisions	
EEIILNRSSSV	silveriness	

EEIILNSSTVY	sensitively	
EEIIILPRSSTT	priestliest	
EEIIILQRSTUV	requisitely	
EEIIILQSTUXY	exquisitely	
EEIILRRSSST	sterilisers	
EEIILRRSSTZ	sterilizers	
EEIILRSSTVY	Sylvester II	
EEIIMMNNTTW	intwinement	
EEIIMMNPRTT	impertinent	
EEIIMNOSSTT	testimonies	
EEIIMNPRRUU	perineurium	
EEIIMNPRSUU	epineuriums	
EEIIMNRSTTW	wintertimes	
EEIIMOPRSST	epitomisers	
EEIIMOPRSTZ	epitomizers	
EEIINNNOSTT	nonentities	
EEIINNNTUVV	uninventive	
EEIINNOOPRT	Pointe-Noire	
EEIINNORRST	reinsertion	
EEIINNORSTV	inventories	
EEIINNPRRWZ	prizewinner	
EEIINNRSSTW	winteriness	
EEIINNRSTTW	intertwines	
EEIINOPRRTT	preterition	
EEIINOPRSTT	petitioners	
	repetitions	
EEIINRSSSST	sensitisers	
EEIINRSSSTZ	sensitizers	
EEIINRSTTUV	investiture	
EEIINRTTTVY	retentivity	
EEIIOPPRRST	proprieties	
EEIIOPPRSTV	prepositive	
EEIIOPRSTTU	repetitious	
EEIIORRRSTT	territories	
EEIIORRSSST	rotisseries	
EEIIPQRSSTU	perquisites	
EEIIRSTTTUV	restitutive	
EEIJMNNNOST	enjoinments	
EEIJNORSSST	jointresses	
EEIKKORSSST	koeksisters	
EEIKLLNRSSW	wrinkleless	
EEIKLMPRTTU	trumpetlike	
EEIKLORRSVW	servile work	
EEIKMNORSSS	irksomeness	
EEIKMORRSTW	timeworkers	
EEILLMMORST	immortelles	
EEILLMNOPRT	Montpellier	
EEILLMPRTUX	multiplexer	
EEILLMPSTUX	multiplexes	
EEILLMRSSUW	Weissmuller	
EEILLNNPSSY	pennilessly	
EEILLNOPQTU	equipollent	
EEILLNOSSSY	noiselessly	
EEILLNPSSSY	spinelessly	
EEILLNPSTTY	pestilently	
EEILLOPSVXY	explosively	
EEILLORRVWY	Yellow River	
EEILLPRRSUW	wirepullers	
EEILLPRSUVY	prelusively	
	repulsively	
EEILLRSUVVY	revulsively	
EEILMMNOPRT	implementor	

EEILMMRSTTU	multimeters	EEIMNRSSTTW	Westminster	EELLMNNORST	enrollments
EEILMNNOSTT	entoilments	EEIMOOOSSTT	osteotomies	EELLNNOSSSW	swollenness
EEILMNNOTVV	involvement	EEIMOOPRSSX	peroxisomes	EELLNOOSTWY	Yellowstone
EEILMNNSSTT	enlistments	EEIMOPPRSSU	superimpose	EELLNOPPRST	propellents
EEILMNOOSST	emotionless	EEIMOPRRRST	misreporter	EELLNOPSTUY	plenteously
EEILMNORSSS	solemnisers		reimporters	EELLNPRTUUV	pulverulent
EEILMNORSSZ	solemnizers	EEIMOPRRSST	spirometers	EELLOPRSSWY	powerlessly
EEILMNOSSSS	lissomeness		temporisers	EELLORRSTTY	storyteller
EEILMNRTTTY	remittently	EEIMOPRRSSV	overimpress	EELMMNOPSTY	employments
EEILMOPRSSY	polymerises	EEIMOPRRSTZ	temporizers	EELMNOOPSTU	Neoptolemus
EEILMOPRSYZ	polymerizes	EEIMPPRSTUV	presumptive	EELMNOSSSUU	emulousness
EEILMOPRTUV	pluviometer	EEIMPRRSSSU	impressures	EELMNPPSSTU	supplements
EEILMOSSSSU	semisoluses	EEIMRSSSSTY	systemisers	EELMOPRSSTU	pulsometers
EEILMPRSSTU	pulsimeters	EEIMRSSSTYZ	systemizers	EELNNSSSSSU	sunlessness
EEILNNOPPTT	plenipotent	EEINNNNORRTU	interneuron	EELNOOPPPRY	polypropene
EEILNNOPSSS	pensionless	EEINNNOSSTTX	nonexistent	EELNOOPPSTW	townspeople
EEILNNOSSST	tensionless	EEINNOPRSTT	pretensions	EELNOORRSUY	erroneously
EEILNNPRTTY	pertinently	EEINNOPRSTT	septentrion	EELNOPPRTTY	prepotently
EEILNNSSSSS	sinlessness	EEINNOPRSTV	preventions	EELNOPRSSSU	leprousness
EEILNOORTVV	overviolent	EEINNORRSTV	intervenors	EELNOPRSTYY	polystyrene
EEILNOPRRST	interlopers	EEINNOSSSUV	enviousness	EELNOPSSSST	toplessness
EEILNORSTVV	intervolves	EEINNOSSTTU	sententious	EELOOPRSSTT	protosteles
EEILNOSSTVY	ostensively	EEINNQSSTUU	unquietness	EELOPPRSSSU	purposeless
EEILNSSSSTW	witlessness	EEINOORRTTX	extortioner	EELORRSSSTU	trouserless
EEILOOPRSST	teliospores	EEINOORRSST	ostensories	EELPRRSSTTU	splutterers
EEILOPPRSTU	superpolite	EEINOOPRSST	peptonisers	EEMNNOPSSTT	pentstemons
EEILOPRSSTY	proselytise	EEINOOPRSTZ	peptonizers	EEMNNRSTTTU	entrustment
EEILOPRSTYZ	proselytize	EEINOPRRSSS	repressions	EEMNOORSTTY	enterostomy
EEILORRSTTW	rottweilers	EEINOPRRSST	interposers	EEMNORSSTTW	westernmost
EEILPPSSTUV	suppletives	EEINOPRRSSV	perversions	EEMOORRSTTU	torturesome
EEILPRRSSUV	pulverisers	EEINOPRSSSX	expressions	EEMOORSSTTU	metoestrous
EEILPRRSUVZ	pulverizers	EEINOPRSTTU	pretentious	EEMOPSSTTUU	tempestuous
EEILPRSSTTU	supertitles	EEINOPSSSTU	piteousness	EENNOOPRRTU	neuropteron
EEIMMNOPRTV	improvement	EEINOQRSSTU	questioners	EENNOORSSSU	onerousness
EEIMMNPRSST	impressment	EEINORRSSUV	overinsures	EENNOORSTTT	rottenstone
EEIMMNRSSSU	summeriness	EEINORRSTUV	enterovirus	EENNOPRSTWW	Newport News
EEIMMPRSUVV	sempervivum	EEINORRSTVW	overwinters	EENNOQRSSTU	quernstones
EEIMMRSSSTY	symmetrises	EEINORRTTVW	overwritten	EENNORSSSUV	nervousness
EEIMMRSSTYZ	symmetrizes	EEINORSSSSU	seriousness	EENNOSSSTUU	tenuousness
EEIMNNNORRTU	environment	EEINPRRRTTU	interrupter	EENOPRSSSTU	Ostpreussen
EEIMNNNRSTT	internments	EEINPRTTTWY	typewritten	EENPRRSSSUU	supernurses
EEIMNNOOSSS	noisomeness	EEINRRSTUWW	wienerwurst	EEOOPRRSSSS	repossessor
EEIMNNOPRST	omnipresent	EEIOPRRSSSU	superioress	EEOORRRSSTV	rootservers
EEIMNNOSSSW	winsomeness	EEIOPRSSTTT	operettists	EEOPPPRRSTW	pepperworts
EEIMNNPSSTU	septenniums	EEIOPSSSSSV	possessives	EEOPPPRSSSU	presupposes
EEIMNNSSTTV	investments	EEIORRRRSST	terrorisers	EEOPPRRSSUW	superpowers
EEIMNOORRST	remontoires	EEIORRRRSTZ	terrorizers	EEOPRRSSSTU	superstores
EEIMNOORSST	eriostemons	EEIPPRSSSUV	suppressive	EEPPRRSSSSU	suppressers
EEIMNOORSTU	neurotomies	EEIPRRRSSSU	pressuriser	EFFFGIKLNRU	kerfuffling
EEIMNOPPRST	preemptions	EEIPRRRSSUZ	pressurizer	EFFGHIINRSS	fishfingers
EEIMNOPRSTU	peritoneums	EEIPRRRSSSU	pressurises	EFFGHILNRSU	reshuffling
EEIMNOQSTUU	Montesquieu	EEIPRRRSSUZ	pressurizes	EFFGILNRSUY	sufferingly
EEIMNORRSSS	sermonisers	EEIPRRSTTWY	typewriters	EFFGLLORTUY	forgetfully
EEIMNORRSSZ	sermonizers	EEIPRSSSSTT	stepsisters	EFFHHINSSSU	huffishness
EEIMNORRSTT	nitrometers	EEJLNOSSSSY	joylessness	EFFILLLMNTU	fulfillment
EEIMNORRSTU	urinometers	EEKKOORRRTV	voortrekker	EFFILOORRSU	floriferous
EEIMNORSSST	monitresses	EEKLOOORRSV	overlookers	EFGGHIINNRT	frightening
EEIMNORSTTT	tintometers	EEKLORRSTTW	trestlework	EFGGHIIRRST	triggerfish
EEIMNORSTZZ	intermezzos	EEKMNNPSSTU	unkemptness	EFGGHINRSTU	gunfighters
EEIMNORTTZZ	mezzotinter	EEKMNOOPSSW	spokeswomen	EFGGIILNNRS	fingerlings
EEIMNPPPRST	peppermints	EEKNNOSSVYZ	Voznesensky	EFGGIINPRRU	prefiguring
EEIMNRSSSTW	westernisms	EEKNOORRSTW	stoneworker	EFGGLOOORST	footslogger

EFGHHOORTTU forethought	**EFHILORRSSU** flourishers	**EGGHIINPSSS** piggishness
EFGHIIIINNRS refinishing	**EFHINOPPSSS** foppishness	**EGGHILNNRUY** hungeringly
EFGHIIKNRSS kingfishers	**EFHLNRSSTUU** hurtfulness	**EGGHLNOORSW** hornswoggle
EFGHIILNSST flightiness	ruthfulness	**EGGIIILNPRV** privileging
EFGHIILOSTW Isle of	**EFHLOOOPRRU** fluorophore	**EGGIIIORRXV** Gregory XIII
Wight	**EFHMORRSTTU** furthermost	**EGGIIILLNNRY** lingeringly
EFGHIINORSV overfishing	**EFHOOOPRRSW** showerproof	**EGGIILNNOOS** neologising
EFGHIIPRSTZ prizefights	**EFHOOOPRRTY** proof theory	**EGGIILNNOOZ** neologizing
EFGHILORSTV overflights	**EFIIIIMNRST** infirmities	**EGGIILNRSTV** greylisting
EFGHIMNORSS fishmongers	**EFIIIINNSTV** infinitives	**EGGIINNOPSW** pigeonwings
EFGHINOORSW foreshowing	**EFIIIILMPRSS** simplifiers	**EGGIINNOSXY** oxygenising
EFGHINORSSU surgeonfish	**EFIIIILNRTTY** infertility	**EGGIINNOXYZ** oxygenizing
EFGHIOORRTT right-footer	**EFIIILORSTV** frivolities	**EGGIINNRRST** restringing
EFGHLLNORSU flugelhorns	**EFIIIINORRTY** inferiority	**EGGILLNORWY** gloweringly
EFGHOOPPRRS froghoppers	**EFIIKNNOPST** knifepoints	**EGGILMMOOST** gemmologist
EFGIIIILLNNR fringilline	**EFIILNPSSTU** pitifulness	**EGGILMOOSST** gemologists
EFGIIIILNNRT interfiling	**EFIILNRSSZZ** frizzliness	**EGGILNNRSSU** gunslingers
EFGIIILNRST fertilising	**EFIILORSSUV** filoviruses	**EGGINOORRVW** overgrowing
EFGIIILNRTZ fertilizing	**EFIILRSSTTU** stultifiers	**EGGINOPRRSS** progressing
EFGIIINPPTT pipefitting	**EFIIMMNNORS** misinformer	**EGGINOSSSTU** suggestions
EFGIIINRVVY revivifying	**EFIIMNOPRST** profeminist	**EGGINOSSTUU** outguessing
EFGIIKNRSTU kitesurfing	**EFIINNORSTU** interfusion	**EGGLNOOORTY** gerontology
EFGIILLLORW gilliflower	**EFIINOPRSSU** spiniferous	**EGHHILOPRSY** hieroglyphs
EFGIILLMORU florilegium	**EFIINORRSSU** uriniferous	hygrophiles
EFGIILLNORV overfilling	**EFIIOPRRSSU** spiriferous	**EGHHILOSSTU** houselights
EFGIILLNSTY stellifying	**EFIKLLNSSSU** skilfulness	lighthouses
EFGIILMNSTT filmsetting	**EFILLLMOSUU** mellifluous	**EGHHLOSSTTU** thoughtless
EFGIILMNSUY emulsifying	**EFILLLNPTUY** plentifully	**EGHHOORSSUU** roughhouses
EFGIIMNNORR reinforming	**EFILLLNSSUW** willfulness	**EGHHOPRSTYY** hygrophytes
EFGIIMNORSS foreignisms	**EFILLNOOSUY** feloniously	**EGHIILLNRSV** shrivelling
EFGIINNORTY renotifying	**EFILLRSSTUY** fruitlessly	**EGHIILLOOST** lithologies
EFGIINNPRRT fingerprint	**EFILMORRTUY** fluorimetry	**EGHIILLNOPRS** repolishing
EFGIINNRSTU interfusing	**EFILNSSSTUW** wistfulness	**EGHIILNPRSY** perishingly
EFGIINNSSTT fittingness	**EFILOOPRRSU** proliferous	**EGHIILNRSSS** girlishness
EFGIINPRRUY repurifying	**EFILPRSTUUY** superfluity	**EGHIILNRTWY** witheringly
EFGIINPRTTY prettifying	**EFIMNNORSSU** uniformness	**EGHIILNSSST** sightliness
EFGIKNNOORW foreknowing	**EFIMNOORSSU** somniferous	**EGHIILOORST** hierologist
EFGILLLORWY gillyflower	**EFIMNORSSTU** misfortunes	**EGHIILPRRST** sprightlier
EFGILMNNSTU ingulfments	**EFINOOOORSUZ** ozoniferous	**EGHIIMMNSTU** thingummies
EFGILMNOORT montgolfier	**EFINOOPRSSS** professions	**EGHIIMNPRSW** whimperings
EFGILNOORVW overflowing	**EFINOOPRSSU** superfusion	**EGHIINNOPSS** sphingosine
EFGILNORSST fosterlings	**EFINORSSSTW** frowstiness	**EGHIINNOPSU** euphonising
EFGILNORSTY fosteringly	**EFINORSSSUU** furiousness	**EGHIINNOPUZ** euphonizing
EFGINNNORRU forerunning	**EFIORRSTTUY** yttriferous	**EGHIINNPSSS** ensignships
EFGINORRSST fortressing	**EFLLNOSSSUU** soulfulness	**EGHIIOPPRSU** Hippo Regius
EFGINORRSUU ferruginous	**EFLLNSSSTUU** lustfulness	**EGHIKNOSTTU** Königshütte
EFGINPRSSUU superfusing	**EFLLRSSSTUY** stressfully	**EGHILLMOSTY** lightsomely
EFGIOPRSSUY gypsiferous	**EFLMNOOORSW** moonflowers	**EGHILLOOPRS** philologers
EFGLNNOSSSU songfulness	**EFLMOORRTUY** fluorometry	**EGHILLSSSTY** sightlessly
EFGNNOORTTU unforgotten	**EFLNNOORRSS** forlornness	**EGHILMNOORT** moonlighter
EFHIIIKLLSS killifishes	**EFLOPRSSUUU** superfluous	**EGHILMOOORS** homologiser
EFHIILRRSTT shirtlifter	**EFMOOPRRSTU** outperforms	**EGHILMOOORZ** homologizer
EFHIINRSSTT thriftiness	**EFNNNORRRTU** frontrunner	**EGHILMOOOSS** homologises
EFHIKLNOSSS folkishness	**EGGGIILNOOS** geologising	**EGHILMOOOSZ** homologizes
EFHIKNRSSTU trunkfishes	**EGGGIILNOOZ** geologizing	**EGHILMOOSTY** mythologies
EFHILLNSSUY unselfishly	**EGGHHHIILRT** highlighter	mythologise
EFHILLSSSTY shiftlessly	**EGGHHIILTTW** lightweight	**EGHILMOOTYZ** mythologize
EFHILNOOSSS foolishness	**EGGHHINORUW** roughhewing	**EGHILNOOOPS** phonologies
EFHILNSSSUW wishfulness	**EGGHHINOSSS** hoggishness	**EGHILNOOPST** nephologist
EFHILOOSTUY Isle of	**EGGHIINOSTT** ghettoising	phenologist
Youth	**EGGHIINOTTZ** ghettoizing	**EGHILNOOSTT** ethnologist
EFHILOPRSST shoplifters	**EGGHIINOTUW** outweighing	**EGHILNOOSTU** lithogenous

EGHILNOSSST	ghostliness	
EGHILOORSST	rheologists	
EGHILOOSSTT	ethologists	
	theologists	
EGHILORSTUY	righteously	
EGHIMNNOOST	smoothening	
EGHINNNOOST	nothingness	
EGHINNOOSSW	snowshoeing	
EGHINNORRST	Sherrington	
EGHINNPSSSU	pushingness	
EGHINOORSUZ	rhizogenous	
EGHINOOSSTT	theogonists	
EGHINOPPRSY	prophesying	
EGHINOPRSST	hotpressing	
EGHINOPRSSU	springhouse	
EGHINORSSST	shoestrings	
EGHINORSSSU	roguishness	
EGHINORSTUU	unrighteous	
EGHINPRSSTU	uprightness	
EGHINRSSTTU	shutterings	
EGHIORRSTTW	ghostwriter	
EGHIORRSSTTW	ghostwrites	
EGHLMOORSTY	mythologers	
EGHLOPPRSTY	petroglyphs	
EGHMOOOSTYZ	homozygotes	
EGHNPRRSTUZ	Hertzsprung	
EGHOORRTUVW	overwrought	
EGIIILLMNPR	imperilling	
EGIIILMNORS	religionism	
EGIIILMSSTT	legitimists	
EGIIILNNNRT	interlining	
EGIIILNNTUZ	luteinizing	
EGIIILNORST	religionist	
EGIIILNRSST	sterilising	
EGIIILNRSTZ	sterilizing	
EGIIILNRTUZ	reutilizing	
EGIIILORRSU	irreligious	
EGIIILORSTY	religiosity	
EGIIIMNNRST	ministering	
EGIIIMNNRTX	intermixing	
EGIIIMNOPST	epitomising	
EGIIIMNOPTZ	epitomizing	
EGIIIMNORSS	isomerising	
EGIIIMNORSZ	isomerizing	
EGIIIMRSSST	mistigrises	
EGIIINNNOSV	envisioning	
EGIIINNOPRT	preignition	
EGIIINNOPTT	petitioning	
EGIIINNRSTW	winterising	
EGIIINNRTWZ	winterizing	
EGIIINNSSST	sensitising	
EGIIINNSSTZ	sensitizing	
EGIIINOPQSU	equipoising	
EGIIINOSSTV	sovietising	
EGIIINOSTVZ	sovietizing	
EGIIJNNOSTT	jettisoning	
EGIIKLLNRSS	reskillings	
EGIIKLNOOSY	kinesiology	
EGIIKNPRSTT	spirketting	
EGIILLMNPSS	misspelling	
EGIILLNNSSW	willingness	
EGIILLNORTU	guillotiner	
EGIIILLNOSTU	guillotines	
EGIIILLNPRUW	wirepulling	
EGIIILLNRSTU	tellurising	
EGIIILLNRTUZ	tellurizing	
EGIIILLOOOPS	oligopolies	
EGIIILLORSUY	religiously	
EGIIILMNNOSS	solemnising	
EGIIILMNNOSZ	solemnizing	
EGIIILMNNSSY	smilingness	
EGIIILMNPRSY	simperingly	
EGIIILMOOSST	semiologist	
EGIIILNNORVV	reinvolving	
EGIIILNNOSTU	lentiginous	
EGIIILNNOSTV	Livingstone	
EGIIILNNOSUY	ingeniously	
EGIIILNNPRST	splintering	
EGIIILNORSUU	unreligious	
EGIIILNPRSUV	pulverising	
EGIIILNPRUVZ	pulverizing	
EGIIILNQRRSU	squirreling	
EGIIILNQRSSU	squirelings	
EGIIILNQRUVY	quiveringly	
EGIIILNRSSST	gristliness	
EGIIILNRTTTY	titteringly	
EGIIILOOSSTT	etiologists	
EGIIIMNNOOPS	empoisoning	
EGIIIMNNORSS	sermonising	
EGIIIMNNORSZ	sermonizing	
EGIIIMNNRTTU	unremitting	
EGIIIMNOPRRT	reimporting	
EGIIIMNOPRST	temporising	
EGIIIMNOPRTZ	temporizing	
EGIIIMNSSSTY	systemising	
EGIIIMNSSTYZ	systemizing	
EGIIIMNSTTTU	Mistinguett	
EGIIINNNNSSW	winningness	
EGIIINNOPPST	peptonising	
EGIIINNOPPTZ	peptonizing	
EGIIINNOPRST	interposing	
EGIIINNOQSTU	questioning	
EGIIINNORSSS	ingressions	
EGIIINNORSUV	souveniring	
EGIIINNOTTUZ	teutonizing	
EGIIINNPRSSS	springiness	
EGIIINNRSSST	stringiness	
EGIIINNRSSTU	unresisting	
EGIIINOPRSSU	serpiginous	
	spinigerous	
EGIIINOPRTTU	pirouetting	
EGIIINORRRST	terrorising	
EGIIINORRRTZ	terrorizing	
EGIIINORRTVW	overwriting	
EGIIINORSSUV	overissuing	
EGIIINORSTUV	vertiginous	
EGIIINPRSSUV	supervising	
EGIIINPRTTWY	typewriting	
EGIIINSSTTTV	vignettists	
EGIIIOPRSSTU	prestigious	
EGIIKLLNNORS	snorkelling	
EGIIKLNOOORV	overlooking	
EGIIKNNNOSSW	knowingness	
EGIIKNNORSTW	networkings	
EGIIKNOORRVW	overworking	
EGILLLNOTXY	extollingly	
EGILLLOOVXY	vexillology	
EGILLLSSTUY	guiltlessly	
EGILLNNOSTW	wellingtons	
EGILLNORTVY	revoltingly	
EGILLNORVVY	revolvingly	
EGILLNPRSSW	wellsprings	
EGILLORSSSY	syllogisers	
EGILLORSSYZ	syllogizers	
EGILMNNOOOS	Mesolóngion	
EGILMNOORTY	terminology	
EGILMNPRSUY	presumingly	
EGILMNRTTUY	mutteringly	
EGILMOOORSU	oligomerous	
EGILMOORSTT	metrologist	
EGILMOOSSTU	museologist	
EGILMOOSTTY	etymologist	
EGILNNNOOSU	unloosening	
EGILNNOPSSS	slopingness	
EGILNNOSUUY	ingenuously	
EGILNNRSTTY	stringently	
EGILNOOOSST	oenologists	
EGILNOOPSST	penologists	
EGILNOORSTU	neurologist	
EGILNOPRRVY	reprovingly	
EGILNOPRSTY	proselyting	
EGILNORTTTY	totteringly	
EGILNPPRSUY	resupplying	
EGILNPRSTTU	spluttering	
EGILNPSTTUY	upsettingly	
EGILNRSSTTU	lutestrings	
EGILNSSSTUU	singultuses	
EGILOOOPRST	tropologies	
EGILOOORSTT	erotologist	
EGILOOORSTY	soteriology	
EGILOOOSSTT	osteologist	
EGILOOPRSTT	petrologist	
EGILOORSSST	serologists	
EGILOOSSSTX	sexologists	
EGIMMNNORSU	resummoning	
EGIMMNNPSTU	impugnments	
EGIMMNNOORRS	ironmongers	
EGIMMNNOORRY	ironmongery	
EGIMMNOORRSV	misgovernor	
EGIMNOORRTT	trimetrogon	
EGIMNOORSST	ergonomists	
EGIMOOPRSST	geotropisms	
EGINNNORRUV	overrunning	
EGINNOORSTU	nitrogenous	
EGINNOPRSTY	trypsinogen	
EGINNORRTUV	overturning	
EGINOOPPRTV	overtopping	
EGINOOPRRSS	progression	
EGINOOPRRST	progenitors	
EGINOOPRSSU	superposing	
EGINOOPSTTU	outstepping	
EGINOPSSTTU	poussetting	
EGINORRSSTW	songwriters	
EGINORSSTUW	outswingers	
EGINPPRSSSU	suppressing	
EGINPRRSSTU	superstring	

EGIOORRSSSU	gressorious	
EGIOPRRSSST	progressist	
EGLMNNOOPRT	prolongment	
EGLOOORRSWW	woolgrowers	
EGMMNOPRSSY	gymnosperms	
EGNOOOPRSSU	sporogenous	
EGOPPRRSSUU	supergroups	
EHHIIMSSTTW	whitesmiths	
EHHIINRSSTW	withershins	
EHHILMOPRST	thermophils	
EHHILOOPPRS	philosopher	
EHHILOPSTTY	lithophytes	
EHHIMOOPRRT	theriomorph	
EHHIMOOPSST	theosophism	
EHHINORSSSW	whorishness	
EHHINORSTTW	whitethorns	
EHHIOOPPRST	phosphorite	
EHHIOOPSSTT	theosophist	
EHHIOPSSTTY	hypothesist	
EHHLOOOPPRS	lophophores	
EHHOOOOPPRST	photophores	
EHHOPPRRTYY	hypertrophy	
EHIIILNPPPS	philippines	
EHIIILNPSST	philistines	
EHIIILOSSTT	hostilities	
EHIIIMOSTTU	Thutmose III	
EHIIIPRSSVZ	vizierships	
EHIIKLNSTTY	kittenishly	
EHIIKMNOOSS	Shimonoseki	
EHIIKMRRSSS	skirmishers	
EHIILLOPSSS	lyophilises	
EHIILLOPSYZ	lyophilizes	
EHIILMOOSTT	lithotomies	
EHIILMRSSTV	silversmith	
EHIILNOOPRT	heliotropin	
EHIILNOOPSS	eosinophils	
EHIILOOPTTX	toxophilite	
EHIILORSTTT	lithotrites	
EHIIMMOPRST	hemitropism	
EHIIMNOSSTT	smithsonite	
EHIIMOORSTZ	rhizotomies	
EHIINNPRSST	internships	
EHIINNSSSSW	swinishness	
EHIINOPRTTY	hyponitrite	
EHIINPRSSST	spinsterish	
EHIINRSSSTT	thirstiness	
EHIIOPRSSST	sophistries	
EHIKMNNOSSS	monkishness	
EHILLMRSSTY	mirthlessly	
EHILLOPPSUY	epiphyllous	
EHILLORSTTU	little hours	
EHILMMNOSTY	semimonthly	
EHILMNOOPTY	entomophily	
EHILMNPSSSU	lumpishness	
EHILMOOPRSU	Hermoupolis	
EHILMORSSTY	thermolysis	
EHILNOOPPSY	polyphonies	
EHILNOORSSZ	horizonless	
EHILNOOSTUW	Wilton House	
EHILNOPRSTU	neutrophils	
EHILNORRSSV	silverhorns	
EHILNOSSSTU	loutishness	

EHILNSSSSTY	stylishness	
EHILOOPRSUX	xerophilous	
EHILOPSSTTY	polytheists	
EHILPRSSSUU	sulphurises	
EHILPRSSUUZ	sulphurizes	
EHIMMOOORST	homoerotism	
EHIMMOOPSTY	mythopoeism	
EHIMMOORSTU	mesothorium	
EHIMMOPSSTU	imposthumes	
EHIMNNOORSS	moonshiners	
EHIMNNORSTU	nourishment	
EHIMNNPSSTU	punishments	
EHIMNOOPSTY	monophysite	
EHIMNOORSTV	von Stroheim	
EHIMNOORTTU	nototherium	
EHIMNOOSSTT	monotheists	
EHIMNORRTUV	erythronium	
EHIMOOPRRST	rheotropism	
EHIMOOPSSTY	mythopoesis	
EHIMOOPSTTY	mythopoeist	
EHIMOPRSTXY	xerophytism	
EHIMORRSSTT	thermistors	
EHINNOOPSTY	hypotension	
EHINOOPRRTT	ornithopter	
EHINOPRSSTY	hypnotisers	
EHINOPRSTYZ	hypnotizers	
EHINRSSSTTU	ruttishness	
EHINSSSSTTY	synthesists	
EHINSSSTTTY	synthetists	
EHIOOOPRTTZ	trophozoite	
EHIOOPRSTTX	thixotropes	
EHIOPPRRSSW	worshippers	
EHIOPQRSSTU	questorship	
EHJMOPRSSUW	showjumpers	
EHLLORSSTWY	worthlessly	
EHLMNOPPSSY	nympholepss	
EHLMNOPPSVY	nympholepsy	
EHLMNOPTUWY	New Plymouth	
EHLMOOOSTTY	toothsomely	
EHLNOOPSSTY	stylophones	
EHLOPRSSUUU	sulphureous	
EHMMOOOORRTT	thermomotor	
EHMNOOOPRST	monostrophe	
EHMOOOPRSTU	homopterous	
EHMOOPSSTTY	photosystem	
EHMOORRSTTW	motherworts	
EHMOORSTTYY	hysterotomy	
EHNNOPRSTWY	pennyworths	
EHNOOOOPRRTT	orthopteron	
EHNOOPPRSTY	phonotypers	
EHOOOPPRRSS	sporophores	
EHOOPPRSSTW	showstopper	
EHOOPPRSSTY	sporophytes	
EHOOPPRSTTY	tropophytes	
EHORRSSTTUV	overthrusts	
EIIIILNSTTU	inutilities	
EIIIINOQSTUV	inquisitive	
EIIILLLMRST	milliliters	
	millilitres	
EIIILLOSSTV	villosities	
EIIILMNNOPS	epilimnions	
EIIILMPRTVY	primitively	

EIIILNNPSTY	insipiently	
EIIILNTTUVY	intuitively	
EIIILORSSST	listeriosis	
EIIILORSSTV	vitriolises	
EIIILORSTVZ	vitriolizes	
EIIIMMNRSTU	ministerium	
EIIIMNORSSV	revisionism	
EIIIMOPRSTX	proximities	
EIIINOPRSTT	peritonitis	
EIIINOQRSTU	requisition	
EIIINORSSTV	revisionist	
EIIINOSSSTU	sinuosities	
EIIINPRRSST	inspiriters	
EIIINSSTTVY	sensitivity	
EIIINSTTTUV	institutive	
EIIIOPRRSST	prioritises	
EIIIOPRRSTZ	prioritizes	
EIIIOPRSSTT	periostitis	
EIIIRSSTTVY	resistivity	
EIIKKNORSSS	kirk session	
EIIKLLNRSTW	winterkills	
EIIKMNORSST	ministrokes	
EIILLLLMSSTY	limitlessly	
EIILLMMNNSU	millenniums	
EIILLMNNSTT	instillment	
EIILLMNORSV	vermillions	
EIILLMOPSVY	implosively	
EIILLMPRSTU	multipliers	
EIILLMPSUVY	impulsively	
EIILLNOPSST	septillions	
EIILLNOSSTX	sextillions	
EIILLOOQSSU	soliloquies	
	soliloquise	
EIILLOOQSUZ	soliloquize	
EIILLMOPRSUY	imperiously	
EIILNNSSTTY	insistently	
EIILNOOPPRT	lipoprotein	
EIILNOPRSTV	silverpoint	
EIILNRSTUVY	intrusively	
EIILNRTTUVY	nutritively	
EIILOSSTVVZ	slivovitzes	
EIILPRRTUVY	irruptively	
EIIMNNOOPRT	premonition	
EIIMNNOPRTU	premunition	
EIIMNNOPSTU	pneumonitis	
EIIMNNORSTU	munitioners	
EIIMNOPRRSS	imprisoners	
EIIMNOPRSSS	impressions	
	permissions	
EIIMNOPSSSU	impiousness	
EIIMNORRTTT	intermittor	
	intromitter	
EIIMOOPPSST	pomposities	
EIIMOORRSTU	meritorious	
EIIMOPPRRTY	impropriety	
EIIMOPRRSSV	improvisers	
EIIMOPRSSST	prestissimo	
EIIMOPSTTUY	impetuosity	
EIIMORRSSTU	moisturiser	
EIIMORRSTUZ	moisturizer	
EIIMORSSSTU	moisturises	
EIIMORSSTUZ	moisturizes	

EIINNOOSTUV	Soviet Union	EIMNNRSTTTU	intrustment	EOPPRRSSSSU	suppressors
EIINNORSSTU	reunionists	EIMNOOPRRTU	premonitory	FFFGIKLNRUU	kurfuffling
EIINOOOPRST	ionotropies	EIMNOOPRSSS	spoonerisms	FFGHIIOPPRS	hippogriffs
EIINOOPPRST	preposition	EIMNOORSTTU	neurotomist	FFGHILLRTUY	frightfully
EIINOOPRRSV	provisioner	EIMNOOSSTTT	tenotomists	FFGIINNOPRT	offprinting
	reprovision	EIMNOPPRSTU	presumption	FFIIRRSSTTU	firstfruits
EIINOOPRSST	repositions	EIMNOPRRSTU	importuners	FGGGHIINNTU	gunfighting
EIINOOPSSTX	expositions	EIMNOPRSSTU	resumptions	FGGHIINOTTU	outfighting
EIINOPRSSUV	supervision	EIMOOPRSTTT	optometrist	FGGHILNORUU	furloughing
EIINORRSSST	sinistrorse	EIMOORRSUVV	vermivorous	FGGIIKLNNOS	folksinging
EIINORSTTTU	restitution	EIMORSSUVXY	myxoviruses	FGGIILNORVY	forgivingly
EIINORSTTWZ	zwitterions	EIMRRSSSTTU	mistrusters	FGGIINNORUV	unforgiving
EIINRSSTTTU	instituters	EINNOOPPRTU	inopportune	FGHIILMNPSY	simplifying
EIINRSSTTTW	intertwists	EINNOORSTUX	neurotoxins	FGHIILNORSU	flourishing
EIIOPPRRRTX	proprietrix	EINNOOSSSUX	noxiousness	FGHIINNRSSU	furnishings
EIIOPPSSTUV	suppositive	EINNOPSSSSU	suspensions	FGHILNORTTY	fortnightly
EIIOPRRSTUV	superiority	EINNOQRSTUU	non sequitur	FGIIILMNPSY	simplifying
EIJKMMRSSUU	Rijksmuseum	EINNORSSSUU	ruinousness	FGIIILNOSSS	fossilising
EIKLLORRSTW	trelliswork	EINNOSSSSUU	sinuousness	FGIIILNOSSZ	fossilizing
EIKNNOSSSTT	stinkstones	EINOOPPRSSS	oppressions	FGIILMNNORY	informingly
EIKNOORRRSW	ironworkers	EINOOPRRSST	resorptions	FGIILNSTTUY	stultifying
EILLMOORSUV	mellivorous	EINOOPSSSSS	possessions	FGIINNOOPSY	opsonifying
EILLNOORRST	ritornellos	EINOORSSSTU	riotousness	FGINOORTTTX	foxtrotting
EILLNOPSSTY	pointlessly	EINOPPRSSST	stroppiness	FGIOORRSUUV	frugivorous
EILLOPRRSUY	prelusorily	EINOPPRSSSU	suppression	FIIIMNNOSSU	infusionism
EILMMNOPRTY	promiliently	EINOPRRRSST	ripsnorters	FIIIMOPRSTT	stipitiform
EILMNNOPRTY	prominently	EINOPRRRTTU	interruptor	FIIINNNOSTU	infusionist
EILMNOOOPRS	monopoliser	EINOPSSTTTY	stenotypist	FIILLNOOSUX	solifluxion
EILMNOOOPRZ	monopolizer	EINOQRSTTUU	tourniquets	FIIMMNOSSTZ	Fitzsimmons
EILMNOOOPSS	monopolises	EINORSSTTUY	strenuosity	FIIORSSTTTU	fortuitists
EILMNOOOPSZ	monopolizes	EIOOPPRRRST	proprietors	FIKLLLNSUUY	unskilfully
EILMNOPRTUY	importunely	EIOOPPRRSST	prepositors	FIKLLOORSST	folklorists
EILMNORSUVY	verminously	EIOORSSTTUZ	zootsuiters	FILLOORSUVY	frivolously
EILMNOSSYYZ	enzymolysis	EIOPRRSSSUV	supervisors	FILMRSSTTUU	mistrustful
EILMOORRSWY	worrisomely	EIOPRRSSUVY	supervisory	FILNOORSSTY	frontolysis
EILMOPRSSTY	proselytism	EIOPRSSTTTU	prostitutes	FLLOORRSUWY	sorrowfully
EILMOPRSTTU	Triptolemus	EIOQRRSTTUU	triquetrous	GGGIILNNNSU	gunslinging
EILMOPRTUVY	pluviometry	EIORRSTTTUY	restitutory	GGHIIINNRSTZ	rightsizing
EILMOPSTUUY	impetuously	EJJMNOOSTUY	jejunostomy	GGHIILLNSTY	slightingly
EILMORSTTUY	multistorey	EJKNOORRUWY	journeywork	GGHIIMNNSTU	gunsmithing
EILNOOPRSST	portionless	EKKOOPPRSVY	Prokopyevsk	GGHINNNOSTU	shotgunning
EILNOOPRTTU	luteotropin	EKLOOPRRSSW	slopworkers	GGIILLNOSSY	syllogising
EILNOORSSTU	resolutions	EKNNNNOSSUW	unknownness	GGIILLNOSYZ	syllogizing
EILNOORSTUV	revolutions	ELLMNNOOSTY	somnolently	GGIILNOPSSY	gossipingly
EILNOOSSTTU	solution set	ELLMORSTUUY	tremulously	GGIINNNRSTU	unstringing
EILNOPRSUUY	penuriously	ELLOQRSUUUY	querulously	GGIINNOPSST	signposting
EILNOQRTUVY	ventriloquy	ELLRSSSTTUY	trustlessly	GGIINNPPRSU	upspringing
EILNPQSTTUU	quintuplets	ELMMNOOSTUY	momentously	GGILLLNOORS	logrollings
EILOOPRRSTY	posteriorly	ELMMOPSSSTY	symptomless	GGILNOOORWW	woolgrowing
EILOOPRSSTY	proteolysis	ELMNOOPSUYY	eponymously	GHHIIINRSTT	nightshirts
EILOPPRRSTW	slipperwort	ELNOOPPRTUY	opportunely	GHHIIPRSSTW	shipwrights
EILOPPRSUVY	purposively	ELNORSSTUUY	strenuously	GHHILOPRTTT	trothplight
EILRRSSTUVW	liverwursts	ELOPPRSSSTU	supportless	GHHINOOPRTU	thoroughpin
EIMMNNORSSW	nonswimmers	EMMOOPRSSTT	postmortems	GHHINOPRSTT	triphthongs
EIMNNOOOPSS	monopsonies	EMNNOOOOSUV	nonvenomous	GHHIOPPPRSY	hippogryphs
EIMNNOOOSST	monotonises	EMNNOOORSTU	motoneurons	GHHMMNOOOPT	monophthong
EIMNNOOOSTZ	monotonizes	EMNOOPPSSSU	pompousness	GHIIIKMNRSS	skirmishing
EIMNNOOPSTT	omnipotents	EMNOOPRSSTW	sportswomen	GHIIKLNNRSY	shrinkingly
EIMNNOOSSSU	ominousness	EMNOPRRSSTU	prosternums	GHIIKNNOTTU	outthinking
EIMNNOSSSYY	synonymises	EMNORRSSTUU	surmounters	GHIILLLNRTY	thrillingly
EIMNNOSSYYZ	synonymizes	EMOOOPRRSST	mosstrooper	GHIILLMRSTW	millwrights
EIMNNRSSTTU	instruments	EMOOORRSSTV	servomotors	GHIILLOOPST	philologist

659

GHIILLOOSTT	lithologist	**GIILNOPSSTY**	stylopising	**HILLOOSTUWW**	Willow South
GHIILMNOOSS	Missolonghi	**GIILNOPSTYZ**	stylopizing	**HILNOOPSTXY**	xylophonist
GHIILNNPSUV	punishingly	**GIILNOSTTUY**	glutinosity	**HIMMOOOPRSZ**	zoomorphism
GHIILNOORST	rhinologist	**GIILOORSSTV**	virologists	**HIMNOOPSSUV**	symphonious
GHIILNOPSTY	philogynist	**GIIMNNOPRSU**	unpromising	**HIMNOPSSSTY**	symphonists
GHIILOOOPST	ophiologist	**GIIMNNOPRTU**	importuning	**HIMOOOPRSSU**	isomorphous
GHIILOOSSTT	histologist	**GIIMNOSSSTY**	misogynists	**HIMOOPRRSTU**	trimorphous
GHIINNOPSTY	hypnotising	**GIIMNRSSTTU**	mistrusting	**HINOOOPRSSS**	sponsorship
GHIINNOPTYZ	hypnotizing	**GIINNOOPTTU**	outpointing	**HINOOOPSTTY**	phonotypist
GHIINNOTTTW	Whittington	**GIINNOPRRST**	ripsnorting	**HINOOPRRTTY**	thyrotropin
GHIINOPPRSW	worshipping	**GIINNOPSSSY**	synopsising	**HINOOPRSTUY**	hyponitrous
GHIJMNOPSUW	showjumping	**GIINNOPSSYZ**	synopsizing	**HINOOPSTTXY**	phytotoxins
GHILLOOOPST	hoplologist	**GIINNPRRSTU**	surprinting	**HIOOPRSSTTT**	orthoptists
GHILLOOPSYY	syphilology	**GIINOORSTUV**	vortiginous	**HLLOOPPRSSY**	sporophylls
GHILMNOOSTY	hymnologist	**GIINOPRRSUU**	pruriginous	**HLNOOOPPSUY**	polyphonous
GHILMOOSTTY	mythologist	**GIINOPRSSTU**	posturising	**HMOOOOPRSSU**	homosporous
GHILNNOOSTY	holystoning	**GIINOPRSTUZ**	posturizing	**HMOOPSTTTUY**	pottymouths
GHILNOOOPST	phonologist	**GIKLNNNOUWY**	unknowingly	**HORRSTTTUWY**	trustworthy
GHILNOOORTY	ornithology	**GIKLNOOPRVY**	provokingly	**IIIILMNNQSU**	inquilinism
GHILNOOPSTY	hypnologist	**GILLLMNOSUU**	slumgullion	**IIIILNNQTUY**	inquilinity
GHILNOOPSUV	philogynous	**GILLMOOPSTY**	polyglotism	**IIIIMMPRSTV**	primitivism
GHILOOOPRTY	oligotrophy	**GILLNOSTUUY**	glutinously	**IIIIMPPSSSS**	Mississippi
GHILOOOORSST	horologists	**GILMMNRRUUY**	murmuringly	**IIIIMPRSTTV**	primitivist
GHILOOPSTTY	phytologist	**GILMNOOOSST**	monologists	**IIIINNOQSTU**	inquisition
GHIMMNOOORSU	mushrooming		nomologists	**IIIILLMNOPST**	pointillism
GHIMNOOPSYY	physiognomy	**GILMOOOPSST**	pomologists	**IIIILLMNOSSU**	illusionism
GHIMOOOSSYZ	homozygosis	**GILMOOSSTYZ**	zymologists	**IIIILLMNOSSTU**	illuminists
GHINOOOSTTU	outshooting	**GILNNNOPSSU**	nonplussing	**IIIILLNNOQTU**	quintillion
GHINOOPPTTY	phototyping	**GILNOOOSSST**	nosologists	**IIIILLNOPSTT**	pointillist
GHLNOOPSSUW	snowploughs	**GILNOPSSTYY**	polygynists	**IIIILLNOSSTT**	tonsillitis
GHNOOOOPRSU	gonophorous	**GILNORRTTUY**	torturingly	**IIIILLNOSSTU**	illusionist
GIIIINNPRST	inspiriting	**GILNRSTTTUY**	struttingly	**IIIILNNOQSSUU**	inquilinous
GIIIILLNORTV	vitriolling	**GILOOOPSSTT**	topologists	**IIIIMNOOPSST**	impositions
GIIIILLOSTUV	litigiously	**GILOOPSSTTY**	typologists	**IIIINNNORTTU**	innutrition
GIIIILNNPRSY	inspiringly	**GIMMNNNRRUUU**	unmurmuring	**IIIINNOSTTTU**	institution
GIIIILNNQORUY	inquiringly	**GIMNNOOSSTY**	monogynists	**IIIINOOPSTUV**	oviposition
GIIIILNNSSTY	insistingly	**GIMNNORSTUU**	surmounting	**IIIINOQRSSTU**	inquisitors
GIIIMNNNOTU	munitioning	**GIMNOOOPRSU**	sporogonium	**IIIOPSSSTTV**	positivists
GIIIMNNOOSU	ignominious	**GINNNOOPRSS**	nonprossing	**IIJLNORSUUY**	injuriously
GIIIMNNOPRS	imprisoning	**GINNNOOPRST**	nonsporting	**IIKKLOOSSTV**	Tsiolkovski
GIIIMNNPRST	imprintings	**GINNOOPRSTT**	strongpoint	**IILLLOPPSSW**	pillowslips
	misprinting	**GINOOPRSTUU**	outpourings	**IILLNOOPSST**	postillions
GIIIMNOPRSV	improvising	**GKMOORSSSUY**	Moussorgsky	**IILLOOQSSTU**	soliloquist
GIIINNNOPPT	pinpointing	**GMNOOORSSTU**	strongrooms	**IILLORSSTUU**	illustrious
GIIINNNPRSU	uninspiring	**GNOOOPRSTUY**	protogynous	**IILMRSSTTUU**	tristimulus
GIIINNOOPST	positioning	**HHIMOOOPPRSS**	phosphorism	**IILNNOOSTUV**	involutions
GIIINNSTTTU	instituting	**HHIMOOPRRSZ**	rhizomorphs	**IILNNOOSUXY**	innoxiously
GIIINOOPSTV	ovipositing	**HHMNOOOOPSU**	homophonous	**IILOOPRRSVY**	provisorily
GIIKLMNOPPS	milksopping	**HHOOOOPPRSU**	phosphorous	**IILOSSSTTXY**	stylostixis
GIIKLNNPRSS	sprinklings	**HHOOOPPRSTT**	phototrophs	**IIMNNNNOOSU**	nonunionism
GIILLLNNUWY	unwillingly	**HIIILLNNNOOT**	nonillionth	**IIMNOOPRSTU**	positronium
GIILLMNOOST	limnologist	**HIIILLNORSTT**	trillionths	**IIMNOPRTTUY**	importunity
GIILLMNOPRY	imploringly	**HIIILLOQRSUV**	liquorishly	**IINNNNOOSTU**	nonunionist
GIILLMNPTUY	multiplying	**HIIILMNNOOPY**	hypolimnion	**IINOOOOPPRST**	proposition
GIILMNOPRSY	promisingly	**HIIILMOOPSUV**	myiophilous	**IINOOOPPSST**	oppositions
GIILMNOPRVY	improvingly	**HIIILMOOSTTT**	lithotomist	**IINOOPPSSTU**	supposition
GIILMNOQRSUY	squirmingly	**HIIILNNPSSST**	shinsplints	**IINOPPQRTUY**	propinquity
GIILMOOSSST	misologists	**HIIILOPRSTTY**	lithotripsy	**IINORSSTTTU**	institutors
GIILNNPQTUU	quintupling	**HIIMMOOPRSS**	isomorphism	**IIOOOPRSSTV**	ovipositors
GIILNNTTUWY	unwittingly	**HIIMMOPRRST**	trimorphism	**ILLORSUUUXY**	luxuriously
GIILNOORSUV	lignivorous	**HIIMNOOPRST**	monitorship	**ILMNNNOOSUU**	nonluminous
GIILNOOSSST	sinologists	**HILLOOPSUXY**	xylophilous	**ILMNOOOPSST**	monopolists

ILMOOSSTTXY	xylotomists	**IMOOOPRSSTU**	impostorous	**IOOPRRSTTTU**	prostitutor
ILNOOOPRSTY	lyosorption	**IMOOPPRSTTU**	pittosporum	**LMNOOOPSUYY**	polyonymous
ILNOOOPSSUV	poisonously	**IMOOPRSSTUU**	imposturous	**LMNOOOSSTUY**	monostylous
ILNOOORSTUY	notoriously	**IMOPSSTTUUY**	sumptuosity	**LMNOORSSTUY**	monstrously
ILNOOPPRSSU	propulsions	**INOOOPPRRST**	proportions	**LMOPSSTUUUY**	sumptuously
ILOOPPRSSST	spoilsports	**INOOOPPRSTU**	opportunist	**LOORRSTTUUY**	torturously
IMNOOPPRSTU	opportunism	**INOOPPRTTUY**	opportunity	**MMNOOOOSSTU**	monostomous
IMNOORSSTTY	monstrosity	**INOOPRRSSTU**	protrusions		
IMOOOPPRRTU	motu proprio	**IOOPPRSSTUY**	suppository		

Twelve Letters

AAAAAALMRSTT	taramasalata		AAABCEERSSSU	scarabaeuses
AAAABCCHILNN	bacchanalian		AAABCEHILLPT	alphabetical
AAAABCLMORST	Malabar Coast		AAABCEHILNPT	analphabetic
AAAABDEGLMNV	Magdalena Bay		AAABCEHIMRSU	Beaumarchais
AAAABDEIKNNR	Bandaranaike		AAABCEHLOPPR	approachable
AAAABDGGHITV	Bhagavad-Gita		AAABCELNRRTU	tabernacular
AAAABDHHMRTY	Madhya Bharat		AAABCGIINNRT	Cantabrigian
AAAABHILNRSS	Hasan al-Basri		AAABDEELLMNT	Matabeleland
AAAACCCCIRTU	acciaccatura		AAABDEILMRST	dramatisable
AAAACDIILPRS	paradisaical		AAABDEILMRTZ	dramatizable
	paradisiacal		AAABDEMRSSSS	ambassadress
AAAACEGGIMNR	Magna Graecia		AAABDIILPTTY	adaptability
AAAACEINRRSV	caravanserai		AAABDIJMNNRS	Bandjarmasin
AAAACGILPSSS	passacaglias		AAABDILLOOPR	paraboloidal
AAAACGIMMNRT	anagrammatic		AAABDILNNSST	Batan Islands
AAAACIMNRSST	antimacassar		AAABEEGILMRR	marriageable
AAAADHNPRRUU	Anuradhapura		AAABEEGLMNNU	unmanageable
AAAADLNPRSSU	Sardanapalus		AAABEEHIMNPS	amphisbaenae
AAAAEGGLNPRU	paralanguage		AAABEEHIRSST	baraesthesia
AAAAEGKKLNNO	Okanagan Lake		AAABEELLNPPU	unappealable
AAAAEGNRTVXZ	extravaganza		AAABEELNPPSU	unappeasable
AAAAEHILMSST	thalassaemia		AAABEHIMNPSS	amphisbaenas
AAAAEHLLNPST	Pallas Athena		AAABEHINRRST	breatharians
AAAAEIKMNORW	Waikaremoana		AAABEHLMOSTT	haematoblast
AAAAEIMMNRRT	armamentaria		AAABEIILMNNT	maintainable
AAAAFGILLNRS	Niagara Falls		AAABEILLMNOT	balletomania
AAAAFINRRSST	rastafarians		AAABEILLNSSU	unassailable
AAAAGGILMMNT	amalgamating		AAABEILNNTTU	unattainable
AAAAGILMMNOT	amalgamation		AAABEINNSSST	San Sebastián
AAAAIILLMNRT	antimalarial		AAABEKLNSSTT	Balkan States
AAAAILLPRRSS	sarsaparilla		AAABELLNPPUY	unappealably
AAAAILNNRSTV	Transvaalian		AAABELLNRSTT	translatable
AAAAILNRSSTU	Australasian		AAABELNOOPTY	palaeobotany
AAAAINNNORTV	Antananarivo		AAABELQSTTUU	absquatulate
AAAALLLOOPSZ	lalapaloozas		AAABEPRRSSUZ	superbazaars
AAABBCEEINRS	Caribbean Sea		AAABGGLNNPRU	Luang Prabang
AAABBCILLRRY	barbarically		AAABGHPPRRSU	subparagraph
AAABBCORRSTY	Barbary Coast		AAABGIILNRRT	Gibraltarian
AAABBEIILLOV	bioavailable		AAABHHIIMPRS	Ibrahim Pasha
AAABBHMMNORT	Rabbath Ammon		AAABHIILNOTT	habitational
AAABBIIMNRRS	barbarianism		AAABHILNPRSU	Ashurbanipal
AAABCCDDIRRY	bradycardiac		AAABHINORSTU	South Arabian
AAABCCEILLMT	acclimatable		AAABIIILLTVY	availability
AAABCDEEINRS	abecedarians		AAABIILLPTTY	palatability
AAABCDEHLNNU	Bechuanaland		AAABIKKLNOTU	Kota Kinabalu
AAABCDEHNOTY	Daytona Beach		AAABILLNQRRU	Barranquilla
AAABCDEIORSS	scarabaeoids		AAABILLNSSUY	unassailably

AAABILNPRSSU	Assurbanipal
	sublapsarian
AAABIMMNRSTU	Ambartsumian
AAACCCCEIRTU	acciaccature
AAACCCDHIRTY	tachycardiac
AAACCCEILSTT	acatalectics
AAACCCISSTTU	catacaustics
AAACCDEEGNRS	Cascade Range
AAACCDEFHNNR	French Canada
AAACCDEIIMNS	academicians
AAACCDEILLMY	academically
AAACCDEILMNO	decalcomania
AAACCDHILORS	saccharoidal
AAACCDIINRRT	intracardiac
AAACCDILLLOP	Dallapiccola
AAACCEGILMTT	metagalactic
AAACCEGIORSU	agaricaceous
AAACCEHINPSU	ipecacuanhas
AAACCEHNOSTU	acanthaceous
AAACCEIINPTT	incapacitate
AAACCEILLNTU	canaliculate
AAACCEILLORS	calceolarias
AAACCEINNQTU	acquaintance
AAACCELNRSSU	crassulacean
AAACCGIINPTT	capacitating
AAACCHILLNRY	anarchically
AAACCHILNNOR	anachronical
AAACCHILNPTY	anaphylactic
AAACCIILMRST	marcasitical
AAACCIINNPTT	incapacitant
AAACCIINOPTT	capacitation
AAACCILMNOST	acclamations
AAACCILNPTTY	anaptyctical
AAACCILORSTU	accusatorial
AAACDEGILMOR	megalocardia
AAACDEHINRST	acidantheras
AAACDEILLMNY	maenadically
AAACDEILMPRS	paramedicals
AAACDEILNRST	cardinalates
AAACDEIMMRSS	macadamisers
AAACDEIMMRSZ	macadamizers
AAACDEINRSTT	tradescantia
AAACDELLLNNW	Welland Canal
AAACDENNOPSU	pandanaceous
AAACDGHNPRTU	Chandragupta
AAACDGIIMMNS	macadamising
AAACDGIIMMNZ	macadamizing
AAACDGIIMMRT	diagrammatic
AAACDGIIMPRT	paradigmatic
AAACDIINNNSV	Scandinavian
AAACDILLMRTY	dramatically
AAACEEEENPPRR	reappearance
AAACEEGHNNRR	carragheenan
AAACEEGNRTVX	extravagance
AAACEEHINSST	East China Sea
AAACEEJKNPSS	jackanapeses
AAACEGGGLOTU	galactagogue
AAACEGHILLPS	cephalalgias
AAACEGHNRSTW	Wasatch Range
AAACEGILLNNS	gallinaceans
AAACEGILMMNO	megalomaniac
AAACEGIMMNSU	Macías Nguema
AAACEGIMNPRT	paramagnetic
AAACEGIRRSWY	carriageways
AAACEGLPRSSW	Pascal's wager
AAACEHHNRTTU	Harthacanute
AAACEHILMMTT	mathematical
AAACEHIMOPPR	pharmacopeia
AAACEHIMRRTT	matriarchate
AAACEHINRSSZ	Arias Sánchez
AAACEHIPRRTT	patriarchate
AAACEHKNSSTW	Saskatchewan
AAACEHLMORTY	haematocryal
AAACEIILMNRT	Latin America
AAACEIJLMNTY	Calamity Jane
AAACEILMOOST	osteomalacia
AAACEILMPRRT	parametrical
AAACEILNORTU	aeronautical
AAACEILORSTT	aerostatical
AAACELMMORST	sarcolemmata
AAACELMNRSST	sacramentals
AAACELMOPRST	paracetamols
AAACELNOSSTU	santalaceous
AAACFIINRRTT	antiaircraft
AAACFIMNRRST	aircraftsman
AAACGGGILLNOV	anagogically
AAACGHHILNWY	Alcan Highway
AAACGHIINNRT	Carthaginian
AAACGHILLNPY	anaglyphical
AAACGHIMNOPS	phagomaniacs
AAACGIIMNSTT	anastigmatic
AAACGILLLNOV	analogically
AAACGILLLNVY	galvanically
AAACGILLMMMO	mammalogical
AAACGILLNPTY	anaglyptical
AAACGILMNNOS	anglomaniacs
AAACHHIKNRTU	Khachaturian
AAACHIKPPRST	apparatchiks
AAACHILLLMTY	thalamically
AAACHILMNRST	charlatanism
AAACHILNOSTU	anacoluthias
AAACHIMNORTU	tauromachian
AAACHIPPRRST	paraphrastic
AAACIIILNNRT	catilinarian
AAACIIILNNOST	canalisation
AAACIILNNOTZ	canalization
AAACIILNNRRT	intracranial
AAACILLLNTYY	analytically
AAACILLMNOTY	anatomically
AAACILLMORTY	aromatically
AAACILMMNNOO	monomaniacal
AAACILMNOPRY	pyromaniacal
AAACILNSTTTY	anticatalyst
AAACIMNNOTTU	catamountain
AAACINPPRSTY	parasynaptic
AAACMMOORSWY	Coomaraswamy
AAADDEGINSTV	disadvantage
AAADDEGLNOPT	Ponta Delgada
AAADDGILLMOV	amygdaloidal
AAADDIJLRSUU	Siraj-ud-daula
AAADDILLNNSS	Åland Islands
AAADEEGKPRSS	Drake Passage
AAADEEGRTTVX	extravagated
AAADEEINRRSV	Sierra Nevada

663

AAADEELNRTTX	Alexandretta
AAADEERSTTVX	extravasated
AAADEFFNNORS	fanfaronades
AAADEGILNRTV	landgraviate
AAADEGILNSSV	Savage Island
AAADEGIMQRSU	Quadragesima
AAADEGLNRSTV	landgravates
AAADEGNOSTUV	advantageous
AAADEILLOPRT	Río de la Plata
AAADEILMNNRS	salamandrine
AAADEIMNNRST	mandarinates
AAADEINOPRTT	readaptation
AAADEINSSSST	assassinated
AAADFIINORST	faradisation
AAADFIINORTZ	faradization
AAADGGINORST	aggradations
AAADGHHIMNSW	Aswan High Dam
AAADGIILLORT	gladiatorial
AAADGINOPRRS	Gran Paradiso
AAADGLNQRRUU	quadrangular
AAADHHMNRSTU	Rhadamanthus
AAADHIILMNOT	amianthoidal
AAADHIINOPRS	anaphrodisia
AAADHILLNRSW	Hadrian's Wall
AAADIILLNOTT	dilatational
AAADIILNORRS	radiolarians
AAADILLLQRTU	Lailat-ul-Qadr
AAADILLNSSTY	All Saints' Day
AAAEEGGLMNTU	metalanguage
AAAEEGILMNRT	Marie Galante
AAAEEGILMSTX	metagalaxies
AAAEEGINNRSX	sexagenarian
AAAEEGMNNPRT	permanganate
AAAEEGRSTTVX	extravagates
AAAEEHIMNSTT	anathematise
AAAEEHIMNTTZ	anathematize
AAAEEHIMRRST	Maria Theresa
AAAEEHIPRSST	paraesthesia
AAAEELLLMNRT	Tell el Amarna
AAAEERSSTTVX	extravasates
AAAEFHIMRRSZ	Mazar-e-Sharif
AAAEFILNRSTT	Santa Fe Trail
AAAEFKLMMSTU	Mustafa Kemal
AAAEGGNNRSTU	Nusa Tenggara
AAAEGHIMMNOS	haemangiomas
AAAEGHIMMNOT	hemangiomata
AAAEGHLOPPRY	palaeography
AAAEGHNPSSTU	agapanthuses
AAAEGIILNRST	egalitarians
AAAEGILLMNRY	managerially
AAAEGILMNNST	galantamines
AAAEGIMNORTV	Moravian Gate
AAAEGIMNPRST	Seringapatam
AAAEGIMRRSTV	margraviates
AAAEGINNNNOR	nonagenarian
AAAEHILNPRST	Rhaetian Alps
AAAEHKORSTUV	katharevousa
AAAEHMOPRRTY	aromatherapy
AAAEHNPRSTTY	parasyntheta
AAAEIILNQRTU	equalitarian
AAAEIINNRSTZ	Saint-Nazaire
AAAEIKLLNNST	antalkalines
AAAEIKNPSSTT	East Pakistan
AAAEILLLNPRT	antiparallel
AAAEILLNPSST	palatialness
AAAEILMNOPPR	paralipomena
AAAEILMRRTTX	extramarital
AAAEILNNNOTX	annexational
AAAEILNPPRRS	prelapsarian
AAAEILNRSTUW	New Australia
AAAEILPPRRSS	reappraisals
AAAEIMNNRSST	transaminase
AAAEIMOOTTUX	autotoxaemia
AAAEINSSSSST	assassinates
AAAEKKLMRTTU	Kemal Atatürk
AAAELLMMMPSS	plasmalemmas
AAAELMNOVVYZ	Novaya Zemlya
AAAELQQRSUUV	quaquaversal
AAAENPPRSSSY	parasynapses
AAAFIILMNNNWY	Flaminian Way
AAAFINRRSTTU	trustafarian
AAAGGHINPPRR	paragraphing
AAAGGINORSTV	aggravations
AAAGGIOPPRTU	appoggiatura
AAAGGLNOSSUV	Volsunga Saga
AAAGGMORRSYZ	Magyarország
AAAGHIKNOSTT	kotahitangas
AAAGHINPPRRS	paraphrasing
AAAGHIRSTTWY	straightaway
AAAGHNOPRSTU	paragnathous
AAAGIILLNPST	palatalising
AAAGIILLNPTZ	palatalizing
AAAGIILNNOTV	navigational
AAAGIINNOPST	paganisation
AAAGIINNOPTZ	paganization
AAAGIINRSSTT	sagittarians
AAAGILLLORRT	grallatorial
AAAGLLMOOTUY	autoallogamy
AAAHHHHNORSS	Rosh Hashanah
AAAHHHJNPRSU	Shahjahanpur
AAAHHNOPSTUX	hapaxanthous
AAAHIILNNOTT	antihalation
AAAHIIMNNRTU	humanitarian
AAAHILMNRRTU	Muralitharan
AAAHLLMNPSYY	phantasmally
AAAHLNNOSTXY	Saxony-Anhalt
AAAIILMNPRSU	marsupialian
AAAIILMPRRTY	paramilitary
AAAIILNNORTT	antirational
AAAIILNNOSST	nasalisation
AAAIILNNOSTZ	nasalization
AAAIILNORTTT	totalitarian
AAAIILNPSSTU	saintpaulias
AAAIINNQRSTU	antiquarians
AAAIINRSTTTW	Taiwan Strait
AAAIKLNNOPRT	National Park
AAAILMNOPSSS	anaplasmosis
AAAILMNORTTU	maturational
AAAILNNOSSTY	analysations
AAAILNNOSTYZ	analyzations
AAAILNNRSTVY	Transylvania
AAAILNOPRSTY	paralysation
AAAILNOPRTYZ	paralyzation
AAAIMNNOOSST	antonomasias

AAAIMNOOPRSS	paronomasias
AAAINNNRRSTU	transuranian
AAAINOOPPSST	appassionato
AAAINPPRSSSY	parasynapsis
AAALLLLOOOPZ	lollapalooza
AABBCCEMOOSU	bombacaceous
AABBCDEHLRRS	hardscrabble
AABBCEEKKRRS	backbreakers
AABBCEGIKKNR	backbreaking
AABBCEGMORSW	cabbageworms
AABBCEGNOSTW	cabbagetowns
AABBCEILNOSZ	Blasco Ibáñez
AABBCEINORST	bicarbonates
AABBCGIKLLLN	blackballing
AABBCIIILMNO	bibliomaniac
AABBCIILLNRY	rabbinically
AABBDEEKRSST	breadbaskets
AABBDEELRSST	beadblasters
AABBDEEORRSV	beaverboards
AABBDEGILNST	beadblasting
AABBDILMNOSU	subabdominal
AABBDNNOORRT	Noordbrabant
AABBEEKLLRRS	ballbreakers
AABBEEKLNNOR	nonbreakable
AABBEELLRSST	barbastelles
AABBEFGLRSST	flabbergasts
AABBEGIINRTV	abbreviating
AABBEIIKLLOS	Bielsko-Biała
AABBEIINORTV	abbreviation
AABBEILNNOTU	unobtainable
AABBEILRTTTU	attributable
AABBEIORRSTV	abbreviators
AABBEIRRSTTU	barbiturates
AABBGHIMNOST	thingamabobs
AABBHIIILTTY	habitability
AABBHIKOSSUZ	bashibazouks
AABBHNNORRTT	North Brabant
AABCCDEIILRT	bactericidal
AABCCDEIKNRR	crackbrained
AABCCDEILLSY	decasyllabic
AABCCEELNPTU	unacceptable
AABCCEILLLNU	incalculable
AABCCEILLMOV	clavicembalo
AABCCEILMNOR	microbalance
AABCCEIMORTY	mycobacteria
AABCCEIRRTUU	bureaucratic
AABCCENOORSU	carbonaceous
AABCCGIIKKNP	pickabacking
AABCCGIJKKLN	blackjacking
AABCCGIKKNRT	backtracking
AABCCHHIIMPR	amphibrachic
AABCCIILLLOT	lactobacilli
AABCCIILOTTY	biocatalytic
AABCCILLLNUY	incalculably
AABCCILMOORT	mobocratical
AABCCILOSSTT	cactoblastis
AABCCINRSTTU	subantarctic
AABCCKLNRRTU	blackcurrant
AABCDDDEEKLS	saddlebacked
AABCDDEEKLLP	backpedalled
AABCDDEENORT	decarbonated
AABCDDEENRSU	Secunderabad
AABCDDEGKLRU	blackguarded
AABCDDEHKLNY	backhandedly
AABCDDEJLORS	Jacob's ladder
AABCDDEKLRRW	bladderwrack
AABCDDIKMNOS	diamondbacks
AABCDEEIILNR	ineradicable
AABCDEEILLPS	displaceable
AABCDEEKNRRS	breakdancers
AABCDEELLLSY	decasyllable
AABCDEELNORV	overbalanced
AABCDEENORST	decarbonates
AABCDEENOSTU	subdeaconate
AABCDEFLNOTU	confabulated
AABCDEGIKLNP	backpedaling
AABCDEGIKNNR	breakdancing
AABCDEHHMNRS	chamberhands
AABCDEHIINRT	dibranchiate
AABCDEHIMMRS	chambermaids
AABCDEHMMNOR	rhabdomancer
AABCDEHORRTY	carbohydrate
AABCDEIILNNS	cannibalised
AABCDEIILNNZ	cannibalized
AABCDEIILNRY	ineradicably
AABCDEILLSTY	syllabicated
AABCDEINOSTU	subdiaconate
AABCDEKNRSSW	backwardness
AABCDELLNNNO	cannonballed
AABCDELLOORT	collaborated
AABCDELMNRSU	candelabrums
AABCDELOPPRR	clapperboard
AABCDELRSTTY	abstractedly
AABCDENOORRT	decarbonator
AABCDEOPRRRS	scraperboard
AABCDEORRSST	broadcasters
	rebroadcasts
AABCDGGIOORS	braggadocios
AABCDGILNOPR	clapboarding
AABCDGINNOOR	carbonadoing
AABCDGINORST	broadcasting
AABCDGKLLRUY	blackguardly
AABCDIILLLOY	diabolically
AABCDIILMNOY	biodynamical
AABCDIIOPRSS	basidiocarps
AABCDIIQRSTU	biquadratics
AABCDKMNOOSW	backwoodsman
AABCEEEFFILN	ineffaceable
AABCEEEGHLNX	exchangeable
AABCEEEGHLRR	rechargeable
AABCEEEHLRRS	researchable
AABCEEENORTT	betacarotene
AABCEEFFILNY	ineffaceably
AABCEEFIPRRT	prefabricate
AABCEEGGPRRT	carpetbagger
AABCEEGHLNNU	unchangeable
AABCEEGHLNXY	exchangeably
AABCEEGINRTX	exacerbating
AABCEEHKLRST	leatherbacks
AABCEEHLMNRT	merchantable
AABCEEHLOPRR	reproachable
AABCEEHMNRST	antechambers
AABCEEIKMNRT	cabinetmaker
AABCEEILLMMT	emblematical

AABCEEILMNSS	amicableness	**AABCENORSSST**	contrabasses
AABCEEINORTX	exacerbation	**AABCEOORSTTZ**	azotobacters
AABCEEKPPRRS	paperbackers	**AABCFIINORST**	fabrications
AABCEELLNOOT	oblanceolate	**AABCFLNOORTU**	confabulator
AABCEELLNPSS	placableness	**AABCGHIILOPR**	biographical
AABCEELLNSSS	scalableness	**AABCGHIOOPRS**	agoraphobics
AABCEELLORRT	correlatable	**AABCGIIKLLMN**	blackmailing
AABCEELNORSV	overbalances	**AABCGIINNNNS**	Canning Basin
AABCEFIILLSS	classifiable	**AABCGIKLNPPS**	backslapping
AABCEFIILLTY	beatifically	**AABCGILLLSUY**	subglacially
AABCEFIILNST	sanctifiable	**AABCGILNNOTU**	outbalancing
AABCEFLNOSTU	confabulates	**AABCGLMNNOUZ**	Guzmán Blanco
AABCEGHILPTY	bathypelagic	**AABCHIILMPST**	amphiblastic
AABCEGHLNNUY	unchangeably	**AABCHIIMORTT**	microhabitat
AABCEGIKNPPR	paperbacking	**AABCHIINOOTT**	cohabitation
AABCEHHPSSTY	bathyscaphes	**AABCHIINORST**	brachiations
AABCEHIIMNPS	amphisbaenic	**AABCIIILNPTY**	incapability
AABCEHILMNRS	chamberlains	**AABCIILLNPPY**	inapplicably
AABCEHILNRTU	uncharitable	**AABCIILLPRSY**	parisyllabic
AABCEHLMNORS	elasmobranch	**AABCIILMRSST**	strabismical
AABCEHLOPRRY	reproachably	**AABCIILNNOTU**	incubational
AABCEHNOORTY	archeobotany	**AABCIILRTTTY**	tractability
AABCEIIILPST	capabilities	**AABCILLLLSYY**	syllabically
AABCEIIILNPP	inapplicable	**AABCILMNOPRY**	incomparably
AABCEIILLOSS	socialisable	**AABCILNORSST**	San Cristóbal
AABCEIILLOSZ	socializable	**AABCILOSSTTY**	biocatalysts
AABCEIILLRTY	laceability	**AABCILRRSUUU**	subauricular
AABCEIILLTVY	cleavability	**AABCINNOORST**	carbonations
AABCEIILMMRS	bicameralism	**AABCINORRSTU**	carburations
AABCEIILMNOT	alembication	**AABCINORSSTT**	abstractions
AABCEIILMRST	bicameralist	**AABCLLOOORRT**	collaborator
AABCEIILNNSS	cannibalises	**AABCLNORSTTY**	contrastably
AABCEIILNNSZ	cannibalizes	**AABCLNORSTUY**	constabulary
AABCEIILRTTY	traceability	**AABCLPRSSSUU**	subscapulars
AABCEIILRTUU	biauriculate	**AABCMNNNOOTT**	noncombatant
AABCEIKLLMRS	blackmailers	**AABDDDENRRST**	standardbred
AABCEILLLORT	bicollateral	**AABDDEEKORST**	skateboarded
AABCEILLNPPU	unapplicable	**AABDDEELRRTW**	Albert Edward
AABCEILLNSSU	suballiances	**AABDDEGGORRS**	daggerboards
AABCEILLNSUV	vulcanisable	**AABDDEHHNRST**	handsbreadth
AABCEILLNUVZ	vulcanizable	**AABDDEHLLMOY**	hebdomadally
AABCEILLPRRY	bicarpellary	**AABDDGHORRTU**	draughtboard
AABCEILLSSTY	syllabicates	**AABDDHIIILMU**	Abdul-Hamid II
AABCEILLTTUV	cultivatable	**AABDEEEGILRS**	disagreeable
AABCEILMNNOT	contaminable	**AABDEEELNRSS**	readableness
AABCEILMNOPR	incomparable	**AABDEEGILRSY**	disagreeably
AABCEILMNRSY	carbylamines	**AABDEEGLNRSS**	gradableness
AABCEILMORRT	barometrical	**AABDEEHHRRSS**	haberdashers
AABCEILNNOST	sanctionable	**AABDEEHHRRSY**	haberdashery
AABCEILORSST	ostracisable	**AABDEEHILPST**	alphabetised
AABCEILORSTZ	ostracizable	**AABDEEHILPTZ**	alphabetized
AABCEILORSUV	vocabularies	**AABDEEHLRSTY**	breathalysed
AABCEILSSTTT	Baltic States	**AABDEEHLRTYZ**	breathalyzed
AABCEIMRSSTT	semiabstract	**AABDEEHORRTW**	weatherboard
AABCEINRRSTT	scatterbrain	**AABDEEILRTTX**	extraditable
AABCEIORSTTT	bacteriostat	**AABDEEJLRSTU**	readjustable
AABCEKLLRRST	trackerballs	**AABDEEKORRST**	skateboarder
AABCEKQRRSTU	quarterbacks	**AABDEELLNSSU**	laudableness
AABCELLOORST	collaborates	**AABDEELMNNSS**	damnableness
AABCELNORSTT	contrastable	**AABDEELMPRTU**	perambulated
AABCELORSSXY	carboxylases	**AABDEFLLNNOR**	flannelboard
AABCELORSTXY	carboxylates	**AABDEGIIMSTU**	disambiguate

AABDEGIKNORW	wakeboarding
AABDEGINORTU	outbargained
AABDEGLLMNOR	balladmonger
AABDEHHIRRST	hairsbreadth
AABDEHILRTHW	withdrawable
AABDEIIKNRSY	bradykinesia
AABDEIILNRST	distrainable
AABDEIKNORST	debarkations
AABDEILLLOSW	disallowable
AABDEILLNOST	labiodentals
AABDEILMNSTU	Ústí nad Labem
AABDEILORRST	bardolatries
	labradorites
AABDEIMNORRS	dermabrasion
AABDEIMNRRSU	barramundies
AABDEIMRRSSS	disembarrass
AABDELNNOPRU	unpardonable
AABDELNRSSST	sandblasters
AABDELOPRRST	plasterboard
AABDFFIILNNS	Baffin Island
AABDGIILNORS	boardsailing
	sailboarding
AABDGIINNOST	bastinadoing
AABDGIINRSST	bastardising
AABDGIINRSTZ	bastardizing
AABDGILNNSST	sandblasting
AABDGINORRST	starboarding
AABDHIOORSUZ	biohazardous
AABDHLOPRSSS	splashboards
AABDHMMOORSY	rhabdomyomas
AABDIIILLTTY	dilatability
AABDIIILSTVY	advisability
AABDIILMQRSU	liquidambars
AABDILOORRSS	boardsailors
AABDIMNORSTU	adumbrations
AABDINOOTTUY	autoantibody
AABDMOORRRST	mortarboards
AABEEEGKMRRS	gamebreakers
AABEEEHKRRRT	heartbreaker
AABEEEILLPRR	irrepealable
AABEEEKRSTVW	basketweaver
AABEEELLNSSS	saleableness
AABEEELMNNSS	amenableness
AABEEELMNRUV	maneuverable
AABEEELMNSST	tameableness
AABEEELNPRTU	unrepeatable
AABEEELNRSST	rateableness
AABEEELNSSSV	saveableness
AABEEFGILLLT	biflagellate
AABEEFGILRRR	irrefragable
AABEEFHINRRT	featherbrain
AABEEFILMNST	manifestable
AABEEFKRRSST	breakfasters
AABEEFLNRRST	transferable
AABEEGGLMORT	mortgageable
AABEEGILMNST	magnetisable
AABEEGILMNTZ	magnetizable
AABEEGLNNTUW	Blaenau Gwent
AABEEGMMORRU	Oberammergau
AABEEHIILRTT	rehabilitate
AABEEHILPRST	alphabetiser
AABEEHILPRTZ	alphabetizer
AABEEHILPSST	alphabetises
AABEEHILPSTZ	alphabetizes
AABEEHLRRSTY	breathalyser
AABEEHLRRTYZ	breathalyzer
AABEEHLRSSTY	breathalyses
AABEEHLRSTYZ	breathalyzes
AABEEIILRSSV	braaivleises
AABEEILLLNPP	inappellable
AABEEILLPRRY	irrepealably
AABEEILMMRSU	immeasurable
AABEEILMNRRST	restrainable
AABEEILNRSSV	variableness
AABEEINRRRST	trainbearers
AABEEINRRSST	brainteasers
AABEEINRSSSV	abrasiveness
AABEEKLMNRRU	unremarkable
AABEEKLMNRTU	unmarketable
AABEEKSSSTTW	wastebaskets
AABEELLMNOST	balletomanes
AABEELLNPPSS	palpableness
AABEELLNSSSV	salvableness
AABEELLNSSUV	valuableness
AABEELMNORUV	manoeuvrable
AABEELMNRSUU	unmeasurable
AABEELMPRSTU	perambulates
AABEELNNORSU	unreasonable
AABEELNNOSSU	unseasonable
AABEELNNRSUW	unanswerable
AABEELNPSSSS	passableness
AABEELNRSTTU	entablatures
	subalternate
AABEELPRSSTT	breastplates
AABEENNRRSTU	subterranean
AABEENNRTUUV	Buenaventura
AABEFGIKNRST	breakfasting
AABEFGILRRRY	irrefragably
AABEFHINRRST	Bairnsfather
AABEFHLMNOTU	unfathomable
AABEFIILNOPS	saponifiable
AABEFIILNQTU	quantifiable
AABEFILLMMNS	inflammables
AABEFLLMMNNO	nonflammable
AABEFLNORUUV	unfavourable
AABEFLNRSSTU	transfusable
AABEGGILLNTU	agglutinable
AABEGHIKNRTT	breathtaking
AABEGHILLOSU	Heliogabalus
AABEGHIMNTTW	bantamweight
AABEGIILMNNU	unimaginable
AABEGIINRRTT	Great Britain
AABEGIINSSUU	Guinea-Bissau
AABEGIKLNRSW	lawbreakings
AABEGILNPPRT	palpebrating
	table-rapping
AABEGIMNRRSS	embarrassing
AABEGIRRRSTU	arbitrageurs
AABEGLLMOSST	megaloblasts
AABEGLMMOPRR	programmable
AABEHIINORTZ	hebraization
AABEHILMNORS	harmonisable
AABEHILMNORZ	harmonizable
AABEHILNQSUV	vanquishable

AABEHILNSSTU	habitualness
AABEHINRRSSW	brainwashers
AABEHIOOPRTT	teratophobia
AABEHLMOSSTT	hematoblasts
AABEIIILLNTY	alienability
AABEIILLLMTY	malleability
AABEIIILLORST	isobilateral
AABEIILLRTTY	alterability
AABEIILNRRST	libertarians
AABEIILPRRTY	reparability
AABEIILPRSTY	separability
AABEIILQTTUY	equatability
AABEIINOORSS	anaerobiosis
AABEIKLMNSTU	unmistakable
AABEIKMNORST	embarkations
AABEILLNRRTU	turbellarian
AABEILLRRSTZ	trailblazers
AABEILMMRSSU	summarisable
AABEILMMRSUY	immeasurably
AABEILMMRSUZ	summarizable
AABEILMORSTU	ambulatories
AABEILNOORST	elaborations
AABEILNPRRST	transpirable
AABEILNRRSTT	rattlebrains
AABEILOORRST	laboratories
AABEILOPPPRR	appropriable
AABEIMNRRSTT	arbitraments
AABEINNQRSTU	barquantines
AABEINSSTTTU	substantiate
AABEJNPSSTTU	Punjab States
AABELMMNOSTU	somnambulate
AABELMNRSTTU	transmutable
AABELMNRSUUY	unmeasurably
AABELMOPRRTU	perambulator
AABELNNORSUY	unreasonably
AABELNNOSSUY	unseasonably
AABELNNRSUWY	unanswerably
AABELNOPRSST	transposable
AABFGIILMORY	fibromyalgia
AABFHLMNOTUY	unfathomably
AABFIILLMMTY	flammability
AABFIILLOTTY	floatability
AABFLLMNOTYY	flamboyantly
AABFLNORUUVY	unfavourably
AABGGGILLNRY	ballyragging
AABGHIIILNTT	habilitating
AABGHIINNRSW	brainwashing
AABGIIILNSST	assibilating
AABGIIILNTVY	navigability
AABGIIINNRRTT	abirritating
AABGIILLNOOT	obligational
AABGIILLNORY	aboriginally
AABGIILLNRTZ	trailblazing
AABGIILMNNUY	unimaginably
AABGIILNOPRS	parabolising
AABGIILNOPRZ	parabolizing
AABGIILNRSTU	tabularising
AABGIILNRTUZ	tabularizing
AABGIMNRSTTU	masturbating
AABGLLMORSSY	syllabograms
AABHIIILNOTT	habilitation
AABHIIILRSSZ	bilharziasis
AABHIIINNOTT	inhabitation
AABHIILNNRTY	labyrinthian
AABHIILORSTT	habilitators
AABHIINOSTTU	habituations
AABHLLLLOOSU	hullaballoos
AABIIILNOSST	assibilation
AABIIILNSTTY	stainability
AABIIINQRTUU	ubiquitarian
AABIILNNTTUU	tintinnabula
AABIILNOORTY	abolitionary
AABIILOPRTVY	vaporability
AABIILRSTTUY	saturability
AABIIMHNNOOST	abominations
AABIINNOORTT	antiabortion
AABIINNORSTU	urbanisation
AABIINNORTUZ	urbanization
AABIINOORRST	arborisation
AABIINOORRTZ	arborization
AABIINORRSTT	arbitrations
AABIKLMNSTUY	unmistakably
AABILLMRSUXY	submaxillary
AABILLNOSTTU	blastulation
AABILNSSSTTU	substantials
AABILNSSTTUV	substantival
AABILOPRRSTU	supraorbital
AABIMNOPRSTY	parasymbiont
AABIMNORSTTU	masturbation
AABINOOPRRTY	probationary
AABLMMNNOSTU	somnambulant
AABLMNRSTTUY	transmutably
AABLORRRSTUY	barratrously
AABMORRSSTTU	masturbators
AABMORRSTTUY	masturbatory
AACCCDHRRSST	scratchcards
AACCCEEHILTT	catechetical
AACCCEFIINOP	Pacific Ocean
AACCCEGNORVY	gynaecocracy
AACCCEHIRSTT	catachrestic
AACCCEIINRSU	inaccuracies
AACCCEJKKRRS	crackerjacks
AACCDDEHIIRS	disaccharide
AACCDDEMMOOT	accommodated
AACCDDHIIRSS	disaccharids
AACCDDIILLTY	didactically
AACCDDIILOPR	diplocardiac
AACCDDIIOTTU	autodidactic
AACCDEEHINOX	hexadecanoic
AACCDEEINRRT	incarcerated
AACCDEEINRTV	revaccinated
AACCDEEKMNRR	cackermander
AACCDEELLRTU	recalculated
AACCDEELNORS	accelerandos
AACCDEENNOTT	concatenated
AACCDEFHIIRS	saccharified
AACCDEHILMOT	machicolated
AACCDEHINORS	archdiocesan
AACCDEHNORRY	archdeaconry
AACCDEIIILNT	dialectician
AACCDEIILMST	acclimatised
AACCDEIILMTZ	acclimatized
AACCDEILLNTY	accidentally
AACCDEILOPSY	cyclopaedias

AACCDEINNTUV	unvaccinated	**AACCEIIINPST**	incapacities
AACCDELNRTUU	carunculated	**AACCEIILLNRT**	anticlerical
AACCDELRTTUU	acculturated	**AACCEIILMRST**	acclimatiser
AACCDEMMOOST	accommodates	**AACCEIILMRTZ**	acclimatizer
AACCDENNORST	contradances	**AACCEIILMSST**	acclimatises
AACCDIIILRST	radicalistic	**AACCEIILMSTZ**	acclimatizes
AACCDIILNOTU	claudication	**AACCEIILPTVY**	capacitively
AACCDIIOPRTT	catadioptric	**AACCEIILLMSTU**	miscalculate
AACCDILLLTYY	dactylically	**AACCEIILLNNOT**	cancellation
AACCDILLNORY	draconically	**AACCEILLNOSS**	neoclassical
AACCEEEILRTV	accelerative	**AACCEILLOPSU**	capillaceous
AACCEEFILNST	calefacients	**AACCEILLPRSS**	preclassical
AACCEEFKRRSS	safecrackers	**AACCEILLSTTY**	ecstatically
AACCEEGHILMP	megacephalic	**AACCEILMMORT**	macroclimate
AACCEEGHOSST	stagecoaches	**AACCEILMNOPS**	complaisance
AACCEEGILNRT	accelerating	**AACCEILMNOPT**	cleptomaniac
AACCEEHILNNP	anencephalic	**AACCEILMOOST**	osteomalacic
AACCEEHIMNOR	aeromechanic	**AACCEILMOSSU**	smilacaceous
AACCEEHIRRST	characteries	**AACCEILMPRST**	malpractices
	characterise	**AACCEILMTUUV**	accumulative
AACCEEHIRRTZ	characterize	**AACCEILNORVY**	clairvoyance
AACCEEHLMNTU	catechumenal	**AACCEILNRRTT**	recalcitrant
AACCEEIILLPR	capercaillie	**AACCEILNRTUY**	inaccurately
AACCEEIILPRZ	capercailzie	**AACCEILORSSV**	slavocracies
AACCEEILNORT	acceleration	**AACCEILSTUVY**	accusatively
AACCEEINRRST	incarcerates	**AACCEIMNNORS**	necromaniacs
AACCEEINRSTV	revaccinates	**AACCEIMNOPRS**	accompaniers
AACCEELLRSTU	recalculates	**AACCEINNORST**	anacreontics
AACCEELORRST	accelerators		transoceanic
AACCEELORRTY	acceleratory	**AACCEINNOTTU**	accentuation
AACCEENNOSTT	concatenates	**AACCEINOORTV**	coacervation
AACCEENRSSTU	accurateness	**AACCEINORRRT**	incarcerator
AACCEFHIIRSS	saccharifies	**AACCEINORRTY**	accretionary
AACCEFHLRRTU	characterful	**AACCEINQSTTU**	acquittances
AACCEFILNRSS	farcicalness	**AACCEIOPRTVY**	overcapacity
AACCEGHIILPR	archipelagic	**AACCEKLLNOSY**	cycloalkanes
AACCEGHIIORS	hagiocracies	**AACCELLPPRSW**	clapperclaws
AACCEGHILMOR	agrochemical	**AACCELNNRSTY**	transcalency
AACCEGHNRSTT	gnatcatchers	**AACCELPRSSTU**	spectaculars
AACCEGHOPRRS	cacographers	**AACCELRSTTUU**	acculturates
AACCEGINNTTU	accentuating	**AACCENOOPSUY**	apocynaceous
AACCEHHIILRR	hierarchical	**AACCENOORSSY**	acrocyanoses
AACCEHHILNTT	chalcanthite	**AACCEORSSTUY**	styracaceous
AACCEHHMOSST	stomachaches	**AACCFIIINOPT**	pacification
AACCEHIILNPS	chaplaincies	**AACCFIILSTTU**	factualistic
AACCEHIIMNNS	mechanicians	**AACCFIINPRST**	transpacific
AACCEHILLMNO	melancholiac	**AACCFIIOPRTY**	pacificatory
AACCEHILLMNY	mechanically	**AACCFIIORRST**	scarificator
AACCEHILMNNU	unmechanical	**AACCFINNORSS**	San Francisco
AACCEHILMOST	machicolates	**AACCFINOORSS**	São Francisco
AACCEHILNPRT	pentarchical	**AACCGHHIKNOW**	Changchiakow
AACCEHILNRSY	saccharinely	**AACCGHHIPRTY**	tachygraphic
AACCEHILOPTU	autocephalic	**AACCGHHLOPRY**	chalcography
AACCEHILORTT	theocratical	**AACCGHIILLOR**	oligarchical
AACCEHILPRTY	archetypical	**AACCGHIILLPR**	calligraphic
AACCEHILRRTT	tetrarchical	**AACCGHIINNNT**	cachinnating
AACCEHIMORTT	metathoracic	**AACCGHIINRSS**	saccharising
AACCEHIMPRTU	pharmaceutic	**AACCGHIINRSZ**	saccharizing
AACCEHINOOSX	hexacosanoic	**AACCGHIMOPRR**	macrographic
AACCEHIOPRTT	cataphoretic	**AACCGHIOPRRT**	cartographic
AACCEHLMOPRY	macrocephaly	**AACCGIILMORT**	tragicomical
AACCEHLPRSTT	scratchplate	**AACCGIINRRTU**	caricaturing

AACCGILLOOPR	carpological
AACCGILLOOST	scatological
AACCGILMNTUU	accumulating
AACCGIMNNOPY	accompanying
AACCHHIMOPSY	psychomachia
AACCHIIINRTT	antirachitic
AACCHIILMSST	schismatical
AACCHIILNOTT	anti-Catholic
AACCHIILTTUX	Ixtaccihuatl
AACCHIILTTUZ	Iztaccihuatl
AACCHIINNNOT	cachinnation
AACCHIINRSTY	saccharinity
AACCHILLLOTY	catholically
AACCHILLORTY	trochaically
AACCHIMNOPRT	panchromatic
AACCHIMOOPRT	apochromatic
AACCHINNORTY	cachinnatory
AACCHIOPRSTT	catastrophic
AACCHLLNORVY	acronychally
AACCIIILPSTT	capitalistic
AACCIILLLMTY	climatically
AACCIILLMSSS	classicalism
AACCIILLSSST	classicalist
AACCIILLSSTY	classicality
AACCIILMORTT	timocratical
AACCIILNNOST	calcinations
AACCIILNRTUV	inarticulacy
AACCIILNTTTY	Atlantic City
AACCIILPRTTY	practicality
AACCIINNOSTV	vaccinations
AACCIINOSSTU	acousticians
AACCIIORRSTT	aristocratic
AACCIIRRSTTU	caricaturist
AACCILLLNOVY	volcanically
AACCILLNNOSS	nonclassical
AACCILLNOOSY	occasionally
AACCILLNORTY	narcotically
AACCILLNOSTU	calculations
AACCILLORSTY	acrostically
AACCILLOSTUY	acoustically
AACCILMNOTUU	accumulation
AACCILMOPRSS	sarcoplasmic
AACCILNNOPRT	nonpractical
AACCILNOOPTU	occupational
AACCIMNOPSST	accompanists
AACCIMNOPSTY	accompanyist
AACCINOORSSY	acrocyanosis
AACCINOORSTT	coarctation
AACCINOPRSTY	pantisocracy
AACCIORRSTTT	stratocratic
AACCLLNOTTUY	contactually
AACCLMORSTUU	accumulators
AACCLNPRTUUU	acupunctural
AACCOQRSTTUY	squattocracy
AACDDDEEEHLOR	dodecahedral
AACDDEEEHHNR	hendecahedra
AACDDEEEHLTY	acetaldehyde
AACDDEELPSTU	decapsulated
AACDDEIIJTUV	adjudicative
AACDDEIILNOT	dedicational
AACDDEIINNNR	incarnadined
AACDDEIINNRT	incardinated

AACDDEEIJRUUZ	Ciudad Juárez
AACDDEEINRSTU	candidatures
AACDDEIORRRTX	dextrocardia
AACDDGIIJNTU	adjudicating
AACDDIIJNOTU	adjudication
AACDDIJORSTU	adjudicators
AACDEEEEFFINT	decaffeinate
AACDEEFHLMSY	shamefacedly
AACDEEFINOST	defaecations
AACDEEGHHINR	headreaching
AACDEEGHLNNO	hendecagonal
AACDEEIINQSU	inadequacies
AACDEEILMMNT	medicamental
AACDEEILNNOW	New Caledonia
AACDEEILNNRS	encarnalised
AACDEEILNNRZ	encarnalized
AACDEEILNRTT	intercalated
AACDEEIMNRTT	readmittance
AACDEEINNNRT	reincarnated
AACDEEINQRTU	reacquainted
AACDEEIPRRTV	prevaricated
AACDEELNPSTU	encapsulated
AACDEELNRSTU	adularescent
AACDEELPSSTU	decapsulates
AACDEEMNNSTV	advancements
AACDEFFHINRS	affranchised
AACDEFILNOST	defalcations
AACDEFILNSTY	fascinatedly
AACDEFINORTT	fractionated
AACDEFMNRTUU	manufactured
AACDEGIILOPR	cardioplegia
AACDEGIINNRT	deracinating
AACDEGIINPTT	decapitating
AACDEGIINTTV	deactivating
AACDEGILLOOP	paedological
AACDEGILMORY	cardiomegaly
AACDEGINNPRS	parascending
AACDEHIILOPP	paedophiliac
AACDEHILLLRY	heraldically
AACDEHILLNTU	hallucinated
AACDEHIMNRTY	diathermancy
AACDEHIMORST	achromatised
AACDEHIMORTZ	achromatized
AACDEHINORSY	hyracoideans
AACDEHINOSTT	anticathodes
AACDEHINPPRS	handicappers
AACDEHLMOSUV	achlamydeous
AACDEHLNOOPP	cephalopodan
AACDEHLOPRRT	procathedral
AACDEHLORRTT	tetrachordal
AACDEHLORSTW	Castle Howard
AACDEHMOORRS	choreodramas
AACDEHNOPRTY	hydnocarpate
AACDEHPRRRSS	cardsharpers
AACDEIIINPRT	pediatrician
AACDEIIIPRST	parasiticide
AACDEIILNRTU	clairaudient
AACDEIILRTVV	divaricately
AACDEIINNNRS	incarnadines
AACDEIINNORT	deracination
AACDEIINNRST	incardinates
AACDEIINOPTT	decapitation

AACDEIINORST	eradications	AACDIILLSSTY	sadistically
AACDEIINORTT	ratiocinated	AACDIILMNOST	disclamation
AACDEIINOTTV	deactivation	AACDIILNORTV	Victoria Land
AACDEIIOSSST	disassociate	AACDIIMNOPSS	dipsomaniacs
AACDEIIPPRTT	participated	AACDIIMNRSTU	traducianism
AACDEIIPRSSU	parasuicides	AACDIINNORRT	doctrinarian
AACDEILLMNOV	demoniacally	AACDIINNOSTY	cyanidations
AACDEILLNOSH	disallowance	AACDIINRSTTU	traducianist
AACDEILLNPTY	pedantically	AACDIIORRSTV	divaricators
AACDEILMMORT	melodramatic	AACDILLNORSY	sardonically
AACDEILMNOST	declamations	AACDILLNSTYY	dynastically
AACDEILMRTTU	matriculated	AACDILLOPRSY	sporadically
AACDEILNORST	declarations	AACDILNOSSTY	anisodactyls
AACDEILNOSTT	anecdotalist	AACDILNPSSST	landscapists
AACDEILNPPRU	appendicular	AACDILORSTTY	artiodactyls
AACDEILNPSTU	incapsulated	AACDIMMNOORT	monodramatic
AACDEILNRSSS	scandalisers	AACDINNOOSTU	coadunations
AACDEILNRSSZ	scandalizers	AACDLLNOSSUY	scandalously
AACDEIMNNOTT	contaminated	AACEEEEFHLOPS	chapel of ease
AACDEIMNORST	demarcations	AACEEEEHLMNPT	metencephala
AACDEIMNORSY	aerodynamics	AACEEEHLMOST	haematoceles
AACDEIMOOSTU	diatomaceous	AACEEFFINOTT	affectionate
AACDEIMORRTV	overdramatic	AACEEFIMNSSS	misfeasances
AACDEINNOSSY	Ascension Day	AACEEFLMRSST	malefactress
AACDEINNQTUU	unacquainted	AACEEGGILLNO	genealogical
AACDEINOPSSU	sapindaceous	AACEEGGIMNOT	agamogenetic
AACDEIOPRSTT	decapitators	AACEEGHILLNR	Carnegie Hall
AACDEIORSTTV	deactivators	AACEEGHIMNOT	haematogenic
AACDELLORSTY	sacerdotally	AACEEGHINORT	archegoniate
AACDELNORSTT	translocated	AACEEGHRRSST	gatecrashers
AACDELOPRSSU	pseudoscalar	AACEEGILLNSV	evangelicals
AACDELORSUVY	cadaverously	AACEEGILNRRV	vicar general
AACDELRSTTTY	tetradactyls	AACEEGINORSU	geraniaceous
AACDENORRSTW	narrowcasted	AACEEGLMORTT	galactometer
AACDFGHINNRT	handcrafting	AACEEGMMORST	macrogametes
AACDFIIILNNT	infanticidal	AACEEHHMPSTY	chamaephytes
AACDFORRRRWY	carryforward	AACEEHIILPRT	perichaetial
AACDGHIINNPP	handicapping	AACEEHIINSTT	aesthetician
AACDGHIIOPRR	radiographic	AACEEHILMRTX	hexametrical
AACDGHILNNRS	crashlanding	AACEEHILMTTT	metathetical
AACDGHINPRRS	cardsharping	AACEEHIMNTTX	exanthematic
AACDGHIOPRRS	cardiographs	AACEEHINSSTT	anaesthetics
AACDGHIOPRRY	cardiography	AACEEHINTTTU	authenticate
AACDGIIINRTV	divaricating	AACEEHIOPRST	apothecaries
AACDGIILLOOR	radiological	AACEEHIPRSTT	paraesthetic
AACDGIILLOOU	audiological	AACEEHLMNOPS	encephalomas
AACDGIILNNSS	scandalising	AACEEHLMPRST	spermatheca
AACDGIILNNSZ	scandalizing	AACEEHLMRTTY	methacrylate
AACDGIILRSTU	gradualistic	AACEEHLNPTTU	pentateuchal
AACDGILLMOTY	dogmatically	AACEEHMNRTTT	reattachment
AACDGLMORSTY	dactylograms	AACEEHMORSTT	metathoraces
AACDHHIKLLRW	Hardwick Hall	AACEEHNNPPST	happenstance
AACDHHILORRY	achlorhydria	AACEEHRRSTTT	tetrarchates
AACDHIILLLNS	Achill Island	AACEEIILPRST	recapitalise
AACDHIILNPRS	cardinalship	AACEEIILPRTZ	recapitalize
AACDHIIOPRSS	aphrodisiacs	AACEEIIMNPTV	emancipative
AACDHINOPQRU	quadraphonic	AACEEIINRSST	sectarianise
AACDHMOPRSSY	psychodramas	AACEEIINRSTZ	sectarianize
AACDIIINORTV	divarication	AACEEIIPPRTV	appreciative
AACDIIJLORTU	judicatorial	AACEEILLMNSS	mesalliances
AACDIILLLTYV	dialytically	AACEEILMMMNY	mecamylamine
AACDIILLNOTY	diatonically	AACEEILMPPRS	preeclampsia

AACEEEILMSTUV	emasculative
AACEEEILNNRSS	encarnalises
AACEEEILNNRSZ	encarnalizes
AACEEEILNORRT	recreational
AACEEEILNRSTT	intercalates
AACEEEILPRTTU	recapitulate
AACEEEIMMNORS	mesoamerican
AACEEEINNNRST	centenarians
AACEEEINNNRST	reincarnates
AACEEEINNNRSSS	necessarians
	renaissances
AACEEEINPRSST	paracentesis
AACEEEIOPRSTT	ectoparasite
AACEEEIPRRSST	separatrices
AACEEEIPRRSTV	prevaricates
AACEEEIRRRRTW	Water Carrier
AACEEEIRRSSTT	secretariats
AACEEKLMPRST	marketplaces
AACEEELNPSSTU	encapsulates
AACEEELNRRTUX	extranuclear
AACEEELNRTTVY	tetravalency
AACEEELRRSTUW	caterwaulers
AACEEEMNORSTU	ramentaceous
AACEENNPPRTU	appurtenance
AACEEENNPRRST	transparence
AACEENPRRSSU	preassurance
AACEENRRSSSU	reassurances
AACEFFHHNSSU	Schaffhausen
AACEFFHINRSS	affranchises
AACEFFIIRSTV	affricatives
AACEFFINOSTT	affectations
AACEFFMORTTT	matter of fact
AACEFGHINNRU	French Guiana
AACEFIIILTTV	facilitative
AACEFIIINORT	aerification
AACEFIINORRT	rarefication
AACEFIMNRRST	aircraftsmen
AACEFINORRST	rarefactions
AACEFINORSTT	fractionates
AACEFLNNORRT	confraternal
AACEFMNRRTUU	manufacturer
AACEFMNRSTUU	manufactures
AACEGGHILOPR	geographical
AACEGGHINRST	gatecrashing
AACEGGIKNPPR	prepackaging
AACEGGHHIMORR	haemorrhagic
AACEGHHNOSTT	chaetognaths
AACEGHHPRRTY	tachygrapher
AACEGHIILPPR	epigraphical
AACEGHILLMPT	phlegmatical
AACEGHILLPRR	calligrapher
AACEGHILMOOT	haematologic
AACEGHILOPRS	archipelagos
AACEGHIMNOPR	anemographic
	phanerogamic
AACEGHIMOPTT	apothegmatic
AACEGHJKNNNU	Kanchenjunga
AACEGHLSSSTW	watchglasses
AACEGHNOOPRY	oceanography
AACEGHNORSTU	autochangers
AACEGHOPRRRT	cartographer
AACEGIIINRRT	geriatrician
AACEGIILLNNT	geanticlinal
AACEGIILLNRT	interglacial
AACEGIILLOOT	aetiological
AACEGIILMNNS	malignancies
AACEGIILMNRS	caramelising
AACEGIILMNRZ	caramelizing
AACEGIILNSTT	elasticating
AACEGIIMMPRT	epigrammatic
AACEGIIMNNPT	emancipating
AACEGIIMNNTT	antimagnetic
AACEGIIMRRSS	miscarriages
AACEGIIMRSST	magistracies
AACEGIINNRST	ascertaining
AACEGIINPPRT	appreciating
AACEGIINRTTV	reactivating
AACEGIKLNPSW	spacewalking
AACEGILLMNTY	magnetically
AACEGILLMSST	Glamis Castle
AACEGILLNORT	reallocating
AACEGILLNOSU	gallinaceous
AACEGILLOPSS	plagioclases
AACEGILLORSU	argillaceous
AACEGILLPRSU	superglacial
AACEGILMNSTU	emasculating
AACEGILMORST	gasometrical
AACEGILNNOTT	cotangential
AACEGILNOOSU	loganiaceous
AACEGILNRTUW	caterwauling
AACEGIMNNRSU	graminaceous
AACEGIMNOSTY	gynecomastia
AACEGINNOORT	octogenarian
AACEGLMNOOPR	campanologer
AACEGLMORTTY	galactometry
AACEGLNOOPSV	galvanoscope
AACEGLNORTTU	congratulate
AACEHHIILMOP	haemophiliac
AACEHIILLPRS	Schiaparelli
AACEHIILLRTY	hieratically
AACEHIILMPRX	alexipharmic
AACEHIILMRTT	arithmetical
AACEHIILNPRS	chaplainries
AACEHIILNTTT	antithetical
AACEHIIMNRRST	matriarchies
AACEHIINPTTT	antipathetic
AACEHIIPRRST	patriarchies
AACEHIIPRSST	parastichies
AACEHILLLTTY	athletically
AACEHILLMPTY	empathically
	emphatically
AACEHILLMTTY	thematically
AACEHILLNSTU	hallucinates
AACEHILLPRSY	seraphically
AACEHILLPTTY	pathetically
AACEHILLRTTY	theatrically
AACEHILMNPRU	alphanumeric
AACEHILMOPRS	semaphorical
AACEHILMOPRT	metaphorical
AACEHILMOTXY	haematoxylic
AACEHILMPSTY	metaphysical
AACEHILOPRRS	archesporial
AACEHILQRRSU	squirearchal
AACEHILRRSTU	chartularies

AACEHILRSTTT	tetrastichal	AACEILMMNORT	commentarial
AACEHIMNORRT	North America		manometrical
AACEHIMORSST	achromatises	AACEILMMRSTY	asymmetrical
AACEHIMORSTT	haematocrits	AACEILMNORST	reclamations
AACEHIMORSTU	South America	AACEILMNOSTU	emasculation
AACEHIMORSTZ	achromatizes	AACEILMNOSTX	exclamations
AACEHIMOSSTT	haemostatics	AACEILMRSTTU	matriculates
AACEHIMPRSTT	metaphrastic	AACEILMSSTTY	systematical
AACEHINOSTTY	thiocyanates	AACEILNNOPTT	placentation
AACEHIOPRSST	cataphoresis	AACEILNNRRTU	intranuclear
AACEHLLPRTYY	archetypally	AACEILNOPRTU	precautional
AACEHMMNNOORT	chromonemata	AACEILNORSTT	altercations
AACEHMNNRSTU	transhumance	AACEILNOSSTV	vacationless
AACEHOPRSSTT	catastrophes	AACEILNPSSTU	incapsulates
AACEHPRRRTTY	charterparty	AACEILNSTTTW	West Atlantic
AACEIIINNRSV	invariancies	AACEILPRSSTU	particulates
AACEIIINPTTV	anticipative	AACEILRSTTTU	straticulate
AACEIIKLLMRT	alkalimetric	AACEILRTTTVY	attractively
AACEIILLMNSS	misalliances	AACEILSTTUUV	auscultative
AACEIILLMRTT	altimetrical	AACEIMMNORTT	commentariat
AACEIILLNRST	lacertilians	AACEIMNNOOPT	companionate
AACEIILLNRSV	incarvilleas	AACEIMNNOSTT	contaminates
AACEIILMNSTX	anticlimaxes	AACEIMNOORST	erotomaniacs
AACEIILNOPPS	episcopalian	AACEIMNOPRST	emancipators
AACEIILNOSTT	elastication	AACEIMNOPRTY	emancipatory
AACEIILNPRTT	antiparticle	AACEIMNRSTUV	aneurysmatic
AACEIILNRTTU	inarticulate	AACEIMOPRSTV	comparatives
AACEIILPRSTU	capitularies	AACEINNNORST	nonsectarian
AACEIIMNNOPT	emancipation	AACEINNORSTT	recantations
AACEIIMNORST	racemisation	AACEINORRTTT	retractation
AACEIIMNORTZ	racemization	AACEINPQRSTU	preacquaints
AACEIIMNRSST	sectarianism	AACEINRTTTUV	unattractive
AACEIIMNRSTU	aneurismatic	AACEIOPPRRST	appreciators
AACEIIMNRSTV	carminatives	AACEIOPPRRTY	appreciatory
AACEIINNNTUV	annunciative	AACEIOPRRRTV	prevaricator
AACEIINOPPRT	appreciation	AACEJNNPRRTU	Japan Current
AACEIINORSTT	ratiocinates	AACEKLNOORRT	Central Karoo
AACEIINORTTV	reactivation	AACEKLQRSSUV	quacksalvers
AACEIINPRSTT	pancreatitis	AACEKNNORSTU	cantankerous
AACEIIOPRSTX	exoparasitic	AACELLLLORTY	collaterally
AACEIIPPRSTT	participates	AACELLMOPSUU	ampullaceous
AACEIIPRSSTT	separatistic	AACELLNNOTVY	covenantally
AACEIJKRSTTT	straitjacket	AACELLNRRUVY	vernacularly
AACEIJLLMSTY	majestically	AACELLOQTTUZ	Quetzalcoatl
AACEIJLNOSTU	ejaculations	AACELMNORSTW	scarlet woman
AACEIJLRSSUU	Julius Caesar	AACELMORSSTU	emasculators
AACEIKLLSTTY	Salt Lake City	AACELMORSTUY	emasculatory
AACEIKLMNOPT	kleptomaniac	AACELNORSSTT	translocates
AACEIKNOPRRT	Tarpeian Rock	AACELOOPPRSS	laparoscopes
AACEILLLLMTY	metallically	AACENNPRRSTY	transparency
AACEILLLLOPV	valpolicella	AACENORRSTVY	contrayervas
AACEILLMMTUY	immaculately	AACFFHIMNNOR	Rachmaninoff
AACEILLMNRUY	unicamerally	AACFFHINOORR	Horn of Africa
AACEILLMNSTY	semantically	AACFFIORRSTT	trafficators
AACEILLNOORT	reallocation	AACFGGILMNOU	camouflaging
AACEILLNOSTT	castellation	AACFGIIILNTT	facilitating
AACEILLNPTUY	paniculately	AACFGIIINNST	fanaticising
AACEILLOPRTY	operatically	AACFGIIINNTZ	fanaticizing
AACEILLPRRST	caterpillars	AACFGIIINOST	gasification
AACEILLRTTUY	articulately	AACFGIILLMNY	magnifically
AACEILLRTUUY	auriculately	AACFHINNORRT	North African
AACEILLSTTUY	eustatically	AACFHINORSTU	South African

AACFIIIILNRT	inartificial
AACFIIILLRTY	artificially
AACFIIILMORR	microfilaria
AACFIIIILNOST	salification
AACFIIIILNOTT	facilitation
AACFIIIMNORT	ramification
AACFIIINNOTZ	nazification
AACFIIINORTT	ratification
AACFIILMNOST	factionalism
AACFIILNOOST	focalisation
AACFIILNOOTZ	focalization
AACFIILNOSTT	factionalist
AACFIILORSTT	facilitators
AACFIINOSSTT	satisfaction
AACFIINSSSTT	antifascists
AACFILLLOSUV	fallaciously
AACFILLNORTY	fractionally
AACFILMORSTT	stalactiform
AACFINOORRTT	fractionator
AACFIORRSTT	fractostrati
AACFIORSSTTV	satisfactory
AACGGHHIIOPR	hagiographic
AACGGHIILLOO	hagiological
AACGGHIMNOTY	gigantomachy
AACGGIILLNTY	gigantically
AACGGILMOSTV	mystagogical
AACGGINORSTU	sugarcoating
AACGHHHIRSTT	Chhattisgarh
AACGHHIKLMNS	hamshackling
AACGHHOPRRTY	chartography
AACGHIILNPST	chaptalising
AACGHIILNPTZ	chaptalizing
AACGHIKMMNRT	matchmarking
AACGHILLNOOT	anthological
AACGHILLOOPT	pathological
AACGHILNOPPR	planographic
AACGHILOOPRZ	zoographical
AACGHIMNOPRT	camphorating
AACGHIMRTTUU	thaumaturgic
AACGHINOPPRT	pantographic
AACGHINOPRRU	uranographic
AACGHLMOOPRY	pharmacology
AACGHLMOORSU	chaulmoogras
AACGHMMOORRT	chromatogram
AACGHMMOOSSU	chasmogamous
AACGHMOOPRSU	macrophagous
AACGHNOOPRRS	coronagraphs
AACGHOOPPRSU	carpophagous
AACGIIILNPST	capitalising
AACGIIILNPTZ	capitalizing
AACGIIILPRST	plagiaristic
AACGIIINNPPT	anticipating
AACGIIINNTTV	inactivating
	vaticinating
AACGIILLMOPX	plagioclimax
AACGIILLNNTT	cantillating
AACGIILMNNTU	calumniating
AACGIILNPTTU	capitulating
AACGIILNRTTU	articulating
AACGIILOPRST	paralogistic
AACGIIMPRSTT	pragmatistic
AACGIINNNNTU	annunciating

AACGIINNOPRS	caparisoning
AACGIINNOSTT	antagonistic
AACGIINNRSST	incrassating
AACGIINOSSTT	castigations
AACGILLMOOST	malacologist
AACGILLOOPRT	patrological
AACGILLOORST	astrological
AACGILLOOTTU	tautological
AACGILLPRSYY	spagyrically
AACGILLRRTUU	agricultural
AACGILNOOSTU	coagulations
AACGILNSTTUU	auscultating
AACGILOSSTTU	cataloguists
AACGIMMOPRRT	programmatic
AACGLMOOSTUU	glaucomatous
AACGLNOOPSVY	galvanoscopy
AACHHIILNPPS	chaplainship
AACHHIIMNPRS	chairmanship
AACHHILMOPTY	hypothalamic
AACHHLNOOTTU	autochthonal
AACHIILMOPRS	parochialism
AACHIILOPRTY	parochiality
AACHIILPRSTY	physiatrical
AACHIIMNNOST	machinations
AACHIINNPPSST	captainships
AACHIINRSSSU	saurischians
AACHIKLMOOTY	Oklahoma City
AACHIKORSTHW	autorickshaw
AACHILLMNORY	harmonically
AACHILLMOPSY	hyaloplasmic
AACHILLNORTU	hallucinator
AACHILMNOOPT	taphonomical
AACHILOPSTTY	hypostatical
AACHIMMNNOPY	nymphomaniac
AACHIMMNOSYY	mythomaniacs
AACHIMNNORSS	anachronisms
AACHIMNOPRRS	parachronism
AACHINOPRTTU	naturopathic
AACHIOPRSSTU	parastichous
AACHIPRSSTTU	parachutists
AACHKMOORRSZ	Ockham's razor
AACHLLNNNOTY	nonchalantly
AACHLLOPPRYY	apocryphally
AACHLMORRSTY	lachrymators
AACHLMORRTYY	lachrymatory
AACHMOORSTTU	trachomatous
AACIIILNNORT	anticlinoria
AACIIILNNOST	laciniations
AACIIILNOSST	laicisations
AACIIILNOSTZ	laicizations
AACIIINNOPTT	anticipation
AACIIINNOTTV	inactivation
	vaticination
AACIIINNRSSU	uncinariasis
AACIIINSSTTT	statistician
AACIIJNOSTTT	jactitations
AACIIILLMNOSY	simoniacally
AACIILLMOTTY	amitotically
AACIILLNNOTT	cantillation
AACIILLNOOST	localisation
AACIILLNOOTZ	localization
AACIILLNOSTV	vacillations

AACIILLNOSTY	antisocially	AACILMNRSTTU	matriculants
AACIILLORSTY	aoristically	AACILMOPSTTY	asymptotical
AACIILLRSTTY	artistically	AACILMORRTTU	matriculator
AACIILMMORSS	commissarial	AACILNNNOSTU	cannulations
AACIILMNNOTU	calumniation	AACILNOOSTUV	vacuolations
AACIILMNORST	lacrimations	AACILNOPSSTU	capsulations
AACIILMNNOST	lancinations	AACILNORSTVY	clairvoyants
AACIILNNOOTV	invocational	AACILNOSTTUU	auscultation
AACIILNOOSTV	vocalisation	AACILOPRSTTU	capitulators
AACIILNOOTVZ	vocalization	AACILOPRTTUY	capitulatory
AACIILNOPPST	applications	AACILORRSTTU	articulators
AACIILNOPTTU	capitulation	AACILORRTTUY	articulatory
AACIILNORTTU	articulation	AACIMMOPSTTY	asymptomatic
AACIILNRSTTU	naturalistic	AACIMNNNOSTT	contaminants
AACIILORSUVY	avariciously	AACIMNNOOPWY	companionway
AACIIMMORSST	commissariat	AACIMNNOORTT	contaminator
AACIIMNNORST	animatronics	AACIMNNOOSTT	antonomastic
AACIIMNNOSTU	acuminations	AACIMNNOOTTU	nonautomatic
AACIIMNOSSTT	mastications	AACIMNOOPRST	paronomastic
AACIIMOTTTUY	automaticity	AACIMOORSSST	sarcomatosis
AACIINNNNOTU	annunciation	AACINNNORSTU	annunciators
AACIINNNOOST	canonisation	AACINNNORTUY	annunciatory
AACIINNNOOTZ	canonization	AACINNOOSTTT	constatation
AACIINNNORST	incarnations	AACINNORSSTT	transactions
AACIINNNOSTT	incantations	AACINORSSTTU	astronautics
AACIINNOPRST	nonparasitic	AACLLNNORTUY	connaturally
AACIINNORSST	incrassation	AACLMOOPRRTY	proclamatory
AACIINOORRTT	ratiocinator	AACLNNOPRTTU	contrapuntal
AACIINOOSSST	associations	AACLNPRSTTYY	cryptanalyst
AACIINOPRSTT	anticipators	AACLORSSTTUU	auscultators
AACIINOPRTTY	anticipatory	AACLORSTTUUY	auscultatory
AACIINOPSTTV	captivations	AACMOOPRSSST	astrocompass
AACIINORRSTU	curarisation	AADDDDEGINRS	granddaddies
AACIINORRTUZ	curarization	AADDDEEHHLRY	hardheadedly
AACIINORSTTV	vaticinators	AADDDEGNNRST	grandstanded
AACIINORTTVY	vaticinatory	AADDDEILRRST	tarradiddles
AACIINOSSTTV	vacationists	AADDDEINRSST	standardised
AACIINPPRSTT	participants	AADDDEINRSTZ	standardized
AACIIOORSSTX	toxocariasis	AADDEEEHHMMR	hammerheaded
AACIIOPPRRTT	participator	AADDEEHHRTXY	hexahydrated
AACIKLMOPRSY	karyoplasmic	AADDEEHNRSVZ	Shevardnadze
AACIKLOPRTYY	karyotypical	AADDEEHNSSWY	Ash Wednesday
AACILLLMORTY	matrilocally	AADDEEILOPRT	Port Adelaide
AACILLLNOPTY	platonically	AADDEEIMNRTV	animadverted
AACILLLOPRTY	patrilocally	AADDEFINORTU	defraudation
AACILLMNORTY	romantically	AADDEGHNRSTU	dreadnaughts
AACILLMNOSTY	monastically	AADDEGINORST	degradations
AACILLMOSTUY	calamitously	AADDEGNNRRST	grandstander
AACILLNNRTYY	tyrannically	AADDEINRRSST	standardiser
AACILLNOOTVY	vocationally	AADDEINRRSTZ	standardizer
AACILLNOPPTY	panoptically	AADDEINRSSST	standardises
AACILLNOPRSS	rapscallions	AADDEINRSSTZ	standardizes
AACILLNPSTYY	synaptically	AADDELNOORTV	Volta Redonda
AACILLOORRTY	oratorically	AADDENNSTUVY	Advent Sunday
AACILLPRRTUY	particularly	AADDGGINNNOR	dragonnading
AACILLQRTUUU	aquicultural	AADDGHINNRST	hardstanding
AACILMNNOPST	complainants	AADDGIIILNPT	dilapidating
AACILMNOOPRT	proclamation	AADDGIMNNRRU	Martin du Gard
AACILMNOORST	astronomical	AADDHIILORRT	diarthrodial
AACILMNORSTU	calumniators	AADDIIILNOPT	dilapidation
AACILMNORSTY	microanalyst	AADDIILLNOTY	additionally
AACILMNORTUY	calumniatory	AADDIILOPRST	dilapidators

AADDILNNSSSU	Sunda Islands
AADDINNRRUUU	Ruanda-Urundi
AADEEEFHHRST	featherheads
AADEEEGHLRRT	largehearted
AADEEEGHRRTT	greathearted
AADEEEGLNNRS	Greenland Sea
AADEEEGMMNNT	endamagement
AADEEEHHLRST	leatherheads
AADEEEHHRTVY	heavyhearted
AADEEELNNRWZ	New Zealander
AADEEFHINRTT	fainthearted
AADEEFLNRSST	East Flanders
AADEEGGGIRST	disaggregate
AADEEGGLMORT	agglomerated
AADEEGHHMORR	haemorrhaged
AADEEGHILNTT	Tintagel Head
AADEEGHINPRS	spearheading
AADEEGILRSTV	Elisavetgrad
AADEEGINRSTU	aguardientes
AADEEGJMNORU	Judaeo-German
AADEEGLPPRSS	glasspapered
AADEEHILNQRU	harlequinade
AADEEHIMNOTZ	diazomethane
AADEEHIMNPTT	amphidentate
AADEEHLMRSTY	headmasterly
AADEEHLNNRST	neanderthals
AADEEHOPRRTZ	trapezohedra
AADEEHQRRSTU	headquarters
AADEEIIILNRX	Alexander III
AADEEIILMMSV	mediaevalism
AADEEIILMRST	materialised
AADEEIILMRTZ	materialized
AADEEIILMSTV	mediaevalist
AADEEIILRRST	arterialised
AADEEIILRRTZ	arterialized
AADEEIIMNNRT	antemeridian
AADEEIKNORRT	Ekaterinodar
AADEEILLNTUV	unalleviated
AADEEILMMORT	material mode
AADEEILMMPST	semipalmated
AADEEILNNRSX	alexandrines
AADEEILNQTUY	inadequately
AADEEILNRSST	Easter Island
AADEEILNRSTU	denaturalise
AADEEILNRTUZ	denaturalize
AADEEIMMNNRR	remainderman
AADEEIMMNNST	misdemeanant
AADEEIMSSSTT	metastasised
AADEEIMSSTTZ	metastasized
AADEEINOPRST	endoparasite
AADEEINOPRTU	deuteranopia
AADEEINORSST	asteroideans
AADEEIRSSTVV	adversatives
AADEELLLNPRU	unparalleled
AADEELLNSTTU	landaulettes
AADEELMNPRTT	departmental
AADEELNRRSTT	retranslated
AADEELOPRTTX	extrapolated
AADEEMMNRSTW	New Amsterdam
AADEEMNNRTUX	extramundane
AADEEMNPRRST	dermapterans
AADEEMQRRSSU	masqueraders

AADEEQRRSTUW	quartersawed
AADEFFIIILST	disaffiliate
AADEFFIILNTU	unaffiliated
AADEFGGILNRT	deflagrating
AADEFGGINRSU	safeguarding
AADEFGHNRRST	grandfathers
AADEFGILNORT	deflagration
AADEFHINNOTU	fountainhead
AADEFIIILMRS	familiarised
AADEFIIILMRZ	familiarized
AADEFIILNSUZ	sulfadiazine
AADEFILMORTY	defamatorily
AADEFILNORTY	deflationary
AADEFILNTTUY	infatuatedly
AADEGGILNNRR	Darling Range
AADEGGILNTTU	agglutinated
AADEGGINRRSS	aggrandisers
AADEGGINRRSZ	aggrandizers
AADEGHILNORU	Dún Laoghaire
AADEGHIMMORX	hexagrammoid
AADEGHINNRVY	Vindhya Range
AADEGHIOPRRR	radiographer
AADEGHNOPRRY	parahydrogen
AADEGIILMNNT	delaminating
AADEGIILMNRS	marginalised
AADEGIILMNRZ	marginalized
AADEGIILNNST	desalinating
AADEGIILPQRU	quadriplegia
AADEGIIMMNST	diamagnetism
AADEGIINPPRS	disappearing
AADEGIKMNRRT	trademarking
AADEGILMNSSU	salmagundies
AADEGILNNRSV	landgravines
AADEGILNPRST	plantigrades
AADEGILNRTTU	adulterating
	triangulated
AADEGIMNNRRT	darraignment
AADEGIMNQRSU	masquerading
AADEGIMNQSTU	desquamating
AADEGINNPPRS	sandpapering
AADEGINOPPRS	propagandise
AADEGINOPPRZ	propagandize
AADEGLNRSTTU	strangulated
AADEGMMNNORS	Grandma Moses
AADEGMNRRSST	grandmasters
AADEGNNPRRST	grandparents
AADEGOPRSTTU	postgraduate
AADEHHIILLPP	Philadelphia
AADEHIKLMORY	holidaymaker
AADEHILMNPRS	aldermanship
AADEHILNORRT	enarthrodial
AADEHINOPRST	Herod Antipas
AADEHIOPRRTY	radiotherapy
AADEHMNNRSTT	Hermannstadt
AADEHPRRSTTU	Uttar Pradesh
AADEIIILNOST	idealisation
AADEIIILNOTZ	idealization
AADEIIILLNUVV	vaudevillian
AADEIIILMNNOT	delamination
AADEIIILNNOST	desalination
	nationalised
AADEIIILNNOTZ	nationalized

AADEIILNNTUV	antediluvian	AADGINOORSTY	Rogation Days
AADEIILNORST	rationalised	AADGINOPPRST	propagandist
AADEIILNORTV	derivational	AADHIIKNSTTZ	Tadzhikistan
AADEIILNORTZ	rationalized	AADHIILMPRSS	admiralships
AADEIILNRSTT	interstadial	AADHIILOPPSY	diapophysial
AADEIILRRTTY	triradiately	AADHIIMOPRSS	adiaphorisms
AADEIIMNNOST	deaminations	AADHIIOPRSST	adiaphorists
AADEIIMNRSTT	administrate	AADHILNOOPRT	anthropoidal
AADEIINNSTTT	instantiated	AADHILNOPSUY	diaphanously
AADEIJKLRRSS	rijksdaalers	AADHIOPRRSTY	parathyroids
AADEIKMNORST	demarkations	AADHJKLMMORS	Hammarskjöld
AADEILNNNORR	noradrenalin	AADHKNNOORTT	North Dakotan
AADEILNNORST	Saint Leonard	AADHKNOOSTTU	South Dakotan
AADEILNNQRSU	quadrennials	AADHLORSTUVY	Holy Saturday
AADEILNNSSTT	Staten Island	AADHNNOORSUZ	nonhazardous
AADEILNORTTU	adulteration	AADIIILNNOPS	Indianapolis
AADEILNOSTUV	devaluations	AADIIILNNOTV	invalidation
AADEILNQRTUV	quadrivalent	AADIIINORRST	irradiations
AADEILNRTUVY	valetudinary	AADIIKLMNNSU	Unimak Island
AADEILORRSTV	advertorials	AADIIKNNRSST	Kristiansand
AADEIMMNRSST	disarmaments	AADIIKNRSSTT	Kristianstad
AADEIMNOQSTU	desquamation	AADIILMNOQRU	quadrinomial
AADEIMNRSSTV	maidservants	AADIILMOPRST	prismatoidal
AADEIMOPPRTX	approximated	AADIILNOOSTV	vasodilation
AADEIMPRRSTY	tryparsamide	AADIILNORSTV	invalidators
AADEINNORTTU	denaturation	AADIINNOSTTX	antioxidants
AADEINNRSSTW	Saint Andrews	AADIINOOTTUX	autoxidation
AADEINOPRSTV	depravations	AADILLMNOOST	amontillados
AADEINORRSTT	retardations	AADILNOPPRST	postprandial
AADEINORSSTT	Soenda Strait	AADILOORSSTV	vasodilators
AADEINORSTTU	desaturation	AADINNORSTTU	transudation
AADEINOSSTTV	devastations	AADLMNNORUWY	laundrywoman
AADEINPQRSSU	pasquinaders	AADLOOOPPPSU	Papadopoulos
AADEIOPPPRRT	appropriated	AADMNOQRSUUU	quadrumanous
AADELMNNRTUU	ultramundane	AADNORRSTTUY	transudatory
AADELNNPRSTT	transplanted	AAEEEGGIRTVX	exaggerative
AADELNNRSTTU	untranslated	AAEEEGMNRSSS	manageresses
AADELNOPRSSU	San Pedro Sula	AAEEEHILRTTY	aethereality
AADELORRSTTU	adulterators	AAEEEHILSSTT	telaesthesia
AADEMNNNRSTU	transmundane	AAEEEHIMMSST	haematemesis
AADEMNNOOTTU	nonautomated	AAEEEHINSSTT	anaesthetise
AADENPRSSTTT	standpatters	AAEEEHINSTTZ	anaesthetize
AADFGHINNSST	handfastings	AAEEEILPRSTT	tapsalteerie
AADFILNNOOTU	foundational	AAEEEMNPRSST	appeasements
AADGGGIINNRS	aggrandising	AAEEENPRSSST	separateness
AADGGGIINNRZ	aggrandizing	AAEEEPRRSSTX	exasperaters
AADGGIINNRRS	disarranging	AAEEFHMRRRSS	sharefarmers
AADGGILMMNOR	Mid Glamorgan	AAEEFNRRSSST	transferases
AADGGJNNNPUU	Ujung Pandang	AAEEGGGINRTX	exaggerating
AADGHHOPRSSW	shadowgraphs	AAEEGGIMNOSS	agamogenesis
AADGHIINPRSU	guardianship	AAEEGGINNRTU	guaranteeing
AADGIIILNNTV	invalidating	AAEEGGINORTX	exaggeration
AADGIIIMNPRS	imparadising	AAEEGGLMORST	agglomerates
AADGIIIMPRRV	primigravida	AAEEGGORRSTX	exaggerators
AADGIILMRSST	madrigalists	AAEEGGORRTXY	exaggeratory
AADGIILMRTUV	multigravida	AAEEGHHMORRS	haemorrhages
AADGIILQRUUV	Guadalquivir	AAEEGHLMOPTY	hepatomegaly
AADGIINNNPST	sandpainting	AAEEGHLRSSTW	weatherglass
AADGIINNPQSU	pasquinading	AAEEGHNNORTU	Haute-Garonne
AADGILLNPPUY	applaudingly	AAEEGHNPPRRS	paperhangers
AADGIMNOPPRS	propagandism	AAEEGHNRSSTT	Eastern Ghats
AADGIMRRSTTU	dramaturgist	AAEEGILLLNSS	selaginellas

AAEEGILLNNST	gentianellas
AAEEGILMNRTY	emarginately
AAEEGILMSSSX	sexagesimals
AAEEGILNNORT	generational
AAEEGILNOTTV	vegetational
AAEEGILNRTUV	reevaluating
AAEEGIMNTTUV	augmentative
AAEEGIMPSSTU	Septuagesima
AAEEGINNORSW	Norwegian Sea
AAEEGINNSTUX	exsanguinate
AAEEGINPRSTX	exasperating
AAEEGINRSSTV	asseverating
AAEEGLMNOPST	planogametes
AAEEGLMNORTV	galvanometer
AAEEGMNNRRST	arrangements
AAEEGMNOPRST	pomegranates
AAEEGMNSSSTU	assuagements
AAEEHHIMPRTT	amphitheater
	amphitheatre
AAEEHHIPSSTY	hypaesthesia
AAEEHHMNRSTW	whatshername
AAEEHIIKNSST	kinaesthesia
AAEEHIILRTVX	exhilarative
AAEEHIIMPRST	hemiparasite
AAEEHILPRSTU	laureateship
AAEEHIMMNPST	amphetamines
AAEEHIMMNPRS	arsphenamine
AAEEHIMNRSTT	metatherians
AAEEHIMOSSST	somaesthesia
AAEEHINNRSTU	neurasthenia
AAEEHINSSSTY	synaesthesia
AAEEHINSSTTT	anaesthetist
AAEEHIPRSSST	paresthesias
AAEEHIRRSSTY	East Ayrshire
AAEEHKMORRTT	katharometer
AAEEHLMOSSTY	haematolyses
AAEEHMNORSUW	warehouseman
AAEEHMORSTTX	metathoraxes
AAEEHOORRSTT	steatorrhoea
AAEEIILLRSTT	lateralities
AAEEIILLRTTV	alliterative
AAEEIILMNRSV	naive realism
AAEEIILMNTTV	alimentative
AAEEIILMORTV	ameliorative
AAEEIILMRRST	materialiser
AAEEIILMRRTZ	materializer
AAEEIILMRSST	materialises
AAEEIILMRSTZ	materializes
AAEEIILRRSST	arterialises
AAEEIILRRSTZ	arterializes
AAEEIIMPRSST	semiparasite
AAEEIINNRRTV	veterinarian
AAEEIINRSSSV	sansevierias
AAEEIIRRSTXX	Artaxerxes II
AAEEIKLLMRST	alkalimeters
AAEEIKNRRTTU	Neturei Karta
AAEEILLMNPST	planetesimal
AAEEILLNORTV	revelational
AAEEILLPPSTV	appellatives
AAEEILLPRSTT	septilateral
AAEEILLQRSTU	equilaterals
AAEEILMNRSST	materialness
AAEEEILMORRST	alstroemeria
AAEEILNNORTV	venerational
AAEEILNORTUV	reevaluation
AAEEILNPRSST	pleasantries
AAEEILNRSTTV	alternatives
AAEEILPRSTVY	separatively
AAEEILQRSSTU	sesquialtera
AAEEIMNORRRS	Sierra Morena
AAEEIMNPPRST	appraisement
AAEEIMSSSSTT	metastasises
AAEEIMSSSTTZ	metastasizes
AAEEINOPRSTX	exasperation
AAEEINORSSTV	asseveration
AAEEINQRRSTU	quaternaries
AAEEIOPRSSTX	exoparasites
AAEEIPPRRSTV	preparatives
AAEEJKMMNRTZ	katzenjammer
AAEEKLNRSSTT	rattlesnakes
AAEELLMNSTTT	mantellettas
AAEELLNOSTVY	Seaton Valley
AAEELLNPRRTY	parenterally
AAEELMMNRTTT	maltreatment
AAEELMNPRSST	malapertness
AAEELNNOSSSS	seasonalness
AAEELNNPSSST	pleasantness
AAEELNRRSSTT	retranslates
AAEELOPRSTTX	extrapolates
AAEEMNNPPRSW	newspaperman
AAEEMNORSSTW	Western Samoa
AAEEMNORSTUX	auxanometers
AAEEMNRSTTTY	testamentary
AAEEMQRSSSTU	marquessates
AAEENNPPRSST	apparentness
AAEENNPRSTUU	superannuate
AAEEPPRRSSTY	state prayers
AAEERRRSSTTUU	restaurateur
AAEFFIIMRSTV	affirmatives
AAEFFILLNSTU	affluentials
AAEFFQRRSTTU	quarterstaff
AAEFGGILLLNT	flagellating
AAEFGHILNRST	farthingales
AAEFGHLLNNPR	flannelgraph
AAEFGIKLNNRR	farnarkeling
AAEFGILLLNOT	flagellation
AAEFGINNORTT	engraftation
AAEFGLLLORST	flagellators
AAEFGLLMNRTY	fragmentally
AAEFGLNNRSST	flagrantness
AAEFHILLLSTV	Festival Hall
AAEFIIILMRRS	familiariser
AAEFIIILMRRZ	familiarizer
AAEFIIILMRSS	familiarises
AAEFIIILMRSZ	familiarizes
AAEFIILMNRSS	familiarness
AAEFIILMORRV	overfamiliar
AAEFIILMPSST	fissipalmate
AAEFIILOPRTV	parvifoliate
AAEFILMNRRST	fraternalism
AAEFILNQRRTU	quarterfinal
AAEFILOPRTTU	fluorapatite
AAEFILORSSTY	forestaysail
AAEFLLLNSSTY	Stanley Falls

AAEGGGINORST	aggregations	AAEGLMOPRSST	ergastoplasm
AAEGGHHIOPRR	hagiographer	AAEGLMOPRSUY	rampageously
AAEGGHILNNOT	halogenating	AAEGLNRSSTTU	strangulates
AAEGGHINNPPR	paperhanging	AAEGORRRSSSW	arrowgrasses
AAEGGHMNOPRT	magnetograph	AAEHHHILMOPTX	exophthalmia
AAEGGILNSTTU	agglutinates	AAEHHIMNSSTW	whatshisname
AAEGGIMNNORV	overmanaging	AAEHHLORSSTT	throatlashes
AAEGGINNPRRR	prearranging	AAEHHOPPSSST	phosphatases
AAEGGIOPPRTU	appoggiature	AAEHIIILNNTV	annihilative
AAEGGLLLOSSS	galloglasses	AAEHIILMMPTU	epithalamium
AAEGHHIKNRST	earthshaking	AAEHIILMNOPT	epithalamion
AAEGHHOPPRRS	phraseograph	AAEHIILNORTX	exhilaration
AAEGHIILNRTX	exhilarating	AAEHIINOPRTZ	azathioprine
AAEGHILNNOOT	halogenation	AAEHIKNOSTTV	stakhanovite
AAEGHIMMNPSS	gamesmanship	AAEHILLMORSV	Villahermosa
AAEGHIMMNSTT	metagnathism	AAEHILMNOTXY	haematoxylin
AAEGHIMNPRST	metaphrasing	AAEHILMNPSSS	salesmanship
AAEGHIMNRRTW	heartwarming	AAEHILMOSSTY	haematolysis
AAEGHIMORRRT	metrorrhagia	AAEHILMRSTUV	amateurishly
AAEGHIOPRSTU	autographies	AAEHILNNOSST	Thessalonian
AAEGHLMNRSTU	manslaughter	AAEHILORRSTX	exhilarators
	slaughterman	AAEHILORRTXY	exhilaratory
AAEGHMNOSTTU	metagnathous	AAEHILPPPSST	slaphappiest
AAEGHMOPRRSS	phraseograms	AAEHILPPRSTY	hyperspatial
AAEGHMRSTTUU	thaumaturges	AAEHIMNOPPRR	paramorphine
AAEGHNOPPRRT	pantographer	AAEHIMNPRSTW	watermanship
AAEGHNOPRRRU	uranographer	AAEHIMNSSTTW	whatsitsname
AAEGHNPRRSST	straphangers	AAEHIMPRSTTW	Matthew Paris
AAEGIIILLNOST	legalisation	AAEHINOPRSST	Aristophanes
AAEGIILLNOTZ	legalization	AAEHINRSSTUV	hantaviruses
AAEGIILLNRTT	alliterating	AAEHLLMOPRSX	morphallaxes
AAEGIILMNORT	ameliorating	AAEHLMNOOTXY	haematoxylon
AAEGIILMNRSS	marginalises	AAEHMNOOPRRT	parathormone
AAEGIILMNRSZ	marginalizes	AAEHMNOOPRSS	anamorphoses
AAEGIILNRSTU	angularities	AAEHMOORSTTU	atheromatous
AAEGIILPRRSS	plagiarisers	AAEHMOPRSSTY	massotherapy
AAEGIILPRRSZ	plagiarizers	AAEHMOPRSTTU	thaumatropes
AAEGIIMMRRSS	mismarriages	AAEIIILMSSTV	assimilative
AAEGIIMNNORT	emargination	AAEIIILNNNTV	Valentinian I
AAEGIINNOSTV	evaginations	AAEIIILPRSTT	partialities
AAEGIINNPPRT	appertaining	AAEIILLLPTVY	palliatively
AAEGIINORSTV	variegations	AAEIILLMMRTY	immaterially
AAEGIINPPRRS	reappraising	AAEIILLMNNRS	millenarians
AAEGIINPRRTT	repatriating	AAEIILLNORTT	alliteration
AAEGIINPRTTX	expatriating	AAEIILLNOSTV	alleviations
AAEGIKMNRRTW	watermarking	AAEIILLNPSTY	sapientially
AAEGILLNNTTY	tangentially	AAEIILMMNNTT	milatainment
AAEGILLNPPRW	wallpapering	AAEIILMMPRST	Maritime Alps
AAEGILMNOORR	oleomargarin	AAEIILMNNOTT	alimentation
AAEGILNPRSSV	palsgravines	AAEIILMNNRRT	interlaminar
AAEGILNRSTTU	triangulates	AAEIILMNOORT	amelioration
AAEGIMNNOTTU	augmentation	AAEIILMNOTTZ	metalization
AAEGIMNNRRST	arraignments	AAEIILMNPTUV	manipulative
AAEGIMNNSTTU	antimutagens	AAEIILMOPRRT	imperatorial
AAEGIMNRRSTT	transmigrate	AAEIILMRSSTT	materialists
AAEGIMRRSTTU	magistrature	AAEIILMRTTUV	multivariate
AAEGLLNORTTY	tetragonally	AAEIILNNOPST	penalisation
AAEGLLNRSUXY	sexangularly	AAEIILNNOPTZ	penalization
AAEGLLOPRSTY	pyrogallates	AAEIILNNOSST	nationalises
AAEGLMNORTVY	galvanometry	AAEIILNNOSTZ	nationalizes
AAEGLMOOPSSU	gamosepalous	AAEIILNOQSTU	equalisation
AAEGLMOOPSTU	gamopetalous	AAEIILNOQTUZ	equalization

AAEIILNORRST	rationaliser
AAEIILNORRTZ	rationalizer
AAEIILNORSST	rationalises
	realisations
AAEIILNORSTT	Aristotelian
	retaliations
AAEIILNORSTV	velarisation
AAEIILNORSTZ	rationalizes
	realizations
AAEIILNORTVZ	velarization
AAEIILNPRSTT	interspatial
AAEIILPPRSVY	appraisively
AAEIIMNNORST	reanimations
AAEIIMNNOSTX	examinations
	examinations
AAEIIMNOSSTV	avitaminoses
AAEIINNOSTTT	tetanisation
AAEIINNOTTTZ	tetanization
AAEIINNRSSST	sanitariness
AAEIINNSSTTT	instantiates
AAEIINOPRRTT	repatriation
AAEIINOPRTTX	expatriation
AAEIINOPSTTX	expatiations
AAEIINQTTTUV	quantitative
AAEIKNPSSTTW	West Pakistan
AAEILLLMNOST	lamellations
AAEILLLMRTTU	multilateral
AAEILLLNRTUY	unilaterally
AAEILLLOOPSS	soapolallies
AAEILLLPRSST	parallelists
AAEILLLRRTTY	trilaterally
AAEILLMNNSUY	semiannually
AAEILLMNRRTY	artilleryman
AAEILLMNRSUY	aneurismally
AAEILLMPRRXY	premaxillary
AAEILLNNNOTW	Antonine Wall
AAEILLNOOSTV	alveolations
AAEILLNOPPST	appellations
AAEILLNOQTUY	equationally
AAEILLNORSTY	senatorially
AAEILLNSSTTU	Saint Austell
AAEILLNSWWYZ	Wislany Zalew
AAEILLOQRTUY	equatorially
AAEILLQRSSTU	aquarellists
AAEILMNNOSTT	lamentations
AAEILMNORSTV	malversation
AAEILMNPRSTU	planetariums
AAEILMNRRSTU	ultramarines
AAEILMNRSSTT	mistranslate
AAEILMOOPRST	laparotomies
AAEILMOORRST	ameliorators
AAEILNNNPSVY	Pennsylvania
AAEILNNOPRTT	replantation
AAEILNNOPSTX	explanations
AAEILNNOPTTX	explantation
AAEILNNORSST	rationalness
AAEILNNORSTT	alternations
AAEILNNPRSST	transalpines
AAEILNNRSTTU	Saint Laurent
	Saint-Laurent
AAEILNOPRRST	proletarians
AAEILNOPSSTY	passionately
AAEILNORSTUV	revaluations
AAEILNPRSSTT	paternalists
AAEILNQRRTTU	Latin Quarter
AAEILNRRSSTU	sertularians
AAEILNRSSSTU	salutariness
AAEILOPRRSTT	proletariats
AAEILORRSTUW	Lower Austria
AAEIMMMOSSTT	metasomatism
AAEIMMNOOPST	Mesopotamian
AAEIMNOOOOPT	onomatopoeia
AAEIMNOPTUUW	Te Waipounamu
AAEIMOPPRSTX	approximates
AAEINNOPRSTT	trepanations
AAEINNOPRSXY	expansionary
AAEINNORSSTU	Austronesian
AAEINNOSTTTU	attenuations
AAEINOOPRSTV	evaporations
AAEINOPPRRST	preparations
AAEINORRSSTT	arrestations
AAEINOSSTTTT	attestations
AAEINPRSSSTU	East Prussian
AAEIOPPPRRST	appropriates
AAEIPPRRSTUU	Upper Austria
AAEKLMNNORTU	nomenklatura
AAEKLOPRSTTY	keratoplasty
AAELLMNNORTY	ornamentally
AAELLMNRSUYY	aneurysmally
AAELLMRRTUXY	extramurally
AAELLNNPSTUY	unpleasantly
AAELLORRSSTT	stellarators
AAELLORSSSUU	allosauruses
AAELMNNNORTU	unornamental
AAELMNNORTTU	ultramontane
AAELMNOOPRTT	protonematal
AAELMOOPRSTZ	spermatozoal
AAELNNPRRSTT	transplanter
AAELNOOPPRSS	aplanospores
AAELNPRRSTUU	supernatural
AAELNRRSSSTV	transversals
AAELNRRSSTUV	transvaluers
AAELNRSSSTTW	stalwartness
AAELNRSSSTUX	transsexuals
AAELOOPRRTTX	extrapolator
AAEMNNNORSTT	transmontane
AAEMNNOORTUY	neuroanatomy
AAEMNNOPRSSS	Montparnasse
AAEMNOOPRSTZ	spermatozoan
AAEMNOPRSTTU	portmanteaus
AAEMNOPRTTUX	portmanteaux
AAEMORSSSTTT	toastmasters
AAENNPPRSTTU	appurtenants
AAEOOPPRRRST	paratroopers
AAFFIIILNOST	affiliations
AAFFIIMNORST	affirmations
AAFGIINNORTT	ingraftation
AAFGIKLMNNOR	frankalmoign
AAFHHLMNNOST	Hofmannsthal
AAFIIILNNOST	finalisation
AAFIIILNNOTZ	finalization
AAFIIILNRTTU	futilitarian
AAFIILLMNRUY	unfamiliarly
AAFIILMMNNOT	inflammation

AAFIILNNORTY	inflationary
AAFIINNOSTTU	infatuations
AAFILMMNOORT	malformation
AAFILMMNORTY	inflammatory
AAFILNNORTTU	Fantin-Latour
AAGGGGILLLNY	lallygagging
AAGGHINNPRST	straphanging
AAGGHINOPRTU	autographing
AAGGHNOOPRRY	organography
AAGGIIILNPRS	plagiarising
AAGGIIILNPRZ	plagiarizing
AAGGIIINNNTV	invaginating
AAGGIIINNRTT	ingratiating
AAGGIIKLLNSS	galligaskins
AAGGIILLNNTV	gallivanting
AAGGIIMNNRRS	misarranging
AAGGIINNNOST	antagonising
AAGGIINNNOTZ	antagonizing
AAGGIINNRTUU	inaugurating
AAGGIKLLNSSY	gallygaskins
AAGGILLMORRS	gorillagrams
AAGGILLNOSST	algolagnists
AAGGLMMOORTY	grammatology
AAGHHIIJNSUZ	Shijiazhuang
AAGHHOPRRRTY	arthrography
AAGHIIILNNNT	annihilating
AAGHIINPSTXY	asphyxiating
AAGHILMOORTY	hamartiology
AAGHILOORSTU	hagiolatrous
AAGHIPRRSTTY	stratigraphy
AAGHLMOOTTUY	thaumatology
AAGHLOOPPRRS	polarographs
AAGHLOOPPRRY	polarography
AAGHOOPPRSSU	saprophagous
AAGIIIILNNST	italianising
AAGIIIILNNTZ	italianizing
AAGIIILMNSST	assimilating
AAGIIILNNSTV	insalivating
AAGIIILNORRT	irrigational
AAGIIIMNNOPR	Parmigianino
AAGIIIMNNOST	imaginations
AAGIIINNNOTV	invagination
AAGIIINNORTT	ingratiation
AAGIIINPRSST	parasitising
AAGIIINPRSTZ	parasitizing
AAGIILLNNUVY	unavailingly
AAGIILMNNPTU	manipulating
AAGIILMRSTTY	magistrality
AAGIILNNRSTU	naturalising
AAGIILNNRSUY	sanguinarily
AAGIILNNRTUZ	naturalizing
AAGIILNPPRSY	appraisingly
AAGIIMNOSTTU	automatising
AAGIIMNOTTUZ	automatizing
AAGIIMNRSTTU	traumatising
AAGIIMNRTTUZ	traumatizing
AAGIINNNNQRTU	quarantining
AAGIINNOORST	organisation
AAGIINNOORTZ	organization
AAGIINNORTUU	inauguration
AAGIINNOSSST	assignations
AAGIINOPSSTT	apostatising
AAGIINOPSTTZ	apostatizing
AAGIINORRTTY	ingratiatory
AAGIINORSTTV	gravitations
AAGILLLORSSY	glossarially
AAGILLMNORSY	organismally
AAGILLMNRTUU	multiangular
AAGILLMNTUWY	mulligatawny
AAGILLNOUVVV	vulvovaginal
AAGILLNRRTUY	triangularly
AAGILMMMOSST	mammalogists
AAGILMNNNNOT	nonmalignant
AAGILNNORSTU	granulations
AAGILNNRSTUV	transvaluing
AAGILNORSTTU	gastrulation
	gratulations
AAGILOOPRSTY	parasitology
AAGIMNNOOSST	anastomosing
AAGIMNNRRSTT	transmigrant
AAGINOOOPRSZ	zoosporangia
AAGINOOPPRST	propagations
AAGINORRSTUU	inaugurators
AAGINORRTUUY	inauguratory
AAGLLOPRSTTU	supraglottal
AAGOPRRRSSSW	sparrowgrass
AAHHIOPPRSTU	phosphaturia
AAHHIPRSSTTW	athwartships
AAHHLMOPSTUY	hypothalamus
AAHIIILLOPRU	ailurophilia
AAHIIILNNNOT	annihilation
AAHIILNNORST	annihilators
AAHIIMMNNSTU	antihumanism
AAHIIMNNOSTU	humanisation
AAHIIMNNOTUZ	humanization
AAHIIMOPPRSS	paraphimosis
AAHIINOPSTXY	asphyxiation
AAHIINPPRSST	partisanship
AAHIINPPRSTZ	partizanship
AAHIKKLNOSSV	kalashnikovs
AAHIKLLNNOPT	haliplankton
AAHIKMMNPRSS	marksmanship
AAHIKMNOSSTV	stakhanovism
AAHILLMOOTXY	homotaxially
AAHILLMOPRSX	morphallaxis
AAHILLNNOPTY	antiphonally
AAHILLOPRSTX	trophallaxis
AAHILLOPSSTT	allopathists
AAHILMMOPRTU	prothalamium
AAHILMNOOPRT	prothalamion
AAHILMPRSSTY	amphistylars
AAHIMMNNOPRSS	anamorphisms
AAHIMMOPPRRS	paramorphism
AAHIMNOOPRSS	anamorphosis
AAHIOPRSSTXY	asphyxiators
AAHKOPRRSSWW	sparrowhawks
AAHLLMMORSSW	marshmallows
AAHLLMMORSWY	marshmallowy
AAHLNORRSTUY	anarthrously
AAHLOPRRSTTY	arthroplasty
AAHMOOPPRRSU	paramorphous
AAIIIKLLLNOU	Liliuokalani
AAIIILMNOSST	assimilation
AAIIILMPRTTY	impartiality

AAIIILNNOSTV	insalivation
AAIIILNNOTTZ	latinization
AAIIILNOPRTT	Tripolitania
AAIIILNOSTTV	visitational
	vitalisation
AAIIILNOTTVZ	vitalization
AAIIILNRSTTU	utilitarians
AAIIILORSTTV	visitatorial
AAIIIMMNOSTX	maximisation
AAIIIMMNOTXZ	maximization
AAIIIMNNRSTU	unitarianism
AAIIIMNOSSTV	avitaminosis
AAIIINNNOSTT	insanitation
AAIIINNOSSTT	sanitisation
AAIIINNOSTTZ	sanitization
AAIIINNRRTTU	Triunitarian
AAIIINORSSTT	satirisation
AAIIINORSTTZ	satirization
AAIIILLMNORTY	minatorially
AAIILLMNPRSU	supraliminal
AAIILLNNOSTT	installation
AAIILLNORRTY	irrationally
AAIILMNNOPRS	paralimnions
AAIILMNNOPTT	implantation
AAIILMNNOPTU	manipulation
AAIILMNOORST	moralisation
AAIILMNOORTZ	moralization
AAIILMNOOTTV	motivational
AAIILMNOPSST	maintopsails
AAIILMNOSSTV	salvationism
AAIILMORSSST	assimilators
AAIILMORSSTY	assimilatory
AAIILNNNOOTT	intonational
AAIILNNNOOTV	innovational
AAIILNNORSTT	transitional
AAIILNNOSSTT	nationalists
AAIILNOOPPST	appositional
AAIILNOOPRST	polarisation
AAIILNOOPRTZ	polarization
AAIILNOORSST	solarisation
AAIILNOORSTV	valorisation
AAIILNOORSTZ	solarization
AAIILNOORTVZ	valorization
AAIILNOOSTTT	totalisation
AAIILNOOTTTZ	totalization
AAIILNOPPSTT	palpitations
AAIILNORRSTU	ruralisation
AAIILNORRTUZ	ruralization
AAIILNORSSTT	rationalists
AAIILNORSTTY	stationarily
AAIILNOSSTTV	salvationist
AAIIMMNNOOST	ammoniations
AAIIMNNOORTZ	romanization
AAIIMNOORSTT	amortisation
AAIIMNOORTTZ	amortization
AAIIMNOPRSTT	impartations
AAIINNOOQSTTU	quantisation
AAIINNOQTTUZ	quantization
AAIINNORSTTU	instauration
AAIINOOPRSTV	vaporisation
AAIINOOPRTVZ	vaporization
AAIKLNSSSTVY	Stanislavsky

AAILLLOSSTWW	swallowtails
AAILLMNOTTUY	mutationally
AAILLMNRRTUY	intramurally
AAILLORSTTUY	salutatorily
AAILMMOPPRSS	malapropisms
AAILMNOPRSTU	manipulators
AAILMNOPRTUY	manipulatory
AAILNNORSSTT	translations
AAILOORSSTTT	totalisators
AAILOORSTTTZ	totalizators
AAILOPRSSSTT	pastoralists
AAIMMNOPSSTT	maintopmasts
AAIMMNOSSSUY	immunoassays
AAIMNNRRSTUU	transuranium
AAIMNOOSSTTT	somatostatin
AAINNOSTTUU	unsaturation
AAINOOORTTTU	autorotation
AAINORRSSTTU	instaurators
AAIOOPPPRRRT	appropriator
AAKLNNNNOOPT	nanoplankton
AALLMOPRSXYY	paroxysmally
AALMNOOPRSTY	trypanosomal
AANNORRSSTUY	tyrannosaurs
ABBBCEHLOPSY	psychobabble
ABBBCIILLTUY	clubbability
ABBBDEEIILSS	Sidi-bel-Abbès
ABBBEHLMORTU	blabbermouth
ABBCCEEHKNRS	backbenchers
ABBCCEEHMORS	beachcombers
ABBCCEGHIMNO	beachcombing
ABBCCEHLMOOR	Colomb-Béchar
ABBCCEKKLORS	backblockers
ABBCDDEEMRRU	breadcrumbed
ABBCDEEIKLRR	blackberried
ABBCDGIIKLNR	blackbirding
ABBCEEHIILOT	bibliothecae
ABBCEEIKLRRS	blackberries
ABBCEHIILOST	bibliothecas
ABBCFIILORST	fibroblastic
ABBDDEEGGORS	Bad Godesberg
ABBDDEEILNSS	biddableness
ABBDDEGIORRS	bridgeboards
ABBDDGINOORY	bodyboarding
ABBDEHIILRSY	hybridisable
ABBDEHIILRYZ	hybridizable
ABBDEIILSSSU	subsidisable
ABBDEIILSSUZ	subsidizable
ABBDEILNNORS	Robben Island
ABBDEINRSSSU	suburbanised
ABBDEINRSUUZ	suburbanized
ABBDEMMNORST	bombardments
ABBEEEILLNUV	unbelievable
ABBEEELMORSY	Melrose Abbey
ABBEEILLNUVY	unbelievably
ABBEEILMRRSU	reimbursable
ABBEEILOPQRU	equiprobable
ABBEEMNSSSTU	subbasements
ABBEENNOTWWY	Newtownabbey
ABBEFHIIRSST	rabbitfishes
ABBEFHIORRSY	Frobisher Bay
ABBEINRSSSUU	suburbanises
ABBEINRSSTUU	suburbanites

ABBEINRSSUUZ	suburbanizes
ABBGHIILOPRY	bibliography
ABBGHIMNOSTU	thingumabobs
ABBGIILNNOTU	obnubilating
ABBIILOPRSST	probabilists
ABBIIMNNOOST	bombinations
ABCCCIILMSTU	subclimactic
ABCCDEEEELPST	bespectacled
ABCCDEEHHKORR	checkerboard
ABCCDEEIIRST	bactericides
ABCCDEHIKSTT	backstitched
ABCCDEHILORU	coachbuilder
ABCCDIILORXY	dicarboxylic
ABCCEEELNORT	concelebrate
ABCCEEENORRS	arborescence
ABCCEEGINNRU	buccaneering
ABCCEEIILNSS	inaccessible
ABCCEEILLNOR	reconcilable
ABCCEELLLOST	collectables
ABCCEEMNNRRU	encumbrancer
ABCCEEMNNRSU	encumbrances
ABCCEHIIMNOS	biomechanics
ABCCEHIKSSTT	backstitches
ABCCEHILLRUY	cherubically
ABCCEHINRSTT	tectibranchs
ABCCEHORRSUY	brachycerous
ABCCEIIILRST	criticisable
ABCCEIIILRTZ	criticizable
ABCCEIILNOOT	coenobitical
ABCCEIILNSSY	inaccessibly
ABCCEIKKLSST	sticklebacks
ABCCEIKLLOSU	cockabullies
ABCCEILLNORY	reconcilably
ABCCEILMMNOU	communicable
ABCCEILNNOOS	conscionable
ABCCEILNORTT	contractible
ABCCEILORSTU	scrobiculate
ABCCEIMNNRSU	incumbrances
ABCCGIKNORSS	backcrossing
ABCCHHIMOORT	bathochromic
ABCCHILLMORU	chlorambucil
ABCCIILLSTUY	cubistically
ABCCIIMOORST	macrobiotics
ABCCILLOOSTY	octosyllabic
ABCCILMMNOUY	communicably
ABCCILNNOOSY	conscionably
ABCCILNORTTY	contractibly
ABCCINOOSSTT	tobacconists
ABCCKLNORTUY	Black Country
ABCCNORSSTTU	subcontracts
ABCDDEEEEERRT	decerebrated
ABCDDEEEINORS	decarbonised
ABCDDEEEINORZ	decarbonized
ABCDDEEIRRSU	decarburised
ABCDDEEIRRUZ	decarburized
ABCDEEEERRST	decerebrates
ABCDEEEHHKSS	backsheeshed
ABCDEEEHILPR	decipherable
ABCDEEEHIRSU	debaucheries
ABCDEEEHLORR	breechloader
ABCDEEEHORSS	cheeseboards
ABCDEEEILNUV	undeceivable

ABCDEEEELNRTU	uncelebrated
ABCDEEFILNOS	Beaconsfield
ABCDEEHOQRRU	chequerboard
ABCDEEIILLNN	indeclinable
ABCDEEIKKSTY	stickybeaked
ABCDEEILMNSS	dissemblance
ABCDEEILMOST	domesticable
ABCDEEILNORS	considerable
ABCDEEILORSV	discoverable
ABCDEEINORRS	decarboniser
ABCDEEINORRZ	decarbonizer
ABCDEEINORSS	decarbonises
ABCDEEINORSZ	decarbonizes
ABCDEEIRRSSU	decarburises
ABCDEEIRRSUZ	decarburizes
ABCDEELMOOPS	decomposable
ABCDEELMRRSS	descramblers
ABCDEENORRST	centreboards
ABCDEFLNNOOU	confoundable
ABCDEGHIILNR	childbearing
ABCDEGILMNRS	descrambling
ABCDEHHLOOOR	bachelorhood
ABCDEHILSSTW	switchblades
ABCDEHIRRSTW	birdwatchers
ABCDEIIILLRT	liberticidal
ABCDEIILLNNY	indeclinably
ABCDEIILRSTT	distractible
ABCDEIIPSSTU	bicuspidates
ABCDEILMORST	blastodermic
ABCDEILNORSY	considerably
ABCDEILNOSTU	discountable
ABCDEINOOPRS	proboscidean
ABCDEINRSSTU	disturbances
ABCDEIORSVYY	Discovery Bay
ABCDEKMNOOSW	backwoodsmen
ABCDELMNOOPU	compoundable
ABCDEOOORRRT	corroborated
ABCDGHIINNRS	disbranching
ABCDGIINNOOT	bandicooting
ABCDHINOOPRS	branchiopods
ABCDHIORSSTW	switchboards
ABCDHNOORRSY	hydrocarbons
ABCDIILLOPST	diploblastic
ABCDIINOOPRS	proboscidian
ABCEEEFNRSST	benefactress
ABCEEEGKNRRS	greenbackers
ABCEEEHHKSSS	backsheeshes
ABCEEEHLNRRT	retrenchable
ABCEEEHLORTT	bachelorette
ABCEEEILPSTT	battlepieces
ABCEEELMNRSS	resemblances
ABCEEEMMNRRR	remembrancer
ABCEEEMMNRRS	remembrances
ABCEEENORSUV	verbenaceous
ABCEEFFIINRT	febrifacient
ABCEEFIILLNY	beneficially
ABCEEFINNOST	benefactions
ABCEEFINORST	sorbefacient
ABCEEFINRSTU	rubefacients
ABCEEFLLOORS	foreclosable
ABCEEGHNRRSU	Rauschenberg
ABCEEGIILNOT	biogenetical

ABCEEGIINNNS	benignancies
ABCEEGIKMNRS	greenbackism
ABCEEGILNORS	recognisable
ABCEEGILNORZ	recognizable
ABCEEHIINRRS	chinaberries
ABCEEHKMOSTT	Thomas Becket
ABCEEHLORSUY	herbaceously
ABCEEHMMNNRT	embranchment
ABCEEHORRRST	torchbearers
ABCEEHORSTTX	chatterboxes
ABCEEIILLNPX	inexplicable
ABCEEIILNNNT	bicentennial
ABCEEIILNRTX	inextricable
ABCEEIILPPRT	precipitable
ABCEEILLSSTU	subcelestial
ABCEEILMMORS	commiserable
ABCEEILNNOTU	unnoticeable
ABCEEILNORST	celebrations
ABCEEILNORSU	ribonuclease
ABCEEILNOSSS	sociableness
ABCEEILRSSTU	resuscitable
ABCEEINNORSV	inobservance
ABCEEINNSSTU	subtenancies
ABCEEINOORRT	cerebrotonia
ABCEEINORRST	cerebrations
ABCEEJKLMRTU	lumberjacket
ABCEEKLNNORU	unreckonable
ABCEELLLNOSU	counsellable
ABCEELLNPSSU	culpableness
ABCEELLOOSST	blastocoeles
ABCEELOPRSTU	prosecutable
ABCEENOPRRTU	protuberance
ABCEEOOPRRRT	baroreceptor
ABCEEORRSSUU	burseraceous
ABCEERRRSTTU	carburetters
ABCEFHNOOPRS	francophobes
ABCEFIIIINOV	Boniface VIII
ABCEGGGIKLLN	blacklegging
ABCEGGILNNOO	Belgian Congo
ABCEGHILORSY	brachylogies
ABCEGHINRSUW	Braunschweig
ABCEGHORRRTU	turbocharger
ABCEGILNORSY	recognisably
ABCEGILNORYZ	recognizably
ABCEGILOORTY	bacteriology
ABCEGINRRTTU	carburetting
ABCEHHINOOPT	technophobia
ABCEHHIOOPST	theophobiacs
ABCEHHKRSSUW	bushwhackers
ABCEHHMOORST	bathochromes
ABCEHIKNRSSS	brackishness
ABCEHILLOPRY	hyperbolical
ABCEHILMNRUU	hibernaculum
ABCEHKLRSSUW	swashbuckler
ABCEHLNOSTUU	untouchables
ABCEEIIILLRST	liberalistic
ABCEIIILTTXY	excitability
ABCEIIILLNPXY	inexplicably
ABCEIILMNOPT	incompatible
ABCEIILNRTXY	inextricably
ABCEIILOORST	borosilicate
ABCEIILORSTT	cristobalite

ABCEIILORTVY	revocability
ABCEIILPRSTY	plebiscitary
ABCEIIMNNOOZ	aminobenzoic
ABCEIINORSTT	obstetrician
ABCEIKNPRSTU	bankruptcies
ABCEILLMOSTY	myeloblastic
ABCEILLNNOOS	inconsolable
ABCEILMMNOTU	incommutable
ABCEILMMOOST	metabolomics
ABCEILMNNOSU	inconsumable
ABCEILMNOPTU	incomputable
ABCEILNNOTUY	unnoticeably
ABCEILNOOPRR	incorporable
ABCEILOOSSTT	osteoblastic
ABCEILOPRRTT	protractible
ABCEILPRTUUV	Tuva Republic
ABCEIMNOORST	embrocations
ABCEINOORSST	obsecrations
ABCEINRRRSST	transcribers
ABCELLLMNOOS	collembolans
ABCELLLNOORT	controllable
ABCELLLOOSTY	octosyllable
ABCELLRRTUUY	tubercularly
ABCELMNNRRSU	unscramblers
ABCELNOPRRUU	unprocurable
ABCELNORSTTU	counterblast
ABCENOPRRTUY	protuberancy
ABCENORSSSSU	scabrousness
ABCENOSSTUUU	subcutaneous
ABCEOOOORRRST	corroborates
ABCEORRRSTTU	carburettors
ABCFIILLMORY	morbifically
ABCFIINORSTU	bifurcations
ABCFINOOSSTU	obfuscations
ABCFLNOOORRU	fluorocarbon
ABCGGGIIKNPY	piggybacking
ABCGGILNNOOT	conglobating
ABCGHHIKNSUW	bushwhacking
ABCGHLOORSUY	brachylogous
ABCGIIKLLNST	blacklisting
ABCGIILLLOOV	biologically
ABCGIINNRRST	transcribing
ABCGIKNOPPST	backstopping
ABCGILLMOOSY	symbological
ABCGILMNNRSU	unscrambling
ABCGILNNOOOT	conglobation
ABCHIIKLOSTY	shockability
ABCHIILNOOPT	haplobiontic
ABCHIILRSTUY	crushability
ABCHIMNORSSU	subharmonics
ABCIIIILRSTY	irascibility
ABCIIILMNOTU	umbilication
ABCIIILNRTUY	incurability
ABCIIIMNORST	imbrications
ABCIILLMNOOY	bionomically
ABCIILMNOPTY	incompatibly
ABCIILNNOTUY	connubiality
ABCIILNOPSTU	publications
ABCIILNORSTU	lubrications
ABCIILNPPRSU	subprincipal
ABCIILORRTUY	orbicularity
ABCIILRSTTUY	scrutability

ABCIIMNNOOST	combinations
ABCIINORRSTU	rubrications
ABCILLLMOSYY	symbolically
ABCILLLOPSYY	polysyllabic
ABCILLMNOOSY	monosyllabic
ABCILLNNOOSY	inconsolably
ABCILMMNOSTU	noctambulism
ABCILMMNOTUY	incommutably
ABCILMNNOSUY	inconsumably
ABCILMNOPTUY	incomputably
ABCILMNOSTTU	noctambulist
ABCILNORSTUU	lucubrations
ABCILOOPSSTU	subapostolic
ABCIMNORSSTU	obscurantism
ABCIMNORSTUU	rambunctious
ABCINNOORSTU	conurbations
ABCINOORSSTU	obscurations
ABCINORSSTTU	obscurantist
	subtractions
ABCLLLNOORTY	controllably
ABCOOOORRRRT	corroborator
ABDDDEEGILRR	griddlebread
ABDDEEEEHLNYZ	benzaldehyde
ABDDEEEEHLORU	doubleheader
ABDDEEEEKORRY	rekeyboarded
ABDDEEEELNNPU	undependable
ABDDEEHLLLUY	bullheadedly
ABDDEEIILRST	detribalised
ABDDEEIILRTZ	detribalized
ABDDEEIILSST	destabilised
ABDDEEIILSTZ	destabilized
ABDDEEILMSSS	disassembled
ABDDEEIMNNST	absentminded
ABDDEELMNRRU	drumbledrane
ABDDEELNORSS	bladdernoses
ABDDEENOORUV	overabounded
ABDDEGINORTU	groundbaited
ABDDEILNOOST	bloodstained
ABDDEINORSTU	subordinated
ABDDELORRSTW	bladderworts
ABDEEEEILMRR	irredeemable
ABDEEEEERRRTV	reverberated
ABDEEEFIILNS	indefeasible
ABDEEEIILMRR	irremediable
ABDEEEIILRTV	deliberative
ABDEEEILLRTY	deliberately
ABDEEEILMMST	emblematised
ABDEEEILMMTZ	emblematized
ABDEEEILMNRT	determinable
ABDEEEILMRRY	irredeemably
ABDEEEINPRRS	prebendaries
ABDEEELMNTTT	battlemented
ABDEEELMNTZZ	bedazzlement
ABDEEELMPRSS	preassembled
ABDEEELPRSSU	supersedable
ABDEEFIIILNT	identifiable
ABDEEFIILNSY	indefeasibly
ABDEEFILLSTT	battlefields
ABDEEFINSTUU	subinfeudate
ABDEEGIILNRT	deliberating
ABDEEGIMNRST	abridgements
ABDEEGKLLNOW	knowledgable

ABDEEEHNPRRSS	sharpbenders
ABDEEIIILTTV	debilitative
ABDEEIIKLRST	East Kilbride
ABDEEIILMRRY	irremediably
ABDEEIILNORT	deliberation
ABDEEIILQRTU	equilibrated
ABDEEIILRSST	detribalises
ABDEEIILRSTZ	detribalizes
ABDEEIILSSST	destabilises
ABDEEIILSSTZ	destabilizes
ABDEEIINORTY	obedientiary
ABDEEIKNRRSW	windbreakers
ABDEEILLNORR	banderillero
ABDEEILMNOPR	imponderable
ABDEEILMNRTY	determinably
ABDEEILMNSST	disablements
ABDEEILMRSSS	disassembler
ABDEEILMSSSS	disassembles
ABDEEILNOSSV	voidableness
ABDEEILNRSSU	undesirables
ABDEEILNRSTY	Libyan Desert
ABDEEILORRST	deliberators
ABDEEILORRUV	boulevardier
ABDEEILPRSTU	disreputable
ABDEEINNORSS	debonairness
ABDEEINNRRSW	breadwinners
ABDEEINNRSTU	Nubian Desert
ABDEEINNSSSU	unbiasedness
ABDEEKMNNOTU	mountebanked
ABDEELLLORRS	rollerblades
ABDEELMNORST	demonstrable
ABDEELNORSSU	labouredness
ABDEENORSSTU	obdurateness
ABDEEOPRRTTU	protuberated
ABDEEORRRSSW	swordbearers
ABDEFFHLORSU	shuffleboard
ABDEFGINORRS	fingerboards
ABDEFIIILLOS	solidifiable
ABDEFIIILNTY	definability
	identifiably
ABDEFLORRTTU	flutterboard
ABDEGHIIOPRS	biographised
ABDEGHIIOPRZ	biographized
ABDEGIIILNTT	debilitating
ABDEGIIKMNRS	disembarking
ABDEGIILLMRU	Millau Bridge
ABDEGIINNNRW	breadwinning
ABDEGIIRRSTU	subirrigated
ABDEGKLLNOWY	knowledgably
ABDEGLNORTTU	battleground
ABDEHHLMOORR	rhombohedral
ABDEHHNOSSUU	househusband
ABDEHIIILMNS	diminishable
ABDEHIILSSST	disestablish
ABDEHILNOORS	dishonorable
ABDEHLLORSVY	hydrolysable
ABDEHLLORYYZ	hydrolyzable
ABDEHMOORRST	motherboards
ABDEIIIILSST	disabilities
ABDEIIILMNSS	inadmissible
ABDEIIILNOTT	debilitation
ABDEIIILRSTY	desirability

ABDEIIILRTVY	driveability
ABDEIIIRSSSU	subsidiaries
ABDEIILNPSTU	indisputable
ABDEIILNRTUY	endurability
ABDEIIMNOSST	demibastions
ABDEIIOOPRSS	basidiospore
ABDEIKORSSTY	keyboardists
ABDEILLLSSSY	dissyllables
ABDEILMNOPRY	imponderably
ABDEILMNOSTU	dismountable
ABDEILPRSTUY	disreputably
ABDEIMORSTUX	ambidextrous
ABDEINORSSTU	subordinates
ABDEINRTTTUU	unattributed
ABDELMNORSTY	demonstrably
ABDELMOORSST	bloodstreams
ABDENNORSSTV	bondservants
ABDENOPRSSUU	superabounds
ABDEOOPPRSTT	bootstrapped
ABDFIILNNRUU	infundibular
ABDFIILNOOOV	bioflavonoid
ABDGHINOOSWX	shadowboxing
ABDGHNNOSUUY	Younghusband
ABDGIILNPRUY	upbraidingly
ABDGIILOOORY	radiobiology
ABDGINNOORSW	snowboarding
ABDGINOPRRSS	springboards
ABDGINORRSST	stringboards
ABDHIIIINRST	British India
ABDHILNOORSY	dishonorably
ABDIIIILNTUY	inaudibility
ABDIIILMNSSY	inadmissibly
ABDIIILRSSUY	subsidiarily
ABDIIIMORSST	trombidiasis
ABDIIIRSSTUY	subsidiarity
ABDIILLMOTUY	modulability
	mouldability
ABDIILNNNOSS	Bonin Islands
ABDIILNPSTUY	indisputably
ABDIINOSSTUU	subauditions
ABDIIRRSTTUY	distributary
ABDIMNNOSSTU	subdominants
ABDLNOOOSSTT	odontoblasts
ABEEEEMNRSTV	bereavements
ABEEEEERRRSTV	reverberates
ABEEEEFILNNSS	fineableness
ABEEEEFILNSSS	feasibleness
ABEEEEFLNQRTU	frequentable
ABEEEEGGILNRU	beleaguering
ABEEEEGILNORT	renegotiable
ABEEEEGILRSSS	Gebrselassie
ABEEEEHHIRRST	heathberries
ABEEEEHKORRSU	housebreaker
ABEEEIILLRRV	irrelievable
ABEEEEIKLLNSS	likeableness
ABEEEILLNRSS	reliableness
ABEEEEILLNSSV	liveableness
ABEEEILLPRSV	replevisable
ABEEEEILMMSST	emblematises
ABEEEEILMMSTZ	emblematizes
ABEEEEILMNPRT	impenetrable
ABEEEEILMNRTX	exterminable
ABEEEEILMRSSS	reassemblies
ABEEEEILNNSSV	enviableness
ABEEEEILNRRST	East Berliner
ABEEEEILNSSSZ	sizeableness
ABEEEINNRRTTV	invertebrate
ABEEEJMMNNST	enjambements
ABEEEELLNOSSV	loveableness
ABEEELMNNSTT	entablements
ABEEEELNNNORW	nonrenewable
ABEEEELNSSSSS	baselessness
ABEEEELQRSSTU	sequestrable
ABEEEMPRSTTU	subtemperate
ABEEEOORRRRTV	reverberator
ABEEEPRRSTTY	presbyterate
ABEEFFGNRSTU	Stauffenberg
ABEEFFILNRSU	insufferable
ABEEFGHILNRT	frightenable
ABEEFIILLMSU	emulsifiable
ABEEFIILLRST	fertilisable
ABEEFIILLRTZ	fertilizable
ABEEFIILNRST	antifebriles
ABEEFIILNRUV	unverifiable
ABEEFILLLNSS	fallibleness
ABEEFKLNOORW	foreknowable
ABEEFLLMNSSU	blamefulness
ABEEFNRRRSTU	afterburners
ABEEGGIILNOR	globigerinae
ABEEGGILNRSS	beggarliness
ABEEGHHIKNSS	baksheeshing
ABEEGHLRSSSU	Burgess Shale
ABEEGIILNSTV	investigable
ABEEGIKNRRTU	Ekaterinburg
ABEEGILMNRSS	reassembling
ABEEGILNNOTU	unnegotiable
ABEEGILNNPUX	inexpugnable
ABEEGILNNSST	tangibleness
ABEEGILNORRS	loganberries
ABEEGILNRSUZ	gaberlunzies
ABEEGINPRSTT	bespattering
ABEEGLNNORUV	ungovernable
ABEEGLNNORVY	Longyearbyen
ABEEHHPRSSTY	bathyspheres
ABEEHIILMPRS	imperishable
ABEEHIKLRSTT	blatherskite
ABEEHILLMORT	thermolabile
ABEEHILLNOSX	Bexhill-on-Sea
ABEEHILOPPRS	prophesiable
ABEEHILPRSST	preestablish
ABEEHILRSSST	establishers
ABEEHIQRRSUU	harquebusier
ABEEHLLRSSTY	breathlessly
ABEEHLMORSTT	thermostable
ABEEHLNNOORR	blennorrhoea
ABEEHLNNORRS	blennorrheas
ABEEHLOPRSST	blastosphere
ABEEHLORRSSU	barrelhouses
ABEEHLORRSWW	wheelbarrows
ABEEHNOPRRSY	hyperboreans
ABEEIIILLRST	liberalities
ABEEIIILSSTT	bestialities
ABEEIIKKMORS	bokmakieries
ABEEIIILLRRSS	liberalisers

ABEEIILLRRSZ	liberalizers	ABEFIILLOSSS	fossilisable
ABEEIILLRSST	sterilisable	ABEFIILLOSSZ	fossilizable
ABEEIILLRSTZ	sterilizable	ABEFIILRTTUV	refutability
ABEEIILMNNRT	interminable	ABEFILNOPRTU	unprofitable
ABEEIILMNSST	imitableness	ABEFILNRSSTU	transfusible
ABEEIILMPRTY	permeability	ABEFLMOORSTT	footlamberts
ABEEIILNNSSV	inviableness	ABEFLNOSSSTU	boastfulness
ABEEIILNPRTX	inextirpable	ABEFLNOSSSUU	fabulousness
ABEEIILNPSST	pitiableness	ABEGGHIINNRR	harbingering
ABEEIILNRTVY	venerability	ABEGGHIOOPRY	biogeography
ABEEIILNRTWY	renewability	ABEGGIILLNST	billingsgate
ABEEIILORTTV	obliterative	ABEGGIILNORS	globigerinas
ABEEIILPRRRS	irrespirable	ABEGGIMNNOOR	boomeranging
ABEEIILQRSTU	equilibrates	ABEGHHKORRTU	breakthrough
ABEEIINORSST	enterobiasis	ABEGHHLOPPRY	phlebography
ABEEIIPRSSTT	baptisteries	ABEGHIILNSST	establishing
ABEEIIRSSTUV	subvarieties	ABEGHIIOPRSS	biographises
ABEEIKLMORRS	boilermakers	ABEGHIIOPRSZ	biographizes
ABEEIILLNNRUV	invulnerable	ABEGHJNNORSU	Johannesburg
	Villeurbanne	ABEGHNNOORTTU	Attenborough
ABEEIILLNNSTU	unlistenable	ABEGIIILLNRS	liberalising
ABEEIILLNOSSV	violableness	ABEGIIILLNRZ	liberalizing
ABEEIILLOPRST	boilerplates	ABEGIIILNSST	bestialising
ABEEIILLORRSV	irresolvable	ABEGIIILNSTZ	bestializing
ABEEIILLPRSUV	pulverisable	ABEGIILLLMNS	mislabelling
ABEEIILLPRUVZ	pulverizable	ABEGIILLNOUV	Bougainville
ABEEIILMMNNSU	immensurable	ABEGIILMNNSU	albumenising
ABEEIILMMOORS	aeroembolism	ABEGIILMNNUZ	albumenizing
ABEEIILMNORSZ	emblazonries	ABEGIILMNOST	metabolising
ABEEIILMNPRTY	impenetrably	ABEGIILMNOTZ	metabolizing
ABEEIILNOPRST	interposable	ABEGIILNORTT	obliterating
ABEEIILNOQSTU	questionable	ABEGIILNPRTY	pregnability
ABEEIILNSSSTU	suitableness	ABEGIINRRSTT	Bering Strait
ABEEIILOPPRRX	expropriable	ABEGIINRSSSU	agribusiness
ABEEIILPRRSTY	presbyterial	ABEGIIRRSSTU	subirrigates
ABEEIINNQRSTU	barquentines	ABEGILLMORSU	semiglobular
ABEEINORRTTV	vertebration	ABEGILLNOOST	balneologist
ABEEINPRRSTY	presbyterian	ABEGILNNPUXY	inexpugnably
ABEEIIQRRSSUU	arquebusiers	ABEGILNNRTTU	table-turning
ABEEIRRRSSTW	strawberries	ABEGINNORRST	interrobangs
ABEEKLMORRTU	troublemaker	ABEGINOOPRTW	powerboating
ABEEKLNORSSW	workableness	ABEGLLNORSSU	globularness
ABEEKLOPRRSW	Parker Bowles	ABEGLLORSSSW	glassblowers
ABEEKORRSSTT	breaststroke	ABEGLMORSSUV	umbrageously
ABEELLMNOPUY	unemployable	ABEGLNNORUVY	ungovernably
ABEELLMNOTTT	ballottement	ABEGLNORSSSU	glabrousness
ABEELLNOSSSV	solvableness	ABEGMORRSSTU	burgomasters
ABEELMMNNOTZ	emblazonment	ABEHIIILNNSU	Husein ibn-Ali
ABEELMNPRSTU	numberplates	ABEHIIILRTTY	heritability
ABEELNNORSTY	Blarney Stone	ABEHIILMOPST	amphibolites
ABEELNNSSSTU	unstableness	ABEHIILMPRSY	imperishably
ABEELOPPRSSU	superposable	ABEHIILNNRTY	labyrinthine
ABEENRSSSSTU	abstruseness	ABEHIILNOPST	inhospitable
ABEEOPRRSTTU	protuberates	ABEHIIMNOOPS	ambiophonies
ABEERRRSSTUU	subtreasurer	ABEHIIMORSSV	behaviorisms
ABEFFHIKRSST	Bashkirtseff	ABEHIIMORSUV	behaviourism
ABEFFIIILNTY	ineffability		misbehaviour
ABEFFILLLMOR	flabelliform	ABEHIINNORST	hibernations
ABEFFILNRSUY	insufferably	ABEHIIORSSTV	behaviorists
ABEFGILNORRY	forbearingly	ABEHIIORSTUV	behaviourist
ABEFGILNORUV	unforgivable	ABEHIKLNNRSU	unshrinkable
ABEFGINNRRTU	afterburning	ABEHILNOPSTY	hypnotisable

ABEHILNOPTYZ	hypnotizable	**ABEINSSSTTUV**	substantives
ABEHILOOPRSU	ailurophobes	**ABELLLLOPSYY**	polysyllable
ABEHINPRSSTU	paintbrushes	**ABELLLMNOOSY**	monosyllable
ABEHIOOPRRSS	barophoresis	**ABELMMNORSUY**	membranously
ABEHLORRSTTY	erythroblast	**ABELMNNORSTU**	submontanely
ABEHMORRRSTX	Marx Brothers	**ABELMNORSTUU**	surmountable
ABEIIILLLMRS	illiberalism	**ABELOOPRSSST**	blastospores
ABEIIILLLRTY	illiberality	**ABELORRRSTUY**	barretrously
ABEIIILLNNRT	brilliantine	**ABELRRSSTTUU**	surrebuttals
ABEIIILLNORS	billionaires	**ABEMNORRRSST**	barnstormers
ABEIIILLNSTY	ensilability	**ABFGIIILNNTU**	infibulating
ABEIIILMMRSS	miserabilism	**ABFGIIILNRTY**	frangibility
ABEIIILMRSST	miserabilist	**ABFGIILLNSYY**	syllabifying
ABEIIILNOSTT	notabilities	**ABFIIILLNORT**	fibrillation
ABEIIILNRRTY	inerrability	**ABFIIILNNOTU**	infibulation
ABEIIILOPRST	bipolarities	**ABFILMNSSTUU**	funambulists
ABEIIILRTVVY	revivability	**ABFILNOPRTUY**	unprofitably
ABEIIINNORST	inebriations	**ABGGGILLNRUY**	bullyragging
ABEIIKLORTVY	revokability	**ABGGHINOORSU**	Gainsborough
ABEIILLLMPTU	multipliable	**ABGGIILNRRSU**	burglarising
ABEIILLMRSTY	bimestrially	**ABGGIILNRRUZ**	burglarizing
ABEIILLMSSTT	bimetallists	**ABGGILLNOSSW**	glassblowing
ABEIILLORTTY	tolerability	**ABGGILOORSST**	garbologists
ABEIILLRSSTT	bristletails	**ABGGINOOSSTT**	tobogganists
ABEIILMMORTY	memorability	**ABGHHOORSSTU**	thoroughbass
ABEIILMNNRTY	interminably	**ABGHIINRSSTT**	brattishings
ABEIILMNOOST	embolisation	**ABGIIIILNTTY**	ignitability
ABEIILMNOOTZ	embolization	**ABGIIILLMNSU**	bilingualism
ABEIILMORTVY	removability	**ABGIILLMRSUW**	Williamsburg
ABEIILNNOSTU	nebulisation	**ABGIILLNNOTU**	antiglobulin
ABEIILNNOTUZ	nebulization	**ABGIILLOORTY**	obligatorily
ABEIILNNTTUY	untenability	**ABGIJNOORSTU**	objurgations
ABEIILNOORTT	obliteration	**ABGIKNRRSSTY**	stringybarks
ABEIILNOPRST	prelibations	**ABGILLNOSTTU**	subtotalling
ABEIILNQRSTU	equilibrants	**ABGILNOOPSST**	spongioblast
ABEIILNRRRTY	interlibrary	**ABGILOOORSTY**	astrobiology
ABEIILOQRRTU	equilibrator	**ABGIMNNORRST**	barnstorming
ABEIILPRSTUY	superability	**ABGINOORSSTU**	subrogations
ABEIILPRTTUY	reputability	**ABHHILOOPSTU**	bathophilous
ABEIIMNRSTUU	subminiature	**ABHIIILORSSZ**	bilharziosis
ABEIIMOQRSTU	Barquisimeto	**ABHIIKMNNPRS**	brinkmanship
ABEIINORSSTU	suberisation	**ABHIILMOPSUY**	amphibiously
ABEIINORSTUZ	suberization	**ABHIILNOPSTY**	inhospitably
ABEIIRSTTTUV	attributives	**ABHIINOPRSTV**	vibraphonist
ABEILLLRSSTY	trisyllables	**ABHIMNNORRTU**	Northumbrian
ABEILLMORSTU	rambouillets	**ABHLLMOPSSTY**	lymphoblasts
ABEILLNNRUVY	invulnerably	**ABHLOOPRSSTT**	trophoblasts
ABEILLNOPPRT	bipropellant	**ABIIIILRRTTY**	irritability
ABEILLNORRTU	interlobular	**ABIIIILLPSTUY**	plausibility
ABEILLOPRRVY	proverbially	**ABIIILMMOTVY**	immovability
ABEILLORRSVY	irresolvably	**ABIIILMMTTUY**	immutability
ABEILMOSSTUY	abstemiously	**ABIIILMNOOST**	abolitionism
ABEILNOQSTUY	questionably		mobilisation
ABEILNORSSUY	Byelorussian	**ABIIILMNOOTZ**	mobilization
ABEILNORTTXY	exorbitantly	**ABIIILMPTTUY**	imputability
ABEILOORRSTT	obliterators	**ABIIILNOOSTT**	abolitionist
ABEIMOORSSTT	strabotomies	**ABIIILNPRTTY**	printability
ABEINOOPRRST	probationers	**ABIIILNRSTUY**	insurability
	reabsorption	**ABIIILSTTTWY**	twistability
ABEINOORSSTV	observations	**ABIIINOPRSTT**	bipartitions
ABEINOOSSTTT	obtestations	**ABIILLLMNSUY**	subliminally
ABEINOPRRTTU	perturbation	**ABIILMOOSTTU**	automobilist

ABIILNOORSTT	strobilation	ACCDEEEENORST	deconsecrate
ABIILNORSSUU	insalubrious	ACCDEEFIILRS	decalcifiers
ABIILNORSTTU	tribulations	ACCDEEFIIRTT	certificated
ABIILOOPPSTY	opposability	ACCDEEFILLMS	Macclesfield
ABIILRSTTTUY	trustability	ACCDEEFLLOTU	deflocculate
ABIIMNNOORST	brominations	ACCDEEHHKLSU	chuckleheads
ABIIMNORSTTU	tambourinist	ACCDEEHIILNP	diencephalic
ABIINOORSSTT	abortionists	ACCDEEHILNOS	chalcedonies
ABIINORSTTTU	attributions	ACCDEEHIORSS	archdioceses
ABIIOPRSTTVY	absorptivity	ACCDEEIIILNS	indelicacies
ABILLORSSUUY	salubriously	ACCDEEIIILNOT	indoleacetic
ABILMMMNOSSU	somnambulism	ACCDEEIILLOPS	peccadilloes
ABILMMNOSSTU	somnambulist	ACCDEEILNOPY	encyclopedia
ABILMNORSTUY	subnormality	ACCDEEILRRTU	recirculated
ABIMNORSSTTU	nimbostratus	ACCDEEINNNST	incandescent
ABINNOORSSTU	subornations	ACCDEEINNORT	concertinaed
ABNOORRSSTUU	brontosaurus	ACCDEEIOPRRT	reciprocated
ACCCDEEEELNS	decalescence	ACCDEEIORSSS	accessorised
ACCCDEHKOPST	spatchcocked	ACCDEEIORSSZ	accessorized
ACCCDENNOORS	concordances	ACCDEEIORSTT	decorticates
ACCCEEEELNRS	recalescence	ACCDEELNNSTY	candescently
ACCCEEEILNNS	incalescence	ACCDEEMORSTU	reaccustomed
ACCCEEEINQSU	acquiescence	ACCDEENNNOTU	countenanced
ACCCEEEELNORS	calorescence	ACCDEENNORTT	concentrated
ACCCEEEELNOSS	coalescences	ACCDEENORTTU	counteracted
ACCCEEHMNOTU	accouchement	ACCDEENOSSUU	succedaneous
ACCCEEHOSSUU	accoucheuses	ACCDEENRSSSU	accursedness
ACCCEEIILSST	ecclesiastic	ACCDEEOOPRRS	Cerro de Pasco
ACCCEEILLLTY	eclectically	ACCDEFGIILNY	decalcifying
ACCCEELMNOPS	complacences	ACCDEFIIMOPT	compactified
ACCCEELNOPST	conceptacles	ACCDEFLLNOTU	deflocculant
ACCCEGIINNOR	carcinogenic	ACCDEGIINNNS	incandescing
ACCCEGINORTY	gynecocratic	ACCDEHHNNRRUW	churchwarden
ACCCEHILMOTY	cytochemical	ACCDEHHORSST	crosshatched
ACCCEHILOORS	ochlocracies	ACCDEHIILOST	catholicised
ACCCEHILOORT	chloroacetic	ACCDEHIILOTZ	catholicized
ACCCEHINORTT	technocratic	ACCDEHILMOPS	accomplished
ACCCEIILMOPS	complicacies	ACCDEHILOPP	cephalopodic
ACCCEIILMRST	climacterics	ACCDEHIOORSU	orchidaceous
ACCCEIMNOOT	concomitance	ACCDEIIILNST	insecticidal
ACCCEIMNRSTU	circumstance	ACCDEIIIPRRT	pericarditic
ACCCEINORRST	acrocentrics	ACCDEIILLOPY	epicycloidal
ACCCELMNOOPU	pneumococcal	ACCDEIILNNOT	coincidental
ACCCENOPPRUY	preoccupancy	ACCDEIILRRSU	circularised
ACCCHHIILLOT	chalcolithic	ACCDEIILRRUZ	circularized
ACCCHIIOPRRT	chiropractic	ACCDEIKLNSST	candlesticks
ACCCHIIOPRSZ	schizocarpic	ACCDEILLNOTY	occidentally
ACCCHILMOTYY	cyclothymiac	ACCDEILNOPTU	conduplicate
ACCCIIILSSST	classicistic	ACCDEILOPSTY	cyclopaedist
ACCCIILNNOTY	anticyclonic	ACCDEIMMNOTU	communicated
ACCCIILNOOST	iconoclastic	ACCDEIMNORTU	undemocratic
ACCCILLLNOVY	cyclonically	ACCDEINNORRT	androcentric
ACCDDEEEIRRT	reaccredited	ACCDEINORRTT	contradicter
ACCDDEEINRTU	unaccredited	ACCDEIOORRTT	decorticator
ACCDDEEIORTT	decorticated	ACCDEMNOSTUU	unaccustomed
ACCDDEHINOOP	dodecaphonic	ACCDFIIINOOT	codification
ACCDDEIINORT	endocarditic	ACCDHILLNOOY	conchoidally
ACCDDEIIRSST	disaccredits	ACCDIIINNOSS	scincoidians
ACCDDEINORSS	discordances	ACCDIIILNOOS	crocodilians
ACCDDEINORTT	contradicted	ACCDIIINOORST	accordionist
ACCDDGIINORS	disaccording	ACCDIIINOSTTY	syndiotactic
ACCDEEEELLNPR	precancelled	ACCDILNNOOTU	conductional

ACCDILNOOSSS	Cocos Islands
ACCDIMOSSSTU	disaccustoms
ACCDINOORRTT	contradictor
ACCDLNNOORTY	concordantly
ACCEEEGINNOT	caenogenetic
ACCEEEHILNPP	epencephalic
ACCEEEHILRST	chelicerates
ACCEEEHLORRT	heterocercal
ACCEEEILSSST	Ecclesiastes
ACCEEEINPSTX	expectancies
ACCEEENOPRSV	vaporescence
ACCEEENORRST	reconsecrate
ACCEEFGIIMNN	magnificence
ACCEEFHMNNORT	Franche-Comté
ACCEEFIIRSTT	certificates
ACCEEFIKRRRS	firecrackers
ACCEEGGIORST	secretagogic
ACCEEGHIKMNN	namechecking
ACCEEGHIMNOS	geomechanics
ACCEEGIINNOT	cainogenetic
ACCEEGILNNPR	precanceling
ACCEEGINNORS	recognisance
ACCEEGINNORZ	recognizance
ACCEEHHILORT	chalicothere
ACCEEHIILNPT	encephalitic
ACCEEHIIORRS	hierocracies
ACCEEHILMOPS	mesocephalic
ACCEEHILNRST	chanticleers
ACCEEHIMORTT	tacheometric
ACCEEHINNPST	catchpennies
ACCEEHIORTTT	heterotactic
ACCEEHIRRTTU	architecture
ACCEEHIRSTVZ	czarevitches
ACCEEHKORSTW	weathercocks
ACCEEHLLORST	electroclash
ACCEEHLMNRSY	sclerenchyma
ACCEEHMNNORT	encroachment
ACCEEIILNRST	electricians
ACCEEIINNORT	interoceanic
ACCEEIINPPRT	precipitance
ACCEEIIOPPSS	episcopacies
ACCEEIKRRSSW	wisecrackers
ACCEEILLLRTY	electrically
ACCEEILLMNUV	ecumenically
ACCEEILNPTTU	centuplicate
ACCEEILNRTTY	tetracycline
ACCEEILRRSTU	recirculates
ACCEEIMNOTTY	actinomycete
ACCEEINOPPRV	Cape Province
ACCEEINORSTV	consecrative
ACCEEIOPRRST	reciprocates
ACCEEIORSSSS	accessorises
ACCEEIORSSSZ	accessorizes
ACCEEIORSTTT	stereotactic
ACCEELLOORTT	collectorate
ACCEELMNNOST	concealments
ACCEELMNOPTU	accouplement
ACCEELNNOPTY	cyclopentane
ACCEELNNOSTV	convalescent
ACCEELNNRSTU	translucence
ACCEELORSTUY	cretaceously
ACCEEMNNORRS	necromancers

ACCEEMNOPPSU	comeuppances
ACCEEMNORTTU	accouterment
	accoutrement
ACCEENNNORTU	countenancer
ACCEENNNOSTU	countenances
ACCEENNORSTT	concentrates
ACCEENNORSVY	conveyancers
ACCEENOPRRSU	precancerous
ACCEFFIIINTY	inefficacity
ACCEFGIIINNS	significance
ACCEFIILLPSY	specifically
ACCEFIIMOPST	compactifies
ACCEFMNNOORS	conformances
ACCEGGILNOOV	gynaecologic
ACCEGHHIOPRR	choregraphic
ACCEGHHIOPRT	hectographic
ACCEGHHISTTW	catchweights
ACCEGHINOPRS	scenographic
ACCEGIIKKKLNP	placekicking
ACCEGIIKNRSW	wisecracking
ACCEGIILMOST	cleistogamic
ACCEGIINNNOZ	incognizance
ACCEGIINRTUX	excruciating
ACCEGILLLOOV	ecologically
ACCEGILLNOOR	necrological
ACCEGILNNOSV	convalescing
ACCEGINNNOVY	conveyancing
ACCEGINNORST	consecrating
ACCEGNOORRTY	gerontocracy
ACCEHHILOSSZ	eschscholzia
ACCEHHLMNORY	chlorenchyma
ACCEHHORSSST	crosshatches
ACCEHIILLMRY	chimerically
ACCEHIILLNST	callisthenic
ACCEHIILNOPR	necrophiliac
ACCEHIILNSST	calisthenics
ACCEHIILNTTY	technicality
ACCEHIILOSST	catholicises
ACCEHIILOSTZ	catholicizes
ACCEHIIMRSTT	chrematistic
ACCEHIIRSTTT	tetrastichic
ACCEHILLLORY	cholerically
ACCEHILLMNOS	melancholics
ACCEHILMOPRS	accomplisher
ACCEHILMOPRY	microcephaly
	pyrochemical
ACCEHILMOPSS	accomplishes
ACCEHILNNNOT	nontechnical
ACCEHILNOOOT	echolocation
ACCEHILOPRTY	chalcopyrite
ACCEHIMNORRS	chiromancers
ACCEHIMNORST	mechatronics
ACCEHIMOORST	mesothoracic
ACCEHINNNOPT	pantechnicon
ACCEHINNRSSU	craunchiness
ACCEHINOPRTY	pyrocatechin
ACCEHINOPSSY	sycophancies
ACCEHINRSSST	scratchiness
ACCEHIOPSTVY	psychoactive
ACCEHKLOOSVZ	Czechoslovak
ACCEHKLRSSTU	saltchuckers
ACCEHLOOPRTY	pyrocatechol

ACCEHLOORSSU	schorlaceous
ACCEHMNORRTU	countermarch
ACCEHMOOORST	motorcoaches
ACCEHOOOPRST	thoracoscope
ACCEHOPRSSST	crosspatches
ACCEIIILNOTV	conciliative
ACCEIIILPSST	specialistic
ACCEIIINNNPS	piccaninnies
ACCEIIINNOST	canonicities
ACCEIIISSTTU	causticities
ACCEIIKKMNRS	camiknickers
ACCEIILLLNTY	enclitically
ACCEIILLLPTY	ecliptically
ACCEIILLMORT	cliometrical
ACCEIILLNNSS	clinicalness
ACCEIILLOSST	solecistical
ACCEIILLRSST	clericalists
ACCEIILMMORT	microclimate
ACCEIILMNNOP	incompliance
ACCEIILMNOPS	compliancies
ACCEIILMOORS	seriocomical
ACCEIILMORRT	calorimetric
ACCEIILMRRSU	semicircular
ACCEIILNOOPS	Ascoli Piceno
ACCEIILNORTV	intervocalic
ACCEIILNRSST	criticalness
ACCEIILNRSTT	centralistic
ACCEIILORRTV	overcritical
ACCEIILOSSTV	viscoelastic
ACCEIILRRRSU	circulariser
ACCEIILRRRUZ	circularizer
ACCEIILRRSSU	circularises
ACCEIILRRSUZ	circularizes
ACCEIILRSSTU	secularistic
ACCEIIMNORRT	craniometric
ACCEIIMNORTT	actinometric
ACCEIIMNOSST	cosmeticians
ACCEIIMORRTT	meritocratic
ACCEIINOPRSS	conspiracies
ACCEIINORTUX	excruciation
ACCEIINOSSTX	exsiccations
ACCEIINPPRTY	precipitancy
ACCEIIPPRSTY	perspicacity
ACCEIJNNOTUV	conjunctivae
ACCEIKLOPRTT	kleptocratic
ACCEILLMMORY	commercially
ACCEILLMNOOY	economically
ACCEILLMOSTY	cosmetically
ACCEILLNNORT	centroclinal
ACCEILLNOTTY	tectonically
ACCEILLOPRRY	reciprocally
ACCEILLOPTYY	ecotypically
ACCEILMMNORU	uncommercial
ACCEILMNNOOU	uneconomical
ACCEILMNORTU	counterclaim
ACCEILNNNOOT	connectional
ACCEILNNOOPT	conceptional
ACCEILNNOOTV	convectional
ACCEILNNOSTY	anticyclones
ACCEILNOORRT	correctional
ACCEILNOPRST	narcoleptics
ACCEILNOSSSU	successional

ACCEILNRRSSU	circularness
ACCEILOOSSTT	osteoclastic
ACCEILOPRSST	ceroplastics
ACCEILOPRSTU	plutocracies
ACCEIMMNOSTU	communicates
ACCEIMNOSTTY	nematocystic
ACCEIMNRTTUU	circumnutate
ACCEINNNNOOS	inconsonance
ACCEINNNOOSS	consonancies
ACCEINNOORST	consecration
ACCEINNORSSU	coinsurances
ACCEINNORSTV	contrivances
ACCEINOOPRRS	pornocracies
ACCEINOOPRTU	reoccupation
ACCEIOOPRRRT	reciprocator
ACCELLMNOPTY	complacently
ACCELLNOPTUY	conceptually
ACCELLOOORSU	corollaceous
ACCELMMNOOPS	commonplaces
ACCELMNORSUU	macronucleus
ACCELMOOSTTY	cyclostomate
ACCELNNRSTUY	translucency
ACCELNOOOPPRY	cyclopropane
ACCELORSUUVY	curvaceously
ACCEMOOSSTUY	ascomycetous
ACCENNOORRTT	concentrator
ACCENOOPRSTU	pococurantes
ACCENOORRSST	consecrators
ACCENOORRSTY	consecratory
ACCENOPRRSTT	precontracts
ACCENOPRRSTU	counterscarp
ACCENORRSTTU	contractures
ACCFGIINNOST	confiscating
ACCFGILLNOTU	flocculating
ACCFIIIINOTT	citification
ACCFIIINOTTY	cityfication
ACCFIIMNNOSU	Confucianism
ACCFIINNOOST	confiscation
ACCFILLNOOTU	flocculation
ACCFILMORTUU	fractocumuli
ACCFINOORSST	confiscators
ACCFINOORSTY	confiscatory
ACCGHHIINOPR	ichnographic
ACCGHHIINTTT	chitchatting
ACCGHHIIOPRR	chirographic
ACCGHHIOOPRR	chorographic
ACCGHIILLNOO	ichnological
ACCGHIILNNOP	Chilpancingo
ACCGHIIMOPRR	micrographic
ACCGHIIMOTTT	thigmotactic
ACCGHIINOOPR	iconographic
ACCGHIINOPRZ	zincographic
ACCGHIIOPPRT	pictographic
ACCGHILLOOPY	phycological
ACCGHIMOOPRS	cosmographic
ACCGHINORRSS	Charing Cross
ACCGIIILNNOT	conciliating
ACCGIIILNSSS	classicising
ACCGIIILNSSZ	classicizing
ACCGIIINORST	organicistic
ACCGIILLMOOT	climatologic
ACCGIILLNOOO	iconological

ACCGIILLOOOS	sociological
ACCGIILMNOPT	complicating
ACCGIINNOOST	consociating
ACCGIKKMMNUU	muckamucking
ACCGILLMOOOS	cosmological
ACCGILMNOOOS	cosmogonical
ACCGILNORTUV	granulocytic
ACCGIOOPRSST	gastroscopic
ACCHHINOOTTU	autochthonic
ACCHHIOPPSTY	psychopathic
ACCHIIINSTUV	chauvinistic
ACCHIILLOOTY	alcoholicity
ACCHIILOPRTY	hypocritical
ACCHIIMMORST	chromaticism
ACCHIIMNOPTY	amphictyonic
ACCHIIMNORST	monarchistic
ACCHIIMOORST	isochromatic
ACCHIIMORRTT	trichromatic
ACCHIIMORTTY	chromaticity
ACCHIINOOPTT	photoactinic
ACCHIIOPRSTY	physiocratic
ACCHILLNNOOO	nonalcoholic
ACCHILLOPTTY	phyllotactic
ACCHILNOPRTY	lycanthropic
ACCHILOOPSSY	psychosocial
ACCHILOPPRTY	prophylactic
ACCHIMOPRSSY	macrophysics
ACCHINOOPSTT	phonotactics
ACCHIOOPRRRT	chiropractor
ACCHIOOPRRST	arthroscopic
ACCHIOORRSSU	chiaroscuros
ACCHJKNNNOUY	Johnny Canuck
ACCIIILNNOOT	conciliation
ACCIIINRSSST	narcissistic
ACCIILLRSTTY	crystallitic
ACCIILMMOORT	microtomical
ACCIILMNNOPY	incompliancy
ACCIILMNOOPT	complication
ACCIILMNOOTV	convictional
ACCIILNNOSTU	inculcations
ACCIILNOORST	conciliators
ACCIILNOORTY	conciliatory
ACCIILNORSTU	circulations
ACCIILOPRSUY	capriciously
ACCIIMNNOSTY	actinomycins
ACCIIMOOPRTT	compatriotic
ACCIINNOOOST	consociation
ACCIJLNNOTUV	conjunctival
ACCIJNNOSTUV	conjunctivas
ACCILLMNOOSU	malocclusion
ACCILLNOOOST	collocations
ACCILNOOSTTU	occultations
ACCIMMNNOSTU	communicants
ACCIMMNOORTU	communicator
ACCIMNNOOSTT	concomitants
ACCIMNOOSTUU	contumacious
ACCIMOORSSTY	macrocytosis
ACCINNOOSTVV	convocations
ACCINNOORSTT	contractions
ACCINOORSSTU	coruscations
ACCIOOPRSSTU	stauroscopic
ACCJLNNORTUU	conjunctural

ACDDDEEHNOOR	dodecahedron
ACDDEEEFNORT	confederated
ACDDEEEHIMST	semidetached
ACDDEEEILNRT	credentialed
ACDDEEEEINNPS	dependancies
ACDDEEEIPRTT	decrepitated
ACDDEEEMMNOR	commandeered
ACDDEEEORTUV	overeducated
ACDDEEFIILSS	declassified
ACDDEEGHNRRU	undercharged
ACDDEEGIINRT	rededicating
ACDDEEGIKLRS	griddlecakes
ACDDEEGKLNOW	acknowledged
ACDDEEHIMNRS	merchandised
ACDDEEHINNST	disenchanted
ACDDEEHLLNOR	candleholder
ACDDEEIINORT	rededication
ACDDEEILPRTU	reduplicated
ACDDEEIMORST	democratised
ACDDEEIMORTZ	democratized
ACDDEEIMOSTT	domesticated
ACDDEEINNRSU	redundancies
ACDDEEIQRSTU	quadrisected
ACDDEELNPTUU	pedunculated
ACDDEENNOSTV	Second Advent
ACDDEGHINRSU	undischarged
ACDDEHLLOSST	saddlecloths
ACDDEIIILMOT	domiciliated
ACDDEIILNORU	radionuclide
ACDDEIILNPTU	induplicated
ACDDEIINNOTV	nonaddictive
ACDDEIINORST	endocarditis
ACDDEILLMOUY	duodecimally
ACDDEILNOOST	consolidated
ACDDEILRSTTY	distractedly
ACDDEINOSTTU	outdistanced
ACDDHIMNORVY	hydrodynamic
ACDDILNORSTY	discordantly
ACDEEEEGINRS	degeneracies
ACDEEEEHLRRS	cheerleaders
ACDEEEFFNSST	affectedness
ACDEEEFLNRST	needlecrafts
ACDEEEFMNNRS	Mendès-France
ACDEEEFNORST	confederates
ACDEEEGHLLNR	rechallenged
ACDEEEGILNRT	decelerating
ACDEEEGINOPT	paedogenetic
ACDEEEGINPRS	predeceasing
ACDEEEHINRUV	underachieve
ACDEEEHIORVV	overachieved
ACDEEEHIRSTT	catheterised
ACDEEEHIRTTZ	catheterized
ACDEEEIIPRTV	depreciative
ACDEEEILNORT	deceleration
ACDEEEILNPRT	precedential
ACDEEEILNRST	decentralise
ACDEEEILNRSU	denuclearise
ACDEEEILNRTV	cantilevered
ACDEEEILNRTZ	decentralize
ACDEEEILNRUZ	denuclearize
ACDEEEILNSST	delicateness
	delicatessen

ACDEEEEIMNOST	adenectomies
ACDEEEEIMRSTV	decemvirates
ACDEEEEINNRTV	inadvertence
ACDEEEEINORTU	auctioneered
ACDEEEEINRSSV	disseverance
ACDEEEEINRSTV	advertencies
ACDEEEEINSSTT	necessitated
ACDEEEEIPRSTT	decrepitates
ACDEEEELNNOSU	endonuclease
ACDEEEELORRST	decelerators
ACDEEEEOORRTV	overdecorate
ACDEEEEOPRTTX	expectorated
ACDEEEEORSTUV	overeducates
ACDEEFFLNTUY	unaffectedly
ACDEEFFNORRT	Fort-de-France
ACDEEFHHIKNR	handkerchief
ACDEEFHILNSS	candlefishes
ACDEEFHINNRS	enfranchised
ACDEEFHINOTT	fianchettoed
ACDEEFHNORRW	henceforward
ACDEEFIILRSS	reclassified
ACDEEFIILRST	federalistic
ACDEEFIILSSS	declassifies
ACDEEFIINRRY	ferricyanide
ACDEEFILMTTU	multifaceted
ACDEEFINORRY	ferrocyanide
ACDEEFNRRSUU	undersurface
ACDEEGHINNRT	interchanged
ACDEEGHLLNNU	unchallenged
ACDEEGHNNRSU	undercharges
ACDEEGHPRRSU	supercharged
ACDEEGIINPRT	depreciating
ACDEEGILLOTY	geodetically
ACDEEGILNRSY	decreasingly
ACDEEGILSTTU	gesticulated
ACDEEGINORRT	redecorating
ACDEEGKLNORW	acknowledger
ACDEEGKLNOSW	acknowledges
ACDEEGNNORTV	Covent Garden
ACDEEGNNOSTT	decongestant
ACDEEHHIMORT	hemichordate
ACDEEHHOPTTY	hypothecated
ACDEEHILMNOR	echinodermal
ACDEEHILMRSS	childermases
ACDEEHILNNOP	diencephalon
ACDEEHIMNRRS	merchandiser
ACDEEHIMNRSS	merchandises
ACDEEHINNRST	disenchanter
ACDEEHINRSTW	windcheaters
ACDEEHINSTTW	Wattenscheid
ACDEEHIORSTT	octahedrites
ACDEEHKKLNSU	knuckleheads
ACDEEHLORTTY	heterodactyl
ACDEEHMMORRTU	routemarched
ACDEEHNNOPRU	unchaperoned
ACDEEHOPPRRS	sharecropped
ACDEEHORRSTT	orchestrated
ACDEEIIINNRS	incendiaries
ACDEEIILLMPY	epidemically
ACDEEIILLNTY	indelicately
ACDEEIILLTTY	dietetically
ACDEEIIMNRRT	recriminated

ACDEEIIMNRTY	intermediacy
ACDEEIINNNST	intendancies
ACDEEIINNOST	neonaticides
ACDEEIINOPRT	depreciation
ACDEEIINQSTU	equidistance
ACDEEIINTTUX	inexactitude
ACDEEIIOPPSS	epidiascopes
ACDEEIIPPRTT	precipitated
ACDEEIKLOOPS	kaleidoscope
ACDEEILLMPRY	premedically
ACDEEILLNNOS	declensional
ACDEEILLNNTY	tendencially
ACDEEILLNRTY	interlacedly
ACDEEILLRTUV	revictualled
ACDEEILMNPST	displacement
ACDEEILMORRS	sclerodermia
ACDEEILMRTUV	vermiculated
ACDEEILNORTU	reinoculated
ACDEEILNPQTU	quindecaplet
ACDEEILNRSTT	decentralist
ACDEEILORRST	clearstoried
ACDEEILORTVY	decoratively
ACDEEILPRSTU	reduplicates
ACDEEILRSSTT	decretalists
ACDEEILRTTVY	detractively
ACDEEIMMORST	commiserated
ACDEEIMNNOPR	predominance
ACDEEIMNNPRS	predicaments
ACDEEIMOPRST	spermatocide
ACDEEIMORRRS	microreaders
ACDEEIMORRTX	xerodermatic
ACDEEIMORSST	democratises
ACDEEIMORSTZ	democratizes
ACDEEIMOSSTT	domesticates
ACDEEINNRTVY	inadvertency
ACDEEINNOORRT	redecoration
ACDEEINOORST	aerodonetics
ACDEEINOPRST	deprecations
ACDEEINOPRTU	deuteranopic
ACDEEINORSTU	reeducations
ACDEEINOSSSU	edaciousness
ACDEEINPRRST	transpierced
ACDEEIOOPRSS	aecidospores
ACDEEIOPPRTU	propaedeutic
ACDEEIOPRRST	depreciators
ACDEEIOPRRTY	depreciatory
ACDEEIORRSTT	directorates
ACDEEIPQRSSU	quadricepses
ACDEEIRSSSTT	dictatresses
ACDEEIRSSTTU	resuscitated
ACDEEKQRRSTU	quarterdecks
ACDEELLNOSTT	constellated
ACDEELMNOPTT	contemplated
ACDEELNRSSSU	underclasses
ACDEEMMMOORT	commemorated
ACDEEMNOPPTY	appendectomy
ACDEEMNRSTTU	traducements
ACDEENNNOPRU	preannounced
ACDEENNNOTUV	uncovenanted
ACDEENNNRSTT	transcendent
ACDEENNORSST	contredanses
ACDEENNORSTT	consternated

ACDEENORRTTU	countertrade
ACDEFFGIINST	disaffecting
ACDEFFIILPST	spifflicated
ACDEFFIINOST	disaffection
ACDEFHIINRSS	disfranchise
ACDEFIIIMOTV	modificative
ACDEFIIINNST	infanticides
ACDEFIIINOST	deifications
ACDEFIILNNOT	confidential
ACDEFIILNSSU	unclassified
ACDEFIINNSTT	disinfectant
ACDEFIINNSTU	unsanctified
ACDEFIINOPTT	pontificated
ACDEFIINORST	fractionised
ACDEFIINORTZ	fractionized
ACDEFIKNORSU	Caudine Forks
ACDEFILLLOTU	folliculated
ACDEFILRTTUX	fluidextract
ACDEGHHNORST	shortchanged
ACDEGHIMOPRS	demographics
ACDEGHIOPRRS	discographer
ACDEGHNNORSU	changerounds
ACDEGIIILMNS	decimalising
ACDEGIIILMNZ	decimalizing
ACDEGIIKNRST	sidetracking
ACDEGIILLNOS	delocalising
ACDEGIILLNOZ	delocalizing
ACDEGIILNOSV	devocalising
ACDEGIILNOVZ	devocalizing
ACDEGIILPQRU	quadriplegic
ACDEGIIMNSTU	miseducating
ACDEGIINNNTU	denunciating
ACDEGIINOTTX	detoxicating
ACDEGIIOOPRT	diageotropic
ACDEGILLOOTY	dialectology
ACDEGILNORTU	edulcorating
ACDEGILNRTTY	detractingly
ACDEGINNNRST	transcending
ACDEGINNOQSU	quindecagons
ACDEGINNORTU	undercoating
ACDEGINNRTTU	detruncating
ACDEGIORRSSU	discouragers
ACDEGKLOORSS	sockdolagers
ACDEHHLOPRYY	hydrocephaly
ACDEHHOOOPTT	photocathode
ACDEHIIINPSS	hispanicised
ACDEHIIINPSZ	hispanicized
ACDEHIILLNOS	Chiloé Island
ACDEHIILMMOT	immethodical
ACDEHIILOPPS	pedophiliacs
ACDEHIIMNNOT	indomethacin
ACDEHIIMORST	radiochemist
ACDEHIINOPRR	perichondria
ACDEHIIOPRST	diaphoretics
ACDEHIIPRTYY	hyperacidity
ACDEHIKLNRST	stickhandler
ACDEHIKLNSST	stickhandles
ACDEHIKMNRSS	scrimshanked
ACDEHILLMOTY	methodically
ACDEHILLPRUY	hyperdulical
ACDEHILMNOTU	unmethodical
ACDEHILORSTY	hydroelastic
ACDEHINOORSS	icosahedrons
ACDEHIOOPRST	orthopaedics
ACDEHKLNNSST	landsknechts
ACDEHLLLOPSY	phylloclades
ACDEHLNPRSTU	thunderclaps
ACDEHLOORSUW	colourwashed
ACDEHMMNNOORS	enchondromas
ACDEHMNORRSY	hydromancers
ACDEHMOORSTW	doomwatchers
ACDEHOORRSTU	urochordates
ACDEHORRSTYY	cryohydrates
ACDEIIIILNSV	civilianised
ACDEIIIILNVZ	civilianized
ACDEIIILMNRS	criminalised
ACDEIIILMNRZ	criminalized
ACDEIIILMOST	domiciliates
ACDEIIILNTVY	indicatively
ACDEIIILORST	cordialities
ACDEIIILRTVY	veridicality
ACDEIIIMMORT	radiomimetic
ACDEIIIMNNOT	nicotinamide
ACDEIIIMNNRS	incendiarism
ACDEIIIMNNRT	incriminated
ACDEIIIMNRST	discriminate
ACDEIIIMORST	isodiametric
ACDEIIINOPRT	antiperiodic
ACDEIIINORST	dictionaries
ACDEIIINPPST	appendicitis
ACDEIIINPSST	aspendicitis
ACDEIIINRTTU	antidiuretic
ACDEIIIOPRTY	aperiodicity
ACDEIIIOSSTV	dissociative
ACDEIIIPRRST	pericarditis
ACDEIIJORSTU	judicatories
ACDEIIKLRSTT	Lake District
ACDEIIKPRSTT	Peak District
ACDEIILLNNTY	incidentally
ACDEIILLNSTT	scintillated
ACDEIILLOPRY	periodically
ACDEIILLOPSY	episodically
ACDEIILLPSTY	septicidally
ACDEIILLRTUY	diuretically
ACDEIILMNOST	maledictions
ACDEIILMNSSU	masculinised
ACDEIILMNSUZ	masculinized
ACDEIILMOORT	iodometrical
ACDEIILMORTT	dilatometric
ACDEIILNNNOT	nonidentical
ACDEIILNNOST	declinations
ACDEIILNORST	discretional
ACDEIILNOSTU	elucidations
ACDEIILNOSTV	valedictions
ACDEIILNPSSS	Spice Islands
ACDEIILOPRST	tropicalised
ACDEIILOPRTZ	tropicalized
ACDEIILRRTUV	diverticular
ACDEIIMNORST	dominatrices
	romanticised
ACDEIIMNORTZ	romanticized
ACDEIIMNOSTU	miseducation
ACDEIIMOPRRT	madreporitic
ACDEIINNNOTU	denunciation

ACDEIINNOORT	incoordinate
ACDEIINNORTT	indoctrinate
ACDEIINNRSTY	tyrannicides
ACDEIINOOPPR	propanedioic
ACDEIINOORTV	coordinative
ACDEIINOOTTX	detoxication
ACDEIINOPRST	predications
ACDEIINORRST	doctrinaires
ACDEIINOSTTU	educationist
ACDEIIORSSTT	siderostatic
ACDEIJORSTUX	coadjutrixes
ACDEILLMOSTY	domestically
ACDEILLNOOST	decollations
ACDEILLNSTYY	syndetically
ACDEILLOPSTU	leucoplastid
ACDEILLOPSTY	despotically
ACDEILLRSSTY	crystallised
ACDEILLRSTYZ	crystallized
ACDEILMMNOSU	communalised
ACDEILMMNOUZ	communalized
ACDEILMNOPRU	unproclaimed
ACDEILMNOSUY	mendaciously
ACDEILMOPSTU	deutoplasmic
ACDEILNOOORT	decoloration
ACDEILNOORTU	edulcoration
ACDEILNOORTY	coordinately
ACDEILNOOSST	consolidates
	disconsolate
ACDEILNORSSW	cowardliness
ACDEILNPRSTY	discrepantly
ACDEILNTTUUV	uncultivated
ACDEILOORRUV	varicoloured
ACDEILOPSTTU	deutoplastic
ACDEILRRTTUU	turriculated
ACDEIMMNNOOT	commendation
ACDEIMMNORTY	dynamometric
ACDEIMNNNOOT	condemnation
ACDEIMNNOPRY	predominancy
ACDEIMOORSTT	domesticator
ACDEINNNOOST	condensation
ACDEINNNOSTU	unsanctioned
ACDEINNORSTU	denunciators
ACDEINNORTTU	detruncation
ACDEINNORTUY	denunciatory
ACDEINOOPRRT	incorporated
ACDEINOOPRSS	scorpaenoids
ACDEINOPRTTV	privatdocent
ACDEINOPRTTY	dictyopteran
ACDEINOSSSTU	decussations
ACDEINOSSTTU	outdistances
ACDEINPSSSSU	scindapsuses
ACDEIOOPRRST	corporatised
ACDEIOOPRRTZ	corporatized
ACDELLOPRRUY	procedurally
ACDELNOORTYY	cotyledonary
ACDELOPRRTTY	protractedly
ACDELOPRSTTY	pterodactyls
ACDEMMMNNOST	commandments
ACDEMMNOORTY	commendatory
ACDEMNNOORTY	condemnatory
ACDEMNNORSTU	countermands
ACDEMOORRSST	ostracoderms

ACDEORSTTTUU	autodestruct
ACDFFGILNOSS	scaffoldings
ACDFFIINORST	diffractions
ACDFGIIIINNT	nidificating
ACDFGIILLNUV	fungicidally
ACDFIIIINNOT	nidification
ACDFIIIMNOOT	modification
ACDFIILNNOTU	difunctional
ACDFIIMOORTY	modificatory
ACDGGIINORSU	discouraging
ACDGHHIOPRRY	hydrographic
ACDGHIIOPRTT	dittographic
ACDGHILLOORY	hydrological
ACDGIIINOSST	dissociating
ACDGIILOORST	cardiologist
ACDGIINNOORT	coordinating
ACDGILMMNNOY	commandingly
ACDGINOOOPRT	gonadotropic
ACDGINOORSVW	woodcarvings
ACDHHINOOPRY	hypochondria
ACDHHINOORTX	xanthochroid
ACDHHIOPRRSS	harpsichords
ACDHIILOOPSU	acidophilous
ACDHIIMMORST	dichromatism
ACDHIIMNOORT	mitochondria
ACDHIIMNORSS	diachronisms
ACDHIIOPRSST	rhapsodistic
ACDHIIOPRSTT	dictatorship
ACDHILLOORTY	trochoidally
ACDHIMNOOPTY	photodynamic
ACDHIMNOORST	trichomonads
ACDHINNORSYY	cyanohydrins
ACDHINOOPQRU	quadrophonic
ACDHIORSSTTY	hydrostatics
ACDHLNOOSSUY	Sunday school
ACDIIILNNPST	disciplinant
ACDIIILNPRSY	disciplinary
ACDIIIMNNRST	discriminant
ACDIIINNOSTV	vindications
ACDIIINOOSST	dissociation
ACDIIIOSSTTU	adscititious
ACDIIILLLOOTY	colloidality
ACDIILLMNPTU	multiplicand
ACDIILLOOPSU	lapidicolous
ACDIILLOPRTY	dioptrically
ACDIILMNNORU	androclinium
ACDIILMNOPTU	undiplomatic
ACDIILNNOOST	conditionals
ACDIILNOOQTU	coloquintida
ACDIILNOOSST	dislocations
ACDIILNOPSTU	duplications
ACDIILNORTTY	doctrinality
ACDIILNOSSSU	discussional
ACDIIMNORRST	doctrinarism
ACDIINNOOORT	coordination
ACDIINNOSSTY	syndications
ACDIINOPRSST	adscriptions
ACDIINOPSSTU	cuspidations
ACDIINORSSTT	distractions
ACDIINORSSYY	idiosyncrasy
ACDILLLMOOSU	molluscoidal
ACDILLMOOORX	loxodromical

ACDILLORSSTY	crystalloids
ACDILMNOOPSU	Pamlico Sound
ACDILMNSSTYY	syndactylism
ACDILMOORSUY	mordaciously
ACDILNOOOORST	consolidator
ACDILNOOPRTU	productional
ACDILORSTTUY	tridactylous
ACDINNORSTTU	transduction
ACDINOOORRST	coordinators
ACDINOOQRSTU	conquistador
ACDLOOOPRSTT	postdoctoral
ACDNOORSSTTU	Sandrocottus
ACEEEEEKPPRS	peacekeepers
ACEEEEEFNRRSS	carefreeness
ACEEEEGIKNPP	peacekeeping
ACEEEEGILPTX	epexegetical
ACEEEEHLPSST	steeplechase
ACEEEEHLNORTT	coelenterate
ACEEEEELNPRRS	real presence
ACEEEENPRRSV	perseverance
ACEEEFFFRSTT	aftereffects
ACEEEFLNNOSV	Anne of Cleves
ACEEEFLNPSSU	peacefulness
ACEEEFLNSSSS	facelessness
ACEEEFNNNRST	transference
ACEEEGGORSTU	secretagogue
ACEEEGHINPRS	cheeseparing
ACEEEGHLLNRS	rechallenges
ACEEEGIILNNS	inelegancies
ACEEEGIKNRRT	racketeering
ACEEEGILLTXY	exegetically
ACEEEGINNOSS	caenogenesis
ACEEEGINNSSW	newsagencies
ACEEEGINRRST	generatrices
ACEEEGLOSTTT	telecottages
ACEEEGNNRRUY	unregeneracy
ACEEEHHIRRST	heterarchies
ACEEEHILSTTT	telaesthetic
ACEEEHIMNQTU	cinematheque
ACEEEHIMNSTV	achievements
ACEEEHINOSST	coenesthesia
ACEEEHIORRVV	overachiever
ACEEEHIORSVV	overachieves
ACEEEHIRSSTT	catheterises
ACEEEHIRSTTZ	catheterizes
ACEEEHKLNRST	leathernecks
ACEEEHLLNRST	chanterelles
ACEEEHLMOPRT	cephalometer
ACEEEHLNNOPP	epencephalon
ACEEEHMNNNST	enhancements
ACEEEHMORSTT	tacheometers
ACEEEHPRRSTU	superteacher
ACEEEILLLNTT	lenticellate
ACEEEILLMRTT	telemetrical
ACEEEILMNPST	mantelpieces
ACEEEILNNNSV	Valenciennes
ACEEEILNORRV	overreliance
ACEEEILNRRSV	irrelevances
ACEEEILRRTVY	recreatively
ACEEEILRTVXY	execratively
ACEEEIMMNNPR	impermanence
ACEEEIMNNPRS	permanencies

ACEEEIMNNPRT	intemperance
ACEEEIMPRSST	masterpieces
ACEEEINRSSTV	creativeness
	reactiveness
ACEEEINSSSTT	necessitates
ACEEEIPPPRTV	apperceptive
ACEEEIPRRTUV	recuperative
ACEEEJKLPSST	steeplejacks
ACEEELLMNOST	metallocenes
ACEEELLOPRTT	electroplate
ACEEELLORSVV	cloverleaves
ACEEELMMNPST	emplacements
ACEEELMNPRST	replacements
ACEEELNNSTVY	evanescently
ACEEELNOSSUX	exonucleases
ACEEELNOTXYY	oxyacetylene
ACEEELNRSSSS	carelessness
ACEEEMNNNRTT	entrancement
ACEEEMNNRSTT	reenactments
ACEEENNORSTW	Western Ocean
ACEEENNRRTTY	tercentenary
ACEEENNRSTXY	sexcentenary
ACEEENNRSSSV	screensavers
ACEEENRSSSST	ancestresses
ACEEEOPPRRTT	preceptorate
ACEEEOPRSTTX	expectorates
ACEEERRSSSTW	watercresses
ACEEFFGINTTU	effectuating
ACEEFFILTTUY	effectuality
ACEEFFINOTTU	effectuation
ACEEFGHIMNST	gemeinschaft
ACEEFGHINNRU	French Guinea
ACEEFGHINORR	forereaching
ACEEFGHLLSST	gesellschaft
ACEEFGHNRTUW	Feuchtwanger
ACEEFGIINRSS	fricasseeing
ACEEFGLNRSSU	gracefulness
ACEEFHHIRRSS	archerfishes
ACEEFHINNRRS	enfranchiser
ACEEFHINNRSS	enfranchises
ACEEFHINOSTT	fianchettoes
ACEEFHIORSTU	chaetiferous
ACEEFHNNRRSTU	furtherances
ACEEFIIIRTVV	verificative
ACEEFIILNQTU	liquefacient
ACEEFIILQTUV	liquefactive
ACEEFIILRSSS	reclassifies
ACEEFIKNNNRS	frankincense
ACEEFILLNORT	reflectional
ACEEFILLNRTY	frenetically
ACEEFILNNORT	conferential
ACEEFILOPRRT	prefectorial
ACEEFILRRTVY	refractively
ACEEFINPRTTU	putrefacient
ACEEFINPSTTU	stupefacient
ACEEFIORRRST	refractories
ACEEFIPRTTUV	putrefactive
ACEEFMNOPRRS	performances
ACEEGGHNPRSS	sprechgesang
ACEEGGINORTV	congregative
ACEEGHHIOPRS	echographies
ACEEGHHOPRRR	choreographer

ACEEGHILLMNO	Michelangelo	ACEEHILLMNOS	melancholies
ACEEGHILOOST	oligochaetes	ACEEHILLMORS	hemerocallis
ACEEGHINNRST	interchanges	ACEEHILLMRTY	hermetically
ACEEGHINOPTT	pathogenetic	ACEEHILLOPPT	leptocephali
ACEEGHINORRV	overreaching	ACEEHILLSTTY	esthetically
ACEEGHINRRRT	rechartering	ACEEHILNORSS	heroicalness
ACEEGHLLNSSY	changelessly	ACEEHILOORST	heterosocial
ACEEGHLOPRRT	electrograph	ACEEHILPRSTY	phylacteries
ACEEGHMMORST	hectogrammes	ACEEHIMMNPST	impeachments
ACEEGHMMNNORV	moneychanger	ACEEHIMMNTTY	enthymematic
ACEEGHNOPRRS	scenographer	ACEEHIMNNNST	enchainments
ACEEGHPRRRSU	supercharger	ACEEHIMNSSTT	chastisement
ACEEGHPRRSSU	supercharges	ACEEHIMOPRTV	overemphatic
ACEEGIIKNNOT	kainogenetic	ACEEHIMOSSTT	somaesthetic
ACEEGIILNNPT	palingenetic	ACEEHINNNOSST	inchoateness
ACEEGIILLNNST	geanticlines	ACEEHINNNRSTU	neurasthenic
ACEEGIILNSTV	evangelistic	ACEEHINPSSTT	pentastiches
ACEEGIIMNORT	geometrician	ACEEHINSSTTY	synaesthetic
ACEEGIINNOSS	cainogenesis	ACEEHIOPRSST	spirochaetes
ACEEGIINPPRV	apperceiving	ACEEHIPRSTTU	therapeutics
ACEEGIINRSTV	eviscerating	ACEEHIRSSTTV	tsarevitches
ACEEGIIOTTVX	excogitative	ACEEHLLOORRU	leucorrhoeal
ACEEGILLLOOT	teleological	ACEEHLMOPRTY	cephalometry
ACEEGILLMOOR	mereological	ACEEHLOPRRST	perchlorates
ACEEGILLNNRT	crenellating	ACEEHMNNNSTT	enchantments
ACEEGILLNTUY	geniculately	ACEEHMOORSST	mesothoraces
ACEEGILSSTTU	gesticulates	ACEEHMORRSTU	routemarches
ACEEGIMMNRST	centigrammes	ACEEHNNOPRRT	Northern Cape
ACEEGIMMORST	microgametes	ACEEHNNORRST	archenterons
ACEEGINNOSSY	cyanogenesis	ACEEHOPPRRRS	sharecropper
ACEEGINNPRRT	carpentering	ACEEHORRSSTT	orchestrates
ACEEGINNRSTV	ingravescent	ACEEIIILLSTX	lexicalities
ACEEGINNSSTX	exactingness	ACEEIIILPSST	specialities
ACEEGINOORST	octogenaries	ACEEIIINNRST	itinerancies
ACEEGINORRTV	overreacting	ACEEIIINRSTV	inveracities
ACEEGINPRRTU	recuperating	ACEEIILLMNSS	miscellanies
ACEEGLMNNOST	congealments	ACEEIILLRTTV	verticillate
ACEEGLMNOORT	conglomerate	ACEEIILMMPRT	metempirical
ACEEGMNORRSS	scaremongers	ACEEIILMPRRT	perimetrical
ACEEGOPRRSSU	supercargoes	ACEEIILMRRSU	mercurialise
ACEEHHILPRTT	terephthalic	ACEEIILMRRUZ	mercurialize
ACEEHHIMNOPR	archiphoneme	ACEEIILNNRST	transilience
ACEEHHIOPTTT	theopathetic	ACEEIILNORST	lectionaries
ACEEHHIPSSTY	hypaesthesic	ACEEIILNOSST	sectionalise
ACEEHHMMOORS	haemochromes	ACEEIILNOSTZ	sectionalize
ACEEHHMOPRTY	chemotherapy	ACEEIILNRSTT	centralities
ACEEHHNNOPRSU	Schopenhauer	ACEEIILRSSTU	secularities
ACEEHHOPRSTU	chapterhouse	ACEEIIMMRSTT	meristematic
ACEEHHOPRTTY	tracheophyte	ACEEIIMNPRSU	epicureanism
ACEEHHOPSTTY	hypothecates	ACEEIIMNRRST	recriminates
ACEEHHORRSTU	Charterhouse	ACEEIINNORST	containerise
ACEEHIIKNSTT	kinaesthetic	ACEEIINNORTZ	containerize
ACEEHIILMNOS	isocheimenal	ACEEIINNRTUV	renunciative
ACEEHIILNPST	encephalitis	ACEEIINNSSTV	inactiveness
ACEEHIILNSST	lecithinases	ACEEIINORSSS	cessionaries
ACEEHIIMOOPT	haemopoietic	ACEEIINORSTV	evisceration
ACEEHIIMSSTT	aestheticism	ACEEIINORTTX	exercitation
ACEEHIINNRST	inheritances	ACEEIIORSSTV	vesicatories
ACEEHIINORTT	theoretician	ACEEIIPPRSTT	peripatetics
ACEEHIINSSTT	estheticians		precipitates
ACEEHIIRRRST	trierarchies	ACEEIJORRSTT	trajectories
ACEEHIKLMNRT	merchantlike	ACEEILLLNTTU	intellectual

ACEEIILLLPTTT	Citlaltépetl	**ACEEIOOPRSTV**	cooperatives
ACEEILLMMRSY	mesmerically	**ACEEIORRSSTV**	eviscerators
ACEEILLMNORY	ceremonially	**ACEEIRSSSTTU**	resuscitates
ACEEILLMNSTY	centesimally	**ACEELLMMNOPT**	complemental
ACEEILLMORTY	meteorically	**ACEELLNOPTUY**	polynucleate
ACEEILLNNNTY	centennially	**ACEELLNORSSV**	Roncesvalles
ACEEILLNNORT	crenellation	**ACEELLNOSSTT**	constellates
ACEEILLNORTY	neoterically	**ACEELLPPRTUY**	perceptually
ACEEILLNRSUV	surveillance	**ACEELMNNORTU**	nomenclature
ACEEILLORSTY	esoterically	**ACEELMNOOSTU**	lomentaceous
ACEEILLORTXY	exoterically	**ACEELMNOPSTT**	contemplates
ACEEILLRTTUY	reticulately	**ACEELMNOPTTU**	outplacement
ACEEILMMNPST	misplacement	**ACEELMNRSTTY**	Clytemnestra
ACEEILMORRST	calorimeters	**ACEELMPRRTUU**	permaculture
ACEEILMRSTUV	vermiculates	**ACEELNOOPRST**	coleopterans
ACEEILNNORST	crenelations	**ACEELNOORRSS**	Eleanor Cross
ACEEILNNORSS	recessionals	**ACEELNOOSTUY**	coetaneously
ACEEILNNORSTU	reinoculates	**ACEELNPRSSST**	spectralness
ACEEILNNRRTU	internuclear	**ACEELNSSSSTT**	tactlessness
ACEEILNOPPRT	perceptional	**ACEELOOPPPTT**	Popocatépetl
ACEEILNOPRRT	precentorial	**ACEELOPPPRST**	copperplates
ACEEILNOPRSS	narcolepsies	**ACEELPRSSSSU**	superclasses
	precessional	**ACEELPSSTUUY**	eucalyptuses
ACEEILNORRST	necrolatries	**ACEEMMMOORST**	commemorates
ACEEILNORSSS	recessionals	**ACEEMMNNORSTU**	commensurate
ACEEILNORSTU	reinoculates	**ACEEMMOPRTTU**	metacomputer
ACEEILNRRSST	centralisers	**ACEEMMNNNOTU**	announcement
ACEEILNRRSTZ	centralizers	**ACEEMNNORRST**	remonstrance
ACEEILOOPSST	Apostolic See	**ACEEMOPRSTTY**	spermatocyte
ACEEILOPPRRT	preceptorial	**ACEENNNOPRSU**	preannounces
ACEEILOPSSTY	caespitosely	**ACEENNOPRSTU**	counterpanes
ACEEILORRSST	clearstories	**ACEENNORRSTV**	contraveners
ACEEILORRSTV	correlatives	**ACEENNORSSTT**	consternates
ACEEILPPSTTU	septuplicate	**ACEENOORSSTT**	cotoneasters
ACEEILPRSSTU	superelastic	**ACEENOPRSTTX**	expectorants
ACEEILPSTTUX	sextuplicate	**ACEENOPRSTUU**	percutaneous
ACEEILRRSSSU	secularisers	**ACEEOOPRRTTT**	protectorate
ACEEILRRSSUZ	secularizers	**ACEEOOPRRTTX**	expectorator
ACEEIMMMNOTT	committeeman	**ACEEOPRRRSTU**	recuperators
ACEEIMMNNPRY	impermanency	**ACEEORRSSTUW**	watercourses
ACEEIMMNORST	commentaries	**ACEFFFHHIRSS**	Frisches Haff
ACEEIMMORSST	commiserates	**ACEFFGHILNRS**	cliffhangers
ACEEIMMOSSTT	mastectomies	**ACEFFGHINRUU**	chauffeuring
ACEEIMNNOORR	oneiromancer	**ACEFFIIILMOS**	semiofficial
ACEEIMMNNOSTT	cementations	**ACEFFIILPSST**	spifflicates
ACEEIMNOPRST	armipotences	**ACEFFILNNSSU**	fancifulness
ACEEIMNOPSTV	compensative	**ACEFFORRSUUU**	furfuraceous
ACEEIMNORRST	craniometers	**ACEFGHIINPRY**	preachifying
ACEEIMNORSTT	actinometers	**ACEFGHILOPRX**	flexographic
ACEEIMNORSVW	servicewoman	**ACEFGHINRSSS**	grassfinches
ACEEIMNQRSTU	acquirements	**ACEFGIIILMNS**	facsimileing
ACEEINNRRTTY	tricentenary	**ACEFGIIILNTT**	felicitating
ACEEINOORRTV	overreaction	**ACEFGIINNRST**	interfacings
ACEEINOPPPRT	apperception	**ACEFGIINORTV**	vociferating
ACEEINOPRRTU	recuperation	**ACEFGILNRSTU**	centrifugals
ACEEINOPRSTT	inspectorate	**ACEFGINNRSTT**	transfecting
ACEEINOPSTTX	expectations	**ACEFHILNOPRS**	francophiles
ACEEINORRSSY	recessionary	**ACEFHLNSSTUW**	watchfulness
ACEEINORRSTY	secretionary	**ACEFHNORSTTU**	countershaft
ACEEINORSTVV	conservative	**ACEFIIIILNST**	finicalities
ACEEINPRRSST	transpierces	**ACEFIIILNOST**	fictionalise
ACEEINRRSSTV	transceivers	**ACEFIIILNOTT**	felicitation
ACEEINRSSTUV	curativeness		

ACEFIIILNOTZ	fictionalize	ACEGHILLNOOT	ethnological
ACEFIIINORST	reifications	ACEGHILLRTUY	theurgically
ACEFIIINORTV	verification	ACEGHILMOPYY	hypoglycemia
ACEFIIILLNNOT	inflectional	ACEGHILNNNTY	enchantingly
ACEFIIILLRRTY	terrifically	ACEGHILNNSTY	chasteningly
ACEFIILMNORS	infomercials	ACEGHILOORST	archeologist
ACEFIILNOQTU	liquefaction	ACEGHILOPPRY	pyelographic
ACEFIILORSTT	felicitators	ACEGHILOPRXY	lexicography
ACEFIILORSTU	laticiferous	ACEGHIMNORTV	overmatching
ACEFIIMNORTV	confirmative	ACEGHIMOOPRT	gametophoric
ACEFIINOORTV	vociferation	ACEGHIMOPRRR	micrographer
ACEFIINOPRTT	petrifaction	ACEGHIMOPTTY	gametophytic
ACEFIINOPSTT	pontificates	ACEGHINOOPRR	iconographer
ACEFIINORSST	fractionises	ACEGHINOOPRRZ	zincographer
ACEFIINORSTZ	fractionizes	ACEGHINOPRST	stenographic
ACEFIIORRTVY	verificatory	ACEGHINORTVW	overwatching
ACEFIIRRTTVY	refractivity	ACEGHINPRRSU	repurchasing
ACEFILLNORSY	forensically	ACEGHIOPPRRR	reprographic
ACEFILLORSUW	cauliflowers	ACEGHIOPPRRT	petrographic
ACEFILNNOOSS	confessional	ACEGHIOPRRST	cerographist
ACEFILORRRTY	refractorily	ACEGHLNOPSTT	plectognaths
ACEFIMNOSTTU	tumefactions	ACEGHMOOPRRS	cosmographer
ACEFINNORSTT	transfection	ACEGHNOOPRSU	necrophagous
ACEFINOORRTT	torrefaction	ACEGHOPPRRST	spectrograph
ACEFINOPRTTU	putrefaction	ACEGHORRSSTU	roughcasters
ACEFINOPSTTU	stupefaction	ACEGIIILLMTY	illegitimacy
ACEFINOSSSTU	factiousness	ACEGIIILLNSX	lexicalising
ACEFIOORRSTV	vociferators	ACEGIIILLNXZ	lexicalizing
ACEFLMOORTTY	olfactometry	ACEGIIILNPSS	specialising
ACEGGGINNORT	congregating	ACEGIIILNPSZ	specializing
ACEGGHINORRV	overcharging	ACEGIIILNSST	elasticising
ACEGGIINNSST	giganticness	ACEGIIILNSTZ	elasticizing
ACEGGIINORST	categorising	ACEGIIINNNRT	incinerating
ACEGGIINORTZ	categorizing	ACEGIIINSTTV	negativistic
ACEGGIINOTTX	excogitating	ACEGIIILLLOTY	collegiality
ACEGGILLLOOY	geologically	ACEGIIILLMOOS	semiological
ACEGGILLMMOO	gemmological	ACEGIIILLNRRV	Invercargill
ACEGGIMNORTY	gyromagnetic	ACEGIIILLOOPT	geopolitical
ACEGGINNOORT	congregation	ACEGIIILLOSTU	eulogistical
ACEGGNOORRST	congregators	ACEGIIILLOSTY	egoistically
ACEGHHIILOPR	heliographic	ACEGIIILNNOTU	geniculation
ACEGHHILOPRS	helicographs	ACEGIIILNNOTY	congeniality
ACEGHHILRSST	searchlights	ACEGIIILNNRST	centralising
ACEGHHINOPRT	ethnographic	ACEGIIILNNRSY	increasingly
ACEGHHIOPRRR	chirographer	ACEGIIILNNRTZ	centralizing
ACEGHHIOPRTY	hyetographic	ACEGIIILNPRSS	Alice Springs
ACEGHHNOPRTY	technography	ACEGIIILNRSSU	secularising
ACEGHHNORRST	shortchanger	ACEGIIILNRSUZ	secularizing
ACEGHHNORSST	shortchanges	ACEGIIILNRTTU	reticulating
ACEGHHOOPRRR	chorographer	ACEGIIILNSTUV	vesiculating
ACEGHHOOPRRS	choreographs	ACEGIIILORSSU	sacrilegious
ACEGHHOOPRRY	choreography	ACEGIIILOTTVY	cogitatively
ACEGHIILLNVY	hygienically	ACEGIIILRSSST	sacrilegists
ACEGHIILLOOR	hierological	ACEGIIMMNOSST	isomagnetics
ACEGHIILNNNS	channelising	ACEGIIMNTTUY	mutagenicity
ACEGHIILNNNZ	channelizing	ACEGIINNPPRT	apprenticing
ACEGHIIMNSST	schematising	ACEGIINNPRST	interspacing
ACEGHIIMNSTZ	schematizing	ACEGIINOOTTX	excogitation
ACEGHIKLLNSS	shellackings	ACEGIINOQTUV	equivocating
ACEGHILLNNOU	hallucinogen	ACEGIKLLNSSS	gallsickness
ACEGHILLNOOP	nephological	ACEGILLLNOOY	neologically
	phenological	ACEGILLMOORT	metrological

ACEGILLMOOSU	museological
ACEGILLMOOTY	etymological
ACEGILLNNOSY	geosynclinal
ACEGILLNNOTY	congenitally
ACEGILLNOORU	neurological
ACEGILLNOORY	orogenically
ACEGILLNRTTY	clatteringly
ACEGILLOOORT	erotological
ACEGILLOOOST	osteological
ACEGILLOOPRT	petrological
ACEGILNNOOST	congelations
ACEGILNNOTTU	conglutinate
ACEGILNOOPRT	organoleptic
ACEGILNOOPTU	unapologetic
ACEGILNSTUUU	unguiculates
ACEGILOOPSST	escapologist
ACEGILORSTTU	gesticulator
ACEGIMMNNOTT	commentating
ACEGIMMNNORSU	commeasuring
ACEGIMMNNOPRS	panicmongers
ACEGIMMNNOPSS	encompassing
ACEGIMMNNOPST	compensating
ACEGIMMNNORST	centimorgans
ACEGIMNOPRTY	pyromagnetic
ACEGINNNORTV	contravening
ACEGINNNORSTT	nonstrategic
ACEGINOPRRSU	superorganic
ACEGINORSSSU	graciousness
ACEGIOOOPPRT	apogeotropic
ACEGIOOORSTTX	excogitators
ACEGLNOOPRSY	laryngoscope
ACEGLNOORSUV	acrogenously
ACEGLNOPRSTY	calyptrogens
ACEGLNORSTUY	granulocytes
ACEGLOORSUUV	courageously
ACEGMOPRRSST	spectrograms
ACEGNOORRSTT	gerontocrats
ACEGOOPRSSST	gastroscopes
ACEHHIIINRST	Chiantishire
ACEHHIILMOPS	hemophiliacs
ACEHHIIMMPTU	amphithecium
ACEHHIINOPRT	hierophantic
ACEHHILMOPTX	exophthalmic
ACEHHILMRTUY	eurhythmical
ACEHHILOOPST	theosophical
ACEHHILOPTTY	hypothetical
ACEHHIMOOOPT	homoeopathic
ACEHHINOPRTT	theanthropic
ACEHHINOSSTX	hexastichons
ACEHHINOSTTY	osteichthyan
ACEHHLNNNORT	North Channel
ACEHHLOOPRTY	orthocephaly
ACEHHMOOPRTU	chemoautroph
ACEHHMORSTTY	chrestomathy
ACEHHNOOSTTU	autochthones
ACEHHOOPRTTY	hypothecator
ACEHIIINPSSS	hispanicises
ACEHIIINPSSZ	hispanicizes
ACEHIIINRSST	christianise
ACEHIIINRSTZ	christianize
ACEHIIKRRSWW	Warwickshire
ACEHIILLMPTY	mephitically

ACEHIILLMRTY	hermitically
ACEHIILLSTTY	theistically
ACEHIILMNNTT	anthelmintic
ACEHIILNPPRS	planispheric
ACEHIILPSTUU	euphuistical
ACEHIILSSTWW	welwitschias
ACEHIIMOORST	rachiotomies
ACEHIINNOPST	phoneticians
ACEHIINORRST	rhetoricians
ACEHIINSSTTU	enthusiastic
ACEHIINTTTUY	authenticity
ACEHIIOPSSTT	sophisticate
ACEHIIPPRRST	periphrastic
ACEHIIQRRSSU	squirarchies
ACEHIKMNOSST	mackintoshes
ACEHIKRRSSSW	kirschwasser
ACEHILLLMNOY	melancholily
ACEHILLLPTYY	phyletically
ACEHILLMNNTU	multichannel
ACEHILLMNOPY	phonemically
ACEHILLNOPST	plainclothes
ACEHILLNOPTY	phonetically
ACEHILLNOPUY	euphonically
ACEHILLORRTY	rhetorically
ACEHILLRSTYY	hysterically
ACEHILMNOOTT	nomothetical
ACEHILMOOPSU	amphicoelous
ACEHILMOOPTY	homeotypical
ACEHILMOPTYY	polycythemia
ACEHILNNNSSS	clannishness
ACEHILNNOTTT	Tenochtitlán
ACEHILNOPPTY	phenotypical
ACEHILNPSSSY	physicalness
ACEHILPPRSTY	hyperplastic
ACEHIMMNORSTU	euchromatins
ACEHIMOOOSTT	homoeostatic
ACEHIMOPRRSU	archesporium
ACEHIMOPRSST	atmospherics
ACEHIMOPSSTY	scyphistomae
ACEHIMORRSST	choirmasters
ACEHIMORSTTT	thermostatic
ACEHINNOOPRT	neoanthropic
ACEHINOOPRTT	epanorthotic
ACEHINOPRRSS	chairpersons
ACEHINOPRRST	chiropterans
ACEHINOPRRTT	trichopteran
ACEHINOPRSTY	hyperactions
ACEHINORRSST	orchestrinas
ACEHIRSSTTWW	wristwatches
ACEHKKRRSSSU	sharksuckers
ACEHKMRRSSTT	stretchmarks
ACEHLLLMOSST	smallclothes
ACEHLLLPRSUY	sepulchrally
ACEHLLMORSYY	lachrymosely
ACEHLLORRSTY	orchestrally
ACEHLMMNOOTW	commonwealth
ACEHLMOORSST	schoolmaster
ACEHLNOOPRTU	photonuclear
ACEHLNOPRSTY	lycanthropes
ACEHLOOPSTUY	polychaetous
ACEHLOOPSUXY	oxycephalous
ACEHLOORSSUW	colourwashes

ACEHLOPSSUXY	psychosexual
ACEHMMNOOORT	monochromate
ACEHMNOOORSU	anemochorous
ACEHMNOORSTTY	tracheostomy
ACEHMOPRRTYY	crymotherapy
ACEHMORRSSTU	chorusmaster
ACEHMOSSSUYY	hyoscyamuses
ACEHNNOOPRST	ctenophorans
ACEHOOPRRSST	arthroscopes
	crapshooters
ACEHOORRRSTT	orchestrator
ACEHOPRRSSSY	chrysoprases
ACEIIIILNSSV	civilianises
ACEIIIILNSVZ	civilianizes
ACEIIIINRSTT	initiatrices
ACEIIIJRSSTU	justiciaries
ACEIIIKNNNPS	pickaninnies
ACEIIILLRSTT	literalistic
ACEIIILMNNSS	inimicalness
ACEIIILMNPSU	municipalise
ACEIIILMNPUZ	municipalize
ACEIIILMNRSS	criminalises
ACEIIILMNRSZ	criminalizes
ACEIIILNNOTT	licentiation
ACEIIILNORTV	Victoria Nile
ACEIIILNOSTT	elicitations
ACEIIILNSTTY	inelasticity
ACEIIILRSTTV	relativistic
ACEIIILRSTVV	revivalistic
ACEIIIMNNRST	incriminates
ACEIIIMNOSST	semioticians
ACEIIIMNPRSS	precisianism
ACEIIINNNORT	incineration
ACEIIINOTTVX	intoxicative
ACEIIIORSSTV	varicosities
ACEIIJLLSTUY	jesuitically
ACEIIJLORSTU	jocularities
ACEIIKKNORTY	karyokinetic
ACEIIKLLMORT	kilometrical
ACEIIKLLOORS	kilocalories
ACEIILLLLPTY	elliptically
ACEIILLMNNSU	illuminances
ACEIILLMNSST	miscellanist
ACEIILLMPTTU	multiplicate
ACEIILLNORTY	collinearity
ACEIILLNOSTV	vellications
ACEIILLNSSTT	scintillates
ACEIILMMNRST	mercantilism
ACEIILMMRRSU	mercurialism
ACEIILMMSSTY	semimystical
ACEIILMNORST	salinometric
ACEIILMNOSST	sectionalism
ACEIILMNRSTT	mercantilist
ACEIILMNSSSU	masculinises
ACEIILMNSSUZ	masculinizes
ACEIILMOPPSS	episcopalism
ACEIILMOPRRT	polarimetric
ACEIILMOPRST	semitropical
ACEIILMOPSTT	metapolitics
ACEIILMPRSTU	implicatures
ACEIILMRRTUY	mercuriality
ACEIILNNNRTU	internuncial
ACEIILNNOPST	inspectional
ACEIILNNORSS	ironicalness
ACEIILNNORST	nonrealistic
	reclinations
ACEIILNOORST	coalitioners
ACEIILNOPRST	inspectorial
	replications
ACEIILNOPSTX	explications
ACEIILNOQSTU	equinoctials
ACEIILNORTTU	reticulation
ACEIILNOSSTT	sectionalist
ACEIILNOSTUV	vesiculation
ACEIILNRSSTT	clarinetists
ACEIILNRSTTT	clarinettist
ACEIILOPRSST	tropicalises
ACEIILOPRSTZ	tropicalizes
ACEIILOQSSUU	siliquaceous
ACEIILOQTUVY	equivocality
ACEIILORRRSV	corrivalries
ACEIILPRRSUY	superciliary
ACEIILPRSSST	plasticisers
ACEIILPRSSTZ	plasticizers
ACEIILRRSSTU	surrealistic
ACEIILRRTTTY	retractility
ACEIILRSTTVY	astrictively
ACEIIMMNORST	cremationism
ACEIIMMORSSS	commissaires
	commissaires
ACEIIMNOORST	craniotomies
ACEIIMNOPRST	imprecations
ACEIIMNORRRT	recriminator
ACEIIMNORSST	miscreations
	romanticises
ACEIIMNORSTT	cremationist
ACEIIMNORSTZ	romanticizes
ACEIIMNRSSTU	insectariums
ACEIIMNSSSTT	semanticists
ACEIIMOORSTV	varicotomies
ACEIINNNORTU	renunciation
ACEIINNNOSST	incensations
ACEIINNNOSTT	Constantine I
ACEIINNNOSTU	enunciations
ACEIINNNSTTV	Saint Vincent
ACEIINNOPSTT	pectinations
ACEIINNORRST	incinerators
ACEIINNORRTY	incretionary
ACEIINNORSTT	interactions
ACEIINNOSSST	ascensionist
ACEIINNOTTUV	continuative
ACEIINNSSTTY	nyctinasties
ACEIINOOQTUV	equivocation
ACEIINOORSTV	viscerotonia
ACEIINOORSTX	excoriations
ACEIINOPRRTT	practitioner
ACEIINOPRSTT	crepitations
ACEIINOPRSTU	pertinacious
ACEIINOPSSTT	pectisations
ACEIINOPSTTZ	pectizations
ACEIINORRSTW	contrariwise
ACEIINORSSTT	creationists
	reactionists
ACEIINPPRSTT	precipitants

ACEIINPRSTTY	antipyretics
ACEIIOPPRRTT	precipitator
ACEIJKLLNOSV	Jacksonville
ACEIJLNOOPRT	projectional
ACEILLLMNORS	lamellicorns
ACEILLMMNNOY	mnemonically
ACEILLMMNOOT	monometallic
ACEILLMNOOPT	compellation
ACEILLMNOOPX	complexional
ACEILLMNOSST	callistemons
ACEILLMNRTUU	multinuclear
ACEILLMNTUVY	multivalency
ACEILLMORRTU	trimolecular
ACEILLMORTUY	molecularity
ACEILLMRRUVY	vermicularly
ACEILLMSSTYY	systemically
ACEILLMTUUVY	cumulatively
ACEILLNNORRU	carillonneur
ACEILLNOOTYZ	enzootically
ACEILLNORTUY	neurotically
ACEILLNOSTTU	scutellation
ACEILLOPTUVY	copulatively
ACEILLRRSSTY	crystalliser
ACEILLRRSTUU	sericultural
ACEILLRRSTYZ	crystallizer
ACEILLRSSSTY	crystallises
ACEILLRSSTTY	crystallites
ACEILLRSSTYZ	crystallizes
ACEILMMMNOSS	commensalism
ACEILMMNOORT	monometrical
ACEILMMNOOST	commonalties
ACEILMMNORSU	communaliser
ACEILMMNORUZ	communalizer
ACEILMMNOSSU	communalises
ACEILMMNOSTY	commensality
ACEILMMNOSUZ	communalizes
ACEILMMORSTT	recommittals
ACEILMNNOOPT	componential
ACEILMNSSSTY	mysticalness
ACEILMOOPSST	leptosomatic
ACEILMOPRRTY	pyrometrical
ACEILMOPRSTT	plastometric
ACEILMOPRSUU	primulaceous
ACEILNNNOOTV	conventional
ACEILNNNOSTT	continentals
ACEILNNNOSTU	antinucleons
ACEILNNOORSV	conversional
ACEILNNORSTU	crenulations
ACEILNNOSSST	sanctionless
ACEILNOOPRSS	processional
ACEILNOOPRST	percolations
ACEILNOOPRTT	lactoprotein
ACEILNOORRST	correlations
ACEILNOORTUY	elocutionary
ACEILNOPSSTU	speculations
ACEILNOPSTUX	exculpations
ACEILNORSTUV	countervails
ACEILNORSUXY	exclusionary
ACEILNOSTTUV	consultative
ACEILOOPPRSS	polariscopes
ACEILOOPRRTY	corporeality
ACEILOOPSSTT	osteoplastic
ACEILOPRRSUY	precariously
ACEILOQSSUUY	sequaciously
ACEILPPRSSTU	superplastic
ACEILRRSSSTY	crystalisers
ACEILRRSSTYZ	crystalizers
ACEIMMNOPRTY	micropayment
ACEIMMNOSTUV	consummative
ACEIMMOORRST	commiserator
ACEIMMORRSTU	crematoriums
ACEIMNNOOPST	compensation
ACEIMNNOOSST	Monte Cassino
ACEIMNNOPRTY	intercompany
ACEIMNNOPRYZ	pancreozymin
ACEIMNOOOOPT	onomatopoeic
ACEIMNORSSTV	conservatism
ACEIMNPSTTUU	mispunctuate
ACEIMNSSTTUY	unsystematic
ACEIMOOPRSTZ	spermatozoic
	zoospermatic
ACEIMOPRRSTY	cryptomerias
ACEIMPRSSSTU	supremacists
ACEINNOORSTV	conservation
	conversation
ACEINNOOSTTT	contestation
ACEINNORRSST	constrainers
	contrariness
ACEINNORRTUY	renunciatory
ACEINNORSSTT	transections
ACEINNORSTTU	counterstain
	encrustation
ACEINOOOPRST	cooperations
ACEINOOPRRST	incorporates
ACEINOORRSTT	retroactions
ACEINOPPRRTU	Port-au-Prince
ACEINOPSSSSU	spaciousness
ACEINOPSSSTU	captiousness
ACEINOSSSTUU	cautiousness
ACEINRRSTUUV	incurvatures
ACEIOOPRRSST	corporatises
ACEIOOPRRSTZ	corporatizes
ACEIOOQRSTUV	equivocators
ACEIOOQRTUVY	equivocatory
ACEIOORSTUUV	overcautious
ACEIORRSSTTU	resuscitator
ACEKLNPRSTTU	planet-struck
ACEKMMNORTUY	mockumentary
ACELLNNOSSUY	consensually
ACELLNNOTUVY	conventually
ACELLNOTTUXY	contextually
ACELMMNOSTUY	consummately
ACELMNNOORST	nomenclators
ACELMNOOPRTT	contemplator
ACELMRSSTUUU	musculatures
ACELNNORSTVY	conversantly
ACELNNRSSUUU	ranunculuses
ACELNOOPRSTU	proconsulate
ACELNOSSSTTU	sansculottes
ACELOORRSTUW	watercolours
ACEMMMOOORRT	commemorator
ACEMMNOOPRRY	common prayer
ACEMMNOORSTT	commentators
ACEMMNOPRSTT	compartments

ACEMNOOPRRTY	contemporary
ACEMNOOPRSST	compensators
ACEMNOOPRSTY	compensatory
ACEMOOPRRSTU	macropterous
ACEMORSSSTTU	scoutmasters
ACENNNORSTUV	unconversant
ACENNOORSSSU	canorousness
ACENNRRRSTTU	transcurrent
ACENOOQRTTTU	quattrocento
ACENOORRSSTV	conservators
ACENOORRSTVY	conservatory
ACENOPRRSTTU	counterparts
ACENOPRRTTUY	counterparty
ACEOOPRSSSTU	stauroscopes
ACEOPRRSSSTT	sportscaster
ACFFGGHIILNN	cliffhanging
ACFFIIINOOST	officiations
ACFFIILLNOUY	unofficially
ACFGGHIMNORR	frogmarching
ACFGIIILNOTU	uglification
ACFGIIILNPST	spiflicating
ACFGIILNRSYY	scarifyingly
ACFGIKNRSSTU	starfuckings
ACFHHLNORSSY	synchroflash
ACFHIIIMNOTU	humification
ACFHIILLORRY	horrifically
ACFIIIILNOTV	vilification
ACFIIIIMNNOT	minification
ACFIIIINOTVV	vivification
ACFIIINNOOTT	notification
ACFIIINNORTT	antifriction
ACFIIINNOSTU	unifications
ACFIIINOOSST	ossification
ACFIIINOPRTU	purification
ACFIIINOPTTY	typification
ACFIIINORSTV	vinificators
ACFIILLLOPRV	prolifically
ACFIILLNOPTY	pontifically
ACFIILNNNOOT	nonfictional
ACFIILOSTTUY	factitiously
ACFIIMNNOORT	confirmation
ACFIINNOORST	fornications
ACFIINORRTTU	trifurcation
ACFIIOPRRSTU	purificators
ACFIIOPRRTUY	purificatory
ACFILLNNOTUY	functionally
ACFILLOORSUU	cauliflorous
ACFILMNNOSTU	malfunctions
ACFILNOSTTUU	fluctuations
ACFIMNNOOORT	conformation
ACFIMNOORRTY	confirmatory
ACFINNOOSTTU	confutations
ACFRRSTUUUUY	usufructuary
ACGGHINORSTU	roughcasting
ACGGIILLOOST	glaciologist
ACGGIILNOTTY	cogitatingly
ACGGILLNOORY	laryngologic
ACGHHHIOPTYY	ichthyophagy
ACGHHIILOPRT	lithographic
ACGHHINOOPPR	phonographic
ACGHHIOOPPRT	photographic
ACGHHIOOPRRT	orthographic

ACGHHIOPPRSY	hypsographic
ACGHHIOPPRTY	phytographic
ACGHHNOOPRRS	chronographs
ACGHIIJKNNNU	Kinchinjunga
ACGHIILLLOOP	philological
ACGHIILLLOOT	lithological
ACGHIILLNOOR	rhinological
ACGHIILLNOOS	alcoholising
ACGHIILLNOOZ	alcoholizing
ACGHIILLOOOP	ophiological
ACGHIILLOOST	histological
ACGHIILMNPTY	lymphangitic
ACGHIILNNORT	chlorinating
ACGHIILNORTY	trichogynial
ACGHIIMNRSSW	scrimshawing
ACGHIINNNOST	stanchioning
ACGHIINPRSTY	scintigraphy
ACGHIIOPPRRS	spirographic
ACGHIIPRSSST	sphragistics
ACGHILLMNOOY	hymnological
ACGHILLMOOTY	mythological
ACGHILLNOOOP	phonological
ACGHILLNOOPY	hypnological
ACGHILLOOPRS	oscillograph
ACGHILLOOPTY	phytological
ACGHILLORTTU	logical truth
ACGHILMOORST	cologarithms
ACGHILMOOSST	logomachists
ACGHILNRSSTT	latchstrings
ACGHILOPRSTY	stylographic
ACGHIMMNOOPR	phonogrammic
ACGHIMOOPRSU	microphagous
ACGHINOOPPRR	pornographic
ACGHIOOPSSTY	phagocytosis
ACGHLMOOORTY	chromatology
ACGHNOOOPRRS	coronographs
ACGHOOOOPPRSU	coprophagous
ACGHOPPRRSTY	cryptographs
ACGHOPPRRTVY	cryptography
ACGIIILLLOTY	illogicality
ACGIIILMNQTU	quitclaiming
ACGIIILNOSST	logisticians
ACGIIILNOSTY	caliginosity
ACGIIILNPRTT	triplicating
ACGIIILNPSST	plasticising
ACGIIILNPSTZ	plasticizing
ACGIIINNOTTX	intoxicating
ACGIIKKLNSTW	walkingstick
ACGIILLLMNOO	limnological
ACGIILLLOSTY	logistically
ACGIILLLRTUY	liturgically
ACGIILLNNNOR	carillonning
ACGIILLNOOST	colligations
ACGIILMNOSUU	mucilaginous
ACGIILMNSSTU	simulcasting
ACGIILNNOSTU	inosculating
ACGIILNOORST	craniologist
ACGIILNPPSTU	supplicating
ACGIILNRSSTY	crystalising
ACGIILNRSTYZ	crystalizing
ACGIILOOPPRT	plagiotropic
ACGIIMMNOOST	monogamistic

ACGIIMNNNOOP	companioning
ACGIIMORRTVY	microgravity
ACGIINNNOOST	consignation
ACGIINNNORST	constraining
ACGIINNOPSTT	constipating
ACGIINNOSTTW	wainscotting
ACGIJNNOOSTU	conjugations
ACGILLLOOORY	orologically
ACGILLMNNOOY	cognominally
	gnomonically
ACGILLMOORSS	oscillograms
ACGILLOOOPRT	tropological
ACGILMOORRTY	martyrologic
ACGILNNNOTTU	conglutinant
ACGILNOOSTUY	contagiously
ACGILNOPSUUY	pugnaciously
ACGILOOPRSST	carpologists
ACGILOOSSSTT	scatologists
ACGIMMNNOSTU	consummating
ACGIMMOOPRRR	microprogram
ACGIMNOOPRTU	compurgation
ACGINOORRSTU	corrugations
ACGLLNOORSUV	clangorously
ACGLNOOPRSYY	laryngoscopy
ACGMOOPRRSTU	compurgators
ACGMOOPRRTUV	compurgatory
ACGMOOPRSTUV	cryptogamous
ACHHIILLPSTV	ithyphallics
ACHHIILMNOPR	philharmonic
ACHHIIMNOPPS	championship
ACHHIIMOSTTY	stichomythia
ACHHIIMOSTYZ	schizothymia
ACHHIIORSTUV	ichthyosauri
ACHHIKOOSSTV	Shostakovich
ACHHILLMRTYV	rhythmically
ACHHILLOOOST	thioalcohols
ACHHILLOPTTY	thallophytic
ACHHILMNRTUY	unrhythmical
ACHHILOOPRST	holophrastic
ACHHILOPRSSS	scholarships
ACHHIOPPRSTU	phosphaturic
ACHHIORSSTUY	ichthyosaurs
ACHHNNOOOPRY	onychophoran
ACHIIIINOSTU	Antiochus III
ACHIIIINRSST	trichiniasis
ACHIIILMSTWY	whimsicality
ACHIIILNORST	histrionical
ACHIIIMNPSSS	hispanicisms
ACHIIIMNPSSU	musicianship
ACHIIINRSTTY	Christianity
ACHIIIRRSSTU	trichuriasis
ACHIIJKNRSSW	jinrickshaws
ACHIIKLMOPTT	machtpolitik
ACHIILLLOSTY	holistically
ACHIILLMOOTT	lithotomical
ACHIILLNOSSU	hallucinosis
ACHIILLORSTY	historically
ACHIILNOORT	chlorination
ACHIILNOPRST	rhinoplastic
ACHIILNPSUVY	picayunishly
ACHIILOPRSTT	cartophilist
ACHIILPSSSTY	physicalists

ACHIIMNOOPRS	anisomorphic
ACHIIMNOPRST	misanthropic
ACHIIMNORSST	chrismations
ACHIINNNORST	non-Christian
ACHIINOPRSTT	antistrophic
ACHIIPRSSTTY	psychiatrist
ACHIKLOOPSST	Chilkoot Pass
ACHIKMORTUUV	kurchatovium
ACHILLNOORSY	isochronally
ACHILLNOPTYY	hypnotically
ACHILLORSUVY	chivalrously
ACHILMORSTYY	lachrymosity
ACHILNOOPPTY	phonotypical
ACHILNOORRST	chlorinators
ACHILNORSUUV	unchivalrous
ACHILOOOPTTV	photovoltaic
ACHILOOPPRRS	corporalship
ACHIMNNOORTY	ornithomancy
ACHIMNNORSSY	asynchronism
ACHIMNOOPRTY	actinomorphy
ACHIMOOOPSST	photomosaics
ACHIMOPRSSSY	symposiarchs
ACHIMOPSSSTY	scyphistomas
ACHINNOOPSTY	apocynthions
ACHINOOPTTUV	autohypnotic
ACHIOOPPRRST	saprotrophic
ACHIOOPPRRST	arthrosporic
ACHIOOPRRSUZ	rhizocarpous
ACHIOPRRSSTU	curatorships
ACHIOPRSSSTY	astrophysics
ACHLLOOPRSST	chloroplasts
ACHLMOOPRSST	chromoplasts
ACHMMNOOORST	monochromats
ACHNNOORSSUY	asynchronous
ACHOOPRRRTTU	Port Harcourt
ACIIIILMRSTT	militaristic
ACIIIILNOSTV	civilisation
ACIIIILNOTVZ	civilization
ACIIILMMNPSU	municipalism
ACIIILMNNOST	nominalistic
ACIIILMNOPST	implications
ACIIILMNPSTU	municipalist
ACIIILMNPTUY	municipality
ACIIILMOPSTT	optimistical
ACIIILNNNOST	inclinations
ACIIILNOOSTT	coalitionist
	solicitation
ACIIILNOPRTT	triplication
ACIIILNOSTVV	convivialist
ACIIILNOTVVY	conviviality
ACIIILNPPRTY	principality
ACIIILQTUYZZ	quizzicality
ACIIIMNNORRT	incriminator
ACIIIMNNORST	criminations
ACIIINNOOTTX	intoxication
ACIIINNOSTTT	nictitations
ACIIINNOSTTU	cutinisation
ACIIINNOTTUZ	cutinization
ACIIINOPSSUU	inauspicious
ACIIINOQSSTU	acquisitions
ACIIJLLRSTUY	juristically
ACIIJLNORSTU	journalistic

ACIIILLMNOOST	collimations	ACILMNOOOPST	cosmopolitan
ACIIILLMNOSTY	monistically	ACILMNOORSTU	matroclinous
ACIIILLNNOOPT	nonpolitical	ACILMOOPPRST	protoplasmic
ACIIILLNOOSST	colonialists	ACILMORSTTUU	cumulostrati
	oscillations		stratocumuli
ACIIILLNOPRVY	provincially	ACILNNNOSTTY	inconstantly
ACIIILLNORSTT	scintillator	ACILNNOOORTT	contortional
ACIIILLNORTTY	tinctorially	ACILNNOOOSST	consolations
ACIIILLNRTUUV	vinicultural	ACILNNOOSTTU	consultation
ACIIILLOOPSTY	isotopically	ACILNNORTTUY	nocturnality
ACIIILLOQTUXY	quixotically	ACILNOOORSTU	colourations
ACIIILLOSSUVY	lasciviously		iconolatrous
ACIIILLPRSTUY	puristically	ACILNOOPRSTU	patroclinous
ACIIILLRTTUUV	viticultural	ACILOOPPRSTT	protoplastic
ACIIILMMNOOSS	commissional	ACILOOPPRTTY	prototypical
ACIIILMNNOOTU	columniation	ACILOPPRSTUY	supplicatory
ACIIILMNNOSTU	culminations	ACIMMNNOOSTU	consummation
ACIIILMNOOPST	compilations	ACIMMNOOSTTU	commutations
ACIIILMNORSTU	matriclinous	ACIMNNOORSTU	mucronations
ACIIILMNSSSTU	masculinists	ACIMNOOPRSTY	trypanosomic
ACIIILNNOOOST	colonisation	ACIMNOOPSTTU	computations
ACIIILNNOOOTZ	colonization	ACIMOOOOPRSTT	somatotropic
ACIIILNNOOSTU	inoculations	ACINNNOOOSTT	connotations
	inosculation	ACINNNORSTTU	unconstraint
ACIIILNNOPSTU	inculpations	ACINNOOPRSTT	contraptions
ACIIILNNOSTUY	insouciantly	ACINNOOPSSTY	syncopations
ACIIILNNOTTUY	continuality	ACINNOORSTTU	continuators
ACIIILNOOORTZ	colorization	ACINNOPSTTUU	punctuations
ACIIILNOORSST	consistorial	ACINOOOOPRRRT	incorporator
ACIIILNOPPSTU	supplication	ACINOOOPRRST	corporations
ACIIILNOPRSTU	patriclinous	ACINOOOPRSTV	provocations
ACIIILNOSTTUV	cultivations	ACINOOPRRSST	conspirators
ACIIILNOSTUUY	incautiously	ACINOOPRRSTT	protractions
ACIIILOPSSUUY	auspiciously	ACINOOPRRSTU	procurations
ACIIILPRSTTUU	apiculturist	ACINOOPRRSTY	conspiratory
ACIIILRSTTUUV	aviculturist	ACINOPRSSTUU	transpicuous
ACIIIMMNNOOST	comminations	ACIOOPRRSSTT	corporatists
ACIIMNOPRTTU	protactinium	ACIORRRSSTTU	cirrostratus
ACIIMNNORSSTT	romanticists	ACKLNNOOPRTY	cryoplankton
ACIINNNOOTTU	continuation	ACLLLPRSTUUY	sculpturally
ACIINNOOPSTT	constipation	ACLLOPRSSTYY	polycrystals
ACIINNOORSST	consistorian	ACLLRRSTTUUY	structurally
ACIINNORSTTU	incrustation	ACLNOORSTTUY	consultatory
ACIINNORSTUV	incurvations	ACMMNOORSSTU	consummators
ACIINOORSSTTX	intoxicators	ACMMNOORSTUY	consummatory
ACIINOPRRSUV	picornavirus	ACMNNOORTUWY	countrywoman
ACIINOPSSUUU	unauspicious	ACMNOOOTTXYY	cytotaxonomy
ACIINORSSTTU	rustications	ACNOOOPPRSTT	contrapposto
ACIJNNOORSTU	conjurations	ADDDDEEEEHLMU	muddleheaded
ACILLLLOOQUY	colloquially	ADDDDEEEEHNRU	dunderheaded
ACILLLMNNOOY	monoclinally	ADDDEEEEHNOOW	woodenheaded
ACILLMNOORTY	microtonally	ADDDEEFIOSTU	eisteddfodau
ACILLMOOOTYZ	zootomically	ADDDEEIMRSSS	misaddressed
ACILLMORSUUY	miraculously	ADDDEEINNRRU	underdrained
ACILLNNOSTYY	syntonically	ADDDEIIINTUV	individuated
ACILLNOOOPST	postcolonial	ADDDEIILLLLY	dillydallied
ACILLNOPSTYY	synoptically	ADDDEMNOOORT	rodomontaded
ACILLOOPPRRTY	proctorially	ADDEEEEFGHRT	featheredged
ACILLOOQSUUY	loquaciously	ADDEEEEGGRST	desegregated
ACILLPRRSTUY	scripturally	ADDEEEEEHLPSY	sleepyheaded
ACILMMNNOOTT	noncommittal	ADDEEEEFGNNOR	Garden of Eden
ACILMMNOSSTU	communalists	ADDEEEEFHLNRY	freehandedly

ADDEEEGGHLOR	loggerheaded
ADDEEEGIMNST	demagnetised
ADDEEEGIMNTZ	demagnetized
ADDEEEGNOTXY	deoxygenated
ADDEEEHINRST	disheartened
ADDEEEHLNNVY	evenhandedly
ADDEEEHLORSY	soreheadedly
ADDEEEIIRSTV	desiderative
ADDEEEILNPRT	interpleaded
ADDEEEILSSUX	desexualised
ADDEEEILSUXZ	desexualized
ADDEEEIMPRTT	premeditated
ADDEEEIORRTT	deteriorated
ADDEEEIORTVV	overdeviated
ADDEEENNRVWY	van der Weyden
ADDEEENOPRVX	overexpanded
ADDEEENPRSSV	depravedness
ADDEEEOPPRSV	eavesdropped
ADDEEFFNRSTU	understaffed
ADDEEFHILPSS	paddlefishes
ADDEEFHLMORY	formaldehyde
ADDEEFHLNORY	forehandedly
ADDEEFHOORSW	foreshadowed
ADDEEFINOORR	foreordained
ADDEEFLNRSSU	dreadfulness
ADDEEFMNRSTU	defraudments
ADDEEGHNORTY	hydrogenated
ADDEEGIINRST	desiderating
ADDEEGILNNST	disentangled
ADDEEGILNTTU	deglutinated
ADDEEGINRRSS	readdressing
ADDEEGIRRRSS	disregarders
ADDEEGMMOPRR	deprogrammed
ADDEEHHIMRTY	hemihydrated
ADDEEHHNRSTU	thunderheads
ADDEEHLNNOPY	openhandedly
ADDEEHMNOTTU	muttonheaded
ADDEEHMORSUY	hydromedusae
ADDEEHOORSVW	overshadowed
ADDEEIIMMNNO	demimondaine
ADDEEIIMNRST	administered
ADDEEIIMNSST	disseminated
ADDEEIINNRST	Indian Desert
ADDEEIINORST	desideration
ADDEEILMSSTT	Middle States
ADDEEILMSTUU	demutualised
ADDEEILMTUUZ	demutualized
ADDEEILNORSV	Slieve Donard
ADDEEILPRSSU	displeasured
ADDEEILRRTVY	daredeviltry
ADDEEIMMNRST	masterminded
ADDEEIMNOPRT	predominated
ADDEEIMRSSSS	misaddresses
ADDEEINOPRST	depredations
ADDEEINPRRSU	underpraised
ADDEEINRSTUV	unadvertised
ADDEELNOSSTT	staddlestone
ADDEEMNORSTT	demonstrated
ADDEENPSSWYY	Spy Wednesday
ADDEENRRRSUW	underdrawers
ADDEFGILRRSU	disregardful
ADDEFHILOPST	feldspathoid
ADDEFIIIINNR	Ferdinand III
ADDEFIIILQSU	disqualified
ADDEFIIINNRV	Ferdinand VII
ADDEFIIISSST	dissatisfied
ADDEFLNNNOUW	Newfoundland
ADDEGGHORSTU	goddaughters
ADDEGGIIIRST	digitigrades
ADDEGGIINRRS	disregarding
ADDEGHHOORTU	daughterhood
ADDEGHNORSTU	dreadnoughts
ADDEGIIMNOSS	misdiagnosed
ADDEGIINORSS	disorganised
ADDEGIINORSZ	disorganized
ADDEGILMNOTU	demodulating
ADDEGIOORUZZ	Guido d'Arezzo
ADDEHLORSSTT	stadtholders
ADDEHMNOORTY	monohydrated
ADDEHMNORSUY	hydromedusan
ADDEHMORSSUY	hydromedusas
ADDEIIILMSST	dissimilated
ADDEIIINSTUV	individuates
ADDEIILLLLSY	dillydallies
ADDEIILLNSSV	Devil's Island
ADDEIILMSSTU	dissimulated
ADDEIILPSSTY	dissipatedly
ADDEIINOPPST	disappointed
ADDEILMNOOTU	demodulation
ADDEILMNOPRS	Promised Land
ADDEILMNSSTW	West Midlands
ADDELMOORSTU	demodulators
ADDEMNOOORST	ròdomontades
ADDENNORSSHW	downwardness
ADDFIILLNSUY	disdainfully
ADDGHILLNNOS	landholdings
ADDGHNORSTUW	downdraughts
ADDGIILNSSTU	studdingsail
ADDGILNNORSW	Darling Downs
ADDGINNOOSSW	Goodwin Sands
ADDHIIILMOPP	amphidiploid
ADDHLLNNOOOR	Noordholland
ADDIIIILLNUVY	individually
ADDIIINORTUV	individuator
ADEEEEFGHRST	featheredges
ADEEEEEGGRSST	desegregates
ADEEEEGINRTV	degenerative
ADEEEEGLNRTY	degenerately
ADEEEEHILRST	etherealised
ADEEEEHILRTZ	etherealized
ADEEEEIKLNRR	Reindeer Lake
ADEEEFFIINRT	differentiae
ADEEEFFORRST	reafforested
ADEEEFGHORRT	foregathered
ADEEEFGIRRRT	refrigerated
ADEEEGGILNRT	lateenrigged
ADEEEGGINNRT	degenerating
ADEEEGGNRSTU	unsegregated
ADEEEGHLMMRS	sledgehammer
ADEEEGIMNRRS	gendarmeries
ADEEEGIMNRST	demagnetiser
	disagreement
ADEEEGIMNRTZ	demagnetizer
ADEEEGIMNSST	demagnetises

ADEEEGIMNSTZ	demagnetizes	ADEEELLMMNRT	entrammelled
ADEEEGINNORT	degeneration	ADEEELLNSSWY	wensleydales
ADEEEGINNRST	tragediennes	ADEEEELNNQRSU	Queenslander
ADEEEGINOPSS	paedogenesis	ADEEEELNOSSST	desolateness
ADEEEGINORTT	renegotiated	ADEEEELNRSTTU	launderettes
ADEEEGINPRRT	peregrinated	ADEEEELOPPRST	tradespeople
ADEEEGINPRST	predesignate	ADEEEELOPRSSS	leopardesses
ADEEEGINRRTT	redintegrate	ADEEEELRSSSTU	adulteresses
	reintegrated	ADEEEEMNORSST	moderateness
ADEEEGLLNOSS	de los Angeles	ADEEEEMNRSSSU	measuredness
ADEEEGLNNNNRW	New Englander	ADEEEEMORRSTV	overmastered
ADEEEGLNORTU	outgeneraled	ADEEEEMOSSTWW	meadowsweets
ADEEEGMNNNRT	endangerment	ADEEEENNNORSX	Andersen Nexø
ADEEEGMNNRST	derangements	ADEEEENOPPRRT	preponderate
ADEEEGNOSTXY	deoxygenates	ADEEEENORRSUV	endeavourers
ADEEEHHLORTW	wholehearted	ADEEEENPPRRSS	preparedness
ADEEEHILPSTT	telepathised	ADEEEENPRRTUV	peradventure
ADEEEHILPTTZ	telepathized	ADEEEENRRTTWW	Derwentwater
ADEEEHIMNRTT	hereditament	ADEEEOPPRRSV	eavesdropper
ADEEEHIMPRSZ	reemphasized	ADEEEOPRRSUV	overpersuade
ADEEEHIMSSTT	metathesised	ADEEEORRSSTV	overasserted
ADEEEHIMSTTZ	metathesized	ADEEEQRSSTTU	sequestrated
ADEEEHINSSSV	adhesiveness	ADEEERSSSSTW	stewardesses
ADEEEHINSSTU	Hauts-de-Seine	ADEEFFIILNRT	differential
ADEEEHINSTTZ	anesthetized	ADEEFGHIIRRT	airfreighted
ADEEEHIRRTTT	tetrahedrite	ADEEFGIILNRS	federalising
ADEEEHLLORSS	leaseholders	ADEEFGIILNRZ	federalizing
ADEEEHLNNNRT	Netherlander	ADEEFGILNORS	freeloadings
ADEEEHMNPRSS	hamperedness	ADEEFGINNNRS	rangefinders
ADEEEHMORSST	homesteaders	ADEEFGINNNRST	freestanding
ADEEEHMORSTV	Mohave Desert	ADEEFGKLNPRS	frankpledges
ADEEEHNNNNORS	enneahedrons	ADEEFHILMSSS	damselfishes
ADEEEHPRSSST	spreadsheets	ADEEFHLOPSST	feldspathose
ADEEEIILMNRS	demineralise	ADEEFHOORRSW	foreshadower
ADEEEIILMNRZ	demineralize	ADEEFILNNSST	inflatedness
ADEEEIILNPTX	expediential	ADEEFILNORTV	overinflated
ADEEEIILORVZ	overidealize	ADEEFILOPRRT	proliferated
ADEEEIIMMRST	semidiameter	ADEEFLMORRTU	reformulated
ADEEEIIMNRTT	intermediate	ADEEFLNRSSTW	West Flanders
ADEEEILLMMOS	mademoiselle	ADEEFLNRTUUV	adventureful
ADEEEILMNORT	radioelement	ADEEFNOPRRTU	unperforated
ADEEEILNPRRT	interpleader	ADEEFNSSSSTT	stedfastness
ADEEEILNRRTT	interrelated	ADEEFOOPRRRS	proofreaders
ADEEEILNRSTX	externalised	ADEEFOOPRRTW	waterproofed
ADEEEILNRTXZ	externalized	ADEEGGHIRSTT	straightedge
ADEEEILSSSUX	desexualises	ADEEGGILNRTU	deregulating
ADEEEILSSUXZ	desexualizes	ADEEGGIRRTTU	regurgitated
ADEEEIMMNNNR	remaindermen	ADEEGGLNOPPR	doppelganger
ADEEEIMNORST	demonetarise		doppelgänger
ADEEEIMNORTZ	demonetarize	ADEEGHHILRTT	lighthearted
ADEEEIMNRTTX	exterminated	ADEEGHIMMOPR	mimeographed
ADEEEIMPRSTT	premeditates	ADEEGHIMNOST	homesteading
ADEEEINOPRSU	europeanised	ADEEGHIMOPRS	demographies
ADEEEINOPRUZ	europeanized	ADEEGHINNPPR	apprehending
ADEEEINPRSTT	predestinate	ADEEGHINNNRT	heartrending
ADEEEIOPPSTX	exopeptidase	ADEEGHINPRSS	grandeeships
ADEEEIORRSTT	deteriorates	ADEEGHINRSTT	straightened
ADEEEIORSTVV	overdeviates	ADEEGHIOPRRV	videographer
ADEEEJMORSTV	Mojave Desert	ADEEGHLORSUV	overslaughed
ADEEEKLLMRSS	Skelmersdale	ADEEGHLRSSTU	daughterless
ADEEEKLLNOST	endoskeletal	ADEEGHMOPRRS	demographers
ADEEEKLRRSST	deerstalkers	ADEEGHNNPRSW	grandnephews

ADEEGHNOPRST	stenographed
ADEEGHNORSTY	hydrogenates
ADEEGHPRSTTU	stepdaughter
ADEEGIIMMNNS	misdemeaning
ADEEGIIMNNRR	remaindering
ADEEGIINRSTT	disintegrate
ADEEGIINSTTV	investigated
ADEEGIJNNRWW	Wandering Jew
ADEEGIKLNRST	deerstalking
ADEEGIKNNRRT	kindergarten
ADEEGIKNPSST	speedskating
ADEEGILLNOPT	Point de Galle
ADEEGILMNNRY	meanderingly
ADEEGILNNRSU	undersealing
ADEEGILNNSST	disentangles
ADEEGILNORTU	deregulation
ADEEGILNSTTU	deglutinates
ADEEGILORTVY	derogatively
ADEEGIMNNRST	deraignments
ADEEGIMORRST	gradiometers
ADEEGIMSSTTU	guesstimated
ADEEGINNNORUV	endeavouring
ADEEGINORRTT	interrogated
ADEEGLLRRSSY	regardlessly
ADEEGLMNOSSS	gladsomeness
ADEEGLNNORSY	General Synod
ADEEGLORRRTY	retrogradely
ADEEGLORRSTU	deregulators
ADEEGLORRTUY	deregulatory
ADEEGMMOPRRS	deprogrammes
ADEEGMNNRRTU	undergarment
ADEEGMNNRRSY	gerrymanders
ADEEGNPRTUUX	unexpurgated
ADEEGNRRSSST	transgressed
ADEEGORRTTXY	dextrogyrate
ADEEHHIKNRRS	headshrinker
ADEEHHIMRSTY	hemihydrates
ADEEHHLORRSS	shareholders
ADEEHHNNPTUY	unhyphenated
ADEEHHNOPRST	heptahedrons
ADEEHIILRRTY	hereditarily
ADEEHIIOPRSS	isodiapheres
ADEEHILMNOOT	endothelioma
ADEEHILMOSSY	hemodialyses
ADEEHILNPRRS	philanderers
ADEEHIMNPPRS	misapprehend
ADEEHIMRSSST	headmistress
ADEEHINPSSSU	dauphinesses
ADEEHIOOPSST	apotheosised
ADEEHIOOPSTZ	apotheosized
ADEEHIRRRSSS	hairdressers
ADEEHKLORSST	stakeholders
ADEEHLLLMOPR	phellodermal
ADEEHLLNOSSW	hallowedness
ADEEHLLORSSV	slaveholders
ADEEHLMMOTUY	mealymouthed
ADEEHLOORSTW	leatherwoods
ADEEHMMNNOSS	handsomeness
ADEEHMNNORRSY	dysmenorrhea
ADEEHMOPRTTY	dermatophyte
ADEEHNNOPRST	pentahedrons
ADEEHNORRSTT	tetrahedrons

ADEEHNORSTTY	stonyhearted
ADEEHORSTTTU	stouthearted
ADEEIIILMRST	demilitarise
ADEEIIILMRTZ	demilitarize
ADEEIIILMTTV	delimitative
ADEEIIILORST	editorialise
ADEEIIILORTZ	editorialize
ADEEIIIMNNPR	Indian Empire
ADEEIIJNOORR	Rio de Janeiro
ADEEIILLNTVY	evidentially
ADEEIILMMNPT	impedimental
ADEEIILMMORS	memorialised
ADEEIILMMORZ	memorialized
ADEEIILMMSSV	medievalisms
ADEEIILMNNSS	maidenliness
ADEEIILMSSTV	medievalists
ADEEIILMTTVY	meditatively
ADEEIILNNOST	delineations
ADEEIILNNRST	internalised
ADEEIILNNRTZ	internalized
ADEEIILNORST	orientalised
ADEEIILNORTZ	orientalized
ADEEIILNPRST	presidential
ADEEIILOPRST	depilatories
ADEEIILRTVVY	derivatively
ADEEIIMMSSTT	misestimated
ADEEIIMNNOTV	denominative
ADEEIIMNRRRT	intermarried
ADEEIIMNRRTY	intermediary
ADEEIIMNSSST	disseminates
ADEEIINORSTT	disorientate
ADEEIINPRSSS	dispensaries
ADEEIINRRSTY	residentiary
ADEEIINRRTVW	water diviner
ADEEIIOPRSST	depositaries
ADEEIKLLNSSY	ladylikeness
ADEEIKMNRSSS	semidarkness
ADEEILLNNTTY	tendentially
ADEEILLNPSSW	Pelew Islands
ADEEILMMORTY	immoderately
ADEEILMNOPRT	redemptional
ADEEILMORRSS	demoralisers
ADEEILMORRSZ	demoralizers
ADEEILMORSTT	dilatometers
ADEEILMPRSST	slipstreamed
ADEEILMSSTUU	demutualises
ADEEILMSTUUZ	demutualizes
ADEEILNNPSTU	peninsulated
ADEEILNNTTUV	unventilated
ADEEILNOPPRT	lepidopteran
ADEEILNOPRSS	personalised
ADEEILNOPRSZ	personalized
ADEEILNOPRTT	interpolated
ADEEILNOTTVY	denotatively
ADEEILNRRSTY	restrainedly
ADEEILOPRRSS	depolarisers
ADEEILOPRRSZ	depolarizers
ADEEILORSSST	idolatresses
ADEEILPRSSSU	displeasures
ADEEIMMNORSS	misdemeanors
ADEEIMMNORSU	misdemeanour
ADEEIMNNRSTT	determinants

	detrainments
ADEEIMNNSTTU	edutainments
ADEEIMNOPRST	impersonated
	predominates
ADEEIMNOSSTU	eudaemonists
ADEEIMNRSTUV	misadventure
ADEEIMOPRRTT	premeditator
ADEEIMORSSTT	stadiometers
ADEEIMSSSTTY	systematised
ADEEIMSSTTYZ	systematized
ADEEINNORSTV	denervations
ADEEINNRRSTU	unrestrained
ADEEINNSSSTU	unsteadiness
ADEEINOPPPRT	preappointed
ADEEINORRSTV	overstrained
ADEEINORSSUV	adenoviruses
ADEEINPRRSSU	underpraises
ADEEIOPPRRTX	expropriated
ADEEJMNRSTTU	readjustment
ADEEKLOPRSSU	loudspeakers
ADEELLLRSSSW	Sadler's Wells
ADEELLMMNRTU	untrammelled
ADEELLNNSSSS	landlessness
ADEELMNOORST	demonolaters
ADEELMNOSTTT	Old Testament
ADEELMNRSUUY	unmeasuredly
ADEELMOPRSTU	deuteroplasm
ADEELMORSSTU	somersaulted
ADEELNPPRRUY	unpreparedly
ADEELNRRSUUV	undervaluers
ADEELOPSTTUX	expostulated
ADEEMMNNORSTY	dynamometers
ADEEMMOSTUXY	myxedematous
ADEEMMNNNORTU	unornamented
ADEEMMNNPRSUU	supermundane
ADEEMMNNPRTUY	underpayment
ADEEMNNORRSTT	remonstrated
ADEEMNNORSSTT	demonstrates
ADEENNNOORRST	androsterone
ADEENNOPPRRT	preponderant
ADEEFFGIMSTUU	suffumigated
ADEEFFILNRSTU	faultfinders
ADEEFFIORSSST	disafforests
ADEEFGHILNSUW	Ludwigshafen
ADEEFGHILRSTY	farsightedly
ADEEFGIINRSTU	disfeaturing
ADEEFGINOOPRR	proofreading
ADEEFGINRRSTU	transfigured
ADEEFHILLORSS	dollarfishes
ADEEFHILLTTWY	halfwittedly
ADEEFHILMNORV	Milford Haven
ADEEFHILOORST	foolhardiest
ADEEFHINRSSSW	dwarfishness
ADEEFIIILNNOT	definitional
ADEEFIIILQRSU	disqualifier
ADEEFIIILQSSU	disqualifies
ADEEFIIISSSST	dissatisfies
ADEEFIILNOOST	defoliations
ADEEFIILNOSTT	deflationist
ADEEFIINNOSTU	infeudations
ADEEFIINRSTTU	unstratified
ADEEFILMNNOSS	manifoldness
ADEEFILMORRSU	formularised
ADEEFILMORRUZ	formularized
ADEEFILNNOOSS	San Ildefonso
ADEEFILNOORST	deflorations
ADEEFIMNOORST	deformations
ADEEFLLNRTUUY	fraudulently
ADEEFLMNORTUU	unformulated
ADEEGGIINNOPX	Deng Xiaoping
ADEEGGIINNRRT	intergrading
ADEEGGIINRTTU	ingurgitated
ADEEGGIJNNPRU	Junggar Pendi
ADEEGGILOORUV	Olduvai Gorge
ADEEGGINORRRT	retrograding
ADEEGGLNRSSSU	sluggardness
ADEEGHHILOPRT	lithographed
ADEEGHHOOPPRT	photographed
ADEEGHHOPRRRY	hydrographer
ADEEGHIILNNPR	philandering
ADEEGHIIMNNSU	dehumanising
ADEEGHIIMNNUZ	dehumanizing
ADEEGHIINRRSS	hairdressing
	sherardising
ADEEGHIINRRSZ	sherardizing
ADEEGHILLNOSV	slaveholding
ADEEGHILNOOST	anthologised
ADEEGHILNOOTZ	anthologized
ADEEGHILOOPTZ	pathologized
ADEEGHIMOPRST	demographist
ADEEGHINNORTY	antihydrogen
ADEEGHINRSSTU	draughtiness
ADEEGHLLNORST	stranglehold
ADEEGHLNORSTY	headstrongly
ADEEGHMNNORRST	grandmothers
ADEEGHNOORRTY	hydrogenator
ADEEGHOOPPRRSX	doxographers
ADEEGHORRSTUV	overdraughts
ADEEGIIILMNTT	delimitating
ADEEGIIILNNSS	desalinising
ADEEGIIILNNST	disentailing
ADEEGIIILNNSZ	desalinizing
ADEEGIIILNRTT	interdigital
ADEEGIIILNSTV	devitalising
ADEEGIIILNTVZ	devitalizing
ADEEGIIJNOPRS	jeopardising
ADEEGIIJNOPRZ	jeopardizing
ADEEGIILLMNSY	misleadingly
ADEEGIILLNNTU	dentilingual
ADEEGIILMNORS	demoralising
ADEEGIILMNORZ	demoralizing
ADEEGIILMNPSS	mispleadings
ADEEGIILNNRRT	interlarding
ADEEGIILNOPRS	depolarising
ADEEGIILNOPRZ	depolarizing
ADEEGIILNORSS	digressional
ADEEGIILNPRSY	despairingly
ADEEGIILNRRRV	Darling River
ADEEGIILNRSSU	singularised
ADEEGIILNRSUZ	singularized
ADEEGIIMNNNOT	denominating
ADEEGIIMNNPRR	reprimanding
ADEEGIIMNOSSS	misdiagnoses
ADEEGIINNOPRR	preordaining

ADEGIINNORST	denigrations
ADEGIINNOSST	designations
ADEGIINNRSTU	denaturising
ADEGIINNRTUZ	denaturizing
ADEGIINOORRT	granodiorite
ADEGIINORRSS	disorganiser
ADEGIINORRSZ	disorganizer
ADEGIINORSSS	disorganises
ADEGIINORSSZ	disorganizes
ADEGIINRSSTT	dissertating
ADEGIKNNRSTU	undertakings
ADEGILNNPRUY	underplaying
ADEGILNNRUUV	undervaluing
ADEGILNOPPTU	depopulating
ADEGILOOPSST	paedologists
ADEGILOORRTY	derogatorily
ADEGILOOSTTU	tautologised
ADEGILOOTTUZ	tautologized
ADEGILRSTTUU	gutturalised
ADEGILRTTUUZ	gutturalized
ADEGIMNORRSS	gormandisers
ADEGIMNORRSZ	gormandizers
ADEGIMNORSSU	gourmandises
ADEGINNOSTUW	Godwin-Austen
ADEGINNRSTTU	understating
ADEGINOPRSTU	outspreading
ADEGINORRSSW	Grosswardein
ADEGINOSSTTU	degustations
ADEGJLMNSTTU	Last Judgment
ADEGMNORSSSU	groundmasses
ADEHHILLPPSU	philadelphus
ADEHHILMOORR	hemorrhoidal
ADEHHIMOORRS	haemorrhoids
ADEHHIOPPSST	phosphatides
	phosphatised
ADEHHIOPPSTZ	phosphatized
ADEHHLMORRTY	hydrothermal
ADEHHOOPPRST	phosphorated
ADEHHOPRRTYV	hydrotherapy
ADEHIILMOSSY	hemodialysis
ADEHIILNSTTT	dilettantish
ADEHIILOPSST	hospitalised
ADEHIILOPSTZ	hospitalized
ADEHIIMNORSS	disharmonies
ADEHIINNRSTY	hydrastinine
ADEHIJLOPSUU	Philo Judaeus
ADEHILLNRSST	disenthralls
ADEHILLOPRSY	spheroidally
ADEHILMNOPSU	sulphonamide
ADEHILMNORSU	malnourished
ADEHINNQSUUV	unvanquished
ADEHINOORSTZ	antherozoids
ADEHINORSTUU	unauthorised
ADEHINORTUUZ	unauthorized
ADEHINPPRSST	transshipped
ADEHINQRRSTU	hindquarters
ADEHINRSSTTW	withstanders
ADEHIOOPRSTT	orthopaedist
ADEHIOPSSSTY	hypostasises
ADEHIOPSSTTY	hypostatised
ADEHIOPSSTYZ	hypostasized
ADEHIOPSTTYZ	hypostatized

ADEHLLLMORSS	smallholders
ADEHLLLORSST	stallholders
ADEHLMNOOPSU	monadelphous
ADEHLORSSTYY	hydrolysates
ADEHMNOORSTY	monohydrates
ADEHOOPSTTTT	photostatted
ADEIIILMNOTT	delimitation
ADEIIILMSSST	dissimilates
ADEIIILORSST	solidarities
ADEIIILORSTT	editorialist
ADEIIIMNORST	dimerisation
ADEIIIMNORTZ	dimerization
ADEIIIMNOSTV	deviationism
ADEIIIMNRSTU	miniaturised
ADEIIIMNRTUZ	miniaturized
ADEIIINNNPPS	pinnipedians
ADEIIINNOOST	deionisation
ADEIIINNOOTZ	deionization
ADEIIINOSTTV	deviationist
ADEIIINSTTTU	attitudinise
ADEIIINTTTUZ	attitudinize
ADEIIIOPSSTV	diapositives
ADEIIILMNORY	meridionally
ADEIIILLOSSTY	disloyalties
ADEIIILLSTUVV	vaudevillist
ADEIIILMMNPRT	malimprinted
ADEIILMMORST	immortalised
ADEIILMMORTZ	immortalized
ADEIILMNSTTT	dilettantism
ADEIILMSSSTU	dissimulates
ADEIILNNORTY	inordinately
ADEIILNOOPST	despoliation
ADEIILNOPRTV	providential
ADEIILNORSST	dilatoriness
ADEIILNQRTUZ	tranquilized
ADEIILORRSTZ	idolatrizers
ADEIILSSSUVY	dissuasively
ADEIIMMNOORT	immoderation
ADEIIMNNNOOT	denomination
ADEIIMNNRSTT	distrainment
ADEIIMNOPRST	postmeridian
ADEIIMNOPRXY	pyridoxamine
ADEIIMNORSSS	readmissions
ADEIIMNORSST	disseminator
ADEIIMOPPRRT	impropriated
ADEIIMORSTTU	audiometrist
ADEIIMRSSTTX	taxidermists
ADEIINNNOSTT	indentations
ADEIINNOPSST	dispensation
ADEIINNORSTT	denitrations
ADEIINNOSSTT	destinations
ADEIINOOPRST	disoperation
ADEIINOOPRTX	peroxidation
ADEIINOPRSTU	repudiations
ADEIINOPRSTV	deprivations
ADEIINORRSVY	diversionary
ADEIINORSSTT	dissertation
ADEIINORSTTX	extraditions
ADEIINOSTTUV	adventitious
ADEIINPRSSSU	prussianised
ADEIINPRSSUZ	prussianized
ADEIINRSSTVY	vineyardists

ADEIIOOOPRST	radioisotope
ADEILLLNOOSY	solenoidally
ADEILLMNRTUV	rudimentally
ADEILLMRRSST	drillmasters
ADEILLNOOTVY	devotionally
ADEILLNOPPRT	dipropellant
ADEILLNPRTUY	prudentially
ADEILMNNNSTU	disannulment
ADEILMNOPSTU	deplumations
ADEILNOOPPTU	depopulation
ADEILNORRSTV	dorsiventral
ADEILNRSSSTW	towardliness
ADEILNRSSTWW	windlestraws
ADEILOPPRSSS	predisposals
ADEIMMOPRSUY	praseodymium
ADEIMNNOORST	denominators
ADEIMNNQRSUU	quadrenniums
ADEIMNOOPRRT	predominator
ADEIMNRRSSUY	nurserymaids
ADEIMOOPRSTZ	spermatozoid
ADEINOOPRSTT	deportations
ADEINOPRSSTY	dispensatory
ADEINRSSTTUV	adventurists
ADEIORRSSSTT	dissertators
ADEJMNNORSTU	adjournments
ADEKOOPRSTVZ	Petrozavodsk
ADELLNORSSUY	slanderously
ADELLOOPRRST	petrodollars
ADELLORSTUUY	adulterously
ADELMNNORUWY	laundrywomen
ADELNOORRSTV	dorsoventral
ADELNORSSTVW	strandwolves
ADELOPRRSSWY	swordplayers
ADEMNOORRSTT	demonstrator
ADEMOPRRSSTU	superstardom
ADENNOPRRSST	transponders
ADENNORSSTUW	untowardness
ADEOORRRTTXY	dextrorotary
ADFFGIIIMNRS	disaffirming
ADFFGIILNNTU	faultfinding
ADFGIILNORTU	fluoridating
ADFGIINORSUV	disfavouring
ADFIIILLNNSU	nullifidians
ADFIIILNNOST	disinflation
ADFIIILNNPTY	pinnatifidly
ADFIIILNOSTU	fluidisation
ADFIIILNOTUZ	fluidization
ADFIILNOORTU	fluoridation
ADFIILOSSTUY	fastidiously
ADGGIIIILNST	digitalising
ADGGIIIILNTZ	digitalizing
ADGGIIMNNORS	gormandising
ADGGIIMNNORZ	gormandizing
ADGHHHIILOSY	High Holidays
ADGHIINNSTTW	withstanding
ADGHIINOPRSS	rhapsodising
ADGHIINOPRSZ	rhapsodizing
ADGHILLLMNOS	smallholding
ADGHILNNOPRY	hydroplaning
ADGHIMRRRSYY	hydrargyrism
ADGIIIIMNNTT	intimidating
ADGIIIINOSTT	digitisation
ADGIIIINOTTZ	digitization
ADGIIILNORST	idolatrising
ADGIIILNORTZ	idolatrizing
ADGIIILOOSSS	idioglossias
ADGIIIMNOSSS	misdiagnosis
ADGIILLNNNSU	disannulling
ADGIILLNNOTU	longitudinal
ADGIILMNNOTY	dominatingly
ADGIILNRSTTU	stridulating
ADGIILOORSST	radiologists
ADGIILOOSSTU	audiologists
ADGIINOPPRSV	disapproving
ADGILNNOSTUY	astoundingly
ADGILNOORSST	andrologists
ADGIMMNORSSU	gourmandisms
ADGIMNNOOOST	Santo Domingo
ADGINNOOOPRT	gonadotropin
ADGLLLNOSUUY	glandulously
ADGOOOOPRSSTU	gastropodous
ADHHIOPRSTTY	hydropathist
ADHHLLNNOORT	North Holland
ADHHLLNOOSTU	South Holland
ADHHLORSTUUY	Holy Thursday
ADHHNOOPRSUY	hydrophanous
ADHIIIMMRSTT	mithridatism
ADHIILMNOPRU	dolphinarium
ADHIIMOPRSST	diastrophism
ADHILLNOSTUY	outlandishly
ADHILMMOOPTY	lymphomatoid
ADHLNOOOOPRT	odontophoral
ADHOOOPRRSTU	arthropodous
ADIIIIMNNOTT	intimidation
ADIIIINNOSTV	divinisation
ADIIIINNOTVZ	divinization
ADIIILLMRSSY	dissimilarly
ADIIILLNOSTT	distillation
ADIIILLNOSVY	divisionally
ADIIILNOQSTU	liquidations
ADIIIMNORSTT	intimidators
ADIIINOPSSST	dissipations
ADIIINORSTTT	traditionist
ADIIKLLNRSSU	Kuril Islands
ADIILLMOPRRY	primordially
ADIILLNOQRSU	quadrillions
ADIILLNOSSUY	sinusoidally
ADIILLNRSTUY	industrially
ADIILLOPPSST	lipidoplasts
ADIILLOPSTUV	postdiluvial
ADIILLORSTTY	distillatory
ADIILMNNOSST	mandolinists
ADIILMOPSSTT	diplomatists
ADIILMORSSTU	dissimulator
ADIILNOORSTT	distortional
ADIILNOPSTUV	postdiluvian
ADIILNORSTTU	stridulation
ADIINOPSSTTU	disputations
ADIIOPSSTTUU	disputatious
ADIIOPSSTTUY	audiotypists
ADILLMNOOOPY	monopodially
ADILLNRSTTUY	stridulantly
ADILLOORSTUY	idolatrously
ADILORRSSTTU	stridulators

ADILORRSTTUY	stridulatory
ADIOOPRRSSUU	sudoriparous
ADLLMOOORSUY	malodorously
ADLLOOOSSWWH	woodswallows
ADMNNOOSSTTU	Santos-Dumont
ADNNOOPRRSST	transpondors
AEEEEGHMORTT	heterogamete
AEEEEGINRRTV	regenerative
AEEEEGNNRRTU	unregenerate
AEEEEHHPRRSS	sheepshearer
AEEEEHILRSST	etherealises
AEEEEHILRSTZ	etherealizes
AEEEEHLNRSST	etherealness
AEEEEHLRSTTT	leatherettes
AEEEEIMNNRST	Seine-et-Marne
AEEEEKLMRRTT	telemarketer
AEEEFFILMNTY	effeminately
AEEEFFKOSSTW	Feast of Weeks
AEEEFGIRRRST	refrigerates
AEEEFHINRRTT	thereinafter
AEEEFILNPRRT	preferential
AEEEFIMNRRTV	fermentative
AEEEFLLNSSSS	leaflessness
AEEEFLMPRSSU	superfemales
AEEEFLNRSSSS	fearlessness
AEEEFLORSTTW	telesoftware
AEEEFMNORSSS	fearsomeness
AEEEGGHLNSTT	snaggleteeth
AEEEGGINNOSS	angiogeneses
AEEEGGINNRRT	regenerating
AEEEGGINRTTV	revegetating
AEEEGGMMNOSU	emmenagogues
AEEEGHIILMRW	whigmaleerie
AEEEGIILNRST	generalities
AEEEGILMMRRS	lammergeiers
AEEEGILMNOSS	amelogenesis
AEEEGILNNPSS	palingeneses
AEEEGILNRRSS	generalisers
AEEEGILNRRSZ	generalizers
AEEEGILNRSSV	evangelisers
AEEEGILNRSVZ	evangelizers
AEEEGILTTVVY	vegetatively
AEEEGIMNNSTV	envisagement
AEEEGINNORRT	regeneration
AEEEGINNRRTTX	exenterating
AEEEGINNSSTV	negativeness
AEEEGINORSTT	renegotiates
AEEEGINORSTV	seronegative
AEEEGINORTTV	revegetation
AEEEGINPRRST	peregrinates
AEEEGINRRSTT	reintegrates
AEEEGIRRSTTV	tergiversate
AEEEGLMMRRSY	lammergeyers
AEEEGLMNNNTT	entanglement
AEEEGLMNNRST	enlargements
AEEEGLNSSSSW	wagelessness
AEEEGMMNORTT	magnetometer
AEEEGMMNOSSS	gamesomeness
AEEEGMNNRSTT	estrangement
AEEEGNORRRST	regenerators
AEEEGOPRRSTU	supererogate
AEEEHHLPSTTT	heptathletes

AEEEHHMNORSX	hexahemerons
AEEEHHNNNPRT	phenanthrene
AEEEHHNOTTXY	ethoxyethane
AEEEHIILNPST	Penthesileia
AEEEHILMPRTY	ephemerality
AEEEHILNNSSV	heavenliness
AEEEHILNRSST	leatheriness
AEEEHILPSSTT	telepathises
AEEEHILPSTTZ	telepathizes
AEEEHIMNNOPP	epiphenomena
AEEEHIMNORSS	Shemona Esrei
AEEEHIMORSTT	metatheories
AEEEHIMPRSSZ	reemphasizes
AEEEHIMSSSTT	metathesises
AEEEHIMSSTTZ	metathesizes
AEEEHINPPRSV	apprehensive
AEEEHINPRSST	parenthesise
AEEEHINPRSTZ	parenthesize
AEEEHINRRTTH	interwreathe
AEEEHINSSTTZ	anesthetizes
AEEEHLMPPRST	pamphleteers
AEEEHLNPSTTT	pentathletes
AEEEHLORSTUX	heterosexual
AEEEHLRRSTTY	Harley Street
AEEEHMNNSTTW	enswathement
AEEEHMNORSUW	warehousemen
AEEEHMOPRSSV	overemphases
AEEEHMORTTTX	methotrexate
AEEEHNOPRRTT	heteropteran
AEEEHNORSSTT	Eratosthenes
AEEEHPRRSSTU	superheaters
AEEEIILMNORT	Maine-et-Loire
AEEEIILMRSTT	semiliterate
AEEEIILNNRTT	interlineate
AEEEIILNPRTX	experiential
AEEEIINNNSTT	Saint-Étienne
AEEEIKNNORST	enterokinase
AEEEILLMMNST	elementalism
AEEEILLMNRTY	elementarily
AEEEILLNPRTT	interpellate
AEEEILMNPRTX	experimental
AEEEILMNRTTY	intemerately
AEEEILNOORST	Saône-et-Loire
AEEEILNRRSTT	interrelates
AEEEILNRSSTV	relativeness
AEEEILNRSSTX	externalises
AEEEILNRSTXZ	externalizes
AEEEILNRTTVY	inveterately
AEEEILRRSTYZ	Eretz Yisrael
AEEEIMNRRTUV	remunerative
AEEEIMNRSTTX	exterminates
AEEEIMOPRRTV	evaporimeter
AEEEIMORSSTT	East Timorese
AEEEIMORSTTV	overestimate
AEEEIMQRRSTU	marqueteries
AEEEINNORTTX	exenteration
AEEEINNRRSTT	entertainers
AEEEINNSSSTV	nativenesses
AEEEINOPRSSU	europeanises
AEEEINOPRSUZ	europeanizes
AEEEINPRSTTV	presentative
AEEEINPRTTVV	preventative

AEEEINRRSTVW	interweavers
AEEEINRRTTUX	extrauterine
AEEEIPRRSTVV	preservative
AEEEIRRSTVVX	extraversive
AEEEJLMNRSUW	New Jerusalem
AEEEKLLPRSSW	sleepwalkers
AEEEKLRRSTTW	streetwalker
AEEELLORSTTT	teetotallers
AEEELLPRSSSU	pleasureless
AEEELMMNNPST	empanelments
AEEELMNNSSSS	namelessness
AEEELMNNSSTV	enslavements
AEEELMNORSYY	eleemosynary
AEEELRRSSSTU	treasureless
AEEEMMNPRSTT	temperaments
AEEEMMNPRTTT	attemperment
AEEEMMNRSSTU	measurements
AEEEMNNNRSST	ensnarements
AEEEMNNPPRSW	newspapermen
AEEEMNNRSTTT	entreatments
AEEEMNNSTTTW	New Testament
AEEEMNRSSSST	reassessment
AEEEMNRSSTTT	restatements
AEEEMOOPRRTV	evaporometer
AEEEMORRSSUV	overmeasures
AEEEMPRRSTTU	temperatures
AEEEMRSSSSST	seamstresses
AEEENOORRSSU	aeroneuroses
AEEENOPRSSTT	stearoptenes
AEEEQRSSSTTU	sequestrates
AEEFFGRSSTTU	suffragettes
AEEFFHLORRTY	forefatherly
AEEFGGIILLNR	fillagreeing
AEEFGHORRSTT	heterografts
AEEFGIKNOPRS	forespeaking
AEEFGILNORRT	foretriangle
AEEFGINRRRST	refrigerants
AEEFGIORRRRT	refrigerator
AEEFGLLPRSUY	presagefully
AEEFGLNRSSTU	gratefulness
AEEFGMNNRSTT	engraftments
AEEFHHHNNOSTU	Hohenstaufen
AEEFHHORSSTU	housefathers
AEEFHIKNRSSS	freakishness
AEEFHILNRSST	fatherliness
AEEFHLMNSSSU	shamefulness
AEEFHLMORRTW	flamethrower
AEEFHOOPRRTW	weatherproof
AEEFHPRRRRSY	Harper's Ferry
AEEFIILMPPRR	preamplifier
AEEFIINRRSTT	fraternities
AEEFILNORSTV	overinflates
AEEFILNRSSUW	wearifulness
AEEFILOPRRST	proliferates
AEEFILOPRSTU	petaliferous
AEEFIMNNORTT	fermentation
AEEFIMNNSSST	manifestness
AEEFIMNORSTU	amentiferous
AEEFIMOPRRTV	performative
AEEFINNORSTT	fenestration
AEEFINRRRSST	fraternisers
AEEFINRRRSTZ	fraternizers

AEEFKNNORSSS	forsakenness
AEEFLLNSSSSW	flawlessness
AEEFLLORRSST	forestallers
AEEFLMNORSTT	forestalment
AEEFLMORRSTU	reformulates
AEEFLNSSSTTU	tastefulness
AEEFLNSSSTUW	wastefulness
AEEFLOPQRSUW	pasqueflower
AEEFNRRRRSST	transferrers
AEEFOOPRRSST	professorate
AEEFOQRRRSTU	forequarters
AEEGGGINNNST	engagingness
AEEGGHIINNRS	garnisheeing
AEEGGHILNPRT	telegraphing
AEEGGHMMMOPR	Memphremagog
AEEGGIILNNRS	generalising
AEEGGIILNNRZ	generalizing
AEEGGIILNNSV	evangelising
AEEGGIILNNVZ	evangelizing
AEEGGIINNNRT	ingenerating
AEEGGIINNOSS	angiogenesis
AEEGGIINORSS	seigniorages
AEEGGILNNORS	sloganeering
AEEGGILNOSST	genealogists
AEEGGILOORST	geratologies
AEEGGILRSSVY	aggressively
AEEGGIMMNOST	geomagnetism
AEEGGINORSST	Saint George's
AEEGGINRSSUV	unaggressive
AEEGGIRRSTTU	regurgitates
AEEGGMNOOSTU	gametogenous
AEEGHHIINNST	heathenising
AEEGHHIINNTZ	heathenizing
AEEGHHILOPRR	heliographer
AEEGHHISTVWY	heavyweights
AEEGHHNOPRRT	ethnographer
AEEGHHOPRRTY	heterography
AEEGHILLMMRT	hellgrammite
AEEGHILORRUV	heliogravure
AEEGHILPRSTT	telegraphist
AEEGHINOPSST	pathogenesis
AEEGHINPRSST	sergeantship
AEEGHINPRSTU	superheating
AEEGHINNRRSTT	straightener
AEEGHIPPRSTW	paperweights
AEEGHLMNNRSTU	slaughtermen
AEEGHLNOPRSS	selenographs
AEEGHLNOPRSY	selenography
AEEGHLOORRTW	woolgatherer
AEEGHLRRSSTU	slaughterers
AEEGHMNOOSTU	hematogenous
AEEGHMOOPRRT	meteorograph
AEEGHMOOPRST	gametophores
AEEGHMOORSTU	heterogamous
AEEGHMOPSTTY	gametophytes
AEEGHNOOPRTV	photoengrave
AEEGHNOOPSTU	hepatogenous
AEEGHNOPRRST	stenographer
AEEGHNPRSSTV	stevengraphs
AEEGHNRSSTTW	Western Ghats
AEEGHOPPRRRT	petrographer
AEEGHOPRRRSX	xerographers

AEEGHOPRRSST	stereographs
AEEGHOPRRSTY	stereography
AEEGIIILLLST	illegalities
AEEGIIILLMTT	illegitimate
AEEGIIILMSTT	legitimatise
AEEGIIILMTTZ	legitimatize
AEEGIIINSTTV	negativities
AEEGIIKNNOSS	kainogenesis
AEEGIIILLMTTY	legitimately
AEEGIILLSSTV	legislatives
AEEGIILLSTTU	aiguillettes
AEEGIILNNORS	legionnaires
AEEGIILNNPSS	palingenesis
AEEGIILNNRST	eternalising
AEEGIILNNRTV	interleaving
AEEGIILNNRTZ	eternalizing
AEEGIILNRSST	gelatinisers
AEEGIILNRSTZ	gelatinizers
AEEGIILRRSTU	regularities
AEEGIINMNNORT	ingeneration
AEEGIINNNRTT	entertaining
	intenerating
AEEGIINNRTVW	interweaving
AEEGIINORRTV	reinvigorate
AEEGIINPRRTV	privateering
AEEGIINSSTTV	investigates
AEEGIJNNRTUV	rejuvenating
AEEGIKLLNPSW	sleepwalking
AEEGIKNNNSSS	sneakingness
AEEGILLMNRTY	regimentally
AEEGILLNSSTT	tessellating
AEEGILLRSSST	legislatress
AEEGILLRSSTU	legislatures
AEEGILLRTUVY	regulatively
AEEGILMNNRST	realignments
AEEGILMNNTTU	integumental
AEEGILNNNOPT	longipennate
AEEGILNNPSSS	pleasingness
AEEGILNNRTTY	entreatingly
AEEGILOORSTT	teratologies
AEEGIMNNOSTT	segmentation
AEEGIMNNRRTU	remunerating
AEEGIMNNRSST	reassignment
AEEGIMNNRSUV	maneuverings
AEEGIMNNOSTTW	witenagemots
AEEGIMNPRTTT	reattempting
AEEGIMNRRSST	mastersinger
AEEGIMSSSTTU	guesstimates
AEEGINNNSSSU	sanguineness
AEEGINOPRRRT	peregrinator
AEEGINORRRSZ	reorganizers
AEEGINORRSTT	interrogates
AEEGINORRTVW	overwatering
AEEGINPPRRTT	perpetrating
AEEGINPPRTTU	perpetuating
AEEGINRRSTTV	tergiversant
AEEGIOPRRSTV	prerogatives
AEEGKNOORSTU	keratogenous
AEEGLLMNOOPR	prolegomenal
AEEGLLMNOPSY	splenomegaly
AEEGLLMNRUWZ	mangelwurzel
AEEGLMNNORTV	governmental

AEEGLNNOORTT	Lot-et-Garonne
AEEGLOORSTVV	overvoltages
AEEGMMNNORTTY	magnetometry
AEEGMNORRSTV	overgarments
AEEGNRRSSSST	transgresses
AEEGPRRSSSSU	supergrasses
AEEHHHILNSTY	heathenishly
AEEHHILMMNTU	helianthemum
AEEHHILNSSTU	helianthuses
AEEHHILNSTTU	unhealthiest
AEEHHILOPRTY	heliotherapy
AEEHHIMNPRSW	New Hampshire
AEEHHIMPRRTY	hyperthermia
AEEHHIRSSTWW	whitewashers
AEEHHLLLMOPS	Pelham Holles
AEEHHLMPRRTY	hyperthermal
AEEHHNOPPRTY	phanerophyte
AEEHHNORSSTT	hearthstones
AEEHHOPPRTTY	phreatophyte
AEEHIIIMNOPT	Amenhotep III
AEEHIIKNPRSY	hyperkinesia
AEEHIIKNSSST	kinaesthesis
AEEHIILMOPST	epitheliomas
AEEHIILRSSTV	shrievalties
AEEHIIMOOPSS	haemopoiesis
AEEHIINORSTT	etherisation
AEEHIINORTTZ	etherization
AEEHIKLMRRSS	sharemilkers
AEEHILLPPRRY	peripherally
AEEHILMMOOST	mesothelioma
AEEHILMPRRSY	hyperrealism
AEEHILNPPRSS	planispheres
AEEHILNSSSTT	stealthiness
AEEHILPRRSTY	hyperrealist
AEEHILPRRTYY	hyperreality
AEEHILPSSTTT	telepathists
AEEHILSTUVXY	exhaustively
AEEHIMNNORTT	nitromethane
AEEHIMNOPRTZ	promethazine
AEEHIMOPRSSV	overemphasis
AEEHIMOSSSST	somaesthesis
AEEHINNNOOST	hootenannies
AEEHINNOPPRS	apprehension
AEEHINOORSTU	heteroousian
AEEHINOPRRTY	erythropenia
AEEHINOPRSTU	neuropathies
AEEHINOPSSTV	topheaviness
AEEHINORSTTT	titanotheres
AEEHINSSSTTT	anesthetists
AEEHIOOPSSST	apotheosises
AEEHIOOPSSTZ	apotheosizes
AEEHIPPRRXYY	hyperpyrexia
AEEHKMPRRSTY	hypermarkets
AEEHKNOORRTY	heterokaryon
AEEHLLMMORWY	yellowhammer
AEEHLLMNNOPY	phenomenally
AEEHLLMNNRTT	enthrallment
AEEHLLMNOOPT	metallophone
AEEHLLMORTXY	exothermally
AEEHLMNNRSTT	enthralments
AEEHLMNORSTT	stenothermal
AEEHLMNRSSSS	harmlessness

AEEHLMORSTTW	Tower Hamlets
AEEHLMPRRSUU	superhumeral
AEEHLNOPRTUY	polyurethane
AEEHLOPRSTTY	heteroplasty
AEEHMMNNORSST	hammerstones
AEEHMMNNRSTUX	xeranthemums
AEEHMMOOPRST	metamorphose
AEEHMNNOPRTY	hymenopteran
AEEHMOORSSTX	mesothoraxes
AEEHMORRSSTW	whoremasters
AEEHMORRSTWY	whoremastery
AEEHMORSSSTU	housemasters
AEEHMORSTTUY	erythematous
AEEHNNOPRSSW	answerphones
AEEHNNORRSTT	northeastern
AEEHNORRSSTT	northeasters
AEEHNORSSTTU	southeastern
AEEHOPRRSSTT	stratosphere
AEEHORSSSTTU	southeasters
AEEIIIILLRSTT	literalities
AEEIIILMRRTZ	remilitarize
AEEIIILNQSTU	inequalities
AEEIIKLMNPRS	marlinespike
AEEIIILLLRTTY	illiterately
AEEIILLMRSTU	mitrailleuse
AEEIILLNOSTV	televisional
AEEIILLNPSTT	pestilential
AEEIILLNSSSV	villainesses
AEEIIILLRRTVY	irrelatively
AEEIILMMORRS	memorialiser
AEEIILMMORRZ	memorializer
AEEIILMMORSS	memorialises
AEEIILMMORSZ	memorializes
AEEIILMNOOST	emotionalise
AEEIILMNOOTZ	emotionalize
AEEIILMNPRSS	imperialness
AEEIILMNRRSS	mineralisers
AEEIILMNRRSZ	mineralizers
AEEIILMNSSST	essentialism
AEEIILMPRTVY	imperatively
AEEIILMRRSST	semitrailers
AEEIILMRSTTU	multiseriate
AEEIILNNPSTT	penitentials
AEEIILNNRSST	internalises
AEEIILNNRSTZ	internalizes
AEEIILNNSSST	inessentials
AEEIILNORSST	orientalises
AEEIILNORSTZ	orientalizes
AEEIILNRRSST	literariness
AEEIILNRSSUV	universalise
AEEIILNRSTTU	neutralities
AEEIILNRSUVZ	universalize
AEEIILNSSSTT	essentialist
AEEIILNSSSTU	sensualities
AEEIILNSSTTY	sensiatility
AEEIILOPTTVX	exploitative
AEEIILPPRSSU	Upper Silesia
AEEIIMMSSSTT	misestimates
AEEIIMNNSSTT	intimateness
AEEIIMNRRRST	intermarries
AEEIINNNORTT	inteneration
AEEIINNOPRSS	pensionaries

AEEIINNNORSTT	eternisation
AEEIINNNORTTZ	eternization
AEEIINNPRTTY	penitentiary
AEEIINNRRTTU	intrauterine
AEEIINOPPRTT	Pointe-à-Pitre
AEEIINORRSTT	reiterations
AEEIINQRSTTU	quaternities
AEEIINRSSTUZ	suzerainties
AEEIINSSTUVV	vesuvianites
AEEIIPRTTUVV	vituperative
AEEIJLOPRTVY	pejoratively
AEEIJMMOPRRS	major premise
AEEIJNNORTUV	rejuvenation
AEEIKMNNSSST	mistakenness
AEEIKMOORSTT	keratotomies
AEEILLLNSTVY	Stanleyville
AEEILLLSTUVY	televisually
AEEILLMNRRTY	artillerymen
AEEILLNNPRTT	interpellant
AEEILLNNPSTY	septennially
AEEILLNNSTTY	sententially
AEEILLNOSSTT	tessellation
AEEILLNOSSTV	volatileness
AEEILLNQSTUY	sequentially
AEEILLNQTUVY	equivalently
AEEILLNRRSTT	interstellar
AEEILLNRRTVY	irrelevantly
AEEILLNSSSST	taillessness
AEEILLNSSSUV	allusiveness
AEEILLOPSTVY	Yelisavetpol
AEEILMMNNPST	impanelments
AEEILMNNNRSS	mannerliness
AEEILMNORSST	salinometers
AEEILMNPSTTU	penultimates
AEEILMNRSSST	masterliness
AEEILMNSSTTU	ultimateness
AEEILMOPRRST	polarimeters
AEEILMORRSST	solarimeters
AEEILMPRRSSU	superrealism
AEEILNNNOSST	nonessential
AEEILNNNRSST	internalness
AEEILNNOPSTX	exponentials
AEEILNNPSSSS	painlessness
AEEILNNPSSTU	peninsulates
AEEILNNSSSTU	unessentials
AEEILNOPRRTT	interpolater
AEEILNOPRSSS	personalises
AEEILNOPRSST	personalties
AEEILNOPRSSX	expressional
AEEILNOPRSSZ	personalizes
AEEILNOPRSTT	interpolates
AEEILNPRRSST	interspersal
AEEILNRRSSTU	neutralisers
AEEILNRRSTUZ	neutralizers
AEEILNRSSTTX	externalists
AEEILPRRSSTU	superrealist
AEEILPRSSTUV	superlatives
AEEILPRSSUVY	persuasively
AEEILRRRSSTT	terrestrials
AEEILRRSTTTU	litterateurs
AEEIMMNORSTT	amortisement
AEEIMMNORTTZ	amortizement

AEEIMMNRSSTU	immatureness	AEELMOOPRSTU	somatopleure
AEEIMMNRSTTT	mistreatment	AEELMOPRSSTT	plastometers
AEEIMMNSSTTT	misstatement	AEELNORSTUXY	extraneously
AEEIMNNNORTT	intermontane	AEELNRRSSTVY	transversely
AEEIMNNNNRSST	insnarements	AEELOOPPRTUV	overpopulate
AEEIMNNNNRSTT	entrainments	AEELOPSSTTUX	expostulates
AEEIMNNORRTU	remuneration	AEELQSSTTUUY	statuesquely
AEEIMNNNORSTT	senarmontite	AEEMNNNNNOPRT	nonpermanent
AEEIMNNNORSTU	enumerations	AEEMNOORTUUV	outmanoeuvre
	mountaineers	AEEMNOPRRSTY	pyranometers
AEEIMNNOSSTT	maisonnettes	AEEMNOQRSTTU	quantometers
AEEIMNNRSTTT	intreatments	AEEMNOQSSSSU	squamoseness
AEEIMNNSSTTT	instatements	AEEMNORRRSTU	remunerators
AEEIMNOPRSST	impersonates	AEEMNORRSSTT	remonstrates
AEEIMNORRTTX	exterminator	AEEMNORSTUUV	outmaneuvers
AEEIMOPRRSTV	vaporimeters	AEEMPQRRTTUV	Empty Quarter
AEEIMRSSSTTY	systematiser	AEENNOPRRSTU	neuropterans
AEEIMRSSTTYZ	systematizer	AEENNORSSSUV	ravenousness
AEEIMSSSSTTY	systematises	AEENNOSSSSUU	nauseousness
AEEIMSSSTTYZ	systematizes	AEENOPRRSSTT	paternosters
AEEINNOOPRTV	nonoperative	AEENORRSSTXY	extrasensory
AEEINNOORSTX	exonerations	AEENQRSSSTTU	sequestrants
AEEINNOPRSTT	penetrations	AEENRRRSSTTV	transverters
	presentation	AEEOOPRSTUUX	autoexposure
AEEINNOSTTUV	eventuations	AEEOPPRRRSTT	perpetrators
AEEINNOSTTUX	extenuations	AEEOPRRSTTTU	tetrapterous
AEEINNPRRRTU	intrapreneur	AEEOQRRSSTTU	sequestrator
AEEINOORRSSU	aeroneurosis	AEFFGILLLMOR	flagelliform
AEEINOORTTTX	extortionate	AEFFGIMSSTUU	suffumigates
AEEINOPPRRTT	perpetration	AEFFGINORSTV	overstaffing
AEEINOPPRTTU	perpetuation	AEFFHILNSSTU	faithfulness
AEEINOPPSSST	appositeness	AEFFIIMNORRS	foraminifers
AEEINOPRRSTV	preservation	AEFFILLMMMRS	flimflammers
AEEINOPRRSTY	arsenopyrite	AEFFILORSSSY	fairyflosses
AEEINORRRSVY	reversionary	AEFFKNRRRSTU	frankfurters
AEEINORRSSST	reassertions	AEFGGGILNOPR	leapfrogging
AEEINORRSSTV	reservations	AEFGGHINORRT	forgathering
AEEINORRSTVX	extraversion	AEFGGILLNNUY	Lingayen Gulf
AEEINPRSSUUV	unpersuasive	AEFGHHINORTY	Fotheringhay
AEEINPRSTUXY	Saint-Exupéry	AEFGHHOORRTU	thoroughfare
AEEINRSSTTTV	transvestite	AEFGHHOORTTU	aforethought
AEEINRSTTTUV	sternutative	AEFGHHORTTTU	afterthought
AEEIOPPRRSTX	expropriates	AEFGHIINNORS	refashioning
AEEIORRSSTTV	restoratives	AEFGHIIRSSTU	guitarfishes
AEEIPRRSSSTT	stripteasers	AEFGIILRTUVY	figuratively
AEEIPRRSSSTU	pasteurisers	AEFGIINNRRST	fraternising
AEEIPRRSSTUZ	pasteurizers	AEFGIINNRRTZ	fraternizing
AEEJNORRSTUV	rejuvenators	AEFGILLMNNUY	meaningfully
AEEKLMNRSSUW	lukewarmness	AEFGILLNORST	forestalling
AEEKLMORRSTW	metalworkers	AEFGILLNRSST	fingerstalls
AEEKMORRSSTT	masterstroke	AEFGILLNRTTY	flatteringly
AEEKMPRRSSTU	supermarkets	AEFGILLNSSUW	wineglassful
AEEKNPRRSSTU	supertankers	AEFGILLOPRTY	profligately
AEELLLMNOTVY	malevolently	AEFGILNNOORS	gonfaloniers
AEELLMNORSTT	reallotments	AEFGILNNRTTU	unflattering
AEELLMNPPSTU	supplemental	AEFGIMNNRSTT	ingraftments
AEELLMORRSST	steamrollers	AEFGINNNNOTT	nonfattening
AEELLNORSSTW	stonewallers	AEFGINNRRRST	transferring
AEELMNRSTTUV	voltammeters	AEFGINRRSSTU	transfigures
AEELMNOPRSST	temporalness	AEFGLLNRTUUY	ungratefully
AEELMNOPRTUY	Merleau-Ponty	AEFGOORRRSTY	agroforestry
AEELMNPRRSTU	premenstrual	AEFHHLOOPSST	photoflashes

AEFHIINNSSST	faintishness
AEFHIOPRRSST	parrotfishes
AEFHKLNNSSTU	thankfulness
AEFHLLMOSSTY	fathomlessly
AEFHLNRSSTUW	wrathfulness
AEFHOOPRRSTT	shatterproof
AEFIIILLRRST	fritillaries
AEFIIILMNSST	semifinalist
AEFIIILNRTTV	infiltrative
AEFIIIMNNOST	feminisation
AEFIIIMNNOTZ	feminization
AEFIILLMOTTU	multifoliate
AEFIILLNOOTU	unifoliolate
AEFIILLNRTUV	interfluvial
AEFIILMNORUV	fluviomarine
AEFIILNOOPRT	perfoliation
AEFIILNOOSTX	exfoliations
AEFIILNORSTT	frontalities
AEFIILRSSUVV	flaviviruses
AEFIIMNNNOTT	infotainment
AEFIINNOSSTT	infestations
	sinfoniettas
AEFIINORSTTU	titaniferous
AEFILLRRSSTTU	ultrafilters
AEFILMMNNOOT	monofilament
AEFILMNOSUVX	fluvoxamines
AEFILMORRRSU	formulariser
AEFILMORRRUZ	formularizer
AEFILMORRSSU	formularises
AEFILMORRSUZ	formularizes
AEFILNNOSSTU	fountainless
AEFILNOOPRSS	professional
AEFILNOOPRTV	flavoprotein
AEFILNORSSTW	satinflowers
AEFILOOPRRSS	professorial
AEFILOPPRSSU	papuliferous
AEFIMNNOOSTT	fomentations
AEFIMNNORRST	frontiersman
AEFIMNNOSSSU	infamousness
AEFIMNOOPRRT	preformation
AEFIMNOORRST	reformations
AEFINNORSSTU	stanniferous
AEFINNRRRSST	transferrins
AEFINOOPRRST	perforations
AEFKLLOORRSW	floorwalkers
AEFLLNNSSUUW	unlawfulness
AEFLMMORSSTY	formal system
AEFLNOOPSSTU	teaspoonfuls
AEFLOQRRSUUY	foursquarely
AEFLORRSSTWW	strawflowers
AEFMNORRRSST	transformers
AEFMOOPRSSTT	foretopmasts
AEFNNORSTTUU	unfortunates
AEGGGIINNRRS	grangerising
AEGGGIINNRRZ	grangerizing
AEGGGILNNOTU	agglutinogen
AEGGGILNRSTY	staggeringly
AEGGGILNRSWY	swaggeringly
AEGGGIMNORRT	remortgaging
AEGGHHILNOST	Golan Heights
AEGGHHIMNORR	hemorrhaging
AEGGHIIJLNNO	Heilongjiang

	Heilong Jiang
AEGGHIILLNNST	nightingales
AEGGHILNRSTU	slaughtering
AEGGHIOORSTU	South Georgia
AEGGHLNOOSTT	snaggletooth
AEGGHLOOPRRS	logographers
AEGGHOOOPRYZ	zoogeography
AEGGIIILLLNS	illegalising
AEGGIIILLLNZ	illegalizing
AEGGIIILMNTT	legitimating
AEGGIIILNNST	gelatinising
AEGGIIILNNTZ	gelatinizing
AEGGIIIMNNNT	ingeminating
AEGGIIIMNNST	enigmatising
AEGGIIIMNNTZ	enigmatizing
AEGGIILLNORS	allegorising
AEGGIILLNORZ	allegorizing
AEGGIILNRRSU	regularising
AEGGIILNRRUZ	regularizing
AEGGIIMNNPRT	impregnating
AEGGIIMNSTTU	guestimating
AEGGIINNNNSU	ensanguining
AEGGIINNORRS	reorganising
AEGGIINNORRZ	reorganizing
AEGGIINNPRSS	preassigning
AEGGIINNPRSY	panegyrising
AEGGIINNPRYZ	panegyrizing
AEGGIINRSTTU	ingurgitates
AEGGILOORSTT	geratologist
AEGGILORRSUY	gregariously
AEGGIMNNNORW	warmongering
AEGGINNPRSSS	graspingness
AEGGINRRSTTU	regurgitants
AEGGLOOORSTY	astrogeology
AEGGMNNOORRT	rontgenogram
AEGHHIIINSTWW	whitewashing
AEGHHILOPRRT	lithographer
AEGHHIPRSUWY	superhighway
AEGHHLOPRSSU	ploughshares
AEGHHMNOPRRY	hymnographer
AEGHHMOPRRST	thermographs
AEGHHMOPRRTY	thermography
AEGHHNOOPPRR	phonographer
AEGHHOOPPRRT	photographer
	rephotograph
AEGHHOOPRRRT	orthographer
AEGHIILMNRST	thermalising
AEGHIILMNRTZ	thermalizing
AEGHIILMNSST	almightiness
AEGHIILNSTTY	hesitatingly
AEGHIILOPPRS	lipographies
AEGHIIMNNRUZ	rehumanizing
AEGHIINNSTTU	unhesitating
AEGHIIPPRSST	epigraphists
AEGHILLMOPSU	melliphagous
AEGHILLMPRST	lamplighters
AEGHILMNNSTU	languishment
AEGHILMOOSTT	hematologist
AEGHILNOOSST	anthologises
AEGHILNOOSTZ	anthologizes
AEGHILNRSTTY	shatteringly
AEGHILOOPSTZ	pathologizes

717

AEGHILQRRTTU	quarterlight
AEGHIMMNOSST	mesognathism
AEGHIMNNRSST	garnishments
AEGHIMNOOPRS	nomographies
AEGHIMNORSUW	housewarming
AEGHIMOOPRST	mastigophore
AEGHIMOPRSSS	seismographs
AEGHIMOPRSSY	seismography
AEGHINNNRSSU	unharnessing
AEGHINOOPRSS	nosographies
AEGHINORSSUW	warehousings
AEGHINRRSSTT	heartstrings
AEGHINRSSSTT	straightness
AEGHIOOPPRST	topographies
AEGHIOPPRRSY	pyrographies
AEGHIRSSTTHW	strawweights
AEGHLMNNOORS	longshoreman
AEGHLMOORTUY	rheumatology
AEGHLOPRRSXY	xylographers
AEGHLORSSTUU	slaughterous
AEGHMNOOOPTT	photomontage
AEGHMNOOPRRS	monographers
	nomographers
AEGHMNOOSSTT	gnathostomes
AEGHMNOOSSTU	mesognathous
AEGHMNOPPRSU	pneumographs
AEGHNNOOPRTY	anthropogeny
AEGHNOOPPRRR	pornographer
AEGHNOOPRRSS	nosographers
AEGHNOOPSSTU	stenophagous
AEGHOOPPRRST	topographers
AEGHOOPRRTUV	photogravure
AEGHOPPRRRSY	pyrographers
AEGHOPPRRSSS	grasshoppers
AEGHOPPRRSTY	typographers
AEGHOPPSSYYZ	zygapophyses
AEGIIIKNNRST	keratinising
AEGIIIKNNRTZ	keratinizing
AEGIIILMNNRS	mineralising
AEGIIILMNNRZ	mineralizing
AEGIIILMNOTT	legitimation
AEGIIILNRSTV	relativising
	revitalising
AEGIIILNRTVZ	relativizing
	revitalizing
AEGIIIMNNNOT	ingemination
AEGIIIMNNNST	inseminating
AEGIIINORTVV	invigorative
AEGIIINRSTVW	West Virginia
AEGIIKLMNPRS	marlingspike
AEGIILLMMMRS	milligrammes
AEGIILLMRRSU	guerrillaism
AEGIILLNNOTW	wellingtonia
AEGIILLNNRST	reinstalling
AEGIILLNPRVY	prevailingly
AEGIILMMNNST	misalignment
AEGIILMNNRST	streamlining
AEGIILMNORSS	regionalisms
AEGIILMNORST	mineralogist
AEGIILMOOPRS	oligospermia
AEGIILNNNSSU	ungainliness
AEGIILNNORTU	urinogenital
AEGIILNNPPRT	interlapping
AEGIILNNPRUV	unprevailing
AEGIILNNRSTU	neutralising
AEGIILNNRTTY	intreatingly
AEGIILNNRTUZ	neutralizing
AEGIILNNSSTV	vigilantness
AEGIILNORRSV	revalorising
AEGIILNORRVZ	revalorizing
AEGIILNORSST	regionalists
AEGIILNPPRTV	livetrapping
AEGIILNPRSTT	earsplitting
AEGIILNRSSSU	singularises
AEGIILNRSSUZ	singularizes
AEGIILOOSSTT	aetiologists
AEGIILRRRTUY	irregularity
AEGIIMMNRSSU	mismeasuring
AEGIIMNNNORT	renominating
AEGIIMNNOPRT	impregnation
AEGIIMNNOPTT	pigmentation
AEGIIMNSSSUV	vaginismuses
AEGIIMRSSSTT	stigmatisers
AEGIIMRSSTTZ	stigmatizers
AEGIINNNOSST	angiotensins
AEGIINNNRSTT	intransigent
AEGIINNOOSTT	negotiations
AEGIINNOPPRT	reappointing
AEGIINNOPTTT	potentiating
AEGIINNORRTV	overtraining
AEGIINNORSST	resignations
AEGIINNORSTT	integrations
AEGIINNPPSTU	unappetising
AEGIINNPPTUZ	unappetizing
AEGIINNRSTTU	intriguantes
AEGIINNSTUXY	exsanguinity
AEGIINOPRRSV	overpraising
AEGIINORRSTT	registration
AEGIINORSTTV	investigator
AEGIINPRSSTU	pasteurising
AEGIINPRSTUZ	pasteurizing
AEGIINPRTTUV	vituperating
AEGIKLMNORTW	metalworking
AEGILLLNPRUY	prelingually
AEGILLMPRSSU	aspergillums
AEGILLMRSTTU	metallurgist
AEGILLNNOSTW	stonewalling
AEGILLNOPRTT	preallotting
AEGILLNOSTUY	gelatinously
AEGILMMNRSTY	stammeringly
AEGILMNNNNOT	nonalignment
AEGILMNNOQTU	magniloquent
AEGILMNOORST	glomerations
AEGILMNOPRSU	pelargoniums
AEGILMNRSTTY	smatteringly
AEGILMOOOSST	somatologies
AEGILMORSSTT	stigmasterol
AEGILNNNOSTU	sanguinolent
AEGILNNOSSTU	langoustines
AEGILNNRSSSU	singularness
AEGILNNRSTTY	astringently
AEGILNOOPRVY	parleyvooing
AEGILNOPPRTU	repopulating
AEGILNRRSSUY	reassuringly

AEGILOORSTTT	teratologist
AEGILOOSSTTU	tautologises
AEGILOOSTTUZ	tautologizes
AEGILORRSSTU	grossularite
AEGILRSSTTUU	gutturalises
AEGILRSTTUUZ	gutturalizes
AEGIMMORSSTU	mesogastrium
AEGIMNNORSUV	manoeuvrings
AEGIMNNRSTTU	menstruating
AEGIMNOPRRST	impregnators
AEGIMOORSSTT	gastrotomies
AEGINNOORRSV	vinegarroons
AEGINNOOSTXY	oxygenations
AEGINNOSSUUX	exsanguinous
AEGINOORRRTT	interrogator
AEGINOORRSTV	overroasting
AEGINOPRSTUX	expurgations
AEGIPRRSTUVY	supergravity
AEGKLORRSSSW	glassworkers
AEGLMNOOPTUV	pneumatology
AEGLNOOSTUUV	autogenously
AEGLNRSSTTUU	gutturalness
AEGLOORSTUUV	outrageously
AEGMNOORRSST	gastronomers
AEGNORRRSSST	transgressor
AEGOOPSSTTUV	steatopygous
AEHHILNOPPRT	philanthrope
AEHHILOPSTTU	thiosulphate
AEHHIMNOPRSS	horsemanship
AEHHIMOOPSTT	homeopathist
AEHHINNNOPSTV	hyphenations
AEHHINNOPTXY	hypoxanthine
AEHHIOPPSSST	phosphatises
AEHHIOPPSSTZ	phosphatizes
AEHHIORSTTTW	whitethroats
AEHHLLOPSTTY	thallophytes
AEHHLMOOPRTT	photothermal
AEHHLMOOPSTX	exophthalmos
AEHHLMOPSTUX	exophthalmus
AEHHLOOOPPRT	lophophorate
AEHHLOOPRSTU	Althorp House
AEHHNOPPRTYY	hypnotherapy
AEHHOOPPRSST	phosphorates
AEHHOOPPRTTY	phototherapy
AEHHOOPRRSST	sharpshooter
AEHHOPRSSTTU	Theophrastus
AEHIIILNOOPS	eosinophilia
AEHIIIMNNOST	thiosinamine
AEHIIIMNNSTU	inhumanities
AEHIIKLNOSST	Thessaloníki
AEHIILLOPRSU	ailurophiles
AEHIILLPSSTT	philatelists
AEHIILNOPRST	relationship
AEHIILOPSSST	hospitalises
AEHIILOPSSTZ	hospitalizes
AEHIILPRRSTT	hairsplitter
AEHIINNOPRTT	trephination
AEHIINOORSTT	theorisation
AEHIINOORTTZ	theorization
AEHIINOPRRSS	parishioners
AEHIINOPRRST	prehistorian
AEHIINRSSTUW	White Russian

AEHIIRRSSTTW	shirtwaister
AEHIKMNNNORS	Krishna Menon
AEHILLMORSTY	isothermally
AEHILLOORSTU	heliolatrous
AEHILLOPRSST	hospitallers
AEHILLOPSTXY	phyllotaxies
AEHILMNNOOPS	aminophenols
AEHILMNOOPSU	anemophilous
AEHILMNOSTXY	hematoxylins
AEHILMNOSSSU	qualmishness
AEHILMOOPRST	photorealism
AEHILMOOPSST	homoplasties
AEHILNOPSTXY	phytoalexins
AEHILNPRRSTY	platyrrhines
AEHILNPRSSST	shinplasters
AEHILOOPRSTT	photorealist
AEHIMMMOPRST	metamorphism
AEHIMMNNNOOT	man in the moon
AEHIMNNOOPRT	enantiomorph
AEHIMMNNOOSSU	Mansion House
AEHIMNNORTTV	North Vietnam
AEHIMNNOSSSW	womanishness
AEHIMNNOSSTT	astonishment
AEHIMNNPRSTT	transhipment
AEHIMNNQSTUV	vanquishment
AEHIMNOPRSST	misanthropes
AEHIMNOSTTUV	South Vietnam
AEHIMOOOSSST	homoeostasis
AEHIMPRSSSTY	sympathisers
AEHIMPRSSTYZ	sympathizers
AEHINNPSSSTY	synthespians
AEHINOOPRRTT	prototherian
AEHINOOPRSST	epanorthosis
AEHINOOPSSTT	photonasties
AEHINOORSTTX	exhortations
AEHINOPRSSTT	antistrophes
AEHINOPRSTTV	attorneyship
AEHINPPRRSST	partnerships
AEHIOOPPRSST	apostrophise
AEHIOOPPRSTZ	apostrophize
AEHIOOPSSTTT	osteopathist
AEHIOOSSSTTU	South Ossetia
AEHIOPQRSSTU	quaestorship
AEHIOPRRSTWV	praiseworthy
AEHIOPSSSSTV	hypostasises
AEHIOPSSSTTV	hypostatises
AEHIOPSSSTYZ	hypostasizes
AEHIOPSSTTYZ	hypostatizes
AEHLLLMOOPRS	allelomorphs
AEHLLLNOPPSY	phylloplanes
AEHLMNPRSUUV	superhumanly
AEHLMOPPRRSV	lamprophyres
AEHLNOPRSSTU	Southern Alps
AEHLNOPRSTUV	polyurethans
AEHLNOPSSTUV	polyanthuses
AEHLOPPRSTUV	pyrosulphate
AEHMMOOOOPRST	ommatophores
AEHMMOOPRSTU	metamorphous
AEHMNOOPRTUX	pneumothorax
AEHNOOPRRSSU	sarrusophone
AEHNOOPRRSTT	orthopterans
AEHNORRSSSTY	synarthroses

AEHOOPRRRSST	arthrospores
AEHOOPRRSSTT	trapshooters
AEIIIILMRSST	similarities
AEIIIILNTTVV	initiatively
AEIIIILRSTTV	trivialities
AEIIIINRSTTX	initiatrixes
AEIIILLMNNOR	millionnaire
AEIIILLMNORS	millionaires
AEIIILLMNTUV	illuminative
AEIIILLNORRT	trillionaire
AEIIILMMORST	immoralities
AEIIILMMPRSS	imperialisms
AEIIILMNNOST	eliminations
AEIIILMNSSST	antimissiles
AEIIILMPRSST	imperialists
AEIIILNPRSST	pleinairists
AEIIILNRSTTT	interstitial
AEIIILPRSSTU	spiritualise
AEIIILPRSTUZ	spiritualize
AEIIILRSTTUV	virtualities
AEIIIMNNNOST	insemination
AEIIIMNORSSS	missionaries
AEIIIMNOSSTT	itemisations
AEIIIMNOSTTZ	itemizations
AEIIIMNRSSTU	miniaturises
AEIIIMNRSTTV	ministrative
AEIIIMNRSTUZ	miniaturizes
AEIIINNOOPTV	opinionative
AEIIINNORSTT	itinerations
AEIIINNRSTTV	intransitive
AEIIINORSTTV	invitatories
AEIIIOPPRTTV	propitiative
AEIIKKNORSSY	karyokinesis
AEIIKLLOPRST	realpolitiks
AEIIKLMNPRSS	marlinspikes
AEIILLLLMNNY	millennially
AEIILLLNTUUX	luxullianite
AEIILLLPRRTU	pluriliteral
AEIILLMMMORY	immemorially
AEIILLMSSTTU	satellitiums
AEIILLMSTUVY	simulatively
AEIILLNNSTTY	intestinally
AEIILLNQRSTU	tranquillise
AEIILLNQRTUZ	tranquillize
AEIILLRSSTTU	Little Russia
AEIILLRSTTUV	illustrative
AEIILMMNOOST	emotionalism
AEIILMMORRST	immortaliser
AEIILMMORRTZ	immortalizer
AEIILMMORSST	immortalises
	memorialists
AEIILMMORSTZ	immortalizes
AEIILMNNOTVY	nominatively
AEIILMNNSSTT	militantness
AEIILMNOORST	meliorations
AEIILMNOOSTT	emotionalist
AEIILMNOOTTY	emotionality
AEIILMNOPRSS	impressional
AEIILMNORSST	misrelations
	orientalisms
AEIILMNOSSTT	testimonials
AEIILMNRSSUV	universalism

AEIILMNRTUVY	ruminatively
AEIILMNSTTUY	simultaneity
AEIILMPRTTTU	multipartite
AEIILMSSTTUV	stimulatives
AEIILNNNQQUU	quinquennial
AEIILNNOOSTV	novelisation
AEIILNNOOTVZ	novelization
AEIILNNOSTTV	ventilations
AEIILNNPRTTY	tripinnately
AEIILNOOPSTX	expositional
AEIILNOOPTTX	exploitation
AEIILNOOSTVW	vowelisation
AEIILNOOTVWZ	vowelization
AEIILNOPPSTY	inappositely
AEIILNOPTTTY	potentiality
AEIILNORSSST	solitariness
AEIILNORSSTT	orientalists
AEIILNQRRTUZ	tranquilizer
AEIILNQRSTUZ	tranquilizes
AEIILNQTTUVY	quantitively
AEIILNRSSTUV	universalist
AEIILNRSTTVY	transitively
AEIILNRSTUVY	universality
AEIILNSTUUXY	unisexuality
AEIILOPPSTSV	appositively
AEIILORRRSTT	territorials
AEIILPRRTTTY	tripartitely
AEIIMMNNSSTT	immanentists
AEIIMMNOORST	memorisation
AEIIMMNOORTZ	memorization
AEIIMMNNNOORT	renomination
AEIIMMNNOOSTT	monetisation
AEIIMMNNOOTTZ	monetization
AEIIMNNOPSSX	expansionism
AEIIMNNORSST	inseminators
	Nestorianism
	nitrosamines
AEIIMNNORSTT	terminations
AEIIMNNORSTV	verminations
AEIIMNNOSSST	sensationism
AEIIMNOOPRST	operationism
AEIIMNOPRSTT	impetrations
AEIIMNRSSSTV	transmissive
AEIIMOOORSTV	ovariotomies
AEIIMOPPRRST	impropriates
AEIIMRRSTTUV	triumvirates
AEIINNNORSTV	innervations
AEIINNNORTTU	antineutrino
AEIINNNQSTTU	Saint-Quentin
AEIINNOOPSTT	anteposition
AEIINNOORSTT	orientations
AEIINNOPRSTU	resupination
AEIINNOPSSTX	expansionist
AEIINNORSTTT	strontianite
AEIINOPPRRST	perspiration
AEIINOPPSSTT	peptisations
AEIINOPPSTTZ	peptizations
AEIINOPRRSTT	partitioners
	repartitions
AEIINOPRSTTX	extirpations
AEIINOPRTTUV	vituperation
AEIINPRSSSSU	prussianises

AEIINPRSSSUZ	prussianizes	AEINNNORSTTU	antineutrons
AEIINRRSSTTVY	intervarsity	AEINNOOPRSST	personations
AEIINSSSSTTUV	antitussives	AEINNOOSSTTT	ostentations
AEIIOOPRSSTV	vaporosities	AEINNORSSSUV	unsavoriness
AEIIORSSSTUV	Soviet Russia	AEINNORSTTTU	sternutation
AEIJLNORRSSU	journalisers	AEINNOSTTTTU	sustentation
AEIJLNORRSUZ	journalizers	AEINOOPPRRST	apportioners
AEIKLNOPSSTT	kinetoplasts		reapportions
AEIKMNNRSTTU	Turkmenistan	AEINOOPRSTTT	protestation
AEIKMRSSSSTT	taskmistress	AEINOOPRSTTX	exportations
AEILLLLPRRRT	pralltriller	AEINOORRSSTT	restorations
AEILLMMMSSTY	symmetallism	AEINOOSSTTTU	ostentatious
AEILLMNNSSTT	installments	AEINOPRSSTTV	transportive
AEILLMNOPRSY	impersonally	AEINOPRSSSSV	vasopressins
AEILLMNPRSUU	superluminal	AEIOOOOPPPRS	prosopopoeia
AEILLNNORTTY	intolerantly	AEIOOOPPPRSS	prosopopeias
AEILLNOOSTTW	wollastonite	AEIOOPRRRTX	expropriator
AEILLNOQRTUV	ventriloqual	AEIOPPRRRSTY	perspiratory
AEILLNORRTTY	torrentially	AEIOPRRRSTTU	portraitures
AEILLNRSSTUV	surveillants	AEIOPRRSSUVV	parvoviruses
AEILMNNNOOOT	nonemotional	AEIOPRRSTTUV	vituperators
AEILMNNOOPST	Neo-Platonism	AEIORRRSSTTT	Torres Strait
AEILMNNORSST	matronliness	AEIPPRSSSTUUV	suppuratives
AEILMNNOSSTU	noumenalists	AEKLMNNOOPRT	meroplankton
AEILMNNOSSTW	Winston-Salem	AEKLNPPRSTTU	splatterpunk
AEILMNNRSTTU	instrumental	AELLLMORSUVV	marvellously
AEILMNOOPRTT	metropolitan	AELLMMNNOTUV	monumentally
AEILMNOOSSTT	molestations	AELLMNOOOSSS	Solomon's seal
AEILMNOPRRST	trampoliners	AELLOOPPSSUV	polysepalous
AEILMNOQSUUV	equanimously	AELLOOPPSTUV	polypetalous
AEILMNOSSTUU	simultaneous	AELMMRSSSTUU	summersaults
AEILMOORSTTT	stromatolite	AELMNOOOPSSU	monosepalous
AEILMOQSSTTU	milquetoasts	AELMNOOOPSTU	monopetalous
AEILMPSSTUVY	assumptively	AELNOPSSSTUU	patulousness
AEILNNQRSSTU	tranquilness	AELOOPRSTTUX	expostulator
AEILNOOPRRTT	interpolator	AEMNNOORSSTY	stonemasonry
AEILNOOPRSTX	explorations	AEMNNOORRSSTT	remonstrants
AEILNOORTUVY	evolutionary	AEMNOOOPRSTZ	spermatozoon
AEILNOPRSSST	personalists	AEMNOOPRSSTY	trypanosomes
AEILNORRSSTU	serrulations	AEMNOORRRSTT	remonstrator
AEILNORRSUVY	revulsionary	AEMNOQSSSSUU	squamousness
AEILOOOPPPRS	prosopopeial	AEMPRRSSTTUU	superstratum
AEILOOPRSTTY	epistolatory	AENOOPRSSSUV	vaporousness
AEILOPPRRRSU	popularisers	AENOPRRRSSTT	transporters
AEILOPPRRRUZ	popularizers	AENORRSSTTTU	sternutators
AEILOPRSTUVV	voluptuaries	AENORRSTTTUY	sternutatory
AEILRRSSTUUV	ultraviruses	AENPPRSSSTUU	suppressants
AEIMMSSSSTTY	systematisms	AEOOPRRSSSSV	vasopressors
AEIMNNOORSTU	Ore Mountains	AEOOPRRSSTTU	tetrasporous
AEIMNNOPPSTT	appointments	AFFGHLOPSSTT	ploughstaffs
AEIMNNORSTTU	menstruation	AFFGIILLMMMN	flimflamming
AEIMNNOOPRRST	impersonator	AFFGIILLNNSTU	insufflating
AEIMNOPRSSTU	reassumption	AFFHILLNTUUY	unfaithfully
AEIMNOPRSTTU	permutations	AFFIILNNOSTU	insufflation
AEIMNRRSSTTT	transmitters	AFFILNORSSTU	insufflators
AEIMNRSSSTTV	transvestism	AFFLLLORUUVY	flavourfully
AEIMOPPRRSSU	appressorium	AFGGHHIILNTU	highfaluting
AEIMOPRRSSSU	aspersoriums	AFGGIILNRTYY	gratifyingly
AEIMPRSSSTTU	suprematists	AFGGIINPPRTW	giftwrapping
AEIMSSSSTTTY	systematists	AFGHIIKNNRST	rankshifting
AEINNNOPRSTT	transpontine	AFGHLOOPRRUY	fluorography
AEINNNORSSTT	nonresistant	AFGIIILNNRTT	infiltrating

AFGIIILLMNORU	anguilliform
AFGIILLOSTUY	flagitiously
AFGIILNNORTU	fluorinating
AFGIILNNOSTU	antifoulings
AFGIILNSSTYY	satisfyingly
AFGIINNOOPRR	rainproofing
AFGIINNSSTUY	unsatisfying
AFGIMNNORRST	transforming
AFGIMNORRSTY	transmogrify
AFIIILMNNOST	inflationism
AFIIILMNNSST	infantilisms
AFIIILNNORTT	infiltration
AFIIILNNOSTT	inflationist
AFIILMNNOSTU	fulminations
AFIILMORSTUU	multifarious
AFIILNNOORTU	fluorination
AFIILNORRSTT	infiltrators
AFIILORRSSST	fissirostral
AFIIMMNNORST	misinformant
AFIIMNNOORST	informations
AFILLMNOPSTU	slumpflation
AFILMNOORSTU	formulations
AFIMMNORRSST	transformism
AFIMNORRSSTT	transformist
AFINNORSSSTU	transfusions
AFINORRSSTTU	frustrations
AGGGGILLLNOY	lollygagging
AGGGIIILMNPR	pilgrimaging
AGGGIIJJNNOU	Jiang Jing Guo
AGGGILLNRSTY	stragglingly
AGGHHLOPPRSY	glyphographs
AGGHHLOPPRYY	glyphography
AGGHHMOPPRSY	sphygmograph
AGGHIIINPRST	graphitising
AGGHIIINPRTZ	graphitizing
AGGHIIKNNSTV	thanksgiving
AGGHIILOOSST	hagiologists
AGGHIIMNNRST	hamstringing
AGGHILMNOOOT	homologating
AGGHILNOPRXY	xylographing
AGGHILOOPRST	graphologist
AGGHIMNNOOPR	monographing
AGGHLNOOPRVY	pharyngology
AGGHLOOPRSSY	glossography
AGGHLOPPRTYY	glyptography
AGGHMMOPRSSY	sphygmograms
AGGIIIILLNNTV	invigilating
AGGIIIMNSSTT	stigmatising
AGGIIIMNSTTZ	stigmatizing
AGGIIINNORTV	invigorating
AGGIILMNORUZ	glamourizing
AGGIKMNOORST	Magnitogorsk
AGGILMNOPRTU	promulgating
AGGILNOOORST	organologist
AGGILOORSSTT	gastrologist
AGGIMMMNNOOR	monogramming
AGGIMNNORRST	strongarming
AGHHILNOPRTT	triphthongal
AGHHIMNOPSTY	hypognathism
AGHHIOPPRSYY	physiography
AGHHNOOPSTUV	hypognathous
AGHHOOPPSTUV	phytophagous

AGHIILMNPSTY	lymphangitis
AGHIIMNPSSTY	sympathising
AGHIIMNPSTYZ	sympathizing
AGHIINNPPRST	transhipping
AGHILMNOOOOT	homologation
AGHILNNOPSTU	sulphonating
AGHILNOOSSTT	anthologists
AGHILNPRSTUU	sulphurating
AGHILOOPSSTT	pathologists
AGHIMNOOPPPT	photomapping
AGHIMNOOPRST	monographist
AGHIMOPRSTUY	hypogastrium
AGHINNOOPRST	trapshooting
AGHINOOPSTTT	photostating
AGHINOOSSSTY	soothsayings
AGHIOPPSSYYZ	zygapophysis
AGHLLMOOPSUY	gamophyllous
AGHLLNOOORTY	orthogonally
AGHLLOOPSSSY	hypoglossals
AGHLMOOOPRSU	lagomorphous
AGHLNOOOPRTY	anthropology
AGHMNOOPRTYY	pharyngotomy
AGIIIIILNNST	initialising
AGIIIIILNNTZ	initializing
AGIIIILMNRST	militarising
AGIIIILMNRTZ	militarizing
AGIIIILNNOTV	invigilation
AGIIIILNRSTV	trivialising
AGIIIILNRTVZ	trivializing
AGIIILLMMNTU	illuminating
AGIIILLNOSTV	volatilising
AGIIILLNOTVZ	volatilizing
AGIIILNORSTV	invigilators
AGIIILNRSSTV	virginalists
AGIIIMMNORST	immigrations
AGIIIMNNOPSS	impassioning
AGIIINNOORST	originations
AGIIINNOORTV	invigoration
AGIIINNOPRTT	partitioning
AGIIINNOSSTT	instigations
AGIIINNPSSST	inspissating
AGIIINOPPRTT	propitiating
AGIIJLNNORSU	journalising
AGIIJLNNORUZ	journalizing
AGIIKLMNSTTU	multitasking
AGIILLLMNTUU	multilingual
AGIILLLNRTUY	trilingually
AGIILLNORTUV	outrivalling
AGIILLNRSTTU	illustrating
AGIILLOPSSSS	salpiglossis
AGIILMNNOPRT	trampolining
AGIILMNOOORU	Giulio Romano
AGIILNNSSTUY	sustainingly
AGIILNOORSUV	vainglorious
AGIILNOPPRSU	popularising
AGIILNOPPRUZ	popularizing
AGIIMNNOPSTU	impugnations
AGIIMNNRSTTT	transmitting
AGIIMNOOSTTU	autotomising
AGIIMNOOTTUZ	autotomizing
AGIINNOOPPRT	apportioning
AGIINOORRSTV	invigorators

AGIJKNNOPRTU	Tanjungpriok	AHINOOPSSTUY	autohypnosis
AGIKLOORSSTY	karyologists	AHINORRSSSTY	synarthrosis
AGILLMNNOOSU	monolinguals	AHKLLNNOOOPT	holoplankton
AGILLMNOPSSY	plasmolysing	AHLMMOOPSTUY	lymphomatous
AGILLMNOPSYZ	plasmolyzing	AHLMNOSTUXYZ	zanthoxylums
AGILLNOOPSTY	palynologist	AHNOOOPRRTTY	prothonotary
AGILLNOORRST	longirostral	AIIIILNORSTV	virilisation
AGILMNNNSSUUY	unassumingly	AIIIILNORTVZ	virilization
AGILMNOOOOSY	onomasiology	AIIIIMMNNOST	minimisation
AGILMNOOPRTU	promulgation	AIIIIMMNNOTZ	minimization
AGILMOOOSSTT	somatologist	AIIILLLNPSTU	lilliputians
AGILMRSSTTUU	gutturalisms	AIIILLMNNOTU	illumination
AGILNNOOOPRT	prolongation	AIIILLNNOSTT	instillation
AGILNPRSSSUY	surpassingly	AIIILLNOSTTT	titillations
AGILOOOPPRSTY	papyrologist	AIIILMNOOSST	isolationism
AGILOOPRSSTT	patrologists	AIIILMPRSSTU	spiritualism
AGILOORSSSTT	astrologists	AIIILNNOOSST	lionisations
AGILOOSSTTTU	tautologists	AIIILNNOOSTZ	lionizations
AGILORSTTUUY	gratuitously	AIIILNOOSSTT	isolationist
AGIMNNNOORRTY	nonmigratory	AIIILNOSSTTU	utilisations
AGIMNOORSSTT	gastronomist	AIIILNOSTTUZ	utilizations
AGINNOPRRSTT	transporting	AIIILPRSSTTU	spiritualist
AGINOOOPRRST	prorogations	AIIILPRSTTUY	spirituality
AGINOOPRSSTT	protagonists	AIIIMMNNOSTU	immunisation
AGINOORRSSTU	surrogations	AIIIMMNNOTUZ	immunization
AGLLMOOPSUVY	polygamously	AIIIMNNORSTT	ministration
AGLLMOORSUUY	glamourously	AIIIMNOOPSTT	optimisation
AGLLNOORSUUY	languorously	AIIIMNOOPTTZ	optimization
AGLMMNOOOSUY	monogamously	AIIIMNRSSTTU	miniaturists
AGLMOOPRRSTU	promulgators	AIIINNNOOSTU	unionisation
AHHIILMOPSTT	ophthalmitis	AIIINNNOOTUZ	unionization
AHHILLLLSSYY	shillyshally	AIIINNNOSSTU	insinuations
AHHILLMMOOST	homothallism	AIIINNOPRSST	inspirations
AHHILNOOPSTU	anthophilous	AIIINNOPSSST	inspissation
AHHILNOORSTU	holothurians	AIIINNOSSTTU	unitisations
AHHILNOPPRTY	philanthropy	AIIINNOSTTUZ	unitizations
AHHIMNOPSSSW	showmanships	AIIINOOPPRTT	propitiation
AHHINNOPRSTT	strophanthin	AIIINOPRRTTT	tripartition
AHHLLNOPSTXY	xanthophylls	AIIINOPRSTTT	partitionist
AHHNOPRSSTTU	strophanthus	AIIINOSTTTTV	tittivations
AHIIILMNOSTU	humiliations	AIIINRSTTTVY	transitivity
AHIIKMNORSUY	Aum Shinrikyo	AIIKMNNOPRSS	parkinsonism
AHIILMMPRSTU	triumphalism	AIIILLLNOOTV	volitionally
AHIILMPRSTTU	triumphalist	AIIILLLNOSUVY	villainously
AHIILRSSSTTY	hairstylists	AIILLMMNOSTU	multinomials
AHIIMNNOORSU	inharmonious	AIILLMNOORTY	monitorially
AHIIMNOOOSSU	homoiousians	AIILLMNORSTU	illuminators
AHILLMMOOPRS	allomorphism	AIILLNNOOTUV	involutional
AHILLNOORTYZ	horizontally	AIILLNORSTTU	illustration
AHILMNOORSUY	harmoniously	AIILLNQRTTUY	tranquillity
AHILMNPRTTUY	triumphantly	AIILMNNORTTU	malnutrition
AHILMOOOPRTY	homopolarity	AIILMNOOPRST	implorations
AHILNOPRSTUU	sulphuration	AIILMNOPRSTT	trampolinist
AHILOPRRSUXY	pyrrhuloxias	AIILMNOSSTTU	stimulations
AHIMMOOPSSTU	amphistomous	AIILNNOTTUUV	invultuation
AHIMNNOORSUU	unharmonious	AIILNOOOPPST	oppositional
AHIMOOPPPSTU	hippopotamus	AIILNOOPRSSV	provisionals
AHIMOOPPRRST	haptotropism	AIILNOPSSTTU	stipulations
AHIMOOPPRSTU	amphitropous	AIILNORRSSST	sinistrorsal
AHINNOPRSSTU	sinanthropus	AIILNORRSTTY	transitorily
AHINOOPSSSTU	sousaphonist	AIILNOSSSTTY	stylisations
AHINOOPSSSTX	saxophonists	AIILNOSSTTYZ	stylizations

AIILOPRSUVVY	viviparously	BBCEILMOSSTU	combustibles
AIILRSSSTUVV	survivalists	BBCEINRSSSUU	unsubscribes
AIIMMNNOSSSU	manumissions	BBCEJKOORSST	stockjobbers
AIIMMNOPSSTT	pantomimists	BBCEJKOORSTY	stockjobbery
AIIMMNOTTUUY	autoimmunity	BBCEKLORSSTU	blockbusters
AIIMMNSSSTTU	numismatists	BBCELLLOOSWY	collywobbles
AIIMNNORSSST	transmission	BBCENOORRSTU	broncobuster
AIIMNOOORSTT	motorisation	BBCGIJKNOOST	stockjobbing
AIIMNOOORTTZ	motorization	BBCGIKLNOSTU	blockbusting
AIIMNOOPRSSU	parsimonious	BBDDGIILNOUY	bodybuilding
AIIMNOOPRSTT	importations	BBDEEGGKLOOO	gobbledegook
AIIMNOOPRSTX	proximations	BBDEEHHLOOSY	hobbledehoys
AIIMNOOQSTTU	misquotation	BBDEGGKLOOOY	gobbledygook
AIIMOOPPRRRT	impropriator	BBDEILLMOOOS	bloodmobiles
AIINNNORRSTT	nonirritants	BBEEGIILLNRS	gibberellins
AIINNOOOPSST	opsonisation	BBEEGILLORRT	Robbe-Grillet
AIINNOOOPSTZ	opsonization	BBEEGILMRSSU	submergibles
AIINNOOOSSTZ	ozonisations	BBEEILLNRSSU	lubberliness
AIINNOOOSTZZ	ozonizations	BBEEILMRSSSU	submersibles
AIINNORRTTUY	nutritionary	BBEFHIINORSS	ribbonfishes
AIINOOPRRSVY	provisionary	BBEGGHIILNOS	bobsleighing
AIINOPRSSSST	inspissators	BBEHIIILLOPS	bibliophiles
AIINOPRSSSTU	suspirations	BBEHINNOSSSS	snobbishness
AIINORRSTTTU	triturations	BBEILNOSSSUU	bibulousness
AIIOOPPRRSTT	propitiators	BBELLNOSTTUY	bellybuttons
AIIOOPPRRTTY	propitiatory	BBENNORSSSTU	stubbornness
AIIOPRRSSTTT	portraitists	BBGHHINOORSY	hobbyhorsing
AIJMNRRSTTUY	Justin Martyr	BBHHMOOOPRSU	ombrophobous
AIKNOPRRSTUU	Sukarnoputri	BBIIILLOOPST	bibliopolist
AILLLNOOPRSU	allopurinols	BCCCEIIMRRSU	circumscribe
AILLLNOPSTUU	pullulations	BCCDEEEIMNSU	decumbencies
AILLMNNOOPRY	pronominally	BCCDEGHIKNOY	bodychecking
AILLMNOOPSTY	polytonalism	BCCEEEEFINNS	beneficences
AILLMOOPRSST	allotropisms	BCCEEEEHKRRRY	checkerberry
AILLNOOPSTTY	polytonalist	BCCEEELNOOSS	obsolescence
AILLNOOPTTYY	polytonality	BCCEEEMNOSTU	obmutescence
AILLORRSSTTU	illustrators	BCCEEHHLORST	breechcloths
AILMNOORSSTT	monolatrists	BCCEEHKLMOOR	checkerbloom
AILMNORSTUVY	voluntaryism	BCCEEHKLORSTU	breechclouts
AILNOOOPPRRT	proportional	BCCEEHNORRSS	crossbencher
AILNOOPSSTTU	postulations	BCCEEHNORSSS	crossbenches
AILNOPPRTUUY	unpopularity	BCCEEIIMNNSU	incumbencies
AILNORSSTTUV	voluntarists	BCCEEILLLOST	collectibles
AILNORSTTUVY	voluntaryist	BCCEHNOOOPRS	bronchoscope
AILOOPRRSUUY	uproariously	BCCEHORSTTTU	butterscotch
AILOORRSTTUY	traitorously	BCCEILMOORTY	motorbicycle
AIMNOOOPRSTT	somatotropin	BCCHIMOORTTY	thrombocytic
AINOOPRRSSTT	prostrations	BCCHNOOOPRSY	bronchoscopy
AIOORRSSTTTU	astrotourist	BCCINOOSSSUU	subconscious
AKLNNOOOPSTZ	zooplanktons	BCCIOOOPRSST	stroboscopic
AKMOOORSSUUY	Yamoussoukro	BCDDEEEEIINOS	disobedience
ALLOORSSTWWW	swallowworts	BCDDEIIILTUV	deducibility
ALMNOOOSTUUY	autonomously	BCDEEEEFIILNT	indefectible
ALMNOOPRSUYY	paronymously	BCDEEEEILNRSS	credibleness
AMOOPRRRSTTY	protomartyrs	BCDEEEEIORRSS	cerebrosides
BBBCEILMORSU	microbubbles	BCDEEEKLNOTT	bottlenecked
BBBEGIIINNSW	winebibbings	BCDEEEKORRST	stockbreeder
BBCCEEEHKLORS	breechblocks	BCDEEEMNNRUU	unencumbered
BBCDEEEEKNRRU	rubbernecked	BCDEEFIIJSTU	subjectified
BBCDEHIRRSTU	butcherbirds	BCDEEFIILNTY	indefectibly
BBCEELNOOSST	cobblestones	BCDEEGIINRRS	redescribing
BBCEGHILNRTU	nightclubber	BCDEEHMNOSTU	debouchments

BCDEEIINNOST	benedictions
BCDEEILOPRRU	reproducible
BCDEEILORRSU	cloudberries
BCDEEILRSTTU	destructible
BCDEEIMNNRUU	unincumbered
BCDEEIMNRSSU	disencumbers
BCDEEINPRRSU	unprescribed
BCDEEIPRRSSU	superscribed
BCDEGHNRRSSU	bergschrunds
BCDEHILORSSU	subchlorides
BCDEIIILRTUY	reducibility
BCDEIILNORTU	introducible
BCDEIKMNRSTU	dumbstricken
BCDEILOPRRUY	reproducibly
BCDEIORRSSTU	subdirectors
BCDEKLOORSSU	bloodsuckers
BCDENORSTTUU	unobstructed
BCDFHIOORSTY	Body of Christ
BCDGIIKMNORS	mockingbirds
BCDIIILNOOPT	diplobiontic
BCDIIRSSSTTU	subdistricts
BCEEEEGHRRSU	cheeseburger
BCEEEEGILLNR	belligerence
BCEEEEHORSTW	Beecher Stowe
BCEEEELNNOSV	benevolences
BCEEEFILNNTY	beneficently
BCEEEGHILNSY	beseechingly
BCEEEGIINORT	bioenergetic
BCEEEGILLNRY	belligerency
BCEEEGMNRSSU	submergences
BCEEEHIKORRS	chokeberries
BCEEEIILLNSU	ebulliencies
BCEEEIIPRRSS	spiceberries
BCEEEINRSSUV	subservience
BCEEEIRRRSVY	serviceberry
BCEEENPPRSTU	prepubescent
BCEEENQSSSUU	subsequences
BCEEFIIJSSTU	subjectifies
BCEEFILNORSS	forcibleness
BCEEGHIILNNR	Berlichingen
BCEEGIILOOOS	bioecologies
BCEEGIMNNOSS	becomingness
BCEEHHNOOPST	technophobes
BCEEHHIIKRRSW	Berwickshire
BCEEHILLNRSU	Brunelleschi
BCEEIIIILMST	imbecilities
BCEEIILLRSTT	belletristic
BCEEIILNNSSV	vincibleness
BCEEIJLSTUVY	subjectively
BCEEIJNNOOTV	nonobjective
BCEEILMNOPTT	contemptible
BCEEILMOPRSS	compressible
BCEEILNORSTV	convertibles
BCEEILPRSSTU	putrescibles
BCEEIMMOSTTU	subcommittee
BCEEIMORRRWY	microbrewery
BCEEINRSSUVY	subserviency
BCEEIPRRSSSU	superscribes
BCEEKKLNNOSU	knucklebones
BCEELMMOORTU	coulombmeter
BCEELMMORSUY	cumbersomely
BCEFGIIINNOR	fibrinogenic

BCEFGIIJNOTY	objectifying
BCEGHIILNTWY	bewitchingly
BCEGHIIMNORS	chemisorbing
BCEGHIMNNOOY	honeycombing
BCEGHIMNOORS	chemosorbing
BCEGIIILNORR	incorrigible
BCEGIILOOOST	bioecologist
BCEGIKLNOSTU	bluestocking
BCEGILMNNOUY	unbecomingly
BCEGILNOOOOY	biocoenology
BCEHIIIOSSTT	bioethicists
BCEHIIMORSTY	biochemistry
BCEHIINOSTTY	biosynthetic
BCEHIKLNOSSS	blockishness
BCEHIMORSTWW	West Bromwich
BCEHLORRSSYY	chrysoberyls
BCEHMOORSTTY	thrombocytes
BCEIIIIMMORS	biomimicries
BCEIIINOSSTT	bioscientist
BCEIIJMSSTUV	subjectivism
BCEIIJOSSTTV	objectivists
BCEIIJSSTTUV	subjectivist
BCEIIJSTTUVY	subjectivity
BCEIIKLLRSST	billstickers
BCEIIKLMOPRU	Komi Republic
BCEIILNRSTTU	instructible
BCEIINORTTUV	contributive
BCEIIPRSSTUV	subscriptive
BCEIJNSSTUUV	subjunctives
BCEIKNNRSUWW	New Brunswick
BCEILLOOPSUY	ebullioscopy
BCEILMNOPTTY	contemptibly
BCEILMOPRSSY	compressibly
BCEILMORSTUU	microtubules
BCEILORSSTUU	tuberculosis
BCEINNNOSTTU	subcontinent
BCEIORSSTTUV	obstructives
BCEKKOORRSST	stockbrokers
BCELSSTTTTUU	scuttlebutts
BCEMNORSSSUU	cumbrousness
BCEOOOPRSSST	stroboscopes
BCERRSSTTUUU	substructure
BCFIIILNORTY	fibrinolytic
BCGIIIKLLNST	billsticking
BCGIIILNORRY	incorrigibly
BCGIILMOOORY	microbiology
BCGIILOOOOSY	sociobiology
BCGIINNORTTU	contributing
BCGIINOOOSTT	gnotobiotics
BCGIKKNOORST	stockbroking
BCGILLNOORUY	cryoglobulin
BCGILNRSTUUU	subculturing
BCHHIIMORSTY	biorhythmics
BCHHIMOOORRT	orthorhombic
BCHIIIOPSSTY	biophysicist
BCHILMOORTTY	thrombolytic
BCIILLORSUUY	lubriciously
BCIILOOOSTUY	bootylicious
BCIINNOORTTU	contribution
BCIINOPRSSTU	subscription
BCIIOOPRSSTY	cryptobiosis
BCIJNNOSSTUU	subjunctions

BCILMMNOSUUU	cumulonimbus
BCINOOPRSTTY	cryptobionts
BCINOORRSTTU	contributors
BCINOORRTTUY	contributory
BCINOORSSTTU	obstructions
BDDDEEEILMORW	middlebrowed
BDDDEEINRRSU	underbidders
BDDDEGIINNRU	underbidding
BDDEEEEFILMN	feebleminded
BDDEEEEFINNRU	unbefriended
BDDEEEEFLMNTU	befuddlement
BDDEEEILMOSW	disemboweled
BDDEEEEIMNRST	debridements
BDDEEEEINNSST	indebtedness
BDDEEEENORRUV	overburdened
BDDEEEFHIORRS	Bedfordshire
BDDEEEIILMORS	disembroiled
BDDEEEILMRSTU	middlebuster
BDDEGIIMNOSY	disembodying
BDDEGIINNRSU	disburdening
BDDEHINRRSTU	thunderbirds
BDDFGIILLNNO	blindfolding
BDDFGIILNORY	forbiddingly
BDDFGIMNNOUU	dumbfounding
BDEEEEILRRRS	elderberries
BDEEEEMMNRRU	unremembered
BDEEEFIILNLNS	indefensible
BDEEEGIILNNR	linebreeding
BDEEEHMORRTU	mouthbreeder
BDEEEIILRSSV	disbelievers
BDEEEIIMORRS	embroideries
BDEEEEILLNRSU	underbellies
BDEEEILMNRTW	bewilderment
BDEEEILMNSTV	bedevilments
BDEEEILNNSSV	vendibleness
BDEEEIMMRRSS	dismemberers
	disremembers
BDEEEEIMNNSTZ	bedizenments
BDEEEIMORRRS	embroiderers
BDEEFIILNNSY	indefensibly
BDEEFIILRSTU	filibustered
BDEEFLLNORSU	bellfounders
BDEEGGHIIRSW	weighbridges
BDEEGGIJRTTU	jitterbugged
BDEEGHHIINRS	Denbighshire
BDEEGHINNORR	herringboned
BDEEGIIILNST	indigestible
BDEEGIIILNSV	disbelieving
BDEEGIIMMNRS	dismembering
BDEEGIIMNORR	embroidering
BDEEGIMMRRUU	Murrumbidgee
BDEEGINORSST	Gibson Desert
BDEEGINORSTU	outbreedings
BDEEGLNNORUY	Glyndebourne
BDEEHILOPRSY	hyperbolised
BDEEHILOPRYZ	hyperbolized
BDEEHINOSTUU	hebetudinous
BDEEHNORSTUX	thunderboxes
BDEEIIILNRTV	indivertible
BDEEIILMNTTW	nimblewitted
BDEEIIMRRTTU	turbidimeter
BDEEIIRRSTTU	redistribute

BDEEIIRSSTTU	distributees
BDEEILLNPRSS	spellbinders
BDEEILORRSSW	bowdlerisers
BDEEILORRSWZ	bowdlerizers
BDEEIMNORSST	disrobements
BDEEIMNRSSTU	disbursement
BDEEIOORSSXY	desoxyribose
BDEFGILNOORY	forebodingly
BDEFLNOSSTUU	doubtfulness
BDEGGGILNRUY	begrudgingly
BDEGGIIMNOSU	disemboguing
BDEGGLNOOORS	boondogglers
BDEGHHINOOOR	neighborhood
BDEGHHOORRTU	thoroughbred
BDEGIIILMNOS	demobilising
BDEGIIILMNOZ	demobilizing
BDEGIIILNSTY	indigestibly
BDEGIILLNNPS	spellbinding
BDEGIILNORSW	bowdlerising
BDEGIILNORUV	overbuilding
BDEGIILNORWZ	bowdlerizing
BDEGIIMNNOST	disentombing
BDEGILLNNRUY	blunderingly
BDEGILLNOOTT	bloodletting
BDEHHMNOOORR	rhombohedron
BDEHHOOORRST	brotherhoods
BDEHIILPRSSU	shipbuilders
BDEHIINOPRTU	unprohibited
BDEHILOOPRSY	hyperboloids
BDEHLNORSTTU	thunderbolts
BDEHMOOORRTU	mouthbrooder
BDEIIIILLNTY	indelibility
BDEIIIILNRTVY	indivertibly
BDEIIIORSTVY	biodiversity
BDEIIIRSTTUV	distributive
BDEIILLNOSSU	indissoluble
BDEIILMRSSUU	subdeliriums
BDEIILNORSST	blindstories
BDEIIRRSSTTU	distributers
BDEILNORSSTY	blindstoreys
BDFIILMNNUUU	infundibulum
BDGGGILNNOOO	boondoggling
BDGHIIILNPSU	shipbuilding
BDGHIIMMNRSU	hummingbirds
BDGIIIIILLRTY	dirigibility
BDGIIINNRSTTU	distributing
BDGIILNOSTUU	outbuildings
BDGIILNRSTUY	disturbingly
BDHILOORSTTY	bloodthirsty
BDIIIIILSTVY	divisibility
BDIIILLNOSUY	libidinously
BDIIINORSTTU	distribution
BDIIINOSSSUV	subdivisions
BDIILLNOSSUY	indissolubly
BDIIORRSSTTU	distributors
BDLMNOOSTTUU	buttonmoulds
BEEEEEFLMNNT	enfeeblement
BEEEEFHINORR	hereinbefore
BEEEEHILPRSS	Peeblesshire
BEEEEIMNSTTW	betweentimes
BEEEELMMNTZZ	embezzlement
BEEEFILLNSSX	flexibleness

BEEEGGGIRRUV	veggieburger	BEEIIILRRSST	irresistible
BEEEGIINNORS	bioengineers	BEEIIINORSST	insobrieties
BEEEGILLNRST	belligerents	BEEIIKLNSSSU	businesslike
BEEEGILMNSTU	beguilements	BEEIILNOSSTU	nebulosities
BEEEGIMNPRSU	Supreme Being	BEEIILRRRSSV	irreversibly
BEEEGIOORRSS	gooseberries	BEEIIORSSTTU	tuberosities
BEEEGLNORSTT	greenbottles	BEEILLLORSUY	rebelliously
BEEEHIINNRTT	terebinthine	BEEILLMORTUY	ebulliometry
BEEEHILLMRSS	embellishers	BEEILMMNORST	embroilments
BEEEHILLNORS	helleborines	BEEILPPRSSSU	suppressible
BEEEHNNNOOPZ	benzophenone	BEEILRSSUVVY	subversively
BEEEHNNOPRRT	Open Brethren	BEEINNNOOQUZ	benzoquinone
BEEEIILNNSTX	inextensible	BEEINNOORSTU	boutonnieres
BEEEIILRRRSV	irreversible	BEEINNORRTUW	winterbourne
BEEEILLMNTTT	belittlement	BEEKNNNORSSU	unbrokenness
BEEEILLMORTU	ebulliometer	BEELLMNRSSUY	numberlessly
BEEEILMORTTY	biotelemetry	BEELLORSSTUY	trolleybuses
BEEEILNNORSV	nonbelievers	BEELNNOSSSUU	nebulousness
BEEEILNNSSSS	sensibleness	BEELNQSSTUUY	subsequently
BEEEILNNSSST	tensibleness	BEELORSTTUVY	oversubtlety
BEEEILNRRSST	terribleness	BEEOOPRRSSTU	obstreperous
BEEEILNRRSTW	West Berliner	BEERRRSSTTUU	surrebutters
BEEEIMMMRRSS	misremembers	BEERRSSSSTTU	stressbuster
BEEEIMMNRTTT	embitterment	BEFGHIINNRSU	refurbishing
BEEEINNNORTZ	nitrobenzene	BEFGHILLRSTU	bullfighters
BEEEIPRRSSTY	presbyteries	BEFGIILMORSZ	gemfibrozils
BEEEIRSSTTTW	bittersweets	BEFGILMNNSSU	fumblingness
BEEELLNNOTVY	benevolently	BEFIILNORRSU	neurofibrils
BEEELNOOSSST	obsoleteness	BEFIILRSTTUY	subfertility
BEEENOPPRSTY	teenyboppers	BEFILLNSSSSU	blissfulness
BEEFGIINNRRT	birefringent	BEFILMOPRSUU	plumbiferous
BEEFGLLOORSW	globeflowers	BEFLLOOPRSTU	bulletproofs
BEEFHIRSSTTU	butterfishes	BEGGHIINNORU	neighbouring
BEEFIILRRSTU	filibusterer	BEGGHILNOORU	Ingleborough
BEEFILMNNOOT	Bloemfontein	BEGGIILNNOSS	obligingness
BEEGHIILLMNS	embellishing	BEGHIILNPRSU	republishing
BEEGHILNORSS	neighborless	BEGHILNOOOTY	ethnobiology
BEEGHINNORRS	herringbones	BEGHINNNRTUU	unburthening
BEEGHLLNOORU	Ellenborough	BEGIIIILLLTY	illegibility
BEEGHOOPRRTU	Peterborough	BEGIIILLLNTY	intelligibly
BEEGIIILLLNT	intelligible	BEGIIKLNNPRS	besprinkling
BEEGIILNNPUX	inexpungible	BEGIILLLNTTY	belittlingly
BEEGIIOORSSU	bourgeoisies	BEGIILLNRSTY	blisteringly
BEEGILNORTTX	letterboxing	BEGIILNNPRTU	blueprinting
BEEGINORRSUY	youngberries	BEGIILOOOSTX	exobiologist
BEEGLOORRTTT	globetrotter	BEGIIMNRSTTU	resubmitting
BEEGNNORRSTV	von Sternberg	BEGILLNRSTUY	blusteringly
BEEHIIILTVXY	exhibitively	BEGILMOORSTY	embryologist
BEEHIIINORTX	exhibitioner	BEGILNOOORUY	neurobiology
BEEHIKLNOSSS	blokeishness	BEGILNPRRTUY	perturbingly
BEEHILLLRSVY	Beverly Hills	BEGIMNNNORTU	outnumbering
BEEHILLMOSTY	blithesomely	BEHHOORSSTTU	toothbrushes
BEEHILMOOPST	phlebotomies	BEHIIILRSSST	British Isles
	phlebotomise	BEHIIIMNSTTU	bismuthinite
BEEHILMOOPTZ	phlebotomize	BEHIINOSSSTY	biosynthesis
BEEHILNORRSS	horribleness	BEHILLRSSTTU	bullshitters
BEEHILOPRSSY	hyperbolises	BEHILMNPSSTU	publishments
BEEHILOPRSYZ	hyperbolizes	BEHILMOOPSTT	phlebotomist
BEEHLORRRTWY	whortleberry	BEHILMOPRSSY	hyperbolisms
BEEHNOOORSSU	Osborne House	BEIIIIILRSST	risibilities
BEEHOPRRSSTT	stepbrothers	BEIIIIILSSTV	visibilities
BEEIIILMRRSS	irremissible	BEIIILLOSSTU	solubilities

BEIIILMMORSS	immobilisers
BEIIILMMORSZ	immobilizers
BEIIILMQRSUU	equilibriums
BEIIILMRRSSY	irremissibly
BEIIILQRSSTU	equilibrists
BEIIILRRSSTY	irresistibly
BEIILLORSTUY	resolubility
BEIILMSSSUVY	submissively
BEIIMNSSSUUV	unsubmissive
BEIINORRSTTU	retributions
BEIISSTTTUUV	substitutive
BEILLMPSSTUU	submultiples
BEILLOORSSTT	stilboestrol
BEILMOOOPRSY	polyribosome
BEILOOQSSUUY	obsequiously
BEILOORSSTUY	boisterously
BEINSSSTTTUU	substituents
BELLMORSSUUY	slumberously
BELLNORTTUWY	Bulwer-Lytton
BELLORSSTUUY	blusterously
BELMNOOPRVYY	polyembryony
BERRSSSTTTUU	trustbusters
BFFIIILLMORR	fibrilliform
BFGGHIILLNTU	bullfighting
BFIIIILNSTUV	infusibility
BFIIIILNORSSY	fibrinolysis
BFKMMNOOOOOR	Book of Mormon
BGGHHLOOORUU	Loughborough
BGHIILLNPPUW	bullwhipping
BGHIILLNSTTU	bullshitting
BGHILLNNSUUY	unblushingly
BGHILNNOOTTU	buttonholing
BGHILOOOOPTY	photobiology
BGIIIIILNTTY	ignitibility
BGIIIILMMNOS	immobilising
BGIIIILMMNOZ	immobilizing
BGIIIIMNNSTU	bituminising
BGIIIIMNNTUZ	bituminizing
BGIIILLNOSSU	solubilising
BGIIILLNOSUZ	solubilizing
BGIIKLLNNNUY	unblinkingly
BGIINSSTTTUU	substituting
BGILLORSUUUY	lugubriously
BGILMOOSSSTY	symbologists
BGINRSSTTTUU	trustbusting
BHIIINOOPRST	prohibitions
BHILMOOOPRSU	ombrophilous
BIIIIILNSTVY	invisibility
BIIILLNOSTUY	insolubility
BIIILNOORSTU	tourbillions
BIILOQSTUUUY	ubiquitously
BIINOSSTTTUU	substitution
BILOORSSTUUY	robustiously
BIMNOPSSSTUU	subsumptions
CCCCEEEENNORS	concrescence
CCCCEHINOOSU	echinococcus
CCCCHHIOPRTU	Coptic Church
CCCDEEEENRSS	decrescences
CCCDEEHKORSS	crosschecked
CCCDEEIINNOS	coincidences
CCCDEEEILNOPY	encyclopedic
CCCDEIIORSTY	cysticercoid

CCCDHIIOOPRS	dichroscopic
CCCEEEENRSSX	excrescences
CCCEEEENORRU	reoccurrence
CCCEEHILORTY	heterocyclic
CCCEEHKNORTU	countercheck
CCCEEIILMSST	eclecticisms
CCCEEIINRTTY	eccentricity
CCCEEILNNOTU	noctilucence
CCCEGIIMNNOO	meningococci
CCCEIIMRRSSU	circumcisers
CCCEILOOTTUY	leucocytotic
CCCEINNOPSTU	concupiscent
CCCEINNSSSTU	succinctness
CCCEIOOPRSTT	streptococci
CCCEKNORSTTU	concertstuck
CCCEMNOOPSUU	pneumococcus
CCCGIIIMNRSU	circumcising
CCCGIKNOORSW	cockcrowings
CCCHHHIRRSTU	Christchurch
CCCHIIORSTTY	trichocystic
CCCHILMOSTYY	cyclothymics
CCCHINOOOOPRS	chronoscopic
CCCIIIMNORSU	circumcision
CCCIIIMORRTU	microcircuit
CCCIOOOPPRST	proctoscopic
CCDDDEEEENNOS	condescended
CCDDEEEENNOPY	codependency
CCDDEEEENORSS	decrescendos
CCDDEEINNOST	disconnected
CCDDEEINORST	disconcerted
CCDDEIMNOSTU	misconducted
CCDEEEEILNST	delitescence
CCDEEEEMNSTU	detumescence
CCDEEEENORRT	retrocedence
CCDEEFFIIINS	deficiencies
CCDEEEFNNORS	frondescence
CCDEEEHIINNS	indehiscence
CCDEEEHNOSTU	escutcheoned
CCDEEEIINRSS	iridescences
CCDEEEIINRSV	viridescence
CCDEEEINOPRV	preconceived
CCDEEEELORTTU	electrocuted
CCDEEENOPRRT	preconcerted
CCDEEENRRSTU	recrudescent
CCDEEGILNSUY	succeedingly
CCDEEGINNORS	crescendoing
CCDEEGINNRSU	recrudescing
CCDEEIIINNSST	insecticides
CCDEEIIMNOSV	misconceived
CCDEEILNNORU	unreconciled
CCDEEILNOSTU	endocuticles
CCDEEIMNRTUV	circumvented
CCDEEINNORST	disconnecter
CCDEEIORRTTU	correctitude
CCDEGIMNNOOS	Second Coming
CCDEHIIINNNO	cinchonidine
CCDEHIIOOPRS	dichroiscope
CCDEHIMOORTY	orchidectomy
CCDEHIOOOPRS	dichrooscope
CCDEHIOOPRSS	dichroscopes
CCDEIIIIRSTV	recidivistic
CCDEIIIRRRTU	circuit rider

CCDEILNOTUVV	conductively	CCEEGINNNORU	incongruence
CCDEILOPSSTY	cyclopedists	CCEEGINNNOST	contingences
CCDEIMNOORSS	microseconds	CCEEGINNNORSU	congruencies
CCDEIORRSSSS	crisscrossed	CCEEGINOSTTY	cytogenetics
CCDENORSSTTU	deconstructs	CCEEGNOORRST	concertgoers
CCDHHILOORRY	hydrochloric	CCEEHHIMOPRS	chemospheric
CCDHILOOPSYV	hypocycloids	CCEEHIILNORT	heliocentric
CCDHIOPRRSTY	cryptorchids	CCEEHIILORTT	heteroclitic
CCDIINOTTUVY	conductivity	CCEEHIMOSTVZ	schizomycete
CCDNNNOOOORTU	nonconductor	CCEEHINNORTT	ethnocentric
CCEEEEHRSTTU	cheesecutter	CCEEHINNOSTU	inescutcheon
CCEEEEIIKKLO	cockieleekie	CCEEHIOPTTUY	hypoeutectic
CCEEEEILLNSX	excellencies	CCEEHKLLLOSS	cockleshells
CCEEEEINPRST	centrepieces	CCEEHKLOORST	electroshock
CCEEEEJNNSUV	juvenescence	CCEEHMOOPRST	chemoceptors
CCEEEFFIIINS	efficiencies	CCEEHMOPSTYY	phycomycetes
CCEEEFHIKNRS	neckerchiefs	CCEEHOPRRRTY	hypercorrect
CCEEEFLNORSU	fluorescence	CCEEIIIORSTV	coercivities
CCEEEGIIMNST	miscegenetic	CCEEIIILLOSTV	collectivise
CCEEEGILNORT	electrogenic	CCEEIIILLOTVZ	collectivize
CCEEEGINNRSS	nigrescences	CCEEIILOOPTU	leucopoietic
CCEEEGNNORSV	convergences	CCEEIIMNORSV	misconceiver
CCEEEHHMORST	homescreetch	CCEEIIMNOSSV	misconceives
CCEEEHIIMNPY	chimneypiece	CCEEIIMOPRSS	microspecies
CCEEEHINNORS	incoherences	CCEEIINNNNOT	incontinence
CCEEEHINOSTT	coenesthetic	CCEEIILLLOTVY	collectively
CCEEEHKLLPRS	spellchecker	CCEEILLNOORT	recollection
CCEEEIIMNNRS	reminiscence	CCEEILLORTTY	electrolytic
CCEEEIINPRSS	resipiscence	CCEEILMORRST	sclerometric
CCEEEIINRSVV	reviviscence	CCEEILNNORTV	conventicler
CCEEEIIKLPPRR	Cripple Creek	CCEEILNNOSTV	conventicles
CCEEEILLORTV	recollective	CCEEILNNOTVY	connectively
CCEEEILMNNRT	encirclement	CCEEILNOORTT	electrotonic
CCEEEILMNNSU	luminescence	CCEEILNORTVY	concretively
CCEEEIMNNOPT	incompetence	CCEEILOPRRTY	pyroelectric
CCEEEIMNNSTU	intumescence	CCEEILORRTVY	correctively
CCEEEIMNOPST	competencies	CCEEILORTTUY	reticulocyte
CCEEEIMORRST	coercimeters	CCEEILSSSUVY	successively
CCEEEINNNOST	consentience	CCEEIMNNNOTV	convincement
CCEEEINNNOSV	conveniences	CCEEIMNNOPTY	incompetency
CCEEEINNORSU	neuroscience	CCEEIMNNSTUY	intumescency
CCEEEINOPRSV	preconceives	CCEEIMNOORST	econometrics
CCEEEINORSSV	coerciveness	CCEEIMNRRTUV	circumventer
CCEEEINOSSTX	coexistences	CCEEIMOSSTTY	cystectomies
CCEEEINRSSTV	vitrescences	CCEEINNNOORT	reconnection
CCEEELNRSTXY	excrescently	CCEEINNNORTT	interconnect
CCEEELOOPRST	electroscope	CCEEINNOORSS	concessioner
CCEEELORSTTU	electrocutes	CCEEINNOSSST	consistences
CCEEELORSTTY	electrocytes	CCEEINOOPRRT	nocireceptor
CCEEEMMMNNOT	commencement	CCEEINOOPRSS	necroscopies
CCEEENNOQSSU	consequences	CCEEIOOPRSST	stereoscopic
CCEEENNORSST	concreteness	CCEEJNORRSTU	conjecturers
CCEEFFIIINNY	inefficiency	CCEEKNORSSSU	cocksureness
CCEEFFIINOST	coefficients	CCEEMNNNORST	concernments
CCEEFGINNNOR	conferencing	CCEENOPSSSTU	conspectuses
CCEEFILMRSUX	circumflexes	CCEENORRRUUV	eurocurrency
CCEEFINNOORT	confectioner	CCEEOOPPRSST	spectroscope
CCEEGGILNOTY	glycogenetic	CCEEOORRRSTV	overcorrects
CCEEGILLNORT	recollecting	CCEEFGIKNNOVY	cockneyfying
CCEEGILLOOSY	ecclesiology	CCEEFHHMOORRU	Church of Rome
CCEEGIMMNNOR	recommencing	CCEEFHINOORSU	conchiferous
CCEEGINNNORT	reconnecting	CCEEFIIINNSTU	unscientific

CCEFILMNRTUU	circumfluent
CCEFKLOOORUW	cuckooflower
CCEFLLLNOTUY	flocculently
CCEFLLSSSUUY	successfully
CCEFLNSSSUUU	unsuccessful
CCEGHIINORTT	ricochetting
CCEGHILMOPYY	hypoglycemic
CCEGIINNNORST	concertising
	concretising
CCEGIINNORTV	reconvicting
CCEGIINNORTZ	concertizing
	concretizing
CCEGIJNNORTU	conjecturing
CCEGIKNORRSW	corkscrewing
CCEGINOPPRUY	preoccupying
CCEHHHOOPSTT	hotchpotches
CCEHHIILMOOR	heliochromic
CCEHHILNRSSU	churchliness
CCEHHIOSSSTT	schottisches
CCEHIILLNOPU	nucleophilic
CCEHIIMORSTT	stichometric
CCEHIINOORRT	rhinocerotic
CCEHIIPRRSTY	hypercritics
CCEHILLLOQRUU	Quiller-Couch
CCEHILNOORTU	technicolour
CCEHILNOPSTY	polytechnics
CCEHIMNOORRT	chronometric
CCEHIMOOPRST	thermoscopic
CCEHIMOPRSTY	psychometric
CCEHINOOPRRT	necrotrophic
CCEHINOPRSTY	pyrotechnics
CCEHIOOPSSTT	stethoscopic
CCEHIORRTTYY	erythrocytic
CCEHKLOSSTTU	shuttlecocks
CCEHLNOOOSTTUY	hectocotylus
CCEHMMOORRYY	myrmecochory
CCEHNNOOPRTUU	counterpunch
CCEHNOOOOPRSS	chronoscopes
CCEHNOOPRSSY	synchroscope
CCEIIILMOPST	complicities
CCEIIIMMORSS	microseismic
CCEIIINNNOST	concinnities
CCEIIINOORRT	oneirocritic
CCEIIILLMOSTV	collectivism
CCEIIILLOSTTV	collectivist
CCEIIILLOTTVY	collectivity
CCEIILMOORRT	colorimetric
CCEIILNNOSUV	inconclusive
CCEIILNOTVVY	convictively
CCEIILPRSTUU	pisciculture
CCEIILRRTTUU	citriculture
CCEIIMOOPSSS	seismoscopic
CCEIINNNNOTY	incontinency
CCEIINNOORTV	reconviction
CCEIINNORSTT	concertinist
CCEIINNOTTVY	connectivity
CCEIINOOPRST	retinoscopic
CCEIINOORSST	coercionists
CCEIINORSTTV	constrictive
CCEIINOSSTUV	viscountcies
CCEIINRSSTTY	syncretistic
CCEIJNNOSTUV	conjunctives

CCEIKLOOTTUY	leukocytotic
CCEILLNOSUVY	conclusively
CCEILLOOOPSS	oscilloscope
CCEILMNORSUU	micronucleus
CCEILOOPRSUY	precociously
CCEILOOSSTUY	leucocytosis
CCEIMNORRTUV	circumventor
CCEINNOOSSTU	consecutions
CCEINNOSTTUY	constituency
CCEINOOPRSSU	preconscious
CCEINORSTTUV	constructive
CCEIOOPSSSTY	cystoscopies
CCEIORRSSSSS	crisscrosses
CCEJNNORSTUU	conjunctures
CCELNNORRTUY	concurrently
CCELNOOOOPSS	colonoscopes
CCENOPRRSTTU	preconstruct
CCENORRRSSTU	crosscurrent
CCENORRSSTTU	constructers
	reconstructs
CCEOOOOPPRSST	proctoscopes
CCEOOOPRRSSS	coprocessors
CCEOOOPPRSSTY	spectroscopy
CCFGGHIIKNOT	cockfighting
CCFGIIMNRSUU	circumfusing
CCFIIINORSUX	crucifixions
CCFIILNNOOST	conflictions
CCFIIMNORSUU	circumfusion
CCFILMORSUUU	circumfluous
CCFILOOOPRSU	fluoroscopic
CCGGHHINORSU	churchgoings
CCGHHIILOOTY	ichthyologic
CCGHIIINNNOS	cinchonising
CCGHIIINNNOZ	cinchonizing
CCGHILNOOOST	conchologist
CCGIIILMNOOR	criminologic
CCGIILNNOVVY	convincingly
CCGIINNNNOUV	unconvincing
CCGIINNOPRST	conscripting
CCGIINNORSTT	constricting
CCGILLNOSTYY	cyclostyling
CCGILMNOORTY	motorcycling
CCGILNNORRUY	concurringly
CCGINNORSTTU	constructing
CCGINORSSTTU	crosscutting
CCHHIIILOTTY	ichthyolitic
CCHHIIMOSTTY	stichomythic
CCHHIIMOSTYZ	schizothymic
CCHHIIOPSTYZ	schizophytic
CCHHIMOOOPRR	chromophoric
CCHHIMOOOPRT	photochromic
CCHHIMOOPRSY	hypsochromic
CCHIIINOPRTU	Pinturicchio
CCHIILNOOPRR	chloropicrin
CCHIIMOPRSSY	microphysics
CCHIIOOPRSTY	hypocoristic
CCHILMNOORSY	chylomicrons
CCHIOOPPRSTY	psychotropic
CCHIOPPRRTYY	cryptophytic
CCIILNNNSTUU	cunnilinctus
CCIILNOOPRSS	ciclosporins
CCIILORSTUUY	circuitously

CCIIMOOPRSST	microscopist	**CDDELLLMOORY**	mollycoddler
CCIINNOOPRST	conscription	**CDDELLLMOOSY**	mollycoddles
CCIINNOORSTT	constriction	**CDDEMNNOOPUU**	uncompounded
CCIIOOTTTTXYY	cytotoxicity	**CDDGIIMMNOOS**	discommoding
CCIJNNNOOSTU	conjunctions	**CDDIIMMOOSTY**	discommodity
CCILMOORSTTY	motorcyclist	**CDDMMNOORSUU**	McMurdo Sound
CCILMORRSUUU	cirrocumulus	**CDEEEEFGLLNO**	Golden Fleece
CCIMNOOPSTUU	compunctious	**CDEEEEGINRST**	detergencies
CCINNOORSTTU	construction	**CDEEEEIILMNT**	telemedicine
CCINOORRSSTT	constrictors	**CDEEEEIINNPX**	inexpedience
CCNOORRSSTTU	constructors	**CDEEEEIINPSX**	expediencies
CDDDEEFIIOST	eisteddfodic	**CDEEEEIKLPRW**	pickerelweed
CDDDEEIMMNOS	discommended	**CDEEEEJNRSUV**	rejuvenesced
CDDDEEMNOOPU	decompounded	**CDEEEELNNPRS**	resplendence
CDDDELLLMOOY	mollycoddled	**CDEEEENPRSSU**	supersedence
CDDEEEEINNNP	independence	**CDEEEFFIINNR**	indifference
CDDEEEEEINNPS	dependencies	**CDEEEFHILRST**	chesterfield
CDDEEEEJNSST	dejectedness	**CDEEEFMNORST**	deforcements
CDDEEEGINNRS	redescending	**CDEEEGIINRSV**	divergencies
CDDEEEGINORS	derecognised	**CDEEEGINORSS**	derecognises
CDDEEEGINORZ	derecognized	**CDEEEGINORSZ**	derecognizes
CDDEEEHMNOPR	comprehended	**CDEEEHILOPRT**	helicoptered
CDDEEEIINNNPY	independency	**CDEEEHIMNPRT**	decipherment
CDDEEEINORRS	reconsidered	**CDEEEHINRRST**	rechristened
CDDEEEIORRSV	rediscovered	**CDEEEHNRSSTW**	wretchedness
CDDEEEIPRSST	disrespected	**CDEEEIINNPXY**	inexpediency
CDDEEEIRRSTT	derestricted	**CDEEEIINNSST**	dissentience
CDDEEEELNSSSU	secludedness	**CDEEEIINPRSS**	presidencies
CDDEEEMNNOPR	precondemned	**CDEEEIINSSSV**	decisiveness
CDDEEEMOPRSS	decompressed	**CDEEEIKNSSSW**	wickednesses
CDDEEHLNNOSU	nonscheduled	**CDEEEILMNORT**	declinometer
CDDEEHLNORTU	underclothed	**CDEEEILNOSST**	deselections
CDDEEIIMOSTZ	domesticized	**CDEEEILNQSTU**	deliquescent
CDDEEIINORST	rodenticides	**CDEEEILORRST**	clerestoried
CDDEEIJNPRUU	unprejudiced	**CDEEEINNNORS**	nonresidence
CDDEEILNNSSU	includedness	**CDEEEINRSSST**	discreetness
CDDEEINNORSU	unconsidered		discreteness
CDDEEINNOSTT	discontented	**CDEEEIRRSSST**	directresses
CDDEEINORRTU	reintroduced	**CDEEELLORSTY**	electrolysed
CDDEEINORSTU	rediscounted	**CDEEELLORTYZ**	electrolyzed
CDDEEINORSUV	undiscovered	**CDEEELMMNOPT**	complemented
CDDEEINPRSUU	superinduced	**CDEEELNNPRSY**	resplendency
CDDEELLNOORT	decontrolled	**CDEEELNPTUXY**	unexpectedly
CDDEEMNNOTUU	undocumented	**CDEEELOPRTTY**	electrotyped
CDDEENOOPRRS	corresponded	**CDEEEMMNORRS**	recommenders
CDDEEOOPRRUV	overproduced	**CDEEEMNNNOTU**	denouncement
CDDEFIIKLSST	fiddlesticks	**CDEEEMOPRSSS**	decompresses
CDDEFIIMNORS	disconfirmed	**CDEEENNORRTU**	rencountered
CDDEFIMOORST	discomforted	**CDEEEOPRRSSS**	predecessors
CDDEFLNNOOUY	confoundedly	**CDEEEOPRRSTT**	retrospected
CDDEGIIINRST	discrediting	**CDEEEOPSSSUY**	pseudocyeses
CDDEHIIMOOST	dichotomised	**CDEEERSSSSTU**	seductresses
CDDEHIIMOOTZ	dichotomized	**CDEEFFGIINNR**	differencing
CDDEHILNOSSS	cloddishness	**CDEEFFIIINOV**	divine office
CDDEHLNORTUU	thundercloud	**CDEEFIIIIKRR**	Frederick III
CDDEIILMNNOO	nondomiciled	**CDEEFILNNNUU**	uninfluenced
CDDEIINNOSTU	discontinued	**CDEEFINNNOSS**	confinedness
CDDEILNOOOTY	cotyledonoid	**CDEEFNNOSSSU**	confusedness
CDDEILNOOPRS	scolopendrid	**CDEEGHILNRSU**	rescheduling
CDDEILNOOSTY	dicotyledons	**CDEEGIILNQSU**	deliquescing
CDDEILOOPSSU	diplodocuses	**CDEEGIILRRTY**	triglyceride
CDDEKORRSSTU	rudderstocks	**CDEEGILNORSS**	girdlescones

CDEEGILNRTTU	decluttering
CDEEGILOPPTY	glycopeptide
CDEEGIMMNNOR	recommending
CDEEGINNNORS	recondensing
CDEEGINNNORSU	unrecognised
CDEEGINNNORUZ	unrecognized
CDEEGINOPRRR	prerecording
CDEEHHKLLOSS	shellshocked
CDEEHILNPRST	stepchildren
CDEEHILOPRRS	perchlorides
CDEEHINNRSTU	unchristened
CDEEHIOPRRRS	recordership
CDEEHIOQSSTU	discotheques
CDEEHKLLNORS	schnorkelled
CDEEHKLNOSUY	honeysuckled
CDEEHLMOOSTU	closemouthed
CDEEHLNORSTU	underclothes
CDEEHORSTTTU	outstretched
CDEEIIILNSVY	indecisively
CDEEIIILOPST	depoliticise
CDEEIIILOPTZ	depoliticize
CDEEIIIMORST	iridectomies
	mediocrities
CDEEIIINNSTV	disincentive
CDEEIIINRTTV	interdictive
CDEEIIKLNSSS	slickensides
CDEEIILNNORV	overinclined
CDEEIILNOPRT	predilection
CDEEIILNORST	derelictions
CDEEIILNRSTY	indiscreetly
	indiscretely
	iridescently
CDEEIILOPSTV	velocipedist
CDEEIILPRTVY	predictively
CDEEIIMNNOSS	diseconomies
CDEEIIMNOPRV	improvidence
CDEEIIMNOSTU	eudemonistic
CDEEIIMORRSS	misericordes
CDEEIIMOSSTZ	domesticizes
CDEEIINNORTV	nondirective
CDEEIINNRSST	indirectness
CDEEIINNSSTY	dissentiency
CDEEIINOPRVW	provincewide
CDEEIINORRST	redirections
CDEEIINOSSSU	dieciousness
CDEEIINRSTTU	incertitudes
CDEEIKLNNOOS	nickelodeons
CDEEIKPPQSTU	quickstepped
CDEEILLLOTUV	Viollet-le-Duc
CDEEILLNPSSU	pellucidness
CDEEILMMNOPT	complimented
CDEEILMNOOPX	complexioned
CDEEILRRSTTY	restrictedly
CDEEIMNNORTU	countermined
CDEEIMNNRSST	discernments
	rescindments
CDEEIMNORSTV	divorcements
CDEEIMOOSSTX	sextodecimos
CDEEIMOPRSTU	computerised
CDEEIMOPRTUZ	computerized
CDEEINNNORSY	nonresidency
CDEEINNOORRT	reconnoitred

CDEEINOOPRSS	processioned
CDEEINOPPRRT	intercropped
CDEEINOPRSTT	introspected
CDEEINORRSST	intercrossed
CDEEINORRSTU	reintroduces
CDEEINPRSSUU	superinduces
CDEEINRRSTTU	unrestricted
CDEEIOPPRRTUV	reproductive
CDEEIOPSSSSUY	pseudocyesis
CDEEIORRSTUV	discoverture
CDEEIORSSTTT	detectorists
CDEEIRRRSSVW	screwdrivers
CDEELMNNOOST	condolements
CDEEMNOOPSSS	composedness
CDEEMNOORSUV	overconsumed
CDEEMNOORTUV	countermoved
	covermounted
CDEENNOOPRST	corespondent
CDEENNRRRTUU	undercurrent
CDEENOOORTXY	deoxycortone
CDEENOORRTTV	controverted
CDEENOORSSSU	decorousness
CDEEOOPRRSUV	overproduces
CDEEOOPRSTUV	pseudovector
CDEERRRSTTUU	restructured
CDEFFIIILSTU	difficulties
CDEFGIIINNST	disinfecting
CDEFIIINNOST	disinfection
CDEFIIMORSST	discomfiters
CDEFIIMORSTU	discomfiture
CDEFIINORSST	disinfectors
CDEGGIILNNNU	indulgencing
CDEGIIIMNRST	misdirecting
CDEGIIINNRTT	interdicting
CDEGIILNNOOS	decolonising
CDEGIILNNOOZ	decolonizing
CDEGIILNNRSY	discerningly
CDEGIILNOORS	decolorising
CDEGIILNOORZ	decolorizing
CDEGINNNRSU	undiscerning
CDEGIINNPRRU	underpricing
CDEGIKNNOORU	undercooking
CDEGILMNNNOY	condemningly
CDEGILNNNOTY	contendingly
CDEGILNNOORU	undercooling
CDEGILNOORUV	overclouding
CDEGINNORRSU	underscoring
CDEGINNRTTUU	undercutting
CDEGINOORRVW	overcrowding
CDEGKLOOORSS	sockdologers
CDEGLMNORUUY	curmudgeonly
CDEHHIIIPRTT	diphtheritic
CDEHHIILNSSS	childishness
CDEHHIIPSTTW	whipstitched
CDEHHIOPRRSY	hydrospheric
CDEHHNOOOPRS	chordophones
CDEHIIILPPSS	discipleship
CDEHIIINNNORS	enchiridions
CDEHIIKNORTY	hydrokinetic
CDEHIIILORRST	trichlorides
CDEHIIMOOSST	dichotomises
CDEHIIMOOSTZ	dichotomizes

CDEHIIMPSSTY	dysphemistic	**CDFGHIINNORY**	chondrifying
CDEHIINOOOPR	conidiophore	**CDFGIIIMNOST**	discomfiting
CDEHIINOORSS	isochronised	**CDFHILOORRUY**	hydrofluoric
CDEHIINOORSZ	isochronized	**CDFINNOSSTUY**	dysfunctions
CDEHIIOPRRST	directorship	**CDGHIKLNOOST**	stockholding
CDEHILLOOPRV	policyholder	**CDGIIIILNNNS**	disinclining
CDEHILMNOOOR	monochloride	**CDGIIIILNNPS**	disciplining
CDEHIMNOOORS	chondriosome	**CDGIIINNNOOT**	conditioning
CDEHINNORSSY	synchronised	**CDGIIILNOORSU**	discolouring
CDEHINNORSYZ	synchronized	**CDGIILOOSSST**	discologists
CDEHIORRTTWY	creditworthy	**CDGIIMMNNOOS**	discommoning
CDEHKLOORSST	stockholders	**CDGIIMNOOPSS**	discomposing
CDEIIIILNNPS	indiscipline	**CDGINNNOOORR**	noncorroding
CDEIIIJRSTUV	jurisdictive	**CDGINOOPRTUU**	outproducing
CDEIIILNPRSS	discipliners	**CDHHILNOORRY**	chlorohydrin
CDEIIILNTVVY	vindictively	**CDHIIIMOOPRS**	isodimorphic
CDEIIIMNORST	misdirection	**CDHIILOSSTUY**	distichously
CDEIIINNORST	indiscretion	**CDHIIMOOSSTT**	dichotomists
CDEIIINNORTT	interdiction	**CDHIIOOPRSST**	chiropodists
CDEIIISSSTUV	vicissitudes	**CDHINOOORSTT**	orthodontics
CDEIIJNSSTUV	disjunctives	**CDIIIJNORSTU**	jurisdiction
CDEIIILLMNOSS	milliseconds	**CDIIILNNSTTY**	indistinctly
CDEIIILMRTUUV	diverticulum	**CDIIIMNNSTTU**	Nunc Dimittis
CDEIIILNNPPRU	unprincipled	**CDIIINNOSSTT**	distinctions
CDEIIILRSSUVY	discursively	**CDIIJNNOSSTU**	disjunctions
CDEIIMMNOOSS	commissioned	**CDIILLORSUUY**	ridiculously
	decommission	**CDIILMORSSTU**	clostridiums
CDEIIMMRSSTY	dissymmetric	**CDIIMMNNOOSU**	condominiums
CDEIIMNORSTU	reductionism	**CDIIMMNOOOSU**	incommodious
CDEIIMPPRSUY	cypripediums	**CDIINNOORTTU**	introduction
CDEIINNNOOSX	disconnexion	**CDIIOPRTTUVY**	productivity
CDEIINNOOPRT	precondition	**CDILMMOOOSUY**	commodiously
CDEIINNOORST	conditioners	**CDILOOORSUUU**	douroucoulis
	reconditions	**CDIMNOOORSTU**	microdontous
CDEIINNORSTU	discontinuer	**CDINNOOPRSTY**	cyprinodonts
CDEIINNOSSTU	discontinues	**CDINOORRTTUY**	introductory
CDEIINNSSSTT	distinctness	**CEEEEEGMNRRS**	reemergences
CDEIINOOPRST	periodontics	**CEEEEEINPRRX**	reexperience
CDEIINOOSSSU	dioicousness	**CEEEEELNPRST**	telepresence
CDEIINOPRSST	descriptions	**CEEEEFFNRSTV**	effervescent
CDEIINORRSTT	interdictors	**CEEEEFINNRRT**	interference
CDEIINORRTTY	interdictory	**CEEEEGHMNORS**	cheesemonger
CDEIINORSTTU	reductionist	**CEEEEHHLORSS**	horseleeches
CDEIILMNOORST	discolorment	**CEEEEHNOPRRY**	honeycreeper
CDEIILNOORSUY	indecorously	**CEEEEHNORSVW**	whencesoever
CDEILOPRTUVY	productively	**CEEEEIINNPRX**	inexperience
CDEIIMNORSSTU	misconstrued	**CEEEEIKKPRTW**	wicketkeeper
CDEIMOOPRSSU	discomposure	**CEEEEILNORST**	electioneers
CDEINNOOORTT	contortioned	**CEEEEILNSSTV**	electiveness
CDEINNOPRSST	nondescripts	**CEEEEINPRSTX**	preexistence
CDEINNRRSTTUU	uninstructed	**CEEEEINRRRSV**	irreverences
CDEINOOPRRTU	reproduction	**CEEEEIORRSVX**	overexercise
CDEINOOPSSST	endoscopists	**CEEEEJNRSSUV**	rejuvenesces
CDEINOPRTUUV	unproductive	**CEEEEELMORRTT**	electrometer
CDEIOORSSTUU	discourteous	**CEEEENNNOPST**	open sentence
CDELLNNOORTU	uncontrolled	**CEEEFFGINRSV**	effervescing
CDELLNOOTUVY	convolutedly	**CEEEFFINNOTV**	noneffective
CDELNNOOPRUY	pronouncedly	**CEEEFFLNORST**	efflorescent
CDELNOOOSTUY	cotyledonous	**CEEEFGHINNRS**	greenfinches
CDENNNOOPRUU	unpronounced	**CEEEFHIIPRSS**	speechifiers
CDENOORRSTUW	counterwords	**CEEEFHLNRSSU**	cheerfulness
CDENRRSTTUUU	unstructured	**CEEEFIIILRRST**	electrifiers

CEEEFIIMPRTV	imperfective
CEEEFILLLMNU	mellifluence
CEEEFILLRTVY	reflectively
CEEEFILNORSU	fluoresceine
CEEEFILNRTUV	unreflective
CEEEFILSTUVX	flexecutives
CEEEFINNRSST	freneticness
CEEEFKLNSSSS	fecklessness
CEEEGGILNOOS	genecologies
CEEEGGNORRRS	greengrocers
CEEEGGNORRRY	greengrocery
CEEEGIILLNNT	intelligence
CEEEGIINNPRX	experiencing
CEEEGIINOPRT	epirogenetic
CEEEGILNPRST	preselecting
CEEEGINNPRRT	Prince Regent
CEEEHHKLNOPS	heckelphones
CEEEHHMOPRSS	chemospheres
CEEEHIIMRSTU	euhemeristic
CEEEHIIPRRSV	receivership
CEEEHIKNSTTT	kitchenettes
CEEEHILLNPRU	Euler-Chelpin
CEEEHILLOPRT	electrophile
CEEEHILORSTT	heteroclites
CEEEHIMNNPRT	encipherment
CEEEHIMNRSTU	hermeneutics
CEEEHINOSSST	coenesthesis
CEEEHINOSSSV	cohesiveness
CEEEHIOORSTU	heteroecious
CEEEHLLPSSSY	speechlessly
CEEEHLNNOTTU	luncheonette
CEEEHLNOOPRT	electrophone
CEEEHLOQQSUU	quelquechose
CEEEHMNNNRTT	entrenchment
CEEEHMNNRRTT	retrenchment
CEEEHMOORRST	stereochrome
CEEEHNOPRRST	centrosphere
CEEEHOOPRRRT	rheoreceptor
CEEEIILLNTTV	intellective
CEEEIIMNNPRT	impertinence
CEEEIIMPPRTV	imperceptive
CEEEIIINPRTTV	interceptive
CEEEIINSSSTZ	citizenesses
CEEEIIPRRSTV	irrespective
CEEEIKNNRSSS	snickersnees
CEEEILLNOPQU	equipollence
CEEEILNNOSTV	nonselective
CEEEILNORSST	reselections
CEEEILORRSST	clerestories
CEEEILPPRTVY	perceptively
	preceptively
CEEEILPRSTVY	respectively
CEEEIMMMNOTT	committeemen
CEEEIMNNNSST	incensements
CEEEIMNNOPRS	omnipresence
CEEEIMNNORST	mesenteronic
CEEEIMNORSTU	neurectomies
CEEEIMNORSVW	servicewomen
CEEEIMORRSTT	stereometric
CEEEINNNOSTX	nonexistence
CEEEINNOSSTV	venesections
CEEEINNOTUVX	nonexecutive

CEEEINNOSSTU	quintessence
CEEEINNRSSSU	insecureness
CEEEINORSTUX	executioners
CEEEINPPRTUV	unperceptive
CEEEINPRRSTT	intercepters
CEEEINRRRSTW	screenwriter
CEEEIOPPRRST	preceptories
CEEEIPPRSSTV	perspectives
CEEEIPRRSSUV	repercussive
CEEEKLNRSSSS	recklessness
CEEELLNPRUUV	pulverulence
CEEELLORRSTY	electrolyser
CEEELLORRTYZ	electrolyzer
CEEELLORSSTY	electrolyses
CEEELLORSTTY	electrolytes
CEEELLORSTYZ	electrolyzes
CEEELMMORTTU	telecommuter
CEEELMNOPSST	completeness
CEEELMORRSST	sclerometers
CEEELMORRTTY	electrometry
CEEELOPRRTTY	electrotyper
CEEELOPRSTTY	electrotypes
CEEELORRSSSU	resourceless
CEEEMNNNORTU	renouncement
CEEEMNNNOSTU	enouncements
CEEEMNOPRRSS	recompensers
CEEEMOPRRSTT	spectrometer
CEEENNNORSTU	encounterers
CEEENNPRTUUV	venepuncture
CEEEOOPRRTTX	exteroceptor
CEEEOOPRSSST	stereoscopes
CEEFFGILNORS	efflorescing
CEEFFIILLOTT	little office
CEEFFLNORSSU	forcefulness
CEEFFNOORRTU	counteroffer
CEEFGGILNNTU	genuflecting
CEEFGHIINPSY	speechifying
CEEFGIILNRTY	electrifying
CEEFGILNNOTU	genuflection
CEEFGILNNRTU	unreflecting
CEEFGLLLNTUY	neglectfully
CEEFGLNORSTU	genuflectors
CEEFHIKRSSSU	suckerfishes
CEEFHILORSSS	Ross Ice Shelf
CEEFHILSSTTU	cuttlefishes
CEEFHKMORRTU	motherfucker
CEEFIIIILNST	infelicities
CEEFIILRTTVY	reflectivity
CEEFIIMNOPRT	imperfection
CEEFIINNORST	reinfections
CEEFIINOPRST	frontispiece
CEEFILLNOSST	flectionless
CEEFILMNRSSU	mercifulness
CEEFILNNORST	inflorescent
CEEFILNOSSUV	voicefulness
CEEFIMNNOOST	confinements
CEEFINORSTTU	counterfeits
CEEFLLOORRTU	electrofluor
CEEFLLPRSTUY	respectfully
CEEFLMOORRST	electroforms
CEEFLOORRSSU	foreclosures
CEEGGILNOSSY	glycogenesis

CEEGHIINORTZ	rhizogenetic	CEEHILOOPRRT	electrophori
CEEGHIINOSTT	histogenetic	CEEHILOPRSST	electorships
CEEGHILNOOST	technologies	CEEHILPRSSTU	lectureships
CEEGHILNOPTY	phylogenetic	CEEHIMMORRTT	thermometric
CEEGHILNPRSU	sepulchering	CEEHIMMOSTTY	thymectomies
CEEGHILOOPRT	herpetologic	CEEHIMMPRSST	sprechstimme
CEEGHIMORSTY	geochemistry	CEEHIMMNNNRTT	intrenchment
CEEGHINNNOPTY	hypnogenetic	CEEHIMNOOSTU	Home Counties
CEEGHINOORTT	orthogenetic	CEEHIMNNOOSTY	homocysteine
CEEGHINOPTTY	phytogenetic	CEEHIMNORSTT	theocentrism
CEEGHINORSTY	hysterogenic	CEEHIMOPRSTT	pitchometers
CEEGHINORTUW	counterweigh	CEEHINNOPRSV	convenership
CEEGHINRRSTT	stretching	CEEHINOOPRST	stereophonic
CEEGHINRSSST	sightscreens	CEEHINOORRSS	rhinoceroses
CEEGIIJNNRTT	interjecting	CEEHINRSSSTT	stretchiness
CEEGIIKNNQRU	requickening	CEEHIOPRSTUX	executorship
CEEGIILLNOTV	vitellogenic	CEEHIPPRRTVY	hyperpyretic
CEEGIINNNSST	enticingness	CEEHKLLNORRS	schnorkeller
CEEGIINNPRST	reinspecting	CEEHKLNOSSUY	honeysuckles
CEEGIINNPRTT	intercepting	CEEHKNORSSUY	honeysuckers
CEEGIINNRSSU	insurgencies	CEEHLMOOPRTU	thermocouple
CEEGIINNRSTT	intersecting	CEEHLOPRSSST	clothespress
CEEGIINOPRTV	precognitive	CEEHMNOOORST	chronometers
CEEGIINORTVX	overexciting	CEEHMNNORSTUX	Herstmonceux
CEEGIINPRSST	stringpieces	CEEHMOOPRSST	thermoscopes
CEEGIJNORRTT	retrojecting	CEEHMOORRSTY	stereochromy
CEEGIKLLNOPS	glockenspiel	CEEHMOPRRSTY	psychrometer
CEEGILMOOORT	meteorologic	CEEHMORSTTYY	hysterectomy
CEEGILNNOSSY	geosynclines	CEEHNOOPPRSS	nephroscopes
CEEGIMNNOPRS	recompensing	CEEHNOORRSTT	orthocenters
CEEGINNNORTU	encountering		orthocentres
CEEGINNOPRRS	precensoring	CEEHOOPRRSTU	urethroscope
CEEGINNOQRRU	reconquering	CEEHOOPSSSTT	stethoscopes
CEEGINNORRTV	reconverting	CEEHORRSTTVY	erythrocytes
CEEGINOPRRSS	reprocessing	CEEHORSSTTTU	outstretches
CEEGINRRRSTU	resurrecting	CEEIIIMNPPRT	impercipient
CEEGIOPRRSTU	picturegoers	CEEIIINNSSSV	incisiveness
CEEGMNOORRST	costermonger	CEEIIINPRRTU	perineuritic
CEEHHIILLLNP	philhellenic	CEEIIINRSSTU	insecurities
CEEHHIINOSTT	henotheistic	CEEIIIOPRSST	preciosities
CEEHHILMOORS	heliochromes	CEEIIIOPSSST	speciosities
CEEHHIMRSSTT	hemstitchers	CEEIIJNNORTT	interjection
CEEHHINPRSTY	hypersthenic	CEEIIJNORTTV	introjective
CEEHHKLRSTTU	kletterschuh	CEEIIKLNNOTU	kinetonuclei
CEEHHLMOOORS	homeschooler	CEEIIKLOOPTU	leukopoietic
CEEHHLOORSST	clotheshorse	CEEIILLNNOTT	intellection
CEEHHMNOOPRS	chromosphere	CEEIILMNNORT	inclinometer
CEEHHOOPPRSS	phosphoresce	CEEIILMOPSTX	complexities
CEEHHOOPRRST	trochosphere	CEEIILMRSTUV	vermiculites
CEEHIIINRRST	inheritrices	CEEIILNNORSV	overinclines
CEEHIIKMNOSS	chemokinesis	CEEIILNNOSSV	insolvencies
CEEHIIKNPRTY	hyperkinetic	CEEIILNNPRSS	princeliness
CEEHIILNNSTT	Lichtenstein	CEEIILNPPRTY	perciipiently
CEEHIINNNPPS	pinchpennies	CEEIILNPSSTX	explicitness
CEEHIKMNOSSS	homesickness	CEEIILOOPSSU	leucopoiesis
CEEHILLNOPSU	nucleophiles	CEEIILOPRTVX	overexplicit
CEEHILLNOSST	clotheslines	CEEIIMNNPRTY	impertinency
CEEHILMMOPRY	myrmecophile	CEEIIMNOPPRT	imperception
CEEHILMNORST	thermoclines	CEEIIMNOSSST	secessionism
CEEHILMOSSTT	Themistocles	CEEIIMOPRSSU	semiprecious
CEEHILNNORTY	incoherently	CEEIIMORRSTU	meretricious
CEEHILNOOSSS	cohesionless	CEEIIMORSSST	esotericisms

CEEIIMORSSTV	viscosimeter
CEEIINNNNNOTV	inconvenient
CEEIINNOPRST	reinspection
CEEIINNOPRTT	interception
CEEIINNORSST	intercession
CEEIINNORSTT	intersection
CEEIINOOPSST	isoteniscope
CEEIINOPRSTT	receptionist
CEEIINORSSTV	insectivores
CEEIINOSSSST	secessionist
CEEIIPPRRSTV	prescriptive
CEEIIPPRTTVY	perceptivity
CEEIJLOPRTVY	projectively
CEEIJNOORRTT	retrojection
CEEIJNORRSTT	interjectors
CEEIJNORRTTY	interjectory
CEEIKKNOPSTV	pocketknives
CEEIKLMNPPRU	pumpernickel
CEEIKLNORRST	interlockers
CEEIKLNOSSSV	lovesickness
CEEILLMNOPTY	incompletely
CEEILLNOPQUY	equipollency
CEEILLORSSTY	electrolysis
CEEILLPRSUVY	preclusively
CEEILMMOPSTU	lumpectomies
CEEILMOOPRSY	copolymerise
CEEILMOOPRVZ	copolymerize
CEEILMOORRST	colorimeters
CEEILMOORSST	sclerotomies
CEEILNNNOTVY	conveniently
CEEILNNNOSUVX	nonexclusive
CEEILNOOPRSS	necropolises
CEEILNOOPSTT	postelection
CEEILNOORRST	intercoolers
CEEILNOPRSTU	neuroleptics
CEEILNORSTTT	electrotints
CEEILOPRTTVY	protectively
CEEILPRSSUVY	percussively
CEEIMMMNORTT	recommitment
CEEIMMMOOSTY	myomectomies
CEEIMNNOPSTT	incompetents
CEEIMNNORSTU	countermines
CEEIMNOOPRST	contemporise
CEEIMNOOPRTZ	contemporize
CEEIMNOORSTT	econometrist
CEEIMNRRSTTU	recruitments
CEEIMOOPSSSS	seismoscopes
CEEIMOPRSSTU	computerises
CEEIMOPRSTUZ	computerizes
CEEINNNOQSTU	inconsequent
CEEINNOORRRT	reconnoitrer
CEEINNOORRST	reconnoiters
	reconnoitres
CEEINNOORRSV	reconversion
CEEINNOOSSTX	coextensions
CEEINNORSSTT	contriteness
CEEINNPRTUUV	venipuncture
CEEINNRRRTTU	intercurrent
CEEINOOPRRTT	interoceptor
CEEINOOPRSTT	stereopticon
CEEINOOPRSTU	counterpoise
CEEINOORRSST	retrocession

CEEINOPPRSSS	sniperscopes
CEEINOPRRSSU	repercussion
CEEINOPRRSTT	interceptors
CEEINOPRSSSU	preciousness
CEEINOPRSSTU	counterspies
	persecutions
CEEINOPSSSSU	speciousness
CEEINORRRSTU	resurrection
CEEINORRSSST	intercessors
	intercrosses
CEEINORRSSTU	intercourses
CEEINORRSSTY	intercessory
CEEINORSTTTU	reconstitute
CEEINPPRRRTU	Prince Rupert
CEEIOOPRRSTT	protectories
	stereotropic
CEEIOORRRSTT	ecoterrorist
CEEKLLNSSSSU	lucklessness
CEEKLNOOSTTY	cytoskeleton
CEEKOOORRRST	retrorockets
CEELLNOORTTV	electronvolt
CEELNNNOQSTUY	consequently
CEELNOOOPRST	coleopterons
CEELNOORSTTU	electrotonus
CEELNORSSSUU	ulcerousness
CEELOOOPRSTU	coleopterous
CEELOPPRSSST	prospectless
CEELPRSSSSTU	sculptresses
CEEMNOORSSUV	overconsumes
CEEMNOORSTUV	countermoves
CEEMNOPRRSTU	procurements
CEEMOPRRSSSU	compressures
CEEMOPRRSTTY	cryptometers
	spectrometry
CEENNOORRSST	cornerstones
CEENNOORRTTU	countertenor
CEENNOQSTUUY	Queen's County
CEENOOOPPRSS	snooperscope
CEENOORRRTTV	controverter
CEENOORRSSTV	seroconverts
CEENOOSSSTUV	covetousness
CEENOPRSTTUY	countertypes
CEENORSSTTTU	stonecutters
CEEOOPRRSTTV	overprotects
CEEOPPRSSSTU	prospectuses
CEERRRSSTTUU	restructures
CEFFGHIINNRY	frenchifying
CEFFHIINNORS	chiffonniers
CEFFHIRSSSTT	festschrifts
CEFFIIINNSTU	insufficient
CEFFIILNSTUY	sufficiently
CEFFIORRSTUU	fructiferous
CEFFIORSSTUU	suffruticose
CEFGGIINNRTU	centrifuging
CEFGIIKLLNRY	flickeringly
CEFGIIMNNORR	reconfirming
CEFHLLLOOOSW	schoolfellow
CEFHLMOOORRU	fluorochrome
CEFIIIILNOSTU	infelicitous
CEFIIILORSSU	siliciferous
CEFIILLOSTUY	felicitously
CEFIILMNNTUY	munificently

CEFIILMORRTU	fluorimetric	CEGIKKNORSTY	skyrocketing
CEFIILNOORRS	ferrosilicon	CEGIKNOORSTV	overstocking
CEFIILNOPRSS	prolificness	CEGILLNRSTUY	clusteringly
CEFIILNOPRTY	proficiently	CEGILNNNOTTY	contingently
CEFIILNORSST	frictionless	CEGILNNOSTTY	contestingly
CEFIILNOSTUY	infectiously	CEGILNOOPRSU	supercooling
CEFIIMNOORST	conformities	CEGILNOOPRTU	glucoprotein
CEFIIMNOOTUZ	Zeno of Citium	CEGILNOOPRTY	glycoprotein
CEFILLMNRUUY	unmercifully	CEGILNOORSST	necrologists
CEFILLMOORSY	frolicsomely	CEGIMNNNOSST	consignments
CEFILLORRTUU	floriculture	CEGIMOOORRSV	microgrooves
CEFILMOORRTU	fluorometric	CEGIMORRRSUY	microsurgery
CEFILNNOSSTU	functionless	CEGINNNNOSTU	unconsenting
CEFILNOORSTU	counterfoils	CEGINNNNORSTT	constringent
CEFILOORSUVY	vociferously	CEGINNORSSTU	countersigns
CEFLNNORSSSU	scornfulness	CEGINNOSTTTU	stonecutting
CEFLOOOPRSSU	fluoroscopes	CEGINNPSSTUU	unsuspecting
CEFMNNNOORTT	confrontment	CEGINOOPPRRV	overcropping
CEFNOOOPRRTU	counterproof	CEGINORRSSTU	stringcourse
CEFNOORRSTTU	counterforts	CEGINPPRTTUU	uppercutting
CEGGIILNNNSS	clingingness	CEGLNOORSTUW	counterglows
CEGGILNOOSTY	gynecologist	CEGLOPRSSUUU	groupuscules
CEGHHIILNRSY	cherishingly	CEGMOOSTUYYZ	zygomycetous
CEGHHIILOPRY	hieroglyphic	CEGNNOOPRSSU	scuppernongs
CEGHHIIMNSTT	hemstitching	CEHHHNOOPRRY	rhynchophore
CEGHHILNOSTT	nightclothes	CEHHIILLOSTV	Cheviot Hills
CEGHIIKNPRSW	shipwrecking	CEHHIILMOPRT	thermophilic
CEGHIILNRSTT	chitterlings	CEHHIILOSTTY	ichthyolites
CEGHIINNRSST	christenings	CEHHIIPSSTTW	whipstitches
CEGHIINOPRTV	overpitching	CEHHILMNORTT	trochelminth
CEGHIIOPSSTY	geophysicist	CEHHILMRSSUY	helichrysums
CEGHIKNNOSSS	shockingness	CEHHILNRSSSU	churlishness
CEGHILNOOORS	chronologies	CEHHILOOPRTY	hypochlorite
CEGHILNOOSTT	technologist	CEHHIMMOOOPR	homeomorphic
CEGHILOOOSTY	stoechiology	CEHHIMOOPRTT	photothermic
CEGHILOOPSSY	psychologies	CEHHIMOOPSTT	photochemist
	psychologise	CEHHIMOPSTTY	phytochemist
CEGHILOOPSYZ	psychologize	CEHHIOOPPRST	photospheric
CEGHINNNORTU	truncheoning	CEHHIOPPRRTY	hypertrophic
CEGHINNNOSSTU	touchingness	CEHHIOPSSTYZ	schizophytes
CEGHINORRTWY	cringeworthy	CEHHLOOOSSSU	schoolhouses
CEGHINSSUWZZ	zwischenzugs	CEHHMMOORRTY	thermochromy
CEGHIOPRRSTY	copyrighters	CEHHMOOOPRRS	chromophores
CEGIIIILMSTT	legitimistic	CEHHMOOPRSSY	hypsochromes
CEGIIJNNORTT	introjecting	CEHHOOOPRRST	trochophores
CEGIIKLNNORT	interlocking	CEHIIILNOOPS	eosinophilic
CEGIIKLNSSST	singlesticks	CEHIIINPSSTZ	citizenships
CEGIILLOOSTX	lexicologist	CEHIIKLNSSST	ticklishness
CEGIILNNOORS	recolonising	CEHIIKNOOPTT	photokinetic
CEGIILNNOORZ	recolonizing	CEHIILLNNORS	Lincolnshire
CEGIILNNPSTY	inspectingly	CEHIILMNOPRS	necrophilism
CEGIILNORSST	sclerotising	CEHIILNQSSSU	cliquishness
CEGIILNORSTZ	sclerotizing	CEHIILOPPRSS	scripophiles
CEGIILOOORST	soteriologic	CEHIILOPSTTY	polytheistic
CEGIIMMNORTT	recommitting	CEHIIMMOOSSS	chemiosmosis
CEGIINNOOPRT	precognition	CEHIIMNOOSTT	monotheistic
CEGIINNOORST	recognitions	CEHIIMNOPRUY	perionychium
CEGIINNRSSTY	syncretising	CEHIIMNOPSST	phonemicists
CEGIINNRSTYZ	syncretizing	CEHIIMNORSTT	trichotomies
CEGIINNRTTTU	intercutting	CEHIINNOPRTY	pericynthion
CEGIINOPTTYY	genotypicity	CEHIINOOPRSS	rhinoscopies
CEGIJKNOOTUY	outjockeying	CEHIINOORSSS	isochronises

CEHIINOORSSZ	isochronizes
CEHIIOPRRSTU	peritrichous
CEHIIOPRSSVY	viceroyships
CEHIKLMORSTY	locksmithery
CEHIKNOSSSST	stockishness
CEHILLNNOPSU	punchinellos
CEHILLNOOPSS	colonelships
CEHILLOPPTYY	polyphyletic
CEHILMMOPRYY	myrmecophily
CEHILMNOOPTY	monophyletic
CEHILMNOOPTY	nympholeptic
CEHILNNOSSSW	clownishness
CEHILOOPRTTU	luteotrophic
CEHILOQSTTUY	coquettishly
CEHILORRTTUU	horticulture
CEHILPPRRSUU	persulphuric
CEHIMMOOPRRT	morphometric
CEHIMMOOPRST	chemotropism
CEHIMNORRTYY	erythromycin
CEHIMOOPRRTT	thermotropic
CEHIMOORSTYZ	zoochemistry
CEHIMOOSSSST	schistosomes
CEHIMOPPRSST	coppersmiths
CEHINNOOPRSV	convenorship
CEHINNORRSSY	synchroniser
CEHINNORRSYZ	synchronizer
CEHINNORSSSY	synchronises
CEHINNORSSYZ	synchronizes
CEHINOOPRRSS	coronerships
CEHINOORRSST	orchestrions
CEHIOOOPPRST	photocopiers
CEHIOOPPRRST	tropospheric
CEHIOOPRSTTY	hyperostotic
CEHILLLOPRSSY	sclerophylls
CEHMNORSTUUX	Hurstmonceux
CEHMOOOOPPST	photocompose
CEHMOOOOPRTY	oophorectomy
CEHMOOSSSTUU	customshouse
CEHNOOOPRRSU	necrophorous
CEHNOOPRRTTU	photocurrent
CEHOOPRRSTUY	urethroscopy
CEHOPPRSTTYY	cryptophytes
CEIIIIILNSTV	incivilities
CEIIIIILMPSST	simplicities
CEIIIIILPRSTT	triplicities
CEIIILLMNPSU	penicilliums
CEIIILLNPTXY	inexplicitly
CEIIILMNPSST	implicitness
CEIIILOPRSTV	proclivities
CEIIIMNOPRSS	precisionism
CEIIINNORSTU	reunionistic
CEIIINNOSSTW	Wisconsinite
CEIIINNOSTTU	continuities
CEIIINOPRSST	precisionist
CEIIINORTTWZ	zwitterionic
CEIIINOSSTVV	vivisections
CEIIIJLNNTUVY	injunctively
CEIIIJNNOORTT	introjection
CEIIIKLLPSSTT	lickspittles
CEIIIKLOOPSTY	poikilocytes
CEIIIKPRSSSTT	spitstickers
CEIIILLNOSTUY	licentiously
CEIIILLRSTUUV	silviculture
CEIIILMNNOOPT	incompletion
CEIIILMNNOSTY	omnisciently
CEIIILMNOSSUX	exclusionism
CEIIILMOPRTUV	pluviometric
CEIIILNOOSTTU	elocutionist
CEIIILNOPRSUY	perniciously
CEIIILNOSSTUX	exclusionist
CEIIILOPRSSUU	supercilious
CEIIILRRTTUUV	viticulturer
CEIIILRSTTUUV	viticultures
CEIIIMMNOORSS	commissioner
CEIIIMMNOPRTU	minicomputer
CEIIIMNOOPSTT	competitions
CEIIIMNORSSTU	neuroticisms
CEIIIMOORSSTT	sociometrist
CEIIIMORRRSTW	microwriters
CEIIINNNORSTU	internuncios
CEIIINNNOSSTT	inconsistent
CEIIINNORRSTU	insurrection
CEIIINOOPRRTY	incorporeity
CEIIINOORSSST	consistories
CEIIINOPPRRST	prescription
CEIIINORRSSTT	restrictions
CEIIINORSSTUX	excursionist
CEIIINORSTTVY	ventricosity
CEIIINOSTTTUV	constitutive
CEIIINRRSSSTU	scrutinisers
CEIIINRRSSTUZ	scrutinizers
CEIIIOPPRRSTV	proscriptive
CEIIIPRRRSTTW	scriptwriter
CEIIIPSSTTUVY	susceptivity
CEIIKLNOORRST	crinkleroots
CEIIKLOOSSTUY	leukocytosis
CEIIKMNNOORST	moonstricken
CEIIKNNORSSTU	countersinks
CEIILLLMNOUUV	involucellum
CEIILLLNOOOSV	violoncellos
CEIILLMOOOTVY	locomotively
CEIILLMOPSUVY	compulsively
CEIILLMOSTUUY	meticulously
CEIILLNOSUVVY	convulsively
CEIILLOPRSSTU	portcullises
CEIILLRSTUUVY	sylviculture
CEIILMNOOOSUY	monoeciously
CEIILMNOOSTUU	contumelious
CEIILMNOPRSTY	polycentrism
CEIILMOOOPSSS	cosmopolises
CEIILMOOOPSST	cosmopolites
CEIILNNOSSTTY	consistently
CEIILNOORRTTU	interlocutor
CEIILNOORSSUY	censoriously
CEIILNOORSTUW	Low Countries
CEIILNOSSSSUU	lusciousness
CEIILNOSSTUUY	incestuously
CEIILOPRRTUVY	corruptively
CEIIMMNNORSTY	nonsymmetric
CEIIMMOOPRRSS	compromisers
CEIIMNNOOPRSU	mispronounce
CEIIMNNOORSTU	conterminous
CEIIMNOOPRSSS	compressions
CEIIMNOOPRSTU	mucoproteins

CEIMNOPRSTTY	streptomycin
CEIMNOPSSTUV	consumptives
CEIMNOPSSTUY	pneumocystis
CEIMNORSSSTU	consumerists
	misconstrues
CEIMOOORRSTV	visceromotor
CEIMOOPRRSTU	micropterous
CEINNOOPRTTU	counterpoint
CEINNOOPRTVW	Provincetown
CEINNOORSSSU	connoisseurs
CEINNOSSTTTU	constituents
CEINOOPRSSTU	prosecutions
CEINORSSTTTU	constituters
CEINPSSSTTUU	intussuscept
CEINRRSSSTTU	instructress
CEIOOOOPRSTT	osteoporotic
CEIOOPRSTTYZ	cryptozoites
CEIPPRRSSSTU	superscripts
CELLLOORSSUY	colourlessly
CELLMOOPRRST	comptrollers
CELMNOPRTUUU	mucopurulent
CELNOOPRSTTU	counterplots
CEMMNNNOOSSU	uncommonness
CEMMOOSTUXYY	myxomycetous
CEMNNOORTUWY	countrywomen
CEMNOOPSTTUU	contemptuous
CENNOSSSTUUU	unctuousness
CEPRRSSSTTUU	superstructs
CFFGINOORSSU	offscourings
CFFGINORRSSU	crossruffing
CFGHIIKNOPRT	pitchforking
CFGIIILMMNOR	microfilming
CFGILMNNOORY	conformingly
CFGILMNOORTY	comfortingly
CFHIILNOOSSS	ichnofossils
CFIIILOSTTUY	fictitiously
CFIIKLLOORST	folkloristic
CFIILLNOOSTU	solifluction
CFIILMOORSSS	microfossils
CFIIMNNOORTY	inconformity
CFILNORSSUUU	furunculosis
CFIMNNOORTUY	unconformity
CFLLOORSSUUY	scrofulously
CGGHIINOPRTY	copyrighting
CGGIINNNORST	constringing
CGHHIINORTUW	witching hour
CGHIIIINNNRST	trichinising
CGHIIIINNNRTZ	trichinizing
CGHIIKLMNOST	locksmithing
CGHIILOOOPRT	oligotrophic
CGHIILOOOSTY	stoichiology
CGHIILOORSTT	trichologist
CGHIIMNOOPSY	physiognomic
CGHIIMOOPRTT	thigmotropic
CGHILMOOPSSY	psychologism
CGHILNOOORST	chronologist
CGHILOOORSST	chorologists
CGHILOOPSSTY	phycologists
	psychologist
CGHIMNOORSST	shortcomings
CGHINOOOPPTY	photocopying
CGHINOOPSSSY	psychognosis

CGHINORSTTTU	shortcutting
CGIIIIILNOPST	politicising
CGIIIIILNOPTZ	politicizing
CGIIIMNOSSTY	misogynistic
CGIIINNRSSTU	scrutinising
CGIIINNRSTUZ	scrutinizing
CGIILMOOSSTU	musicologist
CGIILNNNOTUY	continuingly
CGIILNNOPRSY	conspiringly
CGIILNOOOSST	iconologists
CGIILOOOSSST	sociologists
CGIILOOOSTTX	toxicologist
CGIIMMNOOPRS	compromising
CGIINNOSTTTU	constituting
CGILMOOOSSST	cosmologists
CGILNOOSTUUY	contiguously
CGILOOOPRSTT	proctologist
CGILOOPRSTTY	cryptologist
CGIMNOOOSSST	cosmogonists
CGINOOPRSSTY	pyrognostics
CGLMOOOOTXYY	mycotoxology
CHHIIOOPPRST	phosphoritic
CHHILMOPRTYY	polyrhythmic
CHHIMOOOPRRT	orthomorphic
CHHIOOOPPRTT	phototrophic
CHHLMOOPRTUY	chlorophytum
CHHLOOOPRSUY	hypochlorous
CHHMMOOOORSU	homochromous
CHIIIORSSSTT	historicists
CHIILNOOPRTY	Trichinopoly
CHIIMNNRSSTY	strychninism
CHIIMNOOPSTY	monophysitic
CHIINNOORTTY	nonrhoticity
CHIINOOPTTYY	hypotonicity
CHILOOOPPRSU	coprophilous
CHILOOPSSTUY	polystichous
CHIMMNOOORST	monochromist
CHIMNNORSSSY	synchronisms
CHIMNOOOPRST	monostrophic
CHIMNOOORSTU	monotrichous
CHIMNOOOSSTU	monostichous
CHIMNOOPRRSS	prochronisms
CHIMNOPRSTYY	chymotrypsin
CHIMOOOPPRRT	protomorphic
CHIMOOOORSTTU	trichotomous
CHINOOOPRSTY	ornithoscopy
CHINOOPPSTYY	posthypnotic
CHIOOOPPRTTT	prototrophic
CHIOOOPRRSTV	Rostropovich
CHKLMOOPRTUY	Plymouth Rock
CHKMNOOORRTT	Throckmorton
CHLMOOOPRSUY	polychromous
CHLOOOPSTUYY	hypocotylous
CHMNOOOSTTTU	cottonmouths
CHNNOORRSSTY	synchrotrons
CHNNOORRTTUY	North Country
CIIIIKKKNNNN	kinnikinnick
CIIIIOPSSTTV	positivistic
CIIIILLMMNORS	millimicrons
CIIIILLMPTTUY	multiplicity
CIIINNOPRSST	inscriptions
CIIILLOOSSTUY	solicitously

CIILMNNORSUY	synclinorium	DDEEENOPRSUX	underexposed
CIILMNOOOPST	monopolistic	DDEEENORSUVZ	rendezvoused
CIILNNNNOOSU	noninclusion	DDEEFHIIIMRU	dehumidifier
CIILNOOPSSTU	liposuctions	DDEEFHIIIMSU	dehumidifies
CIILOORSTUVY	victoriously	DDEEFIIINNTU	unidentified
CIILOPSSSUUY	suspiciously	DDEEGHHOOPRS	Good Shepherd
CIIMMNNOOSTU	comminutions	DDEEGHIILMTW	middleweight
CIIMMOORSSTT	microtomists	DDEEGHINORSY	hydrogenised
CIIMNOOOPSST	compositions	DDEEGHINORYZ	hydrogenized
CIIMNOPRSTTY	nyctitropism	DDEEGILMNOST	dislodgement
CIIMNRSSSTTU	misinstructs	DDEEGILNORUV	overindulged
CIIMOPRRSSTU	scriptoriums	DDEEGNOPRSSU	groundspeeds
CIINOOPPRRTU	incorruption	DDEEHIIINRST	disinherited
CIINNOOSTTTU	constitution	DDEEHIIIPPPS	Pheidippides
CIINNORSSTTU	instructions	DDEEHIILNOOT	endothelioid
CIINOOPPRRST	proscription	DDEEHINOPSTY	dehypnotised
CIJLNORSSTUU	jurisconsult	DDEEHINOPTVZ	dehypnotized
CILLMOOPRSUY	compulsorily	DDEEIILMMNPS	simpleminded
CILLORRSSUUY	scurrilously	DDEEIILQSTUY	disquietedly
CILNNOOOSTUV	convolutions	DDEEIKNNRRUW	wunderkinder
CILNNOOSTUUY	continuously	DDEEILNNPSSS	splendidness
CILNOOOOPRSTU	colourpoints	DDEEILNOPSSS	lopsidedness
CIMMNNNOOSTU	noncommunist	DDEEIMNNOSTW	disendowment
CIMMOOORSSTU	microstomous	DDEEINNRRSSU	underinsured
CIMOOOPRRSSU	microsporous	DDEEINORRSTV	overstridden
CINOORSSTTTU	constitutors	DDEEINRSSTUU	understudies
CLLOPRSSUUUY	scrupulously	DDEEIOPSSSSS	dispossessed
CLNOPRSSUUUU	unscrupulous	DDEELNNOPSTY	despondently
DDDDEEEEEFIL	fiddledeedee	DDEEMNOOSSTU	outmodedness
DDDEEEILMNRT	intermeddled	DDEEMNPRRTUU	undertrumped
DDDEEEENRRSSU	underdressed	DDEEENOPPPRRU	underpropped
DDDEEFHIIIMU	dehumidified	DDEFNOOOPRSU	soundproofed
DDDEEFHILRSU	Huddersfield	DDEGGIINNRRU	undergirding
DDDEEIIIMPSY	epididymides	DDEGHILNRSUY	shudderingly
DDDEEINRSTUU	understudied	DDEGILMNOSST	dislodgments
DDDEHNNOOORR	rhododendron	DDEGILNNOPSY	ploddingness
DDEEEEGIRRST	deregistered	DDEGILNNOPSY	despondingly
DDEEEEIMNRRT	redetermined	DDEGILNOORST	dendrologist
DDEEEEMNNSST	dementedness	DDEGLNOOORSU	dendrologous
DDEEEENNSSTX	extendedness	DDEGNNORRSUU	undergrounds
DDEEEENORTVX	overextended	DDEHIIIMNNSU	undiminished
DDEEEENRRSTU	understeered	DDEHILNNOOPR	philodendron
DDEEEENRSSSV	deservedness	DDEIIIILPRSTY	dispiritedly
DDEEEFGINNRU	underfeeding	DDEIIJLNOSTY	disjointedly
DDEEEFMNORSS	deformedness	DDEIILNNOORR	liriodendron
DDEEEGINOSXY	deoxygenised	DDEIINRSTUWY	industrywide
DDEEEGINOXYZ	deoxygenized	DDEILNOPRUVY	unprovidedly
DDEEEHLMNRUW	underwhelmed	DDEIMOOPPSUU	pseudopodium
DDEEEIINSSST	desensitised	DDEINNOOSSTT	endodontists
DDEEEIINSSTZ	desensitized	DDEJKLNNOORS	Nordenskjöld
DDEEEILMNRST	intermeddles	DDENNORSTTUV	von Rundstedt
DDEEEILMNRTY	determinedly	DDINOOOPRSTT	diprotodonts
DDEEEIMNNRTU	undetermined	DEEEEFHILNSS	needlefishes
DDEEEIMOPRSW	disempowered	DEEEEGMNNNRT	engenderment
DDEEEINNNPST	independents	DEEEEHILRSSW	sidewheelers
DDEEEINNPRST	interdepends	DEEEEHLNSSSS	heedlessness
DDEEEIOPPRST	predeposited	DEEEEHNPRRRS	reprehenders
DDEEELLMMOSY	meddlesomely	DEEEEIILRRSV	redeliveries
DDEEELNOPPRU	underpeopled	DEEEEIMNPRRT	predetermine
DDEEELNOPRRT	Old Pretender	DEEEEIMNPRTX	experimented
DDEEELNOPRUV	underdevelop	DEEEEIMNRRST	redetermines
DDEEENOPRRUW	underpowered	DEEEELNNSSSS	needlessness

DEEEELOPRRSV	redevelopers
DEEEEMOPRSST	speedometers
DEEEENRRRVVY	Very Reverend
DEEEENRRSSSV	reservedness
DEEEFIINNSST	definiteness
DEEEFINPRRSU	superrefined
DEEEFNNQRTUU	unfrequented
DEEEGGHILNRT	greenlighted
DEEEGHHOPPRS	hedgehoppers
DEEEGHINNPRR	reprehending
DEEEGHIORTVW	overweighted
DEEEGHNNRSTT	strengthened
DEEEGIIILMST	delegitimise
DEEEGIIILMTZ	delegitimize
DEEEGIILNRRV	redelivering
DEEEGIIMNSST	disesteeming
DEEEGILNOPRV	redeveloping
DEEEGIMNNRTU	unregimented
DEEEGINNORST	roentgenised
DEEEGINNORTZ	roentgenized
DEEEGINNRSSS	resignedness
DEEEGINOSSXY	deoxygenises
DEEEGINOSXYZ	deoxygenizes
DEEEGINRRSTU	unregistered
DEEEGJMNPRTU	prejudgement
DEEEGORRRSST	retrogressed
DEEEHILMNSTV	dishevelment
DEEEHIMOPRSV	empowerished
DEEEHIMPRSST	deemstership
DEEEHMNNORTT	dethronement
DEEEIILNORRT	Indre-et-Loire
DEEEIIMNPRSV	Midi-Pyrénées
DEEEIINRSSST	desensitiser
DEEEIINRSSSV	derisiveness
DEEEIINRSSTZ	desensitizer
DEEEIINSSSST	desensitises
DEEEIINSSSTZ	desensitizes
DEEEIIORRSTX	exteriorised
DEEEIIORRTXZ	exteriorized
DEEEIKLNOSST	skeletonised
DEEEIKLNOSTZ	skeletonized
DEEEILMOPRSY	depolymerise
DEEEILMOPRYZ	depolymerize
DEEEILMPRTVV	redemptively
DEEEILNNOPST	needlepoints
DEEEILNRSSSW	wildernesses
DEEEILNRSTTY	interestedly
DEEEILNSSSUV	delusiveness
DEEEILPRSSVY	depressively
DEEEIMNOPRRT	redemptioner
DEEEIMNORSTT	densitometer
DEEEIMNRRSTW	Midwesterner
DEEEIMNRSSTV	disseverment
DEEEIMOPRSTX	extemporised
DEEEIMOPRTXZ	extemporized
DEEEIMPRRTTT	pretermitted
DEEEIINNRSTTU	uninterested
DEEEINOPPRTU	neuropeptide
DEEEINORRTVW	overwintered
DEEEINPRRSST	interspersed
DEEEINPRSTUX	expenditures
DEEEINRRSSSV	vinedressers

DEEEIPPRSSST	sidesteppers
DEEEIPRRSSSU	depressurise
DEEEIPRRSSUZ	depressurize
DEEEKLNNOOST	endoskeleton
DEEELLNRRSSU	undersellers
DEEELMNNORSY	moneylenders
DEEELMNOPRTY	redeployment
DEEELMNOPSTV	developments
DEEELMNOSTVV	devolvements
DEEELMNPPSTU	supplemented
DEEELNORSSSV	resolvedness
DEEELNRRSTTU	underletters
DEEELNRRSUVY	unreservedly
DEEELOOPRSVV	overdevelops
DEEEMNNORSST	endorsements
DEEEMNORRSTV	Most Reverend
DEEEMPRSTTUW	trumpetweeds
DEEENOPRSSUX	underexposes
DEEENRRRRSSU	surrenderers
DEEENRRSSTTT	trendsetters
DEEEOPPRRSUW	superpowered
DEEEOPPRSSSS	prepossessed
DEEFFFGINSTU	feedingstuff
DEEFFHINRRSU	undersheriff
DEEFGHHORSTU	feedthroughs
DEEFGIIINPRS	presignified
DEEFGJMNORTU	forejudgment
DEEFHIIIMNSS	semifinished
DEEFHIINNSSS	fiendishness
DEEFHJLNNOOY	John of Leyden
DEEFIIIILNST	infidelities
DEEFIIIILNNTY	indefinitely
DEEFIIIILNTVY	definitively
DEEFIIIMNNRS	indemnifiers
DEEFIIIRRSSV	diversifiers
DEEFIILMRSSU	demulsifiers
DEEFIILNNRRU	unfriendlier
DEEFIILNNRSS	friendliness
DEEFIILNRSTU	unfertilised
DEEFIILNRTUZ	unfertilized
DEEFILLPSTUY	despitefully
DEEFILOPRSTT	potter's field
DEEFLOORSTUY	surefootedly
DEEFMOOPRRTU	outperformed
DEEGGHHINOPP	hedgehopping
DEEGGIINNPRS	predesigning
DEEGGIINPRST	predigesting
DEEGGIMNORST	disgorgement
DEEGHIILLNSV	dishevelling
DEEGHIINNNSTW	winding sheet
DEEGHIINSTUX	extinguished
DEEGHINNORTY	heterodyning
DEEGHINORSSY	hydrogenises
DEEGHINORSYZ	hydrogenizes
DEEGHINRSSST	nightdresses
DEEGHNORSSTU	groundsheets
DEEGIIIINNST	indigenities
DEEGIILMNNRT	intermingled
DEEGIILMHOOPY	epidemiology
DEEGIILNNRSS	slenderising
DEEGIILNNRSZ	slenderizing
DEEGIILNNSSY	yieldingness

DEEGIILOOPPT	oligopeptide
DEEGIILOPSTT	epiglottides
DEEGIILRSSVY	digressively
DEEGIIMNNOST	demonetising
DEEGIIMNNOTZ	demonetizing
DEEGIIMNPRST	distempering
DEEGIINNORST	nitrogenised
DEEGIINNORTZ	nitrogenized
DEEGIINNPRST	predestining
DEEGIINOPRST	predigestion
	redepositing
DEEGIINORSST	redigestions
DEEGIINPPSST	sidestepping
DEEGIJMMNSTU	misjudgement
DEEGILLNNRSU	underselling
DEEGILLNRSSW	well dressing
DEEGILMNNNOY	moneylending
DEEGILMNOOOS	demonologies
DEEGILMNSTUV	divulgements
DEEGILMOOSTY	etymologised
DEEGILMOOTYZ	etymologized
DEEGILNNRTTU	underletting
DEEGILNORSUV	overindulges
DEEGILNPRSSY	depressingly
DEEGINNNPRTU	unpretending
DEEGINNNRSSU	enduringness
DEEGINNOPRSV	overspending
DEEGINNNRRSU	surrendering
DEEGINNNRSTT	trendsetting
DEEGINNNRSTTU	undersetting
DEEGINORRSSV	overdressing
DEEGLLOOSTYY	dysteleology
DEEGLNNOOSUY	endogenously
DEEHHIIMOPRS	hemispheroid
DEEHHIOPPRSW	horsewhipped
DEEHHIOPSSTY	hypothesised
DEEHHIOPSTYZ	hypothesized
DEEHHLOORSSU	householders
DEEHIILNQRSU	relinquished
DEEHIILNSSSV	devilishness
DEEHIIMOPRSV	impoverished
DEEHIINOSSST	dishonesties
DEEHIINPRSST	residentship
DEEHILLORSTT	titleholders
DEEHILMMNOST	demolishment
DEEHILOOPRST	heteroploids
DEEHILPRSSUU	desulphurise
DEEHILPRSUUZ	desulphurize
DEEHIMMNORST	endothermism
DEEHINOPSSTY	dehypnotises
DEEHINOPSTYZ	dehypnotizes
DEEHIOPPRTTY	pteridophyte
DEEHKNOOOSUW	Kenwood House
DEEHLPRSTTUU	sulphuretted
DEEHMOORRSTY	hydrometeors
DEEHNNORSTTU	thunderstone
DEEIIILLRSST	distilleries
DEEIIIMNRTTV	divertimenti
DEEIIINORRST	interiorised
DEEIIINORRTZ	interiorized
DEEIIINSSSVV	divisiveness
DEEIIKLLNRTW	winterkilled

DEEIIKNNRTTT	interknitted
DEEIILMNSSSU	disseminules
DEEIILNNSSUW	unwieldiness
DEEIILNOPRSS	lepidosirens
DEEIILNRSSTU	unsterilised
DEEIILNRSTUZ	unsterilized
DEEIILOPRSSY	erysipeloids
DEEIILPRSSVY	dispersively
DEEIIMNNRSTT	disinterment
DEEIIMNORSTT	endometritis
DEEIIMNORTTV	divertimento
DEEIIMNPSSST	dissepiments
DEEIIMNRRSST	irredentisms
DEEIIMNRSSTT	determinists
DEEIIMORRTTU	dumortierite
DEEIINNPRSST	intrepidness
DEEIINNSSSTT	dissentients
DEEIINOOPRST	repositioned
DEEIINPRSSST	spiritedness
DEEIINQSSSTU	disquietness
DEEIINRRSSTT	irredentists
DEEIINRSSSTT	disinterests
DEEIINRSTTTW	intertwisted
DEEIIOOPRSST	depositories
DEEIIOQSSSUX	sesquioxides
DEEIIRRSSSTW	weird sisters
DEEIIRSSTTUV	divestitures
DEEIJNORRRSU	surrejoinder
DEEIKMNPPSSU	pumpkinseeds
DEEILLLLOOPV	Léopoldville
DEEILLNNQTUY	delinquently
DEEILMNNSSSS	mindlessness
DEEILNNOOPRS	prednisolone
DEEILNNSSSSW	windlessness
DEEILNOOPPRT	lepidopteron
DEEILOPPPSTY	polypeptides
DEEILOPPRSUV	oversupplied
DEEILOPRSSTY	proselytised
DEEILOPRSTYZ	proselytized
DEEIMNNORSST	indorsements
DEEIMNNPSSTU	impudentness
DEEIMNNRSTTU	instrumented
DEEIMNOOPRSS	monodisperse
DEEIMNORSTTY	densitometry
DEEIMOOPRSTT	dioptometers
DEEIMOPPRRST	pteridosperm
DEEIMOPPRSSU	superimposed
DEEIMOPRRSTT	Redemptorist
DEEINNNORSST	nonresidents
DEEINNOQSTUU	unquestioned
DEEINNPRSSTU	superintends
DEEINNRRTTUW	underwritten
DEEINORSSSSU	desirousness
DEEINPRSSUUV	unsupervised
DEEINRRSTUUW	underwriters
DEEIOOPRSSTU	eurodeposits
DEEIOOORSTTV	detritovores
DEEIOPSSSSSS	dispossesses
DEELMNORSTUY	tremendously
DEELMOORSTVY	overmodestly
DEELNORSSSSW	wordlessness
DEELNOSSSSUU	sedulousness

DEENNNOSSTUW	unwontedness
DEENOOPRSSST	dessertspoon
DEENOOPRSSTU	uprootedness
DEENOPPPRRRU	underpropper
DEENORRSSTUY	understoreys
DEENORSSSTUX	dextrousness
DEENPPRSSSUU	unsuppressed
DEFGHILLLTUY	delightfully
DEFGIIIMNNNY	indemnifying
DEFGIIINNNRTY	denitrifying
DEFGIIINNSST	disinfesting
DEFGIIINRSSV	diversifying
DEFGIIINRTVY	devitrifying
DEFGIILMNSUY	demulsifying
DEFGIILNNORT	interfolding
DEFGIIMNSTYY	demystifying
DEFGIIINORSST	disforesting
DEFGINNOPTUY	typefounding
DEFGJMNORSTU	forjudgments
DEFHINPRSSTT	spendthrifts
DEFIIILMSTUY	semifluidity
DEFIILNOORSX	dorsiflexion
DEFIILOPRSUY	perfidiously
DEFINNOPRSTU	profundities
DEFIOORRSSUU	sudoriferous
DEFNNOOPRSSU	profoundness
DEGGHLNOORSW	hornswoggled
DEGGHLOOORYY	hydrogeology
DEGGKLLRSUUY	skullduggery
DEGHHIINOPST	diphthongise
DEGHHIINOPTZ	diphthongize
DEGHHIORSSTT	shortsighted
DEGHIIILNRSS	disrelishing
DEGHIILLNOTT	titleholding
DEGHILMOOSTY	mythologised
DEGHILMOOTYZ	mythologized
DEGHILNNRTUY	thunderingly
DEGHNORRSTUW	undergrowths
DEGIIILNNSTT	disentitling
DEGIIILNPPSS	sideslipping
DEGIIIMNNNOS	dimensioning
DEGIIINNNRTW	interwinding
DEGIIINNNSTW	disentwining
DEGIIINNORST	disorienting
DEGIIINNNRST	disinterring
DEGIIINNSSTV	disinvesting
DEGIIKNNORRV	overdrinking
DEGIILLOOSTT	deltiologist
DEGIILNNOSUY	indigenously
DEGIILNNSSTY	dissentingly
DEGIILNORSSV	redissolving
DEGIINNNNPRU	underpinning
DEGIINNOSSUU	disingenuous
DEGIINNRRTUW	underwriting
DEGIINOPPRSS	predisposing
DEGIINORRSTV	overstriding
DEGIJMMNSSTU	misjudgments
DEGIKMNOPRSU	superkingdom
DEGILMNOOOST	demonologist
DEGILNNORSUY	resoundingly
DEGILNOOOSTT	deontologist
DEGILOOPRSTT	proglottides
DEGINNOQRTUU	underquoting
DEGINOOPPRST	doorstepping
DEGLLNORSSUW	groundswells
DEGLLNORSSUY	groundlessly
DEHHIIILMOOP	hemophilioid
DEHHILOSSSTU	South Shields
DEHHIOPRRTYY	hyperthyroid
DEHHLNOSSTUU	sleuthhounds
DEHIIILNOPRS	siderophilin
DEHIIIMMNNST	diminishment
DEHIIKLLNOOU	unlikelihood
DEHIILPRSSTU	trisulphides
DEHILLOPPSUY	polysulphide
DEHILNOPSSSS	slipshodness
DEHILOOPRRSV	overlordship
DEHIMMNOOPRS	endomorphism
DEHINNOOQRUY	hydroquinone
DEHINNORRSUU	undernourish
DEHINOOPRSST	spinsterhood
DEHINOORRSSU	dishonourers
DEHIOOOPPRST	photoperiods
DEHIOOPRSSTT	orthopedists
DEHLLOORRTWY	otherworldly
DEHLNOORRSSU	horrendously
DEHLNOORSTTW	Old Northwest
DEHLNORSTUUY	thunderously
DEHMMNORRSTTU	thunderstorm
DEHMOOPPRSSU	pseudomorphs
DEHNOOOOPRST	odontophores
DEHNOOOORTXY	neoorthodoxy
	neo-orthodoxy
DEHNOOOORSTUW	southernwood
DEHNRRSSTTUU	underthrusts
DEIIIILSSTTU	disutilities
DEIIILMNTUVY	diminutively
DEIILLOOQSSU	soliloquised
DEIILLOOQSUZ	soliloquized
DEIILPRSTUVY	disruptively
DEIIMORSSSTT	dosimetrists
DEIJNPRRSTUU	jurisprudent
DEILMNOOOPTU	leontopodium
DEIMNOPSTUYY	pseudonymity
DEINOOOPPRRT	proportioned
DEINOSSSSTUU	studiousness
DEIOOPRSSSSS	dispossessor
DELLMNOOSSTU	modus tollens
DELNNOOPSTYY	polysyndeton
DELNOOORSSSU	dolorousness
DELNOPSSTUUY	stupendously
DEMNOOPSSUUY	pseudonymous
DENNOORSSSUW	wondrousness
DFGHIINNOSTW	downshifting
DFGHIMNOORRY	hydroforming
DGGGILNNRUUY	ungrudgingly
DGGHINNOTTUU	doughnutting
DGGIILNNRSTU	disgruntling
DGGIILNSSTUY	disgustingly
DGHIINNOORSU	dishonouring
DGHILOORSSTY	hydrologists
DGIIILOORSST	iridologists
DGIILOOPRSUY	prodigiously
DGILNOOOOSTT	odontologist

743

DGINNORRSSUU	surroundings
DHHIILOOPPPS	phospholipid
DHHILOOPRSUY	hydrophilous
DHHIOOPRSTYY	hypothyroids
DHIIIMMOOPRS	idiomorphism
DHILNOOQRSUY	hydroquinols
DHIMOOPRRSTY	hydrotropism
DHINOOOORSTTT	orthodontist
DHIOOORSTTUW	withoutdoors
DHLNOOOPPTYY	polyphyodont
DHLNOOORTUXY	unorthodoxly
DIIIINOQSSTU	disquisition
DIIIINOSSSTV	divisionists
DIIILLNOSSSU	disillusions
DIIINOOPSSST	dispositions
DIILMNOSTUWW	multiwindows
DIILNOOSSSTU	dissolutions
DIILNOOSSTUU	solitudinous
DILLORSSTUUY	stridulously
EEEEEFGINRRS	Friese-Greene
EEEEFGHILNRW	freewheeling
EEEEEFILQRSTU	teleferiques
EEEEEGIILNPSS	spiegeleisen
EEEEEGILLNPSU	Eulenspiegel
EEEEEGILMNRTT	telemetering
EEEEEHILPQRTU	telepherique
EEEEEHIMNPRST	hemiterpenes
EEEEEHINPRRSV	reprehensive
EEEEEHKOPRSSU	housekeepers
EEEEEHLMNOPRT	nephelometer
EEEEEHLNRSSTV	nevertheless
EEEEEHNNSSTTV	seventeenths
EEEEEIINRSTVW	interviewees
EEEEEIISSTVWW	sweetiewives
EEEEEIMNPRRTX	experimenter
EEEEEIMNPRST	presenteeism
EEEEEIMNPRSSW	minesweepers
EEEEEIMNRSTTX	extensimeter
EEEEEINNQRSTU	equestrienne
EEEEEINSSSTWY	eyewitnesses
EEEEEIPRSSTTU	repetiteuses
EEEEEKOPRRSST	storekeepers
EEEEELMNRSTTT	resettlement
EEEEELNRSSSST	treelessness
EEEEELRRSSTTT	trestletrees
EEEEEMNOPRRTT	penetrometer
EEEEEMNORSTTX	extensometer
EEEEENNPRRRTU	entrepreneur
EEEEENNRRSSTV	reverentness
EEEEENPRRSSSV	perverseness
EEEEFFFMNNOST	enfeoffments
EEEEFFHILRSTW	whiffletrees
EEEEFFIMORSTU	effusiometer
EEEEFFINORRST	effronteries
EEEEFFINSSSUV	effusiveness
EEEEFFLLNNORW	fennelflower
EEEEFGILNNSST	fleetingness
EEEEFGLLNRUVY	revengefully
EEEEFGLNNSSUV	vengefulness
EEEEFGNNOORSS	foregoneness
EEEEFHIKNRRST	freethinkers
EEEEFHINRRRSW	Renfrewshire

EEEEFHINRSSSV	feverishness
EEEEFHMNRRSST	refreshments
EEEEFIIKLLNSS	lifelikeness
EEEEFIILLLLMU	millefeuille
EEEEFIILMPRSX	exemplifiers
EEEEFIILNRRTT	interfertile
EEEEFIIMNNNSS	feminineness
EEEEFILLNSSSS	lifelessness
EEEEFILNNORVX	nonreflexive
EEEEFILNSSTTX	self-existent
EEEEFINOORSST	festooneries
EEEEFINPRRSSU	superrefines
EEEEFLLNSSSSU	selflessness
EEEEFLNNSSTUV	eventfulness
EEEEFNNQRSSTU	frequentness
EEEEGHIIMNRSU	euhemerising
EEEEGHIIMNRUZ	euhemerizing
EEEEGHIKNOPSU	housekeeping
EEEEGHILNNRST	enlighteners
EEEEGHILRTTWW	welterweight
EEEEGHIMNOSTU	meeting house
	meetinghouse
EEEEGHLNOPSSY	phylogeneses
EEEEGHNNRRSTT	strengthener
EEEEGHNOORSTU	heterogenous
EEEEGHNORSSTT	togetherness
EEEEGHOORTTYZ	heterozygote
EEEEGIILMNNTV	inveiglement
EEEEGIIMNNPSW	minesweeping
EEEEGIINNORRT	orienteering
EEEEGIINORSST	generosities
EEEEGIINPSSST	epigenesists
EEEEGIKNOPRST	storekeeping
EEEEGILLNOOSS	selenologies
EEEEGILNOPRSV	oversleeping
EEEEGILNRSSTW	swingletrees
EEEEGILRRSSVY	regressively
EEEEGIMNRSSSU	messeigneurs
EEEEGINNORSST	roentgenises
EEEEGINNORSTZ	roentgenizes
EEEEGINNPRRST	representing
EEEEGINNPSSSW	sweepingness
EEEEGINOOSSST	osteogenesis
EEEEGINORRSTV	oversteering
EEEEGINORRTVX	overexerting
EEEEGINQRSSTU	sequestering
EEEEGIOQRSSTU	grotesquerie
EEEEGIPRRRSST	preregisters
EEEEGLNOORSTT	etonogestrel
EEEEGMNORSSSU	gruesomeness
EEEEGMOPRRSTY	pyrgeometers
EEEEGNNORSSSU	generousness
EEEEGNOOPRRST	progesterone
EEEEGNOORRSUV	overgenerous
EEEEGNOORSSST	stereognoses
EEEEGORRRSSST	retrogresses
EEEEHHILLLNPS	philhellenes
EEEEHHINPSSSS	sheepishness
EEEEHHMOPRRST	thermosphere
EEEEHILNPRRSS	replenishers
EEEEHILPPRSTW	whippletrees
EEEEHILRSSSTV	shirtsleeves

EEEHIMNNNRST	enshrinement
EEEHIMNRSTTU	hermeneutist
EEEHIMOPRRSV	empoverisher
EEEHIMOPRSSV	empoverishes
EEEHIMORSSTX	heterosexism
EEEHINNOPRRS	reprehension
EEEHINOPRRSU	superheroine
EEEHINPRSTVY	hypertensive
EEEHIORSSTTX	heterosexist
EEEHLLNOPTYY	polyethylene
EEEHLLNPSSSS	helplessness
EEEHLMNOPRTY	nephelometry
EEEHLMNOSSSS	homelessness
EEEHLNOPSSSS	hopelessness
EEEHMMORRSTT	thermometers
EEEHMNNNNORTT	enthronement
EEEHMOORRSTU	heteromerous
EEEHMOPRRSST	spherometers
EEEHNOPRRRSY	reprehensory
EEEHOPPRSSST	prophetesses
EEEIIKLNORSY	Kyrie eleison
EEEIILPPRSTX	perplexities
EEEIILPRTTVY	repetitively
EEEIIMNRSSTT	mesenteritis
EEEIINPRRTTV	interpretive
EEEIINPRSSVX	inexpressive
EEEIINRRSTVW	interviewers
EEEIIORRSSTX	exteriorises
EEEIIORRSTXZ	exteriorizes
EEEIIPPRSTTU	perpetuities
EEEIIPQRRSTU	prerequisite
EEEIIPRRSSTV	perversities
EEEIJLNNSSUV	juvenileness
EEEIKLNORSTU	leukotrienes
EEEIKLNOSSST	skeletonises
EEEIKLNOSSTZ	skeletonizes
EEEILLLOPPTT	little people
EEEILMMNPRST	implementers
EEEILMNNPRTY	preeminently
EEEILMNNSSSU	unseemliness
EEEILMNNSTTT	entitlements
EEEILMNSSSST	timelessness
EEEILMPPRTVY	preemptively
EEEILNNPRTVY	preveniently
EEEILNPRRSTT	teleprinters
EEEILNPRTVVY	preventively
EEEILNRRRTVY	irreverently
EEEILNRSSSST	tirelessness
EEEILNRSSSTW	westerliness
	Western Isles
EEEILPRRSSVY	repressively
EEEILPRSSVXY	expressively
EEEIMNNNSSTW	entwinements
EEEIMNNPRSTT	presentiment
EEEIMNNPRSTU	supereminent
EEEIMNNRRSTT	reinterments
EEEIMNOORSTT	enterotomies
EEEIMNORSSST	tiresomeness
EEEIMNORSSTT	sensitometer
	tensiometers
EEEIMNPRRSST	misrepresent
EEEIMNQQRSUU	quinqueremes
EEEIMNQRRSTU	requirements
EEEIMNQRSTTU	requitements
EEEIMOORRSST	stereoisomer
EEEIMOORSSTT	stereotomies
EEEIMOPRRSTX	extemporiser
EEEIMOPRRTXZ	extemporizer
EEEIMOPRSSTX	extemporises
EEEIMOPRSTXZ	extemporizes
EEEIMPRRRTTT	pretermitter
EEEINNPRSSTX	inexpertness
EEEINNPRSTUV	supervenient
EEEINNRSSSTV	inventresses
EEEINORRRSSV	reversioners
EEEINPRRRSST	enterprisers
EEEINPRRRSTT	interpreters
	reinterprets
EEEINPRRSSST	intersperses
EEEINPRSSTUV	eruptiveness
EEEINPRSSUVX	unexpressive
EEEINRRTTTUX	intertexture
EEEIORRSTVVX	extroversive
EEEKLNOOSSTX	exoskeletons
EEEKLOOPPSSS	spokespeople
EEEKLORRSSTW	steelworkers
EEELLLNRSSTY	relentlessly
EEELLMORRTTU	tellurometer
EEELLNOSSSSV	lovelessness
EEELMMNOPRTY	reemployment
EEELMNNOOSSS	lonesomeness
EEELMNNOPSTV	envelopments
EEELMNNSTTTU	unsettlement
EEELMNPPRSTU	supplementer
EEELMOPPRRTT	teleprompter
EEELNNOSSSST	tonelessness
EEELNNSSSSTU	tunelessness
EEELNOPRSSSS	responseless
EEELNORSSSTU	resoluteness
EEELNRSSSSST	restlessness
EEELOOPRSTTU	teleutospore
EEELPRRSSSSU	pressureless
EEEMNNPRSSTT	presentments
EEEMPRSSSSST	sempstresses
EEENOORSSTTT	testosterone
EEEOOPRRSUVX	overexposure
EEEOPPRSSSSS	prepossesses
EEEOPRRRSSUV	overpressure
EEEFFGHIIRRST	firefighters
EEFFLLORSSTY	effortlessly
EEFGGIOPRSTT	pettifoggers
EEFGGIOPRTTY	pettifoggery
EEFGHIIKNNRT	freethinking
EEFGHIILNRRT	freightliner
EEFGHIILNRTT	Ferlinghetti
EEFGHIILRTTW	weightlifter
EEFGHIIPRRTZ	prizefighter
EEFGHILNRRSY	refreshingly
EEFGIIINPRSS	presignifies
EEFGIILMNPXY	exemplifying
EEFGIIMNNNRT	infringement
EEFGIINNORRV	overrefining
EEFGIINOPRRT	profiteering
EEFGIINSSTUV	fugitiveness

EEFGIKNNOORT	foretokening
EEFGILLNSSUU	guilefulness
EEFGILNNOSUX	genuflexions
EEFGIMORSTTU	fugitometers
EEFGINOPPRST	Epping Forest
EEFHIILRSSSV	silverfishes
EEFHNOORRSST	foreshortens
EEFIIINNNSST	infiniteness
EEFIIINNRSST	intensifiers
EEFIILMOPPRT	epileptiform
EEFIIMNOPRST	mifepristone
EEFIIMNORSSU	seminiferous
EEFIINOPRRSS	personifiers
EEFIINORRSSU	resiniferous
EEFILLORSSTU	stelliferous
EEFILMOOORST	tomfooleries
EEFILMORRSTU	fluorimeters
EEFILMORSTTU	flittermouse
EEFILNNQRTUY	infrequently
EEFILNOORRTX	retroflexion
EEFILNPSSSTU	spitefulness
EEFILOOPRRST	profiteroles
EEFIMNNORRST	frontiersmen
EEFLLMORRSUY	remorsefully
EEFLLNNTUUVY	uneventfully
EEFLMNORRSUU	unremorseful
EEFLMNORSSSS	formlessness
EEFLMOORRSTU	fluorometers
EEFLNOPRSSUW	powerfulness
EEFNOOORSSST	footsoreness
EEGGHIILNNNT	enlightening
EEGGHIINORVW	overweighing
EEGGIILNNRSS	gingerliness
EEGGIIMNORST	geometrising
EEGGIIMNORTZ	geometrizing
EEGGILSSTUVY	suggestively
EEGGLLOOOPSX	googolplexes
EEGGNOOPRSST	progestogens
EEGGNOORSSSU	gorgeousness
EEGHHILRSTWW	wheelwrights
EEGHHINOORSS	horseshoeing
EEGHIILLMRST	limelighters
EEGHIILNNPRS	replenishing
EEGHIILNPSST	slipsheeting
EEGHIIMNNRST	intermeshing
EEGHIINOSSST	histogenesis
EEGHIINRSSST	tigerishness
EEGHIINRSTUX	extinguisher
EEGHIINRTTWW	winterweight
EEGHIINSSTUX	extinguishes
EEGHILMNORVW	overwhelming
EEGHILNOPPST	teleshopping
EEGHILNOPSSY	phylogenesis
EEGHILOORSST	theologisers
EEGHILOORSTZ	theologizers
EEGHILRSSTTT	streetlights
EEGHIMMRSTUW	summerweight
EEGHIMNOORSS	homogenisers
EEGHIMNOORSZ	homogenizers
EEGHIMOORSST	isogeotherms
EEGHINNOPSSY	hypnogenesis
EEGHINNOSSTT	ethnogenists
EEGHINNPSTWY	pennyweights
EEGHINOORSST	orthogenesis
EEGHINOPSSTY	phytogenesis
EEGHLMNNOORS	longshoremen
EEGHLOOORSTU	heterologous
EEGHMNOORRSW	whoremongers
EEGHMNOORRWY	whoremongery
EEGHMNOORSTU	thermogenous
EEGHNOOORSTU	heterogonous
EEGHNOORSTUY	heterogynous
EEGHOORSTUYZ	heterozygous
EEGIIINNRTVW	interviewing
EEGIILLNNNST	sentinelling
EEGIILMNNNPT	implementing
EEGIILMNNRST	intermingles
EEGIILMOOSST	semeiologist
EEGIILNOSTTT	stilettoeing
EEGIILOPSSTT	epiglottises
EEGIIMMNNPST	impingements
EEGIIMNNNRSS	minnesingers
EEGIIMNNORST	remonetising
EEGIIMNNORTZ	remonetizing
EEGIINNORSST	nitrogenises
EEGIINNORSTZ	nitrogenizes
EEGIINNPRRST	enterprising
EEGIINNPRRTT	interpreting
EEGIINNRSSTW	westernising
EEGIINNRSTWZ	westernizing
EEGIINNSTTTW	Wittgenstein
EEGIKLLNNNNU	unkennelling
EEGIKLNORSTW	steelworking
EEGILLNOOSST	selenologist
EEGILLNRSTWY	swelteringly
EEGILLOOPSST	speleologist
EEGILLOOSSTT	teleologists
EEGILMNOOOST	entomologise
EEGILMNOOOTZ	entomologize
EEGILMNOORSU	numerologies
EEGILMNORRSS	mongrelisers
EEGILMOOPSTY	epistemology
EEGILMOOSSTY	etymologises
EEGILMOOSTYZ	etymologizes
EEGILNNORTUV	volunteering
EEGILNNSSSSW	winglessness
EEGILNOORRSW	lower regions
EEGILOPRSSTT	poltergeists
EEGIMNNPSSTT	temptingness
EEGIMNNRRSTU	interregnums
EEGIMNORSSTW	swingometers
EEGINNNRRSSU	unerringness
EEGINNPRSSSS	pressingness
EEGINOOPRRVW	overpowering
EEGINOOPRSSS	sporogenesis
EEGINOOPRSVX	overexposing
EEGINOORSSST	stereognosis
EEGINOPPRSTV	overstepping
EEGINOPRSSSS	repossessing
EEGINOPRSTTY	stereotyping
EEGINORSSSUV	grievousness
EEGINOSSSUUX	exiguousness
EEGINPRRSSST	prestressing
EEGINPRSSTTU	guttersnipes

EEGIOPRRSSSV	progressives
EEGKLLMNSSUU	muskellunges
EEGKPPRSTYYZ	Kyrgyz Steppe
EEGLMNNOOOPR	prolegomenon
EEGMNNORSSST	engrossments
EEGNNOORRSUU	neurosurgeon
EEGNORRRSUUY	neurosurgery
EEGNORSSSSST	songstresses
EEHHIIMMOPRT	hemimorphite
EEHHIINSSSTV	thievishness
EEHHILLNOPTY	theophylline
EEHHILMOPRST	thermophiles
EEHHILNNORTY	Henry the Lion
EEHHINRSSSSW	shrewishness
EEHHIOPPRRSW	horsewhipper
EEHHIOPRSSTY	hypothesiser
EEHHIOPRSTYZ	hypothesizer
EEHHIOPSSSTY	hypothesises
EEHHIOPSSTYZ	hypothesizes
EEHHLLNNOORZ	Hohenzollern
EEHHLLOPPRSY	phyllosphere
EEHHLLOPRTYY	heterophylly
EEHHMNOOPRSY	hymenophores
EEHHMOOPRRTY	heteromorphy
EEHHMOORSSTU	housemothers
EEHHOOPRRSTT	heterotrophs
EEHIIIKLNSSU	kleinhuisies
EEHIIINRRSTX	inheritrixes
EEHIIKKLRRSS	Selkirkshire
EEHIIKNPRSSY	hyperkinesis
EEHIILNOOPSS	eosinophiles
EEHIILNPRSTY	prehensility
EEHIILNQRRSU	relinquisher
EEHIILNQRSSU	relinquishes
EEHIILNRSSSV	liverishness
EEHIIMNPPRRU	perinephrium
EEHIIMOPRRSV	impoverisher
EEHIIMOPRSSV	impoverishes
EEHIIMPPRRSS	premierships
EEHIINNSSSVX	vixenishness
EEHIIOPRRSST	prehistories
EEHIKMNNOSSY	monkeyshines
EEHILMMOSSTU	mesotheliums
EEHILMNNPSST	plenishments
EEHILMNORSST	motherliness
EEHILMOORSTT	lithometeors
EEHILMOPPRSS	spermophiles
EEHILNNPSTWY	pennywhistle
EEHILNOOPSST	siphonostele
EEHILNOPRSTU	neutrophiles
EEHILNOPSSTT	telephonists
EEHILOPRSSTU	upholsteries
EEHIMNOOPRST	nephrotomies
EEHIMOPPRRSS	emperorships
EEHINNOPRSTY	hypertension
EEHINRSSSSTY	synthesisers
EEHINRSSSTYZ	synthesizers
EEHIPRSSSTTU	trusteeships
EEHKOORRSSUW	houseworkers
EEHLMNOSTTVW	twelvemonths
EEHLNRSSSSTU	ruthlessness
EEHLOPRRSSTU	reupholsters

	upholsterers
EEHMMORSSSUU	summerhouses
EEHMNNOOORRU	neurohormone
EEHMNNOOORSY	honeymooners
EEHMNNOOPRTY	hymenopteron
EEHMNOOORSTU	heteronomous
EEHMNOORSTUY	heteronymous
EEHMOPPRRTYY	hypermetropy
EEHMOPPRSSTY	spermophytes
EEHMORRSTUUY	eurythermous
EEHNNORRSTTW	northwestern
EEHNORRSSTTW	northwesters
EEHNORSSTTUW	southwestern
EEHOOOOPRSTTU	heterotopous
EEHOOPPSTTTY	phototypeset
EEHOOPRRSSTU	porterhouses
EEHOOPRSSSTY	hyperostoses
EEHOOPRSSTTT	photosetters
EEHORSSSTTUW	southwesters
EEIIIJLNSTUV	juvenilities
EEIIIMNRSSTV	intermissive
EEIIIMOOPSST	episiotomies
EEIIINORRSST	interiorises
EEIIINORRSTZ	interiorizes
EEIIINPRRSTU	perineuritis
EEIIINRSSTUV	universities
EEIIKLLNNSSU	unlikeliness
EEIIKLOOPSSU	leukopoiesis
EEIIKNQRSSSU	quirkinesses
EEIILLNSSSUV	illusiveness
EEIILLPPRSST	pipistrelles
EEIILMNNPTTY	impenitently
EEIILMNNSSTU	untimeliness
EEIILMNOPSST	impoliteness
EEIILMNRSSST	minstrelsies
EEIILMPRSSVY	impressively
	permissively
EEIILNNRSSTW	winterliness
EEIILNPPRSSS	slipperiness
EEIILNPRSSST	priestliness
EEIILNPSSSST	pitilessness
EEIILNRSSSST	sisterliness
EEIILNRSSTUV	lentiviruses
EEIILOPSTVXY	expositively
EEIIMMNNNSST	imminentness
EEIIMMNOPRRS	minor premise
EEIIMNNNSTTW	intwinements
EEIIMNNRTTTT	intermittent
EEIIMNNOPRRSS	reimpression
EEIIMNOSSSSV	omissiveness
EEIIMNPRRSTT	misinterpret
EEIIMNPRSSUV	unimpressive
EEIIMNPRSTTY	sempiternity
EEIIMNRRTTUX	intermixture
EEIIMORSSTUV	semivitreous
EEIINNNORTTV	intervention
EEIINNNOSSTV	nonsensitive
EEIINNORRSST	reinsertions
EEIINNORSTTT	retentionist
EEIINNPPSSST	snippetiness
EEIINNPRRSWZ	prizewinners
EEIINNPSSTUV	punitiveness

EEIINNRSSSST	sinisterness	EEIMNORSTTZZ	mezzotinters
EEIINOORSSSTV	stereovision	EEIMOPPRSSSU	superimposes
EEIINOPPRSST	propensities	EEIMOPRRRSST	misreporters
EEIINOPRRSSV	irresponsive	EEINNNORRSTU	interneurons
EEIINOPSSSTV	positiveness	EEINNOPRSSUV	unresponsive
EEIINORRSTVV	introversion	EEINNOPRSTUV	supervention
EEIINORRTTVV	introvertive	EEINNORSSSSU	resinousness
EEIINPRRTTUV	interruptive	EEINOOPPSSST	oppositeness
EEIINRSSTTUV	investitures	EEINOOPRRSSS	responsories
EEIIOOPRRSST	repositories	EEINOOPRSSSS	repossession
EEIIOOPRSSTV	seropositive	EEINOORRRSTV	retroversion
EEIIOPPRSSTV	prepositives	EEINOORRSTTX	extortioners
EEIIPRSSTVXY	expressivity	EEINOORRSTVX	extroversion
EEIKLMNNOSTY	Milton Keynes	EEINOORSSSTU	interosseous
EEIKLNNNORSV	Vernoleninsk	EEINOPPRSSUV	unoppressive
EEIKOPRRRSTW	worker-priest	EEINOPRSSSSU	supersession
EEILLMOSSTVY	motivelessly		suspensories
EEILLMPRSTUX	multiplexers	EEINOPRSSSTV	sportiveness
EEILLNNOQTUY	ineloquently	EEINOPRSSSUV	perviousness
EEILLNNOSSSV	slovenliness		previousness
EEILLNNOSSUV	unloveliness	EEINORSSSTUV	vitreousness
EEILLNSSSSST	listlessness	EEINPRRRSTTU	interrupters
EEILLORRSTUV	irresolutely	EEINRRSSTUWW	wienerwursts
EEILLRSSSSTY	resistlessly	EEIOPPRRRSST	proprietress
EEILMMNNOPRST	implementors	EEIOPRSSTTTY	stereotypist
EEILMNNOSTVV	involvements	EEIORRRSSTUV	retroviruses
EEILMNOOSSST	toilsomeness	EEIORRSSSTWW	Swiss Re Tower
EEILMNOOSSTZ	Simon Zelotes	EEIPRRRSSSSU	pressurisers
EEILMNORSTUV	volunteerism	EEIPRRRSSSUZ	pressurizers
EEILMOOPRSST	metropolises	EEKKOORRRSTV	voortrekkers
EEILMOOPRSTU	pleurotomies	EEKLNORSSSSW	worklessness
EEILMOPPRRTY	peremptorily	EEKNNOORSTTT	Stoke-on-Trent
EEILMOPRSTUV	pluviometers	EEKNOOPPRSSS	spokesperson
EEILMORSSSTU	moistureless	EEKNOORRSSTW	stoneworkers
EEILMPRSTUVY	resumptively	EELLNNOORSSV	lovelornness
EEILNNOOPSVX	nonexplosive	EELLNOSSSSSU	soullessness
EEILNOOORSSU	oleoresinous	EELLORRSSTTY	storytellers
EEILNOOPPRSY	polyisoprene	EELMMNNOPTUY	unemployment
EEILNOORRSTU	resolutioner	EELMOPPRRSUY	superpolymer
EEILNOPRSSSU	perilousness	EELNOOPPPRSY	polypropenes
EEILNOPRSSVY	responsively	EELNOPRRSTUU	seropurulent
EEILNOQSSSTU	questionless	EELNOPSSSSTT	spotlessness
EEILNPRSSTTY	persistently	EEMNNOOPPSTT	postponement
EEILNPSSSUVY	suspensively	EEMNNOORSSSU	enormousness
EEILOPPRSSUV	oversupplies	EEMNNOOSSSUV	venomousness
EEILOPPRSSVY	oppressively	EEMNNORSSSUU	numerousness
EEILOPRRSSTY	proselytiser	EEMNNRSSTTTU	entrustments
EEILOPRRSTYZ	proselytizer	EENNOOPRRSTU	neuropterons
EEILOPRSSSTY	proselytises	EENNOSSSSSUU	sensuousness
EEILOPRSSTYZ	proselytizes	EENOOPRRSTUU	neuropterous
EEILOPSSSSVY	possessively	EENOPRRSSSUY	supersensory
EEIMMNNOOPST	empoisonment	EEOOPPRRSSTU	preposterous
EEIMMNOPRSTV	improvements	EEOOPRRSSSSS	repossessors
EEIMMNPRSSST	impressments	EFFGGHIIINRT	firefighting
EEIMMPRSSUVV	sempervivums	EFFGIINOOPRR	fireproofing
EEIMNNNORSTV	environments	EFFGIINORRTY	refortifying
EEIMNNOOPPRS	perispomenon	EFFGINORSTUV	overstuffing
EEIMNNOORSTV	normotensive	EFFILNRSSTUU	fruitfulness
EEIMNNOPSSTT	impotentness	EFGGGIINOPTT	pettifogging
EEIMNOPPRRSS	improperness	EFGGLOOORSST	footsloggers
EEIMNOQRSUUU	equinumerous	EFGHHILNTTTW	Twelfth Night
EEIMNORSSTTY	sensitometry	EFGHHOORSTTU	forethoughts

EFGHIINNRRSU	refurnishing
EFGHILNRSSTU	rightfulness
EFGIIINNNSTY	intensifying
EFGIILLLORSW	gilliflowers
EFGIILMNNOSY	solemnifying
EFGIILNNORTW	interflowing
EFGIILNNRSST	triflingness
EFGIILNORSUV	griseofulvin
EFGIILNRRTYY	terrifyingly
EFGIINNOPRSY	personifying
EFGIINNPRRST	fingerprints
EFGIINORRTTT	retrofitting
EFGILLLORSWY	gillyflowers
EFGILLNRTTUY	flutteringly
EFGILMNOORST	montgolfiers
EFGILNPSTUYY	stupefyingly
EFGLNNORSSUW	wrongfulness
EFHHILLOOOSY	holy of holies
EFHIILQRRSSU	squirrelfish
EFHIILRRSSTT	shirtlifters
EFHILLRSSTTY	thriftlessly
EFHILMNRSSTU	mirthfulness
EFHIMNPRSSSU	frumpishness
EFHLLNOSSSTU	slothfulness
EFHLNOSSTUUY	youthfulness
EFHLNRSSTTUU	truthfulness
EFHLOOOPRRSU	fluorophores
EFIIIILNNTVY	infinitively
EFIIIMNORSTU	uniformities
EFIILMOPRSVY	oversimplify
EFIIMMNORRSS	misinformers
EFIIMNOPSSTT	postfeminist
EFIINNORSSTU	interfusions
EFIINOPRSSTU	perfusionist
EFIKLLLNSSSU	skillfulness
EFILNOOPSSTT	toploftiness
EFILNRSSSTTU	tristfulness
EFIOOOPRRSSU	soporiferous
EFLLOPPRSUUY	purposefully
EFLMNNORSSUU	mournfulness
EFLNOPRSSSTU	sportfulness
EFLNRSSSTTUU	trustfulness
EFNNNORRRSTU	frontrunners
EFNNOORRSSSW	forswornness
EGGHHHIILRST	highlighters
EGGHHIILSTTW	lightweights
EGGHIILNNOOP	pigeonholing
EGGHIILNOOST	theologising
EGGHIILNOOTZ	theologizing
EGGHIIMNNOOS	homogenising
EGGHIIMNNOOZ	homogenizing
EGGHIINNORTV	overnighting
EGGHIINPRSSS	priggishness
EGGHILNSSSSU	sluggishness
EGGHLNOORSSW	hornswoggles
EGGHLOOOOPTY	photogeology
EGGIIIIILMNST	legitimising
EGGIIIIILMNTZ	legitimizing
EGGIILLMMNRY	glimmeringly
EGGIILLNNSTY	glisteningly
EGGIILLNRSTY	glisteringly
EGGIILLNRTTY	glitteringly

EGGIILMNNORS	mongrelising
EGGIILMNNORZ	mongrelizing
EGGIIMNNORSV	misgoverning
EGGIINNNORST	rontgenising
EGGIINNNORTZ	rontgenizing
EGGIINNNSSST	stingingness
EGGILLLNORVY	grovellingly
EGGILMMOOSST	gemmologists
EGGIMNOOPRSS	gossipmonger
EGGINORSTYYZ	Szent-Györgyi
EGGLNNOOORTY	rontgenology
EGHHHOORRTTU	throughother
EGHHILNOSSSU	ghoulishness
EGHHMORRTTUY	merrythought
EGHHNOORSSTU	thoroughness
EGHIIKLNNSST	knightliness
EGHIIKNNPRRS	preshrinking
EGHIILMMNRSY	shimmeringly
EGHIILMNOPRS	negrophilism
EGHIILMNPRWY	whimperingly
EGHIILNOSTTU	silhouetting
EGHIILOORSST	hierologists
EGHIILPRSSTT	sprightliest
EGHIIMNNOPRS	premonishing
EGHIINNSSSTY	synthesising
EGHIINNSSTTY	synthetising
EGHIINNSSTYZ	synthesizing
EGHIINNSTTYZ	synthetizing
EGHIINORSTWW	Wigtownshire
EGHILMNOORST	moonlighters
EGHILMOOOPRS	morphologies
EGHILMOOORSS	homologisers
EGHILMOOORSZ	homologizers
EGHILMOORSTY	mythologiser
EGHILMOORTYZ	mythologizer
EGHILMOOSSTY	mythologises
EGHILMOOSTYZ	mythologizes
EGHILNOOPRST	nephrologist
	phrenologist
EGHILNOOPSST	nephologists
	phenologists
EGHILNOOSSTT	ethnologists
EGHILNOPRSTU	upholstering
EGHILNPRSTUU	sulphureting
EGHILOOPPSST	psephologist
EGHIMNNNOOOY	honeymooning
EGHIMNPRSSSU	grumpishness
EGHINNOOSSST	soothingness
EGHINOOORSTV	overshooting
EGHINOOPRRSV	governorship
EGHINOOPSTTT	photosetting
EGHINOORRTVW	overthrowing
EGHINOPRSSSU	springhouses
EGHINORRTTUW	interwrought
EGHINORSTTTW	ghostwritten
EGHIORRSSTTW	ghostwriters
EGHMNOOPRSTY	Grey-Thompson
EGIIIKLNNRT	interlinking
EGIIILNNNRST	interlinings
EGIIILNORSST	religionists
EGIIIMNNRTTT	intermitting
EGIIIMNOPSTU	impetiginous

EGIIINNNPRWZ	prizewinning
EGIIINNNRTTW	intertwining
EGIIINNNSSTV	invitingness
EGIIINNOPSSW	Winnipegosis
EGIIKKLNRRSS	Kriss Kringle
EGIIKLNPPRRS	klipspringer
EGIIKNNNSSST	stinkingness
EGIIKNNORRTW	interworking
EGIIKNNRSSST	strikingness
EGIIKNPRSSTT	spirkettings
EGIILLMNPSSS	misspellings
EGIILLMNPTUX	multiplexing
EGIILLNOPRSV	overspilling
EGIILLNORSTU	guillotiners
EGIILLNPRSUW	wirepullings
EGIILLNQRRSU	squirrelling
EGIILMMNOPSY	misemploying
EGIILMNOPRSY	polymerising
EGIILMNOPRYZ	polymerizing
EGIILMOOSSST	seismologist
	semiologists
EGIILNNOORSU	nonreligious
EGIILNNORTVV	intervolving
EGIILNOOOPSS	oligopsonies
EGIILNPPRRSY	perspiringly
EGIIMMNRSSTY	symmetrising
EGIIMMNRSTVZ	symmetrizing
EGIIMNNOPSSS	imposingness
EGIIMNNOTTZZ	mezzotinting
EGIIMNOOPRRT	primogenitor
EGIIMNOORRST	risorgimento
EGIIMNOPRRST	misreporting
EGIIMRSSSTTU	Trismegistus
EGIINNNORTVY	inventorying
EGIINNOPRRTV	overprinting
EGIINNORRSUV	overinsuring
EGIINNORRTTV	introverting
EGIINNPRRTTU	interrupting
EGIINPRRSSSU	pressurising
EGIINPRRSSUZ	pressurizing
EGIKLLMNOORY	kremlinology
EGILLNORSTTY	storytelling
EGILMNNORTTY	tormentingly
EGILMNOOOSTT	entomologist
EGILMNOORSTU	numerologist
EGILMNOOSTYZ	enzymologist
EGILMOORSSTT	metrologists
EGILMOOSSSTU	museologists
EGILMOOSSTTY	etymologists
EGILNOOPRSUY	pyroligneous
EGILNOORSSSU	gloriousness
EGILNOORSSTU	neurologists
EGILNOPPRSSY	oppressingly
EGILNOPRSTTY	protestingly
EGILNRSTTTUY	stutteringly
EGILOOORSSTT	erotologists
EGILOOOSSSTT	osteologists
EGILOOPRSSTT	petrologists
EGIMMNOOPRSU	spermogonium
EGIMNOORRSSV	misgovernors
EGIMNOORRTTY	trigonometry
EGIMNOPRRTUV	overtrumping
EGINNOPRSTTU	unprotesting
EGINNRSSSTTU	trustingness
EGINOOPRRSSS	progressions
EGINOORRSSSU	rigorousness
EGINOORSSSUV	vigorousness
EGINOPPPRSSU	presupposing
EGIOPRRSSSST	progressists
EGLMNNOOPRST	prolongments
EHHIILOOPPSS	philosophies
	philosophise
EHHIILOOPPSZ	philosophize
EHHIIMMMOPRS	hemimorphism
EHHILOOPPRSS	philosophers
EHHILOPPSTUY	hyposulphite
EHHIMMOOORTY	homoiothermy
EHHIMMOOPRRS	rheomorphism
EHHIMMOOPRST	theomorphism
EHHIMNOOPRST	thermosiphon
EHHIMOOPRRST	theriomorphs
EHHINOOOPPRS	siphonophore
EHHIOOPPRSST	phosphorites
EHHIOOPSSSTT	theosophists
EHHIOPSSSTTY	hypothesists
EHHMNOOOPRTY	phytohormone
EHHOOPPRSSSU	phosphoruses
EHIIILORSTTT	lithotrities
EHIIIMNPRSST	ministership
EHIIKNOOPSST	photokinesis
EHIIKNORRSSS	Kinross-shire
EHIIKNSSSSTT	skittishness
EHIILLMNPSTU	phillumenist
EHIILLNOPSTT	septillionth
EHIILLNOSTTX	sextillionth
EHIILMOOPRST	heliotropism
EHIILMRSSSTV	silversmiths
EHIILOOPSTTX	toxophilites
EHIILOPRRTTT	lithotripter
EHIIMMOPPRRS	perimorphism
EHIIMNPRSTUX	xiphisternum
EHIIMOOPPRSS	epimorphosis
EHIINOPRSTTY	hyponitrites
EHIILLOPPRTYY	pyrophyllite
EHIILMMOOPPRS	pleomorphism
EHILNNOSSTYZ	Solzhenitsyn
EHILNOOPRTTU	luteotrophin
EHILNOOPSUUY	euphoniously
EHILNOORTTWY	noteworthily
EHILNPPRSSSU	purplishness
EHILNSSSSTTU	sluttishness
EHIMMMOOPRSS	mesomorphism
EHIMMOORSSTU	mesothoriums
EHIMNOOPSSTY	monophysites
EHIMNOORSTTU	nototheriums
EHIMNORRSTUY	erythroniums
EHIMOOPPRRSU	perimorphous
EHIMOOPPRRTY	pyromorphite
EHIMOOPRSTTT	photometrist
EHIMOOPSSTTY	mythopoeists
EHIMOPRSSTTY	hypsometrist
EHINNORSSTUW	unworthiness
EHINOOPRRSTT	ornithopters
EHIOOOPRSTTZ	trophozoites

EHIOOPRSSSTY	hyperostosis
EHIOPQRSSSTU	questorships
EHIOPRRSSUVY	surveyorship
EHLLMOOPSSUY	mesophyllous
EHLMOOOPPRTY	photopolymer
EHMMOOOPRSSU	mesomorphous
EHMMOOORRSTT	thermomotors
EHMNNOORRSTT	northernmost
EHMNOOOPRSST	monostrophes
EHMNOORSSSUU	humorousness
EHMNOORSSTTU	southernmost
EHMOOPSSSTTY	photosystems
EHNNOOOPRTTU	photoneutron
EHOOOPRRSTTU	orthopterous
EIIIILMNOPSST	postliminies
EIIIILMNOSSTU	luminosities
EIIIMMMNORSS	immersionism
EIIIMMNORSST	immersionist
EIIIMNNORSST	intermission
EIIIMNNPRSTT	inspiritment
EIIIMNOOPRST	reimposition
EIIIMNORSSTV	intromissive
EIIIMPRTTTVY	permittivity
EIIINNNOTTUV	nonintuitive
EIIINNOORSTT	isotretinoin
EIIINOQRSSTU	requisitions
EIIINORSSSTV	revisionists
EIIILLNORSSSU	illusoriness
EIIILLOOQRSSU	soliloquiser
EIIILLOOQRSUZ	soliloquizer
EIIILLOOQSSSU	soliloquises
EIIILLOOQSSUZ	soliloquizes
EIIILLPRSSSTY	spiritlessly
EIIILMNOOSTUV	evolutionism
EIIILMOOPPRST	pleiotropism
EIIILMOPRSUVY	imperviously
EIIILMRSTTUVY	multiversity
EIIILNOOPPRST	lipoproteins
EIIILNOORRSTU	irresolution
EIIILNOOSTTUV	evolutionist
EIIILNOPRSSTV	silverpoints
EIIILNOPRSTUY	polyneuritis
EIIILOOPRSTXY	expositorily
EIIIMMNNOPRST	imprisonment
EIIIMMOOPRSTV	overoptimism
EIIIMNNNQQUUU	quinquennium
EIIIMNNOOPRST	premonitions
EIIIMNNORTTTT	intromittent
EIIIMNORRSTTT	intermittors
	intromitters
EIIIMOOPRSTTV	overoptimist
EIIIMOPRSSSST	prestissimos
EIIIMORRSSSTU	moisturisers
EIIIMORRSSTUZ	moisturizers
EIIINNOORSTV	introversion
EIIINNOPRRTTU	interruption
EIIINNOPRSSTU	interspinous
EIIINOOPPRSST	prepositions
EIIINOOPRRSSV	provisioners
	reprovisions
EIIINOORSTTTX	extortionist
EIIINOPRSSTTU	superstition

EIIINORSSTTTU	restitutions
EIIIOOPPSSTTV	postpositive
EIIIOORSSTTTU	tortuosities
EIIIOPPSSSTUV	suppositives
EIIJLOPRRSUUY	perjuriously
EIILLMNOOSSTY	motionlessly
EIILLOPPRSTUY	suppletorily
EIILMNNOOPTTY	omnipotently
EIILMNNOSSSUU	luminousness
EIILMNOOOPRSS	monopolisers
EIILMNOOOPRSZ	monopolizers
EIILMOPPRSTUU	multipurpose
EIILMORSSTTUY	multistoreys
EIILMORSSTUVY	mysteriously
EIILNOOPRRSTU	retropulsion
EIILOORRSSTUY	roisterously
EIILOPPRSTUVY	supportively
EIILOPRSTUVVY	protrusively
EIIMNNOSSSTUU	mutinousness
EIIMNNRSSTTTU	intrustments
EIIMNOOOPRRST	promontories
EIIMNOOORRSST	sensorimotor
EIIMNOOOSSSTU	isostemonous
EIIMNOORSSSTU	timorousness
EIIMNOORSSTTU	neurotomists
EIIMNOPPRSSTU	presumptions
EIIMOOPRSSTTT	optometrists
EIIMOPRSSSSTT	postmistress
EIINOORSSSUUX	uxoriousness
EIINOPPRSSSSU	suppressions
EIINOPRRRSTTU	interruptors
EIINOPRSSSSUU	spuriousness
EIINOPSSSTTTY	stenotypists
EIINORSSSTUUV	virtuousness
EIOOOOPRSSST	osteoporosis
EKKNNOOSTUVZ	Novokuznetsk
ELNOOPPSSSUU	populousness
ELNOOPRSTTUY	portentously
ELOOPPRRSSUY	prosperously
ELOORRSSTTUY	stertorously
EMMMNOORSTYY	monosymmetry
EMMNOOOPRSSU	monospermous
EMOOOPRRSSST	mosstroopers
EMOPPRSSTTUU	presumptuous
ENNOOORSSSSU	sonorousness
ENOOPPRRSSST	sportsperson
ENOORSSSTTUU	tortuousness
FFGIILNORTYY	fortifyingly
FFILLNRTUUUY	unfruitfully
FGGGILNOOOST	footslogging
FGHHILORRTTY	forthrightly
FGHHLLOTTUUY	thoughtfully
FGHHLNOTTUUU	unthoughtful
FGHIILNORRYY	horrifyingly
FGHIMNOOOPRT	mothproofing
FGIIIMMNNORS	misinforming
FGIILLNOSUUY	fuliginously
FGIILMNORTYY	mortifyingly
FGIILMNSTYYY	mystifyingly
FGILOORSTTUU	futurologist
FGINNNNORRTU	frontrunning
FGINOOPSSTUY	pussyfooting

FHILLOPRSUWY	worshipfully
FHLLNRTTUUUY	untruthfully
FIIINNOSSSTU	infusionists
FIIILMMORTTUY	multiformity
FIKLLLLNSUUY	unskillfully
FILOORSTTUUY	fortuitously
GGGHHHIIILNT	highlighting
GGGILLNRSTUY	strugglingly
GGHHINOORSUU	roughhousing
GGHIILMNNOOT	moonlighting
GGHIILMNOOOS	homologising
GGHIILMNOOOZ	homologizing
GGHIILNOPSTT	spotlighting
GGHIINORSTTW	ghostwriting
GGIIILLNNOTU	guillotining
GGIIIILNNRTUY	intriguingly
GGIILLOORTUY	liturgiology
GGILLOOOSSST	glossologist
GHHILOOPRSUY	hygrophilous
GHHILOPRSTTT	trothplights
GHHINOOPRSTU	thoroughpins
GHHMNNOOOPST	monophthongs
GHHOOORRTTUW	thoroughwort
GHIIIILLLNRS	Nilgiri Hills
GHIIIILLNOPSY	lyophilising
GHIIIILLNOPYZ	lyophilizing
GHIIKLNNNTUY	unthinkingly
GHIILLOOPSST	philologists
GHIILLOOSSTT	lithologists
GHIILNNORSUY	nourishingly
GHIILNOORSST	rhinologists
GHIILNOPSSTY	philogynists
GHIILNPRSSUU	sulphurising
GHIILNPRSUUZ	sulphurizing
GHIILOOOPSST	ophiologists
GHIILOOPSSTY	physiologist
GHIILOOSSSTT	histologists
GHIIMNOPSSTY	physostigmin
GHILLOOOPSST	hoplologists
GHILMNOOSSTY	hymnologists
GHILMOOOPRST	morphologist
GHILMOOSSTTY	mythologists
GHILNOOOPSST	phonologists
GHILNOOPSSTY	hypnologists
GHILOOPSSTTY	phytologists
GHIMMOOPRSYZ	zygomorphism
GHIMNOOPSSTY	gymnosophist
GHLMNOOOOSUY	homogonously
GHLMOOOSUYYZ	homozygously
GHMOOOPRSUYZ	zygomorphous
GIIIIKLLNNNS	Inniskilling
GIIIILNORSTV	vitriolising
GIIIILNORTVZ	vitriolizing
GIIIINOPRRST	prioritising
GIIIINOPRRTZ	prioritizing
GIIIMNNORTTT	intromitting
GIIIMNORSSTU	moisturising
GIIIMNORSTUZ	moisturizing
GIIINNOOPRSV	provisioning
GIILLMNOOSST	limnologists
GIILLNOORSUY	ingloriously
GIILMMNOOSTU	immunologist

GIILMNNOOOPS	monopolising
GIILMNNOOOPZ	monopolizing
GIILNPRRSSUY	surprisingly
GIIMNNNOOOST	monotonising
GIIMNNNOOOTZ	monotonizing
GIIMNNNOSSYY	synonymising
GIIMNNNOSYYZ	synonymizing
GIINNOPRSTTU	outsprinting
GIINOPPRSTTU	outstripping
GIINOPRSTTTU	prostituting
GILLLMNOSSUU	slumgullions
GILLMOOPSTTY	polyglottism
GILLNNNOOPTU	nonpolluting
GINNOOPRSSTT	strongpoints
GLLNOOSTTUUY	gluttonously
GLMMOOOPSTYY	symptomology
GLOOOOOPRTYZ	protozoology
HHIILNOOPRTY	ornithophily
HHILMMOOPRSY	hylomorphism
HHILOOOPPSTU	photophilous
HHIMMMOOOPRS	homomorphism
HHINOOPRRTTY	thyrotrophin
HHMMOOOOPRSU	homomorphous
HIIIILMNPSST	philistinism
HIILLMNOOPSU	limnophilous
HIILLNNNOOST	nonillionths
HIILLOOPPRWW	whippoorwill
HIILMNNOOPSY	hypolimnions
HIILMOOSSTTT	lithotomists
HIILNOOPRSTU	nitrophilous
HIIOPRRSSUVV	survivorship
HIKLOOORSSVV	Voroshilovsk
HILMMOOPPRSY	polymorphism
HILNOOPSSTXY	xylophonists
HILOOOPPRSTU	tropophilous
HIMMMNOOOPRS	monomorphism
HIMOOOOPPRSTT	phototropism
HIMOOOPRRSTT	orthotropism
HINOOOPPPRRSY	porphyropsin
HINOOPPRSSSS	sponsorships
HINOOPPSSTTY	phonotypists
HIOOOPRRSTTY	protohistory
HJKNNNOOOSTX	Knox-Johnston
HLLMNOOOPSUY	monophyllous
HLLOPRSSUUUY	sulphurously
HLMOOOPPRSUY	polymorphous
HLMOOPSSTUUY	posthumously
HMMNOOOOPRSU	monomorphous
HMOOOPSSSTUY	physostomous
HOOOOPRRSTTU	orthotropous
IIIIMMNNOSTT	intuitionism
IIIIMPRSSTTV	primitivists
IIIINNOQSSTU	inquisitions
IIIINNOSTTTU	intuitionist
IIILLNNOQSTU	quintillions
IIILLNOPSSTT	pointillists
IIILLNOSSSTU	illusionists
IIILMMNOPSTU	postliminium
IIILNOQSTUUY	iniquitously
IIIMNNOORSST	intromission
IIIMNOORTTUV	vomiturition
IIINNORSTTTU	nutritionist

IIINNORSTTUU	innutritious		**IINOOPPSSSTU**	suppositions
IIINNOSSTTTU	institutions		**IINOOPRSTTTU**	prostitution
IIINOOOPSSTV	ovipositions		**IIOOPPSSSTUU**	suppositious
IIIOPRSSTTUY	spirituosity		**ILLMNOOOSTTY**	tonsillotomy
IILLOOQSSSTU	soliloquists		**ILLMNOOSUUVY**	voluminously
IILMNOOQSSTU	somniloquist		**ILMNOOOQSSUU**	somniloquous
IILMNOOSTUVY	voluminosity		**ILMNOOORSUVY**	omnivorously
IILNORSSSTUY	sinistrously		**ILOOPSTTUUVY**	voluptuosity
IILNORSTTUUY	nutritiously		**INNNOOOOPSSU**	nonpoisonous
IILOOPPRSTUY	propitiously		**INOOPPRSSTTU**	opportunists
IIMNOOPRSSTU	positroniums		**IOOPRRSSTTTU**	prostitutors
IINNNNOOSSTU	nonunionists		**LLMOSTTUUUUY**	tumultuously
IINOOOOPPRSST	propositions		**LLOOPSTUUUVY**	voluptuously
IINOOOOPPSSTT	postposition		**LMNNOOOOSTUY**	monotonously
IINOOPPRSTUU	unpropitious		**LMNNOOSSUYYY**	synonymously

Thirteen Letters

AAAAACILNNSTT	Santa Catalina
AAAAACINNRSTT	Santa Catarina
AAAABCCEELRTU	baccalaureate
AAAABCCHILMRR	Hamilcar Barca
AAAABDILMORSS	ambassadorial
AAAABEFGKLLLS	Kabalega Falls
AAAACCCCIRSTU	acciaccaturas
AAAACCDIIKLLS	lackadaisical
AAAACCINRSSTU	Transcaucasia
AAAACCLMNORST	malacostracan
AAAACDDGINUUY	Ciudad Guayana
AAAACDEEMRSTT	Atacama Desert
AAAACEGRSSTUU	Caesaraugusta
AAAACEIMMNORS	American Samoa
AAAACEINRRSSV	caravansaries
	caravanserais
AAAACGHILPPRR	paragraphical
AAAACILLLNPTY	aplanatically
AAAACIMNRSSST	antimacassars
AAAADEGHLMNOP	alpha and omega
AAAADGINNOSVY	Sivananda yoga
AAAAEEGNRTUWW	turangawaewae
AAAAEGHIMMNOT	haemangiomata
AAAAEGIMMNRST	anagrammatise
AAAAEGIMMNRTZ	anagrammatize
AAAAEGNRSTVXZ	extravaganzas
AAAAEHILNPPRR	paraphernalia
AAAAGHHIKLSWY	Alaska Highway
AAAAGILMMNOST	amalgamations
AAAAGIMMMNRST	anagrammatism
AAAAGIMMNRSTT	anagrammatist
AAAAHHINPRSSS	Spanish Sahara
AAAAHHKLLMNNU	Amanullah Khan
AAAAHIKMNPSTV	Visakhapatnam
AAAAIILLMNRST	antimalarials
AAAAILLPRRSSS	sarsaparillas
AAAALLPPSSSTU	Uspallata Pass
AAABBIINORRST	barbarisation
AAABBIINORRTZ	barbarization
AAABCCEINORTY	cyanobacteria
AAABCCENNRSSU	bancassurance
AAABCCILLOTY	catabolically
AAABCCILLORTY	acrobatically
AAABCDEHINRTU	chateaubriand
AAABCDIKNORTW	backwardation
AAABCEEEHKPSY	Chesapeake Bay
AAABCEEILNRST	ascertainable

AAABCEEIMNPRZ	carbamazepine
AAABCEFILNOTT	labefactation
AAABCEGILLLRY	algebraically
AAABCEHILNPST	analphabetics
AAABCEHNOORTY	archaeobotany
AAABCEIILNRTT	antibacterial
AAABCEILLNORY	anaerobically
AAABCEILNOOPT	palaeobotanic
AAABCEILNRSTY	ascertainably
AAABCHHINOOPR	arachnophobia
AAABCIKLLLOTY	katabolically
AAABCILLLOPRY	parabolically
AAABDEEINRRST	Arabian Desert
AAABDEELNPSST	adaptableness
AAABDEGIILMTY	damageability
AAABDELQSTTUU	absquatulated
AAABDFILNNORS	Baranof Island
AAABDHMMOORTY	rhabdomyomata
AAABEEEEGKLRRT	Great Bear Lake
AAABEEGLNSSTU	Augean stables
AAABEEILLNSSV	availableness
AAABEELLNPSST	palatableness
AAABEGIILMNTY	manageability
AAABEGILNNOST	antagonisable
AAABEGILNNOTZ	antagonizable
AAABEHLMOSSTT	haematoblasts
AAABEILLMNPTU	manipulatable
AAABELNNRRTUW	unwarrantable
AAABELQSSTTUU	absquatulates
AAABGHPPRRSSU	subparagraphs
AAABHILLMPSTU	amphiblastula
AAABIIILLNOST	labialisation
AAABIIILLNOTZ	labialization
AAABIIILNTTTY	attainability
AAABIIKLNNOST	balkanisation
AAABIIKLNNOTZ	balkanization
AAABILNPRSSSU	sublapsarians
AAABLNNRRTUWY	unwarrantably
AAACCCGHILOPR	cacographical
AAACCDEIINPTT	incapacitated
AAACCDEILLNTU	canaliculated
AAACCDHIILNOR	archidiaconal
AAACCEGILRTTX	extragalactic
AAACCEHILMOPR	macrocephalia
AAACCEIINPSTT	incapacitates
AAACCEILNNOTT	Atlantic Ocean
AAACCEINNQSTU	acquaintances

AAAACCELLPRSTY	Crystal Palace
AAAACCFINNNRSS	San Franciscan
AAAACCGILLLMOO	malacological
AAAACCHIILMRRT	matriarchical
AAAACCHILLRTTY	cathartically
AAAACCHLORSSTY	thalassocracy
AAAACCHLORTTTY	thalattocracy
AAAACCIILLNSST	anticlassical
AAAACCIILLSTTT	stalactitical
AAAACCIINNPSTT	incapacitants
AAAACCIINOPSTT	capacitations
AAAACCILLLTTYY	catalytically
AAAACCILLMNORY	macaronically
AAAACCILLRSSTY	sarcastically
AAAACDDEGHHHILT	Gaidhealtachd
AAAACDEEILMNNO	Lacedaemonian
AAAACDEEINPPRS	disappearance
AAAACDEGIMNNPR	Campina Grande
AAAACDEHHIKRSV	Chevra Kadisha
AAAACDEHHKNRRS	Chandrasekhar
AAAACDEHIMNRTY	adiathermancy
AAAACDEIIINPRT	paediatrician
AAAACDEIINNRRV	Canadian River
AAAACDEIIORTTV	radioactivate
AAAACDEILLOPSV	Palacio Valdés
AAAACDEINRSSTT	tradescantias
AAAACDELLNOOST	Llano Estacado
AAAACDGHIIMPRT	diaphragmatic
AAAACDGILMRRTU	dramaturgical
AAAACDHHHINRRS	Harishchandra
AAAACDHHILMNST	Chatham Island
AAAACDHIINOPRS	anaphrodisiac
AAAACDHILNOPTY	anaphylactoid
AAAACDIIILPRST	parasiticidal
AAAACDIILMNOPS	dipsomaniacal
AAAACDILLOPRXY	paradoxically
AAAACDILMNNSSY	Cayman Islands
AAAACDILNNRSSY	Canary Islands
AAAACDMMNNOSTU	Muscat and Oman
AAAACEEENPPRRS	reappearances
AAAACEEGHILLNP	encephalalgia
AAAACEEGHNNNRS	carragheenans
AAAACEEGNRSTVX	extravagances
AAAACEEHILLLPX	Aix-la-Chapelle
AAAACEEHLMNOPT	encephalomata
AAAACEENNNOPPR	nonappearance
AAAACEEOPPRSUV	papaveraceous
AAAACEFILNORRT	rarefactional
AAAACEGGGLOSTU	galactagogues
AAAACEGHIILNPR	archipelagian
AAAACEGHILOPPR	palaeographic
AAAACEGILMMNOS	megalomaniacs
AAAACEGILMTTUY	Guatemala City
AAAACEGIMNOSTY	gynaecomastia
AAAACEGIMQRRUZ	García Márquez
AAAACEHIIMMNTT	mathematician
AAAACEHILLPTTY	apathetically
AAAACEHIMOOPPR	pharmacopoeia
AAAACEHIMOPPRS	pharmacopeias
AAAACEHIMRRSTT	matriarchates
AAAACEHIPRRSTT	patriarchates
AAAACEIILMNNRT	Latin American
AAAACEILLMNNOTX	exclamational
AAAACEILLMOOST	osteomalacial
AAAACEILNNSSST	satanicalness
AAAACEILNSSTTT	Caltanissetta
AAAACELLMNRSTY	sacramentally
AAAACELLNORRTT	contralateral
AAAACELNNORSSY	narcoanalyses
AAAACELOSSTTUY	autocatalyses
AAAACELRRSTUVX	extravascular
AAAACFIILLLMOX	maxillofacial
AAAACFILLMNSTY	fantasmically
AAAACFILLNSTTY	fantastically
AAAACFIMNORRTW	aircraftwoman
AAAACGGHIIMNOT	gigantomachia
AAAACGGILLOPRY	paragogically
AAAACGHILOPRTU	autographical
AAAACGIILLMSTT	stalagmitical
AAAACGILLMMRTY	grammatically
AAAACGILLMPRTY	pragmatically
AAAACGILLMMNRTU	ungrammatical
AAAACGILNNOTTU	anticoagulant
AAAACHIILLPRSY	pharisaically
AAAACHILLMSTTY	asthmatically
AAAACHILLNOPRY	anaphorically
AAAACHILLPRRTY	patriarchally
AAAACHILNRSSSU	Halicarnassus
AAAACIILLMOTXY	axiomatically
AAAACIILLPRSTY	parasitically
AAAACIILLSTTVY	atavistically
AAAACIILNNNOTT	incantational
AAAACIILNOSSTU	casualisation
AAAACIILNOSTTU	actualisation
AAAACIILNOSTUZ	casualization
AAAACIILNOTTUZ	actualization
AAAACIIMNRRSTT	Tractarianism
AAAACILLLNOTTY	lactationally
AAAACILLLPRTYY	paralytically
AAAACILLMNOPRY	panoramically
AAAACILLMOTTUY	automatically
AAAACILLMRTTUY	traumatically
AAAACILNNORSSY	narcoanalysis
AAAACILNNORSTT	transactional
AAAACILNNRSTTT	transatlantic
AAAACILNORSTTU	astronautical
AAAACILNPRRSTU	intracapsular
AAAACILNSSTTTY	anticatalysts
AAAACILOSSTTUY	autocatalysis
AAAACIMNNOSTTU	catamountains
AAAACLMNPRSTUY	sanctuary lamp
AAADDDEGINSTV	disadvantaged
AAADDEGINSSTV	disadvantages
AAADDEHHMPRSY	Madhya Pradesh
AAADDEHHNPRRS	Andhra Pradesh
AAADEEGILNNSS	Aegean Islands
AAADEEGLMMNRY	Mary Magdalene
AAADEEHIMNSTT	anathematised
AAADEEHIMNTTZ	anathematized
AAADEGILMQRSU	quadragesimal
AAADEGILNRSTV	landgraviates
AAADEHHIMNNRT	rhadamanthine
AAADEHHNPRSSZ	haphazardness
AAADEHIIINPRTT	antiapartheid

AAADEILLMPTVY	maladaptively	**AAAHIKNRSSTUV**	Ratushinskaya
AAADEILLQRRTU	quadrilateral	**AAAHILMMOPSTT**	amphistomatal
AAADEINOPPRTT	preadaptation	**AAAHINRRSTTUZ**	Zarathustrian
AAADEINOPRSTT	readaptations	**AAAIIILMNNOST**	animalisation
AAADELMMOPSST	plasmodesmata	**AAAIIILMNNOTZ**	animalization
AAADFGKKNOORS	Sargon of Akkad	**AAAIILLNORTVY**	variationally
AAADGILLNORTY	gradationally	**AAAIILNNNORTT**	intranational
AAADGIMNOORST	Good Samaritan	**AAAIILNNOSTTT**	tantalisation
AAADHHILNRRSU	Harun al-Rashid	**AAAIILNNOTTTZ**	tantalization
AAADIIMNORSTT	dramatisation	**AAAIIMNNOOSTT**	anatomisation
AAADIIMNORTTZ	dramatization	**AAAIIMNNOOTTZ**	anatomization
AAADKLMRRSTTX	Karl-Marx-Stadt	**AAAIIMNOORSTT**	aromatisation
AAAEEGGLMNSTU	metalanguages	**AAAIIMNOORTTZ**	aromatization
AAAEEGHLOPPRR	palaeographer	**AAAIINNORSTTV**	intravasation
AAAEEGINNRSSX	sexagenarians	**AAAIINNOSSSST**	assassination
AAAEEGKLLRSTT	Great Salt Lake	**AAAIINORRSTTT**	tartarisation
AAAEEGNRSTTVX	Extravagantes	**AAAIINORRTTTZ**	tartarization
AAAEEHIMNSSTT	anathematises	**AAAILLLNOTUVY**	valuationally
AAAEEHIMNSTTZ	anathematizes	**AAAILLNNORSTT**	translational
AAAEEHIPRSSST	paraesthesias	**AAAILLNNORTTU**	ultranational
AAAEEHNNRRSSTW	Western Sahara	**AAAILLNORRSTT**	translatorial
AAAEEILRSTTVV	salva veritate	**AAAILMNORSTVY**	Salvation Army
AAAEFIILMMRST	materfamilias	**AAAILNNNORSTT**	transnational
AAAEFIILMPRST	paterfamilias	**AAAILNNOPRSTU**	supranational
AAAEFILNNPRUZ	parainfluenza	**AAAILNOPRSSTY**	paralysations
AAAEFINNORSTU	Anne of Austria	**AAAILNOPRSTYZ**	paralyzations
AAAEGGIMNOPRS	megasporangia	**AAALLLLOOOPSZ**	lollapaloozas
AAAEGGINRTTVX	extravagating	**AABBBIILORSTY**	absorbability
AAAEGIILMMNOR	Emilia-Romagna	**AABBCEILNRRST**	transcribable
AAAEGIILMMNRS	managerialism	**AABBCIIILMNOS**	bibliomaniacs
AAAEGIILMNRST	managerialist	**AABBCIINRRSUU**	suburbicarian
AAAEGILMNORSU	megalosaurian	**AABBCILLMOSTY**	bombastically
AAAEGIMMNPRST	paramagnetism	**AABBDDEEGILOR**	biodegradable
AAAEGINNNNORS	nonagenarians	**AABBDEEFGLRST**	flabbergasted
AAAEGINORTTVV	extravagation	**AABBDEEINRTUV**	unabbreviated
AAAEGINRSTTVX	extravasating	**AABBDIILORSTY**	adsorbability
AAAEGLLLMOPRR	parallelogram	**AABBDIINOOQSS**	Qaboos bin Said
AAAEGLNRTTVXY	extravagantly	**AABBEEHILNSST**	habitableness
AAAEHIMNOPRTY	hyponatraemia	**AABBEEILLMOST**	metabolisable
AAAEHIOSSSTTU	Southeast Asia	**AABBEEILLMOTZ**	metabolizable
AAAEIIKNPSSTT	East Pakistani	**AABBEEILRUVXY**	Rievaulx Abbey
AAAEIILMNNOTX	examinational	**AABBEHIILNNTU**	uninhabitable
AAAEIILNQRSTU	equalitarians	**AABBEHILNOPRT**	phenobarbital
AAAEILMNPRRTY	parliamentary	**AABBEIILLOSSU**	bouillabaisse
AAAEIMMMNRRTU	armamentarium	**AABBEIINORSTV**	abbreviations
AAAEIMNRNSSST	transaminases	**AABBENORRSSSU**	barbarousness
AAAEINORSTTVX	extravasation	**AABBIIILNOTTY**	obtainability
AAAGGIOPPRSTU	appoggiaturas	**AABCCCEEHKRRST**	backscratcher
AAAGHIRSSTTWY	straightaways	**AABCCDHLRTYYY**	brachydactyly
AAAGHMNOPRSTY	phantasmagory	**AABCCEEFIILRS**	sacrificeable
AAAGIIILMNNOT	imaginational	**AABCCEEIRRSSU**	bureaucracies
AAAGIIKMOORST	Saigo Takamori	**AABCCEEHHLPRYY**	brachycephaly
AAAGIILNNOSTV	galvanisation	**AABCCEEHINOOPR**	cancerophobia
AAAGIILNNOTVZ	galvanization	**AABCCEEIILMPRT**	impracticable
AAAGIILNORTTV	gravitational	**AABCCEEIILPTTY**	acceptability
AAAGIINNOPSST	paganisations	**AABCCEEILLMOSV**	clavicembalos
AAAGIINNOPSTZ	paganizations	**AABCCEEILMNORS**	microbalances
AAAGIINNSSSST	assassinating	**AABCCEEILMOTUU**	bioaccumulate
AAAGILNOOPPRT	propagational	**AABCCEEILNPRTU**	unpracticable
AAAHIIMNNRSTU	humanitarians	**AABCCEEIORSSSU**	brassicaceous
AAAHIINORRTTU	authoritarian	**AABCCEELMOPRTY**	campylobacter
AAAHIIOPPRRUW	pipiwharauroa	**AABCCEELNNOTUU**	unaccountable

AABCCGIKKNRST	backtrackings	AABCEGHIIINRV	Virginia Beach
AABCCIIILNNST	cannibalistic	AABCEGHIILNTY	changeability
AABCCIILLLTUV	calculability	AABCEGHIILRTY	chargeability
AABCCIILMPRTY	impracticably	AABCEGIIKMNNT	cabinetmaking
AABCCILLLOSTU	lactobacillus	AABCEGILLLNOO	balneological
AABCCKLNRRSTU	blackcurrants	AABCEGILLMOST	megaloblastic
AABCCLNNOTUUY	unaccountably	AABCEGILNNORV	overbalancing
AABCDDEKLRRSW	bladderwracks	AABCEGILOPSSY	abyssopelagic
AABCDDIILORUV	Ciudad Bolívar	AABCEGINOORSU	boraginaceous
AABCDEEEFNRSS	barefacedness	AABCEHHHORSTV	Sheva Brachoth
AABCDEEFFHIIN	dieffenbachia	AABCEHIKLPRSU	Sakha Republic
AABCDEEFIPRRT	prefabricated	AABCEHILLLMNR	lamellibranch
AABCDEEGHILRS	dischargeable	AABCEHILMNPUY	unimpeachably
AABCDEEHLNNOT	nondetachable	AABCEHILMOSTT	hematoblastic
AABCDEELLLSSY	decasyllables	AABCEIILLMRRY	irreclaimably
AABCDEELORSXY	decarboxylase	AABCEIILLPRTU	Altai Republic
AABCDEENNORUV	overabundance	AABCEIILMRSST	bicameralists
AABCDEEENOSSTU	subdeaconates	AABCEIILNPPRY	inappreciably
AABCDEGIKLLNP	backpedalling	AABCEIINORRTT	nitrobacteria
AABCDEGINNORT	decarbonating	AABCEIIRSTTTY	tetrabasicity
AABCDEHIILTTY	detachability	AABCEILLLMOTY	metabolically
AABCDEHIIMORT	thiocarbamide	AABCEILLMOPRT	problematical
AABCDEHIINRST	dibranchiates	AABCEILLOORTV	collaborative
AABCDEHMNORRS	rhabdomancers	AABCEILLRSSTY	crystalisable
AABCDEHORRSTY	carbohydrates	AABCEILLRSTTY	tetrasyllabic
AABCDEIILTTUV	educatability	AABCEILLRSTYZ	crystalizable
AABCDEILOPRRT	particleboard	AABCEILMNNOOP	companionable
AABCDEINNOORT	decarbonation	AABCEILPRRTTU	Tatar Republic
AABCDEINORRTU	decarburation	AABCEILRSTTVY	abstractively
AABCDELOPPRRS	clapperboards	AABCEIMORSSUU	simarubaceous
AABCDENOORRST	decarbonators	AABCEIMRRSTUU	bureaucratism
AABCDEOPRRRSS	scraperboards	AABCEINRRSSTT	scatterbrains
AABCDGGIKLNRU	blackguarding	AABCEIORSSTTT	bacteriostats
AABCDGGIOORSU	braggadocious	AABCELMMNNOSU	somnambulance
AABCDGIKLMRSU	blackguardism	AABCELNOOPRTY	polycarbonate
AABCDINNORSTT	contrabandist	AABCFGILNNOTU	confabulating
AABCDKMNORSSW	backswordsman	AABCFIILORTTY	factorability
AABCEEEELNPSS	peaceableness	AABCFILNNOOTU	confabulation
AABCEEEGHLLLN	challengeable	AABCFILORRSUV	fibrovascular
AABCEEEILLPRR	irreplaceable	AABCFLNOORSTU	confabulators
AABCEEELLNPRU	unreplaceable	AABCFLNOORTUY	confabulatory
AABCEEELNRSST	traceableness	AABCGIIILNNNS	cannibalising
AABCEEFIPRRST	prefabricates	AABCGIIILNNNZ	cannibalizing
AABCEEGGPRRST	carpetbaggers	AABCGIILLNSTY	syllabicating
AABCEEGHIOPRT	bacteriophage	AABCGIILLOTUY	coagulability
AABCEEHILMNPU	unimpeachable	AABCGILLNNNNO	cannonballing
AABCEEHLLRRST	Charles Albert	AABCGILLNOORT	collaborating
AABCEEIILLMRR	irreclaimable	AABCHIIILMNTY	machinability
AABCEEIILNPPR	inappreciable	AABCHIIMORSTT	microhabitats
AABCEEIKMNRST	cabinetmakers	AABCHIINOOSTT	cohabitations
AABCEEILLPRRY	irreplaceably	AABCHIMNOPRRS	marsipobranch
AABCEEILMNRSV	vraisemblance	AABCHIORRSSUU	brachiosaurus
AABCEEILNNPSS	incapableness	AABCIIILLMPTY	implacability
AABCEEIRRSTUU	bureaucratise	AABCIIILLNSTT	antiballistic
AABCEEIRRTUUZ	bureaucratize	AABCIIILLPPTY	applicability
AABCEELMMORSU	commeasurable	AABCIIILMNORT	antimicrobial
AABCEELNRSSTT	tractableness	AABCIILLLLSTY	ballistically
AABCEEMMNORSU	membranaceous	AABCIILLNORTU	lubricational
AABCEFFGHNRSU	Aschaffenburg	AABCIILLNOSTY	syllabication
AABCEFIIINOTT	beatification	AABCIILLOSTTY	biostatically
AABCEFIINORTT	abortifacient	AABCIILLRSTYY	sybaritically
AABCEFIOPRRRT	prefabricator	AABCIILMNNOOT	combinational

AABCIILMNOORT	combinatorial
AABCIILMOPRTY	comparability
AABCIIMOPRSTY	parasymbiotic
AABCIINNOORST	carbonisation
AABCIINNOORTZ	carbonization
AABCIINORRSTU	carburisation
AABCIINORRTUZ	carburization
AABCIKLMNNOTU	Black Mountain
AABCILLNOOORT	collaboration
AABCILMNNOOPY	companionably
AABCINORSSSTT	contrabassist
AABCLLOOORRST	collaborators
AABCMNNNOOSTT	noncombatants
AABCNNOOORSST	contrabassoon
AABDDDENRRSST	standardbreds
AABDDEGIILRTY	degradability
AABDDEGIIMSTU	disambiguated
AABDDEGINNPRS	bandspreading
AABDDEILMNRRY	Marie Byrd Land
AABDDGHORRSTU	draughtboards
AABDEEFGIILNT	indefatigable
AABDEEHIILRTT	rehabilitated
AABDEEHORRSTW	weatherboards
AABDEEILLNSST	dilatableness
AABDEEILNSSSV	advisableness
AABDEEKORRSST	skateboarders
AABDEELMRRSSY	embarrassedly
AABDEEMNRRSSU	unembarrassed
AABDEFGIILNTY	indefatigably
AABDEFLLNNORS	flannelboards
AABDEGIIMSSTU	disambiguates
AABDEGIKNORST	skateboarding
AABDEGLLMNORS	balladmongers
AABDEGLLNRTUY	Argyll and Bute
AABDEIIILMNST	damnabilities
AABDEIILNRTUY	unreadability
AABDEIILPRSTY	spreadability
AABDEILMRTUVY	adumbratively
AABDEINNNORRS	San Bernardino
AABDEINSSTTTU	substantiated
AABDELMMNOSTU	somnambulated
AABDENNPRSTUU	superabundant
AABDFFIILORTY	affordability
AABDGLNOORUWY	Albury-Wodonga
AABDHIMNORSTT	rhabdomantist
AABDIIILLSTYY	dialysability
AABDIIILLTYYZ	dialyzability
AABDIILNSSSTU	Tubuai Islands
AABDKMNOORSTU	Dumbarton Oaks
AABEEEEGLNRSS	agreeableness
AABEEEEHKRRRST	heartbreakers
AABEEEKRSSTVW	basketweavers
AABEEELLLMNSS	malleableness
AABEEELNORSST	elaborateness
AABEEEELNPRSSS	separableness
AABEEELOORRTV	overelaborate
AABEEFHIMNNOO	Anne of Bohemia
AABEEFHINRRST	featherbrains
AABEEFILNNOTU	Fontainebleau
AABEEFLNORSSV	favorableness
AABEEFLNRRRST	transferrable
AABEEGHIKNRRT	heartbreaking
AABEEGHLLNSSU	laughableness
AABEEGILMNPRT	impregnatable
AABEEGILNNSSV	navigableness
AABEEHIILRSTT	rehabilitates
AABEEHILPRSST	alphabetisers
AABEEHILPRSTZ	alphabetizers
AABEEHINSSTTW	Bassenthwaite
AABEEHLNOPRTY	balneotherapy
AABEEHLRRSSTY	breathalysers
AABEEHLRRSTYZ	breathalyzers
AABEEIILLNNPX	inexplainable
AABEEIILLRTVY	revealability
AABEEIILNNSSV	Évian-les-Bains
AABEEIILPRTTY	repeatability
AABEEIKLMNSTU	unmistakeable
AABEEILLNNPUX	unexplainable
AABEEELLLRSTTY	tetrasyllable
AABEEELMNNORSU	nonmeasurable
AABEEEMMNNRRSST	embarrassment
AABEFHILNNOSU	unfashionable
AABEFIILLNQUU	unqualifiable
AABEFILLMMNNU	uninflammable
AABEFILMORSSU	balsamiferous
AABEFLMNORRST	transformable
AABEGHIILNPST	alphabetising
AABEGHIILNPTZ	alphabetizing
AABEGHILNRSTY	breathalysing
AABEGHILNRTYZ	breathalyzing
AABEGHIMNSTTW	bantamweights
AABEGIILLNOUV	bougainvillea
AABEGIJKLNRWY	jawbreakingly
AABEGILMNPRTU	perambulating
AABEGILNORRTU	gubernatorial
AABEHIINORSTZ	hebraizations
AABEHLMOPPRSS	blepharospasm
AABEIIKLMRRTY	remarkability
AABEIIKLMRTTY	marketability
AABEIILLLOSTV	volatilisable
AABEIILLLOTVZ	volatilizable
AABEIILLNNPXY	inexplainably
AABEIILMNORST	abnormalities
AABEIILMRSTUY	measurability
AABEIILMSTTTY	metastability
AABEIILNORSTV	verbalisation
AABEIILNORTVZ	verbalization
AABEIILNPTTTY	patentability
AABEIILNRSTWY	answerability
AABEIILOPRTVY	evaporability
AABEIIMNNRSTU	antisubmarine
AABEIINRRRSST	arbitrariness
AABEIKLMNSTUY	unmistakeably
AABEILLLRSTTU	illustratable
AABEILLNRRSTU	turbellarians
AABEILMNNOTTU	Table Mountain
AABEILMNOPRTU	perambulation
AABEILMNRSTTT	transmittable
AABEILNOOPPRT	apportionable
AABEILNOORSTV	observational
AABEILOQRSTUU	subequatorial
AABEIMOPRSSSY	parasymbioses
AABEINSSSTTTU	substantiates
AABELMMNOSSTU	somnambulates

AABELMOPRRSTU	perambulators
AABELMOPRRTUY	perambulatory
AABELNOPRRSTT	transportable
AABELNPRSSSUU	unsurpassable
AABELNRRSTTUU	subternatural
AABFIIMMSSUUX	Fabius Maximus
AABGGIINNORTU	outbargaining
AABGHIIINRSTU	British Guiana
AABGHIINNRSSW	brainwashings
AABGHIOOPRTUY	autobiography
AABGHLLOPRSYY	syllabography
AABGIIILNORTY	aboriginality
AABGIIILNSSTY	assignability
AABGIILLNOOST	globalisation
AABGIILLNOOTZ	globalization
AABGIILOPPRTY	propagability
AABGILLMNRSUY	submarginally
AABHIIILNOSTT	habilitations
AABHIIILNPRRS	librarianship
AABIIIILNRTVY	invariability
AABIIIILNSTTY	insatiability
AABIIILLMPPTY	impalpability
AABIIILMPSSTY	impassability
AABIIILNOSSST	assibilations
AABIIILNOSSTT	stabilisation
AABIIILNOSTTZ	stabilization
AABIIINQRSTUU	ubiquitarians
AABIILNNNRTTU	tintinnabular
AABIILNNSSTTU	insubstantial
AABIILNORSTTU	brutalisation
AABIILNORTTUZ	brutalization
AABIILOPRTUVY	vapourability
AABIILOSTTTUY	autostability
AABIIMOPRSSSY	parasymbiosis
AABIINNNOORTW	rainbow nation
AABIINNORSSTU	urbanisations
AABIINNORSTUZ	urbanizations
AABIINOORRSST	arborisations
AABIINOORRSTZ	arborizations
AABILLNOOPRTY	probationally
AABILLNOSSTTU	blastulations
AABILLNSSTTUY	substantially
AABILMNOOPRST	malabsorption
AABILNNSSTTUU	unsubstantial
AABIMNOPRSSTY	parasymbionts
AABINORSSTTTU	substantiator
AABINORSSTTUU	subsaturation
AABLMMNNOSSTU	somnambulants
AABLMMNOORSTU	somnambulator
AACCCEEILNRRT	recalcitrance
AACCCEENNNOPT	nonacceptance
AACCCEGINORTY	gynaecocratic
AACCCEHIILSTT	catechistical
AACCCEHILMOPR	macrocephalic
AACCCEIILLMRT	climacterical
AACCCFIIILNOT	calcification
AACCCGHHILOPR	chalcographic
AACCCIIIILMNTT	anticlimactic
AACCCIILLLMTY	climactically
AACCCIILMMORT	macroclimatic
AACCDDEHIIRSS	disaccharides
AACCDEEELNRSU	adularescence

AACCDEEHINOPT	heptadecanoic
AACCDEEHIRRST	characterised
AACCDEEHIRRTZ	characterized
AACCDEEIILNRU	clairaudience
AACCDEEILNOPY	encyclopaedia
AACCDEEKMNRRS	cackermanders
AACCDEELLPPRW	clapperclawed
AACCDEENNTTUU	unaccentuated
AACCDEHIILMOR	radiochemical
AACCDEHIIRRST	trisaccharide
AACCDEIIILMRT	acidimetrical
AACCDEIIILNST	dialecticians
AACCDEIILLLTY	dialectically
AACCDEIINORTT	accreditation
AACCDEILLMSTU	miscalculated
AACCDEILNNNOT	nonaccidental
AACCDEILNOOTU	coeducational
AACCDEIMMOOTV	accommodative
AACCDEIMNNOPU	unaccompanied
AACCDFIIIINOT	acidification
AACCDGHIIOPRR	cardiographic
AACCDGIILLOOR	cardiological
AACCDGIMMNOOT	accommodating
AACCDIIILLRTY	diacritically
AACCDIILLOPTY	apodictically
AACCDIILNOSSS	Caicos Islands
AACCDIIMNOORT	carcinomatoid
AACCDIMMNOOOT	accommodation
AACCEEEHMNTTU	catechumenate
AACCEEFHINNOR	French Oceania
AACCEEFILORST	calefactories
AACCEEGIORRST	ergatocracies
AACCEEHILMNOT	catecholamine
AACCEEHIMNORS	aeromechanics
AACCEEHIMRRST	saccharimeter
AACCEEHIRRRST	characteriser
AACCEEHIRRRTZ	characterizer
AACCEEHIRRSST	characterises
AACCEEHIRRSTZ	characterizes
AACCEEHLMNPRY	macrencephaly
AACCEEHLRRSST	characterless
AACCEEHMORRST	saccharometer
AACCEEIILLPRS	capercaillies
AACCEEIILPRSZ	capercailzies
AACCEEILNORST	accelerations
AACCEEINRSSSS	accessariness
AACCEELLNSTUZ	Culzean Castle
AACCEELLPPRRW	clapperclawer
AACCEFIIINOTT	acetification
AACCEFILLSTUY	fasciculately
AACCEFILORRSU	calcariferous
AACCEGHHLOPRR	chalcographer
AACCEGHILLOOR	archeological
AACCEGHILMORS	agrochemicals
AACCEGHILOPRR	cerographical
AACCEGHINOOPR	oceanographic
AACCEGIIILNST	Cilician Gates
AACCEGIILNRTT	intergalactic
AACCEGIINNRRT	incarcerating
AACCEGIINNRTV	revaccinating
AACCEGILLNRTU	recalculating
AACCEGILLOOTU	autecological

AACCEGILLORTY	categorically	**AACCFIIINOPRT**	caprification
AACCEGILLOTTY	geotactically	**AACCFIIINOPST**	pacifications
AACCEGINNNOTT	concatenating	**AACCFIIINORST**	scarification
AACCEGINOQRSU	quangocracies	**AACCFIIILLLORY**	calorifically
AACCEHHLOPPSY	scaphocephaly	**AACCFIILLSSTY**	fascistically
AACCEHIILMMNS	mechanicalism	**AACCFIILNOSTU**	fasciculation
AACCEHIILORRT	hierocratical	**AACCFIIORRSST**	scarificators
AACCEHIILRSTU	eucharistical	**AACCGGIILLLOO**	glaciological
AACCEHIINOSTT	catechisation	**AACCGHHIOPRRT**	chartographic
AACCEHIINOTTZ	catechization	**AACCGHIILMNOT**	machicolating
AACCEHILLMNOS	melancholiacs	**AACCGHIKOPRRT**	Croagh Patrick
AACCEHILLMRSV	clishmaclaver	**AACCGHILLNOOT**	Anglo-Catholic
AACCEHILLMSTY	schematically	**AACCGIIILMNST**	acclimatising
AACCEHILMNNNO	nonmechanical	**AACCGIIILMNTZ**	acclimatizing
AACCEHILMORTT	tachometrical	**AACCGIIILLNOOR**	craniological
AACCEHILMRTTY	tachymetrical	**AACCGIILLOPST**	plagioclastic
AACCEHILOSSTT	scholasticate	**AACCGILLLNTUY**	calculatingly
AACCEHILRRTTU	architectural	**AACCGILNOOPSV**	galvanoscopic
AACCEHIMMORTT	metachromatic	**AACCGILNRTTUU**	acculturating
AACCEHIMOOPPR	pharmacopoeic	**AACCHHHLNRSUU**	Shulchan Aruch
AACCEHIMPRSTU	pharmaceutics	**AACCHIIINRSTT**	antirachitics
AACCEHIMRRSTY	saccharimetry	**AACCHIILMNOOT**	machicolation
AACCEHLNNOPSU	Nonsuch Palace	**AACCHIILMSSST**	schismaticals
AACCEHLPRSSTT	scratchplates	**AACCHIILPRSTY**	psychiatrical
AACCEIILLMNTY	cinematically	**AACCHIILQRRSU**	squirarchical
AACCEIILLMSSS	semiclassical	**AACCHIIMORTTY**	achromaticity
AACCEIILLNRST	anticlericals	**AACCHIINNNOST**	cachinnations
AACCEIILMNOST	encomiastical	**AACCHIINNNORST**	anachronistic
AACCEIILMRSST	acclimatisers	**AACCHILLMNORY**	monarchically
AACCEIILMRSTZ	acclimatizers	**AACCHILLMORTY**	chromatically
AACCEIINNORRT	incarceration	**AACCHILLOPRTT**	trophallactic
AACCEIINNORTV	revaccination	**AACCHILMNOORT**	Roman Catholic
AACCEIIOPRSTT	ectoparasitic	**AACCHILNNOORU**	canonical hour
AACCEIIORRSST	aristocracies	**AACCIIINNOOST**	cocainisation
AACCEILLMRTUV	circumvallate	**AACCIIINNOOTZ**	cocainization
AACCEILLMSSTU	miscalculates	**AACCIIINORSTT**	cicatrisation
AACCEILLNNOST	cancellations	**AACCIIINORTTZ**	cicatrization
AACCEILLNSSSS	classicalness	**AACCIILLMPRTY**	impractically
AACCEILLNSTUY	encaustically	**AACCIILLMSSSS**	classicalisms
AACCEILMMORST	macroclimates	**AACCIILLSSSST**	classicalists
AACCEILMNOPSS	complaisances	**AACCIILLSSTUY**	casuistically
AACCEILMNOPST	cleptomaniacs	**AACCIILMNOOSS**	occasionalism
AACCEILNOPRST	plantocracies	**AACCIILMNORTY**	microanalytic
AACCEILNPRSST	practicalness	**AACCIILNNOPTY**	platinocyanic
AACCEILNRRSTT	recalcitrants	**AACCIIRRSSTTU**	caricaturists
AACCEILNRTTUU	nutraceutical	**AACCILLMORSTU**	miscalculator
AACCEIMMNNOPT	accompaniment	**AACCILLNPRTUY**	unpractically
AACCEINNNOOTT	concatenation	**AACCILLNSTTYY**	syntactically
AACCEINOORSTV	coacervations	**AACCILLOPRTTU**	plutocratical
AACCEINOPSSSU	capaciousness	**AACCILLOPSSTT**	postclassical
AACCEINORRRST	incarcerators	**AACCILMNOSTUU**	accumulations
AACCEIOORSSTU	aeroacoustics	**AACCILNNOOOTV**	convocational
AACCEIORRSSTT	stratocracies	**AACCILNORTTUU**	acculturation
AACCEKNORTTTU	counterattack	**AACCILNPRTTYY**	cryptanalytic
AACCELLPRSTUY	spectacularly	**AACCIMNOORSTU**	carcinomatous
AACCELNPRSTUU	unspectacular	**AACCIMNOPSSTY**	accompanyists
AACCELORSSSUU	crassulaceous	**AACCINORSSTTY**	sacrosanctity
AACCFFILNOPRY	cycloparaffin	**AACCLLNORTTUY**	contractually
AACCFGHIINRSY	saccharifying	**AACDDEEEFFINT**	decaffeinated
AACCFIIILLRSY	sacrificially	**AACDDEEEHLLRY**	clearheadedly
AACCFIIILNORT	clarification	**AACDDEEIIIMMR**	Maria de' Medici
AACCFIIINNORT	carnification	**AACDDEEIILMMR**	Middle America

AACDDEEIQSUUX	Duque de Caxias
AACDDEIIOSSST	disassociated
AACDDFIIINNOT	dandification
AACDDIIJNOSTU	adjudications
AACDEEEFFINST	decaffeinates
AACDEEEFIMNRR	Marie de France
AACDEEEHLNPSS	Passchendaele
AACDEEGHNNORR	Chandernagore
AACDEEGIMNNOY	cyanogenamide
AACDEEGINRRRU	undercarriage
AACDEEHINTTTU	authenticated
AACDEEHKLORRV	Hradec Králové
AACDEEIILPRST	recapitalised
AACDEEIILPRTZ	recapitalized
AACDEEIINRSST	sectarianised
AACDEEIINRSTZ	sectarianized
AACDEEILLRTVY	declaratively
AACDEEILNQRUV	quadrivalence
AACDEEILPRTTU	recapitulated
AACDEEIMMNRTY	medicamentary
AACDEEIMNNOTT	decontaminate
AACDEEIMNRSTT	readmittances
AACDEEINPPRTU	unappreciated
AACDEEINPQRTU	preacquainted
AACDEENNNNOTT	nonattendance
AACDEFFIIMNRS	disaffirmance
AACDEFINNOSTY	Ancient of Days
AACDEGGILLMOV	demagogically
AACDEGGILLOPY	pedagogically
AACDEGHHIMNOS	hochmagandies
AACDEGHIILMOPR	demographical
AACDEGHILRSTT	straightlaced
AACDEGHIOPRRR	cardiographer
AACDEGIILOPRS	cardioplegias
AACDEGILNPSTU	decapsulating
AACDEGJLNOSUU	juglandaceous
AACDEGLMNNORS	scandalmonger
AACDEGLNORTTU	congratulated
AACDEHIILOPPS	paedophiliacs
AACDEHIIMNRRT	archimandrite
AACDEHIORRSTT	trisoctahedra
AACDEHLNOOPPS	cephalopodans
AACDEHLOPRRST	procathedrals
AACDEHMNNOORT	enchondromata
AACDEHNOPRSTY	hydnocarpates
AACDEIIILNRST	cardinalities
AACDEIIINPRST	pediatricians
AACDEIIIPRSST	parasiticides
AACDEIIJLRTUX	extrajudicial
AACDEIILLMRTY	diametrically
AACDEIILLNNOT	declinational
AACDEIILLOPRV	aperiodically
AACDEIILNORTV	valedictorian
AACDEIILORTVV	radioactively
AACDEIILRSTTU	disarticulate
AACDEIINNORST	deracinations
AACDEIINNPPTTU	unanticipated
AACDEIINNRSTT	transactinide
AACDEIINOPRST	endoparasitic
AACDEIINOPSTT	decapitations
AACDEIINOSTTV	deactivations
AACDEIIOSSSST	disassociates
AACDEILLMORTY	declamatorily
AACDEILLNORRU	Claude Lorrain
AACDEILLNOSSW	disallowances
AACDEILLNOTUY	educationally
AACDEILLNSTYY	asyndetically
AACDEILLORRTY	declaratorily
AACDEILMMORST	melodramatics
AACDEILMOPRST	spermatocidal
AACDEILMORSST	sacerdotalism
AACDEILNOPSTU	decapsulation
AACDEILNOSTTST	anecdotalists
AACDEILNQRUVY	quadrivalency
AACDEILNRSTTU	ultradistance
AACDEILNRTTUU	unarticulated
AACDEILORSSTT	sacerdotalist
AACDEILPQRTUU	quadruplicate
AACDEIMNNNOTT	decontaminant
AACDEINNORSUU	arundinaceous
AACDEINOSSSUU	audaciousness
AACDELMNNRSSU	underclassman
AACDELOPRSSSU	pseudoscalars
AACDFIIIMNNOT	damnification
AACDFMNOORSTW	woodcraftsman
AACDFORRRRSWY	carryforwards
AACDGHLOPRTYY	dactylography
AACDGIIILLOST	dialogistical
AACDGIIINNNNR	incarnadining
AACDGIIINNNRT	incardinating
AACDGIIINNOST	diagnostician
AACDHHILOPRTY	hydropathical
AACDHIIIOPRST	adiaphoristic
AACDHIILNPRSS	cardinalships
AACDHIINNRSST	Christiansand
AACDHIKMNOOSU	Cahokia Mounds
AACDHILLLRUVY	hydraulically
AACDHILLOPRSY	rhapsodically
AACDHILMNOORT	trichomonadal
AACDHILORSTTY	hydrostatical
AACDHIMMOOSSS	sadomasochism
AACDHINOPQRSU	quadraphonics
AACDIIILLMOTY	idiomatically
AACDIIILMOPST	idioplasmatic
AACDIIILPQRTU	quadricipital
AACDIIINNNORT	incardination
AACDIIINORSTV	divarications
AACDIIIORTTVY	radioactivity
AACDIILLLSTUY	dualistically
AACDIILLMPRYY	pyramidically
AACDIILLORTTY	dictatorially
AACDIILMNOSST	disclamations
AACDIILNNOPTU	pandiculation
AACDIILNOOORT	radiolocation
AACDIIMNOPSST	antispasmodic
AACDIINNORRST	doctrinarians
AACDIINRSSTTU	traducianists
AACDILLLORSTY	crystalloidal
AACDILLMOPSSY	spasmodically
AACDIMNORSSTY	astrodynamics
AACEEEHJKLRTT	leatherjacket
AACEEEHLLMNPY	myelencephala
AACEEFILOPRRT	praefectorial

AACEEFMNRRTUU	remanufacture
AACEEGGILMNOT	gamogenetical
AACEEGHILOPRS	archipelagoes
AACEEGHLLMOPY	megalocephaly
AACEEGHLMNOPR	encephalogram
AACEEGHLMOPSU	megacephalous
AACEEGHNOOPRR	oceanographer
AACEEGILLLNVY	evangelically
AACEEGILMMRTT	telegrammatic
AACEEGINNNOSTU	gentianaceous
AACEEGLLOOOPY	palaeoecology
AACEEGLMORSTT	galactometers
AACEEHHILNNPR	rhinencephala
AACEEHIILNPST	elephantiasic
AACEEHIINSSTT	aestheticians
AACEEHILLSTTY	aesthetically
AACEEHILMPRTT	heptametrical
AACEEHILNPRTT	parenthetical
AACEEHIMNNOPT	acetaminophen
AACEEHINSTTTU	authenticates
AACEEHLLMRRST	Charles Martel
AACEEHLMRSTTY	methacrylates
AACEEHLNOPPRS	prosencephala
AACEEHMNNOPSUY	nymphaeaceous
AACEEHMNRSTTT	reattachments
AACEEHNNPPSST	happenstances
AACEEHOPRRTXY	archaeopteryx
AACEEIILLMRTT	Little America
AACEEIILNRTTV	intercalative
AACEEIILPRSST	recapitalises
AACEEIILPRSTZ	recapitalizes
AACEEIINNRSST	necessitarian
AACEEIINORRST	reactionaries
AACEEIINRSSST	sectarianises
AACEEIINRSSTZ	sectarianizes
AACEEILLMMRTY	metamerically
AACEEILMMNORT	anemometrical
AACEEILNNPPSU	Cape Peninsula
AACEEILNNRSTW	Saint Lawrence
AACEEILNQRSUV	carnivalesque
AACEEILPRSTTU	recapitulates
AACEEIMNNRSTT	ascertainment
AACEEINSSSTUV	causativeness
AACEEIOPRSSTT	ectoparasites
AACEELLLRRTUX	extracellular
AACEELMRSSSST	masterclasses
AACEELNNOPRTV	convertaplane
AACEELNOPRRTU	palaeocurrent
AACEEMNORSSTU	sarmentaceous
AACEENNPPRSTU	appurtenances
AACEENNPRRSST	transparences
AACEENPRRSSSU	preassurances
AACEFGILNORTV	conflagrative
AACEFIIIILRST	artificialise
AACEFIIIILRTZ	artificialize
AACEFIIILMORR	microfilariae
AACEFIIINORST	aerifications
AACEFIILLNRTY	interfacially
AACEFIILORSSS	Clare of Assisi
AACEFIINORRST	rarefications
AACEFIINRRSVX	Francis Xavier
AACEFILLTTUVY	facultatively

AACEFILMNRSST	Massif Central
AACEFIMNORRTW	aircraftwomen
AACEFIMNORSTU	manufactories
AACEFMNRRSTUU	manufacturers
AACEGGHJKNNNU	Kangchenjunga
AACEGGILLOORT	geratological
AACEGHHIIKKNS	Chiang Kai-shek
AACEGHHOPRRRT	chartographer
AACEGHHPRRSTY	tachygraphers
AACEGHILLLRTY	lethargically
AACEGHILLMOOT	hematological
AACEGHILLMPRY	graphemically
AACEGHILLPRRS	calligraphers
AACEGHILMOPYY	hypoglycaemia
AACEGHILNPRSS	graphicalness
AACEGHILOORST	archaeologist
AACEGHIMNOPRT	cinematograph
AACEGHOPRRRST	cartographers
AACEGHOPRSSSU	sarcophaguses
AACEGIIINRRST	geriatricians
AACEGIILLMNOR	mineralogical
AACEGIILLMNTY	enigmatically
AACEGIILLNNTY	antigenically
AACEGIILLNRST	interglacials
AACEGIILMRRTV	gravimetrical
AACEGIILNNNRS	encarnalising
AACEGIILNNNRZ	encarnalizing
AACEGIILNNRTT	intercalating
AACEGIINNNRRT	reincarnating
AACEGIINNQRTU	reacquainting
AACEGIINPRRTV	prevaricating
AACEGILLLLORY	allegorically
AACEGILLLMRTU	metallurgical
AACEGILLMTUYZ	zeugmatically
AACEGILLNPRYY	panegyrically
AACEGILLOORTT	teratological
AACEGILLRSTTY	strategically
AACEGILMNOOSU	magnoliaceous
AACEGILMNORTV	galvanometric
AACEGILNNPSTU	encapsulating
AACEGINNOORST	octogenarians
AACEGINOSSSSU	sagaciousness
AACEGLLNRRTUY	rectangularly
AACEGLLOOPSUY	polygalaceous
AACEGLMNOOPRS	campanologers
AACEGLNOOPSSV	galvanoscopes
AACEGLNORSTTU	congratulates
AACEHHIILMOPS	haemophiliacs
AACEHHIIMPRTT	amphitheatric
AACEHHILNOPRZ	rhizocephalan
AACEHHINOSSTU	South China Sea
AACEHHLOOPRTX	cephalothorax
AACEHHLORSTTT	throatlatches
AACEHIIIMNRTT	arithmetician
AACEHIIIMPRST	hemiparasitic
AACEHIILLNTUV	hallucinative
AACEHIILLSTTY	atheistically
AACEHIILMPRSX	alexipharmics
AACEHIILNOPST	cephalisation
AACEHIILNOPTZ	cephalization
AACEHIILNPSTT	pantheistical
AACEHIILRTTTY	theatricality

AACEHIIMNNOST	mechanisation
AACEHIIMNNOTZ	mechanization
AACEHIIMNPSTY	metaphysician
AACEHIIOPSSST	associateship
AACEHILLMRTUY	rheumatically
AACEHILLNTTUY	authentically
AACEHILMOPRST	atmospherical
AACEHILMOPTYY	polycythaemia
AACEHILNNORTT	nontheatrical
AACEHIMNNNORRT	North American
AACEHIMNORSTU	South American
AACEHIMPRSTTU	pharmaceutist
AACEHINOPRTTY	actinotherapy
AACEHINORTTTU	authenticator
AACEHINPRSTTY	parasynthetic
AACEHLNOPSSYY	psychoanalyse
AACEHLNOPSYYZ	psychoanalyze
AACEHLOOPSTUU	autocephalous
AACEHMSSSSTTU	Massachusetts
AACEHNOPPRRTY	parthenocarpy
AACEIIILMRSTT	materialistic
AACEIIIMPRSST	semiparasitic
AACEIIINORTTV	ratiocinative
AACEIIKLLMNTY	kinematically
AACEIILLLNSTY	inelastically
AACEIILLLRSTY	realistically
AACEIILLMNPRT	planimetrical
AACEIILLMNSSY	messianically
AACEIILLMOPTT	metapolitical
AACEIILLNRRTY	intercalarily
AACEIILLPPTVY	applicatively
AACEIILMMNNRSU	unicameralism
AACEIILMNNNRST	manneristical
AACEIILMNRSTT	maternalistic
AACEIILMNRSTU	unicameralist
AACEIILNNORTT	interactional
	intercalation
AACEIILNOPPRT	reapplication
AACEIILNOPPSS	episcopalians
AACEIILNORSTT	cartelisation
AACEIILNORTTZ	cartelization
AACEIILNPRSTT	antiparticles
	paternalistic
AACEIILNRSSST	satiricalness
AACEIILPRRSTU	particularise
AACEIILPRRTUZ	particularize
AACEIIMMOSTTU	semiautomatic
AACEIIMNNOPST	emancipations
AACEIIMNNOTTV	contaminative
AACEIIMOPRRST	microparasite
AACEIIMORSSTT	masticatories
AACEIINNNORRT	reincarnation
AACEIINOPPRST	appreciations
AACEIINOPRRTV	prevarication
AACEIINORSTTU	cauterisation
AACEIINORSTTV	reactivations
AACEIINORTTUZ	cauterization
AACEIJKRSSTTT	straitjackets
AACEIKLMNOPST	kleptomaniacs
AACEIKLOPRSTT	keratoplastic
AACEILLLNRRTU	intracellular
AACEILLMMPRST	metrical psalm
AACEILLMNPTUY	pneumatically
AACEILLMMORTXY	exclamatorily
AACEILLMPRSTY	spermatically
AACEILLNOORRT	correlational
AACEILLNOORST	reallocations
AACEILLNOSSTT	castellations
AACEILMNORSSY	microanalyses
AACEILMNOSSTU	emasculations
AACEILMNRRSUV	vernacularism
AACEILMOPRTVY	comparatively
AACEILMORRSTT	astrometrical
AACEILNNOPSTU	encapsulation
AACEILNOSSSSU	salaciousness
AACEILNSSSUUV	Cassivelaunus
AACEILOOPPRSS	laparoscopies
AACEILRSSTTTU	Trucial States
AACEIMMNNORST	commentariats
AACEIMMNORTUU	communautaire
AACEIMNNOPRRT	nonparametric
AACEIMNNRSTTT	transmittance
AACEIMNOOPSST	compassionate
AACEINOPRRSST	procrastinate
AACEINOPRRTUY	precautionary
AACEINOPRSSSU	rapaciousness
AACEINORRSTTT	retractations
AACEINPRRSSTT	transcriptase
AACEIOPRRRSTV	prevaricators
AACELLMNORSSW	lowerclassman
AACELMMNOPRTT	compartmental
AACELNORRSUUV	neurovascular
AACELNRSSTTUU	sustentacular
AACELOPRRSTUX	Castrop-Rauxel
AACEMNNOORSTT	entomostracan
AACFFGHIINNRS	affranchising
AACFFIIILNOST	falsification
AACFGIIIMNNOT	magnification
AACFGIIINORTT	gratification
AACFGIILNNSTY	fascinatingly
AACFGIIINNORTT	fractionating
AACFGILNNOORT	conflagration
AACFGILRSTUVX	Carl XVI Gustaf
AACFGIMNNRTUU	manufacturing
AACFHIMNPRSST	craftsmanship
AACFIIIILRTTY	artificiality
AACFIIILMNOPT	amplification
AACFIIILNOQTU	qualification
AACFIIIMNORST	ramifications
AACFIIINORSTT	ratifications
AACFIILLORSTV	Victoria Falls
AACFIILNOSSTT	factionalists
AACFIILOQRTUY	qualificatory
AACFIINNOORTT	fractionation
AACFIINOORSTT	factorisation
AACFIINOORTTZ	factorization
AACFIINOSSSTT	satisfactions
AACFINOORRSTT	fractionators
AACFINORSTTUY	anfractuosity
AACFORRSSTTTU	fractostratus
AACGGHILLOOPR	graphological
	logographical
AACGGHINOOPRR	organographic
AACGGILLLLOOY	algologically

AACGGILLNOOOR	organological
AACGGILLOORST	gastrological
AACGGILMMOORT	logogrammatic
AACGGILNRSTYZ	crystal gazing
AACGHHILMOOPR	homalographic
AACGHHIPRSTTY	tachygraphist
AACGHIILLMORT	logarithmical
AACGHIILLNNTU	hallucinating
AACGHIILLPRST	calligraphist
AACGHIIMNORST	achromatising
AACGHIIMNORTZ	achromatizing
AACGHIIPRRSTT	stratigraphic
AACGHILLNNOTY	gnathonically
AACGHILLOPRXY	xylographical
AACGHILMNOOPR	nomographical
AACGHILNOORST	arachnologist
AACGHILOOPPRR	polarographic
AACGHILOOPPRT	topographical
AACGHILOPPRTY	typographical
AACGHMMOORRST	chromatograms
AACGHMNOOPRSY	pharmacognosy
AACGIIILLMSTY	imagistically
AACGIIILLNOTZ	gallicization
AACGIIILNNOST	anglicisation
AACGIIILNNOTZ	anglicization
AACGIIINNORTT	ratiocinating
AACGIIINPPRTT	participating
AACGIILLLNTVY	vacillatingly
AACGIILLLOOXY	axiologically
AACGIILLNNORY	inorganically
AACGIILMNRTTU	matriculating
AACGIILNNPSTU	incapsulating
AACGIILNORSTU	cartilaginous
AACGIILNPTTVY	captivatingly
AACGIIMNNNOTT	contaminating
AACGIJLNNOOTU	conjugational
AACGILLLNOOPY	palynological
AACGILLLNOSTY	nostalgically
AACGILLMNSTYY	gymnastically
AACGILLMOOOST	somatological
AACGILLMOOSST	malacologists
AACGILLOOPPRY	papyrological
AACGILMNNOOPST	campanologist
AACGILMNNOORST	gastronomical
AACGILNNORSTT	translocating
AACGILNOOPRTV	galvanotropic
AACGIMMMNNOORT	monogrammatic
AACGINNORRSTW	narrowcasting
AACGLNOORRTTU	congratulator
AACHHHIMORSTT	Simchath Torah
AACHHIILNPPSS	chaplainships
AACHHIIMNPRSS	chairmanships
AACHHILPSTXYY	tachyphylaxis
AACHHIMNPSSTY	yachtsmanship
AACHIIINNRSTT	antichristian
AACHIILLNNOTU	hallucination
AACHIIMMOPSTT	amphistomatic
AACHIKORSSTUW	autorickshaws
AACHILLLMPTYV	lymphatically
AACHILLMOOPSU	malacophilous
AACHILLNOPPSY	pansophically
AACHILLNORRTU	Carrantuohill
AACHILLNORSTU	hallucinators
AACHILLNORSTY	thrasonically
AACHILLNORTUY	hallucinatory
AACHILNNOORRT	North Carolina
AACHILNNOPTYY	hypnoanalytic
AACHILNOORSTU	South Carolina
AACHILOPRSSTY	astrophysical
AACHIMMNNOPSY	nymphomaniacs
AACHIMMNOPRST	panchromatism
AACHIMMOOPRST	apochromatism
AACHIMNOPRRSS	parachronisms
AACHIMOPRSSTT	catastrophism
AACHINNOPRRTT	Pontchartrain
AACHIOPRSSTTT	catastrophist
AACHLMMOOPRSY	lymphosarcoma
AACHLNOPSSTYY	psychoanalyst
AACHLOOPRSTTY	thoracoplasty
AACIIIILNOSTT	italicisation
AACIIIILNOTTZ	italicization
AACIIILLMNOPT	implicational
AACIIILLNNNOT	inclinational
AACIIILLNOPTT	antipolitical
AACIIILLPPRTY	participially
AACIIILNNNOST	nationalistic
AACIIILNOOSST	socialisation
AACIIILNOOSTZ	socialization
AACIIILNORSTT	rationalistic
AACIIINNOORTT	ratiocination
AACIIINNOPSTT	anticipations
AACIIINNOSTTV	vaticinations
AACIIINOPPRTT	participation
AACIIINSSSTTT	statisticians
AACIILLMNNOTY	antinomically
AACIILLMORTTY	matrilocality
	triatomically
AACIILLMOSTTY	atomistically
AACIILLMPRSTY	prismatically
AACIILLNNOSTT	cantillations
AACIILLNOOSST	localisations
AACIILLNOOSTZ	localizations
AACIILLNPRTUY	puritanically
AACIILLNPTTYY	antitypically
AACIILLOPRSTY	piscatorially
AACIILLOPRTTY	patriotically
AACIILLPRSTTY	patristically
AACIILLSSTTTY	statistically
AACIILMNORSSY	microanalysis
AACIILMNORTTU	matriculation
AACIILMPRRSTU	particularism
AACIILNNOOSTV	volcanisation
AACIILNNOOTVZ	volcanization
AACIILNNOPSTU	incapsulation
AACIILNNOSTUV	vulcanisation
AACIILNNOTUVZ	vulcanization
AACIILNOOSSTV	vocalisations
AACIILNOOSTVZ	vocalizations
AACIILNOPSTTU	capitulations
AACIILNORSTTU	articulations
AACIILOPPRSTT	procapitalist
AACIILPRRSTTU	particularist
AACIILPRRTTUY	particularity
AACIIMMNNORTU	communitarian

AACIIMMORSSST	commissariats	**AADDGIINNRSST**	standardising
AACIIMNNNOOTT	contamination	**AADDGIINNRSTZ**	standardizing
AACIIMNNORTUU	actinouranium	**AADDHILLNNOSW**	Howland Island
AACIINNNOSTU	annunciations	**AADDIIILNOTTY**	additionality
AACIINNNOOSST	canonisations	**AADDIILMNSSWY**	Midway Islands
AACIINNNOOSTZ	canonizations	**AADEEEGGLRTXY**	exaggeratedly
AACIINNOORSTT	narcotisation	**AADEEEGGNRTUX**	unexaggerated
AACIINNOORTTZ	narcotization	**AADEEEGMMNNST**	endamagements
AACIINNORSSST	incrassations	**AADEEEHINSSTT**	anaesthetised
AACIINOORRSTT	ratiocinators	**AADEEEHINSTTZ**	anaesthetized
AACIINORRSSTU	curarisations	**AADEEEIILMRST**	dematerialise
AACIINORRSTUZ	curarizations	**AADEEEIILMRTZ**	dematerialize
AACIIOPPRRSTT	participators	**AADEEEIMNNRRT**	mediterranean
AACIIOPPRRTTY	participatory	**AADEEELPRSTXY**	exasperatedly
AACILLLOOPSTY	apostolically	**AADEEEMMNNRSTU**	admeasurement
AACILLMNOOTUV	autonomically	**AADEEFFHHLLRTY**	halfheartedly
AACILLMNOOTXY	taxonomically	**AADEEFHKLLOTY**	Lady of the Lake
AACILLMNOPSTY	complaisantly	**AADEEFKMNNNOR**	Anne of Denmark
AACILLMPRSTYY	sympatrically	**AADEEFNSSSSTT**	steadfastness
AACILLNORTVYY	clairvoyantly	**AADEEGGHILNRT**	Edgar Atheling
AACILMNOOPRST	proclamations	**AADEEGILMORRT**	radiotelegram
AACILMNOOPTTU	computational	**AADEEGILMQRSU**	madrigalesque
AACILMNORSSTY	microanalysts	**AADEEGILRSTVY**	Yelisavetgrad
AACILMNRRSTUU	intramuscular	**AADEEGIMNPRST**	disparagement
AACILMOOPSSTT	somatoplastic	**AADEEGINNSTUX**	exsanguinated
AACILMORRSTTU	matriculators	**AADEEHILMOSSY**	haemodialyses
AACILNNOORSTT	translocation	**AADEEHILNQRSU**	harlequinades
AACILNOSSTTUU	auscultations	**AADEEHIMMMNOZ**	Mohammedanize
AACILNPRSSTYY	cryptanalysis	**AADEEHLLRRTTY**	tetrahedrally
AACILOOPRRRTU	procuratorial	**AADEEHLOPRRTZ**	trapezohedral
AACIMNNOOPSWY	companionways	**AADEEHLORRTTT**	tetartohedral
AACIMNNOORSTT	contaminators	**AADEEHMNNSSSU**	unashamedness
AACIMNNRSTTTY	transmittancy	**AADEEHPRSSSTT**	spatterdashes
AACIMOPRSTTTU	posttraumatic	**AADEEIILMMSSV**	mediaevalisms
AACINNOOSSTTT	constatations	**AADEEIILMSSTV**	mediaevalists
AACLLNNNOOSTY	consonantally	**AADEEIILNNOST**	denationalise
AACLNPRSSTTYY	cryptanalysts	**AADEEIILNNOTZ**	denationalize
AADDEEEEFHHRT	featherheaded	**AADEEIIMNNRSU**	neuraminidase
AADDEEEHQRRTU	headquartered	**AADEEIKNNORRTY**	Yekaterinodar
AADDEEGGILLRT	draggletailed	**AADEEILLNPPRS**	Apple Islander
AADDEEGINNRRU	underdrainage	**AADEEILLOPRSY**	Pays de la Loire
AADDEEGNRRTUU	undergraduate	**AADEEILMMORST**	melodramatise
AADDEEHHLRRTY	hardheartedly	**AADEEILMMORTZ**	melodramatize
AADDEEHHMMMMO	Mohammed Ahmed	**AADEEILNNNORR**	noradrenaline
AADDEEHLORSTT	stadholderate	**AADEEILNRSSTU**	denaturalises
AADDEEIILNRSTU	denaturalised	**AADEEILNRSTUZ**	denaturalizes
AADDEEIILNRTUZ	denaturalized	**AADEEIMMNNSST**	misdemeanants
AADDEELMNNQUU	Queen Maud Land	**AADEEIMNNOSUV**	Madison Avenue
AADDEELNRTTUU	unadulterated	**AADEEIMNOPRRT**	panradiometer
AADDEFFIIILST	disaffiliated	**AADEEIMORRSTV**	overdramatise
AADDEGGHNRRTU	granddaughter	**AADEEIMORRTVZ**	overdramatize
AADDEGINOPPRS	propagandised	**AADEEINOPRSST**	endoparasites
AADDEGINOPPRZ	propagandized	**AADEEINPRSSST**	disparateness
AADDEGNNRRSST	grandstanders	**AADEENNPRSTUU**	superannuated
AADDEHIMNSSSU	Saddam Hussein	**AADEEORRSTTUV**	oversaturated
AADDEIIMNRSTT	administrated	**AADEFFIIILSST**	disaffiliates
AADDEILNNOSSS	Soenda Islands	**AADEFGHLNRRTY**	grandfatherly
AADDEILNRSSST	dastardliness	**AADEFGILNORST**	deflagrations
AADDEINRRSSST	standardisers	**AADEFHINNOSTU**	fountainheads
AADDEINRRSSTZ	standardizers	**AADEFIILNOSTU**	feudalisation
AADDFIMNNOOSU	Usman dan Fodio	**AADEFIILNOTUZ**	feudalization
AADDGGINNNRST	grandstanding	**AADEFILMNOORS**	Maid of Orléans

AADEFILNSSSTY	Safety Islands
AADEFLLMNNTUY	fundamentally
AADEGGHHIMNOU	houghmagandie
AADEGHIIOPPRR	Herod Agrippa I
AADEGHIMMORSX	hexagrammoids
AADEGHIOPRRRS	radiographers
AADEGIIIMPRRV	primigravidae
AADEGIIMNNRTV	animadverting
AADEGILLNNRSW	Wrangel Island
AADEGILNSTTVY	devastatingly
AADEGIMNNRRST	darraignments
AADEGIMNRRSTT	transmigrated
AADEGINOPPRSS	propagandises
AADEGINOPPRSZ	propagandizes
AADEGLMNORSSW	De Morgan's laws
AADEGOPRSSTTU	postgraduates
AADEHHILMOORR	haemorrhoidal
AADEHIILMOSSY	haemodialysis
AADEHIILNPSUZ	sulphadiazine
AADEHIKLMORSY	holidaymakers
AADEHILLLLOTW	Allhallowtide
AADEHILNORSUY	hyaluronidase
AADEHIMMMMNOS	Mohammedanism
AADEHIMNORSTU	diathermanous
AADEHNORRSTTW	northeastward
AADEHNORSSSUZ	hazardousness
AADEHORRSSSUU	hadrosauruses
AADEHORSSTTUW	southeastward
AADEIIILNOSST	idealisations
AADEIIILNOSTZ	idealizations
AADEIIIMNNOST	deaminisation
AADEIIIMNNOTZ	deaminization
AADEIIIMNOSTT	mediatisation
AADEIIIMNOTTZ	mediatization
AADEIIILLMORTY	mediatorially
AADEIIILLMPRXY	maxillipedary
AADEIIILLNRRTY	interradially
AADEIIILLNSUVV	vaudevillians
AADEIILMNNRST	maladminister
AADEIILMNNOST	delaminations
AADEIILMNSSTU	unassimilated
AADEIILNNSTUV	antediluvians
AADEIIMNNORSV	animadversion
AADEIIMNRRSTT	administrates
AADEIINOPSSST	dispassionate
AADEIIPQRRTTU	quadripartite
AADEIKLNNOORS	Roanoke Island
AADEIKMNNRRST	Denmark Strait
AADEILLMNRRTY	intradermally
AADEILLNNQRUY	quadrennially
AADEILMMORSTT	melodramatist
AADEILMNNPTUU	unmanipulated
AADEILMNORSST	maladroitness
AADEILMNRSSTT	mistranslated
AADEILNORSTTU	adulterations
AADEILNRSSTTW	Stewart Island
AADEIMPRRSSTY	tryparsamides
AADEINNORSTTU	denaturations
AADEINORRRTXY	extraordinary
AADEINRRSTTWW	Witwatersrand
AADEJLMMNSTTU	maladjustment
AADEKKLNORSSV	Aleksandrovsk

AADEKLLNOOPRS	Aleksandropol
AADELMOOORRST	mater dolorosa
AADELMOPRSTTY	dermatoplasty
AADEMNORSTTUY	tetradynamous
AADFGHIIMPRST	paradigm shift
AADFHIMNPRSST	draftsmanship
AADFINNOORTUY	foundationary
AADGGIILNPRSY	disparagingly
AADGHIINPRSSU	guardianships
AADGHINORSTTT	Saint Gotthard
AADGHMNORSTUW	draughtswoman
AADGIIIMPRRSV	primigravidas
AADGIILLNNSTW	Watling Island
AADGIILMRSTUV	multigravidas
AADGIIMNOOSTT	dogmatisation
AADGIIMNOOTTZ	dogmatization
AADGILLNNOOSS	Lagoon Islands
AADGILNNOPRST	prostaglandin
AADGIMRRSSTTU	dramaturgists
AADGINOPPRSST	propagandists
AADHILNORRSTY	synarthrodial
AADIIILLLRSUV	Livia Drusilla
AADIIILLNPRSS	Lipari Islands
AADIIILNNNOSS	Ionian Islands
AADIIILNNOSTV	invalidations
AADIIINOOSTTZ	diazotisation
AADIIINOOTTZZ	diazotization
AADIIILLNTTUY	latitudinally
AADIILLNOORST	dollarisation
AADIILLNOORTZ	dollarization
AADIILLNOPRTY	traditionally
AADIIILLOSUUVY	audiovisually
AADIILMNOOQRSU	quadrinomials
AADIIMNNOORST	randomisation
AADIIMNNOORTZ	randomization
AADIIMNORRSTT	administrator
AADILMNSSTUUU	Aldus Manutius
AADINNOPSSSUY	Passion Sunday
AADINNORSSTTU	transudations
AAEEEEKKMRRWW	amakwerekwere
AAEEEGILLRSTT	Tate Galleries
AAEEEGMNNRRRT	rearrangement
AAEEEHIILLSSS	Haile Selassie
AAEEEHINSSSTT	anaesthetises
AAEEEHINSSTTZ	anaesthetizes
AAEEEILNNORRS	Sierra Leonean
AAEEEKMNNPPRT	Petermann Peak
AAEEELMNPRTT	temperamental
AAEEFIIMNSTTV	manifestative
AAEEFIKLLRSTU	Kaieteur Falls
AAEEGGGJNRRUW	Wagner-Jauregg
AAEEGGILMORTV	agglomerative
AAEEGGILNORST	segregational
AAEEGGINORSTX	exaggerations
AAEEGGORSSTTY	Ortega y Gasset
AAEEGHILLMNNT	mental healing
AAEEGHMNOOSTU	haematogenous
AAEEGIIILNUVZ	Venezia Giulia
AAEEGIIMMPRST	epigrammatise
AAEEGIIMMPRTZ	epigrammatize
AAEEGIIMNNRRT	intermarriage
AAEEGIIMNNRSTV	vegetarianism

AAEEGILMNOORR	oleomargarine
AAEEGIMMMNNST	mismanagement
AAEEGIMNRTTUV	argumentative
AAEEGIMNSTTUV	augmentatives
AAEEGINNSSTUX	exsanguinates
AAEEGINOPRSTU	eusporangiate
AAEEGLMNORSTV	galvanometers
AAEEGNNNORRTT	Tarn-et-Garonne
AAEEHHIMPRSTT	amphitheaters
	amphitheatres
AAEEHHLMMORTT	hematothermal
AAEEHHMOPPSTT	metaphosphate
AAEEHIILMOPTT	epitheliomata
AAEEHIILNPSST	elephantiasis
AAEEHIIMPRSST	hemiparasites
AAEEHILLNNNPY	phenylalanine
AAEEHILNPRSST	phalansteries
AAEEHILPRSSTU	laureateships
AAEEHINNRRSTY	Tyrrhenian Sea
AAEEHINSSSTTT	anaesthetists
AAEEHIPPRRSTY	hyperparasite
AAEEHKMORRSTT	katharometers
AAEEHMNOSTTUX	exanthematous
AAEEHMOPRRRST	spermatorrhea
AAEEHNOPPRSTU	Parthenopaeus
AAEEIIILMMRST	immaterialise
AAEEIIILMMRTZ	immaterialize
AAEEIILMNNNRT	interlaminate
AAEEIILMRRSST	materialisers
AAEEIILMRRSTZ	materializers
AAEEIILNPRRTT	interparietal
AAEEIILNSSSUV	Aeneas Silvius
AAEEIIMNNNSST	inanimateness
AAEEIIMNNORTX	reexamination
AAEEIIMPRSSST	semiparasites
AAEEIINNRRSSV	anniversaries
AAEEIINNRRSTV	veterinarians
AAEEIINNSSSTT	insatiateness
AAEEIKLMNSSTT	statesmanlike
AAEEIKLNORSTV	Ekaterinoslav
AAEEIKLNSSTTV	talkativeness
AAEEILLLPPTVY	appellatively
AAEEILLLQRTUY	equilaterally
AAEEILLMNPSST	planetesimals
AAEEILLNRTTVY	alternatively
AAEEILMORRSST	alstroemerias
AAEEILNNNOPPT	peneplanation
AAEEILNORSTUV	reevaluations
AAEEILNRRSTTT	transliterate
AAEEILOPRTTVX	extrapolative
AAEEILPPRRTVY	preparatively
AAEEILQRSSSTU	sesquialteras
AAEEIMNPPRSST	appraisements
AAEEIMNPRRSTV	privateersman
AAEEINORSSSTV	asseverations
AAEEJKMMNRSTZ	katzenjammers
AAEELNPRRRTTU	preternatural
AAEEMQRRRSTTU	quartermaster
AAEENNPRSSTUU	superannuates
AAEEQRRSSTTUV	quarterstaves
AAEERRRSSTTUU	restaurateurs
AAEFFIILMNORR	foraminiferal

AAEFFIILMRTVY	affirmatively
AAEFFIIMNORRT	reaffirmation
AAEFFINOORSTT	afforestation
AAEFGHLLNNPRS	flannelgraphs
AAEFGIILLMNRSU	gallimaufries
AAEFGIKLNNRRS	farnarkelings
AAEFGILLLMNST	flagellantism
AAEFGILLLNOST	flagellations
AAEFGILMNNRTY	fragmentarily
AAEFGIMNNORTT	fragmentation
AAEFGINNNORSTT	engraftations
AAEFHILLOSTUZ	sulfathiazole
AAEFHLMORSSTTW	Waltham Forest
AAEFIIIILMRST	familiarities
AAEFIIILMRRSS	familiarisers
AAEFIIILMRRSZ	familiarizers
AAEFIILNNORRU	Alain-Fournier
AAEFIIMNNOSTT	manifestation
AAEFILLOPRRTY	prefatorially
AAEFILMNOORRT	reformational
AAEFILMNPRTUZ	flunitrazepam
AAEFILNQRRSTU	quarterfinals
AAEFILORSSSTY	forestaysails
AAEGGGILMNORT	agglomerating
AAEGGHHIIOPRS	hagiographies
AAEGGHHIMNORR	haemorrhaging
AAEGGHHIOPRRS	hagiographers
AAEGGHMNOPRST	magnetographs
AAEGGIILNTTUV	agglutinative
AAEGGIIMNNORT	aggiornamenti
AAEGGILMNOORT	agglomeration
AAEGGILNPPRSS	glasspapering
AAEGGIMNNOORT	aggiornamento
AAEGGLLLOSSSW	gallowglasses
AAEGGLMNORSTW	West Glamorgan
AAEGGLNOOPRTU	protolanguage
AAEGHHILOPPRS	haplographies
AAEGHHMOOPSTU	hematophagous
AAEGHHOPPRRSS	phraseographs
AAEGHHOPPRRSY	phraseography
AAEGHIINNPSSU	Spanish Guinea
AAEGHIKMNOPRT	kinematograph
AAEGHILMOOSTT	haematologist
AAEGHILNNOOST	halogenations
AAEGHILNOPPRS	planographies
AAEGHIOPRRRTY	arteriography
AAEGHIPRRRSTT	stratigrapher
AAEGHLLMOPRTY	metallography
AAEGHLOPPSYYZ	zygapophyseal
AAEGHLOPRTTUY	telautography
AAEGHLPRTTUUV	truth-value gap
AAEGHMMNOOPRSU	phanerogamous
AAEGHMORRTTUV	Great Yarmouth
AAEGHNNNOPRSY	nasopharynges
AAEGHNOOPPRRTY	organotherapy
AAEGHNOPPRRST	pantographers
AAEGHNOPRRRSU	uranographers
AAEGIIILMNRST	materialising
AAEGIIILMNRTZ	materializing
AAEGIIILMNTVY	imaginatively
AAEGIIILNRRST	arterialising
AAEGIIILNRRTZ	arterializing

AAEGIIIMMNNST	magnanimities
AAEGIIIMNNRSS	imaginariness
AAEGIIIMNNTUV	unimaginative
AAEGIIILLLORST	legislatorial
AAEGIILLMRSTY	magisterially
AAEGIILLNOSST	legalisations
AAEGIILLNOSTZ	legalizations
AAEGIILNNTTTY	tangentiality
AAEGIIMMMPRST	epigrammatism
AAEGIIMMPRSTT	epigrammatist
AAEGIIMNNORTZ	germanization
AAEGIIMNNOSTT	magnetisation
AAEGIIMNNOTTZ	magnetization
AAEGIIMNQQSUU	Quinquagesima
AAEGIIMNSSSTT	metastasising
AAEGIIMNSSTTZ	metastasizing
AAEGILLMNOOPT	megalopolitan
AAEGILLNRRTUY	triangulately
AAEGILMNNOPST	Leamington Spa
AAEGILMNOORRS	oleomargarins
AAEGILNNRRSTT	retranslating
AAEGILNOPRTTX	extrapolating
AAEGILOPRRTUX	expurgatorial
AAEGIMNNORTTU	argumentation
AAEGIMNNOSTTU	augmentations
AAEGIMNOOPRST	spermatogonia
AAEGIMNRRSSTT	transmigrates
AAEGIMRRSSTTU	magistratures
AAEGINNNOORSTV	Stanovoi Range
AAEGINOORSTTY	geostationary
AAEGINQRRSTUW	quartersawing
AAEGLLNOOOPTY	palaeontology
AAEGLLOOOOPYZ	palaeozoology
AAEGLNNOOSSSU	analogousness
AAEHHILMOPRTX	xerophthalmia
AAEHIIILMNSSS	leishmaniasis
AAEHIIIMNNSTT	antihistamine
AAEHIILNORSTX	exhilarations
AAEHIIMNOSTTT	thematisation
AAEHIIMNOTTTZ	thematization
AAEHIINNOPRST	antiphonaries
AAEHIIORTTTUV	authoritative
AAEHIKMMOPSST	Thomas à Kempis
AAEHIKNOSSTTV	stakhanovites
AAEHILMNOSTXY	haematoxylins
AAEHILNNOSSST	Thessalonians
AAEHIMNPSSSTT	statesmanship
AAEHINNNOQRTU	anthraquinone
AAEHINOPRSTTU	naturopathies
AAEHINPRSSSTY	parasynthesis
AAEHLMNOOSTXY	haematoxylons
AAEHNNOPRSSXY	nasopharynxes
AAEHNNOPRSTTY	parasyntheton
AAEIIIILNNNTV	Valentinian II
AAEIIIILMMMRST	immaterialism
AAEIIILLMMRSTT	immaterialist
AAEIIILMMRTTY	immateriality
AAEIIILNNOSTT	nationalities
AAEIIILNORSST	serialisation
AAEIIILNORSTT	rationalities
AAEIIILNORSTZ	serialization
AAEIIIMNNPPRT	imparipinnate
AAEIIKLMNPSST	Semipalatinsk
AAEIILLLLMNRTY	matrilineally
AAEIILLLNPRTY	patrilineally
AAEIILLMNOSTT	metallisation
AAEIILLMNOTTZ	metallization
AAEIILLMNRSTU	unilateralism
AAEIILLNOPSTT	palletisation
AAEIILLNOPTTZ	palletization
AAEIILLNORSTT	alliterations
AAEIILLNPRRTY	patrilinearly
AAEIILLNRTTUV	unilaterality
AAEIILLQTTUVV	qualitatively
AAEIILMMNNSTT	milatainments
AAEIILMMNOSTT	lemmatisation
AAEIILMMNOTTZ	lemmatization
AAEIILMNNORTT	terminational
AAEIILMNOORST	ameliorations
AAEIILMNOSTTZ	metalizations
AAEIILMNPRSST	impartialness
AAEIILNNNORTT	international
AAEIILNNOORTT	orientational
AAEIILNNOPSST	penalisations
AAEIILNNOPSTZ	penalizations
AAEIILNNORSTV	vernalisation
AAEIILNNORTVZ	vernalization
AAEIILNOPRRST	respirational
AAEIILNOQSSTU	equalisations
AAEIILNOQSTUZ	equalizations
AAEIILNORRSST	rationalisers
AAEIILNORRSTZ	rationalizers
AAEIILNORRTTT	trilateration
AAEIILNOSSTUX	sexualisation
AAEIILNOSTUXZ	sexualization
AAEIIMNNNOSTX	annexationism
AAEIIMNOOPRST	anisometropia
AAEIIMOPPRTVX	approximative
AAEIINNNOSTTX	annexationist
AAEIINNNSTTTY	instantaneity
AAEIINNOSSTTT	tetanisations
AAEIINOPPPRRT	inappropriate
AAEIINOPRRSST	repatriations
AAEIINOPRSSTT	separationist
AAEIIOPPPRRTV	appropriative
AAEIKLLNNOPSU	Kola Peninsula
AAEILLMNNNOPRY	praenominally
AAEILLNNOSSTY	sensationally
AAEILLNOOPRTY	operationally
AAEILLNOPRTXY	explanatorily
AAEILMNNORSTU	mensurational
AAEILMNOPRTTU	permutational
AAEILMNRSSSTT	mistranslates
AAEILMNRSSTUX	transexualism
AAEILMOPPRTXY	approximately
AAEILNNNNPSVY	Pennsylvanian
AAEILNNOPRSTT	replantations
AAEILNNOPRSTU	supernational
AAEILNNOPSTTX	explantations
AAEILNNORRSTT	retranslation
AAEILNOOORTTV	laevorotation
AAEILNOOPRTTX	extrapolation
AAEILOPPPRRTY	appropriately
AAEILOPPRRRTY	preparatorily

AAEILORSSTTVY	assortatively
AAEIMMOOSSSTT	metasomatosis
AAEIMNNNOORTT	ornamentation
AAEIMNORSSTTT	stationmaster
AAEIMNRSTTTUV	transmutative
AAEINNNOSSTTU	instantaneous
AAEINNOPRSTTU	supernatation
AAEKLOPRRSTUX	Kastrop-Rauxel
AAELLMOOPRSTU	somatopleural
AAELLNRRSSTVY	transversally
AAELMNNOOSSSU	anomalousness
AAELMNNORSTTU	ultramontanes
AAELNNNRSSTUU	unnaturalness
AAELNNPRRSSTT	transplanters
AAELNNPRRSTTY	transparently
AAELOOORPRTTVY	laevorotatory
AAELOOPRRSTTX	extrapolators
AAELOOPRRTTXY	extrapolatory
AAEMNNNORSSTT	transmontanes
AAFFGHINPRSSU	suffraganship
AAFFIINNOPRRT	nitroparaffin
AAFGIIIILMNRS	familiarising
AAFGIIIILMNRZ	familiarizing
AAFGIINNORSTT	ingraftations
AAFHIJNOORSTU	John of Austria
AAFIIIILMNRTUY	unfamiliarity
AAFIIILNNOSST	finalisations
AAFIIILNRSTTU	futilitarians
AAFIIIMNRRSTU	fruitarianism
AAFIILMMNNOST	inflammations
AAFIILMNNOORT	informational
AAFIILMNNOOST	Nation of Islam
AAFIILMNOORST	formalisation
AAFIILMNOORTZ	formalization
AAFILMMNOORST	malformations
AAFILNOOSSSUU	Louis of Nassau
AAFIMOORRSSTT	Formosa Strait
AAGGGIILNNTTU	agglutinating
AAGGHHIIOPRST	hagiographist
AAGGIIILMNNRS	marginalising
AAGGIIILMNNRZ	marginalizing
AAGGIILNNOTTU	agglutination
AAGGIILNNRTTU	triangulating
AAGGILNNRSTTU	strangulating
AAGHHINOOPPRT	anthropophagi
AAGHHNOOPPRTY	anthropophagy
AAGHIILMNORTT	antilogarithm
AAGHIINNNOSTW	Washingtonian
AAGHIMNOOPRST	mastigophoran
AAGHINOPRRSTU	uranographist
AAGIIILMMNORT	immigrational
AAGIIILNNNOST	nationalising
AAGIIILNNNOTZ	nationalizing
AAGIIILNNORST	rationalising
AAGIIILNNORTZ	rationalizing
AAGIIINNNOSTV	invaginations
AAGIIINNNSTTT	instantiating
AAGIIINNORSTT	granitisation
	ingratiations
AAGIIINNORTTZ	granitization
AAGIIJNNOORST	jargonisation
AAGIIJNNOORTZ	jargonization

AAGIIKLNNPSTY	painstakingly
AAGIIILLMOORST	malariologist
AAGIIILLNNOPST	Gallinas Point
AAGIIILLNNSTTY	tantalisingly
AAGIIILLNNTTYZ	tantalizingly
AAGIILMNOORST	glamorisation
AAGIILMNOORTZ	glamorization
AAGIILNNORTTU	triangulation
AAGIILNORSTUV	vulgarisation
AAGIILNORTUVZ	vulgarization
AAGIILNRRTTUY	triangularity
AAGIIMNOPPRTX	approximating
AAGIINNOORSST	organisations
AAGIINNOORSTZ	organizations
AAGIINNORSTUU	inaugurations
AAGIINOPPPRRT	appropriating
AAGIKLNNOPQRU	Algonquin Park
AAGIKNNSSUUUY	Aung San Suu Kyi
AAGILLOPRRTUY	purgatorially
AAGILMMNNOSUY	magnanimously
AAGILNNNPRSTT	transplanting
AAGILNNORSTTU	strangulation
AAGILNOOOPRSZ	zoosporangial
AAGILNORSSTTU	gastrulations
AAGIMNNNRRSSTT	transmigrants
AAGIMNORRRSTT	transmigrator
AAGINOOOOPPRSS	prosopagnosia
AAGIRRSSTTTUU	Tsugaru Strait
AAGLMNOORSTUU	granulomatous
AAHHNOOPPRTTY	anthropopathy
AAHIIILNNNOST	annihilations
AAHIILNNPRRTY	platyrrhinian
AAHIIMNNOORST	harmonisation
AAHIIMNNOORTZ	harmonization
AAHIIMNNOSSTU	humanisations
AAHIIMNNOSTUZ	humanizations
AAHIINOORSTTU	authorisation
AAHIINOORTTUZ	authorization
AAHIINOPSSTXY	asphyxiations
AAHIKLLNNOPST	haliplanktons
AAHILNNOPSSYY	hypnoanalysis
AAIIILMNORRST	irrationalism
AAIIILMNOSSST	assimilations
AAIIILNNOPRST	inspirational
AAIIILNNOPRTT	Tripolitanian
AAIIILNNOPSTT	platinisation
AAIIILNNOPTTZ	platinization
AAIIILNNOSTTZ	latinizations
AAIIILNOORSTV	variolisation
AAIIILNOORTVZ	variolization
AAIIILNORRTTY	irrationality
AAIIILNOSSTUV	visualisation
AAIIILNOSTUVZ	visualization
AAIIILNPRSTTU	antispiritual
AAIIIMMNNNOST	antinomianism
AAIIIMMNOSSTX	maximisations
AAIIIMMNOSTXZ	maximizations
AAIIINNNOSTTT	instantiation
AAIIINOPRSTTV	privatisation
AAIIINOPRTTVZ	privatization
AAIIINORSSSTT	satirisations
AAIIILLMMNORTY	matrimonially

AAIILLMNNOTTU	multinational
AAIILLMNOPRTY	patrimonially
AAIILLNNOSSTT	installations
AAIILLNOPRSTU	pluralisation
AAIILLNOPRTUZ	pluralization
AAIILMNNOORST	normalisation
AAIILMNNOORTZ	normalization
AAIILMNNOPSTT	implantations
AAIILMNNOPSTU	manipulations
AAIILMNOOPTTT	totipalmation
AAIILMNOORSST	moralisations
AAIILMNOORSTZ	moralizations
AAIILMNOSTTUU	mutualisation
AAIILMNOTTUUZ	mutualization
AAIILNOOPRSST	polarisations
AAIILNOOPRSTZ	polarizations
AAIILNOORSSTV	valorisations
AAIILNOORSTVZ	valorizations
AAIILNOOSSTTT	totalisations
AAIILNOOSTTTZ	totalizations
AAIILNORRSSTU	ruralisations
AAIILNORRSTUZ	ruralizations
AAIILNOSSSTTV	salvationists
AAIIMMNNORSSTU	summarisation
AAIIMMNORSTUZ	summarization
AAIIMNNOORSTZ	romanizations
AAIIMNOOPPRTX	approximation
AAIIMNOORSSTT	amortisations
AAIIMNOORSTTZ	amortizations
AAIIMNORRSTTY	martyrisation
AAIIMNORRTTYZ	martyrization
AAIINNOPRRSTT	transpiration
AAIINNOQSSTTU	quantisations
AAIINNOQSTTUZ	quantizations
AAIINNORRSSTTY	transitionary
AAIINNORSSTTU	instaurations
AAIINOOPPPRRT	appropriation
AAILLMOOPPSTU	papillomatous
AAILMNNNORSTU	non-naturalism
AAILMNNORSTUU	Ural Mountains
AAILNNOPPSTTU	supplantation
AAILNOOOPRRTT	protonotarial
AAIMNNORSTTTU	transmutation
AAINNOORSSTTUU	unsaturations
AAINOOORSTTTU	autorotations
AAINOPRRRSTTY	transpiratory
AAIOOPPPRRRST	appropriators
AAKLNNNNNOOPT	nannoplankton
AALMOOPSSTTTY	stomatoplasty
AANNORRSSTUUY	tyrannosaurus
ABBBEHLMORSTU	blabbermouths
ABBCDEEIILNRS	indescribable
ABBCDEGIMNNRU	breadcrumbing
ABBCDEIILNRSY	indescribably
ABBCEEIJKORSW	jabberwockies
ABBCEEIJLNOOT	objectionable
ABBCEGIKLNRRY	blackberrying
ABBCEIJLNOOTY	objectionably
ABBCEILNORTTU	contributable
ABBCGHIIILOPR	bibliographic
ABBCIIILMNOTY	combinability
ABBCIIILOPRST	probabilistic

ABBDEGIINORRW	Rainbow Bridge
ABBDEIILRSTTU	distributable
ABBDILOOOOSSU	Bobo-Dioulasso
ABBEEIIILLTVY	believability
ABBEEILLMNRTY	Blantyre-Limbe
ABBEEILMPRRTU	imperturbable
ABBEEILMSSSSU	subassemblies
ABBEELMMNOOTZ	bamboozlement
ABBEFHILLNOTY	Fonthill Abbey
ABBEGHIILOPRR	bibliographer
ABBEIIILOPRST	probabilities
ABBEIILORSTVY	observability
ABBEILMPRRTUY	imperturbably
ABBEILSSTTTUU	substitutable
ABBGIINNRSSUU	suburbanising
ABBGIINNRSUUZ	suburbanizing
ABBIIILMOPRTY	improbability
ABCCDDEHIIIKS	chickabiddies
ABCCDEEEELNRT	credence table
ABCCDEEELNORT	concelebrated
ABCCDEEHKORRS	checkerboards
ABCCDEHILORSU	coachbuilders
ABCCDEILORSTU	scrobiculated
ABCCDENORSTTU	subcontracted
ABCCEEELNORST	concelebrates
ABCCEEIILNNVO	inconceivable
ABCCEEJLNORTU	conjecturable
ABCCEELNORRTU	uncorrectable
ABCCEEMNNRRSU	encumbrancers
ABCCEGIILLOOO	bioecological
ABCCEHIILLMOY	biochemically
ABCCEIIILLLMY	imbecilically
ABCCEIIILMPTY	impeccability
ABCCEIIILSSTY	accessibility
ABCCEIIINOSTV	biconcavities
ABCCEIILNNOVY	inconceivably
ABCCEIILORTTY	bacteriolytic
ABCCEIIMMNRTU	circumambient
ABCCEIMMORTUY	mycobacterium
ABCCEJLNORTUY	conjecturably
ABCCGHIIKNSTT	backstitching
ABCCHHIIOPRRS	archbishopric
ABCCIILLLNSUY	subclinically
ABCCIILORRTXY	tricarboxylic
ABCCIIMNOORST	combinatorics
ABCCIINORSTTU	antiscorbutic
ABCCILLORSTUY	scorbutically
ABCCNOORSTTU	subcontractor
ABCDDEEEHNSSU	debauchedness
ABCDDEEHKLLOY	blockheadedly
ABCDDEEIILRST	discreditable
ABCDDEIILRSTY	discreditably
ABCDEEEGHNRST	Berchtesgaden
ABCDEEEGINRRT	decerebrating
ABCDEEEHLORRS	breechloaders
ABCDEEEILNRRS	candleberries
ABCDEEEINORRT	decerebration
ABCDEEELMMNOR	recommendable
ABCDEEHOQRRSU	chequerboards
ABCDEEIIILTVY	deceivability
ABCDEEIILLTTY	delectability
ABCDEEIIMOSTY	basidiomycete

ABCDEEILNNNOS	incondensable
ABCDEEILNPRTU	unpredictable
ABCDEEINORRSS	decarbonisers
ABCDEEINORRSZ	decarbonizers
ABCDEELMMNNOU	uncommendable
ABCDEFIILSSSU	subclassified
ABCDEGIINNORS	decarbonising
ABCDEGIINNORZ	decarbonizing
ABCDEGIINRRSU	decarburising
ABCDEGIINRRUZ	decarburizing
ABCDEHIILNNRR	brainchildren
ABCDEIIILLNPS	disciplinable
ABCDEIIILNORT	bidirectional
ABCDEIIILNLTUY	ineducability
ABCDEIIILPRTY	predicability
ABCDEIIILPSTY	despicability
ABCDEIIILRTTY	creditability
ABCDEIIILLOQTU	quodlibetical
ABCDEILNPRTUY	unpredictably
ABCDEINOOPRSS	proboscideans
ABCDEKMNORSSW	backswordsmen
ABCDIIIILNTVY	vindicability
ABCDIIILLPTUY	duplicability
ABCDIIIILNNOOT	biconditional
ABCDIINOOPRSS	proboscidians
ABCDILNOOOSTT	odontoblastic
ABCEEEELNRSSX	execrableness
ABCEEEEFIIINRS	beneficiaries
ABCEEEFIILLRT	electrifiable
ABCEEEFILLNNU	influenceable
ABCEEEIINNRST	bicentenaries
ABCEEEILNOPTX	exceptionable
ABCEEEILNRSUV	unserviceable
ABCEEEILNSSTX	excitableness
ABCEEEILORRRV	irrecoverable
ABCEEEILORTVX	overexcitable
ABCEEELMNOPRS	recompensable
ABCEEELNSSSUX	excusableness
ABCEEEMMNNRRS	remembrancers
ABCEEFFIINRST	febrifacients
ABCEEFINORSST	sorbefacients
ABCEEGHHIKNSS	backsheeshing
ABCEEGHLMRRSU	schlumbergera
ABCEEGILNOSTT	blastogenetic
ABCEEGIORSSTU	subcategories
ABCEEHILORSTT	heteroblastic
ABCEEHIMNRSTY	chimneybreast
ABCEEHKLLPRTY	Bletchley Park
ABCEEHLNOSSTU	touchableness
ABCEEHMMNNRST	embranchments
ABCEEIILNNNST	bicentennials
ABCEEIILNPRSU	republicanise
ABCEEIILNPRUZ	republicanize
ABCEEIILNRSSS	irascibleness
ABCEEILLORSTV	Belvoir Castle
ABCEEILLSSSTU	subcelestials
ABCEEILMOORSU	bromeliaceous
ABCEEILNNOSTT	incontestable
ABCEEILNNRSSU	incurableness
ABCEEILNOPRRS	cerebrospinal
ABCEEILNOPTXY	exceptionably
ABCEEILNORSSU	ribonucleases
ABCEEILORRRVY	irrecoverably
ABCEEIMNOSSTV	combativeness
ABCEEJKLMRSTU	lumberjackets
ABCEELLRTTUUY	tuberculately
ABCEELMMNORSU	commensurable
ABCEELNNOOPRU	pronounceable
ABCEELNSSSSTU	substanceless
ABCEENNNOORSV	nonobservance
ABCEENOPRRSTU	protuberances
ABCEEOOPRRRST	baroreceptors
ABCEFGHKNOOOS	Book of Changes
ABCEFHIILLMRU	liebfraumilch
ABCEFIIINORTV	verbification
ABCEFIILSSSSU	subclassifies
ABCEFINOORRSU	carboniferous
ABCEFLMNNOORU	unconformable
ABCEFLMNOORTU	uncomfortable
ABCEGHHOORRTU	thoroughbrace
ABCEGHILOPRTY	copyrightable
ABCEGHORRRSTU	turbochargers
ABCEGIIKKNSTY	stickybeaking
ABCEGIINNOOSU	bignoniaceous
ABCEGILLMOORY	embryological
ABCEHIIIORSTV	behavioristic
ABCEHIILMNTTY	bathylimnetic
ABCEHILLMOOPT	phlebotomical
ABCEHILNOPSST	constableship
ABCEHIMPRRSTY	brachypterism
ABCEHKLRSSSUW	swashbucklers
ABCEHLOOPRSTU	claustrophobe
ABCEHOPRRSTUY	brachypterous
ABCEIIILNOTTY	noticeability
ABCEIIKNNRSSS	brainsickness
ABCEIIILLLMPTU	multiplicable
ABCEIIILLMNOPU	pneumobacilli
ABCEIIILLMORTY	biometrically
ABCEIIILMMRSTY	bisymmetrical
ABCEIIILMNOPST	incompatibles
ABCEIIILMNPRSU	republicanism
ABCEIIILNOPRTU	republication
ABCEIIILNRSTUY	censurability
ABCEIIILOORSST	borosilicates
ABCEIIILORSSTY	bacteriolysis
ABCEIIIMMNOORT	recombination
ABCEIIIMNNOOSZ	aminobenzoics
ABCEIIINOORTTX	bacteriotoxin
ABCEIIINORSSTT	obstetricians
ABCEIKLPRTUUY	Yakut Republic
ABCEIILLMNORYY	embryonically
ABCEIILLORSTTY	obstetrically
ABCEIILNNOSTTY	incontestably
ABCEIILNORTTUU	tuberculation
ABCEIILOORSSTU	strobilaceous
ABCEIILORRRTUU	arboriculture
ABCEINORRSSTU	subcontraries
ABCEIOOORRRTV	corroborative
ABCELLLOOSSTY	octosyllables
ABCELMMNNORSU	commensurably
ABCELNORSSTTU	counterblasts
ABCFIILNOSTUY	confusability
ABCFLMNNOORUY	unconformably
ABCFLMNOORTUY	uncomfortably

ABCFLNOOORRSU	fluorocarbons
ABCGHHNOOPRRY	bronchography
ABCGHIKLNSSUW	swashbuckling
ABCGIIKLLNSST	blacklistings
ABCGIILLNNOOO	nonbiological
ABCGILLLNOOTU	lactoglobulin
ABCGILLMNOORU	macroglobulin
ABCGILNNOOOST	conglobations
ABCGINOOORRRT	corroborating
ABCHHINOOPRST	opisthobranch
ABCHIILLOPSYY	biophysically
ABCHILLMOPSTY	lymphoblastic
ABCHILOOPRSTT	trophoblastic
ABCIIILLNOTUY	inoculability
ABCIIIILLNPTUY	inculpability
ABCIIILLTTUVY	cultivability
ABCIIILMNOSTU	umbilications
ABCIIILMOPTTY	compatibility
ABCIIIILNOSTUY	unsociability
ABCIILLOORTUY	colourability
ABCIILLOPRSTT	triploblastic
ABCIILMMOTTUY	commutability
ABCIILMOPTTUY	computability
ABCIILNPPRSSU	subprincipals
ABCILMMNOSSTU	noctambulisms
ABCILMNOSSTTU	noctambulists
ABCILNOORSTTU	obstructional
ABCINOOOORRRT	corroboration
ABCINORSSSTTU	obscurantists
ABCLRRSSTTUUU	substructural
ABCOOOORRRRST	corroborators
ABCOOOORRRRTY	corroboratory
ABDDDEEEEFHRT	featherbedded
ABDDDEEGILRRS	griddlebreads
ABDDDEILMNORY	broadmindedly
ABDDEEEGHINSS	bigheadedness
ABDDEEEEHLORSU	doubleheaders
ABDDEEEIKLMRR	middlebreaker
ABDDEEFINSTUU	subinfeudated
ABDDEEHLRTUVY	butyraldehyde
ABDDEEIILNPTY	dependability
ABDDEEEIILLNOSS	Bedloe's Island
ABDDEELMNRRSU	drumbledranes
ABDDEENOPRSUU	superabounded
ABDEEEEHINRRS	Aberdeenshire
ABDEEEEEHLNPRR	reprehendable
ABDEEEGKLLNOW	knowledgeable
ABDEEEEHILRSST	reestablished
ABDEEEEHKNORRT	brokenhearted
ABDEEEEHLORRHW	wheelbarrowed
ABDEEEIILMRTY	redeemability
ABDEEEEILMNNST	disenablement
ABDEEEEILNPRST	predestinable
ABDEEEEILNRSSS	desirableness
ABDEEEELMNSTZZ	bedazzlements
ABDEEEELNNRSSU	endurableness
ABDEEEELNRSSSS	beardlessness
ABDEEELRSSSTT	battledresses
ABDEEEFGHINRRT	fingerbreadth
ABDEEFIIILRSV	diversifiable
ABDEEFIIILSTY	defeasibility
ABDEEFINSSTUU	subinfeudates
ABDEEGIILNRST	disintegrable
ABDEEGIKNORRY	rekeyboarding
ABDEEGKLLNOWY	knowledgeably
ABDEEHILNSSTU	unestablished
ABDEEIILMSSSU	disassemblies
ABDEEIILNNPSS	indispensable
ABDEEIILNNSSU	inaudibleness
ABDEEIILNORST	deliberations
ABDEEIILNPTXY	expendability
ABDEEIILNTTXY	extendability
ABDEEIILSTTTY	detestability
ABDEEIIMRTTXY	ambidexterity
ABDEEIKMMNRST	disembarkment
ABDEEIILLNORRS	banderilleros
ABDEEIILMNOPRS	imponderables
ABDEEIILMRSSSU	disassemblers
ABDEEILORRSUV	boulevardiers
ABDEEINNSSSSU	unbiassedness
ABDEEMNPRSTTU	subdepartment
ABDEFFHLORSSU	shuffleboards
ABDEFIILLORRT	defibrillator
ABDEFIILMORTY	deformability
ABDEFIILNNTUU	infundibulate
ABDEFLORRSSTU	flutterboards
ABDEGHINOORSU	boardinghouse
ABDEGIIILNRST	detribalising
ABDEGIIILNRTZ	detribalizing
ABDEGIIILNSST	destabilising
ABDEGIIILNSTZ	destabilizing
ABDEGIILMNSSS	disassembling
ABDEGINNOORUV	overabounding
ABDEGLNORSTTU	battlegrounds
ABDEHHNOSSSUU	househusbands
ABDEHILMNNSST	blandishments
ABDEHILNOORSU	dishonourable
ABDEIIILNOSTT	debilitations
ABDEIIILLNRSTY	Liberty Island
ABDEIIILLOPRTY	deplorability
ABDEIIILNNPSSY	indispensably
ABDEIIILNOPRTY	ponderability
ABDEIIILPRRTUY	perdurability
ABDEIINNORSTU	insubordinate
ABDEIIINORSSU	subordinaries
ABDEIINORSTUV	subordinative
ABDEIIOOPRSSS	basidiospores
ABDEILMNNORRU	ordinal number
ABDEILNORSTUY	subordinately
ABDELNNOPTUUW	unputdownable
ABDFIIIILMOTY	modifiability
ABDFIIIILMORTY	formidability
ABDFIILNOOOSV	bioflavonoids
ABDGGIINNORTU	groundbaiting
ABDGIINNORSTU	subordinating
ABDGILMINNORSU	bildungsroman
ABDHIIINORSTY	hybridisation
ABDHIIINORTYZ	hybridization
ABDHILNOORSUY	dishonourably
ABDIIIILMSSTY	admissibility
ABDIIILNOSSUV	subdivisional
ABDIIILOPSSTY	disposability
ABDIIILPSTTUY	disputability
ABDIIINOSSSTU	subsidisation

ABDIIINOSSTUZ	subsidization
ABDIINNOORSTU	subordination
ABEEEEEFLNORSU	unforeseeable
ABEEEEEILMMPRS	semipermeable
ABEEEEEIRRRTVV	reverberative
ABEEEEELMNPRSS	permeableness
ABEEEEELNNRSSV	venerableness
ABEEEEELNPRRST	representable
ABEEEEFFILNNSS	ineffableness
ABEEEEFIILLMPX	exemplifiable
ABEEEEGINRRRTV	reverberating
ABEEEEGLMMNNNRT	embranglement
ABEEEEHILNPPRS	apprehensible
ABEEEEHILRSSST	reestablishes
ABEEEEHKORRSSU	housebreakers
ABEEEEIIKLMNRS	Berkeleianism
ABEEEEIILLPRRV	irrepleviable
ABEEEEIILRRRTV	irretrievable
ABEEEEIKKRRRST	strikebreaker
ABEEEEILMNRSSS	miserableness
ABEEEEILMNSSST	estimableness
ABEEEEILNNRRSS	inerrableness
ABEEEEILNPRRTT	interpretable
ABEEEEILNQSSTU	equitableness
ABEEEEILNRSSTV	veritableness
ABEEEEILNSSSST	beastlinesses
ABEEEEINORRRTV	reverberation
ABEEEEINRRSTTV	invertebrates
ABEEEJLNNOSSY	enjoyableness
ABEEEELLMNSSSS	blamelessness
ABEEEELLNORSST	tolerableness
ABEEEELMMNORSS	memorableness
ABEEEELMNORSSV	removableness
ABEEEELNNNSSTU	untenableness
ABEEEELNNPRSTU	unpresentable
ABEEEELNPRSSSU	superableness
ABEEEELNRRRTVY	reverberantly
ABEEEELNRSSTTU	utterableness
ABEEEEMMNPRRSU	supermembrane
ABEEEENOSSSTUU	beauteousness
ABEEEEORRRRSTV	reverberators
ABEEEEORRRRTVY	reverberatory
ABEEEEPRRSSTTY	presbyterates
ABEEEFGIILNRRR	irrefrangible
ABEEEFGILNNRSS	frangibleness
ABEEEFGLNORTTU	unforgettable
ABEEEFIILNOPRS	personifiable
ABEEEFIILPRRTY	preferability
ABEEEFILNSSTUU	beautifulness
ABEEEGHIKNORSU	housebreaking
ABEEEGHILNRSST	rightableness
ABEEEGIILMMNST	emblematising
ABEEEGIILMMNTZ	emblematizing
ABEEEGIILMNNRS	Negri Sembilan
ABEEEGIKNRRTUY	Yekaterinburg
ABEEEGILNNNOOT	nonnegotiable
ABEEEGILNORRVY	overbearingly
ABEEEGILNOSSST	blastogenesis
ABEEEHIILNSTUX	inexhaustible
ABEEEHIKLRSSTT	blatherskites
ABEEEHILMNSSTT	establishment
ABEEEHILNPPRSY	apprehensibly

ABEEEHILOPRTTZ	Port Elizabeth
ABEEEHIQRRSSUU	harquebusiers
ABEEEHKLNORRTY	heartbrokenly
ABEEEHLNNOORRS	blennorrhoeas
ABEEEHLNNOORSS	honorableness
ABEEEHLOPRSSST	blastospheres
ABEEEIIIILLMNRS	bimillenaries
ABEEEIIILRSSTU	reusabilities
ABEEEIILLLNRSS	illiberalness
ABEEEIILLMNORS	neoliberalism
ABEEEIILLMNSST	limitableness
ABEEEIILLRRSUV	Aubervilliers
ABEEEIILMPRTTY	temperability
ABEEEIILNNORTV	inventoriable
ABEEEIILNPRTTY	penetrability
ABEEEIILNNRSSU	irritableness
ABEEEIILRRRTVY	irretrievably
ABEEEIIOOPRRRT	Ribeirão Prêto
ABEEEILLNPSSSU	plausibleness
ABEEEILMMNOSSV	immovableness
ABEEEILMMNSSTU	immutableness
ABEEEILMNNNOTU	unmentionable
ABEEEILMNORRSS	salmonberries
ABEEEILMNPSSTU	imputableness
ABEEEILNNPRSST	printableness
ABEEEILNNRSSSS	brainlessness
ABEEEILNNSTTUU	sublieutenant
ABEEEILNPRRTTY	interpretably
ABEEEILOPRRTVY	reprobatively
ABEEEINORRSTTV	vertebrations
ABEEEINPRRSSTY	presbyterians
ABEEEIOORRSSTV	observatories
ABEEEIRRSSSTUU	subtreasuries
ABEEEKLMORRSTU	troublemakers
ABEEEKMNNORTUY	mountebankery
ABEEEKORRSSSTT	breaststrokes
ABEEELLMNOSTTT	ballottements
ABEEELMMNNOSTZ	emblazonments
ABEEELNNNORRTU	nonreturnable
ABEEENORRSSTUU	subterraneous
ABEEERRRSSSTUU	subtreasurers
ABEFFIIMOPRST	baptism of fire
ABEFGIILNRRRY	irrefrangibly
ABEFGLNORTTUY	unforgettably
ABEFIIIILNSTY	infeasibility
ABEFIIIILLRTTY	filterability
ABEFIIJLNSTUU	unjustifiable
ABEFIILNORRRU	neurofibrilar
ABEFLLNOOPSTU	tablespoonful
ABEGHHKORRSTU	breakthroughs
ABEGHIILMOOPS	amphibologies
ABEGIIILNOTTY	negotiability
ABEGIIIILNQRTU	equilibrating
ABEGIIIILNRTTY	integrability
ABEGIILNORTVY	governability
ABEGIILOOORST	aerobiologist
ABEGIKLMNORTU	troublemaking
ABEGIKMNNNOTU	mountebanking
ABEGILLNOOSST	balneologists
ABEGIMNOSSSUU	ambiguousness
ABEGINOPRRTTU	protuberating
ABEHIIIILPRSTY	perishability

ABEHIILNSTUXY	inexhaustibly
ABEHIIMORSSUV	behaviourisms
ABEHIIORSSTUV	behaviourists
ABEHIKLNNNORS	nonshrinkable
ABEHIKMNOORST	thrombokinase
ABEHIKMNQRRTU	Khirbet Qumran
ABEHINNOOSTTT	ethnobotanist
ABEHLLMOPSSUV	blasphemously
ABEHLORRSSTTY	erythroblasts
ABEIIIILLMNTY	eliminability
ABEIIIILNRSST	rinsabilities
ABEIIIILNSSTT	instabilities
ABEIIIILNTTVY	inevitability
ABEIIIILLNSTTY	listenability
ABEIIILMMOTVY	immoveability
ABEIIILMNRTTY	terminability
ABEIIILMRSSST	miserabilists
ABEIIILNOPRTY	inoperability
ABEIIILNOQRTU	equilibration
ABEIIILNORSTT	liberationist
ABEIIILNORTXY	inexorability
ABEIIILNPSTXY	expansibility
ABEIIILPRRSTY	respirability
ABEIILLMOPTVY	employability
ABEIILLNRTUVY	vulnerability
ABEIILLORSTVY	resolvability
ABEIILMNOOSST	embolisations
ABEIILMNRSSST	transmissible
ABEIILMNRSTTT	transmittible
ABEIILMNRSTUY	mensurability
ABEIILMPRTTUY	permutability
ABEIILNNOSSTU	nebulisations
ABEIILNNOSTUZ	nebulizations
ABEIILNOORSTT	obliterations
ABEIILNORSSTV	vibrationless
ABEIILNRRTTUY	returnability
ABEIILOPRTTXY	exportability
ABEIILOQRRSTU	equilibrators
ABEIILRTTTUVY	attributively
ABEIIMNOSSSTU	ambitiousness
ABEIIMOORSTUV	overambitious
ABEIINSSSTTVU	substantivise
ABEIINSSTTUVZ	substantivize
ABEIKKNNSSTUZ	Kuznetsk Basin
ABEILLNOOSSSY	obsessionally
ABEILLNOPPRST	bipropellants
ABEILLOOPRSST	ballistospore
ABEILMNNNOTUY	unmentionably
ABEILMNNOSTUU	Blue Mountains
ABEILNNORSTVY	inobservantly
ABEILNOORSSSU	laboriousness
ABEILNOPPRSTU	insupportable
ABEILNSSTTUVY	substantively
ABEIMNNOSSSUW	businesswoman
ABEINNORSTUVY	subventionary
ABEINOOPRRSST	reabsorptions
ABELLLLOPSSYY	polysyllables
ABELLLMNOOSSY	monosyllables
ABELMMNOORTWY	Melton Mowbray
ABELNOPPRSTUU	unsupportable
ABELNOPRRTTUY	protuberantly
ABFIIIILLLMNS	infallibilism

ABFIIIILLLNST	infallibilist
ABFIIIILLLNTY	infallibility
ABFIIIILLNORST	fibrillations
ABFIIILNNOSTU	infibulations
ABFIIIILOPRTTY	profitability
ABFIIJLNSTUUY	unjustifiably
ABGGHIIINOPRS	biographising
ABGGHIIINOPRZ	biographizing
ABGGIIINRRSTU	subirrigating
ABGGIILOOORST	agrobiologist
ABGIIIILNNTTY	intangibility
ABGIIINORRSTU	subirrigation
ABGIILLNNOSTU	antiglobulins
ABGIIMNNORRST	brainstorming
ABGILNOOPSSST	spongioblasts
ABGINOOPPRRST	bootstrapping
ABHIIIILNPSTUY	punishability
ABHIIIILNRSTTY	labyrinthitis
ABHIIINOORSTV	vasoinhibitor
ABHIINOPRSSTV	vibraphonists
ABHLLMOOTUWYZ	Lützow-Holm Bay
ABIIIIILMNTTY	inimitability
ABIIIIILLNOTV	inviolability
ABIIIILMPRTTY	impartibility
ABIIIILMPSSTY	impassibility
ABIIIILLNOSTVY	insolvability
ABIIILMNOOSST	mobilisations
ABIIILMNOOSTZ	mobilizations
ABIIILMOPRTTY	importability
ABIIILMOPRTVY	improvability
ABIIILNOOSSTT	abolitionists
ABIIILNOSSTTU	subtilisation
ABIIILNOSTTUZ	subtilization
ABIIILRSTUVVY	survivability
ABIIKLNNOTUWY	unknowability
ABIILMNNNTTUU	tintinnabulum
ABIILMNOOSSTY	symbolisation
ABIILMNOOSTYZ	symbolization
ABIILMOOSSTTU	automobilists
ABIILMORRTTUV	multivibrator
ABIIMNORSSTTU	tambourinists
ABILLMMNOOSSY	monosyllabism
ABILMMNOSSTU	somnambulists
ABILNOOPPSTUU	subpopulation
ABILNOPPRSTUY	insupportably
ACCCDEEEELNSS	decalescences
ACCCDEEEINNNS	incandescence
ACCCDEEILNOPY	encyclopaedic
ACCCDEEINNNSY	incandescency
ACCCDEHILNOSY	synecdochical
ACCCDEIMNRSTU	circumstanced
ACCCDGIILLOOO	codicological
ACCCEEEILNNSS	incalescences
ACCCEEEELNNOSV	convalescence
ACCCEEGINORSY	gynecocracies
ACCCEEHINORST	technocracies
ACCCEEHMNNOSTU	accouchements
ACCCEEIILSSST	ecclesiastics
ACCCEEILLNRTY	eccentrically
ACCCEEILMNOPS	complacencies
ACCCEEMOPRRSU	eccremocarpus
ACCCEGILMNNOO	meningococcal

ACCCEHIILMMOR	microchemical
ACCCEHIILMOPR	microcephalic
ACCCEHIINORTT	architectonic
ACCCEHIOOPRST	ptochocracies
ACCCEIMMNOOOR	macroeconomic
ACCCEIMNNOOST	concomitances
ACCCEIMNRSSTU	circumstances
ACCCELOOPRSTT	streptococcal
ACCCGHIKNOPST	spatchcocking
ACCCGHILLNOOO	conchological
ACCCHILMOSTYV	cyclothymiacs
ACCCHILOOPSTY	staphylococci
ACCCIIILMMORT	microclimatic
ACCCIILMMOORS	microcosmical
ACCCIILMOOPRS	microscopical
ACCCIIMNOOTTY	actinomycotic
ACCCILOPRSTTY	cryptoclastic
ACCDDDEEIIRST	disaccredited
ACCDDEEEHHKLU	chuckleheaded
ACCDDEEENORST	deconsecrated
ACCDDEEFLLOTU	deflocculated
ACCDDEEIINORSS	discordancies
ACCDDEIMOSSTU	disaccustomed
ACCDEEEFINORS	confederacies
ACCDEEEGLLORS	Sacred College
ACCDEEEHKORTW	weathercocked
ACCDEEENNNRST	transcendence
ACCDEEENORRRT	catercornered
ACCDEEENORRST	reconsecrated
ACCDEEEORSST	deconsecrates
ACCDEEFLLOSTU	deflocculates
ACCDEEGIINRRT	reaccrediting
ACCDEEHHRSSSU	archduchesses
ACCDEEHILLOPR	Delphic oracle
ACCDEEIILNOST	occidentalise
ACCDEEIILNOTZ	occidentalize
ACCDEEIINPRSS	discrepancies
ACCDEEILNOPSY	encyclopedias
ACCDEEILNPTTU	centuplicated
ACCDEENNNRSTY	transcendency
ACCDEENNORSTU	unconsecrated
ACCDEENOPRRTT	precontracted
ACCDEFHIRRRTU	Crutched Friar
ACCDEFLLNOSTU	deflocculants
ACCDEGIINORTT	decorticating
ACCDEGILNOORT	Angelic Doctor
ACCDEGILNOOTY	accidentology
ACCDEHHILOPRY	hydrocephalic
ACCDEHHNNRRSUW	churchwardens
ACCDEHIMOOSST	homoscedastic
ACCDEIIKLOOPS	kaleidoscopic
ACCDEIILNNOOT	codeclination
ACCDEIINOORTT	decorication
ACCDEIINORTTV	contradictive
ACCDEILLMOPTY	complicatedly
ACCDEILMNOPTU	uncomplicated
ACCDEILOPSSSU	pseudoclassic
ACCDEILOPSSTY	cyclopaedists
ACCDEIMNNOORT	nondemocratic
ACCDEIMNRRTTUU	circumnutated
ACCDEINORRSTT	contradicters
ACCDEIOORRSTT	decorticators

ACCDFIIILNOTU	dulcification
ACCDFIIINOOST	codifications
ACCDGIINNORTT	contradicting
ACCDHHINOOPRV	hypochondriac
ACCDHHIOORRTY	hydrothoracic
ACCDHIILORSTV	clavichordist
ACCDHILLOOPYV	hypocycloidal
ACCDHILOOPRSV	hydroscopical
ACCDHIMNOPSYV	psychodynamic
ACCDIIILNSSTY	syndicalistic
ACCDIIINORSTY	idiosyncratic
ACCDIILLLNRYV	cylindrically
ACCDIIMMNNOOU	incommunicado
ACCDIINNOORTT	contradiction
ACCDIINOORSST	accordionists
ACCDINOORRSTT	contradictors
ACCDINOORRTTY	contradictory
ACCEEEELMORRT	accelerometer
ACCEEEFINOPPR	Prince of Peace
ACCEEEGINNNRSV	ingravescence
ACCEEEHILLNPT	telencephalic
ACCEEEHILLNRS	chancelleries
ACCEEEHILMNPS	mesencephalic
ACCEEEHILMNPT	metencephalic
ACCEEEILLORST	ecclesiolater
ACCEEEILNRSTX	excrescential
ACCEEENNORRTT	reconcentrate
ACCEEENORRSST	reconsecrates
ACCEEFIIIPSTV	specificative
ACCEEGHIKLORT	Greek Catholic
ACCEEGHNNORTU	counterchange
ACCEEGHNORTU	countercharge
ACCEEGILLNNPR	precancelling
ACCEEGILLNOTY	ectogenically
ACCEEGINNNORSS	recognisances
ACCEEGINNNORSZ	recognizances
ACCEEHHILORST	chalicotheres
ACCEEHHLOORST	schoolteacher
ACCEEHHNNRRSTU	Eastern Church
ACCEEHIILMMOS	semiochemical
ACCEEHILLNORS	chancellories
ACCEEHILLNOTY	acetylcholine
ACCEEHILLOPPT	leptocephalic
ACCEEHILMOPRT	cephalometric
	petrochemical
ACCEEHILMOPSS	mesocephalics
ACCEEHILNNSST	technicalness
ACCEEHIMMNSTU	catechumenism
ACCEEHIRRSTTU	architectures
ACCEEHLNNOOXY	cyclohexanone
ACCEEHMMNNORST	encroachments
ACCEEHORRSTTY	oystercatcher
ACCEEIILLNRTV	interclavicle
ACCEEIILMMNSU	ecumenicalism
ACCEEIILMMORS	commercialise
ACCEEIILMMORZ	commercialize
ACCEEIIMORRST	meritocracies
ACCEEIIOPRRTV	reciprocative
ACCEEILLMNOUV	oecumenically
ACCEEILLORSTV	ecclesiolatry
ACCEEILMNOORT	econometrical
ACCEEILNOPSTU	conceptualise

ACCEEILNOPTUZ	conceptualize
ACCEEILNPSTTU	centuplicates
ACCEEILNQSTUY	acquiescently
ACCEEILORSTTT	electrostatic
ACCEEIMMNOTUX	excommunicate
ACCEEIMNOSTTY	actinomycetes
ACCEEINNORSSV	conservancies
ACCEEINNORTTV	concentrative
ACCEEINOPRTTV	contraceptive
ACCEEINORSSSS	accessoriness
ACCEEINORTTUV	counteractive
ACCEEKLMRRSSU	musselcracker
ACCEELLMMOORU	macromolecule
ACCEELLOORSTT	collectorates
ACCEELMNOPSTU	accouplements
ACCEELNNOSSTV	convalescents
ACCEEMNORRSTT	concertmaster
ACCEEMNORSTTU	accouterments
	accoutrements
ACCEENNNORSTU	countenancers
ACCEENNOORTTY	octocentenary
ACCEEOORRSSTU	stercoraceous
ACCEFFIIINOSU	inefficacious
ACCEFFIIINPRS	infraspecific
ACCEFFIILOSUY	efficaciously
ACCEFGIIINNSS	significances
ACCEFGIIINRTT	certificating
ACCEFGIKRRRSU	Carrickfergus
ACCEFIIINOPST	specification
ACCEFIIINORTT	certification
	rectification
ACCEFIIINPRST	intraspecific
ACCEFIIORRTTY	certificatory
ACCEFINNOORTY	confectionary
ACCEGGILLNOOY	gynecological
ACCEGHHIOOPRR	choreographic
ACCEGHIILOPRX	lexicographic
ACCEGHILLNOOT	technological
ACCEGHILMOPYV	hypoglycaemic
ACCEGHILNNORY	encroachingly
ACCEGHIOPRRVY	cervicography
ACCEGIILLLOOX	lexicological
ACCEGIILNRRTU	recirculating
ACCEGIINNNORT	concertinaing
ACCEGIINOPRRT	reciprocating
ACCEGIINORSSS	accessorising
ACCEGIINORSSZ	accessorizing
ACCEGILLLOOOY	oecologically
ACCEGILLNOOSY	synecological
ACCEGIMNORSTU	reaccustoming
ACCEGINNNNOTU	countenancing
ACCEGINNNORTT	concentrating
ACCEGINNORTTU	counteracting
ACCEGINOORRTT	gerontocratic
ACCEHHIILMOST	histochemical
ACCEHHIINSSTT	chainstitches
ACCEHHILMOOPT	photochemical
ACCEHHILOOPRT	orthocephalic
ACCEHHILOSSSZ	eschscholzias
ACCEHHILOSSTZ	eschscholtzia
ACCEHHIMORSTT	chrestomathic
ACCEHIILLNSST	callisthenics

ACCEHIILNOPRS	necrophiliacs
ACCEHIILPRRTY	hypercritical
ACCEHIIMRSSTT	chrematistics
ACCEHIIOPRSSY	physiocracies
ACCEHILLNOPRT	phallocentric
ACCEHILMOPRSS	accomplishers
ACCEHILNOOOST	echolocations
ACCEHILNOPRTY	pyrotechnical
ACCEHIMMNOORT	chromonematic
ACCEHIMNORSST	chromaticness
ACCEHINNNOPST	pantechnicons
ACCEHIOOPSSTT	tachistoscope
ACCEHOOOPRSST	thoracoscopes
ACCEIIILMNORT	cliometrician
ACCEIIINORSTT	creationistic
ACCEIIKLNOSTW	anticlockwise
ACCEIIILLMNORT	clinometrical
ACCEIIILMMMORS	commercialism
ACCEIIILMMORRT	micrometrical
ACCEIIILMMORST	commercialist
	microclimates
ACCEIIILMMORTY	commerciality
ACCEIIILMNOSSS	neoclassicism
ACCEIIILMNORSTV	viscometrical
ACCEIIILNOSSST	neoclassicist
ACCEIIILOPRRTY	reciprocality
ACCEIIILPRRSTU	supercritical
ACCEIIILRRRSSU	circularisers
ACCEIIILRRRSUZ	circularizers
ACCEIIMMNOTUV	communicative
ACCEIINNNOSST	inconstancies
ACCEIINOOPRRT	reciprocation
ACCEIINORSTUX	excruciations
ACCEIIOPPRSSU	perspicacious
ACCEILLLNNOUY	nucleonically
ACCEILLMNOPSU	nucleoplasmic
ACCEILMMNNNOOR	noncommercial
ACCEILMNNNOOP	noncompliance
ACCEILMNOPSTU	conceptualism
ACCEILMNORSTU	counterclaims
ACCEILNNOSSTU	consultancies
ACCEILNOPSTTU	conceptualist
ACCEILNORTTVY	contractively
ACCEIMNRSTTUU	circumnutates
ACCEINNNNOOSS	inconsonances
ACCEINNNOORTT	concentration
ACCEINNOOPRTT	contraception
ACCEINNOORRTY	concretionary
ACCEINNOORSST	consecrations
ACCEINNOORSSY	concessionary
ACCEINNOORTTU	counteraction
ACCEINOOPPRTU	preoccupation
ACCEINOOPRSTU	reoccupations
ACCEIOOPRRRST	reciprocators
ACCEIOOPRRRTY	reciprocatory
ACCEJLLNORTUY	conjecturally
ACCEKMMORRTUW	Crummock Water
ACCENNOORRSTT	concentrators
ACCENOPRRSSTU	counterscarps
ACCFGIIMNOPTY	compactifying
ACCFHIIORRSTV	Vicar of Christ
ACCFIIIINOSTT	citifications

ACCFIIINOORST	scorification
ACCFIIINOSTTY	cityfications
ACCFIILNOOPRX	ciprofloxacin
ACCFIINNOOSST	confiscations
ACCFLMORSTUUU	fractocumulus
ACCGHHINOOPRR	chronographic
ACCGHHINORSST	crosshatching
ACCGHIIILNOST	catholicising
ACCGHIIILNOTZ	catholicizing
ACCGHIILLOORT	trichological
ACCGHIILMNOPS	accomplishing
ACCGHILLNOOOR	chronological
ACCGHILLOOPSY	psychological
ACCGHIOPPRRTY	cryptographic
ACCGIIILNRRSU	circularising
ACCGIIILNRRUZ	circularizing
ACCGIILLMOOSU	musicological
ACCGIILLOOOTX	toxicological
ACCGIILMORRSU	microsurgical
ACCGIIMMNNOTU	communicating
ACCGILLLOOTYY	cytologically
ACCGILLOOOPRT	proctological
ACCGILNOOPRSY	laryngoscopic
ACCHHHIMNPRSU	churchmanship
ACCHHIMMOOORT	homochromatic
ACCHIIILPSSTY	physicalistic
ACCHIILMOPRSY	microphysical
ACCHIILMOSSST	scholasticism
ACCHIIMNOOPRT	actinomorphic
ACCHIIMORRSSU	chiaroscurism
ACCHIINOPSTTY	antipsychotic
ACCHIIORRSSTU	chiaroscurist
ACCHILLOOPRST	chloroplastic
ACCHILLOPSTYY	psychotically
ACCHILMMNOOOR	monochromical
ACCHILMOOPRTY	polychromatic
ACCHILOPPRSTY	prophylactics
ACCHIMMNOOORT	monochromatic
ACCHIMOOPSSTY	psychosomatic
ACCHIOOPRRRST	chiropractors
ACCHIOOPRSSUZ	schizocarpous
ACCHLNOOOPSUV	cacophonously
ACCIIILNNOOST	conciliations
ACCIIIMMNOOST	iconomaticism
ACCIILLNNQUUY	quincuncially
ACCIILLPRSTUU	piscicultural
ACCIILMMNOSTU	communalistic
ACCIILMNOOPST	complications
ACCIILNORTTTY	contractility
ACCIIMMNNOOTU	communication
ACCIIMNOOSSTY	actinomycosis
ACCIINNOOOSST	consociations
ACCIINOORRSTY	Socratic irony
ACCIJLNNNOOTU	conjunctional
ACCILMNNOOTTY	concomitantly
ACCIMMNOORSTU	communicators
ACCIMMNOORTUY	communicatory
ACCIMNOOOTTXY	cytotaxonomic
ACCIMNOOPRSTU	pococurantism
ACCINPRSTTUUU	acupuncturist
ACDDDEEEENRTUU	undereducated
ACDDDEEHNOORS	dodecahedrons

ACDDEEEEFHNRSU	schadenfreude
ACDDEEEEHHNNOR	hendecahedron
ACDDEEEEHINRUV	underachieved
ACDDEEEEHKKLNU	knuckleheaded
ACDDEEEEILNRST	decentralised
ACDDEEEEILNRSU	denuclearised
ACDDEEEEILNRTZ	decentralized
ACDDEEEEILNRUZ	denuclearized
ACDDEEEEOORRTV	overdecorated
ACDDEEEFFILSTY	disaffectedly
ACDDEEEHLLNORS	candleholders
ACDDEEEHLLORTY	coldheartedly
ACDDEEEIINORST	rededications
ACDDEEEIMNOOTY	adenoidectomy
ACDDEEEMNNORTU	countermanded
ACDDEEENORRTTU	countertraded
ACDDEEFHIINRSS	disfranchised
ACDDEEGHILNNRR	grandchildren
ACDDEEGILLNOOR	dendrological
ACDDEEGINORSUU	undiscouraged
ACDDEEHILMOSUY	dichlamydeous
ACDDEEHIMNOOPS	dodecaphonism
ACDDEEHINOOPST	dodecaphonist
ACDDEEIIIMNRST	discriminated
ACDDEEIILLNRTY	dendritically
ACDDEEIILNORSU	radionuclides
ACDDEEIINNORTT	indoctrinated
ACDDEEIINOSSTU	undissociated
ACDDEEINNOORTU	uncoordinated
ACDDHIMNORSYY	hydrodynamics
ACDEEEEEHLPSST	steeplechased
ACDEEEEFINORTV	confederative
ACDEEEEHINNRSS	Niedersachsen
ACDEEEEHINRRUV	underachiever
ACDEEEEHINRSUV	underachieves
ACDEEEEILNORST	decelerations
ACDEEEEILNRSST	decentralises
ACDEEEEILNRSSU	denuclearises
ACDEEEEILNRSTZ	decentralizes
ACDEEEEILNRSUZ	denuclearizes
ACDEEEEILNSSST	delicatessens
ACDEEEEILPRTVY	deprecatively
ACDEEEEINNRSTV	inadvertences
ACDEEEEIOSSTTV	videocassette
ACDEEEELLOPRTT	electroplated
ACDEEEELNOPRST	preadolescent
ACDEEEELNPRSUV	supercalender
ACDEEEELOPRSST	Apostles' Creed
ACDEEEENNOPPRR	preponderance
ACDEEEEOORRSTV	overdecorates
ACDEEEFFGINNORT	confederating
ACDEEEFHHIKNRS	handkerchiefs
ACDEEEFHNORRSW	henceforwards
ACDEEEFHNORRTW	thenceforward
ACDEEEFIINRRSY	ferricyanides
ACDEEEFINNOORT	confederation
ACDEEEFINORRSY	ferrocyanides
ACDEEEFNRRSSUU	undersurfaces
ACDEEEGHHOOPRR	choreographed
ACDEEEGHIMNNNU	machinegunned
ACDEEEGIIMORST	tragicomedies
ACDEEEGIINPRTT	decrepitating

ACDEEGILNPRTY	deprecatingly
ACDEEGIMMNNOR	commandeering
ACDEEGINORTUV	overeducating
ACDEEGKLNORSW	acknowledgers
ACDEEGLMNOORT	conglomerated
ACDEEGNNOSSTT	decongestants
ACDEEHHIMORST	hemichordates
ACDEEHILNNOPS	diencephalons
ACDEEHILORRTT	tetrachloride
ACDEEHIMNNRSS	merchandisers
ACDEEHIMOPRRT	Arc de Triomphe
ACDEEHINNNRSST	disenchanters
ACDEEHLORSTTY	heterodactyls
ACDEEIIILMNRS	decriminalise
ACDEEIIILMNRZ	decriminalize
ACDEEIIILMHSTV	medievalistic
ACDEEIIIMPRTV	impredicative
ACDEEIILLLNSS	Ellice Islands
ACDEEIILMORTU	eudiometrical
ACDEEIILMRRSU	mercurialised
ACDEEIILMRRUZ	mercurialized
ACDEEIILNNNQU	quindecennial
ACDEEIILNNOSST	identicalness
ACDEEIILNOSST	sectionalised
ACDEEIILNOSTZ	sectionalized
ACDEEIILNPSSU	unspecialised
ACDEEIILNPSUZ	unspecialized
ACDEEIILORSTV	valedictories
ACDEEIILPRTUV	reduplicative
ACDEEIILPRTVY	predicatively
ACDEEIIMNNRTY	indeterminacy
ACDEEIIMNOPRT	premedication
ACDEEIIMNOSTU	eudaemonistic
ACDEEIIMOSTTV	domesticative
ACDEEIINNORST	containerised
	inconsiderate
ACDEEIINNORTZ	containerized
ACDEEIINNOSST	Ascensiontide
ACDEEIINOPRTT	decrepitation
ACDEEIKLOOPSS	kaleidoscopes
ACDEEILLNNSTY	clandestinely
ACDEEILLNTTUY	denticulately
ACDEEILMNPSST	displacements
ACDEEILNNPTUV	Vincent de Paul
ACDEEILNOORST	reconsolidate
ACDEEILNORSTY	considerately
ACDEEILNORTUV	countervailed
ACDEEILNPPRRU	perpendicular
ACDEEILNPQSTU	quindecaplets
ACDEEILNRSSTT	decentralists
ACDEEILOPRRTY	deprecatorily
ACDEEILPSTTUX	sextuplicated
ACDEEIMNORSTU	documentaries
ACDEEIMOPRSST	spermatocides
ACDEEINNORSSS	secondariness
ACDEEINOORRST	redecorations
ACDEEIOPPRSTU	propaedeutics
ACDEEJORSSSTU	coadjutresses
ACDEELMNNRSSU	underclassmen
ACDEELNPRSSTU	Pure Land sects
ACDEEMNNOPSTU	uncompensated
ACDEENNNRSSTT	transcendents
ACDEENNOPPRRY	preponderancy
ACDEENORRSSTTU	countertrades
ACDEFFIILRTVY	diffractively
ACDEFGIILNSSY	declassifying
ACDEFGILLRSUY	disgracefully
ACDEFHIINRSSS	disfranchises
ACDEFIIILMSSS	misclassified
ACDEFIIILNOST	fictionalised
ACDEFIIILNOTZ	fictionalized
ACDEFIIIMMOSS	fideicommissa
ACDEFIIILNNOSS	nonclassified
ACDEFIINNSSTT	disinfectants
ACDEFILMNNOTU	malfunctioned
ACDEFILRSTTUX	fluidextracts
ACDEFMNOORSTW	woodcraftsmen
ACDEGGHINNRRU	undercharging
ACDEGGIKLNNOW	acknowledging
ACDEGHHOOPRTU	thoroughpaced
ACDEGHIIMNNRS	merchandising
ACDEGHIINNNST	disenchanting
ACDEGHIIOPRSS	discographies
ACDEGHIMNORTY	hydromagnetic
ACDEGHIOPRRSS	discographers
ACDEGIILLLOOY	ideologically
ACDEGIILLMRUY	demiurgically
ACDEGIILNPRTU	reduplicating
ACDEGIILPQRSU	quadriplegics
ACDEGIIMNORST	democratising
ACDEGIIMNORTZ	democratizing
ACDEGIIMNOSTT	domesticating
ACDEGIIMNOSTY	geodynamicist
ACDEGIINQRSTU	quadrisecting
ACDEGILLMNOOO	demonological
ACDEGILLNOOOT	deontological
ACDEGILLOOSTY	dactylologies
ACDEGILNNOTTU	conglutinated
ACDEHHIOPRRTY	hydrotherapic
ACDEHHLOPRSUY	hydrocephalus
ACDEHHOOOPSTT	photocathodes
ACDEHIIINRSST	christianised
ACDEHIIINRSTZ	christianized
ACDEHIILNOPRR	perichondrial
ACDEHIIMORSST	radiochemists
ACDEHIIOPSSTT	sophisticated
ACDEHIKLNRSST	stickhandlers
ACDEHILMNOPTY	endolymphatic
ACDEHILMORRTY	hydrometrical
ACDEHIMMNOPRS	commandership
ACDEHIMMNORTY	thermodynamic
ACDEHIMOPRTTY	dermatophytic
ACDEHLMOOPRSY	chlamydospore
ACDEHLOOOPPSU	cephalopodous
ACDEHOOOPRRTT	protochordate
ACDEIIILMNPSU	municipalised
ACDEIIILMNPUZ	municipalized
ACDEIIILNOSST	idioticalness
ACDEIIIMMNNOST	nicotinamides
ACDEIIIMNORST	dosimetrician
ACDEIIIMNRSST	discriminates
ACDEIIINOPRST	antiperiodics
ACDEIIINRSTTU	antidiuretics
ACDEIIJLLPRUY	prejudicially

ACDEIILLORRTY	directorially
ACDEIILNNOTTU	denticulation
ACDEIILNOOSTV	consolidative
ACDEIILNOPRTU	reduplication
ACDEIILRSTTVY	distractively
ACDEIIMNNOSTW	ancient wisdom
ACDEIIMNOOSTT	domestication
ACDEIINNNOSTU	denunciations
ACDEIINNOORST	consideration
ACDEIINNORSTT	indoctrinates
ACDEIINOQRSTU	quadrisection
ACDEIINORRSTY	discretionary
ACDEIINOSSTTU	educationists
ACDEIKNNNORRT	Dark Continent
ACDEILLOPSSTU	leucoplastids
ACDEILLPPSTYY	dyspeptically
ACDEILMNORTUY	documentarily
ACDEILNNOPTUU	pedunculation
ACDEILNNORSTY	constrainedly
ACDEILNNOTTUV	noncultivated
ACDEILNOOORST	decolorations
ACDEILOPRSSTY	perissodactyl
ACDEIMMNNOOST	commendations
ACDEIMMOOSTTY	mastoidectomy
ACDEIMNNNOOST	condemnations
ACDEIMNNOOTTU	documentation
ACDEIMNNNORRST	androcentrism
ACDEIMNPSTTUU	mispunctuated
ACDEIMOORSSTT	domesticators
ACDEINNNOOSST	condensations
ACDEINNNORSTU	unconstrained
ACDEINNORSTTU	detruncations
ACDEINOPRSTTV	privatdocents
ACDEINOPRSTTY	dictyopterans
ACDELNOOOSTUY	acotyledonous
ACDEMMNNOSTUU	unconsummated
ACDEOOPPRSSUU	pseudocarpous
ACDEORSSTTTUU	autodestructs
ACDFIIIINNOST	nidifications
ACDFIIIMNOOST	modifications
ACDFIILNNOSTU	difunctionals
ACDFILNNOSTUY	dysfunctional
ACDGHINOOOPRT	gonadotrophic
ACDGIIIILMNOT	domiciliating
ACDGIILNNOOST	consolidating
ACDGIILNRSTTY	distractingly
ACDGIILOORSST	cardiologists
ACDGIINNOSTTU	outdistancing
ACDGILLLOOOXY	doxologically
ACDGILLNOOOOT	odontological
ACDGILLOORTTY	troglodytical
ACDGILMOSTYYZ	zygodactylism
ACDGLOOSTUYYZ	zygodactylous
ACDHIILMNOORT	mitochondrial
ACDHIINOPSSTU	custodianship
ACDHIIOPRSSTT	dictatorships
ACDHILMNOOORS	chondriosomal
ACDHILOORSSUU	dolichosaurus
ACDHIMNOOPSTY	photodynamics
ACDHINOOPQRSU	quadrophonics
ACDHMNOOORSTU	chondromatous
ACDIIILNNOPTU	induplication

ACDIIILNNNPSST	disciplinants
ACDIIIMNNRSST	discriminants
ACDIIIMNORRST	discriminator doctrinairism
ACDIIINOOSSST	dissociations
ACDIIIOOOPRST	radioisotopic
ACDIILLMNPSTU	multiplicands
ACDIILLNNOOTY	conditionally
ACDIILMNNOOPT	nondiplomatic
ACDIILNNNOOTU	unconditional
ACDIILNNOOOST	consolidation
ACDIILNOOORST	discoloration
ACDIILNOOQSTU	coloquintidas
ACDIILPQRTUUY	quadruplicity
ACDIINNOORRTT	indoctrinator
ACDILNOOORSST	consolidators
ACDINOOQRSSTU	conquistadors
ACDLLOOPSTUYY	polydactylous
ACDLMNOOOSTUY	condylomatous monodactylous
ACEEEEHLPRSST	steeplechaser
ACEEEEHLPSSST	steeplechases
ACEEEELNORSST	coelenterates
ACEEEFFGINOPR	peace offering
ACEEEFFINSSTV	affectiveness
ACEEEFFLNSSTU	effectualness
ACEEEFILNORRT	coreferential
ACEEEFMORRRTT	refractometer
ACEEEFNNRRSST	transferences
ACEEEGGORSSTU	secretagogues
ACEEEGHIMNOTT	hematogenetic
ACEEEGHIMORTT	heterogametic
ACEEEGHINPRSS	cheeseparings
ACEEEGILLLNTY	telegenically
ACEEEGILLNRTY	energetically
ACEEEGILLOPRT	precollegiate
ACEEEGLMNORTT	electromagnet
ACEEEGLNRSSSS	gracelessness
ACEEEGMNNORTU	encouragement
ACEEEHIKLLMNO	chameleonlike
ACEEEHILMNRTU	hermeneutical
ACEEEHIMNQSTU	cinematheques
ACEEEHIORRSVV	overachievers
ACEEEHLLNNOPT	telencephalon
ACEEEHLMNNOPS	mesencephalon
ACEEEHLMNNOPT	metencephalon
ACEEEHLMOPRST	cephalometers
ACEEEHLMPSSSY	Champs-Elysées
ACEEEHMMORTTY	hemacytometer
ACEEEHNNRSSST	enchantresses
ACEEEHPRRSSTU	superteachers
ACEEEIILNNSTU	lieutenancies
ACEEEIILNRRSV	irrelevancies
ACEEEIINSSTTV	necessitative
ACEEEILLMPRST	capellmeister
ACEEEILMNNRTT	interlacement
ACEEEILNNNRTT	tercentennial
ACEEEIMNNOSST	amniocenteses
ACEEEIMNNRRSS	mercenariness
ACEEEINNOPRVX	Aix-en-Provence
ACEEEINOSSTVV	evocativeness
ACEEEIRSSSTTV	state services

779

ACEEEELLNORTTV	electrovalent
ACEEEELLOPRRTT	electroplater
ACEEEELLOPRSTT	electroplates
ACEEEMNNNRSTT	entrancements
ACEEEOPPRRSTT	preceptorates
ACEEFFHINNPRS	affenpinscher
ACEEFFILLNTUY	ineffectually
ACEEFGHLNNSSU	changefulness
ACEEFGIIMNRRT	ferrimagnetic
ACEEFGIMNORRT	ferromagnetic
ACEEFHHIRSTTT	featherstitch
ACEEFHIMNNRST	franchisement
ACEEFHINNRRSS	enfranchisers
ACEEFHMNOSTUV	vouchsafement
ACEEFIILNQSTU	liquefacients
ACEEFILNOPRSW	Prince of Wales
ACEEFINOSSSTU	facetiousness
ACEEFINPSSTTU	stupefacients
ACEEFLLLNRSTY	crestfallenly
ACEEFMNORSTUU	frumentaceous
ACEEFMORRRTTY	refractometry
ACEEGGHILLNNR	rechallenging
ACEEGGINNOORT	organogenetic
ACEEGHHIOPRRS	choregraphies
ACEEGHHIOPRRT	heterographic
ACEEGHHLLNORS	Öhlenschläger
ACEEGHHOOPRRR	choreographer
ACEEGHHOPRRRS	choregraphers
ACEEGHIINORVV	overachieving
ACEEGHIINRSTT	catheterising
ACEEGHIINRTTZ	catheterizing
ACEEGHILMPRVY	hyperglycemia
ACEEGHILNOPRS	selenographic
ACEEGHILNORSU	clearinghouse
ACEEGHILNSTTW	angletwitches
ACEEGHILOPRRX	lexicographer
ACEEGHINNRSSS	searchingness
ACEEGHIOPRRST	stereographic
ACEEGHLOPRRST	electrographs
ACEEGHLOPRRTY	electrography
ACEEGHMNNORSY	moneychangers
ACEEGHNOPRRSS	scenographers
ACEEGHOOOPPSS	esophagoscope
ACEEGHPRRRSSU	superchargers
ACEEGIILLMOOS	semeiological
ACEEGIILNNRTV	cantilevering
ACEEGIILSTTUV	gesticulative
ACEEGIIMNNOST	miscegenation
ACEEGIIMNOPTZ	piezomagnetic
ACEEGIIMNORST	geometricians
ACEEGIIMNOSTV	vaginectomies
ACEEGIINNNRST	intransigence
ACEEGIINNORTU	auctioneering
ACEEGIINNSSTT	necessitating
ACEEGILLLNOOS	selenological
ACEEGILLLOOPS	speleological
ACEEGILLMORTY	geometrically
ACEEGILLNNOOT	noncollegiate
ACEEGILMNNOQU	magniloquence
ACEEGILNNNOSS	congenialness
ACEEGILNNNORRT	Central Region
ACEEGIMMNORTT	magnetometric
ACEEGIMORSSTT	gastrectomies
ACEEGINNNSSSU	unceasingness
ACEEGINOPRTTX	expectorating
ACEEGINORRSTT	gastroenteric
ACEEGJNNOSSTU	conjugateness
ACEEGLMNOORST	conglomerates
ACEEHHIILMPRS	hemispherical
ACEEHHILLORTT	heterothallic
ACEEHHIMNOPRS	archiphonemes
ACEEHHOPRSSTU	chapterhouses
ACEEHHOPRSTTY	tracheophytes
ACEEHIILLMORT	heliometrical
ACEEHIILNPSST	Sistine Chapel
ACEEHIIMOOPTT	hematopoietic
ACEEHIIMPSSTY	metaphysicise
ACEEHIIMPSTYZ	metaphysicize
ACEEHIINORSTT	theoreticians
ACEEHIIQRRSSU	squirearchies
ACEEHIJKPPRRT	Jack the Ripper
ACEEHIKNRSSST	heartsickness
ACEEHILLNPRTY	phrenetically
ACEEHILLORTTY	theoretically
ACEEHILMPRRTY	hypermetrical
ACEEHILNPRSSS	sphericalness
ACEEHILOPRRST	terpsichoreal
ACEEHILOPRSTT	heteroplastic
ACEEHILOPRTTY	heterotypical
ACEEHIMNORSSS	marchionesses
ACEEHIMNSSSTT	chastisements
ACEEHIMOORSTT	tracheotomies
ACEEHIMORRSTT	arthrectomies
ACEEHINOPRRST	terpsichorean
ACEEHINORSSTT	thoracentesis
ACEEHIPRRSSTY	secretaryship
ACEEHIPRSSTTY	cryptesthesia
ACEEHLLMOOORT	alcoholometer
ACEEHLLOPPSTU	leptocephalus
ACEEHLMNORRTU	thermonuclear
ACEEHLMNSSSST	matchlessness
ACEEHLORRSTUY	treacherously
ACEEHMNOPPRRT	rapprochement
ACEEHNNOORSTU	Southern Ocean
ACEEHOORSTTTU	heterotactous
ACEEHOPPRRRSS	sharecroppers
ACEEIIIKKLLNR	Killiecrankie
ACEEIIILPRSTU	peculiarities
ACEEIIILRSTTV	verticalities
ACEEIIIMNRRTV	recriminative
ACEEIIIPPRRTTV	precipitative
ACEEIILLLNPTY	penicillately
ACEEIILLLNRTY	rectilineally
ACEEIILLLPPTY	epileptically
ACEEIILLMNRTT	intermetallic
ACEEIILLMPSTY	epistemically
ACEEIILLNRRTY	rectilinearly
ACEEIILMMNORS	ceremonialism
ACEEIILMMNOST	laminectomies
ACEEIILMNOPRS	semiporcelain
ACEEIILMNORST	ceremonialist
ACEEIILMNPRSS	empiricalness
ACEEIILMRRSSU	mercurialises
ACEEIILMRRSUZ	mercurializes

ACEEIILNNNRTT	tricentennial
ACEEIILNNTUVY	enunciatively
ACEEIILNORSTT	intersocietal
ACEEIILNOSSST	sectionalises
ACEEIILNOSSTZ	sectionalizes
ACEEIILORSTVY	viceroyalties
ACEEIILPPRTTY	precipitately
ACEEIIMMORSTV	commiserative
ACEEIIMNNOSST	amniocentesis
ACEEIIMNORRST	mercerisation
ACEEIIMNORRTZ	mercerization
ACEEIIMNPRSSU	epicureanisms
ACEEIIMOORSTV	ovariectomies
ACEEIINNORSST	containerises
ACEEIINNORSTZ	containerizes
ACEEIINNOSSTT	necessitation
ACEEIINNRSSTT	intricateness
ACEEIINNRSTTU	uncertainties
ACEEIINORRSTT	contrarieties
ACEEIINORSSTV	eviscerations
ACEEIINORSTTX	exercitations
ACEEIIRSSTTUV	resuscitative
ACEEIJLNRRTTU	interjectural
ACEEIKLLSSTVW	Sackville-West
ACEEIKLNPSSST	skepticalness
ACEEILLLNOTUV	involucellate
ACEEILLLNPSTY	splenetically
ACEEILLLNRRTU	intercellular
ACEEILLLNSTTU	intellectuals
ACEEILLMNOSSU	miscellaneous
ACEEILLMNTTUU	multinucleate
ACEEILLMOQRUU	equimolecular
ACEEILLNNNSSU	uncleanliness
ACEEILLNNNORST	crenellations
ACEEILLNOPTXY	exceptionally
ACEEILLNOSSTY	coessentially
ACEEILLNPRTTY	centripetally
ACEEILLORRTVY	correlatively
ACEEILLPSTUVY	speculatively
ACEEILLRRSSTY	recrystallise
ACEEILLRRSTYZ	recrystallize
ACEEILMNNSSSU	masculineness
ACEEILMNOPTTV	contemplative
ACEEILMNRRSSU	mercurialness
ACEEILNNOPRTV	convertiplane
ACEEILNNOPTUX	unexceptional
ACEEILNNOQSTU	consequential
ACEEILNNRSSUY	unnecessarily
ACEEILNOQSSUV	equivocalness
ACEEILNORSTTU	interosculate
ACEEILNOSTTUX	contextualise
ACEEILNOTTUXZ	contextualize
ACEEILNRSSTUV	lucrativeness
ACEEILNRTTUUV	enculturative
ACEEILOOPRTVY	cooperatively
ACEEILOPRSTTY	stereotypical
ACEEILORRTTVY	retroactively
ACEEILPPSSTTU	septuplicates
ACEEILPSSTTUX	sextuplicates
ACEEIMMMOORTV	commemorative
ACEEIMMNORRTY	Amrit Ceremony
ACEEIMNNOORRS	oneiromancers

ACEEINNNORSST	nonresistance
ACEEINNNOSTTY	consentaneity
ACEEINNNQRTUY	quincentenary
ACEEINNNRSSTU	uncertainness
ACEEINNNSSSST	incessantness
ACEEINNOORSVZ	conversazione
ACEEINNOSSSTU	tenaciousness
ACEEINOOPRRRT	reincorporate
ACEEINOOPRSTU	proteinaceous
ACEEINOOPRTTX	expectoration
ACEEINOOPRTUV	uncooperative
ACEEINOORRSTV	conservatoire
	overreactions
ACEEINOPPPRST	apperceptions
ACEEINOPRRSTU	recuperations
ACEEINOPRSSTT	inspectorates
ACEEINORSSSUV	veraciousness
ACEEINORSSTVV	conservatives
ACEEKLNRSSSST	tracklessness
ACEELLMNORSSW	lowerclassmen
ACEELLNOOPRSU	porcellaneous
ACEELLNSSSSSS	classlessness
ACEELLOORRRST	rollercoaster
ACEELMMNOPRTY	complementary
ACEELMNNOOPRTV	convertoplane
ACEELNOOPRRSS	corporealness
ACEEMMNNOPSST	encompassment
ACEEMMNNNOSTU	announcements
ACEEMMNNORRSST	remonstrances
ACEEMOPRSSTTY	spermatocytes
ACEEENNNOOSSTU	consentaneous
ACEEOOPRRSTTT	protectorates
ACEEOOPRRSTTX	expectorators
ACEEORRRSTTUU	aerostructure
ACEFFHLSSTTUZ	schutzstaffel
ACEFGHIINNNRS	enfranchising
ACEFGHIINNOTT	fianchettoing
ACEFGIIIINSTV	significative
ACEFGIILMNNTY	magnificently
ACEFGIILNRSSY	reclassifying
ACEFGIINORTUV	configurative
ACEFGILLNRTUY	centrifugally
ACEFGINOSSSUU	fugaciousness
ACEFHHIIINPST	chieftainship
ACEFHLLOPRRUY	reproachfully
ACEFHNORSSTTU	countershafts
ACEFIIIJLLNOT	jellification
ACEFIIIJSTTUV	justificative
ACEFIIILMSSSS	misclassifies
ACEFIIILNOSST	fictionalises
ACEFIIILNOSTT	felicitations
ACEFIIILNOSTZ	fictionalizes
ACEFIIINNORTU	reunification
ACEFIIINOPRTT	petrification
ACEFIIINORSTV	verifications
	versification
ACEFIIINOSTTT	testification
ACEFIILLPRSUY	superficially
ACEFIILMMNORT	microfilament
ACEFIILNOQSTU	liquefactions
ACEFIILNORSTY	forensicality
ACEFIINNOOTTU	autoinfection

ACEFIINNORSTU	functionaries
ACEFIINOORSTV	vociferations
ACEFILNNOOSSS	confessionals
ACEFINNOORSSY	confessionary
ACEFINNORRTTY	confraternity
ACEFINORSSSTU	fractiousness
ACEGGHIINNNRT	interchanging
ACEGGHINPRRSU	supercharging
ACEGGHIOOOPRZ	zoogeographic
ACEGGIILNSTTU	gesticulating
ACEGGILNNORUY	encouragingly
ACEGGILNOOSTY	gynaecologist
ACEGGINNOORST	congregations
ACEGGLLRSSSTU	class struggle
ACEGHHIINOPRS	ichnographies
ACEGHHIMOPRRT	thermographic
ACEGHHINOPTTY	hypothecating
ACEGHHIOOPRRS	chorographies
ACEGHHIOPRRRS	chirographers
ACEGHHNOOPRRR	chronographer
ACEGHHNORRSST	shortchangers
ACEGHHOOPRRRS	chorographers
ACEGHIIMOPRSS	seismographic
ACEGHIINOOPRS	iconographies
ACEGHILLLOOTY	ethologically
	theologically
ACEGHILLNNOSU	hallucinogens
ACEGHILLNOOPR	phrenological
ACEGHILLOOPPS	psephological
ACEGHILOORSST	archeologists
ACEGHILOOSSTT	eschatologist
ACEGHIMNORRTU	routemarching
ACEGHIMOPRRRS	micrographers
ACEGHINNOOPRT	anthropogenic
ACEGHINOOPRRS	iconographers
ACEGHINOPPRRS	sharecropping
ACEGHINOPRRSZ	zincographers
ACEGHINORRSTT	orchestrating
ACEGHIOPRRSST	cerographists
ACEGHIORRSSTT	gastrotriches
ACEGHLOOOORYZ	archeozoology
ACEGHMOOPRRSS	cosmographers
ACEGHMOOPSTUV	mycetophagous
ACEGHNOOPPRSY	pharyngoscope
ACEGHOPPRRRTY	cryptographer
ACEGHOPPRRSST	spectrographs
ACEGHOPPRRSTY	spectrography
ACEGIIILNOOPT	geopolitician
ACEGIIIMNNRRT	recriminating
ACEGIIINORTTY	iatrogenicity
ACEGIIINPPRTT	precipitating
ACEGIILLLNOSS	illogicalness
ACEGIILLLOOTY	etiologically
ACEGIILLMOOSS	seismological
ACEGIILLNOOST	neologistical
ACEGIILLNRTUV	revictualling
ACEGIILLOSTTY	egotistically
ACEGIILMNOORT	goniometrical
ACEGIILMNRTUV	vermiculating
ACEGIILNNORTU	reinoculating
ACEGIILNNOSTU	geniculations
ACEGIILNOSTTU	gesticulation
ACEGIIMMNNORST	commiserating
ACEGIIMNNOOTT	metacognition
ACEGIINNNNRSTY	intransigency
ACEGIINNPRRST	transpiercing
ACEGIINOORSST	cosignatories
ACEGIINOOSTTX	excogitations
ACEGIINOPRSTY	saprogenicity
ACEGIINRSSTTU	resuscitating
ACEGILLLNOOPY	penologically
ACEGILLMNOOOT	entomological
ACEGILLMNOORU	numerological
ACEGILLMNOOYZ	enzymological
ACEGILLNNOOTY	ontogenically
ACEGILLNNOSTT	constellating
ACEGILLNOPTYY	genotypically
ACEGILLOOPRTY	geotropically
ACEGILLSTYYYZ	syzygetically
ACEGILMNNOPTT	contemplating
ACEGILMNOPSTY	salpingectomy
ACEGILMOOSSTU	cleistogamous
ACEGILNNNOSUY	sanguinolency
ACEGILNNOORSS	congressional
ACEGILNNOSTTU	conglutinates
ACEGILNORRSUU	neurosurgical
ACEGILOOPSSST	escapologists
ACEGILORSSTTU	gesticulators
ACEGILORSTTUY	gesticulatory
ACEGIMMMNOORT	commemorating
ACEGIMNOPRSTU	pneumogastric
ACEGINNNNOPRU	preannouncing
ACEGINNNORSTT	consternating
ACEGINOOPRSTT	prognosticate
ACEGIOOPRSSST	gastroscopies
ACEGLNOOOPSUY	polygonaceous
ACEGLNOOPRSSY	laryngoscopes
ACEGMNNOORSSW	congresswoman
ACEGMOOPRSSSY	gyrocompasses
ACEHHIILMNNTT	anthelminthic
ACEHHIINOPRSX	hieracosphinx
ACEHHIINOPRSZ	schizophrenia
ACEHHILMOPRTX	xerophthalmic
ACEHHILPPRSYY	hyperphysical
ACEHHINOPTTY	hypothecation
ACEHHINOSSTTY	osteichthyans
ACEHHINSSSTUZ	schizanthuses
ACEHHIOPPSSTY	psychopathies
ACEHHMMNRSTUY	chrysanthemum
ACEHHMOOOPRRT	chromatophore
ACEHHMOOPRSTU	chemoautrophs
ACEHHMOOPRTTU	chemautotroph
ACEHHOOPRSTTY	hypothecators
ACEHHOPPRSTYY	psychotherapy
ACEHIIILRSTTT	tritheistical
ACEHIIINRRSST	christianiser
ACEHIIINRRSTZ	christianizer
ACEHIIINRRSSS	christianises
ACEHIIINRSSTZ	christianizes
ACEHIILLLMOTY	homiletically
ACEHIILLPPTYY	epiphytically
ACEHIILLRSTUY	heuristically
ACEHIILMNSSSW	whimsicalness
ACEHIILOOPPRT	apheliotropic

ACEHIILOPRRST	prehistorical
ACEHIIMNOPSTY	amphictyonies
ACEHIIMORRSST	chrismatories
ACEHIIMPSSTTY	metaphysicist
ACEHIIOPSSSTT	sophisticates
ACEHIIPRTTVVY	hyperactivity
ACEHILLLOPRTY	plethorically
ACEHILLMMOPRV	morphemically
ACEHILLNORSSS	scholarliness
ACEHILLNSTTVY	synthetically
ACEHILLOOPRTY	orthoepically
ACEHILLOPPRTY	prophetically
ACEHILLOPRTTY	prothetically
ACEHILMNOOPRT	phonometrical
ACEHILMOOOPTY	homoeotypical
ACEHILMOPRSTT	thermoplastic
ACEHILMOPRSTY	hypsometrical
ACEHILNOOPPRS	cephalosporin
ACEHILPPRSSUV	superphysical
ACEHIMNOPRRTY	hyperromantic
ACEHIMNPSTTUY	unsympathetic
ACEHIMOOORSTT	thoracotomies
ACEHIMORSSTTT	thermostatics
ACEHINOORRSTT	orchestration
ACEHINOPPRRST	copartnership
ACEHINOPRRSTT	trichopterans
ACEHIOOPRRSST	arthroscopies
ACEHIOPRRSSTT	stratospheric
ACEHIORSSTTTU	tetrastichous
ACEHLMOORSSST	schoolmasters
ACEHLNOORTTTW	Charlottetown
ACEHMMNOOORST	monochromates
ACEHMMOPSTTYY	sympathectomy
ACEHMMORRSSSTU	chorusmasters
ACEHOORRRSSTT	orchestrators
ACEIIIILMNRST	criminalities
ACEIIIILMPRST	imperialistic
ACEIIIILLMOPST	semipolitical
ACEIIILLMPTVV	implicatively
ACEIIILLNNOPT	penicillation
ACEIIILMNPSSU	municipalises
ACEIIILMNPSUZ	municipalizes
ACEIIILMPSSST	pessimistical
ACEIIILNOSTVV	vivisectional
ACEIIILLQSTUVY	acquisitively
ACEIIIMNNORRT	recrimination
ACEIIINNNOSTT	Constantine II
ACEIIINOORSTT	eroticisation
ACEIIINOORTTZ	eroticization
ACEIIINOPPRTT	precipitation
ACEIIINOQRSTU	reacquisition
ACEIIINRTTTVY	interactivity
ACEIIILLLNOSVV	Silicon Valley
ACEIIILLMNSSST	miscellanists
ACEIIILMORSTY	isometrically
ACEIIILLNNOORT	intercolonial
ACEIIILLNORRTY	acrylonitrile
ACEIIILLNRRTTU	intratelluric
ACEIIILLNRRUVY	curvilinearly
ACEIIILLNRSTXY	extrinsically
ACEIIILLOOPTYZ	epizootically
ACEIIILMMNOOST	commonalities

ACEIIILMNOPSST	neoplasticism
ACEIIILMNORTUV	vermiculation
ACEIIILMNOSSSU	maliciousness
ACEIIILMNPRRSU	supercriminal
ACEIIILMNRSSTT	mercantilists
ACEIIILNNOORTU	reinoculation
ACEIIILNNOPSST	nonspecialist
ACEIIILNOPRRTT	intertropical
ACEIIILNOPRSST	personalistic
ACEIIILNORSTTU	reticulations
ACEIIILNOSSSTT	sectionalists
ACEIIILNOSSTUV	vesiculations
ACEIIILNPPRTTY	precipitantly
ACEIIILNPQTTUU	quintuplicate
ACEIIILNRSSTTT	clarinettists
ACEIIILORRTTVY	correlativity
ACEIIIMMNOORST	commiseration
ACEIIIMMNRSTTY	antisymmetric
ACEIIIMNNOOOST	economisation
ACEIIIMNNOOOTZ	economization
ACEIIIMNORRRST	recriminators
ACEIIIMNORRRTY	recriminatory
ACEIIIMNORRSTT	craniometrist
ACEIIIMNORSSTT	cremationists
ACEIIIMOORSTTU	autoeroticism
ACEIIINNNORSTU	renunciations
ACEIIINNNOSTTX	Constantine XI
ACEIIINNOOPSST	preconisation
ACEIIINNOOPRTZ	preconization
ACEIIINNOORSVZ	conversazioni
ACEIIINNOSSSST	ascensionists
ACEIIINNOSTTUV	continuatives
ACEIIINOOPRRTV	incorporative
ACEIIINOOQSTUV	equivocations
ACEIIINOORRSTV	anticorrosive
ACEIIINOORSSTV	viscerotonias
ACEIIINOPRRSTT	practitioners
ACEIIINORSSSUV	vicariousness
ACEIIINORSSTTU	resuscitation
ACEIIINOSSSUVV	vivaciousness
ACEIIINPRRSTTV	transcriptive
ACEIIIOOPRTTVV	cooperativity
ACEIIIOPPRRSTT	precipitators
ACEIIIORRRSTTV	cirrostrative
ACEIIIORRTTTVV	retroactivity
ACEIILLLLPSTYY	sylleptically
ACEIILLMMNOTYY	metonymically
ACEIILLMMRSTYY	symmetrically
ACEIILLMNNORTY	conterminally
ACEIILLMNOOPST	compellations
ACEIILLNNNOSSY	nonsensically
ACEIILLNNNOTTY	continentally
ACEIILLNNOOSTT	constellation
ACEIILLNNORRSU	carillonneurs
ACEIILLNOOPRRY	incorporeally
ACEIILLNOQUUVY	unequivocally
ACEIILLRRSSSTY	crystallisers
ACEIILLRRSSTYZ	crystallizers
ACEIILMMNOPRTY	complimentary
ACEIILMMNORSSU	communalisers
ACEIILMMNORSUZ	communalizers
ACEIILMMNRSTUY	unsymmetrical

ACEILMMOTTUVY	commutatively	ACFGIIIINNOST	signification
ACEILMNNOOPSS	companionless	ACFGIIIILNNSTY	significantly
ACEILMNNOOPTT	contemplation	ACFGIIIILNOORT	glorification
ACEILMNNOPSST	compliantness	ACFGIIIINNOPTT	pontificating
ACEILMNNORRTU	intercolumnar	ACFGIIINNNORST	fractionising
ACEILMNNSSSUU	unmusicalness	ACFGIIINNNORTZ	fractionizing
ACEILMOOPRSTU	somatopleuric	ACFGIINNOORTU	configuration
ACEILNNNOOSTV	conventionals	ACFHIIIILNOTT	lithification
ACEILNNNOSSTU	continualness	ACFHIIIMNOSTU	humifications
ACEILNNOOTTVY	connotatively	ACFHIIIINOORRT	horrification
ACEILNNORRTTUU	enculturation	ACFHIILLNOORY	honorifically
ACEILNOOPRSSS	processionals	ACFIIIILNOSTV	vilifications
ACEILNOOPRSTT	lactoproteins	ACFIIIINNORTT	nitrification
ACEILNOORRSTV	controversial	ACFIIIINORTTV	vitrification
ACEILNOPRRSTU	pronuclearist	ACFIIIINOSTVV	vivifications
ACEILNORSTTVY	contrastively	ACFIIIJLLNOOT	jollification
ACEILOOPRTVVY	provocatively	ACFIIIJNOSTTU	justification
ACEILOORRSTTW	watercolorist	ACFIIILLMNOOT	mollification
ACEILPPRSSSTU	superplastics	ACFIIILLNNOTU	nullification
ACEIMMMNOOORT	commemoration	ACFIIIMMMNOTU	mummification
ACEIMMOORRSST	commiserators	ACFIIIMNOORTT	mortification
ACEIMNNOOPSST	compensations	ACFIIIMNOSTTY	mystification
ACEIMNNORRTTU	macronutrient	ACFIIINNOOSTT	notifications
ACEIMNNOSSTTY	nonsystematic	ACFIIINOPPTUY	yuppification
ACEIMNOOOOPTT	onomatopoetic	ACFIIINOPRSTU	purifications
ACEIMNORSSSTU	customariness	ACFIIINOPSTTY	typifications
ACEIMNPSSTTUU	mispunctuates	ACFIIJORSTTUY	justificatory
ACEINNNOOORSTT	consternation	ACFIILLLORSTY	floristically
ACEINNNOORTTV	contravention	ACFIILLOOPRSY	soporifically
ACEINNOORRSVY	conversionary	ACFIILMNNOSTU	functionalism
ACEINNOORSSTV	conversations	ACFIILNNOSTTU	functionalist
ACEINNOORSTTW	Coniston Water	ACFIILNNOTTUY	functionality
ACEINNORSSTTU	counterstains	ACFIIMNNOORST	confirmations
	encrustations	ACFILLLORRTUU	floricultural
ACEINOOPRRSSY	processionary	ACFILNNNNOOTU	nonfunctional
ACEINOOORRSTUV	nectarivorous	ACFIMNNOOORST	conformations
ACEINOORSSSTU	atrociousness	ACFINNNOOORTT	confrontation
ACEINOORSSSUV	voraciousness	ACGGHHILOPPRY	glyphographic
ACEIORRSSSTTU	resuscitators	ACGGHHINNORST	shortchanging
ACELLMMNOOORU	monomolecular	ACGGHIKLNOSTU	laughingstock
ACELLNNRSTTUY	translucently	ACGGHILOPPRTY	glyptographic
ACELLNOORSTTY	constellatory	ACGGIILLOOSST	glaciologists
ACELLOOPRSSSU	supercolossal	ACGGILLLOOOSS	glossological
ACELMNOOPRSTT	contemplators	ACGHHHINNSUUU	Hung Hsiu-ch'uan
ACELMNOORSSSU	clamorousness	ACGHHIIOPPRSY	physiographic
ACELMNOPRRSUU	supercolumnar	ACGHHILMOOOPR	homolographic
ACELMNORRSUUU	neuromuscular	ACGHIIIINNPSS	hispanicising
ACELNOOPRSSTU	proconsulates	ACGHIIIINNPSZ	hispanicizing
ACELNOPRSSSUU	crapulousness	ACGHIIKMNNRSS	scrimshanking
ACELOOPPRRSUU	pleurocarpous	ACGHIIILLOOPSY	physiological
ACEMMMOOORRST	commemorators	ACGHILLLMOOOY	homologically
ACEMMMOOORRTY	commemoratory	ACGHILLMOOOPR	morphological
ACEMOOPRSTTTY	prostatectomy	ACGHILLOOPRSS	oscillographs
ACENNOOOOPRRT	noncooperator	ACGHILLOOPRSY	oscillography
ACENNOORRSSSU	rancorousness	ACGHILNOORSUW	colourwashing
ACEOPPRRSSTTU	streptocarpus	ACGHIMNNOOOPT	pathognomonic
ACEOPRRSSSSTT	sportscasters	ACGHIMOOPRSST	cosmographist
ACFFGIIIILNPST	spifflicating	ACGHNOOPPRSYY	pharyngoscopy
ACFFGILNOSTUY	suffocatingly	ACGIIIIILNNSV	civilianising
ACFFIIINOORTT	fortification	ACGIIIIILNNSV	civilianizing
ACFGIIIILNNOT	lignification	ACGIIIILMNNRS	criminalising
ACFGIIIINNNST	insignificant	ACGIIIILMNNRZ	criminalizing

ACGIIIIMNNNRT	incriminating
ACGIIIILLNNSTT	scintillating
ACGIIILMNNSSU	masculinising
ACGIIILMNNSUZ	masculinizing
ACGIIILNOPRST	tropicalising
ACGIIILNOPRTZ	tropicalizing
ACGIIIMNNORST	romanticising
ACGIIIMNNORTZ	romanticizing
ACGIIILLLOSSTY	syllogistical
ACGIILLMMNOOU	immunological
ACGIILLMNNOPY	complainingly
ACGIILLMOOSTT	climatologist
ACGIILLNRSSTY	crystallising
ACGIILLNRSTYZ	crystallizing
ACGIILMMNNOSU	communalising
ACGIILMMNNOUZ	communalizing
ACGIILMNNNOPU	uncomplaining
ACGIILMNOORSU	graminicolous
ACGIILNOORSST	craniologists
ACGIILRRSTTUU	agriculturist
ACGIIMMNOORRS	microorganism
ACGIINNNOOSST	consignations
ACGIINNNOPRST	nonpractising
ACGIINNNOPRSTUY	consanguinity
ACGIINNOOPRRT	incorporating
ACGIINOOPRRST	corporatising
ACGIINOOPRRTZ	corporatizing
ACGILLLMNOOOV	nomologically
ACGILLLMOOOPY	pomologically
ACGILLLNOOOSY	nosologically
ACGILLLNOOOTY	ontologically
ACGILLLOOOPTY	topologically
ACGILLLOOPTYY	typologically
ACGILLNOOOSTV	volcanologist
ACGILLNOOSTUV	vulcanologist
ACGILLNOOSTYY	glycosylation
ACGIMMOOPRRRS	microprograms
ACGIMNOOPRSTU	compurgations
ACGINNNOOOSTU	noncontagious
ACGIOOPRSSSTT	gastroscopist
ACHHIIINNORST	ornithischian
ACHHIILLOOPPS	philosophical
ACHHIILMNOPRS	philharmonics
ACHHIILNOPPRT	philanthropic
ACHHIIMNOPPSS	championships
ACHHIIMOPRSTU	amphitrichous
ACHHILMMOORSS	schoolmarmish
ACHHIMNOORSTX	xanthochroism
ACHHIMNOOSTTU	autochthonism
ACHHIORSSTUUY	ichthyosaurus
ACHHLLNOOOSTU	allochthonous
ACHHNNOOOOPRSY	onychophorans
ACHHNOOOSTTUU	autochthonous
ACHIIIJPRSSTU	justiciarship
ACHIIILNPPPRS	principalship
ACHIIIMNOSTTY	mythicisation
ACHIIIMNOTTYZ	mythicization
ACHIILLOPSSTY	sophistically
ACHIILMOOOSTY	homosociality
ACHIILNNOORST	chlorinations
	nonhistorical
ACHIILNNRSTUY	unchristianly

ACHIILOPRSSTT	cartophilists
ACHIIMMORRSTT	trichromatism
ACHIIMNNOOPPS	companionship
ACHIIOOPRSSTT	sophisticator
ACHIIPRSSSTTY	psychiatrists
ACHILLMNOPSYY	symphonically
ACHILLORRTTUU	horticultural
ACHILMOORSSTY	chromatolysis
ACHILMOPSTTYY	sympatholytic
ACHILOOPPRRSS	corporalships
ACHIMNNORSSSY	asynchronisms
ACHIMNOOPRRST	promonarchist
ACHIMOOOPRSTT	somatotrophic
ACHLLMMOOORSY	chromosomally
ACHMMNOOOORRT	monochromator
ACIIIILNOSSTV	civilisations
ACIIIILNOSTVZ	civilizations
ACIIIIMNNNORT	incrimination
ACIIIIMNOSTTV	victimisation
ACIIIIMNOTTVZ	victimization
ACIIIILLNNOSTT	scintillation
ACIIIILLNNRSTY	intrinsically
ACIIILMNNORTU	anticlinorium
ACIIILMNOPRSV	provincialism
ACIIILMNPSSTU	municipalists
ACIIILNOPRST	inscriptional
ACIIILNOOSSTT	coalitionists
	solicitations
ACIIILNOPRSTT	triplications
ACIIILNOPRTVY	provinciality
ACIIILNOSSTVV	convivialists
ACIIIMNNORRST	incriminators
ACIIIMNNORRTY	incriminatory
ACIIINNOOSTTX	intoxications
ACIIINNOSSTTU	cutinisations
ACIIINNOSTTUZ	cutinizations
ACIILLLMOOOQSU	colloquialism
ACIILLLNNSTTY	scintillantly
ACIILLLRSTUUV	silvicultural
ACIILLLSSTTYY	stylistically
ACIILLMNNOPTY	incompliantly
ACIILLNNSTTUY	instinctually
ACIILLNOORTUY	illocutionary
ACIIILLNORSSTT	scintillators
ACIIILLNRSTTYY	crystallinity
ACIILLOOPRSTY	isotropically
ACIILMNNOOSTU	columniations
ACIILMNOOOPST	compositional
ACIILMNOORSUY	acrimoniously
ACIILMNOORTTY	microtonality
ACIILMOOOPRST	compositorial
ACIILMOORSTTT	stromatolitic
ACIILNNOOOSST	colonisations
ACIILNNOOOSTZ	colonizations
ACIILNNOOSSTU	inosculations
ACIILNNORSTTU	instructional
ACIILNOOORSTU	colourisation
ACIILNOOORSTZ	colorizations
ACIILNOOORTUZ	colourization
ACIILNOPPSSTU	supplications
ACIILNORSTTUV	voluntaristic
ACIILPRSSTTUU	apiculturists

ACIILQRSTTUUU	aquiculturist
ACIILRSSTTUUV	aviculturists
ACIIMMNNOOSTU	communisation
ACIIMMNNOOTUZ	communization
ACIIMMNOORSSY	commissionary
ACIIMMOOPRSTT	compatriotism
ACIIMNNOOSSTU	sanctimonious
ACIIMNOOPRTTU	protoactinium
ACIINNNOOPRTU	pronunciation
ACIINNNOOSTTU	continuations
ACIINNOOOPRRT	incorporation
ACIINNOPRRSTT	transcription
ACIINNORSSTTU	incrustations
ACILLLMRTTUUU	multicultural
ACILLMMNNOOUY	communionally
ACILLNNOOOTUV	convolutional
ACILMMOOPSSSY	mycoplasmosis
ACILMNOOOPSST	cosmopolitans
ACILMNOSSSTTU	sansculottism
ACILMRRSSTTUU	structuralism
ACILNNNNOOSTY	inconsonantly
ACILNNOORSUVY	convulsionary
ACILNNOOSSTTU	consultations
ACILNOORRSTUY	contrariously
ACILNOORRSUVY	carnivorously
ACILNOSSSTTTU	sansculottist
ACILRRSSTTTUU	structuralist
ACIMMNNOOSSTU	consummations
ACINNOPRSTTTU	contrapuntist
ACINOOOPRRRST	incorporators
ACLMORSSTTUUU	cumulostratus
	stratocumulus
ACLNNORRSTTUU	nonstructural
ACNOOOPPRSSTT	contrappostos
ADDDEEHLNNRUY	underhandedly
ADDDEFHIILOSV	Shield of David
ADDEEEEEHNRRTT	tenderhearted
ADDEEEGHINPSS	pigheadedness
ADDEEEGHNORSY	dehydrogenase
ADDEEEGHNORTY	dehydrogenate
ADDEEEGINPRST	predesignated
ADDEEEGINRRTT	redintegrated
ADDEEEGMNRRRY	gerrymandered
ADDEEEGNNRRST	transgendered
ADDEEEHHNOSST	hotheadedness
ADDEEEHINNPSS	pinheadedness
ADDEEEIILMNRS	demineralised
ADDEEEIILMNRZ	demineralized
ADDEEEIILORVZ	overidealized
ADDEEEIIMNRTT	intermediated
ADDEEEIIRSSTV	desideratives
ADDEEEILMNRST	Middle Eastern
ADDEEEIMNORST	demonetarised
ADDEEEIMNORTZ	demonetarized
ADDEEEINOPPST	endopeptidase
ADDEEEINPRSTT	Painted Desert
	predestinated
ADDEEENOPPRRT	preponderated
ADDEEEOPRRSUV	overpersuaded
ADDEEFFHNNOSS	offhandedness
ADDEEFFIORSST	disafforested
ADDEEGGHIRSTT	straightedged

ADDEEGGINNRSS	degradingness
ADDEEGHLNORWY	wrongheadedly
ADDEEGIINRSTT	disintegrated
ADDEEGIMNNNSS	maddeningness
ADDEEGNNRSSUU	unguardedness
ADDEEHIKLNRTY	kindheartedly
ADDEEHILLNRST	disenthralled
ADDEEHLNORTWY	downheartedly
ADDEEIIILMRST	demilitarised
ADDEEIIILMRTZ	demilitarized
ADDEEIIILORST	editorialised
ADDEEIIILORTZ	editorialized
ADDEEIIMMNNOS	demimondaines
ADDEEIINORSST	desiderations
ADDEEIINORSTT	disorientated
ADDEEIMNRSTUV	misadventured
ADDEEINNSSSUV	unadvisedness
ADDEELNOSSSTT	staddlestones
ADDEEMNOOPSSU	pseudomonades
ADDEENNNSSTUU	undauntedness
ADDEFGJMNOTUY	Day of Judgment
ADDEFIIILMNSU	sulfadimidine
ADDEGIIMNRSSS	misaddressing
ADDEGIINNNRRU	underdraining
ADDEGINNNRSTU	understanding
ADDEHHIKNOOSS	Dhodhekánisos
ADDEIIIILNSUV	individualise
ADDEIIIILNUVZ	individualize
ADDEIIINOOSTX	deoxidisation
ADDEIIINOOTXZ	deoxidization
ADDEIIINSTTTU	attitudinised
ADDEIIINTTTUZ	attitudinized
ADDEIINOOORST	deodorisation
ADDEIINOOORTZ	deodorization
ADDEIINOPRSTU	superaddition
ADDEILMNOOSTU	demodulations
ADDEIMNNRSSTU	misunderstand
ADDGIIIINNTUV	individuating
ADDGIILLLLNVY	dillydallying
ADDGIILNSSSTU	studdingsails
ADDGIMNNOOORT	rodomontading
ADDHIIILMOPPS	amphidiploids
ADDIIIILMNSUV	individualism
ADDIIIILNSTUV	individualist
ADDIIIILNTUVY	individuality
ADDIIIINNOTUV	individuation
ADDIIINORSTUV	individuators
ADEEEEFHLRRTY	freeheartedly
ADEEEEGNNRRTU	unregenerated
ADEEEEHLMPPRT	pamphleteered
ADEEEENPRSSST	desperateness
ADEEEFFIINRTT	differentiate
ADEEEFILLNRTY	deferentially
ADEEEFNRRRRST	retransferred
ADEEEGGGINRST	desegregating
ADEEEGGIMNNST	disengagement
ADEEEGGINORST	desegregation
ADEEEGGNNOORST	nonsegregated
ADEEEGHLMMRSS	sledgehammers
ADEEEGILMNRSY	semilegendary
ADEEEGIMNRSST	demagnetisers
	disagreements

ADEEEGIMNRSTZ	demagnetizers	ADEEFGLNRRSSU	regardfulness
ADEEEGIMORSTU	deuterogamies	ADEEFHLORSTTY	softheartedly
ADEEEGINNNRSS	engrainedness	ADEEFHOORRSSW	foreshadowers
ADEEEGINNNORST	degenerations	ADEEFIILOQRUV	overqualified
ADEEEGINPRSST	predesignates	ADEEFINOORSTT	deforestation
ADEEEGINRRSTT	redintegrates	ADEEGGGINSSZZ	zigzaggedness
ADEEEGIRRSTTV	tergiversated	ADEEGGHIRSSTT	straightedges
ADEEEGLLNORTU	outgeneralled	ADEEGGIIMMNNST	demagnetising
ADEEEGMNNNRST	endangerments	ADEEGGIIMMNNTZ	demagnetizing
ADEEEGOPRRSTU	supererogated	ADEEGGINNOTXY	deoxygenating
ADEEEGOPRRTUY	daguerreotype	ADEEGGLNOPPRS	doppelgangers
ADEEEHINPRSST	parenthesised	ADEEGHIINNRST	disheartening
ADEEEHINPRSTZ	parenthesized	ADEEGHILNRSTY	nearsightedly
ADEEEHINRRTTW	interwreathed	ADEEGHNOOPRTV	photoengraved
ADEEEHLNNNRTW	New Netherland	ADEEGHPRSSTTU	stepdaughters
ADEEEHLNOPRTY	openheartedly	ADEEGIIILMSTT	legitimatised
ADEEEHLNSSSST	deathlessness	ADEEGIIILMTTZ	legitimatized
ADEEEIILMNRSS	demineralises	ADEEGIIINRTTT	interdigitate
ADEEEIILMNRSZ	demineralizes	ADEEGIILNNPRT	interpleading
ADEEEIILNNRTT	interlineated	ADEEGIILNSSUX	desexualising
ADEEEIILORSVZ	overidealizes	ADEEGIILNSUXZ	desexualizing
ADEEEIIMMNSST	immediateness	ADEEGIIMNPRTT	premeditating
ADEEEIIMMRSST	semidiameters	ADEEGIINNNRSS	ingrainedness
ADEEEIIMNNRTT	indeterminate	ADEEGIINNRRTT	intergradient
ADEEEIIMNRSTT	intermediates	ADEEGIINORRTT	deteriorating
ADEEEIIMNRTTV	determinative	ADEEGIINORRTV	reinvigorated
ADEEEIIMPRTTV	premeditative	ADEEGIINORSTY	Tayside Region
ADEEEIINPRSST	pedestrianise	ADEEGIINORTVV	overdeviating
ADEEEIINPRSTZ	pedestrianize	ADEEGIINRSSTT	disintegrates
ADEEEIIORRTTV	deteriorative	ADEEGIKNNNRST	kindergartens
ADEEEILLNPRTT	interpellated	ADEEGILNORSTU	deregulations
ADEEEILMNORST	radioelements	ADEEGIIMORSTTU	deuterogamist
ADEEEILMNRTTY	determinately	ADEEGINNOOTXY	deoxygenation
ADEEEILNOPRSS	depersonalise	ADEEGINNOPRVX	overexpanding
ADEEEILNOPRSZ	depersonalize	ADEEGINOPPRSV	eavesdropping
ADEEEILNPRRST	interpleaders	ADEEGINOPRRSV	overspreading
ADEEEILOPRTTY	radioteletype	ADEEGINORSTTU	deuteragonist
ADEEEIMNNORTU	mountaineered	ADEEGLNNOORRT	Greater London
ADEEEIMNORSST	demonetarises	ADEEGMNNNRRSTU	undergarments
ADEEEIMNORSTZ	demonetarizes	ADEEGNNORSSSU	dangerousness
ADEEEIMNRSTTU	underestimate	ADEEGOPRRTUYY	daguerreotypy
ADEEEIMNRSTTV	advertisement	ADEEHHIKNRRSS	headshrinkers
ADEEEIMNRTTVZ	advertizement	ADEEHHIMOPRRT	hermaphrodite
ADEEEIMORSTTV	overestimated	ADEEHHOOORSUW	Harewood House
ADEEEINNRSSST	sedentariness	ADEEHIILMNNPY	diphenylamine
ADEEEINNRSSUW	unweariedness	ADEEHIILNSTTT	dilettanteish
ADEEEINOPQRTU	equiponderate	ADEEHIIMNORTT	trimethadione
ADEEEINPRSSTT	predestinates	ADEEHIMNPPRSS	misapprehends
ADEEEIOPPSSTX	exopeptidases	ADEEHIMRSSSTY	headmistressy
ADEEELLMNOPTV	developmental	ADEEHINNORRTY	nonhereditary
ADEEELLMORRST	steamrollered	ADEEHKLLLNOST	Kedleston Hall
ADEEELMNRSSSS	dreamlessness	ADEEHLMNORRSY	dysmenorrheal
ADEEEMNORSTUV	adventuresome	ADEEHMMOOPRST	metamorphosed
ADEEEMNORTUUV	outmaneuvered	ADEEHMNOORRSY	dysmenorrhoea
ADEEENOPPRRST	preponderates	ADEEHMOPRSTTY	dermatophytes
ADEEENRSSSTUV	adventuresses	ADEEHNNOOSSTU	Southend-on-Sea
ADEEEOPPRRSSV	eavesdroppers	ADEEHNOOPRRTZ	trapezohedron
ADEEEOPRRSSUV	overpersuades	ADEEHORSSTUVY	Shrove Tuesday
ADEEFFIILNRST	differentials	ADEEIIIILMRTZ	remilitarized
ADEEFGGILNRRS	self-regarding	ADEEIIILMRSST	demilitarises
ADEEFGILMNNUV	Van Diemen Gulf	ADEEIIILMRSTZ	demilitarizes
ADEEFGILNNRRS	Flinders Range	ADEEIIILORRST	editorialiser

ADEEIIILORRTZ	editorializer
ADEEIIILORSST	editorialises
ADEEIIILORSTZ	editorializes
ADEEIIIMNSSTV	disseminative
ADEEIIINPRSST	stipendiaries
ADEEIIILLNRSTV	residentially
ADEEIILMNNSTT	disentailment
ADEEIILMNOOST	emotionalised
ADEEIILMNOOTZ	emotionalized
ADEEIILMNPSST	dissepimental
ADEEIILMNRSTY	sedimentarily
ADEEIILMNSTTT	dilettanteism
ADEEIILNRSSUV	universalised
ADEEIILNRSUVZ	universalized
ADEEIIMMNPRTY	impedimentary
ADEEIIMNNORTT	determination
ADEEIIMNNOSTT	sedimentation
ADEEIIMNOPRTT	premeditation
ADEEIIMNORRTT	intermediator
ADEEIIMOPRRRV	Primo de Rivera
ADEEIINNORSTT	tenderisation
ADEEIINNORTTZ	tenderization
ADEEIINOORRTT	deterioration
ADEEIINOPRRTT	repartitioned
ADEEIINOPRTXY	expeditionary
ADEEIINORSSTT	disorientates
ADEEIINORSSTV	disseveration
ADEEILLMNRTTY	detrimentally
ADEEILLNNRTTY	interdentally
ADEEILMMNNSTT	dismantlement
ADEEILMNOORST	demonolatries
ADEEILMNOORTZ	metronidazole
ADEEILMNOPRTY	predominately
ADEEILNNRTTVY	inadvertently
ADEEILNOPPRST	lepidopterans
ADEEIMMNORSSU	misdemeanours
ADEEIMNORSTTV	demonstrative
ADEEIMNRRSTTT	retransmitted
ADEEIMNRSSTUV	misadventures
ADEEIMOPRRSTT	premeditators
ADEEINNOPQRTU	equiponderant
ADEEINOOPPRRT	reapportioned
ADEEINOPRRSST	predatoriness
ADEEINOPRRSTU	superordinate
ADEEINPRSSTUU	unpasteurised
ADEEINPRSTUUZ	unpasteurized
ADEEJMNRSSTTU	readjustments
ADEELMMRSSTUU	summersaulted
ADEELMOPRSSTU	deuteroplasms
ADEELNNSSSSTU	dauntlessness
ADEELOOPPRTUV	overpopulated
ADEEMMOOSTUXY	myxoedematous
ADEEMNNPRSTUY	underpayments
ADEEMNOORTUUV	outmanoeuvred
ADEEMOORRSTUX	xerodermatous
ADEENPPRRRSTU	understrapper
ADEEORRRSTTUW	Wardour Street
ADEFFHIORRSST	Staffordshire
ADEFGHINOORSW	foreshadowing
ADEFGIINNOORR	foreordaining
ADEFHILNNPRTT	Pentland Firth
ADEFHILNOORSS	foolhardiness
ADEFIIILQRSSU	disqualifiers
ADEFIILLNQUUV	unqualifiedly
ADEFIILNOSSTT	deflationists
ADEFIJMMORRSU	Reform Judaism
ADEFILLSSTTUV	distastefully
ADEFLLOOPSTVY	splayfootedly
ADEFMNNORRSTU	untransformed
ADEGGHINNORTV	hydrogenating
ADEGGIILNNNST	disentangling
ADEGGIILNNRSS	niggardliness
ADEGGIILNNTTU	deglutinating
ADEGGIMMNOPRR	deprogramming
ADEGHHOPRRRSV	hydrographers
ADEGHIIOPRSTT	dittographies
ADEGHIMOPRSST	demographists
ADEGHINNOORTV	hydrogenation
ADEGHINNOPPRS	pendragonship
ADEGHINNOPRSS	androsphinges
ADEGHINOORSVW	overshadowing
ADEGHLLNORSST	strangleholds
ADEGHLMNORRTY	grandmotherly
ADEGHMNORSTUW	draughtswomen
ADEGHNOORRSTY	hydrogenators
ADEGIIIMNNRST	administering
ADEGIIIMNNSST	disseminating
ADEGIILLNNSTU	dentilinguals
ADEGIILLNPSSY	displeasingly
ADEGIILMNSTUU	demutualising
ADEGIILMNTTUY	unmitigatedly
ADEGIILMNTUUZ	demutualizing
ADEGIILNNOTTU	deglutination
ADEGIILNPRSSU	displeasuring
ADEGIIMMNNRST	masterminding
ADEGIIMNNOPRT	predominating
ADEGIIMOOPRST	diageotropism
ADEGIINNNPRTU	underpainting
ADEGIINNPRRSU	underpraising
ADEGIINORRSSS	disorganisers
ADEGIINORRSSZ	disorganizers
ADEGIINORRSTT	disintegrator
ADEGILMOORSTT	dermatologist
ADEGILNNOQRTU	grandiloquent
ADEGILNOOPRTT	proglottidean
ADEGIMNNORSTT	demonstrating
ADEGJLMNNNOTU	nonjudgmental
ADEGLLMNORUWZ	mangoldwurzel
ADEHHIIILMOOP	haemophilioid
ADEHHLOPRSTUY	hydrosulphate
ADEHIIIMRSTTV	Mithridates VI
ADEHIILMNPSTY	lymphadenitis
ADEHIIMNOOSTT	methodisation
ADEHIIMNOOTTZ	methodization
ADEHIINNRSSTY	hydrastinines
ADEHIKLNNPSSS	spindleshanks
ADEHILMNOPSSU	sulphonamides
ADEHILMNORXYV	hydroxylamine
ADEHILNNOPRSW	landownership
ADEHIMOOPRRST	moderatorship
ADEHINNNORRTV	Northern Dvina
ADEHINNOPRSSX	androsphinxes
ADEHINNRSSTWW	withdrawnness
ADEHIOOPPRSST	apostrophised

ADEHIOOPPRSTZ	apostrophized
ADEHIOOPRSSTT	orthopaedists
ADEHLLOOPPSUY	polyadelphous
ADEHNORRSTTWW	northwestward
ADEHORSSTTUWW	southwestward
ADEIIIILMSSTV	dissimilative
ADEIIIILMNOSTT	delimitations
ADEIIILMSSTUV	dissimulative
ADEIIILNPSTTU	platitudinise
ADEIIILNPTTUZ	platitudinize
ADEIIILNRSSTU	industrialise
ADEIIILNRSTUZ	industrialize
ADEIIILORSSTT	editorialists
ADEIIILPRSSTU	spiritualised
ADEIIILPRSTUZ	spiritualized
ADEIIIMNNOSST	dissemination
ADEIIINNOOSST	deionisations
ADEIIINOOPRST	periodisation
ADEIIINOOPRTZ	periodization
ADEIIINOSSTTV	deviationists
ADEIIINRSTTTU	attitudiniser
ADEIIINRTTTUZ	attitudinizer
ADEIIINSSTTTU	attitudinises
ADEIIINSTTTUZ	attitudinizes
ADEIILLMNNOSY	dimensionally
ADEIILLMNNTUU	unilluminated
ADEIILLNQRSTU	tranquillised
ADEIILLNQRTUZ	tranquillized
ADEIILLSSTUVV	vaudevillists
ADEIILMNOORST	Tirso de Molina
ADEIILMNOPSSY	impassionedly
ADEIILMNRRTUY	rudimentarily
ADEIILNNOOPTY	opinionatedly
ADEIILNOOTTVY	devotionality
ADEIILNORSSTT	traditionless
ADEIILNPRRSTU	preindustrial
ADEIILNQSTTUY	equidistantly
ADEIILPSTTUVY	disputatively
ADEIIMNNNOOST	denominations
ADEIIMNNOOPRT	predomination
ADEIIMNNOORST	modernisation
ADEIIMNNOORTZ	modernization
ADEIIMNNOPSSU	unimpassioned
ADEIIMNNORSTT	antimodernist
ADEIIMNNRSSTT	distrainments
ADEIIMNORSSST	disseminators
ADEIIMORSSTTU	audiometrists
ADEIINNOOPRRT	preordination
ADEIINNOPSSST	dispensations
ADEIINOOPRSST	disoperations
ADEIINORSSSTT	dissertations
ADEIIOOOPRSST	radioisotopes
ADEILLMNRTTYY	tyndallimetry
ADEILLNOPPRST	dipropellants
ADEILLNRSTTUU	unillustrated
ADEILMNNNSSTU	disannulments
ADEILMNNOPRTY	predominantly
ADEILNOOPPSTU	depopulations
ADEILNOORTUVY	devolutionary
ADEIMNNOORSTT	demonstration
ADEIMNNOPRSTU	superdominant
ADEIMNOOPRRST	predominators
ADEIMOOPRSSTZ	spermatozoids
ADEINOSSSSSUU	assiduousness
ADELNORSTUUVY	adventurously
ADEMNNOORRSST	demonstrators
ADENNORSTUUUV	unadventurous
ADFFHILNOSSTY	standoffishly
ADFGIIILNQSUY	disqualifying
ADFGIIINORSTU	disfiguration
ADFGIIINSSSTY	dissatisfying
ADFHHKLLNOOOO	Hook of Holland
ADFIIIILMNOSS	solifidianism
ADFIILNOORSTU	fluoridations
ADFIKLLNNOORS	Norfolk Island
ADGGIIIMNNOSS	misdiagnosing
ADGGIIINNORSS	disorganising
ADGGIIINNORSZ	disorganizing
ADGHILLLMNOSS	smallholdings
ADGHINNOOOOPRT	gonadotrophin
ADGHMNNOOPRRY	gynandromorph
ADGIIIILMNSST	dissimilating
ADGIILMNSSTU	dissimulating
ADGIIILNNRSSV	Virgin Islands
ADGIIILNPRSSY	dispraisingly
ADGIIINNOPPST	disappointing
ADGIIMNNOSTUU	magnitudinous
ADGIJKNNOPRTU	Tandjungpriok
ADGIJLNOPPRWY	jawdroppingly
ADGILNNOSTTUY	outstandingly
ADGINNOOOOPRST	gonadotropins
ADHHIOPRSSTTY	hydropathists
ADHIILLNOQRTU	quadrillionth
ADHIILMNOPRSU	dolphinariums
ADHIIMNOORSSU	disharmonious
ADHILNOORSTYY	hydrolysation
ADHILNOORTYYZ	hydrolyzation
ADHIMNOPRSSSW	swordsmanship
ADIIIILMNOSST	dissimilation
ADIIIILMNPRTU	platiniridium
ADIIIILMRSSTY	dissimilarity
ADIIIIMNNOSTT	intimidations
ADIIIILLNOSSTT	distillations
ADIIILMNOSSTU	dissimulation
ADIIILMNRSSTU	industrialism
ADIIILMOPRRTY	primordiality
ADIIILMORSSTY	dissimilatory
ADIIILNOOPSST	dispositional
ADIIILNRSSTTU	industrialist
ADIIINORSSTTT	traditionists
ADIILMORSSSTU	dissimulators
ADIILNNNORSTU	nonindustrial
ADIILNOOOPSST	podsolisation
ADIILNOOOPSTZ	podsolization
	podzolisation
ADIILNOOOPTZZ	podzolization
ADIILNOPSSTUV	postdiluvians
ADIILNOPSTTUU	platitudinous
ADIINNRSTTUYY	Trinity Sunday
ADIKLNRSSUUYY	Ryukyu Islands
ADILLLLOOOPPY	allopolyploid
ADILLOOOPPTUY	autopolyploid
AEEEEGHMORSTT	heterogametes
AEEEEGNNRRSTU	unregenerates

AEEEEHHHNNSTVV	seventh heaven
AEEEEHHPRRSSS	sheepshearers
AEEEEHLMNPRSS	ephemeralness
AEEEEILNRRSST	rensselaerite
AEEEEIMNPRSST	passementerie
AEEEEKLMRRSTT	telemarketers
AEEEEMMNRRSTU	remeasurement
AEEEEMMNPRSST	temperateness
AEEEFGHHIRTTW	featherweight
AEEEFGIIRRRTV	refrigerative
AEEEFINQRTTUV	frequentative
AEEEGGIMNOSST	gametogenesis
AEEEGHHINPRSS	sheepshearing
AEEEGHIILMRSW	whigmaleeries
AEEEGHIILNRST	etherealising
AEEEGHIILNRTZ	etherealizing
AEEEGHIMNOSST	hematogenesis
AEEEGHINORSST	atherogenesis
AEEEGHLNOPRRS	selenographer
AEEEGHMNOPRST	magnetosphere
AEEEGIINRSTTV	reinvestigate
AEEEGIKLMNRTT	telemarketing
AEEEGIKMNQRTU	Quaker meeting
AEEEGILLNSTTV	televangelist
AEEEGILNNRSSV	revealingness
AEEEGIMNNSSTV	envisagements
AEEEGIMNPRRTY	prayer meeting
AEEEGINNORRST	regenerations
AEEEGINORRRTT	reinterrogate
AEEEGINORSTTV	revegetations
AEEEGIRRSSTTV	tergiversates
AEEEGLMNNNSTT	entanglements
AEEEGMMNORSTT	magnetometers
AEEEGMNNRSSTT	estrangements
AEEEGOPRRSSTU	supererogates
AEEEGPPPRRSSS	peppergrasses
AEEEHHIMRSSTT	thermesthesia
AEEEHHIPRSSTY	hyperesthesia
AEEEHHNOPRSST	asthenosphere
AEEEHILMNNOPP	epiphenomenal
AEEEHILNRSSTW	weatherliness
AEEEHIMOPRSSV	overemphasise
AEEEHIMOPRSVZ	overemphasize
AEEEHINPRSSST	parenthesises
AEEEHINPRSSTZ	parenthesizes
AEEEHINRRSTTW	interwreathes
AEEEHLMNSSSSS	shamelessness
AEEEHLNPSSSSS	shapelessness
AEEEHLNRSSSST	heartlessness
AEEEHLOPPRSTY	speleotherapy
AEEEHLORSSTUX	heterosexuals
AEEEHMNNSSTTW	enswathements
AEEEHMNORSSST	heartsomeness
AEEEIIILLLNTV	Ille-et-Vilaine
AEEEIIIMMNRST	Seine-Maritime
AEEEIILNNRSTT	interlineates
AEEEIILNRRRTV	irreverential
AEEEIILNRSTTX	externalities
AEEEIILNSTTUV	eventualities
AEEEIILRRTTVY	reiteratively
AEEEIIMNRTTVX	exterminative
AEEEIINRSSTTV	iterativeness
AEEEIKLLMPRST	kapellmeister
AEEEILLNPRSTT	interpellates
AEEEILLNRRTVY	reverentially
AEEEILMNPRSSX	exemplariness
AEEEILMNPRTTY	intemperately
AEEEILNNPRSUY	Eyre Peninsula
AEEEILNNSSSST	essentialness
AEEEIMMNNPRST	semipermanent
AEEEIMNNNRTTT	entertainment
AEEEIMNNRSTTT	reinstatement
AEEEIMNORSSSW	wearisomeness
AEEEIMNPRRSTV	privateersmen
AEEEIMOPRRSTV	evaporimeters
AEEEIMORSSTTV	overestimates
AEEEINNNSSSST	insensateness
AEEEINNPSSSVX	expansiveness
AEEEINNSSTTTV	attentiveness
	tentativeness
AEEEINOPRRSTV	perseveration
AEEEINOPRSSTV	operativeness
AEEEINORTTTVV	overattentive
AEEEINPRSSSVV	pervasiveness
AEEEINRSSSSTV	assertiveness
AEEEIORRSSTVV	overassertive
AEEEIPRRSSTVV	preservatives
AEEEKLRRSSTTW	streetwalkers
AEEELLMRSSSUY	measurelessly
AEEELLNSSSSUV	valuelessness
AEEELLNNPRSSTV	prevalentness
AEEELNSSSSSTT	statelessness
	tastelessness
AEEEMMNOPRTTU	pneumatometer
AEEEMNORSTTTV	overstatement
AEEEMNPRRSSTU	prematureness
AEEEMNRSSSSST	reassessments
AEEEMOOPRRSTV	evaporometers
AEEFFGHIMNRTT	affreightment
AEEFFGINORRST	reafforesting
AEEFGGHINORRT	foregathering
AEEFGGIINRRRT	refrigerating
AEEFGIINORRRT	refrigeration
AEEFGIIPRRTUV	prefigurative
AEEFGILNORRST	foretriangles
AEEFGINORRSTU	argentiferous
AEEFGIORRRRST	refrigerators
AEEFGIORRRRTY	refrigeratory
AEEFHHLLNSSTU	healthfulness
AEEFHILNSSSST	faithlessness
AEEFHLMORRSTW	flamethrowers
AEEFHOOPRRSTW	weatherproofs
AEEFIILLNNRTY	inferentially
AEEFIILMPPRRS	preamplifiers
AEEFIILMPRSSU	superfamilies
AEEFIILOPRRTV	proliferative
AEEFIINNORSTT	reinfestation
AEEFILLMORSTU	metalliferous
AEEFILLMOSSTY	Yosemite Falls
AEEFIMNNORSTT	fermentations
AEEFIMNORSSTV	formativeness
AEEFIMOORRRST	reformatories
AEEFINNOQRTTU	frequentation
AEEFINNORSSSU	nefariousness

AEEFINNORSSTT	fenestrations
AEEFINOORRSTT	reforestation
AEEFINOPRSTTU	superfetation
AEEFIOOPRRSST	professoriate
AEEFLLMNORSTT	forestallment
AEEFLLNSSSSTU	faultlessness
AEEFLMNRSSSTU	masterfulness
AEEFLNPRRSSUY	prayerfulness
AEEFLOPQRSSUW	pasqueflowers
AEEFNNORSSTTU	fortunateness
AEEFOOPRRSSST	professorates
AEEGGHOOOPRRZ	zoogeographer
AEEGGIINNORTT	renegotiating
AEEGGIINNPRRT	peregrinating
AEEGGIINNRRTT	reintegrating
AEEGGILNNORTU	outgeneraling
AEEGGINNOORSS	organogenesis
AEEGGMNNOORRT	roentgenogram
AEEGHHILOPRRS	heliographers
AEEGHHMOPRRRT	thermographer
AEEGHHNOPRRST	ethnographers
AEEGHIILNPSTT	telepathising
AEEGHIILNPTTZ	telepathizing
AEEGHIIMNPRSZ	reemphasizing
AEEGHIIMNSSTT	metathesising
AEEGHIIMNSTTZ	metathesizing
AEEGHIINNSTTZ	anesthetizing
AEEGHILMOORST	isogeothermal
AEEGHILNNRTTY	threateningly
AEEGHILOOPRSS	phraseologies
AEEGHILORRSUV	heliogravures
AEEGHILPRSSTT	telegraphists
AEEGHIMOPRRSS	seismographer
AEEGHINOOPTTV	photonegative
AEEGHINOPRSST	taphrogenesis
AEEGHINRRSSTT	straighteners
AEEGHLLNOOSTU	Longleat House
AEEGHLOORRSTW	woolgatherers
AEEGHMOOPRRST	meteorographs
AEEGHNOOPRRTV	photoengraver
AEEGHNOOPRSTV	photoengraves
AEEGHNOPRRSST	stenographers
AEEGHOPPRRRST	petrographers
AEEGIIILLMSTT	illegitimates
AEEGIIILMSSTT	legitimatises
AEEGIIILMSTTZ	legitimatizes
AEEGIIINSTTVV	investigative
AEEGIILLLSTVY	legislatively
AEEGIILMNORSS	generalissimo
AEEGIILNNORRT	interregional
AEEGIILNNRRTT	interrelating
AEEGIILNNRSTX	externalising
AEEGIILNNRTXZ	externalizing
AEEGIIMNNORTT	regimentation
AEEGIIMNNRSTT	mainstreeting
AEEGIIMNNRTTX	exterminating
AEEGIINNNNORST	ingenerations
AEEGIINNOORTT	renegotiation
AEEGIINNOPRRT	peregrination
AEEGIINNOPRSU	europeanising
AEEGIINNOPRUZ	europeanizing
AEEGIINNORRTT	reintegration
AEEGIINNORRSTV	reinvigorates
AEEGIINORRTTV	interrogative
AEEGIKLNRSTTW	streetwalking
AEEGILLMMNNRT	entrammelling
AEEGILLMNNSSY	meaninglessly
AEEGILLNRSTVY	everlastingly
AEEGILLOOPSST	spelaeologist
AEEGILLOPRSSS	aspergilloses
AEEGILNNPRTTY	penetratingly
AEEGIMMNOOTTV	magnetomotive
AEEGIMNNNNSSU	unmeaningness
AEEGIMNNOSSTT	segmentations
AEEGIMNNRSSST	reassignments
AEEGIMNNRTTUY	integumentary
AEEGIMNORRSTV	overmastering
AEEGIMNRRSSST	mastersingers
AEEGINNPPRSTT	stepparenting
AEEGINOORSSST	astereognosis
AEEGINOPRRRST	peregrinators
AEEGINORRSSTV	overasserting
AEEGINQRSSTTU	sequestrating
AEEGINRRSSSTV	transgressive
AEEGINRRSSTTV	tergiversants
AEEGIORRRSTTV	tergiversator
AEEGLLMNNNTUV	ungentlemanly
AEEGLLMNNOTWY	gentlewomanly
AEEGLLMNRSUWZ	mangelwurzels
AEEGNNOOPQRTU	rontgenopaque
AEEGOOPRRRSTU	supererogator
AEEGORSSSSTUU	stegosauruses
AEEHHIINNOPTZ	phenothiazine
AEEHHILLMNSVW	Wilhelmshaven
AEEHHILMMNNTT	nemathelminth
AEEHHILMMNSTU	helianthemums
AEEHHILNNSSTU	unhealthiness
AEEHHINOPRRST	tenorrhaphies
AEEHHKMPPRSUY	Humphreys Peak
AEEHHMOPRRTTY	thermotherapy
AEEHHNOPPRSTY	phanerophytes
AEEHHOPPRSTTY	phreatophytes
AEEHIIILNPPPS	Philippine Sea
AEEHIIIMMNRST	Hammerstein II
AEEHIILLNNOTZ	hellenization
AEEHIIMOOPSST	hematopoiesis
AEEHIINORSSTT	etherisations
AEEHIINORSTTZ	etherizations
AEEHILMMNNOPS	phenomenalism
AEEHILMMOOSST	mesotheliomas
AEEHILMNNOPST	phenomenalist
AEEHILNLNNSSTU	unearthliness
AEEHILPPRRXYY	hyperpyrexial
AEEHIMNNPSSSS	misshapenness
AEEHIMNORSSTT	thermonasties
AEEHIMNQSSSSU	squeamishness
AEEHIMOPPRRTY	hypermetropia
AEEHINNOPPRSS	apprehensions
AEEHINOORSSTU	heteroousians
AEEHINORSSSTV	overhastiness
AEEHINORSSSTW	seaworthiness
AEEHIOPPRRSXY	hyperprosexia
AEEHIPRRRSSTU	treasurership
AEEHKLNNSSSST	thanklessness

791

AEEHKNOORRSTY	heterokaryons
AEEHLLMMORSWY	yellowhammers
AEEHLLMNNRSTT	enthrallments
AEEHLLMNOOPST	metallophones
AEEHLMNOOSSST	loathsomeness
AEEHLMPRRSSUU	superhumerals
AEEHLNOPRSTUY	polyurethanes
AEEHLNORRSTTY	northeasterly
AEEHLNOSSTUWW	New South Wales
AEEHLORSSTTUY	southeasterly
AEEHMMOOPRSST	metamorphoses
AEEHMMOPSSTUU	emphysematous
AEEHMNNOPRSTY	hymenopterans
AEEHMNOOPPRTU	pneumatophore
AEEHMOOPPRRST	spermatophore
AEEHMOPPRSTTY	spermatophyte
AEEHNOOPPRRST	parthenospore
AEEIIILMNPRRS	preliminaries
AEEIIILMRRSTZ	remilitarizes
AEEIIILRSSTTV	versatilities
AEEIIIMNSSTTV	imitativeness
AEEIIINRSSSTT	initiatresses
AEEIIKLMNPRSS	marlinespikes
AEEIILLLMNNPR	premillennial
AEEIILLLMOSST	lamellosities
AEEIILLLNNRTY	interlineally
AEEIILLNNPTTY	penitentially
AEEIILLNNRRTY	interlinearly
AEEIILLNSTTXY	existentially
AEEIILMMORRSS	memorialisers
AEEIILMMORRSZ	memorializers
AEEIILMNOOSST	emotionalises
AEEIILMNOOSTZ	emotionalizes
AEEIILMNOPRSS	impersonalise
AEEIILMNOPRSZ	impersonalize
AEEIILMOPRSTT	temporalities
AEEIILNNORRTT	interrelation
AEEIILNNOSSTV	inviolateness
AEEIILNNPSSTV	plaintiveness
AEEIILNNTTTVY	inattentively
AEEIILNOPQTTU	equipotential
AEEIILNOPRSST	personalities
AEEIILNOPRTTV	interpolative
AEEIILNORSTTV	revelationist
AEEIILNORSTVY	televisionary
AEEIILNQRRTTU	interquartile
AEEIILNQSTTUY	sequentiality
AEEIILNRSSSUV	universalises
AEEIILNRSSUVZ	universalizes
AEEIILNSSSSTT	essentialists
AEEIILORRRTTX	exterritorial
AEEIIMMNORSST	mesmerisation
AEEIIMMNORSTZ	mesmerization
AEEIIMNNORTTX	extermination
AEEIIMNPSSSSV	impassiveness
AEEIIMNQRSSTU	equestrianism
AEEIIINNNORSTT	intenerations
AEEIINNOORRTT	reorientation
AEEIINNOPSSTT	spontaneities
AEEIINNOQRSTU	questionnaire
AEEIIOPPRRRST	proprietaries
AEEIJNNORSTUV	rejuvenations

AEEIKNOPRSSTT	streptokinase
AEEIILLMNNSTTY	sentimentally
AEEIILLMNPRSTY	sempiternally
AEEIILLNNOPPST	Lepontine Alps
AEEIILLNNOPTXY	exponentially
AEEIILLNNORSSU	Lons-le-Saunier
AEEIILLNNOSTXY	extensionally
AEEIILLNNPRSTT	interpellants
AEEIILLNNSSTUY	unessentially
AEEIILLNOPRRTT	interpellator
AEEIILLNORRSVY	reversionally
AEEIILLNOSSSTT	tessellations
AEEIILLNRSTUXY	intersexually
AEEIILLPRSTUVY	superlatively
AEEIILLRRRSTTY	terrestrially
AEEIILMMNNPRTY	impermanently
AEEIILMNNNORTV	environmental
AEEIILMNNNSTTU	unsentimental
AEEIILMNOOORTV	overemotional
AEEIILMOPRRTXY	extemporarily
AEEIILMORSTTUV	overstimulate
AEEIILNNNOOPPS	Peloponnesian
AEEIILNNNOPRST	antipersonnel
AEEIILNNNOQTUV	nonequivalent
AEEIILNNNOSSST	nonessentials
AEEIILNNOPRRST	interpersonal
AEEIILNNOPRSTT	septentrional
AEEIILNNOSSSST	sensationless
AEEIILNNQQTUUV	quinquevalent
AEEIILNNRSSSUV	universalness
AEEIILNOORRSTV	lateroversion
AEEIILNOPRRSTT	interpolaters
AEEIILNPRRSSST	interspersals
AEEIILOOPSSSTT	osteoplasties
AEEIILOPRSSTUY	erysipelatous
AEEIILOPSTTUVX	expostulative
AEEIILPRRSSSTU	superrealists
AEEIMMNNORSST	momentariness
AEEIMMNORSSTT	amortisements
AEEIMMNORSTTZ	amortizements
AEEIMMNSSSTTT	misstatements
AEEIMNNOPPRTT	reappointment
AEEIMNNORRSTU	remunerations
AEEIMNNORSSTV	normativeness
AEEIMNOPRRSST	temporariness
AEEIMNOPRSSTX	proximateness
AEEIMNORRSTTV	remonstrative
AEEIMNORRSTTX	exterminators
AEEIMNORRTTXY	exterminatory
AEEIMRSSSSTTY	systematisers
AEEIMRSSSTTYZ	systematizers
AEEINNOOPRSVX	overexpansion
AEEINNOPRSSTT	presentations
AEEINNPRRRSTU	intrapreneurs
AEEINOOPRRTTX	reexportation
AEEINOORRSSTV	overassertion
AEEINOORRSTUV	arteriovenous
AEEINOPPRRSTT	perpetrations
AEEINOPRRSSTV	preservations
AEEINOQRSSTTU	sequestration
AEEINOSSSTUVX	vexatiousness
AEEINRSSSTTTV	transvestites

AEEINRSSTTTUV	sternutatives
AEEIOOPPRSTTV	postoperative
AEEKMORRSSSTT	masterstrokes
AEELLMNPPSSTU	supplementals
AEELLMOQRRSUY	quarrelsomely
AEELMNORSSSUV	marvelousness
AEELMNPPRSTUY	supplementary
AEELNOOPSSTTU	stenopetalous
AEELOOPPRSTUV	overpopulates
AEEMMNOPRTTUY	pneumatometry
AEEMNOOPRSTTU	treponematous
AEEMNOORSTUUV	outmanoeuvres
AEEMNPRRRSUUY	supernumerary
AEEOQRRSSSSTTU	sequestrators
AEFFGHILOSSTT	Feast of Lights
AEFFGIMRSSTTU	suffragettism
AEFGGHIIINRRT	airfreighting
AEFGHHOORRSTU	thoroughfares
AEFGHHORSTTTU	afterthoughts
AEFGHIILMOPRS	filmographies
AEFGHINNRRSTU	nursing father
AEFGIILLORRSU	argilliferous
AEFGIILNNNSSU	unfailingness
AEFGIILNNORTV	overinflating
AEFGIILNOPRRT	proliferating
AEFGIINOPRRTU	prefiguration
AEFGILLNSSSUW	wineglassfuls
AEFGILMNORRTU	reformulating
AEFGILNNORRWY	forewarningly
AEFGINOOPRRTW	waterproofing
AEFIIIILMNNST	infinitesimal
AEFIIIILNNSTT	infantilities
AEFIIIILMNORST	informalities
AEFIIILMNSSST	semifinalists
AEFIIILNORSTT	fertilisation
AEFIIILNORTTZ	fertilization
AEFIILLLNNOXY	inflexionally
AEFIILLLNNTUY	influentially
AEFIILLNNNTUU	uninfluential
AEFIILMNORSUU	aluminiferous
AEFIILMNORTVY	informatively
AEFIILNOOPRRT	proliferation
AEFIILNOPRSTU	platiniferous
AEFIIMNNORTUV	uninformative
AEFIIMNOOPRRT	imperforation
AEFIIMNORSSTU	staminiferous
AEFIINRRSTTTY	interstratify
AEFILMMNNOOST	monofilaments
AEFILMNOORRTU	reformulation
AEFILMORRRSSU	formularisers
AEFILMORRRSUZ	formularizers
AEFILNOOPRSSS	professionals
AEFILNOOPRSSW	passionflower
AEFILNOOPRSTV	flavoproteins
AEFIMNOOPRRST	preformations
AEFIOQRRSTUUZ	quartziferous
AEFLNNORTTUUY	unfortunately
AEGGGIINRRTTU	regurgitating
AEGGGILNNOSTU	agglutinogens
AEGGHHLOPPRRY	glyphographer
AEGGHIILMNNTU	hemagglutinin
AEGGHIIMMNOPR	mimeographing

AEGGHIINNOPST	Teng Hsiao-ping
AEGGHIINNRSTT	straightening
AEGGHILNOORTW	woolgathering
AEGGHILNORSUV	overslaughing
AEGGHINNOPRST	stenographing
AEGGHINOORSTU	South Georgian
AEGGHLOOPRRSS	glossographer
AEGGHLOPPRRTY	glyptographer
AEGGHNNOOPRRT	rontgenograph
AEGGIIINNSTTV	investigating
AEGGIIMNSSTTU	guesstimating
AEGGIINNORRTT	interrogating
AEGGIINORRTTU	regurgitation
AEGGILOORSSTT	geratologists
AEGGINNNOORSS	nonaggression
AEGGINNNORTYZ	Tenzing Norgay
AEGGINNRRSSTT	transgressing
AEGGMNNOORRST	rontgenograms
AEGHHILOPRRST	lithographers
AEGHHIOOPRRST	orthographies
AEGHHIOPPRRSY	physiographer
AEGHHIPRSSUWY	superhighways
AEGHHMNOPRRSY	hymnographers
AEGHHNOOPPRRS	phonographers
AEGHHOOPPRRST	photographers
	rephotographs
AEGHHOOPRRRST	orthographers
AEGHIILNNOORT	Lothian Region
AEGHIILNPRTVY	hypervigilant
AEGHIINNSTTUX	extinguishant
AEGHIINOOPSST	apotheosising
AEGHIINOOPSTZ	apotheosizing
AEGHIINOOSTTT	ghettoisation
AEGHIINOOTTTZ	ghettoization
AEGHIIPRRRSST	registrarship
AEGHILMOOSSTT	hematologists
AEGHILOOPRSST	phraseologist
AEGHILQRRSTTU	quarterlights
AEGHIMNORSSUW	housewarmings
AEGHIMNORTTUW	mouthwatering
AEGHIMOOPRSST	mastigophores
AEGHIOPRRSSTU	surrogateship
AEGHLLMOOORTY	moral theology
AEGHLMMOORTTY	thremmatology
AEGHMNOOOPSTT	photomontages
AEGHMNOOOPSTU	entomophagous
AEGHNOOPPRRRS	pornographers
AEGHOOPRRSTUV	photogravures
AEGIIIILNORST	originalities
AEGIIILMMNORS	memorialising
AEGIIILMMNORZ	memorializing
AEGIIILNNNRST	internalising
AEGIIILNNNRTZ	internalizing
AEGIIILNNORST	orientalising
AEGIIILNNORTZ	orientalizing
AEGIIILNORSTU	antireligious
AEGIIILNRSSTU	singularities
AEGIIIMMNSSTT	misestimating
AEGIIIMMNNOST	ingeminations
AEGIIINNOSTTV	investigation
AEGIIINNPPRRS	Pierian Spring
AEGIIINNRSTVW	West Virginian

AEGIIKLMNPRSS	marlingspikes
AEGIILLNNOSTW	wellingtonias
AEGIILLOPRSSS	aspergillosis
AEGIILMMNNSST	misalignments
AEGIILMNNNOOR	Inner Mongolia
AEGIILMNORSST	mineralogists
AEGIILMNORSYY	syringomyelia
AEGIILMNPRSST	slipstreaming
AEGIILMOOSSST	semasiologist
AEGIILNNNPSTU	peninsulating
AEGIILNNOPRSS	personalising
AEGIILNNOPRSZ	personalizing
AEGIILNNOPRTT	interpolating
AEGIIMNNOPRST	impersonating
AEGIIMNNRRRTY	intermarrying
AEGIIMNOPPRRTY	primogenitary
AEGIIMNSSSTTY	systematising
AEGIIMNSSTTYZ	systematizing
AEGIINNNRSSTT	intransigents
AEGIINNOORRTT	interrogation
AEGIINNOPPPRT	preappointing
AEGIINNORRSTV	overstraining
AEGIINNORRTUV	genitourinary
AEGIINOPPRRTX	expropriating
AEGIINORRSSTT	registrations
AEGIINORSSTTV	investigators
AEGIINORSTTVY	investigatory
AEGILLMRSSTTU	metallurgists
AEGILMMOPRSUV	gemmiparously
AEGILMNNNNOST	nonalignments
AEGILMNOOORTU	Outer Mongolia
AEGILMNOORSTY	laryngotomies
AEGILMNORSSTU	somersaulting
AEGILMOORRSTY	martyrologies
AEGILNNNORSUV	unreasoningly
AEGILNNOOOSTT	neonatologist
AEGILNOOPRRSS	progressional
AEGILNOPSTTUX	expostulating
AEGILOORSSTTT	teratologists
AEGIMNNNOORSTU	Regiomontanus
AEGIMNNORRSTT	remonstrating
AEGIMNOOPRSSU	angiospermous
AEGIMOOOPPRST	apogeotropism
AEGIMOORRRRST	agroterrorism
AEGIMOORSSSTT	gastrostomies
AEGINNNNPRSSSU	unsparingness
AEGINNNORSSST	transgression
AEGINOORRRSTT	interrogators
AEGINOOORRRTTY	interrogatory
AEGKNPPRSTUUU	Upper Tunguska
AEGLMNOORSSSU	glamorousness
AEGLMOOSSTTYY	systematology
AEGLNORRSSSUU	garrulousness
AEGNORRRSSSST	transgressors
AEHHHINOPRRRY	herniorrhaphy
AEHHHOOPPPSTY	hypophosphate
AEHHIIILMNSST	helminthiasis
AEHHILLMNPTTY	platyhelminth
AEHHILNOPPRST	philanthropes
AEHHILOPSSTTU	thiosulphates
AEHHIMNOPRSTT	theanthropism
AEHHIMOOOPSTT	homoeopathist
AEHHIMOOPSSTT	homeopathists
AEHHINOPRSTTT	theanthropist
AEHHINORRRSTY	North Ayrshire
AEHHIOPPRSTVY	physiotherapy
AEHHIORRSSTUV	South Ayrshire
AEHHLOOPPRSSY	phosphorylase
AEHHNOOOPPRTY	anthropophyte
AEHHNOOPSTTTY	photosynthate
AEHHOOOPPPRSTY	pyrophosphate
AEHHOOPRRSSST	sharpshooters
AEHIIILMNOSSS	leishmaniosis
AEHIIILOPSSTT	hospitalities
AEHIILLMNNOPY	aminophylline
AEHIILNOPRSST	relationships
	rhinoplasties
AEHIILNORSSSU	hilariousness
AEHIILPRRSSTT	hairsplitters
AEHIIMOPPRRST	imperatorship
AEHIINNOPRSTT	trephinations
AEHIINOORSSTT	theorisations
AEHIINOORSTTZ	theorizations
AEHIINOPRRSST	prehistorians
AEHIINORRSSTW	airworthiness
AEHIIRRSSSTTW	shirtwaisters
AEHILMMNORTUY	aluminothermy
AEHILMOOSTUXY	homosexuality
AEHILMOPPRSTY	amphiprostyle
AEHILOOPRSSTT	photorealists
AEHIMMMOPRSST	metamorphisms
AEHIMMNOPRTUY	immunotherapy
AEHIMMOOPRSST	metamorphosis
AEHIMNNOOPRST	enantiomorphs
AEHIMNNOSSSTT	astonishments
AEHIMNNPRSSTT	transhipments
	transshipment
AEHIMNPRSTUUY	superhumanity
AEHINOOPRRSTT	prototherians
AEHINOPRSSTTY	attorneyships
AEHIOOPPRSSST	apostrophises
AEHIOOPPRSSTZ	apostrophizes
AEHIOOPSSSTTT	osteopathists
AEHLLNNOORRTT	Northallerton
AEHLMNOOPRTVW	Wolverhampton
AEHLOPPRSSTUY	pyrosulphates
AEHMNOOPRRTTY	anthropometry
AEHMNOOPRSSSU	amorphousness
AEHNOOPRRSSSU	sarrusophones
AEIIILLLMNNST	millennialist
AEIIILLMNNORS	millionnaires
AEIIILLMNORSS	millionairess
AEIIILLMNPRRY	preliminarily
AEIIILLMNRSTY	ministerially
AEIIILLMRRSVY	verisimilarly
AEIIILMNPRTTY	amitriptyline
AEIIILNORSSTT	sterilisation
AEIIILNORSTTZ	sterilization
AEIIILNORTTUZ	reutilization
AEIIILNRSSTTT	interstitials
AEIIILPRRSSTU	spiritualiser
AEIIILPRRSTUZ	spiritualizer
AEIIILPRSSSTU	spiritualises
AEIIILPRSSTTU	spiritualties

AEIIILPRSSTUZ	spiritualizes
AEIIIMMNOSSTT	misestimation
AEIIIMNNNOSST	inseminations
AEIIIMNNOOPSTT	epitomisation
AEIIIMNOOPTTZ	epitomization
AEIIIMNOORSST	isomerisation
AEIIIMNOORSTZ	isomerization
AEIIINNORSSSV	visionariness
AEIIINNNORSTTW	winterisation
AEIIINNORTTWZ	winterization
AEIIINNOSSSTT	sensitisation
AEIIINNOSSTTZ	sensitization
AEIIINOOSSTTV	sovietisation
AEIIINOOSTTVZ	sovietization
AEIIINOPQRTTU	equipartition
AEIILLNNNOSTY	intensionally
AEIILLNNNOTTY	intentionally
AEIILLNNORTVY	inventorially
AEIILLNOQRTUV	ventriloquial
AEIILLNQRRSTU	tranquilliser
AEIILLNQRRTUZ	tranquillizer
AEIILLNQRSSTU	tranquillises
AEIILLNQRSTUZ	tranquillizes
AEIILLORRRTTY	territorially
AEIILMMORRSST	immortalisers
AEIILMMORRSTZ	immortalizers
AEIILMNNOOPRS	pronominalise
AEIILMNNOOPRZ	pronominalize
AEIILMNNOOSST	solemnisation
AEIILMNNOOSTZ	solemnization
AEIILMNOORSTT	tolerationism
AEIILMNOOSSTT	emotionalists
AEIILMNOPRSTY	impersonality
AEIILMNRSSSUV	universalisms
AEIILNNNNOTTU	unintentional
AEIILNNNNORTTU	interlunation
AEIILNNNQQSUU	quinquennials
AEIILNNOOPRTT	interpolation
AEIILNNOOSSTV	novelisations
AEIILNNOOSTVZ	novelizations
AEIILNNOOTTUV	antievolution
AEIILNOOPPRST	prepositional
AEIILNOOPSTTX	exploitations
	sexploitation
AEIILNOORSTTT	tolerationist
AEIILNOPPSTTU	Pontius Pilate
AEIILNOPRSTUV	pulverisation
AEIILNOPRTUVZ	pulverization
AEIILNPRSSSTU	spiritualness
AEIILNQRRSTUZ	tranquilizers
AEIILNRSSSTUV	universalists
AEIILOOPPRRRT	proprietorial
AEIILOPPRRRTY	proprietarily
AEIIMNNNOORST	renominations
AEIIMNNOOPRST	impersonation
AEIIMNOOPRRTT	reimportation
AEIIMNOOPRSTT	temporisation
AEIIMNOOPRTTZ	temporization
AEIIMNOSSSTTY	systemisation
AEIIMNOSSTTYZ	systemization
AEIINNNORSTTU	antineutrinos
AEIINNNORSTTV	nontransitive
AEIINNOOPPSTT	peptonisation
AEIINNOOPPTTZ	peptonization
AEIINNOOPSSTT	antepositions
AEIINNOPSSSTX	expansionists
AEIINOOPPRRTX	expropriation
AEIINOOPRSSTT	Espírito Santo
AEIINOOPRSTTX	extraposition
AEIINOORRRSTT	terrorisation
AEIINOORRRTTZ	terrorization
AEIINOPRSSTTU	Espíritu Santo
AEIINOPRSSTTV	transpositive
AEIINOPRSTTUV	vituperations
AEIINOPRRSTTT	antiterrorist
AEIINORRSSSTT	transistorise
AEIINORRSSTTZ	transistorize
AEIKKLMNNORUW	unworkmanlike
AEIKLMNOPRSST	sportsmanlike
AEILLLLPRRRST	pralltrillers
AEILLLMNOOSSS	salmonellosis
AEILLMMMNOOST	monometallism
AEILLMMNOOSTT	monometallist
AEILLNNOOOPSU	Louis Napoleon
AEILLNOPSSSSY	passionlessly
AEILLNORSSUUV	Universal Soul
AEILLOOPRRRTY	reportorially
AEILMMNNORSTU	neutral monism
AEILMMNNOTTUY	monumentality
AEILMNNOOQUYZ	Quezon y Molina
AEILMNNRSSTTU	instrumentals
AEILMNOOPRSTT	metropolitans
AEILMNOPRTTUY	importunately
AEILMNOPSSTUY	pneumatolysis
AEILMOORSSTTT	stromatolites
AEILNNORSSTUV	voluntariness
AEILNNORSTUVY	intravenously
AEILNOOPRRSTT	interpolators
AEILNOOPSTTUX	expostulation
AEILNOORRTUVY	revolutionary
AEILNRSSSTUUU	laurustinuses
AEILOOOOPPPRS	prosopopoeial
AEIMNNNOSSSUU	unanimousness
AEIMNNOOPPRTT	apportionment
AEIMNNOORRSTT	remonstration
AEIMNNORSSTTU	menstruations
AEIMNOOPRRSST	impersonators
AEIMNOPRSSSTU	reassumptions
AEIMNOPRSSTTT	Protestantism
AEIMORSSSSTTT	toastmistress
AEINNORSSSUUV	unsavouriness
AEINNORSSTTTU	sternutations
AEINOOOPPRRTT	proportionate
AEINOOOPPRRST	protonotaries
AEINOOPRSSTTT	protestations
AEIOOOOPPPRSS	prosopopoeias
AEIOOPPRRRSTX	expropriators
AEKLNPPRSSTTU	splatterpunks
AEKLOOPPRSTVV	Petropavlovsk
AELLMNOPRRSUY	supernormally
AELMNOPRSSTTU	postmenstrual
AELNNOOPSSTUY	spontaneously
AELOOPRSSTTUX	expostulators
AELOOPRSTTUXY	expostulatory

AEMMNOOORSTTU	monotrematous
AEMNNNOOSSSSUY	anonymousness
AEMNOORRRSSTT	remonstrators
AEMPRRSSSTTUU	superstratums
AENNNORSSSTUY	tyrannousness
AENOOOPPRRTXY	proparoxytone
AENOPRRSSSTUU	rapturousness
AFFGGIIMNSTUU	suffumigating
AFFGIIMNOSTUU	suffumigation
AFFIILNNOSSTU	insufflations
AFGGIINNRRSTU	transfiguring
AFGIIILNNRTUY	infuriatingly
AFGIILMNORRSU	formularising
AFGIILMNORRUZ	formularizing
AFIIIILLNNTVY	infinitivally
AFIIILNNORSTT	infiltrations
AFIIILNNOSSTT	inflationists
AFIIILNOOSSST	fossilisation
AFIIILNOOSSTZ	fossilization
AFIILLNOOOPRS	Florianópolis
AFIILLORSTTUY	flirtatiously
AFIILMNOORSUY	omnifariously
AFIILNNOORSTU	fluorinations
AFIILNORSSTUU	sulfurisation
AFIILOPRSSSUY	fissiparously
AFIIMMNNORSST	misinformants
AFILNOPPRRUUV	flavopurpurin
AFIMNORRSSSTT	transformists
AGGGIIINNRRTTU	ingurgitating
AGGHHIILNOPRT	lithographing
AGGHHINOOPPRT	photographing
AGGHHMOPPRSSY	sphygmographs
AGGHHMOPPRSYY	sphygmography
AGGHIIKNNSSTV	thanksgivings
AGGHIILLNNSUY	languishingly
AGGHIILNNOOST	anthologising
AGGHIILNNOOTZ	anthologizing
AGGHILNOOPTZ	pathologizing
AGGHILOOPRSST	graphologists
AGGIIILNNOSTU	isoagglutinin
AGGIIILNNRSSU	singularising
AGGIIILNNRSUZ	singularizing
AGGIIILNNSTTY	instigatingly
AGGIIINNORTTU	ingurgitation
AGGIIJNNRUUXY	Xinjiang Uygur
AGGIILNOOSTTU	tautologising
AGGIILNOOTTUZ	tautologizing
AGGIILNRSTTUU	gutturalising
AGGIILNRTTUUZ	gutturalizing
AGGILLNOORSTY	laryngologist
AGGILNOOORSST	organologists
AGGILOORSSSTT	gastrologists
AGHHIILMNRSTY	nightmarishly
AGHHIINOPPSST	phosphatising
AGHHIINOPPSTZ	phosphatizing
AGHHILMNOPPSU	ploughmanship
AGHHIMNOORSTT	orthognathism
AGHHINOOPPRST	phonographist
	phosphorating
AGHHINOOPRSST	sharpshooting
AGHHIOOPRRSTT	orthographist
AGHHLLMOOOPTV	ophthalmology

AGHHLMNNOOOPT	monophthongal
AGHHNOOORSTTU	orthognathous
AGHIIILLMNTUY	humiliatingly
AGHIIILNOPSST	hospitalising
AGHIIILNOPSTZ	hospitalizing
AGHIIILNPRSTT	hairsplitting
AGHIILNNOSSTY	astonishingly
AGHIINNPPRSST	transshipping
AGHIINOPSSSTY	hypostasising
AGHIINOPSSTTY	hypostatising
AGHIINOPSSTYZ	hypostasizing
AGHIINOPSTTYZ	hypostatizing
AGHILMNOOOOST	homologations
AGHIMNOOPRSST	monographists
AGHIMSSSTTUUU	tsutsugamushi
AGHINOOPSTTTT	photostatting
AGHNNOOOPSUUV	Souphanouvong
AGHOOOPPPRRSY	prosopography
AGIIIILNNOSTV	invigilations
AGIIIIMNNRSTU	miniaturising
AGIIIIMNNRTUZ	miniaturizing
AGIIILLLNTTTY	titillatingly
AGIIILLMNNRSTU	trilingualism
AGIIILMNNNPRT	malimprinting
AGIIILMMNORST	immortalising
AGIIILMMNORTZ	immortalizing
AGIIILNNQRTUZ	tranquilizing
AGIIIMNOPPRRT	impropriating
AGIIINNPRSSSU	prussianising
AGIIINNPRSSUZ	prussianizing
AGIILLMNSTTUY	stimulatingly
AGIILLNOOSSTY	syllogisation
AGIILLNOOSTYZ	syllogization
AGIILMOOPPRST	plagiotropism
AGIILMOOPRSTT	primatologist
AGIILNNOPRSTY	patronisingly
AGIILNNOPRTYZ	patronizingly
AGIIMNOORRSUV	graminivorous
AGILLNOOPSSTY	palynologists
AGILMMNOOSTUY	numismatology
AGILMNOOPRSTU	promulgations
AGILMOOOSSSTT	somatologists
AGILMOORRSTTY	martyrologist
AGILNNOOOPRST	prolongations
AGILOOPPRSSTY	papyrologists
AGIMMNOOPRSUZ	zoosporangium
AGIMNOORSSSTT	gastronomists
AGLLOOOSTTUUY	tautologously
AHHMMNOOOPPRT	anthropomorph
AHHNOOOPPRSTY	anthroposophy
AHIIIILNOOPRRT	horripilation
AHIIILNOPSTTY	inhospitality
AHIILMPRSSTTU	triumphalists
AHIILNOORTTYZ	horizontality
AHIIMNOPRSSTT	misanthropist
AHIINNOOPSTTY	hypnotisation
AHIINNOOPTTYZ	hypnotization
AHIIOPPRRTTUVY	hypopituitary
AHIJNNOPRSTUZ	zinjanthropus
AHILLMMOOPRSS	allomorphisms
AHILLNOOPSSUY	anisophyllous
AHILNOPPSSTTU	postulantship

AHIMNOOOPRSTT	somatotrophin	BBCENOORRSSTU	broncobusters
AHIMNOPPRSSST	sportsmanship	BBCGIINNRSSUU	unsubscribing
AHINOOPSSSSTU	sousaphonists	BBCIILMNOSTUY	incombustibly
AHKLNNOOPPTTY	phytoplankton	BBDEEIIKNOORS	bookbinderies
AHMMOOOOPRSTU	ommatophorous	BBDEELNRSSSUU	blunderbusses
AHOOOOPRRRSSTU	arthrosporous	BBEEEEINORRSSY	boysenberries
AIIIILNNOQSTU	inquisitional	BBEEHLORSSTTU	bottlebrushes
AIIIILNOQRSTU	inquisitorial	BBEGGIMNNORUY	moneygrubbing
AIIIIMNPPSSSS	Mississippian	BBHIIIILLMOPS	bibliophilism
AIIILLMNNOSTU	illuminations	BBIIILLOOPSST	bibliopolists
AIIILLMNPSTUY	pusillanimity	BCCCDEIIMRRSU	circumscribed
AIIILLNNOTTUY	intuitionally	BCCCEEHILPRUZ	Czech Republic
AIIILNNOSTTTU	institutional	BCCCEIIMRRRSU	circumscriber
AIIILNOOSSSTT	isolationists	BCCCEIIMRRSSU	circumscribes
AIIILPRSSSTTU	spiritualists	BCCCHINOOOPRS	bronchoscopic
AIIIMMNNOSSTU	immunisations	BCCEEGNOORTUW	Concertgebouw
AIIIMMNNOSTUZ	immunizations	BCCEEHKLMOORS	checkerblooms
AIIIMNNORSSTT	ministrations	BCCEEHNORRSSS	crossbenchers
AIIIMNOOPPRRT	impropriation	BCCEEIILORRTT	triboelectric
AIIIMNOOPRSTV	improvisation	BCCEEIINRSTTY	cyberneticist
AIIIMNOOPSSTT	optimisations	BCCEEIKKKNORR	knickerbocker
AIIIMNOOPSTTZ	optimizations	BCCEEILORRTTU	turboelectric
AIIINNNOOSSTU	unionisations	BCCEFIIIINOST	bioscientific
AIIINNNOOSTTV	innovationist	BCCEHNOOOPRSS	bronchoscopes
AIIINNNOOSTUZ	unionizations	BCCEIIIJOSTTV	objectivistic
AIIINOOPPRSTT	propitiations	BCCEIIILNNNOV	inconvincible
AIIINOPRSSTTT	partitionists	BCCEIILLOOPSU	ebullioscopic
AIIIOOPPRSTTU	propitiatious	BCCEILMOORSTY	motorbicycles
AIIIOOPRTVVVY	ovoviviparity	BCCEILNORSTTU	constructible
AIIJNOOPSTTUX	juxtaposition	BCCGIIIILMOOOR	microbiologic
AIIILLMNOPSSUU	pusillanimous	BCCGIILLMNOOU	symbolic logic
AIIILLNNOOPTTU	antipollution	BCCIIILNNNOVY	inconvincibly
AIIILLNNORTTUY	nutritionally	BCDDEEEEIINOSS	disobediences
AIIILLNNORTUVY	involuntarily	BCDDEEEEILNSSU	deducibleness
AIIILLNOOPRSVY	provisionally	BCDDEEEEIMNRSU	disencumbered
AIIILLNORSSTTU	illustrations	BCDDEEEILNNOTU	nondeductible
AIIILMMNOPPSSU	Numa Pompilius	BCDDEFIINORTY	Forbidden City
AIIILMNOPRSSTT	trampolinists	BCDDEIIIILTTUY	deductibility
AIIILNNOSTTUUV	invultuations	BCDDGILLNOORU	bloodcurdling
AIIILNOOOPPRST	propositional	BCDEEEKORRSST	stockbreeders
AIIILNOOPPSSTU	suppositional	BCDEEGIKNORST	stockbreeding
AIIILNOOPSSSTU	San Luis Potosí	BCDEEGINORRSS	crossbreeding
AIIMNNORSSSST	transmissions	BCDEEIIILNNRS	indiscernible
AIIMNOOQSSTTU	misquotations	BCDEEIILNNNOS	incondensible
AIIMOOPPRRRST	impropriators	BCDEIIIILNRTY	incredibility
AIIMOOPRRSTVY	improvisatory	BCDEIIILNNRSY	indiscernibly
AIINNNOPSSTUU	Antoninus Pius	BCDEIILNORTUY	indolebutyric
AIINNOOOPSSST	opsonisations	BCDEIIMNOOSTY	endosymbiotic
AIINNOOOPSSTZ	opsonizations	BCDIIILOORRTY	corrodibility
AIINNOOPRSSTT	transposition	BCDIIILOPRTUY	producibility
AIIOOOPRSUVVV	ovoviviparous	BCEEEEFFILRSV	effervescible
AILLNOOPSSTTY	polytonalists	BCEEEEGHRRSSU	cheeseburgers
AILMNNOOSTUUY	mountainously	BCEEEFGIINNRR	birefringence
AILMOOOPSSSTX	toxoplasmosis	BCEEEGIINORST	bioenergetics
AILNOOOPPRRST	proportionals	BCEEEGILLNORT	cobelligerent
AILNORSSTTUVY	voluntaryists	BCEEEHIKLRRSU	huckleberries
AIMNNNOOSTUWY	Snowy Mountain	BCEEEHILMOPST	phlebectomies
AIOORRSSSTTTU	astrotourists	BCEEEHLNNOORZ	chlorobenzene
BBCEEGIKNNRRU	rubbernecking	BCEEEIILMORTT	biotelemetric
BBCEEIORRSSUV	oversubscribe	BCEEEIILMPPRT	imperceptible
BBCEGHILNRSTU	nightclubbers	BCEEEIJNOSSTV	objectiveness
BBCEIILMNOSTU	incombustible	BCEEEILMMOOST	embolectomies

BCEEEEIMMORSTY	embryectomies
BCEEEIRRSSSTT	bittercresses
BCEEENPPRSSTU	prepubescents
BCEEGHHNOORST	Hertogenbosch
BCEEGIKLNNOTT	bottlenecking
BCEEGILMNNRUY	encumberingly
BCEEHIKLMPRRU	Khmer Republic
BCEEIILMPPRTY	imperceptibly
BCEEIILNNORTV	inconvertible
BCEEIILNPSSTU	insusceptible
BCEEIILPPRRST	prescriptible
BCEEILNPSSTUU	unsusceptible
BCEEIMMOSSTTU	subcommittees
BCEELLNOOSSTY	obsolescently
BCEELMMOORSTU	coulombmeters
BCEFGIIJNSTUY	subjectifying
BCEGHILNOOOTY	biotechnology
BCEGIIILNORRS	incorrigibles
BCEGIILMNNRUY	incumberingly
BCEGIILOOOSST	bioecologists
BCEGIINPRRSSU	superscribing
BCEGIKLNOSSTU	bluestockings
BCEHIIILPRRSU	Irish Republic
BCEIIIILQRSTU	equilibristic
BCEIIINOSSSTT	bioscientists
BCEIIJSSSTTUV	subjectivists
BCEIILNNORTVY	inconvertibly
BCEIILNOPRRTU	incorruptible
BCEIILNPSSTUY	insusceptibly
BCEIINNOOORSV	bioconversion
BCEIJLNSTUUVY	subjunctively
BCEILMNOOPRVY	polyembryonic
BCEILORSTTUVY	obstructively
BCEINNNOSSTTU	subcontinents
BCELLORSTUUUY	tuberculously
BCERRSSSTTUUU	substructures
BCGHILNOOOORY	chronobiology
BCGHILOOOPSYY	psychobiology
BCGIIIILORRTY	corrigibility
BCGIILOOORSTY	cryobiologist
BCHIIILNOORST	bronchiolitis
BCHIIIOPSSSTY	biophysicists
BCIIIIILMMSTY	immiscibility
BCIIIIILNNTVY	invincibility
BCIIILNOPRRTUY	incorruptibly
BCIIMMNOOSSSU	subcommission
BCIINNOORSTTU	contributions
BCIINOPRSSSTU	subscriptions
BDDEEEEIMMRRS	disremembered
BDDEEEGINNRRU	underbreeding
BDDEEEEILLMOSW	disembowelled
BDDEEIILNOSTY	disobediently
BDDEEIIMMNOST	disembodiment
BDDEEIIRRSTTU	redistributed
BDDEEILMRSSTU	middlebusters
BDDEEILNNRSSU	unbridledness
BDDEEIMNNRSTU	disburdenment
BDDEENNNOSSUU	unboundedness
BDDEGHILMORSU	Middlesbrough
BDDEIILMMORSW	middlebrowism
BDDEIINRSTTUU	undistributed
BDEEEEIMMMRRS	misremembered

BDEEEEFGIKRRRS	Frederiksberg
BDEEEEGHINNSST	benightedness
BDEEEEGIINNRRT	interbreeding
BDEEEEHIINNRRS	Inner Hebrides
BDEEEEHILLMNSU	unembellished
BDEEEEHIORRSTU	Outer Hebrides
BDEEEEHMORRSTU	mouthbreeders
BDEEEEIILLNSS	indelibleness
BDEEEEIMMMNRST	dismemberment
BDEEEELNNSSSSU	unblessedness
BDEEFIIIILNSTY	defensibility
BDEEFILLNORSU	bellfoundries
BDEEFLLOOPRTU	bulletproofed
BDEEGGHIILMRT	thimblerigged
BDEEGIILLNRWY	bewilderingly
BDEEGIILMNOSW	disemboweling
BDEEGIILNRSSV	Blessed Virgin
BDEEGINNNNSSU	unbendingness
BDEEGINNOORRUV	overburdening
BDEEGINNOORRRS	Borders Region
BDEEHIILMTTTW	thimblewitted
BDEEHILMOOPST	phlebotomised
BDEEHILMOOPTZ	phlebotomized
BDEEIIILNSSVW	divisibleness
BDEEIIILNTTXY	extendibility
BDEEIIMRRSTTU	turbidimeters
BDEEIIRRSSTTU	redistributes
BDEEIMNRSSSTU	disbursements
BDEELLNOOSSSS	bloodlessness
BDEELNNOSSSSU	boundlessness
BDEELNOSSSSTU	doubtlessness
BDEFGGHIIORSS	Bridge of Sighs
BDEFHILOORSTW	Bosworth Field
BDEGHHINOOORS	neighborhoods
BDEGHHINOOORU	neighbourhood
BDEGHHOORRSTU	thoroughbreds
BDEGIIIILSTTY	digestibility
BDEGIIILMNORS	disembroiling
BDEGIILLMNSSY	dissemblingly
BDEGILLNOOSTT	bloodlettings
BDEHHIIILLOPPT	Philip the Bold
BDEHHMMNOOOORRS	rhombohedrons
BDEHMOOORRSTU	mouthbrooders
BDEHNOOOPRSTU	boustrophedon
BDEIIIIILLNTUY	ineludibility
BDEIIIRSSTTUV	distributives
BDEIIMNOOSSSY	endosymbiosis
BDEILLOOPRSSW	possible world
BDFFIIIILSTUY	diffusibility
BDGGIIILLNOSY	disobligingly
BDHIIIIINNOST	disinhibition
BDIIILLOSSTUY	dissolubility
BDIIINORSSTTU	distributions
BEEEEEFLMNNST	enfeeblements
BEEEEHILNPRRS	reprehensible
BEEEEHILNSTWW	betweenwhiles
BEEEELMMNSTZZ	embezzlements
BEEEGGGIRRSUV	veggieburgers
BEEEGIILLLNSS	illegibleness
BEEEGIMNNORSSY	embryogenesis
BEEEHIKMOPRRS	Pembrokeshire
BEEEHIKRRSSTW	West Berkshire

BEEEEHILLMMNST	embellishment
BEEEEHILLMORSV	overembellish
BEEEEHILNPRRSY	reprehensibly
BEEEEIILNPRSSX	inexpressible
BEEEEIILPRRRSS	irrepressible
BEEEEILLMNSTTT	belittlements
BEEEEILLMORSTU	ebulliometers
BEEEEILNPRSSSU	supersensible
BEEEEILNRSSSTT	brittlenesses
BEEEEIMMNRRSTU	reimbursement
BEEEEINNNORSTZ	nitrobenzenes
BEEEEINOSSSSSV	obsessiveness
BEEEEINRSSSTTU	butterinesses
BEEEELLNORSSSU	resolubleness
BEEEENNORSSSTU	tenebrousness
BEEFGINRRSTTU	butterfingers
BEEFHIMNRRSTU	refurbishment
BEEFIIIILLRTXY	reflexibility
BEEFIILNNSSSU	infusibleness
BEEFIILRRSSTU	filibusterers
BEEFILLMORSUU	umbelliferous
BEEGGHIILMRRT	thimblerigger
BEEGHHLORSUUY	Burghley House
BEEGHILNORSSU	neighbourless
BEEGIILLNNUVY	unbelievingly
BEEGILMNNRSSU	lumberingness
BEEGLOORRSTTT	globetrotters
BEEHIIINORSTX	exhibitioners
BEEHILMOOPSST	phlebotomises
BEEHILMOOPSTZ	phlebotomizes
BEEHILNOOORTZ	Belo Horizonte
BEEHILNORRSST	brotherliness
BEEHIMMNNOPRS	nonmembership
BEEHINNOPPRRU	buprenorphine
BEEIIIILNSSST	sensibilities
BEEIIILMMPRSS	impermissible
BEEIIILNNSSSV	invisibleness
BEEIIILNSTTXY	extensibility
BEEIIILRRSTVY	reversibility
BEEIILNOPRRSS	irresponsible
BEEIILNPRRTTU	interruptible
BEEIILNPRSSXY	inexpressibly
BEEIILPRRRSSY	irrepressibly
BEEIILRRTTUVY	retributively
BEEILLNNOSSSU	insolubleness
BEEILNPRSSSUY	supersensibly
BEEILNRSSTUVY	subserviently
BEEIMNNOSSSUW	businesswomen
BEEINNORRSTUW	winterbournes
BEEINORSSSTUV	obtrusiveness
BEELLMOORSTUY	troublesomely
BEENNOOSSSTUU	bounteousness
BEERRSSSSSTTU	stressbusters
BEFFGINNNORRTU	burnt offering
BEFGHIINRRSSU	refurbishings
BEFGIIILNRSTU	filibustering
BEFGIINNOORSU	fibrinogenous
BEFGILLOORSUU	globuliferous
BEFIIIILLNTXY	inflexibility
BEFIIILMRSSTU	filibusterism
BEFIIOOORRSST	osteofibrosis
BEFILNNOSSTUU	bountifulness
BEGGGIIJNRTTU	jitterbugging
BEGGHIINNNORR	herringboning
BEGGIIIIILLNTY	negligibility
BEGGILNOORTTT	globetrotting
BEGGINNNOORUU	bourguignonne
BEGHHIORRRSUX	Roxburghshire
BEGHIILLNORTT	Little Bighorn
BEGHIILNOPRSY	hyperbolising
BEGHIILNOPRYZ	hyperbolizing
BEGHILMNOOOXY	oxyhemoglobin
BEGHILNNORUUY	unneighbourly
BEGIIIIILLLNTY	ineligibility
BEGIILOOOSSTX	exobiologists
BEGILMOORSSTY	embryologists
BEGINRSSSSTTU	stressbusting
BEHIIIIMNOSTX	exhibitionism
BEHIIIINOSTTX	exhibitionist
BEHIIILOPRTVY	prohibitively
BEHIMMRSSTUU	British Museum
BEHILMOOPSSTT	phlebotomists
BEHILOORRSUVY	herbivorously
BEHIMNOOSSSTY	tomboyishness
BEIIIIILNRSST	rinsibilities
BEIIIILMRSSTY	remissibility
BEIIIILNNSSTY	insensibility
BEIIIILNRTTVY	invertibility
BEIIIILOPSSST	possibilities
BEIIIILORSSTT	torsibilities
BEIIIILRSSTTY	resistibility
BEIIILMMPRSSY	impermissibly
BEIIILMNORSST	intromissible
BEIIILNOSSTTY	ostensibility
BEIIILNOOSSSUV	obliviousness
BEIILNOPRRSSY	irresponsibly
BEIIOPRSSTTUU	subreptitious
BEILMOOOPRSSY	polyribosomes
BEILNORSTUUVY	unobtrusively
BEIMNOPSSSTUU	bumptiousness
BEINNOOOSSSUX	obnoxiousness
BELNOORSSSTUU	troublousness
BFILLOORSTUUU	tubuliflorous
BIIIILMOPSSTY	impossibility
BIINOSSSTTTUU	substitutions
BILMORSSTUUUY	rumbustiously
BILOOOPPRRSUY	opprobriously
CCCCEEINNOPSU	concupiscence
CCCCEIOOPRSTT	streptococcic
CCCDEEEENNRRSU	recrudescence
CCCDEEHIIOPRT	cercopithecid
CCCDEIIMNRSUU	uncircumcised
CCCDEIIORSSTY	cysticercoids
CCCDHIIIOOPRS	dichroiscopic
CCCDHIIOOOPRS	dichrooscopic
CCCEEEEINRSSX	excrescencies
CCCEEEFIMNRRU	circumference
CCCEEEIORSTUX	coexecutrices
CCCEEEENORRRSU	reoccurrences
CCCEEFILMNRUU	circumfluence
CCCEEHKNORSTU	counterchecks
CCCEEILNNOSTU	noctilucences
CCCEEILOOPRST	electroscopic
CCCEENNNOORRU	nonoccurrence

CCCEFHMNOOORR	French Morocco
CCCEGHIKNORSS	crosschecking
CCCEGIMNNOOSU	meningococcus
CCCEHIIMOSTYZ	schizomycetic
CCCEIIILORSUV	vicious circle
CCCEIIMMNOOOR	microeconomic
CCCEIIMNOOOOS	socioeconomic
CCCEIINNORTTY	concentricity
CCCEILMPRSTUY	circumspectly
CCCEIOOPPRSST	spectroscopic
CCCEKNORSSTTU	concertstucks
CCCEOOPRSSTTU	streptococcus
CCCIIIMNORSSU	circumcisions
CCCIIIIMORRSTU	microcircuits
CCCIIOOOPRRTT	corticotropic
CCDDEEGINNNOS	condescending
CCDDEENORSTTU	deconstructed
CCDEEEEEFNRSV	defervescence
CCDEEEEILNQSU	deliquescence
CCDEEEEILNSST	delitescences
CCDEEEEMNSSTU	detumescences
CCDEEEINNOSST	conceitedness
CCDEEEINOPSSU	pseudoscience
CCDEEELLNOSST	collectedness
CCDEEENNNORSS	concernedness
CCDEEEOORRRTV	overcorrected
CCDEEHIILNNPY	phencyclidine
CCDEEHILORRTY	hydroelectric
CCDEEHKLOSTTU	shuttlecocked
CCDEEIILLOSTV	collectivised
CCDEEIILLOTVZ	collectivized
CCDEEIINNOSTV	disconnective
CCDEEILMNOPSY	encyclopedism
CCDEEILNOPSTY	encyclopedist
CCDEEIMOORRTT	microdetector
CCDEEINNNOOSS	condescension
CCDEEINNORSST	disconnecters
CCDEEINNOSSUV	conduciveness
CCDEELNNNORUY	unconcernedly
CCDEELNNNOTUY	unconnectedly
CCDEENORRSTTU	reconstructed
CCDEENORSSSTU	conductresses
CCDEGIINNNOST	disconnecting
CCDEGIINNORST	disconcerting
CCDEHIIOOPRSS	dichroiscopes
CCDEHIOOOPRSS	dichrooscopes
CCDEIINNNOOST	disconnection
CCDEIINNOORST	disconcertion
CCDEIMNOORSTU	semiconductor
CCDEINNNOOTUV	nonconductive
CCDEINNORSTTU	unconstricted
CCDGIIMNNOSTU	misconducting
CCDHINOOPRSTU	conductorship
CCDNNNOOORSTU	nonconductors
CCEEEEEFFNRSV	effervescence
CCEEEEEFFLNORS	efflorescence
CCEEEEEGIINRSV	vicegerencies
CCEEEEEJNNSSUV	juvenescences
CCEEEEFILNNORS	inflorescence
CCEEEFILORRRT	ferroelectric
CCEEEFNOORRRT	ferroconcrete
CCEEEHHIKORRS	chokecherries

CCEEEHIIMNPSY	chimneypieces
CCEEEEHIINNORS	incoherencies
CCEEEHIPRTTUY	hypereutectic
CCEEEHKLLPRSS	spellcheckers
CCEEEHMOOPRRT	chemoreceptor
CCEEEIIIMNPPR	impercipience
CCEEEIILOPRTZ	piezoelectric
CCEEEIIMNNRSS	reminiscences
CCEEEIINNNNOV	inconvenience
CCEEEILLRRSSU	Euler's circles
CCEEEILMNNORT	reconcilement
CCEEEILMNNRST	encirclements
CCEEEILMORRTT	electrometric
CCEEEIMMNSSUU	Science Museum
CCEEEIMNNSSTU	intumescences
CCEEEINNNOQSU	inconsequence
CCEEEINNRRRTU	intercurrence
CCEEEELOOPRSST	electroscopes
CCEEEMMMNNOST	commencements
CCEEFFIIINNSU	insufficience
CCEEFFIIINSSU	sufficiencies
CCEEFIIINOPRS	proficiencies
CCEEFIIINPRST	interspecific
	prescientific
CCEEFINNOORST	confectioners
CCEEFINNOORTY	confectionery
CCEEGHIINOSTZ	schizogenetic
CCEEGHILMPRYY	hyperglycemic
CCEEGHINOPSTY	psychogenetic
CCEEGIINNNOST	contingencies
CCEEGIINNOPRV	preconceiving
CCEEGIINORTTY	egocentricity
CCEEGILNORTTU	electrocuting
CCEEGINNNORST	constringence
CCEEGINNOPRRT	preconcerting
CCEEHHNNRRSTUW	Western Church
CCEEHIIILLOPRT	electrophilic
CCEEHILNOOPRT	electrophonic
CCEEHILOOPRTT	photoelectric
CCEEHIMOSSTYZ	schizomycetes
CCEEHINNOSSTU	inescutcheons
CCEEHINORSSTT	crotchetiness
CCEEHLNOSSSTU	scutcheonless
CCEEIIIOPRRST	reciprocities
CCEEIILLOSSTV	collectivises
CCEEIILLOSTVZ	collectivizes
CCEEIILNOORST	isoelectronic
CCEEIIMNORSSV	misconceivers
CCEEIIMNRTUVV	circumventive
CCEEIINNOSSST	consistencies
CCEEIINNOSTUV	inconsecutive
CCEEIINNQSTTU	cinquecentist
CCEEIJMNORSTU	misconjecture
CCEEILLNNNORT	Lincoln Center
CCEEILLNOORST	recollections
CCEEILLORSTTY	electrolytics
CCEEILNNORSTV	conventiclers
CCEEILNOORTTU	electrocution
CCEEILNOSSSUV	occlusiveness
CCEEILNOSTUVY	consecutively
CCEEILOPRRSTY	pyroelectrics
CCEEILORSTTUY	reticulocytes

CCEEEIMNRRSTUV	circumventers
CCEEIMHOPRRSTT	spectrometric
CCEEEINNNOORST	reconnections
CCEEEINNNORSTT	interconnects
CCEEEINNOOPPRT	preconception
CCEEEINNOORSSS	concessioners
CCEEEINNORRSST	incorrectness
CCEEEINOOPRRST	nocireceptors
CCEEEOOPPRSSST	spectroscopes
CCEEFFIIINNSUY	insufficiency
CCEEFIIINNNOST	nonscientific
CCEEFIILMNORUX	circumflexion
CCEEFKLOOORSUW	cuckooflowers
CCEEGIIIMNNOSV	misconceiving
CCEEGIIMNNRTUV	circumventing
CCEEGILMOOOSTY	cosmeticology
CCEEGINNNORSTY	constringency
CCEEHHIINOPRSZ	schizophrenic
CCEEHHIMMOORRT	thermochromic
CCEEHHIMOOPRRS	chromospheric
CCEEHIIKNOPSTY	psychokinetic
CCEEHIILOSSTTY	cholecystitis
CCEEHIIMORSSTW	microswitches
CCEEHILLOOPRST	collectorship
CCEEHIMOPRSSTY	psychometrics
CCEEHIMORSTTYY	cytochemistry
CCEEHINOPRSSTU	succentorship
CCEEHIOOPRRSTU	urethroscopic
CCEEHIORRSSSST	christcrosses
CCEEHMOOPSTUVY	phycomycetous
CCEEHNOOPRSSSY	synchroscopes
CCEEIIINOORRST	oneirocritics
CCEEIILLOSSTTV	collectivists
CCEEIIMNNNOOST	connectionism
CCEEIIMNNOOPST	misconception
CCEEIIMNNORTUV	circumvention
CCEEIIMNOOSSSU	semiconscious
CCEEIINNNOSSTY	inconsistency
CCEEIINNOOPRTV	preconviction
CCEEIINNOORSTV	reconvictions
CCEEIINNOOSSTU	conscientious
CCEEIINNORSSTT	concertinists
CCEEIJLNNOTUVY	conjunctively
CCEEILLOOOPSSS	oscilloscopes
CCEEILNOOOOPSS	colonoscopies
CCEEIMMOOPRRTU	microcomputer
CCEEIMNORRSTUV	circumventors
CCEEINNOOSSSUV	consciousness
CCEEIOOOPPRSST	proctoscopies
CCENNNNOORRTU	nonconcurrent
CCENOORRRSTTU	reconstructor
CCENOPRRSSTTU	preconstructs
CCENORRRSSSTU	crosscurrents
CCFGIILLNNOTY	conflictingly
CCFIIIMMORRST	form criticism
CCFIIMNORSSUU	circumfusions
CCGHILNOOOSST	conchologists
CCGHINOOPSSTY	psychognostic
CCGIIIILNRSTY	criticisingly
CCGIIIILNRTYZ	criticizingly
CCGIINORRSSSS	crisscrossing
CCHHHIIIMNOTY	Ho Chi Minh City

CCHHIILOPPRSY	psychrophilic
CCHHIOPPSSSVY	psychophysics
CCHIILNOOPRSU	councilorship
CCHIINNORSSTY	synchronistic
CCHIINNORSTYY	synchronicity
CCHIIOPRRSSTU	Corpus Christi
CCHILMOOPTTYY	lymphocytotic
CCIIMOOPRSSST	microscopists
CCIINNOOPRSST	conscriptions
CCIINNOOPSSUU	inconspicuous
CCIINNOORSSTT	constrictions
CCILMOORSSTTY	motorcyclists
CCILNNOOSSUUY	unconsciously
CCILNOOPSSUUY	conspicuously
CCINNOORSSTTU	constructions
CDDDEEEINNSSU	undecidedness
CDDEEEELLOPTU	leucodepleted
CDDEEEENNPRTU	unprecedented
CDDEEEIINNRRT	inner-directed
CDDEEEELNOORS	enclosed order
CDDEEEMMNNOOU	unrecommended
CDDEEIIILOPST	depoliticised
CDDEEIIILOPTZ	depoliticized
CDDEEIINNOORT	reconditioned
CDDEEILNOOTUY	eudicotyledon
CDDEEINOSSSUU	deciduousness
CDDEGIIMMNNOS	discommending
CDDEGIMNNOOPU	decompounding
CDDEHHILOORRY	hydrochloride
CDDEHLNORSTUU	thunderclouds
CDDEIIILNNPSU	undisciplined
CDDEIINNNOOTU	unconditioned
CDDEILMOOPSSY	discomposedly
CDDEILNOOPRSS	scolopendrids
CDDELLLMOORSY	mollycoddlers
CDDGILLLMNOOY	mollycoddling
CDDIIMMOOOSSU	discommodious
CDEEEEEILNORT	electioneered
CDEEEEEINPRRX	reexperienced
CDEEEEELMORRT	decelerometer
CDEEEEFINSSTV	defectiveness
CDEEEEFLLNSSY	defencelessly
CDEEEEHIILMNW	medicine wheel
CDEEEEINNPRRX	inexperienced
CDEEEEIKLPRSW	pickerelweeds
CDEEEEINNPRUX	unexperienced
CDEEEEINPSSTV	deceptiveness
CDEEEEIORRSVX	overexercised
CDEEEFHILRSST	chesterfields
CDEEEFILNNSST	inflectedness
CDEEEFILNSSTU	deceitfulness
CDEEEFINORTTU	counterfeited
CDEEEFLMOORRT	electroformed
CDEEEGILNORRT	telerecording
CDEEEGLOORRRT	Torre del Greco
CDEEEHMOORRST	stereochromed
CDEEEHORRSTTV	overstretched
CDEEEIIINRSVV	divine service
CDEEEIILNNQSU	delinquencies
CDEEEIIORRSSV	rediscoveries
CDEEEILMNORST	declinometers
CDEEEIMOPRSSV	decompressive

CDEEEINNOORRT	reconnoitered	CDEEELLNOSSSSU	cloudlessness
CDEEEINNOPRVW	New Providence	CDEEELNORSSSUU	credulousness
CDEEEINNORSST	reconditeness	CDEELNPSSTUUY	unsuspectedly
CDEEEINSSSTUV	seductiveness	CDEENNOOPRRST	correspondent
CDEEEMNNNOSTU	denouncements	CDEENNOOPRSST	corespondents
CDEEEMNNOPRSU	unrecompensed	CDEENNOORSSTT	contortedness
CDEEEENNNOSSTT	contentedness	CDEENNRRRSTUU	undercurrents
CDEEEENOORRSTV	seroconverted	CDEENOOORSTXY	deoxycortones
CDEEEOOPRRTTV	overprotected	CDEEOOPRSSTUV	pseudovectors
CDEEFHKMOOORT	Dome of the Rock	CDEEPRRSSTTUU	superstructed
CDEEFILPRSSTU	disrespectful	CDEFGIINNNOSS	confidingness
CDEEFIMNNORSS	confirmedness	CDEFIIINNOSST	disinfections
CDEEFINNOORTV	overconfident	CDEFIINOOPRRT	indirect proof
CDEEGGIINNORS	derecognising	CDEGHILNNORTU	underclothing
CDEEGGIINNORZ	derecognizing	CDEGHILOOPSSY	psychologised
CDEEGHIMNNOPR	comprehending	CDEGHILOOPSYZ	psychologized
CDEEGIILRRSTY	triglycerides	CDEGIIIMNOSTZ	domesticizing
CDEEGIINNOORT	derecognition	CDEGIIMOOOPSS	sigmoidoscope
CDEEGIINNORRS	reconsidering	CDEGIINNNOSTT	discontenting
CDEEGIINORRSV	rediscovering	CDEGIINNORRTU	reintroducing
CDEEGIINPRSST	disrespecting	CDEGIINNORSTU	rediscounting
CDEEGIINRRSTT	derestricting	CDEGIINPRSSUU	superinducing
CDEEGILOPPSTY	glycopeptides	CDEGIINOOOSUY	gynodioecious
CDEEGIMNNNOPR	precondemning	CDEGILLNNOORT	decontrolling
CDEEGIMNOPRSS	decompressing	CDEGILNNOOORY	endocrinology
CDEEGINNNORSTU	countersigned	CDEGINNOOPRRS	corresponding
CDEEGLOORSTUX	dextroglucose	CDEGINOOPRRUV	overproducing
CDEEHHIILNORX	chlorhexidine	CDEHHIOOORRST	rhodochrosite
CDEEHHOOOPPRSS	phosphoresced	CDEHIIILPPSSS	discipleships
CDEEHIINOPRTY	dryopithecine	CDEHIIIOPRSTY	spheroidicity
CDEEEHILLNSSSS	childlessness	CDEHIIKNORSTY	hydrokinetics
CDEEHIOOPTTUY	hypoeutectoid	CDEHIIMNOPRRU	perichondrium
CDEEHNNOOOPPS	phonendoscope	CDEHIINOOOPRS	conidiophores
CDEEIIIIILMSVZ	semicivilized	CDEHIIOOOPPRT	photoperiodic
CDEEIIIILOPSST	depoliticises	CDEHIIOPPRTTY	pteridophytic
CDEEIIILOPSTZ	depoliticizes	CDEHIIOPRRSST	directorships
CDEEIIIMNRSTT	deterministic	CDEHILLOOPRSY	policyholders
CDEEIIIMOSSTT	domesticities	CDEHILMNOOOORS	monochlorides
CDEEIIINNSSTV	disincentives	CDEHIMNOOORSS	chondriosomes
CDEEIIILNOPRST	predilections	CDEHIMOOOPPRSU	pseudomorphic
CDEEIILNOSSSU	deliciousness	CDEHIMOORTTYY	thyroidectomy
CDEEIIILOPSSTV	velocipedists	CDEHKNRRSTTUU	thunderstruck
CDEEIILPRSTVY	descriptively	CDEHMOOOOPPST	photocomposed
CDEEIIMNORSTT	densitometric	CDEIIIINNSTTV	indistinctive
CDEEIINNSSSTUV	inductiveness	CDEIIILLNSUVY	uncivilisedly
CDEEIINOOSSSU	dioeciousness	CDEIIILLNUVYZ	uncivilizedly
CDEEIINORRSTT	derestriction	CDEIIILNSTTVY	distinctively
CDEEIIORSSSTU	discourtesies	CDEIIIMMNOOST	incommodities
CDEEIJNPRRSUU	jurisprudence	CDEIIIMNORSST	misdirections
CDEEILMOOPRSY	copolymerised	CDEIIIMOOOPRS	Piero di Cosimo
CDEEILMOOPRYZ	copolymerized	CDEIIIMPRSSTV	descriptivism
CDEEILNNOOPRS	scolopendrine	CDEIIINNORSST	indiscretions
CDEEILNNOSTUY	tendenciously	CDEIIINNORSTT	interdictions
CDEEILRSTTUVY	destructively	CDEIIIPRSSTTV	descriptivist
CDEEIMMOORTTV	overcommitted	CDEIIJLNSTUVY	disjunctively
CDEEIMNOOPRSS	decompression	CDEIIJNOSSSUU	judiciousness
CDEEIMNOOPRST	contemporised	CDEIIMMNOOSSS	decommissions
CDEEIMNOOPRTZ	contemporized	CDEIIMNOOOPST	decomposition
CDEEINNNORRST	nonrestricted	CDEIIMNORSSTU	reductionisms
CDEEINOOPRSTU	counterpoised	CDEIIMNRSSTTU	misinstructed
CDEEINORSTTTU	reconstituted	CDEIINNNOOSSX	disconnexions
CDEEKKLNRSTUU	knuckleduster	CDEIINNOOPRST	preconditions

CDEIINNORSSTU	discontinuers
CDEIINORSSTTU	reductionists
CDEIIRSTTTUVY	destructivity
CDEILLMOORTUU	multicoloured
CDEILLNORSUUY	incredulously
CDEILMNOOPRSU	scolopendrium
CDEILMNOOPSUY	compendiously
CDEILMNOORSST	discolorments
CDEILMNOORSTU	discolourment
CDEILNORSSSUU	ludicrousness
CDEIMNNOOPRSU	mispronounced
CDEIMOOPRSSSU	discomposures
CDEINNOOPRTUV	nonproductive
CDEINOOPPRRTU	preproduction
CDEINOOPRRSTU	reproductions
CDELLNOOOPTYY	polycotyledon
CDELMNNOOOOTY	monocotyledon
CDFGIIIMNNORS	disconfirming
CDFGIIMNOORST	discomforting
CDFIIMNOORSTY	disconformity
CDGHIIIMNOOST	dichotomising
CDGHIIIMNOOTZ	dichotomizing
CDGHIKLNOOSST	stockholdings
CDGIIINNNOSTU	discontinuing
CDGIIMOOOPSSY	sigmoidoscopy
CDHHILNOORRSY	chlorohydrins
CDHHIMNOOPRUY	hypochondrium
CDHIIMNNOOORT	mitochondrion
CDHILMOOOSTUY	dichotomously
CDHIMOOORSSTY	Dio Chrysostom
CDIIIJLNOSUUY	injudiciously
CDIIIJNORSSTU	jurisdictions
CDIIINNOSTTUY	discontinuity
CDIINNOORSTTU	introductions
CDIINNOOSSTUU	discontinuous
CEEEEEEINPRRSX	reexperiences
CEEEEFFINSSTV	effectiveness
CEEEEFINNRRST	interferences
CEEEEFLMORRTT	reflectometer
CEEEEGHINORTT	heterogenetic
CEEEEGHMNORSS	cheesemongers
CEEEEGIINOPRT	epeirogenetic
CEEEEHLNRSSSS	cheerlessness
CEEEEIKKPRSTW	wicketkeepers
CEEEEILNSSSTV	selectiveness
CEEEEIMNNPRSU	supereminence
CEEEEIMNORSTT	enterectomies
CEEEEINNPRSUV	supervenience
CEEEEINPRSSTV	receptiveness
CEEEEINPRSSTX	preexistences
CEEEEINRSSSSV	recessiveness
CEEEEINRSSSTV	secretiveness
CEEEEINSSSSVX	excessiveness
CEEEEIOPRTTVX	exteroceptive
CEEEEIORRSSVX	overexercises
CEEEEJNNRSTUV	rejuvenescent
CEEEEELMORRSTT	electrometers
CEEEEPPRRSSST	preceptresses
CEEEFFIILNTVY	ineffectively
CEEEFFINNOSTV	noneffectives
CEEEFIIMPRSTV	imperfectives
CEEEFIINNSSTV	infectiveness
CEEEFIMNNORRT	reinforcement
CEEEFIMNPRSST	imperfectness
CEEEFINORRTTU	counterfeiter
CEEEGHIKLNNRS	Gelsenkirchen
CEEEGHILLNOPT	phellogenetic
CEEEGHIMNORTT	thermogenetic
CEEEGIILLNNRT	intelligencer
CEEEGIILLNNST	intelligences
CEEEGIILNOPPT	epileptogenic
CEEEGIJNNRSUV	rejuvenescing
CEEEGIKNNRSSS	greensickness
CEEEHHIPRSTTY	hyperesthetic
CEEEHHKLRSTTU	kletterschuhe
CEEEHIILNNSTT	Liechtenstein
CEEEHILLLMOSU	hemicellulose
CEEEHILLOPRST	electrophiles
CEEEHILMNOPRT	nephelometric
CEEEHIMNOPRST	nephrectomies
CEEEHIMNOPRSV	comprehensive
CEEEHIMNPRSST	phreneticness
CEEEHLNNOSTTU	luncheonettes
CEEEHLNOOPRST	electrophones
CEEEHLOQQSSUU	quelquechoses
CEEEHMMOORTTY	hemocytometer
CEEEHMNNNRSTT	entrenchments
CEEEHMNNRRSTT	retrenchments
CEEEHMOORRSST	stereochromes
CEEEHNOPRRSST	centrospheres
CEEEHOOPRRRST	rheoreceptors
CEEEHORRSSTTV	overstretches
CEEEIIMNNPRST	impertinences
CEEEIIMNNRTTT	intermittence
CEEEIIMNPRSSS	impreciseness
CEEEIINNSSTVV	invectiveness
CEEEIINOPRTTV	interoceptive
CEEEILMMORRST	electromerism
CEEEILMNNNSST	inclementness
CEEEILMNOPSST	splenectomies
CEEEILMNRSSSS	mercilessness
CEEEILMOORTTV	electromotive
CEEEILNOSSSSV	voicelessness
CEEEILNOSTVXY	coextensively
CEEEILNPPRRSU	pluripresence
CEEEILNPRSSSS	pricelessness
CEEEILNSSSSUV	seclusiveness
CEEEILNSSSUVX	exclusiveness
CEEEILPPRSTVY	perspectively
CEEEIMMNOPSTU	pneumectomies
CEEEINNOORRRT	reconnoiterer
CEEEINNRRRSSTW	screenwriters
CEEEINRRSSSTW	wintercresses
CEEEINRSSSUVX	excursiveness
CEEEIOPRRSTTV	retrospective
CEEELLORRSSTY	electrolysers
CEEELLORRSTYZ	electrolyzers
CEEELMORSTTTU	telecommuters
CEEELMNNOSSUW	unwelcomeness
CEEELOPRRSTYY	electrotypers
CEEEMNNNORSTU	renouncements
CEEEMNNOPSSTT	competentness
CEEEMOPRRSSTT	spectrometers
CEEENNPRSTUUV	venepunctures

CEEEOOPRRSTTX	exteroceptors
CEEEOPRRSSSTT	protectresses
CEEFFHINRRSSTT	festschriften
CEEFFIIILLNNTY	inefficiently
CEEFFIJNORSTY	Jefferson City
CEEFFNOORRSTU	counteroffers
CEEFGIINNNOTU	eigenfunction
CEEFGILNNOSTU	genuflections
CEEFGINNOORTT	frontogenetic
CEEFHKMORRSTU	motherfuckers
CEEFIIKLNORSU	nickeliferous
CEEFIIMNOPRST	imperfections
	perfectionism
CEEFIINOPRSST	frontispieces
CEEFIINOPRSTT	perfectionist
CEEFILNOORRTT	retroflection
CEEFINOORSSSU	ferociousness
CEEFLLOORRSTU	electrofluors
CEEFLLORRSUUV	resourcefully
CEEGHIILNOPRT	helicoptering
CEEGHIIMOORST	isogeothermic
CEEGHIINNRRST	rechristening
CEEGHIINOSSSZ	schizogenesis
CEEGHIIRRSTUW	cruiserweight
CEEGHIMNOOPRT	morphogenetic
CEEGHINOPSSSY	psychogenesis
CEEGHINORSTUW	counterweighs
CEEGHINORTTUW	counterweight
CEEGIIMMNNOTU	immunogenetic
CEEGIINORRTVX	Vercingetorix
CEEGIKLLNOPSS	glockenspiels
CEEGILLNORSTY	electrolysing
CEEGILLNORTYZ	electrolyzing
CEEGILMMNNOPT	complementing
CEEGILMMNOTTU	telecommuting
CEEGILMOOSSST	glossectomies
CEEGILNOPRTTY	electrotyping
CEEGINNNORRTU	rencountering
CEEGINOPRRSTT	retrospecting
CEEGMNNOORSSW	congresswomen
CEEGMNOORRSST	costermongers
CEEGNNOOOPRST	rontgenoscope
CEEHHIMMORSTT	thermochemist
CEEHHIMOOPRRT	heteromorphic
CEEHHIOOPRRTT	heterotrophic
CEEHHLLOPRSUY	Holy Sepulchre
CEEHHLOORSSST	clotheshorses
CEEHHMNORSSSY	synchromeshes
CEEHHMOOPRRSS	chromospheres
CEEHHOOPPRRSS	phosphoresces
CEEHHOOPRRSST	trochospheres
CEEHIIKLNRSSS	lickerishness
CEEHILMMOPRSY	myrmecophiles
CEEHIMMRSSSTT	Messerschmitt
CEEHIMNNNRSTT	intrenchments
CEEHIMNNOOPRS	comprehension
CEEHIMNNORSTT	ethnocentrism
CEEHIMOORSTTY	stoechiometry
CEEHIMOPPRRTY	hypermetropic
CEEHINNOPRSSV	convenerships
CEEHINOOPPRSS	nephroscopies
CEEHINOPPRRST	precentorship

CEEHIOPPPRRST	preceptorship
CEEHIOPRSSTUX	executorships
CEEHKLLNORRSS	schnorkellers
CEEHLMOOPRSTU	thermocouples
CEEHLNOOOPRTT	photoelectron
CEEHLOOOPRRSTU	electrophorus
CEEHMOPRRSSTY	psychrometers
CEEHOOOOPPRRTT	photoreceptor
CEEHOOPRRSSTU	urethroscopes
CEEIIIIINNRSST	insincerities
CEEIIIILRSTTUV	reluctivities
CEEIIIMMPRSTT	metempiricist
CEEIIIMORSTTT	meteoriticist
CEEIIJNNORSTT	interjections
CEEIIILLNNOSTT	intellections
CEEIILMNNORST	inclinometers
CEEIILMNNRSTY	reminiscently
CEEIILMOPTTVY	competitively
CEEIILNNSSSUV	inclusiveness
CEEIILNOORSTT	enterocolitis
CEEIILRRSTTVY	restrictively
CEEIIMNNRTTTY	intermittency
CEEIIMNOPPRST	misperception
CEEIIMNOPTTUV	uncompetitive
CEEIIMORSSSTV	viscosimeters
CEEIINNOPRSST	reinspections
CEEIINNOPRSTT	interceptions
CEEIINNORSSST	intercessions
CEEIINNORSSTT	intersections
CEEIINOOPRSST	retinoscopies
CEEIINOOPSSST	isoteniscopes
CEEIINOPRSSTT	receptionists
CEEIINOPRSTTV	introspective
CEEIINOSSSSST	secessionists
CEEIIOPPRRRST	proprietrices
CEEIJNOORRSTT	retrojections
CEEIKLNNOSTUU	kinetonucleus
CEEILMNNOPTTY	incompetently
CEEILMNOORSUY	ceremoniously
CEEILMOOPRSSY	copolymerises
CEEILMOOPRSTY	pylorectomies
CEEILMOOPRSYZ	copolymerizes
CEEILMOPRSSVY	compressively
CEEILNNOOPRTU	nucleoprotein
CEEILNNOOPRXY	clinopyroxene
CEEILNOOPRRST	scleroprotein
CEEILNOORSSSV	venosclerosis
CEEILNOSSSTUY	necessitously
CEEILOOPRSTTU	teleutosporic
CEEILOPPRSTVY	prospectively
CEEILPQRSTUUY	picturesquely
CEEIMMMNORSTT	recommitments
CEEIMMNNOOPTT	omnicompetent
CEEIMNNOORSUU	unceremonious
CEEIMNOOPRSST	contemporises
CEEIMNOOPRSTZ	contemporizes
CEEIMNOOPSSST	compositeness
CEEIMNOORSSTT	econometrists
CEEINNOORRRST	reconnoitrers
CEEINNOORRSSV	reconversions
CEEINNORSTTTU	reconstituent
CEEINNPRSTUUV	venipunctures

CEEINOOPRRSTT	interoceptors
	retrospection
CEEINOOPRSSTT	stereopticons
CEEINOOPRSSTU	counterpoises
CEEINOORRSSST	retrocessions
CEEINOORRSSSV	corrosiveness
CEEINOORRSSTV	controversies
CEEINOPRRSSSU	repercussions
CEEINORRRSSTU	resurrections
CEEINORSSTTTU	reconstitutes
CEEINOSSSSTUV	viscountesses
CEEIOOPRSSSTT	stereoscopist
CEEIOORRRSSTT	ecoterrorists
CEEKLNOOSSTTY	cytoskeletons
CEEKNOORRRTUW	counterworker
CEELLNOORSTTV	electronvolts
CEELPQRSSTUUU	sculpturesque
CEEMMNNOOPTUY	pneumonectomy
CEEMNNNOOPRTU	pronouncement
CEEMNOOPRRTUU	neurocomputer
CEEMOPPRRSTUU	supercomputer
CEENNOORRSTTU	countertenors
CEENOOOPPRSSS	snooperscopes
CEENOORRRSTTV	controverters
CEENOORSSSTUU	courteousness
CEFFIINOOSSSU	officiousness
CEFHIMMOORRRU	ferrochromium
CEFHLLLOOOSSW	schoolfellows
CEFHLMOOORRSU	fluorochromes
CEFIINNNOOSTU	noninfectious
CEFILNOPRRTUY	perfunctorily
CEFLLMOORSSTY	comfortlessly
CEFLLNOORSSUU	colourfulness
CEFMNNNOORSTT	confrontments
CEFNOOOPRRSTU	counterproofs
CEFNORSSSTUUU	fructuousness
CEGGHLNOOOORY	geochronology
CEGGILNOOSSTY	gynecologists
CEGGIMOOORSTU	cogito, ergo sum
CEGHHIILOPRSY	hieroglyphics
CEGHIILOOOSTY	stoicheiology
CEGHIIOPSSSTY	geophysicists
CEGHIKLLNNORS	schnorkelling
CEGHILNOOSSTT	technologists
CEGHILOOOPSVY	ecophysiology
CEGHILOOOPSSSY	psychologises
CEGHILOOPSSYZ	psychologizes
CEGHINNOOSTUU	countinghouse
CEGHINORSTTTU	outstretching
CEGHOPRRSSUYY	psychosurgery
CEGIIILNNNORV	overinclining
CEGIIILNOORST	coreligionist
CEGIINNORSTU	incongruities
CEGIIKNPPQSTU	quickstepping
CEGIILLOOSSTX	lexicologists
CEGIILMMNNOPT	complimenting
CEGIILMNORSYY	syringomyelic
CEGIILNNORRTY	nitroglycerin
CEGIIMHNNNORTU	countermining
CEGIIMNOORRTT	trigonometric
CEGIIMNOPRSTU	computerising
CEGIIMNOPRTUZ	computerizing

CEGIINNNNOORRT	reconnoitring
CEGIINNOOPRSS	processioning
CEGIINNOPPRRT	intercropping
CEGIINNOPRSTT	introspecting
CEGIINNORRSST	intercrossing
CEGILMMOORSTY	myrmecologist
CEGILNNNORTUY	incongruently
CEGILNOOPRSTU	glucoproteins
CEGILNOOPRSTY	glycoproteins
CEGIMNNOORSUV	overconsuming
CEGIMNNOORTUV	countermoving
	covermounting
CEGINNOORRTTV	controverting
CEGINRRRSTTUU	restructuring
CEGNNOOOPRSTY	rontgenoscopy
CEGNNOORSSSUU	congruousness
CEHHHNOOPRRSY	rhynchophores
CEHHIILLLNRST	Chiltern Hills
CEHHIIMMOOORT	homoiothermic
CEHHIIMOOPRRT	theriomorphic
CEHHIINORSSTY	ichthyornises
CEHHIIOORSSTT	orthostichies
CEHHILMNORSTT	trochelminths
CEHHILOOPRRSTY	hypochlorites
CEHHIMMOOOOPR	homoeomorphic
CEHHIMOOPSSTT	photochemists
CEHHIMOPSSTTY	phytochemists
CEHIIKNOPSSSY	psychokinesis
CEHIILMOOPPTY	lymphopoietic
CEHIILMOSSUVY	mischievously
CEHIILNOOPSST	siphonostelic
CEHIIMMOOORST	homoeroticism
CEHIIMNOOPRST	chemisorption
CEHIIMOORSTTY	stoichiometry
CEHIINNOPRSTY	pericynthions
CEHIINOPPRSST	inspectorship
CEHIINOPRTTYY	hypertonicity
CEHIIOOPRSSST	spirochetosis
CEHILNOOPRSSU	counselorship
CEHILNOPSTTVY	polysynthetic
CEHILOPRRSTUY	Holy Scripture
CEHIMMOOPRRST	morphometrics
CEHIMNOOOPRRT	chromoprotein
CEHIMOOPRSTTY	topochemistry
CEHIMOPRSSTTY	psychometrist
CEHINNOOPRSSV	convenorships
CEHINNORRSSSY	synchronisers
CEHINNORRSSYZ	synchronizers
CEHIOOPRRSTTU	trichopterous
CEHMOOOOPPRST	photocomposer
CEHMOOOOPPSST	photocomposes
CEHNOOPRRSTTU	photocurrents
CEIIILMNOPSST	impoliticness
CEIIIILNNSTTVY	instinctively
CEIIILNPRSTVY	inscriptively
CEIIIMNOPSTUY	impecuniosity
CEIIIMOPRSSTU	promiscuities
CEIIINOPRSSST	precisionists
CEIIJNNOORSTT	introjections
CEIIJNOOPRSTT	projectionist
CEIILLLNOOSTV	violoncellist
CEIILMNOPSUUY	impecuniously

CEIILNNNNOTTY	incontinently	CGIIILLOOOPST	oligopolistic
CEIILNNOORTTU	interlocution	CGIIILMNOORST	criminologist
CEIILNOOSSTTU	elocutionists	CGIIILMOOSTTV	victimologist
CEIILNOPRRTUV	proventriculi	CGIIILNOOSSTU	sociolinguist
CEIILNOPSSSSU	suspicionless	CGIIIMMNNOOSS	commissioning
CEIILNORRTTUX	interlocutrix	CGIIINPRRSTTW	scriptwriting
CEIILNOSSSTUX	exclusionists	CGIILMOOSSSTU	musicologists
CEIILNRSTTUVY	instructively	CGIILOOOSSTTX	toxicologists
CEIILOPPRSTUY	precipitously	CGIIMNNORSSTU	misconstruing
CEIILRRSSTTUU	sericulturist	CGILNNOORSUUY	incongruously
CEIILRRSTTUUV	viticulturers	CGILOOOPRSSTT	proctologists
CEIIMMNOORSSS	commissioners	CGLOOOOPRTYYZ	cryptozoology
CEIIMMNOPRSTU	minicomputers	CHHIILOPRSTUU	thiosulphuric
CEIIMNNORRTTU	micronutrient	CHHIMOOPRRSTY	hystricomorph
CEIIMNOOOPRST	recomposition	CHHIOOORSSTTU	orthostichous
CEIIMNOOPRSTT	protectionism	CHHIOOPRSSTYY	psychohistory
CEIIMOORSSSTT	sociometrists	CHHLMOOPRSSTU	chlorophytums
CEIINNOOPRSTT	introspection	CHHMOOOOPRRSU	chromophorous
CEIINNORRSSTU	insurrections	CHIIILOOPRSST	solicitorship
CEIINNORSSSUU	incuriousness	CHIIOOOPRRSTT	protohistoric
CEIINNRSTTUUV	uninstructive	CHILMMNNOOOUV	Holy Communion
CEIINOOPRSSTT	retinoscopist	CHILMOOPSSTYY	lymphocytosis
CEIINOOPRSTTT	protectionist	CHILNNOOOPRST	Port Nicholson
CEIINOORSSTUV	insectivorous	CHILNOOORSSUY	isochronously
CEIINOPPRRSST	prescriptions	CHILNOOPPRSSU	proconsulship
CEIINOPRSSSTU	percussionist	CHILOOPSSSTUY	physoclistous
CEIINORSSSTUX	excursionists	CHILOPPRRSUUY	pyrosulphuric
CEIIPRRRSSTTW	scriptwriters	CHIMMNOOORSST	monochromists
CEIILLMNOOSTTY	tonsillectomy	CHLNNOORSSUYY	synchronously
CEIILMNNOOOSSU	mononucleosis	CHMNNOOOOPRRUY	Murphy-O'Connor
CEILMNOORSTUY	coterminously	CIIIIIMPRSTTV	primitivistic
CEILMNOPSTUVY	consumptively	CIIIILLNOSSTU	illusionistic
CEILNNOOSTTUY	contentiously	CIIIILNRSTTUUV	viniculturist
CEILNNOSTTTUY	constituently	CIIIILRSTTTUUV	viticulturist
CEILNOORRSTTU	interlocutors	CIILLNOPSTUUY	punctiliously
CEILNOORRTTUY	interlocutory	CIILMMOOOOPSST	cosmopolitism
CEILOPPRSSUUY	perspicuously	CIIMNNOOOPSST	monopsonistic
CEIMMMNOORSTY	monosymmetric	CIINNOOORSTTT	contortionist
CEIMNNOOPRSSU	mispronounces	CIINNOOSSTTTU	constitutions
CEINNNOOSSSUU	innocuousness	CIINOOPPRRSST	proscriptions
CEINNOOPRSTTU	counterpoints	CIINOOPPRSTTU	opportunistic
CEINNOPRRSSTU	incorruptness	CIINOOPRRSTTU	corruptionist
CEINPSSSSTTUU	intussuscepts	CIJLNORSSSTUU	jurisconsults
CEIOOOPPPRRRT	proprioceptor	CILMOOPRSSUUY	promiscuously
CELLNOOSSUUVV	convolvuluses	CILMOPRSSTUUY	scrumptiously
CFFIIILNOOSUY	inofficiously	CIMMNNNOOSSTU	noncommunists
CFGHIILLNNNUY	unflinchingly	DDDEEEEINNPRT	interdepended
CFGHIMNNOORTU	unforthcoming	DDDEEEGIMOSSS	demigoddesses
CFHINNORTTTUU	truth-function	DDDEHHNNOOORRS	rhododendrons
CFIILMNNOTTUU	multifunction	DDEEEEIMNPRRT	predetermined
CFIMMNNNOOORS	nonconformism	DDEEEELOOPRVV	overdeveloped
CFIMNNNOOORST	nonconformist	DDEEEEENNOPRTV	overdependent
CFIMNNNOOORTY	nonconformity	DDEEEEGHILNSST	delightedness
CGHHIIINPSTTW	whipstitching	DDEEEEGHINORSY	dehydrogenise
CGHHIILLOOSTTY	ichthyologist	DDEEEEGHINORYZ	dehydrogenize
CGHIIINNOORSS	isochronising	DDEEEEIILLMOTT	Little Diomede
CGHIIINNOORSZ	isochronizing	DDEEEEIINRSSTT	disinterested
CGHIILOORSSTT	trichologists	DDEEEEILMNRSTW	Middle Western
CGHIINNNORSSY	synchronising	DDEEEEILMOPRSY	depolymerised
CGHIINNNORSYZ	synchronizing	DDEEEEILMOPRYZ	depolymerized
CGHILNOOORSST	chronologists	DDEEEEILNNNPTY	independently
CGHILOOPSSSTY	psychologists	DDEEEEINNPRSTU	superintended

DDEEEIPRRSSSU	depressurised
DDEEEIPRRSSUZ	depressurized
DDEEEELMNOPRUY	underemployed
DDEEEELNOPRSUV	underdevelops
DDEEFGIIINNSS	dignifiedness
DDEEFHIIIMRSU	dehumidifiers
DDEEFIIIIMNST	misidentified
DDEEFIIINRSUV	undiversified
DDEEFNNNOSSUU	unfoundedness
DDEEGHHINRTUW	hundredweight
DDEEGHIILMSTW	middleweights
DDEEGIILMNNRT	intermeddling
DDEEGILMNOSST	dislodgements
DDEEGINNNPRSU	underspending
DDEEGINSSSSTU	disgustedness
DDEEHILPRSSUU	desulphurised
DDEEHILPRSUUZ	desulphurized
DDEEIIKMNNRRST	Kidderminster
DDEEILNPPRSUU	undersupplied
DDEEIMNNOSSTW	disendowments
DDEEINORSSSTT	distortedness
DDEFGHIIIMNUY	dehumidifying
DDEGHHIINOPST	diphthongised
DDEGHHIINOPTZ	diphthongized
DDEGHHLOOOSSU	household gods
DDEGHIIINSSTU	distinguished
DDEGIIKMNNOTU	United Kingdom
DDEGILNOORSST	dendrologists
DDEGINNNRSTUUY	understudying
DDEHHILOPRSUY	hydrosulphide
DDEHIIKNOORZZ	Ordzhonikidze
DDEHILNNOOPRS	philodendrons
DDEIIIILMSSTU	dissimilitude
DDEIIILLNOSSU	disillusioned
DDEIILNNOORRS	liriodendrons
DDEIMNOORSSTU	misunderstood
DEEEEFINNSSSV	defensiveness
DEEEEFLLNSSSY	defenselessly
DEEEEGIPRRRST	preregistered
DEEEEHHPRSSSS	shepherdesses
DEEEEIMNPRRRT	predeterminer
DEEEEIMNPRRST	predetermines
DEEEEINPRRRTT	reinterpreted
DEEEELMNOPRTV	redevelopment
DEEEENNPRRSTU	unrepresented
DEEEENPRRSSTV	pervertedness
DEEEFFINNRSST	differentness
DEEEFGIINNRTW	winterfeeding
DEEEFGJMNORTU	forejudgement
DEEEFGKLNOORW	foreknowledge
DEEEFHHIORRRS	Herefordshire
DEEEFHNOORRST	foreshortened
DEEEFIILOPRRT	Porţile de Fier
DEEEFINPRRSSV	perfervidness
DEEEGGIINRRST	deregistering
DEEEGHILNNNTU	unenlightened
DEEEGHINRRRTV	Right Reverend
DEEEGIIMNNRRT	redetermining
DEEEGILLORSTU	Rouget de Lisle
DEEEGINNNORTVX	overextending
DEEEGINNNRRSTU	understeering
DEEEGINNRSSSV	deservingness
DEEEHIMPRSSST	deemsterships
DEEEHLOPRRSTU	reupholstered
DEEEIILNNORSV	nondeliveries
DEEEIILNNPTXY	inexpediently
DEEEIINRSSSST	desensitisers
DEEEIINRSSSTZ	desensitizers
DEEEIKOORSTTU	deuterotokies
DEEEILLORSTUY	deleteriously
DEEEILMOPRSSY	depolymerises
DEEEILMOPRSYZ	depolymerizes
DEEEIMNOPRRST	redemptioners
DEEEIMNORSSTT	densitometers
DEEEIMOPRRSSV	overimpressed
DEEEINOPPRSTU	neuropeptides
DEEEINSSSTTTU	destituteness
DEEEIPRRSSSSU	depressurises
DEEEIPRRSSSUZ	depressurizes
DEEEKLMMRRTTU	kettledrummer
DEEEKLNNOOSST	endoskeletons
DEEELLNNPRSTY	resplendently
DEEELMNOPRSTY	redeployments
DEEELNNSSSTTU	unsettledness
DEEENOPRRSUUX	underexposure
DEEENORSSSTUX	dexterousness
DEEFFHINRRSSU	undersheriffs
DEEFFIILNNRTY	indifferently
DEEFFIINSSSUV	diffusiveness
DEEFFLNNRSSUU	unruffledness
DEEFGHILORSTY	foresightedly
DEEFGIIMNRSTU	disfigurement
DEEFGIIINNPRRT	fingerprinted
DEEFGJMNORSTU	forejudgments
DEEFHHIORRRST	Hertfordshire
DEEFHIIMRRSSU	Dumfriesshire
DEEFHIMNORSTT	Thetford Mines
DEEFIIIIMNSST	misidentifies
DEEFIILNNRSTU	unfriendliest
DEEFILNOPRSSU	splendiferous
DEEFLNNORSSUW	wonderfulness
DEEGGHHINOPPS	hedgehoppings
DEEGGIINNOSXY	deoxygenising
DEEGGIINNOXYZ	deoxygenizing
DEEGGIMNORSST	disgorgements
DEEGHILMNNRUW	underwhelming
DEEGHILMOOOST	methodologies
DEEGHILMOOSTY	demythologise
DEEGHILMOOTYZ	demythologize
DEEGIIINNSSST	desensitising
DEEGIIINNSSTZ	desensitizing
DEEGIILMNNORY	domineeringly
DEEGIILOOPPST	oligopeptides
DEEGIIMNOPRSW	disempowering
DEEGIINOPPRST	predepositing
DEEGIJMMNSSTU	misjudgements
DEEGILMNOOOST	entomologised
DEEGILMNOOOTZ	entomologized
DEEGILMNOOSTY	sedimentology
DEEGILNNORTUV	overindulgent
DEEGINNOPRSUX	underexposing
DEEGINNORSTTW	Downing Street
DEEGINNORSUVZ	rendezvousing
DEEHHIIMOPRSS	hemispheroids

DEEHHIINNOSSS	hoidenishness
DEEHHINNOSSSY	hoydenishness
DEEHHIOPPRRTY	hypertrophied
DEEHHNORRSTUW	thundershower
DEEHIINNPRSTU	indentureship
DEEHIINNPRSST	presidentship
DEEHIINPRSSST	residentships
DEEHIKKNNRSUV	Verkhne-Udinsk
DEEHILMMNOSST	demolishments
DEEHILPRRSSUU	desulphuriser
DEEHILPRRSUUZ	desulphurizer
DEEHILPRSSSUU	desulphurises
DEEHILPRSSUUZ	desulphurizes
DEEHINNORSTTY	North Tyneside
DEEHINOSSTTUY	South Tyneside
DEEHIOPPRSTTY	pteridophytes
DEEHNNORSSTTU	thunderstones
DEEIIIMMNNRST	indeterminism
DEEIIIMNNRSTT	indeterminist
DEEIIINOQRSTU	derequisition
	requisitioned
DEEIIILLNNSSUW	unwieldliness
DEEIIILLNORSSS	soldierliness
DEEIILMNNOSSS	dimensionless
DEEIILMNNSSTU	unlimitedness
DEEIILNNSSTTY	dissentiently
DEEIILNORSSSU	deliriousness
DEEIILOPPRSST	spoiled priest
DEEIILOPPRSTT	lepidopterist
DEEIILOPSTUXY	expeditiously
DEEIIMMRSSSTY	dissymmetries
DEEIIMNNRSSTT	disinterments
DEEIIMNNSSTTV	disinvestment
DEEIIMNOORSST	endometriosis
DEEIIMOORRSTU	demeritorious
DEEIINOOPRRSV	reprovisioned
DEEIINOPRSSTU	serendipitous
DEEIINOSSSSTU	seditiousness
DEEIIORRSTVVY	overdiversity
DEEIJNORRRSSU	surrejoinders
DEEILMNOOSSSU	melodiousness
DEEILNNOSTTUY	tendentiously
DEEILNOOPPRST	lepidopterons
DEEILNORSSSTU	desultoriness
DEEILNOSSSSTU	dissoluteness
DEEILNPPRSSUU	undersupplies
DEEILNPRRTTUY	interruptedly
DEEILOOPPRSTU	lepidopterous
DEEIMNOORSTTU	Deuteronomist
DEEIMNOPRSSST	Simpson Desert
DEEIMOPPRRSST	pteridosperms
DEEINNPRRTTUU	uninterrupted
DEELNNOPSSSUU	pendulousness
DEELNNOSSSSSU	soundlessness
DEEMNORRSSSUU	murderousness
DEEMOOOPRRSST	depressomotor
DEENNOOPRSSSU	ponderousness
DEENNOPSSSTTU	unspottedness
DEENOOPRSSSST	dessertspoons
DEENOPPPRRRSU	underproppers
DEFHIILLOPSSW	disfellowship
DEFHILMRRTTYY	Merthyr Tydfil
DEFHIMORRRTUU	rutherfordium
DEFIILNOORSSX	dorsiflexions
DEFIILPRSTUUY	superfluidity
DEFILLRSSSTUY	distressfully
DEFILMNNNSSUU	unmindfulness
DEFILOOORRSUY	odoriferously
DEFLNNOOOORTW	Tower of London
DEGGHIINNORSY	hydrogenising
DEGGHIINNORYZ	hydrogenizing
DEGGIILNNORUV	overindulging
DEGGHHIILOOPPT	Philip the Good
DEGGHHIINOPSST	diphthongises
DEGGHHIINOPSTZ	diphthongizes
DEGGHHILOPRTTT	trothplighted
DEGGHHNOOOORRTY	orthohydrogen
DEGHIIIINNRST	disinheriting
DEGHIIINRSSTU	distinguisher
DEGHIIINSSSTU	distinguishes
DEGHIINNOPSTY	dehypnotising
DEGHIINNOPTYZ	dehypnotizing
DEGHILMOOOSTT	methodologist
DEGHINNOORSTU	undershooting
DEGHINNORSSTW	downrightness
DEGIIILNPSSTT	sidesplitting
DEGIIILNQSTUY	disquietingly
DEGIILLOOSSTT	deltiologists
DEGIILNRSSSTY	distressingly
DEGIILOOPRSTT	pteridologist
DEGIINNNNPRSU	underpinnings
DEGIINOPSSSSS	dispossessing
DEGIKMNOPRSSU	superkingdoms
DEGILMNOOOSST	demonologists
DEGILNOOOSSTT	deontologists
DEGIMNNPRRTUU	undertrumping
DEGINNOPPPRRU	underpropping
DEHHIILOOPPSS	philosophised
DEHHIILOOPPSZ	philosophized
DEHHIIOPRRSSY	hyperhidrosis
DEHHILOPRSTUY	hydrosulphite
DEHHIOPRRSTYY	hyperthyroids
DEHHLOOOORSUY	Holyroodhouse
DEHIIILNOPRSS	siderophilins
DEHIINOOPPSST	deipnosophist
DEHILLOPPSSUY	polysulphides
DEHMNORRSSTTU	thunderstorms
DEIIILMNOOSTT	demolitionist
DEIIINNOSSSTU	insidiousness
DEIIINNOSSSUV	invidiousness
DEIILMNOPRTVY	improvidently
DEIILNOOSTTUV	devolutionist
DEIINOOOPPRST	propositioned
DEIINOOPSSSSS	dispossession
DEIIJNPRRSSTU	jurisprudents
DEIILLNNORSSUW	unworldliness
DEIILMNOOOPSTU	leontopodiums
DEIIMMNOOPRSST	postmodernism
DEIIMNOOPRSSTT	postmodernist
DEIOOPRSSSSSS	dispossessors
DEIOOPRSSSSSY	dispossessory
DFGGHIILLNOOT	floodlighting
DFGHIINNOSSTW	downshiftings
DFGHIMNOORRSV	hydroformings

DFGINNOOOPRSU	soundproofing
DFIINOORSTTUU	fortitudinous
DFILLRSSTTUUY	distrustfully
DGHIIIILMNNSY	diminishingly
DGIIIILNPRSTY	dispiritingly
DGIINNOPPRRTU	roundtripping
DGILNOOOOSSTT	odontologists
DGLMNOOOOSSTU	odontoglossum
DHHIILOOPPPSS	phospholipids
DHIIIMMOOPRSS	isodimorphism
DHIIMOOOPRSSU	isodimorphous
DHILOOPPRSTYY	lipodystrophy
DHINOOORSSTTT	orthodontists
DHNOOOOOPRSTU	odontophorous
DIIIINNOOPSST	indisposition
DIIIINOQSSSTU	disquisitions
DIILMNOSTTUUU	multitudinous
DIILNORSSTUUY	industriously
DIINOOOOPPRST	disproportion
DILNOOOPSSSUY	isospondylous
DLNOOOOPPRTTY	polyprotodont
EEEEEELNPRSSSV	Seven Sleepers
EEEEFILNRSSVX	reflexiveness
EEEEGGIINNNNR	reengineering
EEEEGHINORSST	heterogenesis
EEEEGHINORTTY	heterogeneity
EEEEGHNOORSTU	heterogeneous
EEEEGIINOPRSS	epeirogenesis
EEEEHILPQRSTU	telepheriques
EEEEHLMNOPRST	nephelometers
EEEEIMNPRRRTT	preretirement
EEEEIMNPRRSTX	experimenters
EEEEIMNRSSTTX	extensimeters
EEEEINNPSSSVX	expensiveness
EEEEINNNQRSSTU	equestriennes
EEEEINNRSSTTV	retentiveness
EEEEINNSSSTVX	extensiveness
EEEEINPQRSSTU	sesquiterpene
EEEELLMOPRRST	Ellesmere Port
EEEEELLNPSSSSS	sleeplessness
EEEELMNRSSTTT	resettlements
EEEELNNRSSSSV	nervelessness
EEEELNNSSSSSS	senselessness
EEEEMNOPRRSTT	penetrometers
EEEEMNORSSTTX	extensometers
EEEENNPRRRSTU	entrepreneurs
EEEFFIMORSSTU	effusiometers
EEEFFINNOSSSV	offensiveness
EEEFGILNNNSSU	unfeelingness
EEEFGIMNPRRTU	prefigurement
EEEFGLNRRSSTU	regretfulness
EEEFHILOPPSSY	Isle of Sheppey
EEEFIILLLLMSU	millefeuilles
EEEFINNPRSSSU	superfineness
EEEFLLNORRTTU	fortune-teller
EEEFLNNRSSSTU	resentfulness
EEEFLNOPRSSSU	reposefulness
EEEGGINORSSSU	egregiousness
EEEGHILMNNNTT	enlightenment
EEEGHILRSTTWW	welterweights
EEEGHIMNORSST	thermogenesis
EEEGHNNRRSSTT	strengtheners

EEEGHOORSTTYZ	heterozygotes
EEEGIILMNNSTV	inveiglements
EEEGIILOPRSSU	Siege Perilous
EEEGIIMNNPRTX	experimenting
EEEGIINORSSTV	sovereignties
EEEGILLNSSSSU	guilelessness
EEEGILNNORVWY	overweeningly
EEEGILNOORSTV	venereologist
EEEGILNPRRSVY	perseveringly
EEEGIOQRRSSTU	grotesqueries
EEEGIORRRSSTV	retrogressive
EEEGNOQRSSSTU	grotesqueness
EEEHHIORRSTVW	whithersoever
EEEHIINRRSSST	inheritresses
EEEHILMNNPRST	replenishment
EEEHILMNORSTT	thermotensile
EEEHILMOPRRTY	pyrheliometer
EEEHIMNNNOOPP	epiphenomenon
EEEHIMNRSSTTU	hermeneutists
EEEHIMOPRRSSV	empoverishers
EEEHINNOPRRSS	reprehensions
EEEHIORSSSTTX	heterosexists
EEEHLLNOPSTYY	polyethylenes
EEEHLMNOOSSSW	wholesomeness
EEEHMNOOPRSSS	mesonephroses
EEEHMOORSSSTU	Somerset House
EEEHOOPRRSTTU	heteropterous
EEEIIILLNRSSU	leisureliness
EEEIILNNPSVXY	inexpensively
EEEIINNNSSSTV	intensiveness
EEEIINNNSSTVV	inventiveness
EEEIINNSSSSTV	sensitiveness
EEEIINORSSTVV	oversensitive
EEEIINOQRSSTU	requisiteness
EEEIINOQSSSTUX	exquisiteness
EEEIIPQRRSSTU	prerequisites
EEEILNNNPSSSS	pennilessness
EEEILNNOSSSSS	noiselessness
EEEILNNPSSSSS	spinelessness
EEEILNOPSSSVX	explosiveness
EEEILNPRSSSUV	repulsiveness
EEEIMNNPRSSTT	presentiments
EEEIMNOOPRTTT	potentiometer
EEEIMNOORSSTT	enterostomies
EEEIMNORSSSTT	sensitometers
EEEIMNPRRSSST	misrepresents
EEEIMOORRSSST	stereoisomers
EEEIMOPRRSSSV	overimpresses
EEEIMOPRRSSTX	extemporisers
EEEIMOPRRSTXZ	extemporizers
EEEIMPRRRSTTT	pretermitters
EEEINORRSSTUV	enteroviruses
EEEINPRRRSSTT	interpretress
EEEINRRSTTTUX	intertextures
EEEIOPRRSSSSU	superioresses
EEELLMORRSSSY	remorselessly
EEELLMORRSTTU	tellurometers
EEELMNPPRSSTU	supplementers
EEELMOPPRRSTT	teleprompters
EEELNNOPSSSTU	plenteousness
EEELNNOSSSSST	stonelessness
EEELNOPRSSSSW	powerlessness

EEELOOPRSSTTU	teleutospores
EEENNOORRSSSU	erroneousness
EEEOOPRRSSUVX	overexposures
EEEOPRRRSSSU	overpressures
EEFFGLNORSSTU	forgetfulness
EEFFIILNNOSVY	inoffensively
EEFGGHIIRRSST	triggerfishes
EEFGGILLMNNOR	fellmongering
EEFGHIILNRRST	freightliners
EEFGHIILRSTTW	weightlifters
EEFGHIIPRRSTZ	prizefighters
EEFGHINORSSSU	surgeonfishes
EEFGIILNNRRTY	interferingly
EEFGIIMNNNRST	infringements
EEFGIINNPRRSU	superrefining
EEFGILLOORSTX	reflexologist
EEFGINNOORSST	frontogenesis
EEFHILNNSSSSU	unselfishness
EEFHILNSSSSST	shiftlessness
EEFIIIINORRST	inferiorities
EEFIILLMNOSTU	feuilletonism
EEFIILLNNOSSX	inflexionless
EEFIILLNOSTTU	feuilletonist
EEFIILPRSSTUU	superfluities
EEFILLLLMNTUY	mellifluently
EEFILLNNPSSTU	plentifulness
EEFILLNOOPRSU	polleniferous
EEFILNNOOSSSU	feloniousness
EEFILNOORRSTX	retroflexions
EEFILNRSSSSTU	fruitlessness
EEFILOPRSSTUY	pestiferously
EEFLNRSSSSSTU	stressfulness
EEFMNOORRSSTT	sternforemost
EEGGGHIILNNRT	greenlighting
EEGGHIINORTVW	overweighting
EEGGHINNNRSTT	strengthening
EEGGHMNOOOPRY	geomorphogeny
EEGGIINNNORST	roentgenising
EEGGIINNNORTZ	roentgenizing
EEGGINORRRSST	retrogressing
EEGGLNNOOORTY	roentgenology
EEGHIIKPPRSTZ	Kirghiz Steppe
EEGHIIMNNOOTY	inhomogeneity
EEGHIIMNOPRSV	empoverishing
EEGHIINRSSTUX	extinguishers
EEGHILMNOSSST	lightsomeness
EEGHILNSSSSST	sightlessness
EEGHILOOPRSTT	herpetologist
EEGHIMNNOOOSU	inhomogeneous
EEGHIMNOOPRSS	morphogenesis
EEGHIMNORSTTT	thermosetting
EEGHINORSSSTU	righteousness
EEGHIOORSSTYZ	heterozygosis
EEGHLMNNOOOPY	phenomenology
EEGHLMNOOOSUY	homogeneously
EEGIIINORRSTX	exteriorising
EEGIIINORRTXZ	exteriorizing
EEGIIKLNNOSST	skeletonising
EEGIIKLNNOSTZ	skeletonizing
EEGIILLLNNTTY	intelligently
EEGIILLNNNTTU	unintelligent
EEGIILLNOSTUV	vitelligenous

EEGIILMNNOORST	terminologies
EEGIILMOOSSST	semeiologists
EEGIILNNRSTTY	interestingly
EEGIILNORSSSU	religiousness
EEGIIMNOPRRTU	primogeniture
EEGIIMNOPRSTX	extemporising
EEGIIMNOPRTXZ	extemporizing
EEGIIMNPRRTTT	pretermitting
EEGIINNNOSSSU	ingeniousness
EEGIINNNRSTTU	uninteresting
EEGIINNORRTVW	overwintering
EEGIINNPRRSST	interspersing
EEGIINORSSTTV	sovereigntist
EEGILLNNNRTUY	unrelentingly
EEGILLNOOSSST	selenologists
EEGILLNSSSSTU	guiltlessness
EEGILLOOPSSST	speleologists
EEGILMNNPPSTU	supplementing
EEGILMNOOOSST	entomologises
EEGILMNOOOSTZ	entomologizes
EEGILMOOORSTT	meteorologist
EEGILOPRRSSVY	progressively
EEGIMMNNORSTV	misgovernment
EEGINNNOSSSUU	ingenuousness
EEGINOORRRSST	retrogression
EEGINOPPRSSSS	prepossessing
EEGINOPPRRSSU	unprogressive
EEGNNOORRSSUU	neurosurgeons
EEHHIILLLMNPS	philhellenism
EEHHIIILLLNPST	philhellenist
EEHHIMNNOOPRSW	homeownership
EEHHINOPPRSTT	Pepin the Short
EEHHIOPPRRSSW	horsewhippers
EEHHIOPPRRSTY	hypertrophies
EEHHIOPRSSSTY	hypothesisers
EEHHIOPRSSTYZ	hypothesizers
EEHHLLOPPRSSY	phyllospheres
EEHHMMNOOOPPR	morphophoneme
EEHHOOPRSTTUW	Petworth House
EEHIIIILLLPPPV	Philippeville
EEHIIKNNSSSTT	kittenishness
EEHIILNQRRSSU	relinquishers
EEHIIMOOPSSTV	photoemissive
EEHIIMOPRRSSV	impoverishers
EEHIINOPSSSTY	hyposensitise
EEHIINOPSSTYZ	hyposensitize
EEHIKORRSSTWY	West Yorkshire
EEHILLOORSSTT	tortoiseshell
EEHILMNOPPSSY	nympholepsies
EEHILMNRSSSST	mirthlessness
EEHILMOOPPSSY	lymphopoieses
EEHILNNORRSST	northerliness
	Northern Isles
EEHILNOOPSSST	siphonosteles
EEHILNORSSSTU	southerliness
EEHIMOORSSTTY	hysterotomies
EEHIMORSSSSTU	housemistress
EEHLLMNOOSUWY	unwholesomely
EEHLMNORSSSSU	humorlessness
EEHLNORRSTTWY	northwesterly
EEHLNORSSSSTW	worthlessness
EEHLOORSSTTUY	heterostylous

EEHLORSSTTUWY	southwesterly
EEHMNNOOORRSU	neurohormones
EEHMNNOOPRSTY	hymenopterons
EEHMNOOOSSSTT	toothsomeness
EEHMNOOPRSTUY	hymenopterous
EEHMNOORRSSTT	North Somerset
EEHNOOOPRRTXY	orthopyroxene
EEHOOOOPRRSSTU	heterosporous
EEHOOPPSSTTTY	phototypesets
EEIIIINSSSTTV	sensitivities
EEIIILNNSSTVY	insensitively
EEIIIMNPRSSTV	primitiveness
EEIIIMOPPRRST	improprieties
EEIIINNSSTTUV	intuitiveness
EEIIIORRRSSTV	Trois-Rivières
EEIIILLMNSSSST	limitlessness
EEIIILMNNPRTTY	impertinently
EEIIILMNPSSSUV	impulsiveness
EEIIILMOOSSTTY	osteomyelitis
EEIIILNNNOSSTV	inventionless
EEIIILNOORSTUV	revolutionise
EEIIILNOORTUVZ	revolutionize
EEIIILNOQRSTUV	ventriloquise
EEIIILNOQRTUVZ	ventriloquize
EEIIILOPPRSTVY	prepositively
EEIIILOPRSTTUY	repetitiously
EEIIMNOPRRSSS	reimpressions
EEIIMNOPRRSST	pretermission
EEIIMNOPRSSSU	imperiousness
EEIIMNOPRSSSX	expressionism
EEIIMNPRRSSTT	misinterprets
EEIIMNRRSTTUX	intermixtures
EEIINNNORSTTV	interventions
EEIINNOPRRSST	interspersion
EEIINNORSSTTT	retentionists
EEIINNRSSSTUV	intrusiveness
EEIINOPRSSSTX	expressionist
EEIJJMNOOSSTU	jejunostomies
EEILLLNOPQTUY	equipollently
EEILMPPRSTUVY	presumptively
EEILNNOPSSSST	pointlessness
EEILNNOSSTTUY	sententiously
EEILNOOPPRSSY	polyisoprenes
EEILNOORSSSTU	resolutioners
EEILNOPRSTTUY	pretentiously
EEILNPRRSTUUV	supervirulent
EEILOOPPRSSST	leptospiroses
EEILOPPRSSSTY	proselytisers
EEILOPRRSSTYZ	proselytizers
EEIMNNNOPRSST	prominentness
EEIMNNOOPPRSS	perispomenons
EEIMNNORSSSUV	verminousness
EEIMNOOPRSSTV	promotiveness
EEIMNOOPRTTTY	potentiometry
EEIMNOPSSSTUU	impetuousness
EEIMOOPRRSSTT	stereotropism
EEINNNOPRSSTT	nonpersistent
EEINNOPRSSSUU	penuriousness
EEINNOPRSTTUU	unpretentious
EEINOOPPRSSSS	prepossession
EEINOOPRSSSSS	repossessions
EEINOORRRSSTV	retroversions
EEINOPPRSSSUV	purposiveness
EEIOPRSSSTTTY	stereotypists
EEKNNOOPSSSTU	outspokenness
EEKNOOPPRSSSS	spokespersons
EELLNOOPPPRYY	polypropylene
EELLOPPRSSSUY	purposelessly
EELMNORSSSTUU	tremulousness
EELMOPPRRSSUY	superpolymers
EELMOPSSTTUUY	tempestuously
EELNOQRSSSUUU	querulousness
EELNRSSSSSTTU	trustlessness
EEMMNNOOSSSTU	momentousness
EEMMPRRSSTUYY	supersymmetry
EEMNNOOPPSSTT	postponements
EENNOOPPRSSTU	opportuneness
EENNORSSSSTUU	strenuousness
EFFGGILNNORSU	longsuffering
EFFGGINOOSTTU	gift of tongues
EFFGHILNRSSTU	frightfulness
EFFIILOORSSSU	fossiliferous
EFGGHIIILNTTW	weightlifting
EFGGHIIINPRTZ	prizefighting
EFGGHIILNNRTY	frighteningly
EFGGIIINNPRSY	presignifying
EFGGIINNORSSV	forgivingness
EFGHIIILNNSTT	thing-in-itself
EFGHIILNORSTT	fortnightlies
EFGIKLNNOORWY	foreknowingly
EFGIMNOOPRRTU	outperforming
EFHIOOPPRRSSS	professorship
EFIILLNOOPRSU	polliniferous
EFIIMNOPSSSTT	postfeminists
EFIINOPRSSSTU	perfusionists
EFIKLLNNSSSUU	unskilfulness
EFILLLLMOSUUY	mellifluously
EFILMNOORSSUY	somniferously
EFILNOOORSSTU	stoloniferous
EFILNOORSSSUV	frivolousness
EFLLOPRSSUUUY	superfluously
EFLNOORRSSSUW	sorrowfulness
EGGHIIINNSTUX	extinguishing
EGGHLMOOOOPRV	geomorphology
EGGIIILMNNNRT	intermingling
EGGIIINNNORST	nitrogenising
EGGIIINNNORTZ	nitrogenizing
EGGIILMNOOSTY	etymologising
EGGIILMNOOTYZ	etymologizing
EGGILNOOORSTT	gerontologist
EGGIMNOOPRSSS	gossipmongers
EGHHIILOPRSTY	hieroglyphist
EGHHIINOPPRSW	horsewhipping
EGHHIINOPSSTY	hypothesising
EGHHIINOPSTYZ	hypothesizing
EGHHILLMNOOTY	helminthology
EGHHLLOSSTTUY	thoughtlessly
EGHHMORRSTTUY	merrythoughts
EGHIIILNNQRSU	relinquishing
EGHIIILNRRSST	Stirlingshire
EGHIIIMNOPRSV	impoverishing
EGHIILMNNOPSY	sphingomyelin
EGHIILNNSSSTU	unsightliness
EGHIILNPRSSST	sprightliness

EGHIILOOOPRST	oligotrophies
EGHIIMNOOPSSY	physiognomies
EGHIIMNOPSSTY	physostigmine
EGHIINPRSSTTU	guttersnipish
EGHILMOORSSTY	mythologisers
EGHILMOORSTYZ	mythologizers
EGHILNOOPRSST	nephrologists
	phrenologists
EGHILNORSTUUY	unrighteously
EGHILNPRSTTUU	sulphuretting
EGHILOOPPSSST	psephologists
EGHIMNNORRSTU	nursing mother
EGHINOOPRRSSV	governorships
EGIIIILNORRST	irreligionist
EGIIIINNORRST	interiorising
EGIIIINNORRTZ	interiorizing
EGIIIKLLNNRTW	winterkilling
EGIIIKNNNRTTT	interknitting
EGIIILLORRSUY	irreligiously
EGIIILNOSSSTU	litigiousness
EGIIINNOOPRST	repositioning
EGIIINNRSTTTW	intertwisting
EGIIKLNPPRSS	klipspringers
EGIILLLOOSTVX	vexillologist
EGIILLNNNSSUW	unwillingness
EGIILLNORSUUY	unreligiously
EGIILMNNRTTUY	unremittingly
EGIILMNOORSTT	terminologist
EGIILMOOSSSST	seismologists
EGIILNNOQSTUY	questioningly
EGIILNOPRSSTY	proselytising
EGIILNOPRSTYZ	proselytizing
EGIILNORSTUVY	vertiginously
EGIILOOOSSTTV	sovietologist
EGIILOPRSSTUY	prestigiously
EGIIMNNNNOPSY	moneyspinning
EGIIMNNNRSTTU	instrumenting
EGIIMNOOPRRST	primogenitors
EGIIMNOPPRSSU	superimposing
EGIIMOPRRSSSV	progressivism
EGIINNNOQSTUU	unquestioning
EGIINNNSSTTUW	unwittingness
EGIINNOORRSST	introgression
EGIIOPRRSSSTV	progressivist
EGILLNNOORSST	Rolling Stones
EGILMNOOOSSTT	entomologists
EGILMNOORSSTU	numerologists
EGILMNOOSSTYZ	enzymologists
EGILNNOSSSTUU	glutinousness
EGILNOPPRSUVY	oversupplying
EGMMNOOPRSSUY	gymnospermous
EHHHIOOPPPSTY	hypophosphite
EHHIILOOPPRSS	philosophiser
EHHIILOOPPRSZ	philosophizer
EHHIILOOPPSSS	philosophises
EHHIILOOPPSSZ	philosophizes
EHHILMOOPRSTU	thermophilous
EHHIMMMOOOPRS	homeomorphism
EHHIMMNOORSTU	Monmouthshire
EHHIMNOOPRSST	thermosiphons
EHHINOOOPPRSS	siphonophores
EHHMMOOOOPRSU	homeomorphous

EHHMMNOOOPRSTY	phytohormones
EHIIILLOPPPSU	Louis Philippe
EHIIIMNPRSSST	ministerships
EHIIKLMOOPRTY	poikilothermy
EHIILLMNPSSTU	phillumenists
EHIILLNOPSSTT	septillionths
EHIILLNOSSTTX	sextillionths
EHIILMOOPPSSY	lymphopoiesis
EHIILNOOOPSSU	eosinophilous
EHIILNOQRSSSU	liquorishness
EHIILOPRRSTTT	lithotripters
EHIIMNOOOPSST	photoemission
EHIINOOOPRSST	iontophoresis
EHIIOOOPPSTTV	photopositive
EHILLNNOOPQUY	phylloquinone
EHILMNOOOPSTU	entomophilous
EHILNOPSSSTYY	polysynthesis
EHIMMOOPRRSTT	thermotropism
EHIMOOPRSSTTT	photometrists
EHIMOPRSSTTYY	hypsometrists
EHLLLOOPPSTUY	leptophyllous
EHLLNOOPSSTUY	stenophyllous
EHLLOPRSSUUUY	sulphureously
EHLMOOOOPPRSTY	photopolymers
EHNNOOOPRSTTU	photoneutrons
EIIIILNQSTUVY	inquisitively
EIIIINNQSTUUV	uninquisitive
EIIIINNSSTTVY	insensitivity
EIIILLMOOPSTY	poliomyelitis
EIIILNSTTTUVY	institutively
EIIIMMNOPRSSS	impressionism
EIIIMMNNORSSST	immersionists
EIIIMNNORSSST	intermissions
EIIIMNNPRSSTT	inspiritments
EIIIMNOOPRSST	reimpositions
EIIIMNOPRSSST	impressionist
EIIIINNOOPRSTT	interposition
EIIJNNORSSSUU	injuriousness
EIILLOOQRSSSU	soliloquisers
EIILLOOQRSSUZ	soliloquizers
EIILMNOQRSTUV	ventriloquism
EIILMOORRSTUY	meritoriously
EIILNOORRSSTU	irresolutions
EIILNOORSSTTU	resolutionist
EIILNOORSTTUV	revolutionist
EIILNOOSSTTUV	evolutionists
EIILNOQRSTTUV	ventriloquist
EIILNORRSSSTY	sinistrorsely
EIILOOPPRSSST	leptospirosis
EIILOPPSSTUVY	suppositively
EIIMMNNOPRSST	imprisonments
EIIMNOORSSSTT	monstrosities
EIIMOOPRSSTTV	overoptimists
EIINNNOOSSSUX	innoxiousness
EIINNOORRSSTV	introversions
EIINNOOSSTTVY	tenosynovitis
EIINNOPRRSTTU	interruptions
EIINOOPPRSSTU	superposition
EIINOOPPRSTTU	opportunities
EIINOORSSTTTX	extortionists
EIINOPRSSSTTU	superstitions
EIIOOPPRSSSTU	suppositories

EIIOOPPSSSTTV	postpositives
EIIOPRRSSTTUU	surreptitious
EIIOPRSSSTTUU	superstitious
EILNNOOPPRTUY	inopportunely
EILNORSSSUUUX	luxuriousness
EINNNOOOPSSSS	nonpossession
EINNOOOPSSSSU	poisonousness
EINNOOORSSSTU	notoriousness
EINNOPSSTUUUX	Pontus Euxinus
EMNNOORSSSSTU	monstrousness
EMNOPSSSSTUUU	sumptuousness
ENOOPPRRSSSST	sportspersons
FGILOORSSTTUU	futurologists
FGLMNNOOOOOSS	Song of Solomon
FILLMRSSTTUUY	mistrustfully
GGGHHINOOORTU	thoroughgoing
GGGHILNNOORSW	hornswoggling
GGHIILMNOOSTY	mythologising
GGHIILMNOOTYZ	mythologizing
GGILLOOOSSSST	glossologists
GHIILLOOPSSTY	syphilologist
GHIILNOOORSTT	ornithologist
GHIILOOPSSSTY	physiologists
GHIIMMOOPRSTT	thigmotropism
GHIIMNOOPSSTY	physiognomist
GHILMOOOPRSST	morphologists
GHIMNOOPSSSTY	gymnosophists
GIIIILNNNPRSTY	inspiritingly

GIIIKLLLMNSTU	multiskilling
GIIILLNOOQSSU	soliloquising
GIIILLNOOQSUZ	soliloquizing
GIIILMNNOOSUY	ignominiously
GIILMMNOOSSTU	immunologists
GIINNOOOPPRRT	proportioning
GILLLMOOPSSYY	polysyllogism
HHIMOOOPRRSUZ	rhizomorphous
HIIILLNNOQTTU	quintillionth
HIIILLOOPPPPS	Philippopolis
HIILLOOPPRSWW	whippoorwills
HIIMMNOOPSSTY	monophysitism
HILMNOOPSSUYY	symphoniously
HILORRSTTTUWY	trustworthily
HLLNOOOPPSUYY	polyphonously
HNORRSTTTUUWY	untrustworthy
IIIINNOSSTTTU	intuitionists
IIIMNNOORSSST	intromissions
IIIMNOORSTTUV	vomituritions
IIINNORSSTTTU	nutritionists
IIINOOOPPSSTT	oppositionist
IILLLORSSTUUY	illustriously
IILMNOOQSSSTU	somniloquists
IILNOOOPSSTTU	lotus position
IIMNOOOPPRRST	misproportion
IINNOOPPRTTUY	inopportunity
IINOOOPPSSSTT	postpositions

Fourteen Letters

AAAAAACCEEMRSZ	Caesarea Mazaca
AAAAAADHMNNRST	Sanatana Dharma
AAAAACGILMMNRT	anagrammatical
AAAAACHHKNRRSY	Shankaracharya
AAAAAGGINNRRTT	rangatiratanga
AAAABBCEILRSTY	sabbatical year
AAAABCCEEHIRRT	archaebacteria
AAAABCCEELRSTU	baccalaureates
AAAABCFIIJLNOR	Baja California
AAAABEHKLLLMRU	Mahalla el Kubra
AAAACCDEINORSU	anacardiaceous
AAAACCILLPRTTY	paratactically
AAAACCINNRSSTU	transcaucasian
AAAACCLMNORSST	malacostracans
AAAACDIILLNNST	Catalina Island
AAAACDIILLPRSY	paradisaically
	paradisiacally
AAAACDIIMMNOST	macadamisation
AAAACDIIMMNOTZ	macadamization
AAAACEGILLMMNO	megalomaniacal
AAAACEHMNORSTU	amaranthaceous
AAAACEIMNNRRST	sacramentarian
AAAACHIILNNRSS	Halicarnassian
AAAADDDGIMNNOU	Goa, Daman, and Diu
AAAADDILMNNNSS	Andaman Islands
AAAADEGIMMNRST	anagrammatised
AAAADEGIMMNRTZ	anagrammatized
AAAADEGINNQRRU	quadragenarian
AAAADELLLNORRV	Andorra la Vella
AAAADIILMNNRSS	Mariana Islands
AAAADIKLLNNSSU	Unalaska Island
AAAAEGIMMNNRSST	anagrammatises
AAAAEGIMMNRSTZ	anagrammatizes
AAAAFIILNNPRRS	infralapsarian
AAAAGGNOORSTUW	Ogasawara Gunto
AAAAGHIMNOPRST	phantasmagoria
AAAAGIMMNRSSTT	anagrammatists
AAAAHHIKMNPSTV	Vishakhapatnam
AAAAHIIMNNNSST	Mina Hassan Tani
AAAAIILLNOPSTT	palatalisation
AAAAIILLNOPTTZ	palatalization
AAAAILLNPRSSTU	Australian Alps
AAAAILNPPRRSSU	supralapsarian
AAABBEEGLLNOOR	Boolean algebra
AAABBHIIJNNRYY	Jabir ibn Hayyan
AAABBLLNNOORTW	Walloon Brabant
AAABCCDLLLMSUU	lambda calculus
AAABCCEIILLMST	acclimatisable
AAABCCEIILLMTZ	acclimatizable
AAABCCILMNNOOV	cyanocobalamin
AAABCDEGINOSTU	Santiago de Cuba
AAABCDILNNOORY	Calydonian boar
AAABCEFLMNRTUU	manufacturable
AAABCEHILLLPTY	alphabetically
AAABCEHILMOSTT	haematoblastic
AAABCEHILNOPPR	inapproachable
AAABCEHLNOPPRU	unapproachable
AAABCEILMNOSSU	balsaminaceous
AAABCHILNOPPRY	inapproachably
AAABCHLNOPPRUY	unapproachably
AAABDEEMRSSSSS	ambassadresses
AAABDHIMOPRSSS	ambassadorship
AAABDIINORSSTT	bastardisation
AAABDIINORSTTZ	bastardization
AAABEEEGLMNNSS	manageableness
AAABEEGILMNRRU	unmarriageable
AAABEEILNNSSTT	attainableness
AAABEGIILLNOUV	bougainvillaea
AAABEIIIILLSTV	availabilities
AAABEILNOOPSTT	palaeobotanist
AAABELLNNPRSTT	transplantable
AAABELLNNRSTTU	untranslatable
AAABGILNQSTTUU	absquatulating
AAABHHNOPSTTUW	Bophuthatswana
AAABIIKLNNOSST	balkanisations
AAABIIKLNNOSTZ	balkanizations
AAABIILLNRRSTV	Brillat-Savarin
AAABIILNOOPRST	parabolisation
AAABIILNOOPRTZ	parabolization
AAABIILNRRTTWY	warrantability
AAACCCEHILRSTT	catachrestical
AAACCCEINNORTT	Antarctic Ocean
AAACCDEHIINORT	archidiaconate
AAACCDEIMNNOOR	adenocarcinoma
AAACCDEIOPPRSU	capparidaceous
AAACCDILORRSUV	cardiovascular
AAACCEEHILMNOR	aeromechanical
AAACCEEHILMNPR	macrencephalia
AAACCEEILMNRRT	Central America
AAACCEEINNQRTU	reacquaintance
AAACCEGHILLOOR	archaeological
AAACCEHILMPRTU	pharmaceutical
AAACCEHLNNNTUY	Yucatán Channel
AAACCEILNNORTX	extracanonical

AAAACCELMNOPSUU	campanulaceous
AAAACCGHILOPRRT	cartographical
AAAACCGIIINNPTT	incapacitating
AAAACCGILLMNOOP	campanological
AAAACCHIILNRSTT	charlatanistic
AAAACCHIINORSST	saccharisation
AAAACCHIINORSTZ	saccharization
AAAACCHILLMORTY	achromatically
AAAACCHILLNNORY	anachronically
AAAACCIIINNOPTT	incapacitation
AAAACCILLORTTUY	autocratically
AAAACCLMOORSSTU	malacostracous
AAAACDDEIIORTTV	radioactivated
AAAACDEEINPPRSS	disappearances
AAAACDEELOPRRTX	Electra paradox
AAAACDEIIINPRST	paediatricians
AAAACDEIIORSTTV	radioactivates
AAAACDEILLNPRSS	Paracel Islands
AAAACDFHIMNNRST	handicraftsman
AAAACDGMNORSSTU	coastguardsman
AAAACDHHILMNSST	Chatham Islands
AAAACDHIINOPRSS	anaphrodisiacs
AAAACDHILNOOPRS	achondroplasia
AAAACDHINNRSTTU	Tristan da Cunha
AAAACDIILNNOSST	scandalisation
AAAACDIILNNOSTZ	scandalization
AAAACDNOOPRRSTX	Cantor's paradox
AAAACEEGIILNSTT	telangiectasia
AAAACEEGILMNOPT	palaeomagnetic
AAAACEEGILNSSTU	Aguascalientes
AAAACEEILLNORRS	Alsace-Lorraine
AAAACEEILNORSUV	valerianaceous
AAAACEENNNOPPRS	nonappearances
AAAACEFGIORSSUX	saxifragaceous
AAAACEFIILNORRT	rarefictional
AAAACEGHILLMOOT	haematological
AAAACEGINSSTUWY	Giant's Causeway
AAAACEHIILNPTTT	antipathetical
AAAACEHIIMMNSTT	mathematicians
AAAACEHIIMNPRSS	Spanish America
AAAACEHILLLMPRY	alphamerically
AAAACEHILLMMTTY	mathematically
AAAACEHILMOOPPR	pharmacopoeial
AAAACEHILMPRSTT	metaphrastical
AAAACEHILNOPPRT	palaeanthropic
AAAACEHIMOOPPRS	pharmacopoeias
AAAACEILLMNNSTY	anamnestically
AAAACEILLMSTTTY	metastatically
AAAACEILLNORTUY	aeronautically
AAAACEILMMNRSST	sacramentalism
AAAACEILMNRSSTT	sacramentalist
AAAACEILMNRSTTY	sacramentality
AAAACFIILLLSTTY	fatalistically
AAAACFIILNSTTTY	fantastically
AAAACFIMNORRSTW	aircraftswoman
AAAACGGHHIILOPR	hagiographical
AAAACGGHIIMNOST	gigantomachias
AAAACGHILLLNPYY	anaglyphically
AAAACGHILNOPRRU	uranographical
AAAACGHIMNOPRST	phantasmagoric
AAAACGIILLMSTTY	astigmatically
AAAACGIILLNPSTY	paganistically
AAAACGIILMPRTTY	pragmaticality
AAAACGILLMNORTY	morganatically
AAAACGILNNOSTTU	anticoagulants
AAAACGIMNOOPRRS	macrosporangia
AAAACGLORRSSTUV	gastrovascular
AAAACHIILMMRRST	matriarchalism
AAAACHIILNOPSTT	chaptalisation
AAAACHIILNOPTTZ	chaptalization
AAAACHILLLLOPTY	allopathically
AAAACHILLMNPSTY	phantasmically
AAAACHILMMNNOPY	nymphomaniacal
AAAACHILMOPRRTU	thaumatropical
AAAACIIILNOPSTT	capitalisation
AAAACIIILNOPTTZ	capitalization
AAAACIIILNPSTTT	anticapitalist
AAAACIILNOSSSTU	casualisations
AAAACIILNOSSTUZ	casualizations
AAAACILLLLOPRTY	allopatrically
AAAADDEELNORRST	Andrea del Sarto
AAAADDEHLLNRRUY	Laurel and Hardy
AAAADDGGIINNSTV	disadvantaging
AAAADEEGIIKKNRR	Kierkegaardian
AAAADEGILMNRRTY	Admiralty Range
AAAADEGILNQRSTU	Griqualand East
AAAADEGLNOSTUVY	advantageously
AAAADEHIMNORSTU	adiathermanous
AAAADEIIILLNNOSS	Aeolian Islands
AAAADEIIILNNRTUV	valetudinarian
AAAADEILLNNPSST	Pleasant Island
AAAADEILLQRRSTU	quadrilaterals
AAAADEILNRSTTTY	Latter-day Saint
AAAADFHNNOOPTUY	Anthony of Padua
AAAADGHIOOPRRTU	autoradiograph
	radioautograph
AAAADGIKLNNOORS	Kangaroo Island
AAAADIIILNNRTTU	latitudinarian
AAAADIILNNSSSVY	Visayan Islands
AAAADIIMNORSSTT	dramatisations
AAAADIIMNORSTTZ	dramatizations
AAAADIJLNNNSSSU	San Juan Islands
AAAADIJNNNORRST	Trans-Jordanian
AAAADILLNRSSSTU	Austral Islands
AAAAEEEGKLLRSTV	Great Slave Lake
AAAAEEGHLOPPRRS	palaeographers
AAAAEEGINNPPUUW	Papua New Guinea
AAAAEEGINNPRSTU	septuagenarian
AAAAEEGLLNPRSTU	Langres Plateau
AAAAEEHHLMMORTT	haematothermal
AAAAEEHIIMNRRTT	Henrietta Maria
AAAAEEIKLMNNRSZ	Mariánské Lázně
AAAAEEJMNNRSTVY	Vestmannaeyjar
AAAAEFGGLLMNORU	formal language
AAAAEFIILMMRSST	matresfamilias
AAAAEFIILMPRSST	patresfamilias
AAAAEGHHMOOPSTU	haematophagous
AAAAEGHIIMNNSTT	anathematising
AAAAEGHIIMNNTTZ	anathematizing
AAAAEGHLNNOPRSY	nasopharyngeal
AAAAEGIIILMNRST	egalitarianism
AAAAEGIILMNRSST	managerialists
AAAAEGILMNORSSU	megalosaurians
AAAAEGINORSTTVX	extravagations

AAAEGLLLMOPRRS	parallelograms	**AABCCEEILMOSTUU**	bioaccumulates
AAAEGMMNNORRTTT	tetragrammaton	**AABCCEEIMNORTUY**	cyanobacterium
AAAEHIMOPRRSTT	aromatherapist	**AABCCIIILPRTTY**	practicability
AAAEHINOSSSTTU	Southeast Asian	**AABCCIILNOTTUY**	accountability
AAAEIIILMPRRST	paramilitaries	**AABCDDEEHKNNSS**	backhandedness
AAAEILLMNNNPSUV	Malay Peninsula	**AABCDDEELLLOSY**	dodecasyllable
AAAEIMMMNRRSTU	armamentariums	**AABCDEEEEHLNRRW**	Hebrew calendar
AAAEIMORRSSTTT	tarsometatarsi	**AABCDEEFIILLSS**	declassifiable
AAAEINORSSTTVX	extravasations	**AABCDEEHNNRUZZ**	nebuchadnezzar
AAAGHINRRSTUUY	Austria-Hungary	**AABCDEEINRRSTT**	scatterbrained
AAAGIILNNNOORST	organisational	**AABCDEEIRRSTUU**	bureaucratised
AAAGIILNNNOORTZ	organizational	**AABCDEEIRRTUUZ**	bureaucratized
AAAGIINNNOOSTT	antagonisation	**AABCDEELNORRST**	labradorescent
AAAGIINNNOOTTZ	antagonization	**AABCDEENNPRSUU**	superabundance
AAAGINOORRSTTV	astronavigator	**AABCDEENRSSSTT**	abstractedness
AAAHIINORRSTTU	authoritarians	**AABCDEGINORRST**	rebroadcasting
AAAHIIOPPRRSUW	pipiwharauroas	**AABCDEHHHLOSUYZ**	Ashby-de-la-Zouch
AAAHILORSSTTUU	South Australia	**AABCDEIILLNOSS**	diabolicalness
AAAIIMMNNQRSTU	antiquarianism	**AABCDEILMNNNRU**	cardinal number
AAAIILMNNOSTTU	Altai Mountains	**AABCDEINORRSTU**	decarburations
AAAIILNNORSTTU	naturalisation	**AABCDELLLORTYY**	Barclay de Tolly
AAAIILNNORTTUZ	naturalization	**AABCDHIKLNOPSU**	Bishop Auckland
AAAIILNNOSSTTT	tantalisations	**AABCDIILNNORSS**	Nicobar Islands
AAAIILNNOSSTTZ	tantalizations	**AABCDINNORSSTT**	contrabandists
AAAIIMNNOOSSTT	anatomisations	**AABCEEEGHLNNSS**	changeableness
AAAIIMNNOOSTTZ	anatomizations	**AABCEEEGHLNRSS**	chargeableness
AAAIIMNOORSSTT	aromatisations	**AABCEEEHILLMNP**	Blenheim Palace
AAAIIMNOOSTTTU	automatisation	**AABCEEGHIOPRST**	bacteriophages
AAAIIMNOOTTTUZ	automatization	**AABCEEHILNRSST**	charitableness
AAAIIMNORSTTTU	traumatisation	**AABCEEHILOPRRR**	irreproachable
AAAIIMNORTTTUZ	traumatization	**AABCEEHLMNNRTU**	unmerchantable
AAAIINNORSSTTV	intravasations	**AABCEEIILLPRTY**	replaceability
AAAIINNOSSSSST	assassinations	**AABCEEILLLMMTY**	emblematically
AAAILLMPRRSUXY	supramaxillary	**AABCEEILLMNPSS**	implacableness
AAAILLNNOOPRSY	Annapolis Royal	**AABCEEILLNPPSS**	applicableness
AAAILMNNORSSTTU	Atlas Mountains	**AABCEEILMNRSSV**	vraisemblances
AAAILNNORSTTUV	transvaluation	**AABCEEIORSSSTT**	bacteriostases
AAAIMNNNOSSTUY	Sayan Mountains	**AABCEEIRRSSTUU**	bureaucratises
AAAIMNNORSTTTU	Tatra Mountains	**AABCEEIRRSTUUZ**	bureaucratizes
AABBCEEFINORST	absorbefacient	**AABCEELMNOPRSS**	comparableness
AABBCEHHISSTTW	witches' Sabbath	**AABCEFGIINPRRT**	prefabricating
AABBDGGIINNNOR	brobdingnagian	**AABCEFIIINOSTT**	beatifications
AABBEEELNNRSSU	unbearableness	**AABCEFIIINOTTU**	beautification
AABBEFGGILNRST	flabbergasting	**AABCEFIINOPRRT**	prefabrication
AABBEFHILMNRST	Flemish Brabant	**AABCEFIINORSTT**	abortifacients
AABBEFINNOSTUY	Fountains Abbey	**AABCEFIOPRRRST**	prefabricators
AABBEIILLOSSSU	bouillabaisses	**AABCEGHILNORST**	branchiostegal
AABBEILNRTTTUU	unattributable	**AABCEGIILLOOOR**	aerobiological
AABBHIIIILNTTY	inhabitability	**AABCEHIIILMPTY**	impeachability
AABCCCDHILRTYY	brachydactylic	**AABCEHIIMMOSTT**	biomathematics
AABCCCEHHILPRY	brachycephalic	**AABCEHILOPRRRY**	irreproachably
AABCCCEHKRRSST	backscratchers	**AABCEHINOORSTT**	archeobotanist
AABCCCGHIKNRST	backscratching	**AABCEIILLORSST**	aeroballistics
AABCCDEILMOTUU	bioaccumulated	**AABCEIILNNPRTU**	antirepublican
AABCCDEILNORTT	contradictable	**AABCEIILRRTTTY**	retractability
AABCCEEEELNPSST	acceptableness	**AABCEIILRTTTXY**	extractability
AABCCEELNNORTU	counterbalance	**AABCEIINOORSTU**	bioaeronautics
AABCCEGHIIOPRT	bacteriophagic	**AABCEIIORSSSTT**	bacteriostasis
AABCCEHILLMOPS	accomplishable	**AABCEILLLRSSTY**	crystallisable
AABCCEHNOOORSU	orobanchaceous	**AABCEILLLRSTYZ**	crystallizable
AABCCEIIORSTTT	bacteriostatic	**AABCEILLMORRTY**	barometrically
AABCCEILMMRTUU	circumambulate	**AABCEILNORSSTU**	constabularies

AABCEIMOORSSUU	simaroubaceous
AABCELNOOPRSTY	polycarbonates
AABCFILNNOOSTU	confabulations
AABCGGIILLOOOR	agrobiological
AABCGHIILLMOOP	amphibological
AABCGHIILLOPRY	biographically
AABCGHIMOOPRRR	microbarograph
AABCHIILPRSTUY	purchasability
AABCHILOOPRSTU	claustrophobia
AABCIIILLMPRSY	imparisyllabic
AABCIIILNRTTTY	intractability
AABCIILLLOPSTY	collapsability
AABCIILLNOSSTY	syllabications
AABCIIMNORSSTT	abstractionism
AABCIINNOORSST	carbonisations
AABCIINNOORSTZ	carbonizations
AABCIINOOSSSTU	subassociation
AABCIINORRSSTU	carburisations
AABCIINORRSTUZ	carburizations
AABCIINORSSTTT	abstractionist
AABCIKLMNNOSTU	Black Mountains
AABCILLLLOPSYY	polysyllabical
AABCILLNOOORST	collaborations
AABCILLORRRTUU	arboricultural
AABCILMNNOOTTU	noctambulation
AABCILNNOSSTTU	consubstantial
AABCINORSSSSTT	contrabassists
AABCNNOOORSSST	contrabassoons
AABDDEEIMRRSSS	disembarrassed
AABDDEELNNRSTU	understandable
AABDDEGIINOORT	biodegradation
AABDDEIILRSSTY	addressability
AABDDELNNRSTUY	understandably
AABDEEEFHINRRT	featherbrained
AABDEEEHHIRRSS	haberdasheries
AABDEEEHNNRRSST	threadbareness
AABDEEELNNRSSU	unreadableness
AABDEEELOORRTV	overelaborated
AABDEEFIIORRRS	barrier of ideas
AABDEEGIKRRSUZ	Gaudier-Brzeska
AABDEEIMNNORSS	Basse-Normandie
AABDEEIMRRSSSS	disembarrasses
AABDEELLMNORSU	Albemarle Sound
AABDEFIIILLQSU	disqualifiable
AABDEGIILMNRSS	Gambier Islands
AABDEIIILMNOPR	imponderabilia
AABDEIIKMNORST	disembarkation
AABDEIILPRSTUY	persuadability
AABDEIINOOSTTU	autoantibodies
AABDGGIIIMNSTU	disambiguating
AABDGIIIMNOSTU	disambiguation
AABDHIMNORSSTT	rhabdomantists
AABDIIIILNSTVY	inadvisability
AABDIIILNOTUVY	unavoidability
AABDIINOOPPRST	disapprobation
AABEEEKLMNRRSS	remarkableness
AABEEEKLMNRSST	marketableness
AABEEEELLMNNSST	lamentableness
AABEEELMNRSSSU	measurableness
AABEEELNNORSSS	reasonableness
AABEEELNNOSSSS	seasonableness
AABEEELNNRSSSW	answerableness
AABEEEELOORRSTV	overelaborates
AABEEFLNNRRSTU	untransferable
AABEEFLNORSSUV	favourableness
AABEEGLMMOPRRR	reprogrammable
AABEEGLNOPPRSS	propagableness
AABEEHIIILRTTV	rehabilitative
AABEEHIILRTTWY	weatherability
AABEEHKLNNSSSU	unshakableness
AABEEIILMNOTTT	antimetabolite
AABEEIILNNRSSV	invariableness
AABEEIILNNSSST	insatiableness
AABEEILLNNSSUV	invaluableness
AABEEILMNPSSSS	impassableness
AABEELLLRSSTTY	tetrasyllables
AABEELNNRRSTUY	subterraneanly
AABEEMMNNRRSSST	embarrassments
AABEFIILMNNQTUU	unquantifiable
AABEFILLMMNNNO	noninflammable
AABEGHIIILNRTT	rehabilitating
AABEGHIKLNRTTY	breathtakingly
AABEGHIOOPRRTU	autobiographer
AABEGIILLNOSUV	bougainvilleas
AABEGILMNRRSSY	embarrassingly
AABEGLMNRSSTUU	Albertus Magnus
AABEHIIILNORTT	rehabilitation
AABEHLLOPPRSTY	blepharoplasty
AABEHLMNOOPRST	nephroblastoma
AABEHLMOPPRSSS	blepharospasms
AABEIIIILLNNTY	inalienability
AABEIIIILLNORST	liberalisation
AABEIIILLNORTZ	liberalization
AABEIIILLNRTTY	inalterability
AABEIIILMNRRST	libertarianism
AABEIIILNPRSTY	inseparability
AABEIIILPRRRTY	irreparability
AABEIILNORSSTV	verbalisations
AABEIILNORSTVZ	verbalizations
AABEIILNSSSTTU	substantialise
AABEIILNSSTTUZ	substantialize
AABEIINSSTTTUV	substantiative
AABEILMNOPRSTU	perambulations
AABEILNNORSTTU	subalternation
AABEINOOPRRRTY	reprobationary
AABFHIIILNOSTY	fashionability
AABFIIILLMMNTY	inflammability
AABFIILLNPPTUY	unflappability
AABGIINNSSTTTU	substantiating
AABGILMMNNOSTU	somnambulating
AABHIIILNPRRSS	librarianships
AABHIIINPPRSST	bipartisanship
AABIIILLMNPTUY	manipulability
AABIIILNOSSSTT	stabilisations
AABIIILNOSSTTZ	stabilizations
AABIILLNOOPTTX	blaxploitation
AABIILLNPRSSUY	Salisbury Plain
AABIILMNSSSTTU	substantialism
AABIILNNNRTTUY	tintinnabulary
AABIILNORSSTTU	brutalisations
AABIILNORSTTUZ	brutalizations
AABIILNSSSTTTU	substantialist
AABIILNSSTTTUY	substantiality
AABIINNOSSTTTU	substantiation

AABILLLNNOPRRU	Nullarbor Plain
AABILLNSSTTUVY	substantivally
AABILMMNNOOSTU	somnambulation
AABINORSSSTTTU	substantiators
AABINORSSSTTUU	subsaturations
AABLMMNOORSSTU	somnambulators
AACCCEEGINORSY	gynaecocracies
AACCCEEHILLTTY	catechetically
AACCCEEHILMNTU	catechumenical
AACCCEEIILLSST	ecclesiastical
AACCCEHHILOPPS	scaphocephalic
AACCCEHIIRRSTT	characteristic
AACCCFIIILNOST	calcifications
AACCCGHHILNNRU	Anglican Church
AACCCHILLNOOPY	cacophonically
AACCCHLLOOPSTY	staphylococcal
AACCCILNOORSTT	social contract
AACCDDEEILMOPR	El Cid Campeador
AACCDDEMMNOOTU	unaccommodated
AACCDDIIIORTUV	Ciudad Victoria
AACCDEEHINORRS	archdeaconries
AACCDEEILNOPSY	encyclopaedias
AACCDEHIIRRSST	trisaccharides
AACCDEHILOPRSY	polysaccharide
AACCDEHIMNOORS	monosaccharide
AACCDEIILLOPTY	apodeictically
AACCDEIILMNTUZ	unacclimatized
AACCDEIIMNORTT	antidemocratic
AACCDEIINNORTT	contraindicate
AACCDEILLMORTY	democratically
AACCDEILLMRTUV	circumvallated
AACCDFIIILNPSS	Pacific Islands
AACCDGHILOPRTY	dactylographic
AACCDHIMOPRSTY	psychodramatic
AACCDIIINRSTTU	traducianistic
AACCDIINNNORTT	contraindicant
AACCDIMMNOOOST	accommodations
AACCEEEHMNSTTU	catechumenates
AACCEEEENORTTUV	overaccentuate
AACCEEGHILLMOP	megalocephalic
AACCEEGIILNTTT	telangiectatic
AACCEEHILMNNSS	mechanicalness
AACCEEHILMNOST	catecholamines
AACCEEHILMORTT	tacheometrical
AACCEEHIMRRSST	saccharimeters
AACCEEHIRRRSST	characterisers
AACCEEHIRRRSTZ	characterizers
AACCEEHMORRSST	saccharometers
AACCEEINNNORSS	reconnaissance
AACCEEINNRSSTU	inaccurateness
AACCEELLPPRRSW	clapperclawers
AACCEFLNORTTUU	counterfactual
AACCEGGILLNOOV	gynaecological
AACCEGHHLOPRRS	chalcographers
AACCEGHIINRRST	characterising
AACCEGHIINRRTZ	characterizing
AACCEGHILLOOST	eschatological
AACCEGHILNOPRS	scenographical
AACCEGIILOOPTT	galactopoietic
AACCEGIIMNRTUV	circumnavigate
AACCEGILLNPPRW	clapperclawing
AACCEGINNOSTUV	nyctaginaceous

AACCEHHIILLRRY	hierarchically
AACCEHHIMNNRRU	Armenian Church
AACCEHIILOPPRS	archiepiscopal
AACCEHIILQRRSU	squirearchical
AACCEHIINOSSTT	catechisations
AACCEHIKLOOSVZ	Czechoslovakia
AACCEHILLORTTY	theocratically
AACCEHILLPRTYY	archetypically
AACCEHINOPPRRT	parthenocarpic
AACCEHLMOOPRSU	macrocephalous
AACCEHLOOPRSSY	polysaccharose
AACCEIIILPRSTT	practicalities
AACCEIIILLMORRT	calorimetrical
AACCEIILMNORRT	craniometrical
AACCEIILMNORTT	actinometrical
AACCEIINNORRST	incarcerations
AACCEIINNORSTV	revaccinations
AACCEIINOPRSST	pantisocracies
AACCEILLLOPPTY	apoplectically
AACCEILLLOPRVY	prevocalically
AACCEILLMRSTUV	circumvallates
AACCEILLMTUUVY	accumulatively
AACCEIMMNNOPST	accompaniments
AACCEINNNOOSTT	concatenations
AACCEIOQRSSTTU	squattocracies
AACCEKNORSTTTU	counterattacks
AACCELLMMOORRU	macromolecular
AACCELNNORSUUU	ranunculaceous
AACCELOOPRSTUU	portulacaceous
AACCENNORSSSST	sacrosanctness
AACCFFILNOPRSY	cycloparaffins
AACCFHILNOOSSU	Nicholas of Cusa
AACCFIIILNORST	clarifications
AACCFIIILNOSST	classification
AACCFIIINNORST	carnifications
AACCFIIINNOSTT	sanctification
AACCFIIINOPRST	caprifications
AACCFIILORSSTY	classificatory
AACCGHHIILNOPR	ichnographical
AACCGHHIILOPRR	chirographical
AACCGHHILOOPRR	chorographical
AACCGHHILOPRST	chalcographist
AACCGHIILLLORY	oligarchically
AACCGHIILNOOPR	iconographical
AACCGHIILNOPRZ	zincographical
AACCGHILMOOPRS	cosmographical
AACCGHILNOPSVY	psychogalvanic
AACCGIILLLMOOT	climatological
AACCGIILLMNSTU	miscalculating
AACCGIILLMORTY	tragicomically
AACCGILLLNOOOV	volcanological
AACCGILLLNOOUV	vulcanological
AACCHHIIMMOPRT	amphichromatic
AACCHHIMNORRUV	Moravian Church
AACCHIILLMSSTY	schismatically
AACCHIILMNOOST	machicolations
AACCHILLLOSSTY	scholastically
AACCHILLOSSTTY	stochastically
AACCHILNOPSTYY	psychoanalytic
AACCIIILMPRTTY	impracticality
AACCIIIMOPRRST	microparasitic
AACCIIINNOOSST	cocainisations

AACCIIINNOOSTZ	cocainizations
AACCIIINORSSTT	cicatrisations
AACCIIINORSTTZ	cicatrizations
AACCIILLMNOSTU	miscalculation
AACCIILMNRSTTU	circumstantial
AACCIILNPRTTUY	unpracticality
AACCIILOOPRSTV	vicar apostolic
AACCIIMNOORSST	carcinomatosis
AACCILLMORSSTU	miscalculators
AACCILLNOOPTUY	occupationally
AACDDEEIILMMNR	Middle American
AACDDEEILOSTVV	devil's advocate
AACDDEEIMNNOTT	decontaminated
AACDDEELLORSSS	Dead Sea Scrolls
AACDDEIILRSTTU	disarticulated
AACDDEILPQRTUU	quadruplicated
AACDDHILMNORYY	hydrodynamical
AACDEEEFHMNSSS	shamefacedness
AACDEEFFGIINNT	decaffeinating
AACDEEFMNRRTUU	remanufactured
AACDEEGIILMORS	cardiomegalies
AACDEEGINRRRSU	undercarriages
AACDEEHIIMNRST	diathermancies
AACDEEHIJLNRSW	Jewish calendar
AACDEEIIILMSTV	mediaevalistic
AACDEEIJKRSTTT	straitjacketed
AACDEEEILOPPRTU	propaedeutical
AACDEEIMNNOSTT	decontaminates
AACDEEJLOQRSUZ	Jaques-Dalcroze
AACDEELLNNSUVY	Lucas van Leyden
AACDEELNNNRSTT	transcendental
AACDEENNNNOSTT	nonattendances
AACDEENORSSSUV	cadaverousness
AACDEFFIIMNRSS	disaffirmances
AACDEFHIMNNRST	handicraftsmen
AACDEFIIIILRST	artificialised
AACDEFIIIILRTZ	artificialized
AACDEFIIINNOTZ	denazification
AACDEFMNNRTUUU	unmanufactured
AACDEGHIOPRRRS	cardiographers
AACDEGHLOPRRTY	dactylographer
AACDEGILLMOORT	dermatological
AACDEGLMNNORSS	scandalmongers
AACDEGMNORSSTU	coastguardsmen
AACDEHIIMNRRST	archimandrites
AACDEHILLNNNSS	Channel Islands
AACDEHILORRSTT	trisoctahedral
AACDEHLNOPSSYY	psychoanalysed
AACDEHLNOPSYYZ	psychoanalyzed
AACDEHMOPRSTUY	pachydermatous
AACDEIIILLLSTY	idealistically
AACDEIIILMNOST	decimalisation
AACDEIIILMNOTZ	decimalization
AACDEIILLNOOST	delocalisation
AACDEIILLNOOTZ	delocalization
AACDEIILLNNOPTY	platinocyanide
AACDEIILNOSTTU	educationalist
AACDEIILPRRSTU	particularised
AACDEIILPRRTUZ	particularized
AACDEIILRSSTTU	disarticulates
AACDEIIMNORSTY	aerodynamicist
AACDEIINNOORTV	nonradioactive
AACDEIINNRSSTT	transactinides
AACDEILLMMORTY	dermatomically
AACDEILMMNORTY	dynamometrical
AACDEILMOPRSTT	dermatoplastic
AACDEILNNNOOST	condensational
AACDEILNOPRSSS	sporadicalness
AACDEILORSSSTT	sacerdotalists
AACDEILPQRSTUU	quadruplicates
AACDEIMNNNOSTT	decontaminants
AACDEIMNNNOTTU	uncontaminated
AACDEIMNNOORTT	decontaminator
AACDEINOPRRSTT	procrastinated
AACDELNNOSSSSU	scandalousness
AACDELORSTTTUY	tetradactylous
AACDFHJMNOOSSU	John of Damascus
AACDFIIIILNOPT	lapidification
AACDFIIIMNNOST	damnifications
AACDGHHILOPRRY	hydrographical
AACDGHIMOOPRRY	myocardiograph
AACDGIIILNRTVY	divaricatingly
AACDGIIINNOSST	diagnosticians
AACDGIIINOSSST	disassociating
AACDGIIILLOORY	radiologically
AACDGIILLLOOUY	audiologically
AACDGIILLNOSTY	diagnostically
AACDHIMOOPRTYY	cardiomyopathy
AACDIIIILNNPRS	disciplinarian
AACDIIILNNPRST	Pitcairn Island
AACDIIILNOPPST	disapplication
AACDIIILNORSTV	Victoria Island
AACDIIINNNORST	incardinations
AACDIIINOOSSST	disassociation
AACDIILLLMOPTY	diplomatically
AACDIILORRSTTU	disarticulator
AACDIIMNOPSSST	antispasmodics
AACDILLNNOOSSV	Volcano Islands
AACDILNOOSSTUY	anisodactylous
AACDILOORSTTUY	artiodactylous
AACEEEFLMRSSST	malefactresses
AACEEEGHIMNOTT	haematogenetic
AACEEEGILNSSTT	telangiectases
AACEEEHJKLRSTT	leatherjackets
AACEEEHLMOSTUY	thymelaeaceous
AACEEEHMMORTTY	haemacytometer
AACEEEFFILNOTTY	affectionately
AACEEEFMNRRSTUU	remanufactures
AACEEGGILLLNOY	genealogically
AACEEGHHLNOPPR	encephalograph
AACEEGHILMPRYY	hyperglycaemia
AACEEGHLMNOPRS	encephalograms
AACEEGHNOOPRRS	oceanographers
AACEEGIILLMNSV	evangelicalism
AACEEGIILNSSTT	telangiectasis
AACEEGILLLOOPS	spelaeological
AACEEGILLNNPTY	pangenetically
AACEEGILMORSTT	galactometries
AACEEHHIRRTTUV	Château-Thierry
AACEEHHLNOPPTY	encephalopathy
AACEEHHMNOPRTY	mechanotherapy
AACEEHIIMOOPTT	haematopoietic
AACEEHILLLPTTY	telepathically
AACEEHILLMPTTY	empathetically

AACEEHILLMRTXY	hexametrically
AACEEHILMMNTTY	enthymematical
AACEEHILNRSSTT	theatricalness
AACEEHILRRTUVX	extravehicular
AACEEHIPRSSTTY	cryptaesthesia
AACEEIIINPPRTV	inappreciative
AACEEIILOPRSTV	overcapitalise
AACEEIILOPRTVZ	overcapitalize
AACEEIILPPRTVY	appreciatively
AACEEIILPRTTUV	recapitulative
AACEEIIMNNRSSS	necessarianism
AACEEIINNRSSST	necessitarians
AACEEIINPPRTUV	unappreciative
AACEEILMMNSSTU	immaculateness
AACEEILNRSSTTU	articulateness
AACEEINNPRRSST	transparencies
AACEEINRSSTTTV	attractiveness
AACEEKLOSSSTTY	Stokesay Castle
AACEELNNOPRSTV	convertaplanes
AACEELNOPRRSTU	palaeocurrents
AACEELOOPRRRTX	extracorporeal
AACEFFHIILORTT	article of faith
AACEFFILNORSSS	Francis of Sales
AACEFIIIILRSST	artificialises
AACEFIIIILRSTZ	artificializes
AACEFIINPRRTTU	parturifacient
AACEFILLNOSSSU	fallaciousness
AACEFIMNORRSTW	aircraftswomen
AACEGGHIIMNOST	gigantomachies
AACEGGHILLOPRV	geographically
AACEGGILNNOORT	congregational
AACEGHHIILLOPR	heliographical
AACEGHHILNOPRT	ethnographical
AACEGHHILOPRTY	hyetographical
AACEGHHIMOPPTT	apophthegmatic
AACEGHHIOPPRRS	phraseographic
AACEGHHOPRRRST	chartographers
AACEGHIILLPPRY	epigraphically
AACEGHIILMOPSU	malpighiaceous
AACEGHIINNTTTU	authenticating
AACEGHIJKRSTTT	straightjacket
AACEGHILLLMPTY	phlegmatically
AACEGHILLMNOPY	megaphonically
AACEGHILLMOPRT	metallographic
AACEGHILLOOPRS	phraseological
AACEGHILLOOPRW	Low Archipelago
AACEGHILNOPRST	stenographical
AACEGHILOORSST	archaeologists
AACEGHILOPPRRT	petrographical
AACEGHILOPRTTU	telautographic
AACEGHIMNOPRST	cinematographs
AACEGHIMNOPRTY	cinematography
AACEGHLNNSTUUW	weltanschauung
AACEGHLOOOORYZ	archaeozoology
AACEGIIILNPRST	recapitalising
AACEGIIILNPRTZ	recapitalizing
AACEGIIINNRSST	sectarianising
AACEGIIINNRSTZ	sectarianizing
AACEGIILLLLSTY	legalistically
AACEGIILLLOOTY	aetiologically
AACEGIILLMOOSS	semasiological
AACEGIILLMOPSX	plagioclimaxes
AACEGIILNPRTTU	recapitulating
AACEGIILOOPSIS	galactopoiesis
AACEGIINNPQRTU	preacquainting
AACEGIINOORSTT	categorisation
AACEGIINOORTTZ	categorization
AACEGILLLMORTY	algometrically
AACEGILLLOOPTY	apologetically
AACEGILLMNOORT	organometallic
AACEGILNOOPSSV	galvanoscopies
AACEGILNORTTUV	congratulative
AACEGILNRRTTUY	rectangularity
AACEGIMNOSSTTT	magnetostatics
AACEHHILNNOPTY	phthalocyanine
AACEHHILNOPRSZ	rhizocephalans
AACEHIIMNRSTT	arithmeticians
AACEHIILLLLPTY	philatelically
AACEHIILLMRTTY	arithmetically .
AACEHIILNOPSST	cephalisations
AACEHIILNOPSTZ	cephalizations
AACEHIIMNOSSTT	schematisation
AACEHIIMNOSTTZ	schematization
AACEHIIMNPSSTY	metaphysicians
AACEHIINNOTTTU	authentication
AACEHIIOPSSSST	associateships
AACEHILLMNNORY	enharmonically
AACEHILLMOPRSY	semaphorically
AACEHILLMOPRTY	metaphorically
AACEHILLMPSTYY	metaphysically
AACEHILMORRSTY	lachrymatories
AACEHIMMMORSTT	metachromatism
AACEHIMOOPPRST	pharmacopoeist
AACEHIMPRSSTTU	pharmaceutists
AACEHINORSTTTU	authenticators
AACEHLNNOORSSU	Chalon-sur-Saône
AACEHLNOPRSSYY	psychoanalyser
AACEHLNOPRSYYZ	psychoanalyzer
AACEHLNOPSSSYY	psychoanalyses
AACEHLNOPSSYYZ	psychoanalyses
AACEHLOOPSSTTY	photocatalyses
AACEHLQRRSTTUU	Urquhart Castle
AACEHMNOOOPPRS	anamorphoscope
AACEHMNOPRSTUY	parenchymatous
AACEIIILLNOSTX	lexicalisation
AACEIIILLNOTXZ	lexicalization
AACEIIILNOPSST	specialisation
AACEIIILNOPSTZ	specialization
AACEIIIILNPTTVY	anticipatively
AACEIIINNOPPRT	inappreciation
AACEIILLLMRTTY	altimetrically
AACEIILLNPSTTY	antiseptically
AACEIILLNRTTUY	inarticulately
AACEIILMNRSSTU	unicameralists
AACEIILNNORSTT	centralisation
	intercalations
AACEIILNNORTTZ	centralization
AACEIILNNRSTTU	antinuclearist
AACEIILNOOPPSU	papilionaceous
AACEIILNOPPRST	reapplications
AACEIILNOPRTTU	recapitulation
AACEIILNORSSTT	cartelisations
AACEIILNORSSTU	secularisation
AACEIILNORSTTZ	cartelizations

AACEIILNORSTUZ	secularization
AACEIILOPPRRTY	appreciatorily
AACEIILPRRRSTU	particulariser
AACEIILPRRRTUZ	particularizer
AACEIILPRRSSTU	particularises
AACEIILPRRSTUZ	particularizes
AACEIIMMOSSTTU	semiautomatics
AACEIIMOPRRSST	microparasites
AACEIINNNORRST	reincarnations
AACEIINOPRRSTV	prevarications
AACEIINORSSSSUV	avariciousness
AACEIINORSSTTU	cauterisations
AACEIINORSTTUZ	cauterizations
AACEILLLNOPSTY	pleonastically
AACEILLMMNORTY	manometrically
AACEILLMMRSTYY	asymmetrically
AACEILLMNORRTU	intramolecular
AACEILLMSSTTYY	systematically
AACEILMNNOOPST	compensational
AACEILMNOSSSTU	calamitousness
AACEILMNRRSSUV	vernacularisms
AACEILNNNRSSTY	tyrannicalness
AACEILNNOORSTV	conservational
	conversational
AACEILNNOPSSTU	encapsulations
AACEILNORSTTUX	exclaustration
AACEILOPRRRTUV	overparticular
AACEILOPRRTTUY	recapitulatory
AACEINNORSTTUU	intracutaneous
AACEINOPRRSSTT	procrastinates
AACEKLNNORSTUY	cantankerously
AACELLLOPPRRVY	polycarpellary
AACELLMNOOPRRY	monocarpellary
AACELLMOPRRSUU	supramolecular
AACEMOOPRSSSST	astrocompasses
AACFFIIILLNOSST	falsifications
AACFGIIIMNNOST	magnifications
AACFGIIIINORSTT	gratifications
AACFGILNNOORST	conflagrations
AACFIIIILLNRTY	inartificially
AACFIIILMNOPST	amplifications
AACFIIILNOQSTU	qualifications
AACFIIIMMNNOOT	ammonification
AACFIIINNOOPST	saponification
AACFIIINNOQTTU	quantification
AACFIIINORSTTT	stratification
AACFIILLMORTTU	multifactorial
AACFIILMNOPSST	Pontifical Mass
AACFIILORSSTTY	satisfactorily
AACFIINNOORSTT	fractionations
AACFIINOORSSTT	factorisations
AACFIINOORSTTZ	factorizations
AACFILMNNOOOORT	conformational
AACFINORSSTTUY	unsatisfactory
AACGGILLLNOORY	laryngological
AACGGILLMOSTYY	mystagogically
AACGGILNNORTTU	congratulating
AACGHHIILLOPRT	lithographical
AACGHHILOOPRRT	orthographical
AACGHHILOPPRSY	hypsographical
AACGHHINOOPPRT	anthropophagic
AACGHHIPRSSTTY	tachygraphists

AACGHHMOOPRRTY	chromatography
AACGHIILLPRSST	calligraphists
AACGHILLLOOPTY	pathologically
AACGHILLMOPRVY	myographically
AACGHILLOOPRRY	orographically
AACGHILLOPRSTY	stylographical
AACGHILMOOPRST	pharmacologist
AACGHILNOORSST	arachnologists
AACGHLOOPPRSYY	parapsychology
AACGIIILNNOSST	anglicisations
AACGIIILNNOSTZ	anglicizations
AACGIIILNPRSTU	paralinguistic
AACGIILLMMOOST	logical atomism
AACGIIMNOOPRRS	microsporangia
AACGILLLOORSTY	astrologically
AACGILLLOOTTUY	tautologically
AACGILLLRRTUUY	agriculturally
AACGILLMOOOSTT	stomatological
AACGILLMOORRTY	martyrological
AACGILLORSTTYY	gyrostatically
AACGILMNOOPSST	campanologists
AACGILMOOPRRTU	compurgatorial
AACGILNNOORTTU	congratulation
AACGINNORRSSTW	narrowcastings
AACGLNOORRSTTU	congratulators
AACGLNOORRTTUY	congratulatory
AACHHINOOPPRTT	anthropopathic
AACHIIILLPRRTU	Tiruchirapalli
AACHIILLNNOSTU	hallucinations
AACHIILLNOOOST	alcoholisation
AACHIILLNOOOTZ	alcoholization
AACHIILMNOPRST	misanthropical
AACHIIMNNORSTT	antimonarchist
AACHIINPRSTTVY	antipsychiatry
AACHILLNOPSTYY	hyponastically
AACHILLOPSTTYY	hypostatically
AACHILLOPTTUYY	autophytically
AACHILNOPSSSYY	psychoanalysis
AACHILOOPSSTTY	photocatalysis
AACHIOPRSSSTTT	catastrophists
AACHLLLMOOPSUY	malacophyllous
AACHLNOPSSSTYY	psychoanalysts
AACIIIILNOSSTT	italicisations
AACIIIILNOSTTZ	italicizations
AACIIILLMMRSTU	multiracialism
AACIIILLNNRSTY	inartistically
AACIIILMNOPPST	misapplication
AACIIILNOPRTTY	anticipatorily
AACIIILNOPSSTT	plasticisation
AACIIILNOPSTTZ	plasticization
AACIIIMNOOSSST	associationism
AACIIINNOORSTT	ratiocinations
AACIILLLLMORSTY	moralistically
AACIILLLRSTTUY	altruistically
AACIILLMMNSTUY	numismatically
AACIILMNORSTTU	matriculations
AACIILNNOPSSTU	incapsulations
AACIILNNOSSTTT	nonstatistical
AACIILNOOPRRST	conspiratorial
AACIILNORSSTTY	crystalisation
AACIILNORSTTTU	straticulation
AACIILNORSTTYZ	crystalization

AACIILOPPRRSSTT	procapitalists
AACIILPRRSSTTU	particularists
AACIIMMNNORSTU	communitarians
AACIIMNNNOOSTT	contaminations
AACILLLLOOPRTY	allotropically
AACILLLNORSTUY	ultrasonically
AACILLMNOORSTY	astronomically
AACILLMOPSTTYY	asymptotically
AACILNNNOSTTUV	anticonvulsant
AACILNNOORSSTT	translocations
AACIMNNOOSSTTU	Coast Mountains
AACINOOPRRRSTT	procrastinator
AACLLNNOPRTTUY	contrapuntally
AADDDEEEHHNNRSS	hardheadedness
AADDDEMNNOORSW	Waddesdon Manor
AADDDFGILMPWVY	Dafydd ap Gwilym
AADDEEEIILMRST	dematerialised
AADDEEEIILMRTZ	dematerialized
AADDEEFLLORRTU	Fort Lauderdale
AADDEEGHLLRTUY	glutaraldehyde
AADDEEGNRRSTUU	undergraduates
AADDEEHLORSSTT	stadholderates
AADDEEHLORSTTT	stadtholderate
AADDEEIILNNOST	denationalised
AADDEEIILNNOTZ	denationalized
AADDEEILLNRSSW	Leeward Islands
AADDEEILMMORST	melodramatised
AADDEEILMMORTZ	melodramatized
AADDEEILMNNNSV	Van Diemen's Land
AADDEEIMORRSTV	overdramatised
AADDEEIMORRTVZ	overdramatized
AADDEENRRSTTUU	undersaturated
AADDEFFINNNRRZ	Franz Ferdinand
AADDEGGHNRRSTU	granddaughters
AADDEHHINPRSVY	Vindhya Pradesh
AADDEILLNNORSS	Ladrone Islands
AADDEILLNNORTV	Torvill and Dean
AADDHILNNOSSTU	Thousand Island
AADDHILNRSSTUY	Thursday Island
AADDHMNRSTUUYY	Maundy Thursday
AADEEEELNNRRTW	Ennerdale Water
AADEEEEFGHLRRTT	Alfred the Great
AADEEEGMNNQRUU	Queen Maud Range
AADEEEIILMRSST	dematerialises
AADEEEIILMRSTZ	dematerializes
AADEEEILNRRSST	parallelepiped
AADEEEILNRRSST	Easter Islander
AADEEEMMNRSSTU	admeasurements
AADEEFGILLLNOT	dinoflagellate
AADEEFIILNORST	federalisation
AADEEFIILNORTZ	federalization
AADEEFMNNOOTTY	Day of Atonement
AADEEGGIMNNRST	aggrandisement
AADEEGGIMNNRTZ	aggrandizement
AADEEGHILOPRRT	radiotelegraph
AADEEGHINQRRTU	headquartering
AADEEGHIPPPRSU	pseudepigrapha
AADEEGIIMMPRST	epigrammatised
AADEEGIIMMPRTZ	epigrammatized
AADEEGILMORRST	radiotelegrams
AADEEGIMNNRRST	disarrangement
AADEEHHIMPRSST	headmastership
AADEEHILMNNOOTT	endotheliomata
AADEEHIMNNORTU	Haute-Normandie
AADEEHNNNOSTTY	Thadentsonyane
AADEEIIILMMRST	immaterialised
AADEEIIILMMRTZ	immaterialized
AADEEIILMNNRTT	interlaminated
AADEEIILNNOSST	denationalises
AADEEIILNNOSTZ	denationalizes
AADEEIILNPQSSU	sesquipedalian
AADEEIILNRSTUV	valetudinaries
AADEEIINNPRRST	predestinarian
AADEEILLLOPPPR	parallelopiped
AADEEILMMORSST	melodramatises
AADEEILMMORSTZ	melodramatizes
AADEEILMNORTTT	tatterdemalion
AADEEILNRRSTTT	transliterated
AADEEIMNOPRRST	panradiometers
AADEEIMORRSSTV	overdramatises
AADEEIMORRSTVZ	overdramatizes
AADEEINNPRSSTT	antidepressant
AADEEINNQSSTTU	antiquatedness
AADEELLMNPRTTY	departmentally
AADEEPRRSSTTUU	supersaturated
AADEFFJLNNORSZ	Franz Josef Land
AADEFHILLNNPRZ	Rheinland-Pfalz
AADEFILLNRSSSU	Fur Seal Islands
AADEFILMMNNSTU	fundamentalism
AADEFILMNNSTTU	fundamentalist
AADEFILMNNTTUY	fundamentality
AADEFILNOOOPRS	Leonardo of Pisa
AADEGGGIINORST	disaggregation
AADEGGHHIMNOSU	houghmagandies
AADEGHIIIOPPRR	Herod Agrippa II
AADEGIILNNRSTU	denaturalising
AADEGIILNNRTUZ	denaturalizing
AADEGIIMRRUUWY	Yerwa-Maiduguri
AADEGIINNORRTT	intergradation
AADEGILNQRSTUW	Griqualand West
AADEGINOORRRTT	retrogradation
AADEHHKLLNNOOV	Hoek van Holland
AADEHIILLMNPSU	sulphanilamide
AADEHIIMNNOSTU	dehumanisation
AADEHIIMNNOTUZ	dehumanization
AADEHIINORRSST	sherardisation
AADEHIINORRSTZ	sherardization
AADEHIIOPRRSTT	radiotherapist
AADEHILLMORTUY	rheumatoidally
AADEHILMORSTUY	Admiralty House
AADEHINNOPSSSU	diaphanousness
AADEHNORRSSTTW	northeastwards
AADEHORSSSTTUW	southeastwards
AADEIIILNNOSST	desalinisation
AADEIIILNNOSTZ	desalinization
AADEIIILNOSTTV	devitalisation
AADEIIILNOTTVZ	devitalization
AADEIIIMNNOSST	deaminisations
AADEIIIMNNOSTZ	deaminizations
AADEIIIMNNRSTTV	administrative
AADEIILMMNRSTT	maladministers
AADEIILMNNNOOT	denominational
AADEIILMNOORST	demoralisation
AADEIILMNOORTZ	demoralization

AADEIILNNOPSST	dispensational
AADEIILNOOPRST	depolarisation
AADEIILNOOPRTZ	depolarization
AADEIILNORSSTT	dissertational
AADEIIMNNORSSV	animadversions
AADEIINNRRSSTT	Transdniestria
AADEIINORRSSTT	radioresistant
AADEILMMORSSTT	melodramatists
AADEILNNORTUUV	undervaluation
AADEILOPRTTTVY	total depravity
AADEINOPPPRRTU	unappropriated
AADEJLMMNSSTTU	maladjustments
AADFFGIIIILNST	disaffiliating
AADFFIIIILNOST	disaffiliation
AADFFIIIIMNORST	disaffirmation
AADFHLLNOOPRST	Parts of Holland
AADFIIIILNNRSSS	Frisian Islands
AADFILLNNOOTUV	foundationally
AADGGIINNOPPRS	propagandising
AADGGIINNOPPRZ	propagandizing
AADGIIIILNOSTT	digitalisation
AADGIIIILNOTTZ	digitalization
AADGIIIMNNRSTT	administrating
AADGIIMNOOSSTT	dogmatisations
AADGILNNOPRSST	prostaglandins
AADIIILMNORSTT	traditionalism
AADIIILNORSTTT	traditionalist
AADIIILNORTTTY	traditionality
AADIIIMNNORSTT	administration
AADIIIMNRRSTTX	administratrix
AADIIINOOSSTTZ	diazotisations
AADIILNNNOORTT	nontraditional
AADIIMNNOORSST	randomisations
AADIIMNNOORSTZ	randomizations
AADIIMNORRSSTT	administrators
AADILLNPRSSSTY	Spratly Islands
AAEEEFGHLLLMOT	hemoflagellate
AAEEEFGMNNORRS	ferromanganese
AAEEEGHIMNOSST	haematogenesis
AAEEEGHLMNRRSY	Hamersley Range
AAEEEGHLRSSSTW	weatherglasses
AAEEEGMNNPRRRT	prearrangement
AAEEEGMNNRRRST	rearrangements
AAEEEHHIMRSSTT	thermaesthesia
AAEEEHHIPRSSTY	hyperaesthesia
AAEEEINPRSSSTV	separativeness
AAEEFGIMNNORRS	ferromagnesian
AAEEFHILMNSTUZ	sulfamethazine
AAEEFILNNRRSTT	transferential
AAEEFINNORSSTT	aftersensation
AAEEGGGILNRTXY	exaggeratingly
AAEEGGHILMNTTU	hemagglutinate
AAEEGHIINNSSTT	anaesthetising
AAEEGHIINNSTTZ	anaesthetizing
AAEEGHIMMNOPSY	hypomagnesemia
AAEEGHLLMOPRRT	metallographer
AAEEGHLLNOOPTY	palaeethnology
AAEEGIILNNORST	generalisation
AAEEGIILNNORTZ	generalization
AAEEGIILNNOSTV	evangelisation
AAEEGIILNNOTVZ	evangelization
AAEEGIIMMPRSST	epigrammatises
AAEEGIIMMPRSTZ	epigrammatizes
AAEEGIIMNRRRST	intermarriages
AAEEGILMNOORRS	oleomargarines
AAEEGILMNTTUVY	augmentatively
AAEEGILNNPPSSU	Gaspé Peninsula
AAEEGILNPRSTXY	exasperatingly
AAEEGIMMNNNRST	misarrangement
AAEEGLMNPRSSTU	suprasegmental
AAEEGLNNORSSTT	tetragonalness
AAEEGMNOPRSSSU	rampageousness
AAEEHHILMNORTT	trihalomethane
AAEEHHMOPPSSTT	metaphosphates
AAEEHIIMOOPSST	haematopoiesis
AAEEHIKKLNOPTT	Alte Pinakothek
AAEEHILMMOOSTT	mesotheliomata
AAEEHILMPPRSSS	plasmapheresis
AAEEHIMNNNOOPZ	aminophenazone
AAEEHIMNRSSSTU	amateurishness
AAEEHIPPRRSSTY	hyperparasites
AAEEHMMOOPRRRST	spermatorrhoea
AAEEIIILMMRSST	immaterialises
AAEEIIILMMRSTZ	immaterializes
AAEEIILLMNNPRR	premillenarian
AAEEIILMMNRSST	immaterialness
AAEEIILMMPRSST	Alpes-Maritimes
AAEEIILMNNRSTT	interlaminates
AAEEIILNNORSTT	eternalisation
AAEEIILNNORTTZ	eternalization
AAEEIILNNOSSST	sensationalise
AAEEIILNNOSSTZ	sensationalize
AAEEIIMNNORSTX	reexaminations
AAEEIKLNORSTVY	Yekaterinoslav
AAEEIKLNRRSSTU	Kaiserslautern
AAEEIKLOPRSSTT	keratoplasties
AAEEILNNNOPPST	peneplanations
AAEEILNNOPRSTT	presentational
AAEEILNNPRRTTY	interplanetary
AAEEILNRRSSTTT	transliterates
AAEEINNOPSSSST	passionateness
AAEEELNNNSSSTU	unpleasantness
AAEEMNNOPPRSWW	newspaperwoman
AAEEMQRRRSSTTU	quartermasters
AAEFFIIMNORRST	reaffirmations
AAEFFINOORSSTT	afforestations
AAEFGIMNNORSTT	fragmentations
AAEFHINNORRRST	Finsteraarhorn
AAEFIIMNNOSSTT	manifestations
AAEFIINNORRSTT	fraternisation
AAEFIINNORRTTZ	fraternization
AAEFIMNORRSSTV	transformative
AAEGGGNOOOORRTY	Góngora y Argote
AAEGGHIILMNNTU	haemagglutinin
AAEGGIIMNNOPRR	Grampian Region
AAEGGIINNNSTUX	exsanguinating
AAEGGIINNORRST	grangerisation
AAEGGIINNORRTZ	grangerization
AAEGGILMMOORST	grammatologies
AAEGGILMNOORST	agglomerations
AAEGGIMMNNOPRSU	megasporangium
AAEGGLNOOPRSTU	protolanguages
AAEGHHIOPRRRST	arthrographies
AAEGHIILLNRTXY	exhilaratingly

AAEGHIIMPRSSTT	magistrateship
AAEGHIIPRRSSTT	stratigraphies
AAEGHIKMNOPRST	kinematographs
AAEGHIKMNOPRTY	kinematography
AAEGHILMOOSSTT	haematologists
AAEGHIPRRRSSTT	stratigraphers
AAEGIIILLLNOST	illegalisation
AAEGIIILLLNOTZ	illegalization
AAEGIIILMRSSTT	magistralities
AAEGIIILNNOSTT	gelatinisation
AAEGIIILNNOTTZ	gelatinization
AAEGIILLNOORST	allegorisation
AAEGIILLNOORTZ	allegorization
AAEGIILNORRSTT	registrational
AAEGIILNORRSTU	regularisation
AAEGIILNORRTUZ	regularization
AAEGIIMMMPRSST	epigrammatisms
AAEGIIMMPRSSTT	epigrammatists
AAEGIIMNNOSSTT	magnetisations
AAEGIIMNNOSTTZ	magnetizations
AAEGIIMNRRSTTV	transmigrative
AAEGIINNNOSTUX	exsanguination
AAEGIINNNRSSSU	sanguinariness
AAEGIINNOORRST	reorganisation
AAEGIINNOORRTZ	reorganization
AAEGIINNSSTTUU	Saint Augustine
AAEGILLMNOOPST	megalopolitans
AAEGILMNOOPRST	spermatogonial
AAEGILNOOPRSTT	progestational
AAEGIMNNORSTTU	argumentations
AAEGINNNPRSTUU	superannuating
AAEGMMNOORRSTU	Gesta Romanorum
AAEHHILLOPSTUZ	sulphathiazole
AAEHHIMOPRRSST	amphiarthroses
AAEHIIIMNNSSTT	antihistamines
AAEHIILMNORSTT	thermalisation
AAEHIILMNORTTZ	thermalization
AAEHIIMNOSSTTT	thematisations
AAEHIIMNOSTTTZ	thematizations
AAEHILOPRRSSTT	arthroplasties
AAEHIMOPRSSSTT	massotherapist
AAEHLMOOPPRRST	spermatophoral
AAEHNNORRSSSTU	anarthrousness
AAEIIIIILNNNTV	Valentinian III
AAEIIIKNNORSTT	keratinisation
AAEIIIKNNORTTZ	keratinization
AAEIIILLMMNNRS	millenarianism
AAEIIILLMSSTVY	assimilatively
AAEIIILMMRSSTT	immaterialists
AAEIIILMNNORST	mineralisation
AAEIIILMNNORTZ	mineralization
AAEIIILNORSSST	serialisations
AAEIIILNORSSTZ	serializations
AAEIIILNORSTTV	relativisation
	revitalisation
AAEIIILNORTTVZ	relativization
	revitalization
AAEIIIMMPRSSST	semiparasitism
AAEIIINNNRSSTU	insanitariness
AAEIIINNPPRTTT	pinnatipartite
AAEIIILLMNOSSTT	metallisations
AAEIIILLMNOSTTZ	metallizations

AAEIIILLMNPTUVY	manipulatively
AAEIIILLMOPRRTY	imperatorially
AAEIIILLNNORSTT	reinstallation
AAEIIILLNPRSTTY	interspatially
AAEIIILMMNOSSTT	lemmatisations
AAEIIILMMNOSTTZ	lemmatizations
AAEIIILMNNOSSST	sensationalism
AAEIIILMNOOPRST	operationalism
AAEIIILMNOPRRST	proletarianism
AAEIIILNNNORSTT	internationals
AAEIIILNNORRSST	irrationalness
AAEIIILNNORSTTU	neutralisation
AAEIIILNNORTTUZ	neutralization
AAEIIILMNOSSSTT	sensationalist
AAEIIILNOORRSTV	revalorisation
AAEIIILNOORRTVZ	revalorization
AAEIIILNORRSTTT	trilaterations
AAEIIILNOSSSTUX	sexualisations
AAEIIILNOSSTUXZ	sexualizations
AAEIIILNQTTTUVY	quantitatively
AAEIIMOPPPRRST	misappropriate
AAEIINNNOSSTTX	annexationists
AAEIINNORSSSTT	stationariness
AAEIINNPPRRSTT	antiperspirant
AAEIINOPRSSSTT	separationists
AAEIINOPRSSTTU	pasteurisation
AAEIINOPRSTTUZ	pasteurization
AAEIKKKLMNRSSU	Kamensk-Uralski
AAEIKKMMMNOPUZ	Kommunizma Peak
AAEILLLLMORRST	lamellirostral
AAEILLLLMRTTUY	multilaterally
AAEILMNRSSSTUX	transsexualism
AAEILMOOPPRSTT	spatiotemporal
AAEILNNNOOOPRT	nonoperational
AAEILNNORRSSTT	retranslations
AAEILNOOORSTTV	laevorotations
AAEILNOOPRSTTX	extrapolations
AAEILNORRRSTTT	transliterator
AAEILNRRSTTUUV	natural virtues
AAEIMNNNOORSTT	ornamentations
AAEIMNNOORSTTU	neuroanatomist
AAEIMNORSSSTTT	stationmasters
AAEINNNOPRSTUU	superannuation
AAEINNOPRSSTTU	supernatations
AAELLNPRRSTUUY	supernaturally
AAELMNOOPPSSTU	postmenopausal
AAELNNNOPRSTTX	xenotransplant
AAFFIINNOPRRST	nitroparaffins
AAFIIIMNNORRTU	uniformitarian
AAFIILLMMNORTY	inflammatorily
AAFIILMNOORSST	formalisations
AAFIILMNOORSTZ	formalizations
AAFILLNNOOPSUU	Paulinus of Nola
AAFIMNNOORRSTT	transformation
AAGGHHIIOPRSST	hagiographists
AAGGHINOOPRRST	organographist
AAGGHLMNOORSTU	South Glamorgan
AAGGIIILNNRTTY	ingratiatingly
AAGGIILNNOSTTU	agglutinations
AAGGIIMNNRRSTT	transmigrating
AAGGILMMOORSTT	grammatologist
AAGHHNOOPPRSTU	anthropophagus

AAGHIIINOPRSTT	graphitisation
AAGHIIINOPRTTZ	graphitization
AAGHIILMNORSTT	antilogarithms
AAGHIIPRRSSTTT	stratigraphist
AAGHIMNOOPRSST	mastigophorans
AAGHINOPRRSSTU	uranographists
AAGIIIMNOSSTTT	stigmatisation
AAGIIIMNOSTTTZ	stigmatization
AAGIIINNORSSTT	granitisations
AAGIIINNORSTTZ	granitizations
AAGIIJNNOORSST	jargonisations
AAGIIJNNOORSTZ	jargonizations
AAGIILLMOORSST	malariologists
AAGIILLNOOSTUV	Ignatius Loyola
AAGIILMNNRSSTT	mistranslating
AAGIILNNORSTTU	triangulations
AAGIILOOPRSSTT	parasitologist
AAGIIMNNORRSTT	transmigration
AAGILMNOOPRSTV	galvanotropism
AAGIMNORRRSSTT	transmigrators
AAGIMNORRRSTTY	transmigratory
AAHHIIMOPRRSST	amphiarthrosis
AAHIILNNPRRSTY	platyrrhinians
AAHIIMNNOORSST	harmonisations
AAHIIMNNOORSTZ	harmonizations
AAHIINOORSSTTU	authorisations
AAHIINOORSTTUZ	authorizations
AAHILMOPPRRSTY	amphiprostylar
AAHILNOOOPRRTT	prothonotarial
AAHLLOPPSSTTYV	staphyloplasty
AAIIIIILMLNNOSTT	initialisation
AAIIIIILLNNOTTZ	initialization
AAIIIILMMNRSTT	antimilitarism
AAIIIILMNORSTT	militarisation
AAIIIILMNORTTZ	militarization
AAIIIILMNRSTTT	antimilitarist
AAIIIILMNRSTTU	utilitarianism
AAIIIILNORSTTV	trivialisation
AAIIIILNORTTVZ	trivialization
AAIIILLLMNNOTU	illuminational
AAIIILLNOOSTTV	volatilisation
AAIIILLNOOTTVZ	volatilization
AAIIILMNORRSST	irrationalisms
AAIIILNNOPSSTT	platinisations
AAIIILNNOPSTTZ	platinizations
AAIIILNOSSSTUV	visualisations
AAIIILNOSSTUVZ	visualizations
AAIIINNNOSSTTT	instantiations
AAIIINNOOOSTTU	autoionisation
AAIIINNNOOOTTUZ	autoionization
AAIIINOPRSSTTV	privatisations
AAIIINOPRSTTVZ	privatizations
AAIIJLNNOORSTU	journalisation
AAIIJLNNOORTUZ	journalization
AAIILLLMNPRSUY	supraliminally
AAIILLLNORSTTU	illustrational
AAIILLMNNOSTTU	multinationals
AAIILLMOOPPSST	papillomatosis
AAIILLNNORSTTY	transitionally
AAIILLNOPRSSTU	pluralisations
AAIILLNOPRSTUZ	pluralizations
AAIILNOOPPRSTU	popularisation

AAIILNOOPPRTUZ	popularization
AAIIMMNOSSSTUY	immunoassayist
AAIIMNNNOSTTUU	Uinta Mountains
AAIIMNOOPPRSTX	approximations
AAIIMNOORRSSTZ	Zoroastrianism
AAIIMNORRSSTTY	martyrisations
AAIIMNORRSTTYZ	martyrizations
AAIINNOPRRSSTT	transpirations
AAIINOOPPPRRST	appropriations
AAIINOOQQSTTUU	quasi-quotation
AAIKMNNOORSTUZ	Ozark Mountains
AAILLLMOORRRYZ	Zorrilla y Moral
AAILMMNNORSTTU	ultramontanism
AAILMNNORSTTTU	ultramontanist
AAILNNOPPSSTTU	supplantations
AAIMNNORSSTTTU	transmutations
AAINNOOPRRSTTT	transportation
ABBCDEEEIORRSU	berberidaceous
ABBCDEILMOOSTU	discombobulate
ABBCEIIJLSTTUY	subjectability
ABBCEILPRRTUUY	Buryat Republic
ABBDDEEEEILNSSS	biddablenesses
ABBDEEGNNNRRUU	Neubrandenburg
ABBDIIIILNTTUY	indubitability
ABBEEEELNORSSSV	observableness
ABBEEHINNOOPRT	phenobarbitone
ABBEEILMNNOPRSS	improbableness
ABBEEINNOOPRTT	pentobarbitone
ABBEGHIIILOPRS	bibliographies
ABBEGHIILOPRRS	bibliographers
ABCCCEEIIMMNRU	circumambience
ABCCCEIIMMNRUY	circumambiency
ABCCCEIORSTUUU	cucurbitaceous
ABCCEEGILNNORT	concelebrating
ABCCEEIIILLNORR	irreconcilable
ABCCEEIILMMNOUX	excommunicable
ABCCEEILNNOORT	concelebration
ABCCEHIINORSST	bronchiectasis
ABCCEIIIILNOTVY	conceivability
ABCCEIIILLNORRY	irreconcilably
ABCCEIILMMNNOU	incommunicable
ABCCEIIILRRSTUV	cruciverbalist
ABCCEILNNNOOSU	unconscionable
ABCCGINNORSTTU	subcontracting
ABCCHHIIOPRRSS	archbishoprics
ABCCHILOOPRSTU	claustrophobic
ABCCIILMMNNOUY	incommunicably
ABCCIINORSSTTU	antiscorbutics
ABCCILLOOPRXYY	polycarboxylic
ABCCILNNNOOSUY	unconscionably
ABCCILOOOPRSST	stroboscopical
ABCCNOORRSSTTU	subcontractors
ABCDDEEILMMNOS	discommendable
ABCDEEEEILNSSV	deceivableness
ABCDEEEELLNSST	delectableness
ABCDEEEHIILNPR	indecipherable
ABCDEEEHILNPRU	undecipherable
ABCDEEEIILRSSV	disserviceable
ABCDEEEILNPRSS	predicableness
ABCDEEEILNPSSS	despicableness
ABCDEEEILNRSST	creditableness
ABCDEEEILPRSST	disrespectable

ABCDEEEEINORRST	decerebrations
ABCDEEGHIIMRRS	Cambridgeshire
ABCDEEGIILPRUV	Adygei Republic
ABCDEEHIILNPRY	indecipherably
ABCDEEIILNNORS	inconsiderable
ABCDEEIILNPRSU	republicanised
ABCDEEIILNPRUZ	republicanized
ABCDEEIIMOSSTY	basidiomycetes
ABCDEFILMOORST	discomfortable
ABCDEGHHOORRTU	thoroughbraced
ABCDEIIILPRTTY	predictability
ABCDEIILNNORSY	inconsiderably
ABCDEIILNNOSTY	condensability
ABCDENOOORRRTU	uncorroborated
ABCDHILNOOOORRT	bronchodilator
ABCDIIIILOSSTY	dissociability
ABCDIIILNNOOST	biconditionals
ABCEEEEEILNPRX	experienceable
ABCEEEEEFNRSSST	benefactresses
ABCEEEEEKLLRSTY	Berkeley Castle
ABCEEELNNRSSSU	censurableness
ABCEEFIILNORTY	enforceability
ABCEEGHLMRRSSU	schlumbergeras
ABCEEGIILLNOTY	biogenetically
ABCEEGIINORSUZ	zingiberaceous
ABCEEGILNNORSU	unrecognisable
ABCEEGILNNORUZ	unrecognizable
ABCEEGKKOORRST	stockbrokerage
ABCEEHIOOPRSUU	euphorbiaceous
ABCEEIIILPRTVY	perceivability
ABCEEIIILRSTUY	serviceability
ABCEEEIILLMPRRU	Mari El Republic
ABCEEIILNPRSSU	republicanises
ABCEEIILNPRSUZ	republicanizes
ABCEEIILORRTVY	recoverability
ABCEEIILPRSTTY	respectability
ABCEEILLMNOPSS	compliableness
ABCEEILLNNPSSU	inculpableness
ABCEEILMNOPSST	compatibleness
ABCEEILNNOSSSU	unsociableness
ABCEEILNNSTUUY	sublieutenancy
ABCEEINOPRRSTU	protuberancies
ABCEEINORRRSST	Cartier-Bresson
ABCEELLNOORSSU	colourableness
ABCEELMMNOSSTU	commutableness
ABCEFIIINORSTV	verbifications
ABCEGHLNORRTTU	Charlottenburg
ABCEGIILOORSTT	bacteriologist
ABCEGINQRSTTUV	cybersquatting
ABCEHIIIORSTUV	behaviouristic
ABCEHIILRSTTTY	stretchability
ABCEHILLLOPRVY	hyperbolically
ABCEHILLNNORST	Bristol Channel
ABCEHILORRSTTY	erythroblastic
ABCEHLOOPRSSTU	claustrophobes
ABCEIIIILLNTTUY	ineluctability
ABCEIIILNSTUXY	inexcusability
ABCEIIIILORRTVY	irrevocability
ABCEIIIILRRTTTY	retractability
ABCEIILNOPPRTU	prepublication
ABCEIILNOPRSTU	republications
ABCEIILNOSTTTY	contestability

ABCEIIMNORRTTU	nitrobacterium
ABCEIIMOSSSTTY	biosystematics
ABCEIINOORSTTX	bacteriotoxins
ABCEILLLMOORTY	bolometrically
ABCEILLLNNOORT	incontrollable
ABCEILLMNOPSUU	pneumobacillus
ABCEILLMNOSSSY	symbolicalness
ABCEILNNNOSTTU	subcontinental
ABCELLLNNOORTU	uncontrollable
ABCELNOSSTUUUY	subcutaneously
ABCEMMMNOORSUU	mucomembranous
ABCFGIILNSSSUY	subclassifying
ABCFIIIMNOORST	bioinformatics
ABCFIILMNOORTY	conformability
ABCGIIIILNOTTY	incogitability
ABCGIILLMOOOTY	bioclimatology
ABCGIILNOOPSST	spongioblastic
ABCGILLLNOOSTU	lactoglobulins
ABCGILLMNOORSU	macroglobulins
ABCHHINOOPRSST	opisthobranchs
ABCHIILNOTTUUY	untouchability
ABCHILMOOPRSTT	thromboplastic
ABCIIIIJLSTTUY	justiciability
ABCIIILLLOPSTY	collapsibility
ABCIIILNRSTTUY	inscrutability
ABCIILLMNOSTYY	symbiontically
ABCIILMMNOSSTU	somnambulistic
ABCIILNORSTTUY	construability
ABCILLLNNOORTY	incontrollably
ABCILMNORSTUUY	rambunctiously
ABCINOOOORRRST	corroborations
ABCLLLNNOORTUY	uncontrollably
ABDDEEEEELNNPSS	dependableness
ABDDEEEFGHINRT	featherbedding
ABDDEEEEHLLNSSU	bullheadedness
ABDDEEEEIKLMRRS	middlebreakers
ABDDEEHIILSSST	disestablished
ABDDEEILMNNSTY	absentmindedly
ABDDEFGIMORRST	Stamford Bridge
ABDEEEEFILNSSS	defeasibleness
ABDEEEEEILNRSST	deliberateness
ABDEEEELNSSSTT	detestableness
ABDEEEFFIILNRT	differentiable
ABDEEEGHINRSST	bigheartedness
ABDEEEHILPRSST	preestablished
ABDEEEIIINNORST	obedientiaries
ABDEEEIILLRTVY	deliberatively
ABDEEEIILMNNRT	indeterminable
ABDEEEIINNOPZZ	benzodiazepine
ABDEEEILMNNSST	disenablements
ABDEEEILNNNSSU	undeniableness
ABDEEEELLNOPRSS	deplorableness
ABDEEEFGHINRRST	fingerbreadths
ABDEEFIIIILNST	definabilities
ABDEEFIIIILNNTU	unidentifiable
ABDEEFIILMNOSS	modifiableness
ABDEEFILMNORSS	formidableness
ABDEEGILNNOOTU	double negation
ABDEEGIPRRRRTY	partridgeberry
ABDEEHIIIILRTTY	hereditability
ABDEEHIILSSSST	disestablishes
ABDEEIIIILLRTVY	deliverability

ABDEEIIIMNOORT	bioremediation
ABDEEIILMNNRTY	indeterminably
ABDEEIILMNSSSS	admissibleness
ABDEEIILNNPSSS	indispensables
ABDEEIILRRSSTY	redressability
ABDEEIKMMNRSST	disembarkments
ABDEEILMNNORST	indemonstrable
ABDEEILNOPSSSS	disposableness
ABDEEILNPSSSTU	disputableness
ABDEELMNNORSTU	undemonstrable
ABDEEMNPRSSTTU	subdepartments
ABDEFGIINNSTUU	subinfeudating
ABDEFIIILLNORT	defibrillation
ABDEFIILLORRST	defibrillators
ABDEFIINNOSTUU	subinfeudation
ABDEFINORSTUUY	subinfeudatory
ABDEGGIKNNORRU	groundbreaking
ABDEGIILLNRSST	Gilbert Islands
ABDEGINNOPRSUU	superabounding
ABDEHINNORRSTU	Dunbartonshire
ABDEHLMNNORRTU	Northumberland
ABDEIIILMNOOST	demobilisation
ABDEIIILMNOOTZ	demobilization
ABDEIILNPSSSTY	dispensability
ABDEIIILNRSTUY	undesirability
ABDEIIINRSSSSU	subsidiariness
ABDEIIIRRSSTTU	distributaries
ABDEIILNOORSTW	bowdlerisation
ABDEIILNOORTWZ	bowdlerization
ABDEIINNORSSTU	insubordinates
ABDEIINSSSTTUV	substantivised
ABDEIINSSTTUVZ	substantivized
ABDEILMNNORSTY	indemonstrably
ABDEILMORSTUXY	ambidextrously
ABDGIIILOOORST	radiobiologist
ABDGILMNNORSSU	bildungsromans
ABDHIIINORSSTY	hybridisations
ABDHIIINORSTYZ	hybridizations
ABDHILNNOORTTY	labyrinthodont
ABDIIIILMNOTTY	indomitability
ABDIIILLOSSTVY	dissolvability
ABDIIILNORSTTU	distributional
ABDIIINOSSSSTU	subsidisations
ABDIIINOSSSTUZ	subsidizations
ABDIIOOOPRSSSU	basidiosporous
ABEEEEFLNPRRSS	preferableness
ABEEEENPRSSSSY	Basses-Pyrénées
ABEEEFIILNNSSS	infeasibleness
ABEEEFIILNRSSV	verifiableness
ABEEEFILLNRSST	filterableness
ABEEEGLMMNNRST	embranglements
ABEEEGLNNORSSV	governableness
ABEEEHIILLLSTV	Élisabethville
ABEEEHILNPRSSS	perishableness
ABEEEHILPRSSST	preestablishes
ABEEEHLNRSSSST	breathlessness
ABEEEIILLPRRSV	irreplevisable
ABEEEIILNNPSSX	inexpiableness
ABEEEIILNNSSTV	inevitableness
ABEEEIKKRRRSST	strikebreakers
ABEEEILMMNOSSV	immoveableness
ABEEEILMNNRRST	terminableness
ABEEEILNNOPRSS	inoperableness
ABEEEEILNNORSSX	inexorableness
ABEEEEILNRRRTTV	intervertebral
ABEEEINORRRSTV	reverberations
ABEEELLNNRSSUV	vulnerableness
ABEEEELLNORSSSV	resolvableness
ABEEEELMNPRSSTU	permutableness
ABEEEELNNOPRSSS	personableness
ABEEEELNORRSSST	restorableness
ABEEEMMNPRRSSU	supermembranes
ABEEFHIMNOORST	Bohemian Forest
ABEEFIIILLLNNSS	infallibleness
ABEEFIILMNRTTY	fermentability
ABEEFILNOPRSST	profitableness
ABEEGHIILNRSST	reestablishing
ABEEGHIILNSTUX	extinguishable
ABEEGHILMMNOOT	methaemoglobin
ABEEGHILNORRHW	wheelbarrowing
ABEEGIIKKNRRST	strikebreaking
ABEEGIILNNNSST	intangibleness
ABEEEGMNORSSSUU	umbrageousness
ABEEGNOORRRTTU	turbogenerator
ABEEHILMNSSSTT	establishments
ABEEHILNOPSSST	hospitableness
ABEEHLNNOORSSU	honourableness
ABEEHLNNOPTUYZ	phenylbutazone
ABEEIIIILLNSST	ensilabilities
ABEEIIILMMPRTY	impermeability
ABEEIIILMNNSST	inimitableness
ABEEIIILRRTTVY	retrievability
ABEEEIILLNNOSSV	inviolableness
ABEEEIILMNOPRSS	impressionable
ABEEIILMNPSSSS	impassibleness
ABEEIILMNRRTUY	remunerability
ABEEIILNPRSTTY	presentability
ABEEIILNPRTTVY	preventability
ABEEIILPRRSTVY	preservability
ABEEIILPRRSTYY	presbyterially
ABEEILMNNNOSTU	unmentionables
ABEEEILMNOPRSSV	improvableness
ABEEILNNOQSTUU	unquestionable
ABEEILNNSSTTUU	sublieutenants
ABEEILRRRSSTTU	subterrestrial
ABEEIMNOSSSSTU	abstemiousness
ABEEKLNNNOSSUW	unknowableness
ABEFGIIILNRRTY	refrangibility
ABEFIIIILRRTTUY	irrefutability
ABEFIIILLNORRRU	neurofibrillar
ABEFLLNOOPSSTU	tablespoonfuls
ABEGHIILMNOORU	hemoglobinuria
ABEGHILMNOOOXY	oxyhaemoglobin
ABEGHLMNRRSSTU	bremsstrahlung
ABEGIIILMNPRTY	impregnability
ABEGIILOOORSST	aerobiologists
ABEGIIILORRSSTY	gyrostabiliser
ABEGIILORRSTYZ	gyrostabilizer
ABEHHIJNOPSTTT	John the Baptist
ABEHHINOOPPSST	bisphosphonate
ABEHIIIILNRTTY	inheritability
ABEHIIILSTTUXY	exhaustibility
ABEHIIMNOPSSSU	amphibiousness
ABEHINNOOSSTTT	ethnobotanists

ABEIIIILMNSTTY	inestimability
ABEIIIILLNORTTY	intolerability
ABEIIILMNNRTUV	innumerability
ABEIIILMORRTVY	irremovability
ABEIIILNORSSTT	liberationists
ABEIIILNPRSTUY	insuperability
ABEIIILPRSSTUY	persuasibility
ABEIIIMNRSSTUU	subminiaturise
ABEIIIMNRSTUUZ	subminiaturize
ABEIIMNOPRRTTU	imperturbation
ABEIIMOPRSSTUU	superambitious
ABEIINSSSSTTUV	substantivises
ABEIINSSSTTUVZ	substantivizes
ABEILLOOPRSSST	ballistospores
ABEILMNNORSTUU	insurmountable
ABEILNNOQSTUUY	unquestionably
ABEILNOOOPPRRT	proportionable
ABEILNORSSSSUU	salubriousness
ABELMNNORSTUUU	unsurmountable
ABENNOOPSSSTUU	subspontaneous
ABENOORRSSSTUU	brontosauruses
ABFGIIIILNNRTY	infrangibility
ABFIIIIILRTTVY	vitrifiability
ABFIIIIJLSTTUY	justifiability
ABFIIIILLLNSST	infallibilists
ABFIIIILNOSSTY	fissionability
ABGGIILOOORSST	agrobiologists
ABGIIIIILMMTTY	immitigability
ABGIIMNNORRSST	brainstormings
ABHIIIKLNNTTUY	unthinkability
ABHIIINOOPRRTY	prohibitionary
ABHIIINOORSSTV	vasoinhibitors
ABHIIINOORSTVY	vasoinhibitory
ABHIILLOPPPRTY	Port Phillip Bay
ABHILMNOOPRSTT	thromboplastin
ABIIIIILLLMTTY	illimitability
ABIIIILLMPSTUY	implausibility
ABIIIILMMNOOST	immobilisation
ABIIIILMMNOOTZ	immobilization
ABIIIIMNNSTTU	bituminisation
ABIIIIMNNOTTUZ	bituminization
ABIILLNORSSUUY	insalubriously
ABIILMNOOSSSTY	symbolisations
ABIILMNOOSSTYZ	symbolizations
ABIILMORRSTTUV	multivibrators
ABIILNNNOSTTUU	tintinnabulous
ABIILOPPRSTTUY	supportability
ABILMNNORSTUUY	insurmountably
ABILNOOOOPPRRTY	proportionably
ABILNOOOPPSSTUU	subpopulations
ACCCCHHHILORTU	Catholic Church
ACCCCHILOOPSTY	staphylococcic
ACCCDEEEINNNSS	incandescences
ACCCEEHINOORSS	onchocerciases
ACCCEEIILSSSTU	Ecclesiasticus
ACCCEEINOPPRSU	preoccupancies
ACCCEEHHILMOPSY	psychochemical
ACCCEHIINOORSS	onchocerciasis
ACCCEHIINORSTT	architectonics
ACCCEILLNNORTY	concentrically
ACCCEIMMNOOORS	macroeconomics
ACCCFIIIKNNOOT	cocknification

ACCCGIIMNNRSTU	circumstancing
ACCCHIIOOPSSTT	tachistoscopic
ACCCHLOOPSSTUU	staphylococcus
ACCDDEEIILNOST	occidentalised
ACCDDEEIILNOTZ	occidentalized
ACCDDEGIIINRST	disaccrediting
ACCDDEINNORTTU	uncontradicted
ACCDEEEELNOPRS	preadolescence
ACCDEEEHHIKNRT	chickenhearted
ACCDEEEINORSST	cardiocenteses
ACCDEEENNORRTT	reconcentrated
ACCDEEGHNNORTU	counterchanged
ACCDEEGHNORRTU	countercharged
ACCDEEGINNNORST	deconsecrating
ACCDEEHMNORRTU	countermarched
ACCDEEIILLLRTY	dielectrically
ACCDEEIILMMORS	commercialised
ACCDEEIILMMORZ	commercialized
ACCDEEIILNOSST	occidentalises
ACCDEEIILNOSTZ	occidentalizes
ACCDEEIINORSST	cardiocentesis
ACCDEEILMNOPSY	encyclopaedism
ACCDEEILMNORTU	counterclaimed
ACCDEEILMNORTY	dynamoelectric
	electrodynamic
ACCDEEILNNNSTY	incandescently
ACCDEEILNOPSTU	conceptualised
ACCDEEILNOPSTY	encyclopaedist
ACCDEEILNOPTUZ	conceptualized
ACCDEEIMMNOTUX	excommunicated
ACCDEEIMNOPPTY	appendicectomy
ACCDEEINNNOSTU	discountenance
ACCDEEINNNOORST	deconsecration
ACCDEEINOPRRTU	unreciprocated
ACCDEFGILLNOTU	deflocculating
ACCDEFIINOORT	recodification
ACCDEFILLNOOTU	deflocculation
ACCDEHHILLOOPY	dolichocephaly
ACCDEHHMNORSY	hydromechanics
ACCDEHILMNOPSU	unaccomplished
ACCDEHIMOORSTT	Socratic method
ACCDEIILLNNOTY	coincidentally
ACCDEIILNNOOST	codeclinations
ACCDEIINNNOSTU	discontinuance
ACCDEIINOORSTT	decortications
ACCDGIIMNOSSTU	disaccustoming
ACCDHHINNORTYY	chondrichthyan
ACCDHHINOOPRSY	hypochondriacs
ACCDHIIIMMORST	dichromaticism
ACCDHIILORSSTV	clavichordists
ACCDHIMNOPSSYY	psychodynamics
ACCDHIOORSSTUY	hydroacoustics
ACCDIIILLNRTYY	cylindricality
ACCDIILNNOOPTU	conduplication
ACCDIINNNOORST	contradictions
ACCDIINOORSTTU	contradictious
ACCEEEELLNORTV	electrovalence
ACCEEEELMORRST	accelerometers
ACCEEEFFIINSTU	efficient cause
ACCEEEHHILMRRS	Schleiermacher
ACCEEEHILLMNPY	myelencephalic
ACCEEEILLORSST	ecclesiolaters

ACCEEEELLNORTVY	electrovalency
ACCEEEELORRTTUY	electrocautery
ACCEEEENNORRSTT	reconcentrates
ACCEEFIMORRRTT	refractometric
ACCEEGHIKNORTW	weathercocking
ACCEEGHILMPRYY	hyperglycaemic
ACCEEGHILOPRRT	electrographic
ACCEEGHNNORSTU	counterchanges
ACCEEGHNORRSTU	countercharges
ACCEEGIINNORSS	carcinogenesis
ACCEEGILLNORTY	geocentrically
ACCEEGINNORRST	reconsecrating
ACCEEGINOORRST	gerontocracies
ACCEEHHIILNNPR	rhinencephalic
ACCEEHHILMMORT	thermochemical
ACCEEHHLOORSST	schoolteachers
ACCEEHIIILNSTT	technicalities
ACCEEHIILMMOSS	semiochemicals
ACCEEHIILMNRSS	chimericalness
ACCEEHILLNORTT	centrolecithal
ACCEEHILMOPRST	petrochemicals
ACCEEHILNOPPRS	prosencephalic
ACCEEHMNORRSTU	countermarches
ACCEEHORRSSTTY	oystercatchers
ACCEEIILLNRSTV	interclavicles
ACCEEIILMMORSS	commercialises
ACCEEIILMMORSZ	commercializes
ACCEEIIMNNOORT	econometrician
ACCEEIINNOORSS	concessionaire
ACCEEILLLNORTY	electronically
ACCEEILLLOPSTY	telescopically
ACCEEILMOOPRTV	overcomplicate
ACCEEILMOPRSTU	proceleusmatic
ACCEEILNOPSSTU	conceptualises
ACCEEILNOPSTUZ	conceptualizes
ACCEEILORSSTTT	electrostatics
ACCEEILORSSTUU	sterculiaceous
ACCEEIMMNOSTUX	excommunicates
ACCEEIINNNOORSS	reconnoissance
ACCEEEINNOORRST	reconsecration
ACCEEINOPRSTTV	contraceptives
ACCEEKLMRRSSSU	musselcrackers
ACCEELLMMOORSU	macromolecules
ACCEELLNNOSTVY	convalescently
ACCEEMNORRSSTT	concertmasters
ACCEFGIIIINNNS	insignificance
ACCEFIIIINNSTT	antiscientific
ACCEFIIIILLNSTY	scientifically
ACCEFIIIINOPSST	specifications
ACCEFIIIINORSTT	certifications
	rectifications
ACCEEGHHILNOOST	schoolteaching
ACCEEGHIILLNNOU	hallucinogenic
ACCEEGHIOPPRRST	spectrographic
ACCEEGIILNPNPTTU	centuplicating
ACCEEGIILNRTUXY	excruciatingly
ACCEEGILLMMOORY	myrmecological
ACCEEGINNOPRRTT	precontracting
ACCEEHHILLNOPRS	chancellorship
ACCEEHHILOSSSTZ	eschscholtzias
ACCEEHIIIMORSTT	chromaticities
ACCEEHIILMORSTT	stichometrical

ACCEEHILLMOPRYY	pyrochemically
ACCEEHILLNNOORR	Iron Chancellor
ACCEEHILMMNOPST	accomplishment
ACCEEHILMNNOORT	chronometrical
ACCEEHILMOOPRST	thermoscopical
ACCEEHILMOOPRSU	microcephalous
ACCEEHILMOPRSTY	psychometrical
ACCEEHILOORSSTU	Horatius Cocles
ACCEEHIMOORRTYZ	ectomycorrhiza
ACCEEHIOOPSSSTT	tachistoscopes
ACCEEHLNNNORTUV	Channel Country
ACCEEIIILMMORSS	microseismical
ACCEEIIILMNNOPS	incompliancies
ACCEEIIILMNORST	cliometricians
ACCEEIIILNNOORT	reconciliation
ACCEEIIILNNOORT	oneirocritical
ACCEEIIILLLOSSTY	solecistically
ACCEEIIILLMOORRT	colorimetrical
ACCEEIIILLMOORSY	seriocomically
ACCEEIIILMRRSUY	semicircularly
ACCEEIIILLOPPRSY	periscopically
ACCEEIILMMORSST	commercialists
ACCEEIIILNNOPTTU	centuplication
ACCEEIIILNOORRTY	reconciliatory
ACCEEIIILNOSSSST	neoclassicists
ACCEEIINNOORSTT	concretisation
ACCEEIINNOORTTZ	concretization
ACCEEIINOOPRRST	reciprocations
ACCEEIINOPRSSSU	capriciousness
ACCEEILLNOSSSUY	successionally
ACCEEILMMNNOOSS	commonsensical
ACCEEILNOPSSTTU	conceptualists
ACCEEIMMNOORTUX	excommunicator
ACCEEIMNOOPRSTU	pococuranteism
ACCEEINNNOORSTT	concentrations
ACCEEINNOORSTTU	counteractions
ACCEEINOOPPRSTU	preoccupations
ACCFFIIINORTTU	fructification
ACCFGIIIINNNSY	insignificancy
ACCFHHILLLLRSU	Churchill Falls
ACCFIIIIIILNOST	silicification
ACCGGHHIIKNNOU	Chiang Ching-kuo
ACCGHHIILLOOTY	ichthyological
ACCGHHIOPPRSSY	psychographics
ACCGHIILLOOPRS	oscillographic
ACCGHILOPRSSUY	psychosurgical
ACCGHINOOPPRSY	pharyngoscopic
ACCGIIILLMNOOR	criminological
ACCGIIILLLOOOSY	sociologically
ACCGIIMNNRRTTUU	circumnutating
ACCGILLLMOOOSY	cosmologically
ACCGILLOOPRSYY	gyroscopically
ACCGILMOOOORSY	macrosociology
ACCHHILOPPSSYY	psychophysical
ACCHHIMOOOPRRT	chromatophoric
ACCHHIMOOORRTT	orthochromatic
ACCHIIILNORSTT	antichloristic
ACCHIIINNNOOST	cinchonisation
ACCHIIINNNOOTZ	cinchonization
ACCHIIILLOPRTYV	hypocritically
ACCHIIMMNNOSTU	Communist China
ACCHIIORRSSSTU	chiaroscurists

ACCHILLNNORSYY	synchronically
ACCHIMMNOOORST	monochromatics
ACCHIMNOOOPRSS	Spanish Morocco
ACCIIILLNOORTY	conciliatorily
ACCIIILLOOOPST	sociopolitical
ACCIIMMNOOSST	iconomaticisms
ACCIIMMNNOOSTU	communications
ACCIIMNNORTTUU	circumnutation
ACCILLOPPRRTYY	procryptically
ACCILMNOOSTUUY	contumaciously
ACCILNNOORSTTU	constructional
ACCINPRSSTTUUU	acupuncturists
ACCLMOOOSSTTUY	cyclostomatous
ACDDEEEHHNNNORS	hendecahedrons
ACDDEEGKLNNOUW	unacknowledged
ACDDEEIIILMNRS	decriminalised
ACDDEEIIILMNRZ	decriminalized
ACDDEEILNOORST	reconsolidated
ACDDEEIMNOSTTU	undomesticated
ACDDEEINRSSSTT	distractedness
ACDDEELOOORRST	Colorado Desert
ACDDEEORSTTTUU	autodestructed
ACDDEFILOOPPRS	apple of discord
ACDDEHHILOOPRY	hydrocephaloid
ACDDEHINOOPSST	dodecaphonists
ACDDEIINOOORSU	androdioecious
ACDDIIJLLORTUU	Ciudad Trujillo
ACDEEEEELLPRRUZ	Pérez de Cuéllar
ACDEEEFFNNSSTU	unaffectedness
ACDEEEHINRRSUV	underachievers
ACDEEEIILNNSST	indelicateness
ACDEEEIINNRSTV	inadvertencies
ACDEEEILLNPRTY	precedentially
ACDEEEIMNOPPST	appendectomies
ACDEEEINNOPQRU	equiponderance
ACDEEEINORSSTV	decorativeness
ACDEEEELNOPRSST	preadolescents
ACDEEEELNPRRSSU	supercalenders
ACDEEENOPRSSSU	predaceousness
ACDEEENRRRSTUY	undersecretary
ACDEEFFIMORRTT	diffractometer
ACDEEFGHOOOOPP	Cape of Good Hope
ACDEEFHIIKRSSU	Fischer-Dieskau
ACDEEFHIINNRSS	disenfranchise
ACDEEFHNORRSTW	thenceforwards
ACDEEFINNOORST	confederations
ACDEEGGILNNORR	Recording Angel
ACDEEGHIINNRUV	underachieving
ACDEEGHINNTUUW	Dutch New Guinea
ACDEEGIILNNRST	decentralising
ACDEEGIILNNRSU	denuclearising
ACDEEGIILNNRTZ	decentralizing
ACDEEGIILNNRUZ	denuclearizing
ACDEEGIILNPRTY	depreciatingly
ACDEEGILNNOQRU	grandiloquence
ACDEEGIMNORSTU	discouragement
ACDEEGINOORRTV	overdecorating
ACDEEGKLMNNOTW	acknowledgment
ACDEEHIIINNRST	disinheritance
ACDEEHIIMPSSTY	metaphysicised
ACDEEHIIMPSTVZ	metaphysicized
ACDEEHILMNOSST	methodicalness
ACDEEHILORRSTT	tetrachlorides
ACDEEHIMNNORTT	disenchantment
ACDEEHLMOORSST	schoolmastered
ACDEEIIIILRSTV	veridicalities
ACDEEIIILMNRSS	decriminalises
ACDEEIIILMNRSZ	decriminalizes
ACDEEIILMNOSTU	eudemonistical
ACDEEIILNNNQSU	quindecennials
ACDEEIILNNNSST	incidentalness
ACDEEIILNRSSTU	diureticalness
ACDEEIIMNOPRST	premedications
ACDEEIINOPRSTT	decrepitations
ACDEEIIORRSTTV	Victoria Desert
ACDEEILLLNNOSY	declensionally
ACDEEILLLNOTUV	involucellated
ACDEEILLRRSSTY	recrystallised
ACDEEILLRRSTVZ	recrystallized
ACDEEILNOORSST	reconsolidates
ACDEEILNORSTTU	interosculated
ACDEEILNOSTTUX	contextualised
ACDEEILNOTTUXZ	contextualized
ACDEEILNPPRRSU	perpendiculars
ACDEEILOPRSSTY	perissodactyle
ACDEEIMMNNOORT	recommendation
ACDEEIMNNOOPST	decompensation
ACDEEIMNNOOSSU	mendaciousness
ACDEEINNNOORST	recondensation
ACDEEINNOORSST	coordinateness
ACDEEINNOPQRUY	equiponderancy
ACDEEINNORSTTU	counterstained
ACDEEINOOPRRRT	reincorporated
ACDEEINOPRSSSU	predaciousness
ACDEELNNNRSTTY	transcendently
ACDEEMMNOORRTY	recommendatory
ACDEENOPRRSSTT	protractedness
ACDEFGHLNNOORT	French Togoland
ACDEFIIIINNOTT	identification
ACDEFIIINOOTTX	detoxification
ACDEFIILLNNOTY	confidentially
ACDEGHILLMOOOT	methodological
ACDEGHIMNORSTY	hydromagnetics
ACDEGHINNORSTU	countershading
ACDEGIILLOOPRT	pteridological
ACDEGIILLOOSTT	dialectologist
ACDEGIIMNOSSTY	geodynamicists
ACDEGILNNNRSTY	transcendingly
ACDEGIMNNORNTU	countermanding
ACDEGINNNORRTU	countertrading
ACDEGINOOPRSTT	prognosticated
ACDEHHIILOORTZ	chlorothiazide
ACDEHHIIMOPRRT	hermaphroditic
ACDEHHILLNOORT	chlorthalidone
ACDEHHIOOPRRST	archpriesthood
ACDEHHLOOPRSUY	hydrocephalous
ACDEHIIKLNORTY	hydrokinetical
ACDEHIILLMMOTY	immethodically
ACDEHIILLOPRSY	spheroidically
ACDEHIIMORRSTY	radiochemistry
ACDEHILLMOPRVY	hypodermically
ACDEHILLNOORRY	hydrocoralline
ACDEHILLNOPTYY	endophytically
ACDEHILMOOPPRR	chlorpropamide

ACDEHIMMNOPRSS	commanderships
ACDEHIMMNORSTY	thermodynamics
ACDEHINNOOPRTY	endocrinopathy
ACDEHINOORRSTT	trisoctahedron
ACDEHLMOOPRSSY	chlamydospores
ACDEHOOOPRRSTT	protochordates
ACDEIIIIMNNRST	indiscriminate
ACDEIIIIMNNRSTV	discriminative
ACDEIIIILMNRSTY	discriminately
ACDEIIILNNORTU	unidirectional
ACDEIIILNORSTT	doctrinalities
ACDEIIILNORTTY	directionality
ACDEIIIMNORSST	dosimetricians
ACDEIIINORSSSY	idiosyncrasies
ACDEIIILLMOORTY	iodometrically
ACDEIIILLNORSTY	discretionally
ACDEIIILMMRSSTY	dissymmetrical
ACDEIIILNNNOORT	nondirectional
ACDEIIILNNOOOST	decolonisation
ACDEIIILNNOOOTZ	decolonization
ACDEIIILNNOSTTU	denticulations
ACDEIIILNOOORST	decolorisation
ACDEIIILNOOORTZ	decolorization
ACDEIIILNOPRSTU	reduplications
ACDEIIILNOSSSTY	Society Islands
ACDEIIILNPQTTUU	quintuplicated
ACDEIIMNOOSSTT	domestications
ACDEIINNOORSST	considerations
ACDEIINOQRSSTU	quadrisections
ACDEILLMNOOSTY	endosmotically
ACDEILLNOOSSTY	disconsolately
ACDEILNNOOPSTUU	pedunculations
ACDEILOPRSSSTY	perissodactyls
ACDFGHIIINNRSS	disfranchising
ACDFGHILMNNTUY	Flying Dutchman
ACDFHIIIIMNOTU	humidification
ACDFIIIILNOOST	solidification
ACDGGIIILNORSUY	discouragingly
ACDGHILLLOORVY	hydrologically
ACDGIIIIMNNRST	discriminating
ACDGIIINNNORTT	indoctrinating
ACDHHIIOPRRSST	harpsichordist
ACDHIIIMNOOPPR	panidiomorphic
ACDHIIOOOPPRTT	diaphototropic
ACDHILLNOOPRVY	hydroponically
ACDIIIIILNNNOST	disinclination
ACDIIIIMMNNORST	discrimination
ACDIIIJLNORSTU	jurisdictional
ACDIIIILNNOOTTY	conditionality
ACDIIIILNNOPSTU	induplications
ACDIIILOSSTTUY	adscititiously
ACDIIIMNORRSST	discriminators
ACDIIIMNORRSTY	discriminatory
ACDIIINNNOOORT	incoordination
ACDIIINNNOORTT	indoctrination
ACDIILNNOOOSST	disconsolation
ACDIILNOOORSTU	discolouration
ACDIINNOORRSTT	indoctrinators
ACDILLLMOOORXY	loxodromically
ACEEEEGILLPTXY	epexegetically
ACEEEEHLPRSSST	steeplechasers
ACEEEEINNRRSTT	tercentenaries
ACEEEFGHIMMNNST	gemeinschaften
ACEEEFGHINNNRSU	French Guianese
ACEEEFGHLLNSST	gesellschaften
ACEEEFGNOORSTT	Congo Free State
ACEEEFINRRSSTV	refractiveness
ACEEEFMORRRSTT	refractometers
ACEEEGHHLLNORS	Oehlenschläger
ACEEEGHILNPSST	steeplechasing
ACEEEGHLNNSSSS	changelessness
ACEEEGIILLNPTY	epigenetically
ACEEEGLMNORSTT	electromagnets
ACEEEGMNNORSTU	encouragements
ACEEEHHIINRSTT	heresthetician
ACEEEHHILLMMOS	Sholem Aleichem
ACEEEHHILLORTT	heterolecithal
ACEEEHHIPRSTTY	hyperaesthetic
ACEEEHHILLMORSS	hemerocallises
ACEEEHILNORSST	cholinesterase
ACEEEHLLMNNOPY	myelencephalon
ACEEEHLLMORRTT	electrothermal
ACEEEHLLNNOPST	telencephalons
ACEEEHLMNNOPSS	mesencephalons
ACEEEHLMNNOPST	metencephalons
ACEEEHLOPRRTTY	electrotherapy
ACEEEHMMOORTTY	haemocytometer
ACEEEHMMORSTTY	hemacytometers
ACEEEIILMNNNST	semicentennial
ACEEEIILOPRSSV	overspecialise
ACEEEIILOPRSVZ	overspecialize
ACEEEIINNRRSTT	tricentenaries
ACEEEIILLLMRTTY	telemetrically
ACEEEIILLMPRSST	capellmeisters
ACEEEIILLOPPPRU	peculiar people
ACEEEIILMNNRSTT	interlacements
ACEEEIILMORRSTT	stereometrical
ACEEEIILNNNOQUV	nonequivalence
ACEEEIILNNNRSTT	tercentennials
ACEEEIILNNQQUUV	quinquevalence
ACEEEIILNRRSSTU	creatureliness
ACEEEILLOPRRSTT	electroplaters
ACEEEILMNOPRTUX	counterexample
ACEEEMNOOPRSTV	overcompensate
ACEEEMNORRSTUU	countermeasure
ACEEENNOOSSSTU	coetaneousness
ACEEFFHINNPRSS	affenpinschers
ACEEFFIILNTTUY	ineffectuality
ACEEFHIIINORTT	etherification
ACEEFHIMNNRSST	franchisements
ACEEFHMNOSSTUV	vouchsafements
ACEEFIIIINORSTT	esterification
ACEEFINORRRSST	refractoriness
ACEEGGIMNNORRS	scaremongering
ACEEGHHILLNNNS	English Channel
ACEEGHHIOOPRRS	choreographies
ACEEGHHOOPRRRS	choreographers

ACEEEGHIKLNNRSU	Recklinghausen
ACEEGHILLNOPRY	hypoallergenic
ACEEGHILLOOPRT	herpetological
ACEEGHILMNPSST	phlegmaticness
ACEEGHILOPRRSX	lexicographers
ACEEGHIMMNORTT	thermomagnetic
ACEEGHIMNOPRST	magnetospheric
ACEEGHIMOOPRRT	meteorographic
ACEEGHINOPRTTU	Pinochet Ugarte
ACEEGHMMMNNOOR	Greenham Common
ACEEGHOOOOPPSS	oesophagoscope
ACEEGIINORTTTY	teratogenicity
ACEEGIINOSSTTV	cogitativeness
ACEEGILLLLOOTY	teleologically
ACEEGILLMOOORT	meteorological
ACEEGILLNOORTY	orogenetically
ACEEGILLNOPRTT	electroplating
ACEEGILLNORSTY	estrogenically
ACEEGILLNRSTVY	synergetically
ACEEGILNNNOSST	congenitalness
ACEEGNOORSSSSU	courageousness
ACEEHHHILNNNOPR	rhinencephalon
ACEEHHIMOPRSTT	chemotherapist
ACEEHHIMORSSTT	chrestomathies
ACEEHIIILNPSTT	licentiateship
ACEEHIILMOOPRR	microaerophile
ACEEHIILPRRSTY	hyperrealistic
ACEEHIIMPSSSTY	metaphysicises
ACEEHIIMPSSTYZ	metaphysicizes
ACEEHIINPPPRST	apprenticeship
ACEEHIKOPRRTTY	hyperkeratotic
ACEEHILLLNOPTY	telephonically
ACEEHILLMNNOSS	melancholiness
ACEEHILLMORTXY	exothermically
ACEEHILLRSTTYY	hysteretically
ACEEHILMMORRTT	thermometrical
ACEEHIMMNORSSV	servomechanism
ACEEHIMOORSSTT	tracheostomies
ACEEHLLMOOORST	alcoholometers
ACEEHLLOOPPSTU	leptocephalous
ACEEHLNNOOPPRS	prosencephalon
ACEEHLNPPRSSTU	Penshurst Place
ACEEHMMNNOSSTU	mesenchymatous
ACEEHMNOPPRRST	rapprochements
ACEEEIIILLLMPST	semielliptical
ACEEIIJLNNORTT	interjectional
ACEEIILLLNPSST	ellipticalness
ACEEIILLRTTVY	verticillately
ACEEIILLMMPRTY	metempirically
ACEEIILLMORSTT	microsatellite
ACEEIILLMPRRTY	perimetrically
ACEEIILLRRSTTV	verticillaster
ACEEIILMNOPSTX	exceptionalism
ACEEIILMNORSST	ceremonialists
ACEEIILNNNNQTU	quincentennial
ACEEIILNNNOPTT	epicontinental
ACEEIILNNNRSTT	tricentennials
ACEEIILNNORSST	intercessional
ACEEIILNNORSTT	intersectional
ACEEIILNORRSST	intercessorial
ACEEIILNOSSTTY	coessentiality
ACEEIINNOSSSTT	necessitations
ACEEIKMMNNORSTU	mockumentaries
ACEEIILLLLNTTUY	intellectually
ACEEIILLLNNTTUU	unintellectual
ACEEIILLMNORRTU	intermolecular
ACEEIILLNOPRSSY	precessionally
ACEEIILLRRSSSTY	recrystallises
ACEEIILLRRSSTYZ	recrystallizes
ACEEIILMNOOOPSU	polemoniaceous
ACEEIILMNOPSTTV	contemplatives
ACEEIILMNSSTUUV	cumulativeness
ACEEIILNNOPRSTV	convertiplanes
ACEEIILNNOPSTUV	nonspeculative
ACEEIILNNQQUUVY	quinquevalency
ACEEIILNORRRSTU	resurrectional
ACEEIILNORSSTTU	interosculates
ACEEIILNORSTVVY	conservatively
ACEEIILNOSSTTUX	contextualises
ACEEIILNOSTTUXZ	contextualizes
ACEEIIMMMNOOTTW	committeewoman
ACEEIIMMNNORSTU	incommensurate
ACEEIIMNOOPRRST	contemporaries
ACEEIIMNOPPRRTU	mercaptopurine
ACEEIINNNORSSST	nonresistances
ACEEIINNOOPRSTV	noncooperative
ACEEIINNOORSSVZ	conversaziones
ACEEIINOOPRRRST	reincorporates
ACEEIINOOPRSTTX	expectorations
ACEEIINOORRSSTV	conservatoires
	conservatories
ACEEIINOPRRSSSU	precariousness
ACEEIINOPRRSTTU	counterparties
ACEEELLLMMNOPTY	complementally
ACEEELMMNORSTUY	commensurately
ACEEELNNOOPRSTV	convertoplanes
ACEEEOORRRSSTTUU	aerostructures
ACEFFHIIJMOOOR	Joachim of Fiore
ACEFFLORRSUUUY	furfuraceously
ACEFGIIINNORTT	gentrification
ACEFGIINNORTTU	centrifugation
ACEFHHIIINPSST	chieftainships
ACEFHHLNORSSSY	synchroflashes
ACEFIIIILMPSTV	simplificative
ACEFIIIINORTVV	revivification
ACEFIIIJLLNOST	jellifications
ACEFIIILMNOSTU	emulsification
ACEFIIILPRSTUY	superficiality
ACEFIIINNORSTU	reunifications
ACEFIIINOPRTTT	prettification
ACEFIIINORSSTV	versifications
ACEFIIINOSSTTT	testifications
ACEFIILLLLNNOTY	inflectionally
ACEFIILMMNORST	microfilaments
ACEFIIMNNOORRT	reconfirmation
ACEFIIINOSSSTTU	factitiousness
ACEFINRRRSSTTUU	infrastructure
ACEFIRRSSTTUUUU	usufructuaries
ACEFLLNOORSTTW	Wollstonecraft
ACEFLNOORSSSTU	colourfastness
ACEGGHHINOOPRR	choreographing
ACEGGHIIMNNNNU	machinegunning
ACEGGILLNOOORT	gerontological
ACEGGILMNNOORT	conglomerating

ACEGGILNOOSSTY	gynaecologists
ACEGHHIILLOPRY	hieroglyphical
ACEGHHNOOPRRRS	chronographers
ACEGHIILLNOSTY	histogenically
ACEGHILLLNOOTY	ethnologically
ACEGHILLNOOPTY	photogenically
ACEGHILLNOORTY	orthogenically
ACEGHILOORRRTY	chloroargyrite
ACEGHILOOSSSTT	eschatologists
ACEGHLMOOPSTYY	metapsychology
ACEGHLNNNOOOTV	nanotechnology
ACEGHMMOOPRSUV	myrmecophagous
ACEGHNOOPPRSSY	pharyngoscopes
ACEGHOOOOPPSSY	oesophagoscopy
ACEGHOPPRRRSTY	cryptographers
ACEGIIIILLLOST	illogicalities
ACEGIIILMNRRSU	mercurialising
ACEGIIILMNRRUZ	mercurializing
ACEGIIILNNOSST	sectionalising
ACEGIIILNNOSTZ	sectionalizing
ACEGIIILNOOPST	geopoliticians
ACEGIIINNNORST	containerising
ACEGIIINNNORTZ	containerizing
ACEGIIKMMNORRT	micromarketing
ACEGIILLLLOSTUY	eulogistically
ACEGIILLMNOORT	terminological
ACEGIILLOOORST	soteriological
ACEGIILLORSSUY	sacrilegiously
ACEGIILNNORTUV	countervailing
ACEGIILNNOTTUV	conglutinative
ACEGIILNOQTUVY	equivocatingly
ACEGIILNOSSTTU	gesticulations
ACEGIILNPSTTUX	sextuplicating
ACEGILLLMOORTY	metrologically
ACEGILLLMOOTYY	etymologically
ACEGILLLOOOSTY	osteologically
ACEGILLLOOPRTY	petrologically
ACEGILMNNOOORT	conglomeration
ACEGILNOOPRSSY	laryngoscopies
ACEGINNNOOSSUU	consanguineous
ACEGINNOOSSSTU	contagiousness
ACEGINNOPSSSUU	pugnaciousness
ACEGINOOPRSSTT	prognosticates
ACEHHIIILMNNTT	antihelminthic
ACEHHIINOPPRTT	pithecanthropi
ACEHHIINOPRRTT	therianthropic
ACEHHIINOPRSSZ	schizophrenias
ACEHHIIPPRRSST	archpriestship
ACEHHILLOOPSTY	theosophically
ACEHHILLOPTTYY	hypothetically
ACEHHILOOPRSUZ	rhizocephalous
ACEHHIMOOPPRST	metaphosphoric
ACEHHINOOPPRST	phosphocreatin
ACEHHINOOPSTTY	hypothecations
ACEHHLMOOOOPST	ophthalmoscope
ACEHHLOOOPRSTU	orthocephalous
ACEHHMMNRSSTUY	chrysanthemums
ACEHHMOOOPRRST	chromatophores
ACEHHMOOPRSTTU	chemautotrophs
ACEHIIIILMSSTW	whimsicalities
ACEHIIINNRRSST	christianisers
ACEHIIINNRRSTZ	christianizers
ACEHIIILLLOPSTY	phyllosilicate
ACEHIILLPSTUUY	euphuistically
ACEHIILNORSSST	historicalness
ACEHIIMNNOOPRT	enantiomorphic
ACEHIIMPSSSTTY	metaphysicists
ACEHIINNOPRSST	anticensorship
ACEHIINNPSSSUV	picayunishness
ACEHIINNSSTTUU	unenthusiastic
ACEHIINOOPRTTU	eutrophication
ACEHIINOPPRSST	spinthariscope
ACEHIIOOPRSSST	spirochaetosis
ACEHIIOORRSTTT	osteoarthritic
ACEHILLMNOPRST	phallocentrism
ACEHILLNOPPTYY	phenotypically
ACEHILLNOPRSTT	phallocentrist
ACEHILLOPPRSTTY	prosthetically
ACEHILLOPRTXYY	xerophytically
ACEHILMNOOPRRZ	chlorpromazine
ACEHILMOPRSSTT	thermoplastics
ACEHILNOOPPRSS	cephalosporins
ACEHILNORSSSUV	chivalrousness
ACEHIMNOOPRRTT	anthropometric
ACEHIMOPPRSTTY	spermatophytic
ACEHIMORRSSTTY	astrochemistry
ACEHINOORRSSTT	orchestrations
ACEHINOPPRRSST	copartnerships
ACEHLLMOORSSTY	schoolmasterly
ACEHLLOPSSUXYY	psychosexually
ACEIIIILMNPSTU	municipalities
ACEIIIILNPPRST	principalities
ACEIIIILQSTUZZ	quizzicalities
ACEIIILLMPTTUV	multiplicative
ACEIIILLNNOPST	penicillations
ACEIIILLNORTTV	verticillation
ACEIIILLOPSSTY	isopiestically
ACEIIILMNOOSTT	emotionalistic
ACEIIILNRRTUVY	curvilinearity
ACEIIILNRSSTUV	universalistic
ACEIIIMMNOORSS	commissionaire
ACEIIIMNNORRST	recriminations
ACEIIIMNNORSTT	interactionism
ACEIIINNNOSTTV	Constantine VII
ACEIIINNOPSSTX	expansionistic
ACEIIINOORSSTT	eroticisations
ACEIIINOORSTTZ	eroticizations
ACEIIINOPPRSTT	precipitations
ACEIIINOPQRSTU	preacquisition
ACEIIINOQRSSTU	reacquisitions
ACEIIINORSSTTU	securitisation
ACEIIINORSTTUZ	securitization
ACEIILLLNRTUUY	unicellularity
ACEIILLMNNOOOS	neocolonialism
ACEIILLNNOOOST	neocolonialist
ACEIILMNNNOSTT	continentalism
ACEIILMNORSTUV	vermiculations
ACEIILMNPRRSSU	supercriminals
ACEIILNNNOSSTY	nonsensicality
ACEIILNNNOSTTT	continentalist
ACEIILNNOOORST	recolonisation
ACEIILNNOOORTZ	recolonization
ACEIILNNOORSTU	reinoculations
ACEIILNNORRSTU	insurrectional

ACEIIILNNORSTTU	nocturnalities
ACEIILNNOTTUUVY	continuatively
ACEIILNOOPPRRTY	incorporeality
ACEIILNOORSSTT	sclerotisation
ACEIILNOORSTTZ	sclerotization
ACEIILNOPRSTUY	pertinaciously
ACEIILNOSSSSUV	lasciviousness
ACEIILNPQSTTUU	quintuplicates
ACEIIMMNNOORTU	immunoreaction
ACEIIMMNOORSST	commiserations
ACEIIMNORRSSTT	craniometrists
ACEIINNORSSTTY	syncretisation
ACEIINNORSTTYZ	syncretization
ACEIINNOSSSTUU	incautiousness
ACEIINOOOPRSTT	cooperationist
ACEIINOOPRSTTV	contrapositive
ACEIINOPSSSSUU	auspiciousness
ACEIINORSSSTTU	resuscitations
ACEILLLMORTUVY	volumetrically
ACEILLLNOOQSSU	colloquialness
ACEILLMMOORSTY	osmometrically
ACEILLMOPRRTYY	pyrometrically
ACEILLNNNOOTVY	conventionally
ACEILLNNOOSSTT	constellations
ACEILLNOOPRSSY	processionally
ACEILLNOPRSSUY	supersonically
ACEILLNOSTTUVY	consultatively
ACEILMNOOORTUV	macroevolution
ACEILMNOOPRRTY	contemporarily
ACEILMNORSSSUU	miraculousness
ACEILNNNNOOTUV	unconventional
ACEILNNNOOPSTT	Constantinople
ACEILNNOOOPRST	spironolactone
ACEILNOOPRRTUY	perlocutionary
ACEILNOOQSSSUU	loquaciousness
ACEILNOPRRTUV	proventricular
ACEILNOPRRSSTU	pronuclearists
ACEILOORRSSTTW	watercolorists
ACEILOORRSTTUW	watercolourist
ACEIMMMNOOORST	commemorations
ACEIMMNNOORSTU	commensuration
ACEIMNNNOOPRTU	pronunciamento
ACEIMNNORRSTTU	macronutrients
ACEIMNOORRSTUV	conservatorium
ACEINNNOOOOPRT	noncooperation
ACEINNNOORSTTV	contraventions
ACEKLMMNOORSTT	Kelmscott Manor
ACELRRRSTTTUUU	ultrastructure
ACEMNOOORSSTTU	entomostracous
ACENNOOOOPRRST	noncooperators
ACFFIIINOORSTT	fortifications
ACFGIIIILLNNOST	fictionalising
ACFGIIIILLNNOTZ	fictionalizing
ACFGIIIINNOSST	significations
ACFGIIIILMNSSSY	misclassifying
ACFGIIIILNOORST	glorifications
ACFGIIINNNNOST	nonsignificant
ACFGIILMNNNOTU	malfunctioning
ACFGIINNOORSTU	configurations
ACFHIIINOORRST	horrifications
ACFIIIILMNOPST	simplification
ACFIIIINNORSTT	nitrifications
ACFIIIINORSTTV	vitrifications
ACFIIIJLLNOOST	jollifications
ACFIIIJNOSSTTU	justifications
ACFIIILNOSTTTU	stultification
ACFIIIMNOORSTT	mortifications
ACFIIIMNOSSTTY	mystifications
ACFIIINNOOOPST	opsonification
ACFIILLNNNOOTY	nonfictionally
ACFIIILLRSTTUUY	futuristically
ACFIILNNOSSTTU	functionalists
ACFINNNOOOORSTT	confrontations
ACGGHHIMOPPRSY	sphygmographic
ACGGIILNNNOTTU	conglutinating
ACGHHHIOOPSTUY	ichthyophagous
ACGHIIIINNRSST	christianising
ACGHIIIINNRSTZ	christianizing
ACGHIIILNOPSTT	antiphlogistic
ACGHIIINOPSSTT	sophisticating
ACGHIILLLLOOPY	philologically
ACGHIILLLLOOTY	lithologically
ACGHIILLLOOSTY	histologically
ACGHIILLNOOORT	ornithological
ACGHIILMNOOPSY	physiognomical
ACGHILLLMOOTVY	mythologically
ACGHILLLNOOOPY	phonologically
ACGHILLLOOPTVY	phytologically
ACGHILMOOORSTT	chromatologist
ACGHHIMOOPRSST	cosmographists
ACGHIOPPRRSTTY	cryptographist
ACGIIIILMNNPSU	municipalising
ACGIIIILMNNPUZ	municipalizing
ACGIIIJLLNOSTY	jingoistically
ACGIIILLLNSTUY	linguistically
ACGIIILLLPSTUY	pugilistically
ACGIIILNNOTTXY	intoxicatingly
ACGIILLLLMNOOY	limnologically
ACGIILLMNOSUUY	mucilaginously
ACGIIILLMOOSSTT	climatologists
ACGIILNNNOOTTU	conglutination
ACGIILRRSSTTUU	agriculturists
ACGIIMMNNOORSS	microorganisms
ACGIIMNNPSTTUU	mispunctuating
ACGILLNOOOSSTV	volcanologists
ACGILLNOOSSTUV	vulcanologists
ACGILNOOPRSSTY	laryngoscopist
ACGINOOOOPRRSTT	prognosticator
ACGIOOPRSSSSTT	gastroscopists
ACHHIIINNORSST	ornithischians
ACHHILLMNOOOPY	homophonically
ACHHIMMMOOORST	homochromatism
ACHHINOOOOPPRST	anthroposophic
ACHHLMOOOOPPSTY	ophthalmoscopy
ACHIIIINNORSTT	trichinisation
ACHIIIINNORTTZ	trichinization
ACHIIIJPRSSSTU	justiciarships
ACHIIILLLPSTVY	syphilitically
ACHIIIILLNORSTY	histrionically
ACHIIILNPPPRSS	principalships
ACHIIIMNOORSST	trichomoniasis
ACHIIINOOPSSTT	sophistication
ACHIILLLMNOOTY	monolithically
ACHIILLLLOSTTYY	histolytically

ACHIIMMOPRSSSY	commissaryship
ACHIIOOPRSSSTT	sophisticators
ACHIIOPRSSSTTY	astrophysicist
ACHILLLNOOPPVY	polyphonically
ACHILLOOPPTTVY	phototypically
ACHILMMOOPRSTY	polychromatism
ACHILMOPSSTTVY	sympatholytics
ACHIMMMNOOORST	monochromatism
ACHIMNOOOPRSTU	actinomorphous
ACHIOOPPRRRSTU	procuratorship
ACHLNNOORSSUVY	asynchronously
ACHMMNOOOORRST	monochromators
ACIIIILNOOPSTT	politicisation
ACIIIILNOOPTTZ	politicization
ACIIIILPRSSTTU	spiritualistic
ACIIIIMNOSSTTV	victimisations
ACIIIIMNOSTTVZ	victimizations
ACIIILLLMPSSTY	simplistically
ACIIILLMNOPTTU	multiplication
ACIIILLMOPSTTY	optimistically
ACIIILLNNOSSTT	scintillations
ACIIILNOPSSUUY	inauspiciously
ACIILLLMOOQSSU	colloquialisms
ACIILNNOOSTTTU	constitutional
ACIILNOOORSSTU	colourisations
ACIILNOOORSTUZ	colourizations
ACIILQRSSTTUUU	aquiculturists
ACIIMMNNOOSSTU	communisations
ACIIMMNNOOSTUZ	communizations
ACIIMMNOOPSTTU	miscomputation
ACIIMNNOPSTTUU	mispunctuation
ACIINNNOOPRSTU	pronunciations
ACIINNOOOPRRST	incorporations
ACIINNOOOPRSTT	contraposition
ACIINNOPRRSSTT	transcriptions
ACIKMNNOORSTUY	Rocky Mountains
ACILLOOPPRTTYY	prototypically
ACILNNOOORTUVY	convolutionary
ACILNOPRSSTUUY	transpicuously
ACILNOSSSSTTTU	sansculottists
ACILRRSSSTTTUU	structuralists
ACIMMOOOORSSTTU	microstomatous
ACIMNOOOSTTTXY	cytotaxonomist
ACINNOPRSSTTTU	contrapuntists
ADDDEEEEHLRRTW	Edward the Elder
ADDDEEEGHNORTY	dehydrogenated
ADDDEEIILMNOSS	Diomede Islands
ADDDEIIIILNSUV	individualised
ADDDEIIIILNUVZ	individualized
ADDEEEEEFHNNRSS	freehandedness
ADDEEEEGHLMMRS	sledgehammered
ADDEEEEHNNNSSV	evenhandedness
ADDEEEEHNORSSS	soreheadedness
ADDEEEEFFIINRTT	differentiated
ADDEEEEFHNNORSS	forehandedness
ADDEEEEFHNOSSST	softheadedness
ADDEEEEGHLNNOSS	longheadedness
ADDEEEEGHNORSSY	dehydrogenases
ADDEEEEGHNORSTY	dehydrogenates
ADDEEEEHIMNPPRS	misapprehended
ADDEEEEHNNNOPSS	openhandedness
ADDEEEEIINPRSST	pedestrianised
ADDEEEEIINPRSTZ	pedestrianized
ADDEEEEILMPRTTY	premeditatedly
ADDEEEEILNOPRSS	depersonalised
ADDEEEEILNOPRSZ	depersonalized
ADDEEEEIMNPRTTU	unpremeditated
ADDEEEEIMNRSTTU	underestimated
ADDEEEEINOPQRTU	equiponderated
ADDEEEFFHLRRUUY	furfuraldehyde
ADDEEEFLNNNORUW	Newfoundlander
ADDEEEGIIINRTTT	interdigitated
ADDEEEHIIMNNRTY	dimenhydrinate
ADDEEEIINPSSSST	dissipatedness
ADDEEEINOPRRSTU	superordinated
ADDEEELNOPPRTUU	underpopulated
ADDEEFGILLRRSUY	disregardfully
ADDEEFIIILSSSTY	dissatisfiedly
ADDEEFIILLNNRSS	Flinders Island
ADDEEFIILNNSSSU	disdainfulness
ADDEEGILNOORRSU	Rio Grande do Sul
ADDEEGINNNRSSTU	understandings
ADDEEHHILOPRSST	stadholdership
ADDEEHILLNOORSW	Lord Howe Island
ADDEEIIIILNRSUV	individualiser
ADDEEIIIILNRUVZ	individualizer
ADDEEIIIILNSSUV	individualises
ADDEEIIIILNSUVZ	individualizes
ADDEEIIILNPSTTU	platitudinised
ADDEEIIILNPTTUZ	platitudinized
ADDEEIIILNRSSTU	industrialised
ADDEEIIILNRSTUZ	industrialized
ADDEEIIINOOSSTX	deoxidisations
ADDEEIIINOOSTXZ	deoxidizations
ADDEEIILNOPPSTY	disappointedly
ADDEEIMNNRSSSTU	misunderstands
ADDIIIILMNSSUV	individualisms
ADDIIIILNSSTUV	individualists
ADDIIIINNOSTUV	individuations
ADEEEEEGNNRSST	degenerateness
ADEEEEHHLMMPST	Hemel Hempstead
ADEEEEIMNPRRTT	predeterminate
ADEEEEFFIINRSTT	differentiates
ADEEEEFGILORRTU	Tierra del Fuego
ADEEEEFGLNNNSSW	newfangledness
ADEEEEFHOOPRRTW	weatherproofed
ADEEEEFIMNNOORT	aforementioned
ADEEEEFIMNRSTTU	disfeaturement
ADEEEEFINNNORST	defenestration
ADEEEEGGIMNNSST	disengagements
ADEEEEGIILHNRST	legerdemainist
ADEEEEGIINRRTTV	redintegrative
ADEEEEGIINRSTTV	reinvestigated
ADEEEEGIKNNRRRT	kindergartener
ADEEEEGINORRTTT	reinterrogated
ADEEEEGLNRRSSSS	regardlessness
ADEEEEGOPRRRTUY	daguerreotyper
ADEEEEGOPRRSTUY	daguerreotypes
ADEEEEHHLLORTWY	wholeheartedly
ADEEEEHIINRRSST	hereditariness
ADEEEEHILNOOPRT	radiotelephone
ADEEEEHIMNNRSTT	disheartenment
ADEEEEHIMNORRSV	Mies van der Rohe
ADEEEEHIMOPRSSV	overemphasised

ADEEEHIMOPRSVZ	overemphasized
ADEEEHIMRSSSST	headmistresses
ADEEEIIIMNRRST	intermediaries
ADEEEIIINRRSST	residentiaries
ADEEEIILLNPTXY	expedientially
ADEEEIILMNRTTY	intermediately
ADEEEIIMMQRSUV	demisemiquaver
ADEEEIIMNRSTTV	determinatives
ADEEEIIMNSSTTV	meditativeness
ADEEEIINPRSSST	pedestrianises
ADEEEIINPRSSTZ	pedestrianizes
ADEEEILMORRTTY	radiotelemetry
ADEEEILNOPRSSS	depersonalises
ADEEEILNOPRSSZ	depersonalizes
ADEEEILOPRSTTY	radioteletypes
ADEEEIMMNORSST	immoderateness
ADEEEIMNRSSTTU	underestimates
ADEEEIMNRSSTTV	advertisements
ADEEEIMNRSTTVZ	advertizements
ADEEEINNRSTTUW	Wiener Neustadt
ADEEEINOPQRSTU	equiponderates
ADEEEELNOPPRRTY	preponderately
ADEEEMNNRSTTTU	understatement
ADEEENNNOSSSSU	unseasonedness
ADEEENNPPRRSSU	unpreparedness
ADEEFFIILLNRTY	differentially
ADEEFFIINORRTT	differentiator
ADEEFGHINRSSST	farsightedness
ADEEFHILNSSTTW	halfwittedness
ADEEFHKLOOOSTW	Lake of the Woods
ADEEFIMNNOORRT	foreordainment
ADEEGGHLNOOSTT	snaggletoothed
ADEEGGIIINNPRST	predesignating
ADEEGGIINNRRTT	redintegrating
ADEEGGILLNNORT	golden triangle
ADEEGGIMNNRRRY	gerrymandering
ADEEGHHILLRTTY	lightheartedly
ADEEGHHOOPPRRT	rephotographed
ADEEGHILNNRRTY	heartrendingly
ADEEGHILNRSSTU	daughterliness
ADEEGHNNORSSST	headstrongness
ADEEGIIILMNNRS	demineralising
ADEEGIIILMNNRZ	demineralizing
ADEEGIIILNORVZ	overidealizing
ADEEGIIIMNNRTT	intermediating
ADEEGIIINRSTTT	interdigitates
ADEEGIIINRSTTV	disintegrative
ADEEGIIKLLNNSS	Keeling Islands
ADEEGIIMNNORST	demonetarising
ADEEGIIMNNORTZ	demonetarizing
ADEEGIINNORRTT	redintegration
ADEEGIINNPRSTT	predestinating
ADEEGIINNRRRVW	Wind River Range
ADEEGIINORRSTT	deregistration
ADEEGIMORSSTTU	deuterogamists
ADEEGINNOPPRRT	preponderating
ADEEGINOORRSST	derogatoriness
ADEEGINOPRRSUV	overpersuading
ADEEGINORSSTTU	deuteragonists
ADEEGJLMNNNOTU	nonjudgemental
ADEEHHIILMOPRS	hemispheroidal
ADEEHHILLPPSSU	philadelphuses

ADEEHHHIMOPRRST	hermaphrodites
ADEEHIIILMPPRY	hyperlipidemia
ADEEHIIMNOORTT	triiodomethane
ADEEHIKLORRSSY	Yorkshire Dales
ADEEHILMNNRSTT	disenthralment
ADEEHILNOOPRTY	radiotelephony
ADEEHIMORRSTTT	tetartohedrism
ADEEHLMNOORRSY	dysmenorrhoeal
ADEEHLORSTTTUY	stoutheartedly
ADEEHNOOPRRSTZ	trapezohedrons
ADEEHOPRRSSSTU	pseudarthroses
ADEEIIILORRSST	editorialisers
ADEEIIILORRSTZ	editorializers
ADEEIIIMNNORTT	intermediation
ADEEIIINORSSTV	radiosensitive
ADEEIILLLLMNSV	Melville Island
ADEEIILLNPRSTY	presidentially
ADEEIILMNNOTVY	denominatively
ADEEIILMNNSSTT	disentailments
ADEEIILMNOPRSS	impersonalised
ADEEIILMNOPRSZ	impersonalized
ADEEIILNNNORST	nonresidential
ADEEIIMNNOOSTT	demonetisation
ADEEIIMNNOOTTZ	demonetization
ADEEIIMNORRSTT	intermediators
ADEEIINNNORSST	inordinateness
ADEEIINNOPRSTT	predestination
ADEEIINOPRSSTY	dispensatories
ADEEIINSSSSSUV	dissuasiveness
ADEEILMMNNSSTT	dismantlements
ADEEILMORSTTUV	overstimulated
ADEEILNNOOSSTV	devotionalness
ADEEILNNRRSTUY	unrestrainedly
ADEEIMNNORRSST	arrondissement
ADEEIMNORSSTTV	demonstratives
ADEEINNOPPRRTO	preponderation
ADEEINOPRRSSTU	superordinates
ADEELNNOPPRRTY	preponderantly
ADEELNNORSSSSU	slanderousness
ADEEMNNNORRUWY	Newry and Mourne
ADEENNPPRRRSSTU	understrappers
ADEFFGIINORSST	disafforesting
ADEFGIIMNORRST	transmogrified
ADEFIIINNOSSTT	disinfestation
ADEFIINNOOORRT	foreordination
ADEFIINOORSSTT	disforestation
ADEFIINOSSSSTU	fastidiousness
ADEFIIOORSSTUV	overfastidious
ADEFILNOPRSSTY	Parts of Lindsey
ADEGGIIINNRSTT	disintegrating
ADEGGILLNRSSSU	sluggardliness
ADEGHHHIILLNRSS	Shire Highlands
ADEGHIILLNNRST	disenthralling
ADEGHIILMNPSTY	lymphangitides
ADEGHINNOOSRTY	hydrogenations
ADEGHNNOOOPRRY	androgynophore
ADEGIIIILMNRST	demilitarising
ADEGIIIILMNRTZ	demilitarizing
ADEGIIIILNORST	editorialising
ADEGIIIILNORTZ	editorializing
ADEGIIINNORSTT	disintegration
	disorientating

ADEGIINNNPRSTU	underpaintings
ADEGIINORRSSTT	disintegrators
ADEGILMOORSSTT	dermatologists
ADEGINNNPSSSTU	upstandingness
ADEGLLMNORSUWZ	mangoldwurzels
ADEHHIILLLLSSY	shillyshallied
ADEHHIMOPRRSTU	Hermaphroditus
ADEHHIOPRRSTTY	hydrotherapist
ADEHHLLMORRTYY	hydrothermally
ADEHHLOPRSSTUY	hydrosulphates
ADEHIILNNOPSSX	Phoenix Islands
ADEHILNNOPRSSW	landownerships
ADEHILNNOSSSTU	outlandishness
ADEHIMOOOPPRSS	paedomorphosis
ADEHIMOOPRRSST	moderatorships
ADEHINOORRSSTW	roadworthiness
ADEHIOPRRSSSTU	pseudarthrosis
ADEHNORRSSTTWW	northwestwards
ADEHORSSSTTUWW	southwestwards
ADEIIILMNNORST	tridimensional
ADEIIILMNNOSTY	dimensionality
ADEIIILNPRSTTU	platitudiniser
ADEIIILNPRTTUZ	platitudinizer
ADEIIILNPSSTTU	platitudinises
ADEIIILNPSTTUZ	platitudinizes
ADEIIILNRSSSTU	industrialises
ADEIIILNRSSTUZ	industrializes
ADEIIIMNNOSSST	disseminations
ADEIIINNOORSTT	disorientation
ADEIIINOOPRSST	periodisations
ADEIIINOOPRSTZ	periodizations
ADEIIINRSSTTTU	attitudinisers
ADEIIINRSTTTUZ	attitudinizers
ADEIILLNOPRTVY	providentially
ADEIILMNNOOPRS	pronominalised
ADEIILMNNOOPRZ	pronominalized
ADEIILNOSTTUVY	adventitiously
ADEIIMNNOORSST	modernisations
ADEIIMNNOORSTZ	modernizations
ADEIIMNNOPPSTT	disappointment
ADEIIMNNORSSTT	antimodernists
ADEIINNOOPRRST	preordinations
ADEIINORRSSSTT	transistorised
ADEIINORRSSTTZ	transistorized
ADEILLNORRSTVY	dorsiventrally
ADEILMMNORRSTU	ultramodernism
ADEILMNNORSTTU	ultramodernist
ADEILNOORSSSTU	idolatrousness
ADEIMNNOORSSTT	demonstrations
ADEIMNNOPRSSTU	superdominants
ADEINOOOPPRRTT	proportionated
ADEINOOORRTTTX	dextrorotation
ADELLNOORRSTVY	dorsoventrally
ADELMNOOORSSSU	malodorousness
ADEOOORRRTTTXY	dextrorotatory
ADFGIIINORSSTU	disfigurations
ADFIIIMNNOORST	disinformation
ADGHILOOORRSVV	Voroshilovgrad
ADGHINNOOOPRST	gonadotrophins
ADGHMNNOOPRRSY	gynandromorphs
ADGHMNNOOPRRYY	gynandromorphy
ADGIIIINNSTTTU	attitudinising

ADGIIIINNTTTUZ	attitudinizing
ADGIILLLNNOTUY	longitudinally
ADGIILNOPPRSVY	disapprovingly
ADHIIMMMMNRTUU	Urim and Thummim
ADHILNOORSSTYY	hydrolysations
ADHILNOORSTYYZ	hydrolyzations
ADIIIILMNOSSST	dissimilations
ADIIIILMNPRSTU	platiniridiums
ADIIIILNOQSSTU	disquisitional
ADIIIILMNOSSSTU	dissimulations
ADIIIILNRSSSTTU	industrialists
ADIIILLOPRRSSTU	Lords Spiritual
ADIILNOPRSSTTU	postindustrial
ADIILOPSSTTUUY	disputatiously
ADILLLLOOOPPSY	allopolyploids
ADILLLLOOOPPYY	allopolyploidy
ADILLMNNOOOSSS	Solomon Islands
ADILLOOOPPSTUY	autopolyploids
ADILLOOOPPTUYY	autopolyploidy
AEEEEFFIMNNSST	effeminateness
AEEEEEGILNORRVZ	overgeneralize
AEEEEEGILNRRTVY	regeneratively
AEEEEEGINSSTTVV	vegetativeness
AEEEEGLNNRRTUY	unregenerately
AEEEEHMNOPPRRT	ephemeropteran
AEEEEHNPRSSTUY	Hautes-Pyrénées
AEEEEEILMNNRSST	elementariness
AEEEEEIMNNRSSTT	intemerateness
AEEEEEIMNNRTTVW	interweavement
AEEEEEINNPRRTTT	interpenetrate
AEEEEEINNRSSTTV	inveterateness
AEEEEEINNRSSTVV	venerativeness
AEEEEEINPRRSTTV	representative
AEEEEEMMNRRSSTU	remeasurements
AEEEEFGHHIRSTTW	featherweights
AEEEEFHIIRRSSTT	Irish Free State
AEEEEFIILNNRRTT	interferential
AEEEEFILLNPRRTY	preferentially
AEEEEFILMNRTTVY	fermentatively
AEEEEFINQRSTTUV	frequentatives
AEEEEGGINRSSSSV	aggressiveness
AEEEEGGIORRSSVV	overaggressive
AEEEEGHHINPRSSS	sheepshearings
AEEEEGHHIOPRRST	heterographies
AEEEEGHILMNPPRT	pamphleteering
AEEEEGIILMNSSTT	legitimateness
AEEEEGIINRSSTTV	reinvestigates
AEEEEGILLNSSTTV	televangelists
AEEEEGILLRSSSST	legislatresses
AEEEEGINORRRSTT	reinterrogates
AEEEGNNOOPQRTU	roentgenopaque
AEEEGNNOORRSTT	enterogastrone
AEEEHHHINNSSST	heathenishness
AEEEHHLMNNOSTY	Henley-on-Thames
AEEEHIIMNRSSST	Shemini Atseres
AEEEHIINNPPRSV	inapprehensive
AEEEHILNPPRSVY	apprehensively
AEEEHILNPRTTVY	hyperventilate
AEEEHILOPRSSTT	heteroplasties
AEEEHIMOPRSSSV	overemphasises
AEEEHIMOPRSSVZ	overemphasizes
AEEEHINNPPRSUV	unapprehensive

AEEEHINSSSTUVX	exhaustiveness
AEEEIIINNPRSTT	penitentiaries
AEEEIILLNPRTXY	experientially
AEEEIILLNRSSTT	illiterateness
AEEEIILMNNSSTT	sentimentalise
AEEEIILMNNSTTZ	sentimentalize
AEEEIILNRRSSTV	irrelativeness
AEEEIIMNPRSSTV	imperativeness
AEEEIINPRRTTTV	interpretative
AEEEILLLNRSSST	Lesser Antilles
AEEEILLMNPRTXY	experimentally
AEEEILMNORRTTV	intervalometer
AEEEILMNRRTUVY	remuneratively
AEEEILNOPRSTUV	superelevation
AEEEIMNNNNRSTTT	entertainments
AEEEIMNNRRTUUV	unremunerative
AEEEIMNNRSSTTT	reinstatements
AEEEINNNPRRTTT	interpenetrant
AEEEINNOPRRSTT	representation
AEEEINOPRRSSTV	perseverations
AEEEINPRSSSSUV	persuasiveness
AEEELMNNNRSSSS	mannerlessness
AEEEMMNOPRSTTU	pneumatometers
AEEEMMNOPPRSWW	newspaperwomen
AEEEMNOOPRSTUX	extemporaneous
AEEEMNORSSSSTV	overassessment
AEEEMNORSSTTTV	overstatements
AEEENNNRSSSSTUX	extraneousness
AEEENNRRSSSSTV	transverseness
AEEENQSSSSTTUU	statuesqueness
AEEFFGHIMNRSTT	affreightments
AEEFGIIMMNRSTT	ferrimagnetism
AEEFGIINRSSTUV	figurativeness
AEEFGILMNNNSSU	meaningfulness
AEEFGIMMNORRST	ferromagnetism
AEEFGINNNRRRST	retransferring
AEEFGLNNRSSTUU	ungratefulness
AEEFHLMNOSSSST	fathomlessness
AEEFIIILNNOPRU	infopreneurial
AEEFIILNOQQTUU	quinquefoliate
AEEFIINNORSSTT	reinfestations
AEEFILMOPRRTVY	performatively
AEEFIOOOPRRSST	professoriates
AEEFNOQRRSSSUU	foursquareness
AEEGGHNNOOOPRRT	roentgenograph
AEEGGHOOOPRRSZ	zoogeographers
AEEGGIINORSSTT	segregationist
AEEGGIINRRSTTV	tergiversating
AEEGGILLNNORTU	outgeneralling
AEEGGINOPRRSTU	supererogating
AEEGGINORRSSSU	gregariousness
AEEGGIOSSTTUUV	autosuggestive
AEEGGMNNNOORRST	roentgenograms
AEEGHHLORSSTUU	slaughterhouse
AEEGHIINNPRSST	parenthesising
AEEGHIINNPRSTZ	parenthesizing
AEEGHIINNRRTTW	interwreathing
AEEGHIIPRRRSST	parish register
AEEGHILNOOSSTY	anesthesiology
AEEGHILNOPRSST	selenographist
AEEGHIMNSSSTTT	steamtightness
AEEGHIMOPRRSSS	seismographers
AEEGHINRSSTTTW	watertightness
AEEGHNOOPRRSTV	photoengravers
AEEGIIILLLMTTY	illegitimately
AEEGIIILLLNNTT	intelligential
AEEGIIILLNNSTT	intelligentsia
AEEGIIILNNNRT	interlineating
AEEGIIILRRRSTU	irregularities
AEEGIILLNNPRTT	interpellating
AEEGIILMNORSSS	generalissimos
AEEGIILNNNRTTY	entertainingly
AEEGIIMMNOPSTZ	piezomagnetism
AEEGIIMNNNNORTU	mountaineering
AEEGIIMNORSTTV	overestimating
AEEGIINNNNRTTU	unentertaining
AEEGIINNOORSTT	renegotiations
AEEGIINNOPRRST	peregrinations
AEEGIINNORRSTT	reintegrations
AEEGIINORRSTTV	interrogatives
	tergiversation
AEEGILLMNORRST	steamrollering
AEEGILLOOPSSST	spelaeologists
AEEGILNNOSSSTU	gelatinousness
AEEGIMNNNORSTU	Green Mountains
AEEGIMNNORTUUV	outmaneuvering
AEEGIMNRRRTUWZ	gewurztraminer
AEEGINOOPRRSTU	supererogation
AEEGIORRRSSTTV	tergiversators
AEEGIORRRSTTVY	tergiversatory
AEEGLLMNNORTVY	governmentally
AEEGNOORSSSTUU	outrageousness
AEEGOOPRRRSSTU	supererogators
AEEGOOPRRRSTUY	supererogatory
AEEHHIINNOPSTZ	phenothiazines
AEEHHILLMORSTT	heterothallism
AEEHHILMMNNSTT	nemathelminths
AEEHHLMNNOPSTU	sulphonmethane
AEEHHOPPPRSSTU	superphosphate
AEEHIILLNNOSTZ	hellenizations
AEEHIJNNOPRSST	Saint-John Perse
AEEHIKOPRRSSTY	hyperkeratosis
AEEHILLMRSSSTW	Wilhelmstrasse
AEEHILMNNOPSST	phenomenalists
AEEHILMNOOPRTY	hyperemotional
AEEHILOOPRRTTY	heteropolarity
AEEHIMNNOPRSST	Pontine Marshes
AEEHIMNORSSTUV	overenthusiasm
AEEHINPPPPRRSW	whippersnapper
AEEHLMNOORRTTT	thermotolerant
AEEHMNNNPRSSSUU	superhumanness
AEEHMNOOPPRSTU	pneumatophores
AEEHMOOPPRRSST	spermatophores
AEEHMOPPRSSTTY	spermatophytes
AEEHNOOPPRRSST	parthenospores
AEEIIILMNSSTTX	existentialism
AEEIIILNNNORTT	interlineation
AEEIIILNNSSTTY	inessentiality
AEEIIILNOPSTTT	potentialities
AEEIIILNSSTTTX	existentialist
AEEIIILORRRSTT	territorialise
AEEIIILORRRTTZ	territorialize
AEEIILLLNOSTVV	televisionally
AEEIILLLNPSTTY	pestilentially

AEEIILLNNNOPRTT	interpellation
AEEIILMMNNOPTT	implementation
AEEIILMMNNSSTT	sentimentalism
AEEIILMNNOSSTX	extensionalism
AEEIILMNNSSTTT	sentimentalist
AEEIILMNNSTTTY	sentimentality
AEEIILMNOORSTT	telomerisation
AEEIILMNOORTTZ	telomerization
AEEIILMNOPRSSS	impersonalises
AEEIILMNOPRSSZ	impersonalizes
AEEIILMNRSSTUX	intersexualism
AEEIILNNNORTTV	interventional
AEEIILNNORRSTT	interrelations
AEEIILNNOSTTXY	extensionality
AEEIILNNQSSTTU	quintessential
AEEIILNORSSTTV	revelationists
AEEIILNRSTTUXY	intersexuality
AEEIILPRTTUVVY	vituperatively
AEEIIMNNOORSTT	remonetisation
AEEIIMNNOORTTZ	remonetization
AEEIIMNNORSTTX	exterminations
AEEIIMNOORSTTV	overestimation
AEEIINNOORRSTT	reorientations
AEEIINNOPPSSST	inappositeness
AEEIINNOPRRTTT	interpretation
AEEIINNOQRSSTU	questionnaires
AEEIINNORSSTTW	westernisation
AEEIINNORSTTWZ	westernization
AEEIINNRSSSTTV	transitiveness
AEEIINPQQRTTUU	quinquepartite
AEEIKLNNOPRSUY	Yorke Peninsula
AEEIKMRSSSSSTT	taskmistresses
AEEILLLNNNPSUY	Lleyn Peninsula
AEEILLNNRSSSTT	slatternliness
AEEILLNOPRRSTT	interpellators
AEEILMNNNNRSSU	unmannerliness
AEEILMNOSSSTUU	simultaneouses
AEEILMORSSTTUV	overstimulates
AEEILNNPPPRSUU	Upper Peninsula
AEEILNOORRSSTV	lateroversions
AEEILNOORTTTXY	extortionately
AEEILNOPRSSTTU	reputationless
AEEIMNNOPPRSTT	reappointments
AEEINNOOPRSSVX	overexpansions
AEEINOOPRRSTTX	reexportations
AEEINOORRSSSTV	overassertions
AEEINOQRSSSTTU	sequestrations
AEEINORRSSTTTU	sternutatories
AEELLLMNPPSTUY	supplementally
AEELLMNORSSSUV	marvellousness
AEFFHILNNSSTUU	unfaithfulness
AEFFIIMNOORRSU	foraminiferous
AEFGGNOORRSSYY	Gregory of Nyssa
AEFGIILNOSSSTU	flagitiousness
AEFGIIMNORRSST	transmogrifies
AEFGIINOPRRSTU	prefigurations
AEFHHLNNOPRTWY	halfpennyworth
AEFHIILNNOPRTY	hyperinflation
AEFIIIILMNNSST	infinitesimals
AEFIIILNORSSTT	fertilisations
AEFIIILNORSTTZ	fertilizations
AEFIILNOOPRRST	proliferations
AEFILLNOOPRSSY	professionally
AEFILLOOPRRSSY	professorially
AEFILMNOORRSTU	formation rules
	reformulations
AEFILNNOOPRSSU	unprofessional
AEFILNOOPRSSSW	passionflowers
AEFIMNNOORRSTW	frontierswoman
AEGGHHLOPPRRSY	glyphographers
AEGGHHOOPPRTYY	phytogeography
AEGGHILOOPRSSS	glossographies
AEGGHILOPPRSTY	glyptographies
AEGGHINNOOPRTV	photoengraving
AEGGHLOOPRRSSS	glossographers
AEGGHLOPPRRSTY	glyptographers
AEGGHNNOOPRRST	rontgenographs
AEGGIIIILMNSTT	legitimatising
AEGGIIIILMNTTZ	legitimatizing
AEGGIIINNORRTV	reinvigorating
AEGGIINORRSTTU	regurgitations
AEGGINOOSSTTUU	autosuggestion
AEGHHIOPPRRSSY	physiographers
AEGHHLMOPPRSTY	plethysmograph
AEGHIILLOPRSST	legislatorship
AEGHIILNNSSTTUY	unhesitatingly
AEGHIILNOOOSTT	theologisation
AEGHIILNOOOTTZ	theologization
AEGHIIMNNOOOST	homogenisation
AEGHIIMNNOOOTZ	homogenization
AEGHIINNSSTTUX	extinguishants
AEGHIINOOSSTTT	ghettoisations
AEGHIINOOSTTTZ	ghettoizations
AEGHIIPRRRSSST	registrarships
AEGHILMOORSTTU	rheumatologist
AEGHILOOPRSSST	phraseologists
AEGHIMMNOOPRST	metamorphosing
AEGHIMNOOPRSTY	pharyngotomies
AEGHLLMOOPPRSY	megasporophyll
AEGHLNOOOPRTUY	neuropathology
AEGHMMOOPRRTTY	photogrammetry
AEGHOOOPPPRRRS	prosopographer
AEGIIIILMNOSTT	legitimisation
AEGIIIILMNOTTZ	legitimization
AEGIIIILMNRRTZ	remilitarizing
AEGIIILMNNOOST	emotionalising
AEGIIILMNNOOTZ	emotionalizing
AEGIIILNNRSSUV	universalising
AEGIIILNNRSUVZ	universalizing
AEGIIILNORTVVY	invigoratively
AEGIIIMNNORRTT	intermigration
AEGIIINNOORRTV	reinvigoration
AEGIIINNOPRRTT	repartitioning
AEGIIINNORSTTT	integrationist
AEGIIINNOSSTTV	investigations
AEGIILMNNOORST	mongrelisation
AEGIILMNNOORTZ	mongrelization
AEGIILMOOSSSST	semasiologists
AEGIILNNNRSTTY	intransigently
AEGIIMNNRRSTTT	retransmitting
AEGIINNNOORSTT	rontgenisation
AEGIINNNOORTTZ	rontgenization
AEGIINNOOPPRRT	reapportioning
AEGIINNOORRSTT	interrogations

AEGILLMNNOQTUY	magniloquently
AEGILMMNRSSTUU	summersaulting
AEGILMNOOORSTU	osmoregulation
AEGILMNOOPSTTU	pneumatologist
AEGILNNNOSSSUU	lanuginousness
AEGILNNOOOSSTT	neonatologists
AEGILNOOPPRTUV	overpopulating
AEGIMMNOOPRSTU	spermatogonium
AEGIMNNNSSSSUU	unassumingness
AEGIMNNOORTUUV	outmanoeuvring
AEGINNORRSSSST	transgressions
AEGINORSSSTTUU	gratuitousness
AEGKKMNOORSSTU	Ust-Kamenogorsk
AEGLLMOPRRTUYY	pyrometallurgy
AEGLMNOORSSSUU	glamourousness
AEGLNNOORSSSUU	languorousness
AEGMMNNOOOSSSU	monogamousness
AEHHHOOOOPPRSTT	orthophosphate
AEHHHOOPPPSSTY	hypophosphates
AEHHIILLLLRSSY	shillyshallier
AEHHIILLLLSSSY	shillyshallies
AEHHIILNOPPRST	philanthropies
AEHHILLMNPSTTY	platyhelminths
AEHHIMOOOPSSTT	homoeopathists
AEHHINOPPRSTTY	hypnotherapist
AEHHINOPRSSTTT	theanthropists
AEHHLLMOOPRTTY	photothermally
AEHHLOOPPRSSSY	phosphorylases
AEHHNOOPPRSTTY	anthropophytes
AEHHNOOPSSTTTY	photosynthates
AEHHOOPPPRSSTY	pyrophosphates
AEHIIKLLMOOPRT	poikilothermal
AEHIILLMNNOPSY	aminophyllines
AEHIILMOOPPRST	apheliotropism
AEHIILOPRRSTWY	praiseworthily
AEHIIMNNOSTTUW	White Mountains
AEHIIMOPPRRSST	imperatorships
AEHIINNOSSTTTY	synthetisation
AEHIINNOSSTTYZ	synthesization
AEHIINNOSTTTYZ	synthetization
AEHIIOORRSSTTT	osteoarthritis
AEHIIPPRRTTUYY	hyperpituitary
AEHILMOPPRSSTY	amphiprostyles
AEHILNNOORSSTZ	horizontalness
AEHIMNNPRSSSTT	transshipments
AEHIMOOOPPPSSTU	hippopotamuses
AEHINNOPRSSSTU	sinanthropuses
AEHINOOOPRRSTT	prothonotaries
AEHLMNOOOOPSSTU	haplostemonous
AEIIIILMNRSSTT	ministerialist
AEIIIILPRSSTTU	spiritualities
AEIIILLLMNNSST	millennialists
AEIIILLMNNORSS	millionnairess
AEIIILLNRSTTTY	interstitially
AEIIILMNPRSTTY	amitriptylines
AEIIILMORRRSTT	territorialism
AEIIILNNNOTTTY	intentionality
AEIIILNNOOPTVV	opinionatively
AEIIILNNRSTTVY	intransitively
AEIIILNORSSSTT	sterilisations
AEIIILNORSSTTZ	sterilizations
AEIIILNORSTTUZ	reutilizations
AEIIIILORRRSTTT	territorialist
AEIIIILORRRTTTY	territoriality
AEIIIILPRRSSSTU	spiritualisers
AEIIIILPRRSSTUZ	spiritualizers
AEIIIMMNOSSSTT	misestimations
AEIIIMNOOPSSTT	epitomisations
AEIIIMNOOPSTTZ	epitomizations
AEIIIMNOORSSST	isomerisations
AEIIIMNOORSSTZ	isomerizations
AEIIINNORSSTTW	winterisations
AEIIINNORSTTWZ	winterizations
AEIIINNOSSSSTT	sensitisations
AEIIINNOSSSTTZ	sensitizations
AEIIINOOPRRSSV	provisionaries
AEIIINOPQRSTTU	equipartitions
AEIIINOQRRSTUV	requisitionary
AEIIIOOPPRRSTT	propitiatories
AEIILLLMNNOPST	postmillennial
AEIILLLLRSTTUVY	illustratively
AEIILLMNOPRSSY	impressionally
AEIILLNNNQQUUY	quinquennially
AEIILLNNOSSSUV	villainousness
AEIILLNQRRSSTU	tranquillisers
AEIILLNQRRSTUZ	tranquillizers
AEIILMNNOOPRSS	pronominalises
AEIILMNNOOPRSZ	pronominalizes
AEIILMNOOPRSTY	polymerisation
AEIILMNOOPRTYZ	polymerization
AEIILMNRSSSTVY	transmissively
AEIILNNNORSTTU	interlunations
AEIILNNOOPRSST	interpolations
AEIILNNOPRSTUY	unipersonality
AEIILNOORSSTTT	tolerationists
AEIILNOPRRSTTY	tripersonality
AEIIMMNORSSTTY	symmetrisation
AEIIMMNORSTTYZ	symmetrization
AEIIMNNOOPRSST	impersonations
AEIIMNNORRSSST	retransmission
AEIIMNOOPRRSTT	reimportations
AEIIMNOORRSSTT	restorationism
AEIIMNOSSSSTTY	systemisations
AEIIMNOSSSTTYZ	systemizations
AEIIMNRSSSTTTV	transvestitism
AEIINNOOPPSSTT	peptonisations
AEIINNOOPPSTTZ	peptonizations
AEIINNORRSSSTT	transitoriness
AEIINOOPPRRSTX	expropriations
AEIINOOPRSSTTX	extrapositions
AEIINOORRSSTTT	restorationist
AEIINOPRRSSSTU	pressurisation
AEIINOPRRSSTUZ	pressurization
AEIINOPRSSSUVV	viviparousness
AEIINORRSSSSTT	transistorises
AEIINORRSSSTTZ	transistorizes
AEIIORRRSTTWYZ	Swazi Territory
AEILLMMMNOOSST	monometallisms
AEILLMMNOOSSTT	monometallists
AEILLMNRSSTTUY	instrumentally
AEILLMNOSSTUUY	simultaneously
AEILMNOPRRSTUY	supernormality
AEILNOOOPPRTUV	overpopulation
AEILNOOPSSTTUX	expostulations

AEILNOOSSTTTUY	ostentatiously
AEIMMNOOOSSTUU	semiautonomous
AEIMNNOOPPRSTT	apportionments
AEIMNNOORRSSTT	remonstrations
AEIMNOPPRRSTTU	superimportant
AEINNOOSSTTTUU	unostentatious
AEINOOOPPRRSTT	proportionates
AEINOOPRRSSSUU	uproariousness
AELLMNNOOOPPRT	monopropellant
AENOOOPPRRSTXY	proparoxytones
AFFGIIMNOSSTUU	suffumigations
AFIIILNOOSSSST	fossilisations
AFIIILNOOSSSTZ	fossilizations
AFIIIMMNNOORST	misinformation
AFIILLMORSTUUY	multifariously
AGGHIILNPRSTUW	Walpurgis Night
AGGHILNOOPRSTY	pharyngologist
AGGIIILNNORTVY	invigoratingly
AGGILLNOORSSTY	laryngologists
AGGLLNOOOORTVY	otolaryngology
AGHHIIOOPRRSTY	historiography
AGHHILOOOPSTTY	histopathology
AGHHINOOPPRSST	phonographists
AGHHIOOPRRSSTT	orthographists
AGHHLOOOPPTTYY	phytopathology
AGHIINOOPPRSST	apostrophising
AGHIINOOPPRSTZ	apostrophizing
AGHILNOOOPRSTT	anthropologist
AGHIMOOOPRSSTU	mastigophorous
AGIIIILNPRSSTU	spiritualising
AGIIIILNPRSTUZ	spiritualizing
AGIIILLLLMNNTUY	illuminatingly
AGIIILLMNNNTUU	unilluminating
AGIIILLNNQRSTU	tranquillising
AGIIILLNNQRTUZ	tranquillizing
AGIIILNOSTUVVV	vulvovaginitis
AGIILMOOPRSSTT	primatologists
AGILMOORRSSTTY	martyrologists
AGLMMOOOPSTTYY	symptomatology
AHHIILNOPPRSTT	philanthropist
AHHLLNOOPSTUXY	xanthophyllous
AHHMNOOOPPRRST	anthropomorphs
AHIILMNNOORSUY	inharmoniously
AHIILMOOPSSSST	histoplasmosis
AHIILNNOOOPSTT	Polish notation
AHIILNOPRSSTUU	sulphurisation
AHIILNOPRSTUUZ	sulphurization
AHIIMNOPRSSSTT	misanthropists
AHIINNOOPSSTTY	hypnotisations
AHIINNOOPSTTYZ	hypnotizations
AIIIILMNNOSTTU	intuitionalism
AIIIILNNOSTTTU	intuitionalist
AIIIILNOORSTTV	vitriolisation
AIIIILNOORTTVZ	vitriolization
AIIIINNRSTTTVY	intransitivity
AIIIINOOPRRSTT	prioritisation
AIIIINOOPRRTTZ	prioritization
AIIIKLLNSSVVYZ	Vislinsky Zaliv
AIIILLMPPSSUUU	Suppiluliumas I
AIIILOOPPRRTTY	propitiatorily
AIIIMNOOPPRRST	impropriations
AIIIMNOOPRSSTV	improvisations
AIIIMNRSSSTTVY	transmissivity
AIIIMNRSTTTTVY	transmittivity
AIIINNNOOSSTTV	innovationists
AIIINNORSTTTUY	institutionary
AIIJNOOPSSTTUX	juxtapositions
AIILLNNOOPSTTU	antipollutions
AIILMNNOOOOPST	monopolisation
AIILMNNOOOOPTZ	monopolization
AIILMNOOPRSSUY	parsimoniously
AIILNOOOPPSSTT	postpositional
AIINNOOPRSSSTT	transpositions
AIKKKMOORRSSVY	Rimsky-Korsakov
AIKMMNNOOSSTUY	Smoky Mountains
AILLNOOOPPRRTY	proportionally
AIMNNNOOSSTUWY	Snowy Mountains
BBCCDEIIMNRSUU	circumbendibus
BBCDEEIORRSSUV	oversubscribed
BBCEEIORRSSSUV	oversubscribes
BBCEIILMNOSSTU	incombustibles
BBCEILMNNOOSTU	noncombustible
BBCIIILMOSTTUY	combustibility
BBDEEGILNOOOSU	Bois de Boulogne
BBEGIIILMRSTUY	submergibility
BBEIIIILMRSTUY	submersibility
BBEIIKLLNOOSSY	Sibylline Books
BCCCEEIIMRRRSSU	circumscribers
BCCCGIIIMNNRSU	circumscribing
BCCCIIMOOPRSSU	submicroscopic
BCCDIIILNOTTUY	conductibility
BCCEEEEHIKRRRS	checkerberries
BCCEEHORSSTTTU	butterscotches
BCCEEIIILORTTY	bioelectricity
BCCEEIILMORRTY	microcelebrity
BCCEEIINRSSTTY	cyberneticists
BCCEEIKKKNORRS	knickerbockers
BCCEEJNORSTTUU	countersubject
BCCEIIIJSSTTUV	subjectivistic
BCCHINOOOPRSST	bronchoscopist
BCCILNOOSSSUUY	subconsciously
BCDEEEIILNRSS	incredibleness
BCDEEGIIMNNRSU	disencumbering
BCDEEHHNOORSUU	Bouches-du-Rhône
BCDEEIILNRSTTU	indestructible
BCDEIIIILRRTUY	irreducibility
BCDEIIILNNOSTY	condensibility
BCDEIILNRSTTUY	indestructibly
BCDEILMPRRTUUU	Udmurt Republic
BCEEEEIIRRRSSV	serviceberries
BCEEEGILLNORST	cobelligerents
BCEEEHILMNOPRS	comprehensible
BCEEEHIOORRRST	Oberösterreich
BCEEEIJNSSSTUV	subjectiveness
BCEEEMMNORSSSU	cumbersomeness
BCEEFIIIILPRTTY	perfectibility
BCEEGIMNNNOSSU	unbecomingness
BCEEHILMNOPRSY	comprehensibly
BCEEIIIILNNNSS	invincibleness
BCEEIIILPPRRTTY	perceptibility
BCEEIILLOOPSSU	ebullioscopies
BCEEIILMNNOSTU	bioluminescent
BCEEIILMNOPRSS	incompressible
BCEEIKNNRRSUWW	New Brunswicker

841

BCEEEILNNNOORTV	nonconvertible
BCEEEILNOORRTTV	controvertible
BCEEIMNNPRSTUU	superincumbent
BCEEIMORRRRSTY	cyberterrorism
BCEGHIILNPRSUU	Ingush Republic
BCEGIINOOPPRST	bioprospecting
BCEIIILNORTTVY	convertibility
BCEIIILPRSTTUY	putrescibility
BCEIIILPSSTTUY	susceptibility
BCEIILMNOPRSSY	incompressibly
BCEIILNORTTUVY	contributively
BCEIINNOOORSSV	bioconversions
BCEIINOORRSTTU	contributories
BCEILMMNOSSUUU	cumulonimbuses
BCEILNOORRTTVY	controvertibly
BCEMNNOOPRTTTU	Compton-Burnett
BCGIIILMOOORST	microbiologist
BCGIIILOOOOSST	sociobiologist
BCGIILOOORSSTY	cryobiologists
BCIIILOPRRTTUY	corruptibility
BCIIMMNOOSSSSU	subcommissions
BCIIMNOORSSTTU	obstructionism
BCIINOORSSTTTU	obstructionist
BDDEEEEFILLMNY	feeblemindedly
BDDEFGIINNORSS	forbiddingness
BDEEEEFILNNSSS	defensibleness
BDEEEFGINRRTTU	butterfingered
BDEEEGIILNSSST	digestibleness
BDEEEGIIMMNRRS	disremembering
BDEEEGIMMNOSTU	disemboguement
BDEEEIINNNORTZ	dinitrobenzene
BDEEEILMMNOSTW	disembowelment
BDEEEIMMMNRSST	dismemberments
BDEEEMNOORRSUV	overburdensome
BDEEFFIILNSSSU	diffusibleness
BDEEFGINNOORSS	forebodingness
BDEEGIIILLNSVY	disbelievingly
BDEEGIILLMNOSW	disembowelling
BDEEGILLNRSTUW	Tunbridge Wells
BDEEIIIIORSSTV	biodiversities
BDEEIIIRRSTTUV	redistributive
BDEEILLNOSSSSU	dissolubleness
BDEGHHINOOORSU	neighbourhoods
BDEGHIILNNNSST	nightblindness
BDEGIIINNRRSTTU	redistributing
BDEHIILOORRSTT	bloodthirstier
BDEIIIIIILSSTV	divisibilities
BDEIIILMQRSUU	disequilibrium
BDEIIIILNSSTTY	distensibility
BDEIIILNNOSSSU	libidinousness
BDEIIILNPSSTUY	suspendibility
BDEIIILRSTTUVY	distributively
BDEIIINORRSTTU	redistribution
BDHIIIINNOSST	disinhibitions
BDHIILLOORSTTY	bloodthirstily
BDIIIIIILNSTVY	indivisibility
BEEEEIILMRSTT	biotelemetries
BEEEEILNNSSSTX	extensibleness
BEEEFIILLNNSSX	inflexibleness
BEEEGIIINNNOR	bioengineering
BEEEGGIILLNNSS	negligibleness
BEEEGIIILLNNSS	ineligibleness

BEEEGIIMMMNRRS	misremembering
BEEEGILLNNNORT	nonbelligerent
BEEEHILLMMNSST	embellishments
BEEEHILMNOSSST	blithesomeness
BEEEHILORRRSTW	whortleberries
BEEEHLORRRSTVY	Everly Brothers
BEEEIILMNRSSSS	remissibleness
BEEEIILNNNSSSS	insensibleness
BEEEILLNORSSSU	rebelliousness
BEEEILORSSTTUV	oversubtleties
BEEEIMMNRRSSTU	reimbursements
BEEEINNORSSSTU	tenebriousness
BEEEINRSSSSUVV	subversiveness
BEEELMNNRSSSSU	numberlessness
BEEENNQSSSSTUU	subsequentness
BEEFHIMNRRSSTU	refurbishments
BEEGGHIILMRRST	thimbleriggers
BEEGHIILNNORSS	neighborliness
BEEGIIILLLNNTU	unintelligible
BEEGILMOOOORTY	biometeorology
BEEHHKNOORSTUW	Knebworth House
BEEHLOOORRSTTU	troubleshooter
BEEIIILNPRTTVY	preventibility
BEEIILMNOPSSSS	impossibleness
BEEIILNPPRSSSU	insuppressible
BEEIIMNSSSSSUV	submissiveness
BEEINNOPRSSSSU	businessperson
BEEINOOQSSSSUU	obsequiousness
BEEINOORSSSSTU	boisterousness
BEELMNORSSSSUU	slumberousness
BEELOOPRRSSTUY	obstreperously
BEFGILLNOOPRTU	bulletproofing
BEGGGHIIILMNRT	thimblerigging
BEGGHILLNOORUW	Wellingborough
BEGGIIILSSTTUY	suggestibility
BEGGILNOORSTTT	globetrottings
BEGHIILMNOOPST	phlebotomising
BEGHIILMNOOPTZ	phlebotomizing
BEGHILNNNSSSUU	unblushingness
BEGIILNOOORSTU	neurobiologist
BEGILNORSSSUUU	lugubriousness
BEHIIIINOSSTTX	exhibitionists
BEIIIILMPRSSTY	permissibility
BEIIILLORRSTUY	irresolubility
BEIIILNOPRSSTY	responsibility
BEIILNPPRSSSUY	insuppressibly
BEIILSSTTTUUVY	substitutively
BEIINOQSSSTUUU	ubiquitousness
BEINOORSSSSTUU	robustiousness
BGHIILOOOOPSTT	photobiologist
BGIILLMMNNOOUU	immunoglobulin
BHIIIMNOOPRST	prohibitionism
BHIIINOOPRSTT	prohibitionist
BIIISSTTTUUVY	substitutivity
CCCDDEEEENNNOS	condescendence
CCCDEEEENRRSSU	recrudescences
CCCDEEEHKNORTU	counterchecked
CCCDEEHIIOOPRT	cercopithecoid
CCCDEEHIIOPRST	cercopithecids
CCCDGIILOOORTU	glucocorticoid
CCCEEEFIMNRRSU	circumferences
CCCEEEHHHIINNR	chincherinchee

CCCEEEIIINRSTT	eccentricities
CCCEEEEILNNOSSS	conscienceless
CCCEEIIMPRSTUV	circumspective
CCCEENNNOORRSU	nonoccurrences
CCCEIIILLOSTTV	collectivistic
CCCEIIILMRSSSU	circumscissile
CCCEIIMMNOOORS	microeconomics
CCCEIIMNOPRSTU	circumspection
CCCHIIOOOPRRTT	corticotrophic
CCCIIIMNNORSUU	uncircumcision
CCCIIIMORRRTUY	microcircuitry
CCCIILMNOORTUU	circumlocution
CCCILMOORRTUUY	circumlocutory
CCDDEEEILNNOSTY	disconnectedly
CCDDEEEILNORSTY	disconcertedly
CCDEEEEEFNRSSV	defervescences
CCDEEEEEILNQSSU	deliquescences
CCDEEEEELNNOSST	closed sentence
CCDEEEEFINNOORV	overconfidence
CCDEEEIINNNNOV	inconvenienced
CCDEEEINNNORTT	interconnected
CCDEEEINOPSSSU	pseudosciences
CCDEEEENNOOPRRS	correspondence
CCDEEHIIMOORST	orchidectomies
CCDEEHILNOORTU	technicoloured
CCDEEHNNOPRTUU	counterpunched
CCDEEIILOORRRV	Crocodile River
CCDEEIJMNORSTU	misconjectured
CCDEEEILNOPSSTY	encyclopedists
CCDEEIMNNORSTT	disconcertment
CCDEEIMOORRSTT	microdetectors
CCDEEINNNOOSSS	condescensions
CCDEENOPRRSTTU	preconstructed
CCDEGIILNNOOOR	endocrinologic
CCDEGINNORSTTU	deconstructing
CCDEIIINORSTTU	reductionistic
CCDEIIINOSTTUV	conductivities
CCDEIILMOORTTY	clitoridectomy
CCDEIIMNNOOSTU	semiconduction
CCDEIINNNOOSST	disconnections
CCDEIINNOORSST	disconcertions
CCDEIIOOORRSTT	corticosteroid
CCDEIMNOORSSTU	semiconductors
CCDEINNOORSTTU	deconstruction
CCDENOOPRRSTUU	superconductor
CCDGIIIMOOOPSS	sigmoidoscopic
CCDHHHOOORRTUX	Orthodox Church
CCDHIIMOPRRSTY	cryptorchidism
CCDHINOOPRSSTU	conductorships
CCDHNOOOOPRTTU	photoconductor
CCEEEEEFLNNORT	teleconference
CCEEEEEJNNRSUV	rejuvenescence
CCEEEEEFFLNORSS	efflorescences
CCEEEEHHMORSST	homescreetches
CCEEEEMMMNNORT	recommencement
CCEEEEFFIIIINNS	inefficiencies
CCEEEEFIIOPRSST	stereospecific
CCEEEFILNNORSS	inflorescences
CCEEEHILMORRTT	electrothermic
	thermoelectric
CCEEEHILMORSTT	electrochemist
CCEEEHMOOPRRST	chemoreceptors

CCEEEIIKLNORTT	electrokinetic
CCEEEIIMNNSSTU	intumescencies
CCEEEIINNNNOSV	inconveniences
CCEEEILLLORTVY	recollectively
CCEEEILLNOSSTV	collectiveness
CCEEEILMNNORST	reconcilements
CCEEEILNNNOOTT	teleconnection
CCEEEIMMNNOOPT	omnicompetence
CCEEEINNRRRSTU	intercurrences
CCEEEINORRRSUU	eurocurrencies
CCEEEINSSSSSUV	successiveness
CCEEFLNSSSSSUU	successfulness
CCEEGHIORRRSUU	churrigueresco
CCEEGIILLOOSST	ecclesiologist
CCEEGIINOSTTTY	cytogeneticist
CCEEGINOORRRTV	overcorrecting
CCEEEHHIMNOSTTY	chemosynthetic
CCEEHIIMNORSTT	theocentricism
CCEEEHIIMOORSTT	stoechiometric
CCEEEHIINORTTTY	theocentricity
CCEEEHNNOPRSTUU	counterpunches
CCEEEIIILLOSTTV	collectivities
CCEEEIILNORRTTU	interlocutrice
CCEEEIINNOSSTTU	constituencies
CCEEEIINNQSSTTU	cinquecentists
CCEEIJMNORSSTU	misconjectures
CCEEILMMOOPRTX	complexometric
CCEEILMNRSSSUU	micronucleuses
CCEEILNNOSSSUV	conclusiveness
CCEEILNOOOPRTT	optoelectronic
CCEEILNOORSTTU	electrocutions
CCEEINNNOOSTUV	nonconsecutive
CCEEINNOOPPRST	preconceptions
CCEEINOOORRRTV	overcorrection
CCEEINOOOORRSTT	corticosterone
CCEEINOOPRSSSU	precociousness
CCEEINORRSTTUV	reconstructive
CCEELNORRTTUUU	counterculture
CCEFIILMNORSUX	circumflexions
CCEFILNNOORTTU	Council of Trent
CCEFLLNSSSUUUY	unsuccessfully
CCEGHIKLNOSTTU	shuttlecocking
CCEGIIILLNOSTV	collectivising
CCEGIIILLNOTVZ	collectivizing
CCEGIINNNNOSSV	convincingness
CCEGINNOOOPRST	rontgenoscopic
CCEGINNORRSTTU	reconstructing
CCEEHHIINOPRSSZ	schizophrenics
CCEEHHIOOPSSUYZ	schizophyceous
CCEEHIIIMOORSTT	stoichiometric
CCEEHIIIMPRRSTY	hypercriticism
CCEEHIIMMORRSTY	microchemistry
CCEEHILLOOPRSST	collectorships
CCEEHIMOOSSTUYZ	schizomycetous
CCEEHINOOPRSSUY	hyperconscious
CCEEHINOOPRSTUY	psychoneurotic
CCEEHINOPRSSSTU	succentorships
CCEEHNNOOOPRSSY	synchronoscope
CCEEIIILMORRSTW	lower criticism
CCEEIILLNNOSUVY	inconclusively
CCEEIILNORSTTVY	constrictively
CCEEIIMNNOOPSST	misconceptions

CCEIIMNNORSTUV	circumventions
CCEIINNOOPRSTV	preconvictions
CCEIINORSSSTUU	circuitousness
CCEILNOOPRSSUY	preconsciously
CCEILNORSTTUVY	constructively
CCEILOOORRSSTU	stercoricolous
CCEIMMOOPRRSTU	microcomputers
CCEIMOOOPRRRSS	microprocessor
CCEIMORRRSTTUU	microstructure
CCEINNOORRSTTU	reconstruction
CCEIOOPPRSSSTT	spectroscopist
CCENOORRRSSTTU	reconstructors
CCFGIILNNNNOOT	nonconflicting
CCGHIILOOPSSTY	psychologistic
CCGHIIOOPRSTYY	hygroscopicity
CCHIILLNOOPRSU	councillorship
CCHIILNOOPRSSU	councilorships
CCHIINOOOPRRTT	corticotrophin
CCIIIJNNOSTTUV	conjunctivitis
CCIIILPRSSTTUU	pisciculturist
CCIIILRRSTTTUU	citriculturist
CCIILMNOORTUUV	circumvolution
CCIIMNORSSTTUV	constructivism
CCIINORSSTTTUV	constructivist
CCILMNOOPSTUUY	compunctiously
CCILMOORRTUUVY	circumvolutory
CDDDDEEEILLMUX	excluded middle
CDDEEEEENNOPRV	overdependence
CDDEEEEIINNNPS	independencies
CDDEEEENNOPRSSY	Ross Dependency
CDDEEFNNNOOSSU	confoundedness
CDDEEIIMMNOOSS	decommissioned
CDDEEIINNOOPRT	preconditioned
CDDEEIJLNPRUUY	unprejudicedly
CDDEEILNNOSTTY	discontentedly
CDDEEILNOOSTUY	eudicotyledons
CDDEEKNOORSSTY	Eddystone Rocks
CDDEHHILOORRSY	hydrochlorides
CDDEIIIMMOOSST	discommodities
CDDEILNOOOSTUY	dicotyledonous
CDEEEEELMORRST	decelerometers
CDEEEEILLLNOST	Leconte de Lisle
CDEEEENNPSSTUX	unexpectedness
CDEEEFHIKNRRRY	Frederick Henry
CDEEEGHINORTUW	counterweighed
CDEEEGILNNORUV	overindulgence
CDEEEHIOPRTTUY	hypereutectoid
CDEEEIIINNSSSV	indecisiveness
CDEEEIINNRSSST	indiscreetness
	indiscreteness
CDEEEILOOPRSTT	electrodeposit
CDEEEINNNOORRU	neuroendocrine
CDEEEINRRSSSTT	restrictedness
CDEEFINNOPRSTU	superconfident
CDEEHIIILPRVYZ	hypercivilized
CDEEHIIMOOPRRT	thermoperiodic
CDEEHKOOORSUYZ	Chudskoye Ozero
CDEEHLLLOORSUY	hydrocellulose
CDEEHNNOOOPPSS	phonendoscopes
CDEEIIIILNRTTVY	interdictively
CDEEIIINNSSTVV	vindictiveness
CDEEIINORRSSTT	derestrictions

CDEEIINRSSSSUV	discursiveness
CDEEIJNPRRSSUU	jurisprudences
CDEEILLNOOPTUY	polynucleotide
CDEEILOPRRTUVY	reproductively
CDEEIMNNNOSTTT	discontentment
CDEEIMNOOPRSSS	decompressions
CDEEINNOOPRTTU	counterpointed
CDEEINNOORSSSU	indecorousness
CDEEINNORSTTUV	nondestructive
CDEEINOPRSSTUV	productiveness
CDEEINPSSSTTUU	intussuscepted
CDEEKKLNRSSTUU	knuckledusters
CDEELNNOOSSTUV	convolutedness
CDEELNOOPRTTTU	counterplotted
CDEENNOOPRRSST	correspondents
CDEFIIIMMMOSSU	fideicommissum
CDEGIIIILNOPST	depoliticising
CDEGIIIILNOPTZ	depoliticizing
CDEGIIINNNOORT	reconditioning
CDEGIIMOOOPSSS	sigmoidoscopes
CDEHINOOOORRSTY	hydrocortisone
CDEIIIIILRSTTUV	diverticulitis
CDEIIIILORSSTUV	diverticulosis
CDEIIINNNOSTTV	nondistinctive
CDEIIINNNSSSTT	indistinctness
CDEIILNORSSSUU	ridiculousness
CDEIINNOORRTTU	reintroduction
CDEIINNOPRSTUU	superinduction
CDEIINORSSTTTU	destructionist
CDEILMNOOPRSSU	scolopendriums
CDEILMNOORSSTU	discolourments
CDEILNOPRTUUVY	unproductively
CDEILOORSSTUUY	discourteously
CDEIMMNOOOSSSU	commodiousness
CDEINOOOPRRTUV	overproduction
CDELLNOOOPSTYY	polycotyledons
CDELMNNOOOOSTY	monocotyledons
CDGIILMNOOPSSY	discomposingly
CDHHILLLOOOPRY	chlorophylloid
CDHIILOOOPRRRS	Polish Corridor
CDHIINNOORTTTU	truth-condition
CDHIINOOOOPRSU	conidiophorous
CDHINOOOPRSSTT	prosthodontics
CDIIJNNNNOOSTU	nondisjunction
CDIILMMNOOOSUY	incommodiously
CDIILNOORRTTUY	introductorily
CDINOOOPPRSTTU	postproduction
CEEEEFFIPRSTUV	supereffective
CEEEEFFLNRSTVY	effervescently
CEEEEFGINNQRUY	eigenfrequency
CEEEEFILNRSSTV	reflectiveness
CEEEEFLMORRSTT	reflectometers
CEEEEGGINORRRS	greengroceries
CEEEEGHINPRRTY	hyperenergetic
CEEEEGIILNNORT	electioneering
CEEEEGIINNPRRX	reexperiencing
CEEEEHIILRRSST	Leicestershire
CEEEEHLNPSSSSS	speechlessness
CEEEEINPPRSSTV	perceptiveness
CEEEEINPRSSSTV	respectiveness
CEEEEFFGILNRSVY	effervescingly
CEEEEFFIINPRSTU	superefficient

CEEEFGLLNNSSTU	neglectfulness
CEEEFIILMPRTVY	imperfectively
CEEEFILLNRTUVY	unreflectively
CEEEFIMNNORRST	reinforcements
CEEEFINORRSTTU	counterfeiters
CEEEFLNPRSSSTU	respectfulness
CEEEGHIIMORSST	geochemistries
CEEEGIILLNNNTU	unintelligence
CEEEGIILLNNRST	intelligencers
CEEEGIIMNOPRST	spermiogenetic
CEEEGIINORRSVX	overexercising
CEEEGILNOPRSST	teleprocessing
CEEEGLORRRSTUY	electrosurgery
CEEEGNNOOOPRST	roentgenoscope
CEEEHIIILRRRUV	Richelieu River
CEEEHIMNOPRSSV	comprehensives
CEEEHIMORSSTTY	hysterectomies
	hysterectomise
CEEEHIMORSTTYZ	hysterectomize
CEEEHINNNNORSST	incoherentness
CEEEHIORRRSSTW	Worcestershire
CEEEHLMNOORRTT	thermoelectron
CEEEHLOPRSSSST	clothespresses
CEEEHMMOORSTTY	hemocytometers
CEEEHMMOPSSSTY	metempsychoses
CEEEIIIMNNPRST	impertinencies
CEEEIIKNNPRSST	pernicketiness
CEEEIILLLNTTVY	intellectively
CEEEIILMPPRTVY	imperceptively
CEEEIILPRRSTVY	irrespectively
CEEEIIMMOORRTT	micrometeorite
CEEEILMMNOPRTZ	complementizer
CEEEILMNNOPSST	incompleteness
CEEEILNOPRSSTU	pleurocentesis
CEEEIMMMNOOTTW	committeewomen
CEEEIMNNORTTUX	extreme unction
CEEEINNOORRRST	reconnoiterers
CEEEINOPRSSTTV	protectiveness
CEEEINPRSSSSUV	percussiveness
CEEEINPSSSSTUV	susceptiveness
CEEEIOOPRRTTVV	overprotective
CEEEIOPRRSSTTV	retrospectives
CEEFGIINNNOSTU	eigenfunctions
CEEFGIINNORTTU	counterfeiting
CEEFGILMNOORRT	electroforming
CEEFIILLNNOSST	inflectionless
CEEFIILNOSSSTU	felicitousness
CEEFIIMNNNSSTU	munificentness
CEEFIINNOSSSTU	infectiousness
CEEFIINOPRSSTT	perfectionists
CEEFIJOOSSSTUY	Society of Jesus
CEEFILMNNRSSUU	unmercifulness
CEEFILMNOORSSS	frolicsomeness
CEEFILNOORRSTT	retroflections
CEEFINOORSSSUV	vociferousness
CEEGHIIRRSSTUW	cruiserweights
CEEGHIMNOORRST	stereochroming
CEEGHINORRSTTV	overstretching
CEEGHINORSSTTU	counterweights
CEEGHLNOOORTTY	terotechnology
CEEGIIINOPSTTY	genotypicities
CEEGIILNNORRTY	nitroglycerine
CEEGIIMMNNOSTU	immunogenetics
CEEGIINNNOORRT	reconnoitering
CEEGILLLLNOOSU	lignocellulose
CEEGINNOORRSTV	seroconverting
CEEGINOOPRRTTV	overprotecting
CEEGNNOOOPRSST	rontgenoscopes
CEEGNNOOOPRSTY	roentgenoscopy
CEEHHIMMORSSTT	thermochemists
CEEHHIMNOSSSTY	chemosynthesis
CEEHHMOOORRSTU	heterochromous
CEEHHNOOPPRSST	phosphorescent
CEEHIILMOPRRTY	pyrheliometric
CEEHIIMNORSTTY	stoicheiometry
CEEHIIMOPRSTYZ	piezochemistry
CEEHIIOOPRRTTY	erythropoietic
CEEHIMMOPSSSTY	metempsychosis
CEEHIMNNOOPRSS	comprehensions
CEEHIMOOOOPRST	oophorectomies
CEEHIMOPRRSTTY	petrochemistry
CEEHINOQSSSTTU	coquettishness
CEEHLNOOOPRSST	photoelectrons
CEEHNOOPRSSSUY	psychoneuroses
CEEHOOOOPPRRST	photoreceptors
CEEIIILNNPSSTX	inexplicitness
CEEIIIHMPRSSTT	metempiricists
CEEIIIMORSSTTT	meteoriticists
CEEIIIMPPRTTVY	imperceptivity
CEEIIILLMNORSTT	scintillometer
CEEIILMORRSTUY	meretriciously
CEEIIILNNNNOTVY	inconveniently
CEEIIILNNOSSSTU	licentiousness
CEEIIILPPRRSTVY	prescriptively
CEEIIMNNOOPTTV	noncompetitive
CEEIIMNOOPRTTT	potentiometric
CEEIINNOPRSSSU	perniciousness
CEEIINNORRSTTV	nonrestrictive
CEEIIOOPPPRRTV	proprioceptive
CEEILLLNOORSTU	nitrocellulose
CEEILMNOOOSSTV	locomotiveness
CEEILMNOPSSSUV	compulsiveness
CEEILMNOSSSTUU	meticulousness
CEEILMOOORSSST	electroosmosis
CEEILNNNOQSTUY	inconsequently
CEEILNNOOPRSTU	nucleoproteins
CEEILNNOOPRSXY	clinopyroxenes
CEEILNNOSSSUVV	convulsiveness
CEEILNNRRRTTUY	intercurrently
CEEILNOOPRRSST	scleroproteins
CEEILNORRSSTTU	interlocutress
CEEIMMOOPRRRTY	micropyrometer
CEEINNNOPRSTTU	supercontinent
CEEINNOOORRSSV	seroconversion
CEEINNOORSSSSU	censoriousness
CEEINNORSSTTTU	reconstituents
CEEINNOSSSSTUU	incestuousness
CEEINOOPRRSSTT	retrospections
CEEINRRSSSSTTU	instructresses
CEEIOOPRSSSSTT	stereoscopists
CEEKKLNOOOSSSV	Československo
CEEKNNOOOSSTTT	Stockton-on-Tees
CEEKNOOORRRSTUW	counterworkers
CEELLNOORSSSSU	colourlessness

CEEMNNNOOPRSTU	pronouncements
CEEMNOOPRRSTUU	neurocomputers
CEEMOPPRRSSTUU	supercomputers
CEEPRRRSSTTUUU	superstructure
CEFFIIILNNSTUY	insufficiently
CEFFILORRSTUUY	fructiferously
CEFGHINOORSSST	sign of the cross
CEFHHJNOOORRST	John of the Cross
CEFIIIILLNOSTUY	infelicitously
CEFIIILNPPRRST	first principle
CEFIIINOSSSTTU	fictitiousness
CEFIIMNNOORSTU	unconformities
CEFLNOORSSSSUU	scrofulousness
CEGGHILMOOOOPR	geomorphologic
CEGGIIINNNORSTU	countersigning
CEGHHINOOPPRSS	phosphorescing
CEGHNNOOORSSUY	geosynchronous
CEGIIILNOORSST	coreligionists
CEGIIKNNNORSTU	countersinking
CEGIILMNOOPRSY	copolymerising
CEGIILMNOOPRYZ	copolymerizing
CEGIIMMNOORTTV	overcommitting
CEGIIMNNOOPRST	contemporising
CEGIIMNNOOPRTZ	contemporizing
CEGIINNNNOOORT	nonrecognition
CEGIINNOOPRSTU	counterpoising
CEGIINNORSTTTU	reconstituting
CEGILMMOORSSTY	myrmecologists
CEGILNNPSSTUUY	unsuspectingly
CEGIMNNOOOOSUY	gynomonoecious
CEGINNOOSSSTUU	contiguousness
CEGINPRRSSTTUU	superstructing
CEHHIIMORSSTTY	histochemistry
CEHHIMMMOORRST	thermochromism
CEHHIMMNOOOOPPR	morphophonemic
CEHHIMNOOPRSTY	phonochemistry
CEHHIMOOPRSTTY	photochemistry
CEHHIMOPRSTTYY	phytochemistry
CEHHINOOPSTTTY	photosynthetic
CEHHOOOOOPPPRSS	phosphoroscope
CEHIIIKLMOOPRT	poikilothermic
CEHIIMNOOPRSST	chemisorptions
CEHIINOPPRSSST	inspectorships
CEHIINOPRRSTTT	streptothricin
CEHIJMNNOORTTU	thermojunction
CEHILLNOOPRRST	controllership
CEHILLNOOPRSSU	counsellorship
CEHILMMOOPRSUY	myrmecophilous
CEHILMOORSSSST	schoolmistress
CEHILNOOPRSSSU	counselorships
CEHIMNOOOOPRRST	chromoproteins
CEHIMOPRSSSTTY	psychometrists
CEHINOOPRSSSUY	psychoneurosis
CEHLLLOOPRSSUY	sclerophyllous
CEHMOOOOPPRSST	photocomposers
CEIIIIILLMPSTTU	multiplicities
CEIIIINOSSTTVV	vivisectionist
CEIIIILNOOSTTUV	evolutionistic
CEIIIMOOPRSTTV	overoptimistic
CEIIIMPPRRSSTV	prescriptivism
CEIIINORRSSTTT	restrictionist
CEIIJNOOPRSSTT	projectionists
CEIILLLNOOSSTV	violoncellists
CEIILLOPRSSUUY	superciliously
CEIILNNNOSSTTY	inconsistently
CEIILNOOORRRST	trinitrocresol
CEIILNOOSSSTTU	solicitousness
CEIILNOSTTTUVY	constitutively
CEIILOOOORSSTUV	oversolicitous
CEIILOPPRRSTVY	proscriptively
CEIILRRSSSTTUU	sericulturists
CEIIMMNNNOORTU	intercommunion
CEIIMMNNORTTUY	intercommunity
CEIIMNNOOOPSSU	pneumoconiosis
CEIIMNNORRSTTU	micronutrients
CEIIMNOOOPRSST	recompositions
CEIINNOOPRSSTT	introspections
CEIINNOORSTTTU	reconstitution
CEIINOOPRSSSTT	retinoscopists
CEIINOOPRSSTTT	protectionists
CEIINOORSSSTUV	victoriousness
CEIINOPPRRSSTU	superscription
CEIINOPRSSSSTU	percussionists
CEIINOPSSSSSUU	suspiciousness
CEIIOOPRSSSUUV	oversuspicious
CEILLMNOOSTUUY	contumeliously
CEILMNNOORSTUY	conterminously
CEILMNOOPRSSSU	compulsoriness
CEILMOOPRRSSTU	multiprocessor
CEILNOPRRSTUUV	proventriculus
CEILNORRSSSSUU	scurrilousness
CEINNNOOSSSTUU	continuousness
CEIOOOOPPPRRRST	proprioceptors
CELMNOOPSTTUUY	contemptuously
CELNOPRSSSSUUU	scrupulousness
CELOOPRRSSUUUV	overscrupulous
CFIILLORRSTTUU	floriculturist
CFIMNNNOOORSST	nonconformists
CGGHIILNOOPSSY	psychologising
CGGHIILNOOPSYZ	psychologizing
CGHHIILOOSSTTY	ichthyologists
CGHIILNOPSSTUY	psycholinguist
CGHILOOOOPSTVY	phytosociology
CGHIMNOOOOPPST	photocomposing
CGIIILMNOORSST	criminologists
CGIIILMOOSSTTV	victimologists
CGIIILNOOOPSST	oligopsonistic
CGIIILNOOSSSTU	sociolinguists
CGIIIMNNNOOSTV	noncognitivism
CGIIIMNNRSSTTU	misinstructing
CGIILMMNOOPRSY	compromisingly
CGIIMMNNOOPRSU	uncompromising
CGIIMNNNOOPRSU	mispronouncing
CGILLNNNNOOORT	noncontrolling
CHHHIOOOPPPRSY	hypophosphoric
CHHILOOOPPPRSY	polyphosphoric
CHHIMOOPRRSSTY	hystricomorphs
CHHIOOOOPPPRRSY	pyrophosphoric
CHHJMNOOORSSTY	John Chrysostom
CHHLLLOOOPRSUY	chlorophyllous
CHIILORRSTTTUU	horticulturist
CHIINOPRRSSTTU	instructorship
CHIIOOOORSSTTXY	thyrotoxicosis
CHILMOOORSTTUY	trichotomously

CHILNOOOPPRSSSU	proconsulships
CHILOOOPPRRSTU	prolocutorship
CIIILLRSSTTUUV	silviculturist
CIIILNRSSTTUUV	viniculturists
CIIILRSSTTTUUV	viticulturists
CIIIMNNORSSTTU	misinstruction
CIINNOOORSSTTT	contortionists
CIINOOPRRSSTTU	corruptionists
CILNOPRSSTUUUY	unscrupulosity
CLLNOPRSSUUUUY	unscrupulously
DDDEEEEELNOPRUV	underdeveloped
DDDEEEGHINORSY	dehydrogenised
DDDEEEGHINORYZ	dehydrogenized
DDEEEEIMNNRSST	determinedness
DDEEEEINNNPRTT	interdependent
DDEEEEELMMNOSSS	meddlesomeness
DDEEEGHINORSSY	dehydrogenises
DDEEEGHINORSYZ	dehydrogenizes
DDEEEGIINNNPRT	interdepending
DDEEEIINQSSSTU	disquietedness
DDEEEILNNNNPRU	Unter den Linden
DDEEEIMNNNORTU	undermentioned
DDEEGHHINRSTUW	hundredweights
DDEEGHILMOOSTY	demythologised
DDEEGHILMOOTYZ	demythologized
DDEEHILNOORRTY	dehydroretinol
DDEEHINNORRSUU	undernourished
DDEEIIINPRSSST	dispiritedness
DDEEIIJNNOSSST	disjointedness
DDEEIIILLMMNPSY	simplemindedly
DDEEIIILNORRSSS	disorderliness
DDEHHILOPRSSUY	hydrosulphides
DDEHIILNOPSSSS	slipshoddiness
DDEIIIILMSSSTU	dissimilitudes
DEEEEHMNORRRTV	Reverend Mother
DEEEEIILNNORSS	Oder-Neisse Line
DEEEEILLMMOSSS	mesdemoiselles
DEEEEIMNPRRRST	predeterminers
DEEEEIMNPRRSST	misrepresented
DEEEEINNRSSSTT	interestedness
DEEEEINPRSSSSV	depressiveness
DEEEEELMNOPRSTV	redevelopments
DEEEEENNRRSSSUV	unreservedness
DEEEFGJMNORSTU	forejudgements
DEEEFIIINNNSST	indefiniteness
DEEEFIIINNSSTV	definitiveness
DEEEFILNNRSSSS	friendlessness
DEEEFILNPSSSTU	despitefulness
DEEEFNOORSSSTU	surefootedness
DEEEGIIMNNPRRT	predetermining
DEEEGIINRSSSSV	digressiveness
DEEEGILNOOPRVV	overdeveloping
DEEEGNNOPRRTUY	Young Pretender
DEEEHIIKLNOOTT	kinetheodolite
DEEEIIMNPRRSTT	misinterpreted
DEEEIIMNRSSTTV	divertissement
DEEEIINORRSSVV	Revised Version
DEEEIINPRSSSSV	dispersiveness
DEEEILNNRSTTUY	uninterestedly
DEEEILNPRRSSTY	interspersedly
DEEEILOPRSSTVX	Prévost d'Exiles
DEEEIMMNOPRSTW	disempowerment
DEEEEINNNPRSTTU	superintendent
DEEEKLMMRRSTTU	kettledrummers
DEEEMNNORSSSTU	tremendousness
DEEENOPRRSSUUX	underexposures
DEEFFHILLOORST	Lord of the Flies
DEEFFIIIMNNRST	indifferentism
DEEFFIIINNRSTT	indifferentist
DEEFGHILLNSSTU	delightfulness
DEEFGIIMNRSSTU	disfigurements
DEEFHOOORRSSTW	Sherwood Forest
DEEFIIILMOPRSY	oversimplified
DEEFIILNNNRSSU	unfriendliness
DEEFIINOPRSSSU	perfidiousness
DEEFMMNOOOORTVX	Oxford Movement
DEEGHIINNSTUUX	unextinguished
DEEGHILMOOSSTY	demythologises
DEEGHILMOOSTYZ	demythologizes
DEEGHLNOORSSYY	hydrogenolyses
DEEGIIILMOOPST	epidemiologist
DEEGIIINNRSSTT	disinteresting
DEEGIILMNOPRSY	depolymerising
DEEGIILMNOPRYZ	depolymerizing
DEEGIINNNOSSSU	indigenousness
DEEGIINNNPRSTU	superintending
DEEGIINPRRSSSU	depressurising
DEEGIINPRRSSUZ	depressurizing
DEEGILLOOSSTTY	dysteleologist
DEEGILMNNRSTTU	disgruntlement
DEEGLNNORSSSSU	groundlessness
DEEHHNORRSSTUW	thundershowers
DEEHIINNPRSSTU	indentureships
DEEHIINOPSSSTY	hyposensitised
DEEHIINOPSSTYZ	hyposensitized
DEEHIINORTTTYY	identity theory
DEEHIINPPRSSST	presidentships
DEEHILPRRSSSUU	desulphurisers
DEEHILPRRSSUUZ	desulphurizers
DEEHINNORRSSUU	undernourishes
DEEIIIILMRSTUV	verisimilitude
DEEIIILNOPRSTV	vespertilionid
DEEIIIMNNRSSTT	indeterminists
DEEIIIMNNSSTUV	diminutiveness
DEEIIINOQRSSTU	derequisitions
DEEIILLNNOPVYY	polyvinylidene
DEEIILNOORSTUV	revolutionised
DEEIILNOORTUVZ	revolutionized
DEEIILNOQRSTUV	ventriloquised
DEEIILNOQRTUVZ	ventriloquized
DEEIILOPPRSSTT	lepidopterists
DEEIJNOPQRSSSU	Josquin des Prés
DEEKNOOPPRRSTV	Dnepropetrovsk
DEEMOOOPRRSSST	depressomotors
DEENNOPSSSSTUU	stupendousness
DEFGIIIIMNNSTY	misidentifying
DEGGHILOOORSTY	hydrogeologist
DEGHHILORSSTTY	shortsightedly
DEGHIIINRSSSTU	distinguishers
DEGHIILNPRSSUU	desulphurising
DEGHIILNPRSUUZ	desulphurizing
DEGHILMOOOSSTT	methodologists
DEGHILNOORSSYY	hydrogenolysis
DEGIILNNOSSUUY	disingenuously

DEGIILOOPRSSTT	pteridologists
DEGIINOOPRSSSU	prodigiousness
DEGILNNPPRSUUY	undersupplying
DEGILNOOOOPRTY	periodontology
DEHIIMOOOPPRST	photoperiodism
DEHIINOOPPSSST	deipnosophists
DEHILNOOPRRXYY	hydroxyproline
DEHIMMOOPPRSSU	pseudomorphism
DEHIOOPPRSTTUY	pteridophytous
DEHLLMMOPRSUUY	Sully-Prudhomme
DEHMOOOPPRSSUU	pseudomorphous
DEIIILMNOOSSTT	demolitionists
DEIIINOOPPRSST	predisposition
DEIIILNOOSSTTUV	devolutionists
DEILMNOOOPSSTU	diplostemonous
DEILNORSSSSTUU	stridulousness
DEIMNOOPRSSSTT	postmodernists
DELMNOOPSSUUYY	pseudonymously
DFGHIIKMNORSST	Kingsford-Smith
DGGHHIIINNOPST	diphthongising
DGGHHIIINNOPTZ	diphthongizing
DGGHIIIINNSSTU	distinguishing
DGHIINNNOOORVZ	Nizhni Novgorod
DGIIIILLNNOSSU	disillusioning
DGLMNOOOOSSSTU	odontoglossums
DHHIIMOOPRSTYY	hypothyroidism
DHINOOOPRSSTTT	prosthodontist
DIIIINNOOPSSST	indispositions
DIINOOOPPRRSST	disproportions
DLNOOOOPPRSTTY	polyprotodonts
EEEEFGLNNRSSUV	revengefulness
EEEEFIMNNORRTV	overrefinement
EEEEFIMNORRRTT	interferometer
EEEEGINRRSSSSV	regressiveness
EEEEHHIMPRRTTT	Peter the Hermit
EEEEHILMNOPRST	nephelometries
EEEEHILNPRRSVY	reprehensively
EEEEIIMMNRRSTT	semiretirement
EEEEIINPRSSTTV	repetitiveness
EEEEEILPRRTTTWV	teletypewriter
EEEEIMNPRRRSST	misrepresenter
EEEEINNPRSSTVV	preventiveness
EEEEINNPRRSSSV	repressiveness
EEEEEINPRSSSSVX	expressiveness
EEEEELLNNRSSSST	relentlessness
EEEEFFHKORRSST	Sheffer's stroke
EEEEFFHLNOORTUW	wheel of fortune
EEEEFFLNORSSSST	effortlessness
EEEEFGIMNPRRSTU	prefigurements
EEEEFIMNORRRTTY	interferometry
EEEEFLMNORRSSSU	remorsefulness
EEEEFLNNNSSTUUV	uneventfulness
EEEEGGIINPRRRST	preregistering
EEEEGGINSSSSTUV	suggestiveness
EEEEGHILNSSSSTW	weightlessness
EEEEGIILLNOSSTV	vitellogenesis
EEEEGIIMNOPRSSS	spermiogenesis
EEEEGIINNPRRRTT	reinterpreting
EEEEGIINNRSSSSV	ingressiveness
EEEEGILNOORSSTV	venereologists
EEEEHHIIMNORRST	Merionethshire
EEEEHHILMOPPSST	Mephistopheles

EEEHIINNNOPPRR	norepinephrine
EEEHIINNRRSSSV	Inverness-shire
EEEHIINPRSSSTY	hypersensitise
EEEHIINPRSSTVY	hypersensitive
EEEHIINPRSSTYZ	hypersensitize
EEEHILMNNPRSST	replenishments
EEEHILMOPRRSTY	pyrheliometers
EEEHIMMNOPRSTV	empoverishment
EEEHINNOPRSTXY	hyperextension
EEEIILMNOPSSST	impolitenesses
EEEIILNPRRTTVY	interpretively
EEEIILNPRSSVXY	inexpressively
EEEIIMNNNPSSTT	impenitentness
EEEIIMNNNRTTTW	intertwinement
EEEIIMNPRRRSTT	misinterpreter
EEEIIMNPRSSSSV	impressiveness
	permissiveness
EEEIINPRSSSTUV	supersensitive
EEEEILLNOSSSTUV	Îles sous le Vent
EEEILMNNPRSTUY	supereminently
EEEILMNOSSSSTV	motivelessness
EEEEILNOPRSSSSX	expressionless
EEEEILNORRSSSTU	irresoluteness
EEEEILORRSTVVXY	extroversively
EEEEIMNOOPRSTTT	potentiometers
EEEEIMNOPPRRSST	peremptoriness
EEEEINNOPRSSSSV	responsiveness
EEEEINNPSSSSSUV	suspensiveness
EEEEINOPPRSSSSV	oppressiveness
EEEEINOPSSSSSSV	possessiveness
EEEEIOPPRRRSSST	proprietresses
EEFGHINNOORRST	foreshortening
EEFGILLOORSSTX	reflexologists
EEFHIILQRRSSSU	squirrelfishes
EEFHILNRSSSSTT	thriftlessness
EEFIIILMOPRSSV	oversimplifies
EEFIIILNRRTTTY	interfertility
EEFIILLNOSSTTU	feuilletonists
EEFIMNNOORRSTW	frontierswomen
EEFLNOPPRSSSUU	purposefulness
EEGHIIMNNSTTUX	extinguishment
EEGHILLMNORVWY	overwhelmingly
EEGHILNOPRRSTU	reupholstering
EEGHILOOPRSSTT	herpetologists
EEGHINOOPPRRTY	porphyrogenite
EEGHLNOOORSTUV	heterogonously
EEGIIILNORRSTU	interreligious
EEGIILMNORTTUU	ultimogeniture
EEGIILMOOPSSTT	epistemologist
EEGIILNNPPRSTY	enterprisingly
EEGIIMNOPRRSSV	overimpressing
EEGIINNNPRRSTU	unenterprising
EEGIINORSSSTTV	sovereigntists
EEGILMOOORSSTT	meteorologists
EEGILNOOPRRVWY	overpoweringly
EEGINNOOPRRSSV	nonprogressive
EEGINOORRRSSST	retrogressions
EEHHIIILLLNPSST	philhellenists
EEHHIIILMNNOTTY	methylthionine
EEHHIMMOOOPRRST	heteromorphism
EEHHLLOOPRSTUY	heterophyllous
EEHHMMNOOOOPPRS	morphophonemes

EEHHMOOOPRRSTU	heteromorphous
EEHIILMNNQRSTU	relinquishment
EEHIILNOPPRSTY	pyelonephritis
EEHIIMMNOPRSTV	impoverishment
EEHIINOOPRRTTY	erythropoietin
EEHIINOOPSSSTT	photosensitise
EEHIINOOPSSSTTV	photosensitive
EEHIINOOPSSTTZ	photosensitize
EEHIINOPSSSSTY	hyposensitises
EEHIINOPSSSTYZ	hyposensitizes
EEHIIOOPRRSSTY	erythropoiesis
EEHIMOOPRRRSTU	mother superior
EEHINNOOPSSSUU	euphoniousness
EEHINNOORSSTTW	noteworthiness
EEHINNORSSSTWW	newsworthiness
EEHLMNOOORSTUY	heteronomously
EEHLMNOORSTUYY	heteronymously
EEHLMNORSSSSUU	humourlessness
EEHMOOOPPRRTTY	pyrophotometer
EEHNOOOPRRSTXY	orthopyroxenes
EEIIIIMPRSTTTV	permittivities
EEIILMNNRTTTTY	intermittently
EEIILMNOSSSTTY	Simeon Stylites
EEIILNOORRSTUV	revolutioniser
EEIILNOORRTUVZ	revolutionizer
EEIILNOORSSTUV	revolutionises
EEIILNOORSTUVZ	revolutionizes
EEIILNPRRSSVVY	irresponsively
EEIILNOQRSSTUV	ventriloquises
EEIILNOQRSTUVZ	ventriloquizes
EEIILNPRRTTUVY	interruptively
EEIILNPRSSSSST	spiritlessness
EEIIMNOPRSSSUV	imperviousness
EEIINNOPRRSSST	interspersions
EEIINOPRSSSSTX	expressionists
EEILLNOQSSSTUY	questionlessly
EEILMNNNNOOTVV	noninvolvement
EEILMNNOOSSSST	motionlessness
EEIMNORSSSSTUY	mysteriousness
EEIMOPRSSSSSTT	postmistresses
EEINOOPPRSSSSS	prepossessions
EEINOPPRSSSTUV	supportiveness
EEINOPRSSSTUV	protrusiveness
EELLNOOPPPRSYY	polypropylenes
EELOOOPPRRSSTUY	preposterously
EENNOOPRSSSTTU	portentousness
EENOOPPRRSSSSU	prosperousness
EENOORRSSSSTTU	stertorousness
EFFGHHLOORTTUU	forethoughtful
EFFGHIIJNORRTY	Griffith-Joyner
EFFILNNRSSTUUU	unfruitfulness
EFGGIIINNNPRRT	fingerprinting
EFGGOOOORRRSTUY	Gregory of Tours
EFGHHINORRSSTT	forthrightness
EFGHHLNOSSTTUU	thoughtfulness
EFGHINOOOPRRSW	showerproofing
EFGIILNNOSSSUU	fuliginousness
EFHILMNOOOSSST	tomfoolishness
EFHILNOPRSSSUW	worshipfulness
EFHIOOPPRRSSSS	professorships
EFHLNNRSSTTUUU	untruthfulness
EFIKLLLNNSSSUU	unskillfulness

EFINOORSSSTTUU	fortuitousness
EGGIILMNNOOOST	entomologising
EGGIILMNNOOOTZ	entomologizing
EGGILNNOOORSTT	rontgenologist
EGGILNOOORSSTT	gerontologists
EGHHIILOPRSSTY	hieroglyphists
EGHHINOPPRRTYY	hypertrophying
EGHIIILMNRSSTV	silversmithing
EGHIIKNNNNSSTU	unthinkingness
EGIIIILNORRSST	irreligionists
EGIIIINNOQRSTU	requisitioning
EGIIILMNNRTTTY	intermittingly
EGIIILNNNRTTWY	intertwiningly
EGIIINNOOPRRSV	reprovisioning
EGIIKLLMNOORST	kremlinologist
EGIILLLOOSSTVX	vexillologists
EGIILMNOORSSTT	terminologists
EGIILNNOORSSSU	ingloriousness
EGIILOOOSSSTTV	sovietologists
EGIIMNOOPRRSSS	progressionism
EGIINNOORRSSST	introgressions
EGIINNPRRSSSSU	surprisingness
EGIINOOPRRSSST	progressionist
EGIIOPRRSSSSTV	progressivists
EGILMMOOOPSSTY	symptomologies
EHHHIOOPPPSSTY	hypophosphites
EHHIILOOPPRSSS	philosophisers
EHHIILOOPPRSSZ	philosophizers
EHHIKNOORRRSTY	North Yorkshire
EHHIKOORRSSTUY	South Yorkshire
EHHIMMMOOOOPRS	homoeomorphism
EHHIMMMOOOPRSS	homoeomorphisms
EHHIMOOOPRRSTU	theriomorphous
EHHINOOOPPPRST	phosphoprotein
EHHINOOPSSSTTY	photosynthesis
EHHLLMOOPRSTUY	thermophyllous
EHHMMOOOOOPRSU	homoeomorphous
EHIILNNOOPRRTT	trinitrophenol
EHIIMNOOOPSSST	photoemissions
EHIIOOPPPRRRST	proprietorship
EHIIOPPRRSSSUV	supervisorship
EHILMNOPSSSTYY	polysynthesism
EHLNOPRSSSSUUU	sulphurousness
EHMOOOPPRRTTYY	pyrophotometry
EIIIMNOPRSSSST	impressionists
EIIINNOOPRSSTT	interpositions
EIIINNOQSSSTUU	iniquitousness
EIIILLMNOOOSSTT	tonsillotomies
EIIILNOOOPPSSST	oppositionless
EIILNOORSSSTTU	resolutionists
EIILNOORSSTTUV	revolutionists
EIILNOQRSSTTUV	ventriloquists
EIILOOPPSSTTVY	postpositively
EIINNOORRRTTUY	union territory
EIINNORSSSTTUU	nutritiousness
EIINOOPPPRSSTU	presupposition
EIINOOPPRSSSTU	propitiousness
EIINOPRSSSSTUU	spirituousness
EILMNNOOSSSUUV	voluminousness
EILOPRRSSUUUUX	superluxurious
EIMNNOOOPPRRTT	proportionment
EIMNNOOORSSSUV	omnivorousness

EINOOOOPPRRRTV	overproportion	**GIIINNOOOPPRST**	propositioning
ELMNOSSSTTUUUU	tumultuousness	**GILLLMOOPSSSYY**	polysyllogisms
ELMOPPRSSTUUUY	presumptuously	**GILOOOOOPRSTTZ**	protozoologist
ELNOOPSSSTUUUV	voluptuousness	**HHIILNOOOPRSTU**	ornithophilous
EMNNNOOOOSSSTU	monotonousness	**HHINOOOOPPRSSU**	siphonophorous
EMNNNOOSSSSUYY	synonymousness	**HHLOOPPRSSUUUY**	hyposulphurous
EMNOPPRSSTUUUU	unpresumptuous	**HINOOOPPPRRRTY**	protoporphyrin
GGHHIILNOPRTTT	trothplighting	**IIIIINNOQSSTTU**	inquisitionist
GHHIIILNOOPPSS	philosophising	**IIINOOOPPSSSTT**	oppositionists
GHHIIILNOOPPSZ	philosophizing	**IIIOOPPSSSTTUU**	supposititious
GHIILLOOPSSSTY	syphilologists	**IILLNOOORRTTTU**	trinitrotoluol
GHIILNOOORSSTT	ornithologists	**IILOOPPSSSTUUY**	supposititiously
GHIIMNOOPSSSTY	physiognomists	**IIMNOOOOPPRRSST**	misproportions

Fifteen Letters

AAAAACELMNNNOPZ   Panama Canal Zone
AAAAACGLMOOPRRY   Macapagal Arroyo
AAAAAGIKMORTTUW   Kitagawa Utamaro
AAAAABBCCIIILLMR   Biblical Aramaic
AAAABCCDEJMSSUU   Judas Maccabaeus
AAAABCEHHIILLTT   Baile Átha Cliath
AAAABCEILLNOOPT   palaeobotanical
AAAABEGNNRRSTTY   Narragansett Bay
AAAABFHILMNOPRS   Plains of Abraham
AAAABIJNNSSTTUU   San Juan Bautista
AAAACCDEILLNNNO   Caledonian Canal
AAAACCDIIKLLLSY   lackadaisically
AAAACCEHHLNNOPT   acanthocephalan
AAAACCILLLLPRTY   parallactically
AAAACDEEHINNRST   Athanasian Creed
AAAACDIIMMNOSST   macadamisations
AAAACDIIMMNOSTZ   macadamizations
AAAACEEHHLLMNPT   thalamencephala
AAAACEGHILLOPPR   palaeographical
AAAACEHIKNNSSTW   Saskatchewanian
AAAACEIIJLLLSTV   Castilla la Vieja
AAAACGHILLPPRRY   paragraphically
AAAADEGINNQRRSU   quadragenarians
AAAAEIILMNNPRRT   parliamentarian
AAAAEIKLLNNPSSU   Alaska Peninsula
AAAAELMORRSSTTT   tarsometatarsal
AAAAFIILNNPRRSS   infralapsarians
AAAAGGIIMMNNNRST   anagrammatising
AAAAGGIIMMNNNRTZ   anagrammatizing
AAAAGHIMNOPRSST   phantasmagorias
AAAAIILLNOPSSTT   palatalisations
AAAAIILLNOPSTTZ   palatalizations
AAAAILNPPRRSSSU   supralapsarians
AAABBIIIILLOTVY   bioavailability
AAABCCEEHILRRST   characterisable
AAABCCEEHILRRTZ   characterizable
AAABCCFINNORSSY   San Francisco Bay
AAABCDEIILLNRSS   Balearic Islands
AAABCEEHINRRTTT   tetrabranchiate
AAABCEEIIMNNRTT   metacinnabarite
AAABCEEILMNSTTU   semantic tableau
AAABCEEILNNRSTU   unascertainable
AAABCEHINOORSTT   archaeobotanist
AAABCEILLLRSTTY   tetrasyllabical
AAABCHIILOPPRTY   approachability
AAABCIIILNNNOST   cannibalisation
AAABCIIILNNNOTZ   cannibalization

AAABDEEGIIILMST   damageabilities
AAABDHIMOPRSSSS   ambassadorships
AAABDIINORSSSTT   bastardisations
AAABDIINORSSTTZ   bastardizations
AAABEGIIILMRRTV   marriageability
AAABEGIILLNOSUV   bougainvillaeas
AAABEHIILNOPSTT   alphabetisation
AAABEHIILNOPTTZ   alphabetization
AAABEHIMNNORRTY   Erymanthian boar
AAABEIKLLNNNPSU   Balkan Peninsula
AAABEILNOOPSSTT   palaeobotanists
AAABIILLNRSTTTY   translatability
AAABIILMNPRSSSU   sublapsarianism
AAABIILNOOPRSST   parabolisations
AAABIILNOOPRSTZ   parabolizations
AAABIKLMNNNOSTU   Balkan Mountains
AAABILNNRSSTTTU   transubstantial
AAACCCGHHILLOPR   chalcographical
AAACCCILLLMSTVY   cataclysmically
AAACCDEEILOPSSU   asclepiadaceous
AAACCDEHIINORST   archidiaconates
AAACCDEIMNNOORS   adenocarcinomas
AAACCDGHIILOPRR   cardiographical
AAACCDHIMMNOPRY   pharmacodynamic
AAACCEEILMNNRRT   Central American
AAACCEEINNQRSTU   reacquaintances
AAACCEEINORRSSU   sarraceniaceous
AAACCEGHILNOOPR   oceanographical
AAACCEHILORSSST   thalassocracies
AAACCEHILORSTTT   thalattocracies
AAACCEHMNORTTTT   chemoattractant
AAACCEILNOPRRST   practical reason
AAACCEMOPPRRSTU   carpometacarpus
AAACCFIILNRRSTU   intrafascicular
AAACCGHHILOPRRT   chartographical
AAACCGHILLMOOPR   pharmacological
AAACCHIILMNNORT   antimonarchical
AAACCIIILMNOSTT   acclimatisation
AAACCIIILMNOTTZ   acclimatization
AAACCIIINNOPSTT   incapacitations
AAACCIILLMNORTY   microanalytical
AAACCILLLOPPTVY   apocalyptically
AAACDDEEILNOPRSS   Nord-Pas-de-Calais
AAACDDIKLLNNSSU   Auckland Islands
AAACDEEHIIMNRST   adiathermancies
AAACDEEHILMMOSU   hamamelidaceous
AAACDEGIILLMNTY   diamagnetically

AAACDEHHHILMPRS	Himachal Pradesh
AAACDEILLLMNNTT	Mittelland Canal
AAACDEILLMNORYY	aerodynamically
AAACDEILLMORSUY	amaryllidaceous
AAACDGIIINORTTV	radioactivating
AAACDGILLMRRTUY	dramaturgically
AAACDGILNNNNORU	Grand Union Canal
AAACDIIINOORTTV	radioactivation
AAACDIILLNOOORT	radiolocational
AAACEEGILLNNPRTY	paragenetically
AAACEEGILNORTTV	lactovegetarian
AAACEEHILLMORTT	Charlotte Amalie
AAACEEHIMMMSTTT	metamathematics
AAACEEHIOPRRSST	acroparesthesia
AAACEELMNNRSSST	sacramentalness
AAACEFILNNSSSTT	fantasticalness
AAACEGILLMNORTV	galvanometrical
AAACEGILMMNRSST	grammaticalness
AAACEGILMNOPRTY	malacopterygian
AAACEHHIILMPRTT	amphitheatrical
AAACEHIIMNNPRSS	Spanish-American
AAACEHIINNNRSSTT	Saint Catharines
AAACEHIKNOPRRTU	Carpatho-Ukraine
AAACEHILMMNNOTT	nonmathematical
AAACEHIMPPRSTTY	parasympathetic
AAACEILMNRSSSTT	sacramentalists
AAACGGHILNOOPRR	organographical
AAACGHIILPRRSTT	stratigraphical
AAACGHILLOPRTUY	autographically
AAACGIILLMRSTTY	magistratically
AAACGIILLOOPRST	parasitological
AAACGIMMORSSTUX	Saxo Grammaticus
AAACHIILLLNNOTU	hallucinational
AAACHIILMNOPRST	sharia-compliant
AAACHIILNOPSSTT	chaptalisations
AAACHIILNOPSTTZ	chaptalizations
AAACHIIMNOORSST	achromatisation
AAACHIIMNOORTTZ	achromatization
AAACIIILNOPSSTT	capitalisations
AAACIIILNOPSTTZ	capitalizations
AAACIIILNPSSTTT	anticapitalists
AAACIILLLMNOSTY	anomalistically
AAACIIILNORSSTUV	vascularisation
AAACIILNORSTUVZ	vascularization
AAACILLNNOORTTV	contravallation
AAACILLNNORSTTY	transactionally
AAACILLNORSTTUY	astronautically
AAADDEGINOSSTUV	disadvantageous
AAADDEGINPRSSWW	Windward Passage
AAADDFIKLLLNNSS	Falkland Islands
AAADDHIMNNOPSTY	Damon and Pythias
AAADDIINNORSSTT	standardisation
AAADDIINNORSTTZ	standardization
AAADEEELNNPRSST	lares and penates
AAADEGIILLNNPSS	Pelagian Islands
AAADEIIILLNNSSTU	Aleutian Islands
AAADEIILNNRSTUV	valetudinarians
AAADFHILNQRRSSU	Farquhar Islands
AAADGHIOOPRRSTU	autoradiographs
	radioautographs
AAADGHIOOPRRTUY	autoradiography
AAADHIJKMMHNRSU	Jammu and Kashmir

AAADHILLLMNRSSS	Marshall Islands
AAADHIMNNORRSTU	Hardouin Mansart
AAADIIILNNRSTTU	latitudinarians
AAAEEEEFGHLLLMOT	haemoflagellate
AAAEEEELMNRSVYYZ	Severnaya Zemlya
AAAEEGGHILMNTTU	haemagglutinate
AAAEEGGHLOOPPRY	palaeogeography
AAAEEGGILNPRTUV	private language
AAAEEGHIMMNOPSY	hypomagnesaemia
AAAEEGILMMNOPST	palaeomagnetism
AAAEEGINNPRSSTU	septuagenarians
AAAEEHILNNORTTT	National Theatre
AAAEEINNORRSSTT	Saorstat Eireann
AAAEEELMMMNORRRT	Moral Rearmament
AAAEFGGLLMNOORV	Vale of Glamorgan
AAAEFGJMNOORRTU	Margaret of Anjou
AAAEFIILMNNOSTT	manifestational
AAAEGGMMMNORRTU	Montague grammar
AAAEGHIMNOPRSST	phantasmagories
AAAEGHLLOOOPPTY	palaeopathology
AAAEGHLNOOPPRTY	palaeontography
AAAEGIIILMNRSST	egalitarianisms
AAAEGIINNNQQRUU	quinquagenarian
AAAEGIKOSTUUWYY	Tokugawa Iyeyasu
AAAEGILLLNNRTY	National Gallery
AAAEGILLNNPRSTU	Transalpine Gaul
AAAEHHLOPRSSTTY	thalassotherapy
AAAEHIMOPRRSSTT	aromatherapists
AAAEIIILMNORSTT	materialisation
AAAEIIILMNORTTZ	materialization
AAAEIIILMNORSTU	equalitarianism
AAAEIIILNORRSTT	arterialisation
AAAEIIILNORRTTZ	arterialization
AAAEIILMMNPRRST	parliamentarism
AAAEILLNNNOPSUV	Avalon Peninsula
AAAEILMNNPRRTUY	unparliamentary
AAAEMORRSSSTTTU	tarsometatarsus
AAAFFIKMMNNNRRTU	Frankfurt am Main
AAAFIIIILMNORST	familiarisation
AAAFIIIILMNORTZ	familiarization
AAAGHIILLMNSUVW	Vaughan Williams
AAAGHINNORRSTUU	Austro-Hungarian
AAAGIIILMNNORST	marginalisation
AAAGIIILMNNORTZ	marginalization
AAAGIILLNORTTVY	gravitationally
AAAGIINNNOOSSTT	antagonisations
AAAGIINNNOOSTTZ	antagonizations
AAAGIINNOORSTTV	astronavigation
AAAGINOORRSSTTV	astronavigators
AAAHIIIMMNNRSTU	humanitarianism
AAAHIIIMNNRSTTU	humanitarianist
AAAHILNORSSTTUU	South Australian
AAAIIIINNNRRTTT	antitrinitarian
AAAIIILLMMNOSST	malassimilation
AAAIIILLMNNORST	antirationalism
AAAIIILMNORSTTT	totalitarianism
AAAIIILNNOOSTT	nationalisation
AAAIIILNNOOTTZ	nationalization
AAAIIILNNNOSTT	antinationalist
AAAIIILNOORSTT	rationalisation
AAAIIILNOORTTZ	rationalization
AAAIIMNOOSSTTTU	automatisations

AAAIINNNPPRRSTTT	antitranspirant
AAAILLNNOPRSTUY	supranationally
AAAILMNNORSTTTU	transmutational
AAAILNNNOPRSTTT	transplantation
AAAILNNORSSTTUV	transvaluations
AABBCEEFINORSST	absorbefacients
AABBCGHIIILLOPR	bibliographical
AABCCCEHHIILOPR	brachiocephalic
AABCCCEHHILPRSY	brachycephalics
AABCCDEEHILLNSY	hendecasyllabic
AABCCDEELNNORTU	counterbalanced
AABCCDEGHHLMNNO	Mönchengladbach
AABCCDEGHHLMNNU	München-Gladbach
AABCCDEILMMRTUU	circumambulated
AABCCDHILMRSTYY	brachydactylism
AABCCDHLORSTUYY	brachydactylous
AABCCEEILNPRSST	practicableness
AABCCEELNNORSTU	counterbalances
AABCCEELORRRSUV	cerebrovascular
AABCCEGIILLOORT	bacteriological
AABCCEGIILMNRUV	circumnavigable
AABCCEHHILMPRSY	brachycephalism
AABCCEHHLOPRSUY	brachycephalous
AABCCEILMMRSTUU	circumambulates
AABCCGIILMNOTUU	bioaccumulating
AABCCIIILLLNTUV	incalculability
AABCCILMMORRTUU	circumambulator
AABCDDEELLLOSSY	dodecasyllables
AABCDEEEGKLLNOW	acknowledgeable
AABCDEEEHLLLNSY	hendecasyllable
AABCDEEHIIILSTT	detachabilities
AABCDEIINNOORST	decarbonisation
AABCDEIINNOORTZ	decarbonization
AABCDEIINORRSTU	decarburisation
AABCDEIINORRTUZ	decarburization
AABCDEILNOORTXY	decarboxylation
AABCDGIIILLOOOR	radiobiological
AABCDHIILLMRTYY	dithyrambically
AABCEEEGHILNNRT	interchangeable
AABCEEEGHLLLNNU	unchallengeable
AABCEEFFIIILNTY	ineffaceability
AABCEEGHIILNTXY	exchangeability
AABCEEGHILNNRTY	interchangeably
AABCEEILNNRSSTT	intractableness
AABCEEINOQRSSTU	sesquicarbonate
AABCEFIINOPRRST	prefabrications
AABCEGGHIILOOPR	biogeographical
AABCEGGHOORSTUX	Saxe-Coburg-Gotha
AABCEGHIOOPRSTU	bacteriophagous
AABCEGIINNRRSTU	bureaucratising
AABCEGIINNRRTUZ	bureaucratizing
AABCEGILMNOPSUU	plumbaginaceous
AABCEHHIILMNPRS	chamberlainship
AABCEHHILNOOPRT	lophobranchiate
AABCEHIKKLPRSSU	Khakass Republic
AABCEHILLMORTTY	bathometrically
AABCEHILLMRTTYY	bathymetrically
AABCEHINOORSSTT	archeobotanists
AABCEHIORRSSSUU	brachiosauruses
AABCEIILNNPRSTU	antirepublicans
AABCEILLLMOPRTY	problematically
AABCEILLLMORSTY	meroblastically
AABCEILMNNNOOPU	uncompanionable
AABCEINNOSSTTTU	consubstantiate
AABCELLOOPRTXYV	polycarboxylate
AABCFIIILLNOSTY	syllabification
AABCGHIMOOPRRRS	microbarographs
AABCHIILLLNRTYY	labyrinthically
AABCHILLLLOOSTY	holoblastically
AABCIIIILLNPPTY	inapplicability
AABCIIILMNOPRTY	incomparability
AABCIILLLLRSTYY	trisyllabically
AABCIINOORSSTTU	bioastronautics
AABCIINOOSSSSTU	subassociations
AABCIINORSSSTTT	abstractionists
AABCILMNNOOSTTU	noctambulations
AABDDEEGHLOOPRT	photodegradable
AABDDEEGIIIILRST	degradabilities
AABDDEGIINOORST	biodegradations
AABDEEGHINORRTW	weatherboarding
AABDEEGIIILRSTY	disagreeability
AABDEEGILMNRRTU	Bermuda Triangle
AABDEEIILNNSSSV	inadvisableness
AABDEEILNNOSSUV	unavoidableness
AABDEFGHHLMOORU	Flamborough Head
AABDEGIIMNRRSSS	disembarrassing
AABDEIIIILNORSTT	detribalisation
AABDEIIIILNORTTZ	detribalization
AABDEIIILNOSSTT	destabilisation
AABDEIIILNOSTTZ	destabilization
AABDEIIKMNORSST	disembarkations
AABDEIILNSSSTTU	substantialised
AABDEIILNSSTTUZ	substantialized
AABDEINNSSTTTUU	unsubstantiated
AABDELLLMMOOSTU	medulloblastoma
AABDIINOOPPRSST	disapprobations
AABEEEGGLLMNRSSY	General Assembly
AABEEEHKLNNSSSU	unshakeableness
AABEEEEIILLNNNSS	inalienableness
AABEEEEILLNNRSST	inalterableness
AABEEEEILNNPRSSS	inseparableness
AABEEEEILNPRRRSS	irreparableness
AABEEEKLNNPSSSU	unspeakableness
AABEEEELLNPRSSSU	pleasurableness
AABEEEELNNORSSST	treasonableness
AABEEFHILNNNOSSS	fashionableness
AABEEFILLMMNNSS	inflammableness
AABEEFLLNNPPSSU	unflappableness
AABEEFLNNNORRST	nontransferable
AABEEFLNNORSSUV	unfavorableness
AABEEGHIKLNRRTY	heartbreakingly
AABEEGIKLLNRRRV	Granville-Barker
AABEEGILNOORRTV	overelaborating
AABEEIIIILLPRRTY	irrepealability
AABEEIILMNOSTTT	antimetabolites
AABEEIILMNRTUVY	maneuverability
AABEEILNOOORRTV	overelaboration
AABEFGIIILRRRTY	irrefragability
AABEFIILNRRSTTY	transferability
AABEGHHMOOPRRRT	thermobarograph
AABEGHIILMNOORU	haemoglobinuria
AABEGHIIOOPRSTU	autobiographies
AABEGHIOOPRRSTU	autobiographers
AABEHIIILNORSTT	rehabilitations

AABEHLNOOPRTTTT	Neath Port Talbot
AABEIIILLNORSST	liberalisations
AABEIIILLNORSTZ	liberalizations
AABEIIILMMRSTUY	immeasurability
AABEIILMNORTUVY	manoeuvrability
AABEIILNORSSSTU	atrabiliousness
AABEIILNSSSSTTU	substantialises
AABEIILNSSSTTUZ	substantializes
AABEILLNOORSTVY	observationally
AABEILNNSSSSTTU	substantialness
AABGGIIILLNTTUY	agglutinability
AABGIILMMOPRRTY	programmability
AABHIIKKMRSSUU	Murasaki Shikibu
AABIIIIMNQRSTUU	ubiquitarianism
AABIIINNOORSTTT	antiabortionist
AABIILLNNSSTTUY	insubstantially
AABIILMNRSTTTUY	transmutability
AABIILNOPRSSTTY	transposability
AABIILNSSSSTTTU	substantialists
AABIINNOSSSTTTU	substantiations
AABILLNNSSTTUUY	unsubstantially
AACCCDEFIIILNOT	decalcification
AACCCEEHILPRTTY	hypercatalectic
AACCCEEHHILOOPRT	cephalothoracic
AACCCEEHIILLSTTY	catechistically
AACCCEHIIOPPRSY	archiepiscopacy
AACCCEHIIRRSSTT	characteristics
AACCCEHILLMOTTY	chemotactically
AACCCEIILLLMRTY	climacterically
AACCCEIILLLSTYV	acetylsalicylic
AACCCILLMMOORSY	macrocosmically
AACCCILLMOOPRSY	macroscopically
AACCDDEIINNORTT	contraindicated
AACCDEEEENORTTUV	overaccentuated
AACCDEEHHLOOPRT	cephalochordate
AACCDEEKNORTTTU	counterattacked
AACCDEFHLLOORUU	La Rochefoucauld
AACCDEGHIILOORS	oligosaccharide
AACCDEGILLLOOT	dialectological
AACCDEGIIMNRTUV	circumnavigated
AACCDEHHILMNORY	hydromechanical
AACCDEHILOPRSSY	polysaccharides
AACCDEHIMNOORSS	monosaccharides
AACCDEIIILLMRTY	acidimetrically
AACCDEIINNORSTT	contraindicates
AACCDEILLNOOTUY	coeducationally
AACCDELMNOOORST	Coromandel Coast
AACCDFGHHIILNOS	Chichagof Island
AACCDGILMMNOOTY	accommodatingly
AACCDGIMMNNOOTU	unaccommodating
AACCDHHILNOOPRY	hypochondriacal
AACCDHIIMOOSSST	sadomasochistic
AACCDHILNOOPRST	achondroplastic
AACCDIILLOOPRSY	radioscopically
AACCDIINNNORSTT	contraindicants
AACCEEEENORSTTUV	overaccentuates
AACCEEGHILMMNOT	magnetochemical
AACCEEGILNORSST	categoricalness
AACCEEHHLOOPRST	cephalothoraces
AACCEEHIIMRRSST	saccharimetries
AACCEEHIIMRRSTZ	mischaracterize
AACCEEHIIOPPRST	archiepiscopate

AACCEEHILMNORSV	servomechanical
AACCEEILLNNOPRT	precancellation
AACCEEILLNORTTY	electroanalytic
AACCEEINNNORSSS	reconnaissances
AACCEFIILNRRSTU	interfascicular
AACCEFIILOOPRSU	caprifoliaceous
AACCEFLNORSTTUU	counterfactuals
AACCEGHIILLOPRX	lexicographical
AACCEGHIIMNOPRT	cinematographic
AACCEGHILLLOORY	archeologically
AACCEGIILOOPSTT	galactopoietics
AACCEGIIMNRSTUV	circumnavigates
AACCEHHILMNOOPT	photomechanical
AACCEHIIKMNOPRT	pharmacokinetic
AACCEHIILLMNSTY	mechanistically
AACCEHIKLNOOSVZ	Czechoslovakian
AACCEHILLLLMNOY	melancholically
AACCEHILLMORTTY	tachometrically
AACCEHILLRRTTUY	architecturally
AACCEHLOOPRSSSY	polysaccharoses
AACCEIIIILLMNRST	anticlericalism
AACCEIILLMNOSTY	encomiastically
AACCEIILLNRRTUV	interclavicular
AACCEIILMNPRSST	impracticalness
AACCEIIMNRSTTTU	circumstantiate
AACCEILLMNOPSTU	nucleoplasmatic
AACCEILMNNORTTU	counterclaimant
AACCEILNLPRSSTU	unpracticalness
AACCEILRRRRTUUX	extracurricular
AACCFIIILNOSSST	classifications
AACCGHHILOPRSST	chalcographists
AACCGHHIMOOPRRT	chromatographic
AACCGHILOPPRRTY	cryptographical
AACCGHIMMNOORRT	chronogrammatic
AACCGHIMNOOPRST	pharmacognostic
AACCGIILLLNOORY	craniologically
AACCGIILLMNRTUV	circumvallating
AACCGIIMNORRTUV	circumnavigator
AACCGILLNNOOSTT	logical constant
AACCHIIILNOOSTT	catholicisation
AACCHIIILNOOTTZ	catholicization
AACCHIIINNORSTT	Christian Action
AACCHIILLMOSSTY	masochistically
AACCHIILLPRSTYY	psychiatrically
AACCHILLNOPSTYY	sycophantically
AACCHIMNNOOPRSS	Spanish Moroccan
AACCIIIILLLOSSTY	socialistically
AACCIIILNORRSTU	circularisation
AACCIIILNORRTUZ	circularization
AACCIIILPRRSTTU	particularistic
AACCIILLMNORTUV	circumvallation
AACCIILLMNOSSTU	miscalculations
AACCILLLOPRTTUY	plutocratically
AACDDEEEEHLNRSS	clearheadedness
AACDDEEGHNPRSSU	Gadsden Purchase
AACDDEGGIINRSST	Giscard d'Estaing
AACDDEHHILNNOPS	Daphnis and Chloe
AACDDEIILNNOORV	Leonardo da Vinci
AACDDHIILNNSSSW	Sandwich Islands
AACDEEGHIMNOPRT	cinematographed
AACDEEHIIORRSTT	icositetrahedra
AACDEEHINNTTTUU	unauthenticated

AACDEEIILMNOSTU	eudaemonistical
AACDEEIILNPRSTU	undercapitalise
AACDEEIILNPRTUZ	undercapitalize
AACDEEIILOPRSTV	overcapitalised
AACDEEIILOPRTVZ	overcapitalized
AACDEEIIMMNOTTV	decontaminative
AACDEGHILLMOPRY	demographically
AACDEGHLOPRRSTY	dactylographers
AACDEGIIMMNNOTT	decontaminating
AACDEGILLMNOUVV	many-valued logic
AACDEGILNOOPRSS	diagonal process
AACDEHHIILNPRST	Christadelphian
AACDEHILMMNORTY	thermodynamical
AACDEIIILMNOSST	idiomaticalness
AACDEIIJLLRTUXY	extrajudicially
AACDEIILLMNRRTY	intradermically
AACDEIILLMORTUV	audiometrically
AACDEIILLNNORSS	Caroline Islands
AACDEIILNNOPSTY	platinocyanides
AACDEIILNORSSTT	dictatorialness
AACDEIILNOSSTTU	educationalists
AACDEIILNRRSTUV	cardinal virtues
AACDEIIMNNNOOTT	decontamination
AACDEIIMNOORSTT	democratisation
AACDEIIMNOORTTZ	democratization
AACDEIIMNORSSTY	aerodynamicists
AACDEILLMORRTTU	courtmartialled
AACDEIMNNOORSTT	decontaminators
AACDEINOOOPRRTT	Pietro da Cortona
AACDFIIIILNOPST	lapidifications
AACDFIIINOSSSTT	dissatisfaction
AACDFIIORSSSTTY	dissatisfactory
AACDGHIMOOPRRSY	myocardiographs
AACDGIIILNRSTTU	disarticulating
AACDGIILNPQRTUU	quadruplicating
AACDHIILLNOOPRY	radiophonically
AACDHIILMNRSSST	Christmas Island
AACDHILLORSTTYY	hydrostatically
AACDIIIILNNPRSS	disciplinarians
AACDIIIILLMNOTUY	unidiomatically
AACDIIIILNOPPSST	disapplications
AACDIIIILNORSTTU	disarticulation
AACDIIINOOSSSST	disassociations
AACDIILNOPQRTUU	quadruplication
AACDIILORRSSTTU	disarticulators
AACDILMNOOPRRUY	cardiopulmonary
AACDLLNOOPRSTUX	Castor and Pollux
AACDMNOORRRSSTY	Ross and Cromarty
AACEEEGHHLRRSTT	Charles the Great
AACEEEGILLMNTTY	metagenetically
AACEEEHHHLNORTX	hexachlorethane
AACEEEHILMORTTT	metatheoretical
AACEEEHMMORSTTY	haemacytometers
AACEEELLNORSSTY	electroanalyses
AACEEEENNQRRTUY	quatercentenary
AACEEFFHIMNNRST	affranchisement
AACEEGGILLMNOTY	gamogenetically
AACEEGHHILOPRRT	heterographical
AACEEGHHLNOPPRS	encephalographs
AACEEGHHLNOPPRY	encephalography
AACEEGHILLLPRTY	telegraphically
AACEEGHILLNOPRS	selenographical
AACEEGHILOPRRST	stereographical
AACEEGHIMMNORST	archeomagnetism
AACEEGHIMNOPRRT	cinematographer
AACEEGHLLMOOPSU	megalocephalous
AACEEGIKMORSTTY	category mistake
AACEEGILLOOOPST	palaeoecologist
AACEEEHHIMNRRST	Carmarthenshire
AACEEHHLOOPRSTX	cephalothoraxes
AACEEHIINORSTTT	catheterisation
AACEEHIINORTTTZ	catheterization
AACEEHILLMORTTY	theorematically
AACEEHILLNPRTTY	parenthetically
AACEEHILLPRTTUY	therapeutically
AACEEHINNORRRSV	Caernarvonshire
AACEEIIILLPPRTTY	peripatetically
AACEEIILOPRSSTV	overcapitalises
AACEEIILOPRSTVZ	overcapitalizes
AACEEILLNORSSTY	electroanalysis
AACEEIMNOPRSSTV	comparativeness
AACEELLLLRRTUXY	extracellularly
AACEENNOOPSSSSU	saponaceousness
AACEFGIMNNRRTUU	remanufacturing
AACEFHHIMRRSSTT	Father Christmas
AACEFHIORSSTTUW	South West Africa
AACEFIILLNOORRW	Lower California
AACEFIINORSSTTU	anfractuosities
AACEFILOOPRSSSU	passifloraceous
AACEGGHILOOOPRZ	zoogeographical
AACEGHHMOOPRRRT	chromatographer
AACEGHIIKMNOPRT	kinematographic
AACEGHIJKRSSTTT	straightjackets
AACEGHILLMOORTU	rheumatological
AACEGHILLOPRRXY	xerographically
AACEGHILLOPRSUU	Sulu Archipelago
AACEGIIJKNRSTTT	straitjacketing
AACEGIILLLMNORY	mineralogically
AACEGIILLMRRTVY	gravimetrically
AACEGIINOORSSTT	categorisations
AACEGIINOORSTTZ	categorizations
AACEGILLLLMRTUY	metallurgically
AACEGILLMNOOPTU	pneumatological
AACEGLNOORSSTUY	agranulocytoses
AACEHHILLMOOPTY	homeopathically
AACEHHILNNOPSTY	phthalocyanines
AACEHIILLNPSTTY	pantheistically
AACEHIINNOSTTTU	authentications
AACEHILLMOPRSTY	atmospherically
AACEHILLMPSTTYY	sympathetically
AACEHILLNOPRTUY	neuropathically
AACEHILLOPSTTUY	osteopathically
AACEHILOOPRSSTT	thoracoplasties
AACEHILOPRRSSTT	stratospherical
AACEHIMOOPPRSST	pharmacopoeists
AACEHLNOPRSSSVY	psychoanalysers
AACEHLNOPRSSYYZ	psychoanalyzers
AACEHMNOOOPPRSS	anamorphoscopes
AACEHMNOOORRSTY	archeoastronomy
AACEHNOOPPRRSTU	parthenocarpous
AACEIIILLMNOSTU	aluminosilicate
AACEIIIILLNOSSTX	lexicalisations
AACEIIILLNOSTXZ	lexicalizations
AACEIIILMNOPPSS	episcopalianism

AACEIIIILNOPSSST	specialisations
AACEIIIILNOPSSTZ	specializations
AACEIIIILNPRSTTT	antiperistaltic
AACEIIIILPRRSTTU	particularities
AACEIIIIMMNOSTTT	metamictisation
AACEIIIIMMNOTTTZ	metamictization
AACEIIIMNNOPSTT	emancipationist
AACEIILLLMNSTTY	mentalistically
AACEIILLLLPRSTTY	peristaltically
AACEIIILLMNNRSTY	manneristically
AACEIILMNOPRRTT	malpractitioner
AACEIIILNNORSTT	centralisations
AACEIIILNNORSTTZ	centralizations
AACEIIILNNPRSSTU	puritanicalness
AACEIILNNRSSTTU	antinuclearists
AACEIIILNOPRSTTU	recapitulations
AACEIIILPRRRSSTU	particularisers
AACEIIILPRRRSTUZ	particularizers
AACEILLLLNRRTUV	intracellularly
AACEILLLLMNOPRTY	planometrically
AACEILLLLNNOOSTT	constellational
AACEILMMMNOOOORT	commemorational
AACEILMNOOPSSTY	compassionately
AACEILMNOOSSSSTY	ancylostomiases
AACEILNOOOORRTTU	autocorrelation
AACEILNORSSTTUX	exclaustrations
AACELLMMNOPRTTY	compartmentally
AACFFIIINORSSSS	Francis of Assisi
AACFGIIIIILNRST	artificialising
AACFGIIIIILNRTZ	artificializing
AACFGIILLNNOORTU	configurational
AACFIIIMMNNOOST	ammonifications
AACFIIIINNOORSTT	fractionisation
AACFIIIINNOORTTZ	fractionization
AACFIIIINNOQSTTU	quantifications
AACFIIIINORSSTTT	stratifications
AACFIILLLMORSTY	formalistically
AACFILNNNOOORTT	confrontational
AACGGHHHILLOPPRY	glyphographical
AACGGHHILNOOPRY	cholangiography
AACGGHILLLOOPRY	logographically
AACGGHILLNOOPRY	pharyngological
AACGGHILLOPPRTY	glyptographical
AACGHHIILOPPRSY	physiographical
AACGHHILLLOOPRY	holographically
AACGHIIILMNORTT	antilogarithmic
AACGHIILLLMORTY	algorithmically
	logarithmically
AACGHILLLOPPRVY	polygraphically
AACGHILLMNOOPRY	monographically
	nomographically
AACGHILLNOOOPRT	anthropological
AACGHILLOOPPRTY	topographically
AACGHILLOPPRTYY	typographically
AACGHILMOOPRSST	pharmacologists
AACGHILNNOPSSVY	psychoanalysing
AACGHILNNOPSYYZ	psychoanalyzing
AACGHIMNOOPRSST	pharmacognosist
AACGHLLOPRRSTYY	crystallography
AACGIIIILNPRRSTU	particularising
AACGIIIILNPRRTUZ	particularizing
AACGIIIILNPRSSTU	paralinguistics
AACGIILLRRSTTUU	agriculturalist
AACGIINNOPRRSTT	procrastinating
AACGIJLLNNOOTUY	conjugationally
AACGILLLMOOOSTY	somatologically
AACGILLMNOORSTY	gastronomically
AACGILLNNORRTUU	nonagricultural
AACGILNNOORSTTU	congratulations
AACGILNOORSSTUY	agranulocytosis
AACGIMMNOOPRRSU	macrosporangium
AACHHIILLNOPPRT	philanthropical
AACHIILLMNORSTY	harmonistically
AACHIILNNNOORRT	North Carolinian
AACHIILNNOORSTU	South Carolinian
AACHIIMNNORSSTT	antimonarchists
AACHILLLMOOPSTY	homoplastically
AACHILLOPPRSTYY	saprophytically
AACHILLOPPSSTTY	staphyloplastic
AACIIIILMNNNORST	criminalisation
AACIIIILMNNNORTZ	criminalization
AACIIILLLRSTTUY	ritualistically
AACIIILMNNOSSTU	masculinisation
AACIIILMNNOSTUZ	masculinization
AACIIILMNOPPSST	misapplications
AACIIILNOOPRSTT	tropicalisation
AACIIILNOOPRTTZ	tropicalization
AACIIIMNNOORSTT	romanticisation
AACIIIMNNOORTTZ	romanticization
AACIILLNOOPRSTY	anisotropically
AACIILLNORSSTTY	crystallisation
AACIILLNORSTTYZ	crystallization
AACIILMMNNOOSTU	communalisation
AACIILMMNNOOTUZ	communalization
AACIILMNOOSSSTY	ancylostomiasis
AACIILNNOOOTTUU	autoinoculation
AACIILNNOPPRRSTT	transcriptional
AACIILNORSSSTTY	crystalisations
AACIILNORSSTTTU	straticulations
AACIILNORSSTTYZ	crystalizations
AACIINNOOPRRSTT	procrastination
AACILLLLMOPSTYY	plasmolytically
AACILLMMOPSTTYY	symptomatically
AACILLMNNRRSTUUY	intramuscularly
AACILNNNOSSTTUV	anticonvulsants
AACILNNOOPRSTTTU	contrapuntalist
AACINOOPRRRSSTT	procrastinators
AACLLRRRSTTTUUU	ultrastructural
AACLNNNOOOPSSTT	postconsonantal
AADDDIILNNRSSSWW	Windward Islands
AADDEEEHHNRRSST	hardheartedness
AADDEEEELMMNNPUY	Eupen and Malmédy
AADDEEHHMRRRTTWY	Edward the Martyr
AADDEEIILMMNRST	maladministered
AADDEIILNOPRSTU	superadditional
AADDHILNNOSSSTU	Thousand Islands
AADEEEFHHLNRSST	halfheartedness
AADEEEGGLNNNNRW	New England Range
AADEEEHMNNRRSSTW	warmheartedness
AADEEEIKLNNRSVX	Alexander Nevski
AADEEEEILLLPPPRS	parallelepipeds
AADEEEEILMNPRSTT	departmentalise
AADEEEEILMNPRTTZ	departmentalize
AADEEFLMNNNSSTU	fundamentalness

AADEEGGHILMNTTU	hemagglutinated	AAEEEGILRRRSTVV	Great Slave River
AADEEGHILOPRRST	radiotelegraphs	AAEEEGMNNPRRRST	prearrangements
AADEEGHILOPRRTY	radiotelegraphy	AAEEEHHIMMMNPTT	methamphetamine
AADEEGIIILMNRST	dematerialising	AAEEEHIILNORSTT	etherealisation
AADEEGIIILMNRTZ	dematerializing	AAEEEHIILNORTTZ	etherealization
AADEEGIIMNNOSTT	demagnetisation	AAEEEHIMNNNOPRS	neoarsphenamine
AADEEGIIMNNOTTZ	demagnetization	AAEEEIIMNNORTTT	Marie Antoinette
AADEEGIMNNRRSST	disarrangements	AAEEEILMNNPTTTU	antepenultimate
AADEEHIIILMPPRY	hyperlipidaemia	AAEEEILNNRSSTTV	alternativeness
AADEEHIIIMNRRST	hereditarianism	AAEEEELLMMNPRTTY	temperamentally
AADEEHLLORRTTTY	tetartohedrally	AAEEFFINOORRSTT	reafforestation
AADEEIILNNOSSST	sensationalised	AAEEFFLNNORSSTT	Feast of Lanterns
AADEEIILNNOSSTZ	sensationalized	AAEEFGILLRRTTVY	Great Rift Valley
AADEEIILNOSSTUX	desexualisation	AAEEFGIMNNRRSST	fragmentariness
AADEEIILNOSTUXZ	desexualization	AAEEFHILPPRSTTY	past life therapy
AADEEIINNPRRSST	predestinarians	AAEEFINNNRSSSTT	aftersensations
AADEEILLLOPPPRS	parallelopipeds	AAEEGGHILMNSTTU	hemagglutinates
AADEEILMMNPRSTT	departmentalism	AAEEGHIKMNOPRRT	kinematographer
AADEEILMNORSTTT	tatterdemalions	AAEEGHILLMORRTY	erythromelalgia
AADEEILMOPRSSTT	dermatoplasties	AAEEGHILNOOSSTY	anaesthesiology
AADEEILNNPRSSUW	Seward Peninsula	AAEEGHLLMOPRRST	metallographers
AADEEINNPRSSSTT	antidepressants	AAEEGIIIMNNSSTV	imaginativeness
AADEELMNNNOPRTT	nondepartmental	AAEEGIIIMNORTVV	overimaginative
AADEFHLLLNRSSTU	Sutherland Falls	AAEEGIILMNRSSST	magisterialness
AADEFILMNNSSTTU	fundamentalists	AAEEGIILNNORSST	generalisations
AADEGHIMNOOORRS	Angra do Heroísmo	AAEEGIILNNORSTZ	generalizations
AADEGIIILNNNOST	denationalising	AAEEGILMNRTTUVY	argumentatively
AADEGIIILNNNOTZ	denationalizing	AAEEGIMMNNRRSST	misarrangements
AADEGIILMMNORST	melodramatising	AAEEGLMNOQRUZZZ	González Márquez
AADEGIILMMNORTZ	melodramatizing	AAEEHHILMNORSTT	trihalomethanes
AADEGIIMNORRSTV	overdramatising	AAEEHIINNOSTTTZ	anesthetization
AADEGIIMNORRTVZ	overdramatizing	AAEEHIMNNNOOPSZ	aminophenazones
AADEGIINNORRSTT	intergradations	AAEEHLMMMNOSSUU	Ashmolean Museum
AADEGINOORRRSTT	retrogradations	AAEEIIILLMNNPRRS	premillenarians
AADEHHLMNOPPTYY	lymphadenopathy	AAEEIILLNOQRTTU	Loire-Atlantique
AADEHIIOPRRSSTT	radiotherapists	AAEEIILNNORSTTX	externalisation
AADEHILNOSSSSTU	South Sea Islands	AAEEIILNNORTTXZ	externalization
AADEHLNORRSTTWY	northeastwardly	AAEEIILNNOSSSST	sensationalises
AADEIILMNOSTTUU	demutualisation	AAEEIILNNOSSSTZ	sensationalizes
AADEIILMNOTTUUZ	demutualization	AAEEIKLMNNSSTTU	unstatesmanlike
AADEIILNOPSSSTY	dispassionately	AAEEILLLMNORRST	lamellirostrate
AADEIILNORRRTXY	extraordinarily	AAEEILLMNNPPRSU	Palmer Peninsula
AADEIIMOPPPRRST	misappropriated	AAEEILNNOPRRSST	proletarianness
AADEILLNOOPRSUX	Alexandroúpolis	AAEEIMNNPRRSSTT	semitransparent
AADEILMNNOORSTT	demonstrational	AAEEINOPPPRRSST	appropriateness
AADEILNNORSTUUV	undervaluations	AAEELLNPRRRTTUY	preternaturally
AADELLOPRRSSSUX	Russell's paradox	AAEENNNPRRSSSTT	transparentness
AADELNOPRSTTUUY	polyunsaturated	AAEFIIILMORRTVY	overfamiliarity
AADEMNNOORSTTUU	monounsaturated	AAEFMNOORRRSTTU	autotransformer
AADFFIIIMNORSST	disaffirmations	AAEGGIIIMMNPRST	epigrammatising
AADFGHILNNNOOSY	laying on of hands	AAEGGIIIMMNPRTZ	epigrammatizing
AADFGHIORRRSTTW	straightforward	AAEGHHINOOPPRTT	anthropophagite
AADFNMOOORRSTTV	Stratford-on-Avon	AAEGHHNOOOPPRST	organophosphate
AADGHHIMNPRSSTU	draughtsmanship	AAEGHILLMOPRSTT	metallographist
AADGIIINNOORSST	disorganisation	AAEGHLLNOORTTUY	natural theology
AADGIIINNOORSTZ	disorganization	AAEGIIIILMMNRST	immaterialising
AADHILLNORRSTYY	synarthrodially	AAEGIIIILMMNRTZ	immaterializing
AADIIILNORSSTTT	traditionalists	AAEGIIILMNNNRTT	interlaminating
AADIIIMNNORSSTT	administrations	AAEGIIILMNNTUVY	unimaginatively
AAEEEEEFGNORRSTT	Orange Free State	AAEGIIILNNOSTTV	investigational
AAEEEEFGHLLLMOST	hemoflagellates	AAEGIIKNNNPSSST	painstakingness
AAEEEEGILLNRRSTT	Greater Antilles	AAEGIIILLNOORSST	allegorisations

AAEGIILLNOORSTZ	allegorizations
AAEGIILNNOORRTT	interrogational
AAEGIILNNRRSTTT	transliterating
AAEGIILNORRSSTU	regularisations
AAEGIILNORRSTUZ	regularizations
AAEGIINNOORRSST	reorganisations
AAEGIINNOORRSTZ	reorganizations
AAEGILLNOOOPSTT	palaeontologist
AAEGILLOOOOPSTZ	palaeozoologist
AAEGIMMNNNOSSSU	magnanimousness
AAEGIMNOPRRSTTU	tetrasporangium
AAEHIIKLMNRSSTU	Karelian Isthmus
AAEHIILORTTTUVY	authoritatively
AAEHIMOPRSSSSTT	massotherapists
AAEIIIILNORRSTT	irrationalities
AAEIIILMMNNOORST	memorialisation
AAEIIILMMNNOORTZ	memorialization
AAEIIILMNNNORTT	interlamination
AAEIIILNNNORSTT	internalisation
AAEIIILNNNORTTZ	internalization
AAEIIILNPRSSSTT	antiperistalsis
AAEIILLMNNRSTTU	transilluminate
AAEIIILLNNNORTTY	internationally
AAEIILLNNORSSTT	reinstallations
AAEIILMNNPRSTUY	Taimyr Peninsula
AAEIILNNOOPSRST	personalisation
AAEIILNNOOPRSTZ	personalization
AAEIILNNORRSTTT	transliteration
AAEIILNNOSSSSTT	sensationalists
AAEIILNOORRSSTV	revalorisations
AAEIILNOORRSTVZ	revalorizations
AAEIILNOPPPRRTY	inappropriately
AAEIIMNOSSSTTTY	systematisation
AAEIIMNOSSTTTYZ	systematization
AAEIIMOPPPRRSST	misappropriates
AAEIINNPPRRRSST	antiperspirants
AAEIKLMNOOSSSTY	ankylostomiases
AAEILLNNOPRSTUY	supernationally
AAEILMNNPRSTUYY	Taymyr Peninsula
AAEILMNPRRSSTUU	supernaturalism
AAEILNNNOSSTTUY	instantaneously
AAEILNORRRSSTTT	transliterators
AAEILNPRRSSTTUU	supernaturalist
AAEIMNNNORRSTTT	Antiremonstrant
AAEIMNNOORSSTTU	neuroanatomists
AAEINNNOPRSSTUU	superannuations
AAEINOPRRSSTTUU	supersaturation
AAELNNNOPRSSTTX	xenotransplants
AAENNORRSSSTUUY	tyrannosauruses
AAFGIINNORRSTTU	transfiguration
AAFIIIILMNRSTTU	futilitarianism
AAFIIIMNNORRSTU	uniformitarians
AAFIILLNORRTTTU	ultrafiltration
AAFIILMNOORRSTU	formularisation
AAFIILMNOORRTUZ	formularization
AAFIMNNOORRSSTT	transformations
AAGGHINOOPRRSST	organographists
AAGGILMMOORRSST	grammatologists
AAGHHNOOOOPPRSTU	anthropophagous
AAGHIIPRRSSSTTT	stratigraphists
AAGHLNOOPRRSTUY	ultrasonography
AAGHMNOOOSSTTTU	gnathostomatous

AAGIIIILNNNORSSTU	singularisation
AAGIIIILNNORSTUZ	singularization
AAGIIIIMNOSSSTTT	stigmatisations
AAGIIIMNOSSTTTZ	stigmatizations
AAGIILNORSTTTUU	gutturalisation
AAGIILNORTTTUUZ	gutturalization
AAGIILOOPRSSSTT	parasitologists
AAGIIMNNORRSSTT	transmigrations
AAGILMNOOPRSSTV	galvanotropisms
AAGIMNNOORSSTUZ	Zagros Mountains
AAHHHLOPPRRSTYY	staphylorrhaphy
AAHHIINOOPPSSTT	phosphatisation
AAHHIINOOPSSTTZ	phosphatization
AAHHIMNOOPPRSTT	anthropopathism
AAHIIIILNOOPSSTT	hospitalisation
AAHIIIILNOOPSTTZ	hospitalization
AAHIINNNOPPRSST	nonpartisanship
AAHIINNNOPPRSTZ	nonpartizanship
AAHIINOOPSSSTTY	hypostasisation
AAHIINOOPSSTTTY	hypostatisation
AAHIINOOPSSTTYZ	hypostasization
AAHIINOOPSTTTYZ	hypostatization
AAIIIIILNNOSSTT	initialisations
AAIIIIILNNOSTTZ	initializations
AAIIIILMNORSSTT	militarisations
AAIIIILMNORSTTZ	militarizations
AAIIIILMNRSSTTT	antimilitarists
AAIIIIMNNORSSTTU	miniaturisation
AAIIIIMNNORTTUZ	miniaturization
AAIIILLNNOPRSTY	inspirationally
AAIIILMMNOORSTT	immortalisation
AAIIILMMNOORTTZ	immortalization
AAIIILMMNOOPRSTV	improvisational
AAIIILNNOQRTTUZ	tranquilization
AAIIINNNOOOSSTTU	autoionisations
AAIIINNNOOOSTTUZ	autoionizations
AAIIJLNNOORSSTU	journalisations
AAIIJLNNOORSTUZ	journalizations
AAIIJLNOOPSSTTUX	juxtapositional
AAIIKLMNOOSSSTY	ankylostomiasis
AAIILNNOOPRSSTT	transpositional
AAIILNOOPPRSSTU	popularisations
AAIILNOOPPRSTUZ	popularizations
AAIIMMNOSSSSTUY	immunoassayists
AAIIMNOOPRSSSTY	trypanosomiasis
AAILMMMNNOOOSSU	anomalous monism
AAILMNNORSSTTTU	ultramontanists
AAIMNNORSSTTUUU	Taurus Mountains
AAINNOOPRRSSTTT	transportations
ABBCCCEIILMRRSU	circumscribable
ABBCDDEILMOOSTU	discombobulated
ABBCDEEGIMNRSUZ	Brześć nad Bugiem
ABBCDEILMOOSSTU	discombobulates
ABBCEEELNNNORYZ	benzenecarbonyl
ABBCEEIILNNRSSS	inscribableness
ABBCEEIJLNNOOTU	unobjectionable
ABBCEHIIKLPRRSU	Bashkir Republic
ABBCHIIILMORSTU	British Columbia
ABBCIKLLMOOOSSY	symbolical books
ABBDEEEELNORSSTU	redoubtableness
ABBDEEIILNNSSTU	indubitableness
ABBEEIIILLNTUVY	unbelievability

ABBEIIIILMOPRST	improbabilities
ABBEIIILOPQRTUY	equiprobability
ABCCEEEEILNNOSSV	conceivableness
ABCCEEEIILLNORRS	irreconcilables
ABCCEEEILNNOORST	concelebrations
ABCCEFIIIJNOOTT	objectification
ABCCEFIIILLPSSUV	subspecifically
ABCCEGIILLLOOOY	bioecologically
ABCCEHHILPRSUUV	Chuvash Republic
ABCCEHHINNRTUYZ	Byzantine Church
ABCCEHHINOORRST	brachistochrone
ABCCEIIIILNSSTY	inaccessibility
ABCCEIIIILLNORTY	reconcilability
ABCCEIKKLLMPRUU	Kalmuck Republic
ABCCGIIILLMOOOR	microbiological
ABCCIIILMMNOTUY	communicability
ABCDDEEEHKLNOSS	blockheadedness
ABCDEEEIILMMNSS	immedicableness
ABCDEEEILNPRSST	predictableness
ABCDEEELMMNNOSS	commendableness
ABCDEEHIIILPRTY	decipherability
ABCDEEHMNORRRTU	Camborne-Redruth
ABCDEEIILNOSSSS	dissociableness
ABCDEIILLLOQTUY	quodlibetically
ABCDEIILMOOPSTY	decomposability
ABCDEIIMOOSSTUV	basidiomycetous
ABCDHILNOOORRST	bronchodilators
ABCDIIIIILRSTTTY	distractibility
ABCEEEEILNRSSSV	serviceableness
ABCEEEEELNPRSSST	respectableness
ABCEEEEILNNOPTUX	unexceptionable
ABCEEEEILNNSSSUX	inexcusableness
ABCEEEEILNORRSSV	irrevocableness
ABCEEEEIMNORRTTU	enterobacterium
ABCEEELNNOQRSSU	conquerableness
ABCEEEELNNORSSSV	conversableness
ABCEEEELNNOSSSTT	contestableness
ABCEEFKLLNORRST	Bracknell Forest
ABCEEFLMNNOORSS	conformableness
ABCEEFLMNOORSST	comfortableness
ABCEEGHHKLNOSSV	Blagoveshchensk
ABCEEHHLMMNNOOPR	rhombencephalon
ABCEEILMMNNORSU	incommensurable
ABCEEILNNOPTUXY	unexceptionably
ABCEEILNNRSSSTU	inscrutableness
ABCEEINOPQRSSUV	Basque Provinces
ABCEELNNNOOPRUU	unpronounceable
ABCEGHHIIKMNRSU	Buckinghamshire
ABCEGHILMPPRSUU	Schaumburg-Lippe
ABCEGIIILNNPRSU	republicanising
ABCEGIIILNNPRUZ	republicanizing
ABCEGIIILNORSTY	recognisability
ABCEGIIILNORTYZ	recognizability
ABCEGIILOORSSTT	bacteriologists
ABCEGILLLMOORYY	embryologically
ABCEHIILMOOPSTT	histocompatible
ABCEIIIILLNPTXY	inexplicability
ABCEIIIILNRTTXY	inextricability
ABCEIIIILPPRTTY	precipitability
ABCEIIILLMMRSTYY	bisymmetrically
ABCEILMMNNORSUY	incommensurably
ABCEILOOORRRTVY	corroboratively
ABCELLLNNNOOORT	noncontrollable
ABCGHHIOOPPRSYY	psychobiography
ABCGHIIILLOOOOPT	photobiological
ABCGIILLNOOOTTY	gnotobiotically
ABCHHIILLMORTYY	biorhythmically
ABCIIIILMNOPTTY	incompatibility
ABCIIIILLNNOOSTY	inconsolability
ABCIIILMMNOTTUY	incommutability
ABCIIILMNOPTTUY	incomputability
ABCIILLLMOSSTYY	symbolistically
ABCIILLLLNOORTY	controllability
ABCIILORRRSTTUU	arboriculturist
ABCILLNOORSTTUY	obstructionally
ABDDDEEIMNNORSS	broadmindedness
ABDDEEELLNNORTV	Oldenbarneveldt
ABDEEEEILMNPRRT	predeterminable
ABDEEEFIILNNNSS	indefinableness
ABDEEEEGKLLNNOUW	unknowledgeable
ABDEEEEHKLNORRTY	brokenheartedly
ABDEEEIIIILMRRTY	irredeemability
ABDEEEEIINNOPSZZ	benzodiazepines
ABDEEEEILNNPSSSS	dispensableness
ABDEEEEILNNRSSSU	undesirableness
ABDEEFIIIILNSTY	indefeasibility
ABDEEGLORRTTUUW	Teutoburger Wald
ABDEEEIILMNNOSST	indomitableness
ABDEEIILLNOSSSSV	dissolvableness
ABDEEEINNORSSSTU	subordinateness
ABDEFIIIILLNORST	defibrillations
ABDEGHHINNOORTV	Brighton and Hove
ABDEGHIIILNSSST	disestablishing
ABDEGHIIIILNSSTU	distinguishable
ABDEIIILMNOOSST	demobilisations
ABDEIIIILMNOOSTZ	demobilizations
ABDEIIIILMNOPRTY	imponderability
ABDEIIIILPRSTTUY	disreputability
ABDEIIIMNRSSTUU	subminiaturised
ABDEIIIMNRSTUUZ	subminiaturized
ABDEIILMNORSTTY	demonstrability
ABDEIILNNORSTUY	insubordinately
ABDEIILNOOORSSTW	bowdlerisations
ABDEIILNOOORSTWZ	bowdlerizations
ABDFIIILLNOPRSS	Pribilof Islands
ABDGHIIIILNSSTUY	distinguishably
ABDGIIILOOOORSST	radiobiologists
ABDHHIINORRSSTU	British Honduras
ABDHHIMOOOPPRSY	dysmorphophobia
ABDHILNNOORSTTY	labyrinthodonts
ABDIIIIILMNSSTY	inadmissibility
ABDIIIIILNPSTTY	indisputability
ABDIIILMNORSTTU	maldistribution
ABDIIINNNOORSTU	insubordination
ABEEEEILMMNPRSS	impermeableness
ABEEEEILNNPRRTT	interpenetrable
ABEEEEEIORRRRSTV	reverberatories
ABEEEEELNNPRSSST	presentableness
ABEEEFGILNNRRSS	refrangibleness
ABEEEFHHLMORSTT	Star of Bethlehem
ABEEEFILNRRSSTU	irrefutableness
ABEEEGILMNNPRSS	impregnableness
ABEEEHIILMNRSSTT	inheritableness
ABEEEHILMNRSSTT	reestablishment

ABEEEEHKNNORRSST	heartbrokenness
ABEEEEHMMOORRRTT	thermobarometer
ABEEEIILMNNSSST	inestimableness
ABEEEIILNNQSSTU	inequitableness
ABEEEEILLNNORSST	intolerableness
ABEEEEILMNNNRSSU	innumerableness
ABEEEEILMNORRSSU	irremovableness
ABEEEEILNNPRSSSU	insuperableness
ABEEEELNNRSSTTUU	unutterableness
ABEEFGIILNNNRSS	infrangibleness
ABEEFIIJLNSSSTU	justifiableness
ABEEFILORSTTTUY	Statue of Liberty
ABEEGHHLLMNNOTW	Bethmann Hollweg
ABEEGHIILNPRSST	preestablishing
ABEEGIIIILNOSTT	negotiabilities
ABEEGINPRRSSTTU	Saint Petersburg
ABEEGNOORRRSTTU	turbogenerators
ABEEHIKLNNNSSTU	unthinkableness
ABEEHILMNORSSTW	blameworthiness
ABEEIIIILLLMNSST	illimitableness
ABEEIIIILLNRSTUV	vulnerabilities
ABEEIIIILMNPRTTY	impenetrability
ABEEIIILLMNPSSSU	implausibleness
ABEEIIMNPRRSSTY	presbyterianism
ABEEIINRSSTTTUV	attributiveness
ABEEILNNNPRSSTU	unprintableness
ABEEINNSSSSTTUV	substantiveness
ABEELNOPPRSSSTU	supportableness
ABEELNORRSSTUUY	subterraneously
ABEFIILLNORRRUY	neurofibrillary
ABEFINNORRRSSUW	Barrow-in-Furness
ABEGIIILNNPTUXY	inexpugnability
ABEGIILORRSSSTY	gyrostabilisers
ABEGIILORRSSTYZ	gyrostabilizers
ABEHHHOOORRRTUY	boo-hurrah theory
ABEHHINOOPPSSST	bisphosphonates
ABEHIIIILMPRSTY	imperishability
ABEHIILMORSTTTY	thermostability
ABEHILMNOOORRTT	tribromoethanol
ABEHMNNORSSTUUY	Sunbury-on-Thames
ABEIIIIILMNNRTTY	interminability
ABEIIILLNNRTUVY	invulnerability
ABEIIIILLORRSTVY	irresolvability
ABEIIIILNOQSTTUY	questionability
ABEIIIMNRSSSTUU	subminiaturises
ABEIIIMNRSSTUUZ	subminiaturizes
ABEIILLMNOPTUVY	unemployability
ABEILMNNORSTUUZ	Elburz Mountains
ABFHIJLNOORSSUY	John of Salisbury
ABFIIILNOPRTTUY	unprofitability
ABGIIINNSSSTTUV	substantivising
ABGIIINNSSTTUVZ	substantivizing
ABHIIILNOPSTTYY	hypnotisability
ABHIIILNOPTTYYZ	hypnotizability
ACCCDEEEIINNNSS	incandescencies
ACCCDEEIIINNNOT	anticoincidence
ACCCDEHHIILLOOP	dolichocephalic
ACCCDEHILLNOSYY	synecdochically
ACCCEEEHILLMORT	electrochemical
ACCCEEEMOPRRSSU	eccremocarpuses
ACCCEEFHILLLOOR	cholecalciferol
ACCCEEGIILLLOOS	ecclesiological
ACCCEEIIILMSSST	ecclesiasticism
ACCCEEILOORSTTU	electroacoustic
ACCCEFIIKNNOOTY	cockneyfication
ACCCEGIIINNORTY	carcinogenicity
ACCCEHHIILMOPSY	physicochemical
ACCCEHHILMOPSSY	psychochemicals
ACCCEHHILOPPRSU	Episcopal Church
ACCCEHIILOORRTT	trichloroacetic
ACCCEIIILMMORST	commercialistic
ACCCEIILNOPSTTU	conceptualistic
ACCCEIKLNOORSTW	contraclockwise
ACCCEILOOPPRSST	spectroscopical
ACCCFIIIKNNOOST	cocknifications
ACCCHIOOPSSSTUY	psychoacoustics
ACCCIIILLMOOPRSY	microscopically
ACCDDEEINNNSTU	discountenanced
ACCDEEEHIORSSTT	heteroscedastic
ACCDEEEILNNOPTY	cyclopentadiene
ACCDEEFIIINORTT	decertification
ACCDEEHILLLPSYY	psychedelically
ACCDEEHINOOOPSU	chenopodiaceous
ACCDEEILMNOPSST	complicatedness
ACCDEEILMNORSTY	electrodynamics
ACCDEEILMOOPRTV	overcomplicated
ACCDEEILNOPSSTY	encyclopaedists
ACCDEEINNNOSSTU	discountenances
ACCDEEINNOORSST	deconsecrations
ACCDEFGHHLNNORU	Church of England
ACCDEFHHIINNNOR	French Indochina
ACCDEFIIINOORST	recodifications
ACCDEFILLNOOSTU	deflocculations
ACCDEHIINNOOPRT	endocrinopathic
ACCDEHILLLOPSYY	psychodelically
ACCDEIIILLNNRSSY	cylindricalness
ACCDEIILNORTTVY	contradictively
ACCDEIINNNOSSTU	discontinuances
ACCDEIINOORRSTT	contradictories
ACCDFHIIINNOORT	chondrification
ACCDFIIIMMNOOOT	commodification
ACCDHHHINNORSTY	chondrichthyans
ACCDIILNNOOPSTU	conduplications
ACCDIILNOORRTTY	contradictorily
ACCEEEELLNORSTV	electrovalences
ACCEEEGILLNNOTY	cenogenetically
ACCEEEGILMNORTT	electromagnetic
	magnetoelectric
ACCEEEHMNOOPRRT	mechanoreceptor
ACCEEEILLMORRTT	electrometrical
ACCEEEINNOORSTT	octocentenaries
ACCEEFFIINOSSSU	efficaciousness
ACCEEFHIIINOPST	speechification
ACCEEFHMNNOOORRS	French Cameroons
ACCEEFIIILNORTT	electrification
ACCEEFIILMNRRTU	circumferential
ACCEEFIINNOORST	confectionaries
ACCEEGIIMOPRSUV	Amerigo Vespucci
ACCEEGILLNOTTYY	cytogenetically
ACCEEGILLORRSTU	electrosurgical
ACCEEGINNNORRTT	reconcentrating
ACCEEHHIMOORRTT	heterochromatic
ACCEEHILLMOPRTY	petrochemically
ACCEEHILLOOPRTT	photoelectrical

ACCEEHILOORRSTT	atherosclerotic
ACCEEHINOORSSTT	thoracocentesis
ACCEEIIILMMORST	commercialities
ACCEEIIMMNOTUVX	excommunicative
ACCEEIIMNNOORST	econometricians
ACCEEIINNOORSSS	concessionaires
	concessionaries
ACCEEIIOPPRRTTY	cryoprecipitate
ACCEEILMOOPRSTV	overcomplicates
ACCEEILMOPRSSTU	proceleusmatics
ACCEEILNNORTTVY	concentratively
ACCEEILNORTTUVY	counteractively
ACCEEILNORTTXYY	oxytetracycline
ACCEEINNNOORRTT	reconcentration
ACCEEINNNOORSSS	reconnoissances
ACCEEINNOORRSST	reconsecrations
ACCEEINNORSSTTV	contractiveness
ACCEELMMNNOOPSS	commonplaceness
ACCEFFIIILNOSUY	inefficaciously
ACCEGGHINNNORTU	counterchanging
ACCEGGHINNORRTU	countercharging
ACCEGHIIILNNORT	anticholinergic
ACCEGHIILLOOOST	stoechiological
ACCEGHIIOPPRRSTY	psychogeriatric
ACCEGHILLLNOOTY	technologically
ACCEGHILLNOPSYY	psychogenically
ACCEGHIMNNORRTU	countermarching
ACCEGIIILMMNORS	commercialising
ACCEGIIILMMNORZ	commercializing
ACCEGIILLLLOOXY	lexicologically
ACCEGIILMNNORTU	counterclaiming
ACCEGIILNNOPSTU	conceptualising
ACCEGIILNNOPTUZ	conceptualizing
ACCEGIIMMNNOTUX	excommunicating
ACCEGILLLNOOSYY	synecologically
ACCEHHILLMNOOPR	chloramphenicol
ACCEHHILLMOOPTY	photochemically
ACCEHHILLNOPRSS	chancellorships
ACCEHHIMOOPRTTU	chemautotrophic
ACCEHIIILMOOPRR	microaerophilic
ACCEHIILLPRRTYY	hypercritically
ACCEHIILNORSSTT	interscholastic
ACCEHIIMNOPRSTY	psychometrician
ACCEHIIMNORSTTY	actinochemistry
ACCEHILLMNOORTY	homocentrically
ACCEHILLMOOPRTY	chemotropically
ACCEHILMMNOPSST	accomplishments
ACCEHINNOOPRRTT	anthropocentric
ACCEHLLMNOOSTUY	collenchymatous
ACCEIIILNNOORST	reconciliations
ACCEIIILOSSTTVY	viscoelasticity
ACCEIIIMMNNOTUV	incommunicative
ACCEIILMMNOTUVY	communicatively
ACCEIILNNOPSTTU	centuplications
ACCEIILOPPRSSUY	perspicaciously
ACCEIIMMNNOOTUX	excommunication
ACCEIIMMNNOTUUV	uncommunicative
ACCEIINNOORSSTT	concretisations
ACCEIINNOORSTTZ	concretizations
ACCEILMOOPRRSTU	ultramicroscope
ACCEIMMNOORSTUX	excommunicators
ACCEIMMNOORTUXY	excommunicatory
ACCELLNOOOSUUVV	convolvulaceous
ACCFIINNOOORTTT	act of contrition
ACCGHIIIILLOOOST	stoichiological
ACCGHILLLNOOORY	chronologically
ACCGHILLLOOPSYY	psychologically
ACCGHILLOOPRSYY	hygroscopically
ACCGIILLLMOOSUY	musicologically
ACCGIILLLOOOTXY	toxicologically
ACCHHILMOOOPPST	ophthalmoscopic
ACCHIIINNNOOSST	cinchonisations
ACCHIIINNNOOSTZ	cinchonizations
ACCHIILNNOORTTY	thyrocalcitonin
ACCIILLLPRSTUUY	pisciculturally
ACCIILLMMNOSTUY	communistically
ACCIIMMNNORSTTUU	circumnutations
ACCIJLLNNNOOTUY	conjunctionally
ACCILMOOPRRSTUY	ultramicroscopy
ACCINOOORRSSTTV	vasoconstrictor
ACDDEEEELNPRRSU	supercalendered
ACDDEEEEFFINSSST	disaffectedness
ACDDEEEHHIKNSST	thickheadedness
ACDDEEEHLNORSST	coldheartedness
ACDDEEEIIMNOOST	adenoidectomies
ACDDEEFHIINNRSS	disenfranchised
ACDDEEHIINSSTTU	Dutch East Indies
ACDDEFLMOOORSSH	Sword of Damocles
ACDDEIIMMNNOOST	discommendation
ACDDIIIIILNSTUV	individualistic
ACDEEEFHHIRSTTT	featherstitched
ACDEEEGKLMNNOTW	acknowledgement
ACDEEEHIINNOPTT	acetophenetidin
ACDEEEIILOPRSSV	overspecialised
ACDEEEIILOPRSVZ	overspecialized
ACDEEEILLORSSTY	electrodialyses
ACDEEEILNNNSSST	clandestineness
ACDEEEINNORSSST	considerateness
ACDEEEMNOOPRSTV	overcompensated
ACDEEFFIINRSSTV	diffractiveness
ACDEEFFIMORRSTT	diffractometers
ACDEEFGILNRSSSU	disgracefulness
ACDEEFHIINNRSSS	disenfranchises
ACDEEFIIINORSTT	desertification
ACDEEFLMNNORRRT	Clermont-Ferrand
ACDEEGGHIMOOPRS	geodemographics
ACDEEGIIILLMOOP	epidemiological
ACDEEGILLLOOSTY	dysteleological
ACDEEGILLOORRTY	Coleridge-Taylor
ACDEEGIMNORSSTU	discouragements
ACDEEGKLMNNOSTW	acknowledgments
ACDEEGNNOPPRSUY	pseudopregnancy
ACDEEHHILMNOORT	dichloromethane
ACDEEHIIIKNNRRS	Kincardineshire
ACDEEHIIINNNRSST	disinheritances
ACDEEHIILNOOPRT	radiotelephonic
ACDEEHILLMNORTY	endothermically
ACDEEHIMNNNSSTT	disenchantments
ACDEEHIMNOORSTU	echinodermatous
ACDEEIIILMNPSTT	simplicidentate
ACDEEIIILLMNORTT	dominical letter
ACDEEIIILLMORTUY	eudiometrically
ACDEEIIILLORSSTY	electrodialysis
ACDEEIIILNNORSTY	inconsiderately

ACDEEIIMMOORRRT	radiomicrometer
ACDEEIIMMOOSSTT	mastoidectomies
ACDEEIIMNNOORTT	codetermination
ACDEEIINNOORRST	reconsideration
ACDEEILLNPPRRUY	perpendicularly
ACDEEILOPRSSSTY	perissodactyles
ACDEEIMMNNOORST	recommendations
ACDEEIMMNNORSTUY	semidocumentary
ACDEEIMNNOOPSST	decompensations
ACDEEINNNOORSST	recondensations
ACDEEIORSTTTUUV	autodestructive
ACDEELMOORRSSTU	sclerodermatous
ACDEEMMMNNNOSTT	Ten Commandments
ACDEFGHIINOOSTZ	sign of the zodiac
ACDEFIIIIMNNNOT	indemnification
ACDEFIIIINNORTT	denitrification
ACDEFIIIINNOSTT	identifications
ACDEFIIIINORSTV	diversification
ACDEFIIIINORTTV	devitrification
ACDEFIIILMNOSTU	demulsification
ACDEFIIILNNOTTY	confidentiality
ACDEFIIIMMORSSY	fideicommissary
ACDEFIIIMNOSTTY	demystification
ACDEFIILNNNNOOT	nonconfidential
ACDEGGHILLOOORY	hydrogeological
ACDEGHIILNNNSTY	disenchantingly
ACDEGHILMOPRSTY	dermatoglyphics
ACDEGIIIILMNNRS	decriminalising
ACDEGIIIILMNNRZ	decriminalizing
ACDEGIILLOOSSTT	dialectologists
ACDEGIILNNOORST	reconsolidating
ACDEGINORSTTTUU	autodestructing
ACDEHHIOOPRRSST	archpriesthoods
ACDEHHLMMOOOSUY	homochlamydeous
ACDEHIILOPSSTTY	sophisticatedly
ACDEHIINOPSSTTU	unsophisticated
ACDEHILLMORRTVY	hydrometrically
ACDEHILLNOOPRTY	polychlorinated
ACDEHILLNOORRSY	hydrocorallines
ACDEHILNNOSSSTU	Schouten Islands
ACDEHILOORSSSUU	dolichosauruses
ACDEHINOORRSSTT	trisoctahedrons
ACDEHLLOOPRSSUY	pseudoscholarly
ACDEHLMMNOOOSUY	monochlamydeous
ACDEHMNNOOORSTU	enchondromatous
ACDEIIIILMNNOORT	omnidirectional
ACDEIIIILNORRSTY	discretionarily
ACDEIIINNNOORST	inconsideration
ACDEIIINNORRSTY	indiscretionary
ACDEIIILLMNORSTY	modernistically
ACDEIIILLNOOPRTY	periodontically
ACDEIIILNOOORST	reconsolidation
ACDEIIILNOOOSST	decolonisations
ACDEIIILNOOOSTZ	decolonizations
ACDEIIILNOOORSST	decolorisations
ACDEIIILNOOORSTZ	decolorizations
ACDEIMNNOOOORSU	andromonoecious
ACDFHIIIIMNOSTU	humidifications
ACDFIIIMNNOORST	disconfirmation
ACDGHIMNNOOPRRY	gynandromorphic
ACDGIILLLOSSTYY	dyslogistically
ACDGILNOOOPRRSS	Colorado Springs

ACDHHIINOOPRSSY	hypochondriasis
ACDHHIIOPRRSSST	harpsichordists
ACDHIIIILLMOOPRY	idiomorphically
ACDHIIIMNOOOSTT	dichotomisation
ACDHIIIMNOOOTTZ	dichotomization
ACDHILLOOPRRTYY	hydrotropically
ACDIIIILNNNOSST	disinclinations
ACDIIIIMNNORSST	discriminations
ACDIIIINRSSTUVY	vicissitudinary
ACDIIINNNOORSTT	indoctrinations
ACDIIINNNOOSTTU	discontinuation
ACDIILLNNNOOTUY	unconditionally
ACDIILNNOOOSSST	disconsolations
ACEEEEGILNORTTV	electronegative
ACEEEEFFILNNSSTU	ineffectualness
ACEEEEFFHHIRSSTTT	featherstitches
ACEEEEFHIMNNNRST	enfranchisement
ACEEEEFIIILMPTVX	exemplificative
ACEEEGHINNNOPRTT	parthenogenetic
ACEEEGIIILLNORTT	intercollegiate
ACEEEEGIKLLNNOTY	kenogenetically
ACEEEEGIMNOPRSTT	spermatogenetic
ACEEEHHHHLNOOPRX	hexachlorophene
ACEEEHHIINRSSTT	herestheticians
ACEEEHILLMNRTUY	hermeneutically
ACEEEHILLMOORST	cholesterolemia
ACEEEHLLMNNOPSY	myelencephalons
ACEEEHMMOORSTTY	haemocytometers
ACEEEHNORRSSSTU	treacherousness
ACEEEIILLLNSTTU	intellectualise
ACEEEIILLLNTTUZ	intellectualize
ACEEEIILMNNNSST	semicentennials
ACEEEIILOPRSSSV	overspecialises
ACEEEIILOPRSSVZ	overspecializes
ACEEEIINNQRSTU	quincentenaries
ACEEEIINPPRSSTT	precipitateness
ACEEEILNNOSSSST	coessentialness
ACEEEILNORRSSTV	correlativeness
ACEEEILNPSSSTUV	speculativeness
ACEEEIMMNOPRSSU	menispermaceous
ACEEEINNNRSSSSU	unnecessariness
ACEEEINOOPRSSTV	cooperativeness
ACEEEINORRSSTTV	retroactiveness
ACEEELLLNORTTVY	electrovalently
ACEEELMNOPRSTUX	counterexamples
ACEEEMNOOPRSSTV	overcompensates
ACEEEMNORRSSTUU	countermeasures
ACEEFFHNOORRSST	father confessor
ACEEFGIIMNNNSST	magnificentness
ACEEFGILNRRTTUU	ultracentrifuge
ACEEFHIIINORSTT	etherifications
ACEEFHILNNOPRSY	French Polynesia
ACEEFHLNOPRRSSU	reproachfulness
ACEEFIIILMNOPTX	exemplification
ACEEFIIINORSSTT	esterifications
ACEEFIILNPRSSSU	superficialness
ACEEFIINNORRSTT	confraternities
ACEEFIILNORSSSTU	lactiferousness
ACEEGHHIINOPRSS	hieracosphinges
ACEEGHINNOOPRTT	anthropogenetic
ACEEGHOOOOPPSSS	oesophagoscopes
ACEEGIIILLMOOPST	epistemological

ACEEGIILMMNNNOTU	immunogenetical
ACEEGIILMNOPSST	salpingectomies
ACEEGIINOPPRRTV	graviperception
ACEEGIINORRSTTT	gastroenteritic
ACEEGILLLNOPTYY	polygenetically
ACEEGILLNNOOTTY	ontogenetically
ACEEGILLNOORSTY	oestrogenically
ACEEHHIINOPRSSX	hieracosphinxes
ACEEHHILNNNOPRS	rhinencephalons
ACEEHHILNOORRTT	trichloroethane
ACEEHHIMNOORRTT	heterochromatin
ACEEHHIMOPRSSTT	chemotherapists
ACEEHHINOOPPRST	phosphocreatine
ACEEHIIILNPSSTT	licentiateships
ACEEHIILLLMORTY	heliometrically
ACEEHIILLMNRSTY	hemicrystalline
ACEEHIILLMPSTUY	euphemistically
ACEEHIILMOOPRRS	microaerophiles
ACEEHIILOORSTTY	heterosociality
ACEEHIINPPPRSST	apprenticeships
ACEEHILMOPPRRTY	hypermetropical
ACEEHILOORRSSST	atherosclerosis
ACEEHIMMNNORSSV	servomechanisms
ACEEHIMMOPSSTTY	sympathectomies
ACEEHINOOPRSTTU	Poitou-Charentes
ACEEIIINQSSSTUV	acquisitiveness
ACEEIILLLMNSTTU	intellectualism
ACEEIILLLNSTTTU	intellectualist
ACEEIILLLNTTTUY	intellectuality
ACEEIILLMOPRTYZ	piezometrically
ACEEIILLRRSSTTV	verticillasters
ACEEIILMMORSTVY	commiseratively
ACEEIILNNNNQSTU	quincentennials
ACEEIILNNNOOSTV	conventionalise
ACEEIILNNNOOTVZ	conventionalize
ACEEIILNNNOQSTU	inconsequential
ACEEIINOSSSSUVV	vivaciousnesses
ACEEIILLLMNOSSUY	miscellaneously
ACEEIILLLNNNOTTU	nonintellectual
ACEEIILLMMNOPRTY	complementarily
ACEEIILLMNOPTTVY	contemplatively
ACEEIILLMNORSSTV	Costermansville
ACEEIILLNNNOPTUXY	unexceptionally
ACEEIILLNNNOQSTUY	consequentially
ACEEIILLNOORSTTY	electrolysation
ACEEIILLNOORTTYZ	electrolyzation
ACEEIILMMMOORTVY	commemoratively
ACEEIILMMNNOOPTT	complementation
ACEEIILMMNOPRRTY	complementarity
ACEEIILMMNRSSSTY	symmetricalness
ACEEIILMMORRRTTU	ultramicrometer
ACEEIILMNNRSSTTU	semitranslucent
ACEEIILNNNNOSSSS	nonsensicalness
ACEEIILNNOQSSUUV	unequivocalness
ACEEIIMNNOOPRTTY	contemporaneity
ACEEIIMOOPRSSTTT	prostatectomies
ACEEINOOPRSTVV	provocativeness
ACEEINORRRRSTUV	resurrectionary
ACEELLOORSSTTUUU	Toulouse-Lautrec
ACEELMNOOQRRSUU	Lourenço Marques
ACEELNNNOOSSTUY	consentaneously
ACEEMNNOOOPRSTU	contemporaneous

ACEEOPPRRSSSTTU	streptocarpuses
ACEFGIIIILNSTVY	significatively
ACEFGIINNORSTTU	centrifugations
ACEFHILNNOPRTUY	hyperfunctional
ACEFIIIINNNOSTT	intensification
ACEFIIIINORSTVV	revivifications
ACEFIIIILMNNOOST	solemnification
ACEFIIINNOOPRST	personification
ACEFIIMNNOORRST	reconfirmations
ACEFINRRRSSTTUU	infrastructures
ACEGGHHIOOPPRTY	phytogeographic
ACEGGILLNNOOORT	rontgenological
ACEGHIIIMNNPSTY	pachymeningitis
ACEGHIIIMNPSSTY	metaphysicising
ACEGHIIIMNPSTYZ	metaphysicizing
ACEGHILLLOOPPSY	psephologically
ACEGHILLMORRTYY	hygrometrically
ACEGHILMNOORSST	schoolmastering
ACEGHILOOOORSTZ	archeozoologist
ACEGHIMMOOPRRTT	photogrammetric
ACEGHLLOOPSUYYZ	zygophyllaceous
ACEGIILLLMOOSSY	seismologically
ACEGIILLLMNOOSTY	neologistically
ACEGIILLMMNNOUY	immunogenically
ACEGIILLMNOORTY	goniometrically
ACEGIILLNRRSSTY	recrystallising
ACEGIILLNRRSTYZ	recrystallizing
ACEGIILLNRSSTYY	synergistically
ACEGIILMNOORRTT	trigonometrical
ACEGIILNNNORSTTU	interosculating
ACEGIILNNOSTTUX	contextualising
ACEGIILNNOTTUXZ	contextualizing
ACEGIIMNNOPRRSSU	superorganicism
ACEGIINNNORSTTU	counterstaining
ACEGIINNOOPRRRT	reincorporating
ACEGIINOOPRSTTV	prognosticative
ACEGIINOPRRSSTU	superorganicist
ACEGILLLLMNOOOTY	entomologically
ACEGILLNNOORSSY	congressionally
ACEGILLNORRSUUY	neurosurgically
ACEGILMNNOOOORST	conglomerations
ACEGILMOORSTUVV	cytomegalovirus
ACEGINOOPRRSSTY	crossopterygian
ACEHHHOORSSTTUW	Chatsworth House
ACEHHIILLMNPTTY	platyhelminthic
ACEHHIIPPRRSSTT	archpriestships
ACEHHILLPPRSYVY	hyperphysically
ACEHHILMOORSSST	schoolmasterish
ACEHHINOPPRSTTU	pithecanthropus
ACEHHINORRSSSTW	crashworthiness
ACEHHIOPPRSSTTY	psychotherapist
ACEHHIORSSSTUUV	ichthyosauruses
ACEHHLMOOOPPSST	ophthalmoscopes
ACEHIILLLLOOPRTY	heliotropically
ACEHIILLLLOPSSTY	phyllosilicates
ACEHIILLOPRRSTY	prehistorically
ACEHIILMMNNOSTT	Mont-Saint-Michel
ACEHIILOOPSTTTY	photoelasticity
ACEHIIMMMOPSTTY	sympathomimetic
ACEHIINOPPRSSST	spinthariscopes
ACEHIIOORRSSTTT	osteoarthritics
ACEHILLLNOORSTY	holocrystalline

ACEHILLMNOOPRXY	xenomorphically
ACEHILLMOOPRTTY	photometrically
ACEHILLMOPRSTYY	hypsometrically
ACEHILLNOPRSSTT	phallocentrists
ACEHILLNOPRSTYY	hypocrystalline
ACEHILMNOOPPTYY	lymphocytopenia
ACEHILOPSSTUXYY	psychosexuality
ACEHINOPRRSTUYY	neuropsychiatry
ACEHMNOOPRSSTUY	prosenchymatous
ACEIIIINNOSTTVV	antivivisection
ACEIIIILLMPSSSTY	pessimistically
ACEIIIILLNORSTTV	verticillations
ACEIIIILLNOSTVVY	vivisectionally
ACEIIILLNNOPRRTV	interprovincial
ACEIIILNPRSSTTU	spiritual incest
ACEIIIMMNOORSSS	commissionaires
ACEIIINOPQRSSTU	preacquisitions
ACEIIINORRRSTVX	Saint Croix River
ACEIILLMMNOPRTY	complimentarily
ACEIILLNNOOOSST	neocolonialists
ACEIILLORSTUVVY	voyeuristically
ACEIILMNNNOOSTV	conventionalism
ACEIILNNNOOSTTV	conventionalist
ACEIILNNNOOTTVY	conventionality
ACEIILNNOOORSST	recolonisations
ACEIILNNOOORSTZ	recolonizations
ACEIILNNOOPRSTT	introspectional
ACEIILNNOORSTTU	interosculation
ACEIILNPRRSTTVY	transcriptively
ACEIILPPRSSTTUY	superplasticity
ACEIIMMNNOORSTU	immunoreactions
ACEIIMNNOORSSSU	acrimoniousness
ACEIIMNOOPRSTTU	computerisation
ACEIIMNOOPRTTUZ	computerization
ACEIINNOOOPRRRT	reincorporation
ACEIINNOORSSTTV	conservationist
	conversationist
ACEIINNORRRSTUY	insurrectionary
ACEIINNORRRTTTU	counterirritant
ACEIINOOOPRSSTT	cooperationists
ACEIINOOPRSSTTV	contrapositives
ACEILLNOORRSTVY	controversially
ACEILMMMNOORSTY	monosymmetrical
ACEILMMNNOPRTUY	uncomplimentary
ACEILMNOOORSTUV	macroevolutions
ACEILNNNNNOOOTV	nonconventional
ACEILNNOORRSTUV	uncontroversial
ACEILOORRSSTTUW	watercolourists
ACEIMNNNOOPRSTU	pronunciamentos
ACEIMNOORRSSTUV	conservatoriums
ACEINNOORRSSSTU	contrariousness
ACEINNOORRSSSUV	carnivorousness
ACELNOOOPPRRSTU	counterproposal
ACELPRRRSSTTUUU	superstructural
ACELRRRSSTTTUUU	ultrastructures
ACEMNNNOOOPRRTY	noncontemporary
ACFFHKLNOORRSTU	Frankfurt School
ACFGIIIILNNNSTY	insignificantly
ACFHIIJLNNOORUW	Julian of Norwich
ACFIIIILMNOPSST	simplifications
ACFIIINNOOOPSST	opsonifications
ACFIILLMNNOTTUU	multifunctional

ACGGIINNNOOPRSTT	prognosticating
ACGHHIIIOOPRRST	historiographic
ACGHHIMOOOOPPRRT	microphotograph
	photomicrograph
ACGHHINOOOPPRTZ	photozincograph
ACGHHLOOOPPSTYY	psychopathology
ACGHIIIILNOPSSTT	antiphlogistics
ACGHIILLLOOPSVY	physiologically
ACGHILLLMOOOPRY	morphologically
ACGHILMOOORSSTT	chromatologists
ACGHIOPPRRSSTTY	cryptographists
ACGIIILLLNNSTTY	scintillatingly
ACGIIILNNPQTTUU	quintuplicating
ACGIIINNNNOOTTX	nonintoxicating
ACGIILLLLOSSTYY	syllogistically
ACGIILLLMMNOOUY	immunologically
ACGIILNNNOOSTTU	conglutinations
ACGIILNNOSSSSUU	Cassius Longinus
ACGIIMMNOOPRRSU	microsporangium
ACGIINNOOOPRSTT	prognostication
ACGILLOOOOPRTZ	protozoological
ACGILNOOPRSSSTY	laryngoscopists
ACGINOOOPRRSSTT	prognosticators
ACHHIILLLOOPPSY	philosophically
ACHHIILLNOOPPSU	unphilosophical
ACHHIMMOOORRSTT	orthochromatism
ACHHIMNOOOPPRRT	anthropomorphic
ACHHIOOPRRSTTYY	orthopsychiatry
ACHHLNOOOSTTUUY	autochthonously
ACHHMOOOOPPRRSTU	chromatophorous
ACHIIIMOOSSSSST	schistosomiasis
ACHIIINOOPSSSTT	sophistications
ACHIILLLOOSTYYZ	hylozoistically
ACHIIMMOPRSSSSY	commissaryships
ACHIINNNOORSSTY	synchronisation
ACHIINNNOORSTYZ	synchronization
ACHIIOPRSSSSTTY	astrophysicists
ACHIKLNNOOPPTTY	phytoplanktonic
ACHILLLORRTTUUY	horticulturally
ACHIOOPPRRRSSTU	procuratorships
ACHMNNNOORRTTUY	northcountryman
ACIIIILLMNOPSTTU	multiplications
ACIIILNNOPQTTUU	quintuplication
ACIILMMNOOOPSST	cosmopolitanism
ACIILMNNOOSSTUY	sanctimoniously
ACIIMMNOOPSSTTU	miscomputations
ACIIMNNOPSSTTUU	mispunctuations
ACIINNOOOPRSSTT	contrapositions
ACIMNOOOSSTTTXY	cytotaxonomists
ADDDEEEHNNNRSSU	underhandedness
ADDDEIIIINNOTUV	deindividuation
ADDEEEEEHLLNSSV	levelheadedness
ADDEEEEEHLNRRTTY	tenderheartedly
ADDEEEEGHNNORSSW	wrongheadedness
ADDEEEHIKNNRSST	kindheartedness
ADDEEEHNNORSSTW	downheartedness
ADDEEEIIJLMMNNT	middelmannetjie
ADDEEEILNNSSSVY	seven deadly sins
ADDEEFIILORRSTT	Distrito Federal
ADDEEGGHINNORTY	dehydrogenating
ADDEEGHINNOORTY	dehydrogenation
ADDEEIIILNRSSTU	deindustrialise

ADDEEIIIILNRSTUZ	deindustrialize
ADDEEEJKLNNOORSS	Nordenskjöld Sea
ADDEFGIKLLLOORS	Kolar Gold Fields
ADDEFIIILLNNRSSY	Friendly Islands
ADDEGGIIINORRST	rigid designator
ADDEGILNNNRSTUY	understandingly
ADDEHHILOPRSSST	stadholderships
ADDEHHILOPRSSTT	stadtholdership
ADDEIIIIILNSTUV	individualities
ADDEIIIIILNRSSUV	individualisers
ADDEIIIIILNRSUVZ	individualizers
ADDGIIIIILNNSSUV	individualising
ADDGIIIIILNNUVZ	individualizing
ADDHIJMOOORSTUX	Orthodox Judaism
ADEEEEGILNORRVZ	overgeneralized
ADEEEEHNNOPRSST	openheartedness
ADEEEEILLLMNRSS	Ellesmere Island
ADEEEEIMNNRSSTT	determinateness
ADEEEEINNPRRTTT	interpenetrated
ADEEEFHNORSSSTT	softheartedness
ADEEEFIMNRSSTTU	disfeaturements
ADEEEFINNORSSTT	defenestrations
ADEEEGGHILMMNRS	sledgehammering
ADEEEEGHINNRSST	nearsightedness
ADEEEGIILMNRSST	legerdemainists
ADEEEGIKNNPRRRT	prekindergarten
ADEEEGIKNNRRTES	kindergarteners
ADEEEGILMNNNSTT	disentanglement
ADEEEGOPRRRSTUV	daguerreotypers
ADEEEHILNNORSST	lionheartedness
ADEEEHILNOOPRST	radiotelephones
ADEEEIIINNNSSST	Seine-Saint-Denis
ADEEEIILMNNRTTY	indeterminately
ADEEEIILMNNSTTS	sentimentalised
ADEEEIILMNNSTTZ	sentimentalized
ADEEEIILMNRTTVY	determinatively
ADEEEIIMMQRSSUV	demisemiquavers
ADEEEIIMOORRSST	diastereoisomer
ADEEEELLLMNOPTVY	developmentally
ADEEEEMNNRSSTTTU	understatements
ADEEFFGIIINNRTT	differentiating
ADEEFFIIINNORTT	differentiation
ADEEFFIINORRSTT	differentiators
ADEEFFIMNORSSTT	disafforestment
ADEEFIIINRRSTTT	interstratified
ADEEFIILNNQSSUU	unqualifiedness
ADEEFILNSSSSTTU	distastefulness
ADEEFIMNNOORRST	foreordainments
ADEEGGMMNORRTTU	Götterdämmerung
ADEEGHIILNNRSTY	dishearteningly
ADEEGHIIMNNPPRS	misapprehending
ADEEGIIINNPRSST	pedestrianising
ADEEGIIINNPRSTZ	pedestrianizing
ADEEGIILNNOPRSS	depersonalising
ADEEGIILNNOPRSZ	depersonalizing
ADEEGIIMNNRSTTU	underestimating
ADEEGIIMNOOORRT	radiogoniometer
ADEEGIINNOPQRTU	equiponderating
ADEEGIINNORRSTT	redintegrations
ADEEGIINOPRSTUU	Portuguese India
ADEEGIINORRSSTT	deregistrations
ADEEGIOPRRSTTUV	daguerreotypist
ADEEHHNOOPPSSYY	adenohypophyses
ADEEHILLMNNRSTT	disenthrallment
ADEEHILMNNRSSTT	disenthralments
ADEEHILNNNORRRT	Northern Ireland
ADEEHILNNORRSTU	Southern Ireland
ADEEHLNNNORSTUY	Ashton-under-Lyne
ADEEIIIILORRRST	territorialised
ADEEIIIILORRRTTZ	territorialized
ADEEIIIMNNNORTT	indetermination
ADEEIIINNOSSSTT	desensitisation
ADEEIIINNOSSTTZ	desensitization
ADEEIIMNNOPRTTU	unpremeditation
ADEEIIMNNOPSSSS	impassionedness
ADEEIIMNNORSTTU	underestimation
ADEEIINNNOOPSST	opinionatedness
ADEEIINPSSSTTUV	disputativeness
ADEEILMNORSTTVY	demonstratively
ADEEIMNNORRSSST	arrondissements
ADEEIMNNORSTTUV	undemonstrative
ADEFFHINOSSSST	standoffishness
ADEFIIINNOSSSTT	disinfestations
ADEFIINNOOORRST	foreordinations
ADEGGIIIINNRTT	interdigitating
ADEGHIINNOORSTY	hydrogenisation
ADEGHIINNOORTYZ	hydrogenization
ADEGHIMNNORSTUY	Mothering Sunday
ADEGHLLMORRTUVY	hydrometallurgy
ADEGHNNOOOOPRRSY	androgynophores
ADEGIIIMNORRSSY	Missionary Ridge
ADEGIIIINNORSTT	disintegrations
ADEGIIIOPRRSTTT	prestidigitator
ADEGIINNOPRRSTU	superordinating
ADEGILLNNOQRTUY	grandiloquently
ADEHHIIMMOPRRST	hermaphroditism
ADEHHINOOPPSSYY	adenohypophysis
ADEHHIOPRRSSTTY	hydrotherapists
ADEHIINNOOPSTTY	dehypnotisation
ADEHIINNOOPTTYZ	dehypnotization
ADEHIKNNOPRRSST	Perth and Kinross
ADEHIMOOPRSSTTY	dermatophytosis
ADEHLNNOPRSSTUU	Southern Uplands
ADEHLNORRSTTWWY	northwestwardly
ADEHLORSSTTUWWY	southwestwardly
ADEIIIIILMRSSST	dissimilarities
ADEIIIILNPRSSTTU	platitudinisers
ADEIIIILNPRSTTUZ	platitudinizers
ADEIIINORSSSTTT	dissertationist
ADEIIJLNPRRSTUU	jurisprudential
ADEIILMNNOORTTU	intermodulation
ADEIIILNORRSSTTX	sinistrodextral
ADEIIILNORRSTTVY	dorsiventrality
ADEIIIMNNOPPSSTT	disappointments
ADEILMNNOPRSSUY	Duplessis-Mornay
ADEILMNORRSSTTU	ultramodernists
ADEILMOPSTTUUUY	pseudomutuality
ADEILNOORRSTTVY	dorsoventrality
ADEINOOORRSTTTX	dextrorotations
ADGHIINNNOSTTTW	notwithstanding
ADGIIIILNNPSTTU	platitudinising
ADGIIIILNNPTTUZ	platitudinizing
ADGIIIILNNRSSTU	industrialising
ADGIIIILNNRSTUZ	industrializing

ADGIIILNNOPPSTY	disappointingly
ADGLMOOOORSSSTU	Mato Grosso do Sul
ADHIILMNOORSSUY	disharmoniously
ADHIIMOOOPPRSTT	diaphototropism
ADHIKMNNOOOORSU	Norodom Sihanouk
AEEEEFKKMNOOPSW	Okefenokee Swamp
AEEEEEFLNRSSSSTU	featurelessness
AEEEEGILNORRSVZ	overgeneralizes
AEEEEHMNOPPRRST	ephemeropterans
AEEEEIILMNPRSTX	experimentalise
AEEEEIILMNPRTXZ	experimentalize
AEEEEILNNPRRRTU	entrepreneurial
AEEEEIMNNPRSSTT	intemperateness
AEEEEIMNNRSTTVW	interweavements
AEEEEINNPRRSTTT	interpenetrates
AEEEEINPRSSTTV	representatives
AEEEELMNRSSSSSU	measurelessness
AEEEEFGIIORRRRST	refrigeratories
AEEEEFIILNPRRTTY	preferentiality
AEEEEFILMMOPRST	Temple of Artemis
AEEEEFKNOPRSSTTV	Parts of Kesteven
AEEEEGHINNOPRSST	parthenogenesis
AEEEEGILLMNNNSST	gentlemanliness
AEEEEGILMNNNSSSS	meaninglessness
AEEEEGILNNRSSSTV	everlastingness
AEEEEGIMNOPRSSST	spermatogenesis
AEEEEHHIMOPRRSTT	thermotherapies
AEEEEHIIMNPPRSSV	misapprehensive
AEEEEHILLMNNOPPY	epiphenomenally
AEEEEHILNORRSSTT	northeasterlies
AEEEEHILORSSSTTU	southeasterlies
AEEEEHILORSTTUXY	heterosexuality
AEEEEHIMNOSSTTUV	South Vietnamese
AEEEEIILMMNPRSTX	experimentalism
AEEEEIILMNNSSSTT	sentimentalises
AEEEEIILMNNSSTTZ	sentimentalizes
AEEEEIILMNPRSTTX	experimentalist
AEEEEIIMNNOPRTTX	experimentation
AEEEEIINNNSSTTTV	inattentiveness
AEEEEIINNOPRSSTV	inoperativeness
AEEEEILMNORRSTTV	intervalometers
AEEEEILMNPPRSSTU	supplementaries
AEEEEILNOPRSSTUV	superelevations
AEEEEILNPRSSSTUV	superlativeness
AEEEEILNRRRSSSTT	terrestrialness
AEEEEIMNNORSSSTV	normativenesses
AEEEEIMNOPRRSSTX	extemporariness
AEEEEIMNPRRRSSUU	supernumeraries
AEEEEINNOPRRSSTT	representations
AEEEELMNNOQRRSSU	quarrelsomeness
AEEEEMNOPRRSSTUW	Weston-super-Mare
AEEEEMNORSSSSSTV	overassessments
AEEEFGHHLLNNOORTT	Angel of the North
AEEEFGHINOOPRRTW	weatherproofing
AEEEFGIILPRRTUVY	prefiguratively
AEEEFGIMNNRRSTTU	transfiguration
AEEEFIIINRRSSTTT	interstratifies
AEEEFIILNOOPRSSS	professionalise
AEEEFIILNOOPRSSZ	professionalize
AEEEFIIMNNORSSTV	informativeness
AEEEFNNNORSSTTUU	unfortunateness
AEEEGGHHOOPPRRTY	phytogeographer
AEEEGGHNNNOOPRRST	roentgenographs
AEEEGGIIINNRSTTV	reinvestigating
AEEEGGIINNORRRTT	reinterrogating
AEEEGGIINORSSSTT	segregationists
AEEEGHHLOOPPRTTY	telephotography
AEEEGHHLORSSSSTUU	slaughterhouses
AEEEGHIIILLPRSTT	Tiglath-pileser I
AEEEGHIIMNOPRSSV	overemphasising
AEEEGHIIMNOPRSVZ	overemphasizing
AEEEGHIKLMNNNORS	Kamerlingh-Onnes
AEEEGHILNOPRSSST	selenographists
AEEEGHINNOOPRSST	anthropogenesis
AEEEGHNNOOPRRTTY	rontgenotherapy
AEEEGIIIILLNNSSTT	intelligentsias
AEEEGIIINNNSTTTW	Wittgensteinian
AEEEGIIINNORSTTV	reinvestigation
AEEEGIILNORRTTVY	interrogatively
AEEEGIINNNOORSTT	roentgenisation
AEEEGIINNNOORTTZ	roentgenization
AEEEGIINNOORRRTT	reinterrogation
AEEEGIINOORRRSTT	interrogatories
AEEEGIINOPRRRSTT	preregistration
AEEEGIINORRSSTTT	gastroenteritis
AEEEGIINORRSSTTV	tergiversations
AEEEGILNRRSSSTVY	transgressively
AEEEGILRRTTTUUXZ	Tuxtla Gutiérrez
AEEEGINNNOSSSSUU	sanguineousness
AEEEGLMNNNNOORTV	nongovernmental
AEEEHHHIINOPRRRS	herniorrhaphies
AEEEHHHILLNNOPPT	phenolphthalein
AEEEHHIJNOSSSTVW	Jehovah's Witness
AEEEHIILMOOPSTTU	epitheliomatous
AEEEHIIMNNOPPRSS	misapprehension
AEEEHIKLNNOPRTUY	phenylketonuria
AEEEHINPPPPRRSSW	whippersnappers
AEEEIIILLMNORSSS	millionairesses
AEEEIIILNSSSTTTX	existentialists
AEEEIIILORRRSSTT	territorialises
AEEEIIILORRRSTTZ	territorializes
AEEEIIINOORRSTTX	exteriorisation
AEEEIIINOORRTTXZ	exteriorization
AEEEIILLNNOPRSTT	interpellations
AEEEIILLORRRTTXY	exterritorially
AEEEIILMNNSSSTTT	sentimentalists
AEEEIILNNOPPRTTY	plenipotentiary
AEEEIILNOORRSTUV	revolutionaries
AEEEIIMNNOPRSSTT	presentationism
AEEEIIMNOOPRSSTTX	extemporisation
AEEEIIMNOOPRTTXZ	extemporization
AEEEIIMNOORSSTTV	overestimations
AEEEIINNOPRSTTT	interpretations
AEEEIINNOPRSSTTT	presentationist
AEEEILLMNNNORTVY	environmentally
AEEEILLMNPPRSTUY	supplementarily
AEEEILMNNOOPPRUU	pleuropneumonia
AEEEILMNNOPPSTTU	supplementation
AEEEILNNOPSSSSSS	passionlessness
AEEEILOOPPRSTTVY	postoperatively
AEEEIMNNOOPPRRTT	reapportionment
AEEEIMNNOPRSSTTU	importunateness
AEEEIMORSSSSSTTT	toastmistresses
AEENNNOOPSSSSSTU	spontaneousness

AEFHHLNNOPRSTWY	halfpennyworths
AEFIIIILLMNNSTY	infinitesimally
AEFIILMNOOPRSSS	professionalism
AEFIILNOOPRSSST	professionalist
AEFIILNORSSSTTU	flirtatiousness
AEFIIMNNOORSSSU	omnifariousness
AEFIINOPRSSSSU	fissiparousness
AEFILNNNOOOPRSS	nonprofessional
AEGGHHINOOPPRRT	rephotographing
AEGGHINNOOPRSTV	photoengravings
AEGGIILNNORRTTY	interrogatingly
AEGHHIIMNNORSTT	Nottinghamshire
AEGHHIIMNNRSSST	nightmarishness
AEGHHIIOOPRRRST	historiographer
AEGHHLMOPPRSSTY	plethysmographs
AEGHIILLOPRSSST	legislatorships
AEGHIIMNNOOOSST	homogenisation
AEGHIIMNNOOOSTZ	homogenizations
AEGHILMOORSSTTU	rheumatologists
AEGHIOOOPPPRRSS	prosopographies
AEGHLLMOOPPRSSY	megasporophylls
AEGHOOOPPPRRRSS	prosopographers
AEGIIILMNNOPRSS	impersonalising
AEGIIIILMNNOPRSZ	impersonalizing
AEGIIIMNNORRSTT	intermigrations
AEGIIINNNOORSTT	nitrogenisation
AEGIIINNNOORTTZ	nitrogenization
AEGIIINNNRSSTTT	intransigentist
AEGIIINNOORRSTV	reinvigorations
AEGIIINNORSSTTT	integrationists
AEGIILMNORSTTUV	overstimulating
AEGIILNOORRRTTY	interrogatorily
AEGIILLNOOPRRSSY	progressionally
AEGILLNOPSTTUXY	expostulatingly
AEGILMNOOPSSTTU	pneumatologists
AEHHHOOOOPPRSSTT	orthophosphates
AEHHHIIILRRSSTWW	Lewis with Harris
AEHHIILLLLRSSSY	shillyshalliers
AEHHIIMNOPRRSTT	therianthropism
AEHHIIOPPRSSTTY	physiotherapist
AEHHINOPPRSSTTY	hypnotherapists
AEHIIMMNNOOOPRST	enantiomorphism
AEHIINNOSSSTTYZ	synthesizations
AEHIINOPRRSSTTT	trainspotterish
AEHIMNOOPRRSTTT	anthropometrist
AEHLMNNOOPRRSTT	Palmerston North
AEIIIILMNRSSSTT	ministerialists
AEIIIKNNSSSTTTV	Saint Kitts-Nevis
AEIIIILORRRSSTTT	territorialists
AEIIILLLNOQRTUVY	ventriloquially
AEIIILLNNNNOTTUV	unintentionally
AEIIILLNOOPPRSTY	prepositionally
AEIIILLNOORRTUVY	revolutionarily
AEIILMMNNRSSTTU	instrumentalism
AEIILMNNOOPRSTT	metropolitanism
AEIILMNNRSSTTTU	instrumentalist
AEIILMNNRSTTTUV	instrumentality
AEIILMNOOPRSSTY	polymerisations
AEIILMNOOPRSTVZ	polymerizations
AEIILNNNORSSTUV	involuntariness
AEIILNOOPRSSTTY	proselytisation
AEIILNOOPRSTTYZ	proselytization
AEIIMMNNORSSSTTY	symmetrisations
AEIIMMNNORSSTTYZ	symmetrizations
AEIIMMNNNORSTTTU	instrumentation
AEIIMMNNORRSSSST	retransmissions
AEIINOORRSSSTTT	restorationists
AEIINOPRRSSSSTU	pressurisations
AEIINOPRRSSSTUZ	pressurizations
AEIKLMMNNOOPRST	Palmer-Tomkinson
AEIKLMNNOPRSSTU	unsportsmanlike
AEILNOOOPPRRTTY	proportionately
AEIMMNNNOORSTUU	Mourne Mountains
AEIMNNNOOSSSTUU	mountainousness
AELLMNNOOOPPRST	monopropellants
AFGGIIMNNORRSTY	transmogrifying
AFGHLMOOOOPRRTU	photofluorogram
AGGHILNOOPRSSTY	pharyngologists
AGHHHILOOOPPRTT	photolithograph
AGHHIILLLLNSSYY	shillyshallying
AGHHIIMNOOPSSTT	opisthognathism
AGHHILLMOOOPSTT	ophthalmologist
AGHHINOOOPSSTTU	opisthognathous
AGHHOOOOPPPRRTTY	phototopography
AGHHOOOOPPPRRTYY	phototypography
AGHIILMNOOOSSTTY	mythologisation
AGHIILMNOOOTTYZ	mythologization
AGHILNOOOPRSSTT	anthropologists
AGIIILMNNNOOPRS	pronominalising
AGIIILMNNNOOPRZ	pronominalizing
AGIIINNORRSSSTT	transistorising
AGIIINNORRSSTTZ	transistorizing
AGIILMNOOSSSTTU	numismatologist
AGIINNOOOPPRRTT	proportionating
AHHIILNOPPRSSTT	philanthropists
AHHILLMOOOPPRSY	moral philosophy
AHHILNOOOPPRSTY	phosphorylation
AHHINOOOPPRSSTT	anthroposophist
AHIIIMOPPRSTTUY	hypopituitarism
AHIJLMNOOOPRSTU	photojournalism
AHIJLNOOOPRSTTU	photojournalist
AHINOOOPRRSSTTT	phototransistor
AIIIIILLNOQRSTUV	inquisitorially
AIIIILNNOSSTTTU	intuitionalists
AIIIILNOORSSTTV	vitriolisations
AIIIILNOORSTTVZ	vitriolizations
AIIIINOOPRRSSTT	prioritisations
AIIILLNNOSTTTUY	institutionally
AIILLLLMNOPSSUUY	pusillanimously
AIILLNOOOPPRSTY	propositionally
AIILLNOOPPSSTUY	suppositionally
AIILMNNOOOOPSST	monopolisations
AIILMNNOOOOPSTZ	monopolizations
AIILNOOOPPRRTTY	proportionality
BBBBEEFGIIILRTT	flibbertigibbet
BBCEEILMNOSSSTU	combustibleness
BBCEGIINORRSSUV	oversubscribing
BBCHIIIIILLOPST	bibliophilistic
BBDDEILMMNOOPRY	mind-body problem
BBEEEGHIILLNNSW	New English Bible
BBEEEIILMMRSSSU	semisubmersible
BBEHILMMMOOORST	thromboembolism
BCCCEEEHHILNPRU	Chechen Republic
BCCDEEEEIJKOSUV	České Budějovice

BCCEEEEIILMNNOSU	bioluminescence
BCCEEEIMNNPRSUU	superincumbence
BCCEEEILNORRSTTU	reconstructible
BCCEEIMNNPRSUUY	superincumbency
BCCEEJNORSSTTUU	countersubjects
BCCHINOOOPRSSST	bronchoscopists
BCDDEEIIIILSTTU	deductibilities
BCDDGILLLNOORUY	bloodcurdlingly
BCDEEEIILNRRSSU	irreducibleness
BCDEEEIMMNNRSTU	disencumberment
BCDEEFIIIILNTTY	indefectibility
BCDEHIOORRSSSTT	Scottish Borders
BCDEIIILOPRRTUY	reproducibility
BCDEIIILRSTTTUY	destructibility
BCEEEEHLLOOPRSSS	phleboscleroses
BCEEEEILNNORSSTV	convertibleness
BCEEEEILNPSSSSTU	susceptibleness
BCEEGHIILNOOOST	biotechnologies
BCEEEHILLOOPRSSS	phlebosclerosis
BCEEEIIILMPPRRST	imperscriptible
	imprescriptible
BCEEEILNOPRRSSTU	corruptibleness
BCEEEINORSSSTTUV	obstructiveness
BCEEGHIILNOOOSTT	biotechnologist
BCEHIIIIINOSTTX	exhibitionistic
BCEIIILMNOPTTTY	contemptibility
BCEIIILMOPRSSTY	compressibility
BCEIIILMPPRRSTY	imprescriptibly
BCEIIMMNOORSSSU	subcommissioner
BCGHIILNOOOORST	chronobiologist
BCGHIILOOOPSSTY	psychobiologist
BCGIIIIILNORRTY	incorrigibility
BCGIIILMOOORSST	microbiologists
BCGIIILOOOOSSST	sociobiologists
BCIINOORSSSTTTU	obstructionists
BCINNNOOORRTTUY	noncontributory
BDDEEIIMRRSTTTU	distributed term
BDEEEEHILLMORSV	overembellished
BDEEEGIMMNOSSTU	disemboguements
BDEEEEIINNNORSTZ	dinitrobenzenes
BDEEEEILMMNOSSTW	disembowelments
BDEEFIIIILNNSTY	indefensibility
BDEEFLMNNOORRUY	ferromolybdenum
BDEEIIIILNNSSSV	indivisibleness
BDEFGILLNOOOORW	Robin Goodfellow
BDEGGIIILNNOSSS	disobligingness
BDEGIIIIILNSTTY	indigestibility
BDEGIILLNOOSSTU	bloodguiltiness
BDEHIILOORSSTTT	bloodthirstiest
BDEIIINORRSSTTU	redistributions
BDFFIIIILMNNORUU	infundibuliform
BDIIIIILLNOSSTUY	indissolubility
BEEEEHILLMORSSV	overembellishes
BEEEGGILNSSSSTU	suggestibleness
BEEEGIILNNNSSUV	unbelievingness
BEEEIINNNORRTTZ	trinitrobenzene
BEEEILNNOPRSSSS	responsibleness
BEEELMNOORSSSTU	troublesomeness
BEEGHIILNNORSSU	neighbourliness
BEEHIINOPRSSTV	prohibitiveness
BEEHINOORRSSSUV	herbivorousness
BEEHLOOORRSSTTU	troubleshooters

BEEIIIILNNSTTXY	inextensibility
BEEIIIILRRRSTVY	irreversibility
BEEINNORSSSTUUV	unobtrusiveness
BEGHHINOOOPTUUY	Houphouet-Boigny
BEGHILNOOORSTTU	troubleshooting
BEGIIIIILLLNTTY	intelligibility
BEGIILNOOORSSTU	neurobiologists
BEGILNNOOORSSTT	Toronto Blessing
BEHIIIIKLLORRSU	Kirribilli House
BEIIIIILMOPSSST	impossibilities
BEIIIIILMRRSSTY	irremissibility
BEIIIIILRRSSTTY	irresistibility
BEIMNORSSSTUUU	rumbustiousness
BEINOOOPPRRSSSU	opprobriousness
BENNNOOPRRTTTUU	Burton-upon-Trent
BGHIILOOOOPSSTT	photobiologists
BGIILLMMNNOOSUU	immunoglobulins
BHIIIINOOPRSSTT	prohibitionists
CCCDDEEEEENNNOSS	condescendences
CCCDEEHIIOOPRST	cercopithecoids
CCCDEIIMNOORTTU	conductiometric
CCCDGIILOOORSTU	glucocorticoids
CCCEEEEHHHIINNRS	chincherinchees
CCCEEEHILNORSTT	electrotechnics
CCCEEEGHIKNNORTU	counterchecking
CCCEEEHLMOOSTTYY	cholecystectomy
CCCEEEIILMNOORRT	microelectronic
CCCEIIIMPPRRSTU	circumscriptive
CCCIIIIMNOPRRSTU	circumscription
CCCIIILMNOORSTUU	circumlocutions
CCDDEEEGILNNNOSY	condescendingly
CCDEEENNNOORSSU	unconcernedness
CCDEEEENNNNOSSTU	unconnectedness
CCDEEEENNOOPRRSS	correspondences
CCDEEEIMNNORSSTT	disconcertments
CCDEEINOPRSTUUV	superconductive
CCDEENNORRSTTUU	unreconstructed
CCDEGIILNNORSTY	disconcertingly
CCDEGINNOPRSTUU	superconducting
CCDEHINOOOPTTUV	photoconductive
CCDEIIOOORRSSTT	corticosteroids
CCDEINNOOPRSTUU	superconduction
CCDEINNNOORSSTU	deconstructions
CCDENOOPRRSSTUU	superconductors
CCDHINNOOOOPTTU	photoconduction
CCDHNOOOOPRSTTU	photoconductors
CCEEEEEFLNNORST	teleconferences
CCEEEEEFILNRRST	Fertile Crescent
CCEEEELOOPRRRTT	electroreceptor
CCEEEEMMMNNORST	recommencements
CCEEEFIINNOORST	confectioneries
CCEEEHHNOOPPRSS	phosphorescence
CCEEEHILMORSSTT	electrochemists
CCEEEEHILOOPRRTT	electrophoretic
CCEEEIIKLNORSTT	electrokinetics
CCEEEEILNNNOOSTT	teleconnections
CCEEEEINNORRSSST	incorrectnesses
CCEEEINNOSSSTUV	consecutiveness
CCEEFFIIIINNSSU	insufficiencies
CCEEGIIINNNNNOV	inconveniencing
CCEEGIILLOOSSST	ecclesiologists
CCEEGIINNNNORTT	interconnecting

CCEEGIINOSSTTTY	cytogeneticists
CCEEGINNOOOPRST	roentgenoscopic
CCEEHIIILMNORST	heliocentricism
CCEEHIIILNORTTY	heliocentricity
CCEEHIIIMOORSTT	stoicheiometric
CCEEHIIMNORSSTT	theocentricisms
CCEEHIINNORTTTY	ethnocentricity
CCEEHINOOPRRRTY	hypercorrection
CCEEHNORRSTTTUU	technostructure
CCEEIIINNNOSSST	inconsistencies
CCEEIILNNOSTUVY	inconsecutively
CCEEIILNORRSTTU	interlocutrices
CCEEIILOPRRTTYY	pyroelectricity
CCEEIINNNNOORTT	interconnection
CCEEILNOOOPRSTT	optoelectronics
CCEEINNOOORRRSTV	overcorrections
CCEELNORRSTTUUU	countercultures
CCEFILNNOOSSSUU	unselfconscious
CCEGHHIIIIMRRST	higher criticism
CCEGHILMNOOORTY	microtechnology
CCEGHINNNOPRTUU	counterpunching
CCEGIIJMNNORSTU	misconjecturing
CCEGINNOPRRSTTU	preconstructing
CCEHIIIMPRRSSTY	hypercriticisms
CCEHIIKLNNOOSTY	cholecystokinin
CCEHIIMMOOPSTTY	psychotomimetic
CCEHNNOOOPRSSSY	synchronoscopes
CCEIILMNOOSSSUY	semiconsciously
CCEIILNNOOSSTUY	conscientiously
CCEIINNNOOSSTUU	unconscientious
CCEIMOOOPRRRSSS	microprocessors
CCEIMORRRSSTTUU	microstructures
CCEINNNOORSTTUV	nonconstructive
CCEINNNOOSSSSUU	unconsciousness
CCEINNOOPSSSSUU	conspicuousness
CCEINNOORRSSTTU	reconstructions
CCEIOOPPRSSSSTT	spectroscopists
CCGIIIILNOOSSTU	sociolinguistic
CCHHIIMOOPRRSTY	hystricomorphic
CCHIILLNOOPRSSU	councillorships
CCIIIILPRSSSTTUU	pisciculturists
CCIIIILRRSSTTTUU	citriculturists
CCIIINNNOOORSTTT	contortionistic
CCIILMNOORSTUUV	circumvolutions
CCIILNNOOPSSUUY	inconspicuously
CCIIMNNOORSSTTU	misconstruction
CCIINNOORSSTTTU	constructionist
CCIINORSSTTTUV	constructivists
CDDEEEEEINNNPRT	interdependence
CDDEEEEINNNPRTY	interdependency
CDDEEEELNNPRTUY	unprecedentedly
CDDEEHIINSSTTUW	Dutch West Indies
CDDEFILLNOOSTTU	Sutton Coldfield
CDDEFINOOSSUUUX	Eudoxus of Cnidus
CDDEINNOOPRRTUU	underproduction
CDDIILMMOOOSSUY	discommodiously
CDDIILOORSSSUUU	Diodorus Siculus
CDEEEEEFLNNSSSS	defencelessness
CDEEEEINNNPRSTU	superintendence
CDEEEGHINORTTUW	counterweighted
CDEEEGILNNORSUV	overindulgences
CDEEEHHILPRSTUW	whited sepulchre
CDEEEHIMORSSTTY	hysterectomised
CDEEEHIMORSTTYZ	hysterectomized
CDEEEIINPRSSSTV	descriptiveness
CDEEEILOOPRSSTT	electrodeposits
CDEEEIMNNPRSTUU	superinducement
CDEEEINNNOSSSTU	tendenciousness
CDEEEINNNPRSTUY	superintendency
CDEEEINRSSSTTUV	destructiveness
CDEEEENNPSSSTUU	unsuspectedness
CDEEFILLPRSSTUY	disrespectfully
CDEEGHIMNNNOPRU	uncomprehending
CDEEGIILLNOOOTU	oligonucleotide
CDEEHIIMOORSTTY	thyroidectomies
CDEEHIKNNRRSTTU	thunderstricken
CDEEHKLNNOOOORST	chondroskeleton
CDEEIIIIMNNRSTT	indeterministic
CDEEIIIILNNSSSSV	uncivilisedness
CDEEIIIILNNSSUVZ	uncivilizedness
CDEEIIINNSSSTTV	distinctiveness
CDEEIINNOPRSTUV	United Provinces
CDEEILLNOOPSTUY	polynucleotides
CDEEILNNORSSSSU	incredulousness
CDEEIMNNOOPSSSU	compendiousness
CDEFIIIMNOORSST	disconformities
CDEGIIIMMNNOOSS	decommissioning
CDEGIIINNNOOPRT	preconditioning
CDEGIILNNOOOORST	endocrinologist
CDEGILNNOOPRRSY	correspondingly
CDEIIIILNNSTTVY	indistinctively
CDEIIIINNNOSSTTU	discontinuities
CDEIIIJNNOSSSUU	injudiciousness
CDEIIMMNNNOOOSS	noncommissioned
CDEIINNOOORRSTTU	reintroductions
CDEIINORSSSTTTU	destructionists
CDHHNNOOOORSTUY	odontorhynchous
CDHIILNOPRSTUUU	pulchritudinous
CDIIIINOSSSTUUV	vicissitudinous
CDIILNNOOSSTUUY	discontinuously
CDIIMOOPPRRSTUU	cryptosporidium
CDIINNOOPRTTUVY	nonproductivity
CEEEEELOOPRSSTT	telestereoscope
CEEEEFFIINNSSTV	ineffectiveness
CEEEEHHLNOOPRRT	perchloroethene
CEEEEHIILLNNRSTT	Liechtensteiner
CEEEEHIMNPRTTXY	hyperexcitement
CEEEFIIMNORRRTT	interferometric
CEEEFLNORRSSSUU	resourcefulness
CEEEGGILNNOOSSU	gluconeogenesis
CEEEGGILNNOOSSY	glyconeogenesis
CEEEGHILORRSSTU	Gloucestershire
CEEEGHIQRRRSSUU	churrigueresque
CEEEGHLLOOOORRTY	electrorheology
CEEEGNNOOOPRSST	roentgenoscopes
CEEEHIIMNNOPRSV	incomprehensive
CEEEHILMNOPRSVY	comprehensively
CEEEHILOOPPRSST	electrophoresis
CEEEHIMORRSSTTY	stereochemistry
CEEEHIMORSSSTTY	hysterectomises
CEEEHIMORSSTTYZ	hysterectomizes
CEEEHLMNOORRSTT	thermoelectrons
CEEEHLOOPRRSSTU	electrophoruses
CEEEIIKNNPRSSST	persnicketiness

869

CEEEIILOOPRSTTV	electropositive
CEEEIIMMOORRSTT	micrometeorites
CEEEIIMNOPSSTTV	competitiveness
CEEEIIMNORSTTUX	excrementitious
CEEEIIMOORRSSTT	stereoisometric
CEEEIINRRSSSTTV	restrictiveness
CEEEIKLNNOSSTUU	kinetonucleuses
CEEEILMNNOPRSTZ	complementizers
CEEEILOPRRSTTVY	retrospectively
CEEEIMMNNOOPSTU	pneumonectomies
CEEEIMNNOORSSSU	ceremoniousness
CEEEINNOPRRSTVW	Western Province
CEEEINPQRSSSTUU	picturesqueness
CEEEMMNNOORTTUV	countermovement
CEEFIIILLNOSTTU	feuilletonistic
CEEFINNOPRRSSTU	perfunctoriness
CEEFLMNOORSSSST	comfortlessness
CEEGGHIINNORTUW	counterweighing
CEEGGHILNOOOORS	geochronologies
CEEGIINNNNORSTT	nonintersecting
CEEHHIMMORRSTTY	thermochemistry
CEEHHIMOPPRTTYY	hemicryptophyte
CEEHIIMNNNOOPRS	incomprehension
CEEHIIMNOSSSSUV	mischievousness
CEEHILLNOORRSXY	hexylresorcinol
CEEHILNLNOSSSTUY	nucleosynthesis
CEEHIMMOPSSSTTY	metempsychosist
CEEIIINOPRSSSTX	expressionistic
CEEIILLMNOOSSTT	tonsillectomies
CEEIILLMNORSSTT	scintillometers
CEEIILNOPRSTTVY	introspectively
CEEIILNORRSTTUX	interlocutrixes
CEEIIMNNOPSSSUU	impecuniousness
CEEIIMNORRRSSTU	resurrectionism
CEEIINNNOORRSTV	interconversion
CEEIINNRSSSTTUV	instructiveness
CEEIINOPPRSSSTU	precipitousness
CEEIINORRRSSTTU	resurrectionist
CEEIINPSSSTTUUV	intussusceptive
CEEIILMNNOORSUUY	unceremoniously
CEEIMMOOPRRRSTY	micropyrometers
CEEIIMNNOPSSSTV	consumptiveness
CEEINNNOOSSSTTU	contentiousness
CEEINNNOPRSSTTU	supercontinents
CEEINOPPRSSSSUU	perspicuousness
CEELLPQRSSTUUUY	sculpturesquely
CEEPRRRSSSTTUUU	superstructures
CEFFIIINNOOSSSU	inofficiousness
CEFGHIMNNOORSST	forthcomingness
CEFIIMMNNNOOORST	nonconformities
CEGHILMNOOOSTUY	ethnomusicology
CEGHLNOOOPRSUYY	neuropsychology
CEGIINNNOOPRTTU	counterpointing
CEGIINNPSSSTTUU	intussuscepting
CEGILNNOOPRTTTU	counterplotting
CEGILOOOOPRSTYZ	cryptozoologies
CEGINNNOORSSSUU	incongruousness
CEHHHILMOOOPRTT	chemolithotroph
CEHHIIOOPRSSSTY	psychohistories
CEHHIMMNOOOPPRS	morphophonemics
CEHHINOPSSSSTYY	psychosynthesis

CEHHOOOOPPPRSSS	phosphoroscopes
CEHIIMMMNNORSTUY	immunochemistry
CEHIINNOOPRSSSU	connoisseurship
CEHIJMNNOORSTTU	thermojunctions
CEHILLMOOPPRRST	comptrollership
CEHILLNOOPRRSST	controllerships
CEHILLNOOPRSSSU	counsellorships
CEHILMOORSSSSTY	schoolmistressy
CEHILOPPRRSUUXY	peroxysulphuric
CEHMNNNOOORRTTUY	northcountrymen
CEHNNNOORSSSSUY	synchronousness
CEIIIIMNOPRSSST	impressionistic
CEIIIINOSSSTTVV	vivisectionists
CEIIILNOQRSTTUV	ventriloquistic
CEIIIMNNORRSSTU	insurrectionism
CEIIINNORRSSTTU	insurrectionist
CEIIINORRSSSTTT	restrictionists
CEIILLNOORRTTUY	interlocutorily
CEIILNNOPSSSTUU	punctiliousness
CEIINNOPSSSTTUU	intussusception
CEIINOPPRRSSSTU	superscriptions
CEILMOOPRRSSSTU	multiprocessors
CEIMNNOOOPRSTUV	overconsumption
CEIMNOOPRSSSSUU	promiscuousness
CEIMNOPRSSSSTUU	scrumptiousness
CFHILMNOOOORRRT	nitrochloroform
CFIILLORRSSTTUU	floriculturists
CGHIILNOPSSTUYS	psycholinguists
CHHHINNOORRSTUY	ornithorhynchus
CHHHIOOOOPPPRST	orthophosphoric
CHIILORRSSTTTUU	horticulturists
CHIINOPRRSSSTTU	instructorships
CHILLMOOOOPPRSY	microsporophyll
CHILOOOPPRRSSTU	prolocutorships
CIIILLRSSSTTUUV	silviculturists
CIIIMNNORSSSTTU	misinstructions

DDEEEEHINOPPRSU	pseudoephedrine
DDEEEEILMNRRSTW	Middle Westerner
DDEEEGIILNPRRUV	underprivileged
DDEEEGILNNOPRUV	underdeveloping
DDEEEIIINOQRSTU	derequisitioned
DDEEEIILNRSSTTY	disinterestedly
DDEEGGHIINNORSY	dehydrogenising
DDEEGGHIINNORYZ	dehydrogenizing
DDEEHILNOORRSTY	dehydroretinols
DDEGHIIINNSSTUU	undistinguished
DDEIINOOOPPRRST	disproportioned
DDEIINOOPSSSUUY	Pseudo-Dionysius
DEEEEEFLNNSSSSS	defenselessness
DEEEEHNOPRRSTUY	superheterodyne
DEEEEILNORSSSTU	deleteriousness
DEEEEELMNOOPRTVV	overdevelopment
DEEEFFIIOPRRSTT	Petrified Forest
DEEEFGHINORSSST	foresightedness
DEEEGIIMNNNORSS	domineeringness
DEEEHIIKLNOOSTT	kinetheodolites
DEEEHIINPRSSSTY	hypersensitised
DEEEHIINPRSSTYZ	hypersensitized
DEEEIIMNRSSSTTV	divertissements
DEEEIINOPSSSTUX	expeditiousness
DEEEIMMNNOPRSSTW	disempowerments

DEEEEINNNOSSSTTU	tendentiousness
DEEEINNNPRSSSTTU	superintendents
DEEELMMNNOPRTUY	underemployment
DEEFFIIINNRSSTT	indifferentists
DEEFILLNOPRSSUY	splendiferously
DEEFILNRSSSSSTU	distressfulness
DEEFINOOORRSSSU	odoriferousness
DEEGGHILNNOSSST	longsightedness
DEEGIIILMOOPSST	epidemiologists
DEEGIILMNOOSSTT	sedimentologist
DEEGILLOOSSSTTY	dysteleologists
DEEHHHILOOPRSSU	householdership
DEEHIIMMOOPRRST	thermoperiodism
DEEHIINOOPSSSTT	photosensitised
DEEHIINOOPSSTTZ	photosensitized
DEEIIIIILMRSSTUV	verisimilitudes
DEEIIILNOPRSSTV	vespertilionids
DEEIILMOORRSTUY	demeritoriously
DEFILNRSSSSTTUU	distrustfulness
DEGGHIILMNOOSTY	demythologising
DEGGHIILMNOOTYZ	demythologizing
DEGGHILOOORSSTY	hydrogeologists
DEGHHIINNNORSTU	Huntingdonshire
DEGHIINNNORRSUU	undernourishing
DEHHIIMOPRRSTYY	hyperthyroidism
DEIIILLMNNOSSTU	disillusionment
DEIIINOOPPRSSST	predispositions
DEIINNORSSSTTUU	industriousness
DFILMNOOOOOSSW	Wisdom of Solomon
DGIILNOOORSSSTY	strongyloidosis
DHHIIMOOPRSSTYY	hypothyroidisms
DHHLOOPRRSSUUUY	hydrosulphurous
DHINOOOPRSSSTTT	prosthodontists
DIIILLMNOSTTUUUY	multitudinously
EEEEEFIMNNNORSTV	overrefinements
EEEEEFIMNORRRSTT	interferometers
EEEEEGHLNOORSTUY	heterogeneously
EEEEEGILNPSTTTTY	teletypesetting
EEEEEGINNNORSSVW	overweeningness
EEEEEIIMMNRRSSTT	semiretirements
EEEEEIINNNPSSSVX	inexpensiveness
EEEEEIINNRRSSTTV	irretentiveness
EEEEEILPRRSTTTWY	teletypewriters
EEEEEIMNPRRRSSST	misrepresenters
EEEEEINPRRRSSSTT	interpretresses
EEEEELMNORRSSSSS	remorselessness
EEEEFFIINNNOSSSV	inoffensiveness
EEEEFHHHILMOORST	Home of the Hirsel
EEEEFHIILNOSSSUW	housewifeliness
EEEEFINOPRSSSSTU	pestiferousness
EEEEGHMNNOOOSSSU	homogeneousness
EEEEGIIMNNPRRSST	misrepresenting
EEEEGIINNNRSSSTT	interestingness
EEEEGIINNOPRSSTV	progenitiveness
EEEEGILNNNNRSSTU	unrelentingness
EEEEGILORRRSSTVY	retrogressively
EEEEGINOPRRSSSSV	progressiveness
EEEEHIINPPRRRSTT	interpretership
EEEEHIINPRSSSSTY	hypersensitises
EEEEHIINPRSSSTYZ	hypersensitizes
EEEEHILNORRSSTTW	northwesterlies
EEEEHILORSSSTTUW	southwesterlies
EEEEHIMORSSSSSTU	housemistresses
EEEEHHINNOPRSSTXY	hyperextensions
EEEEHLMNNOOSSSUW	unwholesomeness
EEEEIIIILNNOPRSTV	vespertilionine
EEEEIIINNNSSSSTV	insensitiveness
EEEEIILLNNRRSSUUY	Neuilly-sur-Seine
EEEEIIMMOORRSSST	stereoisomerism
EEEEIIMNNNRSTTTW	intertwinements
EEEEIIMNPRRRSSTT	misinterpreters
EEEEIINOPRSSSTTU	repetitiousness
EEEEIMNPPRSSSTUV	presumptiveness
EEEEINNNOSSSSTTU	sententiousness
EEEEINNOPRSSSTTU	pretentiousness
EEEELNOPPRSSSSSU	purposelessness
EEEEMNOPSSSSTTUU	tempestuousness
EEFFILLLMNOSSSUU	mellifluousness
EEFLNOPRSSSSUUU	superfluousness
EEGGGILNNOOORSTT	roentgenologist
EEGGHHLNOSSSSTTU	thoughtlessness
EEGGHILMNNOOOPST	phenomenologist
EEGGHIMMNOORRSTY	Montgomeryshire
EEGGHINNORSSSTUU	unrighteousness
EEGGHINOOPPRRSTY	porphyrogenites
EEGGIIILNORRSSSU	irreligiousness
EEGGIIIMNNPRRSTT	misinterpreting
EEGGIIILLLNNNTTUY	unintelligently
EEGGIILMOOPSSSTT	epistemologists
EEGGIIMNNNRSSTTU	unremittingness
EEGGIINNORSSSTUV	vertiginousness
EEGGIINOPRSSSSTU	prestigiousness
EEGGILNOPPRSSSSY	prepossessingly
EEGGIMOOPRRSTTUU	Portuguese Timor
EEGGINNOPPRSSSSU	unprepossessing
EEHHIINOOPSSSTTY	photosynthesise
EEHHIINOOPSSTTYZ	photosynthesize
EEHHHNNOOPRSSUVY	neurohypophyses
EEHIINOOPSSSSTT	photosensitises
EEHIINOOPSSSTTZ	photosensitizes
EEHLNOPRSSSSUUU	sulphureousness
EEHMOOOPPRRSTTY	pyrophotometers
EEIIIIINNOQSSSTUV	inquisitiveness
EEIIIHMNNNORSTTV	interventionism
EEIIIINNNORSTTTV	interventionist
EEIIINNRRSTTUUVY	interuniversity
EEIIILNNOORRTTTU	trinitrotoluene
EEIIILNNOORRSSTUV	revolutionisers
EEIIILNOORRSTUVZ	revolutionizers
EEIIMNOORRSSSTU	meritoriousness
EEIINNNNNOORTTV	nonintervention
EEINNNOOPPRSSTU	inopportuneness
EFGIIIILMNOPRSVY	oversimplifying
EFILMNRSSSSTTUU	mistrustfulness
EGGILNNOOORSSTT	rontgenologists
EGHHIIILLMNOOSTT	helminthologist
EGHIIINNOPSSSTY	hyposensitising
EGHIIINNOPSSTYZ	hyposensitizing
EGHILNOOOPRSUVY	neurophysiology
EGIIILNNOORSTUV	revolutionising
EGIIILNNOORTUVZ	revolutionizing
EGIIILNNOQRSTUV	ventriloquising
EGIIILNNOQRTUVZ	ventriloquizing
EGIIIMNNNOOSSSU	ignominiousness

EGIINOOPRRSSSST	progressionists
EHHIMMMOOOOPRSS	homoeomorphisms
EHHINOOOPPPRSST	phosphoproteins
EHHINOOPPRSSUYY	neurohypophysis
EHIIIKLMMOOPRST	poikilothermism
EHIIILMNNPRSSUY	hyperinsulinism
EHIILLMOOPPRTTU	photomultiplier
EHIIOOPPPRRRSST	proprietorships
EHINORRSSSTTTUW	trustworthiness
EIIIMNOOPPRSSTU	superimposition
EIIKLLMNPRSSTTU	Rumpelstiltskin
EIILLMMNNOOORTT	montmorillonite
EIIILLNORSSSSTUU	illustriousness
EIILNOOPPSSSSTU	suppositionless
EIILOPRRSSTTUUY	surreptitiously
EIILOPRSSSTTUUY	superstitiously
EIINOOOPPPRSSSTU	presuppositions
EINOOOOPPRRRSTV	overproportions
GGGHHILNOOORTUY	thoroughgoingly
GILOOOOOPRSSTTZ	protozoologists
HHHOOOOOPPPRSSUY	hypophosphorous
IIIIINNOQSSSTTU	inquisitionists
IIILLOOPRSTUUVV	Vitruvius Pollio
ILNNOORRRSSSTUU	Snorri Sturluson

Supplement

Word Play

Contents

Internet Resources for Word Games 3

Introduction to Cryptic Crosswords 8

Anagrams and Other Grams 14

Short Words 23

J, Q, X, and Z 28

Internet Resources for Word Games

RESOURCES FOR SOLVING CROSSWORDS

Collins English Dictionary is available online at:
http://www.collins.co.uk/wordexchange/

GENERAL CROSSWORD SITES

The Crossword Centre
www.crossword.org.uk
Crossword resource centre with puzzles, history,
competitions, features and book reviews.

About.com Crosswords
www.crosswords.about.com
American daily crossword and puzzle site
including tutorials.

Crossword Tournament
www.crosswordtournament.com
From the New York Times Puzzle Editor, a site which
includes puzzles and crosswords, links and histories.

Lexcentrics
www.lexcentrics.com/Crosswords/
Cryptic crosswords, wordgames and tutorials.

Thinks.com
www.thinks.com
Includes a daily crossword and other puzzles such
as jigsaws and wordsearches.

The Tantalus Crossword
http://tantalus-crossword.co.uk/

Crossword Compiler
http://crossword-compiler.com/Scrabble
Software for compiling 'everyday' crosswords.

Crossword Maestro
http://crosswordmaestro.com/
Software for solving cryptic crosswords.

CROSSWORD CLUBS

The Times Crossword Club
www.timesonline.co.uk/section/0,,252,00.html
An annual fee allows you to access the Listener
crossword and many others.

The Crossword Club
www.thecrosswordclub.co.uk/
Cryptic crossword site with monthly magazine
for subscribers.

The Australian Crossword Club
http://crosswordclub.org/

ONLINE CROSSWORDS

The Guardian
www.guardian.co.uk/
The Guardian Annual registration allows
you to access Araucaria, Bunthorne & co.

The Independent
http://enjoyment.independent.co.uk/crosswords/cryptic/
The Independent Annual subscription. Good
cryptic puzzles by an increasingly well-respected
team of compilers.

The Atlantic Monthly
www.theatlantic.com/doc/200506
The Atlantic Monthly US cryptic puzzles by Emily
Cox and Henry Rathvon

The Telegraph
www.telegraph.co.uk/arts/main.jhtml
Access the puzzles online.

Private Eye
www.privateeye.co.uk/content/showitem.cfm/issue.1131/section.xword
Fun puzzles with typically scurrilous clues.

Auctor
http://mysite.wanadoo-members.co.uk/Classical_Studies
Puzzles to test your Latin

The Scotsman
http://thescotsman.scotsman.com/games.cfm?id=501162005

Free Crosswords
http://quicksitebuilder.cnet.com/neilshepherd/
Alberich's crossword site

Pub Crosswords
www.pubcrosswords.com/
Fun puzzles and cash prizes

Globe and Mail (Canada)
Crosswords are available online to subscribers at:
www.theglobeandmail.com/

The Toronto Star
www.thestar.com/cgibin/star_static.cgi?section=AandE&page=/
 Third_Party/xword/index.html

A1 Puzzles
www.a1puzzles.com
Subscription site with interactive crosswords, jigsaw
puzzles and trivia. Twenty-five new crosswords and puzzles
added every month.

LINKS FOR SCRABBLE®

MATTEL's official Scrabble site
www.mattelscrabble.com/en/adults/index.html

SCRABBLE CLUBS AND ASSOCIATIONS

Association of British Scrabble Players
www.absp.org.uk/index.html

Scottish Scrabble Association
www.scottishscrabble.org/

Singapore Scrabble Association
www.toucanet.com/

South African Scrabble Players' Association
www.geocities.com/sanspa/home.html

Australian Scrabble Players' Association
www.scrabble.org.au/

New Zealand Association of Scrabble Players
www.scrabble.co.nz/

Scrabble in Nigeria
www.nigerianscrabble.com/

Bahrain Scrabble League
http://mywebpage.netscape.com/bahrainscrabble/main.html

Netherlands English Scrabble Club
www.nesc.nl/

Maltese Scrabble Club
www.maltascrab.net.tf/

National Scrabble Association (North America)
www.scrabble-assoc.com/

Scrabble in Canada
www.scrabble-assoc.com/canada/

OTHER WORDGAMES

Countdown
www.channel4.com/entertainment/tv/showcards/C/countdown.html
www.thecountdownpage.com/

Introduction to
Cryptic Crosswords

Many people who enjoy quick crosswords find the
cryptic variety daunting. This is a shame, as cryptic
crosswords require very much the same attributes
as quick ones; a good vocabulary and an ability to
think laterally. If you have been put off by cryptic
crosswords before, it's well worth giving them another
try – once you have learned how to speak their language.
While the compilers of cryptic puzzles have infinite
depths of devilish cunning, they tend to rely on a fairly
limited set of clue structures with which to torment
crossword addicts.

Cryptic clues generally come in two parts: the first
element is a literal definition of the answer, while the
second is a play on words that is used to work the
answer out. Of course, it can be difficult to work out
which is which, but that is part of the fun! The following
are some of the more common clue structures.

Compilers often use 'trigger' words, or anagram
indicators, to suggest that the solution can be found
in the form of an anagram. The list of these words is
virtually endless; any word that suggests change, upset
or disorder can be used. Here is a list of some examples:

about
adjust
annoy
another
anyhow
anyway
arrange
awkward
badly
bend
blend
broken
chaotic
cocktail
crazy
deform
derange
devastated
different
disfigure
distress
doctor
garble
jumble
mixed
order
strange
transform
wild

Whenever you encounter an anagram indicator, look at the length of the solution. This will help you narrow down the elements of the clue that may be an anagram of the answer. For example, consider the following:

Meat merchant who blends cut herb (7)

Here, *blends* indicates that an anagram of the solution may be contained in the clue. As the solution has seven letters, the next step is to look for one or more consecutive words that contain exactly seven letters. Here, the obvious candidates are *cut* and *herb*. We can then look for a hint in the first part of the clue, which leads us easily from *Meat merchant* to an anagram of *cut herb* – *butcher*.

REVERSALS

A common compiler's ruse is to indicate (cryptically of course!) that a word in the clue should be reversed to provide the solution. Often, the reversal indicator depends on whether the required word is Down or Across in the crossword grid. The following is a Down clue:

Rising evil may breathe (4)

If evil is written so that it 'rises', rather than descends, the grid, we are left with a synonym for breathe – live. Other reversal indicators include:

returning
retreating
turning
going back
climbing
northwards
westwards

Some clues work like a game of charades, with one part
of the clue describing the solution and others indicating
words that can be put together to form it. For example:

Goblin Lima comes out in force (5)

Another word for *goblin* is *imp*, while Lima stands for L in the Nato
Phonetic Alphabet. *Imp* plus *L* "comes out in" a synonym
for *force* – *impel*. It's always worth examining a clue to see if
there is a word or phrase – like 'comes out in' in this
instance – that suggests that certain elements work together
to form another.

READ-THROUGHS

A common clue type is that which includes the solution
within other words in the clue, either 'hidden' in the middle
of a longer word, or spelt out by adjacent letters in two or
more consecutive words. These clues are often indicated
by words such as:

buried
embedded
hidden
in
inside
swallowed

When you find any word that hints at one thing inside
another, it's a good idea to scan the other parts of the clue
to see if you can spot a complete word nestling inside others.
Here's an example of a relatively simple 'read-through':

Item of clothing found in dog-lover's wardrobe (5)

'Found in' is a signal that a read-through may be involved,
and the clue structure tells us that we should be looking
for an item of clothing in *dog-lover's wardrobe*. As *wardrobe*
seems to continue the clothing imagery of the first part of
the clue, we can deduce that we should look at *dog-lover's*.
And here we find the answer – *glove*.

Crossword clues sometimes divide into two sections, each of which defines the solution in a different way. Awareness of this makes clues like the following appear much less baffling:

Assault the pancake mix (6)

A synonym for the verb *assault* is, of course, *batter* – which also happens to be a synonym for *pancake mix*. It's therefore a good idea to see if you can break a given clue into two constituent parts; if no common word springs to mind, try checking one of the parts in this dictionary – you may find that the book points out a sense of the word that previously eluded you.

DELETIONS

One kind of crossword clue is solved by simply removing a letter from one of its constituent words. The compiler will usually hint at this obliquely by using words such as the following:

tailless
headless
beheaded
eviscerated
gutless
heartless
topless
endless

Each of these words indicates that another word in, or suggested by, the clue will yield the solution if a letter is removed from within the word, or from its beginning or end, as in the following:

Great Scots endless noisy fight (4)

Once you have worked out that a noisy fight is a *brawl*, the word *endless* should encourage you to remove the L, leaving you with the Scots word for 'great', *braw*.

&LIT

An important type of clue is the '&lit', short for 'and literally so'. This is perhaps the most satisfying clue to solve, as it represents a perfect composition on the part of the compiler. Often indicated by an exclamation mark, the &lit consists of a phrase that can be read literally to provide the solution – but is also one of the other types of cryptic clue. Probably the most famous example of this sort of clue is:

Terribly angered! (7)

Here, terribly is an anagram indicator; if the letters of angered are terribly messed up, we get enraged – for which the whole clue is also a literal definition. Most '&lit' clues are far trickier than this, however, but the principle remains the same.

Anagrams and other -grams

Here are some more anagrams which transform
the names of contemporary figures and events.
Some of the transformations are most appropriate!

Elvis Aaron Presley	>	Seen alive? Sorry, pal!
Madonna Louise Ciccone	>	one cool dance musician
Albert Einstein	>	ten elite brains
William Butler Yeats	>	a really sublime twit
Diego Maradona	>	an adored amigo
Elle MacPherson	>	her men collapse
Arnold Schwarzenegger	>	he's grown large'n'crazed
Clint Eastwood	>	Old West Action
President Boris Yeltsin	>	tipsiness done terribly
Florence Nightingale	>	angel of the reclining
The Houses of Parliament	>	loonies far up the Thames

There are some anagrams which are quite uncanny
in their coincidental meanings, such as the one below:

'To be or not to be? That is the question.
Whether 'tis nobler in the mind to suffer the
slings and arrows of outrageous fortune.'

Which becomes:

'In one of the Bard's best-thought-of tragedies,
our insistent hero, Hamlet, queries on two fronts
about how life turns rotten.'

The following poem is a very clever anagram.
See if you can guess what it refers to and remember,
the clue is in the title!

Viva United States of America
Monk? Hmm . . . jivin', man!
Honk, known champ – damn!
Calmly twirl, mystic vox,
And dancing skyward, waltz.

ANAGRAM (1)

You should have between two and six players. Prepare
100 cards with a letter of the alphabet written on each.
There should be four of the majority of letters such as
C and M, seven or eight of very common letters such as
A and E, and only one each of rare letters such as X and Z.
The cards should be placed down, and turned over one at a
time by each player in turn. When a word is spotted from
the letters showing, the first player to shout it out claims the
points. So it pays to be quick-thinking! The minimum length
of word is four letters. So, for example, if the letters L, E, A,
and P are turned over one by one, the fastest player to shout
out 'Leap!', 'Pale!', or 'Peal!' will win the points. A player may
also add a letter to the list of words already declared, to form
a new word, or they may rearrange an existing word.

ANAGRAM (2)

This game asks you to solve anagrams set by other players.
Going round a group one by one, each player says an anagram
to the next person, who then attempts to solve it. For example:

> **Barbara:** (*to Ray*) Ok, I'll start with *team.*
>
> **Ray:** *Meat.* (*to Milo*): *Trap.*
>
> **Milo:** *Part.* (*to Lizzie*): *Face.*
>
> **Lizzie:** *Café!* Ok, now for some more difficult ones! (*to Jessie*) *Nectar.*
>
> **Jessie:** Ummm, *train?*
>
> **Lizzie:** Wrong, you're out! It's *trance.* (*to Maggie*) How about *auction?*
>
> **Maggie:** *Caution.*

Try to compose phrases comprising two words that are anagrams of each other, then give your fellow players a clue to the phrase and see if they can guess what you're thinking of. Here are some examples to get you started:

Clue: current snake
Answer: present serpent

Clue: aircraft to Asian kingdom
Answer: Nepal plane

Clue: leftover autumn fruit
Answer: spare pears

Clue: impeccable school monitor
Answer: perfect prefect

Clue: hidden gift
Answer: latent talent

Clue: Teutonic horse trough
Answer: German manger

Clue: Oriental seriousness
Answer: Eastern earnest

Clue: conceited herb
Answer: arrogant tarragon

A *pangram* is a short phrase formed using all 26 letters of the alphabet. The very best pangrams use each letter only once. Here is an example of one formed from the minimum 26 letters:

Mr Jock, TV quiz PhD, bags few lynx.

As most 26-letter pangrams have to resort to using obscure or dubiously valid words, the result can be a little difficult to decipher, as in the example below:

Pyx vang quiz: komb crwth fjelds.

This, roughly explained, means 'A quiz about coin chest nautical rope tackle: German combination ancient Celtic string instrument, high Scandinavian rocky plateau.' Much clearer now!

Using just a few extra letters, normally vowels, can
make your pangram a lot more comprehensible,
as these examples show:

How quickly daft jumping zebras vex. (30 letters)

The five boxing wizards jump quickly. (31 letters)

Probably the best-known of these more 'coherent' pangrams is:

The quick brown fox jumps over a lazy dog.

This sentence is often used in to practice typing, as it uses
every letter key on the keyboard, and is easy to remember.

Try making up your own pangrams. The 'perfect' pangram,
which has not yet been devised, would contain 26 letters only,
make complete grammatical sense and avoid resorting to proper
names or abbreviations. As the twenty-six letters of the alphabet
can be put together in over 403,000,000,000,000,000,000,000,000
different ways, this may keep you occupied for some time!

As well as devising your own pangrams, try making up a themed sentence containing 26 words, each word beginning with a different letter of the alphabet. You may use a certain degree of artistic licence, as you will be unable to use words like *a* and *the* more than once, and allowances are made for words starting with the letter X, as there are not many possibilities to choose from!

How about:

Dog breeding
All British Crufts dog enthusiasts favour gestation; however, I jest; keen Labrador minders never order poor quadrupeds, rightly sceptical, to undertake vexing whelping. X-cellent yearling zealots!

or

Finding Nirvana
Adults bicker concerning discovering enlightenment, for good honest Indians joke kindly: love must nourish. Oriental philosophy quite right. Serene tai-chi uncovers Vishnu; with x-citing yoga – Zen.

(For more of these, see: http://puzzles.about.com/library/weekly)

ANTIGRAMS

An antigram is an anagram which means the opposite
to the starting phrase. They are difficult to deliberately
devise, and most are simply discovered by chance. They
are often witty and apt, as you will see from the examples below:

filled	>	ill-fed
Santa	>	Satan
misfortune	>	it's more fun
funeral	>	real fun!
infection	>	fine tonic
militarism	>	I limit arms
saintliness	>	entails sins
antagonist	>	not against
a picture of health	>	oft pale, I ache, hurt
evangelists	>	evil's agents
within earshot	>	I won't hear this
sweltering heat	>	the winter gales
the man who laughs	>	he's glum, won't ha-ha
the Oscar Nominations	>	It's not a cinema honor

A lipogram is a piece of writing from which all examples of a certain letter have been omitted. It is simple to devise one of these when the letter is, for example, Q or Z, but more difficult when you are trying to avoid using a common letter. Work out which letter is missing from the passage below, then have a go yourself:

> Alas, for lack of application, lipogrammatists can slip up and with what upshot? Inclusion of that symbol you had sought to avoid. Oh my, my, such a pity. A shambolic lipogram! Sham! So that you do not miss my point: all of this stuff and rubbish was a Q-lipogram. But, no, it isn't! What is still missing is that symbol twixt I and K! But is it just that symbol? Oh, no! A slip up! This is as difficult as writing a dictionary! My typing digits, in pain, must follow my brain's commands, and no slip-ups must occur if I want to do this right!
> (from http://en.wikipedia.org/wiki/Lipogram)

An *anugram* is an anagram, both parts of which are mutually true. The best-known of these is:

> *Eleven plus two*   >   *twelve plus one*

These are very rare – well done if you can come up with one of your own!

Short Words

In certain word games, such as Scrabble®, Hangman and crosswords, it is useful to be aware of the many two-letter words that you can play, as these will help you gain an advantage over your opponent, or complete a tricky puzzle. Most of these terms are uncommon in everyday speech and writing, so their meanings are given here for interest and to help you memorize the words.

aa	rough volcanic rock
ad	advertisement
ae	*Scot* one
ai	three-toed sloth
aw	*Scot* all
ax	*US* axe
ba	*myth* a bird with a human head, representing the soul in Egyptian mythology.
di	diameter, didymium
ee	*Scot* eye
el	*US* elevated railroad
em	a print measurement
en	print measurement, half the length of an em
es	einsteinium
ex	a former partner
fa	*music* the fourth note in a scale
gi	judo or karate suit
id	*psychoanal* unconscious instincts
io	ionium
ja	*S Afr* yes
jo	*Scot* sweetheart
ka	*myth* a guardian spirit in Egyptian mythology
la	*music* the sixth note in a scale
li	Chinese unit of length: The li is approximately equal to 590 yards.

mi	*music* the third note in a scale
mo	molybdenum
mu	the twelfth letter of the Greek alphabet
ne	neon
nu	the thirteenth letter of the Greek alphabet
od	a force supposedly responsible for many natural phenomena
om	a sacred symbol of Hinduism, repeated as a mantra
os	*anat* bone
ou	*S Afr* man or chap
ox	type of male cattle
pa	a Maori village
pi	the sixteenth letter of the Greek alphabet
po	chamber pot
qi	vital bodily energy flow
re	with reference to
si	silicon
te	*music* the seventh note in a scale
ti	plant with reddish flowers
ut	a note in medieval music
wo	old spelling of woe
xi	the fourteenth letter of the Greek alphabet
yo	informal greeting
zo	a Tibetan breed of cattle

There are many hundreds of well-known three-letter words available to choose from when playing word games, but here we list some of the more unusual ones that you may not be familiar with. Knowledge of unusual three-letter words can be very useful for solving crossword puzzles or in word games such as Hangman. Challenge your opponent with the word *cwm*, for example, and watch as the noose is drawn tighter and tighter ...

aba	a type of cloth from Syria
adz	a heavy tool with a steel blade
ala	*zoology* a winglike structure
alb	a long white robe worn by priests
alt	*music* high in pitch
ani	a black tropical American bird
awn	a bristle on certain types of grass
bel	a unit of power
ben	*Scot* the inner room in a cottage
bey	a title used in the Ottoman Empire
bon	a Japanese Buddhist religion
caz	*slang* short for casual
col	a mountain pass connecting two peaks
cos	a type of lettuce
cru	in France, a wine-producing region
cwm	*Welsh* a valley
dag	*Aust & NZ* an eccentric person
dak	in India, a system of mail delivery
dal	an Indian lentil dish
dan	a black-belt grade in karate
daw	*archaic* jackdaw
dop	*S Afr* a small drink, usually alcoholic
dor	a type of dung beetle
dun	a brownish-grey colour
duo	a pair of performers
dzo	a Tibetan breed of cattle

edh	a character in the Runic alphabet
eft	*archaic* newt
ell	an obsolete unit of length
erg	a unit of work or energy
ern	the European sea eagle
eta	the seventh letter in the Greek alphabet
gam	a school of whales
hap	*archaic* luck, chance
hoy	*naut* a freight barge
hui	*NZ* a Maori social gathering
ide	a small silver European fish
iff	*logic* if and only if
ism	an unspecified doctrine
jol	*S Afr slang* a party
jot	to write a brief note of
jus	*cookery* a type of sauce
kai	*NZ* food
kat	a white-flowered evergreen shrub
kea	*NZ* a large native parrot
ked	a sheep parasite
kex	a large hollow-stemmed plant
kif	another name for marijuana
kir	a drink made from white wine and cassis
lox	a type of smoked salmon
max	*informal* the greatest or most significant
nix	*mythol* a friendly water sprite
nth	*maths* of an unspecified number
pax	a Christian greeting
pyx	a chest used at the British Mint to check coin weights

qat	a white-flowered evergreen shrub
qua	*prep* by virtue of being
rad	formerly, a unit of radiation
rai	a type of Algerian popular music
raj	in India, government; rule
rav	*Judaism* a religious mentor
reo	NZ a language
ret	to moisten or soak fabric
rex	part of a king's official title
roy	*Austral slang* a trendy male
sax	a tool resembling a small axe
sik	*Austral slang* excellent
ska	type of West Indian pop music
suq	in Muslim countries, an open-air marketplace
tay	*Irish dialect* tea
ted	to shake and loosen hay in order to dry it
tef	a type of grass with edible grain
teg	a two-year-old sheep
tor	a high rocky hill
tux	*US* dinner jacket
vex	to anger or annoy
vie	to contend for superiority with
wat	a Thai Buddhist monastery
wha	*Scot* who
wok	a large Chinese cooking pot
xis	plural of *xi*
zax	a variant of *sax*
zen	a Japanese school of Buddhism
zho	a Tibetan breed of cattle

J, Q, X , and Z

Did you know that J, Q, X, and Z are the least-used letters in the English alphabet? This fact was discovered in a highly scientific manner by a certain Alfred Butts, the inventor of Scrabble®, when he was devising one of the forerunners of the game. He scoured the front page of the New York Times, counted the occurrence of each letter, and concluded a frequency for each, on which the value of the letter tiles in his 'Lexiko' game were based. Here is a list of some of the more unusual words that use J, Q, X and Z, which are helpful in many different word games. Try some of these out the next time you play Hangman!

J

dojo	a room or hall for the practice of martial arts
haji	a Muslim who has made a pilgrimage to Mecca
hajj	the pilgrimage to Mecca that every Muslim should make at least once
jake	*Aust & NZ* slang all right; satisfactory
jamb	the vertical side of a door or window frame
jape	a joke
jarl	a Scandinavian chieftain or noble
jato	*aeronautics* jet-assisted takeoff
jazz	a type of popular music of African-American origin
jess	a short leather strap used in falconry
jebel	a hill or mountain in an Arab country
ajiva	in the Jain philosophy, an object without a soul
ajuga	a type of plant with medicinal uses
bijou	something small but often elegant
djinn	supernatural beings or spirits (in Muslim belief)
hadji	a Muslim who has made a pilgrimage to Mecca
jabot	a frill or ruffle on the neck of a garment
abjure	to solemnly renounce or retract

qadi	a variant spelling of cadi, a judge in a Muslim community
qoph	the nineteenth letter in the Hebrew alphabet
quag	another word for quagmire, a soft wet area of land
quay	a wharf, typically built parallel to the shoreline
quod	*Brit slang* jail
faqir	a variant spelling of *fakir*, a member of any religious order of Islam
maquis	shrubby aromatic vegetation found in Mediterranean areas
pique	a feeling of resentment or irritation
qanat	an underground irrigation system, mostly found in Iran
qorma	a variant spelling of korma, a type of Indian dish made with cream
quaff	to drink heartily or in one draught
quale	*philosophy* an essential property or quality
quist	*West Midland and southwestern English dialect* a wood pigeon
barque	a sailing ship with three or more masts
bisque	a thick soup made from shellfish
claque	a group of people hired to applaud
loquat	an ornamental evergreen tree with small yellow plumlike fruits
aliquot	*maths* relating to an exact divisor of a number
bezique	a card game similar to whist

axel	a type of jump used in skating
axon	the part of a nerve cell that conducts impulses
calx	a powdery metal oxide formed when an ore or mineral is roasted
coxa	the technical name for the hipjoint
doxy	opinion or doctrine, especially concerning religious matters
ixia	a plant with ornamental funnel-shaped flowers
oryx	a large African antelope with long straight horns
addax	a large light-coloured antelope with spiralling horns
auxin	a type of plant hormone which promotes growth
ataxia	lack of muscular coordination
calyx	the part of a flower that protects the developing bud
coccyx	a small triangular bone at the base of the spine
extant	still in existance; surviving
magnox	an alloy consisting mostly of magnesium
oxalis	a plant with cloverlike leaves and white, pink, red or yellow flowers
axolotl	a North American aquatic salamander
bandbox	a lightweight box used for small items such as hats
bauxite	a claylike substance containing aluminium oxides
coaxial	*maths* mounted on a common axis

z

adze	a heavy hand tool with a steel blade
azan	*Islam* the call to prayer
lutz	a type of jump used in skating
meze	a starter eaten in Greece and other Mediterranean countries
zarf	an ornamental holder for a hot coffee cup
zebu	a domesticated ox used in India and East Asia
zein	a protein found in maize used to make plastics, adhesives etc
zila	an administrative district in India
azote	*obsolete* nitrogen
gloze	*archaic* to explain away; minimize the importance of
kudzu	a fast-growing climbing plant with purple fragrant flowers
matzo	a thin biscuit of unleavened bread, traditionally eaten at Passover
winze	*mining* a steeply inclined shaft for ventilation
zenith	the highest point; peak
zephyr	a light breeze
zinnia	a brightly-coloured flower native to America
zorbing	*informal* the activity of travelling downhill inside a large ball
zydeco	a type of Black Cajun music
zymase	a mixture of enzymes that ferments sugars